CASSELL'S NEW LATIN DICTIONARY

CASSELL'S NEW
LATIN-ENGLISH
ENGLISH-LATIN
DICTIONARY

BY

D. P. SIMPSON, M.A.

Assistant Master and Head of
Classical Department at Eton College

CASSELL · LONDON

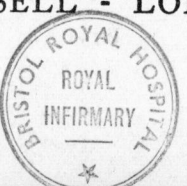

CASSELL & COMPANY LTD
35 Red Lion Square · London WC1
and at
MELBOURNE · SYDNEY · TORONTO · CAPE TOWN
JOHANNESBURG · AUCKLAND

———

© Cassell & Company Ltd, 1959

First published 1959

Printed in Great Britain
by Jarrold & Sons Ltd, Norwich

F.159

PREFACE

CASSELL'S LATIN DICTIONARY first appeared in 1854, as the work of John Relly Beard (1800–76) and his son Charles Beard (1827–88). Both men were eminent Unitarian divines; the father in particular was well known as a minister and teacher in Manchester and the author or editor of many books, several of which were published by Cassell. From the outset the general form and scope of the book were very much the same as they are now.

The Latin-English section was compiled wholly by Charles Beard. In his preface he names the thirty-four Latin authors whose words have been his concern; in the main we should still accept these as the standard or 'classical' authors, though two or three of them are nowadays seldom read. He claims also to have included some 'mythological notices' and 'short biographies of distinguished Romans'. He acknowledges his indebtedness to various scholars, notably to two Germans, Dr Wilhelm Frank (whose Latin-German dictionary was also a main source of the standard work of Lewis and Short) and Dr Karl Ernst Georges, whose *Lateinisch-Deutsches Handwörterbuch* was then available in the tenth edition (Leipzig 1848). The length of the Latin-English text is perhaps two-thirds of that in the present volume. The articles are simple in structure, with no elaborate sub-division and no etymological notes except on words derived from the Greek.

Dr J. R. Beard takes over from his son at the beginning of the English-Latin section. In a fresh preface he tells us of his general aim 'to present a Latin equivalent for every English word and phrase now in current use'; the Latin offered is to be Ciceronian or as nearly as may well be. Modestly he admits that he has done no more than skim the cream of 'the best scholarship of Germany'. Of the non-German sources which he cites, the oldest and most attractive-sounding is *Calliepeia, or A Rich Storehouse of Proper Choyce and Elegant Latine Words and Phrases, collected for the most part out of Tullies Works, by Thomas Drax* (London, 1631). His English-Latin text is almost exactly as long as his son's Latin-English, and has the same simplicity to commend it; the Ciceronian strain is on the whole well maintained, though some of the more technical articles offer ecclesiastical, medical, and other special terms which we should not now wish to hear in school.

The subsequent history of the Dictionary, extending for now just over a century, seems clear enough in its main outline, though the loss of the Publisher's records during the Second World War has made it partly a matter of research and conjecture. In 1869 a second edition appeared, which was in fact a stereotype reprint, bound in the green boards and red back which remained for many years afterwards the regular livery of the book. In text no change was made until nearly the end of the Victorian period.

In 1886 appeared 'CASSELL'S LATIN-ENGLISH DICTIONARY Revised, enlarged and in part rewritten by J. R. V. Marchant, M.A.' This was a new version of the first half of the 1854 book. James Robert Vernam Marchant had gone up from the City of London School to Wadham College, Oxford, as a scholar in 1872. He had taken a 'first in Greats' in 1876 and taught for a short time at St Paul's School. He was called to the Bar in 1884, and in 1920 became County Court Judge on the East Anglian Circuit. He died in 1936. What he sought to do for C. Beard was to make his work 'suited for the middle forms of public schools'. This aim involved him both in pruning and in amplification. Stressing his concern with 'classical' Latin, he set out to cover a narrower field than Beard, omitting much that was 'archaic or post-Augustan'; thus he gives short shrift to Varro and Plautus, to Seneca and Vitruvius. But words which he retains are treated more fully than before, with more frequent notes on etymology (though 'of an un-ambitious kind'), typographical improvements such as the use of 'bold' letters in headings, more explanatory remarks in English and notably more illustrative quotations in Latin. Marchant acknowledges that his revision 'closely follows and in many points is based on the invaluable Dictionary of Professor Georges'. This standby was the 1879 edition of the 'Handwörterbuch' previously used by C. Beard, and comparison indeed confirms that nearly all that Marchant adds to Beard is drawn from this copious source; much of his English is a direct translation from the German of Georges, many of his new quotations from Latin authors are similarly inspired, and above all the somewhat elaborate apparatus of figures and letters with which he divides up even a short article wears a Teutonic look that points, quite justly, to the same origin. The effect of Marchant's changes as a whole was to increase the length of the Latin-English section by about one-third.

By 1892 a similar task of revision had been carried out on Dr J. R. Beard's English-Latin section, and in that year a new edition of the whole work became available in thirty-four successive instalments, of which all but the last were sold for 3d., the last for 2d. The title page gave the credit for the double revision jointly to Marchant and to Joseph Fletcher Charles, B.A. The Latin-English section remained exactly as printed in 1886 under Marchant's name. It is therefore clear that the English-Latin had been overhauled either by the two scholars together or by Mr Charles alone. This fresh recruit had been for a short time, in 1871, a fellow-pupil of Marchant at the City of London School. He was afterwards an exhibitioner at University College, London, and a postmaster at Merton College, Oxford. After taking his degree he taught first at the High School, Gateshead, and then at his own (and Marchant's) old school from 1886 until shortly before his death in 1901. He published a book on *Modern Thought and Modern Thinkers* and several works of fiction. The general tendency of the changes which he made or helped to make in the Latin Dictionary was towards a more modern English and greater brevity. The English-Latin section now became little more than half as long as the Latin-English, whereas the two Beards had produced sections of equal length. The new proportion seems justified by the wholesome stress which it lays on the longer and more informative section, and is retained in the present volume.

After 1892 the Dictionary continued for sixty years to be reprinted at short intervals in the form which it had now reached.

In 1953 I was asked to undertake a complete overhaul of both sections of the work, and I now lay before the reader what is in many respects a new book. My aim has been to conform to the fashions of the present day, both in English idiom and in Latin spelling; to introduce fresh material from various sources; and in matters of explanation and arrangement to go part of the way back to the simplicity of the first edition. Yet while rewriting much, I have tried to adhere throughout to the traditional principle that 'classical' Latin, the language of what we still consider the best period, should be the prime concern of both parts of CASSELL'S NEW LATIN DICTIONARY. The first part is intended primarily to help the student in the reading of such Latin, the second part to help him in the writing of it, or rather in the writing of Latin prose in the manner of Cicero, Caesar or Livy; for the writing of Latin verse more specialized help is needed and should be sought elsewhere. But even for the limited purposes of Latin Prose composition (an exercise which may be called artificial certainly, but has long been regarded in England as an integral part of classical scholarship) the student should refer constantly to the Latin-English for further illumination.

Fuller information can be found at need in a number of other works. I would chiefly recommend the following, in addition to the Latin authors themselves.

DICTIONARIES

Thesaurus Linguae Latinae. An exhaustive work begun by five German academies in 1900, which has now (1958) been taken as far as the letter M.

A Latin Dictionary, by Charlton T. Lewis and Charles Short (1879). Still the standard Latin-English work, pending the completion of that now in hand at Oxford, which will supersede it.

Smith's Smaller Latin-English Dictionary. Revised edition by J. F. Lockwood (1933).

Smith's Smaller English-Latin Dictionary (1870).

Dictionnaire Etymologique de la Langue Latine, by A. Ernout and A. Meillet (Third edition, 1951).

SPECIALIZED WORD-LISTS

Thesaurus Poeticus Linguae Latinae, by L. Quicherat. Third edition, by E. Chatelain (1895). A most convenient authority on the quantities of syllables in Latin words.

English-Latin Gradus or Verse Dictionary, by A. C. Ainger and H. G. Wintle (Second edition, 1891). This, rather than any other English-Latin word-list, should be used for the purpose of Latin verse composition.

Latin Phrase-Book. Originally by C. Meissner; translated from the German by H. W. Arden (1895). The phrases, mainly Ciceronian, are grouped according to subject-matter, but there is an English as well as a Latin index.

Horae Latinae: Studies in Synonyms and Syntax, by R. Ogilvie (1901). Occasional notes (arranged alphabetically) on the translation of certain English words and phrases into Latin prose.

ON GENERAL ANTIQUITIES

A Companion to Latin Studies. Edited by Sir J. Sandys (Third Edition, 1921).

The Oxford Classical Dictionary (1949).

ON LATIN PROSE COMPOSITION

Hints towards Latin Prose Composition, by A. W. Potts (Sixth Edition, 1902).

Latin Prose Composition, by W. R. Hardie (1908).

Sermo Latinus, by J. P. Postgate (New Edition, 1913).

'Bradley's Arnold' Latin Prose Composition, revised by J. F. Mountford (1938).

Without the constant help given to me by most of these books, and others besides, I should have been lost indeed. Hardly smaller is my debt to generous and patient friends, at Eton, at Oxford and—not least—in the office of the publishers.

D. P. S.

ADVICE TO THE USER

Latin-English Section

VOCABULARY. This section contains articles on most of the words used by 'classical' authors from about 200 B.C. to A.D. 100. A number of proper names have also been included, especially those that figure prominently in Roman history and Roman writings.

ORDER OF WORDS. Alphabetical order has been followed in the main, but where two Latin words are very closely connected one article has been placed below the other, at the cost of taking a word out of its ordinary turn. Thus adverbs appear under the adjective from which they are derived, and participles (if their use as adjectives needs description) under the parent verb; in the same way proper names that are related together have been arranged in a group. But wherever this system has involved a wide departure from alphabetical order, cross-references have been inserted. Small figures have been prefixed to words which are different but spelt alike, such as *¹bēta* (=beet) and *²bēta* (=β).

SPELLING OF LATIN WORDS. The aim has been to follow the general tendencies shown by modern editors of Latin texts. Thus the 'unassimilated' forms of compound words have been preferred to the assimilated, for example—*adsiduus* to *assiduus*; here again the cross-references should prevent mystification. I, i replaces J, j throughout, but V, v is retained.

DECLENSION, CONJUGATION, ETC. The Latin word printed in bold type at the head of an article is followed, first, by any alternative form in which it may be found (e.g. *caussa*, as alternative to *causa*). Next come, if the word is a noun, its genitive and gender and further details of its declension if not regular; if the word is an adjective, the feminine and neuter forms of the nominative singular, or else its genitive singular; if the word is a verb, either its present infinitive active or whatever else the user will need in order to be sure of the conjugation. There follows, for many words, a simple indication of origin, enclosed in brackets; in such notices an oblique stroke is often used to distinguish between separate elements in the derivation; for instance *aliunde* is shown to have come from *alius* and *unde* by means of the etymological note '(alius/unde)'.

QUANTITY. The natural length of vowels has been indicated by means of the usual symbols (˘ short, ‾ long) wherever this seemed helpful, and especially at the beginning of an article. But vowels short by nature, which are followed by two consonants, commonly (not always) become 'long by position'. Most of these have been left unmarked here. So have many vowels in final syllables, provided that they conform to some regular type of declension or conjugation; for example, -*a* is not marked short in *mensa*, nor -*o* long in *amo*, nor -*e* short at the end of any active infinitive.

STRUCTURE OF ARTICLES. In many of the articles a distinction is drawn between the 'literal' and the 'transferred' uses of a word. The kind of difference meant is that between the uses of the English word 'sea' in the two phrases 'lost at sea' and

viii

'a sea of troubles'. Consequently an article, or a part of an article, often falls into two sections, prefaced by the two keywords 'LIT.' and 'TRANSF.'. The abbreviation 'Fig.' (=figurative) is used in much the same sense as 'TRANSF.', but generally to describe occasional rather than regular uses of a word. 'Hence' introduces senses and uses which follow naturally from what has already been described.

Arabic numbers in brackets, (1), (2), (3), etc., are used as a separate means of classification, to introduce senses of a word which are parallel and not to be distinguished from each other as literal and transferred. Where an item prefaced by such a number requires to be divided again into parallel members, lower-case letters, **a**, **b**, **c**, etc., are used.

Fresh paragraphs have been introduced on no rigid principle, but only to break up some of the longer articles as seemed desirable.

LATIN AUTHORS. Authors' names have been abbreviated throughout according to the list given below (p. xi). Some classical authority is adduced for every word, and for every separate sense of a word, which appears in this section of the dictionary, but such notes are intended to be representative rather than exhaustive, and simply to suggest how widely a word (or special sense of a word) was used during the classical period, and by what kind or kinds of author.

English-Latin Section

PURPOSE. This section is intended chiefly as an aid to Latin Prose composition, by which is meant the conversion of English prose of various styles and periods into Latin prose of a 'classical' type. Most of the English words treated here are therefore such as might well arise in this form of exercise, and such as can be turned without excessive distortion into classical Latin, whether literary or colloquial. Words like 'madhouse', because they correspond to no genuine Roman idea or institution, have been omitted. There is another kind of word which has necessarily been treated, but not without misgivings. This is the abstract or general term, such as 'passion' or 'politics', which depends on the particular context in which it occurs for its exact meaning, so that the student who meets it in an actual 'prose' should be in a better position to evaluate it and to find an appropriate equivalent than the lexicographer who grapples with it in isolation. For such words some of the more common and useful equivalents are offered here, but for general guidance only and with no hope of saving the student from the need for careful thought and discriminating choice.

The comparatively small scope of this section will make it advisable to refer to the Latin-English section for fuller information about many of the Latin words offered.

ORDER OF WORDS. Alphabetical order has been followed strictly in this section. Words which are different but look alike are distinguished from each other by a reference to parts of speech, e.g. 'subst.', 'adj.'.

LATIN EQUIVALENTS. These are taken as far as possible from Cicero, Caesar and Livy, and may be understood to have been used by at least one of those three, if no particular authority for them is cited. A very small proportion of Latin words are shown to belong quite outside the classical period, by such indications as 'leg.' (i.e. used only by the late writers on law) or 'eccl.' (i.e. used only by Christian writers).

ix

SPELLING OF LATIN WORDS. This is the same as in the Latin-English section.

DECLENSION AND CONJUGATION. Nouns of the fourth declension are followed by a reference to their genitive singular, in the form '(-ūs)', in order to distinguish them from nouns of the second. Similar notes give warning of other unexpected modes of declension. Verbs are cited in the present infinitive active (if they have one), in order to show their conjugation; but their principal parts should be checked in the Latin-English section.

QUANTITY. These are given more sparingly than in the Latin-English section, and chiefly to indicate either declension (as in the fourth-declension genitive -ūs) or conjugation (as in the second- and third-conjugation infinitives -ēre and -ĕre).

STRUCTURE. The same general principles are followed here as in the Latin-English section.

USE OF BRACKETS. Round brackets, ( ), are used not only for the ordinary purposes of parenthesis, such as further explanation or qualification, and the citing of authorities, but also to suggest that some word may be omitted in a Latin phrase, or that both the simple and the compound forms of a Latin word are available for use (e.g. (per)suadēre represents both suadēre and persuadēre).

USE OF homo AND res. To illustrate uses of Latin words, homo (=a person) and res (=a thing) have been introduced in preference to aliquis and aliquid. The following are the forms that will most often be found:

Nom.	singular	homo	res
Acc.	,,	hominem	rem
Genit.	,,	hominis	rei (genit.)
Dat.	,,	homini	rei (dat.)
Abl.	,,	homine	re

LATIN AUTHORS

Acc. L. Accius, tragic poet (170–*c.* 85 B.C.).

App. L. Appuleius, philosopher (2nd cent. A.D.).

Att. T. Pomponius Atticus, friend of Cicero (109–32 B.C.).

Auct. B. Afr.

Auct. B. Alex.

Auct. B. Hisp. } the unknown authors of three prose works, Bellum Africanum, Bellum Alexandrinum, Bellum Hispaniense, written *c.* 45 B.C.

Caes. C. Iulius Caesar, historian (100–44 B.C.).

Cat. C. Valerius Catullus, poet (1st cent. B.C.).

Cato M. Porcius Cato, orator, historian, etc. (234–149 B.C.).

Cels. A. Cornelius Celsus, encyclopaedist (1st cent. A.D.).

Cic. M. Tullius Cicero, orator and philosopher (106–43 B.C.).

Cic. L. The published letters of Cicero.

Col. L. Iunius Moderatus Columella, writer on farming (1st cent. A.D.).

Curt. Q. Curtius Rufus, historian (1st cent. A.D.).

Enn. Q. Ennius, poet (239–169 B.C.).

Gell. Aulus Gellius, grammarian (2nd cent. A.D.).

Hirt. Aulus Hirtius, historian (died 43 B.C.).

Hor. Q. Horatius Flaccus, poet (65–8 B.C.).

Juv. D. Iunius Iuvenalis, satirical poet (1st–2nd cent. A.D.).

Liv. T. Livius ('Livy'), historian (59 B.C.–A.D. 17).

Luc. M. Annaeus Lucanus, epic poet (A.D. 39–65).

Lucil. C. Lucilius, satirical writer (2nd cent. B.C.).

Lucr. T. Lucretius Carus, philosophical poet (1st cent. B.C.).

Manil. M. Manilius, poet (1st cent. A.D.).

Mart. M. Valerius Martialis, poet (1st cent. A.D.).

Nep. Cornelius Nepos, writer of biographies (1st cent. B.C.).

Ov. P. Ovidius Naso, poet (43 B.C.–*c.* A.D. 17).

Pers. A. Persius Flaccus, satirical poet (A.D. 34–62).

Petr. Petronius Arbiter, satirist (1st cent. A.D.).

Phaedr. Phaedrus, writer of fables in verse (1st cent. A.D.).

Pl. T. Maccius Plautus, writer of comedies (died 184 B.C.).

Plin. C. Plinius Secundus maior ('Pliny the Elder'), writer on natural history, etc. (*c.* A.D. 23–79).

Plin. L. The published letters of C. Plinius Caecilius Secundus minor ('Pliny the Younger'), (*c.* 61–*c.* 110).

Prop. Sextus Propertius, poet (*c.* 50–*c.* 16 B.C.).

Q. Cic. Quintus Tullius Cicero (102–43 B.C.), brother of M. Tullius.

Quint. M. Fabius Quintilianus, educationalist (1st cent. A.D.).

Sall. C. Sallustius Crispus ('Sallust'), historian (86–*c.* 34 B.C.).

Sen. L. Annaeus Seneca, philosopher (died A.D. 65).

Stat. P. Papinius Statius, poet (1st cent. A.D.).

Suet. C. Suetonius Tranquillus, biographer (*c.* 69–140).

Tac. Cornelius Tacitus, historian (*c.* 55–*c.* 120).

Ter. P. Terentius Afer, writer of comedies (died 159 B.C.).

Tib. Albius Tibullus, poet (died 19 B.C.).

Val. Fl. C. Valerius Flaccus, epic poet (died *c.* A.D. 90).

Varr. M. Terentius Varro, writer on agriculture and other subjects. (116–27 B.C.).

Vell. C. Velleius Paterculus, historian (1st cent. A.D.).

Verg. P. Vergilius Maro ('Virgil'), poet (70–19 B.C.).

Vitr. Vitruvius Pollio, writer on architecture (1st cent. B.C.).

LIST OF SPECIAL TERMS

abl. ablative.

absol. absolute, absolutely; i.e. without qualification, alone.

abstr. abstract.

acc. or *accus.* accusative.

access. accessory.

act. active.

adj. adjective.

adv. adverb.

adversat. adversative.

ap.=apud; when followed by a proper noun (e.g. ap. Cic.)=in the works of.

appell. appellative (the use of the particular to denote the general, e.g. of a proper name to denote a type of person).

arith. arithmetic or arithmetical.

Aug. Augustan.

c. common, both masculine and feminine.

causat. causative.

cf. compare.

class. classical.

collect. collective or collectively.

Com. Comedy.

compar. comparative.

concr. concrete.

conj. conjunction.

constr. construction.

contr. contraction or contracted.

correl. correlative.

dat. dative.

demonstr. demonstrative.

dep. deponent.

desider. desiderative.

dim. diminutive.

dissyll. etc. dissyllabic, etc.

distrib. distributive.

eccl. ecclesiastical.

e.g. exempli gratia (for example).

ellipt. elliptical, elliptically.

enclit. enclitic.

Eng. English.

esp. especially.

etc. et cetera.

eth. dat. ethic dative.

euphem. euphemism or euphemistic.

exclam. exclamatory.

f. feminine.

fig. figurative or figure.

fl. floruit (flourished).

foll. followed.

Fr. French.

freq. frequently or frequentative

fut. future.

gen. general or generally.

genit. genitive.

geogr. or *geograph.* geographical.

Germ. German.

Gr. Greek.

gram. or *grammat.* grammatical, or writers on grammar.

heterocl. heteroclite.

i.e. id est (that is).

imper. or *imperat.* imperative.

imperf. imperfect.

impers. impersonal.

inanim. inanimate.

inch. or *inchoat.* inchoative, inceptive.

indecl. indeclinable.

indef. indefinite.

indic. indicative.

ind., or *indir.*, *quest.* indirect question.

infin. infinitive.

Inscr. Inscriptions.

instr. instrument or instrumental.

intens. intensive.

interj. interjection.

interrog. interrogative.

intransit. intransitive.

irreg. irregular.

It. Italian.

Lat. Latin.

leg. legal or legal writers.

lit. literal.

locat. locative.

log. logical.

m. masculine.

mathemat. mathematical.

med. medical or medically.

Med. Lat. Latin of the Middle Ages.

met. or *metaph.* metaphorically.

LIST OF SPECIAL TERMS

meton. by metonymy (where a word takes on the meaning of a word related to it).
mid. middle.
milit. military.
myth. or *mythol.* mythological.
n. or *neut.* neuter.
naut. nautical.
neg. negative.
nom. nominative.
num. or *numer.* numeral.
object. objective or objectively.
occ. occasionally.
onomatop. onomatopoeia or onomatopoeic.
opp. opposite to.
or. obliq. oratio obliqua (indirect speech).
ord. or *ordin.* ordinal.
p. page.
p. adj. participial adjective.
partic. participle.
partit. partitive.
pass. passive.
perf. perfect.
pers. person, personal, or personally.
person. or *personif.* personified.
philosoph. philosophical or philosophy.
phr. phrase
pl. or *plur.* plural.
pluperf. pluperfect.
poet. poetic or poetically.
polit. political or politically.
posit. positive.
possess. possessive.
post-Aug. post-Augustan.

predic. predicative.
prep. preposition.
pres. present.
prob. probably.
pron. pronoun.
pronom. pronominal.
prop. properly.
prov. proverb or proverbially.
q.v. quod vide, quae vide (i.e. refer to the article on the word(s) mentioned).
refl. or *reflex.* reflexive.
reg. regular or regularly.
rel. or *relat.* relative.
relig. religious.
rhet. rhetoric, rhetorical, or rhetorically.
Rom. Roman.
sc. scilicet (that is to say, namely).
sing. singular.
subj. or *subjunc.* subjunctive.
subject. subjective or subjectively.
subst. substantive.
suff. suffix.
sup. supine.
superl. superlative.
syncop. syncope or syncopated.
synonym. synonymous.
t. t. technical term.
transf. transferred (i.e. used in an altered or metaphorical sense).
transit. transitive.
trisyll. trisyllabic.
v. verb or vox.
voc. vocative.

* indicates that a word (in the particular form given) is not used in classical Latin.
—, or -, stands for a word, or part of a word, which is to be supplied from the context.
˘, printed over a vowel, indicates that it is *short*.
¯, printed over a vowel, indicates that it is *long*.

xiii

STANDARD LATIN ABBREVIATIONS

A. Aulus, absolvo, antiquo.

A.D. Ante diem (in dates).

App. Appius.

A.U.C. Anno urbis conditae (reckoned from 753 B.C.).

B.D. Bona Dea.

B.M. Bene merenti.

C. Gaius, condemno.

C. As numeral=centum.

Cn. Gnaeus.

Corn. Cornelius.

Cos. Consul.

D. Decimus, Divus, Deus, Dominus.

D.D. Dono dedit.

D.M. Dis manibus.

D.O.M. Deo optimo maximo.

D.N. Dominus noster.

E. Egregius, emeritus, evocatus.

E.M.V. Egregiae memoriae vir.

E.Q.R. Eques Romanus.

F. Filius, fecit.

F.C. Faciendum curavit.

G. Gallica, Germania.

H. Hic, etc., habet, heres, honor.

H.S.E. Hic situs est.

HS. (Not a true H), sestertius.

Id. Idus.

Imp. Imperium, imperator.

I.O.M. Iovi Optimo Maximo.

K. Kaeso.

Kal. Kalendae.

L. Lucius, locus, libra.

L. As numeral=50.

M. Marcus.

M'. Manius.

M. As numeral=mille.

N. Natus, nepos.

N.L. Non liquet.

Non. Nonae.

O. Optimus, omnis.

P. Publius.

P.C. Patres conscripti (title of the assembled Senate).

P.M. Pontifex Maximus.

P.P. Pater patriae.

P.R. Populus Romanus.

P.S. Pecuniā suā.

Prid. Pridie.

Q. Quintus, quaestor, que.

R. Romanus, Rufus, recte, regnum, reficiendum.

R.P. Respublica.

R.R. Rationes relatae.

S. Sacrum, semis.

Ser. Servius.

Sp. Spurius.

S.C. Senatus consultum.

S.P.Q.R. Senatus populusque Romanus.

T. Titus.

Ti. Tiberius.

Tr. Tribunus.

T.P. Tribunicia potestas.

V. Vale, vir, vivus, voto.

V. As numeral=quinque.

X.=10; also denarius.

THE ROMAN CALENDAR

YEARS. From the earliest times the official method of referring to a particular year was to give the names of the consuls of that year. Antiquarians, especially Varro, sought for a more convenient method, and eventually 753 B.C. was accepted as the date of the foundation of Rome, and subsequent events were related to that. Thus:

A.U.C. 1 (the first year *ab urbe condita*, i.e. after the foundation of Rome)=753 B.C.

A.U.C. 2=752 B.C.; and so on; for the whole B.C. era, subtract the A.U.C. number from 754 to obtain the B.C. number.

A.U.C. 753=1 B.C.

A.U.C. 754=A.D. 1.

A.U.C. 755=A.D. 2; and so on; for the whole A.D. era, subtract 753 from the A.U.C. number to obtain the A.D. number.

MONTHS. The year originally consisted of ten months, and began with March; later the number was fixed at twelve. The following are used as adjectives with *mensis, Kalendae*, etc.; also in the masculine as substantives (sc. *mensis*):

Ianuarius	Maius	September
Februarius	Iunius	October
Martius	Quinctilis (later called Iulius)	November
Aprilis	Sextilis (later called Augustus)	December

DAYS. Until the reforms of Julius Caesar, the normal year consisted of 355 days only, but was from time to time lengthened by the addition of intercalary months. The irregular working of this system caused great uncertainty and confusion. Caesar first gave the special length of 445 days to the year 46 B.C. (called by Macrobius *annus confusionis*), and then in 45 B.C. instituted a regular cycle of four years, such as we have now, of which three contained 365 days and the fourth, the leap-year, 366.

L.D.—I **

The following words and phrases indicate *on* a certain date (according to the Calendar of Caesar, which was used from 45 B.C. onwards):

Days of the month	January, August, December (31 days)		March, May, July, October (31 days)		April, June, September, November (30 days)		February (28 days)	
1	Kalendis	Ian. Aug. Dec.	Kalendis	Mart. Mai. Iul. Oct.	Kalendis	Apr. Iun. Sept. Nov.	Kalendis	Feb.
2	a.d. (ante diem) IV Nonas	Ian. Aug. Dec.	a.d. VI Nonas	Mart. Mai. Iul. Oct.	a.d. IV Nonas	Apr. Iun. Sept. Nov.	a.d. IV Nonas	Feb.
3	a.d. III	,,	a.d. V	,,	a.d. III	,,	a.d. III	,,
4	pridie	,,	a.d. IV	,,	pridie	,,	pridie	Feb.
5	Nonis	Ian. Aug. Dec.	a.d. III	,,	Nonis	Apr. Iun. Sept. Nov.	Nonis	Feb.
6	a.d. VIII Idus	Ian. Aug. Dec.	pridie	,,	a.d. VIII Idus	Apr. Iun. Sept. Nov.	a.d. VIII Idus	Feb.
7	a.d. VII	,,	Nonis	Mart. Mai. Iul. Oct.	a.d. VII	,,	a.d. VII	,,
8	a.d. VI	,,	a.d. VIII Idus	Mart. Mai. Iul. Oct.	a.d. VI	,,	a.d. VI	,,
9	a.d. V	,,	a.d. VII	,,	a.d. V	,,	a.d V	,,
10	a.d. IV	,,	a.d. VI	,,	a.d. IV	,,	a.d. IV	,,
11	a.d. III	,,	a.d. V	,,	a.d. III	,,	a.d. III	,,
12	pridie	,,	a.d. IV	,,	pridie	,,	pridie	,,
13	Idibus	Ian. Aug. Dec.	a.d. III	,,	Idibus	Apr. Iun. Sept. Nov.	Idibus	Feb.

Days of the month	January, August, December (31 days)		March, May, July, October (31 days)		April, June, September, November (30 days)		February (28 days)		February in leap-year (29 days) ends thus:	
14	a.d. XIX	Kalendas Feb. Sept. Ian.	pridie	Idus Mart. Mai. Iul. Oct.	a.d. XVIII	Kalendas Mai. Iul. Oct. Dec.	a.d. XVI	Kalendas Mart.		
15	a.d. XVIII	"	Idibus	Mart. Mai. Iul. Oct.	a.d. XVII	"	a.d. XV	"		
16	a.d. XVII	"	a.d. XVII	Kalendas Apr. Iun. Aug. Nov.	a.d. XVI	"	a.d. XIV	"		
17	a.d. XVI	"	a.d. XVI	"	a.d. XV	"	a.d. XIII	"		
18	a.d. XV	"	a.d. XV	"	a.d. XIV	"	a.d. XII	"		
19	a.d. XIV	"	a.d. XIV	"	a.d. XIII	"	a.d. XI	"		
20	a.d. XIII	"	a.d. XIII	"	a.d. XII	"	a.d. X	"		
21	a.d. XII	"	a.d. XII	"	a.d. XI	"	a.d. IX	"		
22	a.d. XI	"	a.d. XI	"	a.d. X	"	a.d. VIII	"		
23	a.d. X	"	a.d. X	"	a.d. IX	"	a.d. VII	"		
24	a.d. IX	"	a.d. IX	"	a.d. VIII	"	a.d. VI	"		
25	a.d. VIII	"	a.d. VIII	"	a.d. VII	"	a.d. V	"	a.d. VI	Kalendas Mart.*
26	a.d. VII	"	a.d. VII	"	a.d. VI	"	a.d. IV	"	a.d. V	Kalendas Mart.*
27	a.d. VI	"	a.d. VI	"	a.d. V	"	a.d. III	"	a.d. IV	"
28	a.d. V	"	a.d. V	"	a.d. IV	"	pridie	"	a.d. III	"
29	a.d. IV	"	a.d. IV	"	a.d. III	"			pridie	"
30	a.d. III	"	a.d. III	"	pridie	"				
31	pridie	"	pridie	"						

* The day thus repeated in a leap-year was called bisextus.

CASSELL'S

LATIN-ENGLISH DICTIONARY

A

A, a, the first letter of the Latin Alphabet.
a s an abbreviation, see table of Latin abbreviations.
a ah, interj. *Ah!* Pl., Verg.
ā, ăb, abs, prep. with abl. (a stands before consonants except h; ab before vowels, h and sometimes consonants; abs only sometimes before c, q, t—esp. te). Ab denotes motion away from a fixed point (opp. ad).
LIT., in space. (**1**) of motion, as with verbs of going or taking, *away from*: ad carceres a calce revocari, Cic. Often with persons: a me, *from me, from my house, from my purse,* etc., Cic. Often strengthened by usque, *all the way from*: usque ab capitolio excitatus, Cic. (**2**) of distance from a point, with actual motion not necessarily involved, *from.* So with measures of distance, adverbs like procul, etc., and such verbs as abesse, distare: ab urbe abesse milia passuum ducenta, Cic. (**3**) of the side from which a thing is viewed, and so of the direction in which it lies: a septentrionibus, *on* or *to the north,* Caes.; a fronte, a tergo, a latere, a dextro cornu, Cic.; ab novissimis, *in the rear,* Caes.
TRANSF., in time, indicating duration or distance *from, after*: ab hora tertia bibebatur, Cic.; cuius a morte hic tertius et tricesimus annus, Cic.; ab urbe condita. Esp. with nouns indicating stages, times of life, etc.: ab initio; ab ovo; a pueris.
TRANSF., of other, analogous relations. (**1**) of separation, difference, change *from*: quantum mutatus ab illo, Verg. So of protection *from,* with such verbs as defendere. Of position or number, counting *from*: quartus ab Arcesila, Cic. Of a part detached or considered separately *from* a whole; *out of, of*: nonnulli ab novissimis, *some of the rear-guard,* Cic. (**2**) of origin. So regularly of agency, especially with passive or intransitive verbs, *by, at the hands of*: reprehendi ab, Cic.; interire ab, Cic.; and of causation generally, *from, because of*: id facinus natum a cupiditate, Cic. With places of origin, *from*: Turnus ab Aricia, Liv.; of ancestry, training, etc.: Zeno et qui ab eo sunt, *Zeno and his school,* Cic. With sources of information, gifts, etc., *from*: so accipere, emere, audire ab. (**3**) corresponding to LIT. (**3**) above, of other relations; *in connexion with, on the side of*: imparati cum a militibus tum a pecunia, *as regards soldiers and money,* Caes. Esp. with terms indicating employment: servus a pedibus, *a footman,* Cic.; a manu servus, *secretary,* Suet.
ăbăcus -i, m. (*ἄβαξ*), *a square board.* Hence (**1**) *a sideboard*: Cic. (**2**) *a counting-board*: Pers. (**3**) *a gaming-board divided into compartments*: Suet. (**4**) in architecture, *a painted ceiling panel*: Vitr., Plin.; or *the square slab on the top of a column*: Vitr.

ăbălĭēnātĭo -ōnis, f. *legal transfer of property*: Cic.
ăbălĭēno -are, *to make alien, separate.* (**1**) of property: agros populi, Cic. (**2**) *to deprive*: abalienati iure civium, Liv. (**3**) *to estrange*: a te iudices, Cic.
Ăbās -antis, m. *king of Argos, father of Acrisius.*
⁋ Hence adj. **Ăbantēus** -a -um: Ov.; subst. **Ăbantĭădes** -ae, m. *a descendant of Abas*; used by Ov. of *Acrisius* (son of Abas), and of *Perseus* (great-grandson of Abas).
ăbăvus -i, m. *a great-great-grandfather*: Cic.; and in general, *forefather*: Plin.
Abdēra -orum, n. pl. (*Ἄβδηρα*); also **Abdēra** -ae, f.: Ov.; *a town in Thrace* (now *Polystilo* or *Asperosa*), *birth-place of Protagoras and Democritus, but noted for the stupidity of its inhabitants*: hic Abdera, *here reigns stupidity,* Cic.
⁋ Hence subst. **Abdērītēs** -ae (abl. -a), m. *an inhabitant of Abdera*: Cic.; and adj. **Abdērītānus** -a -um: Mart.
abdĭcātĭo -ōnis, f. (**1**) *disowning of a son*: Plin. (**2**) *renouncing of an office*: dictaturae, Liv.
¹abdĭco -are, *to renounce, reject.* Esp. (**1**) of relatives (post-Aug. use): filium, Quint. (**2**) of magistracies, *to abdicate,* commonly with reflexive object and ablative of the office vacated: se non modo consulatu sed etiam libertate, Cic.; also, in historians, with simple accusative: magistratum, Sall.; dictaturam, Liv.; absol.: ut abdicarent consules, Cic.
²abdĭco -dīcĕre -dixi -dictum, t. t. of augury, *to refuse assent to, disapprove of* (opp. addico): cum tres partes (vineae) aves abdixissent, Cic.
abdĭtīvus -a -um, *removed, separated*: Pl.
abdo -dĕre -dĭdi -dĭtum. In gen., *to put away, withdraw, remove*: copias ab eo loco abditas, Caes.; reflex.: abdere se in aliquem locum, *to withdraw oneself, to retire*: in intimam Macedoniam, Cic.; in bibliothecam; in litteras (or litteris), Cic.
Esp. *to secrete, to hide*: ferrum veste, Liv.; se in scalarum tenebras, Cic.
⁋ Hence partic. **abdĭtus** -a -um, *concealed, secret*: vis abdita quaedam, Lucr.; res abditae et obscurae, Cic.; neut. plur., abdita, as subst., *secrets*: Lucr., Hor.
⁋ Adv. **abdĭte,** *secretly*: Cic.
abdōmĕn -inis, n. *the belly*: Pl.; esp. as seat of the appetite, *gluttony*: manebat insaturabile abdomen, Cic.; natus abdomini suo, *whose god is his belly,* Cic.; abdominis voluptates, *pleasures of appetite,* Cic.
abdūco -dūcĕre -duxi -ductum, *to lead* or *take away.*
LIT., aliquem e foro, Cic.; conlegam vi de foro, Liv.; in lautumias, Cic. Esp. of theft and elopement: filiam mimi Isidori, Cic.; mancipia, Cic.; armenta, Ov.
TRANSF., (**1**) *to seduce* a person from his allegiance: equitatum Dolabellae ad se, Cic.
(**2**) *to relieve*: animum a sollicitudine, Cic.

(3) *to bring down, to lower*: artem ad mercedem atque quaestum, Cic.

Ăbella -ae, f. *town in Campania* (now *Avella Vecchia*). Adj. **Ăbellānus** -a -um.

ăbĕo -ire -ii -itum, *to go away*.

LIT., (1) in gen.: ex agris atque urbibus, Cic.; ab urbe, Liv.; de Sicilia, Cic.; comitio, Liv.; si abis periturus, *if you go to death*, Verg.; imper., abi (or abin, for abisne), *be off with you*: abi in malam rem, *go to the devil*, Pl.; abi hinc cum tribunatibus ac rogationibus tuis, Liv. Of things: abeuntia vela, Ov.; sol abit, Pl.; cornus sub altum pectus abit, Verg. (2) esp., *to come off in a certain state* (e.g. from a battle): Romani semper victores certamine abire, Liv.; nemo non donatus abibit, Verg.

TRANSF., (1) of persons: **a**, *to retire* from a public office: consulatu, Cic.: **b**, of the dying, *to depart*: ad deos, Cic.; ad plures, *to 'the great majority'*, Petr.; e vita, Cic.: **c**, of a discussion, *to digress*: illuc, unde abii, redeo, Hor.; quid ad istas ineptias abis? Cic.: **d**, *to change*: sic deus in flammas abiit, Ov. (2) of things: **a**, of time, *to pass away*: abiit ille annus, Cic.: **b**, of diseases: iam abiit pestilentia, Cic.: **c**, of other things, *to disappear, vanish*: sensus abit, Cic.; timor, fides abiit, Liv.: **d**, of the consequences of an action: non posse istaec sic abire, *be without consequences*, Cic.: **e**, with notion of transference from one person or thing to another, *pass over* to: ad sanos abeat tutela propinquos, Hor.; vigor ingenii velocis in alas et pedes abiit, Ov.

ăbĕquĭto -are, *to ride off*: Liv.

ăberrātĭo -ōnis, f. *an escape* or *relief from anything irksome*: Cic.

ăberro -are, *to wander, lose one's way*.

LIT., pecore, Liv.; aberrantes ex agmine naves, Liv.

TRANSF., (1) *to deviate from*: a proposito, Cic. (2) *to free oneself from something irksome*: a miseria quasi aberrare, Cic.

ăbhinc, adv. of time. (1) (ante-class. use), *hereafter*; so, perhaps, aufer abhinc lacrimas, Lucr. (where some take it as *hence*, like hinc). (2) *backward from the present time, ago*: annos tres, triennium, annis tribus abhinc, *three years ago*, Cic.

ăbhorrĕo -ēre.

LIT., *to shrink back from, to be disinclined to*: a pace, Caes.; a ducenda uxore, Cic.; with abl. alone: spectaculorum oblectamentis, Tac.; absol.: omnes aspernabantur, omnes abhorrebant, Cic.

TRANSF., *to be inconsistent with* or *opposed to*: oratio abhorret a persona hominis gravissimi, Cic.; a fide, *to be incredible*, Liv.; spes ab effectu haud abhorrens, *hope capable of being realized*, Liv.; orationes abhorrent inter se, *are inconsistent with one another*, Liv.; with simple abl.: neque abhorret vero, Tac.; with dat.: huic tam pacatae profectioni abhorrens mos, Liv. Pres. partic., as adj., *unseasonable, inappropriate*: absurdae atque abhorrentes lacrimae, Liv.

ăbicio -icere -iēci -iectum (ab/iacio), *to throw down*, or *away*.

LIT., (1) scutum, arma, Cic.; se ad pedes alicuius, Cic. (2) *to throw down violently*: aliquem ad tribunal, ad pedes tuos, ad terram virgis et verberibus, Cic.; so in battle, *to strike to the ground*: Verg.

TRANSF., (1) *to pronounce carelessly, to break off abruptly*: versum, Cic.; ambitus non est abiciendus, *the period must not be broken off abruptly*, Cic. (2) *to get rid of, to dispose of*: pecuniam, Cic. (3) *to give up, to let go*: memoriam beneficiorum, Cic.; *to abandon*: Scaurum, Cic. (4) *to dash to the ground, to deprive of all power*: senatus auctoritatem, Cic.; with reference to character, *to dishearten*: se perculsum atque abiectum esse sentit, Cic.; abiecta metu filia, *desponding*, Cic. (5) fig., *to throw away*: cogitationes in rem tam humilem, Cic.; se abicere, *to degrade oneself*, Cic.

¶ Hence partic. (with compar. and superl.) **abiectus** -a -um. (1) of position, *low, common*: familia abiecta atque obscura, Cic. (2) of character, *cowardly, mean-spirited*: animus, Cic. (3) *despicable*: contemptus atque abiectus Cic. (4) *without force, prosaic*: versus, Cic.; oratio humilis et abiecta, Cic.

¶ Adv. **abiectē**, *abjectly, without spirit*: Cic.; *meanly*: Tac.

abiectio -ōnis, f. (abicio), *a throwing away*.

TRANSF., animi, *despondency, despair*, Cic.

ăbiēgnus -a -um (abies), *made of fir wood* or *deal*.

ăbiēs -ĕtis, f. (abietis, abiete trisyll. in poetry). (1) *the silver fir* (Pinus picea, Linn.): Liv. (2) meton., *anything made of deal; a letter*, because formerly written on wood: Pl.; *a ship*: Verg.; *a spear*: Verg.

ăbĭgo -ĕre -ēgi -actum (ab/ago), *to drive away*.

LIT., volucres et feras, Cic. Esp. of cattle: pecus, *to steal cattle*, Cic.

TRANSF., in gen., *to banish, be rid of*: pauperiem, Hor.; in special senses: partum medicamentis, *to procure abortion*, Cic.; uxorem, *to divorce*, Suet.

ăbĭtĭo -ōnis, f.=abitus; q.v.

ăbĭto -are, *to go away*: Pl.

ăbĭtus -ūs, m. (abeo). (1) *a going away, departure*: post abitum huius, Cic. (2) *place of egress* (opp. aditus): Verg., Tac.

abiūdĭco -are, *to take away by a judgment*: aliquid ab aliquo, Cic.; sibi libertatem, Cic.

abiungo -iungĕre -iunxi -iunctum, *to unharness*: iuvencum, Verg.

TRANSF., *to estrange, detach*: abiuncto Labieno, Caes.; se ab hoc dicendi genere, *to keep from*, Cic.

abiuro -are, *to abjure, deny on oath*: creditum, Sall.

ablātīvus -a -um (aufero), *ablative*. With casus (expressed or understood), *the ablative*: Quint.

ablēgātĭo -ōnis, f. *a sending away*: iuventutis ad bellum, Liv. Occasionally, *banishment* (=relegatio): Plin.

ablēgo -are. LIT., *to send away, remove to a distance*: honestos homines, Cic.; pueros venatum, Liv.; aliquem a penatibus suis, Liv. TRANSF., haec (legatio) a fratris adventu me ablegat, *prevents me from being present on my brother's arrival*, Cic.

ablĭgūrĭo -ire, *to lick away, to consume in luxury*: patria bona, Ter.

ablŏco -are, *to let on lease*: Suet.

ablŭdo -ĕre, *to be out of tune with.* Hence *to be unlike:* haec a te non multum abludit imago, Hor.

ablŭo -lŭĕre -lŭi -lūtum, *to wash.* (1) in the sense of cleansing: pedes alicuius, Cic.; pass.: ablui, *to be washed clean,* Cic. (2) in the sense of removing, *to wash away.* LIT., maculas e veste, Plin.; lacrimas, Tac. TRANSF., omnis perturbatio animi placatione abluatur, Cic.; sitis de corpore abluitur, Lucr.

abnĕgo -are, *to deny, refuse:* alicui coniugium et dotes, Verg.; nec comitem se abnegat, Hor.; absol.: abnegat, Verg.

abnĕpos -ōtis, m. *great-great-grandson:* Suet.

abneptis -is, f. *a great-great-granddaughter:* Suet.

Abnŏba -ae, m. *a range of mountains in Germany, where the Danube rises.*

abnocto -are, *to stay out all night:* Sen.

abnormis -e (ab/norma), *irregular, unconventional:* abnormis sapiens, *a philosopher of no particular school,* Hor.

abnŭo -nŭĕre -nŭi -nŭitūrus, *to refuse by a motion of the head* or *eye, deny:* manu abnuit quidquam opis in se esse, *gave a sign with his hand that he could not help,* Liv.; regi pacem, Sall.; nemo abnuit a se commissum esse facinus, Cic.; spes abnuit, *it does not admit of hope,* Tib.; of soldiers, *to refuse to fight:* Liv.

abnūto -are, *to deny* (by a nod) *repeatedly:* Pl.

ăbŏlĕo -ēre -ēvi -ĭtum (alo), *to destroy.* LIT., Poppaeae corpus non igni abolitum, Tac. TRANSF., *to do away with:* magistratum, Liv.; dedecus armis, Verg.; ritus, sacrificandi disciplinam, Liv.

ăbŏlesco -ĕre -ēvi, no sup. (alo), *to perish:* non abolescet gratia facti, Verg.; nomen vetustate abolevit, Liv.

ăbŏlĭtĭo -ōnis, f. *a removing, abrogating, annulling, abolition:* legis, *repeal,* Suet.; tributorum, Tac.; facti, *amnesty,* Suet.

ăbolla -ae, f. (ἀμβολή, ἀναβολή), *a cloak of thick woollen cloth,* worn by soldiers, peasants and certain philosophers: facinus maioris abollae, Juv.

ăbōmĭno=abominor; q.v.

ăbōmĭnor -ari, dep. (ab/omen). (1) *to deprecate an unfavourable omen:* Liv.; quod abominor, *God forbid,* Ov. (2) *to hate, detest, abominate* (opp. optare): Liv.; abominandus, *detestable,* Liv.; abominatus, *detested,* Hor.

Ăbŏrīgĭnes -um, m. *the Aborigines,* an Italian tribe from whom the Latins were said to be descended; hence *original inhabitants of a country* (=αὐτόχθονες): Cic.

ăbŏrior -oriri -ortus, dep. (1) of the heavenly bodies, *to set, to disappear:* Varr. (2) *to perish by untimely birth:* Plin. (3) poet., of the voice, *to fail:* Lucr.

ăbŏriscor -i=aborior; q.v.: Lucr.

ăbortĭo -ōnis, f. *an untimely birth, miscarriage:* Cic.

ăbortīvus -a -um, *prematurely born:* Sisyphus, Hor.; ovum, *addled,* Mart. N. as subst. **ăbortīvum** -i (sc. medicamentum), *drug for procuring abortion:* Juv.

ăbortus -ūs, m. *a miscarriage:* Cic.

abrādo -rādĕre -rasi -rasum. LIT., *to scrape off, shave:* supercilia, Cic. TRANSF., *to squeeze money out of a person, to extort:* nihil

se ab A. Caecina posse litium terrore abradere, Cic.

abrĭpio -ripĕre -rĭpŭi -reptum (ab/rapio), *to snatch away, drag off.* LIT., abripi vi fluminis, Caes.; filios e complexu parentum, Cic. TRANSF., *to remove, detach:* te aestus ingenii tui abripuit, Cic.

abrōdo -dĕre -si -sum, *to gnaw off, away:* Plin.

abrŏgātĭo -ōnis, f. *an annulling* or *repealing:* legis, Cic.

abrŏgo -are. LIT., *to repeal a law wholly, to annul:* legem, Cic.; huic legi nec obrogari fas est, neque derogari ex hac aliquid licet neque tota abrogari potest, Cic. TRANSF., *to remove, take away:* fidem, Cic.; of an office: magistratum, Cic.

abrŏtŏnum -i, n. and **abrŏtŏnus** -i, m. (ἁβρότονον), *southern-wood, an aromatic herb:* Lucr., Hor.

abrumpo -rumpĕre -rūpi -ruptum, *to break off, sever.* LIT., ramos, Ov.; vincula, Liv. TRANSF., (1) *to remove, dissociate:* se latrocinio Antonii, *to break with A.'s gang,* Cic. (2) *to violate:* fas, Verg. (3) *to break off prematurely, to destroy:* vitam, Verg.; medium sermonem, *to break off in the middle of a speech,* Verg.

¶ Hence partic. (with compar. and superl.) **abruptus** -a -um, *torn off.* LIT., *steep, precipitous.* N. as subst. **abruptum** -i, *a steep ascent* or *descent:* sorbet in abruptum fluctus, Verg. TRANSF., *abrupt, rough:* contumacia, Tac.

¶ Adv. **abruptē:** Quint.

abruptĭo -ōnis, f. (abrumpo), *a tearing away:* corrigiae, *of a shoe-latchet,* Cic. TRANSF., *divorce:* Att. ap. Cic.

abscēdo -cedĕre -cessi -cessum, *to go away, depart.*
LIT., of persons: a curia, e foro, Liv. As milit. t. t., *to withdraw, retire:* a Capua, Liv.; impers.: Regio abscessum est, Liv. Of things, *to retire:* quantum mare abscedebat, Liv.
TRANSF., of persons. (1) *to retire from* an office or employment: non militaribus modo sed civilibus quoque muneribus, Liv. (2) *to desert* one: Pallada abscessisse mihi, Ov. Of things. (1) *to go away:* somnus ut abscessit, Ov. (2) *to desert:* cives earum urbium quae regno abscedunt, Liv.

abscessĭo -ōnis, f. (abscedo), *a going away, a separation:* Cic.

abscessus -ūs, m. (abscedo), *a going away.* (1) of persons, *going away, withdrawal:* Rutulum, Verg.; continuus abscessus, Tac. (2) of inanimate objects: solis, Cic.

abscīdo -cīdĕre -cīdi -cīsum (abs/caedo), *to cut off.*
LIT., funes, Caes.; aquam, Liv.; caput, Liv.
TRANSF., (1) *to separate:* intersaeptis munimentis hostis pars parti abscisa erat, Liv.; abscisus in duas partes exercitus, Caes. (2) *to take away:* regibus spem auxilii sui, Liv.

¶ Hence partic. **abscīsus** -a -um, *cut off.* So (1) *precipitous:* rupes, Liv. (2) *abrupt, short:* voce, Quint.

abscindo -scindĕre -scidi -scissum, *to tear off, wrench away.*

LIT., tunicam a pectore, Cic.; vestem humeris, Verg.; venas, *to open the veins*, Tac.; poet.: abscissa comas, *with her hair torn*, Verg.
TRANSF., (1) *to divide*: terras Oceano, Hor. (2) *to separate*: inane soldo, Hor. (3) *to take away*: reditūs dulces, Hor.

abscondo -condĕre -condi (-condĭdi) -condĭtum (-consum). (1) *to conceal, obscure*: gladios, Cic.; galea frontem abscondit, Juv.; hence pass. of stars, *to set*: Verg. (2) *to lose sight of*: Phaeacum arces, Verg.
¶ Hence, from partic. absconditus, adv. **abscondĭtē**, *obscurely, abstrusely*: Cic.

absens -entis, *absent*, pres. partic. of absum; q.v.

absentĭa -ae, f. (absum), *absence*: Cic.

absĭlĭo -ire, -ii or -ui (ab/salio), *to spring forth* or *away*: Lucr.

absĭmĭlis -e, *unlike*: non absimili forma, Caes.

absinthĭum -i, n. (ἀψίνθιον), *wormwood*: Lucr.

absĭsto -sĭstĕre -stĭti. (1) *to go away*, followed by ab or the abl. alone: limine, Verg.; ab signis, Caes.; absol., tandem abstiterunt, Liv.; of things, ab ore scintillae assistunt, Verg. (2) *to desist from*; with abl.: obsidione, spe, Liv.; with infin., absiste moveri, *cease to be moved*, Verg.; with gerund: sequendo, *from following*, Liv.; accusator abstitit, *the accuser withdrew* (i.e. from his accusation), Tac.

absŏlūtĭo -ōnis, f. (absolvo). (1) *acquittal*: maiestatis, *on the charge of treason*, Cic. (2) *perfection*: virtus quae rationis absolutio definitur, Cic.

absŏlūtōrius -a -um, *relating to acquittal*: tabella, *the voting-tablet that acquits*, Suet. N. as subst. **absŏlūtōrĭum** -i (sc. remedium), *means of escape from*: Plin.

absolvo -solvĕre -solvi -solūtum.
LIT., *to loosen*.
TRANSF., (1): **a**, *to free*: se a Fannio iudicio, Cic.; aliquem regni suspicione, Liv.: **b**, *to acquit*: improbitatis, Cic.; capitis, Nep.; reos culpa, Ov.; de praevaricatione, Cic. (2) *to dispose of in narration, to relate*: de Catilinae coniuratione paucis absolvam, Sall. (3) *to complete, to finish*: tectum, Cic.; opera, Caes.; absolve beneficium tuum, Liv.
¶ Hence partic. (with compar. and superl.) **absŏlūtus** -a -um. (1) *perfect, complete*: vita, Cic. (2) *unfettered, unconditional, absolute*: causa, Cic.
¶ Adv. **absŏlūtē**, *perfectly, completely*: vivere feliciter, absolute, Cic.

absŏnus -a -um. LIT., *inharmonious*: vox, Cic.
TRANSF., *disagreeing with, not corresponding with*: absoni a voce motus, Liv.; with dat.: nihil absonum fidei divinae originis fuit, Liv.

absorbĕo -ēre -ŭi, *to swallow, to gulp down*.
LIT., placentas, Hor.; Oceanus vix videtur tot res absorbere potuisse, Cic.
TRANSF., hunc absorbuit aestus gloriae, *carried him off*, Cic.; tribunatus absorbet meam orationem, *absorbs, engrosses*, Cic.

absque, prep. with abl. *without*: absque argumento, Cic.

abstēmius -a -um (abs/temetum), *abstaining from intoxicating liquors, temperate, abstemious, moderate*: Ov., Hor.

abstergĕo -tergēre -tersi -tersum, *to wipe off, to dry by wiping*.

LIT., cruorem, Liv.
TRANSF., *to remove something disagreeable*: omnes senectutis molestias, Cic.

absterrĕo -ēre, *to frighten away, to drive away by fear*.
LIT., hostes saxis, Liv.; neminem a congressu meo, Cic.; eos a tam detestabili consilio, Liv.; animos vitiis, *from vices*, Hor.; aliquem bello, Tac.
TRANSF., *to remove, withdraw*: Lucr.

abstĭnens -entis, partic. from abstineo; q.v.

abstĭnentĭa -ae, f. *abstinence, continence, self-denial, temperance*: Cic.; esp. (in later authors) *fasting*: abstinentiā vitam finire, Tac.

abstĭneo -tinēre -tĭnŭi -tentum (abs/teneo), *to hold back, to keep away from.*
(1) transit., with acc. and abl., or ab and abl.; the acc. often being manūs, and very often a reflexive pronoun: se scelere, Cic.; aliquos ab legatis violandis, Liv.
(2) intransit., *to abstain from*; with abl.: iniuria, Cic.; with ab and abl.: Caes.; with genit. (Greek use): irarum, Hor.; also absol., Verg., or with ne, quin, or quominus.
¶ Hence present partic. (with compar. and superl.) **abstĭnens** -entis, *abstinent, temperate*: Cic.; with genit.: pecuniae, Hor.
¶ Adv. **abstĭnenter**: Cic.

absto -are, *to stand at a distance, stand aloof*: Hor.

abstrăho -trahĕre -traxi -tractum.
LIT., *to drag away*: aliquem de matris complexu, Cic.; naves e portu, Liv.; aliquem a penetralibus, Liv.; liberos in servitutem, Caes.
TRANSF., *to exclude, estrange, restrain*: aliquem ex tanto comitatu clarissimorum virum, Cic.; animus a corpore abstractus, Cic.; copias a Lepido, Cic.; ingressos in castra ab direptione abstrahere non poterat, Liv.

abstrūdo -trudĕre -trūsi -trūsum, *to push away from any place, to hide*: se in silvam densam, Cic.; semina flammae abstrusa in venis silicis, Verg.
¶ Hence partic. (with compar.) **abstrūsus** -a -um, *concealed, secret*: insidiae, Cic.; disputatio abstrusior, *more abstruse*, Cic.; homo abstrusus, *reserved*, Tac.

absum ăbesse ăfui; fut. infin., ăfore; fut. partic., ăfuturus.
(1) *to be away, to be absent.*
LIT., ab urbe, Cic.
TRANSF., **a**, *to take no part in*: ab hoc concilio, Caes.; ab his studiis, Cic.; toto bello, Caes.: **b**, *not to help*: quo plus intererat, eo plus aberas a me, *the more I needed you, the less you helped me*, Cic.; longe iis paternum nomen populi Romani afuturum, *would be of no avail*, Caes.: **c**, *to be wanting*: studium semper sit, cunctatio absit, Cic.; semper aves quod abest, Lucr.; neque corpus neque animus a vobis aberit, Sall.; abest historia nostris litteris, Cic.
(2) *to be far away, to be distant.*
LIT., ab urbe milia passuum ducenta, Cic.; quatridui iter Laodicea, Cic.
TRANSF., **a**, *to be far from*: longe a spe, Cic.; so the impers. phrase, tantum abest ut...ut, e.g. tantum abest ab eo ut malum sit mors ut verear, *so far is death from being an evil that I fear*, etc., Cic.; so haud multum, or procul abest, or paulum abest, or minimum

abest quin, etc.: haud multum afuit quin interficeretur, *he was nearly killed*, Liv.: **b**, *to be free from* (a fault): a culpa, Cic.; a cupiditate pecuniae, Nep.: **c**, *to be far removed* (esp. in phrases expressing a wish): procul absit gloria vulgi, Tib.; nomen ipsum crucis absit non modo a corpore civium Romanorum, etc., Cic.: **d**, *to be firmly opposed to*: a consilio fugiendi, Cic.: **e**, *to be inconsistent with*: quod certe abest a tua virtute et fide, Cic.

absūmēdo -inis, f. *consumption*: Pl.

absūmo -sumĕre -sumpsi -sumptum, *to reduce, consume*. LIT., absumptis frugum alimentis, Liv., Verg. TRANSF., (1) *to waste*: res paternas, Hor.; tempus, Liv., Cic. (2) *to destroy*: multos pestilentia absumpsit, Liv.; leto, Verg.

absurdus -a -um.
LIT., *that which offends the ear, unmelodious, harsh*: vox, Cic.
TRANSF., *foolish, unreasonable*. (1) of things: vestrae istae absurdae atque abhorrentes lacrimae, Liv.; haud absurdum est, *it is not out of place*, Sall. (2) of persons, *incapable*: homo, Cic.; ingenium haud absurdum, Sall.; absurdus ingenio, Tac.
¶ Hence adv. **absurde**. (1) *harshly, discordantly*: canere, Cic. (2) *absurdly*: absurde et aspere respondere verbis vultuque, Cic.

Absyrtus -i, m. ("Αψυρτος), *brother of Medea, killed by his sister on her flight from Colchis*.

ăbundantĭa -ae, f. (1) *abundance, richness, plenty*: omnium rerum quas natura desiderat, Cic.; voluptatum, Cic. (2) *riches, wealth*: Cic., Tac.

ăbundē, adv. *copiously, abundantly*: promittere, Lucr.; satisfacere, Cic.; with adj.: abunde magnus, Sall.; tibi abunde est, *you are more than satisfied*, Plin. Subst. with genit.: terrorum ac fraudis abunde est, Verg.

ăbundo -are, *to overflow*.
LIT., flumina, Lucr.; abundat aqua, Liv.
TRANSF., (1) *to grow in abundance*: de terris abundant herbarum genera, Lucr. (2) *to abound, be rich in*, esp. with abl.: divitiis, Ter.; ingenio et doctrina, Cic.; absol., *to be rich*: cum ex reliquis vel abundare debeam, cogor mutuari, Cic.
¶ Hence partic. (with compar. and superl.) **ăbundans** -antis. LIT., of rivers, *overflowing*: amnis abundantissimus, Cic. TRANSF., (1) *abundant, numerous*: abundante multitudine, Liv.; abundantes voluptates, Liv. (2) *abounding in*, usually with abl.: fontibus, consilio, Cic.; occasionally with genit.: lactis, Verg.
¶ Adv. **abundanter**, *abundantly*; of discourse, *copiously*: loqui, Cic.

ăbūsĭo -ōnis, f. (abutor), in rhetoric, *a false use of tropes*: Cic.

ăbusquĕ, prep. with abl.=usque ab, *from*. (1) as regards position: Oceano abusque, Tac. (2) as regards time: Tiberio abusque, Tac.

ăbūsus -ūs, m. (abutor), *using up, wasting*: Cic.

ăbūtor -ūti -ūsus sum, dep., with abl., *to make full use of, to use fully*. (1) in a good, or neutral, sense: nisi omni tempore, quod mihi lege concessum est, abusus ero, Cic.;

sagacitate canum ad utilitatem nostram, Cic. (2) in a bad sense, *to abuse, to waste*: militum sanguine, Cic.; insolenter et immodice indulgentia populi Romani, Liv. Esp., *to use a word wrongly*: verbo, Cic.

Ăbўdus (Abydos) -i, f. ("Αβυδος). (1) *a town in Asia Minor, on the Hellespont*. (2) *a town in Egypt*.
¶ Hence adj., **Abydēnus** -a -um: iuvenis, or absol., *Leander*, Ov.; m. pl. **Abydēni** -orum, *the inhabitants of Abydos*: Liv.

Ăbўla -ae, f. ('Αβύλη), *a mountain on the African side of the Straits of Gibraltar, forming one of the so-called Pillars of Hercules* (now *Sierra Zimiera*).

ac, *see* atque.

Ăcădēmīa -ae, f. ('Ακαδήμεια), *the Academy*, *a grove near Athens where Plato taught*. Hence, meton., *the Academic school of philosophy*: Cic. Hence also Cicero's use of this term for two of his estates, one near Puteoli and another at Tusculum.

Ăcădēmĭcus -a -um ('Ακαδημικός), *belonging to the Academy at Athens*: philosophi, Cic. M. pl. as subst. **Ăcădēmĭci** -orum, *the Academic philosophers*. N. pl. **Ăcădēmĭca** -orum, *a treatise of Cicero on the Academic philosophy*.

Ăcădēmus -i, m. ('Ακάδημος), *a Greek hero, after whom the Academia was named*.

ăcălanthis -ĭdis, f. (ἀκαλανθίς)=acanthis; q.v.: Verg.

Ăcămās -antis, m. ('Ακάμας). (1) *son of Theseus and Phaedra*: Verg. (2) *a promontory in Cyprus*: Plin.

ăcanthis -ĭdis, f. (ἀκανθίς), *a small singing bird*, perhaps *the siskin*: Plin.

¹**ăcanthus** -i, m. (ἄκανθος). (1) *bear's foot, a plant*: Verg. (2) *a thorny evergreen Egyptian tree*: Verg.

²**Ăcanthus** -i, f. ("Ακανθος), *a town of Chalcidice*.

ăcapnŏs -ŏn (ἄκαπνος), *without smoke*: ligna, *burning without smoke*, Mart.

Ăcarnānĭa -ae, *Acarnania, a country on the west of Greece, between Epirus and Aetolia*.
¶ Hence adj. **Acarnānĭcus** -a -um, *Acarnanian*: Liv.; subst. **Acarnān** -ānis, *an Acarnanian*: Verg., Ov.

Ăcastus -i, m. ("Ακαστος). (1) *son of the Thessalian king Pelias, father of Laodamia, brother of Alcestis*. (2) *a slave of Cicero*.

Acca Lārentia, *a Roman goddess whose festival* (Larentalia) *was on Dec. 23*; *according to one legend, the wife of the herdsman Faustulus, and the nurse of Romulus and Remus*.
¶ Hence **Lārentalia** or **Accālia** -ĭum, n. *her festival at Rome in December*.

accēdo -cēdĕre -cessi -cessum (ad/cedo), *to approach, to come near*.
LIT., of persons, with the accusative and ad: ad urbem, Cic.; alicui ad aurem et dicere, *to approach anyone to whisper*, Cic.; with in: in aedes, Cic.; in funus, *to join the funeral procession*, Cic.; with simple acc.: scopulos, Verg.; Iugurtham, Sall.; absol., *to approach*: Cic. Esp. (1) *to come as a suppliant*: senatus supplex accedit ad Caesarem, Cic.; quo accedam aut quos appellem, Sall. (2) *to come as an enemy*: usque ad castra, Caes.; with simple acc.: loca hostiliter, Sall. (3) *to come to an auction to bid*: ad illud scelus sectionis, Cic.; ad hastam, Liv.

TRANSF., (1) of persons: ad amicitiam Philippi, Nep.; sed propius accedam, de his nostris testibus dicam, Cic. (2) of lifeless subjects: febris accedit, Cic.; accedit manus extrema operibus, Cic.; fervor accedit capiti, *the wine mounts to his head*, Hor. (3) of time, *to approach*: quo propius ad mortem accedam, Cic. (4) *to enter upon work*: ad rem publicam, *to begin public life*, Cic.; ad vectigalia, *to engage in the collection of the taxes*, Cic. (5) *to assent to*: ad condiciones, Cic. (6) *to be added*: ad eas (naves) captivae Massiliensium accesserunt sex, Caes.; quo plus aetatis ei accederet, *the older he became*, Cic.; iis tantum fiduciae accessit ut, Caes.; hence the phrases, huc accedit, eo accedit, often followed by ut and quod, with the meaning of simply *moreover*. (7) of things, *to fall to one's share, to come to one*: num tibi stultitia accessit, Pl.; alicui animus accedit, Cic. (8) *to approach, to become like*: propius ad deos, Cic.

accĕlĕro -are. (1) transit., *to quicken, to accelerate*: iter, Caes.; consulatum alicui, Tac. (2) intrans., *to hasten*: si accelerare volent, Cic.; accelera, signifer, Liv.

accendo -cendĕre -cendi -censum (ad/*cando, causat. of candeo), *to kindle, to set on fire.* LIT., faces, Cic.; tus, Liv. Also of light without reference to fire, *to light up*: luna radiis solis accensa, Cic. TRANSF., *to kindle, fire, inflame, excite,* esp. of feelings: plebis animum, Sall.; animos bello, *to excite to war*, Verg.; ira accensus, Liv.; studia Numidarum in Iugurtham accensa, *the enthusiasm of the N. for I.*, Sall.; also of other forces: cum eo magis vis venti accensa esset, Liv.

accensĕo -censēre -censum, *to reckon in addition*: accenseor illi, *I am his comrade*, Ov.

¶ Hence partic. **accensus** -a -um, *reckoned with.* M. as subst. (1) *an attendant*, esp. on a magistrate. (2) in plural, **accensi**; originally perhaps the *fifth class of Roman citizens*; hence *reserve troops, supernumeraries*, without regular arms, often employed in building roads: Liv.

acceptĭo -ōnis, f. *a reception, acceptance*: Cic.; frumenti, Sall.

accepto -are (freq. of accipio), *to receive*: Pl., Quint.

acceptor -ōris, m. *one who approves*: Pl.

acceptrix -īcis, f. *she who receives*: Pl.

acceptus -a -um, partic. from accipio; q.v.

accerso=arcesso; q.v.

accessĭo -ōnis, f. (accedo), *a going* or *coming to.* LIT., suis accessionibus, Cic. TRANSF., (1) *increase*: dignitatis, Cic.; pecuniae, Nep. (2) *a thing added, appendage*: accessionem adiunxit aedibus, Cic.; minima accessio semper Epirus regno Macedoniae fuit, Liv.

accessus -ūs, m. (accedo), *an approach to.* (1) of movement. LIT., ad urbem nocturnus, Cic.; accessus stellarum et recessus, Cic.; accessus et recessus aestuum, *ebb and flow*, Cic. TRANSF., ad causam, Cic. (2) *opportunity of approach, access*: dare alicui accessum, Ov. (3) *means of approach, entrance*: omnem accessum lustrare, Verg.

¹**accīdo** -cīdĕre -cīdi -cisum (ad/caedo). LIT., *to hew* or *hack at*: aut ab radicibus

subruere aut accidere arbores, Caes. TRANSF., *to weaken, ruin*: Latinorum etsi pariter accisae copiae sint, Liv.; res accisae, Cic.

²**accĭdo** -cĭdere -cĭdi (ad/cado), *to fall down, to fall to.* LIT., ad terram, Pl. Esp. (1) of missiles: tela ab omni parte accidebant, Liv. (2) *to fall at the feet of*, *to ask assistance*: ad pedes omnium, Cic. (3) *to come to the ears* or *notice of*: vox accidit ad hostes, Liv. TRANSF., (1) *to happen* (generally of misfortunes, opposed to evenio): si quid adversi accidisset, Caes.; si quid alicui accidat, *if anything happens*, i.e. *if he dies*, Cic.; often impers., followed by ut: casu accidit ut id primus nuntiaret, Cic.; by quod: accidit perincommode quod eum nusquam vidisti, Cic. L.; by infin.: nec acciderat mihi opus esse, Cic. L. (2) *to fall out*: ut omnia contra opinionem acciderent, Caes.

acciĕo -ēre, obs. form of accio; q.v.

accingo -cingĕre -cinxi -cinctum. LIT., *to gird to* or *on*: ensem lateri, Verg.; miles non accinctus, *unarmed*, Tac. TRANSF., *to equip, to arm*; reflex., se accingere, and pass., accingi. (1) *to arm oneself*: studio popularium accinctus, Tac.; magicas accingier artes, Verg. (2) *to make oneself ready*: accingi ad consulatum, *to strive for the consulship*, Liv.; in audaciam, Tac.; praedae, Verg.; with infin.: Verg., Tac.; accingunt operi=se accingunt operi, Verg.

accĭo -ire -īvi (-ii) -ītum, *to call to, summon, fetch*: haruspices ex Etruria, Cic.; aliquem in adoptionem, Tac.

accĭpĭo -cĭpĕre -cēpi -ceptum (ad/capio), *to take, receive* a person or thing. So: accipere pecuniam, Cic.; alvus omne quod accepit cogit atque confundit, Cic.; aliquem gremio, Verg. Also in a number of special significations. (1) of the senses, *to hear*: orationem, Cic.; pronis auribus accipi, *to be willingly listened to*, Tac.; *to feel*: dolorem, Cic. (2) *of the understanding, to grasp*: quae parum accepi, Cic.; *to learn*: primas artes ab iisdem magistris, Ov.; usum ac disciplinam, Caes.; of the judgment, *to take*: aliquid in bonum partem, *to take in good part*, Cic.; verisimilia pro veris, Liv.; with double acc.: beneficium contumeliam, *to take a kindness for an insult*, Cic. (3) *to accept, not reject*: pacem, Liv.; omen, Cic.; legem, Cic. (4) *to receive persons in a friendly manner*: Romanos in arcem, Liv.; in amicitiam, Cic.; in deditionem, Caes.; *as a guest*: hospitio, Cic. (5) *to treat a person in any way*: leniter clementerque, Cic.; miseris modis, Pl. (6) of business transactions: aliquid (alicui) acceptum referre, *to enter on the credit side* of an account book, Cic.; and so generally, *to consider oneself indebted to someone for a thing*: Cic., Caes.; acceptum refero versibus esse nocens, Ov.

¶ Hence partic. (with compar. and superl.) **acceptus** -a -um, *welcome, pleasant, agreeable.* (1) of persons, with the dat.: qui maxime plebi acceptus erat, Caes. (2) of things: nihil est deo acceptius quam, etc., Cic.

accĭpĭter -tris, m. LIT., *a hawk*: Cic., Hor., Verg. TRANSF., pecuniae, *an avaricious person*, Pl.

accĭtus -ūs, m. *a summons*: Cic., Verg.

Accius -a -um, *name of a Roman* gens, *the most famous member of which was L. Accius, the tragic poet* (170–c. 85 B.C.), *junior to and rival of Pacuvius.* Adj. **Accīānus** -a -um, *of Accius*: versus, Cic.

acclāmātĭo -ōnis, f. (acclamo), *a loud cry.* (1) *an outcry against*: non modo ut acclamatione sed ut convicio et maledictis impediretur, Cic. (2) *a cry of approbation*: Liv., Suet.

acclāmo -are (ad/clamo). (1) *to cry out at* (in derision or disapproval): alicui, Cic.; populus cum risu acclamavit ipsa esse, Cic. (2) *to cry out* in approval: omnes acclamarunt gratias se inter cetera etiam ob hoc agere, quod, Liv. (3) with acc. of person, *to name by acclamation*: aliquem servatorem liberatoremque, Liv.; si nocentem acclamaverant, Tac.

acclāro -are, *to make clear, to reveal* (of omens): Liv.; uti tu signa nobis certa acclarassis (for acclaraveris), Liv.

acclīnis -e. LIT., *leaning on anything*: trunco arboris, Verg. TRANSF., *inclined to*: acclinis falsis animus, Hor.

acclino -are (ad/*clino). LIT., *to lean on anything*: se in illum, Ov.; castra tumuli sunt acclinata, Liv. TRANSF., *to incline to*: haud gravate se acclinaturos ad causam senatus, Liv.

acclivis -e (ad/clivus), *inclined upwards*: pars viae, Cic.; collis leniter ab infimo acclivis, Caes.

acclivĭtas -ātis, f. *acclivity, inclination upwards*: Caes.

acclivus -a -um, *see* acclivis.

accŏla -ae, m. or f. (ad/colo), *one who lives near, a neighbour*: Oceani, Liv.; Cereris, *near the temple of Ceres*, Cic.; as adj.: pastor accola eius loci, *dwelling near that place*, Liv.; accolae fluvii, *neighbouring rivers*, Tac.

accŏlo -cŏlĕre -cŏlŭi -cultum, *to live near*: locum, Cic.; gentes quae Macedoniam accolunt, Liv.

accommŏdātĭo, adv. from accommodo; q.v.

accommŏdātĭo -ōnis, f. (1) *a proportion* or *adjusting of one thing to another*: verborum et sententiarum ad inventionem, Cic. (2) *courteousness, complaisance*: ex liberalitate atque accommodatione magistratuum, Cic.

accommŏdātus -a um, partic. from accommodo; q.v.

accommŏdo -are (ad/commodo), *to fit, put on.* LIT., insignia, Caes.; coronam sibi ad caput, Cic.; lateri ensem, Verg. TRANSF., *to make suitable, to adjust*: testes ad crimen, Cic.; orationem auribus auditorum, Cic.; in omnem eventum consilia, Liv.; se accommodare *or* accommodari, *to adapt oneself*: ad voluntatem alicuius et arbitrium et nutum totum se fingere et accommodare, Cic.

¶ Hence partic. (with compar. and superl.) **accommŏdātus** -a -um, *adapted, suitable to.* (1) of things, with ad and the acc.: puppes ad magnitudinem fluctuum tempestatemque accommodatae, Caes.; with dat.: oratio hominum sensibus ac mentibus accommodata, Cic. (2) of persons, with ad and the acc.: homo ad Verris flagitia libidinesque accommodatus, Cic.; with dat.: servus vilissimus nec cuiquam serio ministerio accommodatus, Tac.

¶ Adv. **accommŏdātē**, *agreeably to*: ad veritatem, Cic.

accommŏdus -a -um, *fit, adapted to*: Verg.

accongĕro -gĕrĕre -gessi, *to bring together*: Pl.

accrēdo -crēdere -credĭdi -creditum (ad/credo), *to believe, give credence to*: alicui, Hor.; absol.: vix accredens, Cic.

accresco -crescĕre -crēvi -crētum (ad/cresco), *to grow, to increase.* LIT., flumen subito accrevit, Cic. TRANSF., cum dictis factisque omnibus ad fallendum instructis varia accresceret fides, Liv.; trimetris accrescere iussit nomen iambeis, *ordered to be joined to*, Hor.

accrētĭo -ōnis, f. (accresco), *increase*: luminis, Cic.

accŭbĭtĭo -ōnis, f. (accubo), *the act of reclining at table*: Cic.

accŭbĭtus -ūs, m.=accubitio; q.v.

accŭbo -are (ad/cubo), *to lie beside.* In gen., with dat. or absol., of persons: Pl., Verg.; of things: cadus Sulpiciis horreis, Hor. Esp., *to recline at table*: in convivio, Cic.; cum aliquo, *next to*, Pl.; apud aliquem, *at the house of* (as a guest), Cic.; accuba, *take your place*, Pl.

accūdo -ĕre, *to hammer together*: Pl.

accumbo -cumbĕre -cŭbui -cŭbĭtum (ad/*cumbo), *to lie down*: in via, Pl. Especially at the dinner table, where each person lay upon a sofa, supported on his left elbow: in sinu alicuius, *to sit next to anyone at table*, Liv.; cum aliquo, *next to*, Mart.; apud aliquem, *at the house of* (as a guest), Cic.

accŭmŭlātē, adv. from accumulo; q.v.

accŭmŭlātor -ōris, m. *one who heaps together*: opum, Tac.

accŭmŭlo -are (ad/cumulo), *to heap up, to accumulate.*
LIT., auget, addit, accumulat, Cic.
TRANSF., (1) *to heap on a person, give in abundance*: alienas res, Liv.; alicui summum honorem, Ov.; also with acc. of person and abl. of thing: animam nepotis his donis, Verg. (2) *to increase*: caedem caede, Lucr.; curas, Ov.
¶ Hence, from partic., adv. **accŭmŭlātē**, *abundantly, copiously*: Cic. L.

accūrātē, adv. from accuro; q.v.

accūrātĭo -ōnis, f. *accuracy, carefulness*: Cic.

accūrātus, partic. from accuro; q.v.

accūro -are (ad/curo), *to take care of, to prepare with care*: Pl.; victum et cultum, Cic.

¶ Hence partic. (with compar. and superl.) **accūrātus** -a -um, *careful, exact, accurate*: oratio, Cic.; accuratiorem delectum habere, Liv.
¶ Adv. **accūrātē**, *carefully, exactly, accurately*: perscribere, Cic.; aedificare, Caes.

accurro -currĕre -curri and -cucurri -cursum (ad/curro), *to run to*: ad praetorem, Cic.; equo admisso ad aliquem, Caes.; of ideas, *to occur*: istae imagines ita nobis dicto audientes sunt, ut, simulatque velimus, accurrant, Cic.

accursus -ūs, m. *a running to, concourse*: Tac.

accūsābĭlis -e, *blameworthy*: Cic.

accūsātĭo -ōnis, f. (1) *an accusation*: accusationem factitare, Cic.; comparare atque constituere, *to prepare with evidence*, Cic.; plur.: acres accusationes, Cic. (2) *an* *indictment* : accusationis quinque libri, *of the orations against Verres*, Cic.

accusātīvus -a -um (accuso), *accusative* : casus, Quint.

accūsātor -ōris, m. (1) *an accuser* (strictly only in regard to state offences, while petitor is a plaintiff in a private suit) : petitoris personam cupere, accusatoris deponere, Cic. (2) *an informer* : Juv.

accūsātōrius -a -um, *pertaining to an accuser* : lex, Cic.; vox, Liv.

¶ Adv. **accūsātōrĭē**, *after the manner of an accuser* : loqui, Cic., Liv.

accūsātrix -īcis, f. *a female accuser* : Pl.

accūsĭto -are (freq. of accuso), *to accuse frequently* : Pl.

accūso -are (ad/causa), *to accuse.*

(1) *to charge before a judge or court* : aliquem ad populum (of the tribunes), Liv. : **a**, with genit., of the offence : aliquem ambitūs, Cic. : **b**, with abl. : de veneficiis, Cic. : **c**, with propter : propter iniurias, Cic. : **d**, with inter : inter sicarios, *of assassination*, Cic. : **e**, with genit., of the punishment : capitis, *on a capital charge*.

(2) *to blame, find fault with* : aliquem aspere in senatu, Cic.; followed by quod or cur with the subj. : Cic.

¹ācer -ĕris, n. *the maple tree* : Plin.; *maple wood* : Plin., Ov.

²ācer -cris -cre (from root ac-, as acuo, acies, etc.), *sharp, cutting.*

LIT., of sharp tools : hastas acri ferro, Tac.

TRANSF., (1) of the senses : **a**, of taste, *biting* : rapula, Hor. : **b**, of touch, *sharp* : dolor corporis cuius morsus est acerrimus, Cic. : **c**, of hearing, *shrill* : vox, Lucr.; flammae sonitus, *crackling*, Verg. : **d**, of smell, *penetrating* : unguenta summa et acerrima suavitate condita, Cic. : **e**, sight, *keen* : acerrimus sensus videndi, Cic.

(2) relating to the mind : **a**, of emotions, *painful* : cura, Lucr. : **b**, of the understanding, *vigorous* : iudicium acrius et certius, Cic. : **c**, of the character, *energetic* : homo ad perdiscendum acerrimus, Cic.; in ferro, *brave in fight*, Cic.; *passionate* : acerrima uxor, Pl.; so of the passions themselves : amor gloriae, Cic.

(3) of other things : egestas, Lucr.; supplicium, Cic.

¶ Hence adv. (with compar. and superl.) **acriter**, *sharply, keenly.* (1) of sight : acriter intueri solem, Cic. (2) of touch : caedunt acerrime virgis, Cic. (3) of the understanding : videre vitia, Cic. (4) of the emotions : exspectare, se morti offerre, Cic. (5) of speech : vituperare, Cic.

ācerbĭtas -ātis, f. *bitterness, harshness.* LIT., fructus magna acerbitate permixtos, Cic. TRANSF., (1) *harshness* : morum, Cic. (2) *painfulness* : temporis Sullani, Cic.; in plur., *calamities* : Cic.

ācerbo -are, *to make bitter, to aggravate* : crimen, Verg.

ācerbus -a -um (from root ac-, as acer, acies, etc.), *bitter.*

LIT., *sour*, used especially of unripe fruit; hence = *raw, unripe, immature* : uva, Phaedr. TRANSF., (1) of sounds, *harsh* : horrorem serrae, Lucr.; acerba sonans, Verg. (2) of the

look, dark, gloomy : vultus acerbi, Ov.; acerba tuens, *with angry look*, Verg. (3) of speech or writing, *bitter* : minaces et acerbae litterae, Cic. (4) of things and events generally, *painful, severe, harsh* : acerbissima tributa, Cic.; incendium, Cic.; frigus, Hor. (5) of persons, *morose* : acerbos e Zenonis schola (of the Stoics), Cic. (6) from the notion of unripeness, *premature* : partus, Ov.; funere, Verg.

¶ Adv. (with compar. and superl.) **ācerbē**, *bitterly, harshly* : accusare, Cic.; acerbius invehi in aliquem, Cic.; acerbissime dicere, Caes.; aliquid ferre, Cic.

ācernus -a -um (¹acer), *made of maple wood* : Verg., Hor.

ācerra -ae, f. *a casket for keeping incense* : Cic., Hor.

Ācerrae -ārum, f. *town in Campania, on the river Clanius* (now *Acerra*).

ācersĕcŏmēs -ae, m. (ἀκερσεκόμης), *having unshorn hair* : Juv.

ācervālis -e, of arguments, *proceeding by accumulation* : Cic. (= Greek σωρείτης).

ācervātim, adv. *by accumulation.* LIT., *in heaps* : Lucr. TRANSF., dicere, *to sum up, to speak comprehensively* : multa acervatim frequentans, *crowding together a number of thoughts*, Cic.

ācervo -are, *to heap up* : promiscue acervati cumuli hominum, Liv. TRANSF., leges, Liv.

ācervus -i, m. *a heap.* LIT., tritici, Cic.; insepulti acervi civium, Cic. TRANSF., (1) *a multitude* : facinorum, Cic. (2) as logical term, *argument by accumulation* : Cic.

ācesco ācescĕre ācŭi (from root ac-, as acerbus, etc.), *to grow sour* : Hor.

Ācesta -ae, f. (᾿Ακέστη), *an old town in the north-west of Sicily*, also called Egesta and Segesta.

¶ Hence subst. **Acestenses** -ĭum, m. pl. *inhabitants of Acesta.*

Ācestes -ae, m. *a king in Sicily, of Trojan descent.*

ācētum -i, n. (from root ac-, as acerbus, etc.). LIT., *vinegar* : Cic. TRANSF., *sharpness, wit* : Italo perfusus aceto, Hor.

Āchāïa -ae, f. (᾿Αχαία), or **Āchāïa** (poet.), *Achaia.* (1) *the Greek country of Achaia*, in the north of the Peloponnese : Ov. (2) *Greece*, in gen. (after Homer's usage) : Prop., Ov. (3) after 146 B.C., *the Roman province of Achaea* (including the whole of Greece except Thessaly) : Cic.

¶ Hence adj. and subst. **Āchaeus** -a -um (᾿Αχαιός), *Achaean, an Achaean.* (1) from Achaia, in Greece : Lucr., Liv. (2) from Greece generally : Plin. (3) from the Roman province of Achaea : Cic. (4) from Achaia, a Greek colony on the Black Sea. F. subst. **Āchāïas** -ădis, *a Greek woman* : Ov. Adj. **Āchāïcus** -a -um, *Achaean, Greek* : Cic., Verg., Hor. F. subst. **Āchāïs** -ĭdos, *an Achaean woman* : Ov.; poet. = *Greece* : Ov. Adj. **Āchāïus** -a -um, *Greek* : Verg. Adj. and subst. **Āchīvus** -a -um, *Achaean, Greek* : Cic., Hor., Ov.

Āchaemĕnēs -is, m. (᾿Αχαιμένης), *ancestor of Cyrus and founder of the Persian line of the Achaemenidae.*

¶ Hence adj. **Achaemĕnĭus** -a -um, *Persian* : Hor., Ov.

Ăcharnae -orum, f. (*'Αχαρναί*), *a town and deme in Attica.*

Ăchātes -ae, m. (*'Αχάτης*). (1) *a river in Sicily.* (2) *a friend of Aeneas.*

Ăchĕlōus -i, m. (*'Αχελῶος*), *the longest river in Greece, rising in Epirus and flowing between Acarnania and Aetolia.* ¶ Hence, f. subst. **Ăchĕlōĭăs** -ădis, *daughter of the river-god Achelous*: Ov. Adj. **Ăchĕlōĭus** -a -um, *belonging to the river-god Achelous*: Ov. F. subst. **Ăchĕlōĭdes** -um, *daughters of Achelous, the Sirens*: Ov.

Ăchĕron -ontis, m. (*'Αχέρων*). (1) *a river in Thesprotia, flowing through the swamp Acherusia* (now *Gurla*, or *river of Suli*). (2) *a river in Brutii, in southern Italy* (now *Mucone* or *Lese*). (3) mythol., *a river in the lower world, hence the lower world itself*: Acheronta movebo, Verg.; fugere Acheronta, *to become immortal*, Hor. ¶ Also found in old Latin form **Ăchĕruns** -untis, m. and f., used esp. by Pl. and Lucr. ¶ Hence adj. **Ăchĕrunticus** -a -um, Pl., Hor.; adj. **Ăchĕrusius** -a -um, Lucr.; f. subst. **Ăchĕrusia** -ae. (1) a swamp in Thesprotia in Epirus. (2) a lake in Campania. (3) a cavern in Bithynia.

Ăchĕrontia -ae, f. *a small town in Apulia*: Hor.

Ăchilles -is, m. (*'Αχιλλεύς*), and **Ăchillēus** -ĕi, m. *a Greek hero, son of Peleus and Thetis.* Hence *any brave, handsome man, a hero*: Pl., Verg. ¶ Hence adj. **Achillēus** -a -um, *relating to Achilles*: Verg., Ov.; m. subst. **Achillīdes** -ae (*'Αχιλλείδης*), *a descendant of Achilles*: Ov.

Achīvus -a -um = Achaeus; q.v.

Achradīna -ae, f. (*'Αχραδινή*), *part of the city of Syracuse*: Cic., Liv.

Ăcīdălĭa -ae, f. (*'Ακιδαλία*), *a surname of Venus, from the fountain Acidalia in Boeotia, where the Graces, daughters of Venus, bathed.* Adj. **Acīdălĭus** -a -um, *belonging to Venus*: nodus, *the girdle of Venus*, Mart.

ăcidus -a -um (from root ac-, as acuo, acetum, etc.), *sharp*. LIT., *sour in taste, acid*: Hor. TRANSF., *sour, disagreeable*: Hor.

ăcĭēs -ēi, f. (ac-, root of acuo), *keenness, edge.* LIT., *of a sharp instrument*: securis, Cic.; falcis, Verg. TRANSF., (1) *of keenness in various senses*: patimur hebescere aciem horum auctoritatis, Cic. Esp. *of the mind, penetration, insight*: animi, ingenii, mentis, Cic.; and *of the eye, as*: **a**, *a piercing look*: ne vultum quidem atque aciem oculorum ferre potuisse, Caes.: **b**, *keen vision*: bonum incolumis acies, malum caecitas, Cic.: **c**, *the pupil of the eye*: Cic.; *the eye itself*: Verg. (2) *of the front of an army as drawn up for battle*: **a**, *a single line*: prima, Caes.; novissima, Liv.: **b**, *the whole army*: aciem instruere, Cic.: **c**, *battle, battlefield*: Pharsalica, Cic.; in acie vincere, Caes.; poet.: Vulcania, *mass of fire*, Verg.; fig., *a battle in words*: Cic.

Ăcīlĭus -a -um, *name of a Roman gens*; esp. of Man. Acil. Glabrio, Consul 192 B.C., *conqueror of Antiochus and the Aetolians.*

ăcīnăcēs -is, m. (ἀκινάκης), *a short Persian sabre*: Hor.

ăcīnus -i, m. and **ăcĭnum** -i, n. *a berry* (esp. *grape*): Plin.; *the stone or seed of the berry*: Cic.

ăcĭpenser -ĕris, also **ăcĭpensis** -is, m. (perhaps from root ac-, as in acuo, etc.), *the sturgeon, a fish prized by the Romans*: Cic., Hor.

Ācis -idis, m. (*"Ακις*). (1) *a river in Sicily, near Etna, famous for its cold water* (now *Fiume di Iaci*): Ov. (2) mythol., *a beautiful shepherd, lover of Galatea*: Ov.

āclys -ўdis, f. (perhaps shortened from ἀγκυλίς), *a small javelin*: Verg.

Acmŏnĭdes -ae, m. (*'Ακμονίδης*), *one of the workmen of Vulcan*: Ov.

ăcŏnītum -i, n. (ἀκόνιτον), *a poisonous herb, monk's hood, aconite*: Plin., Ov., Verg.; in poetry, *a strong poison* generally: Ov., Juv.

acq. = adq.; q.v.

Acrae -arum, f. *a city in Sicily, near Syracuse.*

Acraeus -a -um (ἀκραῖος), *that which is upon a height, surname of Jupiter and Juno*: Liv.

Acragas -antis, m. (*'Ακράγας*); also **Agrigentum** -i, n. *a Doric colony in S.W. Sicily* (now *Agrigento*). ¶ Hence adj. **Acragantinus** -a -um: Lucr.

acrātŏphŏrum -i, n. (ἀκρατοφόρον), *a vessel for holding unmixed wine*: Cic.

ăcrēdŭla -ae, f. Cicero's translation of Aratus' ὀλολυγών; *a bird*, perhaps *the thrush, or the owl, or the nightingale.*

ăcrĭcŭlus -a -um (¹acer), *somewhat sharp in temper*: ille acriculus, senex, Cic.

ăcrĭmōnĭa -ae, f. *sharpness, keenness.* LIT., *of flavours and smells*: Plin. TRANSF., *of speech and action*: Cic.

Ācrĭsĭus -i, m. (*'Ακρίσιος*), *a king of Argos, father of Danaë.* ¶ Hence, f. subst. **Acrĭsĭōnē** -ēs, *Danaë*; m. subst. **Ācrĭsĭōnĭădes** -ae, *Perseus, son of Danaë*; adj. **Acrĭsĭōnēus** -a -um: arces = *Argos*, Ov.

ăcrĭtĕr, adv. from acer; q.v.

ăcrŏāma -ătis, n. (ἀκρόαμα), *that which is heard with pleasure.* Esp. (1) *an entertainment at table of reading or music*: Cic. (2) *the person who conducts such an entertainment, a reader, actor, or singer*: Cic.

ăcrŏāsis -is, f. (ἀκρόασις), *a reading aloud, recitation*: Cic. L.

Ăcrŏcĕraunĭa -orum, n. pl. (1) *part of the Ceraunian mountains, see* Ceraunius. (2) *any dangerous place*: haec Acroceraunia vita, Ov.

Ăcrŏcŏrinthus -i, f. (*'Ακροκόρινθος*), *the citadel of Corinth*: Liv.

¹acta -ae, f. (ἀκτή), *the sea-shore, the beach, especially as a place of recreation*: Cic., Verg.; hence, meton., *the pleasures of life at the seaside*: Cic.

²acta -ōrum. n. subst. from partic. of ago; q.v.

Actaeōn -ŏnis, m. (*'Ακταίων*), *son of Aristaeus, a hunter, who for seeing Diana while bathing was turned into a stag, and torn to pieces by his hounds.*

actarius -i, m. (adj., with subst. scriba understood), *a registrar or short-hand writer*: Suet.

Actē -ēs, f. (*'Ακτή*), *coast land, an old name of Attica.* ¶ Hence adj. and subst. **Actaeus** -a -um, *from Attica or Athens*: Verg., Ov. F. adj. **Actĭăs** -ădis, *Attic*: Verg.

Actiacus ... ad

Actĭacus -a -um, adj. from Actium; q.v.

actĭo -ōnis, f. (ago), *action, doing*: gratiarum, *giving of thanks*, Cic.; primas eius actiones horreo, Cic.
Often also of particular forms of action, such as (1) *the action of any magistrate, proposal*: consularis, Cic.; actio de pace sublata est, Liv. (2) *action in the theatre, plot*: Cic. (3) *action in a court of law*: **a**, *the bringing of an action*: inquieta urbs actionibus, Tac.: **b**, *the action itself*: actionem instituere, constituere, intendere, Cic.; and so: **c**, *the formula used in bringing an action*: actiones componere, *to draw statements of claim*, Cic.; and gen., *a legal formula*: actiones Hostilianae, Cic.: **d**, *the speech on an indictment*: actiones Verrinae, Cic.: **e**, *the permission or right to bring an action*: actionem habere, postulare, dare, accipere, restituere, Cic.

actĭto -are (freq. of ago), *to be busy in pleading or acting*, used of the theatres and courts of law: causas multas, Cic.; tragoedias, Cic.

Actĭum -i, n. (Ἄκτιον). (1) *a promontory in Acarnania*, on which stood a temple of Apollo; nearby was fought the naval battle (31 B.C.) in which Augustus conquered Antony and Cleopatra. (2) *a roadstead near Corcyra.*
¶ Hence adj. **Actĭacus** -a -um: frondes, *the leaves of the bay tree*, sacred to Apollo, Ov.; legiones, *those that fought at Actium*, Tac. Adj. **Actĭus** -a -um: bella, *the battle of Actium*, Verg.

actor -ōris, m. (ago). (1) *a driver*: pecoris, Ov. (2) *a doer* of anything: rerum, Cic.; esp.: **a**, *a dramatic actor, player*: Cic.: **b**, *a public speaker*: Cic.: **c**, *the plaintiff in an action*: Cic.: **d**, *the manager of property or finances*: actor publicus, *one who manages public property*, Tac.

Actŏrĭdēs -ae, m. (Ἀκτορίδης), *a descendant of Actor*; e.g., Menoetius (son of Actor), or *Patroclus* (grandson of Actor): Ov.

actuarĭolum -i, n. (dim. of actuarius), *a small skiff*: Cic.

actŭārĭus -a -um (ago), *easily moved, swift*: actuaria navis, *a swift-sailing vessel*, Caes.; navigium actuarium, Caes. F. as subst. **actŭārĭa** -ae: Cic.

actŭōsus -a -um, *active*: virtus, Cic. Adv. **actŭōsē**, *actively, with energy*: Cic.

actus -ūs, m. (ago). (1) *driving, moving, movement*: fertur magno mons improbus actu, Verg.; esp. of the driving of cattle: levi admonitu, non actu, inflectit illam feram, Cic.; hence *right of way for driving cattle, carts, etc.*: Cic. (2) *doing, action*, esp. on the stage: so: **a**, as the *presentation of a piece on the stage*: fabellarum, Liv.: **b**, *division of a piece, an act*: in extremo actu corruere, Cic.; fig., extremus actus aetatis, Cic.

actūtum, adv. (actus), *immediately, directly*: Pl., Liv., Verg.

ăcŭla -ae (dim. of aqua), *a rivulet*: Cic.

ăcŭlĕātus -a -um (aculeus), *provided with prickles or stings*. Lit., of plants and animals: Plin. Transf., *sharp pointed, stinging*: litterae, Cic.; sophisma, *hair-splitting, subtle*, Cic.

ăcŭlĕus -i, m. (dim. of acus), *sting, point*. Lit., esp. of plants and animals, also of missiles, *sting, painful thoughts, cutting*

remarks: sagittae, Liv. Transf., especially in plur.: aculei in C. Caesarem, Cic.; sollicitudinum, Cic.; orator cum delectatione aculeos relinquit in animis, Cic.

ăcūmen -ĭnis, n. (acuo), *the sharp point of anything*. Lit., stili, Cic. Transf., (1) *point* (of something witty): etiam interpretatio nominis habet acumen, Cic. (2) *sharpness of understanding*: ubi est acumen tuum? Cic. (3) *cunning, trickery*: argutiae et acumen eius, Cic.

ăcŭo -ŭĕre -ŭi -ūtum (ac-, root of acus and acies), *to sharpen to a point*. Lit., *to whet* (a cutting instrument): gladios, Liv., Cic., Verg. Transf., (1) *to sharpen, practise*: linguam exercitatione dicendi, *to make more fluent*, Cic.; ingenia adulescentium, Cic. (2) *to inflame*: iram hostis ad vindicandas iniurias, Liv. (3) *to encourage, incite*: iuventutem ad dicendum, Cic.
¶ Hence partic. (with compar. and superl.) **ăcūtus** -a -um, *sharpened, pointed, acute*. Lit., sagitta, Ov.; of anything pointed: cornua lunae, Cic. Transf., (1) of physical sensations: **a**, of hearing, *shrill*: vox, Cic.; acc. neut. as adv.: resonare triste et acutum, Hor.: **b**, of touch, *piercing*: gelu, Hor.: **c**, more generally, *painful*: morbus, Hor.; poet.: acuta belli, *the hardships of war*, Hor. (2) of mental perceptions: **a**, *sharp, keen*: populi Romani oculos esse acres atque acutos, Cic.; acc. neut. as adv.: cernis acutum, *you have keen sight* (for the failings of others), Hor.: **b**, of persons, *keen-sighted, intelligent*: homo acutus magis quam eruditus, Cic.; of orators, *effective*: orator, Cic.
¶ Adv. **ăcūtē**, *keenly*. (1) of the senses: cernere, Lucr.; of the voice, *shrilly*: sonare, Cic. (2) of the understanding, *intelligently*: acute argute responderre, Cic.

ăcus -ūs, f. (ac-, root of acuo and acies), *a needle, a bodkin*: vulnus, quod acu punctum videtur, Cic.; acu pingere, *to embroider*, Verg.; acu rem tetigisti, *you have hit the nail on the head*, Pl.

ăcūtŭlus -a -um (dim. of acutus), *somewhat subtle*: Cic.

ăcūtus -a -um, partic. from acuo; q.v.

ad, prep. with acc., expressing primarily direction *towards, to* a point (opp. ab); also secondarily presence *at* it.
Lit., in space. (1) of motion, such as going or sending, *to*: ad Dianae (sc. aedem) venire, *to come to Diana's temple*, Ter.; concurrere ad curiam, Cic.; ad me, *to my house*, Cic. Often strengthened by usque: usque ad castra, Caes. Also of writing to, and of looking towards; and of extension: ab unguibus usque ad verticem, Cic. (2) of rest *at* or *near*: sedere ad latus eius, Cic.; esse ad portas, Cic.; ad iudicem, *before a judge*, Cic.; pugna ad Cannas, Liv.
Transf., of time. (1) *to, until*: ab hora octava ad vesperum, Cic.; ad hoc tempus, *till now*, Cic.; quem ad finem? *how long?* Cic.; ad summam senectutem, Cic. (2) *at, about*: nos te hic ad mensem Ianuarium exspectamus, Cic.; ad lucem, *in the morning*, Cic.; ad tempus, *in due time*, Cic.
Transf., of other relations, some suggesting movement towards, others rest at. (1) of aim or purpose, *towards, for*: adiutorem

[10]

ad iniuriam, Cic.; ad id, *for that object*, Liv.; servos ad remum, Liv.; so natus ad, *born to*, *born for*, and aptus ad, *fit for*. (2) of concern, *to*, *in relation to*: ad rem, *to the point*; quid ad me? *what is that to me?* Cic. So esp. with attineo and pertineo. Similarly in qualification and limitation: impiger ad labores belli, Cic. (3) of comparison, *compared with*: scuta ad amplitudinem corporum parum lata, Liv. (4) of extent, figuratively, *to*, *up to*, *down to*: virgis ad necem caedi, Cic.; homo non ad extremum perditus, Liv.; ad unum, *to a man*. (5) of addition: ad cetera, Cic.; ad omnia, *to crown all*, Liv.; ad hoc, *besides*, Sall., Liv. (6) of conformity or correspondence, *according to*: ad istorum normam, Cic.; ad verbum, *literally*, Cic.   (7) of approximation, *about*, very often with numerals: ad ducentos, Cic.; so sometimes adverbially, without acc.   (8) of occasion, *at*, *on*, *in consequence of*: ad famam belli novas legiones scribere, Liv. (9) of accompaniment, *to the sound of*, *by the light of*: ad tibiam, Cic.

ădactĭo -ōnis, f. (adigo), *a driving to*, *compulsion*: iurisiurandi (*obligation*), Liv.

ădactus -ūs, m. (adigo), *a bringing to*: dentis, *a bite*, Lucr.

ădaequē, adv. *in like manner*: Pl.

ădaequo -are (ad/aequus).   (1) transit., *to make equal with*. LIT., moles moenibus, Caes. TRANSF., cum virtute fortunam, Cic.; se virtute nostris, Cic.; so *to compare*: formam, aetatem, genus mortis magni Alexandri fatis, Tac.

    (2) intransit., *to match*, *come near to*: altitudinem muri, Caes.; deorum vitam, Cic.

ădămantēus -a -um, *hard as steel*: Ov.

ădămantĭnus -a -um (ἀδαμάντινος), *made of hard steel*, *adamantine*: Hor.

ădămas -antis, m. (ἀδάμας).   (1) *the hardest steel*, *adamant*: nexae adamante catenae, Ov.; poet., *anything that is firm*, *unyielding*, *and durable*: in pectore ferrum aut adamanta gerit, Ov.; voce sua adamanta movere, *a heart of steel*, Mart.   (2) *the diamond*: Plin.

ădambŭlo -are, *to walk by* or *near anything*: Pl.

ădămo -are, *to fall in love with*, *to find pleasure in*: equos, Cic.; gloriam, Cic.

ădăpĕrĭo -ăpĕrire -ăpĕrŭi -ăpertum, *to open fully*: adapertae fores portae, Liv.

ădăpertĭlis -e, *that which is capable of being opened*: latus tauri, Ov.

ădapto -are, *to fit to*, *adapt*: Suet.

ădăquo -are, *to supply with water*, *to give to drink*: Plin.

ădauctus -ūs, m. (adaugeo), *an increase*: Lucr.

ădaugĕo -ēre -auxi -auctum.   (1) *to increase*, *to augment*: bonum, Cic.   (2) of sacrifices, *to devote*: Pl.

ădaugesco, -ĕre, *to begin to increase*: Lucr.

ădbĭbo -bibĕre -bĭbi -bĭbĭtum. LIT., *to drink*, *drink in*: Pl., Ter. TRANSF., of the ears: verba puro pectore, Hor.

adbĭto -ĕre, *to go near*: Pl.

addĕcet -ĕre, v. impers. *it becomes*, *suits*: Pl.

addensĕo -ēre, and addenso -āre, *to make thick* or *compact*: extremi addensent acies, Verg.

addīco -dīcĕre -dixi -dictum, *to assent to*.

    (1) as t. t. in augury, *to promise favourably* (of the omens of birds): Liv.

    (2) *to award*: **a**, of a judge, especially the praetor (whose formula was do, dico, addico): alicui bona, Cic.; liberum corpus in servitutem, Liv.; esp., *to award a debtor as a slave to his creditor*: ob creditam pecuniam addici, Liv.; addictus, *a debtor thus adjudged a slave*, Liv.: **b**, of an auctioneer, *to knock down to a bidder*: fundum alicui, Cic.; alicui aliquid nummo sestertio, or simply nummo, *to give* (by a fictitious sale), Cic., Hor.; *to put up for sale* (of the vendor): aedes, Cic. TRANSF., regna pecunia, Cic.

    (3) in gen., *to give up* or *over*; *to doom*, *dedicate*, *surrender*: aliquem perpetuae servituti, Caes.; so addictus, *bound*, *pledged*: nullius addictus iurare in verba ministri, Hor.; se alicui, in a bad sense, *to give oneself up to slavishly*: se senatui, Cic.

addictĭo -ōnis, f. (addico), *the judge's award*: bonorum possessionumque, Cic.

addictus -a -um, partic. from addico; q.v.

addisco -discĕre -didĭci, *to learn in addition*: artem, Cic., Ov.

addĭtāmentum -i, n. *an addition*: Ligus, additamentum inimicorum meorum, Cic.

addo addĕre addĭdi addĭtum.   (1) *to give to*, *to bring to*, *to place*. LIT., epistolas in fasciculum, Cic.; soleam pedi, Ov.; of persons: alicui comitem, Verg. TRANSF., *to inspire*, *to cause*, *produce*: mihi alacritatem scribendi, Cic.   (2) *to add*, *join*. LIT., unum granum, Cic.; addendo deducendoque (*by addition and subtraction*) videre quae reliqui summa fiat, Cic. TRANSF., hunc laborem ad cotidiana opera, Caes.; sceleri scelus, Liv. Esp. of speech, writing, and thought: in orationem quaedam, *to make some additions*, Cic; addunt etiam de Sabini morte, *they speak also about the death of S.*, Caes.; with acc. and infin.: addit etiam illud, equos non optimos fuisse, Cic.; adde, or adde huc, or eo, with acc. subst. or quod, *add to this*: adde eo exsilia, luctus, Cic.

addŏcĕo -ēre, *to teach in addition*: Hor.

addŭbĭto -are, *to incline to doubt*, *to begin to doubt*; usually followed by de, in, or indirect question; also transit.: res addubitata, *a question undecided*, Cic.

addūco -dūcĕre -duxi -ductum, *to draw to*.

    (1) *to bring* or *lead* a person or thing *to* a place. LIT., in conspectum populi, Liv.; in ius, or in iudicium, *to bring to justice*, Cic.; aurum secum, Liv.; esp. of bringing water (by an aqueduct, etc.): aquam, Cic. TRANSF., **a**, *to bring to a certain condition*: aliquem in vituperationem, invidiam, Cic.; eo adduxit eos ut, Cic.; se suumque regnum in ultimum discrimen, Liv.: **b**, *to bring a person to a certain state of mind*: in fletum, in metum, Cic.; adduci ad suspicandum, Cic.; followed by ut and the subj.: adducis me ut tibi adsentiar, Cic.; with genit.: in spem adductus conficiendi belli, Sall.; so adductus, *influenced*: spe mercedis, Cic.; absol.: adducor igitur et prope modum adsentior, Cic.

    (2) *to draw to oneself*, *pull in*: parvis colla lacertis (of children embracing their mother), Ov.; funem, Caes.; arcum, Verg. So *to contract*: adducit cutem macies, Ov.

¶ Hence partic. **adductus** -a -um, *contracted*, *taut*; of persons, *strict*: Tac.

¶ Compar. adv. **adductius**: Tac.

ădĕdo -esse -ēdi -ēsum, *to nibble, to gnaw.*
LIT., adesi favi, Liv. TRANSF., scopulus
adesus aquis, Ov.; also in gen., *to consume,
waste away*: non adesa iam sed abundante
etiam pecunia, Cic.

ădemptĭo -ōnis, f. (adimo), *a taking away*:
civitatis, Cic., Tac.

¹**ădĕō**, adv. (ad/eo, old locative case of is), *to
that point, so far*; often strengthened by
usque. (**1**) of space, *so far*: Ter. (**2**) of time,
so long; followed by dum, donec, quoad: Cic.
(**3**) of degree: **a**, *so much, so*; often looking
forward to a consecutive clause with ut: Cic.:
b, *to such an extent, so*, looking back to what
has already been said: adeo prope omnis
senatus Hannibalis fuit, Liv.: **c**, *even, what
is more*: ducem hostium intra moenia atque
adeo in senatu videmus, Cic.: **d**, used encliti-
cally with pron., *just.*: id adeo, Cic.; also
with conj., si, nisi, sive, aut, vel: Cic.:
e, (post-Aug.), *much more*; with a negative,
much less: Tac.

²**ădĕo** -īre -īī -ītum, *to go or come to, approach.*
LIT., ad istum fundum, Cic.; curiam, Liv.
Esp., *to approach for a particular purpose.*
(**1**) adire in praetorem in ius (or, simply, in
ius), *to go to law*, Cic. (**2**) *to travel to, to visit*:
casas aratorum, Cic. (**3**) *to appeal to or consult*: praetorem, magos, aras, Cic. (**4**) *to
approach as an enemy*: ad quemvis numerum
ephippiatorum equitum adire audere, Cic.
TRANSF., (**1**) *to undertake some business*:
ad causas privatas et publicas, Cic.; ad
rempublicam, *to enter public life*, Cic. (**2**) *to
come to some condition, to undergo, incur*:
periculum capitis, Cic. (**3**) legal t. t.: adire
hereditatem, *to enter on an inheritance*, Cic.

ădeps -ipis, c. (connected with ἄλειφα), *the
soft fat of animals*; meton.: Cassii adipes,
the corpulent Cassius, Cic.

ădeptĭo -ōnis, f. (adipiscor), *attainment,
obtaining*: commodi, Cic.

ădēquĭto -are, *to ride to*; with dat.: ipsis
portis, Liv.; with ad: ad nostros, Caes.;
absol.: Liv.

ădesdum, or **ades dum**, *come hither*: Ter.

ădēsŭrĭo -ire, *to hunger after anything*: Pl.

adfābĭlis -e, adj. with compar. (adfor), *easy
to be spoken to, affable*: in omni sermone
adfabilem et iucundam esse velle, Cic.; Verg.

adfābĭlĭtas -ātis, f. (adfabilis), *affability*:
comitas adfabilitasque sermonis, Cic.

adfābrē, adv. (ad/faber), *in a workmanlike
way, skilfully*: factus, Cic.

adfătim, adv. (ad/ obs. fatis), *sufficiently,
enough*: satisfacere alicui, Cic. Subst. with
genit.: copiarum adfatim esse, Liv.

adfātus -ūs, m. (adfor), *an address, speech*: Verg.

adfectātĭo -ōnis, f. (adfecto), *a striving after*:
Germanicae originis, *eagerness to pass for
Germans*, Tac.; imperii, Suet. Esp. *a
striving after effect*: Quint.

adfectātor -ōris, m. (adfecto), *one who strives
after anything*: Quint.

adfectĭo -ōnis, f. (adficio), *manner of being
affected*, and so (**1**) *relation of one thing to
another*: quaedam ad res aliquas adfectio,
Cic. (**2**) *change*: adfectio est animi aut
corporis aliqua de causa commutatio, ut
laetitia, Cic. (**3**) *state, condition*: caeli, Cic.;
firma corporis adfectio, *good health*, Cic.
(**4**) *favourable state of mind, good-will*: Tac.

adfecto -are (adficio), *to strive after.* (**1**) of
material things, *to make for, grasp at*: viam,
Ter.; iter, Cic.; ubi nulla datur dextra
affectare (navem) potestas, Verg. (**2**) of
immaterial things, *to aim at, aspire to*:
regnum, Liv.; famam, Tac.; munditiam,
non adfluentiam, Nep.; bellum Hernicum,
to try to get the command of the war, Liv.;
esp. politically, *to try to win over*: civitates,
Sall. (**3**) *to affect*: in verbis effusiorem cultum, Quint.

¶ Hence partic. **adfectatus** -a -um,
studied: Quint.

¹**adfectus** -ūs, m. (adficio), *a condition, disposition*; esp. of the mind, *a feeling*: animi,
Cic.; veri adfectus, Tac.; often (like adfectio)
friendly feeling, good-will: Tac., Juv.; in
Lucan, plur., objects of such feeling, *loved
ones.*

²**adfectus** -a -um, partic. from adficio; q.v.

adfero adferre attuli adlatum, *to carry* or
bring to.
LIT., aliquid domum, Cic.; epistulam,
litteras, *to bring a letter*, Cic.; is qui litteras
attulit, *the bearer of this letter*, Cic.; si
tantum notas odor attulit auras, Verg.
Esp. of messages, and so also of the news
contained: alicui non iucundissimum nuntium, Cic.; hence absol., *to bring news,
report*: eo de Hortensii morte mihi est
adlatum, *news was brought me*, Cic.; foll. by
acc. and infin.: Caelium ad illum attulisse se
quaerere, etc., Cic.
TRANSF., *to bring*, with physical movement
not necessarily implied. (**1**) *to apply, bring
to bear*: animum vacuum ad res difficiles
scribendas, Cic.; more often with acc. and
dat.: alicui vim, *to offer violence to*, Cic.;
manus, *to lay hands upon*, Cic. (**2**) *to cause,
bring about, occasion*: populo Romano pacem,
tranquillitatem, otium, concordiam, Cic.
(**3**) *to bring forward* by way of excuse or
reason: rationes, cur hoc ita sit, Cic.;
aetatem, Cic. (**4**) *to bring* by way of help,
to contribute: quidquid ad rempublicam
attulimus, Cic.

adfĭcĭo -fĭcĕre -fēci -fectum (ad/facio), *to
influence, to work upon.* (**1**) with adverbs,
to affect in certain ways: exercendum corpus
et ita adficiendum est ut, etc., Cic.; litterae
tuae sic me adfecerunt ut, etc., Cic.; res
quae quodammodo adfectae sunt ad id de
quo quaeritur, *related to*, Cic. (**2**) with
abl. of nouns, *to affect by, treat with,
visit with, present with*; esp. of persons
aliquem maxima laetitia, *to please greatly*,
Cic.; sepultura, *to bury*, Cic.; poena, *to
punish*, Cic.; so in passive: magna difficultate
adfici, *to be placed in a very difficult position*,
Caes.; beneficio, *to be benefited*, Cic.; morbo
gravi et mortifero, Cic.; occasionally of
things: medicamine vultum, Ov. (**3**) absol.,
of the body, *to affect adversely, weaken*:
ut aestus, labor, fames sitisque corpora
adficerent, Liv.

¶ Hence partic. **adfectus** -a -um, *affected,
influenced.* (**1**) with adverbs, *num
manus recte adfecta est cum in tumore est,
Cic.; quomodo sim adfectus, Cic.; eodem
modo erit sapiens adfectus erga amicum,
quo in se ipsum, Cic. (**2**) with abl.,
affected by, furnished with, afflicted by:

virtutibus, Cic.; vitiis, Cic.; senectute, Cic.; vulnere, Liv. (**3**) absol., in two special senses: **a**, of the body, *weakened, sick*: corpus adfectum, Liv.; transf., *respublica*, Liv.: **b**, of undertakings, *worked upon*, and so *nearly* finished: bellum adfectum videmus et, ut vere dicam, paene confectum, Cic.

adfigo -fīgĕre -fixi -fixum (ad/figo), *to fasten to, affix.* Lit., litteram illam (K) ita vehementer ad caput, ut, etc., *to brand*, Cic.; Prometheum Caucaso, Cic.; cruci, Liv.; of trophies of war: signa adfixa delubris, Hor. Transf., Ithaca illa in asperrimis saxis tamquam nidulus adfixa, Cic.; alicui adfixum esse tamquam magistro, *not to leave the side of*, Cic.; ea maxime adfigi animis nostris, *be imprinted*, Cic.

adfingo -fingĕre -finxi -fictum (ad/fingo), *to form in addition.* Lit., esp. of artists: partem corporis, Cic.; ei manus, Cic. Transf., *to invent in addition*: ut intellegatis quid error adfinxerit, Cic.; multa rumore adfingebantur, Caes.

adfinis -e (ad/finis). Lit., *neighbouring*: gens adfinis Mauris, Liv. Transf., (**1**) *related by marriage*: alter mihi adfinis erat, Cic. As subst.: cognati et adfines, *blood relations and connexions by marriage*, Cic. (**2**) *connected with, privy to*: huius suspicionis, Cic.; huic facinori, Cic.

adfinitas -ātis, f. (adfinis), *relationship by marriage.* Lit., adfinitate sese devincire cum aliquo, Cic.; in adfinitatem alicuius pervenire, Cic.; plur.: coniunctio hominum inter homines serpit sensim foras, cognationibus primum, deinde adfinitatibus, deinde amicitiis, Cic. Transf., (**1**) meton., *relations by marriage*: Pl. (**2**) *union* of any kind: litterarum, Quint.

adfirmātio -ōnis, f. *asseveration, positive assertion*: Cic.

adfirmo -are (ad/firmo). (**1**) *to strengthen*: societas iureiurando adfirmatur, Liv. (**2**) *to support a statement, to prove*: quod breviter dictum est rationibus adfirmatum, Cic. (**3**) *to assert as true*: quis rem tam veterem pro certo adfirmet? Liv.; omni adseveratione tibi adfirmo (followed by acc. and infin.), Cic.; with de and the abl.: quid opus est de Dionysio tam valde adfirmare? Cic.
¶ Hence, from partic., adv. **adfirmātē**, *positively*: Cic.

adflātus -ūs, m. (adflo), *a blowing* or *a breathing on.* Lit., ex terra, Cic.; maris, *sea breeze*, Plin.; deneget adflatus ventus et aura suos, Ov.; used of the breath of men and animals: Ov. Transf., *inspiration*: sine aliquo adflatu divino, Cic.

adfleo -flēre -flēvi -flētum (ad/fleo), *to weep at*: Pl., Hor.

adflictātio -ōnis, f. (adflicto), *bodily pain, torture*: Cic.

adflicto -are (freq. of adfligo), *to agitate, to knock about.* Lit., naves tempestas adflictabat, Caes. Transf., *to harass, to distress*: gravius vehementiusque, Cic.; esp. adflictare se, or adflictari, *to be upset*: de quibus vehementer adflictor, Cic.; mulieres adflictare sese, Sall.

adflictor -ōris, m. (adfligo), *a subverter*: dignitatis et auctoritatis, Cic.

adflīgo -flīgĕre -flixi -flictum. Lit., *to dash one thing against another, knock down*, or *knock about*: vasa parietibus, Liv.; statuam, Cic.; equi virique adflicti, *struck down in battle*, Sall.; fusti caput alicuius, Tac.; naves quae gravissime adflictae erant, Caes. Transf., *to weaken, discourage, injure*: non vitium nostrum sed virtus nostra nos adflixit, Cic.; non plane me enervavit nec adflixit senectus, Cic.; causam susceptam, *to drop a law suit*, Cic.; vectigalia bellis adfliguntur, *suffer through war*, Cic.; animos adfligere et debilitare metu, Cic.
¶ Hence partic. **adflictus** -a -um. (**1**) *damaged, shattered*: fortuna, amicitia, Cic. (**2**) of spirits, *broken down, spiritless, desponding*: aegritudine adflictus, debilitatus, iacens, Cic. (**3**) of character, *vile, contemptible*: homo adflictus et perditus, Cic.

adflo -are, *to blow on* or *breathe on*; either transit., with what is breathed or what is breathed on as object of active (or subject of passive); or intransit. Lit., of air, breath, scents: velut illis Canidia adflasset, Hor.; nosque ubi primus equis Oriens adflavit anhelis, Verg.; adflabat acrior frigoris vis, Liv.; adores qui adflarentur e floribus, Cic.; esp. of heat: saucii adflatique incendio, Liv. Transf., of inspiration, influence, rumour, etc.: adflata est numine quando iam propiore dei, Verg.; felix cui placidus leniter adflat amor, Tib.; laetos oculis adflarat honores, Verg.; rumoris nescioquid adflaverat commissione Graecorum frequentiam non fuisse, Cic.

adfluentia -ae, f. (adfluens), *overflow, abundance*: omnium rerum, Cic.

adfluo -flŭĕre -fluxi -fluxum, *to flow, flow to, flow near.* Lit., of water: Aufidus amnis utrisque castris adfluens, Liv.; so of the concourse of atoms in the Epicurean philosophy, Lucr.; esp. of men, *to stream, to flock together*: adfluente cotidie multitudine ad famam belli spernque praedae, Liv.; of immaterial things: nihil ex istis locis non modo litterarum, sed ne rumoris quidem adfluxit, *came in*, Cic. Transf., *to flow freely*; so *to be abundant*, or, with abl., *to abound in*: cum domi otium et divitiae adfluerent, Sall.; divitiis homines adfluere, Lucr.; voluptatibus, Cic.
¶ Hence partic. **adfluens** -entis, *rich, affluent, abounding in*: opibus et copiis, Cic.; omni scelere, Cic.; ex adfluenti, *in abundance*, Tac. Compar. adv. **adfluentius**, *more richly, abundantly*: voluptate adfluentius haurire, Cic.; Tac.

adfor -ari, dep. (**1**st pers. of pres. indic. not found; only used in the other persons of the pres. indic., the **1**st pers. imperf. indic., the **2**nd pers. imper., the infin., and partic.), *to accost, address*: versibus aliquem, Cic. Esp. (**1**) *to say farewell* to the dead: adfari extremum, Verg. (**2**) *to pray to*: deos, Verg.

adformīdo -are, *to be in fear*: Pl.

adfrico -fricare -fricŭi -fricātum, *to rub*: Plin. Transf., *to rub in*: Sen.

adfrictus -ūs, m. (adfrico), *a rubbing on*: Plin.

adfulgeo -fulgēre -fulsi, *to shine, glitter.* Lit., Venus (*the planet*), adfulsit, Ov. Transf., *to shine upon, favour*: vultus ubi tuus adfulsit, Hor.; consuli rei maioris spes adfulsit, Liv.

adfundo -fundĕre -fūdi -fūsum, *to pour upon.*
Lit., venenum vulneri, Tac.; colonia amne
adfusa, *washed by a river*, Plin. Transf., (1)
to throw in, pour in: equitum tria millia
cornibus adfunderentur, Tac. (2) adfundere
se, *or* adfundi, *to prostrate oneself on the
ground*: adfusaque poscere vitam, Ov.

adgĕmo -ĕre, *to groan at, to weep at,* with
dat. : Ov.

adgero -gĕrĕre -gessi -gestum, *to carry to,
bring to.* Lit., luta et limum, Cic.; with dat. :
adgeritur tumulo tellus, Verg. Transf., *to
bring forward*: probra, Tac.

adgestus -ūs, m. (adgero), *a carrying to,
accumulation*: pabulae, materiae, lignorum,
Tac.

adglŏmĕro -are, *to wind on a ball, to add*;
hence of the movement of persons: addunt
se socios et lateri adglomerant nostro,
throng to our side, Verg.

adglūtino -are, *to glue to, fasten to*: Pl., Cic.

adgrăvesco -ĕre, *to become severe, to grow
worse* (of sickness): Ter.

adgrăvo -are, *to make heavier.* Lit., pondus,
Plin. Transf., *to increase, to make worse*: inopiam sociorum, Liv.; summam invidiae
eius, *to heighten*, Liv.

adgrĕdio -ĕre, active form of adgredior; q.v. : Pl.

adgrĕdior -grĕdi -gressus sum, dep. (ad/
gradior), *to go to.*
Lit., *to approach*: ad aliquem, Pl.; non
repellitur quo adgredi cupiet, Cic. Esp. (1)
to approach with words, proposals, etc.; with
acc.: quem ego Romae adgrediar, Cic.;
aliquem pecunia, Sall.; Venerem dictis, *to
address*, Verg. (2) *to approach aggressively,
to attack*: eos impeditos et inopinantes, Caes.;
murum, Sall.
Transf., *to begin, to undertake, to attempt
a thing*; with acc.: ancipitem causam, Cic.;
facinus, *to begin*, Liv.; with ad and the acc. :
ad causam, ad crimen, ad disputationem, ad
historiam, Cic.; with ad and the gerund:
ad dicendum, Cic.; with infin.: oppidum
altissimis moenibus oppugnare, Caes.

adgrĕgo -are, *to add to the flock* (grex); so *to
attach, associate*; with adv.: eodem ceteros
undique collectos naufragos, Cic.; with in
and the acc.: ego te in nostrum numerum
adgregare soleo, Cic.; with ad and the acc. :
se ad eorum amicitiam, Caes.; with dat. : se
Romanis, Liv.

adgressĭo -ōnis, f. (adgredior), *the introduction to a speech*: prima adgressione
animos occupare, Cic.

ădhaerĕo -haerēre -haesi -haesum, *to hang to,
stick to, adhere.*
Lit., manus oneri adhaerentes, *frozen to*,
Tac.; saxis, Liv.
Transf., (1) of place, *to border on, to be
near*: modica silva adhaerebat, Tac. (2) of
various kinds of proximity or attachment:
lateri adhaerere gravem dominum, Liv.; so:
nulli fortunae adhaerebat animus, *depended
upon*, Liv.; of things: cui canis cognomen
adhaeret, *the nickname clings to him*, Hor.;
of an appendage: summusque in margine
versus adhaesit, *was written on the edge for
want of room*, Ov.; so, of persons: te vix
extremum adhaesisse, Cic.

ădhaeresco -haerescĕre -haesi -haesum, *to
hang to, to adhere.*

Lit., gravis lateri craterae limus adhaesit,
Hor.; of burning missiles: ad turrim, Caes.;
fig. : in me uno consulares faces . . . in me
omnia coniurationis tela adhaeserunt; of
shipwrecks: ad saxa sirenum, Cic.; fig. : ad
quamcumque sunt disciplinam quasi tempestate delati, ad eam tamquam ad saxum
adhaerescunt, Cic.
Transf., (1) *to cling to, to remain*: in his
locis adhaerescere, Cic. L.; iustitiae honesta-
tique, *not to swerve from*, Cic.; ad omnium
vestrum studium, *sympathize with*, Cic.
(2) of oratory, *to stick fast, stop*: Cic.

ădhaesĭo -ōnis, f. (adhaereo), *clinging to*:
atomorum, Cic.

ădhaesus -ūs, m. (adhaereo), *an adhering*:
Lucr.

ădhĭbĕo -ēre -ŭi -ĭtum (ad/habeo), *to bring
one thing to another, to apply to.*
Lit., manus genibus, Ov.; manus vectigalibus, *to lay hands on, to seize*, Cic.
Transf., (1) generally, *to apply, bring to
bear*: alicui vim, Cic.; morbis remedia, Cic.;
iambum in fabulis, Cic.; fidem, Cic.;
adhibete animos et mentes vestras, non
solum aures, Cic. (2) *to employ* or *call in* a
person for a purpose: in consilium, Cic.; in
convivium, *to invite*, Cic.; medicum, Cic.;
with double acc.: aliquem patronum, Cic.;
Siciliam testem, Cic. (3) with adv., *to treat*:
aliquem liberaliter, Cic.

ădhinnĭo -ire, *to neigh after.* Lit., Ov.
Transf., sic ad illius orationem adhinnivit,
neighed with joy at, Cic.

ădhortātĭo -ōnis, f. *an exhortation*: Cic.

ădhortātor -ōris, m. *one who exhorts*: operis,
Liv.

ădhortor -ari, dep. *to exhort, encourage* (especially of soldiers): omnes cohortes ordinesque,
Caes.; in bellum, Tac.; ad defendendam
rempublicam, Cic.

ădhūc, adv. *thus far, hitherto.*
(1) of time, *hitherto, up to this* (or *that*)
time: fluctuans adhuc animo, Liv. With neg.,
not yet: adhuc non, Cic. Often with idea of
continuation, *still, even now*: adhuc de
consuetudine exercitationis loquor; nondum
de ratione et sapientia, Cic. Sometimes
strengthened by usque.
(2) in other relations (mainly before and
after the Ciceronian period): a, *besides, also*:
addam minam adhuc, Pl., Tac.: b, in
comparison, *even, still*: adhuc difficilior,
Quint., Tac.: c, =adeo, *so*: Liv.

Ădĭăbēnē -ēs, f. (Ἀδιαβηνή), *a region in north
Mesopotamia.* Adj. **Adĭăbēnus** -a -um,
Adiabenian.

adiăcĕo -ĕre, *to lie by the side of, to be
adjacent*: ad ostium Rhodani, Caes.; with
acc. alone: Etruriam, Liv.; with dat: agro
Romano, Liv.; absol.: adiacente Tibri, Tac.
¶ N. pl. of partic. as subst. **adiăcĕntĭa**,
the neighbourhood: Tac., Plin.

adicio -icĕre -iēci -iectum (ad/iacio). (1) *to
throw to.* Lit., telum in litus, Caes. Transf.,
to cast, direct, apply: oculum hereditati, Cic.;
dictis mentem, Ov. (2) *to add*: aggerem ad
munitiones, Caes.; ad belli laudem doctrinae
et ingenii gloriam, Cic. Special senses: a, *to
add* to what has been said: Liv.: b, *to
outbid* at an auction: supra adiecit Aeschrio,
Cic.

adiectĭo -ōnis, f. (adicio), *an adding to*: adiectione populi Albani, Liv.; inliberali adiectione, *a paltry advance*, Liv.; Hispaniensibus familiarum adiectiones dedit, *gave the right to add*, Tac.

adiectus -ūs, m. (adicio), *an adding to*: Lucr.

ădĭgo -ĭgĕre -ēgi -actum (ad/ago), *to drive to, force to*. LIT., (1) of cattle: pecus e vicis longinquioribus, Caes. (2) of men: aliquem fulmine ad umbras, Verg. (3) of things: triremes per aestuaria, Tac.; quodam loco turri adacta, Caes. TRANSF., *to drive to, to compel to*: ad mortem, Tac.; as legal t. t.: arbitrum adigere aliquem, *bring before an arbiter*, Cic.; as legal and milit. t. t.: aliquem ad iusiurandum, Caes.; iureiurando, *or* sacramento, *to put a man on his oath, to swear in*, Liv.

ădĭmo -ĭmĕre -ēmi -emptum (ad/emo), *to take away*. (1) something painful: vincula canibus, Ov.; dolores, Hor. (2) property: alicui pecuniam, vitam, Cic.; with a and the abl.: Cic. (3) persons: aliquem alicui, Cic.; esp. of death, hence partic. **ademptus** -a -um, poet., *dead*: Hor.

ădĭpātus -a -um (adeps). LIT., *fatty, greasy*. N. pl. as subst. **ădĭpāta** -orum, *pastry made with grease*: Juv. TRANSF., of style, *bombastic*: adipatae dictionis genus, Cic.

ădĭpiscor -ipisci -eptus, dep. (ad/apiscor). LIT., *to come up to, to overtake*: fugientem, Liv. TRANSF., *to obtain*: laudem, Cic.; gloriam ex aliqua re, Nep.; quod adeptus est per scelus, Cic.; with genit.: rerum adeptus, Tac. Perf. partic. adeptus, used passively: eandem accusant adeptam, *when reached*, Cic.

ădĭtĭo -ōnis, f. *a going to, an approach*: Pl.

ădĭtus -ūs, m. (²adeo), *a going to, an approach, access*. LIT., (1) difficiles aditūs habere ad pastum, Cic. (2) *right* or *possibility of entrance to*: aditus in id sacrarium non est viris, Cic.; of audience or a person: homo rari aditus, *difficult of access*, Liv.; faciles aditus ad eum privatorum, Cic.; aditus ad aliquem intercludere, Cic.; ad aliquem postulare, Tac. (3) *entrance to a place, approach*: aditūs insulae muniti, Cic.; aditus templi, Cic., Ov., Liv. TRANSF., *opportunity of obtaining*: ad honorem, Cic.; laudis, Cic.

adiūdĭco -are, *to award as a judge*. LIT., causam alicui, *in favour of anyone*, Cic.; regnum Ptolemaeo, *to assign the kingdom to Ptolemy*, Cic. TRANSF., Italis adiudicat armis, *assigns to the Roman power*, Hor.; alicui salutem imperii huius atque orbis terrarum, Cic.

adiūmentum -i, n. (adiuvo), *help, assistance*: alicuius rei, ad aliquid, alicui rei, in aliqua re, Cic.

adiunctĭo -ōnis, ˉf. (adiungo), *a joining to, addition, union*: naturae ad hominem, Cic.; verborum, Cic. As rhet. t. t.: a, *a limitation, restriction*: Cic.: b, *repetition*: Cic.

adiunctor -ōris, m. (adiungo), *one who joins, connects*: ille Galliae ulterioris adiunctor (i.e., Pompeius, who caused Gallia Transalpina to be added to Caesar's province), Cic.

adiungo -iungĕre -iunxi -iunctum, *to join to*. LIT., of animals: plostello mures, Hor.; of plants: ulmis vites, Verg.

TRANSF., *to connect*. (1) of material things: parietem ad parietem communem, Cic.; adiunctus fundus, *neighbouring*, Cic.; Ciliciam ad imperium populi Romani, Cic.; agros populo, Cic. (2) of immaterial things, *to associate, impart*: iuris scientiam eloquentiae tamquam ancillulam pedisequamque, Cic.; verba ad nomen adiuncta, *epithets*, Cic.; rebus praesentibus adiungere atque adnectere futuras, Cic.; fidem visis, Cic.; sibi auxilium, Cic.; animum ad aliquod studium, Ter. (3) of persons and communities, *to attach*, esp. as partner, helper or friend: aliquem ad suos sermones, Cic.; urbem ad amicitiam, Liv; aliquem sibi socium, or simply socium, Cic.; se comitem fugae, Cic. ¶ Hence partic. (with compar.) **adiunctus** -a -um, *bound to, belonging to*: propiora huius causae et adiunctiora, Cic. N. pl. as subst. **adiuncta**, *collateral circumstances*: Cic., Hor.

adiūro -are (1) *to swear in addition*: Liv. (2) *to swear to, promise on oath*: qui omnia adiurant, Cic.; with acc. and infin.: adiuras id te invito me non esse facturum, Cic.; with per and the acc.: per Iovem, Pl.; with the simple acc.: adiuro Stygii caput implacabile fontis, Verg.

adiūtābĭlis -e, *full of help, serviceable*: Pl.

adiūto -are, *to be serviceable, to help*: Pl., Ter.

adiūtor -ōris, m. (adiuvo), *a helper*: victoriae populi Romani, Cic.; with in and the abl.: in re gerenda, Cic.; with ad and the acc.: adiutores ad iniuriam, Cic.; with contra and the acc.: his adiutor contra patriam inventus est nemo, Cic. Esp., (1) *one who played secondary parts on the stage*: Hor. (2) *the assistant of a public officer, deputy*: P. Manlius in Hispaniam citeriorem adiutor consuli datus, Liv.; Caes.

adiūtrix -īcis, f. (adiutor). (1) of persons, *she that helps, a female assistant, a helper*: Minerva adiutrix consiliorum meorum, Cic. (2) of things, *aid*: quae res Plancio in petitione fuisset adiutrix, Cic. (3) *name for reserve legions under the empire*: Tac.

adiŭvo -iuvare -iūvi -iūtum, *to help, assist, support*: nihil te Neronis iudicium adiuvat, Cic.; nihil igitur adiuvat procedere et progredi in virtute, Cic.; maerorem nationis lacrimis suis, Cic.; aliquem in aliqua re, Cic.; ad bellum, Liv.; followed by ut and subj.: Cic.

adlābor -labi -lapsus, dep. *to glide to, come to, flow to*: angues duo ex occulto adlapsi, Liv.; with dat or acc.: antiquis adlabimur oris, *we land on*, Verg.; fama adlabitur auris, Verg.

adlaboro -are, *to labour at*; also *to add to by labour*: Hor.

adlacrimo -are, *to weep at*: Verg.

adlapsus -ūs, m. (adlabor), *a gliding approach*: serpentium, Hor.

adlatro -are, *to bark at*; fig., *to rail at*: magnitudinem Africani, Liv.

adlaudābĭlis -e, *praiseworthy*: Pl., Lucr.

adlaudo -are, *to praise*: Pl.

adlecto -are (adlicio), *to entice*: Cic.

adlēgātĭo -ōnis, f. (¹adlego), *a sending of a person on a mission*: cum sibi omnes ad istum adlegationes difficiles viderent, Cic.

¹**adlĕgo** -are. Lit., *to send on private business, to commission* (lego, if on state business): si adlegassem aliquem ad hoc negotium, Pl. (and frequently in Pl.); aliquem ad aliquem, *or* alicui, Cic.; patrem adlegando fatigare, *by sending messages*, Cic.; adlegati, *deputies,* Cic. Transf., (1) *to instigate, to suborn* : Ter. (2) *to adduce* or *allege in excuse* : munera, preces, mandata regis sui Scyrothemidi adlegant, Tac.

²**adlĕgo** -lĕgĕre -lēgi -lectum, *to choose, to elect* : de plebe omnes, Liv.; *with in and the* acc.: aliquem in senatum, Suet.

adlĕvāmentum -i, n. (adlevo), *a means of alleviation* : Cic.

adlĕvātĭo -ōnis, f. (adlevo). Lit., *a lifting up* : Quint. Transf., *alleviation* : doloris, Cic.

adlĕvo -are. Lit., *to lift up, to erect* : circumstantium humeris, Tac. Transf., *to lighten, to alleviate* : sollicitudines, Cic.; pass., adlevari, *to be cheered* : adlevor, cum loquor tecum absens, Cic. L.

adlĭcĕfăcĭo -ĕre, *to entice* : Sen.

adlĭcĭo -lĭcĕre -lexi -lectum (ad/*lacio), *to allure, entice, draw to oneself* : ad se adlicere et attrahere ferrum (of the magnet), Cic. Transf., oratione benigna multitudinis animos ad benevolentiam, Cic.

adlīdo -līdĕre -līsi -līsum (ad/laedo). Lit., *to strike against, dash against* : adlidi ad scopulos, Caes. Transf., adlidi, *to suffer damage* : in quibus (damnationibus) Servius adlisus est, Cic.

adlĭgo -are, *to tie to, bind to.*
Lit., aliquem ad palum, *bind a criminal to the stake for punishment*, Cic.; of ships, *to make fast* : unco dente velut manu ferrea iniecta adligavit alterius proram, Liv.; unco non adligat (naves) ancora morsu, Verg.; *to bind up* a wound: vulnus, Cic.; *to bind in fetters* : Tac.
Transf., in gen., *to fetter, bind* : tristi palus inamabilis unda adligat, *confines, imprisons,* Verg. Esp., (1) *to bind by friendship* or *obligations* : non modo beneficio sed etiam benevolentia adligari, Cic. (2) *to bind by promise, oath,* etc.: lex omnes mortales adligat, Cic. (3) adli, *to become an accomplice in, make oneself responsible for* : furti, Ter.; scelere, Cic.; perf. partic. adligatus, *implicated* or *involved in* a crime : Cic.

adlīno -līnere -lēvi -lĭtum, *to smear on, to bedaub.* Lit., Plin. Transf., Cic., Hor.

adlŏcūtĭo -ōnis, f. (adloquor), *an address, a speaking to* : Plin.; esp., *a word of comfort* : Cat.

adlŏquĭum -i, n. (adloquor), *exhortation, encouragement, consolation* : benigni voltus et adloquia, Liv.; adloquio firmare militem, Tac.

adlŏquor -lŏqui -lŏcūtus sum, dep. *to address* : Cic. Esp. *to encourage, appeal to* : aliquem benigne, leniter, Liv.; patriam maesta ita voce miseriter, Cat.

adlŭbesco -ĕre (ad/lubet), *to begin to please* : Pl.

adlūcĕo -lūcēre -luxi, *to shine at*, or *upon.* Lit., Sen. Transf., fortuna faculam tibi adlucet, *offers you a favourable opportunity,* Pl.

adlūdĭo, -are, *to play* : Pl.

adlūdo -lūdĕre -lūsi -lūsum, *to jest at, to sport*

with. Lit., Galba adludens varie et copiose, Cic. Transf., of waves, *to play* or *dash upon* : mare litoribus adludit, Cic.; adludentibus undis, Ov.; quae fluctus salis adludebant, Cat.

adlŭo -lŭere -lŭi, *to wash*; used of the sea: adluuntur a mari moenia, Cic. Transf., Massilia cum barbariae fluctibus adluatur, *exposed to barbarians,* Cic.

adlŭvĭēs -ēi, f. (adluo), *a pool caused by the overflow of a river* : Liv.

adlŭvĭo -ōnis, f. (adluo), *alluvial land, earth deposited by water* : Cic.

admātūro -are, *to hasten* : admaturari defectionem, Caes.

admētĭor -mētiri -mensus, dep. *to measure out to* : frumentum alicui, Cic.

Admētus -i, m. (Ἄδμητος). (1) *ruler of Pherae, in Thessaly, husband of Alcestis, who died for* him. (2) *king of the Molossi, friend of Themistocles.*

admigro -are, *to wander to, to come to* : Pl.

admĭnĭculor -ari, dep. *to support, prop* : vitem, Cic.

admĭnĭcŭlum -i, n. (ad/*mineo). Lit., *a prop, a support, the pole on which a vine is trained* : Cic. Transf., *aid, help* : ad aliquod tamquam adminiculum adniti, Cic.; egere adminiculis, Tac.

admĭnister -stri, m. *an attendant, an assistant* : Iovi se consiliarium atque adminstrum datum, Cic.; in a bad sense, audaciae satelles atque administer tuae, Cic.

admĭnistra -ae, f. (administer), *she that helps* : artes huius administrae comitesque virtutis, Cic.

admĭnistrātĭo -ōnis, f. (1) *the giving of help* : sine hominum administratione, Cic. (2) *direction, government* : navis, Caes.; belli, Cic.; mundi, rerum, reipublicae, Cic.

admĭnistrātŏr -ōris, m. *an administrator, manager* : quidam belli gerendi, Cic.

admĭnistro -are. (1) *to help, assist* : Pl. (2) *to manage, direct, administer* : navem, *to steer,* Caes.; of war, bellum cum Cimbris, Cic.; exercitum, Cic.; provinciam, Cic.; leges et iudicia, Cic.; rempublicam, Cic.; omnem mundum, Cic.

admīrābĭlis -e. (1) *worthy of admiration, admirable* : admirabilis et singularis sapientia, Cic. (2) *astonishing, strange* (n. pl.=Gr. παράδοξα) : Cic.
¶ Adv., in the corresponding senses, **admīrābĭlĭter** : Cic.

admīrābĭlĭtas -ātis, f. *admirableness*; also *admiration* : haec animi despicientia magnam admirabilitatem facit, Cic.

admīrātĭo -ōnis, f. (1) *admiration* : summam hominum admirationem excitare, Cic.; habere, Cic.; in magna admiratione esse, Cic.; plur., admirationes, *outbursts of admiration* : clamores et admirationes efficere, Cic. (2) *wonder, astonishment* : tam atrocis rei, *at so cruel a deed,* Liv.; admiratio consulem incessit quod, Liv.; admiratio orta est, followed by acc. with infin., Liv.; fit clamor et admiratio populi, followed by acc. with infin., Cic.

admīror -ari, dep. (1) *to admire* : res gestas, Cic. (2) *to be astonished at, to wonder* : aliquid, Cic.; in aliqua re, de aliquo, Cic.; with acc. and infin.: Cic.; with quod, cur, quo pacto, unde : Cic.

¶ Hence gerundive **admirandus** -a -um, *admirable* : homo, Cic.

admisceō -miscēre -miscŭi -mixtum (-mistum), *to mix with*. LIT., aquae admixtus calor, Cic.; aer multo calore admixtus, Cic. TRANSF., *to join* : admiscerenturne plebeii, Liv.; ad id consilium admiscear, Cic.; urbes maritimae admiscentur novis sermonibus ac disciplinis, *become familiar with*, Cic.

admissārĭus -i, m. (admitto), *a stallion*; fig., *a lascivious man* : Cic.

admissĭo -ōnis, f. *an audience*, esp. with a royal person : Plin., Suet.

admitto -mittĕre -mīsi -missum, *to send to, admit*. LIT., *to let in, to give access to* : aliquem ad capsas, Cic.; aliquem ad consilium, Cic. Esp. of horses, *to let go, put to a gallop* : equo admisso, Cic.; admisso passu, Ov. TRANSF., (1) of words, entreaties, etc., *to allow to reach* : eas condiciones vix auribus, Liv. (2) *to allow* : litem, Cic.; of omens : admittunt aves, *the auguries allow it*, Liv. (3) of an act, *to admit it to oneself* or *to one's record*, so *to commit* a crime : in te tantum facinus, Cic.

¶ N. sing. of partic. as subst. **admissum** -i, *a crime* : Cic.

admixtĭo -ōnis, f. (admisceo), *an admixture* : corporis, Cic.

admŏdĕrātē, adv. *appropriately* : Lucr.

admŏdĕror -ari, dep. *to moderate* : Pl.

admŏdum adv. (ad/modum), *up to the measure, up to the mark*; hence, *completely, quite*. (1) with adjectives and other parts of speech : *wholly, quite* : forma admodum impolita et plane rudis, Cic.; admodum raro, Cic.; litterarum admodum nihil sciebat, *was entirely ignorant of*, Cic.; of age : puer admodum, *a mere boy*, Liv.; non admodum grandis natu, Cic.; me admodum diligunt, Cic. (2) with numbers, *just about* : turres admodum cxx, Caes. (3) in affirmative answer, *certainly* : Pl., Ter.

admoenĭo -ire, *to besiege* : Pl.

admōlĭor -iri, dep. (1) transit., *to bring to, lay on* : manus, Pl. (2) intransit., *to struggle to* : Pl.

admŏnĕo -ēre -ŭi -ĭtum, *to admonish, remind*. (1) of a fact : aliquem alicuius rei, *or* de aliqua re, Cic.; aliquem haec, eam rem, multa, Cic.; often followed by acc. and infin., or by indirect question clause. (2) of a duty, *to advise to do something*, followed by ut or ne and the subj., or by the simple subj., by ad or in and the acc., or by the infin. : Cic.; ad thesaurum reperiundum admoneri, Cic. (3) *to urge* or *incite* : telo biiugos, Verg.

¶ N. of partic. as subst. **admonitum** -i, *an admonition* : Cic.

admŏnĭtĭo -ōnis, f. *a reminding*; esp. *a friendly admonition* : admonitio in consilio dando familiaris, Cic.; in plur. : nec precibus nec admonitionibus nostris reliquit locum, Cic.

admŏnĭtor -ōris, m. *one who reminds* : Cic.

admŏnĭtrix -tricis, f., *she who reminds* : Pl.

admŏnĭtus -ūs, m. (used only in abl.), *a reminding, warning* : locorum admonitu, Cic.; amici tali admonitu, Cic.; mortis, Ov.

admordĕo -mordēre -morsum. (1) *to bite at, to gnaw* : Prop., Verg. (2) *to fleece* : Pl.

admōtĭo -ōnis, f. *a moving to* : digitorum, *playing* (on the harp), Cic.

admŏvĕo -mŏvēre -mōvi -mōtum, *to move to, bring to*.

(1) of material things : fasciculum ad nares, Cic.; alicui stimulos, Cic.; manum operi, *to engage in a work*, Ov.; manus nocentibus, *to lay hands on the guilty*, Liv.; so : manus vectigalibus, Cic.; aspidem ad corpus, Cic.; angues curribus, *to yoke*, Ov.; with acc. alone : ignem, Cic.; aurem, Cic. Esp. as milit. t. t., *to bring up* war-machines : opus ad turrim hostium, Caes.; *to bring up* soldiers : armatos muris, Liv.

(2) of immaterial things, *to apply, direct, devote* : mentes suas, non solum aures, ad haruspicum vocem, Cic.; curationem ad aliquem, Cic.; orationem ad sensus animorum atque motus inflammandos, Cic.

(3) of persons : se applicare et propius admovere, Cic.

admūgĭo -ire, *to bellow after* : Ov.

admurmŭrātĭo -ōnis, f. *a murmuring* : Cic.

admurmŭro -are, *to murmur at* (in approval or disapproval) : Cic.

admūtĭlo -are, *to shear, shave*; hence, transf., *to fleece* : Pl.

adnăto -are. (1) *to swim to* : Plin. (2) *to swim by the side of* : Sen.

adnāvĭgo -are, *to voyage to* : Plin.

adnecto -nectĕre -nexui -nexum, *to bind to, connect with*. LIT., stomachus ad linguam adnectitur, Cic.; animos corporibus, Lucr. TRANSF., *to connect* : rebus praesentibus futuras adiungere atque adnectere, Cic.

adnexus -ūs, m. (adnecto), *a binding to, a connexion* : Tac.

adnītor -nīti -nīsus or -nixus, dep. *to press against* or *towards*. LIT., *to lean upon* : ad aliquod tamquam adminiculum, Cic. TRANSF., *to strive after* : de triumpho, Cic. L.; ad obtinendum hesternum decus, Liv.; also used by Liv. with ut (*or* ne) and subj.; with infin.; with pro and abl.

adno -are. (1) *to swim to*, or *near*; absol. : Hor.; with ad : Gell.; with acc. : naves, Caes.; with dat. : vestris oris, Verg. TRANSF., *to come to* : ad eam urbem, Cic. (2) *to swim with*, or *alongside of* : pedites adnantes equis, Tac.

adnŏtātĭo -ōnis, f. (adnoto), *remark, annotation* : Plin. L.

adnŏtātor -ōris, m. (adnoto), *one who remarks, an observer* : Plin.

adnŏto -are, *to note, remark on* : pauca adnotabo, Quint.; adnotatum est, with acc. and infin., Tac.; librum, *to make remarks on a book*, Plin.

adnŭmĕro -are. (1) *to count out, pay* : tibi denarios, Cic. (2) *to reckon with*; with dat. : aliquem his duobus, Cic.; with in and the abl. : aliquem patronorum in grege, Cic.

adnuntio -are, *to announce, tell* : Plin.

adnŭo -nŭĕre -nŭi -nūtum. (1) *to nod to* : simul atque sibi adnuisset, Cic.; Pl., Verg. (2) *to nod assent to* : id toto capite, Cic.; hence, in gen., *to agree, agree with, agree to*; with dat. of person : petenti, Verg.; of the thing : adnue coeptis, *be favourable to our undertaking*, Verg. Also *to agree to give* or *do* : caeli quibus adnuis arcem, Verg.; cum adnuisset se venturum, Liv. (3) *to point out by a sign* : quos iste adnuerat, Cic.

adnūto -are (freq. of adnuo), *to nod to, make a sign to* : Pl.

¹**ădŏlĕo** -ēre -ŭi, *to magnify*; hence, in the language of religion, *to worship, to offer sacrifice, to burn a sacrifice*: honores Iunoni, *to honour by burning sacrifices to*, Verg.; flammis Penates, Verg.; so of the altar itself: altaria flammis, Lucr.; cruore captivo aras, Tac.; of the sacrifice burnt: viscera tauri flammis, Ov.
TRANSF., in gen., *to burn*: Ov.

²**ădŏlĕo** -ēre, *to give a smell, to smell*: Pl.

ădŏlescens=adulescens; q.v.

ădŏlesco -ŏlescĕre -ŏlĕvi (adoleo). (1) *to grow up*: **a**, of men and their attributes: is qui adoleverit, Cic.; cum matura adoleverit aetas, Verg.; ratio cum adolevit atque perfecta est, Cic.; ea cupiditas adolescit una cum aetatibus, Cic.: **b**, of plants: viriditas herbescens quae sensim adolescit, Cic.: **c**, of seasons: ver donec adolesceret, Tac.
(2) *to be heaped up*, or perhaps *to burn* (cf. adoleo): adolescunt ignibus arae, Verg.
¶ Hence partic. (with compar.) **adultus** -a -um, *grown up, adult*. LIT., (1) of living things and their attributes: virgo, Cic.; puer aetate adulta, Cic.; fetus apum, Verg. (2) of times and seasons: aestas, Sall., Tac. TRANSF., Athenae, Cic.; pestis, Cic.; coniuratio, Tac.

Ădōneus -ĕi, m.=Adonis; q.v.: Pl.

Ădōnis -is or -ĭdis (Ἄδωνις and Ἄδων), *a beautiful youth, son of Cinyras, king of Cyprus; beloved of Venus, slain by a wild boar.*

ădŏpĕrĭo -ŏpĕrīre -ŏpĕrŭi -ŏpertum, gen. used in past partic. (1) *to cover*: capite adoperto, Liv.; humus floribus adoperta, Ov. (2) *to close*: adoperta lumina somno, Ov.; foribus, Suet.

ădŏpīnor -ari, dep. *to guess*: Lucr.

ădoptātĭo -ōnis, f. (adopto), *adopting*: Cic., Sall.

ădoptĭo -ōnis, f. *the adoption of a child*: emancipare filium alicui in adoptionem, *to give in adoption*, Cic.; ascire aliquem in or per adoptionem, *to adopt*, Tac.

ădoptīvus -a -um, *relating to adoption*. LIT., filius, pater, frater, soror, *adopted son*, etc., Suet.; sacra, *the rites of the family into which the person was adopted*, Cic.; nobilitas, Ov.
TRANSF., of plants, *grafted*: Ov.

ădopto -are. In gen., *to choose for oneself*: sibi aliquem patronum, Cic.; of things: Etruscas opes, *to take to one's aid*, Ov.
Esp., *to adopt* as child or grandchild (per aes et libram, *by a fictitious sale*, or testamento, *by will*): sibi filium, Cic.; aliquem ab aliquo, *from the natural father*, Cic.; in regnum, Sall.
TRANSF., (1) of persons and names: C. Stalenus qui ipse se adoptaverat et de Staleno Aelium fecerat, *had changed his name by adopting himself*, Cic.; frater, pater adde; ut cuique est aetas, ita quemque facetus adopta, *adopt him by calling him brother, father*, Hor.; nomen or cognomen adoptare, Mart. (2) of plants, *to graft*: fac ramus ramum adoptet, Ov.

ădŏr -oris, n. *a species of grain, spelt*: Hor.

ădōrātĭo -ōnis, f. (adoro), *a praying to, adoration*: Plin.

ădōrĕus -a -um (**ador**), *of spelt*: liba, Verg. F. as subst. **ădōrĕa** -ae, *reward of valour* (originally a gift of corn), *glory*: ille dies . . . qui primus alma risit adorea, Hor.

ădōrĭor -ŏrīri -ortus, dep. *to rise up at*. (1) *to attack*: fustibus, gladiis, Cic.; a tergo, Cic.; pagum, Caes.; so fig.: aliquem minis, Tac.; aliquem tumultuosissime, Cic. (2) *to attempt, undertake*: hoc ipsum, Cic.; maius nefas, Verg.; followed by infin.: Cic., Ov., Liv.

ădorno, -are. (1) *to prepare, furnish, provide*: naves onerarias, Caes.; Italiae duo maria maximis classibus firmissimisque praesidiis, Cic.; accusationem, Cic. (2) *to adorn*. LIT., forum magno ornatu, Cic.; aliquem insigni veste, Liv. TRANSF., iusti honores aliquem adornant, Liv.

ădōro -are, *to speak to*. Esp., *to address* a deity, *to entreat*; also *to ask* a deity *for*, with a second acc. of the thing asked: pacem deum, Liv.; or with an ut clause: Liv. Also *to honour, worship*: Phoebum, Ov.

adp-, *see* under app-.

adquĭesco -quiescĕre -quiēvi -quiētum, *to rest, repose.*
(1) physically, of persons: tres horas, Cic.; euphem., *to die*: anno adquievit sexagesimo, Nep.; of things: aures in eo adquiescant, Cic.; rem familiarem adquiescere, *not to be seized*, Liv.
(2) mentally: **a**, absol.: mentis agitatio quae numquam adquiescit, Cic.: **b**, *to find comfort in, be pleased with*: in his (litteris tuis) adquiesco, Cic.; in adulescentium caritate, Cic.; Clodii morte, Cic.

adquīro -quirĕre -quisīvi -quisītum (ad/quaero), *to acquire, get*, esp. in addition to previous possessions: dignitatem, Cic.; vires adquirit eundo, Verg.; triumphos de populis, Tac. Often of money: Juv., Quint.

adrādo -rādĕre -rāsi -rāsum, *to scrape, shave*: adrasum quendam, Hor.

Adrămyttēum -i, n. (Ἀδραμύττειον), *a town on the coast of Mysia, not far from the foot of Mount Ida* (now *Edremit*).
¶ Hence adj. **Adramyttēnus** -a -um: Cic.

Adrastus -i, m. (Ἄδραστος), *king of Argos, father-in-law of Polynices and Tydeus, one of the Seven against Thebes, and the only one who escaped; afterwards one of those who destroyed Thebes in the war of the Epigoni.* Adj. **Adrastĕus** -a -um.

adrectus -a -um, partic. from adrigo; q.v.

adrēpo -rēpĕre -repsi -reptum, *to creep to, to glide gently to*; fig.: quibus rebus non sensim atque moderate ad amicitiam adrepserat, Cic.; Hor.

Adria=Hadria; q.v.

adrīdĕo -rīdēre -risi -rīsum, *to laugh to, to smile upon*: ridentibus adrident, Hor.; vix notis familiariter adridere, Liv.; with acc. of the thing: video quid adriseris, Cic. TRANSF., (1) *to be favourable*: cum tempestas adridet, Lucr. (2) *to please*: 'inhibere' illud tuum quod valde mihi adriserat, Cic. L.

adrĭgo -rĭgĕre -rexi -rectum (ad/rego), *to erect, lift up*: aures, comas, Verg. TRANSF., *to excite, arouse*: adrexere animos Itali, Verg.; animos ad bellandum, Liv.; aliquem oratione, Sall.

adrĭpĭo -rĭpĕre -rĭpui -reptum (ad/rapio), *to seize on, lay hold of, snatch.*
LIT., arma, Liv.; cibum unguium tenacitate, Cic.; aliquem manu, Liv.; aliquem medium, Liv.; tabulam de naufragio, Cic.;

cohortes adreptas in urbem inducere, Liv.; terram velis, *to sail quickly to*, Verg.

Transf., (1) where the object is not material, to *appropriate, take*: facultatem laedendi, quaecumque detur, Cic.; maledicta ex trivio, Cic. (2) *to grasp mentally, to comprehend quickly*: celeriter res innumerabiles, Cic.; litteras Graecas, Cic. (3) where the subject is not personal, *to seize upon*: dolor, qui simul adripuit interficit, Cic. (4) as legal t. t., *to arrest, bring to court, accuse*: Cic. (5) *to satirize*: primores populi populumque, Hor.

adrīsor -ōris, m. *one who smiles approvingly, a flatterer*: Sen.

adrōdo -rōdĕre -rōsi -rōsum, *to gnaw at*: mures Antii coronam auream adrosere, Liv.; fig., ut illa ex vepreculis extracta nitedula rempublicam conaretur adrodere, Cic.

adrogans, partic. from adrogo; q.v.

adrŏgantia -ae, f. *assumption*: ingenii atque eloquentiae molestissima, Cic.; hence *pride, haughtiness*: avaritia et adrogantia praecipue validorum vitia, Tac.

adrŏgo -are. (1) as legal and polit. t. t.: **a**, *to question*: Pl.: **b**, *to associate one public officer with another*: cui unico consuli dictatorem adrogari haud satis decorum visum est patribus, Liv.

(2): **a**, *to take to oneself* (sibi), *to claim, assume*: sibi sapientiam, Cic., Hor., Tac.: **b**, *to adjudge, grant to another* (dat.): decus imperiis, Hor.

¶ Hence partic. (with compar. and superl.) **adrŏgans** -antis, *assuming, arrogant, haughty*: Indutiomarus iste minax atque adrogans, Cic.; consilium, Cic.

¶ Adv. **adrŏganter**, *arrogantly, haughtily*: dicere, Cic.; scribere, Cic.; facere, Caes.

adrōsor -ōris, m. *one who gnaws at*: Sen.

Adrūmētum (Hadrūmētum) -i, n. *a town on the coast of the Roman province of Africa*.

adsc-, *see* under asc-.

adsectātĭo -ōnis, f. *respectful attendance*, e.g., of a client on a patron: Cic.

adsectātor -ōris, m. *a companion, follower*: cum ducibus ipsis, non cum comitatu adsectatoribusque configant, Cic.; philosophiae, Plin.

adsector -ari, dep. *to follow, attend assiduously* (esp. of friends of candidates): cum aedilitatem P. Crassus peteret eumque Ser. Galba adsectaretur, Cic.

adsecula (adsecla) -ae, m. (adsequor), *a follower, servant, sycophant*: adsentatores eorum atque adseculae, Cic.

adsensĭo -ōnis. (1) *assent, agreement, applause*: popularis, Cic.; rem adsensione comprobare, Cic.; plur.: crebrae adsensiones, Cic. (2) as philosoph. t. t., *belief in the reality of sensible appearances* (Gr. συγκατάθεσις): Cic.

adsensor -ōris, m. *one who assents or agrees*: te unum in tanto exercitu mihi fuisse adsensorem, Cic. L.

adsensus -ūs, m. (1) *assent, agreement*: adsensu omnium dicere, Cic., Liv., Ov., Tac. (2) philosoph. t. t., *belief in the reality of sensible appearances*: adsensum retinere, Cic. (3) poet., *echo*: nemorum, Verg.

adsentātĭo -ōnis, f. *a flattering assent or applause, flattery*: faceta parasitorum, Cic.; plur.: blanditiae et adsentationes, Cic.

adsentātĭuncŭla -ae f. (dim. of adsentatio), *trivial flattery*: Pl., Cic. L.

adsentātor -ōris, m. (adsentor), *a flatterer*: cavendum est ne adsentatoribus patefaciamus aures, Cic.

adsentātōrĭē, adv. (adsentator), *flatteringly*: Cic. L.

adsentātrix -trīcis, f. (adsentator), *a female flatterer*: Pl.

adsentĭo -sentire -sensi -sensum, and **adsentĭor** -sentiri, -sensus sum, dep. (ad/sentio), *to assent to, agree with*.

(1) deponent form: de Vennonianis rebus tibi adsentior, Cic.; ut ego adsentior orationi, Cic.; ego illud adsentior Theophrasto, Cic.

(2) active form: cavendum est ne his rebus temere adsentiamus, Cic.; pass.: neque percepta neque adsensa, Cic.

adsentor -ari, dep. (intens. of adsentior).

(1) *to assent constantly*: Ter. (2) *to flatter*: benevolentiam civium blanditiis et adsentando conligere, Cic.; ut nihil nobis adsentati esse videamur, Cic.; Baiae tibi adsentantur, Cic.

adsĕquor -sĕqui -sĕcūtus sum, dep. (1) *to follow after*: Porcius deinde adsecutus cum levi armatura, Liv. (2) *to reach by following, come up to, attain*: aliquem, Cic. Transf., **a**, *to reach*: merita alicuius non adsequi, Cic.; esp., *to attain to something for which one strives*: eosdem honorum gradus, Cic.; immortalitatem, Cic.; foll. by ut or ne with the subj., Cic.: **b**, of the mind, *to grasp, comprehend*: aliquid cogitatione, Cic.

¹**adsĕro** -sĕrĕre -sēvi -sĭtum (ad/sero), *to plant at* or *near*: populus adsita limitibus, Hor.

²**adsĕro** -sĕrĕre -sĕrŭi -sertum (ad/sero), *to join to oneself*.

Lit., as legal t. t.: **a**, *to lay hold of a slave, and thereby declare him free*: aliquem in libertatem, Liv.; aliquem manu liberali causa, Pl.; aliquem in liberali causa, Cic.; adserui iam me, *I have freed myself*, Ov.: **b**, *to claim as a slave*: aliquem in servitutem, Liv.

Transf., **a**, *to set free from, protect*: se a mortalitate, Plin.: **b**, *to claim*: alicui regnum, Liv.; aliquem caelo, *declare the celestial origin of a person*, Ov.

adsertĭo -ōnis, f. *a formal declaration as to freedom*: Suet.

adsertor -ōris, m. (²adsero). (1) *one who asserts that another person is free*. Lit., adsertor libertatis, Plin. Transf., *a liberator, protector*: Ov., Tac. (2) *one who asserts that another is a slave*: adsertor puellae, Liv.

adservĭo -ire, *to assist, help*: toto corpore contentioni vocis, Cic.

adservo -are, *to preserve, guard, watch*: tabulas negligentius, Cic.; aliquem domi suae, Cic.; oram, Caes.; ius negligentius, Cic.

adsessĭo -ōnis, f. (adsideo), *a sitting by the side of one* (to console): quae tua fuerit adsessio, oratio, confirmatio animi mei fracti, Cic.

adsessor -ōris, m. (adsideo), *one who sits by, or assists*: Lacedaemonii regibus suis augurem adsessorem dederunt, Cic. Esp., *an assistant, a judicial assessor*: Suet.

adsessus, abl. -ū, m. (adsideo), *a sitting by the side of*: Prop.

adsĕvērātĭo -ōnis, f. (adsevero). (1) *earnestness, vehemence, in action*: multa adseveratione coguntur patres, Tac. (2) *vehement assertion, asseveration*: omni adseveratione tibi adfirmo (foll. by acc. with infin.), Cic.

adsĕvēro -are (ad/severus). (1) *to act with earnestness*: bella ironia, si iocaremur; sin adseveramus, vide ne, etc., Cic.; also transit., defensionem, Cic. (2) *to assert confidently, strongly*: idque se facturum adseveravit, Cic.; nemo de ulla re potest contendere neque adseverare, Cic.

¶ Hence, from pres. partic., adv. (with compar.) **adsĕvērantĕr**, *earnestly, emphatically*: loqui, Cic. L.

adsĭdeo -sĭdēre -sedi -sessum (ad/sedeo), *to sit near*, or *by the side of*. Lit., Sthenius est, is qui nobis adsidet, Cic. Esp., *to sit at a person's side, to give comfort, advice, protection, etc.*: in carcere mater noctes diesque adsidebat, Cic.; adsidere aegro conlegae, *to sit at the bedside of*, Liv.; cum Cn. Pompeius Lentulo frequens adsideret, Cic.; iudiciis adsidebat, *frequented*, Tac. Transf., (1) *to devote oneself to*: totā vitā litteris, Plin. L. (2) milit. t. t., *to besiege, blockade*, with dat.: intactis muris, Liv.; adsidens Casilino, Liv. (3) *to approximate to*: parcus insano, Hor.

adsĭdo -sīdere -sēdi -sessum, *to sit down*: in bibliotheca, Cic.; super aspidem, Cic.; propter Tuberonem, Cic.; esp., of an orator on finishing a speech: Cic.

adsĭdŭĭtās -ātis, f. (adsiduus). Lit., *continual presence, attention of friends, clients, candidates*: cotidiana amicorum adsiduitas et frequentia, Cic.; medici, Cic. Transf., (1) *constancy*: id adsiduitate et virtute consequere, Cic. (2) *constant repetition*: epistularum, *regular correspondence*, Cic.; molestiarum, Cic.; bellorum, Cic.

¹**adsĭdŭus** -a -um (adsideo). (1) *continuously in one place*, or *engaged in one occupation*: ruri adsiduum semper vivere, Cic.; audivi Romae esse hominem et fuisse adsiduum, Cic.; esp. of the friends who attended candidates and magistrates: mecum fuit adsiduus praetore me, Cic. (2) *constant, persistent*; of persons: qui filios suos agricolas adsiduos esse cupiunt, Cic.; of things: imbres, Cic.; homines labore adsiduo et cotidiano adsueti, Cic.

¶ Hence adv. **adsĭdūē**, *continuously, without remission*: voces quas audio adsidue, Cic.; quibus (litteris) adsidue utor, Ter., Verg. Also **adsĭdŭō**: Pl.

²**adsiduus** -i, m. *a taxpaying citizen* (member of Servius Tullius' upper classes, opp. proletarii): Cic. Hence gen., *a well-to-do citizen*: Pl.

adsignātĭo -ōnis, f. *assignment, allotment*: agrorum, Cic.

adsigno -are. (1) *to assign to anyone, allot*: inferiorem aedium partem alicui, Cic.; esp., of allotting lands to colonists: loca, Cic.; agros colonis, Cic.; agrum militibus, Cic.; munus humanum a deo adsignatum, Cic. (2) *to impute, to ascribe*: aliquid homini, non tempori, Cic.; tuo consilio, Liv. (In Cic., always in a bad sense.) (3) *to seal*: Pl.; hence fig., to *impress upon*: Quint.

adsĭlio -sĭlire -sĭlŭi (ad/salio), *to leap to*, or *on*; of persons: moenibus, Ov.; of water, *to dash up*: adsiliens aqua, Ov. Transf., *to jump to*: neque adsiliendum statim est ad genus illud orationis, Cic.

adsĭmĭlis -e, *like, similar*; with dat.: adsimilis spongiis mollitudo, Cic., Verg.; with genit.: Ov.

Adv. **adsĭmĭlĭtĕr**, *in like manner*: Pl.

adsĭmŭlātĭo -ōnis, f. (adsimulo). (1) *resemblance*: Plin. (2) *rivalry*: Tac.

adsĭmŭlo, -are, *to make like*. Lit., deos in humani oris speciem, Tac.; litterae lituraeque omnes adsimulatae, Cic.; formam totius Britanniae auctores oblongae scutulae vel bipenni adsimulavere, *have compared*, Tac. Transf., *to imitate, counterfeit, pretend*: anum, Ov.; with acc. and infin.: Pl., Ter.; with quasi and subj.: Pl., Ter.

¶ Hence partic. **adsĭmŭlātus** -a -um. (1) *similar*: Lucr. (2) *feigned, pretended, simulated*: virtus, Cic.

adsisto adsistĕre adstĭti *or* astĭti, *to place oneself, to stand by*. Lit., ad fores, Cic.; foribus principum, Cic.; ad epulas regis, Cic. Transf., *to stand by* in a court of law, *to defend*: Tac., Plin. L.

adsŏlĕo -ēre, *to be accustomed*; used only in the third person, sing. and plur.: ponite hic quae adsolent, Pl., Liv.; esp. in phrase, ut adsolet, *as is usual*, Cic.

adsŏno -are, *to answer with a sound*: plangentibus adsonat echo, Ov.

adsp-, *see* under asp-.

adsterno -ĕre, *to strew upon*; pass., *to lie stretched upon*: adsternuntur sepulcro, Ov.

adstĭpŭlātĭo -ōnis, f. *an assenting to, con firmation of*: Plin.

adstĭpŭlātor -ōris, m. Legal t. t., at Rome, *one who joined another* (the stipulator) *in the Roman contract* called stipulatio. Transf., *a supporter*: Stoici et eorum adstipulator Antiochus, Cic.

adstĭpŭlor -ari, dep. *to join in a contract with*. Transf., *to agree with*: Liv.

adstĭtŭo -tŭĕre -tŭi -tūtum, m. (ad/statuo), *to put near*: Pl.

adsto -stare -stĭti, *to stand by*. Gen.: alicui, Pl.; adstante et inspectante ipso, Caes.; adstat in conspectu meo, Cic. Esp., *to stand by the side to help, to assist*: Pl.; *to wait for*: Lucr.; *to stand upright*: Verg.

adstrĕpo -ĕre, *to make a noise at*: adstrepebat vulgus, Tac.; esp., *to applaud*: haec dicenti, Tac.

adstrictus -a -um, partic. of adstringo; q.v.

adstringo -stringĕre -strinxi -strictum, *o tighten, draw together, compress, contract, bind together*. Lit., vincula, Ov.; aliquem ad statuam, Cic.; of cold, *to contract*: Ov. Transf., (1) *to draw tight, to bind, secure*; fig.: ad adstringendam fidem, Cic.; pater nimis indulgens quidquid ego adstrinxi relaxat, Cic. (2) of writing or speech, *to compress*: breviter argumenta, Cic. (3) *to bind, oblige*: vel armis vel legibus totam Galliam sempiternis vinculis, Cic. (4) se adstringere, *to commit oneself to, become guilty of*: furti, Pl.; scelere, Cic.

¶ Hence partic. (with compar.) **adstrictus** -a -um, *tight, compressed, drawn together*.

LIT., limen, *shut*, Ov.; soccus, Hor.; frons, *wrinkled*, Mart.; aquae, *frozen*, Ov.
TRANSF., (**1**) *close-fisted, avaricious*: pater, Prop.; mos, Tac. (**2**) of oratory, *concise*: contracta et adstricta eloquentia, Cic.
Adv. (with compar.) **adstrictē**, *concisely*: Cic., Plin. L., Quint.

adstrŭo -strŭĕre -struxi -str⎯ctum. LIT., *to build to* or *near, to build in addition*: cum veteri adstruitur recens aedificium, Col. TRANSF., *to add to*: formae animum, Ov., Tac

adstŭpĕo -ēre, *to be astonished at*, with dat.: Ov

adsuēfăcio -făcĕre -fēci -factum (adsuetus), *to accustom to*: ad supplicia patrum plebem, Liv.; with abl.: quorum sermone qui adsuefacti erant, Cic.; with dat.: pedites operi aliisque iustis militaribus, Liv.; with infin.: equos eodem remanere vestigio, Caes.

adsuesco -suescĕre -suēvi -suētum. (**1**) intransit., *to grow accustomed*: adsuevi, *I am accustomed*, Cic.; genus pugnae quo (abl.) adsuerant, Liv.; adsuescere ad homines, Caes.; ut quieti (dat.) adsuescerent, Tac.; adsuesce vocari, Verg. (**2**) transit., *to accustom*: qui pluribus adsuerit mentem, Hor. In a different construction, *to make familiar*: ne tanta animis adsuescite bella, Verg.

¶ Hence partic. **adsuētus** -a -um. (**1**) *customary, usual*: cultores, Liv., Ov. (**2**) *accustomed to*, with the same constructions as follow the intrans. finite verb: in omnia familiaria iura adsuetus, Liv.; homines labore adsiduo et cotidiano adsueti, Cic.; quaestui, Liv.; with infin.: adsueti vinci, Liv.

adsuētūdo -inis, f. *custom, use*: Liv., Ov., Tac.

adsuētus -a -um, partic. from adsuesco; q.v.

adsulto -are (intens. of adsilio), *to leap violently upon*: feminae adsultabant ut sacrificantes aut insanientes Bacchae, Tac. Esp., *to attack, assault*: tergis pugnantium, Tac.; latera et frontem (agminis), Tac.

adsultus -ū, m. (adsilio), *a leaping upon, assault* (in plur.): Verg., Tac.

adsum adesse adfui, *to be present, to be at* or *near*. (**1**) gen., of bodily presence: heri cum non adessetis, Cic.; omnes qui aderant, Caes.; mane ad portam adesse, Cic.; in foro, Liv.; ante oculos, Verg.; portis (dat.), Verg.; huc ades, *come here*, Verg. (**2**) *to be present and ready, to stand by*: primum me ipsum vigilare, adesse, Cic.; adversus hostes, Sall; iam omnes feroces aderant, Sall.; pugnae, Liv.; num ades ad parendum vel ad imperandum potius? Cic.; of deities: adsis placidusque iuves, Verg.; hence, *to be favourable to*: rebus Romanis, Liv.; si fortuna coeptis adfuerit, Tac.; so of persons, *to support, help*: Camulogeno suis aderat, Caes. (**3**) *to be present for a special purpose*, esp. political or legal: ad suffragium, Cic.; with dat.: comitiis, Cic.; adesse scribendo senatus consulto or decreto, *to witness*, Cic.; alicui adesse in consilio, *to be an assessor to*, Cic.; *to support* or *defend in the law-courts*: adesse Quinctio, Cic.; contra Satrium, Cic.; *to be present in a court of justice, as the accused*: adesse iuberi, Cic.; or *as the accuser*: adesse in iudicio, Cic. (**4**) of the mind, in the phrase adesse animo or animis, *to attend*: adestote

omnes animis, Cic.; also, *to be of good courage*: ades animo et omitte timorem, Cic. (**5**) of things, *to be near, at hand*: frumentum conferri, comportari, adesse, Caes.; tanti aderant morbi, Cic.; esp. of time: adesse Romanis ultimum diem, Liv.

adsūmo -sūmĕre -sumpsi -sumptum, *to take to oneself*.
LIT., novas umeris alas, Ov.; plura sibi adsumunt quam de se corpora mittunt, Lucr. Also, *to take in addition*: si quis in aliqua arte excellens aliam quoque artem sibi adsumpserit, Cic.
TRANSF., (**1**) *to take persons to help one*: legiones in Italia, Cic.; aliquem in societatem armorum, Liv.; aliquem in nomen familiamque, Tac. (**2**) *to take, appropriate, things*: aliquantum noctis, Cic.; adsumpta verba, *words borrowed, epithets, from another source*, Cic.; auxilia extrinsecus, Cic.; regni insignia, Tac.; Cereris sacra de Graecia, Cic. (**3**) *to claim*: in eo sibi praecipuam laudem adsumere, Liv., Cic. L. (**4**) logical t. t., *to state the minor premises of a syllogism*: Cic.

adsumptĭo -ōnis, f. (adsumo). (**1**) *choice, adoption*: Cic. (**2**) *the minor premises of a syllogism*: Cic.

adsumptīvus -a -um (adsumo), *which derives a defence from an extraneous cause*: causa, Cic.

adsŭo -ĕre, *to sew on*: unus et alter adsuitur pannus, Hor.

adsurgo -surgĕre -surrexi -surrectum, *to rise up, stand up*.
LIT., adsurgentem regem umbone resupinat, Liv.; quae dum recitatur, vos quaeso, qui eam detulistis, adsurgite, Cic.; esp.: adsurgere alicui, *to rise up in the presence of*, as a sign of respect, Cic.; pass., impers.: haec ipsa sunt honorabilia, salutari, adpeti, decedi, adsurgi, Cic.; fig.: firmissima vina, Tmolius adsurgit quibus et rex ipse Pnanaeus, *yields the preference*, Verg.; also, *to rise from a sick-bed*: ne adsurrexisse quidem ex morbo, Liv.
TRANSF., (**1**) with reference to feelings, *to rise, be aroused*: adsurgunt irae, Verg.; querellis haud iustis adsurgis, *break out into*, Verg. (**2**) of style, *to become elevated*: Quint. (**3**) of material things, *to rise up*: colles adsurgunt, Liv.; non coeptae adsurgent turres, Verg.

adt- see under att-.

Adŭātŭci -ōrum, m. *a people in Gallia Belgica*: Caes.

ădūlātĭo -ōnis, f. *fawning*. LIT., of dogs: canum, Cic. TRANSF., in gen., *cringing, flattery*: Cic., Liv.; so of oriental prostration: humi iacentium adulationes, Liv.; adversus superiores, Tac.; patrum in Augustum, Tac.

ădūlātor -ōris, m. *a flatterer*: Suet.

ădūlātōrĭus -a -um, *flattering*: dedecus, Tac.

ădŭlescens (adolescens) -entis (adolesco), *young, growing*.
Adj. (with compar.), *young*: filia, Cic.; admodum adulescens, Cic.; adulescentior academia, Cic.
Subst., *a young man* or *young woman* (without reference to any particular age): puer sive iam adulescens, Cic.; adulescens vel puer potius, Cic.; sometimes used to distinguish a person from someone of the same name, but older: P. Crassius adul., Caes.

ădŭlescentĭa -ae, f. *youth* : citius adulescentiae senectus quam pueritiae adulescentia obrepit, Cic.; ineunte adulescentia, Cic.; ab adulescentiā, a primā adul., ab ineunte adul., *from youth upward*, Cic.

ădŭlescentŭla -ae, f. *a very young girl*, used as a term of endearment : Pl.

ădŭlescentŭlus -i, m. *a very young man*; applied by Cic. to himself in his 27th year, and by Sallust to Caesar when Caesar was about 33 or 35 : ab adulescentulo, *from youth upward*, Cic.

ădŭlo -are, *to fawn* : gannitu vocis adulant (of dogs), Lucr. Pass., *to be fawned upon* : Cic.

ădŭlor -ari, dep. LIT., *to fawn* (of dogs and other animals) : ferae adulantes, Ov. TRANSF., *to flatter, to cringe before*; with acc. : omnes, Cic.; plebem, Liv.; fortunam alterius, Cic.; with dat. : plebi, Liv.; absol. : aperte adulans, Cic. So of oriental prostration : more adulantium procumbere, Liv.

¹ădulter -ĕri, m., **ădultĕra** -ae, f. *an adulterer, adulteress* : Dardanius adulter, *Paris*, Verg.; Lacaena adultera, *Helen*, Hor.; poet., *a gallant* : Hor.

²adulter -era -erum, adj. *adulterous* : virgo, Ov.; crines, *the locks of an adulterer*, Hor.; mens, Ov.; clavis, Ov.

ădultĕrīnus -a -um (adulter), *adulterous* : Plin. TRANSF., *not genuine, forged* : nummus, Cic.; signum, *a forged seal*, Cic.; clavis, *a double key*, Sall.

ădultĕrĭum -i, n. *adultery* : in adulterio deprehendi, Cic.; Mutiliae, *adultery with*, Tac.

ădultĕro -are, *to commit adultery, to defile*, transit., or absol.
  LIT., of persons : Cic.; also of animals : adulteretur et columba miluo, *let the kite wed the dove*, Hor.
  TRANSF., *to falsify, defile, corrupt* : ius civile pecunia, Cic.; faciem arte (of Proteus), changes his form, Ov.

ădultus -a -um, partic. from adolesco; q.v.

ădumbrātim, adv. *in outline* : Lucr.

ădumbrātĭo -ōnis, f. *a sketch* : Cic.

adumbro -are (umbra), *to shade in, to sketch*, esp. in words : fictos luctus dicendo, Cic.
  ¶ Hence partic. **ădumbrātus** -a -um, *sketched*; hence *imperfect, shadowy, unreal* : imago gloriae, Cic.; adumbratae intellegentiae rerum, *confused notions*, Cic.; opinio, Cic.; laetitia, Tac.

ăduncĭtas -ātis, f. *bending, curvature* : rostrorum, Cic.

ăduncus -a -um, *bent inwards, crooked* : unguis, Cic.; nasus, *an aquiline nose*, Ter.

ădurgĕo -ēre, *to press to, or against*; poet., *to pursue closely* : aliquem remis, Hor.

ădūro -ūrēre -ussi -ustum, *to set fire to, to kindle, to singe* : sine gemitu aduruntur, Cic.; candente carbone sibi capillum, Cic.; panis adustus, Hor.; of frost or wind, *to nip* : Verg.; fig., of love : Venus non erubescendis adurit ignibus, Hor.
  ¶ Hence partic. **ădustus** -a -um, *burnt* : hominum color, *sunburnt*, Liv.

ădusquĕ=usque ad.   (1) prep. with acc., *as far as* : Verg. (2) adv.=usque, *thoroughly, entirely* : Ov.

advectīcĭus -a -um, *that which is brought from a distance, foreign* : vinum, Sall.

advecto -are (freq. from adveho), *to convey often* : rei frumentariae copiam, Tac.

advectus -ūs, m. *a conveying, carrying* : Tac.

advĕho -vĕhĕre -vexi -vectum, *to carry, bring, convey to a place*. Act. : frumentum ex agris Romam, Cic.; ultrices unda advehit rates, Ov.; frumentum Romam, Cic. Pass., advehi, *to be borne to* a place (on horseback, in a chariot, on a ship, etc.) : advecta classis, Verg.; e Pompeiano navi in Luculli hospitium, Cic.; citato equo in eam partem, Liv. With acc. : Corcyram insulam advehitur, *reaches*, Tac.; Dardanos, Verg.; ut quosque advectus erat, Tac.

advēlo -are, *to veil* : tempora lauro, Verg.

advĕna -ae, c. (advenio), *a stranger, foreigner* (opp. indigena); often in apposition to another noun.
  LIT., of living things : indigenae advenaeque, Tac.; dei advenae, Cic.; advenam gruem (as a bird of passage), Hor.
  TRANSF., of other things : Tibris, Ov.; amor, *love for a foreigner*, Ov.

advĕnĭo -vĕnire -vēni -ventum, *to come to*.
  LIT., (1) of men : advenis modo? Cic.; ex Hyperboraeis Delphos, Cic.; in provinciam belli gerendi causa, Cic.; with acc. only : Tyriam urbem, Verg. (2) of things, esp. of ships : a quibus adveniat navis Miletida sospes ad urbem, Ov.
  TRANSF., (1) of time, *to come* : interea dies advenit, Cic. (2) of events, *to happen, to come near, to break out* : urbi periculum advenit, Sall.; morbi advenientes, Cic. (3) of acquisitions, *to come to* : res sua sponte mox ad eum advenit, Liv.; Sall.

adventīcĭus -a -um (advenio), *coming from without, from outside sources* : externus et adventicius tepor, Cic.; pecunia, *unearned*, Cic. Esp. *coming from abroad, foreign* : auxilia, Cic.; doctrina transmarina atque adventicia, Cic.

advento -are (freq. of advenio), *to approach, arrive at*, gen. with notion of haste : ad Italiam, Cic.; with dat. of person : Parthis, Tac.; in subsidium, Tac.; of things and abstractions : quod fere iam tempus adventat, Cic.

adventor -ōris, m. (advenio), *one who arrives, a visitor* : Pl.

adventus -ūs, m. (advenio), *an arrival* : nocturnus ad urbem, Cic.; in plur. : invitationes adventusque nostrorum hominum, Cic.; of things : veris, Hor.; in animos et introitus imaginum, Cic.
  TRANSF., malorum, Cic.

adversārĭus -a -um (adversus).
  (1) *turned towards*; n. pl. as subst. **adversāria** -orum (sc. scripta), *a book that lies in front of one*, so *a day-book, journal, memorandum* : adversaria negligenter scribere, Cic.
  (2) *turned against, opposed, contrary*; with dat. : Cic.; factio, Nep. As subst. m. **adversārius** -i, and f. **adversāria** -ae, *an antagonist, rival* : Cic.; also n. pl. **adversāria** -orum, *the assertions of an opponent* : adversaria evertere, Cic.

adversor -ari, dep. (adversus), *to oppose, resist*, of persons or things. Absol. : non adversante conlega, Cic.; adversante fortuna, Cic. Otherwise usually with dat. : alicui infestius, Cic.; legi, Cic., Liv.; cum duae causae perspicuis et evidentibus rebus adversentur, Cic.

¹adversus -a -um, partic. from adverto; q.v.

²adversus, adversum (adverto), adv. and prep., *opposed to.*

  Adv., *against, opposite, to meet*: nemo adversus ibat, Liv.; adversum ire *or* venire, *go to meet*: Pl., Ter.

  Prep with acc.: **a,** as regards place, *towards*: adversus clivum, Caes.; *opposite*: adversus aedes publicas, Liv.: **b,** of action, etc., *against*: adversus quem ibatur, Liv.; adversus rempublicam facere, Caes.; respondere adversus ea, *to answer to,* Liv.; adversus legem, Cic.; adversus quod . . . convenisset, *against the agreement,* Liv.; adversus blanditias incorruptus, Tac.; munitus adversum aliquem *or* aliquid, Sall.: **c,** of behaviour, *towards*: quonam modo me gererem adversus Caesarem, Cic.; reverentia adversus homines, Cic.: **d,** of comparison: quid autem esse duo prospera in tot saeclis bella Samnitium adversus tot decora populi Romani, *compared with,* Liv.

adverto (advorto) -vertĕre -verti -versum, *to turn towards.*

  LIT., agmen urbi, Verg. Esp. of ships, *to steer*: classem in portum, Liv.; pass.: notae advertuntur arenae, *they steer to,* Verg.; Scythicas advertitur oras, Ov.

  TRANSF., **(1)** of the senses, thoughts, etc., *to direct* towards an object: lumina in quamcunque aedis partem, Ov.; aures ad vocem, Ov.; of the gods: malis advertite numen, *direct your powers to,* Verg. Esp. of the mind, animum, and (sometimes) mentem advertere: **a,** *to direct one's attention to*: animos ad religionem: Lucr.; with dat.: animos monitis, Ov.; followed by ne and the subj.: animum animadvertant ne quos offendant, *take care not to,* etc., Cic.; absol.: Cic.: **b,** *to perceive*: aliquem in contione stantem, Cic.; followed by acc. and infin.: Cic.; or relative clause: Cic.: **c,** *to punish*: in aliquem, Tac. **(2)** of the object of attention, *to attract*: adverterat ea res Sabinos, Liv.; gemitus militum aures oraque advertere, Tac.

  ¶ Hence partic. **adversus** -a -um, *turned towards.*

  LIT., *fronting, opposite*: dentes, *the front teeth,* Cic.; adversa vulnera, *wounds in the front,* Cic.; solem adversum intueri, *to look straight at the sun,* Cic.; adversos concitare equos, *to ride towards,* Liv.; adversis hostibus occurrere, *to meet the enemy,* Caes.; adverso colle, *on the front of the hill,* Caes.; adverso flumine, *against the stream,* Caes.; venti adversi, *contrary winds,* Liv.; with prep.: in adversum, *against,* Verg., Liv.; ex adverso, *over against,* Liv.

  TRANSF., **(1)** of persons, *opposed*: adversus alicui, Cic.; adverso Marte, Verg.; adverso senatu, *against the will of the senate,* Liv. **(2)** of things: **a,** *unfavourable, unpropitious*: adversis auribus, Liv.; valetudo, *ill health,* Liv.; bellum, *cruel,* Hor.; proelium, *unsuccessful,* Caes.; res adversae, Cic., fortuna adversa, Verg., *misfortune*; with dat.: res plebi adversa, Liv.: **b,** *hated*: quis omnia regna adversa sunt, Sall.

N. as subst. **adversum** -i, *misfortune*: si quid adversi acciderit, Cic.

advespĕrascit -āvit (impers. and inch.), *evening approaches*: Ter., Cic.

advĭgĭlo -are, *to watch by, to guard.* LIT., parvo nepoti, Tib.; ad custodiam ignis, Cic. TRANSF., *to be vigilant*: Pl.

advŏcātĭo -ōnis, f. *a calling to one's aid*; hence t. t., *legal assistance*: in advocationibus, Cic. L. Hence **(1)** *chance to obtain legal assistance*: advocationes postulent, Cic. **(2)** concr., *the bar*: Cic.

advŏco -are, *to summon, to call*; esp. *to call to one's aid*: contionem populi, Cic.; aliquem in consilium, Cic.; advocare ad obsignandum, Cic.; non desiderat fortitudo iracundiam advocatam, *called to its aid,* Cic.; advocari aegro, Ov.; advocare deum sibi, Cat.; deos, Liv. Hence legal t. t., *to call in as adviser, to consult an advocate*: aliquem contra aliquem, Cic.; aliquem sibi, Pl.

  ¶ Hence m. of partic. as subst. **advocatus** -i, m. *one called in to help,* esp. (legal t. t.) as *witness* or *adviser in a lawsuit* (in republican times): Cic.; or as *advocate* (under the empire): Tac.

advŏlātus, abl. -ū, m. *a flying to*: poet. ap. Cic.

advŏlo -are, *to fly to.* LIT., of birds and insects: ad eas aves quae, Cic. TRANSF., *to hasten towards, to fly to*; of persons: advolone an maneo, Cic.; ad urbem, Cic.; rostra, Cic.; of things: fama mali tanti advolat Aeneae, *flies to the ears of,* Verg.

advolvo -volvĕre -volvi -vŏlūtum, *to roll to*: robora focis, *to the hearth,* Verg. Hence of suppliants, advolvi, *or* se advolvere, *to throw oneself at the feet of*: genibus alicuius, Liv.; genua alicuius, Sall.

advorsum, advorsus, advorto=**adversum, adversus, adverto**; q.v.

ădўtum -i, n. (ἄδυτον=not to be entered). LIT., gen. in plur., *the inmost and holiest portion of a temple, the shrine*: Verg., Hor. Also of a grave: adytis ab imis, Verg. TRANSF., ex adyto tamquam cordis, *from the bottom of the heart,* Lucr.

Aeăcus -i, m. (Αἰακός), *a mythical king of Aegina, father of Peleus and Telamon, grandfather of Ajax and Achilles; after his death judge in the infernal regions.*

  ¶ Hence subst. **Aeăcĭdes** -ae, m. *a male descendant of Aeacus, such as one of his sons*: Ov.; his grandson, *Achilles*: Verg.; *his greatgrandson, Pyrrhus* (Neoptolemus): Verg.; *one of his remote descendants, Pyrrhus* (king of Epirus): Enn.; *Perseus, king of Macedonia*: Liv.

  ¶ Hence adj. **Aeăcĭdēĭŭs** -a -um: regna (Aegina), Ov.; also **Aeăcĭdīnus** -a -um (of Achilles): Pl.

Aeaea -ae, f. (Αἰαίη), *the island of the sorceress Circe, or of Calypso.*

  ¶ Hence adj. **Aeaeus** -a -um, *Aeaean.* **(1)** *of Circe*: Aeaeae artes, Aeaea carmina, *sorceries,* Ov.; Aeaeus Telegonus, *son of Circe,* Prop. **(2)** *of Calypso*: puella, Prop.

Aeās -antis, m. (Αἴας), *a river in Greece, flowing by Apollonia.*

Aebura -ae, f. *a town in Hispania Tarraconensis* (now *Cuerva*): Liv.

Aeculānum -i, n. *a town of the Hirpini in Samnium*: Cic.

aedēs (aedis) -is, f. originally, *a building*
(1) sing.: a, *a room*: Pl.: b, *a temple* (of
less elaborate buildings than templum): aedes
sacra, Cic.; aedes Minervae, Cic.; in plur.:
complures aedes sacrae, Cic.; aedes alone,
the temple of the Palatine Apollo: Hor.
(2) plur. Lit., *rooms*, or *a house*: Pl., Cic.,
Verg.; aedes liberae, *empty*, Liv. Hence,
household: Pl. Transf., a, *the cells of bees*:
Verg.: b, *the chambers of the ears, the ears*: Pl.

aedĭcŭla -ae, f. (dim. of aedes), *a small building*.
(1) *a small temple*: Victoriae, Liv.; also *a
niche*, or *shrine* for the image of a god: Cic.
(2) *a little room*: Pl.; in plur., *a little house*:
Cic.

aedĭfĭcātĭo -ōnis, f. (aedifico), *building*. (1)
abstr., *the act of building*: consilium aedifica-
tionis, Cic.; aedificationem deponere *or*
abicere, *to give up building*, Cic. (2) concr.,
the building itself: domus tua et aedificatio
omnis, Cic. L.

aedĭfĭcātĭuncŭla -ae, f. (dim. of aedificatio),
a small building: Cic. L.

aedĭfĭcātŏr -ōris, m. (aedifico). (1) *a builder*,
architect. Transf., mundi, Cic. (2) *one
who has a passion for building*: Juv.

aedĭfĭcĭum -i, n. (aedifico), *a building*:
aedificia publica privata, sacra profana, Cic.;
sometimes opposed to inhabited houses:
aedes aedificiaque, Liv.; opposed to a palace:
plebis aedificiis obseratis, patentibus atriis
principum, Liv.

aedĭfĭco -are (aedes/facio). Lit., *to build*,
erect, establish: villam, porticum, domum,
urbem, navem, hortos, Cic.; also absol.
Transf., aedificare mundum, *to create*, Cic.;
rempublicam, *to frame*, Cic. L.

aedīlĭcĭus -a -um (aedilis), *relating to the
aediles*: munus, Cic.; vectigal, *tax paid by the
provinces for the shows of the aediles*, Cic.
M. as subst. **aedīlĭcĭus** -i, *one who has been
aedile*: Cic.

aedīlis -is, m. (aedes), *an aedile*, *a public
officer at Rome who had charge of the streets,
traffic, markets, and public games*. There were
originally two aediles; then, after 367 B.C.,
four, two patrician (aediles curules) and two
plebeian (aediles plebeii). Aedilis is once used
as adj.: aediles ludi, Pl.

aedīlĭtās -ātis, f. (aedilis), *the aedileship*:
aedilitate fungi, Cic.

aedĭtĭmus (aeditumus) -i, m., old form of
aedĭtŭus; q.v.

aedĭtŭens -entis, m., Lucr.=aedituus; q.v.

aedĭtŭus -i, m. (aedes), *keeper of a temple*,
sacristan: Cic. Transf., Hor.

Aedŭi (Haedŭi) -ōrum, *a Gallic people living
in modern Burgundy*, whose chief town was
Bibracte.

Aeēta and **Aeētēs** -ae, m. (Αἰήτης), *king of
Colchis, father of Medea*.
¶ Hence subst. **Aeētĭas** -ădis, f. and
Aeētĭne -ēs, f., *daughter of Aeetes=Medea*:
Ov.; adj. **Aeētaeus** -a -um, *belonging to
Aeetes*: fines, Colchis, Cat.

Aegae -ārum, f. (Αἰγαί). (1) *a town in Euboea*.
(2) *an early capital of Macedonia* (now
Vodena). (3) *a town in Cilicia*.

Aegaeŏn -ŏnis, m. (Αἰγαίων). (1) *another name
for the giant Briareus*: Verg. (2) *a sea-god*: Ov.

Aegaeus -a -um (Αἰγαῖος), *Aegean*: mare,
the Aegean Sea, the Archipelago, Cic.

N. as subst. **Aegaeum** -i, *the Aegean Sea*:
Hor.

Aegātēs -um, f. pl. (with or without insulae),
*a group of three islands off the west coast of
Sicily*, near which the decisive battle of the
first Punic war was fought (241 B.C.).

aeger -gra -grum, *sick, ill*.
(1) of *physical illness*: a, of persons:
homines aegri gravi morbo, Cic.; ex vulnere,
Cic.; pedibus, Sall.; oculis, Liv.; manum,
Tac.; m. as subst. **aeger** -gri, *an invalid*:
Cic.: b, of bodies or parts of the body:
corpus, Cic.; dens, Mart.: c, of bodily
conditions: valetudo, Cic.; anhelitus, Verg.
Also of plants: seges, Verg.
(2) of *mental ailments, ill* from any cause,
love, hope, fear, sorrow, etc.: a, of persons:
mortales aegri, Verg.; aegra amans, Verg.;
animo magis quam corpore aeger, Liv.;
amore, Liv.; animi, *in mind*, Liv.; consilii,
infirm of purpose, Sall.: b, of conditions,
states of mind, etc.: amor, Verg.; so of looks:
aegris oculis, *with envious eyes*, Tac.
(3) of *political trouble, unsound*: pars
reipublicae, Cic.; civitas, Liv.; municipia,
mutinous, Tac.
¶ Hence adv. (with compar. and superl.)
aegrē. (1) with mental pain, so *with regret,
with reluctance* or *vexation*, esp.: aegre ferre,
to take it hard, used absol. or with acc. or
with acc. and infin.; also aegre est, with dat.
of person. (2) *with difficulty*: aegre divelli,
aegrius depelli, Cic. (3) *hardly, scarcely*
(cf. vix): se tenere, Cic.

Aegeus -ĕi, m. (Αἰγεύς), *king of Athens, father
of Theseus*.
¶ Hence **Aegīdēs** -ae, m. *Theseus*, or *any
one of the descendants of Aegeus*.

Aegīna -ae, f. (Αἰγινα), *an island near Athens*.
¶ Hence subst. **Aegīnēta** -ae, m. *an
Aeginetan*; adj. **Aegīnētĭcus** -a -um.

Aegīnĭum -i, n. (Αἰγίνιον), *a town in Thessaly*.
¶ Hence **Aegīnĭenses** -ium, m. *the
inhabitants of Aeginium*: Liv.

Aegĭon (Aegĭum) -i, n. (Αἴγιον), *one of the
twelve Achaean towns*.

aegis -idis, f. (αἰγίς), *an aegis*, or *shield*. Lit.,
(1) *of Jupiter*: Verg. (2) *of Minerva with the
Medusa's head*: Ov. Transf., *a protection*,
bulwark: Ov.

Aegisthus -i, m. (Αἴγισθος), *son of Thyestes,
murderer of Agamemnon, afterwards husband
of Clytemnestra, himself murdered by Orestes*:
Cic.

Aegium=Aegion; q.v.

Aeglē -ēs, f. (Αἴγλη), *a nymph, daughter of
Jupiter and Neaera*.

Aegŏcĕrōs -ōtis, m. (αἰγοκέρως), *a sign of the
Zodiac, Capricorn*: Lucr.

aegrē, adv. from aeger; q.v.

aegrĕo -ēre (aeger), *to be sick*: Lucr.

aegresco -ĕre (aegreo), *to fall ill*. Lit., morbis,
Lucr. Transf., (1) *to become worse, more
violent*: violentia Turni aegrescit medendo,
Verg. (2) *to be disturbed in mind, to trouble
oneself*: longiore sollicitudine, Tac.

aegrĭmōnĭa -ae, f. (aeger), *grief, trouble of
mind*: Cic. L., Hor.

aegrĭtūdo -ĭnis, f. (aeger), *sickness*. Lit., of the
body: Pl., Tac. Transf., of the mind, *grief*:
se totum aegritudini dedere, Cic.; aegritudine
emori, Cic.; in aegritudinem incidere, Cic.;

aegritudinem levare, lenire, sedare, adimere alicui, depellere, efficere, Cic.; plur.: aegritudines leniores facere, Cic.
aegror -ōris, m. (aeger), *sickness*: Lucr.
aegrŏtātĭo -ōnis, f. (aegroto), *sickness, of body or of mind*: Cic.
aegrŏto -are (aegrotus), *to be sick* or *ill*.
    LIT., *of the body*: graviter, vehementer diuque, leviter, periculose, Cic.; *of cattle*: Hor.; *of plants*: Plin.
    TRANSF., *of the mind*: ea res ex qua animus aegrotat, Cic., Hor. *Of other things*: aegrotat fama vacillans, Lucr.
aegrōtus -a -um (aeger), *sick, ill.* LIT., *in body*: Cic. TRANSF., *in mind*: Ter.; *of other things*: respublica, Cic.
Aegyptus -i (Αἴγυπτος). (1) mythol., m. *a king of Egypt, son of Belus, brother of Danaus.* (2) geogr., f. *Egypt.*
    ¶ Hence adj. **Aegyptĭus** and **Aegyptĭăcus** -a -um, *Egyptian.*
aelĭnos -i, m. (αἴλινος), *a dirge*: Ov.
Aemilĭus -a -um, gens, *name of one of the oldest and most distinguished patrician families of Rome*: Aemilia via, and simply Aemilia, *a road made by the consul M. Aem. Lepidus,* leading from Ariminum to Placentia; pons, *a bridge near the Pons Sublicius,* Juv.; ratis, *the ship in which the spoils of Perseus were brought home by Aem. Paulus,* Prop.; ludus, *a gladiatorial school founded by P. Aemilius Lepidus,* Hor.
    ¶ Hence adj. **Aemĭlĭānus** -a -um, *relating to the gens Aemilia; a surname of Scipio Africanus minor,* the son of L. Aemilius Paulus, adopted by the elder Scipio Africanus.
Aemōnia=Haemōnia; q.v.
aemŭlātĭo -ōnis, f. (aemulor), *a striving after* or *up to, emulation.* In a good sense: laudis, Nep.; gloriae, Liv. In a bad sense, *jealousy, envy, ill-natured rivalry*: Cic., Tac.; plur., *rivalries*: Cic.
aemŭlātor -ōris, m. (aemulor), *a rival*: Catonis aemulator, *an imitator,* Cic. L.
aemŭlātus -ūs, m. (aemulor), *rivalry*: Tac.
aemŭlor -ari, dep. (aemulus), *to rival, emulate.* (1) in a good sense, *with acc.*: instituta, Cic.; Pindarum, Hor. (2) in a bad sense, *to envy; with dat.*: alicui, Cic.; cum aliquo, Liv.; inter se, Tac.; with infin.: Tac.
aemŭlus -a -um, *emulous, vying with, rivalling in.*
    (1) in a good sense; with genit.: mearum laudium, Cic.; with dat.: dictator Caesar summis oratoribus aemulus, Tac.
    (2) in a bad sense, *zealous, rivalling*: Carthago aemula imperii Romani, Sall.; aemula senectus, *jealous,* Verg. As subst. **aemŭlus** -i, m. and **aemŭla** -ae, f. *a rival in love*: Cic., Ov.; in gen., *a rival*: Cic. Also used of things, in poetry and late prose: tibia tubae aemula, Hor.
Aemus=Haemus.
Aenārĭa -ae, f. *the landing-place of Aeneas, a volcanic island on the west coast of Italy, opposite Campania* (now *Ischia*).
Aenēa -ae, f. (Αἴνεια), *a town in Chalcidice.*
    ¶ Hence subst. **Aenēātes** -um, m. (Αἰνεᾶται), *inhabitants of Aenea.*
Aenēas -ae, m. (Αἰνείας), *son of Venus and Anchises, hero of Vergil's Aeneid, myth. ancestor of the Romans*: Aeneae mater, *Venus,* Ov.; Aeneae urbs, *Rome,* Ov.

¶ Hence subst. **Aenĕădes** -ae, m. *descendant of Aeneas; his son Ascanius*: Verg.; also used of remoter descendants, as of *Augustus*: Ov.; also of *the companions of Aeneas*: Verg.; or *the Trojans* or *the Romans in general*: Verg.
    Subst. **Aenēis** -idos, f. *Vergil's Aeneid.*
    Adj. **Aenēius** -a -um, *relating to Aeneas.*
    Subst. **Aenīdēs** -ae, m. *a son of Aeneas*: Verg.
ăēnĕător -ōris, m. (aeneus), *a trumpeter*: Suet.
ăēnĕus and **ăhēnĕus** -a -um (aenum, ahenum), *made of copper* or *bronze*: Cic., Hor.
    TRANSF., (1) *of a bronze colour*: Suet. (2) *hard as bronze*: murus, Hor.; proles, *the brazen age,* Ov.
Aenīānes -um, m. *a Greek tribe in the south of Thessaly.*
aenigma -ātis, n. (αἴνιγμα), *a riddle, mystery*: somniorum, Cic.
ăēnĭpēs -pĕdis (ăēnĕus/pes), *brazen-footed*: Ov.
¹**ăēnus** (**ăhēnus**) -a -um (aes), *made of copper* or *bronze*: Verg. N. as subst., *a bronze vessel*: Verg. TRANSF., *hard as bronze*: manus, Hor.
²**Aenus** (**Aenŏs**) -i, f. (Αἶνος), *a town in Thrace, at the mouth of the Hebrus* (now *Enez*).
    ¶ Hence **Aenii** -orum, m. *its inhabitants.*
³**Aenus** -i, m. *a river between Vindelicia and Noricum* (now *the Inn*).
Aeŏles -um, m. *the Aeolians, one of the chief tribes of the Greeks, living in Greece and Asia Minor.*
    ¶ Hence adj. **Aeŏlĭcus** -a -um, and **Aeŏlĭus** -a -um, *Aeolic,* with especial reference to Sappho, the Lesbian poetess.
Aeŏlĭa -ae, f. (Αἰολία). (1) *the north part of the coast of Asia Minor, inhabited by the Aeolians.* (2) *a group of volcanic islands off the north coast of Sicily* (the *Lipari isles*).
    ¶ Hence adj. **Aeŏlĭus** -a -um: insulae, Plin.
Aeŏlis -ĭdis, f. (Αἰολίς)=Aeolia; q.v.
Aeŏlus -i, m. (Αἰολος), *son of Jupiter* or *of Hippotas, ruler of the Aeolian islands and of the winds.*
    ¶ Hence subst. **Aeŏlĭdes** -ae, m. *a descendant of Aeolus; his son Sisyphus*: Ov.; *Athamas*: Ov.; *Salmoneus*: Ov.; *his grandson Cephalus*: Ov.; *Ulysses*: Verg. **Aeŏlis** -ĭdos, f. *female descendant of Aeolus; his daughter Canace*: Ov.; *Alcyone*: Ov. Adj. **Aeŏlĭus** -a -um, *belonging to Aeolus* or *his descendants*: virgo, *his daughter Arne,* Ov.; tyrannus, *Aeolus,* Ov.; antra, *the caves where the winds were kept,* Ov.; procellae, Verg.
aequābĭlis -e (aequo), *like, similar, equal.* LIT., praedae partitio, Cic. TRANSF., (1) *equal to itself, uniform, equable, consistent*: fluvius, Cic.; cunctis vitae officiis aequabilis, Tac. (2) *fair, impartial*: nihil ea iurisdictione aequabilius, Cic.; of persons: in suos, Tac.
    ¶ Hence adv. (with compar.) **aequābĭlĭtĕr,** *equably, uniformly, fairly*: praedam dispertire, Cic.; aequabilius provinciae regentur, Tac.
aequābĭlĭtās -ātis, f. (aequabilis), *uniformity, equability*: motus, Cic. Hence of *evenness in style and of impartiality in law*: Cic.
aequaevus -a -um (aequus/aevum), *of equal age*: Verg., Suet.
aequālis -e (aequo), *even.* LIT., *of places, level*: loca, Sall., Tac. TRANSF., *equal*; with

dat.: pars pedis aequalis alteri parti, Cic.; with inter: virtutes sunt inter se aequales et pares, Cic. Esp. of time, *of the same age*, *contemporary*, *coexistent*; with genit.: sacrificium aequale huius urbis, Cic.; Philistus aequalis temporum illorum, Cic.; calo quidam aequalis Hieronymi, Liv.; with dat.: cui si aequalis fuerit Livius, Liv.; exercitus aequalis stipendiis suis, *that had served as many campaigns as he himself*, Liv.; absol.: aequali corpore nymphae, *of the same age and growth*, Verg. As subst. **aequālis** -is, c. *a comrade, person of the same age*: P. Orbius meus fere aequalis, Cic.
¶ Hence adv. **aequālĭtĕr**, *evenly*, *equally*: collis ab summo aequaliter declivis, Cic.; distribuere, Cic.

aequālĭtās -ātis, f. (aequalis), *evenness*. LIT., of places, *smoothness*: Sen., Plin. TRANSF., *equality*: similitudo aequalitasque verborum (of a pun), Cic.; *equality of age*: Cic.; *equality of political privileges*: Tac.

aequănĭmĭtās -ātis, f. (aequus/animus). (1) *impartiality*: Ter. (2) *calmness*: Plin.

aequātĭo -ōnis, f. (aequo), *a making equal*: bonorum, *communism*, Cic.; iuris, Liv.

aequē, adv. from aequus; q.v.

Aequi -ōrum, m. *a people of central Italy*, with whom the Romans waged frequent wars.
¶ Hence adj. **Aequicŭlus** and **Aequĭcus** -a -um, *Aequian*.

aequĭlībrĭtās -ātis, f. *the equal distribution of natural forces*=ισονομία: Cic.

Aequĭmaelĭum -i, n. *an open space in Rome, on the west side of the Capitol.*

aequĭnoctĭālis -e (aequinoctium), *equinoctial, relating to the equinox*: Sen., Plin.

aequĭnoctĭum -i, n. (aequus/nox), *the equinox*: Cic., Caes., Liv.

aequĭpăro (**aequĭpĕro**) -are (aequus/paro). (1) *to compare*; with and the acc.: suas virtutes ad tuas, Pl.; with dat.: mari tranquillo quod ventis concitatur multitudinem Aetolorum, Liv. (2) *to equal*: aliquem, Cic.; nec calamis solum sed voce magistrum, Verg.

aequĭtās -ātis, f. (aequus), *uniformity, evenness*. LIT., membrorum, Suet. TRANSF., *equanimity* (with or without animi): Cic. Also *impartiality, equity, fairness, justice*: causae, Cic.; condicionum, Caes.; servare aequitatem, Cic.

aequo -are (aequus).
(1) *to make level*: locum, Caes.; aequata agri planities, Cic.; aequare frontem, milit. t. t., *to form a line*, Liv.
(2) *to make equal*: pecunias, Cic.; aequato omnium periculo, Cic.; sortes, *to adjust the lots fairly*, Cic. Also *to make equal to*; with cum and abl.: inventum est temperamentum quo tenuiores cum principibus aequari se putarent, Cic.; but usually with dat., often in fig. senses: solo aequare, *to level with the ground*, Suet.; fig.: solo aequandae sunt dictaturae consulatusque, *must be abolished*, Liv.; machina aequata caelo, *as high as the heavens*, Verg.; fig.: aliquem caelo laudibus, *to extol to the heavens*, Verg.; per somnum vinumque dies noctibus, *to turn day into night by sleeping and drinking*, Liv.; nocti ludum, *to spend the whole night in play*, Verg.
(3) *to compare*: Hannibali Philippum, Liv.

(4) *to equal, to come up to*: Appii odium, Liv.; sagitta aequans ventos, Verg.; aliquem passibus, Verg.; aliquem equestri gloria, Liv.

aequor -ōris, n. (aequus), *a flat level surface*: speculorum, Lucr. Esp. (1) *the flat surface of a plain*: camporum patentium aequor, Cic.; poet. (without campi): immensum aequor, *of a desert*, Verg. (2) mainly poet., *the flat surface of the sea, the sea*; with ponti or maris: vastum maris aequor, Verg.; oftener without maris, etc.: Ionium, Lucr.; vastum, Verg.; plur.: saeva aequora, Verg.; rarely, *the surface of a river*, as the Tiber: Verg.

aequŏrĕus -a -um (aequor), *belonging to the sea*: genus, *fishes*, Verg.; rex, *Neptune*, Ov.; Britanni, *sea-girt*, Ov.; Achilles, *a son of Thetis*, Luc.

aequus -a -um, adj. (with compar. and superl.), *equal*.
LIT., (1) *equal in itself, even*; of the surface of the ground, *level*: aequus et planus locus, Cic.; ex aequo loco loqui, *to speak in the senate* (opp. to ex inferiore loco, *in the presence of the judges*, and ex superiore loco, *in the presence of the people*), Cic.; ex superiore et ex aequo loco sermones habitos, *public and private conversations*, Cic. Also of other things, *level*: aequa frons, milit. t. t., *a straight line*, Liv.
(2) *equal to something else*, in amount, in dimensions, or generally: aequo fere spatio abesse, Caes.; sequitur patrem non passibus aequis, *with shorter steps*, Verg.; foll. by dat.: urbs nubibus aequa, *as high as the clouds*, Ov.; also by atque, quam, cum: aequo et pari cum civibus iure vivere, Cic.; aequam partem tibi sumpseris atque populo Romano miseris, Cic. Phrases: ex aequo, in aequo, *on even terms*, Liv., Ov., etc.

TRANSF., (1) of places or times, *favourable, advantageous*: locum se aequum ad dimicandum dedisse, Caes.; et tempore et loco aequo instructos, Liv. (2) of battles, *even*, and so *indecisive*: pugna, Liv.; aequo proelio, aequo marte discedere, Caes.; aequa manu, Liv., Tac. (3) of temper, *even, contented, easy*: concedo et quod animus aequus est et quia necesse est, Cic.; aequam rebus in arduis servare mentem, Hor.; esp. in the phrase aequo animo, *patiently, with resignation*; pati *or* ferre with acc., and acc. with infin.: Cic.; tolerare, Sall.; accipere, Sall.; spectare, Cic.; animo aequissimo mori, Cic. (4) of behaviour, etc., *equal, impartial*; of persons, *fair*: se alicui aequum praebere, Cic.; praetor, iudex, testis, Cic.; of things: iudicia, Cic.; lex, Cic.; aequum est, *it is just*; with the acc. and infin.: aequum esse eum et officio meo consulere et tempori, Cic.; per aequa per iniqua, *by fair means or foul*, Liv.; gravius aequo, *than is right*, Sall.; as a legal formula: quod *or* quantum aequius melius, *as is more equitable*, Cic.; non aequa Pallas, Verg.; minus aequis animis auditus est Scipio, Liv.
¶ N. as subst. **aequum** -i. LIT., *level ground*: in aequo campi, Liv. TRANSF., *fairness, equity*: quid in iure aut in aequo verum aut esset aut non esset, Cic.; esp. associated with bonum: reus magis ex bono aequoque quam ex iure gentium, Sall.; aequi bonique facere, *to consider right and proper*, Ter., Cic.

¶ Hence adv. **aequē,** *in like manner, equally.* (1) duae trabes aeque longae, Caes.; aeque dolere, Cic.; with adv.: aeque lubenter, Cic. Esp. in comparisons, *just as, equally with*; foll. by et, atque, ac si, quam, quam ut, etc.: eosdem labores non esse aeque graves imperatori et militi, Cic.; hi coluntur aeque atque illi, Cic.; with cum and the abl.: ut aeque mecum haec scias, Pl.; with abl. alone: Pl.
(2) *fairly, justly*: societatem condicionis humanae munifice et aeque tuens, Cic.

āēr āĕris, m. (*ἀήρ*), *the lower air, the atmosphere around us*: crassus, Cic.; purus et tenuis, Cic.; temperatus, Cic.; aer summus arboris, *the airy summit of a tree,* Verg.; aere saeptus obscuro, *surrounded by a cloud,* Verg.

aerāmentum -i, n. *bronze or copper ware*: Plin.

aerārĭus -a -um. (1) *of or belonging to bronze or copper*: metallum, fornaces, Plin.; structurae, *copper mines,* Caes. (2) *belonging to* (*copper*) *money*: ratio, *standard of coinage,* Cic.; tribuni, *paymasters*; illa vetus aeraria fabula, *the old tale about the copper coin that Vettius gave to Clodia,* Cic.
M. as subst. **aerārĭus** -i. (1) *a copper-smith*: Plin. (2) gen. in plur., aerarii, *the citizens of the lowest class in Rome, who had no votes, but had to pay a certain sum for the expenses of the state,* a class to which citizens of the higher ranks might be degraded by the censors for punishment: aliquem aerarium facere, *to degrade,* Liv.; aliquem in aerarios referri iubere, Cic.
N. as subst. **aerārĭum** -i, *a treasury,* esp. *the public treasury,* at Rome, under or behind the temple of Saturn, where the treasures and archives of the state were kept: pecuniam in aerarium referre, inferre, deferre, redigere, Cic.; decreta patrum ad aerarium deferre, Tac. Also used of *the money in the treasury*: Cic., and of special funds: sanctius, *reserve fund,* Caes., Liv.; militare, *military chest,* Tac.

aerātus -a -um (aes). (1) *made of or fitted with copper or bronze*: navis, Caes.; lecti, *with bronze feet,* Cic.; poet.: acies, *an armed line of troops,* Verg. (2) *provided with money, rich*: tribuni non tam aerati, quam ut appellantur aerarii (with a play on the words, vide aerarius), Cic.

aerĕus -a -um (aes), *made of or fitted with copper or bronze*: signa aerea et marmorea, Liv.; puppis, Verg.

aerĭfĕr -fĕra -fĕrum (aes/fero), *bearing brazen cymbals*: Ov.

aerĭpēs -pĕdis (aes/pes), *brazen-footed*: Verg., Ov.

āĕrĭus (āĕrĕus) -a -um (aer). (1) *belonging to the air, airy*: alterum (animantium genus), pennigerum et aerium, *living in the air,* Cic.; domus, *the heavens,* Hor.; aerias vias carpere, *to fly through the air,* Ov.; mel (from the belief that honey fell in dew from the sky), Verg. (2) *high in the air, lofty*: Alpes, Verg.

Āĕrŏpē -ēs, f. and **Āĕrŏpa** -ae, f. (*Ἀερόπη*), *the wife of Atreus and mother of Agamemnon and Menelaus.*

aerōsus -a -um (aes), *rich in copper*: aurum, mixed with copper, Plin.

aerūgĭnōsus -a -um (aerugo), *covered with verdigris* or *copper-rust*: Sen.

aerūgo -inis, f. (aes). LIT., *the rust of copper, verdigris*: Cic. Meton.=*rusty money*: Juv. TRANSF., (1) *envy*: Hor. (2) *avarice*: Hor.

aerumna -ae, f. *hard labour, toil, hardship*: Herculis perpeti aerumnas, Cic., Pl., Lucr.

aerumnābĭlis -e (aerumna), *calamitous, pitiable*: Lucr.

aerumnōsus -a -um adj. (with compar. and superl.) (aerumna), *full of hardship and calamity*: Pl., Cic.

aes, aeris, n. *copper.*
LIT., *copper ore,* and *the alloy of copper, bronze*: pedestris ex aere statua, Cic.; poet., of the brazen age: ut inquinavit aere tempus aureum, Hor.
TRANSF., *something made of bronze,* etc. In gen. (esp. in poets), *a vessel, statue,* etc., made of bronze, etc.: aes cavum, *kettle,* Ov.; aera aere repulsa, *cymbals,* Ov.; Corybantia, *cymbals used in the service of Cybele,* Verg.; eius aera refigere, *the brazen tablets on which the laws were engraved,* Cic.; aes publicum, *public inscriptions,* Tac.; aere ciere viros, *with the trumpet,* Verg.; dempto aere, *the helmet,* Ov. Esp. *money.* (1) *copper or bronze money*; aes grave, *the as,* which was weighed instead of counted: denis millibus aeris gravis reos condemnavit, Liv.; quinquaginta millia aeris (for assium), Liv.; aes signatum, *coined money,* Cic.; *small change* (cf. Engl., *coppers*): aera dabant olim, Ov. (2) *money* generally: gravis aere dextra, Verg.; esp.: **a,** aes meum, *my property*: est aliquis in meo aere, *he is bound to me,* Cic.: **b,** aes alienum, *debt*: facere, contrahere, in aes alienum incidere, esse in aere alieno, Cic.; solvere, Cic.; so: aes mutuum, Sall.: **c,** *pay*: Juv.; often *soldiers' pay*: aera militibus constituere, dare, Liv.

Aesācŏs and **Aesācus** -i, m. (*Αἴσακος*), *son of Priam, husband of Asterope* or *Hesperia.*

Aesăr -āris, m. *a river in Bruttii in southern Italy* (now *Esaro*).
¶ Hence adj. **Aesărĕus** -a -um, *belonging to the river Aesar.*

Aeschĭnes -is and -i, m. (*Αἰσχίνης*). (1) *an Athenian philosopher, disciple of Socrates.* (2) *the celebrated Athenian orator, opponent of Demosthenes.*

Aeschўlus -i, m. (*Αἰσχύλος*). (1) *the Athenian tragic poet* (525 or 524–456 B.C.). (2) *a rhetorician of Cnidos, contemporary with Cicero.*

Aescŭlāpĭus -i, m. (*Ἀσκληπιός*), *the god of medicine, son of Apollo and Coronis, worshipped at Epidaurus and at Rome.*
¶ Hence subst. **Aescŭlāpĭum** -i, n. *a temple of Aesculapius.*

aescŭlētum -i, n. (aesculus), *an oak forest*: Hor.

aescŭlĕus -a -um (aesculus), *relating to the* (*winter*) *oak*: Ov.

aescŭlus -i, f. *the winter or Italian oak*: Verg., Hor.

Aesernĭa -ae, f. *a town in Samnium* (now *Isernia*).
¶ Hence adj. **Aesernīnus** -a -um, *belonging to Aesernia*; also *a surname of M. Marcellus, who was taken prisoner at Aesernia*; also *the name of a celebrated gladiator*: Cic.

Aesis -is, m. *a river*, and f. *a town, in Umbria*.
Aesōn -ŏnis, m. (Αἴσων), *a Thessalian prince, father of Jason*.
¶ Hence subst. **Aesŏnĭdes** -ae, m. *a descendant of Aeson (Jason)*: Ov.; adj. **Aesŏnĭus** -a -um, *relating to Aeson*: heros, *Jason*, Ov.
Aesōpus -i, m. (Αἴσωπος). (1) *a celebrated Greek fabulist of Phrygia, supposed to have lived in the 6th cent.* B.C. (2) Claudius (Clodius) Aesopus, *a tragic actor in Rome, contemporary and friend of Cicero.*
aestās -ātis, f. (connected with αἴθω = to burn), *summer*. LIT., ineunte, Cic.; novā, *at the beginning of summer*, Verg.; mediā, Cic.; adultā, Tac.; summā, Cic.; exactā, *at the end of*, Sall.; esp. used of the summer as *the time for military operations*: unis litteris totius aestatis (*summer campaign*) res gestas ad senatum perscribere, Cic.; so: quae duabus aestatibus gesta, Tac. TRANSF., *clear summer weather*: Verg.; *summer heat*: Hor.
aestĭfĕr -fĕra -fĕrum (aestus/fero), *heat-bringing*: ignis, Lucr., Verg.
aestĭmābĭlis -e (aestimo), *valuable*: Cic.
aestĭmātĭo -ōnis, f. (aestimo).
   LIT., *an appraising according to value in money*: aequam aestimationem facere, Caes.; census, *the valuation of the census*, Cic.; frumenti, *valuation of the corn allowance* for the governor of a province, or the amount to be paid by the aratores of the province instead of this allowance, Cic.; litis, *assessment of damages*, Cic.; so: multae, Liv.; possessionis, *valuation of property*, Cic.; praedia in aestimatione ab aliquo accipere, *to take estates at the higher valuation that prevailed before the civil war*, according to a law of Caesar, Cic.
   TRANSF., (1) *the valuation* of a thing or person, *according to intrinsic value*: honoris, Liv. (2) *actual worth or value*: Cat.
aestĭmātor -ōris, m. (aestimo). (1) *one who estimates, an appraiser*: frumenti, Cic. (2) *one who values a thing according to its worth*: rerum, Cic.
aestĭmo (**aestŭmo**) -are (aes), *to appraise, estimate the value of anything*.
   LIT., *to rate*, esp. in terms of money (cf. aestimatio): frumentum, Cic.; with abl. or genit., of value: aliquid ternis denariis, Cic.; ut liceat, quanti quisque velit, tanti aestimet, Cic.; with adv.: tenuissime, *at a very low rate*, Cic.; aliquid ex artificio, *according to the standard of workmanship*, Cic.; litem alicui, *or* alicuius, legal t. t., *to assess the damages in a law-suit*, Cic.; pugnatum est ut lis haec capitis aestimaretur, *should be held a capital charge*, Cic.
   TRANSF., in a wider sense, *to value* a thing or person, with constructions as above: magno, Cic.; virtutem annis, Hor.; magni, Cic.; carius, Cic.; levius tempestatis quam classis periculum, Caes.; vulgus ex veritate pauca, ex opinione multa aestimat, Cic.; satis aestimare, *to estimate at full value*, Tac.; hence generally, *to judge*: sicuti ego aestimo, Sall.
aestīvo -are (aestivus), *to pass the summer*: Plin., Suet.
aestīvus -a -um (aestus), *relating to summer*: tempora, Cic.; aura, Hor.; saltus, *summer pastures*, Liv.; aestivum tonat, *it thunders as in summer*, Juv.
   N. pl. as subst. **aestīva** -orum. (1) *a summer camp*: Cic.; meton. (because the ancients generally waged war only in the summer), *a campaign*: Cic. (2) *summer pastures for cattle*: Plin.; meton., *the cattle in summer pastures*: Verg.
¶ Adv. **aestīvē**, *in summer fashion*: Pl.
aestŭārium -i, n. (aestus). (1) *low ground covered by the sea at high water*: itinera aestuariis concisa, Caes. (2) *a firth, creek*, or *part of the river up which the tide flows*: in aestuario Tamesae, Tac. (3) *in mines, an air-shaft*: Plin.
aestŭo -are (aestus), *to boil, be agitated, seethe*.
   LIT., (1) of fire, of persons, of solid objects, *to burn, be hot*: aestuat ignis, Verg.; ventis pulsa aestuat arbor, Lucr.; si dixeris 'aestuo' (*I am warm*) sudat, Juv. (2) of liquids, *to boil, seethe*: gurges aestuat, Verg.
   TRANSF., (1) of emotional excitement, *to burn*: ut desiderio te nostri aestuare putarem, Cic.; nobilitas invidia aestuabat, Sall.; so of love: rex in illa aestuat, *burns with love for*, Ov. (2) of perplexity, *to waver*: aestuabat dubitatione, Cic.
aestŭōsus -a -um, adj. (with superl.) (aestus). (1) *hot*: via, Cic. (2) *agitated*: freta, Hor.
¶ Hence adv. (with compar.) **aestuōsē**, *hotly*: Pl., Hor.
aestus -ūs, m. (αἴθω), *boiling, agitation, seething*.
   LIT. (cf aestuo). (1) *heat*: propiusque aestūs incendia volvunt, Verg.; of the sun: meridiei aestus, Liv.; plur., *hot days*: Verg.; of fever: aestu febrique iactari, Cic. (2) of liquids, esp. of the sea, *seething, raging*: ferventes aestibus undae, Ov.; minuente aestu, *the storm lessening*, Caes.; also of the sea's *tide*, and *spray*: Lucr.
   TRANSF., of persons. (1) *dizziness*: Lucr. (2) *emotional excitement, heat, fury*: gloriae, Cic.; civilis belli, Hor.; irarum, Verg. (3) *perplexity, anxiety*: qui tibi aestus, qui error, quae tenebrae erant, Cic.; magno curarum fluctuat aestu, Verg.
aetās -ātis, f. (contr. from aevitas, from aevum), *age*.
   (1) *of human life*: **a**, *a lifetime*: aetatem agere, degere, conterere, consumere, Cic.; sometimes *a generation*: tertiam iam aetatem hominum vivebat, Cic.: **b**, *a time of life, age*: id aetatis, *of that age*, Cic.; aetate inutiles, Caes.
   So of particular times of life; of *youth*: iniens aetas, Cic.; bona, Cic.; flos aetatis, Cic., Liv.; so aetas alone: carus eris Romae donec te deseret aetas, Hor.; of *manhood*: in aetatem pervenire, Liv.; of *particular stages in manhood*: ad petendum (magistratum) legitima aetas, Cic.; aetas militaris, *the seventeenth year*, Sall.; quaestoria, *the twenty-fifth*, Quint.; senatoria, *the twenty-fifth*, Tac.; consularis, *the forty-third*, Cic.; of *old age*: aetas ingravescens, Cic.; provecta, Cic.; mala, Pl.; so aetas alone: Pl., Liv.: **c**, *the persons of a particular age*: vestra, Cic.; puerilis, *boys*, Cic.; senilis, *old men*, Cic.
   (2) *time, age* in gen.: omnia fert aetas, Verg. Esp. *a period of time, epoch*: clarissimus imperator suae aetatis, Liv.; nostra aetas, *the men of our time*, Liv.; verborum vetus

aetas, *obsolete words*, Hor.; aurea, *the golden age*, Ov.

aetătŭla -ae, f. (dim. of aetas), *youthful age*: prima illa aetatula sua, Cic.

aeternĭtās -ātis, f. (aeternus), *eternity, immortality*. Lit., ex omni aeternitate verum esse, Cic.; animorum, Cic.; mihi populus Romanus aeternitatem immortalitatemque donavit, Cic. Transf., in imperial times, *a title of the emperor*, similar to maiestas, divinitas, etc.: Plin. L.

aeterno -are (aeternus), *to make eternal, to immortalize*: Hor.

aeternus -a -um adj. (with compar.) (contr. from aeviternus), *eternal, everlasting*, with reference to past or future or both: bellum, Cic.; urbs, Rome, Tib.; amore aeterno, Cic.; ex aeterno tempore, *from eternity*, Lucr.; in aeternum, *for ever*, Liv.; so: aeternum, Verg.; aeterno, *everlastingly*, Plin.

aether -ĕris, acc. -ĕra, m. (αἰθήρ), *the upper air*: Cic.; Iuppiter aethere summo despiciens, Verg.; poet, *heaven*: super aethera notus, Verg.; also *the upper world* (opposed to the infernal regions): aethere in alto, Verg. Personified, **Aether**: Cic., Lucr., Verg.

aethĕrĭus -a -um (αἰθέριος), *belonging to the upper air*, or in gen. *of the air*: natura, Cic.; aqua, *rain*, Ov.; esp., *relating to the heavens as the abode of the gods, heavenly*: domus, *heaven*, Hor.; ignes, *heavenly inspiration*, Ov.; equi, *the horses of the sun*, Ov.; poet., *belonging to the upper world* (as opposed to the lower world): vesci aura aetheria, *to live*, Verg.

Aethĭŏpĭa -ae, f. (Αἰθιοπία), *Ethiopia*, an ill-defined area south of Egypt.

¶ Hence adj. **Aethĭŏpĭcus** -a -um, *Ethiopian*: Plin. Adj. and subst. **Aethĭops** -ŏpis, *Ethiopian*; also used of any *black person*: Juv., and to denote stupidity: cum stipite Aethiope, *stupid blockhead*, Cic.

¹Aethra -ae, f. (Αἴθρα). (1) *daughter of king Pittheus of Troezen, mother of Theseus by Aegeus*. (2) *daughter of Oceanus, mother of Hyas*.

²aethra -ae, f. (αἴθρα), *the upper air, the clear sky*: Verg.

Aetna -ae and Aetnē -ēs, f. (Αἴτνη). (1) *Etna*, a volcano in Sicily; according to one legend, the mountain that Jupiter cast on the giant Typhoeus (or Typhon), or Enceladus: so proverb.: onus Aetna gravius, Cic.; according to another legend, the interior was the workshop of Vulcan and the Cyclopes, who there forged Jupiter's thunderbolts. Hence adj. **Aetnaeus** -a -um, *belonging to Etna*: fratres, *the Cyclopes*, Verg.; pastor, *the Cyclops Polyphemus*, Ov.; meton.: tellus, *Sicily*, Ov.

(2) *a town at the foot of Mount Etna*, also called *Innesa*; hence adj. **Aetnensis** -e, *belonging to the town of Etna*.

Aetōlĭa -ae, f. (Αἰτωλία), *Aetolia, a country in the west of Greece, between Ozolian Locris and Acarnania*.

¶ Hence adj. **Aetōlus** -a -um (Αἰτωλός), *Aetolian*: plagae (alluding to Meleager and the hunt of the Calydonian boar), Hor.; arma, cuspis (of the Aetolian Diomedes), Verg.; urbs, *Arpi*, a town in Apulia, said to have been founded by Diomedes, Verg.

Adj. **Aetōlĭcus** -a -um, *Aetolian*: bellum, Liv.; **Aetōlĭus** -a -um, *Aetolian*: heros, Diomedes, Ov. Subst. **Aetōlis** -ĭdis, f. *an Aetolian woman*; of Deianira, *daughter of Oeneus, king of Aetolia*.

aevĭtās -ātis, f. old form of aetas; q.v.

aevum -i, n.; also aevus -i, m. in Pl. and Lucr. (cf. αἰών).

Lit., *eternity*: per aevom, Lucr.; in aevum, Hor.

Transf., in the same senses as aetas, *time*. (1) *life-time*: degere, Cic.; ter aevo functus, Hor. (2) *time of life*: flos aevi, *youth*, Lucr.; integer aevi, *in the bloom of youth*, Verg.; primo exstingui in aevo, *in early youth*, Ov.; of old age: aevo macieque senescunt, Lucr.; aevi maturus, *far advanced in years*, Verg. (3) *a period of time*: omnis aevi clari viri, *of every age*, Liv. (4) *time* in gen.: vitiata dentibus aevi, Ov.

Āfĕr -fra -frum, *African, from Africa*, especially in the narrow sense of the district round Carthage. As subst.: dirus Afer, *Hannibal*, Hor.; sitientes Afri, Verg. As adj.: aqua, *sea between Sicily and Africa*, Ov.; avis, *guinea-fowl*, Hor.; sorores, *the Hesperides*, Juv.

¶ Hence subst. **Āfrĭca** -ae, f. (1) in wider sense, *the continent of Africa*: Sall. (2) in narrower sense, Africa propria or Africa provincia, *the country around and formerly belonging to Carthage*; after 146 B.C., *the Roman province of Africa*.

Adj. **Āfrĭcānus** -a -um, *belonging to Africa*: bellum, *Caesar's war against the Pompeians in Africa*, Cic.; gallinae, *guinea-fowl*, Varr. As a surname, conferred upon two of the Scipios: *see* under Cornelius. F. pl. as subst. **Africanae** -arum (sc. ferae), *African wild beasts*, i.e. *panthers*: Liv.

Adj. **Āfrĭcus** -a -um, *African*: bellum, *the second Punic war*, Liv.; *Caesar's war against the Pompeians*, Caes.; mare, *south-west part of the Mediterranean sea*, Sall.; ventus Africus, *or simply* Africus, *the S.W. stormy rain-wind*: praeceps, Hor.; creber procellis, Verg.

aff-, *see* under adf-.

Āfrānĭus -a -um, *name of a Roman plebeian gens*. Its most famous members were:
(1) L. Afranius, *a comic poet* (born probably about 130 B.C.), *contemporary of Terence*.
(2) L. Afranius, *dependent and legate of Cn. Pompeius, killed after the battle of Thapsus*.

Agămemnon -ŏnis, m. (Ἀγαμέμνων), *a king of Mycenae, leader of the Greek expedition to Troy*.

¶ Hence subst. **Agamemnŏnĭdes** -ae, m. *a son or descendant of Agamemnon, Orestes*: Juv. Adj. **Agamemnŏnĭus** -a -um, *belonging to Agamemnon*: puella, *Iphigenia*, Prop.

Ăgănippē -ēs, f. (Ἀγανίππη), *a fountain in Boeotia, sacred to the Muses*: Verg.

¶ Hence adj. **Ăgănippeus** -a -um, *belonging to Aganippe, sacred to the Muses*: lyra, Prop.; also f. adj. **Ăgănippis** -ĭdis: Ov.

ăgāsō -ōnis, m. (ago), *a horse-boy, groom*: Liv. In gen., *a lackey*: Hor.

Ăgăthŏclēs -is m. (᾿Αγαθοκλῆς).
(1) *a tyrant of Syracuse* (361–289 B.C.).
(2) *a Greek historian.*

Ăgăthyrsi -ōrum, m. (᾿Αγάθυρσοι), *a Scythian people living on the Maris, who tattooed themselves blue*: picti, Verg.

Ăgāvē or **Agaue** -ēs, f. (᾿Αγαύη), *daughter of Cadmus, mother of Pentheus, whom she killed in a Bacchic frenzy.*

Ăgĕlastus -i, m. (ἀγέλαστος, never laughing), *surname of M. Crassus, grandfather of the triumvir, said to have laughed only once in his life.*

ăgellus -i, m. (dim. of ager), *a little field*: Cic.

ăgēmă -ătis, n. (ἄγημα), *a corps in the Macedonian army*: Liv.

Ăgendĭcum -i, n. *capital of the Senones, in Gallia Lugdunensis* (now *Sens*).

Ăgēnor -ŏris, m. (᾿Αγήνωρ), *a king of Phoenicia, father of Cadmus and Europa*: urbs Agenoris, *Carthage*, Verg.; Agenore natus, *Cadmus*, Ov. ¶ Hence adj. **Ăgēnŏrĕus** -a -um, *relating to Agenor*: domus, *house of Cadmus*, Ov.; bos, *the bull that bore away Europa*, Ov.; aenum, *the kettle used for the Phoenician purple dye*, Mart. Subst. **Ăgēnŏrĭdēs** -ae, m. *a male descendant of Agenor*; *Cadmus*, his son: Ov.; also *Perseus*, as grandson of Danaus, descended from Agenor: Ov.

ăgens -entis, partic. of ago; q.v.

ăger, agri, m. (ἀγρός), *land.* (1) *land with reference to ownership, territory*: ager publicus, Liv.; Hirpinus, Cic.; Helvetius, Caes. (2) *land in cultivation, a field*: colere, Cic.; homo ab agro remotissimus, *knowing nothing of agriculture*, Cic. (3) *open country in opposition to the town*: vastati agri sunt, urbs adsiduis exhausta funeribus, Liv. (4) *the land, opposed to the sea*: arx Crotonis una parte imminens mari, altera parte vergente in agrum, Liv. (5) in agrum, *in depth* (opp. in frontem, *in length*), Hor.

Ăgēsĭlāus -i, m. (᾿Αγησίλαος), *a king of Sparta* (444–360 B.C.).

agg- (except agger and aggero -are); *see* adg-.

agger -ĕris, m. (1) *material brought together to form a heap or mound*: aggerem comportare, petere, Caes.; paludem aggere explere, Caes.; fossas aggere complent, Verg. (2) *a mound formed from such material*; esp. *a rampart, for siege or defence*: apparare, iacere, facere, instruere, Caes.; agger Tarquinii, or simply agger, *a rampart said to have been built by Tarquinus Superbus to protect Rome*; also *a mole*: Caes.; *the bank of a river*: gramineus ripae agger, Verg.; *the causeway of a road*: agger viae, Verg., Tac. Poet., *any pile or high place*: aggeres Alpini, Verg.; aggeres nivei, Verg.; armorum, Tac.

aggĕro -are (agger), *to form a mound, to heap up*. LIT., cadavera, Verg.; ossa, Tac. TRANSF., *to increase*: dictis iras, Verg.

ăgĭlis -e (ago). (1) *of things, easily moved, light*: classis, Liv.; rivus agilior, *quicker*, Plin. (2) *of persons, light, nimble*: dea, Diana, Ov.; Cyllenius, *Mercury*, Ov.; oderunt agilem gnavumque remissi, *active*, Hor.; nunc agilis fio, *busy*, Hor.

ăgĭlĭtās -ātis, f. (agilis), *quickness, agility, lightness*: navium, Liv.; naturae, Cic.

Ăgis -ĭdis, m. (᾿Αγις), *name of several kings of Sparta.*

ăgĭtābĭlis -e (agito), *easily moved, light*: aer, Ov.

ăgĭtātĭo -ōnis, f. (agito), *movement, agitation.* LIT., anceps telorum armorumque, Liv.; agitatio et motus linquae, Cic.; agitationes fluctuum, Cic. TRANSF., *activity*: numquam animus agitatione et motu esse vacuus potest, Cic.; rerum magnarum, *management*, Cic.; virtutum, *exercise*, Sen.

ăgĭtātor -ōris, m. (agito), *one who sets in motion, a driver*: aselli, Verg.; esp. *a charioteer contending in the circus*: Cic.

ăgĭto -are (freq. of ago), *to put in constant motion, to drive about* (cf. ago in most senses). LIT., quod pulsu agitatur externo, Cic.; of animals, *to drive*: spumantem equum, Verg.; or *to hunt*: aquila insectans alias aves et agitans, Cic.; of the action of wind or water, *to toss*: mare ventorum vi agitari atque turbari, Cic. TRANSF., (1) *to vex, agitate, harry*: ut eos agitent insectenturque furiae, Cic.; Tyrrhenam fidem aut gentes agitare quietas, *to trouble*, Verg.; seditionibus tribuniciis atrociter res publica agitabatur, Sall.; *to ridicule*: quas personas agitare solemus, non sustinere, Cic. (2) *to keep in movement, be engaged upon*: **a**, *to treat of* a subject; in speech, *to argue, discuss*: agraria lex vehementer agitabatur, Cic.; in thought, *to think about, consider, turn over in the mind*: rem mente, Cic.; in animo bellum, Liv.; bellum, Tac.; de inferendo bello, Liv.; poet., with infin.: aliquid iamdudum invadere magnum mens agitat mihi, Verg.: **b**, *to perform, see to, be busy with, maintain*: imperium, Sall.; custodiam, Pl.; pacem, Sall.; dies festos, *to keep*, Cic.; esp. of time, *to spend*: vita agitabatur, Sall.; aevum agitare, Verg.; so absol., *to live*: laeti neque procul Germani agitant, Tac.; Libyes propius mare agitant, Sall.

Ăglăĭa -ae or **Ăglăĭē** -ēs, f. (᾿Αγλαΐα and ᾿Αγλαΐη), *one of the Graces*: Verg.

agmĕn -ĭnis, n. (ago). (1) *a driving movement*: agmine remorum celeri, *plying of oars*, Verg.; leni fluit agmine Thybris, Verg. Esp. of troops on the *march*: agmine impeditos, Caes. (2) *a mass in movement*: **a**, of things and persons generally, esp. in orderly movement (cf. **b**, below); *a stream, band, train*; of water: immensum agmen aquarum, Verg.; of atoms: Lucr.; of clouds: Lucr.; of stars: stellae quarum agmina cogit Lucifer, Verg.; of birds: aligerum agmen, Verg.; decedens agmine magno corvorum exercitus, Verg.; of ants: graniferum agmen, Ov.; but esp. of persons: agmine patriciorum, Liv.; mulierum, Liv.; Eumenidum, Verg.: **b**, as military t. t., *an army on the march*: phalanx agmen magis quam acies (acies, *the army in line of battle*), Liv.; agmine instructo, *ready for march*, Liv.; agmine facto, *in close marching order*, Verg.; tripartito agmine, *in three columns*, Tac.; agmen iustum, *an army in close marching order*, Tac.; quadratum, *an army marching in a hollow square*, Sall.; primum, *the vanguard*, Caes.; medium, *the centre*, Caes.; extremum or novissimum, *the rear*, Cic.; ducere, *to lead*, Cic.; cogere, *to act as rearguard*, Caes.; so fig.: ut nec duces sumus nec agmen cogamus, Cic.; also of particular arms: agmen equitum, Liv.; of baggage: impedimentorum, Tac.; of a fleet: navium, Liv. TRANSF., of *military service* generally: rudis agminum, Hor.

agna -ae, f. (agnus), *a ewe lamb*: Hor.

Agnālĭa -ium = Agonalia; q.v.

agnascor -nasci, nātus, dep. (ad/gnascor = nascor), *to be born in addition to.* (1) as legal t. t., of children born after their father's will, either in his lifetime or after his death: Cic. (2) *to grow on,* or *grow in addition*: Plin. ¶ Hence m. of partic. as subst. **agnatus** -i. (1) *a relation descended from a common ancestor in the male line*: Cic. (2) *a child born into a family where a regular heir already exists*: Tac.

agnātĭo -ōnis, f. (agnascor), *relationship reckoned through males only*: Cic.

agnellus -i, m. (dim. of agnus), *a lamb*: Pl.

agnīnus -a -um (agnus), *relating to a lamb*: Pl. F. as subst. **agnīna** -ae (sc. caro), *lamb's flesh*: Hor.

agnĭtĭo -ōnis, f. (agnosco). (1) *recognition*: cadaveris, Plin. (2) *knowledge*: animi, *of the nature of the mind*, Cic.

agnōmen (ad/gnomen = nomen) -ĭnis, n. *surname, name given to a man for some service,* e.g. Africanus, Asiaticus.

agnosco -noscere -nōvi -nĭtum (ad/gnosco = nosco), *to recognize.* (1) *to know again from previous acquaintance*: veterem Anchisen agnoscit amicum, Verg.; parvam Troiam, Verg. (2) *to know by inference* or *from report, understand*: deum ex operibus suis, Cic. (3) *to express such knowledge, to admit, to acknowledge*: filium quem ille natum non agnorat, eundem moriens suum dixerat, Nep.; me ducem, Liv.; of things: crimen, Cic.; quod meum quoddammodo agnosco, Cic.; with acc. and infin.: et ego ipse me non esse verborum admodum inopem agnosco, Cic.

agnus -i, m. (cf. ἀμνός), *a lamb,* collect.: abundare agno, Cic.; prov.: agnum lupo eripere velle, *to wish for the impossible*, Pl.

ago agĕre ēgi actum (ἄγω), *to set in motion* (cf. in most senses, agito).

LIT., *to drive.* (1) of animals: equum, Tac.; esp. of cattle: boves Romam, Liv.; often in the sense of plundering cattle, and combined with fero (or porto) which is used of the portable plunder: res quae ferri agique possunt, Liv.; also of hunting: apros, Verg. (2) of human beings: agmen agere, Liv.; se agere, *to go*, Pl., Verg.; esp. of violent driving: turba fugientium actus, Liv.; glebis aut fustibus aliquem de fundo, Cic. (3) of things: carpentum, Liv.; naves, Liv.; vineas turresque, *bring up*, Caes.; nubes ventus agens, Lucr.; animam agere, *to give up the ghost*, Cic. Esp. *to drive forward while producing*: scintillas, Lucr.; fundamenta, Cic.; radices, *to strike root*, Ov., Plin.; so fig.: vera gloria radices agit, Cic.

TRANSF., (1) *to drive* or *incite to action*: aliquem in fraudem, Verg.; in arma, Liv. (2) *to keep in movement, be engaged upon*: **a,** *to treat of* a subject, in speech, thought, etc.: hoc agere, *to attend to the matter in hand*, Lucr., Juv.; aliud agere, *not to attend.* Hence pass., *to be concerned*: agitur populi

Romani gloria, *is at stake*, Cic.; also impers.: qua de re agitur, *the point in dispute*, Cic.; in perf.: actum est de, *it is settled about*, so *it is all over with*: **b,** intransit., *to have dealings, behave, do*; esp. with adverbs, and with cum and abl.: male, bene, praeclare agere cum aliquo, *to treat a person*, Cic. Imperat.: age, *come on! to action!*: **c,** transit., *to do, perform*: quid agam? Ter.; nihil agere, Cic.; quid agis? (often in the sense *How are you?*). Esp. with particular nouns as objects: grates, gratias, *to express thanks*; bellum, Liv.; vigilias, Cic.; pacem, *to keep*, Sall.; festos dies, Cic.: **d,** of time, *to spend*: aetatem in litteris, Cic.; quartum annum ago et octogesimum, *I am in my eighty-fourth year*, Cic. Sometimes absol., *to spend time, live*: **e,** on the stage, *to act, to play*: fabulam, Cic.; nunquam agit Roscius hunc versum eo gestu quo potest, Cic.; ministrum imperatoris, *to represent, play the part of*, Tac.; esp. primas partes agere, *to play the leading part* (often fig.): **f,** in legal and political spheres, *to take a matter up publicly*: agere cum populo, Cic.; in senatu, Ov.; agere absol., or with iure or lege, *to go to law*, Cic.; agere causam, *to plead a cause*, Cic.; occ. with person as object, *to accuse*: furti, *of theft*, Cic. ¶ Hence pres. partic. **agens** -entis, as adj., *effective*: Cic.

agōn -ōnis, m. (ἀγών), *a contest in the public games*: Plin., Suet.

Ăgōnālĭa -ium and -ōrum, n. *a festival of Janus*. ¶ Hence adj. **Ăgōnālis** -e, *relating to the Agonalia*: Agonalis lux, *the day of the Agonalia*, Ov.

agōnĭa -ōrum, n. (1) *the animals for sacrifice.* (2) = Agonalia: Ov.

ăgŏrănŏmus -i, m. (ἀγορανόμος), *a market inspector in Greece*: Pl.

ăgrārĭus -a -um (ager), *relating to land*: lex, *law relating to the division of the public land*, Cic.; res, *the division of public lands*, Cic.; triumvir, *an officer who presided over the division*, Liv. M. pl. as subst. **agrārĭi** -ōrum, *the agrarian party*, who proposed to distribute the public land among the people: Cic., Liv.

agrestis -e (ager). LIT., *belonging to the fields* or *country*; *wild, rustic*: hospitium, Cic.; poma, Verg. M. as subst. **agrestis** -is, *a countryman*: Verg., Tac. TRANSF., *countrified, boorish, clownish*: servi agrestes et barbari, Cic.; rustica vox et agrestis, Cic.; vultus, *brutish*, Ov.

¹agrĭcŏla -ae, m. (ager/colo), *a tiller of the fields, farmer*: agricola et pecuarius, Cic.; also of patrons of farming: deus agricola, Silvanus, Tib.; caelites agricolae, *the gods of the country*, Tib.

²Agrĭcŏla -ae, m. *Gnaeus Julius* (A.D. 40–93), *governor of Britain, and father-in-law of Tacitus, who wrote his biography.*

agrĭcultĭo -ōnis, f.; *see under* cultio.

agrĭcultor -ōris, m.; *see under* cultor.

agrĭcultūra -ae, f.; *see under* cultura.

Agrĭgentum -i, n.; also **Acrăgās** -antis, m. (q.v.); *a Doric colony in S.W. Sicily* (now *Agrigento*). ¶ Hence adj. **Agrĭgentīnus** -a -um, *Agrigentine*.

agrĭpĕta -ae, m. (ager/peto), *a land-grabber, squatter*: Cic.

Agrippa -ae, m.
  (1) *a Roman family name.* Esp.: **a**, Menenius Agrippa, *the author of the fable of the belly and the members, by which he was said to have reconciled the plebeians and patricians*: Liv. ii. 32: **b**, M. Vipsanius Agrippa, (63–12 B.C.), *the friend and adviser of Augustus, whose niece, Marcella, and daughter, Julia, he successively married, a celebrated general and statesman, who adorned Rome with many large buildings*: **c**, Agrippa Postumus, *son of the above, banished to Planasia by Augustus, said to have been murdered there at the beginning of Tiberius' reign.*
  (2) *a surname of several kings of the Herod family in Judaea.*

Agrippīna -ae, f. *the name of several Roman women.* (1) *daughter of M. Vipsanius Agrippa, by Julia, the daughter of Augustus; wife of Germanicus; mother of the emperor Gaius; banished to Pandataria after her husband's death.* (2) *the granddaughter of Agrippa, daughter of Germanicus and Agrippina.* (3) *wife of Domitius Ahenobarbus and then of her uncle, the emperor Claudius; murdered by order of her son, the emperor Nero.* Hence **Colonia Agrippinensis**, *a town of Germany* (now *Cologne*), *named in honour of Agrippina; and subst.* **Agrippinenses** -ium, m. pl. *its inhabitants*: Tac.

Ăgyīeus -ĕi or -ĕos, m. (Ἀγυιεύς), *surname of Apollo, as protector of streets*: Hor.

Ăgylla -ae, f. (Ἄγυλλα), *Greek name of the Etruscan town Caere.*
  ¶ Hence adj. **Agyllīnus** -a -um, *of Agylla.*

Agȳrium -i, n. (Ἀγύριον), *a town in Sicily, birth-place of the historian Diodorus.*
  ¶ Hence adj. **Agȳrinensis** -e, *of Agyrium.*

āh or **ā**, interj., *ah! oh!* Pl., Ter., Verg.

Ăhāla -ae, m., C. Servilius, *the master of the horse under the dictator Cincinnatus*, 439 B.C., *who slew Sp. Maelius.*

Ahenobarbus, see Domitius.

ai (*ai*), *ah!* an interjection of grief: Ov.

Āiax -ācis, m. (Αἴας), *the name of two Homeric heroes.* (1) Aiax Telamonius, *son of Telamon, king of Salamis, who committed suicide because he failed in the contest with Ulysses for the arms of Achilles.* (2) Aiax Oileus, *son of Oileus, king of the Locri.*

āio, defective verb, mainly used in pres. and imperf. indic. (1) *to say yes, to affirm* (opp. nego): Pl., Cic. (2) *to say, to assert, to state*: ut aiunt, *as the saying goes*, Cic.; quid ais? *what do you say?* Pl., Ter.; ain' (= ais-ne)? or ain tu? *do you really mean it? you don't say!* Cic.
  ¶ Hence pres. partic. **aiens** -entis, *affirmative*: Cic.

Āius Lŏquens or **Āius Lŏcūtius**, m. (aio/loquor), *the voice which is said to have warned the Romans just before the battle of the Allia of the coming of the Gauls; afterwards honoured as a god in a temple erected to it*: Cic.

āla -ae, f. (1) *a wing*; of birds: galli plausu premunt alas, Cic.; of gods: hic paribus nitens Cyllenius alis constitit, Verg.; poet., of the oars of a ship: classis centenis remiget alis, Prop.; of the sails: velorum pandimus alas,

Verg.; *and to express anything swift*: fulminis ocior alis, Verg.; *used of death*: Hor.; *of sleep*: Tib. (2) *the armpit of a man*: sub ala fasciculum portare librorum, Hor. (3) milit. t. t., *a wing, squadron* (originally Roman cavalry, disposed on both sides of the legions like wings; later allied troops, esp. cavalry).

Ălăbanda -ae, f., and -orum, n. (ἡ and τὰ Ἀλάβανδα), *a town in Caria, near the Maeander, famous for its wealth and luxury, founded by Alabandus, son of Eurippus and Callirrhoe.*
  ¶ Hence subst. **Ălăbandenses** -ium, m. pl. *inhabitants of Alabanda*; adj. **Ălăbandēus** -a -um, *born at Alabanda.*

ălăbaster -stri, m., with pl. **alabastra** (ἀλάβαστρος). (1) *a pear-shaped perfume casket*: Cic. (2) *a rose-bud*: Plin.

ălăcer -cris -cre and (rarely) **ălăcris** -e, adj. (with compar.), *quick, lively, animated*; used of men, animals and things: Catilina alacer atque laetus, Cic.; with ad and the gerund: ad bella suscipienda Gallorum alacer et promptus est animus, Caes.; voluptas, Verg.; equus, Cic.

ălăcrĭtās -ātis, f. (alacer), *quickness, eagerness, animation*; of men: quae alacritas civitatis fuit? Cic.; with genit.: reipublicae defendendae, Cic.; mira alacritate ad litigandum, Cic.; of animals: canum tanta alacritas in venando, Cic.

Ălămanni = Alemanni; q.v.

ălăpa -ae, f. *a box on the ear*: Juv. Given by a master to his slave on the manumission of the slave; hence: multo maioris alapae mecum veneunt, *I sell freedom at a much higher price*, Phaedr.

ālārĭus -a -um, and **ālāris** -e (ala; q.v.), *belonging to the wings of an army*: equites, Liv.; cohortes, Cic. M. pl. as subst. **ālāriī** -orum, *allied troops*: Caes.

ālātus -a -um (ala), *winged*: Verg., Ov.

ălauda -ae, f. (a Celtic word). (1) *a lark*: Plin. (2) *the name of a legion formed by Caesar in Gaul*: Suet.
  ¶ Hence in pl. **Alaudae** -arum, *the soldiers of this legion*: Cic.

ălăzōn -ōnis, m. (ἀλάζων), *a braggart, boaster*: Pl.

Alba -ae, f. (albus). (1) *Alba Longa*, the oldest Latin town, according to the legend built by Ascanius on a ridge of the Mons Albanus, the mother city of Rome, said to have been destroyed by Tullus Hostilius. Hence adj. **Albānus** -a -um, *Alban*: mons, *a holy mountain of the Latins* (now *Monte Cavo*); lacus, *the lake at the foot of mons Albanus* (now *Lago Albano*). As subst., m. pl. **Albani**, *the Albans*: Liv.; n. **Albanum** -i, *an estate at Alba*: Cic., Suet. (2) *Alba Fucens, a town N.W. of Lacus Fucinus, near the Marsi.*

albātus -a -um (albus), *clothed in white*: Cic., Hor.

albĕo -ēre (albus), *to be white*: membra in eum pallorem albentia, Tac.; albente caelo, *at daybreak*, Caes.

albesco -ĕre (albeo), *to become white*: albescens capillus, Hor.; lux albescit, *day dawns*, Verg.

albĭcĕrātus -a -um, or **albĭcĕris** -e, or **albĭcĕrus** -a -um, *whitish yellow*: Plin.

albĭco -are (albus), *to be white*: prata canis albicant pruinis, Hor.; Cat., Plin.

albĭdus -a -um (albus), *whitish*: Ov.

Albĭnŏvānus -i, m. (1) Albinovanus Pedo, *an epic poet, contemporary and friend of Ovid.* (2) Celsus Albinovanus, *to whom Horace addressed one of his Epistles.*

Albīnus -i, m. *the name of a family of the* gens Postumia. Esp. Aulus Postumius Albinus, *consul* 151 B.C., *writer of a Roman history in Greek.*

Albĭon -ōnis, f. (albus), *old name of Great Britain*: Plin.

Albis -is, m. *the Elbe*: Tac.

albĭtūdo -ĭnis, f. (albus), *whiteness*: Pl.

Albĭus -i, m. *name of a Roman gens*; esp. Albius Tibullus, *the celebrated Roman elegiac poet* (see under Tibullus).
¶ Hence adj. **Albĭānus** -a -um, *relating to Albius.*

albŭlus -a -um (dim. of albus), *whitish*: columbus, Cat.; freta, *foaming,* Mart. F. as subst. **Albŭla** -ae (sc. aqua), *old name of the Tiber*: fluvius Albula quem nunc Tiberim vocant, Liv.; Verg.

album -i, m. *see* albus.

Albŭnĕa or **Albuna** -ae, f. *a fountain at Tibur*; also *the nymph supposed to dwell there.*

Alburnus -i, m. *a high mountain of Lucania, near Paestum.*

albus -a -um (connected with ἀλβός), *white, dead white* (opp. ater, whereas candidus= *glittering white*). (1) *white*: barba, Pl.; equi, Liv. Often in proverbial phrases: nuper in hanc urbem pedibus qui venerat albis, *a slave who came to Rome with feet chalked to show he was for sale,* Juv.; alba avis, *a white bird, a rarity,* Cic.; albis dentibus deridere, *to laugh at so as to show the teeth,* i.e. *deride,* Pl.; filius albae gallinae, *a lucky fellow,* Juv.; albis equis praecurrere, *to surpass greatly* (referring to the triumphing general whose car was driven by a white horse), Hor.; albus an ater sit nescio, *I know nothing about him.* (2) *pale*: albus ora pallor inficit, Hor. (3) *bright*: admisso Lucifer albus equo, Ov.; so *making bright*: notus, Hor.; fig., *fortunate*: stella, Hor.
N. as subst. **album** -i. (1) *white colour*: sparsis pellibus albo, Verg.; columnas albo polire, Liv. (2) *a white tablet*; esp.: **a**, *the tablet on which the pontifex maximus at Rome published the events of the year*: Cic.: **b**, album (praetoris), *the tablet on which the praetor published his edict*: **c**, *a list of names*: album senatorium, *the list of senators,* Tac.; album iudicum, *the jury-list,* Suet.

Alcaeus -i, m. (Ἀλκαῖος), *a Greek lyric poet of Mytilene, flourishing about* 600 B.C., *contemporary of Sappho and inventor of the Alcaic metre, imitated by Horace.*
¶ Hence adj. **Alcăĭcus** -a -um, *Alcaic.*

Alcămĕnēs -is, m. (Ἀλκαμένης), *a Greek sculptor, perhaps a pupil of Phidias.*

Alcăthŏē -ēs, f. (Ἀλκαθόη), *a mountain in Megara named after Alcathous.* Poet., *for Megara*: Ov.

Alcăthŏus -i, m. (Ἀλκάθοος), *son of Pelops, founder of Megara,* hence: urbs Alcathoi, *Megara,* Ov.

Alcē -ēs, f. (Ἀλκη), *town in Hispania Tarraconensis.*

alcēdo -ĭnis and **alcўōn** -onis, f. (ἀλκυών), *the kingfisher*: Pl. Hence n. pl. as subst. **alcēdŏnĭa** -ōrum. LIT., *the fourteen days of winter, during which the kingfisher is hatching its eggs, and the sea was believed to be calm.* TRANSF., *quietness, calm*: Pl.

alcēs -is, f. *the elk*: Caes., Plin.

Alcestis -is, f. and **Alcestē** -ēs, f. (Ἄλκηστις or Ἀλκήστη), *wife of Admetus, king of Pherae, who saved her husband's life by dying for him, but was rescued from Hades by Hercules.*

Alcēus -ĕi and -ĕos, m. (Ἀλκεύς), *father of Amphitryon, and grandfather of Jason.*
¶ Hence **Alcīdēs** -ae, m. *a descendant of Alceus,* generally *Hercules*: Verg., Hor., Ov.

Alcĭbĭădēs -is, m. (Ἀλκιβιάδης). (1) *an Athenian general, prominent in the Peloponnesian war, pupil of Socrates.* (2) *a Lacedaemonian living at the time of the war of the Romans with the Achaeans.*

Alcĭmĕdē -ēs, f. (Ἀλκιμέδη), *wife of Aeson and mother of Jason.*

Alcĭnŏus -i, m. (Ἀλκίνοος), *king of the Phaeacians, the host of Odysseus,* noted for his gardens and orchards. Hence: poma dare Alcinoo, *to carry coals to Newcastle,* Ov.; Alcinoi sylvae, *orchards,* Verg.; iuventus, *luxurious young men,* Hor.

Alcmaeo and **Alcmaeōn** -ŏnis (Ἀλκμαίων); also **Alcmaeus** -i, m.
(1) *son of Amphiaraus and Eriphyle,* who murdered his mother at the wish of his father and with the approval of the oracle, and was afterwards driven mad. Adj. **Alcmaeŏnĭus** -a -um.
(2) *a Greek philosopher and physician of Croton, pupil of Pythagoras.*

Alcmēna and **Alcumena** -ae; also **Alcmēnē** -ēs, f. (Ἀλκμήνη), *wife of the Theban Amphitryon, and mother of Hercules by Jupiter.*

alcўōn = alcedo; q.v.

Alcўŏnē -ēs, f. (Ἀλκυόνη), *daughter of Aeolus, who jumped into the sea on seeing her husband, Ceyx, drowned, and was changed with him into a kingfisher.*

ālĕa -ae, f. *a game with dice, game of hazard.* LIT., ludere aleā, Cic.; aleam exercere, Tac.; de aleā condemnatus (dice-playing being forbidden at Rome by the Lex Titia et Publicia et Cornelia, except during the Saturnalia), Cic.
TRANSF., *chance, risk, uncertainty*: rem in aleam dare, *to risk,* Liv.; subire, Cic.; in dubiam imperii servitiique aleam ire, Liv.; iacta alea est, *the die is cast* (exclamation of Caesar on crossing the Rubicon), Suet.

ālĕātor -ōris, m. (alea), *a dicer, gambler*: Pl., Cic.

ālĕātōrĭus -a -um (aleator), *relating to a gambler*: damna, *losses at play,* Cic.

ālec = allec; q.v.

Alectō = Allecto; q.v.

Alemanni or **Alamanni** -orum, m. pl. *a confederation of German tribes on the Upper Rhine and Danube.*

ālĕo -onis, m. (alea), *a gambler*: Cat.

ālĕs ālĭtis (ala). Adj., *winged.* LIT., Pegasus, Ov.; deus, *Mercury,* Ov.; puer, *Cupid,* Hor. TRANSF., *swift, quick*: auster, Verg.; passu volat alite virgo, Ov.
As subst., m. and f. *a bird*; used mostly of large birds: regia, *the eagle,* Ov.; Phoebeius, *the raven,* Ov.; Daulias, *the nightingale,* Ov.;

Iunonia, *the peacock,* Ov.; *imitatrix rara, the parrot,* Ov.; *sacer, the hawk,* Verg.; *cristatus, the cock,* Ov.; *Palladis, the owl,* Ov.; *Caystrius, the swan,* Ov. Sometimes of other *winged beings*: ales Maeonii carminis, *a poet of Homeric strain,* Hor. In augury, *a bird whose flight was significant* (oscines=birds whose note was significant): Cic.; hence poet., *a sign, an omen*: bonā, *or* secundā, alite, *with favourable omen,* Hor.

ălesco -ĕre (alo), *to grow up*: Lucr.

Ălĕsĭa -ae, f. *town of the Mandubii in Gallia Lugdunensis* (now *Alise*).

Ălētrĭum (Alatrĭum) -i, n. *an old town of the Hernici in Latium,* afterwards a Roman colony and municipium (now *Alatri*).

¶ Hence adj. **Ălētrīnās** -ātis, *of Aletrium.*

Ăleuas -ae, m. (᾽Αλεύας), *a descendant of Hercules, who ruled in Larissa.*

Ălexander -dri, m. (᾽Αλέξανδρος), *name of several Greek historical and mythological persons,* esp. (1) *Paris, son of Priam, king of Troy.* (2) *Alexander of Pherae, tyrant in Thessaly* 370–357 B.C. (3) *Alexander, son of Neoptolemus, king of Epirus, uncle of Alexander the Great.* (4) *Alexander the Great* (356–323 B.C.), *king of Macedonia.*

¶ Hence subst. **Alexandrīa** or **-ēa** -ae, f. (᾽Αλεξάνδρεια), *the name of several cities founded by Alexander, the most famous of which was the Egyptian city, at the Canopic mouth of the Nile, capital of the kingdom of the Ptolemies.*

¶ Hence adj. **Alexandrīnus** -a -um, *of Alexandria.*

alga -ae, f. *sea-weed*: vilior algā, Hor.; Verg.

algĕo algēre alsi, *to be cold*: Juv. TRANSF., probitas laudatur et alget, i.e. *is neglected,* Juv.

¶ Hence partic. **algens** -entis, *cold.*

algesco algescĕre alsi (algeo), *to catch cold*: Ter.

¹**algĭdus** -a -um (algeo), *cold*: Cat.

²**Algĭdus** -i, m. *a high mountain in Latium, south-east of Rome* (now *Monte Compatri*).

¶ Hence adj. **Algĭdus** -a -um, *belonging to Algidus.*

algor -ōris, m. (algeo), *cold*: Pl., Lucr., Tac.

algōsus -a -um (alga), *abounding in sea-weed*: Plin.

algus -ūs, m. or **algu**, n., old form of algor (q.v.), found usually in abl. sing: Pl., Lucr.

alias, *see under* alius.

ălĭātum -i, n. (ālium), *food seasoned with garlic*: Pl.

ălĭbī, adv. (alius/ubi). (1) *elsewhere, at another place*: Cic.; alibi . . . alibi, *here* . . . *there,* Liv.; alibi alius, *one here, the other there,* Liv. (2) *otherwise, in other respects*: Liv.

ălĭca -ae, f. (1) *spelt, a kind of grain*: Cato, Plin. (2) *a drink prepared from spelt*: Mart.

ălĭcārĭus (hălĭcārĭus) -a -um, *belonging to spelt.* F. as subst. **ălĭcārĭa** -ae, f. *a prostitute, one who sat before the spelt-mills*: Pl.

ălĭcŭbī, adv. (aliquis/ubi), *anywhere, somewhere*: Cic.

ălĭcŭla -ae, f. (ala), *a light upper garment*: Mart.

ălĭcundĕ, adv. (aliquis/unde), *from anywhere, from somewhere, from some source*: Cic.

ălĭēnātĭo -ōnis, f. (alieno), *a transference or alienation of property.* LIT., sacrorum,

transfer of the sacra gentilicia *from one gens to another,* Cic. TRANSF., (1) *a separation between persons, a desertion, alienation of feeling*: tua a me alienatio, Cic.; Caes., Tac. (2) esp. with mentis, *aberration of mind*: Plin., Sen.

ălĭēnĭgĕna -ae, m. (alienus/gigno). Adj., *strange, foreign*: hostis, Cic. Subst., *a foreigner*: quid alienigenae de vobis loqui soleant, Cic.

ălĭēnĭgĕnus -a -um (alienus/gigno), *of different elements, heterogeneous*: Lucr.

ălĭēno -are (alienus), *to make something another's.*

LIT., of property or persons, *to take away, to let go, to transfer*: usus fructus iam mihi harum aedium alienatus est, Pl.; vectigalia, Cic.; *to sell a child or slave to a new family,* Liv.

TRANSF., (1) alienare mentem, etc., *to cause a person to lose his reason*: Iunonis iram ob spoliatum templum alienasse mentem ferebant, Liv.; oftener in pass., alienari, *to go out of one's mind*: mente alienata, Caes.; velut alienatis sensibus, Plin. (2) *to remove from the mind, to banish*: alienatis a memoria periculi animis, *having forgotten danger,* Liv. (3) *to estrange, put at variance*: omnes a se bonos, Cic.; with dat.: alienati Romanis, Liv.; alienari ab interitu, *to have a repugnance to, to shun,* Cic.

ălĭēnus -a -um, adj. (with compar. and superl.) (alius), *that which belongs* or *relates to another* (opp. meus, tuus, suus, proprius).

(1) of ownership: domus, Cic.; aes, *another's money,* and so *debt,* Cic.; nomina, *debts contracted in the names of others,* Sall.; alieno vulnere, *a wound meant for another,* Verg. N. as subst. **ălĭēnum** -i, *another man's property*: Cic.

(2) of more general relations, *strange, foreign, unrelated*: non alienus sanguine regibus, Liv.; alienissimus a Clodio, Cic.; domi atque in patria mallem, quam in externis atque alienis locis, Cic. M. as subst. **ălĭēnus** -i, *a stranger*: cives potiores quam peregrini, propinqui quam alieni, Cic.

(3) *foreign to, unsuitable, averse*: **a**, of persons, *not at home in, not acquainted with, strange to*: in physicis totus alienus est, Cic.; also *estranged, unfriendly*; with ab and the abl.: ab aliquo *or* ab aliqua re, Cic.; with dat.: homo mihi alienissimus, Cic.: **b**, of things, *unfavourable*: alieno loco proelium committere, *in a disadvantageous place,* Caes.; aliena verba, *unsuitable,* Cic.; non alienum est, followed by the infin., *it is not out of place to,* etc., Cic.; aliena loqui, *to talk nonsense,* Ov.; with ab and the abl.: labor alienus non ab aetate solum nostra, verum etiam a dignitate, Cic.; with simple abl.: dignitate imperii, Cic.; with dat.: quod maxime huic causae est alienum, Cic.; with genit.: aliena firmae et constantis adsensionis, Cic.; with ad and the acc.: ad committendum proelium tempus alienum, Cic.

ălĭgĕr -gĕra -gĕrum (ala/gero), *winged*: amor, Verg.

ălĭmentārĭus -a -um, *relating to food*: lex, *relating to a distribution of food among the poor,* ap. Cic.

alimentum

ălĭmentum -i, n. (alo). (1) *food* (gen. used in the plural): alimenta corporis, Cic.; alimenta arcu expedire, *to get food by the bow*, Tac.; used of fire: ignis, *fuel*, Liv.; fig.: seditionis, Tac. (2) *maintenance*; hence (like Gr. τροφεῖα), *the return due from children to their parents for their bringing up*: Cic.

alimonia -ae, f., Pl., and **ălĭmōnĭum** -i, n., Tac. (alo), *nourishment*.

alio, *see* under alius.

ălĭōquī and **ălĭōquĭn**, adv. (alius/quis), *in another way*. (1) *otherwise, in other respects*: nunc pudore a fuga contineri, alioquin pro victis haberi, Liv.; triumphatum de Tiburtibus, alioquin mitis victoria fuit, Liv. (2) *in general, in most respects*: Caesar validus alioquin spernendis honoribus, Tac. (3) *otherwise, else, in other conditions*: et puto nondum: alioqui narrasses mihi, Plin. L., Quint.

ălĭorsum and **ălĭorsus**, adv. (contr. from aliovorsum and aliovorsus). (1) *in another direction, elsewhere*: mater ancillas iubet aliam aliorsum ire, *in different directions*, Pl. (2) *in another manner*: Ter.

ālĭpēs -pĕdis (ala/pes), *having wings on the feet*. LIT., deus, or absol., *Mercury*: Ov. TRANSF., *swift of foot*: cervi, Lucr.; equi, Verg.; also absol., *horses*: Verg.

Alĭphēra -ae, f. ('Ἀλίφηρα or 'Ἀλίφειρα), *a town of Arcadia*.

ălipta -ae, m., and **ăliptēs** -ae, m. (ἀλείπτης), *the anointer in the westling-school or the baths*. Hence *the master of the wrestling-school*: Cic.

ălĭquā, *see* under aliquis.

ălĭquamdĭū, *see* under aliquis.

ălĭquammultus, *see* under aliquis.

ălĭquandŏ, adv. (aliquis/quando), *at some time*. (1) *at any time, once*: sero, verum aliquando tamen, Cic.; si forte aliquando, *if by chance ever*, Cic.; dicendum aliquando est, Cic. (2) *sometimes, occasionally*: scribe aliquando ad nos quid agas, Cic.; aliquando ... aliquando, *sometimes ... at other times*, Cic. (3) *at last*: finem aliquando fecit, Cic.; often with tandem: tandem aliquando L. Catilinam ex urbe eiecimus, Cic.

ălĭquantillum (aliquantulus), *a very little*: Pl.

ălĭquantispĕr, adv. (aliquantus/per), *a moderately long time*: Pl.

ălĭquantŭlus -a -um (dim. of aliquantus), *little, small*. N. as adv. **ălĭquantŭlum**, *a little*: Cic., Liv.

ălĭquantus -a -um (alius/quantus), *of some size, moderate, not small*: timor aliquantus, spes amplior, Sall. N. as subst. **ălĭquantum** -i, *a good deal*: nummorum, Cic.; temporis, Liv.; acc. aliquantum, *considerably, somewhat*: qui processit aliquantum ad virtutis aditum, *had made considerable progress towards*, Cic.; aliquantum commoveri, Cic.; abl. aliquanto, esp. with compar.: aliquanto maiorem locum occuparis, Cic.; aliquanto post *or* ante, *some time after or before*, Cic.

ălĭquātēnus, adv. (aliquis/tenus), *to a certain degree, in some measure*: Sen., Quint.

ălĭqui, aliquae, or aliqua, aliquod, adj. indef. (alius/qui), *some*: si est aliqui sensus in morte, Cic.; aliquod nomenque decusque, Verg.; with numerals: aliquos viginti dies, *some twenty days*, Pl.

alius

ălĭquis aliquid, pron. indef. (alius/quis), *someone, something, anyone, anything*. (1) in gen.: quisquis est ille, si modo aliquis, *if he be anyone at all*, Cic. Occasionally used as adj.: aliquis deus, Cic. Often accompanied by alius: aliquid aliud videbimus, Cic.; by unus: aliquis unus pluresve divitiores, Cic.; by an adj.: aliquid divinum, Cic.; by a numeral, like the Gr. τις (Engl. *some*), to express an unascertained number: tres aliqui aut quattuor, Cic. Partitive, with ex, de *or* genit.: aliquis ex vobis, Cic.; esp. aliquid with genit. of a subst. *or* adj.: aliquid virium, Cic.; falsi aliquid, Cic. N. as adv., aliquid, *in any respect*: si in me aliquid offendistis, Cic. (2) esp. *somebody* or *something great or significant*: si nunc aliquid adsequi se putant, Cic.; esse aliquem *or* aliquid, *to be somebody, to be something*, Cic.; est aliquid nupsisse Iovi, Ov.; dicere aliquid, *to say something weighty*, Cic.

¶ Hence adv. **ălĭquō**, *some whither*: aliquem secum rus aliquo educere, *in some direction or other*, Cic.; aliquo concedere ab eorum oculis, Cic.; adv. **aliqua**, *by some road* or *in some manner*: evolare, Cic.; nocere, Verg.; adv. **aliquam diu** *or* **aliquamdiu** (with acc. fem. of aliquis as adv.), *for some time*: Caes., Cic., Liv.; adj. **aliquam multus** *or* **aliquammultus**, *considerable* in number or quantity: vestrum aliquam multi, *a good many of you*, Cic.

ălĭquŏt, numer. indecl., *some, several*: aliquot epistulae, Cic.; aliquot diebus ante, Cic.

ălĭquŏtĭēns or **ălĭquŏtĭēs**, adv. (aliquot), *several times*: aliquoties ex aliquo audisse, Cic.

ălis, alid, old form of alius, aliud; q.v.

ălĭtĕr, *see* under alius.

ălĭŭbi, adv. (alius/ubi), *elsewhere*: Plin.

ālĭum or **allium** -i, *garlic*: Pl., Hor., Verg.

ălĭundĕ, adv. (alius/unde), *from some other direction*: alii aliunde coibant, *from different directions*, Liv.; aliunde quam, *from a different direction from*, Cic.; aliunde ... aliunde, Liv.

ălĭus -a -ud (old form alis, alid, Lucr., Cat.), adj. and pronoun, *another, other, different* (usually of more than two, unlike alter=one or other of two).

(1) in gen., *other, another*, so used by most authors; with partitive genit.: aliud commodi, Cic.; n. pl. like adv.: alia clarus, *in other respects*, Tac.

(2) distributively, *one, another*: aliud est maledicere, aliud accusare, Cic.; alii ... alii, *some ... others*, Cic.; also: alii ... reliqui, Cic.; alii ... quidam, Liv.; alii ... pars, Sall.; aliud alio melius, *one is better than the other*, Cic.; alius alia via, *the one in this way, the other in that*, Liv.; alius ex alio, Cic.; super alium, Liv.; post alium, *one after another*, Sall.; alius atque alius, *now this, now that*, Cic.

(3) with a comparison expressed, *other than*, followed by ac, atque, et; after a negative by nisi, quam, praeter, or the abl.: lux longe alia est solis et lychnorum, *there is a great difference between the light of the sun and of lamps*, Cic.; alius essem atque nunc sum, Cic.; nec quidquam aliud

[35]

philosophia est praeter studium sapientiae, Cic.; nec quidquam aliud libertate quaesisse, *anything else but liberty*, Cic.; tribunatus Sestii nihil aliud nisi meum nomen causamque sustinuit, Cic.)
(4) *of another nature, different*: alium facere, *to change, transform*, Pl.; alium fieri, *to be transformed*, Cic. L.; in alia omnia ire, discedere, transire, *to dissent from a proposition, be of a contrary opinion* (in the Roman senate), Cic.
(5) *all other, the rest*: Divitiaco ex aliis (Gallis) maximam fidem habebat, Caes.; Liv.
(6) =alter, *one of two*: alius Ariovistus *a second Ariovistus*, Tac.; duo Romani super alium alius corruerunt, Liv.
¶ Hence adv. **ălĭās**. (1) *at another time*: Cic.; alias ... alias, *at one time ... at another time*, Cic.; alius alias, *one person at one time, another at another*, Cic. (2) *elsewhere*: Plin. (3) *otherwise*: non alias quam, *on no other condition than*, Tac.; non alias nisi, *not otherwise than, as if*, Tac.
¶ Adv. **ălĭō**, *to another place*. Lit., si offendet me loci celebritas, alio me conferam, Cic.; alius alio, *one in this direction, the other in that*, Cic. Transf., (1) *to another person*: quo alio nisi ad nos socios confugerent, Liv. (2) *for another end*: nusquam alio natus quam ad serviendum, *born only for slavery*, Liv. (3) *to another object*: si placet sermonem alio transferemus, *to another topic*, Cic.
¶ Adv. **ălĭtĕr**. (1) *otherwise, in another way*: a, absol.: non fuit faciendum aliter, Cic.; alius aliter, *in different ways*, Cic.; quod certe scio longe aliter esse, *is far from being the case*, Cic.; aliter evenire, *to turn out wrongly*, Sall.: b, with a comparison expressed; aliter ... atque: aliter rem cecidisse atque opinatus sis, *in a different way from what you expected*, Cic.; so: aliter ... quam, Cic.; aliter ... atque ut, Cic.; non aliter ... nisi, Cic. (2) *otherwise, else, in other conditions*: ius semper est quaesitum aequabile neque enim aliter ius esset, Cic.
ălĭusmŏdi or **ălĭus mŏdi** (alius/modus), *of another kind*: Cic.
all-, *see also under* adl-.
āllēc or **ālēc** -ēcis, n. *fish-pickle*: Hor.
Allecto or **Alecto** (found only in nom. and acc.), *one of the three Furies*.
Allĭa (**Alĭa**) -ae, f. *river in Latium, flowing into the Tiber*, near which the Romans were defeated by the Gauls, July 18, 390 B.C.: infaustum Allia nomen, Verg. Adj. **Allĭensis** -e: dies Alliensis (a 'dies nefastus'), Liv.
Allifae -ārum, f. *a town of the Samnites on the left bank of the Vulturnus* (now *Alife*).
¶ Hence adj. **Allĭfānus** -a -um, *of Allifae*. N. pl. as subst. **Allĭfāna** -ōrum (sc. pocula), *earthenware drinking-vessels*: Hor.
Allobrox -ŏgis, and pl. **Allŏbrŏges** -um, m. *the Allobroges, a Gallic people occupying the present Dauphiné and Savoy*: Ciceronem Allobroga (i.e. *a speaker of bad Latin*) dixit, Juv. Adj. **Allŏbrŏgĭcus** -a -um: Plin.; also as *a surname of* Q. Fabius Maximus, conqueror of the Allobroges.
Almo -ōnis, m. *a small brook on the south side of Rome* (now *Aquataccia*).
almus -a -um (alo), *nourishing, kind*: nutrix, Pl.; Venus, Lucr.; ager, Verg.

alnus -i, f. *the alder*: Verg., Plin. Meton., *anything made of alderwood*, esp. *a ship of alderwood*: tunc alnos primum fluvii sensere cavatas, Verg.
ălo ălĕre ălŭi altum (or ălĭtum), *to nourish, support*.
(1) *to rear, feed, keep* a living creature: altus educatusque inter arma, Liv.; alere anseres in Capitolio, Cic.; magnum numerum equitatus suo sumptu, Caes.; se alere or ali, with abl., or ex and the abl., *to support oneself*: se suosque latrociniis, *to live by brigandage*, Caes. (2) of land, etc., *to support, maintain*: cum agellus eum non satis aleret, Cic.; venatus viros pariter ac feminas alit, Tac. (3) in gen., *to strengthen, increase, make to grow*; of vegetation: umida maiores herbas alit, Verg.; gramen erat circa quod proximus umor alebat, Ov.; of water: amnis imbres quem super notas aluere ripas, *have swollen*, Hor.; idem (Libanus mons) amnem Iordanem alit funditque, Tac.; of fire: flammas, Ov. (4) in gen., *to promote, advance*: honos alit artes, Cic.; hos successus alit, *encourages*, Verg.; civitatem, *promote the good of the state*, Caes.; alere spem mollibus sententiis, Cic.
¶ Hence partic. (with compar. and superl.) **altus** -a -um, *grown, great*. So (1) as seen from below, *high*. Lit., Cic., Caes.; with acc. of measure: signum septem pedes altum, Liv. Transf., a, of the voice, *shrill*: altiore voce, Quint.: b, of dignity or rank, *high, noble*: altior dignitatis gradus, Cic.; Apollo, Verg.; Caesar, Hor.; Aeneas, *high-born*, Verg.: c, of elevation of character or speech: nimis altam et exaggeratam (orationem), Cic.; te natura excelsum quendam et altum genuit, Cic.; vultus, *a lofty mien*, Hor. (2) as seen from above, *deep*. Lit., flumen, Caes.; with acc. of measure: quinquaginta cubita altum mare, Plin. Transf., a, of quiet, *deep*: somnus altus, Liv.: b, of thoughts and feelings, *secret, deep-seated*: pavor, Tac.; si altior istis sub precibus venia ulla latet, Verg. (3) of time, *reaching far back, ancient*: altior memoria, Cic.
N. as subst. **altum** -i, generally used with prepositions. (1) *height*: aedificia in altum edita, Tac.; esp. *high heaven*: ab alto, Verg.; sometimes also perhaps *the high seas*. (2) *depth*, esp. *the deep sea*: in portum ex alto provehi, Cic. Transf., ex alto dissimulare, Ov.
¶ Hence adv. **altē**. (1) *on high, highly*. Lit., cadere, *from a height*, Cic. Transf., spectare, *to have high aims*, Cic. (2) *deeply*. Lit., sulcus altius impressus, Cic. Transf., quod verbum in Iugurthae pectus altius quam quisquam ratus erat descendit, Sall; altius perspicere, *to look deeper*, Cic.
ălŏē -ēs, f. (ἀλόη), *the aloe*. Lit., Plin. Transf., *bitterness*: plus aloes quam mellis habet, Juv.
Alōeūs -ĕi or -ĕos, m. ('Αλωεύς), *a giant, son of Neptune*.
¶ Hence subst. **Alōĭdae** -arum, m. *sons of Aloeus* (Otus *and* Ephialtes), *giants who tried to storm heaven*.
Alpēs -ium, f. (rare sing. **Alpis** -is; perhaps connected with albus) *the Alps*.
¶ Hence adj. **Alpīnus** and **Alpĭcus** -a -um, *Alpine*.

alpha, indecl. n. (ἄλφα), *the name of the first letter in the Greek alphabet*: Juv. Transf., *the first*: Mart.

Alphēus or **Alphēos** -i, m. (Ἀλφειός), *the principal river of the Peloponnese, flowing through Arcadia and Elis, partly underground*; hence the river-god Alpheus was said to have dived under the sea in pursuit of the nymph Arethusa, and to have come up in Sicily. ¶ Hence subst. **Alphēïas** -ădis, f. *the nymph and fountain Arethusa*: Ov. Adj. **Alphēus** -a -um, *belonging to the river Alpheus*: Verg.

Alsĭum -i, n. *one of the oldest towns in Etruria,* near which Pompeius had an estate. ¶ Hence adj. **Alsĭensis** -e, *belonging to Alsium*: villa (*of Pompeius*), Cic.

alsĭus (alsus) -a -um, *frosty, cold*: Lucr., Cic.

altānus -i, m. *a S.W. wind*: Suet.

altārĭa -ium, n. pl. (altus). Lit., *an erection upon an altar (ara), on which the fire is lighted*: structae diris altaribus arae, Lucr.; Quint. Transf., *high altars*, or *a high altar*: ecce duas tibi, Daphni, duas altaria Phoebo, Verg.; Cic., Liv., Tac.

altĕr -tĕra -tĕrum (genit. altĕrīus, in poetry also altĕrĭus; dat. alteri), *one of two, the one, the other.*

(1) in gen.: consulum alter, Liv.; alter . . . alter, *the one . . . the other*; so: alter . . . ille or hic or iste, or a subst.; in plur.: alteri dimicant, alteri victorem timent, Cic.; with the second alter in a different case: alter alterius ova frangit, Cic.

(2) as a numeral, *second*: altera die, Caes.; altera die quam a Brundisio solvit, Liv.; altero vicesimo die, *on the twenty-second day,* Cic.; unus et alter, *one or two,* Ter., Hor.; in plur., of a *second set.*

(3) of quality: **a,** *second, next best*: fortunate puer, tu nunc eris alter ab illo, *you will be second to him,* Verg.; **b,** of similarity, *another, a second*: me sicut alterum parentem diligit, *a second parent,* Cic.; tamquam alter idem, *a second self,* Cic.; **c,** of difference, *other, changed*: quoties te speculo videris alterum, Hor.; also *another*, in the sense of *a neighbour, fellow-creature*: qui nihil alterius causa facit, Cic.

altercātĭo -ōnis, f. (altercor), *a dispute, wrangling, debate*: magna non disceptatio modo, sed etiam altercatio, Liv.; esp. *cross-examination* in a court of justice: Cic. L.

altercātor -ōris, m. (altercor), *a disputant*: Quint.

altercor -ari, dep. (alter), *to dispute, contend in words, quarrel*: altercari cum Vatinio, Caes. Esp. *to cross-examine, to cross-question*: in altercando invenit parem neminem, Cic. Transf., poet., *to contend with*: altercante libidinibus pavore, Hor.

alterno -are (alternus), *to do first one thing, then another.* (1) transit., *to interchange, change about*: fidem, *make at one time credible, at another not,* Ov.; vices, Ov. (2) intransit., *to alternate, to change about*: illi alternantes magna vi proelia miscent, *changing sides,* Verg.; haec alternanti potior sententia visa est, *hesitating,* Verg.

alternus -a -um (alter), *one after the other, by turns, alternate, interchanging.* In gen.: sermones, *dialogue,* Hor.;

versibus, *in alternate song,* Verg.; alterni metus, *mutual fear,* Liv.; alterno pede terram quatiunt, *first with one foot then with another,* Hor.; alterna loqui cum aliquo, *to hold a conversation with,* Hor.; alternis (sc. vicibus), *by turns,* Lucr. Esp. (1) of metre, *elegiac verse,* where hexameter and pentameter alternate: pedes alternos esse oportebit, Cic.; canere alterno carmine, Ov. (2) as legal t. t.: reicere alterna consilia or alternos iudices (of plaintiff and defendant), *to challenge a number of jurors in turn,* Cic.

altĕrŭter, alterutra (altera utra), alterutrum (alterum utrum); genit., altĕrutrius; *one of two*: Cic., Hor.

Althaea -ae, f. (Ἀλθαία), *wife of Oeneus, king of Calydon, mother of Meleager.*

alticinctus -a -um (altus/cingo), *high girt*; hence *busy*: Phaedr.

altĭlis -e (alo). Lit., *of domestic animals, fattened, fed up.* F. as subst. **altĭlis** (sc. avis), *a fowl*: Hor. Transf., *rich*: Pl.

altĭsŏnus -a -um (altus/sono), *sounding from on high*: Iuppiter, Cic. Transf., *high-sounding, sublime*: Maronis altisoni carmina, Juv.

altĭtŏnans -tis (altus/tono), *thundering from on high*: Lucr.

altĭtūdo -ĭnis, f. (altus). (1) *height.* Lit., montium, Cic.; in concrete sense, *heights*: Liv. Transf., *sublimity*: orationis, Cic. (2) *depth.* Lit., fluminis, Caes. Transp., altitudo animi, *depth, secrecy, reserve,* Cic.

altĭuscŭlus -a -um (altus), *a little too high*: Suet.

altĭvŏlans -antis (altus/volo), *flying high*: Lucr.

altor -ōris, m. (alo), *a nourisher, a foster-father*: omnium rerum seminator et sator et parens, ut ita dicam, atque educator et altor est mundus, Cic.; Ov., Tac.

altrinsĕcŭs, adv. (alter/secus), *on the other side*: Pl.

altrix -ĭcis, f. (alo), *a nurse, foster-mother*: terra altrix nostra, Cic.; Verg., Hor., Ov.

altrōvorsum, adv. (alter/versus), *on the other side*: Pl.

altus -a -um, alte, etc., *see* under alo.

ălūcĭnor -ari, dep. (connected with ἀλύω), *to wander in mind, dream, talk idly*: ego tamen suspicor, hunc, ut solet, alucinari, Cic.

ălumnus -a -um (alo), adj. used as noun, m., f., or n., *a nursling, a foster-child.* Masc. Lit., Italia alumnum suum videret, Cic.; sutrinae tabernae, *a cobbler,* Tac.; of legionum, *brought up in the camp,* Tac.; of animals: parvi alumni, *the young of the flock,* Hor. Transf., Platonis, *pupil,* Cic.; ego, ut ita dicam, pacis alumnus, Cic. Fem., *foster-daughter*: nostra haec alumna et tua profecto filia, Pl.; aquae dulcis alumnae, *frogs,* Cic. poet. Transf., bene constitutae civitatis quasi alumna quaedam eloquentia, Cic. Neut.: numen alumnum, Ov.

Ălūntĭum (Hăluntĭum) -i, n. (Ἀλούντιον), *a town in the north of Sicily.* Adj. **Ăluntīnus** -a -um.

ălūta -ae, f. *a kind of soft leather*: Caes. Hence meton., *a shoe*: Ov.; *a purse*: Juv.; *an ornamental patch on the face*: Ov.

alvĕārĭum -i, n. *a beehive*: Cic., Verg.

alvĕŏlus -i, m. (dim. of alveus). (**1**) *a little hollow, a tray, trough, bucket*: Juv., Liv. (**2**) *a gaming board*: Cic.

alvĕus -i, m. (alvus). (**1**) *a hollow, cavity*: vitiosae ilicis, Verg. (**2**) *a trough*: Liv. (**3**) *a boat*: Verg.; also *the hold of a ship*: Sall. (**4**) *a bath-tub*: Cic. (**5**) *the bed of a stream*: quia sicco alveo transiri poterat, Liv.; Verg., Hor. (**6**) *a beehive*: Plin. (**7**) *a gaming-table*: Plin., Suet.

alvus -i, f. (cf. αὐλός, αὐλών), *the belly*. Lit., purgatio alvi, Cic.; also of *the womb*: Cic.; of *the stomach*: Cic. Transf., (**1**) *the hold of a ship*: Tac. (**2**) *a beehive*: Plin.

Ălўattēs -is or -ĕi, m. (᾽Αλυάττης), *king of Lydia, father of Croesus.*

Alyzĭa -ae, f. (᾽Αλυζία), *a small town in Acarnania*, with a temple of Hercules.

ămābĭlis -e (amo), *amiable, lovable*: amabilior mihi Velia fuit, quod te ab ea amari sensi, Cic.; amabile carmen, *lovely*, Hor.
  ¶ Adv. **ămābĭlĭter**, *amiably, lovingly*: Cic., Hor.

ămābĭlĭtās -ātis (amabilis), *lovableness*: Pl.

Ămalthēa -ae, f. (᾽Αμάλθεια), *a nymph, the nurse of Jupiter in Crete*; according to others, the goat on the milk of which Jupiter was reared, one of whose horns, broken off by accident, was placed among the stars as the Cornu Amaltheae or Cornu copiae.
  ¶ Hence **Amalthēa** -ae, f. and **Amalthēum** -i, n. *a sanctuary of Amalthea in Epirus*, near the estate of Atticus.

āmandātĭo -ōnis, f. (amando), *a sending away*: Cic.

āmando -are, *to send away, to send to a distance*: aliquem Lilybaeum, Cic. Transf., natura res similis procul amandavit a sensibus, Cic.

amans = partic. of amo; q.v.

Amantĭa -ae, f. (᾽Αμαντία), *name of two towns in Illyricum.*
  ¶ Hence **Amantĭāni** -ōrum, m. pl. *the inhabitants of Amantia.*

āmānŭensis -is, m. = a manu servus, *a secretary, clerk*: Suet.

Ămānus -i, m. (᾽Αμανός), *a range of mountains in Asia Minor, dividing Cilicia from Syria.*
  ¶ Hence subst. **Amānĭenses** -ĭum, m. pl. *its inhabitants.*

ămărăcĭnus -a -um, *made of marjoram*: Plin. N. as subst. **ămărăcĭnum** -i (sc. unguentum), *marjoram ointment*: Lucr.

ămărăcus -i, m. and **ămărăcum** -i, n. (ἀμάρακος), *marjoram*: Verg.

ămărantus -i, m. (ἀμάραντος, *unfading*), *the amaranth*: Ov.

ămărĭtĭēs -ei, f. (amarus), *bitterness*: Cat.

ămărĭtūdo -ĭnis, f. (amarus). Lit., *bitterness of taste*: Varr. Transf., *bitterness, sorrow*: Plin. L. As rhet. t. t.: vocis, *harshness of voice*, Quint.

ămăror -ōris, m. (amarus), *bitterness*: Lucr., Verg.

ămărus -a -um, *bitter*. Lit., of taste: Lucr., Verg.; n. as subst. **amarum** -i: Cic.; of smell, *pungent*: fumus, Verg. Transf., (**1**) *disagreeable, unpleasant*: amores, Verg.; curae, Ov. N. pl. as subst. **amara** -orum, *unpleasantnesses*: Hor. (**2**) of persons, *irritable*: amariorem me senectus facit, Verg. (**3**) of speech, *biting, acrimonious*: lingua, Ov.
  ¶ Adv. **ămārē**, *bitterly*: Pl., Sen.

Ămăryllis -ĭdis, acc. -ĭda, f. (᾽Αμαρυλλίς), *name of a shepherdess*: Verg.

Ămărynthĭs -ĭdis, f. *surname of Diana*, from Amarynthus, a place in Euboea where Diana was worshipped.

Ămăsēnus -i, m. *a small river in Latium* (now *Amaseno*).

Ămăsis -is or -ĭdis, m. (῎Αμασις), *an Egyptian, who became pharaoh about* 569 B.C.

ămāsius -i, m. (amo), *a lover*: Pl.

Ămastris -ĭdis, f. (῎Αμαστρις), *a town in Paphlagonia* (now *Amasserah*).
  ¶ Hence adj. **Amastrĭācus** -a -um, *belonging to Amastris*: orae, *coasts of Pontus*, Ov. Subst. **Amastrĭāni** -orum, m. pl. *the inhabitants of Amastris.*

Ămāta -ae, f. myth. *wife of king Latinus, mother of Lavinia.*

Ămăthūs -untis, f. (᾽Αμαθοῦς), *a city of Cyprus, sacred to Venus.*
  ¶ Hence **Ămăthūsĭa** -ae, f. = *Venus*; adj. **Ămăthūsĭăcus** -a -um, *Amathusian.*

ămātĭo -ōnis, f. (amo), *love-making, intrigue*: Pl.

ămātor -ōris, m. (amo). (**1**) *one who loves, a friend*: vir bonus amatorque noster, Cic.; amatores huic (Catoni) desunt, *admirers, readers of his works*, Cic.; so of a thing: puri sermonis, Caes.; sapientiae, pacis, Cic. (**2**) *the lover of a woman, paramour*: virginem ab amatorum impetu prohibere, Cic.; Pl., Hor.

ămātorcŭlus -i, m. (dim. of amator), *a little lover*: Pl.

ămātōrĭus -a -um (amator), *loving, amorous*: sermo, Cic.; poesis (Anacreontis), Cic.; frui voluptate amatoriā, Cic. N. as subst. **ămātōrĭum** -i, *a love philtre*: Plin., Sen.
  ¶ Adv. **ămātōrĭē**, *amorously*: Pl., Cic.

ămātrix -īcis, f. (amator), *a mistress, sweetheart*: Pl.

Ămāzon -ōnis, f., gen. in plur. **Ămāzŏnes** -um (᾽Αμαζόνες), myth. *nation of female warriors*, supposed to have lived in Pontus.
  ¶ Hence subst. **Ămāzŏnis** -ĭdis, f. = Amazon: Verg. Adj. **Ămāzŏnĭcus** and **Ămāzŏnĭus** -a -um, *Amazonian*: vir, Hippolytus, son of an Amazon by Theseus, Ov.

amb, ambi, am, an (cf. ἀμφί), an inseparable prefix to certain words, giving the sense *on both sides*, and so *around, round about.*

ambactus -i, m. (from Celtic amb), *a vassal*: Caes.

ambāges, abl. -e, f. (of sing. only abl. found; complete in the plur.), *going round, roundabout way, winding.*
  Lit., variarum ambage viarum, *of a labyrinth*, Ov.
  Transf., (**1**) *circumlocution*: missis ambagibus, *without circumlocution*, Hor. (**2**) *obscurity, ambiguity*: ambages canere, of the Sibyl, Verg.; immemor ambagum, of the Sphinx, Ov.; esp. of the language of oracles.

ambĕdo -esse -ēdi -ēsum, *to eat round, consume*: Verg., Tac. Transf., of the action of fire: Verg.; of wasting money: Pl.

ambĭgo -ĕre (amb/ago).
  Lit., *to go about or round*: patriam, Tac.
  Transf., (**1**) *to doubt, hesitate, be uncertain*: ius quod ambigitur, Cic; ambigitur, *it is in doubt*, impers.; followed by de and

the abl.: Plin.; or by indirect question : Cic.,
Hor.; by accus. and infin.: Tac. (2) *to
dispute, contend,* at law or otherwise : cum eo
qui heres est, Cic.; de hereditate, Cic.

ambĭgŭĭtās -ātis, f. (ambiguus), *ambiguity*:
verborum, Cic.

ambĭgŭus -a -um (ambigo). LIT., *moving
from side to side, of doubtful nature*: Proteus,
Ov.; virgo, Siren or Sphinx, Ov.; viri,
Centaurs, Ov.; ambiguam promisit Salamina,
a second Salamis, Hor.

TRANSF., (1) *uncertain, doubtful*: haud
ambiguus rex, Liv.; with gen.: ambiguus
tanti certaminis heres, Ov.; imperandi, *not
resolved on,* Tac. N. as subst., *uncertainty*:
non habui ambiguum, *I had no doubt,* Cic.;
relinquere in ambiguo, Lucr. (2) *uncertain,
untrustworthy*: fides, Liv.; res possessionis
haud ambiguae, *with a clear title,* Liv.; res,
insecure, Tac.; aquae, *changing,* Ov. (3) of
speech, *ambiguous, obscure*: oracula, Cic.
N. as subst., *ambiguity*: ex ambiguo dicta,
Cic.; ambiguorum complura sunt genera,
Cic.

Adv. **ambĭgŭē.** (1) *ambiguously*: scribere,
Cic. (2) *indecisively*: equites ambigue certa-
vere, Tac.

ambĭo -īre -īvi *or* -ii -ītum (amb/eo; but con-
jugated regularly according to the 4th conjug.
except imperf. ambibat: Ov.), *to go round.*

LIT., ut terram lunae cursus proxime
ambiret, Cic.; Ov.

TRANSF., (1) *to surround*: silvas profunda
palus ambibat, Tac.; vallum armis ambirent,
Tac. (2) *to go round canvassing for votes,* or
help: ad id quod agi videbatur ambientes,
Liv.; pass.: populus facit eos a quibus est
maxime ambitus, Cic. (3) *to address individuals, entreat*: reginam adfatu, Verg.; te
pauper ambit sollicita prece ruris colonus,
approaches with prayer, Hor.

Ambĭŏrix -rīgis, m. *chief of the Eburones in
Gallia Belgica.*

ambĭtĭo -ōnis, f. (ambio).

LIT., *a canvassing for office in a lawful
manner* (opp. ambitus; q.v.): me ambitio et
forensis labor ab omni illa cogitatione
abstrahebat, Cic.

TRANSF., *striving after honours.* (1) *desire
for office*: me ambitio quaedam ad honorum
studium duxit, Cic. (2) in gen., *desire for
popularity, fame, display, pomp*: funerum
nulla ambitio, *no empty pomp,* Tac.

ambĭtĭōsus -a -um (adj. with compar.)
(ambitio). (1) *twining around*: lascivis
hederis ambitiosior, Hor. (2) *eager for public
office, ambitious*: ita ambitiosus, ut omnes
cottidie persalutet, Cic. (3) in gen., *ingrati-
ating, eager to win favour, seeking popularity*:
dux indulgens ambitiosusque, Liv.; Musa
nec in plausus ambitiosa mea est, Ov.; mors,
ostentatious, Tac.

¶ Adv. (with compar.) **ambĭtĭōsē,** *am-
bitiously, ostentatiously*: non vulgariter nec
ambitiose scribere, Cic.; petere regnum,
Liv.

ambĭtus -ūs, m. (ambio), *a going round,
circuit, revolution, orbit.*

LIT., stellarum rotundi ambitus, Cic.

TRANSF., (1) from the idea of circular
movement: **a,** *circumlocution*: multos circa
unam rem ambitus facere, Liv.: **b,** *border,*

edge: extremus ambitus campi, Tac.; esp. *the
space left round a house*: Cic.: **c,** *extent*: castra
lato ambitu, Tac. (2) from the idea of
approaching or canvassing people: **a,** *illegal
canvassing for office, bribery*: lex de ambitu,
Cic.; ambitus aliquem accusare, damnare,
Cic.: **b,** in gen., *striving after popularity*:
Tac.; *after effect*: Sen., Quint.

Ambĭvăreti -ōrum, m. *a Gallic people, allies
of the Aedui.*

Ambĭvăriti -ōrum, m. *a Gallic people,* near
modern Breda.

Ambĭvĭus -i, m. (L. Turpio), *a celebrated
actor in Rome,* contemporary of Terence.

ambō -ae -ō (ἄμφω), *both, two together*: hic qui
utrumque probat, ambobus debuit uti, Cic.

Ambrăcĭa -ae, f. ('Αμβρακία), *town on the
south border of Epirus, on the gulf of the same
name* (now *Arta*).

¶ Hence adj. **Ambrăcĭensis** -e and
Ambrăcĭus -a -um, *Ambracian*; subst.
Ambrăcĭōtēs -ae, m. *an inhabitant of
Ambracia.*

ambrŏsĭa -ae, f. (ἀμβροσία). (1) *ambrosia, the
food of the gods*: orator ambrosia alendus,
of a distinguished orator, Cic. (2) *the unguent
of the gods*: Verg., Ov.

ambrŏsĭus -a -um (ἀμβρόσιος), *divine, immortal, ambrosial*: dapes, Mart.; comae, Verg.

Ambrўsus -i, f. *a town in Phocis.*

ambūbāia -ae, f. (Syrian abbūb, a flute), *a
Syrian flute-girl*: Hor., Suet.

ambŭlācrum -i, n. *a walk shaded with trees*:
Pl.

ambŭlātĭo -ōnis, f. (ambulo). (1) *a walk*: Cic.
(2) *a place for walking, a promenade*: Cic. L.

ambŭlātĭuncŭla -ae, f. (1) *a little walk*:
Cic. L. (2) *a little promenade*: Cic. L.

ambŭlātŏr -ōris, m. (ambulo), *one who walks
about, a lounger*: Cato; *a pedlar*: Mart.

ambŭlātŏrĭus -a -um (ambulo), *movable*:
Plin.

ambŭlātrix -īcis, f. *a female lounger*: Cato.

ambŭlo -are. (1) *to go backwards and forwards,
to walk*: defessus sum ambulando, Ter.
Esp. *to walk about, go for a walk*: in hortis
cum Galba, Cic. (2) *to travel, proceed, march*:
bene ambula, 'bon voyage', Pl.; ambulare in
ius, go *to law,* Pl.; septingenta milia passuum,
Cic.; with acc., *to traverse*: cum (Xerxes)
maria ambulavisset, Cic. Of things: Nilus
immenso longitudinis spatio ambulans, Plin.

ambūro -ūrĕre -ussi -ustum, *to burn round,
to scorch.*

LIT., ille domi suae vivus exustus est, hic
sociorum ambustus incendio tamen ex illa
flamma periculoque evasit, Cic.; ambusta
tigna, Liv.; of lightning, *to scorch*: ambustus
Phaethon, Hor. N. of past partic. as subst.
ambustum -i, *a burn*: Plin.

TRANSF., (1) of cold, *to nip, numb*: ambusti
multorum artus vi frigoris, Tac. (2) *to
injure*: ambustas fortunarum mearum reliquias, Cic.; damnatione conlegae prope
ambustus evaserat, Liv.

ămellus -i, m. *the purple Italian starwort*:
Verg.

Ămēnānus -i, m. ('Αμένανος), *a river of Sicily*;
also used as adj.: Amenana flumina, Ov.

āmens -entis adj. (with compar. and superl.),
mad, insane, senseless. LIT., metu, Liv.;
animi, *in mind,* Verg. TRANSF., *very foolish*:

homo audacissimus atque amentissimus, Cic.; consilium amentissimum, Cic.

āmentĭa -ae, f. (amens), *insanity, madness, folly*: in istam amentiam incidere, Cic.; Hor., Ov.

āmento -are (amentum), *to furnish with a strap*. LIT., hastae amentatae, Cic.; the same phrase is used fig. by Cic. of *prepared arguments*. TRANSF., *to hurl by means of a strap*: iaculum, Lucr.

āmentum -i, n. (connected with aptus), *a strap, thong*: Caes.; *a shoe-lace*: Plin.

Ămĕrĭa -ae, f. *a town in Umbria* (now *Amelia*).

¶ Hence adj. **Ămĕrīnus** -a -um, *belonging to Ameria*.

āmĕs -ĭtis, m. *a forked pole*, for suspending fowlers' nets: Hor.

Ămestrātus -i, f. *a town near the north coast of Sicily* (now *Mistretta*).

¶ Hence adj. **Amestrătīnŭs** -a -um, *belonging to Amestratus*.

ămĕthystĭnus -a -um, *amethyst-coloured*: vestes, Mart. N. pl. as subst. **ămethystĭna** -ōrum (sc. vestimenta), *dresses of that colour*: Juv.

ămĕthystus -i, f. (ἀμέθυστος), *an amethyst*: Plin.

amfractus=anfractus; q.v.

ămĭcĭo -īcīre -īcui *or* -ixi -ictum, *to clothe, wrap round*. LIT., amictus toga, laena, pallio, Cic. TRANSF., *to cover, conceal, wrap up*: nube cava amictus, Verg.; piper et quidquid chartis amicitur ineptis, Hor.

ămīcĭtĭa -ae, f. (amicus), *friendship*. (1) *friendship between persons*: est mihi amicitia cum aliquo, Cic.; amicitiam facere, iungere, gerere, dimittere, dissociare, dissolvere, Cic. In plur., sometimes in the concrete sense *friends*: Tac., Suet. (2) in politics, *friendship between states*: omni tempore in fide atque amicitia civitatis Aeduae fuisse, Caes.; in amicitiam populi Romani venire, Liv. (3) of inanimate things, *sympathy*: Plin.

ămīcĭtĭēs -ēi, f.=amicitia; q.v.: Lucr.

ămictus -ūs, m. (amicio). LIT., *the putting on of a garment*: Cic. Esp. *the manner of wearing the toga*: nihil est facilius quam amictum imitari alicuius aut statum aut motum, Cic. TRANSF., (1) *a garment*: Verg., Ov. (2) in gen. *a covering*: nebulae amictus, Verg., Lucr.

ămīcŭla -ae, f. (dim. of amica), *a little mistress*: Cic., Plin.

ămĭcŭlum -i, n. (amicio), *a mantle, cloak*: Cic., Liv.

ămĭcŭlus -i, m. (dim. of amicus), *a dear friend*: Cic., Cat., Hor.

ămīcus -a -um (amo).

Adj. (with compar. and superl.), *friendly, well-wishing, inclined, favourable to*. Absol., or with dat., or with prepositions: amicissimus animus, Cic.; homines sibi conciliare amiciores, Cic.; velim ut tibi amicus sit, Cic.; civitates amicae, Caes.; amica luto sus, Hor.; silentia lunae, Verg.; amicum est mihi, *it pleases me*: secundum te nihil est mihi amicius solitudine, Cic.

Subst. **amīcus** -i, m. *a friend*: intimus, Cic.; veritatis, Cic.; of a patron: amicus potens, Hor.; in politics: socius atque amicus, Cic.; esp. plur., *the retinue of a Roman governor*: Suet.; *the courtiers of the emperor*: Suet.; **amīca** -ae f. *a friend* or *a mistress*: Cic.

¶ Adv. (with superl.) **ămīcē**, *in a friendly manner*: amice facis, Cic.; amice pauperiem pati, *willingly*, Hor.

Also adv. **ămīcĭtĕr** in same sense: Pl.

āmigro -are, *to emigrate*: Liv.

Ămīnaeus -a -um, *belonging to Aminaea, a district of Picenum, famous for its wine*: Verg.

Amīsĭa -ae. (1) m. *a river in North Germany* (now the *Ems*). (2) f. *a Roman fortress on the Ems*.

āmissĭo -ōnis, f. (amitto), *a loss*: oppidorum, Cic. Esp. *a loss through death*: liberorum, Cic.

āmissus -ūs, m.=amissio; q.v.: Nep.

Ămīsus -i, f. (Ἀμισός) and **Ămīsum** -i, n. *a town in Pontus* (now *Samsun*).

ămĭta -ae, f. *a father's sister* (opp. matertera; q.v.), *an aunt*: Cic.

Ămĭternum -i, n. *a town in the Sabine country*, birth-place of the historian Sallust.

¶ Hence adj. **Amĭternīnus** -a -um, and (poet.) **Amĭternus** -a -um, *Amiternian*.

āmitto -mittĕre -mīsi -missum, *to send away, to let go*. LIT., hunc servum, Pl., Ter. TRANSF., *to let go, to let slip*: praedam de manibus, Cic. Esp. of time and opportunity: occasionem, Cic.; tempus, Cic. Also in gen., *to lose* (accidentally or negligently, opp. perdo): vitam, Cic.; litem, Cic.; mentem, Cic.; fidem, *credit*, Phaedr.; esp. *to lose by death*: filium consularem, Cic.

Ammĭānus Marcellīnus -i, m. *historian of the fourth century* A.D., who wrote a history of Rome from Nerva to Valens (96–378 A.D.), the first books of which are lost.

Ammōn (**Hammon**) -ōnis, m. (Ἄμμων), *a Libyan deity*, with a temple in the Oasis of Siwa, represented as a ram and worshipped by Romans under the name of Jupiter Ammon: Cic. Adj. **Ammōnĭăcus** -a -um.

amnĭcŏla -ae, c. (amnis/colo), *dwelling by the river-side*: salix, Ov.

amnĭcŭlus -i, m. (dim. of amnis), *a little river*: Liv.

amnis -is, m. *a stream of water, a river*: non tenuis rivulus sed abundantissimus amnis, Cic., Liv. Sometimes of a mountain torrent: ruunt de montibus amnes, Verg. Poet., *current*: Verg.; *river water*: Verg.

ămo -are, *to love passionately* or *fondly* (diligo=to esteem). (1) in personal relations: me non diligi solum, verum etiam amari, Cic.; aliquem mirifice, Cic.; amare se, *to be selfish* or *pleased with oneself*, Cic. Colloquially used as a form of thanks: te multum amamus, quod ea abs te diligenter parvoque curata sunt, Cic.; also as a form of request, amabo te, *or* amabo, *please, be so good*: amabo te, advola, Cic.; as a form of oath: ita me di ament, Ter. (2) of love towards, or between, things: amavi amorem tuum prout ipse amabat litteras, Cic.; amat ianua limen, *clings to*, Hor. (3) with infin., *to like to*: hic ames dici pater atque princeps, Hor.; also (cf. Gr. φιλέω) *to be wont, be accustomed to*: quae ira fieri amat, Sall.

¶ Hence partic. **ămans** -antis, *loving, fond, affectionate*. As adj. (with compar. and superl.): pater amantissimus, Cic.; esp. with genit.: amantissimus reipublicae, Cic.; of things: mea fidelissima atque amantissima consilia, Cic. As subst., *a lover*: Ter., Verg., Ov.

Adv. (with compar. and superl.) **ămantĕr**, lovingly: Cic.

ămoenĭtās -ātis, f. (amoenus), *pleasantness*. Esp. of places: hortorum, Cic.; urbium, Liv.; plur.: amoenitates orarum ac litorum, Cic. Also of other things: vitae, Tac. As a term of endearment: mea amoenitas, Pl.

ămoenus -a -um, *pleasant, delightful to look at*. Esp. of places: locus, Cic.; so n. pl. as subst. amoena -orum, *pleasant places*: Tac. But also more gen.: vita, Tac.; cultus, *attractive*, Liv.

Adv. **ămoenē**, *pleasantly*: Pl.

āmōlĭor -iri, dep. *to remove by an effort*. LIT., obiecta onera, Liv.; se, *to take oneself off*, Pl. TRANSF., *to set aside, to get rid of*: Octaviam uxorem, Tac.; dedecus, Tac.; amolior et amoveo nomen meum, Liv.

ămōmum -i, n. (ἄμωμον), *a shrub from which a costly balsam was prepared*: Verg., Ov.

ămŏr (amos) -ōris, m. (amo), *love* (fond or passionate, unlike caritas).

LIT., (1) in personal relations: noster in te amor, Cic.; amplecti *or* prosequi aliquem amore, Cic.; habere aliquem in amore, Cic.; habere amorem erga aliquem, Cic.; in amore esse alicui, *to be loved by someone*, Cic.; ancillae amor, *love for a servant girl*, Hor.; plur.: amores hominum in te, Cic. In a bad sense, *passion*: amore perdita est, Pl.; amores et hae deliciae quae vocantur, Cic. (2) *love for things, longing, desire*: consulatūs, Cic.; auri, Verg.; scribendi, Hor. TRANSF., (1) *an object of love, darling*: amor et deliciae generis humani (Titus), Suet.; esp. in plur.: amores et deliciae tuae, Cic. (2) *Love* (personified), *Cupid* (Ἔρως): Cic., Verg., Ov.

āmōtĭo -ōnis, f. (amoveo), *a removing*: doloris, Cic.

ămŏvĕo -mŏvēre -mōvi -mōtum, *to move away, withdraw*.

LIT., of things or persons: neque in amovendo neque in exportando frumento, Cic.; aliquem ex istis locis, Cic.; aliquem ab altaribus, Liv.; amoto patre, *in the absence of the father*, Tac.; se amovere, *to depart*, Ter., Liv. Esp. (1) euphem., *to steal*: boves per dolum amotae, Hor. (2) *to banish*: in insulam, Tac.

TRANSF., *to put aside ideas* or *feelings*: amoto metu, Ter.; sensum doloris mei a sententia dicenda amovebo, Cic.; ab se culpam, Liv.

Amphĭārāus -i, m. (Ἀμφιάραος), *a celebrated Argive seer, husband of Eriphyle, father of Alcmaeon and Amphilochus*.

¶ Hence adj. **Amphĭārēus** -a -um, *belonging to Amphiaraus*; subst. **Amphĭarāĭdēs** -ae, m. *son of Amphiaraus* = Alcmaeon: Ov.

amphĭbŏlĭa -ae, f. (ἀμφιβολία), *ambiguity, double meaning*: Cic.

Amphictўŏnes -um, m. (Ἀμφικτύονες), *the Amphictyons, religious representatives of the Greek states*, who met first at Thermopylae and afterwards at Delphi.

¶ Hence subst. **Amphĭlŏchi** -orum, m. pl. *the Amphilochians*; also adj. **Amphĭlŏchĭus** or **Amphĭlŏchĭcus** -a -um,

Amphilochian: Argos Amphilochium *or* Amphilochicum, *Argos, the chief town in Amphilochia*.

Amphīōn -ōnis, m. (Ἀμφίων), *king of Thebes, and husband of Niobe*; said to have raised the walls of Thebes by the magical power of his lyre: arces Amphionis, i.e. *Thebes*, Ov.

¶ Hence adj. **Amphīŏnĭus** -a -um, *belonging to Amphion*: Prop.

Amphĭpŏlis, acc. -im, f. (Ἀμφίπολις), *an Athenian colony in Macedonia, on the Strymon*.

amphisbaena -ae, f. (ἀμφίσβαινα), *a kind of African snake*: Plin.

Amphissa -ae, f. (Ἄμφισσα), *a town of the Ozolian Locrians*, modern Salona.

¶ Hence adj. **Amphissĭus** -a -um: Ov.

amphĭthĕātrālis -e (amphitheatrum), *belonging to the amphitheatre*: spectaculum, Plin.

amphĭthĕātrĭcus -a -um = amphitheatralis; q.v.

amphĭthĕātrum -i, n. (ἀμφιθέατρον), *an amphitheatre, an oval or circular building for gladiatorial shows and public spectacles*: Tac.

Amphītrītē -ēs, f. (Ἀμφιτρίτη), *the wife of Neptune, goddess of the sea*. Hence, *the sea*: Ov., Cat.

Amphitrўōn and **Amphitrŭo** -ōnis, m. (Ἀμφιτρύων), *king of Thebes, and husband of Alcmene*.

¶ Hence subst. **Amphītrўōnĭădēs** -ae, m. *the son of Amphitryon*, i.e. *Hercules*: Verg.

amphŏra -ae, f. (ἀμφορεύς). (1) *a two-handled, narrow-necked jar*, generally made of clay, used for liquids, esp. for wine: Hor.; meton., *wine*: Hor.; used also for honey: Hor.; for oil: Cato. (2) *a measure*: a, *a measure for liquids*, 2 urnae or about 6⅔ gallons: b, *measure of the tonnage of a ship*, about 1/25 of our ton: naves onerariae quarum minor nulla erat duum milium amphorum, ap. Cic. L.

amphŏrālis -e (amphora), *containing an amphora*: Plin.

Amphrўsus or **Amphrўsŏs** -i, m. (Ἀμφρυσός), *a stream in Phthiotis*, near which Apollo kept the flocks of Admetus: pastor ab Amphryso, *Apollo*, Verg.

¶ Hence adj. **Amphrўsĭus** -a -um: Amphrysia vates, *the Sibyl*, Verg.

amplē, adv. from amplus; q.v.

amplector -plecti -plexus sum, dep. *to embrace*.

LIT., (1) *to twine round, clasp* or *grasp* a person or thing: genua, Pl.; aram, Tac.; dextram, Verg. (2) *to enclose, surround*: hostium aciem, Liv.; of fire: ignis proxima quaeque et deinceps continua amplexus, Liv.; of areas enclosed: spatium, Tac.; quattuor milia passuum, Tac.

TRANSF., (1) *to welcome, love, esteem*: amicum, Cic.; aliquem amore, Cic.; tanto amore suas possessiones, Cic. (2) *to embrace in thought, to consider*: si iudex non omnia amplectetur consilio, Cic. (3) *to embrace, in the sense of to include* or *comprise*: quod idem interdum virtutis nomine amplectimur, Cic. (4) *to embrace* or *touch on* in discourse: argumentum pluribus verbis, Cic.; omnia communiter, Liv.

amplexor -ari, dep. (freq. of amplector; also in rare act. form **amplexo** -are). LIT., *to embrace*: Pl., Ter. TRANSF., *to welcome, love, esteem*: Appius totum me amplexatur, Cic.; aequabilitatem iuris, Cic.

amplexus -ūs, m. (amplector), *a surrounding, encircling*: terrarum, Lucr.; serpentis, Cic. Esp. of human beings, *an embrace*: Verg., Ov., Tac.

amplĭfĭcātĭo -ōnis, f. (amplifico), *an enlarging, increasing.* LIT., rei familiaris, Cic. TRANSF., *an enlarging, heightening*: honoris et gloriae, Cic.; esp. in rhetoric, *enlargement, amplification*: Cic.

amplĭfĭcātor -ōris, m. (amplifico), *one who enlarges*: dignitatis, Cic.

amplĭfĭco -are (amplus/facio), *to enlarge.* LIT., civitatem, Cic.; divitias, Cic. TRANSF., *to increase*: voluptatem, Cic.; esp. in rhetoric, *to dilate upon, magnify*: aliquid dicendo amplificare atque ornare, Cic.

amplĭo -are (amplus), *to make wide, enlarge, increase*, rem, Hor.; equitum centurias, Liv. TRANSF., *to glorify*: nomen, Mart.; legal t. t., *to adjourn the hearing of a case*: causam, Cic.; virginem, i.e. *the hearing of her case*, Liv.

amplĭtūdo -ĭnis, f. (amplus), *breadth, size.* LIT., simulacrum modica amplitudine, Cic.; in plur.: amplitudines quaedam bonorum, Cic. TRANSF., *greatness, dignity, grandeur*: nominis, Cic.; maxima cum gloria ad summam amplitudinem pervenire, Cic.; esp. rhet., *dignity of expression*: Platonis, Cic.

amplus -a -um, adj. (with compar. and superl.), *large, spacious, ample.*
LIT., of space, size, number, etc.: domus, Cic.; pecunia amplissima, Cic.; ampliores copiae, Caes.
TRANSF., (1) *great, important*: occasio, Cic.; ampla spes, Sall. (2) *honourable*: praemia, Cic.; amplum Tuscis ratus, *thinking it an honour for the Etruscans*, Liv. (3) *eminent, distinguished*: amplae et honestae familiae, Cic.; amplissimi viri, *men of the highest position*, Cic.; esp. of public offices: amplissimus honor, *the consulship*, Cic. (4) of rhetoric, *grand, full*: orationis genus, Cic.
Adv. **amplē**, *fully, grandly, abundantly*: amplissime dare agrum, exornare triclinium, Cic.; of oratory: elate et ample loqui, Cic.
Adv. **amplĭter**, in same senses: Pl.
Compar. adv. **amplius**, *more* (in some contexts this may rather be taken as neuter of compar. adj.).
(1) *more*, with no comparison expressed. Sometimes in the sense *longer*: non luctabor tecum amplius, Cic.; or *more times*: felices ter et amplius, Hor. Most often as *further, besides, in addition*, esp. with pronouns and negatives: quid est quod iam amplius exspectes, Cic.; nihil amplius, *I say no more*, Cic. Common in judicial and political phraseology: **a**, as a formula of adjournment in court: cum consules re audita amplius de consilii sententia pronuntiavissent, Cic.; **b**, amplius non petere, *to make no further claim*: **c**, adding to a motion: Servilio adsentior et hoc amplius censeo, Cic.
(2) *more than*, with comparison expressed: **a**, with abl.: lamentari amplius aequo, Lucr.;

amplius horis sex, Caes.: **b**, with quam (mainly post-Aug.): amplius quam septem horas, Suet: **c**, most commonly, as with quam but with the word omitted: amplius centum cives Romani, Cic.; amplius ducenti, Liv.; non amplius pedum DC, Caes.

Ampsanctus -i, m. *a lake in Italy*, known for its pestiferous exhalations, and so said to be one of the entrances to the lower world (now *Le Mofete*).

ampulla -ae, f. (dim. of amphora), *a flask, bottle.* LIT., Pl., Cic. TRANSF., *bombast*: Hor.

ampullācĕus -a -um (ampulla), *bottle-shaped*: Plin.

ampullārĭus -i, m. (ampulla), *a bottle-maker*: Pl.

ampullor -ari, dep. (ampulla), *to speak bombastically*: Hor.

ampŭtātĭo -ōnis, f. (amputo), *a cutting off, pruning*: Cic. Also *a cutting* (i.e. what is cut off): Plin.

ampŭto -are, *to cut off.*
LIT., (1) of plants or trees, *to lop* or *prune*: ramos inutiles, Hor.; fig.: non solum ramos amputare miseriarum, Cic. (2) *to cut off a part of the body*: caput, Tac.; as medical t. t., *to amputate*: in corpore quidquid est pestiferum, Cic.
TRANSF., *to remove* or *diminish*: amputata inanitas omnis, Cic.; numerum legionum, Tac.; amputata loqui, *to speak disconnectedly*, Cic.

Ampўcus -i, m. (Ἄμπυκος). (1) *son of Iapetus, a singer and priest of Ceres*, killed at the wedding of Perseus by Pettalus. (2) *the father of Mopsus.*
Hence **Ampўcĭdēs** -ae, m. *a descendant of Ampycus*, i.e. *Mopsus*: Ov.

Ampyx -pўcis, m. (Ἄμπυξ). (1) *a comrade of Phineus*, turned into stone by the Medusa's head at the wedding of Perseus. (2) *one of the Lapithae.*

ămŭlētum -i, n. (Arab. hamalet), *a charm, amulet*: Plin.

Āmūlĭus -i, m. *king of Alba Longa, who drove his elder brother, Numitor, from the throne, and exposed in the Tiber Numitor's grandsons, Romulus and Remus.*

ămurca -ae, f. (ἀμόργη), *the oil-lees*: Verg., Plin.

ămussis (acc. -im), f. *a carpenter's rule*: ad amussim, *exactly*, Varr. Cf. examussim.

Amўclae -arum, f. (Ἀμύκλαι). (1) *a town in Laconia*, about three miles south of Sparta; myth., *home of Tyndareus and birth-place of the Dioscuri.* (2) *an old town in Latium*, said to have been founded from Amyclae (1).
¶ Hence adj. **Amўclaeus** -a -um, *belonging to Amyclae* (1), *Amyclaean*: fratres, *the Dioscuri*, Verg.; hence poet. *Laconian*: canis, Verg.

ămygdălum -i, n. (ἀμύγδαλον), *an almond*: Ov.

Amўmōnē -ēs, f. (Ἀμυμώνη), *daughter of Danaus*, beloved by Neptune, who in her honour caused a fountain to spring out of the rock near Argos, which was named after her.

Amyntās -ae, m. (Ἀμύντας), *name of several Macedonian kings*, the most famous of whom was Amyntas II, *father of Philip of Macedon, and grandfather of Alexander the Great.*
¶ Hence subst. **Amyntĭădēs** -ae, m.
(1) *a descendant of Amyntas* = *Philip*: Ov.
(2) *name of a shepherd in Vergil.*

Ămyntŏr -ŏris, m. (*Ἀμύντωρ*), *king of the Dolopians, father of Phoenix.* ¶ Hence subst. **Ămyntŏrĭdēs** -ae, m. *a son of Amyntor=Phoenix*: Ov.

ămystis -ĭdis, f. (*ἄμυστις*), *the emptying of a goblet at a draught*: Hor.

Ămȳthāŏn -ŏnis, m. (*Ἀμυθάων*), *father of Melampus.* ¶ Hence adj. **Ămȳthāŏnĭus** -a -um, *of Amythaon*: Verg., Prop.

ăn, conj. *or, or whether,* introduces the second (or any subsequent) clause of a direct or indirect double question, or of a sentence implying doubt.

(1) in direct questions: **a,** where both alternatives are expressed: utrum hoc tantum crimen praetermittes an obicies? Cic.; often followed simply by non: **b,** elliptically, where the first alternative is suppressed, often to express irony or astonishment, *or then?*: an etiam id dubium est? Cic.; an censes nihil inter nos convenire? Cic.

(2) in indirect questions, after verbs of asking, etc., and also with other expressions implying doubt or uncertainty: **a,** where both alternatives are expressed: id utrum Romano more locutus sit an quo modo Stoici dicunt, postea videro, Cic.; honestumne factu sit an turpe, dubitant, Cic.; here an non is rare, being replaced usually by necne: **b,** with the first alternative suppressed (cf. (1) **b,** above). Esp. with the expressions of doubt dubito, haud scio, nescio, incertum (est); here the suggestion is that the clause which follows states the truth: haud scio an satis sit, eum qui lacesserit, iniuriae suae paenitere, *I think that perhaps* . . ., Cic. So: quis scit an adiciant hodiernae crastina summae tempora di superi? Hor.

ănăbathrum -i, n. (*ἀνάβαθρον*), *a raised seat*: Juv.

Ănăcharsis -is, m. (*Ἀνάχαρσις*), *a Scythian who, it was said, visited Athens in the time of Solon.*

Ănăcrĕŏn -ontis, m. (*Ἀνακρέων*), *a Greek lyric poet of Teos* who flourished c. 540 B.C. Adj. **Anacrĕontĭus** -a -um, *Anacreontic.*

ănădēma -ătis, n. (*ἀνάδημα*), *an ornament* or *fillet for the head*: Lucr.

Ănagnĭa -ae, f., *a town in Latium, capital of the Hernici* (now *Anagni*). Adj. **Ănagnīnus** -a -um, *belonging to Anagnia.*

ănagnostēs -ae, m. (*ἀναγνώστης*), *a reader*: Cic. L.

ănălecta -ae, m. (*ἀναλέγω*), *a slave whose duty it was to collect and remove crumbs after a meal*: Mart.

ănălŏgĭa -ae, f. (*ἀναλογία*), *proportion, comparison, analogy*: Varr., Quint.

ănancaeum -i, n. (*ἀναγκαῖον, unavoidable*), *a large drinking cup, bumper, to be drained at a draught*: Pl.

ănăpaestus -a -um (*ἀνάπαιστος*): pes, *a metrical foot, an anapaest* (‿ ‿ —), Cic. N. as subst. **anapaestum** -i, *a poem in anapaestic verse*: Cic.

Ănăphē -ēs, f. (*Ἀνάφη*), *an island east of Thera, one of the Sporades* (now *Namfi*).

ănăphŏră -ae, f. (*ἀναφορά*). (1) *the rising of the heavenly bodies*: Plin. (2) in rhetoric, *the repetition of a word at the beginning of several sentences* (as in Cic. Verr. 2.2.10).

Ănāpis -is or **Ănāpus** -i, m. *a river in Sicily, near Syracuse* (now *Anapo*).

Anartes -ium, m. pl. *a people in Dacia.*

¹Ănās -ae, m. (*Ἄνας*), *a river in Spain* (now *Guadiana*).

²ănas ănătis, f. *a duck*: Cic., Ov.

ănătīcŭla -ae, f. (dim. of anas), *a little duck*: Cic. As a term of endearment: Pl.

ănătŏcismus -i, m. (*ἀνατοκισμός*), *compound interest*: Cic. L.

Ănaxăgŏras -ae, m. (*Ἀναξαγόρας*), *a Greek philosopher of Clazomenae, friend and teacher of Pericles and Euripides.*

Ănaxarchus -i, m. (*Ἀνάξαρχος*), *a philosopher of Abdera, in the fourth century* B.C.

Ănaxĭmander -dri, m. (*Ἀναξίμανδρος*), *a philosopher of Miletus, born* 610 B.C.

Ănaxĭmĕnēs -is, m. (*Ἀναξιμένης*), *a philosopher of Miletus, who flourished c.* 550 B.C.

anceps -cĭpĭtis, abl. sing. -cipiti (amb-/caput), *two-headed.* LIT., *with two heads*: Ianus, Ov.; similarly *with two peaks*: acumen montis, Ov.; *with two edges*: securis, Ov. TRANSF., in various senses. (1) *coming on both sides, behind and before*: cum anceps hostis et a fronte et a tergo urgeret, Liv.; anceps proelium, *a battle where the enemy attack on both sides*, Caes.; anceps metus et ab cive et ab hoste, Liv. (2) *of two natures*: bestiae quasi ancipites, *amphibious*, Cic.; anceps faciendi dicendique sapientia, Cic. (3) *ambiguous*: oraculum, Liv. (4) *uncertain, undecided*: belli fortuna, Cic.; proelium, Liv.; Lucanus an Apulus anceps, *uncertain whether a Lucanian or an Apulian*, Hor. (5) *dangerous* (post-Aug. use): viae, Ov.; anceps erat, Liv. N. as subst., *danger*: Tac.

Anchīsēs -ae, m. (*Ἀγχίσης*), *son of Capys and father of Aeneas.* ¶ Hence adj. **Anchīsēus** -a -um, *belonging to Anchises*; subst. **Anchīsĭădēs** -ae, m. *a descendant of Anchises, i.e. Aeneas*: Verg.

ancile -is, n., genit. pl. anciliorum: Hor. (perhaps from amb-/caedo), *a shield which fell from heaven in the time of Numa, on the preservation of which the safety of the Roman empire was supposed to depend*: Verg., Liv., Tac. Also in Juv. as adj.: clipeis ancilibus.

ancilla -ae, f. *a maid-servant, female slave*: Pl., Cic., Hor.

ancillārĭŏlus -i, m. (ancilla), *a lover of maid-servants*: Mart.

ancillāris -e (ancilla), *relating to a maid-servant*: artificium, Cic.

ancillor -ari, dep. (ancilla), *to serve as a maid-servant*; so, in gen., *to serve*: Plin.

ancillŭla -ae, f. (dim. of ancilla), *a little maid-servant*: Pl., Ter., Ov.; fig.: idcirco istam iuris scientiam tamquam ancillulam pedisequamque adiunxisti, Cic.

ancīsus -a -um (amb/caedo), *cut round*: Lucr.

Ancōn -ōnis, f. (*Ἀγκών, elbow*), and **Ancōna** -ae, f. *a town of the Piceni in Italy, with a harbour on the Adriatic coast.*

ancŏra -ae, f. (*ἄγκυρα*), *an anchor*: ancoram iacere, Caes.; figere, pangere, *to cast anchor*, Ov.; tollere, *to weigh anchor*, Caes.; consistere ad ancoram, in ancoris, *to lie at anchor*, Caes. Fig.: ancora iam nostram non tenet ulla ratem, Ov.

ancŏrāle -is, n. (ancora), *a cable*: Liv.

ancŏrārĭus -a -um (ancora), *belonging to an anchor*: funis, Caes.

Ancus (Marcius) -i, *fourth king of Rome.*

Ancȳra -ae, f. (Ἄγκυρα), *capital of Galatia* (now *Ankara*). ¶ Hence adj. **Ancȳrānus** -a -um, *belonging to Ancyra*: Ancyranum monumentum, *an inscription put up by Augustus at the entrance to his temple at Ancyra (and elsewhere) giving his account of his achievements.*

andăbătă -ae, m. *a kind of gladiator who fought with a helmet that had no openings for the eyes*: Cic.

Andanĭa -ae, f. (Ἀνδανία), *an old town in Messenia, between Megalopolis and Messene* (now *Andorossa*).

Andecavi -ōrum, m. and **Andes** -ium, m. pl. *a Gallic people on the Loire, with a town of the same name* (now *Angers*).

¹Andes, *see Andecavi.*

²Andēs -ium, f. *town in the Mantuan country, birth-place of Vergil* (now *Pietola*).

Andraemōn -ŏnis, m. (Ἀνδραίμων). (**1**) *father of Amphissus, husband of Dryope.* (**2**) (also Andremon), *king of Calydon, father of Thoas.*

Andriscus -i, m. (Ἀνδρίσκος), *a slave who gave himself out to be the son of the Macedonian king Perseus. He caused the third Macedonian war, which ended with the reduction of Macedonia into a Roman province by Metellus.*

Andrŏgĕōs, or **Andrŏgĕus** -i, m. (Ἀνδρόγεως), *son of the Cretan king Minos, killed by the Athenians, who were consequently attacked and subdued by Minos, and forced to pay a tribute of youths and maidens to the Minotaur.*

andrŏgȳnus -i, m. (ἀνδρόγυνος), or **andrŏgȳne** -es, f. *a hermaphrodite*: Cic., Liv.

Andrŏmăchē -ēs and **-cha** -ae, f. (Ἀνδρομάχη), *wife of Hector, and, after the capture of Troy, the captive of Pyrrhus and subsequently wife of Helenus.*

Andrŏmĕdē -ēs, f. and **-da** -ae, f. (Ἀνδρομέδη), *daughter of the Ethiopian king Cepheus and of Cassiopeia, exposed to a sea-monster, but rescued and married by Perseus.*

andrōn -onis, m. (ἀνδρών), *a corridor*: Plin. L.

Andrŏnicus -i, m. *surname of several Romans, esp. L. Livius, the earliest of the Roman dramatic and epic poets*; flourished *c.* 240 B.C.

Andrŏs and **Andrus** -i, f. (Ἄνδρος), *the most northerly of the Cyclades.* ¶ Hence adj. **Andrĭus** -a -um, *Andrian*; f. as subst. **Andria** -ae, *the Woman of Andros, the name of one of Terence's comedies.*

ānellus -i, m. (dim. of anulus), *a little ring*: Hor.

ănēthum -i, n. (ἄνηθον), *dill, anise*: Verg.

anfractus -ūs, m. (frango), *a turning, a bend.* LIT., of physical objects, *a turning, bending*: solis, *revolution,* Cic.; anfractus curvus vallis, *winding*, Verg.; recta regione, si nullus anfractus intercederet, Caes. TRANSF.: **a**, *legal intricacies*: iudiciorum, Cic.: **b**, *circumlocution, digression*: Cic.

angellus -i, m. (dim. of angulus), *a little corner*: Lucr.

angīna -ae, f. (angor), *the quinsy*: Pl.

angĭportum -i, n. and **angĭportus** -ŭs, m. (ang-, as in angustus/portus), *a narrow street*: Cic., Hor.

Angĭtĭa -ae, f. *a goddess worshipped by the Marsi*: nemus Angitiae, *a grove sacred to her.*

Angli -orum, m. pl. *a branch of the Suevi, living in Lower Germany.*

ango -ĕre (root ang-; cf. angustus, and Gr. ἄγχω), *to press tightly.* (**1**) of the throat, *to strangle, throttle*: guttur, Verg. (**2**) in gen., *to hurt, distress*: collisio mistorum omnis generis animantium odore insolito urbanos et agrestem confertum in arta tecta aestu ac vigiliis angebat, Liv. (**3**) of the mind, *to torment, make anxious*: alicuius animum *and* aliquem, Cic.; angebant ingentis spiritus virum Sicilia Sardiniaque amissae, Liv.; pass., angi animi *or* animo *or* simply angi, *to be grieved* or *troubled*: alicuius decessu, Cic.; de Statio manumisso et nonnullis aliis rebus, Cic.; me angit *or* angor, followed by quod, or the acc. and the infin.: Cic.

angor -ōris, m. (ango). (**1**) *compression of the throat, so suffocation*: Liv.; *the quinsy*: Plin. (**2**) *mental distress, anguish, trouble*, distinguished by Cic. from anxietas, as a more transitory state: anxius angor, Lucr.; confici angoribus, Cic.

Angrivarĭi -ōrum, m. pl. *a German tribe on the Weser.*

anguĭcŏmus -a -um (anguis/coma), *having snaky hair*: Ov.

anguĭcŭlus -i, m. (dim. of anguis), *a little snake*: Ov.

anguĭfer -fĕra -fĕrum (anguis/fero), *snakebearing*: Gorgo, Prop.; caput, Ov.

anguĭgĕna -ae, m. (anguis/gigno), *snake-born*: Ov.

anguilla -ae, f. (anguis), *an eel*: Juv. TRANSF., *a 'slippery customer'*: anguilla est, elabitur, Pl.

anguĭmănus -a -um (anguis/manus), *snakehanded*: elephantus (so called from the snake-like movements of its trunk), Lucr.

anguĭnĕus -a -um (anguis), *pertaining to a snake, snaky*: Ov.

anguīnus -a -um (anguis), *snaky*: Cat., Plin.

anguĭpes -pĕdis (anguis/pes), *snake-footed*: Ov.

anguis -is, c. *a snake*: Pl., Cic., Verg.; prov.: latet anguis in herba, *there is concealed danger*, Verg.; often also an emblem of terror, of rage, or of wisdom. In astronomy: **a**, *the constellation Draco*: Verg., Ov.: **b**, *the Hydra*: Ov.: **c**, *the Serpent*, which Anguitenens carries in his hand: Ov.

Anguĭtĕnens -entis, m. (anguis/teneo, translation of Gr. Ὀφιοῦχος), *the Snake-holder*; the *constellation Ophiuchus*: Cic.

angŭlātus -a -um (angulus), *angular, cornered*: Cic.

angŭlōsus -a -um (angulus), *full of corners*: Plin.

angŭlus -i, m. (root ang-; cf. ango, angustus, ἄγχω), *a corner, angle.* (**1**) *an angle in mathematics*: ad paris angulos, *at right angles*, Cic. (**2**) *a corner of anything*: castrorum, Caes. (**3**) *a quiet corner, a retired spot,* esp. in the country: extremus angulus agri Bruttii, Liv.; in ullo angulo Italiae, Cic.; ille terrarum mihi praeter omnes angulus ridet, Hor. (**4**) *an awkward corner, a strait*: ad istas verborum angustias et ad omnes litterarum angulos, Cic.

angŭstĭae -ārum, f. pl. (angustus), *narrowness* (the sing. is rare in class. Latin).

LIT., of space, *a strait, a narrow place*: itineris, Caes.; Corinthus posita in angustiis, Cic.; of other physical restriction: spiritus, *shortness of breath*, Cic. TRANSF., (1) of time, *shortness*: angustiae temporis, Cic. (2) of supplies, *shortness, poverty*: pecuniae, aerarii, rei familiaris, Cic. (3) *difficulty, distress*: in angustias adduci, Cic. (4) of disposition, *narrow-mindedness*: Cic. (5) of reasoning, *subtle, minute*: tantas in angustias et stoicorum dumeta (orationem) compellimus, Cic.

angusticlāvius -a -um (angustus/clavus), *wearing a narrow stripe of purple on his tunic*, epithet of a plebeian tribune: Suet.

angusto -are (angustus), *to make narrow*: Luc., Sen.

angustus -a -um, adj. (with compar. and superl.) (root ang-; cf. ango, ἄγχω, angulus), *narrow*. LIT., of space, *narrow, confined* (opp. latus): pons, Cic.; of other physical restriction: habenae, *tightly drawn reins*, Tib.; spiritus angustior, *constricted breath*, Cic. N. as subst. **angustum** -i, *a narrow space*: in angusto tendere, *to encamp in a narrow space*, Liv.; angusta viarum, Verg. TRANSF., of other kinds of restriction, *limited, confined*. (1) in gen., often in n. as subst.: in angustum deducere perturbationes, *to bridle*, Cic.; in angustum concludere, *to confine, limit*, Cic. (2) of time, *short*: nox, Ov. (3) of supplies, *short, scarce*: res frumentaria, Caes; angustas civium domos, Tac.; liberalitas angustior, Cic. (4) of circumstances, *precarious, critical, uncertain*: res angustae, Cic.; fides angustior, Caes.; n. as subst.: res est in angusto, Caes. (5) of mind or speech, *narrow, petty, limited*: alii minuti et angusti, Cic.; of perception: sensus, Cic. (6) of style, *brief, simple*: Cic., Prop. ¶ Hence adv. (with compar. and superl.) **angustē**, *narrowly*. LIT., of space, quantity, etc.: sedere, Cic.; uti re frumentaria, *sparingly*, Caes. TRANSF., (1) *in a narrow, confined manner*: angustius apud Graecos valere, Cic. (2) *briefly*: dicere, Cic.

ănhēlātio -ōnis, f. (anhelo), *panting*: Plin.

ănhēlātor -ōris, m. (anhelo), *one who breathes with difficulty*: Plin.

ănhēlitus -ūs, m. (anhelo), *short, quick breathing, puffing, panting*. LIT., anhelitum ducere, Pl.; anhelitus moventur, Cic.; aeger anhelitus, Verg.; *asthma*: Plin. TRANSF., (1) in gen., *breath*: Ov. (2) *exhalation, vapour*: terrae, Cic.

ănhēlo -are, *to draw a heavy breath, puff, pant*. (1) intransit., of living creatures, *to pant*: Lucr., Verg.; of lifeless objects, *to roar*: fornacibus ignis anhelat, Verg. (2) transit., *to produce with panting*: verba inflata et quasi anhelata gravius, Cic. TRANSF., *to pant for, desire eagerly*: scelus, Cic.

ănhēlus -a -um (anhelo), *puffing, panting*: equi, Verg. TRANSF., *causing to pant*: febris, Ov.

ănicŭla -ae, f. (dim. of anus), *a little old woman*: haec ne aniculae quidem existimant, Cic.

Ănĭēn -ēnis, *see* Anio.

Ănigrŏs -i, m. (Ἄνιγρος), *a river in Elis*.

ănīlis -e (anus), *belonging to* or *like an old woman*: vultus, Verg.; rugae, Ov.; esp. with the notion of superstition or folly: fabellae, *old wives' tales*, Cic. ¶ Hence adv. **ănīlĭtěr**, *like an old woman*: id dicitis superstitiose atque aniliter, Cic.

ănīlĭtās -ātis, f. (anilis), *old age* (of women): Cat.

ănĭma -ae, f. (connected with ἄημι), *something breathing* or *blowing*. LIT., *wind*: impellunt animae lintea Thraciae, *the north winds*, Hor.; quantum ignes animaeque valent, of Vulcan's bellows, Verg. Hence also (1) *air as an element*: Cic., Verg. (2) *breath*: animam ducere, Cic.; continere, Cic.; in plur.: Verg., Ov. TRANSF., *the breath of life, the vital principle, soul* (anima, *physical*; animus, *spiritual*): neque in homine inesse animum vel animam nec in bestia, Cic.; animam edere, *to give up the ghost*, Cic.; animam agere, *to be in the agonies of death*, Cic.; trahere, *to drag on existence*, Liv.; dum anima est, *as long as he is alive*, Cic.; of the blood as the source of life: purpuream vomit animam, *life-blood*, Verg.; of the *vital principle* in plants: Plin. Also used in other senses of the English 'soul'. (1) as a *living being*: Verg., Tac. (2) as a term of endearment: vos meae carissimae animae, Cic.; egregiae animae, Verg. (3) (like animus), as *the rational soul*: anima rationis consiliique particeps, Cic., Sall.

ănĭmadversĭo -ōnis, f. (animadverto), *perception, observation*: excitare animadversionem et diligentiam, Cic.; animadversio in civem quid fecerit, Liv. TRANSF., (1) *censure, blame*: Cic. (2) *punishment*: censoria, Cic.; Dolabellae in audaces sceleratos, Cic.; vitiorum, Cic.

ănĭmadversor -ōris, m. (animadverto), *an observer*: Cic.

ănĭmadverto (**ănĭmadvorto**) -vertěre -verti (-vorti) -versum (-vorsum); (animum/adverto), *to turn* or *give the mind to*. LIT., (1) *to take notice of, attend to*: non animadverti in pace, Cic.; ut animadvertam quae fiant, Cic.; animadvertant ne callida adsentatione capiantur, Cic.; t. t., of the lictor, *to clear the road for the consul*: consul animadvertere proximum lictorem iussit, Liv. (2) *to perceive, observe*: ecquid animadvertis horum silentium? Cic.; his animadversis, Verg.; animadvertit Caesar unos Sequanos nihil earum rerum facere, Caes. TRANSF., *to take notice of* a fault, so (1) *to blame, censure*: Cic. (2) *to punish*; often followed by in: in iudices quosdam, Cic.; res animadvertenda, Cic.; euphem., *to punish with death*: Tac.

ănĭmăl -ālis, n. (anima), *a living being, animal*: cum inter inanimum atque animal hoc maximum intersit, quod animal agit aliquid, Cic. Sometimes including man: animal providum et sagax homo, Cic.; but also as *animal*, excluding man: Cic. Occ. contemptuously, of a particular man: funestum illud animal, Cic.

ănĭmālis -e (anima). (1) *consisting of air, airy*: natura, Cic. (2) *belonging to life, living*: corpora, Lucr.; intellegentia, Cic.

animans   annus

ănĭmans -antis (animo), *living.* Adj.: mundus, Cic. Subst., *a living being, animal*; masc.: alius animans, Cic.; fem.: ceterae animantes, Cic.; neut.: animantia omnia, Cic.

ănĭmātĭo -ōnis, f. (animo), *an animating*; hence, usually, *a living being*: divinae animationis species, Cic.

¹ănĭmātus -a -um, partic. from animo; q.v.

²ănĭmātus -ūs, m. (animo), *life, animation*: Plin.

ănĭmo -are. (1) (anima), *to animate, give life to*: omnia animat, format, alit, Cic.; guttas animavit in angues, Ov. (2) (animus), *to endow with a particular disposition*: pueros orientis animari atque formari, Cic.; acrius animantur, *are made more spirited*, Tac.
¶ Hence partic. **ănĭmātus** -a -um. (1) *endowed with life, alive*: Lucr., Cic. (2) *endowed with a disposition, inclined, disposed*: Pompeius animatus melius quam paratus, Cic.; hoc animo, Pl.; in amicum, Cic.; with infin.: facere, Pl. Esp. *endowed with courage, spirited*: Pl.

ănĭmōsus -a -um. (1) (anima), *full of breath, wind* or *life*: ventus, Ov.; Euri, Verg. (2) (animus), *full of spirit* or *courage*: fortis et animosus vir, Cic.; equus, Ov.; in a bad sense: animosus corruptor, Tac. Poet., with abl., *proud of*: spoliis, Ov.
¶ Hence adv. **ănĭmōsē**, *eagerly, courageously*: animose et fortiter facere, Cic.

ănĭmŭla -ae, f. (dim. of anima) *a little soul, a little life*: tuae litterae quae mihi quidquam quasi animulae instillarunt, Cic.

ănĭmŭlus -i, m. (dim. of animus), *a term of endearment*: mi animule, *my life*, Pl.

ănĭmus -i, m. (connected with anima; q.v.).
(1) *the spiritual* or *rational principle of life in man*, opposed to corpus, *the body*, and to anima, *the principle of physical life*: credo deos immortales sparsisse animos in corpora humana, Cic.; rarely of animals: bestiae quarum animi sunt rationis expertes, Cic.
(2) more specifically, *the soul as*: **a**, *the seat of feeling, the heart*: animus aeger, Cic.; ex animo, *from the heart*, Cic., Hor.; aequo animo, *calmly*; animi causa, *for pleasure*, Caes., Cic. Often in locative or genit. animi, *at heart*: aeger animi, Liv.; infelix animi, Verg.; animi excruciare, Pl., Ter.: **b**, *character, disposition*: apertus et simplex, Cic.; alacer et promptus, Caes.; esse angusti animi atque demissi, Cic.; bono animo esse in aliquem, Caes.; exuerint silvestrem animum, Verg. Esp. of particular traits of character, *courage, confidence, spirit*: fac animo magno fortique sis, Cic.; neutris animus est ad pugnandum, Liv. So esp. in plur.: animi cadunt, *courage sinks*, Cic.; of *fire* or *vivacity* in a speech: quae vis, qui animus, quae dignitas illi oratori defuit, Cic.; poet., of a top: dant animos plagae, Verg. Also unfavourably, of *pride, arrogance* (here too esp. in plur.): uxor, inflata adhuc regiis animis et muliebri spiritu, Liv.; iam insolentiam noratis hominis, noratis animos eius et spiritus tribunicios, Cic.; pone animos, Verg.: **c**, *the seat of the will*: ad omnia et animo et consilio paratus, Cic.; eo ad te animo venimus ut, *with the resolve to*, Cic.; habeo in animo, with infin., *I am resolved*, Cic.; so also: est mihi in animo,

Cic.; inclinat animus, with ut and the subj., Liv.: **d**, *the seat of thought, intellect, mind*: complecti animo et cogitatione, Cic.; animum adhibere, applicare, Cic., etc.; cf. animadverto. So of *opinion*: meo animo, Pl.; of *memory*: Cic., Verg.; of *consciousness*: linqui animo, *to faint*, Suet.; relinquit animus aliquem, *he faints*, Caes., Ov.

Anĭo -ēnis (original nom. was Anien), m.; also poet., **Anĭēnus** -i, m. *the Anio, a river, tributary to the Tiber* (now the *Aniene*). Adj. **Anĭensis** -e and **Anĭēnus** -a -um, *belonging to the Anio.*

Ănĭus -i, m. *priest of Apollo, and king of the island of Delos, friend of Aeneas.*

Anna -ae, f. (1) *sister of Dido.* (2) Anna Perenna, *an Italian goddess, with a festival on March* 15.

annālis -e (annus). Adj.: **a**, *lasting a year*: Varr.: **b**, *relating to a year*: lex, *the law which determined the minimum age for Roman magistracies*, Cic.
¶ M. as subst., sing. **annālis** -is (sc. liber) and more often plur. **annālēs** -ium (libri), *yearly records, annals*, in early times kept by the Pontifices (hence annales pontificum or annales maximi, Cic.); also in gen., of historical compilations, such as the epic of Ennius and the works of Q. Fabius Pictor and Tacitus.

Annĭcĕrĭi -ōrum, m. (Ἀννικέριοι), *a sect of Cyrenaic philosophers.*

annĭcŭlus -a -um (annus), *one year old*: Cato, Varro.

Annĭus -a, *name of a Roman gens*, of which T. Annius Milo was a member; *see* Milo. Adj. **Annĭānus** -a -um, *belonging to that family.*

annĭversārĭus -a -um (annus/verto), *recurring every year*: sacra, Cic.; arma, Liv.

annōna -ae, f. (annus). (1) *yearly produce, crop*: salaria, *of salt*, Liv. Esp. of grain: Cic., Liv., Tac. (2) *the price of provisions*, esp. corn: annonae caritas, Cic.; vilitas, Cic.; varietas, Cic.; annona cara, Pl., Ter., Cic. Esp. *high price of corn*: solatium annonae, Cic.; annonam queri, *to complain of the high price of corn*, Liv. TRANSF., vilis amicorum annona, *friends are to be had cheap*, Hor.

annōsus -a -um (annus), *full of years, long-lived*: cornix, Hor.

annōtĭnus -a -um (annus), *a year old, belonging to last year*: naves, Caes.

annus -i, m. *a circuit*; esp. *a circuit of the sun, a year.*
LIT., exeunte anno, Cic.; anno superiore, Cic.; omnibus annis, *annually*, Caes.; tempus anni, *time of the year, season*, Cic. Adv. phrases: (1) anno, *last year*, Pl.; *for a whole year*: Liv.; *in each year, yearly*: Liv. (2) in anno, *in each year*, Cic. (3) in annum, *for a year*, Liv. (4) ad annum, *for next year*, Cic. (5) intra annum, *within the space of a year*, Liv. Often as a measure of age: annos LXX natus, *seventy years old*, Cic.; Hannibal annorum ferme novem, *when nine years old*, Caes.; habere annos viginti, Cic.; annum agere quartum et octogesimum, Cic.; hence, like aetas, *old age*: confectus annis, Sall.
TRANSF., (1) *the year of a person's life at which he could stand for a magistracy*: is enim erat annus quo per leges ei consulem fieri

[46]

liceret, Caes.; annus meus, tuus, suus, Cic.;
so, *the year of office*: prorogare annum, Cic.
(2) in gen., *time of life*: Prop. (3) poet., *time
of year, season*: nunc formosissimus annus,
Verg.; pomifer, *autumn*; hibernus, *winter*,
Hor. (4) *the produce of the year*: Luc., Tac.

annŭus -a -um (annus). (1) *lasting for a year*:
magistratus, Caes. (2) *returning every year,
annual*: labor agricolarum, Cic.; commutationes, Cic.
    N. as subst. **annŭum** -i, more often pl.
annŭa -orum, *a yearly salary, pension*:
Plin. L., Suet.

anquīro -quīrĕre -quīsīvi -quīsītum (quaero),
to seek carefully, to inquire after. LIT., omnia
quae sunt ad vivendum necessaria anquirere
et parare, Cic. TRANSF., *to investigate*: mens
semper aliquid anquirit aut agit, Cic. Esp. as
legal t. t., *to set an inquiry on foot*: de perduellione, Liv.; capite *or* capitis, *on a charge
involving capital punishment*, Liv.

ansa -ae, f. *a handle, haft*. LIT., ansa poculi,
Verg.; crepidae, *the eye through which a
shoe-tie is passed*, Tib., Plin. TRANSF. (like
English *handle*), *occasion, opportunity*: habere
reprehensionis ansam aliquam, Cic.

ansātus -a -um (ansa), *provided with a handle*.
TRANSF., homo, *a man with handles*, i.e., *with
arms akimbo*, Pl.

¹**anser** -ĕris, m. *a goose*: Cic., Liv.

²**Anser** -ĕris, m. *a wanton poet, friend of the
triumvir Antonius.*

ansĕrīnus -a -um (anser), *relating or belonging
to a goose*: Plin.

Antaeus -i, m. (Ἀνταῖος), *a powerful giant of
Libya, who compelled all strangers coming to
his country to wrestle with him; at last
Hercules, wrestling with him and finding that
each time Antaeus fell on the earth he gained
new force, held him aloft in the air and so
killed him.*

Antandros (us) -i, f. (Ἄντανδρος), *a town of
Mysia.*
  ¶ Hence adj. **Antandrĭus** -a -um, *of
Antandros.*

antĕ (old form **anti**; connected with ἀντί;
prep. and adv. *before.*
    Adv., *before.* (1) of place: ante aut post
pugnare, Liv.; of motion, *forwards*: non
ante sed retro, Cic. (2) of time: de quo ante
dixi, Cic.; with abl. of measure: multis
ante saeculis, Cic.; for ante followed
(immediately or otherwise) by quam, and so
forming a conjunction, see under antequam.
The adv. is very rarely used as adj.: neque
ignari sumus ante malorum (=τῶν πρὶν
κακῶν), *of former sufferings*, Verg.
    Prep., *before.* (1) of place. LIT., ante
pedes, Cic.; causam ante aliquem dicere,
before a judge, Cic. TRANSF., of preference:
quem ante me diligo, *whom I love more than
myself*, Cic.; so, commonly: ante alios, ante
omnes. (2) of time: ante lucem, Cic.; ante
me, *before my time*, Cic.; often with a partic.:
ante urbem conditam, *before the founding
of the city*, Cic.; often also (like the adv.)
with abl. of measure. Esp. in certain phrases:
ante tempus, *before the right time*, Liv.;
ante diem, *before the appointed or the fated
day*, Ov.; ante certam diem, *within a fixed
time*; equites ante certam diem decederent,
Cic.; also in giving dates: ante diem quartum

Idus Martias (A.D. IV. Id. Mart.), *the fourth
day before the Ides of March*, i.e. *the twelfth
of March*, Cic.

antĕā (ante), adv. *before, formerly, before then*:
Cic., Liv.; followed by quam: Cic. (*see under*
antequam).

antĕambŭlo -ōnis, m. (ante/ambulare), *a
footman to clear the way ahead*: Mart., Suet.

antĕcăpio -căpĕre -cēpī -ceptum. LIT., *to
seize beforehand*: pontem Mosae fluminis,
Tac.; locum castris, Sall. TRANSF., (1) *to
anticipate, not to wait for*: noctem, Sall.
(2) *to prepare beforehand*: quae bello usui
forent, Sall. (3) philosoph. t. t.: anteceptam
animo rei quandam informationem, *innate
idea*, Cic.

antĕcēdo -cēdĕre -cessi -cessum, *to go before,
precede.*
    LIT., in space: Pompeius antecesserat
legiones, Cic. L.; absol.: stellae tum antecedunt, tum subsequuntur, Cic.
    TRANSF., (1) in time, *to precede* (with dat.):
Ter. (2) in gen., *to excel*, with dat. or acc. of
what is surpassed, abl. (or in with abl.) of
respect: quantum natura hominis pecudibus
reliquisque bestiis antecedat, Cic.; aliquem
scientiā atque usu nauticarum rerum, Caes.;
et auctoritate et aetate et usu rerum, Cic.
  ¶ Hence partic. **antĕcēdens** -entis,
preceding. Esp., as philosoph. t. t.: antecedens
causa, *the antecedent cause*; n. pl. as subst.
in same sense: antecedentia, Cic.

antĕcello -ĕre, no perf. or sup., *to be outstanding, excel*; used of persons and of things,
with dat. or acc. of what is surpassed, abl. of
respect in which: militari laude, Cic.;
omnibus ingenii gloria, Cic.; duae aedes
sacrae quae longe ceteris antecellant, Cic.;
omnes fortuna, Tac.

antĕcessĭo -ōnis, f. (antecedo). (1) *a preceding
or going before*: quae in orbibus conversiones
antecessionesque eveniunt, Cic. (2) *the
antecedent cause*: homo causas rerum videt
earumque praegressus et quasi antecessiones
non ignorat, Cic.

antecessor -oris, m. (antecedo), *a forerunner*;
in pl., *advanced guard*: Suet.

antĕcursor -ōris, m. (antecurro), *a forerunner*;
in pl., *pioneers, advanced guard of an army*:
Caes.

anteĕo -īre -ii (the e of ante often not scanned
as a syllable, and sometimes not written, as
in anteat, pres. subj.: Ov.; antibo, fut.: Tac.),
to go before. LIT., in space: alicui, Cic.;
aliquem, Hor. TRANSF., (1) *to go before* in
time: si anteissent delicta, *had happened
before*, Tac.; damnationem veneno, *to
anticipate*, Tac. (2) *to excel*: alicui sapientiā,
Cic.; omnes intellegentiā, Cic.; absol., *to
distinguish oneself*: operibus, *by actions*, Cic.

antĕfĕro -ferre -tŭli -lātum. LIT., *to carry
before*: viginti clarissimarum familiarum
imagines, Tac. TRANSF., (1) *to prefer*: longe
omnibus unum Demosthenem, Cic.; iniquissimam pacem iustissimo bello, Cic. (2) *to
anticipate, consider beforehand*: quod est dies
adlatura, id consilio anteferre debemus, Cic.

antĕfixus -a -um (ante/figo), *fastened in front*:
truncis arborum antefixa ora, Tac. N. pl. as
subst. **antefixa** -ōrum, *ornaments fixed on
roofs*: antefixa fictilia deorum Romanorum,
Liv.

antĕgrĕdĭor -grĕdi -gressus, dep. (ante/
gradior), *to go before.* LIT., stella Veneris
antegreditur solem, Cic. TRANSF., *causae
antegressae, antecedent causes,* Cic.

antĕhăbĕo -ēre, *to prefer:* incredibilia veris,
Tac.

antĕhāc, adv. *before this time, formerly:* Pl.,
Cic. L., Tac.

antĕlūcānus -a -um (ante/lux), *happening
before daybreak:* tempus, Cic.; cena, Cic.

antĕmĕrīdĭānus -a -um, *before noon:* Cic.

antĕmitto -mittĕre -misi -missum, *to send
before:* Caes.

antemna or **antenna** -ae, f. *a sail-yard:*
antennas ad malos destinare, Caes.; Liv.,
Verg.

Antemnae -ārum, f. *Sabine town at the
junction of the Anio with the Tiber.*
¶ Hence subst. **Antemnātes** -ĭum, m.
pl. *the inhabitants of Antemna.*

Antēnor -ŏris, m. (Ἀντήνωρ), *a Trojan, the
legendary founder of Patavium* (Padua).
¶ Hence adj. **Antēnŏrĕus** -a -um,
belonging to Antenor, Patavian; subst.
Antēnŏrĭdes -ae, m. *a male descendant of
Antenor.*

anteoccupātĭo -ōnis, f. rhet. t. t., *an exception:*
Cic.

antĕpēs -pĕdis, m. *the forefoot:* Cic., poet.

antĕpīlāni -ōrum, m. (pilum), *the soldiers who
fought in front of the pilani* or *triarii,* i.e. *the
hastati and principes:* Liv.

antĕpōno -pōnĕre -pŏsŭi -pŏsĭtum. LIT., *to
place before:* alicui prandium, Pl.; equitum
locos sedilibus plebis, Tac. TRANSF., *to
prefer:* se alicui, Cic.; amicitiam omnibus
rebus humanis, Cic.; Tac.

antĕpŏtens -entis, *very powerful, very fortunate:* Pl.

antequam (also **ante . . . quam** and **antea
quam**), conjunction, *before;* used with
indic., esp. in pres. and perf. tenses; also
with subjunc. to suggest deliberate timing
of the action in the main clause, e.g. to
anticipate or prevent other action: antequam
de meo adventu audire potuissent, in
Macedoniam perrexi, Cic.

Antērōs -ōtis, m. (Ἀντέρως). (1) *an avenger of
slighted love:* Cic. (2) *a kind of amethyst:*
Plin.

antes -ium, m. pl. *rows* or *ranks,* e.g. of vines:
Verg.

antĕsignānus -i, m. (ante/signum), gen. plur.
antesignani, *chosen Roman soldiers who
marched and fought before the standards:*
Caes., Liv.; hence, sing., *a leader:* Cic.

antesto (antisto) -stāre -stĕti, *to stand before.*
TRANSF., *to surpass;* usually with dat. of
person and abl. of respect: multum omnibus
(dat.) corporum viribus (abl.), Cic.; absol.,
to be prominent: Cic.

antestor -āri, dep. (contr. from antetestor),
legal t. t., *to call as a witness:* Hor. The
formula used to a possible witness was 'licet
antestari?'; if willing to come forward he
allowed the tip of his ear to be touched.
Once in Cicero without reference to judicial
proceedings.

antĕvĕnĭo -vĕnire -vēni -ventum. LIT., *to
come before, to get the start of:* per tramites
occultos exercitum Metelli, Sall. TRANSF.,
(1) *to anticipate, prevent:* consilia et insidias

hostium, Sall. (2) *to excel:* per virtutem
nobilitatem, Sall.; amor omnibus rebus
(dat.), Pl.

antĕverto (**antĕvorto**) -vertĕre -verti -versum.
LIT., *to come* or *go before, to precede:* stella
tum antevertens tum subsequens, Cic.
TRANSF., (1) *to anticipate, prevent:* atque id
ipsum cum tecum agere conarer, Fannius
antevertit, Cic. (2) *to prefer:* Caesar omnibus
consiliis antevertendum existimavit ut Narbonem proficisceretur, Caes.

Anthēdōn -ōnis, f. (Ἀνθηδών), *a town and
harbour in Boeotia.*

anthĭās -ae, m. (ἀνθίας), *a sea-fish:* Ov., Plin.

anthŏlŏgĭca, n. (ἀνθολογικά), *an anthology,
a collection of extracts and small poems:* Plin.

Antĭānus, Antĭas, *see Antium.*

Antĭcāto -ōnis, m. *the Anticato, a work of
C. Jul. Caesar in two books,* in answer to
Cicero's Cato, which praised Cato of Utica:
Juv., Quint.

antĭcĭpātĭo -ōnis, f. (anticipo), *a preconception,
innate idea:* Cic.

antĭcĭpo -are (ante/capio), *to take* or *receive
before, anticipate:* quod ita sit informatum
anticipatumque mentibus nostris, Cic.;
viam, *to travel over before,* Ov.; ludos, *to
celebrate before their time,* Suet.

Antīclēa and -clīa -ae, f. (Ἀντίκλεια), *daughter
of Autolycus, wife of Laertes, mother of
Ulysses.*

anticus -a -um (ante), *forward, in front* (opp.
posticus): pars, Cic.

Antĭcȳra -ae, f. (Ἀντίκυρα), *a town in Phocis,
famous for its hellebore* (now *Aspra Spitia*):
Hor. Two other towns of the same name,
one in Thessaly and one in Locris, seem also
to have been noted for this product.

antĭdĕā, antĭdĕō, antĭdhāc, *see* antea,
anteo, antehac, of which they are old forms.

antĭdŏtum -i, n. (ἀντίδοτον), *an antidote:* Suet.

Antĭgŏnē -ēs, f. and **Antĭgŏna** -ae, f. (Ἀν-
τιγόνη). (1) *daughter of Oedipus, sister of
Polynices and Eteocles, put to death for
burying her brother against the command of
the king of Thebes.* (2) *daughter of Laomedon,
king of Troy, changed into a stork by Hera.*

Antĭgŏnēa -ae, f. (Ἀντιγόνεια or Ἀντιγονία),
*name of several towns, the most important of
which were one in Epirus and another in
Macedonia.*
¶ Hence adj. **Antĭgŏnensis** -e, *belonging
to Antigonea.*

Antĭgŏnus -i, m. (Ἀντίγονος), *name of several
of the successors of Alexander the Great, the
most celebrated of whom were:* Antigonus I,
father of Demetrius Poliorcetes, killed 301 B.C.;
Antigonus Gonatas, *son of Demetrius
Poliorcetes, king of Macedon;* Antigonus
Doson, *brother of Gonatas.*

Antĭlĭbānus -i, m. (Ἀντιλίβανος), *a mountain
range in Phoenicia.*

Antĭlŏchus -i, m. (Ἀντίλοχος), *son of Nestor,
killed before Troy.*

Antĭmăchus -i, m. (Ἀντίμαχος), *a Greek poet,
contemporary with Plato.*

Antĭŏchēa or **Antĭŏchēa** -ae, f. (Ἀντιόχεια),
Antioch; name of several towns; esp. (1)
capital of Syria, on the river Orontes (now
Antakia). (2) *a town of Caria, on the Maeander.*
¶ Hence adj. **Antĭŏchensis** -e, *belonging
to Antioch.*

Antĭŏchus -i, m. (᾽Αντίοχος). (1) *name of several Syrian kings, the most important of whom were*: Antiochus III, Magnus, *protector of Hannibal in his exile, conquered by L. Corn. Scipio; and* Antiochus IV, Epiphanes, *who was deterred by the Roman envoy, L. Popillius, from seizing Egypt.* (2) Antiochus of Ascalon, *philosopher of the Academic school, teacher of Brutus and Cicero.*
¶ Hence adj. **Antĭŏchīnus** -a -um, *belonging either to King Antiochus III or to the philosopher Antiochus;* **Antĭŏchīus** -a -um, *belonging to the philosopher.*
Antĭŏpa -ae, f. and **Antĭŏpē** -ēs, f. (᾽Αντιόπη). (1) *daughter of Nycteus, mother of Amphion and Zethus.* (2) *name of a tragedy by Pacuvius;* q.v.
Antĭpătĕr -tri, m. (᾽Αντίπατρος). (1) *name of several kings of Macedonia, the most important of whom was the general (397–319 B.C.) who succeeded Alexander the Great.* (2) *name of several Greek philosophers;* esp. Antipater Cyrenaicus, *a disciple of the elder Aristippus,* and Antipater of Tarsus, *a Stoic, teacher of Panaetius.* (3) L. Caelius Antipater, *see* Caelius.
Antĭpătria -ae, f. (᾽Αντιπατρία), *a town in Macedonia, on the border of Illyria.*
Antĭphătēs -ae, m. (᾽Αντιφάτης). (1) *ruler of the cannibal Laestrygones.* (2) *a son of Sarpedon, killed by Turnus.*
Antĭphōn -ontis (᾽Αντιφῶν). (1) *a celebrated Athenian orator, c.* 480–411 B.C. (2) *a sophist, contemporary of Socrates.*
Antĭpŏlis -is, f. (᾽Αντίπολις), *a town of the Massilians in Gallia Narbonensis* (now *Antibes*).
antĭquārĭus -a -um (antiquus), *belonging to antiquity.* As subst. **antĭquārĭus** -i, m.: Tac., Suet.; and **antĭquārĭa** -ae, f.: Juv., *an antiquary.*
antĭquē, *see* antiquus.
antĭquĭtās -ātis, f. (antiquus), *antiquity, ancient times*: Cic. TRANSF., (1) *the history of ancient times*: Cic. (2) plur., *the ancients*: Cic. (3) *the good old times, primitive virtue, integrity*: Cic. (4) *great age*: generis, Cic.
antĭquĭtŭs, *see* antiquus.
antĭquo -are (antiquus), *to leave in its former state;* hence, *to reject a bill*: legem, rogationem, Cic.
antĭquus -a -um (for anticus, from ante), *coming before.*
(1) in compar. and superl., *preferred, more important*: id antiquius consuli fuit, Liv.; ne quid vita existimem antiquius, Cic.; nihil ei fuisset antiquius quam (followed by the infin.), Cic.; navalis apparatus ei semper antiquissima cura fuit, Cic.
(2) *before in point of time*: **a**, relative, *previous, earlier*: antiquae munitiones, Caes.; causa antiquior memoria tua, Cic.; nam illa nimis antiqua praetereo, Cic.: **b**, absol., *old, ancient, primitive*: urbs, Verg. Esp. with the notion of what is *simple, pure, innocent*: antiqui homines, Cic.
M. pl. as subst. **antĭqui** -orum, *the people of old time,* esp. *ancient authors*: Cic. N. as subst. **antĭquum** -i, *an old custom.*
¶ Hence adv. (with compar.) **antĭquē,** *in the ancient manner*: Hor., Tac.; also **antĭquĭtus,** *from of old* or *long ago*: Caes., Liv.

Antissa -ae, f. (᾽Αντισσα), *a town on Lesbos.*
¶ Hence subst. **Antissaei** -orum, m. pl. *the Antissaeans.*
antistēs -stĭtis, c. (antisto), *a presiding priest* or *priestess*: sacrorum, Cic., Liv. TRANSF., *master in any art*: artis dicendi, Cic., Ov.
Antisthĕnēs -is and -ae, m. (᾽Αντισθένης), *a Greek philosopher, founder of the Cynic school.*
antistĭta -ae, f. (antistes), *a presiding priestess*: Pl., Cic., Ov.
antisto, *see* antesto.
antĭthĕton -i, n. (ἀντίθετον), rhet. t. t., *antithesis, opposition*: Cic.
Antĭum -i, n. (᾽Αντιον), *an old town of Latium on the sea-coast* (now *Anzio*).
¶ Hence adj. **Antĭānus** -a -um and **Antĭas** -ātis, *belonging to Antium.*
antlĭa -ae, f. (ἀντλίον), *a pump*: Mart.
Antōnĭaster -tri, m. *an imitator of the oratory of Antonius*: Cic.
Antōnīnus -i, m. *a name of several Roman emperors,* esp. (1) Antoninus Pius, ruled A.D. 138–161. (2) M. Aurelius Antoninus Philosophus, *son-in-law and adopted son of the former,* ruled A.D. 161–180. (3) M. Aurelius Antoninus Heliogabalus, ruled A.D. 204–222.
Antōnĭus -a -um, *the name of a Roman gens. Its most famous members were*:
(1) M. Antonius, *surnamed Orator, born* 143 B.C., *put to death by Marius and Cinna* 87 B.C.; *introduced by Cicero as a speaker in the dialogue* De Oratore.
(2) M. Antonius Creticus, *son of* (1): *dispatched against the pirates of the eastern Mediterranean in* 74 B.C.
(3) C. Antonius, *second son of the preceding, the accomplice of Catiline, colleague with Cicero in the consulship,* 63 B.C..
(4) M. Antonius Triumvir, *Mark Antony, son of* (2), *born about* 83 B.C.; *the bitter enemy of Cicero; after Caesar's death triumvir with Octavianus and Lepidus; defeated by Octavianus at the battle of Actium,* 31 B.C.; *killed himself shortly after.*
¶ Hence adj. **Antōnĭānus** -a -um, *of Antonius.*
antrum -i, n. (ἄντρον), *a cave*: Ov., Verg. TRANSF., *the hollow of a tree*: exesae arboris antro, Verg.; *of a litter*: vehi clauso antro, Juv.
Anūbis -bis or -bĭdis, m. (᾽Ανουβίς; Egyptian origin), *an Egyptian god, represented with a jackal's head*: latrator Anubis, Verg.
ānŭlārĭus -a -um (anulus), *belonging to a ring*: scalae, *a place in Rome,* Suet. M. as subst. **anularius** -i, *a ring maker*: Cic.
ānŭlātus -a -um (anulus), *beringed, ornamented with rings*: aures, Pl.
ānŭlus -i, m. (¹anus), *a finger* or *signet ring.*
LIT., in eiusmodi cera centum sigilla imprimere hoc anulo, Cic.; vilissima utensilium anulo clausa, Tac.; anulus equestris, *the gold ring which was the sign of a knight in Rome,* Hor.; anulum invenire, *to be raised to the rank of a knight,* Cic.
TRANSF., of objects similar in form. (1) *a curtain ring*: Plin. (2) *the link of a fetter*: Plin. (3) *a ringlet of hair*: Mart.
¹ānus -i, m. *the fundament*: Cic. L.
²ānŭs -ūs, f. *an old woman*: Cic.; anus Cumaea, *the Sibyl,* Ov.; often like adj., *old,* in opposition to f. noun; of persons: sacerdos, Verg.;

of animals and things: cerva, Ov.; amphora, Mart.; Appia via, Prop.

anxĭĕtās -ātis, f. (anxius), *anxiety, anxiousness,* strictly as a lasting state of mind, whereas angor is the transitory feeling: Cic.; also =angor, *grief, anguish*: Ov. TRANSF., *painful accuracy*: Quint.

anxĭfer -fĕra -fĕrum (anxius/fero), *causing anxiety*: Cic.

anxĭtūdo -ĭnis, f. (anxius), *anxiousness*: Cic.

anxĭus -a -um (ango), *anxious, uneasy*: anxii senes, Cic.; anxium habere aliquem, *to make anxious*, Tac.; anxius animi, Sall. The cause of anxiety is expressed by an abl.: irā et metu, Sall.; by a genit.: furti, Ov.; by de: de successore, Suet.; by pro: pro mundi regno, Ov.; or by a subjunctive clause, introduced by ne *or* an: Sall., Tac. TRANSF., *causing anxiety or anguish*: aegritudines, Cic.

¶ Adv. **anxĭē**, *anxiously*: Sall., Suet.

Anxŭr -ŭris, n. *an old town of the Volsci, on the sea-coast, afterwards called Tarracina* (now *Terracina*).

¶ Hence adj. **Anxŭrus**, applied to Jupiter as worshipped at Anxur: Verg.; also adj. **Anxŭras** -ātis, *belonging to Anxur*.

Āŏnes -um, acc. -as (Άονες), m. pl., adj. and subst. *Boeotian, Boeotians*. **Āŏnĭa** -ae, f. *part of Boeotia, in which were the mountain Helicon and the spring Aganippe, the resort of the Muses*.

¶ Hence adj. **Āŏnĭdĕs** -um, f. *the Boeotian women*, i.e. *the Muses*; adj. **Āŏnĭus** -a -um (Άόνιος), *belonging to Aonia*: vertex, Helicon, Verg.; vir, *Hercules, born at Thebes*, Ov.; iuvenis, *Hippomenes*, Ov.; deus, *Bacchus*, Ov.; fons *and* aquae, *Aganippe*, Ov.; sorores, *the Muses*, Ov.; vates, *a poet*, Ov.: subst. **Āŏnĭdĕs** -ae, m. *a Theban* or *Boeotian*.

Āornos -i, m. (άορνος, *without birds*), *the lake of Avernus*: Verg.

Āŏus -i, m. *a river in Illyria* (now *Vijosë*).

ăpăgĕ, interj. (Gr. imperat ἄπαγε), *take away! remove!* Used as transit., or intransit.=*away with you! be off!* Pl., Ter.

Ăpămēa and -īa -ae, f. (Άπάμεια). (**1**) *a town of Syria on the Orontes* (now *Famieh*). (**2**) *a town of Phrygia on the Maeander*. (**3**) *a town of Bithynia*. Adj. **Ăpămensis** -e and **Ăpămēnus** -a -um, *belonging to Apamea*.

Ăpellēs -is, m., voc. Apella (Άπελλῆς), *one of the greatest Greek painters, friend of Alexander the Great*. Adj. **Ăpellēus** -a -um.

ăper apri, m. *a wild boar*: Cic., Verg.; prov.: uno saltu duos apros capere, *to kill two birds with one stone*, Pl.; apros immittere liquidis fontibus, *to do something absurd and perverse*, Verg.

Ăpĕrantĭa -ae, f. (Άπεραντία), *a province in Thessaly*.

¶ Hence subst. **Ăpĕrantii**, m. pl. *its inhabitants*.

ăpĕrio ăpĕrire ăpĕrui ăpĕrtum (probably from ab-pario).

(**1**) *to uncover, to lay bare, to expose to view.* LIT., caput, *to uncover*, Cic.; so, often of scenes revealed by daylight: novam aciem dies aperuit, Tac. TRANSF., in gen., *to reveal*: occulta, Cic.; sententiam suam, *to pronounce*, Cic.; casus futuros, *to predict*, Ov.; refl., se aperire and middle aperiri, *to reveal*

one's true character: studioque aperimur in ipso, Ov.; memet ipse aperio quis sim, Liv.

(**2**) *to open what was shut, to unclose.* LIT., fores, Cic.; epistulam, Cic.; fundamenta templi, *to excavate*, Liv. TRANSF., *to open up, give access to*, or *start* a thing: fontes eloquentiae, Cic. Esp. *to open up a country, render it accessible*: Pontum, Cic.; Syriam, Tac.; *to open an institution for use*: asylum, Liv.; ludum, *to open a school*, Cic.; annum, *to begin the year* (poet., of the constellation Aries), Verg.

¶ Hence partic. (with compar. and superl.) **ăpertus** -a -um. (**1**) *open, uncovered.* LIT., aether, caelum, *clear*, Verg.; naut. t. t.: naves undecked, Cic. TRANSF., *clear, unconcealed, manifest*: apertum latrocinium, Cic.; apertum est, *it is clear*, followed by acc. and infin.: esse aliquod numen praestantissimae mentis, Cic.; in aperto esse, *to be evident*: quo ad cognoscendum omnia inlustria magis magisque in aperto sint, Sall. Esp. of speech, *clear, intelligible, frank*: narratio aperta, Cic.; apertis *or* apertissimis verbis, Cic.; of character, *frank, straightforward, open*: animus, Cic.; homo, Cic. (**2**) *open, unclosed, accessible.* LIT., vastum atque apertum mare, Caes.; oculi, Lucr.; ostium, Cic.; humerus, *exposed, undefended*, Caes.; campi ad dimicandum aperti, Liv. TRANSF., gen., *available*: beate vivendi via, Cic. N. as subst. **ăpertum** -i, *an open space*: in aperto castra locare, Liv., Lucr., Hor.

Adv. (with compar. and superl.) **ăpertē**, *openly, frankly, without concealment*: mentiri, Cic.; scribere, Cic.

ăperto -are (freq. of aperio), *to lay bare*: Pl.

ăpex -ĭcis, m. *the top.*

Esp. *the top of the conical cap of the Roman flamines*, hence *the cap itself*: lanigeri apices, Verg.; apicem Dialem alicui imponere, *to make a person flamen of Jove*, Liv.

TRANSF., (**1**) *of other distinctive headgear, a crown, tiara, helmet,* etc.: regum apices, Hor. (**2**) fig., *highest honour, crown*: apex senectutis est auctoritas, Cic. (**3**) in gen., *the top* or *summit* of anything: montis, Ov.; flammae, Ov. (**4**) gram. t. t., *the long mark over a vowel*: Quint.

ăphaerĕma -ătis, n. (ἀφαίρεμα), *a coarse kind of grits*: Plin.

Ăphărēus -ěi, m. (Άφαρεύς).

(**1**) *a king of the Messenians, father of Lynceus and Idas*; hence adj. **Ăpharēĭus** -a -um, *belonging to Aphareus*.

(**2**) *a Centaur, whose arm was broken by Theseus at the wedding of Pirithous*.

aphractus -i, f. (ἄφρακτος), *a long undecked boat*: Cic.

Ăphrŏdīsĭa -ōrum, n. (Άφροδίσια), *the festival of Aphrodite*: Pl.

ăpiācus -a -um (apium), *like parsley*: Cato.

ăpĭanus -a -um (apis), *belonging to bees*: Plin.

ăpĭārĭus -i, m. (apis), *a bee-keeper*: Plin.

ăpĭcātus -a -um (apex), *adorned with the priest's cap*: Ov.

¹ăpīcĭus -a -um (apis), *sought by bees*, hence *sweet*: Cato, Varr.

²Ăpīcĭus -i, m. *a celebrated epicure in the time of Augustus and Tiberius*.

ăpĭcŭla -ae, f. (dim. of apis), *a little bee*: Pl.

Ăpĭdănus -i, m. ('Απιδανός), *a river in Thessaly, tributary of the Peneus.*

ăpīnae -arum, f. *trifles*: Mart.

apio, verb found only in participle aptus; q.v.

Apiŏlae -arum, f. *a town in Latium.*

¹ăpis or **ăpes** -is, f. (genit. pl. apium *or* apum), *a bee*: Cic., Verg.

²Ăpis -is, m. ('Απις), *Apis, the ox worshipped by the Egyptians as a god.*

ăpiscor ăpisci aptus, dep. (apio), *to reach after* and so *to attain, come to, come by*: hominem, Pl.; hereditatem, Pl.; mare, Cic. L.; summum honorem, Liv.; once, in Tac., with genit.: dominationis.

ăpĭum -i, n. *parsley* or *celery*, often used for garlands by the ancients: Verg., Hor.

ăplustrĕ -is, n. (ἄφλαστον), generally plur. aplustria -ium, n. and aplustra -ōrum, n. *the carved stern of a ship, with its ornaments*: Lucr., Cic.

ăpŏclēti -ōrum, m. (ἀπόκλητοι), *the supreme council of the Aetolian League*: Liv.

ăpŏdўtērĭum -i, n. (ἀποδυτήριον), *the undressing-room in a bath*: Cic.

Ăpollo -ĭnis (-ōnis), m. ('Απόλλων), *Apollo, son of Jupiter and Latona, brother of Diana, god of archery, music, poetry, prophesying, and the sun, born at Delos*; hence: Delius vates, Verg.; and simply: Delius, Cic.; ad Apollinis (sc. aedem), *to the temple of Apollo*, Liv.; aperitur Apollo, *the temple of Apollo becomes visible*, Verg.; promontorium Apollinis, *a promontory near Utica.*

¶ Hence adj. **Ăpollĭnāris** -e, *sacred to Apollo*: ludi, *games held in honour of Apollo on the 5th of July*, Cic.; also **Ăpollĭnĕus** -a -um, *pertaining to Apollo*: urbs, Delos, Ov.; proles, Aesculapius, Ov.; vates, Orpheus, Ov.; ars, *prophecy* or *medicine*, Ov.

Ăpollŏdōrus -i, m. ('Απολλόδωρος). (1) *a rhetorician of Pergamum, teacher of Augustus.* (2) *a learned and prolific Athenian scholar, born* c. 180 B.C.

Ăpollōnĭa -ae, f. ('Απολλωνία), *Apollonia, name of several towns, esp.* (1) *near Naupactus*: Liv. (2) *in Illyria*: Cic. (3) *in Macedonia*: Liv.

¶ Hence subst. **Ăpollōnĭātēs** -ae, m. *an inhabitant of Apollonia*; adj. **Ăpollōnĭensis** -e, *belonging to Apollonia.*

Ăpollōnis -idis, f. ('Απολλωνίς), *a town in Lydia.*

¶ Hence adj. **Ăpollōnĭdensis** -e, *belonging to Apollonis.*

Ăpollōnĭus -is, m. ('Απολλώνιος), *Apollonius, name of several scholars, esp.* (1) *a famous rhetorician of Rhodes.* (2) Apollonius Rhodius, *author of the 'Argonautica' in the third century* B.C.

ăpŏlŏgus -i, m. (ἀπόλογος), *a narrative*; esp. *a fable in the manner of Aesop*: Cic.

ăpŏphŏrēta -ōrum, n. (ἀποφόρητα), *presents given to guests, especially at the time of the Saturnalia*: Suet.

ăpŏprŏēgmĕna -ōrum, n. plur. (ἀποπροηγμένα), in the philosophy of the Stoics, *that which is to be rejected* (opp. to proēgmena): Cic.

ăpŏthēca -ae, f. (ἀποθήκη), *a store-room, especially for wine*: Cic.

appărātē, adv. from apparo; q.v.

appărātĭo -ōnis, f. (apparo), *preparation*: popularium munerum, Cic.

appărātus -ūs, m. (apparo). (1) abstr., *a preparation, preparing*: operis, Cic.; belli, Liv. (2) concr., *preparation, provision, equipment, apparatus*: totius belli apparatum, Caes.; omnis apparatus oppugnandarum urbium, Liv. Esp. *brilliant preparations, splendour, magnificence, pomp*: regio apparatu, Cic.; Persicos apparatus, Hor. Of a speech, *display, parade*: dixit causam illam nullo apparatu pure et dilucide, Cic.

appārĕo -ēre -ŭi -ĭtum, *to become visible, to appear.*

LIT., equus mecum demersus rursum apparuit, Cic.; with dat. of person: anguis ille, qui Sullae apparuit immolanti, Cic.; apparent rari nantes, Verg.

TRANSF., *to be visible, to show oneself* or *itself, be manifest*: animosus atque fortis appare, Hor.; non apparere labores nostros, Hor.; res apparet, and apparet, *it is clear, plain*, followed by acc. and infin. or by indir. quest.: Cic., Liv. Esp. *to appear as a servant* to some person in authority, or deity, *to serve*: saevi in limine regis apparent, Cic.; with dat. of person: consulibus, Liv.; with dat. of thing: quaestioni, Cic.

appārĭo -ēre, *to get, obtain*: Lucr.

appārĭtĭo -ōnis, f. (appareo), *a waiting upon, serving*: Cic. L.; meton., plur.=apparitores, *servants*: Cic. L.

appārĭtor -ōris, m. (appareo), *a servant*; esp. *a public servant, e.g. a lictor*: Cic., Liv.

appăro -are, *to prepare, get ready, provide*: convivium, Cic.; bellum, iter, ludos, Cic.; crimina in aliquem, *get up charges*, Cic. Apparare, or se apparare, with infin. or ut: Pl.; apparare, with infin.: Caes.

¶ Hence partic. (with compar. and superl.) **appărātus** -a -um, *prepared, well supplied* or *sumptuous*: Cic.

Adv. **appărātē**, *sumptuously*: apparate edere et bibere, Cic.

appellātĭo -ōnis, f. (¹appello). (1) *an addressing of a person*: hanc nactus appellationis causam, Caes. Esp. as legal t. t., *an appeal*: tribunorum, *to the tribunes*, Cic. (2) *a naming*: nominum, Plin.; hence, meton.= *nomen, name, title*: inanis, Cic.; plur.: regum appellationes, Cic. (3) *a pronunciation*: litterarum, Cic.

appellātor -ōris, m. (¹appello), *an appellant*: Cic.

appellĭto -are (freq. of ¹appello), *to be accustomed to name*: Tac.

¹appello -are.

(1) *to address, accost, with words*: singulos appellare, Cic.; nominatim, Caes. Special senses: **a**, *to ask a person to do something, approach, entreat*: aliquem, Cic.; aliquem de proditione, Liv.: **b**, legal t. t., *to appeal to*: praetorem, Cic.; tribunos, Liv.; a praetore tribunos, Cic.: **c**, *to apply to for payment*: aliquem de pecunia, Cic.: **d**, *to sue*: cavendum est ne iisdem de causis alii plectantur, alii ne appellentur quidem, Cic.

(2) *to name, entitle*: aliquem sapientem, Cic.; appellata est ex viro virtus, Cic.; (Scipio) Africanus ob egregiam victoriam de Hannibale Poenisque appellatus, Liv.;

hence, *to mention by name*: quos idcirco non appello hoc loco, Cic.; aliquem nutu significationeque, *to make known*, Cic.

(3) *to pronounce*: litteras, Cic.

²appello -pellĕre -pŭli -pulsum, *to drive to, bring to.*

(1) in gen. LIT., turris ad opera Caesaris, Caes. TRANSF., animum *or* mentem ad aliquid, *to direct the mind to something*: mentem ad philosophiam, Cic.

(2) nautical t. t., *to bring to land*: navem ad ripam, Cic.; classem in insulam, Liv.; poet., aliquem, with dat.: hinc me digressum vestris deus appulit oris, Verg.; pass., appelli, of the ship: navis appellitur ad villam, Cic.; of the persons in the ship: alios ad Siciliam appulsos esse, Cic.; absol.: huc appelle, *put in here*, Hor.

appendĭcŭla -ae, f. (dim. of appendix), *a little addition*: Cic.

appendix -ĭcis, f. (appendo), *an appendage, addition, an appendix to anything*: vidit enim appendicem animi esse corpus, Cic.; exigua appendix Etrusci belli, Liv.

appendo -pendĕre -pendi -pensum, *to weigh to*: aurum alicui, Cic. TRANSF., non enim ea verba me annumerare, lectori putavi oportere, sed tamquam appendere, i.e. *to deal them out by weight, not by number.*

Appennĭnĭcŏla -ae, c. (Appenninus/colo), *an inhabitant of the Appennines*: Verg.

Appennĭnĭgĕna -ae, c. (Appenninus/gigno), *one born upon the Appennines*: Ov.

Appennīnus -i, m. (connected with Celtic Pen, a mountain-top), *the chain of the Appennines*, a mountain range running down through the centre of Italy.

appĕtens -entis, partic. from appeto; q.v.

appĕtentĭa -ae, f. (appetens), *desire, longing*: laudis, Cic.; effrenata, Cic.

appĕtītĭo -ōnis, f. (appeto), *a longing for, desire*; with genit.: principatus, Cic.

appĕtītus -ūs, m. (appeto), *a longing, appetite*; with genit.: voluptatis, Cic.; in pl., *the passions*: Cic.

appĕto -ĕre -ivi *or* -ii -itum, *to make for, to grasp*. (1) LIT., solem manibus, Cic.; esp. *to grasp a hand to kiss it*: appetere manum osculis, Plin.; so: salutari, appeti, Cic. (2) in gen., *to desire, seek*: regnum, Cic.; with infin.: ut appetat animus aliquid agere semper, Cic. (3) *to make for* or *go to, arrive at*: Europam, Cic.; mare terram appetens, *pressing on the land*, Cic. (4) *to attack*: aliquem lapidibus, Cic. TRANSF., ignominiis omnibus appetitus, Cic. (5) intransit., *to draw near*, of time: dies appetebat, Caes., Verg., Liv.

¶ Hence partic. (with compar. and superl.) **appĕtens** -entis, *eager, desirous*; with genit.: gloriae, Cic.; also absol.=*desirous of gold, avaricious*: homo non cupidus neque appetens, Cic.

Adv. **appĕtentĕr**, *greedily*: Cic.

Appĭa, fem. of Appius; q.v.

appingo -pingĕre -pinxi -pictum, *to paint to*, or *upon*. LIT., delphinum silvis, Hor. TRANSF., *to write in addition*: aliquid novi, Cic. L.

Appĭus -i, m., **Appĭa** -ae, f. *a Roman praenomen, common in the gens Claudia, see Claudius.* As adj. **Appĭus** -a -um, *Appian*: Appia via,

the Appian Way, a road begun by the censor Appius Claudius Caecus, which led from Rome to Capua, and was afterwards extended to Brundisium; Appia aqua, *an aqueduct constructed by the same*, Liv.

¶ Hence **Appĭas** -ādis, f. *a nymph associated with this aqueduct*: Ov.; Appiades deae, *statues of the nymph*, Ov.

¶ Hence also adj. **Appĭānus** -a -um, *belonging to an Appius, Appian*: libido (of the Decemvir App. Claudius), Liv.

Appĭĕtās -ātis, f. *the antiquity of the Appian family*, a word invented by Cicero.

applaudo -plaudĕre -plausi -plausum. (1) *to strike upon, to clap*: cavis applauso corpore palmis, Ov. (2) *to applaud*: Pl.

applĭcātĭo -ōnis, f. (applico), *attachment, application*: animi, Cic.; ius applicationis, *the rights springing from the relation of patron and client*, Cic.

applĭco -are -āvi -ātum (Cic.) and -ŭi -ĭtum (post-Cic.), *to apply to, place to* or *near, join to, put to.*

LIT., se ad flammam, Cic.; oscula feretro, *to kiss*, Ov.; ensem capulo tenus, *to drive in*, Verg.; corpora corporibus, *to close up the ranks*, Liv. In passive, esp. in partic. perf., *lying near, situated near, built near*: Leucas colli applicata, Liv. Esp. as nautical t. t., *to bring* or *lay a ship to* or *beside*: naves ad terram, Caes.; navem ad naufragum, Cic.; pass.: ad oras applicor, Ov.; absol., *to land*: quocumque litore applicuisse naves hostium audissent, Liv.

TRANSF., *to attach, to connect*: voluptatem ad honestatem, Cic.; esp. with reflex. object, se ad, and se alicui, *to attach oneself to, devote oneself to*: se ad aliquem quasi patronum, Cic.; se ad alicuius familiaritatem, *or* amicitiam, *or* societatem, Cic.; se ad eloquentiam, Cic.

applōro -are, *to lament, deplore*: Hor.

appōno -pōnĕre -pŏsŭi -pŏsĭtum, *to place near, to put to.*

In gen.: aer omnibus appositus, Lucr.; columnae machina apposita deiectae, Cic. Esp. *to serve, put on the table*: patellam, Cic.; apposita secunda mensa, Cic.; also in writing, *to place near*: notam ad versum, *or* epistulis, Cic.

TRANSF., (1) *to appoint to a duty*: custodem me Tullio, Cic.; calumniatores, Cic. (2) *to put to, add to*: tibi annos, Hor.; *to add a command*: aqua et igni interdictum reo appositumque, ut teneretur insula, Tac. (3) *to put down to, count as* (rare): appone lucro, Hor.

¶ Hence partic. (with compar. and superl.) **appŏsĭtus** -a -um, *placed near.* LIT., *situated*, or *lying near*: castellum flumini, Tac. TRANSF., (1) *approaching, near to*: audacia fidentiae non contrarium sed appositum et propinquum, Cic. (2) *fit, appropriate, apposite*: menses appositi ad agendum, Cic.; homo bene appositus ad istius audaciam, Cic. Adv. **appŏsĭtē**, *appropriately, appositely*: dicere apposite ad persuasionem, Cic.

apporrectus -a -um (ad/porrigo), *extended near*: draco, Ov.

apporto -are, *to carry, bring to*: signa populo Romano, Cic. TRANSF., morbos, Lucr.

apposco -ĕre, *to ask in addition*: Ter., Hor.

appōtus -a -um, *drunk*: Pl.

apprĕcor -ari, dep. *to worship, pray to*: rite deos, Hor.

apprĕhendo -prĕhendĕre -prĕhendi -prĕhensum, and poet. **apprendo** -prendĕre -prendi -prensum, *to seize, lay hold of*.
LIT., claviculis adminicula tamquam manibus, Cic.
TRANSF., (1) *to take possession of*: Hispanias, Cic. (2) *of discourse, to take hold of, employ*: ut quidquid ego apprehenderam, statim accusator extorquebat, Cic.

apprīmē (apprimus), adv., *above all, exceedingly*: Pl., Ter.

apprīmo -prīmĕre -pressi -pressum (ad/ premo), *to press to* (post-Aug.): scutum pectori, Tac.

approbātio -ōnis, f. (approbo), *approbation, approval, assent*: Cic., Liv. Esp., philosoph. t. t., *proof*: quae (propositio) non indiget approbatione, Cic.

approbātor -ōris, m. (approbo), *one who approves* or *assents*: profectionis meae, Cic. L.

approbē, adv., *very well*: Pl.

approbo -are. (1) *to approve of, assent to*: consilium alicuius, Cic.; esp. of a deity, *to bless, approve of*: quod actum est dii approbent, Cic. (2) *to prove, to establish*: propositionem approbare et firmare, Cic. (3) *to make acceptable to* another: rudimenta duci approbavit, Tac.

apprōmitto -mittĕre -mīsi -missum, *to promise in addition*: Cic.

apprŏpĕro -are. (1) transit., *to hasten*: coeptum opus, Liv., Tac. (2) intrans., *to hasten*: approperate, Cic.; approperare ad cogitatum facinus, Cic.

appropinquātio -ōnis, f. (appropinquo), *approach*: mortis, Cic.

appropinquo -are, *to approach, draw near*.
LIT., of place: ad summam aquam, Cic.; with dat: Oceano, Caes.; ianuae, Liv.
TRANSF., (1) of time: hiems appropinquat, Caes.; illi poena, nobis libertas appropinquat, Cic. (2) of stages, rank, etc.: qui iam appropinquat ut videat, *is near to seeing*, Cic.

appugno -are, *to assault, fight against*: castra, Tac.

Appŭlēius or **Āpŭlēius** -i, m. *a Roman name*, esp. of (1) L. Appuleius Saturninus, *a turbulent tribune of the people*, c. 100 B.C. (2) *a Roman writer, born* c. A.D. 123 *at Madaura, in Africa, author of the 'Golden Ass'*.
¶ Hence adj. **Appuleius** -a -um, *of or belonging to Appuleius*: lex (de maiestate), introduced by the tribune Appuleius.

Appūlĭa see Apulia.

appulsus -ūs, m. (²appello), *a driving towards*; hence *approach, influence*: quod pars earum (regionum) appulsu solis exarserit, Cic.; caloris, Cic. Esp. nautical, *landing on, landing*: ab litorum appulsu arcere, Liv.

aprīcātio -ōnis, f. (apricor), *a basking in the sun*: Cic.

aprīcĭtās -ātis, f. (apricus), *sunniness, sunshine, warmth*: Plin.

aprīcor -ari, dep. (apricus), *to sun oneself*: Cic.

aprīcus -a -um, adj. (with compar. and superl.) (aperio). (1) of places, *open to the sun, sunny*:

locus, Cic.; fig.: in apricum proferre, *to bring to light*, Hor. (2) *loving the sun*: flores, Hor.; mergi, Verg.; senes, Pers.

Aprīlis -e (aperio), adj., *belonging to April*; m. as subst. (understanding mensis), *the month of April*: Cic.

aprīnus -a -um (aper), *relating* or *belonging to a wild boar*: Plin.

aprūgnŭs -a -um (aper), *belonging to a wild boar*: Pl.

apsūmēdō -ĭnis, f. (absumo), *a consuming*: Pl.

Apsus -i, m. ("Αψος), *a river of Illyria* (now *Osum*).

apto -are (aptus), *to fit to, adapt to*. LIT., (1) *to adjust*: corpori arma, Liv.; enses dexteris, Hor. (2) *to prepare, get ready, equip with*: arma, Liv.; classem velis, Verg.; se armis, Liv. TRANSF., *to make fit* or *appropriate*: hoc verbum est ad id aptatum quod ante dixerat, Cic.

aptus -a -um (partic. of obsolete verb, apio).
(1) as partic.: **a**, *fitted to, fastened to*: gladius e lacunari seta equina aptus, Cic. TRANSF., *depending upon*: honestum ex quo aptum est officium, Cic.; with abl. alone: rudentibus apta fortuna, Cic.: **b**, *fitted together, fastened together*: omnia inter se connexa et apta, Cic.; so *prepared, fitted out*: omnia sibi esse ad bellum apta et parata, Cic.: **c**, *fitted up with, equipped with*, with abl.: caelum stellis fulgentibus aptum, Verg.
(2) as adj. (with compar. and superl.), *suitable, appropriate, fitting*; with ad and the acc.: milites minus apti ad huius generis hostem, Cic.; id pallium esse aptum ad omne anni tempus, Cic., Liv.; with in and the acc.: in quod (genus) minus apti sunt, Liv.; with dat.: haec genera dicendi aptiora sunt adolescentibus, Cic., Liv.; with qui and subjunc.: Cic.; with infin.: Ov.; absol. (esp. of style): verbis quam maxime aptis, Cic., Liv.
Adv. (with compar. and superl.) **aptē**. (1) *closely, tightly*: Cic., Liv. (2) *suitably, fitly*: Cic., Ov., Liv.; with ad and the acc.: Cic., Liv.

ăpŭd (aput), prep., with acc., *at, near, by, with, among*; used of states of rest, and chiefly in relation to persons.
(1) of physical proximity: apud aliquem sedere, *near*, Cic.; apud me, *at my house*, Cic.; apud Alyziam, *near Alyzia* (and often so with place-names after Cic.); apud exercitum esse, *to be serving as a soldier*, Cic. Esp. *before, in the presence of*: apud iudices, Cic.; apud aliquem queri, Cic.
(2) of analogous relations: **a**, apud se, *in one's senses*, Pl.: **b**, of judgment and feeling: plus apud me auctoritas valet, Cic.; consequi gratiam apud bonos viros, Cic.: **c**, *in the time of*: apud patres nostros, Cic.: **d**, of an author, *in the works of*: apud Xenophontem, Cic.

Apuleius, see Appuleius.

Āpūlĭa or **Appūlia** -ae, f. *Apulia, a region in S. Italy*.
¶ Hence adj. **Apūlĭcus** -a -um: mare Apulicum, *the Adriatic*, Hor.; also **Āpŭlus** -a -um: gens, Hor.

ăqua -ae (old genit. aquai), f. *water*.
(1) *water* in gen.: pluvia, Cic.; marina, Cic.; plur.: aquae dulces, Cic. Special

phrases: aspergere alicui aquam, *to re-animate*, Pl.; aquam praebere, *to entertain*, Hor.; aqua et ignis, *the necessaries of life*: non aqua, non igni, ut aiunt, locis pluribus utimur quam amicitia, Cic.; aqua et igni interdicere alicui, *to make life impossible for a person in a place*, and so *to banish him*, Cic.; so also: aqua et igni aliquem arcere, Tac.; aquam terramque petere *or* poscere ab aliquo, *to demand submission from the enemy*, a Persian custom, Liv.; in aqua scribere, *to write in water* (of futile achievement), Cat. (2) *water in narrower senses*: **a**, *the sea*: ad aquam, *on the sea-coast*, Cic.: **b**, *a lake*: Albanae aquae deductio, Cic.: **c**, *a river*: secunda aqua, *down stream*, Liv.: **d**, *rain*: Hor.: **e**, plur.: aquae, *springs*, Verg.: **f**, plur., *hot medicinal springs*: ad aquas venire, Cic.; hence in proper names, Aquae Sextiae, etc.: **g**, of an aqueduct: aquam ducere non longe e villa, Cic.: **h**, *water in the water-clock*; hence: aquam dare, *to give time*, Plin.; aquam perdere, *to lose time*, Quint.; aqua haeret, *there is a hitch*, Cic.: **i**, *tears*: Prop.

ăquaeductus -ūs, m. (1) *an aqueduct*: Cic. (2) *the right of conveying water to a place*: Cic.

ăquālĭcŭlus -i, m. (dim. of aqualis), *a small water-vessel*; hence, *the belly*: Pers.

ăquālis -e (aqua), *watery*. As subst. **ăquālis** -is, c. *a wash-bowl*: Pl.

ăquārĭus -a -um (aqua), *belonging to water*: provincia, *superintendence of the supply of water*, Cic. M. as subst. **ăquārĭus** -i. (1) *a water-carrier*: Juv. (2) *an inspector of conduits*: ap. Cic. L. (3) *the constellation so called*, one of the signs of the Zodiac: Hor.

ăquātĭcus -a -um (aqua). (1) *living in water, aquatic*: lotos, Ov. (2) *full of water, watery*: auster, *bringing rain*, Ov.

ăquātĭlis -e (aqua), *living* or *growing in the water*: bestiae, Cic.

ăquātĭo -ōnis, f. (aquor), *a fetching of water*: Caes. Meton., *a place whence water may be fetched, a watering-place*: Cic.

ăquātor -ōris, m. (aquor), *a person that fetches water*: Caes.

ăquĭla -ae, f. (perhaps fem. of aquilus), *an eagle*. LIT., Cic., Hor., Verg.; esp. poet. as the bearer of the lightning of Jove. TRANSF., (1) military t. t., *an eagle as the standard of each Roman legion*: Cic. Meton., *a legion*: Lucr.; *the post of standard-bearer*: Juv. (2) *the Eagle, a constellation*: Cic. (3) architect. t. t. (cf. Gr. ἀετός), *a gable* or *pediment*: Tac.

Ăquĭlēia -ae, f. *a town in north-east Italy* (still so called). ¶ Hence adj. **Ăquĭlēiensis** -e, *of Aquileia*.

aquĭlĭfer -fĕri (aquila/fero), m. *an eagle-* or *standard-bearer*: Cic.

ăquĭlīnus -a -um (aquila), *relating to an eagle*: Pl.

Ăquĭlĭus -a -um, *name of a Roman gens. Its most celebrated members were* (1) C. Aquilius Gallus, *friend of Cicero, a famous orator and jurist*. (2) Aquilius Regulus, *an informer under the empire*. ¶ Hence adj. **Ăquĭlĭānus** -a -um, *belonging to Aquilius*.

ăquĭlo -ōnis, m. (aqua or aquilus). (1) *the north wind*: Cic. Meton., *the north*: Cic. (2) *Aquilo, as a myth. person, husband of Orithyia, father of Calais and Zetes*.

Ăquĭlōnĭa -ae, f. *a town in the country of the Hirpini* (now *Lacedogna*).

ăquĭlōnĭus -a -um. (1) *northern*: Cic. (2) *belonging to Aquilo*: proles, *Calais and Zetes*, Prop.

ăquĭlus -a -um, *dark-coloured, blackish*: Pl.

Aquīnum -i, n. *town in Latium* (now *Aquino*). Adj. **Aquīnās** -ātis, *belonging to Aquinum*.

Ăquītānĭa -ae, f. *Aquitania, the south-west part of Gaul, between the Loire and the Pyrenees*. ¶ Hence adj. **Aquītānus** -a -um, *Aquitanian*.

ăquor -ari, dep. (aqua), *to fetch water*: Caes., Sall.

ăquōsus -a -um, adj. (with compar. and superl.) (aqua), *full of water, watery*: nubes, Ov.; Eurus, *rain-bringing*, Hor.; mater, *Thetis*, Ov.

ăquŭla -ae, f. (dim. of aqua), *a little water, a small stream*: Pl., Cic.

āra -ae, f. *an altar*. LIT., aram consecrare deo, Cic.; pro aris et focis, *for hearth and home*, Cic.; as a sanctuary: tamquam in aram confugitis, Cic.; as an altar tomb: ara sepulcri, Verg. TRANSF., (1) *a refuge, protection*: legum, Cic. (2) *a constellation*: Cic. poet. (3) arae, *name of certain rocks at sea*: Verg.

Ărăbarchēs -ae, m. (Ἀραβάρχης), *an Egyptian magistrate, a superior tax-collector*: Juv.; used sarcastically of Pompey (who by his conquests increased the tribute paid to Rome): Cic. L.

Ărăbĭa -ae, f. (Ἀραβία), *the country of Arabia, in Asia*, divided by the ancients into *Petraea, Deserta*, and *Felix*. ¶ Hence adj. **Ărăbĭus** -a -um and **Ărăbĭcus** -a -um, *Arabian*; also adj. and subst. **Arabs** -abis and **Arabus** -a -um, *Arabian, an Arabian*.

ărăbĭlis -e (aro), *that can be ploughed, arable*: Plin.

Ărachnē -ēs, f. (Ἀράχνη), *a Lydian maiden who entered into a contest in spinning with Minerva and was turned into a spider*.

ărănĕa -ae, f. (ἀράχνη). (1) *a spider*: Ov., Verg. (2) *the spider's web*: Pl., Ov.

ărănĕŏla -ae, f. (dim. of aranea), *a little spider*: Cic.

ărănĕŏlus -i, m. (dim. of aranea), *a little spider*: Verg.

ărănĕōsus -a -um (aranea). (1) *full of cobwebs*: Cat. (2) *like a cobweb*: Plin.

¹**ărănĕus** -i, m. *a spider*: Lucr.

²**ărănĕus** -a -um, *relating to a spider*: Plin. N. as subst. **ărănĕum** -i, *a cobweb*: Phaedr.

Ărăr and **Ărăris** -is, m. *a river in Gaul, the Saône*.

ărātĭo -ōnis, f. (aro). (1) *ploughing, agriculture*: Cic. (2) meton., *a ploughed field*: Pl.; esp. arationes, *the public domains let at a rent of one-tenth of their produce*: Cic.

ărātĭuncŭla -ae, f. (dim. of aratio), *a little estate*: Pl.

ărātor -ōris, m. (1) *a ploughman, a husband-man*: Cic., Ov. (2) aratores, *tenants of the arationes*; q.v.: Cic.

ărātrum -i, n. *the plough*: aratrum circum-ducere, Cic.; aliquem ab aratro arcessere, Cic., Verg.

Ărātus -i, m. (Ἄρατος).

(1) *a Greek poet, born in Cilicia, whose astronomical poem Φαινόμενα was translated into Latin by Cicero.* Adj. **ărātēus** and **Ărātīus** -a -um, *belonging to Aratus*: nostra quaedam Aratea=Cicero's translation of the poem, Cic.

(2) *a celebrated Greek general, founder of the Achaean League* (271–213 B.C.).

Ăraxēs -is, m. (Ἀράξης), *a river in Armenia*.

arbĭtĕr -tri, m. (from ar=ad, and bitere, *to go*). LIT., (1) in gen., *a witness, spectator, hearer*: locus ab arbitris remotus, Cic.; remotis arbitris, Cic. (2) as legal t. t., *an umpire, arbitrator*: arbiter litis, Cic.; aliquem arbitrum adigere, Cic.; arbitrum dare, Cic.; sumere, Cic.; esse in aliquam rem arbitrum, Cic.; ad arbitrum confugere, Cic.; uti aliquo arbitro, Cic.

TRANSF., (1) *a judge of any matter*: formae (of Paris), Ov.; inter antiquam Academiam et Zenonem, Cic. (2) *a ruler, lord, master*: bibendi, Hor.; Hadriae, *the south wind*, Hor.; elegantiae, Tac.

arbitra -ae, f. (arbiter), *a female witness*: Hor.

arbitrārĭus -a -um, *arbitrary, uncertain*: Pl. Abl. as adv. **arbitrārĭo**, *uncertainly*: Pl.

arbitrātus -ūs, m. *will, choice, decision, direction*: tuo arbitratu, Cic.; cuius arbitratu sit educatus, Cic.

arbĭtrĭum -i, n. (arbiter). LIT., *the function of an* arbiter. Hence (1) *the presence of witnesses*: Sen. (2) *the decision of an arbitrator*: aliud est iudicium, aliud arbitrium; iudicium est pecuniae certae, arbitrium incertae, Cic. TRANSF., *any decision, judgment, authority*: arbitrium eligendi, Tac.; libera arbitria de aliquo agere, Liv.; res ab opinionis arbitrio seiunctae, Cic.; arbitrio suo, *on his own authority, under his own control*, Cic.; arbitria funeris, *the expenses of a funeral* (as fixed by arbitration), Cic.

arbĭtro -are, rare act. form of arbitror; q.v.: Pl., Cic.

arbĭtror -ari, dep. (arbiter). (1) *to witness, perceive*: Pl. (2) *to bear witness*: Cic. (3) *to arbitrate, judge*: fidem alicui, *to adjudge, grant*, Pl. So in gen., *to decide, judge, think that*: qui se natos ad homines iuvandos arbitrantur, Cic.; ut arbitror, *as I think*, Cic.

arbŏr (arbos) -ōris, f. *a tree*. LIT., fici, *a fig-tree*, Cic.; Iovis, *the oak*, Ov.; Phoebi, *the laurel*, Ov.; Palladis, *the olive*, Ov. TRANSF., of things made of wood: arbor infelix, *the gallows*, Cic.; mali, *a mast*, Verg.; arbor, *an oar*, Verg.; *a ship*: Pelias, *the Argo*, Ov.

arbŏrĕus -a -um, *relating to trees*: Verg., Ov.; cornua, *branching*, Verg.

arbustus -a -um (arbor), *planted with trees*. N. as subst. **arbustum** -i, *a plantation, a vineyard planted with trees*: Cic., Hor. In plur., used by poets as a metrically convenient substitute for arbores: Lucr., Verg.

arbŭtĕus -a -um, *relating to the arbutus*: Verg., Ov.

arbŭtum -i, n. (1) *the fruit of the wild straw-berry* or *arbutus tree*: Verg. (2) *its leaves or shoots*: Verg.

arbŭtus -i, f. *the wild strawberry* or *arbutus tree*: Verg., Hor., Ov.

arca -ae, f. (arceo), *a chest, box*. Esp. *a money coffer*: Cic.; sometimes=*the money in the coffer*: arcae nostrae confidito, Cic.; *a coffin*: Hor., Liv. TRANSF., *a cell for close imprison-ment*: Cic.

Arcădĭa -ae, f. (Ἀρκαδία), *a mountainous region of the Peloponnesus*. Adj. **Arcădĭus** -a -um and **Arcădĭcus** -a -um: deus, *Pan*, Prop.; iuvenis, *a simpleton*, Juv.; virgo, *Arethusa*, Ov. See also Arcas.

arcānus -a -um (arca), *shut, closed*. (1) *silent, able to keep a secret*: dixisti arcano satis, Pl.; nox, Ov. (2) *secret*: Cic.; arcana consilia, Liv.; sacra, Ov.; Cereris arcanae, *whose mysteries are secret*, Hor.

¶ N. as subst. **arcānum** -i, *a secret*: Cic., Liv., Verg.

Adv. **arcānō**, *secretly*: Pl., Cic. L.

Arcăs -ădis, m. (Ἀρκάς). (1) *son of Jupiter and Callisto, placed in the heavens as the con-stellation Arctophylax; progenitor of the Arcadians.* (2) as adj. and subst., *Arcadian, an Arcadian*; esp. of Mercury: Mart.

arcĕo -ēre -ui (connected with ἀρκέω). (1) *to shut in, shut up*: alvus arcet et continet quod recipit, Cic. (2) *to keep at a distance, to hinder, prevent*: copias hostium, Cic.; followed by ne or quin with subj., Liv. The thing or action from which one is restrained is expressed by ab with the abl.: aliquem ab urbe, Cic.; or by the abl. alone: hostem Gallia, Cic.; hostis transitu, Liv. or the dat.: oestrum pecori, Verg. Poet. use, *to protect, keep safe from*: aliquem periclis, Verg.

Arcĕsĭlās -ae, m. (Ἀρκεσίλας) and **Arcĕsĭlāus** -i, m. (Ἀρκεσίλαος), *a Greek philosopher of Pitane in Aeolia* (c. 316–241 B.C.), *founder of the Middle Academy.*

Arcēsĭus -i, m. (Ἀρκείσιος), *father of Laertes, and grandfather of Ulysses.*

arcessītor -ōris, m. *one who calls* or *fetches*: Plin. L.

arcessītū abl. sing. as from arcessitus, m. (arcesso), *by calling for, at the summons*: ipsius rogatu arcessituque, Cic.

arcesso (accerso) -ere -īvi -ītum (causat. of accedo), *to fetch* or *call to a place, to summon*. LIT., aliquem litteris Capua, Cic.; aliquem in senatum, Cic.; sacra ab exteris nationibus asciscere et arcessere, Cic. As legal t. t., *to summon, bring before a court of justice*: innocentem iudicio capitis, Cic.; aliquem capitis, Cic.

TRANSF., *to fetch, derive, obtain anything*: quies molli strato arcessita, Liv.; argumen-tum usque a capite, Cic.

Hence partic. **arcessītus**, *strained, far-fetched*: dictum, Cic.

Archĕlāus -i, m. (Ἀρχέλαος). (1) *a Greek philosopher of Miletus in the fifth century* B.C. (2) *a king of Macedonia*, c. 400 B.C., *friend of Euripides*. (3) *a general of Mithridates in the first century* B.C. (4) *the last king of Cappadocia.*

archĕtўpus -a -um (ἀρχέτυπος), *original*: Juv. N. as subst., *an original*: Plin. L.

Archĭās -ae, m. (Ἀρχίας). (1) Aulus Licinius, *a Greek poet of Antioch, defended by Cicero*. (2) *a celebrated cabinet-maker.*

¶ Hence adj. **Archĭăcus** -a -um, *made by him*: Hor.

archĭgallus -i, m. *a high priest of Cybele*: Plin.

Archĭlŏchus -i, m. (Ἀρχίλοχος), *a Greek satiric poet of Paros, inventor of iambic verse.* Adj. **Archĭlŏchĭus** -a -um, *Archilochian*; appell., *sharp, biting*: edicta, Cic.

archĭmăgīrus -i, m. (ἀρχιμάγειρος), *head cook*: Juv.

Archĭmēdēs -is, m. (Ἀρχιμήδης), *a celebrated mathematician and inventor, killed on the capture of Syracuse by Marcellus* (212 B.C.).

archĭmīmus -i, m. (ἀρχίμιμος), *chief mime or buffoon*: Suet.

archĭpīrāta -ae, m. (ἀρχιπειρατής), *chief pirate*: Cic., Liv.

archĭtectōn -ŏnis, m. (ἀρχιτέκτων), *master-builder*: Pl. TRANSF., *a master in cunning*: Pl.

archĭtector -ari, dep. *to build.* TRANSF., *to devise*: voluptates, Cic.

architectūra -ae, f. *architecture*: Cic.

architectus -i, m. (ἀρχιτέκτων), *an architect, master-builder*: architecti operum, Cic. TRANSF., *an inventor, author, maker*: huius legis, Cic.; quasi architectus beatae vitae, Cic.

archōn -ontis, m. (ἄρχων), *an archon, one of the chief magistrates of Athens*: Cic.

Archȳtās -ae, m. (Ἀρχύτας), *a philosopher of Tarentum and friend of Plato.*

arcĭtĕnens -entis (arcus/teneo), *holding the bow, epithet of Apollo and Diana*: Verg., Ov.

Arctŏs -i, f. (ἄρκτος), *the Great and Little Bear*: Verg., Ov.; hence (1) *the north*: iuncta Aquilonibus Arctos, Ov.; opacam excipere Arcton, *to be towards the north*, Hor. (2) *the night*: Prop.

arctōus -a -um (ἀρκτῷος), *belonging to the Bear* (Arctos); hence, *northern*: Mart., Lucr.

Arctūrus -i, m. (ἀρκτοῦρος). (1) *the brightest star of the constellation Bootes*: Cic. (2) *Bootes itself*: sub ipsum arcturum, Verg.

arcŭla -ae, f. (dim. of arca), *a casket for money, jewels, or perfume*: arculae mulieribus, Cic.; TRANSF., *rhetorical ornament*: omnes (Isocrati) discipulorum arculae, Cic. L.

arcŭlārĭus -i, m. *a casket-maker*: Pl.

arcŭo -are, *to bend or shape like a bow*: Plin L.

¶ Hence partic. **arcŭatus** -a -um, *bow-shaped*: currus, Liv.

arcŭs -ūs, m. (1) *a bow*: arcum intendere, Cic.; adducere, Verg. (2) *the rainbow*: Cic., Verg. (3) *an arch, vault, triumphal arch*: Ov., Suet. (4) *anything else that is arched or curved*, e.g. a serpent's coils: Ov.; *a mathematical arc*: Sen.; *the parallel circles which bound the zones of the earth*: Ov.

¹**ardĕa** -ae, f. *a heron*: Verg.

²**Ardĕa** -ae, f. (Ἀρδέα), *town of the Rutuli in Latium.* Adj. **Ardĕās** -ātis and **Ardĕātīnus** -a -um, *of Ardea.*

ardēlio -ōnis, m. *a busybody*: Mart.

ardĕo ardēre arsi, *to burn, glow, be on fire.*
LIT., faces, Cic.; domus, Cic.; mare arsit eo anno, Liv.; iam proximus ardet Ucalegon, *the house of U.*, Verg.; ardent altaria, Verg.
TRANSF., (1) of bright objects, *to gleam*: oculi, Pl., Cic.; ardebat murice laena, Verg. (2) of physical sensation, *to smart*: cum omnes artus ardere viderentur, *be in pain*, Cic. (3) of emotions, *to burn*: amore, dolore, furore, Cic.; ardere in proelia, Verg. Esp. in

poets, *to burn with love*: ardere aliquā, *or in aliquā, or aliquam*, Hor., Verg., Ov.; ardere invidiā, Cic. (4) of political disorder, *to be ablaze*: cum arderet coniuratio, Cic.; cum arderet Syria bello, Cic.

¶ Hence partic. (with compar. and superl.) **ardens** -entis, *hot, glowing, burning.* LIT., lapides, Liv. TRANSF., of bright objects, *gleaming*: oculi, Verg.; apes ardentes auro, Verg.; of strong flavours: Falernum, *fiery Falernian wine*, Hor.; of passions, etc., *burning, eager, hot*: odium, Liv.; avaritia, Cic.; studia, Ov.; ardentes equi, *spirited*, Verg.; of speech, *fiery*: orator, Cic.; oratio, Cic.
Adv. (with compar. and superl.) **ardentĕr**, *hotly, violently*: cupere, Cic.

ardĕŏla -ae, f. (dim. of ¹ardea), *a little heron*: Plin.

ardesco -ĕre (inch. of ardeo), *to take fire*: ardescunt caelestia templa, Cic. TRANSF., *to glitter*: fulmineis ignibus ardescunt undae, Ov.; of the passions, *to become inflamed*: tuendo, Verg.; libidinibus, Tac.; of strife, *to blaze up*: pugna, Verg.

ardor -ōris, m. (ardeo), *flame, burning, heat.* LIT., solis, Cic. TRANSF., (1) *the gleam of bright objects*: oculorum, Cic.; stellarum, Cic. (2) *of the feelings or passions, ardour, heat, eagerness*: cupiditatum, Cic.; pugnandi, *for fighting*, Liv.; mentis ad gloriam, Cic.; ad bellum armaque, Liv.; esp. *the passion of love*: Ov.; virginis, *for a maiden*, Ov. Meton., *the object of love, the loved one*: Ov.

Ardŭenna -ae, f. *a forest in Gallia Belgica* (now *the forest of the Ardennes*).

ardŭus -a -um, adj. (with compar. and superl. in Cato), *steep, towering, lofty.*
LIT., collis, Liv.; ascensus difficilis atque arduus, Cic.; aether, *high*, Ov.; nubes, Hor.; sese arduus infert (Turnus), *erect, upright*, Verg. N. as subst.: per arduum scandere, Hor.; ducere, Liv.
TRANSF., *difficult to undertake or reach*: res arduae ac difficiles, Cic.; rebus in arduis, *in adversity*, Hor.; arduum videtur, *or est* followed by infin., Sall., Liv. N. as subst., *difficulty*: fuit in arduo, *was difficult*, Tac.

ārĕa -ae, f. *a level or open space*, esp. in a town: quaerenda est area primum, Hor.; collemqua super planissima campi area, Ov.; praeclare area, *a good site for a house*, Cic.; *court-yard*: Liv.; *threshing-floor*: Cic. Esp. *a playground*; and so fig., *play, scope*: area scelerum, Cic.; Ov.

ārĕfăcĭo -făcĕre -fēci -factum, *to make dry*: Lucr., Suet.

Ărĕlătĕ, n. and **Ărĕlās** -atis, f. *a town in Gallia Narbonensis* (now *Arles*). Adj. **Ărĕlātensis** -e.

ărēna = harēna; q.v.

ārĕo -ēre, *to be dry*: aret ager, Verg. Esp., *to be dry with thirst or drought*: Liv., Verg.

¶ Hence partic. **ārens** -entis, *dry, thirsty*: rivus, Verg.; ora, Ov.; sitis, Ov.

ārĕŏla -ae, f. (dim. of area), *a little open space*: Plin.

Ărĕŏpăgus -i, m. (Ἄρειος πάγος), *Mars' hill at Athens, upon which the court called Areopagus held its sittings*: Cic.

¶ Hence **Ărĕŏpăgītēs** -ae, m. *a member of the court*: Cic.

Ărēs -is, m. (Ἄρης), *the Greek god of war,* corresponding to Latin *Mars;* appell., *a warrior:* Pl. Adj. **Ărēus** -a -um, *of Ares* or *Mars:* iudicium, *the Areopagus,* Tac.

ăresco -ĕre (inch. of areo), *to become dry:* cito arescit lacrima, Cic.

Ărestŏrĭdēs -ae, m. (Ἀρεστορίδης), *a descendant of Arestor,* i.e., *Argus, his son:* Ov.

ărĕtălŏgus -i, m. (ἀρεταλόγος), *a babbler about virtue, a kind of philosophical buffoon:* Juv., Suet.

Ărĕthūsa -ae, f. (Ἀρέθουσα), *a fountain in the island of Ortygia at Syracuse;* myth. *a nymph in Elis beloved by the river Alpheus, who chased her under the sea to Sicily.* Adj. **Ărĕthūsis** -ĭdis and **Ărĕthūsĭus** -a -um, *of* or *belonging to Arethusa.*

Ărētĭum -i, n. *a town in Etruria* (now *Arezzo*).

Arganthōnĭus -i, m. (Ἀργανθώνιος), *a king of Tartessus, who lived to a great age.*

Argēi -ōrum, m. (1) *chapels of local deities in Rome.* (2) *figures of men, thrown into the Tiber every year on the Ides of May,* apparently in place of earlier human sacrifices.

Argentānum -i, n. *a town in Bruttium* (now *Argentino*).

argentārius -a -um. (1) *relating to silver:* metalla, *silver mines,* Plin. (2) *relating to money:* inopia, Pl.; taberna, *a banker's stall,* Liv.
　　As subst. **argentārĭus** -i, m. *a money-changer, banker:* Cic., Liv.; **argentārĭa** -ae, f. (1) (sc. taberna), *a banker's office:* Liv. (2) (sc. ars), *a banker's trade:* Cic. (3) (sc. fodina), *a silver mine:* Cic.

argentātus -a -um (argentum). (1) *ornamented with silver:* milites, *with silvered shields,* Liv. (2) *provided with money:* Pl.

argentĕŏlus -a -um (dim. of argenteus), *of silver:* Pl.

argentĕus -a -um, *of silver.* LIT., aquila, Cic.; nummus, Varr.; denarius, Plin.
　　As subst. **argenteus** (sc. nummus), Pl. TRANSF., (1) *ornamented* or *covered with silver:* scaena, Cic. (2) *of the colour of silver:* anser, Verg. (3) *belonging to the Silver Age:* proles, Ov.

argentĭfŏdīna -ae, f. *a silver mine:* Varr., Plin.

argentōsus -a -um, *full of silver, rich in silver:* Plin.

argentum -i, n. (ἄργης, ἀργυρίον), *silver:* signatum, *stamped with a pattern,* Cic. Esp. (1) *silver plate:* Cic., Hor. (2) *silver coin,* and generally *money:* Pl., Hor.

Argīlētum -i, n. *a part of Rome where there were many booksellers and workmen.* Adj. **Argīlētānus** -a -um, *of Argiletum.*

argilla -ae, f. (ἄργιλλος), *white clay, potter's clay:* Cic.

argillācĕus -a -um, *clayey, of clay:* Plin.

Argĭnūsae (**Argĭnūssae**) -arum, f. (Ἀργινοῦσαι), *islands in the Aegean Sea near Lesbos, scene of a naval victory of the Athenians over the Spartans.*

Argō, acc. Argo, genit. Argūs, f. (Ἀργώ), *the ship Argo, in which many Greek heroes sailed to Colchis, under Jason, to fetch the Golden Fleece.* **Argŏnautae** -ārum, m. (Ἀργοναῦται), *the Argonauts, the heroes who sailed in the Argo.* Adj. **Argōus** -a -um.

Argŏs, n. and **Argi** -ōrum, m. *Argos, the capital of Argolis in the Peloponnese.* Adj. **Argēus** -a -um and **Argīvus** -a -um: Argivus augur, *Amphiaraus,* Hor.; plur. subst. **Argīvi** -orum, and poet. -um, m. *the Argives* or *Greeks;* **Argŏlis** -ĭdis, f. (1) f. adj., *Argive.* (2) subst., *the district Argolis.*
　　¶ Hence adj. **Argŏlĭcus** -a -um, *Argolic.*

argūmentātĭo -ōnis, f. *the bringing forward of a proof:* argumentatio est explicatio argumenti, Cic.

argūmentor -ari, dep. *to bring forward a proof:* quid porro argumenter, qua de re dubitare nemo possit, Cic. Transit. *to allege as a proof:* Cic., Liv. Rarely *to argue from, conclude from:* de voluntate, Cic.

argūmentum -i, n. (arguo). (1) *an argument, proof:* Cic.; adferre argumenta, Cic.; multis argumentis deos esse docere, Cic.; argumenta atque indicia sceleris, Cic. (2) *subject, contents, matter:* **a,** of a literary work: epistulae, Cic.; fabulae, Ter.; sometimes as the work itself: explicare argumenti exitum, Cic.: **b,** *subject of a work of art:* ex ebore diligentissime perfecta argumenta erant in valvis (*bas-reliefs*), Cic.

argŭo -ŭĕre -ŭi -ūtum (connected with ἀργός, ἄργυρος), *to put in clear light.*
　　(1) *to declare, prove.* LIT., speculatores non legatos venisse, Liv. TRANSF., *to betray, prove:* degeneres animos timor arguit, Verg.; laudibus arguitur vini vinosus Homerus, Hor.
　　(2) *to accuse, blame:* **a,** of persons, *to charge, expose, convict;* with genit.: summi sceleris, Cic.; with abl.: hoc crimine te non arguo, Cic.; with double acc.: id quod me arguis, Cic.; with infin.: Roscius arguitur occidisse patrem, Cic.: **b,** of things, *to censure, complain of:* culpa, quam arguo, Liv.
　　¶ Hence partic. (with compar. and superl.) **argūtus** -a -um. (1) in relation to the senses: **a,** to the eye, *expressive, lively:* manus, oculi, Cic.: **b,** to the ear, *piercing, penetrating, shrill:* hirundo, Verg.; forum, *noisy,* Ov.; poeta, *melodious,* Hor.; but civem, *prattling,* Pl., Hor. (2) relating to the mind: **a,** *significant, clear;* of omens: argutissima exta, Cic.: **b,** in a good sense, *sagacious, acute:* argutus orator, Cic.; poema, Cic.; in a bad sense, *sly, cunning:* meretrix, Hor.
　　Adv. (with compar. and superl.) **argūtē,** *sagaciously, acutely:* callide arguteque dicere, Cic.

Argus -i, m. (Ἄργος), *the hundred-eyed guardian of Io, slain by Mercury.*

argūtatĭo -ōnis, f. *a rustling:* Cat.

argūtĭae -ārum, f. (argutus). (1) *liveliness, animation:* digitorum, *quick movement of the fingers,* Cic.; of works of art: Plin. (2) of mental qualities, *cleverness, sagacity:* huius orationes tantum argutiarum, tantum urbanitatis habent, Cic.; in a bad sense, *subtlety, quibbling:* Cic.

argūtor -ari, dep. *to chatter:* Pl.

argūtŭlus -a -um, *somewhat acute:* libri, Cic.

argūtus -a -um, partic. from arguo; q.v.

argyraspĭdes -pĭdum, m. (ἀργυράσπιδες), *name of a picked corps in the Macedonian army, the wearers of the silver shield:* Liv.

Arĭadna -ae and **Ărĭadnē** -ēs, f. (*'Ᾱριάδνη*), *daughter of Minos of Crete; she helped Theseus to slay the Minotaur and went with him to Naxos, but was deserted by him there.*

Arīcĭa -ae, f. (1) *an old town in Latium on the Appian Way* (now *Ariccia*). Adj. **Ārīcīnus** -a -um, *belonging to Aricia.* (2) *a nymph, wife of Hippolytus.*

ārĭdŭlus -a -um (dim. of aridus), *somewhat dry*: Cat.

ārĭdus -a -um, adj. (with compar. and superl.) (areo), *dry, arid.*
   LIT., (1) folia, Cic.; poet.: sonus, *a dry, crackling sound*, Verg. (2) *dry with thirst*: viator, Verg.; febris, *parching*, Verg. (3) *shrivelled, fleshless*: crura, Ov.; exsiccati atque aridi, Cic. N. as subst. **aridum** -i, *dry ground*: naves in aridum subducere, Caes.
   TRANSF., (1) *of manner of living, poor, meagre*: vita, Cic. (2) *intellectually dry, jejune*: genus orationis, Cic. (3) *avaricious*: Ter.

ărĭēs -ĭĕtis, m. (the poets sometimes treat the i as a consonant; word perhaps connected with Gk. *ἄρην*). LIT., *a ram*: Pl. TRANSF., (1) *a battering ram*: Caes., Liv. (2) *a prop, beam*: Caes. (3) *one of the signs of the Zodiac*: Cic., Ov.

ărĭĕtātĭo -ōnis, f. *a butting like a ram*: Sen.

ărĭĕto -are, *to butt like a ram*; transit., Pl.; intransit., Verg.

Arīmĭnum -i, n. *town in Umbria on the Adriatic coast* (now *Rimini*). Adj. **Arīmĭnensis** -e, *belonging to Ariminum.*

Arĭŏbarzānēs -is, m. (*'Ᾱριοβαρζάνης*), *name of several kings of Cappadocia.*

Ărīŏn or **Ārĭo** -ŏnis, m. (*'Ᾱρίων*). (1) *a cithara player, saved from drowning by a dolphin.* Adj. **Ārīŏnĭus** -a -um, *belonging to Arion*: Ov., Prop. (2) *a horse able to speak, which Neptune gave to Adrastus.*

Ariovistus -i, m. *a Germanic prince, conquered by Caesar.*

Ărĭsba -ae and **Ărĭsbē** -ēs, f. (*'Ᾱρίσβη*), *a town in the Troad.*

ărista -ae, f. *the beard of an ear of grain*: Cic., Ov. Meton., *the ear itself*: Verg.; *a harvest*: Verg.; of an *ear of spikenard*: Ov.; of *human hair*: Pers.

Ăristaeus -i, m. (*'Ᾱρισταῖος*), *son of Apollo and Cyrene, legendary introducer of bee-keeping and olive-culture.*

Ăristarchus -i, m. (*'Ᾱρίσταρχος*), *a celebrated grammarian and critic of Alexandria* (c. 215–145 B.C.); appell. *a severe critic*: Cic.

Ăristīdēs -is, m. (*'Ᾱριστείδης*). (1) *a celebrated Athenian statesman and general, rival of Themistocles.* (2) *a poet of Miletus.*

Ăristippus -i, m. (*'Ᾱρίστιππος*), *a philosopher of Cyrene, disciple of Socrates, and founder of the Cynic school.* Adj. **Aristippēus** -a -um, *of or belonging to Aristippus.*

Ăristo -ōnis, m. (*'Ᾱρίστων*), *a philosopher of Chios, pupil of Zeno, contemporary with Caesar.*
   ¶ Hence adj. **Aristōnēus** -a -um, *of or belonging to Aristo.*

Ăristŏdēmus -i, m. (*'Ᾱριστόδημος*), *a tyrant of Cumae in Campania, in the 6th century* B.C.

aristŏlŏchĭa -ae, f. (*ἀριστολοχία*), *a plant useful in childbirth*: Cic.

Ăristŏphănēs -is, m. (*'Ᾱριστοφάνης*). (1) *the great Athenian comic dramatist.* Adj. **Ăristŏphănēus** -a -um, *of* or *relating to Aristophanes.* (2) *a celebrated grammarian, pupil of Eratosthenes.*

Ăristŏtĕlēs -is and -i, m. (*'Ᾱριστοτέλης*), *the celebrated Greek philosopher, pupil of Plato, founder of the Peripatetic school.* Adj. **Ăristŏtĕlĭus** -a -um and **Ăristŏtĕlius** -a -um, *of* or *relating to Aristotle.*

¹ărithmētĭca -ae and -ē -ēs, f. (*ἀριθμητική*, sc. *τέχνη*), *arithmetic*: Sen., Plin.

²ărithmētĭca -ōrum, n. *arithmetic*: Cic.

ārĭtūdo -ĭnis, f. *dryness*: Pl.

arma -ōrum, n. (root ar- as in Gr. *ἀραρίσκω*, Latin ars, artus), *defensive arms, armour* (opp. tela, *offensive weapons*), esp. *shields*; but also in wider sense, *weapons of war.*
   LIT., arma his imperata, galea, clypeum, ocreae, lorica, omnia ex aere, Liv.; arma capere, sumere, Cic.; ad arma ire, Cic.; armis decertare *or* decernere, Cic.; in armis esse *or* stare, *to be under arms*, Liv.; CL milia habere in armis, Liv.; arma deponere, Liv.; tradere, Liv.; ad arma, '*to arms*', Caes.
   TRANSF., (1) *war*: arma civilia, Cic.; silent leges inter arma, Cic.; in armis spes, Liv. (2) *soldiers, military power*: Romana arma ingruere, Liv.; levia, *light-armed troops*, Liv. (3) fig., *protection, defence*: arma prudentiae, Cic.; senectutis, Cic. (4) gen., *tools, equipment*: arma equestria, *the fittings of a horse*, Liv.; cerealia, *implements for grinding and baking corn*, Verg.; *building tools*: Cic.

armāmenta -ōrum, n. *implements, tackle*; esp. of a ship: vela armamentaque, Caes., Ov.

armāmentārĭum -i, n. *an armoury*: Cic., Liv.

armārĭŏlum -i, n. (dim. of armarium), *a little cupboard*: Pl.

armārĭum -i, n. *a cupboard, chest*: Pl., Cic.

armātūra -ae, f. *equipment, armour*: Numidae levis armaturae, *light-armed*, Caes. Meton., *armed soldiers*: armatura levis, *light-armed troops*, Cic. Also fig., of discourse: tamquam levis armaturae prima orationis excursio, Cic.

armātus -a -um, subst. found only in abl., armatu, m. *armour.* LIT., haud dispari armatu, Liv. Meton., *armed troops*: gravi armatu, *heavy-armed troops*, Liv.

Armĕnĭa -ae, f. (*'Ᾱρμενία*), *a country in Asia.*
   ¶ Hence adj. and subst. **Armĕnĭus** -a -um, *Armenian, an Armenian*: Cic., Verg., Ov.; also adj. **Armĕnĭacus** -a -um: Plin.

armentālis -e (armentum), *belonging to a herd*: equa, Verg.

armentārĭus -i, m. *a herdsman*: Verg.

armentum -i, n. (aro), *cattle for ploughing*; collectively, *a herd* (of oxen): Pan erat armenti custos, Ov.; greges armentorum reliquique pecoris, Cic. Also of animals other than cattle; of *horses*: Verg.; of *stags*: Verg.

armĭfĕr -fĕra -fĕrum (arma/fero), *bearing arms, warlike*: Ov.

armĭgĕr -gĕra -gĕrum (arma/gero), *bearing arms.* As adj.: Prop. As subst., *an armour-bearer.* (1) m.: armiger, Cic.; Iovis, *the eagle*, Verg.; Catilinae, *adherent*, Cic. (2) f.: armigera, Ov.

armilla -ae, f. *a bracelet*, worn by both men and women: Cic., Liv.

armillātus -a -um (armilla), *adorned with a bracelet*: Suet., Prop.

Armĭlustrĭum -i, n. (arma/lustro), *a festival at which arms were consecrated*, celebrated at a spot in Rome called Armilustrum.

Armĭnĭus -i, m. *a Germanic prince who defeated the Roman Varus in* A.D. 9.

armĭpŏtens -entis (arma/potens), *mighty in arms, warlike*: Mars, Verg.; diva, Verg.

armĭsŏnus -a -um (arma/sono), *resounding with arms*: Verg.

armo -are (arma), *to provide with arms*: aliquem in rempublicam, Cic.; milites, Caes.; servum in or contra dominum, Cic.; equum bello, *for battle*, Verg.; gladiis dextras, Liv. TRANSF., (1) fig., *to arm*: multitudinem auctoritate publica, Cic.; sese eloquentia, Cic. (2) gen., *to equip, fit out*: naves, Caes.; classem, Liv.
¶ Hence partic. (with superl.) **armatus** -a -um, *armed, equipped*. LIT., armatus togatusque, *both in war and in peace*, Liv.; armatae classes, Verg.; m. pl. as subst. **armati**, *armed men*: Liv. TRANSF., erat incredibili armatus audacia, Cic.

Armŏrĭcae -arum, f. pl. *part of N.W. Gaul, corresponding to Brittany and part of Normandy*.

armus -i, m. (ἁρμός). (1) *the shoulder where it is fitted to the shoulder-blade*: latos huic hasta per armos tremit, Verg.; more often of animals: ex umeris armi fiunt, Ov. (2) *the side of an animal*: Verg.

Arnus -i, m. (Ἄρνος), *the chief river of Etruria* (now the *Arno*). Adj. **Arnĭensis** -e.

ăro -are (ἀρόω), *to plough*. LIT., arare terram et sulcum altius imprimere, Cic.; prov.: non profecturis litora bubus aras, *to labour uselessly*, Ov.; hence gen., *to farm, cultivate*: Falerni mille fundi iugera, Hor.; absol.: cives Romani qui arant in Sicilia, *tenants of the domain-lands* (cf. aratio), Cic. TRANSF., (1) *to furrow, wrinkle*: rugae quae tibi corpus arent, Ov. (2) *of ships, to plough the sea*: vastum maris aequor, Verg.

Arpi -ōrum, m. *a town in Apulia*. Adj. **Arpīnus** -a -um, *of or belonging to Arpi*.

Arpīnum -i, n. *a Volscian hill-town, birth-place of Marius and Cicero* (now *Arpino*).
¶ Hence adj. and subst. **Arpīnas** -ātis, *of Arpinum, an inhabitant of Arpinum*; also adj. **Arpīnus** -a -um, *of Arpinum*.

arquātus -a -um (arcus), *relating to jaundice* (because of the colours of the rainbow); m. as subst., *a sufferer from jaundice*: Lucr.

arrha -ae, f. and **arrhăbo** -ōnis, m. *earnest money*: Pl., Ter. TRANSF., amoris, Pl.

Arrūns=Aruns; q.v.

ars -tis, f. (root ar-, as in Gr. ἀραρίσκω), *skill, way, method*.
(1) *an occupation, profession, art*: disserendi, dialectics, Cic.; artes sordidae, *mean occupations*, those of slaves, Cic.; ingenuae, liberales, *honourable occupations*, Cic.; urbanae, *jurisprudence and rhetoric*, Liv.; civiles, Tac.; rhetorica, Quint.; artem aliquam factitare, Cic.; exercere, *to practise, pursue*, Hor.
(2) *skill, knowledge*, as shown in arts: ex arte (dicere, scribere, etc.), *according to the rules of art*, Cic.; hence as title of treatises on a subject: artes oratoriae, Cic.; opus est vel arte vel diligentia, Cic.; arte laboratae vestes, Verg.; arte canere, Ov.; sometimes in bad

sense, *cunning*: Liv., Verg.; sometimes opposed as *technique* to *inspiration* (ingenium): Cic.; or as *theory* to *practice* (facultas): Cic.
(3) in special concrete senses: **a**, artes, *works of art*, Cic.: **b**, Artes, *the Arts*, person., Phaedr.
(4) TRANSF., *conduct, character, method of acting*, good or bad: bonae artes, *good qualities*, Sall.; hac arte Pollux attigit arces igneas, Hor.; Tac.

Arsăcēs -is, m. (Ἀρσάκης), *the first king of the Parthians*.
¶ Hence **Arsăcĭdes** -ae, m. *a descendant of Arsaces*; **Arsăcĭus** -a -um, *Parthian*.

Artaxăta -ōrum, n. (-a -ae, f.: Tac.), *capital of Armenia, on the Araxes*.

Artaxerxēs -is, m. (Ἀρταξέρξης), *name of several Persian kings*.

artē, adv. from artus; q.v.

artērĭa -ae, f. (ἀρτηρία). (1) *the wind-pipe*: Cic.; n. plur., heterocl.: arteria, Lucr. (2) *an artery*: Cic.

arthrīticus -a -um (ἀρθριτικός), *gouty*: Cic.

artĭcŭlāris -e (articulus), *relating to the joints*: morbus, gout, Suet., Plin.

artĭcŭlātim, adv. (articulus), *piecemeal, joint by joint*: Pl. TRANSF., *in a manner properly divided, distinctly*: articulatim distincteque dici, Cic.

artĭcŭlo -are, *to articulate, speak distinctly*: Lucr.

artĭcŭlus -i, m. (dim. of artus).
LIT., (1) *a small joint*: articulorum dolores, *gouty* or *rheumatic pains*, Cic.; meton., *the fingers* or *the limbs*: Lucr., Ov. (2) of plants, *a knob, knot*: sarmentorum, Cic.
TRANSF., (1) *a division of a discourse*: articuli membraque, Cic.; also *an article, as part of speech*: Quint. (2) of time, *a moment, crisis*: in ipso articulo temporis, *in the nick of time*, Cic. (3) of other abstractions, *part, division, point*: per eosdem articulos et gradus, Suet.

artĭfex -fĭcis, m. (ars/facio).
Adj. (1) act., *skilled, clever*: homines talis negotii artifices, Sall.; artifex, ut ita dicam, stilus, Cic. (2) pass., *skilfully made*: boves, Prop.
Subst. (1) *a worker, craftsman* in a particular art, used absol. or with qualifying word: artifices scaenici, *actors*, Cic. (2) in gen., *a maker, master of, expert at* anything, with sphere indicated usually by genit.: probus eius (mundi) artifex, *creator*, Cic.; artifex conquirendae et comparandae voluptatis, Cic.; tractandi animos, Liv.; artifices ad corrumpendum iudicium, Cic.

artĭfĭcĭōsus -a -um. (1) *skilful, accomplished*: rhetores artificiosissimi, Cic. (2) *skilfully made*: operis, Cic.; hence *artificial* (opp. to natural): ea genera divinandi non naturalia, sed artificiosa dicuntur, Cic.
Adv. (with compar.) **artĭfĭcĭōsē**, *skilfully*: id multo artificiosius efficere, Cic.

artĭfĭcĭum -i, n. (artifex).
(1) *the work of an* artifex, *an occupation, craft, art*: ancillare, Cic. Esp. in concrete senses: **a**, *theory, system of an art* as formulated: componere artificium de iure civili, Cic.: **b**, *a work of art*: haec opera atque artificia, Cic.

(2) in gen., *cleverness, skill, art*: simulacrum Dianae singulari opere artificioque perfectum, Cic.; in a bad sense, *cunning, craft*: artificio simulationis, Cic.

arto -are (artus). (1) *to press together, reduce to small compass*: Lucr. (2) *to abridge, curtail*: in praemiis, in honoribus omnia artata, Liv.

artŏlăgănus -i, m. (ἀρτολάγανον), *a cake made of meal, wine, milk, oil, lard, and pepper*: Cic.

artopta -ae, m. (ἀρτόπτης). (1) *a baker*: Juv. (2) *a baker's vessel, bread pan*: Pl.

¹artus (arctus) -a -um, adj. (with compar. and superl.) (root ar- as in Gr. ἀραρίσκω, Latin arma), *narrow, tight, close.*

  LIT., catena, Ov.; regionibus, Lucr.; vallis, Liv. N. as subst. **artum** -i, *a narrow space*: pugna in arto, Tac.; Liv.

  TRANSF., (1) *tight, close*: religionum nodis, Lucr.; vinculum ad astringendam fidem artius, Cic.; somnus, *fast, sound*, Cic. (2) *small, meagre*: numerus, Tac.; commeatus, Liv. (3) *difficult, distressing*: res, Ov., Tac. N. as subst. **artum** -i, *difficulty, constraint*: cum in arto res esset, Liv.

  Adv. (with compar. and superl.) **artē**, *narrowly, tightly, closely.* LIT., artius complecti aliquem, Cic.; signa artius conlocare, Sall.; fig.: artius astringere rationem, Cic. TRANSF., arte et graviter dormire, *soundly, fast*, Cic.; artius appellare aliquem, *to cut a name short*, Ov.; aliquem arte diligere, *strongly*, Plin. L.

²artus -ūs, m. (root ar-, as in Gr. ἀραρίσκω, ἄρθρον), normally plur., artūs -ŭum, *the joints*: dolor artuum, *gout*, Cic.; omnibus artubus contremisco, *I tremble in all my limbs*, Cic.; fig., nervi atque artus sapientiae, Cic. Gen., esp. in poets, *the limbs*: salsusque per artus sudor iit, Verg.; Lucr., Ov.

ārŭla -ae, f. (dim. of ara), *a little altar*: Cic.

arund-, *see harund-.*

Aruns, *an Etruscan name for a younger son* (opp. Lar *or* Lars, an elder son): Liv.

Arverni -orum, m. *a Gallic people in Aquitaine, in what is now Auvergne.* Adj. **Arvernus** -a -um, *Arvernian.*

arvīna -ae, f. *fat, lard*: Verg.

arvus -a -um (aro), *ploughed*: Pl., Cic.
  N. as subst. **arvum** -i, *ploughed land, a field*: Cic., Verg., Hor., Ov. TRANSF., *land, region, country*: Verg., Ov.; arva Neptunia, *the sea*, Verg.

arx -cis, f. (from root of arceo), *a fortress, citadel, stronghold.*

  LIT., (1) in the narrow sense: ne quando arx hostium esset, Liv.; at Rome the *arx* was part of the Capitoline hill: ne quis patricius in arce aut in Capitolio habitaret, Liv.; used also of the whole hill: Capitolina, Liv.; also as *the stronghold* or *chief place of any town*: amisso oppido fugerat in arcem, Cic.; prov.: arcem facere e cloaca, *to make a mountain of a mole-hill*, Cic. (2) in wider sense, *the height of heaven*: siderea arx, Ov.; arces igneae, Hor.; of other high places: beatae arces, *Corinth*, Hor.; Parnassi arx, Ov.

  TRANSF., (1) *refuge, bulwark, protection*: haec urbs arx omnium gentium, Cic.; Liv. (2) *headquarters, chief place*: ubi Hannibal sit, ibi caput atque arcem totius belli esse, Liv.; arx aeternae dominationis, Tac.

as, assis, m., *a whole, a unit*, divided into 12 parts (unciae), the various fractions being expressed as follows: uncia ¹⁄₁₂, sextans ⅙, quadrans ¼, triens ⅓, quincunx ⁵⁄₁₂, semis ½, septunx ⁷⁄₁₂, bes ⅔, dodrans ¾, dextans ⅚, deunx ¹¹⁄₁₂.

  (1) in gen., esp. in terms relating to inheritance: haeres ex asse, *sole heir*, Plin.

  (2) as a coin, the *as*, which originally consisted of a pound of copper, but was frequently reduced later; hence prov.: (omnia) ad assem perdere, *to the last farthing*, Hor.; non assis facere, *not to estimate at a farthing*, Cat.

  (3) as a weight, *a pound*: Ov.

  (4) as a measure of land, *an acre*: Plin.

Ascănĭus -i, m. *son of Aeneas and Creüsa, founder of Alba Longa*: Verg.

ascaules -is, m. (ἀσκαύλης), *a bagpiper*: Mart.

ascendo -scendĕre -scendi -scensum (ad/scando), *to mount, ascend, go up.*

  LIT., intransit.: in murum, Cic.; in equum, Cic.; in contionem, *to go up to speak to the people*, Cic. L.; ad Gitanas, Liv.; transit.: murum, Caes.; ripam equo, Cic.

  TRANSF., (1) *to rise*: in tantum honorem, Cic.; ad maiora, Cic.; altiorem gradum, Cic.; gradatim ascendere vocem, *the voice rising higher and higher*, Cic. (2) with super *or* supra, *to rise above, surpass*: Tac.

ascensĭo -ōnis, f. *an ascent*: Pl. TRANSF., oratorum, *lofty flight*, Cic.

ascensus -ūs, m. (1) *a going up, climbing up, ascent.* LIT., in Capitolium, Cic. TRANSF., primus ad honoris gradum, Cic. (2) meton., *the place for ascending.* LIT., difficilis atque arduus, Cic. TRANSF., in virtute, Cic.

ascĭa -ae, f. (1) *a carpenter's axe*: Cic., quoting the Twelve Tables. (2) *a mason's trowel*, often shown and named in inscriptions.

ascĭo -scire, *to take to oneself, adopt as one's own*: socios, Verg.; asciri per adoptionem, Tac.

ascisco asciscĕre ascīvi ascītum, *to receive, admit.*

  (1) of persons, *to adopt, take to oneself*: aliquem in numerum civium, Cic.; inter patricios, Tac.; with dat.: superis ascitus, Caesar, Ov.; with double acc.: aliquem patronum, Cic. Also of unofficial association: ad sceleris foedus, Cic.; ad spem praedae, Liv.

  (2) of things, *to adopt*; formally, of measures, *to approve*: quas (leges) Latini voluerunt, asciverunt, Cic.; in gen.: hanc consuetudinem, Cic.; nova verba, Hor. Also *to assume, claim*: sibi sapientiam, Cic.

  ¶ Hence partic. **ascītus** -a -um, *foreign, acquired*: Nep., Ov.

ascŏpēra -ae, f. (ἀσκοπήρα), *a leather bag*: Suet.

Ascra -ae, f. (Ἄσκρα), *a small town in Boeotia, near Mount Helicon, the home of Hesiod.* Adj. **Ascraeus** -a -um, *Ascraean, of Ascra.* (1) with reference to Hesiod: poeta, Prop.; senex, Verg.; carmen, Verg.; m. as subst., *the man of Ascra=Hesiod*: Ov. (2) with ref. to Helicon: fontes, *Heliconian*, Prop.

ascrībo -scrībĕre -scripsi -scriptum (ad/scribo), *to write in, add in writing.*

  (1) of things. LIT., with dat.: poenam foederibus, Cic.; with in and the acc.: aliquid in eandem legem, Cic.; diem non

ascribis, *you do not add the date,* Cic. TRANSF., *to attribute, impute*: alicui incommodum, Cic.

(2) of persons, *to enrol, put on an official list*: aliquem in civitatem, Cic.; *as a colonist*: colonos, Liv.; with acc., of the colony: colonos Venusiam, Liv.; *as a soldier*: urbanae militiae ascribi, Tac.; of appointments generally: aliquem tutorem liberis, Cic. TRANSF., *to reckon under a class, include*: tu vero me ascribe in talem numerum, Cic.; aliquem ordinibus deorum, Hor.; opinio socium me ascribit tuis laudibus, Cic.; Tac.

ascripticius -a -um, *enrolled as a member of a community*: Cic.

ascriptio -ōnis, f. *an addition in writing*: Cic.

ascriptivus -a -um, *enrolled as a supernumerary*: Pl.

ascriptor -ōris, m. (ascribo), *one who approves of*: legis agrariae, Cic.

Asculum -i, n. *chief town of Picenum* (now *Ascoli Piceno*). Adj. **Asculānus** -a -um, *of or belonging to Asculum*.

asella -ae, f. (dim. of asina), *a little she-ass*: Ov.

asellus -i, m. (dim. of asinus), *an ass*: Cic. Prov.: narrare fabellam surdo asello, *to preach to deaf ears,* Hor.

Asia -ae, f. (᾿Ασία). (1) *a town in Lydia near the river Cayster*; later *the region round it.* (2) *the continent of Asia.* (3) *the peninsula of Asia Minor*; sometimes used specially for the kingdom of *Pergamum* (Liv.), or of *the Troad* (Ov.). (4) in the narrowest sense (the ordinary meaning of the word), *the Roman province of Asia, formed in* 133 B.C. *out of the kingdom of Pergamum*.

¶ Hence **Asiagĕnes** -is, m. *surname of L. Corn. Scipio.* **Asiānus** -a -um, adj. and subst., *belonging to the province of Asia,* or *an inhabitant of it.* **Asiāticus** -a -um, *Asiatic, surname of L. Corn. Scipio*: Asiatici oratores, *ornate, florid,* Cic. **Asis** -idis, poet., *Asia*: Ov. **Asius** -a -um, *Asiatic,* in the various senses of Asia (see above), esp. sense (1): Asia palus, *the marshes of the Cayster,* Verg.

asilus -i, m. *the gad-fly*: Verg.

asina -ae, f. *a she-ass*: Varr., Plin.

asininus -a -um, *belonging to an ass*: Plin.

Asinius -a -um, *name of a Roman gens, of which the most celebrated member was C. Asinius Pollio, friend of J. Caesar and Augustus, statesman, poet, historian.*

asinus -i, m. *an ass*: Cic. TRANSF., *a dolt, blockhead*: quid nunc te, asine, litteras doceam? Cic.

Asōpus -i, m. (᾿Ασωπός), *a river in Boeotia*; person., *the river-god Asopus.*

¶ Hence **Asōpiădēs** -ae, m. *a male descendant of Asopus* (his grandson Aeacus): Ov. **Asōpis** -idis, f. *daughter of Asopus.* (1) *Aegina, mother of Aeacus by Jupiter*: Ov. (2) *Euadne*: Ov. (3) *Euboea.*

asōtus -i, m. (ἄσωτος), *a sensualist, libertine*: Cic.

asparăgus -i, m. (ἀσπάραγος), *asparagus*: Juv., Suet.

aspargo, *see* aspergo.

Aspăsia -ae, f. (᾿Ασπασία), *a Milesian woman of exceptional intelligence, the mistress of Pericles.*

aspectābilis -e (aspecto), *visible*: Cic.

aspecto -are, *to look at earnestly*: quid me aspectas? Cic. TRANSF., *to observe, attend to*: iussa principis, Tac.; of place, *to lie towards, to face*: mare quod Hiberniam insulam aspectat, Tac.

aspectus -us, m. (1) act.: **a,** *a seeing, looking, sight*: uno aspectu, Cic.; oculi mobiles ut aspectum quo vellent facile converterent, Cic.; aspectum hominum vitare, Cic.: **b,** *range or power of vision*: orbes qui aspectum nostrum definiunt, Cic.; omnia quae sub aspectum cadunt, Cic. (2) pass.: **a,** *sight, power of being seen*: patriam privare aspectu tuo, Cic.; situs Syracusarum laetus ad aspectum, Cic.: **b,** *look, aspect, appearance*: pomorum iucundus aspectus, Cic.

aspello -ĕre, *to drive away*: Pl., Ter.

Aspendos -i, f. (῎Ασπενδος), *a Greek town in Pamphylia.* Adj. **Aspendius** -a -um, *of or belonging to Aspendus.*

asper -ĕra -ĕrum (aspra=aspera: Enn.; aspris=asperis: Verg.), *rough*.

(1) to the senses: **a,** to the touch: lingua, Lucr.; loca, *uneven,* Caes. N. as subst. **asperum** -i, *roughness, a rough place*: Lucr., Hor., Tac.: **b,** to the taste, *pungent, sour*: vinum, Ter.; sapor maris, Plin.: **c,** to the hearing, *harsh, grating*: Cic.; littera aspera, *the letter R,* Ov.: **d,** of weather, *rough*: mare, *stormy,* Liv.; aspera caelo Germania, Tac.

(2) of the character of living creatures, *rough, wild, harsh*: homo asper et durus, Cic.; anguis asper siti, Verg.

(3) of other things, *harsh, difficult*: res, tempora, Cic.; sententia, *severe,* Liv.; doctrina, *austere,* Cic.; facetiae, *bitter,* Cic.

¶ Hence adv. **asperē**, *roughly*: loqui, Cic.; scribere, Cic., Liv.

¹aspergo (**aspargo**) -spergĕre -spersi -spersum (ad/spargo), *to sprinkle upon* or *besprinkle with.* LIT., guttam bulbo, Cic.; virus pecori, Verg.; sapores huc, Verg.; olivam sale, Plin.; aram sanguine, Cic.

TRANSF., alicui molestiam, Cic.; splendorem vitae maculis, Cic.; aliquid mendaciunculis, Cic.

²aspergo (**aspargo**) -ĭnis, f. *a sprinkling, besprinkling, spray*: aquarum, Ov.; salsa aspargo, Verg.

asperĭtās -ātis, f. *roughness.* (1) to the senses: **a,** to the touch, *unevenness*: saxorum, Cic.: **b,** to the taste, *sourness*: vini, Plin.: **c,** to the ear, *harshness*: soni, Tac.: **d,** of weather, *roughness*: hiemis, Tac. (2) of character, *harshness, fierceness, severity, austerity*: Stoicorum, Cic. (3) of other things, *harshness, difficulty*: rerum, Cic.; iudicialis verborum, Cic.

aspernātio -ōnis, f. *contempt*: Cic.

aspernor -ari, dep. *to despise, reject, spurn*: aspernatur dolorem ut malum, Cic.; amicitiam alicuius, Cic.; consilia, Liv.; honorem, Tac.

aspĕro -are, *to make rough.* LIT., **a,** glacialis hiems aquilonibus asperat undas, *make stormy,* Verg.: **b,** *to sharpen, whet*: sagittas ossibus, Tac. TRANSF., *to excite, arouse*: aliquem in saevitiam, Tac.

aspersio -ōnis, f. *a sprinkling*: aquae, Cic.

aspersus -ūs, m. *a sprinkling*: Plin.

aspĭcĭo -spĭcĕre -spexi -spectum (ad/specio).
(1) *to look at, behold.* LIT., lucem aspicere vix possum, *endure the light of day, live,* Cic.; absol.: aspice, *look,* Verg.; esp. *to survey, inspect*: tabulas, Cic.; also *to look straight in the face, to withstand, confront*: aliquem in acie, Nep.; hostem aspicere non possunt, Cic.
TRANSF., **a,** *to investigate, consider*: neque tanta est in rebus obscuritas, ut eas non penitus vir ingenio cernat, si modo aspexerit, Cic.; res sociorum, Liv.: **b,** of places, *to look towards, face*: ea pars Britanniae quae Hiberniam aspicit, Tac.
(2) inch., *to catch sight of, perceive*: simulac Lentulum aspexit, Cic.; Pl., Ov.

aspīrātĭo -ōnis, f. (1) *a breathing*: aëris, Cic. (2) *exhalation*: terrarum, Cic. (3) *the pronunciation of the letter H, aspiration*: Cic., Quint.

aspīro -are, *to breathe, blow upon.*
(1) intransit. LIT., pulmones se contrahunt aspirantes, *exhaling,* Cic.; aspirant aurae in noctem, *towards evening,* Verg.; tibia aspirat choro, Hor. TRANSF., **a,** *to be favourable to, assist*: aspiravit nemo eorum, Cic.; vos aspirate canenti, Verg.: **b,** *to climb up to, to endeavour to obtain, to reach to*: bellica laude ad Africanum aspirare nemo potest, Cic.; nec equis aspirat Achillis, Verg.
(2) transit. LIT., Iuno ventos aspirat eunti, *gives them a favourable wind,* Verg. TRANSF., *to infuse*: divinum amorem dictis, Verg.; Quint.

aspis -idis, f. (ἀσπίς), *an adder, asp*: Cic.

asportātĭo -ōnis, f. *a taking away, carrying off*: signorum, Cic.

asporto -are (abs/porto), *to carry off, take away*: multa de suis rebus secum, Cic.; abreptam ex eo loco virginem secum, Cic.

asprēta -orum, n. pl. (asper), *rough, uneven places*: Liv.

Assărăcus -i, m. (Ἀσσάρακος), *a mythical king of Phrygia, son of Tros, brother of Ganymede, grandfather of Anchises*: Assaraci nurus, *Venus,* Ov.; Assaraci tellus, *Troy,* Hor.

asser -ĕris, m. (connected with ²adsero), *a stake, a pole*: Pl., Caes. Esp. *a pole for carrying a litter*: Suet.

assŭla -ae, f. *a shaving, chip*: Pl., Cat.

assŭlātim, adv. (assula), *in shivers or splinters*: Pl.

assŭlōsē, adv. (assula), *splinter-wise*: Plin.

assus -a -um (perhaps connected with areo), *dried.* LIT., *roasted*: Pl.; assum vitulinum, *roast veal,* Cic. TRANSF., (1) of bathing: sol, *basking in the sun* without being anointed, Cic.; n. pl. as subst. **assa,** *a sweating bath*: Cic. (2) nutrix, *a dry-nurse,* Juv.

Assўrĭa -ae, f. (Ἀσσυρία), *a country in Asia, between Media, Mesopotamia, and Babylonia.* Adj. and subst. **Assўrĭus** -a -um, *Assyrian, an Assyrian*; poet. for *Median, Phrygian, Indian,* etc.

ast=at; q.v.; used in old laws, also in Pl., Verg., Juv.; esp. before a word beginning with a vowel.

Asta -ae, f. (Ἄστα), *a town in Hispania Baetica* (now *Mesa de Asta*).
¶ Hence adj. **Astensis** -e, *of* or *belonging to Asta.*

Astăcus -i, m. *father of Melanippus.*
¶ Hence **Astăcĭdēs** -ae, m. *son of Astacus,* i.e. *Melanippus.*

Astăpa -ae, f. *a town in Hispania Baetica* (now *Estepa*).

Astērĭa -ae, f. and **-ĭē** -ēs, f. (Ἀστερίη). (1) *daughter of Polus and Phoebe.* (2) *daughter of the Titan Coeus, who was changed into a quail and then into an island* (*called Ortygia because of her, and later Delos*). (3) (Asterie), *a woman's name*: Hor.

Astraea -ae, f. (Ἀστραία), *Astraea, goddess of justice, who left the earth in the iron age, and was placed among the stars under the name Virgo.*

astrŏlŏgĭa -ae, f. (ἀστρολογία), *astronomy*: Cic.

astrŏlŏgus -i, m. (ἀστρολόγος). (1) *an astronomer*: Cic. (2) *an astrologer*: Cic., Juv.

astrum -i, n. (ἄστρον), *a star, a constellation.*
LIT., cognitio astrorum, Cic.; with reference to fortune: astrum natale, Hor.
TRANSF., (1) poet., of *any great height*: turris educta ad astra, Verg. (2) of *glory, immortality*: tollere in astra, Cic.; ex astris decidere, Cic.; sic itur ad astra, *thus is immortality gained,* Verg.

astu, n. indecl. (ἄστυ), *a city,* esp. *Athens*: Ter., Cic.

Astūra -ae (Ἄστυρα), *a river in Latium, with an island of the same name at its mouth.*

asturco -ōnis, m. *an Asturian horse*: Plin., Sen.

Astŭrĭa -ae, f. *a region in Hispania Tarraconensis*; adj. **Astŭrĭcus** -a -um, *Asturian*; **Astŭrĭca** -ae, f. *the capital of Asturia* (now *Astorga*); adj. and subst. **Astur** -uris, *Asturian, an Asturian.*

astus -ūs, m. (generally used in abl. sing.), *cleverness, adroitness, cunning*: Pl., Verg., Tac.

astūtĭa -ae, f. (astutus), *adroitness, craft*; in plur. *cunning tricks*: Pl., Cic.

astūtus -a -um (astus), *adroit, clever*; esp. in bad sense, *cunning, crafty*: Pl., Cic., Hor.
¶ Hence adv. (with compar. and superl.) **astutē,** *cunningly*: Pl., Cic. L.

Astўăgēs -is, m. (Ἀστυάγης). (1) *King of Media, grandfather of the elder Cyrus.* (2) *an enemy of Perseus, changed by him into stone.*

Astўănax -actis, m. (Ἀστυάναξ). (1) *son of Hector and Andromache.* (2) *a tragic actor of Cicero's time.*

Astўpalaea -ae, f. (Ἀστυπάλαια), *an island near Crete.*
¶ Hence **Astўpălaeensis** -is, m. *an inhabitant of the island*; adj. **Astўpălaeĭcus** -a -um or **Astўpălēĭus** -a -um, *belonging to Astypalaea.*

ăsȳlum -i, n. (ἄσυλον), *a sanctuary, place of refuge, asylum*: Cic.; templa quae asyla Graeci appellant, Liv.; lucus asyli, Tac.

ăsymbŏlus -a -um (ἀσύμβολος), *contributing nothing to the cost of an entertainment*: Ter.

at (ast), conj., *but, moreover.*
(1) to introduce an idea different from, but not entirely opposed to, one that has gone before: una (navis) cum Nasidianis profugit, at ex reliquis una praemissa Massiliam, Caes. Esp. to mark a surprising development in narrative, or transition to an appeal, expression of emotion, etc.: at videte hominis intolerabilem audaciam, Cic.;

at per deos immortales quid est quod dici possit? Cic.

(2) to express an idea entirely opposed to the preceding one: brevis a natura nobis vita data est; at memoria bene redditae vitae sempiterna, Cic.; strengthened: at contra, Lucr., Cic.; at etiam, Pl., Cic.; at vero, Cic. Esp.: **a**, to introduce an imaginary objection in an argument, *but, you may say*: At sumus, inquint, civitatis participes, Cic.; strengthened: at enim, Cic. Also: **b**, to answer an imaginary objection, *but, I reply*: factumne sit? at constat, Cic.

(3) restrictive, esp. after a negative, *but at least, yet at least*: si minus in praesens, at in posteritatem, Cic.

Ătābŭlus -i, m. *a hot wind in Apulia, the sirocco*: Hor., Plin.

Ătălanta -ae and -ē -ēs, f. ('Αταλάντη), *a maiden of Boeotia, famous for her speed in running; Milanion, or, according to other accounts, Hippomenes, finally beat her in a race and married her.* Adj. **Ătălantaeus** or -tēus -a, m. *of or belonging to Atalanta.*

ătăt, attat, attatae, attattatae, etc. (ἀτταται), an interjection expressive of pain, astonishment, fear, warning, etc., *oh! ah! alas!* Pl., Ter.

ătăvus -i, m. (**1**) *the father of the great-great-grandfather (abavus) or great-great-grandmother*: Cic.; (opp. adnepos). (**2**) gen., atavi, pl., *ancestors*: Maecenas atavis edite regibus, Hor.

Ātella -ae, f. *a very ancient city of Campania.* Adj. **Ātellānus** -a -um; esp. Atellana fabella, or simply **Ātellāna** -ae, f. *a species of popular farce, long popular in Rome*: Liv., Juv.

¶ Hence subst. **Ātellānus** -i, m. *a player in these farces*, and adj. **Ātellānius** -a -um or **Ātellānĭcus** -a -um, *pertaining to them.*

āter atra atrum, *black, dark (dead black*, opp. albus, while niger is *shining black).*

LIT., nemus, Verg.; dens, Hor.; mare, *stormy*, Hor.; alba discernere et atra non posse, Cic.; poet.=atratus, *clothed in black*: lictores, Hor.

TRANSF., (**1**) *dark, gloomy, sad, unfortunate*: mors, cura, Hor.; atri dies, *in the Roman calendar, those on which the republic had suffered a great misfortune*, Liv. (**2**) *malicious, poisonous*: atro dente petere aliquem, Hor.

Ăthāmānĭa -ae, f. ('Αθαμανία), *a region in Epirus.*

¶ Hence **Ăthāmānes** -um, m. *the inhabitants of Athamania.*

Ăthāmās -antis, m. ('Αθάμας), *son of Aeolus and king of Thessaly, father of Phrixus and Helle, Melicerta and Learchus.*

¶ Hence **Ăthāmantēus** -a -um: aurum, *the golden fleece of Phrixus*, Mart.; **Ăthămantĭădes** -ae, m. *son of Athamas*: Ov.; **Ăthămantis** -idis, f. *daughter of Athamas*, i.e. *Helle*: Ov.

Ăthēnae -ārum, f. ('Αθῆναι), *Athens*; meton., *learning*: Juv.

¶ Hence adj. **Ăthēnaeus** -a -um, *Athenian*; n. as subst. **Athēnaeum** -i, *a temple of Minerva (Athene) at Athens*; adj. and subst. **Ăthēnĭensis** -e, *Athenian, an Athenian.*

Ăthēnĭo -ōnis, m. *a Sicilian shepherd, leader of slaves in a rebellion about* 100 B.C.

ăthĕos and **ăthĕus** -i, m. (ἄθεος), *an atheist*: Cic.

Ăthĕsis, acc. -sim, abl. -si, m. ("Αθεσις), *a river in N. Italy (now Adige.)*

athlēta -ae, m. (ἀθλητής), *one who contends in the public games, wrestler, athlete*: Cic., Liv.

athlētĭcus -a -um (ἀθλητικός), *relating to an athlete*: Cels.; adv. **athlētĭcē**, *athletically*: Pl.

Ăthŏs or **Ăthō** or **Ăthōn**, acc. -ō or -on or -ōnem, dat. -ō, abl. -ōne, m. *a mountain at the end of the peninsula of Chalcidice, on the Strymonian gulf.*

Ătīlĭus -a -um, *name of a Roman gens*, esp. M. Atilius Regulus (*see* Regulus). Adj. **Ătīlĭānus** -a -um.

Ătīna -ae, f. ("Ατινα), *a town in Latium* (still called *Atina).*

¶ Hence adj. and subst. **Ătīnas** -ātis, *belonging to Atina, or an inhabitant of it.*

Ătlās -antis, m. ("Ατλας). (**1**) *a high mountain of Mauretania, in Africa, on which the sky was supposed to rest.* (**2**) *a mythical king and giant, son of Iapetus and Clymene, king of Mauretania, changed into Mount Atlas by Perseus.* (**3**) meton., *a very tall man*, or (ironically) *a dwarf* (Juv.).

¶ Hence **Atlantĭădēs** -ae, m. *a descendant of Atlas*; esp. *Mercury (son of Maia, grandson of Atlas)*, or *Hermaphroditus (son of Mercury and great-grandson of Atlas)*; **Atlantis** -idis, f. *a female descendant of Atlas*; esp. *Electra*: Ov.; *Calypso*: Tib.; adj. **Atlantĭcus** -a -um, *connected with Mount Atlas*: mare, *the Atlantic ocean*; also **Atlantēus** -a -um: finis, *Libyan*, Hor.

ătŏmus -i, f. (ἄτομος), *that which is incapable of division, an atom*: Cic.

atque (usually before vowel or h) and **ac** (usually before consonant), *and, and also.*

Joining single words. (**1**) in gen.: **a**, between closely related words: spargere ac disseminare, Cic.; or contrasted words: nobiles atque ignobiles, Sall.: **b**, *and moreover, and even*, adding a new point: alii intra moenia atque in sinu urbis sunt hostes, Sall.; with the pron., hic, is, idem, etc.: negotium magnum est navigare atque id mense Quintili, *and especially*, Cic.; so: atque etiam, Cic. (**2**) with comparisons: **a**, with words expressing similarity, as aeque, aequus, idem, item, iuxta, par, proxime, similis, similiter, talis, totidem, as: pariter hoc atque alias res, Pl., Cic.: **b**, with words expressing dissimilarity, as aliter, aliorsum, alius, contra, contrarius, dissimilis, secus, *than, from*: aliter atque est, Ter., Cic.: **c**, with comparatives, for quam, *than*: artius atque hedera procera astringitur ilex, Hor.: **d**, simul atque, *as soon as*, Cic.; *see also* under simul.

Joining sentences or clauses, *and indeed, and so*. (**1**) in gen.: atque illi omnes sine dubitatione condemnant, Cic. (**2**) to join a more important thought, *and even*: id estne numerandum in bonis? Ac maximis quidem, Cic. (**3**) to introduce a wish, usually preceding utinam: Cic. (**4**) to introduce an adversative clause, alone or preceding tamen: dissimilis inter se ac tamen laudandos, Cic.

(5) to introduce a final clause: ac ne sine causa videretur edixisse, Cic. (6) in narration, *and then*; sometimes *and suddenly*: Pl., Verg. (7) at the end of a speech or treatise: ac de primo quidem officii fonte diximus, Cic.

In particular connexions and phrases. (1) alius atque alius, *now this, now that*, Liv.; also: unus atque alter, Sall., Tac. (2) etiam atque etiam, *again and again*, Lucr. (3) with other conjunctions; after et: non minis et vi ac metu, Cic.; after que: submoverique atque in castra redigi, Liv.; with nec: Mart.; repeated in poetry: atque deos atque astra, Verg.

atqui, conj. (at/qui), *nevertheless, notwithstanding*. (1) gen.: atqui non ego te frangere persequor, Hor.; sometimes confirmatory rather than adversative, *indeed, certainly*: Cic. Often introducing a conditional clause: atqui si, *but if*, Ter., Cic.; or an answer in conversation, *but in fact*: Hor., Cic. (2) in logical conclusions, to introduce the minor premise, *but now, now*: Cic.

ātrāmentum -i, n. (ater), *any black fluid*: sepiae, Cic.; *ink*: Cic.; *shoemaker's black*: sutorium atramentum, Cic.

ātrātus -a -um (ater), *clothed in black, in mourning*: Cic., Tac.

Atrax -ācis (Ἄτραξ), *a city in Thessaly*.
¶ Hence **Atrăcīdēs** -ae, m. *the Thessalian Caeneus*: Ov.; **Atrăcis** -ĭdis, f. *Hippodamia*: Ov.

Atrĕbătes -um, m. *a people in Gallia Belgica*; sing. **Atrĕbas** -bătis, m.: Caes.

Atrēus -ei, m. (Ἀτρεύς), *son of Pelops, king of Argos and Mycenae, father of Agamemnon and Menelaus*.
¶ Hence **Atrīdēs** or **Atrīdă** -ae, m. *a son of Atreus*; plur. Atridae, *Agamemnon and Menelaus*.

ātriensis -is, m. (atrium), *overseer of the atrium, head slave, steward*: Pl., Cic.

ātriŏlum -i, n. (dim. of atrium), *a little atrium, an ante-chamber*: Cic. L.

ātrĭtās -ātis, f. (ater), *blackness*: Pl.

ātrĭum -i, n. (perhaps connected with ater, as a place blackened by the smoke of the fire), *the hall or entrance room in a Roman house, into which opened the* ianua. Poet. plur. for sing.: Verg.; meton., *a house*: atria nostra, Ov.
TRANSF., of other halls, esp. *the hall of a temple or public building*: atrium Libertatis, Cic.; auctionarium, *an auctioneer's sale-room*, Cic.

ătrōcĭtās -ātis, f. (atrox). LIT., *frightfulness, cruelty*: ipsius facti atrocitas aut indignitas, Cic. TRANSF., of human character, speech, etc., *severity, harshness, barbarity*: invidiosa atrocitas verborum, Cic.; atrocitas ista quo modo in veterem Academiam inruperit, Cic.

Atrŏpŏs -i, f. (ἄτροπος, *not to be averted*), *one of the three Parcae or Fates, supposed to have the duty of cutting the thread of human life.*

ătrox -ōcis (from ater, as ferox from ferus), adj., with compar. and superl.
LIT., *terrible, fearful, cruel, horrible*: res scelesta, atrox, nefaria, Cic.; of war: proelium, Liv.; of the seasons: hora flagrantis Caniculae, Hor.

TRANSF., of human character; *harsh, fierce, morose, severe*: Agrippina semper atrox, Tac.; animus Catonis, *unbending*, Hor. So of speech, etc.: imperium, Liv.; atrocissimae litterae, Cic.; vehemens atque atrox orationis genus, Cic.
¶ Hence adv. (with compar. and superl.) **ătrōcĭtĕr**, *severely, harshly, cruelly*: Verri nimis atrociter minitans, Cic.

Atta -ae, m. *a Roman surname*; esp. *of the poet* T. Quinctius Atta (d. 77 B.C.).

attactus -ūs, m. (attingo), used only in abl. sing., *a touching, touch, contact*: Verg.

attăgēn -ēnis, m. (ἀτταγήν), *a bird, the black partridge*: Hor.; also **attăgēna** -ae, f.: Mart.

Attălus -i, m. (Ἄτταλος), *the name of several kings of Pergamum, the last of whom*, Attalus III, *left his territory to the Romans*.
¶ Hence adj. **Attălĭcus** -a -um, *belonging to Pergamum*: urbes, Hor. TRANSF., (1) *woven* or *adorned with gold*: vestes, tori, Prop. (2) in gen., *rich, splendid*: condiciones, Hor.

attămĕn or **at tămĕn**, conj. *but yet*: Caes., Cic., Ov.

attĕgĭa -ae, f. *a hut*: Juv.

attempĕro -are (ad/tempero), *to fit to, adjust to*: Sen.
¶ Hence adv. **attempĕrātē**, *in a fit or appropriate manner*: Ter.

attendo -tendĕre -tendi -tentum (ad/tendo). LIT., *to stretch to*. Usually transf., with animum (animos) or absol., *to direct the attention towards, attend to*. (1) with animum (animos): attendite animos ad ea quae consequuntur, Cic. (2) absol.: **a**, in gen.: diligenter attendite, Cic.: **b**, with what is attended to as object, or subject in passive: primum versum legis, Cic.; extrema pars attenditur, Cic.: **c**, with acc. and infin.: non attendere superius illud ea re a se esse concessum, Cic.: **d**, with ind. quest.: si paulo diligentius, quid de his rebus dicat attenderis, Cic.: **e**, with de and the abl.: animus tamen erit sollicitus, ut nihil possit de officiis legationis attendere, Cic.: **f**, with dat.: Plin. L., Suet.
¶ Hence partic. (with compar. and superl.) **attentus**, *attentive*: animus, Cic.; cogitatio, Cic.; auditor, Cic.; iudex, Cic.; esp. *careful of one's affairs or property*: attentus quaesitis, Hor.; paterfamilias, Hor.; attenta vita et rusticana, Cic.
Adv. (with compar. and superl.) **attentē**, *attentively, carefully*: audire, Cic.; cogitare, Cic., Hor.

attentĭo -ōnis, f. (attendo), *attentiveness, attention*: animi, or absol., Cic., Quint.

attento or **attempto** -are, *to try, test, essay*: ut praeteriri omnino fuerit satius quam attentatum deseri, Cic.; esp. (1) *to tamper with, try to corrupt*: classem, Cic. (2) *to attack*: aliquid lingua, Cic.; aliquem vi, Tac.

attĕnŭo -are, *to make thin, reduce*. LIT., corpus, Ov.; of number, *to lessen*: legio proeliis attenuata, Caes.; of strength, *to weaken*: vires diutino morbo attenuatae, Liv. TRANSF., curas, *diminish*, Ov.; insignem, *degrade*, Hor.
¶ Hence partic. **attĕnŭātus**, *made weak*. TRANSF., of style. (1) *abbreviated*: ipsa illa pro Roscio iuvenilis abundantia multa habet

attenuata, Cic. (2) *over-refined*: eius oratio nimia religione attenuata, Cic. (3) *unadorned, meagre.*

Adv. **attĕnŭātē**, *simply, without ornament*: dicere, Cic.

attĕro -tĕrĕre -trīvi (-tĕrŭi) -trītum. LIT., (1) *to rub against*: leniter caudam, Hor. (2) *to rub* or *wear away*: surgentes herbas, Verg. TRANSF., *to weaken, ruin*: opes, Sall.
¶ Hence partic. (with compar.) **attrītus** -a -um, *rubbed away, worn out*: Cic. TRANSF., frons, *shameless*: Juv.

attestor -ari, dep. *to attest, bear witness to*: Phaedr.

attexo -texĕre -texŭi -textum, *to weave* or *plait on* or *to.* LIT., loricae ex cratibus attexuntur, Caes. TRANSF., *to add*: vos ad id, quod erit immortale, partem attexitote mortalem, Cic.

Atthis -ĭdis, f. (Ἀτθίς), adj., *Attic, Athenian*: Mart.; as f. subst., *Attica*: Lucr.; *nightingale* or *swallow*: Mart.; *a friend of Sappho*: Ov.

Attĭca -ae, f. (Ἀττική), *Attica, the district of Greece containing Athens.*

atticisso -are (ἀττικίζω), *to imitate the Athenian mode of speaking*: Pl.

¹Attĭcus -a -um (Ἀττικός), *belonging to Attica* or *Athens, Attic, Athenian*: pelex, Philomela, Mart. Plur. as subst. **Attĭci** -orum, m. *the Athenians*: Phaedr.
Hence appell., with reference to art and literature, *of the Athenian school* or *standard*: stilus, Cic.; lepos, Mart. Plur. as subst. **Attĭci** -orum, m. *orators of the Attic school*: Cic.
Adv. **Atticē**, *in the Attic* or *Athenian manner*: dicere, Cic.

²Attĭcus, T. Pomponius, *the intimate friend of Cicero*, who received his surname of Atticus from his long residence in Athens.

attĭneo -tĭnēre -tĭnŭi -tentum (ad/teneo).
(1) transit., *to hold, keep.* LIT., dextram, Tac.; aliquem castris, carcere, publica custodia, Tac. TRANSF., simul Romanum et Numidam spe pacis, *to detain, amuse*, Sall.
(2) intransit., *to pertain to,* or *concern*, only in third person: quid istuc ad me attinet? Pl.; cetera quae ad colendam vitem attinebunt, Cic.; esp. in the expression, quod attinet ad aliquem or aliquid, *in respect to*: qui omnes, quod ad me attinet, vellem viverent, *as far as I am concerned*, Cic.; nihil attinet me plura scribere, *it is of no use*, Cic.

attingo -tingere -tĭgi -tactum (ad/tango), *to touch.*
LIT., (1) digito se caelum attigisse putare, Cic. (2) *to arrive at a place*: Italiam, Cic.; arces igneas, Hor. (3) of places, *to touch upon, border upon*: Cappadocia regio ea quae Ciliciam attingit, Cic. (4) *to attack, to strike*: Sulla quem primum hostes attigerant, Sall.; si digito quem attigisset, poenas dedisset, Cic. (5) *to touch,* in the sense, *to appropriate*: de praeda mea nec teruncium attigit, Cic.
TRANSF., (1) *to touch, affect*, of sensations: voluptas aut dolor aliquem attingit, Cic., Liv. (2) *to have to do with, to concern, resemble*: corporis similitudo attingit naturam animi, Cic.; attingere aliquem necessitudine, *to be closely connected with*, Cic. (3) *to handle, manage*: rempublicam, Cic.; Graecas litteras, Cic.; rem militarem, Caes. (4) in writing or speech, *to touch upon,* to *mention*: illam iniuriam non attingere, Cic.

Attis (**Atthis** and **Atys**) -ĭdis, m. *a Phrygian shepherd, beloved by Cybele.*

Attĭus=Accius; q.v.

attollo -tollĕre, *to raise up, lift up.*
LIT., vix prae lacrimis oculos, Liv.; minas, iras (of a snake raising its head in anger), Verg.; se attollere, *or* attolli, *to raise oneself,* Verg.; of buildings, *to erect, raise*: molem, Verg.; terra se attollere tandem visa, *to rise, appear*, Verg.
TRANSF., (1) *to elevate, excite*: animos ad spem consulatus, Liv. (2) *to exalt*: rempublicam bello armisque, Tac.

attondĕo -tondēre -tondi -tonsum. LIT., *to cut, clip*: vitem, *to prune*, Verg.; virgulta, *to crop*, Verg. TRANSF., (1) *to make less, diminish*: Cic. poet. (2) *to cheat, fleece*: Pl.

attŏno -tŏnare -tŏnŭi -tŏnĭtum, *to strike with thunder, stun, make senseless*: Ov.
¶ Hence partic. **attŏnĭtus** -a -um, *struck by thunder*; hence (1) *stunned, terrified, senseless*: magna pars integris corporibus attoniti concidunt, Liv. (2) *inspired, frantic*: vates, Hor.; attonitae Baccho matres, Verg.

attorquĕo -ēre, *to whirl, swing upward*: Verg.

attrăho -trăhĕre -traxi -tractum, *to draw to, attract.*
LIT., of things: magnes lapis, qui ferrum ad se adliciat et attrahat, Cic. Of persons, *to drag*: tribunos attrahi ad se iussit, Liv.
TRANSF., *to attract*: nihil esse quod ad se rem ullam tam adliciat et tam attrahat quam ad amicitiam similitudo, Cic.

attrectātus -ū, m. (attrecto), *a handling, touching*: Pacuvius ap. Cic.

attrecto -are (ad/tracto), *to touch, handle.*
LIT., esp.: **a**, *to touch unlawfully, in an improper manner*: libros (Sibyllinos) contaminatis manibus attrectare, Cic.: **b**, *to lay hands on, to appropriate*: gazas, Liv.
TRANSF., blanditia popularis aspicitur, non attrectatur, Cic.

attrĕpĭdo -are, *to stumble along*: Pl.

attrĭbŭo -ŭĕre -ŭi -ūtum, *to allot to, assign to.*
LIT., (1) in gen.: servos, pastores armat atque iis equos attribuit, Caes. (2) of money, *to assign*: si modo attribuetur, quantum debetur, Cic.; esp. of money paid from the public treasury: pecunia attributa, numerata est, Cic. (3) of business, duties, etc., *to assign*: attribuit nos trucidandos Cethego, Cic.; of a military command: oppidum civibus Romanis, Caes. (4) of a country, *to annex, subject*: insulae, quae erant a Sulla Rhodiis attributae, Cic.
TRANSF., (1) *to give, cause*: summus timor quem mihi natura pudorque meus attribuit, Cic. (2) *to add*: ad amissionem amicorum miseriam nostram, Cic. (3) *to ascribe, impute*: bonos exitus diis immortalibus, Cic. (4) *to impose* as a tax: Liv.
¶ Hence n. of passive partic. as subst. **attrĭbūtum** -i, *a predicate, attribute*: Cic.

attrĭbūtĭo -ōnis, f. (attribuo). (1) *the assignment of a debt*: Cic. L. (2) rhet. t. t., *an attribute*: Cic.

attrītus -a -um, partic. from attero; q.v.

Ătÿs (**Attÿs**) -ўos, m. (Ἄτυς, Ἄττυς). (1) *a son of Hercules and Omphale, father of Tyrrhenus and Lydus, myth. ancestor of the Lydian kings.* (2) *the founder of the gens Atia.* (3) *a son of Alba, king of the Albani.*

au, interj., *oh!* Pl.

auceps -cŭpis, m. (for aviceps, from avis and capio). LIT., *a fowler, bird-catcher*: Pl., Hor. TRANSF., (**1**) *a spy, eavesdropper*: nostris dictis, Pl.; voluptatum, Cic. (**2**) *a quibbling critic, caviller*: syllabarum, Cic.

auctārĭum -i, n. (augeo), *an increase*: Pl.

auctĭfĭcus -a -um, *increasing*: Lucr.

auctĭo -ōnis, f. (augeo), *an increasing*; hence, from the bidding, *an auction*: auctionem facere, constituere, *to appoint an auction*, Cic.; praedicare, proscribere, Cic.; proponere, *to announce publicly*, Quint.; proferre, *to put off*, Cic.

auctĭōnārĭus -a -um (auctio), *relating to an auction*: atrium, *auction-room*, Cic.

auctĭōnor -ari, dep. (auctio), *to hold an auction*: Cic.

auctĭto -are (freq. of augeo), *to increase very much*: pecunias, Tac.

aucto -are=auctito: Pl., Lucr.

auctŏr -ōris, m. (augeo), *one that gives increase*. So (**1**) *an originator, causer, doer*. LIT., *progenitor, ancestor, founder of a family*: praeclarus auctor nobilitatis tuae, Cic.; also *producer of a work of art or literature*: templi, *architect*, Liv.; carminis, *author*, Hor. TRANSF., *cause, author*: incendii, Cic.; vulneris, Verg.; esp.: **a**, *the originator of a proposal or undertaking, leader, beginner*: nec auctor quamvis audaci facinori deerat, Liv.; me auctore, *at my request*, Cic.; auctor interficiendi alicuius, Cic.; ille legibus (dat.) contra auspicia ferendis auctor, Cic.; ad instituendam (rem), Cic.; in restituendo auctorem fuisse, Cic.; alicui auctorem esse, *to advise, recommend*: semper senatui auctor pacis fui, Cic.; foll. by ut *or* ne with the subj.: Cic.: **b**, *the author of a piece of information, warrant for its truth, authority*: certis auctoribus comperisse, Cic.; malus auctor Latinitatis, Cic.; Cratippo auctore, *on the authority of Cratippus*, Cic.; Homerus optimus auctor, Cic.; auctor rerum Romanarum, *historian*, Cic.; hence, auctorem esse, *to answer for, state positively*: nec pauci sunt auctores Cn. Flavium scribam libros protulisse, Cic.

(**2**) *a backer, supporter*. Esp.: **a**, of public measures: le;is, Liv.; multarum legum aut auctor aut dissuasor, Cic.; auctores fiunt patres, *the senators sanction a law*, Cic.: **b**, *bail, surety, or guarantee of a right*: a malo auctore emere, Cic.: **c**, of a trustee, guardian, etc., *approver, sanctioner*: quod mulier sine tutore auctore promiserit, *without the approval of her guardian*, Cic.: **d**, fig., *champion*: civitatis, salutis, Cic.

auctōrāmentum -i, n. (auctoro). (**1**) *a contract*: Sen. (**2**) *wages*: Cic.

auctōrĭtās -ātis, f. (auctor), *giving of increase*; hence, *origination, responsibility, support, power*.

(**1**) *support, backing, example, lead*: maiorum auctoritas, Cic.; auctoritatem sequi, Cic.; hominum consilia et auctoritates, Cic.; auctoritate Orgetorigis permoti, *advice*, Caes. Esp.: **a**, *authority, warrant for views or information*: auctoritatem esse in eo testimonio, Cic.; meton., *authoritative records*: auctoritates ac litteras, Cic.: **b**, political *sanction*: populi Romani, Cic.;

conlegii, Liv.; esp. auctoritas senatus, either gen., *sanction of the senate*: sine auctoritate senatus, Cic.; or t. t., *a resolution agreed by the senate, but less official than a* senatus consultum: si quis huic senatus consulto intercessisset, auctoritas perscriberetur, Cic.

(**2**) *power conferred, rights, command*: legatos cum auctoritate mittere, *authorization*, Cic.; of legal *title*: usus et auctoritas fundi, Cic.

(**3**) (most often) gen., *influence, authority, prestige*: of a person: auctoritatem habere apud aliquem, Cic.; auctoritatem restituere, levare, amittere, Cic.; meton., *a person in authority, an influential person*: Cic.

(**4**) of things: legum, Cic.; honestatis, Cic.; orationis, Cic.

auctōro -are (auctor), *to bind* or *hire for money*; esp. with reflex. object or in pass., *to bind* or *hire oneself*: necari auctoratus, Hor.; eo pignore velut auctoratum sibi proditorem ratus est, Liv.

auctumnus=autumnus; q.v.

auctus -ūs, m. (augeo), *an increase, enlargement, growth*: corporis, Lucr.; fluminum, Tac.; imperii, Tac.; maximis auctibus crescere, Liv.

aucŭpātĭo -ōnis, f. (aucupor), *fowling, bird-catching*: Quint.

aucŭpātōrĭus -a -um (aucupor), *relating to fowling*: Plin.

aucŭpĭum -i, n. (auceps), *bird-catching, fowling*. LIT., vitam propagare aucupio, Cic. Meton., *the birds caught*: Cat. TRANSF., *hunting after anything*: delectationis, *after pleasure*, Cic.; esp. (**1**) *eavesdropping*: Pl. (**2**) aucupia verborum, *cavilling, quibbling*, Cic.

aucŭpo -are=aucupor; q.v.: Pl.

aucŭpor -ari, dep. (auceps). LIT., *to catch birds*: Varr. TRANSF., *to watch out for, lie in wait for*: verba, Cic.; errores hominum, Cic.; inanem rumorem, Cic.; tranquillitates, *calm weather*, Cic. L.

audācĭa -ae, f. (audax). (**1**) in good sense, *courage, daring*: audacia in bello, Sall., Liv., Tac. (**2**) (more often) in bad sense, *audacity, impudence, temerity*: audacia et impudentia fretus, Cic.; alicuius audaciam debilitare, Cic.; frangere, Liv.; contundere et frangere, Cic.; plur.: audaciae, *audacious deeds*, Cic.

audax -ācis, adj. (with compar. and superl.) (audeo), *bold*, in a good or bad sense, of persons or things. (**1**) in a good sense, *daring, courageous*: audacibus adnue coeptis, Verg. (**2**) (more often) in bad sense, *audacious, rash, foolhardy*: **a**, of persons: Verres homo audacissimus atque amentissimus, Cic.; audax in convocandis hominibus et armandis, Cic.: **b**, of things: audax facinus, Ter. TRANSF., of language, *bold, unusual*: verba, Quint.

Adv. **audactĕr** (sometimes **audācĭtĕr**) (with compar. and superl.), *boldly*, in good or bad sense: Pl., Cic.

audentĭa -ae, f. (audens), *boldness, courage*, in good sense: Tac.

audĕo audēre ausus sum (connected with avidus), *to be daring*, *to dare, venture, bring oneself to*. Absol., *to be daring*: quod sperant, quod audent, omne Caesari acceptum referre possunt, Cic.; adversus **Neronem** ausus, Tac.; audere in proelia, Verg. More often *to dare*, etc., followed by (**1**) infin.: aude contemnere opes, Verg.; audeo dicere, *I venture to assert*, Cic. (**2**) object in acc. (esp. pronoun in neuter): tantum facinus, Liv.; nihil, Caes.; proelium, aciem, Tac.; ausurum se in tribunis, quod princeps familiae suae ausus in regibus esset, Liv.; pro vita maiora audere probavi, Verg. ¶ Hence partic. (with compar. and superl.) **audens** -entis, *daring, bold*: Verg. Adv. in compar. **audentius**, *more boldly*: Tac.

audĭentĭa -ae, f. (audio), *hearing, listening, attention*: alicui audientiam facere, *to get a hearing for anyone*, Cic., Liv.

audĭo -ire (connected with auris), *to hear*.

(**1**) in gen.: **a**, *to have the power of hearing*: audiendi sensu carere, Cic.: **b**, *to hear a thing* (acc.) or *a person* (acc.): clamorem, Caes.; galli cantum, Cic.; multa falsa de me audierunt, Cic.; with double acc., te, ut spero, propediem censorem audiemus, Cic. With acc. of person and infin.: saepe hoc maiores natu dicere audivi, Cic.; with acc. and partic.: idque Socratem audio dicentem, Cic. So pass., *to be heard*: nihil habeo praeter auditum, *beyond what I have heard*, Cic.: **c**, *to learn by hearing*; with acc. and infin.: hoc idem fuisse, Cic.; with ind. quest. clause: audire enim cupio quid non probes, Cic.; the person from whom a thing is heard is put in the abl. with ab or de: Cic. So pass., with infin.: Bibulus nondum audiebatur esse in Syria, Cic. L.; audito venisse nuntium, *it having been heard that*, Tac.

(**2**) *to listen to*: **a**, gen.: aliquem lubenter studioseque, Cic.; of judges, *to hear a case*: audire de ambitu, Cic.; of pupils, *to listen to a master, to attend the classes or lectures of a professor*: annum iam audire Cratippum, Cic.: **b**, *to listen to* (*and grant*) *requests*: preces, Cic.: **c**, *to listen to, and believe* a person or thing: si fabulas audire volumus, Cic.; audio, *I believe it*, Cic.: **d**, *to obey, to follow*: aliquem amicissime monentem, Cic. TRANSF., audit currus habenas, Verg.

(**3**) *to be called* (like Gr. ἀκούω): Matutine pater, seu Iane libentius audis, Hor.; bene audire, *to be well spoken of*; a propinquis, Cic. ¶ Hence partic. **audiens** -entis. (**1**) as adj., *obedient*, esp. in phrase: dicto audientem esse, *to obey*, Caes., Cic., Liv. (**2**) as subst., *a hearer*: Cic., Liv.

audītĭo -ōnis, f. (audio). (**1**) *hearing, listening*: aliquid multa lectione atque auditione adsequi, Cic. (**2**) *hearsay report*: levem auditionem habere pro re comperta, Cic.; plur.: fictae auditiones, Cic.

audītor -ōris, m. (audio), *a hearer, listener, scholar*: alicui auditorem venire, Cic.

audītōrĭum -i, n. (audio), *a place of audience, lecture-room, court of justice*, etc.: Tac.; *a school*: Quint.; *circle of listeners*: Plin. L.

audītus -ūs, m. (audio). Gen., *hearing, the sense of hearing*: Cic. Esp., *something heard, a report*: Tac.

aufĕro auferre abstŭli ablātum (ab/fero).

(**1**) in gen., *to carry away, carry off, remove*. LIT., inter manus e convicio tamquam e proelio auferri, Cic.; se e conspectu alicuius,

Cic.; auferor in scopulos, Ov. TRANSF., **a**, *to draw away, seduce*: ne te auferant aliorum consilia, Cic.: **b**, *to carry off, to obtain*: tantum abstulit quantum petiit, Cic.; responsum ab aliquo, Cic.: **c**, *to put aside, cease from*: aufer abhinc lacrimas, Lucr.

(**2**) in a bad sense, *to make away with, carry off, steal*. LIT., of persons: multa palam domum, Cic.; pecuniam de aerario, Cic. L. TRANSF., hi ludi xv dies auferent, Cic.; mors Achillem abstulit, Hor.; spem, Tac.; somnos, Hor.; sometimes in favourable sense: curas, Hor.

Aufīdēna -ae, f. *a town in Samnium* (now *Alfidena*).

Aufĭdĭus -a -um, *name of a Roman gens*, esp. *Cn. Aufidius, author of a Greek History*. Adj. **Aufĭdĭānus** -a -um.

Aufĭdus -i, m. *a river in Apulia* (now *Ofanto*).

aufŭgĭo -fŭgĕre -fūgi (ab/fugio), *to flee away*: Cic., Liv., Tac.; with acc. object, *to flee, escape from*: Cic.

Augē -ēs, f. (Αὔγη), *daughter of Aleus and Neaera, mother of Telephus by Hercules*.

Augēas or **Augĭas** -ae, m. (Αὐγείας), *king of Elis*, the cleansing of whose stable, which had not been cleansed for thirty years, was one of the labours of Hercules.

augĕo augēre auxi auctum (connected with αὔξω and αὐξάνω), *to make grow, to increase*.

(**1**) *to enlarge*. LIT., cibus corpus, Lucr.; rem, *property*, Hor., Cic.; numerum legatorum, Cic.; has munitiones, Caes.; of rivers, *to cause to rise*, gen. in pass., augeri= *to be swollen*: amnis nimbis hiemalibus auctus, Ov. TRANSF., vitium ventris et gutturis, Cic.; populi Romani imperium, Cic.; benevolentiam, Cic.; luctum, Cic.; in speech, *to extol, set forth*: hostium vim et copias et felicitatem, Cic.

(**2**) *to enrich with, furnish with*: aer umorem conligens terram auget imbribus, Cic.; cives suos copia rerum, Cic.; augeri cognomento Augustae, Tac.

(**3**) (rare), intransit., *to grow, increase*: Sall., Cat. ¶ Hence partic. **auctus** -a -um, used as adj. only in compar., *increased, enlarged, enriched*: maiestas auctior, Liv.; socii honore auctiores, Caes.

augesco -ĕre (inch. of augeo), *to begin to grow, to increase*: quae (uva) et suco terrae et calore solis augescens primo et peracerba gustu, Cic. TRANSF., *to increase in strength*: cum hostium res tantis augescere rebus cerneret, Liv.

augmĕn -ĭnis, n. (augeo), *an increase, growth*: Lucr.

augur -ŭris, c. (avis), *an augur, soothsayer, seer*. LIT., *member of a special college at Rome*: Cic. TRANSF., acquae augur annosa cornix, *prophetess of rain*, Hor.; nocturnae imaginis augur, *interpreter*, Ov.

augŭrālis -e (augur), *relating to an augur or augury*: cena, Cic. N. as subst. **augŭrāle** -is, *the part of the Roman camp where the auspices were taken*: Tac. TRANSF., *the general's tent*: Quint.

augŭrātĭo -ōnis, f. (auguro), *divining, soothsaying*: Cic.

augŭrātus -ūs, m. (auguro), *the office of an augur*: Cic., Tac.

augŭrĭum -i, n. (augur), *the office and work of an augur, the observation and interpretation of omens, augury.* LIT., agere, Cic.; capere, Suet.; salutis, *an augury in time of peace* (to inquire if it were permitted to pray to the gods *de salute reipublicae*), Cic. Also of the *omen* obtained: accipere, Liv.; nuntiare, Liv.
TRANSF., *any kind of prophecy*: o mea frustra semper verissima auguria rerum futurarum, Cic.; Apollo augurium citharamque dabat, Verg.; *presentiment*: inhaeret in mentibus quasi saeculorum quoddam augurium futurorum, Cic.; Ov.

augŭrĭus -a -um (augur), *relating to an augur*: ius, Cic.

augŭro -are (augur). LIT., *to act as an augur, take auguries for*: sacerdotes salutem populi auguranto, Cic.; locus auguratur, *the place is consecrated by auguries*, Cic.; augurato (abl. absol.), *after taking the auguries*, Liv. TRANSF., oculis investigans astute augura, Pl.; esp. *to have a foreboding* or *presentiment*: praesentit animus et augurat quodammodo, quae futura sit suavitas, Cic.

augŭror -ari, dep. (augur). LIT., *to act as an augur, to foretell by auguries*: ex passerum numero belli Troiani annos, Cic. TRANSF., (1) *to foretell*: alicui mortem, Cic. (2) *to guess*: quantum auguror coniectura aut opinione, Cic.; cum ex nomine istius, quid in provincia facturus esset, perridicule homines augurarentur, Cic.

Augusta -ae, f. (1) *a name for the wife, daughter, mother*, or *sister of the Roman emperor*. (2) *name of several towns named after the emperor*, esp. Augusta Taurinorum (*Turin*), Augusta Praetoria (*Aosta*), Augusta Treverorum (*Trier, Trèves*), Augusta Emerita (*Mérida*), Augusta Vindelicorum (*Augsburg*).

Augustālis -e (Augustus), *belonging to or in honour of the Emperor Augustus*: ludi, Tac.; sodales, *priests of his cult*, Tac.

Augustŏdūnum -i, *town of the Aedui in Gaul* (now *Autun*).

¹augustus -a -um, adj. (with compar. and superl.) (augeo). (1) *consecrated, holy*: Eleusis sancta illa et augusta, Cic.; Verg., Liv., Ov. (2) *majestic, dignified*: vestis augustissima, Liv.; species, Liv.
Adv. (with compar.) **augustē**, *reverentially*: auguste et sancte venerari deos, Cic.

²Augustus -i, m. *a name granted to Octavianus as emperor in 27 B.C., and later to all subsequent Roman emperors*.

³Augustus -a -um, *relating to Augustus*: pax, Ov.; mensis, *August*, formerly called Sextilis, changed to Augustus in honour of the emperor.

¹aula -ae, f. (αὐλή). LIT., *the fore-court of a Greek house*: Hor.; *a yard for cattle*: Prop.; like atrium, *an inner court*: Verg.
TRANSF., *a palace*: aula Priami, Hor.; so of the dwellings of the gods: illa se iactet in aula Aeolus, Verg.; of the lower world: immanis ianitor aulae (of Cerberus), Verg.; of a beehive: Verg. Meton. (1) *the court, courtiers*: puer ex aula, Hor.; divisa et discors aula erat, Tac. (2) *princely power*: auctoritate aulae communita, Cic. L.

²aula=olla; q.v.

aulaeum -i, n. (αὐλαία), usually plur., *embroidered work, tapestry*; of *bedclothes*: aulaea superba, Verg.; of a *canopy*: Hor.; of *elaborate dress*: Juv.; esp. *the curtain of a theatre*, let down below the stage at the beginning of a play, and drawn up at the end; aulaea premuntur, *the performance begins*, Hor.; aulaeum tollitur, *it ends*, Cic.

Aulerci -orum, m. *a people of Gallia Celtica, divided into three branches.* (1) Aulerci Eburovīces, in modern Normandy. (2) Aulerci Cenomani, in modern Dép. de la Sarthe. (3) Aulerci Brannovīces, on the Loire.

aulĭcus -a -um (αὐλικός), *belonging to the court, princely*: Suet. M. pl. as subst. **aulici** -orum, *courtiers*: Nep.

Aulis -ĭdis, f. (Αὐλίς), *a port in Boeotia*, where the Greek fleet collected before sailing to Troy.

auloedus -i, m. (αὐλῳδός), *one who sings to the flute*: Cic.

Aulōn -ōnis, m. *a celebrated wine-district near Tarentum*.

Aulŭlārĭa -ae, f. ²(aula=olla), sc. fabula, *the play about a little pot, title of a comedy of Plautus*.

aura -ae, old genit. auraï (αὔρα), *air.* (1) *air breathed* or *blowing, breath, wind*: auris vitalibus vesci, *to breathe*, Verg.; nocturna aura uti (of ships), Caes.; venti et aurae cient mare, Liv. TRANSF., **a**, fig., *breath*: rumoris, Cic.; aura popularis, *the breath of popular favour*, Cic.: **b**, *smell*: Verg.: **c**, *glitter*: auri, Verg.: **d**, *echo*: Prop. (2) (poet.) gen., *air, heaven*: cursum per auras dirigere, Verg.; stat ferrea turris ad auras, Verg.; as opposed to the underworld, *the world above*: venire superas ad auras, *the light of day*, Verg.; ferre sub auras, *to make known*, Verg.

aurārĭus -a -um (aurum), *golden, relating to gold*: Plin. Subst. **auraria** -ae, f. (sc. fodina), *a gold-mine*: Tac.

aurātus -a -um (aurum), *golden* or *ornamented with gold*: tecta, Cic.; vestis, Ov.

Aurēlĭus -a -um, *name of à Roman plebeian gens*; for the emperor, M. Aurelius Antoninus *see* Antoninus.

aurĕŏlus -a -um (dim. of aureus). LIT., *of small objects, golden*: Pl. TRANSF., *glittering, splendid*: libellus, Cic.

aurĕus -a -um (aurum), *golden.* LIT., (1) *made of gold*: anulus, Cic.; nummus, and absol., *a golden coin*, Cic., Juv. (2) *gilt, ornamented with gold*: amiculum, Cic.; sella, Cic.; cingula, Verg.; Pactolus, *with golden sands*, Ov. (3) *of the colour of gold*: lumina solis, Lucr.; color, Ov.; caesaries, Verg. TRANSF., *excellent, beautiful*: Venus, Verg.; mediocritas, Hor.

aurichalchum=orichalcum; q.v.

auricŏmus -a -um (aurum/coma), *golden-haired.* TRANSF., *golden-leaved*: fetus (arboris), Verg.

aurĭcŭla -ae, f. (dim. of· auris), *the lobe of the ear.* LIT., sine te prendam auriculis, Pl.; prov.: auriculā infimā mollior, Cic. Hence gen., *the ear*: praeceptum auriculis instillare, Hor., Lucr., Pers.

aurĭfer -fĕra -fĕrum (aurum/fero), *gold-bearing, gold-producing*: arbor (of a tree in the garden of the Hesperides), Cic. poet.; amnis, *bringing gold* (of Pactolus), Tib.

aurĭfex -fĭcis, m. (aurum/facio), *a goldsmith*: Pl., Cic.

aurĭfŏdīna -ae, f. *a gold-mine*: Plin.

aurīga -ae, c. (from old aurea=*reins*, and ago), *charioteer, driver*: Verg., Caes.; esp. *one who contends in the chariot race in the circus*: Cic. TRANSF., *a helmsman*: Ov.; as a constellation, *the Waggoner*: Cic.

Aurĭgĕna -ae, c. (aurum/gigno), *begotten of gold*; epithet of Perseus, son of Danaë: Ov.

aurĭger -gĕra -gĕrum (aurum/gero), *gold-bearing*: tauri, *with gilt horns*, Cic. poet.

aurīgo -are (auriga), *to be a charioteer, contend in the chariot race*: Suet.

aurĭpigmentum -i, n. *orpiment*: Plin.

auris -is, f. (connected with audio), *the ear*. LIT., aures erigere, Cic., adrigere, Ter., *to prick up the ears*; adhibere, admovere, Cic.; applicare, Hor., *to listen*: praebere aures conviciis adulescentium, Liv., dare, Cic.; *to give a hearing to*: accipere auribus, Cic.; aliquem admonere ad aurem, *to whisper advice in the ear*, Cic.; dicere in aurem alicui aliquid, Cic.; insusurrare ad aurem *or* in aures, Cic.; offendere aures, Cic.; aures refercire sermonibus, Cic.; claudere aures alicui, Cic.; aures respuunt aliquid, Cic.; servire alicuius auribus, *to speak according to the wish of*, Caes.; dormire in utramvis aurem, *to sleep soundly, be without anxiety*, Ter. TRANSF., (1) *the hearing*, as judging the merits of a speech*: Atticorum aures teretes et religiosae, Cic. (2) *hearers*: Hor. (3) *the earth- or mould-board of a plough*: Verg.

auriscalpĭum -i, n. *an ear-pick*: Mart.

aurītŭlus -i, m. (dim. of auritus), *the little long-eared one*, i.e., *the ass*: Phaedr.

aurītus -a -um (auris). LIT., *long-eared*: lepus, Verg.; asellus, Ov. TRANSF., *attentive*: quercus, Hor.; testis auritus, *a hearsay witness*, Pl.

aurōra -ae, f. (connected with ἠώς), *dawn, break of day*. LIT., Pl., Lucr., Liv. Personified, *Aurora, goddess of morning*. Meton., *the east*: Verg., Ov.

aurum -i, n. *gold*: Lucr., Cic., Ov.; prov.: montes auri polliceri, Ter. Meton., *something made of gold, gold plate*: Lucr.; *a golden goblet*: Verg.; *chain, necklace*: Verg.; *ring*: Juv.; *bit*: Verg.; *the golden fleece*: Ov.; *gold coin, money*: Cic., Verg., Liv. TRANSF., (1) *the colour or glittering of gold*: Verg., Ov. (2) *the golden age*: Hor., Ov.

Aurunca -ae, f. *Suessa Aurunca, a town in Campania*. Adj. **Auruncus** -a -um, *Auruncian*.

auscultātĭo -ōnis, f. (ausculto). (1) *a listening*: Sen. (2) *obedience*: Pl.

auscultātor -ōris, m. (ausculto), *a listener*: Cic.

ausculto -are (mainly ante-class.), *to hear attentively*: populum, Cat. Esp. (1) *to listen in secret, to overhear*: Pl. (2) of servants, *to attend, wait at the door*: Hor. (3) *to obey*: mihi ausculta; vide ne tibi desis, Cic.

Ausētāni -ōrum, m. *a Spanish people in modern Catalonia*.

ausim, often as subjunctive of audeo; q.v.

Ausŏnes -um, m. (Αὔσονες), *ancient name for original inhabitants of central and southern Italy*.

¶ Hence **Ausŏnĭa** -ae, f. *Ausonia, Lower Italy*: Ov.; gen., *Italy*: Verg., Ov. Adj. and subst. **Ausŏnĭus** -a -um; poet., *Italian, an Italian*: Verg. **Ausŏnĭdae** -ārum, m. *the inhabitants of Ausonia, or generally of Italy*: Verg. **Ausŏnis** -ĭdis, f. adj., *Ausonian, Italian*: Verg.

auspex -ĭcis, c. (for avispex, from avis/specio). LIT., *one who observes the habits of birds for purposes of divination*: latores et auspices legis curiatae (Caesar and Pompeius), Cic.; providus auspex, Hor. TRANSF., (1) gen., *protector, leader*: Teucro duce et auspice Teucro, Hor. (2) t. t., *a person who witnessed the marriage contract, and performed duties at the ceremony* (cf. Gr. παρανύμφιος, Engl. best man): Cic., Liv.

auspĭcĭum -i, n. (auspex), *divination by means of birds*. LIT., of magistrates in peace, of the commander-in-chief in war: in auspicio esse, *to act as augur*, Cic.; praeesse auspiciis, Cic.; adhibere aliquem in auspicium, Cic.; auspicio uti, Cic.; auspicia dissolvere, Cic.; esp., *the right to take auspices*: propraetores auspicia non habent, Cic.; auspicia ponere, *to lay down a magistracy*, Cic.; imperio atque auspicio alicuius, *under the command of*, Liv. TRANSF., (1) *control, protection, guidance*: suis auspiciis ducere vitam, Verg. (2) *an omen, sign*: optimum, Cic.; aves auspicium ratum fecere, Cic.; auspicium facere, *to give a sign*, Pl., Cic., Liv.

auspĭco -are (auspex), *to take the auspices*: mustelam, *to accept as an omen*, Pl.

¶ Hence partic. **auspĭcātus** -a -um. (1) as partic., *consecrated by auguries*: auspicato in loco, Cic.; Liv. (2) as adj. (with compar. and superl.), *favourable, auspicious*: initium, Tac. Hence abl. absol. **auspĭcātō**. LIT., *after taking auspices*: Cic., Tac.; in gen. as adv., *in a fortunate hour*: Pl., Cic.

auspĭcor -ari, dep. (auspex), *to take the auspices*: auspicari oblitus est, Cic. TRANSF., *to begin under good auspices, to begin well*: Tac., Suet.

auster -stri, m. LIT., *the south wind*: vehemens, Cic. L.; Hor., Verg. Meton., *the south*: Cic., Verg.

austērĭtās -ātis, f. (austerus). LIT., *harshness, sourness of taste*: Plin.; *darkness of colour*: Plin. TRANSF., *strictness, severity*: Quint., Plin. L.

austērus -a -um (αὐστηρός). LIT., *sour, harsh in taste*: Plin.; *pungent in smell*: Plin.; *dark in colour*: Plin. TRANSF., (1) *strict, severe, stern*: illo austero more ac modo, Cic. (2) *sad, gloomy, burdensome*: labor, Hor. Adv. **austērē**, *severely*: Cic.

austrālis -e (auster), *southern*: Cic., Ov.

austrīnus -a -um (auster), *southern*: Verg., Plin.

ausum -i, n. (audeo), *a daring deed, undertaking*, in good or bad sense: Verg.

aut, conj. disjunct., *or*; generally (unlike vel) introducing a second alternative which positively excludes the first. (1) gen., *or*: vinceris aut vincis, Prop. Repeated: aut . . . aut . . ., *either . . . or . . .*, Cic., Tac. (2) *or else* (failing the first alternative): nec nasci potest nec mori, aut concidat omne caelum, Cic. (3) *or at least*; esp. aut certe, Cic.

(4) *or rather, or even*; esp. aut etiam, aut potius, etc., Cic. (5) neque . . . aut . . . for neque . . . neque . . . (poet.).

autem, conj. adversat., *but, on the other hand, however, moreover*; never used at the beginning of a clause, seldom in poetry. (1) adversat., *but*: e principio nascuntur omnia; ipsum autem nulla ex re alia nasci potest, Cic.; esp. with pronouns. (2) adding a fresh point without contrast, *moreover*: atque haec in moribus. De benevolentia, autem . . . , Cic. (3) gen., in any transition, *now*; in repetitions; resuming after parenthesis; in questions, sometimes with sed: sed quid ego haec autem? Verg.; in corrections=*did I say?* num quis testis Postumum appellavit? Testis autem? Num accusator? Cic.

authepsa -ae, f. (αὐτός/ἕψω), *a cooking-stove*: Cic.

autŏgrăphus -a -um (αὐτόγραφος), *written with one's own hand*: Suet.

Autŏlўcus -i, m. (Αὐτόλυκος), *son of Mercury, famous for his thefts.*

autŏmătus (-ŏs) -a -um (-ŏn), adj. (αὐτόματος), *self-acting*: Petr. N. as subst. **automaton** or **-um**, *an automaton*: Suet.

Autŏmĕdōn -ontis, m. (Αὐτομέδων), *the charioteer of Achilles*; appell., *a charioteer*: Cic., Juv.

Autŏnŏĕ -ēs, f. (Αὐτονόη), *mother of Actaeon.* Adj. **Autŏnēius** -a -um: heros, *Actaeon*, Ov.

autumnālis -e (autumnus), *autumnal*: Liv., Ov.

¹**autumnus** -i, m. (perhaps from augeo), *autumn*. Lit., Caes., Cic., Hor.; autumno vergente, *towards the end of autumn*, Tac. Transf., septem autumni=*seven years*, Ov.

²**autumnus** -a -um (¹autumnus), *autumnal*: frigus, Ov.

autŭmo -are (orig. aitumo, from aio), *to say, assert*: Pl., Ter.; usually of doubtful statements.

auxĭliāris -e (auxilium), *giving help, assisting, auxiliary*. Gen.: Ov. Esp.: auxiliares (sc. milites, cohortes), *auxiliary* or *allied troops*, Caes., Tac.; hence, *belonging to the allied troops*: auxiliaria stipendia, Tac.

auxĭliārĭus -a -um (auxilium), gen., *helping, auxiliary*: Pl.; esp. milit. t. t.: milites, *auxiliary troops*, Liv.; cohors, Cic.

auxĭliātor -ōris, m. (auxilior), *a helper*: Tac.

auxĭliātus -ūs, m. (auxilior), *help, assistance*: Lucr.

auxĭlĭor -ari, dep. (auxilium), *to help, assist, support*: alicui, Pl., Cic. L.; esp. used of medical aid, with dat. or with contra and acc.: Ov., Plin.

auxĭlĭum -i, n. (augeo), *help, aid, assistance.* In gen.: adiungere sibi auxilium, Cic.; ad auxilium convenire, Caes.; dare adversus aliquem auxilium, Liv.; expetere auxilium ab aliquo, Cic.; expectare vestrum auxilium, Cic.; ferre alicui auxilium contra tantam vim, Cic.; polliceri auxilium alicui rei, Cic.; plur.: illorum auxiliis uti, Cic. Esp. in predicative dat., *to be, etc., a source of help to*: esse auxilio alicui, Caes.; alicui nemo auxilio est, quin, Liv.; venire auxilio alicui, Caes.; mittere, Cic. In concrete sense, esp. plur., *sources of help*: Liv.

Esp. as milit. t. t., often plur. (1) auxilia, *auxiliary troops* (mainly foreign allies and

light-armed troops), Cic., Caes., Tac. (2) gen., *military power*: infimis auxiliis proficisci, Caes.

Avārĭcum -i, n. *a fortified town in Gaul* (now *Bourges*).

ăvārĭtĭa -ae (**ăvārĭtĭĕs** -ei: Lucr.), f. *avarice, cupidity, covetousness*, sometimes for food (Pl.), but usually for money: ardere avaritia, Cic.; avaritia perire, Cic.; plur.: omnes avaritiae, *all kinds of avarice*, Cic.

ăvārus -a -um (aveo), adj. (with compar. and superl.), *desirous, covetous, greedy*: homo avarus et furax, Cic.; semper avarus (subst.) eget, Hor.; with genit.: publicae pecuniae avarus, Tac. Transf., of inanimate objects: mare, Hor. Sometimes without any reproach: agricola, Verg. Adv. **ăvārē**: Ter., Cic., and **ăvārĭtĕr**: Pl., *greedily.*

ăvĕho -vĕhĕre -vexi -vectum, *to carry off, bear away*: frumentum, Caes., Verg., Liv.; pass. *to ride off*: Liv.; *sail off*: Verg.

ăvello -vellĕre -velli and -vulsi (-volsi) -vulsum (-volsum), *to tear away, pluck away*. Lit., poma ex arboribus, cruda si sint, vi avelluntur, Cic.; sive secetur aliquid sive avellatur a corpore, Cic. Transf., in gen., *to take away with violence, separate*: de matris complexu avellere atque abstrahere, Cic.; ex complexu avelli, Cic.; avulsus a meis, Cic. Fig.: hunc a tanto errore, Cic.

ăvēna -ae, f. (1) *oats*: Verg. (2) *wild oats*: Cic.; steriles, Verg. (3) *any stalk, straw*: Ov., Plin. (4) *an oaten pipe, the shepherd's pipe*: tenui meditaris avenā, Verg.; plur.: iunctae avenae *or* structae avenae, Ov.

ăvēnācĕus -a -um (avena), *oaten*: farina, Plin.

Āventīnum -i, n. and **Āventīnus** -i, m. *the Aventine, one of the seven hills of Rome*: Cic. Adj. **Āventīnus** -a -um, *of or belonging to the Aventine.*

¹**ăvĕo** -ēre (cf. Sanskr. av, *to wish*), *to long for, desire*: aveo genus legationis, Cic. L.; gen. with infin.: valde aveo scire quid agas, Cic.; Hor., Tac.

²**ăvĕo** (**hăvĕo**) -ēre, *to be well*; found only in imperat. and infin., as a greeting or at a leave-taking: ave, aveto, avete, *hail!* or *farewell!* Coel. ap. Cic., Sall., Suet.; Marcus avere iubet, Mart. To the dead: atque in perpetuum, frater, ave atque vale, Cat.

Āvernus -i, m. (sc. lacus) (ἄορνος, *without birds*; or else avis), *a lake near Puteoli* (now *Lago d'Averno*). It was said that it was an entrance to the infernal regions, and that birds flying over it were killed by its exhalations. Poet., gen., *the infernal regions*: Ov., Mart.

¶ Hence adj. **Āvernus** -a -um, and **Āvernālis** -e, *relating to Avernus*, or *the lower world*: loca, Lucr.; stagna, freta, Verg. N. pl. as subst. **Āverna** -orum (sc. loca), Verg., Ov.

ăverrunco -are, old relig. t. t., *to turn away, avert*: iram deorum, Liv.

āversābĭlis (aversor), *from which one must turn away, horrible*: Lucr.

¹**āversor** -ari, dep. (averto), *to turn away* (on account of shame, disgust, etc.): aversari advocati, vix etiam ferre posse, Cic.; with acc., *to turn away from*: filium, Liv. Transf., *to repel, avoid, shun*: principes Syracusanorum, Liv.; preces, Liv.; aliquem ut parricidam liberum, Liv.

²**āversor** -ōris, m. (averto), *an embezzler*: pecuniae publicae, Cic.

āversus -a -um, partic. from averto; q.v.

averto (**āvorto**) -vertĕre (-vortĕre) -verti (-vorti) -versum (-vorsum), *to turn away, turn off, remove.*

LIT., in gen.: Lepidus se avertit, Cic.; aliquid ab oculis, Cic.; flumina, *divert*, Cic.; iter, Caes., Liv.; hence pass., averti (as middle): aversus ab suo itinere, *turning away*, Liv.; active sometimes intrans., *to turn away, retire*: prora avertit, Verg. Esp. (1) *to drive away by violence*: barbaros a portis castrorum, Caes. (2) *to carry off, appropriate to oneself, embezzle*: pecuniam publicam, Cic.; hereditatem, Cic.; quattuor a stabulis tauros, Verg.

TRANSF., (1) *to keep off anything dangerous*: pestem ab Aegyptiis, Cic.; quod omen dii avertant, Cic. (2) *to turn away, divert* (thoughts, wishes, etc.): a spe, Cic., Liv.; animum a pietate, Cic.; cogitationem a miseriis, Cic. (3) *to estrange*: civitates ab alicuius amicitia, Caes.; Cic.; mentem deorum, Cat.

¶ Hence partic. **aversus** -a -um, *turned away, backward, behind* (opp. adversus). LIT., aversum hostem videre nemo potuit, Caes.; adversus et aversus impudicus es, *before and behind*, Cic.; quendam actorem aversum (*turning his back on the people*) solitum esse dicere, Cic.; aversos boves in speluncam traxit, *backwards*, Liv. N. pl. as subst. **āversa** -orum, *the back parts*: urbis, Liv. TRANSF., *disinclined, unfavourable, hostile*: aversus a vero, Cic.; with dat.: aversus mercaturis, Hor.; absol.: aversos soliti componere amicos, Hor.

āvia -ae, f. (avus), *a grandmother*: Pl., Cat.

āviārius -a -um (avis), *relating to birds*: rete, Varr. N. as subst. **āviārium** -i, *a place where birds are kept, an aviary*: Cic. L.; also *the haunts of wild birds in the woods*: Verg.

āvĭdĭtās -ātis (avidus), f. Gen., *vehement desire, longing for*: cibi, pecuniae, *for food, money*, Cic.; legendi, Cic.; imperandi, Tac. Esp. *desire for money, avarice*: Pl., Cic.

āvĭdus -a -um (¹aveo), *vehemently desiring, longing for*, in a good or a bad sense (unlike avarus; q.v.).

LIT., of persons, etc., with genit.: cibi, Ter.; laudis, Cic.; novarum rerum, Liv.; belli gerendi, Sall.; also with infin.: committere pugnam, Ov.; with in and the acc.: in novas res, Liv.; with dat.: Tac. Also absol., with various objects of desire understood; esp. *greedy for money, avaricious*: heres, Hor.; convivae, *gluttonous*, Hor.; leones, *bloodthirsty*, Ov.; aures avidae, *eager to hear*, Cic.; libido, *insatiable*, Cic.; legiones, *eager to fight*, Tac.

TRANSF., of inanimate objects: mare, Hor.; ignis, Ov.; avido complexu quem tenet aether, *capacious*, Lucr.

Adv. (with compar. and superl.) **āvĭdē**, *eagerly, greedily*: Cic., Hor.

āvis -is, f. (abl. sing. avī or avĕ), *a bird*. Gen.: Pl., Lucr., Cic. Esp. *a bird of omen*, the favourite Roman means of divination (cf. augur, auspex); hence in gen., *an omen*: avibus bonis, Ov.; secundis, Liv., *with good omens*; avi malā, Hor.; sinistrā, Pl.; adversā, *with bad omen*, Cic.

āvītus -a -um (avus), *relating to a grandfather, ancestral*: bona paterna et avita, Cic. TRANSF., merum, *very old*, Ov.

āvĭus -a -um (a/via). (1) of places, *out of the way, untrodden*: avii saltus montesque, Liv.; avia Pieridum peragro loca, Lucr. N. as subst., usually pl., **avia** -orum, *by-ways, solitary places*: avia dum sequor, Verg.

(2) poet., of persons. LIT., *wandering, remote*: in montes se avius abdidit altos, Verg. TRANSF., *astray, lost*: a vera ratione, Lucr.

āvŏcātĭo -ōnis, f. (avoco), *a calling away, diversion* (very rare): a cogitanda molestia, Cic., Sen.

āvŏco -are, *to call away*, or *off*. LIT., populum ab armis, Liv. TRANSF., (1) *to withdraw, remove, divert*: Socrates videtur primus a rebus occultis avocasse philosophiam, Cic.; senectus avocat a rebus gerendis, Cic. (2) *to relieve*: luctum lusibus, Sen.

āvŏlo -are, *to fly away*. LIT., per umbras, Cat. TRANSF., *to hasten away*: experiar certe ut hinc avolem, Cic. L.; Verg.; citatis equis Romam, Liv.

āvuncŭlus -i, m. (dim. of avus), *a mother's brother, uncle* (patruus=*a father's brother*): magnus, *a grandmother's brother, a great-uncle*, Cic.

āvus -i, m. *a grandfather*: Pl., Cic., Hor.; generally *an ancestor*: Verg., Hor.

Axēnus (ἄξενος, *inhospitable*), *earlier name of the Pontus Euxinus*: Ov.

axis (or **assis**) -is, m. (Gr. ἄξων), *an axle*. (1) *the axle of a wheel*: Verg. Meton., *a chariot, waggon*: Ov. (2) *the axis of the earth*: terra circum axem se convertit, Cic. Meton.: a, *the north pole*: Lucr., Cic., Verg.: b, gen., *the heavens*: sub axe, *in the open air*, Verg.: c, *a region, clime*: boreus, *the north*, Ov. (3) *a board, plank*: Caes., Luc., Plin.

Axŏna -ae, m. *a river in Gallia Belgica* (now *the Aisne*).

B

B, b, the second letter of the Latin Alphabet, corresponding to the Greek beta (β).

băbae or **papae** (βαβαί or παπαί), an exclamation of astonishment or joy, *wonderful!* Pl., Ter.

Băbȳlōn -ōnis, f., acc. -ōna (Βαβυλών), *the chief city of Babylonia, on the Euphrates*.

¶ Hence **Băbȳlōnĭa** -ae, f. *Babylonia, the southern part of the ancient Mesopotamia, between the Euphrates and the Tigris*. Adj. **Băbȳlōnĭcus** -a -um, *Babylonian*: Babylonica peristromata, *embroidered tapestry*, Pl. Adj. and subst. **Băbȳlōnĭus** -a -um, *of Babylon, of Babylonia*, or *a Babylonian*: numeri, *astrological calculations, for which the Babylonians were noted*, Hor. Adj. **Băbȳlōnĭensis** -e, *Babylonian*: Pl.

bāca (**bacca**) -ae, f. *a berry*. LIT., in gen.: lauri bacae, Verg. Esp., *the fruit of the olive*: bicolor baca Minervae, Ov. TRANSF., (1) *the fruit of any tree*: arborum bacae, Cic. (2) *anything of the shape of a berry*, esp. *a pearl*: Hor., Ov.

bacatus -a -um (baca), *set with pearls*: monile, Verg.

baccar (bacchar) -āris, n. and **baccaris** -is, f. (βάκχαρις), *a plant which yielded a kind of oil*; possibly *sowbread*: Verg.

Baccha -ae, f. *a Bacchante, female worshipper of Bacchus*: Pl., Ov., Prop.; the worship was a wild revel, for which the Bacchante had her hair loose, a wand wreathed with ivy in her hand, an ivy crown on her head, and a fawnskin on her shoulder: Bacchis aliquem initiare, *to initiate anyone into the festival of Bacchus*, Liv.

Bacchānal -is, n. *the place where the festival of Bacchus was held*: Pl., Liv.; plur. **Bacchānālia** -ium, *the (Greek) festival of Dionysus* or *Bacchus* (not to be confounded with the Roman feast of Liber), celebrated at Rome every three years and suppressed by a decree of the senate, 186 B.C. LIT., Cic., Liv.; sing.: Bacchanal facere, Pl. TRANSF., poet.: Bacchanalia vivere, *to live riotously* or *wantonly*, Juv.

bacchātio -ōnis, f. *revelling in Bacchanalian fashion*: Cic.

Bacchiädae -ārum, m. (Βαχχιάδαι), *the Bacchiadae, an ancient royal family of Corinth, which, expelled by Cypselus, migrated and founded Syracuse.*

bacchor -ari, dep. (Bacchus).
  LIT., *to celebrate the festival of Bacchus*: Pl., Cat.; hence partic. Bacchantes = Bacchae: Ov.; sometimes as a passive, of places, *to be made the scene of Bacchic revels*: bacchata iugis Naxos, Verg.; virginibus bacchata Lacaenis Taygeta, Verg.
  TRANSF., *to rage, rave like a Bacchante*: tum baccharis, tum furis, Cic.; quanta in voluptate bacchabere, Cic.; totam per urbem, Verg.; of prophetic inspiration: in antro, Verg.; of the wind: Hor.; of rumour: bacchatur fama per urbem, Verg.; of an enthusiastic manner of speech: Cic.

Bacchus -i, m. (Βάκχος), *the god of wine, son of Jupiter and Semele.* Meton. (1) *the vine*: Verg. (2) more frequently, *wine*: Verg. (3) *the Bacchic cry* (Io Bacche): Baccho audito, Verg.
  Adj. **Bacchēus** -a -um (Βάγχειος), *Bacchic*: sacra, Ov.; ululatus, Ov. **Bacchïcus** -a -um: Ov., Mart. **Bacchïus** -a -um: Ov.

Băcēnis -is, f. *a forest in Germany*, probably the west part of the Thuringian Forest.

bacïfer -fēra -fērum (baca/fero), *bearing berries*: Sen.; esp. *bearing olive berries*: Pallas, Ov.

băcillum -i, n. (dim. of baculum), *a little staff*: esp. *the lictor's staff*: Cic.

Bactra -ōrum, n. pl. (Βάχτρα), *the chief city of Bactria* (now *Balkh*).
  ¶ Hence **Bactri** -ōrum, m. *inhabitants of Bactria*: Plin.; adj. and subst. **Bactriānus** -a -um, *of Bactra, of Bactria*, or *a Bactrian*: Plin.; adj. **Bactrius** -a -um, *Bactrian*: Ov.

băcŭlum -i, n. and **băcŭlus** -i, m. (connected with βάκτρον), *a staff, walking-stick*: Cic., Liv., Ov.; also *an augur's staff*: Liv.

bădisso -are (βαδίζω), *to walk, march*: Pl.

Baebïus -a -um, adj., *name of a Roman gens*; hence: lex Baebia (de praetoribus creandis), Liv.

Baecŭla ae, f. *name of two towns in Spain*, one near Baetica, the other on the Ebro.

Baetis -is, m. *a river in Spain* (now *the Guadalquivir*).
  ¶ Hence adj. **Baetĭcus** -a -um, *relating to the Baetis*; esp. Baetica provincia or subst. **Baetica** -ae, f. *the Roman province of Baetica on the Baetis* (now *Andalusia and a part of Granada*); m. pl. as subst. **Baetĭci** -ōrum, *inhabitants of Baetica.* Adj. **Baetĭcātus** -a -um, *clothed in Baetican wool*: Mart.; **Baetĭcŏla** -ae, *living near the Baetis*; **Baetĭgĕna**, *born on the Baetis.*

Băgōus -i, m. and **Băgōas** -ae, m. (Βαγώας), *a eunuch at the Persian court*; hence *any person set to guard women*: Ov.

Băgrăda -ae, m. (Βαγράδας), *a river near Carthage.*

Bāiae -ārum, f. *a town on the coast of Campania, a favourite holiday resort of the Romans.* Meton., *any watering place*: Cic., Mart. Adj. **Bāiānus** -a -um, *belonging to Baiae.*

bāiŭlo -are (baiulus), *to carry a burden*: Pl.

bāiŭlus -i, m. *a porter*: Pl., Cic.

bālaena -ae, f. (φάλαινα), *a whale*: Pl., Ov.

bălănātus -a -um (balanus), *anointed with balsam*: Pers.

bălănus -i, f. rarely m. (βάλανος), (1) *an acorn*: Plin. (2) *any fruit of similar form*, e.g. *a kind of large chestnut*: Plin.; *a date*: Plin.; esp. *the Arabian ben-nut*, from which balsam was extracted: Hor. (3) *a kind of shell-fish*: Pl., Plin.

bălătro -ōnis, m. (connected with blatero), *a buffoon, jester*: Hor.

bālātus -us, m. (balo), *the bleating of sheep*: Lucr., Verg., Ov.; *of goats*: Plin.

¹**balbus** -a -um (connected with barbarus), *stammering* (opp. planus): cum (Demosthenes) ita balbus esset ut, etc., Cic.; verba balba, Hor.
  Adv. **balbē**, *in a stammering manner*: Lucr.

²**Balbus** -i, m. *a Roman cognomen.*

balbūtio -ire (balbus). LIT., *to stammer, stutter*: Cels.; transit., *to stammer out, pronounce with a stammer*: illum balbutit Scaurum, Hor. TRANSF., *to speak obscurely*: desinant balbutire, aperteque et clara voce audeant dicere, Cic.

Bălĭāres (Bălĕāres) -ium, f. (Βαλιαρεῖς), insulae, or absol., *the Balearic Islands, Majorca, Minorca.*
  ¶ Hence adj. **Bălĭāris** -e, **Bălĭārĭcus** -a -um.

bălĭnĕum or **balnĕum** -i, n. (βαλανεῖον), esp. in pl. **bălĭnĕa** or **balnĕa** -ōrum, n.; also heteroclite pl. **bălĭnĕae** or **balnĕae** -ārum, *a bath, bathing place*: Cic.; a balineo or a balineis, *after bathing*, Plin.

Ballio -ōnis, m. *a worthless fellow*, from a character so named in the Pseudolus of Plautus: Cic.

ballista -ae, f. (βάλλω), *a military engine for throwing large stones*: Cic., Caes., Liv. TRANSF., *the missile thrown*: Pl.

ballistārĭum -i, n. = ballista; q.v.: Pl.

balnĕae, see balineum.

balnĕārĭus -a -um (balneum), *belonging to the bath*: fur, *lurking about baths*, Cat. N. as subst. **balnĕāria** -ōrum, *baths, bathing-rooms*: Cic. L.

balnĕātor -ōris, m. (balneum), *the keeper of a bath*: Pl., Cic.

balnĕŏlum -i, n. (dim. of balneum), *a little bathroom*: Sen., Juv.

balnĕum, *see* balineum.

bālo -are, *to bleat*: Pl., Ov.; partic. **balantes**= oves: Lucr.; balantum grex, Verg.

balsămum -i, n. (βάλσαμον). (1) *the sweet-smelling gum of the balsam-tree*: Verg. (2) *the tree itself*: Tac., Plin.

baltéus -i, m. and **baltĕum** -i, n. esp. in pl. baltea, *a girdle*; esp. as serving to hold a weapon: sutilis, Verg.; also *a woman's girdle*: Ov., Mart. TRANSF., of *blows with a belt*: Juv.

Bandūsĭa -ae, f. *a fountain near Venusia, the birth-place of Horace.*

Bantĭa -ae, f. (Βαντία), *town of Apulia, near Venusia.* Adj. **Bantinus** -a -um.

Baptae -arum, m. (Βάπται), *priests of the Thracian goddess Cotytto*: Juv.

baptistērĭum -i, n. (βαπτιστήριον), *a cold plunging bath*: Plin. L.

bărăthrum -i, n. (βάραθρον), *a pit, an abyss*: Pl., Lucr., esp. of *the lower world*: Lucr., Verg.; barathro donare, *to squander*, Hor. TRANSF., barathrum macelli (of a greedy man), *a great hole in the market*, Hor.

barba -ae, f. *the beard.* LIT., (1) of men: promittere barbam, *to let the beard grow*, Liv.; barbam tondere, Cic.; sapientem pascere barbam, *to study the Stoic philosophy*, Hor. (2) of animals: lupi, Hor. TRANSF., of plants: nucum, Plin.

barbărĭa -ae, f. and **barbărĭēs**, acc. -em, abl. -e, f. (barbarus). LIT., *a foreign country*, as opposed to Greece and Rome: a quo non solum Graecia et Italia sed etiam omnis barbaria commota est, Cic. So of particular countries, *Persia*: Cic.; *Phrygia*: Hor.; *Gallia*: Cic.; *Scythia* and *Britannia*: Cic.; even of *Italy* (from the Greek point of view): Pl. TRANSF., (1) *want of culture, rudeness, roughness*: haec turba et barbaria forensis, Cic.; esp. in speech: nec eos aliqua barbaries domestica infuscaverat, Cic. (2) *savageness*: inveteratam quandam barbariam ex Gaditanorum moribus disciplina delevit, Cic.

barbărĭcus -a -um (βαρβαρικός), *foreign*, i.e., not Greek or Roman: supellex, Liv. So of particular countries: esp. *Phrygian, oriental*: aurum, Verg.; ope barbarica, Verg.; manus (of the Phrygian Briseis), Ov.; *German*: Suet.; from the Greek point of view, *Italian*: Pl.

barbărus -a -um βάρβαρος). Adj. and subst., *foreign, strange, a foreigner, a stranger.* LIT., of all but Greeks and Romans: neque noster . . . nec barbarus, Lucr.; Cic., Tac. So referring to particular countries; *Phrygian*: carmen, Hor.; even of *Rome* (from the Greek point of view): barbarus poeta= Naevius, Pl. TRANSF., (1) *uncultivated, rough*: homines barbari atque imperiti, Caes., Cic. (2) *morally rough, savage*: homines feri ac barbari, Caes.; consuetudo hominum immolandorum, Cic.; pirata, Cic. Adv. **barbărē**. LIT., *like a foreigner* (unlike a Greek or Roman); or *like a Roman* (from the Greek point of view): Pl. TRANSF., (1) *roughly*: loqui, Cic. (2) *cruelly, barbarously*: laedere oscula, Hor.

barbātŭlus -a -um (dim. of barbatus), *with a slight beard*: iuvenis, Cic. TRANSF., of fish: Cic.

barbātus -a -um (barba), *bearded.* LIT., of gods: Iovem barbatum, Cic.; of men: quos aut imberbes aut bene barbatos videtis, Cic.; si quem delectet barbatum, *a man grown up*, Hor.; esp. of men of the old Roman time, when the beard was worn: unus aliquis ex barbatis illis, Cic.; barbatus magister, *a philosopher*, Juv., Pers.; of animals: hirculus, Cat.; of fish: Cic. L.

TRANSF., of plants: nux, Plin ; of books, *worn*: Mart.

barbĭgĕr -gĕra -gĕrum (barba/gero), *wearing a beard*: Lucr.

barbĭtŏs, m. and f. (βάρβιτος), found in nom., in voc. barbite, in acc. barbiton; *the lyre*: Hor. Meton., *the song sung to the lyre*: Ov.

barbŭla -ae, f. (dim. of barba), *a little beard*: Cic. TRANSF., of plants: Plin.

Barcās -ae, m. (Βάρκας, connected with Hebrew barak, *lightning*), *the founder of the Barcine family of Carthage, to which belonged Hannibal and Hamilcar.*

¶ Hence adj. **Barcĭnus** -a -um, *Barcine.*

Barcē -ēs, f. (Βάρκη), *town in Cyrenaica*; **Barcaei** -ōrum, m. *the inhabitants of Barce.*

Bardaei -orum, m. *a people of Illyria.* Adj. **Bardaĭcus** -a -um, calceus, or absol., *a kind of soldier's boot*; hence poet., *the soldiery*: Juv.

bardŏcŭcullus -i, m. *a Gallic overcoat, with a hood made of wool*: Mart.

bardus -a -um (βραδύς), *stupid, slow, dull*: Pl., Cic.

Bargўlĭae -ārum, f. and **Bargўlĭa** -ōrum, n. (Βαργύλια), *a town in Caria.*

¶ Hence **Bargўlētae** -ārum, m. *the inhabitants of Bargyliae*; **Bargўlĭētĭcus** -a -um, *relating to Bargyliae.*

bāris -ĭdos, f. *an Egyptian barge*: Prop.

barītus (or **barrītus**) -ūs, m. *a war-cry of the Germans*: Tac.

Bārĭum -i, n. (Βάριον), *a port in Apulia, on the Adriatic* (now *Bari*).

bāro -ōnis, m. *a blockhead, simpleton*: Cic., Pers.

barrus -i, m. (an Indian word), *the elephant*: Hor.

bascauda -ae, f. *a basket*: Mart., Juv.

bāsĭātĭo -ōnis, f. (basio), *kissing, a kiss*: Cat.

bāsĭātor -is, m. (basio), *a kisser*: Mart.

băsĭlĭcus -a -um (βασιλικός).

Adj., *royal, kingly, princely*: Pl.; vitis, *a kind of vine*, Plin.

Hence adv. **băsĭlĭcē**, *royally, splendidly*: exornatus, Pl.

Subst. **băsĭlĭcus** -i, m. (sc. iactus), *the best cast of the dice*: Pl.; **băsĭlĭca** -ae, f. (βασιλική, sc. οἰκία or στοά), *a basilica, the name of a building* (in Rome and other towns) *with double colonnades, situated near the forum and used as a meeting-place of merchants and for the administration of justice*: qui forum et basilicas non spoliis provinciarum, sed ornamentis amicorum ornarent, Cic.; basilicam habeo, non villam, frequentia Formianorum (of a much-frequented place), Cic.; Tac.; **băsĭlĭcum** -i, n. *a splendid robe*: Pl.

bāsĭo -are, *to kiss*: Cat., Mart.

băsis -is and -ĕos, f. (βάσις). (1) gen., *a pedestal, base*: statuae, Cic.; villae, *foundation-wall*, Cic. L. (2) mathemat. t. t.: trianguli, *base*, Cic.

băsium -i, n. *a kiss*: Cat., Mart., Juv.

Bassăreus -ei, m. (Βασσαρεύς, from βασσάρα, *a fox-skin*, as forming part of the clothing of the Bacchantes), *a name of Bacchus*: Hor.

¶ Hence **Bassărĭcus** -a -um, adj.: Prop.

Bastarnae and **Basternae** -ārum, m. *a German people on the lower Danube.*

Bătăvus -a -um, adj. and subst., *of Batavia* or *an inhabitant of Batavia (now Holland)*: Mart., Tac.

bătillum (or **vatillum**) -i, n. (1) *a chafing-dish*: Hor. (2) *a shovel*: Plin.

bătĭŏla -ae, f. *a drinking-cup*: Pl.

battŭo (**bātuo**) -ĕre, *to beat, knock*: Pl.; also *to fence*: Suet.

Battus -i, m. (Βάττος), *the founder of the African city Cyrene.*

¶ Hence **Battĭădes** -ae, m. *an inhabitant of Cyrene*; especially applied to the poet Callimachus, a native of Cyrene: Ov.

baubor -ari, dep., *to bark gently*: Lucr.

bĕātĭtās -ātis, f. (beatus), *happiness, blessedness*: Cic.

bĕātĭtūdo -ĭnis, f. (beatus), *happiness, blessedness*: Cic.

bĕātŭlus -a -um (dim. of beatus); as subst., *the blessed little one*: Pers.

bĕātus -a -um, partic. from beo; q.v.

Bebrўces -um, m. (Βέβρυκες), *a people in Bithynia.* Adj. **Bebrўcĭus** -a -um, *Bebrycian.*

Belgae -ārum, m. *the Belgae, a warlike people of German and Celtic race, inhabiting the north of Gaul.* Adj. **Belgĭcus** -a -um, *Belgic*; hence, Gallia Belgica, or simply Belgica, *the country between the Rhine, the Seine, the Marne, and the North Sea.*

bellārĭa -ōrum, n. (bellus), *dessert, including fruit, nuts, confectionery, sweet wine*: Pl.

bellātor -ōris, m. (bello), *a warrior*: Cic., Ov., Liv. Also used as adj., *warlike, courageous*: deus, *Mars*, Verg.; equus, Verg.; also absol., *a war-horse*: Juv.

bellātōrĭus -a -um (bellio), *warlike*: stilus, *a pugnacious, controversial style*, Plin. L.

bellātrix -īcis, f. (bellator), *a female warrior*; also used (like bellator) as adj., *warlike*: diva, Pallas, Ov.; Roma, Ov.; iracundia, Cic.

Bellĕrŏphōn -ontis, m. (Βελλεροφῶν), or **Bellĕrŏphontēs** -ae, m. (Βελλεροφόντης), *the slayer of the Chimaera and rider of Pegasus.* Adj. **Bellĕrŏphontēus** -a -um: equus, Pegasus, Prop.

bellĭātŭlus -a -um (dim., jocosely formed from bellus), *pretty*: Pl.

bellĭcōsus -a -um (bellicus), *warlike, bellicose*: gentes immanes et barbarae et bellicosae, Cic. Transf., differre sibi consulatum in bellicosiorem annum, *a more warlike year*, Liv.

bellĭcus -a -um (from bellum; old form duellicus: Pl., Lucr.), *relating to war*: disciplina, virtus, Cic.; also *warlike*: dea, Ov. N. as subst. **bellĭcum** -i, *the signal for march* or *attack.* Lit., canere, Cic., Liv. Transf., alter (Thucydides) incitatior fertur et de bellicis rebus canit etiam quodammodo bellicum, Cic.

bellĭger -gĕra -gĕrum (bellum/gero), *waging war, warlike*: gentes, Ov.; hasta, Mart.; manus, Ov.

bellĭgĕro -are (bellum/gero), *to wage war.* Lit., Liv., Tac. Transf., cum fortuna, Cic.

bellĭpŏtens -entis (bellum/potens), *mighty in war.* Poet. subst.=*Mars*: Verg.

bello -are (bellor, dep.: Verg.), *to wage war*: Caes., Cic., Hor.; cum Poenis, Cic.; adversus Gentium, Liv.; impers. pass., Liv. Transf., gen., *to struggle*; poet.: Ov.

Bellōna -ae, f. (bellum), *the goddess of war, sister of Mars*: Verg.

Bellŏvăci -ōrum, m. *a people in Gallia Belgica, near modern Beauvais.*

bellŭa, see belua.

bellŭlus -a -um (dim. of bellus), *pretty, elegant*: Pl.

bellum -i, n. (old form, **duellum**, *a contest between two*), *war.*

Lit., domesticum, Cic.; Punicum, Cic.; sociale, Liv.; piraticum, Cic.; civile, Cic.; navale, Cic.; terrestre, Liv.; iustum, *regular*, Cic.; *against* whom, expressed by genit.: Cic.; cum, Cic.; contra, Cic.; adversus, Liv. With verbs, of *starting* a war: movere, commovere, conflare, Cic.; parare, comparare, Cic.; instruere, Cic.; suscipere, Cic.; alicui inferre, Cic.; inferre contra patriam, Cic.; of *declaring it*: denuntiare, Cic.; indicere, Cic.; of *conducting it*: gerere, Caes., Cic., Liv.; administrare, Cic.; of *prolonging it*: trahere, Cic., Liv.; ducere, Cic.; of *ceasing from* it: deponere, Cic., Liv.; ponere, Sall., Tac.; componere (by agreement), Cic.; conficere (by victory), Cic., Caes., Liv.; ad bellum, *to the war*, Cic.; in bello, *in time of war*, Cic.; locative, belli, *in time of war*: vel domi vel belli, Cic.

Transf., (1) in gen., *fighting, struggle*: tribunicium, Liv.; bellum indicere philosophis, Cic. (2) of a particular *battle*: Verg. (3) personified: Verg.

bellus -a -um (contr. from benulus, dim. of benus, i.e., bonus), colloq., *pretty, handsome, charming*; of persons: homo, Cic. L.; *cheerful from good health*: fac bellus revertare, Cic.; of things: locus, Cic. L.; fama, Hor.; passer, Cat.; quam sit bellum cavere malum, Cic.

Adv. **bellē**, *finely, prettily, elegantly, neatly*: scribere, Cic.; dicere, Cic.; negare, *politely*, Cic.; superl., bellissime navigare, Cic. L.; esp.: belle se habere, belle habere, belle esse, *to be in good health*, Cic. L.

bēlŭa -ae, f. (perhaps connected with fera and θήρ), *a beast.* Lit., *any very large animal*: quantum natura hominis pecudibus reliquisque beluis antecedat, Cic.; belua fera et immanis, Cic.; centiceps, Hor.; esp. of the *elephant*: Ov., Juv. Transf., (1) term of reproach, *monster, brute, beast*: Pl.; in hac immani belua, Cic. (2) of abstract things: avaritia, Sall.; imperium, Suet.

bēlŭātus -a -um (belua), *covered with figures of animals*, of tapestry: Pl.

bēlŭōsus -a -um (belua), *full of monsters*: Oceanus, Hor.

Bēlus -i, m. myth. *an Asiatic king, founder of Babylon, father of Danaus and Aegyptus.*

¶ Hence **Bēlĭdes** -ae, m. *a male descendant of Belus*; **Bēlis** -idis, f. *a female descendant*

of him, esp. plur., **Bēlĭdĕs** -um, *the grand-daughters of Belus, the Danaides*: Ov.
bĕnĕ, adv. (from benus for bonus), comp. **melius**, superl. **optime**, *well.*
  (1) in gen.: **a**, with verbs, *well, in the right or in a good way, honourably, properly*; esp.: rem gerere, *to succeed*, Caes., Cic.; mereri, *to deserve well*, Pl., Cic., Liv.; sentire, *to have good intentions* or *sound views*, Cic.; vivere, *to lead a good life*, Cic., or *a comfortable one*, Pl.; vendere, emere, *advantageously*, Pl.: **b**, with adj. and adv., *thoroughly, very*: bene robustus, Cic.; bene penitus, Cic.; bene sanus, Cic., Hor.
  (2) in particular phrases: **a**, as an exclamation, *good, excellent*: Cic.; with acc. or dat., *good health to you*: Pl.: **b**, bene est, with dat., *it is well with*: Pompeio melius est factum, *P. is better*, Cic.; also absol.: bene est or bene habet, *all is well, all right, I am satisfied*, Cic., Juv.: **c**, bene dicere (post-class. **benedico**), *to speak well*: bene dicere, id est, Attice dicere, Cic.; also *to speak words of good omen* (εὐφημεῖν): Pl.; and esp. with dat., *to speak well of* a person, *praise* him: Cic.: **d**, bene facere, *to do well*; with dat., *to do good to*: Liv.; bene facis, *I am obliged to you*, Pl., Cic.; bene facta (or **benefacta**), *good deeds*, esp. *benefits*, Cic.
bĕnĕdĭcē, adv., *with friendly speech*: Pl.
bĕnĕdĭco, *see* bene.
bĕnĕfăcĭo, *see* bene.
bĕnĕfĭcentĭa -ae, f. (beneficus), *kindness, beneficence*: Cic., Tac.
bĕnĕfĭcĭārĭus -a -um (beneficium), *relating to a favour*: Sen. Subst. **bĕnĕfĭcĭārĭi** -ōrum, m. *soldiers who by favour of their commanders were exempt from the severer military labours*, as throwing up entrenchments, fetching wood, water, etc.; *privileged soldiers*: Caes., Plin. L.
bĕnĕfĭcĭum -i, n. (bene/facio), *a kindness, favour, benefit, service.*
  In gen.: alicui beneficium dare, tribuere, Cic.; in aliquem conferre, Cic.; apud aliquem conlocare, Cic.; aliquem beneficio adficere, *to do anyone a service*, Cic.; beneficium accipere, *to receive a kindness*, Cic.; beneficium tueri, *to be mindful of a service*, Cic.; in beneficii loco, beneficii causa, per beneficium, *as a kindness, service*, Cic.; beneficio tuo, *by your kindness*, Cic.; deorum beneficio, sortium beneficio, Caes.
  Esp. in political life. (1) *a favour, grant, distinction, promotion*: populi, *favour of the people*, Cic.; in beneficiis delatus est, *among those recommended for promotion*: Cic; esp. of military promotions: tribuni militum quae antea dictatorum fuerant beneficia, Liv.; centuriones sui beneficii, *his creatures*, Suet. (2) *privilege, exemption*: liberorum, *exemption from the judicial office in consequence of having a specified number of children*, Suet.
bĕnĕfĭcus -a -um, comp. -entior, superl. -entissimus (bene/facio), *kind, generous, obliging*: Cic.
Bĕnĕventum -i, n. *a town of the Hirpini in Samnium, seat of a Roman colony* (modern *Benevento*).
  ¶ Hence **Bĕnĕventānus** -a -um, *belonging to Beneventum*.
bĕnĕvŏlē, adv. from benevolus; q.v.

bĕnĕvŏlens -entis, comp. -entior, superl. -entissimus (bene/volo), *well-wishing, benevolent, obliging*: Pl., Cic.
bĕnĕvŏlentĭa -ae, f. (benevolens), *good-will, friendly disposition, kindness*: alicui praestare, conferre, Cic.; conligere, Caes.; erga aliquem habere, conferre, Cic.; declarare, Cic. L.
bĕnĕvŏlus -a -um (with comp. and superl. from benevolens; q.v.) (bene/volo), *kind, obliging, well disposed*: alicui, Cic.; erga aliquem, Pl.; servus benevolus domino, *a faithful slave*, Cic.
  Adv. **bĕnĕvŏlē**, *kindly*: Cic.
bĕnignĭtās -ātis, f. (benignus). (1) *kindness, mildness*: Cic. (2) *liberality, generosity*: Cic.
bĕnignus -a -um, adj. (with compar. and superl.) (connected with bonus and gigno).
  (1) gen., *kind, friendly*: animus, Ter.; oratio, Cic.; homines benefici et benigni, Cic.; vultus benigni, Liv.; dies, *fortunate*, Stat.
  (2) in action, *liberal, generous*: erga aliquem, Pl.; alicui, Hor.; in timore benigni, Cic.; vini somnique benignus, *indulging in wine and sleep*, Hor.; also of things, *abundant, fruitful*: ager, Ov.; dapis, Hor.
  Adv. **bĕnignē**. (1) *kindly, in a friendly manner*: benigne respondere, Liv.; benigne attenteque audire, Cic.; arma capere, *willingly*, Liv.; benigne dicis, *or* absol., benigne, *much obliged*, a colloquial phrase used either in accepting or refusing an offer, Pl., Cic., Hor. (2) in action, *generously*: pecuniam praebere, Pl.; benigne facere alicui, *to confer benefits on a person*, Cic.
bĕo -are (connected with bonus), *to bless, make happy*: beas *or* beasti, *that pleases me, I'm glad of it*, Pl., Ter.; with abl., *to bless, enrich, gladden with*: munere te parvo, Hor.
  ¶ Hence partic. **bĕātus** -a -um, *happy, blessed.* In gen. (1) of persons: qui beatus est, non intellego quid requirat, ut sit beatior; si est enim quod desit, ne beatus quidem est, Cic.; agricolae parvo beati, *happy on little means*, Hor. (2) of events or circumstances: beata mors, Cic.; vitam, Cic. N. as subst. **bĕātum** -i, *happiness*: Cic. M. pl. as subst. **bĕāti** -orum, *the blessed ones*: Cic., Hor.
  Esp. *wealthy, prosperous*: of persons: qui se locupletes, honoratos, beatos putant, Cic.; of states: Dionysius tyrannus opulentissimae et beatissimae civitatis, Cic.; of possessions: gazae beatae Arabum, Hor.
  Adv. **bĕātē**, *happily*: bene et beate vivere, Cic.
Bĕrĕcyntus -i, m. *a mountain of Phrygia, sacred to Cybele.*
  ¶ Hence adj. **Bĕrĕcyntĭus** -a -um: mater, *Cybele*, Verg.; heros, *Midas, son of Cybele*, Ov.; tibia, *the flute used at the festivals of Cybele*, Hor. F. also as subst. **Bĕrĕcyntia** -ae = *Cybele*: Verg., Ov.
Bĕrĕnīcē -ēs, f. (Βερενίκη). (1) *queen of Ptolemy Euergetes, whose hair was placed among the stars as a constellation.* (2) *daughter of the Jewish king Agrippa I, mistress of Titus.*
Bĕroea -ae, f. (Βέροια), *a town in Macedonia.*
bēryllus -i, m. (βήρυλλος), *a beryl, a precious stone, of a sea-green colour, found in India*: Juv. Meton., *a ring set with a beryl*: Prop.
Bērȳtus -i, f. (Βηρυτός), *an old Phoenician town, afterwards a Roman colony* (now *Beirut*). Adj. **Bērȳtĭus** -a -um.

bēs bessis, m. (from as; q.v.), *two-thirds* (=*eight* unciae) of any whole composed of twelve parts. (**1**) in gen., esp. in terms relating to inheritance : Plin. (**2**) of the as (as a coin): faenus ex triente factum erat bessibus, *the interest was raised from one-third per cent for the month to two-thirds per cent*—i.e., from 4 per cent for the year to 8 per cent, Cic. L. (**3**) of the as (as weight), *two-thirds of a pound*: Plin.

Bessi -ōrum, m. (*Βέσσοι*), *a people in Thrace.* Adj. **Bessĭcus** -a -um.

Bessus -i, m. *satrap of Bactria, who murdered Darius Codomannus.*

bestia -ae, f. (perhaps connected with belua and fera), *an animal without reason* (opp. homo), *beast*. (**1**) gen.: bestiae mutae, Cic.; mala bestia, as a term of reproach, Pl. (**2**) esp. of the animals exhibited at Roman public spectacles, fighting with gladiators or criminals: aliquem ad bestias mittere, *to condemn to the beasts*, Cic.

bestĭārĭus -a -um (bestia), *belonging to animals*: ludus, *a fight with wild beasts at a show*, Sen. M. as subst. **bestĭārĭus** -i, *one who fought with wild beasts at the public shows*: Cic., Sen.

bestĭŏla -ae, f. (dim. of bestia), *a small animal*: Cic.

¹**bēta** -ae, f. *a vegetable, beet*: Cic. L.

²**bēta**, n. indecl. (*βῆτα*), *the beta, the second letter in the Greek alphabet*; sometimes used prov. for anything that comes *second*: Mart.

Bĭās -antis, m. (*Βίας*), *a philosopher of Priene in Ionia, one of the so-called seven wise men of Greece.*

bĭblĭŏpōla -ae, m. (*βιβλιοπώλης*), *a book-seller*: Mart., Plin.

bĭblĭŏthēca -ae, f. and **bĭblĭŏthēcē** -ēs, f. (*βιβλιοθήκη*), *a collection of books, a library*; also *the place where books are kept*: Cic.

bĭbo bĭbĕre bibi bĭbĭtum, *to drink*. LIT., aquam, Cic.; lac, Ov.; pocula, Tib.; cyathos, Pl.; gemmā, *from a cup set with jewels*, Verg.; dare bibere, *to give to drink*, Pl., Liv.; impers. pass., Cic. Particular phrases: aut bibat aut abeat (transl. of Gr.: *ἢ πῖθι ἢ ἄπιθι*), Cic.; Graeco more, *to drink to one's health*, Cic.; poet.: bibere flumen, *to live on the banks of a river*, Verg.; Danuvium, *of the Danube*, Hor.; bibere aquas, *to be drowned, wrecked*, Ov. TRANSF., (**1**) of things, *to drink in*: sat prata biberunt, Verg.; hortus aquas bibit, Ov.; arcus bibit, *the rainbow draws up water*, Verg. (**2**) of persons, fig.: amorem, Verg.; aure (of attentive listeners), *to drink in*, Hor.

Bibractĕ -is, n. *a town in Gaul, capital of the Aedui* (now *Autun*).

Bibrax -actis, f. *fortress of the Remi in Gaul.*

bĭbŭlus -a -um (bibo), *fond of drinking.* LIT., Hor.; with genit.: Falerni, Hor. TRANSF., of inanimate things: harena, Lucr., Verg.; lana, Ov.; nubes, Ov.; charta, *blotting paper*, Plin. L.

bĭceps -cĭpĭtis (bis/caput), *having two heads, two-headed*: puer, Liv.; Ianus, Ov. Poet., *double-peaked*: Parnassus, Ov.

bĭclīnĭum -i, n. (bis/*κλίνη*), *a dining sofa for the use of two persons*: Pl.

bĭcŏlor -ōris (bis/color), *of two colours*: equus, Verg.; myrtus, Ov.

bĭcorniger -gĕri, m. (bis/corniger), *two-horned*, an epithet of Bacchus: Ov.

bĭcornis -e (bis/cornu), *two-horned*: Ov.; poet.: luna, *the new moon*, Hor.; furcae bicornes, *two-pronged forks*, Verg.; Rhenus, *with two mouths*, Verg.

bĭcorpor -ōris (bis/corpus), *having two bodies*: Cic. poet.

bĭdens -entis (bis/dens), *having two teeth*. LIT., Plin. TRANSF., forfex, Verg.; ancora, Plin. As subst. (**1**) m. *a hoe with two crooked teeth for breaking clods*: Verg., Ov. (**2**) f. *an animal for sacrifice whose two rows of teeth were complete*: Verg., Ov.; hence *a sheep*: Phaedr.

bĭdental -ālis, n. (bidens), *a place struck with lightning; perhaps so called because it was afterwards consecrated by the sacrifice of a sheep* (bidens), *and enclosed*: Hor.

Bidis -is, f. *a town in Sicily, north-west of Syracuse.* ¶ Hence adj. **Bidīnus** -a -um, *belonging to Bidis.*

bĭduum -i, n. (bis/dies), *a space of two days*: in iis operibus consiliisque biduum consumitur, Caes.; aliquem biduum cibo tectoque prohibere, Cic.; abl.: biduo, *in the course of two days*, Cic.; eo biduo, *in the course of these two days*, Cic.; biduo aut summum triduo, *in two days or three at the most*, Cic.; biduo post, *two days afterwards*, Caes.; biduo quo haec gesta sunt, *two days after this was done*, Caes.; bidui iter abesse, *to be two days' march distant*, Caes.; so bidui by itself: castra quae aberant bidui, Cic. L.

bĭennĭum -i, n. (bis/annus), *a space of two years*: biennio iam confecto fere, Cic.; biennium iam factum est postquam abii domo, *it is now two years since I left home*, Pl.; acc., biennium, *for the space of two years*: biennium provinciam obtinere, Cic.; abl., biennio, with compar.: biennio maior natu Domitius, *older by two years*, Tac.; biennio proximo, *in the course of two years*, Tac.; biennio ante, *two years before*, Cic.

bĭfārĭam, adv. (acc. f. of bifarius, *double*), *in two parts*: distribuere, Cic.; castra bifariam facta sunt, Liv.

bĭfer -fĕra -fĕrum (bis/fero), of a tree, *bearing fruit twice a year*: Verg.

bĭfĭdus -a -um (bis/findo), *split into two parts*: Ov.

bĭfŏris -e (bis/foris), *having two doors or openings*: valvae, Ov. TRANSF., *from two openings*: ubi biforem dat tibia cantum, *the different notes of the double flute*, Verg.

bĭformātus -a -um: Cic. poet.=biformis; q.v.

bĭformis -e, *of double form*: Ianus, Ov.; vates, *the poet turned into a swan*, Hor.

bĭfrons -frontis (bis/frons), *with double forehead or countenance*, epithet of Janus: Verg.

bĭfurcus -a -um (bis/furca), *having two prongs or forks*: valli, Liv.; ramus, Ov.

bĭgae -ārum, f. pl., and post-Aug. sing. **biga** -ae (contr. from biiugae or biiuga), *a pair of horses, or a chariot drawn by a pair*: Cat., Verg.

bīgātus -a -um (bigae), *stamped with the effigy of a pair of horses*: argentum, Liv. M. as subst. **bīgatus** -i (sc. nummus), *a silver coin so marked.*

biiŭgis -e and **biiŭgus** -a -um (bis/iugum), *yoked two together*: equi, Mart.; certamen, *a race between two-horse chariots*, Verg. M. pl. as subst. **biiugi** -orum (sc. equi), *a pair of horses or a chariot drawn by a pair*: Verg.

bĭlībra -ae, f. (bis/libra), *two pounds weight*: Liv.

bĭlībris -e (bis/libra). (**1**) *weighing two pounds*: offae, Plin. (**2**) *containing two pounds*: cornu, Hor., Pl.

bĭlinguis -e (bis/lingua), *having two tongues.* LIT., humorously, of kissing: Pl. TRANSF., (**1**) *speaking two languages*: Canusini more bilinguis, Hor. (**2**) *double-tongued, treacherous*: Pl., Verg.

bīlis -is, f. *gall, bile.* LIT., Lucr., Cic.; suffusa, *jaundice*, Plin. TRANSF., (**1**) *anger, displeasure*: movere, Pl.; commovere, Cic. (**2**) atra (*or* nigra) bilis (Gr. μελαγχολία), *black bile*, i.e., *melancholy*: Cic.; *madness*: Pl., Sen.

bĭlix -īcis (bis/licium), *having a double thread*: lorica, Verg.

bĭlustris -e (bis/lustrum), *lasting ten years*: bellum, Ov.

bĭmăris -e (bis/mare), *lying on two seas*: Corinthus, Hor.; Isthmus, Ov.

bĭmārītus, m. (bis/maritus), *the husband of two wives*: ap. Cic.

bimātris -e (bis/mater), *having two mothers*, epithet of Bacchus: Ov.

bĭmātus -ūs, m. (bimus), *the age of two years* (of plants and animals): Plin.

bĭmembris -e (bis/membrum), *having two kinds of limbs*; esp. of the Centaurs: forma, Ov. Plur. as subst. **bimembres**, *Centaurs*, Ov.

bĭmestris -e (bis/mensis), *lasting two months*: consulatus, ap. Cic.; porcus, *a pig two months old*, Hor.; stipendium, *pay for two months*, Liv.

bĭmŭlus -a -um (dim. of bimus), *two years old*: Cat., Suet.

bīmus -a -um (bis/hiems), *two years old or lasting two years*: equus, Plin.; legio, *a legion that had served for two years*, ap. Cic.; merum, Hor.; nix, *snow lying for two years*, Ov.; honor, *office conferred for two years*, Ov.; sententia, *a vote of the senate prolonging a governor's time for two years*, Cic. L.

bīni -ae -a (sing., bīnus -a -um: Lucr.), *twofold.* (**1**) *two apiece*, sometimes simply *two*: unicuique binos pedes adsignare, *two feet each*, Cic.; binos imperatores, *two consuls a year*, Sall.; with subst. that are used only in the plur., or that have a different meaning in the plur., *two*: bina castra, Cic.; binae litterae, Cic.; with other numerals: bina millia passuum, *two miles*, Quint. (**2**) of things that match: boves, *a yoke of oxen*, Plin.; scyphi, *a pair of goblets*, Cic.; aures, Verg.; n. pl. subst.: findi in bina, *to be cleft in twain*, Lucr.: si bis bina quot essent didicisset, *if he had learnt that twice two is four*, Cic.

bĭnoctĭum -i, n. (bis/nox), *a space of two nights*: Tac.

bĭnōmĭnis -e (bis/nomen), *having two names*: Ascanius (because also called Iulus), Ov.; Ister (because also called Danuvius), Ov.

Bĭōn -ōnis, m. (Βίων), *a satirical philosopher from Scythia, of the Cyrenaic school.* ¶ Hence adj. **Bĭōnēus** -a -um: sermones, *witty, caustic*, Hor.

bĭŏs -ii, m. (βίος, *life*, cf. eau de vie), *a celebrated Greek wine*: Plin.

bĭpalmis -e (bis/palmus), *two palms or spans long or broad*: Liv.

bĭpartītus or **bĭpertītus** -a -um (bis/partio), *divided in two*; esp. in abl., used as adv., **bĭpartītō** or **bĭpertītō**, *in two parts, in two ways*: distribuere, Cic.; inferre signa, Caes., Liv., Ov.

bĭpătens -entis (bis/patens), *doubly open, open in two directions*: portis bipatentibus, Verg.

bĭpĕdālis -e, *two feet long, broad, thick*, or *high*: trabes, Caes.; Cic., Hor.

bĭpennĭfer -fĕra -fĕrum, *armed with a two-edged axe* (bipennis): Ov.

bĭpennis -e (bis/penna). (**1**) *having two wings*: Plin. (**2**) *double-edged*: ferrum, Verg. As subst. **bipennis** -is, f. (sc. securis), *a double-edged axe*: Verg., Hor., Tac.

bĭpēs -ĕdis (bis/pes), *having two feet*: equi, Verg., Juv., Plin. As subst., *biped*, esp. used contemptuously of human beings: omnium non bipedum solum, sed etiam quadrupedum impurissimus, Cic.

bĭrēmis -e (bis/remus), *two-oared*: Hor., Liv. As subst. **bĭrēmis** -is, f. (**1**) *a boat with two oars*: Lucr. (**2**) *a ship with two banks of oars*: Caes., Cic.

bĭs, adv., *twice, in two ways*: bis terque, i.e. *often*, Cic. L.; bis terve, i.e. *seldom*, Cic. L.; bis die, Cic.; bis consul, *a man who has been consul twice* (iterum consul, *a man who is consul for the second time*), Cic.; bis tanto *or* tantum, *twice as great*, Pl.; with distributive numerals: bis bina, Cic.; with cardinal numerals, only in poet.: bis quinque viri (the decemviri), Hor.; prov.: bis ad eundem (sc. lapidem offendi), *to make the same mistake twice*, Cic.

Bistōnes -um, m. (Βίστονες), *the Bistones, a Thracian people settled not far from Abdera*; used poet. for *Thracians.* ¶ Hence adj. **Bistŏnĭus** -a -um, *Bistonian* or *Thracian*: tyrannus, Diomedes, Lucr.; chelys, *the lyre of Orpheus*, Claud.; turbo, *violent north wind*, Luc.; Minerva, *goddess of the warlike Thracians*, Ov. Subst. **Bistŏnĭa** -ae, f. *Thrace.* **Bistŏnis** -idis, f. adj., *Thracian*: ales, Procne, *wife of the Thracian king Tereus*, Sen. poet. As subst., *a Thracian woman*, i.e. *a Bacchante*: Hor.

bĭsulcĭlingua -ae, f. adj., *with a cloven tongue.* TRANSF., *of a double-tongued person, a hypocrite*: Pl.

bĭsulcus -a -um (bis/sulcus), *two-furrowed, split into two parts*: lingua, *forked*, Ov.; ungula, *cloven hoof*, Plin.; pes, Lucr., Plin. N. pl. as subst. **bĭsulca** -ōrum, *animals with cloven hoofs* (opp. solidipedes): Plin.

Bĭthŷnĭa -ae, f. (Βιθυνία), *a country in north-west Asia Minor.* ¶ Hence adj. **Bĭthŷnĭcus** -a -um, *of Bithynia*, esp. as *title of Q. Pompeius, conqueror of the Bithynians, and of his son*: Cic.; adj. and subst. **Bĭthŷnĭus** and **Bĭthŷnus** -a -um, *Bithynian, a Bithynian*; **Bĭthŷnis** -idis, f. *a Bithynian woman*: Ov.

bīto (baeto, bēto) -ere, *to go*: Pl.

bĭtūmen -ĭnis, n. *asphalt, bitumen*: Verg., Ov.
bĭtūmĭnĕus -a -um (bitumen), *bituminous*: Ov.
Bĭtŭrĭges -um, m. *a people of Aquitanian Gaul, near the modern towns of Bourges and Bordeaux.*
bĭvĭus -a -um, *having two ways or passages*: fauces, Verg. N. as subst. **bĭvĭum** -i, *a place where two roads meet*: Verg. TRANSF., *a twofold way in anything*: in bivio distineri, *to be distracted by a love for two persons*, Ov.
blaesus -a -um (βλαισός), *lisping, indistinct*: lingua, sonus, Ov.; used of the talk of a parrot: sonus, Ov. Subst., madidi et blaesi, *drunken men*, Juv.
blandē, adv. from blandus; q.v.
blandĭdĭcus -a -um (blandus/dico), *flattering in speech*: Pl.
blandĭlŏquentŭlus -a -um (blandus/loquor) =blandidicus: Pl.
blandĭlŏquus -a -um (blandus/loquor)= blandidicus: Pl.
blandīmentum -i, n. (blandior), *flattery.* LIT., usually plur.: blandimentis corrumpere, Cic.; blandimenta muliebria, Tac. TRANSF., *whatever pleases the senses, an allurement*: sine blandimentis expellunt famem, *without sauces, delicacies*, Tac.
blandĭor -iri, dep. *to flatter, caress, coax*; governing the dative.
    LIT., mihi et per se et per Pompeium blanditur Appius, Cic.; Hannibalem pueriliter blandientem patri Hamilcari, ut duceretur in Hispaniam, Liv.; auribus nostris, Plin.; sibi, *to deceive oneself*, Sen.; votis meis, *to delude oneself into believing what one wishes*, Ov.
    TRANSF., of things: blandiebatur coeptis fortuna, *fortune favoured his undertakings*, Tac.; voluptas sensibus blanditur, Cic.; blandiente inertia, *idleness pleasing him*, Tac.
    ¶ Hence past. partic. **blandītus** -a -um, *charming*: Prop., Plin.
blandĭtia -ae, f. (blandus), *flattery, coaxing*; used in both good and bad senses, unlike adulatio. LIT., popularis, Cic.; often in plur.: benevolentiam civium blanditiis et adsentando conligere, Cic.; adhibere, Ov.; muliebres, Liv. TRANSF., of things, *charm, attraction*: blanditiae praesentium voluptatum, Cic.
blandītim, adv., *flatteringly*: Lucr.
blandus -a -um, adj. (with compar. and superl.), *flattering, fondling, caressing.* (1) of persons: blandum amicum a vero secernere, Cic.; scis me minime esse blandum, Cic. L.; with dat.: blandiores alienis quam vestris, Liv. (2) of things, *enticing, alluring, tempting*: oratio, Cic.; voluptas, Cic.; soni, Ov.; oculi, Plin.; otium consuetudine in dies blandius, *ease becoming by habit every day more attractive*, Liv.
    Adv. (with compar. and superl.) **blandē** (also **blandĭter**: Pl.), *flatteringly*: adloqui, Ter.; rogare, Cic.; dicere, Quint.
blătĕro -are, *to chatter, babble*: Hor.
blătĭo -ire, *to talk idly, babble*: nugas, Pl.
blatta -ae, f. *a cockroach*: Verg., Hor., Plin.
blennus -i, m. (βλεννός), *a stupid fellow*: Pl.
blĭtĕus -a -um (blitum), *insipid, silly*: Pl.
blĭtum -i, n. (βλίτον), *a tasteless herb used in salad*: Pl.

bŏārĭus and **bŏvārĭus** -a -um (bos), *relating to cattle*: forum, *the cattle market*, Cic., Liv.
Bocchar -āris, m. *a king of Mauritania at the time of the second Punic war.* TRANSF., *an African*: Juv.
Bocchus -i, *king of Mauritania, the father-in-law and afterwards the betrayer of Jugurtha.*
    ¶ Hence **bocchus** -i, m. *a plant named after him*: Verg.
Boebe -ēs, f. (Βοίβη), *a village in Thessaly.*
Boeōtarchēs -ae, m. (Βοιωτάρχης), *a Boeotarch, one of the chief magistrates of Boeotia*: Liv.
Boeōti -ōrum or -um, m. pl. (Βοιωτοί), and **Boeōtii** -ōrum, m. *the inhabitants of Boeotia, a district in Greece to the west of Attica, proverbial for their dullness.*
    ¶ Hence **Boeōtĭa** -ae, f. *their district*; adj. **Boeōtĭus** -a -um and **Boeōtus** -a -um, *Boeotian.*
Bŏēthĭus -i, m. Anicius Manlius Severinus, *a distinguished Roman philosopher*; born c. A.D. 480; beheaded A.D. 524 in prison where he wrote his most celebrated work, De Consolatione Philosophiae Libri V.
Bōgud -ūdis, m. *son of Bocchus and king of Mauritania*; ally of Julius Caesar and Antony; killed in battle, 31 B.C.
boia -ae, f., gen. pl. **boiae** -ārum, *a species of collar*: Pl.
Bōii -ōrum, m. *a Celtic people, settled partly in north Italy, partly in central Germany, partly in central Gaul.* Sing. **Bōius** -i, m. *one of the Boii*; **Bōia** -ae, f. *a woman of the Boii.*
    ¶ Hence **Boiēmi, Boihemi, Boihēmum,** *names given to the Boii as established in Germany* (cf. modern Bohemia, Bohemians).
Bōla -ae, f. *a town of the Aequi in Latium.* Adj. **Bōlānus** -a -um.
bōlētus -i, m. (βωλίτης), *a mushroom*: Pl., Mart., Juv.
bōlus -i, m. (βόλος), *a throw* (classical iactus). (1) of dice: Pl. (2) of a fishing net, and hence: **a**, *what is caught at one throw*: bolum emere, Suet.: **b**, fig., *any good haul, gain*: is primus bolu 'st, Pl.; bolo tangere, *or* multare aliquem, *to cheat a man of his gains*, Pl.
bombax, interj. (βόμβαξ), *an exclamation of astonishment, is it possible?* Pl.
bombus -i, m. (βόμβος), *a boom, a deep hollow noise*, esp. of trumpets: Lucr., Cat.
bombȳcĭnus -a -um (bombyx), *silken*: Juv., Plin. N. pl. as subst. **bombȳcĭna** -ōrum, *silken garments*: Mart.
bombyx -ȳcis, m. and f. (βόμβυξ). (1) *the silkworm*: Plin. (2) *silk*: Prop., Plin.
Bŏna Dĕa, *the good goddess*, the deity of chastity and fertility, worshipped by Roman wom∷n.
bŏnĭtās -ātis, f. (bonus), *goodness, excellence.* (1) gen.: **a**, of material things: agrorum, praediorum, vocis, Cic.: **b**, of abstract things: naturae bonitate, Cic.; bonitas et aequitas causae, Cic.; bonitas verborum, Cic.
    (2) *moral goodness, kindness, integrity*: bonitas et beneficentia, Cic.; facit parentes bonitas (*parental love*), non necessitas, Phaedr.; with in *or* erga followed by the acc.: bonitas in suos, Cic.; divina bonitate erga homines, Cic.
Bŏnōnĭa -ae, f. (Βονωνία). (1) *a town in Cisalpine Gaul* (now Bologna); hence adj. **Bŏnōnĭensis** -e. (2) *a port in Gallia Belgica* (now Boulogne).

bŏnus -a -um (old form, **duonus**), compar.
mĕlĭor -ius, gen. -ōris, superl. **optĭmus**
-a -um, *good.*

(1) in gen., *good in itself, good of its kind:*
a, of material objects, *good to look at, to use,*
etc.: nummi boni, *genuine coin,* Cic.; forma
bona, Ter.; cervix, Suet.; color, *good
complexion,* Lucr.; res, *delicacies,* Nep.:
b, of immaterial circumstances, events, etc.:
bono genere natus, Cic.; valetudo, Cic.; tempestas, *weather,* Cic.; fama, *good news,*
Cic.; navigatio, Cic.; mors, Plin.; res,
fortune, Cic.; dies, *lucky,* Verg.; auspicium,
Cic.; occasio, Pl.; quod bonum felix faustumque sit, *fortunate,* Cic.; aetas, *youth,*
Cic.: **c**, of human speech, action, character:
indoles, Cic.; bona dicta, *witty sayings,*
Enn.; mens, Liv.; animus, *courage,* Cic. L.,
Liv.; exemplum, Tac.; bonā veniā tuā, *with
your kind permission,* Cic.; in bonam partem
accipere, *to take in good part,* Cic.; bona
verba, *words of good omen,* Ov., Tib.: **d**, of
persons in particular functions and relations,
able, efficient, etc.: servus, Pl., Cic.; uxor, Cic.;
imperator, Cic.; poeta, Cic.: **e**, of quantity,
substantial, considerable: bona pars hominum,
Hor.; bonam partem sermonis, Cic.

(2) more specifically, *good, useful, efficient*
in some particular respect: **a**, with abl. of
respect: iaculo, *good with, at using,* Verg.;
bonus militia, Sall.; vir pace belloque bonus,
Liv.: **b**, with dat.: pecori alendo, *for keeping,*
Liv.: **c**, with ad: ad proelium, Tac.

(3) morally *good, virtuous, honest,* etc.:
a, gen.: viri boni est misereri, Cic.; often
ironical: homines optimi, Cic.; bona atque
honesta amicitia, Cic.; in voc., as a
familiar greeting: O bone! *my good fellow,*
Hor.: **b**, esp. towards the state, *patriotic,
loyal:* bonus et fortis civis, Cic.; and often
in Cic. and Sall. boni=*conservatives, the
supporters of the existing system:* **c**, *kind:*
bonus atque benignus, Hor.; di boni,
gracious gods! Cic.; with dat.: tuis, Verg.;
with in and the acc.: in me, Cic.

N. as subst. **bŏnum** -i, *good,* material or
moral. (1) gen., *profit, advantage:* bonum
publicum, *the common weal,* Liv.; bono esse
alicui, *to profit one,* Cic.; cui bono fuisset, *for
whose advantage,* Cic.; bona pacis, *the
blessings of peace,* Tac.

(2) material *good;* usually plur., *goods,
property:* bona fortunaeque, Cic.; bonorum
omnium heres, *sole heir,* Liv.; esse in bonis,
to be in possession, Cic.

(3) moral *good,* a *good:* bonum mentis est
virtus, Cic.; summum bonum, *the supreme
good* (in philosoph. sense), Cic.; esp. associated with aequum; q.v.

bŏo -are (βοάω), *to shout, roar;* esp. of places,
to echo: Pl., Ov.

Bŏōtēs -ae, m., also voc. Bootē, acc. Bootēn,
genit. Bootī (βοώτης, *the ox-driver*), *a constellation,* also called Arctophylax.

Bŏrĕās -ae, m. (Βορέας). (1) *the north wind:*
Verg. (pure Lat. aquilo). (2) meton., *the
north:* Hor. (3) mythol., *the husband of
Orithyia, and father of Calais and Zetes.*
Adj. **Bŏrēus** or **Bŏrĭus** -a -um, *northern.*

bŏria -ae, f. *a kind of jasper:* Plin.

Bŏrysthĕnēs -is, m. (Βορυσθένης), *a large
river in Scythia* (now *the Dnieper*).

¶ Hence **Bŏrysthĕnĭdae** or -ītae -ārum,
m. *dwellers on the Borysthenes;* **Bŏrysthĕnis**
-idis, f. *a Greek colony on the Borysthenes;*
Bŏrysthĕnĭus -a -um, *belonging to the
Borysthenes.*

bōs bŏvis, c. (βοῦς). (1) *ox, bullock, cow:* Pl.,
Cic., Liv.; bos Lucas, *an elephant,* Lucr.;
prov.: bovi clitellas imponere, *to saddle an ox,*
i.e. *to impose on anyone an office for which he
is not fit,* poet. ap. Cic. TRANSF., *a strap or
whip of hide:* Pl. (2) *a kind of flat fish:* Ov.,
Plin.

Bospŏrus (or **Bosphŏrus**), -i, m. (Βόσπορος,
'heifer's ford', because of Io's passage as a
heifer), *name of various straits,* esp. (1)
Bosporus Thracius, *the straits between
Thrace and Asia Minor* (now *the Straits of
Constantinople*); hence adj. **Bospŏrĭus** -a -um.
(2) Bosporus Cimmerius, *off the Crimea*
(now *the Straits of Yenikale*); adj. and subst.
Bospŏrānus -a -um, *belonging to this
Bosphorus, a dweller by it.*

Bostra -ae, f. *Bozra, capital of the Roman
province of Arabia.*
¶ Hence adj. and subst. **Bostrēnus** -a
-um, *belonging to Bostra, an inhabitant of it.*

Bottĭaea -ae, f. (Βοττιαία), *a district of Macedonia.*
¶ Hence **Bottĭaei** -ōrum, m. pl. *the
inhabitants of the district.*

bŏtŭlus -i, m. *a sausage:* Mart.

Boudicca -ae, f. *queen of the Iceni, a British
tribe.*

Bŏvĭānum -i, n. (Βοϊανον), *town in Samnium.*
¶ Hence adj. **Bŏvĭānĭus** -a -um.

bŏvĭle=bubile; q.v.

Bŏvillae -ārum, f. *a town in Latium, about
twelve miles from Rome, near which Clodius
was murdered by Milo.*
¶ Hence adj. **Bŏvillānus** -a -um: pugna
(with a play on the word bovillus), *the
murder of Clodius,* Cic.

bŏvillus -a -um (bos), an old form of bubulus,
relating to oxen: grex, ap. Liv.

brăbeuta -ae, m. (βραβευτής), *a judge, umpire
in the public games:* Suet.

brācae (braccae) -ārum, f. pl. (sing. once in
Ov.), *breeches, trousers;* originally worn by
Persians, Gauls, and Germans: Tac., Ov.

brācātus (braccātus) -a -um (bracae),
wearing breeches. LIT., Cic., Prop. TRANSF.,
as geograph. term=transalpinus: Gallia
Bracata, *Gaul on the north side of the Alps,
the old name of Gallia Narbonensis,* Plin.;
cognatio bracata, *connexion with people of
Transalpine Gaul,* Cic. M. pl. as subst.
bracati -orum, *Transalpine Gauls:* Juv.

brăcchĭālis -e (bracchium), *belonging to the
arm:* nervus, Pl.

brăcchĭŏlum -i, n. (dim. of bracchium), *a
small delicate arm:* Cat.

brăcchĭum -i, n. (less correctly brachium,
from βραχίων), *an arm.*
LIT., strictly, *the forearm, arm from the
elbow to the wrist,* whereas lacertus=the
upper arm: brachia et lacerti, Ov.; hence
gen., *the whole arm:* bracchium frangere,
Cic.; diu iactato bracchio scutum emittere,
Caes.; collo dare bracchia circum, *to embrace,*
Verg.; as used in speaking: porrectio
bracchii, Cic.; in dancing: bracchia numeris
movere, Ov.; prov.: bracchia sua praebere

sceleri, *to assist in a crime*, Ov.; levi (*or* molli) bracchio agere, *to act without energy*, Cic.; dirigere bracchia contra torrentem, *to swim against the stream*, Juv.

TRANSF., (1) *the limbs of animals*; *the claw of a crab*: Ov.; *the thigh of an elephant*: Plin.; *the leg of a lion*: Plin.; *the claw of the nautilus*: Plin.; used of the sign Cancer: Ov., and Scorpio: Verg. (2) *of things resembling the arm*; *the branch of a tree*: Verg.; *arm of the sea*: Ov.; *the spur of a mountain chain*: Plin.; *the yard of a sail*=antenna: Verg.; *an outwork connecting two points of a fortification*: muro bracchium iniunxerat, Liv.; *mole of a harbour*: Liv., Plin. L.

bractĕa (brattĕa) -ae, f. *a thin plate of metal, gold leaf*: Lucr., Verg., Ov.

bractĕātus -a -um, *covered with gold leaf.* TRANSF., *glittering, unreal, delusive*: felicitas, Sen.

bractĕŏla -ae, f. (dim. of bractea), *a thin leaf of gold*: Juv.

Branchus -i, m. (Βράγχος), *a son of Apollo.*

¶ Hence **Branchidae** -ārum, m. (Βραγχίδαι), *descendants of Branchus, the hereditary caste of priests at the temple of Apollo at Miletus.*

brassĭca -ae, f. *cabbage*: Pl.

Bratuspantium -i, n. *town in Gallia Belgica*, at or near modern *Breteuil.*

Brennus -i, m. (Βρέννος). (1) *leader of the Gauls, who defeated the Romans at the river Allia*, 390 B.C. (2) *leader of a Gallic horde who invaded Greece in* 279 B.C. Adj. **Brennĭcus** -a -um.

brĕvĭārium -i, n. (brevis), *a short summary, report, epitome*: imperii, officiorum, Suet.

brĕvĭcŭlus -a -um (dim. of brevis), *somewhat short or little*: Pl.

brĕvĭlŏquens -entis (brevis/loquor), *brief in speech*: Cic. L.

brĕvĭlŏquentĭa -ae, f. (brevis/loquor), *brevity of speech*: Cic. L.

brĕvis -e (connected with βραχύς), adj. (with compar. and superl.), *short*, in space or time.

(1) in space. LIT., **a**, as to length (opp. to longus), *short*: via, Verg.; in breve cogere, *to contract into a small space*, Hor.: **b**, as to height (opp. to longus, altus): iudex brevior quam testis, *of shorter stature*, Cic.: **c**, as to depth (opp. to profundus), *shallow*: brevia vada, Verg; hence n. pl. as subst. **brevia** -ium, *shallows, shoals*: Verg., Tac. TRANSF., *slight*: pondus, Hor.; impensa, Ov.

(2) in time (opp. to longus): **a**, *of a period, short*: ad breve tempus, *for a short time*, Cic.; brevi post, *shortly afterwards*, Liv.; brevi, *soon*, Cic.: **b**, *of short duration*: fructus, Lucr.; vitae curriculum, Cic.; rosae flos, lilium, *blooming only for a short time*, Hor.; breves populi Romani amores, *short-lived*, Tac.: **c**, *of the quantity of syllables, short*: syllaba, Cic.: **d**, of discourse or writing, *short, concise*: breves litterae tuae, Cic.; brevis narratio, Cic.; brevi, *in a few words*, Cic.; breve faciam, *I will make it short*, Cic.; so meton. of persons: cum se breves putent esse, longissimi sint, Cic.; brevis esse laboro, Hor.

Adv. (with compar. and superl.) **breviter**, *shortly*. (1) in space: Tib., Tac. (2) in time. TRANSF., **a**, of the quantity of syllables:

breviter dicitur, Cic.: **b**, in speech or writing, *briefly*: rem breviter narrare, Cic.

brĕvĭtās -ātis, f. (brevis), *shortness.* (1) in space, in regard to length: spatii, Caes.; of height: brevitas nostra, *our short stature*, Caes.

(2) in time: **a**, lit. of a period: temporis, diei, Cic.: **b**, shortness of syllables: syllabarum, Cic.: **c**, of speech and writing, *brevity, conciseness*: litterarum, Cic.; orationis, Cic.; brevitati servire, *to study brevity*, Cic.; est brevitate opus, Hor.

Brĭăreus (trisyl.) -ei, m. (Βριαρεύς), also called Aegaeon, *a giant with a hundred arms*: centumgeminus, Verg.; adj. **Brĭărēïus** -a -um.

Brĭgantes -um, m. *a tribe in the north of Britain*; adj. **Brĭganticus** -a -um.

Brīmo -ūs, f. (Βριμώ), *the angry one*, epithet of Proserpina: Prop.

Brĭtanni -orum, m. pl. *the Britons*: Caes., Verg., Hor.; term used for the *inhabitants either of the British Isles* or *of Great Britain.*

¶ Hence **Brĭtannĭa** -ae, f. *Britain*, i.e. either *the British Isles* or *Great Britain*; sometimes in plur. **Brĭtannĭcus** -a -um, adj., *British*: Cic., Tac.; also in m. sing. *a title commemorating successes in Britain*, given to various Romans in imperial times, esp. to the son of Claudius and Messalina who was murdered by Nero. **Brĭtannus** -a -um, poet. adj., *British*: Prop.

Brĭtŏmartis -is, f. (Βριτόμαρτις), *a Cretan nymph, daughter of Zeus and Carme; pursued by Minos, she threw herself into the sea.*

Brixĭa -ae, f. *a town in Cisalpine Gaul* (now *Brescia*); adj. **Brixĭānus** -a -um, *of or relating to Brixia.*

Brŏmĭus -i, m. (Βρόμιος, *the noisy*), *a surname of Bacchus*: Ov., Luc.

Bructĕri -ōrum, m. *a people of North Germany.*

brūma -ae, f. (for brevima, old form of brevissima, sc. dies), *the time of the shortest day of the year, the winter solstice.* LIT., ante brumam, Cic.; sub bruma, Caes. Poet., *winter, wintry cold*: bruma recurrit iners, Hor., Verg. TRANSF., *a year*: Mart.

brūmālis -e (bruma). (1) *relating to the shortest day*: dies, Cic.; signum, *Capricorn*, Cic. (2) *wintry*: horae, Ov.; frigus, Verg.

Brundĭsium -i, n. (Βρεντέσιον), *a town in Calabria, with an excellent harbour, the port most used by the Romans for journeys to Greece and the East* (now *Brindisi*).

¶ Hence adj. **Brundĭsīnus** -a -um, *Brundisian.*

Bruttii (Brūtii, Brittii) -ōrum, m. *the Bruttii, the inhabitants of the southern extremity of Italy*; adj. **Bruttĭus** -a -um, *Bruttian.*

¹**brūtus** -a -um (connected with βαρύς and βριθύς), *heavy, immovable.* LIT., pondus, Lucr. TRANSF., *dull, insensible, without feeling or reason*: adulescentiam, Sen.

²**Brūtus** -i, m. *a cognomen of the Roman gens Iunia.*

Esp. (1) L. Iunius Brutus, *relative of Tarquinius Superbus, who freed Rome from its kings.* (2) M. Iunius Brutus, *nephew of Cato Uticensis, one of the murderers of Julius Caesar.* (3) D. Iunius Brutus, *fellow conspirator with* (2). Adj. **Brūtīnus** -a -um, *belonging to Brutus*: consilia Brutina, Cic.

Būbastis -is, f. (*Βούβαστις*), *an Egyptian goddess, represented with the head of a cat.*

būbīle -is, n. (bos), *an ox-stall*: Pl.

būbo -ōnis, m. (*βύας, βύζα*), *the owl* (the cry of which was thought a bad omen): Lucr., Verg.

būbulcĭtor -ari, dep. *to drive* or *keep oxen*: Pl.

būbulcus -i, m. (bos), *one who ploughs with oxen*: Cic., Ov.

būbŭlus -a -um (bos), *relating to cows* or *oxen*: fimum, Liv. F. as subst. **būbŭla** -ae, f. (sc. caro), *beef*: Pl.

būcaeda -ae, m. (bos/caedo), *one who is beaten with thongs of ox-hide*: Pl.

bucca -ae, f. *the cheek,* esp. when puffed out.
    LIT., buccas inflare, *to puff out the cheeks* (esp. in anger), Hor.; prov.: quod (*or* quidquid) in buccam venerit, *whatever comes uppermost,* Cic. L., Mart.
    TRANSF., (**1**) *a declaimer, bawler*: Juv. (**2**) *one who fills his mouth full, a parasite*: Petr. (**3**) *a mouthful*: Mart. (**4**) *a person with swollen cheeks* (of a trumpeter): Juv.

buccella -ae, f. (dim. of bucca), *a little mouthful*: Mart.

buccĭna, buccĭnator, etc., *see* bucina, etc.

bucco -ōnis, m. (bucca), *a babbling foolish fellow*: Pl.

buccŭla -ae, f. (dim. of bucca). LIT., *a small cheek*: Suet. TRANSF. (in plur.), *the beaver, the visor, the part of a helmet which covers the cheeks*: Liv.

buccŭlentus -a -um (bucca), *puffy-cheeked*: Pl.

Būcĕphălās -ae, acc. -an (*βοῦς/κεφαλή*), *the horse of Alexander the Great.*
    ¶ Hence **Būcĕphăla** -ae, f. and **Būcĕphălē** -ēs, f. (*βουκέφαλα*), *a town founded in its honour on the Hydaspes.*

būcĕrus and **būcĕrĭus** -a -um (*βούκερως*), *having ox's horns*: Lucr., Ov.

būcĭna -ae, f. *a crooked trumpet* (whereas *tuba* is usually straight).
    LIT., (**1**) *the shepherd's horn*: Prop. (**2**) *a military trumpet*: Cic., Verg. Used as a signal for relieving guard, etc.; hence: ad tertiam bucinam (=vigiliam), Liv. (**3**) *the trumpet used to summon the popular assemblies*: Cic., Prop.
    TRANSF., (**1**) *Triton's horn*: Ov. (**2**) famae, Verg.

būcĭnātŏr -ōris, m. *a trumpeter*: Caes. TRANSF., existimationis, ap. Cic. L.

būcĭnum -i, n. (**1**) *the sound of a trumpet*: Plin. (**2**) *a shell-fish, whelk*: Plin.

būcŏlĭca -orum, n. pl. (*βουκολικός*), *pastoral poems*: Verg.

būcŭla -ae, f. (dim. of bos), *a heifer*: Cic., Verg.

būfo -ōnis, m. *a toad*: Verg.

bulbus -i, m. (*βολβός*), *an onion*: Ov.; gen., *a bulb*: Plin.

būlē -es, f. (*βουλή*), *the (Greek) council*: Plin. L.

būleuta -ae, m. (*βουλευτής*), *a councillor*: Plin. L.

būleutērĭon -i, n. (*βουλευτήριον*), *the place of meeting of a Greek council*: Cic.

bulla -ae, f. *a round swelling.* Hence (**1**) *a water bubble*: ut pluvio perlucida caelo surgere bulla solet, Ov. (**2**) *a boss, stud*; on girdles: aurea bullis cingula, Varr.; on doors: bullas aureas omnes ex his valvis non dubitavit auferre, Cic. (**3**) bulla aurea, *a golden ornament, an amulet* (of Etruscan origin), worn by triumphing generals and also by

boys of good family, who laid it aside on assuming the toga virilis; hence: dignus bulla=*childish,* Juv.

bullātus -a -um (bulla). (**1**) *inflated, bombastic,* or perhaps *perishable, transitory*: Pers. (**2**) *furnished with a* bulla, in the sense of *a boss, knob*: cingulum, Varr. (**3**) *wearing the* bulla, i.e. *not grown up*: heres, Juv.

bullĭo -ire and **bullo** -are (bulla), *to well up, bubble up, boil up*: Pers., Plin.

Bullis (Byllis) -idis, f. *a town in Illyria.*
    ¶ Hence **Bullĭdenses** -ium, m. *inhabitants of Bullis;* also **Bulĭenses** -ium, m. and **Bullīni** -ōrum, m.

būmastus -i, f. (*βούμαστος*), *a kind of vine bearing very large grapes*: Verg.

Burdĭgăla -ae, f. *a town in Aquitania* (now *Bordeaux*).

būris -is, m. *the crooked hinder part of the plough*: Verg.

Būsīris -rĭdis, m. (*Βούσιρις*), *a king of Egypt who sacrificed all foreigners who came to his country, and was himself killed by Hercules.*

bustĭrāpus -i, m. (bustum/rapio), *a robber of tombs*: Pl.

bustŭārĭus -a -um (bustum), *belonging to the place where corpses were burned*: gladiator, *one who fought at a funeral pile in honour of the dead,* Cic.

bustum -i, n. (perhaps from buro, old Lat. for uro). LIT., *the place where corpses were burned and buried*: Lucr., Verg. TRANSF., gen., *a grave, sepulchre*: Cic.; fig.: tu bustum reipublicae, *the destroyer of the State,* Cic.; bustum miserabile nati, *Tereus who ate his own son,* Ov.

Buthrōtum -i, n. and **-tŏs** -i, f. (*βουθρωτόν* and -*τός*), *a town on the coast of Epirus, opposite Corcyra* (now *Vutrinto*).

būthȳsĭa -ae, f. (*βουθυσία*), *a sacrifice of oxen*: Suet.

Butrōtus -i, m. *a river in Bruttium* (now *Bruciano*).

Buxentum -i, n. *a town in Lucania* (now *Policastro*).

buxĭfĕr -a -um (buxus/fero), *producing the box-tree*: Cat.

buxus -i, f. and **buxum** -i, n. LIT., *the evergreen box-tree*: Ov.; *box-wood*: Verg. TRANSF., *articles made of box-wood*—e.g., *flute*: Verg.; *top*: Verg.; *comb*: Ov.; *writing-tablets*: Prop.

Byrsa -ae, f. (*Βύρσα*), *the citadel of Carthage.*

Byzantĭum -i, n. (*Βυζάντιον*), *Byzantium, a Greek city in Thrace on the Bosphorus, opposite the Asiatic Chalcedon* (now *Istanbul*). Adj. **Byzantīnus** -a -um, **Byzantĭus** -a -um, *Byzantine.*

C

C, c, the third letter of the Latin Alphabet, corresponding in place and originally in sound to the Greek *Γ, γ*. At an early period it was substituted for K, which, except in a few instances, disappeared from the language.

căballīnus -a -um, *belonging to a horse*: fons (in jest)=*Hippocrene,* Pers.

căballus -i, m. (καβάλλης), *a pack-horse, nag, hack*: Hor., Juv.

Căbillonum -i, n. *a town of the Aedui in Gallia Lugdunensis* (now *Chalons-sur-Saône*).

Căbiri -ōrum, m. (Κάβειροι), *gods honoured by secret rites in Lemnos and Samothrace.*

căchinnātĭo -ōnis, f. (cachinno), *a violent laughing, cachinnation*: Cic.

¹**căchinno** -are (cachinnus), *to laugh aloud*: ridere convivae, cachinnare ipse Apronius, Cic.

²**căchinno** -ōnis, m. (cachinnus), *one who laughs heartily, a jester, scoffer*: Pers.

căchinnus -i, m. *loud laughter*, esp. of derision: cachinnos inridentium commovere, Cic.; tollere, Hor. TRANSF., poet., *the splashing of the sea*: Cat.

căco -are (κακάω). (1) *to void the excrement*: Hor. (2) *to defile with excrement*: Cat.

căcŏēthĕs -is, n. (κακόηθες), *an obstinate disease.* LIT., Plin. TRANSF., scribendi, *an incurable itch to write*, Juv.

căcŭla -ae, m. *a servant*, esp. *a soldier's servant*: Pl.

căcūmen -ĭnis, n. *the extreme point, top, tip, summit, zenith*; esp. of trees: arboris, Verg.; ramorum, Caes., Lucr.; and of mountains: Lucr., Cat., Verg., Hor., Liv. TRANSF., alescendi, *the limit of growth*, Lucr.

căcūmĭno -are (cacumen), *to point, make pointed*: Ov.

Cācus -i, m. (Κάκος), *son of Vulcan, a giant Italian cattle-robber, slain by Hercules.*

cădāver -ĕris (cado), n. *a dead body, carcass*, of men or animals. LIT., Lucr., Cic., Caes., Verg. TRANSF., (1) as a term of reproach: ab hoc eiecto cadavere quidquam mihi aut opis aut ornamenti expetebam, Cic. (2) of the ruins of towns: cadavera oppidum, Sulpicius ap. Cic. L.

cădāvĕrōsus -a -um (cadaver), *like a corpse, cadaverous*: Ter.

Cadmus -i, m. (Κάδμος), *the son of Agenor, king of Tyre, and brother of Europa; father of Polydorus, Ino, Semele, Autonoë, and Agave; founder of Thebes in Boeotia.*
   Adj. **Cadmēus** -a -um: Thebae, Prop.; f. as subst. **Cadmēa** -ae, (sc. arx), *the citadel of Thebes*: Nep.; **Cadmēïs** -ĭdis, f. adj.: arx, Theban, Ov.; and subst., *a female descendant of Cadmus*: Ov.

cădo cădĕre cĕcĭdi (cāsum), *to fall.*
   LIT., (1) gen., *to fall down, drop*: **a**, of persons or things dropped or thrown: si prolapsus cecidisset, Liv.; in terram, Cic.; de equo, Cic.; arma alicui cadunt de manibus, Cic.; of weapons: levius, *are thrown with less violence*, Caes.; of thunderbolts: caelo cadunt fulmina, Petr.; of dice: ut (talus) cadat rectus, Cic.; of sails: vela cadunt, *are furled*, Verg.: **b**, of fluids poured or flowing: guttae, Cic.; imbres, Lucr., Verg.; flumen, Liv.: **c**, of things which naturally fall: altis de montibus umbrae, Verg.; esp. of the *shedding* of fruit, leaves, etc.: motis poma cadunt ramis, Ov.; and of the *setting* of heavenly bodies: iuxta solem cadentem, *in the west*, Verg. (2) esp. in death, *to fall, to perish*: pauci de nostris cadunt, Caes.; in acie, Cic.; sua manu, *to commit suicide*, Tac.; of the victims of a sacrifice: ovis cadit deo, Ov.; hence fig. of nations, etc., *to be destroyed*: tota Troia, Ov.

TRANSF., (1) of power, feeling, natural forces, *to subside, sink, flag*: ira, Liv.; vis venti, Liv.; cadere animis, *to lose heart*, Cic. (2) *to fail*, esp. in a law-suit: causa, in iudicio, Cic.; or on the stage (opp. stare): Hor. (3) *to come under, be subject to*; of jurisdiction: in unius potestatem, Cic.; sub imperium Romanum, Cic.; of perception: sub oculos, Cic.; of classification: in idem genus orationis, Cic. (4) *to agree with, be consistent with*: non cadit in hos mores, non in hunc hominem ista suspicio, Cic. (5) *to fall out, to happen*: si quid adversi casurum foret, Liv.; fortuito, Cic.; male, Caes.; cadere ad (or in) inritum, *to become of no effect*, Liv.; insperanti mihi cecidit ut, Cic. (6) of payments, *to fall due*: in eam diem cadere nummos qui a Quinto debentur, Cic.

cādūcĕātor -ōris, m. (caduceus), *a herald*: Liv.

cādūcĕus -i, m. and **cādūcĕum** -i, n. (1) *a herald's staff*: Cic. (2) *the wand* or *staff of Mercury*: Suet.

cādūcĭfĕr -fĕra -fĕrum (caduceus/fero), *bearing the caduceus*, surname of Mercury: Ov.

cădūcus -a -um (cado).
   (1) *fallen* or *falling.* LIT., bello, *fallen in war*, Verg.; frondes, Verg. TRANSF., as legal t. t., bona: *a legacy rendered void by the death or legal incapacity of the legatee, which fell to other heirs or to the exchequer*, Cic.; n. as subst.: legatum omne capis necnon et dulce caducum, Juv.
   (2) *inclined* or *destined* or *ready to fall.* LIT., vitis, Cic.; flos, Ov.; esp. *destined to die, devoted to death*: iuvenis, Verg. TRANSF., *frail, perishable, transitory*: res humanae fragiles caducaeque, Cic.

Cădurci -ōrum, m. *a Gaulish people in Aquitania, famous for their linen manufactures.*
   ¶ Hence adj. **Cădurcus** -a -um, *of the Caduci*; n. as subst. **Cădurcum** -i (sc. stragulum), *a coverlet of Cadurcian linen*; meton., *a bed so covered*: Juv.

cădus -i, m. (κάδος), *a jar*, esp. (1) *a wine jar*: capite sistere, *to overturn*, Pl.; meton., *wine*: Hor. (2) *a jar for other liquids*, e.g. for honey: Mart. (3)=urna, *a funeral urn*, Verg.

Cadūsii -ōrum, m. (Καδούσιοι), *a warlike nation on the Caspian Sea.*

caecĭas -ae, m. (καικίας), *a north-east wind*: Plin.

caecĭgĕnus -a -um (caecus/gigno), *born blind*: Lucr.

Caecĭlĭus -a -um, *name of a celebrated plebeian gens, of which the most famous members were*:
   (1) Qu. Caec. Metellus, *praetor* 148 B.C. *surnamed Macedonicus for his conquests in Macedonia.*
   (2) his son, Qu. Caec. Metellus, *consul* 123 B.C., *surnamed Balearicus for his victories over the Baleares.*
   (3) Caecilius Statius, *Roman comic poet contemporary of Ennius.*
   ¶ Hence adj. **Caecĭlĭānus** -a -um: fabula *of Caecilius Statius*, Cic.; senex, *in a play of the same*, Cic.

caecĭtās -ātis, f. (caecus), *blindness*: Cic.; fig. of the mind: an tibi luminis obesset caecitas plus quam libidinis? Cic.

caeco -are, *to make blind*: Lucr.; fig.: largitione mentes imperitorum, Cic.; celeritate caecata oratio, *made obscure*, Cic.

Caecŭbum -i, n. and **Caecŭbus ager**, *a marshy district in Latium, famed for its wine.* ¶ Hence adj. **Caecŭbus** -a -um, *Caecuban*: vinum Caecubum, and absol. Caecubum, *Caecuban wine*, Hor.

caecus -a -um, adj. (with compar.: Hor.). (1) act., *blind, not seeing.* LIT., ille qui caecus factus est, Cic.; as subst.: apparet id etiam caeco, Liv. TRANSF., *intellectually or morally blind, blinded*; of persons: caecus animi, Cic.; caecus furore, Verg.; of passions: timor, Cic.; hence *blind, uncertain, objectless*: caeca exspectatione, Cic. (2) pass., *unseen, hidden, obscure, dark*: nox, Lucr.; domus, Cic.; vulnus, Lucr.; pericula, Cic.; and in gen., *unknown*: fata, Hor.; causas, Lucr.

caedēs -is, f. (caedo), *a cutting.* LIT., *a cutting down, killing, slaughter, carnage*: caedes et occisio, Cic.; caedem facere, Caes., Tac.; plur.: multae et atroces inter se caedes, Liv.; esp. *killing of victims for sacrifice*: bidentium, Hor. TRANSF., (1) *persons slain*: caedis acervi, Verg. (2) *blood shed in slaughter*: (currus) respersus fraterna caede, Cat.; Verg., Ov.

caedo caedĕre cĕcīdi caesum, *to cut, to cut down, strike, beat.* (1) *to cut*: arbores, Verg.; silvam, Caes.; nemus, Ov.; securibus umida vina, *the wine now frozen*, Verg. (2) *to beat*: ianuam saxis, Cic.; aliquem virgis, Cic. TRANSF., testibus caedi, *to be hard pressed*, Cic. (3) *to kill*: consulem exercitumque, Liv.; poet.: caesi acervi, *heaps of the slain*, Cat.; caesus sanguis, *the blood of the slain*, Verg.; esp. of sacrificial victims: hostias, Cic.

caelāmĕn -inis (caelo), n. *a bas-relief*: Ov.

caelātor -ōris, m. (caelo), *a chaser, graver, or carver*: Cic., Juv.

caelātūra -ae, f. (caelo), *the art of engraving or chasing*, esp. in metals: Quint.; meton., *an engraving*: Suet., Quint.

caelebs -lĭbis, *unmarried, single.* (1) of men: se rectius viduam et illum caelibem esse futurum, Liv.; Cic.; meton.: vita, *single life*, Hor. (2) of animals: columba, Plin. TRANSF., of trees: platanus, *to which no vine is trained*, Hor., Ov.

caelĕs -itis, usually in pl. **caelĭtēs** -ĭtum (caelum), *heavenly*: regna, Ov. As subst., *a dweller in heaven, a god*: Pl., Cic., Ov.

caelestis -e (caelum), *belonging to heaven, heavenly, coming from heaven.* LIT., fulminis ignis, Lucr.; aqua, *rain*, Hor.; arcus, *rainbow*, Plin. N. pl. as subst. **caelestia** -ium, *things in heaven, the heavenly bodies*: Cic., Tac. TRANSF., *belonging to heaven as the seat of the gods, celestial, divine*: sapientia, Cic.; quem prope caelestem fecerint, *whom they almost deified*, Liv.; irae, Liv.; as subst., esp. in plur., *the gods*: Cic., Verg., Ov., Tac.; hence, in gen., of what is excellent, *glorious, superhuman*: ingenium, Ov.; mens, Liv.

caelĭbātus -ūs, m. (caelebs), *celibacy*: Suet.

caelĭcŏla -ae, adj. (caelum/colo), *dwelling in heaven*; as subst., poet., *a god*: Verg., Ov.

caelĭfĕr -fĕra -fĕrum, *bearing the heavens*: Atlas, Verg.

caelĭpotens -entis (caelum/potens), *powerful in heaven*: Pl.

Caelĭus -a -um. (1) *name of a Roman plebeian gens, the most celebrated members of which were*: a, L. Caelius Antipater, *annalist of the second Punic war, contemporary of the Gracchi*: b, M. Caelius Rufus, *intimate friend and protégé of Cicero.* (2) Caelius Mons, *a hill in Rome south of the Palatine and east of the Aventine.*

caelo -are (¹caelum), *to engrave or chase metals or ivory, to carve in bas-relief*: speciem caelare argento, Cic.; vasa caelata, Cic., Verg.; sometimes of working on other materials, e.g. *wood*: Verg. TRANSF., of poetry: caelatum novem Musis opus, *fashioned by*, Hor.

¹caelum -i, n. (caedo), *the burin or engraving-tool*: Mart., Quint.

²caelum -i, n. (m. pl. caeli in Lucr.) (connected with Gr. κοῖλος and Latin cavus, *hollow*), *the heavens, the sky.* (1) in gen.: caelum totum astris distinctum et ornatum, Cic.; e caelo ictus, *struck by lightning*, Cic.; de caelo servare, of augury, Cic.; caelum nocte atque nubibus obscuratum, Sall.; de caelo cadere, of meteors, Liv.; it clamor caelo, Verg.; minari in caelum, Verg.; prov.: caelum ac terras miscere, Liv.; findere caelum aratro, *to do something impossible*, Ov. (2) *air, climate*: caelum liberum, Cic.; gravitas huius caeli, *unhealthiness*, Cic.; crassum, Cic.; caelum non animum mutant qui trans mare currunt, Hor. (3) fig., *heaven* as the height of joy, renown, etc.: esse in caelo, Cic. L.; ferre ad (or in) caelum, *to extol*, Cic.; so: caelo exaequare, Lucr.; aequare, Tac. (4) *heaven* as the home of the gods: de caelo delapsus, *a messenger of the gods*, Cic.; non ad mortem trudi, verum in caelum videri escendere, Cic.; quid me caelum sperare iubebas? i.e. *marriage with a god*, Verg.

caementum -i, n. (caedo), *rough unhewn stone from the quarry*, usually in plur.: Cic., Hor.

Caenēus -ĕi and -eos, m. (Καινεύς), *a Lapith; according to one story originally a girl but changed by Neptune into a boy.*

Caenīna -ae, f. (Καινίνη), *a town in Latium.* ¶ Hence adj. **Caenīnensis** -e and **Caenīnus** -a -um, *of or belonging to Caenina.*

caenōsus -a -um (caenum), *muddy*: Juv.

caenum -i, n. *mud, dirt, filth* (always with offensive associations). LIT., male olere omne caenum, Cic. TRANSF., (1) *disgrace, degradation*: Pl.; in tenebris volvi caenoque, Lucr.; plebeio, Liv. (2) as a term of reproach: labes illa atque caenum, Cic.

caepa (cēpa) -ae, f. and **caepe** (cēpe) -is, n. *an onion*: Hor., Ov.

Caerĕ, n. indecl. (genit. Caerĭtis f. and abl. Caerēte: Verg.), *a very old city of Etruria* (now *Cervetri*), *whose inhabitants received the Roman citizenship, except the right of voting.* ¶ Hence adj. **Caerēs** -itis and -ētis, *belonging to Caere*: Caerite cera (i.e., tabula) digni=*deserving of civic degradation*, Hor. M. pl. as subst. **Caerĭtes** or **Caerētes** -um, *the inhabitants of Caere.*

caerĭmōnĭa -ae, f. (1) *holiness, sacredness*: deorum, Cic.; legationis, Cic., Tac. (2) *holy awe, reverence*, esp. as shown outwardly: summa religione caerimoniaque sacra conficere, Cic. (3) *religious usage, sacred ceremony* (gen. in plur.): Cic., Liv., Tac.

Caeroesi -ōrum, m. *a people in Gallia Belgica, near modern Luxemburg.*

caerŭlēus (poet. also **caerŭlus**) -a -um (connected with caelum), *blue*. (1) of the sky: Enn.; n. pl. as subst., caerula caeli, *or* simply caerula, *the azure of the sky*: Lucr., Ov. (2) of the sea: aquae, Ov.; pontus, Cat., Ov.; n. pl. as subst., caerula: Verg.; hence, of sea-gods: deus, *Neptune*, Ov.; mater, *Thetis*, Ov.; equi, *of Triton*, Ov. (3) of rivers: Thybris, Verg. (4) of other blue-coloured things: oculi, Cic., Tac.; Germanorum pubes, *blue-eyed*, Hor. (5) gen., of *dark* things: angues, Verg.; imber, nubes, Verg.; ratis fati, Prop.
N. sing. as subst. **caerŭleum** -i, *a blue colour*: Plin.

Caesar -ăris, m. *a Roman family name of the gens Iulia.* Esp. of:
(1) C. Iulius Caesar, *general, author, and statesman who conquered Pompey, overthrew the power of the senate, was made Dictator with supreme power, and was murdered by Brutus and Cassius,* 44 B.C. Hence adj. **Caesareus, Caesariānus, Caesarīnus** -a -um, *of* or *relating to Julius Caesar*; as subst. **Caesariānī** -orum, m. *adherents of Julius Caesar.*
(2) C. Iulius Caesar Octavianus Augustus, *relative and successor of* (1), *who established the empire.* After him all the emperors bore the name of Caesar, with the title Augustus, till, under Hadrian, a distinction was made, and the reigning emperor was called Caesar Augustus, and the appointed heir Caesar.

Caesarēa -ae, f. (Καισάρεια), *name of several towns, including* (1) *in Palestine.* (2) *in Mauritania.* (3) *in Cappadocia.* (4) *in Phoenicia.*

caesărĭātus -a -um (caesaries), *long-haired*: Pl.

caesărĭēs -ēi, f., poet. and usually sing., *hair, a head of hair*: Pl., Verg., Hor.; barbae, *the hair of the beard*, Ov.

caesīcĭus -a -um (caesius), *bluish grey*: Pl.

caesim, adv. (caedo), *with cutting.* LIT., *with the edge of the sword* (opp. to punctim, *with the point*): petere hostem, Liv. TRANSF., of discourse, *in short sentences*: membratim adhuc, deinde caesim diximus, Cic.; Quint.

caesĭus -a -um, *bluish grey*, esp. of the eyes: caesios oculos Minervae, caeruleos Neptuni, Cic.; leo, *with grey eyes*, Cat.

caespĕs (ce‌ⁿpĕs) -ĭtis, m. (caedo), *a turf, a sod.*
LIT., *turf*, used for altars, tombs, mounds: primum exstruendo tumulo caespitem Caesar posuit, Tac.; plur.: gladiis caespites circumcidere, Caes.; non esse arma caespites neque glebas, Cic.
TRANSF., (1) *a hut of turf*: Hor. (2) *an altar of turf*: Hor., Tac. (3) *grassy sward*: gramineus, Verg.

caestus -ūs, m. (caedo), *gauntlet for boxers*, made of leathern thongs: Cic., Verg.

caetra (cetra) -ae, f. *a short Spanish shield*: Verg., Liv., Tac.

caetratus -a -um (caetra), *armed with the* caetra: Caes., Liv.

Cāīcus -i, m. (Κάϊκος), *a river in Mysia.*

Cāiēta -ae (and -ē -ēs), f. (1) *the nurse of Aeneas.* (2) *a town on the sea-coast, on the borders of Latium and Campania* (now *Gaëta*).

Caius=Gaius; q.v.

Călabrĭa -ae, f. *the peninsula at the south-east extremity of Italy.*
¶ Hence adj. and subst. **Călăber** -bra -brum, *belonging to Calabria, a Calabrian.*

Călactē -ēs, f. (Καλὴ ἀκτή), *a town on the north coast of Sicily.*
¶ Hence **Călactīnus** -a -um, *of* or *belonging to* Calacte.

Călăis -is, m. (Κάλαϊς), *son of Boreas and Orithyia, brother of Zetes, and companion of the Argonauts.*

Călămis -mĭdis, m. (Κάλαμις), *one of the great Greek sculptors of the fifth century* B.C.

călămister -tri, m. and **călămistrum** -tri, n. (calamus), *a curling-iron for the hair*: frons calamistri notata vestigiis, Cic. TRANSF., *excessive ornament* or *flourish in discourse*: Cic.; calamistri Maecenatis, Tac.

călămistrātus -a -um (calamister), *curled with the curling-iron*: Pl.; coma, Cic.; saltator, Cic.

călămĭtās -ātis, f. *loss, failure*, esp. in agriculture: Pl., Ter.; fructuum, Cic. Hence in gen., *misfortune, damage, calamity, loss*: calamitatem tolerare, Cic.; calamitate prohibere aliquem, Cic.; plur.: calamitates reipublicae; often of *reverse in war*: Cannensis illa calamitas, Cic.; calamitatem inferre, Caes.

călămĭtōsus -a -um (calamitas) adj. (with compar. and superl.). (1) act., *causing loss, destructive*: tempestas, Cic.; bellum, *calamitous*, Cic. (2) pass., *suffering great loss, miserable*: agri, Cic.; homines miseri et fortuna magis quam culpa calamitosi, Cic. L.
Adv. **călămĭtōsē**, *disastrously*: Cic.

călămus -i, m. (κάλαμος), *a reed.* LIT., Plin. TRANSF., (1) of various articles made of reed; *a writing reed, pen*: Cic. L., Hor.; *a reed-pipe, Pan-pipe*: Lucr., Verg.; *an arrow*: Hor.; *a fishing-rod*: Ov.; *a limed twig for fowling*: Prop. (2) *any reed-shaped stalk*: Verg.

călăthiscus -i, m. (καλαθίσκος), *a small wicker basket*: Cat.

călăthus -i, m. (κάλαθος). LIT., *a wicker basket*, used for fruit or flowers: Verg.; for spinning: Ov. TRANSF., *a vessel of similar form* of metal or wood; *a milk-pail*: Verg.; *a wine-bowl*: Verg.

Călātĭa -ae and **Călātĭae** -ārum, f. *a town in Campania.* Adj. **Călātīnus** -a -um, *Calatine.*

călātor -ōris, m. (¹calo), *an attendant*, esp. *upon priests*: Suet.; also gen., *a servant*: Pl.

calcănĕum -i, n. (¹calx), *the heel*: Verg.

calcar -āris, n. (¹calx), *a spur*; usually in pl. LIT., equo calcaria subdere, Liv.; equum calcaribus concitare, Liv.; prov.: addere calcaria sponte currenti, *to spur the willing horse*, Plin. TRANSF., gen., *stimulus, incitement*: admovere, Cic.; alter frenis eget, alter calcaribus, Cic.; calcaria adhibere, Cic.

calcĕāmentum -i, n. (calceo), *a covering for the foot*: calceamentum solorum callum, Cic.

calcĕārĭum -i, n. (calceus), *shoe-money*: Suet.

calcĕātus -ūs, m. (calceo), *a covering for the foot*: Plin., Suet.

calcĕo -are, *to shoe, provide with shoes*: homines non satis commode calceati et vestiti, Cic.; Suet.; of animals: Suet.

calcĕŏlārĭus -i, m. (calceolus), *a shoemaker*: Pl.

calcĕŏlus -i, m. (dim. of calceus), *a small shoe*: Cic.

calcĕus -i, m. (calx, *the heel*), *a shoe*, distinguished from the sandal (solea) as covering the whole foot: habiles, Cic.; laxus, Hor.; calceos poscere, *to rise from table* (as the Romans took off their shoes when reclining at dinner), Plin. L.; calceos mutare, *to become a senator* (from a particular kind of shoe worn only by senators), Cic.

Calchās -antis, acc. -antem and -anta, m. (Κάλχας), *son of Thestor, soothsayer to the Greeks before Troy.*

Calchedon = Chalcedon; q.v.

calcĭtrātus -ūs, m. *a kicking*: Plin.

¹calcĭtro -are (¹calx), *to strike with the heel, kick.* LIT., Plin. TRANSF., (1) *to resist obstinately*: Cic. (2) *to writhe the feet about*, at death: Ov.

²calcĭtro -ōnis, m. (¹calcitro), *a kicker.* LIT., of a horse: Varr. TRANSF., of men, *a bully, blusterer*: Pl.

calco -are (¹calx), *to tread upon, to trample on.* LIT., vipera, Ov.; morientum acervos, Ov.; of a road: calcanda via leti, Hor.; esp. of grapes: uvam, Ov.
    TRANSF., (1) *to trample under foot*: amorem, Ov.; libertatem, Liv. (2) *to insult*: Prop.

calcŭlātor -ōris, m. *a computer*: Mart.

calcŭlus -i, m. (dim. of ²calx), *a little stone, pebble.*
    In gen.: Cic., Quint.; collectively, *gravel*: Verg.
    Esp. (1) *a piece used in the Roman game of draughts* (*called* Duodecim scripta): calculum reducere, *to retract a move*, Cic. (2) *a voting pebble*, a white one being thrown into the urn to acquit or to affirm, a black one to condemn or to negative: album calculum adiicere errori, Plin. L. (3) *a counter for reckoning*, hence *a calculation*: ad calculos vocare, *to subject a matter to a strict reckoning*, Cic.; *to settle accounts with a person*, Liv.

caldārĭus -a -um (calidus), *concerned with warming* or *warm water*: cella, Plin. L.

caldus = calidus; q.v.

Călēdŏnĭa -ae, f. *the highlands in the north of Scotland.* Adj. **Călēdŏnĭus** -a -um, *Caledonian.*

călĕfăcĭo (**calfacio**) -facere -fēci -factum, pass. calefio, etc. (caleo/facio), *to make warm, heat.* LIT., balineum calfieri iubebo, Cic.; corpus, Cic.; igne focum, Ov. TRANSF., *to disturb, excite*: Gabinium luculente calefecerat Mummius, Cic. L.; calefacta corda tumultu, Verg.

călĕfacto -are (freq. of calefacio), *to make warm, heat.* LIT., Pl., Hor. TRANSF., virgis, Pl.

Calendae = Kalendae; q.v.

călĕo -ēre -ui, *to be warm, hot, to glow.*
    LIT., ignis calet, Cic.; centum Sabaeo ture calent arae, Verg.; terrae alio sole calentes, Hor. Sometimes of animal heat: os calet tibi, Pl.
    TRANSF., (1) of persons, *to be inflamed, aroused, excited*: calebat in agendo, *he was all*

fire in acting, Cic.; Romani calentes adhuc ab recenti pugna, Liv.; cupidine laudis, Ov.; so of love: amore, Ov.; or with the beloved in abl.: femina, Hor. (2) of things, *to be urged on zealously*: indicia calent, Cic.; Veneris bella, Tib. (3) of things, *to be yet warm, fresh, of interest*: nisi dum calet hic agitur, Pl.

Călēs -ium, f. *town in Campania, famous for its wine* (now *Calvi*). Adj. **Călēnus** -a -um, *of* or *belonging to Cales.* N. as subst. **Călēnum** -i, *wine of Cales*: Juv.

călesco -ĕre (inch. of caleo), *to become warm, to grow hot.* LIT., calescere vel apricatione vel igni, Cic.; tunc primum radiis gelidi caluere triones, Ov. TRANSF., of love: quo propior nunc es, flamma propiore calesco, Ov.

Calēti -ōrum and **Calētes** -um, m. *a Gallic tribe in Normandy, on the Seine.*

călĭdus (**caldus**) -a -um, *warm, hot* (caleo).
    LIT., ignis, Lucr.; vapor, Lucr., Cic. F. sing. as subst. **călĭda** (**calda**) -ae (sc. aqua), *warm water*: Tac., Plin. N. sing. as subst. **călĭdum** -i, *warm wine and water*: Pl.
    TRANSF., (1) *hot, fiery, passionate, violent*: equus, Verg.; calidus iuventa, Hor.; consilium calidum, Cic. (2) *quick, speedy*: mendacium, Pl.
    Adv. **călĭdē**, *speedily*: Pl.

călĭendrum -i, n. (κάλλυντρον), *a head-dress of Roman women, built up with false hair*: Hor.

călĭga -ae, f. (connected with calceus), *a stout shoe*, esp. *soldier's boot*: Cic. L., Suet., Juv.

călĭgātus -a -um (caliga), *wearing heavy boots*: Juv. M. as subst., *a private soldier*: Suet.

călĭgĭnōsus -a -um (caligo). LIT., *foggy, misty*: caelum nebulosum et caliginosum, Cic. TRANSF., *dark*: nox, *the unknown future*, Hor.

¹călīgo -ĭnis, f. *fog, mist, vapour.* LIT., fulvae nubis caligo crassa, Verg.; densa, Liv. Hence pen., *darkness*: caeca noctis, Lucr.; tetrae tenebrae et caligo, Cic.; esp. *mist before the eyes*: aliquid cernere quasi per caliginem, Cic.
    TRANSF., (1) *mental darkness, dullness*: haec indoctorum animis offusa caligo, Cic. (2) *calamity, affliction, gloom*: superioris anni caligo et tenebrae, Cic.

²călīgo -are (¹caligo). (1) transit., *to spread a dark mist around*: Verg.; meton.: caligantes fenestrae, *making dizzy*, Juv. (2) intransit., *to be dark*: caligans lucus, Verg.; esp. of the eyes, *to be misty*: caligant oculi, Lucr.
    TRANSF., *to be in darkness*: Plin.; prov.: caligare in sole, *to grope in daylight*, Quint.

Călĭgŭla -ae, m. (dim. of caliga). LIT., *a little soldier's shoe; nickname given by the soldiers to Gaius, the Roman emperor, when as a boy in the camp of his father Germanicus he was dressed in soldier's costume.*

călix -ĭcis, m. (κύλιξ). (1) *a goblet, drinking vessel*: calix mulsi, Cic. (2) *a cooking vessel*: Ov.

callĕo -ēre (callum), *to be thick-skinned.* LIT., plagis, Pl. TRANSF., (1) intransit., *to be hard, insensible*: Sulpicius ap. Cic. L. (2) intransit., *to be practised, experienced*: Pl.; usu alicuius rei, Liv. (3) transit., *to know by experience, understand*: iura, Cic.; res, Liv.; with infin.: Lucr., Hor., Juv.

callĭdĭtās -ātis, f. (1) in a good sense, *expertness, cleverness*: vincere omnes calliditate et celeritate ingenii, Nep.

(2) more frequently in a bad sense, *cunning, craft, artifice*: scientia quae est remota ab iustitia calliditas potius quam sapientia appellanda, Cic.; *stratagem in war*, Liv.; in oratory, *artifice*: genus eiusmodi calliditatis atque calumniae, Cic.; in pl., *artful dodges*: Ter.

callĭdus -a -um (calleo), adj. (with compar. and superl.), *clever by reason of experience, dexterous, skilful*; also in bad sense, *sly, cunning*.

(1) of persons: agitator (equi), Cic.; artifex, Cic.; legum scriptor peritus et callidus, Cic.; of skill in the arts: Hor. The nature of the skill is indicated by ad: ad fraudem, Cic.; by genit.: rei militaris, Tac., Cic., Liv.; by infin.: Hor.

(2) of things, esp. in bad sense: audacia, Cic.; nimis callida iuris interpretatio, *too subtle*, Cic.; ingenium (of Tiberius), Tac.

Adv. **callĭdē**, *cleverly, cunningly*: Pl.; dicere, Cic.; occultare, Sall.

Callifae -ārum, f. *a town in Samnium.*

Callĭmăchus -i, m. (Καλλίμαχος), *a celebrated Greek poet and grammarian from Cyrene, active at Alexandria about 270 B.C.*

Callĭŏpē -ēs and **Callĭŏpēa** -ae, f. (Καλλιόπη, *the beautiful-voiced), Calliope, the Muse of epic poetry, or of poetry in general*: Hor., Ov. Meton.: vos, O Calliope, etc., *all the Muses collectively*, Verg.; also for *poetry*: Ov.

Callĭpŏlis -is, f. (Καλλίπολις). (1) *a town on the Thracian Chersonese (now Gallipoli).* (2) *a town on the Tauric Chersonese.*

Callĭrrhŏē (poet. **Callĭrhŏē**) -es, f. (Καλλιρ- ρόη). (1) *daughter of the river Achelous, wife of Alcmaeon.* (2) *a well at Athens, on the south side of the Acropolis.*

callis -is, m. (f. in Liv.). Lit., *a narrow track, footpath, cattle track*: invius, Liv.; Ov., Verg. Transf., *upland pastures*: Italiae calles et pastorum stabula, Cic., Liv., Tac.

Callistō -ūs, f. (Καλλιστώ), *daughter of the Arcadian king Lycaon, mother of Arcas by Jupiter, punished by one of the goddesses, and placed by Jupiter among the stars as Ursa Major or Helice.*

callōsus -a -um (callum), *having a hard skin, hard, solid*: ova, Hor.

callum -i, n. *hard skin or flesh on animals or plants*: calceamentum callum solorum, Cic.; aprugnum, Pl.; pedum, Plin.; pirorum, Plin. Transf., *toughness, insensibility*: ipse labor quasi callum quoddam obducit dolori, Cic.; quorum animis diuturna cogitatio callum vetustatis obduxerat, Cic.; Quint.

¹călo (**kălo**) -are (καλῶ), *to call, summon*; t. t. of religious ceremonies, esp.: comitia calata, *an assembly called to consecrate a priest or king*; hence, sarcastically: calatis granis, Cic.

²călo -ōnis, m. *a soldier's servant, camp-menial*: Caes., Liv.; gen., *a drudge*: Cic., Hor.

¹călor -ōris, m. (caleo), *warmth, heat, glow.* Lit., vis frigoris et caloris, Cic.; ignis, vitalis, Lucr.; esp. of weather: vitandi caloris causa, Cic.; calores austrini, Verg.; mediis caloribus, *in full summer*, Liv. Transf., *passion, excitement, ardour*: cogitationis, Quint.; esp. *the fire of love*: Ov., Hor.

²Călŏr -ōris, m. *a river in Samnium* (now *Calore*).

Calpē -ēs, f. (Κάλπη), *one of the pillars of Hercules* (now *Gibraltar*).

Calpurnĭus -a -um, *name of a Roman plebeian gens, the families of which bore the names of* Flamma, Asprenas, Piso, Bestia, Bibulus. Adj. **Calpurniānus** -a -um, *belonging to a Calpurnius.*

The most famous members of this gens were (1) C. Calp. Piso, *praetor and propraetor in Spain*, 186 B.C. (2) L. Calp. Piso, *consul in* 112 B.C. (3) L. Calp. Bestia, *tribune* 121 B.C., *consul* 111 B.C., *and general against Jugurtha.* (4) Calpurnia, *wife of Julius Caesar.*

caltha -ae, f. *a plant*, prob. *the common marigold*: Verg.

calthŭla -ae, f. (caltha), *a woman's robe of a yellow colour*: Pl.

călumnĭa (kalumnia) -ae, f. *trick, artifice, chicanery, craft*; gen.: inimicorum calumnia, Cic.; religionis calumnia, *deceitful pretence*, Cic.; calumniam adhibere, Cic.; Academicorum, *misrepresentation*, Cic.

Esp. at law. (1) *a false accusation, malicious prosecution*: calumnia litium alienos fundos petere, Cic.; calumniam iurare, *to swear that an accusation is not malicious*, Cic. (2) *an action for false accusation*: calumniam privato iudicio non effugere, Cic.; Tac.

călumnĭātor (kalumniator) -ōris, m. (calumnior), *a false accuser, pettifogger*: scriptum sequi calumniatoris esse; boni iudicis, voluntatem scriptoris auctoritatemque defendere, Cic.

călumnĭor (kalumnior) -ari, dep. (calumnia), *to accuse falsely, misrepresent* a person or thing: se, Quint.; festinationem, Quint.; absol., *to bring false accusations, to practise trickery*: iacet res in controversiis isto calumniante biennium, Cic.

calva -ae, f. (calvus), *the bald scalp of the head*: Liv., Mart.

calvĕo -ēre, *to be bare of hair, bald*: Plin.

Calvīsĭus -ii, m. *Roman name.* (1) C. Calv. Sabinus, *legate of Caesar.* (2) Calvisius, *the accuser of Agrippina, the mother of Nero.*

calvĭtĭēs -ēi, f. (calvus), *baldness*: Suet.

calvĭtĭum -i, n. (calvus), *baldness*: Cic.

calvor -ī, dep. *to form intrigues, deceive*: Pl.

calvus -a -um, *bald, without hair*: Suet.; of plants: Mart.

Calvus, *a Roman cognomen, see* Licinius.

¹calx -cis, f. *the heel*: certare pugnis, calcibus, Cic.; calcem terere calce, *to tread close on the heels*, Verg.; caedere calcibus, *to kick*, Pl.; accipe calcem, *take a kicking*, Juv. Prov.: adversus stimulum calces (sc. iactare), *to kick against the pricks*, Ter.

²calx -cis, f., rarely m. *a stone.* Hence (1) *a pebble used as a counter in various games*: Pl. (2) *limestone, lime, chalk*: lintribus in eam insulam materiam, calcem, caementa convehere, Cic.; viva, *quicklime*, and exstincta, *slaked lime*, Vitr. (3) meton., *since the goal in a racecourse was marked with chalk, a goal, end* (opp. carceres, *the starting-point)*: quibuscum tamquam e carceribus emissus sis, cum iisdem ad calcem, ut dicitur, pervenire, Cic.; ad carceres a calce revocari, *to turn back from the end to the beginning*, Cic.

Călўdōn -ōnis, f. (Καλυδών), *a very ancient city in Aetolia.* ¶ Hence adj. **Călўdōnius** -a -um, *Calydonian*: heros, *Meleager of Calydon*, Ov.; amnis, *the Achelous*, Ov.; sus, aper, *the boar sent to Calydon by Diana, slain by Meleager*, Mart.; f. adj. and subst. **Călўdōnis** -ĭdis = *Deianira*: Ov.

Călypsō -ūs, acc. -o, f. (Καλυψώ), *a nymph, daughter of Atlas* (or *Oceanus*), *who entertained Ulysses in the island of Ogygia.*

cămăra = camera; q.v.

Cămărīna (Cămĕrina) -ae, f. (Καμάρινα), *a town on the southern coast of Sicily.*

Cambūnii montes, m. *mountains forming the boundary between Thessaly and Macedonia.*

Cambȳsēs -is, m. (Καμβύσης). (1) *husband of Mandane, father of the elder Cyrus.* (2) *son and successor of the elder Cyrus, king of Persia from 529 to 521 B.C.*

camēlla -ae, f. (dim. of camera), *a goblet*: Ov.

cămēlus -i, m. and f. (κάμηλος), *a camel or dromedary*: Cic., Hor., Tac.

Cămēna -ae, f. (orig. casmena, connected with carmen), usually in pl., *Latin goddesses of poetry*, in later times identified with the Greek Muses; meton., *poetry*: Hor.

cămĕra (camara) -ae, f. (καμάρα). (1) *a vaulted chamber, vault*: Lucr., Cic. L. (2) *a kind of flat covered boat*: Tac.

Cămĕrĭa -ae, f. and **Cămĕrĭum** -i, n. *a town in Latium.* Adj. **Cămĕrīnus** -a -um, *of or belonging to Cameria.*

Cămĕrīnum -i, n. *a town in Umbria* (now *Camerino*). ¶ Hence adj. and subst. **Cămers** -ertis, *of Camerinum, an inhabitant of it*; adj. **Cămertīnus** -a -um.

Cămillus -i, m. *cognomen of several members of the gens Furia, the most famous of whom*, M. Furius Camillus, *took Veii, and freed Rome from the Gauls.*

cămīnus -i, m. (κάμινος). (1) *a forge*: Ov.; semper ardente camino, *with ceaseless industry*, Juv. (2) *a fire-place*: Hor.; meton., *fire*: luculentus, Cic. L.; prov.: oleum addere camino, *to aggravate an evil*, Hor.

cammărus -i, m. (κάμμαρος), *a crustacean, regarded as a poor man's food; perhaps crayfish*: Juv., Mart.

Campănĭa -ae, f. (campus, cf. Fr. champagne, *the level country*), *a district of central Italy, the capital of which was Capua.* Adj. **Campănicus, Campănius** -a -um, *Campanian*; also adj. and subst. **Campānus** -a -um, *Campanian, a Campanian*: via, *a by-road connected with the Via Appia*, Suet.; morbus, *a kind of wart on the face common in Campania*, Hor.; pons, *the bridge over the Savo* (*Saona*), Hor.; colonia, *Capua*, Cic.; adrogantia, Cic.

campester -tris -tre (campus). (1) *of level country, flat*: loca campestria, Liv.; iter, *march in level country*, Caes.; n. pl. as subst. **campestria** -ium, *a plain*: Tac. (2) *relating to the Campus Martius and its exercises*: ludus, Cic.; n. sing. as subst. **campestre** -is (sc. velamentum), *a covering worn by wrestlers round their loins*: Hor. (3) *relating to the comitia held in the Campus Martius*: certamen, Liv.; quaestus, Cic.

campus -i, m. *a level space, a plain, field.* LIT., (1) in gen.: campos et montes peragrare, Cic.; herbidus aquosusque, Liv., Lucr., Verg., Hor.; *field of battle*: Liv. (2) esp. of *the Campus Martius at Rome, as a place for various exercises, and for meetings of the assembly of the Roman people* (*comitia*); hence meton., *the comitia*: fors domina campi, Cic.; curiam pro senatu, campum pro comitiis, Cic. (3) of other *Campi*, in Rome and elsewhere. TRANSF., (1) *any free space, field*, or *theatre of action*: cum sit campus, in quo exsultare possit oratio, Cic. (2) *any level surface* (like aequor); esp. of *the sea*: caeruleos, Pl.; natantes, Lucr.; liquentes, Verg., Ov.

Camulōdūnum -i, n. *a town of the Trinobantes in Britain* (now *Colchester*).

cămŭr -a -um (probably connected with κάμπτω), *hooked, curved*: cornua, Verg.

Cănăcē -ēs, f. (Κανάκη), *daughter of Aeolus.*

cănālis -is, m. *a waterpipe, channel, canal*: Verg., Caes.

cănārĭus -a -um (canis), *relating to a dog, canine*: Plin. Adj. prop. **Cānāria** (insula), *one of the Happy Islands in the Atlantic*: Plin.

cancelli -ōrum, m. pl. (dim. of cancer), *a lattice, railing, grating.* LIT., fori, Cic.; circi, Ov. TRANSF., *bounds, limits*: extra cancellos egredi, Cic.

cancer -cri, m. (connected with καρκίνος), *a crab.* LIT., Plin., Verg. TRANSF., (1) *the Crab, the sign of the Zodiac in which the sun is at the summer solstice*: Ov. Hence meton., *the south*: Ov.; *summer heat*: Ov. (2) *the disease cancer*: Ov.

Candāvĭa -ae, f. *a mountainous district of Illyria.*

candēfăcĭo -facere -fēcī -factum (candeo/facio), *to make of a shining white*: Pl.

candēla -ae, f. (candeo). (1) *a wax or tallow candle, taper*: candelae, cuius dispenso et tempero filum, Juv.; candelam apponere valvis, *to set the house on fire*, Juv. (2) *a cord coated with wax to preserve it from decay*: fasces involuti candelis, Liv.

candēlābrum -i, n. (candela), *a candle-stick, candelabrum*: Cic., Mart.

candĕo -ēre -ŭi, *to be of a shining white, to shine, glitter.* LIT., candet ebur soliis, Cat., Hor. TRANSF., *to glow with heat*: candente carbone, Cic.; Hor.

candesco -ĕre -ui (inch. of candeo), *to begin to shine*: Ov. TRANSF., *to begin to glow with heat*: Lucr., Ov.

candĭdātōrĭus -a -um (candidatus), *relating to a candidate*: munus, Cic. L.

candĭdātus -a -um (candidus), *clothed in white*: Pl. M. as subst. **candĭdātus** -i, *a candidate for office, who, among the Romans, was always clothed in white*: consularis, *for the consulship*, Cic.

candĭdŭlus -a -um (dim. of candidus), *shining, dazzling*: dentes, Cic.

candĭdus -a -um (candeo), *shining white, glittering white* (whereas albus = *dead white*). LIT., (1) in gen.: barba, Verg.; luna, Verg.; lilia, Verg.; tunicae linteae, Liv.; tentoria, Ov.; dies, Ov.; candidum altā nive Soracte, Hor.; n. as subst. **candidum** -i, *white colour*: Ov., Plin. Prov.: candida de nigris facere, Ov. (2) *of the complexion or*

limbs, often with the suggestion of beauty, *fair* : corpora (Gallorum), Liv.; bracchia, Ov.; puer, Hor.; Bassareus, Hor.
    TRANSF., (1) of time or fortune, *happy* : hora, Ov.; pax, Tib. (2) of writing, *clear, lucid* : genus dicendi, Cic., Quint. (3) of character, *honest, straightforward* : pauperis ingenium, Hor.; pectore candidus, Ov. (4) *clothed in white*, after the fashion of candidates for offices: turba, Tib.; pompa, Ov. (5) *signifying acquittal*, as white voting-stones did : sententia, Ov.
    Adv. **candĭdē**. (1) *in white* : vestibus, Pl. (2) *clearly, candidly* : Quint.
candor -ōris, m. (candeo), *dazzling white colour, whiteness, lustre.* LIT., candor marmoreus, Lucr.; solis, Cic.; of the Milky Way : via candore notabilis ipso, Ov.; esp. of the body: candor huius et proceritas, Cic. TRANSF., (1) of character, *sincerity, candour* : animi, Ov. (2) of writing, *clarity, simplicity* : Quint.
cānĕo -ēre -ŭi (canus), *to be white* or *hoary* : temporibus geminis canebat sparsa senectus, Verg.; gramina canent, *of dew*, Verg.; partic. **cānens**, *hoary.*
Cănēphŏros, f. (Κανηφόρος), usually in plur. **Cănēphŏroe** (Κανηφόροι). LIT., *basket-bearers; statues by Greek sculptors representing Athenian maidens bearing sacrificial baskets.*
cānesco -ēre (inch. of caneo), *to become white* or *hoary.* LIT., canescunt aequora, Ov. TRANSF., *to become old* : Cic., Ov.; hence fig., of discourse: cum oratio nostra iam canesceret, Cic.
cănīcŭla -ae, f. (dim. of canis), *a dog.* LIT., Plin. Appell., *of a violent woman* : Pl. TRANSF., (1) *the Dog-star, Sirius* : canicula exoritur, Cic.; sitiens, Hor. (2) *the worst throw upon the dice* : Pers. (cf. canis).
cānīnus -a -um (canis), *relating to a dog, canine.* LIT., lac, Ov. TRANSF., (1) littera, *the letter R,* Pers. (2) gen., *snarling, spiteful* : latrare canina verba in foro, Ov.; eloquentia, Quint.
cănis (**cănes** : Pl.) -is, c. (connected with κύων), *a dog, hound.*
    LIT., venaticus, Cic.; alere canes in Capitolio, Cic.; cave canem, *beware of the dog,* inscription on a house-door, Varr.; prov.: cane peius et angue vitare, Hor.
    TRANSF., (1) of persons, as a term of reproach, *a low* or *spiteful person;* of accusers: Cic.; *a parasite, hanger-on* : Clodianus canis, Cic. (2) as a constellation: canis maior, Verg.; canis minor, Ov. (3) of other creatures: *the dog-fish* or *the shark* : Plin.; canes, *the dogs of Scylla,* Lucr., Verg. (4) in dice, *the worst throw* : canes damnosi, Prop.
cănistra -ōrum, n. pl. (κάναστρα), *bread, fruit,* or *flower baskets* : Cic. L., Verg.
cānĭtĭēs, acc. -em, abl. -e, f. (canus), *a whitish-grey colour,* esp. of the hair: Ov.; hence meton., *grey hair* : Verg.; *old age* : Hor.
canna -ae, f. (κάννα), *a reed* : palustris, Ov. TRANSF., (1) *a reed-pipe* : Ov. (2) *a small boat* : Juv.
cannābis -is, acc. -im, abl. -i, f. (κάνναβις), and **cannăbum** -i, n. *hemp* : Plin., Pers.
Cannae -ārum, f. pl. *a small town in Apulia, near the River Aufidus, scene of a defeat of the Romans by Hannibal* 216 B.C. Adj. **Cannensis**

-e, *of* or *belonging to Cannae,* appell. : pugna, *any disastrous slaughter* (e.g. *the proscription of Sulla*), Cic.
căno cănĕre cĕcĭni cantum, *to sing* or *play.*
    (1) intransit.: **a**, of men, *to sing* : voce, Cic.; ad tibicinem, Cic.; in oratory of a sing-song delivery: inclinata ululantique voce more Asiatico canere, Cic.: **b**, of birds and of animals: volucres, Prop.; of the cock, *to crow* : Cic.; of frogs, *to croak* : Plin.: **c**, of men, *to play on an instrument* : tibiā, Lucr.; citharā, Tac.; fidibus, Cic.; milit. t. t.: canere receptui, *to sound the signal for retreat,* Liv.: **d**, of instruments, *to sound* : tubae cornuaque cecinerunt, Liv.; classicum canit, Liv.
    (2) transit.: **a**, *to sing with the voice* : carmen, Cic.; cantilenam eandem, *the old sweet song,* Ter.; hoc carmen hic tribunus plebis non vobis, sed sibi intus canit, *thinks only of his own advantage,* Cic.: **b**, *to sing of, to celebrate in song* : ad tibiam clarorum virorum laudes atque virtutes, Cic.; arma virumque cano, Verg.; with indirect quest.: quae sit causa canamus, Lucr.; with acc. and infin.: anser Gallos adesse canebat, Verg.: **c**, *to sound* or *play an instrument,* esp. as milit t. t.: classicum, Caes.; bellicum, Cic.; signum, Verg.: **d**, *to prophesy* : ut haec quae fiunt canere di immortales viderentur, Cic.; with acc. and infin.: te mihi mater, veridica interpres deum, aucturum caelestium numerum cecinit, Liv.
Cănōpus -i, m. (Κάνωβος), *a city in Lower Egypt, on the western mouth of the Nile;* hence meton., *Lower Egypt* : Verg., and *Egypt generally* : Luc. Adj. **Cănōpēus** -um, *of* or *belonging to Canopus* ; **Cănōpītae** -arum, m. pl. *inhabitants of Canopus* : Cic.
cănor -ōris, m. (cano), *melody, song, sound* : cycni, Lucr.; lyrae, Ov.; Martius aeris rauci, Verg.
cănōrus -a -um (canor), *melodious, harmonious, sweet-sounding;* used both of sounds and of the sources of sounds: orator, Cic.; ales, *the swan,* Hor.; gallus, Cic.; aes, *the trumpet,* Verg.; profluens quiddam habuit Carbo et canorum, Cic.; so of a fault in delivery, *of a sing-song pronunciation* : vox nec languens nec canora, Cic. N. as subst. **cănōrum** -i, *harmonious sound,* Cic.
Cantabria -ae, f. *a region in north-west Spain, not subdued till the reign of Augustus;* hence subst. **Cantăber** -bri, m. *a Cantabrian* (usually in plur.); and adj. **Cantăbrĭcus** -a -um, *Cantabrian.*
cantāmen -ĭnis, n. (canto), *incantation* : Prop.
cantātor -ōris, m. *a singer* : Mart.
canthăris -ĭdis, f. (κανθαρίς), *a beetle* : Plin.; esp. *the Spanish fly* : Cic., Ov.
canthărus -i, m. (κάνθαρος). (1) *a large goblet with handles, a tankard* : Pl., Hor., Verg. (2) *a kind of sea-fish, the black bream* : Ov., Plin.
canthērīnus (**cantērīnus**) -a -um (canterius), *of a horse* : Pl.
canthērius (**cantērius**) -i, m. (κανθήλιος), *a gelding, nag* : Pl., Cic.; prov.: cantherium in fossam, of 'putting on the shelf', Liv.; meton., *an impotent man* : Pl.
canthus -i, m. (κανθός), *the tire of a wheel* : Quint.; meton., *a wheel* : Pers.

cantĭcum -i, n. (cano). (**1**) *a scene in the Roman comedy, enacted by one person and accompanied by music and dancing*: Cic. L.; canticum agere, Liv. (**2**) *a song*: Quint. (**3**) *a sing-song delivery in an orator*: Cic., Plin. L.

cantĭlēna -ae, f. *an old song, twaddle, chatter*: ut crebro mihi insusurret cantilenam suam, Cic. L.; Ter.

cantĭo -ōnis, f. (cano). (**1**) *a song*: Pl., Suet. (**2**) *an incantation, enchantment*: veneficia et cantiones, Cic.

cantĭto -are (freq. of canto), *to sing* or *play repeatedly*: Ter.; carmina in epulis, Cic.

Cantĭum -i, n. *a district in Britain* (now Kent).

cantĭuncŭla -ae, f. (dim. of cantio), *a flattering, enticing song*: si cantiunculis tantus vir inretitus teneretur, Cic.

canto -are -āvi -ātum (freq. of cano), *to sing* or *play*.
  (**1**) intransit.: **a**, of men, *to sing*: ad manum histrioni, *to sing to the dumb-show of an actor*, Liv.: **b**, of birds: cantantes aves, Prop.; of the cock, *to crow*: Cic.: **c**, of men, *to play on an instrument*: avenis, Ov.; fidibus, Pl.: **d**, of instruments, *to sound*: bucina cantat, Ov.; tibia, Ov.
  (**2**) transit.: **a**, *to sing*: carmina, Hor.: **b**, *to sing of, to celebrate in singing*: convivia, Hor.; cantari dignus, *worthy to be celebrated in song*, Verg.: **c**, of an actor, *to play a part*: Orestem, Suet.: **d**, *to reiterate, continually mention*: harum mores, Ter.; Caesarem, Cic. L.: **e**, *to predict*: vera cantas, Hor.: **f**, *to sing an incantation*: carmen, Ov.; hence, *to bewitch*: cantata luna, Prop.

cantor -ōris, m. (cano). (**1**) *a singer, poet, musician*: cantor Apollo, *player on the lyre*, Hor.; contemptuously: cantor formularum, Cic.; cantores Euphorionis, *eulogists*, Cic. (**2**) *an actor*, esp. *the actor who cried* plaudite *at the end of the piece*: Cic., Hor.

cantrix -īcis, f. (cantor), *a female singer* or *musician*: Pl.

cantus -ūs, m. (cano). (**1**) *song, melody, poetry*: **a**, of persons: Sirenum, Cic.: **b**, of birds and animals: galli, Hor.; avium, Cic.: **c**, of instruments, *playing*: vocum et nervorum et tibiarum, Cic. (**2**) *prophecy*: veridici cantus, Cat. (**3**) *incantation*: Verg., Ov.

Canulēius -i, m. *name of a Roman gens, to which belonged* C. Canuleius, *tribune of the people* 445 B.C., *author of the law permitting marriages between plebeians and patricians.*

cānus -a -um, *whitish-grey, grey.*
  LIT., fluctus, Lucr.; lupus, Ov.; esp. of hair: cano capite, Pl.; capilli, Hor.
  Hence m. pl. as subst. **cāni** -ōrum (sc. capilli), *grey hair*: Cic.
  TRANSF., *old, aged*: senectus, Cat.; Fides, Verg.

Cănŭsium -i, n. *a town of Apulia* (now Canosa).
  ¶ Hence adj. and subst. **Cănŭsīnus** -a -um, *Canusian, a Canusian*: Canusina lana, *Canusian wool*, which was very celebrated: Plin.
  ¶ Hence f. as subst. **Cănŭsīna** -ae (sc. vestis), *a garment of Canusian wool*: Mart.; **Cănŭsīnātus** -a -um, *clothed in such a garment*: Suet.

căpācĭtas -ātis, f. (capax), *breadth, capacity*: Cic.

Căpāneus (trisyll.) -ĕi; acc. -ĕa, voc. -eu, m. (Καπανεύς), *one of the seven warriors who attacked Thebes, killed by Jupiter with a thunderbolt.*

căpax -ācis (capio), *able to hold much, broad, wide, roomy.*
  LIT., mundus, Lucr.; urbs, Ov.; with genit.: circus capax populi, Ov.; cibi vinique capacissimus, Liv.
  TRANSF., in gen., *receptive, able to grasp, capable, fit for*: aures avidae et capaces, Cic.; with genit.: capax imperii, Tac.; with ad: animus ad praecepta capax, Ov.

căpēdo -ĭnis, f. (capis), *a bowl used in sacrifices*: Cic.

căpēduncŭla -ae, f. (dim. of capedo), *a small bowl used in sacrifices*: Cic.

căpella -ae, f. (dim. of capra). (**1**) *a she-goat*: Verg., Hor., Cic. (**2**) *a star in the constellation Auriga*: Ov.

Căpēna -ae, f. *a town in Etruria, at the foot of Mount Soracte.*
  ¶ Hence adj. and subst. **Căpēnās** -ātis, *of Capena, an inhabitant of Capena*; adj. **Căpēnus** -a -um, *of* or *belonging to Capena*: porta Capena, *a gate in Rome at the beginning of the Via Appia.*

căper -ri, m. (κάπρος). LIT., *a he-goat*: Verg., Hor., Ov. TRANSF., *the smell under the arm-pits*: Ov.

căpĕro -are, *to be wrinkled*: Pl.

căpesso -ĕre -īvi and -ii -ītum (desider. of capio), *to seize, lay hold of eagerly.* LIT., arma, Verg.; cibum oris hiatu et dentibus (of animals), Cic. Esp. of places, *to strive to reach, to make for*: omnes mundi partes medium locum capessentes, Cic.; Melitam, Cic.; Italiam, Verg. With reflex., *to betake oneself to a place*: se in altum, Pl.
  TRANSF., *to take up, take upon oneself, undertake*: fugam, Liv.; libertatem, Cic.; iussa, Verg.; rempublicam, *to enter public life*, Cic.; so: magistratus, imperium, honores, provincias, Tac.; bellum, Liv.

Căphāreus and **Căphēreus** (trisyll.) -ĕi; acc. -ĕa, voc. -eu; m. (Καφαρεύς), *a dangerous promontory on the south coast of Euboea, where the Greek fleet on returning from Troy was shipwrecked.* Adj. **Căphārēus** -a -um, *of* or *belonging to Caphareus.*

căpillātus -a -um (capillus), *hairy, having hair*: adulescens bene capillatus, Cic.; vinum capillato diffusum consule, *made when long hair was worn* (i.e., *very old*), Juv.

căpillus -i, m. (connected with caput, and κεφαλή). (**1**) *the hair of the head or of the beard*: compositus, Cic.; promissus, Caes. (**2**) *a hair*; seldom sing., often plur.: compti, Cic.; Hor., Ov.

căpio căpĕre cēpi captum (old fut. capso: Pl.), *to take.*
  (**1**) in gen. LIT., *to take, to seize*: arma, Caes., Cic.; saxa manu, Verg.; esp. of places, *to take possession of*, as milit. t. t.: collem, Caes.; *to arrive at*, esp. of ships: portum, Caes.; *to select a place*: locum oculis, Verg.; locum castris, Liv.; so for auguries: templa ad inaugurandum, Liv. TRANSF., **a**, *to take in hand, to take up, adopt* a thing: fugam, Caes.; consulatum, Cic.; of an opportunity:

satis scite et commode tempus ad aliquem
adeundi, Cic.; as an example: documentum
ex aliquo, Cic.; of a quality: avi prudentiam,
Cic.: **b**, *to take* or *choose* a person; as a
companion: aliquem consiliis socium, Verg.;
to select out of a number: in singulos annos
sacerdotem Iovis sortito, Cic.; aliquem
flaminem, *as a flamen*, Liv.

(**2**) *to catch, take possession of by force, in a
hostile manner.* LIT., by hunting, etc.: pisces,
Cic.; in politics: lubido reipublicae capiun-
dae, Sall.; esp. in war: agros de hostibus,
Cic.; urbem, castra hostium, Cic.; belli
nefarios duces, Cic.; partic. as subst. captus
-i, m. (=captivus), *a captive*: Nep. TRANSF.,
a, *to seize, take possession of*: admiratio,
metus capit aliquem, Liv.; nos post reges
exactos servitutis oblivio ceperat, Cic.;
dementia cepit amantem, Verg.: **b**, *to attack,
to injure* in some specified way; pass. capi,
to be injured or *diseased*: oculis et auribus
captus, *blind and deaf*, Cic.; captus mente,
distracted, Cic.: **c**, *to charm, captivate,
deceive*: adulescentium animos dolis, Sall.;
adversarium, Cic.; capere aliquem sua
humanitate, Nep.: **d**, at law, *to convict*:
Cic.

(**3**) *to receive.* LIT., cibum, Sall.; esp. of
money: honores aut divitias, Cic.; pecuniam,
to take money by force or *bribery*; legal t. t.,
to take as heir: ex hereditate nihil, Cic.; of
tribute, pay, etc.: stipendium iure belli,
Caes. TRANSF., *to receive, suffer, undergo,
take on*; esp. in the formula: videant consules ne quid respublica detrimenti capiat,
Cic.; laetitiam, Cic.

(**4**) *to take in, to hold, to contain.* LIT., una
domo capi non possunt, Cic., Ov., Verg.
TRANSF., **a**, *to grasp, to comprehend*: nullam
esse gratiam tantam quam non capere
animus meus posset, Cic.; Liv.: **b**, *to contain,
keep in*: irarum fluctus, Lucr.

căpis -ĭdis, f. (capio), *a one-handled vessel*, used
in sacrifices: Liv.

căpistro -are (capistrum), *to fasten with a
halter*: Ov., Plin.

căpistrum -i, n. *a halter*: Verg. TRANSF.,
maritale, Juv.

căpĭtālis -e (caput). LIT., *relating to the head*,
or *to life*: periculum, Pl. Esp. as legal t. t.,
that which imperils a man's life or caput (i.e.,
social position and *civil rights* in Rome);
of capital crimes: res, Cic.; flagitia, Ter.; of
punishment: poena, Suet.
TRANSF., (**1**) *deadly, mortal*: inimicus, Pl.;
odium, Cic.; oratio, *dangerous*, Cic. (**2**) *first,
chief, distinguished*: Siculus ille capitalis,
creber, acutus, Cic. L.; ingenium, Ov.
As subst. **căpĭtal** (also in post-Aug. form
căpĭtāle), n. *a capital crime*: Pl., Cic., Plin.

căpĭto -ōnis, m. (caput), *a man with a large
head*: Cic.

Căpĭtōlĭum -i, n. (caput). LIT., *the temple of
Jupiter built upon the Tarpeian rock at Rome,
the Capitol*; used often of the whole hill or
mons Capitolinus. Adj. **Căpĭtōlīnus** -a -um,
Capitoline: clivus, Cic.; ludi, *games in honour
of Jupiter Capitolinus*, Liv.; m. pl. as subst.
Căpĭtōlīni -ōrum, *the superintendents of these
games*: Cic.

căpĭtŭlātim, adv. (capitulum), *briefly, summarily*: Nep.

căpĭtŭlum -i, n. (dim. of caput), *a little head*.
LIT., Pl. TRANSF., in comedy, of a *person*:
Pl., Ter.

Cappădŏcĭa -ae, f. *a district of Asia Minor,
north of Cilicia.*
¶ Hence adj. **Cappădŏcus** -a -um,
Cappadocian; subst. **Cappădox** -ŏcis, *a
Cappadocian.*

capra -ae, f. (caper), *a she-goat.* LIT., Cic.;
ferae, Verg. TRANSF., (**1**) *a star in the
constellation Auriga*: Hor. (**2**) *the odour
under the arm-pits*: Hor. (**3**) Caprae palus, *the
place in Rome where Romulus disappeared*,
Liv.

căprĕa -ae, f. (capra), *a roe*: Verg.; prov.:
iungere capreas lupis, of an impossibility,
Hor.

Caprĕae -ārum, f. *small island off the Campanian coast, to which Tiberius retired for the
last ten years of his life* (now *Capri*).

caprĕŏlus -i, m. (caper). (**1**) *a roebuck*: Verg.
(**2**) meton., plur., *props, supports*: Caes.

Căprĭcornus -i, m. (caper/cornu), *Capricorn,
a sign of the Zodiac*: Cic., Hor.

căprĭfīcus -i, m. (caper/ficus), *the wild
fig-tree, and its fruit*: Ter., Hor., Plin.

căprĭgĕnus -a -um (caper/gigno), *born of
goats*: Pl., Verg.

căprĭmulgus -i, m. (caper/mulgeo), *a goat-
milker*—i.e., *a countryman*: Cat.

caprīnus -a -um (caper), *relating to a goat*:
pellis, Cic.; grex, Liv.; prov.: de lana
caprina rixari, *to contend about trifles*, Hor.

căprĭpēs -pĕdis (caper/pes), *goat-footed*:
satyri, Lucr., Hor.

¹**capsa** -ae, f. (capio), *a box* or *case*, esp. *for
books*: Cic., Hor.

²**Capsa** -ae, f. (Κάψα), *a town in Byzacium* (now
Kafsa, south of Tunis).
¶ Hence **Capsenses** -ĭum, m. *the in-
habitants of Capsa.*

capsārĭus -i, m. (capsa), *a slave who carried
to school his young master's satchel*: Suet.

capsŭla -ae, f. (dim. of capsa), *a little chest*:
Cat.

captātĭo -ōnis, f. (capto), *an eager seizing, a
catching at*: verborum, *quibbling, logomachy*,
Cic., Quint.

captātor -ōris, m. (capto), *one who eagerly
seizes*: aurae popularis, *eager after favour of
the people*, Liv.; absol., *a legacy-hunter*: Hor.,
Juv.

captĭo -ōnis, f. (capio), *a taking.* TRANSF., (**1**)
a cheat, deception: in parvula re captionis
aliquid vereri, Cic. (**2**) *harm, loss*: mea captio
est, si, Cic. L. (**3**) *a fallacy, sophism*: quanta
esset in verbis captio, Cic.; captiones
discutere, explicare, repellere, Cic.

captĭōsus -a -um (captio), adj. (with compar.
and superl.). (**1**) *deceitful*: societatem captio-
sam et indignam, Cic. (**2**) *sophistical,
captious, insidious*: captiosissimo genere
interrogationis uti, Cic.; n. pl. as subst.
captĭōsa -ōrum, *sophistries*: Cic.
Adv. **captĭōsē**, *insidiously*: interrogare,
Cic.

captĭuncŭla -ae, f. (dim. of captio), *fallacy,
quibble*: omnes captiunculas pertimescere,
Cic.

captīvĭtās -ātis, f. (captivus), *captivity*: Tac.
TRANSF., (**1**) collectively, *a number of captives*:
Tac. (**2**) *capture*: urbium, Tac.

captīvus -a -um (captus, capio), *taken,
captured.* LIT., naves, Caes.; agri, Tac.;
pisces, Ov.; esp. *taken in war, captive*: cives
Romani, Cic.; as subst. **captīvus** -i, m.;
captīva -ae, f. *a captive*: Cic., Verg.
    TRANSF., *relating to a prisoner*: sanguis,
Verg.; crines, Ov.

capto -are (freq. of capio), *to seize, catch at,
lay hold of, hunt.*
    LIT., feras, Verg.; volucres, pisces, Tib.
    TRANSF., (**1**) gen. *to strive after, desire,
seek*: sermonem alicuius, Pl.; plausus, risus,
Cic.; with infin.: Ov. (**2**) *to entrap, entice,
allure*: insidiis hostem, Liv.; testamenta, *to
hunt for legacies*, Hor.

captūra -ae, f. (capio). LIT., *capture,* esp. of
animals: Plin. TRANSF., *prey*: Plin., Suet.;
gen. *gain*: Suet.

captus -ūs, m. (capio). (**1**) *a catching, taking;*
meton., *that which is taken*: Plin. (**2**) *power
of comprehension, manner of comprehension,
idea*: ut est captus hominum, Cic.; Germanorum, Caes.

Căpŭa -ae, f. *chief town of Campania* (now
Santa Maria di Capua).

căpŭlāris -e (capulus), *fit for a coffin*: Pl.

căpŭlus -i, m. (capio). (**1**) *a coffin*: ire ad
capulum, *to go to the grave*, Lucr. (**2**) *a
handle*: aratri, Ov. Esp. *the hilt of a sword*:
Cic., Verg.

caput -ĭtis, n. (connected with κεφαλή), *the head.*
    (**1**) LIT., *the head* of a living creature: belua
multorum capitum, Hor. Esp. of human
beings: capite operto, obvoluto, involuto,
Cic.; caput alicui auferre, abscidere, praecidere, percutere, Liv.; capita conferre, *to
put their heads together* (of secret conversation), Liv.; per caputque pedesque ire
praecipitem in lutum, *to go over head and
heels*, Cat.; prov.: nec caput nec pedes,
neither beginning nor end; supra caput esse,
to be imminent, to threaten, Cic.; caput
extollere, *to raise one's head again*, Cic.; poet.
as the *seat of understanding*: Hor.
    (**2**) meton., *a living individual, a head* of
cattle: bina boum capita, Verg. Esp. of
human beings, *a person*: caput liberum, Cic.;
carum caput, Verg.; in counting numbers:
capitum Helvetiorum milia cclxiii, Caes.;
exactio capitum, *poll-tax*, Cic.; capite censi,
reckoned by the head, Cic.
    (**3**) a person's *life, existence*: coniuratio in
tyranni caput facta, Liv.; capitis periculum,
danger to life, Ter., Liv.; esp. in Rome, *a
man's political and social rights*: iudicium
capitis, *a sentence involving loss of* caput, so:
capitis damnare, Cic.; capite damnari, Cic.;
capitis minor, *a person who has suffered a loss*
of caput, Hor.; so: capite deminui or minui,
*to lose caput, to suffer a loss of status, to suffer
a loss of political or social rights*, Cic.
    (**4**) of things without life, *the top, summit,
extremity*: papaveris, Liv.; arcus capita, *the
ends*, Verg.; capita aspera montis, Verg.; of
rivers, *the source*: amnis, Verg.; Rheni, Caes.;
fig., *the source*: quo invento ab eo quasi
capite disputatio ducitur, Cic.; in ea est fons
miseriarum et caput, Cic.
    (**5**) of persons and things, *the head, leader,
chief, headquarters, chief point*: omnium
Graecorum concitandorum, Cic.; cenae, *the
main dish*, Cic.; civilis prudentiae, *leading*

principle, Cic.; legis, *heading*, Cic.; of money,
capital: de capite ipso demere, Cic.; of
places, *the capital*: Roma caput orbis
terrarum, Liv.

Căpўs -ўos, m. (Κάπυς). (**1**) *son of Assaracus,
father of Anchises*. (**2**) *a king of Alba*. (**3**) *a
companion of Aeneas*. (**4**) *a king of Capua*.

Cār Cāris, m. (Κάρ), *an inhabitant of Caria.*
    ¶ Hence **Cāria** -ae, f. (Καρία), *a district
in the south-west of Asia Minor.* Adj.
Cāricus -a -um, *Carian*; f. as subst. **Cārica**
-ae (sc. ficus), *a kind of dried fig*: Cic.

Căracalla -ae, m. *the Roman emperor* Antoninus
Caracalla (A.D. 211–217).

Cărālis -is, f. (Κάραλις), and plur. **Cărāles**
-ium, f. *a town in Sardinia* (now *Cagliari*).
    ¶ Hence adj. **Cărălītānus** -a -um, *of* or
belonging to Caralis.

Caratācus -i, m. *a British leader, son of
Cunobelinus, defeated by the Romans*, A.D. 51.

carbāsĕus -a -um (carbasus), *made of canvas*:
vela, Cic., Verg.

carbāsus -i, f. (κάρπασος), plur. heterocl.;
    carbăsa -ōrum, n. *fine Spanish flax.* LIT.,
Plin. TRANSF., of things made of flax;
garments: Verg., Ov.; *curtains*: Lucr.; and
esp. *sails*: Verg.

¹**carbo** -ōnis, m. *burning* or *burnt wood*: Ter.,
Pl., Lucr., Cic.; fig., carbone notare, *to mark
with black*, i.e. *think ill of anyone*, Hor.;
prov.: carbonem pro thesauro invenire, *to
be disappointed*, Phaedr.

²**Carbo** -onis, m. *a Roman cognomen in the* gens
Papiria.

carbōnārius -i, m. (carbo), *a charcoal burner*:
Pl.

carbuncŭlus -i, m. (dim. of carbo), *a little
coal.* TRANSF., (**1**) of a *sorrow*: Pl. (**2**) *a
precious stone*: Plin. (**3**) *a kind of sandstone*:
Plin. (**4**) *a carbuncle*: Plin.

carcer -ĕris, m. *a prison, jail, cell.*
    LIT., in carcerem ducere, condere,
conicere, contrudere, includere, Cic.; emitti
e carcere, Cic.; qui e corporum vinculis
tamquam e carcere evolaverunt, Cic.
    TRANSF., (**1**) meton., *the prisoners confined
in a jail*: in me carcerem effudistis, *you have
emptied the prison on me*, Cic. (**2**) gen. used
in plur. carceres, *the starting-place of a
racecourse* (opp. meta, calx): e carceribus
emitti cum aliquo, Cic.; fig.: ad carceres a
calce revocari, *to go right back to the beginning*,
Cic.

carcērārius -a -um (carcer), *belonging to a
prison*: Pl.

Carchēdŏnius -a -um (Καρχηδόνιος), *Carthaginian*: Pl.

carchēsium -i, n. (καρχήσιον), *a goblet with
handles, contracted in the middle*: Verg., Ov.
TRANSF., from its similar shape, *the top of a
mast, scuttle*: Luc.

Cardăces -um, m. (Persian carda, *brave,
warlike*), *a Persian troop*: Nep.

cardiăcus -a -um (καρδιακός), *pertaining to the
stomach*; of persons, *suffering from a disease
of the stomach*: amicus, Juv. M. as subst.
cardiăcus -i, *one who so suffers*: Cic., Hor.,
Plin.

cardo -ĭnis, m. (connected with Gr. κραδαίνω,
to swing), *a hinge.*
    LIT., of a door: cardinem versare, *to open*
a door, Ov.

TRANSF., (1) *the point round which anything turns, a pole*: cardo duplex, *the ends of the earth's axis*, Cic.; quattuor cardines mundi, *the four cardinal points*, Quint. (2) fig. *a chief circumstance*, or *consideration upon which many others depend*: haud tanto cessabit cardine rerum, Verg.

cardŭus -i, m. *a thistle*: Verg.

cărē, adv. from carus; q.v.

cārectum -i, n. (carex), *a sedgy spot*: Verg.

cărĕo -ēre -ŭi -itūrus, *to be without*; gov. the abl. in classical period. (1) *to be without* what is not wanted, *be free from*: culpa, Pl.; dolore, Cic.; morte, Hor. (2) *to do without, abstain from, make no use of*: vino, Pl.; hence, of a place, *to absent oneself from*: foro, senatu, publico, Cic.; patria, *to leave Rome*, Tac. (3) *to be without* something desirable, *need, miss*: consuetudine amicorum, Cic.; libertate, Hor.; lege carens civitas, *lawless*, Cic.; absol.: quamquam non caret is qui non desiderat, Cic.

cārex -icis, f. *rush* or *sedge*: Verg.

căriēs, acc. -em, abl. -e (other cases not found), f. *rottenness, decay*: Ov.

cărīna -ae, f. *the keel of a ship*. LIT., carinae aliquanto planiores quam nostrarum navium, Caes.; Liv., Tac., Ov. TRANSF., (1) meton., *a ship, vessel*: Verg., Hor., Ov. (2) in plur. **Cărīnae** -ārum, f. *the Keels; a district in Rome between the Coelian and Esquiline Hills, where Pompey's house stood.*

cărīnārius -i, m. *a dyer of yellow*: Pl.

cărĭōsus -a -um (caries), *rotten, decayed*: dentes, Plin. TRANSF., senectus, Ov.

căris -idis, f. (καρίς), *a kind of crab*: Ov.

cārĭtas -ātis, f. (carus), *dearness, high price.* LIT., nummorum, *scarcity of money*, Cic.; annonae, *high price of corn*, Cic.; absol. (sc. annonae), *high cost of living*: annus in summa caritate est, *it is a very dear year*, Cic. TRANSF., *affection, love, esteem*: in caritate et honore esse, Liv.; complecti aliquem amicitia et caritate, Cic.; benevolentiā devincire homines et caritate, Cic.; civium, *esteem of the citizens*, Cic.; in pastores, Cic.; inter natos et parentes, Cic.; liberorum, *for one's children*, Cic.; erga patriam, Liv.; in plur.: omnes omnium caritates patria una complexa est, Cic.

carmen -ĭnis, n. (connected with cano; old form casmen). (1) *a song, tune*, either vocal or instrumental: carmina vocum, Ov.; citharae, Lucr.; also of birds; *the swan's*: Ov.; *the owl's*: Verg. (2) *poetry, a poem of any kind*: fundere, condere, contexere, Cic.; componere, fingere, scribere, Hor.; facere, Verg.; esp. of *lyric poetry*: carmine tu gaudes, Hor.; amabile, *erotic verse*, Hor.; also of *a part of a poem*: Lucr., Cic.; *a poetic inscription*: Verg., Ov. (3) *a prediction, oracular declaration*: Verg., Liv. (4) *an incantation*: Hor., Verg. (5) *a religious* or *legal formula*, in ancient times composed in verse: cruciatus, Cic.; lex horrendi carminis erat, Liv.

Carmentis -is, f. and **Carmenta** -ae, f. (carmen = *oracle*), *a prophetess, the mother of Evander, who came with him to Latium, prophesied on the Capitoline hill, and was afterwards reverenced as a deity.*

¶ Hence adj. **Carmentalis** -e, *of* or *belonging to Carmentis*: porta, *a gate of Rome near the temple of Carmentis, the right arch of which was called the* porta scelerata, *because the Fabii went through it on their journey to Cremera, where they were destroyed.*

Carmo -ōnis, f. *town in Hispania Baetica* (now *Carmona, in Andalusia*).

Carna -ae, f. (apparently the same as Carda and Cardea), *the goddess of hinges, and so of family life.*

carnărĭum -i, n. (caro), *the larder, pantry*: Pl.; also *a frame provided with hooks to which provisions were hung*: Pl.

Carnĕădēs -is, m. (Καρνεάδης), *philosopher of Cyrene, founder of the New Academy at Athens.* Adj. **Carnĕădēus** -a -um.

carnĭfex -fĭcis, m. (²caro/facio), *an executioner, hangman*: Pl., Cic.; used also as a term of reproach; either as *murderer, tormentor*: carnifex civium sociorumque, Cic.; or gen. as *scoundrel*: Pl., Cic.

carnĭfĭcīna -ae, f. (carnifex). (1) *the hangman's office*: Pl. (2) *execution, torture*: Cic.; or *the place where it is done*: Liv. TRANSF., *torture*: Cic.

carnĭfĭco -are (carnifex), *to behead*, or *mangle*: Liv.

carnosus -a -um (caro), *fleshy*, of animals and plants: Plin.

Carnūtes -um, m. *a people in the middle of Gaul*: Caes.

¹**căro** -ĕre, *to card*: lanam, Pl.

²**căro** carnis, f. *flesh.* LIT., lacte et carne vivere, Cic.; plur.: carnes vipereae, Ov. TRANSF., (1) contemptuously, of a man: ista pecus et caro putida, Cic. (2) *the pulpy parts of fruit*: Plin.

Carpăthus -i, f. (Κάρπαθος), *an island in the Aegean Sea* (now *Scarpanto*). Adj. **Carpăthĭus** -a -um: vates, senex, *Proteus*, Ov.

carpătĭna -ae, f. (καρπατίνη), *a rustic shoe*: Cat.

carpentum -i, n. *a two-wheeled carriage*, especially used by the women of Rome: carpento in forum invehi, Liv.; also used by other nations: carpenta Gallica multa praeda onerata, Liv.

Carpetāni -ōrum, m. *the Carpetani, a Spanish tribe in modern Castile and Estremadura, with chief town Toletum* (now *Toledo*).

carpo carpĕre carpsi carptum (connected with καρπός and ἁρπάζω), *to pluck, pluck off.* LIT., (1) *to pluck* fruit, flowers, etc.: flores ex arbore, Ov.; uvam de palmite, Verg. (2) *to pull off* other things: summas media inter cornua saetas, Verg.; pensum, *to card*, Hor., Verg. (3) of animals, *to take something as food*: gramen, *to graze*, of a horse, Verg.; thyma, of bees, *to suck*, Hor. TRANSF., (1) *to select, choose out*: flosculos, Cic.; paucos ad ignominiam, Cic. (2) *to enjoy*: diem, Hor.; auras vitales, Verg. (3) *to proceed on* a journey: viam, Verg., Hor.; iter, Hor., Ov.; and of places, *to pass over, hasten over*: prata fuga, Verg.; mare, Ov. (4) *to carp at, slander, calumniate*: aliquem maledico dente, Cic. (5) *to consume, weaken*: vires paulatim, Verg.; hence as milit. t. t., *to annoy, harass*: equitatu agmen adversariorum, Caes. (6) *to break up, to separate, divide*: in multas parvasque partes exercitum, Liv.

carptim, adv. (carptus, carpo). (1) *in pieces, in single portions, in small parts*: Sall. (2) *in different places*: adgredi, Liv. (3) *at different times*: dimissi carptim et singuli, Tac.

carptor -ōris, m. (carpo), *one who carves food*: Juv.

Carrhae -arum, f. pl. *a town in Mesopotamia where Crassus was defeated by the Parthians*, 53 B.C. (now *Charran*).

carrūca -ae, f. *a kind of four-wheeled carriage*: Mart., Suet.

carrus -i, m. (carrum -i, n.), *a kind of four-wheeled baggage-waggon*: Caes., Liv.

Carsĕŏli (**Carsĭŏli**) -ōrum, m. *a town in Latium.*
 ¶ Hence **Carsĕŏlānus** -a -um, *of or belonging to Carseoli.*

Cartĕia -ae, f. (1) *a town in Hispania Baetica.* (2) *town of the Olcades in Hispania Tarraconensis.*

Carthāgo (**Karthāgo**) -ĭnĭs, f. (1) *the city of Carthage in N. Africa.* (2) Carthago (Nova), *colony of the Carthaginians in Hispania Tarraconensis, founded by Hasdrubal in* 242 B.C. (now *Cartagena*).
 Adj. **Carthāgĭnĭensis** -e, *Carthaginian* (of either Carthage).

cărunculă -ae, f. (dim. of caro), *a small piece of flesh*: Cic.

cārus -a -um, adj. (with compar. and superl.), *high-priced, dear.* LIT., *costly*: pisces, agninam, bubulam, Pl.; annona, Pl., Cic.; with abl. of price: quod non opus est, asse carum est, Cato. TRANSF., *dear, beloved*: dis, Hor.; populo, Cic.; patria, quae est mihi vita mea multo carior, Cic.; carum habere, *to love, esteem*, Cic.
 Adv. **cārē**, *dearly, at a high price*: aestimare, ap. Cic.

Cărўae -arum, f. (Καρύαι), *a village in Laconia, with a temple to Artemis* (Diana).
 ¶ Hence **Cărўātĭdes**, acc. -ĭdas, f. *the Laconian maidens who served in the temple of Artemis; hence, in architecture, figures of women used instead of columns*: Vitr.

Cărўstŏs -i, f. (Κάρυστος), *town on the south coast of Euboea, famous for its marble.*
 ¶ Hence adj. **Cărўstēus** -a -um, *of or belonging to Carystos*; adj. and subst. **Cărўstĭus**, *of Carystos, an inhabitant of Carystos.*

căsa -ae, f. (from same root as castrum), *a hut, cottage, cabin*: Cic., Verg.

cascus -a -um (an Oscan word), *old*: Cic.

căsĕŏlus -i, m. (dim. of caseus), *a little cheese*: Verg.

căsĕus -i, m. (**căsĕum** -i, n.: Pl.), *cheese*: Cic., Ov.; caseum premere, *to make cheese*, Verg.

căsia -ae, f. (κασία). (1) *a tree with an aromatic bark, like cinnamon*: Verg. (2) *the sweet-smelling mezereon*: Verg., Ov.

Căsĭlīnum, -i, n. *a town in Campania on the Vulturnus.*
 ¶ Hence **Căsĭlīnenses** -ĭum, m. *inhabitants of Casilinum.*

Căsīnum -i, n. *a town in Latium.* Adj. **Căsīnas** -ātis, *of or belonging to Casinum.*

Caspium mărĕ or **pĕlăgus**, and **Caspĭus ōcĕănus** (τὸ Κάσπιον πέλαγος), *the Caspian Sea.* Also with other nouns, adj. **Caspĭus** -a -um = *Caspian.*

Cassandra -ae, f. (Κασσάνδρα), *daughter of Priam, on whom the gift of prophecy was conferred by Apollo, with the reservation that no one should believe her.*

Cassandrēa and -īa, ae, f. (Κασσάνδρεια), *the town of Potidaea in Chalcidice, destroyed by Philip, re-built and re-named by Cassander.*
 ¶ Hence **Cassandrenses** -ĭum, m. *the inhabitants of Cassandrea*; **Cassandreus** -ei, m. (Κασσανδρεύς) = *Apollodorus, tyrant of Cassandrea*: Ov.

cassēs -ium, m. pl. (abl. sing. casse: Ov.), poet., *a net.* (1) *a hunter's net, snare*: Verg., Tib.; ponere, Ov. TRANSF., *a trap, snare*: Ov. (2) *a spider's web*: Verg.

cassĭda -ae, f. = cassis; q.v.

¹**Cassĭŏpē** -ēs, f. (Κασσιόπη), *wife of Cepheus, mother of Andromeda, changed into a constellation.*

²**Cassĭŏpē** -ēs, f. (Κασσιόπη), *town in Corcyra.*

cassis -ĭdis (**cassĭda** -ae: Verg.), f. *a metal helmet*: Pl., Caes., Verg. Meton., *war*: Juv.

cassĭtĕrum -i, n. (κασσίτερος), *tin.*
 ¶ Hence **Cassĭtĕrĭdes** -um, f. (Κασσιτερίδες), *the tin islands, the Scilly Isles*: Plin.

Cassĭus -a -um, *name of a Roman gens.* Its most notable members were (1) L. Cassius Longinus Ravilla, *celebrated as an upright judge, author of the* lex tabellaria Cassia (137 B.C.), *that jurymen should vote by ballot.* Hence **Cassĭānus** -a -um, *Cassian*: iudex, *an upright judge*, Cic. (2) *the consul* L. Cassius, *conquered and killed by the Helvetii*, 107 B.C. (3) C. Cassius Longinus, *one of the murderers of Caesar.* (4) C. Cassius Longinus, *a celebrated lawyer in the first century* A.D.

cassus -a -um, *empty, hollow.* LIT., nux, Pl.; with abl., *devoid of*: lumine cassus, *or* aethere cassus, *dead*, Verg. TRANSF., *worthless, useless, vain*: cassum quiddam et inani vocis sono decoratum, Cic.; copia verborum, Lucr. N. pl. as subst. **cassa** -orum, *vanities*: Pl. In **cassum** or **incassum**, adv., *in vain*: Lucr., Verg., Liv.

Castālĭa -ae, f. (Κασταλία), *a spring on Mount Parnassus, sacred to Apollo and the Muses.* Adj. **Castālĭus** -a -um and **Castālis** -ĭdis, f. *Castalian*: sorores, *the Muses*, Mart.; also **Castalides** -um, plur., as subst. in same sense.

castănĕa -ae, f. (1) *the chestnut-tree*: Verg., Plin. (2) *the chestnut*: Verg., Plin.

castellānus -a -um (castellum), *relating to a fortress*: triumphi, *on the capture of fortresses*, Cic. M. pl. as subst. **castellāni** -ōrum, *the garrison of a fortress*: Sall., Liv.

castellātim, adv. (castellum), *in single fortresses*: dissipati, Liv.

castellum -i, n. (dim. of castrum), *a castle, fortress, fort.* LIT., Caes., Cic., Hor.; poet., *a dwelling on a height*: Verg. TRANSF., *a shelter, refuge*: Cic.; omnium scelerum, Liv.

castērĭa -ae, f. *a portion of a ship, used as a resting-place for rowers*: Pl.

castīgābĭlis -e (castigo), *worthy of punishment*: Pl.

castīgātĭo -ōnis, f. (castigo), *punishment* (usually verbal), *reproof*: adficere aliquem castigationibus, Cic.; verborum, Liv.

cāstīgātor -ōris, m. (castigo), *one who reproves or corrects*: Pl., Hor., Liv.

castĭgātŏrĭus -a -um (castigo), *correcting*: Plin. L.

castīgo -are (castus/ago), *to set* or *keep right*. (1) *to reprove, chasten, punish*: pueros verbis, verberibus, Cic., Liv. (2) *to check, restrain*: castigatus animi dolor, Cic., Liv., Tac.

¶ Hence partic. **castīgātus** -a -um, *checked, restrained*; hence *small, neat*, as a term of praise: pectus, Ov.

castĭmōnĭa -ae, f. (castus). (1) *purity, morality*: Cic. (2) *ceremonial purity*: Cic., Liv.

castītās -ātis, f. (castus), *chastity*: Cic., Hor., Tac.

¹**castor** -ŏris, m. (κάστωρ), *the beaver*: Cic.

²**Castor** -ŏris, m. (Κάστωρ), *the son of Tyndarus and Leda, twin-brother of Pollux and brother of Helen.*

¶ Hence **ecastor** and **mecastor**, *By Castor!*, common forms of oath in Rome, esp. among women.

castŏrĕum -i, n. *an aromatic secretion obtained from the beaver*: Lucr., Verg.

castrensis -e (castra), *pertaining to a camp*: Cic., Prop.

castro -are, *to castrate*. LIT., Pl. TRANSF., *to enervate*: Sen., Mart.

castrum -i, n. (from same root as casa).

(1) sing., *a castle, fort, fortress*: Nep., Liv.; oftener in sing. as a proper name, e.g., Castrum Inui, in Latium.

(2) plur. **castra** -ōrum, n. *a camp, encampment*. LIT., *a camp fortified by a ditch* (fossa) *and a mound* (agger) *surmounted by palisades* (vallum): stativa, *permanent*, Cic.; aestiva, *summer quarters*, Cic., Suet.; hiberna, *winter quarters*, Caes., Liv.; navalia, *a naval encampment*, when the ships were drawn up on the beach and protected by an entrenchment, Caes.; ponere, Liv.; locare, facere, *to encamp*, Cic.; movere, *to break up the camp*, Caes.; promovere, *to advance*, Caes.; removere, *or* movere retro, *to retreat*, Liv.; esp. *the camp of the praetorian guard* at Rome: praetoriana, Suet.; and in proper names, e.g., Castra Cornelia, *a height near Utica*. TRANSF., **a,** *a day's march*: tertiis castris pervenit, Liv.: **b,** *martial service*: magnum in castris usum habere, Caes.: **c,** fig., like the English *camp*, of a party: in Epicuri nos adversarii nostri castra coniecimus, Cic.: **d,** of a beehive: cerea castra, Verg.

castus -a -um (connected with Gr. καθαρός), adj. (with compar. and superl.), *clean, pure*, of persons and things. (1) *morally pure, temperate*: homo castissimus, Cic.; homo castus ac non cupidus, Cic.; M. Crassi castissima domus, Cic. (2) *chaste*: matronarum castissima, Cic.; cubile, Cat. (3) of religion, *pious, religious, holy*: hac casti maneant in religione nepotes, Verg.; castam contionem sanctum campum defendo, Cic.

Adv. (with compar. and superl.), **castē**. (1) *purely, spotlessly*: caste et integre vivere, Cic. (2) *innocently, chastely*: Cic.; *piously, religiously*: caste ad deos adire, Cic., Ov.

căsŭla -ae, f. (dim. of casa), *a little hut, cottage*: Juv.

cāsus -ūs, m. (cado), *a falling, fall*.

LIT., nivis, Liv.; graviore casu decidunt turres, Hor.

TRANSF., (1) *fall*: cum gravis casus in servitium ex regno foret, Sall. (2) in grammar,

case: casus rectus, *the nominative*, Cic. (3) *occasion, opportunity*: aut vi aut dolis se casum victoriae inventurum, Sall.; navigandi, Caes. (4) *anything that befalls, an accident, event, occurrence*: novi casus temporum, Cic.; abl. casu, *by chance*: evenire non temere nec casu, Cic. (5) *misfortune, mishap*: meus ille casus tam horribilis, tam gravis, etc., Cic.; reipublicae, Sall.; casus nostros, Verg. (6) *destruction, downfall*, of things or persons: Saturnini atque Gracchorum casus (plur.), Caes.; urbis Troianae, Verg. (7) gen., *end*: extremae sub casum hiemis, Verg.

cătădrŏmus -i, m. (κατάδρομος), *a rope for rope-dancing*: Suet.

Cătădūpa -ōrum, n. (Κατάδουπα), *the Nile cataracts near Syene.*

cătăgĕlāsĭmus -a -um (καταγελάσιμος), *serving as a subject of jest*; as subst., *a banterer*: Pl.

cătăgrăphus -a -um (κατάγραφος), *painted, parti-coloured*: Cat.

Cătămītus -i, m. *the Latin name for Ganymedes.*

Catăŏnĭa -ae, f. *a district of the Roman province Cappadocia.*

cătăphractes -ae, m. (καταφρακτής), *a breastplate of iron scales*: Tac.

cătăphractus -a -um (κατάφρακτος), *mail-clad*: Liv., Prop.

cătăplŭs -i, m. (κατάπλους), *the arrival of a ship*; hence meton., *a ship that is arriving*: Cic., Mart.

cătăpulta -ae, f. (καταπέλτης), *an engine of war for throwing arrows*, etc., *a catapult*: Caes., Liv.; hence meton., *a missile*: Pl.

cătăpultārĭus -a -um (catapulta), *belonging to a catapult*: Pl.

cătăracta (**cătarracta**) -ae, f. and **cătăractes** -ae, m. (καταρράκτης). (1) *a waterfall*, esp. *a cataract of the Nile*: Sen. (2) *a sluice* or *flood-gate*: Plin. L. (3) *a portcullis*: Caes.

cătasta -ae, f. (κατάστασις), *a stage upon which slaves were exposed in the market*: Tib., Pers.

cătēia -ae, f. *a kind of spear*: Verg.

¹**cătellus** -i, m. and **cătella** -ae, f. (dim. of catulus), *a little dog, puppy*: Pl., Cic., Juv.; as a term of endearment: Pl., Hor.

²**cătellus** -i, m. and **cătella** -ae, f. (dim. of catena), *a little chain*: Pl., Liv., Hor.

cătēna -ae, f. *a chain, fetter*. LIT., aliquem catenis vincire, Liv.; in catenas conicere, Liv.; alicui catenas inicere, Cic.; in catenis tenere, Caes.; catenas rumpere, Hor. TRANSF., (1) *restraint*: legum catenae, Cic., Hor., Liv. (2) *a series*: Lucr.

cătēnātus -a -um (catena), *chained, bound*. LIT., Britannus, Hor. TRANSF., labores, *unremitting*, Mart.; versus, *connected*, Quint.

căterva -ae, f. *crowd, troop*. (1) of men, gen.: magna togatorum, Cic. Esp.: **a,** *a troop of soldiers*, esp. of barbarian soldiers, or mercenaries as opp. to Roman legionaries: Verg., Tac.: **b,** *a company of actors*: Cic. (2) of animals: pecudum, Lucr.; avium, Verg.

cătervārĭus -a -um (caterva), *belonging to a troop*: Suet.

cătervātim, adv. (caterva), *in troops, in masses*: Sall., Lucr., Verg.

căthĕdra -ae, f. (καθέδρα). (1) *an easy chair*, principally used by ladies: Hor.; also, *a sedan chair*: Juv. Meton.: cathedrae molles, *luxurious women*, Juv. (2) *a professor's chair*: Juv.

Cătĭlīna -ae, m. L. Sergius, *a Roman of noble birth, who headed a conspiracy against the state, which Cicero exposed. He was killed in battle,* 62 B.C. ¶ Hence adj. **Cătĭlīnārĭus** -a -um, *Catilinarian.*

cătillo -are (catillus), *to lick plates:* Pl.

[1]**cătillus** -i, m. (dim. of catinus), *a small dish or plate:* Hor.

[2]**cătillus** -i, m. *son of Amphiaraus, one of the legendary founders of Tibur.*

Cătĭna or **Cătăna** -ae, f. (Κατάνη), *a town on the east coast of Sicily, at the foot of Mount Etna (now Catania).* Adj. **Cătĭnensis** -e, *of or belonging to Catina.*

cătīnus -i, m. (κάτινον), *a deep dish or bowl:* Hor.

Căto -ōnis, m. (1) *a cognomen belonging to members of the gens Porcia, esp.:* a, M. Porcius Cato, *Cato the Censor* (234–149 B.C.), *celebrated for his uprightness and strenuous support of the old Roman simplicity and discipline, author of the* Origines *and* De Re Rustica. *Hence adj.* **Cătōnĭānus** -a -um: b, M. Porcius Cato Uticensis, *Cato the younger* (95–46 B.C.), *Stoic and enemy of Julius Caesar, who killed himself at Utica after the battle of Thapsus. Hence subst.* **Cătōnīni** -orum, m. *the party of the younger Cato.* (2) *a cognomen belonging to members of the gens Valeria, esp. to* M. Valerius Cato, *a freedman of Gaul, grammarian and poet in the time of Sulla.*

cătōnĭum i, n. (κάτω), *the lower world;* with a play on the word Cato: vereor ne in catonium Catoninos, Cic. L.

cătŭlīnus -a -um (catulus), *relating to a dog:* caro, Pl.; f. as subst. **cătŭlīna** -ae (sc. caro), *dog's flesh:* Plin.

Cătullus -i, m. C. Valerius (c. 85–55 B.C.), *the Roman lyric and epigrammatic poet, born at Verona.* Adj. **Cătullĭānus** -a -um.

[1]**cătŭlus** -i, m. *a young animal:* suis, Pl.; leonis, Hor.; lupi, Verg.; ursae, Ov.; esp. *a young dog, whelp, puppy:* Cic., Lucr., Verg.

[2]**Cătŭlus** -i, m. *a cognomen in the gens* Lutatia, esp. of (1) C. Lutatius Catulus, *consul* 242 B.C., *who brought the first Punic war to a close by his victory at the Aegates islands.* (2) Q. Lutatius Catulus, *consul with Marius,* 102 B.C., *defeated the Cimbri at the battle of Vercellae; perished in the proscription of Sulla,* 87 B.C. (3) Q. Lutatius Catulus, *son of the preceding, aristocratic statesman, contemporary with Cicero; consul* 78 B.C.; *died* 60 B.C.

cătus -a -um, *sharp, esp. of intellect, both in good and in bad sense:* cata est et callida, Pl.; prudens et, ut ita dicam, catus, Cic.; with infin.: iaculari, Hor. Adv. **cătē**, *skilfully, cleverly:* Cic.

Caucăsus -i, m. (Καύκασος), *the Caucasus mountains between the Black and Caspian Seas.* Adj. **Caucăsĭus** -a -um, *Caucasian.*

cauda (**cōda**) -ae, f. *the tail of an animal:* leonis, Cic.; caudam trahere, *to wear a tail, a fool's cap,* Hor. In Cic., humorously: cauda Verrina, *the appendage to the name of Verres which changed it to Verrucius,* with a play on the word verres (*boar*).

caudĕus -a -um (caudex), *wooden:* Pl.

caudex=codex; q.v.

caudĭcālis -e (caudex), *relating to wood:* Pl.

Caudĭum -i, n. *an old city in Samnium, near the pass of the Caudine Forks, in which the Roman army was enclosed by the Samnites,* 321 B.C. Adj. **Caudīnus** -a -um, *Caudine:* furculae, Liv.; proelium, Cic.

caulae -ārum, f. pl. (cavus). (1) *a hole, opening:* Lucr. (2) *a sheep-fold:* Verg.

caulis (colis) -is, m. (connected with καυλός), *the stalk of a plant:* Verg.; esp. *the cabbage-plant:* Cic., Hor.

Caulōn -ōnis, m. and **Caulōnĭa** -ae, f. *a town on the east coast of Bruttium in Italy.*

Caunus (**Caunōs**) -i, f. (Καῦνος), *a town on the coast of Caria.* Adj. and subst. **Caunēus** or **-ĭus** -a -um, *Caunian, a Caunian;* esp. f. as subst. **Caunea** (sc. ficus), *a Caunian dried fig.*

caupo -ōnis, m. *a small shopkeeper,* or *inn-keeper:* Pl., Cic., Hor.

caupōna -ae, f. (caupo), *a tavern, inn:* Cic., Hor.

caupōnĭus -a -um (caupo), *belonging to an innkeeper:* Pl.

caupōnor -ari, dep. (caupo), *to trade in any-thing:* non cauponantes bellum, sed belligerantes, Enn.

caupōnŭla -ae, f. (dim. of caupo), *a little inn:* Cic.

Caurus (**Cōrus**) -i, m. *the north-west wind:* Verg., Caes.

causa (**caussa**) -ae, f. *a cause,* in the various senses of the English word. (1) *a reason, motive, inducement:* magna, levis, iusta, Cic.; cum causa, *with good reason,* Cic.; sine causa, *without reason,* Cic.; with genit.: causa belli, Cic.; rerum, Verg.; with infin. (poet.): quae causa fuit consurgere, in arma, Verg.; usually followed by quia, quod, cur, ut, ne: Cic., Hor.; also, as *reason why not,* by quin: Ter., Cic.; or quominus: Liv.; adferre causam, Cic.; causam dare, Cic.; causae esse, Caes.; sometimes in the sense of *pretext* or *excuse:* causam accipere, Cic.; causas novarum postulationum quaerere, Cic.; fingere causam, Cic.; per causam, with genit., *under the pretext of,* Caes. (2) *interest:* causa plebis, *the people's cause,* Liv.; esp. abl., causā, *on account of, for the sake of:* ioci causa, Cic.; verbi causa, *for example,* Cic.; mea causa, Cic.; so tua, nostra, etc. (3) *a case at law, a law-suit:* causa privata, publica, Cic.; capitis, Cic.; causae dictio, *pleading,* Cic.; causam defendere, Cic.; causam dicere, *to plead,* Cic.; causam cognoscere, *to examine, try,* Caes.; causam perdere or causa cadere, *to lose a suit,* Cic. (4) *case,* in other, kindred senses: a, *a contention, claim:* armis inferiores, non causa, Cic.: b, *situation, condition:* erat in meliore causa, Cic.: c, *a subject of discussion:* Cic.

causārĭus -a -um (causa), *sickly, diseased:* Sen. M. pl. **causāriī** -orum, as milit. t. t., *invalided, discharged on account of illness:* Liv.

causia -ae, f. (καυσία), *a white broad-brimmed Macedonian hat:* Pl.

causidicus   cedo

causĭdĭcus -i, m. (causa/dico), *an advocate, barrister,* often used contemptuously to denote one who pleads for money and without skill; distinguished from *orator*: Cic.

causĭfĭcor -ari, dep. (causa/facio), *to bring forward a pretext*: Pl.

causor -ari, dep. (causa), *to give as a reason, or pretext; to plead, pretend*: multa, Lucr.; consensum patrum, Liv.; valetudinem, Tac. Absol.: causando, Lucr., Verg. With acc. and infin.: Liv.

caustĭcus -a -um (καυστικός), *burning, caustic.* Subst. **caustĭcum** -i, n. *caustic*: Plin.

causŭla -ae, f. (dim. of causa). (1) *a little law-suit*: Cic. (2) *a slight occasion*: Auct. B. Afr.

cautēs -is, f. *a rough sharp rock*: Caes., Verg.

cautĭo -ōnis, f. (caveo). (1) *caution, care, foresight, precaution*: cautio est=cavendum est, *one must take care*, Pl., Ter.; cautionem adhibere, Cic.; res cautionem habet, *the affair needs caution*, Cic.; or *allows of foresight*, Cic. L. (2) legal t. t., *security, bail, bond*: Cic.; chirographi, *written*, Cic.

cautor -ōris, m. (caveo). (1) *one who is on his guard*: Pl. (2) *one who gives bail for another*: Cic.

cautus -a -um, partic. from caveo; q.v.

căvaedĭum -i, n.=cavum aedium, *the open quadrangle formed by the inner walls of a house*: Plin. L.

căvĕa -ae, f. (cavus), *a hollow place, cavity*: Plin. Esp. (1) *an enclosure, a den for animals, a birdcage*: Cic. *a beehive*: Verg. (2) *the seats in a theatre or amphitheatre*: prima, *the first tier, the place of honour where the nobility sat*; media, summa, *less distinguished seats*, Cic.; sometimes of *the whole theatre*: Pl., Cic.

căvĕo căvēre căvi cautum (poet. imperat. căvĕ), *to be on one's guard.*
(1) *to guard against, beware*; absol.: cavetis, Cic.; esp. in imperat.: cave, *take care!* Ter., Hor.; with ab: ab aliquo, Pl., Cic.; with acc. of person or thing, *to be on one's guard against*: me, Cic.; omnia, Cic.; pass.: cavenda etiam gloriae cupiditas, *we must be on our guard against*, Cic.; sometimes with infin.: in quibus cave vereri, Cic. L.; more often with ne (*or* ut ne) and subj.: cavet ne decipiatur, Pl.; quod ut ne accidat cavendum est, Cic.; with subj. alone: cave ignoscas, *take care not to*, Cic.; with ut and the subj., *to take care that*: Pl., Cic.
(2) *to take care for, provide*, with dat. of persons for whom: qui in Oratore tuo caves tibi per Brutum, Cic.; with ad: satis cautum tibi ad defensionem, Cic. Esp. as commercial and legal t. t.: **a**, *to give security for*: praedibus (abl.) et praediis populo, Cic.: **b**, *to get security*: ab sese caveat, Cic.: **c**, *to provide, to order*; by will: heredi velle cavere, Cic.; in a treaty: de quibus cautum sit foedere, Cic.; in a law: cautum est in legibus Scipionis ne, Cic.
¶ Hence partic. (with compar. and superl.) **cautus** a um. (1) *cautious, wary, careful, circumspect*: parum putantur cauti providique fuisse, Cic.; in scribendo, Cic.; consilia cautiora, Cic.; vulpes, *sly*, Hor. (2) of property, *made safe, secured*: quo mulieri esset res cautior, Cic., Hor.

Adv. (with compar. and superl.) **cautē**. (1) *cautiously*: caute pedetemptimque dicere, Cic., Caes. (2) *with security*: Cic. Also adv. **cautim**, *cautiously*: Ter.

căverna -ae, f. (cavus), *a hollow place, grotto, cavern*: Verg., Cic.; navis, *the hold*, Cic.; caeli, *the vault of heaven*, Lucr.

căvilla -ae, f. *jesting, raillery, scoffing*: Pl.

căvillātĭo -ōnis, f. (cavillor), *raillery, jesting, irony*: Cic., Liv. Transf., *sophistry*: Quint.

căvillātor -ōris, m. (cavillor), *a jester, joker*: Pl., Cic. Transf., *a quibbler*: Sen.

căvillor -ari, dep. *to jest, joke, jeer*: cavillor ac iocor, Cic. L.; transit., *to satirize*: togam praetextam, Cic. L.; tribunos, Liv. Transf., *to quibble*: Liv.

căvo -are (cavus), *to hollow, make hollow, excavate*: naves ex arboribus, Liv.; oppida cuniculis, *to undermine*, Plin.; parmam gladio, *to pierce*, Verg.; luna cavans cornua, *waning*, Plin.
¶ Hence partic. **căvătus** -a -um, *hollowed out, hollow*: rupes, Verg.

căvum -i, n. and **cavus** -i, m. (cavus), *a hollow, hole, cavity*: Verg., Hor., Liv.

căvus -a -um, *hollow, concave*: vena, Cic.; vallis, Liv.; nubes, Verg.; flumina, *deep-channelled*, Verg.; luna, *waning*, Plin.

Căystros or **Căystrus** -i, m. (Κάυστρος), *a river in Lydia, famous for its swans.*
¶ Hence adj. **Căystrĭus** -a -um, *Caystrian*: ales, *the swan*, Ov.

cĕ, an inseparable demonstrative particle joined on to pronouns and adverbs—e.g., hisce, Cic. It is often shortened to **c**, as in hic, nunc; and before ne becomes **ci**, as in sicine.

Cēa or **Cīa** -ae, f. and **Cēōs**, acc. Ceo (Κέως), *one of the Cyclades Islands, birth-place of the poet Simonides.*
¶ Hence adj. and subst. **Cēus** -a -um, *Cean, a Cean*: Ceae Camenae, *the poetry of Simonides*, Hor.

Cebrēn -ēnis, m. (Κεβρήν), *a river-god in Troas, father of Oenone and Hesperie.*
¶ Hence **Cēbrēnis** -idos, f. *the daughter of Cebren*, i.e. *Hesperie*: Ov.

Cecrops -ŏpis, m. (Κέκροψ), *the mythical first king of Athens.*
¶ Hence adj. **Cecrŏpĭus** -a -um, *Cecropian*: arx, Ov.; f. as subst. **Cecrŏpĭa** -ae, *the citadel of Athens*: Plin.; meton., *Athens*: Cat. Subst. **Cecrŏpĭdēs** -ae, m. *a male descendant of Cecrops*, e.g. Theseus: Ov.; plur., *the Athenians*: Verg.; **Cecrŏpis** -ĭdis, f. *a female descendant of Cecrops*, e.g. Aglauros, daughter of Cecrops: Ov.; Procne and Philomela, daughters of Pandion: Ov. As f. adj., *Cecropian or Attic*: terra, Attica, Ov.; ales, Procne, Ov.

¹cēdo cēdĕre cessi cessum.
(1) in gen., *to go, proceed.* Lit., per ora, Hor. Transf., **a**, *to come to something, to turn out, to happen*: Hor., Verg., Tac.; alicui male, Ov.: **b**, *to fall to the lot of*: ut etiam is quaestus huic cederet, Cic.; res omnis Albana in Romanum cedit imperium, Liv.: **c**, *to change to, to become*: huc omnis aratri cessit honos, Verg.; poena in vicem fidei, Liv.: **d**, *to go for, be equivalent to*: epulae pro stipendio, Tac.

[96]

(**2**) *to go away, withdraw, give ground, retire.* LIT., cedam atque abibo, Cic.; e patria, *or* (simply) patria, Cic.; ab *or* de oppido, Cic. TRANSF., **a**, *to depart*: e vita *or* vita, Cic.; horae cedunt et dies, Cic.; e memoria *or* memoria, Liv.: **b**, *to give ground to, to submit, yield*: infenso hosti, Liv.; minis, Cic.; tempori, Cic.; precibus, Cic.: **c**, *to be inferior to*: alicui virtute, Caes., Cic., Verg.: **d**, *to give up a right* or *some property*; with abl. and dat.: alicui possessione bonorum, Cic.: **e**, transit., esp. with n. object, *to grant, yield*: multa multis de iure, Cic.; *permitto* aliquid iracundiae tuae, *do* adulescentiae, *cedo* amicitiae, *tribuo* parenti, Cic.; so: cedo ut, *grant that*, Liv.

²cĕdŏ and plur. **cettĕ** (ce/do), colloquial imperat., *give here.* LIT., of things or persons: cedo aquam manibus, Pl.; cedo ut bibam, Pl. TRANSF., (**1**) *out with it! let us hear, tell us*: Pl., Ter., Cic.; often followed by dum: Ter. (**2**) to call attention, *see here*: cedo mihi leges Atinias, Cic.

cĕdrus -i, f. (κέδρος), *the cedar*: Plin. Meton., *cedar-wood*: Verg.; *cedar oil*: carmina linenda cedro, *worthy of immortality* (as the cedar oil preserved from decay), Hor.

Cĕlaenae -ārum, f. (Κελαιναί), *a town in Phrygia, on the Maeander*: Liv. Adj. **Cĕlaenaeus** -a -um, *Celaenean.*

Cĕlaeno -ūs, f. (Κελαινώ). (**1**) *daughter of Atlas, placed in the sky as one of the Pleiades.* (**2**) *one of the Harpies.* Appell., *a covetous woman*: Juv.

cēlātor -ōris, m. (celo), *a concealer*: Luc.

cĕlĕber -bris -bre (masc. **cĕlebris**: Tac.), *filled, crowded.* LIT., of places, *frequented*: locus, Cic.; forum, Cic.; celeberrima fontibus Ide, *many-fountained* Ida, Ov.

TRANSF., (**1**) of occasions, *well attended*: funus fit regium, magis amore civium et caritate quam cura suorum celebre, Liv. (**2**) *celebrated, famous, renowned*; of things: res tota Sicilia celeberrima atque notissima, Cic.; of persons: clarissimarum urbium excidio celeberrimi viri, Liv. (**3**) *often repeated*: vox celeberrima, Ov.

cĕlĕbrātĭo -ōnis, f. (celebro). (**1**) *a numerous assembly*: quae celebratio quotidiana, Cic. (**2**) *numerous attendance upon a festival, celebration*: ludorum, Cic. L.; annua, Tac.

cĕlĕbrātor -ōris, m. (celebro), *one who praises* or *extols*: Mart.

cĕlĕbrĭtās -ātis, f. (celeber). (**1**) *a crowd, multitude*: virorum ac mulierum, Cic. (**2**) *a numerous attendance at*: loci, Cic.; of a festival, *celebration*: supremi diei, *at a funeral*, Cic. (**3**) *fame, renown*: celebritatem sermonis hominum consequi, Cic.

cĕlĕbro -are (celeber).

LIT., *to visit frequently*, or *in large numbers*: domum alicuius, Cic.; forum, Sall., Ov.

TRANSF., (**1**) *to fill*: contiones convicio cantorum, Cic.; ripas carmine, Ov. (**2**) *to celebrate, solemnize*: festos dies ludorum, Cic.; celebratur omnium sermone laetitiaque convivium, Cic. (**3**) *to publish, make known*: factum esse consulem Murenam nuntii litteraeque celebrassent, Cic. (**4**) *to sing the praises of, to honour*: egressum alicuius ornare atque celebrare, Cic.; nomen alicuius scriptis, Cic.; domestica facta, Hor.; honores

alicuius, Verg.; memoriam, Tac. (**5**) *to practise often, repeat, exercise*: artes, Cic.; nec unum genus est divinationis publice privatimque celebratum, Cic.

¶ Hence partic. **cĕlĕbrātus** -a -um. (**1**) of places, *much frequented*: forum rerum venalium totius regni maxime celebratum, Sall. (**2**) of festivals, *kept solemn, festive*: dies festus celebratusque per omnem Africam, Liv. (**3**) *famous, celebrated*: res celebratissimae omnium sermone, Cic.; eloquentia, Tac.

Cĕlemna -ae, f. *a town in Campania.*

cĕler -ĕris -ĕre, adj. (with compar. celerior and superl. celerrimus), *swift, quick, rapid.*

LIT., of persons and things: motus, Lucr.; Mercurius, Hor.; navis, Cat.; with infin.: Hor.

TRANSF., mens qua nihil est celerius, Cic.; in a bad sense, *hasty, rash, precipitate*: consilia celeriora, *over hasty plans*, Liv.; celeres iambos, Hor.

Adv. **cĕlĕrĕ**, *quickly, swiftly*: Pl.; also **cĕlĕrĭtĕr**: Pl., Caes., Cic.; compar. celerius, superl. celerrime.

Cĕlĕres -um, m. (perhaps connected with κέλης), *early name for Roman nobles*, esp. *the body-guard of the kings*: Liv.

cĕlĕrĭpēs -pēdis (celer/pes), *swift-footed*: Cic. L.

cĕlĕrĭtās -ātis, f. (celer), *quickness, swiftness.* LIT., equorum, Cic.; also plur.: Cic. TRANSF., orationis, Cic.; actionis, Cic.; animorum, Cic.

cĕlĕro -are (celer). (**1**) transit., *to make quick, hasten, accelerate*: fugam, Verg. (**2**) intransit., *to hasten*: Lucr., Cat., Tac.

Cĕlĕus -i, m. (Κελεός), *king of Eleusis, father of Triptolemus.*

cella -ae, f. *a room.* (**1**) *a store-room*: in cellam dare, imperare, emere, *to give out, order, buy things for the house*, Cic. Sometimes qualified by adj.: cella penaria, *for corn*, olearia, *for oil*, vinaria, *for wine*, Cic. TRANSF., Capua cella atque horreum Campani agri, Cic.; apium, *a cell in a beehive*, Verg. (**2**) *a garret, a mean apartment*: Ter., Mart.; esp. for the use of slaves: Cic. (**3**) in a temple, *the shrine of the god's image*: Cic., Liv.

cellārĭus -a -um (cella), *relating to a store-room*: Pl. M. as subst. **cellārĭus** -i, *a store-keeper, cellarer*: Pl.

cellŭla -ae, f. (dim. of cella), *a little chamber*: Ter.

cēlo -are, *to hide, conceal, keep secret*; of persons or material things and also, transf., of thoughts, feelings, etc.: se tenebris, Verg.; aurum, Hor.; factum, Verg.; sententiam suam, Cic.; dolorem vultu tegere et taciturnitate celare, Cic.

Normally with acc. of the thing concealed and acc. of person from whom it is concealed: non te celavi sermonem T. Ampii, Cic.; sometimes in pass. with personal subject, the thing concealed remaining in acc. or being expressed by de with abl.: nosne hoc celatos tam diu, Ter.; te maximis de rebus a fratre esse celatum, Cic. L.

cĕlox -ōcis, adj. m. and f. (connected with celer), *swift, quick*: Pl.; f. as subst. **cĕlox** -ōcis (sc. navis), *a swift vessel, yacht*: Liv.; publica, *packet-boat*, Pl.

¹celsus -a -um (from *cello), *upraised, high, lofty.*
LIT., (deus homines) humo excitatos celsos et erectos constituit, Cic.
TRANSF., (1) of rank, *eminent*: celsissima sedes dignitatis et honoris, Cic. (2) morally, *lofty, elevated*: celsus et erectus, Cic., Quint. (3) in a bad sense, *proud, haughty*: Cic.; celsi Ramnes, Hor.

²Celsus -i, m. *a Roman cognomen*; esp. A. Cornelius, *a Latin writer on medicine of the first century* A.D.

Celtae -ārum, m. pl. *the Celts*, esp. those of Central Gaul. Adj. **Celticus** -a -um, *Celtic.*

Celtĭbēri -ōrum, m. *the Celtiberians, a people in the middle of Spain.* Adj. **Celtĭbēr** -ēra -ērum and **Celtĭbērĭcus** -a -um, *Celtiberian.* Subst. **Celtĭbērĭa** -ae, f. *the land of the Celtiberi.*

cēna -ae, f. *the principal meal of the Romans, taken about three or four o'clock in the afternoon.*
LIT., cena recta, *a complete dinner of three courses*, Suet.; caput cenae, *the chief dish*, Cic.; inter cenam, *during dinner*, Cic.; invitare ad cenam, *to ask to dinner*, Cic.; obire cenas, itare ad cenas, Cic.; cenam alicui dare, *to give anyone a dinner*, Cic. L.; venire ad cenam, Cic.; redire a cena, Cic.
TRANSF., (1) *a dish, course at a dinner*: prima, altera, tertia, Mart. (2) *the company invited*: ingens cena sedet, Juv. (3) *the place where the dinner is given*: Plin.

cēnācŭlum -i, n. (ceno), *literally an eating-room*: Varr.; and as these were often in the upper storey, *the upper storey of a house, the garret, attic*: Roma cenaculis sublata atque suspensa, Cic.; mutat cenacula, Hor.

Cēnaeum -i, n. (Κηναῖον ἄκρον), *the north-western promontory of Euboea, on which was a temple of Jupiter.*
¶ Hence adj. **Cēnaeus** -a -um, *of Cenaeum*: Iuppiter, Ov.

cēnātĭcus -a -um (cena), *relating to dinner*: spes, Pl.

cēnātĭo -ōnis, f. (cena), *an eating-room, dining-hall*: Plin. L., Juv., Mart.

cēnātōrĭus -a -um (cena), *relating to dinner.* N. pl. as subst. **cēnātōrĭa** -ōrum, *clothes to dine in*: Petr., Mart.

cēnātŭrĭo -ire (ceno), *to wish to dine*: Mart.

Cenchrĕae -ārum, f. (Κεγχρέαι), *one of the harbours of Corinth, on the Saronic gulf.* Adj. **Cenchrĕus** -a -um, *Cenchrean.*

cēnĭto -are (freq. of ceno), *to dine often, be accustomed to dine*: apud aliquem, Cic. L., Suet.

cēno -are (cena).
(1) intransit., *to dine, sup*: cenare bene, Cic.; cenare apud aliquem, Cic.; cum aliquo, Hor.; impers.: cum cenaretur apud Vitellios, Liv. Perf. partic., with a middle meaning, **cenatus**, *having dined, after dinner*: cenati discubuerunt ibidem, Cic.; Pl., Hor.
(2) transit., *to dine on, to eat*: cenam, Pl.; aves, Hor. Once in the sense *to spend in dining*: cenatae noctes, Pl.

Cenomāni -ōrum, *a Celtic people in Gaul.*

cēnsĕo cēnsēre cēnsŭi cēnsum, *to estimate, to form or express an opinion or valuation.*
(1) *to appraise, estimate*: **a**, of the censor at Rome, *to take an account of the names and*

property of Roman citizens: censores populi aevitates, suboles, familias pecuniasque censento, Cic.; capite censi, *the lowest class of Roman citizens*, whose persons only were counted, Sall.; sintne ista praedia censui censendo? *are those estates fit to be put on the censor's list?* (as the property of the possessors), Cic.: **b**, *to make a return to the censor*: in qua tribu denique ista praedia censuisti? Cic.: **c**, gen.: si censenda atque aestimanda res sit, Cic.; censeri de aliquo, *to be regarded as belonging to a certain person*, Ov.; unā victoriā Carius censebatur, Tac.
(2) *to express an opinion, be of an opinion*: **a**, gen.: ita prorsus censeo, Cic.; tibi igitur hoc censeo, Cic.; with ut and the subj. or subj. alone: magno opere censeo desistas, *I advise*, Cic.: **b**, of one in authority, *to vote, recommend by vote* or *advice*: captivos reddendos in senatu non censuit, Cic.; pars deditionem, pars eruptionem censebant, Caes.: **c**, of the senate (as iubere for the populus), *to resolve*: senatus censuit uti, Caes.; censuere patres duas provincias Hispaniam fieri, Liv.

censĭo -ōnis, f. (censeo), *an assessment, estimate, expression of opinion.* TRANSF., in jest: bubula, *a scourging*, Pl.

censor -ōris, m. (censeo), *the censor.* LIT., *a Roman magistrate*, of whom there were regularly two, responsible esp. for *the census*; q.v. TRANSF., *a severe judge, a rigid moralist, a censurer*: Cic.; castigator censorque minorum, Hor.; Ov.

censōrĭus -a -um, *relating to the censor.* LIT., homo, *one who has filled the office of censor*, Cic.; tabulae, *the censor's lists*, Cic.; lex, locatio, *a contract relating to building* or *to the public revenue*, Cic.; opus, *a fault which was punished by the censor*, Cic. TRANSF., *rigid, severe*: Quint.

censūra -ae, f. (censor), *the censor's office, censorship.* LIT., censuram gerere, Cic., Liv., Ov. TRANSF., *judgment, in gen.*: Ov., Juv.

census -ūs, m. (censeo), *the enrolment of the names and the assessment of the property of all Roman citizens, the census.*
LIT., censum habere, Cic.; agere, *to take a census*, Liv.; censu prohibere, Cic.; censu excludere, *to refuse to enrol in the census*, Liv.; censum perficere, Liv.; censum accipere, Liv.
TRANSF., (1) *the censor's list*: Cic. (2) *the amount of property necessary for enrolment in a certain rank*: senatorum = 800,000 sesterces, Suet.; equester = 400,000 sesterces, Suet. (3) in gen., *property, wealth*: homo sine censu, *a poor man*, Cic.; dat census honores, Ov.; Hor., Liv.

centaurĕum and **centaurĭum** -i, n. (κένταυρειον), *the plant centaury*: Lucr., Verg.

Centaurus -i, m. (Κένταυρος), *a centaur, a supposed monster of Thessaly, half man and half horse*: Verg.; nobilis, Chiron, Hor.; also as *the name of a ship*: Verg. Adj. **Centaurēus** -a -um.

centēnārĭus -a -um (centenus), *containing a hundred, relating to a hundred*: Varr., Plin.

centēni -ae -a; poet. also sing., centena arbore, Verg.; (centum), *a hundred together*, esp. distributively, *a hundred each*: centeni quemque sequuntur, Verg.; often also in

centesimus   **cerebrum**

giving large numbers: viciens centena milia passuum, Caes.

centēsimus -a -um, num. ordin. (centum), *the hundredth*: lux ab interitu Clodii, Cic. F. sing. as subst. **centēsima** -ae (sc. pars), *the hundredth part*; hence (1) *a tax of one per cent.*: Cic. (2) *as interest on money, one per cent.* (reckoned at Rome by the month, therefore = 12 per cent. per annum); binae centesimae = 24 per cent.; quaternae, Cic.; perpetuae, *compound interest*, Cic.

centiceps -cipitis (centum/caput), *hundred-headed*: belua, Cerberus, Hor.

centiens or **centiēs**, adv. (centum), *a hundred times*: HS. centies (sc. centena milia), *ten million sesterces*, Cic.; fig.: centiens eadem imperare, Pl.

centimănus -a -um (centum/manus), *hundred-handed*: Hor. Ov.

cento -ōnis, m. (κέντρων), *patchwork*: Juv.; in war, *coverings to ward off missiles or extinguish fires*: Caes.; prov.: centones sarcire alicui, *to deceive with a tissue of lies*, Pl.

centum, indecl. numer. (1) *a hundred*: Cic. (2) hyperbol., *any indefinitely large number*: centum puer artium, Hor.; linguae, Verg.

centumgēmīnus -a -um, *hundred-fold*: Briareus, *hundred-armed*, Verg.

centumpondium -i, n. (centum/pondus), *a weight of a hundred pounds*: Pl.

centumvirālis -e (centum viri), *relating to the centumviri*: causa, *heard before the centumviri*, Cic.

centum viri or **centumviri** -ōrum, m. pl. *a bench of judges* (first 105; under the emperors 180) appointed annually at Rome to deal with civil suits.

centuncŭlus -i, m. (dim. of cento), *a little piece of patchwork*: Sen.; as a saddle-cloth: Liv.

centŭplex -icis (centum/plico), *a hundred-fold*: Pl.

centŭria -ae, f. (centum), *a division of 100.* (1) *a company of soldiers*, esp. as milit t. t., *a century, one-sixtieth of a legion*: Caes., Liv. (2) *a century, one of the 193 divisions into which Servius Tullius distributed the Roman people*: Cic., Liv.; praerogativa, *the century which obtained by lot the privilege of first voting*, Cic.

centŭriātim, adv. (centuria), *by centuries or companies*: Caes., Cic.

centŭriātus -ūs, m. (centurio). (1) *a division into companies or centuries*: Liv. (2) *the centurion's office*: Cic.

¹**centŭrio** -are (centuria), *to divide into centuries*: iuventutem, Liv.; comitia centuriata, *the assembly in which the whole Roman people voted in their centuries* (e.g., at the election of a consul, Cic.; lex centuriata, *a law passed in such an assembly*, Cic.

²**centŭrio** -ōnis, m. (centuria), *a commander of a century, a centurion*: Caes., Cic., Liv.

centŭriōnātus -ūs, m. (²centurio), *an election of centurions*: Tac.

Centŭrīpae -ārum, f. and **Centŭripa** -ōrum, n. (τὰ Κεντόριπα), *a town in Sicily* (now *Centuripe*).
¶ Hence adj. and subst. **Centŭrīpīnus** -a -um, *of or belonging to Centuripa; an inhabitant of it.*

centussis -is, m. (centum/as), *a hundred asses*: Pers.

cēnŭla -ae, f. (dim. of cena), *a little meal*: Cic., Mart.

cēnum, see caenum.

Cēōs, see Cea.

Cěphallēnia -ae, f. (Κεφαλληνία), *island in the Ionic Sea* (now *Cefalonia*).
¶ Hence **Cěphallēnes** -um, m. *inhabitants of Cephallenia.*

Cěphăloedis -is, f. *a small town in Sicily.* Adj. and subst. **Cěphăloedītānus** -a -um, *of or belonging to Cephaloedis, an inhabitant of it.*

Cēphēnes -um, m. pl. (Κηφῆνες), *a people of Ethiopia.*
¶ Hence adj. **Cēphēnus** -a -um, *Cephenian.*

Cēpheus (dissyl.) -ĕi, m. (Κηφεύς), *a mythical king of Ethiopia, husband of Cassiope, father of Andromeda.* Adj. **Cēphēīus** -a -um, *of or belonging to Cepheus*: virgo, *Andromeda*, Ov.; arva, *Ethiopia*, Ov.; **Cēphēus** -a -um, *Ethiopian*: Prop., Ov.; also **Cēphēīs** -idis, f. = *Andromeda*: Ov.

Cēphisus (-os) -i, m. (Κηφισός). (1) *a river in Boeotia*, and, as a river-god, *the father of Narcissus*; hence **Cēphīsius** -i, m. = *Narcissus*: Ov. F. adj. **Cēphīsis** -idis, *of or belonging to Cephisus*: undae, Ov. (2) *a river of Attica*: Ov. Adj. **Cēphīsias** -ădis, f. *of or belonging to the Cephisus.*

cēra -ae, f. (connected with κηρός), *wax.* LIT., mollissima, Cic.; ceras excudere (of bees making their hive), Verg. TRANSF., of articles made of wax; *a writing-tablet coated with wax*: Cic., Ov.; *a wax seal*: Cic.; *a waxen image of an ancestor*: Sall., Ov.

Cěrāmīcus -i, m. (Κεραμεικός), *the name of two places at Athens, one inside the walls, the other outside, used as cemeteries; in the latter, statues were erected to those who fell in war.*

cērārium -i, n. (cera), *a fee for sealing a document*: Cic.

cěrastēs -ae, m. (κεράστης), *the horned snake*: Prop., Plin.

cěrăsŭs -i, f. (κέρασος). (1) *a cherry-tree*: Ov. (2) *a cherry*: Prop.

Cěrăsūs -untis, f. (Κερασοῦς), *a town in Pontus, from which Lucullus brought the cherry to Italy.*

cěraunius -a -um (κεραύνιος): ceraunia gemma, *a kind of precious stone*, Plin.; **Cěraunii montes** and alone **Cěraunia** -ōrum, n. *mountains in Epirus.*

Cerbĕrus -i, m. (Κέρβερος), *the three-headed* (or *hundred-headed*) *dog guarding Hades.* Adj. **Cerbĕrěus** -a -um, *of or belonging to Cerberus.*

cercŏpĭthēcus -i, m. (κερκοπίθηκος), *a kind of long-tailed ape*: Mart., Juv.

cercūrus -i, m. (κέρκουρος). (1) *a light species of vessel peculiar to Cyprus*: Pl., Liv. (2) *a kind of sea-fish*: Ov.

Cercyōn -ōnis, m. (Κερκύων), *a brigand in Attica, killed by Theseus.* Adj. **Cercyŏnēus** -a -um, *of or belonging to Cercyon.*

cerdo -ōnis, m. (κέρδος), *a workman, artisan*: Juv.; sutor cerdo, *a cobbler*, Mart.

cěrěbellum -i, n. (dim. of cerebrum), *a small brain*: Plin.

cěrěbrōsus -a -um (cerebrum), *hot-headed, hot-tempered*: Hor.

cěrěbrum -i, n. *the brain.* LIT., Cic., Verg. TRANSF., (1) *the understanding*: Pl., Hor. (2) *hot temper*: Pl.; cerebri felicem, Hor.

Cĕrēs -ĕris, *the Roman goddess of agriculture, the daughter of Saturn and Ops, sister of Jupiter and Pluto, and mother of Proserpine.* TRANSF., *bread, grain, corn*: Verg., Hor.; sine Cerere et Libero friget Venus, Ter.

Adj. **Cĕrĕālis** -e, *relating to Ceres, relating to cultivation and agriculture*: Ov.; papaver, *the emblem of Ceres*, Verg.; cenae, *splendid, fit for Ceres*, Pl.; aediles, *who superintended the supply of provisions.* N. pl. as subst. **Cĕrĕālia** -ium, *the festival of Ceres on April* 10.

cēreus -a -um (cera), *waxen.* LIT., Cic.; castra, *the cells of a hive*, Verg. M. as subst., *a wax taper*: Cic. TRANSF., *wax-coloured*: pruna, Verg.; *flexible like wax*: cereus in vitium flecti, Hor.

cērintha -ae, f. (κηρίνθη), *the wax flower, a plant of which bees are fond*: Verg.

cērīnus -a -um (κήρινος), *wax-coloured*: Plin.; n. pl. as subst. **cērina** -orum, *wax-coloured garments*: Pl.

cerno cernĕre crēvi crētum (see also certus; connected with κρίνω), *to separate, sift.*

LIT., in cribris, Ov.

TRANSF., (**1**) *to distinguish*: **a**, with the senses: ut non sensu, sed mente cernatur, Cic.; esp. with the eyes: acies ipsa, qua cernimus, quae pupula vocatur, Cic.; with acc.: Pompeianum non cerno, Cic.; with acc. and infin.: cernebatur novissima illorum premi, Caes.: **b**, with the mind, *to perceive*: animus plus cernit et longius, Cic.; often in pass. *to be distinguished*: fortis animus et magnus duobus rebus maxime cernitur, Cic. (**2**) *to decide*: **a**, in battle: ferro, Verg.; magnis in rebus inter se, Lucr.: **b**, *to resolve, determine*: quodcumque senatus creverit, agunto, Cic.; quid de Armenia cernerent, Tac.: **c**, as legal t. t., *to decide to accept an inheritance*: hereditatem cernere, Cic.; fig., hanc quasi falsam hereditatem alienae gloriae, Cic.

cernŭus -a -um, *falling headlong, with the face towards the ground*: equus, Verg.

cēro -are, *to smear or cover with wax*, gen. in perf. partic. pass.: cerata tabula, Pl.; tabella, Cic.; taedae, Ov.

cērōma -ătis, n. (κήρωμα), *an ointment of oil and wax used by wrestlers*: Juv. TRANSF., *a place for wrestling*: Plin.; *wrestling*: Mart.

cērōmăticus -a -um (κηρωματικός), *anointed with the ceroma*: Juv.

cerrītus -a -um (contracted from cerebritus, from cerebrum), *frantic, mad*: Pl., Hor.

certāmen -inis, n. (²certo), *a contest, struggle.*

LIT., (**1**) in games, etc.: biiugum, Verg.; pedum, Ov. (**2**) in battle: vario certamine pugnatum, Caes.; navale certamen, Liv., Verg.

TRANSF., *any contention or rivalry*: honoris et gloriae, Cic.; in certamen virtutis venire, Cic.; est mihi tecum pro aris et focis certamen, Cic.

certātim, adv. (²certo), *emulously, eagerly*: Cic., Liv., Verg.

certātĭo -ōnis, f. (²certo), *a contest.* LIT., in games: corporum, Cic. TRANSF., in gen., *rivalry*: honesta inter amicos, Cic.; relinquitur . . . virtuti cum voluptate certatio, Cic.; esp. *a legal contest*: poenae, *as to the amount of a fine to be inflicted*, Cic.

certē, adv. from certus; q.v.

¹certo, adv. from certus; q.v.

²certo -are (connected with cerno), *to settle by contest*; hence *to contend, struggle.*

LIT. (**1**) in games: cursu, Sall.; sagitta, Verg. (**2**) in battle: armis, Cic., Tac.; acie, Verg.: de imperio cum populo Romano, Cic.

TRANSF., in gen. *to contend, to vie with*: officiis inter se, Cic.; ioco, Hor.; verbis, oratione, Liv.; foll. by infin.: vincere, Verg.; esp. in law, *to dispute*: inter se, Cic.; foro si res certabitur, Hor.

certus -a -um, adj. (with compar. and superl.) (originally partic. of cerno).

(**1**) *settled, resolved, decided*: certum est mihi consilium, Pl.; certum est mihi, *I am resolved*; sibi certum esse a iudiciis causisque discedere, Cic.; of persons: certus mori, *determined to die*, Verg.; certus eundi, *determined to go*, Verg., Tac.

(**2**) *definite, certain, fixed*: certus ac definitus locus, Cic.; dies, Cic., Liv., Tac., Verg.; signum, *agreed upon*, Caes.; also indef. (like quidam, but emphatic): certi homines, *certain men*, Cic.

(**3**) *sure, to be depended on*: bona et certa tempestate, Cic.; certissima populi Romani vectigalia, Cic.; of persons: homo certissimus, *to be depended upon*, Cic.; certissimus auctor, Verg.

(**4**) of things as known, *undoubted, sure*: res, Caes., Liv.; argumentum, Cic.; si quicquam humanorum certi est, Liv.; certum scio, *I know for certain*, Ter., Cic.; certum habeo or pro certo habeo, *I consider it certain, I feel sure*, Cic. L., Liv.; pro certo nego, Cic.; polliceor, Cic.; dico, Cic.; adfirmo, Liv.; pono, Liv.

(**5**) of persons knowing, *sure, certain of a thing*: certi sumus perisse omnia, Cic. L.; with genit.: spei, Tac.; with de: de genitura, Suet.; esp. in prose in the phrase: certiorem facere aliquem, *to inform*; with genit.: sui consilii, Cic.; with de: de Germanorum discessu, Caes.; with acc. and infin.: Caes.; with ind. quaest.: quid egerim, Cic.

Adv. **certē**, *certainly, assuredly*: certe scio, Cic.; ea quae certe vera sunt, Cic.; in answers, *without doubt*: Cic.; also in a restrictive sense, esp. after a concessive clause, or with a pronoun, *at least, at all events*: res fortasse verae, certe graves, Cic.

Adv. **certō**, *certainly, assuredly*: nihil ita exspectare quasi certo futurum, Cic.; esp. in phrase: certo scio, *I am convinced*, Pl., Ter., Cic.; in answers, *certainly*: Pl., Ter.

cērŭla -ae, f. (dim. of cera), *a little piece of wax*: miniata, *a kind of red pencil for marking errors*, Cic. L.

cērussa -ae, f. *white lead*, used by painters and as a cosmetic: Ov., Mart., Plin.

cērussatus -a -um (cerussa), *painted with white lead*: buccae, Cic.; cutis, Mart.

cerva -ae, f. (cervus), *a hind*: Ov.; poet., gen., *deer*: Cat., Verg.

cervārius -a -um (cervus), *relating to deer*: Plin.

cervīcal -ālis, n. (cervix), *a cushion for the head, a pillow, bolster*: Juv.

cervīcŭla -ae, f. (dim. of cervix), *a little neck*: Cic., Quint.

cervīnus -a -um (cervus), *relating to a stag*: pellis, Hor.; senectus, *extreme old age*, because the stag was believed to be very long-lived, Juv.

cervix -īcis, f. *the nape of the neck, the neck*; in Sall. and Cic., always plur., cervices. Lɪᴛ., of living beings: Cic., Verg., Hor., Liv.; alicui cervices frangere, *to break a person's neck*, Cic.; dare cervices alicui, *to submit to the executioner*, Cic.; so also: cervices securi subicere. Esp. fig., from the bearing of a yoke: imposuistis in cervicibus nostris sempiternum dominum, Cic.; bellum ingens in cervicibus erat, *they had on hand*, Liv.; so of endurance or effort: suis cervicibus rempublicam sustinent, Cic.

Tʀᴀɴsꜰ., of inanimate things: amphorae, Mart.; Peloponnesi, *the Isthmus of Corinth*, Plin.

cervus (formerly cervos) -i, m. *a stag, a deer*. Lɪᴛ., Lucr., Hor., Verg., Ov. Tʀᴀɴsꜰ. milit. t. t.: cervi, *stakes stuck in the ground as a palisade, chevaux-de-frise*, Caes., Liv.

cespes, *see* caespes.

cessātĭo -ōnis, f. (cesso), *a delaying*: Pl.; hence, in gen., *inactivity, laziness*: libera atque otiosa, Cic.

cessātor -ōris, m. (cesso), *one who loiters*: cessatorem esse solere, praesertim in litteris, Cic. L., Hor.

cessĭo -ōnis, f. (cedo), *a giving up, a cession*; legal t. t.: in iure cessio, *a surrender*, Cic.

cesso -are (freq. of cedo), *to give over, leave off*.

(1) *to be slack, delay* or *cease work* at a particular task: si tabellarii non cessarint, Cic.; quid cessas? Ter.; in suo studio atque opere, Cic.; ab opere, Liv.; nullo officio, Liv.; in vota precesque, Verg. With infin: adloqui, adoriri, Ter.; de nobis detrahere, Cic., Pl., Hor. Also in impers. pass.

(2) gen., of persons, *to do nothing, be idle, rest*: deos nihil agere et cessare patitur, Cic. (of Epicurus' philosophy); cessare et ludere, Hor.

(3) gen., of things, *to be left alone, to be at rest, do nothing*: opus, Tib.; arma, Prop.; cessasse Letoidos aras, *remained unvisited*, Ov.; of land, *to lie fallow*: alternis cessare novales, Verg.

(4) as legal t. t., *to default*: Suet.

cestrosphendŏnē -ēs, f. (κεστροσφενδόνη), *an engine for hurling stones*: Liv.

¹cestus and **cestos** -i, m. (κεστός), *a girdle*, esp. *the girdle of Venus*: Mart.

²cēstus -ūs, m. *see* caestus.

cētārĭum -i, n. (cetus), *a fish-pond*: Hor.

cētārĭus -i, m. (cetus), *a fishmonger*: Ter., Cic.

cēte, *see* cetus.

cētĕrōqui or **cētĕrōquin**, adv., *otherwise, else*: Cic.

cētĕrus -a -um (connected with ἕτερος), *the other, the rest*; nom. sing. m. not found; sing. otherwise used collectively: cetera classis, Liv.; usually found in the plur. **cētĕri** -ae -a: omnes ceterae res, *all the other*, Cic.; also as subst., *the others*: cetera de genere hoc, Hor.; esp. in phrase: et cetera, *or* ceteraque, *or* cetera, *and so on*, Cic.

Acc. n. sing. as adv. **cētĕrum**, *for the rest, otherwise*: praeterquam quod sine te, ceterum satis commode, Cic. L.; also used, esp. after Cicero, in the senses of *moreover*: Liv., and *but*: Liv., Suet.

Acc. n. pl. as adv. **cētĕră**, *otherwise*: excepto quod non simul esses, cetera laetus, Hor.; Verg., Liv.

Cĕthēgus -i, m. *a Roman cognomen in the gens Cornelia*; esp. of C. Cornelius Cethegus, *a conspirator with Catiline, put to death by Cicero in 63 B.C.*

cētra, *see* caetra.

cētrātus, *see* caetratus, Liv.

cette, *see* cĕdo.

cētus -i, m. and **cētos**, n., plur. cēte (κῆτος), *any large sea-creature, such as the whale, seal, dolphin*: Pl., Verg., Plin.

ceu, adv., *as, like as*; used for comparisons, esp. in poetry and late prose: fugit ceu fumus, Verg.; ceu cum, *as when*, Verg.; ceu si, *as if*, Lucr. Also in conditional sense by itself, *as if*: per aperta volans, ceu liber habenis, aequora, Verg.; and so with subjunc.: ceu cetera nusquam bella forent, Verg.

Cēy̆x -y̆cis, m. (Κήϋξ), *husband of Alcyone, changed with her into a kingfisher*: Ov. Plur., appell. **cēyces** -um, m. *the male kingfishers*: Plin.

Chaerōnēa -ae, f. (Χαιρώνεια), *a town in Boeotia, scene of a victory of Philip of Macedon over the Athenians and Thebans*, 338 B.C.

Chalcēdon (**Calchēdon**) -ŏnis, f. (Χαλκη-δών), *a town in Bithynia on the Bosporus, opposite Byzantium*. Adj. and subst. **Chal-cēdŏnĭus** -a -um, *Chalcedonian, a Chalcedonian*.

Chalcĭoecŏs -i, f. (Χαλκίοικος, *with the brazen house*, name of the Greek Athena), *a temple of Minerva*: Liv.

Chalcĭŏpē -ēs, f. (Χαλκιόπη), *daughter of Aeetes, sister of Medea, wife of Phrixus*.

Chalcis -ĭdis or -ĭdos, f. (Χαλκίς), *the chief city of Euboea, on the banks of the Euripus*.

¶ Hence adj. **Chalcĭdĭcus** -a -um, *Chalcidian*: versus, *poems of Euphorion, born at Chalcis*, Verg.; arx, *Cumae, said to have been a colony of Chalcis*, Verg.; **Chalcĭdensis** -e, *Chalcidian*.

Chaldaei -orum, m. pl. (Χαλδαῖοι), *the Chaldaeans, an Assyrian people, famous as astronomers and astrologers*; hence gen., *astrologers*: Cic.

Adj. **Chaldaeus** -a -um: grex, *band of astrologers*, Juv.; **Chaldăĭcus** -a -um, Cic.

chăly̆bēĭus -a -um, *of steel*: Ov.

Chăly̆bes -um, m. (Χάλυβες), *a people in Pontus, famous for their steel*.

chăly̆bs -y̆bis, m. (χάλυψ), *steel*: vulnificus, Verg., Prop. Tʀᴀɴsꜰ., *articles made of steel*; *a sword*: Sen.; *a horse's bit*: Luc.; *the tip of an arrow*: Luc.

chamaelĕon -ōnis and -ontis, m. (χαμαιλέων), *the chameleon*: Plin.

chănē or **channē** -es, f. (χάνη, χάννη), *a fish, the sea perch*: Ov., Plin.

Chāŏnes -um, m. (Χάονες), *a people of north-western Epirus*.

¶ Hence **Chāŏnĭa** -ae, f. *their district*; adj. **Chāŏnĭus** -a -um, *Epirote*: pater, *Jupiter, whose oracle was at Dodona*, Verg.; f. adj. **Chāŏnis** -ĭdis, *Chaonian*: arbos, *an oak at Dodona*, Ov.

Chăos, acc. Chaos, abl. Chao (other cases not found), n. (χάος), *boundless empty space*. Hence (1) *the lower world*: Ov.; personified, *Chaos, the father of Night and Erebus*: Verg.

(2) *the shapeless mass out of which the universe was made*: Ov.; a Chao, *since the world began*, Verg.

chara -ae, f. *an edible root*: Caes.

Chăristĭa -ōrum, n. (χαρίστια), *a festival celebrated among the Romans on February 22, the chief object of which was the reconcilement of family disagreements*: Ov.

Chărĭtes -um, f. pl. (Χάριτες), *the Graces* (pure Lat. Gratiae), *Aglaia, Euphrosyne, and Thalia*: Ov.

Chăron -ontis, m. (Χάρων), *Charon, the ferryman, who took the souls of the dead over the river Styx.*

Chărondās -ae, m. (Χαρώνδας), *a celebrated legislator of Catana.*

charta -ae, f. (χάρτης), *a leaf of the Egyptian papyrus, paper.*
   LIT., Plin., Lucr., Hor.; charta dentata, *smoothed*, Cic.
   TRANSF., (1) *the papyrus plant*: Plin. (2) *that which is written upon paper, a letter, poem*, etc.: ne charta nos prodat, Cic.; Lucr., Hor. (3) *a thin leaf of any substance*: plumbea, Suet.

chartŭla -ae, f. (dim. of charta), *a little paper, a small piece of writing*: Cic. L.

Chărybdis -is, f. (Χάρυβδις), *a dangerous whirlpool in a narrow channel* (commonly *identified with the Straits of Messina*) *opposite the rock Scylla*: Cic.; fig., *anything voracious, greedy or destructive*: Charybdim bonorum, voraginem potius dixerim, Cic.; quanta laborabas Charybdi, Hor.

Chatti (**Catti**) -ōrum, m. (Χάττοι), *a Germanic people.*

Chauci -ōrum, m. *a Germanic people on the coast of the North Sea.*

chēlē -ēs, f. (χηλή), plur. chelae, *the arms of the Scorpion in the signs of the Zodiac, and* (since these reach into the constellation of Libra) *Libra*: Verg.

chēlȳdrus -i, m. (χέλυδρος), *an amphibious snake*: Verg.

chēlys, acc. -yn, voc. -y, f. (χέλυς), *the tortoise*: Petr.; and hence, *the lyre made of its shell* (pure Latin, testudo): Ov.

chĕragra and **chirāgra** -ae, f. (χειράγρα), *the gout in the hands*: Hor., Mart.

Cherrŏnēsus and **Chersŏnēsus** -i, f. (Χερρόνησος and Χερσόνησος), *a peninsula*: esp. (1) Cher. Thracia (or absol. Cherronesus), *the Thracian Chersonese* (now *Gallipoli*). (2) Cher. Taurica (or absol. Cherronesus), *the Crimea.*

Chĕrusci -ōrum, m. *a people in North Germany.*

chīlĭarchēs -ae and **chīlĭarchus** -i, m. (χιλιάρχης and χιλίαρχος), *a commander of 1,000 soldiers*; among the Persians, *the chancellor, or prime minister*: Nep.

Chĭmaera -ae, f. (χίμαιρα, *a goat*), *a fire-breathing monster with the fore parts of a lion, the middle of a goat, and the hind parts of a dragon, killed by Bellerophon*; also *the name of a ship*: Verg. Adj. **Chĭmaerēus** -a -um.

chĭmaerĭfĕr -fĕra -fĕrum (Chimaera/fero), *producing the Chimaera*. F. as epithet of Lycia: Ov.

Chĭonē -ēs, f. (Χιόνη). (1) *mother of Eumolpus by Neptune.* (2) *mother of Autolycus by Mercury.*

Chĭos or **Chĭus** -i, f. (Χίος), *an island in the Aegean Sea, famous for its wine and marble.*

¶ Hence adj. **Chīus** -a -um, *Chian*: vinum, Pl.; n. also as subst. **Chīum** (sc. vinum), *Chian wine*: Hor.; **Chīi** -orum, m. *the Chians*: Cic.

chīrŏgrăphum -i, n. (χειρόγραφον), *an autograph, a person's own handwriting*: alicuius chirographum imitari, Cic. TRANSF., (1) *a document so written*: Cic. (2) *a bond*: Suet.

Chīrōn -ōnis, m. (Χείρων), *a centaur, son of Saturn and Philyra, tutor of Aesculapius, Jason, and Achilles; he was finally transformed into a constellation.*

chīrŏnŏmos -i, c. and **chīrŏnŏmōn** -untis or -ontis, m. (χειρονόμος, χειρονομῶν), *one who uses the hands skilfully, a mime*: Juv.

chīrurgĭa -ae, f. (χειρουργία), *surgery*; fig.: sed ego diaetâ curare incipio, chirurgiae taedet, *violent remedies*, Cic. L.

chlămȳdātus -a -um (chlamys), *dressed in a* chlamys: Pl., Cic.

chlămys -ȳdis, f. (χλαμύς), *a large upper garment of wool*, Greek in origin, sometimes purple and inwrought with gold, worn mainly but not exclusively by soldiers: Pl., Cic., Verg., Ov.

Chlōris -idis, f. (Χλῶρις)=Flora, *the goddess of flowers*, Ov.; also as a Greek *female name*: Hor.

Choerīlus -i, m. (Χοιρίλος), *a bad poet of Iasus who accompanied Alexander the Great on his Persian expedition.*

chŏrāgĭum -i, n. (χορηγία), *the training and production of a chorus*: Pl.

chŏrāgus -i, m. (χορηγός), *he who pays for the production of a chorus*: Pl.

chŏraulēs -ae, m. (χοραύλης), *a flute-player, accompanying the dance of the chorus*: Juv., Mart.

chorda -ae, f. (χορδή), *cat-gut*; usually as the *string* of a musical instrument: Cic., Lucr., Hor.

chŏrēa (poet. also **chŏrea**) -ae, f. (χορεία), *a dance, a dance in a ring*: Verg., Hor., Ov.

chŏrēus -i, m. and **chŏrīus** -i, m. (χορείος), *the metrical foot* -⌣, *afterwards called a trochee*: Cic.

chŏrŏcĭthărista -ae, m. (χοροκιθαριστής), *one who accompanies a chorus on the cithara*: Suet.

chŏrus -i, m. (χορός), *a dance in a circle, a choral dance.*
   LIT., agitare, exercere, Verg., Hor.
   TRANSF., (1) *the persons singing and dancing, the chorus*: Cic.; Dryadum, Verg.; Nereidum, Verg.; *the chorus of a tragedy*: Hor. (2) *a crowd, troop of any kind*: Catilinam stipatum choro iuventutis, Cic.

Chrĕmēs -ētis, -is, or ī, m. *name of an old miser in Roman comedy*: Ter., Hor.

Christus -i, m. (Χριστός), *Christ*: Plin. L.; **Christĭānus** -i, m. (Χριστιανός), *a Christian*: Tac., Suet., Plin. L.

chrŏmis -is, c. (χρόμις), *a sea-fish*: Ov.

Chrȳsa -ae, f. and **Chrȳsē** -ēs, f. (Χρύση), *a town on the Troas coast, with a temple of Apollo.*

chrȳsanthus -i, m. (χρυσός ἄνθος), *a flower, perhaps the marigold*: Verg.

Chrȳsās -ae, m. *a river in Sicily* (now *Dittaino*).

Chrȳsēs -ae, m. (Χρύσης), *a priest of Apollo at Chrysa.*
¶ Hence **Chrȳsēis** -idis, f. (Χρυσηίς), *his daughter, carried off by Agamemnon.*

Chrȳsippus -i, m. (Χρύσιππος), *Stoic philosopher of the third century* B.C., *from Soli in Cilicia, pupil of Cleanthes and Zeno*. Adj. **Chrȳsippēus** -a -um, *of or belonging to Chrysippus*.

chrȳsŏlĭthos -i, m. and f. (χρυσόλιθος), *chrysolite, or topaz*: Plin., Prop., Ov.

chrȳsŏphrys, acc. -yn, f. (χρύσοφρυς), *a kind of sea-fish with a golden spot over each eye*: Ov.

chrȳsos -i, m. (χρυσός), *gold*: Pl.

cĭbārĭus -a -um (cibus), *relating to food*. LIT., res, Pl.; uva, *used for eating only, not for wine*, Pl. N. pl. as subst. **cĭbārĭa** -orum, *food, rations, corn allowed to provincial magistrates*: Cic.; *for soldiers*: Caes.
    TRANSF. (from the food of slaves), *ordinary, common*: panis, *black bread*, Cic.

cĭbātus -ūs, m. (cibo), *food, nourishment*: Pl., Lucr.

cĭbo -are (cibus), *to feed* (animals): Suet.

cĭbōrĭum -i, n. (κιβώριον), *a large drinking-vessel shaped like the seed-pod of the Egyptian bean*: Hor.

cĭbus -i, m. *food for man and beast, nourishment, fodder*. LIT., capere, Pl.; capessere (of animals), Cic.; sumere, Nep.; cibus animalis, *nourishment that the lungs draw from the air*, Cic.; fallax, *bait*, Ov.
    TRANSF., *sustenance*: quasi quidam humanitatis cibus, Cic.

Cĭbȳra -ae, f. (Κιβύρα), *a town in Magna Phrygia, near Caria.*
    ¶ Hence **Cĭbȳrāta** -ae and **Cĭbȳrātĭcus** -a -um, *of or belonging to Cibyra.*

cĭcāda -ae, f. *a cicada, or tree cricket*: Verg.; expectate cicadas, *wait for summer*, Juv.

cĭcātrĭcōsus -a -um (cicatrix), *covered with scars*: Pl., Quint.

cĭcātrix -īcis, f. *a scar, cicatrice*. LIT., Cic., Hor., Ov.; adversae or corpore adverso, *wounds received in front*, and therefore *honourable*, Cic. TRANSF., (1) *on plants, a mark of incision*: Verg. (2) *the patch upon an old shoe*: Juv. (3) fig.: refricare obductam iam reipublicae cicatricem, Cic.

ciccus -i, m. (κίκκος), *the core of a pomegranate*; hence *something worthless*: ciccum non interduim, Pl.

cĭcer -ĕris, n. *a chick-pea*: Pl., Hor.

Cĭcĕro -ōnis, m. *a cognomen in the* gens Tullia, esp. of:
    (1) M. Tullius Cicero, *Roman statesman, orator, and writer, born* 106 B.C. *at Arpinum, murdered at the command of Antony*, 43 B.C.; adj. **Cĭcĕrōnĭanus** -a -um, *Ciceronian.*
    (2) Q. Tullius Cicero, *brother of the above.*

cĭchōrēum -i, n. (κιχόριον), *succory or endive*: Hor.

cicilendrum and **cicimandrum** -i, n. *fanciful names for spice*: Pl.

cĭcōnia -ae, f. *a stork*: Hor., Ov.

cĭcur -ūris, *tame*: bestia, Cic.

cĭcūta -ae, f. *hemlock*: Ov. TRANSF., (1) *poison extracted from the hemlock*: Lucr., Hor. (2) *a shepherd's pipe, made from the hemlock stalk*: Lucr., Verg.

cĭĕo ciēre cīvi cĭtum (connected with κίω, κινέω), *to cause to move, to move, stir.*
    LIT., (1) gen., *to move*: natura omnia ciens et agitans motibus et mutationibus suis, Cic.; puppes sinistrorsum citae, Hor.; in stronger sense, *to disturb, agitate*: mare venti et aurae cient, Liv. (2) *to rouse* for a specific purpose,

to incite, to summon: aliquem ad arma, Liv.; *to summon to help*: nocturnos manes carminibus, Verg.
    TRANSF., (1) gen. *to give rise to, to excite, to arouse*: procellas proelia atque acies, Liv.; seditiones, Liv.; motūs, Lucr., Cic.; gemitus, *to utter*; sometimes *to intensify*: pugnam ciere, *to give new impulse to the battle*, Liv. (2) *to call by name*: aliquem magna voce, Verg.; patrem, *name one's father*, i.e. *prove one's free birth*, Liv.
    ¶ Hence partic. **cĭtus** -a -um, *quick, speedy*: navis, Ov., Verg., Hor., Tac. TRANSF., mors, Hor.; vox, Cic.; pes, *the iambus*, Ov.
    Adv. **cĭtŏ**, compar. citius, superl. citissime, *quickly, speedily*: Pl., Cic., Hor. Esp. in phrases: non cito, *not easily*, Cic.; serius aut citius, *sooner or later*, Ov.; citius quam, *sooner than, rather than*, Cic., Hor.

Cĭlĭcĭa -ae, f. (Κιλικία), *a region in Asia Minor.*
    ¶ Hence adj. and subst. **Cĭlix** -ĭcis, *Cilician, a Cilician*; f. adj. **Cĭlissa** -ae, *Cilician*: spica, saffron, Ov.; adj. **Cĭlĭcĭus** -a -um, *Cilician*; n. as subst. **Cĭlĭcĭum** -i, *a coarse garment, originally made of Cilician goats' hair*; and adj. **Cĭlĭcĭensis**, *Cilician.*

cĭlĭum -i, n. *the eyelid*: Plin.

Cilnĭus -a -um: Cilnia gens, *a distinguished Etruscan family, from which Maecenas was descended.*

Cimber -bri, m.; usually pl. **Cimbri** -ōrum (Κίμβροι), *the Cimbrians, a German tribe who invaded Italy and were defeated by Marius.* Adj. **Cimbrĭcus** -a -um, *Cimbrian.*

cimex -ĭcis, m. *a bug*: Cat.; as a term of reproach: Hor.

Cĭmĭnus -i, m. and **Cĭmĭnĭus lacus**, *a lake in Etruria near to a mountain of the same name.*

Cimmĕrĭi -ōrum, m. (Κιμμέριοι). (1) *a Thracian people, living on the Dnieper.* Adj. **Cimmĕrĭus** -a -um, *Cimmerian.*
    (2) *a mythical people, living in caves between Baiae and Cumae, in eternal darkness.* Adj. **Cimmĕrĭus** -a -um, *Cimmerian* = *dark*: lacus, *the lower world*, Tib.

Cĭmōn -ōnis, m. (Κίμων), *an Athenian statesman and general, son of Miltiades.*

cĭnaedĭcus -a -um (cinaedus), *unchaste*: Pl.

cĭnaedus -i, m. (κίναιδος). (1) *one who indulges in unnatural lust*: Pl., Cat.; as adj., *wanton, shameless*: Cat., Mart. (2) *a wanton dancer*: Pl. (3) *a fish of inelegant habits, the wrasse*: Plin.

Cĭnāra -ae, f. (Κινάρα). (1) *an island in the Aegean Sea.* (2) *a woman's name*: Hor.

¹**cincinnātus** -a -um (cincinnus), *having curled hair*: Pl., Cic.

²**Cincinnātus** -i, m. *a cognomen in the* gens Quinctia, esp. of L. Quinctius Cincinnatus, *a type of old Roman honesty and simplicity, called from the plough to be dictator in* 458 B.C.

cincinnus -i, m. (κίκιννος), *curled hair, a lock of hair*: Pl., Cic. TRANSF., *artificial rhetorical ornament*: Cic.

Cincĭus -a -um, *name of a Roman gens*, esp. (1) L. Cincius Alimentus, *Roman historian at the time of the second Punic war.* (2) M. Cincius Alimentus, *tribune of the people*, 204 B.C., *author of the* lex Cincia *forbidding advocates to receive pay.*

cincticulus -i, m. *a little girdle*: Pl.
cinctūra -ae, f. (cingo), *a girdle*: Suet., Quint.
cinctus -ūs, m. (cingo), *a girding.* LIT., cinctus Gabinus, *a particular way of wearing the toga*, at religious festivals, so as to make it look like a girdle, Liv., Verg. TRANSF., *a girdle*: Suet.
cinctūtus -a -um (cinctus), *girded*: Hor., Ov.
cĭnĕfactus -a -um (cinis/facio), *turned to ashes*: Lucr.
cĭnĕrārĭus -i, m. (cinis), *an attendant who heated in hot ashes the irons for curling the hair*: Cat.
Cinga -ae, m. *a tributary of the Iberus in Hispania Tarraconensis* (now *Cinca*).
Cingĕtŏrix -rīgis, m. (1) *a chief of the Treveri in Gaul.* (2) *a British chief.*
cingo cingĕre cinxi cinctum, *to surround, to encircle.*
(1) in a narrow sense: **a**, *to surround* or *equip the body, to gird*; esp. pass., cingi, as middle, *to gird oneself*; *with clothing*: zona, Pl.; often *with a weapon*: ense, Ov.; gladio, Liv.; poet. with acc.: inutile ferrum cingitur, Verg.; *in a particular manner*: alte, Hor.; Gabino cinctu, Liv.; absol., *to prepare, gird oneself*: Pl., Verg.: **b**, *to crown* or *wreathe the head*: tempora floribus, Hor.; comam lauro, Hor.
(2) in a wider sense, *to surround*: **a**, of places: tellus oras maris undique cingens, Lucr.; colles cingunt oppidum, Caes.; esp. as milit. t. t., *to surround* with hostile intent, or for protection: hiberna castra vallo, Caes.; urbem obsidione, Verg. TRANSF., Sicilia multis undique cincta periculis, Cic.: **b**, of persons, *to escort, to accompany*: cingere alicui latus, Liv., Ov.
cingŭla -ae, f. (cingo), *a girdle*: Ov.
¹**cingŭlum** -i, n. (cingo), *a girdle, a sword-belt*: Petr.; usually pl.: Verg.
²**Cingŭlum** -i, n. *a town in Picenum.*
cingŭlus -i, m. (cingo), *a girdle of the earth, a zone*: Cic.
cĭnĭflo -ōnis, m.=cinerarius, Hor.
cĭnis -ĕris, m., rarely f. (connected with κόνις), *ashes.*
LIT., gen.: in cinerem dilabi, *to become ashes*, Hor.; from the use of ashes for scouring came the prov.: huius sermo cinerem haud quaeritat, Pl. Esp. *the ashes, remains* of some particular thing; *of a corpse after cremation*: cinis atque ossa alicuius, Cic.; *of a city that has been burnt*: patriae cineres, Verg.
TRANSF., *as a symbol of destruction*: Troia virum acerba cinis, *the grave*, Cat.
Cinna -ae, m. *a Roman cognomen*, esp. of (1) L. Cornelius Cinna, *partisan of Marius in the civil war against Sulla, noted for his cruelty.* Adj. **Cinnānus** -a -um.
(2) *his son, one of Caesar's murderers.*
(3) C. Helvius Cinna, *a poet, friend of Catullus.*
cinnămōmum or **cinnămum** -i, n. (κιννάμωμον, κίνναμον), *cinnamon*: Ov.; *as a term of endearment*: Pl.
Cinyps -ȳphis, m. (Κίνυψ), *a river in Libya, between the two Syrtes.*
¶ Hence adj. **Cĭnȳphĭus** -a -um, *relating or belonging to the Cinyps*: Verg.; in gen., *African*: Ov.

Cĭnȳras -ae, m. (Κινύρας), *a mythical king of Cyprus, father of Myrrha, and by her of Adonis.* Adj. **Cĭnȳrēĭus** -a -um, *relating or belonging to Cinyras*: virgo, Myrrha, Ov.; iuvenis, Adonis, Ov.
cippus -i, m. *a pale, stake*; esp. (1) *a tombstone*: Hor. (2) plur. milit. t. t., *palisades*: Caes.
circā (alternative form for circum; possibly from circum ea), adv. and prep.
Adv., *around, round about*: gramen erat circa, Ov.; sometimes directly connected with the subst. without esse: multarum circa civitatum, Liv.; omnia circa, *all things around*, Liv.; circa undique, *all around*, Liv.
Prep. with acc. (1) of space: **a**, *around, near*: templa circa forum, Cic.: **b**, *around to*: legatos circa vicinas gentes misit, Liv. (2) of persons, *around* or *with*: trecentos iuvenes circa se habebat, Liv. (3) of time, *about*: circa eandem horam, Liv.; lucem, Suet.; Demetrium, *about the time of Demetrius*, Quint. (4) of number (like circiter), *about*: ea fuere oppida circa septuaginta, Liv. (5) *about, in respect to*: circa bonas artes publica socordia, Tac.
circāmoerĭum -i, n. (circa/muras), *the space around a wall* =pomerium; q.v., Liv.
Circē -ēs and -ae; acc. -am and -ēn; abl. -a, f. (Κίρκη), *an enchantress, daughter of the Sun and Perse, said to have lived at one time near Circeii.*
¶ Hence adj. **Circaeus** -a -um, *Circean*: poculum, *enchanted*, Cic.; moenia, *Tusculum, said to have been built by her son Telegonus*, Hor.; litus, *the promontory of Circeii*, Ov.
Circēii -ōrum, m. *the town of Circeii, on the promontory of the same name in Latium.* Adj. **Circēiensis** -e, *of* or *belonging to Circeii.*
circensis -e (circus), *belonging to the circus*: ludi, *the games in the circus*, Cic., Liv. M. pl. as subst. **circenses** -ium, m. (sc. ludi), *the circus games*: Verg., Juv.
circĭno -are (circinus), *to make round, to form into a circle*: Plin.; poet.: easdem circinat auras, *flies through in a circle*, Ov.
circĭnus -i, m. (κίρκινος), *a pair of compasses for describing a circle*: Caes.
circĭtĕr (circus). (1) adv., *about*; of time: media circiter nocte, Caes.; of number: circiter CCXX naves, Caes. (2) prep. with acc., *about*; of time: circiter Kalendas, Cic. L., Caes., Hor.; of place (very rare): loca haec circiter, Pl.
circlus =circulus; q.v.
circŭeo, see circumeo.
circŭĭtĭo and **circŭmĭtĭo** -ōnis, f. (circueo, circumeo), *a going round.* LIT., esp. as milit. t. t., *patrol*: Liv. TRANSF., *a roundabout way of speaking*: quid opus est circumitione et anfractu? Cic.
circŭĭtus (circŭmĭtus), -ūs, m. (circueo, circumeo), *a going round in a circle, circuit.* LIT., of physical movement: circuitus orbis, Cic.; hence *a roundabout way, circuitous course*: longo circuitu petere aliquem locum, Caes., Liv.; also *compass, circumference, extent*: eius munitionis circuitus XI milia passuum tenebat, Caes.
TRANSF., (1) rhet., *a period*: Cic. (2) *a roundabout way of speaking*: Quint.; *of acting*: Petr.

circŭlātim, adv. (circulor), *in circles* or *groups*: Suet.

circŭlātor -ōris, m. (circulor), *a stroller, a pedlar;* of certain philosophers: Sen.

circŭlor -ari, dep. (circulus). (1) *to gather in groups for conversation:* Caes. (2) *to collect a group around oneself:* Sen.

circŭlus (syncop. **circlus**: Verg.) -i, m. (dim. of circus), *a circle, circular figure, circuit.* LIT., circulus aut orbis, qui κύκλος Graece dicitur, Cic.; priusquam hoc circulo excedas, Liv.; muri, Liv.; of *the orbit of a planet:* stellae circulos suos orbesque conficiunt celeritate mirabili, Cic.
TRANSF., (1) *any circular body:* flexilis obtorti circulus auri, poet. = *a golden collar,* Verg. (2) *a circle* or *group for conversation:* circulos aliquos et sessiunculas consectari, Cic.; Tac., Mart.

circum (prob. acc. of circus = κίρκος, *in a circle*), adv. and prep.
Adv., *round about, around:* quae circum essent, Caes.; stant circum, Verg.; circum undique, *round about, on all sides,* Verg.
Prep. with acc. (sometimes following its noun, esp. in poetry). (1) *round, around:* terra circum axem se convertit, Cic.; hence *round about, near:* circum haec loca commorabor, Cic.; urbes quae circum Capuam sunt, Cic.; circum pedes, *in attendance,* Cic.; often of persons: circum aliquem esse, Cic.; habere aliquem circum se, Sall. (2) *around to:* legatio circum insulas missa, Liv.

circŭmăgo -ăgĕre -ēgi -actum, *to drive* or *turn round, to drive in a circle.*
(1) *to turn round.* LIT., equos frenis, Liv.; se, Liv.; corpora, Tac.; also as a technical term for the manumission of a slave, because his master took him by the right hand, and turned him round: Sen. TRANSF., of time, circumagi *or* circumagere se, *to pass away, to be spent:* annus se circumegit, Liv.; Lucr.; of changing the feelings, *to influence, bring round:* facile circumegit et flexit, Suet.
(2) *to drive about from one place to another.* LIT., huc illuc clamoribus hostium circumagi, Tac.; nil opus est te circumagi, Hor. TRANSF., *to distract:* rumoribus vulgi circumagi, Liv.

circŭmăro -are, *to plough round:* Liv.

circumcaesūra -ae, f. *the external outline of a body:* Lucr.

circumcīdo -cīdĕre -cīdi -cīsum (circum/caedo), *to cut round, to cut, trim.* LIT., ars agricolarum quae circumcidat, Cic.; caespitem gladiis, Caes. TRANSF., *to make less, by cutting, diminish, cut off:* multitudinem, Cic.; sumptus, Liv.
¶ Hence partic. **circumcīsus** -a -um. (1) of localities, *abrupt, steep, inaccessible:* saxum, Cic.; collis ex omni parte circumcisus, Caes. (2) *abridged, brief:* Plin. L.

circumcircā, adv., *all round about:* ap. Cic. L., Pl.

circumclūdo -clūdĕre -clūsi -clūsum, *to shut in, enclose on all sides, surround:* cornua argento, Caes.; esp. *to surround* in a hostile manner: circumcludi duobus exercitibus, Caes. TRANSF., Catilina meis praesidiis, meā diligentiā circumclusus, Cic.

circumcŏlo -ĕre, *to dwell around, dwell near:* Liv.

circumcurso -are (intens. of circumcurro), *to run round:* Pl., Lucr., Cat.

circumdo -dare -dĕdi -dătum, *surround.*
(1) *to put something round something else;* with acc. of the thing placed, and dat. of the thing round which it is placed: tectis ac moenibus subicere ignes circumdareque, Cic.; arma umeris, Verg.; equites cornibus, Liv.; in tmesis: collo dare bracchia circum, Verg. TRANSF., *to supply:* paci egregiam famam, Tac.
(2) *to surround something with something else;* with acc. and abl. (rarely double acc.). LIT., animum corpore, Liv.; tempora vittis, Ov.; regio insulis circumdata, Cic. Esp. in a hostile sense: oppidum coronā, Liv. TRANSF., exiguis quibusdam finibus totum oratoris munus, Cic.

circumdūco -dūcĕre -duxi -ductum, *to lead round, move* or *drive round.*
LIT., exercitum, Pl.; aratrum (of the founding of a colony when a plough was driven around the site of the wall), Cic.; flumen ut circino circumductum, Caes.; cohortes quattuor longiore itinere, Caes.; absol.: praeter castra hostium circumducit, *he marches round,* Liv.; with two accusatives: aliquem omnia sua praesidia, *to take him round them,* Caes.
TRANSF., (1) *to cheat:* Pl. (2) of discourse, *to extend, amplify:* Quint.

circumductĭo -ōnis, f. (circumduco). (1) *cheating:* Pl. (2) rhet. t. t., *a period:* Quint.

circŭmĕo (circŭeo) circu(m)ire, circu(m)ii *or* -īvi, circuitum, *to go round.*
LIT., (1) in gen.: flagrantes aras, Ov.; hostium castra, Caes.; metam ferventi rotā, Ov.; esp. milit., *to surround:* aciem, cornu, urbem, Caes. (2) *to go all round, to visit:* urbem, Liv.; plebem, Liv.; praedia, Cic.; oram maris, Cic.; vigilias, Liv. Esp. *to go round to canvass* or *solicit:* senatum cum veste sordida, Liv.; circumire ordines et hortari, Caes.
TRANSF., (1) *to cheat, circumvent:* Pl., Verg. (2) *to express by circumlocution:* Vespasiani nomen suspensi et vitabundi circumibant, *avoided mentioning,* Tac. (3) fig., *to surround, beset:* circumiri totius belli fluctibus, Cic.

circŭmĕquĭto -are, *to ride round:* moenia, Liv.

circŭmerro -are, *to wander round:* Sen.

circŭmfĕro -ferre -tŭli -lātum, *to carry round, take round.*
LIT., in gen.: circumferuntur tabulae inspiciendi nominis causa, Cic.; poculum circumfertur, Liv.; circa ea omnia templa infestos ignes, Liv.; esp. of the eyes, *to turn them all round:* acies, Verg.; oculos, Liv.; as religious t. t., *to lustrate, purify,* by carrying round consecrated objects: socios pura circumtulit unda, Verg.
TRANSF., in gen., *to spread:* incendia et caedes et terrorem, Tac.; bellum, Liv.; esp. *to spread news:* quae se circumferat esse Corinnam, Ov.

circumflecto -flectĕre -flexi -flexum, *to bend round, to turn about:* longos cursus, Verg.

circumflo -are, *to blow round;* fig.: ut ab omnibus ventis invidiae circumflari posse videatur, Cic.

circumflŭo -fluĕre -fluxi -fluxum, *to flow round.*
LIT., utrumque latus circumfluit aequoris unda, Ov.
TRANSF., (**1**) intransit., *to overflow, abound*: nec ea redundans tamen nec circumfluens oratio, *diffuse,* Cic.; with abl., *to abound in*: circumfluere omnibus copiis, Cic.; gloria, Cic. (**2**) transit., *to encompass*: Luc.

circumflŭus -a -um (circumfluo). (**1**) act., *flowing round, circumfluent*: umor, Ov. (**2**) pass., *flowed round, surrounded by water*: insula, Ov., Tac.

circumfŏrānĕus -a -um (circum/forum). (**1**) *round the forum*: aes, *money borrowed from the bankers whose shops were round the Forum,* Cic. (**2**) *attending at markets*: pharmacopola, Cic.

circumfundo -fundĕre -fūdi -fūsum.
(**1**) *to pour around.* LIT., usually in pass., circumfundi, or reflexive, se circumfundere, *to be poured round=to surround*; with dat.: amnis circumfunditur parvae insulae, Liv. TRANSF., of persons or abstract things: equites Hannoni Afrisque se circumfudere, Liv.; undique circumfusis molestiis *or* voluptatibus, Cic.
(**2**) act., *to surround, encompass,* and pass., *to be surrounded*; usually with instrumental abl. LIT., mortuum cera, Nep.; parva quaedam insula est circumfusa illo mari quem oceanum appellatis, Cic. TRANSF., of persons, etc.: praefectum castrorum et legionarios milites circumfundunt, Tac.; multis circumfusus Stoicorum libris, Cic.

circumgĕmo -ĕre, *to growl round about*: ovile, Hor.

circumgesto -are, *to carry round*: epistulam, Cic. L.

circumgrĕdĭor -grĕdi -gressus sum (circum/gradior), *to go round, travel round,* esp. with hostile intent: exercitum, Sall.; terga, Tac.

circumiăcĕo -ēre, *to lie round about, adjoin*: absol. or with dat.: circumiacent Europae, Liv.

circumicio -icere -iēci -iectum (circum/iacio).
(**1**) *to throw round, put round*; with acc. alone: vallum, Liv., Tac.; or with acc. of thing thrown and dat. of thing round which: multitudinem hominum moenibus, Caes.
(**2**) *to surround* one thing with another; with acc. and instrumental abl.: extremitatem caeli rotundo ambitu, Cic.
¶ Hence partic. **circumiectus** -a -um, in sense (**1**) of the verb, *thrown round,* so *surrounding, adjacent*: nationes, Tac.; with dat.: aedificia circumiecta muris, Liv.

circumiectus -ūs, m. (circumicio), *a surrounding, enclosing*: qui (aether) tenero terram circumiectu amplectitur, Cic.; ut ita munita arx circumiectu arduo niteretur, Cic.

circumĭtĭo=circuitio; q.v.

circumlĭgo -are. (**1**) *to bind round, bind to*: natam mediae hastae, Verg. (**2**) *to bind round with*: ferrum stuppa, Liv.; circumligatum esse angui, Cic.

circumlĭno -lĭnĕre, no perf., -lĭtum (also **circumlĭnĭo** -īre: Quint.). (**1**) *to smear one thing over another*: circumlita taedis sulfura, Ov. (**2**) *to besmear with, bedaub*: circumlitus

auro, Ov.; poet., gen., *to cover*: circumlita saxa musco, Hor.

circumlŭo -lŭĕre, *to wash round, flow round*: quo (mari) in paeninsulae modum pars (arcis) circumluitur, Liv.

circumlŭvĭo -ōnis, f. (luo), *alluvial land*: Cic.

circummitto -mittĕre -mīsi -missum, *to send round*: legationes, Caes.; tribuno cum duorum signorum militibus circummisso, Liv.

circummūnĭo (circummoenio: Pl.), -ire, *to fortify round, to wall round, to shut in by lines of circumvallation*: Uticam vallo, Caes.

circummūnītĭo -ōnis, f. (circummunio), *the investing* or *circumvallation of a fortress*: Caes.

circumpădānus -a -um (circum/Padus), *round about the Po, near the river Po*: campi, Liv.

circumpendeo -ēre, *to hang around*: Ov.

circumplaudo -ĕre, *to clap* or *applaud on all sides*: aliquem, Ov.

circumplector -plecti -plexus, dep. *to embrace, enclose, surround*: domini patrimonium circumplexus quasi thesaurum draco, Cic.; collem opere, Caes.

circumplĭco -are, *to fold round, wind round*: si anguem vectis circumplicavisset, Cic.

circumpōno -pōnĕre -pŏsŭi -pŏsĭtum, *to place* or *put round*: nemus stagno, Tac.; piper catillis, Hor.

circumpōtātĭo -ōnis, f. (circum/poto), *drinking round in succession*: ap. Cic.

circumrētĭo -ire (circum/rete), *to enclose in a net, ensnare.* TRANSF., aliquem, Lucr.; te circumretitum frequentiā populi Romani video, Cic.

circumrōdo -rōdĕre -rōsi, *to gnaw round*: escam, Plin. TRANSF., dudum enim circumrodo quod devorandum est, *I have long hesitated to speak out,* Cic.; dente Theonino circumroditur, *is slandered,* Hor.

circumsaepĭo -saepire -saeptus, *to hedge round, enclose*: stagnum, Suet. TRANSF., ignibus, Cic.; corpus armatis, Liv.

circumscindo -ĕre, *to tear off, round, to strip*: quo ferocius clamitabat, eo infestius circumscindere et spoliare lictor, Liv.

circumscrībo -scrībĕre -scripsi -scriptum, *to describe a circle round, to enclose in a circular line.*
LIT., orbem, Cic.; stantem virgula, Cic.
TRANSF., (**1**) *to draw the outline of an object, to fix the boundaries of*: locum habitandi alicui, Cic.; vitae spatium, Cic. (**2**) *to confine, limit, restrict,* esp. of the powers of magistrates: tribunum plebis, Cic., Caes. (**3**) *to set aside, exclude*: sententias, Cic. (**4**) *to take in, deceive, ensnare*: fallacibus et captiosis interrogationibus circumscripti, Cic.; adulescentulos, *to defraud,* Cic.; vectigalia, *to embezzle,* Quint.
¶ Hence partic. **circumscriptus** -a -um, as rhet. t. t. (**1**) *rounded, periodic*: verborum ambitus, Cic. (**2**) *concise*: explicatio, Cic. Adv. **circumscriptē**. (**1**) *in rhetorical periods*: circumscripte numeroseque dicere, Cic. (**2**) *fully*: complecti singulas res, Cic.

circumscriptĭo -ōnis, f. (circumscribo), *an encircling*; hence *circumference*: Cic. TRANSF., (**1**) *outline, boundary*; gen.: terrae, Cic.; temporis, *limit,* Cic.; in rhetoric, *a period*: Cic. (**2**) *swindling, defrauding*: adulescentium, Cic.

circumscriptor -ōris, m. (circumscribo), *a cheat, swindler*: Cic., Juv.

circumsĕco -sĕcāre -sectum, *to cut round*: aliquid serra, Cic.

circumsĕdĕo -sĕdĕre -sēdi -sessum, *to sit round*: Sen. Esp. *to surround with hostile intent, besiege, beleaguer*: aliquem vallo, Cic. TRANSF., lacrimis omnium circumsessus, assailed, Cic.; blanditiis, Liv.

circumsessĭo -ōnis, f. (circumsedeo), *an encircling, a beleaguering*: Cic.

circumsīdo -ĕre, *to sit down before a place, besiege*: Liv., Tac.

circumsilĭo -ire (circum/salio), *to leap* or *jump round*: (passer) circumsiliens, Cat. TRANSF., circumsilit agmine facto morborum omne genus, Juv.

circumsisto -sistĕre -stĕti, or (more rarely) -stĭti, *to place oneself round, to surround*, esp. with hostile intent: me, Pl.; plures paucos circumsistebant, Caes.; sex lictores circumsistunt, Cic.; curiam, Liv.

circumsŏno -sonare -sonui. (1) transit.: a, *to sound all around*: clamor hostes circumsonat, Liv., Sen.: b, *to make to resound*: murum armis, Verg.

(2) intransit., *to resound, to echo with*: locus circumsonat ululatibus, Liv.; aures tuas vocibus undique circumsonare, Cic.

circumsŏnus -a -um (circumsono), *sounding all around*: turba canum, Ov.

circumspectātrix -īcis, f. (circumspecto), *one who looks about her, a female spy*: Pl.

circumspectĭo -ōnis, f. (circumspicio), *a looking about*. TRANSF., *circumspection, caution*: circumspectio aliqua et accurata consideratio, Cic.

circumspecto -are (freq. of circumspicio), *to look around*.

(1) intransit., *to look round repeatedly*: bestiae in pastu, Cic., Liv.: fig.: dubitans, circumspectans, haesitans, Cic.

(2) transit.: a, *to look round at*, esp. with anxiety or suspicion: omnia, Cic.; patriciorum vultus, Liv.: b, *to look round to seek for something* or *somebody*: circumspectare omnibus fori partibus senatorem raroque usquam noscitare, Liv.: c, gen., *to wait for, watch for*: defectionis tempus, Liv.

¹**circumspectus** -a -um, partic. from circumspicio; q.v.

²**circumspectus** -ūs, m. (circumspicio). (1) *looking round*: Plin. TRANSF., *attention to*: detinere aliquem ab circumspectu rerum aliarum, Liv. (2) *prospect, view on every side*: Cic.

circumspĭcĭo -spĭcĕre -spexi -spectum, *to look round*.

(1) intransit.: qui in auspicium adhibetur nec suspicit nec circumspicit, Cic.; esp. *anxiously*: circumspicit, aestuat, Cic.; diversi circumspiciunt, Verg. TRANSF., *to consider*: circumspicite celeriter animo qui sint rerum exitus consecuti, Cic.

(2) transit., *to look round at, to survey*: cornua sua, Liv.; lucos, Ov.; *to look round and see*: saxum ingens, Verg. TRANSF., *to consider carefully*: consilia, Caes.; omnia pericula, Cic.; also *to look about for, seek for*: externa auxilia, Tac.

¶ Hence partic. **circumspectus** -a -um. (1) pass., of things, *deliberate, well considered*:

verba circumspecta, Ov., Quint. (2) act., of persons, *circumspect, cautious*: Suet., Quint., Sen.

circumsto -stare -stĕti, *to stand round* or *in a circle*.

(1) intransit.: Caes., Verg.; hence partic. as subst. **circumstantes**, *the bystanders*: Liv.

(2) transit., *to surround*: equites senatum, Cic.; sellam, Liv., Verg., Ov.; esp. with hostile intent, *to beleaguer*: circumstare tribunal praetoris urbani, obsidere cum gladiis curiam, Cic. TRANSF., cum tanti undique terrores circumstarent, Liv.; also transit.: Cic., Liv., Verg.

circumstrĕpo -ĕre, *to make a noise round, shout clamorously around*: legatus clamore seditiosorum circumstrepitur, Tac.; also with what is said as object: quidam atrociora circumstrepebant, Tac.

circumstrŭo -struĕre -struxi -structum, *to build round*: Suet.

circumsurgens -entis, *rising round*: iuga, Tac.

circumtĕro -tĕrĕre, *to rub against on all sides*; poet., *to crowd round*: Tib.

circumtextus -a -um (texo), *woven all round*: circumtextum croceo velamen acantho, Verg.

circumtŏno -tŏnare -tŏnŭi, *to thunder round*; poet., *to make a loud noise around*: hunc circumtonuit Bellona, Hor.

circumtonsus -a -um (tondeo), *shaven or shorn all round*: Suet. TRANSF., of discourse, *artificial*: Sen.

circumvādo -vādĕre -vāsi, *to attack from every side, to surround*. LIT., immobiles naves circumvadunt, Liv. TRANSF., cum terror circumvasisset aciem, Liv.

circumvăgus -a -um, *wandering round, flowing round*: Oceanus, Hor.

circumvāllo -are, *to surround with a fortification, to blockade, beleaguer*: oppidum, Caes.; Pompeium, Cic.; fig.: tot res repente circumvallant, Ter.

circumvectĭo -ōnis, f. (circumvehor). (1) *a carrying round of merchandise*: portorium circumvectionis, *transit dues*, Cic. L. (2) *circuit, revolution*: solis, Cic.

circumvector -ari (intens. of circumvehor). (1) *to ride or sail round*: Ligurum oras, Liv. (2) poet., *to go through, describe*: singula dum circumvectamur, Verg.

circumvĕhor -vehi -vectus, *to be carried round*.

(1) *to ride or sail round*: iubet circumvectos (equites), ab tergo Gallicam invadere aciem, Liv.; navibus circumvecti, Caes.; with acc.: cum classe Corsicae oram, Liv.

(2) poet., *to describe*: frustra circumvehor omnia verbis, Verg.

circumvēlo -are, *to veil round, envelop*: aurato circumvelatur amictu, Ov.

circumvĕnĭo -vĕnire -vēni -ventum, *to come round, surround, encircle*.

LIT., homines circumventi flamma, Caes.; Cocytos sinu labens circumvenit atro, Verg.; Rhenus modicas insulas circumveniens, Tac. Esp. *to surround with hostile intent*: hostes a tergo, Caes.; cuncta moenia exercitu, Sall.

TRANSF., (1) *to beset, oppress, assail*: aliquem iudicio capitis, Cic. (2) *to cheat, defraud*: innocentem pecunia, Cic.

circumvertor (-vortor) -verti, *to turn oneself round*: Pl.; with acc.: rota perpetuum qua circumvertitur axem, Ov.

circumvestĭo -ire, *to clothe all round*, poet.: ap. Cic.

circumvincĭo -ire, *to bind all round*: aliquem virgis, Cic.

circumvīso -ĕre, *to look around at*: Pl.

circumvŏlĭto -are, *to fly round*: lacus circumvolitavit hirundo, Verg. TRANSF., *to rove about, hover round*: circumvolitant equites, Lucr.

circumvŏlo -are, *to fly round*: turba praedam circumvolat, Verg. TRANSF., nox atra caput, Verg.; alis (of death), Hor.

circumvŏlvo -volvĕre -volvi -vŏlūtum, *to roll round*; usually pass., *to revolve*: sol magnum circumvolvitur annum, *completes its annual course*, Verg.

circus -i, m. (κίρκος), *a ring*.

(1) in gen., *a circle, orbit*: candens, *the Milky Way*, Cic.

(2) *an oval course for races*; esp. *the* Circus Maximus, *or* Circus, *the great circus or racecourse in Rome, surrounded by galleries which accommodated over* 100,000 *spectators*: Liv., Cic., Tac., Ov.; also the Circus Flaminius and Circus Maritimus.

cīris -is, f. (κεῖρις), *a mysterious bird, into which Scylla, daughter of Nisus, was transformed*: Ov., Verg.

cirrātus -a -um (cirrus), *curly-haired*: Mart.

Cirrha -ae, f. (Κίρρα), *a city of Phocis, near Delphi, sacred to Apollo*.

¶ Hence adj. **Cirrhaeus** -a -um, *relating to Cirrha or Apollo*.

cirrus -i, m. (1) *a lock, curl, or ringlet of hair*: Juv. (2) *the fringe of a garment*: Phaedr.

Cirta -ae, f. (Κίρτα), *a town in Numidia*.

cis, prep., with acc., *on this side of*. (1) of place: cis Taurum, Cic. (2) of time: cis dies paucos, *within a few days*, Pl.

Cisalpīnus -a -um, *on this* (the Roman) *side of the Alps*: Gallia, Caes., Cic., Liv.

cisĭum -i, n. *a light two-wheeled vehicle*: Cic.

Cisrhēnānus -a -um, *on this* (the Roman) *side of the Rhine*: Germani, Caes.

Cisseūs -ĕi, m. (Κισσεύς), *king of Thrace, father of Hecuba*.

¶ Hence **Cissēis** -ĭdis, f. *daughter of Cisseus, Hecuba*.

cista -ae, f. (κίστη), *a chest, box*, for keeping money, fruit, books, etc.: Cic.; for sacred utensils: Cat., Ov., Tib.; *a ballot-box*: Plin.

cistella -ae, f. (dim. of cista), *a little chest or box*: Pl., Ter.

cistellātrix -īcis, f. (cistella), *the female slave whose business it was to keep the cash-box*: Pl.

cistellŭla -ae, f. (dim. of cistella), *a little chest or box*: Pl.

cisterna -ae, f. *a subterranean reservoir, a cistern*: piscinae cisternaeque sevandis imbribus, Tac.

cistĭfer -fĕri, m. (cista/fero), *one who carries a box or chest*: Mart.

cistŏphŏrus -i, m. (κιστοφόρος), *an Asiatic coin worth about four drachmae, so called from the impression of* a cista *upon it*: in cistophoro in Asia habeo ad HS. bis et vicies, *in Asiatic coinage*: Cic. L.; Liv.

cistŭla -ae, f. (dim. of cista), *a little chest or box*: Pl.

cĭtātus -a -um, partic. from ²cito; q.v.

cĭtĕr -tra -trum (cis), *on this side*; positive found in Cato; usually compar. **cĭtĕrĭor** -us, genit. -ōris. LIT., *on this side*: Gallia, Cic. TRANSF., *nearer*: ad haec citeriora veniam et notiora nobis, *more closely concerning us*, Cic.

Superl. **cĭtĭmus** -a -um, *nearest*: terris, Cic.

Abl. f. **citrā** as adv. and prep.; q.v.

Cĭthaerōn -ōnis, m. (Κιθαιρών), *a mountain in the south-west of Boeotia, scene of the Bacchic orgies*.

cĭthăra -ae, f. (κιθάρα), *a stringed instrument, lyre, lute*: Lucr., Verg., Hor., Tac. Meton., *the art of playing the cithara*: Hor., Verg.

cĭthărista -ae, m. (κιθαριστής), *a player on the cithara*: Cic.

cĭthăristrĭa -ae, f. (κιθαρίστρια), *a female player on the cithara*: Ter.

cĭthărizo -are (κιθαρίζω), *to play the cithara*: Nep.

cĭthăroedĭcus -a -um (κιθαρῳδικός), *relating to the citharoedus*: Suet.

cĭthăroedus -i, m. (κιθαρῳδός), *one who plays the cithara, with voice accompanying*: Cic., Hor.

Cĭtĭum -i, n. (Κίτιον), *a city on the coast of Cyprus, birth-place of the Stoic philosopher, Zeno*.

¶ Hence **Cĭtĭensis** -e and **Cĭtĭēus** -a -um, *belonging to Citium, a Citian*.

¹**cĭtŏ**, adv. from cieo; q.v.

²**cĭto** -are (freq. of cieo).

(1) *to put into violent motion*: arma, Stat. (mainly post-Aug., except in partic. citatus; see below). TRANSF., *to excite, start up*: motum (animi), Cic.

(2) *to summon, call forward*; esp.: **a**, for political or military purposes; so *to summon the senate*: patres in curiam, Liv.; *the people to vote*: in campo Martio centuriatim populum, Liv.; *the citizens to take the oath of military allegiance*: citati milites nominatim apud tribunos militum in verba P. Scipionis iuraverunt, Liv.: **b**, at law: si Lysiades citatus iudex non responderit, Cic.; citat reum, non respondet; citat accusatorem, Cic.; omnes ii ab te capitis C. Rabirii nomine citantur, Cic.; in hanc rem te, Naevi, testem citabo, Cic.: **c**, fig., from the summoning of witnesses, *to appeal to, point to* authorities, supporting facts, etc.: quamvis citetur Salamis clarissimae testis victoriae, Cic.: **d**, *to call upon a god for help*: aliquem falso, Ov.

¶ Hence partic. (with compar. and superl.: Liv.) **cĭtātus** -a -um, *quick, rapid, speedy*: Rhenus per fines Trevirorum citatus fertur, Caes.; citato equo, *at full gallop*, Liv.; gradu, agmine, Liv.

Adv. **cĭtātim**, *quickly, hastily*: Auct. B. Afr.

citrā (abl. f. from citer). (1) adv., *on this side, nearer* than some particular point: Ov., Liv., Tac. (2) prep. with acc., *on this side of, nearer than*: citra Veliam, Cic.; citra Rhenum, Caes.; of time, *since*: citra Troiana tempora, Ov. TRANSF., *short of, not extending to*: scelus, necem, Ov.; hence post-Aug. (esp. Quint. and Plin.), *without*: usum, Quint.; vulnus, Plin.

---

cĭtrĕus -a -um (citrus). (1) *belonging to the citrus-tree*: mensa, *made of citrus-wood*, Cic. (2) *belonging to the citron-tree*: Plin.

cĭtrō, adv. (dat. from citer), *to this side*; found only in combination with ultro: ultro et citro, ultro citroque, ultro citro, *up and down, hither and thither, backwards and forwards*, Cic.

cĭtrus -i, m. (1) *the citrus, a kind of African cypress* with an aromatic timber used in making furniture: Luc., Plin. (2) *the citron-tree*: Plin.

cĭtus -a -um, partic. from cieo; q.v.

cīvĭcus -a -um (civis), *relating to a citizen, civic*: bella, *civil war*, Ov.; esp. civica corona, or absol. **cīvĭca** -ae, f. *the civic crown, a chaplet of oak leaves awarded to one who had saved the life of a Roman citizen in war, bearing the inscription* ob civem servatum: Cic.

cīvīlis -e (civis), *of a citizen.*
(1) *relating to a citizen, civic, civil*: bellum, Cic.; discordia, Sall.; irae, Tac.; quercus= corona civica (*see* civicus), Verg. Esp.: ius civile, *the civil law of the Romans*, Cic.; or *civil rights*: Cic.; or *the Roman forms of procedure in law*: Liv.
(2) *becoming a citizen, befitting a citizen*: nulli civilis animus, Liv.; hence, *popular, affable, courteous*: quid civilius illo? Ov., Tac., Suet.
(3) *relating to public life* or *the state*: scientia, Cic.; ratio, Cic.; civilium rerum peritus, Tac.; esp. *civil* as opp. to military: non militaria solum sed civilia quoque munera, Liv.
Adv. **cīvīlĭtĕr.** (1) *like a citizen*: Liv., Juv., Tac. (2) *politely*: Ov., Tac.

cīvīlĭtās -ātis, f. (civilis). (1) *the science of politics*, used by Quint. as a translation of ἡ πολιτική. (2) *politeness, civility*: Suet.

cīvis -is, c. *a citizen*; esp. of Rome (opp. hostis or peregrinus): civis Romanus, Cic.; aliquem civem asciscere, Cic.; fieri civem Romanum, Cic.; also *a fellow citizen*: cives mei, Cic.
Outside Rome, *a citizen* of some other country: civis Attica, f., Ter.; *a subject* under a king: imperare corpori ut rex civibus suis, Cic.; *a citizen of the world*: totius mundi, Cic.

cīvĭtās -ātis, f. (civis).
(1) abstr., *citizenship, the condition* or *rights of a citizen*: civitatem dare alicui, Cic.; amittere, Cic.; aliquem civitate donare, Cic.; aliquem in civitatem asciscere, Liv.; in populi Romani civitatem suscipi, Cic.; civitatem consequi, adipisci, habere, impetrare, adimere, Cic.; civitate mutari, Cic.
(2) concr.: **a**, *a union of citizens, a state, commonwealth*: concilia coetusque hominum iure sociati, quae civitates appellantur, Cic.; civitates aut nationes, *civilized states* or *barbarous tribes*, Cic.; civitatem instituere, administrare, Cic.; civitates condere, Cic.: **b**, *the inhabitants of a city, townsfolk*: Caes., Cic.: **c**, (rarely) *a city, town*: expugnare civitatem, Quint., Tac.

clādēs -is, f. (connected with κλάω). LIT., *destruction, material damage* or *loss*: dextrae manus, Liv.; of plague: Lucr.; of fire: Suet., Tac.
TRANSF., in gen., *disaster, injury*: civitatis, Cic. Esp., *misfortune in war, defeat*: cladem

inferre, Liv.; facere, Sall.; accipere, Cic., Liv.; hosti inferre, Cic. Meton., *of persons that cause disaster*: militum clades, Cic.; geminos Scipiadas, cladem Libyae, Verg.

clam (connected with celo). (1) adv., *secretly* (opp. palam), *in secret*: esse, *to remain unknown*, Liv.; plura clam removere, Cic.; clam ferro incautum superat, Verg.
(2) prep., *unknown to, without the knowledge of*: **a**, with abl.: clam vobis, Caes.: **b**, (more often) with acc.: clam matrem, Pl.; clam me est, *it is unknown to me*, Cic.

clāmātor -ōris, m. (clamo), *a shouter, a bawler, noisy declaimer*: Cic.

clāmĭtātĭo -onis, f. (clamito), *a shouting, bawling*: Pl.

clāmĭto -are (freq. of clamo), *to cry loudly* or *often, shout violently.* LIT., Cauneas clamitabat, *cried figs of Caunus*, Cic.; ad arma! clamitans, Liv.; foll. by acc. and infin.: saepe clamitans liberum se esse, Caes.; foll. by jussive subjunc.: Tac., or ut or ne: Tac.; *to call* a person something: aliquem sycophantam, Ter. TRANSF., *to proclaim, declare*: nonne ipsum caput et supercilia illa penitus abrasa clamitare calliditatem videntur, Cic.

clāmo -are (connected with καλέω), *to call, shout, cry aloud.*
LIT., (1) in gen. of men: loqui omnes et clamare coeperunt, Cic.; de suo et exoris interitu clamant, Cic.; of animals: anseres qui tantummodo clamant, nocere non possunt, Cic. (2) *to call to* or *upon*: comites, Ov.; morientem nomine, Verg. (3) *to shout* something: hoc de pecunia, Cic.; with words quoted: Io triumphe! clamasse, Liv.; with acc. and infin.: clamare ille cum raperetur, nihil se miserum fecisse, Cic.; with ut and the subj.: clamare coeperunt sibi ut haberet hereditatem, Cic.; *to proclaim*: aliquem furem, Hor.
TRANSF., *to proclaim, declare*: eum clamat virtus beatiorem fuisse, Cic.

clāmor (old form **clāmos**) -ōris, m. *a loud shouting, cry.*
LIT., of men: clamor populi infestus atque inimicas, Cic.; clamorem edere, tollere, Cic., Liv., Verg.; excitare, Liv.; clamor oritur, Sall.; auditur, Caes. Esp. (1) *shout of applause*: haec sunt, quae clamoris et admirationes in bonis oratoribus efficiunt, Cic.; *of disapproval*: aliquem clamoribus et conviciis et sibilis consectari, Cic. (2) *war-cry*: clamorem tollere, Caes., Liv. (3) *cry of sorrow*: lamentantium militum, Liv. (4) *of birds*: gruum, Lucr.
TRANSF., of lifeless things, *echo, reverberation*: montium, Hor., Verg.

clāmōsus -a -um (clamo). (1) act., *noisy, clamorous*: Quint., Juv. (2) pass., *filled with noise*: circus, Mart., Juv.

clanculum (clam). (1) adv., *secretly, in secret*: Pl., Ter. (2) prep. with acc., *unknown to*: clanculum patres, Ter.

clandestīnus -a -um (clam), *secret, concealed, hidden, clandestine*: conloquia cum hostibus, Cic.; Pl., Caes., Lucr.
Adv. **clandestīnō**, *secretly*: Pl.

clango -ere, *to sound, resound*: Stat.

clangor -ōris, m. (clango), *a sound, clang, noise*: Liv.; *of birds*: Ov.; *of a trumpet*: Verg.

Clānĭus -i, m. *a river of Campania.*

clārē, adv. from clarus; q.v.

clārĕo -ēre (clarus). LIT., *to be bright, to shine*: Enn., Cic. poet. TRANSF., (1) *to be clear to the mind, be evident*: Lucr. (2) *to be distinguished, illustrious*: Enn.

clāresco clārescĕre clārŭi (inch. of clareo).
LIT., to the sight, *to become clear, bright*: Tac.; to the hearing, *to sound or resound clearly*: clarescunt sonitus, Verg.; Quint.
TRANSF., (1) *to become clear to the mind, become evident*: Lucr. (2) *to become illustrious*: Tac.; ex gente Domitiā duae familiae claruerunt, Suet.

clārigātio -ōnis, f. (clarigo). (1) *the demand for satisfaction and ultimatum delivered by the Fetialis*: Quint., Plin. (2) *the fine imposed on one caught beyond prescribed limits*: Liv.

clārigo -are (clarus), *to demand satisfaction*, used of the Fetialis: Plin.

clārisŏnus -a -um (clarus/sono), *clearly sounding*: vox, Cat.

clārĭtās -ātis, f. (clarus). LIT., to the sight, *clearness, brightness*: Plin; to the hearing: in voce, Cic.; vocis, Quint. TRANSF., (1) *clearness to the mind, plainness*: Quint. (2) *fame, celebrity, renown*: num claritatis, num gloriae paenitebat? Cic.; Herculis, Tac.

clārĭtūdo -ĭnis, f. (clarus), *clearness, brilliancy*. LIT., to the sight: deae (i.e., lunae), Tac. TRANSF., *fame, renown, celebrity*: Sall., Tac.

clāro -are (clarus). LIT., to the sight, *to make bright or clear*: Cic. poet. TRANSF., (1) *to make plain to the mind*: animi naturam versibus, Lucr. (2) *to make illustrious, renowned*: labor Isthmius clarabit pugilem, Hor.

Clărŏs -i, f. (Κλάρος), *a small town in Ionia, on a promontory near Colophon, famous for a temple and oracle of Apollo.*
¶ Hence adj. **Clārĭus** -a -um (Κλάριος), *Clarian, surname of Apollo*: Ov.; poeta, *the poet Antimachus of Colophon.*

clārus -a -um (connected with clamo and obs. calo), *clear, distinct.*
LIT., of sound, *clear, loud*: clamor, Pl.; vox, Caes., Cic., Liv.
TRANSF., (1) to the sight, *bright, shining, brilliant*: lumina mundi, Verg.; lucerna, Hor.; clarissimae gemmae, Cic.; poet., of the wind, *making clear, bringing fair weather*: aquilo, Verg. (2) to the understanding: *clear, evident, plain*: certa et clara, Ter.; luce sunt clariora nobis tua consilia, Cic. (3) of reputation: **a**, in a good sense, *illustrious, renowned, distinguished*: vir clarissimus, Cic.; clarus gloria, Cic.; clarus in philosophia et nobilis, Cic.; ex doctrina nobilis et clarus, Cic.; clarus ob obscuram linguam, Lucr.; of things: pugna, Pl.; oppidum, Cic.; victoria clarissima, Cic.: **b**, in a bad sense, *notorious*: illa oppugnatio fani antiquissimi quam clara apud omnes, Cic.; populus luxuriā superbiāque clarus, Liv.
¶ Hence adv. **clārē**, *clearly*. LIT., as regards sight, *clearly, brightly*: videre, Pl.; fulgere, Cat. As regards hearing, *aloud, distinctly*: plaudere, dicere, Pl.; gemere, Cic. L. TRANSF., (1) of understanding, *clearly, distinctly*: apparere, ap. Cic.; ostendere, Quint. (2) *illustriously*: explendescere, Nep.

classiārius -a -um (classis), *of the fleet*: centurio, Tac. More often m. pl. as subst. **classiārii**, *marines, naval forces*: Caes., Tac.

classĭcŭla -ae, f. (dim. of classis), *a little fleet, flotilla*: Cic. L.

classĭcus -a -um (classis). (1) *relating to the classes into which the Roman citizens were divided*: Varro. Esp. *of the highest classis*: Cato.
Hence Gellius' distinction between *scriptor classicus* ('classical') and *scriptor proletarius.*
(2) *relating to the armed forces*, esp. to the fleet: milites, Liv.; bella, *naval war*, Prop.; so m. pl. as subst. **classĭci** -ōrum, *marines*, Tac. N. sing. also as subst. **classĭcum** -i, *the signal for battle given by a trumpet*: classicum canit, Liv.; meton., *the trumpet itself*: classicum inflare, Verg., Liv.

classis -is, f. (connected with κλέω and calo, *to summon*), *a summoning*; hence *a group as summoned, a division, class.*
(1) *one of the divisions into which Servius Tullius divided the whole Roman people*: Cic., Liv.; hence fig.: quintae classis, *of the lowest rank*, Cic.
(2) *the armed forces*: **a** (archaic), *a land army*: Hortinae classes, Verg.: **b** (usual sense), *the fleet*: classem facere, Caes.; comparare, aedificare, *to build a fleet*, Cic.; instruere atque ornare, *to fit out a fleet*, Cic.; classem appellere, *to land*, Cic.; armare, deducere, Verg.
(3) in gen., *a class, group*: Quint., Suet., Petr.

Clastĭdĭum -i, n. *a town in Gallia Cisalpina* (now *Chiasteggio*).

Clăterna -ae, f. *a fortress in Gallia Cisalpina, near Bononia.*

clātri -ōrum, m. (κλῆθρα), *a trellis* or *grating*: Hor.

clatro -are (clatri), *to provide* or *cover with a trellis* or *grating*: Pl.

claudĕo -ēre and **claudo** -ĕre (claudus), *to limp, halt, be lame*: used fig.: si (beata vita) una ex parte clauderet, Cic.; of orators: in quacunque enim una (parte) plane clauderet, orator esse non posset, Cic.

Claudiānus -i, m. (Claudius), *a Roman poet of Alexandria* (c. A.D. 400).

claudĭcātĭo -ōnis, f. (claudico), *a limping*: Cic.

claudĭco -are (claudus), *to limp, be lame*: graviter claudicare ex vulnere ob rempublicam accepto, Cic. TRANSF., (1) *to incline, be deflected*: claudicat axis mundi, Lucr. (2) fig., *to halt, waver, be defective*: tota res vacillat et claudicat, Cic.; of speech: nihil curtum, nihil claudicans, Cic.

claudĭtās -ātis, f. *lameness*: Plin.

Claudius (**Clōdius**) -a -um, *the name of two Roman gentes, one patrician and the other plebeian, of whom the most celebrated members were*:
(1) Appius Claudius Crassus, *the most notorious of the decemvirs of* 451 B.C.
(2) Appius Claudius Caecus, *censor* 312 B.C., *the builder of several great public works.*
(3) Publius Clodius Pulcher, *tribune of the people, enemy of Cicero, killed by Milo*, 52 B.C.
(4) *the emperor Claudius* (10 B.C.–A.D. 54).
Adj. **Claudiānus** -a -um, **Claudiālis** -e, **Clōdiānus** -a -um, *Claudian.*

¹**claudo** claudĕre clausi clausum and **clūdo** clūdĕre clūsi clusum (connected with clavis and κλείς).

(1) in gen. *to shut, close* (opp. aperire). LIT., forem cubiculi, Cic.; portas alicui, Caes.; Ianum, *to close the gates of the temple of Janus*, Liv. TRANSF., *to stop, to close*: claudere aures alicui rei, Cic.; in ipsius consuetudinem, quam adhuc meus pudor mihi clausit, me insinuabo, Cic.; horum ferocia vocem Evandri clausit, Liv.

(2) *to close up a passage* or *place, to make inaccessible*: omnes aditus claudentur, Cic.; quod clausae hieme Alpes essent, Liv.; adhuc clausum fuisse mare scio, Cic.; rivos, *to dam*, Verg.

(3) *to conclude, bring to an end*: opus, Ov.; octavum lustrum, Hor.; esp. as milit. t. t.: agmen claudere, *to bring up the rear*, Caes.

(4) *to shut in, shut up*. LIT., aliquem in curiam *or* in curia, Liv.; urbs loci natura terra marique clauditur, *is enclosed*, Cic.; n. as subst. **clausum** -i, *an enclosed place*: Verg., Sall. Esp. as milit. t. t., *to blockade, invest*: oppidum undique, Sall.; of hunting: nemorum saltus, Verg. TRANSF., in gen., *to confine, hide*: aliud clausum in pectore, aliud in lingua promptum habere, Sall.; of character: clausus, *close, reserved*, Tac.; of rhythm in speech or writing: sententias numeris, Cic.; pedibus verba, Hor.

¹claudo = claudeo; q.v.

claudus (cludus) -a -um, *limping, halting, lame*. LIT., Volcanus, Cic.; claudus altero pede, *lame on one foot*, Nep.; claudi ac debiles equi, Liv.; prov.: iste claudus pilam, *one who can make proper use of nothing*, Cic. TRANSF., *crippled, defective, wavering*: naves, Liv.; clauda nec officii pars erit ulla tui, Ov.; poet.: carmina alterno versu, *elegiac verse*, Ov.

claustrum -i, n. (claudo), gen. plur., *a means of closing* or *shutting in*.
LIT., of physical objects: **a**, *a bolt, bar*: claustra revellere, Cic.; laxare, Verg.; relaxare, Ov.: **b**, *an enclosure, prison, den*: venti circum claustra ferunt, Verg.; diu claustris retentae ferae, Liv.: **c**, *a barricade, dam, fortress*: claustra loci, Cic.; montium, Tac.; milit. t. t., *the key to a position*: claustra Aegypti, Liv.
TRANSF., arta claustra portarum naturae effringere, *to break into her secrets*, Lucr.; vitai claustra, 'the fastnesses of life', Lucr.; claustra ista nobilitatis refregissem, Cic.

clausŭla -ae, f. (claudo), *the end, conclusion*: epistulae, Cic.; in quo (mimo) cum clausula non invenitur, Cic.; esp. in rhetoric, *the close of a period*: Cic.

clāva -ae, f. (clavus), *a knotty staff* or *cudgel*: Pl., Cic., Verg.; also *a foil for teaching the use of weapons*: Cic.; *the club of Hercules*: Verg., Ov.

clāvārĭum -i, n. (clavus), *an allowance to Roman soldiers for the purchase of shoe-nails*: Tac.

clāvātor -ōris, m. (clava), *one who carries a cudgel*: Pl.

clāvĭcŭla -ae, f. (dim. of clavis), *the twig* or *tendril by which the vine clings to its prop*: Cic.

¹clāvĭger -gĕri, m. (clava/gero), *the club-bearer*, epithet of Hercules: Ov.

²clāvĭger -gĕri, m. (clavis/gero), *the key-bearer*, epithet of Janus as god of doors: Ov.

clāvis -is; acc. clavem *or* -im; abl. clave *or* -ī; f. (connected with κλείς), *a key*: Pl., Liv.;

adulterina portarum, *a false* or *skeleton key*, Sall.; claves adimere uxori, *to separate from one's wife*, Cic. TRANSF., clavis adunca trochi, *a stick for trundling a hoop*, Prop.

clāvus -i, m. (cf. κλείς).
(1) *a nail*. LIT., clavis ferreis confixa transtra, Caes.; clavus trabalis, *a spike*, as a sign of firmness, an attribute of Necessitas, Hor.; prov.: trabali clavo figere, *to fix firmly*, Cic.; annalis, *the nail which on the ides of September every year was driven into the wall of the temple of Jupiter Capitolinus at Rome*; hence fig.: ex hoc die clavum anni movebis, *reckon the beginning of the year*, Cic. TRANSF., *a tiller, helm, rudder*: Verg.; fig.: clavum imperii tenere, Cic.
(2) *a stripe of purple on the tunic, worn broad by the senators* (latus), *narrow by the knights* (angustus): latum clavum a Caesare impetravi, *I have become a senator*, Plin.; also worn by sons of senators or knights: Ov., Liv. TRANSF., clavus = *a tunic*, with either the broad or the narrow stripe: Hor.

Clāzŏmĕnae -ārum, f. (Κλαζομεναί), *a town on the coast of Asia Minor*.

Clĕanthēs -is, m. (Κλεάνθης), *a Stoic philosopher, pupil of Zeno*.
¶ Hence adj. **Clĕanthēus** -a -um, *Stoic*: Pers.

clēmens -entis, adj. (with compar. and superl.), *mild, placid, kind, merciful*.
LIT., of persons: Pl., Liv.; clementes iudices et misericordes, Cic.; ab innocentia clementissimus, Cic.
TRANSF., of things: castigatio, Cic.; esp. of wind, water, weather, *calm, mild*: flamen, Cat.; amnis clementissimus, Ov.
¶ Hence adv. **clēmentĕr**. LIT., *mildly, gently, mercifully*: clementer ferre aliquid, Pl., Lucr., Cic. L.; clementer et moderate ius dicere, Caes.; clementer ductis militibus, *without plundering*, Liv. TRANSF., *gently, gradually*: clementer editum iugum, *gently rising*, Tac.

clēmentĭa -ae, f. (clemens). LIT., *mildness, mercy, clemency*: Ter., Ov.; clementia mansuetudoque, Cic.; confugere in clementiam alicuius, Cic.; clementia uti, Cic. TRANSF., of weather, *mildness*: aestatis, Plin.

Clĕōnae -ārum, f. (Κλεωναί), *a city in Argolis, near Nemea*.
¶ Hence adj. **Clĕōnaeus** -a -um, *Cleonean*.

Clĕŏpātra -ae, f. (1) *the daughter of Philip of Macedon and wife of Alexander, king of Epirus*. (2) *the daughter of Ptolemy Auletes, queen of Egypt, the mistress of Antony, whose forces allied with hers were overthrown by Augustus at Actium*.

clĕpo clĕpĕre clepsi cleptum (κλέπτω), *to steal*: ap. Cic.; se, *to conceal oneself*, Sen.

clepsydra -ae, f. (κλεψύδρα), *a water clock*, esp. as used to measure the time allotted to orators: ad clepsydram latrare, Cic. Hence of the time so allotted: binas clepsydras petere, *to wish to speak for the length of two clepsydrae*, Plin.; dare, *to give leave to speak*, Cic.

clepta -ae, m. (κλέπτης), *a thief*: Pl.

clībănus -i, m. (κλίβανος), *an earthen* or *iron vessel used for baking bread*: Plin.

cliens -entis, m. (archaic cluens, from clueo, κλύω, *to hear*; lit. *a listener*). In Rome, *a client, dependent, one under the protection of a* patronus (q.v.); in Gaul and Germany, *a vassal*; used of entire nations, *allies*: Caes. Transf., cliens Bacchi, Hor.

clĭenta -ae, f. (cliens), *a female client*: Pl., Hor.

clĭentēla -ae, f. (cliens), *clientship*.

(1) at Rome, *the relation between the client and his patron*: esse in alicuius clientela, Cic.; in alicuius clientelam se conferre, Cic. Transf. (gen. in plur.), *clients*: Caes., Cic., Tac.

(2) elsewhere, *the relation of a weaker nation to a more powerful one, dependence*: dicare se alicui in clientelam, Caes.

clĭentŭlus -i, m. (dim. of cliens), *a little client*: Tac.

clīnāmen -ĭnis, n. (*clino), *inclination, swerving aside*: Lucr.

clīnātus -a -um (partic. from obsolete verb clino=κλίνω), *inclined, bent, leaning*: Cic. poet.

Clīnĭas -ae, m. (Κλεινίας), *the father of Alcibiades*.

¶ Hence **Clīnĭădes** -ae, m. *Alcibiades*.

Clīō -ūs, f. (Κλειώ). (1) *the Muse of history*. (2) *a daughter of Oceanus*.

clĭpĕo -are, *to arm with a shield*; ante-class. except in partic. **clĭpĕatus** -a -um, *armed with a shield*: agmina, Verg., Ov.; m. pl. as subst. clipeati -orum, *soldiers with shields*: Pl., Liv.

clĭpĕus -i, m. and **clĭpĕum** -i, n. *the (round) bronze shield of the Roman soldiers*.

Lit., Pl., Cic., Verg., Hor.; prov.: clipeum post vulnera sumere, *to do anything too late*, Ov. Transf., of objects resembling a shield in shape. (1) *the disk of the sun*: Ov. (2) (gen. clipeum), *a medallion portrait of a god or distinguished man*: Liv., Tac.

Clisthĕnēs -is, m. (Κλεισθένης), *an Athenian statesman of the sixth century* B.C.

Clītarchus -i, m. (Κλείταρχος), *a Greek historian who accompanied Alexander the Great on his expeditions*.

clītellae -ārum, f. *a pack-saddle, a pair of panniers*: Pl., Hor., Cic. L.

clītellārĭus -a -um (clitellae), *belonging or relating to a pack-saddle*: Pl.

Clīternum -i, n. *a town of the Aequi*.

Clītŏmāchus -i, m. (Κλειτόμαχος), *an Academic philosopher, pupil of Carneades*.

Clītŏr -ŏris, m. (Κλείτωρ) and **Clītŏrĭum** -i, n. *a town in Arcadia*. Adj. **Clītŏrĭus** -a -um, *Clitorian*.

Clītumnus -i, m. *a river in Umbria* (now *Clitunno*).

clīvosus -a -um (clivus), *hilly, steep, precipitous*: rus, Verg.; Olympus, Ov.

clīvus -i, m. (*clino), *a slope, rise, gradient*.

Lit., lenis ab tergo clivus erat, Liv.; clivum mollire, Caes.; Verg., Hor. Transf., *an ascent, rising road*, esp.: clivus Capitolinus, *the ascent from the Forum up the Capitoline hill*, Cic. L., Liv.; so: clivus sacer, Hor. Prov. of the early stages of a task: clivo sudamus in imo, Ov.

clŏāca -ae, f. (from *cluo, *I cleanse*), *a sewer or drain*: fossas cloacasque exhaurire, Liv., Cic., Hor. Esp.: cloaca maxima, *the sewer* (*attributed to Tarquinius Priscus*) *which drained the Forum and discharged into the Tiber*, Liv.

Clŏācīna -ae, f. (from *cluo, *I cleanse*), *the cleanser*, surname of Venus whose image stood

where the Romans, after the Sabine war, purified themselves with myrtle boughs.

Clōdius = Claudius; q.v.

Cloelĭus (**Cluīlĭus**) -a -um, *name of a Roman gens*, of which the most famous member was **Cloelĭa** -ae, f. *a Roman girl, given as a hostage to Porsenna, who swam back across the Tiber to Rome*.

Clōthō f. (nom. and acc. only) (Κλωθώ), *the spinner, one of the Parcae*.

clŭĕo -ēre (κλύω), *I hear myself called, I am called, am named*: quaecunque cluent, *whatever has a name*, Lucr.; Pl.

clūnis -is, m. and f. (usually pl.), *the buttocks, hinder parts*: Pl., Hor., Liv.

clūrīnus -a -um, *of or pertaining to apes*: Pl.

Clūsĭum -i, n. *a town of Etruria* (now *Chiusi*). Adj. **Clūsīnus** -a -um, *of Clusium*.

Clūsĭus -ii, m. (cludo), *the shutter*, epithet of Janus.

Clymĕne -ēs, f. (Κλυμένη), *the wife of the Ethiopian king Merops, and mother of Phaëthon*.

¶ Hence adj. **Clymĕnēius** -a -um: proles, Phaëthon, Ov.

clystēr -ēris, m. (κλυστήρ). (1) *a clyster*: Suet. (2) *syringe*: Suet.

Clytaemnestra -ae, f. (Κλυταιμνήστρα), *daughter of Leda, sister of Helen, Castor, and Pollux, wife of Agamemnon and mother of Orestes, Electra, and Iphigenia. She killed her husband with the help of Aegisthus, and was herself killed by Orestes*.

Clytĭē -ēs, f. (Κλυτίη), *daughter of Oceanus, beloved by Apollo, changed into the plant heliotropium*.

Cnĭdus (-ŏs), or **Gnĭdus** (-ŏs), -i, f. (Κνίδος), *a town in Caria, famed for the worship of Venus*. Adj. **Cnĭdĭus** -a -um, *Cnidian*.

Cnossus = Gnossus; q.v.

cŏăcervātĭo -ōnis, f. (coacervo), *a heaping up* (of proofs): Cic., Quint.

cŏăcervo -are, *to heap up, accumulate*: pecuniae coacervantur, Cic. Transf., argumenta, Cic.

cŏăcesco -ăcescĕre -ăcŭi, *to become sour*: ut enim non omne vinum, sic non omnis natura vetustate coacescit, Cic.; fig.: quam valde eam (gentem Sardorum) putamus tot transfusionibus coacuisse, Cic.

cŏactĭo -ōnis, f. (cogo), *a collecting*: coactiones argentarias factitavit, Suet.

cŏacto -are (intens. of cogo), *to compel*: Lucr.

cŏactor -ōris, m. (cogo). (1) *a collector of rents, money at auctions*, etc.: Cic., Hor. (2) coactores agminis, *the rear-guard*, Tac. (3) *one who compels*: Sen.

cŏactū, abl. sing. as from coactus, m. (cogo); *by force, under compulsion*: coactu atque efflagitatu meo, Cic.; Caes., Lucr.

cŏactum -i, n. (cogo), *a coverlet of thick cloth*: Caes.

cŏaedĭfĭco -are, *to build on*: campum Martium, Cic.

cŏaequo -are, *to level, make plain, even*. Lit., montes, Sall. Transf., ad libidines tuas omnia coaequasti, *placed on the same footing*, Cic.

cŏagmentātĭo -ōnis (coagmento), *a connexion, binding together*: corporis, Cic.

cŏagmento -are (coagmentum), *to fix together, stick together, join together*. Lit., opus ipsa suum eadem, quae coagmentavit, natura dissolvit, Cic. Transf., verba compone et quasi coagmenta, Cic.; pacem, *to conclude*, Cic.

cŏagmentum -i, n. (cogo), *a joining together, a joint* : Pl.; lapidum, Caes.

cŏagŭlum -i, n. (cogo), *that which causes to curdle, rennet* : Ov., Plin.; meton., *curds* : Plin.

cŏālesco -ălescĕre -ălŭi -ălĭtum.

(1) *to grow together, to become one in growth* : saxa vides sola coalescere calce, Lucr. TRANSF., *to coalesce, unite* : sic brevi spatio novi veteresque (milites) coaluere, Sall.; ut cum patribus coalescerent animi plebis, Liv.; in hunc consensum, Tac.
(2) *to take root, grow.* LIT., of plants : novus in viridi coalescit cortice ramus, Ov.; grandis ilex coaluerat inter saxa, Sall. TRANSF., *to become established* or *firm* : dum Galbae auctoritas fluxa, Pisonis nondum coaluisset, Tac.; so in perf. partic. : coalita libertas, Tac.

cŏangusto -are, *to narrow, limit, confine* : haec lex coangustari potest, Cic.

coarcto, etc.=coarto, etc.; q.v.

cŏargŭo -ŭĕre -ŭi (cum/arguo), *to show in a clear light.*

(1) in gen., *to demonstrate fully, to prove by evidence* : certum crimen multis suspicionibus, Cic.; perfidiam alicuius, Cic.; sin autem fuga laboris desidiam, repudiatio supplicum superbiam coarguit, Cic.
(2) *to prove false* or *wrong* : **a,** of things : (legem) coarguit usus, Liv.: **b,** of persons, *to prove to be wrong, to convict of error, to confute* : quo (decreto) maxime et refelli et coargui potest, Cic.: **c,** of persons, *to prove to be guilty, to convict of a crime* : criminibus coarguitur, Cic.; with genit. of crime : aliquem avaritiae, Cic.

cŏartātĭo -ōnis, f. (coarto), *a drawing together, a confining in a small space* : Liv.

cŏarto -are, *to confine, draw together* (opp. laxare, dilatare).

LIT., Thermopylarum saltum, ubi angustae fauces coartant iter, Liv.; Cic. L., Tac.
TRANSF., (1) of discourse, *to compress, abbreviate* : ut quae coartavit, dilatet nobis, Cic.
(2) of time, *to shorten* : consulatūs aliorum, Tac.

cŏaxo -are (onomatop.; cf. κοάξ), *to croak* (of a frog) : Suet.

coccĭnātus -a -um (coccinus), *clad in scarlet* : Suet., Mart.

coccĭnĕus -a -um (coccum), *scarlet-coloured* : Petr.

coccĭnus -a -um (coccum), *scarlet-coloured* : Juv., Mart. N. pl. as subst. **coccĭna** -orum, *scarlet clothes* : Mart.

coccum -i, n. (κόκκος), *the berry of the scarlet oak* (*Quercus coccifera* Linn.), used as a scarlet dye by the ancients (the real source of the dye has since been discovered to be an insect) : Plin.
TRANSF., (1) *scarlet dye* : Verg., Hor. (2) *scarlet cloth* or *garments* : Suet.

coclĕa (cochlĕa) -ae, f. (κοχλίας), *a snail* : Pl., Cic., Hor. Meton. *the snail-shell* : Mart.

coclĕāre (cochlĕāre) -is, n. and **coclĕārium** -i, n. (coclea), *a spoon* (in the form of a snail-shell) : Mart., Plin.

cocles -itis, m. *a one-eyed man* : Pl.; also *a Roman cognomen,* esp. of Horatius Cocles, *the Roman who defended the bridge over the Tiber against the army of Porsenna.*

coctĭlis -e (coquo), *baked* : lateres, Varr.; muri (Babylonis), *made of burnt brick,* Ov.

Cōcȳtŏs and **-ŭs,** -i, m. (Κωκυτός, *the stream of wailing*), *a river of the lower world.* Adj. **Cōcȳtĭus** -a -um, *Cocytian* : virgo, *Alecto,* Verg.

cōda=cauda; q.v.

cōdex (older form **caudex**) -dĭcis, m. *the trunk of a tree* : Verg., Ov. TRANSF., (1) *a block to which men were bound for punishment* : Pl., Juv. (2) as a term of abuse, *dolt, blockhead* : Ter. (3) *a book, made up of wooden tablets, covered with wax*; hence gen., *a book* : Cic., Quint. Esp. *an account-book, a ledger* (adversaria=*a day-book,* the accounts from which were entered into the codex every month) : in codicem referre, Cic.

cōdĭcārĭus (caudĭcārĭus) -a -um (codex), *made of tree trunks* : naves, Sall.

cōdĭcilli -ōrum, m. (dim. of codex), *little trunks, logs* : Cato. TRANSF., (1) *small tablets upon which to make memoranda* : Plin. (2) *something written on tablets, a letter* : Cic.; *a petition* : Tac.; *a codicil* : Tac.; *an imperial rescript* or *order* : Suet.

Codrus -i, m. (Κόδρος). (1) *the last king of Athens.* (2) *a bad poet, mentioned by Vergil.*

coel-, see cael-.

cŏēmo -ĕmĕre -ēmi -emptum, *to buy in large quantities, buy up* : te quae te delectarint coemisse, Cic.; Hor.

cŏemptĭo -ōnis, f. (coemo), legal t. t. (1) *a form of marriage which consisted in a mock sale of the parties to one another* : Cic. (2) *a fictitious sale of an estate,* to rid it of sacrificial duties attached to it.

cŏemptĭōnālis -e (coemptio), *relating to a* coemptio : senex, *an old man used for a fictitious marriage*; hence gen., *poor, worthless,* Pl.

coen-, see caen-.

cŏĕo -īre -ii (rarely -īvi) -ĭtum (cum/eo), *to go together, come together, assemble.*

LIT., of the actual movement of persons. (1) gen. : populus coibat, Hor.; ad solitum locum, Ov. as enemies, *to engage* : inter se coiisse viros et cernere ferro, Verg.; Ov. (3) *to unite so as to form a whole, to combine* : coire inter se, Caes.; in unum, Liv.; in orbem, Liv.; esp. *to unite in marriage, cohabit* : Ov.; cum uxore, Quint.
TRANSF., (1) of other associations of persons, esp. political : cum hoc tu coire ausus es, Cic.; adversus rempublicam, Liv. As transit. verb, with noun societas; act., *to form an alliance* : societatem vel periculi vel laboris, Cic.; pass. : societas coitur, Cic. (2) of things, *to unite, come together* : ut placidis coeant immitia, Hor.; of wounds : neve retractando nondum coeuntia rumpam vulnera, Ov.; coit formidine sanguis, Verg.; mentiar, an coeat duratus frigore pontus, *freezes,* Ov.

coepĭo coepĕre coepi coeptum (the present-stem tenses ante-class., being replaced by those from incipio; the perfect-stem tenses, supine, etc., are class.; derived from the obs. verb apio), *to begin, commence.*

(1) act., coepi=*I have begun* or *I began* ; fut. partic. coepturus; absol. : dies coepit, Sall.; with acc. : orationem, Tac.; Romanos coepturos bellum, Liv.; usually with infin. act. : ire, Lucr.; oppugnare, Caes.; dicere, Cic.; with dicere understood : coepit cum talia vates, Verg., Liv.; with infin. pass. : rapinae fieri, Cic.

(2) pass., in past partic., perf. tense, etc.: coeptum bellum, Sall.; nocte coepta, Tac. With infin. (esp. pass. infin.): lapides iaci coepti sunt, Caes.; postquam armis disceptari coeptum sit, Cic. N. as subst. **coeptum** -i, *a thing begun* or *undertaken*: Lucr., Verg., Liv.

coepto -are (intens. of coepi). (1) transit., *to begin* or *undertake eagerly*; with infin.: coercere seditionem, Tac.; appetere ea, Cic.; with acc.: Ter.; fugam, Tac. (2) intransit.: coeptantem coniurationem disiecit, Tac.

coeptum -i, n. from coepio; q.v.

coeptus -ūs, m. (from coepi; rare and only in plur.), *a beginning*: appetendi, Cic.

coëpŭlōnus -i, m. *a fellow-reveller, companion at a feast*: Pl.

cŏërcĕo -cēre -cŭi -cĭtum (arceo), *to enclose, shut in.*
LIT., physically, *to encompass, enclose*: mundus omnia complexu suo coercet et continet, Cic.; Lucr., Ov. Hence *to confine, restrain*: (aqua) iubetur coerceri Cic.; quibus (operibus) intra muros coercetur hostis, Liv.; *to keep in order*: virgā aureā turbam, Hor.; *to prune*: vitem ferro amputans coercet, Cic.
TRANSF., in gen., *to limit, confine, restrain*: cupiditates, Cic.; seditionem, Liv.; magistratus noxium civem multā, vinculis verberibusque coerceto, Cic.; Caes., Hor.; of speech or writing: Cic., Hor.

cŏërcĭtĭo -ōnis, f. (coerceo), *a confining, restraint*: profusarum cupiditatum, Tac.; hence *punishment*: magistratus, Liv.; *the right to punish*: Suet.

coeruleus=caeruleus; q.v.

coetus (**cŏĭtŭs**) -ūs, m. (coeo). LIT., *a meeting together*: Lucr.; esp. (coitus only), *sexual union*: Ov. TRANSF., *a meeting, assemblage*: in omni coetu concilioque, Cic.; coetus nocturni, Liv.; coetum *or* coetus celebrare, *to assemble in large numbers*, Verg., Cic. poet.

Coeus (dissyll.) -i, m. (Κοῖος), *a Titan, father of Latona.*

cōgĭtātĭo -ōnis, f. (cogito), *thinking.*
LIT., in gen., *the act* or *faculty of thinking, conception*: homo solus particeps rationis et cogitationis, Cic.; dicebas, speciem dei percipi cogitatione, non sensu, Cic.; ea quae cogitatione depingimus, Cic.; on a particular topic, *reflection, meditation, consideration, reasoning*: ad hanc causam non sine aliqua spe et cogitatione venerunt, Cic.; ad reliquam cogitationem belli se recepit, Caes.
TRANSF., *a thought, idea*: num ullam cogitationem habuisse videantur ii, etc., Cic.; esp. in plur.: mandare litteris cogitationes suas, Cic.; posteriores enim cogitationes sapientiores solent esse, Cic. Esp. *a thinking of, intention, design*: accusationis cogitatio, Cic.

cōgĭtātus -a -um, partic. from cogito; q.v.

cōgĭto -are (cum/agito), *to turn over in the mind, to think, reflect, consider.*
(1) in gen.: cui vivere est cogitare, Cic.; with acc.: rem, Ter.; beneficia alicuius, Cic.; Scipionem, Cic.; with acc. and infin.: homines ea si bis accidere posse non cogitant, Cic.; with de and the abl.: de deo, Cic.; with indir. quest.: cogita qui sis, Cic.; with ad and the acc.: ad haec igitur cogita, Cic.; with ut or ne and the subj.: Caes. (2) more

particularly: **a**, *to think of, intend, plan*: nihil cogitant nisi caedes, nisi incendia, Caes.; qui nocere alteri cogitat, Cic.; de parricidio, Cic.; ellipt.: inde ad Taurum cogitabam, *I intended to go*, Cic. L.: **b**, with adv., *to be disposed towards*: si humaniter et sapienter et amabiliter in me cogitare vis, Cic.
¶ Hence partic. **cōgĭtātus** -a -um, *considered, deliberate*: Cic.; n. pl. as subst. **cōgĭtāta** -ōrum, *thoughts, reflections, ideas*: Cic.; adv. **cōgĭtātē**, *carefully, thoughtfully, with consideration*: rem tractare, Pl.; scribere, Cic.

cognātĭo -ōnis, f. (cognatus).
LIT., *relationship, connexion by blood*: cognatio quae mihi tecum est, Cic.; cognatione cum aliquo coniunctum esse, Cic.; aliquem cognatione attingere, Cic.; propinqua cognatione Hannibali iunctus, Liv.
TRANSF., (1) meton., *persons related, kindred, family*: cognationis magnae homo, *with a large connexion*, Caes.; tota cognatio advehatur, Cic. (2) in gen., *connexion, agreement, resemblance*: studiorum et artium, Cic.; Quint.

cognātus -a -um (gnatus=natus, from nascor), *related, connected by blood.*
LIT., Ter., Cic.; m. and f. often as subst. **cognātus** -i, m., **cognāta** -ae, f. *a relation either on the father's* or *mother's side.*
TRANSF., (1) (poet.) of objects and animals, *kindred, akin*: urbes, sanguis, Verg. (2) in gen., *related, similar, cognate*: nihil est tam cognatum mentibus nostris quam numeri, Cic.; Hor.

cognĭtĭo -ōnis, f. (cognosco), *getting to know, study, knowledge of* or *acquaintance with* a person or thing.
(1) in gen.: aliquem cognitione atque hospitio dignum habere, Cic.; cognitio contemplatioque naturae, Cic.; plur., meton., *an idea, a conception*: insitas deorum vel potius innatas cognitiones habemus, Cic.
(2) in certain special senses (cf. cognosco): **a**, *recognition*: Ter.: **b**, *a legal inquiry, investigation*: consulibus cognitionem dare, Cic.; cognitionem de existimatione alicuius constituere, Cic.; rerum capitalium, Liv.; de libellis, Tac.

cognĭtor -ōris, m. (cognosco), *a knower.* As legal t. t. (1) *a witness to the identity of a Roman citizen in a foreign country*: Cic. (2) *an attorney, advocate*: Cic. Hence in gen., *a supporter*: huius sententiae, *voucher for*, Cic.; Liv., Hor.

cognōmĕn -ĭnis, n. (gnomen=nomen).
LIT., *a surname, family name, the name following the name of the gens* (e.g., Cicero): quorum alteri cognomen Capitoni est, Cic.; Liv.; cognomen habere sapientis, Cic.; cognomen sumere *or* trahere *or* sibi adripere ex aliqua re, Cic.
TRANSF., in gen., *a name*: Hesperiam Grai cognomine dicunt, Verg.

cognōmentum -i, n. *a surname*: Pl., Tac.
TRANSF., in gen., *a name*: Tac.

cognōmĭnātus -a -um (gnomen=nomen). (1)=συνώνυμος, *of the same meaning*: verba, *synonyms*, Cic. (2) *surnamed*: Suet.

cognōmĭnis -e (cognomen), *having the same name*: Pl., Verg.; with dat.: cognomine Insubribus pago, Liv.

cognosco -gnoscĕre -gnōvi -gnĭtum (cum/ gnosco=nosco), *to become acquainted with, get to know, learn*; and in the perf. tenses, *to know.*

(1) in gen., through the senses or the understanding; with acc.: regiones, Caes.; amnem, Verg.; cognoscere naturam rerum, Cic.; aliquem bene cognovisse, Cic.; aliquid experiendo magis quam discendo, Cic.; aliquem ex litteris alicuius, Cic.; aliquem hominem pudentem et officiosum, Cic.; with acc. and infin.: Attici nostri te valde studiosum esse cognovi, Cic. L.; Lucr., Caes.; abl. absol. cognito, *it being known*: cognito vivere Ptolemaeum, Liv.; with indir. quest.: cognoscite nunc, quae potestas decemviris et quanta detur, Cic.

(2) in certain special senses: **a,** *to know again, recognize*: cum eum Syracusis amplius centum cives Romani cognoscerent, Cic.: **b,** of judges, *to examine, hear, decide*: causa cognita, Cic.; cognoscere de actis Caesaris, Cic. ¶ Hence partic. **cognĭtus** -a -um (with compar. and superl., poet.), *known, proved*: homo virtute cognitā, Cic.

cōgo cōgĕre cŏēgi cŏactum (cum/ago), *to bring, drive,* or *draw to one point.*

Lit., (1) in gen., *to bring together, collect*; of cattle: pecudes, Verg.; of men: vi et necessario in portum coacti, Cic.; of troops: exercitum magnasque copias, Caes.; of political or legal gatherings: senatum, Cic.; comitium, Caes.; iudices, Cic.; of lifeless objects: pecuniam ex decumis, Cic.; Ter., etc. (2) esp. *to bring close together, compress*: in artissima ripas cogitur amnis, Liv.; so *to thicken,* of liquids or of a thin material: frigore mella cogit hiems, Verg.; lac coactum, *curdled,* Ov.; n. of partic. as subst. **cŏactum** -i, *thick woven cloth, felt*: Caes.; as milit. t. t.: agmen cogere, *to bring up the rear,* Caes.; hence fig., *to be the last*: ut nec duces simus nec agmen cogamus, Cic.

Transf., (1) in gen., *to bring together, restrict, confine*: ius civile in certa genera, Cic.; Boios in ius iudiciumque populi Romani, Liv. (2) esp., *to compel to do something*: aliquem ad militiam, Sall; ad bellum, Liv.; with infin.: te emere coegit, Cic.; Lucr., Verg., Liv.; with ut and the subj.: cogere incipit eos ut absentem Heraclium condemnarent, Cic.; with acc. of the thing one is compelled to do: cogi aliquid, Liv., Quint.; quid non mortalia pectora cogis? Verg.; partic. **cŏactus**, *constrained*: invitus et coactus, Cic. (3) as t. t. in logic, *to infer, conclude*: Cic.

cŏhaerentĭa -ae, f. (cohaereo), *coherence*: mundi, Cic.

cŏhaerĕo -haerēre -haesi -haesum, *to cling together.*

Lit., (1) of a whole, *to have coherence, subsist, hold together*: mundus ita apte cohaeret, ut dissolvi nullo modo queat, Cic. (2) of one thing, *to cling to, adhere to* another thing: nec equo mea membra cohaerent, Ov.

Transf., (1) *to be coherent* or *consistent, to hang together*: vix diserti adulescentis cohaerebat oratio, Cic. (2) *to be connected* in any way to a person or thing: haec ratio implicita est cum illis pecuniis et cohaeret, Cic.

cŏhaeresco -haerescĕre -haesi (inch. of cohaereo), *to hang together, mutually adhere*: atomi inter se cohaerentes, Cic.

cŏhērēs -ēdis, m. *a coheir*: Cic., Hor.

cŏhĭbĕo -ēre -ŭi -ĭtum (cum/habeo). (1) *to hold in, contain, hold together*: brachium togā, Cic.; omnes naturas ipsa (natura) cohibet et continet, Cic.; auro lacertos, Ov. (2) *to confine, restrain.* Lit., ventos carcere, Ov.; crinem nodo, *to tie,* Hor. Transf., *to hinder, hold back, control, repress*: conatus alicuius, Cic.; manūs, oculos, animum ab auro gazaque regia, Cic.; iras, Verg.; spes, Tac.

cŏhŏnesto -are, *to do honour to*: exsequias, Cic.; statuas, Cic.; Liv., Tac.

cŏhorresco -horrescĕre -horrŭi, *to shudder* or *shiver*: quo (sudore) cum cohorruisset, Cic.; quem ubi agnovi, equidem cohorrui, Cic.

cŏhors (chors) -tis, f. (connected with χορτός and hortus).

Lit., *an enclosure, yard,* esp. for cattle, poultry, etc.: Ov., Mart.

Transf., *a troop, company, throng*: fratrum stipata, Verg.; gigantum, Hor.; of things: febrium, Hor. Esp. (1) as milit. t. t., *a cohort, a division of the Roman army, being the tenth part of a legion*: Caes.; often, as opposed to legiones, *the auxiliary forces of the allies*: Sall., Tac. (2) praetoria cohors, *the retinue of the governor of a province,* Cic.

cŏhortātĭo -ōnis, f. (cohortor), *an exhortation, encouragement*: cohortatio quaedam iudicum ad honeste iudicandum, Cic.; Caes., Tac.

cŏhortĭcŭla -ae, f. (dim. of cohors), *a little cohort*: ap. Cic. L.

cŏhortor -ari, dep. *to encourage, incite, exhort*; esp. of the general's speech to his soldiers before a battle, but also in gen.: Caes., Cic., Tac. Followed (1) by ad: aliquem ad virtutem, Cic.; exercitum more militari ad pugnam, Caes. (2) by ut or ne with the subj.: Caes., Tac. (3) by ad and the gerund: aliquem ad honorandum Serv. Sulpicium, Cic.

cŏinquĭno -are, *to pollute, defile*: Col.

cŏĭtĭo -ōnis, f. (coeo). (1) *a coming together, meeting*: Ter. (2) *a faction, party, coalition, conspiracy*: suspicio coitionis, Cic.; coitiones tribunorum adversus nobilium iuventutem ortae, Liv.

cŏĭtus -ūs, *see* coetus.

cōlăphus -i, m. (κόλαφος), *a cuff, blow, box on the ear*: colapho icere, Pl.; colaphos infringere, Ter.; incutere, Juv.

Colchis -ĭdis, f. (Κολχίς), *Colchis, a country on the eastern shore of the Black Sea*: ¶ Hence adj. **Colchĭcus** -a -um, *of Colchis*: Hor.; f. adj. **Colchis** -ĭdis, *Colchian*; used as subst., esp. of *Medea*: Hor.; adj. and subst. **Colchus** -a -um, *of Colchis, a Colchian*: Hor., Ov.

cōleus -i, *see* culleus.

cōlĭphĭa (cōlȳphĭa) -ōrum, n. *a kind of nourishing food used by athletes*: Pl., Juv.

cōlis=caulis; q.v.

collāre -is, n. (collum), *a chain for the neck*: Pl.

Collātĭa -ae, f. *a town in Latium.* ¶ Hence **Collātīnus** -a -um, *belonging to Collatia*; esp. as *surname of L. Tarquinius, the husband of Lucretia, native of Collatia.*

collīnus -a -um (collis), *hilly, relating to a hill, situated on a hill.* Esp. *of* or *on the Quirinal*

Hill: tribus, Cic.; esp.: porta Collina, *a gate
of Rome near the Quirinal Hill*, Liv.; herbae,
growing near the Porta Collina, Prop.
collis -is, m. *a hill, high ground*: Cic., Caes.,
Verg., Liv.
collum -i, n. (**collus** -i, m.), *the neck*. LIT., of
men and animals: in collum invasit, *fell on
his neck*, Cic.; collum torquere, *to arrest,
take prisoner*, Liv.; posuit collum in pulvere,
Hor. TRANSF., *the neck* of a bottle: Phaedr.;
of a poppy: Verg.
collȳbus -i, m. (κόλλυβος), *exchange* of money:
Cic. L.; *the rate of exchange*: Cic.
collȳra -ae, f. (κολλύρα), *a kind of pastry broken
into broth, vermicelli*: Pl.
collȳricus -a -um: ius, *vermicelli broth*, Pl.
collȳrium -i, n. (κολλύριον), *eye-salve*: Hor.
cŏlo cŏlĕre cŏlui cultum, *to cultivate, till, tend*.
LIT., (1) of agriculture: agrum, Cic.;
praedia studiose, Cic.; vitem, Cic.; Hor.,
Verg. (2) *to dwell in* a place, *inhabit*: hanc
domum, Pl.; nemora, Lucr.; urbem, Cic.;
insulas, Liv.; absol.: circa utramque ripam
Rhodani, Liv.; Tac.
TRANSF., in gen., *to take care of, attend to*.
(1) of physical objects: formam augere
colendo, Ov. (2) of a quality, study, or way
of life, *to foster, cultivate, practise, study*:
studium philosophiae a prima adulescentia,
Cic.; fidem virtutem, sapientiam, Cic.;
amorem, Verg.; vitam, Pl., Cic. L. (3) *to pay
respect to, honour, worship*; of deities: deos,
Cic.; of religious objects: Musarum delubra,
Cic.; templum miro honore, Verg.; of men,
to honour, reverence, court: aliquem summa
observantia, Cic.; donis, Liv.
¶ Hence partic. (with compar. and
superl.) **cultus** -a -um, *cultivated, tilled,
planted*. LIT., loci culti, Cic.; ager cultissi-
mus, Cic. N. pl. as subst. **culta** -orum,
cultivated land: an culta ex silvestribus facere
potui? Liv.; Lucr., Verg.
TRANSF., (1) physically; *tidy, well-dressed,
smart*: femina cultissima, Ov.; sonum
linguae et corporum habitum et nitorem
cultiora quam pastoralia esse, Liv. (2)
mentally; *refined*: Cic., Ov.
¶ Adv. (with compar.) **cultē**, *elegantly*:
Ov., Quint., Tac.
cŏlŏcāsia -orum, n. pl. (κολοκάσιον), *the
Egyptian bean*: Verg., Mart.
cŏlōna -ae, f. (colonus), *a country-woman*: Ov.
Cŏlōnae -ārum, f. (Κολωναί), *a town in Troas*.
Cŏlōnēus -a -um (Κολώνειος), *belonging to the
Attic deme Colonus*: Oedipus Coloneus, *a
tragedy of Sophocles*.
cŏlōnia -ae, f. (colonus). (1) *a farm, estate,
dwelling*: Pl., Col. (2) *a colony*. LIT., constituere coloniam, Cic.; colonos deducere in
colonias, Cic., Liv. Often as part of a proper
name; e.g. Colonia Agrippina *or* Agrippinensis, now *Cologne*: Tac. TRANSF., *the
colonists*: deducere, Cic.; mittere in locum,
Cic., Caes., Liv.
cŏlōnicus -a -um (colonus). (1) *relating to
agriculture*: leges, Varr. (2) *relating to a
colony, colonial*: cohortes, *levied in Roman
colonies*, Caes., Suet.
cŏlōnus -i, m. (colo). (1) *a farmer*: Cic., Verg.,
Hor.; sometimes *a tenant farmer*: Caes., Cic.
(2) *a colonist, inhabitant of a colony*: Caes.,
Cic.; poet. gen.=*inhabitant*: Verg.

Cŏlŏphōn -ōnis, f. (Κολοφών), *one of the twelve
Ionian towns on or near the coast of Lydia,
famed for its cavalry*. Adj. **Cŏlŏphōniăcus**
-a -um, **Cŏlŏphōnĭus** -a -um, *Colophonian*.
cŏlor (old form **colos**) -ōris, m. *colour, tint, hue*.
LIT., in gen.: Pl., Cic.; colorem ducere, of
the grape, *to become coloured*, Verg. Esp. (1)
complexion: verus, *real*, Ter.; fucatus,
artificial, Hor.; mutare, *to change colour*,
Hor., Ov. (2) *beautiful complexion, beauty*:
nimium ne crede colori, Verg.
TRANSF., like English 'colour'. (1) *outward
show, external appearance*: colorem et
speciem pristinam civitatis, Cic. (2) esp. of
style in speech or writing, *cast, character,
tone*: color urbanitatis, Cic.; tragicus, Hor.
(3) *an artful excuse* or *colouring of a questionable action*: Juv., Quint.
cŏlōro -are (color), *to colour*. LIT., corpora,
Cic.; cum in sole ambulem natura fit ut
colorer, *get tanned*, Cic. TRANSF., *to give
tone* or *colour to*: urbanitate quadam quasi
colorata oratio, Cic.
¶ Hence partic. **cŏlōrātus** -a -um,
coloured: arcus, Cic.; esp. of complexion,
tanned, dark: Verg., Tac., Quint.
cŏlosserōs -ōtis, m. (Κολοσσός/Ἔρως), *appellation of a large handsome man*: Suet.
cŏlossēus -a -um (κολοσσιαῖος), *colossal,
gigantic*: Plin., Suet.
cŏlossĭcus -a -um (κολοσσικός), *colossal,
gigantic*: Plin.
cŏlossus -i, m. (κολοσσός), *a colossus, a statue
larger than life*; esp. applied to the gigantic
statue of Apollo at the entrance of the harbour
of Rhodes: Plin.
cŏlostra -ae, f. (**cŏlostrum** -i, n.), *the first
milk after calving, beestings*: Mart., Plin.;
used as a term of endearment: Pl.
cŏlŭber -bri, m. *a serpent, snake*: Verg., Ov.
cŏlŭbra -ae, f. *a female serpent, a snake*: Hor.,
Ov.
cŏlŭbrĭfer -fĕra -fĕrum (coluber/fero), *snakebearing, snaky-haired*, epithet of Medusa: Ov.
cŏlŭbrīnus -a -um (coluber), *snake-like*.
TRANSF., *cunning, wily*: Pl.
cŏlum -i, n. *a colander, sieve, strainer*: Verg.
cŏlumba -ae, f. (columbus), *a pigeon, dove*: Pl.,
Cic.; Cythereiades (as sacred to Venus), Ov.;
as a term of endearment: Pl.
cŏlumbar -āris, n. (columba), *a kind of collar
for slaves like a pigeon-hole*: Pl.
cŏlumbārium -i, n. (columba). (1) *a dove-
cot*: Plin. (2) *a tomb with niches to carry urns
of ashes*: Inscr.
cŏlumbīnus -a -um (columba), *relating or
belonging to a pigeon*: pulli, Cic. L., Hor.;
also as subst., *a little dove*: Mart.
cŏlumbŭlus -i, m. (dim. of columbus), *a little
pigeon*: Plin. L.
cŏlumbus -i, m. *a male dove* or *pigeon*: Pl., Hor.
¹**cŏlŭmella** -ae, f. (dim. of columna), *a little
column*: Caes., Cic.
²**Cŏlŭmella** -ae, m. *a Roman cognomen*, esp. of
L. Iunius Moderatus, *a Roman writer upon
agriculture, native of Cadiz, contemporary of
Seneca and Celsus*.
cŏlŭmen -ĭnis, n. (*cello), *that which is raised on
high, a height, summit, ridge*.
LIT., sub altis Phrygiae columinibus,
mountains, Cat.; of buildings, *roof, gable*:
Cato, Sen.

TRANSF., (**1**) *chief, summit, crown*: audaciae, Pl.; columen amicorum Antonii Cotyla
Varius, Cic. (**2**) *support*: familiae, Ter.;
reipublicae, Cic.; rerum, Hor.
cŏlumna -ae, f. (connected with columen),
a pillar, column.
  LIT., marmorea, Cic.; prov.: incurrere
amentem in columnas, *to run one's head
against a stone wall*, Cic. Esp. of particular
columns. (**1**) columna rostrata, *a column
adorned with beaks of ships, erected in honour
of the victory of Duilius over the Carthaginians*,
Quint. (**2**) columna Maeniana, *a pillar in
the Roman Forum to which thieves and slaves
were tied to receive punishment*, Cic.; hence:
adhaerescere ad columnam, Cic.; ad columnam pervenire, Cic. (**3**) columnae, *pillars as
signs of booksellers' shops in Rome*, Hor.
(**4**) columnae Protei, *the boundaries of Egypt*
(columns being used to mark boundaries),
Verg. (**5**) columnae Herculis, *the pillars of
Hercules*, i.e. *Calpe and Abyla at the Straits of
Gibraltar*, Tac., Plin.
  TRANSF., (**1**) *a support, pillar of the state*:
iniurioso ne pede promas stantem columnam,
Hor. (**2**) *a water-spout*: Lucr.
cŏlumnārĭus -a -um (columna), *belonging to
a pillar*; used only as subst. (**1**) **cŏlumnārĭus**
-i, m. *one punished at the* columna Maeniana
(*see* columna), *a rascal, thief*: ap. Cic. L.
(**2**) **cŏlumnārĭum** -i, n. *a tax on pillars*:
Cic. L., Caes.
cŏlumnātus -a -um (columna), *supported on
columns*: Varr.; os, *resting on the hand*, Pl.
cŏlurnus -a -um (for corulnus, from corulus),
made of hazel-wood: hastilia, Verg.
cŏlus -i and -ūs, f. (m.: Cat., Prop., Ov.),
a distaff: Verg., Stat.
cŏlūtea -orum, n. pl. (κολουτέα), *a pod-like kind
of fruit*: Pl.
cŏma -ae, f. (κόμη), *the hair of the head.*
  LIT., of men: Cic., Verg., Hor.; often in
plur.; also of animals: aureā comā, of the
golden fleece, ap. Cic.
  TRANSF., (**1**) *the leaves of trees*: Hor.,
Verg. (**2**) of *rays* of light: Cat.
cŏmans -antis (coma), *hairy*: colla equorum,
Verg.; galea, *crested*, Verg. TRANSF., stella,
a comet, Ov.; narcissus sera comans, *putting
out late leaves*, Verg.
cŏmarchus -i, m. (κώμαρχος), *the mayor* or
chief officer of a village: Pl.
cŏmātus -a -um (coma), *hairy*. LIT., tempora,
Mart.; hence Gallia Comata, as a name for
Transalpine Gaul: Cic., Plin. TRANSF., silva,
in full leaf, Cat.
¹**combĭbo** -bibĕre -bĭbi. (**1**) *to drink with
another*: Sen. (**2**) *to drink in, suck up, imbibe*:
venenum corpore, Hor.; fig.: quas (artes) si
dum est tener combiberit, Cic.
²**combĭbo** -ōnis, m. (from ¹combibo), *a boon
companion, comrade in drinking*: Cic. L.
combūro -ūrĕre -ussi -ustum, *to burn up,
consume entirely.*
  LIT., libros, Caes.; aliquem vivum, Cic.;
of the burning of the dead: aliquem in foro,
Cic.
  TRANSF., aliquem iudicio, *to ruin*, Cic.;
diem, *to consume*, Pl.; combustus, *consumed
by passion*, Prop.
  ¶ Hence, from past partic. pass. **combu-
stum** -i, n. *a burn* or *scald*: Plin.

Cōmē -ēs, f. (κόμη, *village*). (**1**) Hiera Come,
a place in Caria. (**2**) Xylina Come, *a place in
Pisidia*. (**3**) Acoridos Come, *a place in
Phrygia.*
cŏmĕdo -esse -ēdi -ēsum or -estum, *to eat up,
consume.*
  LIT., ex se natos (of Saturn), Cic.; Pl.,
Ter., Hor.
  TRANSF., (**1**) gen., *to consume*: aliquem
oculis, *to devour with one's eyes*, Mart.; se,
to consume oneself in grief, Cic. (**2**) of property,
to waste, squander: patrimonium, Cic., Hor.;
so, comically, of the owner, *to eat him out of
house and home*: Pl., Ter.
cŏmes -itis, c. (cum/eo), *a fellow-traveller,
companion on a journey.*
  ¶ Hence (**1**) *a companion, comrade,
associate*; mainly used of persons, often with
genit. of the enterprise shared: fugae, Cic.;
victoriae, Caes.; seditionum, Tac.; aliquem
comitem habere, Cic.; non praebere se
comitem illius furoris sed ducem, Cic. Fig.
of things and abstractions: mortis comes
gloria, Cic.
  (**2**) *one who attends for a particular purpose,
an attendant*, esp.: **a**, *the tutor of a boy*: Verg.,
Suet.: **b**, usually in plur., comites, *the retinue
which accompanied a Roman magistrate*:
comites omnes magistratuum, Cic.: **c**, usually
in plur., in later times, *courtiers, the imperial
court*: Suet.
cŏmētēs -ae, m. (κομήτης), *a comet*: Cic., Verg.;
in apposition to sidus: Tac.
cŏmĭcus -a -um (κωμικός), *relating to comedy,
comic*: poeta, Cic.; res, Hor.; esp. *represented
in comedy*: adulescens, Cic. M. as subst.
cŏmĭcus -i, m. (**1**) *an actor in comedy*: Pl.
(**2**) *a writer of comedy*: Cic.
  Adv. **cŏmĭcē**, *in the manner of comedy*:
comice res tragicas tractare, Cic.
cominus=comminus; q.v.
cŏmis -e, *courteous, kind, friendly, obliging,
amiable*; of persons: dominus, Cic.; in
amicis tuendis, Cic.; erga aliquem, Cic.; in
uxorem, Hor.; of things: comi hospitio
accipi, Liv.; sermo, Tac.
  Adv. **cŏmĭter**, *courteously, kindly*: Pl.,
Cic., Ov.
cŏmissābundus -a -um (comissor), *revelling,
rioting*: temulento agmine per Indiam
comissabundus incessit, Liv.
cŏmissātĭo -ōnis, f. (comissor), *a revel,
riotous procession*: Cic., Liv.
cŏmissātor -ōris, m. (comissor), *a reveller*:
Cic., Liv. TRANSF., comissatores coniurationis, of those involved in Catiline's
conspiracy, Cic. L.
cŏmissor (κωμάζω) -ari, dep. *to make a joyful
procession, to revel*: comissatum ire, Pl.,
Liv.; comissari in domum Pauli, Hor.
cŏmĭtās -ātis, f. (comis), *courtesy, friendliness,
obligingness, civility*: comitas adfabilitasque
sermonis, Cic.; Pl., Tac.
cŏmĭtātus -ūs, m. (comitor), *a train, retinue,
following*: optimorum et clarissimorum
civium, Cic.; praedonis societas atque
comitatus, Cic.; Caes., Verg.; esp. (**1**) in
imperial times, *the court, imperial suite*: Tac.
(**2**) *a caravan, convoy*: Caes., Cic., Liv.
TRANSF., tanto virtutum comitatu (opus est),
Cic.
cŏmĭtĕr, adv. from comis; q.v.

cŏmĭtĭa, *see* comitium.

cŏmĭtĭālis -e (comitia), *relating to the comitia* : dies, mensis, *when the comitia were held*, Cic.; homines, *men constantly in attendance on the comitia, and ready to sell their votes*, Pl.; morbus, *epilepsy, so called because its occurrence put a stop to the comitia*, Sen., Cels.

¶ Hence subst. **cŏmĭtĭālis** -is, m. *one afflicted with epilepsy* : Plin.

cŏmĭtĭātus -ūs, m. (comitia), *the assembly of the people in the comitia* : Cic.

cŏmĭtĭum -i, n. (cum/eo).

(1) sing. *a place of assembly, esp. one at Rome, at the end of the* forum.

(2) plur. **cŏmĭtĭa** -ōrum, n. *the assembly of the Roman people for the election of magistrates*, etc.; hence *the elections*. There were three official forms of comitia : centuriata, *an assembly according to the centuriae instituted by Servius Tullius*; curiata, *an assembly of the curiae, in later times rarely held except formally*; tributa, *the assembly of the people in their tribes*; of these the centuriata is the form usually referred to. Comitia habere, *to hold an assembly of the people*, Cic., Liv.; consulum *or* consularia, *assembly for the purpose of electing a consul*, Liv.; tribunicia, quaestoria, Cic.; comitia conficere, dimittere, Cic. L.; differre, Liv. Sometimes used of elections outside Rome : Cic., Liv. Fig. : de capite meo sunt comitia, Pl.

cŏmĭto -are (comes) *to accompany* : Prop., Ov. Esp. as partic. **cŏmĭtātus** -a -um, *accompanied* : alienis viris, Cic.; dolore, Ov.; with adverbs : bene, parum, Cic.

cŏmĭtor -ari, dep. (comes), *to attend, to accompany, to follow*; absol. : magnā comitante catervā, Verg.; with acc. : matrem, Lucr.; eos, Caes.; nautas fuga, Verg.; esp. *to follow to the grave* : Verg.; with dat., esp. fig. : tardis mentibus virtus non facile comitatur, Cic.

commăcŭlo -are, *to spot all over, pollute* : manus sanguine, Verg.; Tac. TRANSF., se isto infinito ambitu, Cic.; Tac.

Commāgēnē -ēs, f. (Κομμαγηνή), *a province in the north of Syria* (capital Samosata). Adj. and subst. **Commāgēnus** -a -um, *of Commagene, an inhabitant of Commagene*.

commănĭpŭlāris -is, m. *a soldier belonging to the same maniple or company, a comrade* : Tac.

commārītus -i, m. *a fellow-husband* : Pl.

comměātus -ūs, m. (commeo), *free passage, going and coming*. (1) *a thoroughfare, communication* : Pl. (2) milit. t. t., *leave of absence, furlough* : sumere, dare, Liv.; in commeatu esse, *to be on furlough*, Liv.; commeatu abesse, Suet. (3) *a transporting, passage, trip* : duobus commeatibus exercitum reportare, Caes. (4) milit. t. t., *supply of provisions, food, forage* : parare, Liv., Sall.; accipere, arcessere, convehere, advehere, portare, Liv.; petere, Caes.; aliquem commeatu prohibere, Caes.; aliquem commeatu et reliquis copiis intercludere, Cic.

commĕdĭtor -ari, dep. *to practise, represent, imitate* : Lucr.

comměmĭni -isse, *to remember fully*; absol. : Pl.; with genit. : Pl.; with infin. : dicere, Pl.; with acc. : hoc, Pl.; hominem, Cic.

comměmŏrābĭlis -e (commemoro), *worthy of mention, memorable* : Pl.; pietas, Cic.

comměmŏrātio -ōnis, f. (commemoro), *reminding, mention* : officiorum, Cic.; Quint., Tac.; posteritatis, *by posterity*, Cic.

comměmŏro -are. (1) *to call to mind, recollect* : quid quoque die dixerim, audierim, egerim, commemoro vesperi, Cic.

(2) *to remind another person of something, so to mention, relate, recount* : gratiam amicitiam cognationemque, Cic.; humanam societatem, Cic.; Critolaus iste, quem cum Diogene venisse commemoras, Cic.; de alicuius virtute, Cic.

commendābĭlis -e (commendo), *commendable, praiseworthy* : nec ullo commendabilis merito, Liv.

commendātīcĭus -a -um (commendatus), *giving recommendation* : litterae, *a letter of introduction*, Cic.

commendātio -ōnis, f. (commendo). (1) *recommendation, commendation* : commendatio nostra ceterorumque amicorum, Cic.; Sall.; fig. : oculorum, *by the eyes*, Cic. (2) *that which recommends, excellence* : ingenii, liberalitatis, Cic., Quint.

commendātor -ōris, m. (commendo), *one that commends* : Plin. L.

commendātrix -īcis, f. (commendo), *one that commends* : legem commendatricem virtutum, Cic.

commendo -are (cum/mando), *to commit to the care, keeping, or protection of anyone*.

LIT., ego me tuae fidei, Ter.; totum me tuo amori, Cic. L.; tibi eius omnia negotia, Cic. L.

TRANSF., (1) *to commit, in gen.* : nomen suum immortalitati, Cic.; aliquid litteris, *to commit to writing*, ap. Cic. L. (2) *to recommend*; hence *to set off, render agreeable* : nulla re una magis oratorem commendari quam verborum splendore et copiā, Cic.; Hor.

¶ Hence partic. **commendātus** -a -um, *recommended, commended* : quae (res) commendatior erit memoriae hominum? Cic.; hence *esteemed, prized, valued* : Plin.

commensus, partic. of commetior; q.v.

commentārĭŏlum -i, n. (dim. of commentarius), *a short treatise* : Cic., Quint.

commentārĭus -i, m. and **commentārĭum** -i, n. (commentus, from comminiscor). (1) *a note, memorandum, or note-book, a diary* : in commentarium referre, Cic. as title of a book, *notes written up, a memoir*, usually plur.; so of Caesar's works on the Civil War and Gallic War : Cic. (3) legal t. t., *a brief* : Cic.

commentātio -ōnis, f. (commentor). (1) *reflection, careful consideration, meditation*; hence *practice* : philosophorum vita commentatio mortis est, Cic.; so of an orator's practising : commentationes cotidianae, Cic. (2) *a dissertation* : Plin.

commentīcĭus -a -um (commentus, from comminiscor), *invented, fictitious* : nominibus novis et commenticiis appellata, Cic.; civitas Platonis, *ideal*, Cic.; crimen, *false*, Cic.

¹**commentor** -ari, dep. (freq. of comminiscor).

(1) *to consider thoroughly, reflect upon deeply* : futuras secum miserias, Cic.; de populi Romani libertate, Cic.; ut ante commentemur inter nos qua ratione nobis traducendum sit hoc tempus, Cic.

(2) *to practise, prepare*: commentabar declamitans saepe cum M. Pisone et cum Q. Pompeio cotidie, Cic.; with acc.: commentari orationem in reum, Cic.; partic. perf. pass.: commentata oratio, Cic.
(3) *to produce as the result of thought and study, to invent*: Pl.; esp. of written works, *to compose, write*: mimos, Cic.

'commentor -ōris, m. (comminiscor), *a discoverer, inventor*: uvae, Bacchus, Ov.

commĕo -are, *to go up and down, come and go, visit frequently*: vulgatum erat inter Veios Romamque nuncios commeare, Liv.; ut tuto ab repentino hostium incursu etiam singuli commeare possent, Caes.; Delos quo omnes undique cum mercibus atque oneribus commeabant, Cic.
So of ships: navis, quae ad ea furta, quae reliquisses, commearet, Cic.; of the heavenly bodies: sursum deorsum, ultro citro, Cic.; of letters: crebro enim illius litterae ab aliis ad nos commeant, *find their way to us*, Cic.

commercĭum -i, n. (commercor).
(1) *trade, commerce*: commercio prohibere aliquem, Sall., Tac., Liv., Plin. Hence, meton.: **a**, *the right to trade*: commercium in eo agro nemini est, Cic.; salis commercium dedit, Liv.: **b**, *an article of traffic, merchandise*: Plin.: **c**, *a place of trade, depot*: Plin.
(2) in gen., *intercourse, communication, correspondence*: commercium habere cum Musis, Cic.; commercium sermonum facere, Liv.; commercium belli, *negotiations as to ransom of prisoners*, etc., Verg., Tac.; plebis, *with the people*, Liv.

commercor -ari, dep. (merx), *to buy together, buy up*: captivos, Pl.; arma, tela alia, Sall.

commĕrĕo -ēre (also **commĕrĕor**, dep.: Pl., Ter.). (1) *to deserve fully*: aestimationem, Cic.; poenam, Ov. (2) *to commit a fault*: noxiam, Pl., Ter., Ov.

commētor -mētiri -mensus, dep. (1) *to measure*: siderum ambitus, Cic. (2) *to measure against something, compare*: negotium cum tempore, Cic.

commĕto -are (freq. of commeo), *to go frequently*: Pl., Ter.

commigro -are, *to remove in a body, to migrate*: huc viciniae, Ter.; Pl., Cic. L.

commilĭtĭum -i, n. (cum/miles), *companionship in war* or *military service*: Tac. Hence, in gen., *companionship, fellowship*: Ov.

commilĭto -ōnis, m. (cum/miles), *a fellow-soldier*: Cic., Suet.

commĭnātĭo -ōnis, f. (comminor), *a threatening, threat*: Cic., Liv.

commingo -mingĕre -minxi -mictum, *to make water on*: Hor. TRANSF., *to defile*: Cat.

commĭniscor -minisci -mentus, dep. (connected with memini and mens), *to think out, contrive, invent*; in gen., of expedients, lies, etc.: mendacium, Pl.; also of philosophical speculation: monogrammos deos, Cic.; of practical devices: litteras, balinearum usum, Suet.; perf. partic. in passive sense, **commentus** -a -um, *feigned, invented*: funera, Ov.; crimen, Liv. N. as subst. **commentum** -i, *a fiction, an invention*: opinionum commenta, *fancies*, Cic.; millia rumorum commenta, Ov.; also *a contrivance, device*: Liv., Suet.

commĭnor -ari, dep. *to threaten*: comminati inter se, Liv.; with acc.: pugnam, obsidionem, oppugnationem, Liv.; necem alicui, Suet.

commĭnŭo -ŭĕre -ŭi -ūtum, *to make small, lessen, break into small pieces, crush to pieces*: Pl.; statuam, anulum, Cic. TRANSF., *to lessen, diminish, to weaken, deprive of strength*: opes civitatis, Cic.; vires ingenii, Ov.; comminuti sumus, Cic. L.

commĭnus, adv. (manus). (1) *hand to hand* (opp. eminus), esp. as milit. t. t., *in close combat*: nec eminus hastis aut comminus gladiis uteretur, Cic.; comminus acriter instare, Sall.; manum comminus conserere, Liv.; of hunting: comminus ire in apros, Ov.; fig.: comminus agamus, Cic. (2) *without the notion of contest, close up, close at hand*: comminus aspicere, Ov.; videre, Tac.

commiscĕo -miscēre -miscŭi -mixtum, *to mix together, to mix up*. LIT., ignem Vestae cum communi urbis incendio, Cic.; commixta frusta mero cruento, Verg.; fumus in auras commixtus, Verg. TRANSF., temeritatem cum sapientia, Cic.; Verg.

commĭsĕrātĭo -ōnis, f. (commiseror), *pity, a pitying*; in rhetoric, *part of an oration intended to excite pity*: Cic.

commĭsĕresco -ĕre, *to pity*: Enn. Impersonal: Ter.

commĭsĕror -ari, dep. *to pity, commiserate, bewail*: fortunam, Nep.; of a speaker, *to excite pity*: cum commiserari, conqueri coeperit, Cic.

commissĭo -ōnis, f. (committo), *a setting together*; hence *the start of games, contests*, etc.: ab ipsa commissione, Cic. L.; ludorum, Suet. TRANSF., *a prize declamation*: Suet.

commissūra -ae, f. (committo), *a joining together, connexion, joint, knot*: molles digitorum, Cic.; navium, Plin. TRANSF., verborum, Quint.

commītĭgo -are, *to make soft*: Ter.

committo -mittĕre -mīsi -missum.
(1) *to unite, connect, combine*. LIT., duas noctes, Ov.; opera, Liv.; nondum commissa inter se munimenta, Liv.; esp. *to bring together in a contest, to match*: pugiles Latinos cum Graecis, Suet.; hence *to compare*: Juv., Prop. TRANSF., *to begin, set on foot, initiate*: **a**, of contests: pugnam cum aliquo, Cic.; proelium, Caes.; bellum, Liv.; ludos, Cic.: **b**, in gen.: iudicium, Cic.; so with ut and the subj., *to bring it about that*: non committam posthac ut me accusare de epistularum negligentia possis, Cic. L.; with cur, Liv.; quare, Caes.; infin.: Ov.: **c**, esp. of crimes, etc., *to commit, perpetrate*: tantum facinus, Cic.; multa et in deos et in homines impie, Cic.; fraudem, Hor.; absol., *to commit a crime, to sin*: nemo enim committeret, Cic.; contra legem, Cic.: **d**, hence of penalties, *to incur*: poenam, Cic.; perf. partic., *forfeited*: hereditas Veneri Erycinae commissa, Cic.
(2) *to entrust, commit*, esp. with reflex. pronoun: se in senatum, Cic.; se urbi, Cic.; aliquem fidei potestatique eius, Cic.; collum tonsori, Cic.; alicui rempublicam, Liv.; committere alicui, ut videat ne quid res publica detrimenti capiat, Cic.

¶ N. of partic. as subst. **commissum** -i.
(1) *something undertaken, an undertaking*: supererat nihil aliud in temere commisso

quam, Liv. Esp. *a crime, fault, transgression*:
factum aut commissum audacius, Cic.; Pl.,
Verg. (2) *something entrusted, a trust, a
secret*: commissa enuntiare, Cic.

commŏdē, adv. from commodus; q.v.

commŏdĭtās -ātis, f. (commodus). (1) *proportion, symmetry*: membrorum, Suet. (2)
fitness, esp. of style: Cic. (3) *a fit occasion*:
commoditas ad faciendum idonea, Cic.
(4) *convenience, advantage*: qui ex bestiis
fructus, quae commoditas percipi potest,
Cic.; ob commoditatem itineris, Liv. (5) of
persons, *kindness*: Ov.; as term of endearment: Pl.

commŏdo -are (commodus). (1) *to make fit,
adapt, accommodate*: Plin. (2) *to adapt oneself to suit another person, to please, oblige,
serve*: ut eo libentius iis commodes, Cic. L.;
tantum ei in hac re, Cic. L.; hence, with acc.,
to furnish, lend, give: nomen suum alicui,
Cic.; aurum, Cic.; reipublicae tempus, Liv.;
alicui aurem, Ov.

commŏdŭlē and **commŏdŭlum,** adv. (from
dim. of ¹commodus), *quite conveniently*: Pl.

¹**commŏdus** -a -um (modus), adj. (with
compar. and superl.).

(1) *to measure, in full, complete*: talentum,
statura, Pl.; cyathis, Hor.

(2) *proper, fit, appropriate, convenient,
satisfactory*: **a,** absol.: valetudine minus
commoda uti, Caes.; litterae satis commodae
de Britannicis rebus, Cic.: **b,** *fit for a
particular purpose*; with dat.: nulla lex satis
commoda omnibus est, Cic.; Verg., Liv.;
with ad: Ov.: **c,** of persons, character, etc.,
friendly, obliging, pleasant: mores commodi,
Cic.

N. as subst. **commŏdum** -i. (1) *a suitable
time, opportunity*; esp. with reference to a
person, *his leisure, convenience*: nostro
commodo, *at our convenience,* Cic.; commodo
tuo, Cic. L.; per commodum, Liv.; quod
commodo valetudinis tuae fiat, Cic. L.;
commodum alicuius exspectare, Cic. (2) *use,
advantage, interest*: pacis, Cic.; reipublicae,
Cic., Liv.; servire, *or* consulere, alicuius
commodis, Cic. (3) *remuneration* for services:
tribunatus (militum) commoda, Cic. L.; Ov.
(4) *a loan*: qui forum et basilicas commodis
hospitum, non furtis nocentium ornarent, Cic.

Accus. of above as adv. **commŏdum.**
(1) *at the right time, opportunely*: Pl.;
commodum enim egeram diligentissime,
Cic. L. (2) *just then,* esp. with temporal
clause: commodum discesseras heri, cum
Trebatius venit, Cic. L.; Ter.

Adv. (with compar. and superl.) **commŏdē.** (1) *rightly, properly, fitly, appropriately*: dicere, Cic., Pl., Ter. (2) *pleasantly,
comfortably*: navigare, Cic. L.; commodius
quam tu vivo, Hor. (3) *kindly*: feceris igitur
commode mihique gratum si, Cic.

²**Commŏdus** -i, m. *Roman emperor from*
A.D. 180 *to* A.D. 192.

commŏlĭor -iri, dep. *to set in motion*: fulmina,
Lucr.

commŏnĕfăcĭo -facĕre -fēci -factum (com-
moneo/facio). (1) *to remind, warn*: aliquem
etiam atque etiam, Cic.; aliquem beneficii
sui, Sall. (2) with acc. of thing, *to call to
mind*: istius turpem calamitosamque praeturam, Cic.; Caes.

commŏnĕo -ēre. (1) *to remind, warn*: quod
vos lex commonuit, Cic.; quin is unoquoque
gradu de avaritia tua commoneretur, Cic.;
non exprobrandi causa, sed commonendi
gratia, Cic.; animos de periculo, Cic.; quin
quidam ex illis amicis commonerent oportere
decerni, Cic. (2) *to call to mind*: amice
aliquid, Quint.

commonstro -are, *to show fully and distinctly*: hominem, Pl., Ter.; aurum alicui,
Cic.

commŏrātĭo -ōnis, f. (commoror), *a delaying,
loitering, lingering*: tabellariorum, Cic. L.;
rhet. t. t., *the dwelling for some time on one
point*: Cic., Quint.

commŏrĭor -mŏri -mortuus, dep. *to die
together with*; with dat.: tibi, Sen.

commŏror -ari, dep. (1) *to linger, make a
stay, remain*: Romae, Cic.; unam noctem ad
Helorum, Cic.; apud aliquem, Cic.; consilium tuum diutius in armis civilibus
commorandi, Cic.; rhet. t. t., *to dwell on*:
pluribus verbis in eo, Cic. (2) transit., *to
delay*: Pl., Sen.

commŏtĭo -ōnis, f. (commoveo), *a violent
movement*: animi, *excitement,* Cic.

commŏtĭuncŭla -ae, f. (dim. of commotio),
a slight indisposition: Cic. L.

commŏvĕo -mŏvēre -mōvi -mōtum (contracted perf. forms commosse, etc.: Cic.),
to move entirely or *violently, to shake, to move
away.*

LIT., of physical movement: magni
commorunt aequora venti, Lucr.; se ex eo
loco, Cic.; castra, Cic.; columnas, *to carry
off,* Cic.; cervum, *to chase,* Verg.; sacra, *to
carry about* (at festivals, etc.) *the sacred
utensils,* Verg.; nummum, *to employ in
commerce,* Cic.

TRANSF., (1) of the mind or the passions,
to move, influence, disturb: commorat omnes
nos, *had upset us,* Ter.; animus commotus
metu, spe, gaudio, Ter.; his omnes, in
quibus est virtutis indoles, commoventur,
Cic.; aut libidine aliqua aut metu commotum
esse, Cic.; nova atque inusitata specie
commotus, Caes.; eiusdem miseriis ac
periculis commovetur, Cic.; with ad, *or* ut,
to incite. (2) *to start up, produce, cause*: risum,
Cic.; magnum et acerbum dolorem, Cic.;
bellum aut tumultum, Cic.; iram, Ov.

¶ Hence partic. (with compar.) **commōtus**
-a -um. (1) *tottering, insecure, unsteady*: aes
alienum, Tac.; genus (dicendi) in agendo, Cic.
(2) *moved in mind, excited*: animus commotior,
Cic.

commūnĭcātĭo -ōnis, f. (communico), *a
communicating, imparting*: consilii, Cic.;
sermonis, Cic. L.; as rhet. t. t. = ἀνακοίνωσις,
*in which the orator pretends to consult the
audience*: Cic.

commūnĭco -are (communis), *to share, divide
out.* (1) in gen., *to share, give a share in*:
iudicia cum equestri ordine communicata
erant, Cic.; rem cum aliquo, Cic. (2) *to
communicate, impart, inform,* by speaking or
writing: consilia, Caes.; de societate multa
inter se, Cic.; so without object, *to take
counsel with, confer with*: cum aliquo de
maximis rebus, Cic. (3) *to join, unite*:
quantas pecunias ab uxoribus dotis nomine
acceperunt, tantas ex suis bonis cum

dotibus communicant, Caes. (4) *to take a share in, participate in*: mecum meam provinciam, Pl.; Cic.

¹**commūnĭo** -ire, *to fortify thoroughly on all sides*: castella, Caes. TRANSF., *to fortify, strengthen*: causam testimoniis, Cic.

²**commūnĭo** -ōnis, f. (communis), *sharing, mutual participation*: inter quos est communio legis, inter eos communio iuris est, Cic.; Tac.

commūnis -e (connected with moenia, munus), *shared, common, general, universal, public* (opp. proprius=*individual, private*).

  In gen.: communia esse amicorum inter se omnia, Ter.; vita, *the customs of society*, Cic.; sensus, *sense of propriety*, Hor.; loca, *public places*, Cic.; loci, *philosophical* or *rhetorical commonplaces*, Cic.; with genit.: communis hominum infirmitas, Cic.; with dat.: mors omni aetati est communis, Cic.; with cum and the abl.: quocum fuit et domus et militia communis, Cic.; with inter se: multa sunt civibus inter se communia, Cic.

  Esp. of persons, *approachable, not pretentious, affable*: Cyrum minorem communem erga Lysandrum atque humanum fuisse, Cic.

  N. as subst. **commūne** -is. (1) *common property*, esp. in plur.: Cic., Hor. (2) *state, commonwealth*: Siciliae, Cic.; hence, adverbial phrase **in commūne**, *for the public good, for common use*: in commune conferre, Cic.; also *in general*: Tac.

  Adv. **commūnĭter**, *in common with others, jointly, generally*: Cic., Hor.

commūnĭtās -ātis, f. (communis), *community, fellowship*: nulla cum deo homini communitas, Cic. TRANSF., (1) *sense of fellowship*: Cic. (2) *condescension, affability*: Nep.

commūnĭtĭo -ōnis, f. (communis), rhet. t. t., *an introduction*: Cic.

commurmŭro -are (Plin.) and **commurmŭror** -ari, dep. *to mutter, murmur*: ut scriba secum ipse commurmuratus sit, Cic.

commūtābĭlis -e (commuto), *changeable*: vitae ratio, Cic.; as rhet. t. t.: exordium, *such as could be easily adapted to a speech on the other side of the question*, Cic.

commūtātĭo -ōnis, f. (commuto), *a change, alteration*: temporum, Cic.; aestuum, Caes.

commūtātus -ūs, m. (commuto), *a change, alteration*: Lucr.

commūto -are. (1) *to change, alter entirely*: iter, consilium, Caes.; cursum, sententiam, Cic.; reipublicae statum, Cic.; tempora in horas commutantur, Cic.; nihil commutari animo, Cic.

  (2) *to exchange, change one thing for another*: gloriam constantiae cum caritate vitae, Cic.; fidem suam et religionem pecuniā, *to barter*, Cic.; captivos, *to interchange*, Cic.

cōmo cōmĕre compsi comptum (contr. from coemo), *to put together*. (1) in partic. comptus only, *formed, framed*: Lucr. (2) *to make tidy* or *beautiful, to arrange, adorn*: esp. of the hair, *to comb, braid, do* the hair: capillos, Cic.; longas compta puella comas, Ov.; praecincti recte pueri comptique, Hor.; of rhetorical ornament: Quint.

  Partic. **comptus** -a -um, also as adj., *adorned, neat*: oratio, Cic., Quint.; comparative: Tac.

cōmoedĭa -ae, f. (κωμῳδία), *a comedy*: Ter., Cic., Hor.

cōmoedĭcē, adv. *as in comedy*: Pl.

cōmoedus (κωμῳδός). (1) subst. -i, m. *a comic actor*: Cic., Quint., Juv. (2) as adj. -a -um, *comic*: natio, Juv.

cŏmōsus -a -um (coma), *hairy*: Phaedr.; of plants, *leafy*: Plin.

compactĭo -ōnis, f. (compingo), *a putting* or *joining together*: membrorum, Cic.

compactum or **compectum** -i, n. (cum/paciscor), *an agreement*: compacto, Cic.; de compecto, Pl.; ex compacto, Suet., *according to agreement*.

compactus -a -um, partic. from compingo; q.v., or=compectus; q.v.

compāges -is, f. (cum/pango). (1) *a joining together, connexion*: lapidum, Ov. (2) *something that joins, a joint, seam*; so of a ship: per se ipsa omnibus compagibus aquam acciperet, Liv.; Verg., Tac. (3) *something joined together, a structure*: inclusi compagibus corporis, Cic.; of the state: Tac.

compāgo -inis, f. (cum/pango), *a joining together* (cf. compages): Ov.

compar -păris, c. an equal; hence *a companion* or *a mate*: Pl., Hor., Ov. (2) as adj., *like, similar*; with dat.: milites militibus compares, Liv.

compărābilis -e (²comparo), *capable of comparison, comparable*: comparabile est, quod in rebus diversis similem aliquam rationem continet, Cic.; Liv.

¹**compărātĭo** -ōnis, f. (²comparo), *a preparing, a providing*: novi belli, Cic.; veneni, Liv.; criminis, *of evidence necessary for an accusation*, Cic.

²**compărātĭo** -ōnis, f. (²comparo), *a putting together*; hence *a comparing, comparison*: orationis suae cum scriptis alienis, Cic.; utilitatum, Cic. Esp. in rhetoric: comparatio criminis, *the weighing of a good motive against a crime*, Cic.

compărātīvus -a -um (²comparo), *relating to comparison, comparative*: iudicatio, Cic., Quint.

comparco (**comperco**) -parcĕre -parsi or -persi. (1) *to scrape together, to save up*: Ter. (2) *to refrain*: Pl.

compārĕo -pārēre -pāruī. (1) *to appear, be visible*: Pl., Lucr.; cum subito sole obscurato non comparuisset (Romulus), Cic. (2) *to be present, be in existence*: Pl.; signa et dona comparere omnia, Cic.; Liv.

¹**compăro** -are (cum/paro), *to prepare, get ready, provide, furnish*. LIT., convivium magnifice et ornate, Cic.; se, *to make oneself ready*, Cic.; insidias alicui, Cic.; classem, Cic.; exercitum, Cic.; rem frumentariam, Caes.; alicui a civitatibus laudationes per vim et metum, Cic.; bellum adversus aliquem, Caes.

  TRANSF., *to arrange, settle, dispose*; of character: sic fuimus semper comparati ut, etc., Cic.; of institutions: iura praeclara atque divinitus a nostris maioribus comparata, Cic.; esp. of the arrangements made by magistrates to share out their duties: inter se comparare provincias, Liv.; comparare ut, Liv.; uter, Liv.

²**compăro** -are (compar), *to couple together, form into pairs*.

compasco

LIT., labella labellis, Pl.; esp. *to bring
together for a contest, to match*: comparari
cum Aesernino Samnite, cum patrono
disertissimo, Cic.
TRANSF., *to liken, to compare*: homo
similitudines comparat, Cic.; Attico Lysiae
Catonem nostrum, Cic.; meum factum cum
tuo comparo, Cic.

compasco -pascere -pastum, *to feed* (cattle)
together: si compascuus ager est, ius est
compascere, Cic.

compascŭus -a -um, *relating to common
pasturage*: ager, *pasturage held in common*,
Cic.

compectus (or **compactus**) -a -um (cum/
paciscor), *in agreement*: Pl.

compĕdĭo -ire (compes), *to fetter*: Pl., Varr.

compellātĭo -ōnis, f. (¹compello), *an accosting,
rebuking, reprimanding*: crebrae vel potius
cotidianae compellationes, Cic. L.

¹compello -pellĕre -puli -pulsum.
(1) *to drive to one place, collect, bring
together*; of cattle: pecus totius provinciae,
Cic.; hence of other things, or of persons:
consules e foro in curiam, Liv.; naves in
portum, Caes.; Romanos in castra, Liv.;
fig.: omne Auruncum bellum Pometiam
compulsum est, *confined to*, Liv.
(2) *to force* or *impel a person to an action*
or *situation, to compel*: aliquem ad bellum,
Ov.; in eundem metum, Liv.; in hunc
sensum et allici beneficiis hominum et
compelli iniuriis, Cic.; with infin.: Ov.,
Tac.

²compello -are (connected with appello).
(1) in gen., *to address, accost, call by name*:
aliquem voce, Verg. (2) *to reproach, chide,
rebuke*: pro cunctatore segnem, pro cauto
timidum, Liv.; ne compellarer inultus, Hor.
(3) legal t. t., *to accuse before a court of justice*:
iudicem qui non adfuerit, Cic. L.; Liv.,
Tac.

compendĭārĭus -a -um (compendium), *short*:
via, Cic.; f. and n. as subst., *a quick method,
short cut*: Sen.

compendĭum -i, n. (cum/pendo), *a weighing
together*; hence (1) *saving*, and hence *gain,
profit, advantage* (opp. dispendium): privato
compendio servire, Caes.; in re uberrima
turpe compendium effugere, Cic. (2) *a
shortening, abbreviation*: fieri dictis compendium volo, Pl.; so: compendi facere, *to
make* or *keep short*, Pl. (3) plur. in concr.
sense, *short ways, short cuts*: per compendia
maris, Tac.; montis, Ov.

compensātĭo -ōnis, f. (compenso), *a balancing
of an account, compensation*: incommoda
commodorum compensatione leniant, Cic.

compenso -are, *to weight together, to reckon
one thing against another, to balance*: laetitiam
cum doloribus, Cic.; summi labores nostri
magnā compensati gloriā, Cic.; bona cum
vitiis, Hor.

comperco = comparco; q.v.

compĕrendĭnātĭo -ōnis, f. (comperendino),
a putting off a trial to the next day but one:
Tac.

compĕrendĭnātus -ūs, m. = comperendinatio;
q.v.: Cic.

compĕrendĭno -are (perendinus), *to remand
to the next day but one*: reum, Cic.; absol.: ut
ante primos ludos comperendinem, Cic.

complano

compĕrĭo -perire -pĕri -pertum (cum/pario),
*to find out, discover, gain certain information
of*: haec certis nuntiis, certis auctoribus
comperisse, Cic.; nihil de hoc comperi, Cic.;
with acc. and infin.: eum posse vivere, Cic.;
so also Ter., Hor. Esp. used in perf. partic.
compertus -a -um. (1) *known, undoubted*:
levem auditionem pro re comperta habere,
for a certainty, Caes.; ea dicimus quae
comperta habemus, quae vidimus, Cic.;
compertum narrare, Sall.; abl. absol.,
comperto, *it having been discovered for certain*: satis comperto Eordaeam petituros
Romanos, Liv. (2) of persons, *convicted*:
probri, Liv.

compĕrĭor = comperio: Ter., Sall., Tac.

compēs -pĕdis, f. *a fetter* or *foot shackle*, gen.
found in the plur.: Pl., Ov. TRANSF., qui in
compedibus corporis semper fuerunt, Cic.;
Telephum tenet puella grata compede
vinctum, Hor.

compesco -pescĕre -pescŭi, *to hold in, restrain,
check, curb*: ramos, Verg.; equum angustis
habenis, Tib.; seditionem exercitus verbo
uno, Tac.; clamorem, Hor.

compĕtītor -ōris, m. (competo), *a rival,
a competitor*: Cic.

compĕtītrix -īcis, f. (competo), *a female rival*
or *competitor*: Cic.

compĕto -petĕre -petīvi and -petĭi -petītum,
to come together, to meet. LIT., Varr. TRANSF.,
(1) *to agree, coincide in point of time*: tempora
cum Othonis exitu competisse, Tac. (2) *to
be equal to, match*; with dat.: animo corpus,
Suet.; absol., esp. with negative, *to be
competent, capable*: ut vix ad arma capienda
aptandaque pugnae competeret animus, Liv.;
neque oculis neque auribus satis compete-
bant, Tac.

compĭlātĭo -ōnis, f. (compilo), *a pillaging*,
hence (contemptuously), *a compilation of
documents*: Chresti, Cic. L.

compĭlo -are, *to bundle together*; hence *to pack
up and take off, to plunder, rob*: aedes, Pl.;
fana, Cic.; templa ornamentis, Liv.; fig.:
consultorum sapientiam, Cic.

compingo -pingĕre -pēgi -pactum (pango),
to put together, construct. TRANSF., *to confine,
lock up, conceal*: aliquem in carcerem, Pl.;
aurum, Pl.; se in Apuliam, Cic. L.; fig.: in
iudicia et contiunculas tamquam in aliquod
pistrinum detrudi et compingi, Cic.
¶ Hence partic. **compactus** -a -um,
constructed, built: Lucr., Cic., Verg.; hence
firm, compact: Plin., Suet.

compĭtālĭcĭus -a -um (compitalis), *relating to
the Compitalia*: dies, Cic. L.; ludi, Cic.

compĭtālis -e (compitum), *relating* or *belonging to cross-roads*: Lares, *the deities who
presided over cross-roads*, Suet.
N. as subst. **Compĭtālĭa** -ium or -iorum,
*the festival in honour of these deities, celebrated
annually at cross-roads on a day appointed
by the praetor, shortly after the Saturnalia*:
Cic. L.

compĭtum -i, n. (competo), *a place where two
or more roads meet, cross-roads*: Cic., Verg.

complăcĕo -cēre -cŭi or -cĭtus sum. (1) *to
please several persons at once*: Ter. (2) *to
please exceedingly*: Pl., Ter.

complāno -are, *to level*: terram, Cato;
domum, *to raze*, Cic.

[122]

complector -plecti -plexus, dep. (cum/plecto), *to embrace, to clasp.*

LIT., *to embrace, encircle, surround, encompass*: aliquem medium, Liv.; aliquem artius, Cic.; of a vine: quidquid est nacta complectitur, Cic.; so: amaracus illum floribus, Verg.; collem opere, Caes.; animum mundi caelo, Cic.

TRANSF., (1) *to hold fast, master*: quam (facultatem) quoniam complexus es, tene, Cic.; so of sleep: me artior somnus, Cic.; sopor artūs, Verg. (2) *to attach oneself to, esteem*: quos fortuna complexa est, *the favourites of fortune*, Cic.; aliquem summa benevolentia, Cic.; Liv., Ov. (3) of the mind, *to embrace, grasp, comprehend*: omnia una comprehensione, Cic.; deum cogitatione, Cic.; Ov., Tac. (4) *to unite in oneself* or *itself*: omnes omnium caritates patria una complexa est, Cic.; esp. *to include*, of speech or writing: omnia istius facta oratione, Cic.

complēmentum -i, n. (compleo), *that which completes* or *fills up, a complement*: inania quaedam verba quasi complementa numerorum, Cic.

compleō -plēre -plēvi -plētum, *to fill up.*

LIT., (1) fossas sarmentis et virgultis, Caes.; paginam, Cic.; multo cibo et potione completi, Cic.; with genit.: convivium vicinorum cotidie compleo, Cic. (2) as milit. t. t.: **a**, *to complete the number of an army, fleet*, etc.: legiones, Caes.; cohortes, Tac.: **b**, *to man, fill with men*, a place, ship, etc.: late loca milite, Verg.; naves, Caes.

TRANSF., (1) *to fill* a place with light, smell, shout, clamour, etc.: omnia clamoribus, Liv.; sol cuncta suā luce lustrat et complet, Cic. (2) *to fill* a person with a feeling: civitatem summa spe et voluntate, Caes.; Cic., Liv. (3) *to fulfil*: fata sua, Ov; centum et septem annos complesse, Cic. (4) of a sum, *to make up*: neque est adhuc ea summa (imperati sumptus) completa, Cic. (5) *to complete, finish* a task: his rebus completis, Caes.

¶ Hence partic. **complētus** -a -um, *perfect, complete*: completus et perfectus verborum ambitus, Cic.

complexiō -ōnis, f. (complector), *connexion, combination.* LIT., complexiones atomorum inter se, Cic. TRANSF., (1) in rhetoric: brevis totius negotii, *a short summary of the whole matter*, Cic.; so: verborum, Cic.; absol., *a period*: Cic. (2) in logic: **a**, *the statement of a syllogism*: Cic.: **b**, *a dilemma*: Cic.

complexus -ūs, m. (complector), *an embrace.*

LIT., (1) of persons, in love or friendship: aliquem de complexu matris avellere, Cic.; currere ad alicuius complexum, Cic. (2) *combat*: complexum armorum vitare, Tac.; Caesaris, Caes. (3) of things, *grasp, compass*: qui (mundus) omnia complexu suo coercet et continet, Cic.

TRANSF., (1) *affection, love*: complexus totius gentis humanae, Cic. (2) in discourse, *connexion*: Quint.

complĭco -are -āvi -ātum (post-Aug. -ŭi -ĭtum), *to fold together, fold up.* LIT., epistulam, Cic. L.; rudentem, Pl. TRANSF., complicata notio, *confused, intricate*, Cic.

complōrātĭo -ōnis, f. (comploro), *a lamentation, a weeping and bewailing*: mulierum, Liv; comploratio sui patriaeque, Liv.

complōrātus -ūs, m. = comploratio; q.v.: Liv.

complōro -are, *to bewail* or *weep, to lament loudly and violently*: mortem, Cic.; desperata complorataque res est publica, Liv., Ov.

complūres, n. complūra (rarely complūrĭa) -ium, *several*; as adj.: Ter., Cic.; as subst.: Cic., Suet.

complūrĭens (complūrĭēs), adv. (complures), *many times, frequently*: Pl.

complusculĭ -ae -a (complures), *a good many*: Pl., Ter.

complūvĭum -i, n. (cum/pluo), *the quadrangular roofless space in the centre of a Roman house, through which the water collected on the roofs found its way to the* impluvium *below*: Varr., Suet.

compōno -pōnĕre -pŏsŭi -pŏsĭtum.

(1) *to put, place, lay, bring together* separate persons or things, whether like or unlike: in quo (loco) erant ea composita, quibus rex te munerare constituerat, Cic.; manibus manus atque oribus ora, Verg. Esp. of unlike persons or things: **a**, *to match, place together as opponents*: pergis pugnantia secum frontibus adversis componere, Hor.: **b**, *to compare*: dignitati alicuius suam, Cic.; parva magnis, Verg.; dicta cum factis, Sall.

(2) *to collect together a whole from several parts, compose*: exercitus eius compositus ex variis gentibus, Sall.; venena, Ov.; aggerem tumuli, Verg.; esp. of writers, *to compose*: volumen de tuenda sanitate, Cic.; oratio ad conciliandos plebis animos composita, Liv.; versus, Hor.; also of plans and agreements, *to form*: pacem, Pl., Liv., Verg.; consilium, Liv.; ex composito, *according to plan*, Liv., Tac.

(3) *to put, arrange, settle* separate persons or things or parts in their right places or right mutual relation: sidera, Cic.; agmen, Liv.; verba, Cic.; cinerem, *ashes of the dead*, Ov.; togam, Hor. Esp. of the body and its parts: se thalamis, Verg.; membra, Verg.; comas, Ov.; composito et delibuto capillo, Cic.; vultum, Tac. TRANSF., **a**, of immaterial things, *to dispose, to settle in a particular way*: itinera sic ut, etc., Cic.; auspicia ad utilitatem reipublicae composita, Cic.: **b**, of strife or disturbance, *to allay, calm, reconcile*: lites, Verg.; controversias regum, Caes.; Armeniam, Tac.; amicos aversos, Hor.

¶ Hence partic. (with compar. and superl.) **compŏsĭtus** -a -um, *placed together.* (1) *constructed, put together* (cf. compono (2) above): crimen, *invented*, Cic.; indignatio, *studied*, Tac.; verba, *compound*, Quint. (2) *arranged in order, settled* (cf. compono (3) above): respublica, Cic.; composito agmine legiones ducere, Tac.; so of oratory: oratio, Cic.; and of the orator himself: orator, Cic.; esp. of the features in feigning an expression: composito vultu, Tac. Hence: **a**, *adapted* to a purpose: in ostentationem, Liv.; historiae, Quint.; adliciendis moribus, Tac.: **b**, of strife or disturbance, *calm, settled*: adfectus, Quint., Tac.

Adv. **compŏsĭtē**, *in an orderly way*: dicere, Cic., Sall., Tac.

comporto -are, *to carry, bring together, collect*: frumentum ab Asia, Caes.; arma in templum, Cic.; Verg.

compŏs -pŏtis (cum/potis), *having the mastery or control of, possessed of, sharing in*: animi, Ter.; mentis, *in full possession of mental faculties*, Cic.; voti, *one whose wish is fulfilled*, Hor., Liv.; scientiae compotem esse, *to be able to know something*, Cic.; rationis et consilii compos, Cic.; qui me huius urbis compotem fecerunt, *enabled me to be in this city*, Cic.; tum patriae compotem me numquam siris esse, Liv.; sometimes also with abl.: Cic., Liv.

compŏsĭtē, adv. from compono; q.v.

compŏsĭtĭo -ōnis, f. (compono), *a putting together*. (**1**) gen. (cf. compono (1) above); so of opponents, *a matching*: gladiatorum compositiones, Cic. (**2**) (cf. compono) *a composing, compounding*: sonorum, Cic.; unguentorum, Cic.; of a book: iuris pontificalis, Cic. (**3**) (cf. compono) *an orderly arrangement*: membrorum, Cic.; anni, *of the calendar*, Cic.; of words: compositio apta, Cic.; also of the *settlement* of differences: pacis, concordiae, compositionis auctor esse non destiti, Cic.

compŏsĭtor -ōris, m. (compono), *an arranger, adjuster*: Cic., Ov.

compŏsĭtūra -ae, f. (compono), *a connexion, joining*: oculorum, Lucr.

compŏsĭtus -a -um, partic. from compono; q.v.

compŏtātĭo -ōnis, f. *a drinking party* (translation of συμπόσιον): Cic.

compŏtĭo -ire (compos), *to make master or partaker of* (ante- and post-class.); with abl. of the thing: Pl.; genit.: App.

compŏtor -ōris, m. *a drinking-companion*: Cic.

compŏtrix -īcis, f. (compotor), *a female drinking-companion*: Ter.

compransor -ōris, m. *a dinner companion*: Cic.

comprĕcātĭo -ōnis, f. (comprecor), *common supplication*: haec sollemnis deorum comprecatio, Liv.

comprĕcor -ari, dep. *to pray to, supplicate*: deos, Ter.; caelestum fidem, Cat.; Cytherea, comprecor, ausis adsit, Ov.; with acc., *to pray for*: Sen., Plin. L.

comprĕhendo -prehendĕre -prĕhendi -prĕhensum and **comprendo** -prendĕre -prendi -prensum, *to grasp*.
   (**1**) *to take together, to unite*: naves, Liv. TRANSF., *to embrace, comprise, include*: multos amicitia, Cic.; quae omnia una cum deorum notione comprehendimus, Cic.; breviter comprehensa sententia, Cic.; ne plura consecter, comprehendam brevi, Cic.; aliquid numero, *to count, express in numbers*, Verg.
   (**2**) *to take firmly, seize*. LIT., **a**, of things and places: quid opus est manibus si nihil comprehendendum est? Cic.; raedas equosque, Caes.; aliis comprehensis collibus, Caes.; esp. of things *catching fire* or of *fire catching* them: ignem, *to catch fire*, Verg.; ignis robora comprendit, *seizes on*, Verg.; avidis comprenditur ignibus agger, Ov.; without igne: comprehensa aedificia, Liv.: **b**, of persons, in supplication: comprehendunt utrumque et orant, Caes.; esp. *to capture, arrest*: tam capitalem hostem, Cic.; vivum in fuga, Caes.; *to catch red-handed*: in furto, Cic.; so of the crime itself: nefandum

adulterium, Cic. TRANSF., with the senses or intellect, *to comprehend, perceive*: sensu *or* sensibus, Cic.; memoria, Cic.; animo intellegentiam alicuius rei, Cic.; intellegere et cogitatione comprehendere qualis sit animus, Cic.; esse aliquid, quod comprehendi et percipi posset, Cic.

comprĕhensĭbĭlis -e (comprehendo), *that which can be comprehended, comprehensible*: natura non comprehensibilis, Cic.

comprĕhensĭo -ōnis, f. (comprehendo), *a grasping, laying hold of*. (**1**) (cf. comprehendo (1) above) *a taking together, uniting*; hence of a rhetorical *period*: verba comprehensione devicta, Cic., Quint. (**2**) (cf. comprehendo (2) above) *a seizing, apprehending*: sontium, Cic. TRANSF., *a perceiving, comprehending, comprehension*: complecti omnia una comprehensione, Cic.

comprendo = comprehendo; q.v.

compressĭo -ōnis, f. (comprimo), *a pressing together*; hence (**1**) *an embrace*: Pl. (**2**) *compression of style, conciseness*: compressione rerum breves, Cic.

compressū, abl. sing. from verbal noun compressus (comprimo), *by pressing together*: Cic.; hence *by embracing*: Pl., Ter.

compressus -a -um, partic. of comprimo; q.v.

comprĭmo -primĕre -pressi -pressum (cum/premo), *to compress*.
   (**1**) *to press together, squeeze together* separate things: dentes, Pl.; digitos compresserat et pugnum fecerat, Cic.; prov.: compressis manibus sedere, *to sit with folded hands, idle*, Liv.; ordines, *to close the ranks*, Liv.
   (**2**) *to press* a thing *tightly*; hence *to embrace*; also *to check, hold back*: animam, hold the breath, Ter. TRANSF., **a**, *to restrain or stop* actions and feelings: delicta magna, Cic.; plausus ipse admiratione compressus est, Cic.; gressum, Verg.; furentis hominis conatum atque audaciam, Cic.; seditionem, Liv.: **b**, *to suppress, hold back* things: frumentum, Cic. L.; famam, Liv.
   ¶ Hence partic. **compressus** -a -um, with compar. adv. **compressius**, *more or rather concisely*: loqui, Cic.

comprŏbātĭo -ōnis, f. (comprobo), *approval*: Cic.

comprŏbātor -ōris, m. (comprobo), *one who approves*: Cic.

comprŏbo -are. (**1**) *to approve fully*: orationem omnium adsensu, Liv.; istam tuam sententiam laudo vehementissimeque comprobo, Cic. (**2**) *to confirm, prove, establish*: patris dictum sapiens temeritas filii comprobavit, Cic.

comprōmissum -i, n. (compromitto), *a mutual agreement to abide by the decision of an arbitrator*: de hac pecunia compromissum facere, Cic.

comprōmitto -mittĕre -mīsi -missum, *to agree to refer a cause to arbitration*: Cic. L.

Compsa -ae, f. *town of the Hirpini in Samnium* (now *Conza*); hence **Compsānus** -a -um, *of or belonging to Compsa*.

¹comptus -a -um, partic. from como; q.v.

²comptus -ūs, m. (**1**) (como), *a head-dress*: Lucr. (**2**) (=coemptio), *a band, tie*: Lucr.

compungo -pungĕre -punxi -punctum, *to prick, puncture on all sides*.

LIT., collum, Phaedr.; hence *to tattoo*: barbarus compunctus notis Threiciis, Cic. TRANSF., (I) gen. *to prick, sting*: ipsi se compungunt suis acuminibus, Cic. (2) of the action of light, or heat and cold: Lucr.

compŭto -are, *to reckon together, calculate, compute*: rationem digitis, Pl.; facies tua computat annos, *shows thy age*, Juv.; absol.: computarat, pecuniam impetrarat, Cic.

compŭtresco -ĕre, *to rot, to putrefy*: Lucr.

Cōmum -i, n. *a lake-side town in Cisalpine Gaul, birth-place of the elder and younger Pliny* (now *Como*). Adj. **Cōmensis** -e, *of or belonging to Comum*.

cōnāmen -mĭnis, n. (conor). (I) *an effort, endeavour*: Lucr., Ov. (2) in concr. sense, *a support*: Ov.

cōnātum -i, n. (conor), *an undertaking*; gen. in plur.: conata efficere, Cic.; Pl., Lucr., Caes.

cōnātus -ūs, m. (conor), *an exertion, effort.* (I) in gen.: hoc conatu desistere, Cic.; tumultus Gallicus haud magno conatu brevi oppressus est, Liv. (2) *an impulse, inclination*: ut (beluae) conatum haberent ad naturales pastus capessendos, Cic. (3) in concr. sense, *an undertaking*: compressi tuos nefarios conatus, Cic.

concăco -are, *to defile all over*: Phaedr.

concaedēs -ium, f. pl. *a barricade of trees*: Tac.

concălĕfăcĭo -făcĕre -fēci -factum, and pass. **concălĕfĭo** -fieri -factus sum, *to warm thoroughly*: bracchium, Cic.; Lucr.

concălĕo -ēre, *to be warm through and through*: Pl.

concălesco -călescĕre -călŭi, *to become thoroughly warm*: corpora nostra ardore animi concalescunt, Cic. TRANSF., *to glow with love*: Ter.

concallesco -callescĕre -callŭi (calleo), *to become thoroughly hard.* TRANSF., (I) *to become practised, expert*: tamquam manus opere, sic animus usu concalluit, Cic. (2) *to become callous* or *without feeling*: Cic. L.

Concăni -ōrum, m. (sing. **Concănus**: Hor.), *a savage tribe in Spain, who drank horses' blood.*

concastīgo -are, *to punish, chastise severely*: Pl.

concăvo -are (concavus), *to hollow out, make hollow* or *concave*: bracchia geminos in arcus, *curves, bends*, Ov.

concăvus -a -um, *hollow, vaulted, arched, concave*: cymbala, Lucr.; altitudines speluncarum, Cic.; aqua, *swelling*, Ov.

concēdo -cēdĕre -cessi -cessum.

    (I) intransit., *to go away, retire, withdraw.* LIT., ex aedibus, Ter.; superis ab oris, Verg.; caelo, Verg.; ab alicuius oculis, Cic.; cum coniugibus ac liberis in arcem Capitoliumque, Liv.; docet unde fulmen venerit, quo concesserit, Cic.; concedere vita, *to die*, Tac.; so absol.: quando concessero, Tac. TRANSF., **a**, *to come over to, join with*, esp. with in and acc., *to submit*: in alicuius ditionem, Liv.; in Attali sententiam, Liv.: **b**, *to yield, give way to*, with dat.: voluptas concedit dignitati, Cic.; concedere naturae, *to die a natural death*, Sall.; so, *to be inferior to*: nemini studio, Cic.; amore nobis, Tac.: **c**, *to give in to, agree to*: tibi, Ter.; alicuius postulationi, Cic.; hence *to pardon*: alienis peccatis, Cic.

(2) transit. (usually with acc. and dat.): **a**, *to yield* a thing, *grant, give up*: alicui libertatem in aliqua re, Cic.; alicui primas in dicendo partes, Cic.; reipublicae dolorem atque amicitias suas, *sacrifice*, Cic.: **b**, *to pardon, overlook*: multa virtuti eorum, Caes.: **c**, *to permit, allow*; with infin.: Caes., Hor., Liv.; with ut clause: Lucr., Cic.: **d**, *to concede, grant that*, with acc. and infin.: Lucr., Cic.

concĕlĕbro -are. LIT., *to visit a place often*, or *in large companies*: Lucr. TRANSF., (I) of any occupation, *to pursue eagerly, assiduously*: studia per otium, Cic. (2) *to celebrate a festivity*: diem natalem, Pl.; triumphum, Cic.; spectaculum, Liv. (3) *to praise, extol*: fama et litteris eius diei victoriam, Cic.

concēnātĭo -ōnis, f. (ceno), *a supping together* (translation of Gr. σύνδειπνον): Cic.

concentĭo -ōnis, f. (concino), *a singing together, harmony*: Cic.

concenturio -are, *to assemble by centuries*; hence *to bring together*: Pl.

concentus -ūs, m. (concino), *a singing together, harmony*: avium, Cic.; tubarum ac cornuum, Liv. TRANSF., *agreement, harmony of opinion, unity, concord*: melior actionum quam sonorum concentus, Cic.; Tac., Hor.

conceptĭo -ōnis, f. (concipio). (I) *conception, a becoming pregnant*: Cic. (2) *the drawing up of legal formulae*: Cic.

conceptus -ūs, m. (concipio). (I) *a conceiving, pregnancy*: hominum pecudumve, Cic.; of plants, *budding*: Plin. (2) *a catching*, of fire: Suet. (3) *a collecting*, or *a collection*: Plin., Sen.

concerpo -cerpĕre -cerpsi -cerptum (carpo), *to pull, pluck, tear in pieces.* LIT., epistulas, Cic. L., Liv. TRANSF., *to abuse*: aliquem ferventissime, ap. Cic. L.

concertātĭo -ōnis, f. (concerto), *contest, strife*: magistratuum, Cic.; esp. *a contest in words, dispute*: sine ieiuna concertatione verborum, Cic.

concertātor -ōris, m. (concerto), *a rival*: Tac.

concertātōrĭus -a -um (concerto), *relating to a contest*: genus dicendi, Cic.

concerto -are, *to strive eagerly*: cum ero, Ter.; proelio, Caes.; esp. of dispute in words: nunquam accidit ut cum eo verbo uno concertarem, Cic.

concessĭo -ōnis, f. (concedo), *a yielding, granting.* (I) agrorum, Cic. (2) as legal t. t., *an admission of a fault*: Cic. (3) as rhet. t. t., *a concession, yielding of a point*: Quint.

concesso -are, *to cease, leave off*: Pl.

concessū, abl. sing. as from concessus, m. (concedo), *by permission, with leave*: concessu omnium, Cic.; Caes., Tac.

concha -ae, f. (κόγχη). LIT., *a sea-shell*: Lucr., Cic., Ov.; and so *a shell-fish*, esp. (I) *a mussel*: Cic. (2) *a pearl-oyster*: Plin.; hence poet.: *pearl*: conchae teretesque lapilli, Ov. (3) *the shell-fish which yielded the purple dye*: Lucr.; poet., *purple dye*: Ov.

    TRANSF., *a vessel in the shape of a shell.* (I) for condiments, etc.: concha salis puri, *salt-cellar*, Hor.; funde capacibus unguenta de conchis, Hor. (2) *a trumpet*: Verg.; esp. *the horn of Triton*: Verg., Hor.

conchis -is, f. (κόγχος), *a kind of bean boiled with its pod*: Juv.

conchīta -ae, m. (κογχίτης), *a mussel-gatherer*: Pl.

conchȳlĭātus -a -um (conchylium). (1) *dyed with purple*: peristromata, Cic. (2) *dressed in purple*: Sen.

conchȳlĭum -i, n. (κογχύλιον). (1) *a mussel*, or gen. *shell-fish*: Cic. (2) *an oyster*: Cic., Hor. (3) *the shell-fish which yielded the purple dye*: Lucr.; meton.: a, *a purple dye*: vestis conchylio tincta, Cic.: b, *a purple garment*: Quint., Juv.

¹concĭdo -cĭdĕre -cĭdi (cado), *to fall down, tumble to the ground, sink down*. Lit., concidat caelum omne necesse est, Cic.; repentinā ruinā pars eius turris concidit, Caes.; equus eius ante signum Iovis Statoris sine causā concidit, Cic.; pronus in fimo, Verg.; esp. in battle: ita pugnans concidit, Caes. Transf., *to sink, collapse, perish, waste away*: neque enim tam facile opes Carthaginis tantae concidissent, Cic.; tum ferocia omnis concidit, Liv.; bellum, Tac.; venti, *subside*, Hor.; so of persons, *to be ruined, to fail*, esp. at law: malas causas semper obtinuit, in optimā concidit, Cic.; iudicum vocibus fractus reus et una patroni omnes conciderunt, Cic.

²concīdo -cīdĕre -cīdi -cīsum (caedo), *to cut up, cut in pieces, cut down, destroy*. Lit., nervos, Cic.; ligna, Ov.; esp. of beating and fighting: virgis, Cic.; pugnis, Juv.; in battle: concisos equites nostros a barbaris nuntiabant, Cic.; Caes. Transf., (1) *to cut through, make breaks in*: magnos scrobibus montes, Verg.; pedestria itinera concisa aestuariis, Cic. (2) in gen., *to ruin, strike down*: Antonium decretis, auctoritatem, Cic. (3) as rhet. t. t., *to divide too minutely*: concidat delumbetque sententias, Cic.

¶ Hence partic. **concīsus** -a -um, *cut up small, brief, concise*: sententiae, Cic., Quint. Transf., of a speaker: Cic.

Adv. **concīsē**, *concisely*: Quint.

concĭĕo -cĭēre -cīvi -cītum and **concio** -ire (Lucr., Liv., Tac.).

(1) *to collect, bring together*: totam urbem, Liv.; exercitum ex tota insula, Liv.; auxilia, Tac.

(2) *to move violently*: concita navis, Ov.; concita flumina, Ov.; concita freta, Verg. Transf., a, *to excite, rouse, stir up*: plebem contionibus, Liv.; immani concitus irā, Verg.: b, *to produce, cause, promote* agitations, etc.: bellum in his provinciis, Liv.; seditionem, Tac.

concĭlĭābŭlum -i, n. (concilio), *a place of assembly*: nundinas et conciliabula obire, Liv., Tac.

concĭlĭātĭo -ōnis, f. (concilio), *a bringing together, a uniting, joining*: communem totius generis hominum conciliationem et consociationem colere, Cic. Transf., (cf. concilio). (1) *a uniting in sentiment, conciliating*: aut conciliationis causā leniter aut permotionis vehementer aguntur, Cic.; as rhet. t. t., *the gaining the favour of the audience*: Cic. (2) *a procuring or causing* (by conciliation): gratiae, Cic. (3) *inclination*: prima est enim conciliatio hominis ad ea, quae sunt secundum naturam, Cic.

concĭlĭātor -ōris, m. (concilio), *one who brings about* or *procures*: nuptiarum, *a match-maker*, Nep.; proditionis, Liv., Tac.

concĭlĭātrīcŭla -ae, f. (dim. of conciliatrix), *that which unites* or *conciliates*: Cic.

concĭlĭātrix -īcis, f. (conciliator), *she who unites*; hence *a match-maker*: Pl., Cic.; vis orationis conciliatrix humanae societatis, *which brings together*, Cic.

concĭlĭātū, abl. sing. of conciliatus, m. (concilio), *by union, by connexion*: Lucr.

concĭlĭātus -a -um, partic. from concilio; q.v.

concĭlĭo -are (concilium), *to bring together, to unite, connect*. Lit., corpora, Lucr. Transf., (1) *to unite in sentiment, win over*: gen.: homines inter se, Cic.; legiones sibi pecuniā, Cic.; animos plebis, Liv.; hence *to recommend, make acceptable*: dictis artes conciliare suas, Ov. (2) *to bring about* (by conciliation): pacem, Cic.; sibi amorem ab omnibus, Cic.; nuptias, Nep. (3) in gen., *to bring about, cause, procure*: pecunias, Cic.; famam clementiae, Liv.

¶ Hence partic. **concĭlĭātus** -a -um, *won over, inclined, favourable*: ut iudex ad rem accipiendam fiat conciliator, Cic.

concĭlĭum -i, n. (cum/calo), *a bringing together*. (1) of things, *a union, connexion*: rerum, Lucr. (2) of persons (sometimes of animals), *a coming together, assembling*: Camenarum cum Egeria, Liv.; hence in concr. sense, *a gathering, an assembly*: pastorum, deorum, Cic.; ferarum, Ov.; esp. *an assembly for deliberation, a council*: constituere diem concilio, Caes.; cogere or convocare concilium, Caes.; aliquem adhibere ad concilium, Caes.; concilium sanctum patrum, Hor.; concilium plebis habere, Liv.; Gallorum, Liv.; Achaicum, *the Achaean League*, Liv.

concinne, adv. from concinnus; q.v.

concinnĭtās -ātis, f. (concinnus), *elegance*, esp. *harmony of style*: verborum or sententiarum, Cic., Sen.

concinnĭtūdo -ĭnis, f. = concinnitas; q.v., Cic.

concinno -are (concinnus), *to put* or *fit together carefully, to arrange*: pallam, Pl.; vultum, Petr. Transf., *to produce, cause*: consuetudo amorem, Lucr.; me insanum verbis concinnat suis, *makes me mad*, Pl.

concinnus -a -um, adj. (with compar.), *well put together, pleasing, on account of harmony and proportion*: sat edepol concinna est virgo facie, Pl.; tectorium, Cic.; Samos, Hor. Transf., (1) in gen., *elegant, neat*: helluo, Cic.; esp. of discourse, *tasteful, polished*: oratio, Cic.; concinnus et elegans Aristo, Cic. (2) *suited, fit, appropriate, pleasing*: concinnus amicis, Hor.; tibi concinnum est, *it suits you*, Pl.

¶ Hence adv. **concinnē**, *elegantly*: vestita, Pl.; rogare, Cic.

concĭno -cĭnĕre -cĭnŭi (cum/cano).

(1) intransit. Lit., *to sing in chorus, play instruments in concert*: concinunt tubae, Liv.; sic ad vada Maeandri concinit albus olor, Ov. Transf., a, *to join together in an utterance, to agree in saying*: ne iuvet vox ista veto, qua concinentes conlegas auditis, Liv.: b, in gen., *to agree together, harmonize*: cum Peripateticis re concinere, verbis discrepare, Cic.

(2) transit. LIT., haec cum concinuntur, Cic.; carmen ad clausas fores, Ov. TRANSF., **a**, *to celebrate*: laetos dies, Hor.: **b**, *to prophesy*: tristia omina, Ov.

¹concĭo=concieo; q.v.

²concĭo -ōnis=contio; q.v.

concĭōn- =contion-; q.v.

concĭpĭo -cĭpĕre -cēpi -ceptum (cum/capio).
   (1) *to take together, hold together*. LIT., *to contain, hold*: multum ignem trullis ferreis, Liv. TRANSF., of words, *to express in a certain form*: quod EX ANIMI SENTENTIA iuraris, sicut concipitur more nostro, *according to our customary form*, Cic.; conceptis verbis iurare, Cic.; vadimonium, Cic.; ius iurandum, Liv.; Qu. Marcio Philippo praeeunte in foro votum, *to repeat formally at his dictation*, Liv.; vota, preces, Ov.; foedus, Verg.
   (2) *to take completely, take in, absorb*. LIT., physically: **a**, of fluids, *to draw in, suck in*: concipit Iris aquas, Ov.; terra caducas concepit lacrimas, Ov.: **b**, of fire, *to catch*: materies, quae nisi admoto igni ignem concipere possit, Cic.; fig., of love: ignem mens mea concipit ignem, Ov.: **c**, of air, *to draw in*: pars (animae) concipitur cordis parte quadam, quem ventriculum cordis appellant, Cic.: **d**, *to conceive*: cum concepit mula, Cic.; with ex and abl.: Cic.; with ab or de: Ov.; fig.: hoc quod conceptum respublica periculum parturit, Cic.: **e**, of physical qualities, *to take, gain*: alias aliasque vires, Ov.
   TRANSF., (1) *to receive, take in, grasp* by senses or intellect: oculis, Pl.; animo ac mente, Cic. (2) *to form inwardly, conceive, imagine*: superstitiosa ista, Cic.; of passions, *to begin to feel*: iram intimo animo et corde, Cic.; spem regni, Liv.; animo iras, Ov.; so of action, *to devise*, esp. in bad sense: scelus in se, Cic.; nefas, Ov.

concīsĭo -ōnis, f. (²concīdo), rhet. t. t., *the breaking up of a clause into divisions*: Cic.

concīsus -a -um, partic. from ²concīdo; q.v.

concĭtātĭo -ōnis, f. (concito), *quick or violent movement*. LIT., remorum, Liv. TRANSF., (1) *tumult, sedition*: plebi contra patres concitatio et seditio, Cic. (2) *disturbance of the mind, passion*: ab omni concitatione animi semper vacare, Cic.; animorum, Liv.

concĭtātor -ōris, m. (concito), *one who excites, stirs up*: seditionis, Cic., Liv., Tac.

concĭto -are (freq. of concieo), *to move quickly or violently, stir up, excite*.
   LIT., of physical movement: equum calcaribus, *to spur to a gallop*, Liv.; navem remis, Liv.; Eurus concitat aquas, Ov.; servos ex omnibus vicis, Cic.; concitare aciem, *to move forward the army*, Liv.; se concitare in hostem, *to rush against the enemy*, Liv.
   TRANSF., (1) in gen., *to stir up, incite, impel*: Etruriam omnem adversus Romanos, Liv.; omnem Galliam ad suum auxilium, Caes.; animi quodam impetu concitatus, Cic.; Tac. (2) of results, *to cause, produce*: seditionem ac discordiam, Cic.; invidiam in aliquem, Cic.; Liv., Ov.
   ¶ Hence partic. (with compar. and superl.) **concĭtātus** -a -um, *quickly* or *violently moved*; hence (1) *quick, rapid*: conversio caeli, Cic.; quam concitatissimos equos

immittere, *spur the horses to a full gallop*, Liv. (2) *excited, violent, passionate*: contio, Cic.; concitatior clamor, Liv.; oratio, Quint.
   Adv. **concĭtātē**, *excitedly*: Quint.

concĭtor -ōris, m. (concieo), *one who excites* or *stirs up*: belli, vulgi, Liv., Tac.

conclāmātĭo -ōnis, f. (conclamo), *a loud shouting* or *shouting together*: universi exercitūs, Caes.; Tac.

conclāmĭto -are (freq. of conclamo), *to shout loudly, cry violently*: Pl.

conclāmo -are. (1) *to shout together* or *shout loudly*: vos universi a me conservatam esse rempublicam conclamastis, Cic.; conclamaverunt, uti aliqui ex nostris ad conloquium prodirent, *demanded*, Caes.; conclamavit, quid as se venirent, *called out to ask*, Caes.; in joy: cum conclamasset gaudio Albanus exercitus, Liv.; conclamare victoriam, Caes.; in grief, *to call upon* the dead, *to bewail*: Verg.
   (2) *to call together*: conclamare socios, Ov.; agrestes, Verg.; esp. as milit. t. t.: ad arma, *to call to arms*, Liv.; vasa, *to give the signal for packing up baggage before a march*, Caes.

conclāve -is, n. (cum/clavis), *a room, chamber*: Pl., Cic., Hor.

conclūdo -clūdĕre -clūsi -clūsum (claudo), *to shut up, enclose, confine*.
   LIT., me in cellam, Pl.; bestias delectationis causā, Cic.; mare conclusum, *an inland sea*, Caes.
   TRANSF., (1) *to include, compress, confine*: aliquem in angustissimam formulam sponsionis concludere, Cic.; quartus ubi hoc libro concluditur, *is comprised*, Cic. (2) *to bring to an end*: epistulam, Cic.; perorationem inflammantem restinguentemve concludere, Cic.; rhet. t. t., *to close rhythmically, to round off in a period*: sententias, Cic. (3) as philosoph. t. t., *to bring to a conclusion, to argue, infer*: deinde concludebas summum malum esse dolorem, Cic.; argumenta ratione concludentia, *reasonable, logical proofs*, Cic.
   ¶ Hence, from partic., adv. **conclūsē**, *with well-turned periods*: concluse apteque dicere, Cic.

conclūsĭo -ōnis, f. (concludo), *a shutting, a closing*; hence in military language, *a blockade*: Caes. TRANSF., *a close, conclusion*: conclusio muneris ac negotii tui, Cic. L.; esp. as rhet. or philosoph. t. t. (1) *conclusion of a speech, peroration*: conclusio est exitus et determinatio totius orationis, Cic. (2) *a period*: verborum quaedam ad numerum conclusio, Cic. (3) *conclusion in a syllogism, consequence*: rationis, Cic.

conclūsĭuncŭla -ae, f. (dim. of conclusio), *a foolish inference*: contortulae quaedam et minutulae conclusiunculae, Cic.

concŏlor -ōris, *similar in colour*: sus, Verg.; with dat.: concolor est illis, Ov.

concŏquo -cŏquere -coxi -coctum.
   LIT., *to boil* or *cook thoroughly* or *together*: Lucr., Sen.; hence *to digest*: cibum, Cic.
   TRANSF., (1) *to bear, endure, stomach*: ut eius ista odia non sorbeam solum sed etiam concoquam, Cic. L.; aliquem senatorem (*as senator*) non concoquere, Liv. (2) *to consider maturely, deliberate upon*: tibi diu concoquendum est utrum, etc., Cic.; clandestina concocta sunt consilia, *have been concocted*, Liv. (3) with reflex., *to waste away*: Pl.

¹**concordĭa** -ae, f. (concors), *agreement, union, harmony, concord.* LIT., of persons: concordiam confirmare cum aliquo, Cic.; conglutinare, Cic.; constituere, Cic.; reconciliare, Liv.; meton.: et cum Pirithoo felix concordia Theseus, *one heart and mind,* Ov. TRANSF., of things: rerum, Hor., Quint., Juv.

²**Concordĭa** -ae, f. *the goddess Concord,* to whom several temples in Rome were dedicated.

concordĭtĕr, adv. from concors; q.v.

concordo -are (concors), *to agree, be in harmony*: Ter.; cum animi iudicia opinionesque concordant, Cic.; with dat.: concordant carmina nervis, Ov.; with cum: Quint.

concors -dis, adj. (with compar. and superl.) (cum/cor), *of one mind* or *opinion, concordant, agreeing, harmonious*: fratres concordissimi, Cic.; secum, Liv., Tac.; so also of things: moderatus et concors civitatis status, Cic.; regnum, Liv.; pax, Ov.

Adv. (with compar. and superl.), **cordĭtĕr,** *harmoniously*: vivere cum aliquo, Cic.; Liv., Ov.

concrēbresco -brescĕre -bruī, *to increase*: Verg.

concrēdo (concrēduo = Pl.) -crēdĕre -crēdĭdi -crēdĭtum, *to entrust, to commit to*: rem et famam suam commendare et concredere alicui, Cic.; Pl., Hor.

concrēmo -are, *to burn down, burn entirely*: omnia tecta, Liv., Suet.

concrĕpo -are -ŭi -ĭtum. (**1**) intransit., *to rattle, creak, clash, grate loudly* or *together*: scabilla concrepant, Cic.; concrepuere arma, Liv.; also *to make a noise by bringing together*: armis concrepat multitudo, Caes.; exercitus gladiis ad scuta concrepuit, Liv.; digitis concrepare, *to snap the fingers,* Pl., Cic. (**2**) transit., *to rattle, strike upon*: aera, Ov.; digitos, Petr.

concresco -crescĕre -crēvi -crētum (perf. infin. concresse: Ov.). (**1**) *to grow, collect, increase, be formed*: de terris terram concrescere parvis, Lucr.; aut simplex est natura animantis aut concreta est ex pluribus naturis, *is compounded,* Cic. (**2**) *to become stiff, to congeal, curdle, harden*: nive pruinâque concrescit aqua, Cic.; frigore sanguis, Verg.

¶ Hence perf. partic. **concrētus** -a -um. (**1**) *compounded.* (**2**) *thickened, congealed, condensed, stiffened*: glacies, Liv.; lac, Verg.; dolor, *hard, tearless,* Ov.

concrētio -ōnis, f. (concresco). (**1**) *a growing together, congealing, condensing*: corporum, Cic. (**2**) *materiality, matter*: mortalis, Cic.

concrŭcio -are, *to torture violently*: Lucr.

concŭbīna -ae, f. (concumbo), *a concubine*: Pl., Cic.

concŭbīnātus -ūs, m. (concubinus), *concubinage*: Pl.

concŭbīnus -i, m. (concumbo), *a man living in a state of concubinage*: Cat., Tac.

concŭbĭtus -ūs, m. (concumbo). (**1**) *lying together* or *reclining together* (at table): Prop. (**2**) *copulation*: Cic., Verg.

concŭbĭus -a -um (concumbo), *relating to sleep,* found only in the phrase concubiâ nocte: Cic., Liv. (or noctu concubiâ = Enn.), *at the time of men's first sleep, at dead of night.*

N. as subst. **concŭbĭum** -i, *the time of the first sleep*: Pl.

conculco -are (cum/calco), *to tread, trample under foot*: Cato. TRANSF., *to misuse, to despise*: miseram Italiam, Cic.; Macedonicam lauream, Cic.

concumbo -cumbĕre -cŭbŭi -cŭbĭtum. (**1**) *to lie together* or *recline together* (at table): Prop. (**2**) *to lie with, have intercourse with*: Ter., Cic., Ov.

concŭpĭens -entis (cupio), *desiring, covetous of*: Enn.

concŭpisco -piscĕre -pīvi or -pĭi -pītum (cupio), *to desire eagerly, covet, to endeavour after, aim at*: eandem mortem gloriosam, Cic.; signa, tabulas, supellectilem, vestem infinite, Cic.; with infin.: ducere aliquam in matrimonium, Cic.; Hor., Liv., Tac.

concurro -currĕre -curri (rarely -cŭcurri) -cursum, *to run together.*

Hence (**1**) *to assemble hurriedly, flock to one spot*: tota Italia concurret, Cic.; ad arma, Caes.; ad curiam, Cic.; ad me restituendum Romam, Cic.

(**2**) *to rush together, run to meet one another*: ne prorae concurrerent, Liv.; esp. *to meet in conflict, attack, engage*: concurrunt equites inter se, Caes.; omnia ventorum concurrere proelia vidi, Verg.; cum acie legionum rectâ fronte, Liv.; with dat.: concurrere equitibus, Sall.; adversus aliquem, Liv.; in aliquem, Sall.; so fig.: concurrentis belli minae, *war on the point of breaking out,* Tac. Also without the idea of conflict: neve aspere (verba) concurrerent neve vastius diducantur, Cic.; concurri dextera laeva, *of clapping the hands for applause,* Hor. TRANSF., *to happen at the same time*: quae ut concurrant omnia, optabile est, Cic.

concursātio -ōnis, f. (concurso). (**1**) *a running together, concourse.* TRANSF., *coincidence*: somniorum, Cic. (**2**) *a running about, rushing hither and thither*: puerorum, Cic.; concursatio regis a Demetriade nunc Lamiam in concilium Aetolorum nunc Chalcidem, Liv.; esp. *skirmishing of light troops*: Liv.

concursātor -ōris, m. (concurso), *a skirmisher* (opp. statarius): Liv.

concursio -ōnis, f. (concurro). (**1**) *a running together, concourse*: atomorum, Cic. (**2**) *a figure of speech in which the same word is frequently repeated* (Gr. συμπλοκή): Cic.

concurso -are, *to run about, rush hither and thither*: tum trepidare et concursare, Caes.; dies noctesque, Cic.; ignes concursant, Lucr.; with object in acc., *to go round visiting*: omnes fere domos omnium, Cic. As milit. t. t., *to skirmish*: inter saxa rupesque, Liv.

concursus -ūs, m. (concurro).

(**1**) *a running together, concourse*: concursus hominum in forum, Cic.; in forum a tota urbe, Liv., Hor., Verg. TRANSF., of abstractions, *union*: honestissimorum studiorum, Cic.

(**2**) *a rushing together, meeting*: corpusculorum, Cic.; verborum, Cic.; calamitatum, Cic.; navium, *a dashing together,* Caes.; esp. *a hostile encounter*: concursus utriusque exercitus, Caes.; fig.: non posse sustinere concursum omnium philosophorum, Cic.

concussū, abl. sing. from concussus, m. (concutio), *by a shaking, by concussion*: Lucr.

concŭtĭo -cŭtĕre -cussi -cussum (cum/quatio), *to shake together* or *violently*, *agitate*.
  LIT., frameas, Tac.; caput, Ov.; of earthquakes: concussae urbes, Lucr.; terra ingenti motu concussa est, Liv.
  TRANSF., (**1**) *to shatter*, *disturb*, *impair*: rempublicam, Cic.; regnum, Liv. (**2**) *to alarm, trouble* : terrorem metum concutientem definiunt, Cic.; casu concussus acerbo, Verg. (**3**) *to arouse, excite* : pectus, Verg. (**4**) (cf. excutio) *to shake the clothes of*, and so *to search the person* : te ipsum concute, *examine yourself*, Hor.

condālĭum -i, n. (κονδύλιον), *a ring for slaves* : Pl.

condĕcet -ēre, impers. *it is proper, fit, decent* : capies quod te condecet, Pl.

condĕcŏro -are, *to adorn carefully* : ludos scaenicos, Ter.

condemnātor -ōris, m. (condemno), *one who causes condemnation, an accuser* : Tac.

condemno -are (cum/damno), *to condemn*.
  LIT., Cic., Tac.; the crime in the genit. : aliquem iniuriarum, Cic.; or with de : aliquem de ala, Cic.; or in abl. : eodem crimine, Cic.; the penalty in the genit. : capitis, Cic.; or abl. : capitali poenā, Suet.; or with ad : ad mortem, Tac.
  TRANSF., (**1**) of an accuser, *to urge* or *effect the condemnation of a person* : condemnare aliquem uno crimine, Cic. (**2**) in gen., *to blame, disapprove* : aliquem inertiae, Cic.; iniquitatis, Caes.; tuum factum non esse condemnatum iudicio amicorum, Cic.

condenso -are, *to make thick, press close together* : Varr.; condenseat (as from condenseo), Lucr.

condensus -a -um, *dense, thick* : puppes litore, Verg.; vallis arboribus condensa, Liv.

condĭcĭo -ōnis, f. (condico), *an arrangement, agreement.*
  Hence (**1**) *a condition, stipulation, provision, proviso* : non respuit condicionem, Caes.; condicionem aequissimam repudiare, Cic.; condicionem accipere, Cic.; ea condicione ut . . . (ne . . .), *on condition that . . .*, Cic.; sub condicionibus iis, Liv.; esp. *conditions of marriage, marriage contract, marriage* : aliam condicionem quaerere, Cic.; condicionem filiae quaerere, Liv.; nullius condicionis non habere potestatem, Nep.; also *relations with a mistress* : Ter., Cic. (**2**) *state, condition, place, circumstances* : infima servorum, Cic.; eā condicione nati sumus ut, Cic.; condicio imperii, Cic.; parem cum ceteris fortunae condicionem subire, Cic.; condicione super communi, Hor.

condĭco -dīcĕre -dixi -dictum, *to make arrangement with, agree to, fix, appoint, settle* : sic condicunt, Tac., Liv.; esp. : alicui condicere cenam or ad cenam, *to engage to dine with somebody*, Pl., Suet.; absol. : cum mihi condixisset, Cic. L.

condignus -a -um, *very worthy* : donum, Pl.; with abl., *very worthy of* : Pl.
  Adv. **condignē** : Pl.

condīmentum -i, n. (condio), *spice, seasoning, sauce, condiment.* LIT., cibi condimentum est fames, potionis sitis, Cic. TRANSF., Pl.; facetiae omnium sermonum condimenta, Cic.; severitas alicuius multis condimentis humanitatis mitigatur, Cic.

condĭo -ire (perhaps from condo).
  (**1**) *of fruits, etc., to pickle, to preserve* : oleas, Cato; hence *to embalm* : mortuos, Cic.
  (**2**) *to season, make savoury* : escas, Pl.; ius, Hor.; unguenta, Cic. TRANSF., *to season, temper* : orationem, Cic.; tristitiam temporum, Cic.
  ¶ Hence partic. **condītus** -a -um, *seasoned, savoury*. LIT., conditiora haec facit venatio, Cic. TRANSF., *seasoned, ornamented* : oratio lepore et festivitate conditior, Cic.

condiscĭpŭla -ae, f. *a female schoolfellow* : Mart.

condiscĭpŭlātus -ūs, m. (condiscipulus), *companionship in school* : Nep.

condiscĭpŭlus -i, m. *a schoolfellow* : Cic.

condisco -discĕre -dīdĭci, *to learn thoroughly* : modos, Hor.; with infin. : mihi paulo diligentius supplicare, Cic.; pauperiem pati, Hor.

condītĭo=condicio; q.v.

condĭtĭo -ōnis (condio). (**1**) *pickling* or *preserving of fruits* : Varr. (**2**) *a seasoning, making savoury* : ciborum, Cic.

condĭtor -ōris, m. (condo), *a founder* : urbis, Liv.; Romanae arcis, Verg. TRANSF., in gen., *contriver, composer, author* : Verg.; Romanae libertatis, Liv.; conditor et instructor convivii, Cic.; conditor Romani anni, of himself, *as author of the Fasti*, Ov.

condĭtōrĭum -i, n. (condo), *the place in which a corpse* or *its ashes are preserved* : Suet., Plin. L.

¹condĭtus -a -um, partic. of condo; q.v.

²condītus -a -um, partic. from condio; q.v.

condo -dĕre -dĭdi -dĭtum.
  (**1**) *to put together.* LIT., *to build, to found* : urbem Romam, Cic.; Liv; arces, Verg. TRANSF., in gen., *to form, establish* : Romanam gentem, Verg.; conlegium ad id novum, Liv.; and esp. *to compose, write* : carmen, Cic.; leges, Liv.; also *to write of* : tristia bella, Verg.; Caesaris acta, Ov.
  (**2**) *to put up, put away* a thing (or person) where it will be safe or unobserved. LIT., a, of things, *to store* : pecuniam, Cic.; litteras publicas in sanctiore aerario conditas habere, Cic.; aliquid domi suae conditum iam putare, Cic.; esp. of wine, fruits, etc. : frumentum, Cic. (cf. condio): b, of things, *to hide, withdraw* : caelum umbra, Verg.; caput inter nubila, Verg.; fig. : ensem in pectore, Verg. : c, of persons, *to hide* : se deserto in litore, Verg.; *to put, place* : aliquem in carcerem, Cic.; *to bury* : aliquem in sepulcro, Cic. TRANSF., of abstractions : a, *to store* : mandata corde, Cat., Cic., Verg. : b, *to hide* : iram, Tac.; conditae res futurae, Cic. : c, of time, *to pass, dispose of* : longos soles cantando, Verg.; Lucr., Hor., Liv.

condŏcĕfăcĭo -facĕre -fēci -factum, *to train, instruct, teach* : beluas, Cic.; animum, Cic.

condŏcĕo -dŏcēre -docui -doctum, *to train, instruct* : Pl.

condŏlesco -dŏlescĕre -dŏlŭi (doleo), *to suffer severely, to feel pain* : si pes condoluit, si dens, Cic.; latus ei dicenti condoluisse, Cic.; Pl., Hor.; also of mental pain : Cic., Ov.

condōnātĭo -ōnis (condono), *a giving away* : bonorum possessionumque, Cic.

condōno -are, *to give away, present.*
  LIT., agros suis latronibus, Cic.; consuli totam Achaiam, Cic.; of the praetor : alicui

hereditatem, *to award the inheritance*, Cic.; sometimes with acc. of gift and of recipient: Pl., Ter.

TRANSF., (1) *to give up to, sacrifice to*: se vitamque suam reipublicae, Sall.; condonari libidini muliebri, Cic. (2) *to forgive a debt*: pecunias creditas debitoribus, Cic.; hence *to overlook, forgive a fault*: alicui crimen, Cic.; *to forgive an injury for the sake of a third party*: praeterita se Divitiaco fratri condonare dicit, Caes.

condormio -ire, *to sleep soundly*: Suet.

condormisco -ĕre, *to go to sleep*: Pl.

Condrūsi -ōrum, m. *a Germanic people in Gallia Belgica.*

condūcĭbĭlis -e (conduco), *profitable, useful*: consilium ad eam rem, Pl.

condūco -dūcĕre -duxi -ductum.

(1) transit.: **a**, *to bring* or *lead together, collect*; of persons: exercitum in unum locum, Caes.; virgines unum in locum, Cic.; of things, *to bring together, unite, connect*: partes in unum, Lucr.; vineas, Cic.; cortice ramos, Ov. TRANSF., propositionem et adsumptionem in unum, Cic.: **b**, as commercial term, *to hire*: aliquem mercede, Cic.; consulem ad caedem faciendam, Cic.; of mercenaries: homines, Caes.; milites Gallos mercede, Liv.; of things: domum, hortum, Cic.; also, *to contract for, farm*: columnam faciendam, Cic.; portorium, Cic., Liv.

(2) intransit. (3rd person only), *to be of use, to profit, to serve*; with dat.: quae saluti tuae conducere arbitror, Cic.; Pl., Hor.; with ad and acc.: ad vitae commoditatem, Cic., Pl.; with in and acc.: in commune, Tac., Pl.

conductīcĭus -a -um (conduco), *hired*: fidicina, Pl.; exercitus, *mercenary*, Nep.

conductĭo -ōnis, f. (conduco). (1) *a bringing together, uniting*: Cic. (2) *hiring, farming*: fundi, Cic.; vectigalium, Liv.

conductor -ōris, m. (conduco). (1) *one who hires*: mercedes habitationum annuas conductoribus donare, Caes. (2) *a contractor*: histrionum, Pl.; operis, Cic. L.

condŭplĭcatio -onis, f. (conduplico), comically, *an embrace*: Pl.

condŭplĭco -are, *to double*: divitias, Lucr.; comically, of an embrace: corpora, Pl.

condūro -are, *to harden*: ferrum, Lucr.

cōnecto -nectĕre -nexŭi -nexum, *to fasten, tie together, connect.*

LIT., illae (apes) pedibus conexae ad limina pendent, Verg.; nodum, Cic., Ov.; Mosellam atque Ararim factā inter utrumque fossā, Tac.

TRANSF., in gen., *to join, unite*: persequere conexos his funeribus dies, *close-following*, Cic.; amicitia cum voluptate conectitur, Cic.; esp. (1) *to unite in discourse*: facilius est enim apta dissolvere quam dissipata conectere, Cic. (2) of logical connexion: omne quod ipsum ex se conexum sit verum esse, Cic. (3) *of personal relationship*: alicui conexus per adfinitatem, Tac.

¶ Hence partic. **cōnexus** -a -um, *joined, connected*; n. as subst. **cōnexum** -i, *logical connexion*: Cic.

cōnexio -onis, f. (conecto), *a binding together*; hence *a logical sequence*: Quint.

cōnexus -ūs, m. (conecto), *connexion, union*: Lucr.

confābŭlor -ari, dep. *to talk, converse*, or *talk over*: Pl., Ter.

confarrĕātĭo -ōnis, f. (confarreo), *an ancient and solemn form of marriage among the Romans, in which* panis farreus *was used*: Plin.

confarrĕo -are (far), *to marry by the ceremony of* confarreatio: patricios confarreatis parentibus genitos, Tac.

confātālis -e, *determined by the same fate*: Cic.

confectĭo -ōnis, f. (conficio). (1) *a producing, composing, completing*: huius libri, Cic.; belli, *successful completion*, Cic.; tributi, *complete exaction of*, Cic. (2) *consumption*: escarum, Cic.

confector -ōris, m. (conficio). (1) *one who produces, completes, finishes*: negotiorum, Cic.; totius belli, *victor in*, Cic. L. (2) *a destroyer, consumer*: confector et consumptor omnium ignis, Cic.; Suet.

confercĭo -fercire -fertum (farcio), *to press close together, compress, cram together*; usually in perf. partic. (with compar. and superl.) **confertus** -a -um. (1) *closely compressed, dense* (opp. *rarus*): confertae naves, Liv.; confertissima turba, Liv.; conferti milites, *in close formation*, Caes. (2) with abl., *stuffed with, full of*: cibo, Cic.; ingenti turbā conferta templa, Liv. TRANSF., vita plena et conferta voluptatibus, Cic.

¶ Hence adv. **confertim**, *compactly*: pugnare, Liv., Sall.

confĕro -ferre -tŭli -lātum.

(1) *to bring* or *put together, collect*. In gen.: sarcinas in unum locum, Caes.; capita, Cic.; gradum, *to walk beside*, Verg.; vires in unum, Liv.

Esp.: **a**, *to bring together money*, etc., *contribute*: tributa quotannis ex censu, Cic.; frumentum, Caes.; quadragena talenta quotannis Delum, Nep.: **b**, as milit. t. t., *to bring into hostile contact* or *collision*: Galli cum Fonteio ferrum ac manus contulerunt, Cic.; pedem cum pede, *or* conferre pedem, *to fight foot to foot*, Liv., Cic.; signa conferre, *to engage*, Cic.; se viro vir contulit, *man fought with man*, Verg.; absol.: mecum confer, ait, *fight with me*, Ov.; fig.: conferre lites, *to contend*, Hor.: **c**, of speech and ideas, *to interchange, discuss*: sermonem cum aliquo, Cic.; consilia, Liv.; iniurias, Tac.; tum si quid res feret, coram conferemus, Cic. L.: **d**, *to compare*: Gallicum cum Germanorum agro, Caes.; cum illius vita P. Sullae vobis notissima, Cic.; parva magnis, Cic.; vitam inter se utriusque, Cic.; Hor., Ov.: **e**, *to bring into a small compass, condense*: rem in pauca, Cic.

(2) *to bring to a particular place*. In gen., *to remove, transfer*: suas rationes et copias in illam provinciam, Cic.; se conferre, *to betake oneself, flee*: se in fugam, Cic., Pl., Caes., Liv.

Esp.: **a**, *to apply, devote*: pecuniam ad beneficentiam, Cic.; curam ad philosophiam, Cic.; so se conferre, *to devote oneself*: ad studium scribendi, Cic.: **b**, *to put off, postpone*: aliquid in longiorem diem, Caes.; Cic. L., Liv.: **c**, *to impute, attribute*: permulta in Plancium quae ab eo dicta non sunt, Cic.; culpam in aliquem, Cic.: **d**, *to transform, change*: aliquem in saxum, Ov

confertim, adv. from confercio; q.v.

confertus, partic. from confercio; q.v.

confervĕfăcĭo -făcĕre, *to make very hot, to melt*: Lucr.

confervesco -fervescĕre -ferbŭi, *to begin to boil, begin to glow.* TRANSF., mea cum conferbuit ira, Hor.

confessĭo -ōnis, f. (confiteor), *a confession, acknowledgment*: errati sui, Cic.; captae pecuniae, Cic.; adducere aliquem ad ignorationis confessionem, Cic.; exprimere ab aliquo confessionem culpae, Liv.; ea erat confessio caput rerum Romam esse, Liv.

confessus -a -um, partic. from confiteor; q.v.

confestim, adv. *immediately, without delay*: confestim huc advolare, Cic.; consequi, Cic.; patres consulere, Liv.; Verg.

confĭcĭens, partic. from conficio; q.v.

conficĭo -fĭcĕre -fēci -fectum (facio), *to make together.*

Hence (**1**) *to finish, make ready, bring about, accomplish*: soccos suā manu, Cic.; litteras, Cic.; sacra, Cic.; tantum facinus, Cic.; bellum, Cic.; his rebus confectis, Caes.; business, *to conclude a bargain* or *transaction*: negotium ex sententia, Cic.; rem sine pugna et sine vulnere, Caes.; fractiones, Cic.; pretium, *settle the price*, Cic.; absol.: confice cum Apella de columnis, *settle, arrange*, Cic. Esp.: **a**, of time or space, *to complete, pass through*: cursum, Cic. L.; iter ex sententia, Cic.; incredibili celeritate magnum spatium paucis diebus, Cic.; prope centum confecisse annos, Cic.; extremum vitae diem morte, Cic.; nondum hieme confecta, Caes.: **b**, *to produce, cause*: alicui reditum, *procure*, Cic.; motus animorum, Cic.; as philosoph. t. t.: ex quo conficitur ut, *it follows from this that*, Cic.

(**2**) *to get together, obtain*: permagnam ex illa re pecuniam confici posse, Caes.; frumentum, Liv.; reliquas legiones, quas ex novo delectu confecerat, Cic.; exercitus maximos, Cic.; tribum suam necessariis, *to gain over*, Cic.

(**3**) *to use up, exhaust, consume*: **a**, of food, *to chew, eat*: escas, Cic.; plures iam pavones confeci, quam tu pullos columbinos, Cic.; also *to digest*: confectus et consumptus cibus, Cic.: **b**, of property, *to waste, destroy*: patrimonium suum, Cic.: **c**, of living creatures, *to destroy, kill*: haec sica nuper ad regiam me paene confecit, Cic.: **d**, in gen., *to weaken, wear out*, esp. of persons and communities: vitae cupiditas, quae me conficit angoribus, Cic.; often in pass.: confici fame, frigore, lacrimis, curis, dolore, Cic.; confectus macie et squalore, Cic.; vulneribus, Caes.; aevo, Verg.; Britanniam, Cic.; praevalentis populi vires se ipse conficiunt, Liv.

¶ Hence partic. **confĭcĭens** -entis, *productive, effecting, efficient*: causae, Cic.; with genit.: cum civitate mihi res est acerrima et conficientissima litterarum, *that notes down everything carefully*, Cic.

confictĭo -ōnis, f. (confingo), *a fabrication, invention*: criminis, Cic.

confĭdens, partic. from confido; q.v.

confĭdentĕr, adv. from confido; q.v.

confĭdentĭa -ae, f. (confidens): **a**, *confidence*: confidentiam adferre hominibus, ap. Cic.: **b**, more frequently, *impudence, boldness,*

shamelessness: confidentia et temeritas tua, Cic.

confīdo -fīdĕre -fīsus sum, *to have complete trust, be assured*, absol.: nimis confidere, Cic.; with dat.: sibi, Cic.; legioni, Caes., Liv.; with abl.: militum virtute non satis, Cic.; with de: de salute urbis, Caes.; with acc. and infin., *to believe firmly*: id ita futurum esse confido, Cic.

¶ Hence partic. (with compar.: Pl., and superl: Verg.) **confĭdens** -entis, *confident, self-reliant*: Pl., Ter.; often in a bad sense, *bold, self-assured*: Cic., Hor.

Adv. **confĭdentĕr**, *confidently, boldly*, in good or bad sense: Pl., Ter.; confidentius dicere, Cic.

configo -fīgĕre -fixi -fixum. (**1**) *to fasten together, nail together*: transtra clavis ferreis, Caes. (**2**) *to pierce through, transfix with a weapon*. LIT., filios suos sagittis, Cic. TRANSF., *to pin down, paralyse*: ducentis confixus senatus consultis, Cic.

confingo -fingĕre -finxi -fictum, *to construct, form, fashion*. LIT., nidos, Plin. TRANSF., *to fabricate, feign, invent*: crimen incredibile, Cic.; crimina in aliquem, Cic., Liv.

confīnis -e. LIT., *having the same boundary, adjacent*: confines erant hi Senonibus, Caes.; caput collo confine, Ov.; m. as subst. **confīnis** -is, *a neighbour*: Mart. TRANSF., *nearly allied, similar*: studio confinia carmina vestro, Ov.

confīnĭum -i, n. (confinis). LIT., *a confine, common boundary, limit, border* (of countries or estates): Trevirorum, Caes.; convenit in omni re contrahenda vicinitatibus et confiniis aequum et facilem esse, *to those living near*, Cic.

TRANSF., *border-line, boundary*: confinia noctis, *twilight*, Ov.; breve confinium artis et falsi, Tac.

confirmātĭo -ōnis, f. (confirmo), *a thorough strengthening*; hence (**1**) of an institution, *a securing, making firm*: confirmatio perpetuae libertatis, Cic. (**2**) *consolation, encouragement, support*: neque enim confirmatione nostrā egebat virtus tua, Cic. L. (**3**) *confirming* or *verifying* of fact or statement: Caes., Cic.; so as rhet. t. t., *adducing of proofs*: Cic.

confirmātor -ōris, m. (confirmo), *one who confirms*: pecuniae, *a surety*, Cic.

confirmo -are, *to make firm, confirm, strengthen.* LIT., hoc nervos confirmari putant, Caes.; valetudinem, *to recover health*, Cic.; se confirmare, *to recover strength*, Cic. L.

TRANSF., (**1**) gen., *to strengthen, make lasting*: pacem, Cic.; consilia, *to support*, Caes.; confirmatis rebus, *firmly established*, Caes.; se transmarinis auxiliis, Caes.; so as polit. t. t., *to ratify*: acta Caesaris, Cic. L.; of the attitudes of persons, *to confirm*, in allegiance, etc.: iure iurando inter se, Caes.

(**2**) *to strengthen in mind, encourage*: confirmare et excitare adflictos animos, Cic.; erige te et confirma, *take courage*, Cic. L.; animos Gallorum verbis, Caes.

(**3**) *to confirm an assertion*; hence: **a**, *to corroborate, establish it*: nostra argumentis ac rationibus, Cic., Caes.: **b**, *to affirm, assert positively*: id omne ego me rei publicae causā suscepisse confirmo, Cic.

¶ Hence partic. (with compar.) **confirmātus** -a -um. (**1**) *encouraged, emboldened*: satis certus et confirmatus animus, Cic., Caes. (**2**) *certain*: in quibus (litteris) erat confirmatius idem illud, Cic.

confisco -are (fiscus). (**1**) *to lay up, preserve in a chest*: Suet. (**2**) *to appropriate to the imperial treasury, to confiscate*: Suet.; also of persons, *to deprive by confiscation*: Suet.

confīsĭo -ōnis, f. (confido), *confidence, assurance*: fidentia, id est firma animi confisio, Cic.

confĭtĕor -fĭtēri -fessus sum, dep. (fateor). (**1**) *to confess, admit, acknowledge*: divitias meas, Pl.; peccatum suum, Cic.; amorem nutrici, Ov.; se victos, Caes.; multa se ignorare, Cic.; aliquid de veneno, Cic.

(**2**) *to reveal, make known*: se, Ov.; vultibus iram, Ov.; confessa deam, *manifesting her divinity*, Verg.

¶ Hence partic. **confessus** -a -um. (**1**) in act. sense, *having confessed*; so m. as subst.: Sall. (**2**) in pass. sense, *undoubted, acknowledged, certain*: res manifesta, confessa, Cic.; hence: ex confesso, *confessedly*, Quint.; in confesso esse, Tac.; in confessum venire, *to be generally acknowledged, universally known*, Plin.

conflagro -are, *to blaze up, be well alight.* LIT., classis praedonum incendio conflagrabat, Cic. TRANSF., amoris flammā, Cic.; incendio invidiae, Cic.; Liv.

conflictĭo -ōnis, f. (confligo), *a striking together, collision, conflict*: corporum, Quint. TRANSF., causarum, Cic.

conflicto -are (intens. of confligo), *to strike together violently*; usually in pass., as (**1**) *to collide with, contend with*: conflictari cum adversā fortunā, Nep.; cum ingeniis eiusmodi, Ter.; once act. in same sense: Ter. (**2**) *to be grievously troubled, to be harassed, tormented*, usually with abl.: iniquissimis verbis, Cic.; magnā inopiā necessariarum rerum, Caes.; duriore fortunā, Cic.; difficultatibus, Liv.; so in act., *to harass*: Tac.

conflictu, abl. sing. from conflictus, m. (confligo), *by a striking together*: lapidum, Cic.

confligo -flīgĕre -flixi -flictum. (**1**) transit., *to strike or throw together*: corpora, Lucr. TRANSF., *to bring together in order to compare*: factum adversarii cum scripto, Cic.

(**2**) intransit., *to collide, clash*: illae (naves) graviter inter se incitatae conflixerunt, Caes.; hence in gen., *to come into conflict*: inter se, Caes.; cum hoste, Cic.; adversus classem, Nep.

conflo -are, *to blow together, to blow up.* Hence (**1**) *to blow into flame, kindle.* LIT., quorum operā id conflatum incendium, Liv. TRANSF., *to excite*: seditionem, Cic.; coniurationem, Suet.

(**2**) *to melt.* LIT., of metals: Plin.; falces in ensem, *to forge*, Verg.; of money, *to coin*: aut flare aut conflare pecuniam, Cic. TRANSF., *to forge, fabricate, put together* (often in bad sense): horum consensus conspirans et paene conflatus, Cic.; ut una ex duabus naturis conflata videatur, Cic.; exercitus perditorum civium clandestino scelere conflatus, Cic.; crimen, Cic.; alicui periculum,

Cic.; iudicia domi conflabant, pronuntiabant in foro, Liv.

conflŭo -flŭĕre -fluxi, *to flow together*: in unum, Cic., Lucr., Liv. TRANSF., *to stream* or *flock together*. (**1**) of persons: Athenas, Cic.; ad haec studia, Cic., Caes. (**2**) of abstractions: ad ipsos laus, honos, dignitas confluit, Cic.; Lucr., Ov.

¶ Hence partic. **conflŭens** -entis, *flowing together*: a confluente Rhodano castra movi, *from the confluence of the Rhône with the Arar*, ap. Cic. L.

So m. sing. or pl. as subst. **conflŭens** -entis or **conflŭentes** -ium, *the confluence* or *place of junction of two rivers*: Mosae et Rheni, Caes., Liv. As place-name **Conflŭentes** -ium, m. pl., *Coblenz*.

confŏdĭo -fŏdĕre -fōdi -fossum. (**1**) *to dig thoroughly*: hortum, Pl. (**2**) *to stab, pierce through*: iacentem, Liv.; (Ciceronem) de improviso domi suae, Sall.; confossus, Verg. TRANSF., tot iudiciis confossi praedamnatique, Liv.

conformātĭo -ōnis, f. (conformo), *a regular forming, conformation*; hence *form, shape.* LIT., lineamentorum, Cic. TRANSF., vocis, *expression*; verborum, *arrangement*, Cic.; esp. (**1**) as philosoph. t. t.: conformatio animi, *or simply* conformatio, *an idea*, Cic. (**2**) as rhet. t. t., *a figure of speech*: Cic., Quint.

conformo -are, *to form, put together.* LIT., mundum a natura conformatum esse, Cic.; ad maiora quaedam nos natura genuit et conformavit, Cic. TRANSF., *to adapt*: vocem secundum rationem rerum, Cic.; se ad voluntatem alicuius, Cic.

confossus -a -um, partic. (with compar.: Pl.) of confodio; q.v.

confrāgōsus -a -um, *rugged, uneven*: via, Liv.; n. pl. as subst., *uneven places*: Liv. TRANSF., rough, hard: Pl., Quint.

confrāgus -a -um=confragosus: Luc.

confrĕmo -frĕmĕre -frĕmŭi, *to murmur, make a noise*: conflremuere omnes, Ov.

confrĭco -frĭcare -frĭcŭi -frĭcātum, *to rub hard*: caput atque os suum unguento, Cic.; fig.: genua, in entreaty, Pl.

confringo -fringĕre -frēgi -fractum (frango), *to break in pieces*: digitos, Cic.; Pl., Liv. TRANSF., *to destroy, bring to naught*: consilia senatoria, Cic.

confŭgĭo -fŭgĕre -fūgi, *to fly to, take refuge with*: ad aliquem, ad *or* in aram, Cic.; in naves, Caes., Verg. TRANSF., *to have recourse to.* (**1**) of external support: ad alicuius misericordiam, Cic.; ad quem iudicum, Cic. (**2**) of expedients: patrias ad artes, Ov.; confugit illuc ut neget, Cic.; Ter.

confŭgĭum -i, n. (confugio), *a place of refuge*: Ov.

confulcio -fulcire -fultus, *to prop up*: Lucr.

confulgeo -ēre, *to shine brightly*: Pl.

confundo -fundĕre -fūdi -fūsum. (**1**) *to pour together, mingle, mix.* LIT., cum alicuius lacrimis lacrimas confundere nostras, Ov.; Pl., Cic., Verg. TRANSF., **a**, *to join together*: tantā multitudine confusā, Caes.; duo populi confusi in unum, Liv.; ea philosophia quae confundit vera cum falsis, Cic.: **b**, *to confuse, throw into disorder*: signa et ordines peditum atque equitum, Liv.; iura gentium, Liv.; particulas minutas primum

confusas, postea in ordinem adductas a
mente divinā, Cic.; vultum Lunae, *to
obscure*, Ov.: **c**, *to confuse, trouble, disturb,
upset*: confusa pudore, Ov.; audientium
animos, Liv.; maerore recenti confusus, Liv.;
quamvis digressu veteris confusus amici, Juv.
   (2) *to pour into*: cruor confusus in fossam,
Hor.; per quas lapsus cibus in eam venam
confunditur, Cic. TRANSF., est hoc quidem
in totam orationem confundendum, nec
minime in extremam, Cic.
   ¶ Hence partic. **confūsus** -a -um,
disorderly, confused: ita confusa est oratio,
ita perturbata, nihil ut sit primum, nihil
secundum, Cic.; strages, Verg.; verba, Ov.;
confusissimus mos, Suet.; esp. of mental
confusion, *embarrassed, troubled*: vultus, Liv.;
confusus animo, Liv.; facies confusior, Tac.
   Adv. (with compar.) **confūsē**, *confusedly*:
loqui, Cic.
confūsĭo -ōnis, f. (confundo). (1) *a mixing,
blending, union*: haec coniunctio confusioque
virtutum, Cic. (2) *confusion, disorder*:
temporum, Cic.; suffragiorum, *voting not in
the centuries, but man by man*, Cic.; religionum, Cic.; oris, *blushing*, Tac., Liv.
confūsus -a -um, partic. from confundo; q.v.
confūto -are, *to check the boiling of a liquid*,
hence TRANSF., (1) *to check, repress*: maximis doloribus adfectus eos ipsos inventorum
suorum memoriā et recordatione confutat,
Cic. (2) esp. by speech, *to put down, silence*:
audaciam alicuius, Cic.; argumenta Stoicorum, Cic.; Lucr., Liv.
congĕlo -are.
   (1) transit., *to freeze thoroughly*. LIT.,
Mart. TRANSF., *to harden, thicken*: rictus in
lapidem, Ov.
   (2) intransit., *to freeze up*. LIT., Ister con-
gelat, Ov. TRANSF., congelasse nostrum amicum laetabar otio, *had become inactive*, Cic.;
lingua, Ov.
congĕmĭno -are, *to double, redouble*: ictus
crebros ensibus, Verg.
congĕmo -gĕmĕre -gĕmŭi. (1) intransit., *to
sigh* or *groan loudly*: congemuit senatus
frequens, Cic., Verg. (2) transit., *to bewail,
lament*: mortem, Lucr.
congĕr -gri, m. (γόγγρος), *a sea* or *conger
eel*: Pl.
congĕrĭēs -ēi, f. (congero). Gen., *a heap,
mass*: lapidum, Liv. Esp. (1) *a heap of wood,
a wood pile*: Ov. (2) *chaos*: Ov. (3) as rhet.
t. t., *accumulation*: Quint.
congĕro -gĕrĕre -gessi -gestum, *to carry
together, bring together, collect.*
   LIT., undique quod idoneum ad muniendum putarent, Nep.; salis magnam viam ex
proximis salinis, Caes.; maximam vim auri
atque argenti in regnum suum, Cic.; undique
saccos, Hor.; hence (1) in gen., *to pile up,
accumulate*: alicui viaticum, Cic.; auri
pondus, Ov.; oscula, Ov. (2) esp., *to build
up*: aram sepulcri acribus; so of birds:
locus aeriae quo congessere palumbes, *have
built their nests*, Verg.
   TRANSF., (1) in discourse, *to bring together,
comprise*: turbam patronorum in hunc
sermonem, Cic.; also *to repeat*: argumenta,
Quint. (2) *to heap upon*: ingentia beneficia
in aliquem, Liv.; omnia ornamenta ad
aliquem, Cic.; maledicta in aliquem, Cic.;

omnes vastati agri periculorumque imminentium causas in aliquem, *to ascribe, impute*,
Cic.
congestīcĭus -a -um (congero), *heaped up,
artificially brought together*: agger, Caes.
congestus -ūs, m. (congero), *a collecting,
heaping together.*
   LIT., municipia congestu copiarum vasta-
bantur, Tac.; of birds, *building nests*: herbam
(exstitisse) avium congestu, Cic.
   TRANSF., *that which is brought together,
a heap, mass*: lapidum, Tac., Lucr.
congiārĭum -i, n. sing. from adj. congiarius
(sc. donum), *a donation among the people*,
originally of a congius of wine, oil, etc., to
each person: Liv. TRANSF., *a donation in
money*. (1) *among the soldiers*: Cic. (2) *among
the people*: Tac. (3) *among private friends*:
ap. Cic. L., Liv.
congĭus -i, m. *a Roman measure for liquids,
containing six sextarii*: Liv.
conglăcĭo -are. Intransit. LIT., *to freeze*:
frigoribus conglaciat aqua, Cic. TRANSF.,
Curioni nostro tribunatus conglaciat, *passes
inactively*, ap. Cic. L.
   Transit., *to turn to ice*: Plin.
conglŏbātĭo -ōnis, f. (conglobo), *a heaping,
pressing, crowding together*: Tac.
conglŏbo -are (globus), *to form into a ball* or
sphere. LIT., mare conglobatur undique
aequabiliter, Cic.; figura conglobata, Cic.
TRANSF., *to press together in a mass* or *crowd*:
catervatim uti quosque fors conglobaverat,
Sall.; se in forum, Liv.; conglobata in unum
multitudo, Liv.; maxime definitiones valent
conglobatae, *accumulated*, Cic.
conglŏmĕro -are, *to roll, twist, entangle
together*: Lucr.
conglūtĭnātĭo -ōnis, f. (conglutino), *a sticking,
cementing together*. LIT., Cic. TRANSF.,
connexion, joining together: verborum, Cic.
conglūtĭno -are, *to stick together, cement
together*. LIT., Plin. TRANSF., *to connect,
bind closely*: amicitias, Cic.; voluntates
nostras consuetudine, Cic.; conglutinare ut,
so to arrange matters that . . ., Pl.
congraeco -are (graecus), *to spend like a Greek*,
i.e. *to squander*: Pl.
congrātŭlor -ari, dep. *to wish one another joy,
congratulate*: congratulantur libertatem con-
cordiamque civitati restitutam, Liv.; Pl.
congrĕdĭor -grĕdi -gressus, dep. (gradior), *to
meet*: cum aliquo, Cic.; inter se, Liv.; locus,
ubi congressi sunt, Cic.; congredi sua sponte
cum finitimis proelio, Cic.; with dat.: impar
congressus Achilli, Verg.; *to dispute in words,
argue*: congredi cum Academico, Cic.
congrĕgābĭlis -e (congrego), *sociable, inclined
to collect*: examina apium, Cic.
congrĕgātĭo -ōnis, f. (congrego), *an assembling
together, society, union*: nos ad congrega-
tionem hominum et ad societatem com-
munitatemque generis humani esse natos,
Cic.
congrĕgo -are (grex).
   (1) *to collect into a flock*: oves, Plin.; refl.,
se congregare, or pass., congregari, in a
middle sense, *to form into flocks*: apium
examina congregantur, *form themselves into
swarms*, Cic.
   (2) of men, *to collect, gather together*:
dispersos homines in unum locum, Cic.;

refl., se congregare, and pass., congregari, in middle sense, *to assemble* : congregari in fano commentandi causa, Cic.

congressĭo -ōnis, f. (congredior). (**1**) *a meeting* : Cic. (**2**) *intercourse, association* : aliquem ab alicuius non modo familiaritate, sed etiam congressione prohibere, Cic.

congressus -ūs, m. (congredior), *a meeting* ; hence (**1**) *a friendly meeting, social intercourse* : alicuius aditum, congressum, sermonem fugere, Cic., Liv.; often in plur. : congressus hominum fugere atque odisse, Cic., Verg. TRANSF., of lifeless things, *combination* : Lucr.

(**2**) *a hostile encounter, combat* : ante congressum, Cic.; primo congressu terga vertere nostros cogere, Caes.; Verg.

congrŭentĭa -ae, f. (congruo), *agreement, harmony, symmetry, proportion* : Suet., Plin. L.

congrŭo -ŭĕre -ŭi, *to run together, come together, meet.*

LIT., ut vicesimo anno ad metam eandem solis, unde orsi essent, dies congruerent, Liv.

TRANSF., (**1**) of time, *to coincide* : qui suos dies mensesque congruere volunt cum solis lunaeque ratione, Cic.; Liv., Tac. (**2**) *to be suited, fitted to, correspond with, agree* : sensus nostri ut in pace semper, sic tum etiam in bello congruebant, Cic.; with cum and the abl. : eius sermo cum tuis litteris valde congruit, Cic.; with dat. : non omni causae nec auditori neque personae neque tempori congruere orationis unum genus, Cic.; with inter se : multae causae inter se congruere videntur, Cic.

¶ Hence partic. **congrŭens** -entis. (**1**) *agreeing, fit, appropriate, suitable* : vultus et gestus congruens et apta, Cic.; with cum : gestus cum sententiis congruens, Cic.; with dat. : actiones virtutibus congruentes, Cic. (**2**) *harmonious, uniform* : is concentus ex dissimillimarum vocum moderatione concors tamen efficitur et congruens, Cic.; clamor congruens, *unanimous*, Liv.

Adv. **congrŭentĕr,** *aptly, agreeably, suitably* : congruenter naturae convenienterque vivere, Cic.

congrŭus -a -um (congruo), *agreeing, fit, suitable* : sermo cum illā, Pl.

conicio -icĕre -iēci -iectum (iacio).

(**1**) *to throw together.* LIT., sarcinas in medium, Liv.; sortes in hydriam, Cic.; sortem conicere, *to cast lots*, Cic.; aggerem in munitionem, Caes. TRANSF., mentally, *to 'put two and two together', to conjecture, guess* : de matre suavianda ex oraculo acute arguteque, Cic.; belle coniecta, *clever surmises*, Cic.; esp. *to interpret dreams* or *omens* : somnium, Pl.; omen, Cic.

(**2**) *to throw, to hurl*, in gen. LIT., of things : tela in nostros, Caes.; gladium in adversum os, Caes.; cum haec navis invitis nautis vi tempestatis in portum coniecta sit, Cic.; of persons : quem in carcerem, Cic.; in vincula, Cic.; in lautumias, Cic.; esp. with refl., se conicere, *to betake oneself, flee* : in portum, in fugam, in castra alicuius, Cic.; in latebras, Verg. TRANSF., naves coniectae in noctem, *benighted*, Caes.; se in noctem, *to hasten away under cover of night*, Cic.; forensem turbam in quattuor tribus, *to divide*, Liv.;

aliquem ex occultis insidiis ad apertum latrocinium, *to force*, Cic.; crimina in tuam diligentiam, *bring against*, Cic.; tantam pecuniam in propylaea, *to spend*, Cic.; haec verba in interdictum, *to introduce*, Cic.

coniectĭo -ōnis, f. (conicio), *a hurling, throwing* : telorum, Cic. TRANSF., *conjectural interpretation* : somniorum, Pl.

coniecto -are (freq. of conicio), *to throw together.* TRANSF., *to 'put two and two together', conclude, infer, conjecture, surmise, guess at* : coniectantes iter, Liv.; rem eventu, Liv.; Caesar coniectans eum Aegyptum iter habere, Caes.; de imperio, Tac.

coniector -ōris, m. (conicio), *an interpreter of dreams* or *riddles* : Isiaci coniectores, *the priests of Isis*, Cic.; Pl.

coniectrix -īcis, f. (coniector), *a female interpreter of dreams* or *riddles* : Pl.

coniectūra -ae, f. (conicio), *a guess, conjecture, inference.* Gen., coniecturam adhibere, Cic.; aberrare coniectura, *to be mistaken in*, Cic.; coniecturam facere (*or* capere) ex (*or* de) aliqua re, Cic.; adferre coniecturam, Cic.; coniectura adsequi *or* consequi, Cic.; quantum coniecturā auguramur, Cic. Esp. *interpretation of dreams and omens, divination, soothsaying* : facilis coniectura huius somnii, Pl.; Cic., Ov.

coniectūrālis -e (coniectura), *relating to conjecture, conjectural* : controversia, Cic.; Quint.

coniectus -ūs, m. (conicio), *a throwing* or *throwing together.* LIT., materiai, Lucr.; lapidum, Cic.; venire ad teli coniectum, *to come within range*, Liv.; ne primum quidem coniectum telorum ferre, Liv.

TRANSF., *casting* or *directing towards* : vester in me animorum oculorumque coniectus, Cic.

cōnĭfĕr -fĕra -fĕrum (conus/fero), *cone-bearing* : cyparissi, Verg.

cōnĭgĕr (conus/gero), *cone-bearing* : pinus, Cat.

cōnītor -nīti -nīsus *or* -nixus sum, dep. LIT., *to lean* or *press hard against* : Cic. poet.

TRANSF., *to make any great effort.* (**1**) *physical* : in summum iugum, *to clamber up*, Caes.; in unum locum conixi, Liv.; with infin. : invadere hostem, Liv.; with ut and the subj. : infantes conituntur, sese ut erigant, Cic.; of offspring, *to bring forth with difficulty* : Verg. (**2**) *mental* : quantum animo coniti potes, Cic.; ad convincendum eum, Tac.

coniŭgālis -e (coniunx), *relating to marriage, conjugal* : amor, Tac.

coniŭgātĭo -ōnis, f. (coniugo), *the etymological connexion of words* : Cic.

coniŭgātor -ōris, m. (coniugo), *one who connects, unites* : boni amoris, Cat.

coniŭgĭālis -e (coniugium), *relating to marriage, conjugal* : festa, Ov.

coniŭgĭum -i̯, n. (coniunx), *a close connexion, union* : corporis atque animae, Lucr. TRANSF., (**1**) *marriage, wedlock* : Tulliae meae, Cic.; tota domus coniugo et stirpe coniungitur, Cic.; poet., of animals : Ov. (**2**) *husband* : Prop.; *wife* : Verg., Tac.

coniŭgo -are, *to bind together, connect* : est ea iucundissima amicitia, quam similitudo morum coniugavit, Cic.; coniugata verba, *words etymologically connected*, Cic.

coniunctĭo -ōnis, f. (coniungo), *uniting, joining together*: portuum, Cic. TRANSF., (1) of things: coniunctio confusioque naturae, Cic.; as rhet. and philosoph. t. t., *connexion of ideas*: Cic.; as grammat. t. t., *a connecting particle, conjunction*: cum demptis coniunctionibus dissolute plura dicuntur, Cic. (2) of persons, *union, association, connexion*: societas coniunctioque humana, Cic.; citius cum eo veterem coniunctionem dirimere quam novam conciliare, Cic.; Pompeium a Caesaris coniunctione avocare, Cic.; summa nostra coniunctio et familiaritas, Cic.; esp. *connexion by blood* or *marriage*: coniunctio sanguinis, Cic.; coniunctio adfinitatis, Cic.

coniungo -iungĕre -iunxi -iunctum, *to join together*, constr. with dat., cum and abl., or inter se; often also with an instrumental abl. LIT., navi onerariae alteram, Caes.; calamos plures cerā, Verg.; dextram dextrae, Ov.; eam epistulam cum hac epistula, Cic.; hunc montem murus circumdatus arcem efficit et cum oppido coniungit, Caes. TRANSF., *to bring into connexion, unite, join*: noctem diei, Caes.; causam alicuius cum communi salute, Cic.; coniungere bellum, *to undertake in common*, Cic.; amicitias, *to form*, Cic.; esp. *to unite persons by marriage, friendship, alliance*, etc.: filias suas filiis alicuius matrimonio, Liv.; me tibi studia communia coniungunt, Cic. ¶ Hence partic. (with compar. and superl.) **coniunctus** -a -um, *connected, joined.* (1) of place: sublicae cum omni opere coniunctae, Caes.; with dat. *bordering on, near*: theatrum coniunctum domui, Caes.; Paphlagonia coniuncta Cappadociae, Nep. (2) of time, *contemporary with*: coniunctus igitur Sulpicii aetati P. Antistius fuit, Cic. (3) of other relations, *connected with, agreeing with, proportioned to*: prudentia cum iustitiā, Cic.; talis simulatio est vanitati coniunctior, *is more nearly allied*, Cic.; continuata coniunctaque verba, Cic.; esp. of persons, *connected by blood* or *marriage* or *friendship*: homines benevolentiā coniuncti, Cic.; homo mihi coniunctus fidissimā gratiā, Cic.; inter se coniunctissimos, Cic.; tam coniuncta populo Romano civitas, Caes.; sanguine coniuncti, Nep.; civium Romanorum omnium sanguis coniunctus existimandus est, Cic. N. as subst. **coniunctum** -i. (1) *an inherent property* or *quality*: Lucr. (2) rhet. t. t., *connexion*: Cic. Adv. **coniunctē** (with compar. and superl.). (1) *conjointly, in connexion*: coniuncte cum reliquis rebus nostra contexere, Cic.; elatum aliquid, *hypothetically* (opp. simpliciter, *categorically*), Cic. (2) *intimately, on terms of friendship*: cum aliquo vivere coniunctissime et amantissime, Cic. Adv. **coniunctim**, *conjointly, in common*: huius omnis pecuniae coniunctim ratio habetur, Caes.; Liv.

coniunx (coniux) -iŭgis, c. (coniungo), *spouse, wife*: Cic., Hor.; more rarely, *husband*: Cic., Verg.; plur. *a married pair*: Cat.; poet. *a betrothed virgin, bride*: Verg., Ov.

coniūrātĭo -ōnis, f. (coniuro), *swearing together*; hence (1) *union confirmed by an oath*: coniuratio Acarnanica, Liv.; coniurationem

nobilitatis facere, Caes. (2) in bad sense, *conspiracy, plot*: coniuratio Catilinae, Sall.; in ea coniuratione esse, *to be implicated in*, Sall.; coniurationem facere contra rempublicam, Cic. Menton. *the conspirators*: voces coniurationis tuae, Cic.

coniuro -are, *to swear together*. (1) in neutral or good sense, *to take an oath, to unite together by oath*: omne coniurat Latium, Verg.; barbari coniurare, obsides inter se dare coeperunt, Caes.; with acc. and infin.: per suos principes inter se coniurant nihil nisi communi consilio acturos, Caes. (2) in bad sense, *to plot, conspire*: coniurasse supra septem millia virorum ac mulierum, Liv.; ii, quibuscum coniurasti, Cic.; principes inter se coniurant, Sall.; contra rempublicam, Cic.; adversus patriam, Liv.; de interficiendo Pompeio, Cic.; cum aliquo in omne flagitium et facinus, Liv.; with infin.: patriam incendere, Sall.; with ut and subj.: urbem ut incenderent, Liv. ¶ Hence perf. partic. (in act. sense) **coniūrātus** -a -um, *sworn, united by an oath*: Cic., Verg., Ov. M. pl. as subst. **coniūrāti** -orum, *conspirators*: Cic.

coniux = coniunx; q.v.

cōnīveo -nīvēre -nīvi or -nixi, *to close the eyes, to wink, blink with the eyes.* LIT., oculis somno coniventibus, Cic.; altero oculo, Cic.; poet., of the sun or moon: quasi conivent, Lucr. TRANSF., *to wink at, let pass unnoticed*: consulibus si non adiuvantibus, at coniventibus certe, Cic.; with in and the abl.: quibusdam etiam in rebus coniveo, Cic.

conlābasco -ĕre (labo), *to begin to fall, to totter*: Pl.

conlăbĕfacto -are, *to cause to totter*: Ov.; used also of the liquefaction of hard bodies: Lucr.

conlăbĕfīo -fĭĕri -factus, *to be made to totter* or *fall*. LIT., altera (navis), praefracto rostro tota conlabefieret, *was dashed to pieces*, Caes.; igni conlabefacta, *melted*, Lucr. TRANSF., a Themistocle conlabefactus, *overthrown*, Nep.

conlābor -labi -lapsus, dep. *to fall down, sink down, collapse.* LIT., of buildings, towns, etc.: conlapsa quaedam ruinis sunt, Liv.; Verg., Tac.; of persons, *to fall down in a swoon* or *death*: cecidit conlapsus in artus, Verg.; Tac. TRANSF., *to fall, sink*: Pl., Verg.

conlăcĕrātus -a -um (lacero), *very much lacerated* or *torn*: corpus, Tac.

conlăcrĭmātĭo -ōnis, f. (conlacrimo), *a weeping together*: Cic.

conlăcrĭmo -are, *to weep together* or *weep much*: Pl., Cic.; transit., *to bemoan, weep for very much*: histrio casum meum totiens conlacrimavit, Cic.

conlactĕus -i, m. **-a** -ae, f. *a foster-brother* or *sister*: Juv.

conlātĭo -ōnis, f. (confero), *a bringing together*. LIT., (1) in war: signorum, *a battle*, Cic. (2) of money, *a contribution, collection*: stipis aut decimae, Liv.; Tac. TRANSF., (1) *a combination*: malitiarum, Pl. (2) *comparison, simile, analogy*: conlatio est oratio rem cum re ex similitudine conferens, Cic.

conlātīvus -a -um (confero), *brought together, united*: Pl.

conlātor -ōris, m. (confero), *a contributor*: Pl.

conlātus -a -um, partic. from confero; q.v.

conlaudātĭo -ōnis, f. (conlaudo), found only in abl. sing.; *strong* or *hearty praise*: Cic.

conlaudo -are, *to praise very much*: orationem satis multis verbis, Cic.; Pl., Ter., Liv.

conlaxo -are, *to widen, extend*: Lucr.

conlecta -ae, f. (¹conligo, partic. conlectus), *a contribution in money*: conlectam a conviva exigere, Cic.

conlectāneus -a -um (¹conligo), *collected*: Plin., Suet.

conlectīcius -a -um (¹conligo), *gathered together*: exercitus, *quickly levied*, Cic. L.

conlectĭo -ōnis, f. (¹conligo), *a collecting, gathering together, collection*: membrorum, Cic.

TRANSF., (1) in rhetoric, *a brief recapitulation*: Cic. (2) in logic, *a conclusion, inference*: Sen., Quint.

conlēga -ae, m. (lĕgo), *one who is chosen with another, a colleague, partner in office*: alicuius conlegam in quaestura fuisse, Cic.; Hor., Tac.

TRANSF., in gen., *an associate*: Pl., Cic., Juv.

conlēgĭum -i, n. (conlega).

(1) abstr., *colleagueship, the connexion between those who jointly fill the same office*: P. Decius per tot conlegia expertus, Liv., Tac.

(2) concr., *persons united in colleagueship, a body, guild, corporation, college*; of magistrates: praetorum, tribunorum, Cic.; of priests: pontificum, augurum, Cic.; *a political club*: innumerabilia quaedam conlegia ex omni faece urbis ac servitio constituta, Cic.; *a trade guild*: mercatorum, Liv.; in gen., *a band, body*: ambubaiarum, Hor.

conlēvo -are, *to make quite smooth*: Sen., Plin.

conlībertus -i, m. *a fellow-freedman*: Pl.

conlĭbet or **conlŭbet** -bēre -bŭit or -bĭtum est (cum/lubet or libet), impers. verb, used only in perfect and tenses formed from perfect; *it pleases, is agreeable*: simul ac mihi conlibitum sit de te cogitare, Cic.; Pl., Ter., Hor.

conlīdo -līdĕre -līsi -līsum (laedo), *to strike together, dash together*.

LIT., umor ita mollis est, ut facile comprimi conlidique possit, Cic.; Lucr., Ov.; esp. in past partic. conlisus: Cic.

TRANSF., *to bring into hostile collision*: Graecia barbariae lento conlisa duello, Hor.

conlĭgātĭo -ōnis, f. (²conligo), *a binding together, connexion*: causarum omnium, Cic.

¹conlĭgo -lĭgĕre -lēgi -lectum (lĕgo), *to gather* or *bring together, collect*.

LIT., (1) of things: radices, Cic.; vasa, *to pack up*, Liv. (2) of persons: ex agris ingentem numerum perditorum hominum, Cic.; milites, Cic., Liv. (3) *to gather into a smaller space, contract*: pallium, Pl.; togam, Mart.; se conlegit in arma, *shrank into cover behind*, Verg.

TRANSF., (1) *to gather together*: causae, Pl.; dicta, Cic.; hence *to gain, acquire*: ex hoc labore magnam gratiam magnamque dignitatem, Cic. (2) conligere se, *or* animum, *or* mentem, *to compose oneself, gain courage*: se ex timore, Caes. (3) in the mind, *to put together*: maximarum civitatum veteres animo calamitates conligo, Cic.; hence *to infer, conclude*: bene etiam conligit haec pueris et mulierculis esse grata, Cic.; ex eo

conligere potes, Cic. L.; in pass., of numbers, *to be reckoned* (post-Aug.): centum et viginti anni ab interitu Ciceronis in hunc diem conliguntur, Tac.

²conlĭgo -are (ligo), *to bind, tie, fasten together*.

LIT., manus, Cic., Liv.; omne conligatum solvi potest, Cic.

TRANSF., (1) in gen., *to connect*: res omnes inter se aptae conligataeque, Cic.; esp. in speech or writing: septingentorum annorum memoriam uno libro, Cic.; ut verbis conligentur sententiae, Cic. (2) *to detain, hinder, stop*: aliquem in Graecia, Cic.; impetum furentis vitae suae periculo, Cic.

conlĭnĕo -are, *to direct in a straight line*: hastam aut sagittam, Cic.; absol.: quis est enim qui totum diem iaculans non aliquando conlineet? *hits the mark*, Cic.

conlĭno -lĭnĕre -lēvi -lĭtum, *to besmear, daub*: crines pulvere, Hor., Ov. TRANSF., Pl.

conlĭquĕfactus -a -um (liquefio), *liquefied, melted*: Cic.

conlŏcātĭo -ōnis, f. (conloco). (1) *a placing, arrangement*: siderum, Cic.; esp. in speech or writing, *arrangement, order*: verborum, Cic.; argumentorum, Cic.; bene structam conlocationem dissolvere, Cic. (2) *a giving in marriage*: filiae, Cic.

conlŏco -are, *to place, lay, set, arrange*.

LIT., (1) of persons: aliquem in curru, Cic.; in latebris, Verg.; as milit. t. t., *to station*: duas legiones et omnia auxilia in summo iugo, Caes.; alicui insidias ante fundum suum, Cic.; *to billet, quarter*: exercitum in hibernis, Caes. (2) of things: tabulas bene pictas in bono lumine, Cic.; simulacrum Victoriae ante ipsam Minervam, Caes.; sedes ac domicilium, Cic.; chlamydem ut pendeat apte, *to settle*, Ov.

TRANSF., (1) of persons, *to settle, place*: in eius tetrarchia unum ex Graecis comitibus suis, Cic.; aliquem in patrimonio suo, Cic.; aliquem in amplissimo consilio et in altissimo gradu dignitatis, Cic.; esp. of women, *to settle in marriage*: aliquam in matrimonium, Cic.; alicuius filio filiam suam, Cic. (2) of things: **a,** *to arrange, settle*: res eae quae agentur aut dicentur, suo loco conlocandae, Cic.; verba diligenter conlocata, Cic.; rem militarem, Cic.: **b,** *to lay out, place, employ*: in aliquo magnam spem, Cic.; adulescentiam suam in amore atque voluptatibus, Cic.; esp. of money, *to spend, invest*: pecuniam in praediis, Cic.; patrimonium in reipublicae salute, Cic.

conlŏcŭplēto -are, *to enrich*: Ter.

conlŏcūtĭo -ōnis, f. (conloquor), *conversation*: conlocutiones familiarissimae cum aliquo, Cic.

conlŏquĭum -i, n. (conloquor), *talk, conversation, colloquy, conference*: ad conloquium evocare, Cic.; congredi, Liv.; conloquia secreta serere cum aliquo, Liv.; clandestina conloquia cum hostibus, Cic.; conloquium expetere, Caes.; dare, Liv.; inter se habere, Caes.; dirimere, Caes.; interrumpere, Caes.; in alicuius congressum conloquiumque pervenire, Cic.

conlŏquor -loqui -locutus, dep. *to speak, talk, converse with anyone, to treat* or *negotiate with*: cum aliquo, Ter., Caes., Cic.; inter se, Cic.; per litteras, Cic.

conlūcĕo -ēre, *to shine on all sides, to be completely illuminated.* LIT., sol qui tam longe lateque conluceat, Cic.; conlucent moenia flammis, Verg. TRANSF., vidi conlucere omnia furtis tuis, Cic.; floribus agri, Ov.

conlūdo -lūdĕre -lūsi -lūsum. LIT., *to play with*: paribus, Hor. TRANSF., *to have a secret understanding with, to act in collusion*: Cic.

conlŭo -lŭĕre -lŭi -lūtum, *to wash thoroughly, rinse*: os, Plin.; ora, *to quench the thirst*, Ov.

conlūsĭo -ōnis, f. (conludo), *collusion, a secret understanding*: cum aliquo, Cic.

conlūsor -ōris, m. (conludo), *a play-fellow*; esp. *a fellow-gambler*: Cic.

conlustro -are, *to illuminate on all sides*: sol omnia clarissima luce conlustrans, Cic.; in picturis alios opaca, alios conlustrata delectant, *brilliant colouring*, Cic. TRANSF., *to survey, look at on all sides*: omnia oculis, Cic.

conlŭtŭlento -are, *to dirty* or *defile all over*: Pl.

conlŭvĭo -ōnis (Cic., Liv.) and **conlŭvĭēs** -ēi (Tac.), f. (conluo), *a flowing together*, or *collection of impurities, filth*: Plin. TRANSF., *rabble, medley, offscourings*: omnium scelerum, Cic.; ex hac turba et conluvione discedam, Cic.; conluvies nationum, Tac.

conm-, *see* comm-.

conn-, *see* cōn-.

Cŏnōn -ōnis, m. (Κόνων). (1) *an Athenian admiral, active about* A.D. 400. (2) *a mathematician and astronomer of Samos, in the third century* B.C.

cōnōpēum -i, n. (κωνωπεῖον) or **cōnōpĭum** -i, n. *a net to keep off gnats* or *mosquitoes*: Hor., Juv.

cōnor -ari, dep. *to undertake, endeavour, attempt, exert oneself, strive*; with acc.: opus magnum, Cic.; rem, Liv.; plurima, Verg.; with infin.: facere id quod constituerant, Caes.; ii qui haec delere conati sunt, Cic.; Hor.

conp-, *see* comp-.

conquassātĭo -ōnis, f. (conquasso), *a violent shaking*: totius valetudinis corporis, Cic.

conquasso -are, *to shake thoroughly, shatter*: conquassatur enim tum mens, Lucr.; Apulia maximis terrae motibus conquassata, Cic. TRANSF., conquassatas exteras nationes illius anni furore, Cic.

conquĕror -quĕri -questus, dep. *to complain loudly of*: fortunas suas, Pl.; bonorum direptiones, Cic.; iniuriam, Liv.; se dissolvi, Lucr.; de istius improbitate, Cic.; conqueror an sileam? Ov.

conquestĭo -ōnis, f. (conqueror), *a loud complaint*: ubi nullum auxilium est, nulla conquestio, Cic.; in rhetoric: conquestio est oratio auditorum misericordiam captans, Cic.

conquestū, abl. sing. as from conquestus, m. (conqueror), *by loud complaint*: Liv.

conquĭesco -quĭescĕre -quĭēvi -quĭētum, *to rest thoroughly, take rest, repose.* LIT., *to rest bodily*: videmus ut conquiescere ne infantes quidem possint, Cic.; haec (impedimenta) conquiescere vetuit, to *rest from a march*, Caes.; conquiescere meridie, *to sleep*, Caes.

TRANSF., *to be still, quiet, to take repose, stop*: imbre conquiescente, Liv.; conquiescit mercatorum navigatio, *is stopped*, Cic.;

conquiescere a continuis bellis et victoriis, Cic.; in nostris studiis libentissime conquiescimus, *we find recreation*, Cic. L.

conquīnisco -ĕre, *to squat, stoop down*: Pl.

conquīro -quīrĕre -quīsivi -quīsitum (quaero), *to seek for, to bring together, to collect, get together.*

LIT., sagittarios, Caes.; naves, Caes.; libros, Liv.; pecuniam, Liv.; also of individual things or persons, *to search for*: aliquem totā provinciā, Cic.

TRANSF., voluptatem conquirere et comparare, Cic.; suavitates, Cic.

¶ Hence partic. **conquīsītus** -a -um, *sought after, selected, chosen, costly*: mensas conquisitissimis epulis exstruere, Cic.

conquīsītĭo -ōnis, f. (conquiro), *search, collection*: pecuniarum, Tac.; talium librorum, Liv.; esp. *a levying of soldiers, conscription*: exercitus durissimā conquisitione confectus, Cic.; Liv.

conquīsītor -ōris, m. (conquiro). (1) *a recruiting officer*: Cic., Liv. (2) *a claqueur*: Pl.

conr-=corr-; q.v.

consaepĭo -saepire -saepsi -saeptum, *to fence round, to hedge in*: Suet.; esp. as partic. **consaeptus** -a -um, *fenced round*: ager, Cic.; n. as subst. **consaeptum** -i, *an enclosure*: Liv.

consălūtātĭo -ōnis, f. (consaluto), *a mutual salutation of several persons*: forensis, Cic. L.; Tac.

consălūto -are, *to greet together, hail, salute*: inter se amicissime, Cic.; with double acc.: aliquem dictatorem, Liv.; eam Volumniam, Cic.; Tac.

consānesco -sānescĕre -sānŭi, *to become healthy, to get well*: illa quae consanuisse videbantur, Cic. L.

consanguĭnĕus -a -um, *related by blood, brotherly, sisterly*: umbrae, Ov. Generally as subst. **consanguĭnĕus** -i, m. *brother*: Cic. L.; fig.: consanguineus Leti Sopor, Verg.; **consanguĭnĕa** -ae, f. *sister*: Cat.; plur. **consanguĭnĕi** -orum, m. *relations*: necessarii et consanguinei Aeduorum, Caes.

consanguĭnĭtās -ātis, f. (consanguineus), *relationship by blood, consanguinity*: Verg., Liv.

consaucĭo -are, *to wound severely*: Suet.

conscĕlĕro -are, *to defile with crime*: miseram domum, Cat.; oculos videndo, Ov.; aures paternas, Liv.

¶ Hence partic. (with superl.), **conscĕlĕrātus**, *wicked, villainous, depraved*: consceleratissimi filii, Cic.; mens, Cic. M. as subst.: Cic.

conscendo -scendĕre -scendi -scensum (scando), *to ascend, mount, go up*; with acc.: equum, to *mount on horseback*, Liv.; vallum, Caes.; aequor navibus, Verg.; with in and the acc.: in equos, Ov. Esp. as naut. t. t., *to go on board ship, embark*; with in and the acc.: in navem, Caes.; with acc.: navem, Caes.; absol., *to embark*: conscendere a Brundisio, Cic.; Thessalonicae (loc.), Liv.; in Siciliam, *for Sicily*, Liv.

conscensĭo -ōnis, f. (conscendo), *an embarking, embarkation*: in naves, Cic.

conscientĭa -ae, f. (conscio).

(1) *a joint knowledge with some other person, being privy to*; with subjective genit.: horum omnium, Cic.; with objective: coniurationis, Tac.; eiusmodi facinorum, Cic.; absol.:

conscindo

consensus

conscientiae contagio, Cic.; aliquem in conscientiam adsumere, Tac.

(2) *consciousness, knowledge in oneself*. In gen.: nostrarum ac suarum, Liv.; absol.: nostra stabilis conscientia, Cic. Esp. *consciousness of right* or *wrong*: conscientia bene actae vitae, Cic.; scelerum et fraudum suarum, Cic.; ex nullā conscientiā de culpā, Sall.; praeclarā conscientiā, Cic.; absol.: **a**, *a good conscience*: mea mihi conscientia pluris est quam omnium sermo, Cic.: **b**, *a bad conscience*: angor conscientiae, Cic.; conscientiā ictus, Liv.

conscindo -scindĕre -scĭdi -scissum, *to tear* or *rend in pieces*: epistulam, Cic. L. TRANSF., conscissi sibilis, *hissed at*, Cic. L.

conscĭo -ire, *to be conscious of guilt*: nil conscire sibi, Hor.

conscisco -sciscĕre -scīvi and -scĭi -scītum (perf. forms conscisse: Liv.; conscisset: Cic.). (1) *to agree on, resolve publicly, decree*: Cic.; bellum, Liv.; ut bellum fieret, Liv., Cic. (2) *to bring* or *inflict upon oneself*: sibi mortem, necem, *to kill oneself*, Cic.; sibi exsilium, Liv.; sibi letum, Lucr. Sometimes sibi is omitted: Liv., Tac.

conscĭus -a -um (scio).

(1) *having joint* or *common knowledge with another, privy to, cognizant of*; with genit.: homo meorum in te studiorum et officiorum maxime conscius, Cic. L.; poet.: conscia fati sidera, Verg.; alicui conscium esse facinoris, Tac.; with dat. of what is known: conscius facinori, Cic.; coeptis, Ov.; with in and the abl.: conscius in privatis rebus, Cic.; with de and the abl.: his de rebus conscium esse Pisonem, Cic.; absol.: Cic. L., Tac., Hor. M. or f. as subst. **conscius** -i and **conscia** -ae, *an accomplice, confidant, fellow-conspirator*: Cic., Tac.

(2) *conscious to oneself*; with genit.: si alicuius iniuriae sibi conscius fuisset, Cic.; mens sibi conscia recti, Verg.; etsi mihi sum conscius me nimis cupidum fuisse vitae, Cic.; absol.: virtus conscia, Verg.; esp. *conscious of guilt*: animus, Sall., Pl., Lucr.

conscrĕor -ari, dep. (screo), *to clear the throat*: Pl.

conscribillo -are (dim. of conscribo), *to scribble* or *scrawl all over*: Varr. TRANSF., nates, *to mark with beating*, Cat.

conscrībo -scrībĕre -scripsi -scriptum, *to write together*.

Hence (1) *to enter on a list, enroll*; as milit. t. t., *to levy*: exercitus, Cic.; legiones, Caes.; as polit. t. t., *to enroll in a colony, class, etc.*: centuriae tres equitum conscriptae sunt, Liv.; Collinam (tribum) novam delectu perditissimorum civium conscribebat, Cic.; esp. *to enroll as a senator*; hence the phrase: patres conscripti (*for* patres et conscripti), *senators*, Cic.; sing., *a senator*: Hor.

(2) *to put together in writing, write, compose*: librum de consulatu, Cic.; epistulam, legem, Cic.; absol., *to write a letter*: de Antonio quoque Balbus ad me cum Oppio conscripsit, Cic.; of physicians, *to prescribe*: pro salutaribus mortifera, Cic. TRANSF., *to write all over*: mensam vino, Ov.

conscriptĭo -ōnis, f. (conscribo), *a writing, composition, written paper*: falsae conscriptiones quaestionum, *forged minutes*, Cic.

consĕco -sĕcare -sĕcŭi -sectum, *to cut in small pieces, dismember*: membra fratris, Ov.

consĕcrātĭo -ōnis, f. (consecro), *a dedication, consecration* (to gods above or gods below): capitis, Cic.; esp. *of the deification of the emperors, apotheosis*: Tac.

consĕcro -are (sacro), *to consecrate, to dedicate to the service of a god*.

LIT., (1) of things: locus consecratus, Caes.; totam Siciliam Cereri, Cic.; diem adventus alicuius, *make a feast-day*, Liv. Sometimes *to consecrate to the gods below*, *to curse*: caput eius, qui contra fecerit, consecratur, Cic.; Liv. (2) of persons, *to deify*: Liber quem nostri maiores consecraverunt, Cic.; esp. of the emperors: consecrare Claudium, Suet.

TRANSF., (1) *to devote, make holy*: vetera iam ista et religione omnium consecrata, Cic. (2) *to make immortal*: amplissimis monumentis memoriam nominis sui, Cic. L.

consectārĭus -a -um (consector), *following logically, consequent*: Cic. N. pl. as subst. **consectāria** -orum, *logical conclusions, inferences*: Cic.

consectātĭo -ōnis, f. (consector), *eager pursuit, desire, striving after*: concinnitatis, Cic.

consectātrix -īcis, f. (consectator), *an eager pursuer, devoted friend*: consectatrices voluptatis libidines, Cic.

consectĭo -ōnis, f. (conseco), *a cutting to pieces*: arborum, Cic.

consector -ari, dep. (freq. of consequor), *to follow, pursue eagerly*. (1) in favourable sense, *to make for, try to join*. LIT., Pl., Ter. TRANSF., tardi ingenii est rivulos consectari, fontes rerum non videre, Cic.; esp. *to strive after, try to imitate* or *gain*: opes aut potentiam, Cic.; ubertatem orationis, Cic.; vitium de industriā, Cic.

(2) in hostile sense, *to chase, hunt*. LIT., redeuntes equites, Caes.; Cic., Liv. TRANSF., omnia mea mala consectantur, Pl.; aliquem et conviciis et sibilis, Cic. L.

consĕcūtĭo -ōnis, f. (consequor). (1) philosoph. t. t., *that which follows, an effect, consequence*: causas rerum et consecutiones videre, Cic. (2) rhet. t. t., *order, connexion, arrangement*: verborum, Cic.

consĕnesco -sĕnescĕre -sĕnŭi, *to become old together*, or simply *to become old*.

In gen.: hac casā, Ov., Liv., Hor.

Esp. *to lose one's strength, to decay*. LIT., insontem, indemnatum in exsilio consenescere, Liv.; consenescere in Siciliā sub armis, Liv.; consenescunt vires atque deficiunt, Cic. TRANSF., invidia habet repentinos impetus, interposito spatio et cognitā causā consenescit, Cic.; omnes illius partis auctores ac socios nullo adversario consenescere, *to lose power*, Cic.

consensĭo -ōnis, f. (consentio), *agreement, harmony, consent*; of persons, *agreement*: omnium gentium, Cic.; nulla de illis magistratuum consensio, Cic.; libertatis vindicandae, Caes.; of things, *harmony*: naturae, Cic. In a bad sense, *a plot, conspiracy*: consensio scelerata, Cic.

consensus -ūs, m. (consentio), *agreement, unanimity, concord, agreement*; of persons: omnium, Cic.; optimus in rempublicam consensus, Cic.; abl., consensu, *unanimously*,

[138]

by general consent: resistere, Liv.; *of things*: mirus quidam omnium quasi consensus doctrinarum concentusque, Cic. In a bad sense, *a secret agreement, conspiracy*: consensus audaciae, Cic.

consentānĕus -a -um (consentio), *agreeing with, consonant with, fit, suitable*: cum iis litteris, Cic. L.; gen. with dat.: Stoicorum rationi, Cic.; impers.: consentaneum est, with ut or infin., *it agrees, is reasonable, suitable*, Pl., Cic.

Consentes Dii (perhaps from cum/sens, pres. partic. of sum), *the twelve chief deities of the Romans, whose gilt statues stood in the forum*; perhaps *the following*: Jupiter, Juno, Vesta, Ceres, Diana, Minerva, Venus, Mars, Mercurius, Neptunus, Vulcanus, Apollo.

Consentia -ae, f. *a town in Bruttii* (now *Cosenza*). Adj. **Consentīnus** -a -um.

consentio -sentire -sensi -sensum, *to share in feeling*.

(1) *of physical sensation, to feel together*: vitalis motus, Lucr.

(2) *of thought or sentiment, to agree.* LIT., *of persons; to agree, to assent, to resolve unanimously*: animi consentientes, Cic.; with dat.: consentire superioribus iudiciis, Cic.; with cum: cum populi Romani voluntatibus consentiant, Cic.; with de *or* in and the abl.: Cic.; ad rempublicam conservandam, Cic.; adversus maleficium, Sen.; with acc.: bellum, *to resolve upon war*, Liv.; with acc. and infin., or infin. alone: Cic., Tac. Also in a bad sense, *to plot, conspire, form an unlawful union*: ad prodendam Hannibali urbem, Liv.; belli faciendi causa, Cic. TRANSF., *of inanimate objects, to agree, harmonize*: vultus cum oratione, Caes.; ratio nostra consentit, Cic.

¶ Hence partic. **consentiens** -entis, *harmonious*: consentiens populi Romani universi voluntas, Cic.; clamore consentienti, Liv.

consēpio = consaepio; q.v.

consĕquentia -ae, f. (consequor), *a consequence, succession*: eventorum, Cic.

consĕquia -ae, f. = consequentia; q.v.: Lucr.

consĕquor -sequi -secūtus, dep.

(1) *to follow, go after.* LIT., aliquem vestigiis, *on foot*, Cic.; in hostile sense, *to pursue*: consequi statim Hasdrubalem, Liv. TRANSF., **a**, *to follow in point of time*: mors, quae brevi consecuta est, Cic.; quia libertatem pax consequebatur, Cic.: **b**, *to follow as an effect or consequence, result from*: quam eorum opinionem magni errores consecuti sunt, Cic.: **c**, *to follow as a logical consequence*: fit etiam quod consequitur necessarium, Cic.: **d**, *to follow a particular object or example*: consequi suum quoddam institutum, Cic.; mediam consilii viam, Liv.

(2) *to come up to by following, attain to, reach, obtain.* LIT., si statim navigas, nos Leucade consequere, Cic.; in hostile sense, *to catch*: reliquos omnes equitatu, Caes. TRANSF., *to attain to, obtain, get*: **a**, in gen.: cuius rei tantae tamque difficilis facultatem consecutum esse me non profiteor; *secutum esse prae me fero*, Cic.; opes quam maximas, Cic.; amplissimos honores, Cic.; regna, Caes.; fructum amplissimum ex reipublicae causa, Cic.; omnia per senatum; fortitudinis

gloriam insidiis et malitia, Cic.; foll. by ut *or* ne with the subj.: Cic. L.: **b**, *of states and events, to befall, happen to* a person: tanta prosperitas Caesarem est consecuta, Nep.: **c**, *to come up to, to equal*: verborum prope numerum sententiarum numero, Cic.; esp. *to express adequately in words*: alicuius laudes verbis, Cic.: **d**, *to come up to in speech or thought, to understand, grasp*: similitudinem veri, Cic.

¶ Hence partic. **consĕquens** -quentis, *appropriate*: in coniunctis (verbis) quod non est consequens vituperandum est, Cic.; esp. *following logically, consequent*: consequens est, *it follows as a logical consequence*, Cic.

N. as subst. **consĕquens** -quentis, *a logical consequence*: Cic.

¹**consĕro** -sĕrĕre -sēvi -sĭtum, *to sow, plant*; either of seeds and plants: arborem, Liv.; or of ground: agros, Cic. TRANSF., lumine arva (of the sun), *to cover*, Lucr.; consitus senectute, Pl.

²**consĕro** -sĕrĕre -sĕrŭi -sertum, *to connect, tie, join, twine together.*

In gen., *of a number of objects or one composite object*: lorica conserta hamis, Verg.; exodia conserere fabellis potissimum Atellanis, Liv.

Esp. *to join in a hostile manner.* (1) as milit. t. t.: manum (*or* manus) conserere, *to engage*, Cic.; cum aliquo, Cic.; inter se, Sall.; conserere pugnam, Liv.; proelium, Liv.; navis conseritur, *the ship is engaged*, Liv.; absol.: conserere cum levi armatura, Liv. (2) as legal t. t.: manum conserere, *to commence an action concerning property by laying hands on it*, Enn., Cic.

¶ Hence adv. from partic. consertus, **consertē**, *connectedly*: Cic.

conserva -ae, f. *a fellow-slave*: Pl. TRANSF., conservae fores, *in the same service*, Ov.

conservātio -ōnis, f. (conservo), *a preservation, keeping, laying up*: frugum, Cic. TRANSF., *a keeping up*: aequabilitatis, Cic.

conservātor -ōris, m. (conservo), *a preserver*: inimicorum, Cic.; reipublicae, Cic.

conservĭtium -i, n. *joint servitude*: Pl.

conservo -are, *to keep, preserve*; of persons or concrete objects: cives suos, Cic.; omnes salvos, Cic.; rempublicam, Cic.; rem familiarem, Cic.; of abstract objects, *to preserve, maintain, observe*: pristinum animum, Liv.; iusiurandum, *to keep*, Cic.; legem, Quint.

Pres. partic. as adj. **conservans** -antis, *preserving*; with genit.: ea quae conservantia sunt eius status, Cic.

conservus -i, m. *a fellow slave*: Pl., Cic., Hor.

consessor -ōris, m. (consido), *one who sits near or with*; in a court of justice, *an assessor*: Cic.; *a neighbour* at a feast or spectacle: Cic., Liv.

consessus -ūs, m. (consido), *an assembly* (of persons sitting together): in ludo talario, Cic.; praeconum, Cic.; ludorum gladiatorumque, Cic.; Verg., Tac.

consīdĕrātio -ōnis, f. (considero), *consideration, contemplation*: considerationem intendere in aliquid, Cic.

consīdĕro -are (cum/sidus; cf. desidero), *to look at, regard carefully, contemplate*: considerare opus pictoris, Cic. TRANSF., *to* consider, weigh, reflect upon: considerare secum eos casus, in quibus, etc., Cic.; consideres quid agas, Cic.; with de and the abl.: nunc de praemiis consideremus, Cic.; absol.: ille (ait) se considerare velle, Cic.

¶ Hence partic. (with compar.) **consĭdĕrātus** -a -um. (1) pass., *thoroughly considered, well weighed, deliberate*: verbum, Cic.; considerata atque provisa via vivendi, Cic. (2) act., of persons, *cautious, wary, circumspect*: homo, Cic., Liv.

Adv. (with compar. and superl.) **consĭdĕrātē**, *thoughtfully, carefully*: agere, Cic.

consĭdo -sĭdĕre -sēdi -sessum, *to sit down, to settle.*

LIT., of persons: hic in umbrā, Cic.; in molli herbā, Cic.; transtris, Verg.; saxo, Ov.; esp. (1) *to sit down in a public assembly or court of justice*: ut primum iudices consederant, Cic.; ad ius dicendum, Liv. (2) milit. t.t.: **a**, *to take up one's position*: triarii sub vexillis considebant sinistro crure porrecto, Liv.; in insidiis, Liv.: **b**, more commonly, *to stop, encamp*: considere non longius mille passibus a nostris munitionibus, Caes. (3) *to stay, settle down*: hic an Antii, Cic.; Tarquiniis, Liv.; vultis an his mecum pariter considere regnis? Verg.

TRANSF., (1) of things, *to fall to the ground, settle, sink, subside*: quae (Alpes) iam licet considant, Cic.; Ilion ardebat neque adhuc consederat ignis, Ov. (2) of ideas, *to sink in*: iustitia in mente, Cic. (3) of feelings, *to subside*: ardor animi consedit, Cic.; ferocia, terror, Liv. (4) *to be overcome, sink down* or *fall into neglect*: totam videmus consedisse urbem luctu, Verg.; consedit utriusque nomen in quaestura, Cic.

consigno -are, *to seal, to affix a seal to*: tabulas signis, Cic., Liv. TRANSF., (1) *to vouch for, authenticate*: antiquitas clarissimis monumentis testata consignataque, Cic. (2) *to record*: litteris aliquid, Cic.

consĭlesco -sĭlescĕre -sĭlui, *to become quite still*: Pl.

consĭlĭārĭus -a -um (consilium), *relating to counsel, deliberating*: senatus, Pl. M. as subst. **consĭlĭārĭus** -i. (1) *an adviser*: consiliario et auctore Vestorio, Cic.; consiliarii regis, Cic. (2) *an assessor in a court of law*: Suet. (3) of an augur, as *interpreter* of the divine will: Cic.

consĭlĭātor -ōris, m. (consilior), *counsellor, adviser*: Phaedr., Plin. L.

consĭlĭor -ari, dep. (consilium). (1) *to hold a consultation, consult, take counsel*: difficilis ad consiliandum legatio, Cic. L.; Hor., Tac. (2) *to give counsel, advise*: amicē, Hor.

consĭlĭum -i, n. (connected with consulo).

(1) act., *a deliberation, consultation, taking counsel*: consilium principum habere, *to hold a consultation with the chiefs*, Liv.; quasi consilii sit res, *as if the matter allowed of consideration*, Caes.; consiliis interesse, Cic.; esp. *the deliberation of a public body*: consilii publici participem fieri, Cic.; consilium habere, Cic.; rem ad consilium deferre, Caes. TRANSF., **a**, *the assembly of persons giving advice, council*: senatus, id est, orbis terrae consilium, Cic.; ex senatu in hoc consilium delecti estis, Cic.; consilium convocare, *a council of war*, Caes.; so: consilio advocato,

Liv.: **b**, of the appropriate mental quality, *judgment, understanding, prudence*: vir maximi consilii, Caes.; mulier imbecilli consilii, Cic.; vis consili expers, Hor.; Tac.

(2) pass.: **a**, the result of deliberation; *a resolution, plan, conclusion*: capere consilium, *to form a resolution*, Cic.; belli renovandi, Caes.; subito consilium cepi, ut antequam luceret exirem, Cic.; consilium consistit, *holds good*, Cic.; est consilium, foll. by infin.: Cic.; quid sui consilii sit proponit, *he explains what his plan is*, Caes.; inire consilium senatus interficiendi, Cic.; abl.: consilio, *intentionally, designedly*, Cic. L., Lucr., Liv., Verg.; privato consilio, privatis consiliis (opp. publico consilio, publicis consiliis), *in the interests of private persons*, Cic.; consilium imperatorium, *the strategic plan*, Cic.: **b**, a contribution to deliberation; *advice, suggestion*: alicui consilium dare, Cic., Hor.; consiliis uti, Cic., Hor.; sequi, Liv.

consĭmĭlis -e, *like in all respects, exactly similar*; with genit.: causa consimilis earum causarum quae, etc., Cic.; with dat.: consimilis fugae profectio, Caes.; absol.: laus, Cic.

consĭpĭo -sĭpĕre (sapio), *to be in one's right mind* or *senses*: Liv.

consĭsto -sĭstĕre -stĭti -stĭtum, *to put oneself in any place.*

In gen., *to take one's stand, place oneself.* LIT., of persons: consistere ad mensam, Cic.; hi proximi constitere, Liv.; tota in illa contione Italia constitit, Cic.; as milit. t. t., *to be posted*: ne saucio quidem eius loci, ubi constiterat, relinquendi facultas dabatur, Cic. TRANSF., of things. (1) *to fall to, come upon, rest on*: in quo (viro) ... ne suspicio quidem potuit consistere, Cic.; so of the fall of dice: quadringentis talis centum Venerios non posse casu consistere, Cic. (2) *to agree with*: videsne igitur Zenonem tuum cum Aristone verbis consistere, re dissidere? Cic. (3) *to consist, to be formed of*: maior pars victus eorum in lacte, caseo, carne consistit, Caes.; Cic., Lucr. So with ex, or plain abl.: Lucr.

Esp. *to stand still*. (1) *to stop, halt.* LIT., of persons (and animals): consistite! Ov.; consistere et commorari cogit, Cic.; viatores etiam invitos consistere cogunt, *stop for conversation*, Caes.; bestiae saepe immanes cantu flectuntur et consistunt, Cic.; esp. as milit. t. t., *to halt*: prope hostem, Caes., Liv.; fig., in speech: in uno nomine, Cic.; with duration indicated, *to halt, stop, stay*: consistere unum diem Veliae, Cic. TRANSF., of lifeless objects: vel concidat omne caelum omnisque natura consistat necesse est, Cic.; of water, *to stop still*: ter frigore constitit Ister, *froze*, Ov.; of abstract things, to cease: labor, Cic.; cum ad Trebiam terrestre constitisset bellum, Liv. (2) *to stand firmly, keep one's ground, footing*: in fluctibus, Caes.; vertice celso aeriae quercus constiterunt, Verg. TRANSF., in forensibus causis praeclare, *to hold one's own*, Cic.; neque mens, neque vox neque lingua consistit, Cic.

consĭtĭo -ōnis, f. (consero), *a sowing, planting*: Cic.

consĭtor -ōris, m. (consero), *a sower, planter*: uvae, Bacchus, Ov.

consĭtūra -ae, f. (consero), *a sowing, planting*: agri, Cic.

consōbrīnus -i, m. and **consōbrīna** -ae, f. *cousin on the mother's side*: Cic.; also, in gen., *cousin*: Cic.; and in a more extended sense, *second, third cousin*: Suet.

consŏcer -cĕri, m. *a joint father-in-law*: Suet.

consŏcĭātĭo -ōnis, f. (consocio), *union, connexion, association*: hominum, Cic., Liv.

consŏcĭo -are, *to unite, connect, share, make common*: consilia cum aliquo, Cic.; iniuriam cum amicis, Cic.; rem inter se, Liv.; nunquam tam vehementer cum senatu consociati fuistis, Cic. TRANSF., to make by union: pinus et populus umbram, Hor.
¶ Hence partic. **consŏcĭātus** -a -um, *united, harmonious*: consociatissima voluntas, Cic.; di, Liv.

consōlābĭlis -e (consolor), *consolable*: dolor, Cic. L.

consōlātĭo -ōnis, f. (consolor), *consolation, encouragement, comfort, alleviation*: communium malorum, Cic. L.; timoris, Cic. L.; adhibere aliquam modicam consolationem, Cic.; adhibere alicui consolationem, Cic.; num me una consolatio sustentat quod, etc., Cic.; uti hac consolatione alicuius (foll. by acc. and infin.), Cic.; meton., *a consolatory treatise or discourse*: Cic., Quint.

consōlātor -ōris, m. (consolor), *a consoler*: Cic.

consōlātōrĭus -a -um (consolator), *relating to consolation, consolatory*: litterae, Cic. L., Suet.

consōlor -ari, dep. (1) of persons, *to console, comfort, to encourage*: se illo solatio quod, etc., Cic.; foll. by acc. and infin.: Cic., Hor.; aliquem de communibus miseriis, Cic.; spes sola homines in miseriis consolari solet, Cic.; absol.: consolando levare dolorem, Cic.; Ter., Caes., Ov. (2) of things, *to alleviate, lighten, solace*: dolorem, Cic. L., Liv.

consŏno -sŏnare -sŏnŭi. (1) *to sound together, sound loudly*: consonante clamore nominatim Quinctium orare, Liv. TRANSF., *to harmonize, agree with*, with cum or dat. (post-Aug.): Sen., Quint. (2) *to resound, echo*: plausu fremituque virum consonat omne nemus, Verg.; Pl., Tac.

consŏnus -a -um, *sounding together, harmonious*. LIT., fila lyrae, Ov. TRANSF., *accordant, fit, suitable*: satis consonum fore ut, Cic. L.

consōpĭo -ire, *to lull to sleep, stupefy*: somno consopiri sempiterno, Cic.; Endymion a Luna consopitus, Cic.; Lucr.

consors -sortis. (1) act., *having an equal share or lot, sharing in, partaking of*: consortes tres fratres, Cic.; usually with genit.: socius et consors gloriosi laboris, Cic.; mecum temporum illorum, Cic.; tribuniciae potestatis, Tac. Poet. as subst., *brother or sister*: consors magni Iovis, *Juno*, Ov.; as adj., *brotherly, sisterly*: sanguis, Ov.
(2) pass., *shared*: consorti vitā, Lucr.; consortia tecta, Verg.

consortĭo -ōnis, f. (consors), *companionship, community, partnership*: humana, Cic., Liv.

consortĭum -i, n. (consors), *partnership*: Suet.; with genit., *participation in*: sis in consortio, si in societate reipublicae esse licet, Liv.; Tac.

¹conspectus -a -um, partic. from conspicio; q.v.

²conspectus -ūs, m. (conspicio), *look, sight, view*.
(1) act. LIT., dare se alicui in conspectum, *to allow oneself to be seen by*, Cic.; in conspectu esse, with genit., *to be within sight of* a person or thing, Cic.; e conspectu abire, Caes.; adimere conspectum oculorum, Liv.; cadere in conspectum, Cic.; conspectus est in Capitolium, *the view is towards the Capitol*, Liv.; conspectum alicuius fugere, Caes.; privare aliquem omnium suorum consuetudine conspectuque, Cic. TRANSF., *mental view, survey*: in hoc conspectu et cognitione naturae, Cic.; Liv.
(2) pass., *appearance*: conspectu suo proelium restituit, Liv.; tuus iucundissimus conspectus, Cic.

conspergo -spergĕre -spersi -spersum (spargo), *to sprinkle* or *moisten by sprinkling*: me lacrimis, Cic. TRANSF., ut oratio conspersa sit quasi verborum sententiarumque floribus, *interspersed with*, Cic.

conspĭcĭo -spĭcĕre -spexi -spectum, *to catch sight of, behold, perceive*.
LIT., conspicere nostros equites, Caes.; infestis oculis omnium conspici, Cic.; milites in summo colle, Caes.; cum inter se conspecti essent, Liv.; Ov.; with acc. and infin.: calones qui nostros victores flumen transisse conspexerant, Caes.; esp. *to look at with attention*: Demetrium ut pacis auctorem cum ingenti favore conspiciebant, Liv.; locum insidiis, *for an ambush*, Verg.; in pass., conspici, *to attract notice, to be gazed at*: vehi per urbem conspici velle, Cic.; Hor.
TRANSF., *to see mentally, understand*: corde, Pl.; mentibus, Cic.
¶ Hence partic. **conspectus** -a -um. (1) in gen., *visible*: tumulus hosti conspectus, Liv. (2) *striking, remarkable, conspicuous*: conspectus elatusque supra modum hominis, Liv.; conspecta mors eius fuit, quia publico funere est elatus, Liv.; victor Tyrio conspectus in ostro, Verg.; compar.: turba conspectior, Liv.
Gerundive **conspiciendus** -a -um, *worth looking at, notable*: opus, Liv.; templam, Ov.

conspĭcor -ari, dep. (conspicio), *to catch sight of, perceive*: quem huc advenientem conspicor, Pl.; ex oppido caedem et fugam suōrum, Caes.; quae res in nostris castris gererentur conspicati, Caes.

conspĭcŭus -a -um (conspicio). (1) in gen., *visible*: conspicuus polus, Ov. (2) *remarkable, striking, conspicuous*: conspicuus late vertex, Hor.; Romanis conspicuum eum novitas divitiaeque faciebant, Liv.; Ov., Tac.

conspīrātĭo -ōnis, f. (conspiro), *a blowing* or *breathing together*. Hence *harmony, agreement, union*: omnium bonorum, Cic.; magnā amoris conspiratione consentientes amicorum greges, Cic.; in a bad sense, *conspiracy, plot*: conspiratio certorum hominum contra dignitatem tuam, Cic.; Tac.

conspīro -are (cum/spiro), *to blow* or *breathe together*.
LIT., of instruments, *to blow together, sound together*: aereaque adsensu conspirant cornua rauco, Verg.
TRANSF., *to agree, harmonize in opinion and feeling*. (1) in a good sense: conspirate nobiscum, consentite cum bonis, Cic. (2) in

a bad sense, *to conspire, to form a plot*: priusquam plures civitates conspirarent, Caes.; in iniuriam, Liv.; in caedem, Tac.; with ad, *or* ut: Suet.

¶ Hence perf. partic. (in act. sense) **conspīrātus** -a -um, *sworn together, united by an oath*: Caes., Phaedr. M. as subst. **conspīrāti** -orum, *conspirators*: Suet.

consponsor -ōris, m. *a joint surety*: Cic. L.

conspŭo -spŭĕre, *to spit upon*: Pl., Juv. TRANSF., cana nive Alpes, Hor. (parodying Bibaculus).

conspurco -are, *to cover with dirt, defile*: Lucr.

conspŭto -are (freq. of conspuo), *to spit upon contemptuously*: nostros, Cic. L.

constans -antis, partic. from consto; q.v.

constantĭa -ae, f. (constans), *steadiness, firmness.* (1) in gen.: cursūs cum admirabili incredibilique constantia (of the stars), Cic.; dictorum conventorumque constantia, Cic. (2) of character, *perseverance, firmness*: pertinacia aut constantia intercessoris, Cic.; animi, Ov.; morum, Tac. (3) *uniformity, harmony*: testimoniorum, Cic.

consternātĭo -ōnis, f. (²consterno). (1) *fear, alarm, dismay, confusion*: pavor et consternatio quadrigarum, Liv.; pavor et consternatio mentis, Tac. (2) *a mutiny, tumult*: vulgi, Tac.; muliebris consternatio, Liv.

¹consterno -sternĕre -strāvi -strātum, *to strew, scatter, cover by strewing*: tabernacula caespitibus, Caes.; omnia cadaveribus, Sall.; cubile veste, Cat.; Verg., Liv.; fig.: forum corporibus civium caede nocturna, Cic.; sometimes of standing objects, *to knock over*: tempestas aliquot signa, Liv.

¶ Hence partic. **constrātus** -a -um, esp. constrata navis, *a decked ship*, Caes., Cic. N. as subst., *flooring, deck*: Liv., Petr.

²consterno -are (connected with ¹consterno). (1) *to throw into confusion, to alarm, to frighten*: procella ita consternavit equos, Liv.; esp. in pass.: equi consternati, *startled*, Liv.; pavida et consternata multitudo, Liv. (2) *to drive to action by fear*, esp. *hasty action*: in fugam consternari, Liv.; metu servitutis ad arma consternati, Liv.; Ov.

constĭpo -are, *to press, crowd together*: tantum numerum hominum in agrum Campanum, Cic.; Caes.

constĭtŭo -stĭtŭĕre -stĭtŭi -stĭtūtum (statuo), *to cause to stand, set up, place, establish.*

LIT., (1) in gen.: hominem ante pedes Q. Manilii, Cic.; taurum ante aras, Verg. (2) as milit. t. t., *to post, station, arrange*: signa ante tribunal, Liv.; legionem Caesar constituit, *drew up*, Caes.; naves in alto, Caes.; intra silvas aciem ordinesque, Caes.; also *to halt*: agmen, Sall., Liv. (3) *to settle* people in homes or quarters: praesidia in Tolosatibus circumque Narbonem, Caes.; plebem in agris publicis, Cic. (4) *to found, set up*, buildings, etc.: turres, Caes.; oppidum, Caes.; nidos, Cic.; hiberna omnium legionum in Belgis, Caes.; moenia, Verg.

TRANSF., (1) of persons, *to appoint to an office*: regem, Cic.; aliquem sibi quaestoris in loco, Cic.; Commium regem ibi, Caes. (2) *to settle, fix upon* an amount, time, etc.: vectigal, Cic.; tempus, diem, Cic., Caes.; mercedem funeris, Cic.; pretium frumento,

Cic.; diem cum aliquo, Caes.; with indir. quest.: armorum quantum quaeque civitas quodque ante tempus efficiat constituit, Caes. (3) in gen., *to settle, arrange*, anything already existing: is cui corpus bene constitutum sit, Cic.; animus bene constitutus, Cic.; rem familiarem, rem publicam, Cic.; controversiam, Cic. (4) *to set up, establish, form*, anything new: quaestionem, Cic.; concordiam, Cic.; exemplum iustitiae, Cic.; tres legiones, Caes. (5) *to decide* about a fact, *decide that* . . . : nondum satis constitui molestiaene an plus voluptatis adtulerit Trebatius noster, Cic. (6) *to decide* on a course of action, *decide* to . . . (very frequent); absol.: ut erat constitutum, Cic.; with acc. object: haec ex re et ex tempore constitues, Cic.; with acc. and infin.: me hodie venturum esse, Cic. L.; with plain infin.: Lucr.; bellum cum Germanis gerere, Caes.; with ut and the subj.: ut pridie Idus Aquini manerem, Cic. L.; ut L. Bestia quereretur, Cic.

¶ Hence partic. **constĭtūtus** -a -um, *arranged, settled.* N. as subst. **constĭtūtum** -i, *anything arranged, settled* or *agreed upon*: constitutum factum esse cum servis, ut venirent, Cic.; ad constitutum experiendi gratiā venire, *the appointment*; naturam per constituta procedere, Sen.

constĭtūtĭo -ōnis, f. (constituo). (1) *the act of settling*: religionum, Cic.; summi boni, *definition*, Cic. (2) *settled condition, disposition*: firma constitutio corporis, Cic.; rei-publicae, Cic.; illa praeclara constitutio Romuli, Cic. (3) *a regulation, order, ordinance*: cogebatur alia aut ex decreto priorum legatorum aut ex novā constitutione senatus facere, Cic. (4) as rhet. t. t., *the issue, point in dispute*: Cic.

consto -stare -stiti -statum.

(1) *to stand together*, i.e. to stand in a fixed relation to some person or thing. LIT., Pl. TRANSF., **a**, *to be composed, consist*: unde omnis rerum nunc constet summa creata, Lucr.; ex animo constamus et corpore, Cic.; **b**, *to depend upon, rest upon*: monuit eius diei victoriam in earum cohortium virtute constare, Caes.: **c**, *to correspond to, be consistent with*; with dat.: sibi, Cic., Hor.; constat humanitati suae, Cic.; absol., of accounts, etc., *to correspond, come right*: ratio constat, Cic., Tac.; hence with abl., *to cost*: ambuli uncula prope dimidio minoris constabit isto loco, Cic.; Caes., Ov.

(2) absol., *to stand firm, stand still.* LIT., nullo loco constabat acies, Liv. TRANSF., **a**, *to remain the same, to be unaltered*: adeo perturbavit ea vox regem, ut non color, non vultus ei constaret, Liv.; postquam cuncta videt caelo constare sereno, Verg.; uti numerus legionum constare videretur, Caes.; esp. of mental attitudes: nec animum eius satis constare visum, Liv.; of resolves, *to be fixed, firm*: animo constat sententia, Verg.; hence alicui constat, *a person is resolved*: mihi quidem constat nec meam contumeliam nec meorum ferre, ap. Cic.; of evidence, facts, etc. *to be established, certain, sure, well-known*: eorum quae constant exempla ponemus, horum quae dubia sunt exempla adferemus, Cic.; hence impers. constat, often with acc.

and infin., *it is agreed*: quod omnibus constabat hiemari in Gallia oportere, Caes.; mihi plane non satis constat, utrum sit melius, Cic.; cum de Magio constet, Cic.; de facto, Quint.: **b**, *to exist*: nullum est genus rerum, quod avulsum a ceteris per se ipsum constare possit, Cic.; often in Lucr.

¶ Hence partic. (with compar. and superl.) **constans** -antis, *steady, firm, unchanging, immovable, constant*. (**1**) in gen.: constanti vultu graduque, Liv.; quae cursus constantes habent, Cic.; pax, Liv.; fides, Hor.; constans iam aetas, quae media dicitur, Cic. (**2**) of character, *firm, resolute, constant*: sunt igitur firmi et stabiles et constantes (amici) eligendi, Cic.; Tac., Ov. (**3**) *consistent, harmonious*: oratio, Cic.; constans parum memoria huius anni, Liv.

Adv. (with compar. and superl.) **constantĕr**, *steadily, firmly*. (**1**) in gen.: constanter in suo manere statu, Cic.; constanter et non trepide pugnare, Caes. (**2**) of character, *firmly, resolutely*: constanter et sedate ferre dolorem, Cic. (**3**) *uniformly, harmoniously*: constanter omnes nuntiaverunt manus cogi, Caes.; constanter sibi dicere, Cic.

constringo -stringĕre -strinxi -strictum.
LIT., (**1**) *to draw, bind together*: sarcinam, Pl. (**2**) *to bind fast, to confine, fetter*: corpora vinculis, Cic.; Pl., Hor.
TRANSF., (**1**) *to bind, restrain, confine*: fidem religione potius quam veritate, Cic.; orbem terrarum novis legibus, Cic. (**2**) of discourse, *to compress, abbreviate*: sententiam aptis verbis, Cic.; Quint.

constructĭo -ōnis, f. (construo). (**1**) *a putting together, building, construction, making*: hominis, Cic. (**2**) rhet. t. t., *the proper connexion of words*: verborum apta et quasi rotunda, Cic.

construŏ -strŭĕre -struxi -structum. (**1**) *to heap up together*: acervos nummorum, Cic.; divitias, Hor. (**2**) *to make by heaping up, to construct, build up*: mundum, navem, aedificium, Cic. (**3**) *to arrange*: dentes in ore constructi, Cic.

constuprātor -ōris, m. *a ravisher, debaucher*: Liv.

constupro -are, *to debauch, to ravish*: matronas, Liv.; fig.: emptum constupratumque iudicium, *corrupt*, Cic. L.

consuādĕo -suādĕre -suāsi -suāsum, *to advise earnestly*: Pl.

Consuālĭa, *see* Consus.

consuāsor -ōris, m. (consuadeo), *an adviser*: Cic.

consūdo -are, *to sweat profusely*: Pl.

consuēfăcĭo -făcĕre -fēci -factum (consuesco/facio), *to accustom, habituate*: ea ne me celet, consuefeci filium, Ter.; multitudinem ordines habere, Sall.

consuesco -suescĕre -suēvi -suētum (perf. forms often contr. consuesti, consuestis, consuemus, consuerunt, consueram, consuerim, consuesse).

(**1**) transit., *to accustom, habituate*: bracchia, Lucr.

(**2**) intransit.: **a**, in gen., *to accustom oneself*; esp. in perf., consuevi, *I am accustomed*; with infin.: qui mentiri solet, peierare consuevit, Cic.; with inanimate things as subjects: naves quae praesidii causā Alexandriae esse consuerant, Caes.; ut consuesti, *as you are accustomed*, Cic.; in teneris consuescere multum est, Verg.: **b**, *to cohabit with*: cum aliquo, cum aliquā, Cic., Ter.

¶ Hence partic. **consuētus** -a -um. (**1**) of persons, *accustomed to* (poet.): Pl., Liv.; with infin.: Lucr. (**2**) of things, *accustomed, usual* (poet.): Ter., Verg., Sall.; superl.: consuetissima verba, Ov.

consuētūdo -inis, f. (consuesco), *custom, usage, habit*.
LIT., in gen.: mos consuetudoque civilis, Cic.; consuetudo populi Romani, Cic.; consuetudo sermonis nostri, Cic.; consuetudo peccandi, Cic.; consuetudo bona, Cic.; adducere aliquem in eam consuetudinem ut, Caes.; ab omnium Siculorum consuetudine discedere, Cic.; non est meae consuetudinis rationem reddere, Cic.; ut est consuetudo, *as is the usual practice*, Cic.; mutare consuetudinem dicendi, Cic.; tenere consuetudinem suam, Cic.; in consuetudinem venire, *to become customary*, Cic.; ex consuetudine, Caes.; consuetudine, *according to custom*, Cic.; ad superiorem consuetudinem reverti, Cic.; sometimes for *manner of speaking*: consuetudo indocta, Cic.
TRANSF., of *habitual dealings with persons*; in gen., *intimacy, familiar acquaintance*: insinuare in consuetudinem alicuius, Cic.; esp. of lovers: stupri vetus consuetudo, *an intrigue of long standing*: Sall.; Ter., Liv., Suet.

consuētus -a -um, partic. from consuesco; q.v.

consul -sŭlis, m. (old forms consol, cosol; abbreviation cos., plur. coss.; etymology doubtful), *a consul*; plur. consules, *the consuls, the two chief magistrates of the Roman state under the republic, chosen annually by the comitia centuriata, originally from patricians only, but after 367 B.C., also from the plebeians*: consul ordinarius, *one elected at the usual time*, opp. consul suffectus, *one chosen in the course of the year to replace a consul deceased or resigned*, Liv.; consul designatus, *consul elect*, so called between the election in July and entrance upon office on the 1st of January, Cic.; consul maior, *the consul who had precedence of his colleague*; consul Flaminius consul iterum, *for the second time*, Cic.; aliquem dicere consulem, Liv.; facere, declarare, Cic.; creare, Cic., Caes.; pro consule, *an officer in the place of the consul, a proconsul*, e.g. *a governor of a province*: pro consule in Ciliciam proficisci, *to go as proconsul to Cilicia*, Cic.

The year was generally called by the consuls' names, e.g.: L. Pisone et A. Gabinio coss. (i.e. consulibus), i.e. 696 A.U.C., Caes.; consule Tullo, Hor.; so was the year of a vintage: Bibuli consulis amphora, Hor.

consŭlāris -e (consul). (**1**) *relating to a consul, consular*: aetas, *the age (namely the forty-third year) at which a man might lawfully be chosen consul*, Cic.; fasces, Liv.; lictor, auctoritas, Cic.; candidatus, Cic.; familia, Cic.; imperium, Cic.; locus, *place in the senate*, Cic. (**2**) *having been a consul*; as adj.: homo, vir, Cic.; m. as subst. **consŭlāris** -is, *an ex-consul*: Cic.; in the imperial period, *a provincial governor of the consular rank*: Tac.

Adv. **consŭlārĭtĕr**, *in a manner worthy of a consul*: vita omnis consulariter acta, Liv.

consŭlātus -ūs, m. (consul), *the office of consul, the consulship*: abdicare se consulatu, Cic.; abdicare consulatum, Liv.; abire consulatu, Liv.; adipisci consulatum, Cic.; adferre consulatum in eam familiam, Cic.; petere consulatum, Cic.; peracto consulatu, Caes.

consŭlo -sŭlĕre -sŭlŭi -sultum (cum/root sed- or root sal-).

(1) *to reflect, consult, consider.* LIT., in gen.: in commune, *for the common good*, Liv.; in longitudinem, *for the future*, Ter.; facto non consulto in tali periculo opus esse, Sall.; re consulta et explorata, Cic.; quid agant consulunt, Caes.; esp. with dat., *to take counsel for some person or thing, to have regard for the interests of, look to*: tuae rei, Pl.; parti civium consulere, Cic.; sibi, Cic.; dignitati alicuius, Cic.; alicui optime, Cic.; suae vitae, Caes. TRANSF., after deliberation, *to come to a conclusion, to take measures*: quae reges atque populi mala consuluerint, Sall.; obsecro ne quid gravius de salute et incolumitate tuā consulas, Caes.; consulere in, *to take measures against*: nihil in quemquam superbe ac violenter, Liv.; aliquid boni (*or* optimi) consulere, *to take in good part*: haec missa, Ov.; Quint.

(2) *to ask the advice of, consult*: nec te id consulo, *consult about that*, Cic.; quod me de Antonio consulis, Cic.; quid mihi faciendum esse censeat, Cic.; esp.: **a**, *to refer to a political body*: senatus a Bestiā consultus est, placeretne legatos Iugurthae recipi moenibus, Sall.; populum de eius morte, Cic.: **b**, *to take legal advice*: qui de iure civili consuli solent, Cic.: **c**, *to consult an oracle or deity*: haruspicem, Cic.; Phoebi oracula, Ov.; exta, Verg.; Apollinem Pythium quas potissimum regiones tenerent, Cic.; id possetne fieri, consuluit, Cic.

¶ Hence partic. (with superl.) **consultus** a- -um. (1) *of things, well considered, deliberated upon, well weighed*: omnia consulta ad nos et exquisita deferunt, Cic. (2) *of persons, experienced*, with genit.: consultissimus vir omnis divini et humani iuris, Liv.; consultus insanientis sapientiae, Hor.; esp. in law, iuris consultus, as adj. *or* m. subst.: Cic.; so **sultus** -i, alone, as m. subst., *a lawyer*: Hor.

N. as subst. **consultum** -i. (1) the act of deliberation, *reflection, consideration*: consulto opus est, Sall. (2) the result of deliberation, *a resolution, plan, decision*: consulto conlegae, virtute militum victoria parta est, Liv.; facta et consulta fortium et sapientium, Cic.; of the *considered answer* of an oracle: dum consulta petis, Verg. Esp. *a decree* of the senate at Rome, senatus consultum (shortened to S.C.): senatus consultum facere, Cic.; S.C. facere in aliquem, Liv.; S.C. facere ut, etc., Cic.; alicui senatus consulto scribendo adesse, Cic.; consulta patrum, Hor.; so of *the decree* of a Sicilian senate (βουλή): Cic.

Abl. as adv. **consultō**, *deliberately, designedly*: consulto fecisse aliquid, Cic.; non consulto sed casu in eorum mentionem incidere, Cic.; Pl., Hor.

Adv. (with compar.) **consultē**, *advisedly, after consideration*: caute ac consulte gerere aliquid, Liv.; Pl., Tac.

consultātĭo -ōnis, f. (consulto). (1) *a full consideration, deliberation*: venit aliquid in consultationem, Cic.; consultationem raptim transigere, Liv.; meton., *a case or subject under consideration*: Quint. (2) *an asking for advice, inquiry*: consultationi alicuius respondere, Cic. L.

consulto -are (freq. of consulo). (1) *to consider maturely, weigh, ponder.* In gen.: quid illaec consultant? Pl.; de officio, Cic.; triduum ad consultandum dare, Liv.; ad eam rem consultandam, Liv.; in longius, *for the future*, Tac.; in medium, *for the common good*, Sall.; consultabat, utrum Romam proficisceretur, an Capuam teneret, Cic.; esp. with dat., *to consult for, provide for*: reipublicae, Sall.

(2) *to consult, ask advice of*: quid me consultas? Pl.; Tib., Plin.

consultor -ōris, m. (consulo). (1) *an adviser*: egomet in agmine, in proelio consultor idem et socius periculi vobiscum adero, Sall.; Tac. (2) *one who asks advice*, esp. legal advice, *a client*: consultoribus suis respondere, Cic.; Hor.

consultrix -īcis, f. (consultor), *she who consults, cares for, provides*: natura consultrix et provida utilitatum, Cic.

consum -futurum -fore, *to be, to happen*; only found in future forms: Pl., Ter.

consummātĭo -ōnis, f. (consummo). (1) *a summing up, adding up*: Plin. (2) *a finishing, completion, consummation*: maximarum rerum, Sen.

consummo -are (summa). (1) *to add together, sum up.* TRANSF., *to form a whole, complete*: quae consummatur partibus, una dies (of an intercalary day), Ov.; in suum decus nomenque velut consummata eius belli gloria, Liv. (2) *to bring to perfection*: ars, Quint.; animus, Sen., Liv.

¶ Hence partic. **consummātus** -a -um, *complete, perfect, consummate*: eloquentia, Quint.; orator, Quint.; ars, Plin.

consūmo -sūmĕre -sumpsi -sumptum, *to take altogether, consume.*

(1) in doing something, *to spend, employ*: pecuniam in agrorum coemptionibus, Cic.; omne tempus in litteris, Cic.; ingenium in musicis, Cic.; omnem laborem, operam, curam, studium in salute alicuius, Cic.; curam in re una, Hor.; tota in dulces consument ubera natos, Verg.

(2) in gen., *to use up, consume, finish.* LIT., omnia tela, *to shoot away*, Caes.; omne frumentum, Caes.; patrimonia, Cic.; omnes fortunas sociorum, Caes.; of effort: multam operam frustra, Cic.; esp. of time, *to spend*, pass: magna diei parte consumpta, Caes.; aestatem in Treviris, Caes.; consumendi otii causa, Cic. TRANSF., *to waste or wear away, destroy*: omnia flammā, Caes.; aedes incendio, Liv.; viscera morsu, Ov.; of life, *to destroy, kill*: si me vis aliqua morbi aut natura ipsa consumpsisset, Cic.; totidem plagis hostem, Hor.; garrulus hunc consumet *will be the death of him*, Hor.; fame consumi *to die of hunger*, Caes.

consumptĭo -ōnis, f. (consumo), *a consuming, destroying*: Cic.

consumptor -ōris, m. (consumo), *a consumer, destroyer*: confector et consumptor omnium, Cic.

consuo

consuo

consŭo -sŭĕre -sŭi -sūtum, *to sew together, stitch together*: Varr. TRANSF., dolos, *to form*, Pl.; os, *to close*, Sen.

consurgo -surgĕre -surrexi -surrectum, *to rise up together*, or simply *rise up, stand up.*
LIT., (1) of persons: triarii consurrexerunt, Liv.; ex insidiis, Caes.; toro, Ov.; ad iterandum ictum, Liv.; senatus cunctus consurgit, Cic.; esp. of an orator, *to rise up to speak*: consurgit P. Scaptius de plebe et inquit, Liv.; also *to rise up in honour of someone*: consurrexisse omnes et senem sessum recepisse, Cic. (2) of things without life: consurgunt geminae quercus, Verg.
TRANSF., (1) of persons, *to be roused to action*: magno tumultu ad bellum, Liv.; ad gloriam, Liv. (2) of things, *to rise, arise, break out*: consurgunt venti, Verg.; novum bellum, Verg.; ira, Quint.

consurrectĭo -ōnis, f. (consurgo), *a general standing up*: iudicum, Cic.

Consus -i, m. (? condo), *an ancient Roman deity, apparently concerned with agriculture*; hence **Consŭālĭa** -ĭum, n. pl., *the festivals of Consus*, on the 19th of August and 15th of December.

consŭsurro -are, *to whisper together*: Ter.

contābĕfăcĭo -făcĕre, *to consume, cause to waste away*: Pl.

contābesco -tābescĕre -tābŭi, *to waste away gradually*: cor, Pl.; Artemisia luctu confecta contabuit, Cic.

contăbŭlātĭo -ōnis, f. (contabulo), *a covering with boards, planking, floor, storey*: Caes.

contăbŭlo -are, *to cover with boards, to equip with floors or storeys*: murum, turrem, Caes.

contactus -ūs, m. (contingo), *contact, touching, touch*: sanguinis, Ov., Verg.; esp. of what is unclean, *contagion*: contactus aegrorum vulgabat morbos, Liv. TRANSF., oculos a contactu dominationis inviolatos, Tac.

contāgēs -is, f. (contingo), *touch, contact*; perhaps with the extra notion of *harmony, fellow-feeling* (Epicurus' συμπάθεια): Lucr.

contāgĭo -ōnis, f. (contingo), *a touching, contact*: cum est somno sevocatus animus a societate et contagione corporis, Cic.; esp. *a touching of something unclean, contagion, infection*: contagio pestifera, Liv. TRANSF., *moral infection, bad companionship, evil example*: turpitudinis, Cic.; furoris, Liv.

contāgĭum -ii, n. (contingo), a word perhaps coined by Lucr. as a convenient metrical alternative to contages and contagio, q.v., *touch, contact*; sometimes in Lucr. with the extra notion of *harmony, fellow-feeling* (Epicurus' συμπάθεια), but esp. *infection, contagion*: contagia morbi, Lucr.; mala vicini pecoris contagia, Verg. TRANSF., *moral infection*: aegrae mentis, Ov.; contagia lucri, Hor.

contāmĭno -are (cum/root tag-, as in tango). (1) *to pollute, to render unclean by contact or mixture, infect*: sanguinem, Liv.; se scelere, Cic.; veritatem aliquo mendacio, Cic. (2) in Ter., describing the methods of Ter., Pl., and others, perhaps *to blend original Greek plays*, perhaps even here *to spoil.*
¶ Hence partic. (with superl.) **contāmĭnātus** -a -um, *polluted, unclean*: Cic., Liv., Hor., Tac.

L.D.—6

contendo

contechnor -ari, dep. (techna), *to devise a trick*: Pl.

contĕgo -tĕgĕre -texi -tectum, *to cover.*
LIT., se corbe, Cic.; caput amictu, Verg.; locum linteis, Liv.; eos uno tumulo, *to bury*, Liv.; esp. *to conceal* or *shield by covering*: corporis partes, quae aspectum sint deformem habiturae, contegere atque abdere, Cic.
TRANSF., libidines fronte et supercilio, non pudore et temperantiā, Cic.

contĕmĕro -are, *to pollute, defile*: Ov.

contemno -temnĕre -tempsi -temptum, *to think meanly of, despise, contemn*: tuum consilium, Ter.; mea dona, Lucr.; dicta, Sall.; humanos, Cic.; Romam prae sua Capua inridere atque contemnere, Cic.; with infin.: contemnere coronari, Hor.; with acc. and infin.: ut ipsum vinci contemnerent, Cic.; se non contemnere, *to have a high opinion of oneself*, Cic.
¶ Hence partic. (with compar. and superl.) **contemptus** -a -um, *despised, despicable, contemptible*: vita contempta ac sordida, Cic.; homo contemptus et abiectus, Cic.; Hor., Tac.

contemplātĭo -ōnis, f. (contemplor), *a surveying, contemplation.* LIT., caeli, Cic. TRANSF., naturae, Cic.; Tac., Plin. L.

contemplātor -ōris, m. (contemplor), *one who surveys or contemplates*: caeli, Cic.

contemplātu, abl. sing. from contemplatus, m. (contemplor), *by surveying, by contemplation*: Ov.

contemplor (contemplo) -ari, dep. (templum), *to mark out a quarter or enclosure* (templum); hence *to look at attentively, survey, regard, contemplate.*
LIT., caelum suspicere caelestiaque contemplari, Cic.; situm Carthaginis, Liv.; Pl., Ter., Hor.
TRANSF., *to consider carefully*: ut totam causam quam maxime intentis oculis, ut aiunt, acerrime contemplemini, Cic.

contemptim, adv. (contemno), *contemptuously*: Pl., Lucr.; de Romanis loquentes, Liv.

contemptĭo -ōnis, f. (contemno), *contempt, scorn, disdain*: pecuniae, Cic.; deorum, Liv.; hostibus in contemptionem venire, Caes.

contemptor -ōris, m. (contemno), adj. and subst., *a despiser* or *contemptuous*: divitiarum, Liv.; divum, Verg.; nemo tam contemptor famae est, Liv.; contemptor lucis animus, Verg.; contemptor animus, Sall.

contemptrix -ricis, f. form of contemptor; q.v.: Pl., Ov., Plin.

¹contemptus -a -um, partic. from contemno; q.v.

²contemptus -ūs, m. (contemno), *contempt, disdain.* (1) act.: operis, Quint.; ambitionis, Tac. (2) pass.: turpis contemptus, Lucr., Liv., Ov.; esp. in dat.: Gallis brevitas nostra contemptui est, Caes.

contendo -tendĕre -tendi -tentum, *to strain, to exert.*
(1) *to strain in relation to some other person or thing*; hence: **a**, transit., *to compare, contrast*: ipsas causas, quae inter se confligunt, Cic.; Hor., Tac.: **b**, intransit., *to strive with another*: cum victore, Caes.; cycnis (dat.), Lucr.; contra Paridem, Verg.; pro vitulis contra leones, Cic.; inter se de principatu,

[145]

Caes.; cum Libone de mittendis legatis, Caes.; at an auction, *to bid against*: Cic.

(2) in gen.: **a**, transit., *to stretch, strain, exert.* Lit., vincla, Verg.; tormenta, Cic.; arcum, Verg.; ballistas lapidum et reliqua tormenta telorum contendere atque adducere, Cic.; and hence of missiles, *to shoot, cast*: tela, Verg. Transf., summas vires, Lucr.; omnes nervos ut, Cic.: **b**, intransit., *to strain, exert oneself.* Lit., of physical exertion: eniti et contendere debet ut vincat, Cic.; fuga salutem petere contendunt, Caes.; esp. *to hasten on a journey, try to reach*: Bibracte ire contendit, Caes.; fig.: si potuissemus, quo contendimus pervenire, Cic. Transf., in gen.: maximis laboribus et periculis ad summam laudem gloriamque, Cic.; ob eam causam contendi, ut plura dicerem, Cic.; esp. *to strive* for a concession, favour, etc.: non erat causa, cur hoc tempore aliquid a te contenderem, Cic.; ab aliquo valde de reditu in gratiam, Cic.; vehementer contendere ab aliquo ut, etc., Cic.; also *to assert with confidence, maintain*: contendentes numquam eam urbem fuisse ex Triphylia, Liv.; Cic., Lucr.

¶ Hence partic. **contentus** -a -um, *strained, stretched, tense.* Lit., funis, Hor.; onera contentis corporibus facilius feruntur, remissis opprimant, Cic.; Lucr., Verg. Transf., *eager, zealous*: ad tribunatum contento studio cursuque veniamus, Cic.; Lucr.

Adv. (with compar.) **contentē**, *eagerly, earnestly*: pro se dicere, Cic.

¹**contentē**, adv. from contendo; q.v.

²**contentē**, adv. from contineo; q.v.

contentĭo -ōnis, f. (contendo), *exertion, effort, striving.* (1) *in relation to some other person or thing*; hence: **a**, *a contrast, comparison*: hominum ipsorum, Cic.; contentionem facere, Cic.; as rhet. t. t., *antithesis, juxtaposition of opposed ideas*: Cic., Quint.: **b**, in competition with others, *combat, contest, strife*: magna contentio belli, Cic.; adversus procuratores contentio dicendi, Cic.; contentiones habere cum aliquo, Caes.; also *competition for*: honorum, Cic.; libertatis, Liv., Quint.

(2) in gen., *exertion, straining*: vocis, Cic.; animi, Cic.

contentĭōsus -a -um (contentio), *pertaining to a contest, contentious, quarrelsome*: oratio, Plin.

¹**contentus** -a -um, partic. from contendo; q.v.

²**contentus** -a -um, partic. from contineo; q.v.

contermĭnus -a -um, *bordering upon, adjacent, near*: contermina stabula ripae, Ov. N. as subst., *an adjoining region, a confine*: Tac., Plin.

contĕro -tĕrĕre -trīvi -trītum, *to rub away, reduce to small portions by rubbing, to grind, pound.*

Lit., cornua cervi, Ov.; Lucr.

Transf., *to destroy, wear away*: omnes iniurias voluntariā quādam oblivione, *to obliterate*, Cic.; reliqua conterere et contemnere, *trample under foot*, Cic.; ferrum, *to wear away by using*, Ov.; se in musicis, geometriā, astris, Cic.; of time, *to consume, spend*: omne otiosum tempus in studiis, Cic.; bonum otium socordiā atque desidiā, Sall.

conterrĕo -ēre, *to terrify, frighten exceedingly*: conterrere loquacitatem alicuius vultu ipso aspectuque, Cic.; his nuntiis senatus conterritus, Liv.; Verg., Ov.

contestor -ari, dep. *to call to witness*: deos hominesque, Cic.; hence as legal t. t., contestari litem, *to inaugurate an action by calling witnesses*, Cic.

¶ Hence partic. **contestātus** -a -um, in pass. sense: lis contestata, Cic. Transf., virtus contestata, *approved*, Cic.

contexo -texĕre -texŭi -textum, *to weave together, twine together.* Lit., lilia amaranthis, Tib.; ovium villis contextis homines vestiuntur, Cic.

Transf., (1) of material things, *to lay together*; hence *to build, construct, put together*: sic deinceps omne opus contexitur, Caes.; equum trabibus acernis, Verg. (2) of abstract things, *to connect, unite*: extrema cum primis, Cic.; hence *to form, devise*: crimen, Cic.; carmen longius, Cic.

¶ Hence partic. **contextus** -a -um, *interwoven, connected, united*: contexta condensaque corpora, Lucr.; perpetuae et contextae voluptates, *an unbroken series of pleasures*, Cic.; contexta historia eorum temporum, *continuous*, Nep.

Adv. **contextē**, *in close connexion*: Cic.

¹**contextus** -a -um, partic. from contexo; q.v.

²**contextus** -ūs, m. (contexo), *uniting, connexion*: contextum dissolvere, *to break up the connexion between atoms* or *the fabric composed of atoms*, Lucr. Transf., mirabilis contextus rerum, Cic.; totus quasi contextus orationis, Cic.; Quint., Tac.

conticesco (**conticisco**) -ticescĕre -tĭcŭi (taceo), *to become silent, to be silent.*

Lit., conscientiā convictus repente conticuit, Cic.; neque ulla aetas de tuis laudibus conticescet, Cic.; Hor., Verg.

Transf., *to become still* or *quiet, to abate, cease*: illae scilicet litterae conticuerunt forenses et senatoriae, Cic.; tumultus, Liv.

contignātĭo -ōnis, f. (contigno), *a constructed floor, storey*: Caes., Liv.

contigno -are (tignum), *to put planks together, to floor*: Caes.

contigŭus -a -um (contingo). (1) act., *that which touches another, contiguous, near*: domus, Ov.; pars circi quae Aventino contigua, Tac.; Cappadoces, Tac. (2) pass., with dat., *within reach of*: contiguus missae hastae, Verg.

continens -entis, partic. from contineo; q.v.

continentĭa -ae, f. (contineo), *self-control, moderation, temperance*: continentia in omni victu cultuque corporis, Cic.; Sall., Caes.

contineo -tĭnēre -tĭnui -tentum (teneo).

(1) *to hold together, to keep together*: cum agger altiore aquā contineri non posset, Caes.; legiones uno in loco, Caes.; so *to connect, join*: quod oppidum Genabum pons fluminis Ligeris continebat, Caes. Transf., nec enim ulla res vehementius rempublicam continet quam fides, Cic.

(2) *to keep in, surround, contain.* Lit., mundus qui omnia complexu suo coercet et continet, Cic.; beluas immanes saeptis, *to confine*, Cic.; se suo loco, Caes.; alvus continet quod recipit, Cic.; milit. t. t., *to shut in*: Pompeium quam augustissime,

Caes.; milites sub pellibus, Caes. TRANSF., in gen.: se in suis perennibus studiis, Cic.; Belgas in officio, *to maintain in allegiance*, Caes.; petimus ab Antonio, ut ea quae continet neque adhuc protulit explicet nobis, Cic.; esp. *to include, comprise*: tales res quales hic liber continet, Cic.; de summo bono quod continet philosophiam, *which is the main point in philosophy*, Cic.; status reipublicae maxime iudicatis rebus continetur, *is involved in, depends upon*, Cic.

(3) *to hold back, restrain.* LIT., naves copulis, Caes.; risum, Cic.; gradum, *to check*, Verg. TRANSF., suos a proelio, Caes.; contineo me ab exemplis, Cic.; omnes cupiditates, Cic. L.; non posse milites contineri quin, Caes.

¶ Hence pres. partic. act. **continens** -entis. (1) *lying near, adjacent, bordering upon*: praedia continentia huic fundo, Cic.; continenti litori, Liv.; continentibus diebus, *in the days immediately following*, Caes. (2) *hanging together, unbroken*: agmen, Liv.; terra continens, *the mainland*, Nep.; so also without terra, as subst., **continens** -entis, f. *a continent*: Caes., Liv.; of time, *continuous, unbroken*: e continenti genere, *in unbroken genealogical succession*, Cic.; totius diei continens labor, Caes.; continenti cursu, Liv. (3) *self-controlled, temperate, continent*: puer, Cic.; continentior in vita hominum, quam in pecuniā, Caes.; superl.: Cic.

N. as subst. (rhet. t. t.) **continens** -entis, *the main point*: causae, Cic., Quint.

Adv. **continenter.** (1) *without break*, of space: sedetis, *close together*, Cat.; of time, *continuously*: totā nocte ierunt, Caes., Liv. (2) *continently, temperately*: vivere, Cic.

¶ Past partic. pass. **contentus** -a um, *contented, satisfied*; with abl.: suis rebus, Cic.; ea victoria, Cic.; paucis, Hor.; contentus quod, Cic.; with infin.: Ov., Quint.

contingo -tingĕre -tīgi -tactum (tango).

(1) transit., *to touch*: **a**, in gen.: terram osculo, Liv.; paene terram (of the moon), Cic.; funem manu, Verg.; dextram, *to grasp*, Liv.; cibos ore, Ov.: **b**, *to touch with* something, *smear* or *sprinkle* with: oras pocula circum mellis liquore, Lucr.; lac sale, Verg. TRANSF., *to affect, infect*; esp. in perf. partic.: contacta civitas rabie iuvenum, Liv.; contactum nullis ante cupidinibus, Prop.; ora nati sacro medicamine, Ov.: **c**, as geograph. t. t., *to border on, touch*: quorum agri non contingunt mare, Cic., Liv.; with dat., or with inter se: Caes.; of personal relationship: aliquem sanguine ac genere, Liv., Hor.: **d**, *to reach*: Italiam, Verg.; avem ferro, Verg.; ex tantā altitudine contingere hostem non posse, Liv.; optatam cursu metam, Hor.; nec contigit ullum vox mea mortalem, Ov. TRANSF., aevi florem, Lucr.; hence *to concern, affect*: Romanos nihil (consultatio) contingit, nisi quatenus, etc., Liv.

(2) intransit., *to happen, to befall* (usually of good luck); with dat.: mihi omnia, quae opto, contingant, Cic.; with infin.: celeriter antecellere omnibus ingenii gloriā contigit, Cic.; non cuivis homini contingit adire Corinthum, Hor.; with ut: quoniam autem, tecum ut essem, non contigit, Cic.

continuātio -ōnis, f. (continuo), *an unbroken continuance* or *succession*: tribunatus, Liv.; imbrium, Caes.; causarum, Cic.; rhet. t. t., *a period*: nimis longa continuatio verborum, Cic.

continuitās -ātis, f. (continuus), *continuity, unbroken succession*: Varr., Plin.

¹**continŭō**, adv. from continuus; q.v.

²**continŭo** -are (continuus), *to connect up, unite, make continuous.* LIT., in space: (aer) mari continuatus et iunctus est, Cic.; fundos, Cic.; binas aut amplius domos, Sall.; aedificia moenibus, Liv.; so: verba, *to form into a sentence*, Cic. Pass. in middle sense, *to join up with*: Cic., Tac.

TRANSF., esp. in time: prope continuatis funeribus, *in almost immediate succession*, Liv.; diem noctemque potando, *continue drinking day and night*, Tac.; iter die et nocte, Caes.; militiam, Liv.; magistratum, *to prolong*, Sall.; alicui consulatum, Liv.

continŭus -a -um (contineo), *connected up, hanging together, continuous, unbroken, uninterrupted.*

LIT., in space: Leucada continuam veteres habuere coloni, *connected with the mainland*, Ov.; Rhenus uno alveo continuus, Tac.

TRANSF., esp. in time, *successive, following on, uninterrupted*: secutae sunt continuos complures dies tempestates, Caes.; superiora continuorum annorum decreta, Cic.; oppugnatio, Liv.; amor, Prop.; with abl. of persons or periods, *continuously occupied with*: Tac.; translationes, *in an unbroken stream*, Cic.

Abl. n. sing. as adv. **continŭo**, *immediately, at once*: Pl., Cic., Caes., Verg.; esp. in conjunction with a temporal clause introduced by ubi, postquam, etc., *immediately after, as soon as*: Pl., Cic., Hor. TRANSF., in argument, *forthwith, necessarily, as an immediate consequence* (usually with neg. or virtual neg.): non continuo, si me in gregem sicariorum contuli, sum sicarius, Cic.

contio -ōnis, f. (contr. from conventio). LIT., *an assembly of the people* or *of the soldiers, a public meeting*: contionem advocare, Cic., Caes., Liv.; populi, militum, Caes.; vocare ad contionem, Liv.; contionem habere, dimittere, Liv.; prodire in contionem, Cic.; producere aliquem in contionem, Liv.; aliquid in contione dicere, Cic.; pro contione, *at a meeting*, Sall., Liv.

TRANSF., (1) *the speech made in such an assembly*: contiones turbulentae Metelli, temerariae Appii, furiosissimae Publii, Cic.; habere contiones in Caesarem graves, Caes.; funebris, *a funeral oration*, Cic., Tac. (2) *the speaker's platform*: in contionem ascendere, Liv., Cic.

contiōnābundus -a -um (contionor), *haranguing, speaking in public*: Liv.

contiōnālis -e (contio), *relating to a public assembly*: contionalis prope clamor senatus, Cic. L.; illa contionalis hirudo aerarii, *that blood-sucker and demagogue*, Cic. L.; senex, Liv.

contiōnārius -a -um (contio), *relating to a public assembly*: ille contionarius populus, Cic. L.

contiōnātor -ōris, m. (contionor), *a popular orator, demagogue*: Cic.

contionor

contiōnor -ari, dep. (contio). (**1**) *to attend an assembly*: nunc illi vos singuli universos contionantes timent, Liv. (**2**) *to speak in public before an assembly*: apud milites, Caes.; superiore e loco, Cic.; also *to proclaim publicly*: C. Cato contionatus est se comitia haberi non siturum, Cic. L.

contiuncŭla -ae, f. (dim. of contio), *a short harangue*: Cic.

contollo -ĕre (obsol. for confero), *to bring together*: gradum, Pl.

contōnat, impers. *it thunders violently*: Pl.

contorquĕo -torquēre -torsi -tortum, *to twist, whirl, turn violently, contort*: gubernaclum, Lucr.; membra quocunque vult, Cic.; proram ad laevas undas, Verg.

Esp. *to whirl in throwing* a spear, etc., so *to hurl*: lit., telum validis contortum viribus ire, Lucr.; contorquere hastam in latus, Verg. TRANSF., verba, *to hurl forth*, Cic., Plin. L.

¶ Hence partic. **contortus** -a -um. (**1**) *intricate, confused, complicated*: contortae et difficiles res, Cic. (**2**) *whirling*; so *powerful, vigorous*: oratio, Cic.

Adv. (with compar.) **contortē**, *intricately*: Cic.

contortĭo -ōnis, f. (contorqueo), *a whirling, twisting*: contortiones orationis, *intricacies of speech*, Cic.

contortor -ōris, m. (contorqueo), *a twister, one who perverts*: legum, Ter.

contortŭlus -a -um (dim. of contortus), *somewhat intricate*: Cic.

contortus -a -um, partic. from contorqueo; q.v.

contrā (from cum, as extra from ex), adv. and prep.

Adv., *opposite, over against, on the opposite side*. LIT., of place: adi contra, Pl.; ulmus erat contra, Ov.; omnia contra circaque plena hostium erant, Liv. TRANSF., in other relations: **a**, of equivalence, *in return, back*: cum hic nugatur, contra nugari lubet, Pl.; amare, Pl.; diligere, Cat.; auro contra constat filius, *is worth his weight in gold*, Pl.: **b**, of difference, *otherwise*: alia aestimabilia, alia contra, Cic.; often foll. by atque, *or* quam: simulacrum Iovis contra atque antea fuerat converteret, Cic.; cum contra fecerint quam polliciti sint, Cic.: **c**, of opposition, *against*: accingere, Lucr.; pugnare, Lucr.; consistere, Caes.; dicere, Cic.

Prep. with acc., *opposite to, over against*. LIT., of place: insula quae contra Brundusinum portum est, Caes. TRANSF., *against, in opposition to, contrary to*: contra opinionem, Cic.; contra ea, *on the contrary, on the other hand*, Caes.; esp. of *hostile* action or speech: contra vim atque impetum fluminis, Caes.; contra populum Romanum coniurasse, Caes.; contra deos disputare, Cic. Contra occasionally is placed after its acc.: quos contra, Cic.; so, in Vergil, after nouns.

contractĭo -ōnis, f. (contraho), *a drawing together, contraction*. LIT., contractio et porrectio digitorum, Cic.; frontis, Cic. TRANSF., (**1**) *abbreviation, shortness*: orationis, Cic.; syllabae, Cic. (**2**) *anxiety, depression*: animi, Cic.

contractiuncŭla -ae, f. (dim. of contractio), *slight depression*: animi, Cic.

contrectabiliter

contractus -a -um, partic. from contraho; q.v.

contrādīco -dīcĕre -dixi -dictum, *to gainsay, speak against, contradict*: sententiis aliorum, Tac.; nec contradici quin amicitia de integro reconcilietur, Liv.

contradictĭo -ōnis, f. (contradico), *a speaking against, contradiction*: Quint., Tac.

contrăho -trăhĕre -traxi -tractum.

(**1**) *to draw together, collect, unite* (opp. dissipare). LIT., omnia in unum locum, Cic. L.; cohortes ex finitimis regionibus, Caes.; magnam classem, Nep.; Luceriam omnes copias, Cic.; Scipionem et Hasdrubalem ad conloquium, Liv. TRANSF., **a**, *to unite*: contrahit celeriter similitudo eos, Liv.: **b**, *to conclude* or *complete a business arrangement*: rem, rationem, negotium, Cic.; contrahere magnam rationem cum Mauritaniae rege, Cic.: **c**, in gen., *to cause, bring on, bring about*: amicitiam, Cic.; offensionem, Cic.; aes alienum, *to contract debt*, Cic.; bellum, Liv.; lites, Cic.; porca contracta, *due to expiate a crime*, Cic.

(**2**) *to draw together by way of shortening* or *narrowing, to contract*. LIT., frontem (in frowning), Pl., Cic., Hor.; castra, Caes.; pulmones se contrahunt, Cic.; contractum aliquo morbo bovis cor, Cic.; orbem (of the moon), Ov.; vela, *to furl one's sails*, fig. *to be moderate*, Cic.; of the action of cold: contracto frigore pigrae, i.e. *numbed*, Verg. TRANSF., *to shorten, reduce, draw in*: orationem in verbum contrahere, Cic.; appetitus omnes contrahere, Cic.; of the spirits, *to depress*: animum, Cic.

¶ Hence partic. as adj. (with compar.) **contractus** -a um, *drawn in, contracted, narrow*. LIT., in space: locus exiguus atque contractus, Verg., Hor., Cic. TRANSF., his iam contractioribus noctibus, Cic.; contractum genus vocis, Cic.; dialectica quasi contracta et astricta eloquentia putanda est, Cic.; of circumstances, *straitened*: paupertas, Hor.; of persons, *retired, quiet*: contractus leget, Hor.

contrārĭus -a -um (contra), *opposite, over against*. LIT., of place: collis adversus huic et contrarius, Caes.; vulnera, *wounds in front*, Tac.; contrarius ictus, Liv.; classi contraria flamina, *contrary winds*, Ov.; also of mutual opposition: in contrarias partes fluere, Cic.; in comparison, followed by atque: qui versantur contrario motu atque caelum, Cic.

TRANSF., *opposed, contrary*: contrariae epistulae, *contradictory*, Cic.; in contrarias partes disputare, disserere, *to speak for and against*, Cic.; with genit.: huius virtutis contraria est vitiositas, Cic.; with dat.: nihil malum esse, nisi quod virtuti contrarium esset, Cic.; in comparison, followed by atque *or* ac: contrarium decernebat ac paulo ante decreverat, Cic.; esp. of *hostile action* or *speech*: arma, Ov., Lucr., Verg.; hence *injurious*: otium maxime contrarium esse, Caes.

N. as subst. **contrārĭum** -i, *the opposite*: Cic., Tac.; also in plur.: Verg., Ov., Cic.; ex contrario, *on the other side*, Caes., Cic.

Adv. **contrārĭē**, *in an opposite direction* or *manner*: sidera contrarie procedentia, Cic.; verba relata contrarie, Cic.

contrectābĭlĭtĕr, adv. (contrectabilis), *with feeling*: Lucr.

[148]

contrectătĭo -ōnis, f. (contrecto), *a touching, handling*: Cic.

contrecto -are (tracto), *to touch, feel, handle.* LIT., vulnus, Ov.; pectora, Ov.; esp. of *familiar handling*: Hor.; and so of *defiling*: Pl., Tac. TRANSF., totaque mente contrectare varias voluptates, *consider*, Cic.

contrĕmisco -trĕmiscĕre -trĕmŭi. (1) intransit., *to tremble violently, to quake*: contremiscere totā mente atque artubus omnibus, Cic.; Lucr., Verg. (2) transit., *to tremble before, be afraid of*: periculum, Hor.

contrĕmo -ĕre, *to tremble violently, quake*: tellus, Lucr.

contrĭbŭo -tribŭĕre -tribŭi -trībutum (tribus), *to put in the same division with, brigade with, incorporate with, unite*: Calagurritani qui erant cum Oscensibus contributi, Caes.; Ambracia quae tum contribuerat se Aetolis, Liv. TRANSF., *to bring together, bring in, contribute*: Ov., Tib.

contristo -are (tristis), *to make sorrowful, sadden*: contristat haec sententia Balbum Cornelium, ap. Cic. L. TRANSF., pluvio frigore caelum, *make gloomy*, Verg.; Hor.

contrītus -a -um, partic. from contero; q.v.

contrŏversĭa -ae, f. (controversus), *a dispute*, properly at law, but also in gen.: hereditatis, *about an inheritance*, Cic.; controversiam habere de fundo, Cic.; componere, Caes.; in controversiā versari, esse, Cic.; rem adducere in controversiam, deducere in controversiam, vocare in controversiam, *to make matter of debate*, Cic. TRANSF., *possible dispute, contradiction, question*: sine controversia, *indisputably*, Ter., Cic.; controversia non erat quin, *there was no doubt that*, Cic.

contrŏversĭōsus -a -um (controversia), *controverted, strongly disputed*: res, Liv.

contrŏversus -a -um (contro, like contra, formed from cum), *that which is a subject of debate, controverted*: res, Cic., Liv., Quint.

contrŭcīdo -are, *to cut in pieces, hew down, slay*: debilitato corpore et contrucidato, Cic.; fig.: rempublicam, Cic.

contrūdo -trūdĕre -trūsi -trūsum, *to thrust, push together*: nubes in unum, Lucr.; aliquos in balneas, Cic.

contrunco -are, *to cut in pieces*: filios, Pl.; cibum, Pl.

contŭbernālis -is, c. (contubernium). LIT., as milit. t. t. (1) *a messmate, comrade, one who shares the same tent*: domi una eruditi, militiae contubernales, Cic. (2) *a young man who accompanied a general to learn the art of war*: fuit in Cretā postea contubernalis Saturnini, Cic.

TRANSF., (1) in gen., *a comrade, mate*: alicui contubernalem in consulatu fuisse, Cic.; habuisses non hospitem sed contubernalem, Cic. (2) *the husband* or *wife of a slave*: Plin.

contŭbernĭum -i, n. (taberna). (1) concr.: **a**, *a tent in which ten men and an officer lodged*: deponere in contubernio arma, Caes.; Tac.: **b**, *the common dwelling of a male and female slave*: Tac.

(2) abstr.: **a**, *a sharing in the same tent, comradeship*: militum, Tac.: **b**, *the attendance of a young man on a general to learn the art of war*: contubernii necessitudo, Cic., Liv.: **c**, fig., in gen.: *companionship, intimacy*,

Suet., Tac.: **d**, esp. *the living together of slaves as man and wife*: Col., Curt.; hence *concubinage*: Cic.

contŭĕor -tŭēri -tŭĭtus sum, dep. (1) *to survey, to look at attentively.* LIT., aspicite ipsum, contuemini os, Cic. TRANSF., *to consider, reflect upon*: a contuendis nos malis avocat, Cic.; Lucr. (2) *to catch sight of*: Pl.

contŭĭtū (contutu), abl. sing. from contuitus, m. (contueor), *by surveying, attentive looking*: Plin., Pl.

contŭmācĭa -ae, f. (contumax), *stubbornness, obstinacy*; gen. in a bad sense: insolentia, superbia, contumacia, Cic., Liv., Tac.; in a good sense, *firmness*: libera contumacia (of Socrates), Cic.

contŭmax -ācis, *stubborn, obstinate*: quis contumacior? quis inhumanior? quis superbior? Cic.; contumaces et inconsultae voces, Tac.; in a good sense, *firm, unyielding*: contumax etiam adversus tormenta servorum fides, Tac.

Adv. **contŭmācĭtĕr**, *stubbornly, obstinately*: Cic., Liv.; in a good sense: Sen., Quint.

contŭmēlĭa -ae, f. *outrage.*

LIT., *physical violence*; from persons: Tac.; from things: naves totae factae ex robore ad quamvis vim et contumeliam perferendam, Caes.

TRANSF., esp. of speech, *insult, affront*: contumeliam iacēre in aliquem, Cic.; facere, Pl., Ter.; lacerare aliquem contumeliis, Cic.; onerare contumeliis, Cic.; vexare omnibus contumeliis, Cic.; contumeliae causa describere, Cic.; contumelia appellare perfugam, *insultingly*, Caes.; vertere aliquid in contumeliam suam, *to take as an insult*, Caes.; Hor.

contŭmēlĭōsus -a -um, adj. (with compar. and superl.) (contumelia), *outrageous, insulting, abusive*: epistulae in aliquem contumeliosae, Cic.; id contumeliosum est plebi (followed by acc. and infin.), Liv.

Adv. (with compar. and superl.) **contŭmēlĭōsē**, *abusively*: dicere, Cic., Ter., Liv.

contŭmŭlo -are. (1) *to heap up in a mound*: Plin. (2) *to bury, inter*: Ov.

contundo -tundĕre -tŭdi -tūsum, *to bruise, crush, pound, break to pieces.*

LIT., allia serpyllumque, Verg.; of persons, *to beat up*: anum saxis, Hor.; pugiles caestibus contusi, Cic.; contusi ac debilitati inter saxa rupesque, Liv.

TRANSF., *to crush, demolish*: ferocem Hannibalem, Liv.; animum, Cic.; audaciam alicuius contundere et frangere, Cic.; calumniam stultitiamque alicuius obterere ac contundere, Cic.

contŭor -i = contueor; q.v., Pl., Lucr.

conturbātĭo -ōnis, f. (conturbo), *disorder, confusion, perturbation*: mentis, Cic.

conturbo -are, *to disturb, throw into disorder, confusion*: ordines Romanorum, Sall.; rempublicam, Sall. TRANSF., (1) *to disturb in mind, cause anxiety*: valetudo tua me valde conturbat, Cic. L.; animum, Lucr. (2) conturbare rationes (or absol., conturbare: Cic.), *to bring a person's finances into confusion, to ruin, make bankrupt*: conturbare putat sibi licere, Cic.

¶ Hence partic. as adj. (with compar.), **conturbātus** -a um, *disordered*: Cic.

contus -i, m. (κοντός). (1) *a pole used for pushing a boat along*: Verg. (2) *a long spear* or *pike*: Tac.

cōnūbiālis -e (conubium), *relating to marriage, connubial*: Ov.

cōnūbium -i, n. (from nubo; in poets sometimes trisyll.), *marriage, intermarriage*. Esp. of *legal Roman marriage*: sequuntur conubia et adfinitates, Cic.; hence ius conubi, *or* simply conubium, *the right to intermarry*: conubium finitimis negare, Liv. In gen., poet., *marriage*: Pyrrhi conubia servare, Verg; *intercourse*: Ov.

cōnus -i, m. (κῶνος), *a cone*: Cic., Lucr. TRANSF., *the apex of a helmet*: Verg.

convādor -ari, dep. *to bind to appear before a court*: Pl.

convălesco -vălescĕre -vălŭi, *to become strong.*
(1) in gen.: postquam pestifer ignis convaluit, *blazed up*, Ov.; cum mala per longas convaluere moras, *have become rooted*, Ov.; so of political power: (Milo) in dies convalescebat, Cic.; his ille (Caesar) rebus ita convaluit ut, Cic.
(2) esp. *to recover from a disease, gain strength, get well*: non aegri omnes convalescunt, Cic.; ex morbo, Cic. TRANSF., ut convalescere aliquando et sanari posset, Cic.; ut tandem sensus convaluere mei, Ov.

convallis -is, f. *a valley shut in on all sides*: Lucr., Cic., Verg.

convāso -are (vasa), *to pack up baggage*: Ter.

convecto -are (freq. of conveho), *to bring together, collect*: praedam, Verg., Tac.

convector -ōris, m. (conveho), *a fellow-traveller*: Cic. L.

convĕho -vĕhĕre -vexi -vectum, *to bring together, carry into one place*: frumentum ex finitimis regionibus in urbem, Caes.; lintribus in eam insulam materiem, calcem, caementa, arma, Cic.; Liv.

convello -vellĕre -velli -vulsum, *to tear, pluck up, pull away, wrench off.*
LIT., repagula, Cic.; gradus Castoris, Cic.; Herculem ex suis sedibus convellere atque auferre, Cic.; viridem ab humo silvam, Verg.; dapes avido dente, *devour*, Ov.; as milit. t. t.: convellere signa, *to pluck up the standards, to decamp*, Cic., Liv.
TRANSF., *to weaken, overthrow, destroy*: cuncta auxilia reipublicae labefactari convellique, Cic.; si eam opinionem ratio convellet, Cic.; quo iudicio convulsam penitus scimus esse rempublicam, Cic.; verbis pectus, Ov.

convĕna -ae, c. adj. (convenio), *coming together*: Pl.; in plur., subst., *a concourse of strangers, assembled multitude*: pastores et convenas congregare, Cic.

convĕniens, partic. from convenio; q.v.

convĕnientia -ae, f. (conveniens), *agreement, harmony, conformity*: quaedam convenientia et coniunctio naturae, Cic.

convĕnĭo -vĕnire -vēni -ventum. (1) *to meet.*
Intransit., *to come together, to assemble*: ex provinciā, Caes.; ad hoc iudicium, Cic.; celeriter ad clamorem hominum circiter millia sex convenerant, Caes.; uno tempore undique comitiorum ludorum censendique causā, Cic.; so, fig., of communities: civitates

quae in id forum conveniunt, *which belong to that district*, Cic.; as legal t. t.: convenire in manum, of the wife, *to come into the power of her husband by marriage*, Cic. Transit., *to visit, meet, call upon*: videre et convenire, Pl.; quotidie plurimos, Cic.; Caes., Liv.
(2) *to fit*. LIT., si cothurni laus illa esset ad pedem apte convenire, Cic. TRANSF., *to agree with, be congenial to, be fitting to*: haec tua deliberatio non convenit cum oratione Largi, Cic.; non in omnes omnia convenire, Cic.; impers.: convenit, *it is fitting*; with infin., or acc. and infin.: illicone ad praetorem ire convenit? Cic.; Ter., Lucr., Hor.
(3) *to agree*; usually in pass. sense, *to be agreed upon*: id signum quod convenerat, *which had been agreed upon*, Caes.; pax convenit, Liv.; impers., convenit, *it is agreed*: mihi cum Deiotaro convenit, ut ille in meis castris esset, Cic.; cum de facto conveniret, Cic.
¶ Hence partic. **conventus** -a -um; n. as subst. **conventum** -i, *an agreement, compact*: pactum, conventum, stipulatio, Cic.
¶ Hence partic. (with compar.: Suet.; superl.: Plin. L.) **convĕniens** -entis. (1) *agreeing, unanimous, concordant*: bene convenientes propinqui, Cic. (2) *fit for, appropriate, suitable*: conveniens decretis eius, Cic.; oratio tempori conveniens, Liv.; nihil est enim tam naturae aptum, tam conveniens ad res vel secundas vel adversas, Cic.; with inter se: Lucr.; with cum: Ov.
Adv. **convĕnĭentĕr**, *agreeably with, suitably to*: convenienter cum naturā vivere, Cic.; constanter convenienterque sibi dicere, Cic.; convenienter ad praesentem fortunae statum loqui, Liv.

conventīcius -a -um (convenio), *to do with coming together*: patres, *assembled*, Pl. N. as subst. **conventīcium** -i (sc. aes)=τὸ ἐκκλησιαστικόν, *the money received by Greek citizens for attendance in the popular assembly*: Cic.

conventĭcŭlum -i, n. (dim. of conventus).
(1) *a coming together, assembly, association*: conventicula hominum, quae postea civitates nominatae sunt, Cic. (2) *a place of meeting*: Tac.

conventĭo -ōnis, f. (convenio). (1) *an assembly*: Varr. (2) *an agreement, compact*: Cic.

conventum -i, n. from convenio; q.v.

conventus -ūs, m. (convenio). LIT., (1) *a coming together, an assembly*: virorum mulierumque celeberrimus, Cic.; in nocturno conventu fuisse apud M. Laecam, Cic.; omnium sociarum civitatum, Liv.; esp. *an assembly of the inhabitants of a province*: conventūs agere, *to hold the assizes*, Cic.; hence *a corporation or company formed in a province*: conventus Syracusanus, Cic. (2) of atoms, *union, combination*: Lucr.
TRANSF., *agreement*: Cic.

converbĕro -are, *to beat violently*: Plin. TRANSF., Sen.

converro (**convorro**) -verrĕre -verri -versum, *to sweep together, brush up*: Pl. TRANSF., (1) *to beat thoroughly*: Pl. (2) *hereditates omnium, scrape together*, Cic.

conversātĭo -ōnis, f. (conversor). (1) *frequent use*: Sen.; esp. *frequent sojourn in a place*: Plin. (2) *dealings with persons*: Sen., Quint., Tac.

conversio -ōnis, f. (converto).
LIT., *a turning round*: caeli, Cic.; mensium annorumque conversiones, *periodical return*, Cic.
TRANSF., in rhetoric. (1) *the rounding off of a period*: ut (oratio) conversiones habeat absolutas, Cic. (2) *the repetition of the same word at the end of a clause*: Cic. (3) *change*: naturales esse quasdam conversiones rerum publicarum, Cic.

converso -are (freq. of converto), *to turn round frequently*: animus se ipse conversans, Cic. Pass. **conversor** -ari, in middle sense, *to live*: Plin.; *to have dealings with*: Sen.

converto (**convorto**) -vertĕre -verti -versum, *to turn round, whirl round*. LIT., (terra) circum axem se summa celeritate convertit et torquet, *revolves*, Cic. Esp. *to turn in the opposite direction*.
(1) *to turn back*: palam anuli ad palmam, Cic.; esp. milit. t. t.: signa convertere, *to wheel round*, Caes.; terga *or* se convertere, *to flee*, Caes.; vox boum Herculem convertit, *makes Hercules turn round*, Liv.; iter convertere, Caes.; reflex.: se ad montes, Caes.; as intransit. verb: cum paucis ad equites, Sall. TRANSF., **a**, *to change, alter*: convertere formas, Lucr.; mirum in modum conversae sunt omnium mentes, Caes.; cavendum ne in graves inimicitias convertant se amicitiae, Cic.; Hecubam in canem esse conversam, Cic.; as intransit. verb: hoc vitium in bonum convertebat, Cic.: **b**, *to translate*: librum e Graeco in Latinum, Cic.
(2) *to turn in any direction, direct towards*. LIT., naves in eam partem, quo ventus fert, Caes.; ferrum in me, Verg.; spelunca conversa ad aquilonem, *facing*, Cic.; video in me omnium vestrum ora atque oculos esse conversos, Cic. TRANSF., *to direct, devote*: omne studium curamque ad hanc scribendi operam, Cic.; reflex., se ad otium pacemque, Cic.; rationem in fraudem malitiamque, Cic.; pecuniam publicam domum, *to embezzle*, Cic.; as intransit. verb, *to turn*: ad sapientiora, Tac.

convestio -ire, *to clothe*: Enn. TRANSF., *to cover, surround*: domus duobus lucis convestita, Cic.; luce, Lucr.

convexĭtās -ātis, f. (convexus), *convexity*: mundi, Plin.

convexus -a -um (conveho). (1) *vaulted, arched, convex*: Verg., Ov.; n. as subst. (sing. or pl.), *an arch*: convexa caeli, Verg. (2) *sloping downwards*: iter, Ov.; vallis, Plin.

convīciātor -ōris, m. (convicior), *a railer, reviler*: Cic., Suet.

convīcior -ari, dep. (convicium), *to rail at, revile*: Liv., Quint.

convīcium -i, n. (cum/vox). (1) *a loud cry, shout, clamour*: mulierum, Cic. (2) *violent reproach, reviling, insult*: clamore et conviciis et sibilis consectari, Cic.; alicui convicium facere, Cic., Pl., Hor., Ov. TRANSF., *censure, reproof*: aurium, Cic.; verberavi te cogitationis tacito dumtaxat convicio, Cic.; meton.: nemorum convicia, picae, *mocking-birds*, Ov.

convictio -ōnis, f. (convivo), *social intercourse, familiarity*: ap. Cic. L.; meton., *familiar friends*: Cic. L.

convictor -ōris, m. (convivo), *one who lives with another, constant associate*: ap. Cic., Hor., Plin. L.

convictus -ūs, m. (convivo). (1) *a living together, constant intercourse*: conventus hominum ac societas, Cic. (2) *entertainment, feast*: Tac., Juv.

convinco -vincĕre -vīci -victum. (1) *to convict of a crime*: aliquem summae negligentiae, Cic.; multis avaritiae criminibus, Cic.; convictus in hoc scelere, Cic.; with infin, or acc. and infin.: Liv., Sall., Tac.
(2) *to prove mistaken*: convincere falsum, Lucr., Cic.
(3) *of things, esp. of crimes or mistakes, to prove conclusively, demonstrate*: errores Epicuri, Cic.; inauditum facinus ipsius qui commisit voce, Cic.; with acc. and infin.: Stoicos nihil de diis explicare convincit, Cic.; Quint.

convīso -ĕre, *to look at attentively, examine*: omnia loca oculis, Lucr.; poet. (of the sun, etc.), *to beam upon*: Lucr.

convīva -ae, m. (cum/vivo), *a table-companion, guest*: hilarus et bene acceptus, Cic.; Pl., Lucr., Hor.

convīvālis -e (conviva), *of a feast*: Liv., Tac.

convīvātor -ōris, m. (convivor), *one who gives a feast, a host*: Hor., Liv.

convīvium i, n. (convivor). (1) *a feast, entertainment, banquet*: accipere aliquem convivio, Cic.; adhibere aliquem convivio *or* in convivium, Cic.; convivium apparare, Cic.; ornare, Cic.; dimittere convivium, Liv.; discedere de convivio, Cic.; inire convivium publicum, Cic.; interesse in convivio, Cic.; producere convivium vario sermone ad multam noctem, Cic.; venire in convivium, Cic., Verg., Hor., Tac.
(2) meton., *the company assembled, guests*: vinosa convivia, Ov.; Sen.

convīvo -vīvĕre -vixi -victum, *to live with*: avaro, Sen. TRANSF., *to feast with*: cum aliquo, Quint.

convīvor -ari, dep. (conviva), *to eat and drink in company, feast*: non solum in publico sed etiam de publico, Cic.

convŏcātio -ōnis, f. (convoco), *a calling together*: populi Romani ad rempublicam defendendam, Cic.

convŏco -are, *to call together, assemble, convoke*: dissipatos homines, Cic.; principes ad se, Caes.; ad contionem, Liv. TRANSF., of the thoughts: consilia in animum, Pl.

convŏlo -are, *to fly together, run together, come together hastily*: cuncta ex Italia ad me revocandum convolaverunt, Cic.; Ter., Liv.

convolvo -volvĕre -volvi -volūtum. (1) *to roll together or roll round*: sol se convolvens, Cic.; of a snake: in lucem lubrica terga, Verg.; of a scroll: Sen. (2) *to intertwine*: testudo convoluta omnibus rebus, quibus ignis iactus et lapides defendi possent, Caes.

convŏmo -ĕre, *to vomit all over*: Cic., Juv.

convulnĕro -are, *to wound severely*: Plin.

convulsus -a -um, partic. of convello; q.v.

cŏōlesco = coalesco; q.v.

cŏ͞opĕrio -ŏpĕrire -operui -opertum, *to cover entirely, envelop, overwhelm*: aliquem lapidibus, *to stone to death*, Cic.; Decii corpus coopertum telis, Liv. TRANSF., nefariis sceleribus, Cic.; flagitiis atque facinoribus, Sall.

cŏoptātĭo -ōnis, f. (coopto), *election of a colleague, co-optation*: conlegiorum, Cic.; censoria, *filling up of the senate by the censors*, Cic., Liv.

cŏopto -are, *to choose, elect*, esp. *to join to oneself in a public office, to co-opt*: senatores, Cic.; tres sibi conlegas, Liv.; aliquem in paternum auguratus locum, Cic.; aliquem magistrum equitum, Liv.

cŏŏrĭor -oriri -ortus sum, *to arise, come forth at once* or *together.*
    Hence (1) in gen., of things, *to appear, break out*: tum subito tempestates sunt coortae maximae, Lucr.; quod pluribus simul locis ignes coorti essent, Liv.; pestilentia coorta, minacior quam periculosior, Liv.; bellum, Caes.; seditio tum inter Antiates Latinosque coorta, Liv.; risus, Nep.; libero conquestu coortae voces sunt, Liv.
    (2) of people, *to rise for insurrection* or *fight*: infensa erat coorta plebs, Liv.; Volscos summa vi ad bellum coortos, Liv.; Tac.

cŏortus -ūs, m. (coorior), *an arising, breaking forth*: Lucr.

Cŏos (Cŏus)=Cōs; q.v.

copa -ae, f. (cf. copo, caupo), *the hostess of a wine-shop*: Verg., Suet.

cŏphĭnus -i, m. (κόφινος), *a basket* or *hamper*: Juv.

cōpĭa -ae, f. (cŏŏpia, from cum/ops), *plenty, abundance.*
    LIT., (1) of things: agri, vectigalium, pecuniae, Cic.; frumenti, Caes.; lactis, Verg.; copia cum egestate confligit, Cic.; in plur.: omnium rerum adfluentes copiae, Cic.; esp. as milit. t. t., *supplies, provisions*: copias Dyrrhachii comparare, Caes. (2) of persons: virorum fortium atque innocentium tanta copia, Cic.; esp. as milit. t. t., *troops, forces*: omnis armatorum copia, Cic.; augebatur illis copia, Caes.; copiae peditum equitumque, Liv.; terrestres navalesque, Liv.; copias magnas cogere, Caes.; comparare, Cic.; contrahere, Cic.; dimittere, Caes. (3) of abstract things: argumentorum, Lucr.; dicendi, Cic.; verborum, Cic., Quint.
    TRANSF., *means, opportunity*: somni, Liv.; dimicandi cum hoste, Liv.; ab hoste copia pugnandi fit, Sall.; facere civibus consilii sui copiam, *to make one's advice available*, Cic.; with genit. of person, *access to*: Pl., Ter.; pro copia, *according to one's ability*, Pl., Liv.

cōpĭōsus -a -um (copia), adj. (with compar. and superl.). (1) *richly provided, wealthy*: urbs celebris et copiosa, Cic.; copiosus a frumento locus, *rich in*, Cic.; opulenti homines et copiosi, Cic. TRANSF., *copious in speech, eloquent*: homo copiosus ad dicendum, Cic.; oratio, Cic.; lingua, Cic.
    (2) *plentiful, abundant*: Caes., Phaedr., Quint.
    ¶ Adv. (with compar. and superl.) **cōpĭōsē**, *abundantly, plentifully*: large et copiose comparare pastum, Cic.; senatorum urna copiose absolvit, *with a large majority*, Cic.; of speech, *copiously*: dicere, Cic.

cōpis -e (cum/ops), *richly provided*: Pl.

cōpo, cōpona=caupo, caupona; q.v.

cŏprĕa -ae, m. (κοπρίας), *a low buffoon*: Suet.

copta -ae, f. (κόπτη), *a hard cake* or *biscuit*: Mart.

cōpŭla -ae, f. (cum/*apio), *a link, bond, tie.*

LIT., *a rope*: Pl.; dura copula canem tenet, *a leash*, Ov.; plur.: copulae, *grapnels*, Caes. TRANSF., *a bond, connexion*: quos inrupta tenet copula, Hor.; Quint.

cōpŭlātĭo -ōnis, f. (copula), *a union, connexion*: atomorum inter se, Cic. TRANSF., *union* socially, or *between abstract things*: Cic., Quint.

cōpŭlo -are (copula), *to join together, connect, unite.* LIT., altera ratis huic copulata est, Liv.; Lucr., Cic. TRANSF., copulare honestatem cum voluptate, Cic.; an haec inter se iungi copularique possint, Cic.; concordiam, Liv.
    ¶ Hence partic. **cōpŭlātus** -a -um (cōplātus: Lucr.), *connected, united, coupled*: quaedam sunt in rebus simplicia, quaedam copulata, Cic. TRANSF., nihil est amabilius neque copulatius quam morum similitudo, Cic.

cŏqua -ae, f. (coquus), *a female cook*: Pl.

cŏquĭno -are (coquo), *to cook*: Pl.

cŏquo coquĕre coxi coctum, *to cook, prepare food.*
    (1) of physical action. LIT., *to cook*: is qui illa coxerat, Cic.; cibaria, Liv. TRANSF., **a**, *to bake, burn*: coquit glebas aestas matutinis solibus, Verg.: **b**, *to ripen*: poma matura et cocta, Cic.; vindemia, Verg.: **c**, *to digest*: cibus confectus coctusque, Cic.
    (2) mentally: **a**, *to think of, meditate, contrive*: consilia secreto ab aliis, Liv.; Pl., Cic.: **b**, *to harass*: ardentem curaeque iraeque coquebant, Verg.; Pl., Quint.

cŏquus (cocus) -i, m. (coquo), *a cook*: Pl., Cic., Liv.

cŏr cordis, n. (connected with κῆρ, καρδία), *the heart.*
    LIT., *the heart*: cor palpitat, Cic.; Lucr.
    TRANSF., (1) *the heart as the seat of the emotions*: corde amare, Pl.; percussit laudis spes magna meum cor, Lucr.; exsultantia corda, Verg.; cordi esse, with dat., *to be to a person's liking*, Pl., Ter., Hor.; idque mihi magis est cordi, Cic.; with infin.: Pl., Liv.
    (2) *the heart as the seat of thought, the mind, judgment*: sapere corde, Pl.; propter haesitantiam linguae stuporemque cordis.
    (3) meton., *a person*: lecti iuvenes, fortissima corda, Verg.

Cŏra -ae, f. *an old town in Latium* (now *Cori*). Adj. **Cŏrānus** -a -um.

cōram (cum/os, *face*). (1) adv., *personally, openly, publicly*: commodius fecissent, si ea coram potius me praesente dixissent, Cic.; intueri aliquid, *to behold with one's own eyes*, Cic.; agere, i.e., *not by letters*, Cic.; ut veni coram, *when I came into the presence*, Hor.
    (2) prep. with abl., *in presence of*: genero meo, Cic.; populo, Hor.; sometimes placed after the noun, esp. in Tac.

Corbĭo -ōnis, f. (1) *a town of the Aequi.* (2) *a town in Hispania Tarraconensis.*

corbis -is, m. and f. *a wicker basket*: messoria, Cic., Pl., Ov.

corbīta -ae, f. (corbis), *a slow-sailing merchant vessel*: Pl., Cic. L.

corbŭla -ae, f. (dim. of corbis), *a little basket*: Pl., Suet.

corcŭlum -i, n. (dim. of cor), *a little heart*; sometimes used as a term of endearment: Pl.

Corcȳra -ae, f. (Κέρκυρα), *Corcyra, an island in the Ionian Sea* (now *Corfu*).

¶ Hence adj. and subst. **Corcȳraeus** -a -um, *Corcyraean, a Corcyraean*: horti, *the gardens of Alcinous*, Mart.

cordātus -a -um (cor), *prudent, sagacious, wise*: Enn., Sen. Adv. **cordātē**, *wisely, prudently*: Pl.

cordax -dācis (κόρδαξ), *a licentious dance*: Petr. TRANSF., of the trochaic rhythm: Cic.

cordŏlĭum -i, n. (cor/doleo), *heartache*: Pl.

Cordŭba -ae, f. *a town in Hispania Baetica, birth-place of Lucan and the Senecas (now Cordova).* Adj. **Cordŭbensis** -e.

cordȳla -ae, f. (κορδύλη). (1) *the fry of the tunny fish*: Mart. (2) *the mackerel*: Mart.

Corfīnĭum -i, n. *the capital of the Paeligni, headquarters of the Italians during the Social War.* Adj. **Corfīnĭensis** -e, *Corfinian.*

cŏrĭandrum -i, n. or **coriandrus** -i, f. (κοριαννον), *coriander*: Pl.

cŏrĭārius -i, m. (corium), *a tanner*: Plin.

Cŏrinna -ae, f. (Κόριννα). (1) *a Greek poetess of Tanagra, contemporary with Pindar.* (2) *the feigned name of Ovid's mistress.*

Cŏrinthus -i, f. (Κόρινθος), *Corinth, a city of Greece on the Isthmus of Corinth.* ¶ Hence adj. (1) **Cŏrinthĭăcus** -a -um. (2) **Cŏrinthĭensis** -e. (3) **Cŏrinthĭus** -a -um, *Corinthian*: aes, *an alloy of gold, silver, and copper,* greatly prized by the ancients, Cic.; vasa, supellex, *made of this alloy,* Cic.; and absol., **Cŏrinthĭa** -orum, n. (sc. vasa): Cic.

Cŏrĭŏli -ōrum, m. pl. *a town of the Volsci in Latium.* ¶ Hence adj. and subst. **Cŏrĭŏlānus** -a -um, *belonging to Corioli*; esp. as cognomen of Cn. or C. Marcius, *the capturer of Corioli.*

cŏrĭum -i, n. (**corius** -i, m.: Pl.). (1) *hide, skin*: animantium aliae coriis tectae sunt, Cic.; petere corium, *to thrash,* Cic.; prov.: canis a corio nunquam absterrebitur uncto, *old dogs will not learn new tricks,* Hor. (2) *leather*; hence *a leathern thong, strap*: Pl. (3) of plants, *rind, bark*: Plin.

Cornēlĭus -a -um, *name of a Roman gens,* the most famous members of which were:
(1) P. Corn. Scipio Africanus maior, the conqueror of Hannibal (236–184 B.C.).
(2) P. Corn. Scipio Aemilianus Africanus minor, son of L. Aemilius Paulus, the destroyer of Carthage (c. 185–129 B.C.).
(3) Cornelia, wife of Ti. Sempronius Gracchus, the mother of the Gracchi.
(4) L. Corn. Sulla, the dictator (138–78 B.C.).
¶ Adj. **Cornēlĭānus** -a -um, *Cornelian.*

Cornelius Nepos, see Nepos.

cornĕŏlus -a -um (dim. of ¹corneus), *horny*: Cic.

¹**cornĕus** -a -um (cornu). (1) *horny, made of horn*: rostrum, Cic., Verg., Ov. (2) *like horn*; so, *hard*: cornea fibra, Pers.; *horn-coloured*: Plin.

²**cornĕus** -a -um (cornus), *of cornel-trees* or *of cornel-wood*: virgulta, Verg.; Liv., Ov.

cornĭcĕn -cĭnis, m. (cornu/cano), *a horn-blower*: Cic., Liv., Juv.

cornĭcor -ari, dep. (cornix), *to caw like a crow*: Pers.

cornĭcŭla -ae, f. (dim. of cornix), *a little crow*: Hor.

cornĭcŭlārĭus -i, m. (¹corniculum), *a soldier decorated with the* corniculum, *and promoted*; e.g. *an adjutant to a centurion*: Suet.

¹**cornĭcŭlum** -i, n. (dim. of cornu). (1) *a little horn*: Plin. (2) *a horn-shaped decoration awarded to brave soldiers*: Liv.

²**Cornĭcŭlum** -i, n. *a town in Latium.* Adj. **Cornĭcŭlānus** -a -um, *Corniculan.*

cornĭger -gĕra -gĕrum (cornu/gero), *horned*: Lucr., Verg., Ov.; n. pl. as subst. **cornĭgĕra** -orum, *horned cattle*: Plin.

cornĭpēs -pĕdis (cornu/pes), *horn-footed, hoofed*: equi, Verg., Cat., Ov.

cornix -īcis, f. (connected with corvus, κορώνη, κόραξ), *the crow*: natura cornicibus vitam diuturnam dedit, Cic.; garrula, Ov.; annosa, Hor.; prov.: cornicum oculos configere, *to give anyone a dose of his own medicine*, Cic.

cornū -ūs (and **cornum** -i: Ov.), n. *a horn.*

LIT., *the horn of animals*, of the bull, ram, goat, stag, etc.: Lucr., Cic., Hor., Verg.; esp.: Cornu Copiae (Cornucopia), *the horn of the goat Amalthea, the sign of plenty,* Hor.

TRANSF., (1) as in Hebrew, poet. for *strength, courage*: tollere cornua in aliquem, Hor.; cornua sumere, Ov.

(2) *of anything made of horn*; esp. *a bow*: Verg.; *a large curved trumpet,* or *horn*: Cic., Verg.; *a lantern*: Pl.; *an oil cruet*: Hor.; *a funnel*: Verg.

(3) *of anything resembling a horn*; esp. *a hoof*: Verg.; *a bird's beak*: Ov.; *the tip* or *cone of a helmet*: Verg.; *the ends of the sail-yards*: Verg.; *the ends of the stick round which parchments were rolled*: Ov.; *the horns of the moon*: Verg., Ov.; *the arm of a river*: Ov.; *the end of a promontory*: Liv.; *the corner* or *extremity of a country*: Liv.; *the wing of an army*: dextrum, sinistrum, Caes.

Cornūcŏpĭa -ae, see cornu.

cornum -i, n. (cornus). (1) *the cornel-cherry*: Verg. (2) meton., *a spear made of cornel-wood*: Ov.

cornus -i (and -ūs), f. (1) *the cornel-tree* (Cornus mascula Linn.): Verg., Plin. (2) *the wood of the cornel-tree* and meton. *a spear made of cornel-wood*: Verg.

cornūtus -a -um (cornu), *horned*: animalia, Varr.

Cŏroebus -i, m. *a Phrygian, son of Mygdon.*

cŏrolla -ae, f. (dim. of corona), *a little crown*: Pl., Cat.

cŏrollārĭum -i, n. (corolla), originally, *a garland of flowers,* then *a garland of gilt* or *silvered flowers given away to actors,* etc.: Varr.; hence *a present, douceur, gratuity*: Cic.

cŏrōna -ae, f. (cf. κορωνίς).

LIT., *garland, chaplet, crown*; in gen. as worn at festivals and ceremonies: Pl., Cic., Hor., Tac.; as a military decoration: corona castrensis, triumphalis, navalis, civica, obsidionalis, muralis, Cic.; sub corona vendere, *to sell into slavery prisoners of war,* who wore chaplets, Cic.; sub corona venire, Liv.; regni corona, *a diadem,* Verg.

TRANSF., of things resembling a crown. (1) *a constellation, the northern crown*: Cic. (2) *a circle, assembly of men, bystanders, audience*: Cic., Hor., Ov. (3) as milit. t. t., *the besiegers of a city*: (urbem) coronā cingere, *to invest,* Caes.; or *the defenders*: coronā vallum defendere, Liv. (4) *the halo round the sun*: Sen.

cŏrōnārĭus -a -um (corona), *relating to a garland* : Plin.; aurum, *the present sent by the provinces to a victorious general*, originally in the form of a golden crown.

Cŏrōnē -ēs, f. (Κορώνη), *a town in Messenia.* Adj. **Cŏrōnaeus** -a -um, *of Corone* : Plin.

Cŏrōnēa -ae, f. (Κορώνεια), *a town in Boeotia.* Adj. **Cŏrōnaeus** -a -um, *of Coronea* : Liv.

Cŏrōnis -ĭdis, f. (Κορωνίς), *daughter of Phlegyas, mother of Aesculapius.*

¶ Hence **Cŏrōnīdes** -ae, m. = *Aesculapius.*

cŏrōno -are (corona).

LIT., *to wreathe, crown with a garland* : aras, Prop.; puppim, Ov.; cratera, Verg.; sequebantur epulae quas inibant propinqui coronati, Cic.; magna coronari Olympia, *to be crowned as conqueror at the Olympic games*, Hor.

TRANSF., *to surround, enclose in the form of a circle* : coronant myrteta summum lacum, Ov.; omnem abitum custode, Verg.

corpŏrālis -e (corpus), *relating to the body, corporeal* : voluptates, Sen.

corpŏrĕus -a -um (corpus). (1) *relating to the body, corporeal* : ille corporeus (ignis), Cic. (2) *fleshy, consisting of flesh* : umerus, Ov.

corpŭlentĭa -ae, f. (corpulentus), *fatness, corpulence* : Plin.

corpŭlentus -a -um, adj. (with compar.) (corpus), *fat, stout, corpulent* : Pl., Quint.

corpus -pŏris, n. *body, substance, matter as perceived by the senses* (opp. mens, animus, anima).

LIT., (1) *body in gen.* : tangere enim aut tangi nisi corpus nulla potest res, Lucr.; also plur., of the *primary particles of matter, atoms* : Lucr., Cic. (2) *the body of* men and animals : animi voluptates et dolores nasci e corporis voluptatibus et doloribus, Cic.; esp. the body as : **a**, *flesh* : ossa subiecta corpori, Cic.; corpus amittere, *to lose flesh*, Cic.; abiit corpusque colorque, Ov. : **b**, *a corpse* : Caes., Liv.; poet. *the shades of the dead* : Verg. : **c**, *the trunk* : Verg., Ov.

TRANSF., (1) *a person, 'a body'*, poet. : delecta virum corpora, Verg.; Liv. (2) *the 'body politic'* : totum corpus reipublicae, Cic.; civitatis, Liv. (3) in gen., *the main mass* of a thing; of a ship, or of military works : Caes.; of the world : universitatis corpus, Cic.; of a book : corpus omnis iuris Romani, Liv.

corpuscŭlum -i, n. (dim. of corpus). (1) *a little particle, corpuscle, atom* : Cic. (2) *a small human body* : Pl., Juv.

corrādo -rādĕre -rāsi -rāsum (cum/rado), *to scrape* or *rake together* : corpora, Lucr.; esp. of money : Pl. TRANSF., *of abstract things* : fidem, Lucr.

correctĭo -ōnis, f. (corrigo), *straightening out, improvement, amendment* : correctio philosophiae veteris et emendatio, Cic.; in rhetoric, *a figure of speech, in which an expression already used is replaced by a stronger one* (Gr. ἐπανόρθωσις) : Cic.

corrector -ōris, m. (corrigo), *an improver, amender, corrector* : corrector atque emendator nostrae civitatis, Cic.; Hor., Liv.

corrēpo -rēpĕre -repsi -reptum (cum/repo), *to creep, to slink* : in onerariam (navem), Cic.; in fear : correpunt membra pavore, *crawl with fear*, Lucr.; Sen.

correptius, compar. adv. from corripio; q.v.

corrīdĕo -ēre (cum/rideo), *to laugh loudly* : Lucr.

corrīgĭa -ae, f. *a shoe-string, boot-lace* : Cic.

corrīgo -rĭgĕre -rexi -rectum, *to put straight, reduce to order, set right.*

LIT., physically : curva, Plin. L.; cursum, Liv.

TRANSF., in gen., *to reform, amend* : praeterita magis reprehendi possunt quam corrigi, Liv.; mores, Cic.; sententiam, Cic.; non modo superiores sed etiam se ipse correxerat, Cic.; esp. of speech or writing, *to correct* : eas epistulas perspiciam, corrigam, Cic. L.; corrige sodes hoc, Hor.; Quint.

corripĭo -rĭpĕre -rĭpŭi -reptum, *to seize violently, lay hold of, take up.*

LIT., hominem corripi iussit, Cic.; arcumque manu celeresque sagittas, Verg.; se corripere, *to hasten off*, Pl., Ter., Verg.; viam, *to hasten on a journey*, Verg.; so : gradum, Hor.; esp. *to snatch away, steal, carry off* : pecuniam, Cic., Verg., Tac.

TRANSF., (1) *of disease, etc., to attack* : nec singula morbi corpora corripiunt, Verg., Lucr., Ov. (2) *of the passions, to overcome* : visae correptus imagine formae, Ov. (3) *to blame, rebuke* : consules, Liv.; voce magistri corripi, Hor. (4) *to accuse, bring to trial* : statim corripit reum, Tac. (5) *to shorten* : numina corripiant moras, Ov.; of syllables : Quint.

¶ Hence partic. **correptus** -a -um, and compar. adv. **correptius**, *more shortly* : Ov.

corrōbŏro -are (cum/roboro), *to strengthen, invigorate* : cum is se corroboravisset et vir inter viros esset, Cic. TRANSF., coniurationem non credendo corroborare, Cic., Tac.

corrōdo -rōdĕre -rōsi -rōsum (cum/rodo), *to gnaw away* : Platonis Politiam nuper apud me mures corroserunt, Cic.; Juv.

corrōgo -are (cum/rogo), *to bring together, collect by begging* : nummulos de nepotum donis, Cic.; auxilia ab sociis, Liv.

corrūgo -are (cum/rugo), *to wrinkle up* : ne sordida mappa corruget nares, *make you turn up your nose in disgust*, Hor.

corrumpo -rumpĕre -rūpi -ruptum, *to break to pieces.*

Hence (1) *to destroy, annihilate* : sua frumenta corrumpere et aedificia incendere, Caes.; vineas igni et lapidibus, Sall.; res familiares, Sall.; libertatem, Tac.; multo dolore corrupta voluptas, Hor.

(2) *to spoil, mar, make worse.* In gen : conclusa aqua facile corrumpitur, Cic.; Ceres corrupta undis, *corn spoiled by seawater*, Verg.; of animals and men, *to weaken* : corrupti equi macie, Caes.; of pronunciation, *to corrupt* : nomen eorum paulatim Libyes corrupere, barbarā linguā Mauros pro Medis appellantes, Sall.; of writings, etc., *to falsify* : tabulas publicas municipii manu suā corrumpere, Cic. Esp. morally, *to corrupt* : mores civitatis, Cic.; huius urbis iura et exempla corrumpere, Cic.; milites soluto imperio licentia atque lascivia corruperat, Sall.; corrumpere pecuniā, *to bribe*, Cic., Hor.

¶ Hence partic. (with compar. and superl.) **corruptus** -a -um, *spoilt, damaged, corrupt*; physically : caelum, Lucr.; iter factum

corruptius imbri, Hor.; morally: homines corruptissimi, Sall.
¶ Adv. (with compar.) **corruptē**, *corruptly, incorrectly*: neque depravate iudicare neque corrupte, Cic.
corrŭo -rŭĕre -rŭi (cum/ruo).
(1) intransit., *to fall to the ground, fall together, sink down.* Lit., corruerunt aedes, Cic.; conclave illud proxima nocte corruit, Cic.; of persons: paene ille timore, ego risu corrui, Cic.; ubi vero corruit telis obrutus, Liv.; of animals: Prop. Transf., illa plaga pestifera qua Lacedaemoniorum opes corruerunt, Cic.; of persons, *to be ruined*: si uno meo fato et tu et omnes mei corruistis, Cic., Liv.
(2) transit.: **a**, *to throw down, overthrow*: hanc rerum summam, Lucr.: **b**, *to heap up*: Pl.
corruptē, adv. from corrumpo; q.v.
corruptēla -ae, f. (corruptus), *the means of corruption; corruption, bribery, seduction*: mores hac dulcedine corruptelaque depravati, Cic.; pecuniosi rei corruptelam iudicii molientes, Cic.; meton., *a corrupter*: Pl., Ter.
corruptĭo -ōnis, f. (corrumpo), *a corrupting or corrupt state*: corporis, Cic.; opinionum, Cic.
corruptor -ōris, m. (corrumpo), *a corrupter, seducer, briber*: iuventutis, Cic.; exercitus, Liv.
corruptrix -īcis, f. (fem. of corruptor), *she that corrupts or seduces*; as f. adj., *corrupting*: tam corruptrice provinciā, Cic.
corruptus -a -um, partic. from corrumpo; q.v.
cors=cohors; q.v.
Corsĭca -ae, f. *the island of Corsica in the Mediterranean Sea.* Adj. **Corsus** -a -um and **Corsĭcus** -a -um, *Corsican.*
cortex -tĭcis, m. and f. *bark, rind, shell*; in gen., of trees and plants: obducuntur libro aut cortice trunci (liber=*the inner bark*), Cic.; esp. *the bark of the cork tree, cork*: Hor., Ov.; prov.: nare sine cortice, *to swim without corks*, i.e. *to need no assistance*, Hor.; levior cortice, Hor.
cortīna -ae, f. *a round kettle* or *cauldron*: Pl.; esp. *the cauldron-shaped Delphic tripod*: cortina Phoebi, *the oracle of Apollo*, Verg. Transf., *a thing in the shape of a cauldron*; *the vault of heaven*: Enn.
Cortōna -ae, f. (Κόρτωνα), *Cortona, a town of Etruria.* Adj. **Cortōnensis** -e, *of Cortona.*
cŏrŭlus=corylus; q.v.
cŏrus=caurus; q.v.
cŏrusco -are (connected with κορύσσω). (1) transit., *to move quickly, swing, shake*: telum, Verg.; of snakes: linguas, Ov.; in butting: frontem, Juv. (2) intransit., *to move quickly, tremble, flutter*: apes pennis, Verg.; abies, Juv.; of butting: agni, Lucr.; esp. of light, *to twinkle, flash*: Verg.
cŏruscus -a -um (corusco), *shaking, trembling*: silvae, Verg.; esp. of light, *twinkling, flashing*: fulgura, Lucr.; sol, Verg.; iuvenes auro corusci, Verg.
corvus -i, m. (cf. κορώνη, κόραξ, cornix), *a raven*: Pl., Cic., Ov.; prov.: in cruce corvos pascere, *to be crucified*, Hor.; perhaps also sometimes *a rook*.
Cŏrўbantes -ĭum, m. pl. from Corybas (Κορύβας), *the priests of Cybele.* Adj. **Cŏrўbantĭus** -a -um, *Corybantian.*

¹**Cōrўcĭus** -a -um (Κωρύκιος), *belonging to the Corycian caves on Mount Parnassus.*
¶ Hence **Cōrўcīdes** Nymphae, *the Muses*: Ov.
²**Cōrўcĭus** -a -um, adj. from Corycos; q.v.
Cōrўcos or **-us** -i, f. (Κώρυκος), *a promontory and city of Cilicia, famous for the cultivation of saffron.*
¶ Hence adj. **Cōrўcĭus** -a -um, *Corycian*: crocum, Hor.
cōrўcus -i, m. (κώρυκος), *a sand-bag in the palaestra, which the athletes used as a punch-ball*; fig.: corycus laterum et vocis meae, Bestia, Cic.
cŏrўlētum -i, n. (corylus), *a hazel copse*: Ov.
cŏrўlus -i, f. (κόρυλος), *a hazel-tree*: Verg., Ov.
cŏrymbĭfĕr -fĕra -fĕrum (corymbus/fero), *carrying bunches of ivy berries*, epithet of Bacchus: Ov.
cŏrymbus -i, m. (κόρυμβος), *a bunch of flowers* or *fruit*, esp. *a cluster of ivy berries*: Verg., Ov.
cŏrўphaeus -i, m. (κορυφαῖος), *a leader, chief, head*: Epicureorum Zeno, Cic.
Cōrўthus -i (Κόρυθος). (1) f. *a town in Etruria* (afterwards *Cortona*). (2) m. *the name of several obscure persons in mythology.*
cōrўtus or **cōrўtos** -i, m. (γωρυτός), *a quiver*: Verg., Ov.
¹**cōs** cōtis, f. *any hard, flinty stone*: Cic., Liv., Verg.; esp. *a whetstone, grindstone*; hence, fig. of any *stimulus*: Cic., Hor.
²**Cōs** or **Cŏus** (**Cŏos**) Coi, f. (Κῶς, Κόως), *a small island in the Aegean Sea, off the coast of Caria.*
¶ Adj. **Cōus** -a -um, *Coan*: poeta, Philetas, Ov.; artifex, Apelles, Ov.; Venus, *the Venus Anadyomene of Apelles*, Cic. As subst. **Cōum** -i, n. *Coan wine*: Hor.; **Cōa** -orum, n. pl. *Coan garments*: Hor., Ov.
cosmēta -ae, m. (κοσμήτης), *the slave who had charge of his mistress's wardrobe and toilet*: Juv.
cosmĭcos -a -um (κοσμικός), *belonging to the world.* M. as subst., *a citizen of the world*: Mart.
Cossўra (**Cōsўra**) and **Cossūra** -ae, f. *a small island between Sicily and Africa* (now Pantellaria).
costa -ae, f. *a rib.* Lit., Pl., Lucr., Verg. Transf., *a side*: aeni, Verg.
costum -i, n. (κόστος), *an eastern aromatic plant, employed in the preparation of unguents*: Hor., Ov.
cŏthurnātus -a -um (cothurnus), *provided with a buskin*, hence *tragic* or *elevated*: Ov.
cŏthurnus -i, m. (κόθορνος). (1) *a large hunting boot, reaching to the calf, and laced up the front*: Verg. (2) *the thick-soled boot worn by tragic actors.* Lit., cothurnus tragicus, Hor.; cothurnus maior, minor, Cic. Transf., *tragedy*: Hor.; *a tragic, elevated style*: sola Sophocleo tua carmina digna cothurno, Verg.
cotid- = quotid-; q.v.
Cotta -ae, m. *a cognomen of a family of the gens Aurelia.*
cottăbus -i, m. (κότταβος), *a game played by throwing heeltaps of wine into a metal basin*; hence, from the similarity of sound, *the strokes of a beating*: Pl.
cottăna (**cotōna, coctōna, coctăna**) -ōrum, n. (κόττανα, from Syrian), *a kind of small fig*: Juv.

Cottĭus -i, m. *name of two successive Alpine kings*; the father was recognized by Augustus, but after the son's death Nero annexed their territory, known as the Alpes Cottiae. Adj. **Cottius** and **Cottiānus** -a -um.

cŏtŭla or **cŏtўla** -ae, f. (κοτύλη), *a measure of capacity, half a sextarius*: Mart.

cŏturnix -īcis, f. *a quail*: Pl., Lucr., Ov.

Cŏtўs -tўis; acc. -tyn, voc. -tў, abl. -tўe, m. (Κότυς). (1) *name of several Thracian princes.* (2) *brother of Mithridates, prince of the Bosporus.*

Cŏtyttō -ūs, f. (Κοτυττώ), *the goddess of unchastity, originally worshipped in Thrace, afterwards in Athens and Corinth also*: Juv.

¶ Hence **Cŏtyttĭa** -ōrum, n. pl. *the festival of Cotytto*: Hor.

cŏvinnārĭus -i, m. (covinnus), *one who fights from a war chariot*: Tac.

cŏvinnus -i, m. (a Celtic word). (1) *the war-chariot of the ancient Britons and Belgae*: Luc. (2) *a travelling-chariot*: Mart.

cŏxa -ae, f. *the hip-bone*: Plin. L.

coxendix -īcis, f. (coxa), *the hip*: Pl., Suet.; *the hip-bone*: Plin.

Crabra or **Aqua Crabra**, *a water conduit between Tusculum and the Tiber.*

crabro -ōnis, m. *a hornet*: Verg., Ov.

crambē -ēs, f. (κράμβη), *cabbage*: Plin. Transf., crambe repetita, *cold cabbage warmed up*, i.e. *stale repetitions*, Juv.

Crannōn -ōnis, f. (Κραννών), *a town in Thessaly.* Adj. **Crannōnĭus** -a -um.

crāpŭla -ae, f. (κραιπάλη), *drunkenness*, and esp. its *after-effects, 'hangover'*: crapulam edormire et exhalare, Cic.; Pl., Liv.

crāpŭlārius -a -um, *to do with drunkenness*: unctio, *to prevent it*, Pl.

cras, adv. *tomorrow*: scies igitur fortasse cras, Cic. L.; Hor.; as n. subst.: cras istud, quando venit? Mart. Transf., poet., *in the future*: quid sit futurum cras, fuge quaerere, Hor.; Ov.

crassĭtūdo -ĭnis, f. (crassus), *thickness*: parietum, Caes.; aëris, *density*, Cic.

¹**crassus** -a -um, adj. (with compar. and superl.), *thick, dense, solid.* Lit., unguentum, Hor.; aër, *misty, heavy*, Cic., Hor.; restis, Pl.; toga, *coarse-grained*, Hor.

Transf., infortunium, *a sound thrashing*, Pl.; esp. of intellect, *dull* or *uneducated*: turba, Mart.; Ofellus rusticus abnormis sapiens crassaque Minerva, Hor.

¶ Adv. **crassē**, *roughly, rudely*: compositum poema, Hor.; Sen.

²**Crassus** -i, m. *name of a family of the gens Licinia*; q.v.

crastĭnus -a -um (cras), *of tomorrow*: dies crastinus, Cic.; die crastina, *tomorrow*, Liv., Verg., Hor. N. as subst. **crastĭnum** -i, *the morrow*: in crastinum differre, Cic.

crātēra -ae, f. and **crātēr** -ēris, m. (κρατήρ), *a large bowl in which wine was mixed with water*: Cic., Hor., Verg., Ov.

Transf., (1) *a receptacle for other liquids; for oil*: Verg. (2) *the crater of a volcano*: Lucr.; or *a volcanic fissure in the earth*: Ov. (3) *a constellation, the Bowl*: Cic., Ov.

Crātĕrus -i, m. (Κρατερός). (1) *a general of Alexander the Great.* (2) *a physician in the time of Cicero*: Cic. L., Hor.

Crāthis -thĭdis, m. (Κρᾶθις), *a river in southern Italy, near Thurii* (now *Crati*).

Crātīnus -i, m. (Κρατῖνος), *an Athenian comic poet, contemporary of Aristophanes*: Hor.

Crătippus -i, m. (Κράτιππος), *a peripatetic philosopher of Athens, teacher of Cicero's son.*

crātis -is, *a frame* or *basket made of wicker-* or *hurdle-work.* Lit., Verg., Hor.; sub crate necari, *to be crushed with stones while lying under a hurdle*, an old method of execution, Pl., Liv., Tac.; also, *a harrow*: Verg.; as milit. t. t., *fascines*: Caes. Transf., favorum, honeycomb, Verg.; spinae, *the joints of the backbone*, Ov.; pectoris, Verg.

crĕātĭo -ōnis, f. (creo), *choice, election*: magistratuum, Cic.

crĕātor -ōris, m. (creo), *the creator, maker, founder*: huius urbis Romulus creator, Cic.; *father*: Ov.

crĕātrix -īcis, f. (creator), *she who creates, a mother*: natura rerum, Lucr.; diva, Verg.

crēber -bra -brum (connected with cresco); compar. crebrior, superl. creberrimus.

(1) *of space, thick, crowded together, close*; esp. of growth: silva, Lucr., Ov.; hence in gen.: a, *crowding, numerous, thick*: hostes, Pl.; creberrima aedificia, Caes.; creberrima grando, Liv.: b, *crowded with, full of*; with abl.: creber arundinibus lacus, Ov.; creber procellis Africus, Verg.; fig.: (Thucydides) creber rerum frequentiā, Cic.

(2) *of time, repeated, numerous, frequent*: crebra inter se conloquia habere, Caes.; crebri ictus, Verg.; creberrimus sermo, Cic.; hence of persons, to signify *repeated* action: creber pulsat, *he beats repeatedly*, Verg.; in scribendo multo essem crebrior quam tu, Cic.

¶ Adv. **crēbrō**, with compar. crebrius and superl. creberrime, *repeatedly, frequently, often*: crebrius litteras mittere, Cic.; crebro respicere Romam, Ov.

crēbresco (**crēbesco**) -ĕre -brŭi (or -bŭi) (creber), *to become frequent, increase, gather strength, extend*: seditio crebrescens, Tac.; horror: Verg.; crebrescunt optatae aurae, Verg.; crebrescit vivere Agrippam, *the report spreads that*, Tac.

crēbrĭtās -ātis, f. (creber), *frequency*: sententiarum, Cic.; officiorum, Cic. L.

crēbrō, adv. from creber; q.v.

crēdĭbĭlis -e (credo), *credible, worthy of belief*: narrationes credibles, Cic.; followed by acc. and infin.: fit credibile deorum et hominum causā factum esse mundum, Cic.; vix credibile est, Hor.

¶ Adv. **crēdĭbĭlĭter**, *credibly*: Cic.

crēdĭtor -ōris, m. (credo), *a creditor*: tabulae creditoris, Cic.; Hor., Liv.

crēdo -dĕre -dĭdi -dĭtum, *to trust.*

(1) with acc. and dat., *to entrust, commit, trust something to someone*; in gen.: arma militi, Liv.; se perfidis hostibus, Ov.; aciem campo, Verg.; esp.: a, *of secrets*: arcana libris, Hor.; alicui arcanos sensus, Verg.: b, *of money, to lend*: pecuniam, Cic.; hence absol., *to lend*: credendi modum constituere, Cic.; often in partic. perf.: pecunia credita or res creditae, *loans*, Cic.; also n. of partic. as subst. **crēdĭtum** -i: Sall., Liv.

(2) with dat., *to trust in, rely upon, place confidence in*: credere nemini, Cic.; praesenti fortunae non credere, Liv.; ne crede colori, Verg.

(3) with dat., *to believe, give credence to* a person or thing: his auctoribus temere credens, Caes.; often parenthetic: mihi crede *or* crede mihi, *believe me, take my advice,* Cic., Hor., Ov.; fabulis, Cic.; lacrimis, Ov.; somniis, Cic.

(4) with acc., *to believe as a fact, to accept as true*: fere libenter homines id quod volunt credunt, Caes.; parenthetic: quod quidem magis credo, Cic.

(5) *to believe, to think, to be of the opinion*; with acc. and infin.: credo ego vos, iudices, mirari, Cic.; in pass., with nom. and infin.: pro certo creditur necato filio vacuam domum scelestis nuptiis fecisse, Sall.; impers., with acc. and infin.: quorum neminem nisi iuvante deo talem fuisse credendum est, Cic.; parenthetic, credo, *I suppose, I believe*: male, credo, mererer de meis civibus, si, Cic.; past potential, in 2nd person, crederes: maesti (crederes victos) redeunt, *you would have thought them beaten men,* Liv.

crēdŭlĭtās -ātis, f. (credulus), *credulity*: Ov., Tac.

crēdŭlus -a -um (credo), *believing easily, credulous, confiding*; with dat.: Verg., Tac.; in vitium, Ov.; stultus et credulus auditor, Cic. TRANSF., of things: spes, Hor.; fama, Tac.

Crĕmĕra -ae, m. *a river in Etruria, near which the Fabii were killed.* Adj. **Crĕmĕrensĭs** -e: Tac.

crĕmo -are, *to burn, consume by fire*: libros in conspectu populi, Liv.; regalia tecta, Ov.; esp. of the burning of the bodies of the dead: Sulla primus e patriciis Corneliis igni voluit cremari, Cic.; corpus alicuius, Cic.; also of sacrifices: crematos igni vitulos, Ov.

Crĕmōna -ae, f. *Cremona, a town in N. Italy.* Adj. and subst. **Crĕmōnensis** -e, *of Cremona, a man of Cremona.*

Crĕmōnis iugum, *a range in the Pennine Alps.*

crĕmor -ōris, m. *the thick juice obtained from animal or vegetable substances, pulp, cream,* etc.: Pl., Ov.

¹crĕo -are (connected with cresco), *to make, create, produce.*

(1) in gen. LIT., natura creet res auctet alatque, Lucr.; quas et creat natura et tuetur, Cic. TRANSF., periculum, Cic.; tribuniciam potestatem, Liv.

(2) *to elect* to an office: consules, Caes., Cic.; with double acc: Ancum Marcium regem populus creavit, Liv.

(3) of parenthood, *to beget, bear*: Hor., Liv., Ov.; hence partic., creatus with abl., of father or mother=*daughter* or *son*: Telamone creatus, Ov.

²Crĕo and **Crĕon** -ontis, m. *king of Corinth, whose daughter Creusa was married to Jason.*

crĕper -pĕra -pĕrum (Sabine word connected with κνέφας), *dark, obscure, uncertain*: Lucr.

crĕpĭda -ae, f. (κρηπίς), *a sandal*: Cic., Liv., Hor.; prov.: ne sutor ultra crepidam, *let the cobbler stick to his last,* Plin.

crĕpĭdātus -a -um (crepida), *wearing sandals*: Cic.

crĕpĭdo -ĭnis, f. (κρηπίς). (1) *a base, foundation, pedestal*: Plin. (2) *a quay, pier, dam,* etc.: Cic., Verg., Liv.

crĕpĭdŭla -ae, f. (dim. of crepida), *a little sandal*: Pl.

crĕpĭtācillum -i, n. (dim. of crepitaculum), *a little rattle*: Lucr.

crĕpĭtācŭlum -i, n. (crepito), *a rattle*: Mart., Quint.

crĕpĭto -are (freq. of crepo), *to rattle, creak, crackle, rustle, clatter*: crepitantia arma, Ov.; lenis crepitans auster, *rustling,* Verg.; multā grandine nimbi culminibus crepitant, Verg.

crĕpĭtus -ūs, m. (crepo), *a rattling, creaking, rustling, clattering*: digitorum, *snapping of the fingers,* Mart.; pedum, Cic.; dentium, Cic.; aeris, Liv.; viridis materiae flagrantis, Liv.; alarum, Liv.

crĕpo -pare -pŭi -pĭtum.

(1) intransit., *to creak, rattle, rustle, crackle*: crepat foris, Pl., Ter.; digiti crepantis signa, *a snapping of the fingers to call a servant's attention,* Mart.; acuto in murice remi obnixi crepuere, *crashed,* Verg.; crepat in mediis laurus adusta foris, *crackle,* Ov.

(2) transit.: **a**, *to cause to resound, rattle*: cum populus frequens laetum theatris ter crepuit sonum, Hor.: **b**, *to talk much of, chatter about, prate about*: publicas res, Pl.; post vina gravem militiam aut pauperiem, Hor.

crĕpundĭa -ōrum, n. pl. (crepo), *a child's plaything, a rattle,* or *amulet*: naevo aliquo aut crepundiis aliquem cognoscere, Cic.; Pl.

crĕpuscŭlum -i, n. (creper), *twilight*. (1) gen.: dubiae crepuscula lucis, Ov. (2) esp. *evening twilight*: inducunt obscura crepuscula noctem, Ov.

Crēs -ētis, m. see ¹Creta.

cresco crescĕre crēvi crētum.

(1) *to come into existence, spring forth, arise*: quaecunque e terrā corpora crescunt, Lucr.; esp. in past partic. cretus, *sprung from*: mortali semine, Ov.; Troiano a sanguine, Verg.

(2) of what exists, *to grow, increase in size*: **a**, of living creatures: fruges, arbusta, animantes, Lucr.; in longitudinem: Plin.; ut cum lunā pariter crescant pariterque decrescant, Cic.; of boys, *to grow up*: toti salutifer orbi cresce puer, Ov.: **b**, of other objects, *to increase in height, number,* etc.: Roma interim crescit Albae ruinis, Liv.; cum Albanus lacus praeter modum crevisset, Cic.; luna crescens, *waxing,* Cic.: **c**, of abstract things: crescit in dies singulos hostium numerus, Cic.; crescentes morbi, Cic.; crescebat in eos odium, Cic.: **d**, of persons, *to grow great, increase in fame, power,* etc.: pater per se crevisset, Caes.; Cic., Liv., Hor.

¹Crēta -ae, f. and **Crētē** -ēs, f. (Κρήτη), *the Mediterranean island of Crete (now Kriti).*
¶ Hence m. adj. and subst. **Crēs** -ētis, *Cretan, a Cretan*; plur. **Crētes** -um, m. *the Cretans*; f. adj. and subst. **Cressa** -ae: Cressa nota, *of Cretan chalk,* Hor.; bos = Pasiphaë, Prop.; as subst.=*Ariadne* or *Aerope*: Ov.; adj. **Crēsĭus** -a -um, *Cretan*; adj. and subst. **Crētaeus** -a -um, *Cretan*; as subst.=*Epimenides*: Prop.; m. subst. **Crētānus** -i, *a Cretan*; adj. **Crētensis** -e, *Cretan*; adj. **Crētĭcus** -a -um, *Cretan*; also *the surname of Q. Metellus, from his conquest of the island.*

²crēta -ae, f. (prop. adj. of ¹Creta), *Cretan earth, chalk,* or *a kind of fuller's earth,* used for whitening garments: Pl.; used also for painting the face: Hor.; for seals: Cic.

crētātus -a -um (²creta), *chalked*: fascia, Cic. L., Juv. TRANSF., ambitio, *canvassing by the white-robed candidates*, Prop.

crētĕus -a -um (²creta), *made of chalk or Cretan earth*: Lucr.

crētĭo -ōnis, f. (cerno), *a declaration by an heir accepting an inheritance*: Cic.

crētōsus -a -um (²creta), *abounding in chalk*: Ov.

crētŭla -ae, f. (dim. of ²creta), *white clay for sealing*: Cic.

Crĕūsa -ae, f. (Κρέουσα). (1) *daughter of Creon, king of Corinth, wife of Jason, killed by Medea*. (2) *daughter of Priam, wife of Aeneas*. (3) *a port in Boeotia*.

crībrum -i, n. (connected with κρίνω and cerno), *a sieve*: Cic.

crīmen -ĭnis, n. (connected with κρίνω and cerno). (1) *an accusation, charge*: esse in crimine, *to be accused*, Cic.; dare alicui aliquid crimini, Cic.; propulsare, defendere, *to repel, confute*, Cic.; meton., *an object of reproach*: perpetuae crimen posteritatis eris, Ov.

(2) *the fault, guilt, crime, with which a person is charged*: foedati crimine turpi, Lucr.; tuum crimen, *your fault*, Prop.; pictas caelestia crimina vestes, Ov.; meton., *cause of crime*: se causam clamat crimenque caputque malorum, Verg.

crīmĭnātĭo -ōnis, f. (criminor), *an accusation, calumny, charge*: illa criminatio quā in me absentem usus est, Cic.; Liv., Tac.

crīmĭnātor -ōris, m. (criminor), *an accuser, calumniator*: Tac.

crīmĭnor -ari, dep. (crimino -are: Pl.) (from crimen), *to bring a charge or accusation*.

(1) with acc. of person, *to accuse, charge*; esp. *to calumniate*: patres apud populum, Liv.; Sistium, Cic.; Q. Metellum apud populum Romanum criminatus est bellum ducere, Cic.; Tac.

(2) with acc. of offence, *to complain of, bring up against*: licet omnia criminari, Cic.; contiones quibus quotidie meam potentiam invidiose criminabatur, Cic.; with acc. and infin.: me esse gratum criminaris, Cic.; Liv.; absol., *to reproach*: argumentando criminari, Cic.

crīmĭnōsus -a -um (crimen), *reproachful, calumnious, slanderous*: ille acerbus criminosus popularis homo ac turbulentus, Cic.; orationes, Liv.; iambi, Hor. ¶ Adv. (with compar. and superl.) **crīmĭnōsē**, *by way of accusation, reproachfully*: qui suspiciosius aut criminosius diceret, Cic.; Liv., Tac.

crīnālis -e (crinis), *relating to the hair*: Verg.; vitta, Ov. N. as subst. **crīnāle** -is, *a hairband*: Ov.

crīnis -is, m. *a hair or the hair*, esp. of the head, and esp. in plur.: Cic.; crines sparsi, Liv.; crinibus passis, Liv., Hor., Verg., Tac. TRANSF., *the tail of a comet*: Verg., Ov.

crīnītus -a -um (crinis), *hairy, with long hair*: Apollo, Verg., Ov. TRANSF., stella crinita, *a comet*, Cic.; galea, *crested*, Verg.

crispĭsulcans -antis (crispus/sulco), *forked, wavy*: igneum fulmen, *forked lightning*, poet. ap. Cic.

crispo -are (crispus), *to curl, crisp*: capillum, Plin. TRANSF., *to move rapidly, brandish*: hastilia manu, Verg. ¶ Hence partic. **crispans** -antis, in intransit. sense, *curled, wavy*: Plin., Pers.

crispŭlus -a -um (dim. of crispus), *curly-haired, curly*: Mart., Sen.

crispus -a -um, *curly, curly-headed*: Pl., Ter. TRANSF., *in trembling motion, trembling, quivering*: latus, Verg.; pecten, Juv.

crista -ae, f. (connected with crinis), *the crest of an animal* or *bird*, such as *the comb of a cock*: Ov., Juv. TRANSF., *the crest* or *plume of a helmet*: Lucr., Verg., Liv.

cristātus -a -um (crista), *crested*: draco, Ov.; aves, *cocks*, Mart. TRANSF., *having a crest* or *plume*: galeae, Liv.; Achilles, Verg.

crītĭcus -i, m. (κριτικός), *a critic*: Cic. L., Hor., Quint.

Crĭtŏlāus -i, m. (Κριτόλαος). (1) *a peripatetic philosopher, ambassador from Athens to Rome*, 155 B.C. (2) *a general of the Achaean League*.

crŏcĕus -a -um (crocus). (1) *of saffron*: odores, Verg. (2) *saffron-coloured, golden, yellow*: flores, Verg., Ov.

crŏcĭnus -a -um (κρόκινος), *belonging to saffron, saffron-coloured, yellow*: tunica, Cat. ¶ N. as subst. **crŏcĭnum** -i, n. (sc. oleum), *saffron oil*: Prop.; as a term of endearment: Pl.

crŏcĭo -ire (κρώζω), *to croak like a raven*: Pl.

crŏcŏdīlus -i, m. (κροκόδειλος), *a crocodile*: Cic.

crŏcŏtārius -a -um (crocus), *of or belonging to the preparation of saffron-coloured garments*: Pl.

crŏcŏtŭla -ae, f. (dim., from crocus), *a saffron-coloured robe*: Pl., Verg.

crŏcus -i, m., **crŏcum** -i, n. (κρόκος). LIT., *the crocus*. TRANSF., (1) *saffron*, prepared from it by the ancients for use in spices, medicines, and perfumes: Lucr., Hor., Ov. (2) *the colour of saffron, yellow*: Verg.

Croesus -i, m. (Κροῖσος), *a king of Lydia, famous for his wealth*; appell.=*a rich man*: Ov. Adj. **Croesĭus** -a -um, *of Croesus*.

crŏtălĭa -ōrum, n. (κροτάλια), *ear-rings*: Petr., Plin.

crŏtălistrĭa -ae, f. *a castanet-dancer*: Prop.

crŏtălum -i, n. (κρόταλον), *a castanet*: Cic.

Crŏton -ōnis, c. (Κρότων), *a Greek colony near the 'toe' of Italy* (now *Cotrone*). ¶ Hence subst. **Crŏtōnĭātes** -ae, m. (Κροτωνιάτης), *an inhabitant of Crotona*; adj. **Crŏtōnĭensis** -e, *of Crotona*.

Crŏtōpĭădes -ae, m. (Κροτωπιάδης), *the poet Linus, grandson, on the mother's side, of Crotopus, king of Argos*: Ov.

crŭcĭābĭlĭtās -atis, f. (crucio); only in plur.: cruciabilitates, *tortures*, Pl.

crŭcĭābĭlĭter, adv. (crucio), *with tortures*: Pl.

crŭcĭāmentum -i, n. (crucio); only in plur.: cruciamenta, *tortures*, Pl., Cic.

crŭcĭātus -ūs, m. (crucio), *torture, torment*: omnes animi cruciatus et corporis, Cic.; per cruciatum interficere, Caes.; quin tu abi in malam pestem malumque cruciatum, *go and be hanged*, Cic. TRANSF., instruments of torture: Cic.

crŭcĭo -are (crux), *to torture, torment*; physically: cum vigiliis atque fame cruciaretur, Cic.; Pl., Ov.; mentally: me deliberatio cruciat, Cic. L.; pass. in middle sense, crucior, sometimes followed by acc. and infin. : Pl., Ter.

crūdēlis -e adj. (with compar.) (crudus), *unfeeling, cruel*; of persons : mulier, Cic.; Lepidus crudelis in liberos, Cic.; in hominis calamitate crudelis, Cic. TRANSF., of things : bellum, Cic.; consilia, Cic.; poena, Verg., Ov.
¶ Adv. (with compar. and superl.) **crūdēlĭter**, *cruelly* : imperare, Caes.; interficere, Cic., Liv.

crūdēlĭtās -ātis, f. (crudelis), *cruelty, inhumanity* : importuna in me crudelitas, Cic.; Caes., Liv.

crūdesco -descĕre -dŭi, *to become hard, violent* : crudescit morbus, Verg.; pugna, Verg.; seditio, Tac.

crūdĭtās -ātis, f. (crudus), *overloading of the stomach, indigestion* : Cic.

crūdus -a -um, adj. (with compar.) (connected with cruor).
LIT., (1) *bleeding* : vulnera, Ov., Plin. L. (2) *uncooked, raw* : exta cruda victimae, Liv.
TRANSF., (1) of material, *fresh, not prepared* : cortice crudo hasta, Verg. (2) of fruit, *unripe* : poma, Cic.; hence of development in gen., *green, immature, untimely* : puella, Mart.; senectus, *still fresh*, Verg., Tac.; servitium, *novel*, Tac. (3) of food, *undigested* : pavo, Juv.; of persons, *stuffed, dyspeptic* : Cic., Mart.; hence of feeling and conduct, *hard, rough, cruel* : Getae, Ov.; ensis, Verg.; of the voice, *harsh* : Cic.

crŭento -are (cruentus), *to make bloody, to stain with blood* : manus sanguine, Nep.; gladium, Cic.; fig. : haec te lacerat, haec cruentat oratio, *wounds*, Cic.

crŭentus -a -um (cruor), *bloody*.
LIT., guttae imbrium quasi cruentae, Cic.; cruentus sanguine civium Romanorum, Cic.; cadaver, Cic.; gaudens Bellona cruentis, *in the shedding of blood*, Hor.
TRANSF., (1) of abstr. things, *bloody* : victoria, Sall.; ira, Hor.; pax, Tac. (2) of character, *bloodthirsty* : Mars, Hor.; Ov. (3) of colour, *blood-red* : myrta, Verg.

crŭmēna -ae, f. *a leathern pouch for money, usually carried by a strap round the neck* : Pl. TRANSF., *store of money, funds* : non deficiente crumenā, Hor.; Juv.

crŭor -ōris, m. (connected with crudus), *the blood which flows from a wound, gore* : cruor inimici recentissimus, Cic.; Hor., Ov., Tac.; rarely of *the blood circulating in the body* : Lucr.
TRANSF., *murder, slaughter* : cruor Cinnanus, *the slaughter of Cinna*, Cic.; castus a cruore civili, Cic.; ad caedem et cruorem abstrahi, Cic.

cruppellārĭi -ōrum, m. pl. *Gaulish gladiators, who fought in full armour* : Tac.

crūrĭfragĭus -i, m. (crus/frango), *one whose legs or shins are broken* : Pl.

crūs crūris, n. *the shin, shin-bone, leg* : frangere alicui crus *or* crura (of persons crucified), Cic.; rigida crura, Cic.; succidere crura equo, Liv. TRANSF., in plur., *the supports of a bridge* : Cat.

crusta -ae, f. (1) *the crust, rind, shell, bark of any substance* : concrescunt subitae currenti in flumine crustae, *coating of ice*, Verg. (2) *inlaid work on walls, bas-relief or embossing on silver plate* : Cic., Juv.

crustŭĭum -i, n. (dim. of crustum), *a little cake* : Hor., Sen.

crustum -i, n. (crusta), *anything baked, bread, cake* : Verg., Hor.

Crustŭmĕrĭa -ae, f.; also **Crustŭmĕrĭum** -i, n.; **Crustŭmĕri** -orum, m. pl. *a town of the Sabines, near the sources of the Allia.*
¶ Hence adj. **Crustŭmĭnus** -a -um and **Crustŭmĭus** -a -um, *of Crustumeria.*

crux crŭcis, f. *a cross* : agere (*or* rapere) aliquem in crucem, Cic.; adfigere cruci, Liv.; detrahere ex cruce, Cic.
TRANSF., (1) *torment, trouble* : abi in malam crucem, *go and be hanged!* Pl., Ter. (2) as a term of abuse, *gallows bird* : Pl.

crypta -ae, f. (κρύπτη), *a covered gallery, vault, crypt, grotto* : Juv., Suet.

cryptoporticus -us, f. *a covered passage* : Plin. L.

crystallĭnus -a -um (κρυστάλλινος), *crystalline, made of crystal* : Plin. N. pl. as subst. **crystallĭna** -ōrum (sc. vasa), *crystal vases* : Juv., Mart.

crystallus -i, f. and **crystallum** -i, n. (κρύσταλλος), *crystal* : Curt., Sen.
TRANSF., (1) *a crystal drinking vessel* : Mart. (2) *a precious stone looking like crystal* : Prop.

Ctēsĭphōn -phontis. (1) m. (Κτησιφῶν), *an Athenian, friend of Demosthenes.* (2) f. (Κτεσιφῶν), *a city on the Tigris.*

cŭbĭcŭlāris -e (cubiculum), *of a bedchamber* : lectus, Cic.

cŭbĭcŭlārĭus -a -um (cubiculum), *of a bedchamber* : Mart. M. as subst. **cŭbĭcŭlārĭus** -i, *a chamber-servant* : Cic.

cŭbĭcŭlum -i, n. (cubo). (1) *a bedchamber, bedroom* : Pl., Cic., Liv. (2) *the emperor's raised seat in the theatre* : Suet., Plin.

cŭbīle (cubo), *a bed* : Lucr., Cic., Hor.; esp. *the marriage-bed*; of animals, *lair, den, nest*; of a mouse, Pl.; ferarum bestiarum, Liv.; rimosa cubilia, of bees, *hives*, Verg.
TRANSF., in gen., *seat, resting-place* : ut omnes mortales istius avaritiae non iam vestigia sed ipsa cubilia videre possint, Cic.

cŭbĭtal -tālis, n. (cubitum), *an elbow cushion* : Hor.

cŭbĭtālis -e (cubitum), *of the elbow*; hence *one cubit long* : cubitalis fere cava, Liv.

cŭbĭto -are (freq. of cubo), *to lie down often, be accustomed to lie* : Pl., Cic., Tac.

cŭbĭtum -i, n. (cubo), *the elbow* : cubito remanere presso, Hor.; Pl., Verg., Ov. TRANSF., *a cubit* : Pl., Cic.

cŭbĭtus -us, m. (cubo), *a lying down* : Verg., Pl.

cŭbo -are -ŭi -ĭtum, *to lie down, recline.* LIT., in lectica, Cic.; esp. *to lie down to sleep* : cubitum ire, *to go to bed*, Cic.; *to recline at table* : quod meminisset quo eorum loco quisque cubuisset, Cic.; *to lie down from illness, to lie in bed ill* : cubantem disputare de aliqua re, Cic.; Pl., Lucr., Hor.
TRANSF., of inanimate objects, *to lie*; esp. in partic. cubans, *sloping* : Lucr., Hor.

cŭcullus -i, m. *a hood, cowl* : Juv., Mart.

cŭcūlus -i, m. (κόκκυξ), *the cuckoo* : Plin.; as a term of reproach : Pl., Hor.

cŭcŭmis -mĕris, m. *a cucumber* : Verg.

cŭcurbĭta -ae, f. *a gourd* : Plin. TRANSF., in medicine, *a cupping-glass* : Juv.

cūdo -ĕre, *to beat, pound*: fabas, *to thresh*; prov.: istaec in me cudetur faba, *I shall suffer for that*, Ter.; of metals, *to forge, stamp, coin*: plumbeos nummos, Pl.; Ter., Quint.

cuicuimodi (for cuius-cuius-modi, from quisquis/modus), *of whatever kind*: Pl., Cic.

cūiās -ātis (cuius), *of what country? whence?* Cic.

cūius (old form **quoius**) -a -um. (1) interrog. pron. *to whom belonging? whose?* cuium pecus? *whose flock?* Verg. (2) relat. pron. *whose*: quoiā causā, *wherefore*, Pl., Cic.

cūiuscĕmŏdi (qui/ce/modus), *of whatever kind*: Cic.

cūiusdam-mŏdi, *of a certain kind*: Cic.

cūiusmŏdi (qui/modus), *of what kind?* Cic.

cūiusquĕmŏdi (quisque/modus), *of every kind*: Cic., Lucr.

culcīta -ae, f. (calco), *a bolster, pillow*: plumea, Cic., Pl.

cŭlĕus = culleus; q.v.

cŭlex -icis, m. *a gnat, midge*: Pl., Lucr., Verg., Hor.

cŭlīna -ae, f. *a kitchen*: tua (philosophia) in culina, mea in palaestra est, Cic. L.; Pl., Hor.; meton., *food, fare, victuals*: Murena praebente domum, Capitone culinam, Hor.

cullĕus (**cūlĕus**) -i, m. (κολεός, Ion. κουλέος, *sheath*). LIT., *a leather sack*: Pl., Nep.; aliquem insuere in culeum (the punishment of parricides), Cic., Juv. TRANSF., (1) *a liquid measure*: Cato. (2) (also in form coleus), *the scrotum*: Cic. L., Mart.

culmen -ĭnis, n. (for columen from *cello). LIT., (1) like culmus, *an upright thing*; *a stalk*: Ov. (2) *the top, summit*: culmen Alpium, Caes.; *the ridge of a roof*: culmen tecti, Verg. TRANSF., in gen., *summit*: summum culmen fortunae, Liv.; Verg.

culmus -i, m. (from *cello, like culmen), *a stalk, haulm*, esp. of grain: Cic., Verg. TRANSF., *thatch*: Romuleoque recens horrebat regia culmo, Verg.

culpa -ae, f. *fault, blame.* LIT., culpa delicti, Cic.; huius culpā, non meā, Ter.; haec mea culpa est, Cic.; culpa est penes aliquem, Ter.; Liv.; esse in culpa, Cic.; extra culpam esse, Cic.; abesse a culpa, Cic.; vacare culpa, Cic.; culpam in aliquem conferre, transferre, Cic.; liberare aliquem culpa, Cic.; in se suscipere istius culpam, Cic.; esp. *the fault of unchastity*: Verg., Ov., Tac. TRANSF., *the cause of error* or *sin*: culpam ferro compesce, Verg.

culpito -are (freq. of culpo), *to blame severely*: Pl.

culpo -are (culpa), *to blame, find fault with, accuse, disapprove*: laudatur ab his, culpatur ab illis, Hor.; Ov., Quint.; fig. of things: arbore nunc aquas culpante, Hor.

cultellus -i, m. (dim. of culter), *a little knife*: Hor.

culter -tri, m. *a knife*: Pl., Cic., Liv.; cultri tonsorii, *razors*, Cic.; *a ploughshare, coulter*: Plin.; prov.: me sub cultro linquit, *leaves me under the knife*, i.e., *in the greatest peril*, Hor.

cultĭo -ōnis, f. (colo), *cultivation*: Cic.

cultor -ōris, m. (colo), *a cultivator, planter, labourer*. LIT., terrae, Cic.; agrorum, Liv.; absol., *husbandman*: Sall., Verg., Liv.; hence, with

genit., *an inhabitant, occupier*: eius terrae, Sall., Verg., Liv. TRANSF., in gen., *a friend, supporter*: bonorum (*of the optimates*), Liv.; veritatis, Cic.; esp. *a worshipper*: deorum, Hor.; religionum, Cic.

cultrārius -i (culter), *a slayer of the victim* (for sacrifice): Suet.

cultrix -īcis, f. (cultor). (1) *she who tends* or *takes care of*: Cic. (2) *inhabitant*: nemorum Latonia virgo, Verg.; Cat., Ov.

cultūra -ae, f. (colo), *tilling, culture, cultivation.* LIT., agri, Cic.; vitis, Cic.; absol., *agriculture, husbandry*: Hor. TRANSF., (1) *mental culture, cultivation*: animi, Cic. (2) *courting*: potentis amici, Cic.

¹cultus -a -um, partic. from colo; q.v.

²cultus -ūs, m. (colo), *tilling, cultivation, tending.* LIT., of agriculture: agrorum, Liv., Cic.; also of cattle-farming: Cic., Verg. TRANSF., (1) physically; *care, tending*: corporis, Cic. (2) mentally: **a**, *culture, training, education*: animi, ingenii, Cic.: **b**, *reverence, respectful treatment*; of the gods: cultus deorum, Cic., Ov.; of men: benevolis officium et diligens tribuitur cultus, Cic.; Tac. (3) of civilization in gen.; *refinement, culture*, physical and mental: a fera agrestique vita ad humanum cultum, Cic.; cultus Punicus, Liv.; Caes., Verg.

cŭlullus -i, m. *a drinking-vessel*: Hor.

cūlus -i, m. *the fundament*: Cat., Mart.

¹cum, conj., less correctly quum; q.v.

²cum (old form com, as seen in compound verbs), as a separate word or suffixed to a pronoun (mecum, quocum, quicum, etc.), is a preposition governing the abl. and meaning *together with.*

(1) of accompaniment in space; by persons: cum Pansa vixi, Cic.; vagamur cum coniugibus, Cic. L.; cenas mecum, Hor.; by things, esp. equipment: cum impedimentis venire, Caes.; cum pallio purpureo versabatur in conviviis, Cic.; fig., abstr.: legatos cum auctoritate mittere, Cic.; mors cum gloria, Cic.

(2) of time, *simultaneously with*: cum prima luce, Cic.

(3) of circumstances or results, *with, among, to*: cum cura, Cic.; cum lacrimis, Caes., Liv.; cum summa tua dignitate, Cic.; hunc abstulit magno cum gemitu civitatis, Cic.; esp. of heaven's blessing or favour: volentibu' cum magnis dis, Enn.; of conditions; cum eo quod, ut, or ne, *on the condition that*: sit sane sed tamen cum eo, credo, quod sine peccato meo fiat, Cic.

(4) of various relations, to complete the sense of a verb, esp. of dealings with persons, whether friendly or hostile: agere cum, bellum gerere cum, Caes., Cic.; of comparison: conferre, comparare cum, Cic.

Cūmae -ārum, f. (Κύμη), *an ancient city on the coast of Campania, famous as the residence of the Sibyl.* Adj. **Cūmānus** -a -um; **Cūmaeus** -a -um, *Cumaean*: virgo, *the Sibyl*, Ov.

cumba (**cymba**) -ae, f. (κύμβη), *a small boat, skiff*: Cic., Ov.; esp. *Charon's boat*: Verg., Hor.; fig.: non est ingenii cumba gravanda tui, Prop.

cŭmĕra -ae, f. *a corn-bin*: Hor.

cŭmīnum -i, n. (κύμινον), *a herb, supposed to make the face pale*: Hor.

cum prīmis, see primus.

cumque (cunque, quomque), an adverb usually found in composition, added to a relative with the force of *-ever, -soever*; thus quicumque, *whoever, whosoever*; sometimes separated by tmesis from the relative (esp. in Lucr.): quae demant cumque dolorem, Lucr.; perhaps used alone in Hor., Odes I, 32: mihi cumque salve rite vocanti, *whenever I call.*

cŭmŭlo -are (cumulus). (1) *to heap up, pile up*: cetera omnis generis arma in acervum, Liv. TRANSF., *to pile on*: cum aliae super alias clades cumularentur, Liv.; omnes in aliquem honores, Tac.; also *to increase, heighten*: invidiam, Liv.; cumulare eloquentiā bellicam gloriam, Cic. (2) *to fill by heaping up, fill up, overload*: fossas corporibus, Tac.; altaria donis, Verg.; Liv. TRANSF., confiteor me cumulari maximo gaudio, Cic.; cumulatus laude, *loaded with praise*, Cic.; also *to crown, bring to perfection*: cumulata erant officia vitae, *perfectly fulfilled*, Cic.; gaudium, Cic.

¶ Hence partic. (with compar. and superl.) **cŭmŭlātus** -a -um. (1) *heaped up, increased, enlarged*: Hesiodus eadem mensurā reddere iubet, quā acceperis, aut etiam cumulatiore, si possis, Cic.; Liv. (2) *crowned, perfected*: hoc sentire et facere perfectae cumulataeque virtutis est, Cic.; Verg.

¶ Adv. (with compar. and superl.) **cŭmŭlātē**, *abundantly, fully*: Cic.

cŭmŭlus -i, m. (connected with κυέω and κῦμα), *a heap, pile, mass.*

LIT., hostium coacervatorum, Liv.; aquarum, Ov.; legum, Liv.

TRANSF., *addition, increase, finishing touch*: commendationis tuae, Cic.; gaudii, Cic.; addit perfidiae cumulum, Ov.

cūnābŭla -ōrum, n. pl. (cunae), *a cradle*: esse in cunabulis, Cic.; *the bed of the young bees*: Verg. Fig., *the earliest abode*: gentis, Verg.

cūnae -ārum, f. pl. *a cradle*: in cunis dormire, Cic.; primis cunis, *in earliest childhood*, Ov.; *the nest of young birds*: Ov.

cunctābundus -a -um (cunctor), *loitering, delaying, dilatory*: Liv., Tac.

cunctātīo -ōnis, f. (cunctor), *a delay, lingering, hesitation*: invadendi, Liv.; sine cunctatione, Cic.; abiecta omni cunctatione, Cic.

cunctātor -ōris, m. (cunctor), *one who delays, lingers, hesitates*: cunctatorem ex acerrimo bellatore factum, Liv.; *a surname of the dictator* Q. Fabius Maximus.

cuncto -are=cunctor; q.v.: Pl.

cunctor -ari, dep. *to delay, linger, hesitate*: cunctari diutius in vitā, Cic.; sedendo et cunctando bellum gerebat, Liv.; with infin.: non est cunctandum profiteri, Cic.; non cunctor, foll. by quin: non cunctandum existimavit, quin pugnā decertaret, *there ought to be no delay in*, etc., Caes.; impers. pass.: nec cunctatum apud latera, Tac.

TRANSF., of things: tardum cunctatur olivum, *moves slowly*, Lucr.; amnis, Verg.

¶ Hence partic. as adj. (with compar.) **cunctans** -antis, *loitering, lingering, slow*: Plin.; ilex glebae, *tenacious*, Verg.

¶ Adv. (with compar.) **cunctantĕr**, *slowly, lingeringly*: Liv.

cunctus -a -um (contr. from coniunctus or coiunctus), *all, all collectively, the whole*; sing.: Gallia, Caes.; senatus, Cic.; orbis terrarum, Verg.; plur.: cuncti cives, Cic.; in poet. sometimes with genit.: hominum cunctos, Ov.; esp. in n. pl.: cuncta terrarum, Hor.

cŭnĕātim, adv. (cuneus), *in shape of a wedge*: Caes.

cŭnĕo -are (cuneus). (1) *to secure with wedges*: Plin., Sen. (2) *to shape like a wedge*; hence partic. (with compar.) **cŭnĕātus** -a -um, *pointed like a wedge*: iugum in angustum dorsum cuneatum, Liv.; Ov.

cŭnĕus -i, m. *a wedge.*

LIT., cuneis scindere fissile lignum, Verg. TRANSF., (1) *a wedge as a triangular figure*: Britannia in cuneum tenuatur, *is narrowed in the shape of a wedge*, Tac. (2) *troops drawn up in the form of a wedge*: cuneum facere, Caes. (3) *the wedge-shaped compartments into which the seats of a theatre were divided*: Verg.; meton.: cuneis omnibus, *to all the spectators*, Phaedr.

cŭnīcŭlōsus -a -um (cuniculus), *full of rabbits or of caverns*: Cat.

cŭnīcŭlus -i, m. *a rabbit, cony*: Cat. TRANSF., *an underground passage*: omne genus cuniculorum apud eos notum atque usitatum est, Caes.; esp. as milit. t. t., *a mine*: agere cuniculum, Caes.; aperire cuniculum, Caes.

cunnus -i, f.=pudendum muliebre; meton., *a prostitute*: Hor.

cūpa -ae, f. *a cask or butt*: Caes., Cic.

cŭpĭdē, adv. from cupidus; q.v.

cŭpĭdĭtās -ātis, f. (cupidus), *eager desire, passionate longing*. In gen.: cupiditas inexplebilis, insana, nimia, Cic.; with objective genit.: pecuniae, Cic.; dominandi, Cic.; with ad: tanta cupiditas ad reditum, Cic.; ardere cupiditate, Cic.; coercere cupiditates, Cic.; explere cupiditates, Cic.; servire cupiditatibus, Cic.

Esp. (1) *ambition*: popularis (of a demagogue), Cic. (2) *desire for money, avarice*: cupiditas et avaritia, Cic. (3) *factiousness, party spirit*: cupiditatis atque inimicitiarum suspicio, Cic. L.

cŭpīdo -ĭnis, f. (m. in some poets; forms cūpēdo and cuppēdo: Lucr.) (from cupio), *longing, desire*. In gen.: Lucr., Hor., Ov., Tac.; with genit.: auri, Tac.; pecuniae, honoris, Sall.; flagrare cupidine regni, Liv.; Hannibalem ingens cupido incesserat Tarenti potiendi, Liv.

Esp. (1) *desire for power, ambition*: honoris, Sall., Liv., Tac. (2) *desire for money, avarice*: cupido sordidus, Hor. (3) *physical desire*: somni, Sall.; most often of *love*: cupido visae virginis, Ov.

¶ Hence personified **Cŭpīdo** -ĭnis, m. *Cupid, the god of love, son of Venus*: Cic.; plur. **Cŭpīdines**, *Cupids*; adj. **Cŭpīdĭnĕus** -a -um.

cŭpĭdus -a -um, adj. (with compar. and superl.) (cupio), *desirous, eager, keen.*

In gen.: consul non cupidus, Cic.; with genit. of object: novarum rerum, Caes., Cic.; te audiendi, Cic.; vitae, Lucr.; mortis, Hor.; with infin.: Prop., Ov.; in perspicienda cognoscendaque rerum natura, Cic.

Esp. (**1**) *eager for power, ambitious*: Caes.
(**2**) *eager for money, avaricious*: homo non
cupidus neque appetens, Cic. (**3**) *physically,
desirous*: vini, Pl.; most often of *love*: Cat.,
Ov. (**4**) *towards persons, attached, partial*;
in a good sense: homo tui cupidus, Cic.; in
a bad sense: quaestores vehementer istius
cupidi, Cic.; absol.: iudex cupidus, Cic.

¶ Adv. (with compar. and superl.)
cŭpĭdē, *eagerly, passionately, keenly, warmly*:
cupide appetere, Cic.; ego vero cupide et
libenter mentiar tuā causā, Cic.

cŭpĭo cŭpĕre cŭpīvi or -ii -ītum, *to desire, long
for, wish for*; with acc.: is quem cupimus
optamusque vestitus, Cic.; pacem, Liv.;
domum, agros, Sall.; with infin.: Ter., Lucr.,
Cic., Caes.; with acc. and infin.: equidem
cupio Antonium haec quam primum audire,
Cic.; with ut: Pl.

Sometimes *to want things on another's
behalf*, and so *to favour him, wish him well*:
cuius causā omnia cupio, Cic.; cupio omnia
quae vis, Hor.

¶ Hence partic. **cŭpĭens** -entis, *desiring,
longing, eager*; absol.: Tac.; as adj. with
genit.: nuptiarum, Pl.; novarum rerum, Tac.

¶ Adv. **cŭpĭenter**, *eagerly*: Pl.

cŭpĭtor -ōris, m. (cupio), *one who desires*:
matrimonii, Tac.

'cuppēdĭa -ae, f. (cuppes), *taste for delicacies*:
Cic.

'cuppēdĭa -orum, n. pl. (cuppes), *delicacies,
tit-bits*: Pl.

cuppēdinarius -i, m. (cuppedia), *a confec-
tioner*: Ter.

cuppēs (cūpēs) -ēdis, m. adj., *fond of
delicacies*: Pl.

cupressētum -i, n. (cupressus), *a cypress
wood*: Cic.

cupressĕus -a -um (cupressus), *made of
cypress wood*: signa Iunonis, Liv.

cupressĭfer -fĕra -fĕrum (cupressus/fero),
cypress-bearing: Ov.

cuprĕssus -i (-ūs), f. (from κυπάρισσος; form
cyparissus in Verg.), *the cypress*, sacred to
Pluto, used at funerals: Verg. Meton., *a
casket of cypress wood*: Hor.

cūr (older form **quor**: Pl.) interrog. adv. *why?
wherefore?* (**1**) in direct questions: Pl., Ter.,
Cic., Hor., etc. (**2**) in indirect questions:
miror cur, Cic.; quid est cur, Cic., Liv.;
esp. with causa: Cic.

cūra -ae, f. (caveo), *care, carefulness, concern*.
(**1**) *care taken, pains, trouble* (opp. negligentia), *attention*. In gen.: magna cum cura
et diligentia scribere, Cic.; with genit.:
rerum alienarum cura, Cic.; cura colendi,
Verg.; with de: studium tuum curaque de
salute mea, Cic.; adhibere curam in capris
et ovibus parandis, Cic.; agere curam civium,
Liv.; conferre magnam curam in alicuius
salutem, Cic.; maxima erat cura duci ne, etc.,
Liv.; curae esse (with dat. of person), *to be
an object of concern* (*to somebody*), Caes.,
Cic., Hor.; imprimis tibi curae sit ne mihi
tempus prorogetur, Cic.; habere curam
rerum divinarum, Liv.; incumbe in eam
curam, *devote yourself to*, Cic.; ponere
curam in aliqua re, *to devote one's attention to*,
Cic.; suscipere curam, Cic.; sustinere maximam curam belli, Cic. Esp., in some specific
business, *attention to, care for, minding*: **a**, in

farming: quae cura boum, Verg.: **b**, in
medicine, *medical care, healing, a cure*, fig.:
simplex illa iam cura doloris tui, Cic. L.:
c, in special personal relations, such as
guardianship: suum sororisque filios in
eadem cura habere, Liv.: **d**, in religion: cura
deorum, Liv.: **e**, in public affairs, *management, administration*: cura reipublicae, Liv.;
cura navium, *of the fleet*, Tac.; meton.,
business, administration: cum sumus necessariis negotiis curisque vacui, Cic. TRANSF.,
a, *an object of care*: tua cura, palumbes,
Verg.: **b**, *a caretaker*: cura fidelis harae, Ov.

(**2**) *care felt, anxiety, worry, disquiet*: sine
cura, Cic.; cura vacare, Cic.; adficere aliquem
curā, Cic.; confici curis, Cic.; metus
hominum curaeque sequaces, Lucr.; atra
cura, Hor.; esp. of the disquiet of love:
iuvenum curas, Hor., Verg. TRANSF., *the
object of love*: tua cura, Lycoris, Verg.; Hor.

cūrābĭlis -e (cura), *to be dreaded, alarming*:
vindicta, Juv.

cūrālĭum -i, n. (Ion. κουράλιον), *coral, esp. red
coral*: Ov., Plin.

cūrātĭo -ōnis, f. (curo), *care*.

In gen., *a taking care, attention, management*; with genit.: curatio corporis, Cic.;
quid tibi hanc curatio est rem? *why need you
concern yourself about this?* Pl.

Esp. (**1**) *medical attention, healing, cure*:
curatio medici, Cic.; curatio valetudinis,
Cic.; adhibere curationem, Cic.; praescribere,
Cic. (**2**) of public affairs, *management,
administration*: curatio Nemeorum, *of the
Nemean games*, Liv.; Asiatica curatio
frumenti, *commission to buy corn*, Cic.;
curatio agraria, *commission to divide land*,
Cic.; aedes Telluris est curationis meae, Cic.

cūrātor -ōris, m. (curo), *one who takes care*;
in gen., *a guardian, overlooker, curator*: viae
Flaminiae, Cic.; sunto aediles coeratores
(=curatores) urbis annonae ludorumque
sollemnium, old law ap. Cic.; legibus agrariis
curatores constituere, Cic.; esp. as legal t. t.
guardian: alicui curatorem dare, Hor.

cūrātus, partic. from curo; q.v.

curcŭlĭo -ōnis, m. *a weevil, corn-worm*: Pl.,
Verg.

curcŭlĭuncŭlus -i, m. (dim. of curculio), *a
little weevil*; comically, for a *worthless
object*: Pl.

Cŭrēs -ium, f. *an ancient town of the Sabines*
meton., *the inhabitants of Cures*: Ov. Adj
Cŭrensis -e, *of Cures*: Ov.; **Cŭrētis**, Prop.

Cūrētes -um, m. (Κουρῆτες), *ancient inhabitants of Crete, who celebrated a noisy
worship of Jupiter, like that of Cybele by the
Corybantes*. Adj. **Cūrētis** -ĭdis, poet.=
Cretan: Ov.

cūrĭa -ae, f. (**1**) *a curia, one of thirty divisions
into which the Roman patricians were divided
by Romulus*: Liv.; hence meton., *the meeting-
place of a curia*: Ov., Tac.

(**2**) *the meeting-place of the senate at Rome
the senate-house*, whether that attributed to
Tullus Hostilius or that begun by Julius
Caesar in 44 B.C.: in curiam introducere, Liv.
Cic., Hor.; so, outside Rome, *of buildings
corresponding to the Roman senate-house
at Salamis*: Cic.; Syracuse: Cic.; Troy: Ov.
at Athens, *the Areopagus*: Juv. Meton., *the
senate itself*: consulenti curiae, Hor.

:ŭrĭālis -e (curia), *belonging to the same curia*: Pl., Cic.

:ŭrĭātim, adv. (curia), *by curiae*: populum consuluit, Cic.

:ŭrĭātii -ōrum, m. *name of an Alban gens, from which three champions fought with three Horatii.*

:ŭrĭātus -a -um (curia). (**1**) *relating to the curiae*: comitia curiata, *the original assembly of the Roman people, in which they voted by curiae*, Cic., Liv. (**2**) lex, *a law passed in the comitia curiata*, Cic.

:cŭrĭo -ōnis, m. (curia), *the priest of a curia*: Varr.; maximus, *the head of the college formed by the thirty curiones*, Liv. TRANSF., *a herald, crier*: Mart.

:cŭrĭo -ōnis, m. adj. (cura), *wasted by cares*: Pl.

:ŭrĭōsĭtās -ātis, f. (curiosus), *inquisitiveness, curiosity*: Cic. L.

:ŭrĭōsus -a -um, adj. (with compar. and superl.) (cura). (**1**) *careful, attentive, diligent*: ad investigandum, Cic.; permulta alia conligit Chrysippus, ut est in omni historia curiosus, Cic. (**2**) *inquisitive, curious*: curiosis oculis perspici, Cic.; Hor.; m. as subst., *a spy, scout*: Suet. (**3**) *wasted by cares*: Pl.

¶ Adv. (with compar.) **cŭrĭōsē**. (**1**) *carefully*: Suet.; *over-carefully*: Quint. (**2**) *inquisitively*: curiosius conquiram, Cic.

:ŭris or **quiris**, f. (a Sabine word), *a spear*: Ov.

:ŭrius -a -um, *name of a plebeian gens; its most famous member was* M'. Curius Dentatus, *the conqueror of the Sabines, Samnites, and of Pyrrhus; he was celebrated for his temperance; hence appell. a brave and temperate man*: Hor.

¶ Adj. **Cŭrĭānus** -a -um, *of or belonging to Curius.*

:ŭro -are (cura).

In gen., *to care for, pay attention to, trouble about*: negotia aliena, Cic.; with gerundive, *to see to* a thing being done: in Sicilia frumentum emendum et ad urbem mittendum curare, *to get bought and sent*, Cic.; with infin.: qui res istas scire curavit, Cic.; esp. with neg.: in Siciliam ire non curat, Cic.; Hor., Ov.; followed by ut, ne, and the subj.: Pl., Cic.; so in letters: cura ut valeas, Cic. L.; by subj. alone: Cic. L.; with de: Quintus de emendo nihil curat hoc tempore, Cic. L.; colloquially, *to bother about*: alia cura, Pl.; aliud cura, *worry about something else—not this*, Ter.

Esp., *to attend to some specific business* (cf. cura). (**1**) in farming: vineam, Cato. (**2**) in medicine, etc., *to rest, cure*: curare corpora, Cic.; vulnus, Liv.; membra, Hor. (**3**) in business, *to provide* or *procure a sum of money*: iube sodes nummos curari, Cic. (**4**) in religion: sacra, Cic. (**5**) of public affairs, *to administer, manage*: res Romae, Liv.; absol. *to command*: curare Romae, Tac.

¶ Hence partic. **cŭrātus** -a -um, *cared for*: sacra, Cic.; vox, Quint.; also *showing care, betraying anxiety*: curatissimae preces, Tac.

¶ Compar. adv. **cŭrātius**, *more carefully*: Tac., Plin. L.

:urrĭcŭlum -i, n. (curro). (**1**) *a running*: Pl.; abl.: curriculo, *at a run*, Pl., Ter.

(**2**) *a contest in running, a race*: Cic., Hor., Liv. TRANSF., **a**, *raceground, course, lap*: athletae se in curriculo exercentes, Cic.; often fig.: exiguum vitae curriculum natura circumscripsit, immensum gloriae, Cic.; also of heavenly bodies: solis et lunae, Cic.: **b**, *a racing chariot*: Tac.

curro currĕre cŭcurri cursum, *to run, hasten.*

LIT., of living creatures: per vias, Pl.; Cic., Hor., Verg.; pass. impers.: curritur, *one runs*, Cic.; pro se quisque currere ad sua tutanda, Liv.; with cognate acc.: eosdem cursus currere, Cic.; prov.: currentem hortari, incitare (or instigare), *to spur the willing horse*, Cic. Esp. (**1**) *to run in a race*: currere bene, Ov.; with acc. of place: qui stadium currit, Cic. (**2**) at sea, *to sail*: per omne mare, Hor.; with acc.: currere cavâ trabe vastum aequor, Verg.

TRANSF., (**1**) of concr. objects: si mea sincero curreret axe rota, Ov.; currentes aquae, Ov.; libera currebant et inobservata per annum sidera, Ov.; of the hem of a garment: quam plurima circum purpura Maeandro duplici Meliboea cucurrit, Verg. (**2**) of abstr. things; of fright, cold, shame, etc.: varius per ora cucurrit Ausonium turbata fremor, Verg.; of time, *to pass*: currit ferox aetas, Hor.; of discourse, *to march easily*: perfacile currens oratio, Cic.

currus -ūs, m. (curro), *a chariot, car.* LIT., Lucr., Cic., Verg. Esp. (**1**) *a triumphal car*: flectere currum de foro in Capitolium, Cic. Meton., *triumph*: quem ego currum aut quam lauream cum tua laudatione conferrem? Cic.; Prop. (**2**) *a war-chariot*: Caes., Tac. (**3**) *a racing car*: Verg.

TRANSF., (**1**) *the horses, the team*: neque audit currus habenas, Verg. (**2**) *a plough with wheels*: Verg. (**3**) *a ship*: Cat.

cursim, adv. (curro), *by running, hastily, quickly*: cursim agmen agere, Liv.; cursim dicere aliena, Cic.

cursĭto -are (freq. of curso), *to run up and down*: huc et illuc, Cic., Hor.

curso -are (freq. of curro), *to run hither and thither*: ultro et citro, Cic.; Ter., Tac.

cursor -ōris, m. (curro), *a runner*. (**1**) in a race: Lucr., Cic.; in a chariot-race: Ov. (**2**) on errands, *a courier, a messenger*: Plin. L., Suet. (**3**) *a slave who ran before his master's carriage, a running footman*: Suet., Mart.

cursus -ūs, m. (curro), *a running, rapid motion.*

LIT., of living creatures: milites cursu exanimatos, Caes.; cursus equorum, Verg.; cursu tendere ad, Liv.; in cursu esse, Cic.; of racing: cursus certamen, Ov.; hence of the *direction* of movement, *course, march, journey*: cursus maritimus, Cic.; mihi cursus in Graeciam per tuam provinciam est, Cic.; cursus dirigere, Liv.; cursum secundum habere, Caes.; cursum tenere, Cic.

TRANSF., of other things: **a**, *movement*; concr.: longarum navium, Caes.; lunae, Lucr., Liv.; abstr.: honorum, Cic., Tac.: **b**, *direction, course*; concr.: amnes in alium cursum contortos et deflexos videmus, Cic.; abstr.: vitae, rerum, Cic.

¹Curtius -a -um, *name of a Roman gens; its most famous member was* Q. Curtius Rufus, *the author of a Latin history of Alexander the Great, in the time of Claudius or Vespasian.*

²Curtius lacus, m. *a pit in the forum at Rome*; hence stories to account for its origin, esp.

that of M'. Curtius leaping armed and on horseback into the chasm.

curto -are (curtus), *to shorten, abbreviate*: Hor.

curtus -a -um, *shortened, mutilated*: dolia, Lucr.; esp. *gelded*: Prop., Hor. TRANSF., *short, defective*: oratio, Cic.; res, Hor.

cŭrūlis -e (currus), *relating to a chariot*: equi, *horses provided out of public funds for the Circus*, Liv.; esp.: sella, *the curule chair*, inlaid with ivory, official seat of consuls, praetors, and curule aediles, Cic., Liv., etc.; absol. as subst. **cŭrūlis** -is, f.: Tac., Suet. Hence of the magistrates: curulis aedilis, *a curule aedile*, Liv.; aedilitas, Cic., Liv.

curvāmen -ĭnis, n. (curvo), *a curving, arching*: Ov.

curvātūra -ae, f. (curvo), *a curving, arching*: Ov.

curvo -are (curvus), *to bend, arch, curve*: bracchia longo circuitu, Ov.; nux plurima curvabit ramos, Verg.; curvare genua sua, Verg.; Hadria curvans Calabros sinus, Hor. TRANSF., *make to bend, move*: nec te vir Pieria pellice saucius curvat, Hor.

curvus -a -um (connected with κυρτός), *bent, bowed, arched, curved*.
LIT., arbor, *bent with the weight of fruit*, Ov.; aratrum, Verg.; naves, Ov.; flumen, *winding*, Verg.; curvus arator, *bent* (with age or toil), Verg.; curva senecta, Ov.
TRANSF., morally, *crooked*: mores, Pers.; n. as subst. **curvum** -i: curvo dignoscere rectum, Hor.

cuspis -ĭdis, f. *a point*, esp. of a spear: asseres cuspidibus praefixi, Caes.; of the *sting* of a bee: Plin.; of a scorpion: Ov.
TRANSF. (1) *a spear, lance*: Hor., Verg., Liv. (2) *Neptune's trident*: cuspis triplex, Ov. (3) *a spit*: Mart.

custōdia -ae, f. (custos), *a watching, guarding, custody, care*.
LIT., canum, Cic.; committere custodiam corporis feris barbaris, Cic.; aliquem diligenti custodia adservare, Liv.; as milit. t. t., *keeping guard, watch*: custodiae classium, Caes.; esp. of prisoners, *custody, safe-keeping*: dare aliquem in custodiam, Cic.; esse in custodia publica, Cic.; necari in custodia, Caes.; custodia libera, *house-arrest*, Liv.; fig.: salutis, iustitiae, Cic.
TRANSF., (1) *persons guarding, guards, sentinels*: custodiam ex suis ac praesidium sex milia hominum unā reliquerunt, Caes.; circumdare horribiles custodias, Cic.; disponere custodias diligentius, Caes.; frequens custodiis locus, Liv. (2) *the station of the guard, post*: haec mea sedes est, haec vigilia, haec custodia, Cic. (3) *prison*: Caes., Cic. (4) *persons guarded, prisoners*: Sen. L.

custōdĭo -ire (custos), *to guard, watch, keep*.
In gen.: tuum corpus domumque, Cic.; se diligentissime, Cic.; salutem alicuius, Cic.; poma, of a dragon, Ov.; fig.: memoria, Cic.
Esp. (1) *to keep in sight, observe, watch*: aliquem custodire ne quid auferat, Cic.; Liv. (2) *to take care of*: liber tuus a me custoditur diligentissime, Cic. L. (3) *to keep in prison, hold captive*: ducem praedonum, Cic.; obsides, Caes.

custos -ōdis, c. *a guardian, watchman, keeper, preserver, attendant*.
LIT., of persons guarding persons or things: custos tabellarum, Cic.; portae, Liv.;

custos defensorque provinciae, Cic.; custos urbis, Cic.; custos incorruptissimus, of a young man's *guardian*, Hor.; nimium serva[.] custos Iunonius Io, Ov.; of *gaolers*: iugular[.] a custodibus, Nep.; as milit. t. t., *a sentinel guard*: custodes dare, Cic.; disponere, Caes.; *a spy*: Caes.
TRANSF., (1) of animal guards, esp. dogs [.] Verg. (2) of receptacles: custos telorum, *a quiver*, Ov. (3) abstract: virtutis, Hor.[.] custos ac vindex cupiditatum, Cic.

cŭtĭcŭla -ae, f. (dim. of cutis), *the skin, cuticle*: Juv.

Cŭtĭlĭae -ārum, f. *an old town in the country of the Sabines*.

cŭtis -is, f. *the skin*, esp. the living skin of a man: Hor. TRANSF., *rind*: Plin.; *hide, leather*: Mart.

Cўănē -ēs, f. (Κυάνη), *a nymph changed into a fountain for her grief at the loss of Proserpine*.

Cўănēē -ēs, f. (Κυανέη), *daughter of Maeander, mother of Caunus and Byblis*.

cўăthisso -are (κυαθίζω), *to ladle out wine*: Pl.

cўăthus -i, m. (κύαθος), (1) *a ladle for filling the goblets* (pocula) *with wine from the bowl* (crater): Hor. (2) *a measure of capacity* = one-twelfth of a sextarius: Hor.

cўbaeus -a -um (κυβή); cybaea navis and absol. **cўbaea** -ae, f. *a merchantman*: Cic.

Cўbĕlē or **Cўbēbē** -ēs, f. (Κυβέλη, Κυβήβη) *originally a Phrygian goddess, afterwards worshipped at Rome under various names* (Rhea, Ops, Magna Mater), *whose priests were called Galli*; adj. **Cўbĕlēïus** -a -um, *belonging to Cybele*.

¹**cyclăs** -ădis, f. (κυκλάς), *a female robe of state having a border of purple* or *gold embroidery*: Prop., Juv.

²**Cyclăs** -ădis, f. (sc. insula), gen. in plur. **Cyclădes** -um, f. (Κυκλάδες), *a group of islands in the Aegean Sea*.

cyclĭcus -a -um (κυκλικός), *cyclic*: scriptor, *a cyclic poet*, a contributor to the series of epics known as the epic cycle, Hor.

Cyclops -clōpis, m. (Κύκλωψ, *round-eyed*) *a Cyclops*, gen. in plur. **Cyclōpes** -clōpum m. *the Cyclopes, a gigantic one-eyed race, the workmen of Vulcan*; in sing. esp. *the Cyclops Polyphemus*: Hor. Adj. **Cyclōpĭus** -a -um saxa, Verg.

cycnēus or **cygnēus** -a -um (κύκνειος), *belonging to the swan*: plumae, Ov.; tamquam cycnea fuit divini hominis vox et oratio, hi[.] *swan's song*, Cic.

¹**cycnus** or **cygnus** -i, m. (κύκνος), *the swan famed in legend for its death-song, sacred to Apollo*: Cic.; meton. = *poet*: Dircaeu[.] cycnus, Pindar, Hor.

²**Cycnus** or **Cygnus** -i, m. (1) *king of Liguria, son of Sthenelus, changed into a swan*. (2) *the son of Neptune by Calyce, changed into a swan*.

Cўdōnĭa or **Cўdōnēa** -ae, f. (Κυδωνία), *an ancient city on the north coast of Crete*.
¶ Hence subst. **Cўdōn** -ōnis, m. *a Cydonean*; **Cўdōnĭātae** -ārum, m. *inhabitants of Cydonea*; adj. **Cўdōnĭus** -a -um: Verg., an[.] **Cўdōnēus** -a -um: Ov., *Cydonian, poet[.] for Cretan*.

cўlindrus -dri, m. (κύλινδρος). (1) *a cylinder* Cic. (2) *a roller for levelling the ground*: Verg[.]

Cyllărus -i, m. (Κύλλαρος). (1) *a Centaur* (2) *the horse of Castor*.

Cyllēnē -ēs and -ae, f. (*Κυλλήνη*), *a mountain in north-east Arcadia, where Mercury was born and reared.* ¶ Hence adj. **Cyllēnĭus** -a -um, *Cyllenian and Mercurian*: proles, of *Mercury*, Verg.; of *Cephalus, son of Mercury*: Ov.; ignis, *the planet Mercury*, Verg.; m. as subst. **Cyllenius** -i, *Mercury*: Verg.; also adj. **Cyllēnēus** -a -um, and f. adj. **Cyllēnis** -idis, *Cyllenian or Mercurian.*

cymba -ae, f.=cumba; q.v.

cymbălum -i, n. (*κύμβαλον*), *a cymbal*, usually found in the plur.: Lucr., Cic., Verg., Liv.

cymbĭum -i, n. (*κυμβίον*), *a small drinking-vessel*: Verg.

Cymē -ēs, f. (*Κύμη*), *a town in Aeolis, on the coast of Asia Minor.* Adj. **Cymaeus** -a -um, *Cymaean.*

Cynĭcus -a -um (*κυνικός*), *Cynic, of the Cynic school*: Tac.; m. as subst. **Cynĭcus** -i, *a Cynic philosopher*: Cic., Hor., Juv. Adv. **Cynĭcē**, *after the manner of the Cynics*: Pl.

cynŏcĕphălus -i, m. *the dog-faced baboon*: Cic. L.

Cynoscĕphălae -ārum, f. (*Κυνὸς κεφαλαί, dog's heads*), *two hills near Scotussa in Thessaly, where the Romans defeated the Macedonians.*

Cynŏsūra -ae, f. (*Κυνόσουρα, dog's tail*), *the constellation Ursa Minor.* ¶ Hence f. adj. **Cynŏsūris** -ĭdis: ursa, Ov.

Cynthus -i, m. (*Κύνθος*), *a mountain in Delos, the birth-place of Apollo and Diana.* ¶ Hence adj. **Cynthius** -a -um *Cynthian*; as subst., m. **Cynthĭus** -i, *Apollo*, f. **Cynthĭa** -ae, *Diana.*

Cypărissus -i, m. *a youth who was changed into a cypress.*

cypărissus, f.=cupressus; q.v.

Cyprus or **Cypros** -i, f. (*Κύπρος*), *the island of Cyprus.* ¶ Hence adj. **Cyprius** -a -um, *Cyprian*: Cyprium aes, or n. as subst. **Cyprium** -i, *copper*, Plin.; f. as subst. **Cypria** -ae, *Venus*, worshipped in Cyprus.

Cypsĕlus -i, m. (*Κύψελος*), *a tyrant of Corinth.*

Cyrēnē -ēs and **Cyrēnae** -arum, f. *a city of north-eastern Africa, birth-place of the poet Callimachus and of the philosopher Aristippus, founder of the Cyrenaic school.* ¶ Hence adj. **Cyrēnaeus** -a -um and **Cyrēnăĭcus** -a -um, *Cyrenaic*; m. pl. **Cyrēnaei** and **Cyrēnăĭci** -orum, *the Cyrenaic philosophers*; adj. and subst. **Cyrēnensis** -e, *Cyrenaic, an inhabitant of Cyrene.*

Cyrnŏs -i, f. (*Κύρνος*), *the Greek name for the island of Corsica.* Adj. **Cyrneus** -a -um, *Corsican.*

Cyrus -i, m. (*Κῦρος*). (1) *the founder of the Persian Empire* (559 B.C.). (2) *Cyrus minor, second son of Ochus, who was killed at Cunaxa* (401 B.C.). (3) *an architect at Rome in the time of Cicero.* ¶ Hence **Cyrēa** -ōrum, n. pl. *his buildings*: Cic. L.

Cytae -ārum, f. *a city in Colchis, reputed birth-place of Medea.* Adj. **Cytaeus** -a -um, *Cytaean=Colchian*; **Cytaeis** -ĭdis, f. *the Cytaean*, i.e., *Medea.*

Cythēra -ōrum, n. (*Κύθηρα*), *the island Cythera, sacred to Venus* (now *Kithira*).

¶ Hence adj. **Cythĕrēus** -a -um and **Cythĕrēĭus** -a -um, *Cytherean*; f. as subst. **Cythērēa** and **Cythĕrēĭa**=*Venus*; **Cythĕrēis** -ĭdis, f.=*Venus*; adj. **Cythēriăcus** -a -um and f. adj. **Cythĕrēĭăs** -ădis, *of Cythera* or *of Venus.*

cytisus -i, c. (*κύτισος*), *a kind of clover* or *lucerne much valued by the ancients*: Verg.

Cytōrus (**Cytōros**), -i m. (*Κύτωρος*), *a mountain and city in Paphlagonia, famous for box-trees.* Adj. **Cytōriăcus** -a -um, *Cytorian*: pecten, *made of boxwood*, Ov.

Cyzĭcus or **Cyzĭcos** -i, f. (*Κύζικος*), *a town on the Propontis.* Adj. **Cyzĭcēnus** -a -um, *Cyzicene.*

D

D, d, the fourth letter of the Latin alphabet, corresponding in sound and alphabetical position with the Greek *Δ, δ*. For its meaning as an abbreviation, see Table of Abbreviations.

Dāci -ōrum, m. *the Dacians, a warlike people on the Lower Danube.* ¶ Hence **Dācĭa** -ae, f. *their country, Dacia*; **Dācus** -i, m., *a Dacian*; **Dācĭcus** -i, m. (sc. nummus), *a gold coin of Domitian, the conqueror of the Dacians.*

dactylĭcus -a -um (*δακτυλικός*), *dactylic*: numerus, Cic.

dactylĭŏthēca -ae, f. (*δακτυλιοθήκη*). (1) *a casket for rings*: Mart. (2) *a collection of seal rings and gems*: Plin.

dactylus -i, m. (*δάκτυλος, a finger*), *a metrical foot, consisting of one long, followed by two short syllables* (- ◡ ◡), *a dactyl*: Cic.

¹**daedălus** -a -um (*δαίδαλος*). (1) act., *skilful*: Circe, Verg.; natura daedala rerum, *the quaint artificer*, Lucr. (2) pass., *curiously wrought, variegated*: carmina, Lucr.; tecta, Verg.

²**Daedălus** -i, m. (*Δαίδαλος*), *a mythical Athenian craftsman, builder of the Cretan labyrinth.* ¶ Hence adj. **Dacdălēus** -a -um (Hor.) and **Daedălĭus** -a -um (Prop.), *Daedalean*: iter, *the labyrinth*, Prop.

Dalmătae (**Delmătae**) -ārum, m. (*Δαλμάται*), *the Dalmatians, inhabitants of Dalmatia.* ¶ Hence **Dălmătĭa** -ae, f. *the country of Dalmatia on the east side of the Adriatic Sea*; adj. **Dălmătĭcus** -a -um, *Dalmatian.*

Dămascus -i, f. (*Δαμασκός*), *the city of Damascus, capital of Coele-Syria.* Adj. **Dămascēnus** -a -um, *Damascene*: pruna, *damsons*, Plin., Mart.

damma (older form **dāma**) -ae, f. (m., Verg.), *a fallow-deer, chamois, antelope*: Verg., Hor., Ov. Transf., *venison*: Ov., Juv.

damnātĭo -ōnis, f. (damno), *condemnation*: ambitūs, *for bribery*, Cic.; tantae pecuniae, *to pay*, etc., Cic.

damnātōrĭus -a -um (damno), *relating to condemnation, condemnatory*: iudicium, Cic.

damno -are (damnum). In gen., *to cause loss or injury to*: divites, Pl. Esp., at law, *to condemn, sentence, punish.*

damnosus   **d**

LIT., with acc. of person: Caes., Cic.,
Liv., Tac.; with acc. of thing: Cic. Often in
pass., with personal subject: damnari inter
sicarios, *to be condemned as an assassin*, Cic.;
damnari per arbitrum, Cic.; damnari nullam
aliam ob causam, Cic.; damnari suā lege,
Cic. The *offence* is expressed by a genit.:
ambitūs, furti, maiestatis, Cic.; sometimes
by abl.: eo crimine, Cic.; by de: de vi, Cic.;
or by a clause, esp. with quod: A. Baebius
unus est damnatus, quod milites Romanos
praebuisset ad ministerium caedis, Liv. The
punishment is expressed by a genit.: octupli,
Cic.; Liv., Verg.; or by abl.: capite, *to loss
of civil rights*, Cic.; in later writers by ad:
ad mortem, Tac. Rarely of the prosecutor,
to effect the condemnation of: hoc uno crimine
illum, Cic.

TRANSF., outside the law; in gen., *to
condemn, disapprove of*; with genit. of
grounds: aliquem summae stultitiae, Cic.;
esp. (1) of deities: damnare aliquem voti
or voto, *to grant a person's wish, and thereby
compel him to discharge his vow*: damnabis
tu quoque votis, Verg.; in pass.: damnari
voti *or* voto, *to attain one's wish*; bis eiusdem
voti damnata republica, Liv. (2) *to assign,
devote*: caput Orco, Verg.; Ilion mihi
castaeque damnatum Minervae, *made over
to us* (for destruction), Hor. (3) of a testator,
to bind an heir to conditions: Hor.

damnōsus -a -um, adj. (with compar. and
superl.) (damnum). (1) act., *causing loss or
damage, ruinous, detrimental*: bellum sumptuo-
sum et damnosum Romanis, Liv.; Hor., Ov.
(2) pass., *damaged, injured*: Pl. (3) middle
sense, *self-injuring*: Pl.

¶ Adv. **damnōsē**, *ruinously*: bibere, *to the
host's loss*, Hor.

damnum -i, n. (old form dampnum; connected with daps and Greek δαπάνη), *loss,
damage, injury* (opp. lucrum).

In gen.: damnum dare, *to cause loss*, Pl.,
Cic.; contrahere, facere, *to suffer loss*, Cic.;
pati, Liv.; ferre, Ov.; damna Romano accepta
bello, Liv.; damna caelestia lunae, *the waning
of the moon*, Hor.; damnum naturae, *a
natural defect*, Liv.; in abuse, of persons:
Pl., Ov.

Esp. at law, *a fine*: Pl., Cic., Liv.

Dămoclēs -is, m. (Δαμοκλῆς), *a courtier of
Dionysius, tyrant of Syracuse, who, on
praising the tyrant's prosperity, was placed
by Dionysius at a feast, but with a sword hung
by a hair over his head.*

Dāmōn -ōnis, m. (Δάμων). (1) *a Pythagorean,
famous for his friendship with Phintias*. (2) *a
celebrated Athenian musician, teacher of
Pericles.*

Dănăē -ēs, f. (Δανάη), *daughter of Acrisius,
mother of Perseus by Jupiter, who visited her
in a shower of gold when she was shut up in a
tower by her father.*

¶ Hence adj. **Dănăēïus** -a -um: heros=
Perseus, Ov.

Dănăus -i, m. (Δαναός), *son of Belus; brother
of Aegyptus, with whom he quarrelled; he left
Egypt for Argos.*

¶ Hence adj. **Dănăus** -a -um, *Argive,
Greek*; esp. in m. pl. **Dănăi** -ōrum, *the
Greeks*; **Dănăïdes** -um, f. *the fifty daughters
of Danaus.*

dănīsta -ae, m. (δανειστής), *a money-lender*: Pl
Adj. **dănīstĭcus** -a -um (δανειστικός): Pl.

dāno=old form of do; q.v.

Dānŭvĭus -i, m. *the Danube* (in the upper par
of its course; the lower part was calle
Hister).

Daphnē -ēs, f. (Δάφνη). (1) *the daughter of th
river-god Peneus, changed into a laurel-tre*
(2) *a park near Antioch in Syria.*

Daphnis -nĭdis; acc. -nim and -nin (Δάφνις
*son of Mercury, a Sicilian shepherd, invento
of pastoral poetry.*

daphnōn -ōnis, m. (δαφνών), *a grove of laurels
Mart., Petr.

daps, dăpis, f. (cf. δαπάνη), *a sacrificial feas
religious banquet*: ergo obligatam redde Iov
dapem, Hor. TRANSF., in gen., *a meal, feas
banquet*: amor dapis, Hor.; humanā dap
(with human flesh) pascere equos, Ov.; plur.
dapibus epulari opimis, Verg.; Tac.

dapsĭlis -e (daps, δαψιλής), *sumptuous, plentiful
Pl.

Dardăni -ōrum, m. (Δάρδανοι), *a warlik
Illyrian people in Upper Moesia.*

Dardănus -i, m. (Δάρδανος), *son of Jupiter an
Electra, the mythical ancestor of the roy
family of Troy.*

¶ Hence adj. **Dardănus** -a -um an
Dardănĭus -a -um, *Trojan*; subst. **Dar
dănĭa** -ae, f. *Dardanus' city*; usually=*Troy
Dardănĭdēs -ae, m. *a descendant of Dardanus
hence *a Trojan*, and esp. *Aeneas*: Verg.
f. adj. and subst. **Dardănis** -ĭdis, *a Troja
woman*: Ov.; *Creusa*: Verg.

Dārēus -i, m. (Δαρεῖος), *name of sever
Persian kings*; esp. (1) *Darius Hystasp*
(ruled 521–486 B.C.). (2) *Darius Noth*
(ruled 424–405 B.C.). (3) *Darius Codomannu
overthrown by Alexander the Great* (rule
336–330 B.C.).

dătārius -a -um (do), *to be given away*: Pl.

dătātim, adv. (do), *by giving alternately*;
games: Pl.

dătĭo -ōnis, f. (do), *a giving*: legum, Cic
TRANSF., *the legal right of alienation*: Liv.

dătīvus -a -um (do), *to do with giving*: casus,
dativus as m. subst., *the dative case*, Quint.

dăto -are (freq. of do), *to keep giving or to gi*
away: Pl.

dător -ōris, m. (do), *a giver*: laetitiae=
Bacchus, Verg.

dătū, abl. sing. as from datus, m. (do), *l*
giving: Pl.

Daulis -ĭdis, f. (Δαυλίς), *a city in Phocis.*

¶ Hence adj. **Daulius** -a -um; and f. ad
Daulĭas -ădis, *Daulian*: ales=*Procne*, Ov
Dauliades puellae=*Procne and Philomel*
Verg.

Daunus -i, m. *a mythical king of Apuli
ancestor of Turnus.*

¶ Hence adj. **Daunĭus** -a -um, *Daunia
heros, Turnus*, Verg.; gens, the Rutulians,
whom Turnus was king, Verg.; caede
Roman, Hor. Subst. **Daunĭas** -ădis,
Apulia: Hor.

dē, prep., with abl., *down from* a certain poi
of departure.

(1) in space. LIT., *down from, away fro*
de alterā parte agri Sequanos deceder
iuberet, Caes.; de manibus effugere, Cic
de digito anulum detrahere, Cic.; de cae
labi, Verg. TRANSF., *from*: a, *coming fr*

[166]

an origin: homo de plebe, Cic.; copo de viā Latinā, Cic.; rabula de foro, Cic.; Libyca de rupe Leones, *African lions*, Ov.: **b**, *taken from* a class, collection, or stock: pauci de nostris, Caes.; hominem misi de comitibus meis, Cic.; de duobus honestis utrum honestius, Cic.; de meo, *from my property*, Cic.; so in such adverbial phrases as: de integro, *anew*, Cic.; de improviso, *unexpectedly*, Cic.: **c**, *made from* a material, or *changed from* a previous state: verno de flore corona, Tib.; de templo carcerem fieri, Cic.: **d**, of information, *from* a source: de patre audivi, Cic.

(2) in time: **a**, *following from, after*: statim de auctione venire, Cic.; diem de die, *day after day*, Liv.: **b**, *in the course of, during*: de nocte venire, Cic.; de die, *in the day-time*, Hor.; de mense Decembri navigare, Cic.

(3) of various analogous relations: **a**, of a starting-point of thought, discussion, strife, etc., *about*: recte non credis de numero militum, Cic. L.; de Samnitibus triumphare, *over* them, Cic.: **b**, of a cause of action, *on account of*: gravi de causa, Cic.; qua de causa, *wherefore*, Cic.: **c**, of a norm or regulation, *according to*: vix de mea sententia, Cic.; de more maiorum, Liv.

d**ĕa** -ae, f. (dat. and abl. pl., usually deābus), *a goddess*: Cic.; triplices, *the Parcae*, Ov.; deae novem, *the Muses*, Ov.

d**ĕalbo** -are, *to whitewash, plaster*: columnas, Cic.

d**ĕambŭlātĭo** -ōnis, f. (deambulo), *a walking about*: Ter.

d**ĕambŭlo** -are, *to take a walk*: Ter., Suet.

d**ĕamo** -are, *to love dearly*: Pl.

d**ĕarmo** -are, *to disarm*: dearmatus exercitus hostium, Liv.

d**ĕartuo** -are (artus), *to tear limb from limb*; fig.: Pl.

d**ĕascio** -are (ascia), *to smoothe with an axe*; fig., *to cheat*: Pl.

d**ēbacchor** -ari, dep. *to rave, revel furiously*: debacchantur ignes, Hor.

d**ēbellātor** -ōris, m. (debello), *a conqueror*: ferarum, Verg.

d**ēbello** -are.

(1) intransit., *to wage war to the end, finish a war*: neque priusquam debellavero absistam, Liv.; proelio uno debellatum est, Liv.

(2) transit.: **a**, *to fight out*: rixa super mero debellata, Hor.: **b**, *to conquer, overcome*: superbos, Verg.; Tac.

d**ēbĕo** -ēre -ŭi -ĭtum (for dehibeo, from de/habeo, *to have from a person*), *to owe*.

LIT., of money and its equivalent: alicui pecuniam, Cic.; talenta cc, Cic.; illi quibus debeo, *my creditors*, Cic.; absol.: ii qui debent, *debtors*, Cic.; n. of perf. partic. pass. as subst. d**ēbĭtum** -i, *a debt*: debitum alicui solvere, Cic.; debito fraudari, Cic.

TRANSF., of other things owed. (1) *to owe* anything that one should pay: alicui gratiam, Cic.; in pass.: honores debitos, *due*, Sall.; praemia debita, Verg. (2) *to owe for* anything that one has, *to be indebted to* somebody *for*: alicui beneficium, Cic.; vitam, Ov. (3) with infin., *to be due to* a thing, *be morally bound to* (cf. English *owe/ought*): num ferre contra patriam arma debuerunt? Cic.; ut iam nunc dicat iam nunc debentia dici, Hor.

(4) with infin., *to be bound by logic* or *necessity* or *natural law to* (poet.): omnia debet enim cibus integrare, Lucr. (5) *to have to pay* because of fate, *to be destined to give*: tu, nisi ventis debes ludibrium, *if you are not bound to become*, Hor.; debitus destinatusque morti, Liv.; vita quae fato debetur, Cic.

d**ēbĭlis** -e, adj. (with compar.), *powerless, feeble, weak*: corpus, Cic.; senex, Cic.; ferrum, Verg. TRANSF., mancam ac debilem praeturam futuram suam, Cic.; ingenio debilior, Tac.

d**ēbĭlĭtās** -ātis, f. (debilis), *weakness, feebleness, debility*: bonum integritas corporis, miserum debilitas, Cic.; linguae, Cic.; membrorum, Liv. TRANSF., animi, Cic.

d**ēbĭlĭtātĭo** -ōnis, f. (debilito), *a weakening, disabling*: animi, Cic.

d**ēbĭlĭto** -are (debilis), *to weaken, enfeeble, disable*.

LIT., membra lapidibus, fustibus, Cic.; gen. in pass., esp. in perf. partic.: debilitatum corpus et contrucidatum, Cic.; poet., of things: quae (hiems) nunc oppositis debilitat pumicibus mare Tyrrhenum, Hor.

TRANSF., *to enervate, break down*: audaciam debilito, sceleri resisto, Cic.; tribunicios furores, Cic.; debilitatus metu, Cic.; Verg.

d**ēbĭtĭo** -ōnis, f. (debeo), *an owing, debt*: pecuniae, Cic.

d**ēbĭtor** -ōris, m. (debeo), *one who owes, a debtor*.

LIT., addicere Futidium creditorem debitoribus suis, Cic.; Caes., Hor.

TRANSF., mercede solutā non manet officio debitor ille tuo, Ov.; vitae, *owing his life to*, Ov.

d**ēbĭtum** -i, subst. from partic. of debeo; q.v.

d**ēcanto** -are. (1) transit., *to sing* or *say repeatedly*: elegos, Hor.; pervulgata praecepta, Cic. (2) intransit., *to leave off singing*: sed iam decantaverant fortasse, Cic.

d**ēcēdo** -cēdĕre -cessi -cessum. (1) *to move away, withdraw, retire*.

LIT., of physical movement: ex nostrā provinciā, Cic.; decedere Italiā, Sall.; as milit. t. t., *to march away, to evacuate*: decedere atque exercitum deducere ex his regionibus, Caes.; pugnā, Liv.; of the magistrate of a province, *to leave on the expiration of his term*: de or ex or (simply) provinciā, Cic.; of actors: decedere de scenā, Cic.; of animals: decedere e pastu, Verg.; esp. with dat., *to make way for*: alicui de via, Pl.; pass.: salutari, appeti, decedi, *to be made way for*, Cic.

TRANSF., **a**, *to retire, give up*: de iure, de bonis, Cic.; with dat., *to yield to, retire in favour of*: vivere si recte nescis, decede peritis, Hor.; serae decedere nocti, Verg.: **b**, *to depart from life, to die*: decedere de vitā, Cic.; or absol.: decedere, Cic.

(2) of things without life, *to retire, abate, cease*: cum decessisse inde aquam nuntiatum esset, Liv.; sol decedens, *setting*, Verg.; alteram quartanam mihi dixit decessisse, Cic.; postquam invidia decesserat, Sall.

(3) *to go astray, deviate*. LIT., of physical movement: de viā decedere, *to depart from one's course*, Cic.; naves paululum suo cursu decesserunt, Cic. TRANSF., se nullā cupiditate inductum de viā decessisse, Cic.; de officio et dignitate, Cic.

Dĕcĕlēa (-īa) -ae, f. (Δεκέλεια), *a town under Mt. Parnes, overlooking the plain of Attica.*

dĕcem (δέκα), indecl. adj. *ten:* Cic. etc.; meton., *for an indefinite number:* decem vitia, Hor.; Pl.

Dĕcember -bris (decem), adj. *of the tenth month of the Roman year reckoned from March;* i.e. *of December:* Kalendae, Cic.; Decembri utere, *the licence of December,* i.e. *of the Saturnalia,* Hor. M. as subst. **December** -bris (sc. mensis), *December:* Cic., etc.; poet., *a completed year:* Hor.

dĕcemiŭgis -is, m. (decem/iugum), adj. used as subst. (sc. currus), *a ten-horse chariot:* Suet.

dĕcempĕda -ae, f. (decem/pes), *a measuring rod ten feet in length:* Cic., Hor.

dĕcempĕdātor -ōris, m. (decempeda), *one who uses the decempeda, a land-surveyor:* aequissimus agri privati et publici decempedator, Cic.

dĕcemplex -icis (decem/plico), *ten-fold:* Nep.

dĕcemprimi -ōrum, m. (often written as two words), *the ten chief men in the senate of a municipium or colonia:* Cic.

dĕcemscalmus -a -um (decem/scalmus), *having ten rowlocks:* actuariola, Cic. L.

dĕcemvir -i, m.; usually plur. **dĕcemvĭri** -orum, m. *a board of ten commissioners at Rome* for various occasional purposes, esp. (1) decemviri legibus scribundis, *those who drew up the 'twelve tables' of laws,* 451-450 B.C. (2) decemviri sacris faciundis, *the guardians of the Sibylline Books, etc.* (3) decemviri stlitibus (litibus) iudicandis, *who judged cases affecting freedom and citizenship.* (4) decemviri agris dividundis, *the commission for dividing public lands.*

dĕcemvĭrālis -e (decemvir), *relating to the decemvirs:* annus, Cic.; potestas, Liv.; leges, Liv.

dĕcemvĭrātus -ūs, m. (decemvir), *the office of a decemvir:* Cic., Liv.

dĕcennis -e, adj. (decem/annus), *of ten years:* Quint.

dĕcens -entis, partic. from decet; q.v.

dĕcentia -ae, f. (decet), *propriety, comeliness:* figurarum venustas atque ordo et, ut ita dicam, decentia, Cic.

dĕcerno -cernĕre -crēvi -crētum (syncop. perf. forms: decrerim, decreram, decrero, decresset, decresse), *to decide, determine, settle.* (1) peacefully, and esp. by authority: a, about facts: rem dubiam, Liv.; with acc. and infin.: qui sine manibus et pedibus constare deum posse decreverunt, Cic.: b, about action; with acc., *to decide to do or to give a thing:* pecunias, Cic.; alicui triumphum, Cic.; with infin., acc. and infin., etc., *to decide* as an individual: Caesar his de causis Rhenum transire decreverat, Caes.; decreram cum eo familiariter vivere, Cic.; also *to decide, decree* as a competent body (e.g. the senate); or, as a member of such a body, *to move, propose:* senatus decrevit, darent operam consules, ne quid respublica detrimenti caperet, Sall.; si hic ordo (*the senate*) placere decreverat te ire in exsilium, obtemperaturum te esse dicis, Cic.; Silanus primus sententiam rogatus supplicium sumendum decreverat, Sall.

(2) by fighting; with the issue in acc.: proelium, Cic.; pugnam, Liv.; or as clause: Samnis Romanusne imperio Italiam regat, Liv.; with the means in abl.: armis, Cic.; ferro ancipiti, Verg.

¶ Hence partic. **dĕcrētus** -a -um; n. as subst. **dĕcrētum** -i, *a resolve;* esp. *of an authority, a resolution, decree:* consulis, Liv.; senatus, Cic.; decreta facere, Cic.; as philosoph. t. t., like δόγμα, *doctrine, principle:* Cic.

dĕcerpo -cerpĕre -cerpsi -cerptum (carpo), *to pluck down.*

LIT., *to pluck off, pluck away:* arbore pomum, Ov.

TRANSF., (1) *to gather:* oscula, Cat., Hor., Cic. (2) *to derive:* humanus animus decerptus ex mente divina, *a scion of,* Cic. (3) *to take away:* ne quid iocus de gravitate decerperet, Cic.

dĕcertātio -ōnis, f. (decerto), *a contest:* rerum omnium, Cic.

dĕcerto -are, *to contend, fight to a finish:* proeliis cum acerrimis nationibus, Cic.; pugnā, Caes.; armis, Caes.; fig.: locus, ubi Demosthenes et Aeschines inter se decertare soliti sunt, Cic.; qua de re iure decertari oporteret, armis non contendere, Cic.

dĕcessio -ōnis, f. (decedo), *a withdrawing, departure* (opp. accessio).

LIT., of physical movement: tua, Cic. L.; esp. *the departure of a governor from his province* after his year of office: Cic.

TRANSF., *deduction, diminution:* non enim tam cumulus bonorum iucundus esse potest quam molesta discessio, Cic.

dĕcessor -ōris, m. (decedo), *one who retires from an office, a predecessor:* successori decessor invidit, Cic.

dĕcessus -ūs, m. (decedo), *a withdrawal, departure:* Dionysii, Nep. Esp. (1) *the retirement of an official:* post M. Bruti decessum, Cic. (2) *death:* amicorum, Cic. (3) *of water, ebb:* aestus, Caes.

dĕcet -ēre -ūit (connected with δοκεῖν), *it is proper, seemly, fitting;* what is fitting is expressed, if at all, by an infin., or sometimes by noun or pronoun, sing. or plur.; the person or thing fitted or suited is usually acc., rarely dat.

(1) physically: quem decet muliebris ornatus, Cic.; quem tenues decuere togae nitidique capilli, Hor.

(2) morally: istue facinus nostro generi non decet, Pl.; oratorem irasci minime decet, Cic.; exemplis grandioribus decuit uti, Cic.; spem habeo nihil fore aliter ac deceat, Cic.; id enim maxime quemque decet, quod est cuiusque maxime suum, Cic.; et quod decet honestum est et quod honestum est decet, Cic.

¶ Hence partic. (with compar. and superl.) **dĕcens** -entis, *proper, fit.* (1) physically: amictus, Ov.; motus, Hor.; hence, *well-formed, comely, handsome:* facies, forma, Ov.; Venus, Hor. (2) morally: quid verum atque decens curo et rogo, Hor.

¶ Adv. (with compar.) **dĕcentĕr**, *properly, fitly:* Hor.

¹**dĕcido** -cidĕre -cidi (de/cado), *to fall down.*

LIT., of persons: equo, Caes.; toro, Ov.; of things: decidunt turres, Hor.; si decidit imber, Hor.; poma, si matura et coeta, decidunt, Cic.

TRANSF., (1) *to fall dead, die*: scriptor abhinc annos centum qui decidit, Hor. (2) in gen., *to sink, fall*; of disappointment: de spe, Ter.; a spe, Liv.; in hanc fraudem, Cic.; ficta omnia celeriter tamquam flosculi decidunt, Cic.

²dēcīdo -cīdĕre -cīdi -cīsum (de/caedo), *to cut down, cut off*.

LIT., aures, Tac.; pennas, Hor.

TRANSF., *to cut short, to settle, to arrange*: post decisa negotia, Hor.; quibus omnibus rebus actis atque decisis, Cic.; per te, C. Aquili, decidit P. Quinctius quid liberis eius dissolveret, Cic.; sine me cum Flavio decidisti, Cic.

dĕcĭens and **dĕcĭēs**, adv. (decem), *ten times*: Cic., Ov. TRANSF., *an indefinite number of times*: Hor.

decima=decuma; q.v.

decimanus=decumanus; q.v.

decimo=decumo; q.v.

dĕcĭmus (older **decumus**) -a -um (decem), *the tenth*: Cic., Liv., etc.; n. as subst., ager cum decimo effecit, *gave a ten-fold yield*, Cic.; as adv.: decimum, *for the tenth time*, Liv., Cic.

dēcĭpĭo -cĭpĕre -cēpi -ceptum (de/capio), *to catch*; hence *to cheat, deceive*: homines honestissimos, Cic.; per conloquium, Caes.; in prima spe, Liv.; poet.: laborum decipitur, *is beguiled into forgetting his toils*, Hor. TRANSF., of things, *to beguile*, esp. of time: diem, Ov.; iudicium non decipit error, Ov.

dēcīsĭo -ōnis, f. (²decido), *a settlement, decision*: decisionem facere, Cic.

Dĕcĭus -a -um *name of a Roman gens; its most famous members were* P. Decius Mus, *supposed to have 'devoted' himself to death in battle in the Latin war* (340 B.C.), *and his son*, P. Decius Mus, *supposed to have done the same at Sentinum* (295 B.C.). Adj. **Dĕcĭānus** -a -um.

dēclāmātĭo -ōnis, f. (declamo). (1) *loud, violent speaking, declamation*: non placet mihi declamatio (candidati) potius quam persalutatio, Cic. (2) *practice in oratory*: quotidiana, Cic.; Quint.; also *a theme for such practice*: Quint., Juv.

dēclāmātor -oris, m. (declamo), *a declaimer*: Cic., Quint., Juv.

dēclāmātōrĭus -a -um (declamator), *relating to declamation, rhetorical*: Cic., Tac.

dēclāmĭto -are (freq. of declamo). (1) *to speak loudly, declaim*: Graece apud Cassium, Cic. (2) *to practise public speaking*: Cic., Hor., Juv.; causas, *to plead for the sake of practice*, Cic.

dēclāmo -are, *to shout downwards*; hence (1) *to speak loudly and violently*: contra me, *to declaim against*, Cic. (2) *to practise speaking in public*: ad fluctum aiunt declamare solitum Demosthenem, Cic.; with object, *to declaim*: quae mihi iste visus est ex alia oratione declamare, Cic.

dēclārātĭo -ōnis, f. (declaro), *a making clear, open expression*: animi tui, Cic. L.

dēclāro -are (clarus), *to make clear or distinct, reveal, declare*.

LIT., of public announcements: praesentiam saepe divi suam declarant, Cic.; esp. of appointments, *to declare, proclaim*: aliquem consulem, Cic.; Numa declaratus rex, Liv.

TRANSF., in gen., *to explain, make clear, declare*: volatibus avium res futuras declarari, Cic.; animi magnitudinem, Cic.; nimirum plus esse sibi declarat inanis, Lucr.; declaravit quanti me faceret, Cic.; verba idem declarantia, *synonyms*, Cic.

dēclīnātĭo -ōnis, f. (declino), *a bending away, a turning aside*.

LIT., tuas petitiones parvā quādam declinatione effugi, Cic.; declinatio atomi, Cic.

TRANSF., (1) *an avoiding, declining, turning away from*: appetitio et declinatio naturalis, Cic. (2) as rhet. t. t., *a digression*: declinatio brevis a proposito, Cic. (3) as grammat. t. t., *inflexion, declension*: Cic.

dēclīno -are (*clino; cf. κλίνω).
(1) transit., *to bend aside, turn away, deflect*. LIT., se, Pl., Lucr.; agmen, Liv.; fig., in pass: metu declinatus animus, Quint. TRANSF., *to avoid, to shun*: urbem unam mihi amoenissimam, Cic.; vitia, Cic.; invidiam, Tac.
(2) intransit., *to deviate, swerve*. LIT., cohortes declinavere paululum, Liv.; declinare de via, Cic.; esp. of atoms: declinare dixit atomum perpaulum, Cic. TRANSF., de statu suo, Cic.; a religione officii, Cic.; of orators, writers, *to digress*: aliquantum a proposito, Cic.

dēclīvis -e (de/clivus), *bent or inclined downwards, sloping*: collis aequaliter declivis ad flumen, Caes.; flumina, Ov.; fig.: iter declive senectae, Ov.

¶ N. as subst. **dēclīve** -is, *a slope, declivity*: per declive se recipere, Caes.; Ov.

dēclīvĭtās -ātis, f. (declivis), *a declivity*: Caes.

dēcocta -ae, f. subst. from decoquo; q.v.

dēcoctor -ōris, m. (decoquo), *a spendthrift, bankrupt*: Cic.

dēcollo -are (de/collum), *to behead*: Suet., Sen.

dēcōlo -are (colum), *to run away as through a sieve*: spes, Pl.

dēcŏlor -ōris (color), *off-colour, pale or discoloured*. LIT., decolor ipse suo sanguine Rhenus, Ov. TRANSF., deterior paulatim ac decolor aetas, Verg.; fama, Ov.

dēcŏlōrātĭo -ōnis, f. (decoloro), *a discolouring*: Cic.

dēcŏlōro -are (decolor), *to discolour*: quod mare Dauniae non decoloravere caedes? Hor.

dēcŏquo -cŏquĕre -coxi -coctum. (1) *to boil thoroughly*: olus, Hor. (2) *to boil down, boil away*. LIT., of metals, *to melt away*: pars quarta argenti decocta erat, Liv. TRANSF., of property, etc.: a, *to waste*: Quint.: b, *to ruin a person*: Pers.: c, *to ruin oneself, to become bankrupt*: tenesne memoria praetextatum te decoxisse? Cic.

¶ Hence partic. **dēcoctus** -a -um, *boiled down*; hence, of style, *insipid*: Cic. F. as subst. **dēcocta** -ae (sc. aqua), *a cold drink invented by Nero*: Juv., Suet.

dĕcor -ōris, m. (decet), *grace, comeliness, beauty*. (1) physical: te decor iste, quod optas, esse vetat, Ov. (2) in gen.: mobilibus decor naturis dandus et annis, Hor.; Verg.; of style: Liv., Quint.

dĕcŏro -are (decus), *to embellish, beautify, adorn*. LIT., physically: oppidum monumentis, Cic.; templa novo saxo, Hor.

TRANSF., haec omnia vitae decorabat dignitas et integritas, Cic.; aliquem honoribus, Cic.; muneribus, Verg.

dĕcōrus -a -um (decor). (1) physically; *graceful, beautiful, comely*: facies, Hor.; membra, Verg.; arma, Sall.; with abl., *adorned with*: Bacchus aureo cornu, Hor.

(2) morally; *proper, fit, becoming*: decorus est senis sermo, quietus et remissus, Cic.; dulce et decorum est pro patria mori, Hor.; ad ornatum decorus, Cic.

¶ N. as subst. **dĕcōrum** -i, *propriety, grace*: πρέπον appellant hoc Graeci, nos dicamus sane decorum, Cic.; Tac.

¶ Adv. **dĕcōrē**. (1) *beautifully*: poet. ap. Cic. (2) *fitly, becomingly*: loqui, Cic.

dĕcrĕpĭtus -a -um (crepo), *infirm, decrepit*: senex, Pl.; aetas, Cic.

dĕcresco -crescĕre -crēvi -crētum, *to grow down*; hence *to become smaller, decrease*: ostreis et conchyliis omnibus contingere, ut cum luna pariter crescant pariterque decrescant, Cic.; decrescentia flumina, Hor.; cornua decrescunt, *become smaller and smaller, disappear*, Ov.; tantum animorum nobis in dies decrescit, Liv.

dĕcrētum -i, n. subst. from decerno; q.v.

dĕcŭma (dĕcĭma) -ae, f. (decimus; sc. pars), *a tenth part, tithe*. (1) as an offering to the gods: Liv. (2) *a tax paid by landowners in the provinces*: decuma hordei, Cic., Liv. (3) *a largess bestowed on the people*: Cic., Tac.

dĕcŭmānus (dĕcĭmānus) -a -um (decimus), *of the tenth*. (1) *relating to the provincial tax of a tenth*: ager, *the land paying a tenth*, Cic.; frumentum, *a tithe of corn*, Cic.; m. as subst. **dĕcŭmānus** -i, *the farmer of such a tax*: Cic.; mulier decumana or simply decumana -ae, f. (sarcastically), *the wife of a farmer of the taxes*: Cic.

(2) *belonging to the tenth legion*: Auct. B. Afr.; m. pl. as subst. **dĕcŭmāni**, *its members*: Tac.

(3) *belonging to the tenth cohort*: porta, *the gate of a Roman camp farthest from the enemy*, so called because the tenth cohorts of the legions were stationed there.

dĕcŭmātes agri (decimus), m. pl. *lands on which the tithe or land-tax was paid* (?), or 'the ten cantons' (?): Tac.

dĕcumbo -cumbĕre -cŭbŭi, (de/*cumbo). (1) *to lie down*, either to sleep or at table: Cic. (2) *to fall, fall down*, used of a vanquished gladiator: Cic.

dĕcŭmo (dĕcĭmo) -are (decimus), *to take a tithe*; as milit. t. t., *to take every tenth man for punishment, to decimate*: Suet., Tac.

dĕcŭria -ae, f. (decem). LIT., *a body of ten men*: Sen. TRANSF., irrespective of number, *a class, division*, esp. of jurors: iudicum, Cic.; scribarum, Tac.; *a party, club*: Pl.

dĕcŭriātĭo -ōnis, f. (¹decurio), *a dividing into decuriae*: Cic.

dĕcŭriātus -ūs, m. (¹decurio), *a dividing into decuriae*: Liv.

¹dĕcŭrio -are (decuria), *to divide into bodies of ten*: equites decuriati, centuriati pedites coniurabant, Liv. TRANSF., *to divide into classes* in gen.: Cic.

²dĕcŭrio -ōnis, m. (decuria). LIT., *head of a body of ten*. (1) as milit. t. t., *company-commander* in the cavalry: decurio equitum

Gallorum, Caes.; Liv., Tac. (2) *a senator of a municipium or colonia*: Cic. (3) *a head-chamberlain*: Suet.

dĕcurro -currĕre -cucurri *or* -curri -cursum.
LIT., *to run down, hasten down*: summa decurrit ab arce, Verg.; ad naves, Caes.; decurro rus, Cic.; esp. as milit. t. t., *to move down*; at practice, *to manœuvre*: pedites ordinatos instruendo et decurrendo signa sequi docuit, Liv.; in action: ex Capitolio in hostem, Liv.; ex omnibus partibus, Caes.
TRANSF., (1) *to run in a race, run towards the goal*; transit., *to run through, traverse*, a set course: nunc video calcem, ad quam cum sit decursum, nihil sit praeterea extimescendum, Cic.; quasi decurso spatio, Cic.; fig.: decurso lumine vitae, Cic.; acta iam aetate decursaque, Cic.; inceptum decurre laborem, Verg. (2) *to have recourse to, take refuge in*: decurrere ad istam cohortationem, Cic.; ad miseras preces, Hor. (3) of the movement of things; of ships, *to sail downstream* or *to land*: Liv.; of water, *to run down*: monte decurrens velut amnis, Hor.

dĕcursĭo -ōnis, f. (decurro), as milit. t. t., *a manœuvre*: Suet.; *a charge*: ap. Cic. L.

dĕcursus -ūs, m. (decurro). LIT., *a running down*: aquāī, Lucr.; aquarum, Ov.; esp. as milit. t. t., *a manœuvre*: alios decursu edere motus, Liv.; Tac.; *a charge, attack*: subitus ex collibus decursus, Liv.; Tac.
TRANSF., *the completion of a course*: honorum, Cic.; rhet., *rhythmical movement*: Quint.

dĕcurtātus -a -um (curtis). LIT., *mutilated*: Sen. TRANSF., of style: mutila senti quaedam et quasi decurtata, Cic.

dĕcus -ŏris, n. (decet), *that which adorns or beautifies, distinction, honour, glory, grace*.
LIT., (1) of things: decora atque ornament fanorum, Cic.; hominis decus ingenium, Cic.; civitatis dignitatem et decus sustinere, Cic.; decus enitet ore, Verg.; vitis ut arboribus decori est, Verg. (2) of persons pride, glory*: imperii Romani decus ac lumen (of Pompey), Cic.; Hor.
TRANSF. (1) plur., decora, *distinguished acts*: militiae, Liv. (2) *moral dignity, virtue*: Cic., Liv.

dĕcusso -are (decussis, *the intersection of two lines), to divide cross-wise in the shape of the letter X*: Cic.

dĕcŭtĭo -cŭtĕre -cussi -cussum (de/quatio), *to shake down, shake off, knock off*. LIT. papaverum capita baculo, Liv.; rorem Verg.; turres fulminibus, Liv.; ariete decuss ruebant muri, Liv. TRANSF., cetera aetat iam sunt decussa, ap. Cic. L.

dĕdĕcet -dĕcēre -dĕcŭit, *it is unbecoming, un suitable, unfitting*: only in 3rd person, sing and plur.; what is fitting is expressed, if all, by an infin., or sometimes by noun or pronoun; the person or thing not fitted, o disgraced, is in the acc. (cf. decet): simulac non dedecet, Cic.; ut ne dedeceat, Cic neque te ministrum dedecet myrtus, Hor Pomponius Atticus Claudiorum imagine dedecere videbatur, Tac.

dĕdĕcŏro -are (dedecus), *to dishonour, brin shame upon*: se flagitiis, Sall.; urbis auctor tatem, Cic.

dēdĕcōrus -a -um, *shameful, dishonourable*: Pl., Tac.

dēdĕcus -ŏris, n. *shame, dishonour, disgrace*.
LIT., alicui dedecori esse *or* fieri, *to bring shame upon*, Cic.; dedecus concipere, Cic.; admittere, Caes.
TRANSF., *a dishonourable act, crime, cause of disgrace*: nullo dedecore se abstinere, Cic.; dedecora militiae, *dishonourable conduct in the field*, Liv.; in gen.: *vice*, Ov., Tac.

dēdĭcātĭo -ōnis, f. (dedico), *a consecration, dedication*: aedis, Liv.

dēdĭco -are. (1) *to dedicate, consecrate*: aedem, Cic.; Iunonem, *to install her in a temple*, Cic.; Hor., Liv. (2) *to specify, indicate*; of property: praedia in censum, Cic.; in gen.: naturam eius, Lucr.; plus in se corporis esse, Lucr.

dēdignor -ari, dep. *to think unworthy*, and so *to scorn, reject*: dedignari maritum, Ov.; Verg.; with infin.: sollicitare, Ov.; Tac.

dēdisco -discĕre -dĭdĭci, *to unlearn, forget*: nomen disciplinamque populi Romani, Caes.; with infin.: eloquentia loqui paene dediscit, Cic.

dēdĭtīcĭus -a -um (dedo), *relating to capitulation or surrender*; plur.: dediticii, *the subjects of Rome, individuals* or *communities who had surrendered unconditionally and had no rights* (opp. socii), Caes., Liv.

ēdĭtĭo -ōnis (dedo), *unconditional surrender, capitulation*: aliquem in deditionem accipere, Caes., Liv.; in deditionem venire, Liv.; facere deditionem, Caes.; deditionis condicio, Liv.; agere de deditione, *to treat*, Caes.; plur.: deditiones cohortium, Tac.

ēdo dēdĕre -dĭdi -dĭtum, *to give up, surrender*.
LIT., aliquem ad supplicium, Liv.; aliquem telis militum, Cic.; aliquem trucidandum populo Romano, Liv.; ad necem, Liv.; neci, Verg., Liv.; esp. of the conquered, *to give up, surrender*: dedere se populo Romano, Caes.; se in arbitrium dicionemque populi Romani, Liv.; se suaque omnia Caesari, Caes.
TRANSF., *to give up to, dedicate, devote*, to good or bad things and causes: aures suas poetis, Cic.; filiam libidini Ap. Claudii, Cic.; se totum Catoni, Cic.; se ei studio, Cic.; se libidinibus, Cic.
¶ Hence partic. **dēdĭtus** -a -um, *given to, devoted to, addicted to*: Coepio nimis equestri ordini deditus, Cic.; mirifice studiis deditus, Cic.; nimis voluptatibus, Cic.; ventri atque somno, Sall.; in pugnae studio, Lucr.; phrase: deditā operā, *intentionally*, Pl., Cic., Liv.

ēdŏcĕo -ēre, *to cause to unlearn, to unteach*: aliquem geometriam, Cic.; aut docendus is est aut dedocendus, Cic.; virtus populum falsis dedocet uti vocibus, *teaches them not to use*, Hor.

ēdŏlĕo -dŏlēre -dŏlŭi, *to make an end of grieving*: Ov.

ēdūco -dūcĕre -duxi -ductum.
(1) *to lead* or *bring down*. LIT., aliquem de rostris, Caes.; ramos pondere suo, *to weigh down*, Ov.; pectine crines, *to comb down*, Ov.; aquam Albanam ad utilitatem agri suburbani, Cic.; esp. as milit. t. t., *to lead down*: aciem in planum, Sall., Caes.; also *to draw a ship down to the sea*: naves in

aquam, Liv.; of enchantment, *to bring down*: Iovem caelo, Ov. TRANSF., *to bring down* in various metaphorical senses: **a**, from general to particular: universitatem generis humani ad singulos, Cic.; rem ad arma, Caes.: **b**, in time, from the past, *to trace downwards* to the present: nomen ab Anco, Ov.: **c**, in amount, *to reduce*, or from an amount, *to subtract*: cibum, Ter.; centum nummos, Cic.
(2) more generally, *to lead* or *draw away*, esp. to a particular place: **a**, in gen., of persons and things: aliquem ex ea via, Cic.; in arcem, Liv.; atomos de via, Cic.: **b**, as milit. t. t.: praesidia de oppidis, Cic.; legiones in hiberna, Caes., Liv.: **c**, *to lead forth, conduct colonists, to found a colony*: coloniam, Cic.; deducere colonos lege Iulia Capuam, Caes.: **d**, *to escort* a person to a place where he is to stay; to his home: me quem luna solet deducere, Juv.; to another's home: ad hospitem, Cic.; to prison: in carcerem, Sall.; esp. magistrates home or to the forum, as a mark of respect: haec ipsa sunt honorabilia adsurgi, deduci, reduci, Cic.; Liv., Hor.; also brides to their new home: uxorem domum, Ter.; Caes., Liv., Tac.: **e**, as legal t. t., *to lead away* a person *from a disputed possession* to procure him the right of action: Cic.: **f**, fig., of persons and things, *to bring out of one state, opinion, etc. into another*: aliquem ab humanitate, Cic.; de sententia, Cic.; ad sententiam, Caes.; in periculum, Caes.: **g**, of things, *to lead, draw*; esp. in weaving: filum, Ov., Cat.; hence, fig., *to draw out, spin out* in speech or writing: tenui deducta poemata filo, Hor.; Ov., Quint.
¶ Hence partic. **dēductus** -a -um. (1) of the nose, *bent inwards*: Suet. (2) *spun out, fine, subtle*: carmen, Verg.

dēductĭo -ōnis, f. (deduco).
(1) *a leading down*: rivorum a fonte, Cic. TRANSF., **a**, in logic: ex hac deductione rationis, Cic.: **b**, *reduction*: Cic.
(2) *a leading away*: **a**, of colonists: in oppida militum crudelis et misera deductio, Cic.; in istos agros deductio, Cic.: **b**, *a fictitious ejectment from disputed property*: Cic.

dēductus -a -um, partic. from deduco; q.v.

deerro (dissyll. in poets) -are, *to wander from the right path, go astray*. LIT., in itinere, Cic.; in navigando a ceteris, Sall.; Verg. TRANSF., magno opere a vero longe, Lucr.; Tac., Quint.

dēfaeco -are (faex), *to clean* or *clear*: Pl.

dēfătīgātĭo -ōnis, f. (defatigo), *exhaustion, weariness, fatigue*: membrorum, Cic.; hostium, Caes.

dēfătīgo -are, *to weary, fatigue, tire*. (1) physically: exercitum quotidianis itineribus, Caes.; defatigatis in vicem integri succedunt, Caes. (2) mentally: te nec animi neque corporis laboribus defatigari, Cic.

dēfătiscor = defetiscor; q.v.

dēfectĭo -ōnis, f. (deficio), *a failure*. Hence (1) *defection, rebellion*: defectio a populo Romano, Cic.; sociorum, Cic.; facere defectionem, Liv.; sollicitare aliquem ad defectionem, Liv.; Caes., Tac. TRANSF., a tota ratione defectio, Cic.

(2) *a weakening, failing, vanishing, disappearing*: virium, Cic.; animi, Cic.; of light: defectiones solis et lunae, *eclipses*, Cic. ¶ Hence partic. **dēfectus** -a -um, *failing, deficient*: Ov., Tac.

dēfector -ōris, m. (deficio), *a rebel, deserter*: Tac., Suet.

¹dēfectus -a -um, partic. of deficio; q.v.

²dēfectus -ūs, m. (deficio), *a failing, ceasing, disappearing*: aquarum, Liv.; esp. *a failing of light, eclipse*: lunae, Cic., Lucr., Verg.

dēfendo -fendĕre -fendi -fensum (de/*fendo).
(1) *to repel, repulse, ward off, drive away*: defendere ictus ac repellere, Caes.; nimios solis ardores (from the vines), Cic.; defendere civium pericula, Cic.; crimen, Cic., Liv.; proximus a tectis ignis defenditur aegre, Ov. (2) *to defend, protect.* LIT., against physical danger: rempublicam, Cic.; se telo, Cic.; vitam ab inimicorum audaciā telisque, Cic.; castra, Caes.; senatum contra Antonium, Cic. TRANSF., in gen., *to defend*: acta illa Caesaris, Cic.; se adversus populum Romanum, Cic.; myrtos a frigore, Verg.; esp.: a, *to defend before a court of law*: Sex. Roscium parricidii reum, Cic.; aliquem de ambitu, *on a charge of*, Cic.; aliquem in capitis periculo, Cic.; hence *to maintain* or *assert in defence*: id aliorum exempla se fecisse defendit, Cic.: b, *to maintain any proposition or statement*: defendere sententiam, Cic.; with acc. and infin.: Cic., Tac.: c, *to sustain a part*: vicem rhetoris atque poetae, Hor.; defendere commune officium censurae, Cic.

dēfensio -ōnis, f. (defendo). (1) *a warding off*: criminum, Liv. (2) *a defence*, physically: castrorum, Caes.; in gen.: defensio miserorum, Cic.; defensionem rei suscipere, Cic.; defensionem causae suae scribere, Cic.

dēfensito -are (freq. of defenso), *to defend frequently*: causas, Cic.; haec non acrius accusavit in senectute quam antea defensitaverat, Cic.

dēfenso -are (freq. of defendo), *to defend vigorously*: Italici, quorum virtute moenia defensabantur, Sall.

dēfensor -ōris, m. (defendo). (1) *one who wards off* or *averts*: periculi, Cic. (2) *a defender*, physically: murus defensoribus nudatus, Caes.; in gen., *a defender, protector*; esp. in a court of law: adoptare sibi aliquem defensorem sui iuris, Cic.; Hor.

dēfĕro -ferre -tūli -lātum.
(1) *to bring down, carry down*: ex Helicone perenni fronde coronam, Lucr.; excipere dolia quae amnis defert, Liv.; acies in campos delata est, Liv.; so with praeceps, of *headlong* movement down: tota prolapsa acies in praeceps deferri, Liv.; praeceps aerii speculā de montis in undas deferor, Verg.
(2) more generally, *to bring* or *carry away*, esp. to a particular place (cf. deduco): a, in gen.: ad causas iudicia iam facta domo, Cic.; commeatum in viam, Liv.; alicui epistulam, Cic.: b, as polit. t. t., *to bring certain things to the appropriate place*: deferre pecuniam in aerarium, Liv.; deferre rationes, *to hand in the accounts*, Cic. deferre censum Romam, *to send the census-lists from the colonies to Rome*, Liv.: c, as naut. t. t., *to drive away, carry*: aliquem ex alto ignotas ad terras et in desertum litus, Cic.: d, fig., of intangible

things, *to offer, hand over, refer*: si quid petet, ultro defer, Hor.; alicui praemium dignitatis, Cic.; totius belli summa ad hunc omnium voluntate defertur, Caes.: e, *to communicate, report*, esp. *to appropriate authority*: deferre falsum equitum numerum, Caes.; te esse sollicitum multi ad nos quotidie deferunt, Cic.; rem ad senatum, Cic.; Liv.: f, as legal t. t., *to report* so that charges may be brought; esp. with nomen, *to inform against* a person, *indict*: deferre nomen alicuius de ambitu, Cic.; nomen venefici cuiusdam, Cic.; deferre crimen, *to bring a charge*, Cic.; deferre aliquem, *to accuse*, Tac. g, *to report favourably on* a person, *recommend for reward*: in beneficiis ad aerarium delatus, Cic.

dēfervesco -fervescĕre -fervi or -ferbŭi, *to cease boiling*; of the heat of passion, *to cease to rage, diminish in violence*: cum adulescentiae cupiditates defervissent, Cic.

dēfessus, see defetiscor.

dēfĕtiscor (**dēfătiscor**) -fĕtisci -fessus, dep. *to become tired, grow weary*; gen. found in perf. partic. **dēfessus** -a -um, *weary, tired*: defessus cultu agrorum, Cic.; with gerund quaeritando, Pl.; with infin.: quaerere, Pl. TRANSF., of things: Cic.

dēfĭcio -fĭcĕre -fēci -fectum (de/facio).
(1) intransit., *to do less than one might*, *to fail*; hence: a, *to desert, rebel, revolt*: a rege, Sall.; a republica, Cic.; ad Poenos, *to go over to the Carthaginians*, Liv. TRANSF., ab amicitia, Cic.; a virtute, Liv.: b, of things *to fail, run short*; esp. of supplies: non materia, non frumentum deficere poterat Caes.; of the sun or moon, *to become eclipsed*: sol deficiens, Cic.; of fire, *to go out*: ignem deficere extremum videbat, Verg.; of water utcumque exaestuat aut deficit mare, *flow or ebbs*, Liv.; deficiunt laesi carmine fonti aquae, Ov.; also of abstr. things: nec ver levitatis Atheniensium exempla deficiunt Cic.; of time: dies deficiat, si velim paupertatis causam defendere, Cic.: c, of strength etc., *to fail, become weak*: ne vox viresque deficerent, Cic.; nisi memoria defecerit, Cic. et simul lassitudine et procedente iam di fame etiam deficere, Liv.; animo deficere *to lose heart*, Caes., Cic.
(2) transit., *to abandon, leave, fail* quoniam me Leontina civitas atque legati deficit, Cic.; ipsos res frumentaria deficer coepit, Caes.; dolor me non deficit, Cic rarely pass. defici, *to be failed by, abandone by*: defici a viribus, Caes.; mulier abund audaciā, consilio et ratione deficitur, Cic. ¶ Hence partic. **dēfectus** -a -um, *feebl* esp. because of age: Ov., Sen., Tac.

dēfīgo -fīgĕre -fixi -fixum, *to fasten dow to fix in.*
LIT., sudes sub aqua, Caes.; sicam consulis corpore, Cic.; tellure hastas, Verg gladium iugulo, Liv.
TRANSF.) in gen., *to secure, plant firml* virtus est una altissimis radicibus defix Cic.; in oculis omnium furta atque flagiti Cic. (2) of sight or thought, *to concentrat fix upon*: omnes vigilias, curas, cogitation in reipublicae salute defigere, Cic.; Liby defixit lumina regnis, Verg.; in cogitation defixus, *deep in thought*, Cic.; defix

lumina, Verg. (3) *to fix, make motionless,*
with astonishment, etc.: defixerat pavor
cum admiratione Gallos, Liv.; partic.
defixus, *astounded*: cum silentio defixi
stetissent, Liv.; obtutu haeret defixus in uno,
Verg. (4) of enchantment, *to bind by a spell*:
regis Iolciacis animum defigere votis, Verg.

dēfingo -fingĕre -finxi, *to form, mould* (perhaps
with the idea of *distortion*): Hor.

dēfīnĭo -ire, *to limit, bound, mark out.*
LIT., imperium populi Romani, Cic.; eius
fundi extremam partem oleae directo ordine
definiunt, Cic.
TRANSF., (1) *to set limits to* anything,
confine: potestatem in quinquennium, Cic.;
so in respect of time, *to limit in length*:
orationem, Cic. (2) *to set as a limit, appoint,
assign*: ut suus cuique locus erat definitus,
Caes.; sibi hortos, Cic.; tempus adeundi,
Caes. (3) *to interpret* ideas or words in
terms of each other, *to understand* one thing
by another: qui mala dolore, bona voluptate
definiunt, Cic.; as logic. t. t., *to define*: rem
verbis, Cic.
¶ Hence partic. **dēfīnītus** -a -um,
definite, distinct: constitutio, Cic.; causa,
Cic. Adv. **dēfīnītē**, *definitely, distinctly*:
Cic.

dēfīnītĭo -ōnis, f. (definio), *a limiting, pre-
scribing*: iudiciorum aequorum, Cic.; as
logic. t. t., *a definition*: verborum omnium
definitiones, Cic.; Quint.

dēfīnītīvus -a -um (definio), *definitive, explanatory*: constitutio, Cic.

dēfit (as from dēfio; cf. deficio); plur. dēfīunt,
infin. dēfiĕri; *fails*: numquamne causa
defiet, cur victi pacto non stetis? Liv.; lac
mihi non defit, Verg.; Pl., Ter.

dēflagrātĭo -ōnis, f. (deflagro), *a burning,
destruction by fire*: terrarum, Cic.; fig.: Cic.

dēflagro -are, *to be burnt down, destroyed by
fire.*
LIT., cum curia Saliorum deflagrasset,
Cic.; Phaethon ictu fulminis deflagravit,
Cic.
TRANSF., (1) in gen., *to be destroyed*:
communi incendio, Cic.; Liv. (2) of passions,
to cease burning, to abate, cool: spes animum
subibat deflagrare iras vestras, Liv.; de-
flagrante paulatim seditione, Tac.
¶ Partic. in pass. sense, **dēflagrātus** -a
-um, *burnt down*: Enn. TRANSF., *destroyed*:
Cic.

dēflecto -flectĕre -flexi -flexum.
(1) transit., *to bend down* or *aside*. LIT.,
tenerum prono pondere corpus, Cat.;
amnes in alium cursum, Cic. TRANSF.,
declinare a proposito et deflectere sententiam, Cic.; tragoediam in risus, Ov.
(2) intransit., *to turn aside, turn away*:
viā, Tac. TRANSF. (often in Cic.), *a veritate*:
Cic.; of speech, *to digress*: oratio redeat
illuc unde deflexit, Cic.

dēflĕo -flēre -flēvi -flētum, *to bewail, weep for*:
impendentes casus inter se, Cic.; alicuius
mortem, Cic.; te cinefactum, Lucr.; absol.:
Prop., Tac.

dēfloccātus -a -um (floccus), *shorn of its
wool*; hence *bald*: Pl.

dēflōresco -flōrescĕre -flōrŭi, *to shed blossom,
to fade.* LIT., (flos) tenui carptus defloruit
ungui, Cat. TRANSF., *to lose bloom, wither*:

cum corporibus vigere et deflorescere
animos, Liv.; amores mature et celeriter
deflorescunt, Cic.

dēflŭo -flŭĕre -fluxi.
(1) *to flow down.* LIT., sudor a capite, Cic.;
umor saxis, Hor.; Rhenus in plures defluit
partes, Caes. TRANSF., a, of physical movement, *to float*: dolia medio amni defluxerunt,
Liv.; secundo amni, Verg.; cum paucis
navigiis secundo amni, Liv.; in gen., *to slip
down, to fall down, descend*; of persons:
moribundus Romanus ad terram, Liv.; of
things, esp. hair and dress: defluebant
coronae, Cic.; pedes vestis defluxit ad imos,
Verg.; toga defluit, *hangs awry*, Hor.: b,
abstr., *to come down*, esp. of the gifts of
heaven: quodsi inest in hominum genere
mens, fides, virtus, concordia, unde haec in
terras nisi a superis defluere potuerunt? Cic.;
also of persons: a necessariis artificiis ad
elegantiora defluximus, Cic.
(2) *to flow away, disappear, be lost*: dum
defluat amnis, Hor.; tristi medicamine
tactae defluxere comae, Ov. TRANSF., of
persons: ex novem tribunis unus me absente
defluxit, *has proved false to me*, Cic.; of
things: vires, tempus, ingenium, Sall.;
numerus Saturnius, Hor.

dēfŏdĭo -fŏdĕre -fōdi -fossum. (1) *to dig down
into*: terram, Hor. (2) *to form by digging,
excavate*: specus, Verg. (3) *to dig in, cover,
bury*: signum septem pedes altum in terram
defodi, Liv.; thesaurum sub lecto, Cic.;
Menucia Vestalis viva defossa est scelerato
campo, Liv. TRANSF., *to conceal*: Hor.

dēfōrmātĭo -ōnis, f. (deformo), *a deforming,
disfiguring*: tantae maiestatis, *degradation*,
Liv.

dēformis -e, adj. (with compar.) (de/forma).
(1) *deformed, misshapen, ugly.* LIT., of
persons or animals, *deformed in body*:
deformem natum esse, Cic.; iumenta parva
atque deformia, Caes.; of things, *ugly,
disgusting*: foeda omnia ac deformia visa,
Liv.; aspectus deformis atque turpis, Cic.
TRANSF., *foul, shameful*: spectaculum, Liv.;
ira, deforme malum, Ov.; obsequium, Tac.
(2) *formless, shapeless*: deformes animae,
Ov.
¶ Adv. **dēformĭter**, *in an ugly fashion*:
Quint., Suet.

dēformĭtās -ātis, f. (deformis), *deformity,
ugliness.* LIT., corporis, Cic.; oris, Tac.
TRANSF., *disgrace, dishonour*: illius fugae
negligentiaeque deformitas, Cic.; Quint.

dēformo -are. (1) *to form, fashion*: marmora,
Quint. TRANSF., ille quem supra deformavi,
whom I have formerly delineated, Cic. (2) *to
put out of proper form* or *shape, disfigure.*
LIT., deformatus corpore, Cic.; parietes
nudos ac deformatos reliquit, Cic. TRANSF.,
to disgrace, dishonour: victoriam clade, Liv.;
homo vitiis deformatus, Cic.

dēfraudo (dēfrūdo) -are, *to deceive, defraud,
cheat*: me drachumā, *out of a drachma*, Pl.;
fig.: aures, Cic.; genium suum, *to deprive
oneself of a pleasure*, Pl., Ter.

dēfrēnātus -a -um (frenum), *unbridled,
unrestrained*: cursus, Ov.

dēfrĭco -fricare -fricŭi -frictum (-fricātum -
Cat.), *to rub down*: dentes, Cic.; fig.: urbem
sale multo, *to satirize, lash.* Hor.

dēfringo -fringĕre -frēgi -fractum (de/frango), *to break down, break off*: ramum arboris, Cic.; ferrum ab hasta, Verg.

dēfrutum -i, n. (from de/ferveo; sc. mustum), *new wine boiled down*: Pl., Verg.

dēfŭgĭo -fŭgĕre -fūgi.
Intransit., *to flee away*: armis abiectis totum sinistrum cornu defugit, Liv.; Caes.
Transit., *to fly from, avoid, get out of the way of*: proelium, Caes.; iudicia, Cic.; auctoritatem consulatus sui, Cic.; eam disputationem, Cic.

dēfundo -fundĕre -fūdi -fūsum, *to pour down, pour out*: vinum, Hor.; aurea fruges Italiae pleno defundit Copia cornu, Hor.

dēfungor -fungi -functus, dep. *to perform, discharge, finish, have done with*: defunctus honoribus, *having filled all public offices*, Cic.; periculis, Cic.; proelio, bello, Liv.; laboribus, Hor.; defunctum bello barbiton, *discharged from the warfare of love*, Hor.; esp.: vitā defungi, *to die*, Verg.; absol.: defungi, *to die*, Ov., Tac.

dēgĕnĕr -ĕris (de/genus), *fallen away from one's origin, unworthy of one's race, degenerate*.
LIT., Neoptolemus, *unworthy of his father*, Verg.; hi iam degeneres sunt, mixti, et Gallograeci vere, quod appellantur, Liv.; with genit.: patriae artis, Ov.
TRANSF., *morally degenerate, unworthy, ignoble*: non degener ad pericula, Tac.; ceterorum preces degeneres fuere ex metu, Tac.

dēgĕnĕro -are (degener). (1) intransit., *to become unlike one's race or kind, to fall off, degenerate*. LIT., a vobis nihil degenerat, Cic.; Macedones in Syros, Liv.; poma degenerant sucos oblita priores, Verg. TRANSF., *to degenerate morally*: ab hac perenni contestataque virtute maiorum, Cic.; in Persarum mores, Liv.; Tac. (2) transit.: **a**, *to cause to degenerate*: ni degeneratum in aliis huic quoque decori offecisset, *his degeneracy*, Liv.: **b**, *to disgrace by degeneracy*: propinquos, Prop.; Ov.

dēgero -ĕre, *to carry off*: ornamenta, Pl.

dēgo dēgĕre dēgi (de/ago), *to pass time*: aetatem, Pl., Ter., Cic.; vitam in egestate, Cic.; in beatorum insulis immortale aevum, Cic.; senectam turpem, Hor.; absol., *to live*: ille potens sui laetusque deget, Hor.; Tac.

dēgrandĭnat, impers., *it hails violently*, or (perhaps), *it ceases to hail*: Ov.

dēgrăvo -are, *to weigh down, bring down, lower*. LIT., degravat Aetna caput, Ov. TRANSF., *to bear down, overpower*: degravabant prope circumventum cornu, Liv.; quia vulnus degravabat, Liv.

dēgrĕdĭor -grĕdi -gressus, dep. (de/gradior), *to step down, march down*: degressus ex arce, Liv.; monte, colle, Sall.; in campum, Liv.; ad pedes, *to dismount*, Liv.

dēgrunnio -ire, *to grunt hard*: Phaedr.

dēgusto -are, *to take a taste from, taste*. LIT., nec degustanti lotos amara fuit, Ov. TRANSF., (1) of fire, *to lick*: celeri flammā tigna trabesque, Lucr. (2) of a weapon, *to graze*: summum vulnere corpus, Verg. (3) in gen., *to try, make a trial of*: eandem vitam, Cic.; imperium, Tac.; litteras primis labris, Quint.; *to sound*: eorum, apud quos aliquid aget aut erit acturus, mentes sensusque degustet, Cic.

dĕhinc, adv. (sometimes monosyll. in poets) *from here, hence*. (1) of space: Tac., Plin. (2) of time: **a**, *from this time, henceforth* quācumque dehinc vi possum, Liv.; Ter. Pl.; also from a time mentioned, *from tha time*: omnes dehinc Caesares, Suet.: **b** *immediately after this* or *that time, thereupon* Eurum ad se Zephyrumque vocat; dehin talia fatur, Verg.; Hor., Tac.; rarely afte primum, as *next*, and *then*: Sall.

dĕhisco -ĕre, *to gape, open, split down*: terr dehiscat mihi, *may the earth swallow me up* Verg.; dehiscens intervallis hostium acies Liv.; Ov.

dĕhŏnestāmentum -i, n. (dehonesto), *blemish, deformity, disgrace*: corporis, Sall. fig.: amicitiarum, Tac.

dĕhŏnesto -are, *to dishonour, disgrace*: famam Liv., Tac.

dĕhortor -ari, dep. *to discourage, to dissuade* res ipsa me, Cic.; me a vobis, Sall.; wit infin.: plura scribere dehortatur me fortuna Sall.; Tac.; with ne: Ter.

Dēĭănīra -ae, f. (Δηάνειρα), *daughter o Oeneus, wife of Hercules*. She killed he husband unintentionally by sending him garment smeared with the blood of Nessus

dēicio -icĕre -iēci -iectum (de/iacio). (1) *to throw, cast, hurl down*. LIT aliquem equo, Caes.; de ponte in Tiberin Cic.; librum in mare, Cic.; sortem (i urnam), Caes., Liv., Verg.; deiecto i pectora mento, Ov.; with reflex., *to rus down*: venti subiti ac procellosi se deiciun Liv.; esp. *to throw to the ground, fel* arbores, Liv.; statuas, Cic.; turrim, Caes hence of persons, *to kill*: paucis deiecti Caes.; Verg. TRANSF., *to bring down*: honore, Cic.; principatu, Caes. (2) more generally, *to fling away* or *asid* as naut. t. t., deici, *to be thrown off cours* classis tempestate vexata ad insulas deicitu Liv.; Caes., Tac.; as milit. t. t., *to dislodg* nostros loco, Caes. TRANSF., **a**, as legal t. t *to eject, dispossess*: aratores, Cic.; aliqu de possessione fundi, Cic.: **b**, *to shift* person from an opinion, attitude, etc.: sententia, Cic.; Tac.: **c**, *to disappoint*: sp Caes.; certo consulatu, Liv.; Cic., Verg **d**, with abstr. object, *to cast aside*: metur vitia, Cic.
¶ Hence partic. **deiectus** -a -um. (1 *low-lying*: equitatus noster deiectis loc constiterat, Caes. (2) *dispirited, dejecte* Verg., Quint.

Dēīdămīa -ae, f. (Δηΐδάμεια), *daughter* Lycomedes, *mother of Pyrrhus or Neoptolem by Achilles*.

dēiectio -onis, f. (deicio), *a throwing dou an eviction* from property: Cic.

¹**dēiectus** -a -um, partic. from deicio; q.v.

²**dēiectus** -ūs, m. (deicio). (1) *a throwing dow* arborum, Liv., Ov. (2) *declivity, steep slop* collis, Caes.

dēiero -are (iuro), *to swear*: per omnes de et deas, Pl.; Ter.

dein, see deinde.

dĕinceps, adv. (from deinde; originally ad cf. princeps; dissyll.: Hor.), *one after anoth successively*. (1) in space: tres deinceps turr cum ingenti fragore prociderunt, Liv.; Cae Cic. (2) in time: deinceps tribunos pleb fore, Cic.; Caes., Liv. (3) in enumerations: primum est officium ut se conservet in naturae statu, deinceps ut, etc., Cic.; combined with deinde, *or* inde: Cic., Liv.

dĕinde and abbrev. **dĕin** (ei often one syllable in poets), adv. (de/inde).
(1) of space, *from that place*: via tantum interest perangusta, deinde paulo latior patescit campus, Liv.; Tac.
(2) of time, *thereafter, thereupon, then, afterwards*: incipe, Damoeta; tu deinde sequere, Menalca, Verg.; Pl., Ter., Caes., Cic., Hor.; often corresponding to primum, principio, prius, inde, post, postremo, etc.: Caesar primum suo, deinde omnium ex conspectu remotis equis, Caes.; with other adverbs: tum deinde, Liv.; deinde postea, Cic., etc.
(3) of other order: **a**, in enumerations, *next, and then*: hoc apparet . . . primum ut . . . deinde ut . . ., Cic.: **b**, of seniority or precedence: Cic.

Dēĭŏnĭdēs -ae, m. (Δηϊονίδης), *son of Deione and Apollo*, i.e. *Miletus*: Ov.

Dēĭŏpēa -ae, f. (Δηϊοπεία), *one of the nymphs of Juno*: Verg.

Dēĭŏtărus -i, m. *a king of Galatia, defended at court at Rome by Cicero.*

Dēïphŏbē -ēs, f. (Δηϊφόβη), *daughter of Glaucus*: Verg.

Dēïphŏbus -i, m. (Δηϊφοβος), *son of Priam, husband of Helen after the death of Paris.*

dēiungo -ĕre, *to disconnect*; fig.: se a labore, Tac.

dēlābor -lābi -lapsus sum, dep. *to glide down, fall down, sink.*
LIT., signum de caelo delapsum, Cic.; ex equo, Liv.; of a deity: caelo, Verg., Liv.; so: de caelo delapsus, of a person *arriving unexpectedly*, Cic.; of liquids, *to flow down*: ex utraque parte tecti aqua delabitur, Cic.
TRANSF., (1) *to sink to, come down to*: in difficultates, Cic.; in vitium scurrile, Tac.; a sapientium familiaritatibus ad vulgares amicitias oratio nostra delabitur, Cic. (2) *to proceed from, be derived from*: illa sunt ab his delapsa plura genera (sc. vocum), Cic. (3) *to fall unawares*: medios in hostes, Verg.

dēlăcĕro -are, *to tear to pieces*; fig.: Pl.

dēlāmentor -ari, dep. *to bewail, lament*: natam ademptam, Ov.

dēlasso -are, *to weary, tire out*: cetera loquacem delassare valent Fabium, Hor.

dēlātĭo -ōnis, f. (defero), *a reporting, a giving information against anyone, accusation, denunciation*: nominis, Cic.; Tac.

dēlātor -ōris, m. (defero), *an informer, denouncer*: criminum auctores delatoresque, Liv.; maiestatis, Tac.; Suet.

dēlēbĭlis -e (deleo), *that can be obliterated or destroyed*: liber, Mart.

dēlēctābĭlis -e (delecto), *delightful, pleasant*: cibus, Tac.

dēlēctāmentum -i, n. (delecto), *delight, pleasure, amusement*: inania ista sunt delectamenta puerorum, Cic.; Ter.

dēlēctātĭo -ōnis, f. (delecto), *delight, pleasure*: mira quaedam in cognoscendo suavitas et delectatio, Cic.; videndi, Cic.

dēlēcto -are (freq. from de/*lacio), *to divert, attract, delight*: ista me sapientiae fama delectat, Cic.; libris me delecto, Cic.; often

in pass., with abl., *to take delight in*: iumentis, Caes.; criminibus inferendis, Cic.; also with ab or in: Cic. In act., with infin. clause as subject: delectabat eum defectiones solis et lunae multo ante nobis praedicere, Cic.; also in pass. with infin., *to delight to*: vir bonus dici delector, Hor.

dēlēctus -ūs, m. (¹deligo), *a choosing, choice*: Cic. In many passages modern editors replace delectus by dilectus; q.v.

dēlēgātĭo -ōnis, f. (²deligo), *an assignment of a debt*: a mancipe annuā die, Cic. L.; Sen.

dēlēgo -are, *to transfer, commit, assign.*
LIT., in Tullianum, Liv.; rem ad senatum, Liv.; in fantem nutricibus, Tac.; hunc laborem alteri, ap. Cic. L.; as mercantile t. t., *to assign a debt* or *to nominate someone else to pay a debt*: alicui, Cic.
TRANSF., *to impute, attribute, ascribe*: crimen alicui, Cic., Tac.; servati consulis decus ad servum, Liv.

dēlēnĭfĭcus -a -um (delenio/facio), *soothing*: Pl.

dēlēnīmentum -i, n. (delenio), *anything that soothes or charms*: delenimentum animis Volani agri divisionem obici, Liv.; Tac.

dēlēnĭo (**delinio**) -ire, *to soften down*; hence *to soothe* or *to charm*: milites, Cic.; mulierem non nuptialibus donis, sed filiorum funeribus, Cic.; aliquem blanditiis voluptatum, Cic.; animos hominum praedā, Liv.

dēlēnītor -ōris, m. (delenio), *one who soothes, cajoles, wins over*: cuius (iudicis) delenitor esse debet orator, Cic.

dēlĕo -lēre -lēvi -lētum.
(1) *to blot out, efface.* LIT., of writing: digito legata, Cic.; Hor., Ov. TRANSF., memoriam discordiarum, Cic.; Volscum nomen, Liv.; improbitatem, Cic.; ignominiam, Liv.
(2) in gen., *to destroy, annihilate*; of things: urbes, Liv.; bella, *to put an end to*, Cic.; leges, Cic.; of persons: paene hostes, Caes.; senatum, Cic.; rarely of a single person: C. Curionem delere voluisti, Cic.

dēlētrix -trīcis, f. (deleo), *that which destroys*: sica paene deletrix huius imperii, Cic.

dēlībĕrābundus -a -um (delibero), *carefully considering, deliberating*: consules velut deliberabundi capita conferunt, Liv.

dēlībĕrātĭo -ōnis, f. (delibero), *consideration, consultation, deliberation*: res habet deliberationem, *admits of*, or *needs*, Cic.; habere deliberationes de republica, Cic.

dēlībĕrātīvus -a -um (delibero), *relating to consideration* or *deliberation*: genus, Cic.; Quint.

dēlībĕrātor -ōris, m. (delibero), *one who deliberates*: Cic.

dēlībĕro -are (de/libra), *to weigh carefully, consider, consult about.*
LIT., re deliberata, Caes.; deliberare maxima de re, Cic.; de Corintho cum imperatore Romano, Liv.; utri potissimum consulendum sit, deliberetur, Cic.
TRANSF., (1) *to ask advice*, esp. of an oracle: Delphos, Nep. (2) *to resolve, decide as a consequence of deliberation*: quod iste certe statuerat ac deliberaverat non adesse, Cic.; deliberata morte ferocior, Hor.
¶ Hence partic. (with compar.) **dēlībĕrātus** -a -um, *resolved, determined*: Cic. L.

dēlībo -are, *to take a little from, to taste*. LIT., sol humoris parvam delibet partem, Lucr.; oscula, Verg. TRANSF., (1) in gen., *to extract*: ex universa mente divina delibatos animos habemus, *derived*, Cic. (2) *to take from* so as to *enjoy*: ut omnes undique flosculos carpam et delibem, Cic.; novum honorem, Liv. (3) *to take from* so as to *lessen* or *spoil*: aliquid de gloria, Cic.; animi pacem, *to mar*, Lucr.

dēlībro -are (de/liber), *to bark, peel the bark off*: Caes.

dēlībūtus -a -um, partic. as from delibuo (cf. λείβω), *steeped*: multis medicamentis delibutus, Cic.; delibutus capillus, Cic.; Pl., Hor.; fig.: gaudio, Ter.

dēlĭcātus -a -um, adj. (with compar. and superl.) (deliciae), *dainty, nice*, in various senses. (1) *soft, tender*: tenellulo delicatior haedo, Cat.; versiculi, Cat. (2) in unfavourable sense; *luxurious* of things, *spoilt, effeminate* of persons: muliebri et delicato comitatu, Cic.; voluptates, Cic.; adulescens, pueri, Cic.; convivium, Cic. L. (3) *fastidious, dainty, nice*: est fastidii delicatissimi, Cic.; aures, Quint.
¶ Hence adv. (with compar.) **dēlĭcātē**, *luxuriously*: delicate ac molliter vivere, Cic.

dēlĭciae -ārum, f. pl. (sing. delicia -ae, f.: Pl.; delicium -i, n.: Phaedr., Mart.; from de/*lacio), *allurements, charms, delights, fancies*. LIT., abstr.: multarum deliciarum comes est extrema saltatio, Cic.; animus deliciarum egens, Hor.; ecce aliae deliciae equitum vix ferendae, *extravagant notions*, Cic.; esse in deliciis alicui, *to be one's favourite*, Cic., Lucr. TRANSF., concr.: *beloved object, darling, sweetheart*: amores ac deliciae tuae Roscius, Cic.; Pl., Cat., Verg.

dēlĭcĭŏlae -ārum, f. pl. (dim. of deliciae), *a darling*: Tullia, deliciolae nostrae, Cic.

dēlictum -i, n. (delinquo), *a fault, crime, delinquency*: quo delictum maius est, eo poena est tardior, Cic.

dēlicuus -a -um (delinquo), *wanting*: Pl.

¹dēlĭgo -lĭgĕre -lēgi -lectum (de/lego). (1) *to pick, pluck*: tenui primam ungue rosam, Ov. (2) *to choose, select*: magistratus, consulem Cic.; aliquem potissimum generum, Cic.; ad eas res conficiendas Orgetorix deligitur, Caes.; optimum quemque, Cic.; locum castris, Caes.

²dēlĭgo -are, *to fasten, bind up*: naviculam ad ripam, Caes.; aliquem ad palum, Cic.

dēlingo -ĕre, *to lick off, lick up*: salem, Pl.

dēlinquo -linquĕre -līqui -lictum, *to fail, be wanting*, esp. *to fail in duty, commit a crime*; intransit. or with n. pronoun as internal object: ne quid delinquam, Pl.; ut nihil adhuc a me delictum putem, Cic.; si quid deliquero, Cic.; (miles) in bello propter hostium metum deliquerat, Cic.; Liv., Tac.

dēlĭquesco -liquescĕre -licŭi, *to melt, dissolve*: ubi delicuit nondum prior (nix) altera venit, Ov. TRANSF., *to vanish, disappear*: nec alacritate futili gestiens deliquescat, Cic.

dēlĭquĭō -ōnis, f. *a failure, want*: Pl.

dēlĭquĭum -i, n. *a failure*: solis, *an eclipse*, Plin.

dēlĭquo and **dēlĭco** -are, *to clarify, strain*; hence *to clear up, explain*: Pl.

dēlīrāmentum -i, n. (deliro), *nonsense*: Pl.

dēlīrātĭo -ōnis, f. (deliro), *folly, silliness, dotage*: ista senilis stultitia, quae deliratio appellari solet, Cic.; Plin. L.

dēlīro -are (de/lira). LIT., *to draw the furrow awry in ploughing*; hence *'to go off the rails'*, *act crazily, rave*: delirat lingua (in old age), Lucr.; delirare et mente captum esse, Cic.; quidquid delirant reges plectuntur Achivi, *the people suffer for the mad acts of their rulers*, Hor.

dēlīrus -a -um (de/lira), *silly, crazy, doting*: senex, Cic.; mater, Hor.; dementit enim deliraque fatur, Lucr.

dēlĭtesco -lĭtescĕre -lĭtui (de/latesco), *to conceal oneself, lurk, lie hid*. LIT., hostes noctu in silvis delituerant, Caes.; in ulva, Verg.; in cubilibus, Cic. TRANSF., *to take refuge*: in alicuius auctoritate, Cic.; in frigida calumnia, Cic.; sub tribunicia umbra, Liv.

dēlĭtĭgo -are, *to scold furiously*: Hor.

Dēlos -i, f. (Δῆλος), *a small island in the Aegean Sea, one of the Cyclades, the supposed birth-place of Apollo and Diana*.
¶ Hence adj. **Dēlĭăcus** -a -um and **Dēlĭus** -a -um, *of Delos*, esp. with reference to Apollo: folia, *the laurel*, Hor.; tellus, Ov.; absol. as subst. **Dēlius** -i, m.= *Apollo*: Ov.; Tib.; **Dēlĭa** -ae, f.= *Diana*: Verg., Ov., Tib.

Delphi -ōrum, m. (Δελφοί), *a small town in Phocis, famous for its oracle of Apollo*.
¶ Hence adj. **Delphĭcus** -a -um, *of Delphi*, esp. with reference to Apollo.

delphīnus -i and **delphin** -īnis, m. (δελφίς) (1) *a dolphin*: Cic., Verg. (2) *a constellation so called*: Ov.

Deltŏton -i, n. (Δελτωτόν), *the constellation called the Triangle*: Cic. poet.

dēlūbrum -i, n. (de/luo), *a shrine*, as a place for expiation; in gen., *a temple*: noctu ex delubro audita vox, Liv.; gen. in plur. deorum templa ac delubra, Cic.; Lucr. Verg.

dēluctor -ari, dep. and **dēlucto** -are, *to wrestle*: Pl.

dēlūdĭfĭco -are, *to make game of*: Pl.

dēlūdo -lūdĕre -lūsi -lūsum, *to mock, cheat, delude*: corvum hiantem, Hor.; et quae sopitos deludunt somnia sensus, Verg.; amantem, Ov.; absol.: lentius agere atque deludere, Cic.

dēlumbis -e (de/lumbus), *nerveless, weak*: Pers.

dēlumbo -are (de/lumbus). LIT., *to lame the loins*: Plin. TRANSF., *to enervate, weaken*: sententias, Cic.

dēmădesco -mădescĕre -mădŭi, *to become wet through*: Ov.

dēmando -are, *to entrust, commit*: puero curae alicuius, Liv.; Suet.

Dēmărātus -i, m. (Δημάρατος), *a Corinthian exile, father of Tarquinius Priscus*.

dēmens -mentis, adj. (with compar. and superl.) (de/mens), *out of one's mind, insane, senseless*. LIT., of persons: summos viros desiperare, delirare, dementes esse dicebas, Cic.; tranquillo tempestatem adversam optar dementis est, Cic.; Verg., Hor. TRANSF., of things: dementissimum cor silium, Cic.; minae, Hor.; Verg.

¶ Adv. **dēmentĕr**, *senselessly, madly*: Cic.

1ēmentĭa -ae, f. (demens), *senselessness, insanity*: Cic., Caes., Verg., Hor.; in plur., *mad actions*: Cic. L.

4ēmentĭo -ire (demens), *to be mad, to rave*: Lucr.

1ēmĕrĕo -ēre and **dēmĕrĕor** -ēri, dep. *to earn thoroughly*. LIT., aliquid mercedis, Pl. TRANSF., *to deserve well of* a person, *to oblige*: demerendi beneficio tam potentem populum occasio, Liv.; servos, Ov.

1ēmergo -mergĕre -mersi -mersum, *to sink, to plunge into, dip under*.

LIT., esp. in water: C. Marius in palude demersus, Cic.; tredecim capere naves, decem demergere, Liv.; dapes avidam in alvum, *to swallow*, Ov.; plebs in fossas cloacasque exhauriendas demersa, Liv.

TRANSF., est enim animus caelestis ex altissimo domicilio depressus et quasi demersus in terram, Cic.; plebs aere alieno demersa, *over head and ears in debt*, Liv.

1ēmētĭor -metiri -mensus, dep. *to measure out*: cibum, Pl.; partic. **dēmensus** -a -um, in pass. sense: ut verba verbis quasi demensa et paria respondeant, Cic.; n. as subst. **dēmensum**, *an allowance*: Ter.

dēmĕto -mĕtĕre -messŭi -messum, *to mow, reap, cut down* or *off*: fructus, Cic.; frumentum, Liv.; agros, Cic.; ense caput, Ov.

dēmigrātĭo -ōnis, f. (demigro), *emigration*: Nep.

dēmigro -are, *to emigrate, depart*: loco, Pl.; ex his aedificiis, Caes.; ex agris in urbem, Liv.; in alia loca, Cic. TRANSF., de meo statu demigro, Cic.; esp. *to die*: Cic.

dēmĭnŭo -mĭnŭĕre -mĭnŭi -mĭnūtum, *to take away from, to diminish, make less, lessen*. LIT., militum vires inopia frumenti deminuerat, Caes.; aequora venti deminuunt, Lucr. TRANSF., in gen.: dignitatem, Cic.; aliquid de iure, de libertate, Cic.; esp. as legal t. t.: capite se deminuere, *to suffer a loss of civil rights*, Cic., Liv.

dēmĭnūtĭo -ōnis, f. (deminuo), *a lessening, diminution*.

LIT., accretio et deminutio luminis, Cic.; vectigalium, Cic.

TRANSF., (**1**) in gen.: libertatis, Cic.; sui, *loss of prestige*, Tac.; capitis, *loss of civil rights*, Caes. (**2**) as legal t. t., *right of alienation*: utique Fecenniae Hispalae datio deminutio esset, Liv.

dēmīror -ari, dep. *to wonder at, to wonder*: quod demiror, Cic.; with acc. and infin.: nihil te ad me postea scripsisse demiror, Cic.; colloquial, with indir. quest., *I wonder*: Pl., Ter.

dēmissĭo -ōnis, f. (demitto), *a sinking, lowering*: storiarum, Caes. TRANSF., *dejection*: animi, Cic.

dēmītĭgo -ari, *to make mild, soften*: nosmet ipsi quotidie demitigamur, Cic. L.

dēmitto -mittĕre -mīsi -missum, *to send down, to lower, let down, put down*.

LIT., (**1**) in gen.: se manibus, *to let oneself down by the hands*, Liv.; aliquem per tegulas, Cic.; equum in flumen, Cic.; imbrem caelo, Verg.; aures, Hor.; tunica demissa, *hanging loosely*, Hor.; vultus, oculos, *to let fall, lower*, Ov.; demissi capilli, *growing long*, Ov.

(**2**) with force, *to thrust down*: sublicas in terram, Caes.; ferrum in pectus, Tac. (**3**) as milit. t. t., *to lead down*: agmen in inferiorem campum, Liv.; demittere se, *to march down*, Caes. (**4**) as naut. t. t.: **a**, *to lower* gear: antemnas, Sall.; cornua, Ov.: **b**, *to bring* a vessel *downstream*: Liv.; or *to land*: Verg.

TRANSF., (**1**) *to sink, bury, plunge*: hoc in pectus tuum demitte, Sall.; se in causam, Cic.; Tac. (**2**) *to lower*, of spirits: se animo, Caes.; animum, Cic.; mentem, Verg.

¶ Hence partic. (with compar.) **dēmissus** -a -um. LIT., (**1**) *hanging down*: aures, Verg.; hence of dress and hair, *long, loose*. (**2**) *deep down, sunken, low-lying*: loca demissa ac palustria, Caes. TRANSF., (**1**) *feeble, weak*: demissā voce loqui, Verg. (**2**) *unassuming, modest*: sermo demissus atque humilis, Cic. (**3**) *down-cast, dispirited*: animus, Cic. (**4**) *poor, needy*: qui demissi in obscuro vitam habent, Sall. (**5**) of origin, *descended*: ab alto demissum genus Aeneae, Verg.

¶ Adv. (with compar. and superl.) **dēmissē**. LIT., *low, near the ground*: volare, Ov. TRANSF., *modestly, lowly, humbly, abjectly, meanly*: suppliciter demisseque respondere, Cic.; humiliter demisseque sentire, Cic.

dēmĭurgus or **dāmiurgus** -i, m. (δημιουργός), *the highest magistrate in certain Greek states*: Liv.

dēmo dēmĕre dempsi demptum (de/emo), *to take away, subtract*.

LIT., Publicola secures de fascibus demi iussit, Cic.; barbam, Cic.; de capite medimna DC, Cic.; clipea de columnis, Liv.; Ov., Hor.

TRANSF., sollicitudinem, Cic.; maerorem e pectore, Lucr.; partem solido de die, Hor.

Dēmocrĭtus -i, m. (Δημόκριτος), *a famous philosopher of Abdera, originator of the atomic theory* (c. 460–370 B.C.).

¶ Hence adj. **Dēmocrĭtĭcus** (-crĭtĭus -crĭtēus) -a -um, *Democritean*; n. pl. as subst. **Dēmocrĭtēa** -orum, *the doctrines of Democritus*: Cic.; also m. plur. subst. **Dēmocrĭtĭi** -orum, *the disciples of Democritus*: Cic.

dēmōlĭor -iri, dep. *to throw down, demolish*: domum, parietem, statuas, Cic. TRANSF., de me culpam hanc, Pl.; Bacchanalia, Liv.

dēmōlītĭo -ōnis, f. (demolior), *a throwing down, demolition*: statuarum, Cic.

dēmonstrātĭo -ōnis, f. (demonstro). LIT., *a pointing out* (by the hand, by gestures, etc.): Cic. TRANSF., *indication, explanation, description*: Cic. Esp. as rhet. t. t., *a branch of oratory concerned with praise and censure*: Cic., Quint.

dēmonstrātīvus -a -um (demonstro), *demonstrative*; as rhet. t. t.: demonstrativum genus, *a branch of oratory concerned with praise and censure*, Cic., Quint.

dēmonstrātor -ōris, m. (demonstro), *one who points out* or *indicates*: Simonides dicitur demonstrator uniuscuiusque sepeliendi fuisse, Cic.

dēmonstro -are, *to indicate, point out, show clearly*.

LIT., with the hand or by gesture: figuram digito, Cic.; itinera, Cic.; esp. as legal t. t.: demonstrare fines, *to show a purchaser the extent of property and hand it over to him*, Cic.

TRANSF., in gen., *to explain, describe, show*: demonstrare rem, Cic.; demonstravi haec Caecilio, Cic.; ad ea castra quae supra demonstravimus contendit, *that indicated above*, Caes.; with acc. and infin.: mihi Fabius demonstravit te id cogitare facere, Cic.; with indir. quest.: quanta praedae faciendae facultas daretur demonstraverunt, Caes.

dēmŏrĭor -mori -mortŭus, dep. *to die, die off* (used of one among a number): cum esset ex veterum numero quidam senator demortuus, Cic.; in demortui locum censor sufficitur, Liv. TRANSF., (1) of things: potationes demortuae, Pl. (2) with acc. of person, *to die for love of*: Pl.

dēmŏror -ari, dep.
   (1) intransit., *to delay, loiter*: ille nihil demoratus exsurgit, Tac.
   (2) transit., *to stop, hinder, delay, retard*: aliquem diutius, Cic.; iter, Caes.; agmen novissimum, Caes.; inutilis annos demoror, *drag on a useless existence*, Verg.; Teucros demoror armis, *restrain from battle*, Verg.

Dēmosthĕnēs -is; also genit. -i: Cic. (Δημοσθένης), *the celebrated Athenian orator* (384–322 B.C.).

dēmŏvĕo -mŏvēre -mōvi -mōtum, *to move away, remove*.
   LIT., demoveri et depelli de loco, Cic.; ex sua sede, Cic.; hostes gradu, Liv.; flumen solito alveo, Tac.
   TRANSF., aliquem de sententia, *make him change his opinion*, Cic.; also *to remove* a person from an office: aliquem praefecturā, Tac.

dēmūgītus -a -um (de/mugio), *filled with the noise of lowing*: paludes, Ov.

dēmulcĕo -mulcēre -mulsi, *to stroke down, caress by stroking*: caput tibi, Ter.; dorsum (of horses), Liv.

dēmum, adv. (perhaps a superl. formed from dē, as summus from sub), *at length, at last*.
   (1) of time, *at a moment and not before it*; esp. strengthening adverbs of time: nunc demum, *now at last*, Pl., Cic., Verg.; tum demum, Caes., Liv., Verg.; iam demum, Ov. TRANSF., post-Aug., to end an enumeration or sum it up, *finally, in short*: Tac.
   (2) to express a climax or emphasis, esp. with pron.: ea demum firma amicitia est, *that and that alone*, Sall.; id demum aut potius id solum, Cic.; hac demum terra, Verg.; hence, post-Aug., in gen., *exclusively*: Quint.

dēmurmŭro -are, *to murmur* or *mutter over*: ter novies carmen magico ore, Ov.

dēmūtātĭo -ōnis, f. (demuto), *change, alteration*, esp. for the worse: morum, *deterioration*, Cic.

dēmūto -are, *to change*. (1) transit., *to change, alter* a thing, esp. for the worse: Pl., Tac. (2) intransit.: **a**, *to change one's mind*: Pl.: **b**, in gen., *to become different*: Pl.

dēnārĭus -a -um (deni), *containing ten*. Esp. denarius; nummus or subst. **dēnārĭus** -i, m. (also n.: Pl.; genit. pl.: denarium, Cic.; denariorum, Cic. L.) *a Roman silver coin, originally equivalent to ten asses, but afterwards to eighteen; equivalent also to an Attic drachma*: Caes., Cic., Liv.

dēnarro -are, *to narrate, tell, relate*: matri denarrat ut, Hor.; Ter.

dēnāso -are (nasus), *to deprive of the nose*: Pl.

dēnăto -are, *to swim down*: Tusco alveo, Ho

dēnĕgo -are. (1) *to deny, say no*: Pl., Ta (2) more frequently, *to deny, refuse, reje a request*: id antea petenti denegavisse, Caes potest mihi denegari occupatio tua, Cic operam reipublicae, Liv.; with infin.: Ter Hor.

dēni -ae -a, distrib. num. adj. (decem), *ten b ten, ten at a time, by tens*: uxores habent de duodenique inter se communes, Caes. denos adducere, *each to bring ten*, Caes.; b denis navibus, *two sets of ten*, Verg.

dēnĭcālis -e (de/nex), *releasing from death* feriae, *a funeral ceremony* (at which th family of the dead was purified), Cic.

dēnĭque, adv. (dē/-ne/-que), *at last*.
   (1) in time; *at last, finally*: mori m denique coges, Verg.; esp. (cf. demum strengthening adverbs of time: nunc deniqu tum denique, Cic.
   (2) in enumerations: **a**, to add a fresh item *again, further*; so generally in Lucr.: **b**, t add a last item, often by way of climax pernegabo atque obdurabo, peiierabo de nique, Pl.: **c**, to summarize, by means of more general expression, *in short, in fine* tota denique Italia, Cic.; qui non civium non denique hominum numero essent, Liv

dēnōmĭno -are, *to name*: hinc (ab Lamic Lamias ferunt denominatos, Hor.; Quint.

dēnormo -are (de/norma), *to make crooked* o si angulus ille proximus accedat, qui nur denormat agellum, Hor.

dēnōto -are. (1) *to mark out for anothe designate precisely*: cives necandos denotavi Cic. (2) *to take note of*, for one's ow purposes: Cic., Tac.

dens dentis, m. *a tooth*.
   LIT., dentes genuini, *the grinders*, Cic. dentibus manditur atque extenuatur cibus Cic.; eburneus, Liv.; aprorum, Ov.
   TRANSF., (1) concr., of things resemblin a tooth: dens ancorae, Verg.; vomeri Verg.; dens uncus, *mattock*, Verg.; Saturn *the sickle*, Verg. (2) abstr., of what i sharp, biting, destructive: dentibus aev Ov.; leti, Lucr.; esp. of envy and calumny hoc maledico dente carpunt, Cic.; den invidus, *the tooth of envy*, Hor.; atro dent aliquem petere, Hor.

denso -are and **densĕo** -ēre (densus), *to mak thick, to thicken, condense, press togethe* LIT., male densatus agger, Liv.; ordine Liv.; catervas, Verg.; in weaving, *to mak thick* with the reed: Ov. TRANSF., mixt senum ac iuvenum densentur funera, a *crowded together*, Hor.; orationem, *to con dense*, Quint.

densus -a -um, adj. (with compar. an superl.), *thick, close, dense* (opp. rarus).
   LIT., in sing. or plur.: silva, Cic.; imbe densissimus, Verg.; aristae, apes, Verg. frutices, Ov.; with abl.: caput densum cae sarie, Ov.; acies densa armis virisque, Tac.
   TRANSF., (1) in time, *following closely upo one another, frequent*: ictus, Verg. (2) i degree, *intense, vehement*: densa frigori asperitas, Ov. (3) in style, of work or autho *condensed*: Quint.
   ¶ Hence adv. (with compar. and superl **densē**. (1) *densely*: Plin. (2) of time, *fre quently*: Cic.

dentālĭa -ĭum, n. pl. (dens), *the share-beam of a plough*: Verg., Pers.

dentātus -a -um (dens). (1) *provided with teeth, toothed.* LIT., si male dentata puella est, Ov.; serrula, Cic. TRANSF., of *biting* speech: Pl. (2) *polished by teeth*: charta, Cic.

dentifrangĭbŭlus (dens/frango), *tooth-breaking*; as subst., **dentifrangibulus** -i, m. of a man: Pl.; **dentifrangibula** -orum, n. pl. *the fist*: Pl.

dentĭlĕgus -i, m. (dens/lego), *one that recovers his teeth by picking them up*: Pl.

dentio -ire (dens), *to cut teeth*: Plin.; of the teeth, *to grow*: Pl.

dentiscalpĭum -i, n. (dens/scalpo), *a tooth-pick*: Mart.

dēnūbo -nūbĕre -nupsi -nuptum, *to be married off to, to marry* (of the woman), esp. *beneath her*: nec Caenis in ullos denupsit thalamos, Ov.; Iulia, quondam Neronis uxor, denupsit in domum Rubellii Blandi, Tac.; of a mock marriage: Tac.

dēnūdo -are, *to lay bare, uncover.* LIT., ne Verres denudetur a pectore, Cic., Suet. TRANSF., (1) of facts: suum consilium, Liv. (2) *to rob, plunder*: cives Romanos, ap. Cic. L.; concesso et tradito (ornatu) spoliare atque denudare, Cic.

dēnuntĭātĭo -ōnis, f. (denuntio), *an announcement, intimation, declaration, threat*: periculi, Cic.; belli, *declaration of war*, Cic.; a dis profecta significatio et quasi denuntiatio calamitatum, Cic.

dēnuntĭo -are, *to announce, give notice, declare, threaten*, esp. with real or assumed authority. In gen.: alicui inimicitias, Cic.; mortem, Cic., Liv.; illa arma, centuriones, cohortes non periculum nobis, sed praesidium denuntiant, Cic.; with indirect statement: Gorgias se ad omnia esse paratum denuntiavit, Cic.; with indirect command: Lupus mihi denuntiavit ut ad te scriberem, Cic. L.; with indirect question: ut denuntiet quid caveant, Cic. Esp. (1) milit. or polit.: bellum denuntiare, *to declare war*, Cic.; with subj., *to order*: ut arma capiant, Liv. (2) legal: a, alicui testimonium denuntiare, *to summon a person as witness*, Cic.: b, denuntiare alicui, *to give notice of an action*: de isto fundo Caecinae, Cic.: c, denuntiare in iudicium, *to give notice to a person to attend a trial.* (3) religious: quibus portentis magna populo Romano bella perniciosaeque caedes denuntiabantur, Cic.

dēnŭo, adv. (for de novo), *anew, again*; sometimes like iterum, *a second time*: Pl., Ter., Cic., Liv.

Dēōis -idis, f. (Δηωΐς), *daughter of Deo* (Δηώ, *Ceres*), i.e. *Proserpine*: Ov. Adj. **Dēōĭus** -a -um, *sacred to Ceres*: quercus, Ov.

dĕonĕro -are, *to unload, disburden.* TRANSF., ex illius invidia deonerare aliquid et in te traicere coepit, Cic.

dĕorsum or **dĕorsus**, adv. (for dēvorsum), *downwards* (opp. sursum), indicating motion: cuncta feruntur, Lucr.; phrase, sursum deorsum, *up and down, backwards and forwards*: naturis sursum deorsum, ultro citro commeantibus, Cic.

dĕoscŭlor -ari, dep. *to kiss warmly*: Pl.

dēpăciscor=depĕciscor; q.v.

dēpactus -a -um, partic. as from depango, *fastened down, firmly fixed*, fig.: vitae depactus terminus alte, Lucr.

dēparcus -a -um, *excessively niggardly*: Suet.

dēpasco -pascĕre -pāvi -pastum and **dēpascor** -pasci, dep. *to feed off.* LIT., of the herd or the shepherd: saltus, Ov.; luxuriem segetum, Verg.; in pass.: Hyblaeis apibus florem depasta salicta saepes, Verg. TRANSF., (1) in gen., *to eat up, consume*: depasta altaria (i.e. *the food on the altars*), Verg. (2) fig.: depascere luxuriem orationis stilo, *to prune down extravagance of language*, Cic.; artus depascitur arida febris, Verg.

dēpĕciscor -pĕcisci -pectus, dep. (paciscor), *to make a bargain for* or *about*: ipse tria praedia sibi, Cic.; cum aliquo ut, Cic. TRANSF., *to settle for, accept* some condition: morte, Ter., Cic. L.

dēpecto -pectĕre -pexum, *to comb down*: crines buxo, Ov.; vellera foliis tenuia, *to comb off*, Verg.; in comedy, *to beat soundly*: Ter.

dēpĕcŭlātor -ōris, m. (depeculor), *one who robs* or *embezzles*: aerarii, Cic.

dēpĕcŭlor -ari, dep. (de/peculium), *to rob, plunder*: fana, Cic.; aliquem omni argento spoliare atque depeculare, Cic.; fig.: qui laudem honoremque familiae vestrae depeculatus est, Cic.

dēpello -pellĕre -pŭli -pulsum. (1) transit., *to drive down, away, out, expel, remove.* LIT., in gen.: simulacra deorum depulsa, Cic.; aliquem ex urbe, Cic.; (Mantuam) teneros fetus, Verg.; nubila caelo, Tib.; esp.: a, as milit. t. t., *to dislodge*: hostem loco, Caes.: b, *to wean*: ab ubere matris, Verg.: c, as naut. t. t., *to drive out of one's course*: aliquem obvii aquilones depellunt, Tac. TRANSF., *to drive away, avert*: a, of things: famem sitimque, Cic.; suspicionem a se, Cic.; pestem, Verg.: b, of persons, *to dissuade*: aliquem de causa suscepta, Cic.; de spe conatuque depulsus, Cic.; ab superioribus consiliis, Caes.; spe, Liv.; with quin: Pl., Tac. (2) intransit., *to deviate*: Lucr.

dēpendĕo -ēre. LIT., *to hang down, hang from*: ex umeris dependet amictus, Verg.; laqueo dependentem invenere, Liv. TRANSF., (1) *to depend upon*: fides dependet a die, Ov. (2) *to be derived from*: huius et augurium dependet origine verbi, Ov.

dēpendo -pendĕre -pendi -pensum, *to weigh out and pay over.* LIT., *to pay*: dependendum tibi est quod mihi pro illo spopondisti, Cic. L. TRANSF., poenas reipublicae, Cic., Luc.

dēperdo -perdĕre -perdĭdi -perditum. (1) *to lose*: non solum bona sed etiam honestatem, Cic.; paucos ex suis, Caes.; Pl., Ov. (2) *to waste, destroy*; only in perf. partic. **deperditus** -a -um: fletu, Cat.; also *desperately in love*: Prop., Suet.

dēpĕrĕo -perire -pĕrii -pĕrĭtūrus, *to perish* or *be ruined utterly*: tempestate deperierant naves, Caes.; si servus deperisset, Cic. TRANSF., *to be desperately in love*: amore mulierculae, Liv.; with acc. of the person loved: Pl., Ter., Cat.

---

dēpĭlo -are, *to strip of hair* or *feathers*: Mart.

dēpingo -pingĕre -pinxi -pictum, *to paint, represent in painting, depict.*
> LIT., pugnam Marathoniam, Nep.
> TRANSF., (**1**) *to embroider* clothes: paenulas, Suet. (**2**) *to portray in words*: formam verbis, Pl.; vitam huius, Cic.; nimium depicta, *too elaborately delineated*, Cic. (**3**) *to picture to oneself*: cogitatione, Cic.

dēplango -plangĕre -planxi, *to bewail, lament*: Ov.

dēplexus -a -um (plector), *clasping*: Lucr.

dēplōrābundus -a -um (deploro), *weeping bitterly*: Pl.

dēplōro -are. Intransit., *to weep bitterly, to lament*: de suis incommodis, Cic. Transit. (**1**) *to lament, bewail*: alicuius interitum, Cic.; Liv., Ov. (**2**) *to regard as lost, give up*: agros, Liv.; spem Capuae retinendae deploratam, Liv.

dēplŭit -plŭere, *rains down*: multus lapis, Tib.

dēpōno -pōnĕre -pŏsŭi (-pŏsīvi: Pl., Cat.) -pŏsĭtum, *to lay down, put down.*
> (**1**) in gen.: mentum in gremio, Cic.; onus, Cic.; arma in contubernio, Caes.; caput terrā, Ov.; comas, *to cut the hair*, Mart.; of childbirth: quam mater deposivit, Cat.; esp. *to lay as a wager* or *as a prize*: vitulam, Verg.
> (**2**) for safe-keeping, *to put down, to deposit*; hence *to commit, entrust.* LIT., pecuniam in delubro, Cic.; obsides apud eos, Caes.; pecuniam apud aliquem, Cic. TRANSF., ius populi Romani in vestra fide ac religione depono, Cic.
> (**3**) *to lay aside, have done with.* LIT., arma, Caes., Liv. TRANSF., of abstract things: simultates, Cic.; adeundae Syriae consilium, Cic.; memoriam alicuius rei, *or* aliquid ex memoria, *to forget*, Cic.; imperium, Cic.; bellum, Ov., Liv., Tac.
> ¶ Hence partic. **dēpŏsĭtus** -a -um. (**1**) *laid out*; hence *dying* or *despaired of* or *dead*: ut depositi proferret fata parentis, Verg.; prope depositus, Ov.; fig.: prope depositam reipublicae partem, Cic. (**2**) *entrusted*; n. as subst. **dēpŏsĭtum** -i, *a deposit*: Cic., Juv.

dēpŏpŭlātĭo -ōnis, f. (depopulor), *a laying waste, ravaging*: aedium sacrarum publicorumque operum, Cic.; Liv.

dēpŏpŭlātor -ōris, m. (depopulor), *one who ravages* or *lays waste*: fori, Cic.

dēpŏpŭlor -ari, dep.; also **dēpŏpŭlo** -are, esp. in partic. **dēpŏpŭlātus** (populus), *to depopulate*, hence *to lay waste, ravage*: Ambiorigis fines, Caes.; agros, Cic.; depopulatis agris, Caes.; late depopulato agro, Liv. TRANSF., *to waste, destroy*: omne mortalium genus vis pestilentiae depopulabatur, Tac.

dēporto -are.
> (**1**) *to carry down*: argentum ad mare ex oppido, Cic.
> (**2**) *to carry off, take away.* In gen.: frumentum in castra, Caes.; Tertiam secum, Cic.; Pleminium legatum vinctum Romam, Liv. Esp.: **a**, *to bring home*: victorem exercitum, Cic.; si nihil aliud de hac provincia nisi illius benevolentiam deportassem, Cic.; so of abstract acquisitions: triumphum, Cic.; lauream, Tac.: **b**, *to banish for life* (with loss of civil rights and property): in insulam Amorgum deportari, Tac.; Italiā, Tac.

dēposco -poscĕre -pŏposci, *to demand, ask for*, usually for a particular purpose. In gen.: certas sibi deposcit naves, Caes.; unum ad id bellum imperatorem deposci atque expeti, Cic.; sibi id muneris, Caes.; sibi partes istas, Cic. Esp. *to demand for punishment*: aliquem ad mortem, Caes.; aliquem morti, Tac.; ducem in poenam, Liv.

dēprāvātĭo -ōnis, f. (depravo), *a perverting, distorting.* LIT., oris, Cic. TRANSF., animi depravity, Cic.

dēprāvo -are (de/pravus), *to make crooked, to pervert, distort, disfigure.* LIT., Cic. TRANSF., (**1**) verbally, *to distort, misrepresent*: depravata imitatio, caricature, Cic.; Ter. (**2**) morally, *to spoil, corrupt, deprave*: puer indulgentiā nostrā depravatus, Cic.; mores dulcedine depravati, Cic.; plebem consiliis, Liv.; Caes.
> ¶ Hence, from partic. depravatus, adv. **dēprāvātē**, *perversely*: iudicare, Cic.

dēprĕcābundus -a -um (deprecor), *earnestly entreating*: Tac.

dēprĕcātĭo -ōnis, f. (deprecor). (**1**) *an attempt to avert by entreaty, deprecating*: **a**, with genit. of what is feared: periculi, Cic.: **b**, with genit. or dat. of the offence for which punishment is feared, *an entreaty for forgiveness*: eius facti, Cic.; meis perfidiis, Pl.
> (**2**) *an entreaty against a person*, for his punishment: deorum (against perjurers), Cic.

dēprĕcātor -ōris, m. (deprecor). (**1**) *one that begs off, an intercessor*: huius periculi, Cic. (**2**) *one that pleads for*: sui, Cic.; causae suae, Tac.

dēprĕcor -ari, dep.
> (**1**) *to try to avert by entreaty, to deprecate*: **a**, in gen.: mortem, Caes.; ab sese calamitatem, Cic.; with ne and the subj.: primum deprecor ne putetis, Cic.; Caes., Liv.; non deprecor, with quominus or quin, Liv.: **b**, with ref. to possible punishment (cf. deprecatio), *to allege in excuse*: errasse regem, Sall.
> (**2**) *to entreat against a person, to curse* him: deprecor illi adsidue, Cat.
> (**3**) *to entreat for, to beg for*, esp. in face of anger or impatience: multorum vitam ab aliquo, Cic.; civem a civibus, Cic.; absol. *to intercede*: pro aliquo, Cic.

dēprĕhendo and **dēprendo** -endĕre -endi -ensum, *to seize upon, catch hold of.*
> LIT., in gen.: tabellarios deprehendere litterasque intercipere, Caes.; naves, Caes.; of storms: deprensis nautis, *caught in a storm*, Verg. Esp., *to surprise, catch, detect*, in a crime or fault: deprehendi in manifesto scelere, Cic.; aliquem in adulterio, Pl., Hor., Quint.; also *to discover* things, esp. evidence of crime: venenum, Cic., Liv.
> TRANSF., *to detect, observe, mark*: res magnas saepe in minimis rebus, Cic.; in Livio Patavinitatem, Quint.

dēprĕhensĭo -ōnis, f. (deprehendo), *detection*: veneni, Cic.

dēprĭmo -prĭmĕre -pressi -pressum (de/premo), *to press down, sink down.*
> LIT., in gen.: altero ad frontem sublato, altero ad mentum depresso supercilio, Cic.; depresso aratro (sc. in terram), Verg. Esp.

(1) *to plant deep in the ground, dig deep*: saxum in mirandam altitudinem depressus, Cic. **(2)** of ships, *to sink*: naves, Caes.; classem, Cic.

TRANSF., *to press down, depress*: fortunam meam, Cic.; spes illius civitatis, Cic.; multorum improbitate depressa veritas, Cic.; Liv.

¶ Hence partic. as adj. (with compar. and superl.) **dēpressus** -a -um, *low-lying, sunk down*: domus, Cic.; convallis, Verg.

dēproelĭans -antis, partic. as from deproelior, *struggling violently*: ventos aequore fervido deproeliantes, Hor.

dēprōmo -prōmĕre -prompsi -promptum, *to take down, produce, fetch out*: pecuniam ex aerario, Cic.; Caecubum cellis, Hor.; Verg., Ov. TRANSF., orationem ex iure civili, Cic.; verba domo patroni, Cic.

dēprŏpĕro, *to hasten*, intransit.: Pl.; transit., *to hasten over, produce'in haste*: coronas, Hor.

dēpŭdet -pŭdĕre -pŭdŭit, *ceases to be ashamed, loses all sense of shame*: Ov., Sen.

dēpūgis -is, adj. (de/puga), *without buttocks*, or *with thin buttocks*: Hor.

dēpugno -are, *to fight hard, fight it out*: ut acie instructā depugnarent, Caes.; cum Hectore, Cic.; Pl., Lucr., Liv. TRANSF., cum fame, Pl.; voluptas depugnat cum honestate, Cic.

dēpulsĭo -ōnis, f. (depello). **(1)** *a driving away*: mali, Cic.; doloris, Cic. **(2)** in rhetoric, *defence*: Cic.

dēpulso -are (freq. of depello), *to push away*: Pl.

dēpulsor -ōris, m. (depello), *one who drives away, an averter*: dominatūs, Cic.

dēpungo -ĕre, *to mark down*: Pers.

dēpurgo -are, *to clean out*: Pl.

dēpŭto -are. **(1)** *to prune, cut off*: umbras, branches, Ov. **(2)** *to count, estimate*: operam parvi preti, Ter.; omne id esse in lucro, Ter.

dēpўgis=depugis; q.v.

dēque, *see* susque deque.

Dercĕtis -is, f. and **Dercĕtō** -ūs, f. (Δερκετώ), *a Syrian goddess*.

dērēlictĭo -ōnis, f. (derelinquo), *a deserting, neglecting*: communis utilitatis, Cic.

dērēlinquo -linquĕre -līqui -lictum, *to forsake, desert, abandon*: totas arationes derelinquere, Cic.; naves ab aestu derelictae, Caes.; derelictus ab amicis, Cic.

dērĕpentĕ, adv. *suddenly*: Tac.

dērēpo -rēpĕre -repsi, *to creep, crawl down*: Phaedr.

dērīdĕo -rīdēre -rīsi -rīsum, *to laugh at, mock, deride*: aliquem, Pl., Cic., Hor.; aliquid, Hor., Juv.; also absol.

dērīdĭcŭlus -a -um (ridiculus), *very ridiculous, very laughable*: Pl., Liv.; n. as subst. **dērīdĭcŭlum** -i, *ridicule, ridiculousness*: esse deridiculo, *to be an object of ridicule*, Tac.; deridiculi causa, *for sport*, Pl.; deridiculo corporis, *by the absurdity*, Tac.

dērīgo -rigĕre -rexi -rectum (rego), *to set straight, to direct.* LIT., **(1)** of directing movement: ad castra Corneliana vela, Caes.; cursum, eo, Cic.; iter ad Mutinam, Cic.; huc gressum, Verg.; esp. of weapons, *to aim, direct*: hastam in aliquem, Ov.; so of the sight: aciem ad aliquem, Cat. **(2)** of placing (also in form dirigo), *to order, dispose*: in

quincuncem ordines (arborem), Cic.; as milit. t. t., *to draw up*: aciem, Caes.; naves in pugnam, Liv.

TRANSF., *to direct, aim, guide* abstr. things: suas cogitationes ad aliquid, Cic.; orationem, Cic.; vatis opus, Ov.; vitam ad certam rationis normam, Cic.; utilitate officium magis quam humanitate, Cic.

dērĭgŭi, perf. as from derigesco, *grew quite stiff, rigid*: deriguere oculi, Verg.; formidine sanguis, Verg.; comae, Ov.

dērĭpĭo -rĭpĕre -rĭpŭi -reptum (de/rapio), *to tear down, snatch away*: aliquid de manu, Cic.; aliquem de provincia, Cic.; ensem vaginā, Verg. TRANSF., quantum de mea auctoritate deripuisset, Cic.

dērīsor -ōris, m. (derideo), *one who derides, a mocker*: Pl., Hor., Quint.

dērīsus -ūs, m. (derideo), *mockery, derision*: Phaedr., Tac.

dērīvātĭo -ōnis, f. (derivo), *a turning away* or *diversion of water*: aquae Albanae, Liv.; fluminum, Cic.

dērīvo -are, *to turn away into another channel, to divert.* LIT., of water: aquam ex flumine, Caes.; Pl. TRANSF., in gen.: in me iram senis, Ter.; crimen, Cic.; responsionem alio, Cic.; culpam in aliquem, Cic.; hoc fonte derivata clades, Hor.

dērŏgo -are.

LIT., *to propose to repeal part of a law; to restrict, modify a law*: huic legi nec *obrogari* fas est neque *derogari* ex hac aliquid licet neque tota *abrogari* potest, Cic.

TRANSF., *to diminish, detract from*: de honestate quiddam, Cic.; fidem alicui, Cic.; certam derogat vetustas fidem, Liv.

dērōsus -a -um, partic. as from derodo, *gnawed away*: clipeos esse a muribus, Cic.

dēruncĭno -are (runcina), *to plane off*; hence *to cheat, fleece*: Pl.

dērŭo -rŭĕre -rŭi -rŭtum, *to cast down, make to fall*: vim aquarum, Sen.; fig.: cumulum de laudibus Dolabellae, Cic.

dēruptus -a -um, partic. (with compar.) as from derumpo, *broken off*; hence of places (cf. abruptus), *precipitous, steep*: ripa, Liv.; collis, Tac.

¶ N. pl. as subst. **dērupta** -orum, *precipices*: Liv., Tac.

dēsaevĭo -ire -ii -ītum, *to rage violently*: pelago desaevit hiems, Verg.; toto Aeneas desaevit in aequore, Verg.; Hor.

dēsalto -are, *to dance the part of*: desaltato cantico, Suet.

dēscendo -scendĕre -scendi -scensum (de/scando), *to climb down, come down, descend* (opp. ascendo).

LIT., **(1)** of persons; in gen.: ex equo, Cic.; equo, Sall.; de rostris, Cic.; monte, Verg.; caelo ab alto, Verg.; ab Alpibus, Liv.; in campos, Liv.; ad umbras, Verg.; esp.: **a**, from the residential quarters of Rome for politics, business, etc: ad forum, Cic., Liv.; hodie non descendit Antonius, Cic.: **b**, milit. t. t., *to march down* from higher ground: ex superioribus locis in planitiem, Caes.; in aequum, Liv. **(2)** of things, *to sink, to pierce, to penetrate*: ferrum in corpus descendit, Liv.; of mountains, *to slope down*: Caelius ex alto quā mons descendit in aequum, Ov.; of the voice, *to sink*: Cic.

TRANSF., (1) of persons to lower oneself, to stoop to, give way to: senes ad ludum adulescentium descendant, Cic.; ad vim atque ad arma, Caes.; in preces omnes, Verg. (2) of things: a, to sink in, penetrate: quod verbum in pectus Iugurthae altius quam quis ratus erat descendit, Sall.; in aures, Hor.: b, to come down, descend in time: usus in nostram aetatem, Quint.

dēscensĭo -ōnis, f. (descendo), a going down, descent: Tiberina, voyage down the Tiber, Cic.

dēscensus -ūs, m. (descendo). (1) a going down, descent: qua illi descensus erat, Sall. (2) a way down: facilis descensus Averno, Verg.

dēscisco -sciscĕre -scīvi or -scii -scītum, to break away from.

LIT., to revolt from, desert to: multae civitates ab Afranio desciscunt, Caes.; a populo Romano, Liv.; a senatu, Cic.; ab Latinis ad Romanos, Liv.

TRANSF., to withdraw, diverge, fall away from: a nobis, Lucr.; a pristina causa, Cic.; a veritate, Cic.; a se, to be untrue to oneself, Cic.

dēscrībo -scrībĕre -scripsi -scriptum.

(1) to transcribe, copy: quintum 'de Finibus' librum, Cic.; carmina, Verg., Hor.

(2) to describe, delineate, represent. LIT., by drawing: geometricas formas in arena, Cic. TRANSF., to represent in words, to describe: hominum sermones moresque, Cic.; regionem aut pugnam, Cic.; flumen Rhenum, Hor.; of persons, to portray: coniugem sine contumelia, Cic.

dēscriptio -ōnis, f. (describo).

(1) a copy: descriptio imagoque tabularum, Cic.

(2) a representation. LIT., by drawing: aedificandi, plans, Cic.; numeri aut descriptiones, geometric figures, Cic. TRANSF., a representation in words, a description: regionum, Quint.

dēsĕco -sĕcare -sĕcŭi -sectum, to hew off, cut off: partes ex toto, Cic.; aures, Caes.; segetem, Liv.

dēsĕro -sĕrĕre -sĕrŭi -sertum (de/sero), to sever one's connexion with, to desert, forsake, abandon, leave.

LIT., (1) as milit. t. t.: exercitum, Caes., Cic.; castra, Liv. (2) in gen., of places: agros latos ac fertiles deserere, Cic.; insulas desertas, Cic.; inamabile regnum, Ov. (3) in gen., of persons: cum amici partim deseruerint me, partim etiam prodiderint, Cic.; pass., sometimes with abl. alone: deseror coniuge, Ov.; desertus suis, Tac.

TRANSF., with abstr. subject or object, to forsake, neglect, disregard: deserere officium, Cic.; curam belli, Liv.; nec fratris preces nec Sextii promissa nec spem mulieris, Cic.; multo tardius fama deseret Curium Fabricium, Cic.; a mente deseri, to lose one's head, Cic. Esp. (1) of religious rites, to neglect: publica sacra et Romanos deos in pace, Liv. (2) as legal t. t.: vadimonium, to fail to appear, Cic.

¶ Hence partic. (with compar. and superl.) **dēsertus** -a -um, forsaken, abandoned, deserted: urbes, Cic.; loca, Caes.; deserta siti regio, Sall.; Hor., Liv. TRANSF.,

vita, Cic. N. pl. as subst. **dēserta** -ōrum, deserts, wildernesses: Verg.

dēsertor -ōris, m. (desero), one who forsakes, abandons: amicorum, Cic.; desertor communis utilitatis, Cic.; as milit. t. t., a deserter: Caes., Liv., Tac.

dēservĭo -ire, to serve zealously, to be a slave to: cuivis, Cic.; corpori, Cic.; divinis rebus, Cic.

dĕsĕs -sĭdis, m.; nom. sing. not found (desideo), idle, lazy, inactive: sedemus desides domi, Liv.; nec rem Romanam tam desidem umquam fuisse atque imbellem, Liv.

dēsicco -are, to dry thoroughly: Pl.

dēsĭdĕo -sīdĕre -sēdi -sessum, to sit idle, to be slothful: Pl., Ter., Suet.

dēsīdĕrābĭlis -e, adj. (with compar.) (desidero), desirable: nihil enim desiderabile concupiscunt, Cic.; Liv., Tac., Suet.

dēsīdĕrātĭo -ōnis, f. (desidero), a desire, longing for: voluptatum, Cic.

dēsīdĕrĭum -i, n. (desidero).

LIT., desire or longing, grief for the absence or loss of a person or thing: miserum me desiderium urbis tenet, Cic. L.; Athenarum, Ter.; esse in desiderio rerum sibi carissimarum, Cic.; desiderium nostri, Lucr.; tam cari capitis, Hor.; meton., as term of endearment: Cat.; desiderium meum, Cic. L.

TRANSF., (1) natural desire: cibi atque potionis, Liv. (2) a request: desideria militum, Tac.

dēsīdĕro -are (sidus), to long for some person or thing that is absent or lost, to wish for: aliquem, Pl., Ter., Cic.; aliquid, Cic., Caes., Hor., Tac.; res non modo tempus sed etiam animum vacuum desiderat, Cic.; with acc. and infin.: quo ullam rem ad se importari desiderent, Caes.

Esp. (1) in criticizing, to miss, find a lack of: ex me audis quid in oratione tua desiderem, Cic.; in Catone eloquentiam, Cic. (2) milit. t. t., to lose: in eo proelio CC milites desideravit, Caes.; ut nulla navis desideraretur, Caes.

dēsĭdĭa -ae, f. (desideo), a sitting still, idleness, inactivity, apathy: ne languori se desidiaeque dedat, Cic., Pl., Lucr., Verg.

dēsĭdĭōsus -a -um, adj. (with superl.) (desidia), slothful, idle, lazy. LIT., qui nolet fieri desidiosus, amet, Ov. TRANSF., involving or causing idleness: delectatio, Cic.; inertissimum et desidiosissimum otium, Cic.; puer (sc. Cupido), Ov.

¶ Hence adv. **dēsĭdĭōsē**, slothfully, idly: Lucr.

dēsīdo -sīdĕre -sēdi, to sink down, subside, settle: terrae, Cic., Liv. TRANSF., to deteriorate: mores, Liv.

dēsignātĭo -ōnis, f. (designo). (1) a marking out, designation, mention: personarum et temporum, Cic. (2) appointment to an office: annua designatio, nomination of consuls, Tac.

dēsignātor -ōris, m. (designo)=dissignator: q.v.

dēsigno -are, to mark out, trace out, plan. LIT., urbem aratro, Verg.; fines templo Iovis, Liv.

TRANSF., (1) in gen., to point out, indicate, signify: aliquem digito, Ov.; notare et designare aliquem oculis ad caedem, Cic.;

hac oratione Dumnorigem designari, Caes.;
turpitudinem, Cic. (2) *to portray, delineate*:
Maeonis elusam imagine tauri Europam, Ov.
(3) as polit. t. t., *to nominate to an office,
elect*: ut ii decemviratum habeant, quos
plebs designaverit, Cic.; esp. partic. **dēsig-
natus**, *elected but not yet in office, designate*:
consul designatus, Cic.; tribunus plebis,
Cic.; fig.: civis (of a child not born), Cic.

dēsĭlĭo -sĭlire -sĭlii -sultum (de/salio), *to leap
down*: de navibus, Caes.; ab equo, Verg.;
curru, Verg.; ad pedes, *dismount*, Caes.,
Liv.; fig.: in artum, Hor.; also of things: ex
alto desiliens aqua, Ov.; Hor., Prop.

dēsĭno -sĭnĕre -sĭi -sĭtum, *to leave off, cease,
give over, desist.*
(1) transit., artem, Cic. L.; versus, Verg.;
dominam, Ov.; esp. with infin.: amare, Pl.;
illud iam mirari, Cic.; pass.: veteres orationes a plerisque legi sunt desitae, Cic.
(2) intransit., *to cease, stop, end*: desierant
imbres, Ov.; bellum, Sall.; with in and acc.,
to end in: cauda desinit in piscem, Ov.;
desinit in lacrimas, Ov.; rhetoric, of the close
of a period: quae similiter desinunt aut
quae cadunt similiter, Cic.; with abl.:
desine quaeso communibus locis, Cic.; with
genit.: tandem mollium querelarum, Hor.

dēsĭpĭentĭa -ae, f. (desipiens), *foolishness*:
Lucr.

dēsĭpĭo -sĭpĕre (de/sapio), *to be foolish, silly,
to act foolishly*: summos viros desipere, Cic.;
dulce est desipere in loco, Hor.

dēsisto -sistĕre -stĭti -stĭtum, *to stand away.*
(1) from a person, *to withdraw*: quid illa
abs te irata destitit? Pl. (2) from an undertaking, attitude, etc., *to desist, leave off,
cease*: with de or ab or plain abl.: de illa
mente, Cic.; a defensione, Caes.; conatu,
Caes.; with dat.: Verg.; with infin.: destiti
stomachari, Cic.; Caes., Hor.

dēsōlo -are (solus), *to leave solitary, to forsake*:
ingentes agros, Verg.; frequently in perf.
partic. **dēsōlātus** -a -um, *forsaken, desolate*:
desolatae terrae, Ov.; also of persons:
desolatio servilibus ministeriis, Tac.

dēspecto -are (freq. of despicio), *to regard
from above, look down upon.* LIT., terras,
Verg. TRANSF., (1) of position, *to overlook*:
quos despectant moenia Abellae, Verg.
(2) *to despise*: liberos ut multum infra, Tac.

dēspectus -a -um, partic. from despicio; q.v.

dēspectus -ūs, m. (despicio). (1) *a looking
down, downward view*: erat ex oppido Alesia
despectus in campum, Caes. (2) *an object
of contempt*: Auct. Her.

dēspērantĕr, adv. from despero; q.v.

dēspērātĭo -ōnis, f. (despero), *hopelessness,
despair*: vitae, Cic.; recuperandi, Cic. L.;
Caes., Liv.

dēspēro -are, *to be without hope, to despair.*
(1) intransit., de pugna, Caes.; de republica, Cic. L.; sibi, Cic.; suis fortunis, Caes.
(2) transit., *to despair of, give up*: honores,
Cic.; rempublicam, Cic.; in pass.: nil
desperandum, Hor.; Cic.; with acc. and
infin.: non despero fore aliquem, Cic.; Hor.,
Ov.
¶ Hence, from pres. partic., adv. **dēspērantĕr**, *despairingly, hopelessly*: loqui, Cic.
¶ Perf. partic. (with compar. and superl.)
dēspērātus -a -um. (1) in pass. sense,

despaired of: aegrota ac paene desperata
respublica, Cic. (2) in middle sense,
desperate: desperatis hominibus, Caes.

dēspĭcātĭo -ōnis, f. (despicor), *contempt*;
in plur.: odia, invidia, despicationes adver-
santur voluptatibus, Cic.

dēspĭcātus -ūs, m. (despicor), *contempt*: si
quis despicatui ducitur, Cic.

dēspĭcĭentĭa -ae, f. (despicio), *looking down
upon, contempt*: rerum humanarum, Cic.

dēspĭcĭo -spĭcĕre -spexi -spectum (specio).
(1) *to look down, regard from above.* LIT.,
a, intransit.: de vertice montis in valles, Ov.;
a summo caelo in aequora, Ov.: b, transit.:
Iuppiter aethere summo despiciens mare,
Verg.; varias gentes et urbes despicere et
oculis conlustrare, Cic. TRANSF., *to look
down upon, despise*: despicere et contemnere
aliquem, Cic.; divitias, Cic.; Caes., Verg.
(2) *to look away*: Cic.
¶ Hence pres. partic. act. **dēspĭcĭens**,
contemptuous: sui, Cic.
¶ Perf. partic. pass. **dēspectus** -a -um,
despised, contemptible: Tac.

despĭcor -ari (specio), dep. *to look down upon,
despise*: Pl. Perf. partic. in pass. sense
despĭcātus -a -um, *despised, contemptible*:
homo despicatissimus, Cic.

dēspōlĭo -are, *to plunder, despoil*: aliquem, Pl.,
Ter., Cic. L.; templum Dianae, Cic.; fig.:
despoliari triumpho, Liv.

dēspondĕo -spondĕre -spondi -sponsum, *to
pledge, to promise.*
LIT., Syriam homini, Cic. L.; consulatum,
Liv.; esp. *to promise in marriage, betroth*:
filiam alicui, Pl.; Cic., Ov.
TRANSF., (1) *to pledge, devote*: spes reipublicae despondetur anno consulatus tui, Cic. L.
(2) with animum or animos, *to give up*;
hence *to lose heart, despair*: Pl., Liv.

dēspūmo -are (spuma). (1) *to skim off*: foliis
undam aheni, Verg. TRANSF., *to digest*:
Pers. (2) *to drop foam*: Luc.

dēspŭo -spŭĕre, *to spit down, spit on the
ground*; esp. as a religious observance for
averting evil: sacellum ubi despui religio est,
Liv. TRANSF., transit., *to reject*: preces
nostras, Cat.; Pl., Sen.

dēsquāmo -are (squama), *to take off the
scales, to scale*: pisces, Pl.

dēsterto -stertĕre -stertŭi, *to finish snoring*;
poet. *to finish dreaming*: Pers.

dēstillo -are, *to drip down, distil*: lentum
destillat ab inguine virus, Verg.; destillant
tempora nardo, *drip with*, Tib.

dēstĭmŭlo -are, *to worry away, waste away*:
bona, Pl.

dēstĭnātĭo -ōnis, f. (destino), *a fixing, determining, appointment*: partium quibus ces-
surus esset, Liv.; consulum, Tac.

dēstĭno -are (connected with στανόω and sto),
to make fast, fix down.
LIT., antemnas ad malos, Caes.
TRANSF., *to fix, determine, settle, appoint*;
in gen.: tempus locumque ad certamen,
Liv.; aliquem ad mortem, Liv.; debiti
destinatique morti, Liv.; with infin., *to resolve
to do*: quae agere destinaverat, Caes.; Liv.,
Ov. Esp. (1) *to appoint* a person to an
office: aliquem consulem, Liv., Tac.;
similarly *to betroth* as wife: Lepida destinata
quondam uxor L. Caesari, Tac. (2) *to aim

at with a missile: locum oris, Liv. (3) *to fix upon, intend to buy*: Pl., Cic. L.

¶ Hence partic. **dēstĭnātus** -a -um, *fixed, determined*: Cic.; destinatum est, with dat. and infin., *one has determined to*, Liv. N. as subst., sing. or pl., *an objective or intention*: Liv., Tac.; in abl. **destĭnātō** or **ex destĭnātō**, *intentionally*: Suet.

dēstĭtŭo -stĭtŭĕre -stĭtŭi -stĭtūtum (de/statuo). LIT., *to set down, place*, esp. *apart, alone*: aliquem ante tribunal regis, Liv.; in convivio, Cic.; nudos in litore pisces, Verg.

TRANSF., *to leave in the lurch, forsake, desert*: aliquem in ipso discrimine periculi, Liv.; nudus paene est destitutus, Cic.; with abl. of separation: deos mercede pactā, *to cheat*, Hor.; fig., with abstr. subject or object: destituere inceptam fugam, Ov.; destitutus ab unica spe, Liv.

dēstĭtūtus -a -um, partic. of destituo.

dēstĭtūtĭo -ōnis, f. (destituo), *a forsaking, abandoning*: Cic.

dēstringo -stringĕre -strinxi -strictum. (1) *to strip.* LIT., Quint.; esp. *to draw* or *bare the sword*: gladium, Caes., Cic., Liv.; ensem, Hor. TRANSF., *to satirize, censure*: aliquem mordaci carmine, Ov.
(2) *to touch lightly, to graze*: aequora alis, Ov.; pectora summa sagittā, Ov.

¶ Hence partic. (with compar.) **dēstrictus** -a -um, *severe*: accusator, Tac.

dēstrŭo -strŭĕre -struxi -structum, *to pull down, dismantle.* LIT., aedificium, Cic.; moenia, Verg. TRANSF., *to destroy, ruin*: ius destruere ac demoliri, Liv.; hostem, Tac.

dēsŭbĭto (or **dē sŭbĭto**), adv. *suddenly*: Pl., Lucr., Cic.

dēsūdasco -ĕre, *to begin to sweat violently*: Pl.

dēsūdo -are, *to sweat violently.* TRANSF., *to exert oneself hard*: in aliqua re, Cic.

dēsŭēfīo -fĭĕri -factum, pass., *to be made unaccustomed*: multitudo desuefacta a contionibus, Cic.

dēsŭesco -suescĕre -suēvi -suētum, *to become unaccustomed*; esp. in partic. **dēsŭētus** -a -um: (1) in pass. sense, *disused*: res desueta Liv.; arma, Verg. (2) in middle sense, *unaccustomed, unused to*: desuetus triumphis, Verg.

dēsŭētūdo -ĭnis, f. (desuesco), *disuse*: armorum, Liv., Ov.

dēsultor -ōris, m. (desilio), *a leaper*; esp. *a circus rider who leaped from one horse to another*: Liv. TRANSF., *an inconstant person*: amoris, Ov., Sen.

dēsultōrĭus -a -um (desultor), *relating to a desultor*: equus, Suet.; m. as subst. (sc. equus): Cic.

dēsum -esse -fŭi -fŭtūrus (ee as one syllable, poet.), *to be down, to fall short, to fail.*
(1) of things: omnia deerant, Caes.; with dat.: tibi nullum officium a me defuit, Cic.; with in and the abl.: desunt (verba) in C. Laenia commendando, Cic.; foll. by quominus: duas sibi res, quominus in vulgus et in foro diceret defuisse, Cic.; with infin.: Prop., Tac.
(2) of persons, *to fail, be wanting*, esp. in a duty: convivio, *to be missing at*, Cic.; officio, Cic.; nullo loco deesse alicui, Cic.; sibi, Cic.; foll. by quin: deesse mihi nolui, quin te admonerem, Cic.; absol.: nos consules desumus, *are wanting in our duty*, Cic.; Tac.

dēsūmo -sūmĕre -sumpsi -sumptum, *to take out, to choose, select*: sibi hostes, Liv.; Hor., Tac.

dēsŭpĕr, adv. *from above*: Caes., Verg., Ov.

dēsurgo -surgĕre -surrexi -surrectum, *to rise from one's place and go down* or *out*: cenā, Hor.; Lucr.

dētĕgo -tĕgĕre -texi -tectum, *to uncover, lay bare.* LIT., aedem, Liv.; caput, Verg.; quia possit fieri, ut (illa) patefacta et detecta mutentur, Cic. TRANSF., *to disclose*: insidias, consilium, cladem, Liv.; culpam, Ov.

dētendo -tendĕre -tensum, *to unstretch*: tabernacula, *to strike the tents*, Caes.; Liv.

dētergĕo -tergĕre -tersi -tersum.
(1) *to wipe off, wipe away*: lacrimas, Ov.; hence, in gen., *to clear away, brush off*: nubila caelo, Hor.; remos, Caes., Liv. TRANSF., *to sweep off, get away*: primo anno octoginta detersimus, Cic.
(2) *to cleanse by wiping*: cloacas, Liv.; Pl. TRANSF., mensam, Pl.

dētĕrĭor -ĭus, genit. -ōris, compar. adj., *with* superl. dēterrĭmus, *lower, inferior, poorer, worse*: vectigalia, Caes.; aetas, Verg.; peditatu, *weaker*, Nep.; homo deterrimus, Cic.; n. as subst., sing. or plur.: in deterius mutare, Tac.

¶ Adv. **dētĕrĭus**, *worse, in an inferior manner*: de male Graecis Latine scripta deterius, Cic.; Pl., Hor., Tac.

dētermĭnātĭo -ōnis, f. (determino), *a boundary, end*: mundi, Cic. TRANSF., orationis, Cic.

dētermĭno -are, *to bound, fix the limits of, determine.* LIT., augur regiones ab oriente ad occasum determinavit, Liv. TRANSF., id quod dicit spiritu non arte determinat, Cic.

dētĕro -tĕrĕre -trīvi -trītum, *to rub down, rub away, wear out.*
LIT., detrita tegmina, Tac.; Lucr.
TRANSF., *to detract from, to weaken*: laudes egregii Caesaris et tuas, Hor.; si quid ardoris ac ferociae miles habuit, popinis et comissationibus et principis imitatione deteritur, Tac.

dēterrĕo -terrēre -terrŭi -territum, *to frighten from anything, deter, discourage.*
LIT., between persons: homines a scribendo, Cic.; Stoicos de sententia, Cic.; a dimicatione, Cic.; multis verbis ne (with subj.), Caes.; non deterrere quominus (with subj.), Cic.; non deterrere quin, Caes.; with infin.: Cic.
TRANSF., (1) with a thing as subject: pudor, Cic. (2) with a thing as object, *to avert, to ward off*: vim a censoribus, Liv.

dētestābĭlis -e, adj. (with compar.) (detestor), *abominable, detestable, horrible*: omen, Cic.; homo, Cic.; Liv.

dētestātĭo -ōnis, f. (detestor). (1) *a cursing, execration*: Liv., Hor. (2) *a warding off, averting*: scelerum, Cic.

dētestor -ari, dep.
(1) *to pray against*: **a**, *to pray for deliverance from* a person or thing: te tamquam auspicium malum, Cic.; invidiam, Cic. **b**, *to pray for harm to come to, to curse, execrate*: omnibus precibus aliquem, Caes. perf. partic. in pass. sense: bella matribus detestata, Hor.; sometimes with the harm invoked in acc.: minas periculaque in caput eorum, Liv.

(2) of the gods' action, *to avert, remove*: dii immortales, avertite et detestamini hoc omen, Cic.

dētexo -texĕre -texŭi -textum, *to plait, make by plaiting*: aliquid viminibus mollique iunco, Verg. Transf., *to finish, complete*: detexta prope retexere, Cic.

dētĭnĕo -tĭnēre -tĭnŭi -tentum (de/teneo), *to hold away, hold back, detain.*
  Lit., novissimos proelio, Caes.; Romano bello in Italia detineri, Liv.; me gratā detinuit compede Myrtale, Hor.
  Transf., (1) in gen., *to prevent*: aliquem ab incepto, Sall.; ab circumspectu aliarum rerum, Liv. (2) *to engage, occupy exclusively*: in alienis negotiis, Cic.; Ov., Tac.

dētŏndĕo -tondēre -totondi and -tondi -tonsum, *to shear, clip.* Lit., crines, Ov. Transf., detonsae frigore frondes, *made leafless*, Ov.

dētŏno -tŏnare -tŏnŭi, *to cease to thunder.* Lit., hic (Iuppiter) ubi detonuit, Ov. Transf., *to cease to rage*: dum detonet omnis (nubes belli), Verg.; Quint.

dētorquĕo -torquēre - torsi -tortum.
  (1) *to turn away, bend aside.* Lit., ponticulum, Cic.; habenas, Verg.; in dextram partem, Cic.; proram ad undas, Verg. Transf., voluptates animos a virtute detorquent, Cic.; Tac., Hor.
  (2) *to twist anything out of its proper shape, distort*: corporis partes detortae, Cic. Transf., calumniando omnia detorquendoque suspecta et invisa efficere, Liv.

dētractio -ōnis, f. (detraho), *a drawing off, withdrawal, taking away*: doloris, Cic.; detractio atque appetitio alieni, *of another person's property*, Cic. Esp. (1) as medic. t. t., *a purging*: Cic. (2) rhet. t. t., *ellipsis*: Quint.

dētracto=detrecto; q.v.

dētractor -ōris, m. (detraho), *a detractor, disparager*: sui, Tac.

dētrăho -trăhĕre -traxi -tractum.
  (1) *to draw down, drag down.* Lit., aliquem de curru, Cic.; aliquem equo, Liv.; muros coloniae, *to demolish*, Tac. Transf., a, of persons, *to persuade to come down*: ab arce hostem, Liv.: b, *to lower, humiliate*: regum maiestatem ab summo fastigio ad medium, Liv.
  (2) *to draw off, drag away.* Lit., alicui de digito anulum, Cic.; torquem hosti, Cic.; vestem, Cic.; pellem, Hor.; spolia hostium templis porticibusque, Liv.; numerically, *to subtract from a sum*: de tota summa binas quinquagesimas, Cic. Transf., a, of persons, *to take away, remove*: inimicum ex Gallia, Cic.; aliquem ad accusationem, Cic.: b, of abstr. things: alicui calamitatem, Cic.; detracta opinione probitatis, Cic.; debitum honorem, Cic.; multa de suis commodis, Cic.; de honestate et de auctoritate alicuius, Cic.; hence *to detract from* a person and so *disparage* or *slander* him: de absentibus, Cic.

dētrectātĭo -ōnis, f. (detrecto), *a refusal*: militiae, Liv.

dētrectātor -ōris, m. (detrecto), *a disparager, detractor*: laudum suarum, Liv.

dētrecto -are (de/tracto). (1) *to have nothing to do with, to decline, refuse*: aratrum, Ov.; esp. of combat: militiam, Caes., Liv.; certamen, Liv.; absol., *to shirk*: Liv.

(2) *to disparage, detract from, depreciate*: virtutes, Liv.; Ov., Tac., Sall.; absol. : Ov.

dētrīmentōsus -a -um (detrimentum), *detrimental, hurtful*: ab hoste discedere detrimentosum esse existimabat, Caes.

dētrīmentum -i, n. (detero), *loss, damage, injury, detriment*; in gen.: detrimentum capere, accipere, facere, *to suffer*, Cic.; alicui ornamento et praesidio, non detrimento, esse, Caes.; esp. in the formula calling upon the consuls to make use of their powers in an emergency: videant consules ne quid respublica detrimenti capiat, Caes., Cic., Liv.; also as milit. t. t., *loss, defeat*: magna detrimenta inferre, Caes.; accipere, Caes.

dētrītus -a -um, partic. from detero; q.v.

dētrūdo -trūdĕre -trūsi -trūsum, *to push down, thrust down.*
  Lit., naves scopulo, Verg.; scutis tegumenta, Caes. Esp. (1) as milit. t. t., *to dislodge an enemy*: impetu conari detrudere virum, Liv. (2) as legal t. t., *to dispossess, eject*: ex praedio vi, Cic.
  Transf., (1) of persons, *to force, compel*: aliquem de sua sententia, Cic.; in tantum luctum, Cic.; ad necessitatem belli civilis, Tac. (2) *to put off in time, to postpone*: comitia in mensem Martium, Cic.

dētrunco -are, *to lop* or *cut off*: arbores, Liv. Transf., *to mutilate*: gladio detruncata corpora, Liv.

dēturbo -are, *to force away, dash down.*
  Lit., aliquem de tribunali, Cic.; aliquem tabula, Cic.; statuam, Cic.; Menoeten in mare, Verg.; esp. as milit. t. t., *to dislodge, drive off*: nostros de vallo lapidibus, Caes.; Cic.
  Transf., verecundiam mi, Pl.; aliquem de sanitate ac mente, Cic.; deturbari ex magna spe, Cic.; as legal t. t., *to eject, dispossess*: aliquem possessione, Cic.

Deucălĭōn -ōnis, m. (Δευκαλίων), *son of Prometheus, king of Phthia in Thessaly.* He and his wife Pyrrha, saved in an ark from a great flood, together repeopled the world by throwing stones behind their backs; Deucalion's stones turned into men, Pyrrha's into women.
  Adj. **Deucălĭōnēus** -a -um, *Deucalionian*: undae, *the deluge*, Ov.

deunx -uncis, m. (de/uncia), *eleven-twelfths* of a fixed unit: heres ex deunce, Cic.

deūro -ūrĕre -ussi -ustum. (1) *to burn down*: agros vicosque, Liv.; Tac. (2) fig., of cold, *to destroy, nip*: hiems arbores deusserat, Liv.

dĕus -i, m.; nom. plur. dei, dii, and di; genit. deorum or deum; dat. deis, diis, and dis (connected with Ζεύς, divus, dies), *a god, a deity.*
  Lit., particular or general: aliquem ut deum colere, Cic.; di hominesque, *the whole world*, Cic.; esp. in phrases, such as: di boni, Cic.; (pro) dii immortales, Cic.; pro deum atque hominum fidem, Ter.; di magni, Cat., Ov.; di meliora (ferant), *God forbid*, Cic., Liv.; si dis placet, *God willing*, Liv.
  Transf., of distinguished or influential persons: audiamus Platonem quasi quemdam deum philosophorum, Cic.; deus ac parens fortunae ac nominis mei, Cic.; deus sum, Pl., Ter.

deūtor -ūti -ūsus, dep. *to misuse, ill-treat*: Nep.

dēvasto -are, *to lay waste, devastate*: agrum, fines, Liv.; Ov.

dēvĕho -vĕhĕre -vexi -vectum, *to carry away or down* from one place to another: carinas, *downstream*, Caes.; legionem equis, Caes.; frumentum in Graeciam, Liv. Pass. used as middle, devehi (sc. navi), *to sail*: Veliam devectus, Cic.; Tiberi devectus, Tac.

dēvello -vellĕre -velli -vulsum, *to pull, pluck, tear away*: ramum trunco, Ov.; Cat., Tac.

dēvēlo -are, *to unveil, uncover*: ora, Ov.

dēvĕnĕror -ari, dep. (**1**) *to worship, revere*: deos prece, Ov. (**2**) *to avert by prayers*: somnia, Tib.

dēvĕnĭo -vĕnire -vēni -ventum, *to come to, arrive at, reach*. LIT., ad senatum, Cic.; in locum, Liv.; poet. with acc.: speluncam,Verg. TRANSF., in victoris manus, Cic.; ad iuris studium, Cic.; in medium certamen, Cic.

dēverbĕro -are, *to thrash soundly*: Ter.

¹dēversor -ari, dep. (freq. of deverto), *to lodge as a guest*: apud aliquem, Cic.; in ea domo, Cic.; Liv.

²dēversor -ōris, m. (deverto), *a guest*: Cic.

dēversōrĭŏlum -i, n. (dim. of deversorium), *a small lodging*: Cic. L.

dēversōrĭus -a -um (deverto), *fit to lodge in*: taberna, Pl.; Suet. N. as subst. **dēversōrĭum** -i, *an inn, lodging*: peropportunum, Cic.; Liv. TRANSF., *a refuge, resort*: studiorum deversorium esse non libidinum, Cic.

dēvertĭcŭlum (**dēvortĭcŭlum**) -i, n. (deverto).

(**1**) *a by-way, by-path*. LIT., deverticula flexionesque quaesivisti, Cic. TRANSF., *a digression*: Liv., Quint., Juv.

(**2**) *an inn, lodging*. LIT., Ter., Liv., Tac. TRANSF., *a refuge, resort*: fraudis, Cic.

dēverto (**dēvorto**) -vertĕre -verti -versum; transit., *to turn aside*: fata, Luc.; usually intransit., either in act. or in pass. with middle sense, *to turn aside*.

In gen.: viā, Liv. TRANSF., *to digress*: redeamus ad illud unde devertimus, Cic.

Esp. *to turn aside to a lodging, to put up at, stay with*: ad hospitem, Cic.; in tabernam, Pl., Cic., Tac.; ut locum publice pararet, ubi deverteretur, Liv. TRANSF., *quid ad magicas deverteris artes, have recourse to*, Ov.

dēvexus -a -um (deveho), *moving downwards, descending*.

LIT., (**1**) of moving objects: amnis devexus ab Indis, Hor.; Orion devexus, *sinking*, Hor. (**2**) of position, *sloping downwards, shelving, steep*: lucus devexus in novam viam, Cic.; Caes., Verg., Ov.

TRANSF., of abstr. things: aetas iam a diuturnis laboribus devexa ad otium, *inclining to*, Cic.

dēvincĭo -vincire -vinxi -vinctum, *to bind, tie fast*.

LIT., servum, Pl.; aliquem fasciis, Cic.

TRANSF., *to bind, attach, connect*: illud vinculum quod primum homines inter se reipublicae societate devinxit, Cic.; membra sopore, Lucr.; urbem praesidiis, Cic.; animos eorum, qui audiant, voluptate, Cic.; aliquem beneficio, Cic.; omni cautione, foedere, exsecratione, Cic.

¶ Hence partic. **dēvinctus** -a -um, *attached, devoted to*: iis studiis, Cic.; devinctior alicui, Hor.

dēvinco -vincĕre -vīci -victum, *to conquer thoroughly, subjugate*. LIT., Galliam Germaniamque, Caes.; Poenos classe, Cic.; devicta bella, *won outright*, Verg. TRANSF., *to prevail, overcome*: sententia devicit, ut in decreto perstaretur, Liv.

dēvītātĭo -ōnis, f. (devito), *an avoiding*: legionum, Cic.

dēvīto -are, *to avoid*: procellam, Cic.; dolorem, Cic.; letum, Lucr.; repulsam, Hor.

dēvĭus -a -um (de/via), *off the beaten track, out of the way*: iter, Cic.; oppidum, Cic.

TRANSF., (**1**) *living out of the way, solitary, retired*: devia et silvestris gens, Liv.; Cic.; mihi devio, *wandering*, Hor.; avis, *the owl*, Ov. (**2**) *erroneous, unreasonable*: homo in omnibus consiliis praeceps et devius, Cic.; Ov.

dēvŏco -are, *to call down* or *away from one* place to another: aliquem de provincia, Cic.; suos ab tumulo, Liv.; Iovem deosque ad auxilium, Liv. TRANSF., philosophiam e caelo, Cic.; ad gloriam Cic.; non avaritia ab instituto cursu ad praedam aliquam devocavit, Cic.; sese suas exercitusque fortunas in dubium non devocaturum, *bring into danger*, Caes.

dēvŏlo -are, *to fly down*. LIT., turdus devolat illuc, Hor.; per caelum (of Iris), Verg. TRANSF., *to hasten down*: alii praecipites in forum devolant, Liv.; ad florentem (amicitiam), Cic.

dēvolvo -volvĕre -volvi -vŏlūtum, *to roll down* LIT., saxa in musculum, Caes.; corpora in humum, Ov.; pensa fusis, *to spin off*, Verg. pass. with middle sense, *to roll down, fall headlong*: veluti monte praecipiti devolutu torrens, Liv.

TRANSF., per audaces nova dithyrambos verba, Hor.; pass., with middle sense, *to sink back, to fall into*: ad spem estis inanem pacis devoluti, Cic.; Liv.

dēvŏro -are, *to swallow, gulp down, devour*. LIT., id quod devoratur, Cic.

TRANSF., (**1**) of the action of things, *to swallow up, absorb*: me Charybdis devoret Ov. (**2**) *to seize upon*: libros, Cic.; spe e opinione praedam, Cic.; oratio a multitudini devorabatur, Cic. (**3**) *to articulate badly, mispronounce*: verba, Sen., Quint. (**4**) *to consume, waste* property: pecuniam publi cam, Cic.; patrimonium, Cic. (**5**) to swallow suppress: lacrimas, Ov.; hence *to accep* anything disagreeable, *put up with*: hominum ineptias ac stultitias, Cic.

dēvortĭcŭlum, *see* deverticulum.

dēvortĭum -i, n. (deverto), *a by-way, by path*: devortia itinerum, Tac.

dēvōtĭo -ōnis, f. (devoveo). (**1**) *a consecrating devoting* (esp. to the infernal gods): vitae o capitis, Cic.; P. Decii consulis, Liv.; plur. Deciorum devotiones, Cic. (**2**) *a cursing* Nep. (**3**) *an enchantment, an incantation*: Tac

dēvōto -are (freq. of devoveo), *to consecrate devote to death*: quae vis patrem Decium quae filium devotavit, Cic.

dēvōtus, partic. from devoveo; q.v.

dēvŏvĕo -vŏvēre -vōvi -vōtum, *to consecrate devote*.

LIT., as religious t. t., *to devote to a deity* Dianae quod in suo regno pulcherrimum natum esset, Cic.; Marti ea quae ceperunt

Caes. *Esp. to devote to the infernal gods*; hence (**1**) *to devote to death*: se dis immortalibus pro republica, Cic.; devota corpora (Deciorum), Liv.; Hor., Verg. (**2**) *to curse, execrate*: aliquem, Nep., Ov., Quint. Sometimes also *to bewitch, enchant*: Tib., Ov. TRANSF., in gen., *to devote, give up*: vobis animam hanc, Verg.; se alicuius amicitiae, Caes.

¶ Hence partic. **dēvotus** -a -um, *devoted*. LIT., to the infernal gods, *accursed*: arbor, Hor. TRANSF., to a person, *attached*: cliens, Juv.; m. pl. as subst. **dēvoti** -orum, *faithful followers*: Caes.

dextans -antis, m. (de/sextans), *five-sixths*: Suet.

dextella -ae, f. (dim. of dextra), *a little right hand*: Quintus filius Antonii est dextella, Cic. L.

dexter -těra -těrum, more freq. -tra -trum; compar. **dextěrĭor** -ĭus: Ov.; superl. **dextĭmus** -a -um: Sall.; *right, on the right hand, on the right side*. LIT., manus, Pl., Cic.; latus, Hor.; ab dextra parte, Caes.; rota dexterior, Ov. TRANSF., (**1**) *dexterous, skilful*: rem dexter egit, Liv.; *propitious* (like an omen from the right), *favourable, opportune*: Verg., Hor., Quint.

¶ F. as subst. **dextera** or **dextra** -ae (sc. manus), *the right hand*. LIT., ad dextram, *to the right*, Cic.; a dextra, *on the right*, Caes.; dexterā or dextrā, *on the right*, Caes. TRANSF., (**1**) as pledge of faith: dextram dare, *to give the right hand*, Liv.; tendere, Cic.; dominorum dextras fallere, *to betray*, Verg. (**2**) *the hand*, in gen.: Hor.

¶ Adv. **dextěrē** or **dextrē**; compar. dexterius; *dexterously, skilfully*: liberaliter dextreque obire officia, Liv.

dextěrĭtās -ātis, f. (dexter), *skilfulness, readiness*: Liv.

dextrorsum and **dextrorsus** (dextrovorsum: Pl.), adv. *on the right hand, towards the right*: Hor., Liv.

Dia -ae, f. (*Δία*). (**1**) *old name of the island of Naxos*: Ov. (**2**) *the mother of Mercury*: Cic.

diabathrārius -i, m. (*διάβαθρα*), *a shoemaker*: Pl.

diădēma -ătis, n. (*διάδημα*), *a royal headband, diadem*: diadema alicui imponere, Cic.; Hor.

diaeta -ae, f. (*δίαιτα*). (**1**) *a way of living prescribed by a physician, regimen, diet*: sed ego diaetā curare incipio; chirurgiae taedet, Cic. L. (**2**) *a living-room*: Plin. L.

diălectĭcus -a -um (*διαλεκτικός*), *relating to discussion, dialectical*: captiones, Cic., Quint.; Pl.

¶ As subst.; m. **diălectĭcus** -i, *a dialectician, logician*: Cic., Quint.; f. **diălectĭca** -ae: Cic., and **diălectĭcē** -es: Quint. (sc. ars), *the art of dialectic, logic*; n. pl. **diălectĭca** -orum, *dialectical discussion*: Cic.

¶ Adv. **diălectĭcē**, *dialectically*: Cic.

diălectos -i, f. (*διάλεκτος*), *a dialect*: Suet.

diălis -e (connected with dies and Iuppiter), *relating to Jupiter*; esp.: flamen dialis, Liv. (and absol.: dialis, Tac.), *the priest of Jupiter* (*most distinguished of the* flamines): coniux sancta dialis, *his wife*, Ov.; diale flaminium, Suet.

diălŏgus -i, m. (*διάλογος*), *a philosophical dialogue* or *conversation*: Cic.

Dĭāna (older form **Dīāna**) -ae, f. *an Italian goddess, identified with the Greek Artemis, daughter of Jupiter and Latona, sister of Apollo, the virgin goddess of the moon and of hunting*: tria virginis ora Dianae, *the three forms of Diana* (*Luna in heaven, Diana on earth, Hecate in the lower world*), Verg.; meton., *the moon*: Ov.; *the chase*: Mart.

¶ Hence adj. **Dĭānĭus** -a -um, *belonging to Diana*: Ov.; n. as subst. **Dĭānĭum** -i. (**1**) *a place dedicated to Diana*. (**2**) *a promontory in Spain* (now *Denia*): Cic.

diārĭa -orum, n. pl. (dies), *a day's allowance of food* or *pay*: Cic. L., Hor.

dĭbăphus -a -um (*δίβαφος*), *double-dyed*: purpura, Plin. F. as subst. **dĭbăphus** -i (sc. vestis), *the purple-striped robe of the higher magistrates at Rome*: dibaphum cogitat, *he is thinking about office*, Cic. L.

dĭca -ae, f. (*δίκη*), *a law-suit, action in a Greek court*: dicam scribere alicui, *to bring an action against*, Pl., Ter., Cic.; dicas sortiri, *to select the jury by lot*, Cic.

dĭcācĭtās -ātis, f. (dicax), *pungent wit, satire, raillery*: Cic.

dĭcăcŭlus -a -um (dim. of dicax), *ready of speech*: Pl.

dĭcātĭo -ōnis, f. (¹dico), *settling as a citizen in another state*: Cic.

dĭcax -ācis, adj. (with compar.) (²dico), *ready of speech*; hence *witty, satirical, ironical, sarcastic*: Demosthenes non tam dicax fuit facetus, Cic.; Pl., Hor., Liv.

dĭchŏrēus -i, m. (*διχόρειος*), *a double trochee*: Cic.

dĭcĭo -ōnis, f. (connected with ²dico), *power, sovereignty, authority*: esse in dicione alicuius, *to be in the power of*, Cic.; redigere bellicosissimas gentes in dicionem huius imperii, Cic.; urbes multas sub imperium populi Romani dicionemque subiungere, Cic.; dicionis suae facere, Liv.; in dicionem venire, Liv.; Ov., Tac.

dĭcis (genit., from root of ²dico), found only in the phrases, dicis causā, dicis gratiā, *for form's sake, for the sake of appearances*: Cic.

¹dĭco -are (connected with ²dico). LIT., as religious t. t., *to consecrate, dedicate, devote to the gods*: donum Iovi dicatum, Cic.; aram, Iovi, Liv.; templum, Cic.; hence (**1**) *to deify, place among the gods*: inter numina dicatus Augustus, Tac. (**2**) *to inaugurate*: nova signa, Tac.

TRANSF., *to devote, give up, set apart*: hunc totum diem tibi, Cic.; se alicui in clientelam, Caes.; se civitati *or* in civitatem, *to become a citizen of another state*, Cic.

²dĭco dīcěre dixi dictum (older form deico; cf. δείκνυμι; syncop. perf. dixti=dixisti: Cic., Ov.), *to indicate*.

Hence (**1**) *to appoint*; of things, esp. in legal terms: diem (esp. for a trial), Cic., Caes., Liv.; pecuniam, multam, Cic.; of persons: dictatorem, Cic.; aliquem dictatorem, Caes., Liv.

(**2**) most commonly, *to say, speak, tell, mention*: **a**, without object, *to say, speak, make a speech*: ut dixi, Cic.; pass.: ut dictum est, Caes., Cic.; ars dicendi, Cic.; pro reo, Cic.; contra aliquem pro aliquo apud centum viros, Cic.: **b**, with the spoken word as object, either quoted or described: 'chommoda' dicebat, Cat.; crudelem, ne dicam 'sceleratum', Cic.; nisi quid dicis, *if you have nothing to say against it*, Cic.; illa quae dixi, Cic.; orationem, Cic.; versus, carmen, Verg., Hor.; often with clause as object, either indir. quest. or acc. and infin.: Cic. etc.; so in pass. with infin., *to be said to*: Aesculapius dicitur obligavisse, Cic., or impersonally, dicitur, *it is said that*, with acc. and infin.: Cic. etc.: **c**, *to express, put something into words*: sententiam, Caes.; quod sentio, Cic.; causam, Caes., Cic., Liv.; ius, *to administer law, give rulings*, Caes., Cic.; phrase, dictum factum, *no sooner said than done*, Ter.; dicto citius, Verg., Hor., Liv.: **d**, *to mention, speak of* a person or thing: ille quem dixi, Cic.; so *to tell of*, relate: bella, laudes, Hor.; facta, Verg.: **e**, *to name, call*: quem dixere chaos, Ov.; pass.: orbis qui κύκλος Graece dicitur, Cic.: **f**, *to mean, refer to*, without having named: Hilarum dico, Cic.

¶ N. of perf. partic. as subst. **dictum** -i, *a word, saying, speech*.

In gen. (often opp. factum): nullum meum dictum intercessit, Cic.; dicta tristia, *complaints*, Ov.; mutua dicta reddere, *to converse*, Liv.; Pl., Verg.

Esp. (1) *a maxim, saying*: Catonis est dictum, Cic. (2) *a witty saying, a bon-mot*: dicta dicere in aliquem, Cic.; Hor., Liv. (3) *a prediction*: Lucr., Verg. (4) *an order, command*: dicto parere, Verg., Ov., Liv.; dicto audientem esse, Cic., Liv.

dicrŏtum -i, n. (from δίκροτος; sc. navigium), *a vessel having two banks of oars*: Cic. L.

dictamnus -i, f. (δίκταμνος), *dittany, a plant found on Mount Dicte and Mount Ida*: Cic., Verg.

dictāta -ōrum, n. from dicto; q.v.

dictātor -ōris, m. (dicto), *a dictator*. (1) in Rome, *an extraordinary magistrate, elected in times of emergency for six months, and granted absolute power*. (2) elsewhere, *a chief magistrate*; in Italian cities: Cic., Liv.; in Carthage, *a suffete*: Liv.

dictātōrĭus -a -um (dictator), *belonging to a dictator, dictatorial*: gladius, Cic.; invidia, *against the dictator*, Liv.; iuvenis, *son of the dictator*, Liv.

dictātrīx -īcis, f. (dicto), *a mistress*: Pl.

dictātūra -ae, f. (dictator), *the office of dictator, dictatorship*: dictaturam gerere, Cic.; dictaturā se abdicare, Caes.; dictaturam abdicare, Liv.

Dictē -ēs, f. (Δίκτη), *a mountain in Crete on which Jupiter was reared.* Adj. **Dictaeus** -a -um: arva, *Cretan*, Verg.; rex=*Jupiter*, Verg.; =*Minos*, Ov.

dictĭo -ōnis, f. (²dico), *a saying, speaking, uttering.* In gen.: sententiae, Cic.; causae, Cic.; iuris, Cic., Liv.

Esp. (1) rhet. t. t., *oratory, speech, diction*: dictioni operam dare, Cic.; Quint.; in concr. sense, *a speech*: dictiones subitae, *extemporized*, Cic.; Quint. (2) *the utterance of an oracle*: Liv. (3) *conversation*: Tac.

dictĭto -are (freq. of dicto). (1) in gen., *to say often, reiterate, assert repeatedly*: ut dictitabat, Caes.; quod levissimi ex Graecis dictitare solent, Liv.; Catilinam Massiliam ire, Cic.

(2) as legal term: dictitare causas, *to plead frequently*, Cic.

dicto -are (freq. of ²dico). (1) *to say often, repeat*: Cic., Hor. (2) *to say over, dictate* a thing to be written: quod non modo Tironi dictare, sed ne ipse quidem auderem scribere, Cic. L.; Hor., Quint.; in teaching pupils, Hor.; hence *to get written down*: versus, Hor.; carmina Livii, Hor.; dictabitur heres, Juv.

dictum -i, n. subst. from dico; q.v.

Dictynna -ae, f. (Δίκτυννα). (1) *a name of the nymph Britomartis*. (2) *a name of Diana*.

¶ Hence **Dictynnēum** -i, n. *a place sacred to Dictynna (near Sparta)*.

¹**Dīdō** -ūs, f. (Διδώ), *the founder of Carthage, daughter of Belus of Tyre, sister of Pygmalion, wife of Sichaeus*; also called Elisa or Elissa.

²**dīdo** dīdĕre dīdĭdi dīdĭtum (dis/do), *to divide, distribute, spread round*: in venas cibum, Lucr.; dum munia didit, Hor.; diditur subito Troiana per agmina rumor, *is spread*, Verg.

dīdūco -dūcĕre -duxi -ductum (dis/duco), *to draw apart, separate*.

LIT., in gen.: pugnum, Cic.; fores, Tac.; esp. as milit. t. t., *to divide, distribute*: copias, Caes.; aciem in cornua, Liv.; also *to scatter, disperse*: adversariorum manus, Caes.; hostem, Tac.

TRANSF., of the separation or division of persons, or of abstr. things: cum diducaris ab eo, Cic.; oratio rivis diducta est, non fontibus, Cic.; vastius diducuntur verba, Cic.; assem in partes centum diducere, Hor.; animus varietate rerum diductus, *distracted*, Cic.

dĭēcŭla -ae, f. (dim. of dies), *a little day, a short time*: Ter., Cic. L.

dĭērectus -a -um, an abusive expression found only in Pl. and Varr., like *go and be hanged*: LIT., of persons: i hinc dierectus, Pl. TRANSF., of things: lembum dierectum, Pl.

dĭēs -ēi, m. except as indicated below (connected with Iuppiter, deus, Ζεύς), *day*.

In gen. (1) *daytime, day* as opp. to night: multo die, *late in the day*, Caes.; ad multum diem (or diei), *till late*, Liv.; die, *by day*, Cic.; noctes et dies, Cic.; dies caelo concesserat, Verg.; videre diem, Ov. (2) *a day, period of twenty-four hours*; sometimes f., esp. in poets: paucos dies, Caes.; hesterno, hodierno, crastino die, Cic.; postero die, Cic.; postera die, Sall.; diem ex die, *from day to day*, Caes., Liv.; in dies, *daily*, esp. of a continuing process of change: magis magis in dies e horas, Cat.; Cic., Caes., Liv.; in diem vivere, *to live for the day*, Cic. (3) meton., *the business or events of the day*: exercere diem the day's work, Verg.; so of *a day's march*: regionem, dierum plus triginta in longitudinem patentem, Liv. (4) *time* in gen.: quod est dies adlatura, Cic.; longa dies, Verg., Pl., Ter.

Esp. *a particular day, fixed date*. (1) *a day appointed* for any purpose; usually f.: dies dicta, Cic.; pecuniae, *pay-day*, Cic.; alio non solvere, aliorum diem nondum esse *day for payment not arrived*, Cic. (2) *a day notable for its events, historic day*: is dies honestissimus nobis, Cic. (3) *day of death*, esp. with suus, or supremus: Cic., Nep.

(4) *anniversary*, esp. *birthday*, with or without natalis: Cic.

Diespĭter -tris, m. (dies/pater), *another name for Jupiter*: Hor.

diffāmo -are (fama), *to spread evil reports about, to defame*: viros illustres procacibus scriptis, Tac.

diffĕrentĭa -ae, f. (differo), *difference, distinction*: honesti et decori, Cic.; in principiis, Cic.

diffĕrĭtās -ātis, f. (differo), *difference*: Lucr.

diffĕro -differre distŭli dīlātum (dis/fero).

Transit., *to carry in different directions, spread abroad, scatter*. Lit., ignem, *to spread*, Caes.; aquilo differt nubila, Verg.; classem vis venti, Hor. Transf., **(1)** of news, etc., *to spread*: famam, Pl.; rumorem, Liv. **(2)** of persons: **a**, in gen., *to harass, disturb*: Pl., Ter.: **b**, by spreading rumours, *to discredit*: dominos variis rumoribus, Tac.; differor invidia, Prop. **(3)** in time: **a**, of events, *to delay, postpone*: tempus, Cic., bellum, Liv.; rem in aliud tempus, Caes.; concilium, Verg.; with infin.: nec differret obsides ab Arretinis accipere, Liv.; with quin: Liv.: **b**, of persons, *to put off*: aliquem in tempus aliud, Cic.; Liv., Verg.

Intransit. (without perf. or supine), *to differ, be different*: inter se, Cic.; with ab and abl., rarely with cum, *to differ from*: Cic.; so with dat.: Hor., Quint.; nihil differt inter deum et deum, *there is no difference*, Cic.

differtus -a -um (dis/farcio), *stuffed full, crammed*: corpus odoribus, Tac.; fig.: provincia differta praefectis atque exactoribus, Caes.

diffĭcĭlis -e adj. (with compar. difficilior and superl. difficillimus) (dis/facilis), *difficult*.

Lit., of actions, and things entailing action: est difficile confundere, Cic.; res arduae ac difficiles, Cic.; iter, Sall.; aditus, Caes.; so of times when, and places where, action is difficult: tempus anni difficillimum, Cic.; valles, Caes.; with ad: difficilius ad eloquendum, Cic.

Transf., of character, *hard to deal with, surly, morose, obstinate*: parens in liberos difficilis, Cic.; vocanti, Hor.; terrae, Verg.

¶ N. as subst.; abl.: in difficili esse, Liv.; acc. difficile as adv., *with difficulty*: Suet.

¶ Adv. **difficĭlĭter** (with compar. difficilius and superl. difficillimē), *with difficulty*, Cic.

¶ Adv. **difficulter**, *with difficulty*: Caes.

difficultās -ātis, f. (difficilis), *difficulty, need, trouble, distress*. Lit., dicendi, navigandi, Cic.; loci, Sall.; magnam haec Caesari difficultatem ad consilium adferebat si, Caes.; nummaria, *pecuniary embarrassment*, Cic.; domestica, *distressed circumstances*, Cic.

Transf., of character, *obstinacy, moroseness*: Cic.

diffīdentĭa -ae, f. (diffidens), *want of confidence, diffidence, distrust, despair*: fidentiae contrarium est diffidentia, Cic.; diffidentiam rei simulare, Sall.; praesentium, Tac.

diffīdo -fīdĕre -fīsus sum (dis/fido), *to have no confidence, mistrust, despair*: sibi, Cic.; suis rebus, Caes.; virtuti militum, Sall.; with acc. and infin., rem posse confici diffido, Cic.; Caes., Liv.; absol.: iacet, diffidit, abiecit hastas, Cic.

¶ Hence partic. **diffīdens** -entis, *distrustful, diffident*: Suet.

¶ Adv. **diffīdentĕr**, *diffidently, without confidence*: timide et diffidenter attingere, Cic.; Liv.

diffindō -findĕre -fīdi -fissum (dis/findo), *to split, cleave*: saxum, Cic.; Hor., Verg.; fig.: portas muneribus, *open*, Hor.; as legal t. t.: diem, *to break off business and postpone it*, Liv.

diffingo -ĕre (dis/fingo), *to form again, forge anew*: ferrum incude, Hor.; fig., *to change*: Hor.

diffĭtĕor -ēri, dep. (dis/fateor), *to deny, disavow*: Ov., Quint.

difflo -are (dis/flo), *to blow apart*: Pl.

difflŭo -flŭĕre -fluxi -fluxum (dis/fluo).

Lit., *to flow in different directions*; of liquids: ut nos quasi extra ripas diffluentes coerceret, Cic.; of solids: a summo diffluat altus acervus, Lucr.; of persons, sometimes *to drip with* liquid: iuvenes sudore diffluentes, Phaedr.

Transf., *to dissolve, melt away*: natura animantum, Lucr.; esp. of moral collapse: uti per socordiam vires, tempus, ingenium diffluxere, Sall.; luxuriā, Cic.

diffringo -fringĕre -fractum (dis/frango), *to shatter*: Pl., Suet.

diffŭgĭo -fŭgĕre -fūgi -fūgitum (dis/fugio), *to fly apart, fly in different directions, to disperse*: metu perterriti repente diffugimus, Cic.; diffugere nives, Hor.

diffŭgĭum -i, n. (diffugio), *a dispersion*: Tac.

diffundito -are (freq. of diffundo), *to scatter*: Pl.

diffundo -fundĕre -fūdi -fūsum (dis/fundo), *to pour in different directions*.

Lit., **(1)** of liquids: vina, Hor.; sanguis per venas in omne corpus diffunditur, Cic. **(2)** of solids, *to spread out*: diffusis capillis, Ov. **(3)** of impalpable things, such as light or scent: lux diffusa toto caelo, Cic.; Lucr., Verg.

Transf., in gen., *to spread, extend*: error longe lateque diffusus, Cic.; Hor., Verg.; esp. *to make to relax*, and so *to brighten up, gladden*: diffundere animos munere Bacchi, Ov.; ut ex bonis amici quasi diffundantur et incommodis contrahantur, Cic.

¶ Hence partic. (with compar.: Plin. L.) **diffūsus** -a -um, *spread out, extensive, wide*. Lit., platanus diffusa ramis, Cic. Transf., ius civile quod nunc diffusum et dissipatum est, in certa genera coacturum, Cic.

¶ Adv. (with compar.) **diffūsē**, *copiously, diffusely*: res dicere, Cic.

diffūsĭlis -e (diffundo), *capable of spreading, elastic*: aether, Lucr.

Dĭgentĭa -ae, f. *a brook flowing through Horace's Sabine farm into the Anio* (now *Licenza*).

dīgĕro -gĕrĕre -gessi -gestum (dis/gero), *to carry apart in different directions, to separate, spread*.

Lit., Nilus septem in cornua digestus, Ov.; esp. of orderly arrangement: capillos, Ov.; vacuos ut sit digesta per agros (arbor), Verg.; so *to digest*: Sen.

Transf., *to spread* anything: mala per annos, Ov.; esp. in orderly fashion, *to arrange*: ius civile in genera, Cic.; rempublicam bene, Cic.; nomina in codicem accepti et expensi, Cic.; Verg., Liv.

dīgestĭo -ōnis, f. (digero), *arrangement*; rhet. t. t. = μερισμός, *distribution*: Cic., Quint.

dīgestus -a -um, partic. from digero; q.v.

dīgĭtŭlus -i, m. (dim. of digitus), *a little finger*; hence *the touch of a finger*: Pl., Ter., Cic.

dīgĭtus -i, m.

(1) *a finger*. LIT., Cic. etc.: digitus pollex, *the thumb*, Caes.; index, *the forefinger*, Hor.; digitos comprimere pugnumque facere, Cic.; digitos extendere, Cic.; concrepare digitis, Cic.; digito caelum attingere, *to be in the seventh heaven*, Cic. L.; digito attingere, *to touch gently*, Pl., Ter., Cic.; liceri digito *or* tollere digitum, *to raise the finger to bid at an auction*, Cic.; ne digitum quidem porrigere, *not to move a finger*, Cic. TRANSF., as a measure, *a finger's breadth, an inch, the sixteenth part of a Roman foot*: quattuor patens digitos, Caes.; prov.: ab hac (regula) mihi non licet transversum, ut aiunt, digitum discedere, *a finger's breadth*, Cic.

(2) *a toe*: insistere digitis, *to tread on the toes*, Ov.; constitit in digitos adrectus, Verg.

dīglădĭor -ari, dep. (gladius), *to flourish the sword*. LIT., *to fight, struggle fiercely*: inter se sicis, Cic. TRANSF., *to dispute in words*: inter se de aliqua re, Cic.; cum aliquo, Cic.

dignātĭo -ōnis, f. (dignor). (1) *esteem*: Suet. (2) *dignity, reputation, honour*: Liv., Tac., Suet.

dignĭtās -ātis, f. (dignus), *worth, worthiness, merit*.

LIT., honos dignitate impetratus, Cic.

TRANSF., (1) *dignified appearance*: **a**, of persons: in formis aliis dignitatem esse, aliis venustatem, Cic.: **b**, of buildings, etc.: porticūs, Cic.: **c**, of *style*: verborum, Cic.; orationis, Tac.; Quint. (2) *dignified position, esteem, reputation, honour*: cum dignitate otium, Cic.; Caes., Liv., Tac.; esp. *official rank*: altus dignitatis gradus, Cic.; aliquem ad summam dignitatem perducere, Caes.; hence plur. dignitates, *persons of rank*: Liv., Quint.

digno -are (dignus), *to consider worthy*: res consimili laude dignentur, Cic.; Verg.

dignor -ari, dep. (dignus), *to consider worthy*; with acc. and abl.: haud equidem tali me dignor honore, Verg.; Ov., Tac.; with double acc.: si quem dignabitur virum, Ov.; with infin., *to deign to*: Lucr., Ov.

dignosco (dinosco) -noscĕre -nōvi (dis/nosco), *to recognize as different, to distinguish*: rectum curvo, Hor.; civem hoste, Hor.; geminos inter se similes, vix ut dignoscere possis, Ov.

dignus -a -um, adj. (with compar. and superl.) (connected with decet), *worthy*.

(1) *worthy to have, deserving*; esp. of persons: **a**, most usually with abl.: laude, Cic.; memoriā, Cic.; Pl., Verg. **b**, with genit.: Pl., Cic. L., Ov. **c**, with verbs: dictu, Liv.; qui aliquando imperet dignus, *worthy to command*, Cic.; quos ut socios haberes dignos duxisti, Liv.; poet. with infin.: puer cantari dignus, Verg. **d**, with prepositions; with ad: amicus dignus huic ad imitandum, Cic.; with pro: Cic., Hor. **e**, absol.: diligere non dignos, Cic.

(2) of things, *worth having, deserved, becoming, suitable, fitting*: qui maeror dignus in tanta calamitate inveniri potest, Cic.;

praemia, Verg.; dignum est, foll. by infin., *it is proper*, Pl., Cic., Verg.

¶ Adv. (with compar.) **dignē**: quis de tali cive satis digne umquam loqueretur? Cic.; Pl., Hor.

dīgrĕdĭor -grĕdi -gressus sum, dep. (dis/gradior), *to go apart, go asunder, separate, depart*.

LIT., luna tum congrediens cum sole, tum digrediens, Cic.; ab aliquo, Cic.; a Corcyra, Liv.; ex loco, Caes.; in urbem, Tac.; viā, Liv.

TRANSF., *to deviate*: officio, Ter.; esp. of discourse, *to digress*: digredi ab eo quod proposueris, Cic.; a causā, de causā, Cic.; Quint.

dīgressĭo -ōnis, f. (digredior), *a separation, departure*. LIT., Cic. L. TRANSF., *a deviation*, esp. *a digression in discourse*: a proposita oratione, Cic.; Quint.

dīgressus -ūs, m. (digredior), *a separation, departure*. LIT., digressus et discessus, Cic.; veteris amici, Juv. TRANSF., *a digression*: Quint.

diiūdĭcātĭo -ōnis, f. (diiudico), *a judging, decision*: Cic.

dīiūdĭco -are (dis/iudico).

(1) *to judge between parties, to decide, determine*: controversiam, Cic.; litem, Hor. TRANSF., *to decide by fighting*: diiudicatā fortunā, Caes.

(2) *to distinguish, find a difference between*: vera et falsa, Cic.; vera a falsis diiudicare et distinguere, Cic.; inter has sententias, Cic.

diiun-, *see* disiun-.

dīlābor -lābi -lapsus sum, dep. (dis/lābor), *to glide apart*.

LIT., (1) of solids, *to fall to pieces, fall down*: aedes Iovi vetustate dilapsa, Liv.; of ice, *to melt, dissolve*: eadem (aqua conglaciata) admixto colore liquefacta et dilapsa, Cic. (2) of liquids, gases, etc., *to flow apart, run away*: Cic., Verg.

TRANSF., (1) of persons in groups, *to break up, to slip away*, esp. of soldiers: exercitus brevi dilabitur, Sall.; nocte in sua tecta, Liv. (2) in gen., *to break up, vanish*: rem familiarem dilabi sinere, Cic.; dilapsa esse robora corporum animorumque, Liv.; sunt alii plures fortasse sed de mea memoria dilabuntur, Cic. (3) of time, *to go by*: dilapso tempore, Sall.

dīlăcĕro -are (dis/lacero), *to tear in pieces*. LIT., aliquem, Ov.; Tac. TRANSF., rempublicam, Cic., Sall.; Ov., Tac.

dīlāmĭno -are (dis/lamina), *to split in two*: Ov.

dīlănĭo -are (dis/lanio), *to tear in pieces*: cadaver, Cic.; Lucr., Ov.

dīlăpĭdo -are (dis/lapis), *to demolish*: Ter.

dīlargĭor -iri, dep. (dis/largior), *to hand round, give liberally*: qui omnia quibus voluit dilargitus est, Cic.

dīlātĭo -ōnis, f. (differo), *a putting off, delaying postponing*: temporis, Cic.; belli, Liv.; sine dilatione, Liv.; res dilationem non recipit, Liv.

dīlāto -are (dilatus), *to spread out, extend*. LIT., manum, Cic.; aciem, Liv. TRANSF., nomen in continentibus terris, Cic.; legem in ordinem cunctum, Cic.; orationem, Cic.; litteras, *to pronounce broadly*, Cic.

dīlātor -ōris, m. (differo), *a dilatory person, a loiterer*: Hor.

dilātus, partic. from differo; q.v.

dilaudo -are (dis/laudo), *to praise highly*: libros, Cic.

dilectus -a -um, partic. from diligo; q.v.

dilectus -ūs, m. (diligo). (1) in gen., *a choosing, choice, selection*: verborum, *a choice of language*, Cic.; sine ullo dilectu, *without any choice*, Cic.
(2) as milit. t. t., *a levy, recruiting of troops, conscription*: dilectum habere, Cic., Caes., Liv.; conficere, Liv.; dilectus provincialis, *a levy in the provinces*, Cic.; meton., of the troops so raised: Tac.

diligens -entis, partic. from diligo; q.v.

diligentia -ae, f. (diligo), *carefulness, attentiveness, accuracy*. In gen., with objective genit.: testamentorum, Cic.; with in and the abl.: pro mea summa in republica diligentia, Cic.; non mediocrem adhibere diligentiam, Caes.; adhibere ad considerandas res et tempus et diligentiam, Cic.; omnia acerbissimā diligentiā perpendere, Cic. Esp. *care in management, economy*: res familiaris conservari (debet) diligentiā atque parsimoniā, Cic.; Suet.

diligo -ligere -lexi -lectum (dis/lego), *to choose out*; hence *to prize, love, esteem highly*: aliquem, Cic., Verg., Hor.; se ipsum, Cic.; inter se, Cic.; of things: hunc locum, Cic.; alicuius consilia, officia, Cic.
¶ Hence pres. partic. (with compar. and superl.) **diligens** -entis.
In gen., *attentive, careful* (opp. neglegens). LIT., of persons: omnibus in rebus, Cic.; with genit.: diligentissimus omnis officii, Cic.; with dat.: Corinthios publicis equis adsignandis fuisse diligentes, Cic.; with ad and the gerund: ad custodiendum, Cic., Quint. TRANSF., of things which bear marks of attention: adsidua ac diligens scriptura, Cic.; Sen., Tac.
Esp., *careful in housekeeping, economical, saving*: homo frugi ac diligens, Cic.; in re hereditaria, Cic.; Quint., Plin. L.
¶ Adv. (with compar. and superl.) **diligenter**, *attentively, carefully, assiduously*: aliquem benigne et diligenter audire, Cic.; iter caute diligenterque facere, Caes.
¶ Perf. partic. **dilectus** -a -um, *beloved*: Ov.

dilorico -are (dis/lorica), *to tear open*: tunicam, Cic.

diluceo -ēre (dis/luceo), *to be clear, evident*: dilucere deinde fraus coepit, Liv.

dilucesco -lūcescere -luxi (diluceo), *to grow light, become day*.
LIT., (1) with subject: omnem crede diem tibi diluxisse supremum, Hor. (2) impers.: cum iam dilucesceret, Cic.
TRANSF., *to become clear*: origo, Lucr.; Ov.

dilucidus -a -um (diluceo) adj. (with compar.), *clear, lucid, plain*: oratio, Cic.; dilucidis verbis uti, Cic.; Quint.
¶ Adv. **dilucide**, *clearly*: plane et dilucide dicere, Cic.; Quint.

diluculum -i, n. (diluceo), *the break of day, dawn*: primo diluculo, Cic.; diluculo, *at dawn*, Cic.

diludium -i, n. (dis/ludus), *an interval between games* or *shows*: diludia posco, *breathing-space, rest*, Hor.

diluo -luere -lui -lutum (dis/luo).
(1) *to wash apart, separate, dissolve*.
LIT., ne canalibus aqua immissa lateres diluere posset, Caes.; sata laeta, Verg.; unguenta lacrimis, Ov.
TRANSF., *to resolve*; of troubles, *to remove*; of puzzles and errors, *to clear up*: molestias, Cic.; curam multo mero, Ov.; crimen, Cic.; diluere aliquid et falsum esse docere, Cic.
(2) *to dilute, temper*. LIT., vinum, Mart.; venenum, Liv. TRANSF., *to weaken, lessen, impair*: vires, Quint.; auctoritatem, Sen.

diluvies -ēi, f. (diluo), *a washing away, inundation*: Lucr., Hor.

diluvio -are (diluvies), *to flood, inundate*: Lucr.

diluvium -i, n. (diluo), *a flood, deluge, inundation*: Verg., Ov.; fig.: diluvio ex illo, of the Trojan War, Verg.

dimano -are (dis/mano), *to flow in different directions, spread abroad*; fig.: meus hic forensis labor vitaeque ratio dimanavit ad existimationem hominum, Cic.

dimensio -ōnis, f. (dimetior), *a measuring*: quadrati, Cic.

dimetior -mētiri -mensus, dep. (dis/metior), *to measure out*.
LIT., caelum atque terram, Cic.; Verg.; perf. partic. often in pass. sense: opere dimenso, Caes.; dimensa atque descripta, Cic.; tigna dimensa ad altitudinem fluminis, Caes.; certis dimensus partibus orbis, Verg.
TRANSF., syllabas, Cic.; audiam civem digitis peccata dimetientem sua, Cic.

dimeto -are and dep. **dimetor** -ari, *to measure out*; pass.: locum castris dimetari iussit, Liv.; dep.: eorum cursús dimetati, Cic.

dimicatio -ōnis, f. (dimico), *a fight, struggle*.
LIT., *a battle*: Caes., Liv.; with genit.: proelii, Cic. TRANSF., *any contest* or *struggle*: vitae, *for life and death*, Cic.; capitis, Cic.; Liv., Quint.

dimico -are -avi (infin. dimicuisse: Ov.; from dis/mico), *to brandish weapons*; hence *to fight, contend, struggle*. LIT., in battle: acie, in acie, Caes.; proelio, Cic.; pro patria, Liv.; cum aliquo, Liv. Impers. pass.: Caes., Cic. TRANSF., of any contest: omni ratione erit dimicandum, Cic.; de fama, de civitate, Cic.

dimidiātus -a -um (dimidius), *halved, divided, half*: mensis, Cic.; partes versiculorum, Cic.; fig.: o dimidiate Menander, addressing Terence, Caes. ap. Suet.

dimidius -a -um (dis/medius), *halved, divided in half*. In ante-Aug. period, only with pars: dimidia pars, *the half*, Lucr., Cic., Caes. In and after Augustans, with any noun (like dimidiatus): luna, Ov.; crus, Juv.; dimidius patrum, dimidius plebis, *half patrician and half plebeian*, Liv.
¶ N. as subst. **dimidium** -i, *the half*: pecuniae, Cic.; Pl., Hor.; dimidio minus, *less by half*, Pl., Caes., Cic., Hor.; prov.: dimidium facti, qui coepit, habet, *well begun is half done*, Hor.

diminutio, see deminutio.

dimissio -ōnis, f. (dimitto). (1) *a sending out*: libertorum ad provincias, Cic. (2) *a dismissing, discharging*: remigum, Cic.

dīmitto -mittĕre -mīsi -missum (dis/mitto).

(1) *to send forth, send in different directions*: pueros circum amicos, Cic.; litteras per omnes provincias, Caes.; nuntios in omnes partes, Caes.; aciem (oculorum) in omnes partes, Ov.; without object, *to send* (*word*) *round*: Caes., Liv.

(2) *to send away, let go.* LIT., **a**, of things, *to let fall*: signa ex metu, Caes.; librum e manibus, Cic.: **b**, of persons: legatos, Liv.; tabellarium, Cic.; hostem ex manibus, *let slip*, Caes.; regem spoliatum, Cic.; as milit. t. t., *to detach*: Caes.: **c**, of a gathering, *to break up, dismiss*: senatum, concilium, Cic.; convivium, Liv.; as milit. t. t., *to disband*: exercitum, Caes. TRANSF., **a**, of material things, *to give up, leave* (without actually causing to move): locum, Caes.; provinciam, Liv.: **b**, of abstr. things, *to give up, renounce, abandon, leave*: oppugnationem, Caes.; quaestionem, Cic.; iniuriam ignominiamque nominis Romani inultam impunitamque, Cic.

dimmĭnŭo -ĕre, *to dash to pieces*: Pl., Ter.

dīmŏvĕo -mŏvēre -mōvi -mōtum (dis/moveo). (1) *to move asunder, part, divide*: terram aratro, *to plough*, Verg.; aquam corpore, Ov.; turbam, Tac. (2) *to separate, remove, to take away.* LIT., sacra suo statu, Liv. TRANSF., spes societatis equites Romanos a plebe dimovet, Sall.

Dindўmus -i, m. and **Dindўma** -ōrum, n. pl. (Δίνδυμος, Δίνδυμα), *a mountain in Mysia, sacred to Cybele.*

¶ Hence **Dindўmēnē** -ēs, f. *Cybele*: Hor.

dīnosco=dignosco; q.v.

dīnŭmĕrātĭo -ōnis, f. (dinumero), *an enumeration*: dierum ac noctium, Cic.

dīnŭmĕro -are (dis/numero), *to count out, enumerate*: stella, Cic.; regis annos, Cic. Esp. *to count money, to pay*: viginti minas illi, Ter.

Dĭŏdōrus -i, m. (Διόδωρος), *Diodorus Siculus, of Agyrium, who wrote a History of the World in Greek* (*c.* 60–30 B.C.).

dĭoecēsis -ĕos and -is, f. (διοίκησις), *a district under a governor*: Cic. L.

dĭoecētēs -ae, m. (διοικητής), *a revenue official or treasurer*: Cic.

Dĭŏgĕnēs -is, m. (Διογένης), *the name of several Greek philosophers, esp. the Cynic philosopher of Sinope, of the fourth century* B.C.

Dĭŏmēdēs -is, m. (Διομήδης). (1) *a hero of the Trojan war, son of Tydeus, and comrade of Odysseus.*

¶ Hence adj. **Dĭŏmēdēus** (-ius) -a -um, *relating to Diomede.*

(2) *king of the Bistones in Thrace, who gave his captives as food to his horses.*

Dĭōnē -ēs, f. and **Dĭōna** -ae, f. (Διώνη). (1) *the mother of Venus.* (2) *Venus.* Adj. **Dĭōnaeus** -a -um, *relating to Dione*: mater, i.e. *Venus*, Verg.; Caesar, (by the legend) *descendant of Aeneas, son of Venus*, Verg.; antrum, *sacred to Venus*, Hor.

Dĭŏnўsĭus -i, m. (Διονύσιος). (1) *the elder, tyrant of Syracuse* 406–367 B.C. (2) *his son and successor, sometime pupil of Plato.*

Dĭŏnўsus (-os) -i, m. (Διόνυσος), *the Greek name of Bacchus.*

¶ Hence **Dĭŏnўsĭa** -ōrum, n. pl. *the feast of Dionysus.*

dĭōta -ae, f. (διώτη), *a two-handled wine-jar*: Hor.

Dĭphĭlus -i, m. (Δίφιλος), *a comic poet of Sinope, contemporary of Menander and Philemon, imitated by Plautus.*

diplōma -ătis, n. (δίπλωμα), literally, *a folded letter.* Hence (1) *a letter of introduction given to travellers by the government to facilitate their journey*: Cic., Tac. (2) *a government document conferring privileges on the person(s) addressed*: Suet.

Dircē -ēs, f. (Δίρκη). (1) *the wife of Lycus, king of Thebes, bound to a bull by Amphion and Zethus, and thrown (or changed) into the fountain named after her.*

(2) *the fountain of Dirce, to the north-west of Thebes.* Adj. **Dircaeus** -a -um, *Dircean, Boeotian*: cycnus=*Pindar*, Hor.

dīremptus -ūs, m. (dirimo), *a separation*: Cic.

dīreptĭo -ōnis, f. (diripio), *a plundering, pillaging*: urbs relicta direptioni, Cic.; bonorum direptio, Cic.; Caes., Liv.

dīreptor -ōris, m. (diripio), *a plunderer, pillager*: Cic., Tac.

dīrĭbĕo -ēre -itum (dis/habeo), *to sort the tablets when taken out of the ballot-box*: tabellas, Cic.

dīrĭbĭtĭo -ōnis, f. (diribeo), *the sorting of the voting tablets*: Cic.

dīrĭbĭtor -ōris, m. (diribeo), *the officer whose duty it was to sort the voting tablets*: Cic.

dīrĭgo -rigĕre -rexi -rectum (dis/rego), *to arrange, direct*: Cic. But in many passages modern editors replace dirigo by derigo (q.v.) which appears to be the older and more popular word.

¶ Hence partic. **dīrectus** -a -um. LIT., *straight, direct*, either in a horizontal or perpendicular direction: paries, Cic.; iter, Cic.; trabes, Caes. TRANSF., *straightforward, plain, simple*: ratio, Cic.; senex, Cic.

¶ Abl. as adv. **dīrectō**, *straight, directly*: Caes., Cic.

¶ Adv. **dīrectē**.

dīrĭmo -imere -ēmi -emptum (dis/emo), *to part, separate, sunder, divide.*

LIT., corpus, Cic.; urbs Volturno flumine dirempta, Liv.

TRANSF., *to break off, interrupt, stop* temporarily or permanently; esp. (1) of fighting: proelium, Pl., Caes., Liv.; bellum, Liv., Verg.; Sabinae mulieres ex transverso impetu facto dirimere infestas acies, dirimere iras, Liv. (2) of peaceful associations and undertakings: ea res conloquium ut diremisset, Caes.; veterem coniunctionem civium, Cic.; consilia, Liv.

dīrĭpĭo -rĭpĕre -rĭpŭi -reptum (dis/rapio), *to snatch apart.*

LIT., (1) *to tear to pieces*: Hippolytum, Ov. (2) *to divide as spoil*; as milit. t. t., *to pillage, lay waste*: bona, Caes.; castra, urbes, Liv.; provincias, Cic.; in gen., *to scramble for*: Quint. (3) *to tear away*: a pectore vestem, Ov.

TRANSF., of mental distress: diripior, Pl.

dīrĭtās -ātis, f. (dirus). (1) *misfortune, disaster*: poet. ap. Cic.; Suet. (2) *cruelty, fierceness*: quanta in altero diritas, in altero comitas, Cic.

dīrumpo -rumpĕre -rūpi -ruptum, *to break apart* or *to pieces, shatter.*

LIT., tenuissimam quamque partem (nubis) dividere atque dirumpere, Tac.; (homo) diruptus, *ruptured*, Cic.

TRANSF., (**1**) *to sever, break up*: amicitiam, societatem, Cic. (**2**) in pass., dirumpi, *to burst with envy, grief, anger*, etc.: dirumpi plausu alicuius, *to burst with envy at the applause given to someone else*, Cic.; dolore, Cic. L.

dirŭo -rŭĕre -ŭi -ŭtum, *to pull apart, pull to pieces, demolish, destroy*.

LIT., urbem, Cic.; Ter., Ov., Verg.

TRANSF., in gen., *to break up*: agmina vasto impetu, Hor.; esp. financially: aere dirutus est, *ruined by gambling*, Cic.; homo diruptus dirutusque, *bankrupt*, Cic.

dīrus -a -um, *fearful, horrible, dire*.

LIT., of unfavourable omens: omen, Ov.; aves, Tac.; Verg. As subst. (**1**) n. pl. dīra -orum and f. pl. dirae -arum (sc. res), *unlucky omens, curses*: diris agam vos, Hor.; Cic., Tac. (**2**) f., generally pl., **Dirae** -arum, as name for the *Furies*: Verg.

TRANSF., *abominable, horrible, cruel, frightful*. (**1**) of things: exsecratio, Verg.; venena, Hor.; Tac. (**2**) of persons: dea, *Circe*, Ov.; Hannibal, Hor., Verg.

¹dis- di- dir- inseparable prefix, meaning *separately, apart, in different directions*.

²Dīs, Dītis, m. *a name of Pluto, god of the Lower World*: Cic.; domina Ditis, *Proserpine*, Verg.

³dīs, dītis, adj. (with compar. and superl.) (contracted from dīves), *rich*. LIT., of persons: dis hostis, Liv.; ditissimus fuit Orgetorix, Caes.; with genit.: ditissimus agri, Verg. TRANSF., *richly endowed, containing* or *bringing wealth*: stipendia, *profitable*, Liv.; fig., of mental resource: Lucr.

discēdo -cēdĕre -cessi -cessum.

(**1**) *to go asunder, part, separate*: in duas partes, Sall.; caelum discedit, *the heavens open*, Cic. TRANSF., omnis Italia animis discedit, *is divided*, Sall.

(**2**) *to depart, go away*.

LIT., e Gallia, Cic.; ab amicis, Cic.; de foro, Cic.; finibus Ausoniae, Ov.; impers. pass.: a contione disceditur, Caes.; Liv., Tac.; esp. as milit. t. t.: **a**, *to march away*: a Brundisio, Caes.; ab signis, *to break the ranks*, Caes., Liv.; ab armis, *to lay down arms*, Caes., Sall., Liv.: **b**, *to come out of a contest, to come off*: victor, Caes.; victus, Sall.; aequo Marte cum Volscis, *to have a drawn battle with*, Liv.; so *to come out of any contest* (e.g., in a court of law): superior discedit, Cic.; turpissime, *with disgrace*, Cic.

TRANSF., **a**, in gen., *to depart, pass away*: ex vita tamquam ex hospitio, Cic.; a vita, Caes.; nunquam ex animo meo discedit illius viri memoria, Cic.: **b**, *to deviate, swerve from*: a re, *to digress*, Cic.; ab officio, Cic.; a consuetudine, Cic.: **c**, polit. t. t., of the senate: in aliquam sententiam discedere, *to support a resolution*; in alia omnia discedere, *to support the opposite opinion*, Cic.: **d**, discedere ab aliquo, *to except*: cum a vobis discesserim, *you excepted*, Cic.

disceptātĭo -ōnis, f. (discepto), *a debate, discussion, controversy*: cum quibus omnis fere nobis disceptatio contentioque est, Cic.; esp. at law, often with genit.: disceptatio iuris, Cic.; Quint.

disceptātor -ōris, m. (discepto), *an arbitrator, judge of a controversy*: domesticus, Cic.; iuris, Cic.; Caes., Liv.

disceptātrix -trīcis, f. (disceptator), *a female arbitrator*: Cic.

discepto -are (dis/capto). LIT., *to take apart*; hence *to discuss*, esp. before an arbitrator. (**1**) *to decide, settle, determine*: controversias, Cic.; inter populum et regem, Liv. (**2**) *to dispute, debate, discuss*: de controversiis apud se potius quam inter se armis, Caes.; de iure publico armis, Cic.; verbis de iure, Liv.

discerno -cernĕre -crēvi -crētum.

LIT., *to sever, separate*: mons qui fines eorum discerneret, Sall.; improbos a nobis, Cic.; duae urbes magno inter se maris terrarumque spatio discretae, Liv.; discretae sedes piorum, *set apart*, Hor.

TRANSF., *to distinguish, discern*: alba et atra discernere non posse, Cic.; animus discernit, quid sit eiusdem generis, quid alterius, Cic.; Caes., Hor., Liv.

discerpo -cerpĕre -cerpsi -cerptum (dis/carpo), *to pluck to pieces, dismember*.

LIT., membra gruis, Hor.; animus nec dividi nec discerpi potest, Cic.

TRANSF., quae complecti tota nequeunt, haec facilius divulsa et quasi discerpta contrectant, *pulled apart*, Cic.; me infestis dictis, *pull to pieces*, Cat.

discessĭo -ōnis, f. (discedo). (**1**) *a going separate ways, separation*; of married people: Ter.; as polit. t. t., *voting, a division in the senate*: senatus consultum facere per discessionem; facta est discessio in sententiam alicuius, Cic. (**2**) *a going away, departure*: Tac.

discessus -ūs, m. (discedo). (**1**) *a parting, separation*: caeli, Cic. (**2**) *a departure, going away*: ab urbe, Cic.; e vita, Cic.; esp. as milit. t. t., *marching off*: Caes.; ab Dyrrhachio discessus exercituum, Cic.; also as euphem., *banishment*: Cic.

discidium -i, n. (discindo), *a tearing apart*.

LIT., nubis, Lucr.; partibus eius discidium parere, Lucr.

TRANSF., (**1**) *separation, division, parting*: corporis atque animai, Lucr.; adfinitatum, Cic.; esp. of parting between man and woman, *divorce*, etc.: coniugis miserae, Cic. L.; Ter., Ov., Tac. (**2**) *separation in feelings, disagreement*: belli discidio, Cic.; deorum odia, discidia, discordiae, Cic.; Liv., Tac.

discīdo -ĕre (dis/caedo), *to cut in pieces*: Lucr.

discindo -scindĕre -scĭdi -scissum (dis/scindo), *to cleave asunder, split*: cotem novaculā, Cic.; tunicam, Cic. TRANSF., amicitias, Cic.

discingo -cingĕre -cinxi -cinctum, *to take off the girdle, ungird*: tunicam, Hor.; districtis gladiis discinctos destituit, Liv.; Afros, *to strip*, Juv.

¶ Hence partic. **discinctus** -a -um, *ungirt*; hence *at ease, careless*: otia, Ov.; also *dissolute*: nepos, Hor.

disciplīna (discĭpŭlīna: Pl.) -ae, f. (discipulus), *instruction, teaching*.

(**1**) through study, as at school. LIT., litterae reliquaeque res quarum est disciplina, Cic.; novum aliquem alicui in disciplinam tradere, Cic.; ab aliquo disciplinam accipere,

Cic.; with. genit.: disciplina maiorum, *the traditional system*, Cic.; virtutis, *instruction in*, Cic. TRANSF., *that which is taught, learning, body of knowledge, science*; in gen.: bellica, Cic.; navalis, Cic.; habere quasdam etiam domesticas disciplinas, Cic.; iuris civilis, Cic. Esp.: **a**, *a philosophical school, a system*: philosophiae disciplina, Cic.: **b**, *a rhetorical school* or *system*: Hermagorae, Cic.

(2) in a wider sense, *training, education*. LIT., disciplina puerilis, *of boys*, Cic.; disciplina familiae, *of slaves*; gravis et constans, Cic.; esp. *military training*: militaris, Liv.; militiae, Cic.; Caes., Tac. TRANSF., *the result of training, discipline, ordered way of life*: disciplinae sanctitas, Liv.; certa vivendi disciplina, Cic.; reipublicae, Cic.; disciplinam dare, Cic.; o morem praeclarum disciplinamque quam a maioribus accepimus, Cic.

discĭpŭla -ae, f. (discipulus), *a female pupil*: Pl., Hor.

discĭpŭlus -i, m. (disco), *a pupil, apprentice*: Pl., Cic.

disclūdo -clūdĕre -clūsi -clūsum (dis/claudo), *to shut up apart, to separate, divide*: Nerea ponto, Verg.; tigna, *keep at the proper distance*, Caes.; mons qui Arvernos ab Helviis discludit, Caes.; morsūs roboris, *to loosen*, Verg.

disco discĕre dĭdĭci (cf. διδάσκω), *to learn, get to know.*

(1) by study, as at school: litteras Graecas, Cic.; ius civile aut rem militarem, Cic.; ab eo Stoico dialecticam didicerat, Cic.; apud aliquem litteras, Cic.; in castris per laborem usum militiae, Sall.; causam, *the facts of the case*, Cic.; with infin.: saltare, Cic.; Latine loqui, Sall.; quinqueremes gubernare didicisse, Cic.; disco fidibus, *learn to play on the lyre*, Cic.; absol.: valent pueri, studiose discunt, diligenter docentur, Cic.

(2) in gen., *to receive information, find out*: didici ex tuis litteris te omnibus in rebus habuisse rationem, Cic. L.; plures discent quem ad modum haec fiant quam quem ad modum huc resistatur, Cic.

(3) *to become acquainted with, learn to recognize*: haec certis signis, Verg.; me peritus discet Hiber Rhodanique potor, Hor.

discŏlor -ōris, adj. (color). (1) *of different colours*: miles, *black and white* (of the men at draughts), Ov. (2) *different from*. LIT., *in colour*: Cic., Verg., Ov. TRANSF., in gen.: matrona meretrici dispar atque discolor, Hor.

discondūco -ĕre, *to be unprofitable*: Pl.

disconvĕnĭo -ire, *to disagree, not to harmonize*: vitae ordine toto, Hor.; impers.: eo disconvenit inter meque et te, Hor.

discordābĭlis -e (discordo), *disagreeing*: Pl.

discordĭa -ae, f. (discors), *dissension, disagreement, discord*: haec discordia non rerum sed verborum, Cic.; Pl., Verg.; esp. of troops, *mutiny, sedition*: Tac.

discordĭōsus -a -um (discordia), *full of discord, mutinous*: vulgus seditiosum atque discordiosum fuit, Sall.

discordo -are (discors), *to be at discord, to disagree*: cum Cheruscis, Tac.; inter se dissidere atque discordare, Cic.; animus a se dissidens secumque discordans, Cic.; of

soldiers, *to be mutinous*: Tac. TRANSF., *to be opposed to, differ from*: quantum discordet parum avaro, Hor.

discors -cordis (dis/cor), *disagreeing, inharmonious, discordant*: civitas secum ipsa discors, Liv.; Cic., Tac.; fig., of inanimate objects: venti, Verg.; bella, Ov. TRANSF., *opposed, different*: tam discordia inter se responsa, Liv.; Verg.

discrĕpantĭa -ae, f. (discrepo), *disagreement, difference*: scripti et voluntatis, Cic.

discrĕpātĭo -ōnis, f. (discrepo), *disagreement, disunion*: inter consules, Liv.

discrĕpĭto -are (freq. of discrepo), *to be quite unlike*: Lucr.

discrĕpo -are -ui, *to differ in sound, to be out of time, to be discordant.*

LIT., in fidibus aut in tibiis, Cic.

TRANSF., *to disagree, be different, be unlike*: facta cum dictis discrepare, Cic.; ab aequitate, Cic.; inter se, Cic.; with dat.: quantum simplex hilarique nepoti discrepet, Hor. Esp. res discrepat, or impers., discrepat. (1) *there is a disagreement, people are not agreed*: discrepat inter scriptores, Liv.; nec discrepat quin dictator fuerit, Liv. (2) with acc. and infin., *it is inconsistent that*: Lucr.

discrībo -scrībĕre -scripsi -scriptum, *to divide up by writing*; hence of a whole or total, *to mark out, arrange, classify, define*; of items, *to allot, fix, appoint*: rationem totius belli, Cic.; ius civile generatim in ordines aetatesque, Cic.; officia, Cic.; civitatibus pro numero militum pecuniarum summas, Cic.; suum cuique munus, Cic.; duodena in singulos homines iugera, Cic.

¶ Hence partic. (with compar.) **discriptus** -a -um, *classified, arranged*: ordo verborum, Cic., Hor.

¶ Adv. **discriptē**: Cic.

discrīmen -ĭnis, n. (discerno), *that which divides.*

LIT., (1) *the dividing line*: cum pertenui discrimine (duo maria) separarentur, Cic.; Verg., Ov. (2) *space between, interval*: aequo discrimine, Lucr.

TRANSF., (1) *distinction, difference*: delectu omni et discrimine remoto, Cic.; nullo discrimine, Verg.; Liv., Tac.; with genit., *distinction between*: septem discrimina vocum (of the lyre with seven strings), Verg.; Liv. (2) *turning-point, critical moment*: ea res nunc in discrimine versatur utrum ... an, Cic.; in discrimen adductum esse, Cic.; belli, Liv.; hence *crisis, hazard, danger*: ad ipsum discrimen eius temporis, Cic.; res esse in summo discrimine, Caes.; in tanto discrimine periculi, Liv.; per tot discrimina rerum, Verg.

discrīmino -are (discrimen), *to separate, sunder, divide*: Etruriam discriminat Cassia, Cic.; vigiliarum somnique nec die nec nocte discriminata tempora, Liv.

discriptĭo -ōnis, f. (discribo), *a division by means of writing*; hence *an arrangement, definition, distribution*: nominis brevis et aperta, Cic.; expetendarum fugiendarumque rerum, Cic.; possessionum, Cic.; magistratuum, civitatis, Cic.

discrŭcĭo -are, *to torture by pulling apart*: discruciatos necare, Cic.; fig., of mental anguish, refl. or pass., *to torment oneself,* *make oneself miserable*: Pl., Ter., Cic.; with acc. and infin., *with the thought that*: Pl., Cic. L.

discumbo -cumbĕre -cŭbŭi -cŭbitum, *to lie down separately*. (1) *to recline at table*: discubuimus omnes praeter illam, Cic. L.; Lucr.; impers. pass.: Cic., Verg. (2) *to go to bed*: cenati discubuerunt ibidem, Cic.

discŭpĭo -cŭpĕre (colloq.), *to long to* do something; with infin.: Pl., Cat.

discurro -currĕre -cŭcurri and -curri -cursum, *to run in different directions, run about, run to and fro*.

    LIT., in muris, Caes.; circa deum delubra, Liv.; ad arma, Liv.; impers. pass.: totā discurritur urbe, Verg.

    TRANSF., of things: (Nilus) diversa ruens septem discurrit in ora, Verg.; mens discurrit utroque, Ov.

discursus -ūs, m. (discurro), *a running up and down, a running about, running to and fro*: militum, Liv.; lupi, Ov.

discus -i, m. (δίσκος), *a quoit*: discum audire quam philosophum malle, Cic.; Hor., Ov.

discŭtĭo -cŭtĕre -cussi -cussum (dis/quatio), *to strike asunder, to shatter*.

    LIT., arietibus aliquantum muri, Liv.

    TRANSF., *to disperse, scatter*; of physical objects: nubem, Ov.; umbras, Verg.; coetūs, Liv.; fig., of abstr. things, *to break up*: terrorem animi tenebrasque, Lucr.; discussa est caligo, Cic.; eorum advocationem manibus, ferro, lapidibus, Cic.

dĭsertus -a -um, adj. (with compar. and superl.) (dissero), *eloquent, expressive*. (1) of a speaker: homo, Cic.; disertissimus orator, Cic.; Ov. (2) of speech: oratio, historia, Cic.; Ov., Quint.

    ¶ Adv. (with compar. and superl.) **dĭsertē**, *clearly, distinctly, eloquently*: Pl., Cic., Liv., Quint.

    ¶ Adv. **dĭsertim**: Pl.

dĭsĭcĭo dĭsĭcĕre disiēci disiectum (dis/iacio), *to throw in different directions, to cast asunder*.

    LIT., in gen.: disiecti membra poetae, Hor.; disiecta comas, *with dishevelled hair*, Ov. Esp. (1) of buildings, etc., *to throw down, lay in ruins*: aedificia, Caes.; disiecta tempestate statua, Liv. (2) of military formations, *to break up, disperse*: phalangem, Caes.; classem, Liv.; Sall.

    TRANSF., of abstr. things, *to break up, frustrate*: consilia ducis, Liv.; Verg.

disiecto -are (freq. of disicio), *to toss about*: Lucr.

¹**disiectus** -a -um, partic. from disicio; q.v.

²**disiectus** -ūs, m. (disicio), *a scattering, dispersing*: Lucr.

disiunctio -ōnis, f. (disiungo), *separation*. LIT., meorum, Cic. TRANSF., in gen., *estrangement*: animorum, Cic.; esp. in logic, *a disjunctive proposition*: Cic.

disiungo (dīiungo) -iungĕre -iunxi -iunctum, *to unbind, loosen, separate*.

    LIT., (1) *to unyoke*: iumenta, Cic.; Hor., Ov. (2) in gen., *to separate, sunder, remove*: intervallo locorum et tempore disiuncti sumus, Cic.; Italis disiungimur oris, Verg.

    TRANSF., *to separate* otherwise than physically. (1) in sympathy, etc.: Pompeium a Caesaris amicitia, Cic.; Liv. (2) logically, *to distinguish*: insaniam a furore, Cic.

¶ Hence partic. (with compar. and superl.) **disiunctus** -a -um, *separated, apart, distant*. LIT., Aetolia procul a barbaris gentibus, Cic. TRANSF., in gen., *remote*, otherwise than physically: homines, Graeci longe a nostrorum hominum gravitate disiuncti, Cic.; esp. (1) of speech, *disconnected*: Cic.; so of a speaker: Tac. (2) as logic. t. t., *disjunctive*: Cic.

¶ Compar. adv. **disiunctius**, *rather in disjunctive fashion*: Cic.

dispālesco -ere (dispālor), *to be divulged*: Pl.

dispālor -ari, dep. *to wander about, to stray*: Nep.

dispando -pandĕre -pandi -pansum or -pessum, *to expand, extend, stretch out*: Pl., Lucr., Suet.

dispār -păris, *unlike, different, dissimilar, unequal*: proelium, Caes.; fortuna, Cic.; tempora, Cic.; with dat.: illa oratio huic dispar, Cic.; Hor.; with genit.: quidquam dispar sui atque dissimile, Cic.

dispărĭlis -e, *unlike, dissimilar, different, unequal*: disparilis aspiratio terrarum, Cic.

dispăro -are, *to separate, part, divide*: seniores a iunioribus divisit eosque disparavit, Cic.; Pl., Caes.

    ¶ Hence n. of partic. as subst. **dispărātum** -i, rhet. t. t., *the contradictory proposition*; e.g.: sapere, non sapere, Cic.

dispartio=dispertio; q.v.

dispello -pellĕre -pŭli -pulsum, *to drive in different directions, to scatter*: pecudes, Cic.; umbras, Verg. TRANSF., ab animo tamquam ab oculis caliginem, Cic.

dispendĭum -i, n. (dispendo), *expenditure, expense, loss*: sine dispendio, Pl., Ter.; plus dispendi faciant. TRANSF., dispendia morae, *loss of time*, Verg.

dispendo -ĕre, *to weigh out*: Varr.

dispenno=dispando; q.v.: Pl.

dispensātĭo -ōnis, f. (dispenso), *weighing out*. LIT., Liv. TRANSF., (1) *management, administration*: aerarii, Cic.; annonae, Liv. (2) *the office of a dispensator*: regia, *the office of treasurer to a king*, Cic.

dispensātor -ōris, m. (dispenso), *a steward, bailiff, treasurer*: Juv., Suet.

dispenso -are (freq. of dispendo), *to weigh out or pay out*.

    LIT., of money or stores: Pl., Cic. L.

    TRANSF., (1) *to distribute*: oscula per natos, Ov.; laetitiam inter impotentes populi animos, Liv. (2) *to arrange*: inventa non solum ordine, sed etiam momento quodam atque iudicio, Cic.; annum intercalariis mensibus interponendis dispensavit, Liv.

dispercŭtĭo -cŭtĕre, *to dash out in all directions*: cerebrum, Pl.

disperdo -dĕre -dĭdi -dĭtum, *to squander*. LIT., rem, Pl.; possessiones, Cic. TRANSF. *to ruin, spoil*: carmen, Verg.

dispĕrĕo -ire -ii, *to perish utterly, to be squandered, ruined*: fundus disperit, Cic.; in exclamations: dispeream si (or nisi), *may I perish if* (or *unless*), Cat., Hor., Prop.

dispergo -spergĕre -spersi -spersum (dis/spargo), *to scatter, disperse*. LIT., of things: nubes dispergunt venti, Lucr.; Cic.; also of persons, esp. of troops: Caes., Cic., Liv. TRANSF., of abstr. things: rumores, Tac.; Cic., Verg.

¶ Hence adv. from perf. partic. **dispersē**, *dispersedly, here and there*: Cic.

dispertĭo -ire, and dep. **dispertior** -iri (dis/partio), *to separate, divide, distribute.* Lit., pecuniam iudicibus, Cic.; exercitum per oppida, Liv.; Sall. Transf., tempora voluptatis laborisque, Cic.; administrationem inter se, Liv.

dispĭcĭo -spĭcĕre -spexi -spectum (dis/specio), *to see clearly,* esp. by an effort.
Lit., of physical sight. (1) intransit.: catuli qui iam dispecturi sint, *about to open their eyes,* Cic. (2) transit., *to make out:* rem, Lucr.; dispecta Thule, Tac.
Transf., mentally. (1) *to discern, perceive:* verum, Cic.; Romanus libertatem ex diutina servitute dispiciens, Cic.; si dispicere quid coepero, Cic. (2) *to reflect upon, consider:* res Romanas, Cic. L.

displĭcĕo -ēre (dis/placeo), *to displease;* with person or thing as subject, or infin., or infin. clause: Cic.; the person displeased in dat., if expressed; esp. in phrase: displicere sibi, *to be dissatisfied with oneself, to be melancholy, out of spirits,* Cic.

displōdo -plōdĕre -plōsi -plōsum (dis/plaudo), *to burst noisily:* Lucr., Hor.

dispōno -pōnĕre -pŏsŭi -pŏsĭtum (dis/pono), *to put in different places, to distribute.*
Lit., signa ad omnes columnas, omnibus etiam intercolumniis, in silva denique disposita sub divo, Cic.; pocula Bacchi, Ov.; bene dispositae comae, Ov.; milit. t. t., *to station at intervals:* portis stationes, Liv.; praesidia ad ripas, Caes.
Transf., *to arrange* abstr. things, *put in order:* verba ita, ut pictores varietatem colorum, Cic.; Homeri libros antea confusos, Cic.; imperii curas, Tac.; Liv., Quint.
¶ Hence partic. **dispŏsĭtus** -a -um, *arranged, orderly:* studia ad honorem disposita, Cic.
¶ Adv. **dispŏsĭtē**, *in proper order, methodically:* Cic., Quint.

dispŏsĭtĭo -ōnis, f. (dispono), *a regular arrangement* or *order in a speech:* Cic., Quint.

dispŏsĭtū abl. sing. from dispositus, m. (dispono), *in* or *by arranging:* Tac.

dispŏsĭtūra -ae, f. (dispono), *arrangement, order:* Lucr.

dispudet -ēre -uit, *it is a great shame:* Pl., Ter.

dispŭtātĭo -ōnis, f. (disputo), *an arguing, debate:* hāc in utramque partem disputatione habitā, Cic.; Caes., Quint.

dispŭtātor -ōris, m. (disputo), *a debater, disputant:* Cic.

dispŭto -are. Lit., *to reckon up:* rationem, Pl. Transf., *to debate, discuss, argue:* aliquid, Pl., Cic.; de aliqua re, Caes., Cic.; pro omnibus et contra omnia, Cic.; in utramque partem, *for and against,* Cic.; ego enim quid desiderem, non quid viderim disputo, Cic.

disquīro -ĕre (dis/quaero), *to inquire into, investigate:* Hor.

disquīsĭtĭo -ōnis, f. (disquiro), *an inquiry, investigation:* Cic., Liv., Tac.

dissaepĭo -saepire -saepsi -saeptum, *to hedge off, separate, divide:* aliquid tenui muro, Cic.; Ov., Lucr.
¶ N. of perf. partic. as subst. **dissaeptum** -i, *a barrier, partition:* Lucr.

dissāvĭor -ari, dep. (suavior), *to kiss violently:* ap. Cic. L.

dissĕco -sĕcare -sĕcui -sectum, *to cut up:* Plin., Suet.

dissēmĭno -are, *to spread abroad, disseminate:* sermonem, Cic.; malum, Cic.

dissensĭo -ōnis, f. (dissentio), *difference in feeling* or *opinion; disagreement, variance.*
Lit., between persons: inter homines de iure, Cic.; dissensio ac discidium, Cic.; dissensio civilis, Caes.
Transf., between things, *conflict, opposition:* utilium cum honestis, Cic.

dissensus -ūs, m. (dissentio), *disunion, disagreement:* Verg.

dissentānĕus -a -um (dissentio), *disagreeing, different* (opp. consentaneus): alicui rei, Cic.

dissentĭo -sentire -sensi -sensum, *to be of different feeling* or *opinion, not to agree.*
Lit., of persons: acerrime dissentientes cives, Cic.; ab aliquo, Caes., Cic.; de aliqua re, Cic.; cum aliquo, Cic., Sen.; inter se, Cic.; with dat.: condicionibus foedis, Hor.
Transf., of things, *to be opposed, different:* a more, Cic.; quid ipsum a se dissentiat, Cic.

dissēpĭo, *see* dissaepio.

dissĕrēnat -are, impers. (dis/serenus), *it is clearing up all round,* of the weather: Liv., Plin.

¹**dissĕro** -sĕrĕre -sēvi -sĭtum, *to scatter seed, sow:* Plin. Transf., *to spread:* Lucr., Caes.

²**dissĕro** -sĕrĕre -sĕrŭi -sertum, *to set in order.* Hence *to examine, treat of, discuss;* with de: quae Socrates supremo vitae die de immortalitate animorum disseruisset, Cic.; with acc. of amount of discussion: nihil de ea rē, Tac.; Cic.; with acc. of matter of discussion: bona libertatis, Tac.; Liv. With acc. and infin.: Cic.; with indir. quest.: Sall., Quint.

disserpo -ĕre, *to creep about, spread:* late disserpunt tremores, Lucr.

dissertĭo -ōnis, f. (sero), *a severance:* iuris humani, Liv.

disserto -are (freq. of ²dissero), *to treat of, discuss, argue:* pacis bona, Tac.

dissĭdĕo -sĭdēre -sēdi -sessum (dis/sedeo), *to sit apart, to be distant, to be separated.*
Lit., (1) of places: quantum Hypanis Veneto dissidet Eridano, Prop.; Verg. (2) of clothes: si toga dissidet impar, *sits unevenly,* Hor.
Transf., *not to agree.* (1) of persons, *to disagree, dissent, be of a different opinion:* inter se, Cic.; ab aliquo, Cic., Ov.; cum aliquo, Cic.; de aliqua, Cic. (2) of things, *to b opposed, contrary:* scriptum a sententia dissidet, Cic.; cupiditates inter se dissident et discordant, Cic.; with cum : Cic.; with dat. : Hor.

dissīdo -sīdĕre -sēdi, *to fall apart, disagree:* a Pompeio, Cic. L.; Suet., Tac.

dissignātĭo -ōnis, f. (dissigno), *arrangement:* operis, Cic.

dissignātor -ōris, m. (dissigno), *one that arranges, a supervisor:* Pl., Hor., Sen.

dissigno -are, *to arrange, regulate, manage:* Pl., Cic., Hor.

dissĭlĭo -silire -sĭlŭi (dis/salio), *to leap apart.*
Lit., haec loca dissiluisse ferunt, Verg.; dissilit omne solum, Ov.
Transf., gratia sic fratrum geminorum dissiluit, *was broken up,* Hor.

dissimilis   distendo

dissĭmĭlis -e, adj. (with superl. dissimillimus), *unlike, dissimilar*; with genit.: verum tamen fuit tum sui dissimilis, Cic.; Hor., Ov.; with dat.: Cic., Verg., Hor.; with inter se: Lucr., Cic., Quint.; with inter se and the genit.: qui sunt et inter se dissimiles et aliorum, Cic.; with atque (ac): Lucr., Cic.; absol.: naturae dissimiles, Cic.

¶ Adv. **dissĭmĭlĭtĕr**, *differently, in a different manner*: Cic., Sall., Liv.

dissĭmĭlĭtūdo -ĭnis, f. (dissimilis), *unlikeness, difference*: locorum, Cic.; habet ab illis rebus dissimilitudinem, Cic.; tanta inter oratores bonos dissimilitudo, Cic.

dissĭmŭlantĕr, adv. from dissimulo; q.v.

dissĭmŭlantia -ae, f. (dissimulo), *a dissembling*: Cic.

dissĭmŭlātĭo -ōnis, f. (dissimulo), *a concealing, dissembling*: Cic., Tac.; esp. *of irony* (in the Socratic sense): Cic.

dissĭmŭlātor -ōris, m. (dissimulo), *a dissembler, concealer*: opis propriae, Hor.; Tac.; as adj.: Sall.

dissĭmŭlo -are, *to conceal, to pretend that things are not as they are.*

(**1**) *to dissemble, disguise, keep secret*: aliquid silentio, Cic.; with acc. and infin.: Pl., Cic. L., Ov.; with indir. quest.: Verg., Quint.; non dissimulare, followed by quin, Cic.; pass. with middle force: dissimulata deam, *concealing her divinity*, Ov. Absol., *to dissemble*: non dissimulat, Cic.; Pl., Verg.

(**2**) *to ignore, leave unnoticed*: Liv., Tac.

¶ Adv. from pres. partic. **dissĭmŭlantĕr**, *in a dissembling manner*: verba non aperte sed dissimulanter conclusa, Cic.; Liv., Ov.

dissĭpābĭlis -e (dissipo), *that can be scattered*: ignis et aër, Cic.

dissĭpātĭo -ōnis, f. (dissipo), *scattering*: civium, Cic.; praedae, Cic.; as rhet. t. t.: Cic.

dissĭpo or **dissŭpo** -are, *to scatter, disperse, spread abroad.*

LIT., in gen.: membra fratris, Cic.; aliud alio, Cic.; esp. as milit. t. t., *to break up, rout*: hostes, Caes., Cic. L.; in fugam, Liv.; dissipata fuga, Liv.; fig.: curas, Hor.

TRANSF., (**1**) *to break up, destroy, squander*: possessiones, Cic., Tac.; patrimonium, Cic.; reliquias reipublicae, Cic. (**2**) *to spread, scatter*: famam, Cic.; bellum, Liv.

¶ Hence partic. **dissĭpātus** -a -um: oratio, *disconnected*, Cic.

dissĭtus, partic. from ¹dissero; q.v.

dissŏcĭābĭlis -e (dissocio). (**1**) act., *that which separates*: oceanus, Hor. (**2**) pass., *that cannot be united*: res, Tac.

dissŏcĭātĭo -ōnis, f. (dissocio), *a separation, parting*: spiritus corporisque, Tac.

dissŏcĭo -are, *to separate, sever, divide.* LIT., physically: partes, Lucr.; ni (montes) dissocientur opacā valle, Hor.

TRANSF., in feeling, *to estrange*: morum dissimilitudo dissociat amicitias, Cic.; disertos a doctis, Cic.; Tac.

dissŏlūbĭlis -e (dissolvo), *dissoluble, separable*: mortale omne animal et dissolubile et dividuum sit necesse est, Cic.

dissŏlūtĭo -ōnis, f. (dissolvo), *breaking up, dissolution, destruction.*

LIT. naturae, *death*, Cic.; navigii, *shipwreck*, Tac.

TRANSF., (**1**) *destruction, abolition*: legum, iudiciorum, Cic. (**2**) *refutation*: criminum, Cic. (**3**) *want of energy, weakness*: remissio animi ac dissolutio, Cic. L., Sen. (**4**) rhet. t. t., *want of connexion*: Cic.

dissŏlūtus -a -um, partic. from dissolvo; q.v.

dissolvo -solvĕre -solvi -sŏlūtum, *to loosen, break up.*

LIT., (**1**) of things: nodos, Lucr.; aes, glaciem, *to melt*, Lucr.; animam, *to die*, Lucr., Cic. (**2**) of persons, *to untie, release*: Pl.

TRANSF., (**1**) in gen., *to break up, destroy*: societatem, amicitiam, Cic.; leges, Cic.; rempublicam, Liv. (**2**) *to refute*: criminationem, Cic.; Tac. (**3**) *to pay, discharge* a debt: aes alienum, Cic.; pecuniam publicam civitati, Cic.; Caes. (**4**) *to release* a person from difficulties: Pl., Ter. (**5**) *to unravel, explain* a difficulty: poterit ratio dissolvere causam, Lucr.; Cic.

¶ Hence partic. (with compar. and superl.) **dissŏlūtus** -a -um. LIT., *loose*: navigium, *leaky*, Cic. TRANSF., (**1**) of style, *disconnected*: Cic., Quint. (**2**) *wanting in energy, lax*: Cic. (**3**) *profligate, dissolute*: dissolutissimus hominum, Cic.; Tac.

¶ Adv. **dissŏlūtē**. (**1**) *disconnectedly, loosely*: dissolute dicere, *without connecting particles*, Cic. (**2**) *carelessly, negligently, without energy*: minus severe quam decuit, non tamen omnino dissolute, Cic.

dissŏnus -a -um, *discordant, inharmonious, dissonant.* LIT., clamores, Liv. TRANSF., *different, disagreeing*: dissonae gentes sermone moribusque, Liv.; Quint.

dissors -sortis, *having a different lot or fate*: ab omni milite dissors gloria, *not shared with*, Ov.

dissuādĕo -suādēre -suāsi -suāsum, *to advise against, oppose by argument*: legem agrariam, Cic.; de capitivis, Cic.; with acc. and infin.: Cic., Quint. Absol.: dissuasimus nos, *I spoke against it*, Cic.

dissuāsĭo -ōnis, f. (dissuadeo), *advising to the contrary, speaking against*: rogationis eius, Cic.; Sen.

dissuāsor -ōris, m. (dissuadeo), *one who advises to the contrary, one who speaks against*: rogationis, Cic.; legis agrariae, Liv.

dissuāvĭor=disuavior; q.v.

dissulto -are (freq. of dissilio), *to leap apart, burst asunder*: nec fulmine tanti dissultant crepitus, Verg.; dissultant ripae, Verg.

dissŭo -sŭĕre -sŭi -sūtum, *to unstitch, undo.* LIT., sinum, Ov. TRANSF., tales amicitiae dissuendae magis quam discindendae, Cic.

distaedet -ēre, *causes boredom* or *disgust to*: me loqui, Ter.; Pl.

distantĭa -ae, f. (disto), *distance*; hence *difference, diversity*: morum studiorumque, Cic.; Quint.

distendo (**distenno**) -tendĕre -tendi -tentum, *to stretch apart, expand, extend.*

LIT., in gen.: aciem, Caes.; bracchia, Ov.; Liv.; esp. *to fill full, distend*: ubera cytiso, Verg.; horrea plena spicis, Tib.

TRANSF., *to distract, perplex*: distendit ea res animos Samnitium, Liv.; in duo bella curas hominum, Liv.

¶ Hence partic. (with compar.: Hor.) **distentus** -a -um, *distended, full*: ubera, Hor.; Ov., Suet.

distermĭno -are, *to separate by a boundary, divide*: quod (flumen) Dahas Ariosque disterminat, Tac.; fig.: Lucr.

distichon distichi, n. (δίστιχον), *a poem of two lines, a distich*: Mart., Suet.

distinctĭo -ōnis, f. (distinguo), *a distinction*. In gen., (1) *a distinction that exists, a difference*: causarum distinctio et dissimilitudo, Cic.; solis lunae siderumque omnium, Cic. (2) *the finding of a difference, the act of distinguishing, discriminating*: facilis est distinctio ingenui et inliberalis ioci, Cic.; lex est iustorum iniustorumque distinctio, Cic. Esp. as rhet. t. t. (1) *a division* in a speech: Cic. (2) *a pause, stop*: Cic., Quint. (3) *a distinguishing between the same word used in different ways*, or *between ideas nearly alike*: Cic., Quint.

¹**distinctus** -a -um, partic. from distinguo; q.v.

²**distinctus** -ūs, m. (distinguo), *difference, distinction*: Tac.

distĭnĕo -tĭnēre -tĭnŭi -tentum (dis/teneo), *to hold asunder, keep apart, separate*. LIT., tigna binis utrimque fibulis distinebantur, Caes.; Ov.; milit. t. t., *to keep from uniting*: Volscos, Liv.; Caes. TRANSF., (1) *to divide in feeling*, etc.: duae factiones senatum distinebant, Liv. (2) *to prevent the concentration of one's thoughts, to distract*: maximis occupationibus distineri, Cic. L.; Liv., Tac. (3) *to keep away, prevent*: victoriam, Caes.; pacem, Liv. ¶ Hence partic. **distentus** -a -um, *distracted, occupied*: Cic. L., Tac.

distinguo -stinguĕre -stinxi -stinctum (from dis and stinguo, connected with στίζω), *to mark off*. Hence *to distinguish, divide*. LIT., (1) *to divide up*: onus inclusum numero distinxit eodem, Ov. (2) *to mark, set off* by distinctive ornament, colouring, etc.: Hor., Ov. TRANSF., (1) *to separate, distinguish*: distinguere voces in partes, Cic.; vera a falsis, Cic.; quid inter naturam et rationem intersit non distinguitur, Cic.; vero falsum, Hor.; fortes ignavosque, Tac.; as grammat. t. t., *to punctuate*, Cic., Quint. (2) *to set off, decorate, adorn*: oratio distinguitur atque illustratur aliquā re, Cic.; historiam varietate locorum, Cic.; Liv. ¶ Hence partic. (with compar.) **distinctus** -a -um. (1) *separate, distinct*: Cic.; of a speaker, *clear*: Cic. (2) *set off, diversified, adorned*: pocula gemmis clarissimis, Cic.; caelum astris, Cic.; Ov. ¶ Adv. (with compar.: Plin. L.) **distinctē**, *clearly, distinctly*: Cic.

disto -are (dis/sto), *to be apart, separate, distant*; usually with inter se or ab. (1) of space: quae turres pedes LXXX inter se distarent, Caes.; Cic., Liv., Ov. (2) of time: quantum distet ab Inacho Codrus, Hor. TRANSF., *to differ, be distinct*: Cic., Quint.; scurrae (dat.), Hor.; impers., distat, *there is a difference*, Hor.

distorquĕo -torquēre -torsi -tortum, *to twist apart, distort*: ora cachinno, Ov.; oculos, Hor. TRANSF., *to torture*: Sen., Suet. ¶ Hence partic. (with compar. and superl.) **distortus** -a -um, *distorted, deformed*. LIT., crura, Hor.; of persons: distortus Gallus,

Cic. TRANSF., of discourse, *perverse*: nullum (genus enuntiandi) distortius, Cic.

distortĭo -ōnis, f. (distorqueo), *distortion*: membrorum, Cic.

distractĭo -ōnis, f. (distraho), *a pulling apart*; hence (1) *separation*: humanorum animorum, Cic.; Pl., Sen. (2) *disunion*: nulla nobis societas cum tyrannis et potius summa distractio est, Cic.

distrăho -trăhĕre -traxi -tractum, *to pull apart* or *pull to pieces*. LIT., in gen.: vallum, Liv.; corpus, Cic.; equis distrahi, Verg.; acies distrahitur, *is divided*, Caes.; fuga distrahit aliquos, Cic.; esp.: a, *to sell up property*: agros, Tac.; b, grammat. t. t., *to leave a hiatus in a verse*: voces, Cic. TRANSF., (1) *to break up, dissolve*: amorem, Ter.; omnem societatem civitatis, Cic.; concilium Boeotorum, Liv.; hanc rem, Caes.; controversias, *to settle*, Cic. (2) *to draw away, estrange*: aliquem a complexu suorum, Cic.; ab aliquo, Cic. (3) *to distract*: oratoris industriam in plura studia, Cic.; Tac.

distribŭo -ŭĕre -ŭi -ūtum, *to distribute, divide*. LIT., argentum, Ter.; pecunias exercitui, Caes. TRANSF., populum in quinque classes, Cic.; causam in crimen et in audaciam, Cic. ¶ Adv. from partic. **distribūtē**, *methodically, with logical arrangement*: scribere, Cic.

distribūtĭo -ōnis, f. (distribuo), *a division, distribution*: criminum, Cic.

distringo -stringĕre -strinxi -strictum, *to draw apart, stretch out*. LIT., radiis rotarum districti pendent, Verg. TRANSF., *to engage at different points, divert, occupy*: in Africam mittere ad distringendos Romanos, Liv. ¶ Hence partic. (with compar.) **districtus** -a -um, *busy, occupied, engaged*: contentione ancipiti, Cic.

distrunco -are, *to hack apart*: Pl.

disturbātĭo -ōnis, f. (disturbo), *destruction*: Corinthi, Cic.

disturbo -are, *to drive apart in confusion*. LIT., contionem gladiis, Cic. TRANSF., (1) *to destroy, raze to the ground*: domum meam, Cic.; aedes, Lucr.; Caes. (2) *to bring to naught, frustrate, ruin*: nuptias, Ter.; societatem, Cic.; legem, Cic.

dītesco -ĕre (dīs, dītis), *to become rich*: Lucr., Hor.

dīthўrambĭcus -a -um (διθυραμβικός), *dithyrambic*: poëma, Cic.

dīthўrambus -i, m. (διθύραμβος), *a dithyrambic poem* (originally in honour of Bacchus): Cic., Hor.

dītĭo, better **dĭcĭo**; q.v.

dītĭor, dītissĭmus, see dis.

dīto -are (dīs, dītis), *to enrich, make wealthy*: praemiis belli socios, Liv.; militem ex hostibus, Liv.; pass., ditari as middle, *to become rich*: Liv. TRANSF., sermonem patrium, Hor.

dĭū, adv. (dies). (1) *by day*: diu noctuque, Tac.; Pl., Sall., Hor. (2) a, *for a long time*: tam diu, iam diu, Cic.; diu multumque, Cic.; Pl., Hor., etc.: b, *a long time ago*: iam diu, Pl., Ter., Cic. L. ¶ Compar. **dĭūtĭus**. (1) *longer*: Cic., Pl., Caes. (2) *too long*: Caes., Sall., Tac. ¶ Superl. **dĭūtissĭmē**: Caes., Cic.

dǐurnus -a -um (dius, dies), *belonging to a day* or *lasting for a day*: lumen, Lucr.; itinera, Caes.; opus, *a day's work*, Cic.; cibus, *rations*, Liv.

¶ N. as subst. **dǐurnum** -i. (1) *a journal, account-book*: Juv.; in plur. diurna, see acta. (2) *a daily allowance*: Sen., Suet.

dǐus -a -um (connected with dies and divus, Gr. δῖος). (1) *divine*: dia dearum, Enn.; *god-like*: dius fidius, Cic.; hence *fine, noble*: dia Camilla, Verg.; sententia dia Catonis, Hor. (2) (probably) *out of doors, in the open air*: pastorum otia dia, Lucr.

dǐūtǐnus -a -um (diu), *lasting a long time, long*: servitus, Cic.; Caes., Liv.

¶ Adv. **dǐūtǐnē**, *for a long time*: Pl.

dǐūtǐus, dǐūtǐssǐmē, see diu.

dǐūturnǐtās -ātis, f. (diuturnus), *long duration*: temporis, Cic.; belli, Caes.

dǐūturnus -a -um (diu) adj. (with compar.), *lasting a long time, of long duration*: gloria, bellum, Cic.; of persons: quae nupsit, non diuturna fuit, *did not live long*, Ov.; non potes esse diuturnus, *you cannot remain long in your position*, Cic.

dǐvārǐco -are, *to stretch apart, spread out, spreadeagle*: hominem, Cic.

dǐvello -vellěre -velli -vulsum (-volsum), *to pluck apart, tear asunder*. LIT., res a natura copulatas, Cic.; suos artus lacero morsu, Ov. TRANSF., (1) *to break up, destroy*: commoda civium, Cic.; somnum, *interrupt*, Hor. (2) *to distract*: divellor dolore, Cic. (3) *to pull away, remove, separate*: liberos a complexu parentum, Sall.; dulci amplexu, Verg.; sapientiam a voluptate, Cic.

dǐvendo -venděre -venditum, *to sell in separate lots*: bona populi Romani, Cic.; Liv., Tac.

dǐverběro -are, *to strike apart, cleave, divide*: volucres auras sagittā, Verg.; Lucr.

dǐverbǐum -i, n. (dis/verbum), *a dialogue on the stage*: Liv.

dǐversǐtās -ātis, f. (diversus). (1) *contrariety, contradiction*: inter exercitum imperatoremque, Tac. (2) *difference, diversity*: supplicii, Tac.; Quint.

dǐversōrǐum, see deversorium.

dǐverto (**dǐvorto**) -vertěre -verti -versum, *to turn different ways*; hence *to differ*: Pl.

¶ Hence partic. (with compar and superl.) **dǐversus** -a -um, *turned in different directions from each other*, or *turned away from a certain point*.

LIT., diversis a flumine regionibus, Caes.; anguli maxime inter se diversi, Cic.; equos in diversum iter concitatos, Liv.; quo diversus abis? Verg.; diversi abeunt, Liv.; plures diversae semitae erant, Liv.; hence *out of the way, remote*: litus, Verg.; oppida, Tac. TRANSF., (1) *fluctuating, irresolute*: metu ac libidine diversus agebatur, Sall. (2) *different, unlike, opposed*; absol.: varia et diversa studia, Cic.; with ab: haec videntur esse a proposita ratione diversa, Cic.; with inter se: diversa inter se mala, luxuria atque avaritia, Sall.; with dat.: Hor.; hence *actively opposed, hostile*: acies, Tac.

¶ Adv. (with compar. and superl.) **dǐversē**, *in different directions, differently, diversely*: inconstans est, quod ab eodem de eadem re diverse dicitur, Cic.

dǐves -vǐtis (compar. dīvǐtior, superl. dīvǐtissimus). *rich, wealthy*.

LIT., of persons: ex pauperrimo dives factus est, Cic.; with abl.: agris, Hor.; with genit: pecoris, Verg.

TRANSF., of things: terra dives amomo, *rich in*, Ov.; so with genit.: Hor.; epistula, *containing much*, Ov.; lingua, *eloquent*, Hor.; divitior fluxit dithyrambus, Cic.; cultus, *costly*, Ov.

dǐvexo -are (dis/vexo), *to tear asunder*; hence (1) *to destroy, plunder*: agros civium optimorum, Cic. (2) *to distract*: Suet.

dǐvǐdǐa -ae, f. (divido), *division, trouble*: Pl.

dǐvǐdo -vǐděre -vīsi -vīsum (from dis and root vid-, whence viduus), *to divide*.

(1) *to divide up, separate into parts*. LIT., in gen.: omne animal secari ac dividi potest, Cic.; exercitum in duas partes, Caes.; Gallia est omnis divisa in partes tres, Caes.; populum in duas partes, Cic.; muros, Verg. Esp. *to divide among persons, distribute, allot*: agros, Lucr., Cic., Verg.; bona viritim, Cic.; praedam per milites, Liv. TRANSF., in gen.: genus universum in species certas partiri et dividere, Cic.; esp. as polit. t. t.: sententiam; *to divide a resolution into parts so that each part can be voted on*, Cic.; in music, *to accompany*: citharā carmina, Hor.

(2) *to separate two wholes from one another*. LIT., a corpore capita, Liv.; Cic.; geograph.: Gallos ab Aquitania Garumna dividit, Caes. TRANSF., a, *to distinguish*: legem bonam a mala, Cic.; Tac.: b, *to set off, to adorn*: gemma fulvum quae dividit aurum, Verg.

¶ Hence partic. (with compar.) **dīvīsus** -a -um, *separate*: Lucr.

dǐvǐdǔus -a -um (divido). (1) *divisible*: Cic. (2) *divided, parted*: aqua, Ov.; Pl.; fig., *distracted*: Ov.

dǐvǐnātǐo -ōnis, f. (divino). (1) *the gift of prophecy, divination*: Cic. (2) legal t. t., *the selection of a prosecutor*: Cic. L., Quint.

dǐvǐnē, adv. from divinus; q.v.

dǐvǐnǐtās -ātis, f. (divinus). (1) *divine nature, divinity*: Cic. (2) *the power of prophecy or divination*: Cic. (3) *excellence, surpassing merit*: Cic., Quint.

dǐvǐnǐtus, adv. (divinus). (1) *divinely, by divine influence*: Lucr., Cic., Verg. (2) *by inspiration, by means of divination*: Cic. (3) *admirably, nobly*: loqui, Cic.

dǐvǐno -are (divinus), *to foretell, prophesy, forebode*; with acc.: hoc, Cic.; Ov., Liv.; with clause: Cic., Liv.; absol.: Pl., Cic., Ov.

dǐvǐnus -a -um, adj. (with compar. and superl.) (divus).

(1) *belonging* or *relating to a deity, divine*: numen, Cic.; res divina, *the service of the gods*, Cic.; often opp. to humanus; so, e.g.: res divinae, *natural law* as opp. to res humanae, *positive law*, Cic. N. as subst. **dǐvǐnum** -i, *a sacrifice*: Liv.; plur.: divina, *divine things*, Liv.; *the attributes of the gods*: Cic.

(2) *divinely inspired, prophetic*: Cic.; vates, a poet, Hor.; m. as subst. **dǐvǐnus** -i, *a seer*: Cic., Hor., Liv.

(3) *noble, admirable*: divinus ille vir, Cic.; Quint.

¶ Adv. (with compar.) **dǐvīnē**, *divinely*. (1) *by divine power*: Pl. (2) *by divine inspiration, prophetically*: Cic. (3) *admirably, excellently*: Cic., Quint.

dīvīsĭo -ōnis, f. (divido), *division*. (**1**) as rhet. t. t., *division of a subject*: Cic., Quint. (**2**) *distribution*: agrorum, Tac.

dīvīsor -ōris, m. (divido), *a divider*; hence *a distributor*, esp. of lands: Cic.; also *a hired bribery agent*: Cic.

dīvīsŭī, dat. sing. as from divisus, m. (divido), *for division*: Macedonia divisui facilis, Liv.

dīvĭtĭae -ārum, f. (dives), *riches, wealth*. LIT., superare Crassum divitiis, Cic. L.; Pl., Hor. TRANSF., *ornaments, rich offerings*: Liv., Ov.; of soil, *richness*: Ov., Plin.; fig.: ingenii, *gifts*, Cic.

dīvortĭum -i, n. (diverto), *a divergence, separation*. (**1**) of things, *a boundary, parting of the ways*: itinerum, Liv.; divortia nota, Verg.; artissimum inter Europam Asiamque divortium, Tac. (**2**) of persons: **a**, *a divorce*: divortium facere cum aliqua, Cic.; Quint.: **b**, *separation generally*: Pl.

dīvorto, *see* diverto.

dīvulgo -are, *to make common* or *public, publish, spread abroad*: librum, Cic.; rem sermonibus, Cic.; with acc. and infin.: Cic. L.

¶ Hence partic. (with superl.) **dīvulgātus** -a -um, *spread abroad, made common*: magistratus levissimus et divulgatissimus, Cic.; Lucr., Tac.

dīvus -a -um (connected with deus, dies; cf. dius).

(**1**) as adj., *divine* or *deified*: Cic., Liv., Verg.

(**2**) as subst. **dīvus** -i, m. *a god* and **dīva** -ae, f. *a goddess*: Pl., Lucr., Cic., Liv., Verg., Hor.; often as epithet of dead and deified emperors; **dīvum** -i, n. *the sky*: sub divo, *in the open air*, Cic., Verg., Hor.

do dăre dĕdi dătum; originally two separate verbs of different derivation, corresponding generally to (**1**) and (**2**) below; in practice commonly confused.

(**1**) *to offer* or *give*. LIT., aliquid, Pl.; donum, Cic.; populo Romano arma, Cic.; esp.: **a**, *to give* for a particular purpose; of letters, *to give for dispatch*: tres epistulae eodem abs te datae tempore, Cic.; in marriage: aliquam in matrimonium, Caes.; natam genero, Verg.; vela dare ventis, *to sail*, Verg.; dare alicui cervices, *to offer the neck for punishment*, Cic.; aliquid deo, *to dedicate*, Hor., Liv., Tac.: **b**, *to give as due, pay*: poenas, *a penalty*, Ov.; verba, *words only*, i.e. *to cheat*, Pl., Cic., Hor. TRANSF., **a**, in gen., *to grant, lend, bestow*: alicui vitam, Cic.; nomen, Liv.; veniam, Cic., Caes., Liv.; facultatem, Caes., Cic.; contionem, Cic.; indutias, Liv.; with infin., or with ut, or ne and subj., *to allow*: Liv., Ov.: **b**, *to hand over, commit, devote*: operam, Pl., Caes., Cic.; se studiis, Cic.; corpori omne tempus, Cic.; urbem excidio ac ruinis, Liv.; aliquem morti, Hor.: **c**, *to tell, communicate*: Ter., Verg.

(**2**) *to cause, bring about, put* (cf. compounds abdo, etc.): alicui dolorem, Cic.; stragem, Lucr., Verg., Liv.; ruinas, Lucr.; impetum in hostem, Liv.; documentum, Cic., Liv.; esp. of sounds: clamorem, sonitum, Verg.

dŏcĕo dŏcēre dŏcŭi doctum (connected with δοκέω), *to teach, instruct*; with acc. of person: aliquem, Caes., Cic., etc.; aliquem equo

armisque, Liv.; aliquem fidibus, Cic.; with adv.: aliquem Latine, Cic.; with acc. of thing: ius civile, Cic.; with double acc.: aliquem litteras, Cic.; Pl., Hor.; so in pass. with acc. of thing: Hor.; with infin.: aliquem sapere, Cic.; Liv., Tac.; with clause, *to inform that* or *how*: Cic.; absol.: doceo et explano, Cic.

Esp. as theatr. t. t.: docere fabulam (like διδάσκειν δρᾶμα), *to teach a play to the actors, to bring out, exhibit*, Cic., Hor.

¶ Hence partic. (with compar. and superl.) **doctus** -a -um, *taught*; hence (**1**) of persons, *learned, instructed, well-informed*: Graecis litteris et Latinis, Cic.; ex disciplina Stoicorum, Cic.; with genit.: fandi, Verg.; m. as subst., esp. plur. docti -orum, *the learned*: Cic.; fig., of things that show learning: ars, Ov.; sermones, Cic. (**2**) *experienced, clever, shrewd*: Pl., Ter.

¶ Adv. (with compar. and superl.) **doctē**. (**1**) learnedly, skilfully: Hor. (**2**) *cleverly, shrewdly*: Pl.

dochmĭus -ii, m. (δόχμιος, sc. πούς), *a species of foot in poetry, the dochmiac* (‿ − − ‿ −): Cic.

dŏcĭlis -e, adj. (with compar.) (doceo), *teachable, docile*: attentus iudex et docilis, Cic.; docilis ad hanc disciplinam, Cic.; with genit.: modorum, Hor.; fig., of things: capilli, Ov.

dŏcĭlĭtās -ātis, f. (docilis), *teachableness, docility*: Cic.

doctor -ōris, m. (doceo), *a teacher*: eiusdem sapientiae doctores, Cic.; Hor., Quint.

doctrīna -ae, f. (doceo). (**1**) *teaching, instruction*: doctrina politos constituat, Lucr.; puerilis, Cic.; honestarum rerum, Cic. (**2**) *that which is imparted by teaching, knowledge, learning*: Piso Graecis doctrinis eruditus, Cic.

doctus -a -um, partic. from doceo; q.v.

dŏcŭmen -inis, n.=documentum; q.v.: Lucr.

dŏcŭmentum -i, n. (doceo), *example, pattern, warning, proof*: documentum fuit hominibus virtutis, Cic.; alicui documento esse, Caes.; documentum sui dare, Liv.; with clause, *a proof how*: Cic., Liv.; *a warning against*: Liv., Hor.

Dōdōna -ae, f. (Δωδώνη), *a city of Epirus, renowned for its sacred oak and oracle of Zeus.* ¶ Hence adj. **Dōdōnaeus** -a -um, and f. **Dōdōnis** -ĭdis, *of Dodona*.

dodrans -antis, m. (de/quadrans), *three-fourths*: aedificii reliquum dodrantem emere, Cic.; heres ex dodrante, *heir to three-fourths of the property*, Nep.; as a measure of length, *nine inches, three-fourths of a foot*: Plin., Suet.

dogma -ătis, n. (δόγμα), *a philosophical doctrine*: Cic., Juv.

Dolabella -ae, m. *a Roman family name in the gens Cornelia*; esp. P. Cornelius Dolabella, *the son-in-law of Cicero*.

dŏlābra -ae, f. (¹dolo), *a pick-axe*: Liv., Tac., Juv.

dŏlĕo dŏlēre dŏlŭi, fut. partic. dŏlĭtūrus, *to suffer pain*.

(**1**) of bodily pain: pes, caput dolet, Cic.; impers.: mihi dolet, Pl.

(**2**) mentally: **a**, of persons, *to be pained, to grieve, bewail*: de Hortensio, Cic.; bonis rebus, Cic.; meum casum luctumque doluerunt, Cic.; with acc. and infin.: se a suis

doliaris   domo

superari, Cic.; foll. by quod.: Caes., Ov.; by si: Hor.; absol.: aeque dolendo, Cic.: **b**, of things, *to cause pain*: nihil cuiquam doluit, Cic.; Pl., Ter.

¶ Hence partic. (with compar.: Ov.) **dolens**, *painful*.

¶ Adv. (with compar.: Cic.) **dŏlenter**, *painfully, sorrowfully*: hoc dicere, Cic.

dōlĭāris -e, adj. (dolium), *tubby*: Pl.

dōlĭŏlum -i, n. (dim. of dolium), *a little cask*: Liv.

dōlĭum -i, n. *a large jar for storing wine*: de dolio haurire, Cic.; Pl., Hor.

¹dŏlo -are, *to hew with an axe*. Lit., robur, Cic.; non est (homo) e saxo sculptus aut e robore dolatus, Cic. Transf., illud opus, *to work roughly*, Cic.; caput fuste, *to cudgel*, Hor.

²dŏlo or **dŏlon** -ōnis, m. (δόλων). (1) *a pike*: Verg.; *sword-stick*: Suet., Verg. Transf., *the sting of a fly*: Phaedr. (2) *a small foresail*: Liv.

Dŏlops -lŏpis; usually plur. **Dŏlŏpes** -um, acc. -as, m. (Δόλοπες), *the Dolopes, a people in Thessaly*.

¶ Hence **Dŏlŏpĭa** -ae, f. *the country of the Dolopes*.

dŏlor -ōris, m. (doleo), *pain, ache, anguish*.
(1) physical: pedum, Cic.; laterum, Hor.
(2) mental *pain, grief, sorrow*. Lit., dolorem accipere, commovere, facere, dare, Cic.; dolore adfici, Cic.; esp. of *disappointment, resentment*: dolore exarsit, Caes.; dolor iniuriae, Caes. Transf., **a**, *the cause of sorrow*: Ov.: **b**, as rhet. t. t., *pathos*: Cic., Quint.

dŏlōsus -a -um (dolus), *crafty, deceitful, cunning*: mulier, Hor.; artes, Ov.

¶ Adv. **dŏlōsē**, *deceitfully, craftily*: agi dolose, Cic.

dŏlus -i, m. (δόλος), *a device, artifice*.
(1) qualified by malus, as legal t. t., *fraud*: cum ex eo quaereretur quid esset Dolus malus, respondebat cum esset aliud simulatum aliud actum, Cic.; Pl., Ter., Liv.
(2) absol., *fraud, deceit, guile*: fraus ac dolus, Cic.; ut magis virtute quam dolo contenderent, Caes.; Pl., Verg. Meton., *an instrument of deception, trap*: dolos (=retia) saltu deludit, Ov.

dŏmābĭlis -e (domo), *that can be tamed, tameable*: Cantaber, Hor.; Ov.

dŏmestĭcus -a -um (domus.) (1) *belonging to the house* or *the family, domestic*: parietes, Cic.; luctus, Cic.; difficultas, *poverty*, Cic.; tempus, *spent at home*, Cic.; domesticus homo, Cic.; m. as subst., esp. plur. **dŏmestĭci** -ōrum, *the inmates of one's house, members of one's family*: Cic.
(2) *domestic, native* (opp. to *foreign*): crudelitas, *towards citizens*, Cic.; si superavissent vel domesticis opibus vel externis auxiliis, Caes.; bellum, *civil war*, Cic.; celebrare domestica facta, Hor.

dŏmĭcĭlĭum -i, n. (domus), *a place of residence, dwelling*. Lit., aliud domicilium, alias sedes parant, Caes.; domicilium conlocare in aliquo loco, Cic. Transf., imperii, *Rome*, Cic.; superbiae, Cic.; Liv.

dŏmĭna -ae, f. (dominus). Lit., *the mistress of a household*: Verg., Ov. Transf., (1) *a wife*: Verg., Ov.; also *a mistress*: Tib. (2) *a goddess*: domina Venus, *Lady Venus*, Ov.;

of Cybele: Verg. (3) *royal lady*: Suet. (4) of abstr. things, *ruler, controller*: iustitia domina virtutum, Cic.; Fors domina campi, Cic.

dŏmĭnātĭo -ōnis, f. (dominor), *mastery, irresponsible power, despotism*. Lit., unius, Cic.; Liv., Tac.; also in plur. Transf., *control, direction*: temperantia est rationis in libidinem firma et moderata dominatio, Cic.

dŏmĭnātor -ōris, m. (dominor), *ruler, governor*: rerum Deus, Cic.

dŏmĭnātrix -īcis, f. (f. of dominator), *a female ruler, mistress*. Transf., caeca ac temeraria dominatrix animi cupiditas, Cic.

dŏmĭnātus -ūs, m. (dominor), *mastery*; esp. *absolute power*: dominatus regius, Cic. Transf., dominatus cupiditatum, Cic.

dŏmĭnĭum -i, n. (dominus). (1) *rule, power, ownership*: Liv. (2) *a feast, banquet*: huius argento dominia vestra ornari, Cic.

dŏmĭnor -ari, dep. (dominus), *to rule, be lord* or *master, to domineer*.
Lit., dominari Alexandriae, Cic.; in suos, Cic.; in nobis, Cic.; in capite fortunisque hominum honestissimorum, Cic.; iudiciis, Cic.; with inter: Caes.; summa arce, Verg.
Transf., dominatur libido, *is supreme*, Cic.; mare, Tac.

¶ Hence partic. (with compar.) **dŏmĭnans** -antis, *dominant*: Lucr., Hor.

dŏmĭnus -i, m. (domus), *the master of a house, head of the household, lord, master*; plur.: domini, *master and mistress*, Cic.
Transf., (1) *a husband* or *lover*: Ov. (2) *a master, owner, possessor*: aedificii, navis, Cic.; as adj., *the master's*: dominae manus, Ov. (3) *an employer*: Pl., Cic. L. (4) *a ruler, lord, controller*: Cic., Verg.; gentium, Cic.; rei (of the judge), Cic.; fig., of a passion: Cic. (5) with or without convivii or epuli, *the person who arranges a feast, host*: Cic., Liv. (6) of an emperor: Suet.

dŏmĭporta -ae, f. (domus/porto), *she who carries her house upon her back, the snail*: poet. ap. Cic.

Dŏmĭtĭānus -i, m. *T. Flavius Domitianus, son of Vespasian, brother of Titus*; born A.D. 51, Emperor from 81 to 96.

Dŏmĭtĭus -a -um, *name of a plebeian gens at Rome, the most famous members of which were*: Cn. Domitius Ahenobarbus, *consul* 122 B.C., *conqueror of the Allobroges*; L. Domitius Ahenobarbus, *consul* 54 B.C., *general and adherent of Pompey*.

¶ Adj. **Dŏmĭtĭānus** -a -um, *of Domitius*: milites, *the soldiers of L. Domitius Ahenobarbus*, Caes.

dŏmĭto -are (freq. of domo), *to tame, subdue, break in*: boves, Verg.

dŏmĭtor -ōris, m. (domo), *a tamer*. Lit., equorum, Cic.; Verg. Transf., *conqueror, victor*: domitor Persarum, Cic.; Saturnius domitor maris alti, Verg.

dŏmĭtrix -īcis, f. (f. of domitor), *she who tames*: Epidaurus domitrix equorum, Verg.; clava domitrix ferarum, Ov.

dŏmĭtus -ūs, m. (domo), *taming*: efficimus domitu nostro quadrupedum vectiones, Cic.

dŏmo dŏmare dŏmŭi dŏmĭtum (connected with domus), *to tame, break in*.
Lit., beluas, Cic.; equos stimulo et verbere, Ov.

[201]

TRANSF., *to conquer, subdue*: (1) men or communities, esp. in war: maximas nationes virtute, Cic.; hasta pugnantem, Ov. (2) concr. things: ipsius fluminis vim, Liv.; arbores multā mercede, Verg.; uvas prelo, *to press*, Hor. (3) abstr. things: domitas habere libidines, Cic.; invidiam, Hor.

dŏmus -ūs, f. (Sing. acc. domum; genit. domūs; dat. domui; abl. domo, occ. domū. Plur. nom. domūs; acc. domos or domūs; genit. domorum or domuum; dat. and abl. domibus; cf. Gr. root δεμ-, δέμω, whence δόμος).
LIT., *a house, a home*: domum aedificare, Cic.; aliquem tecto et domo invitare, Cic.; locative: domi, *at home, in the house*, Cic.; meae domi, *at my house*, Cic.; alienae domi, *in the house of another*, Cic.; domi aliquid habere, *to have at home, to possess, be provided with*, Cic.; domum, *home, homewards*, Cic.; domo, *from home, out of the house*, Cic.
TRANSF., (1) poet. *a dwelling, abode*; of birds: Verg.; of the gods: Verg., Ov.; *the body*, as home of the soul: Ov.; *the labyrinth*: Verg. (2) *home, native country*; locative: domi, *at home, in one's own country*, Cic.; domi militiaeque, Cic.; belli domique, Liv., *in peace and in war*. (3) *a household*: Cic. L. (4) *a philosophical school* or *sect*: Cic., Sen.

dōnārĭum -i, n. (donum). LIT., *a place in a temple for offerings*: Luc. TRANSF., (1) *a temple, shrine, altar*: Verg., Ov. (2) *a votive offering*: Liv.

dōnātĭo -ōnis, f. (dono), *a giving, donation*: Cic.

dōnātīvum -i, n. (dono), *an imperial largess* or *donative to the soldiery*: Tac., Suet.

dōnĕc, conj. (shortened from donique, Lucr., which is from done/que). (1) *up to the time when, until*; with indic.: Cic., Verg., Liv.; with subj.: Verg., Hor., Tac.; often preceded by usque, usque eo, eo usque, Pl., Cic. etc. (2) *so long as, while*; with indic.: donec gratus eram tibi, Hor.; Liv., Tac.; with subj.: Liv., Tac.

dōnĭcum = donec; q.v.: Pl.

dōno -are (donum).
(1) (alicui aliquid), *to give as a present, to present to*. LIT., non pauca suis adiutoribus, Cic.; Pl., Caes., Hor., Verg. TRANSF., **a**, *to grant, bestow*: alicui aeternitatem, Cic.; poet., with infin.: alicui divinare, Hor.: **b**, *to sacrifice, give up to*: amicitias reipublicae, Cic. L.: **c**, esp. *to remit a debt* or *obligation*: alicui aes alienum, Cic.: **d**, *to forgive, pardon* (for the sake of someone else): noxae damnatus donatur populo Romano, Liv.; Ov.
(2) (aliquem aliquā re), *to present with*: cohortem militaribus donis, Caes.; Pl., Cic., Hor.

dōnum -i, n. (dare), *a gift, present*: gen.: dona nuptialia, Cic.; dona ferentes, Verg.; dono dare, *to give as a present*, Ter.; esp. *a gift to the gods, a votive offering*: Cic., Verg.

dorcas -ădis, f. (δορκάς), *a gazelle, antelope*: Mart.

Dōres -um, m. (Δωριεῖς), *the Dorians*, one of the Hellenic tribes.
¶ Hence adj. **Dōrĭcus** and **Dōrĭus** -a -um, *Dorian*; poet. = *Greek*: Verg.; **Dōris** -ĭdis, f., as adj., *Dorian*; as subst. (1) *the country of*

the Dorians. (2) *the wife of Nereus, and mother of fifty sea-nymphs*. (3) meton., *the sea*: Verg.

dormĭo -ire, *to sleep*. LIT., se dormitum conferre, Cic.; ad dormiendum proficisci, Cic.; dormientem excitare, Cic.; nox dormienda, *to be slept through*, Cat. TRANSF., (1) of the sleep of death: Pl. (2) *to rest, be inactive*: beneficia dormientibus deferuntur, Cic.; Prop.

dormītātor -ōris, m. (dormito), *a dreamer*: Pl.

dormīto -are (freq. of dormio), *to be sleepy, to begin to sleep*. LIT., dormitanti mihi epistula illa reddita, Cic. TRANSF., (1) *to dream, be lazy*: ista oscitans et dormitans sapientia Scaevolarum, Cic.; quandoque bonus dormitat Homerus, nods, Hor. (2) of a lamp: iam dormitante lucernā, *just going out*, Ov.

dormītor -ōris, m. (dormio), *a sleeper*: Mart.

dormītōrius -a -um (dormio), *for sleeping*: Plin. L.

dorsum -i, n. (dorsus -i, m.: Pl.), *the back*, either of men or animals. LIT., dorso onus subire, Hor.; dorsum demulcere equis, Liv. TRANSF., *any elevation of similar form*: duplex dentalium, *the back of the sharebeam of a plough*, Verg.; immane dorsum mari summo, *a reef*, Verg.; *a mountain ridge, 'hog's back'*: Caes., Liv., Verg.

Dŏrўlaeum -i, n. (Δορύλαιον), *a town in Phrygia*.
¶ Hence **Dŏrўlenses** -ĭum and **Dŏrўlaei** -orum, m. *the inhabitants of Dorylaeum.*

Dŏrўphŏrŏs -i, m. (δορυφόρος), *the lance-bearer*, the name of a celebrated statue by Polycletus: Cic.

dōs dōtis, f. (do), *a dowry, marriage portion*. LIT., accipere pecuniam ab uxore dotis nomine, Caes.; filiae nubili dotem conficere non posse; Cic.; Hor. TRANSF., *a gift*: cuius artem cum indotatam esse et incomptam videres, verborum eam dote locupletasti et ornasti, Cic.; esp. *a quality, endowment*: dotes ingenii, Ov.

dōtālis -e (dos), *belonging to* or *forming a dowry*: praedium, Cic. L.; Hor., Verg.

dōto -are (dos), *to provide with a dowry, endow*: sanguine Troiano et Rutulo dotabere, virgo, Verg.
¶ Hence partic. **dōtātus** -a -um, *richly endowed*. LIT., Aquilia, Cic. TRANSF., Chione dotatissima formā, Ov.

drachma (**drachuma**: Pl.) -ae, f. (δραχμή). (1) *a drachma, a small Greek coin, about equal in value to a Roman denarius*: Pl., Cic., Hor. (2) as a weight, ⅛ *of an uncia*: Plin.

¹drăco -ōnis, m. (δράκων), *a kind of snake, dragon*. LIT., Cic. TRANSF., *a constellation so called*: Cic. poet.

²Drăco -ōnis, m. (Δράκων), *Draco, an Athenian who drew up in 621 B.C. a code of laws afterwards famous for its severity.*

drăcōnĭgĕna -ae, c. (draco/gigno) = δρακοντογενής, *dragon-born, sprung from dragon-seed*: urbs, *Thebes*, Ov.

drāpĕta -ae, m. (δραπέτης), *a runaway slave*: Pl.

Drĕpănum -i, n. (Δρέπανον) and **Drĕpăna** -ōrum, n. (Δρέπανα), *a town on the west coast of Sicily* (now *Trapani*).
Adj. **Drĕpănĭtānus** -a -um, *of* or *belonging to Drepanum.*

drŏmas -ădis, m. (δρομάς), *a dromedary*: Liv.

drŏmos -i, m. (δρόμος), *the race-course of the Spartans*: Liv.

Drŭentĭa -ae, f. *a river in Gaul flowing into the Rhône* (now *the Durance*).

Drŭĭdēs -um, m. and **Drŭĭdae** -ārum, m. (Celtic word), *the Druids, the priests and wise men of the Gauls and Britons*: Caes., Tac.

Drūsus -i, m. *a cognomen of the gens Livia*; esp. of (1) M. Livius Drusus, *tribune in* 91 B.C., *murdered for attempting to revive some of the Gracchan laws*. (2) Nero Claudius Drusus, *son of Livia Drusilla and Tiberius Claudius Nero*.

¶ Hence adj. **Drūsĭānus** -a -um and **Drūsīnus** -a -um, *of or belonging to Drusus*; subst. **Drūsīlla** -ae, f. *name of several females of the gens Livia*.

¹**Drŷas** -ădis, f. (Δρυάς), *a wood nymph, Dryad*; gen. plur.: Dryades, Verg.

²**Drŷas** -antis, m. (Δρύας), *father of Lycurgus, king of Thrace*.

¶ Hence **Drŷantīdes** -ae, m. *the son of Dryas*, i.e. *Lycurgus*: Ov.

Drŷopes -um (Δρύοπες), *a people of Epirus*.

Dŭbis -is, m. *river in Gallia Belgica* (now *the Doubs*).

dŭbĭtābĭlis -e (dubito), *doubtful, uncertain*: Ov.

dŭbĭtantĕr, adv. from dubito; q.v.

dŭbĭtātĭo -ōnis, f. (dubito).

(1) *wavering in opinion, doubt, uncertainty*: sine ulla dubitatione, *certainly*, Cic.; res non habet dubitationem, *the matter admits of no doubt*, Cic.; with objective genit.: dubitatio adventūs legionum, *doubt as to the coming*, Cic.; Caes., Quint.; with de: illa Socratica dubitatio de omnibus rebus, Cic.; with indir. quest.: si quando dubitatio accidit, quale sit, Cic.; with quin, after a neg.: nulla dubitatio est quin, Cic.

(2) *wavering as to action, hesitation, irresolution*: nullā interpositā dubitatione, Caes.; aestuabat dubitatione, Cic.

dŭbĭto -are (freq. of old verb dubo; cf. dubius).

(1) *to doubt, waver in opinion, be uncertain*: de hoc, Cic.; with n. acc.: haec, Cic.; utrum sit utilius an, Cic.; honestumne factu sit an turpe, Cic.; non dubito quin, *I have no doubt that*, Pl., Cic., Ov.; with acc. and infin.: Lucr., Liv.; in pass.: Ov.

(2) *to waver as to action, be irresolute, hesitate*: quid dubitas? Caes.; foll. by infin.: Pl., Cic., Verg.; non dubito, foll. by quin: Caes., Cic.

¶ Hence, from partic., adv. **dŭbĭtanter**. (1) *doubtingly*: dubitanter unum quodque dicemus, Cic. (2) *hesitatingly*: illud verecundi et dubitantes recepisse, Cic.

dŭbĭus -a -um (from duo, through old verb dubo), *doubtful*.

(1) act., *wavering*: a, *in opinion, doubting, doubtful, uncertain*: Cic.; with genit.: sententiae, Liv.; salutis, Ov.; with indir. quest.: Lucr., Verg., Liv.; with acc. and infin.: Liv.: b, *as to action, hesitating, uncertain, irresolute*: dubius an transiret, Liv.

(2) pass., *uncertain, doubted, doubtful*: genus causae, Cic.; victoria, Caes.; lux, caelum, Ov. Esp. n. dubium: dubium est, non dubium est, absol., or with de, or with clause, Pl., Ter., Cic., Liv.; also

n. as subst.: in dubium vocare, *to call in question*, Cic.; in dubio esse, Ter., Lucr.; sine dubio, Cic.; procul dubio, *without doubt*, Liv.

(3) fig. *doubtful, dubious, dangerous, critical*: res, Pl., Verg., Liv.; tempora, Hor.

¶ Adv. **dŭbĭē**, *doubtfully*: ut aliquod signum dubie datum pro certo sit acceptum, Cic.; hence: haud dubie, nec dubie, non dubie, *certainly, without doubt*, Cic. L., Liv.

dŭcēni -ae -a (ducenti), *a group of two hundred, or two hundred each*: Liv.

dŭcentēsĭma -ae, f. (f. of ducentesimus, from ducenti, sc. pars), *the two hundredth part, one-half per cent*, Tac., Suet.

dŭcenti -ae -a (duo/centum), *two hundred*: Liv. TRANSF., *an indefinitely large number*: Pl., Hor.

dŭcentiens or **dŭcentĭēs**, adv. (ducenti), *two hundred times*: Cic. TRANSF., *many times*: Cat.

dūco dūcĕre duxi ductum.

(1) *to draw*: a, in gen., *to draw along, from place to place*. LIT., plaustra, Ov.; sidera crinem ducunt, Verg.; os, *to strain, distort*, Cic.; hence *to shape anything long, to construct*: parietem, Cic.; murum, Liv.; vallum, Caes.; ocreas argento, Verg.; so in spinning: lanas, Ov. TRANSF., of a poet: carmina, *to make verses*, Hor.; and esp of time, either *to spend*: aetatem in litteris, Cic.; or to *delay, protract*: bellum, Cic.; aliquem diem ex die, *to put off*, Caes.: b, *to draw towards oneself*. LIT., frena manu, Ov.; remos, Ov.; hence *to attract, take on*: colorem, Verg.; silvas carmine, Ov. TRANSF., *to charm, influence, mislead*: fabellarum auditione ducuntur, Cic.; errore duci, Cic.; me ad credendum tua ducit oratio, Cic.: c, *to draw into the body*. LIT., aera spiritu, *to inhale*, Cic.; pocula, *to quaff*, Hor. TRANSF., somnos, Verg.: d, *to draw out or away*. LIT., sortes, Cic.; ferrum vagina, Ov. TRANSF., *to derive*: nomen ex aliqua re, Cic.

(2) *to lead*: a, in gen.: ducere equum, Liv.; aliquem in ius, Liv.; in carcerem, in vincula, Cic.; suas mulierculas secum, Cic.; fig., of a road: duxit via in leniter editum collem, Liv.: b, in marriage, *to marry* a wife; with in matrimonium or absol.: Caes., Cic., Liv.; ducere ex plebe, *to marry a plebeian*, Liv.: c, as milit. t. t., either *to lead on the march*: cohortes ad munitiones, Caes.; or *to command*: exercitum, Cic.; turmas, Verg.

(3) *to calculate, count, reckon*: faenus quaternis centesimis, Cic. TRANSF., *to esteem, consider*: aliquem in hostium numero, Caes.; aliquid parvi, Cic.; pluris, Cic.; pro nihilo, Cic.; aliquem despicatui, *to despise*, Cic.; with acc. and infin.: qui se regem esse ducebat, Cic.; Caes., Verg.

ductim, adv. (duco), *by drawing*; *in a stream*: Pl.

ductĭto -are (freq. of duco), *to lead, esp. to lead home* a wife: Pl. TRANSF., *to cheat*: Pl.

ducto -are (freq. of duco), *to draw or lead, esp. to lead home*: Pl. TRANSF., *to cheat*: Pl.

ductor -ōris, m. (duco), *a leader*. (1) *a commander*: exercitūs, Cic. (2) *a guide*: itineris, Liv.

[203]

ductus -ūs, m. (duco). (**1**) *drawing*; hence: **a**, *shape*: oris, *the lineaments of the face*, Cic.; muri, *line of a wall*, Cic.: **b**, *drawing off*: aquarum, Cic.
(**2**) *leading, command, leadership*: alicuius ductu, Cic.; se ad ductum Pompeii applicare, Cic.

dūdum, adv. (dum), *some time ago*; hence (**1**) *a little while ago, not long since*: quod tibi dudum (*just now*) videbatur, Cic.; Pl., Verg. (**2**) *a long while ago* or *for a long time*: quam dudum nihil habeo quod ad te scribam, Cic. L.; esp. with iam: quem iam dudum Cotta et Sulpicius expectat, Cic.; Verg.

dŭellum, dŭellĭcus, dŭellātor=bellum, bellicus, bellator; q.v.

Dŭīlĭus -a -um, *name of a Roman gens, of which the most famous member was* C. Duilius, *consul* 260 B.C., *who gained a great naval victory over the Carthaginians off Sicily*; this was commemorated by a column in the forum, adorned with the prows of captured ships (columna rostrata).

dulcēdo -ĭnis, f. (dulcis), *sweetness*. TRANSF., *pleasantness, charm*: dulcedine quadam gloriae commoti, Cic.; dulcedine orationis, Cic.; Liv., Tac.

dulcesco -ĕre (dulcis), *to become sweet*: Cic.

dulcĭcŭlus -a -um (dim. of dulcis), *somewhat sweet*: potio, Cic.

dulcĭfer -era -erum (dulcis/fero), *sweet*: Pl.

dulcis -e, adj. (with compar. and superl.) (connected with γλυκύς), *sweet* (opp. amarus). LIT., to the taste: vinum, Hor.; unda, *fresh water*, Ov. TRANSF., (**1**) in gen., *pleasant, delightful, agreeable*: nomen libertatis, Cic.; poemata, Hor.; orator, Cic. (**2**) of persons, *friendly, dear, beloved*: amici, Cic.; used in addresses: dulcissime Attice, Cic. L.
  ¶ N. acc. **dulcĕ** as adv., *sweetly*: Cat., Hor.
  ¶ Adv. **dulcĭter** (with compar. dulcius, superl. dulcissime), *sweetly*: Cic., Quint.

dulcĭtūdo -ĭnis, f. (dulcis), *sweetness*: Cic.

Dūlĭchĭum -ii, n. (Δουλίχιον), *an island in the Ionian Sea, forming part of the kingdom of Ulysses*. Adj. **Dūlĭchĭus** -a -um, *Dulichian, poet., belonging to Ulysses*: rates, Verg.; dux, Ulysses, Ov.

dum (evidently an accusative indicating duration), adv. and conj.
(**1**) adv., joined as an enclitic with other words: **a**, in the sense *yet*, with non, nullus, haud, vix, etc.: nondum, *not yet*, Cic.; so: necdum, Liv.; nequedum, Cic.; nullusdum, *no one yet*, Liv.; vixdum, *scarcely yet*, Cic.; nihildum, *nothing yet*, Cic.; nedum, *not to say*, Cic.: **b**, in the sense *now, for a moment*, with imperat.: age dum, Pl., Ter., Cic.; itera dum, Cic.
(**2**) conj.: **a**, *while, during the time that*, with indic., usually present: Pl., Caes., Cic., Verg., Liv.: **b**, *while, throughout the time that*, with indic.: Pl., Cic., Caes., Liv.: **c**, *so long as, provided that*, with subj., often strengthened by modo: dummodo, Pl., Cic., Ov.; neg.: dum ne, Pl., Cic. L. or dummodo ne, Cic.: **d**, *until*, usually with subj.: Pl., Caes., Cic., Verg.; also with indic., esp. perf. indic.: Cic.

dūmētum -i, n. (dumus), *a thorn brake, thicket*: Cic., Verg., Hor.; fig.: cur eam tantas in angustiae et Stoicorum dumeta compellimus? Cic.

dummŏdo, see dum.

dūmōsus -a -um (dumus), *covered with thorn bushes, bushy*: Verg., Ov.

dumtaxăt, adv. (dum/taxo), *exactly*; *'as far as applies'* or perhaps *'as far as one estimates'*; hence (**1**) *at least, not less than*: nos animo dumtaxat vigemus, Cic.; Hor., Quint. (**2**) *at most, not more than*: dissita sunt dumtaxat, Lucr.; Caes., Cic.

dūmus -i, m. *a thorn bush, bramble*: Cic., Verg.

dŭŏ -ae -ŏ (acc. m.: duo or duos; Gr. δύο), *two*: Cic., etc.

dŭŏdĕcĭens or **dŭŏdĕcĭēs**, adv., *twelve times*: Cic., Liv.

dŭŏdĕcim (duo/decem), *twelve*: duodecim tabulae (sometimes simply duodecim), *the Twelve Tables of laws*, Cic.

dŭŏdĕcĭmus -a -um (duodecim), *the twelfth*: Caes.

dŭŏdēni -ae -a, *twelve at a time* or *twelve each*: uxores habent deni duodenique inter se communes, Caes.; Cic., Verg., Liv.

dŭŏdēquādrāgēsĭmus, *thirty-eighth*: Liv.

dŭŏdēquādrāginta, *thirty-eight*: Cic.

dŭŏdēquinquāgēsĭmus -a -um, *the forty-eighth*: Cic.

dŭŏdētrīcĭens (-trīcĭēs) adv., *twenty-eight times*: Cic.

dŭŏdētrīginta, *twenty-eight*: Liv.

dŭŏdēvīcēni -ae -a, *eighteen each*: Liv.

dŭŏdēvīginti, *eighteen*: Pl., Caes., Cic.

dŭŏetvīcēsĭmāni -ōrum, m. *soldiers of the 22nd legion*: Tac.

dŭŏetvīcēsĭmus -a -um, *the twenty-second*: Tac.

duplex -plĭcis (duo/plico), *double, doubled, two-fold*. LIT., amiculum, Nep.; pannus, Hor.; murus, Caes.; quaestio, Cic. TRANSF., (**1**) plur., *both*: oculi, Lucr.; palmae, Verg. (**2**) *two-faced, deceitful, equivocal*: Hor.

duplĭcārĭus -a -um (duplex): miles, *a soldier who gets double pay*, Liv.

duplĭcĭter, adv. (duplex), *doubly*: Cic.

duplĭco -are (duplex), *to double*. LIT., numerum dierum, Cic.; Caes.; duplicare verba, *to repeat*, Cic.; but also *to form compound words*: Liv.
TRANSF., (**1**) *to bend double*: virum dolore, Verg. (**2**) in gen., *to lengthen, increase*: sol decedens duplicat umbras duplicari sollicitudines, Cic.

duplus -a -um (Gr. διπλόος), *twice as much, double*: pars, Cic.; pecunia, Cic.; n. as subst. **duplum** -i, *the double*, esp. *a double penalty*: poenam dupli subire, *or* in duplum ire, Cic.; f. as subst. **dupla** -ae: Pl.

dupondĭus -i, m. (duo/pondo), *a coin of two asses*: Cic.

dūrābĭlis -e (duro), *lasting, durable*: Ov., Quint.

dūrāmen -ĭnis, n. (duro), *hardness*: aquarum, ice, Lucr.

dūrătĕus -a -um (δουράτεος), *wooden, of the Trojan horse*: Lucr.

dūrē, adv. from durus; q.v.

dūresco dūrescĕre dūrŭi (durus), *to grow hard*: frigoribus durescit umor, *freezes*, Cic., Verg., Tac.

dūrēta -ae, f. (Spanish-Celtic), *a wooden bath-tub*: Suet.

dūrĭtās -ātis, f. (durus), *harshness, unfriendliness*: Cic.

dūrĭter, adv. from durus; q.v.

dūrĭtĭa -ae, f. and **dūrĭtĭēs** -ēi, f. (durus), *hardness.* LIT., atrae pellis, Ov. TRANSF., (1) *hardness, austerity*: duritia virilis, Cic.; ab parvulis labori ac duritiae studere, Caes. (2) *harshness, severity, oppressiveness*: animi, Cic.; operum, Tac.; caeli militiaeque, Tac.

dūro -are (durus).
(1) transit., *to make hard.* LIT., caementa calce, Liv.; enses in scopulos, Ov.; terram, Verg.; Albanam fumo uvam, Hor. TRANSF., **a,** physically, *to make hardy, inure*: se labore, Caes.: **b,** mentally, *to harden*: ad omne facinus duratus, Tac.
(2) intransit., *to become hard* or *dry.* LIT., durare solum, Verg. TRANSF., **a,** physically, *to endure, hold out*: sub Iove, Ov.; occasionally with acc.: laborem, Verg.; aequor, Hor.: **b,** mentally, *to be hard* or *callous*: in nullius unquam suorum necem duravit, Tac.: **c,** in gen., *to last, remain, continue*: durat simulacrum, Verg.; totidem durare per annos, Verg.; Tac.

dūrus -a -um, adj. (with compar. and superl.), *hard.*
LIT., (1) *hard to the touch*: ferrum, Hor. (2) *harsh to other senses*: sapor Bacchi, Verg.; vocis genus, Cic.; oratio, Cic.
TRANSF., (1) *tough, strong, enduring*: Scipiadae duri bello, Verg. (2) in demeanour or tastes, *rough, rude, uncouth*: ut vitā sic oratione durus, incultus, horridus, Cic.; signa dura sed tamen molliora quam Canachi, Cic.; C. Marius, qui durior ad haec studia videbatur, Cic. (3) in character, *hard, austere*: homo durus ac priscus, Cic.; also *stern, severe*: Varius est habitus iudex durior, Cic.; sometimes *brazen, shameless*: os, Ter. (4) of things, *hard, awkward*; so of weather, *severe*: tempestates, Caes.; of the soil, *difficult to work*: glebae, Verg.; of a task, *hard, difficult*: subvectio, Caes.; of circumstances, *unfavourable, adverse*: condicio durior, Verg.; pauperies, Hor.
¶ Adv. **dūrē** and **dūrĭter** (with compar. durius), *hardly*; hence (1) *hardily*: Ter. (2) *roughly, rudely*: membra moventes duriter, Lucr.; Hor.; durius incedit, Ov. (3) *harshly, unpleasantly, severely*: durius in deditos consulere, Liv.; dure dicere, Hor.

dŭumvir and **dŭŏvir** -vĭri, m. (duo/vir), usually pl., duumviri or duoviri, *a pair of magistrates, a commission of two.* (1) duumviri perduellionis, *a criminal court, trying cases of* perduellio, Cic., Liv. (2) duumviri sacrorum, *keepers of the Sibylline books* (afterwards increased to ten, and then to fifteen), Liv. (3) duumviri aedi faciendae (or locandae, or dedicandae), *a commission for building* or *dedicating a temple*, Liv. (4) duumviri navales, *a commission for looking after the fleet*, Liv. (5) in the Roman municipia: duumviri (iuri dicundo), *the highest magistrates*, Cic., Caes.

dux dŭcis, c. (connected with dūco).
(1) *a guide, conductor*: locorum, Liv.; armenti, Ov. TRANSF., impietatis, Cic.; diis ducibus, *under the direction of the gods*, Cic.; dux femina facti, Verg.
(2) *a leader, ruler*: superum, *Jupiter*, Verg.; pecoris, Tib. Esp. *a military* or *naval*

commander: dux praefectusque classis. Cic.; Caes., Liv.

Dўmās -mantis, m. (*Δύμας*), *father of Hecuba.*
¶ Hence Dymantis probes, or subst. **Dўmantis** -tĭdis, f. *Hecuba*: Ov.

Dўmē -ēs, f. (*Δύμη*) and **Dўmae** -ārum, f. *a town in Achaea.* Adj. **Dўmaeus** -a -um, *of* or *belonging to Dyme.*

dўnastes -is, m. (*δυνάστης*), *ruler, prince*: Caes., Cic.

Dyrrhăchĭum -i, n. (*Δυρράχιον*), *later name of Epidamnus, in Illyria, the port where ships landed coming from Brundisium to Greece* (now *Durrës*).
¶ Hence **Dyrrhăchīni** (-ēni) -ōrum, m. *the people of Dyrrhachium.*

E

E, e, indecl. n. or (sc. littera) f., the fifth letter of the Latin Alphabet, corresponding in the Greek Alphabet both to *ε* and *η*. For the meaning of E. as an abbreviation, see Table of Abbreviations.

ē, prep. = ex; q.v.

ĕā, adv. = abl. of is; q.v.

ĕādem, adv. (abl. f. of idem, sc. viā, parte, etc.), *by the same way, likewise*: Pl., Cic., Liv.

ĕāpropter = propterea: Ter.

ĕātĕnus = ea tenus (parte), adv., *so far*; foll. by quoad: Cic.; by ut and the subj.: Cic.

ĕbĕnus -i, m. = hebenus; q.v.

ēbĭbo -bĭbĕre -bĭbi, *to drink up*: poculum, Pl.; Nestoris annos, *to drink as many cups as the years of Nestor's age*, Ov.; of the sea, ebibit amnes, Ov. TRANSF., *to squander on drink*: Hor.

ēbĭto -ĕre, *to go out*: Pl.

ēblandĭor -iri, dep. *to obtain by flattery*: unum consulatūs diem, Tac.; omnia, Liv.; partic. as pass.: eblandita illa non enucleata esse suffragia, Cic.

ēbrĭĕtās -ātis, f. (ebrius), *drunkenness*: Cic., Ov.

ēbrĭŏlus -a -um (dim. of ebrius), *tipsy*: Pl.

ēbrĭōsĭtas -ātis, f. (ebriosus), *the love of drink, habit of drunkenness*: Cic.

ēbrĭōsus -a -um (ebrius), *drink-loving*: Cic. TRANSF., of a grape: Cat.

ēbrĭus -a -um, *drunk*; rarely *that has drunk enough*: Pl., Ter.; usually *intoxicated*: Pl., Cic., Ov.; so also of words, actions, etc.: Tib., Prop. TRANSF., *intoxicated with, full of*: dulci fortunā, Hor.

ēbullĭo -ire, *to boil up.* TRANSF., *to boast of*: virtutes, Cic.

ēbŭlum -i, n. (-us -i, m.), *the dwarf elder* (Sambucus ebulus, Linn.): Verg.

ĕbur -ŏris, n. *ivory*: signum ex ebore, Cic. TRANSF., (1) *of things made of ivory; a statue*: Verg.; *a flute*: Verg.; *the sheath of a sword*: Ov.; *the curule chair*: Hor., Ov. (2) *the elephant*: Juv.

ĕburnĕŏlus -a -um (dim. of eburneus), *made of ivory*: fistula, Cic.

ĕburnĕus (prose) or **ĕburnus** (poet.) -a -um (ebur), *made of ivory, ivory*: signum, Cic.; dens (of the elephant): Liv. Meton., *white as ivory*: bracchia, cervix, Ov.

Ebŭrōnes -um, m. *a German people in Gallia Belgica.*

Ēbŭsus and **-ŏs** -i, f. *an island in the Mediterranean, off the Spanish coast* (now *Iviza*).

ĕcastor, *see* Castor.

eccĕ, adv. (?/-ce), *behold! lo! see!* used to indicate a thing or person present, or to draw attention to a point; sometimes with nom. or acc.: ecce hominem, Pl.; ecce tuae litterae, Cic.; ecce tibi exortus est Isocrates, Cic.; ecce autem, Cic.

Sometimes combined with pronouns; as ecca (=ecce ea), eccum (=ecce illum): Pl.

eccĕrē, interj. 'there you are!': Pl., Ter.

eccheuma -atis, n. (ἔκχευμα), *a pouring out*: Pl.

ecclesia -ae, f. (ἐκκλησία), *an assembly of the* (Greek) *people*: Plin. L.

ecdĭcus -i, m. (ἔκδικος), *a solicitor for a community*: Cic. L.

Ēcētra -ae, f. *capital of the Volsci.*

¶ Hence **Ēcetranus** -i, m. *an inhabitant of Ecetra.*

ecf-, *see* eff-.

Ĕchecrătēs -ae, m. (Ἐχεκράτης), *a Pythagorean philosopher, contemporary of Plato.*

ĕchĕnēis -idis, f. (ἐχενηΐς), *a sucking fish, the remora* (Echeneis remora, Linn.): Ov.

Ĕchidna -ae, f. (1) *the Lernaean hydra killed by Hercules*: Ov. (2) *a monster of the lower world, half woman, half serpent, mother of Cerberus and of the Lernaean hydra*: Ov.

¶ Adj. **Ĕchidnēus** -a -um: canis echidneus, Cerberus, Ov.

ĕchīnus -i, m. (ἐχῖνος). (1) *an edible sea-urchin* (Echinus esculentus, Linn.): Hor. (2) *a copper dish*: Hor.

Ĕchīōn -ŏnis, m. (Ἐχίων). (1) *one of the Theban heroes who sprang from the dragon's teeth sown by Cadmus, husband of Agave, father of Pentheus*: Echione natus, Pentheus, Ov.

¶ Hence **Ĕchīŏnīdes** -ae, m. *a son of Echion*, i.e. *Pentheus*: Ov.; **Ĕchīŏnīus** -a -um, *Echionian*; poet.=*Cadmeian, Theban*: Verg.

(2) *son of Mercury, one of the Argonauts, who joined the Calydonian boar-hunt.*

¶ Hence adj. **Ĕchīŏnīus** -a -um, *of or belonging to Echion.*

ēchō -ūs, f. (ἠχώ). (1) *an echo*: Plin. (2) personif., *Echo, a wood-nymph*: Ov.

eclŏga -ae, f. *a selection of passages or a short poem*: Varr., Stat.

eclŏgărĭi -ōrum, m. pl. (ecloga), *select passages* or *extracts*: Cic. L.

ecquando, adv. *ever? at any time?* (sometimes with -ne added); used in passionate interrogation: ecquando te rationem factorum tuorum redditurum putasti? Cic.

ecqui, ecquae or ecqua, ecquod, interrog. adj., *is there any . . . that? does any . . .?* (sometimes with -nam added); used in passionate interrogation: ecqui pudor est? ecquae religio, Verres? Cic.

ecquis, ecquid, interrog. pron., *is there any that? does anyone?* (sometimes with -nam added); used in passionate interrogation: ecquis retulit aliquid ad coniugem ac liberos, praeter odia? Liv.; ecquisnam tibi dixerit,

Cic.; as adj.=ecqui: ecquis Latini nominis populus defecerit ad nos? Liv.

Used adverbially. (1) **ecquid** (acc.) or **ecqui** (abl.), *at all?* or *whether?*: fac sciam ecquid venturi sitis, Cic. (2) **ecquo,** *whither?* ecquo te tua virtus provexisset? Cic.

ĕcŭlĕus i, m. (dim. of equus), *a little horse, colt*: Liv.; so of *model horses*: Cic. TRANSF., *a rack, instrument of torture*: Cic.

ĕdācĭtās -ātis, f. (edax), *greediness, gluttony*: Pl., Cic. L.

ĕdax -ācis, f. (¹edo), *greedy, gluttonous*: hospes, Cic. TRANSF., *destructive, consuming*: ignis, Verg.; curae edaces, Hor.; tempus edax rerum, Ov.

edento -are (dens), *to knock out the teeth*: Pl.

edentulus -a -um (dens), *toothless*: Pl.

ĕdĕpol (Pollux), an exclamation, *by Pollux, indeed, truly*: Pl., Ter.

Ēdessa -ae, f. (Ἔδεσσα). (1) *town in Macedonia, residence of the old Macedonian kings, also called Aegae.*

¶ Hence adj. **Ēdessaeus** -a -um, *of or belonging to Edessa.* (2) *capital of the province of Osroene in Mesopotamia.*

ēdīco -dīcĕre -dixi -dictum, *to say out.* In gen., *to announce, declare*; with dir. object or clause: Pl., Cic., Hor. Esp. of a magistrate, *to publish openly, to decree, ordain by proclamation*: diem comitiis, Liv.; iustitium, Cic.; Liv.; with acc. and infin.: Cic.; with ut or ne and the subj.: Cic., Liv.; with subj. alone: Cic. L., Verg.

¶ Hence n. of partic. as subst. **ēdictum** -i, *a decree, edict*; esp. of a magistrate: edicta Bibuli, Cic.; edictum constituere, proponere, Cic.; praemittere, Caes.; most commonly, the proclamation by a praetor on his entering office in which he published the principles that would govern his judicial decisions: Cic.

ēdictio -ōnis, f. (edico), *an edict*: Pl.

ēdicto -are (freq. of edico), *to proclaim*: Pl.

ēdisco -discĕre -didĭci, *to learn thoroughly.* (1) *to learn off by heart*: aliquid ad verbum, word for word, Cic.; magnum numerum versuum, Caes. (2) in gen., *to learn, study*: istam artem, Cic.; Hor., Ov.

ēdissĕro -sĕrĕre -sĕrŭi -sertum, *to explain, set forth, relate fully*: res gestas, Liv.; neque necesse est edisseri a nobis, quae finis funestae familiae fiat, Cic.; Verg.

ēdisserto -are (freq. of edissero), *to explain exactly*: neque adgrediar narrare quae edissertanda minora vero faciam, Liv.

ēdĭtīcĭus -a -um (²edo), *put forth, announced, proposed*: iudices, *a panel of jurors chosen by a plaintiff*, Cic.

ēdĭtĭo -ōnis, f. (²edo), *a putting forth*; hence (1) *the publishing of a book*: maturare libri huius editionem, Tac. (2) *a statement*: in tam discrepante editione, Liv. (3) legal t. t.: editio tribuum, *the proposal of four tribes by a plaintiff, out of which the jury were to be chosen.*

ēdĭtus -a -um, partic. from ²edo; q.v.

¹ĕdo edere or esse ēdi ēsum (class. contracted forms es, est, estis, subj. essem; old pres. subj. edim; cf. Gr. ἔδομαι), *to eat.*

LIT., nec esuriens Ptolemaeus ederat iucundius, Cic.; multos modios salis simul edendos esse ut amicitiae munus expletum sit, Cic.

TRANSF., *to devour, consume, waste*; of persons: Pl.; of inanimate things: culmos est robigo, Verg.; si quid est animam, Hor.

²**ēdo** -děre -dĭdi -dĭtum, *put forth, give out.*

In gen.: animam, extremum vitae spiritum, *to breathe one's last, to die*, Cic.; cuniculus armatos repente edidit, *brought to light*, Liv.; clamorem, *to utter*, Cic.; Ov. Esp. (1) *to bring into the world, to bring forth, give birth to*: partum, Cic.; aliquem, Tac.; edi in lucem, *to be brought into the world*, Cic.; Maecenas atavis edite regibus, *descended from*, Hor.; of things, *to produce*: (terra) edit innumeras species, Ov. (2) *to make known*: **a**, of writings, *to publish*: illos de republica libros, Cic.: **b**, of ideas and information, *to divulge, spread*: quae opinio erat edita in vulgus, Cic.; ede illa quae coeperas, Cic.; consilia hostium, Liv.: **c**, of official pronouncements, *to proclaim*: Apollo oraculum edidit Spartam perituram, Cic.; as legal t. t., *to fix, determine*: iudicium, Cic.; tribus, *to nominate the tribes out of which the jury were to be chosen*, Cic.; ederet consul quid fieri vellet, Liv.; hence n. of partic. as subst. **ēdĭta** -ōrum, *commands*: Ov. (3) *to bring about, cause, produce*: ruinas, Cic.; annuam operam, *to serve for a year*, Liv.; magnam caedem, Liv.; of magistrates, *to provide games for the people*: ludos, spectaculum, Tac.

¶ Hence partic. (with compar. and superl.) **ēdĭtus** -a -um, *raised, high, lofty*: collis, Caes.; locus, Cic. TRANSF., viribus editior, Hor.; n. as subst. **ēdĭtum** -i, *a high place, eminence*: Tac., Suet.

ēdŏcĕo -dŏcēre -dŏcŭi -doctum, *to teach, instruct thoroughly, to inform fully*; what is taught is expressed by infin., or by clause, or by acc.: omnia venalia habere edocuit, Sall.; edocuerat quae fieri vellet, Caes.; omnia ordine, Liv.; the person taught also acc.: iuventutem multa facinora, Sall.; or as subject in pass.: edoctus artes belli, Liv. TRANSF., with abstr. subject: edocuit ratio ut videremus, Cic.

ēdŏlo -are, *to hew out with an axe, to bring into shape, complete*: quod iusseras edolavi, Enn. ap. Cic.

ēdŏmo -dŏmare -dŏmŭi -dŏmĭtum, *to tame thoroughly, entirely subdue*: vitiosam naturam doctrina, Cic.; orbem (terrarum), Ov.

Ēdōni -ōrum (᾽Ηδωνοί), *a Thracian people, famed for the worship of Bacchus.*

¶ Hence adj. **Ēdōnus** -a -um, poet., *Thracian*: Verg.; **Ēdōnis** -nĭdis, f. poet. adj., *Thracian*: Ov.; as subst., *a Bacchanal*: Prop.

ēdormĭo -ire, *to have one's sleep out.*

Intransit., *to sleep away, to sleep one's fill*: cum (vinolenti) edormiverunt, Cic. Transit., (1) *to sleep off*: crapulam, Cic. (2) Fufius Ilionam edormit (of an actor), *sleeps through the part of Iliona*, Hor.

ēdormisco -ěre (edormio) *to sleep off a thing*: Pl., Ter.

ēdŭcātĭo -ōnis, f. (¹educo), *bringing up, training, education*; of children: educatio liberorum, Cic.; institutus liberaliter educatione doctrināque puerili, Cic.; of animals: Cic.

ēdŭcātor -ōris, m. (¹educo), *one who trains or brings up*; hence *a foster-father*: Cic.; *a tutor*: Tac.

ēdŭcātrix -ĭcis, f. (educator), *a foster-mother, nurse*. TRANSF., earum (rerum) parens est educatrixque sapientia, Cic.

¹**ēdūco** -are (connected with duco), *to bring up, rear, educate*. LIT., of human beings: aliquem, Cic.; caelum quo natus educatusque essem, Liv.; homo ingenuus liberaliterque educatus, Cic.; ad turpitudinem educatur, Cic. TRANSF., (1) of animals and plants: in educando perfacile apparet aliud quiddam iis (bestiis) propositum, Cic.; florem imber, Cat. (2) of abstr. things: educata huius nutrimentis eloquentia, Cic.

²**ēdūco** -dūcěre -duxi -ductum.

(1) *to draw out, lead out*. In gen.: gladium e vagina, Cic.; lacum (i.e. *to drain*), Cic.; sortem, Cic.; equos ex Italia, Liv.; hominem de senatu, Cic.; aliquem in provinciam, Cic. TRANSF., *to spend time*: pios annos, Prop.; esp.: **a**, milit. t. t., *to march troops out*: cohortes ex urbe, Caes.; exercitum in expeditionem, Cic.; Liv., Verg.: **b**, legal t. t., *to bring before a court of law*: aliquem in ius, Cic.; ad consules, Cic.: **c**, naut. t. t., *to take a ship out of port*: naves ex portu, Caes. (2) *to raise up*: **a**, of persons: aliquem superas sub auras, Verg.; fig.: in astra, *to praise sky high*, Hor.: **b**, of buildings: turrim summis sub astra eductam tectis, Verg.; Ov., Hor., Tac. (3) *to bring up, rear a child*: Cic., Verg., Tac.

ēdūlis -e (¹edo), *eatable*: Hor.

ēdūro -are, *to last, endure*: Tac.

ēdūrus -a -um, *very hard*: pirus, Verg. TRANSF., eduro ore negare, Ov.

Ēĕtĭōn -ōnis, m. (᾽Ηετίων), *father of Andromache, prince of Thebe in Cilicia.*

¶ Hence adj. **Ēĕtĭōnēus** -a -um, *of or belonging to Eetion.*

effarcio=effercio; q.v.

effātum -i, n. from partic of effor; q.v.

effectĭo -ōnis, f. (efficio), *a doing, practising*: artis, Cic. TRANSF., *an efficient cause*: Cic.

effectīvus -a -um (efficio), *productive, practical*: Quint.

effector -ōris, m. (efficio), *one who produces, causes, originates*: effector mundi molitorque deus, Cic.; of things: stilus optimus et praestantissimus dicendi effector ac magister, Cic.

effectrix -trīcis, f. (effector), *she that causes or produces*: terra diei noctisque effectrix, Cic.

¹**effectus** -a -um, partic. of efficio; q.v.

²**effectus** -ūs, m. (efficio). (1) *doing, effecting, execution, performance*: conatus tam audax traiciendarum Alpium et effectus, Liv.; in effectu esse, Cic.; postquam ad effectum operis ventum est, Liv. (2) *effect, result*: quarum (herbarum) causam ignorares, vim et effectum videres, Cic.; effectus eloquentiae est audientium approbatio, Cic.; sine ullo effectu, Liv.

effēmĭno -are (ex/femina), *to make into a woman.* (1) by representation: effeminarunt eum (aërem), Cic. (2) in character, etc., *to make effeminate, to enervate*: virum in dolore, Cic.; animos, Caes.

¶ Hence partic. **effēmĭnātus** -a -um, *effeminate, womanish*: opinio, Cic.; effeminatissimus languor, Q. Cic. ap. Cic. L.

¶ Adv. **effēmĭnātē**, *effeminately*: Cic.

effercĭo or **effarcio** (also ecf-: Pl.), -fercire,
-fertum (ex/farcio), *to stuff full*: intervalla
grandibus saxis, Caes.
¶ Hence partic. (with superl.) **effertus**
(ecf-), *stuffed*: Pl.

effĕrĭtās -ātis, f. (efferus), *wilderness, savagery*:
Cic.

¹**effĕro** -are (ferus), *to make wild, make savage.*
LIT., barba et capilli efferaverant speciem
oris, Liv.; terram immanitate beluarum
efferari, Cic. TRANSF., gentem, Cic.; animos,
Liv.; odio iraque efferati, Liv.
¶ Hence partic. **efferātus** -a -um, *wild,
savage*: Cic.; compar.: Liv.

¹**effĕro** (**ecfĕro**) efferre extŭli ēlātum (ex/fero).
(1) *to carry out, bring out.* In gen.: tela
ex aedibus alicuius, Cic.; pedem portā non
efferre, *not to stir outside*, Cic. L.; as milit.
t. t.: efferre signa (vexilla, arma), *to march
out*, Liv. Esp.: **a**, *to carry to the grave,
bury*: aliquem, Pl., Cic., Hor.; pass.: efferri,
to be borne out, buried, Cic.; fig.: ingens periculum manet ne libera respublica efferatur,
Liv.: **b**, of the earth, *to bring forth, bear*:
uberiores fruges, Cic.; Verg.: **c**, of words,
to utter, express: verba, Ter.; si graves
sententiae inconditis verbis efferuntur, Cic.;
hence of ideas or information, *to publish,
make known*: aliquid in vulgus, Cic.; ne has
meas ineptias efferatis, Cic.
(2) *to carry off.* LIT., Messium impetus
per hostes extulit ad castra, Liv. TRANSF.,
to carry away: si me efferet ad gloriam animi
dolor, Cic.; esp. pass.: efferri (laetitiā,
dolore, studio, iracundiā), *to be carried away
by*, Caes., Cic.
(3) *to raise up, lift up.* LIT., scutum super
caput, Liv.; lucem, Verg.; Tac. TRANSF.,
a, *to raise*: aliquem ad summum imperium,
Cic.: **b**, *to praise, extol*: aliquem *or* aliquid
laudibus, Cic.: **c**, esp. as efferri *or* se efferre,
to pride oneself, to be puffed up: efferre se
insolenter, Cic.; partic. elatus, *puffed up*:
resenti victoriā, Caes.
(4) *to endure to the end*: laborem, Lucr.
¶ Hence partic. **ēlātus** -a -um, *elevated,
exalted*; of discourse: verba, Cic.; of the
mind: animus magnus elatusque, Cic.
¶ Adv. **ēlātē.** (1) *loftily*: loqui, Cic.
(2) *arrogantly*: se gerere, Nep.

effertus -a -um, partic. from effercio. q.v.

effĕrus -a -um (ex/ferus), *very wild, savage*:
facta tyranni, Verg.; Lucr.

effervesco -fervescĕre -fervi, *to boil up,
foam up, effervesce.* LIT., aquae quae
effervescunt subditis ignibus, Cic. TRANSF.,
Pontus armatus, effervescens in Asiam atque
erumpens, *bursting forth*, Cic.; of an orator,
to be passionate: Cic.; poet. of the stars, at
the creation of the world, *to swarm forth,
to break out into a glow*: Ov.

effervo -ĕre (ex/fervo), *to boil up* or *over*: effer-
vere in agros vidimus undantem Aetnam,
Verg. TRANSF., *to swarm forth*: Lucr., Verg.

effētus -a -um (ex/fetus), *weakened by giving
birth, effete*: corpus, Cic.; vires, Verg.;
innumeris effetus laniger annis, Ov.; effeta
veri senectus, *now incapable of truth*, Verg.

effĭcācĭtās -ātis, f. (efficax), *efficacy*: Cic.

effĭcax -ācis, adj. (with compar and superl.)
(efficio), *effective, efficient, efficacious*: Hercules, Hor.; scientia, Hor.; maxime efficaces

ad muliebre ingenium preces, Liv.; in
quibus (rebus) peragendis continuatio ipsa
efficacissima esset, Liv.; with infin.: amara
curarum eluere efficax, Hor.
¶ Adv. (with compar. and superl.)
effĭcācĭter, *effectually*: Tac., Plin. L.

effĭcĭens -entis, partic. from efficio; q.v.

effĭcĭentĭa -ae, f. (efficiens), *efficiency*: Cic.

effĭcĭo -fĭcĕre -fēci -fectum (ex/facio), *to do,
produce, effect, make.*
(1) of material things; in gen.: mundum,
Cic.; columnam, *to build*, Cic.; esp. of the
produce of the ground, *to yield, bear*: cum
octavo, *eightfold*, Cic.
(2) of abstr. things; in gen.: omne opus
Caes.; officium, Cic.; magnas rerum commutationes, Caes.; so with clause as object
efficere ut (*or* ne) with subj., *to bring it about
that*, Caes., Cic., Verg., Liv., Tac.; esp.: **a**, of
numbers, *to make up, amount to*: ea tribut
vix in fenus Pompeii quod satis est efficiunt
Cic.; magnum cratium numerum, Caes.; dua
legiones, Caes.: **b**, as philosoph. t. t., *to
prove, show*: minutis interrogationibus quod
proposuit efficit, Cic.; with acc. and infin.
Cic.: **c**, of appointments and changes, *to
make*: Catilinam consulem, Cic.; hostes ae
pugnam alacriores, Caes.
¶ Hence partic. **efficiens** -entis, *effective
res*, Cic.; causa, *efficient cause*, Cic.; wit
genit.: efficiens voluptatis, *cause of*, Cic.
¶ Adv. **efficĭentĕr**, *efficiently, powerfully*: Cic.

effĭgĭēs -ēi, f. or **effĭgĭa** -ae, f.: Pl., Lucr
(effingo), *an image, likeness, effigy.* LIT., deu
effigies hominis, Cic.; hanc pro Palladic
effigiem statuere, Verg.; also of *a shade
ghost*: effigies, immo umbrae hominum, Liv
TRANSF., *an ideal*: et humanitatis et probi
tatis, Cic.; iusti imperii, Cic.; Liv.

effingo -fingĕre -finxi -fictum (ex/fingo). (1
to wipe: e foro sanguinem spongiis effingere
Cic.; manūs, Ov. (2) *to mould, form, fashion*
in gen.: oris lineamenta, Cic.; esp. *to form
one thing like another*, and so *to copy, repre
sent it*: (natura) speciem ita formavit oris u
in ea penitus recondito mores effingeret
Cic.; hence *to express in words*: aliciuii
mores, Cic.; sensūs mentis, Tac.; also *t
conceive* in thought: ea effingenda animo
Cic.

effĭo (ecf-) -fĭĕri, old pass. of efficio; q.v.: Pl
Lucr.

efflāgĭtātĭo -ōnis, f. (efflagito), *an urgen
demand*: Cic. L.

efflāgĭtātū, abl. as from efflagitatus, n
(efflagito), *at an urgent request*: coactu atqu
efflagitatu meo, Cic.

efflāgĭto -are (ex/flagito), *to ask earnestl
demand, entreat*: nostram misericordiar
Cic.; epistulam, Cic. L.; ab ducibus signu
pugnae, Liv.; ut se ad regem mitteret, Ver
Verg.

efflīgo -flīgĕre -flixi -flictum (ex/fligo),
destroy: Pompeium, Cic. L.

efflo -are (ex/flo), *to blow out.* Transit., *t
breathe out*: ignes ore et naribus, Ov
animam, extremum halitum, *to die*, Ci
Intransit.: Lucr.

efflōresco -flōrescĕre -flōrŭi (ex/floresco),
blossom, break into bloom. TRANSF., ex reru
cognitione oratio, Cic.

ffluo (ecflŭo) -flŭĕre -fluxi (ex/fluo), *to flow out.*
Lit., una cum sanguine vita, Cic.; aër effluens huc et illuc ventos efficit, Cic.
Transf., (1) *to vanish, drop off*: tanta est enim intimorum multitudo, ut ex iis aliquis potius effluat quam novo sit aditus, Cic.; of time, *to pass away*: ne effluat aetas, Cic. (2) *to pass out of mind. to be forgotten*: effluere ex animo alicuius, Cic.; absol.: quod totum effluxerat, Cic.; with mens as subject: alicui ex tempore dicenti solet effluere mens, Cic. (3) *to come to light, become known*: effluunt multa ex vestra disciplina, quae etiam ad nostras aures saepe permanant, Cic.

ffluvĭum -i, n. (effluo), *flowing out, outlet*: convivium effluvio lacus appositum, Tac.

ffŏdĭo -fŏdĕre -fŏdi -fossum (ex/fodio), *to dig out.* Lit., ferrum e terra, Cic.; also *to make by digging, to excavate*: lacum, Suet.
Transf., (1) *to gouge out*: oculos, Pl., Caes., Cic. (2) *to gut, to rummage*: domibus effossis, Caes.

ffor (ecfor) -fāri -fātus, dep. (ex/for). In gen., *to speak out, express, speak*: verbum, Cic.; nefanda, Liv.; tum ferunt ex oraclo ecfatam esse Pythiam, Cic.; Verg.
Esp. (1) in logic, *to state a proposition*: Cic. (2) as religious t. t., *formally to dedicate a place*: templum, Cic. L.
¶ Hence partic. (in pass. sense) **effātus** -a -um. (1) *pronounced*: verba, Liv. (2) *dedicated*: locus templo, Liv. N. as subst. **effātum** -i: Cic.

ffrēnātĭo -ōnis, f. *unbridled impetuosity*: animi impotentis, Cic.

ffrēno -are (frenum), *to unbridle, let loose*; post-Aug. except in past partic. (with compar. and superl.) **effrēnatus** -a -um, *unbridled.* Lit., equi, Liv. Transf., *unrestrained, unchecked, violent*: furor, cupiditas, homo, Cic.; effrenatior vox, Cic. Adv. (with compar.) **effrēnatē**, *unrestrainedly*: Cic.

ffrēnus -a -um (frenum), *unbridled.* Lit., equus, Liv. Transf., *unrestrained*: amor, Ov.; Verg.

ffringo -fringĕre -frēgi -fractum (ex/frango), *to break open*: fores, Cic., Pl., Ter.; ianuam, Cic.; naturae portarum claustra, Lucr.; cerebrum, Verg.

ffŭgio -fŭgĕre -fūgi -fŭgĭtum (ex/fugio).
(1) intransit., *to flee, fly away, escape, get off*: e proelio, Cic.; a quibus (ludis) vix vivus effugit, Cic.; Liv., Verg.; with ne and subj.: Liv., Tac.
(2) transit., *to escape from, avoid, flee from, shun*: equitatum Caesaris, Caes.; alicuius impias manus, Cic.; mortem, Caes.; scopulos, Verg.; me effugit, *it escapes me, escapes my observation*, Cic.

ffŭgium -i, n. (effugio), *a flying away, flight.* Lit., Lucr., Cic., Verg., Tac. Transf., *the means or opportunity of flight*: effugia pennarum habere, Cic.; dare alicui, Liv.

ffulgĕo -fulgēre -fulsi (ex/fulgeo), *to shine out, glitter*, Lit., nova lux oculis effulsit, Verg.; auro, *glitter with gold*, Verg. Transf., *to be distinguished, conspicuous*: effulgebant Philippus ac magnus Alexander, Liv.

ffultus -a -um (fulcio), *resting upon, supported by*: velleribus, Verg.

---

effundo (ecf-: Pl.) -fundĕre -fūdi -fūsum (ex/fundo), *to pour out, pour forth, shed.*
Lit., (1) of liquids: lacrimas, Cic.; Tiberis effusus super ripas, Liv.; imber effusus nubibus, Verg. (2) of solids, *to fling out, empty out*: saccos nummorum, Hor.; tela, Verg.
Transf., (1) with access. idea of violence, *to throw off, fling down*: aliquem solo, Verg.; esp. of horses, *to throw their riders*: effundere consulem super caput, Liv.; of weapons, *to discharge*: Verg., Liv.; excutiat Teucros vallo atque effundat in aequum, *drive forth*, Verg.; spiritum extremum, *to die*, Cic.; vinolentum furorem, *to give vent to*, Cic.; reflex.: se effundere, and middle, effundi, *to stream forth, pour forth*: cunctum senatum, totam Italiam esse effusam, Cic.; Celtiberi omnes in fugam effunduntur, Liv.; esp. of sounds, *to utter*: tales voces, Verg.; vox in coronam turbamque effunditur, Cic.; effudi vobis omnia quae sentiebam, Cic.
(2) with access. ideas of generosity, waste, freedom from restraint, *to pour out freely*: segetes effundunt fruges, Cic.; patrimonia effundere largiendo, *to squander*, Cic.; laborem, vires, Verg.; habenas, *to slacken*, Verg.; sinum togae, Liv.; reflex. and middle, *to give oneself up to, indulge in*: effundere se in aliqua libidine, Cic.; nimio successu in tantam licentiamque socordiamque effusus, Liv.
¶ Hence partic. (with compar. and superl.) **effūsus** -a -um, *poured out*; hence (1) *widespread, extensive*: mare late effusum, Hor.; Tac. (2) *extravagant, wasteful*: in largitione, Cic. (3) *unrestrained*: comae, Ov.; effuso cursu, agmine, Liv.; licentia, Liv.
¶ Adv. (with compar. and superl.) **effūsē**. (1) *far and wide*: ire, *in disorder*, Sall.; vastare, Liv. (2) *profusely, lavishly*: donare, Cic. (3) *unrestrainedly, immoderately*: exsultare, Cic.

ffūsĭo -ōnis, f. (effundo), *a pouring forth.*
Lit., tutantur se atramenti effusione sepiae, Cic.
Transf., (1) *violent movement*: effusiones hominum ex oppidis, Cic. (2): a, *extravagance, prodigality*: hae pecuniarum effusiones, Cic.; absol.: liberalitatem effusio imitatur, Cic. b, *exuberance of spirits*: effusio animi in laetitia, Cic.

ffūsus -a -um, partic. from effundo; q.v.

effūtĭo -ire (connected with fundo), *to blab out, chatter*: aliquid, Cic.; de mundo, Cic.; absol.: ex tempore, Cic.

effŭtŭo -fŭtŭĕre -fŭtŭi -fŭtūtum, *to squander in debauchery*: Cat.

ĕgĕlĭdus -a -um, *with the chill off, lukewarm, tepid*: tepores, Cat.; flumen, *rather cold*, Verg.

ĕgens -entis, partic. from egeo; q.v.

ĕgēnus -a -um (egeo), *needy, destitute*; with genit., *in need of*: omnium, Verg., Liv.; with abl.: Tac.; in rebus egenis, *in poverty*, Verg.

ĕgĕo -ēre -ŭi, *to want, be in need, be destitute.*
Lit., absol.: egebat? immo locuples erat, Cic.; more often, *to be in want of* something; with abl.: medicinā, Cic.; Caes.; with genit.: auxilii, Caes.; Ov.
Transf., (1) *to be without, not to have*; with abl.: auctoritate, *to have no authority,*.

Cic.; with genit.: audaciae, Sall. (2) *to desire, wish for, want*; with abl.: pane, Hor.; with genit.: Pl., Hor.

¶ Hence partic. (with compar. and superl.) **ĕgens** -entis, *needy, destitute*: egens quidam calumniator, Cic.; with genit., *in need of*: verborum non egens, Cic.; Ov.

Ēgĕrĭa -ae, f. *an Italian nymph, the instructress of Numa Pompilius.*

ēgĕro -gĕrĕre -gessi -gestum, *to bear out, carry out.* Lit., tantum nivis, Liv.; esp. *to carry off* as plunder: praedam ex hostium tectis, Liv. Transf., expletur lacrimis egeriturque dolor, *is expelled*, Ov.

ĕgestās -ātis, f. (egeo), *poverty, indigence, need.* Lit., ista paupertas vel potius egestas ac mendicitas, Cic.; with genit., *want of, deficiency in*: frumenti, Sall.; Tac. Transf., animi, Cic.; patrii sermonis, Lucr.

ĕgestio -onis, f. (egero), *wasting*: Plin. L.

ĕgŏ (ἐγώ) personal pronoun, *I.* Forms: sing., acc. me, genit. mei (usually objective), dat. mihi, abl. mē; plur., nom. nōs, acc. nos, genit. nostri (usually objective) and nostrum (usually partitive), dat. nobis, abl. nobis; -met or -pte added to several of these forms to give emphasis, -cum to abl. me and nobis for *with me, with us.*

Special senses and uses: alter ego, *my second self, the other self*; nos *for* ego: nobis consulibus, Cic.; ad me, *to my house*, Cic. L.; apud me, *at my house*, also *in my senses*, Ter.; a me, *from my property*, Cic.; dat. mihi and nobis often 'ethic' in senses *please, tell me*, etc.

ēgrĕdĭor -grĕdi -gressus, dep. (ex/gradior), *to step out.*

(1) intransit.: **a**, *to go out, pass out*. Lit., in gen., with ex or ab: Pl., Caes., Cic., Liv.; esp. as milit. t. t., *to march out*: e castris, Caes.; or, simply, castris: Caes.; ad proelium, Caes.; as naut. t. t.: egredi ex navi, Caes., Cic.; or, simply, navi: Caes.; *to disembark*, so: egredi in terram, Cic.; absol.: Caes.; egredi ex portu, *to sail away*, Cic. L. Transf., in discourse, *to digress*: a proposito, Cic.

b, *to go up, ascend*: ad summum montis, Sall.; Liv., Tac.

(2) transit., *to go out of, to pass beyond.* Lit., munitiones, fines, Caes. Transf., *to overstep, pass*: modum, Tac.

ēgrĕgĭus -a -um (ex/grex), *not of the common herd*; so *admirable, excellent, extraordinary, distinguished*: civis, Cic.; with in and the abl.: Laelius in bellica laude, Cic.; with ad: vir ad cetera egregius, Liv.; with abl.: bello, Verg.; with genit.: animi, Verg. Subst. **ēgrĕgĭa** -ōrum, n. *distinguished actions*: Sall.; *honours*: Tac.

¶ Adv. **ēgrĕgĭē**, *excellently, admirably*, with verbs: pingere, loqui, Cic.; Liv.; with adjectives: egregie fortis imperator, Cic.; Caes.; compar. egregius: Juv.

ēgressus -ūs, m. (egredior), *a going out, departure.*

Lit., vester, Cic.; ventos custodit et arcet Aeolus egressu, Ov.; esp. *a landing from a ship, disembarkation*: egressus optimus, Caes.

Transf., (1) *a passage out*: egressūs obsidens, Tac.; poet., *the mouth of a river*: Ov. (2) *a digression*: Quint., Tac.

ēgurgĭto -are (gurges), *to pour forth*: Pl.

ehem, interj., *expressing pleased surprise*, oho!: Ter., Pl.

ĕheu, interj., *expressing grief or pain, alas! woe!*: Pl., Hor., Ov.

ēhŏ, interj., used in questions, commands, etc., hi!: Pl., Ter.

ei (hei), interj., *expressing pain or fear, ah! woe!*: ei mihi conclamat, Ov.; Pl., Verg.

eiă and **heiă**, interj. (1) expressing joy or surprise, oho! well!: Pl., Ter.; sometimes heia vero, Pl., Cic. (2) in exhortation, come on!: Pl., Ter.; eia age, Verg.

ēiăcŭlor -ari, dep. *to throw out, hurl out*: aquas, Ov.

ēicĭo -icĕre -iēci -iectum (ex/iacio), *to throw out, cast out, eject.*

Lit., in gen.: corpus, Cic.; vocem, *to utter*, Cic.; linguam, *to thrust out*, Cic. armum, *to dislocate*, Verg.; esp.: **a**, with reflex.: se eicere, *to rush out*, Caes., Cic. Liv.: **b**, as naut. t. t., *to bring to shore* navem in terram, Caes.; in pass., *to be cast ashore, stranded*: classis ad Baleares eicitur Liv.; eici in litore, Caes.; eiectus, *a ship wrecked person*, Cic.

Transf., (1) *to drive out, expel, dispossess* a person: aliquem ex oppido, Caes.; domo, *to divorce*, Cic.; ex patria, *to banish*, Cic.; d conlegio, e senatu, Cic.; multos sedibus a fortunis, Cic. (2) *to hiss an actor off th stage*: Cic.; so *to reject*: Cynicorum rati tota est eicienda, Cic. (3) *to cast out, pu aside* feelings, etc.; curam ex animo, Pl amorem, Cic.; Liv.

ēiectāmentum -i, n. (eiecto), *that which thrown up*, in plur.: maris, Tac.

ēiectĭo -ōnis, f. (eicio), *banishment, exile* Cic. L.

ēiecto -are (freq. of eicio), *to hurl out, ejec* harenas, favillam, Ov.; cruorem ore, Verg.

ēiectus -ūs, m. (eicio), *a casting out*: Lucr.

ēiŭlātĭo -ōnis, f. (eiulo), *wailing, a lamentatio* illa non virilis, Cic.; Pl.

ēiŭlātus -ūs, m. (eiulo), *a wailing, lamentin* eiulatus ne mulieri quidem concessus es Cic.

ēiŭlo -are, *to wail, lament*: magnitudine dol rum eiulans, Cic.

ēiūro and **ēiĕro** -are, *to refuse or deny on oat* (1) legal t. t.: bonam copiam, *to swear th one is insolvent*, Cic.; forum (*or* iudicem) s iniquum, *to declare by oath that a court* (*judge*) *is partial, to challenge*, Cic.; magistratum, imperium, *to resign*, abdica Tac. (3) in gen., *to give up, disown*: patria Tac.

ēiusdemmŏdi or **ēiusdem mŏdi** (ide modus), *of the same kind*: Cic.

ēiusmŏdi or **ēius mŏdi** (is/modus). (1 *this kind, such*: genus belli est eiusmodi, C (2) =ita, *so*: quam viam tensarum atq pompae eiusmodi exegisti ut, Cic.

ēlābor -lābi -lapsus, dep. *to glide out or aw* Lit., in gen.: anguis ex columna lign elapsus, Liv.; cum se convolvens elaberetur et abiret, Cic.; Verg.; esp. *to s away, escape*: e manibus curantium, Li animi corporibus elapsi, Cic.; with ac custodias, Tac.; Verg.

Transf., (1) of abstr. things, *to gl away, disappear*: vita, Lucr.; aliqu memoriā, Cic.; disciplina elapsa est manibus, Cic. (2) of persons, fig. *to get away, escape*: ex tot tantisque criminibus, Cic.

lăbōro -are.
  (1) intransit., *to labour hard, strive, take pains*; with in: in litteris, Cic.; with ut and the subj.: Cic.; impers. pass.: Cic.
  (2) transit., *to labour on, work out, elaborate*, esp. in pass. partic. **ēlăbōrātus** -a -um: causae diligenter elaboratae et tanquam elucubratae, Cic.; versus ornati elaboratique, *carefully worked out*, Cic.; elaborata concinnitas, *artificial, not natural*, Cic.

lāmentābĭlis -e, *very lamentable*: gemitus, Cic.

languesco -guescĕre -gŭi, *to become weak, be relaxed*: alienā ignaviā, Liv.; Tac.; fig.: differendo deinde elanguit res, Liv.

largĭor -iri, *to lavish, give liberally*: Pers.

ătēius -a -um, *of or belonging to Elatus, a Lapith*; m. as subst., *son of Elatus*, i.e. *Caeneus*.

ātĭo -ōnis, f. (²effero), *a lifting up*; hence fig., *exaltation*: elatio et magnitudo animi, Cic.; elatio atque altitudo orationis suae, Cic.

ātro -are, *to bark out, cry out*: Hor.

ātus -a -um, partic. from ²effero; q.v.

ĕa or **Vĕlĭa** -ae, f. (᾽Ελέα), *a town in Lucania, birth-place of Parmenides and Zeno, the founders of the Eleatic school of philosophy.*
  ¶ Hence subst. **Ēlĕătēs** -ae, m. *Zeno*: Cic.; adj. **Ēlĕātĭcus** -a -um, *Eleatic*: philosophi, Cic.

ectĭo -ōnis, f. (eligo), *choice, selection*; of persons: senatus electionem (legatorum) Galbae permiserat, Tac.; of things: verborum, Cic.; trium condicionum, Liv.

ecto -are (freq. of eligo), *to choose*: Pl.

ectra -ae, f. (᾽Ηλέκτρα). (1) *daughter of Atlas, one of the Pleiades, mother of Dardanus by Jupiter.* (2) *daughter of Agamemnon, wife of Pylades, sister of Orestes and Iphigenia.*

ectrum -i, n. (ἤλεκτρον). (1) *amber*: Verg.; plur. *amber balls*: Ov. (2) *an alloy of gold and silver, resembling amber in colour*: Verg.

lectus -a -um, partic. from eligo; q.v.

lectus -ūs, m. (eligo), *choosing, choice*: necis, Ov.

ĕgans -antis, adj. (with compar. and superl.) (as from elego=eligo).
  (1) in good sense, *choice, fine, neat*: **a**, of persons: non parcus solum, sed etiam elegans, Cic.; subst. elegantes, *fine folk*: Cic.: **b**, of things, *tasteful*: artes, Cic.; epistula elegantissima, Cic. L.
  (2) (ante-class.), in bad sense, *fastidious, fussy*: Pl., Ter.
  ¶ Adv. (with compar. and superl.) **ēlĕganter**, *tastefully, choicely, neatly*: scribere, Cic.; scribere, psallere et saltare elegantius quam necesse est, Sall.; Latine loqui elegantissime, Cic.

ĕgantĭa -ae, f. (elegans). (1) in good sense, *taste, refinement, grace*: integritas et elegantia alicuius, Cic.; elegantia vitae, Cic.; doctrinae, Cic.; loquendi, disserendi, Cic. (2) (ante-class.), in bad sense, *fastidiousness*: Pl.

ĕgi -ōrum, m. (ἔλεγοι), *elegiac verses*: Hor., Ov., Tac.

ĕlĕgīa and **ĕlĕgēa** -ae, f. (ἐλεγεία), *an elegy*: Ov., Quint.

Ēlĕleus -ĕi, m. (from ἐλελεῦ, the Bacchic cry), *a surname of Bacchus*: Ov.
  ¶ Hence **Ēlĕlēĭdĕs** -um, f. *Bacchantes*: Ov.

ĕlĕmentum -i, n. *an element, first principle*; usually in plur. elementa.
  Lit., *physical elements*: Lucr., Cic., Ov.
  Transf., (1) *the letters of the alphabet*: Lucr., Suet. (2) *the elements of any science or art*: rationis, Lucr.; loquendi, Cic. (3) *the beginnings of other things*: prima Romae, Ov.

ĕlenchus -i, m. (ἔλεγχος), *a pearl pendant worn as an ear-ring*: Juv., Plin.

Ēlĕphantīnē -ēs, f. (᾽Ελεφαντίνη), **Ēlĕphantĭs** -tĭdis, f. (᾽Ελεφαντίς), *an island in the Nile, below the first cataract.*

ĕlĕphantus -i, c. (in class. prose commoner than elephas, esp. in oblique cases), *an elephant*: elephanto beluarum nulla prudentior, Cic.; Pl., Ter., Liv.
  Transf., *ivory*: Verg.

ĕlĕphās (-ans) -phantis, m. (ἐλέφας). Lit., *the elephant*: Lucr., Sen., Luc. Meton., *the disease elephantiasis*: Lucr.

Ēlĕus -a -um, *see* Elis.

Ēleusīn -īnis, f. (᾽Ελευσίν), *Eleusis, an ancient city in Attica, famous for the worship of Demeter (Ceres), and for the mysteries there celebrated.* Adj. **Ēleusīnus** -a -um: Eleusina mater, *Ceres*, Verg.

Ēleuthĕrĭus -a -um (᾽Ελευθέριος), *making free, a surname of Jupiter.* N. pl. as subst. **Ēleuthĕrĭa** -ōrum (sc. sacra), *a festival of Jupiter Liberator*: Pl.

ĕlēvo -are (ex/levo). Lit., *to lift up, raise, elevate*: contabulationem, Caes. Transf., *to make light of.* (1) in a bad sense, *to weaken, impair, disparage*: adversarium, Cic.; res gestas, auctoritatem, Liv. (2) in a good sense, *to alleviate, lighten*: suspiciones offensionesque, Cic.

ēlĭcĭo -licĕre -licŭi -lĭcĭtum (ex/*lacio), *to lure out, entice out.*
  Lit., hostem ex paludibus silvisque, Caes.; aliquem ad disputandum, Cic.; ad pugnam, Caes.; in proelium, Tac. Esp. by magic: inferorum animas, *to conjure up*, Cic.
  Transf., of things, *to elicit, call forth, produce*: lacrimas, Pl.; causam alicuius rei, Cic.; sententiam meam, Cic.; misericordiam, Liv.

Ēlĭcĭus -i, m. (elicio), *a surname of Jupiter* (in connexion with incantations): Liv., Ov.

ēlīdo -līdĕre -līsi -līsum (ex/laedo).
  (1) *to strike, knock, thrust out*: aurigam e curru, Cic.; oculos, Verg. Transf., morbum, *to expel*, Hor.
  (2) *to dash to pieces, shatter*: naves, Caes.; caput pecudis saxo, Liv. Transf., aegritudine elidi, Cic.

ēlĭgo -ligĕre -lēgi -lectum (ex/lego), *to pluck out*; hence (1) *to pick out, to choose, select*: amicos, Cic.; ex multis Isocratis libris triginta fortasse versus, Cic.; hunc urbi condendae locum, Liv. (2) fig., *to root out*: nervos urbis, Cic.; superstitionis stirpes omnes, Cic.
  ¶ Hence partic. (with superl.) **ēlectus** -a -um, *chosen, select*: Cic. Adv. **ēlectē**, *choicely*: Cic.

ēlīmĭno -are (ex/limen), *to carry out of doors*:
dicta foras, *to blab*, Hor.
ēlīmo -are (ex/lima), *to file off, smooth, polish.*
LIT., graciles ex aere catenas retiaque et
laqueos, Ov. TRANSF., *to elaborate, perfect*:
σχόλιον aliquod ad aliquem, Att. ap. Cic. L.
ēlinguis -e (ex/lingua). (1) *speechless*: Cic.,
Liv. (2) *without eloquence*: Cic., Tac.
Ēlĭs (or Ālĭs) -ĭdis, f. (*Ἦλις), *a territory in the
western part of Peloponnesus, containing
Olympia.*
¶ Hence adj. Ēlēus -a -um, *Elean, Olympic*: amnis, *the Alpheus*, Ov.; f. adj. Ēlĭăs
-ădis, *Elean, Olympic*: equae, Verg.
Ēlissa (Ēlīsa) -ae, f. (*Ἔλισσα), *another name
of Dido.*
ēlixus -a -um, *boiled.* LIT., Pl., Hor., Juv.
TRANSF., *sodden*: Mart., Pers.
ellĕbŏrus (hellĕbŏrus) -i, m. (ἐλλέβοϱος and
ἐλλέβοϱος) and ellĕbŏrum (hellĕbŏrum)
-i, n. *hellebore*, a plant supposed to be a
remedy for madness: expulit elleboro morbum bilemque meraco, Hor.; Pl., Verg.
ēlŏco -are, *to let, hire out*: fundum, Cic.
ēlŏcūtĭo -ōnis, f. (eloquor), *oratorical delivery,
elocution*: Cic., Quint.
ēlŏgĭum -i, n. (1) *a short saying, maxim*:
Solonis, Cic. (2) *an inscription*, esp. *on a
gravestone, epitaph*: Cic. (3) *a clause in a
will, a codicil*: Cic. (4) *a record* of a case:
Suet.
ēlŏquentĭa -ae, f. (eloquens), *eloquence*: Cic.
ēlŏquĭum -i, n. (eloquor), *eloquence*: qui licet
eloquio fidum quoque Nestora vincat, Ov.;
Verg., Hor., Juv.
ēlŏquor (ex/lŏquor) -lŏqui -lŏcūtus, dep. *to
speak out, express*: id quod sentit, Cic.;
cogitata praeclare, Cic.; also absol., *to speak
and esp. to speak eloquently*: Cic.
¶ Hence partic. (with compar. and superl.)
ēlŏquens -entis, *eloquent*: Cic., Quint.,
Tac. Adv. ēlŏquenter (with compar. and
superl.): Plin. L.
ēlūcĕo -lūcēre -luxi (ex/luceo), *to beam forth,
shine out, glitter.* LIT., splendidissimo candore inter flammas elucens circulus, Cic.
TRANSF., quae (scintilla ingenii) iam tum
elucebat in puero, Cic.; Lucr., Quint.
ēluctor -ari, dep.
(1) intransit., *to struggle out.* LIT., aqua
eluctabitur omnis, Verg. TRANSF., velut
eluctantia verba, Tac.
(2) transit., *to struggle out of, surmount a
difficulty.* LIT., cum tot ac tam validae
manus eluctandae essent, Liv.; nives, Tac.
TRANSF., locorum difficultates, Tac.
ēlūcubro -are, *to compose by lamplight*:
causae diligenter elaboratae et tanquam elucubratae, Cic.; Tac. Dep. form ēlūcubror
-ari: epistulam, Cic. L.
ēlūdo -lūdĕre -lūsi -lūsum (ex/ludo).
(1) intransit., *to finish playing*; esp. of the
waves of the sea: ipsum autem mare sic terram
appetens litoribus eludit, Cic.; litus qua
fluctus eluderet, Cic.
(2) transit.: **a**, *to parry a blow*: hastas,
Mart.; absol.: quasi rudibus eius eludit
oratio, Cic.; hence in gen., *to ward off,
evade*: bellum, pugnam, Liv.; Tac.: **b**, *to
beat* an opponent in play: Pl.; hence in
gen., *to delude, mock*: aliquem, Cic.; nos
contumeliis, Liv.; gloriam alicuius, Liv.

ēlūgĕo -lūgere -luxi, *to mourn for the pre
scribed period.* Transit.: Cic. L. Intransit.
Liv.
ēlumbis -e (ex/lumbus), *weak in the loin.*
TRANSF., of orators, *weak, feeble*: Tac.
ēlŭo -lŭĕre -lŭi -lūtum, *to wash out, was
clean, rinse, cleanse.* LIT., corpus, Ov.
sanguinem, Cic.; colorem, Lucr. TRANSF
(1) *to squander*: Pl. (2) *to wash away, effac
remove*: maculas furtorum, Cic.; crimer
Ov.; scelus, Verg.; amicitias, Cic.
¶ Hence partic. (with compar.) ēlūtus -
-um, *washed out, watery, insipid*: inrigu
nihil est elutius horto, Hor.
ēlŭvĭes -ēi, f. (eluo). (1) *a flowing ou
discharge*: siccare eluviem, Juv. (2)
flowing over, flood: eluvie mons est deductu
in aequor, Ov.; fig.: illa labes atque eluvie
civitatis, *impurity*, Cic. (3) *a ravine*: Curt.
ēlŭvĭo -ōnis, f. (eluo), *an inundation*: Cic;
plur.: aquarum eluviones, Cic.
Ēlўsĭum -i, n. (*Ἠλύσιον), *Elysium, the abode
the blessed.*
¶ Hence adj. Ēlўsĭus -a -um, *Elysian*
campi, Verg.; m. as subst. Ēlўsĭi (sc. campi
the Elysian fields: Mart., Luc.
¹em=hem; q.v.
²em, interj. (emo), *here! hi!*: Pl., Ter., Cic.
ēmācĭtās -ātis, f. (emax), *fondness for buying
Plin. L.
ēmancĭpātĭo -onis, f. (emancipo), *emancip
tion or transfer*: Quint., Plin. L.
ēmancĭpo (ēmancŭpo) -are. (1) *to release
emancipate a son from the patria potestas
Liv.; filium alicui in adoptionem, Cic. (2)
transfer or make over property*: Quint., Suet
fig., of persons, *to make over, give up
emancipatum esse alicui, Cic.; Pl., Hor.
ēmāno -are (ex/mano), *to flow out.* LIT., Luc
TRANSF., (1) *to arise, spring, emanate from
alii quoque alio ex fonte praeceptor
dicendi emanaverunt, Cic. (2) *to sprea
abroad*: mala quae a Lacedaemoniis profec
emanarunt latius, Cic.; of speech: ne per
his sermo tum emanet, Cic.; consilia tu
emanare, Liv.; emanabat, foll. by acc. an
infin., Liv.
Ēmăthĭa -ae, f. (*Ἠμαθία), *a district of Mac
donia*: Liv.; also a name for *Macedon
itself, or for Thessaly*: Verg.
¶ Hence adj. Ēmăthĭus -a -um, *Emathia
Macedonian*: dux, *Alexander*, Ov.; f. adj. an
subst. Ēmăthĭs -idis, *Macedonian*; henc
Emathideš, *the Muses*, Ov.
ēmātūresco -tūrescĕre -tūrŭi, *to becon
mature.* LIT., *to ripen*: Plin. TRANSF.,
become mild, be softened: ira, Ov.
ĕmax -ācis (emo), *fond of buying*: Cic., Ov.
emblēma -ātis, n. (ἔμβλημα), *inlaid or mosa
work*: Cic.
embŏlĭum -i, n. (ἐμβόλιον), *a dramatic inte
lude*: Cic.
ēmendābĭlis -e (emendo), *that may
amended*: error, Liv.
ēmendātĭo -ōnis, f. (emendo), *improveme
emendation, amendment*: correctio phi
sophiae veteris et emendatio, Cic.; Quint.
ēmendātor -ōris, m. (emendo), *an amend
corrector*: quasi emendator sermonis usita
Cic.; nostrae civitatis, Cic.
ēmendātrix -ícis, f. (emendator), *she u
corrects or amends*: vitiorum emendatrice

legem esse oportet, Cic.; o praeclaram emendatricem vitae poeticam, Cic.

ēmendo -are (ex/mendum), *to free from errors, emend, correct, improve.* (**1**) intellectually: alicuius annales, Cic. (**2**) morally: civitatem, Cic.; conscius mihi sum corrigi me et emendari castigatione posse, Liv.; consuetudinem vitiosam, Cic.; res Italias legibus, Hor.

¶ Hence partic., *free from mistakes, correct, faultless*: **a**, intellectually: locutio, Cic.; carmina, Hor.: **b**, morally: mores, Cic.; superl.: Plin. L.

Adv. **ēmendātē**, *correctly, faultlessly*: pure et emendate loqui, Cic.; compar.: Quint.

ēmentior -iri -ītus, dep. *to devise falsely, feign, counterfeit*: auspicia, Cic.; falsa naufragia, Liv.; with acc. and infin.: eo me beneficio obstrictum esse ementior, Cic.; Liv., Tac.; absol., *to make false statements*: in aliquem, Cic.; perf. partic. in pass. sense: auspicia ementita, Cic.

ēmercor -ari, dep. *to buy up*: Tac.

ēmĕrĕo -ēre -ŭi -itum and **ēmĕrĕor** -ēri -itus, dep. *to obtain by service, earn completely.*

LIT., with acc.: Pl., Prop.; with infin.: Ov.; also *to deserve well of a person*: aliquem, Tib., Ov.; esp. milit. t. t., *to earn pay, to serve*; with stipendia: Cic., Sall., Liv.

¶ Hence partic. as subst. **ēmĕrĭtus**, *a soldier that has served his time, a veteran*; in plur.: Tac.

TRANSF., of other service: annuum tempus (sc. magistratūs), Cic. L.: annuae operae emerentur, Cic. L.; partic. **ēmĕrĭtus** -a -um, *worn out, finished with*: equi, Ov.

ēmergo -mergĕre -mersi -mersum (ex/mergo).

(**1**) transit., *to cause to rise up*: emergere se *or* emergi, *to rise up, emerge.* LIT., serpens se emergit, Cic.; emersus e flumine, Cic., Liv., Tac. TRANSF., *to free oneself, to rise*: sese ex malis, Ter.; emersus ex tenebris, Cic.; Liv.

(**2**) intransit., *to come forth, come up, emerge.* LIT., equus ex flumine emersit, Cic.; Liv.; so of sun, moon, plants, *to come out*: Cic., Liv. TRANSF., **a**, *to extricate oneself, get clear, emerge*: emergere ex iudicio peculatus, Cic.; ex paternis probris ac vitiis, Cic.: **b**, *to rise, come to the top*: Lucr., Juv.: **c**, *to come to light, appear*: ex quo magis emergit quale sit decorum illud, Cic.

ēmĕrĭtus -a -um, partic. from emereo; q.v.

ēmĕtĭca -ae, f. (ἐμετική), *an emetic*: ap. Cic. L.

ēmētĭor -mētiri -mensus sum, *to measure out.*

LIT., spatium oculis, Verg. TRANSF., (**1**) *to pass over, traverse*: una nocte aliquantum iter, Liv.; freta, terras, Verg.; past partic. emensus -a -um in pass. sense: toto emenso spatio, Caes.; Verg., Liv. (**2**) *to pass through a space of time*: tres principes, *live through the reigns of*, Tac.; partic. as pass.: emensae in lucem noctes, Ov. (**3**) *to measure out, bestow*: ego autem voluntatem tibi profecto emetiar, Cic.; Hor.

ēmĕto -ĕre, *to reap away*: plus frumenti agris, Hor.

ēmĭco -micare -micŭi -micātum. (**1**) *to spring out, leap forth*; of persons: in litus, Verg.; solo, Verg.; of things: e corpore

sanguis, Lucr.; telum excussum velut glans emicabat, Liv.

(**2**) *to gleam forth.* LIT., flamma ex oculis, Ov. TRANSF., *to shine forth, be conspicuous*: inter quae verbum emicuit si forte decorum, Hor.; pavor, Tac.

ēmĭgro -are, *to move from a place, migrate*: huc ex illa domo praetoria emigrabat, Cic.; domo, Caes. TRANSF., e vita, *to die*, Cic.

ēmĭnentĭa -ae, f. (emineo), *standing out, prominence*: nec habere ullam soliditatem nec eminentiam, Cic.; in painting, *the lights* of a picture: Cic.

ēmĭnĕo -mĭnēre -mĭnŭi (ex/mineo), *to project, stand out.*

LIT., ex terra, Cic.; eminentibus oculis, *with projecting eyes*, Cic.; iugum directum eminens in mare, Caes.; of the lights of a picture, *to stand out*: magis id quod erit illuminatum exstare atque eminere videatur, Cic.

TRANSF., *to stand out, be conspicuous, remarkable*: toto ex ore crudelitas eminebat, Cic.; Demosthenes unus eminet inter omnes in omni genere dicendi, Cic.; tantum eminebat peregrina virtus, Liv.

¶ Hence partic. (with compar. and superl.) **ēmĭnens** -entis, *outstanding, projecting.* LIT., promontoria, Caes.; oculi, *standing out*, Cic.; genae leniter eminentes, Cic. TRANSF., *distinguished, eminent*: oratores, Tac. As subst., m. pl. **ēmĭnentes**: Tac.; n. pl. **ēmĭnentĭa**: Quint.

ēmĭnor -ari, *to threaten*: Pl.

ēmĭnus, adv. (e/manus, opp. comminus). (**1**) milit. t. t., *at a distance, from a distance*: eminus hastis aut comminus gladiis uti, Cic.; eminus pugnare, Caes. (**2**) in gen., *at a distance, from afar*: Ov.

ēmĭror -ari, dep. *to wonder at exceedingly, be astonished at*: aequora, Hor.

ēmissārĭum -i, n. (emitto), *an outlet for water*: Cic. L.

ēmissārĭus -i, m. (emitto), *an emissary, a spy*: Cic.

ēmissĭo -ōnis, f. (emitto), *a sending forth.* (**1**) of missiles: ballistae lapidum et reliqua tormenta eo graviores emissiones habent, quo sunt contenta atque adducta vehementius. (**2**) *letting loose*: anguis, serpentis, Cic.

ēmissus -ūs, m. (emitto), *sending forth*: Lucr.

ēmitto -mittĕre -mīsi -missum (ex/mitto), *to send forth, send out.*

(**1**) *to dispatch, send on a chosen course*; of things: hastam in fines eorum, Liv.; aquam ex lacu Albano, Liv.; varios sonitus linguae, *to utter*, Lucr.; of starting races between animals: ex porta leporem, Pl.; so fig.: tanquam e carceribus emissus, Cic.; esp. of troops: equitatus pabulandi causa emissus, Caes.; cohortes ex statione et praesidio, Caes.; equites in hostem, Liv. TRANSF., of books, *to publish*: si quando aliquid dignum nostro nomine emisimus, Cic.

(**2**) *to let go, let loose, free*: manu arma, Caes.; nubium conflicta ardor coruscans, Cic.; anguem, Cic.; aliquem ex obsidione, Liv.; e carcere, Cic.; legal t. t., of slaves: aliquem manu, *to free*, Pl., Liv., Tac.; of a debtor: libra et aere liberatum emittit, Liv.; so in gen., *to let slip* a person or matter: Catilinam ex urbe, Cic.; emissa de manibus res est, Liv.

ĕmo ĕmĕre ēmi emptum, *to buy, purchase.*
Lit., domum de aliquo, Cic.; aedes ab
aliquo, Cic.; with abl. of price: emere grandi
pecunia, Cic.; magno, *dear,* Cic.; parvo,
cheap, Cic.; with genit. (of some adjectives
and pronouns): tanti, quanti, Pl., Cic.;
minoris, pluris, Cic.; with adv.: emere
domum prope dimidio carius quam aestima-
batur, Cic.; bene, *cheap,* Cic.; male, *dear,*
Cic.; carē, Hor.
Transf., *to bribe, buy*: emptum iudicium,
Cic.; empta dolore voluptas, Hor.

ēmŏdĕror -ari, dep. *to moderate*: dolorem
verbis, Ov.

ēmŏdŭlor -ari, dep. *to put to music*: Musam per
undenos pedes, Ov.

ēmōlior -iri, dep. *to achieve by effort*: negotium,
Pl.

ēmollĭo -ire -īvi -ītum (ex/mollio), *to soften.*
Lit., fundas et amenta, Liv. Transf., (**1**) in
a good sense, *to make mild, soften*: mores,
Ov. (**2**) in a bad sense, *to make effeminate*:
exercitum, Liv.; Tac.

ēmŏlo -ĕre, *to grind away*: Pers.

ēmŏlŭmentum -i, n. (emolo), *the result of
effort, gain, advantage*: emolumento esse,
Cic.; emolumenta rerum, Liv.; pacis, Tac.

ēmŏnĕo -ēre, *to warn, admonish*: aliquem ut,
Cic. L.

ēmŏrĭor -mŏri -mortŭus sum, dep. *to die off.*
Lit., of persons: pro aliquo, Cic.; non mise-
rabiliter, Cic.; per virtutem, *bravely,* Sall.
Transf., *to perish*: laus emori non potest,
Cic.; amor, Ov.

ēmortŭālis -e, adj. (emorior), *of death*: Pl.

ēmŏvĕo -mŏvēre -mōvi -mōtum, *to move out,
move away, remove.* Lit., multitudinem e
foro, Liv.; aliquos senatu, Liv.; muros
fundamentaque, *to shake,* Verg. Transf.,
curas dictis, Verg.

Empĕdŏclēs -is, m. ('Εμπεδοκλῆς), *a poet and
philosopher of Agrigentum, of the fifth century*
B.C.
¶ Hence adj. **Empĕdŏclēus** -a -um,
Empedoclean: sanguis (according to the
doctrines of Empedocles), *the soul,* Cic.; n.
pl. as subst. **Empĕdŏclēa** -ōrum, *the doctrines of Empedocles*: Cic.

emphasis -is, f. (ἔμφασις), *emphasis*: Quint.

empīrĭcus -i, m. (ἐμπειρικός), *an unscientific
physician, empiric*: Cic.

Empŏrĭae -ārum, f. ('Εμπορίαι), *a town in
Hispania Tarraconensis.*

empŏrĭum -i, n. (ἐμπόριον), *a place of trade,
market*: celebre et frequens, Liv.; Pl., Cic. L.

emptĭo -ōnis, f. (emo), *a buying, purchasing.*
Lit., ista falsa et simulata emptio, Cic.; Tac.
Meton., *a purchase*: prorsus ex istis emptio-
nibus nullam desidero, Cic. L.; Plin. L.

emptĭto -are (freq. of emo), *to buy up, to buy*:
Tac., Plin. L.

emptor -ōris, m. (emo), *a buyer, purchaser*:
emptor fundi, Cic.; emptores bonorum,
Cic. Transf., dedecorum pretiosus emptor,
Hor.

ēmūgĭo -ire, *to bellow*: Quint.

ēmulgĕo -mulgēre -mulsum, *to drain out, to
exhaust*: paludem, Cat.

ēmungo -mungĕre -munxi -munctum (connected with mucus), *to clean a nose.* Lit.,
with reflex. or pass. in middle sense; *to wipe
one's nose*: Suet., Juv. Transf., *to cheat* a

person: Pl., Hor.; with abl., *out of* a thing:
Pl., Ter.
¶ Hence partic. **ēmunctus** -a -um:
emunctae naris, *with a clean nose,* i.e. *shrewd,
discerning,* Hor., Phaedr. Transf., homo
emunctae naris, *with a keen scent for other
persons' faults,* Hor.

ēmūnĭo -ire. (**1**) *to fortify, strengthen, make
safe*: locum, Liv.; postes, Verg. (**2**) *to build
up*: murum, Liv. (**3**) *to clear*: silvas ac
paludes, Tac.

ēn (sometimes **em**: Pl., Ter.). (**1**) interj., *lo!
behold! see!* used like ecce to call attention
to a person or thing present or to a point
made; often with nom. or acc.: en ego vester
Ascanius, Verg.; en quattuor aras, Verg.;
en causa, Cic.; en cui tu liberos committas,
Cic.; en aspice, Ov. (**2**) interrog., *look, say*:
en, quid ago? Verg.; esp. with unquam: en
unquam futurum, Liv.; Pl., Verg. (**3**) with
imperat., *come!*: Pl., Verg.

ēnarrābĭlis -e (enarro), *that can be narrated
or told*: Verg., Sen., Quint.

ēnarrātĭo -ōnis, f. (enarro), *exposition*:
Quint.; *scansion*: Sen.

ēnarro -are, *to narrate* or *explain*: alicui somnium, Cic.; Pl., Ter., Liv.

ēnascor -nasci -nātus sum, dep. *to grow out of,
spring forth, arise from*: capillus, Liv.;
cornua, Plin.

ēnāto -are, *to swim away, escape by swimming.*
Lit., si fractis enatat exspes navibus, Hor.
Transf., *to extricate oneself*: reliqui habere
se videntur angustius; enatant tamen, Cic.

ēnāvĭgo -are, *to sail away*; with acc.: undam,
over the waves, Hor.; Plin. Transf., tanquam e scrupulosis cotibus enavigavit
oratio, Cic.

Encĕlădus -i, m. ('Εγκέλαδος), *one of the giants,
slain by the lightning of Jupiter, and buried
beneath Etna.*

endo, archaic=in.

endrŏmis -ĭdis, f. (ἐνδρομίς), *a rough cloak worn
by athletes* (*male* or *female*) *after exercise*:
Mart., Juv.

Endўmĭōn -ōnis, m. ('Ενδυμίων), *a beautiful
young man, loved by the Moon*; appell., *a
beautiful youth*: Juv.

ēnĕco (**ēnĭco**) -nĕcare -nĕcŭi -nectum, *to kill
off.* Lit., Pl. Transf., *to wear out, exhaust,
torture*: siti enectus Tantalus, Cic.; fame
frigore, inluvie, squalore enecti, Liv.; hence
colloq., *to fag*: Pl., Ter.

ēnervis -e (nervus), *powerless, weak*: orator
Tac.; Quint.

ēnervo -are (nervus), *to remove the sinews from*
hence *to weaken.* Lit., aliquem, Cic.;
corpora animosque, Liv.; Hor. Transf., u
enervetur oratio compositione verborum
Cic.
¶ Hence partic. **ēnervātus** -a -um
weakened, powerless. Lit., Cic. Transf.
mollis et enervata oratio, Cic.; enervata
muliebrisque sententia, Cic.

ēnĭco=eneco; q.v.

ĕnim, conj. (generally second or third word
in its clause). (**1**) corroborating a previous
statement, *indeed, truly, certainly*: Caes.
Cic., Verg., Liv.; sometimes ironical: Pl.
Cic. (**2**) in conjunction with other particles
at enim, *but you may object* . . ., Cic.; sed enim
but indeed, Cic., Verg.; enimvero as one word

q.v. (3) explanatory, *namely, for instance*: Pl., Ter., Cic. (4) (most commonly) explanatory, *for*: de corpusculorum (ita enim appellat atomos) concursione fortuita, Cic.; often where a point has not been expressed but understood: tum Socrates, non enim paruisti mihi revocanti, *that is not to be wondered at for*, Cic.

nimvēro, *to be sure, certainly*: Cic., Liv.

nīpeūs -pĕi, m. ('Ενιπεύς). (1) *a river in Thessaly*; also *the river-god there.* (2) *a river in Pieria*: Liv.

nīsus, partic. from enitor; q.v.

nītĕo -ēre -ŭi, *to shine out, shine forth.* LIT., enitet campus, Verg. TRANSF., *to be conspicuous*: quo in bello virtus enituit egregia M. Catonis, Cic.; Liv.

nītesco -ĕre (inch. of eniteo), *to gleam, shine forth.* LIT., enitescit pulchrior multo, Hor. TRANSF., bellum novum exoptabat, ubi virtus enitescere posset, Sall.; Quint., Tac.

nītor -niti -nīsus or -nixus, dep.

(1) *to work one's way up, to struggle up, ascend.* LIT., in ascensu, Caes.; per adversos fluctus ingenti labore remigum, Liv.; in editiora, Tac.; with acc., *to climb*: aggerem, Tac. TRANSF., Hor.

(2) in gen., *to strive, struggle, make an effort*: in aliqua re, Cic.; ad dicendum, Cic.; with n. acc.: quod quidem certe enitar, Cic. L.; with ut and subj.: Caes., Cic., Liv., Sall; with ne and the subj.: Sall., Cic. L.; with infin.: Ter., Sall., Hor.

(3) transit., *to bring forth, bear*: partus plures, Liv.; Verg., Tac.; also absol., *to bear*: Quint., Tac.

¶ Hence partic. **ēnixus** -a -um, *strenuous, eager*: enixo studio, Liv.; compar., Sen.

¶ Adv. (with compar. and superl.) **ēnixe**, *eagerly, strenuously*: iuvare, Caes.; operam dare, Liv.; Cic.

nna = Henna; q.v.

nnĭus -i, m. Q. (239–169 B.C.), *the 'father of Roman poetry' in most of its forms, esp. epic, born at Rudiae in Calabria.*

nnŏsĭgaeus -i, m. ('Εννοσίγαιος), *the Earthshaker, surname of Neptune*: Juv.

no -are, *to swim out, escape by swimming.* LIT., e concha, Cic.; in terram, Liv. TRANSF., *to fly away*: insuetum per iter gelidas enavit ad Arctos, Verg.

ēnōdātĭo -ōnis, f. (enodo), *an untying*; hence *an explanation*: explicatio fabularum et enodatio nominum, Cic.

ēnōdis -e (ex/nodus), *without knots*: truncus, Verg.; abies, Ov. TRANSF., *clear, plain*: Plin. L.

ēnōdo -are, *to free from knots*; hence *to make clear, explain, expound*: nomina, Tac.

¶ Hence, from partic., adv. (with compar.) **ēnōdātē**, *clearly, plainly*: narrare, Cic.

ēnormis -e (ex/norma). (1) *irregular, unusual*: vici, Tac. (2) *very large, immense, enormous*: hasta, gladius, Tac.

ēnormĭtās -ātis, f. (enormis), *irregular shape*: Quint.

ēnōtesco -nōtescĕre -nōtŭi, *to become known, be made public*: quod ubi enotuit, Tac.; Plin. L.

ensĭcŭlus -i, m. (dim. of ensis), *a little sword*: Pl.

ensĭfĕr -fĕra -fĕrum (ensis/fero), *swordbearing*: Orion, Luc.

ensĭgĕr -gĕra -gĕrum (ensis/gero), *swordbearing*: Orion, Ov.

ensis -is, m. *a sword*: Lucr., Liv., Verg.

Entella -ae, f. ('Έντελλα), *a town in Sicily.*

¶ Hence adj. and subst. **Entellīnus** -a -um, *of Entella, an inhabitant of it.*

enthȳmēma -ătis, n. (ἐνθύμημα), *a thought, line of thought, argument*: Cic., Quint.; esp. *a kind of syllogism*: Cic., Quint.

ēnūbo -nūbĕre -nupsi -nuptum, of a woman, *to marry out of her rank*: e patribus, Liv.; also *to marry and leave home*: Liv.

ēnuclĕo -are (ex/nucleus), *to take out the kernel.* TRANSF., haec nunc enucleare non ita necesse est, *explain in detail*, Cic.

¶ Hence partic. **ēnuclĕātus** -a -um, *straightforward, simple, clear*: suffragia, honest, Cic.; genus dicendi, *plain*, Cic.

¶ Adv. **ēnuclĕātē**, *clearly, plainly*: Cic.

ēnŭmĕrātĭo -ōnis, f. (enumero), *a counting up, enumeration*: singulorum argumentorum, Cic.; in rhetoric, *recapitulation*: Cic., Quint.

ēnŭmĕro -are, *to reckon, count up, enumerate.* LIT., dies, Caes.; pretium, *to pay out*, Cic. TRANSF., *to recount, recapitulate*: multitudinem beneficiorum, Cic.; Verg., Liv.

ēnuntĭātĭo -ōnis, f. (enuntio), in rhetoric, *an enunciation, proposition*: Cic., Quint.

ēnuntĭo -are, *to tell, divulge, disclose.* LIT., consilia adversariis, Cic.; enuntiare mysteria, Cic.; silenda, Liv.; rem Helvetiis per indicium, Caes.; with indir. quest., plane quid sentiam enuntiabo apud homines familiarissimos, Cic.

TRANSF., (1) *to declare, announce, express in words*: aliquid verbis, Cic.; esp. as logic. t. t., *to state a proposition, to predicate*: Cic. (2) *to pronounce clearly*: litteras, Quint.

¶ N. of partic. as subst. **ēnuntiātum** -i, *a proposition*: Cic.

ēnuptĭo -ōnis, f. (enubo), *a woman's marrying out*: gentis, *out of her gens*, Liv.

ēnūtrĭo -ire, *to nourish, rear, bring up*: puerum Ideis sub antris, Ov.; ingenia, Quint.

¹**ĕo** ire ȋvi and ȋi ȋtum (connected with Gr. εἶμι), *to go.*

LIT., of physical movement. (1) by living beings; in gen.: domum, Pl.; ad forum, Pl.; subsidio suis, Caes.; novas vias, Prop.; Viā Sacrā, Hor.; pedibus, equis, Liv.; puppibus, *to make a voyage*, Ov.; with supine: cubitum, *to go to bed*, Cic.; with infin.: visere, Ter.; esp.: a, milit. t. t.: ire ad arma, ap. Cic.; ad saga, Cic., *to fly to arms*; maximis itineribus, Liv.; contra hostem, Caes.; in hostem, Liv.; Verg.: b, polit. t. t.: ire (*or* pedibus ire) in sententiam, *to support a motion*, Liv., Cic.; in alia omnia, *to oppose a motion, vote against*, Cic. (2) by things: it clamor caelo, Verg.; iit hasta, Verg.; it naribus ater sanguis, Verg.

TRANSF., of metaphorical movement, *to pass, proceed*, etc. (1) of persons: ire in poenas, *to start punishing*, Ov.; in scelus, *to commit a fault*, Ov.; in duplum, *to give a double penalty*, Cic.; ierat in causam praeceps, Liv.; ire per laudes tuorum, *to go over*, Ov.; in exclamations, i, *go to*: i nunc et cupidi nomen amantis habe, Ov. (2) of things: pugna it ad pedes, Liv.; incipit res melius ire, *to go better*, Cic. L.; sic eat quaecunque Romana lugebit hostem, Liv.; eunt anni, *pass,* Ov.; ire in aliquid, *to be changed to*; sanguis it in sucos, Ov.

²ĕō, adv. (is). (1) old dat., *thither, to that point*: **a,** in space: eo pervenire, Cic.; Caes., Hor., Liv., etc.: **b,** in time: usque eo dum, Cic.: **c,** in other relations; of addition: accedit eo, Cic. L.; of tendency: eo spectare, Cic.; esp. of degree, *so far, to such a pitch*: eo rem adducam ut, etc., Cic.; with genit.: eo consuetudinis adducta res est, Liv. (2) locative, *there*; esp. with loci (partitive genit.): Cic. L., Tac. (3) abl.: **a,** *for that, on that account*: eo quod, Cic.; eo quia, Cic.; eo ut, Cic.; non eo, dico, quo, Cic.: **b,** with comparatives, esp. as correl. to quo, *the more . . . the more . . .*: eo gravior est dolor, quo culpa maior, Cic. L.

ĕōdem, adv. (idem). (1) old dat., *to the same place*: eodem mittere, Caes. TRANSF., *to the same point* or *person*: eodem pertinet, Caes., Cic. L. (2) locative, *in the same place*: Liv. TRANSF., res est eodem loci ubi reliquisti, *in the same condition*, Cic.

Ēos (ἠώς) (occurs only in nom.), f. *dawn.*

¶ Hence adj. **Ēous** and **Ēŏus** -a -um, *belonging to the morning,* or *eastern.* M. as subst. **Ēŏus** -i. (1) *the morning star*: Verg. (2) *a dweller in the East*: Ov. (3) *one of the horses of the sun*: Ov.

ĕpastus -a -um (pasco), *eaten up*: escae, Ov.

ĕphēbus -i, m. (ἔφηβος), *a young man between eighteen and twenty* (generally of Greeks): Ter., Cic., Ov.

ĕphēmĕris -ĭdis, f. (ἐφημερίς), *a journal, diary*: Cic., Ov.

Ĕphĕsus -i, m. (Ἔφεσος), *one of the twelve Ionian towns in Asia Minor,* famous for its temple of Diana and school of rhetoric.

¶ Hence adj. and subst. **Ĕphĕsĭus** -a -um, *Ephesian, an Ephesian.*

ĕphippĭātus -a -um (ephippium), *provided with a saddle*: Caes.

ĕphippĭum -i, n. (ἐφίππιον), *a horse-cloth, saddle*: Caes., Cic.; prov.: optat ephippia bos piger, optat arare cabellus, *no one is content with his condition,* Hor.

¹**ĕphŏrus** -i, m. (ἔφορος), *an ephor, a Spartan magistrate*: Cic.

²**Ĕphŏrus** -i, m. (Ἔφορος), *a Greek historian of Cyme in Asia Minor, flourishing about* 340 B.C.

Ĕphȳra -ae and **Ĕphȳrē** -ēs (Ἐφύρα), f. *the ancient name of Corinth.*

¶ Hence **Ĕphȳrēïus** -a -um, *Corinthian*: Verg.

Ĕpĭcharmus -i, m. (Ἐπίχαρμος), *a philosopher and comic poet of the fifth century* B.C., *disciple of Pythagoras.*

epichysis -is, f. (ἐπίχυσις), *a vessel for pouring*: Pl.

ĕpĭcōpus -a -um (ἐπίκωπος), *provided with oars*: phaselus, Cic. L.

ĕpĭcrŏcus -a -um (ἐπίκροκος), *transparent, fine*: Pl.

Ĕpĭcūrus -i, m. (Ἐπίκουρος), *an Athenian philosopher, founder of the Epicurean school* (342–270 B.C.).

¶ Hence adj. and subst. **Ĕpĭcūrēus** -a -um, *Epicurean, an Epicurean.*

ĕpĭcus -a -um (ἐπικός), *epic*: poëta, Cic.; poëma, Cic.

Ĕpĭdaurus -i, f. (Ἐπίδαυρος), *a town in Argolis, on the Saronic Gulf, with a temple of Aesculapius.*

¶ Hence adj. **Ĕpĭdaurĭus** -a -um, *Epidaurian*; m. as subst. **Ĕpĭdaurĭus** -i, *Aesculapius*: Ov.

ĕpĭdictĭcus -a -um (ἐπιδεικτικός), *for display*: genus dicendi, Cic.

ĕpĭdipnis -idis, f. (ἐπιδειπνίς), *dessert*: Petr., Mart.

Ĕpĭgŏni -ōrum, m. (Ἐπίγονοι), *the after-born, sons of the Seven against Thebes, who renewed the war of their fathers; name of a tragedy of Aeschylus, translated into Latin by Accius.*

ĕpĭgramma -ătis, n. (ἐπίγραμμα). (1) *an inscription*: Cic. (2) *an epigram*: Cic., Quint.

ĕpĭlŏgus -i, m. (ἐπίλογος), *a conclusion, peroration, epilogue*: Cic., Quint.

ĕpĭmēnia -orum, n. pl. (ἐπιμήνια), *a month's rations*: Juv.

Ĕpĭmētheus -ĕi, m. (Ἐπιμηθεύς), *father of Pyrrha, son of Iapetus and brother of Prometheus.*

¶ Hence **Ĕpĭmēthis** -thĭdis, f. (Ἐπιμηθίς), *Pyrrha*: Ov.

ĕpĭrēdĭum -ii, n. (ἐπί/raeda), *the strap by which a horse was fastened to a vehicle; trace*: Juv., Quint.

Ĕpīrus -i, f. (Ἤπειρος), *a region in north-west Greece.*

¶ Hence adj. **Ĕpīrensis** -e, *of Epirus*; subst. **Ĕpīrōtes** -ae, m. (Ἠπειρώτης), *an Epirote*; adj. **Ĕpīrōtĭcus** -a -um, *of Epirus.*

ĕpistŏlĭum -ii, n. (ἐπιστόλιον), *a little letter, note*: Cat.

ĕpistŭla (or **ĕpistŏla**) -ae, f. (ἐπιστολή), *a written communication, letter, epistle*: epistula ab aliquo, Cic.; ad aliquem, Cic.; epistulam dare, *to send off,* Cic.; epistula Graecis litteris conscripta, Caes.; epistulam inscribere alicui, Cic.; ab epistulis, *to do with correspondence,* of secretaries, etc., Suet.

TRANSF., *a sending of letters, post*: Cic. L.

ĕpĭtaphĭum -i, m. (ἐπιτάφιον), *a funeral oration*: Cic.

ĕpĭthălămium -i, n. (ἐπιθαλάμιον), *a nuptial song*: Quint.

ĕpĭthēca -ae, f. (ἐπιθήκη), *an addition*: Pl.

ĕpĭtŏma -ae and **ĕpĭtŏmē** -ēs, f. (ἐπιτομή), *an abridgment, epitome*: Cic. L.

ĕpŏdes -um, m. pl. *a kind of salt-water fish*: Ov.

Ĕpōna -ae, f. *the protecting goddess of horses and asses*: Juv.

ĕpops -ŏpis, m. (ἔποψ), *the hoopoe*: Verg., Ov.

Ĕpŏrĕdĭa -ae, f. *a Roman colony in Gallia Cisalpina* (now Ivrea).

ĕpos, nom. and acc. only, n. (ἔπος), *an epic poem*: Hor.; plur. epē, Prop.

ĕpōtus -a -um (poto), *drunk up, drained.* LIT., poculo epoto, Cic.; medicamento, Liv. TRANSF., (1) *spent on drink*: Pl. (2) *swallowed up*: terreno Lycus est epotus hiatu, Ov.

ĕpŭlae -ārum, f. *food, dishes of food.* In gen.: Pl., Cic., Verg.; esp. *banquet, feast*: mensae conquisitissimis epulis exstruebantur, Cic.; funestas epulas fratri comparare, Cic.; also at festivals: Cic., Hor. TRANSF., oculis *feast for the eyes,* Pl., Cic.

ĕpŭlāris -e (epulae), *belonging to a banquet*: accubitio amicorum, Cic.; sacrificium, Cic.

ĕpŭlātĭo -ōnis, f. (epulor), *feasting*: Suet.

ĕpŭlo -ōnis, m. (epulum), *a feaster*: Cic.; esp. Tresviri (subsequently Septemviri) epulones

epulor   **ergo**

a college of priests who had charge of the sacrificial feasts, Cic., Liv.; so simply epulones: Cic.

ĕpŭlor -ari, dep. (epulum), *to feast.*
(1) intransit.: unā, *together*, Cic.; cum aliquo, Cic.; modice, Cic.; Saliarem in modum, *splendidly*, Cic.; with abl.: dapibus opimis, Verg.
(2) transit., *to feast on, eat*: aliquem epulandum ponere mensis, *to place on the table to be eaten*, Verg.; Liv.

ĕpŭlum -i, n. *a banquet, feast*, esp. on special public occasions: epuli dominus, Cic.; epulum populi Romani, Cic.; alicui epulum dare nomine alicuius, Cic.

ĕqua -ae, f. (dat. and abl. pl. generally equabus; from equus), *a mare*: Cic., Verg., Hor.

ĕquĕs -ĭtis, m. (equus), *a horseman, rider.*
In gen.: illum equitem sex dierum spatio transcurrisse longitudinem Italiae, Liv.; Ov. Esp. (1) *a horse-soldier*: Caes., Liv.; (opp. pedes), and used collectively, *cavalry*: Liv., Tac. (2) equites, *the knights, a distinct order in the Roman commonwealth, between the senate and the plebs*, Cic., Ov.; collectively in sing.: Hor., Tac.

ĕquester -stris -stre (eques), *relating to horsemen, equestrian.* In gen.: statua, Cic. Esp. (1) *relating to horse-soldiers and cavalry*: proelium, Caes.; pugna, Cic.; Liv. (2) *relating to the knights*: ordo, Cic.; locus, Cic.; census, Cic., Liv.

ĕquĭdem (quidem strengthened by demonstrative prefix e-), a particle, generally used with the first person. (1) *indeed, truly, for my part*: nihil, inquit, equidem novi, Cic.; equidem ego, Cic.; certe equidem, Pl., Verg. (2) in a concessive sense, *of course, certainly*; *admittedly*; with sed, verum, tamen: Cic., Liv.

ĕquĭlĕ -is, n. (equus), *a stable*: Cato, Suet.

ĕquīnus -a -um (equus), *relating to horses*: seta, Cic.; nervus, Verg.; Hor.

ĕquīria -ōrum, n. (equus), *horse-races in honour of Mars, which took place every year at Rome, in the Campus Martius*: Ov.

ĕquĭtātus -ūs, m. (equito), *cavalry* (opp. peditatus): Caes., Cic., Sall.

ĕquĭto -are (eques), *to ride on horseback.* Lit., Cic., Hor., Liv.; esp. of cavalry: Cic. Transf., of winds, *to rush*: Eurus per Siculas equitavit undas, Hor.

ĕquŭlĕus = eculeus; q.v.

ĕquus -i, m. (older forms equos and ecus; genit. pl. equum: Verg.) (connected with ἵππος), *a horse.*
Lit., equorum domitores, Cic.; equus bellator, *a war-horse*, Verg.; equus publicus, *given by the state*, Liv.; equum conscendere, Liv.; in equum ascendere, Cic.; in equum insilire, Liv.; sedere in equo, Cic.; vehi in equo, Cic.; equis insignibus et aurato curru reportari, *to ride in triumph*, Cic.; merere equo, *to serve in the cavalry*, Caes.; equis virisque (*or* equis viris), *with horse and foot*, hence prov., *with all one's might*, Cic., Liv.; ad equum rescribere, *to make someone a knight*, Caes.; equus Troianus, *the Trojan horse*, Verg.; fig., of a conspiracy: Cic.
Transf., (1) equus ligneus, *a ship*, Pl. (2) plur.: equi, *a chariot*, Verg. (3) equus

bipes, *the sea-horse*, Verg. (4) *the constellation* Pegasus: Cic. poet.

Equus Tūtĭcus -i, m. *a small town in the country of the Hirpini in Lower Italy.*

ĕra -ae, f. (erus), *a mistress.* Lit., of a house: Pl., Ter. Transf., (1) used of a goddess, *Lady*: Pl., Cat. (2) of a sweetheart: Cat., Ov.

ērādīco -are (radix), *to root out*: Pl., Ter.

ērādo -rādĕre -rāsi -rāsum, *to scratch out*: aliquem albo senatorio, *from the senatorial list*, Tac.; in gen., *to destroy, get rid of*: elementa cupidinis pravi, Hor.

Ĕrătō (found only in nom.), f. ('Ερατώ), *the Muse of lyric and love-poetry*: Ov.; appell., *any Muse*: Verg.

ercisco, erctum = hercisco; herctum; q.v.

Ĕrĕbus -i, m. ("Ερεβος). (1) *a god of the lower world, son of Chaos and brother of Nox*: Cic. (2) *the lower world*: Verg. Adj. **Ĕrĕbēus** -a -um, *belonging to the lower world.*

Ĕrechtheus -ĕi, m. ('Ερεχθεύς), *a mythical king of Athens, father of Orithyia and Procris.*
¶ Hence adj. **Ĕrechthēus** -a -um, m. *Athenian*: Ov.; subst. **Ĕrechthīdae** -arum, m. *the Athenians*: Ov.; subst. **Ĕrechthis** -ĭdis, f. *daughter of Erechtheus, i.e. Orithyia or Procris*: Ov.

ērectus, partic. from erigo; q.v.

ērēpo -rēpĕre -repsi -reptum. (1) *to creep out*: Pl. (2) *to creep up* or *over*; with acc.: montes quos nunquam erepsemus (=erepsissemus), Hor.; agrum, Juv.

ērēptĭo -ōnis, f. (eripio), *a taking by force, seizure*: Cic.

ēreptor -ōris, m. (eripio), *one who takes away by force, a robber*: bonorum, Cic.; libertatis, Cic.; Tac.

Ĕrĕtria -ae, f. ('Ερετρία). (1) *chief town in the island of Euboea.* (2) *a town in Thessaly.*
¶ Hence subst. **Ĕretrĭcus** -i, m. *an Eretrian*; esp. in plur. Eretrici, *philosophers of the Eretrian school*: Cic.; so **Ĕretrĭăci** -ōrum, m., Cic.; adj. and subst. **Ĕretrĭensis**, *Eretrian, an Eretrian*: Liv.

Ĕrētum -i, n., *an old Sabine town on the Tiber.* Adj. **Ĕrētīnus** -a -um, *Eretine*: Tib.

ergā, prep. with acc. (perhaps connected with rego), *towards.* Lit., of place: Pl. Transf., of personal relations, *towards, in relation to.* (1) in a good sense: amor erga te suus, Cic.; benevolentia erga aliquem, Cic.; Pl., Caes. (2) in a bad sense: odium erga aliquem, Nep.; invidia erga aliquem, Tac.; Pl., Ter. (3) (post-Aug.) more generally, *about*: anxii erga Seianum, Tac.; sometimes of relation to things: erga memoriam filii sui, Tac.

ergastŭlum -i, n. (ἐργάζομαι), *a workhouse for debtors* or *slaves*: ille ex compedibus atque ergastulo, Cic.; aliquem in ergastulum dare *or* ducere, Liv.; apud aliquem in ergastulo esse, Cic. Transf., in plur., *the inmates of an ergastulum*: ergastula solvere, Caes.; Juv.

ergō (poet. sometimes ergŏ), prep. and adv. (perhaps connected, like erga, with rego).
As prep., preceded by genit., *because of, on account of*: formidinis ergo, Lucr.; illius ergo, Verg.
As adv., *consequently, therefore, accordingly, then*; esp. (1) of logical consequences; *therefore*: dissolvitur, interit ergo, Lucr.; Pl., Cic., Liv.; itaque ergo, Liv. (2) with questions, *then*: quid ergo? why then? Pl.,

L.D.—8*   [217]

Caes. Cic. (3) with imperatives, *then, now*: Cic. (4) to resume a point, *well then, as I was saying*: Cic.

Ĕrichthō -ūs, f. ('Εριχθώ), *a Thessalian witch consulted by Pompey*. TRANSF., *any witch*: Ov.

Ĕrichthŏnĭus -i, m. ('Εριχθόνιος).

(1) *a mythical king of Athens*.

¶ Hence adj. **Ĕrichthŏnĭus** -a -um, *Athenian*.

(2) *a mythical king of Troy, son of Dardanus, father of Tros*.

¶ Hence adj. **Ĕrichthŏnĭus** -a -um, *Trojan*.

ērĭcĭus -i, m. *a hedgehog*; as milit. t. t., *a beam thickly studded with iron spikes, chevaux de frise*: Caes.

Ērĭdănus -i, m. ('Ηριδανός), *the Greek name of the river Padus* (now *Po*).

ĕrĭfŭga -ae, m. (erus/fugio), *a runaway slave*: Cat.

ērĭgo -rĭgĕre -rexi -rectum (ex/rego), *to set up, place upright, lift up, erect*.

LIT., scalas ad moenia, Liv.; mālum, *a mast*, Cic., Verg.; oculos, *to raise*, Cic.; aures, *to prick up the ears*, Cic.; with reflex., or in pass. with middle sense, *to rise*: insula Sicanium iuxta latus erigitur, Verg.; Caes., Cic. Esp. (1) *to erect a building*: turrem, Caes. (2) milit. t. t., *to march a body of soldiers up a height*: agmen in adversum clivum, Liv.; aciem in collem, Tac.

TRANSF., (1) *to arouse, excite*: animum ad audiendum, Cic.; auditor erigatur, *be attentive*, Cic. (2) *to raise up, encourage, cheer*: aliquem, Cic.; aliquem ad spem belli, Tac.; animum, Cic.; erigere se in spem legis, Liv.

¶ Hence partic. (with compar.) **ērectus** -a -um, *raised, upright, erect*. LIT., status, Cic.; Caes., Ov. TRANSF., (1) *high, elevated*: **a**, in a good sense: celsus et erectus, Cic.: **b**, in a bad sense, *proud*: erectus et celsus, Cic. (2) *alert, anxious, intent, with minds on the stretch*: iudices, Cic.; exspectatione erecta, *in suspense*, Liv. (3) *resolute, cheerful*: alacri animo et erecto, Cic.

Ērĭgŏnē -ēs, f. ('Ηριγόνη), *the daughter of Icarus, transformed into the constellation Virgo*.

¶ Hence adj. **Ērĭgŏnēĭus** -a -um, *belonging to Erigone*: canis, *the dog of Icarus, Maera, changed into the constellation Canicula*.

ĕrīlis -e (erus, era), *of a master or mistress*: Pl., Verg., Hor., Ov.

Ĕrīnys -ўos, f. ('Ερινύς), *one of the Furies*; plur. Erinyes, *the Furies*. TRANSF., *scourge, curse*: patriae communis Erinys, *of Helen*, Verg.

Ĕrĭphўla -ae, f. and **Ĕrĭphўlē** -es, f. ('Εριφύλη), *daughter of Talaus and Lysimache, wife of Amphiaraus, whom she betrayed to Polynices for a golden necklace, for which she was slain by her son Alcmaeon*.

ērĭpĭo -rĭpĕre -rĭpŭi -reptum (ex/rapio), *to snatch away, tear out*; constr. with ex, ab, de and abl., or poet. with abl. alone, or with dat. (usually of person).

(1) in gen. *to snatch*, esp. violently and wrongly. LIT., ensem vaginā, Verg.; aliquem ex equo, Liv.; aliquem ex manibus populi Romani, Cic.; hereditatem ab aliquo, Cic.; aurum Gallis, Liv. TRANSF., of abstr. things: alicui vitam, Sall.; omnem usum

navium, Caes.; fugam, Verg.; sometimes of undesirable things: alicui timorem, Cic.

(2) in a good sense, *to free, rescue*: aliquem e manibus hostium, Caes.; filium a morte, Cic.; se ab illa miseria, Cic.; aliquem ex servitute, Sall.; eripe te morae, *away with delay*, Hor.

¶ Hence partic. **ēreptus** -a -um, *snatched away* or *rescued*; also in special sense, *snatched away by death*: fato, Verg., Liv.; fatis, Ov.

ērōdo -rōdĕre -rōsi -rōsum (ex/rodo), *to gnaw away, eat into*: Plin.

ĕrŏgātĭo -ōnis, f. (erogo), *payment, expenditure*: pecuniae, Cic.

ĕrŏgĭto -are (freq. of erogo), *to keep asking*: Pl.

ĕrŏgo -are (ex/rogo), *to ask for and obtain for some purpose*; used in the sense to *pay out* money, esp. from public funds: pecuniam ex aerario, Cic.; pecuniam in classem, Cic.; pecuniam in Tigellinum, *to bequeath*, Tac.

errābundus -a -um (¹erro), *wandering*: nunc errabundi domos suos pervagarentur, Liv.; vestigia bovis, Verg.; odor, Lucr.

errātĭcus -a -um (¹erro), *wandering, erratic*: Delos, Ov.; vitis serpens multiplici lapsu et erratico, Cic.

errātĭo -ōnis, f. (¹erro), *a wandering, straying*: nulla in caelo erratio, Cic.; Pl., Ter.

errātus -ūs, m. (¹erro), *wandering about, straying*: longis erratibus actus, Ov.

¹erro -are, *to wander, stray, rove*.

LIT., of persons and things: vagus et exsul erraret, Cic.; stellae errantes, Cic.; sparsos errare capillos. As transit. verb, *to wander over*: terrae erratae, *wandered over*, Ov.; litora errata, Verg. Esp. *to wander from the right path, lose one's way*: errare viā, Verg.; Lucr.

TRANSF., (1) *to waver*: ne vagari et errare cogatur oratio, Cic.; ne tuus erret honos, Ov.; sententia errans et vaga, *uncertain*, Cic. (2) *to err, be in error, be mistaken*: errat animus, Lucr.; de nostris verbis, Ter.; si quid erro, Pl.; errabant tempora, *in chronology*, Ov.; impers. pass.: si erratur in nomine, Cic.

¶ N. of perf. partic. as subst. **errātum** -i, *a fault, error*. (1) technically: erratum fabrile Cic. (2) morally: errata aetatis meae, *of my youth*, Cic. L.

²erro -ōnis, m. (¹erro), *a wanderer, vagabond*; esp. of slaves: Hor.; of unfaithful lovers: Ov.

error -ōris, m. (¹erro), *a wandering about*.

LIT., of persons and things: error ac dissipatio civium, Cic.; Verg., Ov.

TRANSF., (1) *wavering, uncertainty*: fluctuat incertis erroribus ardor amantum, Lucr.; errore viarum, Liv. (2) *error, mistake*: errore duci, Cic.; in errorem induci, rapi, Cic.; ferendus tibi in hoc meus error, Cic.; demere, Hor.; also *source of error, deception*: Verg., Liv., Tac.

ērŭbesco -rūbescĕre -rŭbŭi, *to grow red, blush*, esp. with shame: erubuere genae, Ov.; with infin. and the abl.: Cic.; with abl.: Liv.; with infin., *to blush to*: Verg., Liv.; with acc., *to blush for*: Prop.; *to respect*: Verg.

¶ Hence gerundive **ērŭbescendus** -a -um, *of which one should be ashamed*: ignes, Hor.; Liv.

ērūca -ae, f. *a colewort*: Hor.

ēructo -are, *to belch forth, throw up, vomit.*
LIT., saniem, Verg. TRANSF., (**1**) *to talk
drunkenly about*: sermonibus suis caedem,
Cic. (**2**) *to cast out, emit, eject*: harenam,
Verg.; Lucr.

ērūdīo -ire (ex/rudis), *to free from roughness*;
hence *to instruct, teach, educate*: aliquem,
Cic.; with abl.: aliquem artibus, Cic.; with
in and the abl.: aliquem in iure civili, Cic.;
filios omnibus artibus ad Graecorum disciplinam, Cic.; with indir. quest.: Ov.; with a
thing as object: Ov.
¶ Hence partic. (with compar. and superl.)
ērūdītus -a -um, *instructed, educated,
trained*: homo, Cic.; eruditior litteris, Cic.;
artibus militiae, Liv.; eruditissimus disciplinā iuris, Cic.; with infin.: Tac. TRANSF.,
of things: saecula, oratio, Cic.
¶ Adv. **ērūdītē**, *learnedly*; used in compar. and superl. only: Cic.

ērūdītīo -ōnis, f. (erudio). (**1**) *teaching,
instruction*: Cic. L., Quint. (**2**) *knowledge,
learning, erudition*: Cic., Quint.

ērūdītūlus -i, m. (dim. of eruditus), *somewhat
skilled*: Cat.

ērūdītus -a -um, partic. from erudio; q.v.

ērumpo -rumpĕre -rūpi -ruptum.
(**1**) transit., *to break open, cause to burst
forth.* LIT., nubem, Verg.; reflex. se erumpere, or pass. erumpi, *to burst forth*: portis
se erumpere foras, Caes.; Verg. TRANSF., *to
vent, discharge*: stomachum in aliquem, Cic.;
iram, Liv.
(**2**) intransit., *to break out, burst forth.*
LIT., ignes ex Aetnae vertice erumpunt, Cic.;
milit. t. t., *to rush forth*: ex castris, Caes.;
impers.: duabus simul portis erumpitur, Liv.
TRANSF., erumpat enim aliquando vera et
me digna vox, Cic.; erupit deinde seditio,
Liv.; coniuratio ex latebris, Cic.; haec quo
sit eruptura timeo, Cic.; ad perniciem
civitatis, Cic.

ērūo -rŭĕre -rŭi -rŭtum, *to tear out, dig up.*
LIT., mortuum, Cic.; aurum terrā, Ov.;
humum, Ov.; aquam remis, Ov.; eruitur
oculos, *his eyes are torn out*, Ov.; esp. *to
raze, demolish*: urbem totam, Verg.
TRANSF., memoriam alicuius ex annalium
vetustate, *to bring to light*, Cic.; si quid
indagaris, inveneris, ex tenebris erueris, Cic.;
with indir. quest.: erues qui decem legati
Mummio fuerint, Cic.; veritatem, Quint.

ēruptīo -ōnis, f. (erumpo), *a bursting* or *breaking forth*: Aetnaeorum ignium, Cic.; as
milit. t. t., *a sally, attack*: eruptio ex oppido
simul duabus portis, Liv.; eruptionem
facere, Caes.

ĕrus -i, m. *a master.* LIT., of a house: Pl., Cic.,
Verg. TRANSF., (**1**) *owner*: Cat., Hor. (**2**) of
a god, *Lord*: Cat.

ervum -i, n. *bitter vetch*: Verg., Hor.

Ērўcīnus, see Eryx.

Ērўmanthus -i, m. (Ερύμανθος). (**1**) *a chain
of mountains in Arcadia, where Hercules slew
the Erymanthian boar.*
¶ Hence adj. **Ērўmanthĭus** -a -um; f.
adj. **Ērўmanthis** -ĭdis: ursa, *Callisto of
Arcadia, changed into a bear and set as a
constellation in the sky.*
(**2**) *a river in Arcadia, flowing into the
Alpheus.*

Ērўsichthōn -thōnis, m. (Ερυσίχθων), *the son
of the Thessalian king Triopas; he was
punished by Ceres with a raging hunger for
having cut down one of her groves.*

Ērўthēa (-ĭa) -ae, f. *a small island near Gades,
where Hercules stole the oxen of Geryon.*
¶ Hence f. adj. **Ērўthēis** -thēĭdis, *Ery-
thean*: praeda, *the oxen of Geryon*, Ov.

ĕrўthĭnus -a -um (ἐρυθῖνος), *a kind of red
barbel* or *mullet*: Ov.

Ērythrae -ārum, f. (Ερυθραί). (**1**) *a town in
Boeotia.* (**2**) *one of the twelve Ionian towns in
Asia Minor.*
¶ Hence adj. **Ērythraeus** -a -um, *Ery-
threan*; f. as subst. **Ērythraea** -ae, *the district
of Erythrae.*

Ēryx -rýcis or **Ērўcus** -i, m. (Ἔρυξ), *a mountain
with a city of the same name, on the west coast
of Sicily, with a famous temple of Venus.*
Adj. **Ērўcīnus** -a -um, *of Eryx*: Venus
Erycina, Cic.; f. as subst. **Ērўcīna** -ae,
Venus: Hor.

esca -ae, f. (¹edo), *food, victuals*: Pl., Cic.,
Verg.; esp. as *bait*: Pl. TRANSF., (**1**) fig.,
bait: voluptas esca malorum, Cic. (**2**) *titbits
of gossip*: Pers.

escārĭus -a -um (esca), *relating to food* or *to
bait*: Pl., Juv.

escendo -scendĕre -scendi -scensum (ex/
scando).
(**1**) intransit., *to climb up, ascend*: in rogum
ardentem, Cic.; in currum, Cic.; in tribunal,
Liv.; esp. *to go up from the sea-coast inland*:
Ilium a mari, Liv.
(**2**) transit., *to ascend*: Oetam, Liv.; rostra,
Tac.

escensĭo -ōnis, f. (escendo), *a movement
inland*, esp. *hostile*: escensionem facere ab
navibus in terram, Liv.

esculetum, esculus, see aesc.

escŭlentus -a -um (esca), *edible, esculent*:
frusta, Cic.

ēsĭto -are (freq. of edo), *to keep eating*: Pl.

Esquĭlĭae -ārum, f. (ex/colere; literally, *the
outer town, the suburb*), *one of the seven hills
on which Rome was built, the Esquiline.*
¶ Hence adj. **Esquĭlĭus** -a -um, also
Esquĭlīnus -a -um, *Esquiline*; f. as subst.
Esquĭlīna -ae, *the Esquiline gate*: Cic.

essĕdārĭus -a -um (essedum). (**1**) *a fighter in a
British* or *Gallic war-chariot*: Caes., Cic. L.
(**2**) *a kind of gladiator*: Suet.

essĕdum -i, n. (a Celtic word), *a war-chariot
used among the Gauls and Britons*: Caes., Cic.,
Verg.

ēsū, abl. sing. from esus, m. (edo), *in the eating*:
Pl.

ēsŭrĭalis -e (esurio), *of hunger*: Pl.

ēsŭrĭo -ire (desider. of ¹edo), *to be hungry,
desire food.* LIT.: Pl., Cic., Hor. TRANSF., *to
desire eagerly, long for*: nil ibi, quod nobis
esuriatur, erit, Ov.

ēsŭrītĭo -ōnis, f. (esurio), *hunger*: Cat.

ēsus -a -um, partic. of ¹edo; q.v.

ĕt, adv. and conj. (cf. Gr. ἔτι).
As adv., *also, even*: timeo Danaos et dona
ferentes, Verg.; addam et illud etiam, Cic.;
Caes., Liv. Also combined with simul,
quoque, quidem: Cic.; with nec non: Verg.
As conj., *and*: Cic., etc. Sometimes *and
indeed*: magna vis est conscientiae, et magna
in utramque partem, Cic.; in narrative, *and*

then: Verg., Tac.; occasionally adversative, *and yet*, esp. in questions: Cic., Verg. After aeque, alius, idem, par, similis, *as* or *than*: Cic. Repeated, et... et... *both* ... *and*...: et audax et malus, Pl.; Cic., etc.; -que ... et ...: Liv., Tac.; also et ... -que, rare but in Cic. With nec (neque), nec ... et, *not only not* ... *but*: nec miror et gaudeo, Cic.; et ... nec, *not only* ... *but also not*: Cic.

ĕtĕnim, conj., usually at beginning of clause, *for indeed*: Pl., Lucr., Cic.; sometimes to introduce an explanatory parenthesis: Cic., Liv.

Ĕtĕoclēs -is and -ĕos, m. (᾽Ετεοκλῆς), myth., son of Oedipus, brother of Polynices, killed in the siege of Thebes.

ĕtēsiae -ārum, m. pl. (ἐτησίαι), *winds which blow for forty days every year about the dog-days, Etesian winds*: Lucr., Cic.

ĕtēsius -a -um (ἐτήσιος), *Etesian*: Lucr.

ēthŏlŏgia -ae, f. (ἠθολογία), *the art of mimicry*: Quint.

ēthŏlŏgus i, m. (ἠθολόγος), *one who mimics the peculiarities of others*: mimi ethologi, Cic.

ĕtĭam, conj. (et/iam).

(1) of time: **a**, *as yet, still*: cum iste etiam cubaret, Cic.; Pl., Ter., Verg. So with negatives: nondum etiam, vixdum etiam, *not yet, scarcely yet*, Cic.: **b**, etiam atque etiam, *again and again*: rogare, Cic.; sometimes to give emphasis: quare etiam atque etiam, *so I repeat*, Lucr.

(2) without reference to time: **a**, *also, besides, even*: voce, motu, forma etiam magnifica, Cic.; non solum (*or* modo) ... sed (*or* verum) etiam, *not only* ... *but also*, Cic.; with comparatives, *still*: dic etiam clarius, Cic.: **b**, in answers, *yes, certainly*: etiam, inquit, beatam, Cic.; aut etiam aut non respondere, *to answer yes or no*, Cic.: **c**, in questions, expressing incredulity, *actually? really?* etiam respicis? Pl.; Ter.

ĕtĭamnum and **ĕtĭamnunc**, adv., *yet, still, till now*: de materia loqui orationis etiamnunc, non ipso de genere dicendi, Cic.; nihil etiamnunc, *nothing further*, Cic.

ĕtĭam-si, conj., used like si, with indic. or subj., *even if, although*: Pl., Cic., Liv.

ĕtĭam-tum and **ĕtĭam-tunc**, adv., used with past tenses, *even then, till that time, till then*: Cic., Tac.

Etrūria -ae, f. *a district in north-west Italy.*

¶ Hence adj. and subst. **Etruscus** -a -um, *Etruscan, an Etruscan.*

et-si, conj., *even if, although*, used like si, with indic. or subj.: Pl., Cic., Verg., Liv.; often followed by tamen, at, certe; sometimes without separate verb: Cic., Liv. Sometimes also elliptically, like quamquam, with the force of *and yet, notwithstanding*: do poenas temeritatis meae; etsi quae fuit ista temeritas? Cic. L.

ĕtўmŏlŏgia -ae, f. (ἐτυμολογία), *etymology*: Cic.

eu (εὖ), interj. *good! well done!*: Pl., Ter., Hor.

Euadnē -ēs, f. (Εὐάδνη), myth., *wife of Capaneus, one of the Seven who fought against Thebes.*

Euan or **Euhan**, m. (εὐάν), *a name of Bacchus*: Iacchus et Euhan, Ov.; Lucr.

euans or **euhans** -antis (εὐάζων), *shouting Euan*, of the Bacchanals; with acc.: euantes orgia, *celebrating the orgies of Bacchus*, Verg.

Euandĕr and **Euandrus** -dri, m. (Εὔανδρος), myth., *son of Carmenta, from Pallantium in Arcadia, who founded Pallanteum at the foot of the Palatine hill.* Adj. **Euandrius** -a -um, ensis, *of Pallas, son of Evander.*

euax, interj., *good!*: Pl.

Euboea -ae, f. (Εὔβοια), *an island off Boeotia and Attica, in the Aegean Sea.*

¶ Hence adj. **Euboïcus** -a -um.

Euclīdēs -is, m. (Εὐκλείδης), Euclid. (1) *a philosopher of Megara.* (2) *a mathematician of Alexandria.*

Euēnus -i, m. (Εὔηνος), myth., *king of Aetolia, father of Marpessa, drowned in the river Lycormas, which received the name of Euenus.* Adj. **Euēnīnus** -a -um, *of the river Euenus.*

Eugănĕi -ōrum, m. *a people in northern Italy.*

euge (εὖγε) and **eugĕpae** (εὖγεπαι), interj., *well done!*, sometimes ironical: Pl., Ter.

Euhēmĕrus -i, m. (Εὐήμερος), *a Greek philosopher*, flourishing about 315 B.C., famous for his rationalizing of myths.

Euïas or **Euhïas** -ădis, f. (εὐιάς), *a Bacchante.*

Euïus or **Euhïus** -i, m. (Εὔιος), *a name of Bacchus.*

Eumĕnĭdes -um, f. (Εὐμενίδες), *Eumenides, the gracious ones*, euphem. name for the Furies.

Eumolpus -i, m. (Εὔμολπος), myth., *son of Poseidon and Chione, a Thracian priest of Demeter, founder of the Eleusinian mysteries.*

¶ Hence **Eumolpĭdae** -ārum, m. (Εὐμολ-πίδαι), *his descendants in Athens, from whom the priests of Demeter were chosen.*

eunūchus -i, m. (εὐνοῦχος), *a eunuch*: Cic., Juv.

euoe, euhoe, interj. (εὐοῖ), *shout of the Bacchantes*: euhoe Bacche, Verg.

Euphorbus -i, m. (Εὔφορβος), *a Trojan, whose soul Pythagoras believed to have descended to himself.*

Euphŏrīon -ōnis, m. (Εὐφορίων), *a Greek poet of Chalcis in Euboea*, flourishing about 220 B.C.

Euphrātēs -is, m. (Εὐφράτης), *the Euphrates, a river in Western Asia, flowing into the Persian Gulf*; meton., *the dwellers on the Euphrates*: Verg.

Eupŏlis -pŏlĭdis, m. (Εὔπολις), *an Athenian comic poet*, flourishing about 420 B.C.

Eurīpĭdēs -is, m. (Εὐριπίδης), *the celebrated Athenian tragic poet* (c. 485–406 B.C.). Adj. **Eurīpĭdēus** -a -um.

Eurīpus -i, m. (εὔριπος). (1) *a channel, strait*, esp. *the strait between Euboea and Boeotia*: Cic. (2) *a canal* or *water-course*: Cic. (3) *the ditch* or *moat constructed round the Circus Maximus*: Suet.

Eurōpa -ae, f. and **Eurōpē** -ēs, f. (Εὐρώπη). (1) myth., *daughter of Agenor, king of Phoenicia; mother of Sarpedon and Minos by Jupiter, who in the form of a bull carried her off to Crete.* (2) geograph., *the continent of Europe, named after Europa.*

¶ Adj. **Eurōpaeus** -a -um, *belonging to Europa* or *to Europe*: Ov., Nep.

Eurus -i, m. (εὖρος), LIT., *the south-east wind*: Verg. TRANSF., *the east wind*: Ov.; poet., *wind in general*: Verg.

¶ Adj. **Eurōus** -a -um, *eastern*: Verg.

Eurўdĭcē -ēs, f. (Εὐρυδίκη), *wife of Orpheus, recovered by him from Hades, but lost again.*

Eurystheus -ĕi, m. (Εὐρυσθεύς), myth., *son of Sthenelus, a king of Mycenae, who imposed on Hercules his twelve labours.*

[220]

Eurȳtus -i, m. (*Εὔρυτος*), myth., *king of Oechalia, father of Iole and Dryope.* ¶ Hence **Eurȳtis** -ĭdis, f. *daughter of Eurytus,* i.e., *Iole.*

euschēmē, adv. (*εὐσχήμως*), *gracefully*: Pl.

Euterpē -ēs, f. (*Εὐτέρπη*), *the Muse of harmony*: Hor.

Euxīnus -a -um (*Εὔξεινος*=*hospitable*), *an epithet of the Black Sea*: mare, aquae, Ov.; esp. with subst. Pontus; also m. alone as subst., *the Black Sea.*

ēvādo -vādĕre -vāsi -vāsum, *to go out, go forth.* (1) intransit. LIT., in gen.: ex balneis, Cic.; oppido, Sall., esp.: **a**, *to climb up* or *out*: per praeruptum saxum in Capitolium, Liv.; Cic., Verg.: **b**, *to escape, get off*: e manibus hostium, Liv.; e periculo, Cic. TRANSF., *to turn out, result*: **a**, of persons: posse oratores evadere, Cic., Liv.: **b**, of things: quo evasura sint, Cic.; Pl., Liv. (2) transit., *to go out through, pass over*: ripam, Verg.; evaserant media castra, Liv.; esp.: **a**, *to climb up*: gradus altos, Verg.; Liv.: **b**, *to escape*: flammam, Verg.; Ov., Liv.

ēvăgor -ari, dep. (1) intransit., *to wander out, stray away.* LIT., effuse, Liv.; as milit. t. t., *to wheel to right and left, manœuvre*: nullo ad evagandum relicto spatio, Liv. TRANSF., appetitūs longius evagantur, Cic.; Liv. (2) transit., *to overstep*: ordinem rectum, Hor.

ēvălesco -vălescĕre -vălŭi, *to grow strong.* (1) in tumultum, *to grow into a tumult,* Tac. (2) *to prevail, come into vogue*: nationis nomen evaluisse paullatim, Tac. (3) in perf., *to have power, be able*; with infin.: sed non Dardanidae medicari cuspidis ictum evaluit, Verg.; Hor.

Evan, *see* Euan.

Evander, *see* Euander.

ēvānesco -vānescĕre -vānŭi, *to vanish, disappear, pass away*: evanescunt vinum et salsamentum vetustate, Cic.; Verg. TRANSF., eorum memoria evanuit, Cic.; spes, Cic.; rumor, Liv.

ēvānĭdus -a -um (evanesco), *vanishing, passing away*: pectora in tenues abeunt evanida rivos, Ov. TRANSF., amor, Ov.

ēvans, *see* euans.

ēvasto -are, *to devastate, lay waste utterly*: agrum, vallem, Liv.

ēvectus -a -um, partic. of eveho; q.v.

ēvĕho -vĕhĕre -vexi -vectum. (1) *to carry out.* LIT., aliquid plaustris ex fanis, Cic.; with reflex. or in pass. with middle sense, of ships, *to sail away*: in altum, Liv.; of riders, *to ride away*: Liv., Tac. TRANSF., evehi in middle sense: e Piraeo eloquentia evecta est, Cic.; spe vanā evectus, Liv. (2) *to carry up*: aliquem ad auras, Ov. TRANSF., ad deos, Hor.; ad consulatum, Tac.; Verg.

ēvello -vellĕre -velli -vulsum, *to tear out, pluck out.* LIT., alicui linguam, Cic.; arborem, Liv.; Hor. TRANSF., consules non modo e memoria sed etiam ex fastis evellendi, Cic.; alicui ex animo scrupulum, Cic.

ēvĕnĭo -vĕnire -vēni -ventum, *to come out, come forth.* LIT., merses profundo, pulchrior evenit, Hor.

TRANSF., (1) of things, *to turn out, result*: alicui feliciter, Caes.; bene, Cic.; vides omnia fere contra ac dicta sint evenisse, Cic.; si adversa pugna evenisset, Liv. (2) *to befall* a person, *fall to* his *lot*: provincia (sorte) evenit alicui, Liv.; Cic. (3) in gen., *to happen, occur*: pax evenerat, ut plerumque evenit, Cic.; forte evenit ut, Cic., Ter., Quint. ¶ Hence n. of perf. partic. as subst. **ēventum** -i. (1) *issue, consequence, result*: causarum cognitio cognitionem eventi facit, Cic. (2) in gen., *an event, occurrence*: causae eventorum magis me movent quam ipsa eventa, Cic. (3) a *person's experience*: aliorum eventis doceri, Tac.; Cic. L.

ēventus -ūs, m. (evenio). (1) *consequence, issue, result*: eventus rei, Caes.; eventus rerum qui acciderunt, Cic.; belli eventus prosper, Liv.; of a drama: semper ad eventum festinat, Hor. (2) in gen., *an event, occurrence*: Cic. (3) a person's *experience* or *fate*: auditur Decii eventus, Liv.; Caes., Cic.

ēverbĕro -are, *to strike violently*: clipeum alis, Verg.; cauda pendentem escam, Ov.

ēverrĭcŭlum -i, n. (everro), *a fishing-net, drag-net*: Varro; fig., quod umquam huiuscemodi everriculum ulla in provincia fuit (with a pun on the name of Verres), Cic.; everriculum malitiarum omnium, *a clean sweep*, Cic.

ēverro -verrĕre -verri -versum, *to sweep out*: Varro. TRANSF., *to plunder*: quod fanum non eversum atque extersum reliquerit (with a pun on the name of Verres), Cic.

ēversĭo -ōnis, f. (everto), *an overturning*: columnae, Cic. TRANSF., *destruction, ruin*: vitae, Cic.; patriae, rerum publicarum, Cic.; Tac.

ēversor -ōris, m. (everto), *an overturner, destroyer*: civitatis, Cic.; Verg.

ēverto -vertĕre -verti -versum. (1) *to turn out, dislodge, eject*: pupillum fortunis patriis, Cic.; Pl. (2) *to turn up, stir*: aequora ventis, Verg. (3) *to overturn, throw down*: navem, Cic.; arborem, Verg.; hence, of a city, *to demolish*: Carthaginem, Cic. TRANSF., *to overthrow, destroy*: funditus civitates, Cic.; philosophiam, Cic.; aliquem, *to ruin*, Cic.; res Asiae, Verg.

ēvestīgātus -a -um, *tracked out, discovered*: ingeniis evestigata priorum, Ov.

Ēvĭas, *see* Euias.

ēvĭdens -entis, adj. (with compar. and superl.) (ex/video), *visible, clear, plain, evident*: res, Cic.; evidentior causa victoriae, Liv.; quid est evidentius? Cic. ¶ Adv. **ēvĭdentĕr**, *visibly, clearly*: evidenter praenitere, Liv.

ēvĭdentĭa -ae, f. (evidens), *distinctness of language*: Cic., Quint.

ēvĭgĭlo -are. (1) intransit.: **a**, *to wake up*: Plin., Quint.: **b**, *to be awake, be vigilant*: in quo evigilaverunt curae et cogitationes meae? Cic. (2) transit.: **a**, *to watch through, pass in watching*: nox evigilanda, Tib.: **b**, *to work hard at, to elaborate*: libros, Ov.; consilia evigilata cogitationibus, Cic.

ēvĭlesco -vīlescĕre -vīlŭi, *to become worthless, contemptible*: Tac., Suet.

ēvincĭo -vincire -vinxi -vinctum, *to bind, bind round*: diademate caput Tiridatis evinxit,

Tac.; esp. in perf. partic.: viridi evinctus oliva, Verg.; Ov.

ēvinco -vincĕre -vīci -victum, *to conquer entirely, utterly subdue.* Lit., imbelles Aeduos, Tac.; evicit omnia miles, Liv. Transf., in gen., *to prevail over.* (1) over physical objects: platanus caelebs evincet ulmos, Hor.; oppositas gurgite moles, *to get through,* Verg. (2) over abstr. things: evicit miseratio iusta superbiam ingenitam, Liv. (3) over or upon persons: lacrimis, dolore, precibus evinci, Verg. (4) *to bring it about that*: summa ope evicerunt, ut M. Furius Camillus crearetur, Liv. (5) *to prove irresistibly*: si puerilius his ratio esse evincet amare, Hor.

ēvĭro -are (ex/vir), *to castrate*: Cat.

ēviscĕro -are (ex/viscus), *to disembowel, tear in pieces*: columbam (of the hawk), Verg.

ēvītābĭlis -e (evito), *that can be avoided*: telum, Ov.

¹**ēvīto** -are (vito), *to avoid, shun*: tela, Cat.; Hor. Transf., causas suspicionum, Cic.

²**ēvīto** -are (vita), *to deprive of life*: Enn.

Ēvĭus, see Euius.

ēvŏcātor -ōris, m. (evoco), *one who calls to arms*: servorum et civium perditorum, Cic.

ēvŏco -are, *to call out.* Lit., in gen.: aliquem foras, Pl.; magna cum contumelia verborum nostros ad pugnam, Caes.; mercatores undique ad se, Caes.; aliquem litteris, Cic. Esp. (1) *to summon the spirits of the dead*: Metellos ab inferis, Cic. (2) *to call forth a deity from a hostile city, promising a temple at Rome*: evocare deos, Liv. (3) as milit. and polit. t. t., *to call out, call up, summon*: aliquem ad se, Cic.; ad conloquium, Liv.; legiones ex hibernis, Caes. Transf., (1) *to draw out, draw on*: ad honorem, Caes.; familiam obscuram tenebris in lucem, Cic. (2) *to call forth, produce*: misericordia tua nullius oratione evocata, Cic.; Liv.

¶ Hence m. pl. of perf. partic. as subst. **ēvŏcāti** -orum, *veteran soldiers recalled to the colours*: Caes.

ēvoe, see euoe.

ēvŏlo -are, *to fly out, fly away.* Lit., ex quercu, Cic.; Ov. Transf., (1) *to come out quickly, rush forth*: ex corporum vinculis tanquam e carcere, Cic.; e senatu, Cic.; evolat ignis, Lucr. (2) of abstr. things: e poena, *to escape,* Cic.; evolavit oratio, *rose,* Cic.

ēvŏlūtĭo -ōnis, f. (evolvo), *the unrolling,* and hence, *reading of a book*: poetarum, Cic.

ēvolvo -volvĕre -volvi -vŏlūtum. (1) *to roll out, roll forth,* esp. with reflex. or pass. with middle sense. Lit., per humum evolvi, Tac.; of a river: se evolvere in mare, Verg. Transf., of news; evolvi, *to spread*: ad aures quoque militum dicta ferocia evolvebantur, Liv. (2) *to unroll, roll open.* Lit., vestes, Ov.; esp. *to unroll a book to read it*: volumen epistularum, Cic. L.; librum Cic.; Ov., Tac. Transf., **a,** *to extricate, disentangle, detach*: evolutus illis integumentis dissimulationis; se ex his turbis, Tac.; illos ex praeda clandestina, *make to disgorge,* Liv.: **b,** *to unravel, disclose,*

explain: naturam rerum, Cic.; seriem fati, Ov.; Lucr., Verg.

ēvŏmo -ĕre -ŭi -itum, *to vomit forth.* Lit., conchas, Cic.; Tac. Transf., quae (urbs) tantam pestem evomuit forasque proiecit, Cic.; in quo tu, acceptā et devorāta pecuniā, evomere non poteras, *disgorge,* Cic.; in me absentem orationem ore impurissimo, Cic.

ēvulgo -are, *to publish, make known*: ius civile, Liv.; Octaviae iniurias, Tac.

ēvulsĭo -ōnis, f. (evello), *a pulling out*: dentis, Cic.

ex or **e,** prep. with abl. (ἐξ, ἐκ), *from* or *out of*; ex before vowels always; e often before consonants.

(1) in space; *out of, from*: exire ex urbe, Cic.; milites ex eo loco deducere, Cic.; delabi ex equo, Liv.; so also: ex equo pugnare, *to fight on horseback* (operating *from* it), Caes.; ex adverso (coming *from*), *opposite,* Liv.; laborare ex pedibus, *to suffer in the feet,* Cic.

(2) in time: **a,** *since*: ex eo tempore, Cic.; esp.: ex quo, *from which time, since,* Liv.: **b,** *immediately after*: Cotta ex consulatu est profectus in Galliam, Cic.; aliud ex alio, *one thing after another,* Cic.; diem ex die, *day after day,* Cic. L., Caes.; hunc iudicem ex Kal. Ian. non habebimus, *from Jan.* 1 *onwards,* Cic.

(3) in other relations: **a,** to denote origin, *from, out of, of*: quidam ex Arcadia hospes, Nep.; ex animo, *heartily,* Cic.; e memoria, Cic.; ex industria, *on purpose*; hence with verbs of taking, perceiving, questioning, and the like—e.g.: sumere, percipere, accipere, auferre, conligere, quaerere, percunctari, discere, intellegere, etc.: **b,** to denote the whole out of which any part is taken: unus ex meis intimis, Cic.; Q. Vettius Vettianus e Marsis, *a Marsian,* Cic.: **c,** to denote the material of which anything is made or compounded: pocula ex auro, Cic.; so of the source from which anything is paid or gained: largiri ex alieno, Liv.; vivere e rapto, Ov.: **d,** to denote the cause or occasion of anything, *from, on account of, by reason of*: ex eadem causa, Cic.; Demetrius e doctrina clarus, Cic.; ex eo factum est quod, *hence it came about that,* Cic.; urbem e suo nomine Romam iussit nominari, Cic.; e vulnere mori, Liv.: **e,** to denote change from one condition or occupation to another: ex oratore arator factus, Cic.: **f,** to denote correspondence, *according to, in accordance with*: ex edicto, Cic.; ex decreto, Cic.; ex foedere, Cic.; ex re et ex tempore, *according to time and circumstance,* Cic.; ex sententia, *as required,* Ter.: **g,** to denote effect: ex re, ex usu, *to a person's advantage*; e republica, *for the benefit of the republic,* Cic.: **h,** to denote relationship in general, *in regard to, with respect to*: e ratione libertatis; laborare ex pedibus, Cic.; ex parte, *in part,* Cic.

exăcerbo -are, *to irritate, provoke, exasperate, embitter*: contumeliis hostes, Liv.

exactĭo -ōnis, f. (exigo). (1) *a driving out, expulsion*: regum, Cic. (2) *a demanding, exacting,* esp.: **a,** *collecting of debts, tribute,* etc.: nominum, Cic.; capitum, *poll-tax,* Cic.: **b,** in gen., *management, direction*: operum publicorum, Cic.

exactor -ōris, m. (exigo). (**1**) *one who drives out, expels*: regum, Liv. (**2**) *one who demands or exacts*, esp.: **a**, *a collector of taxes*: Caes.: **b**, in gen., *a superintendent, overseer*: supplicii, Liv.; Tac., Quint.

exactus -a -um, partic. from exigo; q.v.

exăcŭo -ŭĕre -ŭi -ūtum, *to sharpen to a point, make sharp*.
    LIT., furcas, Verg.; fig.: mucronem aliquem tribunicium in nos, Cic.
    TRANSF., (**1**) of perceptions: ut oculorum, sic ingenii aciem, Cic. (**2**) of passions, *to intensify, stir up, inflame*: aliquem, Cic.; animos in bella, Hor.; irā exacui, Nep.

exadversum or **exadversŭs**, *opposite*. Adv.: Pl., Ter. Prep. with acc.: exadversus eum locum, Cic.

exaedĭfĭcātĭo -ōnis, f. (exaedifico), *a building up*; fig., of an oration: ipsa autem exaedificatio posita est in rebus et verbis, Cic.

exaedĭfĭco -are, *to build, build up, erect, finish building*. LIT., Capitolium, Cic.; domos et villas, Sall.; Liv. TRANSF., *to finish*: exaedificare id opus quod instituisti, Cic.

exaequātĭo -ōnis, f. (exaequo), *a making equal, equality*: Liv.; Pl.

exaequo -are, *to make level* or *equal*. LIT., argentum, Pl. TRANSF., (**1**) *to level up, make equal, relate*: facta dictis sunt exaequanda, Sall.; aliquem secum, Caes.; se cum aliquo, Cic.; vetus miles tironi exaequari, Liv. (**2**) *to equal, be like*: tetricas Sabinas, Ov.

exaestŭo -are, *to be hot, to boil up, foam up*. LIT., mare, Liv.; unda ima verticibus, Verg.; with internal acc.: largos exaestuat aestus, Lucr. TRANSF., mens exaestuat irā, Verg.

exaggĕrātĭo -ōnis, f. (exaggero), *heaping up*; hence *elevation, exaltation*: amplitudo et quasi quaedam exaggeratio quam altissima animi, Cic.

exaggĕro -are, *to heap up*. LIT., Curt., Plin. TRANSF., (**1**) *to enlarge, increase*: rem familiarem, Cic. (**2**) *to heighten, exalt, magnify*: beneficium verbis, Cic.; virtutem, Cic.

exăgĭtātor -ōris, m. (exagito), *one who blames, a censurer*: omnium rhetorum, Cic.

exăgĭto -are, *to chase about*.
    LIT., et lepus hic aliis exagitatus erit, Ov.; vis (venti) exagitata foras erumpitur, Lucr.
    TRANSF., (**1**) *to harass, disquiet, disturb*: exagitati istius iniuriis, Cic.; ab Suebis complures annos exagitati bello premebantur, Caes.; quos illa quaestio exagitabat, Sall. (**2**) *to scold, blame, reproach, censure, criticize*: aliquem, convicio, Caes.; omnes eius fraudes, Cic. (**3**) *to excite, irritate*: plebem, Sall.; maerorem, Cic. L.

exăgŏga -ae, f. (ἐξαγωγή), *export*: Pl.

exalbesco -bescĕre -bŭi, *to grow white, turn pale*: Cic.

exāmen -ĭnis, n. (ex/ago). (**1**) *a swarm*. LIT., of bees: Cic.; of wasps: Liv. TRANSF., *a throng, crowd, shoal*: servorum, Cic. (**2**) *the tongue of a balance*. LIT., Verg. TRANSF., *testing, consideration*: examina legum servare, Ov.

exāmĭno -are (examen), *to weigh*.
    LIT., ad certum pondus, Caes.; non aurificis staterā, sed quādam populari trutinā examinari, Cic.
    TRANSF., *to weigh, consider*: diligenter verborum omnium pondera, Cic.; haec meis

ponderibus, Cic.; male verum examinat omnis corruptus iudex, Hor.

exāmussim, *according to the square* or *rule, exactly*: Pl.

exanclo -are (ex/ἄντλος), *to drain, exhaust, empty*. LIT., vinum poculo, Pl. TRANSF., *to bear to the end, endure*: labores, Cic.; Enn.

exănĭmālis -e (ex/anima). (**1**) *dead*. (**2**) *deadly*: Pl.

exănĭmātĭo -ōnis, f. (exanimo), *want of breath*, esp. from fright: Cic.

exănĭmis -e and **exănĭmus** -a -um (ex/anima). (**1**) *lifeless, dead*: Verg., Liv. (**2**) (exanimis only), *breathless*, esp. from fright: Verg., Hor., Liv.

exănĭmo -are (ex/anima), *to deprive of breath*. LIT., (**1**) *to take away the breath of, to wind*: duplici cursu exanimari, Caes.; milites cursu exanimati, *breathless*, Caes. (**2**) *to deprive of life, to kill*: gravi vulnere, Cic.; Caes., Hor., Liv.
    TRANSF., *to make breathless* or *weak* with emotion, esp. fright; *to stun*: te metus exanimat, Cic.; cur me querelis exanimas tuis? Hor.; Verg.

exantlo = exanclo; q.v.

exardesco -ardescĕre -arsi -arsum, *to blaze up*.
    LIT., materia facilis ad exardescendum, Cic.; also *to become hot, to glow*: aetherioque recens exarsit sidere limus, Ov.
    TRANSF., (**1**) of persons, *to be excited, inflamed*: iracundiā ad stomacho, Cic.; ad spem libertatis, Cic.; of lovers: imis tota exarsit medullis, Cat. (**2**) of things, *to break out*: exarsit bellum, Cic.; dolor, Verg.

exāresco -ārescĕre -ārŭi, *to dry, become quite dry*. LIT., exarescunt amnes, Cic.; fontes, Caes.; lacrimae, Cic. TRANSF., *to dry up, become exhausted*: exaruit facultas orationis, Cic.; vides enim exaruisse iam veterem urbanitatem, Cic.

exarmo -are, *to disarm, deprive of arms*: cohortes, Tac.

exăro -are.
    (**1**) *to plough up, dig up*: puerum, Cic.; sepulcra, Cic.
    (**2**) *to produce by ploughing*: tantum frumenti, Cic. TRANSF., **a**, of wrinkles: frontem rugis, Hor.: **b**, *to write on waxen tablets*: exaravi ad te harum exemplum in codicillis, Cic. L.

exascĭātus -a -um (ascia), *hewn out*: Pl.

exaspĕro -are, *to make rough*. LIT., Plin.; of the sea: exasperato fluctibus mari, Liv.; Ov. TRANSF., *to irritate*: durati tot malis exasperatique, Liv.; animos, Liv.

exauctōro -are, *to dismiss from military service, discharge*: se exauctorare, *to leave the service*, Liv.; Tac.; in a bad sense, *to cashier*: Tac.

exaudĭo -ire. (**1**) *to hear plainly*: maximā voce, ut omnes exaudire possint, dico, Cic.; non exaudito tubae sono, Caes.; Liv. (**2**) *to hear favourably, listen to*: vota precesque, Verg.; monitor non exauditus, Hor.

exaugĕo -ēre, *to increase much*: ictum, Lucr.; Pl., Ter.

exaugŭrātĭo -ōnis, f. (exauguro), *profanation, desecration*: sacellorum exaugurationes, Liv.

exaugŭro -are, *to desecrate, profane*: fana, Liv.

exauspĭco -are, *to take an augury from*: Pl.

exballisto -are (ballista), *to finish off with the ballista*: Pl.

excaeco -are, *to make quite blind.* LIT., Cic.
TRANSF., *to stop up* a river or channel:
flumina, Ov.
excalceo -are, *to take the shoes from*: pedes,
Suet.; esp. in drama, *to take the tragic
cothurnus from* an actor: Sen.
excalfăcio -făcĕre -factum, *to heat up*: Plin.
excandescentĭa -ae, f. (excandesco), *heat,
irascibility*: Cic.
excandesco -descĕre -dŭi, *to become hot, to
glow.* LIT., Cato. TRANSF., *to grow hot* with
passion: nisi ira excanduit fortitudo, Cic.
excanto -are, *to charm out, bring forth by
incantations*: sidera excantata voce Thessalā,
Hor.
excarnĭfĭco -are, *to tear to pieces*: aliquem,
Cic., Sen. TRANSF., *to torment*: Ter.
excăvo -are, *to hollow out*: ex una gemma
praegrandi trullā excavatā, Cic.
excēdo -cēdĕre -cessi -cessum.
  (1) intransit.: **a,** *to go out, go away, go
from.* LIT., via, Liv.; oppido, Caes.; urbe,
Cic.; ex proelio, proelio, Caes. TRANSF., e
pueris, *to pass out of the age of boyhood*, Cic.;
e memoria, *to pass out of memory*, Liv.; e vitā,
to die, Cic.; so: vitā, Cic., Tac.; and absol.
excedere, Tac.; excedere palmā, *to resign
the prize*, Verg.: **b,** *to go beyond* a point or
limit, esp. fig.: ut nulla (pars) excederet
ultra, Cic.; cum libertas non ultra vocem
excessisset, Cic.; hence *to proceed* to a further
point, *attain to, result in*: ne in altercationem
excedet res, Liv.; eo laudis excedere, Tac.
  (2) transit.: **a,** in gen., *to leave*: curiam,
urbem, Liv.: **b,** *to pass beyond, exceed*:
modum, Liv.; tempus finitum, Liv.; fidem,
Ov.
excellens -entis, partic. from excello; q.v.
excellentĭa -ae, f. (excello), *eminence, distinction*: animi excellentia magnitudoque,
Cic.; propter excellentiam, *pre-eminently*, Cic.
excello -ĕre (cf. antecello, celsus), *to stand out,
to excel, be distinguished, be eminent*: illud
excellit regium nomen, Cic. Sphere of
excellence in the abl.: animi magnitudine,
Cic.; Caes.; or with in: in qua parte excello
ipse, Cic. Persons excelled with a prep.: inter
quos posset excellere, Cic.; in eo genere
praeter ceteros, Cic.; quia super ceteros
excellat, Liv.; or else in dat.: ita figuratum
esse corpus ut excellat ceteris, Cic.; in
quibus tu longe aliis excellis, Cic.
  ¶ Hence partic. (with compar. and superl.)
excellens, *high, lofty, eminent, distinguished,
remarkable*: Brutus excellens omni genere
laudis, Cic.; excellens pulchritudo muliebris
formae, Cic.; Caes., Liv., Verg.
  ¶ Adv. **excellentĕr**, *eminently*: quae
magno animo fortiter excellenterque gesta
sunt, Cic.; compar. excellentius: Cic.
excelsĭtās -ātis, f. (excelsus), *height*. TRANSF.,
animi, *elevation*, Cic.
excelsus -a -um, adj. (with compar. and
superl.) (celsus), *lofty, high, elevated.*
  LIT., mons, Caes.; locus, Cic.
  TRANSF., *distinguished, eminent*: in excelso
et industri loco sita laus tua, Cic.; of mind or
character: magnus homo et excelsus, Cic.;
animus excelsus, Cic.; of style: orator
grandior et quodammodo excelsior, Cic.
  ¶ N. as subst. **excelsum** -i. LIT., *a
height*: in excelso conlocare, Cic.; Ov.

TRANSF., *eminence*: in excelso vitam agere,
Sall.; plur.: excelsa et alta sperare, Liv.
  ¶ Adv. (with compar.) **excelsē**, *loftily*: Cic.
exceptĭo -ōnis, f. (excipio), *an exception,
restriction, limitation*; in gen.: cum exceptione, Cic.; sine exceptione, Cic.; quodsi
exceptionem facit ne, Cic.; esp. as legal t. t.,
*an exception by the defendant to the plaintiff's
statement of a case*: exceptionem alicui dare,
Cic.
excepto -are (freq. of excipio). (1) *to take up,
catch*: barbatulos mullos de piscina, Cic.;
auras, *to snuff up*, Verg. (2) *to take in
succession*: singulos, Caes.
excerno -cernĕre -crēvi -crētum, *to separate,
sift, sort*: Saguntinos ex captorum numero,
Liv.; haedi excreti, *separated from their
mothers*, Verg.
excerpo -cerpĕre -cerpsi -cerptum (ex/carpo),
to pick out. LIT., semina pomis, Hor.
TRANSF., (1) *to gather out, choose*: excerpere
ex malis si quid inesset boni, Cic.; excerpere
nomina ex tabulis, Liv. (2) *to put on one
side, separate*: de numero, Cic.; se numero
illorum, Hor.
  ¶ N. of partic. as subst. **excerptum** -i,
an extract: Sen., Quint.
excessus -ūs, m. (excedo), *a departure*; hence
(1) *departure from life*, i.e. *death*: vitae, Cic.;
e vita, Cic.; absol.: laeti excessu principes,
Tac. (2) *departure from subject*, i.e. *digression*:
Quint., Plin. L.
excētra -ae, f. *a snake*: Cic. poet. TRANSF., as
term of abuse, *viper*: Pl., Liv.
excīdĭum -i, n. (exscindo), *overthrow,
destruction*: Libyae, Verg.; urbium relicta-
rum, Liv.; legionum, Tac.
¹**excĭdo** -cidĕre -cĭdi (ex/cado), *to fall out,
fall from.*
  LIT., sol excidisse mihi e mundo videtur,
Cic.; gladii de manibus exciderunt, Cic.;
Verg.; esp. of a lot, *to fall out*: ut cuiusque
sors exciderat, Liv.
  TRANSF., (1) in gen., *to be lost, fall away*:
ut quodammodo victoria e manibus ex-
cideret, *slipped out*, Cic.; in vitium libertas
excidit, *degenerated*, Hor.; excidit illa metu,
lost consciousness, Ov. (2) *of words, to slip
out unawares, escape*: verbum ex ore alicuius
(*or* alicui), Cic.; libellus me imprudente et
invito excidit, Cic.; vox ore, Verg. (3) *of
ideas, to pass from memory* or *thought, be
forgotten*: at mihi ista exciderant, Cic.;
Carthaginem excidisse de memoria, Liv.;
nomen tuum mihi excidit, Ov.
²**excĭdo** -cidĕre -cĭdi -cīsum (ex/caedo), *to cut
out.* LIT., lapides e terra, *to quarry*, Cic.;
arbor excisa non evulsa, Cic.; Verg.
  TRANSF., (1) *to destroy, demolish*: portas,
force open, Caes.; domos, Cic. (2) *to root
out, banish*: illud tristissimum tempus ex
anno, Cic.; causas bellorum, Tac.
excĭĕo and **excĭo** -cīre -cīvi and -cĭi -cītum
and cĭtum, *to call out, arouse.*
  LIT., in gen.: ea res ab stativis excivit
Mettium, Liv.; artifices e Graecia, Liv.;
animas imis sepulcris, Verg. Esp. (1) *to
awaken*: somno, Sall.; ex somno, Liv. (2) *to
summon to help*: Romanos ad auxilium urbis
obsessae, Liv.; auxilia e Germania, Tac.
  TRANSF., (1) of persons, *to excite, arouse*:
hostem ad dimicandum acie, Liv.; *to alarm*:

conscientia mentem excitam vastabat, Sall.
(2) of feelings, *to call forth, excite, produce*:
tumultum in portis, Liv.; timorem, Liv.
(3) of material things, *to stir, shake*: pulsuque
pedum tremit excita tellus, Verg.

excĭpĭo -cĭpĕre -cēpi -ceptum (ex/capio).
(1) *to take out.* LIT., aliquem e mari, Cic.;
Pl. TRANSF., a, *to rescue*: servitute, Liv.:
b, *to except*: hosce homines excipio et
secerno, Cic.; excepto quod non simul esses,
cetera laetus, Hor.
(2) *to take up, catch.* LIT., a, of persons:
servos in pabulatione, Caes.; moribundum,
Liv.; incautum, Verg.: b, of things: sanguinem paterā, Cic. TRANSF., a, *to receive,
greet, welcome* a person: excipi ab omnibus
clamore, Cic.; aliquem hospitio, Ov.; Verg.,
Liv., Tac.: b, *to pick up* news or ideas by
listening: rumores, Cic.; motus futuros,
Verg.: c, of events and states, *to take people,
come upon* them: qui quosque eventūs
exciperent, Caes.; except deinde eum bellum,
Liv.
(3) more passively, *to receive*: vulnera,
labores, Cic.; tela, Caes., Cic.; gentem,
Verg.; porticus excipit Arcton, *faces north*,
Hor. TRANSF., *to follow, succeed*: orationem
Tullii exceperunt preces multitudinis, Liv.;
Herculis vitam immortalitas excipit, Cic.;
hunc excipit Labienus, *speaks next*, Caes.;
absol., *to succeed, come later*: Caes., Liv.

excīsĭo -ōnis (excido), *destruction*: urbium, Cic.
excĭto -are.
(1) *to rouse forth, arouse.* LIT., feras, Cic.;
aliquem e somno, Cic.; somno, Liv.;
clamore excitatum praesidium Romanorum,
Liv.; aliquem a mortuis *or* ab inferis, Cic.
TRANSF., of things, *to provoke, call forth,
cause*: fletum alicui, amores, Cic.; iras, Verg.
(2) *to rouse up, raise up.* LIT., universi
rursus prociderunt, tandem excitati curiā
excesserunt, Liv.; testes, Cic. TRANSF., (1)
of persons, *to console, cheer, inspire*: animum
iacentem, Cic.; adflictos, Cic.; trepido nuntio
excitatus, Liv.; aliquem ad laborem et
laudem, Cic. (2) of buildings, *to raise, erect*:
turrem, Caes.; sepulcrum, Cic. (3) of a fire,
to kindle, inflame: ignem, Caes.; incendium,
Cic.
¶ Hence partic. (with compar.: Liv.,
and superl.: Plin.), **excĭtātus** -a -um, *lively,
vigorous, loud*: sonus, Cic.

exclāmātĭo -ōnis, f. (exclamo), in rhetoric, *an
exclamation*: Cic., Quint., Tac.
exclāmo -are. (1) intransit., *to shout, cry
aloud*: in stadio cursores exclamant quam
maxime possunt, Cic.; Pl., Quint. (2) *to
shout* something, *exclaim*; with words quoted:
mihi libet exclamare: pro Deum, Cic.; with
clause, acc. and infin. for statement, ut and
subj. for command: Cic., Liv. (3) *to call*
somebody *by name*: Ciceronem, ap. Cic.
exclūdo -clūdĕre -clūsi -clūsum (ex/claudo),
to shut out, exclude.
LIT., (1) of persons: aliquem a domo sua,
Cic.; aliquem moenibus, Cic., Verg. (2) of
things, *to knock out*: oculum, Pl., Ter.
(3) of birds, *to hatch*: pullos suos in nido, Cic.
TRANSF., *to exclude, keep away, prevent*: ab
hereditate paterna, Cic.; his praemiis et
honoribus, Cic.; aliquem a republica, Cic.;
Romanos ab re frumentaria, Caes.; Liv.

exclūsĭo -ōnis, f. (excludo), *a shutting out,
exclusion*: Ter.
excōgĭtātĭo -ōnis, f. (excogito), *a contriving,
devising*: illa vis, quae investigat occulta,
quae inventio atque excogitatio dicitur,
Cic.
excōgĭto -are, *to think out, devise, contrive, invent*: mira quaedam genera furandi, Cic.;
with purpose expressed by ad: excogitare
multa ad avaritiam, Caes.; by dat.: tuendis
urbibus; absol.: ad haec igitur cogita, mi
Attice, vel potius excogita, Cic. L.
excŏlo -cŏlĕre -cŏlŭi -cultum, *to tend or
cultivate carefully.*
LIT., arva, Mart.; lanas rudes, *to spin*, Ov.
TRANSF., (1) *to adorn, polish, ennoble, refine*:
Tuditanus omni vitā atque victu excultus,
Cic.; animos doctrinā, Cic.; vitam per artes,
Verg. (2) *to serve, honour*: ut te non excolat
ipsum, Ov.
excŏquo -cŏquĕre -coxi -coctum. (1) *to boil
down, boil away*; fig., *to purge away*: omne
per ignes vitium, Verg. (2) *to cook, bake,
make hard*: terram sol excoquit, Lucr.;
ferrum, Ov.; harenas in vitrum, Tac.; fig.,
to cook up: malum, Pl.
excors -cordis (ex/cor), *foolish, silly, without
intelligence*: anus, Cic.; hoc qui non videt,
excors est, Hor.; Pl.
excrēmentum -i, n. (excerno), *excrement*:
oris, *spittle*, Tac.; narium, Tac.
excresco -crescĕre -crēvi -crētum, *to grow up,
spring up*: in hos artus, in haec corpora,
quae miramur, excrescunt, Tac.
excrētus -a -um, partic. of excerno or of
excresco.
excrŭcĭābĭlis -e (excrucio), *deserving of
torture*: Pl.
excrŭcĭo -are, *to torture, torment exceedingly.*
LIT., servos fame vinculisque, Caes.; excruciare vinculis ac verberibus atque omni
supplicio, Cic. TRANSF., of mental torture:
meae me miseriae magis excruciant quam
tuae, Cic.; Pl.
excŭbĭae -ārum, f. (excubo), *a lying out*; in
gen.: Pl.; esp. milit., *keeping watch, keeping
guard*: o excubias tuas, o flebiles vigilias,
Cic.; excubias agere, Tac.; of animals:
excubiae vigilum canum, Hor.
TRANSF., (1) *watchfires*: excubias divum
aeternae, Verg. (2) *the persons who keep
watch, watchmen, guard*: Tac., Suet.
excŭbĭtor -ōris, m. (excubo), *a sentinel,
watchman, guard*: Caes.; of birds: excubitor
ales, *the cock*, Verg.
excŭbo -bare -bŭi -bĭtum, *to lie or sleep out of
doors.*
LIT., in gen.: in agris, Cic.; esp. milit., *to
keep watch*: in armis, pro castris, ad portum,
Caes.; Verg.
TRANSF., *to be watchful, vigilant*: excubabo
vigilaboque pro vobis, Cic.; cupido excubat
in genis, Hor.
excūdo -cūdĕre -cūdi -cūsum, *to strike out,
beat out.*
LIT., in gen.: scintillam silici, Verg.;
esp. (1) *to hammer, forge*: spirantia mollius
aera, Verg. (2) *to hatch*: pullos ex ovis,
Cic.
TRANSF., (1) of bees, *to mould*: recentes
ceras, Verg. (2) of writers, *to compose*:
Cic. L., Tac., Plin. L.

exculco -are (ex/calco), *to trample firm, tread hard, stamp firm*: singuli ab infimo solo pedes terra exculcabantur, Caes.

excūrātus -a -um (curo), *carefully seen to*: Pl.

excurro -currĕre -cŭcurri and -curri -cursum, *to run out, hasten forth*.
    Lit., in gen.: Pl., Cic.; esp. milit. t. t., *to attack, make a sortie*: omnibus portis, Liv.; ex Africa: Cic.
    Transf., in gen.: quorum animi spretis corporibus evolant atque excurrunt foras, Cic.; with acc., *to run over*: spatium, Ter.; esp. (1) fig., *to run out, move freely*: campus in quo excurrere virtus possit, Cic. (2) of places, *to run out, to project*: promontorium in altum excurrens, Liv.

excursĭo -ōnis, f. (excurro), *a running out*.
    (1) as rhet. t. t.: a, *stepping forwards while speaking*: excursio moderata eaque rara, Cic.: b, fig., *outset* of a speech: prima excursio orationis, Cic.
    (2) milit. t. t., *an attack, assault, sally*: excursionem facere ex oppido, Caes.; excursiones et latrocinia hostium, Cic.

excursor -ōris, m. (excurro), *a scout, skirmisher*: Cic.

excursus -ūs, m. (excurro), *a running out*.
    (1) rhet. t. t., *a digression*: Quint. (2) milit. t. t., *an attack, sally, assault*: excursus militum, Caes.; Tac.; fig., of bees: Verg.

excūsābĭlis -e (excuso), *excusable*: delicti pars, Ov.

excūsātĭo -ōnis (excuso), *an excuse, plea, defence*; with subjective genit.: Pompeii, Cic.; with objective genit.: peccati, Cic.; with both: excusatio Ser. Sulpici legationis obeundae, *his plea to be excused it*, Cic.; with causal genit.: excusationem oculorum accipere, Cic.; excusatione uti temporis *or* valetudinis, Cic.; Caes., Pl.; stultitia excusationem non habet, *finds no excuse*, Cic.; excusationem probare, Cic.; with cur: Cic. L.

excūso -are (ex/causa), *to exempt from blame or accusation, to excuse*. (1) *to excuse* a person: se apud aliquem, *or* se alicui, Cic.; se de aliqua re, Caes.; with quod: Caes., Cic.; pass.: excusatus, Hor.; cui excusari mallet, *from which he preferred to be excused*, Cic. (2) *to make excuses for* a thing: tarditatem litterarum, Cic. L.: Ov., Tac. (3) *to allege in excuse, to plead*: morbum, Cic.; valetudinem, aetatem, Liv., Ov.; with acc. and infin.: Pl., Liv.; si Lysiades excusetur Areopagites esse, *if it is said in L.'s defence that he is*, Cic.
    ¶ Hence partic. **excūsātus** -a -um, *free from blame*. Adv. (with compar.) **excūsātē**, *excusably*: Quint.

excussus -a -um, partic. of excutio; q.v.

excŭtĭo -cŭtĕre -cussi -cussum (ex/quatio), *to shake out*.
    Lit., (1) of actual shaking: caesariem, Ov.; litteras in terram, Cic.; esp. *to shake out* clothes to find anything hidden: Pl.; hence *to search, examine* a person: non excutio te, Cic.; fig., *to investigate*: omnes ineptias, Cic. (2) *to strike off, throw out, knock away*: equus excussit equitem, Liv.; agnam ore lupi, Ov.; Teucros vallo, Verg.; of missiles: glandem, Liv.
    Transf., *to shake off, put away, drive out*: conceptum foedus, Verg.; excussus patriā, Verg.; studia de manibus, Cic.; excutior somno, Verg.

exdorsŭo -are (dorsum), *to fillet* a fish: Pl.

exec-, see exsec-.

exĕdo -esse -ēdi -ēsum, *to eat up, devour, consume*. Lit., Pl., Ter.
    Transf., (1) of the action of time, rust, etc.: exesis posterioribus partibus versiculorum, Cic.; exesa robigine pila, Verg. (2) fig., of troubles, *to wear down, exhaust*: aegritudo exest animum, Cic.; Pl. (3) in gen., *to destroy*: Tac.

exĕdra -ae, f. (ἐξέδρα), *a hall for conversation* or *debate*: Cic., Quint.

exedrĭum -i, n. (ἐξέδριον), *a sitting-room*: Cic. L.

exemplāris -e (exemplum), *serving as a copy*: (litteras) exemplares omnium litterarum, Tac.
    ¶ N. as subst. **exemplar** -āris (exemplārĕ: Lucr.). (1) *a copy, transcript* (cf. exemplum): rerum magnarum, Lucr., Plin. L. Transf., *a likeness*: alicuius, Cic. (2) *a pattern, ideal*: reipublicae, Cic.; Hor., Quint., Tac.

exemplum -i, n. (eximo), originally *something chosen from a number of things, a sample*.
    Hence (1) *an example*. In gen.: iracundiae, Cic.; exempli causā (*or* gratiā), *for instance*, Cic., Quint. Esp.: a, *a general character, manner, fashion* (as shown by examples): isto exemplo vivere, Pl.; quaestionem haberi eodem exemplo quo M. Pomponius praetor habuisset, Liv.; Caes., Cic.: b, *an example to be followed, model*: exemplum innocentiae, pudicitiae, Cic.; exemplum ad imitandum, Cic.; petere ab aliquo, Liv.; capere, Cic.: c, *a precedent*: Cic., Liv.: d, *an example of what may happen, warning, object-lesson*: exemplo esse, Caes., Liv.; in exemplo esse, Ov.; exemplum severitatis edere, Cic.; exemplum statuere in aliquo, Tac.; hence *a punishment intended to deter*: habet aliquid ex iniquo omne magnum exemplum, Tac.
    (2) *a copy, transcript*: Caesaris litterarum exemplum tibi misi, Cic. L.; Ov.

exemptus -a -um, partic. of eximo; q.v.

exentĕro -are (ἐξεντερίζω), *to disembowel*: Pl.

exĕo -īre -ii (-īvi) -itum.
    (1) intransit., *to go out, go away, go forth*. Lit., of persons: ex urbe, Cic.; ab urbe, Liv.; de triclinio, Cic.; domo, Cic.; castris, Caes.; ad pugnam, Liv., Verg.; of things: cum de consularibus mea prima sors exisset, Cic.; ad caelum arbos, *spring up*, Verg. Transf., a, *to pass from* a previous state: e vita, de vita, to die, Cic.; ex potestate, Cic.; e patriciis, *to lose one's rank as a patrician*, Cic.: b, *to pass into another state, come out changed*: Hor., Cic. L.: c, *to get out, to become known*: exit oratio, Cic.: d, of time, *to come to an end, pass away*: quinto anno exeunte, Cic.; Liv., Sen.
    (2) transit.: a, *to pass over, beyond*: Avernas valles, Ov.; Ter. Transf., modum, Ov.: b, *toward off* vim viribus, Verg.; Lucr.

exeq-, see exseq-.

exercĕo -ēre -ŭi -ĭtum (ex/arceo; cf. ἀρχεῖν) *to make strong, to keep at work, exercise, train*.
    Lit., copias, Caes.; corpus, Cic.; se in curriculo, Cic.; equos aequore campi, Verg.; adsiduis bracchia telis, Ov.; famulas a lumina longo penso, Verg.
    Transf., (1) of physical objects, *to work at, use*: solum presso sub vomere, *to cultivate*

Verg.; arma, Verg.; praedia rustica, Liv.;
metalla auri atque argenti, Liv. (2) of
abstr. things, *to employ, exploit*: diem,
Verg.; victoriam, Sall., Liv. (3) of feelings,
arts, and processes, *to practise, exercise*:
medicinam, Cic.; iudicium, Cic.; quaestiones, Liv.; legem, Liv.; facilitatem et
lenitudinem animi in aliquo, Cic.; graves
inimicitias cum aliquo, Sall.; libidinem et
avaritiam in socios, Liv. (4) of the mind, *to
train*: se cotidianis commentationibus, Cic.;
ingenium, Quint. (5) *to overwork, harass,
trouble*: meos casus in quibus me fortuna
vehementer exercuit, Cic.; exerceri poenis,
Verg.
¶ Hence partic. **exercĭtātus** -a -um.
(1) *trained, schooled*: bello, Tac. (2) *harassed*:
Cic. L. (3) *severe, vexatious*: Tac.
exercĭtātĭo -ōnis, f. (exercito). (1) *practice,
exercise*. Lit., of the body: corpora nostra
motu atque exercitatione recalescunt, Cic.
Transf., of the mind: dicendi, Cic.; iuris
civilis, Cic.; Quint. (2) *experience*: Caes.,
Cic.
exercĭtātus -a -um, partic. from exercito; q.v.
exercĭtĭum -i, n. (exerceo), *practice, exercise*:
equitum, Tac.
exercĭto -are (freq. of exerceo), *to train hard,
keep at work*: Sall., Quint.
¶ Hence partic. **exercĭtātus** -a -um.
(1) *trained, practised, exercised*: homines in
armis exercitati, Cic.; exercitatus in uxoribus
necandis, Cic.; in arithmeticis satis exercitatus, Cic.; bello, Liv. (2) *troubled, harassed*:
curis agitatus et exercitatus animus, Cic.;
Syrtes Noto, Hor.
exercĭtus -a -um, partic. of exerceo; q.v.
exercĭtus -ūs, m. (exerceo).
Lit., *training*: Pl.
Transf., *a trained body of soldiers, army*:
exercitus terrestris, navalis, Liv.; exercitum,
conscribere, comparare, ducere, alere, Cic.;
cogere, Caes.; esp., *the infantry*: exercitus
equitatusque, Caes.; sometimes of a civil
gathering: Pl.; poet. in gen., *a crowd,
swarm*: corvorum, Verg.
exēsor -ōris, m. (exedo), *one who gnaws or eats
away*: Lucr.
exhālātĭo -ōnis, f. (exhalo), *an exhalation,
vapour*: exhalationes terrae, Cic.
exhālo -are. (1) transit., *to exhale, breathe
out*: of things: nebulam, Verg.; odores, Lucr.;
of persons: vitam, Verg.; animam, Ov.;
crapulam, Cic.
(2) intransit., of things, *to steam*: Lucr.; of
persons, *to expire*: Ov.
exhaurĭo -haurire -hausi -haustum.
(1) *to draw out*. Lit., of fluids: sentinam,
Cic.; also in gen., *to remove, take out*: terram
manibus, Caes.; pecuniam ex aerario, Cic.
Transf., *to take away* abstr. things: vitam,
Cic.; partem ex tuis laudibus, Cic.
(2) *to drain dry, empty out*. Lit., fossas
cloacasque, Liv.; puteos, poculum, vinum,
to empty by drinking, Cic.; also in gen. *to
empty*: aerarium, Cic. Transf., **a**, *to impoverish*: facultates patriae, Cic.; homines,
Cic.: **b**, *to finish, bring to an end*: amorem,
Cic.; sermo hominum exhaustus est, Cic. L.:
c, *to endure, suffer*: labores, Liv.; bella, Verg.
exhērēdo -are (ex/heres), *to disinherit*: aliquem, Cic., Quint.

exhērēs -ēdis, *disinherited*; with genit.:
paternorum bonorum exheres, Cic.; Pl.,
Quint. Transf., vitae, Pl.
exhĭbĕo -hĭbēre -hĭbŭi -hĭbĭtum (ex/habeo), *to
hold out*.
Lit., *to produce*, esp. in court: pupillum,
fratres, Cic.; exhibe librarium illud legum
vestrarum, Cic.; omnia integra, Cic.
Transf., (1) *to show, display, exhibit*: dea
formam removit anilem Palladaque exhibuit,
Ov.; populo Romano philosophiam, *set forth,
present*, Cic.; humanitatem, Plin. L. (2) *to
offer, allow*: toros, Ov.; exhibe liberam
contionem vel Argis vel Lacedaemone, Liv.
(3) *to produce* by making, *to cause*: alicui
molestiam, Cic. L.; Pl.
exhĭlăro -are, *to make cheerful*: miraris tam
exhilaratam esse servitutem nostram, Cic. L.
exhorresco -horrescĕre -horrŭi. Intransit., *to
shudder exceedingly, be terrified*: aequoris
instar, Ov.; metu, Cic. Transit., *to tremble
at, to dread*: vultus, Verg.; Liv.
exhortātĭo -ōnis, f. (exhortor), *exhortation,
encouragement*: ducum, Tac.; Quint.
exhortātīvus -a -um (exhortor), *of exhortation*:
Quint.
exhortor -ari, dep. *to exhort, encourage*: natum,
Verg.; foll. by ut and subj.: Tac., Quint.
exĭgo -ĭgĕre -ēgi -actum (ex/ago).
(1) *to drive out*. Lit., reges ex civitate,
Cic.; sacer admissas exigit Hebrus aquas,
pours into the sea, Ov.; ensem per iuvenem,
Verg. Transf., **a**, fig., *to drive away*:
fabulam, Ter.; uxorem, Ter.; otium, Hor.:
b, *to force out, exact, demand*: pecunias,
Caes., Cic.; poenas, Ov.; litteras, Cic. L.;
viam, *its buildings*, Cic.; veritatem a teste,
Cic.; with ut and subj.: Cic.: **c**, *to sell*:
agrorum fructūs, Liv.
(2) *to drive through*; hence: **a**, *to complete,
finish*, of work: monumentum aere perennius,
Hor.; opus, Ov.; of time: exacta aetate, Cic.;
annos, Hor., Verg.; exacto die, Tac.: **b**, *to
determine, settle*; objectively, *to adjust,
regulate*: columnas ad perpendiculum, Cic.;
ad illam summam veritatem legitimum ius,
Cic.; subjectively, *to consider, reflect upon*:
tempus secum ipsa opusque exigit, Verg.;
also *to ascertain, decide*: non satis exactum
quid agam, *not certain*, Cic.
¶ Hence partic. (with compar. and superl.)
exactus -a -um, *accurate, precise, exact*:
numerus, Liv.; with genit.: morum, Ov.
exĭgŭĭtās -ātis, f. (exiguus), *littleness, smallness*:
castrorum, Caes.; copiarum, Cic.; ut temporis
exiguitas postulabat, Caes.
exĭgŭus -a -um (exigo), *small, little, scanty*.
(1) of quantity, in size, *small*: castra, Caes.;
pars terrae, Cic.; toga, Hor.; in number,
scanty: numerus oratorum, Cic.; in time,
short: vita, Cic.; Caes., Verg.
(2) of quality, *meagre*: facultates, Caes.;
laus, Cic.; ingenium, Cic.
N. as subst. **exĭgŭum** -i, *small extent*:
Liv.
¶ Adv. **exĭgŭē**, *sparingly, scantily, scarcely*:
frumentum exigue dierum xxx habere,
Caes.; nimis exigue et exiliter ad calculos
revocare amicitiam, *too narrowly*, Cic.; exigue scripta est (epistula), Cic.
exĭlis -e (?ex/ilia), *little, thin, slender, meagre*:
legiones, Cic.; solum, Cic.; femur, Hor.

TRANSF., (1) in possessions, *poor*: domus, Hor.; with genit., *without*: Pl. (2) of style, *dry, dreary*: genus sermonis, Cic.; Quint.

¶ Adv. **exīlĭtĕr**, *thinly, poorly, meagrely*: nimis exigue et exiliter ad calculos revocare amicitiam, Cic.; annales sane exiliter descripti, Cic.; nolo verba exiliter exanimata exire, Cic.

exīlĭtās -ātis, f. (exilis), *thinness, meagreness, weakness*: in dicendo, Cic.; Quint.

exim = exinde; q.v.

exĭmĭus -a -um (eximo), *excepted*. LIT., te illi unum eximium cui consuleret fuisse, Cic.; hence *selected*: Verg., Liv. TRANSF., *exceptional, distinguished*: virtus, Caes.; facies, ingenium, spes, Cic.; ironical, istae vestrae eximiae pulchraeque virtutes, Cic.

¶ Adv. **exĭmĭē**, *uncommonly, exceptionally*: diligere, Cic.; templum eximie ornatum, Liv.

exĭmo -ĭmĕre -ēmi -emptum (ex/emo), *to take out, take away*.

LIT., spinis de pluribus unam, Hor.; Ov.

TRANSF., (1) *to take off* a list, *take out* of a group: aliquid ex rerum natura, Cic.; unum diem ex mense, Cic.; aliquem ex (*or* de) reis, Cic. (2) *to free, release*: agrum de vectigalibus, Cic.; aliquem ex culpa, Cic.; aliquem servitute, Liv. (3) *to take away, remove* an abstr. thing: curas, Hor.; moram certaminis hosti, Liv.; of time, *to take and use* for some different purpose, i.e. *to waste*: diem dicendo, Cic.; Liv.

exin = exinde; q.v.

exĭnānĭo -ire, *to empty*: navem, Cic.; agros, gentes, *to plunder*, Cic.

exinde (exin, exim), adv., *from there, thence*. (1) in space, *thence, next*: mari finitimus aër, Cic. (2) in time, *thereupon, after that, then*: Cic., Verg., Liv.; also in the enumeration of a series of facts, *then, next*: Verg., Liv., Tac. (3) in other relations, *consequently, accordingly*: Pl.

existĭmātĭo -ōnis, f. (existimo). (1) *the opinion that a man has of a thing or person, judgment*: hominum, Caes., Cic.; non militis de imperatore existimationem esse, Liv. (2) *the opinion that others have of a man*, esp. morally, *reputation, good name, honour, character*: bona, integra, magna, Cic.; alicuius existimationem offendere, Cic.; venisse in eam existimationem, Cic.; in finance, *credit*: Caes.

existĭmātŏr -ōris, m. (existimo), *one who forms or gives an opinion, a critic*: Cic.

existĭmo (existumo) -are (ex/aestimo), *to judge a thing according to its value.*

LIT., to value at a price: vitam tanti, Cic.; Pl., Liv.

TRANSF., in gen., *to form a judgment* about a person or thing; hence (1) *to judge that, hold* a particular *opinion, consider, regard, deem*; with predic. acc.: existumare aliquem avarum, Cic.; in pass.: homo, ut existimabatur, avarus et furax; with in and the abl.: in hostium numero existimari, Cic.; with acc. and infin.: non possum existimare plus quemquam a se ipso quam me a te amari, Cic.; in pass.: Africano vim attulisse existimatus est, Cic.; with pronoun acc.: quod ego nullo modo existimo; with adv.: ita intellegimus vulgo existimari, Cic. (2) to form some opinion unspecified, *to judge*,

decide, pass judgment, esp. on literary works: de scriptoribus, qui nondum ediderunt, existimare non possumus, Cic.

exĭtĭābĭlis -e (exitium), *deadly, destructive*: bellum, Cic. L.; Ov., Liv., Tac.

exĭtĭālis -e (exitium), *destructive, fatal, deadly*: exitus, Cic.; donum Minervae, Verg.

exĭtĭo -ōnis, f. (exeo), *a going out*: Pl.

exĭtĭōsus -a -um (exitium), *destructive, fatal, deadly*: exitiosum esse reipublicae, Cic.; compar.: Tac.

exĭtĭum -i, n. (exeo). LIT., *a going out or away*; hence *destruction, ruin*: huius urbis, Cic.; omnia exitia publica, Cic.; Pl., Verg., Tac. TRANSF., *a cause of destruction*: exitio esse, with dat. of person, Cic. L., Tac.

exĭtus -ūs, m. (exeo), *a going out, a going forth*.

LIT., reditum mihi gloriosum iniuria tua dedit, non exitum calamitosum, Cic.; omni exitu et pabulatione interclusi, Caes.; ne exitus inclusis ab urbe esset, Liv.

TRANSF., (1) *a means of going out, exit*: Caes., Cic., Liv.; fig.: quae plurimos exitus dant ad eiusmodi digressionem, *opportunities for digression*, Cic. (2) *end, finish*: adducta ad exitum quaestio est, Cic.; hic fuit exitus oppugnationis, Caes.; of a drama: explicare argumenti exitum non potestis, Cic.; of life: humanus, Cic. (3) *issue, result*: eventus atque exitus rerum, Cic.; exitus futuri temporis, Hor.; Caes., Liv.

exlex -lēgis (ex/lex). (1) *bound by no law*: exlegem esse Sullam, Cic. (2) *lawless, reckless*: Hor.

exmŏvĕo = emoveo; q.v.

exobsecro -are, *to entreat earnestly*: Pl.

exŏcŭlo -are (oculus), *to deprive of eyes*: Pl.

exŏdĭum -i, n. (ἐξόδιον), *a comic afterpiece*: Liv., Juv., Suet.

exŏlesco -ŏlescĕre -ŏlēvi -ŏlētum (alo), *to grow old and weak, decay, fade out*; fig.: ne vetustissima Italiae disciplina per desidiam exolesceret, Tac.; Liv.

¶ Hence pass. partic. **exŏlētus** -a -um, *worn out*; fig.: exoletum iam vetustate odium, Liv.; m. as subst. **exŏlētus** -i, *a dissolute person of mature age*: Pl., Cic., Tac.

exŏnĕro -are, *to unload, disburden*. LIT., navem, Pl.; plenas colos, Ov. TRANSF., *to free, release, relieve*; in gen.: civitatem metu, Liv.; Tac.; esp. by dispersal of people: regnum multitudine, Liv.; multitudinem proximas in terras, Tac.

exopto -are, *to desire eagerly, long for*: exoptare ea maxime, Cic.; Samnitium adventum, Liv.; tibi pestem exoptant, *wish you*, Cic.; with infin.: Cic. L.; with ut and the subj.: Cic. L.

¶ Hence partic. (with compar. and superl.: Cic. L.) **exoptātus** -a -um, *desired, longed for*: Pl., Cic., Verg.

exŏrābĭlis -e, adj. (with compar.) (exoro), *able to be entreated, placable*: Cic. L., Hor., Liv.

exŏrābŭla -orum, n. pl. (exoro), *means of entreaty*: Pl.

exŏrātŏr -ōris, m. (exoro), *one who entreats successfully*: Ter.

exordior -ordiri -orsus sum, dep. *to lay a warp, begin to weave*; fig.: pertexe quod exorsus es, Cic. TRANSF., in gen., *to begin*: bellum ab causa tam nefanda, Liv.; with infin.: dicere, Cic.; absol., of orators, *to begin*: Cic., Quint., Tac.

¶ Partic. in pass. sense **exorsus** -a -um, *begun*: Pl., Cic.; n. pl. as subst. **exorsa** -ōrum, *the beginning*: Verg.

exordium -i, n. (exordior), *the warp of a web*: Quint. TRANSF., in gen., *a beginning*: vitae, Cic.; plur.: revocare exordia prima pugnae, Verg.; esp. *the beginning of a speech*: in dicendi exordio permoveri, Cic.; as a part of a speech, *the introduction*: Cic., Quint.

exŏrĭor -ŏriri -ortus sum, dep. *to rise, rise up*. LIT., omnes exorti, *sprang up*, Liv.; e terrā arbusta, Lucr.; esp. of the sun, moon, and stars: post solstitium Canicula exoritur, Cic. TRANSF., *to arise, issue, appear, come forward*: repentinus Sulla nobis exoritur, Cic.; exortus est servus, *as an accuser*, Cic.; exoritur Antipatri ratio ex altera parte, Cic.; honestum quod ex virtutibus exoritur, Cic.; discordia, Verg.; bella, Liv.

exornātĭo -ōnis, f. (exorno), *adorning, ornament*: Cic.

exornātor -ōris, m. (exorno), *one who adorns, an embellisher*: ceteri non exornatores rerum, sed tantummodo narratores fuerunt, Cic.

exorno -are, *to furnish, provide plentifully*. LIT., nuptias, navem, Pl.; vicinitatem armis, Sall.; also *to ornament, adorn*: domum, Cic. TRANSF., *to adorn* abstr. things: Graeciam praestantissimis artibus, Cic.; philosophiam falsā gloriā; orationem, Cic.

exŏro -are, *to entreat successfully, obtain by entreaty, prevail upon*; with acc. of person: deos, Ov.; Cic.; in pass.: viri non esse neque exorari neque placari, Cic.; with ut and the subj.: denique exoravit tyrannum ut abire liceret, Cic., with acc. of what is obtained: pacem divum, Verg.

exorsus -a -um, partic. of exordior; q.v.

exorsus -ūs, m. (exordior), *a beginning*: orationis meae, Cic.

exortus -ūs, m. (exorior), *a rising*: solis, Suet. TRANSF., *the East*: Liv.

exos -ossis, *without bones*: Lucr.

exoscŭlor -ari, dep. *to kiss*: alicuius manum, Tac.

exosso -are (exos), *to bone, take out the bones*: Ter.; exossatum pectus, *boneless, flexible*, Lucr.

exostra -ae, f. (ἐξώστρα), *a theatrical machine, by which the inside of a house was revealed to the spectators*: Cic.

exōsus -a -um (ex/odi), *hating exceedingly*: exosus Troianos, Verg.; templa oculos exosa viriles, Ov.

exōtĭcus -a -um (ἐξωτικός), *foreign, outlandish, exotic*: Pl.

expallesco -pallescĕre -pallŭi, *to become very pale*: toto ore, Ov.; Pl.; poet., with acc.: Pindarici fontis haustus, *to dread*, Hor.

expalliātus -a -um (pallium), *robbed of his cloak*: Pl.

expallĭdus -a -um, *very pale*: Suet.

expalpo -are, *to coax out*: Pl.

expando -ĕre, *to stretch out, expand, spread out*. LIT., pass. in middle sense; of the Nile: Plin. L. TRANSF., *to explain*: rerum naturam dictis, Lucr.

expatro -are, *to squander*: Cat.

expăvesco -păvescĕre -pavi, *to grow very frightened*: ad id, Liv.; with acc.: ensem, *to dread exceedingly*, Hor.; Tac.

expĕdĭo -ire -īvi and -ĭi -ītum (ex/ped-), *to free from a snare, disengage, disentangle, set free*. LIT., se ex laqueo, Cic.; Verg., Hor. TRANSF., (1) physically, *to clear, free, get out, get ready for action*: naves, classem, aditūs, Caes.; legiones, Caes.; virgas, Cic.; Cererem canistris, Verg.; se ad pugnam, Liv.; iaculum trans finem, *to throw*, Hor. (2) fig., *to release, clear, set free, set straight*: se ab omni occupatione, Cic.; negotia, Cic.; frumentariam, Caes.; esp. in speech, *to clear up* a point, *explain*: omnem expediat morbi causam, Verg.; priusquam huiusmodi rei initium expediam, Sall.; ea de re quam verissime expediam, Tac.; with indir. quest.: Tac., Juv. (3) res expedit, or impers. expedit, *it is expedient, useful, advantageous*; nihil nec expedire nec utile esse, Cic.; with acc. and infin., or infin. simply: omnibus bonis expedit salvam esse rempublicam, Cic.; Hor., Quint.; with ut and the subj.: Tac.

¶ Hence partic. (with compar. and superl.) **expedītus** -a -um, *unshackled, unimpeded*.
(1) of persons. LIT., Caes., Cic., Hor.; esp. milit. t. t., *lightly equipped*: copiae, Caes.; Sall., Liv.; m. as subst.: Caes., Liv. TRANSF., *free, ready*: expeditus proficisci, Cic.; expeditus homo et paratus, Cic.; ad dicendum, Cic.
(2) of material things, *clear, free, ready for action*: locus, Caes.; via, Liv.; n. as subst. **expedītum** -i, *clear ground*: in expedito habere integras copias, Liv.
(3) of abstr. things, *clear, settled, ready*: res frumentaria, Caes.; ad suos receptus, Caes.; victoria, Caes.; negotia, Cic.; expedita et facile currens oratio, Cic.

¶ Adv. (with compar. and superl.) **expedītē**, *freely, easily*: Pl., Cic.

expĕdītĭo -ōnis, f. (expedio), *a military operation* with lightly equipped troops, *expedition*: milites ex hibernis in expeditionem evocare, Sall.; milites equitesque in expeditionem mittere, Caes.; in expeditionem exercitum educere, Cic.

expello -pellĕre -pŭli -pulsum, *to drive out, expel*.
LIT., (1) of living beings: pecus portā Esquilinā, Liv.; aliquem ex oppido, Caes.; Romanos castris, Caes.; aliquem domo suā, bonis, regno, patriā, Cic.; ex urbe, Cic.; filiam ex matrimonio, Cic.; fig.: naturam furcā, Hor. (2) of other material things, *to drive forth, thrust forth*: ab litore naves in altum, Liv.; sagittam arcu, Ov. TRANSF., metaphorically: aliquem vitā, Cic.; omnem dubitationem, Caes.; somnum, quietem, Verg.

expendo -pendĕre -pendi -pensum, *to weigh out*.
LIT., ut iam expendantur non numerentur pecuniae, Cic.; esp. *to weigh out in payment, pay out, put down money*: Cic., Pl. TRANSF., (1) *to value, rate*: hominem auro, Pl. (2) in gen., *to weigh up, consider*: expendere atque aestimare voluptates, Cic.; testem, Cic.; expende Hannibalem, Juv.; Tac.; with indir. quest., Cic. (3) *to pay* a penalty: poenas scelerum, Verg.; Tac.

¶ Hence partic. **expensus** -a -um, *weighed out*, hence *paid out*; esp. in phrase:

ferre alicui expensum aliquid, *to note* a thing
as paid to a person, *charge* to, Cic., Liv.
N. as subst. **expensum** -i, *payment*: Pl., Cic.
expergĕfăcĭo -făcĕre -fēci -factum, *to
awaken.* Lit., Suet. Transf., *to rouse,
excite*: se, Cic.; Pl.
expergiscor -pergisci -perrectus sum, dep. *to
wake up.* Lit., si dormis, expergiscere, Cic.;
Hor. Transf., *to arouse oneself*: experrecta
nobilitas, Cic.; Pl.
expergo -pergĕre -pergi -pergĭtum, *to awaken.*
Lit., Tac. Transf., from death: expergitus
exstat, Lucr.
expĕrĭens -entis, partic. from experior; q.v.
expĕrĭentĭa -ae, f. (experior), *trial, testing.*
Lit., of the process of trying: veri, Ov.;
hence *a trying to do* something; with genit.:
patrimonii amplificandi, Cic. Transf., of
the result of trying, *knowledge gained by
experience*: multarum rerum experientiā
cognitus, Tac.; hominum, Verg.
expĕrīmentum -i, n. (experior), *experience*:
Metello experimentis cognitum erat genus
Numidarum perfidum esse, Sall.; also *proof
from experience*: hoc maximum est experimentum, Cic.; Tac.
expĕrĭor -pĕriri -pertus sum, dep. (connected
with peritus, periculum; cf. πειράω), *to try,
test, prove, put to the test.*
 Hence (1) *to make trial of* a person or
thing; with acc.: rei eventum, Caes.;
alicuius amorem, Cic.; vim veneni in servo,
Cic.; amicos, Cic.; imperium, Liv.; absol.,
in battle: si iterum experiri velint, iterum
paratum esse decertare, Caes.; with indir.
quest.: Pl., Cic., Liv.; esp. at law: experiri
ius, *to go to law*, Cic.; experiri iudicium
populi Romani, *to leave it to the decision of the
Roman people*, Liv.
 (2) usually in perf., *to know by having
tried, know by experience*; with predic. acc.:
deos constantes inimicos, Ov.; with acc. and
infin.: iam antea expertus sum parum fidei
miseris esse, Sall.; Caes., Cic., Verg.
 (3) *to try to do* a thing: omnia de pace,
Caes.; ultima, Liv.; with ut and subj.:
experiar certe ut hinc avolem, Cic. L.
 ¶ Hence pres. partic. **expĕrĭens** -entis,
enterprising, venturesome: promptus homo et
experiens, Cic.; with genit.: laborum, Cic.
 ¶ Perf. partic. **expertus** -a -um. (1)
pass., *tested, tried, approved*: virtus, Cic.,
Liv. (2) act., *with experience, experienced*;
with genit.: expertus belli, Verg., Tac.; with
abl.: expertus tribuniciis certaminibus, Liv.
experrectus -a -um, partic. of expergiscor;
q.v
ȝxpers -pertis (ex/pars), *having no part in,
not sharing in*; with genit.: periculorum,
publici consilii, Cic. Transf., *wanting in,
destitute of*; with genit.: omnis eruditionis,
Cic.; viri, *without a husband*, Ov.; with
abl.: famā atque fortunis, Sall.; Lucr.
expertus -a -um, partic. from experior; q.v.
expĕtesso -ĕre (expeto), *to desire, wish for*: Pl.
expĕto -ĕre -īi and -īvi -ītum.
 (1) transit. *to desire, strive after, make for*:
vi am alicuius, Cic.; auxilium ab aliquo,
Cic.; esp. of things due, *to demand, require*:
pecuniam, poenas, Cic.; Liv.; with infin.,
to seek to do: Pl., Ov., Liv.; with acc. and
infin.: nostram gloriam tuā virtute augeri

expeto, Cic. L.; with ut and the subj., Tac.;
with a thing as subject: mare medium terrae
locum expetens, *encroaching on*, Cic.
 (2) intransit., *to fall upon*: ut in eum omnes
expetant huiusce clades belli, Liv.; Pl.
expĭātĭo -ōnis, f. (expio), *atonement, expiation*:
scelerum, Cic.; Liv.
expĭlātĭo -ōnis, f. (expilo), *a plundering,
robbing*: sociorum, Cic.
expĭlātor -ōris, m. (expilo), *a plunderer,
robber*: Cic. L.
expĭlo -are, *to plunder, rob*: aerarium, Cic.
expingo -pingĕre -pinxi -pictum. (1) *to paint
over*: Plin., Mart. (2) fig., *to describe, depict
in writing*: Cic.
expĭo -are. (1) *to propitiate, appease* an
offended or threatening power: poenis manes
mortuorum, Cic.; prodigium, Liv. (2) *to
purify* what is defiled: forum a sceleris vestigiis, Cic.; religionem aedium suarum, Cic.
(3) *to atone for* an offence: scelus supplicio,
Cic.; tua scelera dii in nostros milites
expiaverunt, Cic.; incommodum virtute, *to
make good*, Caes.
expiscor -ari, dep. *to fish out.* Transf., *to
search out, find out*: omnia ab aliquo, Cic. L
explānātĭo -ōnis, f. (explano), *a making clear
explanation*: naturae, Cic.; portentorum
Cic.; as rhet. t. t., *illustration*: Cic., Quint.
also *clear articulation*: Quint.
explānātor -ōris, m. (explano), *one wh[o]
explains, an interpreter*: oraculorum e[t]
vaticinationum, Cic.
explānātus -a -um, p. adj. (from explano)
clear, plain: vocum impressio, Cic.
explāno -are (ex/planus), *to make quite level
smooth out*; hence (1) *to explain, make clear*
ille tibi omnia explanabit, Cic.; carmen, Liv
(2) *to set out clearly*: de cuius hominu[m]
moribus pauca prius explananda sunt, Sall.
Cic. (3) *to articulate clearly*: Plin.
explaudo = explodo; q.v.
explēmentum -i, n. (expleo), *filling, stuffing*
Pl., Sen.
explĕo -plēre -plēvi -plētum, *to fill, fill up.*
 Lit., paludem cratibus atque aggere, Caes.
rimas, Cic.
 Transf., (1) in gen., *to fill*: sententias mol[-]
lioribus numeris, Cic. (2) *to fill up, complete*
required amount, either by including or b[y]
being included in it: numerum, legiones
Caes.; centurias, tribūs, Liv.; aurum quo[d]
summam talenti Attici expleret, Liv. (3) *to
make good* losses, etc.: damna, Liv.; Cic
(4) in quality, *to complete, perfect*: vitam bea[-]
tam cumulate, Cic. (5) of time, *to complete
finish*: expletum annum habeto, Cic.; Tac
(6) of duties, *to fulfil, discharge*: munus, Cic
(7) of wants, *to satisfy, quench, appease*: sitim
avaritiam, Cic.; desiderium, Liv.; se caede
Liv.; animum ultricis flammae, Verg.
 ¶ Hence partic. **explētus** -a -um, *perfect
complete*: expletus omnibus suis partibus, Cic
explētĭo -ōnis, f. (expleo), *satisfying*: naturae
Cic.
explĭcātē, adv. from explico; q.v.
explĭcātĭo -ōnis, f. (explico), *an unfolding
uncoiling*: rudentis, Cic. Transf., *explana[-]
tion, interpretation*: in disserendo mir[a]
explicatio, Cic.; explicatio fabularum, Cic.
explĭcātor -ōris, m. (explico), *an interpreter
explainer*: rerum explicator prudens, Cic.

explĭcatrix -īcis, f. (explico), *she that explains*: Cic.

explĭcātus -a -um, partic. from explico; q.v.

explĭcātus -ūs, m. (explico), *explanation*, *exposition*: difficiles habere explicatus, Cic.

explĭcĭtus -a -um, partic. from explico; q.v.

explĭco -are -āvi -ātum and -ŭi (after Cic.) -ĭtum (rare in Cic.), *to unfold, unroll, disentangle*.
LIT., volumen, Cic.; suas pennas, Ov.; frontem, sollicitam, Hor.; hence in gen., *to spread out, extend, expand*: forum laxare et usque ad atrium Libertatis explicare, Cic.; Capua planissimo in loco explicata, Cic.; esp. as milit. t. t., *to extend the ranks, deploy*: agmen, aciem, ordinem, Liv.; Caes., Verg.
TRANSF., (1) *to disentangle, put in order*: explica atque excute intellegentiam tuam, Cic.; rem frumentariam, Caes.; rationes meas, *accounts*, Cic.; alicuius negotia, Cic.; of a debt, *to pay off*: nomen, Cic. (2) *to explain in discourse, expound, interpret*: causas rerum, Cic.; explicare breviter quae mihi sit ratio et causa cum Caesare, Cic.; de rerum natura, Cic.; Verg., Liv. (3) *to set free*: Cic., Liv.
¶ Hence partic. (1) **explĭcātus** -a -um: a, *ordered, arranged*: provincia quam maxime apta explicataque, Cic.: b, *made plain, clear*: litterae tuae, quibus nihil potest esse explicatius, Cic. L. (2) **explĭcĭtus** -a -um, *straightforward, easy*: ex duobus consiliis propositis explicitius videbatur Ilerdam, reverti, Caes.
¶ Adv. **explĭcātē**, *plainly, clearly*: Cic.

explōdo (explaudo) -plōdĕre -plōsi -plōsum, *to drive off by clapping*; hence *to hiss an actor off the stage*: histrionem exsibilare et explodere, Cic.; Hor. TRANSF., *to scare off, to reject*: sententiam, Cic.; Lucr.

explōrātĭo -ōnis, f. (exploro), *investigation*: occulta, Tac.

explōrātor -ōris, m. (exploro), *one who investigates, an explorer, scout, spy*: Caes., Tac.; also *a forerunner*: Suet.

explōro -are, *to search out, investigate, explore*. LIT., Africam, Cic.; iter, Ov.; esp. as milit. t. t., *to spy out, reconnoitre*: hostium iter, Caes.; loca, Caes., Sall., Cic.; in abl. absol.: explorato (or explorato ante), *after intelligence had been gained*, Liv.
TRANSF., (1) in gen., *to search out, examine, investigate*: rem totam, Cic.; fugam domini, Cic.; Liv. (2) *to test, try, put to proof*: explorat robora fumus, Verg.; secundae res animos, Tac.
¶ Hence partic. (with compar.) **explōrātus** -a -um, *established, confirmed, certain, sure*: spes, Cic.; victoria, Caes.; exploratum habeo, mihi exploratum est, *I am convinced, am sure*, foll. by acc. and infin., Cic.
¶ Adv. (with compar.) **explōrātē**, *certainly, surely, definitely*: ad te explorate scribo, Cic.

explōsĭo -ōnis, f. (explodo), *a hissing off the stage*: ap. Cic. L.

expŏlĭo -īre -ii and -īvi -ītum, *to smooth, polish*. LIT., libellum pumice, Cat. TRANSF., *to polish, refine*: Dionem Plato doctrinis omnibus expolivit, Cic.
¶ Hence partic. **expŏlītus** -a -um. LIT., *smooth, polished*: dens expolitior, Cat.

TRANSF., *polished, refined*: vir omni vitā excultus atque expolitus, Cic.

expŏlītĭo -ōnis, f. (expolio), *a smoothing, polishing*. LIT., urbana, *of a town-house*, Cic. L. TRANSF., of discourse, *polishing, embellishing*: inventi artificiosa, Cic.

expōno -pōnĕre -pŏsŭi -pŏsĭtum, *to put out*.
Hence (1) *to put outside, cast out*: aliquem ictu, Pl.; esp.: a, *to expose* a child: in proxima alluvie pueros, Liv.: b, as naut. t. t., *to land, disembark*: exponere frumentum, Cic.; milites navibus, Caes.; in terram, Caes., Liv.; de puppibus, Verg.: c, of places, esp. in partic. expositus -a -um; see below.
(2) *to put on view, display*. LIT., aliquid venditioni, Tac.; vasa Samia, Cic.; aliquem populo videndum, Ov.; copias in omnibus collibus, *place openly*, Caes. TRANSF., *to show, place before one*: praemia alicui, Cic.; orationem, Cic.; esp. in words, *to set forth, exhibit, explain*: vitam alicuius totam, Cic.; Caes., Liv., Tac.; with acc. and infin. or indir. quest.: Cic.
¶ Hence partic. **expŏsĭtus (expostus)** -a -um, *exposed, open, accessible*: domus patens atque adeo exposita cupiditati et voluptatibus, Cic.; expositae prope in ipsis litoribus urbes, Liv.; rupes exposta (=exposita) ponto, Verg.; mare nimiā propinquitate ad pericula classium externarum expositum, Liv.; sometimes also of abstract nouns: libertas exposita ad iniurias Masinissae, Liv.; of persons, *affable*: Plin. L.; in a bad sense, *vulgar*: Juv.

exporrĭgo -rĭgĕre -rexi -rectum, *to stretch out, expand, smooth out*: Ter., Pers.

exportātĭo -ōnis, f. (exporto), *exportation*: earum rerum quibus abundaremus, Cic.

exporto -are, *to carry out*; in gen.: omnia signa ex fanis plaustris evecta exportataque, Cic.; esp. *to export*: aurum ex Italia quotannis Hierosolyma, Cic.

exposco -poscere -pŏposci, *to implore, entreat earnestly*; in gen.: signum proelii, Caes.; victoriam ab diis, Caes.; misericordiam, Cic.; with infin.: Verg.; precibus exposcere plebem, unum sibi civem donarent, Liv.; absol.: exposcentibus militibus, Caes.; esp. *to demand the surrender* of a person: eum ad poenam, Tac.; Liv.

exposĭtīcĭus -a -um (expono), *exposed* (of a child): Pl.

expŏsĭtĭo -ōnis, f. (expono), *a putting out*; hence *a statement, exposition, narration*: sententiae suae, Cic.; plur.: expositiones rerum, Cic.

expŏsĭtus -a -um, partic. from expono; q.v.

expostŭlātĭo -ōnis, f. (expostulo), *a complaint, expostulation*: expostulationem facere, Cic.; expostulationes cum absente Pompeio, Cic. L.; Liv., Tac.

expostŭlo -are. (1) *to demand earnestly*: aliquid ab aliquo, Cic.; foll. by ut and the subj.: Tac.; by acc. and infin.: Tac.; esp. *to demand the surrender* of a person: aliquem ad supplicium, Tac.
(2) *to make a claim* or *complaint, to expostulate*: cum aliquo de aliqua re, Ter., Cic.; aliquid, Ter.; foll. by acc. and infin.: Pl.

expōtus=epotus; q.v.

expressus -a -um, partic. from exprimo; q.v.

exprĭmo -prĭmĕre -pressi -pressum (ex/ premo). (1) *to press out, force out.* LIT., sudorem de corpore, Lucr.; sucina solis radiis expressa, Tac.; corporis pondere conisa tenuem iam spiritum expressit, Tac.; vestis exprimens singulos artus, *showing,* Tac. TRANSF., *to extort, squeeze out*: nummulorum aliquid ab aliquo blanditiis, Cic. L.; deditionem, Liv.
(2) *to mould* or *form* one thing in imitation of another: expressa in cera imago, Pl.; hence *to copy* that other thing, *to express, portray, represent*: ungues exprimet, Hor.; in pass.: expressi vultus per aenea signa, Hor.; esp.: **a**, *to express in words, describe*: mores alicuius oratione, Cic.; diligenter oportere exprimi, quae vis subiecta sit vocibus, Cic.: **b**, *to translate*: aliquid Latine, Cic.; verbum e verbo, Cic.; ad verbum de Graecis, Cic.: **c**, *to articulate*: litteras, Cic.; Quint.
(3) *to raise up*: quantum has (turres) cottidianus agger expresserat, Caes.
¶ Hence partic. (with compar.) **expressus** -a -um, *made clear, prominent*: litterae lituraeque, Cic.; fig.: sceleris vestigia, Cic.; of pronunciation, *distinct*: Cic., Quint.

exprobrātĭo -ōnis, f. (exprobro), *reproach, upbraiding*: alicui veteris fortunae, Liv.

exprobro -are (ex/probrum), *to reproach, lay to the charge of*; with acc. of thing, dat. of person: haec hosti, Liv.; Pl., Cic.; with de: de uxore mihi exprobrare, Nep.; with acc. and infin.: exprobrare nihilo plus sanitatis in curia quam in foro esse, Liv.; with quod: quasi exprobrare quod in vita maneam, Cic.; absol.: Liv.; sometimes *to bring up* a thing *against* a person as constituting a claim upon him, e.g. one's own services: officia, Cic.; virtutem suam, Liv.

exprōmo -prōmĕre -prompsi -promptum, *to bring forth, produce.* LIT., omnes apparatus supplicii, Liv.; Pl. TRANSF., (1) *to fetch out, utter*: maestas voces, Verg. (2) *to exhibit, display*: crudelitatem suam in aliquo, Cic. (3) *to disclose, set forth, state*: occulta apud amicum, Ter.; leges de religione, Cic.; causas et ordinem belli, Liv.; with indir. quest.: quanta vis sit (eius) eloquentiae expromere, Cic.; Liv.; with acc. and infin.: Tac.

expugnābĭlis -e (expugno), *that may be taken by storm*: urbs, Liv.; Tac.

expugnācĭŏr -ōris, compar. adj. (expugno), *more effective*: Ov.

expugnātĭo -ōnis, f. (expugno), *the taking of any place by storm*: urbis, Caes.; plur.: expugnationes urbium, Cic.; aedium, Cic. L.

expugnātŏr -ōris, m. (expugno), *a taker, capturer*: urbis, Cic. TRANSF., pudicitiae, *violator,* Cic.

expugno -are, *to take by storm, capture.* LIT., urbes, naves, Caes.; urbem obsidione, Caes.; tyrannos eius, non ipsam urbem, Liv.; of things: fames obsessos expugnavit, *compelled to surrender,* Liv.
TRANSF., (1) *to overcome, subdue*: animum, Cic.; pudicitiam, Cic.; pertinaciam legatorum, Liv. (2) *to gain forcibly, extort*: legationem, Cic.; with ut and the subj., bring

it *about that*: Cic. (3) *to accomplish*: coepta, Ov.

expulsĭo -ōnis, f. (expello), *a driving out, expulsion*: Laenatis, Cic.; plur.: expulsione vicinorum, Cic.

expulso -are (freq. of expello), *to drive out*: Mart.

expulsor -ōris, m. (expello), *one who drive out* or *expels*: iste homo acerrimus, bonorum possessor, expulsor, ereptor, Cic.

expultrix -trīcis, f. (expulsor), *she who expels* philosophia expultrix vitiorum, Cic.

expungo -pungĕre -punxi -punctum, *to prick out*; hence *to cancel, expunge*: Pl., Suet.

expurgātĭo -ōnis, f. (expurgo), *a vindication justification*: Pl.

expurgātŭ, abl. from expurgatus, m. (expurgo) *in the justifying*: Ter.

expurgo -are, *to cleanse, purify.* Hence (1) *to cure*: quae poterunt unquam satis expurgare cicutae? Hor. (2) fig., *to purify*: expurgandus est sermo, Cic. (3) *to justify, defend*: dissimulandi causa aut sui expurgandi, Sall. Pl., Tac.

expūtesco -ĕre, *to rot away*: Pl.

expŭto -are, *to lop away*; hence (1) *to consider* Pl. (2) *to comprehend*: ap. Cic. L.

exquaero = exquiro; q.v.

exquīro -quīrere -quīsīvi -quīsītum (ex/ quaero), *to search out, seek out.* LIT., antiquam matrem, Verg.; iter, Caes TRANSF., (1) *to search for, look for, ask for* veritatem, verum, Cic.; a te nihil certi, Cic.; palam pretia; with indir. quest.: quid in omni genere vitae optimum et verissimum sit exquirere, Cic. (2) *to search through, examine*: vescendi causā mari terraque omnia, Sall.; facta alicuius ad antiquae religionis rationem, Cic.; aliquem, Pl.
¶ Hence partic. (with compar. and superl.) **exquīsītus** -a -um, *carefully sought or worked out, choice, exquisite*: sententiae, Cic.; exquisitius dicendi genus, Cic.; exquisitissimis verbis laudare, Cic.; sometimes in bad sense, *artificial*: munditia exquisita nimis, Cic.; Quint.
¶ Adv. (with compar.) **exquīsītē,** *accurately, carefully*: de eo crimine accurate et exquisite disputare, Cic.

exrādīcĭtŭs, adv. (radix), *from the roots*: Pl.

exsacrĭfico -are, *to sacrifice*: Enn.

exsaevĭo -ire, *to rage to an end, cease to rage*: dum reliqua tempestas exsaeviret, Liv.

exsanguis -e, *bloodless, without blood.* LIT., umbrae, Verg.; corpora mortuorum, Cic. TRANSF., (1) *deathly pale*: color, Sall.; metu Ov. (2) of a *bloodless style*: Calvus exsanguis et aridus, Tac. (3) act., *making pale* cuminum, Hor.

exsarcĭo -sarcire -sartum, *to patch up, make good, repair*: Ter.

exsātĭo -are, *to satisfy thoroughly, satiate* LIT., vino ciboque, Liv. TRANSF., morte alicuius exsatiari, Liv.; Ov., Tac.

exsātŭrābĭlis -e (exsaturo), *that can be satiated*: non exsaturabile pectus, Verg.

exsātŭro -are, *to satisfy, satiate.* LIT., belua exsaturanda visceribus meis, Ov. TRANSF., eius cruciatu atque supplicio pascere oculos animumque exsaturare, Cic.

exscendo = escendo; q.v.

exscensio = escensio; q.v.

exscensus = escensus; q.v.

exscindo -scindĕre -scĭdi -scissum, *to tear out*; hence *to destroy utterly*: Numantiam, Cic.; Verg., Liv.; *of persons*: hostem, Tac.

exscrĕo -are, *to cough out*: totiens clausas ante fores, Ov.; Pl.

exscrībo -scrībĕre -scripsi -scriptum, *to write out*; hence (**1**) *to copy*: tabulas, Cic.; fig., not by writing: Plin. L. (**2**) *to note down, register*: ei sacra omnia exscripta exsignataque attribuit, Liv.; Pl.

exsculpo -sculpĕre -sculpsi -sculptum. (**1**) *to scratch out, erase*: versus, Nep. (**2**) *to carve or scoop out*: aliquid e quercu, Cic. L.; fig.: verum, Ter.

exsĕco -sĕcare -sĕcŭi -sectum, *to cut out*. LIT., linguam, Cic.; esp. *to castrate*: Cic. TRANSF., vitiosas partes reipublicae, Cic.; quinas hic capiti mercedes exsecat, *deducts from the principal*, Hor.

exsecrābĭlis -e (exsecror), *cursing, execrating*: carmen, Liv.; ira atque odium, *deadly*, Liv.

exsecrātĭo -ōnis, f. (exsecror), *a curse, execration*: Cic., Tac. TRANSF., *an oath containing an imprecation*: Cic., Liv., Tac.

exsecrātus -a -um, p. adj. (from exsecror), *cursed, execrated*: exsecratus populo Romano, Cic.

exsecror -ari, dep. (ex/sacer), *to curse, execrate*. LIT., aliquem, Cic.; consilia Catilinae, Sall.; in caput alicuius, Liv.; exsecratur primum ut naufragio pereat, Cic. TRANSF., *to swear with an imprecation*: haec exsecrata civitas, Hor.

exsectĭo -ōnis, f. (exseco), *a cutting out*: linguae, Cic.

exsĕcūtĭo -ōnis, f. (exsequor), *performance, accomplishment*: negotii, Tac.; executio Syriae, *administration*, Tac.; *of speech*, *a discussion*: Quint.

exsĕquĭae -ārum, f. (exsequor), *a funeral procession*: iusta exsequiarum, Cic.; exsequias alicuius funeris prosequi, Cic.; exsequias celebrare, Liv.; ire, Ter., Ov.

exsĕquĭālis -e (exsequiae), *belonging to a funeral procession*: carmina, Ov.

exsĕquor -sĕqui -sĕcūtus sum, dep. (**1**) *to follow a corpse to the grave*: Cic. poet. (**2**) *to follow to the end*; in gen.: suam quisque spem, sua consilia exsequentes, Liv. Esp.: **a**, *to maintain, keep up*: sermonem, Pl.; ius suum armis, Caes.; orationem, Cic.: **b**, *to carry out, accomplish, execute*: mandata vestra, Cic.; officia, Cic.; praecepta, Verg.: **c**, *to follow revengefully, to avenge, punish*: iura violata, dolorem, Liv.; rem tam atrocem, Liv.: **d**, *to relate, describe, explain*: ea vix verbis exsequi posse, Cic. L.; viam consili scelerati, Liv.; exsequebatur inde, quae sollemnis derivatio esset, Liv.: **e**, *to suffer, endure*: egestatem, Pl.; fatum, Cic. L.

exsĕro -sĕrĕre -sĕrŭi -sertum, *to stretch out, thrust out*. LIT., linguam, Liv.; caput ponto, Ov.; bracchia, Ov.; esp. in perf. partic. **exsertus** -a -um, *bared, protruding*: dextris umeris exsertis, Caes.; unum exserta latus pugnae, Verg. TRANSF., *to put forth, assert*: ius, Plin. L.

exserto -are (freq. of exsero), *to stretch out*: ora, Verg.

exsertus -a -um, partic. of exsero; q.v.

exsībĭlo -are, *to hiss*; esp. an actor *off the stage*: Cic., Suet.

exsicco -are. (**1**) *to dry thoroughly*: arbores, Cic. (**2**) *to drain dry, to empty* by drinking: vina culullis, Hor.

   ¶ Hence partic. **exsiccātus** -a -um, of style, *dry, jejune*: genus orationis, Cic.

exsigno -are, *to mark out*: sacra omnia exscripta exsignataque, Liv.

exsĭlĭo -silire -silŭi (ex/salio), *to leap out* or *up*: de sella, Cic.; gaudio, *for joy*, Cic.; in siccum (of a snake), Verg.; exsiluere loco silvae, Ov.; oculi exsiluere, Ov.

exsĭlĭum -i, n. (exsul), *banishment, exile*. LIT., exsilii poena, Cic.; aliquem exsilio adficere, multare, Cic.; in exsilium ire, pergere, eicere, pellere, Cic.; in exsilium mittere, Liv.; aliquem reducere de exsilio, Cic. L.; revocare, Liv. TRANSF., (**1**) *place of exile*: Cic.; Tac., Verg. (**2**) plur. = exsules, *exiles*: plenum exsiliis mare, Tac.

exsisto (**existo**) -sistĕre -stĭti -stĭtum.

   (**1**) *to stand forth, come forth, appear*: ab ara, Cic.; e latebris, Liv.; vox ab aede Iunonis ex arce, Cic.

   (**2**) *to spring forth, arise, come into existence*. LIT., vermes de stercore, Lucr.; dentes, Cic. TRANSF., inter eos controversia, Caes.; ut tyranni existerent, Cic.; ex luxuria existit avaritia, Cic.; ego huic causae patronus exstiti, Cic.; with ut and the subj. (of logical consequence): ex quo existet, ut de nihilo quippiam fiat, Cic.

exsolvo -solvĕre -solvi -sŏlūtum.

   (**1**) *to loosen, unloose, untie, unbind*. LIT., restim, Pl.; catenas, Tac.; bracchia ferro, *to open*, Tac.; glaciem, *to dissolve*, Lucr.; *of persons, to disentangle, free*: se corpore, Verg.; Lucr., Tac. TRANSF., **a**, *to loosen, put aside*: exsoluti plerique legis nexus, Tac.: **b**, *to explain*: Lucr.: **c**, *to free*: plebem aere alieno, Liv.; animos religione, Liv.; Verg., Tac.

   (**2**) *to pay off*: pretium, Pl.; nomina, Cic.; stipendium praeteritum cum fide, Tac. TRANSF., *to discharge* any obligation, *perform* anything due: quod promiserat, Cic.; poenas morte, Tac.

exsomnis -e (ex/somnus), *sleepless, wakeful*: Verg.

exsorbĕo -ēre, *to suck up, suck dry*. LIT., pectora, Ov. TRANSF., gustaras civilem sanguinem vel potius exsorbueras, Cic.; multorum difficultatem, Cic.; quantas iste Byzantiorum praedas exsorbuit, Cic.

exsors -sortis, *without lot*; hence (**1**) *for which no lot has been cast, specially chosen*: ducunt exsortem Aeneae (equum), Verg. (**2**) *having no share in, deprived of*; with genit.: dulcis vitae, Verg.; amicitiae, Liv.; Hor., Tac.

exspătĭor -ari, dep. *to deviate from the course*: exspatiantur equi, Ov.; exspatiata ruunt per apertos flumina campos, Ov.; fig., *to digress*: Quint.

exspectābĭlis -e (exspecto), *that is to be expected, probable*: Tac.

exspectātĭo -ōnis, f. (exspecto), *a waiting for, looking for, expectation*; with objective genit.: exspectationem sui facere, concitare, Cic.; with de: quantum tu mihi moves exspectationem de sermone Bibuli, Cic. L.; with indir. quest.: summa omnium exspectatio,

quidnam sententiae ferrent iudices, Cic.;
absol.: obscurā spe et caecā exspectatione
pendere, Cic.; in exspectatione esse, Pl., Caes.

exspecto -are, *to look out for, wait for.*

In gen., *to await, wait to see*: transitum
tempestatis, Cic.; me tranquilla senectus
exspectat, *is in store for*, Hor.; with indir.
quest.: exspecto quid tribunus plebis
excogitet, Cic.; Pl., Caes.; with dum:
exspectas fortasse dum dicat, Cic.; Caes.,
Hor.; with quoad: Nep.; with si: Pl., Caes.;
with ut and the subj.: nisi forte exspectatis
ut illa diluam, Cic.; Caes., Liv.; non exspectare foll. by quin.: Caes.; absol., *to wait,
loiter*: ad portam, Cic.

Esp. *to wait with longing, fear, hope, desire,*
etc., *to hope for, dread*: testamenta, Cic.;
aliquid ab (*or* ex) with abl.: Caes., Cic., Liv.;
a te hoc civitas vel potius omnes cives non
exspectant solum sed etiam postulant, Cic.;
with acc. and infin.: cum exspectaret effusos
omnibus portis Aetolos in fidem suam
venturos (esse), Liv.

¶ Hence partic. (with compar. and superl.)
exspectātus -a -um, *awaited, wished for,
welcome*: carus omnibus exspectatusque
venies, Cic. L.; expectate venis, Verg.;
phrase: ante exspectatum, *before it was
expected*, Verg., Ov.

exspergo -spergĕre -spersum (ex/spargo), *to
sprinkle, scatter*: Lucr., Verg.

exspēs, adj. (only in nom. sing.), *without hope,
hopeless*: erret inops, exspes, Ov.; with genit.:
exspes vitae, Tac.

exspīrātĭo -ōnis, f. (exspiro), *an exhalation*:
terrae, Cic.

exspīro -are. (1) transit., *to breathe out, exhale*: flammas pectore, Verg. TRANSF., *to
emit*: Lucr. (2) intransit.: **a**, *to blow forth,
rush forth*: vis ventorum exspirare cupiens,
Ov.; Lucr.: **b**, *to give up the ghost, to die*: in
pugna et in acie, Liv.; fig.: quid? si ego
morerer, mecum exspiratura respublica
erat, Liv.

exspŏlĭo -are, *to plunder, rob, despoil*: fana
atque domos, Sall.; exercitu et provinciā
Pompeium, Cic. L.; Caes.

exspŭo -spŭĕre -spŭi -spūtum, *to spit out*:
vina, Juv. TRANSF., *to get rid of, cast away*:
hamum (of fishes), Ov.; rationem ex animo,
Lucr.

externo -ēre, *to frighten, terrify*: Ov., Cat.

exstillo -are, *to drop moisture, drip, trickle*:
Pl., Ter.

exstĭmŭlātor -ōris, m. (exstimulo), *an inciter,
instigator*: rebellionis, Tac.

exstĭmŭlo -are, *to goad, to excite, instigate*:
virum dictis, Ov.; Tac.

extinctĭo -ōnis, f. (exstinguo), *annihilation,
extinction*: Cic.

exstinctor -ōris, m. (exstinguo). (1) *one who
extinguishes*: incendii, Cic.; fig.: belli, Cic.
(2) *one who destroys, annihilates*: patriae, Cic.

exstinguo -stinguere -stinxi -stinctum (syncop.
forms exstinxti, exstinxem: Verg.), *to put
out, extinguish.*

LIT., lumen, Lucr.; incendium, Cic. L.;
consumptus ignis exstinguitur, Cic.

TRANSF., (1) of persons, *to kill*: Cic., Verg.;
invictum bello iuvenem fortuna morbo
exstinxit, Liv. (2) in gen., *to abolish, destroy,
annihilate*: gratiam alicuius, Cic.; memoriam

publicam, Cic.; rumor exstinguitur, Cic.;
exstinguere famam, Liv.; sitim, Ov.

exstirpo -are (ex/stirps), *to tear up by the root*:
pilos, Mart. TRANSF., *to root out, extirpate*:
vitia, Cic.; humanitatem ex animo, Cic.

exsto (exto) -are, *to stand out, project.*

LIT., milites capite solo ex aqua exstant,
Caes.; quo altius ab aqua exstaret, Liv.;
Verg., Ov.

TRANSF., (1) in gen.: quo magis id quod
erit illuminatum exstare atque eminere
videatur, Cic. (2) *to be visible, show itself,
appear*: exstant huius fortitudinis vestigia,
Cic.; exstat, impers. with acc. and infin.,
Cic.; apparet atque exstat, utrum . . . an,
Cic. (3) *to be still in existence, to be extant*:
exstant epistulae Philippi, Cic.; non exstat
alius, Liv.; Pl., Hor.

exstructĭo -ōnis, f. (exstruo), *a building up,
erection*: exstructiones tectorum, Cic.

exstrŭo -strŭere -struxi -structum.
(1) *to heap up, pile up.* LIT., divitias in
altum, Hor.; focum lignis, Hor.; mensae
conquisitissimis epulis exstruebantur, Cic.
TRANSF., exstrue animo altitudinem ex-
cellentiamque virtutum, *build up*, Cic.
(2) *to build up*: rogum, acervum librorum,
Cic.; Tac.

exsuctus -a -um, partic of exsugo; q.v.

exsūdo -are. (1) intransit., *to come out in
sweat, exude*: inutilis umor, Verg. (2)
transit., *to sweat out.* LIT., Plin. TRANSF.,
*to sweat through, toil through, perform with
great labour*: novum de integro laborem,
Liv.; certamen ingens, Liv.; Hor.

exsūgo -sūgĕre -suxi -suctum, *to suck out, suck
up, suck dry*: sanguinem, Pl.; ostrea vacuis
exsucta medullis, Juv.

exsul -sūlis, c. (ex/solum), *a banished* or *exiled
person, an exile.* LIT., cum vagus et exsul
erraret, Cic.; exsules reducuntur, Cic.; with
genit.: patriae, Hor.; with abl.: exsul patriā,
domo, Sall. TRANSF., *deprived of*; with
genit.: exsul mentisque domusque, Ov.

exsŭlo (exŭlo) -are (exsul), *to be banished,
live in exile.* LIT., Romae, *at Rome*, Cic.;
apud Prusiam, Cic.; in Volscos exsulatum
abire, Liv. TRANSF., meo discessu exsulasse
rempublicam, Cic.; Pl.

exsultātĭo -ōnis, f. (exsulto), *a leaping up.*
LIT., Plin. TRANSF., *exultation, excessive
rejoicing*: Sen., Tac.

exsultim, adv. (exsilio), *friskingly*: Hor.

exsulto (exulto) -are (freq. of exsilio), *to leap
up frequently* or *violently.*

LIT., (1) of living subjects: equi ferocitate
exsultantes, Cic.; in numerum, Lucr.;
medias inter caedes exsultat Amazon, Verg.
(2) of things: vada exsultant, *dash up*, Verg.

TRANSF., (1) *to rejoice exceedingly, exult,
triumph*: laetitiā, gaudio, Cic.; in ruinis alterius, Cic.; Graeci exsultant quod, Cic.;
Verg., Liv., Tac. (2) of orators and of discourse, *to run riot, range freely*: audacius,
Cic.; verborum audaciā exsultans, Cic.;
campus in quo exsultare possit oratio, Cic.;
Quint., Tac.

exsŭpĕrābĭlis -e (exsupero), *that can be
overcome*: non exsuperabile saxum (of
Sisyphus), Verg.

exsŭpĕrantĭa -ae, f. (exsupero), *superiority,
pre-eminence*: virtutis, Cic.

exsŭpĕro -are.
(1) intransit. LIT., *to mount up, appear above*: flammae, Verg. TRANSF., *to be prominent, excel*: quantum feroci virtute exsuperas, Verg.; si non poterunt exsuperare, cadant, Ov.; Lucr.
(2) transit. LIT., *to surmount*: iugum, Verg.; omnes angustiae exsuperatae, Liv. TRANSF., **a,** *to surpass, exceed*: magnitudo sceleris omnium ingenia exsuperat, Sall.; omnes Tarquinios superbiā, Liv.; Ov.: **b,** *to overcome*: consilium caecum, Verg.; Ov.

exsurdo -are (ex/surdus), *to deafen.* LIT., Plin. TRANSF., of taste, *to make dull* or *blunt*: palatum, Hor.

exsurgo -surgĕre -surrexi, *to rise up, lift oneself up, stand up.*
LIT., (1) of persons, esp. when rising and then going out: foras, Pl.; cum exsurgeret, simul adridens, Cic.; exsurgit facem attollens, Verg.; altior exsurgens (to give force to a blow), Verg. (2) of things rising: (Roma) tota simul exsurgere aedificiis, Liv.
TRANSF., (1) *to rise up, to regain strength*: exsurgere atque erigere se, Cic.; auctoritate vestrā respublica exsurget, Cic. L. (2) of political risings: invidiā eorum exsurgere rursus plebem, Liv.; Tac.

exsuscĭto -are, *to arouse.*
LIT., (1) *to awaken from sleep*: te gallorum, illum bucinarum cantus exsuscitat, Cic. (2) of fire, *to kindle* or *fan*: flammam aurā, Ov.; Liv.
TRANSF., mentally, *to excite, arouse*: quae cura etiam exsuscitat animos, Cic.; se exsuscitare, *to make an effort*, Cic.

exta -ōrum, n. pl. *the entrails of animals*, esp. *the heart, lungs, liver*, used by the Romans for divination *to* inspicere, Cic.; si est in extis aliqua vis, quae declaret futura, Cic.; Verg., Liv.

extābesco -tābescĕre -tābŭi, *to waste away entirely.* LIT., corpus macie extabuit, poet. ap. Cic. TRANSF., *to vanish, disappear*: opiniones diuturnitate extabuisse, Cic.

extāris -e (exta), *used for cooking*: exta, Pl.

extemplo, adv. (ex/templum), *immediately, directly, forthwith*: Pl., Cic., Verg., Liv.

extempŏrālis -e (ex/tempus), *extemporary, unrehearsed*: oratio, actio, Quint.

extempŭlo=extemplo; q.v.

extendo -tendĕre -tendi -tensum and -tentum, *to stretch out, expand, extend.*
LIT., (1) *to stretch out a body* or *thing to its fullest extent*: bracchium, Cic.; extentum funem, *tight rope*, Hor.; rigidā cervice et extento capite currere (of horses), Liv.; toto ingens extenditur (Cerberus) antro, Verg.; as milit. t. t., *to extend in order of battle*: aciem in radicibus montis, Liv. (2) *to increase*: agros, Hor.; itinera, Liv.
TRANSF., (1) *to strain, to exert*: se supra vires, Liv.; Caes. (2) of abstr. things, *to increase, extend*: nomen in ultimas oras, Hor.; in Asiam quoque cognitionem, Liv.; famam factis. (3) in time, *to extend, prolong*: ab hora tertia ad noctem pugnam, Liv.; aevum, Hor.; Pl., Verg.
¶ Hence partic. (with superl.) **extentus** -a -um, *wide, extensive*: Lucr.; castra quam extentissimā potest valle locat, Liv.

extento -are (freq. of extendo), *to stretch out, to strain.* LIT., nervos, Lucr. TRANSF., vires, Pl.

extentus -a -um, partic. from extendo; q.v.

extĕnŭātĭo -ōnis, f. (extenuo), *a thinning.* LIT., Plin. TRANSF., as a figure of speech, *a diminution, lessening* (Gr. μείωσις, opp. exaggeratio): Cic., Quint.

extĕnŭo -are, *to make thin* or *small, to reduce, diminish.*
LIT., aër extenuatus, *rarefied*, Cic.; dentibus extenuatur et molitur cibus, Cic.; extenuari in aquas, *dissolves into*, Ov.; as milit. t. t., *to extend*: angustiae extenuabant agmen, Liv.; extenuatā suorum acie, Sall.
TRANSF., *to lessen, weaken, diminish*: sumptus, Cic.; spem, crimen, Cic.; vires, Hor.; curas, Ov. Esp. in speech, *to disparage, depreciate*: suum munus, Cic.; famam belli, Liv.
¶ Hence partic. (with superl.) **extĕnŭātus** -a -um, *weak, poor, slight*: vestigia, Cat.; copiolae extenuatissimae, ap. Cic. L.

exter and **extĕrus** -a -um (from ex), *outward, foreign, strange.*
(1) posit.: ius nationum exterarum, Cic.; hostis, Cic.; Lucr., Caes.
(2) compar. **extĕrĭor,** -ĭus, genit. -ōris, *outer*: orbis, Cic.; hostis, Cic.; exteriorem ire alicui, *to go on the left side*, Hor.
(3) superl. **extrēmus** -a -um, *outermost.* LIT., in space: Caes., Cic., Hor., Liv.; n. as subst. extremum -i, *outer edge, extreme*: caelum quod extremum atque ultimum mundi est, Cic.; Lucr. TRANSF., **a,** in time, *last*: vitae dies, Cic.; Hor., Liv. N. as subst.: extremum habet, *has an end*, Cic.; extremum aestatis, Sall.; extrema pati, Verg., Tac. Adverbial uses of neuter: extremum, acc., *for the last time*, Verg., Ov.; ad extremum, *to the end*; ad extremum reservatus, Cic.; also *at the end*: Caes., Cic., Ov.; extremo, *at the end*, Nep.: **b,** *in degree* or *quality*; in gen., *extreme*: famem, Caes.; senatus consultum (used in great emergency), Caes.; tempora, *extreme need*, Cic.; extremum bonorum, malorum, *the highest good, evil*, Cic.; n. as subst.: vitam ipsam in extremum adductam, Tac.; ad extrema ventum foret, Liv.; esp. *lowest, worst*: haud Ligurum extremus, Verg.; extremi ingenii est, Liv.
(4) superl. **extĭmus** -a -um, *outermost*: orbis, Cic.; Pl., Lucr.

extĕrebro -are, *to bore out, extract by boring*: ex eo auro, quod exterebratum esset, Cic. TRANSF., *to extort*: Pl.

extergĕo -tergēre -tersi -tersum, *to wipe off, wipe clean.* LIT., Pl. TRANSF., *to strip clean, plunder*: quod fanum non eversum atque extersum reliqueris? Cic.

extĕrĭor, exterius, see exter.

extermĭno -are (ex/terminus), *to drive beyond the boundaries*; hence LIT., *to drive out, expel, banish*: aliquem ex urbe, Cic.; urbe atque agro, Cic.; de civitate, Cic. TRANSF., *to put aside, remove*: auctoritatem senatus e civitate, Cic.

externus -a -um (exter), *that is outside, external.* In gen.: tepor, Cic.; Hor., Ov. Esp. *foreign, strange*: auxilia, Caes.; hostis, Cic.; amor (of a foreigner), Ov.; timor, terror (of a foreign enemy), Liv.; Tac.
¶ M. as subst. **externus** -i, *a foreigner, a stranger*: canum odium in externos, Cic.; Liv.

¶ N. pl. as subst. **externa** -ōrum, *outward* or *foreign things*: externa libentius in tali re quam domestica recordor, Cic.; externa moliri, Tac.

extĕro -tĕrĕre -trīvi -trītum. (**1**) *to rub out*: extritus viribus ignis, Lucr. (**2**) *to wear away*: Ov.

exterrĕo -terrēre -terrŭi -terrĭtum. (**1**) *to frighten out of*: somno, Enn. (**2**) *to frighten badly, scare, terrify*: periculo suo aliquem, Liv.; esp. in pass.: praeter modum exterreri, Cic.; exterritus aspectu, Cic.; Caes., Lucr., Tac.; of a snake: Verg.

extĕrus, *see* exter.

extexo -ĕre, *to unweave*; hence *to cheat*: Pl.

extĭmesco -tĭmescĕre -tĭmŭi.

(**1**) intransit., *to be greatly afraid, to be terrified*: de fortunis communibus extimescere, Cic.; foll. by ne and the subj.: Cic.; Hor., Tac.

(**2**) transit., *to be greatly afraid of, to dread*: periculum, Cic.; unum illud extimescebam ne quid turpiter facerem, Cic.; magistrum, Hor.

extĭmus, *see* exter.

extispex -spĭcis, m. (exta/*specio), *a soothsayer who predicts from the entrails of victims*: Cic.

extispĭcĭum -i, n. (extispex), *an inspection of entrails*: Suet.

extollo -ĕre, *to lift up, raise up.*

LIT., cruentum pugionem, Cic.; of buildings, *to raise, erect*: Pl.

TRANSF., (**1**) *to raise, elevate, exalt*: extollere animos, Cic.; se extollere, Cic.; aliquem secundā oratione, Sall.; esp. in words, *to praise*: fortunam alicuius, Cic.; aliquem ad caelum, Cic.; aliquid verbis in maius, *to exaggerate*, Liv.; sometimes *to adorn*: hortos a Lucullo coeptos insigni magnificentiā extollere, Tac. (**2**) *to defer, postpone*: Pl.

extorquĕo -torquēre -torsi -tortum, *to twist out, wrest away, wrench out.*

LIT., in gen.: arma e manibus civium, Cic.; alicui sicam de manibus, Cic.; esp. *to dislocate*: servilem in modum, Liv.; prava extortaque puella, *deformed*, Juv.

TRANSF., *to obtain by force, extort.* (**1**) of material things: Caesare per Herodem talenta Attica L, Cic. (**2**) of abstr. things: alicui veritatem, errorem, Cic.; ex animis cognitiones verborum, Cic.; Lucr., Hor., Liv.; with ut and the subj.: extorsisti ut faterer, Cic.

extorris -e (ex/terra), *driven from the country, exiled, banished*: huic CXXXII patres familias extorres profugerunt, Cic.; with abl.: agro Romano, Liv.; patriā, Sall.

extortŏr -ōris, m. (extorqueo), *an extorter*: Ter.

extrā, adv. and prep. (perhaps abl. f. sing. of exterus), *outside.*

Adv. LIT., *outside* (opp. intus): quae extra sunt, Cic.; cum extra et intus hostem haberent, Caes.; with verb of motion: Cic. with compar.: exterius sitae (urbes), Ov. TRANSF., *except*: extra quam, extra quam si, *except, unless*, Cic.; Liv.

Prep. with acc., *beyond, outside of, without.* LIT., in space: provinciam, Caes.; Cic., Hor.; with verb of motion: Caes., Cic. TRANSF., (**1**) *beyond, without* abstr. things: extra modum,

Cic.; extra ordinem, Cic.; extra iocum, *joking apart*, Cic. L.; esse extra culpam, Cic.; extra numerum, Pl., Cic., Hor. (**2**) *except for*: extra ducem, Cic. L.; Pl., Liv.

extrăho -trăhĕre -traxi -tractum, *to draw out, drag out, extract.*

LIT., telum e corpore, Cic.; telum de vulnere, Ov.; vivum puerum ex, Hor.; aliquem domo, Cic.; aliquem vi in publicum, Liv.; velut ab inferis extractus, Liv.

TRANSF., (**1**) fig., *to bring out, remove, extricate*: urbem ex periculis, Cic.; religionem ex animis, Cic.; scelera in lucem, Liv. (**2**) fig., *to bring forward*: aliquem ad honorem, Liv.; hostes invitos in aciem, Liv. (**3**) in time, *to draw out, prolong, protract*: res variis calumniis, Cic.; certamen usque ad noctem, Liv.; sometimes, *to waste*: aestatem sine ullo effectu, Liv.; triduum, Caes.

extrănĕus -a -um (extra), *that is outside.* In gen., *extraneous*: res extraneae, Cic.; ornamenta, Cic. Esp. *not belonging to a commumity* or *place, foreign, strange*: exercitatio forensis et extranea, Cic.

M. as subst. **extrănĕus** -i, *a foreigner, stranger*: si extraneus deest, domi hostem quaerunt, Liv.

extrāordĭnārĭus -a -um, *extraordinary, anomalous, irregular*: petitio consulatus, Cic.; imperium, Cic.; pecunia, *obtained by gift, legacy*, etc., Cic.; fig.: cupiditates, *unnatural*, Cic. As milit. t. t.: equites, cohortes, *picked troops of the auxiliary forces*, Liv.

extrārĭus -a -um (extra), *outward, external, extrinsic*: utilitas aut in corpore posita est aut in extrariis rebus, Cic.; hence *strange, unrelated, foreign*: Ter., Quint.

extrēmĭtās -ātis, f. (extremus), *the end, farthest portion, extremity*: mundi, Cic.

extrēmus -a -um, *see* exter.

extrīco -are (extricor -ari, dep.: Pl.) (from tricae), *to disentangle, extricate.* LIT., cervam plagis, Hor. TRANSF., (**1**) *to procure with difficulty*: nummos, Hor. (**2**) *to clear up, unravel*: Pl.

extrinsĕcŭs, adv. (exter/secus). (**1**) *from without, from the outside*: Cic.; Liv. (**2**) *on the outside, outwardly*: columna extrinsecus inaurata, Cic.; Suet.

extrūdo -trūdĕre -trūsi -trūsum, *to push out, thrust forth.* LIT., aliquem ex aedibus, Pl.; te in viam, Cic.; extrudi a senatu in Macedoniam, Cic. TRANSF., of things in fig. senses: mare aggere, Caes.; merces, *to get sold*, Hor.

extundo -tundĕre -tŭdi -tūsum, *to beat out.*

(**1**) *to form by beating with a hammer*: lapsa ancilia caelo extuderat, Verg. TRANSF., *to invent, devise*: artem, Verg.; librum, Tac.

(**2**) *to beat out violently*: Phaedr. TRANSF., **a**, *to drive away*: labor extuderit fastidia, Hor.: **b**, *to extort*: Pl., Suet.

exturbo -are, *to drive away, thrust out.*

LIT., homines e possessionibus, Cic.; aliquem provinciā, Cic.; aliquem e fortunis omnibus, Cic.; matrimonio, Tac.; alicui oculos, Pl.

TRANSF., omnem spem pacis, *to drive out*, Liv.; mentem, *to agitate*, Cic. L.

exūbĕro -are, *to grow thickly, abound*: alte spumis exuberat amnis, Verg.; luxuriā foliorum exuberat umbra, Verg.; pomis exuberat annus, Verg.; fig.: eloquentia, Tac.

exul, see exsul.

exulcĕro -are. LIT., to make sore: Plin. TRANSF., (1) to make worse, aggravate: ea quae sanare nequeunt, exulcerant, Cic. (2) to irritate, embitter: ut in exulcerato animo facile fictum crimen insideret, Cic.

exŭlŭlo -are, to howl out, howl loudly: Ov.
¶ Hence partic. **exŭlŭlātus** -a -um, invoked with howlings: mater Cybeleia, Ov.

exundo -are, to overflow, to flow out or over. LIT., tura balsamaque vi tempestatum in adversa litora exundant, Tac. TRANSF., to overflow, abound: largus et exundans ingenii fons, Juv.

exungo -ungĕre -unctum, to anoint, smear with unguents: Pl.

exŭo -ŭĕre -ŭi -ūtum (cf. ind-uo), to take off.
(1) to lay aside, put off a thing. LIT., of coverings, equipment, etc.: serpens vestem, Lucr.; ensem, Verg.; Hor., Ov. TRANSF., torvam faciem, Verg.; hominem, human shape, Ov.; humanitatem omnem, Cic.; servitutem, Liv.; magistros, Tac.; in pass. with clause as subject: mihi ex animo exui non potest esse deos, I cannot but believe, Cic.
(2) to strip, deprive of a thing: aliquem agro paterno, Liv.; hostem impedimentis, Caes.; ex his te laqueis, to deliver, Cic.

exūro -ūrĕre -ussi -ustum. (1) to burn out: aliis scelus exuritur igni, Verg. (2) to burn up, consume entirely: aliquem vivum, Cic.; classem, Verg.; also to dry up: exustus ager, Verg.; sitis exurat miseros, Lucr.; fig.: exustus flos siti veteris ubertatis exaruit, Cic. (3) to heat: antra positis exusta caminis, Ov.; fig., with love: Tib.

exustĭo -ōnis, f. (exuro), a burning up, conflagration: terrarum, Cic.

exŭvĭae -ārum, f. pl. (exuo), that which is taken off.
(1) of men: **a**, dress: has enim exuvias mihi perfidus ille reliquit, Verg.; Pl.: **b**, spoils taken from the enemy, arms, etc.: nauticae, Cic.; tu ornatus exuviis huius, Cic.; Verg.
(2) of animals: **a**, the skin or slough which is laid aside (naturally): exuvias ponere, Verg.: **b**, the skin taken off, the hide: leonis, Verg.; bubulae, a hide whip, Pl.

F

F, f, the sixth letter of the Latin Alphabet, corresponding in form with the Greek digamma (F), though in sound most nearly represented by Φ, φ. For the meaning of this letter when used as an abbreviation, see Table of Abbreviations.

făba -ae, f. the broad bean: Pl., Cic., Verg.; prov.: isthaec in me cudetur faba, I shall have to suffer for this, Ter.

făbālis -e (faba), of beans: stipulae, Ov.

Făbāris -is, m. a tributary of the Tiber in the Sabine country, also called Farfarus (now Farfa).

făbella -ae, f. (dim. of fabula), a little story, little narrative. In gen.: fabellarum auditione duci, Cic. Esp. (1) a fable: Hor. (2) a little drama: Cic.

făber -bra -brum, ingenious, skilful: ars, Ov.
¶ M. as subst. **făber** -bri. (1) a worker, esp. in any hard material: tignarius, a carpenter, Cic.; ferrarius, a blacksmith, Pl.; milit.: fabri, the engineers, Caes.; praefectus fabrum, commander of the engineers, Caes. (2) a fish, perhaps the dory: Ov.
¶ Adv. **fabrē**, skilfully: Pl.

Făbĭus -a -um, name of a Roman gens, of which the most famous members were:
(1) Q. Fabius Pictor, who wrote a history of Rome in Greek about the time of the second Punic war. (2) Q. Fabius Maximus Cunctator, the opponent of Hannibal in the second Punic war. (3) Q. Fabius Maximus Aemilianus, son of L. Aemilius Paullus, adopted by the Fabii, consul 145 B.C. (4) Q. Fabius Maximus Allobrogicus, son of the preceding, consul 121 B.C., conqueror of the Allobroges and builder of a triumphal arch (fornix Fabii, fornix Fabius, fornix Fabianus: Cic.).
¶ Adj. **Făbĭus** -a -um, Fabian, of a Fabius; also **Făbĭānus** -a -um.

fabrĕfăcio -făcĕre -fēci -factum, to make or fashion skilfully: ex aere multa fabrefacta, Liv.

fabrĭca -ae, f. (faber), the art of a faber: pictura et fabrica, architecture, Cic. TRANSF., (1) the production of a faber: membrorum animantium, Cic.; fig., a device, trick: Pl., Ter. (2) the workshop of a faber: Cic.

fabrĭcātĭo -ōnis, f. (fabrico), making, framing, construction. LIT., hominis, Cic. TRANSF., of style: ne illa quidem traductio in verbo quandam fabricationem habet, Cic.

fabrĭcātor -ōris, m. (fabrico), a maker, artificer: tanti operis, Cic.; ipse doli fabricator Epēos, Verg.; fig.: leti, Lucr.

Fabrĭcĭus -a -um, name of a Roman gens; esp. of C. Fabricius Luscinus, consul 282 and 278 B.C., conqueror of the Samnites, and opponent of Pyrrhus.
¶ Adj. **Fabrĭcĭanus** -a -um, Fabrician: pons, a bridge in Rome; also **Fabrĭcĭānus** -a -um.

fabrĭco -are (faber), to form, make, forge: arma, Hor.; pocula fago fabricata, Ov.; Verg.

fabrĭcor -ari, dep. (faber), to form, make, forge: gladium, fulmen, signa, Cic.; Capitolii fastigium, Cic.; Tac. TRANSF., hominem, Cic.; verba, invent new words: Cic.

fabrīlis -e (faber), relating to an artificer: erratum, Cic. L.; scalprum, Liv.; opera, Verg.; n. pl. as subst. **fabrīlia** -ium, tools: Hor.

fābŭla -e, f. (fari). (1) talk, conversation: fabulam fieri, to get talked about, Hor.; fabulae conviviales, Tac.; prov.: lupus in fabula, of one who appears while being spoken about, Ter., Cic. L.
(2) a tale, story, fable. In gen.: fabula narratur, Hor.; fabula tantum sine auctore edita, Liv. Esp.: a, an untrue story, myth; hence: fabulae! nonsense! Ter.; fabulae manes, the mythical shades, Hor.: b, a play, a drama: in iis quae ad scenam componuntur fabulis, Cic.; Ter., Hor.

fābŭlaris -e (fabula), *mythical*: Suet.
fābŭlātor -ōris, m. (fabulor), *a story-teller*: Sen., Suet.
fābŭlor -ari, dep. (fabula). (1) *to talk, converse, chatter*: quid Ser. Galba fabuletur, Liv. (2) *to tell an untruth*: Liv.
fābŭlōsus -a -um (fabula), *renowned in story, fabled*: Hydaspes, Hor.; palumbes, Hor.
făcesso făcessĕre făcessi făcessītum (intens. of facio). (1) transit., *to do eagerly, perform, fulfil, accomplish*: iussa, Verg.; in bad sense: negotium, *to give trouble to*, Cic.; innocenti periculum, Cic.; Pl., Tac. (2) intransit., *to make off, go away, depart*: ab omni societate, reipublicae, Cic.; ex urbe, Liv.; urbe finibusque, Liv.; Pl.
făcētĭa -ae, f. (facetus). (1) sing., *wit*: Pl. (2) plur., *wit, facetiousness, drollery, humour*: Scipio omnes sale facetiisque superabat, Cic.
făcētus -a -um, adj. (with superl.). (1) *fine, elegant*; of things and persons: orator, Cic.; of behaviour: Pl., Hor.; of style: sermo, Cic. (2) *witty, facetious*: Cic., Juv.
¶ Adv. (with compar. and superl.) făcētē. (1) *elegantly*: Pl., Cic. (2) *wittily, humorously*: si (contumelia) facetius iactatur, urbanitas dicitur, Cic.; Quint.
facĭēs -ēi, f. *shape, form, figure.*
LIT., of physical characteristics. (1) in gen., *shape as seen, outward appearance*: Tyndaridis, Verg.; se in omnes facies vertere, Verg.; Hor., Ov. (2) esp. *face, countenance*: quem ne de facie quidem nosti, Cic.; Hor., Verg., Ov.
TRANSF., (1) *character, nature*: ceterum facies totius negotii varia, incerta, foeda atque miserabilis, Sall.; in faciem hederae frondescere, Ov.; non una pugnae facies, Tac.; Cic. (2) *seeming, pretence*: Tac.
făcĭlis -e (facio) (compar. facilior; superl. facillimus).
LIT., *easy to do, easy.* (1) of tasks, undertakings, etc.: ascensus, Caes.; aditus, Cic.; with ad and the acc., esp. gerund: illud autem facile ad credendum est, Liv.; Cic.; with abl. of verbal noun in -u: res cognitu facilis, Cic.; with infin. as subject: facile est perficere, Cic.; n. as subst. with prep.: in facili esse, *to be easy*, Liv.; ex facili, *easily*, Ov., Tac. (2) of other things, places, circumstances, etc., *easy to manage, convenient, favourable*: angustiae ad receptum faciles, Liv.; campus operi, Liv.; facili feminarum credulitate ad gaudia, Tac.; res et fortunae faciliores, Cic. L. (3) of movements, *easy, mobile*: Verg., Ov.
TRANSF., of persons. (1) in act. sense, *facile, dexterous, clever*: facilis et expeditus ad dicendum T. Iunius, Cic. (2) in pass. sense, of character, *affable, easy, good-natured*: facilis et liberalis pater, Cic.; mores facillimi, Cic.; with ad and the gerund: facilis ad concedendum, Cic.; with in and the abl.: facilis in hominibus audiendis, Cic.; with in and the acc.: si faciles habeas in tua vota deos, Ov.; with dat.: si mihi di faciles et sunt in amore secundi, Ov.
¶ N. acc. as adv. făcĭlĕ (compar. facilius; superl. facillime). (1) *easily, without difficulty*: haec facile ediscere, Cic; Caes., etc. (2) *easily, indisputably, certainly*: facile primus facile princeps, *indisputably first*,

Cic.; facile doctissimus, Cic.; non facile, haud facile, *not easily, hardly*, Cic. (3) *willingly*: pati, Ter., Cic.; facillime audiri, Cic.
făcĭlĭtās -ātis, f. (facilis), *easiness, ease*; esp. in speech: verborum, Quint.; facilitatem, non celeritatem, Sen.; of a site: camporum, Tac. TRANSF., of character. (1) *willingness, friendliness, affability, good-nature*: facilitas in audiendo, Cic.; morum, Cic. (2) *levity*: Suet.
făcĭnŏrōsus -a -um (facinus), adj. (with superl.) *wicked, criminal*: vir, Cic.; vita, Cic.; Liv.
făcĭnus -ŏris, n. (facio), *a deed, action.*
(1) in gen., good or bad, as qualified by adj., etc.: pulcherrimum, Cic.; indignum, Cic.; Pl., Caes., Tac.
(2) esp. *a bad deed, crime, villainy*: facinus est vinciri civem Romanum, scelus verberari, Cic.; facinus facere, obire committere, Cic.; in se admittere, Caes.; patrare, Sall. TRANSF., **a**, *the instrument of crime*: facinus excussit ab ore, *the poisoned cup*, Ov.: **b**, in plur., *criminals*: omnium flagitiorum atque facinorum circum se stipatorum catervae, Cic.
făcĭo făcĕre fēci factum (old forms: fut. indic. faxo: Verg., Liv.; subj. faxim: Pl., Cic., Hor.; the pass. of facio is fio; q.v.).
Transit., *to make, do.* (1) of material things, *to make, form*: castra, pontem, Caes.; ignem ex lignis viridibus, Cic.; alicui anulum, Cic.; orationem, litteras ad aliquem, Cic.; carmen, Verg.; lucrum, *to make money*, Cic.; auxilia mercede, *to raise* troops, Tac. (2) of actions, *to do, perform*: **a**, with noun as object: facinus, Pl.; caedem, furtum, fraudem, res divinas, indutias, pacem, bellum, Cic.; fugam, Sall., Liv.; iter, Cic., Liv.; gradum, Cic.; impetum in hostes, Cic., Liv.; mercaturas, *to trade*, Cic.; stipendia, *to serve in war*, Sall.; scelus, *to commit*, Tac.: **b**, with n. pronoun or adj. as object: ego plus quam feci facere non possum, Cic.; esp. interrog., with quid? as object and person or thing affected in abl. or dat: quid hoc homine facias? Cic.; quid tu huic homini facias? Cic.; Pl., Hor.; so in pass.: quid fiet? Pl., Cic. L., Ov. (3) of feelings and circumstances, *to cause, bring about*: **a**, with noun as object: alicui dolorem, spem, Cic.; metum, timorem, Liv.; orationi audientiam, Cic.; silentium, Liv.; esp. copiam or potestatem, *to give a chance, grant permission*: **b**, with clause as object; with ut and subj.: facis ut rursus plebes in Aventinum sevocanda esse videatur, Cic.; with subj. alone: di faverent, sine patre forem! Cic.; fac sciam, *let me know*, Cic. L.; with ne and subj.: Cic.; in neg., with quin: facere non possum quin ad te mittam, *I cannot but*, Cic.; poet. with acc. and infin.: illum forma timere facit, Ov. (4) *to experience, suffer*: fecere ruinas, Lucr.; naufragium, damnum, detrimentum facere, Cic. (5) with double acc., *to make, appoint, change into*: aliquem consulem, Cic.; Pl., Caes., Verg.; so in pass.: hi consules facti sunt, Cic.; Liv. (6) with genit., *to make something the property of* a person or thing, *to bring into the power of*: tota Asia populi Romani facta est, Cic.; facere aliquid potestatis, ditionis suae, Cic.; sui muneris rempublicam, Tac. (7) with genit., mentally *to put into a category, to*

regard, to esteem, value: parvi, minimi, pluris, maximi, nihili, Cic.; aequi bonique facere aliquid, *to be content with*, Cic. (8) *to take it, assume* that a thing is so: esse deos faciamus, Cic.; fac velle, Verg. (9) *to make out, represent* to others that a thing is so: quem Homerus apud inferos conveniri facit ab Ulysse, Cic. (10) *to do,* referring to another verb: me ut adhuc fecistis audiatis (where fecistis=audivistis), Cic.

Intransit., *to act.* (1) in gen., with adverbs, *to behave*: humaniter, bene, amice, Cic.; Caes., Liv. (2) facere cum, *or* ab, aliquo, *to act on the side of, support, be of the same party*: contra nos, *to be of the opposite party*, Cic. (3) *to sacrifice*: Iunoni Sospitae, Cic.; Verg., Liv. (4) *to be serviceable, to suit, to help, be of service*: nec caelum nec aquae faciunt nec terra nec aurae, Ov.; esp. with dat. or ad and acc.: Medeae faciunt ad scelus omne manus, Ov. (5) used instead of repeating another verb, *to do so*: me ut adhuc fecistis audiatis, Cic.; Hor.

¶ Hence partic. **factus** -a -um, *done, wrought*; n. of compar., factius, *nearer to achievement*: Pl.; n. of positive as subst. **factum** -i, *a deed, act, exploit*: Pl., Cic., Verg.; esp. with adverbs: recte, male facta, Cic.; Caes., Liv.

¶ **factĕon**, a word jestingly formed from facio, in imitation of the Greek=faciendum: Cic.

factĭo -ōnis, f. (facio). (1) *a making, doing*: Pl.; also *the right of making* or *doing*: factionem testamenti non habere, *to be incapable of making a will*, Cic. (2) *a party, group* of people; esp.: a, *a political party, faction, side*: populus paucorum factione oppressus, Caes.; triginta illorum consensus et factio, Cic.; Caes., Liv., Tac.: b, *the parties into which the charioteers in the circus and their supporters were divided*: Suet.

factĭōsus -a -um (factio). (1) *busy*: Pl. (2) *factious, associated with a faction*: adulescens nobilis, egens, factiosus, Sall.; exsistunt in republica plerumque largitores et factiosi, Cic.

factĭto -are (freq. of facio). (1) *to make, do frequently, be accustomed to make* or *do*: verba compone ut quasi coagmenta, quod ne Graeci quidem veteres factitaverunt, Cic.; versus, Hor.; esp. *to practise* as a profession, *make a trade of*: accusationem, Cic.; delationem, Cic. (2) *to appoint openly*: quem palam heredem semper factitarat, Cic.

factus -a -um, partic. from facio; q.v.

făcŭla -ae, f. (dim. of fax), *a little torch*: Prop.

făcultās -ātis, f. (Old Lat. facul=facile), *feasibility, possibility, opportunity, power, means.*

Lit., esp. with genit.: Miloni manendi nulla facultas, Cic.; dare alicui facultatem inridendi sui, Cic.; habere efficiendi facultatem, Cic.; res mihi videtur esse facultate (*in practice*) praeclara, mente (*in theory*) mediocris, Cic.; alicui facultatem dare, offerre, concedere with ut and the subj., Cic.

Transf., (1) *capacity, ability*: facultas dicendi et copia, Cic.; ingenii, Cic. (2) *resources, stock, abundance*: omnium rerum in oppido summa facultus, Caes.; Cic.; esp. in plur., *means*: Cic.

fācundĭa -ae, f. (facundus), *eloquence, readiness of speech*: Memmi facundia clara pollensque fuit, Sall.; Hor., Tac.

fācundus -a -um (fari), *eloquent, fluent, ready of speech*: ingenia hominum sunt ad suam cuique levandam culpam nimio plus facunda, Liv.; oratio, Sall.; vox, Ov.; compar. and superl.: Quint.

¶ Adv. **fācundē**, *eloquently*: Pl., Liv., Tac.

faecĕus -a -um (faex), *impure*: Pl.

faecŭla -ae, f. (dim. of faex), *the lees of wine*: Lucr., Hor.

faenebris -e (faenus), *relating to interest*: leges, Liv.; Tac.

faenĕrātĭo -ōnis, f. (faeneror), *lending at interest, usury*: Cic.

faenĕrātō, adv., *with interest*: Pl.

faenĕrātor -ōris, m. (faeneror), *one who lends money at interest, money-lender, usurer*: acerbissimus, Cic., Hor.

faenĕror -ari, dep. and **faenĕro** (fēnĕro) -are (faenus), *to lend at interest*: pecuniam binis centesimis, *at two per cent per month*, or *twenty-four per cent per annum*, Cic. Transf., provincias, *to despoil by usury*, Cic.; beneficium, *to trade in*, Ter., Cic.

faenĕus -a -um (faenum), *made of hay*: homines, *men of straw*, Cic.

faenīlĭa -ium, n. pl. (faenum), *a hay-loft*: Verg., Ov.

faenīsĕca -ae, m. (faenum/seco), *a mower*; hence *a countryman*: Pers.

faenum (fēnum) -i, n. *hay*; prov.: faenum habet in cornu, *he is dangerous* (the horns of vicious cattle were bound with hay), Hor.

faenus (fēnus) -ŏris, n. (connected with fecundus), *that which is produced*; hence *interest on money.*

Lit., pecuniam alicui dare faenore, *to lend at interest*, Cic.; pecuniam accipere faenore, *to borrow*, Liv.; nummos in faenore ponere, Hor.

Transf., (1) *debt, indebtedness*: faenore obrui, mersum esse, laborare, Liv. (2) *capital*: duas faenoris partes in agris conlocare, Tac.; Pl., Cic. L. (3) *usury*: Tac.

Faesŭlae -ārum, f. *town in Etruria, at the foot of the Apennines* (now *Fiesole*).

¶ Hence adj. **Faesŭlānus** -a -um, *of Faesulae.*

faex faecis, f. *the dregs* or *lees of any liquid*: Lucr., Hor.; esp. *of wine*: Hor.; *the brine of pickles*: Ov. Transf., socially, *the dregs, the lower orders*: faex populi, Cic. L.; Lucr., Juv.

fāgĭnĕus -a -um (fagus), *of beech, beechen*: frons, Ov.

fāgĭnus -a -um (fagus), *beechen*: pocula, Verg.; Ov.

fāgus -i, f. (φηγός), *the beech-tree*: Caes., Verg., Ov.

fāla (**phăla**) -ae, f. (1) *a wooden tower from which missiles were thrown into a besieged city*: Enn., Pl. (2) in plur., *wooden pillars in the circus*: Juv.

fălārĭca (**phălārĭca**) -ae, f. *a missile covered with tow and pitch*: Enn., Verg., Liv.

falcārĭus -i, m. (falx), *a sickle-maker*: inter falcarios, *in the sickle-makers' quarter*, Cic.

falcātus -a -um (falx). (1) *furnished with sickles*: currus, quadrigae, Liv. (2) *sickle-shaped*: ensis, Ov.; sinus, *a bay*, Ov.

falcĭfer -fĕra -fĕrum (falx/fero), *carrying a scythe or sickle*: senex, *Saturnus*, Ov.; Lucr.

Fălĕrĭi -ōrum, m. *the capital of the Falisci.*

Fălernus ager, *the Falernian country, between the Volturnus and Mount Massicus, in Campania.* Adj. **Fălernus** -a -um, *Falernian*: vites, uvae, Hor.; n. as subst. **Fălernum** -i, *Falernian wine*: Hor.

Fălisci -ōrum, m. *a people in Etruria.* Adj. **Făliscus** -a -um, *Faliscan.*

fallācĭa -ae, f. (fallax), *deceit, trick, fraud*: sine fuco ac fallaciis, Cic.; Pl., Ter.

fallācĭlŏquus -a -um (fallax/loqui), *speaking falsely or deceitfully*: Acc. ap. Cic.

fallax -ācis, adj. (with compar. and superl.) (fallo), *deceitful, treacherous, false, fallacious*: homines, Cic.; herbae non fallaces, *not disappointing the farmer*, Cic.; spes, Cic.; nuntius, Liv.; arva, Ov.

¶ Adv. **fallācĭtĕr**, *deceitfully, craftily*: Cic.

fallo fallĕre fĕfelli falsum (perhaps connected with σφάλλω), *to deceive.*

(1) in gen., *to put wrong, lead astray, cause to be mistaken*: a, with person as object: nisi me forte fallo, Cic.; fallit me tempus, Cic.; pass.: nisi fallor, *unless I am mistaken*, Cic., Verg., Hor.; also impers.: me fallit, *I am wrong*, Cic.: b, with thing as object: glacies fallit pedes, Liv.; more often of abstr. things, *to disappoint, fail in*: alicuius spem, Cic.; fidem hosti datam, Cic.; Liv.

(2) *to deceive deliberately, cheat*: a, with person as object: Pl., Cic., Verg.: b, poet., *to beguile, wile away*: infandum amorem, Verg.; curam vino et somno, Ov.

(3) *to escape the notice of, be concealed from*: custodias, Liv.; absol.: aetas labitur occulte fallitque, Ov. Esp. impers.: (non) fallit me, *I am* (*not*) *unaware*, Pl.; with acc. and infin.: Ter., Cic. L., Liv.; with indir. quest.: Lucr., Cic.; aliquem non fallit quin, Caes.

¶ Hence partic. **falsus** -a -um. (1) *wrong, mistaken, misled*: opinio, spes, Cic.; gaudia, Verg.; Hor., Ov., Liv. N. as subst. falsum -i, *a mistake*: ad te falsum scripseram, Cic. L.; abl. as adv.: falso, *falsely*, i.e. *mistakenly*, Cic., Liv. (2) *made wrong, false, untrue, spurious*: rumores, Caes.; litterae, Cic., Liv.; ora non falsa, Ov. (3) in act. sense, *deceitful, lying*: testes, Cic.; vates, Liv. N. as subst. falsum -i, *a lie*: Cic., Ov.; abl. as adv.: falso, *falsely*, i.e. *fraudulently*, Pl., Caes., Cic.

¶ Adv. **falsē**, *falsely*: Pl., Cic.

falsĭdĭcus -a -um (falsus/dico), *lying*: Pl.

falsĭfĭcus -a -um (falsus/facio), *fraudulent*: Pl.

falsĭiūrĭus -a -um (falsus/iuro), *swearing falsely*: Pl.

falsĭlŏquus -a -um (falsus/loquor), *lying*: Pl.

falsĭmōnĭa -ae, f. (falsus), *a deception*: Pl.

falsĭpărens -entis (falsus/parens), *having a putative father*: Amphitryoniades, *Hercules*, Cat.

falsus -a -um, partic. from fallo; q.v.

falx falcis, f. (1) *a sickle, bill-hook, pruning-hook*: Cic., Verg., Hor. (2) *a sickle-shaped implement of war, used for tearing down stockades*, etc.: Caes., Tac.

fāma -ae, f. (fari).

(1) *talk*; hence *what is talked, report, rumour, tradition*: famā accipere, Caes.; nulla adhuc fama venerat, Cic.; fama est, *there is a rumour*, Liv.; fama ferebat, Cic., Ov., Liv. Personif.: Fama, *a goddess, daughter of Terra*, Verg.

(2) *public opinion*, as expressed by common talk: Caes.; contra famam opinionemque omnium, Cic.; Caes., Verg., Liv. (3) *standing in public opinion, repute*: bona fama, Pl., Cic.; mala fama, Sall.; fama sapientiae, Cic.; often without such qualification, as either: a, *good name*: famae consulere, Cic.; famam sororis defendere, Cic.; Hor., Liv.; or: b, *ill fame, bad repute*: moveri famā, Verg.; Ter., Sall., Tac.

fămēlĭcus -a -um (fames), *suffering hunger, hungry, famished*: armenta, Juv.; Pl., Ter.

fămes -is, f. *hunger.*

Lit., cibi condimentum esse famem, Cic.; aliquā re famem tolerare, Caes.; aliquā re famem depellere, *to satisfy*, Cic.; explere, Cic.; famem ab ore civium propulsare, Cic. Sometimes *famine, time of famine*: in fame frumentum exportare, Cic.

Transf., (1) *insatiable desire*: auri sacra fames, Verg.; Hor. (2) *poverty of expression*: ieiunitas et fames, Cic.

fāmĭgĕrātĭo -ōnis, f. (fama/gero), *rumour*: Pl.

fāmĭgĕrātor -ōris, m. (fama/gero), *a rumour-monger*: Pl.

fămĭlĭa -ae (old genit. in -as after the words pater, mater, filius, filia), f. (famulus), *a household of slaves, household.*

Lit., familiam intellegamus quae constet ex servis pluribus, Cic.; emere eam familiam a Catone, Cic.; Pl., Caes. Also of the *dependents, vassals of a noble*: Caes.; *of the slaves of a temple*: Martis, Cic. Esp.: pater familias or paterfamilias, *the head of the household*, Cic.; materfamilias, *a married woman or an unmarried woman whose father was dead*, Cic.; filiusfamilias, *a son still under his father's power*, Cic.

Transf., (1) *a family estate*: Ter., Cic. (2) *a family*, as a subdivision of a *gens*: Laeliorum et Muciorum familiae, Cic.; Liv. (3) *any fraternity, group, sect*: tota Peripateticorum, Cic.; ducere familiam, Cic.

fămĭlĭāris -e (familia). Lit., (1) *belonging to the slaves of a house*; only as subst. **fămĭlĭāris** -is, m. *a servant, slave*: Pl., Liv. (2) *belonging to a family or household*: lares, Cic.; copiae, Liv.; res familiaris, Pl., Caes., Cic.; funus, *a death in the family*, Cic.

Transf., (1) (with compar. and superl.), *known in the house or family, intimate, friendly*: sermones, Cic.; aditus familiarior, Liv.; esp. as subst. **fămĭlĭāris** -is, m. and f. *a familiar friend*: Caes., Cic. (2) as t. t. of augury: fissum familiare, *or* pars familiaris, *the part of the entrails relating to the persons sacrificing*, Cic., Liv.

¶ Adv. (with compar. and superl.) **fămĭlĭārĭtĕr**, *familiarly, intimately*: familiariter cum aliquo vivere, Cic.; Pl., Quint.

fămĭlĭārĭtās -ātis, f. (familiaris), *confidential friendship, intimacy, familiarity*. Lit., in alicuius familiaritatem venire, intrare, se dare, Cic.; mihi cum aliquo familiaritas est, Cic.; inter mulieres, Liv. Transf., *familiar friends*: e praecipua familiaritate Neronis, Tac.; Suet.

fāmōsus -a -um (fama). (1) pass., in a good or neutral sense, *much spoken of, renowned*: urbs (of Jerusalem), Tac.; mors, Hor.; in a bad sense, *infamous, notorious*: largitio, Sall.; Pl., Ov., Tac. (2) act., *libellous, defamatory*: versus, Hor.; libelli, Tac.

fămŭl, fămŭla, *see* famulus.

fămŭlāris -e (famulus), *relating to servants* or *slaves*: vestis, Cic.; iura famularia dare, *to make slaves*, Ov.

fămŭlātus -ūs, m. (famulor), *servitude, slavery*: Cic. Transf., (1) fig., *service*: quam miser virtutis famulatus servientis voluptati, Cic. (2) *an establishment of slaves*: Tac.

fămŭlor -ari, dep. (famulus), *to be a servant, to serve anyone*: Cic.; alicui, Cat.

fămŭlus -a -um, *serving, servile*: vertex, Ov. Usually as subst. (1) m. **fămŭlus** -i (fămŭl: Lucr.), *a house-servant, slave*: Pl., Cic., Verg. Transf., *an attendant* of a god: Cic., Liv., Ov. (2) f. **fămŭla** -ae, *a female slave, handmaid*: Verg., Ov. Transf., virtus famula fortunae est, Cic.

fānāticus -a -um (fanum), *inspired by a deity, enthusiastic*. Lit., of persons: Galli fanatici, Liv.; isti philosophi superstitiosi et paene fanatici, Cic. Transf., of things, *frenzied*: vaticinantes carmine fanatico, Liv.; fanaticus error, Hor.; cursus, Liv.

Fannius -a -um, *name of a Roman* gens.

¶ Hence adj. **Fanniānus** -a -um, *of* or *relating to* Fannius.

*fānum -i, n. *a place solemnly consecrated to a god*; hence *a temple with the land round it, a holy place*: Lucr., Cic.

*Fānum -i, n. *a town on the coast of Umbria* (now *Fano*).

fār farris, n. *spelt* (Triticum spelta, Linn.). Lit., farris seges, Liv.; farris acervus, Verg.; in plur., *grain*: Verg., Ov. Transf., *meal*: percontor quanti olus et far, Hor.; esp. as used in sacrifices: far pium, Hor.

farcio farcire farsi fartum (cf. φράσσω), *to fill full, stuff full*: pulvinus rosā fartus, Cic.; Cat.

fărfărus -i, m. the plant *colt's foot*: Plin.

fărīna -ae, f. (far), *meal, flour*: Plin.; hence *dust* or *powder of any kind*: Plin.; fig.: nostrae farinae, *of our kind* or *sort*, Pers.

fărīnārius -a -um (farina), *relating to meal, made of meal*: Plin.

farrācĕus (-ius) -a -um (far), *of* or *belonging to* spelt: Plin.

farrāgo -inis, f. (far), *mixed fodder for cattle, mash*. Lit., Verg. Transf., (1) *a medley, mixture*: nostri libelli, Juv. (2) *a trifle*: Pers.

farrārius -a -um (far), *relating to* spelt or *to grain generally*: Cato.

farrātus -a -um (far). (1) *provided with grain*: Pers. (2) *made of corn*: Juv.

farrĕus -a -um (far), *made of spelt* or *corn*; n. as subst. **farrĕum** -i, *a spelt-cake*: Plin.

fartim (fartem), acc. sing. (farcio), *stuffing, mincemeat*: Pl.

fartor -ōris, m. (farcio), *a fattener of fowls*: Ter., Cic., Hor.

*ās, n. indecl. *divine command, divine law* (opp. *ius, human law and right*).

Lit., ius ac fas omne delere, Cic.; contra ius fasque, Cic.; personif.: audi Iuppiter, audite fines, audiet fas, Liv.; sometimes *fate, destiny*: fas obstat, Verg.; si cadere fas est, *if I am destined to fall*, Ov.

Transf., in gen., *right, that which is allowed,*

lawful (opp. nefas): per omne fas et nefas aliquem sequi, Liv.; esp. fas est, *it is allowed, is lawful*: quod aut per naturam fas esset aut per leges liceret, Cic.; Pl., Hor.; hoc fas est dictu, Cic.; fas putare, Caes.; ultra fas, Hor.

fascia -ae, f. *a bandage, band*. Lit., *a surgical bandage*: Cic.; *a woman's girdle*: Ov.; *a bed-girth*: Cic. Transf., *a streak of cloud in the sky*: Juv.

fascĭcŭlus -i, m. (dim. of fascis), *a little bundle* or *packet*: epistularum, Cic.; librorum, Hor.; florum, *a nosegay*, Cic.

fascĭno -are (fascinum), *to bewitch*: agnos, Verg.; hence *to envy*: Cat.

fascĭnum -i, n. and **fascĭnus** -i, m. (cf. βάσκανος), *the evil eye, witchcraft, an enchanting, bewitching*: Plin. Transf., = membrum virile: Hor.

fascĭŏla -ae, f. (dim. of fascia), *a little bandage*: Cic., Hor.

fascis -is, m. *a bundle, packet*. In gen.: sarmentorum, Liv.; ego hoc te fasce levabo, Verg. Esp. plur. fasces, *bundles of sticks with an axe projecting, carried by lictors before the chief Roman magistrates*: fasces habere, Cic.; praeferre, Liv.; summittere fasces, *to lower as a sign of respect*, Liv.; hence fig.: alicui, *to yield to* a person, Cic. Transf., *high office*, esp. *the consulate*: Verg., Hor.

fasti -ōrum, m. *see* fastus -a -um.

fastīdĭo -ire (fastidium), *to loathe, feel distaste* or *disgust*.

Lit., of physical loathing: olus, Hor.; omnia praeter pavonem rhombumque, Hor. Transf., in gen., *to be averse to, dislike, loathe*: etiam in recte factis saepe fastidiunt, Cic.; with acc.: preces alicuius, Liv.; with genit.: Pl.; with infin.: ne fastidieris nos in sacerdotum numerum accipere, Liv.

fastīdĭōsus -a -um, adj. (with compar. and superl.) (fastidium), *full of loathing, squeamish*. Lit., Pl., Varr. Transf., (1) *nice, dainty, fastidious*: Antonius facilis in causis recipiendis erat, fastidiosior Crassus, sed tamen recipiebat, Cic.; with genit., *sick of, disgusted with, impatient of*: terrae, Hor. (2) in act. sense, *causing loathing, disgusting, loathsome*: Hor.

¶ Adv. (with compar.) **fastīdĭōsē**, *squeamishly, fastidiously, with disgust*: huic ego iam stomachans fastidiose, immo ex Sicilia, inquam, Cic.; quam diligenter et quam paene fastidiose iudicamus, Cic.

fastīdĭum -i, n. *loathing, squeamishness, disgust*. Lit., for food: cibi satietas et fastidium, Cic.

Transf., in gen. (1) *dislike, aversion, disgust, fastidiousness*: delicatissimum, Cic.; audiendi, Cic.; domesticarum rerum, Cic. (2) *scorn, haughtiness, disdain*: fastidium et superbia, fastidium adrogantiaque, fastidium et contumacia, Cic.; fastidium alicuius non posse ferre, Cic.; plur. fastidia: Hor.

fastīgātus -a -um (fastigium). (1) *pointed*: collis est in modum metae in acutum cacumen a fundo satis lato fastigatus, Liv. (2) *sloping down*: collis leniter fastigatus, Caes.; Liv.

¶ Adv. **fastīgātē**, *slantingly*: Caes.

fastīgĭum -i, n. *the gable end, pediment* of a roof.

LIT., Cic., Verg., Liv.; fig.: operi inchoato, prope tamen absoluto, tamquam fastigium imponere, *put the last touch to*, Cic.

TRANSF., (1) *a slope*, either up or down: ab oppido locus tenui fastigio vergebat, Caes.; Cic., Liv. (2) of measurements, looking up, *height*: colles pari altitudinis fastigio, Caes.; looking down, *depth*: Caes., Verg. (3) *high rank, dignity*: dictaturae altius fastigium, Liv.; Tac., Quint. (4) *principal point* in a subject: summa sequar fastigia rerum, Verg.

¹**fastus** -ūs, m. *pride, haughtiness, arrogance*: stirpis Achilleae fastus (plur.), Verg.; fastu erga patrias epulas, Tac.

²**fastus** -a -um (fas), dies fastus, plur. dies fasti, *or* simply fasti, *days on which the praetor could administer justice, court-days*. LIT., fastus erit per quem lege licebit agi, Ov. TRANSF., *a list of these days, with festivals*, etc., *the Roman calendar*: fasti memores, Hor.; esp. *a poetical form of this calendar composed by Ovid*; also *a register of events, record*: Cic., Hor.; *a list of magistrates*: Cic., Liv.

fātālis -e (fatum), *relating to destiny or fate*. In gen.: necessitas, Cic.; libri, *the Sibylline books*, Liv.; deae, *the Fates*, Ov. Esp. (1) *fated, destined by fate*: annus ad interitum huius urbis fatalis, Cic.; hora, Liv. (2) in a bad sense, *deadly, fatal*: telum, Verg.; iaculum, Ov.

¶ Adv. **fātālĭtĕr**, *according to fate*: definitum esse, Cic.; Ov., Tac.

fătĕŏr fătēri fasus sum, dep. (cf. fari), *to confess, admit, allow*: verum, Cic.; de facto turpi, Cic.; with acc. and infin.: si quis se fecisse fateatur, Cic.; Pl., Hor., Ov. TRANSF., *to reveal, make known*: iram vultu, Ov.; mors sola fatetur, Juv.

fātīcănus -a -um and **fātīcĭnus** -a -um (fatum/cano), *prophetic*: Ov.

fātĭdīcus -a -um (fatum/dico), *announcing fate, prophetic*: vates, Verg.; anus, Cic.; m. as subst., *a prophet*: Cic.

fātĭfĕr -fĕra -fĕrum (fatum/fero), *death-bringing, deadly, fatal*: arcus, Verg.; Ov.

fātīgātĭo -ōnis, f. (fatigo), *weariness, fatigue*: cum fatigatione equorum atque hominum, Liv.; Tac.

fātīgo -are (connected with adfatim), *to weary, tire, fatigue*. LIT., se atroci pugnā, Liv.; itinere, magno aestu fatigati, Caes.; cervos iaculo cursuque, Verg.; Cic., Ov. TRANSF., (1) *to vex, harass*: verberibus, tormentis, igni fatigati, Cic.; verbis, Cic.; animum, Sall.; se, Sall. (2) *to tease, importune, worry*: aliquem precibus, Liv.; Vestam prece, Hor.; Tac.

fātĭlŏqua -ae, f. (fatum/loquor), *a prophetess*: Carmenta mater . . . quam fatiloquam miratae hae gentes fuerant, Liv.

fātisco -ĕre (**fātiscor** -i, dep.: Lucr.; cf. Gr. χατέω, χάσμα). (1) *to gape, crack, open, part asunder*: naves rimis fatiscunt, Verg.; Liv. (2) *to become weak, droop*: seditio fatiscit, Tac.; dum copiā fatiscunt, Tac.; Lucr.

fātŭĭtās -ātis, f. (fatuus), *foolishness, silliness*: Cic.

fātum -i, n. (fari), *an utterance*.

LIT., *a divine utterance, expressed will of a god*: fata Sibyllina, Cic.

TRANSF., (1) *destiny, fate; the appointed order of the world; the fate, lot, or destiny of*

man: omnia fato fieri, Cic.; fato rerum prudentia maior, Verg.; alicuius *or* alicui, fatum est, with acc. and infin., Cic.; fuit hoc sive meum sive rei publicae fatum ut, Cic. (2) *the will of a god*: sic fata Iovis poscunt, Verg. (3) *a cause of fate*: duo illa reipublicae paene fata, Gabinius et Piso, Cic.; personif.: Fata, *the Parcae or Fates*, Prop. (4) *doom, fate, natural death*: maturius exstingui quam fato suo, Cic.; fato cedere, Liv.; fato fungi, Ov.; fato obire, Tac.; fata proferre, *to prolong life*, Verg. (5) *misfortune, ruin, calamity*: impendet fatum aliquod, Cic.

fătŭus -a -um, *foolish, idiotic, silly*; of persons and things: fatuus et amens es, Cic.; Pl., Ter. As subst. **fătŭus** -i, m. and **fătŭa** -ae, f. *a male or female fool, jester*: Sen.

faucēs, plur. from faux; q.v.

Faunus -i, m. (faveo), *a mythic deity of the forests, also of herdsmen*; sometimes identified with Pan; hence plur. **Fauni** -orum, *Fauns, forest gods*: Ov.

faustĭtās -ātis, f. (faustus), *prosperity*; personif. as a goddess: Ceres almaque Faustitas, Hor.

Faustŭlus -i, m. (faveo), myth., *the herdsman of the Alban king Amulius, who saved and brought up Romulus and Remus*.

¹**faustus** -a -um (faveo), *favourable, lucky, auspicious*: dies faustus alicui, Cic.; Lucr., Ov., Liv.

¶ Adv. **faustē**, *favourably*: evenire, Cic.

²**Faustus** -i, m. and **Fausta** -ae, f. *a Roman surname*, esp. of L. Cornelius Sulla, *son of the dictator Sulla*; and of *the dictator's daughter, wife of Milo*.

fautor -ōris, m. (originally favitor, from faveo), *a favourer, patron, promoter, partisan*: regis, Sall.; dignitatis, Cic.; bonorum, Liv., Pl., Hor.

fautrix -trīcis, f. (fautor), *a patroness*: voluptatum, Cic.; regio suorum fautrix, Ter., Ov.

faux, f.; sing. abl. only, **fauce**; usually plur. **fauces** -ium; *the throat, gullet*.

LIT., arente fauce, Hor.; sitis urit fauces, Hor.; Pl., Ov.,

TRANSF., (1) fig., *throat, jaws*: cum inexplebiles populi fauces exaruerunt libertatis siti, Cic.; Catilina cum exercitu faucibus urguet, *is at our throats*, Sall.; premit fauces defensionis tuae, *strangles, makes impossible*, Cic.; urbem ex belli ore ac faucibus ereptam esse, Cic. (2) *a chasm*: patefactis terrae faucibus, Cic.; Verg. (3) *a gorge, narrow pass, defile*: angustissimae, Caes.; angustae, Liv.; artae, Tac.; Cic., Verg. (4) *an isthmus, neck of land*: artae fauces (Isthmi), Liv. (5) *straits*: Hellesponti, Liv.

făvĕo făvēre făvi fautum, *to favour, be favourable to, help, support*; with dat. of person, cause, etc.: faveas tu hosti, Cic.; si tibi dei favent, Cat.; favere enim pietati fideique deos, Liv.; honori et dignitati, Caes.; Cic.; isti sententiae, Cic.; impers.: non modo non invidetur illi aetati, verum etiam favetur, Cic.; absol.: dum favet nox et Venus, Hor.; multitudo audiens favet, odit, Cic.; with infin., *to be inclined to*; hence *to desire to*: Enn., Ov.

Esp., as religious t. t., *to speak no words of bad omen*; hence *to be silent*: favete linguis, Hor.; ore favete, Verg.; linguā, Juv.

făvilla -ae, f. *glowing ashes*: Ter., Lucr., Verg.; esp. *the still glowing ashes of the dead*: reliquias vino et bibulam lavēre favillam, Verg.; Hor. Transf., *ashes*: Verg.; *spark*: Prop.

făvitor -ōris, m.=fautor; q.v.: Pl.

Făvōnĭus -i, m.=Zephyrus, *the west wind which blew at the beginning of spring*: Cic.

făvor -ōris, m. (faveo), *favour, good-will, support, partiality, inclination.*
   In gen.: with subjective genit.: populi, Cic.; with objective genit.: nominis, Liv.; amplecti aliquem favore, Liv.; in favorem alicuius venire, Liv.; favor in aliquem, Tac.
   Esp. (1) *applause at the theatre, approbation, acclamation*: quod studium et quem favorem in scenam attulit Panurgus, Cic.; Verg., Quint. (2) *as religious t. t.* (cf. faveo): pium praestare et mente et voce favorem, Ov.

făvōrābĭlis -e (favor), *in favour, popular*: oratio, Tac.; compar.: Plin. L.

făvus -i, m. *a honeycomb*: fingere favos, Cic.; Verg.

fax făcis, f.
   (1) *a torch.* In gen.: Cic., Hor., Verg., Liv. Esp. as carried: **a**, at weddings, before the bride: faces nuptiales, Cic.; Verg.: **b**, in funeral processions: Verg. Transf., alicui ad libidinem facem praeferre, *to show the way*, Cic.; also as symbol of *marriage* or *death*: Hor., Ov., Prop.
   (2) *a fire-brand*: faces incendere, Cic.; Caes., Tac.; as an attribute of Cupid and the Furies: Ov., Verg. Transf., **a**, of persons, *instigator*: omnium incendiorum fax, of Antonius, Cic.: **b**, of things, *stimulus*: subicere faces invidiae alicuius, Cic.
   (3) *light, flame*, in gen. Lit., esp. of heavenly bodies; of the moon: canentes rite crescentem face noctilucam, Hor.; of a fiery meteor, shooting-star: faces caelestes, Cic.; Lucr., Verg. Transf., dicendi faces, *of eloquence*, Cic.; of love: me torret face mutuā Calais, Hor.

faxim, faxo, *see* facio.

fĕbrĭcŭla -ae, f. (dim. of febris), *a slight fever, feverishness*: febriculam habere, Cic. L.

fĕbrĭcŭlōsus -a -um (febricula), *feverish*: Cat.

fĕbris -is, f. (acc. -em or -im; abl. -e or -i; for ferbris from ferveo), *fever*: in febrim subito incidere, Cic. L.; febri carere, Cic. L.; Romam venisse cum febre, Cic. L.; plur.: Lucr., Hor. Febris personif. as a goddess, with three temples in Rome: Cic.

Fĕbruārĭus -i, m. or **Februārĭus mensis** (februus), *the cleansing month* (so called because of the festival Februa; *see* februum), *February*; up to 450 B.C. the last month of the year, afterwards the second: Cic., Sall., Ov. As adj., qualifying days of the month: Kalendae Februariae, *the 1st of February*, Cic.

fĕbruum -i, n. *religious purification*: Ov.
  ¶ Hence **Februa** -ōrum, n. pl. *the Roman feast of purification held on the 15th of February.*

fĕciālis=fetialis; q.v.

fēcundĭtās -ātis, f. (fecundus), *fruitfulness, fecundity.* Lit., of persons: mulieris, Cic.; of the earth: aquarum inductionibus terris fecunditatem damus, Cic. Transf., of style: volo se efferat in adulescente fecunditas, Cic.

fēcundo -are (fecundus), *to fructify, fertilize*: viridem Aegyptum nigrā harenā, Verg.

fēcundus -a -um, adj. (with compar. and superl.) (connected with fētus), *fruitful, prolific.*
   Lit., terra, Cic.; coniunx, Hor.; Verg., Tac.
   Transf., (1) *abundant, full, plentiful*: calices, Hor.; fons, Ov. (2) *rich in, abounding in*; with genit.: saecula fecunda culpae, Hor.; with abl.: gens inter accolas latrociniis fecunda, Tac. (3) *making fruitful*: fecundae verbera dextrae, Ov.; imber, Verg.

fĕl fellis, n. *the gall-bladder, gall, bile.* Lit., fel gallinaceum, Cic.; esp. as the supposed seat of anger: atrum fel, Verg. Transf., (1) *poison, venom*: vipereo spicula felle linunt, Ov.; Verg. (2) *bitterness*: Pl., Ov.

fēles -is, f. *a cat*: Cic., Ov. Transf., *a thief*: Pl.

fēlĭcĭtās -ātis, f. (felix). Lit., *fertility*: Plin. Transf., *happiness, good fortune, success*: perpetuā quādam felicitate usus ille excessit e vita, Cic.; Caes.; plur.: incredibiles felicitates, Cic.; personif.: Felicitas, *Good Fortune as a goddess*, with a temple in Rome, Cic., Suet.

fēlix -īcis, adj. (with compar. and superl.).
   Lit., *fruitful, fertile*: arbor, Liv.; regio, Ov.; Verg.
   Transf., (1) *of good omen, favourable, bringing good luck*: omen, Ov.; so the formula: quod bonum, faustum, felix fortunatumque sit, Cic. (2) *fortunate, lucky, successful*: Sulla felicissimus omnium, Cic.; saecula, Ov.; seditio, Liv.; with genit.: cerebri, *in your bad temper*, Hor.; with in and abl. of gerund: si minus felices in diligendo fuissemus, Cic.; with infin.: felicior unguere tela manu, Verg.; Felix, *the Lucky One*, surname of Sulla, Liv.
  ¶ Adv. (with compar. and superl.) **fēlīcĭtĕr.** Lit., *fruitfully*: illic veniunt felicius uvae, Verg. Transf., (1) *auspiciously, favourably*: precatus sum ut ea res mihi, populo plebique Romanae bene atque feliciter eveniret, Cic.; Pl., Caes. (2) *luckily, successfully*: vivere, Cic.; Pl., Caes., Ov.

fēmella -ae, f. (dim. of femina), *a young woman, a girl*: Cat.

fĕmĕn=femur; q.v.

fēmĭna -ae, f. (connected with fētus), *one that bears young, a female.* (1) of human beings, *a woman*: Cic., Verg. (2) of gods and animals, *the female*; used as adj.: porcus femina, Cic.; Ov.

fēmĭnĕus -a -um (femina). (1) *relating to a woman, female, feminine*: amor, Ov.; vox, Ov.; Kalendae, *the 1st of March, when the Matronalia were celebrated*, Juv. (2) *womanish, effeminate*: amor praedae, Verg.; fuga, Ov.

fĕmur -ŏris or -ĭnis, n. *the thigh*: Cic.; femur utrumque, Caes.; Pl., Cic., Verg.

fĕnestra -ae, f. (connected with φαίνω), *a window.* Lit., Pl., Cic. L., Hor., Prop. Transf., of other openings. (1) physical: lato dedit ore fenestram, *a breach*, Verg.; fenestras ad tormenta mittenda in struendo reliquerunt, *loopholes*, Caes.; molles in aure fenestrae, Juv. (2) abstr.: Ter., Cic.

fĕra -ae, f. *see* ferus.

fĕrācĭus, *see* ferax.

fērālis -e, *relating to the dead.* LIT., *funereal*: cupressus, Verg.; tempus *or* dies=feralia, Ov. N. pl. as subst. **fērālĭa** -ium (fĕr-: Ov.), *the festival of the dead, in February*: Cic. L., Liv.
    TRANSF., (1) *deadly, fatal*: dona, Ov.; annus, Tac. (2) *mournful*: Verg., Tac.

fĕrax -ācis (fero), *fruitful, fertile, prolific.* LIT., agri, Cic.; with genit.: Iberia ferax venenorum, Hor.; with abl.: feracior uvis, Ov.; Verg. TRANSF., nullus feracior in philosophia locus est quam de officiis, Cic.; with genit.: illa aetate qua nulla virtutum feracior fuit, Liv.
    ¶ Hence compar. adv. **fĕrācĭus,** *more fruitfully*: velut ab stirpibus laetius feraciusque renata urbs, Liv.

fercŭlum -i, n. (fero), *a frame, litter, bier, tray*; esp. (1) for carrying the trophies at a triumph, the images of the gods in processions, etc.: Cic., Liv. (2) for serving food; hence *a course or dish*: Hor., Juv., Mart.

fĕrē, adv. (perhaps connected with firmus). (1) *almost, nearly*: totius fere Galliae legati, Caes.; omnes fere, Cic.; quintā fere horā, Cic.; eādem fere horā quā veni, *about the same hour*, Cic.; with negatives, *scarcely, hardly*: aetates vestrae nihil aut non fere multum differunt, Cic. (2) *just, exactly*: paria esse fere peccata, Hor.; circa hanc fere consultationem disceptatio omnis, Liv. (3) *as a rule, generally, usually*: fit fere ut, Cic.; nigra fere terra, Verg.

fĕrentārĭus -i, m. *a light-armed soldier who fought with missiles*: Sall., Tac. TRANSF., *an active body*: Pl.

Fĕrentīnum -i, n. (1) *a town of the Hernici on the Via Latina* (now *Ferentino*): Liv.; adj. **Fĕrentīnās** -ātis, *Ferentine.*
    (2) *a town in Etruria* (now *Ferento*).

Fĕretrĭus -i, m. (feretrum or ferio), *a surname of Jupiter.*

fĕretrum -i, n. (φέρετρον), *a bier for carrying a corpse to the grave*: Verg., Ov.

fērĭae -ārum, f. pl. (cf. festus), *festivals, holidays.* LIT., novendiales, Cic.; ferias agere, Liv. TRANSF., *rest*: Hor.

fērĭātus -a -um, p. adj. (feriae), *keeping holiday, idle, at leisure*: deus feriatus torpet, Cic.; feriatus a negotiis publicis, Cic.; of things, *idle*: Pl.

fĕrīnus -a -um (ferus), *relating to a wild beast, wild*: caro, Sall.; vellera, Ov.; f. as subst. **fĕrīna** -ae, *flesh of wild animals, game*: Verg.

fĕrĭo -ire, *to strike, knock, smite.*
    LIT., in gen.: murum arietibus, Sall.; frontem, Cic.; ferire mare, *to row*, Verg.; sublimi feriam sidera vertice, Hor.; ferit aethera clamor, Verg.; esp. *to strike dead, slay, kill*: hostem, Sall.; particularly as a sacrifice: humilem agnam, Hor.; hence: foedus ferire, *to make a treaty*, Cic., Verg.
    TRANSF., (1) *to hit*: multa patent in eorum vita quae fortuna feriat, Cic.; medium ferire, *to keep the middle of the road*, Cic.; verba palato, Hor. (2) *to cheat*: Pl., Ter., Prop.

fĕrĭtās -ātis, f. (ferus), *wildness, savageness*: hominis, Cic.; leonis, Ov.; loci, Ov.

fermē, adv. (superl. of fere=ferime). (1) *almost, nearly*: haec ferme gesta, Liv.; sex

millia ferme passuum, Liv.; Pl., Caes., Tac. (2) with negatives, *hardly, scarcely*: nihil ferme, *hardly anything*, Cic.; Pl., Liv. (3) *usually*: quod ferme evenit, Cic.; Pl., Liv., Tac.

fermento -are (fermentum), *to cause to ferment*: Plin.

fermentum -i, n. (ferveo). LIT., (1) *that which causes fermentation, leaven, yeast*: Tac. (2) *a kind of beer*: Verg. TRANSF., *anger, passion*: Pl.; *its cause*: Juv.

fĕro ferre (connected with φέρω), borrowed perf. tŭli and supine lātum (originally tetuli; Pl., Ter. and tlatum, both connected with tollo), *to bear, bring, carry.*
    (1) in gen. LIT., faces in Capitolium, Cic.; cervice iugum, Hor.; ventrem, *to be pregnant*, Liv.; arma, Caes., Cic., Verg. TRANSF., *to bear*: a, of names, etc.: nomen Aemilii Pauli, Liv.; prae se ferre, *to display, make public*, Cic.; obscure ferre, *to conceal*, Cic.: b, *to endure, submit to*; (i) without adv. or adverbial phrase: contumaciam alicuius, Cic.; ea vina quae vetustatem ferunt, *which keep for a long time*, Cic.; with personal objects: optimates quis ferat? Cic.; with acc. and infin.: ferunt aures hominum illa laudari, Cic.; absol.: non feram, non patiar, non sinam, Cic.; (ii) with adv. or adverbial phrase: aliquid ferre aegre, moleste, graviter molesteque, *to take ill, be vexed at*, Cic.; aequo (*or* iniquo) animo, Cic.; facile, clementer, fortiter ac sapienter, Cic.; with acc. and infin.: si quis aegre ferat se pauperem esse, Cic.
    (2) *to bear, bring forth, produce.* LIT., terra fruges ferre potest, Cic.; Hor., Liv. TRANSF., Cic.
    (3) *to bring to* a place or person, *fetch, offer.* LIT., alicui venenum, Liv.; osculum, Ov.; sacra divis, Verg. TRANSF., a, in gen.: *to bring*: opem, auxilium, Cic.; alicui fraudem, Cic.; ferre responsa Turno, Verg.; condicionem, Caes.: b, as polit. or legal t.t.: suffragium, sententiam, *to vote*, Cic.; legem ferre, *to propose a law*, Cic.; so: ferre de aliqua ut, *to propose that*, Cic.; (alicui) iudicem, of the prosecutor, *to propose a judge to the defendant*, Cic.: c, as commercial t. t.: expensum ferre, *to set down in an account-book as paid*: d, *to cause, bring about*: alicui luctum lacrimasque, Liv.; Verg., Ov.: e, *to report to others, to spread abroad, speak of*: ferre haec omnibus sermonibus, Caes.; fama fert, *the story goes*, Liv.; esp. *to publish* a person's *praises*: nostra laus feretur, Cic. Verg.; also *to extol with praises*: aliquem ad caelum laudibus ferre, Liv.; Cic.; most frequently of actual assertions, with a clause introduced by ferunt, *they say that*, fertur, etc.: Caes., Cic., Hor., Verg.
    (4) *to bear away, carry off.* LIT., ferre et agere, *to plunder*, Liv.; Verg.; te fata tulerunt, Verg. TRANSF., *to win, get*: fructus e republica, Cic.; gratiam (*thanks*) alicuius rei, Liv.; repulsam (a populo), Cic.; centuriam tribus, *to gain the votes of*, Cic.
    (5) *to bear along, move forward, put in motion.* LIT., inde domum pedem, Verg.; milit. t. t.: signa ferre, *to march*, Liv.; se ferre alicui obviam, Cic.; ad eum omni celeritate ferri, Caes.; Rhenus citatus fertur, *rush quickly*, Caes. TRANSF., *to move, impe-*

act. with object: qua quemque animus fert, Liv.; pass.: eloquentia quae cursu magno sonituque fertur, *rushes on*, Cic.; crudelitate et scelere, *to be carried away by*, Cic.; act. without object, *to lead, tend*: via fert Verruginem, Liv.; ut mea fert opinio, Cic.

ĕrōcĭa -ae, f. (ferox). (1) in a good sense, *high spirit, courage*: Cic., Sall., Liv. (2) in a bad sense, *arrogance, ferocity*: Cic., Ov., Tac. TRANSF., vini, *harshness, roughness*, Plin.

ĕrōcĭtās -ātis, f. (ferox). (1) in a good sense, *courage, untamed spirit*: Cic. (2) in a bad sense, *arrogance*: Pl., Cic.

ĕrōcĭtĕr, adv. from ferox; q.v.

ĕrōnĭa -ae, f. *an old Italian goddess, patroness of freedmen.*

ĕrox -ōcis (connected with ferus), adj. (with compar. and superl.).

(1) in a good sense, *courageous, high-spirited, warlike, brave*: iuvenis ferocissimus, Liv.; feroces ad bellandum viri, Liv.; Pl., Hor., Tac.

(2) in a bad sense, *wild, unbridled, arrogant*; with abl.: stolide ferox viribus suis, Liv.; with genit.: linguae, Tac.; absol.: victoria eos ipsos ferociores impotentioresque reddit, Cic.; of things: ferox aetas, Hor.; oratio, Cic.

¶ Adv. (with compar. and superl.) **fĕrōcĭtĕr**. (1) in a good sense, *courageously, bravely*: Liv., Tac. (2) in a bad sense, *arrogantly, fiercely*: Pl., Cic., Liv.

errāmenta -orum, n. pl. (ferrum), *tools made of*, or *shod with, iron*, esp. for agriculture: Caes., Cic., Hor.

errārĭus -a -um (ferrum), *of iron*: faber, *a blacksmith*, Pl. M. as subst. **ferrārĭus** -i, *a blacksmith*: Sen.; f. pl. as subst. **ferrārĭae** -arum, *iron-mines*: Caes., Liv.

errātĭlis -e (ferratus), *in irons*; of slaves: Pl.

errātus -a -um (ferrum), *furnished* or *covered with iron*: hasta, Liv.; agmina, *iron-clad*, Hor.; sudes, Verg.; servi, *in irons*, Pl. M. pl. as subst. **ferrāti** -orum, *soldiers in armour*: Tac.

errĕus -a -um (ferrum), *of iron*. LIT., *made of iron*: clavi, Caes. Meton., *like iron*. (1) *hard, stern, unfeeling, cruel*: Aristo Chius, praefractus, ferreus, Cic.; os, Cic.; Ov. (2) *immovable, unyielding, firm*: corpus animusque Catonis, Liv.; sors vitae, Ov.; somnus, *death*, Verg.

erricrĕpĭnus -a -um (ferrum/crepo), *with clanking fetters*: Pl.

errĭtĕrĭum -i, n. (ferrum/tero), *fetters-galling-house*=ergastulum: Pl.

errĭtĕrus -i, m. (ferrum/tero), *one galled with fetters*: Pl.

errĭtrībax -ācis, adj. (ferrum/τρίβω), *galled with fetters*: Pl.

errūgĭnĕus -a -um (ferrugo), *rust-coloured, dusky*: hyacinthus, Verg.; cymba, Verg.

errūgĭnus=ferrugineus; q.v., Lucr.

errūgo -ĭnis, f. (from ferrum, as aerugo from aes). LIT., *iron rust*: Plin. TRANSF., *the colour of iron rust, dusky* or *dark colour*: Verg., Ov.

errum -i, n. *iron.*

LIT., Lucr., Cic.; fig.: in pectore ferrum gerere, Ov.

TRANSF., *any iron instrument; the plough*: Verg.; *an axe*: Hor.; *a stylus for writing*: Ov.; *scissors for hair-cutting*: Ov.; *curling-irons*: Verg. Esp., *a sword*: ferrum stringere, Liv.;

aliquem cum ferro invadere, Cic.; urbes ferro atque igni vastare, Liv.; haec omnia flamma ac ferro delere, Cic.

ferrūmen -ĭnis, n. *cement*: Plin.

ferrūmĭno -are (ferrumen), *to cement, bind together*: Plin.

fertĭlis -e (fero) adj. (with compar. and superl.), *fruitful, prolific, fertile*. LIT., agri, Cic., Ov., Liv.; with genit.: multos fertiles agros alios aliorum fructuum, Cic. TRANSF., (1) *productive*: pectus, Ov. (2) *fertilizing, making fruitful*: dea, Ceres, Ov.; Bacchus, Hor.

fertĭlĭtās -ātis, f. (fertilis), *fruitfulness, fertility*: loci, Caes.; agrorum, Cic.; of persons: indoluit fertilitate suā, Ov.

fertum (ferctum) -i, n. *a kind of sacrificial cake*: Pers.

fĕrŭla -ae, f. (fero). (1) *the herb fennel*: Verg. (2) *a stick, cane*, esp. as used *to punish slaves and children*: Hor.; as *a goad for cattle*: Ov.

fĕrus -a -um (connected with θήρ), *wild*.

LIT., *untamed, uncultivated*: bestiae, Cic.; silvae, Hor.; fructus, Verg. As subst. (1) m. **ferus** -i, *a wild animal*; of a horse: Verg.; of a boar: Ov. (2) f. **fera** -ae (sc. bestia), *a wild animal*: ferarum ritu, Liv.; feras agitare, Cic. Fig., of constellations: magna minorque ferae, *the Great and Little Bear*, Ov.

TRANSF., *wild, rough, savage, uncivilized, cruel*: gens, Verg.; hostis, Cic.; mores, Cic.; hiems, Ov.

fervĕfăcĭo -făcĕre -fēci -factum (ferveo/facio), *to make hot, heat, boil, melt*: pix fervefacta, Caes.; iacula fervefacta, Caes.; Pl.

fervens -entis, partic. from ferveo; q.v.

fervĕo fervēre ferbŭi (and fervo fervēre fervi: Pl., Lucr., Verg.), *to be boiling hot, to boil, seethe, glow.*

LIT., validum posito medicamen aeno fervet, Ov., Lucr., Hor., Verg.

TRANSF., (1) *to be in quick movement, to seethe*, esp. of crowds, armies, etc.: fervēre cum videas classem lateque vagari, Lucr.; so of bees: Verg.; hence: fervet opus, Verg. (2) *to be excited by passion, rage*: fervet avaritiā pectus, Hor.; Cic., Verg.

¶ Hence partic. **fervens** -entis, *glowing, hot, heated*. LIT., aqua, Cic.; rota, Ov. TRANSF., of character or feelings, *heated, fiery*: fortis animus ferventior est, Cic.; Cassi rapido ferventius amni ingenium, Hor.

¶ Adv. **fervĕntĕr**, *hotly, warmly*: loqui, ap. Cic.; superl.: Cic. L.

fervesco -ĕre (ferveo), *to become hot, begin to glow, begin to boil*: Lucr.

fervĭdus -a -um (ferveo), adj. (with compar.), *boiling, seething, foaming.*

LIT., pars mundi, Cic.; sol, Lucr.; aequor, Hor.

TRANSF., of character or feelings, *fiery, passionate, excited*: paulo fervidior erat oratio, Cic.; fervidi animi vir, Liv.; with abl.: fervidus irā, Verg.

fervo=ferveo; q.v.

fervor -ōris, m. (ferveo), *boiling heat, seething, foaming*. LIT., mediis fervoribus, *in the heat of noon*, Verg.; mundi, Cic. TRANSF., *ardour, passion*: mentis, animi, Cic.; pectoris, Hor.

Fescennĭa -ae, f. *a town in Etruria famous for its outspoken verse dialogues*. Adj. **Fescennīnus** -a -um, *Fescennine*: licentia Fescennina, Hor.

fessus -a -um (fatisco), *weary, tired, exhausted*: de via, Cic.; militiā, Hor.; plorando, Cic.; corpus fessum vulnere, Liv.; with genit.: fessi rerum, Verg. Transf., fessa aetas, *old age*, Tac.; res fessae, *distress*, Verg.

festīnātio -ōnis, f. (festino), *haste, speed, hurry*: festinatio praepropera, Cic.; adipiscendi honoris, Cic.; Liv.; plur.: quid adferebat festinationum, Cic.

festīno -are. (1) intransit., *to hasten, hurry*: plura scripsissem nisi tui festinarent, Cic. L.; with ad and the acc.: ad effectum operis, Liv. (2) transit., *to hasten, accelerate*: profectionem, Sall.; fugam, Verg.; iter, Ov.; with infin.: tanto opere migrare, Cic.; defungi proelio, Liv.; Hor., Verg.

¶ Hence adv. (from pres. partic.) (with compar.) (Tac., Suet.) **festīnantěr**, *hastily, rapidly, quickly*: nimium festinanter dictum, Cic.

¶ Also adv. (from past partic.) **festīnātō**, *hastily*: Quint., Suet.

festīnus -a -um (festino), *hastening, hasty*: cursu festinus anhelo, Ov.; Verg.

festīvĭtās -ātis, f. (festivus), *gaiety, jollity*: Pl.; of speech or writing, *cheerfulness, humour*: lepos et festivitas, festivitas et facetiae, Cic.; plur., *humorous passages*: Cic.

festīvus -a -um (festus), *of a holiday, festive.* Lit., ludi, Pl. Transf., *merry, good-humoured, cheerful*: homo, puer, Cic.; of speech or writing: oratio, Cic.; poema, Cic.; copia librorum, Cic.

¶ Adv. **festīvē**, *in holiday mood, gaily, humorously*: Pl., Cic.

festūca -ae, f. (fero). Lit., *a stalk, straw, stem*: Plin. Transf., *the rod with which slaves were touched in the ceremony of manumission*: Pl.

¹**festus** -a -um (connected with feriae), *of a holiday, festive*: dies, Cic.; lux (=dies), Ov.; tempus, Hor.; dies festos anniversarios agere, Cic. N. as subst. **festum** -i, *a feast*: Ov.; in plur.: Hor., Ov. Transf., *keeping holiday, on holiday*: plebs, Tac.

²**Festus** -i, m. Sext. Pompeius, *a Latin grammarian of uncertain date* (A.D.), *author of a work in twenty books*, 'De Verborum Significatione'.

fētĭālis -is, m. *one of a college of priests responsible for formally making peace or declaring war*: Cic., Liv. Also as adj. **fētĭālis** -e, *belonging to the fetiales*: ius fetiale, Cic.; Liv.

fētūra -ae, f. (fetus), *the bearing* or *bringing forth of young, breeding*: Cic. Meton., *the young brood, offspring*: Cic., Ov.

¹**fētus** -a -um. (1) *pregnant.* Lit., pecus, Verg.; vulpes, Hor. Transf., *fruitful, fertile*: terra feta frugibus, Cic.; Ov.; hence in gen., *teeming with, full of*: machina feta armis, Verg. (2) *that has brought forth, newly delivered*: ursa, lupa, Ov.; Verg.

²**fētus** -ūs, m. (¹fetus), *the bearing, bringing forth* or *hatching of young.*

Lit., labor bestiarum in fetu, Cic.; of the soil, *bearing, producing*: quae frugibus atque baccis terrae fetu profunduntur, Cic.; fig.: nec ullā aetate uberior oratorum fetus fuit, Cic.

Transf., *that which is brought forth*: **a**, *offspring, brood*: Germania quos horrida parturit fetus, Hor.; avium, apium, Verg.:

b, of plants, *fruit, produce, shoot*: nucis, Verg.; meliores et grandiores fetus edere (of land), Cic.; fig.: ex quo triplex ille animi fetus exsistet, Cic.

fīber -bri, m. *a beaver*: Plin.

fibra -ae, f. (1) *a fibre, filament*, in animals or plants: stirpium, radicum, Cic.; Verg., Ov. (2) *the entrails of an animal*: bidentis, Ov.

Fībrēnus -i, m. *a river in Latium, near Arpinum* (now *Fibreno*).

fibrīnus -a -um (fiber), *of* or *belonging to the beaver*: Plin.

fībŭla -ae, f. (figo). (1) *a buckle, brooch, clasp*: Verg., Liv. (2) *an iron clamp fastening beams together*: Caes.

Fīcāna -ae, f. *a town in Latium, on the road to Ostia.*

fīcēdŭla -ae, f. (ficus), *a small bird, the becafico*: Plin., Juv.

fictĕ, adv. from fingo; q.v.

fictĭlis -e (fingo), *shaped; hence earthen, made of clay*: vasa, Cic.; figurae, Cic.; Liv., Ov. N. as subst. **fictĭle** -is, usually plur., *earthenware, earthen vessels*: omnia (ponuntur) fictilibus, Ov.; Juv.

fictĭō -onis, f. (fingo), *a forming, feigning* or *assumption*: Quint.

fictor -ōris, m. (fingo). (1) *an image-maker, a moulder*: pictores fictoresque, Cic. (2) in gen., *a maker, contriver*: fandi fictor Ulysses, *master in deceit*, Verg.

fictrix -īcis, f. (fictor), *she that forms* or *fashions*: materiae fictrix et moderatrix divina est providentia, Cic.

fictūra -ae, f. (fingo), *a forming, fashioning*: Pl.

fictus, partic. from fingo; q.v.

fīcŭlus -i, m. (dim. of ficus), *a little fig*: Pl.

Fīcŭlĕa (Fīcŭlnĕa) -ae, f. *town in the country of the Sabines.*

fīculnus (fīculnĕus) -a -um (ficus), *of the fig-tree*: truncus, Hor.

fīcus -i and -ūs, f. (1) *a fig-tree*: arbor fici, Cic. (2) *a fig*: Pl., Cic., Hor.

fĭdĕicommissum -i, n. (fides/committo), *lega t. t., a trust*: Quint., Suet.

fĭdēlĭa -ae, f. *an earthenware pot* or *vase*: Pl. prov.: duo parietes de eadem fidelia dealbare, *to kill two birds with one stone*, ap Cic. L.

fĭdēlis -e (¹fides) adj. (with compar. and superl.), *that can be trusted* or *relied upon, true steadfast, faithful.*

Lit., of persons: socius, amicus, Cic. alicui, Cic., Hor.; in aliquem, Cic., Sall M. as subst., esp. pl. **fĭdēles** -ium, *confidants faithful friends*: Cic. L.

Transf., of inanimate objects: consilium fidele, Cic.; opera, Caes., Cic.; cura, Lucr. lorica, *dependable*, Verg.

¶ N. sing. as adv. **fĭdēlĕ**, *faithfully*: Pl.

¶ Adv. **fĭdēlĭtěr** (compar.: Ov.; superl. Plin.). (1) in relation to a person, *faithfully* Cic., Ov. (2) in relation to a task, *soundly thoroughly*: didicisse fideliter artes, Ov (3) *securely, without danger*: per quorum loca fideliter mihi pateret iter, ap. Cic. L.

fĭdēlĭtās -ātis, f. (fidelis), *faithfulness, trust worthiness, fidelity*: Pl., Cic.

fĭdēlĭtěr, adv. from fidelis; q.v.

Fĭdēnae -ārum, f. and **Fĭdēna** -ae, f. *a tow in Latium* (now *Castel Giubileo*). Adj **Fĭdēnās** -ātis, *of Fidenae*: Liv.

fidens

fĭdens -entis, partic. from fido; q.v.

fīdentĭa -ae, f. (fido), *confidence, boldness*: Cic.

¹fĭdes -ĕi, f. (fido), *trust, confidence, reliance, credence, belief, faith.*

Lit., (1) in gen.: fidem decipere, Liv.; fallere, Cic.; fidem habere, *to place confidence in*, with dat., Pl., Lucr., Cic.; fidem tribuere, adiungere, Cic.; fidem facere, *to create confidence, cause belief*, Caes., Cic.; with acc. and infin.: Cic.; nuntiabantur haec eadem Curioni; sed aliquamdiu fides fieri non poterat, Caes. (2) as mercantile t. t., *credit*: cum fides totā Italiā esset angustior, *impaired*, Caes.; fidem moliri, Liv.; fides concidit, *has fallen*, Cic.; fides de foro sublata est, Cic.; often in contrast with res, *property*: res et fides, Sall.; ubi res eos iam pridem, fides nuper deficere coepit, Cic.; homo sine re, sine fide, sine spe, Cic.; fig.: segetis certa fides meae, Hor.

Transf., *that which produces confidence.* (1) in gen., *faithfulness, fidelity, conscientiousness, honesty*: exemplum antiquae probitatis ac fidei, Cic.; fidem praestare, *to be loyal*, Cic.; pro vetere ac perpetua erga Romanum fide, Caes.; as legal t. t.: ex bona fide *or* bonā fide, *in good faith, sincerely, honestly*, Cic.; iudicia de mala fide, *dishonesty*, Cic.; also of things, *credibility, trustworthiness*: Cic.; sometimes *actuality, fulfilment*: dicta fides sequitur, Ov. Fides personif. as a goddess: Cic., Verg., Hor. (2) esp. *a promise, assurance, word of honour, engagement*: fidem fallere, frangere, violare, prodere, *to break a promise*, Cic.; dare alicui, Pl., Cic., Verg.; obligare, *to make an engagement*, Cic.; servare, *to keep a promise*, Pl., Cic., Tac.; fide meā, *on my word of honour*, Cic. Often fides (*or* fides publica) is specifically *a promise of protection in the name of the state, a safe-conduct*: fidem publicam postulare, Cic.; Lusitani contra interpositam fidem interfecti, Cic.; fide acceptā venerat in castra Romana, Liv. Hence, without the notion of promise, *faithful protection, constant help*: conferre se in alicuius fidem et clientelam, in alicuius amicitiam et fidem, Cic.; se suaque omnia in fidem atque potestatem populi Romani permittere, Cic.; venire in alicuius fidem, Liv.; in alicuius fidem ac potestatem, Caes.; alicuius fidem sequi, Caes.; aliquem in fidem recipere, Cic.

²fĭdes -is, f., usually plur. **fĭdēs** -ium (σφίδη, or perhaps from findo). Lit., *a gut-string for a musical instrument*; hence *a lyre, lute, harp*: discere, Cic.; fidibus Latinis Thebanos aptare modos, Hor.; sing.: fides Teïa, Hor.

fĭdĭcĕn -cĭnis, m. (²fides/cano), *a player on the harp, lyre, lute*: Cic.; poet., *a lyric poet*: lyrae Romanae, Hor.; Ov.

fĭdĭcĭna -ae, f. (fidicen), *a female player on the lute or harp*: Pl., Ter.

fĭdĭcĭnus -a -um (fidicen), *relating to lute-playing*: Pl.

fĭdĭcŭla -ae, f., usually plur. **fĭdĭcŭlae** -ārum, f. (dim. of ²fides). (1) *a little lyre or lute*: Cic. (2) *an instrument for torturing slaves*: Suet.

³fĭdĭus -i, m. (¹fides), *a surname of Jupiter*; esp. in phrase: medius fidius! (ellipt.=ita me Dius Fidius iuvet), *So help me God!*: Cic. L., Sall., Plin.

fīdo fīdĕre fīsus sum, *to trust, believe, confide in*; with dat.: sibi, Cic. L., Hor.; nocti, Verg.; Liv.; with abl.: prudentiā, Cic.; fugā, Verg.; Ov.; with acc. and infin.: Hor., Luc.

¶ Hence partic. **fīdens** -entis, *without fear, confident, courageous*: homo, animus, Cic.; Verg., Tac.

¶ Adv. **fīdentĕr**, *confidently, boldly*: Cic.; compar.: Cic. L.

fīdūcĭa -ae, f. (fido). Lit., *confidence, trust, reliance, assurance*: alicuius, *in someone*, Cic.; arcae nostrae, Cic.; esp. with suī or absol., *self-confidence, self-reliance, courage, bravery*: Pl., Caes., Ov. Transf., (1) *fidelity*: Pl. (2) as legal t. t., *trust*: formula fiduciae, Cic.; fiducia accepta, Cic.

fīdūcĭārĭus -a -um (fiducia), *entrusted, committed, given in trust*: urbs, Liv.; opera, Caes.

fīdus -a -um (fido) adj. (with compar. and superl.), *true, faithful, trusty, sure.*

Lit., of persons: amici fidi, Cic.; with dat.: Abelux fidus ante Poenis, Liv.; with genit.: regina tui fidissima, Verg.

Transf., of inanimate objects: tam fida canum custodia, Cic.; pax, Liv.; statio male fida carinis, *an insecure anchorage for ships*, Verg.

¶ Superl. adv. **fīdissĭmē**, *most faithfully*: Cic. L.

figlīnus (**figŭlīnus**) -a -um (figulus), *of a potter*: Plin. F. as subst. **figlīna** -ae. (1) *the potter's art*: Plin. (2) *the potter's workshop*: Plin.; n. as subst. **figlīnum** -i, *earthenware*: Plin.

fīgo fīgĕre fixi fixum. (1) *to fix, fasten, make fast, make firm, attach, affix.* Lit., aliquem in cruce, Cic.; legit in poste curiae, Cic.; arma ad postem, Hor. Transf., esp. with oculos, *to fix the gaze*: Verg., Liv.; oscula, *to imprint*, Verg.; vestigia, Verg.; nequitiae modum suae, *to set a limit*, Hor.; omnia mea studia, Cic. L. (2) *to thrust home* a weapon, etc. so as to stick fast: palum in parietem, Pl.; mucronem in hoste, Cic. (3) *to transfix*: aliquem sagittā, Tac.; Verg. Transf., aliquem maledictis, *attack with reproaches*, Cic.

¶ Hence partic. **fixus** -a -um, *firm, fixed, immovable*: vestigia, Lucr.; decretum, Cic.

fĭgŭlāris -e (figulus), *of a potter*: rota, Pl.

fĭgŭlīnus=figlinus; q.v.

fĭgŭlus -i, m. (fingo), *a worker in clay, a potter*: a figulis munitam urbem, *Babylon, made of brick*, Juv.

fĭgūra -ae, f. (fingo), *form, shape, figure, size.* Lit., hominis, Cic.; Lucr., Caes., Ov.; esp. (1) *an atom*: Lucr. (2) *shade of a dead person*: Verg.

Transf., *kind, nature, species, form*: negotii, Cic.; in rhetoric, *a figure of speech*: Cic.

fĭgūrātus -a -um, partic. from figuro; q.v.

fĭgūro -are (figura), *to form, mould, shape.* Lit., ita figuratum corpus ut excellat aliis, Cic.; Ov., Tac. Transf., os tenerum pueri balbumque poeta figurat, Hor.; rhet. t. t., *to adorn with figures*: Quint.

fīlātim, adv. (filum), *thread by thread*: Lucr.

fīlĭa -ae, f. (dat. and abl. pl. often filiābus) (from filius), *a daughter*: virgo filia, Cic.; poet.: pinus silvae filia nobilis, Hor.

[247]

fīlĭcātus -a -um (filix), *adorned with ferns*: paterae, *embossed* or *chased with fern leaves*, Cic.

fīlĭŏla -ae, f. (dim. of filia), *a little daughter*: Pl., Cic.; sarcastically of an effeminate man: duce filiolā Curionis, Cic.

fīlĭŏlus -i, m. (dim. of filius), *a little son*: Pl., Cic. L.

fīlĭus -i (voc. sing. fīlī), m. *a son*: Pl., Cic., Hor.; special phrases: filius terrae, *a nobody*, *an unknown person*: Cic.; filius fortunae, *a child of fortune*: Ov.

fīlix -icis, f. *fern*: Verg., Hor.

fīlum -i, n. *a thread*. LIT., (1) of wool, linen, etc.: velamina filo pleno, Ov.; prov.: pendere filo (tenui), *to hang by a thread, be in great danger*, Ov. (2) *a woollen fillet round the cap of the flamen*: capite velato filo, Liv. (3) *any thread* or *cord*: deducit aranea filum pede, Ov. (4) *the thread of life* spun by the Parcae: sororum fila trium, Hor. TRANSF., *form, shape*: Pl., Lucr.; of speech or writing, *texture, thread*: orationis Cic.; Hor.

fimbrĭae -ārum, f. pl. *fringe, border, edge*: madentes cincinnorum fimbriae, *extremities*, Cic.

fimbrĭātus -a -um (fimbriae), *fringed*: Suet.

fīmus -i, m. (and **fīmum** -i, n.), *dung, excrement, dirt*: Verg., Liv.

findo findĕre fĭdi fissum, *to split, cleave*. LIT., lignum, Verg.; findere agros sarculo, Hor.; hāc insulā quasi rostro finditur Fibrenus, Cic. TRANSF., *to divide, halve*: Hor.

¶ Hence partic. **fissus** -a -um, *split, cloven*; n. as subst. **fissum** -i, *a split, cleft*; in augury, *a divided liver*: Cic.

fingo fingĕre finxi fictum, *to shape, fashion, form, mould*.

LIT., mollissimam ceram ad nostrum arbitrium formare et fingere, Cic.; imago ficta, *a statue*, Cic.; natura fingit hominem, Cic.; also *to arrange, put in order* what already exists: crinem, Verg.

TRANSF., (1) *to form*: oratorem, Cic.; se totum ad arbitrium alicuius, Cic.; carmina, Hor.; *to form for a purpose*: ad honestatem, Cic.; *to form into* something: miserum fortuna Sinonem finxit, Verg. (2) *to represent, imagine, conceive*: fingite igitur cogitatione imaginem huius condicionis meae, Cic.; with acc. and infin.: finge aliquem fieri sapientem, Cic. (3) *to feign, invent, fabricate, devise*: crimina, opprobria in aliquem, Cic.; nihil fingam, nihil dissimulem, Cic.; fingere vultum, *to put on an artificial expression*, Caes., Ov.

¶ Hence partic. **fictus** -a -um, *feigned, false*; of things: fabula, Cic.; gemitus, Ov.; of persons: Hor. N. as subst. **fictum** -i, *a falsehood*: Verg., Ov.

fīnĭo -ire (finis), *to bound, limit, enclose within limits*.

LIT., imperium populi Romani, Caes.; lingua finita dentibus, Cic.; Ov., Liv.

TRANSF., (1) *to enclose within bounds, restrain*: an potest cupiditas finiri? Cic. (2) *to define, determine, prescribe, appoint*: sepulcris novis modum, Cic.; with ne and the subj.: potuisse finire senatus consulto ne, Liv. (3) *to put an end to, conclude, end, finish*; and pass., *to end, cease*: bellum, Caes.; labores, Cic.: omnia finierat (of a speaker), Ov.;

finitā Claudiorum domo, *having become extinct*, Tac.; ut sententiae verbis finiantur, Cic. (4) *without an object, to finish* doing something: illi philosopho placet ordiri a superiore paeone, posteriore finire, Cic.; sic Tiberius finivit, *died*, Tac.; finierat Telamone satus, *had finished speaking*, Ov.

¶ Hence pres. partic. **fīnĭens** -entis; as adj.: finiens orbis, *the horizon*, Cic.

¶ Perf. partic. **fīnītus** -a -um; of a phrase, *well-rounded*: Cic. Adv. **fīnītē**, *moderately, within bounds*: Cic.

fīnis -is, m. (sometimes f. in sing.; old abl. sing. fīnī: Lucr.) (perhaps connected with findo), *boundary, limit, border*.

LIT., eius loci, Cic.; provinciae Galliae, Liv.; plur., *enclosed area, territory*: iter in Santonum fines facere, Caes.; Cic., Verg.

TRANSF., (1) *bound, limit*: mihi fines terminosque constituam, extra quos egredi non possum, Cic.; ad eum finem, *so far*, Cic.; abl. fine, with genit., *as far as*: fine genūs, Ov. (2) *end*: finis vitae, Cic.; ad finem venire, Liv.; finem facere, with genit. of noun or gerund: Lucr., Caes., Cic.; with dat.: Ter., Caes., Cic.; absol.=*death*: Neronis, Tac.; Hor. (3) *summit, extremity*: bonorum, malorum, *greatest good, greatest evil*, Cic.; Tac. (4) *object, end, aim*: domus finis et usus, Cic.

fīnĭtĭmus (**fīnĭtŭmus**) -a -um (finis), *neighbouring, adjacent*.

LIT., Galli Belgis, Caes.; aër mari finituma, Cic. M. pl. as subst. **fīnĭtĭmi** -ōrum, *neighbours*: Caes., Cic., Liv.

TRANSF., *related to, resembling, similar*: vicina eius atque finitima dialecticorum scientia, Cic.; with dat.: huic generi historia finitima est, Cic.

fīnĭtor -ōris, m. (finio), *one who determines boundaries, a land surveyor*: Pl., Cic. TRANSF., *the horizon*: Sen., Luc.

fīo fĭĕri factus sum (connected with φύω), used as pass. of facio.

(1) of persons and things, *to be made, come into existence*: nullam rem e nilo fieri, Lucr.; fit clamor, Caes.; id ei loco nomen factum, Liv.; with predicate *to become, be appointed*: consules facti sunt, Cic.; with genit., *to be valued*: me a te plurimi fieri, Cic. L.

(2) of actions, *to be done*; of events, *to happen*; with abl.: quid illo fiet? *what will happen to him?* Cic.; with de: quid de Tulliola mea fiet? Cic.; often without subject expressed: ut fit, ut fit plerumque, Cic.; often followed by clause: fit saepe ut non respondeant ad tempus, Cic.; potest fieri ut fallar, *I may be deceived*, Cic.; ita fit ut sapientia sanitas sit animi, *so it follows that*, Cic.; fieri non potest quin, *it must be that*, Cic.; per aliquem fit quominus, Cic.

firmāmen -inis, n. (firmo), *support, prop*: Ov.

firmāmentum -i, n. (firmo), *a means of support, a prop*. LIT., transversaria tigna, quae firmamento esse possint, Cic.; Caes. TRANSF., in gen.: reipublicae, Cic.; in rhetoric, *the main point* in an argument: Cic.

firmātor -ōris, m. (firmo), *one who makes firm* or *establishes*: Tac., Plin.

firmĭtās -ātis, f. (firmus), *firmness, stability*. LIT., corporis, Cic. TRANSF., *strength of mind, constancy*: animi, Cic.

firmĭtūdo -dinis, f. (firmus), *firmness, stability.* Lit., operis, Caes. Transf., *strength, firmness, constancy*: animi, Pl., Cic., Tac.

firmo -are (firmus), *to make firm, strengthen.* Lit., corpora, Cic., Liv.; urbem colonis, Cic.; castra munimentis, Liv. Transf., (1) in gen., *to make durable, make secure*: pacem, Caes., Liv.; rempublicam, Cic.; vocem, Cic.; animum adulescentis nondum consilio et ratione firmatum, Cic. (2) esp. *to encourage, cheer, animate*: nostros, Caes.; cunctos adloquio, Tac. (3) *to prove, establish*: aliquid rationibus, iure iurando, Cic. (4) *to assert, maintain*: Lucr., Tac.

Firmum -i, n. *a town in Picenum* (now *Fermo*). Adj. **Firmānus** -a -um, *of Firmum.*

firmus -a -um, *firm, strong, stout.* Lit., rami, Caes.; carina, Ov.; vina, Verg.; with dat.: area firma templis ac porticibus sustinendis, Liv.; of health, *strong, healthy*: corpus Cic. Transf., (1) in gen., *strong*: equitatus et peditatus Cic.; ad dimicandum, Caes.; acta Caesaris, *lasting, valid*: Cic.; spes, litterae, Cic. (2) esp. *morally strong*: animus, Cic.; accusator, Cic.; contra pericula, Sall.; firmior in sententia, Cic.; copiae et numero et genere et fidelitate firmissimae, Cic.; Verg., Liv., Tac.

¶ Adv. **firmē**, *firmly, steadfastly*: aliquid comprehendere, Cic.; firmissime adseverare, Cic.

¶ Adv. (with compar. and superl.) **firmĭtĕr**, *firmly, strongly*: firmiter insistere, Caes. firmiter stabilire aliquem, Cic.; Pl., Ov.

fiscella -ae, f. (dim. of fiscina), *a small basket*: Cic.

fiscĭna -ae, f. (fiscus), *a small basket*: Pl., Cic., Verg.

fiscus -i, m. originally *a basket*; hence *a moneybag, purse*: Cic. Transf., (1) *the state treasury*: Cic. (2) under the empire, *the emperor's privy purse* (opp. aerarium, *the state treasury*): Tac., Suet. (3) *money*: Juv.

fissĭlis -e (findo). (1) *that can be cloven or split*: lignum, Verg. (2) *split*: Pl.

fissĭo -ōnis, f. (findo), *a splitting, cleaving, dividing*: glebarum, Cic.

fistūca -ae, f. *a rammer, mallet*: Caes.

fistŭla -ae, f. *a tube, pipe.* (1) *a water-pipe*, usually of lead: fistulas, quibus aqua suppeditabatur Iovis templis, praecidere, Cic.; Ov., Liv. (2) *a reed-pipe, a shepherd's pipe*: eburneola, *a pitch-pipe of ivory*, Cic. (3) *a kind of ulcer, fistula*: Nep.

fistŭlātor -ōris, m. (fistula), *one who plays upon the reed-pipe*: Cic.

fixus -a -um, partic. from figo; q.v.

flābellĭfĕra -ae, f. (flabellum/fero), *a girl with a fan*: Pl.

flābellum -i, n. (dim. of flabrum), *a small fan*: Ter., Prop.; fig.: cuius linguā quasi flabello seditionis illa tum est egentium contio ventilata, Cic.

flābilis -e (flo), *airy*: Cic.

flābrum -i, n. (flo), used in plur. **flābra** -ōrum, *blasts of wind, breezes*: Lucr., Verg.

flaccĕo -ēre (flaccus), *to be flabby.* Transf., *to fail or flag*: Messala flaccet, Cic. L.

flaccesco flaccescĕre flaccŭi (flacceo), *to begin to flag become flabby*: flaccescebat oratio, Cic.

flaccĭdus -a -um (flaccus), *flabby*; hence *weak, languid*: Lucr.

¹**flaccus** -a -um, *flabby*: Varr. Transf., of men, *flap-eared*: Cic.

²**Flaccus**, Q. Horatius, *see* Horatius.

³**Flaccus**, C. Valerius, *see* Valerius.

flăgello -are (flagellum), *to whip, scourge, beat*: Ov., Mart., Suet.

flăgellum -i, n. (dim. of flagrum), *a whip.* Lit., *a scourge*: Cic., Hor.; *a riding-whip*: Verg. Transf., (1) *the thong of a javelin*: Verg. (2) *a young sprout, vine-shoot*: Verg. (3) plur.: flagella, *the arms of a polypus*, Ov. (4) fig., *the sting* of conscience: Lucr., Juv.; of love: Hor.

flăgĭtātĭo -ōnis, f. (flagito), *an earnest demand or entreaty*: Cic.

flăgĭtātor -ōris, m. (flagito), *one who earnestly demands or entreats*: Pl., Cic.; with genit.: pugnae, Liv.

flăgĭtĭōsus -a -um (flagitium), *shameful, disgraceful, infamous*: flagitiosa atque vitiosa vita, Cic.; flagitiosum est, with acc. and infin., Sall.; fama, Tac.

¶ Adv. (with superl.) **flăgĭtĭōsē**, *shamefully, infamously*: impure ac flagitiose vivere, Cic.

flăgĭtĭum -i, n. (connected with flagito and flagro), *a disgraceful action, shameful crime*: flagitia et adulteria, Tac.; ista flagitia Democriti, *shameful expressions*, Cic. Transf., (1) *shame, disgrace*: dedecus et flagitium, Cic.; Liv. (2) *a scoundrel, rascal*: Pl., Sall.

flăgĭto -are (perhaps connected with flagro), *to entreat, ask, demand earnestly.* In gen.: stipendium, Caes.; alicuius auxilium, Cic.; mercedem gloriae ab aliquo, Cic.; with double acc.: aliquem frumentum, Cic.; with ut and the subj.: semper flagitavi ut convocaremur, Cic.; with infin.: Hor.; of abstr. subjects: quae tempus flagitat, Cic. Esp. (1) *to demand to know*: posco atque adeo flagito crimen, Cic. (2) *to summon before a court of justice*: aliquem ut peculatorem, Tac.

flagrans -antis, partic. from flagro; q.v.

flagrantĭa -ae, f. (flagro), *a burning, blazing, glittering*: oculorum, Cic.

flagritrība -ae, m. (flagrum/τϱίβω), *one that wears out whips, a whipping boy*: Pl.

flagro -are (connected with φλέγω), *to blaze, burn, glow, flame.* Lit., onerariae flagrantes, Cic.; Verg., Ov.; also *to glitter*: flagrant lumina nymphae, Ov. Transf., (1) *to glow or burn with passion*: desiderio, amore, cupiditate, odio, studio dicendi, Cic.; Hor., Liv. (2) *to suffer from*, with abl.: invidiā, Cic.; Hor., Tac. (3) with abstr. thing as subject: flagrabant vitia libidinis apud illum, Cic.; Sall.

¶ Hence partic. (with compar. and superl.) **flagrans** -antis, *blazing, burning.* Lit., telum, Verg.; aestus, Liv.; also *glittering*: oculi, Cic.; Verg. Transf., *passionate, ardent*: cupiditas, Cic.

¶ Adv. **flagrantĕr**, *passionately, ardently*: Tac.

flagrum -i, n. *a scourge, whip*, esp. as used for punishing slaves: flagro caedi, Liv.; Pl., Juv.

¹**flāmen** -inis, m. *the priest of some particular deity*; there were three flamines maiores,

Dialis *of Jupiter* (the highest in rank), Martialis, *of Mars*, and Quirinalis, *of Romulus*, and twelve flamines minores (Vulcani, Florae, etc.): flaminem inaugurare, Liv.

²flāmen -inis, n. (flo), *a blowing, blast.* (1) of wind: flamina venti, Lucr.; ferunt sua flamina classem, Verg. (2) on a wind instrument: flamina tibiae, *the notes of a flute*, Hor.

flāmĭnĭca -ae, f. (¹flamen), *the wife of a flamen*: flaminica Dialis, Tac.; Ov.

Flāmĭnīnus, *a surname in the patrician gens* Quinctia; *see* Quinctius.

flāmĭnĭum -i, n. (¹flamen), *the office of a flamen*: Cic., Liv., Tac.

Flāmĭnĭus -a -um, *name of a Roman gens; its most famous member was C. Flaminius Nepos, who was defeated by Hannibal at Lake Trasimenus.* As adj., *Flaminian, of a Flaminius*; esp. via Flaminia, *the road built by the above.*

flamma -ae, f. (flagro), *a flame, blaze, blazing fire.*

LIT., solis, Lucr.; se flammā eripere, Cic.; flammam concipere, *to catch fire*, Caes.; prov.: prius undis flamma miscebitur, *sooner will fire mingle with water*, of something impossible, poet. ap. Cic.

TRANSF., (1) *a source of light, a torch, star, lightning*: Cic., Verg. (2) *lustre, glitter*: galea flammas vomens, Verg. (3) fig., *the fire or glow of passion*, esp. of love: amoris, Cic.; Hor., Ov.; gulae, *raging hunger*, Ov. (4) *devouring flame, destruction*: civilis belli, Cic. L.; invidiae, Cic.

flammĕŏlum -i, n. (dim. of flammeum), *a small bridal veil*: Juv.

flammesco -ĕre (flamma), *to become inflamed*: Lucr.

flammĕus -a -um (flamma), *fiery, flaming.* LIT., stellae, Cic. TRANSF., *flashing, flame-coloured, fiery-red*: corpora, Lucr., Ov.

¶ N. as subst. **flammĕum** -i, *a (flame-coloured) bridal veil*: flammeum capere, Cat.; Juv.

flammĭfer -fĕra -fĕrum (flamma/fero), *flame-bearing, flaming, fiery*: Ov.

flammo -are (flamma). (1) intransit., *to flame, blaze, burn*: flammantia lumina, *glittering*, Verg. (2) transit., *to set on fire, inflame*. LIT., ut interirent crucibus adfixi aut flammandi, Tac. TRANSF., flammato corde, *with angry passion*, Verg.; Tac.

flammŭla -ae, f. (dim. of flamma), *a little flame*: Cic.

flātus -ūs, m. (flo), *a blowing, blast, breathing.* LIT., Alpini boreae, Verg.; equorum, Verg. TRANSF., (1) of fortune: prospero flatu fortunae utimur, Cic. (2) *haughtiness, arrogance*, gen. in plur.: Verg., Ov.

flāvens -entis (flavus), *yellow* or *gold-coloured*: coma, Verg.; harena, Verg.; Ov.

flāvesco -ĕre (flavus), *to become yellow* or *gold-coloured*: campus flavescet aristā, Verg.; Ov.

Flāvĭus -a -um, *name of a Roman gens, to which the emperors Vespasian, Titus, and Domitian belonged.* As adj., *Flavian, of a Flavius*; so also adj. **Flāvĭālis** -e and **Flāvĭānus** -a -um.

flāvus -a -um (connected with flagro), *golden-yellow, gold-coloured, yellow*: arva, Verg.; crines, Verg.; aurum, Verg.; decem flavos, *ten gold pieces*, Mart.

flēbĭlis -e (fleo). Pass., *lamentable, wretched, deserving tears*: illa species, Cic.; multis ille bonis flebilis occidit, Hor. Act., *tearful, doleful*, of persons: Ino, Hor.; Ov.; of things: gemitus, Cic.; Hor., Ov., Liv.

¶ Adv. **flēbĭlĭter**, *tearfully, dolefully*: Cic., Hor., Liv.

flecto flectĕre flexi flexum, *to bend.*

(1) *to alter the shape of, to bow, twist, curve.* LIT., membra, Cic.; arcūs, Verg., Ov. TRANSF., *to change, alter, influence*: vitam, Cic.; fata deum, Verg.; (animus) flectitur a medicina, Lucr.; flecti misericordiā, Liv.; nihil flexerunt animos quin collem defenderent, Liv.

(2) *to alter the direction of, to turn, wheel.* LIT., equos, Caes.; currum de foro in Capitolium, Cic.; plaustrum, Ov.; oculos, Verg.; vocem, *to modulate*, Cic.; esp. with iter, viam, cursum as object expressed or understood: Verg., Liv.; pass. as middle: flecti in gyrum, *to turn round in a circle*, Ov.; so with reflex.: hinc (silva) se flectit sinistrorsus, Caes. TRANSF., in gen., *to turn in a certain direction*: aliquem a proposito, Liv.; a studio ad imperium, Cic.; sometimes without object expressed, *to turn, resort*: ad sapientiam, Tac.

flĕo flēre flēvi flētum (syncop. perf. forms: flesti, Ov.; flerunt, Verg.; flesse, Liv.).

(1) intransit., *to weep*: de filii morte, Cic.; lapides flere et lamentari cogere, Cic.; Pl., Caes., Hor. TRANSF., *to drip, trickle*: Lucr.

(2) transit., *to weep for, lament, bewail*: aliquem, Pl., Cat., Hor., Ov.; meum casum, Cic.; filii necem, Tac.; flendus, *worthy of being lamented*, Ov.; fletus, *wept for, lamented*, Verg.

¹flētus -a -um, partic. of fleo; q.v.

²flētus -ūs, m. (fleo), *a weeping, bewailing*: clamore et fletu omnia complere, Cic.; urbe totā fletus gemitusque fieret, Cic.; Verg., Ov.

flexănimus -a -um (flecto/animus). Act., *moving, affecting*: oratio, Pac. ap. Cic. Pass., *affected, touched, moved*: Pac. ap. Cic.

flexĭbilis -e (flecto), *that can be bent, flexible.* LIT., materia rerum, Cic. TRANSF., (1) of speech or the voice, *adaptable*: vocis genus, Cic.; nihil est tam flexibile quam oratio, Cic. (2) in a bad sense, *fickle, changeable*: animus, Cic.

flexĭlis -e (flecto), *flexible, pliant, supple*: cornu, Ov.

flexĭlŏquus -a -um (flexus/loquor), *having two meanings, equivocal, ambiguous*: Cic.

flexĭo -ōnis, f. (flecto), *a bending*: virili laterum flexione, Cic.; vocis or modorum, *modulation of the voice*, Cic. TRANSF., deverticula flexionesque, *twists and turns*, Cic.

flexĭpēs -pĕdis (flexus/pes), *crooked-footed*: hederae, *twining*, Ov.

flexŭōsus -a -um (flexus), *full of windings and turnings, crooked*: iter (of the ear), Cic.

flexūra -ae, f. (flecto), *a bending*: Lucr., Suet.

¹flexus -a -um, partic. of flecto; q.v.

²flexus -ūs, m. (flecto), *a bending, turning.* LIT., duros introitus habent (aures) multis cum flexibus, Cic.; flexus vallium, Liv.; in quo flexus est ad iter Arpinas, *turn of the road*, Cic. L.; of the voice, *modulation*: Quint. TRANSF., in gen., *change, alteration*: itinera flexūsque rerum publicarum, Cic.

flictus -ūs, m. (fligo), *a striking together,
dashing against*: cavae dant sonitum flictu
galeae, Verg.

fligo -ĕre, *to beat* or *dash down*: Lucr.

flo flāre flāvi flātum, *to blow*. (**1**) intransit., of
winds: qui ventus in his locis flare consuevit,
Cic.; of persons: scintillam levem flando
accenderunt, Liv.; of the flute: protinus
inflexo Berecyntia tibia cornu flabit, Ov. (**2**)
transit.: **a**, *to blow, blow forth*: flammam,
Lucr.: **b**, *to blow on* an instrument: furiosa
tibia flatur, Ov. (**3**) *to cast metals, to coin*:
flare pecuniam, Cic.

floccus -i, m. *a flock of wool*: Varr.; prov., as a
measure of indifference, *a trifle, straw*: Pl.,
Ter.; esp. in genit. with facere, and in neg.:
flocci non facere, *to think nothing of*, Cic. L.

Flōra -ae, f. (flos), *the goddess of flowers and
Spring*. Adj. **Flōrālis** -e, *belonging to Flora*;
n. pl. as subst. **Flōrālia** -ium, *the festival of
Flora*; **Flōrālīcius** -a -um, *relating to the
festival of Flora*.

flōrens -entis, partic. from floreo; q.v.

Flōrentia -ae, f. *a town in Etruria* (now
Florence). Adj. **Flōrentīnus** -a -um, *Floren-
tine*.

flōrĕo -ēre -ŭi (flos), *to bloom, flower*.
LIT., haec arbor ter floret, Cic.; Lucr.,
Verg., Ov.
TRANSF., (**1**) *to be in one's prime, to prosper,
flourish, be in high repute*: floret Epicurus,
Cic.; verborum vetus interit aetas, et
iuvenum ritu florent modo nata virentque,
Hor.; with abl.: gratiā et auctoritate, Cic.;
honoribus, Cic. (**2**) *to be bright with, abound
in, swarm with*: mare velivolis puppibus,
Lucr.; urbes pueris, Lucr.; Cic.
¶ Hence partic. (with compar. and
superl.) **flōrens** -entis, *blooming, flourishing*.
LIT., cytisus, Verg.; arva, Ov. TRANSF.,
florens orationis genus, Cic.; aetas, Lucr., Cic.,
Liv.; fortuna, Caes.; res publica florentis-
sima, Cic.; florentes aere catervae, *glittering*,
Verg.; urbs, Liv.; with abl.: gratiā atque
hospitiis florens hominum nobilissimorum,
Cic.

flōresco -ĕre (floreo), *to begin to blossom, come
into flower*. LIT., Lucr., Cic. TRANSF., *to
begin to flourish*: Sulpicius ad summam
gloriam florescens, Cic.; Lucr., Plin.

flōreus -a -um (flos). (**1**) *made of flowers*: serta,
Tib.; Pl. (**2**) *rich in flowers, flowery*: rura,
Verg.

flōrĭdŭlus -a -um (dim. of floridus), *somewhat
blooming*: Cat.

flōridus -a -um (flos), *flowery*. LIT., (**1**)
blossoming: ramuli, Cat. (**2**) *made of flowers*:
serta, Ov. (**3**) *rich in flowers*: Hybla, Ov.
TRANSF., (**1**) *of age, fresh, blooming*: novitas
mundi, Lucr.; aetas, Cat. (**2**) *of speech,
flowery, florid*: Demetrius est floridior, Cic.

flōrifer -fĕra -fĕrum (flos/fero), *flower-bearing*:
Lucr., Cic.

flōrĭlĕgus a -um (flos/lego), *culling flowers*:
apes, Ov.

Flōrus -i, m. *a Roman historian of the second
century A.D., who composed an epitome of
Roman military history*.

flōs flōris, m. *a flower, blossom*.
LIT., florum omnium varietas, Cic.; Lucr.,
Verg., etc.; meton.: flores, *the juice of
flowers*, Verg.

TRANSF., (**1**) *the prime, flower* of anything,
the best, the pride; esp. of youth: flos aetatis,
the flower of youth, Cic.; flos iuventae, Liv.;
flos=*first beard, down*: Verg.; of other things:
flos totius Italiae ac robur, Cic.; virium, Liv.;
vini, *bouquet*, Pl., Lucr.; flammai, Lucr.
(**2**) of speech, *ornament*: Cic., Quint.

floscŭlus -i, m. (dim. of flos), *a little flower*.
LIT., ficta omnia tamquam flosculi decidunt,
Cic. TRANSF., (**1**) *best part, pride*: vitae, Juv.
(**2**) of speech, *ornament*: omni ex genere
orationis flosculos carpam, Cic.; Quint.

fluctĭfrăgus -a -um (fluctus/frango), *wave-
breaking*: Lucr.

fluctŭātĭo -ōnis, f. (fluctuo), *a moving backwards and forwards, fluctuation*. TRANSF., *indecision*: animorum, Liv.

fluctŭo -are (fluctus), *to be in wave-like motion,
move up and down*. LIT., mare, Pl.; Lucr.,
Cic. TRANSF., (**1**) of a *glittering* effect:
fluctuat omnis aere renidenti tellus, Verg.
(**2**) of persons and passions, *to be tossed about,
to waver*: animus, Pl.; ira, Verg.; in suo
decreto, Cic.; of speech: oratio quasi
fluctuans, Cic.

fluctŭor -ari -ātus sum, dep. *to toss about,
waver*; cf. fluctuo. LIT., Sen., Plin. TRANSF.,
fluctuatus animo est, Liv.

fluctŭōsus -a -um (fluctus), *full of waves,
stormy*: mare, Pl.

fluctus -ūs, m. (fluo). LIT., *a streaming, flowing*: Lucr.; hence *a wave, wave of the sea,
billow*: Cic., Verg., esp. in plur.; prov.: excitare fluctus in simpulo, *to raise a storm in a
teacup, make much ado about nothing*, Cic.
TRANSF., *commotion, disturbance*: fluctus
contionum, Cic.; irarum, Lucr., Verg.

flŭens -entis, partic. from fluo; q.v.

flŭentĭsŏnus -a -um (fluentum/sono), *resounding with waves*: Cat.

flŭentum -i, n. (fluo), used in plur.; *running
water, a stream*: rauca Cocyti, Verg.; Lucr.

flŭĭdus -a -um (fluo), *flowing, fluid*. LIT.,
cruor, Verg.; Lucr., Ov. TRANSF., (**1**) *lax,
languid*: frondes, Lucr.; pendere lacertos,
Ov. (**2**) *relaxing*: calor, Ov.

flŭĭto -are (freq. of fluo), *to flow hither and
thither*.
LIT., (**1**) of moving liquids: fusile per
rictus aurum fluitare videres, Ov. (**2**) of
objects in or on a liquid, *to float, swim, sail,
move up and down, be tossed about*: navem
fluitantem in alto tempestatibus, Cic.; Verg.,
Ov., Liv.
TRANSF., (**1**) *to flutter, flap about*: fluitantia
vela, Ov.; Lucr., Tac. (**2**) *to waver, vacillate*:
mobilia et caeca fluitantia sorte, Hor.; fides,
Tac.

flūmen -ĭnis, n. (fluo), *a flowing*; hence *a
stream*. LIT., flumine vivo, *running water*,
Verg.; flumine secundo, *downstream*, Caes.;
flumine adverso, *upstream*, Caes. Esp. *one
particular stream, a river*: Garumna flumen,
Caes. TRANSF., (**1**) *a stream of anything*;
of blood: Lucr.; of tears: Verg. (**2**) *of words,
flood, flow, stream*: flumen orationis aureum,
Cic.; Quint.

Flūmentāna porta (flumen), *the river-gate,
a gate in Rome near the Campus Martius*: Liv.

flūmĭnĕus -a -um (flumen), *of a river*: Ov.

flŭo flŭĕre fluxi fluxum, *to flow*.
LIT., (**1**) of water and other fluids, *to flow*:

ut flumina in contrarias partes fluxerint, Cic.;
fluit de corpore sudor, Ov. (2) of a solid
object, *to flow, drip with any liquid*: cruore,
Ov.; sudore, Ov.
  TRANSF., (1) of moving bodies in gen., *to
flow, stream, pour*: venti fluunt, Lucr.;
ramos compesce fluentes, Verg.; of a crowd:
turba fluit castris, Verg. (2) of abstr.
things, *to proceed, issue, spread*: Pythagorae
doctrina cum longe lateque flueret, Cic.;
haec omnia ex eodem fonte fluxerunt, Cic.
(3) of circumstances, *to tend*: in rebus
prosperis et ad voluntatem fluentibus, Cic.;
res fluit ad interregnum, Cic. (4) of language,
to flow: oratio, Cic.; carmen, Ov. (5) *to sink,
droop*: mollitiā, Cic.; fluent arma de manibus,
Cic.; fluit voluptas corporis, Cic.; ad terram
cervix, Verg.; tempora, Hor.
  ¶ Hence pres. partic. **flŭens** -entis,
flowing; hence (1) *lax*: Campani fluentes
luxu, Cic. (2) of speech, *fluent*: oratio, Cic.;
also in bad sense, *diffuse*: ut ne aut dissoluta
aut fluens sit oratio, Cic.; Quint.
  ¶ Adv. **flŭentĕr**, *in a flowing manner*:
Lucr.
  ¶ Past. partic. **fluxus** -a -um, *flowing*;
hence *leaky*: Lucr. TRANSF., (1) of solid
objects, *waving, fluttering, loose*: crines, Tac.;
habena, Liv. (2) of character, *lax, loose,
weak*: animus, Sall. (3) of abstr. things,
fleeting, unstable: gloria, Sall.; fides, Pl.,
Sall., Liv.
flŭto -are (for fluito), *to flow, float, swim*: Lucr.
flŭviālis -e (fluvius), *of a river*: undae, Verg.;
anas, Ov.
flŭviātilis -e (fluvius), *of a river*: testudo, Cic.,
Liv.
flŭvĭdus -a -um (fluo)=fluidus; *flowing, fluid*:
Lucr.
flŭvĭus -ĭi, m. (fluo), *flowing water, a stream,
river*: fluvius Eurotas, Cic.; Verg.
¹**fluxus** -a -um, partic. from fluo; q.v.
²**fluxus** -ūs, m. (fluo), *a flowing*: Plin.
fŏcāle -is, n. (for faucale, from fauces), *a
wrapper for the neck*: Hor., Quint.
fŏcillo -are, *to warm up, refresh by warmth*.
LIT., Plin. TRANSF., Sen., Suet.
fŏcula -orum, n. pl. *stoves*: Pl.
fŏcŭlus -i, m. (dim. of focus), *a brazier*: Liv.,
Juv.
fŏcus -i, m. *a fireplace*; esp. (1) *the fireplace
in a house, hearth*: Pl., Cic., Verg.; meton.,
house, family, home: domo et focis patriis
eicere, Cic.; Ter., Hor. (2) *an altar-fire*: Ov.
(3) *a funeral pyre*: Verg.
fŏdico -are (fodio), *to dig*: latus, *to dig in the
ribs*, Hor. TRANSF., fodicantibus iis rebus
quas malas esse opinemur, *pricking, jogging*,
Cic.
fŏdĭo fŏdĕre fōdi fossum, *to dig*.
  LIT., fodit, invenit auri aliquantum, Cic.;
humum, Verg.; also *to dig out*: argentum,
Liv.; *to excavate*: puteum, Caes.; fossam, Liv.
  TRANSF., *to prick, prod*. (1) physically:
pectora telis, Ov.; aversos (elephantos) sub
caudis, Liv.; Verg., Tac. (2) mentally: cor
stimulo, Pl.; pungit dolor, vel fodiat sane,
Cic.
foecundus, foecundo=fecundus, fecundo;
q.v.
foedĕrātus -a -um (²foedus), *confederate,
allied*: civitates, Cic.

foedĭfrăgus -a -um (²foedus/frango), *treaty-
breaking*: Poeni, Cic.
foedĭtās -ātis, f. (¹foedus), *foulness, hideousness,
filthiness*. LIT., physical: odoris intolerabilis
foeditas, Cic.; vestitus, Cic. TRANSF., moral:
turpificati animi, Cic.; decreti, Liv.
foedo -are (¹foedus), *to make foul, make filthy,
defile, deform, disfigure*. LIT., physically:
pectora pugnis, Verg.; canitiem pulvere, Ov.;
aliquid sanguine, Ov.; agri foedati, *laid
waste*, Liv. TRANSF., morally, *to dishonour,
disgrace*: aliquem nefario scelere, Cic.; Lucr.
¹**foedus** -a -um, adj. (with compar. and superl.),
foul, filthy, horrible, abominable.
  LIT., physically: monstrum foedissimum,
Cic.; foedi oculi, *bloodshot*, Sall.; Lucr.
Verg., Hor.; with dat.: pestilentia foeda
homini, Liv.; with supine: rem non modo
visu foedam sed etiam auditu, Cic.
  TRANSF., morally: bellum foedissimum,
Cic. L.; consilium, Liv.; Verg., Hor.; with
supine: foedum inceptu, Liv.
  ¶ Adv. (with compar. and superl.) **foedē**,
foully, horribly, cruelly: foede exercere victoriam, Liv.; foedius pulsi, Liv.; foedissime
agere causam, Cic.
²**foedus** -ĕris, n. *a league*.
  LIT., (1) between states: foedus facere
cum aliquo, *or* icere, *or* ferire, Cic.; foedus
frangere, rumpere, violare, Cic.; Caes., Liv.,
Verg. (2) *a compact, covenant, agreement
between individuals*: amorum, Cic.; inter se
facere, Cic.; thalami, Ov.
  TRANSF., *a law*: naturae, Lucr.; Verg., Ov.
foen-. *see* faen-.
foetĕo -ēre, *to have a bad smell, to stink*: Pl.
foetĭdus -a -um (foeteo), *having a bad smell,
stinking, fetid*: os, Cic.; Pl., Suet.
foetor -ōris, m. (foeteo), *a bad smell, stink*: Cic.
foetus, *see* fetus.
Fōlĭa -ae, f. *a witch of Ariminum*: Hor.
fŏlĭātus -a -um (folium), *leafy*: Plin.; n. as
subst. **fŏlĭātum** -i (sc. unguentum), *a salve
or oil of spikenard leaves*: Juv.
fŏlĭum -i, n. (connected with φύλλον), *a leaf*:
Pl., Cic., Hor., Verg.
follĭculus -i, m. (dim. of follis), *a little sack
or bag*: Cic., Liv.; esp. *an inflated ball*: Suet.
follis -is, m. *a leather bag*. Esp. (1) *a pair of
bellows*: Cic., Verg.; follis fabrilis, Liv. (2) *a
purse*: Juv. (3) *puffed-out cheeks*: folles
spirant mendacia, Juv.
fōmentum -i, n. (foveo), *a poultice, fomentation*: Hor., Tac., Suet. TRANSF., *alleviation*:
summorum malorum, Cic.; Hor., Tac.
fōmes -ĭtis, m. (foveo), *touchwood, tinder*:
Verg., Luc.
fons fontis, m. *a spring, fountain*: Cic., Hor.,
Liv.; meton., *fresh or spring water*: Verg.
TRANSF., *spring, origin, fountain-head, source*:
philosophiae, Cic.; mali, Liv.; ingenii, Juv.
fontānus -a -um (fons), *of a spring or fountain*:
unda, Ov.
Fontēius -a -um, *name of a Roman gens*.
fonticulus -i, m. (dim. of fons), *a little fountain
or spring*: Hor.
Fontĭnālis -e (fons), *of a spring*: porta, *a gate
in Rome on the Quirinal, near the Campus
Martius*, Liv.
for fāri fātus, dep. (cf. φημί, φάσκω; the forms
in use are: pres., fatur, fantur; fut., fabor,
fabitur; imperat., fare; pres. partic., **fans**,

etc.; gerund, fandi, fando; infin., fari and (Verg.) farier; perf. partic., fatus -a -um, giving perf. tense, etc.), *to speak, say*: ad eos deus fatur, Cic.; sic fatus, Verg.; ne fando quidem auditum est, Cic.; with object: delira, Lucr.; ea, talia, Verg.; also *to speak of*: Tarpeium nemus fabor, Prop.

fŏrābĭlis -e (foro), *that can be bored through, penetrable*: Ov.

fŏrāmen -ĭnis, n. (foro), *a hole, opening, aperture*: foramina terrae, Lucr.; foramina illa quae patent ad animum a corpore, Cic.; foramina retis, Ov.

fŏras, adv. (from old noun fora; cf. θύρα), *(moving) out of doors, forth, out*: exit foras, Pl.; aliquem proicere foras, Cic.; portis se foras erumpere, Cic.; quae (vestigia) ubi omnia foras versa vidit, Liv.; (scripta) foras dare, *to publish*, Cic. L.

forceps -cĭpis (*formus/capio), m. and f. *a pair of tongs, pincers*: Verg., Ov.

forda -ae (fero), *a cow in calf*: Ov.

fŏre fŏrem, used as fut. infin. and imperf. subj. of sum; q.v.

fŏrensis -e (forum), *relating to the market* or *forum*. (1) in gen.: factio, turba, Liv. (2) *relating to the business of the Roman forum*, esp. *legal*: causa, res, certamen, Cic.; vestitus, Cic., Liv.; Mars, *eloquence*, Ov.

Fŏrentum -i, n. *a town in Apulia* (now *Forenza*): Hor.

forfex -fĭcis, f. *a pair of shears* or *scissors*: Mart.

fŏrĭca -ae, f. *a privy*: Juv.

¹fŏris -is, f. (connected with foras and ²foris), *a door*; more often plur. fores, *folding-doors*: claudere forem cubiculi, Cic.; fores aperire, Cic.; ad fores adsistere, Cic.; Pl., Hor., Ov. TRANSF., *any opening, entrance*: equi aenei, Cic.; quasi amicitiae, Cic. L.

²fŏris, adv. (from old noun fora; cf. θύρα). (1) *(situated) out of doors, outside, without* (opp. domi, intus): foris cenare, Pl., Cic.; foris valde plauditur, *among the people*, Cic.; Pl., Ter.; sometimes = *abroad, outside Rome*: Cic. (2) *from without, from abroad*: consilium petere foris potius quam domo, Cic.; Hor.

fŏrma -ae, f. *form, figure, shape*.

LIT., (1) in gen.: corporis, Cic.; Verg., Hor. (2) *beauty*: Hor., Verg. (3) *figure, image, likeness*: formae virorum, Cic.; formae quas in pulvere descripserat, Liv.; Hor., Tac. (4) *a shape serving as model*; hence *a shoemaker's last*: Hor.; *a mould, stamp*: Ov.

TRANSF., (1) *form, manner, type*: forma rerum publicarum, Cic.; in formam provinciae redigere, Liv.; forma insolitae pugnae, Liv.; in logic, *species*: Cic. (2) form as briefly indicated, *outline, general notion*: totius negotii, Cic.

fŏrmālis -e (forma), *formal, having a set form*: Suet.

fŏrmāmentum -i, n. (formo), *conformation*: Lucr.

fŏrmātor -ōris, m. (formo), *a fashioner*: Plin. L.

fŏrmātūra -ae, f. (formo), *forming, shaping*: Lucr.

Formiae -ārum, f. *town on the coast of Latium* (now *Mola di Gaeta*). Adj. **Formĭānus** -a -um, *of Formiae*. N. as subst. **Formĭānum** -i (sc. praedium), *an estate near Formiae*: Cic.

formīca -ae, f. *an ant*: Cic., Verg.

formīdābĭlis -e (formido), *exciting terror, fearful, formidable*: lumen, Ov., Sen.

¹formīdo -are (²formido), *to be terrified, to dread*; absol.: Pl., Cic.; with object: omnia, Cic.; with the infin.: naribus uti, Hor.; with ne *or* si and the subj.: Pl.

²formīdo -ĭnis, f. *dread, terror*: Stoici definiunt formidinem metum permanentem, Cic.; formidinem alicui inicere, Cic.; with objective genit.: Cic., Hor.; in plur.: horribiles formidines, Cic. Meton., *that which causes fear, dreadfulness, awfulness*: Verg., Tac.; *a scarecrow*: Hor., Verg.

formīdŏlōsus -a -um (²formido). Act., *causing dread, terrible, fearful*: tempora, Cic.; bellum formidolosissimum, Cic.; ferae, Hor. Pass., *fearful, timid*; with objective genit.: formidolosior hostium, Tac.

¶ Adv. **formīdŏlōsē**, *dreadfully, terribly*: Cic.

formo -are (forma), *to form, shape, fashion*. LIT., materiam, Cic.; signum in muliebrem figuram, Cic.; classem, Verg. TRANSF., *to arrange, order, regulate, dispose*: orationem, Cic.; formatis omnibus ad belli et pacis usus, Liv.; novos conlegas in suos mores, Liv.; in personam novam, of actors, *to represent*, Hor.

formōsĭtās -ātis, f. (formosus), *beauty*: Cic.

formōsus -a -um (forma), adj. (with compar. and superl.), *beautifully formed, beautiful*: virgines formosissimae, Cic.; Verg., etc. TRANSF., of abstr. things: tempus, spring, Ov.; virtute nihil est formosius, Cic.; Verg.

¶ Adv. **formōsē**, *beautifully*; compar.: formosius, Quint.

formŭla -ae, f. (dim. of forma). (1) *physical beauty*: Pl. (2) *legal t. t., set form, formula*: testamentorum, Cic.; cognitionis, Cic.; esp. *the form of an alliance*: Lampsacenos in sociorum formulam referre, Liv. (3) in gen., *rule, principle*: Stoicorum, Cic.; disciplinae, Cic.

fornācālis -e (fornax), *of an oven*: dea, *the goddess of ovens* (Fornax), Ov. N. pl. as subst. **Fornācālĭa** -ĭum, *the festival of the goddess Fornax*.

fornācŭla -ae, f. (dim. of fornax), *a little oven*: Juv.

fornax -ācis, f. (1) *an oven, furnace, kiln*: ardens, Cic.; Lucr., Verg. TRANSF., Aetnae, crater, Lucr., Verg. (2) personif.: Fornax, *the goddess of ovens*, Ov.

fornicātus -a -um (fornix), *arched, vaulted*: paries, Cic.; via, Liv.

fornix -ĭcis, m. *an arch, vault*. LIT., parietis, Cic.; Sall., Verg.; *an arcade*: Liv.; esp. Fornix Fabii, *a triumphal arch erected by Q. Fabius Maximus*; as milit. t. t., *an arched sally-port*: Liv. TRANSF., *a brothel*: Hor.

fornus = furnus; q.v.

fŏro -are, *to bore, to pierce*: Pl.

fors, abl. forte, f. (fero), only in nom. and abl. sing., *chance, luck*. In gen.: sed haec ut fors tulerit, Cic.; Hor., Liv. Esp. as adv. in both cases: (1) nom. **fors**, also **forsit** (fors sit), **forsăn** (fors an), and **forsĭtăn** (fors sit an), *perhaps, perchance*: Verg., Hor., Liv.; with subj., sometimes indic. (2) abl. **fortĕ**, *by chance, accidentally, as it happened*: Pl., Cic.,

Hor., etc.; often after si, nisi, ne, etc., *by any chance*: Pl., Cic., etc.
  Personif. as a deity: dea Fors, Ov.; esp. Fors Fortuna, Liv.
forsăn, adv. from fors; q.v.
forsit, adv. from fors; q.v.
forsĭtăn, adv. from fors; q.v.
fortassĕ (fortassis), adv. (fors), *perhaps*; in gen.: dolent fortasse et anguntur, Cic.; res fortasse verae, Cic.; incondite fortasse, Cic.; Pl.; also with acc. and infin.: Pl., Ter., Cic.; esp. with numbers and other indications of amount: triginta fortasse versus, Cic.; nimis fortasse, Cic.
fortĕ, *see* fors.
fortĭcŭlus -a -um (dim. of fortis), *tolerably bold*: Cic.
fortis -e (old form forctis) adj. (with compar. and superl.). (1) physically, *strong, powerful, robust, stout*: ligna fortissima, Caes.; coloni, Verg.; equus, Verg. (2) morally, *brave, courageous, stout, steadfast*: **a**, of persons: horum omnium fortissimi sunt Belgae, Caes.; fortior in dolore, Cic.; vir fortissimus contra audaciam, Cic.; fortis ad pericula, Cic.; prov.: fortes fortuna adiuvat, *fortune favours the brave*, Cic.; with infin.: Hor.: **b**, of things, *courageous, energetic*: sententia, Cic.; genus dicendi, Cic.; Hor., Liv., Ov.; sometimes in bad sense, *bold, audacious*: Liv., Ov.
¶ Adv. (with compar. and superl.) **fortĭtĕr**. (1) physically, *strongly*: fortius attrahere lora, Ov. (2) morally, *bravely*: ferre dolorem, Cic.; Caes., Hor.
fortĭtūdo -inis, f. (fortis). (1) physical *strength*: Phaedr. (2) moral *bravery, courage*: Caes., Cic.; plur.: fortitudines, *deeds of bravery*, Cic.
fortŭĭtus -a -um (fors), *accidental, casual, fortuitous*: concursus atomorum, Cic.; subita et fortuita oratio, *unpremeditated*, Cic.; Hor., Tac. N. pl. as subst. **fortŭĭta** -ōrum, *chance occurrences*: Tac., Quint.
¶ Abl. sing. as adv. **fortŭĭto**, *by chance, by accident, fortuitously*: Cic.
fortūna -ae, f. (fors), *chance, fate, lot, luck, fortune*.
  In gen.: fortuna prospera, secunda, *good fortune*, Cic.; adversa, *misfortune*, Cic.; fortunae se committere, Cic.; plur.: fortunae secundae, Cic. Personif., *chance*: gubernans, Lucr.; Pl., Cic., Hor. Esp. (1) *good fortune*: dum fortuna fuit, Verg.; fortunam sibi facere, Liv.; Pl., Cic., Hor. (2) (rarely) *misfortune*: contra fortunam paratus armatusque, Cic.
  TRANSF., (1) *lot, condition, state, mode of life*: infima servorum, Cic.; magna, *high position*, Liv. (2) *property, possessions*; usually plur.: alicui bona fortunasque adimere, Cic.; Caes., Hor.
fortūnātus -a -um, partic. from fortuno; q.v.
fortūno -are (fortuna), *to make happy, bless, prosper*: tibi patrimonium dei fortunent, Cic. L.; Pl., Hor., Liv.
¶ Hence partic. (with compar. and superl.) **fortūnātus** -a -um, *blessed*. (1) in gen. sense, *lucky, fortunate*: homo, Cic.; respublica, Cic.; with genit.: laborum, Verg. (2) *well off, wealthy, rich*: Cic.
¶ Adv. **fortūnātĕ**, *happily, fortunately*: vivere, Cic.; Pl., Liv.

¹fŏrŭli -ōrum, m. (dim. of forus), *a bookcase*: Juv., Suet.
²Fŏrŭli -ōrum, m. *a place in the Sabine country*.
fŏrum -i, n. *an open square, market-place*.
  LIT., (1) as primarily a *market-place*: **a**, in Rome: forum bovarium, *or* boarium, *the cattle-market*, Cic.; forum holitorium, *vegetable-market*, Liv., Tac.; forum piscarium, *or* piscatorium, *fish-market*, Liv.: **b**, of market-towns other than Rome: Vacca, forum rerum venalium totius regni maxime celebratum, Sall. Hence the names of several towns: Forum Appii, *on the Via Appia in Latium*; Forum Aurelium, *in Etruria, on the Via Aurelia*; Forum Cornelii, *in Gallia Cispadana*; Forum Iulii *or* Iulium, *in Gallia Narbonensis* (now *Fréjus*); Forum Voconii, *in Gallia Narbonensis*. (2) in a wider sense, as a place of public business, commercial, political and judicial; usually of the original forum in Rome: forum Romanum, *or* magnum, *or* vetus, *or* simply forum, *an open place at the foot of the Palatine and Capitoline hills*: Pl., Cic., Hor., etc.; also of others in Rome built later, such as forum Caesaris, *founded by J. Caesar*: Suet.; forum Augusti, *built by Augustus*: Ov.; forum Traiani, *built by Trajan*.
  TRANSF., of the business transacted in a forum: sublata erat de foro fides, *credit*, Cic.; forum agere, *to hold an assize*, Cic.; forum attingere, *to begin to apply oneself to public business*, Cic. L.
fŏrus -i, m. (1) *the gangway of a ship*: Cic., Verg. (2) *a block of seats in the theatre*: Liv. (3) plur., *tiers of cells* in a beehive: Verg.
fossa -ae, f. (fodio), *a ditch, trench, channel*: fossam ducere, Caes.; facere, fodere, Liv.; vallo et fossā cingere, Cic.; Rheni, Cic.; fossas implere, Cic.; fossae Cluiliae, Liv.
fossĭo -ōnis, f. (fodio), *a digging, excavation*: Cic.
fossor -ōris, m. (fodio), *a digger, delver*: Verg., Hor.; contemptuously, *a boor, clown*: Cat.
fossūra -ae, f. (fodio), *a digging*: Suet.
fōtus, partic. of foveo; q.v.
fŏvĕa -ae, f. *a pit*, esp. *as a trap for catching game, a pitfall*: in foveam incidere, Cic.; Pl., Lucr., Verg.
fŏvĕo fŏvēre fōvi fōtum, *to warm, keep warm*.
  LIT., of a bird: pullos pennis, Cic.; ignibus aras, Ov.; vulnus lymphā, *to foment*, Verg.
  TRANSF., (1) physically, *to tend, caress*: gremio puerum; fig., *to stay constantly in a place*: castra, Verg. (2) in gen., *to foster, cherish, support*: spem, Liv.; voluntatem patrum, Liv.; Cic., Ov., Tac.; aliquem, *to encourage*, Cic., Liv.
fractus -a -um, partic. from frango; q.v.
frāga -ōrum, n. *strawberries*: Verg., Ov.
frăgĭlis -e (frango). (1) *crackling*: lauri, Verg. (2) *easily broken, fragile*. LIT., rami, Verg.; Hor., Ov. TRANSF., **a**, *fleeting, transitory*: res humanae, Cic.; gloria, Sall.: **b**, *weak, feeble*: corpus, Cic.; Lucr., Hor.
frăgĭlĭtās -ātis, f. (fragilis), *frailty, weakness*: humani generis, Cic.
fragmen -mĭnis, n. (frango), *a breaking*; hence, usually plur., *fragments, remains, ruins*: silvarum, Lucr.; navigii, Ov., Verg., Tac.

fragmentum -i, n. (frango), *a piece broken off, fragment*; usually plur.: fragmenta saeptorum, Cic.; Verg.

frăgor -ōris, m. (frango), *a breaking*: Lucr.; hence *a noise of breaking, crack, crash*: tectorum, Liv.; pelagi, Verg.; of thunder: Ov.; fragorem dare, *to crash*, Ov.; Cic.

frăgōsus -a -um (fragor). (1) *crashing, roaring*: torrens, Verg. (2) *fragile*: Lucr. (3) *broken, rough*: Ov.

fragro -are, *to emit a smell*, esp. *a sweet smell*: Mart.; usually in pres. partic. **fragrans** -antis, *sweet-smelling, fragrant*: Cat., Verg.

frăgum, *see* fraga.

frango frangĕre frēgi fractum, *to break, break in pieces, shatter.*

LIT., bracchium, Cic.; domum lapidum coniectu, Cic.; compluribus navibus fractis, *dashed to pieces*, Caes.; gulam laqueo, *to strangle*, Sall.; glebas rastris, *to break small*, Verg.; fruges saxo, *to grind*, Verg.

TRANSF., (1) of things: fidem, foedus, Cic.; diem morantem mero, *to shorten*, Hor. (2) of persons, their spirit, their passions, etc., *to master, tame, subdue, humble*: nationes, cupiditates, impetum, Cic.; frangi animo, *to be discouraged*, Cic.; te ut ulla res frangat? Cic.

¶ Hence partic. **fractus** -a -um, *broken, humbled, enfeebled*: fractiorem esse animo, Cic. L.

frāter -tris, m. (cf. Gr. φράτωρ), *a brother.*

LIT., fratres gemini, *twin-brothers*, Cic.; =*Castor and Pollux*, Ov.; fratres gemelli, Ov.; germanus, *own brother*, Cic.; fratres (like ἀδελφοί), *brothers and sisters*, Tac.; sometimes also *a cousin*: Cic., Ov., Tac.; or *a brother-in-law*: Liv.

TRANSF., (1) of a person in any close relation, *a comrade*: Cic., Hor.; *a compatriot*: Verg.; *an ally*: Caes. (2) of a thing similarly related to another thing: aspicies illic positos ex ordine fratres (of writings), Ov.

frāterculus -i, m. (dim. of frater), *a little brother*: Cic., Juv.

frāternĭtas -ātis, f. (fraternus), *brotherhood, fraternity*: Tac.

frāternus -a -um (frater), *of a brother, brotherly, fraternal.*

LIT., amor, Cic.; hereditas, *coming from a brother*, Cic.; lyra, *received by Apollo from his brother Mercury*, Hor.; nex, *murder of a brother*, Hor.; sometimes *of a cousin*: fraterna peto, *the arms of my cousin*, Ov.

TRANSF., (1) *of some related person, as of a brother*: amor in nos, Cic. (2) *of some thing related to another*: maerentem abiungens fraterna morte iuvencum, Verg.

¶ Adv. **frāternē**, *in a brotherly manner, like a brother*: facere, Cic. L.; ab aliquo armari, Cic. L.

frātrĭcīda -ae, m. (frater/caedo), *one who kills a brother, a fratricide*: Cic.

fraudātĭo -ōnis, f. (fraudo), *deceit, fraud, swindling*: Pl., Cic.

fraudātor -ōris, m. (fraudo), *a deceiver, swindler*: creditorum, Cic.

fraudo -are (fraus), *to cheat, defraud, deceive, swindle*; usually with acc. of person and abl. of thing: Caecilium magnā pecuniā, Cic.; milites praedā, Liv.; creditores, Cic.; aliquem in hereditaria societate, Cic.; also with

acc. of thing, *to steal, embezzle*: stipendium equitum, Caes.; fraudata restituere, Caes.

fraudŭlentĭa -ae, f. (fraudulentus), *deceitfulness*: Pl.

fraudŭlentus -a -um (fraus), *deceitful, fraudulent*: Carthaginienses, Cic.; venditio, Cic.; Pl., Hor.

fraus, fraudis, f. (genit. pl. fraudium and fraudum), *deceit, deception, fraud.*

LIT., (1) act., fraus odio digna maiore, Cic.; sine fraude, *honourably*, Caes.; fraudem facere legi, Pl., Cic. L., Liv.; contra legem, Liv. (2) pass., *delusion, error*: in fraudem incidere, delabi, Cic.; Pl., Verg.

TRANSF., (1) act., in gen., *a crime, offence*: fraudem suscipere, Cic.; fraudem capitalem admittere, Cic. (2) pass., *damage, harm*: alicui fraudem ferre, alicui fraudi esse, *to cause loss to*, Cic.; esp. in phrase: sine fraude, *without harm*, Hor., Liv.

fraxĭnĕus -a -um (fraxinus), *of ash-wood, ashen*: trabes, Verg., Ov.

¹**fraxĭnus** -a -um=fraxineus: Ov.

²**fraxĭnus** -i, f. *an ash-tree*: Verg., Hor.; meton., *a spear* or *javelin, the shaft of which was made of ash-wood*: Ov.

Frĕgellae -ārum, f. *town of the Volsci, in Latium, on the Liris* (now *Ceprano*). Adj. and subst. **Frĕgellānus** -a -um, *Fregellan, a Fregellan.*

frĕmĕbundus -a -um (fremo), *roaring, murmuring*: Ov.

frĕmĭtus -ūs, m. (fremo), *a roaring, murmuring, growling*: murmurantis maris, terrae, Cic.; virum, apum, Verg.; castrorum, equorum, Liv.

frĕmo -ĕre -ŭi -ĭtum (βρέμω), *to roar, murmur, growl*: leo, equus, Verg.; fremunt ripae, rustle, Verg.; venti, Ov.; of persons: laetitiā fremunt, Verg.; adversus iniuriam decreti fremere, Liv.; also with acc., *to murmur out something, grumble, complain*: uno omnes eadem ore fremebant, Verg.; with acc. and infin.: falsas esse at a scriba vitiatas (litteras) fremebant, Liv.; Arrius consulatum sibi ereptum fremit, Cic. L.

frĕmor -ōris, m. (fremo), *a roaring, murmuring*: varius, Verg.

frendo -ĕre. (1) intransit., with or without dentibus, *to gnash the teeth*, Cic., Liv. (2) transit., *to crush, bruise, grind*: fabam, Varr.

frēni -ōrum, m. *see* frenum.

frēnĭger -era -erum (frenum/gero), *bearing a bridle*: Stat.

frēno -are (frenum), *to bridle, curb.* LIT., equos, Verg.; Liv., Ov. TRANSF., *to curb, restrain, check, hold in*: cursus aquarum, Verg.; furores, Cic.; Liv.

Frentāni -ōrum, m. *an Italian tribe on the Adriatic coast.*

¶ Hence adj. **Frentānus** -a -um, *Frentanian.*

frēnum -i, n., usually plur. **frēna** -ōrum, n.; also **frēni** -ōrum, m. (frendo), *bridle, reins, bit, curb.*

LIT., frena remittere, dare, *to slacken*, Ov.; frenos inhibere, *to draw in*, Liv.

TRANSF., *restraint*: frenos dare impotenti naturae, *to give rein to*, Liv.; alicui frenos adhibere, *to bridle*, Cic.; frenos recipere, *to submit to the rein*, Cic.; frenum mordere, *to chafe against restraint*, Cic. L.

frĕquens -entis, adj. (with compar. and superl.), *crowded*.
  Lit., of number, *numerous, full*. (1) of persons and groups: senatus, Cic.; legatio, Liv.; populus, Hor. (2) of places, *full, frequented, populous*: theatrum, Cic.; municipium, Cic.; with abl.: frequens custodiis locus, Liv.; with genit.: Tac.
  Transf., of time, *repeated, frequent, constant*. (1) of persons, *often doing* a thing: Platonis auditor, Cic.; adesse senatui, Tac.; in ore frequens posteritatis eris, Ov. (2) of things, *often done* or *used*: pocula, Cic.; opera, Pl.; Liv.
  ¶ Adv. (with compar. and superl.) **frĕquentĕr**. (1) *in large numbers*: Romam inde frequenter migratum est, Liv.; Cic. L. (2) *frequently, often*: adhibenda frequentius etiam illa ornamenta rerum sunt, Cic.; Quint.

frĕquentātĭo -ōnis, f. (frequento), *frequency, crowding*: argumentorum, Cic.

frĕquentĭa -ae, f. (frequens). (1) of persons, *a large concourse, numerous assembly*: civium, Cic.; frequentiā crescere, *to increase in population*, Liv. (2) of things, *a large number, abundance*: sepulcrorum, Cic.

frĕquento -are (frequens), *to crowd*.
  Lit., of number. (1) *to collect in large numbers*; of persons: de domo scribas ad aerarium, Cic.; of things: multa acervatim, Cic. (2) *to fill* a place; with people: urbes, Cic.; templa, Ov.; with things: luminibus orationem, Cic. (3) *to do* a thing *in crowds* or *with a crowd*: Marium, *to visit*, Sall.; sacra, *to celebrate*, Ov.; festos dies, Tac.
  Transf., of time, *to do* or *use* a thing *frequently*: domum, *to visit often*, Cic.; Hymenae! frequentant, *they repeat*, Ov.; memoriam alicuius, *to dwell upon the thought of*, Sen.

frĕtensis -e (fretum), *of straits*: Cic.

frĕtum -i, n. Lit., *a strait, sound, estuary, firth, channel*: Verg., Cic. Esp.: fretum Siciliae, Caes., or Siciliense, Cic., or absol. fretum, Cic., *the Straits of Messina*; nostri maris et oceani, *the Straits of Gibraltar*, Sall. Transf., (1) *the sea* in gen., usually plur.: Verg., Ov. (2) fig., *disturbance, turmoil*: aetatis, Lucr.

¹frētus -a -um, *relying on, confiding in, trusting, depending on*; with the abl.: vobis, Cic.; intellegentiā vestrā, Cic.; iuventā, Verg.; with dat.: nulli rei, Liv.; with acc. and infin.: satis fretus esse etiamnunc tolerando certamini legatum, Liv.

²frētus -ūs, m. (cf. fretum). Lit., *a strait*: Lucr. Transf., (1) *an interval, difference*: Cic. (2) *spring*: fretus ipse anni, Lucr.

frĭco fricare frĭcŭi frictum and frĭcātum, *to rub, rub down*: (sus) fricat arbore costas, Verg.; Pl., Juv.

frīgĕo -ēre (ῥιγέω), *to be cold*. Lit., corpus frigentis (of a dead person), Verg. Transf., (1) *to be inactive, lifeless, dull*: vires in corpore, Verg.; consilia, Liv.; Ter., Cic. L. (2) *to be coldly received, fall flat*: itaque (contio) frigebat, Cic. L.; Ter.

frīgĕro -are (frigus), *to cool, refresh*: Cat.

frigesco -ĕre (frigeo), *to become cold*. Lit., pedes manusque, Tac. Transf., *to become dull*: ap. Cic. L.

frĭgĭdŭlus -a -um (dim. of frigidus), *somewhat cold*: Verg. Transf., *somewhat faint*: singultus, Cat.

frīgĭdus -a -um (frigeo), adj. (with compar. and superl.), *cold, cool, chilly*.
  Lit., flumen, Cic.; rura, Verg.; annus, *winter*, Verg.; also of the chill of death or fright: Verg., Ov.; f. sing. as subst. (sc. aqua), *cold water*: Pl., Plin. L.
  Transf., (1) in act. sense, *chilling, causing cold*: sidera, Ov.; mors, Verg.; fig.: rumor, Hor. (2) fig., *cold, dull, lifeless*: accusatoribus frigidissimis, Cic. L.; bello dextera, Verg. (3) of speech, *flat*: calumnia, Cic.
  ¶ Adv. **frīgĭdē**, *coldly*; hence, *languidly, feebly*: aliquid agere, ap. Cic.

frīgo frīgĕre frixi frictum (φρύγω), *to roast, parch*: Pl., Hor.

frīgus -ŏris, n. (ῥῖγος), *cold, coolness, coldness*.
  Lit., *physical cold*: vis frigoris et caloris, Cic.; Pl., Verg. Esp. (1) *the cold of winter*: non aestate, non frigore, Verg. (2) *a cold place*: frigus non habitabile, Ov. (3) *the cold of death*: Verg., Lucr., Ov.; *of fright*: Verg.
  Transf., (1) *coldness in action, dullness, indolence, remissness*: ap. Cic. L., Ov. (2) *a cold reception, coolness, disfavour*: Hor., Quint.

frīguttĭo -ire, *to stammer*: Pl.

frĭo -are, *to rub, crumble*: Lucr.

Frīsĭi -ōrum, m. *the Frisians*. Adj. **Frīsĭus** -a -um, *Frisian*.

frītillus -i, m. *a dice-box*: Juv.

frīvŏlus -a -um (frio), *trifling, worthless*: Suet., Plin. N. pl. as subst. **frīvŏla** -ōrum, *sticks of furniture*: Juv.

frondātor -ōris, m. (¹frons), *one who cuts off leaves, a pruner of trees*: Verg.

frondĕo -ēre (¹frons), *to be in leaf, be leafy*: nunc frondent silvae, Verg.

frondesco -ĕre (frondeo), *to come into leaf, put forth leaves*: Cic.

frondĕus -a -um (¹frons), *leafy*: nemus, Verg.; tecta, *leafy coverts*, Verg.; casa, Ov.

frondĭfer -fĕra -fĕrum (¹frons/fero), *leaf-bearing, leafy*: Lucr.

frondōsus -a -um (¹frons), *full of leaves, leafy*: ramus, Ov.; Verg.

¹frons frondis, f. *a leaf, foliage*: via interclusa frondibus et virgultis, Cic.; Verg., Ov., etc. Meton., *a chaplet* or *crown of leaves*: Hor., Verg., Ov.

²frons frontis, f. *the forehead, brow*.
  Lit., frontem contrahere, *to frown*, Cic.; explicare, *to look cheerful again*, Hor.; frontem ferire, percutere, Cic.; fronte occultare sententiam, Cic.; frons urbana, *shameless*, Hor.; laeta parum, Verg.
  Transf., (1) in gen., *the front, forepart*: castrorum, Caes.; frons adversa (montis), Verg.; as milit. t. t., *the van*: et a fronte et a tergo circumire hostem, Caes.; a fronte instare, Liv.; frontem aequare, Liv. (2) *the outside end of a book roll*: Tib., Ov. (3) *frontage* (in measuring land): Hor.

frontālĭa -ium, n. pl. (²frons), *the frontlet of a horse*: Liv.

fronto -ōnis, m. (²frons), *a man with a broad forehead*: Plin.

fructŭārĭus -a -um (fructus), *fruit-bearing, fruitful*: agri quos fructuarios habent civitates, *with payment levied on the produce*, ap. Cic. L.

ructŭōsus -a -um (fructus), adj. (with compar.
and superl.), *fruit-bearing, fruitful, fertile.*
LIT., ager, Cic. TRANSF., tota philosophia
frugifera et fructuosa, Cic.; Quint.

ructus -ūs, m. (fruor). (1) abstr., *enjoyment,
enjoying*: Pl., Lucr. TRANSF., ad animi mei
fructum, *for my intellectual enjoyment*, Cic.
(2) concr., *proceeds, profit, produce, fruit,
income*; in gen.: praediorum, Cic.; pecuniae,
Cic.; verae virtutis, Cic.; fructūs ferre,
capere, percipere ex aliqua re, Cic.; magno
fructui esse alicui, Liv.; esp. of *the fruits of
the earth*: fructūs serere, demetere, Cic.;
rami fructus tulere, Verg.

rūgālis -e (frux), *frugal, economical, honest*: ut
frugalior sim, Ter.; colonus frugalissimus,
Cic. (posit. not used in class. Latin; frugi
instead).
    ¶ Adv. frūgālĭtĕr: Pl., Cic., Hor.

rūgālĭtas -ātis, f. (frugalis), *frugality, economy,
honesty*: Cic.; frugalitatem, id est modestiam
et temperantiam, Cic.; of style, *restraint*:
Quint.

rūgi, *see* frux.

rūgĭfer -fĕra -fĕrum (frux/fero), *fruit-bearing,
fruitful, fertile.* LIT., ager, Cic.; numen,
making fruitful, Ov. TRANSF., *profitable,
advantageous*: tota philosophia frugifera et
fructuosa, Cic.; Liv.

rūgĭfĕrens -entis (frux/fero), *fruitful, fertile*:
Lucr.

rūgĭlĕgus -a -um (frux/lego), *collecting grain*:
formicae, Ov.

rūgĭpărus -a -um (frux/pario), *fruitful,
prolific*: Lucr.

rūĭtus, frūĭtūrus, *see* fruor.

rūmentārĭus -a -um (frumentum), *of grain*
or *corn*: res, *the supply of corn*, Caes., Cic.;
lex, *relating to its distribution*, Cic.; navis,
Caes. M. as subst. frūmentārĭus -i, *a
corn-merchant*: Cic., Liv.

rūmentātĭo -ōnis, f. (frumentor). (1) *a
foraging*: Caes. (2) *a distribution of corn*: Suet.

rūmentātor -ōris, m. (frumentor), *a forager*
or *a provider of corn*: Liv.

rūmentor -ari, dep. (frumentum), *to forage,
fetch corn*: frumentari in propinquo agro,
Liv.; Caes., Sall.

rūmentum -i, n. (frux, fruor), *corn, grain*:
Caes., Cic., Hor., etc.

rŭor frŭi fructus and frŭĭtus sum (cf. frux),
to have the benefit of, to enjoy, a person,
physical object, or abstr. thing. In early Latin,
with acc. object: ea quae fructus cumque
es, Lucr. Later with abl.: immortali aevo,
Lucr.; vitā, Cic., Tac.; voluptate, Cic.;
votis, *to obtain one's wishes*, Ov.; amicitiae
recordatione, *to take delight in*, Cic.; as legal
t. t., *to have the use and enjoyment of*: fundis
certis, Cic.; absol.: iucundius est carere quam
frui, Cic.

rŭsino -ōnis, m. *town in Latium* (now
Frosinone). Adj. and subst. Frŭsĭnās -ātis,
of Frusino, an inhabitant of it.

rustillātim (frustillum, dim. of frustum),
bit by bit: Pl.

rustrā (perhaps connected with fraudo).
LIT., *in error*: frustra esse, *to be deceived,
mistaken*, Pl., Sall. TRANSF., (1) *in vain,
without effect*: frustra tempus contero, Cic.;
Pl., Verg., Hor. (2) *wantonly, without
reason*: Cic., Verg., Suet.

frustrāmen -inis, n. (frustror), *deception*:
Lucr.

frustrātĭo -ōnis, f. (frustror), *a deception,
disappointment, frustration*: Pl., Liv.

frustro -are (Pl.) and dep. frustror -ari
(frustra), *to disappoint, deceive, trick*: nos
falsā atque inani spe, Liv.; Lucr., Cic., Verg.

frustum -i, n. (fruor), *a bit, piece, morsel.* LIT.,
of food: frusta esculenta, Cic.; in frusta
secare, Verg. TRANSF., in gen.: Pl., Sen.,
Quint.

frŭtex -tĭcis, m. *a shrub, bush*: Lucr., Verg.,
Ov. TRANSF., as a term of reproach, *blockhead*: Pl.

frŭtĭcētum -i, n. (frutex), *a thicket*: Hor.,
Suet.

frŭtĭco -are and frŭtĭcor -ari, dep. (frutex),
to shoot out, become bushy: Cic. L., Juv.

frŭtĭcōsus -a -um (frutex), *bushy* or *full of
bushes*: Ov.

frux frūgis, f. (cf. fruor), usually plur. frūgēs
-um, *fruits of the earth.* LIT., non omnem
frugem neque arborem in agro reperire, Cic.;
terrae fruges bacaeve arborum, Cic.; Verg.,
Hor., Ov. TRANSF., in gen., *fruits, success*:
fruges industriae, Cic.; bonam frugem
libertatis ferre, Liv.; ad bonam frugem se
recipere, *to improve oneself*, Cic.; Pl., Hor.
    ¶ Dat. sing. frūgī, used as indecl. adj.,
useful, honest, discreet, moderate, temperate:
homo, Cic.; Hor.; strengthened by bonae:
permodestus et bonae frugi, Cic. L.; Pl.

Fūcĭnus -i, m. *a lake in central Italy* (now
Lago Fucino).

fūco -are (¹fucus), *to colour, paint, dye*: originally *to paint red*: Assyrio lana veneno, Verg.;
to rouge: Ov.; in gen. *to paint any colour*:
Verg., Hor., Tac. TRANSF., *to colour,
embellish*: iisdem ineptiis fucata sunt illa
omnia, Cic.; lepido fucata sonore, Lucr.
    ¶ Hence partic. fūcātus -a -um, *painted*;
hence *counterfeited, simulated*: nitor, Cic.;
omnia fucata et simulata a sinceris atque
veris (secernere), Cic.

fūcōsus -a -um (¹fucus), *painted*; hence
simulated, counterfeited: merces, Cic.; amicitiae, Cic.

¹fūcus -i, m. (φῦκος). LIT., *red* or *purple dye*,
obtained from a rock lichen: Hor., Quint.;
hence the colour obtained, *red* or *purple*:
Hor., Ov.; also of other colouring-matter,
esp. *rouge*: Pl., Cic.; in gen., *paint, dye* of any
colour: Prop.; sometimes=propolis, *the
reddish substance with which bees stop up the
entrance to their hives, bee-glue*, Verg.
TRANSF., *deceit, dissimulation, pretence*: sine
fuco ac fallaciis, Cic.; Pl., Ter., Hor.

²fūcus -i, m. *a drone bee*: Verg.

Fūfĭus -i -um, *name of a Roman gens.*

fŭga -ae, f. (cf. fugio, Gr. φυγή). *flight, running
away.*
    LIT., fuga ab urbe turpissima, Cic.; ex
fuga se recipere, Caes.; esse in fuga, Cic.;
hostes in fugam convertere, dare, conicere,
Caes.; in fugam se dare, se conferre, se
conicere, Cic.; fugae se mandare, Caes.;
fugam dare, *to flee*, Verg., or *to let flee*, Verg.,
Hor.; fugam facere, *to flee*, Sall., Liv., or
to make to flee, Cic., Liv.; fugam sistere,
to stop, Liv.; plur.: quantae in periculis
fugae proximorum, Cic.; esp. *flight from one's
country, exile, banishment*: fuga Metelli, Cic.;

fugax

dura fugae mala, Hor.; meton., *the place of exile*: Ov.

Transf., (**1**) *swift course* in gen., *speed*: facilem fugam exspectare, Verg.; fuga temporum, Hor. (**2**) *avoiding*, with genit.: laborum, Cic.; Verg., Hor.

fŭgax -ācis (fugio), *ready to flee, flying.* Lit., Parthus, Ov.; fugacissimus hostis, Liv.; Verg., Hor. Transf., (**1**) *speeding* in gen.: volucri fugacior aurā, Ov.; hence *fleeting, transitory*: anni, Hor.; haec omnia brevia, fugacia, caduca existima, Cic. (**2**) with genit., *avoiding*: condicionis, Ov.

¶ Hence compar. adv. **fŭgācĭus**, *in a manner more inclined to flight*: utrum a se audacius an fugacius ab hostibus geratur bellum, Liv.

fŭgĭo fŭgĕre fūgi fŭgĭtum (φεύγω), *to flee.*

Intransit., *to take to flight, run away.* Lit., (**1**) of persons, esp. of soldiers: ex proelio, Cic. L.; of exiles: a patria, Ov.; of slaves: Hor. (**2**) of animals: omne animal appetit quaedam et fugit a quibusdam, Cic. (**3**) of things: nubes, Hor. Transf., *to pass away, disappear*: fugiunt cum sanguine vires, Ov.; of time: fugit inreparabile tempus, Verg.

Transit., *to flee from.* Lit., *to run away from*: cerva fugiens lupum, Liv.; velut qui currebat fugiens hostem, Hor.; as an exile: patriam, Verg.; Acheronta, *to escape from*, Hor. Transf., (**1**) of persons, *to avoid, shun, be averse from*: concilia conventusque hominum, Caes.; ignominiam et dedecus, Cic.; laborem, Verg.; aliquem iudicem, *to reject*, Liv.; neque illud fugerim dicere, Cic.; with infin.: fuge quaerere, *do not seek*, Hor. (**2**) of things, *to escape*: vox Moerim fugit, Verg.; esp.: aliquid aliquem fugit, *escapes the notice of*, Cic.; with infin.: de Dionysio fugit me ad te antea scribere, Cic. L.

¶ Hence partic. **fŭgĭens** -entis, *fleeing.* Lit., Lucr. Transf., (**1**) *avoiding*, with genit.: laboris, Caes. (**2**) *fleeting*; hence *deteriorating*, of wine: Cic.

fŭgĭtivus -a -um (fugio), *flying, fugitive*: a dominis, Cic.; servi, Liv.; m. as subst., a *fugitive*, esp. a *runaway slave*: Pl., Cic., Hor.

fŭgĭto -are (freq. of fugio). Intransit., *to flee*: Ter. Transit., *to fly from, avoid, shun*: erum, Pl.; fig.: quaestionem, Cic.; with infin.: Ter., Lucr.

¶ Hence partic. **fŭgĭtans** -antis, *fleeing*; with genit., *avoiding*: litium, Ter.

fŭgo -are (fuga), *to put to flight, chase away, drive away.* Lit., homines inermes, Caes.; fundere atque fugare, Sall.; esp. *to drive into exile*: Lucr., Ov. Transf., *to dismiss, avert*: Hor., Ov.

fulcīmĕn -ĭnis, n. (fulcio), a *prop, support, pillar*: Ov.

fulcĭo fulcire fulsi fultum, *to prop up, support.* Lit., porticum, Cic.; vitis fulta, Cic.; Verg., Hor.

Transf., (**1**) physically, *to strengthen, secure*: postes, Verg.; ianuam serā, Ov. (**2**) morally, *to support, stay, uphold*: amicum, Cic.; labantem rempublicam, Cic.; subsidiis fulta acies, Liv.

fulcrum -i, n. (fulcio), *the post* or *foot of a couch*: Verg. Transf., a *couch*: Juv.

fulgĕo fulgēre fulsi, *to flash, to lighten.*

Lit., Iove fulgente, caelo fulgente, Cic.;

Lucr., Verg.; fig., of Pericles: fulgere, tonare, permiscere Graeciam, Cic.

Transf., (**1**) in gen., *to shine, gleam, glitter*: auro, Cic.; gladii, Liv.; oculi, Hor.; fulgebat luna, Hor. (**2**) fig., *to be distinguished, to shine*: virtus intaminatis fulget honoribus, Hor.; Liv., Tac.

fulgĭdus -a -um (fulgeo), *shining, gleaming, glittering*: Lucr.

fulgo -ĕre=fulgeo; q.v.: Lucr., Verg.

fulgor -ōris, m. (fulgeo), *lightning*: fulgores et tonitrua, Cic.; Verg., Ov. Transf., (**1**) in gen., *glitter, brightness*: armorum, Hor.; candelabri, Cic. (**2**) fig., *brightness, glory*: nominis, Ov.; honoris, Tac.

fulgŭr -ŭris, n. (fulgeo), a *flash of lightning*: Cic., Ov., Tac.; also a *stroke of lightning*: Verg., Hor., or *an object which has been struck by lightning*: Juv. Transf., in gen., *brightness*: solis, Lucr.; Ov.

fulgŭrālis -e (fulgur), *relating to lightning*: libri, *treating of lightning*, Cic.

fulgŭrātor -ōris, m. (fulguro), a *priest who interpreted the omens from lightning*: Cic.

fulgŭrītus -a -um (fulgur), *struck by lightning*: Pl.

fulgŭro -are (fulgur), *to lighten*: Iove fulgurante, Cic. Transf., of oratory: Quint.

fŭlĭca -ae, f. a *coot*: Verg., Ov.

fūlīgo -ĭnis, f. *soot*: Pl., Cic., Verg. Transf., a *powder used for darkening the eyebrows*: Juv.

fŭlix -ĭcis, f.=fulica; q.v.: Cic. poet.

fullo -ōnis, m. a *fuller, cloth-fuller*: Pl., Plin.

fullōnĭca -ae, f. (fullo), *the art of fulling*: Pl.

fullōnĭus -a -um (fullo), *of a fuller*: Pl.

fulmen -ĭnis, n. (originally fulgmen, from fulgeo), a *stroke of lightning, a thunderbolt.*

Lit., fulmine percussus, Cic.; ictu fulminis deflagrare, Cic.; Verg., etc.

Transf., (**1**) a *thunderbolt, crushing calamity*: fortunae, Cic.; duo fulmina domum perculerunt, Liv. (**2**) *mighty* or *irresistible power*: verborum, Cic.; esp. of *the Scipios*: duo fulmina belli, Lucr.; imperi nostri, Cic.

fulmenta -ae, f. (fulcio), a *support*; of the heel of a shoe: Pl.

fulmĭnĕus -a -um (fulmen), *of lightning.* Lit., ignes, Ov.; ictus, Hor. Transf., *like lightning*, i.e. *rapid* or *destructive*: ensis Verg.; os apri, Ov.

fulmĭno -are (fulmen), *to lighten.* Lit., Iuppiter fulminans, Hor.; impers.: fulminat Verg. Transf., Caesar fulminat bello, Verg. Prop.

fultūra -ae, f. (fulcio), a *support, prop, stay* of food: Hor.

Fulvĭus -a -um, *name of a Roman* gens; it most famous members were M. Fulvius Flaccus supporter of C. Gracchus, and Fulvia, *wife o* Clodius and afterwards of M. Antony.

fulvus -a -um, *tawny, yellowish brown*; of lions wolves, sand, gold: Verg.; Ov.

fūmĕus -a -um (fumus), *smoky, full of smoke* Verg.

fūmĭdus -a -um (fumus), *smoky, full of smoke* taeda, Verg.; altaria, Ov.

fūmĭfer -fĕra -fĕrum (fumus/fero), *smoke bearing, smoky*: ignes, Verg.

fūmĭfĭcus -a -um (fumus/facio), *causin smoke*: Ov.

[258]

fŭmo -are (fumus), *to smoke, steam*: agger fumat, Caes.; domus fumabat, *reeked with the odours of feasts*, Cic.; equum fumantia colla, Verg.

fŭmōsus -a -um (fumus), *smoked*: imagines, *figures of ancestors*, Cic.; perna, Hor.

fŭmus -i, m. (θυμός), *smoke, steam, vapour*: fumus ganearum, Cic.; fumo excruciari, Cic.; fumo dare signum, Liv.; plur.: fumi incendiorum procul videbantur, Caes.; prov.: vertere omne in fumum et cinerem, *to squander, consume*, Hor.

fŭnālis -e (funis), *attached to a rope*: equus, *a trace-horse*, Suet. N. as subst. **fūnāle** -is. (1) *the thong of a sling*: Liv. (2) *a wax-torch*: Cic., Verg., Hor.

fŭnambŭlus -i, m. (funis/ambulo), *a rope-dancer*: Ter., Suet.

fŭnctĭo -ōnis, f. (fungor), *a performance, performing, executing*: muneris, Cic.

fŭnda -ae, f. (cf. σφενδόνη), *a sling*: Caes., Verg.; fundā mittere glandes et lapides, Liv. TRANSF., (1) *a sling-stone*: Caes., Liv. (2) *a casting-net*: Verg.

fŭndāmen -ĭnis, n. (¹fundo), usually plur., *a foundation, base*: ponere, Verg.; Ov.

fŭndāmentum -i, n. (¹fundo), usually plur., *a foundation*. LIT., fundamenta iacere, Cic., Liv.; locare, Verg.; a fundamentis diruere Pteleum, Liv. TRANSF., *basis*: pietas fundamentum est omnium virtutum, Cic.; fundamenta libertatis, Cic.; Quint.

Fŭndānĭus -a -um, *name of a Roman* gens.

fŭndātor -ōris, m. (¹fundo), *a founder*: urbis, Verg.

fŭndĭto -are (funda), *to sling*: Pl.

fŭndĭtor -ōris, m. (funda), *a soldier furnished with a sling, a slinger*: Caes., Sall.

fŭndĭtŭs, adv. (fundus). (1) *from the bottom.* LIT., monumenta delere, Cic. TRANSF., *completely, entirely*: evertere amicitiam, Cic.; Lucr., Tac. (2) *at the bottom, below*: Lucr.

fŭndo -are (fundus), *to lay the foundation of, to found.* LIT., arces, Verg.; urbem colonis, Verg.; dente tenaci ancora fundabat naves, *fastened to the ground*, Verg. TRANSF., *to found*: accurate non modo fundata verum etiam extructa disciplina, Cic.; also *to make firm, to strengthen*: urbem legibus, Verg.; nostrum imperium, Cic.

¶ Hence partic. (with superl.) **fundatus** -a -um, *founded, firm*: fundatissima familia, Cic.

fŭndo fundĕre fūdi fūsum, *to pour, pour out.* LIT., (1) of liquids: sanguinem e patera, Cic.; liquorem de patera, Hor.; lacrimas, Verg.; ingentibus procellis fusus imber, Liv. (2) of metals, *to melt, cast*: quid fusum durius, Hor.

TRANSF., (1) with emphasis on quantity, *to pour out, shower, give abundantly*: terra fundit fruges, Cic.; segetem in Tiberim, Liv.; tela, Verg.; plenis se portis, *to rush out*, Verg.; quem Maia fudit, *gave birth to*, Verg.; opes, *to squander*, Hor.; luna per fenestram se fundebat, *streamed through*, Verg.; multo vitam cum sanguine, Verg.; esp. of sounds, *to utter*: sonos inanes, Cic.; of compositions: versus, Cic.; Verg. (2) with emphasis on distribution, *to spread, extend, scatter*: ne vitis nimia fundatur, Cic.; fusi per agros, Cic.; utrumque eorum fundi quoddamodo et quasi dilatari, Cic.; fig.: tum se latius

fundet orator, Cic.; esp.: **a**, on the ground: fusus in herba, Ov.; Verg.: **b**, as milit. t. t., *to rout, defeat, scatter, put to flight*: hostes, Liv.; Caes., Cic.; pass. as middle, *to rush away*: turpi fugā fundi, Liv.

¶ Hence partic. **fūsus** -a -um, *spread out, extended*: campi fusi in omnem partem, Verg.; fusa et candida corpora, *fleshy*, Liv.; crines, *flowing free*, Verg.; fig., of discourse, *diffuse*: genus sermonis, Cic.; Quint.

¶ Adv. (with compar.) **fūsē**, *widely, copiously*: dicere, Cic.

fundus -i, m. *ground.* (1) *the bottom* or *base of anything*, Cic., armarii, Cic.; aequora ciere fundo, *from the bottom*, Verg. TRANSF., largitio non habet fundum, *knows no bounds*, Cic.; fundum fieri legis, *to sanction, authorize*, Cic. (2) *soil; a farm, estate*: Pl., Cic., Hor.

fūnebris -e (funus), *of a funeral, funereal*: epulum, contio, Cic.; cupressi, Hor. TRANSF., *deadly, destructive*: bellum, Hor.; munera, Ov.

fūnĕrĕus -a -um (funus), *of a funeral, funereal*: faces, Verg. TRANSF., *that causes* or *betokens death*: dextra, Ov.; bubo, *ill-omened*, Ov.

fūnĕro -are (funus), *to bury solemnly, inter with funeral rites*: Plin., Suet.

¶ Hence partic. **fūnĕrātus** -a -um, *done to death*: Hor.

fūnesto -are (funestus), *to defile* or *pollute with death*: aras ac templa hostiis humanis, Cic.; gentem, Juv.

fūnestus -a -um (funus). (1) pass., *filled with mourning, defiled by death*: agros funestos reddere, Lucr.; familia funesta, *in mourning*, Liv.; Cic. (2) act., *fatal, disastrous, deadly*: tribunatus, Cic.; funestior dies, Cic.; Verg.; with dat.: funesta reipublicae pestis, Cic.

fungīnus -a -um (fungus), *of a mushroom*: Pl.

fungor fungi functus sum, dep. *to occupy oneself with anything, to perform, execute, undergo.* In early Latin with acc. object: Pl., Ter., Lucr.; and so found in gerundive: muneris fungendi gratiā, Cic. Usually with abl.: muneribus corporis, Cic.; munere aedilicio, *discharge the office of aedile*, Cic.; vice cotis, *to serve as*, Hor.; virtute, laboribus, Hor.; dapibus, *to take food*, Ov.; sumptu, Tac. Absol., in special sense, *to be affected, suffer*: Lucr.

fungus -i, m. (σφόγγος, σπόγγος), *a mushroom, fungus*: Pl., Hor. TRANSF., (1) as a term of reproach applied to a dull, stupid fellow: Pl. (2) *a 'thief' in the wick of a candle, a candle-snuff*: Verg.

fūnĭcŭlus -i, m. (dim. of funis), *a thin rope, cord, string*: funiculus a puppi religatus, Cic.; Quint.

fūnis -is, m. (f.: Lucr. 2, 1154), *a rope, cord, line*: per funem demitti, Verg.; of ship's ropes: ancorarius funis, Caes.; funes qui antennas ad malos religabant, Caes.; *the rope of a rope-dancer*: per extentum funem ire, Hor.; prov.: ne currente retro funis eat rota, *that all your labour may not be wasted*, Hor.; ducere, *to guide the rope*—i.e., *to command*, Hor.; sequi, *to follow, obey*, Hor.; reducere, *to change one's mind*, Pers.

fūnus -ĕris, n. *a funeral, burial.*

LIT., funus quo amici conveniunt ad exsequias cohonestandas, Cic.; funus alicui facere, Cic.; ducere, Cic.; in funus venire,

Cic.; funus celebrare, Liv.; also plur.: Cic., Verg.

TRANSF., (1) *the corpse*: lacerum, Verg. (2) *death*: crudeli funere exstinctus, Verg.; edere funera, *to kill*, Verg.; Hor. (3) in gen., *destruction, ruin*: reipublicae, Cic.; Hor.; meton., *persons who cause ruin*: paene funera reipublicae, *destroyers*, Cic.

fŭo fŭi fŭtūrus, etc., *see* sum.

fŭr fūris, c. (φώρ), *a thief*: non fur sed ereptor, Cic.; fur nocturnus, Cic.; Pl., Hor.; as a term of reproach to slaves: Pl., Ter., Verg.

fŭrax -ācis (¹furor) adj. (with compar. and superl.), *inclined to steal, thievish*: homo avarus et furax, Cic.

¶ Hence superl. adv. **fŭrācissĭmē**, *most thievishly*: domos scrutari, Cic.

furca -ae, f. (fero), *a (two-pronged) fork*.

LIT., *a pitch-fork*: furcā detrudere aliquem, Liv.; prov.: naturam expellas furcā, tamen usque recurret, Hor.

TRANSF., (1) *a fork-shaped prop* or *pole*: valli furcaeque bicornes, Verg.; furcae duodenos ab terra spectacula alta sustinentes pedes, Liv.; Ov. (2) *an instrument of punishment, with two prongs to which the arms were tied*: Pl., Cic., Liv.; fig.: ire sub furcam, Hor. (3) *a narrow pass*: Furcae Caudinae, *see* Caudium.

furcĭfer -fĕra -fĕrum (furca/fero), *that carries the* furca *as a punishment*; a term of reproach usually applied to slaves, *gallows-bird*: Pl., Cic., Hor.

furcilla -ae, f. (dim. of furca), *a little fork*; prov.: furcillā extrudi, *to be expelled by force*, Cic. L.

furcillo -āre (furcilla), *to support*: Pl.

furcŭla -ae, f. (dim. of furca), *a little fork*; hence (1) *a fork-shaped prop*: Liv. (2) *a narrow pass*, esp.: furculae Caudinae, *the Caudine forks*, Liv.

fŭrentĕr, adv. from furo; q.v.

furfur -ŭris, m. (1) *bran*: Pl. (2) *scales, scurf on the skin*: Plin.

fŭrĭa -ae, f., usually plur. (furo), *rage, frenzy, madness, passion, fury*: muliebres furiae, Liv.; ventorum furiae, Verg.; iustis furiis, Verg.; tauri, Mart. Personif. **Fŭrĭa** -ae, f., usually plur. **Fŭrĭae** -ārum, f. *the mythological Furies* (Allecto, Megaera, Tisiphone), *the deities who avenged crimes and tormented criminals, esp. parricides*: eos (parricidas) agitent Furiae, Cic.; Verg., Hor.

TRANSF., of persons: illa Furia, *Clodius*, Cic.; hunc iuvenem tamquam furiam facemque huius belli, Liv.

fŭrĭālis -e (furia). (1) *furious, raging, frenzied*: vox, Cic.; carmen, Liv.; Erichtho, *inspired with Bacchic fury*, Ov. (2) *belonging to the Furies*: membra, Verg.; Cic., Ov.

¶ Adv. **fŭrĭālĭtĕr**, *furiously, madly*: Ov.

fŭrĭbundus -a -um (furo). (1) *raging, furious*: furibundus homo ac perditus, Cic.; Hor. (2) *inspired*: praedictio, Cic.

fŭrĭo -are (furia), *to make furious, madden*: matres equorum, Hor.; partic., furiatus, *raging*: mens, Verg.

fŭrĭōsus -a -um, adj. (with compar. and superl.) (furia), *raging, raving, mad, furious*; of persons: mulier iam non morbo sed scelere furiosa, Cic.; Hor.; of things: cupiditas, Cic.; tibia, *maddening*, Ov.

¶ Adv. **fŭrĭōsē**, *furiously, madly*: aliquid furiose facere, Cic. L.

Fūrĭus -a -um, *name of a Roman gens*; *its most famous member was M. Furius Camillus, who freed Rome from the Gauls.*

furnārĭa -ae, f. (furnus), *the trade of a baker*: Suet.

furnus -i, m. *an oven, a bakehouse*: Pl., Hor., Ov.

fŭro -ĕre (cf. φύρω), *to rage, rave, be mad*.

LIT., furere se simulavit, Cic.; Hor.

TRANSF., (1) of impassioned persons, *to rave, be frantic*: Catilina furens audaciā, Cic.; libidinibus inflammatus et furens, Cic.; furere aliquā, *to be madly in love with*, Hor.; furens Neptunus, *the raging waves*, Hor.; with acc.: furorem, Verg.; with acc. and infin.: (Clodius) furebat a Racilio se contumaciter urbaneque vexatum, Cic. L. (2) of a passion: ardor edendi, Ov. (3) of physical objects: ventus, Lucr.; animate objects: tempestas, ignis, Verg.

¶ Hence from partic. furens, adv **fŭrentĕr**, *furiously*: irasci, Cic. L.

¹fŭror -ari, dep. (fur), *to steal, pilfer*. LIT., quae rapuit et furatus est, Cic.; librum ab aliquo (of plagiarists), Cic. L. TRANSF., (1) fig., *to steal away, withdraw*: oculos labori Verg. (2) *to counterfeit, personate*: civitatem Cic.; speciem, Prop.

²fŭror -ōris, m. (furo), *madness, raving, insanity* LIT., ira furor brevis est, Hor.; Cic.

TRANSF., (1) of strong passions: esp.: a *furious anger, martial rage*: versatur mih ante oculos aspectus Cethegi et furor ir vestra caede bacchantis, Cic.; Iuno act furore gravi, Verg.; sic animis iuvenum furor additus, Verg.; personif.: Furor, as ar attendant of Mars, Verg.: **b**, *passionate love* intus erat furor igneus, Ov.; meton., *th object of passion*: sive mihi Phyllis sive esse Amyntas seu quicumque furor, Verg (2) *inspiration, poetic* or *prophetic frenzy* negat sine furore Democritus poetan magnum esse posse, Cic.; Ov. (3) of physica objects: furores caeli marisque, Verg. Cat.

furtĭfĭcus -a -um (furtum/facio), *thievish*: P

furtim, adv. (furtum), *by stealth, stealthily secretly*: Pl., Cic., Hor., Liv., Tac.

furtīvus -a -um (furtum). (1) *stolen*: strigilis Hor.; Pl., Liv. (2) *secret, concealed, furtive* iter per Italiam, Cic.; amor, Verg.; Ov.

¶ Adv. **furtīvē**, *stealthily, secretly*: Pl. Ov.

furtum -i, n. (fur), *a theft, robbery*. LIT. furtum facere alicuius rei, Cic.; fur damnari, Cic. TRANSF., (1) in plur., *stole property*: Cic., Hor. (2) *underhand methods trick, deceit*: furto laetatus inani, Verg.; furt et fraude, Liv. (3) *secret* or *stolen love*: Verg Ov.

fūruncŭlus -i, m. (dim. of fur), *a sneak thie pilferer*: Cic.

furvus -a -um (cf. fuscus), *dark-coloured dark, black*. LIT., equus, Ov.; Juv. TRANSF of the lower world: antrum, Ov.; Proserpin Hor.

fuscĭna -ae, f. *a three-pronged fork, trident* Cic., Juv.

fusco -are (fuscus), *to darken, blacken*: dente Ov.; Luc.

---

fuscus -a -um (cf. furvus), *dark-coloured, dark, black.* Lit., cornix, Cic.; purpura paene fusca, Cic.; Verg., Ov. Transf., of the voice, *indistinct*: genus vocis, Cic.

fūsē, adv. from ²fundo; q.v.

fūsĭlis -e (²fundo), *molten, liquid, soft*: aurum, Ov.; ferventes fusili, ex argilla glandes, Caes.

fūsĭo -ōnis, f. (²fundo), *a pouring-out, out-pouring*: mundum esse eius (dei) animi fusionem universam, Cic.

fustis -is; abl. -i and -e; m. *a stick, staff, cudgel, club*: Pl., Cic., Hor., Tac.

fustĭtūdĭnus -a -um (fustis/tundo), *cudgel-walloping*: Pl.

fustŭārĭum -i, n. (fustis), *cudgelling to death,* a military punishment: Cic., Liv.

¹fūsus -a -um, partic. from ²fundo; q.v.

²fūsus -i, m. *a spindle*: fusum versare, Ov.; as an attribute of the Parcae: suis dixerunt, currite fusis, Verg.

fūtātim, *abundantly*: Pl.

futtĭlis and **fūtĭlis** -e (connected with ²fundo). (1) *brittle*: glacies, Verg. (2) *vain, worthless, futile, good for nothing*: haruspices, Cic.; sententiae, Cic.; auctor, Verg.

futtĭlĭtās and **fūtĭlĭtās** -ātis, f. (futtilis), *worthlessness, folly, silliness*: Cic.

fŭtŭo -ŭĕre -ŭi -ūtum, *to have intercourse with* a woman: Cat., Mart.

fŭtūrus -a -um, used as future partic of sum; q.v.

G

G, g, the seventh letter of the Latin Alphabet, originally represented by C, introduced into the Latin Alphabet about the time of the second Punic war. For the use of this letter in abbreviations, see Table of Abbreviations.

Găbăli -ōrum, m. *a people in the south-east of Gallia Aquitania.*

Găbii -ōrum, m. *a very ancient city of Latium, between Rome and Praeneste.* Adj. **Găbīnus** -a -um, *Gabinian*: via, *from Gabii to Rome,* Liv.; Iuno, *honoured in Gabii,* Verg.; cinctus, *a particular mode of wearing the toga,* Liv.

Găbīnĭus -a -um, *name of a Roman gens; its most famous member was* A. Gabinius, *who restored the Egyptian king Ptolemaeus Auletes to his kingdom.* As adj. = *of a Gabinius,* esp. lex, *a law giving extraordinary military power to Pompeius,* Cic.; also adj. **Găbīnĭānus** -a -um.

Gādēs -ium, f. *a town in Hispania Baetica* (now *Cadiz*). Adj. and subst. **Gādītānus** -a -um, *of Gades, a man of Gades.*

gaesum -i, n. *a long heavy javelin, originally a Gaulish weapon*: Caes., Liv., Verg.

Gaetūli -ōrum, m. *a people in north-west Africa.* Adj. **Gaetūlus** -a -um and **Gaetūlicus** -a -um.

Gāius -i, m. (abbrev. C.) and **Gaia** -ae, f. *a common praenomen among the Romans.* At a wedding, the bride and bridegroom were called by these names, and the bride said 'Ubi tu Gaius, ego Gaia'.

Esp. (1) *the name of the emperor Gaius Caesar or Caligula.* (2) *the name of a celebrated Roman jurist* (A.D. 110–180).

Gălaesus -i, m. *a river in the south of Italy* (now *Galaso*).

Gălătae -ārum, m. (Γαλάται) *a Celtic people settled in Asia Minor, the Galatians.*

¶ Hence **Gălătĭa** -ae, f. *the country of the Galatae.*

Galba -ae, m. *a cognomen of the Sulpician gens*; esp. of Ser. Sulpicius, *emperor* A.D. 68–69.

galbănĕus -a -um (galbanum), *of galbanum*: Verg.

galbănum -i, n. (χαλβάνη), *the resinous sap of a Syrian plant* (Bubon galbanum, Linn.): Plin., Suet.

galbĕum -i, n. or **galbĕus** -i, m. *an arm-band* or *bandage for the arm*: Suet.

galbĭnus -a -um, *greenish-yellow*: Mart.; n. pl. as subst., *greenish-yellow garments*: Juv.

gălĕa -ae, f. *a helmet*; originally *of leather*: Pl., Caes.; later *of metal* also: aenea, Cic.; aerea, Verg.

gălĕo -are, *to cover with a helmet*; usually partic., **gălĕātus** -a -um, *armed with a helmet*: Minerva, Cic.; Juv.

Gălĕōtae -ārum, m. (Γαλεῶται), *a body of Sicilian seers*: Cic.

gălērĭcŭlum -i, n. (dim. of galerum). (1) *a skull-cap*: Mart. (2) *a wig*: Suet.

gălērītus -a -um (galerus), *wearing a hood* or *skull-cap*: Prop.

gălērum -i, n. (**gălērus** -i, m.: Verg.). (1) *a skull-cap*: Verg., Juv., Suet. (2) *a wig*: Juv., Suet.

galla -ae, f. *the gall-nut, oak-apple*: Verg.

Gallaeci (**Callaeci**) -ōrum, m. *a people in the north-west of Spain.*

¶ Hence **Gallaecĭa** -ae, f. *the country of the Gallaeci*; adj. **Gallaecus** -a -um and **Gallaïcus** -a -um.

Galli -ōrum, m. *the Gauls, a Celtic people, living to the west of the Rhine and in the north of Italy*; sing. **Gallus** -i, m. *a Gaul* and **Galla** -ae, f. *a Gaulish woman.*

¶ Hence **Gallĭa** -ae, f. *Gaul, the land of the Gauls*; Cisalpina = *Northern Italy*; Trans-alpina = *France*; adj. **Gallĭcānus** -a -um and **Gallĭcus** -a -um, *Gaulish*: canis, *a grey-hound*, Ov.; f. as subst., gallica (sc. solea), *a kind of slipper*: Cic.

gallĭambus -i, m. *a song of the priests of Cybele*: Mart.

gallĭca -ae, f. *see* Galli.

gallīna -ae, f. (¹gallus), *a hen*: Pl., Cic., Hor.

gallīnācĕus -a -um (gallina), *relating to poultry*: gallus, *a poultry-cock*, Pl., Cic.

gallīnārĭus -a -um (gallina), *relating to poultry*; m. as subst., *a poultry-farmer*: Cic.

Gallograeci -orum, m. pl. = Galatae; q.v.

¶ Hence **Gallograecĭa** -ae, f. = Galatia; q.v.

¹gallus -i, m. *a cock, dunghill cock*: gallorum cantus, cock-crow, Cic.; Hor.

²Gallus, *a Gaul, see* Galli.

³Gallus -i, m. usually plur. **Galli** -ōrum, m. *a priest of Cybele.*

¶ Hence adj. **Gallĭcus** -a -um, *of the priests of Cybele.* Transf., *of the priests of Isis* whose worship resembled that of Cybele: turba, Ov.

'Gallus -i, m., C. Cornelius (69–26 B.C.), *a poet and orator, friend of Vergil.*

gānĕa -ae, f. and gānĕum -i, n. (Pl., Ter.), *a brothel* or *a low eating-house*: Cic., Liv., Tac.

gānĕo -ōnis, m. (ganea), *a debauchee*: Ter., Cic., Tac.

Gangărĭdae and Gangărĭdes -um, m. *a people in India, on the Ganges.*

Gangēs -is, m. (Γάγγης), *the river Ganges in India.* Adj. Gangēticus -a -um; f. adj. Gangētis -ĭdis = *Indian*: Ov.

gannĭo -ire, *to yelp, to snarl, growl*; originally of dogs; of persons: Ter., Cat., Juv.

gannītus -ūs, m. (gannio), *a yelping, snarling*; of dogs: Lucr.; of persons: Mart.

Gănўmēdēs -is, m. (Γανυμήδης), *son of the Trojan king Tros, carried off on account of his beauty by an eagle, and made the cup-bearer of Jove*; adj. Ganymēdēus -a -um.

Gărămantes -um, m. (Γαράμαντες), *a people in the interior of Africa.*

¶ Hence f. adj. Gărămantis -ĭdis: Verg.

Gargānus -i, m. *a mountain of Apulia* (now *Monte di S. Angelo*). Adj. Gargānus -a -um, *of* or *belonging to Garganus.*

Gargettus -i, m. (Γαργηττός), *a deme in Attica, birth-place of Epicurus, hence called Garget-tius.*

Gargīlĭus -a -um, *name of a Roman gens.*

garrĭo -ire (connected with γῆρυς, Doric γᾶρυς), *to chatter, prate, babble*; with object: nugas, Pl.; fabellas, Hor.; Cic. L.; absol.: in iis philosophi garrire coeperunt, Cic. TRANSF., of frogs: Mart.

garrŭlĭtās -ātis, f. (garrulus), *chattering*; of magpies: garrulitas rauca, Ov.

garrŭlus -a -um (garrio), *talkative, garrulous, chattering, babbling.* LIT., of persons: Pl., Hor.; garrula lingua, Ov. TRANSF., (1) of animals: cornix, Ov.; hirundo, Verg. (2) of inanimate objects, *noisy*: rivus, Ov.; lyra, Tib. (3) of abstr. things: hora, Prop.

gărum -i, n. (γάρος), *a fish-sauce*: Hor., Mart.

Gărumna -ae, f. *a river in Gaul* (now *Garonne*).

¶ Hence Gărumni -ōrum, m. *a people living on the Garonne.*

gaudĕo gaudēre gāvīsus sum (cf. γηθέω), *to rejoice, be glad.*

LIT., of persons; in gen.: si est nunc ullus gaudendi locus, Cic.; poet. with partic.: gaudent scribentes, *write with pleasure*, Hor.; gen. with abl. of cause, *to delight in*: correctione gaudere, Cic.; Hor., Liv., etc.; with internal acc.: gaudium, Ter., Cat.; with acc. and infin.: quae perfecta esse gaudeo, Cic.; Pl., Caes.; with infin. alone: laedere gaudes, Hor.; Tac.; with quod: sane gaudeo quod te interpellavi, Cic.; Hor. Esp. (1) in sinu gaudere, *to rejoice in secret*, Cic., Tib.; so: in se, Cat. (2) like salvere, in a salutation: Celso gaudere refer, *take my greeting to Celsus*, Hor.

TRANSF., of inanimate objects, *to delight in*: scena gaudens miraculis, Liv.; Verg., Prop.

gaudĭum -i, n. (gaudeo), *joy, gladness, delight* (esp. as an inward feeling; laetitia denotes external expression). LIT., gaudio exclamare, Ter.; triumphare, exsultare, Cic.; aliquem gaudio adficere, Liv.; gaudia corporis, Sall. Meton., *that which produces*

---

delight: gaudio esse, Pl.; Clytium, nova gaudia, Verg.; Liv.

Gaurus -i, m. *a mountain in Campania.*

gausăpĕ -is, n. and gausăpum -i, n. (γαυσάπης), *a woollen cloth with a long nap, frieze*: Ov., Hor. TRANSF., of a beard: Pers.

gāza -ae, f. (Persian word), originally *the royal treasure of Persia*; hence in gen., *treasure, riches, wealth*: regia, Cic.; agrestis, Verg.; Hor., Liv.

Gĕla -ae, f. (Γέλα), *a town on the south coast of Sicily.*

¶ Hence adj. Gĕlōus -a -um, *of Gela*; subst. Gĕlenses -ĭum, m. *the inhabitants of Gela.*

gĕlăsīnus -i, m. (γελασῖνος), *a dimple on the cheek*: Mart.

gĕlĭdus -a -um (gelu), *cold, icy-cold, frosty, icy.*

LIT., aqua, Cic.; humor, Verg.; Lucr., Liv.; f. as subst. gĕlĭda -ae (sc. aqua), *cold water*: Hor., Juv.

TRANSF., applied to the chill of old age, fear, death, etc. (1) pass.: sanguis, Verg. (2) act., *chilling*: tremor, Verg.; mors, Hor.; metus, Ov.

¶ Adv. gĕlĭdē, *coldly, feebly*: Hor.

Gellĭus -a -um, *name of a Roman gens*; its most famous member was A. Gellius, *a grammarian of the second century* A.D.

gĕlo -are (gelu). (1) transit., *to cause to freeze, to freeze.* LIT., Mart. TRANSF., of fear: pavido gelantur pectore, Juv. (2) intransit., *to freeze*: Plin., Luc.

Gĕlōni -ōrum, m. (Γελωνοί), *a Scythian people on the Borysthenes in Russia.* Sing. Gĕlōnus -i, m. collect. *the Geloni*: Verg.

gĕlu -ūs, n. (earlier gĕlus -ūs, m. and gĕlum -i, n.), *frost, icy cold*; usually abl. sing. LIT., rura gelu claudit hiems, Verg.; Hor., Liv. TRANSF., *the chill of age, death, fear*, etc.: Verg.

gĕmĕbundus -a -um (gemo), *groaning, sighing*: Ov.

gĕmellĭpăra -ae, f. adj. (gemellus/pario), *twin-bearing*: dea, or diva, Latona, Ov.

gĕmellus -a -um (dim. of geminus), *twin, double.*

LIT., (1) *twin*: fratres, proles, Ov.; m. as subst., *a twin*: Cat.; plur.: gemelli, *twins*, Verg., Hor., Ov. (2) *paired, double*: quam (legionem) factam ex duabus gemellam appellabat, Caes.

TRANSF., *resembling each other like twins, similar*: par nobile fratrum nequitiā et nugis pravorum et amore gemellum, Hor.

gĕmĭnātĭo -ōnis, f. (gemino), *a doubling*: verborum, Cic.

gĕmĭno -are (geminus).

(1) transit., *to double*: victoriae laetitiam, Liv. Hence partic. gĕmĭnātus -a -um, *doubled*: sol, Cic.; Liv. TRANSF., a, *to join together*: tigribus agni, Hor.; aera, *strike together*, Hor.: b, *to repeat*: vulnus, Ov.; Verg., Liv.

(2) intransit., *to be double*: Lucr.

gĕmĭnus -a -um, *twin, double.*

LIT., (1) *twin, twin-born*: fratres, Cic.; m. pl. as subst. gĕmĭni -ōrum, *twins, esp. the twins Castor and Pollux*: Cic., Liv. (2) *double; paired* or *half-and-half*: geminae nuptiae, Ter.; acies, Verg.; aures,

Ov.; Chiron, *the Centaur, half man and half horse*, Ov.; Cecrops, *half Greek and half Egyptian*, Ov.
TRANSF., *similar, alike*: geminus et simillimus nequitiā, Cic.

ᵹĕmĭtus -ūs, m. (gemo), *a sigh, groan*. LIT., of persons: gemitus fit, Cic.; gemitum dare, tollere, Verg. TRANSF., of things, *a groaning, roaring*: pelagi, Verg.

ᵹemma -ae, f. (probably connected with gigno), *a bud* or *eye of a plant*: Cic., Verg.
TRANSF., *a jewel, gem, precious stone*: Cic., Ov. Hence meton. (1) *a thing made of* or *adorned with jewels, a goblet*: bibere gemmā, Verg.; *a seal-ring, seal*: gemmā signare, Ov. (2) gemmae, *the eyes in a peacock's tail*, Ov. (3) *a literary gem*: Mart.

ᵹemmātus -a -um (gemma), *set* or *adorned with jewels*: monilia, Ov.; Liv.

ᵹemmĕus -a -um (gemma), *made of* or *set with jewels, gemmed*: trulla, Cic.; Ov. TRANSF., *bright*: Plin. L., Mart.

ᵹemmĭfer -fĕra -fĕrum (gemma/fero), *bearing* or *producing jewels*: mare, Prop.

ᵹemmo -are (gemma), *to bud*: vites, Cic. TRANSF., in pres. partic. **gemmans** -antis, *set with jewels*: sceptra gemmantia, Ov.; fig., *glittering like jewels*: herbae gemmantes rore recenti, Lucr.

ᵹĕmo gĕmĕre gĕmŭi gĕmĭtum.
(1) intransit., *to sigh, groan*; of persons: desiderio alicuius, Cic. TRANSF., **a**, of animals; of the lion, *to roar*: Lucr.; of the turtle-dove, *to coo*: Verg.: **b**, of inanimate objects, *to groan, creak*: gementis litora Bospori, Hor.; gemuit sub pondere cymba, Verg.
(2) transit., *to sigh* or *groan over, lament, bemoan*: aliquid, Cic.; Ityn, Hor.; with infin., or acc. and infin.: Hor.

ᵹĕmōnĭae -ārum, f. (sc. scalae); more rarely Gemoniae scalae, *a flight of steps from the Aventine hill to the Tiber, down which the dead bodies of malefactors were thrown*.

ᵹĕna -ae, f. usually plur. (cf. γένυς), *cheek* or *cheeks and chin*: Cic., Verg. TRANSF., (1) *the eye-sockets*: Ov. (2) *an eye* or *the eyes*: et patiar fossis lumen abire genis, Ov.; Prop.

ᵹĕnābum -i, n. *a town in Gaul, the capital of the Carnutes* (now *Orléans*). Adj. **Gĕnābensis** -e, *of Genabum*.

ᵹĕnauni -ōrum, m. *a people in Rhaetia*.

ᵹĕnāva -ae, f. *a town of the Allobroges* (now *Geneva*).

ᵹĕnĕălŏgus -i, m. (γενεαλόγος), *a genealogist*: Cic.

ᵹĕner -ĕri, m. (connected with gigno), *a son-in-law*: Pl., Cic., Ov.; also *a prospective son-in-law*: Verg., Hor.; *a grand-daughter's husband*: Tac.; *a brother-in-law*: Nep.

ᵹĕnĕrālis -e (genus). (1) *belonging to a kind, generic*: constitutio, Cic.; Lucr. (2) *universal, general*: quoddam decorum, Cic.; Quint.
¶ Adv. **gĕnĕrālĭtĕr**, *in general, generally*: Cic.

ᵹĕnĕrasco -ĕre (genero), *to be produced, come to birth*: Lucr.

ᵹĕnĕrātim, adv. (genus). (1) *according to kinds* or *classes*: generatim saecla propagent, Lucr.; Cic., Verg. (2) *in general, generally*: singillatim potius quam generatim loqui, Cic.

gĕnĕrātor -ōris, m. (genero), *a begetter, producer*: nosse generatores suos optime poterant, Cic.; Acragas equorum, Verg.

gĕnĕro -are (genus), *to beget, produce, bring to life*. LIT., of living beings: deus hominem generavit, Cic.; Herculis stirpe generatus, Cic.; quale portentum nec lubae tellus generat, Hor. TRANSF., of inanimate objects: Verg., Quint.

gĕnĕrōsus -a -um (genus), adj. (with compar. and superl.), *of noble birth, noble*.
LIT., (1) of persons: Cic., Verg. (2) of animals, plants, etc., *well-bred*: pecus, Verg.; vinum, Hor. (3) of a place, *producing well*: insula generosa metalli, Verg.
TRANSF., of character, *noble, magnanimous*: virtus, Cic.; mens, Ov.
¶ Adv. **gĕnĕrōsē**, *nobly*: perire, Hor.

gĕnĕsis -is, f. (γένεσις), *the constellation which presides over one's birth*: Juv., Suet.

gĕnĕtīvus -a -um (geno=gigno). (1) *inborn, innate*: imago, Ov.; nomina, *family names*, Ov. (2) casus, *the genitive case*, Suet.

gĕnĕtrix -tricis, f. (genitor), *one who brings forth*; *a mother*: Aeneadum, *Venus*, Lucr.; magna deum, *Cybele*, Verg. TRANSF., *she that produces*: frugum, *Ceres*, Ov.; Cic.

gĕniālis -e (genius), *belonging to the genius of a person*; hence (1) *relating to marriage*: lectus, *the marriage-bed*, Cic., Hor., Liv. (2) *relating to enjoyment; joyful, gay*: festum, Ov.; hiems, Verg.
¶ Adv. **gĕniālĭtĕr**, *jovially, gaily*: Ov.

gĕnĭcŭlātus -a -um (geniculum), *knotty, full of knots*: culmus, Cic.

gĕnĭcŭlum -i, n. (dim. of genu). (1) *the knee*: Varr. (2) *a knot in a plant*: Plin.

gĕnista (**gĕnesta**) -ae, f. *the plant broom*: Verg.

gĕnĭtābĭlis -e (geno=gigno), *fruitful, productive*: Lucr.

gĕnĭtālis -e (geno=gigno), *belonging to birth*; hence (1) *creative, fruitful*: Lucr., Verg. (2) dies, *birthday*, Tac. (3) *of Diana, as presiding over births*: Hor.
¶ Adv. **gĕnĭtālĭtĕr**, *in a fruitful manner*: Lucr.

gĕnĭtīvus, see gĕnĕtīvus.

gĕnĭtor -ōris, m. (geno=gigno), *a begetter, father*: deum, *Jupiter*, Ov. TRANSF., *producer*: quae genitor produxerit usus, Hor.; Ov.

gĕnĭtura -ae, f. (geno=gigno), *a begetting, engendering*: Plin. TRANSF., *the constellation which presides over a birth*: Suet.

gĕnĭus -i, m. (geno=gigno), *the guardian spirit of a man* or *place, a genius*: genium piare, placare, Hor.; loci, Verg.; urbis Romae, Liv. Esp. as *a spirit of enjoyment, one's taste, inclination*: genium curare vino, *to enjoy oneself with*, Hor.; December geniis acceptus (because of rest from toil in the fields), Ov. TRANSF., *talent, genius*: Juv.

gĕno=gigno; q.v.

gens gentis, f. (geno, old form of gigno).
(1) *a gens, a clan, a number of families connected by a common descent and the use of the same gentile name*. LIT., vir patriciae gentis, Cic.; gens Cornelia, Liv.; sine gente, *of low origin*, Hor.; patricii maiorum gentium (*senators appointed by Romulus*), minorum gentium (*appointed by Tarquin*), Cic. L.

TRANSF., **a**, of gods: maiorum gentium dii, *superior gods*, Cic.: **b**, of beasts, *a stock*: Verg., Ov.

(2) *an offspring, descendant*: vigilasne, deum gens, Aenea? Verg.

(3) more generally, *a people, tribe, nation*. LIT., exterae nationes et gentes, Cic.; Suevorum, Caes. TRANSF., **a**, *a district, country*; esp. in partitive genit.: ubi gentium? *where in the world?* Pl.; minime gentium, *not the least bit in the world*, Ter.: **b**, plur.: gentes, *foreigners*, Tac.

genticus -a -um (gens), *belonging to a nation, national*: Tac.

gentilicius -a -um (gentilis), *belonging to a particular gens*: sacra, Liv.

gentilis -e (gens), *belonging to a gens*. LIT., nomen, Suet.; manus, *of the 300 Fabii*, Ov.; m. as subst., *a clansman, a person of the same gens*: Cic., Liv., Suet. TRANSF., *belonging to a country, national*: religio, Tac.

gentilitas -ātis, f. (gentilis), *the relationship between the members of a gens*: Cic.

genu -ūs, n. (γόνυ), *the knee*: advolvi genibus alicuius, Liv., Tac.; genibus minor, *kneeling*, Hor.; Cic.

Genŭa -ae, f. *coast-town in Liguria* (now *Genoa*).

genŭalia -ium, n. pl. (genu), *garters*: Ov.

¹**genŭinus** -a -um (geno=gigno), *natural, innate*: genuinae domesticaeque virtutes, Cic.

²**genŭinus** -a -um (genae), *relating or belonging to the cheek or jaw*: dentes, *the jawteeth*, Cic.; so m. as subst. **genŭinus** -i, *a jaw-tooth*: Verg., Juv.

¹**genus** -ěris, n. (geno=gigno and γένος), *kind*.

LIT., (1) *birth, descent, origin*: genus patricium, plebeium, Liv.; maternum, paternum, Cic.; Verg.; esp. *of high birth*: genus et virtus, Hor. (2) *race, stock, family, house*: genus Aemilium, Fabium, Liv.; Hispanum, Liv.; genere regio natum esse, Cic.; Hor.; hence *offspring, descendant*, and collectively, *descendants*: genus deorum (of Aeneas), Verg.; *sex*: genus virile, muliebre, Cic.

TRANSF., (1) *of living beings, class, kind*: genus humanum, Cic.; omnis generis homines, Cic.; Caes., Hor.; also *of animals*: multa genera ferarum, Caes.; Lucr., Cic. (2) *of things, kind, variety, sort*: armorum, Caes.; omne genus frugum, Liv.; id genus imperii, Cic. (3) *as philosoph. t. t., genus* in logic: genus universum in species certas partiri, Cic. (4) *in gen., fashion, manner, way*: tota domus in omni genere diligens, Cic.

²**genus** -ūs=genu; q.v.

geōgraphia -ae, f. (γεωγραφία), *geography*: Cic.

geōmetrēs -ae, m. (γεωμέτρης), *a geometer*: Cic., Quint., Juv.

geōmetria -ae, f. (γεωμετρία), *geometry*: Cic., Quint.

geōmetricus -a -um (γεωμετρικός), *geometrical*: formae, *figures*, Cic. As subst. m. **geōmetricus** -i, *a geometer*: Quint.; n. pl. **geōmetrica** -ōrum, *geometry*: geometrica didicisse, Cic.

geōrgicus -a -um (γεωργικός), *agricultural*; n. pl.as subst. **Geōrgica** -ōrum, *the Georgics of Vergil*: Gell.

Gergŏvia -ae, f. *town of the Averni in Gallia Aquitania*.

Germāni -ōrum, m. pl. *the Germans*.
¶ Hence **Germānus** -a -um, adj. *German*. **Germānia** -ae, f. *Germany*: superio, inferior, Tac.; plur.: Germaniae, Tac. **Germānicus** -a -um, adj. *German*; m. a subst. **Germānicus** -i, surname (o account of victories in Germany) of *Augustu son-in-law Tiberius Drusus*, of *Drusus' so* of the *emperor Domitian*, and others.

germānitās -ātis (germanus). LIT., *the rela tionship between brothers and sisters, brother hood, sisterhood*: Cic.; Liv. TRANSF., (1) *th connexion between cities which are colonies o the same mother-city*: Liv. (2) *in gen similarity*: Plin.

¹**germānus** -a -um (like germen, from geno= gigno), *having the same parents*: frater, soro Cic.; Pl., Ter. As subst. m. **germānus** -i, *own brother*; f. **germāna** -ae, *own sister*: Verg

TRANSF., (1) *brotherly, sisterly*: in germa num modum, Pl. (2) *genuine, real, true*: sci me asinum germanum fuisse, Cic. L.; Pl. superl.: Cic.

¶ Adv. **germānē**, *faithfully, honestly* rescribere, Cic.

²**Germānus** -a -um, *see* Germani.

germen -inis, n. (from geno=gigno, or els from gero). LIT., *an embryo*: Ov. TRANSF (1) *a bud, shoot or graft*: Verg. (2) fig., *ger* (of madness): Lucr.

germĭno -are (germen), *to sprout forth*: Hor TRANSF., *to put forth*: Plin.

¹**gěro** gěrěre gessi gestum, *to carry, bear*.

LIT., (1) *to carry about*: hastam, Verg esp. *to wear*: vestem, Ov. (2) *to carry a thin, somewhere*: saxa in muros, Liv. (3) *to bear give birth to*; of human beings: Plin.; of th earth, plants, etc.: platani malos gessere Verg.; violam terra, Ov.

TRANSF., (1) *to carry about, display a appearance*: virginis os habitumque gerens Verg.; or a quality: fortem animum, Sall. prae se utilitatem, Cic.; personam gerere, t *act a part*, Cic.; se gerere, *to show oneself* in *certain light, conduct oneself*; with adv. honeste, Cic.; with adj.: dis te minorem Hor.; with phrase: pro cive, Cic.; mor maiorum, Sall. (2) *to carry about, entertai* a feeling: iras, Pl.; inimicitias, Cic.; pro m curam, Verg. (3) *to carry on, conduct manage* public or private business: rem benc male gerere, Cic.; res gestae, *exploits*, esp. *warlike exploits*, Cic.; rempublicam gerer atque administrare, Cic.; magistratum, Cic. negotium, Cic. L.; bellum, Caes., Cic., Liv

²**gěro** -ōnis, m. (¹gero), *a carrier*: Pl.

gerrae -ārum, f. pl. (γέρρα), *wattled twigs* Varr. TRANSF., *trifles, nonsense*: Pl.

gerro -ōnis, m. (gerrae), *a trifler, idler*: Ter.

gěrŭlifĭgŭlus -i, m. (gerulus/figulus), *a abettor*: Pl.

gěrŭlus -i, m. (¹gero), *a porter, carrier*: Pl Hor., Suet.

Gēryōn -ŏnis, m. and **Gēryŏnēs** -ae, m (Γηρυών and Γηρυόνης), myth., *a king in Spai with three bodies, killed by Hercules*.

gestāmen -ĭnis, n. (gesto). (1) *that which carried*: clipeus gestamen Abantis, Verg (2) *that by which anything is carried; a carriag* or *litter*: Tac.

gesticŭlātio -ōnis, f. (gesticulor), *pantomime gesticulation*: Quint., Suet.

gestĭcŭlor -ari, dep. (from gesticulus, dim. of gestus), *to make pantomimic gestures, gesticulate* : Suet.

¹gestĭo -ōnis, f. (¹gero), *management, performance* : negotii, Cic.

²gestĭo -ire (¹gero). (1) *to exult, to be excited, run riot*; esp. with abl.: laetitiā, Cic.; voluptate, Cic.; animus gestiens rebus secundis, Liv. (2) *to desire eagerly, to long*; with infin.: scire omnia, Cic.; Pl., Hor.

gestĭto -are (freq. of gesto), *to carry often, wear often* : Pl.

gesto -are (freq. of ¹gero), *to carry, bear about.* Lɪᴛ., caput in pilo, Cic.; clavos manu, Hor.; pectora, Verg.; pass. as middle, *to ride about* : Sen., Juv.

gestor -ōris, m. (¹gero), *a tale-bearer, gossip* : Pl.

gestus -ūs, m. (¹gero), used in sing. and plur., *the carriage of the body, posture* : gestum imitari, Lucr.; Cic.; esp. *the studied gestures of an actor* or *orator* : histrionum nonnulli gestus, Cic.; Quint., Juv.

Gĕta -ae, m. and **Gĕtēs** -ae, m.; usually plur. **Gĕtae** -ārum, m. (*Γέται*), *a people of Thrace living near the Danube.* Adj. **Gĕtĭcus** -a -um, poet.=*Thracian*; adv. **Gĕtĭcē**, *after the Getic fashion* : loqui, Ov.

Gētŭlus, etc.=Gaetulus, etc.; q.v.

gibba -ae, f. (cf. gibbus), *a hump, hunch* : Suet.

gibber -ĕra -ĕrum, *hump-backed* : Suet.

gibbus -i, m. (connected with *κύπτω, κυφός*), *a hump, hunch* : Juv.

Gĭgās -gantis, m. (*Γίγας*), *a giant*; usually plur., Gigantes, *sons of Earth and Tartarus, who in an attempt to storm heaven were killed by the lightning of Jupiter.* Adj. **Gĭgantēus** -a -um : Verg.

gigno gignĕre gĕnŭi gĕnĭtum (originally geno), *to beget, bear, bring forth.* Lɪᴛ., Herculem Iuppiter genuit, Cic.; pass., with plain abl. of origin: Verg., Liv.; or ex: Ov.; de: Ov.; ab: Tac. Tʀᴀɴsғ., *to cause* : virtus amicitiam, Cic.; Hor.

gilvus -a -um, *pale yellow* : Verg.

gingīva -ae, f. *gum (of the mouth)* : Cat., Juv.

glăber -bra -brum, *without hair, bald* : Pl.; m. as subst., *a page* : Cat.

glăcĭālis -e (glacies), *icy* : hiems, Verg.; frigus, Ov.

glăcĭēs -ēi, f. *ice* : dura et alte concreta glacies, Liv.; plur.: glacies Hyperboreae, Verg. Tʀᴀɴsғ., *hardness* : aeris, Lucr.

glăcĭo -are (glacies), *to freeze* : nives, Hor.

glădĭātor -ōris, m. (gladius), *one hired to fight at public shows, a gladiator,* Cic.; as a term of reproach, *bandit, brigand* : Cic. Meton., gladiatores=*gladiatorial exhibition* : dare, Cic.; Liv., Tac.; abl.: gladiatoribus, *at a show of gladiators,* Cic. L.

glădĭātōrĭus -a -um (gladiator), *pertaining to gladiators, gladiatorial* : animus, Ter.; ludus, Cic.; familia, *a troop* or *band of gladiators,* Cic.; locus, *the place of exhibition,* Cic.; consessus, *the assembled spectators,* Cic.; munus, spectaculum, Cic. Tʀᴀɴsғ., totius corporis firmitas, Cic.

    N. as subst. **glădĭātōrĭum** -i, *the pay of gladiators* : Liv.

glădĭātūra -ae, f. (gladiator), *the profession of gladiator* : Tac.

glădĭus -i, *a sword.*

    Lɪᴛ., gladium stringere, Caes., Cic., Verg.,

Liv.; nudare, Ov.; alicui gladium intentare, Liv.; recondere in vaginam, Cic.; prov.: plumbeo gladio iugulari, *to be defeated with little trouble,* Cic.

    Tʀᴀɴsғ., (1) *the work of the sword* : tanta gladiorum impunitas, *of murder,* Cic. (2) *a gladiatorial combat* : Sen.

glaeba=gleba; q.v.

glaesum (**glēsum**) -i, n. *amber* : Tac.

glandĭfer -fĕra -fĕrum (glans/fero), *acorn-bearing* : quercus, Cic.

glandium -i, n. (glans), *a delicate glandule in meat* : Pl.

glans glandis, f. (cf. *βάλανος*), *mast; an acorn, chestnut,* etc.: Cic., Verg., Hor. Tʀᴀɴsғ., *an acorn-shaped bullet shot from a sling* : glandes fundis in casas iacere, Caes.; Verg.

glārĕa -ae, f. *gravel* : Cic. L., Verg., Liv.

glārĕōsus -a -um (glarea), *gravelly, full of gravel* : saxa, Liv.

glaucōma -ătis, n. (also -ae, f.: Pl.) (from *γλαύκωμα*), *a disease of the eye, cataract* : Pl.

¹glaucus -a -um (*γλαυκός*), *bluish-* or *greenish-grey* : undae, Lucr.; salix, Verg.

²Glaucus -i, m. (*Γλαυκός*). (1) *a fisherman of Anthedon, changed into a sea-god.* (2) *son of Sisyphus, torn to pieces by his own horses.* (3) *leader of the Lycians at the Trojan war.*

glēba (**glaeba**) -ae, f. *a lump* or *clod of earth* : Lucr., Cic., Verg. Tʀᴀɴsғ., (1) *land, soil* : terra potens ubere glebae, Verg. (2) *a piece, lump* of any substance : picis, Caes.; turis, Lucr.

glēbŭla -ae, f. (dim. of gleba), *a little clod.* Tʀᴀɴsғ., (1) *a little farm* or *estate* : Juv. (2) *a small lump* of anything : Plin. L.

glēsum=glaesum; q.v.

glīs glīris, m. *a dormouse* : Plin., Mart.

glisco -ĕre, *to grow up, swell up, blaze up.* Lɪᴛ., ignis sub pectore gliscens, Lucr. Tʀᴀɴsғ., ad iuvenilem libidinem copia voluptatum gliscit illa, ut ignis oleo, Cic.; violentia, Verg.; ne glisceret negligendo bellum, Liv.; gliscente in dies seditione, Liv.; multitudo gliscit immensum, *increases very much,* Tac.

glŏbo -are (globus), *to form into a ball* : Plin. Tʀᴀɴsғ., *to form into a mass, to crowd together* : Plin.

glŏbōsus -a -um (globus), *spherical* : terra, Cic.; Liv.

glŏbus -i, m. *a round ball, globe, sphere.* Lɪᴛ., stellarum, Cic.; terrae, Cic.; Lucr., Verg., Tac. Tʀᴀɴsғ., *a troop, crowd, mass of people* : globus circumstans consulis corpus, Liv.; Verg., Tac.

glŏmĕrāmen -inis, n. (glomero), *a round mass, globe* : Lucr.

glŏmĕro -are (glomus), *to form into a sphere, or rounded heap.* Lɪᴛ., lanam in orbes, Ov.; frusta mero glomerata, Ov. Tʀᴀɴsғ., in gen., *to gather together, collect, form into a mass* : agmina, Verg.; glomerantur aves, Verg.

glŏmus -ĕris, n. (akin to globus), *clue, skein, ball of thread* : lanae, Lucr., Hor.

glōrĭa -ae, f. *fame, renown, glory.*

    Lɪᴛ., doctrinae et ingenii, Cic.; belli, in summam gloriam venire, Cic.; gloriam habere, consequi, capere, acquirere, Cic.; aliquem gloriā adficere, *to honour,* Cic.

    Tʀᴀɴsғ., (1) plur.: gloriae, *glorious deeds,* Tac. (2) *of an outstanding member of a group, the pride, glory* : armenti gloria, taurus, Ov. (3) *desire of glory, ambition, boastfulness*: vana, Liv.; Cic., Hor.

glŏrĭātĭo -ōnis, f. (glorior), *a glorying, boasting*: Cic.

glŏrĭŏla -ae, f. (dim. of gloria), *a little glory*: hisce eum ornes gloriolae insignibus, Cic. L.

glŏrĭor -ari, dep. (gloria), *to glory, boast, pride oneself.*

(1) absol.: hic tu me gloriari vetas, Cic.; with adverbs: nimis, Cic.; insolenter, Cic.; with adversus and the acc.: ne adversus te quidem gloriabor, Liv.

(2) *to glory in, boast of* something; with plain abl.: nominibus veterum, Cic.; suā victoriā tam insolenter, Caes.; Liv., Ov.; with de: de tuis beneficiis intolerantissime gloriaris, Cic.; with in: in victoria vel ignavis gloriari licet, Sall.; Cic.; with acc. and infin.: is mihi etiam gloriabitur se omnes magistratus sine repulsa adsecutum, Cic.; Caes., Hor.; with acc. of n. pron.: vellem equidem idem posse gloriari quod Cyrus, Cic.; gerundive, gloriandus, *glorious, to be boasted of*: beata vita glorianda et praedicanda est, Cic.

glŏrĭōsus -a -um (gloria). (1) objective, *famous, glorious*: mors, Cic.; gloriosissimum factum, Cic.; Liv., Tac. (2) subjective, *ambitious, pretentious, boastful*: miles, Ter., Cic.; ostentatio, Cic.

¶ Adv. glŏrĭōsē. (1) *with glory, gloriously*: aliquid gloriosissime et magnificentissime conficere, Cic. L. (2) *vauntingly, boastingly*: mentiri, Cic.; Pl.

glūbo -ĕre (cf. γλύφω), *to peel, take off the rind or bark*: Varr. TRANSF., *to rob*: magnanimos Remi nepotes, Cat.

glūtĕn -tīnis, n. glue: Lucr., Verg.

glūtĭnātor -ōris, m. (glutino), *one who glues together books, a bookbinder*: Cic. L.

glūtĭno -are (gluten), *to glue or paste together*: Plin.

glūtĭo (gluttĭo) -ire, *to swallow, gulp down*: epulas, Juv.

glūto (glutto) -ōnis, m. (glutio), *a glutton*: Pers.

Glýco and Glýcōn -ōnis, m. (Γλύκων). (1) *a wrestler*: Hor. (2) *a physician*: Cic.

Gnaeus -i, m. *a Roman* praenomen, shortened Cn.

gnārĭtās -ātis, f. (gnarus), *knowledge*: Sall.

gnārus -a -um (connected with nosco).

(1) act., *knowing, acquainted with, expert in*; with genit.: reipublicae, Cic.; Latinae linguae, Liv.; with indir. quest.: eum gnarum fuisse, quibus orationis modis quaeque animorum partes pellerentur, Cic.; with acc. and infin.: Liv., Tac.; with acc. alone: hanc rem, Pl.

(2) pass., *known*: gnarum id Caesari, Tac.

Gnătho -ōnis, m. *the name of a parasite in the Eunuchus of Terence*; hence in gen.=*parasite*: Cic.; subst. Gnāthōnĭci -ōrum, m. *parasites of Gnatho's school*: Ter.

Gnātĭa=Egnatia, *a town in Apulia.*

gnātus, gnāvus=natus, navus; q.v.

Gnĭdus=Cnidus; q.v.

Gnossus (Gnōsus) -i, f. (Κνωσσός), *an ancient city of Crete, the residence of Minos.*

¶ Hence adj. Gnōsĭus -a -um, *Gnosian, Cretan*; f. as subst. Gnōsĭa -ae, *Ariadne*: Prop.; adj. Gnōsĭăcus -a -um, *Gnosian*:

rex, *Minos*, Ov.; f. adj. Gnōsĭas -adis, *Gnosian*, poet.=*Cretan*; as subst.=*Ariadne*; f. adj. Gnōsĭs -ĭdis: corona, *the constellation of Ariadne's crown*, Ov.; as subst.=*Ariadne*.

gōbĭus (cōbĭus) -i, m. and gōbĭo -ōnis, m. (κωβιός), *a gudgeon*: Ov., Juv.

gonger, *see* conger.

Gordĭum -i, n. (Γόρδιον), *a town in Phrygia.*

Gordĭus -i, m. (Γόρδιος), *a king of Gordium* (q.v.), *famed for a knot on the yoke of his chariot, cut by Alexander the Great.*

Gorgĭās -ae, m. (Γοργίας). (1) *a Greek sophist of Leontini, contemporary of Socrates.* (2) *a rhetorician at Athens, contemporary of Cicero.*

Gorgō -gŏnis, f. (Γοργώ), *daughter of Phorcus, also called Medusa, who had snakes for hair, and whose look turned persons to stone. She was slain by Perseus, and her head set in Minerva's shield*; in plur. Gorgones, *all three daughters of Phorcus*; Medusa, Stheno, and Euryale. Adj. Gorgŏnĕus -a -um: equus, *the horse Pegasus*, Ov.

Gortȳna -ae, f. (Γόρτυνη), *an ancient city in Crete.* Adj. Gortȳnius -a -um, and Gortȳnĭăcus -a -um, *Gortynian.*

grăbātus -i, m. (κράβατος, orig. Macedonian), *a low couch, camp-bed*: Cic., Cat., Verg.

Gracchus -i, m. *a cognomen in the* Gens Sempronia, esp. of Ti. Sempronius Gracchus, *husband of Cornelia, and their two sons,* Tiberius *and* Gaius, *the 'Gracchi'.* Adj. Gracchānus -a -um, *Gracchan.*

grăcĭlis -e, *slender, thin, slim.* LIT., puer, Hor.; capella, Ov. TRANSF., (1) *meagre*: Plin. (2) of discourse, *simple, without ornament*: materia, Ov.

grăcĭlĭtās -ātis, f. (gracilis), *thinness, slimness, slenderness*: corporis, Cic. TRANSF., of discourse: Quint.

grăcŭlus -i, m. *a jackdaw*: Phaedr., Mart.

grădārĭus -a -um (gradus), *going step by step*; fig.: Sen.

grădātim, adv. (gradus), *step by step, by degrees*: Cic., Plin. L.

grădātĭo -ōnis, f. (gradus), in rhetoric, *climax*: Cic., Quint.

grădĭor grădi gressus sum, dep. *to step, walk*: Pl., Cic., Verg. TRANSF., of sound: Lucr.

Grădīvus -i, m. (gradior, *he that walks in battle*), *a surname of Mars*: Liv., Verg., Ov.

grădus -ūs, m. *a step.*

(1) *a step as made, a pace.* LIT., suspenso gradu, *on tiptoe*, Ter.; gradum facere, *to make a step*, Cic.; celerare, Verg.; corripere, Hor.; addere, *to hasten*, Liv.; gradu citato, pleno, *at quick march*, Liv.; gradum referre, *to go back*, Liv.; gradum inferre in hostes, *to advance against*, Liv. TRANSF., **a**, *a step towards something*: primus gradus imperii factus est, Cic.; gradum fecit ad censuram, Liv.; hence *approach*: quem mortis timuit gradum, Hor.; **b**, as milit. t. t., *station, position, post*: aliquem gradu movere, demovere, Liv.; Ov., fig.: aliquem de gradu deicere.

(2) *a step as climbed, a stair, rung of a ladder.* LIT., usually plur.: gradus templorum, Cic.; Verg., Liv. TRANSF., **a**, physical: of things resembling steps, or rising in stages, *a braid of hair*: Juv., Suet.; as music. t. t., *gradations of sound*: sonorum gradus, Cic.: **b**, abstr.: *degree, stage*: a virtute ad

rationem video te venisse gradibus, *by stages*, Cic.; omnes gradus aetatis, Cic.; necessitudinum gradus, of relationship, Cic.; also *rank, position*: gradus senatorius, Cic.; infimo fortunae gradus, Cic.

Graeci -ōrum, m. *the Greeks*; sing. **Graecus** -i, m. *a Greek*: Cic. and **Graeca** -ae, f. *a Greek woman*: Liv.

¶ As adj. **Graecus** -a -um, *Greek*; n. as subst. **Graecum** -i, *Greek language*; adv. **Graecē**, *in the Greek language*.

¶ **Graecĭa** -ae, f. (1) *Greece*. (2)=*Magna Graecia, the Greek colonies in the south of Italy.*

¶ Dim. adj., usually contemptuous, **Graecŭlus** -a -um; m. as subst. **Graecŭlus** -i, *a little Greek*, used of Greek hangers-on in Roman society: Cic., Juv.

graecisso -are (Graecus), *to imitate the Greeks*: Pl.

graecor -ari, dep. (Graecus), *to imitate the Greeks*: Hor.

Graecostăsis -is, f. (Γραικόστασις), *a building in the Roman forum, erected for the purpose of lodging Greek and other foreign ambassadors*: Cic.

Grāii -ōrum (and poet. -um), m.=Graeci, *the Greeks*: Cic.; also sing. **Grāius** -i, m. *a Greek*, and as adj. **Grāius** -a -um, *Greek*.

Grāiŭgĕna -ae, m. (Graius/geno=gigno), *a Greek by birth*: Verg.

grallae -arum, f. pl. (gradior), *stilts*: Varr.

grallātor -ōris, m. (grallae), *one that walks on stilts*: Pl., Varr.

grāmen -ĭnis, n. *grass, turf*, used in sing. and plur. LIT., Verg., Hor., Liv. TRANSF., any *plant* or *herb*: Verg., Ov.

grāmĭnĕus -a -um (gramen), *of grass, grassy*. LIT., campus, Verg.; corona obsidionalis, Liv. TRANSF., *made of cane* or *bamboo*: hasta, Cic.

grammătĭcus -a -um (γραμματικός), *concerned with reading and writing; literary, grammatical*: tribus grammaticas adire, *the company of grammarians*, Hor.

¶ As subst. m. **grammătĭcus** -i, *a philologist, grammarian*: Cic., Hor., Quint.; f. **grammătĭca** -ae (and **grammătĭcē** -ēs), *grammar, philology*: Cic., Suet.; n. pl. **grammătĭca** -ōrum, *grammar, philology*: Cic.

grammătista -ae, m. (γραμματιστής), *a teacher of grammar, teacher of languages*: Suet.

grānārium -i, n. (granum), usually plur., *a granary*: Pl., Cic., Hor.

grandaevus -a -um (grandis/aevum), *very old*: Nereus, Verg.; Ov., Tac.

grandēsco -ěre (grandis), *to become great, to grow*: Lucr.

grandĭcŭlus (dim. of grandis), *rather large*: Pl., Ter.

grandĭfer -fěra -fěrum (grandis/fero), *producing great profits* or *returns*: Cic.

grandĭlŏquus -a -um (grandis/loquor), *speaking grandly*: Cic.; in a bad sense, *boastful, grandiloquent*: Cic.

grandĭnat -are, impers. (grando), *it hails*: Sen.

grandĭo -ire (grandis). Transit., *to make great, increase*: Pl. Intransit., *to become great, grow*: Cato.

grandis -e adj. (with compar.), *full-grown, great, large.*

LIT., physically, esp. of living beings; in stature, *tall*: puer, Cic.; in years, *old*: Lucr., and often so with natu *or* aevo: Cic., Hor., Tac.; of plants: frumenta, Verg.; of other objects: saxa, Lucr., Caes.; epistula, Cic. L., Juv.

TRANSF., *great, important*: res grandiores, Cic.; decus, Hor. Esp. of style, *high, lofty, grand, sublime*: genus dicendi, Cic.; so of speakers: oratores grandes verbis, Cic.

grandĭtās -ātis, f. (grandis), of style, *loftiness, sublimity*: verborum, Cic.

grando -ĭnis, f. *hail, hail-storm*: Cic., Verg.

grānĭfer -fěra -fěrum (granum/fero), *grain-carrying*: agmen, ants, Ov.

grānum -i, n. *a grain* or *seed*: tritici, Pl.; uvae, Ov.; fici, Cic.

grăphĭārĭus -a -um (graphium), *relating to the graphium*: Suet.

grăphĭcus -a -um (γραφικός), *concerned with painting.* LIT., only as subst. **grăphĭcē** -ēs, f. (sc. τεχνή), *the art of painting*: Plin. TRANSF., of persons, *masterly*: Pl.

¶ Adv. **grăphĭcē**, *skilfully*: Pl.

grăphĭum -i, n. (γραφεῖον), *a stilus, a pointed instrument for writing on waxen tablets*: Ov., Suet.

grassātor -ōris, m. (grassor). (1) *an idler*: Cato. (2) *a footpad*: Cic., Juv.

grassor -ari, dep. (gradior), *to walk about.* LIT., esp. *to loiter about idly* or *for sinister purposes*: iuventutem grassantem in Subura, Liv.; Tac. TRANSF., (1) *to proceed, go about an undertaking*: ad gloriam virtutis viā, Sall.; in possessionem agri publici, Liv.; iure, non vi, Liv.; veneno, Tac.; obsequio, Hor. (2) *to proceed against somebody*: in te, Liv.; absol.: ut paucorum potentia grassaretur, Tac.

grātē, adv. from gratus; q.v.

grātes, acc. grates, abl. gratibus, f. pl. (gratus), *thanks*, esp. to the gods: alicui grates agere, *to express thanks*, Pl., Cic., Liv.; habere, *to feel gratitude*, Pl., Liv., Tac.

grātĭa -ae, f. (gratus), *agreeableness, pleasantness.*

(1) *that which is pleasing, charm, attraction*: formae, Ov.; gratia non deest verbis, Prop.; personif. **Grātĭae** -arum (=χάριτες), *the three Graces* (Euphrosyne, Aglaia, and Thalia): Hor., Ov.

(2) *favour with* others; *esteem, regard, popularity*: gratiam alicuius sequi, Caes.; sibi conciliare, Cic.; gratiam inire ab aliquo, Cic.; in gratia esse, *to be beloved*, Cic.; in gratiam redire cum aliquo, Cic. L.; Liv.

(3) *a favour done, a service, kindness*: petivit in beneficii loco et gratiae, Cic.; gratiam dicendi facere, *to allow to speak*, Liv.; in gratiam alicuius, *to please someone*, Liv.; esp. abl. gratiā, *on account of*: meā gratiā, *for my sake*, Pl.; hominum gratiā, Cic.; exempli gratiā, *for example*, Quint.

(4) *indulgence* towards an offence: delicti gratiam facere, *to be indulgent to*, Sall.

(5) *thankfulness, thanks*; in sing. and plur.: gratiam persolvere diis, Cic.; gratias agere, with dat., *to express thanks*, Cic., Liv.; pro suo summo beneficio, Cic.; gratiarum actio, *giving of thanks*, Cic.; gratias habere, *to feel grateful*, Pl., Cic., Liv.; gratiam reddere, Sall.; in abl. plur. **grātiīs** or **grātīs**, *without*

recompense, for nothing, gratis: noctem gratiis dono dabo, Pl.; gratis reipublicae servire, Cic.

grātĭfĭcātĭo -ōnis, f. (gratificor), *complaisance, obligingness, showing of kindness*: Sullana, *of Sulla to his soldiers*, Cic.; gratificatio et benevolentia, Cic.

grātĭfĭcor -ari, dep. (gratus/facio), *to act so as to please anyone, to oblige, gratify, do a favour to*: gratificatur mihi gestu accusator, Cic.; Tac.; also with acc. of the favour done, *to do for, give to, present to*: tibi hoc, Cic. L.; populo aliena et sua, Cic.; Sall.

grātĭis, see gratia.

grātĭōsus -a -um (gratia). (1) *enjoying favour, favoured, beloved*: apud omnes ordines, Cic.; in provincia, Cic.; rogatio gratiosissima, Cic. (2) *showing favour, complaisant*: gratiosi scribae sint in dando et cedendo loco, Cic.

grātis, see gratia.

Grātĭus -a -um, *name of a Roman gens.*

grātor -ari, dep. (gratus). (1) *to wish joy to, to congratulate*: invicem inter se, Liv.; with dat.: sorori, Verg.; sibi, Ov.; with acc. and infin.: Verg., Tac. (2) *to give thanks*: Iovis templum gratantes ovantesque adire, Liv.; Ov.

grātŭĭtus -a -um (gratus), *not paid for* or *not provoked, gratuitous, spontaneous*: comitia, *unbribed*, Cic. L.; amicitia, Cic.; liberalitas, Cic.; furor, Liv.
¶ Abl. sing. n. as adv. **grātŭĭto**, *gratuitously*: alicui gratuito civitatem impertire, Cic.; Sall., Liv., Tac.

grātŭlābundus -a -um (gratulor), *congratulating*: Liv., Suet.

grātŭlātĭo -ōnis, f. (gratulor). (1) *a wishing joy, congratulation*: civium, Cic.; laudis nostrae, *because of*, Cic.; plur.: Caes. (2) *a thanksgiving festival*: reipublicae bene gestae, Cic.; Liv.

grātŭlor -ari, dep. (gratus). (1) *to wish a person joy, congratulate*; with dat. of person: mihi de filiā, Cic. L.; tibi in hoc, Cic.; with acc. of grounds: alicui victoriam, Cic.; also with quod clause: Cic.; or acc. and infin.: Cic., Ov., Liv. (2) *to give solemn thanks*, esp. to the gods: Ter.

grātus -a -um, adj. (with compar. and superl.). (1) *pleasing, welcome, agreeable*: **a**, of persons: conviva, Hor.; donec gratus eram tibi, Hor.: **b**, of things: victoria, Cic.; tellus, Verg.; carmina, tempus, Hor.; Ov., Liv.; gratum alicui facere, *to do a favour*, Caes., Cic. (2) of things, *deserving thanks*: veritas etiamsi iucunda non est, mihi tamen grata est, Cic. (3) of persons, *thankful, grateful*: gratus alicui, *or* in, *or* erga, aliquem, Cic.; Sall., Hor.
¶ Adv. **grātē**. (1) *willingly, with pleasure*: Cic. (2) *thankfully*: et grate et pie facere, Cic.; Hor.

grăvantĕr, adv. from gravo; q.v.

grăvātē, adv. from gravo; q.v.

grăvātim, *reluctantly*: Lucr., Liv.

grăvēdĭnōsus -a -um (gravedo), *subject to colds*: Cic.

grăvēdo -ĭnis, f. (gravis), *heaviness of the head, cold, catarrh*: Cic.

grăvĕŏlens -lentis (gravis/oleo), *strong-smelling, rank*: Verg.

grăvesco -ĕre (gravis), *to become heavy*. LIT., fetu nemus omne, Verg. TRANSF., *to grow worse*: aerumna, Lucr.; Tac.

grăvĭdĭtās -ātis, f. (gravidus), *pregnancy*: Cic.

grăvĭdo -are (gravidus), *to load, burden*; hence *to impregnate*: terra gravidata seminibus, Cic.

grăvĭdus -a -um (gravis), *heavy*; hence *pregnant*. LIT., puero, Pl.; uxor, Cic.; Verg. TRANSF., *laden, filled, full*; with abl.: pharetra sagittis, Hor.; urbs bellis, Verg.; tempestas fulminibus, Lucr.

grăvis -e (cf. βαρύς), adj. (with compar. and superl.), *heavy, weighty* (opp. levis).
(1) intrinsically, *heavy*. LIT., onus armorum, Caes.; cibus, *heavy, hard to digest*, Cic.; agmen, *heavy-armed*, Liv.; aes grave, *heavy coin*, according to the old reckoning, in which an *as* weighed a pound, Liv. TRANSF., **a**, of sound, *low, deep, bass* (opp. acutus): vox, sonus, Cic.: **b**, of persons or things, *weighty, important*: testis, auctor, Cic.; exemplum, Hor.: **c**, of character, *dignified, serious*: civitas, Cic., Liv.; virum, Verg.; of style, *elevated, dignified*: genus epistularum severum et grave, Cic.
(2) *burdened, loaded, laden*. LIT., naves spoliis, Liv.; agmen praeda, Liv.; esp. *pregnant*: Verg. TRANSF., graves somno epulisque, *weighed down, heavy*, Liv.; morbo, Verg.; aetate, *stricken in years*, Liv.
(3) causally, *burdensome, oppressive*. LIT., physically: cibus, tempestas anni tempus, Cic.; vulnus, Caes.; odor caeni, Verg. TRANSF., of persons or things, *grievous, painful, harsh, severe, unpleasant*: hostis, Liv.; noverca, Tac.; senectus, supplicium, Cic.; ne quid gravius in fratrem statueret, Caes.
¶ Adv. (with compar. and superl.) **grăvĭtĕr**, *heavily*. (1) *with weight*: Lit., cadere, Lucr.; Verg., Liv. TRANSF., orationem habere, ferre, vivere, Cic. (2) *as a burden, reluctantly*: ferre, Cic.; accipere, Cic., Liv., Tac. (3) *grievously, harshly, severely*: ictus, Caes.; aegrotare, Cic.; queri, dissentire, Cic.

Grăviscae -ārum, f. *a town in Etruria.*

grăvĭtās -ātis, f. (gravis), *weight, heaviness*.
(1) as an intrinsic quality, *weight*. LIT., armorum, Caes.; Cic., Ov. TRANSF., **a**, *weight, consequence, importance*: sententiarum, Cic.; Caes.: **b**, of character, *dignity, authority, seriousness*: cum gravitate et constantia vivere, Cic.; Liv.; of style: dicendi, Cic.
(2) as an effect, *heaviness*; esp.: **a**, *pregnancy*: Ov.: **b**, *dullness, heaviness, faintness*: corporis, linguae, Cic.; Lucr.
(3) as a cause, *weight, pressure*: **a**, physically: caeli, Cic. L., Liv.; odoris, Tac.: **b**, fig.: annonae, Tac.; belli, Liv.; Cic.

grăvĭtĕr, adv. from gravis; q.v.

grăvo -are (gravis), *to load, burden*.
LIT., arbores fetu, Lucr.; aliquem sarcinis, Tac.; esp. in perf. partic. **grăvātus** -a -um, *weighed down*: cibo, vino somnoque, Liv.; Verg.
TRANSF., (1) *to heighten, exaggerate, increase*: invidiam matris, Tac.; Ov., Liv. (2) *to oppress, burden, trouble*: officium quod me gravat, Hor.; Liv.; esp. pass., gravor used as dep., *to feel burdened* or *troubled by a thing* Pl., Cic., Tac.; with acc. object: Hor., Tac.; with infin., *to make heavy weather of* doing a thing: rogo ut ne graveris exaedificare id opus quod instituisti, Cic.; Caes., Liv.
¶ Adv. (from pres. partic.) **grăvantĕr**, *reluctantly*: haud gravanter venerunt, Liv.

¶ Adv. (from perf. partic.) **grăvātē**, *reluctantly*: Cic., Liv.

grĕgālis -e (grex), *belonging to a herd* or *flock*: Varr., Plin.
TRANSF., (1) *belonging to the same company*; as subst., plur. **grĕgāles** -ium, m. *companions, associates, accomplices*: Catilinae, Cic. (2) *common, of a common kind*: amiculum, *of a private soldier*, Liv.; Tac.

grĕgārĭus -a -um (grex), *belonging to a herd* or *flock*. TRANSF., miles, *a private soldier*, Cic., Liv., Tac.

grĕgātim, adv. (grex), *in flocks* or *herds*: Plin. TRANSF., *in troops* or *crowds*: videtis cives gregatim coniectos, Cic.

grĕmĭum -i, n. LIT., (1) *lap, bosom*: in gremio matris sedere, Cic.; Cat., Verg.; fig.: abstrahi e gremio patriae, Cic. (2) *womb*: Ter.
TRANSF., *centre, middle*: medio Graeciae gremio, Cic.

gressus -ūs, m. (gradior), *a step*: gressum tendere ad moenia, Verg. TRANSF., *of a ship, course*: huc dirige gressum, Verg.

grex grĕgis, m. *a herd, flock, drove*. LIT., of animals: equarum, Cic.; avium, Hor.; Verg. TRANSF., (1) of human beings, *a troop, band, company*, sometimes contemptuously, *a herd*: amicorum, Cic.; praedonum, Cic.; esp.: a, *a philosophical sect*: philosophorum, Cic.; Epicuri de grege porcus, Hor.; Cic.: b, of soldiers, *a troop*: grege facto, *in close order*, Sall., Liv. (2) of things without life: virgarum, Pl.

grunnĭo (grundĭo) -ire, *to grunt like a pig*: Plin., Juv.

grunnītus -ūs, m. (grunnio), *the grunting of a pig*: Cic.

grus grŭis, m. and f. (cf. γέρανος), *a crane*: Lucr., Cic., Hor.

grȳ, n. indecl. (γρῦ), *a scrap, crumb*: Pl.

gryllus -i, m. (γρύλλος), *a cricket, grasshopper*: Plin.

Grȳnīa -ae, f. (Γρύνεια) and **Grȳnĭum** -i, n. (Γρύνιον), *a town in Aeolis*, with a temple of Apollo. Adj. **Grȳnēus** -a -um, *Grynean*: Verg.

gryps, grȳpis, m. (γρύψ), *a griffin*: Verg.

gŭbernācŭlum (gŭbernāclum) -i, n. (guberno), *a rudder, helm*. LIT., ad gubernaculum accedere, Cic.; Verg. TRANSF., *direction, management, government*; esp. in plur. of the state: accedere ad regendula gubernacula, Liv.; ad aliquem gubernacula reipublicae deferre, Cic.; gubernacula reipublicae tractare, Cic.; senatum a gubernaculis deicere, Cic.

gŭbernātĭo -ōnis, f. (guberno). LIT., *steering*: Cic. TRANSF., *direction, government*: tantarum rerum, Cic.

gŭbernātor -ōris, m. (guberno), *helmsman, steersman, pilot*: Cic. TRANSF., *director*: governor*: civitatis, Cic.

gŭbernātrix -īcis, f. (gubernator), *she that directs, governs*: ista praeclara gubernatrix civitatum, eloquentia, Cic.

gŭberno -are (κυβερνῶ), *to steer a ship*: Cic.; prov.: e terra, *from a place of safety to direct those who are in danger*, Liv. TRANSF., *to be at the helm*: gubernare me taedebat, Cic.; with object, *to steer, direct, govern*: rempublicam, Cic.

gŭbernum -i, n.=gubernaculum; q.v.: Lucr.

gŭla -ae, f. (cf. gluttio), *the gullet, throat*: obtorta gula, Cic.; gulam laqueo frangere, *to strangle*, Sall. Meton., *greediness, gluttony*: inritamenta gulae, Sall.; o gulam insulsam, Cic.; Hor.

gŭlōsus -a -um (gula), *gluttonous, dainty*: Mart., Juv.

gŭmĭa -ae, c. *a glutton, gourmand*: Lucil. ap. Cic.

gummi, n. indecl. (κόμμι), *gum*: Plin.

gurgĕs -itis, m. *a whirlpool, eddy, abyss*.
LIT., Rheni, Cic.; Verg., Liv.
TRANSF., (1) poet., *troubled water* in gen.; *a stream, flood, sea*: Carpathius, Verg.; Ov. (2) fig., *abyss, depth*: gurges libidinum, Cic.; gurges ac vorago patrimonii, *squanderer*, Cic.; tu gurges atque helluo, Cic.; Liv .

¹**gurgŭlĭo** -ōnis, f. *the windpipe*: Pl., Cic.

²**gurgŭlĭo** -ōnis, m., *see* curculio.

gurgustĭum -i, n. (gurges), *a hut, hovel*: Cic.

gustātus -ūs, m. (gusto), *taste, as one of the senses*: Cic. TRANSF., (1) *taste, appetite for*: verae laudis gustatum non habere, Cic. (2) *the taste, flavour* of anything: pomorum, Cic.

gusto -are (cf. γεύω), *to taste, take a little of*.
LIT., aquam, Cic. L.; anserem, Caes.; absol.: quorum nemo gustavit cubans, Cic.; Plin. L.
TRANSF., *to partake of, enjoy*: amorem vitae, Lucr.; lucellum, Hor.; partem voluptatis, Cic.

gustus -ūs, m. (cf. gusto), *tasting*. LIT., gustu explorare cibum, potum alicuius, Tac. TRANSF., (1) *a whet* or *relish taken before a meal*: Mart. (2) *taste* or *flavour*: Plin. Hence, fig., *taste* or *foretaste*: Quint., Plin. L.

gutta -ae, f. *a drop*. LIT., guttae imbrium quasi cruentae, Cic.; Pl., Verg., Ov. TRANSF., (1) guttae, *spots* or *marks on animals*, Verg., Ov. (2) *a drop* of anything, *a little*: Pl., Lucr.

guttātim, adv. (gutta), *drop by drop*: Pl.

guttŭla -ae, f. (dim. of gutta), *a little drop*: Pl.

guttur -ŭris, n. *the windpipe, throat*. LIT., guttur alicui frangere, *to break a person's neck*, Hor.; Pl., Ov. TRANSF., *gluttony*: Cic., Juv.

guttus -i, m. (gutta), *a narrow-necked jug*: Hor., Juv.

Gÿăros -i, f. (Γύαρος) and **Gÿăra** -ōrum, n. (Γύαρα), *a barren island in the Aegean Sea*, used *as a place of exile under the empire*.

Gÿās -ae, acc. -an (Γύης). (1) *a giant with a hundred arms*. (2) *a companion of Aeneas*.

Gÿgēs -is and -ae, acc. -en, m. (Γύγης), *a king of Lydia, famous for his ring*. Adj. **Gÿgaeus** -a -um, *of* or *belonging to Gyges*.

gymnăsĭarchus -i, m. (γυμνασίαρχος), *the master of a gymnasium*: Cic.

gymnăsĭum -i, n. (γυμνάσιον), *a public school of gymnastics, gymnasium* (among the Greeks): Pl., Cic., Ov. TRANSF., since the gymnasia in Greece were frequented by philosophers and sophists, *a place for philosophical discussion*: Cic.; Liv., Juv.

gymnastĭcus -a -um (γυμναστικός), *gymnastic*: Pl.

gymnĭcus -a -um (γυμνικός), *gymnastic*: ludi, Cic.; certamen, Cic.

gy̆naecēum -i, n. and **gy̆naecīum** -i, n.
(γυναικεῖον), *the women's apartments in a
Greek house*: Pl., Ter., Cic.
gy̆naecōnītĭs -ĭdis, f. (γυναικωνῖτις)=gynae-
ceum; q.v.: Nep.
gypso -are (gypsum), *to cover with gypsum*;
esp. in partic. **gypsātus** -a -um, *covered
with gypsum*: pes (the feet of slaves for sale
being marked with gypsum), Tib., Ov.;
gypsatissimis manibus, *with hands whitened
with gypsum* (of actors who played women's
parts), Cic. L.
gypsum -i, n. (γύψος), *gypsum*: Plin. Meton., *a
plaster figure*: Juv.
gy̆rus -i, m. (γῦρος), *a circle, ring.*
  LIT., gyrum trahere (of a snake), Verg.;
gyros per aera ducere, *to wheel through the
air* (of birds), Ov.; volat ingenti gyro
(telum), Verg.; esp. of a horse: gyros dare,
to career, curvet, Verg.
  TRANSF., (1) *a course* for training horses:
Prop.; fig.: ex ingenti quodam oratorem
immensoque campo in exiguum gyrum
compellere, Cic.; gyro curre, poeta, tuo, Ov.
(2) *orbit, circuit*: bruma nivalem interiore
diem gyro trahit, Hor.

H

H, h the eighth letter of the Latin Alphabet,
partly corresponding to the Greek rough
breathing.
  In combination, h before t is sometimes
changed into c, as traho, tractus, and with
following s forms x, as traxi, vexi.
ha! also **hahae!** and **hahahae!**, exclamations,
esp. indicating joy or amusement: Pl., Ter.
hăbēna -ae, f. (habeo), *that by which anything
is held.*
  Hence (1) *a strap*; of a sling: Verg.; of **a**
javelin: Luc.; for whipping: Verg., Hor.
(2) *a bridle, reins* (gen. in plur.). LIT.,
habenas fundere, dare, *to give the rein, loosen
the rein*, Verg.; adducere, premere, *to
tighten*, Verg.; Liv., Ov. TRANSF., **a**, of
sails: immittit habenas classi, *crowds on sail*,
Verg.; Ov.: **b**, fig., in gen.: amicitiae habenas
adducere, remittere, Cic.; rerum, *control of
the state*, Verg.; Lucr.
hăbĕo -ēre -ŭi -itum, *to have, hold.*
  LIT., of the physical possession of things
or persons. (1) of immediate contact, *to have
about one, carry, wear*: feminae duplices
papillas habent, Cic.; coronam in capite,
Cic.; vestis bona quaerit haberi, *to be worn*,
Ov.; often with dat. of reflex.: habeant sibi
arma, Cic.; hence the formula of divorce: res
tuas tibi habeas (habe), Pl.; Cic.; with thing
as subject, *to hold, contain*: altera vestes ripa
meas habuit, Ov.; Tartara habent Panthoiden,
Hor.; so of the contents of a letter or book:
Cic. (2) in a more general sense, *to possess,
hold, have power over*: **a**, of goods: aurum,
Pl.; pecuniam, Cic.; argentum, Hor.; pecus,
to keep, Verg.; absol., *to possess property,
to be wealthy*: habere in Bruttiis, Cic.;

habet idem in nummis, habet in praediis
urbanis, Cic.; habendi amor, Verg.: **b**, of
places, *to hold, own, inhabit*, or *rule over*:
Capuam, Liv.; hostis habet muros, Verg.;
urbem Romam a principio reges habuere,
Tac.: **c**, of persons, *to keep*, esp. in a certain
place, state, or relation: domi divisores, Cic.;
senatum in curia inclusum, Cic.; aliquem
in vinculis, Sall; catervas flagitiosorum
circum se, Sall.; milites in castris, Liv.
  TRANSF., (1) *to have* an abstr. thing: a,
in gen.: aliquid in manibus, *on hand*, Cic.;
aliquid in animo, *to have in the mind, intend*;
with infin.: Caes., Cic.; aliquem in animo,
to have in one's thoughts, Sall.; animus habet
cuncta neque ipse habetur, Sall.; dimidium
facti qui coepit habet, Hor.; hoc habet, *or*
habet, of a fighter, '*he's had it*', Verg.; habes
consilia nostra, *you know of*, Cic.; habeo
dicere, *I have it in my power to say*, Cic.;
nihil habeo quod incusem senectutem, Cic.:
b, of physical or mental states: vulnus, *to be
wounded*, Ov.; febrem, Cic.; bonum animum,
to be of good courage, Sall.; odium in aliquem,
to cherish hatred, Cic.; invidiam, *to experience*,
Cic.: **c**, of qualities: modestiam, Sall.;
habebat hoc omnino Caesar, *that was Caesar
all over*, Cic.: **d**, *to have as a result, to involve,
to cause*: beneficium habet querelam, Cic.;
misericordiam, *to cause pity*, Cic. (2) with
an abstract noun to complete the sense of the
verb; *to hold* a function, *carry out* an action,
etc.: concilium plebis, *to hold a council of the
people*, Cic.; contionem, comitia, Caes., Cic.,
Liv.; iter Aegyptum, *to go to Egypt*, Cic.;
orationem, *to make a speech*, Caes., Cic., Liv.;
sermonem, *to hold a conversation*, Cic.;
habere verba, *to speak*, Cic.; alicui honorem,
to pay honour to, Cic. (3) *to keep* a person or
thing *in a certain condition* (without actual
possession): mare infestum, Cic.; aliquem
in honore, Caes.; esp. with perf. partic.:
domitas habere libidines, Cic. So with
reflex., *to keep oneself, be*, in a condition; of
persons: graviter se habere, *to be ill*, Cic.;
singulos ut se haberent rogitans, Liv.; of
things: ut nunc res se habet, Liv.; Cic.;
sometimes intransit.: bene habet, *all right*,
Cic., Juv. (4) *to use, manage, treat*: aliquem
liberalissime, Cic.; exercitum luxuriose,
Sall. (5) *to hold, consider, regard in a certain
light*: plebes servorum loco habetur, Cic.;
aliquem ludibrio habere, Ter., Cic.; rempublicam quaestui, Cic.; aliquem parentem,
in the light of a parent; Cic.; aliquem pro
hoste, *as an enemy*, Liv.; aliquid pro certo,
Caes., Cic.; aliquid religioni, *to make a
matter of conscience of*, Cic.; paupertas probro
haberi coepit, *to be considered a disgrace*, Sall.
  ¶ Hence partic. **hăbĭtus** -a -um, *disposed*;
mentally: Ter.; esp. *in good condition*;
physically, compar.: habitior, Pl.
hăbĭlis -e (habeo), *easily managed, handy*.
  LIT., gladii, Liv.; arcus, Verg.; currus, Ov.
  TRANSF., *suitable, fit, convenient*. (1) of
things; with ad: calceus habilis et aptus ad
pedem, Cic.; with dat.: gens equis tantum
habilis, Liv. (2) of persons: in aliqua re,
Cic.; habilis capessendae reipublicae, Tac.;
Hor.
hăbĭlĭtās -ātis, f. (habilis), *aptitude, suitability*
Cic.

ăbĭtābĭlis -e (habito), *habitable*: regio, Cic.; Hor., Ov.

ăbĭtātĭo -ōnis, f. (habito), *a dwelling, habitation*: sumptus habitationis, Cic.; Pl., Caes.

ăbĭtātor -ōris, m. (habito), *one who dwells in* or *inhabits*: habitatorem in hac caelesti ac divina domo, Cic.; Liv., Juv.

ăbĭto -are (freq. of habeo).
(1) transit., *to inhabit*: urbes, Verg.; in pass., *to be inhabited*: vix pars dimidia (urbis) habitabatur, Liv.; Cic., Verg., Hor.
(2) intransit., *to dwell.* LIT., in aedibus, Pl.; cum aliquo, Cic.; in via, Cic.; impers. pass.: habitari, ait Xenocrates, in luna, Cic. Pres. partic. as subst.: habitantes, *inhabitants*, Ov., Quint. TRANSF., *metus habitat in vita beata*, Cic.; in foro, *to be always in the forum*, Cic.; quorum in vultu habitant oculi mei, Cic.; in eo genere rerum, *to dwell on*, Cic.

ăbĭtūdo -ĭnis, f. (habeo), *condition*: corporis, Ter.

ɪăbĭtus -a -um, partic. from habeo; q.v.

ɪăbĭtus -ūs, m. (habeo), *the condition, habit, bearing.* LIT., physical: corporis, oris, Cic.; hominis, Hor.; of dress, *style*: Romanus, Hor.; pastorum, Liv., Suet.; of places, *lie of the land*: locorum, Verg.; Liv. TRANSF., abstr., *nature, character, disposition*: virtus est animi habitus naturae modo atque rationi consentaneus, Cic.; orationis, Cic.; provinciarum, *attitude, morale*, Tac.

ăc, adv. from hic; q.v.

actēnus, adv. (hāc/tenus), *as far as this, so far.* (1) in space: hactenus dominum est illa secuta suum, Ov.; Verg. (2) in time, *hitherto*: Verg., Ov., Liv., Tac. (3) fig., in discussion, etc., *up to this point*: hactenus mihi videor de amicitia quid sentirem potuisse dicere, Cic.; often elliptically: sed haec hactenus; nunc ad ostenta veniamus, Cic.; hactenus arvorum cultūs, Verg.; Hor. (4) of degree, indicating or introducing a restriction; *only so far*: hactenus respondisse, 'ego me bene habeo', Tac.; esp. followed by clause, *only so far as*; with quoad, quod: Cic. L.; with ut *or* ne: Cic., Hor., Ov.

ɪadrĭa -ae, (1) f. *a town in the north of Italy, on the Adriatic coast* (now *Adria*); hence (2) m. *the Adriatic Sea.* Adj. Hadrĭăcus -a -um and Hadrĭātĭcus -a -um, *Adriatic*.

ɪadrĭānus -i, m., P. Aelius, *Roman emperor from* A.D. 117 *to* 138.

ɪadrūmētum, see Adrumetum.

aedilĭa -ae, f. (dim. of haedus), *a little kid*: Hor.

aedillus -i, m. (dim. of haedus), *a little kid*: Pl.

aedinus -a -um (haedus), *of a kid*: pellicula, Cic.

aedŭlus -i, m. (dim. of haedus), *a little kid*: Juv.

aedus -i, m. *a kid, young goat*: Cic., Verg., Hor. TRANSF., Haedi, *the Kids, two stars of the constellation Auriga*, Verg., Ov.

ɪaemŏnĭa -ae, f. (Αἱμονία), Haemonia, *an old name of Thessaly.* Adj. Haemŏnĭus -a -um, *Thessalian*: puppis, *the ship Argo*, Ov.; iuvenis, *Jason*, Ov.; puer, heros, *Achilles*, Ov.; meton., as Thessaly was notorious for witches, artes, *arts of enchantment*, Ov. Subst. Haemŏnis -nĭdis, f. *a Thessalian woman*: Ov.

haerĕo haerēre haesi haesum.
(1) *to stick, cleave, adhere* to somebody or something. LIT., haerere in equo, Cic.; with abl.: equo, Hor.; terra ima sede, Cic.; pede pes, Verg.; with dat.: capiti, Hor. TRANSF., *to hang on, linger, stick to, attach to* a person or thing: visceribus civitatis tyrannus, Liv.; in sententia, Cic.; haerere in iure ac praetorum tribunalibus, Cic.; memoria rei in populo haerebit, Cic.; milit. t. t.: haerere tergis, *or* in tergis, hostium, *to hang upon the rear of an enemy*, Liv.
(2) *to come to a standstill, get stuck.* LIT., aspectu territus haesit continuitque gradum, Verg. TRANSF., **a**, *to be checked, to cease*: Hectoris manu victoria Graium haesit, Verg.: **b**, *to be in perplexity, to be embarrassed*: haerere homo, versari, rubere, Cic.; Pl., Hor.

haeresco -ĕre (haereo), *to adhere, stick*: Lucr.

haerĕsis -ĕos, f. (αἵρεσις), *a philosophical sect*: Cic.

haesĭtantĭa -ae, f. (haesito), *a faltering*: linguae, *stammering*, Cic.

haesĭtātĭo -ōnis, f. (haesito), *a sticking fast*; hence (1) in speech, *hesitation, stammering*: quanta haesitatio tractusque verborum, Cic.; Quint. (2) mentally, *hesitation, indecision*: Cic. L., Tac.

haesĭto -are (freq. of haereo), *to stick fast, remain fast.* LIT., in vadis, Liv.; Lucr., Caes. TRANSF., *to hesitate*. (1) in speech: linguā, *to stammer*, Cic. (2) mentally, *to be undecided, be at a loss*: non haesitans respondebo, Cic.; Liv.

Hălaesa (Hălēsa) -ae, f. (Ἅλαισα), *a town on the north coast of Sicily.* Adj. Hălaesīnus -a -um.

Hălaesus (Hălēsus) -i, m. *a son of Agamemnon, ally of Turnus.*

hălăgŏra -ae, f. (ἅλς/ἀγορά), *the salt-market*: Pl.

halcēdo, see alcedo.

halcўon, see alcyon.

Halcўōnē, see Alcyone.

hālec, see alec.

hălĭaeĕtos -i, m. (ἁλιαίετος), *the sea-eagle, osprey*: Verg., Ov.

Hălĭartus -i, f. (Ἁλίαρτος), *a town in Boeotia.*
¶ Hence Hălĭartĭi -ōrum, m. *the inhabitants of Haliartus.*

Hălĭcarnassus -i, f. (Ἁλικαρνασσός), *town in Caria, birth-place of Herodotus.*
¶ Hence Hălĭcarnassenses -ium, m. and Hălĭcarnassĭi -ōrum, m. *inhabitants of Halicarnassus*; m. adj. Hălĭcarnassēus -ei and -eos: Cic.

Hălĭcўae -ārum, f. (Ἁλικύαι), *town in Sicily.*
¶ Hence adj. Hălĭcўensis -e, *of Halicyae*: Cic.

Hălĭeutĭca -orum, n. (ἁλιευτικά), *the title of a poem of Ovid's on fishing.*

hālĭtus -ūs, m. (halo), *breath, exhalation, vapour*: Lucr., Verg.

hallex -ĭcis, m. *the thumb* or *big toe*: Pl.

hālo -are, *to breathe out, exhale.* Intransit.: arae sertis halant, Verg.; Ov. Transit.: nectar, Lucr.

hălŏphanta -ae, m. (ἁλοφάντης), *a scoundrel*: Pl.

hălūc-. *see* aluc-.

Hălўs -lўos; acc. -lyn; m. (Ἅλυς), *a river in Asia Minor.*

hăma (ăma) -ae, f. (ἄμη), *a bucket, esp. a fireman's bucket*: Juv., Plin. L.

Hămādrўas -ădis, f. (´Αμαδρυάς), *a wood-nymph, hamadryad*: Verg., Prop.

hāmātus -a -um (hamus), *provided with hooks, hooked.* LIT., ungues, Ov. TRANSF., *curved like a hook, crooked*: corpora, Cic., Ov.

hămaxo -are (ἄμαξα), *to yoke to a waggon*: Pl.

Hămilcăr -căris, m. *name of several Carthaginians,* esp. Hamilcar Barca, *general in the first Punic war, father of Hannibal.*

hămĭōta -ae, m. (hamus), *an angler*: Pl.

Hammon, *see* Ammon.

hămŭlus -i, m. (dim. of hamus), *a small hook*: Pl.

hāmus -i, m. *a hook.* LIT., in gen.: hami ferrei, Caes.; lorica hamis auroque trilix, *a coat of mail,* Verg.; esp. *a fish-hook*: Pl., Cic. TRANSF., *the talons of a hawk*: Ov.; *a thorn*: Ov.

Hannĭbăl -bălis, m. *name of several Carthaginians,* esp. Hannibal, *son of Hamilcar Barca, leader of the Carthaginians in the second Punic war, defeated by Scipio at Zama.*

hăra -ae, f. *a pen* or *coop for domestic animals*; esp. *a pig-sty*: Ov. TRANSF., abusively: Pl., Cic.

hărēna -ae, f. *sand.*
    LIT., saxa globosa harenae immixta, Liv.; harenae carae, *the sands of Pactolus,* Ov.; prov.: harenae mandare semina, *to sow the sand,* of a fruitless work, Ov.
    TRANSF., (1) *desert* or *sandy ground*: harenam aliquam aut paludes emere, Cic. (2) *the sea-shore*: optata potiri harena, Verg. (3) *the arena in the amphitheatre* (covered with sand): promittere operas harenae, Tac.; hence, *the scene of any contention* or *struggle*: Plin. L., Luc.

hărēnārius -a -um, *relating to sand, sandy.* As subst. **hărēnāria** -ae, f. (sc. fodina), *a sand pit*: Cic.

hărēnōsus -a -um, *sandy*: Verg., Ov.

hărĭŏlātĭo -ōnis, f. (hariolor), *soothsaying*: Enn.

hărĭŏlor -ari, dep. (hariolus), *to divine, utter prophecies*: Cic. TRANSF., *to talk nonsense, foolishness*: Pl., Ter.

hărĭŏlus -i, m. *a soothsayer, prophet*: Pl., Ter., Cic.; f. **hărĭŏla** -ae: Pl.

¹**harmŏnĭa** -ae, f. (ἁρμονία), *the agreement of sounds, melody*: Lucr., Cic.; fig., in gen., *concord, harmony*: Lucr.

²**Harmŏnĭa** -ae, f. (´Αρμονία), *daughter of Mars and Venus, wife of Cadmus, mother of Semele and Ino.*

harpăgo -ōnis, m. (ἁρπάγη), *a large hook, a drag, a grappling-iron*: Caes., Liv. TRANSF., *a rapacious person*: Pl.

harpē -ēs, f. (ἅρπη), *a sickle-shaped sword, scimitar*: Ov., Luc.

Harpŏcrătēs -is, m. (´Αρποκράτης), *an Egyptian deity, the god of silence*: aliquem reddere Harpocratem, *to impose silence upon,* Cat.

Harpy̆iae (trisyll.) -ārum, f. (´Αρπυιαι, *the snatchers*), *the Harpies, mythical monsters, half-bird and half-woman.*

hărundĭfer -fěra -fěrum (harundo/fero), *reed-bearing*: caput, Ov.

hărundĭnĕus -a -um, *reedy*: silva, Verg.; carmen, *a shepherd's song,* Ov.

hărundĭnōsus -a -um, *full of reeds*: Cat.

hărundo -inis, f. *a reed.* LIT., crines umbrosa tegebat harundo, Verg.; casae ex harundine textae, Liv. Meton., for an object made of

reed. (1) *a fishing-rod*: moderator harundinis, *a fisherman,* Ov. (2) *limed twigs for catchin birds*: Pl., Prop., Mart. (3) *a pen*: tristis, *severe style,* Mart. (4) *the shaft of an arrow* Ov.; poet., *the arrow itself*: Verg., Ov. (5) *shepherd's pipe*: Verg. (6) *a flute*: Ov (7) *a weaver's comb*: Ov. (8) *a plaything fo children, a hobby-horse*: Hor.

hăruspex -spĭcis, m. (Etruscan haru/*specio), *a soothsayer, one who foretold the future from the inspection of entrails*: Pl., Cic., Verg TRANSF., in gen., *a seer, prophet*: Prop., Juv.

hăruspĭca -ae, f. (haruspex), *a female soothsayer*: Pl.

hăruspĭcīnus -a -um (haruspex), *concerned with divination by the inspection of entrails*: Cic. F. as subst. **hăruspĭcĭna** -ae (sc. ars), *the art of so inspecting entrails*: haruspicinam facere, *to practise the art o haruspex,* Cic.

hăruspĭcĭum -i, n. (haruspex), *the inspection of entrails, divination*: Cat.

Hasdrŭbăl (**Asdrŭbăl**) -bălis, m. *name o several Carthaginians,* esp. (1) *son-in-law o Hamilcar Barca, general in Spain.* (2) *son o Hamilcar Barca, brother of Hannibal, killed at the battle of the Metaurus.* (3) *Carthaginian general in the third Punic war.*

hasta -ae, f. *a spear, pike, javelin.* (1) in milit. use: amentata, *furnished with a thong to assis in throwing it,* Cic.; eminus hastis aut comminus gladio uti, Cic.; fig.: hastas abicere, *to 'throw up the sponge',* Cic. (2) in ceremonial use: **a,** as sign of a public auction; hence: sub hasta vendere, *to sell by auction,* Liv.; emptio ab hasta, Cic.; hasta venditionis, Cic.: **b,** of the centumviral court: Suet. **c,** *a miniature spear, with which the bride' hair was parted on the wedding-day*: Ov.

hastātus -a -um (hasta), *armed with a spear* Tac.; esp. m. pl. as subst. **hastāti** -ōrum *the first line of the Roman army when draw up in order of battle, the first rank, vanguard* Liv., Ov.; hence: primus, secundus, etc. hastatus (sc. ordo), *the first, second,* etc., *o the companies into which the* hastati *wer divided,* Caes., Cic., Liv.

hastīlĕ -is, n. (hasta), *the shaft of a spear* Cic., Liv. TRANSF., (1) *the spear itself* Verg., Ov., Juv. (2) *wood in the form of shaft; a shoot, prop for vines,* etc.: Verg.

hau, interj. *oh!* an exclamation of pain o grief: Pl., Ter.

haud (**haut**), adv., *an emphatic negative, use with single words; not, not at all, by no means* (1) with verbs: haud dubito, Cic.; haud scio Cic.; haud scio an, Cic. (2) with adjectives haud mediocris, Cic.; Liv. (3) with pro nouns: haud alius, Liv.; Pl., Ter. (4) wit adverbs: haud dubie, Sall.; haud sane, Cic. haud secus, Liv.; haud longe, Caes.

hauddum (**hautdum, haud dum**), adv. *n at all as yet, not yet*: Liv.

haudquāquam (**hautquāquam, haud quā quam**), adv. *by no means, not at all*: Cic Verg.

haurĭo haurīre hausi haustum (fut. partic hausurus: Verg.), *to draw up, draw out.*
    LIT., of physical action. (1) *to draw an fluid from a source*: aquam de puteo, Cic sanguinem, *to shed,* Cic., Liv.; esp. to *drin up, absorb, drain*: alveus haurit aquas, Ov

fig.: hauris de faece, *you use the worst*, Cic. (2) of solid objects: **a**, *to drain, empty* what contains fluid: pocula ore, Ov.; latus gladio, Verg.: **b**, *to swallow up* things or persons: ventus arbusta, Lucr.; pulverem, Ov.; altitudine nivis nauriebantur, Tac. (3) of light, air, and sound, *to draw in*: lucem, Verg.; suspiratus, Ov.; vocem auribus, Verg.

TRANSF., fig. (1) *to derive* from a source: sumptum ex aerario, Cic.; fontes adire et praecepta haurire, Hor. (2) *to take in, absorb* a feeling or experience: voluptates, calamitates, Cic.; supplicia, animo spem inanem, Verg.; oculis gaudium, Liv. (3) *to exhaust, weaken, waste*: sua, Tac.; Italiam et provincias immenso faenore, Tac.; caelo medium sol igneus orbem hauserat, Verg.; exsultantia haurit corda pavor pulsans Verg.

ustrum -i, n. (haurio), *a machine for drawing water*: Lucr.

ustus -ūs, m. (haurio). (1) *a drawing of water*: Juv.; as legal t. t.: aquae, *the right of drawing water*, Cic. (2) *drawing in*: **a**, of air, *inhaling*: apibus esse haustus aetherios, Verg.: **b**, of fluids, *drinking* and concr., *a draught*: aquae, Liv.; fontis Pindarici, Hor.: **c**, of solids, *a handful*: arenae, Ov.

ut = haud; q.v.

vĕo, see aveo.

autontīmōrūmĕnos -i, m. (ἑαυτὸν τιμωρούμενος), *the self-tormentor*, the title of one of Terence's comedies.

bdŏmas -ădis, f. (ἑβδομάς), *the seventh day of a disease* (supposed to be a critical period): Cic. L.

bē -ēs, f. (Ἥβη, *youth*), *the daughter of Jupiter, cup-bearer of the gods, wife of Hercules*.

bĕnus -i, f. (ἔβενος), *the ebon-tree, ebony*: Verg.

bĕo -ēre (hebes), *to be blunt, dull*: ferrum, Liv. TRANSF., *to be dull, heavy, inactive*: anguis hebet, Verg.; sic mihi sensus hebet, Ov.

bĕs -ĕtis, *blunt, dull*.

LIT., mucro, Lucr.; tela, Cic.; gladius, Ov.; hence: hebeti ictu, Ov.

TRANSF., (1) physically, *faint, sluggish*; of action, *sluggish, weak*: hebes ad sustinendum laborem miles, Sall.; of colour, *dull*: color, Ov.; esp. of the senses: aures, Cic.; acies oculorum, Cic. (2) mentally, *dull, heavy, stupid*: homines hebetes, Cic.; compar.: hebetiora ingenia, Cic.; Tac., Quint.

besco -ĕre (hebeo), *to become dull, blunt, dim*; of the senses: mentis acies, Cic.; fig.: auctoritatis acies, Cic.

bĕto -āre (hebes), *to make blunt*. LIT., hastas, Liv. TRANSF., *to make dull, blunt, deaden, dim*: flammas, Ov.; alicui visus, Verg.; ingenium, Plin. L.

braeus -a -um, *Hebrew, Jewish*: Tac.

brus -i, m. (Ἕβρος), *the chief river of Thrace, flowing into the Aegean* (now *Maritza*).

călē -ēs, f. (Ἑκάλη), *a poor old woman who entertained Theseus*.

cătē -ēs, f. (Ἑκάτη), *the goddess of magic and enchantment, often identified with Diana and Luna*.

¶ Hence adj. **Hĕcătēius** -a -um and adj. **Hĕcătēis** -ĭdis, *Hecatean*; hence = *magical*: Ov.

---

hĕcătombē -ēs, f. (ἑκατόμβη), *a hecatomb*. LIT., *sacrifice of a hundred oxen*: Juv.

Hectŏr -tŏris, m. (Ἕκτωρ), *son of Priam, husband of Andromache, the bravest of the Trojans, killed by Achilles*. Adj. **Hectŏrĕus** -a -um (Ἑκτόρεος), *belonging to Hector*; poet. = *Trojan*: Verg.

Hĕcŭba -ae, f. and **Hĕcŭbē** -ēs, f. (Ἑκάβη), *wife of Priam*.

hĕdĕra -ae, f. *ivy, a plant sacred to Bacchus*: Verg., Hor., Ov.

hĕdĕrĭger -gĕra -gĕrum (hedera/gero), *ivy-bearing, ivy-crowned*: Cat.

hĕdĕrōsus -a -um (hedera), *ivied, full of ivy*: Prop.

hĕdychrum -i, n. (ἡδύχροον), *a fragrant ointment*: Cic.

hei, interj. = ei; q.v.

Hĕlĕna -ae, f. and **Hĕlĕnē** -ēs, f. (Ἑλένη), *daughter of Leda and Jupiter, sister of Castor, Pollux, and Clytemnestra, mother of Hermione, wife of Menelaus. She was carried off by Paris to Troy, and so caused the Trojan war*.

Hĕlĕnus -i, m. (Ἕλενος), *son of Priam, a soothsayer*.

Hĕlĭădes -um, f. (Ἡλιάδες), *the daughters of the Sun, who, at the death of their brother Phaëthon, were changed into poplars* (or *alders*), *and their tears into amber*; hence: nemus Heliadum, *a poplar* (or *alder*) *grove*, Ov.; Heliadum lacrimae, *amber*, Ov.; gemmae, *amber*, Mart.

Hĕlĭcē -ēs, f. (Ἑλίκη) (1) *a town in Achaia*. (2) *a constellation, the Great Bear*: Cic., Ov.

Hĕlĭcon -ōnis, m. (Ἑλικών), *a hill in Boeotia, sacred to Apollo and the Muses*: Heliconis alumnae, *the Muses*, Ov.

¶ Hence adj. **Hĕlĭcōnĭus** -a -um, *Heliconian*; subst. **Hĕlĭcōnĭădes** -um, f. and **Hĕlĭcōnĭdes** -um, f. *the Muses*.

Hĕlĭöpŏlis -ĕos, f. (Ἡλιόπολις), *a town in Lower Egypt*: Cic.

Hellē -ēs, f. (Ἕλλη), *daughter of Athamas and Nephele, who fled from her step-mother Ino on a golden ram; and was drowned in the Hellespont, so named after her*.

hellĕborus, see elleborus.

Hellespontus -i, m. (Ἑλλήσποντος), *the Hellespont, Dardanelles*. TRANSF., *the coast on both sides of the Hellespont*: Cic., Liv.

¶ Hence adj. **Hellespontĭus** -a -um and **Hellespontĭăcus** -a -um, *of the Hellespont*.

Hĕlōrus -i, m. (Ἕλωρος) and **Hĕlōrum** -i. n. (Ἕλωρον), *a river on the east coast of Sicily and a town of the same name*. Hence adj. **Hĕlōrĭus** -a -um, *of Helorus*; subst. **Hĕlōrīni** -ōrum, m. *inhabitants of the town*.

hellŭo (hēlŭo) -ōnis, m. *a glutton, squanderer*: Ter., Cic.

hellŭor (hēlŭor) -ari, dep. (helluo), *to guzzle, gormandize*: Cic. TRANSF., libris: Cic.; reipublicae sanguine, Cic.

hĕlops (ĕlops, ellops) -ōpis, m. (ἔλλοψ), *a savoury fish, perhaps the sturgeon*: Ov.

helvella -ae, f. *a small pot-herb*: Cic. L.

Helvētii -ōrum, m. *the Helvetii, a people of Gallia Lugdunensis, in what is now Switzerland*. Adj. **Helvētĭus** and **Helvētĭcus** -a -um, *Helvetian*.

Helvii (Helvi) -ōrum, m. *a people in* Gallia Narbonensis.

hem, interj. of surprise; *well! just look!*: hem causam, Cic.; Pl., Ter.

hēmĕrodrŏmus -i, m. (ἡμεροδρόμος), *a special courier, express*: Liv.

hēmĭcillus -i, m. (ἥμισυς/κιλλός), *a mule*, as a term of reproach: Cic. L.

hēmĭcyclĭum -i, n. (ἡμικύκλιον), *a semi-circle*: Plin. L. Transf., *an arrangement of seats in a semi-circle*: Cic., Suet.

hēmĭna -ae, f. (ἡμίνα), *a measure of capacity*, half a sextarius=nearly a pint English: Pl.

hēmĭnārĭa -orum, n. pl. (hemina), *presents of the measure of a hemina*: Quint.

hendĕcăsyllăbi -ōrum, m. (ἐνδεκασύλλαβοι), *verses of eleven syllables, hendecasyllables*: Cat., Plin. L.

Henna (Enna) -ae, f. (*Έννα*), *an ancient city of Sicily* (now *Enna*), *with a famous temple of Ceres*.
¶ Hence adj. **Hennensis** -e and **Hennaeus** -a -um, *of Henna*.

hēpătārĭus -a -um, *of the liver*: Pl.

hepteris -is, f. (ἑπτήρης), *a galley with seven banks of oars*: Liv.

¹**hĕra=ĕra**; q.v.

²**Hēra** -ae, f. (*Ήρα*), *the Greek goddess identified with the Roman Juno*.
¶ Hence **Hēraea** -ōrum, n. (*Ήραῖα*), *the festival of Hera*: Liv.

Hēraclēa (-ĭa) -ae, f. (*Ήράκλεια*), *the city of Heracles* (Hercules), *name of several Greek towns*. (1) *a colony of the Tarentines in the south of Italy, on the river Siris*. (2) *a town in Phthiotis, near Thermopylae*. (3) *a town in Bithynia on the Black Sea* (now *Erekli*). (4) *a town in Sicily on the Halycos, also called Minoa*. (5) Heraclea Sintica, *a town in Paeonia on the Strymon*.
¶ Hence subst. **Hēraclĕenses** -ĭum, *the inhabitants of Heraclea*; m. adj. **Hēraclĕōtes** -ae, *belonging to Heraclea*; plur. as subst. **Hēraclĕōtae** -ārum, *the inhabitants of Heraclea*.

Hēraclĕum -i, n. (*Ήράκλειον*), *a town in Macedonia, on the borders of Thessaly*.

Hēraclĭdēs -ae, m. (*Ήρακλείδης*), Ponticus, *a Greek philosopher, pupil of Plato*.

Hēraclītus -i, m. (*Ήράκλειτος*), *a Greek philosopher of Ephesus, about* 500 B.C., *known as* 'The Obscure'.

¹**Hēraea** -ōrum, see Hera.

²**Hēraea** -ae, f. (*Ήραῖα*), *a town in Arcadia on the Alpheus*.

herba -ae, f. (cf. φορβή), *springing vegetation, a stalk*. Hence (1) *a blade* or *stalk*, esp. of corn or grass: frumenta in herbis erant, Caes.; Verg., Ov. (2) *a green plant*: stirpes et herbae, Cic.; esp. *grass*: Cic., Verg. (3) *a weed*: officiant laetis ne frugibus herbae, Verg.

herbesco -ĕre (herba), *to grow into blades* or *stalks*: Cic.

herbĕus -a -um (herba), *grass-green*: Pl.

herbĭdus -a -um (herba), *full of grass, grassy*: campus, Liv.; Ov.

herbĭfer -fĕra -fĕrum (herba/fero), *full of herbage, grassy*: colles, Ov.

herbĭgrădus -a -um (herba/gradior), *going through the grass*: poet. ap. Cic.

Herbĭta -ae, f. (* Έρβιτα*), *a town in Sicily*.
¶ Hence adj. **Herbĭtensis** -e, *of Herbita*.

herbōsus -a -um (herba), *of grass* or *full of grass*: Verg., Hor., Ov.

---

herbŭla -ae, f. (dim. of herba), *a little herb*: Cic., Quint.

Hercēus -a -um (*Έρκεῖος*), *a surname of Jupiter as the protector of the house, courtyard* etc.

hercisco (ercisco) -ĕre (herctum), *to divide an inheritance*: Cic.

Hercle, see Hercules.

herctum -i, n. (probably connected with heres), *an inheritance*, found only in the phrase herctum ciere, *to divide an inheritance*: Cic.

Hercŭlānĕum -i, n. *a town in Campania destroyed by an eruption of Vesuvius in* A.D. 79.
¶ Hence, adj. **Hercŭlānensis** -e and **Hercŭlānēus** -a -um, *of Herculaneum*.

Hercŭlēs -is and -i, m. (*Ήρακλῆς*), *the son of Jupiter and Alcmena, husband of Deianira and* (after his deification) *of Hebe; the performer of twelve labours imposed upon him by Eurystheus; regarded as the giver of riches and the guide of the Muses*. Vocat. sing. **Hercŭle** or **Hercŭle** or **Hercle**; all these forms were used as an oath, *by Hercules*: Cic.; also **mēhercŭles** and **mēhercŭle**: Cic., and **mēhercle**: Ter.
¶ Hence adj. **Hercŭlĕus** -a -um *Herculean*: arbor, *the poplar*, Verg., and **Hercŭlānēus** -a -um.

Hercўnĭa silva -ae, f. *the Hercynian forest in central Germany*: Caes., Tac.; also with saltus: Tac., Liv.; and absol.: Tac.

Herdōnĭa -ae, f. *a town in Apulia*.

hĕrē=heri; q.v.

hērēdĭtārĭus -a -um (hereditas). (1) *relating to an inheritance*: auctio, Cic. (2) *inherited, hereditary*: cognomen, Cic.; controversia, Cic.

hērēdĭtās -ātis, f. (heres), *inheritance*. Lit. (1) abstr.: hereditate possidere, Cic. (; concr.: hereditatem capere, adire, cernere, Cic.; Pl., Tac. Transf., hereditas gloriae, Cic.

Hērennĭus -a -um, *name of a Roman gens*. Adj. **Hērenniānus** -a -um, *Herennian*: Cic. L.

hērēdĭum -i, n. (heres), *a patrimony*: Nep.

hērēs (haeres) -ēdis, c. *an heir, heiress*. Lit., heres esse alicui or alicuius, Cic.; aliquem heredem scribere, facere, instituere, *to make a person one's heir*, Cic.; secundus, *a person named to receive the inheritance the original heir cannot inherit*, Cic., Hor., Quint.
Transf., (1) *owner*: Pl. (2) *successor*: veteris Academiae, Cic.; Ov.

hĕrī (hĕrĕ), adv. (χθές), *yesterday*: Pl., Cic., Hor., Ov. Transf., *lately*: Cat.

hĕrĭfūga=erifuga; q.v.

hĕrĭlis -e=erilis; q.v.

hermaphrŏdītus -i, m. (ἑρμαφρόδιτος), *hermaphrodite*: Ov.

Hermăthēna -ae, f. (*Έρμῆς/Άθηνᾶ*), *a double bust of Hermes and Athena, on the same pedestal*: Cic. L.

Hermēraclēs -is, m. (*Έρμῆς/Ήρακλῆς*), *double bust of Hermes and Hercules*: Cic. L.

Hermēs or **Herma** -ae, m. (*Έρμῆς*), *the Hermes, identified with the Roman Mercury*; hence *a post, the top of which was carved into a head, placed in the streets, esp. of Athens*

ermĭŏnē -ēs, f. and **Hermĭŏna** -ae, f. (Ἑρμιόνη). (1) *daughter of Menelaus and Helen, wife of Orestes.* (2) *a town in Argolis* (now *Kastri*).

¶ Hence adj. **Hermĭŏnĭcus** -a -um, *of Hermione.*

ermĭŏnes -um, m. *a people of Germany.*

ermundūri -ōrum, m. *a Germanic tribe.*

ernĭci -ōrum, m. *a people in Latium.* Adj. **Hernĭcus** -a -um, *Hernican.*

ērō -ūs, f. (Ἡρώ), *a priestess of Aphrodite at Sestos, loved by Leander.*

ērŏdēs -is, m. (Ἡρώδης), *Herod*; esp. *Herod the Great, king of Judea.*

ērŏdŏtus -i, m. (Ἡρόδοτος), *the first great Greek historian, born 484 B.C.*

ērŏĭcus -a -um (ἡρωϊκός), *relating to the heroes, heroic:* tempora, Cic.; Quint., Tac.

ērŏĭna -ae, f. (ἡρωΐνη), *a demigoddess, heroine:* Prop.

ērŏis -ĭdis, f. (ἡρωΐς), *a demigoddess, heroine:* Ov. (Gr. dat. plur., heroisin: Ov.).

ērŏs -ŏis, m. (ἥρως), *a demigod, hero:* Cic., Verg., Ov. TRANSF., *a distinguished man, hero:* noster Cato, Cic.

ērŏus -a -um (ἡρῷος), *relating to a hero, heroic:* pes, versus, *epic verse* (hexameter), Cic.; absol. herous -i, m. *a hexameter:* Ov.

ersĭlia -ae, f. *wife of Romulus.*

erus = erus; q.v.

ēsĭŏdus -i, m. (Ἡσίοδος), *an early Greek poet of Boeotia.* Adj. **Hēsĭŏdēus** or **-ĭus** -a -um, *Hesiodean.*

ēsĭŏna -ae, f. and **Hēsĭŏnē** -ēs, f. (Ἡσιόνη), *daughter of Laomedon, king of Troy, rescued by Hercules from a sea-monster.*

espērus or **-os** -i, m. (Ἕσπερος), *the Evening Star*; myth., either *son of Cephalus and Aurora or son of Iapetus and Asia.*

¶ Hence adj. **Hespĕrĭus** -a -um (ἑσπέριος), *western:* terra, *Italy*, Verg.; subst. **Hespĕria** -ae, f. *the western land; Italy:* Verg.; *Spain:* Hor.; f. adj. **Hespĕris** -ĭdis (Ἑσπερίς), *western:* aquae, *Italian*, Verg.; subst. **Hespĕrĭdes** -um, f. *the Hesperides, daughters of Hesperus, living in the extreme west, watching a garden with golden apples.*

esternus -a -um (cf. heri), *of yesterday:* dies, Cic., Cat.

ētairia -ae, f. (ἑταιρία), *a secret society:* Plin. L.

ētairĭcē -ēs, f. (ἑταιρική), *Band of Brothers,* name of a troop in the Macedonian army: Nep.

ēu, interj. expressing grief or pain, *oh! alas!:* heu me miserum, Pl., Ter., Cic.

ēurētēs -ae, m. (εὑρετής), *an inventor:* Pl.

ēus! interj. *hallo! ho there! hark!:* heus tu quid agis! Cic.; Pl., Verg.

ēxămĕtĕr -tri, m. adj. (ἑξάμετρος), *with six feet* (of metre): hexameter versus, *or* absol. hexameter, *a hexameter, verse of six feet,* Hor.

ēxēris -is, f. (ἑξήρης), *a galley with six banks of oars:* Liv.

iātus -ūs, m. (hio), *a cleft, opening.* LIT., oris, Cic.; terrae, Cic.; absol., *the opening of the mouth, the open jaws:* Lucr., Ov.; in plur.: Verg. TRANSF., (1) *of style:* quid dignum tanto feret hic promissor hiatu? *of such pompous language,* Hor. (2) *gaping after, desire for:* praemiorum, Tac. (3) in grammar, *a hiatus, the meeting of two vowels:* Cic.

Hĭbĕr -ēris, m. (Ἴβηρ), *an Iberian, Spaniard;* usually plur. **Hĭbĕrēs** -ērum, *Spaniards;* also **Hĭbĕri** -orum, m. *Spaniards;* **Hĭbĕrus** -i, m. *the river Ebro;* **Hĭbĕria** -ae (Ἰβηρία), *Spain;* adj. **Hĭbĕrĭcus** -a -um and **Hĭbĕrus** -a -um, *Spanish:* gurges (of the western ocean), Verg.; piscis, *the scomber,* Hor.; pastor triplex, *Geryon,* Ov.; vaccae, *or* boves, *belonging to Geryon,* Ov.

hĭberna -ōrum, n., *see* hibernus.

hĭbernācŭlum -i, n. (hiberno), plur.: hibernacula, *tents* or *huts for winter quarters,* Liv., Caes., Tac.

Hĭbernĭa -ae, f. *Ireland.*

hĭberno -are (hibernus), *to winter, spend the winter:* in sicco (of ships), Liv.; esp. as milit. t. t., *to keep in winter quarters:* Cic.

hĭbernus -a -um (hiems), *wintry, of winter.* LIT., tempus, mensis, Cic.; annus, *time of winter,* Hor. TRANSF., (1) *like winter; cold* or *stormy:* Alpes, mare, Hor.; Verg. (2) *wintering, for the winter:* legiones, Suet.; esp.: castra, *winter quarters;* n. pl. as subst. **hĭberna** -ōrum (sc. castra), *winter quarters:* dies hibernorum, *time for going into winter quarters,* Caes.; hiberna aedificare, Liv.; cohortes in hiberna mittere, Cic.; ibi hiberna habere, Liv.; ex hibernis discedere, egredi, Cic.

hĭbiscum -i, n. (ἰβίσκος), *the marsh-mallow:* Verg.

hĭbrĭda (hybrĭda) -ae, c. of animals, *a hybrid:* Plin. TRANSF., of men, *the offspring of a Roman by a foreign woman or of a freeman by a slave:* Hor.

¹hĭc, haec, hōc, pron. or pronom. adj. *this,* of persons and things either physically present or present in thought. (1) in space, *this . . . here:* Pl., Cic., etc.; often: hic homo = ego, I, Pl., Hor. (2) in thought, *this, the one referred to:* haec cum Scipio dixisset, Cic.; Pl., Verg., etc. (3) in relation to another pronoun or to a clause; opp. iste, in the courts, *my client:* Cic.; opp. ille = *the former,* hic = *the latter* (sometimes *vice versa*): Sall., Liv.; as antecedent of relative clause: quam quisque norit artem, in hac se exerceat, Cic.; n. hoc referring to a clause that follows: hoc commodi est quod, *there is this advantage, that . . . ,* Cic. (4) in time, *the present, modern:* his temporibus, Cic.; haec, *the present state of affairs,* Cic.; his annis viginti, *in the last twenty years,* Cic.

¶ Strengthened form **hice, haece, hoce** (hic/ce): Pl., Ter., Cic.; also further strengthened by interrog. -ne, **hicine, haecine, hocine:** huncine solem tam nigrum surrexe mihi, Hor.; Pl., Cic.

²hĭc and heic, adv. *here.* LIT., *in this place:* Pl., Cic., Verg. TRANSF., *herein, in this matter:* Caes., Cic. Also of time, *hereupon, here:* Cic., Verg., Liv. Strengthened forms **hīce** and interrog. **hīcĭne.**

Hĭcĕtāon -ŏnis, m. (Ἰκετάων), *son of Laomedon, king of Troy.* Adj. **Hĭcĕtāŏnĭus** -a -um: Thymoetes, *son of Hicetaon,* Verg.

hĭcĭne, see ¹hic and ²hic.

hĭĕmālis -e (hiems), *wintry, of winter:* tempus, Cic., Verg. TRANSF., *like winter, stormy:* navigatio, Cic. L.

hĭĕmo -are (hiems). (1) *to winter, spend the winter:* mediis in undis, Hor. Esp. of

[275]

soldiers, *to keep in winter quarters*: hiemare
in Gallia, Caes. (**2**) *to be stormy*: mare
hiemat, Hor.

hǐems (hǐemps) -ĕmis, f. (cf. χειμών), *winter*.
LIT., initā hieme, Caes.; Arabes campos
hieme et aestate peragrantes, Cic.; also in
plur. Personif.: glacialis Hiems, Ov.; Verg.
TRANSF., (**1**) *stormy weather, storm*:
hiemis magnitudo, Cic.; dum pelago desaevit
hiems, Verg. (**2**) *cold*: letalis hiems in
pectora venit, Ov. (**3**) fig.: mutati amoris
hiems, Ov.

Hǐĕro -ōnis, m. ('Ιέρων), *the name of two
famous rulers of Syracuse.* Adj. **Hǐĕrŏnǐcus**
-a -um, *of Hiero.*

Hǐĕrŏcles -is, m. ('Ιεροκλῆς), *a Greek rhetorician, contemporary of Cicero.*

Hǐĕrŏnўmus -i, m. ('Ιερώνυμος). (**1**) *a ruler
of Syracuse*: Liv. (**2**) *a Greek peripatetic
philosopher*: Cic.

Hǐĕrŏsŏlўma -ōrum, n. pl. ('Ιεροσόλυμα),
Jerusalem, capital of Judea.

¶ Hence **Hǐĕrŏsŏlўmārǐus**, *a name given
to Pompey, after his capture of Jerusalem.*

hǐĕto -are (freq. of hio), *to gape*: Pl.

hǐlāris -e and **hǐlārus** -a -um, adj. (with
compar.; and superl.: Pl.), *cheerful, merry,
blithe, gay*: animus, Cic. L.; vita, Cic.; esse
vultu hilari atque laeto, Cic.; dies, Pl., Ter.;
Hor.

¶ N. acc. sing. as adv. **hǐlārē**, *cheerfully,
merrily*: vivere, Cic.; loqui, Cic.; compar.:
hilarius, Cic.

hǐlārĭtās -ātis, f. (hilaris), *cheerfulness, mirth,
gaiety*: Cic., Quint.

hǐlārĭtūdo -ĭnis, f.=hilaritas; q.v.: Pl.

hǐlāro -are (hilaris), *to make joyful, to cheer up*:
huius suavitate maxime hilaratae Athenae
sunt, Cic.; multo convivia Baccho, Verg.

hǐlārŭlus -a -um (dim. of hilarus), *gay,
cheerful*: Cic.

hillae -arum, f. pl. (dim. of hira), *the smaller
intestines of animals.* TRANSF., *a kind of
sausage*: Hor.

Hǐlōtae and **Ilōtae** -ārum, m. (Εἱλῶται), *the
Helots, slaves of the Spartans.*

hǐlum -i, n. *a trifle*; usually with neg.: neque
(nec) hilum, *not a whit, not in the least*, Lucr.

Hǐmella -ae, f. *a stream in the Sabine country.*

Hǐmĕra -ae, f. ('Ιμέρα), *name of a river and
town in Sicily.*

hinc, adv. (¹hic), *from here, hence.*
LIT., a nobis hinc profecti, Cic.
TRANSF., (**1**) *from this side, on this side*:
hinc atque illinc, *on this side and on that*, Liv.;
hinc . . . illinc, Cic.; Verg. (**2**) *of causation,
from this cause*: hinc illae lacrimae, Ter.;
Cic., Verg. (**3**) *of time*: **a**, *henceforth*:
quisquis es, amissos hinc iam obliviscere
Graios, Verg.: **b**, *thereupon*: hinc toto
praeceps se corpore ad undas misit, Verg.

hinnǐo -ire, *to neigh, whinny*: Lucr., Quint.

hinnītus -ūs, m. (hinnio), *a neighing*: Lucr.,
Cic., Verg.

hinnǔlĕus -i, m. (hinnus), *a young roebuck,
a fawn*: Hor.

hinnus -i, m. (ἵννος), *a mule, the offspring of a
stallion and a she-ass* (mulus=*the offspring of
a he-ass and a mare*): Varr.

hǐo -are, *to open, stand open, gape.*
LIT., oculi, Pl.; concha hians, Cic.; leo
hians, Verg.

TRANSF., (**1**) *of speech, to be badly pu[t]
together, hang together badly*: hiantia loqui[?]
Cic.; Quint., Tac. (**2**) *to desire with ope[n]
mouth, long for*: Verrem avaritiā hiant[e]
atque imminente fuisse, Cic.; Hor. (**3**) *t[o]
open the mouth in astonishment*: Verg., Tac
(**4**) with acc. object, *to pour forth*: carme[n]
lyrā, Prop.

hippăgōgi -orum, f. pl. (ἱππαγωγοί), *transport
for cavalry*: Liv.

Hippǐas -ae, m. ('Ιππίας). (**1**) *son of Pisistratus
tyrant of Athens.* (**2**) *a sophist of Elis
contemporary with Socrates.*

Hippo -ōnis, m. ('Ιππών), *name of several cities
esp. a port in Numidia* (now *Bône*).

hippŏcentaurus -i, m. (ἱπποκένταυρος),
centaur: Cic.

Hippŏcrătēs -is, m. ('Ιπποκράτης), *a physicia[n]
of Cos* (flourishing about 430 B.C.).

Hippŏcrēnē -ēs, f. (ἵππου κρήνη), *a founta[in]
on Mount Helicon, produced by a blow fro[m]
the hoof of Pegasus.*

Hippŏdămē -ēs, f. and **Hippŏdămēa** or -[ī]
-ae, f. ('Ιπποδάμη, -δάμεια). (**1**) *daughter [of]
Oenomaus, king of Elis.* (**2**) *wife of Pirithou[s].*

Hippŏdămus -i, m. ('Ιππόδαμος), *the hors[e]-
tamer, epithet of* Castor: Mart.

hippŏdrŏmos -i, m. (ἱππόδρομος), *a hippodro[n]
or racecourse for horses and chariots*: Pl., Ma[r]

Hippŏlўtē -ēs, f. and **Hippŏlўta** -ae,
('Ιππολύτη). (**1**) *Queen of the Amazons, tak[en]
prisoner by Theseus.* (**2**) *wife of Acastu[s]
King of Magnesia.*

Hippŏlўtus -i, m. ('Ιππόλυτος), *son of These[us]
and Hippolyte, falsely accused by his ste[p]
mother Phaedra.*

hippŏmănes, n. (ἱππομανές). (**1**) *a sli[m]
humour which flows from a mare when in hea[t]*:
Verg., Tib., Prop. (**2**) *a membrane on t[he]
head of a new-born foal, used for lov[e]
potions*: Juv.

Hippŏmĕnēs -ae, m. ('Ιππομένης). (**1**) *son [of]
Megareus and husband of Atalanta.* (**2**)
Athens, father of Limone; whence **Hipp[?]
mĕnēis** -nēidis, f.=Limone.

Hippōnax -nactis, m. ('Ιππώναξ), *a Gre[ek]
satirical poet of the sixth century B.C.*
¶ Hence adj. **Hippōnactēus** -a -u[m]
biting, satirical: praeconium, Cic. L.; m.
subst. (sc. versus), *an iambic line as written [by]
Hipponax*: Hipponacteos effugere vix pos[?]
Cic.

hippŏpŏtămus -i, m. (ἱπποπόταμος), *a riv[er]
horse, hippopotamus*: Plin.

Hippŏtădēs -ae, m. ('Ιπποτάδης), *descend[ant]
of Hippotes=Aeolus* (grandson of Hippot[es])
Ov.

hippŏtoxŏta -ae, m. (ἱπποτοξότης), *a moun[ted]
archer*: Caes.

hippūrus -i, m. (ἵππουρος), *a fish*, perhaps
goldfish: Ov.

hǐr, indecl. n. (connected with χείρ), *the ha[nd]*
Lucil. ap. Cic.

hǐra -ae, f. *a gut, intestine*: Pl.

hircīnus -a -um (hircus), *of a he-goat*:
folles, *made of goat-skins*, Hor.

hircōsus -a -um (hircus), *smelling like a g[oat]*
Pl.

hircus -i, m. *a he-goat*: Verg., Hor. TRAN[SF]
(**1**) *a goat-like smell*: Pl., Hor. (**2**) as a t[erm]
of reproach, an old goat: Pl., Cat.

hirnĕa -ae, f. *a can* or *jug*: Pl.

irpini -ōrum, m. *a Samnite people of central Italy*; adj. **Hirpinus** -a -um, *Hirpine*: Cic.

irquus, hirquinus=hircus, hircinus; q.v.

irsūtus -a -um, *covered with hair, rough, shaggy, prickly*: supercilium, Verg.; crines, Ov.; aliae (animantium) spinis hirsutae, Cic. TRANSF., *rough, unadorned*: nihil est hirsutius illis (annalibus), Ov.

iirtius -a -um, *name of a Roman gens; its most famous member was* A. Hirtius, *the friend and follower of* C. *Julius Caesar, slain at the battle of Modena, the author of the eighth book of Caesar's* Bell. Gall.
¶ Hence adj. **Hirtīnus** -a -um, *of Hirtius*.

irtus -a -um, *shaggy, rough, hairy, prickly*: setae, capellae, Ov. TRANSF., *rough, uncultivated*: ingenium, Hor.

irūdo -inis, f. *a leech*: Pl., Plin. TRANSF., aerarii, Cic. L.; Hor.

irundininus -a -um (hirundo), *of swallows*: Pl.

irundo -dinis, f. (χελιδών), *a swallow*: Pl., Lucr., Verg.

isco -ere (hio). (1) *to open, split open, gape*: tellus, Ov. (2) *to open the mouth*: respondebisne ad haec aut omnino hiscere audebis? Cic.; Verg., Liv.

iispālis -is, f. *town in Spain* (now *Seville*).
¶ Hence **Hispālienses** -ium, *the inhabitants of Seville*: Tac.

iispāni -ōrum, m. *the Spaniards*.
¶ Hence subst. **Hispānia** -ae, f. *the whole of the Spanish peninsula (including Portugal) divided into* citerior, *the eastern part* (later Hisp. Tarraconensis), *and* ulterior, *the southern and western part* (later Lusitania and Baetica); also in plur., Hispaniae.
¶ Adj. **Hispāniensis** -e and **Hispānus** -a -um, *Spanish*.

ispidus -a -um, *rough, hairy, bristly*: facies, Hor. TRANSF., agri, Hor.

hister=histrio; q.v.

Hister (**Ister**) -tri, m. (Ἴστρος), *name of the lower part of the Danube* (the upper part being called Danuvius): Ov.

istōria -ae, f. (ἱστορία), *inquiry*; hence *the results of inquiry*. (1) *learning in gen.*: Cic. (2) *historical narrative, history*: historia Italici belli et civilis, Cic.; historiam scribere, Cic.; quidquid Graecia mendax audet in historia, Juv. (3) *in gen., narrative, a story*: historiā dignum, *worthy of narration*, Cic. L.; Hor. (4) *the subject of a story*: Prop.

istōricus -a -um (ἱστορικός), *relating or belonging to history, historical*: sermo, Cic.; m. as subst. **histōricus** -i, *an historian*: Cic., Quint., Juv.

Iistri -ōrum (Ἴστροι), *Istrians, inhabitants of Istria*.
¶ Hence subst. **Histria** -ae, f. (Ἱστρία), *Histria, a country near Illyria*; adj. **Histrīcus** -a -um, *Histrian*.

istrīcus -a -um (hister), *of actors*: Pl.

istriō -ōnis, m. *an actor*: Pl., Cic., Liv.

istriōnālis -e (histrio), *of or for an actor*: Tac.

iulco -are (hiulcus), *to cause to gape, to split*: Cat.

iulcus -a -um (hio), *gaping, cleft, open*. LIT., hiulca siti arva, Verg. TRANSF., (1) *of discourse, ill put together, with hiatus*: concursus verborum, Cic.; Quint. (2) *eager, longing*: Pl.
¶ Adv. **hiulcē**, *with hiatus*: loqui, Cic.

hŏdĭē, adv. (=hoc die), *today*. LIT., hodie sunt nonae Sextiles, Cic.; Pl., Hor. TRANSF., (1) *at the present time*: Cic., Juv. (2) *still, even now*: si hodie hanc gloriam atque hoc orbis terrae imperium teneremus, Cic.; quem vivere hodie aiunt, Cic.; Liv., Tac. (3) *at once*: Pl., Cic., Hor.

hŏdĭernus -a -um (hodie), *of today*: dies, edictum, Cic. TRANSF., ad hodiernum diem, *up to this time*, Cic.

hŏlĭtor -ōris, m. (holus), *a kitchen-gardener*: Pl., Cic. L., Hor.

hŏlĭtōrĭus -a -um (holitor), *of herbs*: forum, *vegetable-market*, Liv.

hŏlus (**ŏlus**) -ĕris, n. *any kind of culinary vegetable, pot-herb*: Verg., Hor., etc.

Hŏmērus -i, m. (Ὅμηρος), *Homer, the Greek epic poet*.
¶ Hence adj. **Hŏmērĭcus** -a -um, **Hŏmērĭus** -a -um, *Homeric*.

hŏmĭcīda -ae, c. (homo/caedo), *a murderer, murderess, homicide*: Cic., Juv.; in special sense (=Gr. ἀνδροφόνος), of Hector, *slayer of men*: Hor.

hŏmĭcīdĭum -i, n. (homicida), *murder, manslaughter, homicide*: Quint., Tac.

hŏmo -ĭnis (connected with humus), *a human being, man*.
In gen., *man, as opp. to beasts and gods* (vir=*man* as opp. to woman): Pl., Cic., Verg., etc.; nemo homo, *not a soul, no one*, Pl., Cic.; odium hominis, *a hateful man*, Cic.; in plur.: homines, *men in general, people*, Cic.; inter homines esse, *to live or to mix in society, be in the world*, Cic.
Esp. (1) *a man, with the implications of humanity*: homo sum, humani nihil a me alienum puto, Ter.; in a good sense: nihil hominis esse, *to be without the better qualities of a man*: si quidem homo esset, *if he had the feelings of a man*, Cic.; virum te putabo ... hominem non putabo, *I must praise your patience but not your taste*, Cic.; in a bad sense, *a man as liable to error, a mortal*: quia homo est, Cic. (2) *used like a pron.*: valde hominem diligo, *the man, him*, Cic.; hic homo=ego, Hor. (3) *rarely, man, as opp. to woman*: Pl. (4) *milit. t. t., plur.*: homines, *infantry* (opp. equites), Caes.

hŏmoeŏmĕria -ae, f. (ὁμοιομέρεια), *similarity of parts* (i.e. to each other and to the whole), as a tenet of Anaxagoras: Lucr.

Hŏmŏlē -ēs, f. (Ὁμόλη), *a mountain in Thessaly*: Verg.

hŏmullus -i, m. (dim. of homo), *a little man, manikin*: Lucr., Cic.

hŏmuncĭo -ōnis, m. (dim. of homo), *a little man, manikin*: Ter., Cic.

hŏmuncŭlus -i, m. (dim. of homo), *a little man, manikin*: Pl., Cic.

hŏnestās -ātis, f. (honestus). (1) *honour as received, repute, respectability*: honestatem amittere, Cic., Liv.; TRANSF., honestates civitatis, *notabilities*, Cic. (2) *worth, virtue, honourable character, probity*: vitae, Cic.; hinc (pugnat) honestas, illinc turpitudo, Cic. TRANSF., *of things, beauty*: testudinis, Cic.

hŏnesto -are (honestus), *to honour, distinguish, adorn, dignify*: aliquem laude, Cic.; domum, Cic.; Liv.

hŏnestus -a -um (honor), adj. (with compar. and superl.).

(1) *honoured, in good repute, respectable*: familia, Cic.; honesto loco natus, Cic.; honestos fascibus et sellis, Hor.; m. as subst. **hŏnestus** -i, *a gentleman*: Hor.; f. as subst. **hŏnesta** -ae, *a gentlewoman*: Ter.

(2) *honourable, proper, virtuous*: vita, homines, Cic.; mores, Juv.; with supine: honestumne factu sit an turpe, Cic.; n. as subst. **hŏnestum** -i, *morality, virtue*: Cic., Hor. TRANSF., *fine, beautiful*: homo, forma, facies, Ter.; caput, equi, Verg. ¶ Adv. (with compar. and superl.) **hŏnestē.** (1) *respectably*: natus, Suet. (2) *honourably, properly*: cenare, Cic.; se gerere, Cic.; in pugna honeste cadere, Cic.; Pl., Hor.

hŏnor=honos; q.v.

hŏnōrābĭlis -e (honor), *respectful*: haec ipsa sunt honorabilia, salutari, appeti, decedi, adsurgi, Cic.

hŏnōrārĭus -a -um (honor), *done* or *given as an honour*: frumentum, Cic.; opera, Cic.; delectare honorarium (est), *done out of respect for the audience*, Cic.; n. as subst.: ap. Plin. L.

hŏnōrātus -a -um, partic. from honoro; q.v.

hŏnōrĭfĭcus -a -um (compar. honorificentior, superl. honorificentissimus) (honor/facio), *causing honour, honouring*: mentio, oratio, Cic. ¶ Adv. **hŏnōrĭfĭcē** (compar. honorificentius, superl. honorificentissime), *with honour, in an honourable* or *respectful manner*: praedicare, Cic.; tractare, Cic. L.; Liv.

hŏnōro -are (honor), *to honour, show honour to, adorn, dignify*: virtutem, Cic.; aliquem sellā curuli, Liv.; tumulum, Ov. ¶ Hence partic. (with compar. and superl.) **hŏnōrātus** -a -um. (1) pass., *honoured, distinguished, respected*: viri, Cic.; nusquam est senectus honoratior, Cic.; Liv., Tac.; esp. *honoured by public office*: honorati quattuor filii, Cic.; consul, Ov. (2) act., *conferring honour*: Liv., Ov., Tac. ¶ Adv. **hŏnōrātē**, *with honour, honourably*: Tac.

hŏnōrus -a -um (honor), *honourable*: Tac.

hŏnōs and **hŏnor** -ōris, m. LIT., *honour, a mark of honour* or *respect, distinction*. In gen.: honorem alicui reddere, Cic., Liv.; tribuere, Cic.; praestare, Ov.; honore aliquem adficere, *to show honour to*, Cic.; honore aliquem augere, Caes.; in honore habere, Cic.; magno esse honore, Caes., Liv., Tac.; honori ducitur, *it is considered an honour*, Sall.; honorem praefari, dicere, *to say 'By your leave'*, Cic.; phrase, honoris causā, *with due respect* or *to honour* or *for the sake of*: quem honoris causā nomino, Cic.; honoris Divitiaci et Aeduorum causā, Caes.; mei honoris causā, *for me*, Pl. Esp. (1) personif., *Honour*: Cic., Liv. (2) frequently, *an office of dignity, a public office*: ad honores ascendere, Cic.; honoribus amplissimis perfunctus, Cic.; honores dare, Hor. (3) of other particular awards to persons: militaris, Liv.; pugnae, Verg.; medico, Cic. L., *supremus honos* (*the last honour*=burial), Verg.; communi in morte honore carere, Cic.; mortis honore carere, Verg. (4) *an offering* to the gods, *sacrifice*, etc.: aris, divum templis, Verg.; dis, Liv.

TRANSF., poet., *beauty, grace*: honorum ruris, *crops*, Hor.; silvarum, *foliage*, Verg.; Hor.

hoplŏmăchus -i, m. (ὁπλομάχος), *a kind of gladiator*: Mart., Suet.

¹**hōra** -ae, f. (ὥρα), *an hour*. LIT., as part (a twelfth) of day or night: hora hiberna, Pl.; quinta fere hora, Cic.; hora amplius, *more than an hour*, Cic.; in hora, *in an hour*, Cic.; in horas, *hourly*, Cat., Hor.; hora quota est? *what's o'clock*? Hor.; horae legitimae, *hours fixed as limits to a speech*, Cic.; phrase: in horam vivere, *to live for the moment*, Cic. TRANSF., (1) *time* in gen.: numquam te crastina fallet hora, Verg.; Hor. (2) *season*: verni temporis, Hor. (3) in plur. **hōrae** -ārum, *a clock, dial*: mittere ad horas, Cic. ¶ Personif. **Hōrae** -ārum, f. ('Ωραι), *the Hours, goddesses who presided over the changes of the seasons and kept watch at the gates of heaven.*

²**Hōra** -ae, f. *the name of Hersilia when deified, the wife of Quirinus* (*Romulus*).

hōraeum -i, n. (ὡραῖον), *fish-pickle*: Pl.

Hŏrātĭus -a -um, *name of a Roman gens, to which belonged*: (1) *the three* Horatii, *who fought against the three Alban Curiatii.* (2) Horatius Cocles, *who defended the bridge over the Tiber against the army of Porsena.* (3) Q. Horatius Flaccus, *son of a freedman of the Horatian gens* (65–8 B.C.), *the poet.*

hordĕācĕus and **-cĭus** -a -um (hordeum), *of barley*: Plin.

hordĕārĭus -a -um (hordeum), *of barley*: Plin.

hordĕum -i, n. *barley*: Liv.

hŏrĭa -ae, f. *a small fishing-boat*: Pl.

hŏrĭŏla -ae, f. (dim. of horia), *a small fishing-boat*: Pl.

hornŏtĭnus -a -um (hornus), *of the present year*: frumentum, Cic.

hornus -a -um, *of this year, this year's*: vina, Hor.; adv. **hornō**, *this year*: Pl.

hŏrŏlŏgĭum -ii, n. (ὡρολόγιον), *a clock; a sun-dial* or *water-clock*: Cic.

hŏroscŏpŏs -ŏn, m. (ὡροσκόπος), *a horoscope*: Pers.

horrendus -a -um, gerundive from horreo; q.v.

horrĕo -ēre, *to bristle*. LIT., physically; in gen., *to be rough*: Caucasus seges aristis, Verg.; echinus, Hor.; esp. with cold: terram uno tempore florere deinde vicissim horrere, Cic.; horrent servo, Juv.; with fright: of the hair, *to stand on end*: comae horrent, Ov.; of the whole body: totus tremo horreoque, Ter.; Ov. TRANSF., fig., in gen., *to be rough*: horrebant saevis omnia verba minis, Ov.; esp. *to shudder at, to dread*; with acc. object: crimen, Cic.; pauperiem, Hor.; with infin.: non horreo in hunc locum progredi, Cic.; Liv. with ne and subj.: Liv. ¶ Gerundive as adj. **horrendus** -a -um. (1) *horrible, frightful, dreadful*: monstrum, Verg.; rabies, Hor., Verg.; n. as internal acc.: horrendum stridens belua, Verg. (2) *awful, worthy of reverence, 'numinous'*: Sibylla, virgo, Verg.

horresco horrescĕre horrŭi (horreo), *to stand on end, bristle, be rough.* LIT., horrueruntque comae, Ov.; mare coepit horrescere, *to be stormy*, Cic.; esp. from fear: Cic. TRANSF., *to tremble, begin to shudder, begin to dread*: Cic.; horresco referens, Verg.; with acc. object: morsus futuros, Verg.

orrĕum -i, n. *a barn, storehouse, granary*: Capua horreum Campani agri, Cic. TRANSF., *a wine-cellar*: Hor.; *a bee-hive*: Verg.; *an ant-hill*: Ov.

orrĭbĭlis -e (horreo), adj. (with compar.). (1) *horrible, frightful, dreadful*: pestis reipublicae, Cic.; species, Caes. (2) colloq., *astonishing, wonderful*: horribili vigilantiā, Cic. L.

orrĭdē, adv. from horridus; q.v.

orrĭdŭlus -a -um (dim. of horridus). LIT., physically, *somewhat rough*: Pl. TRANSF., fig., *somewhat rough, unadorned*: orationes, Cic.

orrĭdus -a -um (horreo), adj. (with compar.), *rough, shaggy, bristly*.
LIT., barba, Cic.; caesaries, Ov.; sus, Verg.; esp. from cold, *shivering*: si premerem ventosas horridus Alpes, Ov.; Verg.
TRANSF., (1) *rough, wild, savage*: campus, Cic.; silva, Verg.; tempestas, Hor. (2) *rough, unpolished, uncouth*: Tubero vitā et oratione horridus, Cic.; modus dicendi, Liv. (3) *frightful, horrible*: vis teli, Lucr.; Verg.; Hor.
¶ Adv. (with compar.) horrĭdē, *roughly*: dicere, Cic.; adloqui, Tac.

orrĭfer -fĕra -fĕrum (horror/fero), *causing shudders of cold or fear*: Boreas, Ov.; Erinys, Ov.

orrĭfĭco -are (horrificus). (1) *to make rough*: Cat. (2) *to terrify*: Verg.

orrĭfĭcus -a -um (horror/facio), *causing terror, dreadful*: letum, Verg. Adv. horrĭfĭcē, *dreadfully*: Lucr.

orrĭsŏnus -a -um (horreo/sono), *sounding dreadfully*: fremitus, Verg.; Lucr.

orror -ōris, m. (horreo), *a bristling, shuddering*.
LIT., physical: comarum, Luc.; esp. from cold or fear: Cic. L., Verg.
TRANSF., (1) *roughness* of speech: Quint. (2) *dread, fright*: qui me horror perfudit, Cic. L.; esp. *religious dread, awe*: perfusus horrore venerabundusque, Liv. (3) *object of dread, a terror*: Lucr.

orsum, adv. (contr. for hŏvorsum), *in this direction, hither*: Ter., Pl.

ortāmen -inis, n. (hortor), *an encouragement, exhortation*: Liv., Ov., Tac.

ortāmentum -i, n. (hortor), *encouragement, incitement*: Sall., Liv., Tac.

ortātĭo -ōnis, f. (hortor), *exhortation, encouragement*: Cic. L., Sall., Liv.

ortātīvus -a -um (hortor), *of encouragement*: Quint.

ortātor -ōris, m. (hortor), *an inciter, encourager*: isto hortatore, Cic.; with genit.: studii, *to study*, Cic.; scelerum, Verg.; with ad: auctores hortatoresque ad me restituendum, Cic.; animorum, *of spirits*, Ov.

ortātus -ūs, m. (hortor), *incitement, encouragement*; in abl. sing. or in plur.: id fecisse aliorum consilio, hortatu, Cic.; Caes., Ov., Tac.

Iortensĭus -a -um, *name of a Roman gens; its most famous member was* Q. Hortensius Hortalus, *an orator of the time of Cicero*. Adj. Hortensĭānus -a -um, *Hortensian*.

ortor -ari, dep. *to exhort, incite, encourage*.
LIT., of a person urging men or animals.

With acc. alone: aliquem, Pl., Cic. L., Ov.; prov.: hortari currentem, *to spur the willing horse*, Cic. L.; esp. *to harangue* troops: suos, Caes. The purpose in view may be expressed by ut and the subj.: Pl., Cic.; by ne and the subj.: hortatur eos ne animo deficiant, Caes.; by subj. alone: hortatur non solum ab eruptionibus caveant, Caes.; Liv.; by infin.: Ov., Suet.; by ad: ad laudem, Cic.; ad vindicandum, Sall.; by in and the acc.: Gentium in amicitiam secum et cum Macedonibus iungendam, Liv.; in proelia, Verg.; by de: de Aufidiano nomine nihil te hortor, Cic. L.; Caes.; by plain acc. object: pacem, Cic.
TRANSF., of inanimate subjects: multae res ad hoc consilium Gallos hortabantur, Caes.; with infin.: reipublicae dignitas minora haec relinquere hortatur, Cic.

hortŭlus -i, m. (dim. of hortus), *a little garden*: Cat., Juv.; plur.: hortuli, *grounds, a small park*, Cic.

hortus -i, m. (cf. χόρτος), *a garden*: Pl., Cic.; plur.: horti, *grounds, park*, Cic., Hor., Tac.; meton., *garden produce*: Hor.

hospĕs -pĭtis, m. and hospĭta -ae, f. (1) *a host, hostess*: Cic., Hor. (2) *a guest*: Cic., Hor.
TRANSF., (1) *a guest-friend, friend*: Caes., Cic. (2) *a stranger*: nec peregrinum atque hospitem in agendo esse debere, Cic.; Hor.; with subst., like adj., *foreign*; f. sing. and n. pl.: hospita, aequora, Verg.; navis, Ov.

hospĭtālis -e (hospes), *relating to a guest or host*. LIT., cubiculum, *guest-chamber*, Liv.; sedes, Cic.; caedes, *murder of a guest*, Liv.; Iuppiter, *protector of guests*, Cic. TRANSF., *friendly, hospitable*: domo hospitalissimus, Cic.; Cimonem in suos curiales Laciadas hospitalem, Cic.; m. as subst., *a guest-friend*: Liv.
¶ Adv. hospĭtālĭtĕr, *hospitably*: Liv.

hospĭtālĭtās -ātis, f. (hospitalis), *hospitality*: Cic.

hospĭtĭum -i, n. (hospes), *hospitality, the relation between host and guest*: mihi cum aliquo hospitium est, Cic.; intercedit, Caes.; alicuius hospitio usus sum, Caes.; hospitium cum aliquo facere, Cic.; iungere, Liv.; sometimes *a hospitable reception*: aliquem hospitio accipere, invitare, Cic.; excipere, Liv. Meton., *a guest-chamber, inn, quarters*: hospitium parare, Cic.; cohortes per hospitia dispersae, *billeted*, Tac.; of animals, *shelter*: Verg.

hostĭa -ae, f. (from ²hostio), lit., *the thing struck*), *an animal slain in sacrifice, a victim*: humana, Cic.; hostias immolare, Cic.; mactare, Hor.

hostĭātus -a -um (hostia), *provided with animals for sacrifice*: Pl.

hostĭcus -a -um (hostis). (1) *foreign*: Pl. (2) *belonging to the enemy, hostile*: ager, Liv.; moenia, Hor.; n. as subst. hostĭcum -i, *the enemy's territory*: in hostico, Liv.

hostīlis -e (hostis). (1) *of or by or for the enemy, hostile*: expugnatio, Cic.; naves, Hor.; metus, Sall. (2) *like an enemy, unfriendly, hostile*: hostili odio et crudelitate, Cic.; n. pl. as subst.: multa hostilia audere, Tac.; Sall.
¶ Adv. hostīlĭtĕr, *like an enemy*: quid ille fecit hostiliter, Cic.; Liv., Ov.

Hostīlĭus -a -um, *name of a Roman* gens; esp. of *Tullus, third king of Rome*; as adj. *Hostilian*: curia, *built by Tullus Hostilius*, Liv.

hostīmentum -i, n. ('hostio), *compensation, requital*: Pl.

¹hostĭo -ire, *to requite, recompense*: Pl.

²hostĭo -ire, *to strike*: Enn.

hostis -is, c. originally *a stranger*, but afterwards *an enemy, a public foe* (opp. inimicus, *a private enemy*).
LIT., cives hostesque, Liv.; omnes nos statuit ille non inimicos sed hostes, Cic.; populo Romano, adversus Romanos, Liv.; hostem aliquem iudicare, *to denounce as an enemy to his country*, Cic.; sing. collect.: capta hostis, *the female captives*, Liv.
TRANSF., (1) in gen., *an opponent, foe*: hostis omnium hominum, Cic.; Pl., Verg. (2) of animals and things: Hor., Ov.

hūc, adv. (older form hōc; from ¹hic), *hither, to this place*. LIT., of space: huc ades, *come hither*, Verg.; esp. contrasted with illuc: nunc huc nunc illuc, Verg.; huc atque illuc, *hither and thither*, Cic. TRANSF., (1) *to this*, with verbs of addition: accedit huc, Caes., Lucr., Cic. (2) *to this pitch, to this degree*: Cic.; with partitive genit.: huc adrogantiae venerat ut, Tac.
¶ Interrog. form **hūcĭne**, *so far? as far as this?*: hucine tandem omnia reciderunt? Cic.; Sall.

hŭi, interj., exclamation of surprise, *eh! hallo!*: hui, quam timeo quid existimes, Cic. L.; Pl., Ter.

hūiusmŏdi or **hūiuscĕmŏdi** (hic/modus), *of this kind, of such a kind, such*: ex huiusmodi principio, Cic.

hūmānē, adv. from humanus; q.v.

hūmānĭtās -ātis, f. (humanus), *humanity, human nature, human feeling*. In gen.: omnem humanitatem exuere, Cic.; humanitatis societas, Cic. Esp., (1) *humanity, human kindness*: summa erga nos, Cic. L.; Caes. (2) *refinement, education, culture*: communium litterarum ac politioris humanitatis expers, Cic.

hūmānĭtĕr, adv. from humanus; q.v.

hūmānĭtŭs, adv. (humanus). (1) *after the manner of men*: si quid mihi humanitus accidisset, i.e. *if I should die*, Cic. (2) *kindly*: Ter.

hūmānus -a -um (homo), adj. (with superl.), *human, relating to human beings*.
In gen.: genus, *the human race*, Cic.; facies, Cic.; res humanae, *human affairs*, Cic.; hostia, *human sacrifice*, Cic.; scelus, *against men*, Liv.; humanum est, *it is human*, Cic.; as subst. m. **hūmānus** -i, *one of the human race*: Ov., Lucr.; n. pl. **hūmāna** -ōrum, *human affairs*: humana miscere divinis, Liv.; Cic.
Esp. of good human qualities. (1) *humane, kind, philanthropic*: erga aliquem, Cic.; Pl., Ter. (2) *educated, civilized, refined*: gens humana atque docta, Cic.
¶ Adv. in two forms, **hūmānē** (Cic., Hor.) and **hūmānĭtĕr** (Cic. L.), compar.: humanius, Cic.; superl.: humanissime, Cic. L. (1) *humanly, in a way becoming human nature*: vivere, Cic.; Ter., Hor. (2) *politely, courteously, kindly*: litterae humaniter scriptae, Cic. L.

hŭmātĭo -ōnis, f. (humo), *a burying, interment*: Cic.

hūmecto, hūmectus, hūmĕo, *see* um-.

hūmĕrus, *see* um-.

hūmesco, hūmidus, *see* um-.

hŭmĭlis -e (humus), adj. (with compar. humilior, superl. humillimus), *on the ground*.
LIT., (1) *not high above ground, low*: arbores et vites et quae sunt humiliora, Cic.; turrim, Caes.; casa, Verg. (2) *not deep below ground, shallow*: fossa, Verg., Tac.
TRANSF., (1) of birth, position, rank, *humble, poor, insignificant*: humilibus parentibus natus, Cic.; humillimus homo de plebe Liv.; m. as subst., *a person of low rank*: Hor. (2) of mind or character, *abject* or *submissive*: humili animo ferre, Cic.; obsecratio humilis Cic.; non humilis mulier, Hor. (3) of circumstances, *poor, mean*: Juv. (4) of language, *mean, without elevation*: oratio humilis et abiecta, Cic.; sermo, Cic., Hor.
¶ Adv. **hŭmĭlĭtĕr**, *humbly, meanly, abjectly*: sentire, Cic.; servire, Liv.

hŭmĭlĭtās -ātis, f. (humilis), *nearness to the ground* (cf. humilis).
LIT., (1) *lowness*: animalium, Cic. (2) *shallowness*: navium, Caes.
TRANSF., (1) of birth, position, rank, *insignificance, obscurity*: alicuius humilitatem despicere, Cic.; Caes., Liv. (2) of mind or character, *submissiveness, abjectness*: humilitas et obsecratio, Cic.; Caes., Liv.

hŭmo -are (humus). (1) *to cover with earth, bury*: aliquem, Cic. (2) TRANSF., *to perform the funeral rites over a corpse* (*burn*, etc.): Nep.

hūmor, *see* um-.

hŭmus -i, f. (akin to χαμαί), *the ground, earth, soil*. LIT., humus iniecta, Cic; abl. sing. humo, either *on the ground*: sedere, Ov., or *from the ground*: surgere, Ov.; fundit hum facilem victum iustissima tellus, Verg. Meton., *land, country*: Punica, Pontica, Ov.

hўăcinthĭnus -a -um (ὑακίνθινος), *belonging the hyacinth*: flos, Cat.

¹Hўăcinthus (-ŏs) -i, m. (Ὑάκινθος), *a beautiful Spartan youth, beloved of and accidentally killed by Apollo; from his blood sprang the flower called by his name*.
¶ Hence **Hўăcinthĭa** -ōrum, n. pl. *festival celebrated at Sparta*.

²hўăcinthus -i, m. (ὑάκινθος), *a flower* perhaps *the martagon lily*: Verg.

Hўădes -um, f. (Ὑάδες), *the Hyades, a group seven stars in the constellation Taurus*: Verg.

hўaena -ae, f. (ὕαινα), *the hyena*: Ov.

hўălus -i, m. (ὕαλος), *glass*: color hyali, *glass green*, Verg.

Hўantes -ium, m. (Ὕαντες), *an old name f the Boeotians*.
¶ Hence adj. **Hўantēus** -a -um, *Boeotia* Ov.; aqua, *Castalia*, Mart.; also adj. **Hўa tĭus** -a -um, *Boeotian*: iuvenis, *Actaeo grandson of Cadmus*, Ov.

Hўās -antis, m. (acc. sing. Hyan, Ov.) (Ὑα son of Atlas and brother (or father) of t Hyades*: sidus Hyantis, *the Hyades*, Ov.

Hўbla -ae, f. and **Hўblē** -ēs, f. (Ὕβλα). (1) *mountain range in Sicily, famed for its be* adj. **Hyblaeus** -a -um, *Hyblaean*. (2) *nar of several towns in Sicily*.
¶ Hence subst. **Hyblenses** -ium, m. *the inhabitants of Hybla*.

Iўdaspēs -pis, m. ('Υδάσπης), *a river in India* (now *Jelum*).

Iўdra -ae, f. ("Υδρα). (**1**) *the many-headed water-snake of the Lernaean Lake, slain by Hercules.* (**2**) *a constellation, also called Anguis.* (**3**) *a monster of the lower world with fifty heads.*

ydraulus -i, m. (ὕδραυλος), *a water-organ*: Cic.

ydria -ae, f. (ὑδρία), *an urn, jug*: Cic.

ydrŏchŏus -i, m. ('Υδροχόος), *the constellation Aquarius*: Cat.

ydrōpicus -a -um (ὑδρωπικός), *dropsical*: Hor.

ydrops -ōpis, m. (ὕδρωψ), *the dropsy*: Hor.

ydrus -i, m. (ὕδρος), *a water-snake*: Verg., Ov., Juv.; *of the hair of Medusa and the Furies*: Verg.

Iўdrūs -druntis, f. ('Υδροῦς) or **Hydruntum** -i, n. *a town near the heel of Italy* (now *Otranto*).

Iўlās -ae, m. ("Υλας), *a beautiful youth, companion of Hercules on the Argonautic expedition, who was carried off by the water-nymphs in Mysia.*

Iyllus (Hŷlus) -i, m. ("Υλλος), *son of Hercules and Deianira.*

ўmēn -ěnis, m. ('Υμήν), *Hymen, the god of marriage*: Ov. TRANSF., *the marriage song*: Ter.

ўmĕnaeŏs or **-ŭs** -i, m. ('Υμέναιος), *Hymen* (cf. Hymen, above), *the god of marriage*: Cat., Ov. TRANSF., (**1**) (often plur.) *wedding*: Verg. (**2**) *of animals, pairing*: Verg. (**3**) *the marriage song*: Pl., Ov.

ўmettŏs and **Hŷmettus** -i, m. ('Υμηττός), *a mountain near Athens, famous for its bees and marble. Adj.* **Hŷmettius** -a -um, *Hymettian.*

ўpaepa -ōrum, n. pl. (τὰ "Υπαιπα), *a town in Lydia.*

ўpănis -is, m. ("Υπανις), *river in Sarmatia* (now *the Bug*).

ўpăta -ae, f. ("Υπατα), *town in Thessaly. Adj.* **Hypataeus** -a -um.

ўperbătŏn -i, n. (ὑπέρβατον), rhet. t. t., *transposition of words*: Quint.

ўperbŏlē -ēs, f. (ὑπερβολή), rhet. t. t., *exaggeration*: Quint.

ўperbŏrĕi -ōrum, m. ('Υπερβόρεοι), *the Hyperboreans, a fabulous people, dwelling in the extreme north*; adj. **Hŷperbŏrĕus** -a -um, *northern*: Verg.

ўpěrion -ŏnis, m. ('Υπερίων). (**1**) *Hyperion, son of a Titan, father of the Sun.* (**2**) *the Sun god himself.*

¶ Hence subst. **Hŷpěriŏnis** -ĭdis, f. *daughter of the Sun; Aurora*: Ov.

ўpermestra -ae, and **-ē** -ēs, f. ('Υπερμήστρα), *the youngest of the Danaides, the only one who did not kill her husband* (*Lynceus*).

ўpŏdĭdascălus -i, m. (ὑποδιδάσκαλος), *an under-teacher*: Cic. L.

ўpomnēma -mătis, n. (ὑπόμνημα), *a memorandum, note*: ap. Cic. L.

ўpsĭpŷlē -ēs, f. ('Υψιπύλη), *Queen of Lemnos; saved her father when the women of Lemnos killed all the men; received the Argonauts.*

ўrcāni -ōrum, m. ('Υρκανοί), *the Hyrcanians, a people on the Caspian Sea*; adj. **Hyrcānus** -a -um, *Hyrcanian.*

ўrĭeus -ěi, m. ('Υριεύς), *father of Orion. Adj.* **Hŷrĭeus** -a -um: proles, *Orion*, Ov.

ўrtăcus -i, m. *father of Nisus*: Verg.; **Hyrtăcĭdēs** -ae, m. *the son of Hyrtacus, i.e. Nisus*: Verg., Ov.

I

I, i, the ninth letter of the Latin Alphabet, used both as a vowel, long or short, and as a consonant, formerly written j and apparently pronounced by the Romans like the English consonant y. For meaning of I. as an abbreviation, see Table of Abbreviations.

Iacchus -i, m. ('Ιακχος), *a god worshipped in the Eleusinian mysteries and associated with Bacchus*; meton., *wine*: Verg.

iăcĕo iacēre iacŭi (akin to iacio), *to lie.*

LIT., in gen.: humi, Lucr., Cic.; in limine, Cic.; super corpus alicuius, Ov.; alicui ad pedes, Cic.; esp. (**1**) *to lie resting or sick*: in lecto, Cic.; Hor., Ov. (**2**) *to lie thrown to the ground*, of men, buildings, etc.: Troia iacet, Ov. (**3**) *to lie dead, be slain*: pro patria, Ov.; telo iacet Hector, Verg.

TRANSF., (**1**) of physical position: **a**, *to remain for a long time*: Brundusii, Cic. L.: **b**, *to lie geographically, be situate*: Nep.: **c**, *to lie low, be flat*: domus depressa, caeca, iacens, Cic.; iacet campus, Liv.; planities, Verg.: **d**, of hair or clothes, *to hang loosely*: praeverrunt latas veste iacente vias, Ov. (**2**) fig.: **a**, *to be idle, neglected*, or *despised*: philosophia iacuit usque ad hanc aetatem, Cic.; pecunia, Cic.; virtutes, Cic.; pauper ubique iacet, Ov.; of prices: iacent pretia praediorum, Cic.: **b**, *to be overthrown, to fall*: iacent hi suis testibus, Cic.; iacet igitur tota conclusio, Cic.: **c**, *to be low in spirits, be cast down, dejected*: animum amici iacentem excitare, Cic.; iacet in maerore, Cic. L.; Liv.

iăcĭo iăcĕre iēci iactum.

(**1**) *to lay*: aggerem, Caes.; fundamenta, Cic., Liv.; muros ,Verg.; Liv.; fig.: fundamenta pacis, Cic.; Tac.

(**2**) *to throw, cast, hurl*. LIT., in aliquem scyphum, Cic.; materiam de muro in aggerem, Caes.; se in profundum, Cic. Esp.: **a**, *to throw dice*: talos, Pl., Cic.: **b**, *to throw out an anchor*: ancoram, Caes.: **c**, *to fling away, shed*: vestem procul, Ov.; cornua, Ov.: **d**, *to scatter, diffuse*: flores, Verg.; semina, Verg., Ov.; de corpore odorem, Lucr. TRANSF., **a**, fig., *to throw, cast*: contumeliam in aliquem, Cic.: **b**, *to let fall in speaking, to utter*: suspicionem, Cic.; fortuitos sermones, Tac.

iactantĭa -ae, f. (iacto), *boasting, bragging*: sui, *about oneself*, Tac.

iactātĭo -ōnis, f. (iacto), *a tossing, shaking*. LIT., vulneris (by careless handling), Liv.; maritima, Liv.; navis, Cic.; of gesticulation: corporis, Cic. TRANSF., (**1**) *violent emotion*: Cic. (**2**) *boasting, ostentation*: Cic., Liv., Tac.

iactātor -ōris, m. (iacto), *a boaster, braggart*: Quint., Suet.

iactātus -ūs, m. (iacto), *a shaking, moving quickly up and down*: pennarum, Ov.

iactĭto -are (freq. of iacto), *to toss about*: inter se ridicula, *to bandy*, Liv.

iacto -are (freq. of iacio), *to throw, cast, fling away* or *about.*

LIT., (**1**) of missiles, etc.: faces in vicinorum tecta, Cic.; hastas, Cic.; lapides, Verg.; vestem de muro, Caes.; arma multa passim, Liv.; odorem late, *to diffuse, spread, scatter*, Verg. (**2**) of the body, in gesticulation: bracchia, Lucr., Ov.; cerviculam, Cic.; manus, Quint.; with reflex., or in pass. as

middle, *to gesticulate*: Cic. (3) of ships and
voyagers, *to toss*: cum adversā tempestate
in alto iactarentur, Cic.; Verg.

TRANSF., (1) *to harass, disturb*: iactari
morbis, Lucr.; Pl., Cic., Liv. (2) in pass. as
middle, *to waver*: iactabatur nummus,
fluctuated, Cic. (3) *to broadcast* words: voces
per umbram, Verg.; hence *to bring up* a
subject, *discuss, speak of*: rem in contione,
Cic.; querimonias, Liv.; pectore curas,
Verg. (4) *to keep bringing up, to boast of*:
gratiam urbanam, Caes.; genus et nomen,
Hor. (5) with reflex., or in pass. as middle,
*to 'throw one's weight about', make oneself
conspicuous, be officious*: se magnificentissime,
Cic.; se in causis centumviralibus, Cic.

¶ Hence partic. (with compar.) **iactans**
-antis, *boastful*: Cic., Verg., Hor.

¶ Adv. **iactantĕr**, *boastfully*; compar.:
Tac.

iactūra -ae, f. (iacio), *a throwing away*. LIT.,
in mari iacturam facere, *to throw goods
overboard*, Cic. TRANSF., *loss, sacrifice*:
iacturae rei familiaris erunt faciendae, Cic.;
suorum, Caes.; sepulcri, Verg.

iactus -ūs, m. (iacio), *a throwing, cast, throw*:
fulminum, Cic.; intra teli iactum, *within
range*, Verg.; tesserarum, Liv.

iăcŭlābĭlis -e (iaculor), *that can be thrown
or cast*: telum, Ov.

iăcŭlātor -ōris, m. (iaculor), *a thrower,
hurler*: Hor.; esp. *a javelin-man, a light-
armed soldier*: Liv.

iăcŭlātrix -īcis, f. (iaculator), *she that hurls,
the huntress* (*Diana*): Ov.

iăcŭlor -ari, dep. (iaculum). LIT., (1) *to throw
a javelin*: totum diem iaculari, Cic.; Liv.
(2) with acc., *to shoot at*: cervos, Hor. (3)
with acc., *to throw, toss, cast, hurl*: ignes,
Verg.; silicem in hostes, Ov.

TRANSF., (1) *to make an attack with words*:
probris procacibus in aliquem, Liv. (2) with
acc., *to aim at, strive after*: multa, Hor.
(3) with acc., *to utter*: verbum, Lucr.

iăcŭlum -i, n. (iacio). (1) *a dart, javelin*:
fervefacta iacula in castra iacere, Caes.; Cic.,
Ov. (2) *a casting-net*: Pl., Ov.

iăcŭlus -a -um (iacio), *thrown, darting*: Pl.,
Luc.

¹**Ĭālўsus** -i, m. (Ἰάλυσος), *a town in Rhodes.*
Adj. **Ĭālўsĭus** -a -um, *Rhodian*: Ov.

²**Ĭālўsus** -i, m. *son of Sol*: Cic.

iam, adv. *now, already.*

(1) temporal; *by this time, by that time*:
a, of present time, *by now, now*: non quia
iam sint, sed quia saepe sint, Cic.; iam nunc,
just now, Cic.; repeated: iam iam intellego,
Cic.; sometimes *now at last*: te aliquando
iam rem transigere, Cic.: **b**, of past time:
iam tum, Cic.; omnes iam istius generis
legationes erant constitutae, Cic.: **c**, of
future time, *immediately, directly, presently,
soon*: quam pulchra sint ipse iam dicet, Cic.;
iam fuerit, Lucr.; repeated: iam iam non
domus accipiet te, Lucr.; also *henceforth*:
Cic., Verg.: **d**, with duration indicated; in
present, *till now, up to the present time*:
septingentos iam annos amplius unis
moribus vivunt, Cic.; iam diu, iam dudum,
iam pridem, *now for a long time*, Cic.; with
imperf.: iam dudum flebam, *I had long been
weeping*, Ov.; so iam pridem; with perf.,

iam dudum and iam pridem, *long ago*, or wit
neg., *not for a long time past*: Cic., Ov.

(2) of other relations: **a**, *in that case, as a
immediate consequence*: da mihi hoc, ian
tibi maximam partem defensionis praecideris
Cic.: **b**, to introduce something new, *further
moreover*: et aures . . . itemque nares . .
iam gustatus, Cic.; iam vero, Cic.; Verg.
c, to emphasize, *just, indeed*: iam illud no
sunt admonendi, Cic.; non scire quider
barbarum iam videtur, Cic.; nec, si iam
possit, *if it actually could*, Lucr.

ĭambēus -a -um (ἰαμβεῖος), *iambic*: Hor.

ĭambus -i, m. (ἴαμβος), *an iambus, a metrice
foot* (⌣ –): Cic., Hor. TRANSF., *an iamb
poem, iambic poetry*: Cic., Hor.

iamdūdum, iamprīdem, *see* iam.

Iānĭcŭlum -i, n. *a hill west of Rome, on th
right bank of the Tiber.*

Iānĭgĕna -ae, c. (Ianus/gigno), *child of Janus*
Ov.

iānĭtor -ōris, m. (ianus), *a door-keeper, porte*
ianitor carceris, Cic.; of Janus: caelest
aulae, Ov.; of Cerberus: ianitor imman
aulae, Hor.

iānĭtrix -īcis, f. (ianitor), *a portress*: Pl.

ĭanthĭnus -a -um (ἰάνθινος), *violet-coloure*
Plin.; n. pl. as subst. **ĭanthĭna** -ōrun
violet-coloured clothes: Mart.

iānŭa -ae, f. (ianus), *a door.*

LIT., properly *the outer door of a hous*
ianuam claudere, Cic.; quaerere aliquem
ianua, *to ask at the door for someone*, Cic.; P
Verg., Ov.

TRANSF., (1) *entrance, 'key'*: maris gemir
of the Bosphorus, Ov.; eam urbem sibi Asi
ianuam fore, Cic. (2) in gen., *approach*: le
Lucr.; quā nolui ianuā sum ingressus
causam, Cic.

iānus -i, m. (root of ire, *to go*), *a cover
passage*: Cic., Liv.; esp. *one of the arcade*
the forum at Rome*, of which there were thre
summus, imus, and medius, where th
merchants, bankers, and booksellers h
their shops: Cic., Hor., Ov.

Personif. **Iānus**, *Janus, an old Itali
deity*, represented with two faces looking
opposite directions.

¶ Hence adj. **Iānālis** -e and **Iānŭālis** -
belonging to Janus; also adj. **Iānŭārius**
-um. (1) *of Janus*. (2) *of January*: Ianuari
mensis, *the month January*, Cic., or simpl
Ianuarius, Caes.; Kalendae Ianuariae, *th
1st of January*, Cic.

Ĭăpĕtus -i, m. (Ἰαπετός), *a Titan, father
Atlas, Epimetheus, and Prometheus*: gen
Iapeti, *Prometheus*, Hor.

¶ Hence **Ĭăpĕtĭönĭdēs** -ae, m. *a son
Iapetus*, i.e. *Atlas*: Ov.

Ĭăpўdes -um, m. (Ἰάπυδες), *a people in Illyr*
¶ Hence **Ĭăpys** -ўdis, *Iapydian*; sub
Ĭăpўdĭa -ae, f. *Iapydia.*

Ĭăpyx -ўgis, m. (Ἰάπυξ), *the son of Daedal
who reigned in a part of southern Ita*
TRANSF., as adj.: *Iapygian*, Verg., Ov.;
subst. (sc. ventus), *a west-north-west wi
favourable for crossing from Brundisium*
Greece.

¶ Hence subst. **Ĭăpўgĭa** -ae, f. (Ἰαπυγ
a district in Apulia, in southern Italy.

Ĭarba and **Ĭarbas** -ae, m. *an African ki
rival of Aeneas.*

¶ Hence subst. **Ĭarbīta** -ae, m. *a Maure-tanian*: Hor.
ardānis -nĭdis, f. *a daughter of Iardanus*, i.e. *Omphale*: Ov.
āsĭus -i, m. (᾿Ιάσιος). (**1**) *a Cretan, beloved by Ceres* (also called Iāsĭōn). (**2**) *an Argive king, father of Atalanta.*
¶ Hence m. subst. **Ĭăsīdes** -ae (᾿Ιασίδης), *a descendant of Iasius*; f. subst. **Ĭăsis** -sĭdos, *a daughter of Iasius*, i.e. *Atalanta.*
āsōn -ōnis, m. (᾿Ιάσων), *Jason.*
  (**1**) *son of Aeson, king of Thessaly, leader of the expedition of the Argonauts to Colchis to fetch the Golden Fleece.* Adj. **Iāsŏnĭus** -a -um, *Jasonian*: carina, *the Argo*, Prop.; remex, *an Argonaut*, Ov.
  (**2**) *a tyrant of Pherae, in the fourth century* B.C.
aspis -idis, f. (ἴασπις), *jasper*: Verg.
āzȳges -um, m. (᾿Ιάζυγες), *a Sarmatian tribe on the Danube.*
ĕr-, *see* Hiber-.
ŏī, adv. *there, at that place.* LIT., of space: Caes., Cic., Ov., etc. TRANSF., (**1**) of time, *then, thereupon*: Pl., Ter., Liv. (**2**) *therein, in that matter*: numquid ego ibi peccavi? Pl.; Cic., Liv. (**3**) rarely, of persons, *in him*, etc.: Ter., Liv., Juv.
ŏīdem, adv. (ibi/suffix -dem, as in i-dem), *in the same place, in that very place.* LIT., of space: Pl., Cic., Verg. TRANSF., (**1**) of time, *at that moment*: Cic. (**2**) *in the same matter*: Cic., Juv.
ŏīs, genit. ibis and ibĭdis, f. (ἴβις), *the ibis, a sacred bird among the Egyptians*: Cic., Ov.
īscum=hibiscum; q.v.
ȳcus -i, m. (῎Ιβυκος), *a Greek lyric poet of Rhegium.*
cădĭus -i, m. (᾿Ικάδιος), *a notorious pirate*: Cic.
cărus or **Ĭcărĭus** -i, m. (῎Ικαρος or ᾿Ικάριος), *the father of Erigone and Penelope, who became the constellation Bootes.*
¶ Hence adj. **Ĭcărĭus** -a -um; f. subst. **Ĭcăris** -ĭdis=*Penelope*; also **Ĭcărĭŏtĭs** -ĭdis, f. subst.=*Penelope* or adj.=*of Penelope.*
cărus -i, m. (῎Ικαρος), *the son of Daedalus, drowned in the Aegean Sea whilst flying from Crete with wings made by his father.*
¶ Hence adj. **Ĭcărĭus** -a -um, *of Icarus*, esp. of *the Icarian Sea, a part of the Aegean.*
circo=idcirco; q.v.
ēni -ōrum, m. *a British people in East Anglia.*
hneumon -ŏnis, m. (ἰχνεύμων), *the ichneumon*: Cic., Mart.
io or **ico** ici ictum, *to strike, hit, smite* (usually in perf. partic. **ictus** -a -um).
  LIT., icimur, Lucr.; lapide ictus, Caes.; e caelo ictus, *struck by lightning*, Cic.
  TRANSF., (**1**) from the sacrificing of victims to mark an agreement, *to strike a bargain*: icere foedus, *to make a treaty*, Cic. (**2**) of feeling, *to strike*: conscientiā ictus, Liv.; desideriis icta, Hor.
ōn -onis, f. (εἰκών), *an image*: Plin.
ŏnĭcus -a -um (εἰκονικός), *of an image*: Plin., Suet.
ŏnĭum -i, n. (᾿Ικόνιον), *town in Lycaonia.*
tĕrĭcus -a -um (ἰκτερικός), *suffering from jaundice, jaundiced*: Juv.
tus -ūs, m. (ico), *a blow, stroke.*
  LIT., lapidum, Caes.; gladiatorius, Cic.;

sagittarum ictus, Liv.; apri, Ov.; pollicis, *the striking of the lyre*, Hor.; fulminis, *lightning-stroke*, Cic.; solis, *a sunbeam*, Ov.; sub ictum dari, *to come within range*, Tac.
  TRANSF., (**1**) *a mental blow*: novae calamitatis, Cic. (**2**) in music, *beating time, beat*: Hor.; so in poetry: Quint.
Īda -ae, f. and **Īdē** -ēs, f. (῎Ιδα, ῎Ιδη). (**1**) *a mountain in Crete, where Jupiter was nursed.* (**2**) *a mountain range in Phrygia, near Troy.*
¶ Adj. **Īdaeus** -a -um. (**1**) *of Mount Ida in Crete.* (**2**) *of Mount Ida in Phrygia*; esp. *of Cybele*: parens deum, Verg.; mater, Cic.; and *of Paris*: pastor, Cic.; iudex, hospes, Ov.
Īdălĭum -i, n. (᾿Ιδάλιον), *a mountain-city in Cyprus, sacred to Venus*; also called **Īdălĭa** -ae, f.
¶ Hence adj. **Īdălĭus** -a -um, poet., *belonging to Cyprus*: Venus, Verg.; f. subst. **Īdălĭē** -ēs, *Venus.*
idcirco (iccirco), adv. (id/circo=circa), *on that account, for that reason, for that purpose*; absol.: Cic., Caes., Hor. Esp. referring to a clause, expressing either a reason or a purpose: hence: quod (or quia) . . . idcirco . . ., idcirco . . . quod (or quia) . . ., Ter., Cic., Hor.; non, si . . . idcirco . . ., Cic., Hor.; ut (or ne) . . . idcirco . . ., idcirco . . . ut (or ne) . . ., Caes., Cic.
īdem, ĕădem, ĭdem, pron. (is/suffix -dem), *the same.* In gen.: non quod alia res esset: immo eadem, Cic.; often with an effect of addition, *also*: suavissimus et idem facillimus, Cic.; or of contrast, *yet*: cum dicat . . . negat idem, Cic.; Lucr.; as subst., masc.: amicus est tamquam alter īdem, *a second self*, Cic.; neut.: idem velle atque idem nolle, Sall.; with partitive genit.: idem iuris, Cic. Esp. *the same as*, with dat.: idem facit occidenti, Hor.; Cic. L.; with cum and abl.: Liv., Cic., Tac.; with relative clause: eadem virtus quae in proavo, Cic.; with ac, atque, *or* et: Caes., Cic.
īdentĭdem, adv. (idem), *repeatedly, again and again*: Pl., Cic., Cat.
ĭdĕō, adv. (id/eo), *on that account, therefore, for that reason, for that purpose*; used like idcirco (q.v.); absol.: Caes., Lucr.; esp. referring to a clause, expressing either a reason or a purpose; hence: ideo quod (or quia, *or* quoniam) . . ., Cic., Hor.; non, si causa iusta est, ideo . . ., Cic.; ideo . . . ut (or ne) . . ., Cic., Liv., Tac.
ĭdĭōta -ae, m. (ἰδιώτης), *an ignorant, uneducated man*: Cic.
Idmōn -mŏnis, m. (῎Ιδμων), *father of Arachne.* Adj. **Idmŏnĭus** -a -um: Arachne, *daughter of Idmon*, Ov.
īdōlon -i, n. (εἴδωλον), *a spectre*: Plin. L.
Īdŏmĕneus -ei, m. (᾿Ιδομενεύς), *son of Deucalion, king of Crete.*
ĭdōnĕus -a -um, *fit, appropriate, suitable*: of persons and things. Absol.: auctor, Cic.; verba minus idonea, Cic. With dat.: castris idoneum locum, Caes.; puellis nuper idoneus, Hor.; with ad *or* in and acc.: ad hoc negotium, Cic.; idoneus in eam rem, Liv.; with infin.: fons rivo dare nomen idoneus, Hor.; with qui and the subj. (like dignus): tibi fortasse nemo fuit quem imitere, Cic.; Pl., Ter.
¶ Adv. **ĭdōnĕē**, *fitly, appropriately*: Cic.

Ĭdūmaea -ae, f. (Ἰδουμαία), *a district in Palestine, bordering on Judea and Arabia Petraea.* Adj. **Ĭdūmaeus** -a -um, *Idumaean.*

Ĭdūs -ŭum, f. *the Ides, a day in the Roman month; the fifteenth day in March, May, July, October; the thirteenth in the other months*: idus Martiae, *the 15th of March,* Cic.; Caes., Hor., etc.

ĭĕcur, genit. iĕcŏris and iŏcĭnĕris, n. *the liver*: Cic., Liv., Hor. TRANSF., *the supposed seat of the passions,* esp. love and anger: fervens difficili bile tumet iecur, Hor.; Juv.

ĭĕcuscŭlum -i, n. (dim. of iecur), *a little liver*: Cic.

ĭĕiūnĭōsior -ius, compar. adj. (ieiunus), *more hungry, fasting more*: Pl.

ĭĕiūnĭtās -ātis, f. (ieiunus), *hungriness, emptiness*: Pl. TRANSF., of style, etc., *poverty, meagreness*: inopia et ieiunitas, Cic.

ĭĕiūnĭum -i, n. (ieiunus), *a fast, abstinence from food.* LIT., ieiunium Cereri instituere, Liv.; Hor., Ov. TRANSF., (1) *hunger*: ieiunia pascere, satiare, solvere, sedare, placare, *to satisfy hunger,* Ov. (2) *leanness*: Verg.

ĭĕiūnus -a -um, *fasting.*
   LIT., ita ieiunus ut ne aquam quidem gustarim, Cic.; meton., *hungry*: Cic. L.; *thirsty*: Prop.
   TRANSF., (1) of material objects: ager, *poor,* Cic.; sanies, *scanty,* Verg. (2) of immaterial things: **a,** *hungry for*: ieiunae huius orationis aures, Cic.: **b,** *poor, mean*: animus, calumnia, Cic.: **c,** of style, *meagre, weak*: oratio, Cic.
   ¶ Adv. (with compar.) **ĭĕiūnē,** of style, *meagrely, without energy* or *taste*: Cic., Plin. L.

ĭentācŭlum -i, n. (iento), *a breakfast*: Pl., Mart., Suet.

ĭento -are, *to breakfast*: Suet.

ĭgĭtur, adv. *then* (avoided by Caes. and most poets; usually second word in clause, or later, in Cic.; often first word in Sall., Liv., Tac.).
   (1) inferential, *so, therefore, then, accordingly*: **a,** in statements: si mentiris, mentiris. Mentiris autem; igitur mentiris, Cic.; Pl., Quint.: **b,** in questions: in quo igitur loco est? Cic.; ironically: haec igitur est tua disciplina? Cic.; Pl., Liv.: **c,** in commands, *then, so then*: fac igitur quod, Cic. (2) after digressions, parentheses, etc. to resume the argument, *so, as I was saying*: scripsi etiam (nam ab orationibus disiungo me fere), scripsi igitur, Cic. (3) to emphasize, *I say*: pro imperio, pro exercitu, pro provincia, etc., pro his igitur omnibus rebus, Cic.

ĭgnārus -a -um (in/gnarus). (1) act., *ignorant of, unacquainted with, inexperienced in*; with genit.: faciendae orationis, Cic.; mariti, *unmarried,* Hor.; with acc. and infin.: non sumus ignari multos studiose contra esse dicturos, Cic., Liv.; with indir. quest.: ignaro populo Romano quid ageretur, Cic.; quid virtus valeret, Cic.; Liv.; absol.: Cic., Verg., Liv.; sometimes of things: flumina, Hor. (2) pass., *unknown*; with dat.: proles ignara parenti, Ov.; regio hostibus ignara, Sall.; absol.: Sall., Ov.

ĭgnāvĭa -ae, f. (ignavus). (1) *idleness, listlessness*: Pl., Sall. (2) *cowardice*: contraria fortitudini ignavia, Cic.; Verg.

ĭgnāvus -a -um (in/gnavus), adj. (wit compar. and superl.), *idle, slothful, listles inactive.*
   LIT., (1) homo, Cic.; with genit.: legione operum et laboris ignavae, Tac.; with ac ignavissimus ad muniendum hostis, Li (2) *cowardly*: miles, Cic.; hostis, Liv.; m. subst. **ĭgnāvus** -i, *a coward, poltroon*: Sall plur.: Cic.
   TRANSF., of inanimate objects. (1) *iner sluggish*: senectus, Cic.; nemora, *unfruitfu* Verg.; lux, *a lazy day,* Juv.; gravitas, *im movable,* Verg. (2) *causing idleness*: frigus, O
   ¶ Adv. **ĭgnāvē** and **ĭgnāvĭtĕr,** *lazily slothfully, without spirit*: dicere, Hor facere, Cic.; compar. **ĭgnāvĭus**: Verg.

ĭgnesco -ĕre (ignis), *to kindle, catch fire*: Cic Ov. TRANSF., *to burn, glow with passion* Rutulo ignescunt irae, Verg.

ĭgnĕus -a -um (ignis), *fiery, burning, glowin with heat.* LIT., sidera, Cic.; sol, Verg vis caeli, Ov. TRANSF., *ardent, glowing wi passion,* etc.: furor, Ov.; vigor, Verg Tarchon, Verg.

ĭgnĭcŭlus -i, m. (dim. of ignis), *a little fir little flame, spark.* LIT., Plin., Juv. TRANSF desiderii, Cic. L.; virtutum, Cic.; ingeni *sparks of talent,* Quint.

ĭgnĭfer -fĕra -fĕrum (ignis/fero), *fire-bearin fiery*: aether, Lucr.; axis, Ov.

ĭgnĭgĕna -ae, m. (ignis/geno=gigno), *bor of fire,* epithet of Bacchus: Ov.

ĭgnĭpes -pĕdis (ignis/pes), *fiery-footed*: equ Ov.

ĭgnĭpŏtens -entis (ignis/potens), *mighty fire, ruler of fire,* epithet of Vulcan: Verg.

ĭgnis -is, m. *fire.*
   LIT., (1) in gen.: ignem concipere, Cic comprehendere, Caes.; *to catch fire*: acces dere, Verg.; ignem ab igne capere, *to kind* Cic.; aliquem igni cremare, necare, inte ficere, Caes. (2) esp.: **a,** *conflagration* pluribus simul locis, et iis diversis, ign coorti sunt, Liv.; Verg.,: **b,** *a watch-fi beacon*: ignibus exstinctis, Liv.; Caes **c,** *a firebrand*: ignibus armata inge multitudo, Liv.: **d,** *the flames of the funer pile*: ignes supremi, Ov.: **e,** *lightning*: ign coruscus, Hor.: **f,** *light of the stars*: ign curvati lunae, Hor.
   TRANSF., (1) *glow, glitter*: solis, Ov oculorum, Cic.; sacer ignis, *St. Anthony fire, erysipelas,* Verg. (2) fig., *fire, flam firebrand*: of war: Liv.; huic ordini novu ignem subieci, Cic. (3) fig., *glow of passion* exarsere ignes animo, Verg.; Hor., Ov meton., *the beloved*: meus ignis, Verg.

ĭgnōbĭlis -e (in/gnobilis=nobilis), *unknow obscure, inglorious*: civitas, Caes.; Pl., Ci Verg. TRANSF., *of humble birth*: famili Cic.; eques, Juv.

ĭgnōbĭlĭtās -ātis, f. (ignobilis), *ingloriou ness, obscurity*: Cic., Ov. TRANSF., *humb birth*: generis, Cic.; Liv.

ĭgnōmĭnĭa -ae, f. (in/gnomen=nomen), *de radation, disgrace, dishonour,* official unofficial: ignominiā notare, Caes., Cic.; a ficere, Cic.; ignominiam accipere, Ci alicui iniungere, inferre, Liv.; inurere, Ci ignominiam habere, Cic.; with geni senatūs, *inflicted by the senate,* Cic.; amiss rum navium, *consisting of the loss,* Caes.

gnōmĭnĭōsus -a -um (ignominia). (**1**) of persons, *disgraced*: Liv., Quint. (**2**) of things, *ignominious, disgraceful*: dominatio, Cic.; fuga, Liv.; Hor.

gnōrābĭlis -e (ignoro), *unknown*: Cic.

gnōrantĭa -ae, f. (ignoro), *want of knowledge, ignorance*: loci, Caes.; with indir. quest.: Tac.

gnōrātĭo -ōnis, f. (ignoro), *want of knowledge, ignorance*: locorum, sui, Cic.; with de: Cic.

gnōro -are. (**1**) *to be ignorant of, not to know*; with acc.: causam, Cic.; alicuius faciem, Sall.; aliquem, Cic.; with acc. and infin.: Cic.; with indir. quest.: cum id quam vere sit ignores, Cic.; with de: Cic. L.; absol.: Cic., Hor. (**2**) rarely, *to neglect, ignore*; with acc.: Pl., Cic.

gnosco -nōvi -nōtum (in/gnosco=nosco), *to take no cognizance of*; *to overlook, forgive, pardon*: Ter., Cic., Juv. The person is regularly in the dat.: mihi ignoscite si appello, Cic. The offence is either in the acc.: ut eis delicta ignoscas, Pl.; hoc, Cic.; or in the dat.: festinationi meae, Cic. L.; vitiis, Hor.; nom. as subject of pass. or with gerundive: Ter., Verg.

¶ Hence partic. as adj. **ignoscens** -entis, *forgiving, placable*: Ter.

ignōtus -a -um, partic. of ignosco; q.v.

ignōtus -a -um (in/gnotus=notus), adj. (with compar. and superl.). (**1**) pass., *unknown*: plurimis ignotissimi gentibus, Cic.; ius obscurum et ignotum, Cic. TRANSF., *ignoble, obscure*: mater, Hor.; hic ignotissimus Phryx, Cic. (**2**) act., *ignorant*: Cic.

gŭvĭum -ii, n. *a town in Umbria* (now *Gubbio*).

¶ Hence **Ĭgŭvīni** -ōrum, m. and **Ĭgŭvīnātes** -ium, m. *the inhabitants of Iguvium.*

lerda -ae, f. *a town in Hispania Tarraconensis* (now *Lerida*).

lergētes -um, m. *a people in Hispania Tarraconensis.*

lex -icis, f. *the holm-oak*: Verg., Hor., Ov.

lĕ -is, n.; usually plur. **ilĭa** -ium (*ĭλια*), *intestines, guts*. LIT., o dura messorum ilia, Hor.; rumpere, Verg. TRANSF., *the loin, flank*: suffodere ilia equis, Liv.; ducere, *to draw the flanks together, to become broken-winded*, Hor.

lĭa -ae, f. *a name of Rhea Silvia, mother of Romulus and Remus.*

¶ Hence subst. **Ĭlĭădēs** -ae, m. *son of Ilia,* i.e. *Romulus* or *Remus*: Ov.

lĭăcus, *see* Ilion.

lĭcet (=ire licet), *let us go, you may go*, an ancient form of dismissal at the close of a meeting; hence (**1**) in gen., *it is all over*: Ter. (**2**) *immediately, forthwith*: Verg.

lĭcētum -i, n. (ilex) *an ilex-grove*: Mart.

lĭcō (illĭco), adv. (in loco), *on the spot, in that very place*: Ter. TRANSF., *on the spot, immediately*: Pl., Cic.

lignum -a -um (ilex), *of ilex* or *holm-oak*: Verg.

lĭŏn or **Ĭlium** -i, n. (*Ἴλιον*) and **Ĭlĭŏs** -i, f. (*Ἴλιος*), *Troy*.

¶ Hence adj. **Ĭlĭus** -a -um and **Ĭlĭăcus** -a -um, *Trojan*; subst. **Ĭlĭensēs** -ium, m. *the Trojans*; m. subst. **Ĭlĭădēs** -ae, *a son of Troy*; esp. *Ganymede*: Ov.; f⋅ subst. **Ĭlĭăs** -ădis. (**1**) *a Trojan woman*: Verg. (**2**) *the Iliad of Homer*: Cic.

Ĭlĭŏna -ae, f. and **Ĭlĭŏnē** -ēs, f. *the eldest daughter of king Priam, wife of Polymnestor, king in Thrace.*

ill-. for words compounded from in/l ..., *see* inl-.

illāc, adv. (ille), *by that way, there*: hac atque illac, hac illac, Ter.; Pl. TRANSF., illac facere, *to stand on that side, belong to that party*, Cic. L.

ille, illa, illud (older forms **olle** and **ollus**), demonstr. pron., *that*.

In gen., alone or agreeing with a noun or pronoun, *that yonder*, of a person or thing at some distance from the speaker in space, time, or thought: hinc illae lacrimae, Ter.; ista beatitas cur aut in solem *illum* aut in *hunc* mundum cadere non potest, Cic.; qui illorum temporum historiam reliquerunt, Cic.; ex illo (tempore), *since then*, Verg.

Esp. (**1**) emphatically, *that well-known*: ille Epaminondas, Cic.; tune ille Aeneas? Verg. (**2**) strengthened by quidem, esp. concessively: philosophi quidam, minime mali illi quidem. (**3**) in contrast with hic: ille=*the former*, hic=*the latter* (sometimes *vice versa*), Sall., Liv. (**4**) indeterminate: ille aut ille, ille et ille, hic et ille, *this or that, one or other*, Cic. (**5**) in relation to a clause; as antecedent of relative clause: ille ego qui ..., Verg.; n. illud referring to a clause that follows: illud acerbissimum est quod, Cic.; illud perlibenter audivi te esse, Cic.

¶ Abl. f. sing. as adv. **illā**, *by that way*: Pl., Tac.

¶ Adv. **illō** (orig. illoi, dat. of ille), *to that place, thither*: Pl., Caes., Cic. TRANSF., *to that matter* or *point*: haec omnia eodem illo pertinere, Caes.

¹illĭc, illaec, illūc, pron. demonstr. (ille/-ce), *that there*: Pl., Ter.; interrog. form: illicine, Pl., Ter.

²illĭc or **illī**, adv. (ille), *there, at that place*: Pl., Caes., Verg. TRANSF., *therein, in that matter*: Ter., Liv.

illim, adv. (ille). (**1**) *from that place*: Pl., Cic. L. (**2**) *from that person*: Cic.

illinc, adv. (illim/-ce). (**1**) *from that place*: Pl., Ter., Ov. (**2**) *on that side*: Pl., Cic., Juv.

illōc, adv. (ille/-ce), *thither*: Pl.

illūc, adv. (ille). LIT., of space, *thither, to that place*: Pl., Cic., Juv.; esp.: huc illuc, Ter., Sall.; huc et illuc, Cic., Hor. TRANSF., *to that matter* or *person*: ut illuc revertar, Cic.; Hor.

Illўrĭi -ōrum, m. pl. *a people on the Adriatic Sea, in the modern Yugoslavia and Albania.*

¶ Hence, adj. **Illўrĭus** -a -um, *Illyrian*; subst. **Illўrĭa** -ae, f. *Illyria*; adj. **Illўrĭcus** -a -um, *Illyrian*; subst. **Illўrĭcum** -i, n. *Illyria*; **Illўris** -idis, f. adj., *Illyrian*; subst. *Illyria*: Ov.

Ĭlōtae -ārum=Hilotae; q.v.

Ĭlus -i, m. (*Ἴλος*). (**1**) *son of Tros, father of Laomedon, builder of Troy*. (**2**)=*Iulus*.

Ilva -ae, f. *an island in the Mediterranean* (now *Elba*).

im=eum, *see* is.

ĭmāgĭnārĭus -a -um (imago), *imaginary*: fasces, Liv.; militia, Suet.

ĭmāgĭnātĭo -ōnis, f. (imaginor), *imagination, fancy*: provincias Orientis secretis imaginationibus agitare, Tac.; Plin.

ĭmāgĭnor -ari, dep. (imago), *to imagine, conceive, picture to oneself*: pavorem, Tac.; Quint., Suet.

ĭmāgo -inis, f. *an image, copy, likeness*.

LIT., physical; in gen., *a representation, portrait, figure, bust, statue*: ficta, picta, Cic.; cereae, Hor.; sometimes *a portrait engraved on a seal-ring*: est signum notum, imago avi tui, Cic. Esp. (1) plur.: imagines (maiorum), *waxen figures, portraits of ancestors*, placed in the atria of Roman houses, and carried in funeral processions, Cic.; Liv. (2) *the shade or ghost of a dead man*: imagines mortuorum, Cic.; Verg. (3) *an echo*: laus bonorum virtuti resonat tamquam imago, Cic.; Verg.

TRANSF., (1) mental: **a**, *a mental picture*: imago venientis Turni, Verg.; illius noctis, Ov.: **b**, *idea, conception*: naturae urbis et populi, Cic.; tantae pietatis, Verg. (2) rhetorical, *a metaphor, simile, image*: hac ego si compellor imagine, Hor.; Cic. (3) abstr., *mere form, appearance, pretence*: pacis, Tac.; decoris, Liv.; imaginem reipublicae nullam reliquerunt, *they left no shadow of the republic*, Cic.

imbēcillĭtās -ātis, f. (imbecillus), *weakness, feebleness*. LIT., physically: corporis, Cic. TRANSF., consilii, Cic.; animi, Caes.; humani generis, Cic.

imbēcillus -a -um, adj. (with compar.), *weak, feeble*. LIT., physically: filius, Cic.; imbecillior valetudine, Cic. L. TRANSF., (1) of the mind.: animus, Cic. (2) in gen.: regnum, Sall.; aetas, Hor.

¶ Hence compar. adv. **imbēcillĭus**, *somewhat weakly, feebly*. adsentiri, Cic.

imbellis -e (in/bellum), *unwarlike*. (1) *not fighting*: multitudo, Liv.; Ov. (2) *not disposed to fight or unable to fight*; of living beings: Cic., Verg., Liv.; of things: telum, feeble, Verg.; annus, *peaceful, quiet*, Liv.; lyra, cithara, Hor.

imber -bris, m. (cf. ὄμβρος), *a shower or storm of rain, pelting rain* (pluvia=*rain* in gen.). LIT., magnus, maximus, Cic.; grandinis, Lucr.; lactis, sanguinis, Cic. TRANSF., (1) *a rain-cloud*: super caput astitit imber, Verg. (2) *water or any fluid*: fluminis imber, Ov.; Lucr. (3) of a shower of missiles: ferreus ingruit imber, Verg.

imberbis -e and **imberbus** -a -um (in/barba), *beardless*: Cic., Hor.

imbĭbo -bĭbĕre -bĭbi (in/bibo), *to drink in*. Hence (1) mentally, *to conceive*: de vobis malam opinionem animo, Cic.; Liv. (2) *to resolve, to determine*: memor eius quod initio consulatus imbiberat, Liv.; with infin.: Lucr., Cic.

imbrex -icis, c. (imber.), *a hollow tile used in roofing*: Pl., Verg. TRANSF., *a mode of applauding with the hands*: Suet.

imbrĭfer -fĕra -fĕrum (imber/fero), *rain-bringing*: ver, Verg.; auster, Ov.

imbŭo -ŭĕre -ŭi -ūtum (perhaps connected with bibo), *to wet, steep, saturate*.

LIT., vestem sanguine, Ov.; imbuti sanguine gladii, Cic.

TRANSF., (1) *to steep, stain, taint*: imbutus maculā sceleris, Cic.; imbutus superstitione, Cic.; mentem imbuit deorum opinio, Cic. (2) *to accustom, initiate, instruct*: imbutus cognitionibus verborum, Cic.; ad quam

legem non instituti sed imbuti sumus, Cic.; litterulis Graecis imbutus, Hor.

ĭmĭtābĭlis -e (imitor), *that can be imitated, imitable*: orationis subtilitas, Cic.; Verg.

ĭmĭtāmen -ĭnis, n. (imitor), *an imitation*: Ov.; plur., *an image*: Ov.

ĭmĭtāmentum -i, n. (imitor), *an imitating, imitation*; in plur.: lacrimae vel dolorum imitamenta, Tac.

ĭmĭtātĭo -ōnis, f. (imitor). (1) *imitation*: virtutis, Cic. (2) *pretence*: Cic.

ĭmĭtātor -ōris, m. (imitor), *an imitator*: principum, Cic.; Hor., Ov.

ĭmĭtātrix -īcis, f. (imitator), *she that imitates*: imitatrix boni, voluptas, Cic.; Ov.

ĭmĭtor -ari, dep. *to imitate, copy*. (1) *to make a copy of*: aliquid penicillo, *to depict*, Cic.; capillos aere, Hor.; poet., *to replace*: pocula vitea acidis sorbis, Verg. (2) in gen., *to be like, act like*: amictum alicuius aut statum aut motum, Cic.; praeclarum factum, Cic.; of things, *to resemble*: ▸umor potest imitari sudorem, Cic.

immădŭi, infin. -isse, perf. as from immadesco (in/madesco), *to have become moist* or *wet*: lacrimis immaduisse genas, Ov.; Plin.

immānis -e (in/manus=bonus), *enormous, immense, monstrous*. LIT., physically: corporum magnitudo, Caes.; ingens immanisque praeda, Cic.; antrum, Verg.; immane quantum, *to an enormous extent*, Hor., Tac. TRANSF., of character, *savage, horrible, inhuman*: hostis, Cic.; belua, Cic.; vitium, Hor.

immānĭtās -ātis, f. (immanis), *savageness, inhumanity, frightfulness*: vitiorum, facinoris, Cic.; in hac tanta immanitate versari, Cic.

immansuētus -a -um (in/mansuetus), *untamed, wild*: ingenium, Ov.; superl.: Ov.

immātūrĭtās -ātis, f. (immaturus). (1) *immaturity*: Suet. (2) *untimely haste*: Cic.

immātūrus -a -um (in/maturus), *unripe, immature*: Plin. TRANSF., *untimely*: consilium, Liv.; esp. of death: mors, Cic.; filius immaturus obiit, Hor.

immĕdĭcābĭlis -e (in/medicabilis), *incurable*: vulnus, Ov.; telum, *wounding fatally*, Verg.

immĕmor -mŏris (in/memor), *unmindful, forgetful*: ingenium, Cic.; mens, Cat.; with genit.: mandati, Cic.; nec Romanarum rerum immemor, *and familiar with Roman history*, Cic.; libertatis, Liv.; equus immemor herbae, *paying no heed to*, Verg.; with infin.: Pl.

immĕmŏrābĭlis -e (in/memorabilis). (1 *indescribable*: spatium, Lucr. (2) *unworthy o, mention*: versus, Pl. (3) *silent, uncommunica tive*: Pl.

immĕmŏrāta -ōrum, n. pl. (in/memoro) *things not yet related*: Hor.

immensĭtās -ātis, f. (immensus), *immeasur ableness, immensity*: latitudinum, Cic.; plur *immense stretches*: Cic.

immensus -a -um (in/metior), *immeasur able, immense, vast, boundless*: magnitud regionum, Cic.; mare, Cic. N. as subst **immensum** -i, *immense size, immensity* altitudinis, *immeasurable depth*, Liv.; i immensum, *to an immense height*, Sall.; a immensum augere, Liv.; immensum e dicere, *it is an endless task to tell*, Ov.

immĕrens -entis (in/mereo), *not deservin, innocent*: Hor.

immergo -mergĕre -mersi -mersum (in/mergo), *to dip into, plunge into, immerse.* LIT., manus in aquam, Plin.; aliquem undā, Verg.; immersus in flumen, Cic. TRANSF., immergere se in consuetudinem alicuius, *to insinuate oneself into,* Cic.

immĕrĭtus -a -um (in/mereo). (1) act., *not deserving (punishment), innocent*: gens, Verg.; Ov.; mori, *that has not deserved to die,* Hor. (2) pass., *undeserved, unmerited*: laudes haud immeritae, Liv.; Ov.
¶ Adv. **immĕrĭto**, *undeservedly*: Ter., Cic., Liv.

immersābĭlis -e (in/merso), *that cannot be sunk*: adversis rerum immersabilis undis, *not to be overwhelmed by,* Hor.

immētātus -a -um (in/meto), *unmeasured*: iugera, Hor.

immigro -are (in/migro), *to remove into.* LIT., in domum et in paternos hortos, Cic. TRANSF., ut ea (translata) verba non inruisse in alienum locum, sed immigrasse in suum diceres, *to have fallen naturally into their place,* Cic.; Liv.

immĭnĕo -ēre (in/mineo), *to project over, overhang.* LIT., quercus ingens arbor praetorio imminebat, Liv.; populus antro imminet, Verg.; collis urbi imminet, Verg.; carcer imminens foro, Liv.; luna imminente, Hor. TRANSF., (1) in time, *to be imminent, hang over*: mors quae cottidie imminet, Cic.; imminentium nescius, *ignorant of the immediate future,* Tac. (2) *to be near with hostile intent, threaten*: castra Romana Carthaginis portis immineant, Liv.; videt hostes imminere, Caes.; gestus imminens, *threatening demeanour,* Cic. (3) *to be on the watch for, to look out for*: in victoriam, Liv.; ad caedem, Cic.

immĭnŭo -ŭĕre -ŭi -ŭtum (in/minuo), *to lessen, diminish.* LIT., copias, Cic. L.; numerum, Liv.; verbum imminutum, *abbreviated,* Cic. TRANSF., (1) *to weaken*: corpus otio, animum libidinibus, Tac.; Lucr., Sall. (2) *to infringe*: maiestatem, Liv.; auctoritatem, Cic. L.

immĭnūtĭo -ōnis, f. (imminuo), *a lessening, diminishing, weakening*: corporis, Cic. TRANSF., dignitatis, Cic.; as rhet. figure, *meiosis* (e.g., non minime for maxime): Cic.

immiscĕo -miscēre -miscŭi -mixtum (in/misceo) *to mix in, intermingle.* LIT., of things: nives caelo prope immixtae, Liv.; poet.: immiscent manus manibus, *they fight hand to hand,* Verg.; of persons: togati immisti turbae militum, Liv.; se mediis armis, Verg. TRANSF., *to join with, unite*; of things: vota timori, Verg.; sortem regni cum rebus Romanis, Liv.; of persons: se conloquiis montanorum, Liv.

immĭsĕrābĭlis -e (in/miserabilis), *unpitied*: Hor.

immĭsĕrĭcors -cordis (in/misericors), *unmerciful*: Cic.; adv. **immĭsĕrĭcordĭtĕr**: Ter.

immissĭo -ōnis, n. (immitto), *a letting grow*: sarmentorum, Cic.

immītis -e (in/mitis), adj. (with compar.), *unripe, sour, harsh.* LIT., uva, Hor. TRANSF., *harsh, cruel, pitiless, stern*: tyrannus, Verg.;

oculi, Ov.; lupus, Ov.; ara, *on which human sacrifices were offered,* Ov.

immitto -mittĕre -mĭsi -missum (in/mitto). (1) *to send in, cause* or *allow to go in.* LIT., tigna machinationibus in flumen, Caes.; aquam canalibus, Caes.; corpus in undam, Ov.; esp.: **a**, *to engraft*: feraces plantas, Verg.: **b**, *to work in*: lentum filis aurum, Ov.; TRANSF., hic corrector in eo ipso loco, quo reprehendit, immittit imprudens ipse senarium, *lets slip in,* Cic. (2) *to let loose, let go free*: iuga, frena, habenas, Verg.; esp. *to let grow*: palmes laxis immissus habenis, Verg.; barba immissa, *long, uncut,* Verg.; capilli, Ov. (3) *to let go against, launch against.* LIT., naves pice completas in classem Pompeianam, Caes.; tela in aliquem, Caes.; se in hostes, *to attack,* Cic.; servos ad spoliandum fanum, Cic.; tu praetor in mea bona quos voles immittes? Cic. TRANSF., *to incite against*: immissis qui monerent, Tac.; of feelings, *to instil*: Teucris fugam atrumque timorem, Verg.

immixtus, partic. from immisceo; q.v.

immŏ, a particle, usually placed first in its sentence and often strengthened by etiam, vero, enimvero, magis, potius, etc., which contradicts or goes beyond what has previously been stated or suggested; *on the contrary, yes indeed, no indeed*: causa non bona est? immo optima, Cic.; familiarem? immo alienissimum, Cic.; nullane habes vitia? immo alia et fortasse minora, *yes, I have,* Hor.; sometimes in the middle of a sentence: simulacra deum, deos immo ipsos, *or rather,* Liv.

immōbĭlis -e (in/mobilis), *immovable*: terra, Cic.; also *hard to move*: Liv. TRANSF., precibus, *inexorable,* Tac.; ardet Ausonia immobilis ante, Verg.

immŏdĕrātĭo -ōnis, f. (immoderatus), *want of moderation, excess*: efferri immoderatione verborum, Cic.

immŏdĕrātus -a -um (in/modero), *immeasurable, endless*: Lucr. TRANSF., *immoderate, unbridled, unrestrained*: libertas, oratio, homo, Cic.; potestas, Liv.
¶ Adv. **immŏdĕrātē**, *without rule* or *measure*: moveri immoderate et fortuito, Cic. TRANSF., *immoderately, intemperately*: vivere, Cic.; compar.: Cic. L.

immŏdestia -ae, f. (immodestus), *want of restraint*: eri, Pl.; publicanorum, Tac.; militum, Nep.

immŏdestus -a -um (in/modestus), *unrestrained, extravagant*: genus iocandi, Cic.; Ter., Tac.
¶ Adv. **immŏdestē**, *extravagantly*: immodice immodesteque gloriari, Liv.; Pl., Quint.

immŏdĭcus -a -um (in/modicus), *immoderate, excessive.* LIT., frigus, Ov. TRANSF., *unrestrained, unbridled.* (1) of persons: in augendo numero, Liv.; immodicus linguā, Liv.; with genit.: laetitiae, Tac. (2) of things: imperia, cupido, Liv.; Ov.
¶ Adv. **immŏdĭcē**, *immoderately*: hac potestate immodice ac superbe usum esse, Liv.

immŏdŭlātus -a -um (in/modulatus), *inharmonious*: Hor.

immoenis, see immunis.

immŏlātĭo -ōnis, f. (immolo), *a sacrificing*: in ipso immolationis tempore, Cic.; Tac.

immŏlātor -ōris, m. (immolo), *a sacrificer*: Cic.

immŏlītus -a -um (in/molior), *built up, erected*: quae in loca publica inaedificata immolitave privati habebant, Liv.

immŏlo -are (in/molo), originally, *to sprinkle with sacred meal*; hence, *to sacrifice, immolate.* Lɪᴛ., bovem Dianae, vitulum Musis, Cic.; with abl. of the victim: Iovi singulis bubus, Liv.; absol.: in Capitolio, Liv. Tʀᴀɴsꜰ., *to devote to death, slay*: Pallas te immolat, Verg.

immŏrĭor -mori -mortŭus, dep. (in/morior), *to die in* or *upon*: sorori, *on his sister's body*, Ov.; Euxinis aquis, Ov. Tʀᴀɴsꜰ., studiis, *to work oneself to death over*, Hor.

immŏror -ari (in/moror), *to stay, remain in* or *upon*: Plin. Tʀᴀɴsꜰ., *to dwell on* a subject: Plin. L.

immorsus -a -um (in/mordeo), *bitten into, bitten*: immorso collo, Prop. Tʀᴀɴsꜰ., *stimulated*: stomachus, Hor.

immortālis -e (in/mortalis), *deathless, immortal.* Lɪᴛ., dii, di, Cic., Liv.; genus, Verg.; as subst., esp. plur.: Lucr., Cic., Liv. Tʀᴀɴsꜰ., (1) *everlasting, imperishable*: memoria et gloria, Cic.; amicitiae immortales, inimicitiae mortales esse debent, Liv. (2) *happy beyond measure, divinely blessed*: Prop.
¶ Adv. **immortālĭtĕr**, *infinitely*: gaudeo, Cic. L.

immortālĭtās -ātis, f. (immortalis), *immortality.* Lɪᴛ., animorum, Cic. Tʀᴀɴsꜰ., (1) *everlasting renown*: gloriae, Cic.; immortalitati commendare, tradere, *to make immortal*, Cic., Liv. (2) *extreme happiness*: Ter.

immōtus -a -um (in/moveo), *unmoved, motionless.* Lɪᴛ., (1) of things: arbores, *undisturbed*, Liv.; dies, *calm, windless*, Tac.; portus ab accessu ventorum immotus, Verg. (2) of persons: stat gravis Entellus nisuque immotus eodem, Verg.; adversus incitatas turmas stetit immota Samnitium acies, Liv. Tʀᴀɴsꜰ., *firm, steadfast*: mens, fata, Verg.; pax, Liv.; animus, Tac.

immūgĭo -ire (in/mugio), *to bellow, roar in* or *on*: immugiit Aetna cavernis, Verg.

immulgĕo -ēre (in/mulgeo), *to milk into*: teneris immulgens ubera labris, Verg.

immundĭtĭa -ae, f. (immundus), *uncleanness, impurity*: Pl.

immundus -a -um (in/¹mundus), *unclean, impure, foul*: humus, Cic.; canis, Hor.; sues, Verg. Tʀᴀɴsꜰ., dicta, Hor.

immūnĭo -ire (in/munio), *to fortify in* a place: Tac.

immūnis -e (in/munus), *without duty, free, exempt.* Lɪᴛ., ager, *tax-free*, Cic.; militiā, *exempt from military service*, Liv.; with genit.: portoriorum, Liv.; immunes militarium operum, Liv. Tʀᴀɴsꜰ., (1) in gen., *not working* or *not contributing*: fucus, Verg.; non ego te meis immunem meditor tingere poculis, Hor.; quem scis immunem Cynarae placuisse rapaci, *without gifts*, Hor.; with genit.: immunis operum, Ov. (2) *free, exempt*: manus, *stainless*, Hor.; with genit.: mali, Ov.

immūnĭtās -ātis, f. (immunis), *exemptio from public offices* or *burdens*; with genit. omnium rerum, Caes.; plur.: immunitate dare, Cic.; Tac. Tʀᴀɴsꜰ., in gen., *immunity exemption*: magni muneris, Cic.

immūnītus -a -um (in/munio). (1) *unfortified* oppida castellaque, Liv.; Ov. (2) *unpaved* via, Cic.

immurmŭro -are (in/murmuro), *to murmu at*: silvis immurmurat Auster, Verg.; Ov.

¹immūtābĭlis -e (in/mutabilis), adj. (wit compar.), *unchangeable*: aeternitas, Cic.; Liv

²immūtābĭlis -e (immuto), *changed*: Pl.

immūtābĭlĭtās -ātis, f. (¹immutabilis), *im mutability*: Cic.

immūtātĭo -ōnis, f. (immuto), *a change alteration*: ordinis, Cic.; rhet. t. t., *metonymy* Cic., Quint.

¹immūtātus -a -um (in/muto), *unchanged* Ter., Cic.

²immūtātus -a -um, partic. from immuto q.v.

immūto -are (in/muto), *to change, alter* ordinem verborum, Cic.; aliquid de in stitutis priorum, Cic.; of persons: prosperi rebus immutari, Cic.; esp. as rhet. t. t., *t use by way of metonymy*: Ennius pro Afri immutat Africam, Cic.; immutata oratio *allegory*, Cic.

impācātus -a -um (in/paco), *restless*: Verg.

impallesco -pallescĕre -pallŭi (in/pallesco), *t turn pale over*: nocturnis chartis, Pers.

impar -păris (in/par), *unequal, uneven* Hence (1) of numbers, *odd*: par et impa ludere, *to play at odd and even*, Hor. (2 *unequal* in quantity or dimensions: imparibu intervallis, Cic.; modi impares, *hexamete and pentameter*, Ov.; si toga dissidet impar sits *unevenly*, Hor. (3) in gen., *unlike discordant*: boves et uri, Verg.; sibi, Hor. pugna, *ill-matched*, Verg. (4) esp. *unequa to, not a match for*: impar congressus Achilli Verg.; in rank: maternum genus impar Tac.
¶ Adv. **impărĭtĕr**, *unevenly, unequally* Hor.

impărātus -a -um (in/paro), adj. (with superl.) *unprepared*: cum a militibus, tum a pecunia *unprovided with*, Cic.; inermis atqu imparatus, Caes.; Pl., Ter.

impartĭo, impartĭor=impertio, impertior q.v.

impastus -a -um (in/pasco), *unfed, hungry* leo, Verg.

impătĭbĭlis=impetibilis; q.v.

impătĭens -entis (in/patior), *unable to bea* or *to endure, impatient.* (1) of persons laborum, Ov.; vulneris, Ov.; solis, Tac. irae, *wrathful*, Ov. (2) of inanimate objects cera impatiens caloris, Ov.
¶ Adv. **impătĭentĕr**, *impatiently*: Tac. Plin. L.

impătĭentĭa -ae, f. (impatiens), *impatienc inability to endure*: silentii impatientian Tac.

impăvĭdus -a -um (in/pavidus), *fearles undaunted*: vir, Hor.; pectora, Liv.; Verg Ov. Adv. **impăvĭdē**, *fearlessly*: Liv.

impĕdīmentum -i, n. (impedio), *a hindranc impediment.* In gen.: impedimentum alic facere, inferre, Cic.; adferre, Tac.; esse alic impedimento, Pl., Ter., Caes.; ad dicendun

Cic. Esp. in plur., *the baggage of an army or traveller*: impedimenta et sarcinas invadere, Liv.; impedimenta exspectanda sunt quae Anagniā veniunt, Cic.; sometimes= *pack-horses*: Caes.

impĕdĭo -ire (connected with pes), *to entangle, ensnare.*
LIT., physically: impediunt vincula nulla pedes, Ov.; equos frenis, Ov.; saltum munitionibus, *to render impassable*, Liv.; poet., *to surround*: caput myrto, Hor.; Verg., Ov.
TRANSF., abstr., (1) *to embarrass*: mentem dolore, Cic.; stultitiā suā, Cic. (2) *to hinder, impede, prevent, obstruct*: aliquem, Cic.; iter, Liv.; navigationem, Caes.; se a suo munere non impedit, Cic.; foll. by ne and the subj.: Cic., Liv.; by quominus: Cic.; in neg., by quin: Cic. L.; by infin.: Cic., Lucr., Verg.
¶ Hence partic. (with compar. and superl.) **impĕdītus** -a -um, *entangled, hindered, impeded.* LIT., physically; of persons: Pl.; esp. as milit. t. t., *hindered by baggage* (opp. expeditus): miles, Caes.; Liv.; of places, *impassable, blocked*: silva, Caes.; saltus, Liv. TRANSF., immaterially. (1) *embarrassed, obstructed*: impeditis animis, Caes., Cic.; tempora reipublicae, Cic. (2) *awkward, complicated*: Caes., Liv., Tac.

impĕdītĭo -ōnis, f. (impedio), *a hindrance*: animus liber omni impeditione curarum, Cic.

impĕdītus -a -um, partic. from impedio; q.v.

impello -pellĕre -pŭli -pulsum (in/pello).
(1) *to drive against, strike upon*: chordas, Ov.; maternas impulit aures luctus Aristaei, Verg.; Liv.
(2) *to set in motion, drive on.* LIT., navem remis, Verg.; aliquem in fugam, Cic., Liv. TRANSF., in gen., *to incite, urge on, impel*: aliquem ad scelus, Cic.; in eam mentem, Cic.; foll. by ut: Caes., Cic., Hor.; by infin.: Verg., Liv., Tac.; esp. *to give a push to one falling* or *tottering*; *to complete a person's ruin*, etc.: praecipitantem, Cic.; animum labantem, Verg.

impendĕo -ēre (in/pendeo), *to hang over, overhang.*
LIT., with dat.: cervicibus, Cic.; saxum impendere Tantalo, Cic.; with acc.: Lucr.
TRANSF., *to hang over, to threaten, be close at hand*: in me terrores impendent, Cic.; with dat.: omnibus terror impendet, Cic.; with acc.: te mala, Ter.; magnum etiam bellum impendet a Parthis, Cic.

impendĭum -i, n. (impendo). (1) *expenditure, outlay, cost*: impendio publico, *at the public expense*, Liv.; sine impendio, Cic.; abl. as adv. **impendĭo**, colloq., *by much, very much*; with comparatives: magis, *far more*, Cic. L.; Pl., Ter. (2) *interest on money*: Cic.

impendo -pendĕre -pendi -pensum (in/pendo), *to weigh out*; hence *to expend, lay out.* LIT., pecuniam in aliquam rem, Cic.; Liv. TRANSF., operam in aliquid, Cic.; curas, Verg.; Tac.
¶ Hence partic. **impensus** -a -um, *freely expended*; hence LIT., of price, *considerable, great*: impenso pretio, Cic.; absol.: impenso, *at a high price*, Hor. TRANSF., *strong, vehement*: voluntas, Cic., Liv.; compar.: Pl., Ov.

¶ Adv. (with compar.) **impensē**, *at great cost*: Pers. TRANSF., *urgently, eagerly, pressingly*: nunc eo facio id impensius, Cic. L.; orare, Liv.; consulere, Verg.

impĕnĕtrābĭlis -e (in/penetrabilis), *impenetrable*: silex impenetrabilis ferro, Liv.; tegimen adversus ictūs impenetrabile, Tac. TRANSF., pudicitia, Tac.

impensa -ae, f. (impendo), *expense, outlay.* LIT., impensam facere in aliquid, Cic. L.; sine impensā, Cic.; Hor., Liv. TRANSF., cruoris, Ov.; operum, Verg.

impensus -a -um, partic. from impendo; q.v.

impĕrātor -ōris, m. (impero), *a commander, leader.*
LIT., (1) milit. t. t., *the commander-in-chief of an army*: Caes., Cic., etc. (2) a title given to a general after a great victory, and added to his name; e.g. Cn. Pompeio Cn. F. Magno imperatori: Cic. (3) after Julius Caesar, a name of the Roman emperors: imperator Augustus, Suet.; absol.=*the Roman emperor*: Suet.
TRANSF., in gen., *leader, chief*: familiae, Pl.; populus est imperator omnium gentium, Cic.; vitae, Sall.; esp. as a name of Jupiter: Cic., Liv.

impĕrātōrĭus -a -um (imperator). (1) *of or relating to a general*: nomen, Cic. L.; ius, laus, labor, Cic. (2) *imperial*: Suet.

impĕrātrix -īcis, f. (imperator), *a female commander*; (sarcastically) *a general in petticoats*: Cic.

imperceptus -a -um (in/percipio), *unperceived, unknown*: fraus, Ov.

impercussus -a -um (in/percutio), *not struck*: impercussos nocte movere pedes, *noiseless*, Ov.

imperdĭtus -a -um (in/perdo), *not slain, undestroyed*: Verg.

imperfectus -a -um (in/perficio), *incomplete, unfinished, imperfect*: reliquum corpus imperfectum ac rude relinquere, Cic. L.; verba, Ov.

imperfossus -a -um (in/perfodio), *unstabbed, unpierced*: ab omni ictu, Ov.

impĕrĭōsus -a -um (imperium), *commanding.*
LIT., of political power: populus, Cic.; virga, *the fasces*, Ov.; dictatura, Liv. TRANSF., in gen.: sibi, *master of oneself*, Hor.; esp. in bad sense, *imperious, tyrannical*: cupiditas, Cic.; aequor, Hor.

impĕrĭtĭa -ae, f. (imperitus), *inexperience, ignorance*: Sall., Tac.

impĕrĭto -are (impero), *to command.* (1) *to command a thing, give an order*: aequam rem imperito, Hor.; Pl. (2) *to be in command*: si Nero imperitaret, Tac.; with dat.: oppido, Liv.; nemori, Verg.

impĕrītus -a -um (in/peritus), adj. (with compar. and superl.), *unskilled, inexperienced, ignorant*: Ter., Cic., Liv.; esp. with genit.: iuris, Cic.; nandi, Liv.
¶ Adv. (with compar. and superl.) **impĕrītē**, *unskilfully, ignorantly*: imperite absurdeque fictum, Cic.

impĕrĭum -i, n. (impero), *command, order.*
(1) *a thing ordered; an order, a command*: parere, Caes.; accipere, Liv.; exsequi, Pl., Verg.
(2) *the right* or *power of ordering*; *power, mastery, command*. In gen.: in suos, Cic.;

domesticum, Cic.; animi imperio, corporis servitio magis utimur, *the mind as a master, the body as a slave,* Sall.; Hor., Liv. Esp., *political power, authority, sovereignty*: totius Galliae, Caes.; sub P. R. imperium redigere, Cic.; de imperio decertare, dimicare, Cic.; tu regere imperio populos, Romane, memento, Verg.; within the Roman state, sovereignty as constitutionally delegated to magistrates, which included military command: in imperio esse, *to hold an office,* Cic.; cum imperio esse, Cic.; summum imperium, Cic.; maritimum, Caes.; imperium, sine quo res militaris administrari, teneri exercitus, bellum geri non potest, Cic.; alicui imperium prorogare, Cic. Meton.: **a**, in plur., *persons exercising authority*: erat plena lictorum et imperiorum provincia, Caes.; imperia et potestates, Cic.: **b**, *an area governed, an empire*: finium imperii nostri propagatio, Cic.; Verg., Tac.

imperiūrātus -a -um (in/periuro), *that by which no one dares to swear falsely*: aquae, *the Styx,* Ov.

impermissus -a -um (in/permitto), *forbidden*: Hor.

impĕro -are (in/paro; old form: imperassit, Cic.), *to impose* a thing upon *a person* or *community.*
    Hence **(1)** *to requisition, order* a thing; with acc. of thing and dat. of person: obsides civitatibus, *hostages from the states,* Caes.; frumentum civitati, Cic.
    (2) *to order* an action *to be done, give orders to* a person. Usually with dat. of person and the action expressed by acc. or by clause (or by nom. as subject of pass.): facere imperatum, *or* imperata, *or* quae imperarentur, Caes.; with ut *or* ne and subj.: mihi ne abscedam imperat, Ter.; Caes., Liv., Ov.; with subj. alone: Caes., Ov., Liv.; with pass. infin.: hãs actuarias fieri, Caes.; Cic.; with act. infin.: flectere iter sociis, Verg.; Ov., Tac. Sometimes with persons as subject of pass.: in easdem lautumias etiam ex ceteris oppidis deduci imperantur, Cic.; Hor.
    (3) *to rule over, govern, command*: Iugurtha omni Numidiae imperare parat, Sall.; fig.: sibi, Cic.; cupiditatibus, Cic.; arvis, Verg.; animo, Liv.

imperterrĭtus -a -um (in/perterreo), *undaunted, fearless*: Verg.

impertĭo -ire (pars), *to share.* **(1)** *to cause* a person *to share in*: aliquem salute, Pl., Ter. **(2)** *to share* a thing *with* a person, *to impart to*: indigentibus de re familiari, Cic.; alicui civitatem, Cic.; tempus cogitationi, Cic.; pass., *to be bestowed*: Cic., Liv.

imperturbātus -a -um (in/perturbo), *undisturbed, calm*: os, Ov.

impervĭus -a -um (in/pervius), *impassable, impervious*: iter, Tac.; annis, Ov.

impĕtĭbĭlis -e (patior), *insufferable*: dolor, Cic.

impĕto -ĕre, *to make for, attack*: Luc.

impetrābĭlis -e (impetro). **(1)** pass., *obtainable*: venia, Liv.; pax, Liv.; compar.: Liv. **(2)** act., *that obtains easily, successful*: orator, Pl. Transf., dies, *on which things go well,* Pl.

impetrātĭo -ōnis, f. (impetro), *an obtaining by asking*: Cic. L.

impetrĭo -ire (impetro), *to seek to obtain by favourable omens*: Pl., Cic.

impetro -are (in/patro), *to get, obtain, accomplish, effect*; in gen., by any effort: Pl.; esp., *to obtain by asking*; with acc. object: optatum, *one's desire,* Cic.; alicui civitatem (*citizenship*) a Caesare, Cic.; with ut *or* ne and the subj.: impetrabis a Caesare, ut tibi abesse liceat, Cic. L.; Pl., Caes.; with subj. alone: Pl.; absol.: haec si tecum patria loquatur, nonne impetrare debeat? Cic.

impĕtus -ūs, m. (from impeto; old genit. sing. impetis: Lucr.; abl. impete: Lucr., Ov.), *a making for; an attack, onset.*
    Lit., impetum facere in hostes, Caes.; excipere, sustinere, ferre, *to receive an attack,* Caes.; impetum dare in aliquem, Liv.; frangere, Cic. L.
    Transf., in gen., *violent impulse, rapid motion.* **(1)** of physical objects: impetus caeli, Lucr., Cic.; in magno impetu maris atque aperto, Caes.; sometimes of *extent* without motion: Lucr. **(2)** mental *impulse, passion, force*: divinus, *inspiration,* Cic.; dicendi, Cic.; impetu magis quam consilio, Liv.; of things: tanti belli impetus, Cic.

impexus -a -um (in/pecto), *uncombed*: Verg., Hor. Transf., *rude, uncouth*: Tac.

impĭē, adv. from impius; q.v.

impĭĕtās -ātis, f. (impius), *disregard for obligation, undutifulness*: in deos, *impiety,* Cic.; *unfilial conduct*: Ov.; political *disloyalty*: Cic., Tac.

impĭger -gra -grum (in/piger), *unslothful, diligent, active*: in scribendo, Cic.; ad labores belli, Cic.; militiā, Liv.; with genit.: militiae, Tac.; with infin.: hostium vexare turmas, Hor.
    ¶ Adv. **impĭgrē**, *actively*: impigre promittere auxilium, Liv.; Pl., Sall.

impĭgrītās -ātis, f. (impiger), *activity*: Cic.

impingo -pingĕre -pēgi -pactum (in/pango), *to pin to, to thrust, dash, drive against.* Lit., pugnum in os, Pl.; huic compedes, Pl.; agmina muris, Verg.; litoribus impactus, Tac. Transf., without physical force, *to press upon, bring upon* a person: alicui calicem mulsi, Cic.; dicam tibi grandem, Ter.; Hor.

impĭo -are (impius), *to make undutiful*: Pl.

impĭus -a -um (in/pius), *regardless of obligation, undutiful, disloyal*; hence *godless, unfilial, unpatriotic,* etc. Lit., civis, Cic.; miles, Verg.; Titanes, Hor. Transf., **(1)** of things: scelerosa atque impia facta, Lucr.; esp. of civil war: bellum, Cic.; arma, Verg. **(2)** of gods, *invoked in curses*: Tac.
    ¶ Adv. **impĭē**, *undutifully, disloyally*: aliquid impie scelerateque committere, Cic.

implācābĭlis -e (in/placabilis), *implacable*: alicui, Cic., Liv.; in aliquem, Cic.; of things: iracundiae, Cic. L.
    ¶ Compar. adv. **implācābĭlius**, *more implacably*: implacabilius alicui irasci, Tac.

implācātus -a -um (in/placo), *unappeased, unsatisfied*: Charybdis, Verg.; Ov.

implācĭdus -a -um (in/placidus), *rough, savage*: genus, Hor.

implĕo -plēre -plēvi -plētum (in/*pleo), *to fill in, fill up, fill full.*
    Lit., in gen.: volumina, Cic.; fossas, Liv.; with abl.: gremium frustis, Cic.; mero pateram, Verg.; with genit.: ollam denariorum, Cic.

legiones equitesque in naves, Caes.; exercitum Brundisii, Cic.; nos cumbae, Hor.

TRANSF., in gen., *to fill*: scopulos vocibus, Verg.; urbem lamentis, Liv.; omnia terrore, Liv.; adulescentem temeritatis, Liv. Esp. **(1)** *to fill up* a measure, *complete* an amount: annum, Ov.; numerum, Juv.; impleta ut essent sex milia armatorum, Liv.; of the moon: luna quater iunctis implerat cornibus orbem, *had completed its circle*, Ov. **(2)** *to satisfy, content*: sese regum sanguine, Cic.; milites praedā, Liv. **(3)** *to fulfil, perform*: officium scribendi, Cic.; fata, Liv.; munia, Tac. **(4)** *to contaminate*: Liv., Juv.

implexus -a -um (plecto), *entwined*. LIT., implexae crinibus angues Eumenides, *with hair interwoven with serpents*, Verg. TRANSF., vidua implexa luctu continuo, *involved in*, Tac.

implĭcātĭo -ōnis, f. (implico), *an entwining, interweaving*. LIT., nervorum, Cic. TRANSF., locorum communium, *weaving together*, Cic.; rei familiaris, *embarrassment*, Cic.

implĭcātus -a -um, partic. from implico; q.v.

implĭciscor -i, dep. (implico), *to become confused, disordered*: Pl.

implĭco -are -āvi -ātum and (esp. post-Aug.) -are -ŭi -ĭtum (in/plico), *to enfold, entwine, entangle*.

LIT., se dextrae, *to cling to*, Verg.; bracchia collo, Verg.; crinem auro, Verg.; implicari remis, Liv.

TRANSF., **(1)** *to involve, entangle*: implicari morbo, *or* in morbum, Caes.; negotiis, Cic.; implicare ac perturbare aciem, Sall.; aliquem incertis responsis, Liv. **(2)** *to associate, unite*: se societate civium, Cic.

¶ Hence partic. **implĭcātus** -a -um; as adj., *confused, entangled*: partes orationis, Cic.

¶ From partic. implicitus, adv. **implĭcĭtē**, *confusedly*: Cic.

implōrātĭo -ōnis, f. (imploro), *an imploring for help*; with subjective genit.: illius, Cic.; with objective genit.: deum, Liv.

implōro -are (in/ploro). **(1)** *to call upon with tears, to beseech, implore*: deos, Cic.; milites ne, etc., Caes. **(2)** *to call for with tears, beg for*: alicuius auxilium, fidem, misericordiam, Cic.; auxilium ab aliquo, Cic., Caes.

implūmis -e (in/pluma), *unfledged*: pulli, Hor.; fetus (avis), Verg.

implŭo -plŭere -plŭi (in/pluo), *to rain upon*. TRANSF., Peneus summis aspergine silvis impluit, Ov.; Pl.

implŭvĭum -i, n. (impluo), *an opening in the roof of the atrium of a Roman house* or *the basin for the rain-water below it*: Pl., Ter., Cic., Liv.

impŏlītus -a -um (in/polio), *rough, unpolished*: lapis, Quint. TRANSF., formam ingenii impolitam et plane rudem, Cic.

¶ Adv. **impŏlītē**, *plainly, without ornament*: dicere, Cic.

impollūtus -a -um (in/polluo), *undefiled*: Tac.

impōno -pōnĕre -pŏsŭi -pŏsĭtum (in/pono) (perf. partic. syncop. impostus= Lucr., Verg.), *to put, set, lay, place in* or *upon*.

LIT., in gen.: dextram in caput, Liv.; aliquem in rogum, Cic.; coloniam in agro Samnitium, Liv.; praesidium Abydi, *at Abydos*, Liv.; commonly with dat.: alicui coronam, Cic.; iuvenes rogis, Verg.; esp. as naut. t. t., *to put on board ship, to embark*:

TRANSF., in gen., *to lay* or *put upon*: reipublicae vulnera, Cic.; invidiam belli consuli, Sall.; manum extremam (summam, supremam) alicui rei, *to put the last touch to*, Verg., Ov.; finem imponere alicui rei, Liv. Esp. **(1)** *to put over as master*: regem Macedoniae, Liv.; consulem populo, Cic. **(2)** *to lay upon as a burden* or *duty, to impose*: alicui onus, Cic.; stipendium victis, Caes. **(3)** *to impose upon, cheat, deceive*; with dat.: Catoni egregie, Cic. L.; Juv.

importo -are (in/porto), *to bring in, import*: vinum ad se importari omnino non sinunt, Caes. TRANSF., **(1)** *to bring in, introduce*: importatis artibus, *foreign*, Cic. **(2)** *to bring upon, cause*: alicui detrimentum, Cic.

importūnĭtās -ātis, f. (importunus), *self-assertion, inconsiderateness, insolence*: animi, Cic.; Pl., Sall.

importūnus -a -um (cf. opportunus). LIT., *unsuitable, ill-adapted*: loca machinationibus, Sall.; of time, *unfavourable*: tempus, Cic. TRANSF., **(1)** *ill-omened*: bubo, Verg.; Hor. **(2)** *troublesome, burdensome*: tempestas, Pl.; pauperies, Hor. **(3)** of character, *assertive, inconsiderate, insolent, savage*: mulier, hostis, libido, Cic.; mors, Ov.

importŭōsus -a -um (in/portus), *without harbours*: mare, Sall.; litus, Liv.

impos -pŏtis (cf. compos), *having no power over*: animi, Pl.

impŏsĭtus (impostus) -a -um, partic. from impono; q.v.

impŏtens -entis (in/potens), adj. (with compar. and supᵉrl.), *feeble, impotent, having no power*.

In gen., with genit., *having no power over, not master of*: equi regendi, Liv.; irae, Liv.; amoris, Tac.

Esp. *unable to command oneself, violent, unrestrained*. LIT., homo, Cic.; animus, Cic.; impotens quidlibet sperare, Hor. TRANSF., of the passions themselves, *unbridled*: iniuria, Liv.; laetitia, Cic.

¶ Adv. **impŏtentĕr**. **(1)** *weakly, powerlessly*: elephantos impotentius regi, Liv. **(2)** *intemperately, passionately*: Quint.

impŏtentĭa -ae, f. (impotens). **(1)** *poverty*: Ter. **(2)** *lack of self-restraint, violent passion*: animi, Cic.; muliebris, Liv.

impraesentĭārum (probably for in praesentiā harum rerum), *in present circumstances, for the present*: Cato, Nep., Tac.

impransus -a -um (in/pransus), *without breakfast, fasting*: Pl., Hor.

imprĕcātĭo -onis, f. (imprecor), *an invoking of harm, curse*: Sen.

imprĕcor -ari, dep. (in/precor), *to invoke harm upon, to call down upon*: litora litoribus contraria, Verg.; alicui diras, Tac.

impressĭo -ōnis, f. (imprimo), *a pressing into* or *upon*. Hence **(1)** *physical pressure, an attack, assault*: non ferre impressionem Latinorum, Liv.; of political contests: me vi et impressione evertere, Cic. **(2)** in rhetoric, *distinct expression, emphasis*: explanata vocum impressio, Cic.; impressiones, *rhythmical beats*, Cic. **(3)** in philosophy, *sense-data, the impressions of outward things received through the senses*: Cic.

imprīmis, adv. (=in primis), *especially, first of all, principally*: Cic., Sall.

imprīmo -prīmēre -pressi -pressum (in/ premo). (1) *to press into* or *upon*: aratrum muris, Hor.; impresso genu, Verg.; sulcum altius, Cic.; signo suo impressae tabellae, *sealed*, Liv.; cratera impressum signis, *chased, embossed*, Verg.; fig.: quasi ceram animum, Cic.; quae cum viderem tot vestigiis impressa, Cic. (2) *to make by pressing, imprint*: vestigium, Cic.; in cera sigilla hoc anulo, Cic.; fig.: in animis notionem, Cic.

imprŏbābĭlis -e (in/probabilis), *not to be approved*: Sen.

imprŏbātĭo -ōnis, f. (improbo), *disapprobation, blame*: improbatione hominis uti, Cic.

imprŏbē, adv. from improbus; q.v.

imprŏbĭtās -ātis, f. (improbus), *badness*; of persons, *depravity*: Cic.; of animals, *roguery*: simiae, Cic.

imprŏbo -are (in/probo), *to disapprove, blame, reject*: multorum opera, Cic.; aliquem testem, Cic.

imprŏbŭlus -a -um (dim. of improbus), *somewhat wicked*: Juv.

imprŏbus -a -um (in/probus), adj. (with compar. and superl.), *not up to standard*. (1) of material things, *inferior, bad*: merces, Pl.; Mart. (2) of persons, or by personification, *morally bad, perverse, wilful*, esp. through intentional breach of standards or rights; the exact sense depends on the context: homo, Cic.; in me, Cic.; m. pl. as subst., improbi, *the unpatriotic*: Cic.; lex, *wicked*, Cic.; labor, *persistent*, Verg.; rabies ventris, *insatiable hunger*, Verg.; anguis, Verg.; less seriously: anser, Verg.; carmina, *naughty*, Ov.; puer (=Amor), *impudent, bold, mischievous*, Verg.

¶ Adv. (with compar. and superl.) **imprŏbē**, *badly*; of human action (1) *wickedly*: dicere, facere, Cic. (2) *impudently, boldly*: Cat.

imprŏcērus -a -um (in/procerus), *small, low of stature*: pecora, Tac.

imprōdictus -a -um (in/prodico), *not postponed*: Cic.

impromptus -a -um (in/promptus), *not ready*: linguā, *slow of speech*, Liv.; Tac.

imprŏpĕrātus -a -um (in/propero), *not hurried, slow*: vestigia, Verg.

imprŏprius -a -um (in/proprius), *unsuitable*: Quint.

improsper -ěra -ěrum (in/prosper), *unfortunate, unprosperous*: claritudo, Tac.

¶ Adv. **improspērē**, *unfortunately*: Tac.

improvĭdus -a -um (in/providus), *without forethought, improvident*: improvidi et creduli senes, Cic.; improvida aetas puerorum, Lucr.; improvidos incautosque hostes opprimere, Liv.; with genit.: improvidus futuri certaminis, Liv.; Tac., Juv.

¶ Adv. **improvĭdē**, *without forethought, improvidently*: Liv.

improvīsus -a -um (in/provideo), *unforeseen, unexpected*: res, Cic.; adventus, Cic.; improvisi aderunt, Verg.; phrases: de improviso, ex improviso, improviso, *suddenly, unexpectedly*, Pl., Cic.

imprūdens -entis (in/prudens). (1) *not foreseeing, not expecting*: imprudentem adgredi,

Caes.; Verg. (2) *not knowing, unaware*: imprudente Sullā, *without the knowledge of Sulla*, Cic.; with genit., *ignorant of*: legis, Cic.; laborum, Verg.; maris, Liv. (3) *unwise, rash, imprudent*: Tac., Quint.

¶ Adv. **imprūdentěr**. (1) *without foresight*: Nep.; *unwittingly, unawares*; compar.: imprudentius, Ter. (2) *unwisely, imprudently*: nihil imprudenter facere, ap. Cic. L.

imprūdentĭa -ae, f. (imprudens). (1) *lack of foresight*: propter imprudentiam labi, Caes. (2) *lack of knowledge*: ne imprudentiam quidem, *not even unconsciously*, Cic. L.; with genit., *ignorance of*: eventus, Liv. (3) *lack of wisdom, imprudence*: teli emissi, Cic.

impūbēs -bĕris and (esp. poet.) **impūbēs** -is, adj. (in/pubes). (1) *below the age of puberty, youthful*: filius, Cic.; anni, Ov.; genae, *beardless*, Verg.; plur. as subst.: impuberes, or impubes, *boys*, Liv., Caes. (2) *unmarried*: qui diutissime impuberes permanserunt, Caes.

impŭdens -entis (in/pudens), adj. (with compar. and superl.), *without shame, shameless, impudent*: tu es impudens! Cic.; Pl., Hor. TRANSF., mendacium, Cic.; impudentissimae literae, Cic.

¶ Adv. (with compar. and superl.) **impŭdentěr**, *shamelessly*: mentiri, Cic.; Pl., Ter.

impŭdentĭa -ae, f. (impudens), *shamelessness, impudence*: Pl., Caes., Cic.

impŭdīcĭtĭa -ae, f. (impudicus), *lewdness, incontinence, unchastity*: Pl., Tac.

impŭdīcus -a -um (in/pudicus), adj. (with compar. and superl.). (1) *shameless*: Pl. (2) *unchaste, lewd, incontinent*: Pl., Cic.

impugnātĭo -ōnis, f. (impugno), *an assault, attack*: Cic. L.

impugno -are (in/pugno), *to attack, assail*. LIT., as milit. t. t.: terga hostium, Liv.; Caes. TRANSF., in gen., *to attack*: regem, Sall.; dignitatem alicuius, Cic.; sententiam, Tac.

impulsĭo -ōnis, f. (impello), *pushing, pressure*. LIT., physical: Cic. TRANSF., mental, *incitement, impulse*: omnis ad omnem animi motum impulsio, Cic.

impulsor -ōris, m. (impello), *an instigator, inciter*: profectionis meae, Cic.; Caesare impulsore atque auctore, Cic.; Ter., Tac.

impulsus -ūs, m. (impello), *pushing, pressure, impulse*. LIT., physical: scutorum, Cic. TRANSF., *incitement, instigation*: impulsu meo, vestro, Cic.; Ter., Caes.

impūnē (in/punio), adv., with compar. (and superl.: Pl.), *with impunity, without punishment*. LIT., facere, Cic.; ferre, *to go unpunished*, Cic.; non impune abire, Caes. TRANSF., *without peril, safely*: in otio esse, Cic.; revisere aequor, Hor.

impūnĭtās -ātis, f. (in/punio), *impunity, exemption from punishment*: alicui veniam et impunitatem dare, Cic.; impunitas non modo a iudicio, sed etiam a sermone, Cic.; Caes.; with genit.: peccandi, flagitiorum, Cic.; Tac.

impūnītus -a -um (in/punio), adj. (with compar.), *unpunished, exempt from punishment*. LIT., multorum impunita scelera Cic.; si istius haec iniuria impunita discesserit, Cic.; aliquem impunitum dimittere,

Sall. TRANSF., *unbridled, unrestrained*: mendacium, Cic.; omnium rerum libertas, Cic.

¶ Adv. **impūnītē**, *with impunity*: Cic.

impūrātus -a -um (impurus), *vile, infamous*: Pl., Ter.; superl.: Pl.

impūrĭtās -ātis, f. (impurus), *moral impurity*: Cic.

impūrĭtĭae -arum, f. pl. (impurus), *moral impurity*: Pl.

impūrus -a -um (in/purus), adj. (with compar. and superl.), *unclean, stained, foul*. LIT., Ov. TRANSF., morally, *impure, vile, infamous*: homo, Cic.; animus, Sall.; historia, Ov.

¶ Adv. (with superl.) **impūrē**, *impurely, vilely, infamously*: multa facere, Cic.; vivere, Cic.

¹**impŭtātus** -a -um (in/puto), *unpruned, untrimmed*: vinea, Ov.

²**impŭtātus** -a -um, partic. from imputo; q.v.

impŭto -are (in/puto), *to lay to a charge, enter in an account*; hence, with dat. of person or personified thing. (1) *to reckon as a merit* or *a fault* in someone, *to impute to*: adversa uni imputantur, Tac. (2) *to reckon as a service done* or *gift given* to someone: hoc solum erit certamen, quis mihi plurimum imputet, i.e. *can have served me best*, Tac.; soles qui nobis pereunt et imputantur, Mart. Without dat., *to take credit for*: Plin. L.

īmŭlus -a -um (dim. of imus), *lowest, little*: oricilla, Cat.

īmus -a -um, superl. from inferus; q.v.

¹**ĭn**, prep., with acc.=*into*, with abl.=*in*.

(1) with acc. LIT., of space, *into, on to, towards, against*: **a**, of actual motion: ad urbem vel potius in urbem exercitum adducere, Cic.; in Britanniam, Caes.; in me convertite ferrum, Verg.: **b**, of direction only, *towards*: spectant in septentriones, Caes.; sex pedes in altitudinem, *upwards, in height*, Caes. TRANSF., **a**, of time: dormire in lucem, *until*, Hor.; more often to indicate intended duration: aliquid in omne tempus perdidisse, *for ever*, Cic.; magistratum creare in annum, Liv.; in multos annos praedicere, Cic.; in diem vivere, *to live for the moment*, Cic.; esp. with comparatives, etc., to denote regular increase: et magis magis in dies et horas, Cat.; Cic., Hor.: **b**, of division, *into*: Gallia est omnis divisa in partes tres, Caes.: **c**, of change, *into*: in villos abeunt vestes, Ov.: **d**, of tendency or purpose or object, *for*: nullam pecuniam Gabinio, nisi in rem militarem datam, Cic.; in eandem sententiam loqui, Cic.; ardere in proelia, Verg.: **e**, of feelings, personal relationships, etc., *towards, against*: amor in patriam, Cic.: **f**, in adverbial phrases indicating manner or extent: servilem in modum, Cic.; in universum, *in general*, Liv.; in vicem, *in turn*, Cic., Caes.: in vices, Ov.

(2) with abl., *in*. LIT., of space, *in, on, among*: esse in Sicilia, Cic.; in equo, Cic.; in oculis, *before one's eyes*, Cic.; esp. of dress, etc.: esse in veste domestica, Ov.; excubare in armis, Caes. TRANSF., **a**, of time: in sex mensibus, *within*, Cic.; in tali tempore, *at*, Liv.; in omni aetate, Cic.; in tempore, *at the right time*, Ter., Liv., Tac.: **b**, with abstract nouns indicating condition, situation, etc., *in*: in hac solitudine, Cic.; in honore, Cic.; in motu, Lucr., Cic.; so of business *in* which

one is employed, esp. with a gerundive: Caes., Cic.: **c**, *in relation to* persons, *in the case of*: in hoc homine non accipio excusationem, Cic.; non talis in hoste, Verg.: **d**, of a class or body including a person or thing, *in, among*: in quibus Catilina, Sall.

²**in-**, inseparable particle, with adjectives, nouns, and participles, *without, not*; e.g. innocens, imberbis (in/barba), indoctus.

ĭnaccessus -a -um (in/accedo), *inaccessible*: lucus, Verg.; Tac.

ĭnăcesco -ăcescĕre -ăcŭi, *to become sour*. TRANSF., haec tibi per totos inacescant omnia sensus, Ov.

Ĭnăchus (Ĭnăchos) -i, m. (Ἴναχος), *a mythical king of Argos, father of Io, after whom the river Inachus in Argolis was named*.

¶ Hence adj. **Ĭnăchĭus** -a -um, *relating to Inachus*: iuvenca, *Io*, Verg.; urbes, *Greek*, Verg.; m. subst. **Ĭnăchĭdēs** -ae, *a descendant of Inachus*; *Perseus*: Ov.; *Epaphus*: Ov.; f. **Ĭnăchis** -ĭdis, as adj., *relating to Inachus*: ripa, *of the river Inachus*, Ov.; as subst., *a daughter of Inachus*; Io: Prop.

ĭnadfectātus -a -um (in/adfecto), *natural, unaffected*: Quint., Plin.

ĭnadsuētus -a -um (in/adsuesco), *unaccustomed*: equi, Ov.

ĭnădustus -a -um (in/aduro), *unsinged*: Ov.

ĭnaedĭfĭco -are. (1) *to build in* or *upon*: sacellum in domo, Cic.; aliquid in locum, Liv. (2) *to build up, block up, barricade*: vicos plateasque, Caes.; Cic., Liv.

ĭnaequābĭlis -e, *uneven*. LIT., physically: solum, Liv. TRANSF., in gen., *unequal*: motus, Cic.

¶ Adv. **ĭnaequābĭlĭtĕr**, *unequally, variously*: Suet.

ĭnaequālis -e. (1) *uneven, unequal, various*. LIT., loca, Tac.; calices, Hor. TRANSF., varietas, Cic. (2) act., *making unequal*: tonsor, Hor.; procellae, *disturbing the level of the sea*, Hor.

¶ Adv. **ĭnaequālĭtĕr**, *unevenly, unequally*: inaequaliter eminentes rupes, Liv.; Tac.

ĭnaequālĭtās -ātis, f. (inaequalis), *unevenness, inequality*: Varr., Quint.

ĭnaequo -are, *to make even, level up*: haec levibus cratibus terráque inaequat, Caes.

ĭnaestĭmābĭlis -e (in/aestimo). (1) *that cannot be estimated*: nihil tam incertum nec tam inaestimabile quam animi multitudinis, Liv. (2) *priceless, inestimable*: gaudium, Liv. (3) *having no value*, Cic.

ĭnaestŭo -are, *to boil, rage in*: si meis inaestuat praecordiis bilis, Hor.

ĭnaffectātus=inadfectatus; q.v.

ĭnămābĭlis -e, *hateful, unlovely*: palus (of the Styx), Verg.; Pl., Ov.

ĭnămaresco -ĕre, *to become bitter*: Hor.

ĭnambĭtĭōsus -a -um, *not ambitious, unpretentious*: Ov.

ĭnambŭlātĭo -ōnis, f. (inambulo), *a walking up and down*: Cat.

ĭnambŭlo -are, *to walk up and down*: cum Cotta in porticu, Cic.; Pl., Liv.

ĭnămoenus -a -um, *unlovely, dismal*: regna umbrarum, Ov.

ĭnānĭae -ārum, f. (inanis), *emptiness*: Pl.

ĭnānĭlŏgista -ae, m. (inanis/λογιστής), *an empty talker*: Pl.

ĭnānīmentum -i, n. (inanio), *emptiness*; plur., *empty spaces*: Pl.

ĭnănĭmus -a -um (in/anima), *lifeless, inanimate*: Cic., Liv., Tac.

ĭnănĭo -ire -īvi -ītum (inanis), *to empty, make void*: Lucr., Plin.

ĭnānis -e, adj. (with compar. and superl.), *empty, void*.
   LIT., physically, in gen.: spatium, Lucr.; vas, domus, Cic.; equus, *without rider*, Cic.; navis, *unloaded*, Caes.; corpus, *soulless, dead*, Cic.; lumina, *blind*, Ov.; galea, *taken from the head*, Verg.; with genit.: Hor., Ov.; n. as subst. **ĭnāne** -is, *empty space*: Lucr., Cic., Verg. Esp. (1) *empty-handed*: redire, Cic.; hence, *poor, indigent*: civitas, Cic. (2) *without substance*: Verg., Ov.
   TRANSF., in abstr. sense, *vain, hollow, idle*: contentiones, Cic.; spes, Cic., Verg.; minae, Hor.; ingenia, Liv.; with genit., *empty of*: inanissima prudentiae, Cic.; with abl.: Cic. L.; n. as subst. **ĭnāne** -is, *vanity, emptiness*: Hor.; plur.: inania, Hor., Tac.
   ¶ Adv. **ĭnānĭtěr**, *emptily, vainly, uselessly*: Cic., Hor., Ov.

ĭnānĭtās -ātis, f. (inanis), *emptiness, empty space*: Cic. TRANSF., *uselessness*: Cic.

¹ĭnărātus -a -um (in/aro), *unploughed, fallow*: Verg., Hor.

²ĭnărātus, partic. from inaro; q.v.

ĭnardesco -ardescĕre -arsi, *to catch fire, burn, glow*. LIT., nubes inardescit solis radiis, Verg.; Hor. TRANSF., of passions: amor specie praesentis inarsit, Ov.; Tac.

ĭnāresco -ārescĕre -ārŭi, *to become dry*: vi solis, Tac. TRANSF., liberalitas, Plin. L.

ĭnāro -are, *to plough in*: Cato, Plin.

ĭnassuētus=inadsuetus; q.v.

ĭnattĕnŭātus (in/attenuo), *undiminished, unimpaired*: fames, *unappeased*, Ov.

ĭnaudax -ācis, *timid, fearful*: Hor.

ĭnaudĭo -ire, *to hear*; particularly, *to hear as a secret*: aliquid de; de aliqua re, Pl., Cic. L.

¹ĭnaudītus -a -um (in/audio). (1) *unheard*; esp. of persons accused, *without a hearing* (before a judge): aliquem inauditum et indefensum damnare, Tac.; Suet.
   (2) *unheard of, unusual*: agger inauditus, Caes.; nomen est, non dico inusitatum, verum etiam inauditum, Cic.

²ĭnaudītus -a -um, partic. from inaudio; q.v.

ĭnauguro -are. (1) intransit., *to take the auguries*: Palatium Romulus, Remus Aventinum ad inaugurandum templa capiunt, Liv.; with indir. quest.: inaugura fierine possit, quod nunc ego mente concipio, Liv. (2) transit., *to consecrate, install, inaugurate*: templum, Cic.; flaminem, Cic.; Liv.
   ¶ Abl. absol. from partic. inauguratus, as adv. **ĭnaugŭrāto**, *after taking the auguries*: Liv.

ĭnaures -ium, f. (in/auris), *earrings*: Pl.

ĭnauro -are, *to gild, cover with gold*. TRANSF., *to gild, enrich*: Cic. L., Hor.
   ¶ Hence partic. **ĭnaurātus** -a -um, *gilt*: statua, Cic.; vestis, *gold-worked*, Ov.

ĭnauspĭcātus -a -um (in/auspicor), *without auspices*: lex, *adopted without auspices*, Liv. TRANSF., *unlucky, inauspicious*: Plin.
   ¶ Abl. absol. as adv. **ĭnauspĭcāto**, *without consulting the auspices*: Cic.

ĭnausus -a -um (in/audeo), *not dared, not*

attempted: ne quid inausum aut intractatum scelerisve dolive fuisset, Verg.; quid inausum vobis? Tac.

incaedŭus -a -um (in/caedo), *not cut, unfelled*: lucus, Ov.

incălesco -călescĕre -călŭi, *to glow, become warm*. LIT., of things: incalescente sole, Liv.; of persons: vino, Liv. TRANSF., *to grow passionate*: vidit et incaluit pelagi deus, Ov.; Tac.

incalfăcĭo -făcĕre, *to heat, warm*: Ov.

incallĭdus -a -um, *not clever, ingenuous*: servus non incallidus, Cic.; Tac.
   ¶ Adv. **incallĭdē**, *unskilfully*: Cic.

incandesco -candescĕre -candŭi, *to begin to whiten*, esp. with *heat*: incandescit eundo (plumbum), Ov.; Verg.

incānesco -cānescĕre -cānŭi, *to become grey*: ornusque incanuit albo flore piri, Verg.

incanto -are, *to enchant*; partic.: incantatus, *enchanted*: vincula, Hor.

incānus -a -um, *quite grey*: menta, Verg.; Pl.

incassum, adv. (*see* cassus), *in vain*: Verg.

incastīgātus -a -um (in/castigo), *unchastised*: Hor.

incautus -a -um, adj. (with compar.). (1) *incautious, careless, unwary*: homo incautus et rusticus, Cic.; with ab and the abl.: incautus a fraude, Liv.; with genit.: futuri, Hor. (2) *not guarded against, unforeseen*: scelus, Lucr. (3) *unguarded*: repente incautos agros invasit, Sall.; iter hostibus incautum, Tac.
   ¶ Adv. (with compar.) **incautē** (in sense (1)), *incautiously, carelessly*: incaute et stulte, Cic. L.; Caes., Liv.

incēdo -cēdĕre -cessi -cessum, *to walk, march, step*.
   LIT., pedes, *on foot*, Liv.; molliter, *with a light step*, Ov.; quācumque incederet, Cic.; esp. of dignified movement: divum incedo regina, Verg.; as milit. t. t., *to march, advance*: usque ad portas, Liv.; Sall., Tac.; with acc.: locos, Tac.
   TRANSF., *to advance, proceed, come on*: postquam tenebrae incedebant, Liv.; incessit in ea castra vis morbi, Liv.; occultus rumor incedebat (with acc. and infin.), Tac.; with dat. of person, *to come over*: exercitui dolor, Caes.; gravis cura patribus, Liv.; with acc. of person: timor patres, Liv.; aliquem valetudo adversa incessit, Tac.

incĕlĕbrātus -a -um (in/celebro), *not spread abroad*: Tac.

incēnātus -a -um (in/ceno), *without dinner, not having dined*: Pl.

incendĭārĭus -a -um (incendium), *fire-raising, incendiary*; m. as subst. **incendĭārĭus** -i, *an incendiary*: Tac., Suet.

incendĭum -i, n. (incendo), *a conflagration, fire*.
   LIT., incendium facere, excitare, restinguere, Cic.; conflare, Liv.; meton., *torch, firebrand*: incendia poscit, Verg.
   TRANSF., (1) *fire, glow, heat* of passions: cupiditatum, Cic.; Pl., Ov. (2) *destruction, ruin*: civitatis, Cic.; Liv.

incendo -cendĕre -cendi -censum (in/*cando), *to kindle, set fire to, burn*.
   LIT., tus et odores, Cic.; lychnos, Verg.; urbem, *to set on fire*, Cic., Liv.; altaria, *to kindle fire upon*, Verg.

TRANSF., (**1**) *to make bright, to illumine*:
solis incensa radiis luna, Cic.; Verg. (**2**) *to
fire with passion, excite, incense*: animos
iudicum in aliquem, Cic.; desine me incendere querelis, Verg.; incendi amore,
desiderio, Cic.; incensus irā, Cic.; of feelings,
to arouse: cupiditatem, odia, Cic.; luctūs,
Verg. (**3**) *to destroy*: genus, Pl.

incensĭo -ōnis, f. (incendo), *a burning*: Cic.

incensus -a -um (in/censeo), *not enrolled by
the censor, unassessed*: Cic., Liv.

incensus, partic. from incendo; q.v.

inceptĭo -ōnis, f. (incipio). (**1**) *a beginning*:
tam praeclari operis, Cic. (**2**) *an enterprise*:
Ter.

incepto -are (freq. of incipio). (**1**) *to begin*: Pl.
(**2**) *to attempt, undertake*: Pl., Ter.

inceptor -ōris, m. (incipio), *a beginner*: Ter.

inceptum -i, n. of partic. of incipio; q.v.

incerno -cernĕre -crēvi -crētum, *to sift upon*:
piper album cum sale nigro incretum, Hor.

incēro -are, *to cover with wax*: genua deorum,
perhaps *to cover with votive wax tablets*, Juv.

incertō, n. abl. of incertus; q.v.

incerto -are (incertus), *to make uncertain* or
doubtful: Pl.

incertus -a -um (in/certus), adj. (with compar.
and superl.), *uncertain, doubtful, not sure.*

(**1**) as to fact: **a**, act., of persons, *not knowing, doubting*: suspensam et incertam plebem,
Cic.; with indir. quest.: ubi esses, Cic. L.;
quo fata ferant, Verg.; with genit.: salutis,
Ov.: **b**, pass., of things, *not known, obscure*:
spes, Ter., Cic.; rumores, Caes.; casus, Cic.;
responsum, Liv.; luna, Verg.; with indir.
quest.: incerti socii an hostes essent, Liv.;
Cic., Tac.; n. as subst. **incertum**, *uncertainty*:
ad (*or* in) incertum revocare, *to make uncertain*, Cic.; in incerto habere, Sall.; plur.:
incerta belli, *the uncertainties of war*, Liv.

(**2**) as to intended action, *undecided*: **a**, of
persons, *hesitating, irresolute*; with indir.
quest.: quid dicam incertus sum, Ter.; Sall.,
Hor.: **b**, of things: incertumst abeam an
maneam, Pl.; incertam securim, *not surely
aimed*, Verg.

incesso -cessĕre -cessīvi (freq. of incedo), *to
attack, assail*. LIT., aliquem iaculis saxisque,
Liv.; Ov. TRANSF., verbally: reges dictis
protervis, Ov.; aliquem criminibus, Tac.

incessus -ūs, m. (incedo). (**1**) *a march, walk*:
a, *manner of walking, gait*: incessus citus
modo, modo tardus, Sall.; et vera incessu
patuit dea, Verg.; Cic.: **b**, *a hostile attack,
assault*: primo incessu solvit obsidium, Tac.
(**2**) *entrance, approach*: alios incessus hostis
claudere, Tac.

incesto -are (incestus). (**1**) *to defile, pollute*:
classem funere, Verg. (**2**) *to dishonour*:
puellam, Pl.; Verg.

¹incestus -a -um (in/castus), *impure, defiled.*
(**1**) ceremonially: Hor., Liv., Tac.
(**2**) morally, *sinful*: incesto addidit integrum,
Hor.; esp.: os, Cic.; manus, Liv.; *unchaste*:
iudex (of Paris), Hor.; flagitium, Cic.;
amores, Hor., Tac.; n. as subst. **incestum**
-i, *unchastity, incest*: incestum facere, Cic.;
Liv.
¶ Adv. **inceste**, *impurely, sinfully*: Cic.

²incestus -ūs, m. (¹incestus), *unchastity, incest*:
Cic., Liv.

inchŏo, see incoho.

---

¹incĭdo -cĭdĕre -cĭdi -cāsum (in/cado), *to fall
in* or *on.*

LIT., of physical movement; in gen.: in
foveam, Cic.; in insidias, Cic.; Lucr., Verg.;
with dat.; ruinae capitibus nostris, Liv.; arae,
Ov.; esp. of personal encounters: cohortes in
agmen Caesaris, *fall in with*, Caes.; in hostem,
to fall upon, Liv.; castris, *to assail*, Liv.

TRANSF., not physically. (**1**) of persons:
in morbum, Cic. L., Liv.; in aes alienum,
to run into debt, Cic.; in eorum mentionem,
Cic., Tac.; in Diodorum, *to fall in with the
opinion of*, Cic. (**2**) of abstr. things; *to
occur, happen, 'crop up'*: aliquid in mentem,
Cic.; mentio, Liv.; terror exercitui, Caes.;
incidunt saepe tempora cum, Cic.; si qua
clades incidisset, Liv.; forte ita inciderat ne,
Liv.; in hunc diem incidunt mysteria, Cic.

²incīdo -cīdĕre -cīdi -cīsum (in/caedo).

LIT., in gen., *to cut into, cut open*: in
arbores, Caes.; pulmo incisus, Cic. Esp. (**1**)
to inscribe, engrave an inscription: leges in
aes, Liv.; notum est carmen incisum in
sepulcro, Cic. (**2**) *to make by cutting*: faces,
Verg. (**3**) *to cut through*: linum, Cic.; funem,
Verg.

TRANSF., *to cut short, bring to an end,
break off*: poema quod institueram, Cic.;
sermonem, Liv.; spem omnem, Liv.

¶ Hence, from partic. incīsus -a -um,
n. subst. **incīsum** -i=incisio; q.v.; adv.
incīsē=incisim; q.v.

incĭens -entis (connected with ἔγκυος),
pregnant, with young: Varr., Plin.

incīle -is, n. (perhaps from ²incido), *a ditch,
trench*: tamquam in quodam incili omnia
adhaeserunt, ap. Cic. L.

incĭlo -are, *to blame, scold, rebuke*: Lucr.

incingo -cingĕre -cinxi -cinctum, *to surround,
engird*: incinctus cinctu Gabino, Liv.;
pellibus, Verg. TRANSF., urbes moenibus,
Ov.

incĭno -ĕre (in/cano), *to sing*: Prop.

incĭpĭo -cĭpĕre -cēpi -ceptum (in/capio),
mainly used in pres., fut. and imperf. tenses
and in perf. partic. (cf. coepi), *to take in
hand, begin, commence*. (**1**) transit.: facinus,
Pl., Sall.; opus, pugnam, Liv.; with infin.:
bella gerere, Pl., Caes., Ov.; in pass.:
Sall., Verg., Tac.; absol.: ut incipiendi ratio
fieret, Cic. Sometimes *to begin to speak*: sic
statim rex incipit, Sall.; Cic., Ov. (**2**)
intransit., *to commence*: tum incipere ver
arbitrabatur, Cic.; Pl., Verg., Liv.

¶ N. of perf. partic. as subst. **inceptum** -i.
(**1**) *a beginning*: Hor. (**2**) *an attempt, enterprise*: inceptum perficere, incepta patrare,
Sall.; incepto desistere, Verg.; absistere,
Liv.; Cic.

incĭpisso -ĕre (incipio), *to begin*: Pl.

incīsim, adv. (²incido), *in short clauses*: Cic.;
cf. incise, sub ²incido.

incīsĭo -ōnis, f. (²incīdo), *a division* or *clause
of a sentence*: Cic.; cf. incisum, sub ²incido.

incītāmentum -i, n. (incito), *an inducement,
incentive*: incitamentum periculorum et
laborum, Cic.; Tac.

incītātĭo -ōnis, f. (incito). (**1**) act., *an inciting,
instigating, exciting*: languentis populi, Cic.
(**2**) pass., *violent motion*: sol tantā incitatione
fertur, Cic. TRANSF., *excitement, vehemence*:
animi, Caes.; mentis, Cic.

incĭto -are, *to put into rapid motion, urge on, hasten.*
Lit., equos, Caes.; prov.: incitare currentem, *to spur the willing horse,* Cic.; reflex. se incitare, or middle incitari, *to quicken one's pace, to hasten*: alii ex castris se incitant, Caes.
Transf., (**1**) *to excite, rouse, spur*: animos, ingenium, Cic.; Caesarem ad id bellum, Caes. (**2**) *to inspire*: terrae vis Pythiam incitabat, Cic. (**3**) *to incite against, make hostile, stir up*: aliquem in aliquem, Cic. (**4**) *to increase*: amnis incitatus pluviis, Liv.; eloquendi celeritatem, Cic.
¶ Hence partic. (with compar. and superl.), *hastened*; hence **incĭtātus** -a -um, *rapid, vehement*: equo incitato, *at full gallop*, Caes., Cic., Liv. Transf., cursus in oratione incitatior, Cic.
¶ Compar. adv. **incĭtātĭus**, *more violently*; in speech: fluere, Cic.

¹**incĭtus** -a -um (in/cieo), *in rapid motion*: Lucr., Verg.

²**incĭtus** -a -um (in/cieo), *unmoved,* of a piece in the game of draughts: Pl.

inclāmĭto -are (freq. of inclamo), *to call out against, scold*: Pl.

inclāmo -are, *to call upon loudly.* In gen.: aliquem nomine, Liv.; comitem suum semet et saepius, Cic.; with dat.: Albanus exercitus inclamat Curiatiis, uti opem ferant fratri, Liv. Esp. *to call out against, scold*: aliquem, Pl.; Hor., Liv.

inclāresco -clārescĕre -clārŭi, *to become famous*: Tac.

inclēmens -entis, *unmerciful, harsh, rough*: dictator, Liv.; inclementiori verbo appellare, Liv.
¶ Adv. (with compar.) **inclēmentĕr**, *harshly*: inclementius invehi in aliquem, Liv.; Pl., Ter.

inclēmentĭa -ae, f. (inclemens), *unmercifulness, harshness*: divum, Verg.

inclīnātĭo -ōnis, f. (inclino), *a leaning, bending, inclination.* Lit., corporis, Cic.; *change of the voice*: Cic. Transf., (**1**) *a tendency, inclination*: ad meliorem spem, Cic. (**2**) *good-will, liking*: voluntatis, Cic.; in hos, Tac. (**3**) *change, alteration*: temporum, Cic. (**4**) *inflexion*: vocis, Cic.

inclīnātus -a -um, partic. from inclino; q.v.

inclīno -are (in/*clino; cf. κλίνω).
(**1**) transit., *to bend, incline.* Lit., genua harenis, Ov.; mālos, *the masts*, Liv.; milit., in pass., *to fall back, waver*: acies inclinatur, Liv., Tac. Transf., without physical movement, *to incline, turn*: omnem culpam in aliquem, Cic.; haec animum inclinant ut credam, *induce me to believe*, Liv.; se ad Stoicos, Cic.; pass.: inclinari timore, Cic.; fraus rem inclinavit, *gave a decisive turn to*, Liv.; sometimes *to change for the worse*: omnia simul inclinante fortunā, Liv.
(**2**) intransit., *to take a turn, verge, incline.* Lit., meridies, Hor.; sol, Juv.; milit. t. t., *to waver, yield*: acies inclinat, Liv.; Tac. Transf., without physical movement: sententia senatūs inclinat ad pacem, Cic.; with ut and the subj.: Liv.; sometimes *to change*: fortuna belli, Liv.
¶ Hence partic. (with compar.) **inclīnātus** -a -um. (**1**) *inclined, prone*: ad pacem, Tac.;

Liv. (**2**) *sinking*: fortuna, Cic. L.; domus, Verg. (**3**) of the voice, *low, deep*: Cic.

inclūdo -clūdĕre -clūsi -clūsum (in/claudo), *to shut in, enclose.* Lit., in gen.: parietibus deos, Cic.; aliquid domi, Cic.; armatos in cella Concordiae, Cic.; emblemata in scaphis aureis, Cic.; suras auro, Verg.; esp. *to block, obstruct*: viam, Cic.; Verg., Liv. Transf., in gen.: in huius me consilii societatem, Cic.; esp. *to confine*: verba versu, Cic.; Liv.

inclūsĭo -ōnis, f. (includo), *a shutting up, confinement*: Cic.

inclŭtus, inclĭtus -a -um (in/clueo; cf. κλυτός), *celebrated, famous, renowned*: populi regesque, Liv.; leges Solonis, Liv.; Lucr., Verg.

¹**incoctus** -a -um (in/coquo), *uncooked, raw*: Pl.

²**incoctus** -a -um, partic. from incoquo; q.v.

incŏgĭtābĭlis -e, *thoughtless, inconsiderate*: Pl.

incŏgĭtans -antis, *inconsiderate*: Ter.

incŏgĭtantĭa -ae, f. (incogitans), *thoughtlessness*: Pl.

incŏgĭtātus -a -um (in/cogito). (**1**) pass., *unstudied*: Sen. (**2**) act., *inconsiderate*: Pl.

incŏgĭto -are, *to contrive, plan*: fraudem socio, Hor.

incognĭtus -a -um (in/cognosco). (**1**) *unexamined*: incognitā re, Cic.. (**2**) *unknown*: incognita pro cognitis habeamus, Cic.; with dat. of person: Caes., Ov. (**3**) *unrecognized, so unclaimed*: Liv.

incŏho -are, *to take in hand, begin*: signum, Cic.; templum, Liv.; aras, Verg.; in discussion, *to begin to treat of*: philosophiam multis locis, Cic.; incohante Caesare de, etc., Tac.
¶ Hence perf. partic. **incŏhātus** -a -um, *only begun, not finished, incomplete*: cognitio, officium, Cic.; Pl.

incŏla -ae, c. (incolo), *an inhabitant.* (**1**) in gen., of persons: Pythagorei incolae paene nostri, *our fellow-countrymen*, Cic.; with genit.: mundi, Cic.; poet.: incola turba, *natives*, Ov.; of animals: aquarum incolae, Cic.; of winds, *native*: aquilones, Hor. (**2**) = μέτοικος, *a foreign resident without full civic rights*: Cic., Liv.

incŏlo -cŏlĕre -cŏlŭi. Transit., *to inhabit, dwell in*: eas urbes, Cic.; of animals: Liv. Intransit., *to dwell*: inter mare Alpesque, Liv.; Pl., Caes.

incŏlŭmis -e, *safe after danger, uninjured, safe and sound*: cives, Cic.; naves, Caes.; with ab and the abl.: incolumis a calamitate, Cic.

incŏlŭmĭtās -ātis, f. (incolumis), *safety, preservation*: mundi, Cic.; incolumitatem deditis polliceri, Caes.

incŏmĭtātus -a -um (in/comitor), *unaccompanied, without retinue, alone*: Verg., Ov.

incommendātus -a -um, *not entrusted*; hence *without protector*: Ov.

incommŏdĭtās -ātis, f. (incommodus), *inconvenience, unsuitableness, disadvantage*: incommoditas alienati, illius animi, Cic. L.; temporis, *unseasonableness*, Liv.; Ter.

incommŏdo -are (incommodus), *to be unpleasant, troublesome*; with dat.: alicui nihil, Cic.; Ter.

incommŏdus -a -um, adj. (with superl.), *inconvenient, troublesome, disagreeable.* (**1**) of things: valetudo, *ill-health*, Cic.; vox, Liv.

(2) of persons, *troublesome, annoying*; with dat.: Pl., Cic.

¶ N. as subst. **incommŏdum** -i, *inconvenience, disadvantage, misfortune*: incommodo tuo, *to your disadvantage*, Cic. L.; incommodo adfici, Cic.; alicui incommodum ferre, Cic.; capere, accipere, Cic.; valetudinis, Cic. L.; plur.: Caes., Cic.

¶ Adv. (with compar. and superl.) **incommŏdē**, *inconveniently, unseasonably*: accidit, Caes.; venire, Cic. L.; incommodissime navigare, Cic. L.

incommūtābĭlis -e, *unchangeable*: reipublicae status, Cic.

incompărābĭlis -e, *incomparable*: Plin., Quint.

incompertus -a -um (in/comperio), *unknown*: inter cetera vetustate incomperta, Liv.

incompŏsĭtus -a -um (in/compono), *not in order, disorderly, irregular*: agmen, Liv.; motus, Verg. TRANSF., of style: nempe incomposito dixi pede currere versus Lucili, Hor.; Quint.

¶ Adv. **incompŏsĭtē**, *in disorder*: hostis negligenter et incomposite veniens, Liv.; of style: Quint.

incomprĕhensĭbĭlis -e, *that cannot be grasped*. (1) metaph. from wrestling, of a *slippery* opponent: Plin. L. (2) mentally, *incomprehensible*: Quint.

incomptus -a -um, *unkempt, untrimmed*. LIT., of the hair: capilli, Hor., Ov.; so: homo, Tac. TRANSF., of style, etc., *rude, rough*: oratio, Cic.; Liv.; versus, Verg.

inconcessus -a -um (in/concedo), *not allowed, forbidden*: hymenaei, Verg.; Ov.

inconcĭlĭo -are, *to deceive*: Pl.; sometimes *to gain by deceit*: Pl.

inconcinnĭtās -atis, f. (inconcinnus), *absurdity*: Suet.

inconcinnus -a -um, *awkward, inelegant, absurd*: qui in aliquo genere inconcinnus et stultus est, Cic.; Hor.

inconcussus -a -um, *unshaken, firm*: sidera, Luc.; pax, Tac.

incondĭtus -a -um (in/condo). (1) *not arranged, disorderly, confused*: acies, Liv.; Tac. TRANSF., ius civile, Liv.; genus dicendi, *rough*, Cic.

¶ Adv. **incondĭtē**, *confusedly*: versus Graecos dicere, Cic.

incongrŭens -entis, *not agreeing, inconsistent*: Plin. L.

inconsĭdĕrātus -a -um. (1) act., *thoughtless, inconsiderate*: Cic. (2) pass., *unadvised, reckless*: cupiditas, Cic. Adv. **inconsĭdĕrātē**, *without consideration*: Cic.

inconsōlābĭlis -e, *inconsolable*. TRANSF., vulnus, *incurable*, Ov.

inconstans -stantis, adj. (with compar.), *changeable, inconsistent*: mihi ridicule es visus esse inconstans, Cic.

¶ Adv. (with superl.) **inconstantĕr**, *inconsistently, capriciously*: loqui, Cic.; Liv.

inconstantĭa -ae, f. (inconstans), *changeableness, inconsistency*: mentis, Cic.

inconsultus -a -um (in/consulo). (1) pass., *not consulted*: inconsulto senatu, Liv. (2) act., *without asking advice, unadvised*: inconsulti adeunt, Verg.; hence *inconsiderate, imprudent, indiscreet*: homo inconsultus et temerarius, Cic.; ratio, Cic.; Hor., Liv.

¶ Adv. (with compar.) **inconsultē**, *without advice, indiscreetly*: inconsulte ac temere, Cic.; Caes., Liv.

inconsultū, abl. sing. from inconsultus, m. (in/consulo): meo, *without asking my advice*, Pl.

inconsumptus -a -um, *unconsumed, undiminished*: Ov.; hence *unfailing*: Ov.

incontāmĭnātus -a -um (in/contamino), *unpolluted*: Liv.

incontentus -a -um (in/contendo), *not stretched*: fides, *untuned*, Cic.

incontĭnens -entis, *incontinent*: homo, Pl.; Tityos, Hor.; manus, Hor.

¶ Adv. **incontĭnentĕr**, *incontinently*: nihil incontinenter facere, Cic.

incontĭnentĭa -ae, f. (incontinens), *incontinence*: Cic.

inconvĕnĭens -entis, *not suiting, dissimilar*: Phaedr.

incŏquo -cŏquĕre -coxi -coctum, *to boil in* or *with*: radices Baccho, Verg.; Hor. TRANSF., *to dye*: vellera Tyrios incocta rubores, Verg.

incorpŏrālis -e (in/corpus), *bodiless*: Quint.

incorrectus -a -um, *unamended, unimproved*: Ov.

incorruptus -a -um, adj. (with superl.), *not corrupted, untainted*. LIT., sanguis, Cic.; templa, Liv.; incorruptā sanitate esse, Cic. TRANSF., in gen., *incorrupt, unspoilt, not tampered with, unimpaired*: testis, Cic.; virgo, *pure*, Cic.; iudicium, *upright*, Liv.; integritas Latini sermonis, Cic.; fides, Hor., Tac.

¶ Adv. (with compar.) **incorruptē**, *incorruptly, justly*: iudicare, Cic.

incrēbresco -crēbrescĕre -crēbrŭi and **increbesco** -crēbescĕre -crēbŭi, *to become frequent, strong, prevalent*; *to increase, prevail*: ventus, Cic.; consuetudo, Cic.; proverbio, *to grow into a proverb*, Liv.

incrēdĭbĭlis -e, *not to be believed, incredible*: memoratu, Sall.; fides, Cic.; vis ingenii, Cic.; Caes.

¶ Adv. **incrēdĭbĭlĭtĕr**, *incredibly, extraordinarily*: delectari, Cic.; pertimescere, Cic.

incrēdŭlus -a -um, *incredulous*: Hor.

incrēmentum -i, n. (incresco), *growth, increase*.
   LIT., *of plants* or *animals*: vitium, Cic.
   TRANSF., (1) in gen.: urbis, multitudinis, Liv. (2) meton., *that from* or *by which anything grows, the makings*: dentes populi incrementa futuri, Ov. (3) meton., *offspring*: Iovis, Verg.

incrĕpĭto -are (freq. of increpo). (1) *to call loudly to anyone*: tum Bitiae dedit increpitans, Verg. (2) *to reproach, chide*: increpitare Belgas qui (with subj.), Caes.; pertinaciam praetoris, Liv.; aestatem seram, Verg.

incrĕpo -are -ŭi (-āvi) -ĭtum (-ātum), *to rustle, rattle, make a noise*.
   LIT., (1) intransit.: discus increpuit, Cic., Verg. (2) with internal acc.: tuba terribilem sonitum, Verg. (3) *to cause to sound*: Iuppiter atras nubes, Ov.; Hor.
   TRANSF., (1) intransit., *to be noised abroad*: simulatque increpuit suspicio tumultūs, Cic.; quicquid increpuerit, Catilinam timeri, Cic. (2) *to speak angrily*: ad contionem, Liv.; with internal acc.: haec in regem, Liv.; with acc. and infin.: simul increpante

qui vulneraverat habere quaestorem, Liv.;
with indir. quest.: cum undique duces, victisne
cessuri essent, increparent, Liv. (**3**) with
person as object, *to chide, reproach, rebuke,
reprove*: filium, Pl.; socios, Verg.; aliquem
graviter quod, Liv.; morantes aeris rauci
canor increpat, Verg. (**4**) with abstr. object:
perfidiam, Cic.; mollitiem, Liv.

incresco -crescĕre -crēvi. (**1**) *to grow in* or
on: squamae cuti increscunt, Ov.; animis dis-
cordibus irae, Verg. (**2**) in gen., *to grow*:
increscit certamen, Liv.

incrētus -a -um, partic. from incerno; q.v.

incrŭentātus -a -um (in/cruento), *not stained
with blood*: Ov.

incrŭentus -a -um, *bloodless*: proelium,
victoria, Liv.; exercitus, *that has lost no
soldiers*, Sall., Tac.

incrusto -are, *to cover with a rind, encrust*: vas
sincerum, *to bedaub*, Hor.

incŭbātĭo -ōnis, f. (incubo), *a sitting upon
eggs, incubation*: Plin.

incŭbĭto -are (freq. of incubo), *to lie in* or *on*:
Pl.

incŭbo -are -ŭi -ĭtum, *to lie in* or *on*; usually
with dat.
    Lɪᴛ., in gen.: stramentis, Hor.; caetris,
Liv.; nidis, Ov.; esp. *to pass the night in a
temple, hoping for a divine message* or *cure
of a disease*: in Pasiphaae fano, Cic.
    Tʀᴀɴsꜰ., (**1**) *to lie over*: ponto nox incubat
atra, Verg. (**2**) *to watch over jealously*:
pecuniae, Cic.; auro, Verg.; Liv. (**3**) *to hang
over, lie heavily upon*: Italiae Hannibal,
Hor. (**4**) *to dwell in*: Erymantho, Ov.

inculco -are (in/calco), *to trample in*; hence (**1**)
to foist in, mix in: Graeca verba, Cic. (**2**) *to
force upon, to impress upon*: se auribus nostris,
Cic.; tradatur vel etiam inculcetur, Cic.;
with acc. and infin.: Cic.

inculpātus -a -um (in/culpo), *unblamed,
blameless*: Cic.

¹incultus -a -um, adj. (with compar.), *uncultivated, untilled*.
    Lɪᴛ., ager, Cic.; Liv.; n. pl. as subst.
inculta -orum, *wastes, deserts*: Verg.; Liv.
    Tʀᴀɴsꜰ., (**1**) of dress, etc., *neglected,
disorderly, untidy*: comae, Ov.; homines
intonsi et inculti, Liv. (**2**) in gen., *unpolished,
unrefined, rude*: homo, *without education*,
Sall.; inculta atque rusticana parsimonia,
Hor.; versus, *rough, unpolished*, Hor.
    ¶ Adv. (with compar.: Sall.) **incultē**,
without refinement, roughly, rudely: vivere,
Cic.; dicere, Cic.

²incultus -ūs, m. *neglect, want of cultivation*:
suos honores desertos per incultum et
neglegentiam, Liv.; Sall.

incumbo -cumbĕre -cŭbŭi -cŭbĭtum, *to lie
upon, lean upon*.
    Lɪᴛ., usually with dat., or in and acc.: toro,
Verg.; cumulatis in aqua sarcinis insuper,
Liv.; in gladium, Cic.; laurus incumbens
arae, *leaning over, overhanging*, Verg.; esp.
to put weight on, throw oneself upon: suo et
armorum pondere in hostem, Liv.; tempestas
incubuit silvis, Verg.; remis, Verg.
    Tʀᴀɴsꜰ., (**1**) *to apply oneself to* a thing,
concentrate upon, 'get down to': in bellum,
Caes.; in studium, Cic.; ad laudem, Cic.;
ad ulciscendas iniurias, Cic.; novae cogitationi, Tac.; with infin.: Verg., Tac.;

with ut and subj.: Liv. (**2**) *to incline to,
favour, further* a cause or movement: eodem
incumbunt municipia, Cic.; fato urguenti,
Verg.

incūnābŭla -ōrum, n. pl. *swaddling-clothes*:
Pl. Tʀᴀɴsꜰ., (**1**) *infancy*: Liv., Ov. (**2**) *birth-
place*: incunabula nostra, ap. Cic. L.; Ov.
(**3**) in gen., *source, origin*: incunabula nostrae
veteris puerilisque doctrinae, Cic.; Caes.

incūrātus -a -um, *uncared-for, unhealed*:
ulcera, Hor.

incūrĭa -ae, f. (in/cura), *carelessness, neglect,
negligence*: rei necessariae, Cic.; Hor., Tac.

incūrĭōsus -a -um. (**1**) act., *careless, negligent*;
with genit.: famae, Tac.; with abl.: serendis
frugibus, Tac. (**2**) pass., *neglected*: finis, Tac.
    ¶ Adv. (with compar.) **incūrĭōse**, *negli-
gently, carelessly*: agere, Liv.

incurro -currĕre -curri (-cŭcurri) -cursum, *to
run into*.
    Lɪᴛ., in gen.: incurrere in columnas,
prov., *to run one's head against a stone wall*,
Cic. As milit. t. t. (**1**) *to assail, attack*: in
Romanos, Liv.; with dat.: levi armaturae
hostium, Liv.; with acc.: hostium latus, Liv.
(**2**) *to make a raid into*: in Macedoniam, Liv.
    Tʀᴀɴsꜰ., (**1**) *to attack* with words, *inveigh
against*: in tribunos militares, Liv. (**2**) *to
come upon* unintentionally, *meet, fall in with*:
incidere in aliquem, Cic.; in morbos, Cic.;
in odia hominum, Cic.; in oculos, *to meet
the eye*, Cic. L.; incurrunt tempora, *occur*,
Cic.; casus qui in sapientem potest incidere;
nec ulla est disputatio, in quam non aliquis
locus incurrat, Cic. (**3**) in space, *to extend
into*: privati agri, qui in publicum Cumanum
incurrebant, Cic. (**4**) in time, *to coincide
with*: Cic. L.

incursĭo -ōnis, f. (incurro), *a running against,
clash, onset*: atomorum, *collision*, Cic. Esp.
as milit. t. t. (**1**) *an attack*: incursio atque
impetus armatorum, Cic. (**2**) *a raid, invasion*:
incursionem facere in fines Romanos, Liv.;
Caes.; esp.: seditionis, Cic.

incursĭto -are (freq. of incurso), *to rush upon,
clash against*: Sen.

incurso -are (freq. of incurro), *to run against,
strike against, attack*. Lɪᴛ., with dat.:
rupibus, Ov.; esp. milit.: in agmen Romanum, Liv.; with acc.: aciem agros Romanos,
Liv. Tʀᴀɴsꜰ., incursabat in te dolor meus,
Cic. L.

incursus -ūs, m. (incurro), *a running against,
an attack, assault*. Lɪᴛ., of things: aquarum,
Ov.; of persons and animals, *hostile attack*:
luporum, Verg.; esp. as milit. t. t.: aditus
atque incursus ad defendendum, Caes.
Tʀᴀɴsꜰ., incursus animus varios habet,
efforts, impulses, Ov.

incurvo -are (incurvus), *to bend, curve, make
crooked*: bacillum, Cic.; arcum, Verg.;
membra incurvata dolore, Ov.

incurvus -a -um, *bent, curved, crooked*:
bacillum, Cic.; Verg., Ov.

incūs -cūdis, f. (in/cudo), *an anvil*: Cic., Verg.,
Hor., Tac.; prov.: uno opere eandem incu-
dem noctem diemque tundere, *to be always
hammering at the same thing*, Cic.

incūsātĭo -ōnis, f. (incuso), *blame, reproach,
accusation*: Cic.

incūso -are (in/causa), *to accuse, blame, find
fault with* a person or thing: eos incusavit

quod, Caes.; aliquem luxūs et superbiae, Tac.; quietem Africani nostri somniantis, Cic.; with acc. and infin.: Liv.

incussū, abl. sing. from incussus, m. (incutio), *by a clash*: armorum, Tac.

incustōdītus -a -um (in/custodio). (**1**) pass., *unwatched, unguarded*: ovile, Ov.; urbs, Tac.; amor, *unconcealed*, Tac. (**2**) act., *incautious, imprudent*: Plin. L.

incūsus -a -um (in/cudo), *forged, fabricated*: Verg.

incūtĭo -cŭtĕre -cussi -cussum (in/quatio), *to strike, dash, beat against*. LIT., scipionem in caput alicuius, Liv.; tela saxaque, *to hurl*, Tac. TRANSF., *to strike into, inspire with*: terrorem alicui, Cic.; religionem animo, Liv.; desiderium urbis, Hor.; in pectus amorem, Lucr.

indāgātĭo -ōnis, f. (¹indago), *an investigation*: veri, Cic.

indāgātor -ōris, m. (¹indago), *an investigator, explorer*: Pl.

indāgātrix -trīcis, f. (indagator), *a female investigator*: philosophia indagatrix virtutis, Cic.

¹indāgo -are (ago), *to track down*, as hounds hunting: canis natus ad indagandum, Cic. TRANSF., *to search out, explore, investigate*: rem, Pl.; indicia, Cic.

²indāgo -ĭnis, f. (ago), *a surrounding and driving of game*, Scott's *tinchel* (Waverley): velut indagine dissipatos Samnites agere, Liv.; saltus indagine cingere, *with a cordon*, Verg. TRANSF., delatores in poenarum indagine inclusos, Plin.

indĕ, adv. (from is, with adverbial ending -de), *thence, from there*.
LIT., of place: non exeo inde ante vesperum, Cic.; hinc . . . inde . . ., *on this side . . . on that . . .*, Tac., Liv.
TRANSF., (**1**) of starting-point, cause, origin: inde (i.e., ex audacia) omnia scelera gignuntur, Cic.; of persons: quod inde oriundus erat, Liv. (**2**) of time: **a**, *then, thereupon*: Caes.: **b**, *from that time forth*: inde usque, Cic.; iam inde a principio, Liv.

indēbĭtus -a -um (in/debeo), *not owed, not due*: non indebita posco, Verg.; Ov.

indĕcens -centis, *unbecoming, unseemly, unsightly*: Quint., Mart. Adv. **indĕcentĕr**, *unbecomingly, indecently*: Mart.; compar.: Sen.; superl.: Quint.

indĕcĕo -ēre, *to be unbecoming to*; with acc.: Plin. L.

indēclīnābĭlis -e (in/declino), *unchangeable*: Sen.

indēclīnātus -a -um (in/declino), *unchanged, firm*: amicitia, Ov.

indĕcŏr -oris or **indĕcŏris** -e, *unbecoming, inglorious, shameful*: Verg.

indĕcŏro -are, *to disgrace, dishonour*: Hor.

indĕcŏrus -a -um, *unbecoming*. (**1**) of outward appearance, *unseemly, unsightly*: motus, Liv.; Tac. (**2**) morally, *indecorous, disgraceful*: si nihil malum, nisi quod turpe, inhonestum, indecorum, pravum, Cic.; indecorum est, with infin.: Cic.; Liv., Tac.
¶ Adv. **indĕcŏrē**, *unbecomingly, indecorously*: facere, Cic.; Tac.

indēfătīgābĭlis -e (in/defatigo), *untiring*: Sen.

indēfătīgātus -a -um (in/defatigo), *not tired*: Sen.

indēfensus -a -um (in/defendo), *undefended, unprotected*: Capua deserta indefensaque, Liv.; Tac.

indēfessus -a -um, *unwearied, indefatigable*: Verg., Ov., Tac.

indēflētus -a -um (in/defleo), *unwept*: Ov.

indēiectus -a -um (in/deicio), *not thrown down*: Ov.

indēlēbĭlis -e (in/deleo), *imperishable*: nomen, Cic.

indēlībātus -a -um (in/delibo), *uninjured, undiminished*: Ov.

indemnātus -a -um (in/damno), *uncondemned*: cives, Cic.; Liv.

indēplōrātus -a -um (in/deploro), *unwept, unlamented*: Ov.

indēprensus -a -um (in/deprendo), *undiscovered*: error, Verg.

indēsertus -a -um, *not forsaken*: Ov.

indēspectus -a -um (in/despicio), *unfathomable*: Luc.

indestrictus -a -um (in/destringo), *untouched, unhurt*: Ov.

indētonsus -a -um (in/detondeo), *unshorn*: Ov.

indēvītātus -a -um (in/devito), *unavoided*: telum, Ov.

index -dĭcis, m. (in/dico), *one that informs or indicates*.
LIT., (**1**) with or without digitus, *the forefinger*: Cic. L., Hor. (**2**) *an informer*: Cic., Tac., Juv.
TRANSF., of things, *that which informs*. (**1**) in gen., *a sign, token*: vox index stultitiae, Cic. (**2**) *a title, superscription*: libri, Cic.; on a statue: Liv. (**3**) *a touch-stone*: Ov.

Indi -ōrum, m. ('Ινδοί), *the inhabitants of India, the Indians*; sing. **Indus** -i, m. *an Indian*; transf., *an Ethiopian*: Verg. (**2**) *an elephant-driver, mahout*: Liv.
Adj. **Indus** -a -um ('Ινδός), *Indian*: dens, *ivory*, Ov.; conchae, *pearls*, Prop. Subst. **India** -ae, f. ('Ινδία), *India*. Adj. **Indĭcus** -a -um ('Ινδικός), *Indian*.

indĭcātĭo -ōnis, f. (¹indico), *a valuing or value*: Pl.

indĭcentĕ, abl. sing. of participle (in/dico), *not saying*: me indicente, *without my saying a word*, Ter., Liv.

indĭcĭum -i, n. (index).
(**1**) *information, disclosure, evidence*. LIT., coniurationis, Cic.; indicia exponere et edere, Cic.; profiteri, Sall.; offerre, Tac.= 'to turn Queen's evidence'. TRANSF., **a**, *permission to give evidence*: indicium postulare, Cic.: **b**, *a reward for giving evidence*: partem indicii accipere, Cic.
(**2**) *a mark, sign, token*: sceleris, Cic.; indicio esse, *to be a sign of, serve to show*, Nep.

¹indĭco -are (index), *to make known, betray, show, indicate*. In gen.: rem dominae, Cic.; dolorem lacrimis, Cic.; vultus indicat mores, Cic. Esp. (**1**) *to inform against, give evidence about*: se, Cic.; de coniuratione, Cic. (**2**) *to put a price on, value*: fundum alicui, Cic.

²indĭco -dīcĕre -dixi -dictum, *to make publicly known, announce, proclaim*: alicui bellum, *to declare war*, Cic.; comitia, Liv.; diem comitiis, Liv.; exercitum Aquileiam, *order to*, Liv.; tributum, Liv.; sibimet exsilium, Liv.; with ut and the subj.: Liv.

¹indictus -a -um (in/dico), *not said, unsaid*:

indictus

indoles

indictis carminibus nostris, *unsung*, Verg.; indictā causā, *without a hearing*, Cic., Liv.

²**indictus** -a -um, partic. from ²indico; q.v.

Indĭcus -a -um, *see* Indi.

indĭdem, adv. (inde/idem), *from the same place*, *from that very place*: indidemne Ameriā? Cic.; Liv. Transf., *from the same matter*: Cic.; Liv.

indifférens -entis (in/differo), *indifferent.* (1) ethically (=ἀδιάφορον), *neither good nor bad*: Cic., Sen. (2) in attitude: Suet.

¶ Adv. **indifférentĕr**: Quint., Suet.

indĭgĕna -ae (indu/geno), *native, born in* an area; as adj.: miles, Liv.; bos, Ov.; as subst., *a native*: ne maiores quidem eorum *indigenas*, sed *advenas* Italiae cultores, Liv.

indĭgens, *see* indigeo.

indĭgentĭa -ae, f. (indigeo). (1) *want, need*: Cic. (2) *insatiable desire*: Cic.

indĭgĕo -ēre -ŭi (indu=in/egeo). (1) *to want, need, stand in need of, require*; with genit.: alterius, Cic.; with abl.: iis rebus quae ad oppugnationem castrorum sunt usui, Caes.; Tac. (2) *to long for, desire*: auri, Cic.

¶ Hence partic. **indĭgens** -entis, *in need*; with genit.: Cic.; m. as subst., *a needy person*: Cic.

¹**indĭgĕs** -gĕtis, m. (indu=in/?ago), *native, indigenous*; of gods and heroes: Verg., Liv.

²**indĭgĕs** -is (indigeo), *needy*: Pac. ap. Cic.

indĭgestus -a -um (in/digero), *disordered, confused, unarranged*: chaos rudis indigestaque moles, Ov.

indignābundus -a -um (indignor), *filled with indignation*: Liv., Suet.

indignandus -a -um, from indignor; q.v.

indignans -antis, partic. from indignor; q.v.

indignātĭo -ōnis, f. (indignor), *indignation*: indignationem movere, Liv.; facit indignatio versum, Juv. Meton. (1) *the rhetorical exciting of indignation*: Cic. (2) *a cause of indignation*: Juv.

indignē, adv. from indignus; q.v.

indignĭtās -ātis, f. (indignus). (1) *unworthiness, vileness*: hominis, accusatoris, Cic.; rei, Caes. (2) *unworthy behaviour* or *treatment of others, indignity*: hominum insolentium, Cic.; omnes indignitates perferre, Caes. (3) *indignation at unworthy treatment*: Cic. L., Liv.

indignor -ari, dep. (indignus), *to consider unworthy, take as an indignity, be offended, indignant at*: aliquid, Cic.; casum amici, Verg.; of things: pontem indignatus Araxes, Verg.; foll. by quod: Caes., Verg.; by acc. and infin.: Caes.; by infin.: Lucr., Ov., Liv.

¶ Gerundive **indignandus** -a -um, *to be scorned*: Ov.

¶ Partic. **indignans** -antis, *impatient, offended*: Verg., Ov.

indignus -a -um, adj. (with compar. and superl.).

(1) of persons, *unworthy, not deserving*; with abl.: omni honore indignissimus, Cic.; with genit.: magnorum avorum, Verg.; with relat.: indigni erant qui impetrarent, *to obtain*, Cic.; with ut and the subj.: Liv.; with infin.: Hor.; with absol.: divitias quivis, quamvis indignus, habere potest, Cic.

(2) of things, *unworthy*; with abl.: vox populi R. maiestate indigna, Caes.; with infin.: fabula non indigna referri, Ov.; relatu,

Verg. Hence, absol., *unworthy, disgraceful, shameful*: facinus, Ter., Cic.; hoc uno sol non quidquam vidit indignius, Cic.; non indignum videtur memorare, *not inappropriate*, Sall.; indignum est a pari vinci aut superiore, *a disgrace*, Cic.

¶ Adv. (with superl.) **indignē.** (1) *unworthily, dishonourably, undeservedly*: indignissime cervices frangere civium Romanorum, Cic.; Pl., Ter., Caes. (2) *impatiently, indignantly*: indigne pati, Cic.

indĭgus -a -um (indigeo), *needing, in want of*; with genit.: nostri, Lucr.; nostrae opis, Verg.; with abl.: auxilio, Lucr.

indīlĭgens -entis, *negligent*; compar.: Caes. Adv. **indīlĭgentĕr**, *carelessly, negligently*: Cic. L.; compar.: Caes.

indīlĭgentĭa -ae, f. (indiligens), *carelessness, negligence*: Aeduorum, Caes.; litterarum amissarum, Cic. L.; veri, *in the investigation of truth*, Tac.

indĭpiscor -dīpisci -deptus sum, dep. and **indĭpisco** -ĕre: Pl. (ind/apiscor). (1) *to reach, attain*: indeptum esse navem manu ferreā iniectā, Liv. (2) *to obtain, get*: Pl.

indīreptus -a -um (in/diripio), *unpillaged*: Tac.

indiscrētus -a -um (in/discerno). (1) *unsevered, undivided*: Tac. (2) *undistinguished*: Tac. (3) *indistinguishable*: proles indiscreta suis, Verg.

indĭsertus -a -um, *ineloquent*: homo, Cic. Adv. **indĭsertē**, *ineloquently*: Cic. L.

indispŏsĭtus -a -um, *disorderly, confused*: Tac.

indissŏlūbĭlis -e, *indissoluble*: immortales et indissolubiles, Cic.

indissŏlūtus -a -um (in/dissolvo), *undissolved*: Cic.

indistinctus -a -um (in/distinguo). (1) *not separated, not arranged*: Cat. (2) *indistinct, obscure*: Tac. (3) *unpretentious*: Quint.

indĭvĭdŭus -a -um (in/divido), *indivisible*: corpora, *atoms*, Cic.; n. as subst. **indĭvĭdŭum** -i, *an atom*: Cic. Transf., of friends, *inseparable*: Tac.

indīvīsus -a -um (in/divido), *undivided*: Plin.

indo -dĕre -dĭdi -dĭtum, *to put in* or *on, place in* or *on*.

Lit., ignem in aram, Pl.; castella rupibus, Tac.; aliquem lecticae, Tac.

Transf., (1) *to introduce*: novos ritus, Tac. (2) *to cause, occasion*: alicui pavorem, Tac. (3) *to give as a name*: urbi nomen, Pl.; sometimes with dat. of the name: Superbo ei Romae inditum cognomen, Liv.

indŏcĭlis -e (in/doceo). (1) *that learns with difficulty, unteachable*: homo, Cic.; with infin.: pauperiem pati, Hor. (2) *untaught*; so: **a**, *ignorant, inexperienced*: genus, Cic.: **b**, *rude, artless*: numerus, Ov. (3) *that cannot be learned*: usūs disciplina, Cic.

indoctus -a -um (in/doceo), *untaught, untrained, unskilled*: Cic.; with genit.: pilae discive, Hor.; with infin.: iuga ferre nostra, Hor.; canet indoctum, *without art*, Hor.; moribus indoctis, Pl.

¶ Adv. **indoctē**, *unskilfully*: Pl., Cic.

indŏlentĭa -ae, f. (in/doleo), *freedom from pain*: Cic.

indŏlēs -is, f. (ind-/alo), *native constitution* or *quality, nature*. In gen.: servare indolem, of plants, Liv.; esp. of men, *natural disposition, character, talents*: adulescens bonā indole praediti, Cic.; virtutis, Cic.; segnis, Tac.

indŏlesco -dŏlescĕre -dŏlŭi (in/doleo), *to be pained, grieved at anything*: Cic.; with acc. and infin.: tam sero se cognoscere, Cic.; with abl.: nostris malis, Ov.; with n. acc.: id ipsum indoluit Iuno, Ov.; with quod *or* quia: Ov.

indŏmābĭlis -e, *untameable*: Pl.

indŏmĭtus -a -um (in/domo), *untamed, wild.* LIT., boves, Varr.; Hor. TRANSF., *un-restrained, wild*; of persons: pastores, Caes.; gens, Liv.; of things: cupiditas, furor, libido, Cic.; mors, Hor.; Falernum, *in-digestible*, Pers.; ira, Verg.

indormĭo -ire -īvi -ītum, *to sleep on* or *over.* LIT., with dat.: congestis saccis, Hor. TRANSF., *to go to sleep over, be negligent about*; with dat.: tantae causae, Cic. L.; with in: in isto homine colendo tam indormi-visse diu, Cic. L.

indōtātus -a -um (in/doto), *without a dowry, portionless.* LIT., soror, Hor. TRANSF., corpora, *without funeral honours*, Ov.; ars, *unadorned, poor*, Cic.

indŭ, archaic form of in; q.v.

indŭbĭtābĭlis -e (in/dubito), *that cannot be doubted*: Quint.

indŭbĭtātus -a -um (in/dubito), *undoubted, not doubtful, certain*: Plin., Quint.

indŭbĭto -are, *to feel doubt*; with dat.: tuis viribus, Verg.

indŭbĭus -a -um, *not doubtful, certain*: Tac., Quint.

indūcĭae=indutiae; q.v.

indūco -dūcĕre -duxi -ductum.

(1) *to draw over* or *on, to spread over* so as *to cover*; also *to cover* one thing with another. In gen.: scuta pellibus, Caes.; tectorium, Cic.; varias plumas membris, Hor.; Pl., Verg. Esp.: **a**, *to put on articles of clothing, arms*, etc.: manibus caestus, Verg.; tunicaque inducitur artus, Verg.: **b**, *to erase writing, to draw a line through*: nomina, Cic. L.; hence *to revoke, make invalid*: senatus consultum, Cic. L.; locationes, Liv.

(2) *to lead* and *bring in.* LIT., in gen.: milites in pugnam, Liv.; in regiam habitandi causā, Caes.; esp.: **a**, *to introduce* or *bring upon the stage* or *circus, produce on the stage*: gladiatores, Cic.: **b**, *to enter in an account-book*: pecuniam in rationes, Cic. TRANSF., **a**, *to introduce*: discordiam in civitatem, Cic.; morem novum iudiciorum in rempublicam, Cic.; also *in speaking* or *writing*: hinc ille Gyges inducitur a Platone, Cic.: **b**, *to lead on, to induce, persuade*: aliquem in errorem, Cic.; ad misericordiam, ad pigendum, Cic.; with ut and the subj.: aliquem ut men-tiatur, Cic.; with infin.: noctes vigilare serenas, Lucr.; Tac.: **c**, with animum *or* in animum: (i) *to bring one's mind to, to resolve*; with infin.: Ter., Cic.; with ut *or* ne and subj.: Pl., Cic., Liv.: (ii) *to take it into one's head that, believe that*; with acc. and infin.: Pl., Ter., Liv.

inductĭo -ōnis, f. (induco), *a leading* or *bringing in.* LIT., iuvenum armatorum, Liv.; inductio-nes aquarum, Cic. TRANSF., (1) animi, *a resolve, intention*, Cic. (2) erroris, *a misleading*, Cic. (3) personarum

ficta inductio, *feigned introduction of persons in a composition*, Cic. (4) in logic, *induction*: Cic., Quint.

inductor -ōris, m. (induco), *one that persuades*; of a whip: Pl.

inductū, abl. sing. from inductus, m. (induco), *by instigation*: huius persuasu et inductu, Cic.

indūcŭla -ae, f. (induo), *an under-garment*: Pl.

indūgrĕdĭor=ingredior; q.v.

indulgens -entis, partic. from indulgeo; q.v.

indulgentĭa -ae, f. (indulgens), *tenderness, indulgence*, with objective genit.: corporis, Cic.; with in and the acc.: in captivos, Liv.; Caes., Tac.

indulgĕo -dulgēre -dulsi.

(1) intransit., *to be forbearing, patient, indulgent.* LIT., with dat. of person or thing: sibi, Cic.; irae, Liv.; ordinibus, *to be generous with*, Verg. TRANSF., *to give oneself up to, indulge in*: novis amicitiis, Cic.; vino, Verg.; somno, Tac.

(2) transit.: **a**, *to indulge* a person: Ter.: **b**, *to grant* a thing, *allow, concede*: alicui sanguinem suum, Liv.; largitionem, Tac.

¶ Hence partic. (with compar.) **indulgens** -entis, *kind, tender, indulgent*: peccatis, Cic.; in captivos, Liv.; irarum indulgentes ministri, Liv.; aleae, *addicted to*, Suet.

¶ Adv. **indulgentĕr**, *kindly, tenderly, indulgently*: nimis indulgenter loqui, Cic.; compar. and superl.: Sen.

indŭo -dŭĕre -dŭi -dūtum, *to put on.* LIT., esp. of dress: galeam, Caes.; alicui tunicam, Cic.; pass. with abl.: socci quibus indutus esset, Cic.; indutus duabus quasi personis, *with two masks*, i.e., *playing a double part*, Cic.; pass. with acc.: virgines longam indutae vestem, Liv.

TRANSF., (1) *to clothe, surround, cover*: dii induti specie humanā, *clothed in human form*; homines in vultus ferarum, *to change*, Verg.; arbor induit se in florem, Verg. (2) *to put on, assume*: personam iudicis, Cic.; sibi cognomen, Cic.; proditorem et hostem, *to assume the part of*, Tac.; societatem, sedi-tionem, *to engage in*, Tac.; sibi cognomen, Cic. (3) se with dat. *or* in and acc., *to fall into, fall on*: venti se in nubem, Cic.; se hastis, Verg.; pass. with acc.: indui confessione suā, Cic.; pass.: indui confessione suā, Cic.

indŭpĕdĭo, indŭpĕrātor=impedio, impera-tor; q.v.

indūresco -dūrescĕre -dūrŭi, *to become hard.* LIT., stiria induruit, Verg. TRANSF., miles induruerat pro Vitellio, *had become confirmed in loyalty to Vitellius*, Tac.

indūro -are, *to make hard, to harden.* LIT., nivem indurat Boreas, Ov. TRANSF., *to harden, to steel*: induratus resistendo hostium timor, Liv.; Tac.

¹**Indus**, see India.

²**Indus** -i, m. (Ἰνδός). (1) *the Indus, a river of India.* (2) *a river of Phrygia and Caria.*

indūsārĭus -i, m. (indusium: Varr.), *a maker of under-garments*: Pl.

indūsĭātus -a -um (indusium: Varr.), *wearing an under-garment*: Pl.

industrĭa -ae, f. (industrius), *industry, dili-gence*: in agendo, Cic.; industriam in aliqua re ponere, Cic.; de industria, Ter., Cic.; ex industria, Liv., *on purpose, intentionally.*

industrĭus -a -um (perhaps from ind-/struo), *diligent, painstaking, industrious*: Cic., Tac., Juv.; compar.: industrior, Pl.
¶ Adv. **industrĭē**, *industriously, diligently*: Caes., Quint.

indūtĭae -ārum, f. pl. *a truce, armistice, suspension of hostilities.* Lit., indutias facere, Cic.; dare, Liv.; violare, Caes.; rumpere, Liv.; postulare, Sall.; per indutias, *during*, Liv. Transf., in quarrels: Pl., Ter.

Indūtĭŏmărus -i, m. *a chief of the Treveri.*

indūtus -ūs, m. (induo), *a putting on, clothing*: ea, quam indutui gerebat, vestis, Tac.

indŭvĭae -ārum, f. (induo), *clothes, clothing*: Pl.

ĭnēbrĭo -are, *to intoxicate.* Lit., Plin., Sen. Transf., *to saturate*: aurem, Juv.

ĭnēdĭa -ae, f. (in/edo), *fasting, abstinence from food*: vigiliis et inediā necatus, Cic.; inediā consumi, Cic.

ĭnēdĭtus -a -um (in/edo), *not published, unknown*: iuvenes, quorum inedita cura (i.e. *writings*), Ov.

ĭneffābĭlis -e, *unutterable*: Plin.

ĭneffĭcax, *ineffective*: Sen.

ĭnēlĕgans -antis, *not choice, tasteless*; esp. with negative: orationis copia, non inelegans, Cic.
¶ Adv. **ĭnēlĕgantĕr**, *tastelessly*: historia non inelenganter scripta, Cic.; ineleganter dividere, *without judgment*, Cic.

ĭnēluctābĭlis -e, *from which one cannot struggle free*: fatum, Verg.

ĭnēmendābĭlis -e, *incorrigible*: Sen., Quint.

ĭnēmŏrĭor -ēmŏri, dep. *to die in* or *at*; with dat.: spectaculo, Hor.

ĭnemptus -a -um (in/emo), *unbought*: dapes, Verg.; Hor., Tac.

ĭnēnarrābĭlis -e, *indescribable, inexpressible*: labor, Liv.; Quint. Adv. **ĭnēnarrābĭlĭtĕr**, *indescribably*: Liv.

ĭnēnōdābĭlis -e (in/enodo), *inextricable,* hence *inexplicable*: res, Cic.

ĭnĕo -īre -ĭi -ĭtum.
(1) intransit., *to go* or *come in, to enter.* Lit., in urbem, Liv. Transf., of time, *to begin, commence*: ab ineunte aetate, *from youth*, Cic.; Verg.
(2) transit., *to go* or *come into, to enter.* Lit., domum, Cic.; urbem, Liv.; viam, *to enter upon, begin a journey*, Cic. Transf., **a**, *to begin on* a period of time: initā aestate, *at the beginning of*, Caes.: **b**, of action, *to begin, to enter upon*: magistratum, proelium, viam, Cic.; societatem cum aliquo, Cic.; gratiam ab aliquo, Cic. L.; consilium, *to form a plan*, Caes., Cic., Ov.; esp. inire numerum, inire rationem, *to go into figures, enter upon a calculation*, Caes., Cic., Liv.

ĭneptĭa -ae, f. (ineptus), *foolish behaviour, silliness, absurdity*: Pl., Ter.; esp. plur.: hominum ineptiae ac stultitiae, Cic.

ĭneptĭo -ire (ineptus), *to talk* or *act foolishly*: Ter., Cat.

ĭneptus -a -um (in/aptus), *unsuitable, out of place, tasteless, silly*, of persons and things: inepte, Ov.; ioca, negotium, Cic.; chartae, *waste-paper*, Hor.
¶ Adv. **ĭneptē**, *unsuitably, absurdly, foolishly*: dicere, Cic.; Pl., Hor.

ĭnermis -e and (Sall.) **ĭnermus** -a -um (in/arma), *unarmed.* Lit., milites, Caes.; inermes palmas, Verg.; ager, *undefended by*

troops, Liv.; gingiva, *toothless*, Juv. Transf. in philosophiae parte, *defenceless, helpless*, Cic.; carmen, *inoffensive*, Ov.

¹ĭnerrans -antis (in/erro), *not wandering, fixed*: stellae inerrantes, Cic.

²ĭnerrans -antis, partic. from inerro; q.v.

ĭnerro -are, *to rove* or *wander about in*: Plin. L.

ĭners -ertis (in/ars), adj. (with compar. and superl.). (1) *untrained, unskilful*: poeta iners, Cic. (2) *inactive, lazy, idle, sluggish*: homo, senectus, otium, Cic.; aqua, *stagnant*, Ov.; aequora, *calm*, Lucr.; terra, Hor. (3) act. *making idle* or *slothful*: frigus, Ov. (4) *ineffective, dull, insipid*: querella, Cic.; caro, Hor. (5) *cowardly*: Cic.; Verg., Hor.

ĭnertĭa -ae, f. (iners). (1) *unskilfulness, want of skill*: Cic. (2) *slothfulness*: laboris, at work, Cic.; operis, Liv.

ĭnērŭdītus -a -um, *illiterate, ignorant*: Cic., Quint.

ĭnesco -are, *to allure with a bait.* Transf., *to entice, deceive*: nos caeci specie parvi beneficii inescamur, Liv.; Ter.

ĭnēvectus -a -um (in/eveho), *borne upon*: Verg.

ĭnēvītābĭlis -e, *unavoidable*: fulmen, Ov.; Tac.

ĭnexcĭtus -a -um (in/excieo), *unmoved, quiet*: Verg.

ĭnexcūsābĭlis -e. (1) *without excuse*: Hor. (2) *inexcusable*: Ov.

ĭnexercĭtātus -a -um (in/exercito), *untrained, unpractised*: miles, *undrilled*, Cic.; prompti et non inexercitati ad dicendum, Cic.; eloquentia, Tac.

ĭnexhaustus -a -um (in/exhaurio), *unexhausted*: metalla, Verg.; pubertas, Tac.

ĭnexōrābĭlis -e, *inexorable, not to be moved by entreaty*; of persons: in ceteros, Cic.; adversus te, Liv.; with dat.: delictis, Tac.; of things: fatum, *stern*, Verg.; disciplina, *severe*, Tac.

ĭnexperrectus -a -um (in/expergiscor), *not awakened*, Ov.

ĭnexpertus -a -um.
(1) act., *inexperienced in, unacquainted with*; with abl.: bonis inexpertus atque insuetus, Liv.; lasciviā, Tac.; with ad: animus ad contumeliam inexpertus, Liv.
(2) pass., *untried, untested, unattempted*: ne quid inexpertum relinquat, Verg.; legiones bello civili inexpertae, Tac.; puppis, Ov.; fides, Liv.

ĭnexpĭābĭlis -e (in/expio), *inexpiable*: religio, Cic. Transf., *implacable, irreconcilable*: odium, bellum, Liv.

ĭnexplēbĭlis -e (in/expleo), *insatiable, that cannot be satisfied.* Lit., Sen. Transf., cupiditas, Cic.; populi fauces, Cic.; epularum foeda et inexplebilis libido, Tac.; vir inexplebilis virtutis veraeque laudis, *with an insatiable desire for*, Liv.

ĭnexplētus -a -um (in/expleo), *unfilled, insatiate.* Lit., Stat. Transf., inexpletus lacrimans, *that cannot be satisfied with weeping*, Verg.

ĭnexplĭcābĭlis -e, *that cannot be untied*; hence (1) *intricate, impracticable, difficult*: inexplicabiles continuis imbribus viae, *impassable*, Liv. (2) *inexplicable, beyond explanation*: res, Cic. L. (3) *without result*: facilitas, Liv.; bellum, Tac.

ĭnexplōrātus -a -um (in/exploro), *unexplored, uninvestigated*: stagni vada, Liv. Abl. sing. n. as adv. **ĭnexplōrātō**, *without exploring, without reconnoitring*: proficisci, Liv.

ĭnexpugnābĭlis -e, *unconquerable, impregnable.* LIT., arx, Liv. TRANSF., volumus eum qui beatus sit tutum esse, inexpugnabilem, Cic.; with dat.: inexpugnabile amori pectus, Ov.

ĭnexspectātus -a -um, *unlooked-for, unexpected*: Cic., Ov.

ĭnexstinctus -a -um (in/exstinguo), *unextinguished, inextinguishable.* LIT., ignis, Ov. TRANSF., fames, libido, *insatiable*, Ov.; nomen, *immortal*, Ov.

ĭnexsŭpĕrābĭlis -e, adj. (with compar.), *that cannot be passed over or crossed, insurmountable.* LIT., Alpes, Liv.; paludes, Liv. TRANSF., vis fati, Liv.

ĭnextrĭcābĭlis -e (in/extrico), *that cannot be disentangled, inextricable*: error, *mazes past unravelling*, Verg.

infabrē, adv. *unskilfully*: vasa non infabre facta, Liv.; Hor.

infabrĭcātus -a -um (in/fabrico), *unwrought, unfashioned*: robora, Verg.

infăcētĭae (infĭcētĭae) -ārum, f. (infacetus), *crudity*: Cat.

infăcētus and infĭcētus -a -um (in/facetus), *dull, crude, without humour or wit*: homo, Pl., Cic.; saeclum, Cat.; mendacium non infacetum, Cic.
¶ Adv. **infăcētē (infĭcētē)**, *crudely, without humour*: Suet.

infācundus -a -um, *not eloquent*: vir acer nec infacundus, Liv.; compar.: quia infacundior sit, Liv.

infāmĭa -ae, f. (in/fama), *ill fame, dishonour, disgrace.*
LIT., alicui infamiam inferre, Cic.; movere, *to cause*, Liv.; infamiā flagrare, Cic. L.; infamiam habere, Caes.; subire infamiam sempiternam, Cic.
TRANSF., *a cause of ill fame, disgrace*: nostri saecli, Ov.; infamia silvae (of Cacus), Ov.

infāmis -e (in/fama), *ill-famed, disgraced, disreputable*: homines vitiis atque dedecore infames, Cic.; vita, Cic.; scopuli, Hor.; Liv., Tac.

infāmo -are (infamis), *to bring into bad repute, put to shame, disgrace*: iniuriam, Cic. L.; infamata dea, Ov.; aliquid, Cic.

infandus -a -um (in/fari), *unutterable, unnatural, abominable*: corpus eius impurum et infandum, Cic.; caedes, Liv.; laborem, bellum, Verg.; n. as exclamation: infandum! *grief unspeakable!* Verg.

infans -fantis (in/fari), adj. (with compar. and superl.), *speechless, unable to speak.*
LIT., esp. of children: pueri, Cic.; Hor.; as subst., *a little child*: infantibus parcere, Caes.; Lucr., Verg.
TRANSF., (1) *without the gift of speech, tongue-tied*: infantes et insipientes homines, Cic.; pudor, *embarrassed*, Hor. (2) *youthful*: pectora infantia, Ov.; ova, *fresh*, Ov. (3) *childish, silly*: omnia fuere infantia, Cic. L.

infantĭa -ae, f. (infans), *inability to speak*: linguae, Lucr. TRANSF., (1) *want of eloquence, slowness of speech*: Cic., Quint. (2) *infancy*: prima ab infantia, Tac.; Quint.

infarcĭo (infercĭo) -ire (in/farcio), *to stuff in, cram in*; fig.: neque inferciens verba quasi rimas expleat, Cic.

infătīgābĭlis -e, *indefatigable*: Plin., Sen.

infătŭo -are (in/fatuus), *to make a fool of*: aliquem mercede publicā, Cic.

infaustus -a -um, *unlucky, unfortunate*; of things: auspicium, Verg.; dies, Tac.; of persons: bellis, Tac.

infector -ōris, m. (inficio), *a dyer*: Cic.

¹**infectus** -a -um (in/facio). (1) *unworked, unwrought*: argentum, *not coined*, Liv.; aurum, Verg. (2) *not done, unfinished, incomplete*: infecta dona facere, *to revoke*, Pl.; rē infectā abire, Liv.; infecto negotio, Sall.; infectā victoriā, Liv.; infectā pace, Ter., Liv.; reddere infectum, *to make void*, Hor.; Verg. (3) *impracticable, impossible*: rex nihil infectum Metello credens, Sall.

²**infectus**, partic. from inficio; q.v.

infēcundĭtās -ātis, f. (infecundus), *barrenness, sterility*: terrarum, Tac.

infēcundus -a -um, *unfruitful, barren, sterile*: ager, Sall.; fig.: fons (ingenii), Ov.

infēlīcĭtās -ātis, f. (infelix), *ill-luck, unhappiness, misfortune*: haruspicum, Cic.; alicuius in liberis, Liv.

infēlīcĭter, adv. (infelix), *unluckily, unfortunately*: totiens infeliciter temptata arma, Liv.

infēlīco -are (infelix), *to make unhappy*: Pl.

infēlix -ĭcis, adj. (with compar. and superl.), *unfruitful, barren.*
LIT., tellus frugibus infelix, Verg.; arbor, *the gallows*, Cic., Liv.
TRANSF., (1) *unhappy, miserable*: homo miserrimus atque infelicissimus, Cic.; infelicior domi quam militiae, Liv.; patria, Verg.; with genit.: animi, *in mind*, Verg.; with abl.: operis summā, Hor. (2) act., *causing unhappiness, bringing trouble*: reipublicae, Cic.; consilium, Liv.; vates, *prophesying woe*, Verg.

infenso -are (infensus), *to attack, ravage*: pabula, Tac.; Armeniam bello, Tac.

infensus -a -um (in/*fendo), *hostile, aggressive.* (1) in action, esp. of weapons, *aimed, ready*: hasta, Verg.; Liv. (2) in spirit, *embittered, dangerous*; of persons: rex irā infensus, Liv.; with dat.: Turno Drances, Verg.; with in and acc.: eo infensioribus in se iudicibus, Liv.; of things: animus, Cic.; opes principibus infensae, *dangerous*, Tac.
¶ Adv. **infensē**, *hostilely, acrimoniously*: infense invectus, Tac.; quis Isocrati est adversatus infensius, Cic.

infer, see **inferus**, **infĕri** -ōrum, see **inferus**.

infĕrĭae -ārum, f. (inferi), *sacrifices or offerings in honour of the dead*: alicui inferias adferre, Cic.; Verg., Hor.

infercĭo, see **infarcio**.

infĕrĭor, see **inferus**.

infĕrĭus, see **infra** and **inferus**.

infernē, adv. (inferus), *on the lower side, beneath, below*: Lucr.

infernus -a -um (infer), *that which is, or comes from, below, lower.* In gen.: stagna, Liv.; mare, *the Tuscan sea*, Luc. Esp. *of the lower world, infernal*: rex, Pluto, Verg.; Iuno, Proserpine, Verg.; palus, *the Styx*, Ov.; umbras, Tac. As subst. m. pl. **inferni** -ōrum, *the inhabitants of the lower world,* the shades: Prop.; n. pl. **inferna** -ōrum, the lower world, infernal regions: Tac.

infĕro inferre intŭli inlātum, to bring, bear, carry in, to put or place on.

LIT., in gen.: templis ignes inferre, to set fire to, Cic.; aliquid in ignem, Caes.; in equum, to put on horseback, Caes.; scalas ad moenia, against the walls, Liv. Esp. (1) to sacrifice, pay: honores Anchisae, Verg. (2) milit. t. t., of hostile action: signa in hostem, to attack, charge, Caes.; pedem, Liv.; hostibus gradum, Liv.; bellum alicui, or contra aliquem, to make war on, levy war against, Cic.; arma, Hor., Liv. (3) reflex., se inferre and pass. as middle, inferri, to betake oneself, to go: lucus quo se persaepe inferebat, Liv.; inferri in urbem, Liv.; Cic.

TRANSF., (1) to bring on, introduce, occasion: spem alicui, Caes.; vim et manūs alicui, Cic.; hostibus terrorem, Cic.; periculum civibus, Cic.; sermonem, Cic.; mentionem, to mention, Liv. (2) in accounts, to enter: sumptum civibus, Cic. (3) in logic, to infer, conclude: Cic., Quint.

infĕrus -a -um, below, lower (opp. superus): limen, Pl.; esp. (1) southern: mare, the Tuscan Sea (opp. mare Superum, the Adriatic), Cic. (2) of the lower world: di, Pl., Cic., Liv. M. pl. as subst. **infĕri** -ōrum, the dead, the lower world: ab inferis exsistere, to rise from the dead, Liv.; apud inferos, in the lower world, Cic.; elicere animas inferorum, Cic.

¶ Compar. **infĕrĭor** -ius, genit. -iōris, lower (opp. superior). LIT., of position: labrum, the under-lip, Caes.; ex inferiore loco dicere, to speak from the body of the court (opp. ex superiore loco, from the tribunal), Cic. L. TRANSF., (1) of time, later, junior: aetate inferiores, Cic. (2) of number, rank, etc.: gradus, Cic.; inferioris iuris magistratus, Liv.; versus, in an elegiac couplet, the pentameter, Ov.; with abl.: inferior animo, Caes.; numero navium, Caes.; fortunā, Cic.; with in: in iure civili, Cic.

¶ Superl. (1) **infĭmus (infŭmus)** -a -um, lowest (opp. summus). LIT., solum, Caes.; ab infimis radicibus montis, Caes.; sometimes indicating the lowest part of a thing (cf. summus): ab infimā arā, from the bottom of the altar, Cic. TRANSF., of position, lowest, meanest: infimo loco natus, Cic.; faex populi, Cic.; precibus infimis, with abject prayers, Liv.

¶ Superl. (2) **imus** -a -um, lowest. LIT., sedes ima, Cic.; sometimes indicating the lowest part of a thing (cf. infimus): ab imis unguibus ad verticem summum, Cic.; gurges, Ov.; n. as subst., the bottom: ab imo, Caes.; ab imo suspirare, to sigh deeply, Ov.; plur., the lower world: Ov. TRANSF., (1) of tone, deepest, lowest: vox ima, Hor. (2) of time, last: mensis, Ov.; n. as subst., the end: Hor.

infervesco -fervescĕre -ferbŭi, to begin to boil, grow hot: hoc ubi confusum sectis inferbuit herbis, Hor.

infesto -are (infestus), to attack, disquiet: latus dextrum, Ov.; Sen.

infestus -a -um (in/*fendo).
(1) act., aggressive, hostile, dangerous: **a**, milit.: ab Tibure infesto agmine profecti,

Liv.; infestis signis, in hostile array, Caes.; hastā infestā, Liv.; infesta tela, Verg.: **b**, in gen.: infestis oculis conspici, Cic.; with dat.: alicui invisus infestusque, Cic.; with in and acc.: infestus in suos, Cic.; Hor., Liv., Tac.

(2) pass., infested, beset, unsafe: iter, Cic.; mare infestum habere, Cic.; with abl.: via illa incursionibus barbarorum infesta, Cic.; senectus, regnum, Liv.

¶ Adv. **infestē**, in a hostile manner: Liv.; compar.: infestius atque inimicius, Liv.; superl.: inimicissime atque infestissime, Cic.

infĭcētus inficētē=infacetus infacete; q.v.

infĭcĭo -fĭcĕre -fēci -fectum (in/facio), to include in the making, work in.

Hence (1) to tinge, dye, stain, colour. LIT., se vitro, Caes.; rivos sanguine, Hor.; ora pallor albus inficit, makes colourless, Hor. TRANSF., to steep, imbue: (puer) infici debet in artibus, Cic.; Verg.

(2) to poison, taint: Gorgoneis Alecto infecta venenis, Verg. TRANSF., to corrupt: ut cupiditatibus principum et vitiis infici solet tota civitas, Cic.

infĭdēlis -e, untrue, disloyal, faithless: Caes., Cic., Hor.; superl.: infidelissimi socii, Cic. L.

¶ Adv. **infĭdēlĭter**, faithlessly: Cic.

infĭdēlĭtās -tātis, f. (infidelis), disloyalty, faithlessness: amicitiarum, Cic.; Caes.

infĭdus -a -um, unfaithful, faithless, untrue; of persons: amici, Cic.; Hor.; of things: societas regni, Liv.; nihil est enim stabile quod infidum est, Cic.

infĭgo -fīgĕre -fixi -fixum, to fix, fasten or thrust in. LIT., gladium hosti in pectus, Cic.; hasta infigitur portae, Verg. TRANSF., to imprint, impress, fix: cura erit infixa animo, Cic.; in hominum sensibus positum atque in ipsā naturā fixum, Cic.; religio infixa animo, Liv.; Tac.

infĭmātis -is, m. (infimus), a person of the lowest rank: Pl.

infĭmus -a -um, superl. of inferus; q.v.

infindo -findĕre -fidi -fissum, to cut into: sulcos telluri, Verg.; poet.: sulcos mari, Verg.

infīnĭtās -tātis, f. (in/finis), infinity, endlessness: infinitas locorum, Cic.; in infinitatem omnem peregrinari, Cic.

infīnĭtĭo -ōnis, f. (infinitus), infinity: Cic.

infīnītus -a -um (in/finio), infinite, unbounded. LIT., of space: altitudo, Cic.; imperium, Cic., Liv.; n. as subst. infinitum -i, infinite space: Lucr. TRANSF., (1) of time, endless, unceasing: tempus, Lucr., Cic. (2) of number, countless: infinita corporum varietas, Cic.; multitudo, Caes., Cic., Tac. (3) of size or degree, boundless, immense: magnitudo, Caes.; spes, Cic. (4) indefinite, general: infinitior distributio, Cic.

¶ Adv. **infīnītē**, infinitely, boundlessly, endlessly: partes secare et dividere, Cic.; concupiscere, Cic.

infirmātĭo -ōnis, f. (infirmo), a weakening; hence (1) a refuting: rationis, Cic. (2) invalidating: rerum iudicatarum, Cic.

infirmĭtās -tātis, f. (infirmus), weakness, feebleness. LIT., physical: corporis, Cic. L. TRANSF., (1) mental weakness: animi, Cic. (2) instability, fickleness: Gallorum, Caes. (3) in concrete sense, the weaker sense: Liv.

nfirmo -are (infirmus), *to weaken.* Lit., legiones, Tac. Transf., (**1**) *to impair, to shake*: fidem testis, Cic. (**2**) *to refute*: res leves, Cic. (**3**) *to annul*: acta illa atque omnes res superioris anni, Cic.; leges, Liv.

nfirmus -a -um, adj. (with compar. and superl.), *weak, feeble.* Lit., physically: vires, Cic.; classis, Cic.; infirmi homines ad resistendum, Caes. Transf., (**1**) mentally or morally, *weak, timorous*: animo infirmo esse, Cic.; Caes., Hor. (**2**) of things: res infirma ad probandum, Cic.; Liv., Tac.

¶ Adv. **infirmē**, *weakly, faintly*: socii infirme animati, Cic. L.

nfit, defective verb, *he* (or *she*) *begins*; with infin.: Pl., Lucr., Verg.; esp. *begins to speak*: Verg., Liv.

nfĭtĭās (in/fateor) **ire**, *to deny*; with acc.: Pl.; with acc. and infin.: infitias eunt mercedem se pactos (esse), Liv.

nfĭtĭālis -e (infitiae), *negative, containing a denial*: quaestio, Cic.; Quint.

nfĭtĭātĭō -ōnis, f. (infitior), *a denying*: negatio infitiatioque facti, Cic.

nfĭtĭātor -ōris, m. (infitior), *a denier*; esp. *one who denies a debt* or *deposit*: Cic.

nfĭtĭor -ari, dep. (in/fateor), *to deny*; in gen., with acc.: verum, Cic.; Pl., Ov.; with acc. and infin.: neque ego in hoc me hominem esse infitiabor unquam, Cic.; esp. *to deny a debt, refuse to restore a deposit*: quid si infitiatur? quid si omnino non debetur? Cic. L.; Ov.

nflammātĭō -ōnis, f. (inflammo), *a setting fire.* Transf., animorum, *inspiration*, Cic.

nflammo -are (flamma), *to kindle, set fire to.* Lit., taedas, Cic.; classem, Cic.; Liv. Transf., *to inflame, excite*: populum in improbos, Cic.; inflammatus ad gloriam, Cic.; aliquem amore, Verg.

nflātĭō -ōnis, f. (inflo), *an inflation*; of the body, *flatulence*: inflationem magnam habere, *to cause severe flatulence*, Cic.

nflātĭus, compar. adv. from inflo; q.v.

nflātus -a -um, partic. from inflo; q.v.

nflātus -ūs, m. (inflo), *a blowing into.* Lit., primo inflatu tibicinis, *at the first blast*, Cic. Transf., *inspiration*: divinus, Cic.

nflecto -flectĕre -flexi -flexum, *to bend, bow, curve.* Lit., bacillum, Cic.; cum ferrum se inflexisset, Caes.; inflectere nullum unquam vestigium sui cursus, Cic.; oculos, Cic.; middle, inflecti, *to curve*: sinus ab litore in urbem inflectitur, Cic. Transf., (**1**) *to warp, change*: ius civile, Cic.; nomen, Cic.; of persons, *to change.* (**2**) *to sway, move, affect*: aliquem leviter, Cic.; sensūs, Verg. (**3**) *to modulate the voice*: inflexā ad miserabilem sonum voce, Cic.

nflētus -a -um (in/fleo), *unwept, unlamented*: Verg.

nflexĭbĭlis -e, *that cannot be bent, inflexible*: Sen., Plin. L.

nflexĭo -ōnis, f. (inflecto), *a bending, swaying*: laterum inflexio fortis ac virilis, Cic.

nflexus -a -um, partic. from inflecto; q.v.

nflexus -ūs, m. (inflecto), *a bending, curving*: Juv.

nflīgo -flīgĕre -flixi -flictum, *to strike, knock, dash against.* Lit., alicui securim, Cic.; puppis inflicta vadis, *dashed on*, Verg. Transf., *to inflict a blow, cause hurt* or

damage: mortiferam plagam, Cic.; alicui turpitudinem, Cic.

inflo -are, *to blow into.*

Lit., (**1**) *to play on wind instruments*: calamos leves, Verg.; tibias, Cic.; absol., *to give a blast*: simul inflavit tibicen, Cic.; sonum, *to produce*, Cic. (**2**) *to blow out, puff out, swell*: buccas, Pl., Hor.

Transf., (**1**) *to inspire*: Cic., Liv. (**2**) *to puff up, elate*: inflatus laetitiā, Cic.; animos falsa spe, Liv.; Hor.

¶ Hence partic. (with compar.) **inflātus** -a -um, *inflated.* Lit., *swollen*: collum, Cic. Transf., *puffed up, pompous*: animus, Cic.; Liv.; of style, *turgid*: Prop., Tac.

¶ Hence compar. adv. **inflātius**. (**1**) *too pompously*: latius atque inflatius perscribere, Caes. (**2**) *on a grander scale*: Caes.

inflŭo -flŭĕre -fluxi -fluxum, *to flow in.*

Lit., non longe a mari, quo Rhenus influit, Caes.; Hypanis in Pontum influit, Cic.

Transf., (**1**) *to steal in*: in aures, Cic.; in animos, Cic. (**2**) *to stream in, rush in*: in Italiam Gallorum copiae, Cic.

infŏdĭo -fŏdĕre -fōdi -fossum, *to dig in, bury*: corpora terrae, Verg.; taleas in terram, Caes.; Hor.

informātĭo -ōnis, f. (informo), *a conception, idea*: dei, Cic.; antecepta animo rei, *an a priori idea*, Cic.

informis -e (in/forma), *formless, shapeless*: Verg., Liv. Transf., *deformed, hideous*: cadaver, Verg.; hiems, Hor.; Tac.

informo -are, *to give form and shape to, to form, fashion.*

Lit., clipeum, Verg.

Transf., mentally, *to form, dispose*: animus a natura bene informatus, Cic.; artes quibus aetas puerilis ad humanitatem informari solet, Cic.; *to form an idea* or *conception of anything*: eos (deos) ne coniecturā quidem informare posse, Cic.; oratorem, Cic.; causam, Cic.

infortūnātus -a -um, *unfortunate, miserable*: nihil me infortunatius, Cic.; Ter.

infortūnĭum -i, n. (in/fortuna), *misfortune, ill luck*; hence *punishment*: Pl., Ter., Liv.

infrā (for inferā from inferus), adv. and prep., *below.*

Adv., *below, underneath.* Lit., innumeros supra infra, dextra sinistra deos esse, Cic.; in writing: earum (litterarum) exemplum infra scripsi, Cic. L.; non seges est infra, *in the lower world*, Tib.; geograph., *to the south*: Caes., Verg. Transf., *below in rank*: nec fere unquam infra ita descenderent ut ad infimos pervenirent, Liv., Tac.

Compar. **infĕrĭus**, *lower down.* Lit., inferius suis fraternos currere Luna admiratur equos, Ov. Transf., in rank, etc.: Sen.

Prep., with acc., *below, under.* Lit., in space: mare infra oppidum, Cic.; infra eum locum ubi pons erat, Caes. Transf., (**1**) of size: hi sunt magnitudine paulo infra elephantos, Caes. (**2**) of time, *later than*: Homerus non infra superiorem Lycurgum fuit, Cic. (**3**) *beneath, below*, in rank, estimation: res humanas infra se positas arbitrari, Cic.; Ter., Plin. L.

infractĭo -ōnis, f. (infringo), *a breaking.* Transf., animi, *dejection*, Cic.

infractus -a -um, partic. from infringo; q.v.

infrăgĭlis -e, *that cannot be broken*: Plin. TRANSF., *strong*: vox, Ov.

infrĕmo -frĕmĕre -frĕmŭi, *to growl*: aper, Verg.

¹infrēnātus -a -um (in/freno), *without bridle*: equites, equi, Liv.

²infrēnātus -a -um, partic. from infreno; q.v.

infrendĕo -ēre, *to gnash with the teeth*; class. only in partic., infrendens -entis, *gnashing*: Verg.

infrēnis -e and **infrēnus** -a -um (in/frenum), *without bridle, unbridled*: equus, Verg.; Numidae, *riding without bridle*, Verg.

infrēno -are, *to bridle, rein in*. LIT., equos, Liv.; currus, *to harness the horses to the chariot*, Verg. TRANSF., *to restrain, hold back, check*: infrenatum conscientiā scelerum et fraudium suarum, Cic.

infrĕquens -entis, adj. (with compar. and superl.), *not crowded*.

LIT., of number, *thin, not numerous.* (1) of persons and groups: copiae infrequentiores, Caes.; senatus infrequens, Cic. L.; hostes, Liv. (2) of places, *not full, scantily populated*: pars urbis infrequens aedificiis erat, Liv.; causa, *attended by few hearers*, Cic.; n. as subst.: infrequentissima urbis, *the least populous parts of the city*, Liv.

TRANSF., of time, *infrequent*; of persons, *not doing a thing often*: deorum cultor, Hor.

infrĕquentĭa -ae, f. (infrequens). (1) of numbers, *fewness, scantiness, thinness*: senatus, Liv. (2) of places, *emptiness, loneliness*: locorum, Tac.

infringo -fringĕre -frēgi -fractum (in/frango), *to break*. LIT., hastam, Liv.; papavera, Ov.; remus, *appearing broken* (through refraction), Cic. TRANSF., *to weaken, impair, cast down*: vim militum, Caes.; conatus adversariorum, Caes.; spem, Cic.; animum, Liv.; Samnitium vires, Liv.

¶ Hence partic. **infractus** -a -um, *broken*. LIT., Plin. TRANSF., *weakened, impaired*: vires, Verg.; animos, Liv.; of speech: loquella, *broken*, Lucr.; infracta loqui, Cic.

infrons -frondis, *leafless*: Ov.

infructŭōsus -a -um, *unfruitful*. TRANSF., *unproductive, fruitless*: militia, Tac.; Plin. L.

infūcātus -a -um (in/fuco), *coloured*; fig.: vitia, Cic.

infŭla -ae, f. *a band, bandage*: Cic.; esp. *a fillet, a heavy band of twisted wool, worn by priests and suppliants, and used to decorate victims for sacrifice*: Caes., Lucr., Cic., Verg., Liv.; fig. (like 'laurels'), *a mark of distinction*: his insignibus atque infulis imperii Romani venditis, of the state lands, Cic.

infŭlātus -a -um (infula), *adorned with the infula*: Suet.

infulcĭo -fulcire -fulsi -fultum, *to stuff in, cram in*: Suet.; fig.: Sen.

infundo -fundĕre -fūdi -fūsum, *to pour in* or *on*.

LIT., (1) of liquids: aliquid in vas, Cic.; largos umeris rores, Verg.; with dat., *to pour out for*, hence *to administer*: alicui venenum, Cic.; alicui poculum, Hor. (2) not of liquids: obruebatur navis infuso igni, Liv.

TRANSF., (1) of persons, reflex., se infundere, or pass. infundi as middle, *to pour in, pour over*: infusus gremio, Verg.; circo infusum populum, Verg.; Cic. (2) in gen.: infundere orationem in aures tuas, Cic.; vitia in civitatem, Cic.

infusco -are, *to make dark, to blacken*. Li vellera, harenam, Verg. TRANSF., *to disfigu stain*: vicinitas non infuscata malevolent Cic.; eos barbaries infuscaverat, Cic.

Ingauni -ōrum, m. *a Ligurian tribe*.

ingĕmĭno -are. (1) transit., *to redouble*: ict voces, Verg.; me miserum! ingeminat, *repeats*, Ov. (2) intransit., *to be redoubl to increase*: imber, clamor, Verg.

ingĕmisco or **ingĕmesco** -gĕmiscere -gemescĕre -gĕmŭi, *to sigh* or *groan over*.

LIT., absol.: nemo ingemuit, Cic.; with and the abl.: in quo tu quoque ingemisc Cic.; with dat.: eius minis, Liv.; Cic.; w acc.: tuum interitum, Verg.; with acc. a infin.: quid ingemiscis hostem Dolabella iudicatum? Cic.

TRANSF., of things: Verg., Ov.

ingĕmo -ĕre, *to sigh, groan over*; with da laboribus, Hor.; aratro, Verg.; agris, Tac.

ingĕnĕro -are, *to implant, generate in*: natu ingenerat amorem in eos, Cic.; ingener familiae frugalitas, Cic.; Liv.

ingĕnĭātus -a -um (ingenium), *disposed nature*: Pl.

ingĕnĭōsus -a -um (ingenium), adj. (w compar. and superl.). LIT., *naturally clev talented, able*: quo quisque est sollertior ingeniosior, Cic.; ad aliquid, Ov. TRANS of things. (1) *requiring talent*: Cic., C (2) *naturally fit for, adapted to*: terra coler Ov.; ad segetes ager, Ov.

¶ Adv. **ingĕnĭōsē**, *cleverly, ingenious* ista tractare, Cic.

ingĕnĭtus -a -um, partic. from ingigno; q.v.

ingĕnĭum -i, n. (in/geno=gigno), *natu natural constitution*.

(1) of persons: **a**, *natural dispositi temperament, character*: redire ad ingeniu to revert to type, Ter.; ingenio suo vive *after one's own inclination*, Liv.; w qualifying adj.: Ter., Liv., Tac.: **b**, *men power, cleverness, ability, talent, geni docilitas*, memoria, quae fere appellan uno ingenii nomine, Cic.; with qualifyi adj.: tardum, acerrimum, acutum, magnu etc., Cic.; Hor., Liv., Ov.; meton.: (i) *a m of genius, a genius*: Cic., Liv., Tac.: (ii) *clever invention*: Plin. L., Tac.

(2) of things, *natural quality*: loci, Sal arvorum, Verg.; terrae, Liv.

ingens -entis (perhaps from in/geno=gign *monstrous, vast, enormous*. LIT., pecun campus, numerus, Cic.; aequor, Ho monstrum horrendum informe ingens, Ve TRANSF., fama, Verg.; bellum, Ov.; virt Hor.; with genit.: femina ingens animi, T

ingĕnŭi, perf. indic. from ingigno; q.v.

ingĕnŭĭtās -tātis, f. (ingenuus), *the condit of a free man, free birth*: ornamenta ingen tatis, Cic. TRANSF., *noble-mindedness, u rightness, frankness*: Cic.

ingĕnŭus -a -um (in/geno=gigno).

LIT., (1) *native, not foreign*: fons, Luc Juv. (2) *natural, innate*: indoles, Pl.; col Prop.

TRANSF., *free-born, of free birth*: Cic., Ho Liv.; hence (1) *worthy of a free man, nob honourable*: vita, artes, Cic.; amor, H (2) *tender, delicate*: Ov.

¶ Adv. **ingĕnŭē**, *like a free man*: ed catus, Cic. TRANSF., *frankly*: confiteri, Ci

ngĕro -gĕrĕre -gessi -gestum, *to carry, throw, put, pour in* or *upon*. LIT., ligna foco, Tib.; hastas in tergum fugientibus, Verg.; saxa in subeuntes, Liv. TRANSF., (1) in speech, *to heap on*: probra, Liv.; convicia alicui, Hor. (2) *to press upon, force upon*: alicui nomen, Tac.; aliquem (*as judge*), Cic.

ngigno. verb found only in perf. indic. **ingĕnŭi**, *I implanted*, and perf. partic. **ingĕnĭtus** -a -um, *implanted*: natura cupiditatem homini ingenuit veri videndi, Cic.; terra ingenito umore egens, Liv.; ingenita caritas liberum, Liv.

nglōrĭus -a -um (in/gloria), *without fame* or *glory, inglorious*: vita, Cic.; rex apum, *undistinguished*, Verg.; imperium, Tac.

nglŭvĭēs -ēi, f. *the crop of birds, the maw of animals*: Verg. Meton., *gluttony*: Hor.

ngrātiīs or ingrātiīs (in/gratia), *unwillingly*: Pl., Lucr., Cic.; tuis, *against your will*, Pl.; amborum, Pl.

ngrātus -a -um. (1) *unpleasant, unpleasing*; of persons or things: ne invisa deis immortalibus oratio nostra aut ingrata esse videatur, Cic.; labor, Verg.; otium, Hor. (2) *unthankful, ungrateful*. LIT., of persons and actions: homo, Cic.; ingrati animi crimen horreo, Cic.; ingratus in Democritum, Cic.; with genit.: salutis, Verg. TRANSF., of things, *ungrateful, unrewarding, thankless*: donum, Pl.; ingluvies, Hor.; labor, Sall.; pericula, Verg.

¶ Adv. ingrātē. (1) *unwillingly*: Ov. (2) *ungratefully*: Cic. L., Tac.

ngrăvesco -ĕre, *to become heavy*. LIT., Plin.; poet., *to become pregnant*: Lucr. TRANSF., (1) *to become a burden, become troublesome*: annona ingravescit, Caes.; ingravescit in dies malum intestinum, Cic. L.; seditio, Liv. (2) *to become weary*: corpora exercitationum defatigatione ingravescunt, Cic.

ngrăvo -are, *to weigh down*: puppem, Stat. TRANSF., *to aggravate*: ingravat haec Drances, Verg.

ngrĕdior -grĕdī -gressus sum, dep. (in/gradior), *to step in* or *into, to enter, go in*.
LIT., in navem, in templum, in fundum, Cic.; intra munitiones, Caes.; with acc.: domum, Cic.; curiam, Liv.; with abl.: campo, *to walk in the plain*, Verg.; absol., *to walk*, Cic. L.
TRANSF., *to enter upon, begin on*: in bellum, Cic.; in eam orationem, Cic.; in spem libertatis, Cic.; with acc.: vitam, pericula, orationem, Cic.; with infin., *to begin to*: dicere, Cic.; Verg.

ngressĭo -ōnis, f. (ingredior). (1) *an entering, going in*. LIT., fori, Cic. TRANSF., *a beginning*: Cic. (2) *gait, pace*: Cic.

ngressus -ūs, m. (ingredior).
(1) *a going into, an entering*. LIT., Cic., Liv.; esp. milit. t., *an inroad*: ingressus hostiles praesidiis intercipere, Tac. TRANSF., *a beginning*: ingressus capere, *to begin*, Verg.
(2) *a walking, going, stepping*: ingressus, cursus, accubitio, inclinatio, sessio, Cic.; ingressu prohiberi, *not to be able to move*, Caes.; Liv.

ngrŭo -ŭĕre -ŭi (connected with ruo), *to fall upon, assail*. LIT., Pl., Tac.; with dat.: ingruit Aeneas Italis, Verg. TRANSF., of unwelcome things, *to come on, attack*:

periculum, bellum ingruit, Liv.; morbi in remiges, Liv.; bellum, Verg., Tac.

inguen -guĭnis, n. (1) *the groin*: Verg., Liv. (2) *the private parts*: Hor., Ov.

ingurgĭto -are (in/gurges). LIT., *to pour in like a flood*: Pl. TRANSF., reflex. (1) *to plunge*: se in tot flagitia, Cic. (2) *to glut* or *gorge oneself, to gormandize*: Cic.

ingustābĭlis -e (in/gusto), *that cannot be tasted*: Plin.

ingustātus -a -um (in/gusto), *untasted, not tasted before*: ilia rhombi, Hor.

ĭnhăbĭlis -e, *that cannot be handled* or *managed, unmanageable*. LIT., navis inhabilis prope magnitudinis, Liv.; telum ad remittendum inhabile imperitis, Liv. TRANSF., *unfit, ill-adapted*: tegimen inhabile ad resurgendum, Tac.; multitudo inhabilis ad consensum, Liv.

ĭnhăbĭtābĭlis -e, *uninhabitable*: maximae regiones inhabitabiles, Cic.

ĭnhăbĭto -are, *to inhabit*: eum secessum, Ov.

ĭnhaerĕo -haerēre -haesi -haesum, *to stick in, cling to, cleave to*. LIT., ad saxa, Cic.; in visceribus, Cic.; with dat.: sidera sedibus suis inhaerent, Cic.; Ov. TRANSF., inhaeret in mentibus augurium, Cic.; virtutes semper voluptatibus inhaerent, Cic.; studiis, Ov.; Liv.

ĭnhaeresco -haerescĕre -haesi -haesum (in-haereo), *to adhere to, begin to cling to*. LIT., Caes., Verg. TRANSF., in mentibus, Cic.

ĭnhālo -are, *to breathe upon*: cum taeterrimam nobis popinam inhalasses, Cic.

ĭnhĭbĕo -ēre -ŭi -ĭtum (in/habeo). (1) *to hold in, hold back, check, restrain*. LIT., tela, Verg.; equos, Ov.; si te illius acerba imploratio et vox miserabilis non inhibebat, Cic.; as naut. t. t.: inhibere remis or navem retro inhibere, *to back water*, Liv. TRANSF., impetum victoris, Liv. (2) *to practise, use, employ*: supplicia nobis, Cic.; imperium in deditos, Liv.

ĭnhĭbĭtĭo -ōnis, f. (inhibeo), *a restraining*: remigum, *backing water*, Cic. L.

inhĭo -are, *to gape, stand agape*: tenuit inhians tria Cerberus ora, Verg.; esp. with wonder and desire: inhians in te, dea, Lucr.; with dat.: Romulus lactens uberibus lupinis inhians, gaping for, Cic.; Verg. TRANSF., *to covet, desire, long for*; with dat.: hortis, opibus, Tac.; with acc.: aurum, Pl.; varios pulchra testudine postes, Verg.

ĭnhŏnesto -are (inhonestus), *to disgrace, dishonour*: palmas, Ov.

ĭnhŏnestus -a -um. (1) morally; of persons, *degraded, dishonoured*: Pl., Hor.; of things, *dishonourable, shameful, disgraceful*: Ov.; inhonestissima cupiditas, Cic.; mors, Liv.; vulnera, Ov. (2) physically, *ugly, unsightly*: homo, Ter.; vulnus, *disfiguring*, Verg.

¶ Adv. ĭnhŏnestē, *dishonourably, disgracefully*: aliquem accusare, Cic. L.

ĭnhŏnōrātus -a -um (in/honoro), adj. (with compar. and superl.: Liv.). (1) *not honoured*: vita, Cic.; honoratus atque inhonoratus, Liv.; inhonoratior triumphus, Liv. (2) *unrewarded*: aliquem inhonoratum dimittere, Liv.; Ov.

ĭnhŏnōrus -a -um, *not respected*: Plin.; signa, *defaced*, Tac.

ĭnhorrĕo -ēre, *to bristle*: haud secus quam vallo saepta inhorreret acies, Liv.

ĭnhorresco -horrescĕre -horrŭi. Lĭt., (**1**) *to begin to bristle, to bristle up*: aper inhorruit armos, Verg.; spicea iam campis messis inhorruit, Verg. (**2**) *to shudder, quiver*: inhorruit unda tenebris, Verg.; tristis hiems aquilonis inhorruit alis, Ov.; agitatus aër, Ov. Transf., *to shudder from fright*, etc.: dicitur inhorruisse civitas, Cic.; domus principis inhorruit, Tac.

ĭnhospĭtālis -e, *inhospitable*: Caucasus, Hor.

ĭnhospĭtālĭtās -tātis, f. (inhospitalis), *want of hospitality*: Cic.

ĭnhospĭtus -a -um, *inhospitable*: tecta, Ov.; Syrtis, Verg.

ĭnhūmānĭtās -tātis, f. (inhumanus). (**1**) *cruelty, inhumanity*: Cic. (**2**) *incivility, discourtesy*: Cic. (**3**) *stinginess, niggardliness*: Cic.

ĭnhūmānus -a -um, adj. (with compar. and superl.). (**1**) *cruel, barbarous, inhuman*: homo, Cic.; quis inhumanior? Cic.; scelus, Liv. (**2**) *rude, discourteous, uncivil*: Cic. (**3**) *uncultured*: aures, Cic.

¶ Adv. (with compar.) **ĭnhūmānē**, *inhumanly*: Ter., Cic.

¶ Adv. **ĭnhūmānĭtĕr**, *uncivilly, discourteously*: Cic.

ĭnhŭmātus -a -um (in/humo), *unburied*: Cic., Verg.

ĭnhŭmo -are, *to cover with earth*: Plin.

ĭnĭbī, adv., *therein, in that place*. Lĭt., of space: Cic. Transf., (**1**) of time, *near at hand*: aut inibi esse aut iam esse confectum, Cic. (**2**) *in that matter*: Pl.

ĭnĭcĭo -icĕre -iēci -iectum (in/iacio).

(**1**) *to throw in* or *into, cast* or *put in* or *into*. Lĭt., se in medios hostes, Cic.; with dat.: manum foculo, Liv.; Verg. Transf., **a**, *to cause, inspire, infuse, occasion*: alicui timorem, Cic.; alicui mentem, ut audeat, Cic.; certamen uxoribus, Liv.; Verg.: **b**, in conversation, *to throw in*: alicui nomen cuiuspiam, Cic.; mentionem, Hor.

(**2**) *to throw* or *cast on* or *over*. Lĭt., pontem (flumini), Liv.; bracchia collo, *to embrace*, Cic.; ei pallium, Cic.; sibi vestem, Ov.; esp.: **a**, of chains: alicui catenas, vincula, Cic.; Verg., Liv.: **b**, as legal t. t., manum inicere, *to lay hands on in order to appropriate, to take possession of*: manum virgini venienti, Liv. Transf., **a**, *to impose* a restraint: frenos, Cic.; frena, Hor.: **b**, with manum, *to lay hands on*: Verg., Plin. L.

iniectĭo -ōnis, f. (inicio), *a laying on*: manus, Quint.

iniectus -ūs, m. (inicio), *a throwing on* or *over*: iniectu multae vestis, Tac.; animi, *projection of the mind*, Lucr.

ĭnĭgo -ĕre -ēgi -actum (in/ago), *to incite*: Sen.

ĭnĭmīcĭtĭa -ae, f. (inimicus), *enmity*: Pl., Cic., often in plur.: cum aliquo mihi inimicitiae sunt or intercedunt, Cic.; inimicitias gerere, Cic.; exercere, Cic.; suscipere, Cic.; Caes., Tac.

ĭnĭmīco -are (inimicus), *to make hostile, set at variance*: ira miseras inimicat urbes, Hor.

ĭnĭmīcus -a -um (in/amicus), adj. (with compar. and superl.), *unfriendly, adverse, hostile*.

Lĭt., inimicus alicui, Cic.; inimicus cenis sumptuosis, Cic.; Liv.

Transf., (**1**) of inanimate objects, *hurtful, prejudicial*: odor nervis inimicus, Hor.; Cic., Verg. (**2**) poet.=hostilis: castra, Verg.

¶ As subst., m. **ĭnĭmīcus** -i, a (*personal*) *enemy, foe*: Cic., Liv.; f. **ĭnĭmīca** -ae, a *female foe*: Cic. So superl.: inimicissimus suus, *his bitterest foes*, Cic.

¶ Adv. (with compar. and superl.) **ĭnĭmīcē**, *in an unfriendly manner*: Cic., Liv.

ĭnĭquĭtās -tātis, f. (iniquus), *unevenness*. Lĭt., loci, Caes.; Liv. Transf., (**1**) *unfavourableness, difficulty*: temporis, Cic.; rerum, Caes. (**2**) *unfairness, injustice, unreasonableness*: hominis, Cic.; iniquitates maximae, Cic.; Caes., Liv.

ĭnĭquus -a -um (in/aequus), adj. (with compar. and superl.), *uneven, unequal*.

Lĭt., (**1**) of ground, *not level*: locus, Liv.; Verg., Ov. (**2**) in amount, *not corresponding*: heminae, Pers.

Transf., (**1**) of things, *excessive* or *unbalanced*: pondus, *too great*, Verg.; sol, *too hot*, Verg.; of contests, *ill-matched*: pugna, Verg.; of terms, *unfair*: pacem iniqua condicione retinere, Cic.; pax, Verg.; lex, Hor.; hence, in gen., *adverse, disadvantageous*: locus, Caes., Liv.; tempus, Liv.

(**2**) of persons and human attitudes, *unfair*: iudices, Ter.; hence: **a**, *perverse, disgruntled*; esp. with animus: animo iniquo pati, Ter.; ferre, Cic., Liv., *to take badly*; so of animals: iniquae mentis asellus, Hor.: **b**, *unfavourable, adverse*: in aliquem, Ter.; omnibus, Cic.; m. pl. as subst. **ĭnīqui** -ōrum, *enemies*: Cic.; aequi iniqui, aequi iniquique, *friends and foes*, Liv.

¶ Adv. (with compar. and superl.) **ĭnīquē**. Lĭt., *unequally*: Ter.; iniquissime comparatum est, Cic. Transf., *unfairly, adversely*: Pl., Cic., Hor., Liv.

ĭnĭtĭāmenta -orum, n. pl. (initio), *an initiation*: Sen.

ĭnĭtĭātĭo -onis, f. (initio), *an initiation*: Suet.

ĭnĭtĭo -are (initium), *to initiate*. Lĭt., into a secret worship: aliquem Cereri, Cic.; Liv. Transf., studiis, Quint.

ĭnĭtĭum -i, n. (ineo), *an entering upon*; hence *a beginning*.

Lĭt., initium capere, Caes.; initium dicendi sumere, Cic.; initium caedis, confligendi facere, Cic.; ab initio, *from the beginning*, Cic.; initio, *in the beginning, at the start*, Cic.

Transf., esp. in plur. (**1**) *the elements* or *first principles of a science*: initia mathematicorum, Cic. (**2**) *the auspices*; hence *the beginning of a reign*: initiis Tiberii auditis Tac. (**3**) *a secret worship, hidden rites mysteries*: Cic., Liv.; meton., *things used in such rites*: Cat.

ĭnĭtus -ūs, m. (ineo). (**1**) *an entrance*: Lucr (**2**) *a beginning*: Lucr.

ĭnĭūcundĭtās -tātis, f. (iniucundus), *un pleasantness*: ne quid habeat iniucunditati oratio, Cic.

ĭnĭūcundus -a -um, *unpleasant*: minime nobi iniucundus labor, Cic.; adversus malo iniucundus, *unfriendly*, Tac.

¶ Compar. adv. **ĭnĭūcundĭus**, *rathe unpleasantly*: res actae, Cic. L.

ĭnĭūdĭcātus -a -um (in/iudico), *undecidea* Quint.

niungo -iungĕre -iunxi -iunctum. LIT., *to join, attach, fasten* to: tigno asseres, Liv.; vineas et aggerem muro, Liv. TRANSF., *to inflict upon, bring upon*: civitatibus servitatem, Caes.; alicui laborem, onus, leges, Liv.; tributum, Tac.

niūrātus -a -um, *unsworn*: Pl., Cic., Liv.

niūrĭa -ae, f. (in/ius), *an injury, injustice, wrong.* LIT., iniuriam alicui inferre, imponere, facere, Cic.; ab aliquo accipere, Cic.; propulsare, Cic.; defendere, Caes.; with genit., *wrong done to*: Caes., Liv.; abl. sing. as adv. iniuriā, *wrongly, without cause*: Pl., Cic.; esp. *an insult*: spretae formae, Verg.; legal t. t.: actio iniuriarum, Cic. TRANSF., (1) *a possession wrongfully obtained*: pertinaces ad obtinendam iniuriam, Liv. (2) *revenge for an affront*: consulis, Liv.; Verg.

niūrĭōsus -a -um (iniuria), *acting wrongfully, unjust*: vita, Cic.; in proximos, Cic. TRANSF., *harmful*: Hor.
¶ Adv. (with compar.) **iniūrĭōsē**, *wrongfully*: in magistratus decernere, tractare, Cic.

niūrĭus -a -um (in/ius), *wrongful, unjust*: quia sit iniurium, Cic.

niūrus -a -um=iniurius; q.v.: Pl.

niussū, abl. sing. from iniussus, m. (in/iubeo), *without orders*: iniussu imperatoris, Cic.; iniussu suo, Cic.; Caes., Liv.

niussus -a -um (in/iubeo), *uncommanded, unbidden, spontaneous*: gramina virescunt, *without cultivation*, Verg.; Hor.

niustĭtĭa -ae, f. (iniustus). (1) *injustice*: totius iniustitiae nulla est capitalior, Cic. (2) *severity*: Ter.

niustus -a -um. (1) *unfair, unjust*: homo, bellum, Cic.; regna, *unjustly acquired*, Ov.; n. as subst. iniustum -i, *injustice*: metu iniusti, Hor. (2) in gen., *harsh, oppressive*: noverca, Verg.; onus, Cic.; fascis, Verg.
¶ Adv. **iniustē**, *unjustly, unfairly*: facere, Cic.

inlăbĕfactus -a -um (in/labefacio), *unshaken, firm*: Ov.

inlābor -lābi -lapsus, dep. (in/labor), *to glide into, fall into.* LIT., si fractus inlabatur orbis, Hor.; Cic. TRANSF., pernicies inlapsa civium in animos, Cic.; Verg.

inlăbōro -are (in/laboro), *to work upon, labour at*: domibus, *at building houses*, Tac.

inlăcessītus -a -um (in/lacesso), *unattacked, unprovoked*: Tac.

inlacrĭmābĭlis -e (in/lacrimabilis). (1) *unwept*: omnes inlacrimabiles urgentur, Hor. (2) *not to be moved by tears, pitiless*: Pluto, Hor.

inlacrĭmo -are (in/lacrimo), *to weep over, bewail*; with dat.: errori, Liv. TRANSF., ebur maestum inlacrimat templis, Verg.

inlacrĭmor -ari, dep. (in/lacrimor), *to weep over, bewail*: morti, Cic.

inlaesus -a -um (in/laedo), *unhurt, uninjured*: Ov., Suet.

inlaetābĭlis -e (in/laetabilis), *gloomy, cheerless*: ora, Verg.

inlăqueo -are (in/laqueo), *to entrap, ensnare*; fig.: munera navium saevos inlaqueant duces, Hor.

inlaudātus -a -um (in/laudo). (1) *unpraised,*

obscure: Plin. L. (2) *not to be praised, abominable*: Busiris, Verg.

inlautus=inlotus; q.v.

inlĕcebra -ae, f. (inlicio), *an allurement, enticement, attraction, charm*: voluptas est inlecebra turpitudinis, *to dishonour*, Cic.; Hor., Liv. Meton., *an enticer, a decoy-bird*: Pl.

inlĕcebrōsus -a -um (inlecebra), *attractive, enticing*; compar.: Pl. Adv. **inlĕcebrōsē**, *enticingly*: Pl.

¹inlectus -a -um (in/lego), *unread*: Ov.

²inlectus -ūs (inlicio), m. *allurement, enticement*: Pl.

³inlectus -a -um, partic. of inlicio; q.v.

inlĕpĭdus -a -um (in/lepidus), *inelegant, rude, unmannerly*: parens avarus, inlepidus, in liberos difficilis, Cic.; Pl., Cat. Adv. **inlĕpĭdē**, *rudely*: Pl., Hor.

¹inlex -lĭcis, c. (inlicio), *a decoy, lure*; of a person or thing: Pl.

²inlex -lēgis (in/lex), *lawless*: Pl.

inlībātus -a -um (in/libo), *undiminished, unimpaired*: divitiae, Cic.; imperium, Liv.

inlībĕrālis -e (in/liberalis), *unworthy of a free man, ungenerous*: te in me inliberalem putabit, Cic. L.; quaestus, Cic.; genus iocandi, Cic.; adiectio, *avaricious, sordid*, Liv.
¶ Adv. **inlībĕrālĭtĕr**, *ignobly, ungenerously, meanly*: patris diligentiā non inliberaliter institutus, Cic.; facere, Cic. L.

inlībĕrālĭtās -ātis, f. (inliberalis), *stinginess, meanness*: inliberalitatis avaritiaeque suspicio, Cic.

inlĭcĭo -licĕre -lexi -lectum (in/*lacio), *to entice, allure, decoy, inveigle*: aliquem in fraudem, Pl.; ad bellum, Sall.; with ut and the subj.: Liv.

inlĭcĭtātor -ōris, m. (licito), *a sham bidder at an auction, a puffer*: Cic.

inlĭcĭtus -a -um (in/licitus), *not allowed, illegal*: exactiones, Tac.; Luc.

inlīdo -līdĕre -līsi -līsum (in/laedo), *to strike, beat, dash against*: caestus effracto inlisit in ossa cerebro, Verg.; dentem, Hor.

inlĭgo -are (in/ligo), *to bind, tie, fasten, attach.* LIT., emblemata in poculis, Cic.; aratra iuvencis, Hor.; Mettium in currus, Liv. TRANSF., (1) *to connect, attach*: aliquem pignoribus, Cic.; familiari amicitiā, Liv.; sententiam verbis, Cic. (2) *to entangle, impede*: inutilis inque ligatus, Verg.; angustis et concisis disputationibus inligati, Cic.

inlīmis -e (in/limus), *free from mud, clear*: fons, Ov.

inlĭno -linĕre -lēvi -lĭtum (in/lino), *to smear, daub, spread.* (1) *to spread something on* a surface: aurum vestibus inlitum, Hor.; quodcumque semel chartis inleverit, *has written, scribbled*, Hor. (2) *to spread a surface with something*: pocula ceris, Ov.; fig.: color venustatis non fuco inlitus, Cic.

inlĭquĕfactus -a -um (in/liquefacio), *molten, liquefied*: Cic.

inlittĕrātus -a -um (in/litteratus), *ignorant, illiterate*; of persons: vir non inlitteratus, Cic. TRANSF., of things: nervi, Hor.; Cic. L.

inlōtus (**inlautus**, **inlūtus**) -a -um (in/lavo), *unwashed, unclean*: Hor.; sudor, *not washed off*, Verg.

inlŭcesco (inlūcisco) -lūcescĕre -luxi (in/
lucesco, lucisco), *to become light, begin to
shine.* LIT., cum tertio die sol inluxisset,
Cic.; inlucescet aliquando ille dies, Cic.;
impers., inlucescit, *it grows light, is daylight*:
ubi inluxit, Liv.; transit., *to shine upon*: Pl.
TRANSF., cum in tenebris vox consulis
inluxerit, Cic.

inlūdo -lūdĕre -lūsi -lūsum (in/ludo).
(1) *to play with, sport with*: chartis, *to play
with paper, amuse oneself with writing*, Hor.;
transit.: inlusas auro vestes, *fancifully
worked*, Verg.
(2) *to mock, laugh at, ridicule*: **a**, with dat.:
capto, Verg.; alicuius dignitati, Cic.; rebus
humanis, Hor.: **b**, transit., with acc. object:
miseros inludi nolunt, Cic.; eam artem, Cic.;
virtutem, Verg.
(3) *to maltreat*: **a**, with dat.: cui (frondi)
silvestres uri inludunt, Verg.; Tac.: **b**,
transit., with acc. object: Ter., Tac.

inlūmĭno -are (in/lumen), *to light up, illuminate*: Cic.; luna inluminata a sole, Cic.
TRANSF., *to make clear, set off, adorn*:
orationem sententiis, Cic.
¶ Hence adv. from perf. partic. **inlūmĭ-
nātē,** *luminously, clearly*: dicere, Cic.

inlūsĭo -ōnis, f. (inludo), *irony, as a rhetorical
figure*: Cic.

inlustris -e (in/lustro), adj. (with compar.),
light, full of light, bright, brilliant. LIT., stella;
lumen; locus, Cic. TRANSF., (1) *clear, plain,
evident*: oratio, res, Cic. (2) *distinguished,
famous*: inlustribus in personis tempori-
busque, Cic.; nomen inlustrius, Cic.; res
inlustrior, Caes.
¶ Hence compar. adv. **inlustrĭus,** *more
clearly, more distinctly*: dicere, Cic.

inlustro -are (in/*lustrum, *lighting), *to light
up, make bright.*
LIT., sol oras, Hor.
TRANSF., (1) *to bring to light, make known
or clear*: consilia, Cic.; ius obscurum, Cic.
(2) *to make illustrious, do honour to*: tuam
amplitudinem, Cic. L.; quid prius inlustrem
satiris? Hor.

inlūtĭlus -e (inlutus, inlotus), *unable to be
washed out*: Pl.

inlŭvĭes -ēi, f. (1) *an inundation, flood*: Tac.
(2) *dirt, mud*: morbo inluvieque peresus,
Verg.; Pl., Tac.

inm-, *see* imm-.

innābĭlis -e (in/no), *that cannot be swum in*:
unda, Ov.

innascor -nasci -nātus, dep. *to be born, grow,
arise in or upon.* LIT., neglectis filix innascitur agris, Hor.; salicta innata ripis, Liv.
TRANSF., *to be produced, arise*: in hac elatione
animi cupiditas innascitur, Cic.
¶ Hence partic. **innātus** -a -um, *innate,
inborn*: insita quaedam vel potius innata cupiditas, Cic.; with dat.: mihi, *in me*, Pl.; Caes.

innăto -are. (1) *to swim into*: in concham
hiantem, Cic. (2) *to swim or float in or upon*;
with dat.: lactuca acri innatat stomacho,
Hor.; unda freto, Ov.; with acc.: undam
innatat alnus, Verg. TRANSF., in partic.:
innatans, *superficial,* Quint.

innātus, partic. from innascor; q.v.

innāvĭgābĭlis -e, *not navigable*: Liv.

innecto -nectĕre -nexŭi -nexum, *to tie in, bind,
fasten, weave together.*

LIT., comas, Verg.; fauces laqueo, Ov.;
palmas armis, Verg.; inter se innexi rami, Liv
TRANSF., (1) causas morandi, *to put together
bring forward one after the other,* Verg. (2) t(
connect, entangle, implicate: innexus conscientiae alicuius, Tac.; Hyrcanis pe(
adfinitatem innexus erat, Tac.

innītor -nīti -nixus sum, dep. *to lean upon,
rest upon, support oneself by.* LIT., scutis
Caes.; hastā, Liv.; alis, *to fly*, Ov. TRANSF.,
uni viro, Messio, fortuna hostium innititur
Liv.

inno -nare, *to swim in or on.* LIT., fluitantes e(
innantes beluae, Cic.; with acc.: fluvium
Verg. TRANSF., (1) *to flow over*: Hor. (2) t(
sail over, navigate; with dat.: aquae, Liv.
with acc.: Stygios lacus, Verg.

innŏcens -entis, adj. (with superl.), *harmless*
LIT., epistula, Cic. L.; innocentis pocul(
Lesbii, Hor. TRANSF., *innocent, harmless,
inoffensive, blameless*: innocens is dicitur qu(
nihil nocet, Cic.; with genit.: factorum, Tac.
¶ Adv. **innŏcentĕr,** *innocently, blame-
lessly*: Quint., Tac.; compar.: innocentius
agere, Tac.

innŏcentĭa -ae, f. (innocens), *harmlessness*:
ferorum animalium, Plin. TRANSF., *innocence, integrity, inoffensiveness, disinterestedness*: Caes., Cic., Liv.; also meton.=*the
innocent*: innocentiam poenā liberare, Cic.

innŏcŭus -a -um. (1) act., *innocuous, harm-
less.* LIT., herba, Ov.; litus, *safe*, Verg.
TRANSF., *innocent, harmless, blameless*: homo,
Ov. (2) pass., *unhurt, unharmed*: carinae,
Verg.
¶ Adv. **innŏcŭē,** *harmlessly*: vivere, Ov.

innōtesco -nōtescĕre -nōtŭi, *to become known
or noted*: nostris innotuit illa libellis, Ov.;
quod ubi innotuit, Liv.

innŏvo -are, *to renew*: se ad suam intempe-
rantiam, *to return*, Cic.

innoxĭus -a -um.
(1) act. LIT., *innoxious, harmless*: anguis,
Verg. TRANSF., *innocent*: criminis, Liv.;
paupertas, Tac.
(2) pass., *unhurt, unharmed*: ipsi innoxii,
Sall.; Lucr.

innūbĭlus -a -um, *unclouded, clear*: Lucr.

innūba -ae, f. adj. (in/nubo), *unmarried,
without a husband*: Sibylla, Ov.; laurus
(because Daphne, while still a virgin, was
changed into a laurel), Ov.

innūbo -nūbĕre -nupsi -nuptum, *to marry
into*: quo innupsisset, Liv.; nostris thalamis,
Ov.

innŭmĕrābĭlis -e, *that cannot be counted,
innumerable*: multitudo, Cic.; Hor.
¶ Adv. **innŭmĕrābĭlĭtĕr,** *innumerably*
Lucr., Cic.

innŭmĕrābĭlĭtās -atis, f. (innumerabilis)
an infinite number: mundorum, Cic.

innŭmĕrālis -e, *countless, innumerable*: Lucr

innŭmĕrus -a -um, *countless, innumerable*
gentes, Verg.; Lucr., Ov., Tac.

innŭo -nŭĕre -nŭi -nūtum, *to give a nod to
make a sign or signal to*: alicui, Pl., Ter.
ubi innuerint, Liv.

innupta -ae, f. adj. (in/nubo), *unmarried*
puellae, Verg.; meton.: nuptiae innupta
(γάμος ἄγαμος), *a marriage that is no marriag(
an unhappy marriage*, poet. ap. Cic. A(
subst., *a maiden*: Cat., Verg.

innūtrĭo -ire, *to bring up in* or *among*: mari, Plin. L.; amplis opibus, Suet.

Īnō -ūs, f. ('Ινώ), *daughter of Cadmus, wife of Athamas*; adj. **Īnōus** -a -um, *of* or *belonging to Ino.*

ĭnoblītus -a -um (in/obliviscor), *mindful, not forgetful*: Ov.

ĭnobrŭtus -a -um (in/obruo), *not overwhelmed*: Ov.

ĭnobservābĭlis -e, *not to be observed, imperceptible*: Cat.

ĭnobservantĭa -ae, f. *negligence, carelessness, inattention*: Suet., Quint.

ĭnobservātus -a -um, *unobserved, unperceived*: sidera, Ov.

ĭnoccĭdŭus -a -um, *never setting*: Luc.

ĭnŏcŭlātĭo -ōnis, f. *an engrafting*: Cato.

ĭnŏdōrus -a -um, *without smell*: Pers.

ĭnoffensus -a -um (in/offendo). LIT., *not struck against*: meta, Luc.; pedem, *not stumbling*, Tib. TRANSF., *unhindered, unobstructed*: vita, Ov.; cursus honorum, *uninterrupted*, Tac.

ĭnoffĭcĭōsus -a -um. (1) *neglectful of duty*: testamentum, *in which the nearest relatives are passed over*, Cic. (2) *disobliging*: in aliquem, Cic. L.

ĭnŏlens -entis, *without smell*: Lucr.

ĭnŏlesco -ōlescĕre -ŏlēvi, *to grow in* or *on.* LIT., udo libro, Verg. TRANSF., penitusque necesse est multa (mala) diu concreta modis inolescere miris, Verg.

ĭnōmĭnātus -a -um (in/omen), *inauspicious, unlucky*: Hor.

ĭnŏpĭa -ae, f. (inops), *want of means, need, poverty.* In gen.: Cic.; frumentaria, Caes.; with genit., *lack of, want of*: frugum, consilii, Cic.; frumenti, Caes., Sall. Esp. (1) of a speaker, *lack of ideas*: Cic. (2) *helplessness*: Cic.

ĭnŏpīnans -antis, *not expecting, unawares*: aliquem inopinantem adgredi, Caes.; Liv.

¶ Adv. **ĭnŏpīnantĕr**, *unexpectedly*: Suet.

ĭnŏpīnātus -a -um. (1) pass., *unexpected, unlooked for*: res, Cic.; malum, Caes.; Liv.; ex inopinato, Cic.; inopinato, Liv., *unexpectedly.* (2) act., *not expecting*: inopinatos invadere, Liv.

ĭnŏpīnus -a -um (in/opinor), *unexpected, unlooked for*: quies, Verg.; visus, Ov.; Tac.

ĭnŏpĭōsus -a -um (inopia), *needy, in want*; with genit.: consilii, Pl.

ĭnops -ŏpis, *without means.*
LIT., of persons, *poor, helpless*: Cic., Verg., Hor., Ov.; esp. with genit., *wanting in, in need of*: amicorum, humanitatis, Cic.; animi, Verg.; pecuniae, Liv.; so with abl.: verbis, Cic.; Liv.
TRANSF., of things: aerarium inops et exhaustum, Cic.; amor, Lucr.; animus, Hor.; with genit.: terra pacis, Ov.; esp. of language, *weak, poor*: lingua, oratio, Cic.

ĭnōrātus -a -um (in/oro), *not formally brought forward and heard*: re inoratā, Cic.

ĭnordĭnātus -a -um, *disorderly, in confusion*: dispersi, inordinati exibant, Liv.; n. as subst. **inordĭnātum** -i, *disorder*: ex inordinato in ordinem adducere, Cic.

ĭnornātus -a -um, *unadorned.* LIT., mulieres, Cic.; Ov. TRANSF., (1) *plain,* orator: Cic. (2) *unpraised, uncelebrated*: Hor.

inp-, *see* **imp-**.

inquam, originally perhaps a present subj.; the other forms found are: pres., inquis, inquit, inquimus, inquitis, inquiunt; imperf., inquibat and inquiebat; fut., inquies, inquiet; perf., inquii, inquisti; imperat., inque, inquito, *I say.*
Used (1) parenthetically, in quoting the words of a speaker: 'misere cupis', inquit, 'abire', Hor.; with dat.: inquit mihi, Cic. L. (2) in repetition, for the sake of emphasis: hunc unum diem, hunc unum, inquam, diem, Cic.; Lucr. (3) in stating objections: non solemus, inquit, ostendere, Cic.; inquiebat, Cic.

¹**inquĭes** -ētis, f. *disquiet, want of rest*: Plin.

²**inquĭes** -ētis, adj. *unquiet, restless*: homo, Sall.; Tac.

inquĭēto -are (inquietus), *to disquiet, disturb*: rumoribus, Plin. L. TRANSF., victoriam, Tac.

inquĭētus -a -um, *unquiet, restless.* LIT., Hadria, *stormy*, Hor.; nox inquieta, Liv. TRANSF., animus, Liv.; tempora, Tac.

inquĭlīnus -i, m. (colo), *one who dwells in a place not his own, a tenant, lodger*: inquilinus civis Romae (of Cicero, who was not born in Rome), Sall.; Cic.

inquĭno -are (connected with caenum), *to befoul, pollute, stain.* LIT., aqua turbida et cadaveribus inquinata, Cic.; aquas venenis, Ov. TRANSF., *to corrupt*: omnem splendorem honestatis, Cic.; se parricidio, Cic.; Hor., Liv.
¶ Hence partic. **inquĭnātus** -a -um, *dirty, foul, polluted, sordid*: homo vita omni inquinatus, Cic.; superl.: sermo inquinatissimus, Cic.
¶ Adv. **inquĭnātē**, *filthily*: loqui, Cic.

inquīro -quīrĕre -quīsīvi -quīsītum (in/quaero), *to seek for, search for.* LIT., corpus alicuius, Liv. TRANSF., (1) *to investigate, inquire into*: diligenter in ea, Cic.; in eum quid agat, quem ad modum vivat, inquiritur, Cic. (2) *to search for, look for*: vitia, Hor.; omnia ordine, Liv.; Cic.; esp. as legal t. t., *to search for evidence* against anyone: in competitores, Cic.

inquīsĭtĭo -ōnis, f. (inquiro). (1) *a searching after, looking for*: corporum, Plin.; esp. as legal t. t., *a search for evidence* against anyone: candidati, *against a candidate*, Cic.; Plin. L. (2) *a looking into, an investigation, inquiry*: veri inquisitio atque investigatio, Cic.

inquīsītor -ōris, m. (inquiro), *an inquirer*; hence (1) *a spy*: Suet. (2) *an investigator*: rerum, Cic.; in law, *one who searches for evidence to support an accusation*: Cic., Tac., Plin. L.

inrāsus -a -um, *unshaved*: Pl.

inrătĭōnālis -e, *without reason, irrational*: Quint.

inraucesco -raucescĕre -rausi (in/raucus), *to become hoarse*: Cic.

inrĕdĭvīvus -a -um, *irreparable*: Cat.

inrĕdux -ŭcis, *not bringing back*: Luc.

inrĕlĭgātus -a -um, *unbound*: croceas inreligata comas, Ov.

inrĕlĭgĭōsus -a -um, *irreligious, impious*: inreligiosum ratus, with infin., Liv.; Plin. L.
¶ Adv. **inrĕlĭgĭōsē**, *irreligiously, impiously*: Tac.

inrĕmĕābĭlis -e, *from which there is no return*: unda, Verg.

inrĕpărābĭlis -e, *that cannot be restored, irrecoverable*: tempus, Verg.; Sen.

inrĕpertus -a -um (in/reperio), *not discovered, not found out*: aurum, Hor.

inrēpo -rēpĕre -repsi -reptum, *to creep, crawl in*. LIT., Suet. TRANSF., *to creep in, insinuate oneself*: in mentes hominum, Cic.; in testamenta locupletium, Cic.; with acc.: Tac.

inreprĕhensus -a -um (in/reprehendo), *unblamed, blameless*: Ov.

inrĕquĭētus -a -um, *restless, troubled*: Charybdis, Ov.

inrĕsectus -a -um (in/reseco), *uncut*: pollex, Hor.

inrĕsŏlūtus -a -um (in/resolvo), *not loosed, not slackened*: vincula, Ov.

inrētĭo -ire (in/rete), *to catch in a net, entangle*; fig.: aliquem corruptelarum inlecebris, Cic.

inrētortus -a -um (in/retorqueo), *not turned or twisted back*: oculo inretorto, Hor.

inrĕvĕrens -entis, *disrespectful*: Plin. L.; adv. **inrĕvĕrenter**, *disrespectfully*: Plin. L.

inrĕvĕrentia -ae, f. *want of respect, irreverence*: iuventutis, Tac.; adversus fas nefasque, Tac.

inrĕvŏcābĭlis -e, *that cannot be called back, irrevocable*. LIT., aetas, Lucr.; verbum, Hor. TRANSF., *unalterable, implacable*: Tac., Plin. L.; compar.: Tac.

inrĕvŏcātus -a -um, *not called back, i.e. not asked to repeat anything*: Hor.

inrīdĕo -rīdēre -rīsi -rīsum. Intransit., *to laugh at, jeer at*: Cic., Tac.; with dat.: Cic. L. Transit., *to mock, ridicule, deride*: deos, Cic.; Hor., Verg.

inrīdĭcŭlo, predicative dat. from adj. inridiculus, *for a laughing-stock*: inridiculo esse, *to be made game of*, Pl.; habere, *to make game of*. Adv. **inrīdĭcŭlē**, *without wit* or *humour*: non inridicule dixit, Caes.

inrĭgātĭo -ōnis, f. (inrigo), *a watering, irrigation*: agri, Cic.

inrĭgo -are.
(1) *to conduct water* or *any other liquid*: imbres, Verg. TRANSF., *to diffuse*: per membra quietem, Verg.
(2) *to water, irrigate, inundate*: Aegyptum Nilus inrigat, Cic.; hortulos fontibus, Cic. TRANSF., fessos sopor inrigat artus, *overspreads*, Verg.; Lucr., Pl.

inrĭgŭus -a -um (inrigo). (1) act., *watering, irrigating*: fons, Verg. TRANSF., somnus, *refreshing*, Pers. (2) pass., *watered*: hortus, Hor.; Liv. TRANSF., corpus mero, *soaked*, Hor.

inrīsĭo -ōnis, f. (inrideo), *a laughing at, mocking, derision*; with subjective genit.: omnium, Cic.

inrīsor -ōris, m. (inrideo), *a laugher, mocker, derider*; with objective genit.: huius orationis, Cic.

inrīsus -ūs, m. (inrideo), *laughter, mockery, derision*: ab inrisu (*in derision*) linguam exserere, Liv.; predicative dat. inrisui, *for a laughing-stock*: esse, Caes., Tac.

inrītābĭlis -e (inrito), *irritable, easily roused*: inritabiles sunt animi optimorum, Cic. L.; genus vatum, Hor.

inrītāmen -ĭnis, n. (inrito), *an incitement, inducement*: amoris, Ov.

inrītāmentum -i, n. (inrito), *incitement, incentive*; with genit.: certaminum, Liv.; libidinum, Tac.; Ov.

inrītātĭo -ōnis, f. (inrito), *a stirring up, provoking, incitement*; with genit.: nullis conviviorum inritationibus, Tac.; inritatio quidem animorum ea prima fuit, Liv.

inrīto -are, *to stir up, stimulate, incite, excite,* esp. to anger: aliquem, Pl., Cic.; aliquem ad certamen, Liv.; animos barbarorum, Liv.; iram et odium, Liv.; quietos amnes, Hor.

inrītus -a -um (in/ratus). (1) *void, invalid*: testamentum facere inritum, Cic. (2) *vain, ineffectual, useless.* LIT., of things: inceptum, Liv.; dona, tela, Verg.; remedium, Tac.; n. as subst.: spes ad inritum cadit, *is disappointed*, Liv. TRANSF., of persons, *without doing anything*: initi legati remittuntur, Tac.; with genit. of the object: legationis, Tac.

inrŏgātĭo -ōnis, f. (inrogo), *the imposing of a fine* or *penalty*: multae, Cic.

inrŏgo -are, *to propose to the people a measure against anyone*: alicui legem, privilegium, Cic.; hence, in gen., *to inflict, impose*: multam alicui, Cic., Liv.; poenas peccatis, Hor.

inrŏro -are, *to moisten (with dew)*: crinem aquis, Ov.; with dat.: lacrimae inrorant foliis, *trickle down upon*, Ov.

inructo -are, *to belch at*: Pl.

inrumpo -rumpĕre -rūpi -ruptum, *to break in, burst in, rush in.* LIT., in castra, Cic.; with dat.: thalamo, Verg.; with acc.: portam, Sall.; limina, Verg. TRANSF., in nostrum patrimonium, Cic.; luxuries quam in domum inrupit, Cic.; imagines in animos per corpus inrumpunt, Cic.

inrŭo -rŭĕre -rŭi. (1) transit., *to fling in*: Ter. (2) intransit., *to rush in.* LIT., in aciem, Cic.; in forum, Liv. TRANSF., in alienas possessiones, Cic.; in odium offensionemque populi Romani, *rush blindly into*, Cic.; ne quo inruas, *in case you make some blunder*, Cic.

inruptĭo -ōnis, f. (inrumpo), *a breaking, bursting into, irruption*: etiamsi inruptio nulla facta est, Cic.; Pl., Tac.

inruptus -a -um (in/rumpo), *unbroken, unsevered*: copula, Hor.

insălūbris -e, *unhealthy*: Plin., Quint.

insălūtātus -a -um, *ungreeted*: in tmesis: inque salutatam linquo, Verg.

insānābĭlis -e, *incurable.* LIT., morbus, Cic.; Hor., Liv. TRANSF., contumeliae, Cic.; ingenium, Liv.

insānĭa -ae, f. (insanus), *madness, frenzy.*
LIT., nomen insaniae significat mentis aegrotationem et morbum, Cic.; concupiscere aliquid ad insaniam, *madly*, Cic.; Verg.
TRANSF., (1) *thought, speech* or *conduct like a madman's, senseless excess, senseless extravagance*: libidinum, Cic.; Liv.; in plur.: Cic. (2) *poetical rapture* or *inspiration*: amabilis, Hor.

insānĭo -ire (insanus), *to be mad, to rage.* LIT., Cic., Hor. TRANSF., (1) *to act like a madman, to rave*: ex iniuriā, Liv.; Verg.; with acc.: similem (errorem), Hor.; sollemnia, Hor. (2) of things, *to rage*: insanientem Bosporum, Hor. (3) *to be inspired*: Cic.

insānĭtas -ātis, f. (insanus), *disease, unsoundness*: Cic.

insānus -a -um, adj. (with compar. and superl.), *of unsound mind, mad, insane.* Lit., Cic., Juv. Transf., (1) *of persons, etc., acting like a madman, raving, senseless*: homo flagitiis insanus, Cic.; contio, Cic.; cupiditas, Cic.; cupido, Verg.; Hor., Liv. (2) *of things, raging, stormy*: fluctus, Verg. (3) *inspired*: vates, Verg.
¶ Adv. (with compar.) **insānē**, *madly*: Pl., Hor.

insătĭābĭlis -e (in/satio). (1) pass., *that cannot be satisfied, insatiable*: cupiditas, Cic.; Liv. (2) act., *that does not satiate, uncloying*: pulchritudo, Cic.; compar.: insatiabilior species, Cic.
¶ Adv. **insătĭābĭlĭtĕr**, *insatiably*: Lucr., Tac., Plin. L.

insătĭĕtās -ātis, f. *insatiateness*: Pl.

insătŭrābĭlis -e (in/saturo), *insatiable*: abdomen, Cic.
¶ Adv. **insătŭrābĭlĭtĕr**, *insatiably*: Cic.

inscendo -scendĕre -scendi -scensum (in/scando), *to climb on, ascend, mount*; intransit.: in rogum ardentem, Cic.; transit.: quadrigas, Pl.

inscensĭo -ōnis, f. (inscendo), *a going on board*: in navem, Pl.

insciens -entis. (1) *not knowing a particular fact, unaware*: me insciente factum, *done without my knowledge*, Cic. L. (2) in gen., *ignorant*: Ter.
¶ Adv. **inscĭentĕr**, *ignorantly, stupidly*: facere, Cic.; Liv.

inscĭentĭa -ae, f. (insciens). (1) *ignorance, inexperience*: inscientia mea, nostra, Cic.; foll. by genit. of the subject: vulgi, Caes.; of the object: locorum, Caes.; dicendi, Cic. (2) *culpable ignorance*: Tac.

inscītĭa -ae, f. (inscitus), *inexperience, want of skill, ignorance*; with genit. of subject: Tac.; of object: rerum negotii gerendi, disserendi, Cic.; veri, Hor.; litterarum, Tac.; erga domum suam, Tac.; absol.: Pl., Liv.

inscītus -a -um, *ignorant, unskilful, stupid*: Pl., Cic.; compar.: quid autem est inscitius, Cic.
¶ Adv. **inscītē**, *clumsily, unskilfully*: Cic,. Liv.

inscĭus -a -um, *ignorant, not knowing*: medici inscii imperitique, Cic.; with genit.: omnium rerum, Cic.; culpae, Verg.; equus inscius aevi, Verg.; with de: Pl.; with indir. quest.: inscii quid in Aeduis gereretur, Caes.; Verg., Hor.

inscrībo -scrībĕre -scrīpsi -scriptum, *to write in or on, inscribe.*
Lit., aliquid in basi tropaeorum, Cic.; nomen monumentis, Cic.; inscripti nomina regum flores, Verg.; epistulam patri, Cic.
Transf., (1) *to mark*, without actual writing: pulvis inscribitur hastā, Verg. (2) fig., *to impress*: orationes in animo, Cic. (3) *to entitle, mark as* something: liber qui Oeconomicus inscribitur, Cic.; sua quemque deorum inscribit facies, Ov.; hence *to ascribe, mark as belonging to*: sibi nomen philosophi, Cic.; deos sceleri, *to charge the gods with a crime*, Ov.

inscriptĭo -ōnis, f. (inscribo), *a writing in or upon*: nominis, Cic.

¹**inscriptus** -a -um (in/scribo), *unwritten*: Quint.

²**inscriptus** -a -um, partic. from inscribo; q.v.

insculpo -sculpĕre -sculpsi -sculptum, *to cut or carve in, engrave.* Lit., summam patrimonii saxo, Hor.; foedus columnā aeneā, Liv.; Cic. Transf., *to impress*: natura insculpsit in mentibus ut, Cic.

insĕcābĭlis -e, *that cannot be cut, indivisible*: Quint., Sen.

insĕco -sĕcare -sĕcŭi -sectum, *to cut into*: Plin.; perf. partic. insectus -a -um, *notched*: Ov.

insectātĭo -ōnis, f. (insector), *a close following, hot pursuit.* Lit., hostis, Liv. Transf., *railing at, abuse*: alicuius, Liv.; Tac.

insectātor -ōris, m. (insector), *a pursuer, persecutor*: plebis, Liv.; Quint.

insecto -are=insector; q.v., Pl.

insector -ari, dep. *to follow closely, pursue.* Lit., aquila insectans alias aves, Cic. Transf., (1) *to pursue with harsh words, reproach, abuse, rail at*: aliquem maledictis, Cic.; audaciam improborum, Cic. (2) herbam rastris, *to harry*, Verg.

insēdābĭlĭtĕr, adv. (in/sedo), *unquenchably, incessantly*: Lucr.

insĕnesco -sĕnescĕre -sĕnŭi, *to grow old at or among*; with dat.: libris et curis, Hor.; Ov., Tac.

insensĭlis -e, *insensible, without sensation*: Lucr.

insĕpultus -a -um (in/sepelio), *unburied*: acervi civium, Cic.; aliquem insepultum proicere, Liv.; sepultura, *burial without the usual rites*, Cic.

insĕquor -sĕqui -sĕcūtus sum, dep.
(1) *to follow after, follow on, succeed.*
Lit., in space: insequitur acies ornata armataque, Liv.; with acc.: temere insecutae Orphea silvae, Hor.
Transf., **a**, in time: insequitur clamor virum, Verg.; with acc.: hunc proximo saeculo Themistocles insecutus est, Cic.; annus insequens, Liv.: **b**, *to pursue a subject*: insequar longius, Cic.
(2) *to follow up, pursue with hostile intent.* Lit., aliquem gladio stricto, Cic.; clamore et minis, Cic.; Liv., Verg. Transf., **a**, *to censure, reproach*: aliquem irridendo, homines benevolos contumeliā, Cic.: **b**, in gen., *to attack, assail*: mors insecuta est Gracchum, *overtook*, Cic.

¹**insĕro** -sĕrĕre -sēvi -sĭtum, *to graft in*: Verg., Ov. Transf., *to implant*: inserit novas opiniones, evellit insitas, Cic.; Hor.
¶ Hence partic. **insĭtus** -a -um. (1) *implanted, innate, inborn*: insitus menti cognitionis amor, Cic.; Liv. (2) *incorporated*: Cic., Tac.

²**insĕro** -sĕrere -sĕrŭi -sertum, *to let in, introduce, insert.*
Lit., collum in laqueum, Cic.; caput in tentoria, Liv.; radiis subtemen, Ov.
Transf., in gen., *to associate, connect, put in or among*: me lyricis ratibus, Hor.; deos minimis rebus, Liv.; se turbae, Ov.; iocos historiae, Ov.

inserto -are (freq. of ²insero), *to insert, put into*: clypeo sinistram, Verg.

inservĭo -ire, *to be a slave, to serve.* Lit., reges inservientes, *vassal kings*, Tac. Transf., (1) *to serve* a person, *to be devoted to*; with dat.: Ter., Cic., Liv.; nihil est inservitum a me temporis causā, Cic. (2) *to serve* a thing: artibus, Cic.; famae, Tac.

insessus, partic. from insido; q.v.

insībĭlo -are, *to hiss, whistle in*: Ov.

insīdĕo -ēre (in/sedeo), *to sit in* or *on*.
LIT., immani et vastae beluae, Cic.; equo, Cic.; with acc., *to occupy, hold*: locum, Liv. TRANSF., (1) insidens capulo manus, *resting upon*, Tac. (2) of abstr. things, *to rest, dwell, remain*: insidet quaedam in optimo quoque virtus, Cic.; Liv.

insĭdĭae -ārum, f. pl. (insideo), *an ambush*.
LIT., insidias locare, Liv.; conlocare, Caes.; componere, Tac.; of the place of ambush: milites in insidiis conlocare, Caes.
TRANSF., *a snare, trap, deceit, plot*: insidias vitae ponere, facere, Cic.; ponere contra aliquem, Cic.; alicui parare, Cic.; conlocare, struere, adhibere, comparare, Cic.; moliri, Verg.; per insidias, ex insidiis, *or* insidiis, *treacherously*, Cic.

insĭdĭātor -ōris, m. (insidior). LIT., *a man in ambush*: Liv. TRANSF., *a spy, waylayer, lurker*: viae, Cic.; Liv.

insĭdĭor -ari, dep. (insidiae), *to lie in ambush, lie in wait*. LIT., with dat.: Clodio, Cic.; hostibus, Ov.; ovili, Verg. TRANSF., (1) *to plot against*: alicui, Cic. (2) *to watch for, wait for*: somno maritorum, Cic.; tempori, Liv.

insĭdĭōsus -a -um (insidiae), *deceitful, treacherous*: insidiosus et plenus latronum locus, Cic.; clementia, Cic. L.; compar.: quis insidiosior? Cic.; verba, Ov.
Adv. (with superl.) **insĭdĭōsē**, *deceitfully, treacherously, insidiously*: Cic.

insīdo -sīdĕre -sēdi -sessum, *to sit, settle, perch upon*.
LIT., (1) in gen.; with dat.: floribus (of bees), Verg.; digitos insidere membris, *sink into*, Ov. (2) *to settle on*: iugis, Verg.; with acc.: cineres patriae, Verg. (3) milit. *to occupy, to beset*; with dat.: silvestribus locis, Liv.; with acc.: tumulos, viam, Liv.; montes insessi, Tac.
TRANSF., *to sink deep*: in animo oratio, Cic.

insignĕ -is, n. (insignis), *a distinguishing mark, token*. LIT., in gen., Caes., Cic.; nocturnum, *a night-signal*, Liv.; esp. *an official badge, decoration*, or *medal*: insigne regium, Cic.; more commonly plur., insignia, *badges, insignia*: imperatoris, Caes.; sacerdotum, Liv.; regia, Cic. TRANSF., in plur. (1) *distinctions*: insignia virtutis, laudis, Cic. (2) in speech: orationis lumina et quoddammodo insignia, *beauties*, Cic.

insignĭo -ire (insignis), *to mark, distinguish*: cum omnis annus funeribus et cladibus insigniretur, *was remarkable for*, Tac.; agros tropaeis, Verg.; clipeum Io auro insignibat, Verg.
¶ Hence partic. **insignītus** -a -um, *marked*; hence (1) *conspicuous*: flagitium, Tac.; compar.: insignitior contumelia, Liv. (2) *clear*: imagines, Cic.; notae veritatis, Cic.
¶ Hence adv. (with compar.) **insignītē**, *remarkably, extraordinarily*: Pl., Cic., Liv.

insignis -e (in/signum), *distinguished, remarkable, notable*.
LIT., (bos) maculis insignis, Verg.; uxores insignes auro et purpurā, Liv.; Phoebus insignis crinibus, Ov.

TRANSF., *eminent, distinguished, extraordinary*: improbitas, Cic.; virtus Scipionis, Cic.; insigne ad inridendum vitium, Cic.; vir, Tac.; Hor., Liv.
¶ Adv. **insignĭtĕr**, *remarkably*: Cic., Plin. L.

insignītus -a -um, partic. from insignio; q.v.

insĭlia n. pl. (? insilio), *the treadles* of a loom, or perhaps *the leash-rods*: Lucr.

insĭlio -sĭlire -sĭlŭi (in/salio), *to leap, spring, jump in* or *on*: in phalangas, Caes.; in equum, Liv.; with dat.: tergo, Ov.; with acc.: Aetnam, Hor.; undas, Ov. TRANSF., in malum cruciatum, Pl.

insĭmŭlātĭo -ōnis, f. (insimulo), *an accusation, charge*: probrorum, Cic.

insĭmŭlo -are, *to charge, accuse*, esp. falsely: insontem, Pl.; aliquem falso, Cic.; falso crimine, Cic., Liv.; with genit. of charge: proditionis, Caes.; se peccati, Cic.; with internal acc.: id quod ego insimulo, Cic.; with acc. and infin.: Ter., Cic., Liv.

insincērus -a -um, *tainted*: cruor, Verg.

insĭnŭātĭo -ōnis, f. (insinuo), rhet. t. t., *the gaining the favour of the audience*: Cic.

insĭnŭo -are, *to introduce by windings* or *turnings, to insinuate*.
LIT., Romani, quacumque data intervalla essent, insinuabant ordines suos, *pushed forward their files into the gaps of the enemy*, Liv.; (anima) nascentibus insinuetur, Lucr.; with reflex, se insinuare, *to penetrate, work one's way in*: se inter equitum turmas, Caes.; qua se inter valles flumen insinuat, Liv.; with acc. of place: lacunas se, Lucr.; so also without reflex.: latebras, Lucr.
TRANSF., with or without reflex., *to penetrate, make one's way*: se in familiaritatem alicuius, Cic.; insinuare se in philosophiam Cic.; penitus in causam, Cic.

insĭpĭens -entis, adj. (with compar.) (in/sapiens), *foolish*: Cic., Cat.
¶ Adv. **insĭpĭentĕr**, *foolishly*: Pl., Cic.

insĭpĭentĭa -ae, f. (insipiens), *foolishness*: Pl., Cic.

insisto -sistĕre -stĭti.
(1) *to set foot on, tread on, place oneself on* LIT., in gen.; with dat.: iacentibus, Caes. digitis, *to stand on tip-toe*, Ov.; with acc. vestigia, Lucr.; limen, Ov.; cineres, Hor. esp.: **a**, *to enter on a journey, road*, etc.: viam Ter.; iter, Liv.; **b**, with dat.: *to follow hard upon, pursue*: fugientibus, Liv. TRANSF., **a**, *to set about* an occupation: totus et mente e animo in bellum insistit, Caes.; with acc. rationem pugnae, Caes.; munus, Cic.; with dat.: ei rei, Liv.
(2) *to stand still in* or *on*. LIT., in iugo Caes.; Cic.; also *to halt*: Cic. TRANSF., **a**, *to stop, pause*, in speech: quae cum dixisse paulumque institisset, 'Quid est', inquit, Cic. **b**, *to dwell upon*: singulis peccatorum gradibus, Cic.: **c**, *to hesitate, to doubt*: ir reliquis rebus, Cic.: **d**, *to persist in*; wit dat.: crudelitati, Tac.; with infin.: Pl.

insĭtĭcĭus -a -um (¹insero), *engrafted, foreign* Plin.

insĭtĭo -ōnis, f. (¹insero). (1) *a grafting* plur.: insitiones, *the kinds of grafting*, Cic (2) meton., *the grafting season*: Ov.

insĭtīvus -a -um (¹insero), *grafted*. LIT., pira Hor. TRANSF., *spurious, not genuine*: Phaedr

nsĭtor -ōris, m. (¹insero), *a grafter*: Prop.

nsĭtus -a -um, partic. from ¹insero; q.v.

nsŏcĭābĭlis -e, *unable to combine with others*: gens, Liv.; with dat.: homines generi humano insociabiles, Liv.; Tac.

nsōlābĭlĭtĕr, adv. (in/solor), *inconsolably*: Hor.

nsŏlens -entis (in/soleo), *contrary to custom.* Hence (1) *contrary to one's own custom*: quid tu Athenas insolens venisti? Ter.; emirabitur insolens, Hor.; hence, with genit., *unaccustomed to, unused to*: infamiae, Cic. L.; so with in: in dicendo, Cic.
(2) *contrary to general custom*: **a**, in gen., *unusual*: verbum, Cic.: **b**, *excessive*: Cic., Hor.; of persons, *extravagant*: non fuisse insolentem in pecunia, Cic.: **c**, *proud, haughty, arrogant, insolent*: exercitus, Hor.
¶ Adv. (with compar.) **insŏlentĕr.** (1) *unusually, contrary to custom*: evenire vulgo soleat, an insolenter et raro, Cic. (2) *immoderately, excessively*: his festivitatibus insolentius abuti, Cic. (3) *haughtily, arrogantly, insolently*: se efferre, Cic.; Caes.

nsŏlentĭa -ae, f. (insolens). (1) *the not being accustomed to a thing, inexperience*: huius disputationis, Cic. (2) *unusual character*: **a**, *novelty of diction*: verborum, Cic.: **b**, *extravagance, excess*: Cic.: **c**, *pride, arrogance, insolence*: Cic., Sall.

nsŏlesco -escĕre (in/soleo), *to become haughty, insolent, elated*: per licentiam insolescere animum humanum, Sall.; Tac.

nsŏlĭdus -a -um, *soft, tender*: herba, Ov.

nsŏlĭtus -a -um. Act., *unaccustomed to*: ad laborem, Caes.; with genit.: rerum bellicarum, Sall.; Cic., Verg. Pass., *unusual, strange, uncommon*: insolita mihi loquacitas, Cic.; verbum, Cic.; Liv., Tac.

nsŏlūbĭlis -e, *incontrovertible*: Quint.

nsomnĭa -ae, f. (insomnis), *sleeplessness, loss of sleep*: Ter.; in plur.: insomniis carere, Cic.

nsomnis -e (in/somnus), *sleepless*: insomnes magis quam pervigiles, Tac.; of things: nox, Verg.

ĭnsomnĭum -i, n. (in/somnus), *sleeplessness*: Plin.

ĭnsomnĭum -i, n. (in/somnus), *a bad dream*; sing.: Tac.; plur.: Verg., Tib.

nsŏno -sōnare -sŏnŭi, *to make a noise in, sound, resound*: insonuere cavernae, Verg.; flagello, *to crack a whip*, Verg.; with internal acc.: verbera, Verg.

nsons -sontis (in/sum), *innocent, guiltless*: insontes sicut sontes circumvenire, Sall.; Verg.; with genit.: fraterni sanguinis, Ov.; Liv.; poet., *harmless*: Cerberus, Hor.

nsŏpītus -a -um (in/sopio), *not lulled to sleep, watchful*: draco, Ov.

nsŏpŏr -ōris (in/sopor), *sleepless*: Ov.

nspectio -ōnis, f. (inspicio), *scrutiny, consideration*: Quint.

nspecto -are (freq. of inspicio), *to look at or on, observe, view*: inspectante exercitu interfici, Cic. L.; Caes., Liv.

nspērans -antis (in/spero), *not hoping, not expecting*: insperanti mihi sed valde optanti, Cic. L.; Ter., Cat.

nspērātus -a -um (in/spero), *unhoped-for, unexpected*: malum, Cic.; pax, Liv. In abl. n.: insperato, Pl.; ex insperato, Liv., *unexpectedly*.

---

inspergo -spergĕre -spersi -spersum (in/spargo), *to sprinkle in or on*: molam et vinum, Cic.; inspersos corpore naevos, Hor.

inspĭcĭo -spĭcĕre -spexi -spectum (in/specio). (1) *to look into, see into.* LIT., intro, Pl.; domos, Verg.
(2) *to contemplate, view, examine, inspect.* LIT., signum publicum, Cic.; candelabrum, Cic.; as milit. t. t., *to inspect*: arma militis, Cic.; viros, Liv. TRANSF., *to consider*: aliquem a puero, Cic.; res sociorum, Liv.

inspĭco -are, *to sharpen to a point*: Verg.

inspīro -are, *to breathe upon, to blow upon.* LIT., with dat.: conchae, Ov. TRANSF., *to breathe into, inspire*: alicui occultum ignem, Verg.

inspŏlĭātus -a -um (in/spolio), *not plundered*: arma, Verg.; Quint.

inspŭo -spŭĕre -spŭi -spūtum, *to spit in* or *upon*: Plin., Sen.

inspūto -are, *to spit upon*: Pl.

instăbĭlis -e.
(1) *that does not stand firm, unstable, tottering.* LIT., cumbae, Verg.; pedes instabilis ac vix vado fidens, Liv. TRANSF., *unsteady, unstable, inconstant*: hostis instabilis ad conferendas manus, Liv.; motus, Caes.; animus, Verg.
(2) *on which it is impossible to stand, insecure*: tellus, Ov.; locus ad gradum, Tac.

instans -antis, partic. from insto; q.v.

instantĕr, adv. from insto; q.v.

instantĭa -ae, f. (insto). (1) *presence*: Cic. (2) *perseverance*: Plin. L.

instar, n. (only nom. and acc. sing.), *an image, likeness*: quantum instar in ipso! *how great a figure!* Verg. Usually with genit., in the sense *the equivalent of, corresponding to, like.* (1) in physical properties, size, weight, etc.: navis cybaea maxima triremis instar, Cic.; instar montis equum, Verg. (2) in number: cohortes quaedam quod instar legionis videretur, Caes. (3) in importance: Plato mihi unus est instar omnium, Cic. (4) in character: idque si accidat, mortis instar putemus, Cic.; exhorruit aequoris instar, Ov.

instaurātĭo -ōnis, f. (instauro), *repetition, renewal*: sacrorum, Liv.

instaurātīvus -a -um (instauro), *renewed, repeated*: ludi, Cic.

instauro -are. (1) *to set up, establish*: novam proscriptionem, Cic. L.; aras, choros, Verg. (2) *to renew, restore*; in gen.: scelus, caedem, Cic.; novum de integro bellum, Liv.; instaurati (sunt) animi, Verg.; esp.: **a**, of recurring ceremonies: sacrificium, Cic.; sacra, ludos, Liv.: **b**, *to repay, requite*: talia Graiis, Verg.

insterno -sternĕre -strāvi -strātum, *to spread over* or *cover over*: equus instratus speciosius, saddled, Liv.; modicis pulpita tignis, Hor.; Verg.

instīgātor -ōris, m. (instigo), *an instigator, stimulator*: sibi quisque dux et instigator, Tac.

instīgātrix -trīcis, f. (instigator), *a female instigator*: Tac.

instīgo -are (in/STIG-o = στίζω), *to goad, incite, stimulate*: instigante te, *at your instigation*, Cic.; Romanos in Hannibalem, Liv.; Caes., Verg.

instillo -are, *to drop in, pour in by drops*: oleum lumini, Cic.; Hor. TRANSF., *to instil*: praeceptum auriculis, Hor.

instĭmŭlātor -ōris, m. (instimulo), *an instigator*: seditionis, Cic.

instĭmŭlo -are, *to incite*: Ov.

instinctor -ōris, m. (*instinguo), *an inciter, instigator*: sceleris, Tac.

instinctū, abl. sing. as from instinctus, m. (*instinguo), *by instigation*: instinctu divino, Cic.

instinctus -a -um (cf. distinguo), *instigated, incited, impelled*: furore, Cic.; furiis, Liv.

instĭpŭlor -ari, dep. *to stipulate* or *bargain for*: Pl.

instĭta -ae, f. (insto), *border* or *flounce on a lady's robe*; meton., *a lady*: nulla, Ov.

instĭtĭo -ōnis, f. (insisto), *a standing still*: stellarum, Cic.

instĭtor -ōris, m. (insto), *a hawker, huckster, pedlar*: mercis, Liv.; Hor., Juv.

instĭtōrĭum -i, n. (institor), *the business of a hawker*: Suet.

instĭtŭo -ŭĕre -ŭi -ūtum (in/statuo), *to put in place*.
LIT., (1) in gen.: vestigia nuda sinistri pedis, Verg. (2) as milit. t. t., *to draw up in order*: aciem, Caes., Cic. (3) *to set up, make ready, build, construct*: turrim, pontes, naves, Caes.; vineas, Cic.; dapes, Verg.
TRANSF., (1) *to implant* an abstr. thing: argumenta in pectus, Pl. (2) *to establish* as an institution, *ordain, introduce*: portorium, Cic.; dies festos, Liv.; ludos, Ov.; with ut and the subj., *to arrange that*, etc.: Cic., Liv. (3) *to settle on* a course of action, *to undertake*: negotium, Pl.; iter, Hor.; with infin., *to resolve, determine*: Caes., Cic. L., Liv. (4) *to appoint* a person: me tutorem, Cic. L. (5) *to instruct, educate, train* a person: aliquem ad dicendum, Cic.; aliquem artibus, Juv.; with infin.: Verg., Hor.

instĭtūtĭo -ōnis, f. (instituo). (1) *arrangement*: rerum, Cic. (2) *regular method, custom*: institutionem suam conservare, *method*, Cic. L. (3) *education, instruction*: doctoris, Cic.

instĭtūtum -i, n. (instituo). (1) *an undertaking, purpose*: non ad nostrum institutum pertinet, Cic. (2) *an arrangement, institution*; in sing. and plur.: maiorum, Cic.; institutum vitae capere, *to adopt a rule of life*, Cic.; ex instituto, *according to the settlement*, Liv. (3) *an instruction, precept*: philosophiae, Cic.

insto -stare -stĭti.
(1) *to stand in* or *on*: iugis, Verg.; with acc.: rectam instas viam, Pl.
(2) *to be close to, follow closely*. LIT., vestigiis, Liv.; Caes.; hence *to press upon, pursue eagerly*; with acc.: me, Pl.; nostros, Caes.; with dat.: adversario, Cic.; hosti, Liv. TRANSF., **a**, *to pursue* or *devote oneself eagerly to*: de indutiis, Caes.; with acc.: currum, Verg.; with dat.: operi, Verg.; with following infin., *to persist, to persevere*: poscere recuperatores, Cic.: **b**, *to insist, ask pressingly*: alicui instare ut, with subj., Cic.: **c**, of time or events, *to approach, impend*: dies instat quo, Cic.; Liv.
¶ Hence partic. **instans** -antis. (1) *present*: Cic. (2) *pressing, urgent*: tyrannus, Hor.; compar.: instantior cura, Tac.

¶ Hence adv. **instantĕr**, *urgently, vehe mently*; compar.: instantius, Tac.

instrātus -a -um, partic. from insterno; q.v.

instrēnŭus -a -um, *inactive, lazy*: Pl., Ter.

instrĕpo -ĕre -ŭi -itum, *to make a noise, rattle, clatter, creak*: sub pondere axi instrepat, Verg.

instructĭo -ōnis, f. (instruo), *a setting in array drawing up in order*: militum, Cic.

instructor -ōris, m. (instruo), *a preparer* convivii, Cic.

¹**instructus** -a -um, partic. from instruo; q.v.

²**instructus** -ūs, m. (instruo), *provision*; henc *matter* (in a speech): quocumque (oratio ingreditur, eodem est instructu ornatuqu comitata, Cic.

instrūmentum -i, n. (instruo), *equipment, tool, an implement*; used in sing. and plur LIT., villae, *implements of husbandry*, Cic. militare, Caes.; belli, Cic., Liv.; instrument anilia, *dress*, Ov. TRANSF., (1) *store, stock* oratoris, Cic. (2) any *means to an end* instrumenta ad obtinendam sapientiam Cic.; virtutis, Cic.; necis, Ov. (3) *publi records*: tribunatūs, Cic.

instrŭo -strŭĕre -struxi -structum, *to build i* or *into*.
LIT., contabulationem in parietes, Caes Also in gen., *to set up, build*: muros, Nep. aggerem, Tac. TRANSF., (1) *to equip furnish with*: domum suam in provincia Cic.; mensas epulis, Verg.; Liv.; hence t *train* a person: aliquem ad omne offici munus, Cic.; Verg. (2) *to prepare, provide* accusationem, Cic.; epulas, fraudem, Liv. consilia, Tac.; milit., *to draw up in order o battle*: aciem, Caes., Cic.; exercitum, Liv.
¶ Hence partic. (with compar. and superl.) **instructus** -a -um, *equipped supplied*: domus, aedes, Cic.; hence o persons, *trained, instructed*: in iure civili Cic.; artibus, Cic.

insuasum -i, n. some *dark colour*: Pl.

insuāvis -e, *not sweet, unpleasant, disagreeable*: littera insuavissima, Cic.; homo, Hor.; vita, Cic.

Insŭbres -ium, m. pl. the *Insubrians, a people in Cisalpine Gaul*, whose capital was Medio lanum (now *Milan*); as adj. **Insŭbĕr** -bri -bre, *Insubrian*.

insūdo -are, *to sweat in* or *at*: libellis insudat manus, Hor.

insuēfactus -a -um, *accustomed to, inured to*: Caes.

insuesco -suescĕre -suēvi -suētum. Intransit. *to accustom oneself to, to become used to*: cor pori, Tac.; ad disciplinam, Liv.; with infin.: victoriā frui, Liv. Transit., *to accustom, habi tuate anyone to*: insuevit pater hoc me, Hor.

¹**insuētus** -a -um (in/suesco). (1) of persons, *unaccustomed to, unused to*; with genit. laboris, Caes.; Cic. L., Liv.; with dat. moribus Romanis, Liv.; with ad: ad stabilem pugnam, Liv.; Caes.; with infin.: vera audire, Liv. (2) of things, *unaccustomed unusual*: solitudo, Liv.; n. pl. as interna acc.: insueta rudentem, Verg.

²**insuētus** -a -um, partic. from insuesco ir transit. sense; q.v.

insŭla -ae, f. *an island*. LIT., Cic., Verg., etc TRANSF., *a detached house* or *block of flats let out to poor families*: Cic., Tac., Suet.

insŭlānus -i, m. (insula), *an islander*: Cic.
insulsĭtās -ātis, f. (insulsus), *insipidity,*
tastelessness, absurdity: Graecorum, Cic.; Pl.
insulsus -a -um (in/salsus), *unsalted, insipid*:
O gulam insulsam! *pleased with tasteless*
food, Cic. TRANSF., *insipid, tasteless, absurd,*
foolish: genus ridiculi, Cic.; adulescens, Cic.;
superl.: Cat.
¶ Adv. **insulsē**, *insipidly, tastelessly,*
absurdly: loqui, Cic.
insulto -are (freq. of insilio), *to leap, prance in*
or *on*. LIT., with dat.: busto Priami, Hor.;
with acc.: nemora, *dance through*, Verg.
TRANSF., *to triumph over, insult*; with dat.:
tibi in calamitate, Cic.; Liv.; with acc.:
multos bonos, Sall.; in rempublicam, Cic.
insultūra -ae, f. (insilio), *a leaping at* or *on*: Pl.
insum -esse -fŭi, *to be in* or *on*.
LIT., in domo, Cic.; with dat.: comae
insunt capiti, Ov.; ferrum quale hastis
velitaribus inest, Liv.
TRANSF., *to be in, to be contained in, to*
belong to: superstitio, in qua inest inanis
timor, Cic.; vitium aliquod in moribus, Cic.;
with dat.: cui virile ingenium inest, Sall.; Ov.
insūmo -sūmĕre -sumpsi -sumptum, *to take*
for a purpose, to expend upon: operam frustra,
Liv.; sumptum in rem, Cic.; with dat.:
paucos dies reficiendae classi, Tac.; with
abl.: Hor.
insŭo -sŭĕre -sŭi -sūtum, *to sew in, sew up*:
aliquem in culeum, Cic.; insutum vestibus
aurum, *embroidered, sewn on*, Ov.; Verg.
insŭpĕr, adv. and prep., *above*.
(**1**) adv. LIT., *above, overhead*: insuper
inicere centones, Caes.; iugum insuper
imminens, Liv.; Verg. TRANSF., *over and*
above, in addition, moreover, besides: insuper
etiam, Liv.; insuper quam, Liv.; Verg.
(**2**) prep., with acc., *over*: Cato.; with abl.,
besides: Verg.
insŭpĕrābĭlis -e. (**1**) *insurmountable, im-*
passable: via, Liv. (**2**) *unconquerable*: genus
insuperabile bello, Verg.; fatum, *inevitable*,
Ov.
insurgo -surgĕre -surrexi -surrectum, *to rise*
up, raise oneself up.
LIT., (**1**) of living beings: insurgens Entellus,
rising to his full height, Verg.; so of a serpent:
arduus insurgens, *rearing up*, Verg.; of
rowers: insurgite remis, *put weight into the*
stroke, Verg. (**2**) of other things: inde colles
insurgunt, Liv.; of the wind: aquilo, Hor.;
of water: vastius insurgens decimae ruit
impetus undae, Ov.
TRANSF., (**1**) *to increase in power* or *force*:
Caesar paulatim insurgere, Tac.; Horatius
insurgit aliquando, Quint. (**2**) *to rise up*
against: suis regnis, Ov.
insŭsurro -are, *to whisper, whisper in the ear*.
Intransit.: alicui, Cic.; in aurem alicuius,
Cic. Transit.: alicui cantilenam, Cic.
intābesco -tābescĕre -tābŭi, *to melt* or *wither*
away gradually: diuturno morbo, Cic.; igne
cerae, Ov.
intactĭlis -e, *that cannot be touched*: Lucr.
¹**intactus** -a -um (in/tango), *untouched*.
LIT., physically: thesaurus, Hor.; nix,
Liv.; cervix iuvencae, *untouched by the yoke*,
Verg.; Britannus, *unconquered*, Hor.; prope
intacti evasere, *unhurt*, Liv.; esp. *virgin*:
Pallas, Hor.

TRANSF., not physically. (**1**) *untried*:
bellum, Sall.; carmen, Hor. (**2**) *unspoilt,*
free from; with abl.: intactus infamiā,
cupiditate, Liv.
²**intactus** -ūs, m. *intangibility*: Lucr.
intāmĭnātus -a -um (in/*tamino, whence con-
tamino), *unstained, unspotted*: honores, Hor.
¹**intectus** -a -um, *uncovered*. LIT., corpora,
unclothed, Sall.; domus, *roofless*, Sall.; Tac.
TRANSF., *open, frank*: Tac.
²**intectus** -a -um, partic. from intego; q.v.
intĕgellus -a -um (dim. of integer). (**1**) *more*
or less pure: Cat. (**2**) *more or less undamaged*:
Cic. L.
intĕger -gra -grum, adj. (with compar.
integrior, superl. integerrimus) (in/TAG from
tango).
(**1**) *complete, whole, entire, intact*. LIT.,
physically: sublicae quarum pars inferior
integra remanebat, Caes.; opes integrae,
Hor.; esp. of health and strength, *fresh,*
sound, unexhausted: integris viribus repugnare, Caes.; valetudo, Cic.; integer aevi,
in the prime of life, Verg.; often of troops:
integros pro saucis accessere, Sall. TRANSF.,
in gen., *intact, entire*: annus, Cic.; dies,
Hor.; n. as subst. in phrase, in integrum
restituere, *to restore a thing to its former*
condition: praedia, Cic.; Ter., Caes.
(**2**) in quality, *unspoilt, pure, fresh*. LIT.,
physically: fontes, Lucr.; vinum, Hor.;
coniuges, Cic. TRANSF., **a**, morally, *innocent,*
uncorrupted: se integros castosque conservare,
Cic.; with genit.: integer vitae scelerisque
purus, Hor.; fides, Tac.; **b**, in thought or
feeling, *balanced, unbiased, impartial, free*
from prejudice: integri testes, Cic.; integrum
se servare, Cic. L.; vultum integer laudo,
Hor.: **c**, of matters for discussion or action,
open, unprejudiced, undecided: rem integram
relinquere, Cic.; causam integram reservare
alicui, Cic.; in integro mihi res est, integrum
est mihi, *I am at liberty*, Cic., sometimes
followed by infin. or ut and the subj.
(**3**) *renewed, begun afresh*: novi et integri
laboris, Liv.; n. as subst. in phrases meaning
afresh: ab integro, Cic., Verg.; de integro,
Cic., Liv.
¶ Hence adv. **integrē** (compar. integrius:
Cic.; superl. integerrĭmē: Plin. L.). (**1**)
wholly: Tac. (**2**) *honestly, uprightly, impar-*
tially: iudicare, Cic.; in privatorum periculis
caste integreque versari, Cic. (**3**) of style,
purely, correctly: dicere, Cic.
intĕgo -tĕgĕre -texi -tectum, *to cover*: turres
coriis, Caes.; Liv. TRANSF., *to protect*: Liv.
integrasco -ĕre (integro), *to break out afresh*:
Ter.
integrātĭo -ōnis, f. (integro), *a renewing*: Ter.
integrē, adv. from integer; q.v.
integrĭtās -ātis, f. (integer). (**1**) *unimpaired*
condition, soundness, health: corporis, valetudinis, Cic. (**2**) *purity*; morally, *uprightness,*
integrity: integritas vitae, Cic.; of style,
purity, correctness: incorrupta quaedam
sermonis Latini integritas, Cic.
integro -are (integer), *to make whole*. LIT.,
amnes integrant mare, Lucr.; elapsos in
pravum artus, *to heal*, Tac. TRANSF., (**1**) *to*
renew, begin afresh: pugnam, Liv.; lacrimas,
Liv.; carmen, Verg. (**2**) *to refresh*: animus
integratur, Cic.

intĕgŭmentum -i, n. (intego), *a covering*:
lanx cum integumentis, Liv. TRANSF., *a*
cloak, disguise: flagitiorum, Cic.; evolutum
illis integumentis dissimulationis tuae, Cic.
intellectus -ūs, m. (intellego). (**1**) *a perceiving,*
perception, sensation: Plin. (**2**) *an under-*
standing, comprehension: boni, mali, Tac.
(**3**) *intellect*: Sen.
intellĕgens -entis, partic. from intellego; q.v.
intellegentĭa -ae, f. (intellego), *perception.*
(**1**) *by the senses*: Cic. (**2**) *mental under-*
standing, knowledge: Ter., Cic.; with genit.:
intellegentiam iuris habere, Cic.; *sometimes*
the knowledge of a connoisseur, taste: Cic.
(**3**) *capacity for understanding, intelligence*:
fretus intellegentiā vestrā, Cic.
intellĕgo lĕgĕre -lexi -lectum (inter/lego)
(intellexti for intellexisti, Ter., Cic. L.), *to*
distinguish, discriminate, perceive. (**1**) by the
senses: Ov. (**2**) mentally, *to understand,*
grasp, become aware of. In gen.; with acc.:
linguam, Cic.; cernere aliquid animo atque
intellegere, Cic.; with indir. quest.: de gestu
intellego quid respondeas, Cic.; with acc.
and infin.: intellexi ex tuis litteris, te audisse,
Cic. L. Esp.: **a**, *to understand thoroughly,*
know as a connoisseur: tamen non multum
in istis rebus intellego, Cic.: **b**, *to understand*
a person's character, judge, appreciate: aliquis
falsus intellegitur, Tac.; Cic.: **c**, *to under-*
stand by a term, take as its meaning: Cic.
¶ Hence partic. **intellĕgens** -entis. (**1**)
intelligent, understanding or *well acquainted*
with anything: vir, Cic.; with genit.:
cuiusvis generis eius intellegens, Cic.; of
things: iudicium, Cic. (**2**) *having good*
taste: homo ingeniosus et intellegens, Cic.;
in hisce rebus intellegens esse, Cic.
¶ Adv. **intellegentĕr**, *intelligently, with*
understanding: audiri, Cic.
Intĕmĕlĭi (**Intĭmĕlĭi**) -ōrum, m. *a people on*
the coast of Liguria.
intĕmĕrātus -a -um (in/temero), *unspotted,*
undefiled, inviolate: fides, Verg.; munera,
Verg.; Penelope: Ov.
intempĕrans -antis, adj. (with compar. and
superl.), *extravagant, unrestrained, intemper-*
ate: intemperans est, with infin., Cic.; in
augendo eo intemperantior, Liv.; of things:
libertas, gloria, Cic.; esp. *incontinent*: in
aliqua re, Cic.; of things: intemperantissimae
perpotationes, Cic.
¶ Adv. (with compar.) **intempĕrantĕr**,
extravagantly, intemperately: opibus suis
uti, Cic.
intempĕrantĭa -ae, f. (intemperans), *want of*
moderation or *restraint, extravagance, excess,*
intemperance: Cic.; with genit.: libidinum,
Cic.; vini, Liv.
intempĕrātus -a -um, *intemperate, im-*
moderate: intemperata quaedam benevolentia,
Cic.
¶ Adv. **intempĕrātē**, *intemperately*: vivere, Cic.
intempĕrĭae -ārum, f. pl. *wildness, raging*; of
weather: Cato; of behaviour: quae te in-
temperiae tenent? Pl.
intempĕrĭēs -ēi, f. *wildness, lack of restraint.*
LIT., of weather: caeli, Liv.; aquarum,
excessive fall of rain, Liv. TRANSF., *intem-*
perate behaviour, outrageous conduct: amici,
Cic. L.; cohortium, Tac.

intempestīvus -a -um, *unseasonable, untimely*;
perhaps sometimes *immoderate*: imbres,
Lucr.; Cic., Ov., Tac.
¶ Adv. **intempestīvē**, *unseasonably*: accedere, Cic.; Ov.
intempestus -a -um (in/tempus). (**1**) *timeless*:
intempesta nox, *the dead of night*, Cic.;
personif.: Nox intempesta, *the mother of*
the Furies, Verg. (**2**) *unwholesome, unhealthy*:
Graviscae, Verg.
intemptātus (intentatus) -a -um, *untried*: sors,
Verg.; iter, Tac.; Hor.
intendo -tendĕre -tendi -tentum.
(**1**) *to stretch, strain.* LIT., arcum, Verg.;
vincula stupea collo, *stretch round*, Verg.;
tabernacula carbaseis velis, *to pitch*, Cic.
TRANSF., **a**, *to spread*: gloriam, Tac.: **b**, *to*
strain: intentis animis, Caes.; vocem, Verg.:
c, *to maintain, try to prove*: id quod intenderat confirmare, Cic.; with acc. and infin.: Ter.
(**2**) *to stretch* in a particular direction, *to*
aim, extend. LIT., dextram ad statuam, Cic.;
of weapons: tela, Cic.; sagittas, Verg.
TRANSF., **a**, *to direct* an abstract thing
against: periculum in aliquem, Cic.; alicui
litem, Cic.; eo bellum, Liv.: **b**, *to direct one's*
course towards; esp. with iter: Liv.; also
without object: quo intenderat in Manliana
castra pervenit, Cic.; Liv.: **c**, *to apply the*
mind, direct the thoughts to: animum eo, Cic.;
animum, mentem in aliquid, Cic.; oculos
mentesque ad pugnam, Caes.; animum
studiis, Hor.; Liv.: **d**, *to intend, aim at*: aliquid, Ter., Sall., Cic.; with infin.: Sall., Liv.
¶ Hence partic. (with compar. and
superl.) **intentus** -a -um, *stretched, tense,*
taut. LIT., arcus, Cic.; Verg. TRANSF., (**1**) of
thought or feeling; *anxious, intent*: omnes
milites intenti pugnae proventum exspecta-
bant, Caes.; in omnem occasionem, Liv.;
with dat., *intent upon*: operi agresti, Liv.;
with abl.: Sall. (**2**) of speech, *earnest*: Cic.
(**3**) *thorough, strict, rigorous*: intentissima
cura, Liv.; disciplina, Tac.
¶ Adv. (with compar.) **intentē**, *earnestly,*
attentively: aliquem intentius admonere,
Liv.; Tac.
¹intentātus -a -um=intemptatus; q.v.
²intentātus -a -um, partic. from intento; q.v.
intentĭo -ōnis, f. (intendo). (**1**) *a stretching,*
straining: corporis, Cic.; of the mind, *an*
effort, exertion: animi cogitationum, Cic.
(**2**) *a directing*; hence: **a**, *attention*: Sen.;
with objective genit.: lusus, Liv.: **b**, *attack,*
accusation: Cic., Quint.
intento -are (freq. of intendo), *to stretch*
towards or *against*, esp. *to stretch out threaten-*
ingly: manus in aliquem, Liv.; sicam alicui,
Cic. TRANSF., arma Latinis, Liv.; viris
mortem, Verg.; Cic., Tac.
¹intentus -ūs, m. (intendo), *a stretching out*:
palmarum, Cic.
²intentus -a -um, partic. from intendo; q.v.
intĕpĕo -ēre, *to be lukewarm*: Prop.
intĕpesco -tĕpescĕre -tĕpŭi, *to become*
lukewarm, grow gradually warm: Verg., Ov.
intĕr, prep. with acc. *between, among, amid*;
sometimes placed after noun or pronoun.
(**1**) in space, *between* two or more points,
objects, or persons; of rest: moror inter aras,
Cic.; cum (Hercules) inter homines esset,
among men, Cic.; inter falcarios, *in the street*

of the sickle-makers, Cic.; inter viam, *on the way,* Pl., Ter., Cic.; of motion: inter stationes hostium emissi, Liv.

(2) in time: a, *between:* inter horam tertiam et quartam, Liv.: b, *during, in the course of*: inter decem annos, Cic.; inter cenam, Cic.; inter noctem, Liv.; inter haec, *meanwhile,* Liv.; inter agendum, Verg.

(3) in other, analogous relations: a, of difference, as in choice or rivalry *between:* inter se differre, Caes.; inter Marcellos et Claudios patricios iudicare, Cic.; certamen inter primores, Liv.: b, of association, *among:* amicitiam nisi inter bonos esse non posse, Cic.; inter sicarios accusare, *to accuse of murder,* Cic.; inter pauca, inter paucos, *especially, particularly,* Liv.; inter cuncta, *before all,* Hor.; esp. with pronouns, inter se, inter nos, inter vos, inter ipsos, *between one another, mutually:* amare inter se, *to love one another,* Cic.; Verg., Liv.

intĕrāmenta -ōrum, n. pl. *the woodwork of a ship:* Liv.

Intĕramna -ae, f. (1) *a town in Umbria (now Terni).* (2) *a town in Latium (now Teramo).* ¶ Hence adj. and subst. **Intĕramnās** -ātis, *belonging to Interamna, an inhabitant of Interamna.*

interaptus -a -um, *joined together:* Lucr.

intĕrāresco -ĕre, *to become dry, to dry up, decay.* TRANSF., Cic.

interātim, *meanwhile:* Pl.

interbĭbo -ĕre, *to drink up:* Pl.

interbīto -ĕre, *to perish:* Pl.

intercălāris -e (intercalo), *inserted, intercalary:* Kalendae, *the first day of an intercalary month,* Cic.

intercălārĭus -a -um (intercalo), *intercalary:* mensis, Cic., Liv.

intercălo -are, *to call out that something is inserted;* hence (1) *to insert or intercalate a day or month in the calendar;* impers. pass.: pugnes ne intercaletur, Cic. L. (2) *to insert anything extra:* intercalatae poenae, Liv.

intercăpēdo -inis, f. (capio), *an interval, intermission, pause, respite:* molestiae, Cic.

intercēdo -cēdĕre -cessi -cessum, *to go between, come between.*

LIT., inter singulas legiones impedimentorum magnum numerum intercedere, Caes.; of places, *to stand or lie between:* palus quae perpetua intercedebat, Caes.

TRANSF., (1) of time, *to intervene:* nox nulla intercessit, Cic.; Liv. (2) of events, *to happen between:* saepe in bello parvis momentis magni casus intercedunt, Caes.; Liv. (3) of relationships, *to exist between:* inter nos vetus usus intercedit, Cic. L. (4) legal t. t., *to interpose, to stand surety:* pro aliquo, Cic.; magnam pecuniam pro aliquo, *in a large sum for,* Cic. (5) *to step between, withstand, protest against;* of the tribunes when they exercised their veto, with dat.: Cic.; alicui, Cic.; Liv.; also in gen., *to interfere, interpose:* cum vestra auctoritas intercessisset ut, Cic. L.; with dat.: Tac.

interceptĭo -ōnis, f. (intercipio), *a taking away:* poculi, Cic.

interceptor -ōris, m. (intercipio), *one who intercepts or takes away, an embezzler:* praedae, Liv.; Tac.

intercessĭo -ōnis, f. (intercedo). (1) legal t. t.,

interposition, a becoming surety, going bail: Cic. (2) polit. t. t., *an exercise by the tribunes of their veto:* Caes., Cic., Liv.

intercessor -ōris, m. (intercedo). (1) legal t. t., *a surety, bail:* Cic. (2) polit. t. t., *one who opposes;* of a tribune in the exercise of his veto, with genit.: legis, Cic.; also in gen., *an obstructor:* rei malae, Cic.

¹**intercīdo** -cīdĕre -cīdi -cīsum (inter/caedo), *to cut asunder:* pontem, *to demolish,* Liv.; montem, *to cut through,* Cic. L.; Tac. ¶ Hence, from partic. intercisus -a -um, adv. **intercīsē,** *piecemeal:* Cic.

²**intercĭdo** -cĭdĕre -cĭdi (inter/cado). (1) *to fall between.* LIT., telum in mari, Liv. TRANSF., *to happen in an interval, intervene:* si qua interciderunt, Cic. (2) *to drop out, be lost, perish:* memoriā, *be forgotten,* Liv.; si intercidit tibi aliquid, *if you have forgotten something,* Hor.

intercĭno -ĕre (inter/cano), *to sing between:* medios actus, Hor.

intercĭpĭo -cĭpĕre -cēpi -ceptum (inter/capio), *to take by the way, intercept.* LIT., litteras, Cic.; commeatūs, Liv.; hastam, *to get in the way of,* Verg.; Caes., Tac. TRANSF., (1) *to embezzle, appropriate:* honorem, Cic.; agrum a populo Romano, Liv. (2) through death, *to cut off, carry off prematurely:* aliquem veneno, Tac. (3) *to block:* iter, Liv.; Tac.

intercīse, adv. from ¹intercīdo; q.v.

interclūdo -clūdĕre -clūsi -clūsum (inter/claudo), *to shut off, block up, hinder.*

LIT., with acc. of thing: fugam, Caes., Cic. L., Liv.; viam, Liv.; with dat. of person also: exitum Romano, Liv.; Cic. With acc. of person: illos, Verg.; with abl., or ab and abl. of thing, *to shut off from:* aliquem ab exercitu, Caes.; aliquem re frumentariā, Caes.; pass.: Caes., Liv.

TRANSF., aliquem in insidiis, *to enclose, shut in,* Cic.; intercludor dolore quominus, *I am prevented by grief,* Cic.

interclūsĭo -ōnis, f. (intercludo), *a stopping or blocking up:* animae, Cic. TRANSF., *a parenthesis:* Quint.

intercŏlumnĭum -i, n. (inter/columna), *the space between two columns:* Cic.

intercurro -currĕre -cŭcurri -cursum. (1) *to run between;* hence: a, *to step between, intercede:* Cic.: b, fig., *to run through:* quin intercurrat quaedam distantia formis, Lucr.: c, *to be among, mingle with:* his laboriosis exercitationibus et dolor intercurrit, Cic. (2) *to hasten in the meanwhile:* Veios ad confirmandos militum animos, Liv.

intercurso -are (freq. of intercurro), *to run between, run among:* Lucr., Liv.

intercursū, abl. sing. as from intercursus, m. (intercurro), *by running between, by the interposition:* intercursu consulum, Liv.

intercus -cŭtis (inter/cutis), *under the skin:* aqua, *the dropsy,* Pl., Cic.

interdīco -dīcĕre -dixi -dictum.

(1) *to stop by interposition, to forbid, prohibit.* In gen.; with dat. of person and abl. of thing: Romanis omni Galliā, Caes.; Cic., Liv.; impers. pass.: Cic., Liv.; also with acc. of thing: alicui orbem, Ov.; Suet.; pass.: praemio interdicto, Cic. Esp. as legal t. t.: interdicere alicui aquā et igni, *to outlaw,* Caes., Cic.

(2) *to make an injunction, to order.* LIT., of the praetor: de vi, Cic.; with ut: praetor interdixit ut unde deiectus esset eo restitueretur, Cic. TRANSF., in gen., with dat. of person and ut *or* ne: interdicit atque imperat Cassivellauno ne Mandubracio noceat, Caes.; familiae valere interdicere ut uni dicto audiens sit, Cic.; impers. pass.: Pythagoreis interdictum ne fabā vescerentur, Cic.

interdictio -ōnis, f. (interdico), *a forbidding, prohibition*: aquae et ignis, *outlawing*, Cic.; Liv.

interdictum -i, n. (interdico). (1) *a prohibition*; with subjective genit.: Caesaris, Cic. (2) *a praetor's interdict* or *provisional order*: Cic.

interdiū (**interdĭus**: Pl.), adv. (dies), *in the daytime, by day*: nocte an interdiu, Liv.; Caes.

interdo -dăre -dătum, *to put between* or *among, distribute*: Lucr.

interductus -ū, m. *interpunctuation*: Cic.

interdum, adv. *sometimes, occasionally, now and then*: Pl., Lucr., Cic., Tac.

interdŭo=interdo; q.v.

intĕrĕā, adv. *in the meantime, meanwhile*: Ter., Lucr., Cic., Verg.; sometimes with the extra sense of *nevertheless, notwithstanding*: cum interea nullus gemitus audiebatur, Cic.

intĕremptor -ōris, m. (interimo): Cic.; *a murderer*: Sen.

intĕrĕo -īre -ĭi -ĭtum, *to be lost from among, to perish.* LIT., muriae stilla interit magnitudine maris, Cic.; of men, *to die*: fame aut ferro, Caes., Liv. TRANSF., of abstr. things: salus urbis, Cic.; Liv.

intĕrĕquĭto -are, *to ride between*: ordines, Liv.

interfātĭo -ōnis, f. (interfari), *a speaking between, interruption*: Cic., Quint.

interfātur -fāri -fātus, dep. forms, as from interfor, *to speak between, interrupt*: aliquem, Liv.; absol.: Liv., Verg.

interfectĭo -ōnis, f. (interficio), *a slaying*: ap. Cic. L.

interfector -ōris, m. (interficio), *a murderer, slayer*: Cic., Liv., Tac.

interfectrix -trīcis, f. (interfector), *a murderess*: Tac.

interfĭcĭo -fĭcĕre -fēci -fectum (nter/facio), *to do away with, destroy, put an end to*; of things: herbas, Cic.; messīs, Verg.; of animals or persons, *to slay, kill*: feras, Lucr.; aliquem insidiis, Cic.; Crassum suāpte interfectum manu, Cic.; Caes., Liv.

interfĭo -fĭĕri (pass. of interficio=interficior), *to perish*: Pl., Lucr.

interflŭo -flŭĕre -fluxi -fluxum, *to flow between*: Naupactum et Patras, Liv.; Tac.

interfŏdĭo -fŏdĕre -fōdi -fossum, *to dig into, pierce*: Lucr.

interfor -fari, dep. *to interrupt a person speaking*: Verg., Liv., Plin. L.

interfŭgĭo -fŭgĕre, *to flee between*: Lucr.

interfulgens -entis, partic. as from interfulgeo, *shining* or *gleaming among*: Liv.

interfūsus -a -um, partic. as from interfundo, *poured between, flowing between*: noviens Styx interfusa, Verg. TRANSF., maculis interfusa genas, *stained here and there*, Verg.

interiăcĕo -ēre, *to lie between* or *among*: interiacebat campus, Liv.; with dat.: campus interiacens Tiberi ac moenibus Romanis, Liv.

interiacio=intericio; q.v.

intĕrĭbi, adv. *meanwhile, in the meantime*: Pl

interĭcĭo -ĭcĕre -ĭēci -ĭectum (inter/iacio), *to throw, cast, put, among* or *between.* LIT., legionarias cohortes, Caes.; with dat.: nasus, quasi murus oculis interiectus, Cic. TRANSF., interiectus inter philosophos e eos, *standing between*, Cic.; of time: anne interiecto, *after an interval of a year*, Cic. moram, Tac.; Liv.

interiectĭo -ōnis, f. (intericio), *an interjection* or *a parenthesis*: Quint.

interiectus -ūs, m. (intericio), *a throwing between*: luna interpositu interiectuque terrae deficit, Cic. TRANSF., of time, *an interval*: interiectu noctis, Tac.

intĕrim, adv. (1) *meanwhile, in the meantime, for the time being*: Pl., Caes., Cic., Tac.; sometimes (like interea) with the extra sense of *however*: Cic. L. (2) *sometimes*: Quint.

intĕrĭmo -ĭmĕre -ēmi -emptum (inter/emo), *to take away out of the midst.* LIT., of things, *to destroy, annihilate, make an end of*: sensum, Lucr.; sacra, Cic.; of persons, *to put out of the way, slay, murder*: aliquem, Cic.; stirpem fratris virilem, Liv.; se, *to commit suicide*, Cic. TRANSF., me examinant et interimunt hae voces Milonis, Cic.

intĕrĭor -ius, genit. -ōris, compar. adj. (superl.=intimus -a -um; q.v.), *inner, interior.*

LIT., in space. (1) in gen.: pars aedium, Cic.; interiore epistulā, *in the middle of the letter*, Cic. L.; Falernum interiore notā, *from the depth of the cellar*, Hor. (2) *remote from the sea, inland*: nationes, Cic.; interiora regni, *the interior of the kingdom*, Liv. (3) *nearer*, esp. in racing, *on the inside of the course*: Hor., Verg., Ov.; interior periculo vulneris, *too near to be in danger of a wound*, Liv.

TRANSF., *more secret, more intimate, more confidential*: interiores et reconditae litterae, Cic.; amicitia, Liv.

¶ Hence adv. **intĕrĭus**, *more inwardly*: Verg., Ov. TRANSF., (1) *short, not far enough*: Cic. (2) *closely*: Juv.

intĕrĭtĭo -ōnis, f. (intereo), *destruction, ruin*: aratorum, Cic.

intĕrĭtus -ūs, m. (intereo), *destruction, ruin, annihilation*; of things: legum, Cic.; of persons: consulum, Cic.; Verg.

interiungo -iungĕre -iunxi -iunctum. (1) *to join together, unite, connect*: dextras, Liv. (2) *to unyoke*: Mart., Sen.

interius, see interior.

interlābor -labi -lapsus, dep. *to glide, flow between*: in tmesis: inter enim labentur aquae, Verg.

interlĕgo -ĕre, *to pluck, gather here and there*: Verg.

interlĭno -lĭnĕre -lēvi -lĭtum, *to daub between*: caementa interlita luto, Liv. TRANSF., *to erase, cancel, to falsify by erasure*: testamentum, Cic.

interlŏquor -lŏqui -lŏcūtus, dep. *to interrupt a person speaking*: Plin. L.; with dat.: Ter.

interlūcĕo -lūcēre -luxi. (1) *to shine* or *gleam between*: terrena quaedam atque etiam volucria animalia plerumque interlucent (in amber), Tac.; duos soles, noctu interluxisse, Liv. TRANSF., quibus inter gradus dignitatis et fortunae aliquid interlucet, Liv. (2) *to be transparent, let light through gaps*: interlucet corona (militum), Verg.

interlūnĭum -i, n. (inter/luna), *the change of the moon, time of new moon*; in plur.: Hor.

interlŭo -lŭĕre, *to wash between*: quod Capreas et Surrentum interluit fretum, Tac.; Verg.

intermenstrŭus -a -um, *between two months*: intermenstruo tempore, *at the time of the change of the moon*, Cic.; n. as subst. **intermenstrŭum** -i (sc. tempus), *the time of the new moon*: Cic.

*¹**intermĭnātus** -a -um (in/termino), *unbounded, boundless*: magnitudo regionum, Cic.

²**intermĭnātus** -a -um, partic. from interminor; q.v.

intermĭnor -āri, dep. *to threaten, forbid with threats*, with dat. of person: Pl.; perf. partic. in pass. sense: cibus interminatus, *forbidden with threats*, Hor.

intermiscĕo -miscēre -miscŭi -mixtum, *to mix with, intermix*; with dat.: turbam indignorum intermiscere dignis, Liv.; intermixti hostibus, Liv.; Verg.

intermissĭo -ōnis, f. (intermitto), *leaving off, interruption*: verborum, Cic.; offici, Cic.; sine ulla temporis intermissione, Cic.; Liv.

intermissus -a -um, partic. from intermitto; q.v.

intermitto -mittĕre -mīsi -missum.

(1) transit., *to leave a space between, leave free*. LIT., in space, *to separate, break off*; esp. in partic. intermissus -a -um: pars oppidi a flumine intermissa, Caes.; loca custodiis intermissa, Liv.; trabes paribus intermissae spatiis, Caes. TRANSF., **a**, in time, *to let pass*: ne quem diem intermitterem, Cic.; with ab: ut reliquum tempus ab labore intermitteretur, Caes.; with ad and the acc.: nulla pars nocturni temporis ad laborem intermittitur, Caes.; neque ullum fere diem intermittebat quin perspiceret, *without examining*, Caes.; Pl., Ter.: **b**, in gen., *to discontinue, interrupt*: studia, Cic.; proelium, Caes.; Hor., Tac.; with infin.: alicui litteras mittere, Cic.; Caes.; vento intermisso, *the wind having dropped*, Caes.

(2) intransit., *to cease, leave off*. LIT., in space: quā flumen intermittit, Caes. TRANSF., in time: Cic.

intermŏrĭor -mŏri -mortŭus, dep. *to die off, perish suddenly*: civitas intermoritur, Liv.

¶ Hence partic. **intermortŭus** -a -um, *swooning, half-dead*: Liv., Suet. TRANSF., contiones intermortuae, *lifeless*, Cic.

intermundĭa -ōrum, n. pl. (inter/mundus), *spaces between the worlds* (according to Epicurus, *the abode of the gods*): Cic.

intermūrālis -e, *between walls*: amnis, Liv.

internascor -nasci -nātus sum, dep. *to grow between* or *among*, esp. in perf. partic.: internata virgulta, Liv.; with dat.: saxis, Tac.

internĕcīnus -a -um, *see internecivus*.

internĕcĭo -ōnis, f. (interneco), *entire destruction, extermination, massacre*: civium, Cic.; ad internecionem redigere, *to annihilate*, Caes.; Liv.

internĕcīvus and **internĕcīnus** -a -um (interneco), *murderous, deadly, internecine*: bellum, Cic., Liv.

internĕco -are, *to destroy utterly, exterminate*: hostes, Pl.

internecto -ĕre, *to bind together, bind up*: ut fibula crinem auro internectat, Verg.

internĭtĕo -ēre, *to shine among, gleam through*: Plin., Curt.

internōdĭum -i, n. (inter/nodus), *the space between two knots* or *joints*: Ov.

internosco -noscĕre -nōvi -nōtum, *to distinguish between*: geminos, Pl., Cic.; quae internosci a falsis non possunt, Cic.

internuntĭa -ae, f. *a female messenger* or *go-between*: Pl., Cic., Juv.

internuntĭo -are, *to send messengers between parties*: Liv.

internuntĭus -i, m. *a messenger, mediator, go-between*: Iovis interpretes internuntiique (of the augurs), Cic.; totius rei, *in the whole matter*, Liv.; Caes.

internus -a -um, *inward, internal*. LIT., arae, Ov. TRANSF., *domestic, civil*: discordia, Tac.

intĕro -tĕrĕre -trīvi -trītum, *to rub, crumble, pound in*: Plin.; fig.: tute hoc intristi, *you made this mess*, Ter.

interpellātĭo -ōnis, f. (interpello), *an interruption*, especially in a speech: Pl., Cic.

interpellātor -ōris, m. (interpello), *an interrupter, disturber*: Cic., Quint.

interpello -are (inter/*pello; cf. appello), *to interrupt a speaker*: crebro dicentem, Cic.; Pl., Quint. TRANSF., in gen., *to disturb, impede, obstruct*: aliquem in iure suo, Cic.; haec tota res interpellata bello, Cic.; poenam, Liv.; Caes.; with ne and subj.: Liv.; with infin.: Hor.

interpōlis -e (inter/polio), *furbished up, vamped up*: Pl., Plin.

interpŏlo -are (cf. interpolis), *to furbish, vamp up*: togam praetextam, Cic. L. TRANSF., *to falsify*: semper aliquid demendo, mutando, interpolando, Cic.

interpōno -pōnĕre -pŏsŭi -pŏsĭtum, *to put, place between* or *among, interpose*.

LIT., elephantos, Liv.; Caes.

TRANSF., (1) of time, *to insert, allow to pass between*: spatium ad recreandos animos, Caes.; spatio interposito, *after some time*, Cic.; intercalariis mensibus interpositis, Liv. (2) of other abstr. things, *to put in, to cause to come between, interpose*: verbum, operam, studium, laborem, Cic.; fidem, *to pledge one's word*, Caes.; iudicium, edictum, *to bring forward*, Cic. (3) with reflex., se interponere in aliquid, *or* alicui, *to engage in, mediate in, interfere with*: se in pacificationem, Cic.; se audaciae alicuius, Cic. (4) *to falsify*: rationes populorum, Cic.

interpŏsĭtĭo -ōnis, f. (interpono). (1) *a bringing forward, introducing*: multarum personarum, Cic. (2) *a putting in, insertion*: Cic. L. (3) rhet. t. t., *a parenthesis*: Quint.

interpŏsĭtū, abl. as from interpositus, m. (interpono), *by putting between, by interposition*: luna interposita terrae deficit, Cic.

interpres -prĕtis, c. (inter/root of pretium). (1) *a negotiator, mediator, messenger*: iudicii corrumpendi, Cic.; divum, Mercury, Verg. (2) *an expounder, explainer*, in gen.: iuris, Cic.; poetarum, Cic.; divum, *prophet, prophetess*, Verg., Liv.; interpretes comitiorum, *the haruspices, who declare whether the* *comitia have been rightly held*, Cic. Esp.: **a**, *an interpreter*: appellare *or* adloqui aliquem per interpretem, Cic.; Caes., Liv.: **b**, *a translator*: nec converti (orationes) ut interpres, sed ut orator, Cic.

interprĕtātĭo -ōnis, f. (interpretor), *explanation, exposition, interpretation*: iuris, Cic.; verborum, Cic.; voluntatis, Liv.; esp. *translation*: Quint. TRANSF., *meaning, signification*: foederis, Cic.

interprĕtor -ari, dep. (interpres). (**1**) *to put an interpretation upon, understand in a certain sense*, with or without imparting to others: ius, fulgura, somnia, Cic.; aliquid mitiorem in partem, Cic.; recte alicuius sententiam, Cic.; with acc. and infin.: reditu in castra liberatum se esse iureiurando interpretabatur, *took it that*, Cic.; Liv. (**2**) *to translate*: Cic.; perf. partic. in pass. sense: Liv.

interprīmo -prĭmĕre -pressi -pressum, *to squeeze*: Pl.

interpunctĭo -ōnis, f. (interpungo), *punctuation*: verborum, Cic.

interpungo -pungĕre -punxi -punctum, *to punctuate*: Sen.; usually in perf. partic. **interpunctus** -a -um, *well-divided*: narratio, Cic.; n. pl. as subst.: clausulae atque interpuncta verborum, *divisions*, Cic.

interquĭesco -quĭescĕre -quĭēvi -quĭētum, *to pause between*: cum haec dixissem et paulum interquievissem, Cic.; Sen., Plin. L.

interregnum -i, n. *a period between two reigns, an interregnum*: Cic., Liv.; under the republic 'at Rome, *the time between the death or retirement of the consuls and the choice of their successors*: Cic. L., Liv.

interrex -rēgis, m. *a regent, temporary king*: Liv.; under the republic at Rome, *the temporary chief magistrate during an inter-*regnum: Cic., Liv.

interrĭtus -a -um (in/terreo), *unterrified, undaunted*: Verg., Ov., Tac.

interrŏgātĭo -ōnis, f. (interrogo), *a question, questioning, interrogation*: Cic.; esp. (**1**) legal t. t., *the examination of witnesses*: testium, Tac.; Quint. (**2**) logic. t. t., *an argument, syllogism*: aptā interrogatione concludere, Cic.; Sen. (**3**) grammat. t. t., *an interrogation*: Quint.

interrŏgātĭuncŭla -ae, f. (dim. of interrogatio), *a short syllogism or argument*: minutae interrogatiunculae, Cic.; Sen.

interrŏgo -are, *to put in a question, to ask, question, interrogate*.
In gen.: te eisdem de rebus, Cic.; interrogabat suos quis esset, Cic.; interrogans solerentne veterani milites fugere, Caes.; with double acc.: pusionem quendam interrogavit quaedam geometrica, Cic.; interrogatus sententiam, *being asked his opinion*, Liv.
Esp. (**1**) *to interrogate judicially, to examine*: testem, Cic. (**2**) *to accuse, bring an action against*: aliquem legibus ambitus, Sall.; Cic., Liv. (**3**) *to argue by syllogism*: Sen.
¶ Hence n. of perf. partic. pass. as subst. **interrŏgātum** -i: ad interrogata respondere, Cic.

interrumpo -rumpĕre -rūpi -ruptum, *to break in the middle, to sever*. LIT., pontem, Caes.; aciem hostium, Liv.; interrupti ignes, Verg.; itinera, Tac. TRANSF., *to interrupt*,

break off, disturb: iter amoris et officii, Cic.; orationem, Caes.; querellas, Tac.
¶ Hence from partic. interruptus -a -um, adv. **interruptē**, *interruptedly, disconnectedly*: non interrupte narrare, Cic.

intersaepĭo -saepire -saepsi -saeptum, *to hedge or fence between, enclose, hem in, block up*: foramina, Cic.; quaedam operibus, Liv.; urbem vallo ab arce, Liv.; Tac.

interscindo -scindĕre -scĭdi -scissum, *to cut or tear asunder*. LIT., pontem, Cic.; venas, *to open*, Tac.; Caes. TRANSF., (**1**) *to cut off, separate*: Chalcis arcto interscinditur freto, Liv. (**2**) *to interrupt*: Sen.

interscrībo -ĕre, *to write between*: Plin. L.

¹intersĕro -sĕrĕre -sēvi -sĭtum, *to sow or plant between*: Lucr.

²intersĕro -sĕrĕre -sĕrui, *to put or place between*: oscula mediis verbis, Ov. TRANSF., causam interserens, Nep.

interspīrātĭo -ōnis, f. *a breathing between, a taking breath*: Cic.

interstinctus -a -um, *marked with spots, speckled*: facies interstincta medicaminibus, Tac.

interstinguo -ĕre, *to extinguish*: ignes, Lucr.

interstringo -ĕre, *to squeeze tight*: alicui gulam, *to throttle*, Pl.

intersum -esse -fŭi.
(**1**) *to be between*. LIT., in space: ut Tiberis inter eos interesset, Cic.; Caes., Liv. TRANSF., **a**, in time, *to intervene*: inter primum et sextum consulatum XLVI anni interfuerunt, Cic.; Liv.: **b**, *to be between as a difference*, of neuter subjects: ut inter eos ne minimum quidem intersit, Cic.; inter hominem et beluam hoc maxime interest, Cic.; Liv.
¶ Hence also impers. **interest**, *it makes a difference, it concerns, it is of importance*. The person or thing concerned is in the genit. or the f. abl. of the possess. pron., meā, tuā, suā, nostrā, vestrā: nam eorum quoque vehementer interest, Cic.; sometimes ad is used: ad nostram laudem non multum interesse, Cic. The degree of importance is expressed by a n. acc., such as multum, quantum, tantum, or by adv. such as maxime, vehementer, magnopere, or by genit. of value, such as magni, parvi, minoris, pluris: Cic. The cause of the concern is expressed by infin., or acc. and infin., or ut, or ne, or indir. quest.; sometimes also by n. pron.: magni interest meā unā nos esse, Cic.; illud magni meā interest ut te videam, Cic.; nunquam enim interest uter sit eorum in pede extremo, Cic.
(**2**) *to be among, be present at, take part in*: with dat.: proelio, Caes.; senatui, Cic.; Verg., Liv.; with in: in convivio, Cic.
(**3**) *to differ, be different*: qui illa visa negant a falsis interesse, Cic.; Ter.

intertextus -a -um, *interwoven*: flores hederis intertexti, Ov.; chlamys auro intertexta, Verg.

intertrăho -trăhĕre -traxi, *to take away*: Pl.

intertrīmentum -i, n. (inter/tero), *loss by friction*. LIT., *loss in working gold and silver* in auro, argenti, Liv. TRANSF., in gen., *loss, damage*: sine ullo intertrimento, Cic.; Ter.

interturbātĭo -ōnis, f. *disturbance, disquiet*: Liv.

interturbo -are, *to confuse*: Pl.
intervallum -i, n. (inter/vallus), *a space between two palisades.* Hence (1) *an intervening space, interval, distance*: pari intervallo, *at an equal distance*, Caes.; locorum, Cic.; Verg., Liv. (2) *an interval of time*: sine intervallo loquacitas, *without intermission*, Cic.; Liv., Tac. (3) in gen., *difference, unlikeness*: Cic.
intervello -vellĕre -vulsi -vulsum, *to pull or pluck out here and there*: Pl., Sen.
intervĕnĭo -vĕnire -vĕni -ventum, *to come between, come up while anything is doing, to intervene.*
  Lit., with dat. of person or thing: verens ne molesti vobis interveniremus, Cic.; huic orationi, Cic.
  Transf., (1) of events, etc., *to occur while something else is being done* and so *to interrupt*; with dat.: nox intervenit proelio, Liv.; intervenit deinde huis cogitationibus avitum malum, Liv. (2) *to delay*, with acc.: Tac.
interventor -ōris, m. (intervenio), *an interrupting visitor*: magis vacuo ab interventoribus die, Cic.
interventus -ūs, m. (intervenio), *intervention, interposition, interference*: hominis, Cic.; noctis, Caes.; Liv.
interverto (-vorto) -vertĕre -verti -versum, *to intercept*; hence (1) *to embezzle, purloin*: regale donum, Cic.; Pl. Transf., of immaterial things: promissum et receptum (consulatum) intervertere et ad se transferre, Cic. (2) *to cheat, rob of*: me muliere, Pl.
intervīso -vīsĕre -vīsi -vīsum. (1) *to look in at*: domum, Pl.; crebro interviso, Cic. L. (2) *to visit from time to time*: aliquem, Cic. L., Tac.
intervŏlĭto -are, *to flit about among*: Liv.
intervŏmo -ĕre, *to pour forth among*: Lucr.
intestābĭlis -e, *disqualified from being a witness*; hence *dishonoured, infamous*; of persons: Sall., Hor., Tac.; of things: periurium, Liv.; compar.: Tac.
intestātus -a -um. (1) *having made no will, intestate*: Juv.; n. abl. as adv. intestato *or* ab intestato, *intestate*: mori, Cic. (2) *not convicted by witnesses*: Pl.
intestātus -a -um (²testis), *castrated*: Pl.
intestīnus -a -um (intus), *inward, internal*: intestinum ac domesticum malum, Cic.; bellum, Cic.; Liv.
  ¶ N. as subst., sing. and plur. **intestīnum** -i and **intestīna** -ōrum, *the intestines*: intestinum medium, Cic.; ex intestinis laborare, Cic.; Juv.
intexo -texĕre -texŭi -textum. (1) *to weave in, plait in, interweave.* Lit., purpureas notas filis, Ov.; intexti Britanni (in needlework), Verg. Transf., venae toto corpore intextae, Cic.; facta chartis, Tib.; Liv. (2) *to weave around, to wind around*: hastas foliis, Verg.; hederae solent intexere truncos, Ov.
intĭbum -i, n. *endive, succory*: Verg., Ov.
intĭmus (intŭmus) -a -um, superl. adj. (in) (compar. interior; q.v.), *innermost, inmost.* Lit., intima Macedonia, *the very centre of Macedonia*, Cic.; Verg. Transf., (1) *deepest, most profound*: philosophia, Cic. (2) *most secret, confidential, intimate*: sermo, Cic.; amici, Tac.; familiaritas, Nep. M. as subst., *an intimate friend*: Pl., Cic.

  ¶ Adv. **intĭmē**. (1) *confidentially, intimately*: Nep. (2) *cordially, strongly*: commendari ab aliquo, Cic. L.
intingo (intinguo) -tingĕre -tinxi -tinctum, *to dip in*: faces in fossā sanguinis, Ov.; Pl., Quint.
intŏlĕrābĭlis -e, adj. (with compar.), *unbearable, intolerable*: frigus, dolor, Cic.; saevitia, Liv.
intŏlĕrandus -a -um, *unbearable, unendurable*: Cic., Liv., Tac.
intŏlĕrans -antis, adj. (with compar. and superl.). Act., *impatient, unable to bear*; with genit.: corpora intolerantissima laboris, Liv.; Tac. Pass., *unbearable, intolerable*: subiectis intolerantior, Tac.
  ¶ Adv. (with compar. and superl.) **intŏlĕrantĕr**, *immoderately, excessively, impatiently*: dolere, Cic.; intolerantius se iactare, Cic.; intolerantissime gloriari, Cic.
intŏlĕrantĭa -ae, f. (intolerans), *insufferable conduct, insolence*: regis, Cic.; superbia atque intolerantia, Cic.
intŏno -tŏnare -tŏnŭi, *to thunder.*
  Lit., pater omnipotens ter caelo clarus ab alto intonuit, Verg.
  Transf., *to make a thundering noise*, especially of a speaker: iam hesternā contione intonuit vox perniciosa tribuni, Cic.; with acc. object: cum haec intonuisset plenus irae, Liv.; minas, Ov.; perf. partic. pass. intŏnātus -a -um, used in act. sense: Eois intonata fluctibus hiems, *raging on*, Hor.
intonsus -a -um (in/tondeo), *unshorn.*
  Lit., caput, Ov.; of animals: intonsa bidens, Verg.; of persons, *with long hair* or *beard*: deus, *Apollo*, Ov.; of the old Romans: intonsi avi, Ov.; Numa, Ov.
  Transf., (1) of persons, *rude, rough*: homines intonsi et inculti, Liv.; intonsi Getae, Ov. (2) of country, *wooded, not cleared of trees*: montes, Verg.
intorquĕo -torquēre -torsi -tortum. (1) *to twist* or *turn round*: paludamentum circum bracchium, Liv.; oculos, Verg.; mentum in dicendo, Cic. (2) *to hurl*: telum in hostem, Verg.; fig.: intorquentur inter fratres gravissimae contumeliae, Cic.
  ¶ Hence partic. **intortus** -a -um, *twisted.* Lit., rudentes, Cat.; intorti capillis Eumenidum angues, Hor. Transf., *tangled*: Pl.
intrā, adv. and prep., *within, inside.*
  Adv., Quint., Suet.
  Prep., with acc. Lit., of space, with or without motion: intra parietes, Cic.; intra moenia compulsus, Liv.; Pl., Caes., Verg., Plin. Transf., (1) of time, *within, during, in the space of*: intra tot annos, Cic.; intra annos XIV, Caes.; foll. by quam: intra decimum diem quam Pheras venerat, *in less than ten days after his arrival*, Liv. (2) with numerals: intra centum, *less than a hundred*, Liv. (3) with other words indicating limit: intra legem epulari, Cic. L.; intra finem iuris, Liv.
intrābĭlis -e (intro), *that can be entered, accessible*: amnis os multis simul venientibus haud sane intrabile, Liv.
intractābĭlis -e, *unmanageable, intractable*: genus intractabile bello, *formidable*, Verg.; bruma, *inconvenient*, Verg.

intractātus -a -um, *not handled.* LIT., equus intractatus et novus, Cic. TRANSF., *unattempted*: scelus, Verg.

intrĕmisco -trĕmiscĕre -trĕmŭi, *to begin to tremble*: undae, Verg.; genua, Ov.

intrĕmo -ĕre, *to tremble, quake*: Verg.

intrĕpĭdus -a -um, *unconfused, calm*: dux, Ov.; with dat.: intrepidus minantibus, Tac. TRANSF., of things: vultus, Ov.; hiems, *undisturbed by war*, Tac.

¶ Adv. **intrĕpĭdē**, *calmly*: Liv.

intrīco -are (in/tricae), *to confuse, entangle*: Chrysippus intricatur, Cic.; Pl.

intrinsĕcŭs, adv. (1) *inside, inwardly*: Lucr. (2) *inwards*: Suet.

¹**intrītus** -a -um (in/tero), *not worn away.* TRANSF., *unexhausted*: cohortes intritae ab labore, Caes.

²**intrītus** -a -um, partic. from intero; q.v.

¹**intrō**, adv. *inwards, within*: intro ire, Caes.; filiam intro vocare, Cic.

²**intro** -are, *to go into, enter*; transit. and intransit. LIT., regnum, pomoerium, Cic.; in Capitolium, Cic.; maria, Verg.; in hortos, Ov.; portas, Liv.; ad munimenta, Liv.; intra praesidia, Caes. TRANSF., in rerum naturam, Cic.; in alicuius familiaritatem, Cic. L.; of things: quo non modo improbitas sed ne imprudentia quidem possit intrare, Cic.; animum cupido, Tac.

intrŏdūco -dūcĕre -duxi -ductum, *to lead or conduct inside.*
    LIT., copias in fines Bellovacorum, Caes.; exercitum in Ligures, Liv.; esp. *to present, introduce*: in senatum, Cic., Liv.
    TRANSF., in gen., *to bring in, introduce*: philosophiam in domos, Cic.; consuetudinem, Cic.; Caes., Liv.; esp. *to introduce in speech*: introducta rei similitudo, Cic.; with acc. and infin., *to bring forward an idea, suggest that*: Cic.

intrŏductĭo -ōnis, f. (introduco), *a bringing in, introduction*: adulescentulorum, Cic. L.

intrŏĕo -īre -ĭi -ĭtum, *to go into, enter*; transit. and intransit. LIT., in urbem, Cic. L.; domum, Cic.; portā, *by the gate*, Cic.; Pl., Liv. TRANSF., in vitam, Cic.

intrŏfĕro -ferre -tŭli -lātum, *to carry in*: liberis cibum, Cic.; Liv.

intrŏgrĕdĭor -grĕdī -gressus sum, dep. (intro/gradior), *to enter*: Verg.

intrŏĭtus -ūs, m. (introeo), *an entrance.* LIT., Smyrnam, Cic.; in urbem, Cic.; primo introitu, Tac. TRANSF., (1) *a place of entrance, passage*: Cic.; Caes., Suet. (2) in gen., *a beginning, introduction*: defensionis, Cic.

intrŏmitto -mittĕre -mīsi -missum, *to send in, allow* or *cause to enter*: legiones, Caes.; Liv., Tac.

introrsŭs (introrsum), adv. (for introversus), *towards the inside, inwards*: Caes., Liv., Tac. TRANSF., *inwardly, internally*: Hor., Liv., Ov.

intrōrumpo -rumpĕre -rūpi -ruptum, *to break into, enter by force*: Caes.

introspĭcĭo -spicĕre -spexi -spectum (intro/specio), *to look into, look within*; transit. and intransit. LIT., domum tuam, Cic. TRANSF., *to look attentively into, observe, examine*: in omnes reipublicae partes, Cic.; introspice in mentem tuam ipse, Cic.; aliorum felicitatem, Tac.

intŭbum -i, n., *see* intibum.

intŭĕor -tŭēri -tŭĭtus sum, dep. *to look at attentively, gaze at*; transit. and intransit. LIT., solem, Cic.; in aliquem contra, *right in the face*, Liv.; Hor. TRANSF., (1) *to consider, contemplate, pay attention to*: veritatem, Cic.; in aliquod malum, Cic.; Liv., Tac. (2) *to look with astonishment* or *admiration at*: Pompeium, Cic.; Liv.

intŭmesco -tŭmescĕre -tŭmŭi, *to swell, swell up.* LIT., intumuit venter, Ov. TRANSF., (1) in gen., *to increase*: vox, Tac.; intumescente motu, Tac. (2) *to swell with pride*: superbiā, Tac. (3) *to swell with anger*: Ov.

intŭmŭlātus -a -um (in/tumulo), *unburied*: Ov.

intŭor -i, dep. = intueor; q.v.

inturbĭdus -a -um, *undisturbed, quiet*: annus Tac.; vir, Tac.

intŭs, adv. (in; cf. ἐντός), *within, inside.* LIT., ea quae sunt intus in corpore, Cic.; Pl. Verg., Liv.; sometimes with verbs of motion, *to the inside*: duci intus, Ov.; Caes., Lucr. Tac.; sometimes *from within*: Pl., Liv. TRANSF., *inwardly, in oneself*: Cic., Pers.

intūtus -a -um. (1) *unprotected*: castra, Liv. n. pl.: intuta moenium, *the unprotected parts of the walls*, Tac. (2) *unsafe, dangerous*: latebrae, Tac.; amicitia, Tac.

ĭnŭla -ae, f. *the plant elecampane*: Hor.

ĭnultus -a -um (in/ulciscor). (1) *unavenged*: iniuriae, Cic.; ne inultus esset, Cic.; Verg. Hor., Liv. (2) *unpunished*: hostis, Sall., Ov. scelus, Sall.; Cic., Hor.

ĭnumbro -are, *to shade, overshadow*: ora coronis, Lucr.; vestibulum, Verg.; inumbrante vesperā, *as the shades of evening were coming on*, Tac.

ĭnundātĭo -ōnis, f. (inundo), *an inundation, flood*: Plin., Suet.

ĭnundo -are.
    (1) transit., *to overflow, inundate.* LIT., hanc (terram) inundat aqua, Cic.; vestro sanguine Enna inundabitur, Liv. TRANSF., *to stream over like a torrent*: multitudo campos, Curt.; cursus inundant Troes Verg.
    (2) intransit., *to overflow with*: inundant sanguine fossae, Verg.

ĭnungo -ungĕre -unxi -unctum, *to anoint*: oculos, Hor.

ĭnurbānus -a -um, *rude, unpolished, boorish*: Cic., Hor.
¶ Adv. **ĭnurbānē**, *inelegantly, without wit* or *humour*: Cic.

ĭnurgĕo -urgēre -ursi, *to push, thrust against*: Lucr.

ĭnūro -ūrĕre -ussi -ustum, *to burn in* or *on, brand.*
    LIT., notam, Verg.
    TRANSF., (1) *to imprint indelibly, brand*: notam turpitudinis vitae alicuius, Cic. (2) *to inflict*: alicui dolorem, Cic. (3) *to crimp* or *curl as with the curling-irons, to adorn elaborately*: aliquid calamistris, Cic.

ĭnūsĭtātus -a -um, adj. (with compar.) *unusual, strange, uncommon*: res inusitata a nova, Cic.; species navium inusitatior, Caes with dat.: inusitatus nostris oratoribus lepo Cic.; inusitatum est, with acc. and infin., Cic.
¶ Adv. (with compar.) **ĭnūsĭtātē**, *unusually, strangely*: inusitate loqui, Cic.

ĭnustus -a -um, partic. from inuro; q.v.

ĭnūtĭlis -e, *useless, unserviceable, unprofitable*: homo, Cic.; with dat.: valetudine aut aetate inutiles bello, Caes.; with ad and the acc.: ad usus civium non inutile, Cic.; naves, Caes.; ferrum, Verg.; Hor., Liv. TRANSF., *injurious, harmful*: seditiosus et inutilis civis, Cic.; oratio inutilis sibi et civitati suae, Liv.
  ¶ Adv. **ĭnūtĭlĭtĕr**, *uselessly, unprofitably*: Liv. TRANSF., *harmfully*: Cic.

ĭnūtĭlĭtās -ātis, f. (inutilis), *uselessness, unprofitableness*: Lucr. TRANSF., *harmfulness*: Cic.

invādo -vādĕre -vāsi -vāsum.
  (**1**) *to go in, enter, get in.* LIT., quocunque ignis invasit, Cic.; in eas urbes, Cic.; with simple acc.: portūs, Verg.; urbem, Liv.; Tac. TRANSF., *to undertake*: aliquid magnum, Verg.
  (**2**) *to attack, assault, fall upon.* LIT., in hostem, in Galliam, Cic.; with simple acc.: agmen, Caes.; urbem, Verg.; Liv. TRANSF., **a**, with words, *to assail, attack*: aliquem minaciter, Tac.: **b**, of disease, passion, etc., *to attack, befall*: pestis in vitam invasit, Cic.; with simple acc.: aliquem lubido invadit, Sall.; pestilentia populum invasit, Liv.: **c**, *to fall upon in order to take*; *to usurp, seize*: in alicuius praedia, Cic.; with simple acc.: Sall., Tac.

invālesco -vălescĕre -vălŭi, *to gather strength, become strong*: tantum opibus invaluit, Cic.; Tac.

invălĭdus -a -um, *weak, powerless, feeble.* LIT., physically: milites, Liv.; ad munera corporis senectā invalidus, Liv.; Verg., Tac. TRANSF., in gen., *weak*: moenia invalida adversus inrumpentes, Tac.

invectio -ōnis, f. (inveho). (**1**) *importation*: Cic. (**2**) *an inveighing against, invective*: Cic.

invĕho -vĕhĕre -vexi -vectum. (**1**) act., in gen., *to carry, bear, bring in.* LIT., pecuniam in aerarium, Cic.; vinum in Galliam, *to import*, Liv. TRANSF., *to introduce*: quae (mala) tibi casus invexerat, Liv.; divitiae avaritiam invexere, Liv.
  (**2**) reflex., se invehere, and pass. as middle, invehi: **a**, *to drive, ride, or travel, on horseback, in a vehicle, in a ship*: curru in capitolium, Cic.; equo, Verg., Ov., Liv.; flumine, *to sail on*, Cic.; in portum, Cic.; with acc.: moenia, Verg.; portum, Liv.: **b**, *to advance against, burst into, attack.* LIT., Romana se invexit acies, Liv.; cum utrinque invehi hostem nuntiaretur, Liv. TRANSF., *to attack with words, assail, inveigh against*: petulanter in aliquem, Cic.; Liv.

invendĭbĭlis -e, *unsaleable*: Pl.

invĕnĭo -vĕnīre -vēni -ventum, *to come upon, find, meet with.*
  LIT., of physical discovery: naves, Caes.; hostem, Liv.; Pl., Verg.
  TRANSF., (**1**) *to find out, discover* abstract things: coniurationem, Cic.; with acc. and infin. or indir. quest., *to find out that, find out why*, etc.: Cic., Lucr., Liv. (**2**) *to invent, devise*: multa divinitus, Lucr., Cic.; artes, Verg. (**3**) *to procure, acquire, get, earn*: cognomen, Cic.; gloriam ex culpa, Sall. (**4**) reflex., se invenire, or pass. as middle, inveniri, *to show oneself*: dolor se invenit, Ov.

inventĭo -ōnis, f. (invenio). (**1**) *an inventing, invention*: Cic., Quint. (**2**) *the inventive faculty*: Cic., Quint.

inventor -ōris, m. (invenio), *an inventor, finder out*: novorum verborum, Cic.; Verg.

inventrix -trīcis, f. (inventor), *she that finds out*: oleae Minerva inventrix, Verg.; illae omnium doctrinarum inventrices Athenae, Cic.
  ¶ Hence partic. **inventus** -a -um, *discovered*; n. as subst. **inventum** -i, *an invention, discovery*: Cic., Ov.

invĕnustus -a -um. (**1**) *not charming, unattractive, ungraceful*: Cat., Cic. (**2**) *unhappy in love*: Pl., Ter.

invĕrēcundus -a -um, *shameless, impudent*: deus, *Bacchus*, Hor.; superl.: Pl.

invergo -ĕre, *to tip* or *pour upon*: fronti vina, Verg.; Pl.

inversĭo -ōnis, f. (inverto). (**1**) verborum, *irony*, Cic. (**2**) *transposition*: Quint. (**3**) *allegory*: Quint.

inversus -a -um, partic. from inverto; q.v.

inverto -vertĕre -verti -versum, *to turn over, turn about.* LIT., in locum anulum, Cic.; vomere terras graves, Verg.; vinaria tota, Hor. TRANSF., *to transpose, alter, pervert*: ordinem, Cic.; verba, Cic.; virtutes, Hor.
  ¶ Hence partic. **inversus** -a -um, *overturned.* LIT., vomer, Hor. TRANSF., verba, Lucr.; mores, Hor.

invespĕrascit -ĕre, impers. *it grows dark, becomes twilight*: Liv.

investĭgātĭo -ōnis, f. (investigo), *an inquiring into, investigation*: veri, Cic.

investĭgātor -ōris, m. (investigo), *an inquirer, investigator*: antiquitatis, Cic.; coniurationis, Cic.

investĭgo -are, *to search out, track out.* LIT., esp. with dogs: canum tam incredibilis ad investigandum sagacitas narium, Cic. TRANSF., coniurationem, Cic.; verum, Cic.; with indir. quest.: Pl., Cic.

invĕtĕrasco -ascĕre -āvi, *to become old in one's place.*
  LIT., inveteraverunt hi omnes compluribus Alexandriae bellis, Caes.
  TRANSF., (**1**) *to become obsolete*: si (res) inveteravit, actum est, Cic.; Tac. (**2**) *to become established, fixed, rooted*: inveteravit iam opinio, Cic.; with dat.: quorum nomen et honos inveteravit et huic urbi et hominum famae et sermonibus, Cic.; Lucr., Caes.

invĕtĕrātĭo -ōnis, f. (invetero), *inveterateness, permanence*: Cic.

invĕtĕrātus -a -um, *of long standing, established, firmly rooted*: amicitia, Cic.; ira, Cic.

invĭcem, adv. (in/vicem). (**1**) *in turn, by turns, alternately*: hi rursus invicem anno post in armis sunt, illi domi remanent, Caes.; Liv. (**2**) *mutually, reciprocally*: invicem inter se gratantes, Liv.; multae invicem clades, Tac.

invictus -a -um (in/vinco), *unconquered, unsubdued, unconquerable, invincible*: imperator, Cic.; a labore, armis, Cic.; ad vulnera, Ov.; adversum gratiam, Tac.; fig.: defensio, *unanswerable*, Cic.

invĭdentia -ae, f. (invideo), *envying, envy*: Cic.

invĭdĕo -vĭdēre -vīdi -vīsum, *to look upon with the evil eye.* LIT., Cat. TRANSF., *to envy,*

grudge, be envious of. Regularly with dat. of person: paribus aut inferioribus, Cic.; often with dat. of thing: honori, Cic.; impers., pass.: superioribus saepe invidetur, Cic.; Pl. Also with acc. of thing grudged: alicui honorem, Hor.; Verg., Liv.; with in and abl. of thing: in qua tibi invideo, Cic.; with abl. of thing: non invideo laude sua mulieribus, Liv.; with genit. of thing: illi ciceris, Hor.; with infin., or acc. and infin.: Liburnis deduci triumpho, Hor.; Pl., Ov.; with ut *or* ne and the subj.: Verg.
¶ Hence partic. **invīsus** -a -um. (1) pass., *hated,* of persons or things: persona, Cic.; negotia, Hor.; with dat., *hated by*: invisus deo, Cic.; iudicium invisum etiam iudicibus, Liv.; compar.: Cic. (2) act., *hostile*: invisum quem tu tibi fingis, Verg.

invidĭa -ae, f. (invidus). (1) act., *envy, grudging, jealousy, ill-will*: Cic., Verg.; with genit.: laudis suae, Caes.; absit verbo invidia, Liv. (2) pass., *odium, unpopularity*: habere, *to be unpopular,* Cic.; in invidiam venire, Cic.; invidiam in aliquem commovere, concitare, excitare, Cic.; conflare, Liv. TRANSF., **a**, personif.: *Envy*: Verg., Hor., Ov.; invidiam lenire, Cic.: **b**, *a source of ill-will*: invidiae erat amissum Cremerae praesidium, Liv.

invĭdĭōsē, adv. (invidiosus), *enviously, jealously, bitterly*: Cic.

invĭdĭōsus -a -um, adj. (with compar. and superl.) (invidia). (1) *envious*: vetustas, Ov. (2) *causing envy, envied*: non invidiosa voluptas, Ov. (3) *hateful, causing hate* or *ill-feeling*: crimen, damnatio, Cic.; with dat.: hoc ipsis iudicibus invidiosissimum futurum, Cic.; nomina, Liv.; Tac.

invĭdus -a -um (invideo), *envious*: Cic., Hor., Ov.; with genit.: laudis, Cic.; m. as subst.: obtrectatores et invidi Scipionis, Cic.; Tac. TRANSF., of things: cura, aetas, Hor.; nox coeptis invida nostris, *unfavourable to,* Ov.

invĭgĭlo -are, *to be watchful* or *wakeful over; give great attention to*; with dat.: reipublicae, Cic.; Verg.

invĭŏlābĭlis -e, *unassailable, that cannot be violated* or *injured*: pignus, Verg.; Lucr., Tac.

invĭŏlātus -a -um. (1) *uninjured, unhurt*: invulnerati inviolatique vixerunt, Cic.; inviolatā vestrā amicitiā, Cic. (2) *inviolable*: tribunus plebis, Liv.; Sall., Caes.
¶ Adv. **invĭŏlātē**, *inviolately*: memoriam nostri pie inviolateque servabitis, Cic.

invīsĭtātus -a -um, *not seen*; hence, *unusual, strange*: magnitudo, forma, Cic.; nova acies, Liv.; Tac.

invīso -vīsĕre -vīsi -vīsum. (1) *to go to see, to visit*: domum, Pl.; aliquem, Cic. L.; suos, Liv.; Delum, Verg. (2) *to inspect*: urbes, Verg.; Cic. (3) *to look at*: Cat.

¹**invīsus** -a -um (in/video), *unseen, secret*: sacra occulta et maribus non solum invisa sed etiam inaudita, Cic.

²**invīsus** -a -um, partic. from invideo; q.v.

invītāmentum -i, n. (invito), *an invitation, attraction, allurement*; with subjective genit.: naturae, Cic.; with objective genit.: temeritatis invitamenta, Liv.; with ad: multa ad luxuriam invitamenta perniciosa, Cic.

invītātĭo -ōnis, f. (invito), *invitation, inducement, reception*; with subjective genit.:

hospitum, Cic.; in Epirum, Cic. L.; ut biberetur, Cic.; ad dolendum, Cic.

invītātū, abl. as from invitatus, m. (invito), *by invitation*: invitatu tuo, Cic. L.

invīto -are, *to invite.* LIT., *to invite as a guest*: aliquem ad cenam, Cic.; aliquem domum suam, Cic.; sometimes *to receive, entertain*: aliquem tecto ac domo, Cic.; Liv.; reflex., invitare se, *to treat oneself*: se cibo vinoque, Sall. TRANSF., (1) *to summon*: aliquem in legationem, Cic. L. (2) *to invite, allure, induce*: aliquem praemiis ad rem, Cic.; somnos, Hor.; with ut and subj.: Pl., Caes.; with infin.: Verg.

invītus -a -um, adj. (with superl.), *unwilling, against one's will.* (1) of persons: invitus facio, Cic.; in abl. absol., me, te, se invito, *against my,* etc., *will*: Caes., Cic., Verg. TRANSF., of things: invitā lege agere, Cic.; invitā ope, Ov.; Hor., Verg.
¶ Adv. (with compar.) **invītē**, *unwillingly, involuntarily, against one's will*: invite cepi Capuam, Cic.; vel pudentius vel invitius ad hoc genus sermonis accedere, Cic.

invĭus -a -um (in/via), *impassable*: saltus, Liv.; maria invia Teucris, Verg.; lorica invia sagittis, *impenetrable,* Mart.; n. pl. as subst. invĭa -orum, *trackless places,* Liv. TRANSF., nil virtuti invium, Tac.; Ov.

invŏcātĭo -ōnis, f. (invoco), *a calling upon, invocation*: deorum, Quint.

¹**invŏcātus** -a -um (in/voco), *uncalled, uninvited*: Pl., Ter., Cic.

²**invŏcātus** -a -um, partic. from invoco; q.v.

invŏco -are, *to call in, call upon for help, invoke*: Iunonem, Cic.; aliquem advocatum ad communem imperatorum fortunam defendendam, Cic.; deos, Pl., Liv.; leges, Tac.

invŏlātū, abl. as from involatus, m. (involo), *by the flight*: Cic.

invŏlĭto -are, *to float* or *wave over*: comae involitant humeris, Hor.

invŏlo -are, *to fly at, seize* or *pounce upon*; transit. and intransit. LIT., equites ab dextera, Pl.; castra, Tac. TRANSF., in possessionem quasi caducam ac vacuam, Cic.; animos cupido, Tac.

invŏlūcre -is, n. (involvo), *a wrap*: Pl.

invŏlūcrum -i, n. (involvo), *a wrap, cover.* LIT., candelabri, Cic. TRANSF., involucris simulationum tegi, Cic.

invŏlūtus -a -um, partic. from involvo; q.v.

involvo -volvĕre -volvi -vŏlūtum. (1) *to roll in, to envelop, wrap up, cover*: sinistras sagis, Caes.; igni suo involvunt, Tac.; Lucr., Verg. TRANSF., se litteris, Cic. L.; se suā virtute, Hor.; bellum pacis nomine, Cic.; nox involvit umbrā diem, Verg. (2) *to roll upon*; with dat.: Olympum Ossae, Verg.
¶ Hence partic. **invŏlūtus** -a -um, *rolled up*; hence *involved*: res involutas definiende explicare, Cic.

invŏlvŭlus -i, m. (involvo), *a caterpillar which wraps itself up in leaves*: Pl.

invulgo -are, *to give information*: Cic. L.

invulnĕrātus -a -um (in/vulnero), *unwounded*: Cic.

¹**ĭō**, interj., *an exclamation of joy, hurrah!*: Hor.; or of pain, *oh!*: Pl.; or a call, *ho!*: Verg., Ov.

²**Īō** (**Īōn**) -ūs (-ōnis), f. (*'Ιώ*), *daughter of the Argive king, Inachus, beloved by Jupiter, who for fear of Juno changed her into a cow*; identified with the Egyptian goddess, Isis. Hence adj. **Īŏnĭus** -a -um, *of the sea between Italy and Greece, across which Io swam*: mare Ionium, Liv.; aequor, Ov.; sinus, Hor., *the Ionian sea*; also simply Ionium, n. (sc. mare): Verg.

iŏcātĭo -ōnis, f. (iocor), *a joke, jest*: Cic. L., Cat.

iŏcor -ari, dep. (also **iŏco** -are, act.: Pl.) (from iocus), *to joke, jest*: cum aliquo per litteras, Cic.; me appellabat iocans, Cic.; Ter., Liv.; with internal acc.: haec iocatus sum, Cic. L.; in faciem permulta, Hor.

iŏcōsus -a -um (iocus), *humorous, sportive, merry, facetious*: Maecenas, Hor.; res, Cic.; imago (vocis), *the sportive echo*, Hor.; Ov.
¶ Adv. (with compar.) **iŏcōsē**, Cic. L., Hor.

iŏcŭlāris -e (iocus), *jocular, laughable*: audacia, Ter.; Cic.; n. pl. as subst. iocularia, *jests*, Hor., Liv.
¶ Adv. **iŏcŭlārĭter**, *jestingly*: Plin., Suet.

iŏcŭlārius -a -um (ioculus), *laughable, droll*: Ter.

iŏcŭlātor -ōris, m. (ioculor), *a joker*: Cic. L.

iŏcŭlor -ari, dep. (ioculus), *to joke, jest, speak jocosely*: quaedam militariter ioculantes, Liv.

iŏcŭlus -i, m. (dim. of iocus), *a little joke*: Pl.

iŏcus -i, m. (plur. ioci and ioca), *a joke, jest*: ioci causā, *for a joke*, Cic.; per iocum, *in jest*, Cic.; extra iocum, remoto ioco, *joking apart*, Cic.; ludus et iocus, *mere sport*, Liv.; Hor., Ov. Personif., **Iŏcus** -i, m. *god of Jests*: Pl., Hor.

Īolcus (-ŏs) -i, f. (*'Ιωλκός*), *town in Thessaly, from which Jason sailed with the Argonauts.*
¶ Hence adj. **Īolcĭăcus** -a -um, *of Iolcus.*

¹**īon** ii, n. (*ἴον*). (**1**) *the blue violet*: Plin. (**2**) *a precious stone of similar colour*: Plin.

²**Īon** -ōnis, f., see Io.

Īōnes -um, m. (*'Ιωνες*), *the Ionians, a people in the west of Asia Minor, originally from Greece.*
¶ Hence subst. **Īōnĭa** -ae, f. *their country, a district in Asia Minor between Caria and Aeolis*; adj. **Īōnĭăcus** -a -um, *Ionian*; adj. **Īōnĭcus** -a -um, *Ionian.*

iōta, n. indecl. (*ἰῶτα*), *the name of the Greek vowel, ι*, Cic.

Īphĭănassa -ae, f. = Iphigenia; q.v.: Lucr.

Īphĭgēnīa -ae, f. (*'Ιφιγένεια*), *daughter of Agamemnon, sacrificed by her father to appease the wrath of Diana*; or, according to another legend, *saved by Diana, and carried away, and made her priestess in Tauris.*

ipse (ipsus: Pl.) -a -um, genit. ipsīus, dat. ipsi (is/-pse), *self*; standing alone to indicate a person or thing, or agreeing with a noun or another pronoun.
In gen.: ego ipse, *I myself*, Cic.; ipse interviso, Cic.; in me ipso probavi, *in myself*, Cic.; ipse Epicurus, Lucr.; ipse frater, Ter.; eaque ipsa causa belli fuit, *and that very thing was the cause of the war*, Liv.; victor ex Aequis in Volscos transiit et ipsos bellum molientes, *who on their side too were preparing war*, Liv.
Esp. (**1**) with numbers, etc., *just, exactly*: ipso vicesimo anno, Cic.; eā ipsā horā, Cic.; Praeneste sub ipsa, Verg. (**2**) of a *master,*

mistress, teacher, etc.: ipse dixit, *the master* (i.e. *Pythagoras*) *has said it*, Cic. (**3**) *spontaneously, of one's own accord*: valvae se ipsae aperuerunt, Cic.; ipsae domum referent capellae ubera, Verg. (**4**) with reflex.: ipsum si quicquam posse in se sistere credis, Lucr.; genitor secum ipse volutat, Verg. (**5**) with suffix -met: Pl., Cic. (**6**) superl.: ipsissimus, *one's very self*, Pl.

īra (eira: Pl.) -ae, f. *wrath, anger, ire.*
LIT., per iram, *in anger*, Cic.; irae indulgere, Liv.; in plur.: irae caelestes, *divine wrath*, Liv.; with genit. of the cause of anger: dictatoris creati, Liv.; ira adversus Romanos, Liv.; veteres in populum Romanum irae, Liv.
TRANSF., (**1**) of things, *violence, rage*: belli, Sall. (**2**) personif., in plur.: Verg. (**3**) *cause of anger*: Verg., Ov.

īrācundĭa -ae, f. (iracundus). (**1**) *an angry disposition, passionateness, irascibility*: Cic., Suet. (**2**) *state of anger, fury, wrath*: iracundiam cohibere, Cic.; excitare, Cic.; Ter., Caes.

īrācundus -a -um (irascor), *inclined to anger, irascible, passionate*: mens, Lucr.; senes, Cic.; in aliquem, Cic.; Hor.
¶ Adv. (with compar.) **īrācundē**, *wrathfully, passionately*: Cic.

īrascor -i, dep. (ira), *to grow angry, wrathful*: Cic.; with dat.: alicui, Cic.; poet., of a bull: in cornua, *to put his rage into his horns*, Verg.
¶ Hence partic. (with compar. and superl.) **īrātus** -a -um, *angry, full of wrath*; with dat.: alicui, *with anyone*, Cic., Ov.; iratus de iudicio, Cic. TRANSF., of things, *raging*: mare, venter, Hor.
¶ Adv. **īrātē**, *angrily*: Phaedr.

Īris -ridis, f. (*'Ιρις*; acc. Irim: Verg.; voc. Iri: Verg., Ov.), *messenger of the gods, and goddess of the rainbow.*

īrōnīa -ae, f. (*εἰρωνεία*), *irony*: Cic.

irr- see inr-.

Īrus -i, m. (*'Ιρος*), *the name of a beggar in Ithaca*; appell. = *a poor man* (opp. to Croesus): Ov.

is, ĕa, ĭd, *he, she, it*; *this* or *that person* or *thing*; demonstrative pronoun, chiefly used to refer to some person or thing already mentioned.
In gen. (**1**) standing alone, *he, she, it*: mihi venit obviam puer tuus; is mihi litteras reddidit, Cic. L. (**2**) with a noun, *that*: in eum locum, Caes.; eam ob rem, Lucr. (**3**) as antecedent, with relat. clause: **a**, of individuals: ea legione quam secum habebat, *that legion which*, Caes.; quod virtute effici debet, id temptatur pecuniā, Cic.: **b**, of classes, one (*of those*) *who, such . . . as*: neque is es, qui quid sis nescias (subj. verb in relat. clause), Cic. L.; also with ut: cuius ea stultitia ut, Cic.
Esp. (**1**) with et, -que, etc., *and that too, and what is more*: cum una legione eaque vacillante, Cic. (**2**) n. sing. id: a, with quod, in apposition to a clause or sentence: si nos, id quod debet, nostra patria delectat, Cic.: **b**, alone, meaning *on that account*: id gaudeo, Cic. L.: **c**, in phrases: id temporis, id aetatis, *at that age*, Cic.; in eo est, *the position is such*, Liv., or, *it depends on this*, Cic.; Liv.; id est, *that is*, in explanation, Cic.

Ĭsăra -ae, f. *a river in Gaul* (now *the Isère*).

Ĭsauri -ōrum, m. (Ἴσαυροι), *the Isaurians*.

¶ Hence subst. **Ĭsaurĭa** -ae, f. (Ἰσαυρία), *their country, a mountainous region in Asia Minor*; adj. **Ĭsaurĭcus** -a -um and **Ĭsaurus** -a -um, *Isaurian*.

Ĭsis -is and -idis, f. (Ἶσις), *the Egyptian goddess Isis*. Adj. **Ĭsĭăcus** -a -um, *of Isis*.

Ismărus -i, m. (Ἴσμαρος) and **Ismăra** -ōrum, n. *a mountain in Thrace*. Adj. **Ismărĭus** -a -um, poet.=*Thracian*: tyrannus, *Tereus*, Ov.

Ismēnus (-ŏs) -i, m. (Ἰσμηνός), *a river in Boeotia*.

¶ Hence f. subst. **Ismēnĭs** -ĭdis, poet.=*a Theban woman*; adj. **Ismēnĭus** -a -um, poet.=*Theban*.

Ĭsocrătēs -is, m. (Ἰσοκράτης), *a famous Athenian orator of the fourth century* B.C. Adj. **Ĭsocrătēus** and **Ĭsocrătĭus** -a -um, *Isocratean*.

Issa -ae, f. (Ἴσσα), *an island in the Adriatic Sea*. Adj. **Issensis** -e, **Issaeus** -a -um, **Issăĭcus** -a -um, *of Issa*.

istāc (iste) adv. *by that way*: Pl., Ter.

istactēnus, adv. *thus far*: Pl.

istĕ ista istŭd, demonstr. pron. or adj. (locative **isti**: Pl., Verg.), *that of yours, that beside you.*

In gen.: adventu tuo ista subsellia, vacuefacta sunt, Cic.; de istis rebus exspecto tuas litteras, Cic. L.

Esp. (**1**) in speeches, referring to parties opposed to the speaker (opp. to hic, *my client*); so, according to context, *the defendant* or *the prosecutor*: Cic. (**2**) in certain contexts, contemptuous: ex quibus generibus hominum istae copiae comparentur, Cic. (**3**) *such, of such a kind*: Cic.

Ister=Hister; q.v.

Isthmus (-ŏs) -i, m. (Ἰσθμός), *the Isthmus of Corinth*: Caes., Liv., Ov. Adj. **Isthmĭus** -a -um, *Isthmian*: labor, *in the Isthmian games*, Hor.; plur. subst. **Isthmĭa** -ōrum, n. *the Isthmian Games*: Liv.

¹istĭc istaec istŏc or istūc (iste/-ce), *that of yours*: istic labor, Pl.; istuc considerabo, Cic.; istaec loca, Cic. L.

²istĭc, adv. (iste/-ce), *over there, there by you.* LIT., scribite quid istic agatur, Cic. L.; Pl., Liv. TRANSF., *therein, in that*: istic sum, *I am all ears*, Ter., Cic.

istim, adv. (iste), *from there*: Enn.

istinc, adv. (istim/-ce), *from over there*. LIT., qui istinc veniunt, Cic. L.; Pl., Ter. TRANSF., *of that thing, from that thing*: Pl., Hor.

istĭusmŏdī or **istĭus mŏdī** or **istĭmodī**, *of that kind, such*: ratio istiusmodi, Cic.; Pl.

istō, adv. (iste), *thither, to that place, to the place where you are*: venire, Cic. L.; Pl. TRANSF., (**1**) *thereunto, into that thing*: admiscere aliquem, Cic. L. (**2**) *therefore*: Pl.

istŏc, adv. (iste/-ce), *thither*: Ter.

istorsum, adv. (isto/vorsum), *thitherwards*: Ter.

Istri, see Histri.

istūc, adv. (isto/-ce), *thither*: venire, Cic.; Pl., Ov. TRANSF., *to that*: Ter.

ĭtă, adv. (is), *so, thus, in this fashion.*

(**1**) absol.; in gen.: quae cum ita sint, Cic.; ita est, Lucr.; ita fecit, Cic. Esp.: **a**, interrog., itane? *really?* Cic.; quid ita? *why*

so? Cic.: **b**, in answers: ita vero, Pl.; ita prorsus, ita plane, *certainly*, Cic.: **c**, in narration, *and so*: Cic., Liv.: **d**, with adj. or adv., *so, so very*; often with neg.: non ita antiqua, *not particularly ancient*, Cic.; Liv.

(**2**) in close relation to a clause: **a**, in a comparison, before or after a clause introduced by ut, quemadmodum, quomodo, *so . . . as, as . . . so*: me consulem ita fecistis quomodo pauci facti sunt, Cic.; ita . . . quasi, *or* tamquam, *just as if*, Liv.: **b**, in solemn assertions and adjurations: ita vivam ut maximos sumptus facio, Cic.; saepe, ita me dii iuvent, te desideravi, Cic.: **c**, with consecutive clause: ita . . . ut, *in such a way that*, Caes., Cic.: **d**, to express condition or limitation, ita . . . ut, *only to the extent that, only on condition that, only that*: ita tamen ut tibi nolim molestus esse, Cic. L.; Liv.: **e**, with final clause, ita . . . ut, *in order that*: duobus consulibus ita missis, ut alter Mithridatem persequeretur, Cic.

Ĭtăli -ōrum and -um, m. *the Italians*.

¶ Hence subst. **Ĭtălĭa** -ae, f. *Italy*; adj. **Ĭtălĭcus** -a -um, **Ĭtălĭus** -a -um, **Ĭtălus** -a -um, *Italian*; f. adj. **Ĭtălĭs** -ĭdis, f. *Italian*; plur. as subst. Italides, *Italian women*, Verg.

ĭtăquĕ, adv. (**1**) *and thus, and so*: Caes., Cic. (**2**) *therefore, for that reason, on that account*: Cic., Hor., Liv.

ĭtem, adv. (is/-em), *also, likewise, in like manner*: Romulus augur cum fratre item augure, Cic.; solis defectiones itemque lunae, Cic.; Pl., Liv. In comparisons: fecisti item uti praedones solent, Cic.

ĭter, ĭtĭnĕris, n. (connected with ire, itum), *a going, walk, way.*

LIT., in diversum iter equi concitati, *in opposite directions*, Liv.; in itinere, ex itinere, *on the way*, Caes.; Cic., Liv.

TRANSF., (**1**) *a journey, march*: iter facere, Caes., Cic., Liv.; conficere, Liv.; flectere, Verg.; instituere, Hor. (**2**) *a march*, considered as a measure of distance: cum abessem ab Amano iter unius diei, *one day's journey*, Cic.; magnis itineribus, Caes. (**3**) *a right of way, permission to march*: negat se posse iter ulli per provinciam dare, Caes. (**4**) concr., *a way, road*: iter angustum et difficile, Caes.; Cic., Liv., Tac.; vocis, *passage*, Verg. (**5**) fig., *way, course, method*: iter amoris nostri et officii mei, Cic.; naturam suo quodam itinere ad ultimum pervenire, Cic.; salutis, Verg.

ĭtĕrātĭo -ōnis, f. (itero), *a repetition, iteration*: verborum, Cic.; Quint.

ĭtĕro -are (iterum), *to do a second time, repeat.* In gen.: pugnam, *to renew*, Liv.; aequor, *to take ship again*, Hor.; Ov., Tac. Esp. (**1**) *to plough again*: agrum non semel arare sed iterare, Cic. (**2**) *to repeat* words: Pl., Cic., Liv.

ĭtĕrum, adv. *again, a second time*: C. Flaminius consul iterum, Cic.; primo . . . iterum, Cic.; semel . . . iterum, Liv.; also of repeated action: iterum atque iterum, *again and again*, Hor., Verg.

Ĭthăca -ae and **Ĭthăcē** -ēs, f. (Ἰθάκη), *an island in the Ionian Sea, the home of Ulysses.*

¶ Hence adj. **Ĭthăcensis** -e and **Ĭthăcus** -a -um, *Ithacan*; m. as subst. **Ĭthăcus** -i, *Ulysses*: Verg.

ĭtĭdem, adv. (ita/-dem), *in like manner, likewise*: Pl., Cic.

ĭtĭo -ōnis, f. (eo), *a going, travelling*: domum itio, Cic.; Ter.

ĭto -are (freq. of eo), *to go*: Ter., Cic. L.

Ĭtūraei -ōrum, m. (*Ἰτουραῖοι*), *a people in the north-east of Palestine*; also adj. **Ĭtūraeus** -a -um, *Ituraean*.

ĭtus -ūs, m. (eo), *a movement, going, departure*: noster itus, reditus, Cic. L.; Lucr., Suet.

Ĭtўs -tўos; acc. -tyn and -tym, m. (*Ἴτυς*), *son of Tereus and Procne, killed by his mother and served up for food to his father.*

¹ĭuba -ae, f. *the mane of any animal*: Caes., Cic., Verg. TRANSF., *the crest of a helmet*: Verg.; *of a serpent*: Verg.

²Ĭuba -ae, m. (*Ἰόβας*), *the name of two Numidian kings.*

ĭubar -āris, n. (connected with ¹iuba), *a beaming light, radiance*, esp. of the morning star and other heavenly bodies; *the light of the sun*: Ov.; *of the moon*: Ov.; *of fire*: Ov. TRANSF., (1) *a heavenly body*, esp. *the sun*: Verg. (2) *the radiance* of a god: Mart.

ĭubātus -a -um (iuba), *having a mane, crested*: anguis, Pl., Liv.

ĭubĕo ĭubēre ĭussi ĭussum, *to order, command, bid.*

In gen. (1) with acc. and infin.: Caesar te sine cura esse iussit, *told you not to be troubled*, Cic.; pontem iubet rescindi, Caes.; in pass. with infin. alone: consules iubentur scribere exercitum, Liv.; Caes.; with infin. alone: receptui canere iubet, Caes. (2) with ut *or* ne and the subj.: iubere ut haec quoque referret, Caes.; Cic., Hor., Liv. (3) with subj. alone: Ter., Ov., Liv. (4) with acc. of the action alone: caedem fratris, Tac. (5) absol.: defessa iubendo est saeva Iovis coniux, Ov.

Esp. (1) in greetings: salvere iubere, *to greet*, Cic. L. (2) in medicine, *to prescribe*: aegrotus qui iussus sit vinum sumere, Cic. (3) political t. t., *to ratify* an order: senatus censuit populusque iussit, Cic.; legem, Cic.; populus iussit de bello, Liv.; with ut *or* ne and subj.: Cic., Liv.

❡ Hence, from perf. partic. iussus -a -um, subst. **iussum** -i, n. (usually plur.), *an order, command*; in gen.: iussa efficere, Sall.; capessere, Verg.; Caes., Tac.; esp. (1) *a medical prescription*: Ov. (2) polit. t. t., *a command of the Roman people*: Cic.

ĭucundĭtās -ātis, f. (iucundus), *pleasantness, agreeableness, delightfulness, pleasure*: vitae, Cic.; dare se iucunditati, *to give oneself up to pleasure*, Cic.

ĭucundus -a -um (iuvo), adj. (with compar. and superl.), *pleasant, agreeable, delightful*: est mihi iucunda in malis vestra erga me voluntas, Cic.; comes alicui iucundus, Cic.; verba ad audiendum iucunda, Cic.; Caes., Hor.

❡ Adv. (with compar. and superl.) **ĭucundē**, *pleasantly, agreeably, delightfully*: vivere, Cic.; iucundius bibere, Cic.; Lucr.

Iūdaea -ae, f. (*Ἰουδαία*), *the country of the Jews, Judea* or *Palestine.*

❡ Hence adj. and subst. **Iūdaeus** -a -um, *Jewish* or *a Jew*; adj. **Iūdăĭcus** -a -um, *Jewish.*

iūdex -ĭcis, m. (ius/dico), *a judge.*

LIT., Cic., Hor., Liv.; in plur., *a panel of jurors*: Cic.; iudex quaestionis, *a judge chosen to preside at a trial*, Cic.; dare iudicem, *to appoint* (said of the praetor), Cic.; iudicem alicui ferre, *to offer, propose*, Cic., Liv.; iudicem dicere, of the defendant, Cic.; iudices reicere, *to object to*, Cic.; apud iudicem causam agere, Cic.; iudicem esse de aliqua re, Cic.

TRANSF., of a person who judges or decides on anything: aequissimus eorum studiorum aestimator et iudex, Cic.; sub iudice lis est, Hor.

iūdĭcātĭo -ōnis, f. (iudico). (1) *a judicial investigation*: Cic., Quint. (2) *a judgment, opinion*: Cic.

iūdĭcātum -i, n. from iudico; q.v.

iūdĭcātus -ūs, m. (iudico), *the office* or *business of a judge*: Cic.

iūdĭcĭālis -e (iudicium), *relating to a court of justice, judicial*: causa, Cic.

iūdĭcĭārĭus -a -um (iudicium), *relating to a court of justice*: quaestus, Cic.

iūdĭcĭum -i, n. (iudex), *a trial, legal investigation.*

LIT., iudicium dare, of the praetor, Cic.; qui iudicium exercet, i.e., *the praetor*, Cic.; inter sicarios, Cic.; vocare in iudicium, Cic.

TRANSF., (1) legal: **a**, *a law-court*: Cic.: **b**, *a decision*: senatūs, Caes.: **c**, *jurisdiction*: Liv. (2) in gen.: **a**, *judgment, considered opinion*: iudicium facere, *to decide*, Cic.; meo iudicio, Cic.: **b**, *the power of judging, discernment, understanding*: intellegens, Cic.; subtile, Hor.; esp. *good judgment*: iudicio aliquid facere, Cic.; Tac.

iūdĭco -are (iudex), *to judge.*

LIT., *to be a judge*: Cic., Hor.; with acc., *to decide as judge*: litem, Pl.; rem, Cic.; aliquid contra aliquem, Cic.; deberi dotem, Cic.; perduellionem Horatio, *to investigate H.'s alleged treason*, Liv. So perf. partic. iudicatus -a -um, of persons, *condemned*: Cic., Liv.; of things, *decided*: iudicata res, Cic.

TRANSF., (1) in gen., *to decide, to judge*: quod ante iudicaram, Cic.; with acc. and infin.: iudicio neminem tanta habuisse ornamenta, Cic.; in pass.: nos bene emisse iudicati sumus, Cic. (2) *to declare openly*: Dolabellā hoste iudicato, Cic.; Caes.

iūgālis -e (iugum), *yoked together*; m. pl. as subst. **iūgālēs** -ium, *a team of horses*: Verg. TRANSF., *matrimonial, nuptial*: vinclum, Verg.; dona, Ov.

Iūgārĭus vīcus, *a part of Rome, near the forum*: Liv.

iūgātĭo -ōnis, f. (iugo), *a binding*; esp. *the training of vines on a trellis*: Cic.

iūgĕrum -i, n., plur. according to the 3rd declension (connected with iungo), *a measure of land*, consisting of 28,000 square feet, about two-thirds of an English acre: Cic., Verg.

iūgis -e (iungo), *joined together*; hence *perpetual, continuous*, esp. of water: aqua, Cic.; puteus, Cic.

iūglans -glandis, f. (=Iovis glans), *a walnut* or *walnut-tree*: Cic.

iūgo -are (iugum), *to bind together, connect, couple*; in gen.: virtutes inter se iugatae sunt, Cic.; esp. in marriage: Verg.

iŭgōsus -a -um (iugum), *mountainous*: Ov.
iŭgŭlae -ārum, f. (iugum), *Orion's belt*: Pl.
iŭgŭlo -are (iugulum), *to cut the throat of, to butcher.* LIT., suem, Cic.; cives optimos, Cic.; Verg., Liv. TRANSF., *to ruin, destroy*: aliquem factis decretisque, Cic.; iugulari suā confessione, Cic.; Ter.
iŭgŭlum -i, n. and **iŭgŭlus** -i, m. (iungo), *the throat*: iugulum dare (alicui), Cic.; porrigere, *to offer one's throat for cutting, as a defeated gladiator,* Hor.
iŭgum -i, n. (root of iungo).

(1) *a yoke* or *collar* on the necks of oxen, horses, etc. LIT., iuga imponere bestiis, Cic.; Verg. TRANSF., **a**, *a team* or *yoke of oxen* or *horses*: Cic., Verg.; hence fig. of men, *a pair, a couple*: impiorum (of Antonius and Dolabella), Cic.; also *a chariot*: Verg.: **b**, *bond, union*: ferre iugum pariter, Hor.; esp. *the bond of love, the marriage-tie*: Hor., Ov.: **c**, *the yoke of slavery*: servitutis iugum depellere, Cic.; iugum accipere, Liv.

(2) *a cross-bar*; esp.: **a**, *the yoke, under which the Romans compelled their vanquished enemies to pass in token of submission*: mittere sub iugum, Caes., Cic., Liv.: **b**, *the beam of a pair of scales*: Liv.; hence *the constellation Libra*: Cic.; *the beam of a weaver's loom*: Ov.: **c**, plur. : iuga, *rowers' benches*, Verg.: **d**, *a ridge* between mountains: Caes., Liv.; plur., poet., *mountain heights*: Verg., Ov.
Iŭgurtha -ae, m. *king of Numidia, who was conquered by Marius in* 106 B.C.
¶ Hence adj. **Iŭgurthīnus** -a -um, *Jugurthine.*
Iūlius -a -um, *name of a Roman gens, including the family of the Caesars; the adj. signifies therefore of a Julius, and esp. of C. Julius Caesar*: lex, *a law of Julius Caesar*, Cic.; mensis Iulius *or*, simply, Iulius, *the month of July*, so called in honour of Julius Caesar, formerly called Quinctilis.
¶ Hence adj. **Iūliānus** -a -um, *of Julius Caesar*; plur. as subst., *his adherents in the civil war.*
Iūlus -i, m. *son of Ascanius and grandson of Aeneas.*
¶ Hence adj. **Iūlēus** -a -um, *of Iulus*: Ov.; also *of Caesar, of the Caesars*: Ov.
iūmentum -i, n. (iungo), *an animal used for carrying* or *drawing, beast of burden*: Caes., Cic., Liv.
iuncĕus -a -um (iuncus). (1) *made of rushes*: vincula, Ov. (2) *like a rush*: Ter.
iuncōsus -a -um (iuncus), *full of rushes, rushy*: litora, Ov.
iunctim, adv. (iungo), *successively*: Suet.
iunctĭo -ōnis, f. (iungo), *a joining, connexion*: eorum verborum, Cic.
iunctūra -ae, f. (iungo), *a joining.* Hence (1) *a joint*: tignorum, Caes.; latorum, Verg. (2) *relationship*: generis, Ov. (3) *rhetorical combination, putting together*: Hor.
iunctus -a -um, partic. from iungo; q.v.
iuncus -i, m. *a rush*: limosus, Verg.; iunci palustres, Ov.
iungo iungĕre iunxi iunctum (connected with ζεύγνυμι, ζυγόν), *to join, unite, connect.*
LIT., physically. (1) *to yoke, harness*: equos, currūs, Verg.; Cic. L., Liv., Ov. (2) *to mate*: aliquam alicui conubio, Verg.; cum impari, Liv.; Ov. (3) in gen., *to connect*:

tigna inter se, Caes.; oscula, *to kiss*, Ov.; fluvium ponte, Liv.; pontem, *to throw a bridge over a river*, Verg., Tac.
TRANSF., not physically, *to unite*: improbitas scelere iuncta, Cic.; indignatio iuncta conquestioni, Cic.; se ad aliquem, Cic.; amicitiam cum aliquo, *to form*, Cic.; foedere, societate alicui iungi, Liv.; amicos, Hor.
¶ Hence partic. as adj. (with compar. and superl.) **iunctus** -a -um, *joined, connected, united.* LIT., physically: corpora inter se, Cic.; Iano loca iuncta, Ov.; Verg. TRANSF., (1) *united* by relationship, friendship, etc.: iunctissimus illi comes, Ov. (2) in gen., *associated*: iunctior cum exitu, Cic.
iūnĭor, see iuvenis.
iūnĭpěrus -i, f. *the juniper-tree*: Verg.
Iūnĭus -a -um, *the name of a Roman gens; its most famous members were the Bruti, including two of the murderers of Caesar.* As adj., Junian: mensis Iunius *or*, simply, Iunius, *the month of June*, Cic., Ov.
iūnix -īcis, f. *a heifer*: Pers.
Iūno -ōnis, f. *the goddess Juno, Greek Hera, daughter of Saturn, sister and wife of Jupiter; guardian deity of women*: Iuno inferna, Proserpine, Verg.; so: Iuno Averna, Ov.; urbs Iunonis, *Argos*, Ov.
¶ Hence **Iūnōnĭcŏla** -ae, c. *a worshipper of Juno*; **Iūnōnĭgĕna** -ae, m. *son of Juno; Vulcan*: Ov.; adj. **Iūnōnālis** -e, *belonging to Juno*: tempus, *the month of June*, Ov.; **Iūnōnĭus** -a -um, *Junonian*: hospitia, Carthage, Verg.; ales, *the peacock*, Ov.; custos, *Argus*, Ov.; mensis, *June*, Ov.
Iuppĭter (and Diespiter), Iovis, m. (connected with dies and divus), *Jupiter, the supreme god among the Romans, brother and husband of Juno, corresponding to the Ζεύς of the Greeks*: Iovis satelles, Cic.; ales, *the eagle*, Ov.; Iuppiter Stygius, *Pluto*, Verg. TRANSF., (1) *the planet Jupiter*: Cic. (2) *air, sky, heavens*: sub Iove, *in the open air*, Hor., Ov.
Iūra -ae, m. *a mountain-chain along the north-west frontier of modern Switzerland*: Caes.
iūrātor -ōris, m. (iuro), *a sworn assessor*: Pl., Liv.
iūrātus -a -um, partic. from iuro; q.v.
iūrĕiūro -are (ius/iuro), *to swear by an oath*: Liv.
iūrĕpĕrītus=iurisperitus; q.v.
iurgĭum -i, n. (ius/ago), *altercation, quarrel, brawl*: iurgio saepe contendere cum aliquo, Cic.; Verg., Ov., Tac.
iurgo -are (ius/ago). Intransit., *to quarrel, contend in words, brawl*: Cic. Transit., *to scold*: Hor.
iūrīdĭcĭālis -e (ius/dico), *relating to right* or *justice*: constitutio, Cic.
iūrisconsultus -i, m. *one learned in the law, a lawyer*: Cic.
iūrisdictĭo -ōnis, f. *the administration of justice*: conficere, Cic. L. TRANSF., *judicial authority*: iurisdictio urbana et peregrina (of the praetor urbanus and peregrinus), Liv.; iurisdictio in libera civitate contra leges senatusque consulta, Cic.
iūrispĕrītus or **iūrĕpĕrītus** -i, m. adj. (with compar. and superl.), *skilled* or *experienced in the law*: Cic., Juv.

iūro -are (²ius), *to swear, take an oath.*
Lit., iuravi verissimum iusiurandum,
Cic.; falsum, Cic.; per deos, Sall.; per Iovem,
Cic.; with plain acc. of deity: Cic. L., Verg.,
Ov.; in verba alicuius, *to swear after a pre-
scribed formula,* Liv.; in certa verba, Cic.;
in legem, *to swear to,* Cic.; but: in me iurare,
to conspire against me, Ov.; with acc. and
infin.: Caes., Cic., Liv.
Transf., *to deny on oath*: calumniam in
aliquem, Liv.
¶ Hence perf. partic. in act. sense **iūrātus**
-a -um, *having sworn, under oath*: si diceret
iuratus, Cic.; iurati iudices, Cic.; Liv., Ov.
Sometimes in pass. sense, *having been sworn*:
Cic.

¹iūs iūris, n. *broth, soup*: Pl., Cic., Hor.
²iūs iūris, n. *right, law.*
Lit., divina ac humana iura, Cic.;
principia iuris, Cic.; ius ac fas omne delere,
Cic.; ius civile, *law binding Roman citizens,*
Cic.; ius gentium, *law binding the world at
large,* Cic.; summum ius, summa iniuria,
of the letter of the law, Cic.; ius dicere, *to
declare the law, to administer justice,* Cic.; so:
ius reddere, Liv.; dare iura, Verg.
Transf., (1) *a court of justice*: in ius vocare,
Cic.; in ius ambulare, Pl., Ter.; adire, Cic.;
rapi, Hor. (2) *jurisdiction*: homines recipere
in ius ditionemque, Liv.; sui iuris esse, *to
be independent,* Cic. (3) *right* as conferred
by law: uxores eodem iure sunt quo viri,
have the same rights as, Cic.; iure optimo,
by the best of rights, Cic.; so iure, alone,
rightly: Lucr., Cic.; ius civitatis, Cic.; ius
agendi cum plebe, Cic.

iusiūrandum iūrisiūrandi (or in two words),
n. *an oath*: accipere, *to take an oath,* Caes.;
conservare, violare, Cic.; fidem adstringere
iureiurando, Cic.; aliquem iureiurando
obstringere, with acc. and infin., Caes.;
populum iureiurando adigere, Liv.

iussum -i, n. subst. from iubeo; q.v.

iussū, abl. sing. as from iussus, m. (iubeo), *by
order, by command*: vestro, Cic.; populi, Liv.

iustĭficus -a -um (iustus/facio), *acting justly*:
Cat.

iustĭtĭa -ae, f. (iustus), *justice, fairness, equity*:
colere, Cic.; erga deos, Cic.; in hostem, Cic.;
Caes.

iustĭtĭum -i, n. (ius/sisto), *a suspension of
business in the courts of law*: edicere, *to
proclaim a suspension of legal business,* Cic.;
so: indicere, Liv.; sumere, Tac.; remittere,
to end such suspension. Transf., in gen.,
pause, cessation: omnium rerum, Liv.

iustus -a -um (ius), adj. (with compar. and
superl.). (1) *just, equitable, fair*; mainly of
persons: Cic., Verg. (2) *lawful, justified,
well-grounded, proper*: uxor, Cic., Liv.;
causa, Caes., Cic.; supplicia, Cic.; ira, Ov.
(3) *regular, perfect, complete, suitable*: bellum,
Cic., Liv.; proelium, Liv.; victoria, Cic. L.;
numerus, Liv.; altitudo, Caes.
¶ N. as subst. (1) sing. **iustum** -i, *justice,
what is right*: Cic.; plus iusto, *more than is
right,* Hor. (2) plur. **iusta** -orum: **a,** *what
is fitting, rights, due*: iusta praebere servis,
Cic.: **b,** *due forms and observances,* esp.
funeral rites: iusta facere alicui, Cic.
¶ Adv. (with compar. and superl.) **iustē**,
justly, rightly: imperare, Cic.; Ov.

Iūturna -ae, f. *a nymph, sister of Turnus, king
of the Rutuli.*

¹iŭvĕnālis -e (iuvenis), *youthful*: corpus, Verg.;
ludus, Liv.

²Iŭvĕnālis -is, m., D. Iunius, *a Roman writer
of satires, contemporary of Domitian and
Trajan.*

iŭvencus -a -um (iuvenis), *young*: equus,
Lucr. As subst., m. **iŭvencus** -i. (1) *a
young man*: Hor. (2) *a young bullock*: Verg.;
f. **iŭvenca** -ae. (1) *a young woman, a
maiden*: Ov. (2) *a young cow, heifer*: Verg.,
Hor., Juv.

iŭvĕnesco iŭvĕnescĕre iŭvĕnŭi (iuvenis). (1)
to grow up: vitulus, Hor. (2) *to become young
again*: iuvenescit homo, Ov.

iŭvĕnīlis -e (iuvenis), *youthful*: licentia, Cic.;
redundantia, Cic.; Verg., Ov.; compar.: Ov.
¶ Adv. **iŭvĕnīlĭtĕr**, *youthfully, like a
youth*: iuveniliter exsultans, Cic.; Ov.

iŭvĕnis -is, adj., *young, youthful*: maritus,
Tib.; anni, Ov.; compar.: iūnior, Cic., Hor.;
also iuvenior, Plin. L.
¶ As subst. **iŭvĕnis** -is, c. *a young man,
young woman, one in the prime of life* (between
the ages of 20 and 45): Cic., Verg., etc.

iŭvĕnor -ari, dep. (iuvenis), *to act like a youth,
act impetuously*: Hor.

iŭventa -ae, f. (iuvenis), *youth*: flos iuventae,
Liv.; iuventa imbellis, docilis, Hor.; Verg.
Personif.: Ov.

iŭventās -ātis, f. (iuvenis), *youth, the time of
youth*: Lucr., Verg., Hor. Personif.: Cic.,
Hor., Liv.

iŭventus -ūtis, f. (iuvenis), *youth, the prime of
life* (between the ages of 20 and 45). Lit.,
ea quae iuventute geruntur et viribus, Cic.
Transf., *young men*: iuventus Romana,
Liv.; legendus est hic orator iuventuti, Cic.;
Caes., Verg.; principes iuventutis, in
republican times, *the first among the knights,*
Cic.; under the empire, *imperial princes,* Tac.

iŭvo -are iūvi iūtum, fut. partic. iŭvātūrus:
Sall. (1) *to help, assist, aid*: aliquem in
aliqua re, Cic.; aliquem auxilio laboris, Cic.;
hostes frumento, Caes.; iuvante deo, diis
iuvantibus, *with God's help,* Cic.; Verg.,
Hor., Ov.; with infin. as subject: Verg., Ov.
(2) *to delight, please, gratify*: ut te iuvit
coena? Hor.; ita se dicent iuvari, Cic.; often
impers., with infin. or acc. and infin. as
subject, *it delights, it pleases*: iuvit me tibi
tuas litteras profuisse, Cic. L.; forsan et
haec olim meminisse iuvabit, Verg.

iuxtā (connected with iungo), adv. and prep.
(1) adv. Lit., of space, *close by, near*: legio
quae iuxta constiterat, Caes.; sellam iuxta
ponere, Sall.; forte fuit iuxta tumulus, Verg.;
Ov. Transf., *in like manner, equally*: vitam
mortemque iuxta aestimo, Sall.; aliaque
castella iuxta ignobilia, Liv.; iuxta ac si
hostes adessent, Liv.; iuxta quam, Liv.;
iuxta mecum omnes intellegitis, Sall.
(2) prep., with acc., *close to, near to, hard
by.* Lit., in space: iuxta murum castra
posuit, Caes.; Verg., Tac. Transf., **a,** in
time; *just before*: iuxta finem vitae, Tac.:
b, in other relations; *near to, just short of*:
Sall., Liv., Tac.

iuxtim, adv. (connected with iungo), *near,
close by*: Lucr., Suet. Transf., *equally*:
Lucr.

Ixion -ŏnis, m. ('Iξίων), *king of the Lapithae in Thessaly, father of Pirithous; for an insult to Juno he was hurled down to Tartarus, and bound to a perpetually revolving wheel.* ¶ Hence adj. **Ixĭŏnĭus** (-ĕus) -a -um, *of Ixion*; m. subst. **Ixĭŏnĭdēs** -ae, *a son of Ixion; Pirithous*: Ov.

J *see* I

The Latin **i**, when used as a consonant, was printed as **j** in earlier dictionaries and classical texts. This practice has become rare. As a consonant, **i** was probably pronounced as y- rather than as j-.

K

The letter **K, k**, corresponding to Greek kappa (*κ*), was a part of the Latin Alphabet, but in some words was eventually replaced by C.

Kălendae (Călendae) -ārum, f. (from calare, *to call*, the Kalends being the day on which the times of the Nones and the festivals were proclaimed).
LIT., *the first day of the Roman month*: Kal. (Cal.) Februariae, *the first of February*; femineae Kalendae, *the first of March, the day of the Matronalia, when Roman matrons sacrificed to Juno Lucina.* On the Kalends, interest was paid; hence: tristes Kalendae— i.e. for debtors—Hor. Prov., as there were no Kalends in the Greek year, ad Graecas Kalendas solvere=*never to pay*, Suet.
TRANSF., *a month*: Ov.
Karthago=Carthago; q.v.

L

L, l, corresponds to the Greek lambda (*Λ, λ*). For its use as an abbreviation, see Table of Abbreviations.

lăbasco -ĕre (labo), *to totter, threaten to fall*: Lucr. TRANSF., *to give way*: Pl., Ter.

lăbēcŭla -ae, f. (dim. of labes), *a little stain, a slight disgrace*: Cic.

lăbĕfăcĭo -făcĕre -fēci -factum, pass. lăbĕfīo -fĭĕri -factus sum (labor), *to cause to totter, shake, loosen.*
LIT., partem muri, Caes.; charta sit a vinclis non labefacta suis, *not opened*, Ov.; Lucr., Verg., Tac.
TRANSF., (1) politically, *to shake, impair*: iura plebis, Liv. (2) mentally, *to cause to shake* or *waver*: quem nulla unquam vis, nullae minae, nulla invidia labefecit, Cic.; Verg., Tac.

lăbĕfacto -are (freq. of labefacio), *to cause to totter, shake violently.* LIT., signum vectibus, Cic. TRANSF., (1) politically: rempublicam, Cic. (2) mentally: animam, Lucr.; alicuius fidem pretio, *to corrupt*, Cic. (3) in gen., *to weaken*: amicitiam aut iustitiam, Cic.; vitas hominum, *to disturb, disquiet*, Cic.

¹lăbellum -i, n. (dim. of ¹labrum), *a little lip*: Pl., Cic., Verg.

²lăbellum -i, n. (dim. of ²labrum), *a small washing-vessel*: Cic.

Lăbĕrĭus -a -um, *name of a Roman gens; its most famous member was D. Laberius, a writer of mimes, contemporary of Julius Caesar.*

¹lābēs -is, f. (¹labor), *a falling in, sinking in.* LIT., esp. of the earth: multis locis labe factae sint, Cic.; terrae, Liv. TRANSF., (1) *fall*: prima labes mali, Verg. (2) *cause of ruin*: innocentiae labes aut ruina, Cic.; applied to a person: labes atque pernicies provinciae Siciliae, Cic.

²lābēs -is, f. *a spot, stain, blemish.* LIT., physical: sine labe toga, Ov.; victima labe carens, Ov. TRANSF., moral, *stain of infamy, disgrace*: alicui labem inferre, Cic.; Verg., Ov., Tac.

lăbia -ae, f., Pl., Ter., and **lăbĭum** -i, n. Quint. (lambo), *a lip.*

Lăbīci (Lăvīci) -ōrum, m. *an old Latin town.* ¶ Hence adj. **Lăbīcānus** -a -um, *of Labici*; as subst. (1) n. sing. **Lăbīcānum** -, *the territory of Labici.* (2) m. pl. **Lăbīcāni** -ōrum, *the inhabitants of Labici.*

Lăbĭēnus -i, m., T. *a legate of Julius Caesar who went over to Pompey at the beginning of the civil war.*

lăbĭōsus -a -um (labium), *with large lips*: Lucr.

lăbĭum -i, n.=labia; q.v.

lăbo -are (connected with lābor), *to totter, waver, be about to fall, begin to sink.* LIT., signum labat, Cic.; labat ariete crebro ianua, Verg.; labantem unā parte aciem, *wavering*, Liv. TRANSF., (1) politically, *to waver, totter*: omnes reipublicae partes aegras et labantes sanare et confirmare, Cic.; fide sociorum labare coepit, Liv.; Ov., Tac. (2) mentally: animus, corda, Verg.; Cic., Liv. (3) in gen.: res, Pl.; omnia, Cic.

¹lābor lābi lapsus sum, dep. *to glide, slide, fall down, slip.*
LIT., of physical movement, esp. downwards: sidera, Cic.; per gradus, Liv.; equo, Liv.; equo, Hor.; umor in gena furtim labitur, Hor.; stellas praecipites cael labi, Verg.; lapsi de fontibus amnes, Ov.; quia continenter laberentur et fluerent omnia, Cic.; labentes aedes deorum, *collapsing*, Hor.; custodiā labi, *to slip away from* Tac.
TRANSF., (1) fig., *to glide, pass, flow*: frigus per artūs, Verg.; of time, *to glide by*: fugace labuntur anni, Hor.; of speech: orati sedate placideque labitur, Cic. (2) *to fall away, decline*: labor eo ut adsentiar Epicuro, *I feel myself drawn to*, Cic.; civitatum mores lapsi ad mollitiem, Cic.; labentem et prop cadentem rempublicam, Cic.; lapsum genus Verg.; spe lapsi, Caes.; Liv. (3) *to be deceived to make a mistake*: erravit, lapsus est, non putavit, Cic.; in aliqua re, Cic.; per errorem Cic.; propter imprudentiam, Cic.; in officio, Cic.; in vitium, Hor.; in errorem Liv.

²lăbor (labos: Pl., Ter.) -ōris, m.
(1) *work, labour, toil, effort.* LIT., quant labore partum, Ter.; res est magni laboris, *difficult*, Cic.; capere tantum laborem, Cic. impenditur labor ad incertum casum, Cic. laborem hominum periculis sublevandis im pertire, Cic.; laborem interponere pro aliquo

[332]

Cic.; labor est, with infin., Liv. TRANSF., a, *industry, capacity for work*: homo magni laboris, Cic.: **b**, *feat, work, result of labour*: multorum mensium labor interiit, Caes.; Herculeus, Hor.; hominum boumque, Verg.

(2) *hardship, fatigue, distress*: cuius erga me benevolentiam vel in labore meo vel in honore perspexi, Cic.; poet.: labores solis, *eclipse of the sun*, Verg.; Lucinae, *pains of labour*, Verg.

lăbōrĭfer -fĕra -fĕrum (labor/fero), *bearing toil*: Hercules, Ov.

lăbōrĭōsus -a -um (²labor), adj. (with compar. and superl.). (1) of things, *toilsome, laborious*: vitae genus laboriosum sequi, Cic.; Liv. (2) of persons, *industrious, undergoing trouble and hardship*: laboriosa cohors Ulixei, Hor.; quid nobis duobus laboriosius? Cic.

¶ Hence adv. (with compar. and superl.) **lăbōrĭōsē**, *laboriously, with toil*: diligentissime laboriosissimeque accusare, Cic.; Pl., Cat.

lăbōro -are (¹labor).

(1) intransit.: **a**, *to work, toil, labour, strive*: sibi et populo Romano, non Verri laborare, Cic.; in aliquid, Liv.; with ut *or* ne and the subj.: Cic.; with infin.: brevis esse laboro, Hor.: **b**, *to be troubled* or *anxious, to care*: quorsum recidat responsum tuum, non magno opere laboro, Cic.; tuā causā, Cic. L.; de aliqua re, Cic.: **c**, *to suffer, labour under anything, be oppressed with, afflicted with*: telis ictuque, Lucr.; morbo, *to be ill*, Cic.; ex intestinis, pedibus, renibus, Cic.; ex invidia, Cic.; ex aere alieno, Caes.; a re frumentaria, Caes.; with plain abl.: domesticā crudelitate, Cic.; Hor., Liv.; absol.: laboranti subvenire, Caes.; fig., of things: quod vehementer eius artus laborarent, Cic.; digitorum contractio nullo in motu laborat, *finds no difficulty*, Cic.; cum luna laboret, *is eclipsed*, Cic.

(2) transit., *to work out, to elaborate, prepare, form*: arte laboratae vestes, Verg.; dona laboratae Cereris, *corn made into bread*, Verg.; Hor., Tac.

labos -ōris, m.=¹labor; q.v.

Lăbrōs -i, m. (Λάβρος), *name of a dog*: Ov.

labrum -i, n. (lambo), *a lip*: superius, *the upper lip*, Caes.; prov.: primus labris gustasse, *to have only a superficial knowledge of*, Cic. TRANSF., in gen., *edge, rim, lip*: fossae, Caes.; Liv.

labrum -i, n. (lavo), *a basin, tub*: Cic. L., Verg., Liv. TRANSF., *a bathing-place*: labra Dianae, Ov.

lăbrusca -ae, f. *the wild vine*: Verg.

lăbruscum -i, n. *the fruit of the wild vine, wild grape*: Verg.

lăbўrinthēus -a -um (labyrinthus), *labyrinthine*: Cat.

lăbўrinthus -i, m. (λαβύρινθος), *a labyrinth*, esp. *the labyrinth in Crete constructed by Daedalus*: Verg., Ov.

lac, lactis, n. (akin to γάλα, γάλακτος), *milk*. LIT., Pl., Cic., Verg. TRANSF., *the milky sap of plants*: Ov.; *milk-white colour*: Ov.

lăcaena -ae, f. adj. (Λάκαινα), *Spartan, Lacedaemonian*: virgo, Verg.; as subst., *a Spartan woman*; esp. *Helen*: Verg.; *Leda*: Mart.

lăcĕdaemon -ŏnis, f. (Λακεδαίμων), *the city Lacedaemon* or *Sparta*.

¶ Hence adj. **Lăcĕdaemŏnĭus** -a -um, *Lacedaemonian*: Tarentum, *built by a colony from Sparta*, Hor.; m. pl. as subst., *the Spartans*.

lăcer -cĕra -cĕrum. Pass., *torn, mangled*: corpus, Sall.; vestis, Tac.; Lucr., Verg., Liv. Act., *tearing to pieces*: morsus, Ov.

lăcĕrātĭo -ōnis, f. (lacero), *a tearing to pieces, mangling*: corporis, Cic.; Liv.

lăcerna -ae, f. *a mantle worn over the toga on a journey* or *in bad weather*: Cic., Ov.

lăcernātus -a -um (lacerna), *clad in the lacerna*: Juv.

lăcĕro -are (lacer), *to tear to pieces, maim, mangle, lacerate*.

LIT., alicuius corpus lacerare atque vexare, Cic.; lacerare aliquem omni cruciatu, Cic.; pontem, Liv.; loricam, Verg.

TRANSF., (1) *to wound deeply, cut up, torture*: lacerare rempublicam, Cic.; patriam scelere, Cic.; meus me maeror lacerat, Cic. L. (2) *to squander*: pecuniam, Cic.; Pl., Sall. (3) *to slander, pull to pieces*: aliquem contumeliis, Cic.; aliquem probris, Liv.

lăcerta -ae, f. (1) *a lizard*: Hor., Ov., Juv. (2) *a sea-fish*: Cic. L.

lăcertōsus -a -um (lacertus), *muscular, powerful*: centuriones, Cic.; Ov.

¹lăcertus -i, m. LIT., *the upper arm* (from the shoulder to the elbow), esp. in respect of its muscles: Milo Crotoniates nobilitatus ex lateribus et lacertis suis, Cic.; Lucr., Verg., Ov. TRANSF., fig. of vigour, in gen.: a quo cum amentatas hastas acceperit, ipse eas oratoris lacertis viribusque torquebit, Cic.; Hor.

²lăcertus -i, m.=lacerta; q.v.

lăcesso -ĕre -īvi and -ii -itum (*lacio), *to provoke, stimulate, excite, exasperate, irritate*. (1) with acc. of the one provoked: virum ferro, Cic.; aliquem proelio, Caes.; bello, Cic., Liv.; aliquem ad pugnam, Liv.; te ad scribendum, Cic. L.; aliquem iniuriā, Cic.; deos precibus, Hor.; pelagus carinā, Hor. (2) with acc. of the response produced, *to bring on*: pugnam, Verg., Liv.; sermones, Cic. L.

Lacĕtāni -ōrum, m. *a people in Hispania Tarraconensis*.

¶ Hence **Lacĕtānĭa** -ae, f. *the country of the Lacetani*.

lăchănisso or **-nizo** -are (λαχανίζω), *to be feeble*: Suet.

Lăchĕsis -is, f. (Λάχεσις), *one of the three Parcae* or *Fates*.

lăcĭnĭa -ae, f. (connected with lacer), *a lappet* or *flap of a garment*: Pl., Suet.; prov.: aliquid obtinere laciniā, *to hold by the extreme end, to have an insecure hold on*, Cic.

Lăcĭnĭum -i, n. (Λακίνιον), *a promontory in Bruttium, near Crotona*, where Juno had a temple.

¶ Hence adj. **Lăcĭnĭus** -a -um, *Lacinian*: diva Lacinia, *the Lacinian goddess (Juno)*, Verg.

Lăcō (**Lăcōn**) -ōnis, m. (Λάκων), *a Spartan, Lacedaemonian*: fulvus Laco, *a Spartan hound*, Hor.

¶ Hence adj. **Lăcōnĭcus** -a -um, *Laconian*; as subst., f. **Lăcōnĭca** -ae or **Lăcōnĭcē** -es (Λακωνική), *the country of Laconia*: Plin., Nep.; n. **Lăcōnĭcum** -i, *a sweating-room* *at baths*: Cic.; f. adj. **Lăcōnĭs** -ĭdis, *Spartan*: mater, Ov.

lacrĭma (lacrŭma) -ae, f. (δάϰϱυ), *a tear*. Lit., multis cum lacrimis, *with a flood of tears*, Cic.; lacrimas profundere, *to shed tears*, Cic.; effundere, Lucr.; fundere, Verg.; lacrimis (*for tears*) loqui non possum, Cic.; lacrimis gaudio effusis, Liv. Transf., *the exudation from certain plants*: turis, Ov.; Heliadum, *amber*, Ov.; Verg.

lacrĭmābilis -e (lacrimo), *deplorable, woeful*: tempus, Ov.; bellum, Verg.

lacrĭmābundus -a -um (lacrimo), *breaking into tears, weeping*: Liv.

lacrĭmo (lacrŭmo) -are, *to weep, shed tears*. Lit., ecquis fuit quin lacrimaret? Cic.; Ter.; Verg. Transf., *to exude, to drip*: lacrimavit ebur, Ov.; perf. partic. pass.: lacrimatas cortice myrrhas, *dripping from*, Ov.

lacrĭmōsus -a -um (lacrima). (1) *tearful, shedding tears*: lumina vino lacrimosa, Ov.; voces, Verg. (2) *causing tears*: fumus, Hor.; hence *mournful, piteous*: bellum, Hor.

lacrĭmŭla -ae, f. (dim. of lacrima), *a little tear*: Ter., Cic., Cat.

lacrŭma, etc., *see* lacrima, etc.

lactans -antis (lac), *giving milk*: ubera, Ov.

lactātĭo -onis, f. (lacto), *enticement*: Cic.

lactens -entis (lac). (1) *sucking milk*: lactens Romulus, Cic.; lactens hostia, Cic.; Ov.; plur. as subst., *sucklings, unweaned animals*, as victims for sacrifice: lactentibus rem divinam facere, Liv. (2) *milky, juicy, full of sap*: frumenta, Verg.; sata, Ov.

lactěŏlus -a -um, adj. (dim. of lacteus), *milk-white*: Cat.

lactēs -ĭum, f. (lac), *the small intestines, guts*: Pl.

lactesco -ěre (lacteo), *to become milk, be changed into milk*: omnis fere cibus matrum lactescere incipit, Cic.

lactěus -a -um (lac), *milky, of milk*. Lit., umor, Lucr., Ov.; ubera, Verg. Transf., (1) *milk-white*: cervix, Verg.; via lactea, Ov.; orbis lacteus, *the Milky Way*, Cic.. (2) of style: Quint.

lacto -are (freq. of *lacio), *to allure, wheedle, dupe, cajole*: Pl., Ter.

lactūca -ae, f. (lac), *a lettuce*: Verg., Hor.

lăcūna -ae, f. (lacus), *a cavity, hollow, dip*; esp. *a pool, pond*. Lit., lacunae salsae, *the salt depths of the sea*, Lucr.; vastae lacunae Orci, Lucr.; cavae lacunae, Verg. Transf., *a gap, deficiency, loss*: ut illam lacunam rei familiaris expleant, Cic.

lăcūnar -āris, n. (lacuna), *a panelled ceiling*: Cic., Hor., Juv.

lăcūno -are (lacuna), *to work in panels, to panel*: Ov.

lăcūnōsus -a -um (lacuna), *full of hollows or gaps*: nihil lacunosum, *defective*, Cic.

lăcus -ūs, m. *a hollow*; hence (1) *a lake*: Lucr., Caes., Cic.; used poet. for *any large body of water*: Verg., Ov. (2) *a trough, basin, tank, vat, tub*: Hor., Ov., Liv.; esp. *a wine-vat*: Verg.; fig.: nova ista quasi de musto ac lacu fervida oratio, Cic.; also *a blacksmith's tank*: Verg., Ov.

Lădās -ae, m. (Λάδας), *a Greek runner in the time of Alexander the Great, whose speed was proverbial*: Mart., Juv.

laedo laedĕre laesi laesum, *to strike, knock*; hence *to hurt, injure, damage*. Lit., physically: cursu aristas, Verg.; frondes laedit hiems, Ov.; zonā laedere collum, *to strangle*, Hor. Transf., (1) *to hurt the feelings of, offend, annoy*: aliquem periurio suo, Cic.; dicto, Pl.; iniuste neminem, Cic.; Hor. (2) *to violate or outrage* an abstr. thing: fidem, Caes., Cic., Hor.; numen, Verg., Hor.

Laelĭus -a -um, *name of a Roman gens*; esp. of C. Laelius, *the friend of Scipio Africanus*.
¶ Hence adj. **Laeliānus** -a -um, *Laelian*.

laena -ae, f. (χλαῖνα), *an upper garment, cloak*: Cic., Verg.

Lāërtēs -ae, m. (Λαέϱτης), *the father of Ulysses*.
¶ Hence adj. **Lāërtĭus** -a -um, *Laertian*: regna, *Ithaca*, Verg.; heros, *Ulysses*, Ov.; subst. **Lāërtĭădēs** -ae, m. *son of Laertes*, i.e. *Ulysses*: Hor.

laesĭo -ōnis, f. (laedo), rhet. t. t., *an oratorical attack*: Cic.

Laestrȳgōn -ŏnis, and plur. **Laestrȳgŏnes** -um, m. (Λαιστϱύγονες), myth., *a race of giants and cannibals in Sicily*: urbs Lami Laestrygonis, i.e. *Formiae*, Ov.
¶ Hence adj. **Laestrȳgŏnĭus** -a -um, *Laestrygonian*: domus, *Formiae*, Ov.

laetābĭlis -e (laetor), *joyful, glad*: Cic., Ov.

laetātĭo -ōnis, f. (laetor), *a rejoicing, joy*: Caes.

laetē, adv. from laetus; q.v.

laetĭfĭco -are (laetificus). (1) *to fertilize*: agros aquā, Cic. (2) *to cheer, gladden, delight*: sol terram laetificat, Cic.; pass. as middle, *to rejoice*: Pl.
¶ Hence partic. **laetĭfĭcans** -antis, *rejoicing*: Pl.

laetĭfĭcus -a -um (laetus/facio), *gladdening, cheering, joyous*: Lucr.

laetĭtĭa -ae, f. (laetus). (1) *fertility*. Transf., *richness, beauty, grace*: orationis, Tac. (2) *joy, unrestrained gladness, delight*: laetitiam capere, percipere ex aliqua re, Cic.; dare alicui laetitiam, Cic.; laetitiā frui, Cic.; Pl., Ter., Caes., Verg.

laetor -ari, dep. (laetus), *to rejoice, be joyful, take delight, be glad*; with abl.: bonis rebus, Cic.; Ter., Juv.; with de: de communi salute, Cic.; with in: Cic.; with acc. of the n. pron.: utrumque laetor, Cic.; Liv.; with acc.: Sall., Verg.; with acc. and infin.: filiolā tuā te delectari laetor, Cic.; Ter., Verg.; with quod clause: Hor.

laetus -a -um, adj. (with compar. and superl.). Lit., *fat, rich*; of animals: boum armenta, Verg.; of plants and land, *fertile*: flores, Cic.; segetes, Verg. Transf., (1) of style, *rich, copious, fluent*: nitidum quoddam genus est verborum et laetum, Cic. (2) of things, *bright, pleasant, fortunate, propitious*: augurium, Tac.; saecula, Verg.; Cic. (3) of persons, *glad, joyful*: hi vagantur laeti atque erecti passim toto foro, Cic.; with abl.: minime laetus origine novae urbis, Liv., Verg.; with genit.: laeta laborum, Verg.
¶ Adv. (with compar.) **laetē**, *gladly, joyfully*: Cic., Liv., Tac.

laevus -a -um (λαιός), *left*. Lit., manus, acc.; amnis, Tac., Verg. Ov. As subst. (1) f. **laeva** -ae (sc. manus or pars), *the left hand, the left*: Pl., Cic., Verg. ad laevam, *to the left*, Cic., Liv. (2) n

laevum -i, *the left side*: in laevum flectere cursus, Ov.; plur. **laeva** -ōrum, *places lying to the left*: Verg., Ov.
    TRANSF., (1) *left-handed, foolish, silly*: mens, Verg.; ego laevus! Hor. (2) *unlucky, unpropitious*: tempus picus, Hor.; Verg. (3) in augury, *favourable*, as the Roman augurs, looking south, had the east, or lucky, side on their left hand: laevum intonuit, *favourably*, Verg.; Ov.
    ¶ Adv. **laevē**, *on the left hand*, hence *awkwardly*: Hor.
lăgānum -i, n. (λάγανον), *a cake made of flour and oil*: Hor.
lăgēos -ēi, f. (λάγειος), *a Greek kind of vine*: Verg.
lăgoena (lăgōna) -ae, f. (λάγηνος), *a large earthen jar with handles and a narrow neck*: Pl., Cic. L., Hor.
lăgōis -idis, f. (λαγωΐς), *a bird*, perhaps *a heathcock* or *grouse*: Hor.
lăguncŭla -ae, f. (dim. of lagoena), *a little bottle* or *flask*: Plin. L.
Lăgus -i, m. *the father of Ptolemy I, king of Egypt.*
    ¶ Hence adj. **Lăgēus** -a -um, poet. = *Egyptian*: Mart.
Lăis -idis and -idos f. (Λαΐς), *the name of two famous Corinthian beauties.*
Lăius -i, m. (Λάϊος), *son of Labdacus, father of Oedipus.*
    ¶ Hence **Lăiădēs** -ae, m. *son of Laius*, i.e. *Oedipus*: Ov.
lāma -ae, f. *a bog, slough*: Hor.
lambo lambĕre lambi, *to lick.* LIT., of animals: tribunal meum, Cic.; Verg., Liv. TRANSF., of rivers, *to wash*: quae loca fabulosus lambit Hydaspes, Hor.; of fire: flamma summum properabat lambere tectum, Hor.
lāmenta -orum, n. pl. *wailing, weeping, lamentation*: se lamentis lacrimisque dedere, Cic.; Lucr., Verg.
lāmentābilis -e (lamentor). (1) *lamentable, deplorable*: regnum, Verg. (2) *expressing sorrow, mournful*: vox, Cic.; mulierum comploratio, Liv.
lāmentārius -a -um (lamenta), *mournful*: Pl.
lāmentātio -ōnis, f. (lamentor), *a lamenting, weeping, wailing*: plangore et lamentatione complere forum, Cic.; Pl.
lāmentor -ari, dep. (lamenta), *to weep, wail, lament*: flebiliter in vulnere, Cic.; Pl. Transit., *to bewail, weep over, lament*: caecitatem, Cic.; Pl., Ter.; with acc. and infin.: Pl., Hor.
lămia -ae, f. (λαμία), *a witch, vampire*: Hor.
Lămia -ae, m. *a cognomen of the Aelian gens.*
Lămia -ae, f. (Λαμία), *a town in Thessaly.*
lāmina, lammina, and **lamna** -ae, f. *a plate* or *thin piece of metal* or *marble*, etc. LIT., aenea, Liv.; laminae ardentes, *iron plates*, *heated and used for torture*, Cic.; *the blade of a sword*: Ov.; *the blade of a saw*: Verg. TRANSF., (1) *coin*: Hor., Ov. (2) *a nutshell*: Ov.
lampas -pădis, acc. sing. -păda, f. (λαμπάς), *a torch.* LIT., Pl., Lucr., Verg.; *a wedding-torch*: Ter., Cic.; also used at the torch-race, when one runner delivered his torch to another; hence: quasi cursores vitai lampada tradunt, Lucr. TRANSF., *brightness*, esp. of the sun: solis, Lucr.; Phoebea, Verg.; also *a meteor*: Luc.

Lampsăcum -i, n. and **Lampsăcus (-os)** -i, f. (Λάμψακος), *a town of Mysia on the Hellespont.*
    ¶ Hence adj. **Lampsăcēnus** -a -um, *of Lampsacus*; m. pl. as subst., *Lampsacenes.*
Lămus -i, m. (Λάμος). (1) *a king of the Laestrygones, founder of the town of Formiae*: urbs Lami, *Formiae*, Ov. (2) *son of Hercules and Omphale.*
lămyrus -i, m. (λάμυρος), *a sea-fish*: Ov.
lāna -ae, f., *wool.*
    LIT., lanam ducere, Ov.; trahere, *to spin*, Juv.; lanam sufficere medicamentis quibusdam, Cic.; Verg.
    TRANSF., (1) *wool-spinning*: lanae dedita, Liv. (2) of things like wool; prov.: rixari de lana caprina, *to quarrel about nothing*, Hor.; *the down on leaves, fruit*, etc.: Verg.; *clouds*: Verg.
lānārius -i, m. *a worker in wool*: Pl.
lānātus -a -um (lana), *wool-bearing, woolly*: capras lanatas, Liv.; f. pl. as subst. **lānātae** -ārum, *sheep*: Juv.
lancĕa -ae, f. *a light spear* or *lance, with a leather thong attached to it*: Verg., Tac.
lancĭno -are (lacer), *to tear to pieces.* LIT., Plin. TRANSF., paterna bona, *to squander*, Cat.
lānĕus -a -um (lana), *made of wool, woollen.* LIT., pallium, Cic.; Pl., Verg. TRANSF., *soft as wool*: Cat., Mart.
Langŏbardi -ōrum, m. *a Germanic people.*
languĕfăcio -făcĕre (langueo/facio), *to make weak* or *faint*: Cic.
languĕo -ēre, *to be faint, weak, languid.* LIT., physically: cum de via languerem, *weary with the journey*, Cic.; corpora, Verg.; of things, *to droop, fall back*: Verg. TRANSF., *to be languid, inert, inactive*: otio, Cic.; languent vires, Cic.; Ov.
    ¶ Hence partic. **languens** -entis, *faint, languid*: vox, Cic.; Caes., Verg.
languesco languescĕre langŭi (langueo), *to become faint, weak, languid.* LIT., physically: corpore, Cic.; senectute, Cic.; nec mea consueto languescent corpora lecto, Ov.; Bacchus languescit in amphora, *becomes milder*, Hor. TRANSF., *to grow inactive, listless*: Cic.
languĭdŭlus -a -um (dim. of languidus), *somewhat faint, languid, limp*: Cic., Cat.
languĭdus -a -um (langueo), adj. (with compar.), *faint, weak, languid, limp.*
    LIT., physically; of persons: vino vigiliisque languidus, Cic.; of animals: Cic.; of other things: ventus, *gentle*, Ov.; aqua, *with gentle current*, Liv.; of wine stored up, *mild, mellow*: Hor.
    TRANSF., (1) *sluggish, inactive, feeble*: animus, Caes.; studium, Cic. (2) act.: languidae voluptates, *enervating*, Cic.
    ¶ Adv. (with compar.), *faintly, feebly*: Caes., Cic.
languor -ōris, m. (langueo), *faintness, languor, weariness, feebleness.* LIT., physical: corporis, Cic.; Pl., Caes.; esp. from disease: aquosus, *dropsy*, Hor. TRANSF., *listlessness, inactivity, idleness, sluggishness*: se languori dedere, Cic.; languorem alicui adferre, Cic.; Hor., Tac.
lănĭātus -ūs, m. (lanio), *a mangling, tearing in pieces*; with subjective genit.: ferarum,

Cic. TRANSF., si recludantur tyrannorum mentes posse adspici laniatus et ictus, Tac.

lănĭēna -ae, f. (lanius), *a butcher's shop*: Liv.

lānĭfĭcus -a -um (lana/facio), *working in wool, spinning* or *weaving wool*: ars, Ov.; sorores, *the Parcae*, Mart.

lānĭger -gĕra -gĕrum (lana/gero), *wool-bearing*: bidens, Verg.; apices, *woollen*, Verg. As subst. **lānĭger** -gĕri, m. *a ram*: Ov.; **lānĭgĕra** -ae, f. *a sheep*: Lucr.

lănĭo -are, *to tear to pieces, mangle, lacerate.* LIT., physically: hominem, Cic.; aliquem bestiis, Liv.; crinem manibus, Ov.; Verg. TRANSF., et tua sacrilegae laniarunt carmina linguae, Ov.

lănista -ae, m. *a trainer of gladiators.* LIT., Cic., Juv., Suet. TRANSF., *an instigator to violence, inciter*: Cic., Liv.

lānĭtĭum -i, n. (lana), *wool*: Verg.

lănĭus -i, m. (lanio), *a butcher*: Pl., Cic., Liv. TRANSF., *an executioner*: Pl.

lanterna -ae, f. (λαμπτήρ), *a lantern, lamp*: Pl., Cic. L., Juv.

lanternārĭus -i, m. (lanterna), *a lantern-bearer*: Catilinae, Cic.

lānūgo -ĭnis, f. (lana), *the down of plants*: Lucr., Verg.; *on the cheeks*: flaventem primā lanugine malas, Verg.; Ov.

Lānŭvĭum -i, n. *a town in Latium on the Via Appia, south-east of Rome.*
¶ Hence adj. **Lānŭvīnus** -a -um, *belonging to Lanuvium*; n. as subst. **Lānŭvīnum** -i, *an estate near Lanuvium*: Cic.

lanx lancis, f. (connected with λεκάνη). (1) *a plate, platter, a large flat dish*: Pl., Cic. L., Hor., Ov. (2) *the scale of a balance*: Cic., Verg.

Lāŏcŏōn -ontis, m. (Λαοκόων), *a Trojan priest, who with his two sons was killed by serpents from the sea.*

Lāŏmĕdōn -ontis, m. (Λαομέδων), *a king of Troy, father of Priam.*
¶ Hence adj. **Lāŏmĕdontēus (-ius)** -a -um, *Laomedontean*, poet. = *Trojan*: Verg.; m. subst. **Lāŏmĕdontĭădēs** -ae, *a male descendant of Laomedon*; *Priam*: Verg.; plur.: Laomedontiadae, *the Trojans*, Verg.

lăpăthum -i, n. and **lăpăthus** -i, f. (λάπαθον, λάπαθος), *sorrel*: Hor.

lăpĭcīdīnae -ārum, f. (lapis/caedo), *stone quarries*: Cic.

lăpĭdārĭus -a -um (lapis), *of* or *relating to stone*: Pl.

lăpĭdātĭo -onis, f. (lapis), *a throwing of stones*: facta est lapidatio, Cic.

lăpĭdātor -ōris, m. (lapido), *a thrower of stones*: Cic.

lăpĭdĕus -a -um (lapis), *made of stone*: murus, Liv.; imber, *a shower of stones*, Cic., Liv. TRANSF., *petrified*: Pl.

lăpĭdo -are (lapis), *to throw stones at*: Suet.; impers. lapidat, *it rains stones*: Veiis de caelo lapidaverat, Liv.; also impers. pass.: Liv.

lăpĭdōsus -a -um (lapis). (1) *full of stones, stony*: montes, Ov. (2) *as hard as stone*: panis, Hor.; Verg.

lăpillus -i, m. (dim. of lapis), *a little stone, pebble.* In gen.: lapilli crepitantes, Ov.; white stones were used to mark lucky, and black stones unlucky days, hence: dies

signanda melioribus lapillis, Mart.; similarly for voting at trials, hence: lapilli nivei atrique, Ov. Esp. *a precious stone, gem*: nivei viridesque lapilli, *pearls and emeralds*, Hor.; Ov.

lăpis -ĭdis, m. *a stone.*
LIT., in gen.: lapidibus aliquem cooperire, obruere, Cic.; lapidibus pluit, *it rains stones from the sky*, Liv.; lapide candidiore diem notare, *to mark a day as lucky* (cf. lapillus), Cat. Esp. (1) *a boundary-stone*: Tib., Liv. (2) *a grave-stone*: Prop. (3) *a precious stone, jewel*: Hor. (4) *marble*: Parius, Verg.; albus, *a table of white marble*, Hor. (5) *a piece of mosaic*: Hor. (6) *a mile-stone*: intra vicesimum lapidem, Liv.; Ov., Tac. (7) *the platform of stone on which the* praeco *stood at slave-auctions*: duos de lapide emptos tribunos, Cic. (8) Iuppiter lapis, *a stone held in the hand as a symbol of Jupiter, and sworn by*: Iovem lapidem iurare, Cic.
TRANSF., *as a symbol of dullness, etc.*: Ter., Pl., Cic., Ov.

Lăpĭthae -arum, m. pl. (Λαπίθαι), *the Lapithae, myth., a savage mountain race in Thessaly, famous for their fight with the Centaurs at the wedding of Pirithöus.*
¶ Hence adj. **Lăpĭthaeus** -a -um and **Lăpĭthēius** -a -um, *of the Lapithae.*

lappa -ae, f. *a burr*: Verg., Ov.

lapsĭo -ōnis, f. (¹labor), *a gliding*; hence, *an inclination, tendency towards*: Cic.

lapso -are (freq. of ¹labor), *to slip, stumble*: Priamus lapsans, Verg.

lapsus -ūs, m. (¹labor), *a gradual movement, esp. downwards; a gliding, sliding, fall.* LIT., terrae, Liv.; si lacus emissus lapsu et cursu suo in mare profluxisset, Cic.; volucrum lapsus atque cantus, Cic.; equi, Verg. TRANSF., *a fault, error*: cum sint populares multi variique lapsus, Cic.; Pl.

lăquĕāre -is, n., esp. plur. **lăquĕārĭa** (connected with lacunar), *a panelled ceiling*: laquearia tecti, Verg.; Sen.

lăquĕātus -a -um (laqueare), *with a panelled ceiling*: laqueata tecta, Cic.; Hor., Liv.

lăquĕus -i, m. *a noose, halter, snare.* LIT. collum inserere in laqueum, Cic.; laqueo gulam frangere, Sall.; premere, Hor.; Caes. Liv., Ov. TRANSF., *a trap*: alicui laqueo ponere, Ov.; laquei legum, interrogationum Cic.

Lar Lăris, m., usually plur. **Lăres** -um (Cic.) -ium (Liv.), *tutelary deities among the Romans*: Lares praestites, Ov.; Lares per marini, Liv.; agri custodes, Tib. Esp. *household deities*: domestici, familiares, privati patrii, Pl., Cic., Ov.; meton., *hearth, dwelling, home*: ad larem suum reverti *home*, Cic.; Hor., Liv., Ov.

Lăra and **Lărunda** -ae, f. *a nymph who had her tongue cut out by Jupiter because she talked too much.*

Larcĭus -a -um, *name of a Roman gens*; *its most famous member was the dictator, T. Larcius Flavus*: Cic., Liv.

lardum (lārĭdum: Pl.) -i, n. (connected with λαρινός), *the fat of bacon, lard*: Hor., Ov. Juv.

Lărentĭa -ae, f., or **Acca Lārentĭa**, *the wife of Faustulus, who brought up Romulus and Remus.*

❡ Hence **Larentālĭa** -ĭum, n. pl. *a feast in her honour on December 23.*

Lăres, *see* Lar.

largē, adv. from largus; q.v.

largĭfĭcus -a -um (largus/facio), *bountiful, liberal:* Lucr.

largĭflŭus -a -um (largus/fluo), *flowing freely:* fons, Lucr.

largĭlŏquus -a -um (largus/loquor), *talkative, loquacious:* Pl.

largĭor -iri, dep. (largus), *to give abundantly, bestow liberally, lavish.* Lit., qui eripiunt aliis quod aliis largiantur, Cic.; Pl., Caes., Tac.; of bribery: Sall., Liv., Quint. Transf., (**1**) in gen., *to give, bestow, grant:* populo libertatem, Cic.; alicui civitatem, Cic.; solamen, Verg. (**2**) *to condone:* Cic., Tac.

largĭtās -ātis, f. (largus), *liberality, bountifulness:* terra cum maxima largitate fruges fundit, Cic.; Ter.

largĭtĕr, adv. from largus; q.v.

largītĭo -ōnis, f. (largior), *a giving freely, spending freely, lavishing:* in cives, Cic.; largitione benevolentiam alicuius consectari, Cic.; prov.: largitio non habet fundum, *giving has no limits,* Cic.; Caes.; of bribery: largitionis suspicionem recipere, Cic. Transf., in gen., *granting, bestowing:* civitatis, Cic.; aequitatis, Cic.

largĭtor -ōris, m. (largior), *a liberal giver or spender:* praedae erat largitor, Liv.; Sall.; in a bad sense, *a briber:* Cic.; also *a waster:* Cic.

largus -a -um, adj. (with compar. and superl.). (**1**) of things, *abundant, plentiful, numerous, copious:* cum sol terras largā luce compleverit, Cic.; imbres, Lucr., Verg.; with genit., *rich in, abounding in:* opum, Verg. (**2**) of persons, *liberal, bountiful, profuse:* Pl., Cic., Tac.; with abl.: largus promissis, *liberal in promises,* Tac.; with infin.: spes donare novas, Hor.

❡ Adv. (**1**) (with compar. and superl.) **largē,** *plentifully, liberally:* dare, Cic.; large atque honorifice aliquid promittere, Cic.; senatus consultum large factum, *with sweeping provisions,* Tac.

❡ Adv. (**2**) **largĭtĕr,** *abundantly, much:* distare, Lucr.; posse, *to be very powerful,* Caes.; Hor.

ārĭdum -i, n.=lardum; q.v.

Lārīnum -i, n. *a town in Italy* (now *Larino*).

❡ Hence adj. **Lārīnās** -ātis, *of Larinum;* m. pl. as subst., *inhabitants of Larinum.*

Lārīsa (Lārīssa) -ae, f. (Λάρισα, Λάρισσα), *a town in Thessaly.*

❡ Hence adj. **Lārīsaeus (Lārīssaeus)** -a -um, *Larissean=Thessalian:* Cic., Verg.; subst. **Lārīsenses** -ĭum, m. pl. *the inhabitants of Larisa.*

Lārĭus -i, m. *name of a lake in north Italy* (now *Lago di Como*). Adj. **Lārĭus** -a -um, *of Lake Como:* Cat.

ārix -icis, f. (Λάριξ), *the larch:* Plin.

Lars Lartis, m. *an Etruscan title or praenomen.* *see* Lara.

Lārunda -ae, *see* Lara.

larva and **lārŭa** -ae, f. *a ghost, spectre:* Pl. Transf., *a mask:* Hor.

larvātus -a -um (larva), *bewitched:* Pl.

ăsănum -i, n. (λάσανον), *a night-commode:* Hor.

ăsarpīcĭfer -fĕra -fĕrum (lasarpicium= laserpicium/fero), *producing asafoetida:* Cat.

---

lascīvĭa -ae, f. (lascivus). (**1**) in a good sense, *playfulness, sportiveness, frolicsomeness:* hilaritas et lascivia, Cic.; Pl., Lucr., Liv. (**2**) in a bad sense, *wantonness, licentiousness, insolence:* quos soluto imperio licentia atque lascivia corruperat, Sall.; Tac., Quint.

lascīvībundus -a -um (lascivio), *wanton, sportive:* Pl.

lascīvĭo -ire (lascivus). (**1**) in a good sense, *to sport, play:* agnus lascivit fugā, Ov.; Cic. (**2**) in a bad sense, *to wanton, run riot:* plebs lascivit, Liv.; Tac.

lascīvus -a -um, adj. (with compar.). (**1**) in a good sense, *playful, sportive, frolicsome:* puella, Verg.; aetas, verba, Hor. (**2**) in a bad sense, *wanton, licentious, insolent:* puella, Ov.; oscula, Tac. Transf., hederae, *luxuriant,* Hor.

❡ Adv. **lascīvē,** *lasciviously, wantonly:* Mart.

lăserpīcĭum -i, n. *a plant, also called silphium, from which asafoetida* (laser) *was obtained:* Pl., Plin.

lassĭtūdo -ĭnis, f. (lassus), *weariness, exhaustion:* lassitudine exanimari, confici, Caes.; Cic., Liv.

lasso -are (lassus), *to make weary, tire, exhaust:* corpus, Ov.; Prop.

lassŭlus -a -um (dim. of lassus), *somewhat weary, rather tired:* Cat.

lassus -a -um, *weary, tired, exhausted;* of persons: itinere atque opere castrorum et proelio fessi lassique erant, Sall.; ab equo indomito, Hor.; with genit.: maris et viarum, Hor.; with infin.: Prop.; also of things: fructibus adsiduis lassa humus, Ov.; lasso papavera collo, *drooping,* Verg.

lātē, adv. from ²lātus; q.v.

lătebra -ae, f. (lateo), usually plur., *a hiding-place, lurking-place, retreat.* Lit., latebrae ferarum, Cic.; Verg.; lunae, *an eclipse of the moon,* Lucr. Transf., (**1**) fig.: cum illa coniuratio ex latebris erupisset, Cic.; Lucr. (**2**) sing., *a subterfuge, loophole:* latebra mendacii, Cic.; latebram dare vitiis, Ov.

lătebrĭcŏla -ae, c. (latebra/colo), *one that lives in hiding:* Pl.

lătebrōsus -a -um (latebra), *full of hiding-places, secret, retired:* via, Cic.; pumex, *porous,* Verg.

❡ Adv. **lătebrōsē,** *secretly, in a corner:* Pl.

lătĕo -ēre (connected with λανθάνω), *to lie hid, be concealed.*

Lit., in occulto, Cic.; abdite, Cic.; latet anguis in herba, Verg.; navis latet portu, Hor.; latet sub classibus aequor, *is concealed, covered,* Verg.; portus latet, *is screened from the winds,* Cic.; esp. *to keep out of sight,* in order not to appear in court: Cic.

Transf., (**1**) *to live in obscurity:* bene qui latuit, bene vixit, Ov. (**2**) *to be sheltered, safe from misfortune:* sub umbra amicitiae Romanae, Liv.; in tutela ac praesidio bellicae virtutis, Cic. (**3**) *to be unknown:* aliae (causae) sunt perspicuae, aliae latent, Cic.; scelus latere inter tot flagitia, Cic.; also with acc.: res latet aliquem, *is concealed from, unknown to,* Verg.; Ov.

❡ Hence partic. **lătens** -entis, *concealed, hidden:* res, Cic.; causa, Verg.; Ov.

❡ Adv. **lătentĕr,** *secretly:* Cic., Ov.

lăter -tĕris, m. *a brick, tile:* Cic., Caes.

lateramen

lătĕrāmen -ĭnis, n. (later), *pottery*: Lucr.

Lătĕrānus -a -um, *family name in the gentes* Claudia, Sextia, *and* Plautia.

lătercŭlus -i, m. (dim. of later), *a small brick, tile*: Caes. TRANSF., *a biscuit*: Pl.

lătĕrīcĭus -a -um (later), *brick, built of brick*: turris, Caes.; Suet.

lāterna, see lanterna.

lāternārĭus, see lanternarius.

lătesco -ĕre (lateo), *to hide oneself, be concealed*: Cic.

lătex -tĭcis, m. *a fluid, liquid*; esp. of water: occulti latices, Liv.; securi latices, Verg.; frugum laticumque cupido, *hunger and thirst*, Lucr.; also of wine: meri, Ov.; Lucr., Verg.; latex absinthi, *wormwood juice*, Lucr.

Lătĭālis -e, see Latium.

Lătĭāris -e, see Latium.

lătĭbŭlum -i, n. (lateo), *a hiding-place, a lurking-place.* LIT., of animals: cum etiam ferae latibulis se tegant, Cic.; of men: latibula locorum occultorum, Cic. TRANSF., latibulum aut perfugium doloris mei, Cic. L.

lătĭclāvĭus -a -um (latus/clavus), *having a broad purple stripe* (the distinguishing peculiarity of senators, equestrian military tribunes, and sons of noble families): tribunus, Suet.

lătĭfundĭum -i, n. (latus/fundus), *a large landed estate*: Plin.

Lătīnē, see Latium.

Lătīnĭtās -ātis, f. (Latinus). (1) *a pure Latin style, Latinity*: Cic. L. (2) *Latin rights (like* ius Lati): Cic. L., Suet.

¹Lătīnus -a -um, see Latium.

²Lătīnus -i, m. *a king of the Laurentians, who received Aeneas hospitably, and gave him his daughter Lavinia in marriage.*

lātĭo -ōnis, f. (fero), *a bringing*: auxili, *a rendering assistance*, Liv.; legis, *a proposing, bringing forward*, Cic.; suffragi, *voting*, Liv.

lătĭto -are (freq. of lateo), *to lie hid, be concealed*: latitandi copia tenvis, Lucr.; extrahitur domo latitans Oppianicus a Manlio, Cic.; invisae atque latitantes res, Caes.; esp. *to conceal oneself, so as not to appear in* court: Cic.

lătĭtūdo -ĭnis, f. (latus), *breadth*: fossae, Caes.; Cic. TRANSF., (1) *extent*: possessionum, Cic. (2) *broad pronunciation*: verborum, Cic.

Lătĭum -i, n. *a district of Italy, in which Rome was situated*; ius Lăti *or* Lătĭum, *Latin rights (like* Latinitas), *a political status, short of Roman citizenship, allowed by the Romans first to Latins, later to others.*

¶ Hence adj. **Lătĭus** -a -um, *belonging to Latium, Latin*; poet.=*Roman*: forum, Ov.; adj. **Lătīnus** -a -um, *Latin*: via, Cic., Liv.; lingua, Cic.; convertere in Latinum, *to translate into Latin*, Cic.; feriae Latinae, *or* simply Latinae, *the Latin games*, Liv.; m. pl. as subst. **Lătīni** -orum, *the Latins*; adv. **Lătīnē**, *in Latin*: Latine loqui, Cic., Liv.; adj. **Lătĭālis** -e *or* **Lătĭāris** -e, *Latin*; n. subst. **Lătĭar** -āris, *the festival of Jupiter Latiaris.*

Latmus -i, m. (Λάτμος), *a mountain in Caria, where Selene kissed the sleeping Endymion.*

¶ Hence adj. **Latmĭus** -a -um, *Latmian.*

Lātō -ūs, f. and **Lātōna** -ae, f. (Λητώ), *the mother of Apollo and Diana, whom she bore on the island of Delos.*

---

latus

¶ Hence adj. **Lātōnĭus** -a -um, *Latonian*: Latonia virgo, *or* simply Latonia, *Diana*, Verg.; subst. **Lātōnĭgĕna** -ae, c. (Latona/gigno), *offspring of Latona*, Ov.; adj. **Lātōĭus** and **Lētōĭus** -a -um, *Latonian*: proles, *Apollo and Diana*, Ov.; as subst., m. **Lātōĭus** -i, *Apollo*, and f. **Lātōĭa** -ae, *Diana*: Ov.; f. adj. **Lātōis** or **Lētōis** -ĭdis, *Latonian*: Calaurea, *sacred to Latona*, Ov.; as subst., *Diana*: Ov.; adj. **Lātōus** -a -um, *Latonian*; m. as subst. **Lātōus** -i, *Apollo*: Hor., Ov.

lātor -ōris, m. (fero), *a bearer*; hence *the proposer of a law*: legis Semproniae, Cic.; Liv.

lātrātor -ōris, m. (¹latro), *a barker*: Anubis, Verg., Ov.

lātrātus -ūs, m. (¹latro), *a barking*: Verg., Ov., Juv.

lātrīna -ae, f. (lavo), *a bath* or *lavatory*: Pl., Suet.

¹lātro -are, *to bark, bay.*
(1) intransit. LIT., quod si luce quoque canes latrent, Cic.; Lucr., Hor. TRANSF., of men, *to bark, rant*: latrare ad clepsydram, Cic.; Hor.; of inanimate objects, *to rumble, roar*: undae, Verg.; stomachus, Hor.
(2) transit.: **a**, *to bark at*: senem, Hor.; **b**, *to bark for*: Lucr., Hor.

²lătro -ōnis, m. (λάτρις). LIT., *a hired servant* or *a mercenary soldier*: Pl. TRANSF., (1) *robber, freebooter, bandit, brigand*: insidiosus et plenus latronum locus, Cic.; Caes., Liv., Juv. (2) *a hunter*: Verg. (3) *a piece on a draught-board*: Ov.

latrōcĭnĭum -i, n. (latrocinor). (1) *military service as a mercenary*: Pl. (2) *highway robbery, brigandage, piracy.* LIT., incursiones hostium et latrocinia, Cic.; Caes., Sall., Liv. TRANSF., **a**, *villainy, roguery*: quid futurum sit latrocinio tribunorum, Cic.: **b**, meton., *a band of robbers*: unus ex tanto latrocinio, Cic.

latrōcĭnor -ari, dep. (²latro). (1) *to serve as a mercenary soldier*: Pl. (2) *to practise robbery, piracy, brigandage*: Cic.

lātruncŭlus -i, m. (dim. of ²latro). (1) *highwayman, freebooter, bandit*: Cic. (2) *a piece on a draught-board*: Suet.

¹lātus -a -um, partic. from fero; q.v.

²lātus -a -um (originally stlatos), adj. (with compar. and superl.), *broad, wide.*
LIT., fossa XV pedes lata, Caes.; via, Cic. in latum crescere, *to grow broad*, Ov.; Verg. Tac.
TRANSF., (1) *extensive, large*: locus, Cic. latissimae solitudines, Caes. (2) of persons *proud, haughty*: latus ut in circo spatiere Hor. (3) of pronunciation, *broad*: cuius tu illa lata non numquam imitaris, Cic. (4) of style *diffuse, copious, full, rich*: oratio, disputatio Cic.; Liv., Quint., Tac.

¶ Hence adv. (with compar. and superl.) **lātē**, *broadly, widely.* LIT., longe lateque *far and wide*, Cic.; vagari, Caes.; populus late rex, Verg.; Liv., Tac. TRANSF., *extensively*: ars late patet, Cic.; fidei bonum nomen latissime manat, Cic.; fuse lateque dicere de aliqua re, Cic.; Caes., Hor.

³lătus -ĕris, n. *the side, flank.*
LIT., of persons and animals: ab alicuius latere numquam discedere, Cic.; latus dare *to expose the side* (*in fencing*), Tib.; malo latus obdere apertum, *to give a handle to*, Hor.

cuius (equi aenei) in lateribus fores essent, Cic.; esp. *the lungs*: lateris, *or* laterum, dolor, Cic., Hor.; neque enim ex te nobilitatus es sed ex lateribus et lacertis tuis, Cic.; meton. =*the body*: latus fessum longā militiā, Hor.; Ov. TRANSF., *the side, flank* of anything (opp. frons, tergum): latus castrorum, Caes.; insula cuius unum latus est contra Galliam, Caes.; prora avertit et undis dat latus, Verg.; as milit. t. t., *the flank of an army*: nostros latere aperto adgressi, Caes.; a latere, a lateribus, *on the flank*, Caes., Cic., Liv.; ex lateribus, Sall., Liv.

ātuscŭlum -i, n. (dim. of ²latus), *a little side*: Lucr., Cat.

audābĭlis -e (laudo), adj. (with compar.), *praiseworthy, laudable*: vita, Cic.; orator, Cic.; Ov., Liv.
¶ Adv. **laudābĭlĭter**, *laudably, in a praiseworthy manner*: vivere, Cic.

audātĭo -ōnis, f. (laudo), *praise, commendation*: laudatio tua, Cic. Esp. (1) in a court of justice, *a testimonial to character*: gravissima atque ornatissima, Cic. (2) *a funeral oration* or *panegyric*: nonnullae mortuorum laudationes, Cic.; Liv., Quint.

audātīvus -a -um (laudo), *laudatory*: Quint.

audātor -ōris, m. (laudo), *a praiser*: temporis acti, Hor.; pacis semper laudator, Cic.; Ov. Esp. (1) *a witness who bears favourable testimony to character*: Cic. (2) *one who delivers a funeral panegyric*: Liv., Plin. L.

audātrix -īcis, f. (laudator), *a female praiser*: vitiorum laudatrix fama popularis, Cic.

audo -are (laus), *to praise, extol, commend*. In gen.: bonos, Cic.; Hor., Ov., Tac.; in pass., with infin.: exstinxisse nefas laudabor, Verg. Esp. (1) *to bear favourable testimony to anyone's character*: Cic. (2) *to deliver a funeral panegyric over*: aliquem, Cic. (3) *to name, mention, cite, quote*: aliquem auctorem, Cic.; Pl.
¶ Hence partic. **laudātus** -a -um, *praiseworthy, esteemed, excellent*: vir, Cic.; vultus, Ov.

ūrĕa -ae, f., *see* laureus.

ūrĕātus -a -um (laurea), *crowned with laurel, laurelled*, esp. as a sign of victory: imago, Cic.; fasces, lictores, Cic.; litterae, *bringing tidings of victory*, Liv.; Tac.

aurentes -um, m. pl. *the Laurentians, inhabitants of a town in Latium, between Ostia and Lavinium*; sing. also as adj. **Laurens** -entis, *Laurentine*.
¶ Hence adj. **Laurentĭus** -a -um, *Laurentine*.

ūrĕŏla -ae, f. (dim. of laurea), *a laurel branch, laurel crown*; meton., *a triumph*: Cic. L.; prov.: laureolam in mustaceo quaerere, *to seek fame in trifles*, Cic. L.

ūrĕus -a -um (laurus), *of laurel*: corona, Liv.; serta, Ov. F. as subst. **laurea** -ae. (1) *the laurel-tree*: Hor., Liv. (2) *the laurel crown, as a sign of victory*: decemviri laureā coronati, Liv.; Hor.; meton., *a triumph, victory*: quam lauream cum tua laudatione conferrem, Cic. L.

ūrĭcŏmus -a -um (laurus/coma), *covered with laurel-trees*: Lucr.

ūrĭfĕr -fĕra -fĕrum (laurus/fero), *crowned with laurels*: Luc.

laurĭgĕr -gĕra -gĕrum (laurus/gero), *crowned with laurels, wearing laurels*: Ov.

laurus -i, f. (abl. laurū: Hor.; nom. and acc. pl. laurūs: Verg.), *the laurel* or *bay-tree, sacred to Apollo, with which poets, triumphant generals, and sometimes priests and ancestral busts were crowned*: Pl., Cic., Verg.; meton., *triumph, victory*: Cic. L.

laus laudis, f. *praise, fame, glory, commendation*. LIT., adipisci laudem, Cic.; canere ad tibiam clarorum virorum laudes, Cic.; capere (*to earn*) ex hac una re maximam laudem, Cic.; celebrare alicuius laudes, Cic.; cumulare aliquem omni laude, Cic.; efferre aliquem laudibus ad caelum, Cic.; in laude vivere, Cic.; hoc in tua laude pono, Cic.; Fabio laudi datum est, quod pingeret, Cic.; laudis immensa cupido, Verg.; Liv. TRANSF., *a praiseworthy action* or *quality*: hae tantae summis in rebus laudes, Cic.; quarum laudum gloriam adamaris, Cic.; Caes., Verg.

lautē, adv. from lavo; q.v.

lautĭa -ōrum, n. pl., *entertainment given to foreign ambassadors at Rome*: Liv.

lautĭtĭa -ae, f. (lautus; see lavo), *splendour, elegance, sumptuous manner of living*: mea nova lautitia, Cic. L.; Sen.

Lautŭlae (**Lautŏlae**) -ārum, f. *a town in Latium*: Liv.

lautŭmĭae (**lātŏmĭae**) -ārum, f. (λατομίαι), *a stone-quarry*: Pl.; esp. *the quarries at Syracuse, used as prisons*: Cic.; also of a similar prison at Rome: Liv.

lautus -a -um, partic. from lavo; q.v.

lăvabrum -i, n. (lavo), *a bath*: Lucr.

lăvātĭo -ōnis, f. (lavo), *a washing, bathing*: Pl. TRANSF., *bathing apparatus*: Cic. L., Phaedr.

Lăverna -ae, f. *the goddess of gain* (just or unjust).
¶ Hence adj. **Lăvernālis** -e, *belonging to Laverna*.

Lăvīci, etc., see Labici.

Lāvīnĭa -ae, f. *daughter of Latinus, wife of Aeneas*.

Lāvīnĭum -i, n. *a town in Latium, built by Aeneas, and named after his wife Lavinia*.
¶ Hence adj. **Lāvīnĭus** -a -um and **Lāvīnus** -a -um, *Lavinian*.

lăvo lavare *or* lavēre lāvi lautum *or* lōtum *or* lăvātum (cf. λούω), *to wash, bathe*. LIT., transit.: manus, Cic.; Pl., Verg.; intransit., lavare and pass. as middle, *to wash oneself, bathe*: lavanti regi, Liv.; lavantur in fluminibus, Caes.; Cic. TRANSF., (1) *to moisten, wet, bathe*: vultum lacrimus, Ov.; Lucr., Verg. (2) of the sea etc., *to wash* a place: villam, Hor.; Ov. (3) *to wash away*: mala vino, *to drive away*, Hor.
¶ Hence partic. (with compar. and superl.) **lautus** -a -um, *washed, bathed*; hence (1) of things, *fine, splendid, elegant, sumptuous*: supellex, Cic. (2) of persons, *refined, grand*: homines lauti et urbani, Cic.; Pl.
¶ Adv. (with compar.) **lautē**, *finely, elegantly*: Pl., Cic.

laxāmentum -i, n. (laxo), *a widening, extending*. TRANSF., *a relaxing, mitigation, respite*: si quid laxamenti a bello Samnitium esset, Liv.; laxamentum dare legi, Cic.

laxē, adv. from laxus; q.v.

laxĭtās -ātis, f. (laxus), *wideness, roominess*: in domo clari hominis adhibenda cura est laxitatis, Cic.

laxō -are (laxus), *to widen* or *loosen*. LIT., (1) *to extend, enlarge*: forum, Cic.; manipulos, Caes. (2) *to undo, unfasten, slacken*: vincula epistulae, Nep.; claustra, rudentes, Verg.; also *to set free*: laxantur cupora rugis, Ov.
TRANSF., (1) *to relieve, release*: animos curamque, Cic.; cum laxati curis sumus, *free from*, Cic.; Liv. (2) *to mitigate, relax, remit*: aliquid laboris, Liv.; ubi laxatam pugnam vidit, Liv.; annonam, *to lower*, Liv.; intransit.: annona haud multum laxaverat, *had not fallen much*, Liv.

laxus -a -um, adj. (with compar. and superl.), *wide, loose, spacious.*
LIT., arcus, Verg., Hor.; ianua, anulus, Ov.; spatium, Liv.
TRANSF., (1) of time: diem statuo satis laxum, *later, postponed*, Cic. L. (2) in gen., *loose, lax, relaxed*: laxissimas habenas habere amicitiae, Cic.; annona laxior, *lower prices*, Liv.; milites laxiore imperio habere, Sall.
¶ Adv. (with compar.) **laxē**, *widely, loosely.* LIT., aliquem vincire, Liv. TRANSF., (1) of time: laxius proferre diem, *to put farther off*, Cic. L. (2) *loosely, without restraint*: vivere, Liv.; Sall.

lĕa -ae, f. (leo), *a lioness*: Lucr., Verg., Ov.

lĕaena -ae, f. (λέαινα), *a lioness*: Cat., Verg., Ov.

Lĕander -dri, m. (Λείανδρος), *a youth of Abydos who swam nightly across the Hellespont to visit Hero at Sestos, till he was drowned in a storm.*

Lĕarchus -i, m. (Λέαρχος), *the son of Athamas and Ino, killed by his father in a fit of madness.* Adj. **Lĕarchēus** -a -um, *of Learchus.*

Lĕbĕdus -i, f. (Λέβεδος), *a town in Ionia, where annual games were held in honour of Bacchus.*

lĕbēs -ētis, m. (λέβης). (1) *a bronze pan or cauldron*: Verg. (2) *a basin for washing the hands*: Ov.

lectĭca -ae, f. (lectus). (1) *a litter*: lecticā octophoro ferri, *in a litter borne by eight slaves*, Cic.; Hor., Tac. (2) *a bier*: Suet.

lecticārius -i, m. (lectica), *a litter-bearer*: Cic., Suet.

lecticŭla -ae, f. (dim. of lectica). (1) *a small litter*: lecticulā in curiam deferri, Cic.; Liv. (2) *a small bier*: Nep. (3) *a settee*: Suet.

lectio -ōnis, f. (¹lego). (1) *a picking out, selecting*: iudicum, Cic. (2) *a reading, perusal*: librorum, Cic.; lectio sine ulla delectatione, Cic. Hence: lectio senatūs, *a reading out* or *calling over of the names of the senators* (by the censor, who at the same time struck from the list the names of those he considered unworthy), Liv.

lectisterniātor -oris, m. (lectisternium), *a slave who arranged the couches round the dining-table*: Pl.

lectisternium -i, n. (lectus/sterno), *a feast offered to the gods, in which their images were placed on couches and food was put before them*: Liv.

lectĭto -are (freq. of ²lego), *to read often* or *with eagerness*: Platonem studiose, Cic.; Tac., Plin. L.

lectiuncŭla -ae, f. (dim. of lectio), *a sh* *reading*: Cic. L.

lector -ōris, m. (²lego), *a reader*: aptus delectationem lectoris, Cic.; Hor., Qui Esp. *a slave who reads aloud*: Quint., Plin.

lectŭlus -i, m. (dim. of lectus). (1) *a sm bed*: in lectulis suis mori, Cic.; Juv. (2) *couch*; for reading: Cic., Ov.; for dinin stravit pelliculis haedinis lectulos Punican Cic. (3) *a funeral bed, bed of state*: Tac.

¹lectus -a -um, partic. from lego; q.v.

²lectus -i, m. (cf. λέχος). (1) *a couch, a be* cubicularis, Cic.; lecto teneri, *to keep on bed*, Cic.; genialis, *the marriage-bed*, C. (2) *a couch* for resting on at meals, *a dinin couch*: Cic.; Hor., Liv. (3) *a funeral couc* Tib., Quint.

Lēda -ae, f. and **Lēdē** -ēs, f. (Λήδη), *the w of Tyndarus, who bore to Zeus Castor, Poll Helen, and Clytemnestra.*
¶ Hence adj. **Lēdaeus** -a -um, *of Led dei, Castor and Pollux*, Ov.; Helena, Verg.

lēgālis -e (lex), *legal*: Quint.

lēgātārius -i, m. (legatum), *a legatee*: Suet.

lēgātĭo -ōnis, f. (¹lego), *the post of deput delegated authority.*
(1) polit. t. t.; *the office of an ambassad an embassy, legation*: legationem susciper *to undertake*, Caes.; obire, Cic.; in legatione proficisci, Liv.; libera legatio, *permissi given to a senator to travel with the privileg yet without the duties, of an ambassad* Cic. L. TRANSF., a, *the result of an embass* legationem renuntiare, Cic.; referre, Liv b, *the persons constituting an embassy*: Cae Liv.
(2) milit. t. t.; *the post of deputy or suboro nate commander under a commander-in-chie* Caes.; esp. *the command of a legio* Tac.

lēgātor -ōris, m. (¹lego), *a testator, one w leaves something by will*: Suet.

lēgātum -i, n. subst. from ¹lego; q.v.

lēgātus -i, m. subst. trom ¹lego; q.v.

lēgĭfer -fĕra -fĕrum (lex/fero), *law-givin* Minos, Ov.; Verg.

lĕgĭo -ōnis, f. (²lego), *a choosing*; hence *chosen body*; esp. (1) *a legion, a division the Roman army, consisting of ten cohorts a comprising between 4,200 and 6,000 men*: Cic duas legiones ibi conscribere, Caes. (2) of t troops of other nations*: Pl., Liv. (3) in ge *an army*: Verg.

lĕgĭōnārius -a -um (legio), *belonging to legion*: milites, Caes.; Liv.

lēgĭtĭmus (lēgĭtŭmus) -a -um (lex), *la ful, legal, legitimate*: dies comitiis habend Cic.; controversiae, *legal, decided by la* Cic.; aetas, Liv.; coniunx, Ov. N. pl subst. **lēgĭtĭma** -ōrum, *legal usages*: Nep.
TRANSF., *right, fit, proper, appropria* numerus, Cic.; poema, Hor.; Ov.
¶ Adv. **lēgĭtĭmē**, *lawfully, legally*: Ci Juv.; in gen., *properly*: Tac., Juv.

lĕgiuncŭla -ae, f. (dim. of legio), *a sm legion*: Liv.

¹lēgo -are (lex), *to ordain, appoint.* (1) *appoint* a person, *make a deputy, delega authority to* (polit. or milit.): ut legati legare tur, Cic.; aliquem Caesari, *make second-command to Caesar*, Cic.; Sall., Liv. (2) *property, to bequeath, leave as a legacy*: alic pecuniam, Cic.; Liv., Quint.; aliquid alicui ab aliquo, *to leave a legacy to be paid to the legatee by the heir*, Cic.

¶ Hence from partic. legatus ‑a ‑um: M. as subst. **lēgātus** ‑i, *a deputy, one bearing delegated authority.* (1) political: **a,** *an ambassador, envoy*: Caes., Cic., Liv., Ov.: **b,** *the deputy* or *second-in-command* to a magistrate: Caes., Cic., Liv.; esp. under the empire, *the governor* set over an imperial province: Tac., Suet. (2) milit.; *a deputy or subordinate commander under a commander-in-chief*, esp. *the commander of a legion*: Caes., Tac.

N. as subst. **lēgātum** ‑i, *a legacy, bequest*: Cic. L., Quint., Juv.

ěgo lěgěre lěgi lectum (λέγω), *to collect, gather together, to pick.*
LIT., in gen.: nuces, Cic.; spolia caesorum, Liv.; mala ex arbore, Verg.; ossa, Ov.; esp.: fila, of the Parcae, *to wind up, spin*, Verg.; vela, *to furl the sails*, Verg.; sacra divum, *to steal*, Hor.
TRANSF., (1) *to pass through, traverse* a place: saltūs legit, Ov.; vestigia alicuius, *to follow the footsteps*, Verg.; esp. of ships, *to coast along*: oram Italiae, Liv. (2) *to survey, scan*: omnes adversos, Verg.; esp. of writing, *to read, peruse*: eos libros, Cic.; Ov., Liv., etc.; apud Clitomachum, *in the works of Clitomachum*, Cic.; with the writer as object: Ov., Quint.; sometimes *to read aloud, recite*: volumen suum, Cic.; hence: senatum legere, *to call over the senate, to go over the list of senators*, Liv. (3) *to choose, select, pick out*: iudices, Cic.; viros ad bella, Ov.; cives, Liv.
¶ Hence partic. (with compar. and superl.) **lectus** ‑a ‑um, *chosen, selected*: pueri, Cic.; Verg., Hor. (2) *choice in quality, excellent*: adulescens, femina, Cic.; Pl., Hor.

ěgŭlěius ‑i, m. (lex), *a pettifogging lawyer*: Cic.

ěgūmen ‑ĭnis, n. (lego), *any leguminous plant; pulse*: Caes., Juv.; *the bean*: Verg.

ělěges ‑um, m. pl. (Λέλεγες), *a people, scattered in different places over Greece and Asia Minor.*
¶ Hence f. adj. **Lělěgēïs** ‑ĭdis, f. *Lelegean*; adj. **Lělěgēïus** ‑a ‑um, *Lelegean.*

ěmannus ‑i, m. (with or without lacus), *a lake in the country of the* Helvetii, *now the Lake of Geneva.*

ěmbus ‑i, m. (λέμβος), *a boat, cutter, pinnace*: Pl., Verg., Liv.

ěmma ‑ătis, n. (λῆμμα), *the theme* or *title* of a composition; also *an epigram*: Mart., Plin. L.

ěmniscātus ‑a ‑um (lemniscus), *adorned with ribbons*: palma, *a palm-branch ornamented with ribbons, token of victory*, Cic.

ěmniscus ‑i, m. (λημνίσκος), *a ribbon attached to a victor's wreath*: Liv.

emnŏs (‑us) ‑i, f. (Λῆμνος), *the island of Lemnos in the Aegean Sea, the abode of Vulcan.*
¶ Hence adj. **Lemnĭus** ‑a ‑um, *Lemnian*: Lemnius pater, Verg.; and subst. **Lemnius**, *Vulcan*, Ov.; adj. **Lemnĭensis** ‑e, *Lemnian*; f. subst. **Lemnĭăs** ‑ădis, *a Lemnian woman*: Ov.; m. subst. **Lemnĭcŏla** ‑ae, *an inhabitant of Lemnos* (of Vulcan): Ov.

ěmŏvīces ‑um, m. *a people of Aquitanian Gaul*: Caes.

lěmŭrēs ‑um, m. *ghosts, spectres*: Hor.
¶ Hence **Lěmŭrĭa** ‑ōrum, n. pl. *a festival held in May to expel ghosts*: Ov.

lēna ‑ae, f. (leno), *a procuress, bawd*: Pl., Ov. TRANSF., natura quasi sui lena, *enticing persons to her*, Cic.

Lēnaeus ‑a ‑um (Ληναῖος), *Bacchic*: latices, *wine*, Verg.; Lenaeus pater, *or* simply Lenaeus, *Bacchus*, Verg.

lēnīmen ‑ĭnis, n. (lenio), *a means of alleviation*: testudo laborum dulce lenimen, Hor.; Ov.

lēnīmentum ‑i, n. (lenio), *a mitigation, alleviation*: Tac.

lēnĭo ‑ire; imperf. lenībant: Verg.), *to make mild, alleviate, mitigate, soothe, relieve.*
LIT., stomachum latrantem, Hor.; vulnera, Prop. TRANSF., se consolatione, Cic.; aliquem iratum, Cic.; dolentem solando, Verg.; Liv. Intransit., *to calm down*: Pl.

lēnis ‑e, adj. (with compar. and superl.), *smooth, soft, mild, gentle.*
LIT., sensus iudicat lene asperum, Cic.; venenum, *slight*, Cic. L.; vinum, *mellow*, Hor.; ventus lenissimus, Cic. L.; stagnum, *flowing gently*, Liv. N. acc. as adv. **lēnĕ**, *gently, softly*: lene sonantis aquae, Ov.
TRANSF., (1) of gradients, *gentle*: clivus, Liv.; Caes. (2) of disposition or tone, *mild*: populus Romanus in hostes lenissimus, Cic.; leniorem sententiam dicere, Caes.; consilium, Hor. (3) of style, *smooth*: oratio placida, submissa, lenis, Cic.
¶ Adv. (with compar. and superl.) **lēnĭtěr**, *softly, gently, mildly, calmly*: adridere, Cic.; collis leniter acclivis, *rising gradually*, Caes.; of disposition, etc., *gently, mildly*: adloqui, Liv.; Cic.; of style or enunciation, *smoothly*: dicere, Cic.; Cat. In a bad sense, *(too) mildly, slackly*: Caes.

lēnĭtās ‑ātis, f. (lenis), *gentleness, softness, mildness.* LIT., vocis, Cic.; Arar in Rhodanum influit incredibili lenitate, *slowness, gentleness*, Caes. TRANSF., (1) of disposition, etc., *gentleness, mildness*: animi, Cic.; legum, Cic. (2) of style, *smoothness*: verborum, Cic.

lēnĭtěr, adv. from lenis; q.v.

lēnĭtūdo ‑ĭnis, f. (lenis), *gentleness, mildness*: in istum, Cic.; of style, *smoothness*: Cic.

lēno ‑ōnis, m. (lenio), *a procurer, pander*: Pl., Cic., Hor. TRANSF., *a go-between*: Cic., Ov.

lēnōcĭnĭum ‑i, n. (leno), *the trade of a procurer* or *bawd.* LIT., facere, Pl.; Suet. TRANSF., *an enticement, allurement*: Cic.; of dress, *finery*: Cic.; of style, *meretricious ornament*: Tac., Quint.

lēnōcĭnor ‑ari, dep. (leno), *to pursue the trade of a procurer.* TRANSF., with dat. (1) *to make up to, to flatter*: alicui, Cic. (2) *to advance, promote*: feritati, Tac.

lēnōnĭus ‑a ‑um (leno), *belonging to a procurer*: Pl.

lens lentis, f. *a lentil*: Verg.

lentē, adv. from lentus; q.v.

lentesco ‑ěre (lentus). LIT., *to become pliant, soft, sticky*: tellus picis in morem ad digitos lentescit habendo, Verg. TRANSF., *to weaken, slacken*: lentescunt tempore curae, Ov.

lentiscĭfer ‑fěra ‑fěrum (lentiscus/fero), *producing the mastic-tree*: Ov.

lentiscus ‑i, f. and **lentiscum** ‑i, n. *the mastic-tree*, poet. ap. Cic. TRANSF., *a mastic toothpick*: Mart.

lentĭtudo -ĭnis, f. (lentus). (1) *slowness, slug-gishness*: Tac. (2) *insensibility, apathy*: Cic.
lento -are (lentus), *to bend*: lentandus remus in unda, *must be plied*, Verg.
¹**lentŭlus** -a -um (dim. of lentus), *somewhat slow*: Cic. L.
²**Lentŭlus** -i, m. *the name of one of the families of the patrician gens Cornelia. Its most famous members were* (1) P. Cornelius Lentulus Sura, *a fellow-conspirator with Catiline.* (2) P. Cornelius Lentulus Spinther, *who proposed the recall of Cicero from exile.*
¶ Hence **Lentŭlĭtās** -ātis, f. *the family pride of the Lentuli*: Cic. L.
lentus -a -um, adj. (with compar. and superl.), *tough, resistant, barely yielding to force.*
Hence LIT., (1) *supple, pliant*: rami, Verg.; lentior salicis virgis, Ov. (2) *sticky, tenacious*: gluten visco lentius, Verg.; lentis adhaerens bracchiis, Hor.; marmor (of the sea), Verg.
TRANSF., (1) *slow, lingering, lasting*: negotium, Cic. L.; pugna, Liv.; lentiorem facere spem, Ov.; in dicendo, *drawling*, Cic.; infitiator, *a bad payer*, Cic. (2) *inactive, apathetic, phlegmatic*: iudex, Cic.; nihil illo lentius, Cic.; lentissima pectora, Ov.; lentus in umbra, Verg.
¶ Adv. **lentē**, *slowly.* LIT., proceditur, Caes.; curritur, Ov. TRANSF., (1) *without animation, calmly, coolly*: aliquid ferre, Cic.; respondere, Cic.; agere, Liv. (2) *leisurely, deliberately*: lente ac fastidiose probare, Cic. L.
¹**lēnuncŭlus** -i, m. (dim. of leno), *a little pander*: Pl.
²**lēnuncŭlus** -i, m. (for lembunculus, dim. of lembus), *a small boat or skiff*: Caes., Tac.
lĕo -ōnis, m. (λέων), *a lion.* LIT., vis leonis, Cic. TRANSF., *the constellation Leo*: Hor.
Lĕōnĭdās -ae, m. (Λεωνίδας), *king of Sparta, killed at the defence of the pass of Thermopylae.*
lĕōnīnus -a -um (leo), *of a lion, leonine*: Pl.
Lĕontīni -ōrum, m. (Λεοντῖνοι), *a town on the east coast of Sicily* (now Lentini).
¶ Hence adj. **Lĕontīnus** -a -um, *Leontine.*
lĕpăs -ādis, f. (λεπάς), *a limpet*: Pl.
¹**lĕpĭdus** -a -um, adj. (with compar. and superl.) (cf. lepor), *pleasant, charming, agreeable, elegant, neat.* (1) of looks: Pl., Ter. (2) of manner: Pl., Ter.; also in a bad sense; *effeminate*: hi pueri tam lepidi ac delicati, Cic. (3) of speech, *witty, polished*: dictum, Hor.; Cat.
¶ Adv. (with compar. and superl.) **lĕpĭdē**, *pleasantly, agreeably, charmingly*; of looks, manner, and speech: Pl., Ter., Cic.; also as an expression of agreement or approval: Pl.
²**Lĕpĭdus** -i, m. *the name of a family of the patrician gens Aemilia. Its most famous members were* (1) M. Aemilius Lepidus, *praetor in Sicily, consul 79 B.C., the bitter enemy of Sulla, whose measures he proposed to annul, and thereby brought about a civil war.* (2) M. Aemilius Lepidus, *triumvir with Antonius and Octavius*, 43 B.C.
lĕpor and **lĕpos** -ōris, m. *pleasantness, agree-ableness, charm.* (1) of looks: Pl., Lucr. (2) of manner: Cic., Cat. (3) of speech, *pleasantry, wit*: scurrilis, Cic.; Pl.
lĕpus -ōris, m. (akin to λαγώς), *a hare*: Verg., Hor., Ov.; prov.: aliis leporem agitare, *to*

labour for another's advantage: Ov. TRANSF., *the constellation Lepus*: Cic.
lepuscŭlus -i, m. (dim. of lepus), *a young hare*: Cic.
Lerna -ae, f. and **Lernē** -ēs, f. (Λέρνη), *a marsh in Argolis, inhabited by the Lernaean Hydra, slain by Hercules*: belua Lernae, Verg.
¶ Hence adj. **Lernaeus** -a -um, *Lernaean.*
Lesbos (-us) -i, f. (Λέσβος), *an island in the Aegean Sea, birth-place of Alcaeus and Sappho.*
¶ Hence adj. **Lesbĭăcus** -a -um, *Lesbian*: Cic.; f. adj. and subst. **Lesbĭas** -ādis; **Lesbĭs** -idis, *Lesbian, a Lesbian woman*: lyra, *of Arion*, Ov.; Lesbis puella, *or simply* Lesbis, *Sappho*, Ov.; adj. **Lesbĭus** -a -um, *Lesbian*: civis, *Alcaeus*, Hor.; plectrum *lyric*, Hor.; pes, *lyric poetry*, Hor.; vates *Sappho*, Ov.; n. as subst. **Lesbĭum** -i, *Lesbian wine*: Hor.; f. as subst. **Lesbĭa** -ae, *pseudonym of Catullus' mistress*; adj. **Lesbōus** -a -um, *Lesbian.*
lessum, acc. sing. as from lessus, m. *a mournful cry, lamentation for the dead*: old law, ap. Cic.
lētālis -e (letum), *deadly, mortal, fatal*: harundo, Verg.; Ov., Suet.
lēthargĭcus -i, m. (ληθαργικός), *a drowsy, lethargic person*: Hor.
lēthargus -i, m. (λήθαργος), *drowsiness, lethargy*: coma: Lucr., Hor., Quint.
Lēthē -ēs, f. (Λήθη), *a river in the infernal regions, the waters of which brought forgetfulness of the past.*
¶ Hence adj. **Lēthaeus** -a -um. (1) *relating to Lethe or the underworld generally*: Lethaea vincula abrumpere, Hor.; Verg. (2) *causing forgetfulness*: somnus, Verg.; sucus, Ov.
lētĭfĕr -fĕra -fĕrum (letum/fero), *death-bringing, deadly*: arcus, Verg.; locus, *a vital spot*, Ov.
lēto -are (letum), *to kill, slay*: Verg., Ov.
Lētōis, **Lētōïus**=Latois, Latoius, see Lato.
lētum -i, n. *death.* LIT., consciscere sibi, Pl., turpi leto perire, Cic.; sibi parĕre manu, Verg.; leto adimere aliquem, *to save from death*, Hor.; Lucr., Liv. TRANSF., of things poet., *ruin, annihilation*: Teucrum res eripe leto, Verg.
Leucădĭa -ae, f. (Λευκαδία) and **Leucăs** -ădis, (Λευκάς), *an island in the Ionian Sea, with a temple to Apollo* (now Levkás).
¶ Hence adj. **Leucădĭus** -a -um, *Leucadian*: deus, *Apollo*, Ov.; aequor, Ov.; plur. as subst. **Leucădĭi** -ōrum, m. *the Leucadians*: Liv.
leucaspĭs -ĭdis, f. (λεύκασπις), *having white shields*: phalanx, Liv.
Leucāta -ae and **Leucātē** -ēs, f. and **Leucă** -cādis, f. *a promontory of the island Leucadi* (now Doukáton).
Leucē -ēs, f. (Λευκή), *a town in Laconia.*
Leuci -ōrum, m. *a people in Gallia Belgica.*
Leucippus -i, m. (Λεύκιππος). (1) myth., *father of Phoebe and Hilaira, who were carried off by Castor and Pollux.*
¶ Hence **Leucippĭs** -ĭdis, f. *a daughter of Leucippus*: Prop.
(2) hist., *a Greek philosopher, disciple of Zeno of Elea.*
Leucopĕtra -ae, f. *a promontory in southern Italy, near Rhegium.*

Leucophryna -ae, f. (λευκοφρύνη), i.e. *with white eyebrows*), *a name of Diana among the Magnesians.*

Leucŏthĕa -ae and **Leucŏthĕē** -ēs, f. (Λευκοθέα, i.e. *the white goddess*), *name of Ino, daughter of Cadmus, after she had been turned into a sea-deity.*

Leucŏthŏē -ēs, f. *daughter of the eastern king Orchamus and Eurynome.*

Leuctra -ōrum, n. pl. (Λεῦκτρα), *a small town in Boeotia, where Epaminondas defeated the Spartans in* 371 B.C.
¶ Hence adj. **Leuctrĭcus** -a -um, *Leuctrian.*

lĕvāmen -ĭnis, n. (¹levo), *a mitigation, alleviation, solace*: quod si esset aliquod levamen, id esset in te uno, Cic. L.; Cat., Verg., Liv.

lĕvāmentum -i, n. (¹levo), *alleviation, mitigation, solace*: miseriarum, Cic.; Tac., Plin. L.

lĕvātĭo -ōnis, f. (¹levo), *a lightening*; hence (1) *an alleviation, mitigation*: invenire levationem doloribus, Cic. (2) *a diminution*: vitiorum, Cic.

lĕvĭcŭlus -a -um (dim. of ¹levis), *somewhat vain, light-headed*: leviculus noster Demosthenes, Cic.

lĕvĭdensis -e (¹levis/densus), *of thin texture*; hence, *slight, poor*: munusculum, Cic. L.

lĕvĭpēs -pĕdis (¹levis/pes), *light-footed*: Varr.
¹lĕvis -e, adj. (with compar. and superl.), *light, not heavy* (opp. gravis).
LIT., (1) in weight: pondus, Ov.; levis armatura, *light armour*, Caes.; and of troops, *light-armed*: Liv., Tac.; of soil: Verg.; of ghosts: Hor.; of sleep: Hor.; in movement, *rapid, swift*: cervus, Verg.; hora, *transitory*, Ov.
TRANSF., (1) *light, trifling, unimportant*: dolor, Cic.; periculum levius, Caes.; auditio, *a trifling, unfounded report*, Caes.; causa, Caes., Liv.; proelium, Caes., Liv.; in levi habere, *to regard as a trifle*, Tac.; of poetry, *light, unambitious*: Musa, Ov. (2) of behaviour, *light, mild, gentle*: reprehensio levior, Cic. (3) of character, *fickle, light-headed, capricious, unstable*: homo, Pl., Cic.; amicitia, Cic.; Hor., Liv.
¶ Adv. (with compar. and superl.) **lĕvĭtĕr**, *lightly, softly*: levius casura pila sperabat, Caes. TRANSF., (1) *slightly, somewhat*: saucius, Cic.; aegrotare, Cic.; Lucr., Hor. (2) *mildly*: ut levissime dicam. (3) *lightly, with equanimity*: ferre, Cic., Liv.
²lĕvis -e (λεῖος), adj. (with compar. and superl.), *smooth* (opp. asper).
LIT., in gen.: corpuscula, Cic.; pocula, *polished*, Verg.; sanguis, *slippery*, Verg.; Hor., Ov.; esp. poet., *smooth, beardless*: iuventas, Hor.; senex, *bald*, Ov.; pectus, Verg.; vir, *effeminate*, Ov.
TRANSF., of style, *flowing, smooth, polished*: oratio, Cic.; Quint.

lĕvĭsomnus -a -um (¹levis/somnus), *lightly sleeping*: Lucr.

¹lĕvĭtās -ātis, f. (¹levis), *lightness* (opp. gravitas).
LIT., (1) in weight: armorum, Caes. (2) in movement: Lucr.
TRANSF., (1) *levity, fickleness, inconstancy*: levitatem alicuius experiri, Cic.; Caes. (2) *vainness*: opinionis, Cic.

²lĕvĭtās -ātis, f. (²levis), *smoothness.* LIT., speculorum, Cic. TRANSF., of style, *smoothness, polish*: Aeschini, Cic.; Quint.

lĕvĭtĕr, adv. from ¹levis; q.v.
¹lĕvo -are (¹levis). (1) *to raise, lift up*: se attollere ac levare, Liv.; de caespite virgo se levat, Ov.; Verg. (2) *to make light, relieve, ease.*
LIT., ego te fasce levabo, Verg.
TRANSF., (1) *to relieve a person from trouble, etc.*: se aere alieno, *to free*, Cic.; aliquem metu, religione animos, Liv. (2) *to relieve a condition or affliction, to alleviate, mitigate*: curam et angorem animi mei, Cic. L.; iniurias, Caes.; morbum, Pl.; ictum, Hor.; Verg. (3) *to diminish, weaken, impair*: auctoritatem, Cic.; fidem, Hor.
²lĕvo -are (²levis), *to make smooth, polish.* LIT., corpus, Cic.; Lucr. TRANSF., of discourse: aspera, Hor.

lēvor -ōris, m. (²levis), *smoothness*: Lucr.
lex lēgis, f. (²lego), *a set form of words.*
LIT., (1) *a contract, covenant, agreement*: lex operi faciundo, *a building contract*, Cic.; legem alicui scribere, Cic.; dicere, Hor., Liv.; pacis, *conditions of peace*, Verg., Liv. (2) *a law as proposed by a magistrate to the people, a bill*: legem ferre, rogare, *to propose a bill to the people*, Cic.; sciscere, iubere (of the people), *to accept* or *pass a bill*, Cic.; repudiare, antiquare, *to reject, throw out a bill*, Cic.; promulgare, *to publish*, Cic., Liv. (3) *a law as passed, a statute*: legem ferre, *to pass a law, enact*, Liv.; abrogare, *to repeal*, Cic.; leges duodecim tabularum, *the laws of the Twelve Tables, drawn up by the decemvirs*, Liv. Phrases: lege, legibus, used adv.=*legally, according to law*, Ter., Nep.; lege agere: **a**, of the lictor, *to execute a sentence*: Liv.: **b**, *to bring an action*: Pl., Ter., Cic.
TRANSF., *law generally, ordinance, rule, precept*: legem sibi statuere, Cic.; leges amicitiae, philosophiae, historiae, Cic.; versibus est certa lex, Cic.; of natural law: homines ea lege natos esse, Cic.; Sen., Ov. Phrase: sine lege, *without restraint, irregularly*; equi sine lege ruunt, Ov.

Lexovii -ōrum, m. *a people of Gallia Lugdunensis.*

lībāmen -ĭnis, n. (libo), *a libation, offering to the gods*: Verg. TRANSF., *a sample, specimen*: tu nova servatae carpes libamina famae, Ov.

lībāmentum -i, n. (libo), *a libation, offering to the gods*: Cic.

lībātĭo -ōnis, f. (libo), *a libation*: Cic.

libella -ae, f. (dim. of libra). (1) *a small coin, a tenth of a* denarius, *equal in value to the* as: Cat.; hence: heres ex libella, *heir to a tenth of a property*, Cic. TRANSF., *a very small sum of money, a farthing, a mite*; hence: ad libellam, *exactly*, Cic. (2) *a carpenter's level, plummet-line*: Lucr.

lībellus -i, m. (dim. of liber), *a little book.*
LIT., scripsi etiam illud quodam in libello, Cic.; Liv., Juv., etc.; plur. meton.=*a bookseller's shop*: Cat. Esp., *a note-book, memorandum-book, diary*: rettulit in libellum, Cic.
TRANSF., (1) *a memorial, a petition*: libellum composuit, Cic. (2) *a programme,*

placard, hand-bill: gladiatorum libelli, Cic.; Juv., Tac. (3) *a letter*: Pl., Cic. L. (4) *a satire, libel*: Suet.

lĭbens and **lŭbens** -entis, partic. from libet; q.v.

lĭbentĭa (**lŭbentia**) -ae, f. (libens, lubens), *delight, cheerfulness, gladness*: Pl.

Lĭbentīna (**Lŭbentīna**) -ae, f. (libens, lubens), *a name of Venus, as the goddess of sensual pleasure.*

¹lĭber -ĕra -ĕrum, adj. (with compar. and superl.), *free*.
(1) absol.: **a**, socially, *free* (opp. servus): aliquem non liberum putare, Cic.; Pl., etc.: **b**, politically, of states, *free, independent*: civitas, Caes.; Cic., Liv.: **c**, in gen., *unrestrained, unencumbered*: tempus, animus, Cic.; agri, *free from tribute*, Cic.; aedes, *uninhabited*, Liv.; ut rei familiaris liberum quidquam sit, *unencumbered with debt*, Cic.; custodia, *house arrest*, Liv.; faenus, *unlimited by law*, Liv.; esp. *free in thought* or *expression*: lingua, Pl.; animus, Cic.; liberiores litterae, Cic. Phrase: liberum est mihi, foll. by infin., *one is free to*, Quint., Plin. L.
(2) *free from* some particular thing, *exempt, without*; with **a**: a delictis, Cic.; Ov.; with simple abl.: omni metu, Liv.; Ov.; with genit.: Verg., Hor.
¶ Adv. (with compar.) **lĭbĕrē**, *freely*. (1) *freely, without restraint, without hindrance*: vivere, Cic.; respirare, Cic.; Quint. (2) *generously, spontaneously*: tellus omnia liberius ferebat, Verg. (3) *frankly, openly, boldly*: loqui, Cic.; Liv., Quint.

²lĭber -bri, m. *the inner bark of a tree.*
LIT., Cic., Verg.
TRANSF., as this was used by the ancients as a material upon which to write: (1) *a book, writing, treatise*: librum incohare, conficere, Cic.; libri Sibyllini, Cic., Liv., Tac., etc. (2) *a book, a division into which a work is divided*: tres libri de Natura Deorum, Cic.; Quint. (3) *a register, catalogue*: Cic., Liv. (4) *a letter*: Nep., Plin. L.

³Lĭber -ĕri, m. *an old Italian deity, presiding over agriculture, later identified with the Greek Bacchus*; meton., *wine*: Hor.
¶ Hence **Lĭbĕrālĭa** -ium, n. pl. *the festival of Liber on the 17th of March, at which youths received the toga virilis*: Cic.

⁴lĭber -ĕri, *see* liberi -ōrum.

Lĭbĕra -ae, f. (³Liber). (1) *Proserpine, daughter of Ceres, sister of Liber.* (2) *Ariadne, wife of Bacchus.*

lĭbĕrālis -e (¹liber), adj. (with compar. and superl.).
LIT., *relating to freedom*: causa, *a law-suit in which the freedom of some person is in dispute*: Pl., Ter., Quint.
TRANSF., *becoming to a freedman, gentlemanlike.* (1) of occupations, etc.: artes liberales, *liberal arts*, Cic.; sumptus, Cic. (2) of character and action, *courteous, generous*: responsum, Cic. L.; with genit.: laudis avidi, pecuniae liberales erant, Sall. (3) of looks, *handsome*: Pl.
¶ Adv. (with compar. and superl.) **lĭbĕrālĭtĕr**, *in a manner becoming a freedman*: vivere, Cic.; Caes. TRANSF., *courteously, generously, kindly*: liberalissime erat pollicitus omnibus, Cic. L.; Caes.

lĭbĕrālĭtās -ātis, f. (liberalis), *courtesy, kindness, liberality, generosity*: Ter., Cic. TRANSF., *a grant*: Tac., Suet.

lĭbĕrātĭo -ōnis, f. (libero), *a setting free*; in gen., *release from*: culpae, Cic.; esp., *a legal acquittal*: Cic.

lĭbĕrātor -ōris, m. (libero), *one who sets free, a liberator*: patriae, Cic.; attrib.: liberator ille populi Romani animus, Liv.

lĭbĕrē, adv. from ¹liber; q.v.

lĭbĕri -ērōrum and -ērum, m. pl. (¹liber), *children*. LIT., liberos procreare, liberis operam dare, Cic.; Pl., Hor., etc. TRANSF., *the young of animals*: Pl.

lĭbĕro -are (¹liber), *to set free, liberate*. (1) absol., socially and politically, *to make free, to manumit*: servos, Caes.; Pl., Cic. (2) *to set free from some particular thing, exempt, deliver, release*: te ab eo vindico ac libero, Cic.; divinus animus liberatus a corpore, Cic.; aliquem culpā, Cic.; aliquem periculo, Caes.; esp. legal, *to set free from a debt* or *engagement*: aliquem eodem illo crimine, Cic.; with genit.: culpae regem, Liv.; templa liberata, *having a free prospect*, Cic. (3) with acc. of the impediment removed: promissa, Cic.; obsidionem urbis, *to raise*, Liv.

lĭberta -ae, f., *see* libertus.

lĭbertās -ātis, f. (¹liber), *freedom*.
(1) socially and polit.: **a**, of an individual, social *freedom, rights, liberty* (opp. slavery): se in libertatem vindicare, Cic.; Pl., Liv.: **b**, polit., *independence*: ad usurpandam libertatem vocare, *to summon to the voting*, Cic.; libertatem eripere, *to take away political privileges*, Liv.: **c**, of a community, *freedom, independence*: libertatem capessere, Cic.; perdere, Cic.; recipere, Cic.; Caes., Liv.
(2) in gen., *freedom, liberty of action, freedom from restraint*: vivendi, loquendi, Cic.; dat populo libertatem ut quod velint faciant, Cic.; Caes., Liv. (3) *freedom of speech, frankness, candour*: Ov., Quint. (4) personif., Libertas, *the goddess of Freedom, having a temple on the Aventine Hill*: Cic.

lĭbertīnus -a -um (libertus), *of the class of freedman*: homo, Cic.; pater, Hor.; mulier, Liv.
¶ As subst., m. **lĭbertīnus** -i, *a freedman*: Cic.; f. **lĭbertīna** -ae, *a freedwoman*: Hor.

lĭbertus -i, m. *a freedman*, and **lĭberta** -ae, f. *a freedwoman*, in relation to the person who freed or manumitted them: Pl., Cic., Liv.

lĭbet (**lŭbet**) -bēre -buit or -bĭtum est, impers., *it pleases, is agreeable*; with dat. of person: mihi, tibi, etc., or absol.: facite quod libet, Cic.; Pl., Ter.; with infin., or acc. and infin. clause, as subject: non libet plura scribere, Cic. L.; Pl., Ter.
¶ Hence partic. (with superl.) **lĭbens** and **lŭbens** -entis, *willing, with good-will, with pleasure*: libens facio, Pl.; tecum obeam libens, Hor.; libenti animo, *willingly*, Cic.; me libente, *with my good-will*, Cic.; *joyful, pleased, glad*: Pl., Ter.
Adv. (with compar. and superl.) **lĭbentĕr** (**lŭbentĕr**), *willingly, with pleasure*: libenter uti verbo Catonis, Cic.; nusquam libentius cenare, *with better appetite*, Cic.; libentissime dare, Cic.; Pl., Caes.

lĭbīdĭnōsus -a -um (libido), adj. (with compar. and superl.), *full of desire*; esp. (1) *wilful, arbitrary, capricious*: libidinosissimae liberationes, Cic. (2) *passionate, lustful*: caper, Hor.; Cic.

¶ Adv. **lĭbīdĭnōsē**, *wilfully, arbitrarily*: Cic., Liv.

lĭbīdo (lŭbīdo) -ĭnis, f. (libet), *violent desire, appetite, longing*. In gen.: est lubido orationem audire, Pl.; Cic., Liv. Esp. (1) *irrational; whim, caprice*: ex libidine, Sall.; ad libidinem militum, Liv. (2) *immoderate; passion, lust*: libidines refrenare, Cic.; Sall., Liv.; meton.: libidines, *obscenities in painting and sculpture*, Cic.

Lĭbītĭna -ae, f. *the goddess of the dead, in whose temple the requisites for a funeral were kept for hire, and the register of deaths was preserved.*

TRANSF., (1) *the requisites for a funeral*: pestilentia tanta erat, ut Libitina vix sufficeret, Liv. (2) *the grave, death*: multaque pars mei vitabit Libitinam, Hor.

lĭbo -are (λείβω), *to take away from.*

LIT., (1) *to taste*: dapes, Verg.; iecur, Liv.; hence, *to touch*: cibos digitis, Ov.; oscula natae, *to kiss*, Verg. (2) *to give a taste of, offer to the gods*: diis dapes, Liv.; frugem Cereri, Ov.; Cic., Verg.

TRANSF., (1) *to extract, derive*: a natura deorum libatos animos habemus, Cic. (2) *to impair, diminish*: vires, Liv.; Lucr., Ov.

lībra -ae, f. (λίτρα).

(1) *a balance, pair of scales*. LIT., librae lanx, Cic.; Caes.; per aes et libram, aere et librā, *a fictitious form of sale used in making wills, adopting sons*, etc.; mercari aliquid aere et librā, *in due form*, Hor., Liv. TRANSF., *the constellation Libra*: Verg., Ov.

(2) *the Roman pound of 12 oz.*: Varr., Liv., Juv.

lībrāmentum -i, n. (libro). (1) *weight as a source of power* or *for balancing*, as used e.g. in a ballista: plumbi, Liv.; aquae, Plin. (2) *a horizontal plane*: Cic.

lībrārĭa -ae, f. (libra), *a female who weighed out wool to slaves for working*: Juv.

lībrārĭŏlus -i, m. (dim. of librarius), *a junior transcriber* or *bookseller*: Cic.

lībrārĭum -i, n., *see* librarius.

lībrārĭus -a -um (¹liber), *of books*: taberna, *a bookshop*, Cic.; scriptor, Hor. As subst. m. **lībrārĭus** -i. (1) *a transcriber of books, a copyist*: Cic., Liv. (2) *a bookseller*: Sen.; n. **lībrārĭum** -i, *a place to keep books in, a bookcase*: Cic.

lībrīlis -e (libra), *of a pound weight*: fundae libriles, *slings throwing one-pound stones*, Caes.

lībrĭtŏr -ōris, m. (libro), *from an engine, an artilleryman*: Tac.

lībro -are (libra), *to balance*; hence (1) *to poise, keep in equilibrium*: terra librata ponderibus, Cic.; Ov., Verg. (2) *to swing, level, brandish*: summā telum librabat ab aure, Verg.; Ov., Liv.; hence, *to hurl*: glandem, Liv.; Verg. (3) *to hold suspended, keep in its place*: vela librantur ab aura, Ov.

¶ Hence partic. (with compar.) **lībrātus** -a -um, *poised, swung, hurled with force*: glans, Liv.; ictus, Liv.; Tac.

Libs Lĭbis, m. (λίψ), *the west-south-west wind*: Plin.

lībum -i, n. *a cake, such as was offered to the gods, especially on a birthday*: Ov., Verg.

Lĭburni -ōrum, m. *the Liburnians, a people of Illyria*; sing., Liburnus -i, m. *a Liburnian slave*: Juv. As adj. **Lĭburnus** -a -um, *Liburnian*; f. as subst. **Lĭburna** -ae, *a light vessel, galley*: Caes., Hor.

¶ Hence subst. **Lĭburnĭa** -ae, *Liburnia*; and adj. **Lĭburnĭcus** -a -um, *Liburnian*.

Lĭbўs -yos, plur. **Lĭbўes** -um, m. *a Libyan, inhabitant of northern Africa.*

¶ Hence subst. **Lĭbўa** -ae and **Lĭbўē** -ēs, f. *Libya*; sometimes in gen., *Africa*; adj. **Lĭbўcus** -a -um; **Lĭbўssus** -a -um; **Lĭbўstīnus** -a -um; **Lĭbўus** -a -um, *Libyan*; f. adj. **Lĭbўstis** -ĭdis, *Libyan.*

Lĭbўphoenīces -um, m. (Λιβυφοίνικες), *a Libyan people in Byzacium, descended from the Phoenicians*: Liv., Plin.

līcens -centis, partic. from licet; q.v.

līcentĕr, adv. from licet; q.v.

līcentĭa -ae, f. (licet), *freedom, leave, liberty*: pueris non omnem ludendi damus licentiam, Cic.; tantum licentiae dabat gloria, Cic.; scribendi, dicendi, Cic.; verborum, Ov.; esp. of the abuse of freedom, *dissoluteness, licentiousness*: comprimere hominum licentiam, Cic.; refrenare, Hor.; coercere, Tac.; personif.: Licentia, as a goddess, *Licence*, Cic.

līcĕo -ēre -ŭi -ĭtum (connected with licet), *to be on sale, to be valued at*: quanti licuisse tu scribis hortos, Cic. L.; Hor.

līcĕor -ēri, dep. (liceo), *to bid, offer a price*: liciti sunt usque eo, Cic.; Pl., Caes.; with acc., *to bid for*: hortos, Cic. L.

līcet līcēre, licŭit or licĭtum est, impers., *it is allowed, one can* or *may.*

» LIT.: the person given permission is in the dat.; the action permitted is expressed by a n. pronoun or by an infin. or clause, acting as subject of the verb; the person giving permission, if expressed, is in the acc. with per: id ei licet, Cic.; licet rogare? (legal formula), *may I ask?* Cic.; licuit semperque licebit . . . producere nomen, Hor.; with acc. and infin.: nos frui liceret, Cic.; with dat. of predicate: Themistocli licet esse otioso, Cic.; with acc. of predicate: per quam non licet esse neglegentem, Cat.; so even when dat. accompanies licet: civi Romano licet esse Gaditanum, Cic.; with subjunctive clause as subject: fremant omnes licet, Cic.; also with ut clause as subject: Cic.

TRANSF., as conjunction, *granted that, although*; with verb in subjunctive: omnia licet concurrant, Cic.; Verg., etc.; without verb.: Ov., Sen.

¶ Hence pres. partic. (with compar.) **līcens** -entis, *free, unrestrained, unbridled*: Lupercus, Prop.; licentior dithyrambus, Cic.

¶ Adv. (with compar.) **līcentĕr**, *freely, without restraint*: Cic., Liv., Tac.

¶ Perf. partic. **līcĭtus** -a -um, *allowed, permitted*: sermo, Verg.; n. plur. as subst., *things permitted*: Tac.

līchēn -ēnis, m. (λειχήν). (1) *moss* or *lichen*: Plin. (2) *ringworm*: Plin., Mart.

Lĭcinĭus -a -um, *name of a Roman gens. Its most famous members were*: (1) L. Licinius

Crassus, *an orator,* 140–91 B.C. (2) M. Licinius Crassus, *the triumvir, killed at Carrhae in* 53 B.C.

lĭcĭtātĭo -ōnis, f. (licitor), *a bidding at a sale or auction*: Cic., Suet.

lĭcĭtor -ari, dep. (liceor), *to bid for*: Pl.

lĭcĭtus -a -um, partic. from licet; q.v.

lĭcĭum -i, n. *the thrum or end of thread left unwoven at the end of the warp;* alternatively perhaps *a leash,* used in dividing the warp for the passage of the shuttle: telae licia addere, Verg.; in gen., *a thread*: Verg., Ov.

lictor -ōris, m. *a lictor, one of the public attendants of the principal Roman magistrates, who bore before them the fasces as emblem of their criminal jurisdiction, and executed the sentences which they pronounced*: Pl., Cic., Liv.

lĭen -ēnis, m. *the milt* or *spleen*: Pl.

lĭēnōsus -a -um (lien), *splenetic*: Pl.

lĭgāmen -ĭnis, n. (¹ligo), *a string, tie, bandage*: Prop., Ov.

lĭgāmentum -i, n. (¹ligo), *a bandage*: Tac.

Lĭgārĭus -a -um, *the name of a Roman gens. Its most famous member was* Q. Ligarius, *a member of the Pompeian party, banished by Caesar, afterwards pardoned, defended by Cicero.*

¶ Hence adj. **Lĭgārĭānus** -a -um, *relating to Ligarius*: oratio, Cic.; or simply Ligariana -ae, f. *Cicero's speech on behalf of Ligarius*: Cic.

Lĭgēa -ae, f. (*Λίγεια*), *name of a wood-nymph*: Verg.

Lĭgĕr -gĕris, m. *a river on the borders of Aquitania and Gallia Lugdunensis* (now the *Loire*): Caes.

lignārĭus -i, m. (lignum), *a carpenter*: inter lignarios, *in the carpenters' quarter,* Liv.

lignātĭo -ōnis, f. (lignor), *a felling of timber, getting of wood*: Caes.

lignātor -ōris, m. (lignor), *a wood-cutter*: Caes.

lignĕŏlus -a -um (dim. of ligneus), *wooden*: Cic. L.

lignĕus -a -um (lignum), *made of wood, wooden*: ponticulus, Cic.; Pl., Caes. TRANSF., *like wood, dry*: coniux, Cat.

lignor -ari, dep. (lignum), *to fetch* or *get wood*: lignari pabularique, Caes.; Pl., Liv.

lignum -i, n. (¹lego), *wood,* esp. plur., *firewood* (opp. materia, *wood used for building*). LIT., ignem ex lignis viridibus in loco angusto fieri iubere, Cic.; prov.: in silvam ligna ferre, *to carry coals to Newcastle,* Hor. TRANSF., (1) *timber,* growing or as material: Verg., Hor. (2) *a writing-table of wood*: Juv.

¹lĭgo -are, *to bind, tie.* LIT., physically: aliquem vinculo, Tac.; manus post terga, Ov.; pisces in glacie ligati, *frozen fast,* Ov.; vulnera veste, *to bind up, bandage,* Ov.; mulam, *to harness,* Hor. TRANSF., *to bind together, connect, unite*: dissociata locis concordi pace ligavit, Ov.; pacta, Prop.

²lĭgo -ōnis, m. *a mattock*: Hor., Ov. TRANSF., *tillage*: Juv.

lĭgŭla (**lingŭla**) -ae, f. (dim. from root of lingo), *a little tongue;* hence (1) *a tongue of land, promontory*: Caes. (2) *a shoe-strap*: Juv.

Lĭgŭrēs -um, m. pl. *the Ligurians, a people living along the north-west coast of Italy;* in sing. **Lĭgŭs** (**Lĭgŭr**) -gŭris, subst. and adj. *a Ligurian, Ligurian.*

¶ Hence **Lĭgŭrĭa** -ae, f. *the country of the Ligures*; adj. **Lĭgustĭcus** -a -um and **Lĭgustīnus** -a -um, *Ligurian.*

lĭgūrĭo (**lĭgurrĭo**) -ire (lingo), *to lick, lick up*: ius, Hor. TRANSF., (1) *to feed upon, gloat over*: furta, Hor. (2) *to lust after, long for*: lucra, Cic.

lĭgūrītĭo (**lĭgurrītĭo**) -ōnis, f. (ligurio), *daintiness*: Cic.

Lĭgus -gŭris, m., *see* Ligures.

lĭgustrum -i, n. *privet*: Verg., Ov.

līlĭum -i, n. (cf. *λείριον*), *a lily.* LIT., Verg., Hor. TRANSF., milit. t. t., *a kind of fortification consisting of pits with stakes in them*: Caes.

Lĭlўbaeōn (**-baeum**) -i, n. (*Λιλύβαιον*), *a promontory and town at the western end of Sicily.* Adj. **Lĭlўbaeus** -a -um, and **Lĭlўbēĭus** -a -um, and **Lĭlўbaetānus** -a -um, *Lilybaean.*

līma -ae, f. (cf. ²levis), *a file*: Pl. TRANSF., limae labor, Hor., *polishing, revision of a composition;* so: defuit et scriptis ultima lima meis, Ov.

līmātŭlus -a -um (dim. of limatus; *see* limo), *rather polished, refined*: opus est huc limatulo et polito tuo iudicio, Cic. L.

līmātus -a -um, partic. from limo; q.v.

līmax -acis, c. *a slug, snail*: Plin.

limbōlārĭus -i, m. (limbus), *a fringe-maker*: Pl.

limbus -i, m. *a border, hem, fringe*: Verg., Ov.

līmen -ĭnis, n. (perhaps connected with ¹limus), *threshold* (strictly, limen inferum= *threshold,* limen superum=*lintel*). LIT., Caes., Verg., etc. TRANSF., (1) *doorway, entrance*: intrare limen, Cic.; Pl., Liv., Verg. (2) *home, house, dwelling*: limine pelli, Verg. (3) *the entrance* or *border of any place*: in limine portus, Verg.; extra limen Apuliae, Hor.; esp. *the starting-point in a race-course*: limen relinquunt, Verg. (4) abstr., *outset, beginning*: belli, Tac.; Lucr.

līmes -itis, m. (¹limus), *a cross path* or *by-way.* LIT., in gen., *a path*: acclivis, Ov.; transversus, Liv.; solitus limes fluminis, *river-bed,* Ov.; esp. *a boundary-path, a boundary-line*: partiri limite campum, Verg.; *a fortified boundary-line*: Tac.

TRANSF., (1) *a course, path, track;* of a comet: Verg.; sectus, *the Zodiac,* Ov.; quasi limes ad caeli aditum patet, Cic. (2) *distinction, difference*: iudicium brevi limite falle tuum, Ov.; Quint.

Limnātis -tidis, f. (*Λιμνᾶτις,* of marshes), *a name of Diana.*

līmo -are (lima), *to file.* LIT., gemmas, Plin.; limare caput, i.e. *to kiss hard,* Pl. TRANSF., (1) *of compositions,* etc., *to polish, finish*: quaedam institui, quae limantur a me politius, Cic. (2) *to investigate accurately*: veritatem, Cic. (3) *to file down, pare down, to diminish*: alteri adfinxit, de altero limavit, Cic.; mea commoda, Hor.

¶ Hence partic. (with compar.) **līmātus** -a -um, *refined, elegant*: vir oratione maxime limatus, Cic.; Hor.

¶ Compar. adv. **līmātĭus,** *more elegantly*: Cic.

līmōsus -a -um (¹limus), *slimy, miry, muddy*: lacus, Verg.; Ov.; iuncus, *growing in mud,* Verg.

limpĭdus -a -um, *clear, limpid*: lacus, Cat.

līmŭlus -a -um (dim. of ¹limus), *squinting*: Pl.

¹līmus -a -um (connected with obliquus), of the eyes, *sidelong, looking sideways*: ocelli, Ov.; Pl., Ter., Quint.

²līmus -i, m. (connected with λίμνη), *slime, mud, mire, filth*: Pl., Verg., Hor., Liv. Transf., malorum, Ov.

³līmus -i, m. *an apron trimmed with purple, worn by a priest when offering sacrifice*: Verg.

linctus, partic. from lingo; q.v.

līnĕa -ae, f. (linum), *a linen thread, string.* Lit., Plin.; linea dives, *a string of pearls*, Mart.; esp. (**1**) *a fishing-line*: Mart. (**2**) *a carpenter's plumb-line*: lineā discere uti, Cic. L.; hence: ad lineam, *perpendicularly*, Cic.; rectis lineis, Caes.
Transf., *a line drawn.* (**1**) *a geometrical line*: Quint. (**2**) *a boundary-line*: si quidem est peccare tanquam transire lineas, Cic.; mors ultima linea rerum est, *the final goal*, Hor.

līnĕāmentum -i, n. (linea), *a line drawn with pen* or *pencil.* Lit., in geometria lineamenta, Cic. Transf., (**1**) plur., *drawing, sketch, outline*: tu operum lineamenta sollertissime perspicis, Cic. (**2**) *a feature, lineament*: corporis, Cic.; also abstr.: animi, Cic.

līnĕo -are (linea), *to make straight*: Pl.

līnĕus -a -um (linum), *made of flax* or *linen, linen*: vincula, Verg.

lingo lingĕre linxi linctum (cf. λείχω), *to lick*: Cat.

Lingŏnes -um, m. pl., *a people in Gaul*, whence the modern *Langres*.

lingua -ae, f. *a tongue.*
Lit., linguam ab inrisu exserere, Liv.; linguam eicere, Cic.; Ov., etc.
Transf., (**1**) in gen., *speech, language*: linguam diligentissime continere, *to restrain*, Cic.; Aetolorum linguas retundere, *to silence*, Liv.; est animus tibi, sunt mores et lingua fidesque, Hor.; in a bad sense, *loquacity*: poenam lingua commeruisse, Ov.; Verg.; poet., of the sounds of animals: linguae volucrum, Verg. (**2**) *a particular language, tongue*: Latina, Graeca, Cic.; Gallica, Caes.; utraque lingua, *Greek and Latin*, Hor. (**3**) of tongue-shaped objects; esp. *a tongue of land, promontory*: Liv.; tribus haec (Sicilia) excurrit in aequora linguis, Ov.

lingŭlāca -ae, f. (lingula, ligula), *a chatterbox*: Pl.

līnĭgĕr -gĕra -gĕrum (linum/gero), *clothed in linen*, applied to Isis and her priests: Ov.

līno linĕre līvi and lēvi lĭtum, *to smear one thing upon another*, or *to besmear, daub one thing with another.*
Lit., medicamenta per corpora, Ov.; spiramenta cerā, Verg.; ferrum pice, Liv.; esp. *to rub over what has been written on waxen tablets*: digna lini, *worthy of being erased*, Ov.
Transf., (**1**) *to cover*: tecta auro, Ov. (**2**) *to befoul, dirty*: splendida facta carmine foedo, Hor.

linquo linquĕre līqui (cf. λείπω), *to leave, abandon, forsake, depart from*: urbem, Cic.; vitam, Pl.; dulces animas, Verg.; linqui, *to faint*, Ov.; linque severa, Hor.; nil intem tatum nostri liquere poetae, Hor.

lintĕātus -a -um (linteum), *clothed in linen*: legio, *a Samnite legion, so called from the canvas covering of the place where they took the military oath*: Liv.

lintĕo -onis, m. (linteum), *a linen-weaver*: Pl.

lintĕŏlum -i, n. (dim. of linteum), *a small linen cloth*: Pl.

linter -tris, f. (**1**) *a boat, skiff, wherry*: Caes., Cic., Liv., Ov. (**2**) *a trough, tub, vat*: Verg., Tib.

lintĕus -a -um (linum), *linen, made of linen*: vestis, Cic.; libri, *written on linen*, Liv. N. as subst. **lintĕum** -i, *linen cloth, linen*: Pl.; esp. *a sail*: dare lintea ventis, Ov.; Verg., Hor.

lintrĭcŭlus -i, m. (dim. of linter), *a small boat*: Cic. L.

līnum -i, n. (λίνον), *flax.* Lit., Verg. Transf., (**1**) *linen*: linum tenuissimum, Cic., Hor. (**2**) *a thread, line*; esp. *the thread with which letters were tied up*: nos linum incĭdimus legimus, Cic. (**3**) *a fishing-line*: Ov. (**4**) *a rope, cable*: Ov. (**5**) *a net for hunting* or *fishing*: Ov., Verg.

Līnus (-ŏs) -i, m. (Λίνος), *Linus, son of Apollo and the Muse Terpsichore, celebrated singer and poet, the teacher of Orpheus and Hercules; Hercules killed him with a blow of the lyre.*

Lĭpăra -ae, f. and **Lĭpărē** -ēs, f. (Λιπάρα), *the largest of the Aeolian islands, north of Sicily* (now *Lipari*); plur. **Lĭpărae** -arum, f. *the Aeolian islands.* Adj. **Lĭpăraeus** -a -um and **Lĭpărensis** -e, *Liparean.*

lippĭo -ire, *to have sore eyes, be blear-eyed*: cum leviter lippirem, Cic. L.; Pl.

lippĭtūdo -inis, f. (lippus), *inflammation in the eyes*: Pl., Cic.

lippus -a -um, *having inflamed* or *watery eyes, blear-eyed*: Pl., Hor. Transf., *half-blind*: Juv.; *mentally blind*: Hor.

lĭquĕfăcĭo -făcĕre -fēci -factum, pass. **lĭquĕfīo** -fĭĕri -factus sum, *to melt, dissolve, make liquid.* Lit., glacies liquefacta, Cic.; Verg., Suet. Transf., (**1**) *to decompose*: viscera liquefacta, Verg.; Ov. (**2**) *to make weak, enervate*: aliquem languidus voluptatibus, Cic.; Ov.

lĭquesco liquescĕre lĭcŭi (liquet), *to become fluid, to melt.*
Lit., cera liquescit, Verg.; Liv.
Transf., (**1**) *to putrefy*: liquescunt corpora, Ov. (**2**) *to become effeminate*: voluptate, Cic. (**3**) *to melt* or *waste away*: liquescit fortuna, Ov.

lĭquet liquēre licuit, originally of liquids, as in pres. partic., liquens (see below), but the classical sense of the finite verb is *it is clear, evident, apparent*: dixit sibi liquere, Cic.; with acc. and infin.: cui neutrum licuerit, nec esse deos nec non esse, Cic.; Liv.; with indir. quest.: Liv., Plin. L. Legal t. t.: non liquet, *not proven*, used by a jury refusing a definite verdict, Cic., Quint.
¶ Hence partic. **līquens** -entis, *fluid liquid*: vina, Verg.; campi, *the sea*, Verg.

lĭquĭdus -a -um (sometimes līquĭdus in Lucr.) (from liquet).
(**1**) *fluid, flowing, liquid.* Lit., odores, Hor.; Nymphae, *nymphs of springs*, Ov. N. as subst. **līquĭdum** -i, *a liquid*: Lucr., Hor., Ov. Transf., genus sermonis, Cic.

(2) *clear, bright, serene.* LIT., fontes, aer, Verg.; color, Hor. TRANSF., **(1)** *calm, pure, clear*: liquida voluptas et libera, Cic.; mens, Cat. **(2)** of sound, *clear, liquid*: vox, voces, Lucr., Verg., Hor. **(3)** *evident, certain*: Pl. N. as subst. **lĭquĭdum** -i, *certainty*: Liv.; abl. sing. as adv. **lĭquĭdo,** *clearly, plainly*: dicere, Cic.

Adv. (with compar.) **lĭquĭdē,** *clearly, plainly*: Cic.

lĭquo -are. **(1)** *to make liquid, melt, liquefy*: Plin. **(2)** *to strain, clarify*: vinum, Hor. TRANSF., Quint.

¹lĭquor -i, dep. (liquet), *to be fluid, flow, melt*: toto corpore sudor liquitur, Verg. TRANSF., *to melt away, pass away*: in partem peiorem liquitur aetas, Lucr.

¶ Hence partic. **lĭquens** -entis, *flowing*: Verg.

²lĭquor -ōris, m. (liquet), *liquidity, fluidity.* LIT., Lucr., Cic. TRANSF., *a liquid, fluid, liquor*: perlucidi amnium liquores, Cic.; Lucr., Verg., Ov.; absol., *the sea*: Hor.

Līris -is, m. (Λεῖρις), *a river of Latium* (now the *Garigliano*).

līs (old form, stlis), lītis, f.

LIT., *a legal controversy, an action, suit*: litem alicui intendere, in aliquem inferre, *to bring an action against,* Cic.; litem habere cum aliquo, Cic.; litem suam facere, said of an advocate who neglects his client's business to defend himself, Cic.; Verg., Hor.

TRANSF., **(1)** *the subject* or *cause of a suit*: litem in rem suam vertere, Liv.; Caes., Cic. **(2)** in gen., *contention, strife, controversy, quarrel*: aetatem in litibus conterere, Cic.; componere, *to settle,* Verg.; sub iudice lis est, Hor.; Pl., Liv., Ov.

Lītāna silva -ae, f. *a forest in Cisalpine Gaul.*

lītātĭo -ōnis, f. (lito), *a successful sacrifice*: hostiae maiores sine litatione caesae, Liv.

Līternum -i, n. *a town in Campania.* Adj. **Līternus** -a -um and **Līternīnus** -a -um, *Liternian*; n. as subst., **Līternīnum** -i, *an estate near Liternum*: Liv.

lītĭgātor -ōris, m. (litigo), *a party in a law-suit, litigant*: Quint., Tac.

lītĭgĭōsus -a -um (litigium), *full of strife, contentious.* **(1)** of persons, *fond of dispute, litigious*: homo minime litigiosus, Cic. **(2)** of things, *full of dispute, quarrelsome*: disputatio, Cic.; of a place: forum, Ov.; also, *contested at law*: praediolum, Cic.

lītĭgĭum -i, n. (litigo), *a quarrel, contention*: Pl.

lītĭgo -are (lis/ago). **(1)** *to go to law*: noli pati fratres litigare, Cic. **(2)** in gen., *to quarrel, dispute, brawl*: acerrime cum aliquo pro aliquo, Cic. L.

līto -are. **(1)** intransit., *to bring an acceptable offering and so to obtain favourable omens*: Pl., Liv.; with dat. of the deity: alicui deo, Cic.; with abl. of the sacrifice: proximā hostiā litatur saepe pulcherrime, Cic.; Verg., Tac.; non auspicato nec litato aciem instruunt, *without having offered an auspicious sacrifice,* Liv.; fig.: litemus Lentulo, *let us appease,* Cic. **(2)** transit., *to sacrifice successfully*: sacris litatis, Verg.; sacra bove, Ov.

lītŏrālis -e (litus), *of the shore*: dii, *gods of the shore,* Cat.

lītŏrĕus -a -um (litus), *of the shore*: aves, Verg.; harena, Ov.

littĕra (**lītĕra**) -ae, f.

LIT., *a letter of the alphabet*: litterarum notae, Cic.; litteras discere, Cic.; scire, Pl. homo trium litterarum=fur, *a thief,* Pl.; tristis (C), used in court for Condemno; salutaris (A), for Absolvo, Cic.; ad me litteram nunquam misit, *not a line,* Cic. litteris parcere, *to be sparing with paper,* Cic. *an epitaph*: Ov.

TRANSF., **(1)** usually plur., poet. also sing. *a letter, dispatch, epistle*: dare alicui littera ad aliquem, *to give a messenger a letter to deliver to a person,* Cic.; signare, Cic. resignare, Pl.; Mycenaeā littera facta manu, Ov. **(2)** plur., *written records, documents, deeds,* etc.: parvae et rarae per eadem tempora litterae fuere, Liv. **(3)** *literature, letters, scholarship*: litteris omnibus a pueritia deditus, Cic.; litteris tinctus, Cic. Graecis litteris studere, Cic.; esp. of *history*: Liv.

littĕrārĭus -a -um (littera), *relating to reading and writing*: ludus, Quint., Tac.

littĕrātor -ōris, m. (littera), *a philologist, grammarian, critic*: Cat.

littĕrātūra -ae, f. (littera). **(1)** *a writing composed of letters, the alphabet*: Tac. **(2)** *grammar*: Sen. L., Quint.

littĕrātus -a -um (littera), adj. (with compar. and superl.), *lettered.* **(1)** *inscribed with letters*: servus, *branded,* Pl. **(2)** *learned, liberally educated*: Canius nec infacetus e satis litteratus, Cic. TRANSF., otium, *learned leisure,* Cic.

¶ Adv. (with compar.) **littĕrātē.** **(1)** *in clear letters, legibly*: litterate et scite per scriptae rationes, Cic. **(2)** *literally, word for word*: respondere, Cic. **(3)** *learnedly*: dicta, Cic.

littĕrŭla -ae, f. (dim. of littera). **(1)** *a letter (of the alphabet) written small*: litterulae minutae, Cic. L. **(2)** plur., *a little letter, note*: Cic. L. **(3)** *a smattering of literature*: Hor.

littus, etc., *see* litus, etc.

lĭtūra -ae, f. (lino), *the smearing of a waxed tablet to erase what has been written, an erasure, correction*: flagitiosa litura tabularum Cic.; Hor. TRANSF., **(1)** *a passage erased*: nomen esse in litura, Cic. **(2)** *a blot*: Prop. Ov. **(3)** *a wrinkle*: Mart.

lītus -tŏris, n. **(1)** *the sea-shore, beach, strand coast*: litus insulae, Cic.; naves agere in litus Liv.; Verg., etc.; prov.: litus arare, *to plough the shore, to labour in vain,* Ov.; in litu harenas fundere, *to carry coals to Newcastle* Ov. **(2)** *the shore of a lake* or *river*: Cic. Cat., Verg., Ov.

lĭtŭus -i, m. **(1)** *the curved staff* or *wand of an augur*: Cic., Verg., Liv. **(2)** *a curved cavalry trumpet, clarion*: Verg., Hor. TRANSF., *signal*: Cic. L.

līvĕo -ēre, *to be of a bluish colour.* LIT., Prop. Ov. TRANSF., *to be envious, to envy*: with dat.: Mart., Tac.

¶ Hence partic. **līvens** -entis, *bluish* plumbum, Verg.; crura compedibus, *livid black and blue,* Ov. TRANSF., *envious* Mart.

līvesco -ĕre (liveo), *to become bluish, grow livid* Lucr.

līvĭdŭlus -a -um (dim. of lividus), *somewhat envious*: Juv.

līvĭdus -a -um (liveo), *bluish, leaden-coloured.* LIT., racemi, Hor.; vada (of the Styx), Verg.; esp. from blows, *livid, black and blue*: bracchia, Hor.; ora, Ov. TRANSF., *envious, spiteful*: differ opus, livida lingua, tuum, Ov.; obliviones, Hor.; Cic.

Līvĭus -a -um, *name of a Roman gens. Its most famous members were*: M. Livius Andronicus, *a freedman and Roman tragic poet, who died in* 204 B.C.; *and* T. Livius Patavinus, *the Roman historian, born* 59 B.C., *died* A.D. 16. ¶ Adj. **Līvĭus** -a -um, *Livian*: lex, Cic.; also **Līvĭānus** -a -um, *Livian*: fabulae, *of Livius Andronicus*, Cic.; exercitus, *of the consul M. Livius*, Liv.

līvor -ōris, m. (liveo). LIT., *a bluish colour, livid spot on the body*: niger livor in pectore, Ov.; Pl., Quint. TRANSF., *envy, spite*: ap. Cic. L., Ov., Tac.

lixa -ae, m. *a sutler*: Liv., Tac. TRANSF., in plur., *camp-followers of every kind*: Sall., Quint.

lŏcātĭo -ōnis, f. (loco), *a placing*; hence (1) *an arrangement*: Quint. (2) *a leasing*: Liv.; also, *a contract of letting and hiring, a lease*: Cic.

lŏcātōrĭus -a -um (loco), *concerned with leases*: Cic. L.

lŏcĭto -are (freq. of loco), *to let out to hire*: Ter.

lŏco -are (locassint for locaverint, Cic.; from locus), *to place, lay, put, set.*
In gen. LIT., castra, Cic.; milites super vallum, Sall.; fundamenta urbis, Verg., Tac. TRANSF., *to place*: homines in amplissimo gradu dignitatis, Cic.
Esp. (1) *to give in marriage, bestow in marriage*: virginem in matrimonium, Pl.; virginem alicui, Pl.; Cic., Tac. (2) in commerce: **a**, *to let out on hire, to farm out, lease, invest*: vectigalia, portorium, fundum, Cic.; agrum fruendum, Liv.; agrum frumento, Liv.; se, operam suam, *to hire out one's services*, Pl.; fig.: beneficia apud gratos, Liv.: **b**, *to contract for* work to be done: statuam faciendam, Cic.
¶ Hence from partic. locatus -a -um, n. as subst. **lŏcātum** -i, *a lease, leasing, contract*: Cic.

lŏcŭlus -i, m. (dim. of locus), *a little place*: Pl. Esp. (1) *a coffin*: Plin. (2) plur., loculi, *a money-box*: nummum in loculos demittere, Hor. (3) phrase, *a school satchel*: Hor.

lŏcŭplēs -plētis (locus/*pleo; abl. sing., locupletī or locupletē; genit. plur., locupletium, Cic.; locupletum, Caes.), adj. (with compar. and superl.), *possessing large landed property*: Cic. Hence, in gen., *rich, wealthy, opulent.* LIT., mulier copiosa plane et locuples, Cic.; urbes, Caes.; with abl., *rich in*: copiis rei familiaris locupletes et pecuniosi, Cic.; annus locuples frugibus, Hor. TRANSF., (1) fig., *rich*: Lysias oratione locuples, Cic. (2) *trusty, sufficient, satisfactory*: auctor, testis, Cic.; tabellarius, Cic. L.; reus, Liv., Tac.

lŏcŭplēto -are (locuples), *to enrich*: homines fortunis, Cic.; templum picturis, Cic.; sapientem locupletat ipsa natura, Cic.; Liv.

lŏcus -i, m. (plur., loci, *single places*; loca, *places connected with one another, neighbourhood, region*). LIT., in space; in gen.: omnes copias in unum locum convenire, Cic.; Caes., Liv.,

etc.; ex (*or* de) loco superiore agere, of a speaker from the *rostra*, or of a judge who gives judgment from the bench: ex aequo loco, of a speaker in the senate, Cic.; ex inferiore loco, from the body of a court, Cic. Esp. (1) milit. t. t., *position, place, ground, post*: locum tenere, relinquere, Caes.; Sall., Verg., Liv. (2) *a seat* or *place* at a gathering: Pl., Cic., Liv. (3) n. pl., loca, *neighbourhood, region*: ea loca incolere, Caes.; Cic., Verg., Liv.
TRANSF., (1) in time: **a**, *a period*, usually in partitive genit.: ad id locorum, *till then*, Sall., Liv.; interea loci, Ter.: **b**, *a moment, the moment*: nec vero hic locus est, ut multa dicantur, Cic.; dulce est desipere in loco, *in the right place*, Hor. (2) in other relations: **a**, *position, condition, situation*: meliore loco erant res nostrae, Cic.; parentis loco, Cic.; hostium, Liv.; quo res summa loco? Verg.; in partitive genit.: eo loci, quo loci, Cic.: **b**, *position, rank, place in order of succession*: secundo loco, *secondly*, Cic.; loco dicere, *in his turn*, Cic.; esse ex equestri loco, Cic.; infimo loco natus, Cic.; Caes., Liv.: **c**, *occasion, cause*: dare suspicioni locum, Cic.: **d**, *passage* or *place in a book*: aliquot locis significavit, Cic.; Hor.: **e**, *ground of argument* or *topic*: Cic., Quint.

¹lŏcusta -ae, f. (1) *a locust*: locustarum examina, Liv.; Pl. (2) *a kind of lobster, crayfish*, or *crab*: Plin.

²Lŏcusta -ae, f. *a woman in Rome, notorious for her skill in poisoning; contemporary and accomplice of Nero.*

lŏcūtĭo -ōnis, f. (loquor). (1) *speaking, speech*: Cic. (2) *pronunciation*: Cic.

lōdix -dīcis, f. *a blanket, rug, counterpane*: Juv.

lŏgĭcus -a -um (λογικός), *logical*; n. pl. as subst. **lŏgĭca** -ōrum, *logic*: Cic.

lŏgos (-us) -i, m. (λόγος), *a word*: Pl.; esp. (1) plur., *mere words*: Pl., Ter. (2) *a joke, jest, bon mot*: Pl., Cic.

lōlīgo, see lolligo.

lōlĭum -i, n. *darnel*: Pl., Verg., Ov.

lollīgo -gĭnis, f. *a cuttle-fish*: Cic., Hor.

lollīguncŭla -ae, f. (dim. of lolligo), *a little cuttle-fish*: Pl.

Lollius -a -um, *name of a Roman gens*; hence adj. **Lolliānus** -a -um, *Lollian*.

lōmentum -i, n. (lavo), *face-cream, made of bean-meal and rice*: Mart. TRANSF., *a means of cleansing*: ap. Cic. L.

Londinium -i, n. *London.*

longaevus -a -um (longus/aevum), *aged, old*: parens, Verg.; manus, Ov.

longē, adv. from longus; q.v.

longinquĭtās -ātis, f. (longinquus). LIT., of space. (1) *length*: itineris, Tac. (2) *distance, remoteness*: Cic. L., Tac. TRANSF., of time, *length, duration*: temporum, Cic.; morbi, Cic.; bellorum, Liv.

longinquus -a -um (longus), adj. (with compar.), *long.*
LIT., of space. (1) *long*: Plin. (2) *distant, far, remote*: hostis, Cic.; Lacedaemon, Cic.; e (ex) longinquo, *from a distance*, Liv., Tac. (3) *living at a distance, foreign*: homo alienigena et longinquus, Cic.; Ov.; m. as subst.: Cic.
TRANSF., of time. (1) *long in duration, long*: observatio, Cic.; Pl., Liv. (2) *distant*:

in longinquum tempus aliquid differre, Cic.;
Liv., Tac.
longĭtĕr, adv. from longus; q.v.: Lucr.
longĭtūdo -inis, f. (longus), *length*. LIT., in
space: itineris, Cic.; Caes. TRANSF., in
time: noctis, orationis, Cic.; Quint.
longĭuscŭlus -a -um (dim. of compar.
longior), *somewhat long*: versus, Cic.
Longŭla -ae, f. *a Volscian city near Corioli*.
longŭlus -a -um (dim. of longus), *somewhat
long*: iter, Cic. L. Adv. **longŭlē**, *somewhat
far, at a little distance*: ex hoc loco, Pl.; Ter.
longŭrĭus -i, m. (longus), *a long pole, rod,
rail*: Caes.
longus -a -um, adj. (with compar. and superl.),
long.
LIT., in space; of things: epistula, Cic. L.;
spatium, Caes.; navis, *a man-of-war*, Caes.;
with acc. of extent: ratis longa pedes centum,
Liv.; of persons: longus homo est, Cat.;
poet., *vast, spacious*: freta, Ov.; pontus, Hor.
TRANSF., in time; in gen., *long, of long
duration*: horae quibus expectabam longae
videbantur, Cic.; longa mora, Caes.; morbus,
caedes, Liv.; with acc. of extent: mensis
XLV dies longus, Cic.; n. as subst. in
phrases: in longum, *for a long time*, Verg.,
Liv.; ex longo, *for a long time back*, Verg.;
of syllables, *pronounced long*: Cic., Quint.;
esp. *too long, tedious*: longum est dicere,
it is tedious to relate, Cic.; ne longum sit, ne
longum faciam, *to cut a long story short*, Cic.;
Hor.; of persons, *prolix, tedious*: nolo esse
longus, Cic.
¶ Adv. (with compar. and superl.) **longē**,
a long way off, far, at a distance.
LIT., in space: longe absum, Cic.; longe
videre, Cic.; discedere, Cic.; longe lateque,
far and wide, Cic.; Caes., Verg., etc.
TRANSF., (1) in time: longe prospicere,
Cic.; Pl., Hor.; so of speaking *at length*: haec
dixi longius, Cic. (2) of metaphorical
distance: longissime abesse a vero, Cic.;
ab aliquo longe abesse, *to be of no help to*,
Caes., Verg.; tam longe repetita principia,
far-fetched, Cic. (3) of degrees of difference,
esp. (with compar. and superl.), *by far*: longe
melior, Verg.; longe maximus, Cic.; longe
aliud, Liv.; longe dissimilis contentio, Cic.
¶ Adv. **longĭtĕr**, *far*: ab leto errare, Lucr.
lŏquācĭtās -ātis, f. (loquax), *talkativeness,
loquacity*: mea, Cic.; Liv.
¶ Adv. **lŏquācĭtĕr**, *loquaciously, talkatively*: respondere, Cic.; Hor.
lŏquācŭlus -a -um (dim. of loquax), *somewhat
talkative*: Lucr.
lŏquax -quācis (loquor), adj. (with compar.
and superl.), *talkative, garrulous, loquacious.*
LIT., of persons: homo omnium loqua-
cissimus, Cic. TRANSF., of animals: ranae,
croaking, Verg.; of things: nidus, *full of
nestlings*, Verg.; stagna, *full of frogs*, Verg.;
lymphae, *babbling*, Hor.; epistula, *gossiping*,
Cic.; vultus, *expressive*, Ov.
lŏquella (**lŏquēla**) -ae, f. (loquor), *speech,
discourse*: fundit has ore loquellas, Verg.; Pl.,
Lucr. TRANSF., *a language*: Graia, Ov.
lŏquĭtor -ari, dep. (freq. of loquor), *to chatter*:
Pl.
loquor lŏqui lŏcūtus sum, dep. *to speak*, esp.
in ordinary conversation.
(1) intransit. LIT., bene loqui de aliqua

re, de aliquo, Cic.; cum aliquo, Cic.; p
aliquo (either=*in defence of* or *in the na*
of someone), Cic.; apud (*before*) alique
Cic.; pure et Latine, Cic. TRANSF., a,
material things, esp. trees, *to rustle*: Ca
Verg.: **b**, of abstr. things, *to indicate*:
consuetudo loquitur, Cic.; Ov.
(2) transit.: **a**, *to say*: quid loquar
militari ratione, Cic.; Pl., Liv.; with acc. a
infin.: Cic. L., Verg., Liv.: **b**, *to talk* .
speak of, tell of: classes, Cic.; proelia, Ho
urbes, Liv.
lōrārĭus -i, m. (lorum), *a flogger*: Pl.
lōrātus -a -um (lorum), *bound with thong*
Verg.
lōrĕus -a -um (lorum), *made of thongs*: Pl.
lōrīca -ae, f. (lorum), *a leather cuirass, corsele*
Cic., Verg.; also *a metal breastplate*: libr
mutare loricis, *to exchange study for w*
Hor. TRANSF., as milit. t. t., *a breastwor*
parapet: Caes., Tac.
lōrīcātus -a -um (lorica), *equipped with*
cuirass: Liv., Quint.
lōrīpēs -pĕdis (lorum/pes), *bandy-legged*: F
Juv.
lōrum -i, n. *a strap* or *thong of leather.*
LIT., cum apparitor Postumium la
vinciret, 'Quin tu', inquit, 'adducis lorum
Liv.; Pl., Hor.
TRANSF., (1) plur., *reins, bridle*: lo
ducere equos, Liv.; lora dare, *to relax t*
reins, Verg.; Ov. (2) *a scourge, whip*: lo
uri, Hor.; loris caedere aliquem, Cic.;
(3) *a leather bulla* (see bulla): Juv.
Lōtŏphăgi -orum, m. (Λωτοφάγοι), myth., *
Lotus-eaters, a people in Africa.
lōtŏs (**-us**) -i, f. (λωτός), *the name of seve*
plants: Verg., Plin.; esp. *of a tree growing*
North Africa, said to have been the food of t
Lotus-eaters.
TRANSF., (1) *the fruit of the lotus*: C
(2) *a flute made of the lotus-tree wood*: Ov.
¹**lōtus** -a -um, partic. from lavo; q.v.
²**lōtus** -i, f.=lotos; q.v.
Lŭa -ae, f. *a goddess to whom arms captured*
war were dedicated.
lŭbet, lubido, etc.=libet, libido, etc.; q.v.
lŭbrĭco -are (lubricus), *to make smooth*
slippery: Juv.
lŭbrĭcus -a -um, *slippery, smooth.*
LIT., glacies, Liv.; Pl.; n. as subs
lubricum -i, *a slippery place*: Verg., Tac.
TRANSF., (1) *smooth, slimy*; hence, *quic*
moving: oculos, Cic.; anguis, Verg.; amn
Hor.; annus, *quickly passing, fleeting*, C
(2) *deceitful*: Verg. (3) *uncertain, insecu*
perilous: aetas puerilis maxime lubrica atc
incerta, Cic.; lubrica defensionis ratio, Ci
poet. with infin.: vultus nimium lubric
aspici, *dangerous to look at*, Hor.; n. as subs
in lubrico versari, Cic.; lubricum adu
scentiae, *the slippery paths of youth*, Tac.
¹**Lūca** -ae, f. *town in Etruria* (now *Lucca*).
¶ Hence adj. **Lūcensis** -e, *of Luca.*
²**Lūca**, see Lucani.
Lūcāni -ōrum, m. pl. *a people in southe*
Italy; meton.=*the country of the Lucar*
Caes.; sing., Lucanus, coll.: Liv.
¶ Hence adj. **Lūcānus** -a -um, *Lucania*
subst. **Lūcānĭa** -ae, f. *the country of t*
Lucani; adj. **Lūcānĭcus** -a -um, *Lucania*
f. as subst. **Lūcānĭca** -ae, *a kind of sausa*

Cic.; phrase **Lūca bōs**, *a Lucanian cow*, i.e. *an elephant*, because the Romans first saw elephants in Lucania, with the army of Pyrrhus: Enn., Lucr.

¹Lūcānus -a -um, *see* Lucani.

²Lūcānus -i, m., **M. Annaeus**, *a poet, native of Corduba in Spain, and author of the Pharsalia, put to death by Nero in* A.D. 65.

lūcar -āris, n. (lucus), *a forest-tax*, used for paying actors: Tac.

lūcellum -i, n. (dim. of lucrum), *a little profit, a small gain*: Apronio aliquid lucelli iussi sunt dare, Cic.; Hor.

Lūcensis, *see* ¹Luca.

lūcĕo lucēre luxi (connected with lux), *to be bright, shine, glitter.* LIT., (stella) lucet, Cic.; lucent oculi, Ov.; Pl., Verg.; impers., lucet, *it is light, it is day*: nondum lucebat, *it was not yet light*, Cic., Pl. TRANSF., *to shine forth*: nunc imperii nostri splendor illis gentibus lucet, Cic.; cum res ipsa tot tam claris argumentis luceat, *is made clear*, Cic.; bombyce puella, Prop.

Lūcĕrēs (Lūcĕrēs: Prop.) -um, m. *one of the three tribes into which Romulus was said to have divided the Roman patricians*: Cic., Liv., Ov.

Lūcĕria -ae, f. *a town in Apulia* (now *Lucera*). ¶ Hence adj. **Lūcĕrinus** -a -um, *of Luceria.*

lūcerna -ae, f. (luceo), *a lamp, oil-lamp*: lumen lucernae, Cic.; Pl., Hor., Juv.

lūcesco (lūcisco) lūcescĕre luxi (luceo), *to begin to shine*: novus sol lucescit, Verg.; cras lucescere Nonas, *appear*, Ov.; impers.: lucescit, *it grows light, day is breaking*, Pl., Cic. L., Liv.

lūci, *see* lux.

lūcĭdus -a -um (lux), adj. (with compar.), *full of light, clear, bright.* LIT., aër, Lucr.; sidera, Hor.; n. as internal acc.: lucidum fulgentes oculi, Hor. TRANSF., *clear, lucid*: ordo, Hor.; Quint. ¶ Adv. **lūcĭdē,** *clearly, plainly, lucidly*: definire verbum, Cic.; compar.: Sen.; superl.: Quint.

lūcĭfĕr -fĕra -fĕrum (lux/fero), *light-bearing, light-bringing*: equi, *the horses of the moon*, Ov.; manus (of Lucina), Ov. M. as subst. **Lūcĭfĕr** -fĕri. (1) *Lucifer, the morning star, the planet Venus*: Cic., Ov. (2) myth., *the son of Aurora, and father of Ceyx*, hence: Lucifero genitus (=*Ceyx*), Ov. (3) meton., *a day*: tot Luciferi, Ov.; Prop.

lūcĭfŭgus -a -um (lux/fugio), *shunning the light*: blatta, Verg. TRANSF., homines, Cic.

Lūcīlius -a -um, *name of a Roman gens. Its most famous member was* C. Lucilius, *born at Suessa Aurunca*, 148 B.C., *died* 103 B.C., *founder of Roman satiric poetry.*

Lūcina -ae, f. (lux), *the goddess of births*: Pl., Cat., Verg. TRANSF., *a bearing of children, birth*: Lucinam pati (of the cow), *to calve*, Verg.; Ov.

lūcisco=lucesco; q.v.

Lūcius -i, m. *a common Roman praenomen* (abbreviated to L.).

lucrātīvus -a -um (lucror), *attended with gain, profitable*: Quint.

Lucrētĭlis -is, m. *a mountain in the Sabine country, part of the modern Monte Gennaro.*

Lucrētĭus -a -um, *name of a Roman gens. Its most famous members were* (1) Sp. Lucretius, *successor of L. Junius Brutus in the consulate,* 508 B.C. (2) *his daughter* Lucretia, *who, being ravished by Sextus Tarquinius, stabbed herself, and thereby led to the expulsion of the kings from Rome.* (3) T. Lucretius Carus, *a Roman poet, contemporary of Cicero, author of* De rerum natura.

lucrĭfăcio=lucri facio, *see* lucrum, *to gain, receive as profit*: pecuniam, Cic.; tritici modios centum, Cic.

lucrĭfĭcābĭlis -e, *gainful, profitable*: Pl.

lucrĭfĭcus -a -um (lucrum/facio), *gainful, profitable*: Pl.

lucrĭfŭga -ae, c. (lucrum/fugio), *one who shuns gain*: Pl.

Lucrīnus -i, m. (with or without lacus), *a lake on the coast of Campania, near Baiae.* ¶ Hence adj. **Lucrīnus** -a -um, *Lucrine*: conchylia, Hor. and n. pl. as subst., Mart., *Lucrine oysters*, celebrated for their flavour; also adj. **Lucrīnensis** -e, *Lucrine*: Cic.

lucror -ari, dep. (lucrum), *to get gain, to gain, profit.* LIT., auri pondo decem, Cic.; stipendium, Cic.; Hor., Tac. TRANSF., nomen ab Africā, *to win*, Hor.; lucretur indicia veteris infamiae, *I will make him a present of*, i.e. *I will say nothing about*, Cic.

lucrōsus -a -um (lucrum), *gainful, profitable*: Ov.

lucrum -i, n. (cf. λαύω), *gain, profit, advantage* (opp. damnum). LIT., lucri causā, Cic.; ad praedam lucrumque revocare, *to turn to one's profit*, Cic.; ponere in lucro, *or* in lucris, *to reckon a gain*, Cic.; so: lucro appone, Hor.; lucra facere ex vectigalibus, Cic.; lucri facere, *or* in one word lucrifacere, *to gain*, Pl., Cic.; de lucro vivere, *to have to thank someone else for being alive*, Cic. TRANSF., (1) *love of gain, avarice*: Hor. (2) *lucre, riches*: Ov.

luctāmen -inis, n. (luctor), *effort, exertion, struggling, toil*: Verg.

luctātĭo -ōnis, f. (luctor), *a wrestling*: Cic. TRANSF., *a struggle, contest, dispute*: magna cum aliquo, Cic.; Liv.

luctātor -ōris, m. (luctor), *a wrestler*: Pl., Ov., Sen.

luctĭfĭcus -a -um (luctus/facio), *causing grief, mournful, baleful*: Allecto, Verg.

luctĭsŏnus -a -um (luctus/sono), *sad-sounding*: mugitus, Ov.

luctor -ari, dep. (and **lucto** -are: Pl., Ter.), *to wrestle.* LIT., luctabitur Olympiis Milo, Cic.; fulvā harenā, Verg. TRANSF., in gen., *to struggle, strive, contend.* (1) physically: in arido solo, Liv.; in turba, Hor.; with infin.: telum eripere, Verg.; Ov.; of things struggling: Verg., Hor. (2) mentally: cum aliquo, Cic.; with infin.: Ov.

luctŭōsus -a -um (luctus), adj. (with compar. and superl.), *mournful.* (1) *causing sorrow, lamentable, doleful*: o diem illum reipublicae luctuosum, Cic.; luctuosissimum bellum, Cic. (2) *feeling or expressing sorrow, mourning*: Hesperia, Ov. ¶ Compar. adv. **luctŭōsius,** *more sorrowfully*: Liv.

luctus -ūs, m. (lugeo), *mourning, lamentation,* especially for a bereavement.
  Lit., luctus domesticus, Cic.; luctus publicus, privatus, Liv.; luctum minuere, levare, Cic.; luctum ex aliqua re percipere, haurire, Cic.; plur., *expressions of sorrow*: in maximos luctus incidere, Cic.
  Transf., (1) *mourning apparel, mourning,* or *a period of mourning*: erat in luctu senatus, Cic.; Liv. (2) meton., *the cause of sorrow*: tu . . . luctus eras levior, Ov. (3) personif.: Luctus, *the god of mourning,* Verg.

lūcubrātĭo -ōnis, f. (lucubro), *a working by night* or *lamp-light, nocturnal study*: vix digna lucubratione anicularum, *scarce fit to be told by old wives while spinning at night,* Cic.; plur.: lucubrationes detraxi et meridiationes addidi, Cic. Transf., *that which is produced by lamp-light*: lucubrationem meam perire, Cic. L.

lūcubrātōrĭus -a -um (lucubro), *for night-study*: Suet.

lūcubro -are (connected with lux). (1) intransit., *to work by night*: inter lucubrantes ancillas sedere, Liv. (2) transit., in perf. partic. pass.: **a**, *composed at night*: parvum opusculum, Cic.: **b**, *spent in work*: nox, Mart.

lūcŭlentus -a -um (lux), adj. (with compar. and superl.), *full of light, bright*: caminus, Cic. L. Transf., *brilliant, distinguished, splendid*: femina, dies, facinus, Pl.; forma, Ter.; patrimonium, Cic.; auctor, Cic. L.; oratio, Sall.
  ¶ Adv. **lūcŭlentē** and **lūcŭlentĕr,** *admirably, splendidly*: opus texere, Cic.; scribere, dicere, Cic.

Lūcullus -i, m. *the name of a family of the gens Licinia. The most distinguished of the Luculli was L. Licinius Lucullus, conqueror of Mithridates, notorious for his riches and lavish expenditure.* Adj. **Lūcullēus** -a -um and **Lūcullĭānus** -a -um, *Lucullan.*

lūcŭlus -i, m. (dim. of lucus), *a little grove*: Suet.

Lŭcŭmo (**Lŭcŏmo** and syncop. **Lucmo**) -ōnis, m. (Etruscan), *title given to Etruscan princes and priests*: Prop., Liv.

lūcus -i, m. (luceo), *a sacred grove* or *wood*: Pl., Cic., Verg.; poet., in gen., *a wood*: Verg.

lūdĭa -ae, f. (ludius). (1) *an actress*: Mart. (2) *a female gladiator*: Juv.

lūdĭbrĭum -i, n. (ludo). (1) *derision, mockery, sport*: per ludibrium auditi dimissique, *heard and dismissed with scorn,* Liv. (2) *an object of derision, a laughing-stock, plaything*: is ludibrium verius quam comes, Liv.; ludibria ventis, Verg.; esp. in predicative dat.: ludibrio esse alicui, Cic., Sall., Liv., Tac.; habere aliquem, Pl., Lucr., Sall., Liv.

lūdĭbundus -a -um (ludo), *playful, sportive*: Pl., Liv. Transf., *without difficulty* or *danger*: caelo sereno in Italiam ludibundi pervenimus, Cic.

lūdĭcer -cra -crum (ludus), *sportive, done for sport*: exercitatio, Cic.; Liv.
  Esp. *relating to the stage*: ars, *acting,* Liv.; Tac.
  ¶ N. as subst. **lūdĭcrum** -i. (1) *a plaything*: Cat. (2) *a theatrical performance, public spectacle*: Liv. (3) *a trifle*: Hor.

lūdĭfĭcātĭo -ōnis, f. (ludifico), *a making game*

of, deriding, deceiving: cum omni mo ludificatione, calumniā, senatus auctori impediretur, Cic.; veri, Liv.

lūdĭfĭcātor -ōris, m. (ludifico), *one who ma game of another, a mocker*: Pl.

lūdĭfĭcātŭi, dat. sing. as from ludificatus, (ludifico), *as an object of derision*: Pl.

lūdĭfĭco -are (ludus/facio), *to make game deride, cheat*: aliquem, Sall.; Pl., Luc absol.: Cic.

lūdĭfĭcor -ari, dep. (ludus/facio), *to ma game of, deride, delude, cheat*: aliquem, Li Pl., Ter.; absol.: Cic. Transf., *to frustr by cunning*: ea quae hostes agerent, Liv.

lūdĭo -ōnis, m. *an actor*: Liv.

lūdĭus -i, m. *an actor*: Pl., Cic., Ov.

lūdo -ōnis, m. *an actor*: Liv.

lūdo -ĕre lūsi lūsum, *to play.*
  Lit., (1) *to play at* a specific game; w abl.: aleā, Cic.; trocho, Hor.; with ac proelia latronum, *chess,* Ov. (2) in gen., *play, sport*: exempla honesta ludendi, Ci in numerum, *to dance,* Verg.; lusisti sat Hor.
  Transf., (1) *to do for amusement, amu oneself with doing, to play with*: causam illa disputationemque, Cic.; carmina pastoru Verg. (2) *to imitate, mimic*: opus, Hor. (*to rally, banter*: Appium conlegam, Cic. (4) *to deceive, delude*: Ter., Hor., Liv.

lūdus -i, m. *play, game, sport, pastime.*
  Lit., in gen.: ludus campestris, Ci novum sibi aliquem excogitant in otio l dum, Cic.; Hor., Liv.: esp. plur., ludi, *pub games* or *spectacles*: ludos facere, *to gi celebrate,* Cic., Liv.; ludis, *at the time of t games,* Cic.; ludos committere, *to begin t games,* Cic.; Verg.
  Transf., (1) *a game, a child's game, trifle*: illa perdiscere ludus esset, Cic.; L (2) *sport, jest, joke*: per ludum et iocum, Cic Verg., Hor.; ludum dare, with dat., *to gi free play to,* Pl., Hor. (3) *a place where bo* or *mind is exercised, a school*: **a**, *for gladiator* Caes., Hor., Juv.: **b**, *for the education of t young*: ludus litterarum, Liv.; in alicui ludum mittere, Hor.

lŭella -ae, f. (luo), *punishment, expiation*: Lu

lŭēs -is, f. (luo), *a plague, pestilence, contagio disease.* Lit., Verg., Ov. Transf., (1) *word of reproach, pest, plague*: Cic. (2) *a widespread calamity, war*: Tac.; *earthquak* Tac.

Lugdūnum -i, n. *a city in Gaul* (now *Lyon* Adj. **Lugdūnensis** -e.

lūgĕo lūgēre luxi.
  (1) intransit., *to mourn, be in mournin* luget senatus, Cic.; lugere pro aliquo, Cic campi lugentes, *places of mourning* (of t lower world), Verg.
  (2) transit., *to bewail, lament, we mourning for*: mortem Treboni, Cic matronae annum, ut parentem, eum lux runt, Liv.; with acc. and infin.: Cic.

lūgubris -e (lugeo). (1) *relating to mournin mournful*: lamentatio, *for the dead,* Cic domus, *a house of mourning,* Liv.; Hor., Ta N. pl. as subst. **lūgubria** -ium, *mourni attire*: Ov.; n. sing. as internal acc.: comet lugubre rubent, Verg. (2) *grievous, caus mourning*: bellum, Hor., Liv. (3) *expressi grief, plaintive*: verba, Ov.; Lucr.

lumbus -i, m. *the loin*: Pl., Hor., Juv.

ūmen -ĭnis, n. (connected with luceo), *light.*
Lit., tabulas conlocare in bono lumine, *in a good light,* Cic.; lumen solis, Cic.; candelae, Juv.; Lucr., Verg.
Transf., (1) *a source of light, lamp, taper*: lumini oleum instillare, Cic.; Liv.; (2) *the light of day, day*: luminis orae, Lucr., Verg.; lumine quarto, Verg. (3) *the light of life, life*: relinquere, Pl., Verg. (4) *the light of the eye, the eye*: luminibus amissis, *being blind,* Cic.; caecitas luminis, Cic.; lumina defixa tenere in aliqua re, Ov.; Verg. (5) *an opening, a light* in a building: luminibus obstruere, Cic.; so, fig.: duo lumina ab animo ad oculos perforata nos habere, Cic. (6) fig., *light, clearness, insight*: ordo maxime est, qui memoriae lumen adfert, Cic. (7) fig., *a shining light, glory, ornament*: Corinthus totius Graeciae lumen, Cic.; lumina civitatis, Cic.; Verg.

ūmĭnāre -āris, n. (lumen), *a window-shutter, window*: plur., Cic.

ūmĭnōsus -a -um (lumen), *full of light*; of discourse, *bright*: Cic.

lūna -ae, f. (connected with luceo), *the moon.*
Lit., plena, *full moon,* Caes.; ortus aut obitus lunae, Cic.; lunae defectus, Liv.; quarta luna, *the fourth day after new moon,* Cic.
Transf., (1) *the night*: roscida, Verg.; Prop. (2) *a month*: Ov. (3) *a crescent-shaped ornament, worn by Roman senators on their shoes*: Juv. (4) personif.: Luna, *the goddess of the Moon,* afterwards identified with Diana.

Lūna -ae, f. *a town on the borders of Liguria and Etruria.*
¶ Hence adj. **Lūnensis** -e, *of Luna.*

ūnaris -e (luna), *of the moon, lunar*: cursus, Cic.; cornua, Ov.

ūno -are (luna), *to bend into a crescent*: arcum, Ov.; esp. in perf. partic. **lūnātus** -a -um, *bent into a crescent, sickle-shaped*: peltae Amazonidum, Verg.

ūo lŭĕre lŭi lŭĭtūrus (λύω), *to loose.* Hence (1) *to expiate, atone for*: stuprum voluntariā morte, Cic.; Verg., Liv. (2) *to pay, make good*; esp. in phrase: luere poenam, *or* poenas, *to pay penalty for,* itaque mei peccati luo poenas, Cic. L.; poenam pro caede, Ov. (3) *to avert,* by expiation or punishment: Liv.

ŭpa -ae, f. (lupus), *a she-wolf*: Liv., Ov. Transf., *a prostitute*: Pl., Cic., Liv.

ŭpānar -āris, n. (lupa), *a brothel*: Pl., Juv.

ŭpātus -a -um (lupa), *provided with wolf's teeth*—i.e., *iron spikes*: frena, Hor. As subst., m. pl. **lŭpāti** -ōrum and (sc. freni, frena) **lŭpāta** -ōrum, *a curb with jagged spikes*: Verg.

Lŭpercus -i, m. (lupus). (1) *an Italian pastoral deity, sometimes identified with the Arcadian Pan.*
¶ Hence subst. **Lŭpercal** -cālis, n. *a grotto on the Palatine Hill, sacred to Lupercus*: Verg.; and n. pl. of adj. **Lŭpercālĭa** -ium and -iorum, *the festival of Lupercus, celebrated in February.*
(2) *a priest of Lupercus*: Cic.

ŭpia -ae, m. *a river in north-west Germany* (now *Lippe*).

ŭpillus -i, m. (dim. of ²lupinus), *a small lupin*: Pl.

¹lŭpīnus -a -um (lupus), *of* or *relating to a wolf, wolfish*: ubera, Cic.

²lŭpīnus -i, m. and **lŭpīnum** -i, n. *the lupin*: Verg.; used on the stage instead of coin: nec tamen ignorat quid distent aera lupinis, Hor.

lŭpus -i, m. (λύκος), *a wolf.*
Lit., genus acre luporum atque canum, Verg.; prov.: lupus in fabula, *or* in sermone, *talk of the devil, and he'll appear,* Pl., Ter., Cic.; hac urget lupus, hac canis angit, *to be between two fires,* Hor.
Transf., (1) *a voracious fish, the pike*: Hor., Mart. (2) *a horse's bit with jagged points*: Ov. (3) *a hook*: ferrei, Liv.

lurco -ōnis, m. *a glutton*: Pl.

lūrĭdus -a -um, *pale yellow, lurid, ghastly.* Lit., dentes, Hor.; pallor, Ov. Transf., *producing paleness*: horror, aconita, Ov.

lūror -ōris, m. *ghastliness, paleness*: Lucr.

luscĭnĭa -ae, f. *the nightingale*: Hor.

luscĭnĭŏla -ae, f. (dim. of luscinia), *a little nightingale*: Pl.

luscĭnĭus -i, m.=luscinia; q.v.: Sen., Phaedr.

luscĭnus -a -um (luscus), *one-eyed*: Plin.

luscĭōsus and **luscĭtĭōsus** -a -um (luscus), *purblind, dim-sighted*: Pl.

luscus -a -um, *one-eyed*: Cic.; dux, Hannibal, Juv.; Pl.

lūsĭo -ōnis, f. (ludo), *play, a game*: Cic.

Lūsĭtānĭa -ae, f. *the modern Portugal, with a part of the modern Spain.*
¶ Hence adj. **Lūsĭtānus** -a -um, *Lusitanian*; m. pl. as subst., *the Lusitanians.*

lūsĭto -are (freq. of ludo), *to play, sport*: Pl.

lūsor -ōris, m. (ludo), *one that plays, a player*: Ov. Transf., (1) *a playful writer*: tenerorum lusor amorum, Ov. (2) *a mocker*: Pl.

lūsōrĭus -a -um (lusor), *relating to play* or *pleasure*: Plin., Sen.

lustrālis -e (²lustrum). (1) *relating to expiation* or *atonement*: sacrificium, Liv.; exta, Verg. (2) *relating to a period of five years* (because of the quinquennial expiatory sacrifice at Rome): Tac.

lustrātĭo -ōnis, f. (lustro), *a purification by sacrifice*: lustrationis sacro peracto, Liv. Transf., *a going round, going over, traversing*: municipiorum, Cic.; solis, Cic.

lustrĭcus -a -um (²lustrum), *of purification*: Suet.

¹lustro -are (connected with luceo), *to make bright, illumine*: sol cuncta suā luce lustrat et complet, Cic.; Lucr., Verg.

²lustro -are (²lustrum), *to purify, cleanse* by sacrifices. Lit., populum, Cic.; Verg., Liv., Ov. Transf., (1) *to go round* (as in ceremonial purification), *go over, traverse*: Aegyptum, Cic.; navibus aequor, Verg., Hor. (2) *to review, observe, examine*: quae sit me circum copia, lustro, Verg.; alicuius vestigia, Verg.; exercitum, Cic. L.; omnia ratione animoque, Cic.

lustror -ari (²lustrum), *to haunt brothels*: Pl.

¹lustrum -i, n. (lutum), *a bog, morass*: Varr.
Transf., (1) in plur., *the den* or *lair of a wild beast*: ferarum, Verg.; and in gen., *woodlands*: Verg. (2) in plur., *brothels*; hence *debauchery*: Pl., Cic., Hor.

²lustrum -i, n. (connected with luo).
Lit., *an expiatory sacrifice,* esp. *that offered every five years by the censors at the close of the census on behalf of the Roman people, at*

which an ox, sheep, and sow were sacrificed (suovetaurilia): lustrum condere, *to offer the expiatory sacrifice*, Cic.; Liv. TRANSF., *a period of five years, a lustrum*: octavum claudere lustrum, Hor.; Cic., Liv., Ov.

lūsus -ū, m. (ludo), *a playing, game, amusement, sport*: per lusum atque lasciviam, Liv.; aleae, Suet.; Tac.; *dalliance*: Ov.

Lŭtātĭus -a -um, *name of a Roman gens*; *see* Catulus.

lūtĕŏlus -a -um (dim. of luteus), *yellow*: caltha, Verg.

Lūtētĭa -ae, f. *a town in Gallia Lugdunensis* (now *Paris*).

¹lūtĕus -a -um (lūtum), *of the colour of the plant* lutum, *saffron-yellow*: Aurora, Verg.; soccus, Cat.; Ov. TRANSF., *pallor, sallow*, Hor.

²lŭtĕus -a -um (lŭtum). (1) *of mud* or *clay*: Hor., Ov. TRANSF., (1) *dirty, covered with dirt*: Vulcanus, Juv. (2) morally *dirty*: homo, negotium, Cic.

lŭto -are (²lŭtum), *to smear with mud* or *dirt*: Mart.

lŭtŭlentus -a -um (²lŭtum), *muddy, dirty.* LIT., sus, Hor.; amnis, Ov. TRANSF., (1) morally *filthy, dirty*: homo, vitia, Cic. (2) of style, *turbid, impure*: Hor.

¹lūtum -i, n. *a plant used for dyeing yellow, dyers' weed*: Verg. TRANSF., *yellow colour*: Verg., Tib.

²lŭtum -i, n. (λύω), *mud, mire, dirt.* LIT., volutari in luto, Cic.; crates luto contegere, Caes.; prov.: in luto esse, haerere, Pl., Ter.; as a term of reproach, *scum*: Pl., Cic., Cat. TRANSF., *loam, clay*: pocula de facili luto componere, Tib.; Mart., Juv.

lux lūcis, f. (connected with luceo), *light.*
LIT., in gen.: solis, Cic.; lunae, Verg.; lychnorum, Cic.; esp., *daylight, day*: cum prima luce, *as soon as it was day*, Cic.; prima luce, Caes.; ante lucem, Cic. Abl., luce, or locative, luci, *by day, by daylight*: Cic.
TRANSF., (1) *a day*: centesima lux ab interitu P. Clodii, Cic.; aestiva, Verg.; brumalis, Ov. (2) *the light* of life: in lucem edi, Cic.; corpora luce carentum, Verg. (3) *the eye, eyesight*: Ov. (4) *the light of day, publicity, the sight of men*: res occultas in lucem proferre, Cic.; Isocrates luce forensi caruit, Cic. (5) *light, illustration, elucidation*: historia testis temporum, lux veritatis, Cic. (6) *light, hope, encouragement*: lucem adferre reipublicae, Cic. (7) *light, ornament*: haec urbs, lux orbis terrarum, Cic.

luxo -are (luxus), *to dislocate*: Plin., Sen.

luxor -ari, dep. (³luxus), *to riot*: Pl.

luxŭrĭa -ae (Pl., Ter., Caes., Cic.), and **luxŭrĭēs** -ēi (Cic., Verg.), f. (³luxus), *rankness, exuberant growth.* LIT., of plants: segetum, Verg.; Cic. TRANSF., *excess, prodigality, dissipation, extravagance*: odit populus Romanus privatam luxuriam, publicam magnificentiam diligit, Cic.; Pl., Ter.; of style: Cic.

luxŭrĭo -are, and **luxŭrĭor** -ari, dep. (luxuria), *to be luxuriant, rank, abundant in growth.*
LIT., of vegetation: humus, seges, Ov. TRANSF., (1) of animal growth, *to swell, grow*: membra, Ov. (2) of animals, *to frisk, be sportive*: ludit et in pratis luxuriatque

pecus, Ov. (3) of men, *to run riot, be solute*: ne luxuriarent otio animi, L Capua luxurians felicitate, Liv.; so of sty Hor., Quint.

luxŭrĭōsus -a -um (luxuria), adj. (w compar.), *luxuriant, rank.* LIT., of veg tion: frumenta, Cic.; Ov. TRANSF., (1) feelings, *immoderate, excessive*: laetitia, L amor, Ov. (2) of life, *luxurious, dissol extravagant*: nihil luxuriosius (homine il Cic.; Sall.
¶ Adv. **luxŭrĭōsē**, *luxuriously, volu ously*: vivere, Cic.

¹luxus -a -um (λοξός), *dislocated*: Cato.

²luxus -ūs, m. (¹luxus), *a dislocation*: Cato.

³luxus -ūs, m. *luxury, excess, extravagance* vino ac luxu, Cic.; Ter., Sall., Verg., Ta

Lўaeus -i, m. (Λυαῖος), *the releaser from c surname of Bacchus*: pater Lyaeus, V TRANSF., *wine*: uda Lyaei tempora, Hor.

Lўcaeus -i, m. (Λύκαιον) *a mountain Arcadia, sacred to Jupiter and Pan. Lўcaeus* -a -um, *Lycaean.*

Lўcambēs -ae, m. (Λυκάμβης), *a Parian, v for refusing his daughter in marriage Archilochus, was attacked by the poet in s sarcastic verses that he and his daug hanged themselves.*
¶ Hence adj. **Lўcambēus** -a - Lycambean.

Lўcāōn -ŏnis, m. (Λυκάων), *king of Arca father of Callisto, transformed by Jupiter a wolf.*
¶ Hence adj. **Lўcāŏnĭus** -a -um: Arc Callisto, *as a constellation*, Ov.; axis, *northern sky*, Ov.; subst. **Lўcāŏnis** -idi Callisto, *daughter of Lycaon*: Ov.

Lўcāŏnes -um, m. (Λυκάονες), *the Lycaoni a people in Asia Minor.*
¶ Hence adj. **Lўcāŏnĭus** -a -um, *Lyca ian*: Verg.; subst. **Lўcāŏnĭa** -ae, f. *country of the Lycaones*: Cic., Liv.

Lўcēum -i, n. and **Lўcīum** -i, n. (Λύκειο *gymnasium at Athens, at which Arist taught.* TRANSF., *a gymnasium with a libr in Cicero's Tusculan villa.*

lychnūchus -i, m. (λυχνοῦχος), *a lamp-st candelabrum*: Cic. L., Suet.

lychnus -i, m. (λύχνος), *a lamp*: Lucr., C Verg.

Lўcĭa -ae, f. (Λυκία), *a country of Asia Mino*
¶ Hence adj. **Lўcĭus** -a -um, *Lyc deus, Apollo*, Prop.; sortes, *the oracle Apollo at Patara*, Verg.; hasta, *of the Ly king Sarpedon*, Ov.; m. pl. as subst. **Lў** -ōrum, *the Lycians.*

Lўcīum=Lyceum; q.v.

Lўcōrĭs -idis, f. *a freedwoman of Volum Eutrapelus, the mistress of the poet L. Corne Gallus.*

Lyctus (-ŏs) -i, f. (Λύκτος), *a town in C* Adj. **Lyctĭus** -a -um=*Cretan*: Verg.

Lўcurgus -i, m. (Λυκοῦργος). (1) Myth., *of Dryas, king of the Edoni in Thrace, prohibited the worship of Bacchus among subjects.* (2) Myth., *son of Aleus and Nea father of Ancaeus, king of Arcadia*; h **Lўcurgĭdēs** -ae, m. *a son of Lycurg Ancaeus*: Ov. (3) Hist. (?), *a Spartan giver.* (4) Hist., *an Athenian orator, fa for his integrity*; hence m. subst. **Lўcur** -ōrum (Λυκούργειοι)=*strict, inflexible citi*

Lўdĭa -ae, f. (*Λυδία*), *a country of Asia Minor, from which according to legend the Etruscans originally came.* ¶ Hence adj. **Lўdĭus** -a -um, *Lydian*: aurifer amnis, *Pactolus*, Tib. TRANSF., Etruscan: fluvius, *the Tiber*, Verg.; adj. **Lўdus** -a -um, *Lydian*: puella, *Omphale*, Verg.; m. pl. as subst. **Lўdi** -orum, *the Lydians or the Etruscans*: Cic.

lympha -ae, f. *water, esp. clear spring or river water*: Lucr., Verg.; personif. **Lymphae** -arum, *Nymphs of the springs*: Hor.

lymphātĭcus -a -um (lympha), *raving, mad, frantic*: pavor, *a panic terror*, Liv.; Pl., Sen.; n. as subst. **lymphātĭcum** -i, *craziness*: Pl.

lymphātus -a -um (perhaps directly from lympha, not through lympho), *raving, mad, frantic*: mentem lymphatam Mareotico, Hor.; lymphati et attoniti, Liv. ¶ Hence, perhaps, **lympho** -are, *to make mad, strike with frenzy*: Plin.

Lynceus (dissyll.) -ĕi or -ĕī, m. (*Λυγκεύς*). (I) *a Messenian hero, one of the Argonauts, renowned for the sharpness of his sight.* ¶ Hence adj. **Lynceus** -a -um, *belonging to Lynceus*: Ov. TRANSF., *sharp-sighted*: Cic. L.; m. subst. **Lyncīdēs** -ae, *a descendant of Lynceus.* (2) *the son of Aegyptus, husband of Hypermnestra.*

Lyncus -i (*Λύγκος*), m. *a king in Scythia, changed by Ceres into a lynx.*

lynx -cis, c. (*λύγξ*), *a lynx*: Verg., Hor., Ov.

lŷra -ae, f. (*λύρα*), *the lyre or lute, a stringed instrument resembling the cithara*: Hor., Ov. TRANSF., (I) *lyric poetry, song*: Aeoliae lyrae amica, Ov.; Hor. (2) *a constellation, the Lyre*: Ov.

lŷrĭcus -a -um (*λυρικός*), *of the lyre, lyric*: vates, *a lyric poet*, Hor. As subst., n. pl. **lŷrĭca** -orum, *lyrics*: Plin. L.; m. pl. **lŷrĭci** -orum, *lyric poets*: Quint.

lyristēs -ae, m. (*λυριστής*), *a lute-player*: Plin. L.

Lyrnēsus -i, f. (*Λυρνησός*), *a town in the Troad, birth-place of Briseis.* ¶ Hence subst. **Lyrnēsĭs** -ĭdis, f. *Briseis*; adj. **Lyrnēsĭus** -a -um, *Lyrnesian.*

Lўsander -dri, m. (*Λύσανδρος*), *a famous Spartan general, conqueror of the Athenians*: Cic.

Lўsĭas -ae, m. (*Λυσίας*), *a famous Athenian orator, contemporary of Socrates.*

Lўsĭmăchus -i, m. (*Λυσίμαχος*), *one of the generals of Alexander the Great, later ruler in Thrace.*

Lўsippus -i, m. (*Λύσιππος*), *a celebrated worker in metal of Sicyon.*

Lўsĭs -ĭdis, m. (*Λῦσις*). (I) *a Pythagorean philosopher of Tarentum, teacher of Epaminondas*: Cic. (2) *a river in Asia Minor*: Liv.

M

M, m, the twelfth letter of the Latin Alphabet, corresponding to the Greek *M, μ*. For M. as an abbreviation, see Table of Abbreviations.

Măcăreus (trisyll.) -ĕi and -ĕos, m. (*Μακαρεύς*), *son of Aeolus, brother of Canace.* ¶ Hence subst. **Măcărēis** -ĭdis, f. *daughter of Macareus*=*Isse*: Ov.

Măcĕdō (-ōn) -dŏnis, m. (*Μακεδών*), *a Macedonian*; plur. **Măcĕdŏnes** -um, m. *the Macedonians.* ¶ Hence subst. **Măcĕdŏnĭa** -ae, f. (*Μακεδονία*), *a country between Thessaly and Thrace*; **Măcĕdŏnĭcus** -a -um and **Măcĕdŏnĭus** -a -um, *Macedonian.*

măcellārĭus -i, m. (macellum), *a victualler, provision-dealer*: Suet.

măcellum -i, n. (cf. *μάκελλον*), *a provision-market*: annonam in macello cariorem fore, Cic.; Pl., Hor.

măcĕo -ēre, *to be lean*: Pl.

¹măcĕr -cra -crum, *lean.* LIT., taurus, Verg.; Hor. TRANSF., *thin, poor*: solum, Cic.; fig.: me palma negata macrum reducit, Hor.

²Măcĕr -cri, m. C. Licinius Macer, *a Roman historian.*

măcĕrĭa -ae, f. (cf. *μάσσω*), *a wall*: Caes., Liv.; esp. *a garden-wall*: Pl., Ter., Cic. L.

măcĕro -are (connected with *μάσσω*), *to soften.* LIT., esp. by soaking: Ter. TRANSF., (I) *to make weak, reduce*: aliquem fame, Liv.; Pl., Hor. (2) *to torment, tease, vex*: quae vos, cum reliqueritis, macerent desiderio, Liv.; Pl., Hor., Ov.

măcesco -ĕre (maceo), *to grow thin, become lean*: Pl.

măchaera -ae, f. (*μάχαιρα*), *a sword*: Pl., Suet.

măchaerŏphŏrus -i, m. (*μαχαιροφόρος*), *a sword-bearer*: Cic. L.

Măchāōn -ŏnis, m. (*Μαχάων*), myth., *son of Aesculapius, celebrated physician.* ¶ Hence adj. **Măchāŏnĭus** -a -um, *of Machaon.*

măchĭna -ae, f. (*μηχανή*), *a machine, any artificial contrivance for performing work.* LIT., esp. *a crane* for moving heavy weights: Cic., Liv.; *a windlass* for drawing ships down to the sea: Hor.; *a military engine, a catapult, ballista*, etc.: Sall., Verg. TRANSF., (I) *fabric*: moles et machina mundi, Lucr. (2) *a device, contrivance, trick, stratagem*: ut omnes adhibeam machinas ad tenendum adulescentulum, Cic.; Pl.

măchĭnāmentum -i, n. (machinor), *a machine, instrument*: Liv.

măchĭnātĭo -ōnis, f. (machinor), *a contrivance, machinery, mechanism.* LIT., machinatione quādam moveri aliquid videmus, Cic. TRANSF., (I) *a cunning device, machination*: Cic. (2) *a mechanical contrivance, a machine*: navalis, Caes., Pl.

măchĭnātor -ōris, m. (machinor), *a maker of machines, engineer*: tormentorum, Liv.; Tac. TRANSF., in a bad sense, *a deviser, contriver, originator*: horum omnium scelerum, Cic.; huius belli, Liv.

măchĭnor -ari, dep. (machina), *to contrive, invent, devise*: opera, Cic.; Lucr. Esp., *to plot evil, contrive*: pestem in aliquem, Cic.; Sall., Liv.

măchĭnōsus -a -um (machina), *equipped with engines*: Suet.

măcĭēs -ēi, f. (maceo), *leanness, thinness.* LIT., of men and animals: corpus macie intabuit, Cic.; Caes., Hor. TRANSF., (I) of soil or crops, *poverty, barrenness*: Ov. (2) *meagreness of expression*: Tac.

măcĭlentus -a -um (macies), *thin, lean*: Pl.

Macra -ae. (1) *a river in Italy (now Magra).*
(2) Macra cōmē (Μαχρὰ κώμη), *a place in
Locris, on the borders of Thessaly.*
macresco -ĕre (¹macer), *to grow lean, become
thin*: Hor.
Macri Campi and **Campi Macri** -ōrum, m.
a valley in Gallia Cispadana.
macrĭtūdo -inis, f. (¹macer), *leanness*: Pl.
Macrŏbĭus -i, m. Aurelius Ambrosius
Theodosius, *a grammarian of about* A.D. 400.
macrŏcollum -i, n. (μαχρόχωλον), *paper of the
largest size, royal paper*: Cic. L.
maciābĭlis -e (²macto), *deadly*: Lucr.
mactātū, abl. sing. as from mactatus, m.
(²macto), *by a sacrificial stroke*: parentis,
Lucr.
macte, *see* ¹mactus.
¹macto -are (¹mactus), *to magnify, honour,
glorify*: aliquem honoribus, Cic.; esp. to
honour a god: puerorum extis deos manes,
Cic.
²macto -are, *to slay, smite.* LIT., esp. in
sacrifice: hostiam, Hor.; se Orco, Liv.; Lucr.,
Verg., Tac. TRANSF., *to afflict, punish*:
aliquem summo supplicio, Cic.; morte, Cic.;
malo, Pl.; Tac.
¹mactus -a -um, *glorified, honoured*; used only
in the voc. m. **macte** as an expression
of goodwill, congratulation, etc., *well done!
bravo! a blessing on you!* Often with abl. of
grounds, sometimes with imperat. of verb
sum: macte virtute! Cic. L.; macte esto
virtute! Hor.; macte nova virtute, puer!
Verg.; as plur.: macte virtute, milites
Romani, este! Liv.; absol.: macte, Cic.
²mactus -a -um (connected with ²macto),
smitten: Lucr.
măcŭla -ae, f. *a spot.* LIT., *a physical spot,
mark*: equus albis maculis, Verg.; esp. *a
stain, blot*: corporis, Cic.; Pl., Ov.; sometimes *the mesh of a net*: Ov. TRANSF.,
a moral blot, stain, blemish, fault: hunc tu
vitae splendorem maculis aspergis tuis? Cic.;
Pl., Liv.
măcŭlo -are (macula), *to spot, to make spotted.*
LIT., physically, *to spot, stain*: terram tabo
maculant, Verg.; candor corporum magis
sanguine atro maculabatur, Liv. TRANSF.,
morally, *to stain, defile, pollute*: rex ille
optimi regis caede maculatus, Cic.; partus
suos parricidio, Liv.; Lucr., Verg.
măcŭlōsus -a -um (macula), *full of spots,
spotted, speckled.* LIT., physically, *spotted,
stained*: lynx, Verg.; vestis, Cic.; sanguine
harenae, Ov. TRANSF., morally, *defiled,
polluted*: senatores, Cic.; nefas, Hor.
mădĕfăcĭo -făcĕre -fēci -factum, and pass.
mădĕfīo -fĭĕri (madeo/facio), *to make wet,
moisten, soak*: gladii sanguine madefacti,
Cic.; sanguis madefecerat herbas, Verg.; Ov.
mădĕo -ēre (μαδάω), *to be wet, moist, to stream.*
LIT., in gen.: natabant pavimenta vino,
madebant parietes, Cic.; sanguine terra
madet, Verg.; Ov. Esp. (1) *to be drunk*: Pl.,
Tib. (2) *to be boiled, to be made soft by
boiling*: Pl., Verg.
TRANSF., *to be steeped in, abound in,
overflow with*: pocula madent Baccho, Tib.;
Socraticis madet sermonibus, Hor.
¶ Hence partic. **mădens** -entis, *wet,
moist*: umor, Lucr.; nix sole, *melting*, Ov.;
vino, *drunk*, Sen.

mădesco mădescĕre mădŭi (madeo), *to beco
moist* or *wet*: semiusta madescunt robo
Verg.; Ov.
mădĭdus -a -um (madeo), *moist, wet.* LIT.,
gen.: fasciculus epistularum totus ac
madidus, Cic. L.; genae, *wet with tears*, C
Esp., (1) *drunk*: Pl., Mart. (2) *boiled so
Pl., Juv. (3) *dyed*: vestis cocco, Ma
TRANSF., *steeped*: Mart.
¶ Adv. **mădĭdē**, *drunkenly*: Pl.
mădor -ōris, m. (madeo), *moisture, wetne
Sall.
mădulsa -ae, m. (madeo), *a drunkard*: Pl.
Maeandĕr and **Maeandrŏs** (-us) -dri,
(Μαίανδρος), *a river of Asia Minor, proverl
for its winding course; in legend, father
Cyane, the mother of Caunus and Byb
TRANSF., *a winding.* (1) of a road: C
(2) *a winding border on a dress*: Verg.
¶ Hence adj. **Maeandrĭus** -a -um,
Maeander: iuvenis, *Caunus*, Ov.
Maecēnās -ātis, m. *an Etruscan name*; esp.
C. Cilnius, *a Roman knight, the friend
Augustus, and the patron of Horace
Vergil.*
Maecĭus -a -um, *name of a Roman* gens;
most famous member was Sp. Maecius Tar
a celebrated critic.
Maedi -ōrum, m. (Μαῖδοι), *a Thracian peo
Adj. **Maedĭcus** -a -um, *belonging to
Maedi*; subst. **Maedĭca** -ae, f. *the coun
of the Maedi.*
Maelĭus -a -um, *name of a Roman* gens.
most famous member was Sp. Maeli
*suspected of aiming at kingly power and ki
by* C. Servilius Ahala, 439 B.C.
maena (**mēna**) -ae, f. (μαίνη), *a kind of sm
sea-fish*, often salted: Cic., Ov.
Maenălus (-ŏs) -i, m. and **Maenăla** -ōr
n. pl. (Μαίναλον), *a mountain-range
Arcadia, sacred to Pan.*
¶ Hence adj. **Maenălĭus** -a -um, *Mae
lian, Arcadian*: deus, *Pan*, Ov.; ver
pastoral poetry, Verg.; f. adj. **Maen
-ĭdis, *belonging to Maenalus*: ursa, *Calli
Ov.; ora, *Arcadia*, Ov.
Maenăs -ădis, f. (μαινάς). (1) *a bacchante*: C
esp. pl. Maenades -um. (2) *a prophe
(Cassandra)*: Prop.
Maenădes, *see* Maenas.
Maenĭus -a -um, *name of a Roman* ge
columna Maenia, *see* columna.
¶ Hence adj. **Maenĭānus** -a -
Maenian; esp. n. as subst. **Maeniānum
a projecting balcony, first introduced b
Maenius: Cic.
Maeŏnes -um, m. (Μαίονες), *the Maeon
or Lydians.*
¶ Hence subst. **Maeŏnĭa** -ae, f. (Μαίο
Maeonia or Lydia, and, as the Etruscans w
said to have come from Lydia=*Etru
Verg.; subst. **Maeŏnĭdēs** -ae, m. (1) *Ho
as a native, according to some, of Colop
or Smyrna*: Ov. (2) *an Etruscan*: Ve
subst. **Maeŏnīs** -ĭdis, f. *a Lydian won
Arachne*: Ov.; *Omphale*: Ov.; adj. **Maeŏn
-a -um, *Maeonian, Lydian*: ripa (of the r
Pactolus), Ov.; senex, *or* vates, *Homer*, C
so *Homeric* or *heroic*: carmen, pes, cha
Ov.; also *Etruscan*: nautae, Ov.
Maeŏtae -ārum, m. (Μαιῶται), *a Scythian pe
on Lake Maeotis.*

¶ Hence adj. **Maeōtĭcus** and **Maeōtĭus** -a -um, *Maeotic*; f. adj. **Maeōtĭs** -idis, *of the Maeotae*; esp. Maeotis palus, *or* lacus (now *the Sea of Azov*).

naerĕo -ēre (cf. maestus).
(1) intransit., *to be sad, mournful, to grieve, mourn, lament*: maeret Menelaus, Cic.; Verg.; with dat., *to grieve over*: suo incommodo, Cic.; with internal acc.: talia, Ov.; partic., maerens, *mournful, sorrowful*: quis Sullam nisi maerentem vidit? Cic.
(2) transit., *to lament, mourn over, bewail*: casum, Cic.; filii mortem graviter, Cic.; with acc. and infin.: Cic.

naeror -ōris, m. (maereo), *mourning, grief, sorrow, sadness*: in maerore iacēre, Cic.; Pl., Ter., Lucr., Sall.

naestĭtĭa -ae, f. (maestus), *sadness, dejection, gloominess*: orationis quasi maestitiam sequi, Cic.; esse in maestitia, Cic.

naestĭtūdo -ĭnis, f. (maestus), *sadness*: Pl.

naestus -a -um (cf. maereo), adj. (with superl.), *sad, sorrowful, dejected.* LIT., of persons: senex, Cic.; Pl., Verg.; oratores, *gloomy,* Tac. TRANSF., (1) of things: urbs, Juv.; Ov., Verg. (2) *causing* or *indicating sorrow*: vestis, Prop.; funera, Ov.
¶ Adv. **maestĭtĕr**, *in mourning fashion*: Pl.

Maevius -i, m. *a bad poet of the time of Vergil and Horace.*

nāgālĭa -ium, n. (a Punic word), *huts*: Sall., Verg.

năgĕ, see magis.

năgĭcus -a -um (μαγικός), *relating to magic, magical*: artes, Verg.; di, *gods invoked in enchantments* (as *Pluto, Hecate, Proserpina*), Tib.; Ov., Tac.

nāgĭs (or **măgĕ** : Pl., Lucr., Verg.), compar. adv. (from root of magnus), *more, to a greater extent, rather.* Used (1) with adj. and adv.: magis apta, Ov.; but esp. with those that have no regular compar.: magis necessarius, Cic. (2) with verbs: tum magis id diceres, Cic.; sometimes in the sense of choice, *preferably, for preference, rather* (like potius): Cic. (3) with nouns and pronouns: magis aedilis esse non potuisset, Cic. Sometimes the *amount* of difference is expressed by an abl.: impendio magis, *considerably more,* Cic.; multo magis, Cic.; nihilo magis, *just as little,* Cic. *Than,* after magis, is expressed usually by quam: magis ratione et consilio quam virtute vicisse, Caes.; sed praeterita magis reprehendi possunt quam corrigi, Cic.; sometimes by atque: Ter.; or by abl.: solito magis, *more than usual,* Liv.; Cic., Verg.
Special combinations: non magis . . . quam, *not more . . . than, just as much . . . as,* Cic.; quo magis . . . eo magis, *the more . . . the more,* Cic.; quo magis . . . eo minus, Cic.; eo magis, *so much the more, all the more,* Cic.; magis magisque, magis et magis, *more and more,* Cic.; magis magis, Cat.; magis est quod . . . quam quod, *or* magis est ut . . . quam ut, *there is more reason why . . . than* . . ., Cic.
Superl. **maxĭmē** (**maxŭmē**), *in the highest degree, most of all, especially, very.*
In gen. (1) with adj. and adv.: maxime fidus, Cic.; esp. with those that have no regular superl.: loca maxime frumentaria,

Caes.; maxime necessarius, Cic.; sometimes to add force to a superl.: aberratio maxime liberalissima, Cic. (2) with verbs: cupere, velle, Cic.; confidere, Caes. (3) with nouns and pronouns: quae ratio poëtas, maximeque Homerum impulit, *and most of all Homer,* Cic.
Particular combinations. (1) with unus, omnium, multo, vel: unus omnium maxime, Nep.; multo maxime, Cic. (2) quam maxime, *as much as possible,* Cic. (3) with tum, cum, *just, precisely*: haec cum maxime loqueretur, Cic.; nunc cum maxime, Cic.; cum saepe, tum maxime bello Punico, Cic.; Pl., Liv. (4) with relat.: ut quisque maxime opis indigeat, ita ea potissimum opitulari, Cic.
In colloquial language, maxime is used to express emphatic assent: vos non timetis eam? Immo vero maxume, Sall.; Pl.

măgister -tri, m. (connected with magis), *master, chief, head, director, superintendent.*
LIT., (1) polit. and relig. t. t.: populi, *dictator,* Cic.; equitum, *master of the horse, the dictator's lieutenant,* Liv.; morum, *the censor,* Cic.; sacrorum, *the chief priest,* Liv. (2) *a schoolmaster, teacher*: ludi, Cic.; artium, religionis, virtutis, Cic.; fig.: usus est magister optimus, Cic. (3) in gen.: societatis, *the director of a company formed for farming the revenue,* Cic.; elephanti, *driver,* Liv.; auctionis, Cic.; cenandi, *the president of a feast,* Cic.; navis, *master* or *helmsman,* Verg., Liv.; gladiatorum, *trainer, fencing-master,* Cic., Liv.; *helmsman*: Verg.
TRANSF., *an instigator, adviser, guide*: magister ad despoliandum Dianae templum, Cic.; Ter., Tac.

măgistĕrĭum -i, n. (magister), *the office* or *power of* a magister; *directorship, magistracy*: morum, *the censorship,* Cic.; sacerdotii, *priesthood,* Liv., Suet.; me magisteria (conviviorum) delectant, Cic. TRANSF., in gen., *direction, guidance*: Pl., Tib.

măgistra -ae, f. (magister), *a mistress, directress*: Ter. TRANSF., lex quasi dux et magistra studiorum, Cic.; arte magistrā, *by the help of art,* Verg.

măgistrātus -ūs, m. (magister), *the office* or *dignity of* a magister, *a magistracy, official dignity, office.*
LIT., magistratum gerere, habere, Cic.; inire, ingredi, Sall.; deponere, Caes.; magistratu abire, Cic.
TRANSF., *a magistrate, state official.* Magistrates in Rome were either ordinarii— e.g., praetors, consuls, etc.; or extraordinarii —e.g., dictator, master of the horse: est proprium munus magistratūs intellegere se gerere personam civitatis, Cic.; creare magistratūs, Liv.

magnănĭmĭtās -ātis, f. (magnanimus), *greatness of soul, magnanimity*: Cic.

magnănĭmus -a -um (magnus/animus), *high-minded, magnanimous*: Cic., Verg.

Magnēs -nētis, see Magnesia.

Magnēsĭa -ae, f. (Μαγνησία). (1) *a district in Thessaly.* (2) *a town in Caria, near the Maeander.* (3) *a town in Lydia under Mount Sipylus.*
¶ Hence adj. and subst. **Magnēs** -nētis, m. (Μάγνης), *Magnesian, a Magnesian*; esp.: lapis Magnes, *a loadstone, magnet*; adj.

Magnēsĭus -a -um, *Magnesian*: saxum, *the magnet*, Lucr.; subst. **Magnessa** -ae, f. *a Magnesian woman*: Hor.; subst. **Magnē-tarchēs** -ae, m. *the chief magistrate of the Magnesians*: Liv.; f. adj. **Magnētĭs** -ĭdis, *Magnesian*: Argo, *built at Pagasae in Magnesia*, Ov.

Magni Campi -ōrum, m. *a place in Africa not far from Utica*.

magnĭdĭcus -a -um (magnus/dico), *boastful*: Pl.

magnĭfĭcentĭa -ae, f. (magnificus). (1) in a good sense; of persons, *loftiness* of thought and action; of things, *grandeur, magnificence, splendour*: odit populus Romanus privatam luxuriam, publicam magnificentiam diligit, Cic.; epularum, villarum, Cic. (2) in a bad sense, *boasting, pomposity*: Ter., Cic.

magnĭfĭco -are (magnificus), *to prize highly, esteem*: Pl., Ter., Plin.

magnĭfĭcus -a -um, compar. **magnĭfĭcentĭor**; superl. **magnĭfĭcentissĭmus** (magnus/facio).

(1) in a good sense, *grand*. Of persons, *great* in thought and action, *splendid, fine*: animo excelso magnificoque, Cic.; in suppliciis deorum magnifici, domi parci, Sall.; *distinguished*: vir factis magnificus, Liv. Of things, *splendid, magnificent, glorious*: villa, Cic.; aedilitas, Cic.; res gestae, Liv.; of style: dicendi genus, Cic.

(2) in a bad sense, *boastful, pompous*: miles, Pl.; verba, Ter.; Sall.

¶ Adv. **magnĭfĭcē**, compar. **magnĭfĭcentĭus**; superl. **magnĭfĭcentissĭmē**. (1) in a good sense, *splendidly, grandly, magnificently*: habitare, vivere, vincere, Cic. (2) in a bad sense, *haughtily, proudly*: loqui de bello, Sall.; incedere, Liv.

magnĭlŏquentĭa -ae, f. (magniloquus). (1) *lofty* or *elevated language*: Homeri, Cic. (2) *pompous, boastful language*: Liv.

magnĭlŏquus -a -um (magnus/loquor). (1) *lofty* or *elevated in language*: Homerus, Stat. (2) *pompous* or *boastful*: os, Ov.; Tac.

magnĭtūdo -ĭnis, f. (magnus), *greatness*. LIT., (1) of size: mundi, Cic.; fluminis, Caes.; Liv. (2) of number or quantity: fructuum, Cic.; pecuniae, Cic. TRANSF., abstr.: reipublicae, Sall.; beneficii, amoris, Cic.; animi, *magnanimity*, Cic.

magnŏpĕrĕ and separately **magno ŏpĕrĕ**, adv. (magnus/opus), used as adv. of magnus; q.v., *greatly, very much*: magnopere delectare, mirari, desiderare, Cic.; Pl., Caes., Liv. Superl.: maximo opere, *very greatly*, Pl., Ter., Cic. L.; but more used is maxime; q.v.

magnus -a -um, compar. **māior**, maius, superl. **maxĭmus (maxŭmus)** -a -um, *great, large*.

LIT., physically. (1) of size, *large, great, tall*: domus, Cic.; montes, Cat.; oppidum maximum, Caes.; aquae, Liv. (2) of number, quantity, etc.: maximum pondus auri, magnum numerum frumenti, vim mellis maximam exportasse, Cic.; multitudo peditatūs, Caes.; magnā comitante catervā, Verg. (3) of sound, *loud*: vox, Cic.; clamor, Caes., Cic., Liv.; murmur, Verg.; n. acc. as adv.: magnum clamat, Pl. (4) of price or value, *high, great*: ornatus muliebris pretii maioris,

Cic.; thus n. abl. sing. magno, and ge magni, *at a high price, dear*: magni aestim; *to esteem highly*, Cic.; magni, maximi fac¢ Cic.; magno emere, Cic.

TRANSF., (1) of time: **a,** *long*: ann Verg.; Cic.: **b,** of age: magno natu, gɪ age, Liv.; esp. in compar. and superl., v or without natu *or* annis, *older*: natu m; frater, Cic.; annos natus maior quadragiɪ Cic.; ex duobus filiis maior, Caes.; max; virgo, *the oldest of the Vestals*, Ov. M. pl compar. as subst. **māiōrēs**, *ancestors*: m; maiorum, Cic.; Pl.

(2) of other abstr. qualities; of deities magni! *great heaven!* Cat.; Iuppiter optin maximus, *supreme*, Liv.; of persons, c *standing, great, powerful, mighty*: proɪ summam nobilitatem et singularem po¹ tiam magnus erat, Cic.; nemo vir mag¡ sine aliquo adflatū divino umquam fuit, C magno animo, Cic.; of states: o ma¡ Carthago! Hor.; of things, *important, grɛ* magna et ampla negotia, Cic.; reipubl¹ magnum aliquod tempus, Cic.; pericul¹ Caes.; infamia, Cic.; laudis spes, Lu magna verba, *proud words*, Verg.

Adverbial phrases; **in maius,** *to a hiɡ degree*: Liv., Tac.; **magno opere,** magnopere. For superl. adv. **maxir** *see* magis.

Māgo (-ōn) -ōnis, m. *brother of Hannibal*.

¹**măgus** -i, m. (μάγος), *a learned man among Persians*: Cic. TRANSF., *a magician*: Ov.

²**măgus** -a -um, adj. (¹magus), *magical*: ar¹ Ov.

Māia -ae, f. (Μαῖα), *the daughter of Atlas*, bore Mercury to Jupiter: Maiā genitus, Ve¹ Maiā natus, Hor.; Maiā creatus, ¢ *Mercury*.

¶ Hence adj. **Māius** -a -um, *of M¢ mensis Maius, or simply Maius, the mo of May*, Cic., Ov.; Kalendae Maiae, Cic. Ov.

māiālis -is, m. *a gelded boar*: Varr.; used ; term of abuse: Cic.

māiestas -ātis, f. (from root of magn¹ *greatness, grandeur, dignity, majesty*; app¹ to gods, persons, and states, esp. the Ror people: dii non censent esse suae maiesta *to be consistent with their majesty*, C consulis, Cic.; patria, *the paternal author* Liv.; matronarum, Liv.; populi Romani, C maiestatem minuere, *to offend against sovereignty of the people*, Cic.; hence: criɪ maiestatis, *treason*, Cic.; so: maiestatis iudicium, Cic.; maiestas=*treason*, Tac.

māior maiores, *see* magnus.

Māius -a -um, adj. from Maia; q.v.

māiuscŭlus -a -um (dim. of maior). (1) so *what greater*: in aliqua maiuscula cura, Cic (2) *somewhat older*: Pl.

māla -ae, f. *the cheek-bone, jaw-bone*, bot¹ men and animals, esp. plur.: Lucr., V¢ TRANSF., *the jaw, the cheek*: malae decen Hor.

mălăcĭa -ae, f. (μαλακία), *a calm at sea*: t; subito malacia ac tranquillitas exstitit, Ca Sen.

mălăcisso -are (μαλακίζω), *to soften, ren pliable*: Pl.

mălăcus -a -um (μαλακός). **1)** *soft, pliable*: (2) *effeminate, delicate*: Pl.

mălĕdīco -dīcĕre -dixi -dictum (from male/ dico; sometimes separately, male dico, *see* male), *to speak ill, abuse*: alicui, Pl., Cic., Hor.

¶ Hence pres. partic. (with compar. and superl.) **mălĕdīcens** -entis, *abusive*: maledicentissima civitas, Cic.; Pl.

¶ N. of perf. partic. as subst. **mălĕdictum** -i, *cursing, abusive language*: maledicta in aliquem dicere, conferre, congerere, Cic.

mălĕdictĭo -ōnis, f. (maledico), *reviling, abuse*: Cic.

mălĕdĭcus -a -um (male/dico), *abusive, scurrilous*: conviciator, Cic.; Quint. Adv. **mălĕdĭcē,** *abusively*: dicere, Cic.; Liv.

mălĕfăcĭo -făcĕre -fēci -factum (from male/ facio; sometimes separately, male facio, *see* male), *to injure*: alicui, Pl., Cic. L.

¶ N. of perf. partic. as subst. **mălĕfactum** -i, *an ill deed, injury*: Cic.

mălĕfactor -ōris, m. (malefacio), *an evildoer, malefactor*: Pl.

mălĕfĭcentĭa -ae, f. (male/facio), *evil-doing*: Plin.

mălĕfĭcĭum -i, n. (maleficus), *wrongdoing*: Caes., Liv. Concr., *an evil deed, crime, mischief*: maleficium committere, admittere, Cic.; sine ullo maleficio, Caes.; Liv.

mălĕfĭcus -a -um (male/facio), *evil-doing, mischievous*: homo, Cic.; Pl., Tac. Adv. **mălĕfĭcē,** *mischievously*: Pl.

mălĕsuādus -a -um (male/suadeo), *illadvising, seductive*: fames, Verg.

Mălĕventum -i, n. *an old town in Samnium, the name of which the Romans changed to Beneventum.*

mălĕvŏlens -entis (male/volo), *spiteful, illdisposed*: Pl.; superl.: malevolentissimae obtrectationes, Cic.

mălĕvŏlentĭa -ae, f. (malevolens), *ill-will, spite, malice*: malevolentia est voluptas ex malo alterius sine emolumento suo, Cic.; Sall.

mălĕvŏlus -a -um (male/volo), *ill-disposed, spiteful, malicious*: alicui, Cic. L.; in aliquem, Cic. L.; malevoli de me sermones, Cic. L. As subst., *an ill-disposed person*: Pl., Cic.

Mălĭăcus sĭnus (κόλπος Μαλιακός), *a gulf in Thessaly, opposite Euboea.* Adj. **Mălĭensis** -e, *Malian.*

mălĭfĕr -fĕra -fĕrum (malum/fero), *applebearing*: Verg.

mălignĭtās -ātis, f. (malignus), *ill-nature, malignity, spite*: Liv.; esp., *stinginess, niggardliness*: malignitas praedae partitae, Liv.; Pl.

mălignus -a -um (opp. benignus; from malus), *ill-disposed, malicious, malignant, wicked*. In gen.: vulgus, Hor.; oculis malignis spectare, Verg.; leges, Ov. Esp., *stingy, niggardly*: caupo, Hor.; Pl. TRANSF., (1) *barren, unfruitful*: collis, Verg. (2) *stinted, scanty*: lux, Verg.; aditus, Verg.; fama, Ov.

¶ Adv. **mălignē,** *maliciously, spitefully, malignantly*: loqui, Liv.; esp., *stingily, sparingly*: dividere, Liv.; laudare, Hor.

mălĭtĭa -ae, f. ([1]malus), *badness of quality*. In gen., *wickedness, vice*: Sall. Esp., *craft, cunning, malice*: malitia est versuta et fallax nocendi ratio, Cic., Pl.; sometimes playful, like our *'roguery'*: tamen a malitiā non discedis, Cic. L.

mălĭtĭōsus -a -um (malitia), *wicked*; esp., *crafty, roguish, knavish*: homo, Cic.; iuris interpretatio, Cic.

¶ Adv. (with compar.) **mălĭtĭōsē,** *wickedly, knavishly*: facere aliquid, Cic.

mallĕŏlus -i, m. (dim. of malleus), *a little hammer.* TRANSF., *a kind of fire-dart*: Cic.

mallĕus -i, m. *a hammer, mallet*: Pl.; esp., *the axe used for slaying animals offered in sacrifice*: Ov.

mālo malle mālŭi (mage/volo), *to wish rather, choose rather, prefer.*

In gen., (1) with acc. of noun or pronoun: ridenda poemata malo quam te, Juv.; Cic., Liv., Ov. (2) with infin.: servire quam pugnare, Cic. (3) with acc. and infin.: malo me vinci quam vincere, Cic.; Hor. (4) with nom. and infin.: esse quam videri bonus malebat, Sall.; Juv. (5) with subj.: mallem cognoscerem, Cic.; Liv., Juv. In these uses malo is sometimes strengthened by multo, or potius, or magis: Uticae potius quam Romae esse maluisset, Cic.

Esp., with dat. of person, *to be more favourable to*: in hac re malo universae Asiae et negotiatoribus, Cic. L.

mălŏbăthrum -i, n. (μαλόβαθρον), *an Indian or Syrian plant, from which a costly ointment was prepared*: Plin. TRANSF., *the oil of the plant*: Hor.

[1]**mālum** -i, n., *see* malus.

[2]**mālum** -i, n. (μῆλον), *an apple*, prov.: ab ovo usque ad mala, *from beginning to end* (as the Roman dinner began with eggs and ended with fruit), Hor. TRANSF., *any similar fruit, as the quince, peach, pomegranate, etc.*: Verg.

[1]**mălus** -a -um; comp. **pēior** -us; superl. **pessĭmus** -a -um, *bad, evil* (physically or morally).

In gen.: malus homo, Pl.; mores, Sall.; consuetudo, Hor.; opinio, Cic.; fama, *ill repute*, Sall.; poeta, Cic.; valetudo, *ill health*, Cic.; mala copia (*excess*) stomachum sollicitat, Hor.; gramina, *harmful*, Verg.

Esp. (1) *unfavourable, unsuccessful*: pugna, Cic.; in peius ruere, *to become worse*, Verg.; auspicium, Cic.; res, Sall.; avis, Hor. (2) *ugly*: Pl., Hor.

N. as subst. **mălum** -i, *an evil*; hence (1) *harm, disaster*: mala civilia, Cic.; cavere malum, Cic. (2) *punishment*: malum dare, Pl.; Cic., Sall., Liv. (3) *mischief, wrong*: Verg. (4) as a term of abuse, *scoundrel*: Pl., Ter., Cic.

Adv. **mălĕ,** compar. **pēius;** superl. **pessĭme,** *badly, ill.* In gen.: male olere, Cic.; male vestitus, Cic.; with some verbs, like a subst., *harm, ill*, etc.: male audire, *to be ill spoken of*, Cic.; male agere, Cic.; alicui male facere, Pl., Cic. L.; male velle, Pl.; L. Antonio male sit, Cic. L.; Pl., Cat.

Esp. (1) *unsuccessfully, unfortunately*: tuos labores male cecidisse, Caes.; Cic., Liv. (2) with words themselves used in bad sense, *bitterly, excessively*: odisse, ap. Cic. L.; male superbus, Caes. (3) with adj. partic., etc., of favourable sense, with negative force: male sanus, Cic. L.; Verg.; civitas male pacata, Cic.; male gratus, *unthankful*, Ov.; Liv., Tac.

[2]**mālus** -i, f. (μηλέα), *an apple-tree*: Verg.

[3]**mālus** -i, m. (1) *the mast of a ship*: malum erigere, Cic.; Verg., Hor. (2) *in the theatre*

or circus, *the pole 'to which awnings were fastened*: Lucr., Liv. (3) *an upright, used in the building of a tower*: Caes.

malva -ae, f. (μαλάχη, from μαλακός), *the mallow*: Cic. L., Hor.

Māmers -mertis, m. *the Oscan name of Mars.* ¶ Hence **Māmertīni** -ōrum, m. (*sons of Mars*), *the name assumed by certain mercenary troops who seized Messana.* Adj. **Māmertīnus** -a -um, *Mamertine*: civitas, Messana, Cic.

Māmilīus -a -um, *name of a Roman gens.*

māmilla -ae, f. (dim. of mamma), *a breast, teat*: Juv.

mamma -ae, f. (μάμμα), *a breast*; of men: mamma et barba, Cic.; of women: mammam matris appetere, Cic.; Pl., Lucr., Verg.; of female animals: suibus mammarum data est multitudo, Cic.; Liv.

mammĕātus -a -um (mamma), *big-bosomed*: Pl.

mammōsus -a -um (mamma), *big-bosomed*: Varr., Lucr.

Māmurra -ae, m. *a Roman knight of Formiae,* praefectus fabrum *in Caesar's army in Gaul, where he amassed great wealth*: urbs Mamurrarum, *Formiae*, Hor.

mānābĭlis -e (mano), *flowing, penetrating*: frigus, Lucr.

manceps -cĭpis, m. (manus/capio), *a person who bought anything at a public auction, and esp., one who contracted to farm state property; a purchaser, farmer, contractor*: praedae, Cic.; manceps fit Chrysogonus, Cic.; Tac. TRANSF., *a surety*: Pl.

Mancīnus -i, m., C. Hostilius, *consul, delivered up to the Numantines because of a dishonourable peace which he tried to make with them.*

mancĭpĭum (mancŭpĭum) -i, n. (manus/capio), *a taking in hand,* an old form of sale and purchase in Rome. Hence, *a formal, legal purchase of anything, conferring full power of possession*: lex mancipi (mancipii), *the contract of sale*, Cic.; mancipio dare, *to sell formally*, Pl., Cic., Lucr.; mancipio accipere, *to buy*, Pl., Cic.; res mancipi, *property which could be acquired by the ceremony of* mancipium, Cic.
TRANSF., *a slave acquired by the process of* mancipium: Hor., Liv.

mancĭpo (mancŭpo) -are (manus/capio), *to transfer by* mancipium *or formal sale, to sell formally*: alienos, Pl.; quaedam mancipat usus, *gives a title to*, Hor. TRANSF., *to give up to*: saginae mancipatus, Tac.

mancus -a -um, *maimed, crippled, lame*: mancus et omnibus membris captus ac debilis, Cic.; Pl., Liv., Ov. TRANSF., *imperfect, incomplete, defective*: virtus, Cic.; praetura, Cic.; Hor.

mandātor -ōris, m. (mando), *one who suborns accusers or informers*: Suet.

mandātū, abl. sing. as from mandatus, m. (mando), *by order*: mandatu meo, Cic. L.; Sullae, Cic.

mandātum -i, n., subst. from mando; q.v.

Mandēla -ae, f. *a town in the Sabine country.*

¹mando -are (manus/do), *to commit to one's charge, entrust.* LIT., (1) of persons and things: filiam viro, Pl.; alicui magistratum, Cic.; aliquem alicui alendum, Verg. (2) of actions, *to order, command, commission*; with

ut *or* ne and the subj.: Caes.; with pᵣ subj.: Caes.; with infin.: Tac. TRANSF. commit: aliquem aeternis tenebris, Cic. fugae, Caes.; aliquid memoriae, *to commᵢ memory*, Cic.; litteris, scriptis, *to commᵢ writing*, Cic.; corpus humo, Verg.
¶ Hence n. of partic. as subst. **mandāt** -i, *a commission, charge, order*: dare aᵢ mandata ut, Cic.; accipere, exsequi, ᵢ efficere, Sall.; perficere, Liv.; negleg fallere, *fail to execute*, Ov. Esp. of impᵉ orders: Plin. L., Tac., Suet.

²mando mandĕre mandi mansum, *to cₐ masticate.* LIT., animalia alia sugunt, carpunt, alia vorant, alia mandunt, ᵢ equi fulvum mandunt sub dentibus aur *champ the bit*, Verg.; humum, *to bite ground* (cf. mordere humum), of those ᵥ fall in battle, Verg. TRANSF., in gen., *to devour, consume*: lora, Liv.; Ov.

mandra -ae, f. (μάνδρα). (1) *a stall, cattle-*ᵢ Mart. (2) *a herd of cattle* (with drover): (3) *a draught-board*: Mart.

Mandūbii -ōrum, m. *a people in Gₑ Celtica.*

mandūcus -i, m. (²mando), *a mask to repre a person chewing*: Pl.

Mandūria -ae, f. *a town in southern Iᵢ between Aletium and Tarentum.*

māně, indecl. n. (1) as subst., *morning*: ᵢ mane novum, Cic.; ad ipsum mane, Hᵣ multo mane, *very early in the morning*, Ciᵣ (2) as adv., *in the morning, early*: hodie mₐ *early this morning*, Cic.; bene mane, ᵣ early in the morning, Cic.; cras mane, Tₑ

mānĕo mānēre mansi mansum (cf. μένω). (1) intransit., *to remain, stay*: seu manₑ seu proficiscantur, Caes.; in patria, Esp., *to stay the night*: apud me, Cic. sub Iove frigido, Hor.; Liv. TRANSF. *remain, endure, last*: nihil suo statu mₐ Cic.; in voluntate, Cic.; in condicionₑ *abide by*, Cic.; promissis, Verg.; of thiᵣ munitiones integrae manebant, Caes.; dat.: manent ingenia senibus, Cic.; Vₑ Liv.
(2) transit., in gen., *to wait for*: host adventum, Liv.; Pl., Ter.; esp., *to awaᵢ fate* or *destiny*: quis me manet exitus? ᵢ Liv.

mānes -ĭum, m. pl. (lit.=*the good*), *shades of the departed, the spirits of the ₐ* esp. as deified and courted with sacrif etc.: deorum manium iura sacra sunto, ᵢ Lucr., Hor., Liv.; of *the shade* of a sᵢ person: patris Anchisae, Verg.; Liv.
TRANSF., (1) poet., *the lower wᵢ infernal regions*: Verg.; Hor. (2) coᵢ *ashes, remains*: accipiet manes parvula ᵢ meos, Prop.; omnium nudatos manes, Lᵢ

mango -ōnis, m. (μάγγανον), *a salesman, esᵢ slave-dealer*: Mart., Juv., Quint.

mangōnĭcus -a -um (mango), *of a salesᵢ* Suet.

mănĭca -ae, f. (manus). (1) *the long sleeᵢ the tunic, reaching to the hand, and servinᵢ glove*: Cic., Verg., Tac. (2) *handᵢ manacles*: Pl., Verg., Hor.

mănĭcātus -a -um (manicae), *having sleeves*: tunica, Cic.

mănĭcŭla -ae, f. (dim. of manus), *a hand*: Pl.

mănĭfestărĭus -a -um (manifestus), *plain, evident, manifest*: Pl.

mănĭfestō, abl. as adv., *see* manifestus.

mănĭfesto -are (manifestus), *to manifest, show clearly, reveal*: aliquem latentem, Ov.

mănĭfestus -a -um (manus/*fendo, lit. *struck with the hand*), *palpable, clear, visible, evident*. In gen.: manifestae et apertae res, Cic.; Pl., Verg. Esp., *caught out, detected.* (1) of offences: manifestum atque deprehensum scelus, Cic. (2) of persons: ut coniuratos quam maxime manifestos habeant, *red-handed*, Sall.; Pl., Ov.; with genit. of crime: rerum capitalium, Sall.; vitae, *giving evident signs of life*, Tac.

¶ Abl. sing. of n. as adv. **mănĭfesto**, *clearly, plainly*: manifesto deprehendere, comprehendere, comperisse, Cic.; Pl. Compar. **mănĭfestĭus**, Verg., Tac.

Mănĭlĭus -a -um, *name of a Roman gens*; esp. of C. Manilius, *tribune of the people*, 67 B.C., *the author of the Lex Manilia, which gave to Pompey the sole command in the Mithridatic war.*

mănĭprētĭum=manupretium; q.v.

mănĭpŭlāris (**mănĭplāris**: Ov.) -e (manipulus), *belonging to a maniple*: iudex, *chosen from a maniple* (from the common soldiers), Cic.

¶ M. as subst. **mănĭpŭlāris** -is. (1) *a private soldier*: Pl., Cic. L., Tac. (2) *a fellow-soldier*: Pl., Caes.

mănĭpŭlārĭus -a -um (manipulus), *belonging to a private soldier*: Suet.

mănĭpŭlātim, adv. (manipulus). (1) *in bundles* or *handfuls*: Plin. (2) milit. t. t., *in maniples*: manipulatim structa acies, Liv.; Pl.

mănĭpŭlus (poet. **mănĭplus**) -i, m. (manus/*pleo), *a handful*. Lit., *a small bundle* or *handful*: filicum manipli, Verg. Transf., milit. t. t., *a company of foot soldiers, a division of the Roman army*, three maniples forming a cohort (so called because in early times the standard was a pole with a bundle of hay at the top): Pl., Caes., Liv., Ov.

Manlĭus -a -um, *name of a Roman gens*. Esp. of (1) M. Manlius Capitolinus, *consul in* 392 B.C., *who repulsed the attack of the Gauls upon the Capitol.* (2) L. Manlius Torquatus, *consul in* 340 B.C.

¶ Hence adj. **Manlĭānus** -a -um, *relating to Manlius*: turba, seditio, Liv.; Manliana imperia, *severe commands*, Liv.

mannŭlus -i, m. (dim. of ¹mannus), *a pony*: Mart., Plin. L.

mannus -i, m. (a Celtic word), *a small fast horse of Gaulish breed, a pony, cob*: Lucr., Hor., Ov.

Mannus -i, m. *a god of the Germans, son of Tuisto*: Tac.

māno -are, *to flow, drip.*

Lit., (1) of fluids, *to drip down*: e toto corpore sudor, Lucr.; fons nigra sub ilice manat, Ov. (2) of solid things, persons, etc., *to drip* (*with*); with abl.: Herculis simulacrum multo sudore manavit, Cic.; with internal acc., *to exude*: lacrimas (of a statue), Ov.; fig.: mella poetica, Hor.

Transf., (1) of things not fluid, esp. air, *to flow, spread*: aer, qui per maria manat, Cic.; Lucr., Tac. (2) of abstr. things, *to*

spread, to proceed, come from: peccata ex vitiis manant, Cic.; malum manavit per Italiam, Cic.; Liv.

mansĭo -ōnis, f. (maneo), *a remaining, stay, sojourn*: in vita, Cic., Ter. Transf., *a station, halting-place, stage*: Suet., Plin.

mansĭto -are (freq. of maneo), *to abide, stay, sojourn*: sub eodem tecto, Tac.

mansuēfăcĭo -făcĕre -fēci -factum, pass. **mansuēfīo** -fĭeri -factus sum (mansues/facio). Lit., of animals, *to tame*: uri mansuefieri non possunt, Caes. Transf., of men, *to soften, pacify, civilize*: a quibus mansuefacti et exculti, Cic.; plebem, Liv.

mansuēs -is or -ētis (manus/sueo), *tame*: Pl., Varr.

mansuesco -suescĕre -suēvi -suētum (manus/suesco). Transit., *to tame*: Varr., Lucr. Intransit., *to grow tame, mild, soft*: nescia humanis precibus mansuescere corda, Verg.

¶ Hence partic. as adj. (with compar. and superl.) **mansuētus** -a -um, *tame*. Lit., of animals: sus, Liv. Transf., *mild, soft, gentle, quiet*: mansuetus in senatu, Cic.; ut mansuetissimus videret, Cic.; Musae mansuetiores (of philosophy, rhetoric, etc.), Cic.; Prop., Liv., Ov.

¶ Adv. **mansuētē**, *mildly, gently, quietly*: Cic.

mansuētūdo -ĭnis, f. (mansuetus), *tameness*: Plin. Transf., *mildness, gentleness*: imperii, Cic.; uti clementiā et mansuetudine in aliquem, Caes.

mansuētus -a -um, partic. from mansuesco; q.v.

mantēlĕ -is, n. (manus), *a towel, napkin*: Verg.

mantēlum (mantellum) -i, n. *a covering, cloak*: Pl.

mantĭca -ae, f. *a wallet, knapsack*: Cat., Hor.

mantĭcĭnor -ari, dep. (μάντις/cano), *to prophesy*: Pl.

¹**manto** -are (freq. of maneo), *to remain, wait*; transit., *to wait for*: Pl.

²**Mantō** -ūs, f. (Μαντώ). (1) *daughter of the Theban seer Tiresias, mother of the seer Mopsus.* (2) *an Italian prophetess, mother of Ocnus, the founder of Mantua.*

Mantŭa -ae, f. *a town in north Italy, on the river Mincius, near to the birth-place of Vergil.*

mănŭālis -e (manus), *fitted to the hand*: saxa, *thrown by hand*, Tac.

mănŭbĭae -ārum, f. (manus), *the money obtained from the sale of booty*; esp. *the share given to the general, who often spent it in erecting some public building*: porticum de manubiis Cimbricis fecit, Cic., Liv. Transf., *the profits of robbery*: Cic., Suet.

mănŭbĭālis -e (manubiae), *relating to booty*: Suet.

mănŭbĭārĭus -a -um (manubiae), *relating to booty*: amicus, *profitable*, Pl.

mănŭbrĭum -i, n. (manus), *a haft, handle*: aurem vasis, Cic.; Pl., Juv.

mănŭf-. *see* manif-.

mănŭlĕātus -a -um (manulea), *with long sleeves*: Pl., Suet.

mănŭlĕus -i, m. and **mănŭlĕa** -ae, f. (manus), *the long sleeve of a tunic*: Pl.

mănŭmissĭo -ōnis, f. (manumitto), *the emancipation of a slave*: Cic.

mănūmitto -mittĕre -mīsi -missum, or as two words, manū mitto (manus/mitto), *to* *manumit, emancipate a slave*: servos, Cic.; Pl., Liv.

mănŭprĕtĭum (mănĭprĕtĭum) -i, n. *wages, hire, pay*: Pl., Liv. TRANSF., *a reward*: perditae civitatis, Cic.; Sen.

mănus -ūs, f. *the hand.*

LIT., and gen. fig. uses: manus dextera, laeva, Cic., etc.; accipere aliquid manibus, Cic.; lavare manūs, Cic.; prehendere alicuius manum, Cic.; aliquem manu, Cic.; ne manum quidem vertere, *not to move a finger, not to take any trouble*, Cic.; manūs adhibere vectigalibus, *lay hands on, rob*, Cic.; manūs dare, *to surrender*, Caes., Hor.; elabi de manibus, Cic.; oratio est in manibus, *can be read, is well known*, Cic.; habeo opus in manibus, *on hand, in preparation*, Cic. L.; ad manum esse, *to be near at hand*, Liv.; servum sibi habere ad manum, *as a private secretary*, Cic.; de manu in manum tradere, *to hand over*, Cic.; plenā manu alicuius laudes in astra tollere, *liberally*, Cic. L.; traditae per manus religiones, Liv.; manibus aequis (*with equal advantage, after a drawn battle*), dirimere pugnam, Liv.; abl. manu, *by manual labour, by art, artificially*: manu sata, *sown by hand*, Caes.; facta manu, Lucr.; urbs manu munitissima, Cic.

TRANSF., (1) *the strong arm, the fist*, as symbol of *force, effort*, etc.: manu capere urbes, Sall.; so of *hand to hand fighting*: res venit ad manus atque ad pugnam, Cic. (2) *power, jurisdiction*: haec non sunt in manu nostra, Cic.; Sall., Liv. (3) *the work of a hand*, esp. *the hand of artist or craftsman*: extrema, *the finishing touch*, Cic.; nos aera, manūs, navalia demus, Verg.; redeo ad meam manum, *I have begun again to write with my own hand*, Cic. L. (4) *a band* or *body of men*: coniuratorum, Cic.; manum facere, Cic.; conducere, Caes.; cogere, Caes.; Verg., Liv. (5) *the trunk of an elephant*: Cic. (6) manus ferrea, *a grappling-iron used in naval warfare*, Caes., Liv.

măpālĭa -ĭum, n. (a Punic word), *huts, hovels, the movable habitations of the African nomads*: Sall., Liv.

mappa -ae, f. (a Punic word), *a table-napkin*: Hor., Juv.; esp., *a napkin thrown down in the circus as a signal for the races to begin*: Juv., Suet.

Mărăthōn -ōnis, f. (Μαραθών), *a coastal village in Attica, where the Persian army was defeated by the Athenians in 490 B.C.*

¶ Adj. **Mărăthōnĭus** -a -um, *Marathonian.*

Marcellus -i, m. *the cognomen of a family of the* gens Claudia.

Esp. (1) M. Claudius Marcellus, *the conqueror of Syracuse, who defeated Hannibal at Nola, and slew Viridomarus king of the Insubres with his own hand.* (2) M. Claudius Marcellus, *nephew, adopted son, and son-in-law of Augustus.*

¶ Hence subst. **Marcellĭa** -ōrum, n. pl. *a festival in honour of the family of Marcellus in Sicily*: Liv.; adj. **Marcellĭānus** -a -um, *of Marcellus.*

marcĕo -ēre, *to wither, to droop, to be feeble.* LIT., marcent luxuriā, Liv.; Lucr. TRANSF., *to slacken*, of appetite: Hor.

marcesco -ĕre (marceo), *to begin to droop, to grow feeble*: vino, Ov.; desidiā, Liv.

marcĭdus -a -um (marceo), *withering, drooping*: lilia, Ov. TRANSF., *enfeebled, languid*: somno aut libidinosis vigiliis, Tac

Marcĭus -a -um, *name of a Roman* gens. *It most famous member was* Ancus Marcius, *fourth king of Rome.* As adj., *Marcian*: aqu an aqueduct begun by Ancus Marcius; saltu (in Liguria, so called from the defeat o Q. Marcius, 188 B.C.), Liv.

¶ Hence, also adj. **Marcĭānus** -a -um *Marcian*: foedus, *made by L. Marcius wit the inhabitants of Cadiz.*

Marcōmāni and **Marcōmanni** -ōrum, m *a powerful Germanic tribe.*

marcor -ōris, m. (marceo), *rottenness, decay* Sen., Plin.

marcŭlus -i, m. *a small hammer*: Plin., Mar

Marcus -i, m. *a common Roman praenomen* abbreviated M.

măre -is, n. (abl. sing. mari or mare), *the se* LIT., mare Aegaeum, Cic.; mare nostru =*the Mediterranean Sea*, Caes.; superun *the Adriatic*, Cic.; inferum, *the Tyrrhenia Sea*, Cic.; conclusum, *inland sea*, Caes mari magno, Lucr.; mare ingredi, *to go* sea, Cic.; mare infestum habere, *to infest th sea* (of pirates), Cic.; terrā marique, *by se and land*, Liv., Juv., etc.; polliceri maria montes, *to make boundless promises*, Sall.

TRANSF., *sea-water*: Chium maris exper *unmixed with sea-water*, Hor.

Mărĕa -ae or **Mărĕōta** -ae, f. (Μαρέα), *a lal and city of Lower Egypt, famous for its wine.*

¶ Hence adj. **Mărĕōtĭcus** -a -um, *M reotic, Egyptian*; n. as subst. **Mărĕōtĭcu** -i, *Mareotic wine*: Hor.; f. adj. **Mărĕōti** ĭdis, poet.=*Egyptian*: vites, Verg.

margărīta -ae, f. and **margărītum** -i, (μαργαρίτης), *a pearl*: Cic.

margĭno -are (margo), *to make a border to, t border*: vias, Liv.

margo -ĭnis, m. and f. *a border, edge*: scut Liv.; fontis, Ov.; libri, Juv. TRANSF *boundary*: imperii, Ov.

Mărĭca -ae, f. *a nymph, supposed to reside c Minturnae*; poet., *a lake near Minturnc named after her*: Hor.

mărīnus -a -um (mare), *of the sea, marine* marini terrenique umores, Cic.; ros, ros mary, Hor.

mărisca -ae, f. *a large fig*: Mart. TRANSF., *th piles*: Juv.

mărīta, *see* maritus.

mărītālis -e (maritus), *relating to marriage o a married pair, matrimonial*: vestis, Ov.; Ju

mărītĭmus (mărītŭmus) -a -um (mare (1) *of the sea, marine, maritime*: fluctus, ora, Caes., Cic., Liv.; praedo, *a pirate*, Cic imperium, *a naval command*, Cic. (2) c *the sea-coast*: civitas, Caes.; silva, Ci N. pl. as subst. **mărītĭma** -ōrum, *mariti regions, the sea-coast*: Cic. L., Liv.

mărīto -are (maritus). LIT., *to marry, give marriage*: principem, Tac.; Suet. TRANSF *of vines, to bind to a tree, to train*: Hor.

mărītus -a -um (mas).

LIT., *of* or *relating to marriage, matr monial, nuptial*: foedus, Ov.; Venus, *conjug love*, Ov.; domus, *houses of married peop* Liv.

TRANSF., of plants, *tied* or *trained togethe* ulmus, Cat.

¶ As subst. (1) **marītus** -i, m. *a husband*: Pl., Cic., Verg. TRANSF., *a lover, suitor*: Prop.; of animals: maritus olens, *the he-goat*, Hor.; Verg. (2) **marīta** -ae, f. *a wife*: Hor., Ov.

Marius -a -um, *the name of a Roman gens. Its most distinguished member was* C. Marius, *seven times consul, conqueror of Jugurtha and the Cimbri, rival of Sulla, leader of the popular party at Rome. As adj., Marian.*
¶ Hence also adj. **Mariānus** -a -um, *Marian.*

Marmarĭdēs -ae, m. *a man of Marmarica, an African*: Ov.

marmor -ŏris, n. (μάρμαρος), *marble*. LIT., Cic., Verg., Hor. TRANSF., (1) *wrought marble,* esp. *a statue*: Ov., Hor. (2) *the white foamy surface of the sea*: marmor infidum, Verg.; Lucr. (3) *stone* generally: Ov.

marmŏrārĭus -a -um (marmor), *of marble*: Sen.

marmŏrĕus -a -um (marmor), *marble, made of marble.*
LIT., signum, Cic.; aliquem marmoreum facere, *or* ponere, *to make a marble statue of,* Verg., Hor.
TRANSF., *like marble in smoothness* or *colour*: cervix, Verg.; gelu, Ov.; aequor, Verg.

Marō -ōnis, m. *the cognomen of the poet* P. Vergilius; *see* Vergilius.

Marobodŭus -i, m. *king of the Suevi, who was defeated by Arminius, fled to Italy, and was received by Augustus.*

Marōnēa (-ĭa) -ae, f. (Μαρώνεια). (1) *a Samnite town.* (2) *a town in Thrace, famous for its wine*; adj. **Marōnēus** -a -um.

Marpessus (Marpēsus) -i, m. *a mountain in Paros.* Adj. **Marpessĭus (Marpēsĭus)** -a -um, *Marpessian, Parian*: Verg.

marra -ae, f. *a hoe for rooting up weeds*: Juv.

Marrŭcĭni -ōrum, m. *a people on the Adriatic coast of Italy.*
¶ Hence adj. **Marrūcīnus** -a -um, *of the Marrucini.*

Marrŭvĭum (Marrŭbĭum) -i, n. *a city in Latium, capital of the Marsi.* Adj. **Marrŭvĭus** -a -um, *of Marruvium.*

Mars Martis, m. (old form, Māvors), *Mars, father of Romulus and ancestor of the Romans; god of agriculture and of war.* Mars pater, Cic., Liv. TRANSF., (1) *war, battle, fight*: Hectoreus, *with Hector*, Ov.; invadunt martem, *begin the fray*, Verg.; suo marte cadunt, *in fight with one another*, Ov.; femineo marte cadere, *in fight with a woman*, Ov.; rex suo marte res suas recuperavit, *by his own exertions*, Cic.; esp., *manner of fighting*: equitem suo alienoque marte pugnare—i.e., *both on horse and on foot*, Liv.; *of the issue* of war: marte aequo, Caes.; aequato, Liv.; incerto, Tac.; mars belli communis, Cic.; *of legal disputes*: mars forensis, Ov. (2) *the planet Mars*: Cic.
Adj. **Martĭus** and poet. **Māvortĭus** -a -um (*see* Mavors), *of Mars, sacred to Mars.*
LIT., Martius mensis *or* simply Martius, *the month of March*: Kalendae Martiae, *the 1st of March*: Cic.; proles, *Romulus and Remus*, Ov.; miles, *Roman*, Ov.; Campus Martius, *the plain of Mars at Rome*, Cic.; Martia legio, *name of a Roman legion*, Cic.

TRANSF., (1) *warlike*: Penthesilea, Verg.; Thebe, *scene of many wars*, Ov. (2) *belonging to the planet Mars*: fulgor rutilus horribilisque terris quem Martium dicitis, Cic.
¶ Adj. **Martĭālis** -e, *of Mars*: flamen, Cic.; lupi, *sacred to Mars*, Hor.; m. as subst.
Martĭālis. (1) *a priest of Mars*: Cic. (2) *a soldier of the Legio Martia*: Cic.

Marsi -ōrum, m. (1) *the Marsians, an ancient people of Latium.* Adj. **Marsĭcus** -a -um, *Marsic*: bellum, *the Social War*, Cic.; adj. **Marsus** -a -um, *Marsian*: nenia, *enchantments*, Hor.
(2) *a people in Germany, between the Rhine, the Lippe, and the Ems.*

marsūppĭum -i, n. (μαρσύπιον), *a purse, pouch*: Pl.

Marsÿās and **Marsÿa** -ae, m. (Μαρσύας). (1) *a satyr, beaten in a musical contest with Apollo, who flayed him alive. A statue of Marsyas stood in the Roman forum, at the spot where lawyers transacted their business.* (2) *a river in Phrygia, flowing into the Maeander.*

¹**Martĭālis** -e, adj. from Mars; q.v.
²**Martĭālis** -is, m. M. Valerius, *a native of Bilbilis in Spain, who wrote Latin epigrams under the emperors Domitian, Nerva, and Trajan.*

Martĭcŏla -ae, m. (Mars/colo), *a worshipper of Mars*: Ov.

Martĭgĕna -ae, m. (Mars/geno=gigno), *begotten of Mars, offspring of Mars*: Ov.

Martĭus -a -um, adj. from Mars; q.v.

mas măris, m. *the male* (opp. femina), applied to men, animals, and plants.
LIT., a prima congressione maris et feminae, Cic.; mas vitellus, *a male yolk,* i.e., *that would produce a male chick*, Hor.; ure mares oleas, i.e., *barren*, Ov.
TRANSF., *manly, vigorous*: animi mares, Hor.; male mas, *unmanly, effeminate*, Cat.

mascŭlīnus -a -um (masculus), *of the male sex and gender, masculine*: Phaedr., Plin.

mascŭlus -a -um (dim. of mas), *of the male sex, male.* LIT., Phaedr., Mart.; m. as subst., *a male*: Liv. TRANSF., *manly, bold, courageous, vigorous*: tura, Verg.; libido, Hor.; proles, Hor.

Măsĭnissa -ae, m. *king of Numidia, grandfather of Jugurtha, first enemy then ally of the Romans.*

massa -ae, f. (μάζα), *a lump, mass*: picis, Verg.; lactis coacti, *of cheese*, Ov.; esp., *of metals; of copper*: Verg.; *of iron* or *gold*: Ov.

Massăgĕtēs -ae, m. (Μασσαγέτης), plur.: Massagetae, *a Scythian people on the east coast of the Caspian Sea.*

Massĭcus -a -um, *Massic*: mons, *a mountain in Campania, famous for its wine* (now Monte Masso *or* Massico); Massicum vinum *or* simply Massicum -i, n. *Massic wine*: Hor.; so: umor Massicus, Verg.

Massĭlĭa -ae, f. (Μασσαλία), *a seaport town in Gallia Narbonensis, colonized from Phocaea in Asia Minor* (now Marseilles). Adj. **Massĭlĭensis** -e, *of Massilia*; m. pl. as subst. **Massĭlĭensēs** -ium, *Massilians.*

Massÿli -ōrum, m. *a people in Numidia.* Adj. **Massÿlus** -a -um, poet.=*African*: equites, Verg.

mastigĭa -ae, m. (μαστιγίας), *a scoundrel*: Pl.

mastrūca -ae, f. (a Sardinian word), *a sheepskin*: Cic.; used as a term of reproach: Pl.

mastrūcātus -a -um (mastruca), *clothed in the* mastruca: Cic.

matăra -ae (Caes.) and **matăris** -is (Liv.), f. (a Celtic word), *a pike or lance.*

mătellĭo -ōnis, m. (dim. of matula), *a small pot, vessel*: Cic.

māter mātris, f. (μήτηρ), *a mother.*
LIT., (1) human: de pietate in matrem, Cic.; materfamilias, Cic.; matrem fieri de Iove, *to become pregnant by*, Ov.; *wife*: Liv.; applied to a nurse: Verg.; to priestesses and elderly women: Pl. (2) of goddesses: Mater Terra, Liv.; magna mater, Cic.; *or simply* mater (sc. deorum), *Cybele*, Verg.; Amorum, *Venus*, Ov. (3) of animals, *dam, parent*: Verg. (4) of plants, *the parent stem*: Verg.
TRANSF., (1) of native towns or countries: Populonia mater, Verg.; haec terra quam matrem appellamus, Liv. (2) in gen., *source, origin*: mater omnium bonarum artium est sapientia, Cic.; utilitas iusti prope mater et aequi, Hor.; Quint.

mătercŭla -ae, f. (dim. of mater), *a little mother*: Pl., Cic., Hor.

mătĕrĭa -ae, f. and **mătĕrĭēs** -ēi, f. *matter, material, stuff of which anything is composed.*
LIT., physical; in gen.: materies opus est ut crescant postera saecla, Lucr.; materia rerum, Cic.; materiam praebet seges arida, *fuel*, Ov.; materiam superabat opus, Ov.; esp., *wood, timber*: delata materia omnis infra Veliam, Liv.; materiam caedere, Liv.; Caes., Lucr., Cic., Tac.
TRANSF., (1) *subject-matter*: artis, Cic.; Hor., Plin. L. (2) *occasion, cause*: gloriae, seditionis, Cic.; aurum summi materies mali, Hor.; Liv., Tac. (3) *natural disposition, abilities*: Catonis, Cic.; Ov.

mătĕrĭārĭus -a -um (materia), *of timber*: Plin. M. as subst. **mătĕrĭārĭus** -i, *a timber merchant*: Pl.

mătĕrĭēs -ēi, f. = materia; q.v.

mătĕrĭo -are (materies), *to build, construct of wood*: aedes male materiatae, *of bad woodwork*, Cic.

mătĕrĭor -ari, dep. (materia), *to fell wood, procure wood*: Caes.

mătĕris = matara or mataris; q.v.

măternus -a -um (mater), *of a mother, maternal*: animus, Ter.; sanguis, Cic.; tempora, *period of pregnancy*, Ov.; nobilitas, *on the mother's side*, Verg.; Caesar cingens materna tempora myrto, Verg.

mătertĕra -ae, f. (mater), *a mother's sister, maternal aunt*: Pl., Cic., Ov.

măthēmătĭcus -a -um (μαθηματικός), *mathematical*: Plin. M. as subst. **măthēmătĭcus** -i. (1) *a mathematician*: Cic., Sen. (2) *an astrologer*: Tac., Juv. F. as subst. **măthēmătĭca** -ae. (1) *mathematics*: Sen. (2) *astrology*: Suet.

Mătīnus -i, m. *a mountain in Apulia, famous for its honey.* Adj. **Mătīnus** -a -um, *Matine.*

Matisco -ōnis, m. *town of the Aedui in Gaul* (now *Mâcon*).

Mătĭus -a -um, *name of a Roman gens.*

Mātrālĭa -ĭum, n. pl. (mater); with or without festa, *the annual festival of the* Mater Matuta, *celebrated on the* 11th *of* June: Ov.

mātrĭcīda -ae, c. (mater/caedo), *a person who murders his mother, a matricide*: Cic. L., Suet.

mātrĭcīdĭum -i, n. (matricida), *the slaying of a mother by her son, matricide*: Cic.

mātrīmōnĭum -i, n. (mater), *marriage, matrimony.* LIT., aliquam in matrimonium ducere, *to marry*, Cic.; dare alicui filiam in matrimonium, Caes.; habere aliquam in matrimonio, Cic.; Pl., Tac. TRANSF., plur.: matrimonia, *married women*, Tac.

mātrīmus -a -um (mater), *having a mother still living*: Liv., Tac.

[1]**mātrōna** -ae, f. (mater), *a married woman, matron*: Pl., Verg., Liv.; esp., *a noble lady*: Pl., Cic., Liv.; of *Juno*: Hor.

[2]**Mātrōna** -ae, m. *a river in Gallia Lugdunensis* (now the *Marne*).

mātrōnālis -e ([1]matrona), *of a married woman, matronly*: decus, Liv.; Ov. N. pl. as subst. **Mātrōnālia** -ium, *a festival held by Roman matrons in honour of Mars on the* 1st *of March*: Ov.

matta -ae, f. *a mat of rushes*: Ov.

mattĕa (mattўa) -ae, f. (ματτύα), *a dainty dish, a dainty*: Sen., Suet., Mart.

Mattĭăcus -a -um, *of Mattiacum, a town near the modern Wiesbaden.*

mătŭla -ae, f. *a vessel, pot*; as a term of reproach, *simpleton*: Pl.

mātūrātē, adv. from maturo; q.v.

mātūrē, adv. from maturus; q.v.

mātūresco mātūrescĕre mātūrŭi (maturus), *to ripen, become ripe*: cum maturescere frumenta inciperent, Caes.; partūs, Cic.; nubilibus maturuit annis, Ov.

mātūrĭtās -ātis, f. (maturus), *ripeness.* LIT., frugum, Cic.; Caes. TRANSF., (1) *full development, ripeness, maturity*: scelerum maturitas in nostri consulatūs tempus erupit, Cic.; aetatis ad prudentiam, Cic. L.; Tac. (2) *the right moment of time, fullness of time*: eius rei maturitas nequedum venit, Cic. L.

mātūro -are (maturus).
Transit., *to make ripe, to ripen.* LIT., uvas, Tib.; maturata omnia, *ripe*, Cic. TRANSF., (1) *to quicken, hasten, accelerate*: huic mortem, Cic.; insidias consuli, Sall.; iter, Caes.; fugam, Verg.; with infin., *to hasten, make haste to*: flumen exercitum transducere maturavit, Caes. (2) *to anticipate, do too soon*: ni Catilina maturasset signum dare, *had been too hasty in giving the signal*, Sall.
Intransit., *to hasten, make haste*: successor tuus non potest ita maturare, Cic.; Liv.

mātūrus -a -um, adj. (with compar. maturior, superl. maturissimus *or* maturrimus), *ripe, mature, perfect.*
LIT., physically, (1) of fruits: poma, Cic., uva, Verg.; Liv. (2) of men and animals, *mature, grown up*: maturus aevi, *grown*, Verg.; aetas, virgo, Hor.; with dat.: virgo matura viro, Verg.; progenies matura militiae, *ripe for*, Liv. (3) of light: maturi sole, Verg.
TRANSF., (1) intellectually and morally, *ripe, mature*: annis gravis atque animi maturus Aletes, Verg.; Cic. (2) of things, *ripe, developed, mature, timely*: gloria, Liv.; maturum videbatur (*it seemed the proper time*) repeti patriam, Liv.; Cic. (3) *quick,*

speedy, *early*: hiems, Caes.; decessio, iudicium, Cic.

¶ Adv. **mātūrē** (with compar. mātūrĭŭs, and superl. mātūrissĭmē *or* mātūrrĭmē). (**1**) *at the right time, seasonably, opportunely*: sentire, Cic.; satis mature occurrere, Caes.; Pl. (**2**) *in good time, betimes, early*: senem fieri, Cic.; maturius proficisci, Caes. (**3**) *too soon, prematurely*: mature decessit, Nep.; Pl.

Mātūta -ae, f. (**1**) *the goddess of the early morn*. (**2**) *an ancient Italian goddess, identified with Ino Leucothea.*

mātūtīnus -a -um (connected with mane), *early in the morning, pertaining to the morning*: tempora, Cic. L.; equi, *horses of Aurora*, Ov.; pater, *Janus, invoked in the morning*, Hor.; like adv.: se matutinus agebat, Verg.

Mauri -ōrum, m. (Μαῦροι), *the Moors, inhabitants of Mauritania*; adj. **Maurus** -a -um, *Moorish*; poet., *African, Carthaginian.*

¶ Hence subst. **Mauritānĭa** -ae, f. *Mauritania, a district in North-west Africa*; adj. **Maurūsĭus** -a -um, *Mauritanian*; poet.: *African.*

Mausōlus -i, m. (Μαύσωλος), *king of Caria, husband of Artemisia, who erected a splendid monument to his memory*. Adj. **Mausōlēus** -a -um, *belonging to Mausolus*: sepulcrum, or as subst. **Mausōlēum** -i, n. *the tomb of Mausolus*, Plin.; in gen., *any splendid sepulchre*: Suet.

māvŏlo=malo; q.v.

Māvors -vortis, m. archaic and poet. for Mars; q.v. Adj. **Māvortĭus** -a -um, *belonging to Mars, Martial*: moenia, *Rome*, Ov.; tellus, *Thrace*, Verg.; proles, *the Thebans*, Ov.; m. as subst. Mavortius, *Meleager, the son of Mars*: Ov.

maxilla -ae, f. (dim. of mala), *the jaw-bone, jaw*: Cic.

maximē, superl. of magis; q.v.

maximĭtās -ātis, f. (maximus), *greatness, size*: Lucr.

maximŏpĕrĕ, see magnopere.

maximus, superl. of magnus; q.v.

māzŏnŏmus -i, m. *or* **māzŏnŏmŏn** -i, n. (μαζονόμος), *a charger, large dish*: Hor.

nĕämet, **nĕäptĕ**, see meus.

mĕātus -ūs, m. (meo), *a going, motion*: aquilae, *flight*, Tac.; Lucr., Verg. TRANSF., *a way, path, course*: Danubius in Ponticum mare sex meatibus (*mouths*) erumpit, Tac.; Luc.

Mēcastor, see Castor.

nēchănĭcus -i, m. (μηχανικός), *a mechanic*: Suet.

neddix -ĭcis, m. (Oscan), *the name of a magistrate among the Oscans*; with the addition, tuticus, meddix tuticus, *chief magistrate*: Liv.

Mēdĕa -ae, f. (Μήδεια), *an enchantress, daughter of king Aeetes in Colchis; she helped Jason to obtain the golden fleece, fled with him, and was afterwards deserted by him.*

¶ Hence f. adj. **Mēdēis** -idis, *magical*: Ov.

nĕdĕor -ēri, dep. *to heal, to cure*.

LIT., ars medendi, Cic.; with dat.: morbo, Cic.; prov.: cum capiti mederi debeam, reduviam curo, Cic.

TRANSF., *to heal, assist, alleviate*: incommodis omnium, Cic.; adflictae et perditae reipublicae, Cic.; Caes., Tac.

Pres. partic. as subst. **mĕdens** -entis, m. *a physician*; esp. in plur.: Lucr., Ov.

Mēdi -ōrum, m. (Μῆδοι), *the Medes*; poet.= the *Persians, Assyrians, Parthians.*

¶ Hence subst. **Mēdĭa** -ae, f. (Μηδία), *Media*, a district of Asia.; adj. **Mēdĭcus** and **Mēdus** -a -um, *Median*; poet.=*Persian, Assyrian.*

mĕdĭastīnus -i, m. (medius), *a drudge*: Cic., Hor.

mēdĭca -ae, f. (Μήδικη), *lucerne, a kind of clover*: Verg.

mĕdĭcābilis -e (medicor), *curable*: nullis amor est medicabilis herbis, Ov.

mĕdĭcāmen -ĭnis, n. (medicor), *a drug, medicine.*

LIT., Cic., Juv., Tac.; also (**1**) *a poison*: Tac. (**2**) *colouring matter, dye*, and esp., *rouge, paint*: Ov.

TRANSF., *a remedy*: iratae medicamina fortia praebe, Ov.

mĕdĭcāmentum -i, n. (medicor), *a drug, medicine, remedy.*

LIT., salutare, Cic.; salubria, Liv.; also (**1**) *a poison*: coquere medicamenta, Liv. (**2**) *a magic potion*: Pl., Ov.

TRANSF., (**1**) *a remedy, cure*: doloris, Cic. (**2**) *embellishment*: fucati medicamenta ruboris et candoris, Cic.

¹**mĕdĭcātus** -a -um, partic. from medico; q.v.

²**mĕdĭcātus** -ūs, m. (medicor), *a means of enchantment, charm*: Ov.

mĕdĭcīna -ae, f., see medicinus.

mĕdĭcīnus -a -um (medicus), *belonging to the art of healing*: Varr.

F. as subst. **mĕdĭcīna** -ae. (**1**) (sc. domus, etc.), *a doctor's house*: Pl. (**2**) (sc. ars), *the art of healing*: medicinam exercere, *to practise medicine*, Cic.; medicinam facere, Phaedr. (**3**) (sc. res), *means of healing, medicine*. LIT., medicinam adhibere, Cic. L.; Pl. TRANSF., *cure*: laboris, Cic.; furoris, Verg.; Ov.

mĕdĭco -are (medicus). (**1**) *to medicate, drug*: semina, Verg. (**2**) *to dye*: capillos, Ov.; Hor. (**3**) *to poison*: Suet.

¶ Hence partic. **mĕdĭcātus**, *steeped, drugged*: somnus, *procured by drugs or magic*, Ov.; as adj. (with compar. and superl.), *healing, medicinal*: Plin.

mĕdĭcor -ari, dep. (medicus), *to heal, cure*; with acc.: cuspidis ictum, Verg.; with dat. of person: senibus, Verg.

¹**mĕdĭcus** -a -um (medeor), *healing, wholesome, medicinal*. Adj.: manus, Verg.; ars, Ov. M. as subst. **mĕdĭcus** -i, *a doctor, physician*: medicum ad aegrum adducere, Cic.; Pl., Suet.

²**Mēdĭcus**, see Medi.

mĕdĭē, adv. from medius; q.v.

mĕdĭĕtās -ātis, f. (medius), *the middle, mean*; *a translation of the Greek* μεσότης.: Cic.

mĕdimnum -i, n. and **mĕdimnus** -i, m. (genit. pl. medimnum: Cic.; from μέδιμνος), *a Greek measure of capacity, containing six Roman modii*: Cic.

mĕdĭocris -e (medius), *moderate, middling, ordinary*: spatium, Caes.; copiae, Caes.; orator, vir, Cic.; eloquentia, Cic.; often with neg., *extraordinary*: Ter., Caes., Cic.

¶ Adv. (with compar.) **mĕdĭocrĭtĕr**. (**1**) *moderately, tolerably, not extraordinarily*: nemo mediocriter doctus. Cic.: in aliqua re

[365]

mediocriter versatum, Cic.; with neg.: Pl.,
Caes., Cic. (2) *with moderation*: aliquid
mediocriter ferre, Cic.

mĕdĭocrĭtās -ātis, f. (mediocris). (1) *moderation, medium, the mean*: mediocritatem illam
tenere quae est inter nimium et parum, Cic.;
auream mediocritatem diligere, *the golden
mean*, Hor.; plur.: mediocritates probabant,
moderation in passion, Cic. (2) *mediocrity,
insignificance*: ingenii, Cic.; Quint.

mĕdĭocrĭtĕr, adv. from mediocris; q.v.

Mĕdĭōlānum -i, n. and **-lānĭum** -i, n. *a town
in Cisalpine Gaul* (now *Milan*).

¶ Hence adj. **Mĕdĭōlānensis** -e, *of
Mediolanum*.

Mĕdĭōmatrīci -ōrum, m. *a people in Gaul,
on the Moselle*.

mĕdĭoxĭmus (**mĕdĭoxŭmus**) -a -um
(medius), *in the middle, mid-most*: dii superi
atque inferi et medioxumi, Pl.

mĕdĭtāmentum -i, n. (meditor), *preparation,
practice*; in plur.: belli meditamenta, Tac.

mĕdĭtātē, adv. from meditor; q.v.

mĕdĭtātĭo -ōnis, f. (meditor). (1) *a thinking
over anything, contemplation*: futuri mali,
Cic. (2) *practice, exercise, preparation*:
obeundi muneris, Cic.; locos multā com-
mentatione atque meditatione paratos atque
expeditos habere, Cic., Sen., Quint.

mĕdĭtātus -a -um, partic. from meditor; q.v.

mĕdĭterrānĕus -a -um (medius/terra), *inland*:
regiones, Caes.; homines, Cic.; n. pl. as
subst. mediterranea, *inland country*: mediterranea Galliae petit, Liv. (Not used in
classical Latin for what is now called the
Mediterranean Sea.)

mĕdĭtor -ari, dep. (connected with μήδομαι
and μέτρον). (1) *to think over, consider*: de sua
ratione, Cic.; with indir. quest.: mecum,
quid dicerem, Cic.; with acc.: Cic. (2) *to
think about doing a thing, to meditate, intend*;
with acc.: Cic. L., Verg.; with infin.: multos
annos regnare, Cic. (3) *to practise, exercise
oneself in*: Demosthenes perfecit meditando
ut, with acc., Verg., Juv.

¶ Hence perf. partic. in pass. sense
mĕdĭtātus -a -um, *meditated, considered,
prepared*: meditatum et cogitatum scelus,
Cic.; oratio, Liv.; Ov., Tac.

¶ Adv. **mĕdĭtātē**, *thoughtfully, thoroughly*: Pl.

mĕdĭum -i, n. *the middle*, see medius.

mĕdĭus -a -um (connected with μέσος -η -ον),
middle, midmost, mid.

LIT., in space; in gen.: medius mundi
locus, Cic.; Caes., Lucr., etc.; esp. as predicative adj., *at its midmost point, in the centre,
by the middle*: in foro medio, Pl.; medium
adripere aliquem, Ter.; Caes., Cic., Verg.

TRANSF., (1) in time; in gen., *intervening,
intermediate*: ultimum, proximum, medium
tempus, Cic.; mediis diebus, Liv.; of age:
media aetas, *middle age*, Cic.; esp. as predicative adj., *mid-*: media nocte, *at midnight*,
Caes.; Cic., Verg., Hor., Liv.

(2) in other relations: a, *central, neutral,
intermediate*: cum inter bellum et pacem
medium nihil sit, *no mean*, Cic.; medium
quendam cursum tenebant, Cic.; medium
se gerere, *to remain neutral*, Cic.; pacis eras
mediusque belli, Hor.; Liv.: b, *ordinary,
common, middling*: gratia non media, Liv.:

c, *ambiguous*: responsum, Liv.: d, *intervening* between parties; *as mediator*: medium
sese offert, Verg.; *as troublemaker*: quos
inter medius venit furor, Verg.: e, *half*:
media pars, Ov.

¶ N. as subst. **mĕdĭum** -i, *the middle*.
LIT., in space: in medio aedium sedens, Liv.;
Lucr., Verg., Liv. TRANSF., (1) in time: iam
diei medium erat, Liv. (2) *the public eye,
everyday life*: voluptates faciles, communes,
in medio sitas, *available to all*, Cic.; tabulae
sunt in medio, *in everyone's view*, Cic.; rem
in medium vocare, Cic.; aliquem tollere de
medio, *to put out of the way, do away with*,
Cic. (3) *the community, the common good*:
in medium, Cic., Verg., Tac.

¶ Adv. **mĕdĭē**, *moderately*: Tac.

mĕdĭus fĭdĭus, see fidius.

medix, see meddix.

mĕdulla -ae, f. (medius). LIT., *the middle*;
esp. *the marrow of bones*;gen. plur.:cum albis
ossa medullis, Ov.; Cic.; Hor. TRANSF.,
marrow, heart, inmost part: mihi haeres in
medullis, *I love you from the bottom of my
heart*, Cic. L.; Pl., Ov.

Mĕdullĭa -ae, f. *a town in Latium*.

¶ Hence adj. **Mĕdullīnus** -a -um, *of
Medullia*.

mĕdullĭtŭs, adv. (medulla), *from the very
marrow*; hence, *inwardly, cordially*: Pl.

mĕdullŭla -ae, f. (dim. of medulla), *marrow*:
Cat.

Mēdus -i, m., see Medi.

Mĕdūsa -ae, f. (Μέδουσα), *the daughter of
Phorcus, one of the Gorgons, mother of the
horse Pegasus by Neptune; Minerva made
everything she looked at turn to stone; she was
slain by Perseus.*

¶ Hence adj. **Mĕdūsaeus** -a -um,
Medusean: equus, *Pegasus*, Ov.; fons,
Hippocrene, Ov.

Mĕgaera -ae, f. (Μέγαιρα), *one of the Furies.*

Mĕgălē -ēs, f. (Μεγάλη), *the Great One*, a
name of Magna Mater *or* Cybele.

¶ Hence adj. **Mĕgălensis** -e, *belonging to
Cybele*; n. pl. as subst. **Mĕgălensĭa** and
Mĕgălēsĭa -ĭum, *the festival celebrated on
the 4th of April, in honour of Cybele.*

¶ Hence adj. **Mĕgălēsĭăcus** -a -um,
relating to this festival.

Mĕgălŏpŏlis, acc. -im, f. and **Mĕgălē pŏlis**
acc. -in, f. (Μεγαλόπολις and Μεγάλη πόλις), *a
town in Arcadia, birth-place of Polybius.*

¶ Hence subst. **Mĕgălŏpŏlītae** -ārum,
m. *the inhabitants of Megalopolis*; adj.
Mĕgălŏpŏlītānus -a -um, *of Megalopolis.*

Mĕgăra -ae, f. and **Mĕgăra** -ōrum, n
(Μέγαρα). (1) *a town in a part of Greece
next to Attica, called* **Mĕgăris** -ĭdis, f
(Μεγαρίς). (2) *a town in Sicily, also calle*
Mĕgăris.

¶ Hence subst. **Mĕgărēus** -i, m.
Megarian; adj. **Mĕgărĭcus** -a -um, *Megarian*; m. pl. as subst. **Mĕgărĭci** -ōrum
disciples of Euclides of Megara; adj. **Mĕgăru**
-a -um, *Megarian.*

¹**Mĕgărēus** (quadrisyll.), see Megara.

²**Mĕgăreus** (trisyll.) -ĕi, m. (Μεγαρεύς), *son o
Neptune, father of Hippomenes.*

¶ Hence adj. **Mĕgărēĭus** -a -um
belonging to Megareus: heros, *Hippomene.*
Ov.

ıĕgistānes -um, m. pl. (μεγιστᾶνες), *grandees, magnates*: Tac.

ıĕhercle, mehercule, mehercules, *see* Hercules.

ıēio mēiěre, *to make water*: Cat., Hor.

ıĕl mellis, n. (μέλι), *honey.* LIT., stilla mellis, Cic.; plur.: roscida mella, Verg.; prov., of a vain attempt: mella petere in medio flumine, Ov. TRANSF., *sweetness, pleasantness*: poetica mella, Hor.; as a term of endearment, *honey*: Pl.

ıĕla -ae, m. Pomponius, *a Roman writer on geography under the Emperor Claudius.*

ıĕlanchŏlĭcus -a -um (μελαγχολικός), *having black bile, melancholy*: Cic.

ıĕlandrўum -ī, n. (μελάνδρυον), *a piece of salted tunny-fish*: Plin., Mart.

ıĕlănūrus -i, m. (μελάνουρος), *a kind of small edible sea-fish*: Ov.

ıelcŭlum -i, n. and **melcŭlus** -i, m. (dim. of mel), *little honey* (a term of endearment): Pl.

ıeldi -ōrum, m. *a people in Gallia Celtica.*

ıĕlĕăgěr and **Mĕlĕagrus** (-ǒs) -i, m. (Μελέαγρος), *son of Oeneus, king in Calydon, and of Althaea.*

¶ Hence **Mĕlĕagrĭdes,** f. pl. *the sisters of Meleager, who, according to the legend, were changed to guinea-fowls on his death.*

ıĕlēs -ētis, m. (Μέλης), *a river near Smyrna, where Homer is said to have been born.*

¶ Hence adj. **Mĕlētēus** -a -um, *of Meles,* poet.; *Homeric*; **Mĕlētīnus** -a -um, *of Meles.*

ıĕlēs -ĭum, f. pl., *a place in Samnium.*

ıĕlĭboea -ae, f. (Μελίβοια), *a town in Thessaly, birth-place of Philoctetes.*

¶ Hence adj. **Mĕlĭboeus** -a -um, *Meliboean*: dux, Philoctetes, Verg.

ıĕlĭcerta (-ēs) -ae, m. (Μελικέρτης), *son of Athamas and Ino; Ino plunged with him into the sea to escape the fury of her husband, and thereupon Melicerta was changed into a sea-god called Palaemon by the Greeks and Portunus by the Romans.*

ıĕlĭcus -a -um (μελικός), *musical*: Lucr.; esp., *lyrical, lyric*: poëma, Cic.

ıĕlĭlōtŏs -i, f. (μελίλωτος), *a species of clover*: Ov.

ıĕlĭmēlă -i, n. pl. (μελίμηλα), *honey-apples, a kind of sweet apple*: Hor.

ıĕlĭor -us, compar. of bonus; q.v.

ıĕlisphyllum and **mĕlissŏphyllŏn** -i, n. (μελίφυλλον and μελισσόφυλλον), *balm, a plant attractive to bees*: Verg.

ıĕlĭta -ae, f. and **Mĕlĭtē** -ēs, f. (Μελίτη). (1) *the island of Malta.* (2) *a sea-nymph.*

¶ Hence adj. **Mĕlĭtensis** -e, *of Malta*: vestis, Cic.; n. pl. as subst. **Mĕlĭtensĭa** -ĭum, *Maltese garments*: Cic.

ıĕlĭuscŭlus -a -um (dim. of compar. melior), *somewhat better*: Pl., Ter.

¶ Adv. **mĕlĭuscŭlē,** *somewhat better, pretty well* (in health): alicui est, Cic. L.

ıĕlla -ae, f. (mel), *mead*: Pl.

ıĕlla -ae, m. *a river in northern Italy, near Brescia.*

ıĕllĭcŭlus -a -um (mel), *honey-sweet*: Pl.

ellĭfěr -fěra -fěrum (mel/fero), *producing honey*: apes, Ov.

ellĭfĭco -are (mel/facio), *to make honey*: Verg.

mellilla -ae, f (dim. of mel), a term of endearment, *little honey*: Pl.

mellītus -a -um (mel), *honeyed*: placenta, *sweetened with honey,* Hor. TRANSF., *as sweet as honey*: Cat., Cic. L.

¹mĕlŏs, n. (μέλος), *a tune, song*: Hor.; plur. **mĕlē**: Lucr.

²Mĕlŏs -i, f. (Μῆλος), *an island in the Aegean Sea.*

¶ Hence adj. **Mēlĭus** -a -um, *Melian.*

Melpŏmĕnē -ēs, f. (Μελπομένη), *the Muse of tragic poetry.*

membrāna -ae, f. (membrum), *a thin skin, film, membrane.* LIT., natura oculos membranis tenuissimis vestivit, Cic. TRANSF., (1) *the skin* or *slough of a snake*: Ov. (2) *skin prepared to write on, parchment*: Hor., Quint. (3) *any film*: coloris, Lucr.

membrānŭla -ae, f. (dim. of membrana), *a little parchment*: Cic. L.

membrātim, adv. (membrum). LIT., *limb by limb* (Shakespeare's 'limb-meal'): deperdere sensum, Lucr. TRANSF., *piecemeal, singly*: quasi membratim gestum negotium, Cic.; of style, *in short sentences*: dicere, Cic., Quint.

membrum -i, n. *a limb* or *member of the body.* LIT., Pl., Cic.; captus (*crippled*) omnibus membris, Liv.
TRANSF., *a limb, member, part of anything*: omnes eius (philosophiae) partes atque omnia membra, Cic.; *of a house*: cubicula et eiusmodi membra, Cic. L.; Lucr.; *a clause* in a sentence: Cic.

mĕmĭni -nisse (connected with moneo, mens; perf. with sense of present, cf. μέμνημαι), *to remember, recollect.*
LIT., with genit.: vivorum memini, Cic.; with acc.: dicta, Cic.; numeros, Verg.; Pl.; with dat.: de Herode et Mettio meminero, Cic. L.; Juv.; with indir. quest.: meministi quanta hominum esset admiratio, Cic.; Ter., Liv.; with acc. and infin.: memini te narrare, Cic.; with infin., *to remember to* do a thing: Pl., Cic. L.; absol.: ut ego meminisse videor, Cic.
TRANSF., *to make mention of, to mention*: de exsulibus, Cic.; with genit.: Cic., Quint.

Memmĭus -a -um, *name of a Roman gens, to which belonged C. Memmius, the friend of Lucretius, who was condemned for bribery and went into exile at Athens.*

¶ Hence subst. **Memmĭădes** -ae, m. *one of the Memmian gens, a Memmius*: Lucr.; adj. **Memmĭānus** -a -um, *of Memmius.*

Memnōn -ŏnis, m. (Μέμνων), *king of Ethiopia, son of Tithonus and Aurora, killed before Troy by Achilles*: mater lutea Memnonis, *Aurora,* Ov.

¶ Hence subst. **Memnŏnĭdes** -um, f. *the birds of Memnon, birds which arose from his ashes*; adj. **Memnŏnĭus** -a -um, *Memnonian*; poet., *eastern, Moorish, black.*

mĕmor -ŏris (memini), *mindful, remembering.*
LIT., in gen.: homo ingeniosus ac memor, *with a good memory,* Cic.; memores animi motūs, Lucr.; memori animo notavi, Ov.; memorem Iunonis ob iram, Verg.; with genit.: beneficii, Cic.; Caes., Hor., etc.; with indir. quest.: Hor. Esp., *thankful, grateful*: nimium memor nimiumque gratus, Cic.; *thoughtful, prudent*: memor provisa repones, Verg.

TRANSF., *reminiscent, reminding*: nota, Ov.; with genit.: nostri memorem querellam, Hor.

mĕmŏrābĭlis -e, adj. with compar. (memoro), *remarkable, worthy of mention, memorable*: vir, Liv.; virtus, Cic.; Verg.

mĕmŏrandus -a -um, gerundive from memoro; q.v.

mĕmŏrātor -ōris, m. (memoro), *a narrator, relater*: Prop.

¹**mĕmŏrātus** -a -um, partic. from memoro; q.v.

²**mĕmŏrātus** -ūs, m. (memoro), *a mention, mentioning*: Pl., Tac.

mĕmŏrĭa -ae, f. (memor).
    LIT., (1) in gen., *memory, the capacity for remembering*: memoria bona, Cic. L.; memoriā tenere, Caes., Cic.; memoriā comprehendere, complecti aliquid, Cic.; excidere de memoriā, Liv. (2) *memory* or *remembrance of* some specific person or thing: primam sacramenti memoriam, Caes.; Pompeii memoriam amisisse, Cic.; memoria alicuius (rei) excidit, abiit, abolevit, *it has fallen into oblivion, has been forgotten*, Liv.; memoriae prodere, Cic.; tradere, Liv.; *to leave on record* (of historians): viri digni memoriā, *worthy of remembrance*, Cic.
    TRANSF., (1) *time of remembrance, recollection*: nostrā memoriā, *in our recollection*, Cic.; post hominum memoriam, *in human memory*, Cic.; Caes. (2) *record of the past, tradition, history, information*: omnium rerum; litterarum memoriam (*written evidence*) flagitare, Cic.; aliquid prodere memoriā, Cic.; Caes., Liv. (3) *notion*, not of the past: belli inferendi memoria, *idea, intention*, Liv.

mĕmŏrĭālis -e (memoria), *relating to memory*: libellus, *a notebook*, Suet.

mĕmŏrĭŏla -ae, f. (dim. of memoria), *memory*: Cic. L.

mĕmŏrĭtĕr, adv. (memor), *by heart, from memory*: orationem memoriter habere, Cic.

mĕmŏro -are (memor), *to mention, call to mind, recount, relate*; with acc.: artibus quas supra memoravi, Sall.; Pl., Cic., Verg.; with de: de magna virtute, Sall.; with acc. and infin.: id factum per ambitionem consulis memorabant, Sall.; Pl., Liv., Tac.; in pass. with nom. and infin.: ubi ea gesta esse memorantur, Cic.; with indir. quest.: Hor.
    ¶ Hence gerundive **mĕmŏrandus** -a -um, *notable, memorable*; of persons: iuvenis memorande, Verg.; of things: proelium, Liv.

Memphis -is and -idos, f. (*Μέμφις*), *a celebrated city of Egypt*.
    ¶ Hence m. adj. **Memphītes** -ae, *belonging to Memphis*: bos, *Apis*, Tib.; adj. **Memphītĭcus** -a -um, *belonging to Memphis*; f. adj. **Memphītis** -idis, *belonging to Memphis*; poet.=*Egyptian*: vacca (of Io), Ov.

Mēnae -ārum, f. (*Μέναι*), *a town in Sicily* (now Meneo). Adj. **Mēnaenus** -a -um, *of Menae*.

Mĕnander and **Mĕnandrŏs** -dri, m. (*Μένανδρος*), *a famous Greek comic poet, imitated by Terence*. Adj. **Mĕnandrēus** -a -um, *Menandrian*.

Mĕnăpĭi -ōrum, m. *a people in Gaul, between the Meuse and the Scheldt*.

menda -ae, f., *see* mendum.

mendācĭum -i, n. (mendax), *a lie, falsehood*:

impudens, Cic.; mendacium alicuius refe lere et redarguere, Cic.; Pl., Ov.

mendācĭuncŭlum -i, n. (dim. of me dacium), *a little lie*: Cic.

mendax -ācis (mentior), adj. (with compa and superl.), *lying, mendacious*.
    LIT., of persons: homo, Cic.; Pl., Hor.
    TRANSF., of inanimate objects, *deceitfu false, untrue*: visa, Cic.; speculum, Ov fundus, *bearing less than the expected cro* Hor.

mendīcābŭlum -i, n. (mendico), *a begga* Pl.

mendīcĭtās -ātis, f. (mendicus), *beggary*: P

mendīco -are and **mendīcor** -ari, de (mendicus), *to beg, go begging*: Pl., Ov., Sen transit., *to beg for*: malum, Pl.; pass mendicatus panis, Juv.

mendīcŭlus -a -um (dim. of mendicus), *b longing to a beggar*: Pl.

mendīcus -a -um, adj. (with superl.), *po as a beggar, beggarly, indigent*.
    LIT., of persons: solos sapientes esse, mendicissimi (sint), divites, Cic. M. subst. **mendīcus** -i, *a beggar*: Cic.; plu mendici, *the begging priests of Cybele*, Hor.
    TRANSF., of things, *paltry, pitiful, beggarl* instrumentum, Cic.

mendōsus -a -um (mendum), adj. (wi compar.). (1) *full of faults*: a, physically: n equi mendosa sub illo deteriorque vi facies, Ov.: b, intellectually, *inaccurat* historia rerum nostrarum est facta mendosic Cic.: c, morally: mendosi mores, O (2) *making a mistake*: cur servus semper Verruci nomine mendosus esset, Cic.
    ¶ Adv. (with superl.) **mendōsē**, *faultil erroneously*: scribere, Cic.

mendum -i, n. and **menda** -ae, f. *a fau* LIT., *a bodily defect, blemish*: Ov. TRANS *a mistake*. (1) *in writing*: quod mendum is litura correxit? Cic. (2) *in reasoning* *calculation*: Cic.

Mĕneclēs -is, m. (*Μενεκλῆς*), *an Asia rhetorician of Alabanda*.
    ¶ Hence adj. **Mĕneclīus** -a -um, *Menecles*.

Mĕnĕlāus -i, m. (*Μενέλαος*), *son of Atre brother of Agamemnon, husband of Helen*.
    ¶ Hence adj. **Mĕnĕlāēus** -a -um, *Menelaus*.

Mĕnēnĭus -a -um, *name of a Roman ge* esp. of Menenius Agrippa, *said to ha reconciled patricians and the plebeians at t secession of* 494 B.C.

Mĕnippus -i, m. (*Μένιππος*). (1) *a Cy philosopher*. (2) *the greatest of the Asia orators of the time of Cicero*.

Mĕnoeceus (trisyll.) -ĕi and -ĕos, m. (*Μ νοικεύς*), *son of the Theban king Creon, u sacrificed his life for his country in obedie to an oracle*.

Mĕnoetĭădēs -ae, m. (*Μενοιτιάδης*), *the s of Menoetius*, i.e., *Patroclus*: Prop.

mens mentis, f. (connected with memini), *mind, understanding, reason, intellect, ju ment*.
    In gen.: mens cui regnum totius anim natura tributum est, Cic.; mente comple aliquid, *to comprehend*, Cic.; mentis su esse, mentis compotem esse, *to be in p session of one's faculties*, Cic.; mente capt

insane, Cic., Liv.; in mentem venire, *of thoughts, to occur to one*, Pl., Cic., Liv.; also impers.: venit in mentem alicui, *with genit.*, *he thinks of, remembers*; *with ut, or infin.*: Pl. Esp. *of certain mental functions.* (1) *feelings, disposition*: mens mollis ad perferendas calamitates, Cic.; mens bona, Liv.; Hor. (2) *courage*: addere mentem, *to inspire courage*, Hor.; demittere mentem, *to lose courage*, Verg.; Caes., Liv. (3) *opinion, thoughts*: Cic., Verg. (4) *intention, resolve*: classem eā mente comparavit, ut, Cic.; muta iam istam mentem, Cic. (5) *personif.*: Mens, *goddess of understanding*, Cic., Liv.

mensa -ae, f. *a table.*
(1) *a table for eating upon.* Lit., mensas cibis exstruere, Cic.; mensam ponere, *to bring in dinner*, Ov.; tollere, Cic.; removere, Verg. Transf., *a course*: mensa secunda, *dessert*, Cic. L.
(2) *a sacrificial table, altar*: Verg.
(3) *the table* or *counter of a money-changer*: Pl., Cic., Hor.

mensārius -i, m. (mensa), *a member of a board regulating payments out of the treasury*: Cic., Liv.

mensio -ōnis, f. (metior), *a measuring*: vocum, Cic.

mensis -is, m. (cf. μήν), *a month*: intercalarius, Cic.; mense primo, Verg.; Hor., Liv., etc.

mensor -ōris, m. (metior), *a measurer*: maris et terrae, Hor.; esp. (1) *a measurer of land, surveyor*: Ov. (2) *an architect*: Plin. L.

menstruālis -e (menstruus), *monthly*: Pl.

menstruus -a -um (mensis). (1) *monthly*: usura, Cic. (2) *lasting for a month*: spatium, Cic. N. as subst. **menstruum** -i, *rations for a month*: Liv.; *a month in office*: Plin. L.

mensula -ae, f. (dim. of mensa), *a little table*: Pl.

mensūra -ae, f. (metior), *a measuring.*
Lit., mensuram alicuius rei facere, *to measure*, Ov.; Caes.
Transf., (1) *amount, proportion, measure*: nosse mensuras itinerum, Caes.; alicui mensuram bibendi dare, Ov. (2) *a measure, standard, that by which anything is measured*: maiore mensurā reddere, Cic. (3) *abstr., standard, capacity*: mensuram nominis implere, Ov.; legati, Tac.

menta (mentha) -ae, f. (μίνθη), *the herb mint*: Ov.

mentio -ōnis, f. (connected with memini and mens), *a speaking of, mention*: mentionem facere, *with genit., or de, to mention*, Pl., Caes., Cic., Liv.; casu in eorum mentionem incidi, *I mentioned them accidentally*, Cic.; alicuius rei mentionem movere, *to mention*, Liv.

mentior -īri, dep. (connected with mens), *to lie.*
(1) *intransit.* Lit., *of persons*: si te mentiri dicis, verumque dicis, mentiris, Cic.; aperte, Cic.; in aliqua re, Cic. L.; de aliqua re, Cic. Transf., *of inanimate objects, to deceive, mislead*: frons, oculi, vultus persaepe mentiuntur, Cic. L.
(2) *transit.*: **a**, *to say falsely, to invent*: tantam rem, Sall.; res quas mentiris, Ov.; auspicium, *to fabricate*, Liv.: **b**, *to deceive, disappoint*: seges mentita spem, Hor.: **c**, *to counterfeit, put on, assume*: centum figuras, Ov., Verg.

¶ Hence pres. partic. **mentiens** -entis, *lying*; m. as subst., *a fallacy, sophism*: Cic. ¶ Perf. partic. **mentitus** -a -um. (1) dep.), *lying*. (2) in pass. sense, *fictitious*: Plin. L., Prop.

Mentor -ōris, m. (Μέντωρ). (1) *a friend of Ulysses.* (2) *a famous artist in metal work.* ¶ Hence adj. **Mentōrĕus** -a -um, *of Mentor.*

mentum -i, n. *the chin*: Cic., Verg.

meo -āre, *to go, pass*; of persons: domus Plutonia, quo simul mearis, Hor.; Tac.; of inanimate objects: meantia sidera, Ov.; Lucr., Tac.

mēphītis -is, f. *a noxious exhalation from the earth, malaria*: Verg.; personif., Mephitis, *the goddess who protects against malaria*, Tac.

merāculus -a -um (dim. of meracus), *tolerably pure*: Pl.

merācus -a -um (merus), *pure, unmixed.* Lit., vinum meracius, Cic.; elleborum, Hor. Transf., libertas, Cic.

mercābilis -e (mercor), *that can be bought*: Ov.

mercātor -ōris, m. (mercor), *a merchant, wholesale trader* (opp. caupo, *a shopkeeper, retailer*): Caes., Cic. Transf., provinciarum, Cic.

mercātōrius -a -um (mercator), *relating to trade*: navis, *a merchant-ship*, Pl.

mercātūra -ae, f. (mercor), *trade, traffic.*
Lit., mercaturas facere, *to carry on trade*, Cic.
Transf., (1) *traffic in abstr. things*: non erit ista amicitia, sed mercatura quaedam utilitatum suarum, Cic. (2) *merchandise*: Pl.

mercātus -ūs, m. (mercor), *trade, traffic, business*: Cic. Transf., *a market, fair, public place of business*: mercatum indicere, habere, Cic.; frequens, *a full market*, Liv.; Pl., Tac.

mercēdula -ae, f. (dim. of merces). (1) *a small reward, low wages*: mercedulā adducti, Cic. (2) *low rent*: praediorum, Cic. L.

mercennārius (mercēnārius) -a -um (merces), *hired, paid, mercenary*: miles, Liv.; testes, *suborned*, Cic.; of things: arma, Liv.; liberalitas, Cic. M. as subst. **mercennārius** -i, *a hired servant*: Pl., Cic.

mercēs -ēdis, f. (merx).
(1) *hire, pay, wages, fee, salary.* Lit., operae, Cic.; conducere aliquem mercede, Liv.; Sall., Caes.; in a bad sense, *bribe*: lingua adstricta mercede, Cic.; Liv. Transf., *wages in a bad sense, cost, punishment*: temeritatis, Cic.; istuc nihil dolere non sine magna mercede contingit, Cic.
(2) *interest, rent, income*: praediorum, Cic.; insularum, rent, Cic.; quinas hic capiti mercedes exsecat, 5 *per cent*, Hor.

mercimōnium -i, n. (merx), *goods, merchandise*: Pl., Tac.

mercor -ari, dep. (merx). Intransit., *to carry on trade, to traffic*: Pl. Transit., *to buy.* Lit., fundum de pupillo, Cic.; aliquid ab aliquo, Cic.; aliquid tanto pretio, Cic. Transf., officia vitā, *with life*, Cic. L.; hoc magno mercentur Atridae, *would give much for*, Verg.

Mercurius -i, m. *Mercury, identified with the Greek Hermes, son of Jupiter and Maia; messenger of the gods; god of oratory; conductor*

*of the souls of the dead to the lower world;
patron of merchants and thieves;* also *the
planet Mercury.*

¶ Hence adj. **Mercŭriālis** -e, *of Mercury:* viri, *lyric poets,* Hor.; m. pl. as subst.
Mercŭriāles -ium, *a corporation of traders
at Rome:* Cic.

merda -ae, f. *excrement:* Hor., Mart.

mĕrē, adv. from merus; q.v.: Pl.

mĕrenda -ae, f. *a luncheon:* Pl.

mĕrĕo -ēre -ŭi -itum and **mĕrĕor** -ēri -ĭtus
sum, dep. *to deserve, earn, obtain.*

    LIT., of money, etc.; in gen.: mereri non
amplius duodecim aeris, Cic.; nardo vina,
to exchange, Hor.; hic meret aera liber Sosiis,
. Hor.; esp., *to earn pay as a soldier, serve as a
soldier;* with stipendia: Caes.; so: mereo
(*or* mereor) alone, Cic.; sub aliquo imperatore, Liv.; equo, *in the cavalry,* Cic.;
pedibus, *in the infantry,* Liv.

    TRANSF., (1) *to deserve, merit, earn* an
abstr. thing, good or bad: praemia,
laudem, Caes.; odium, Caes.; poenam, Ov.;
fustuarium, Liv.; with ut clause: ut
honoribus decoraretur, Cic.; with infin.:
meruisse mori, Ov. (2) intransit., *to deserve:*
si mereor, Cic.; esp. with adv. and de, *to
deserve of:* bene, optime de republica, Cic.;
male de civibus suis, Cic.; ita se de populo
Romano meritos esse ut, Caes.; si quid bene
de te merui, Verg.

    ¶ Hence perf. partic. **mĕrĭtus** -a -um.
(1) dep., *deserving:* meriti iuvenci, Verg.
(2) in pass. sense, *deserved:* iracundia, Cic.;
dona, Liv.

    N. as subst. **mĕrĭtum** -i, *desert, merit.*
LIT., (1) *a good action, benefit, service:* dare
et recipere merita, Cic.; Liv., Tac. (2)
demerit, blame, fault: nullo meo merito, Cic.;
nullo meo in se merito, *though I am guilty
of no offence against him,* Liv.; Tac. TRANSF.,
grounds, reason: quo sit merito quaeque
notata dies, Ov.

    ¶ Abl. as adv. **mĕrĭtō,** *deservedly, rightly:*
merito sum iratus Metello, Cic.; merito ac
iure laudari, Cic. Superl.: meritissimo, Cic.

mĕretrīcius -a -um (meretrix), *of a harlot:*
amores, Cic.; Pl., Ter.

    ¶ Adv. **mĕretrīciē,** *after the manner of
a harlot:* Pl.

mĕretrīcŭla -ae, f. (dim. of meretrix), *a little
harlot:* Cic., Hor.

mĕretrix -īcis, f. (mereo), *a harlot:* Pl., Cic.,
Ov.

mergae -ārum, f. (cf. ἀμέργω), *a two-pronged
fork:* Pl.

mergĕs -gĭtis, f. (mergae), *a sheaf of corn:*
Verg.

mergo mergĕre mersi mersum, *to dip, plunge
into liquid, immerse.*

    LIT., aves quae se in mari mergunt, Cic.;
nec me deus aequore mersit, Verg.; naves
in alto, *to sink,* Liv.

    TRANSF., (1) in gen., *to sink, plunge in:*
canes mersis in corpora rostris dilacerant
dominum, Ov.; caput in terram, Liv.; middle:
mergi, of stars, *to sink,* Ov. (2) fig., *to sink,
overwhelm:* me his malis, Verg.; se in
voluptates, Liv.; vino somnoque mersi
iacent, Liv.

mergus -i, m. (mergo), *a sea-bird,* esp. *a
shearwater* or *gull:* Verg., Hor.

---

mĕrīdiānus -a -um (meridies), *of* or *at
midday, meridian:* tempus, Cic.; sol, Liv.
TRANSF., *southern:* regio, vallis, Liv.

mĕridiātio -ōnis, f. (meridio), *a midday
sleep, siesta:* Cic.

mĕridiēs -ēi, m. (medius/dies), *midday,
noon:* Pl., Cic. TRANSF., *the south:* inflectens
sol cursum tum ad septentriones, tum ad
meridiem, Cic.; Caes., Tac.

mĕridio -are (meridies), *to take a siesta:* Cat.
Suet.

¹**mĕrito** -are (freq. of mereo), *to earn regularly:*
fundus qui sestertia dena meritasset, brough
in, Cic.

²**mĕritō,** adv. from mereo; q.v.

mĕrītōrius -a -um (mereo), *hired:* rheda
a hackney-coach, Suet. N. pl. as subst
mĕrītōria -ōrum, *lodgings:* Juv.

mĕrītum -i, n., subst. from mereo; q.v.

mĕrŏbĭbus -a -um (merum/bibo), *drinking
wine unmixed:* Pl.

Mĕrŏpē -ēs, f. (Μερόπη), *daughter of Atlas,
wife of Sisyphus, one of the Pleiades; her star
is dimmer than the others because she married
a mortal.*

¹**Mĕrops** -ŏpis, m. (Μέροψ), *king of Ethiopia
husband of Clymene, who bore Phaethon to
Apollo.*

²**mĕrops** -ŏpis, f. (μέροψ), *a bird, the bee-eater*
Verg.

merso -are (freq. of mergo), *to dip in, immerse*
gregem fluvio, Verg.; Tac. TRANSF., mersar
civilibus undis, Hor.; Lucr.

mĕrŭla -ae, f. (1) *a blackbird:* Cic. (2) *a fish
the sea-carp:* Ov.

mĕrus -a -um, *pure, unmixed.*

    LIT., argentum, Pl.; undae, Ov.; esp. o
wine, *undiluted:* vinum, Ov.; n. as subst
mĕrum -i, *wine unmixed with water:* Pl.
Hor., Quint.

    TRANSF., *pure, complete, sheer:* meran
hauriens libertatem, Liv.; merum bellum
loqui, *to talk of nothing but war,* Cic.; mer
monstra nuntiare, Cic. L.

merx (**mers**) mercis, f. *merchandise, goods
wares:* fallaces et fucosae, Cic.; femineae
for women, Ov. TRANSF., of a person: mal
merx, *a bad lot,* Pl.

Mĕsembria -ae, f. (Μεσημβρία), *a town i
Thrace at the foot of Mount Haemus.*

    ¶ Hence adj. **Mĕsembriācus** -a -um, *o
Mesembria.*

Mĕsŏpŏtămĭa -ae, f. (Μεσοποταμία), *a countr
of Asia, between the Euphrates and the Tigri*

Messalla (**Messāla**) -ae, m. *a cognomen o
the gens* Valeria; esp. of M. Valerius Messall
Corvinus, *the patron of Tibullus, a skille
orator.*

Messāna -ae, f. *a town in Sicily, on the strai
between Italy and Sicily* (now *Messina*).

Messāpĭa -ae, f. *old name of a part of souther
Italy.*

    ¶ Hence adj. **Messāpĭus** -a -um, *Mes
sapian;* m. pl. as subst., *Messapians.*

Messēnē -ēs, f. (Μεσσήνη), *the chief town i
the district of Messenia in the Peloponnese.*

    ¶ Hence adj. **Messēnius** -a -um, *Mes
senian.*

messis -is, f. (meto), *harvest.*

    LIT., messem amittere, Cic.; Verg., Liv.
    TRANSF., (1) *the gathering of honey:* Verg
(2) *grain gathered in, harvest:* illius immensa

ruperunt horrea messes, Verg. (3) *the standing crop*: Ov. (4) *the time of harvest, harvest-tide*: Verg.; poet., *the year*: sexagesima messis, Mart. (5) fig., *harvest, crop*: illa Sullani temporis messis, Cic.

messor -ōris, m. (meto), *a reaper, mower*: Cic., Hor., Juv.

messōrius -a -um (messor), *of a reaper*: corbis, Cic.

mēta -ae, f. *a post, mark*, on a race-course; in the Roman circus, *a pyramidal column* used as turning-post or winning post. LIT., metaque fervidis evitata rotis, Hor.; collis in modum metae in acutum cacumen fastigatus, conical, Liv.; Verg. TRANSF., (1) *a turning-point*: in flexu aetatis haesit ad metas, Cic.; metas lustrare Pachyni, Verg. (2) *a goal, end, term, boundary*: mortis, aevi, Verg.; vitae metam tangere, Ov.

mětallum -i, n. (μέταλλον). (1) *a metal; gold, silver, iron*, etc.: potior metallis libertas, Hor. (2) esp. plur., *a mine, quarry*: reditus metallorum, *income*, Liv.; damnare in metallum, Plin. L.

mětămorphōsis -is, f. (μεταμόρφωσις), *a transformation, metamorphosis*; plur. **Mětămorphōses** -ěōn, *the title of a poem by Ovid*.

mětăphŏra -ae, f. (μεταφορά), *a metaphor*: Quint.

Mětăpontum -i, n. (Μεταπόντιον), *a Greek colony in southern Italy*.

¶ Hence adj. **Mětăpontīnus** -a -um, *Metapontine*.

mētātor -ōris, m. (metor), *a measurer, one who marks out*: castrorum, urbis, Cic.

Mětaurus -i, m. *a river in Umbria, where Hasdrubal was defeated and slain in* 207 B.C. (now *the Metauro*). Adj. **Mětaurus** -a -um.

Mětellus -i, m. *a cognomen in the gens Caecilia*; esp. of (1) Qu. Metellus Macedonicus, *who made Macedonia a Roman province*. (2) Qu. Caecilius Metellus Numidicus, *general in the war against Jugurtha*. (3) C. Caecilius Metellus Celer, *a contemporary of Cicero*.

¶ Hence adj. **Mětellīnus** -a -um, *relating to Metellus*: oratio, *against Metellus Nepos, brother of Celer*, Cic. L.

Mēthymna -ae, f. (Μήθυμνα), *a town in Lesbos*.

¶ Hence adj. **Mēthymnaeus** -a -um and f. adj. **Mēthymniăs** -ădis, *of Methymna*.

mētīor mētiri mensus sum, dep. (cf. μέτρον), *to measure*.

LIT., agrum, Cic.; pedes syllabis, Cic.; Hor., Liv.; with dat., *to measure out, distribute*: frumentum militibus, Cic.

TRANSF., (1) *to traverse, pass over*: aequor curru, Verg.; iter annuum, Cat. (2) mentally, *to measure, estimate, judge*: sonantia auribus, Cic.; omnia quaestu, *everything with reference to gain*, Liv.; odium aliorum suo odio, Liv.; fidelitatem ex mea conscientia, Cic.; Hor.

mēto mētěre messŭi messum, *to reap, mow, gather, harvest*. LIT., in metend oocupati, Caes.; prov.: ut sementem feceris, ita et metes, *as a man sows, so shall he reap*, Cic.; with acc.: arva, Prop.; farra, Ov.; of bees: apes metunt flores, Verg. TRANSF., *to mow down, cut off*: virgā lilia summa metit, Ov.; barbam fortice, Mart.; in battle: proxima quaeque metit gladio, Verg.

mētor -ari, dep. (and **mētō** -are: Verg.; cf. metior), *to measure off, lay out*: castra, Caes.; regiones, Liv.; frontem castrorum, Liv.; Verg. Perf. partic. in pass. sense: Hor., Liv.

metrēta -ae, f. (μετρητής), *a Greek liquid measure, containing about nine English gallons*: Pl.

metrĭcus -a -um (μετρικός). (1) *of measuring*: Plin. (2) *metrical*: Quint.

Mětrŏpŏlis, acc. -im, f. (Μητρόπολις), name of several towns, esp. *a town in Thessaly, between Pharsalus and Gomphi*.

¶ Hence subst. **Mětrŏpŏlītae** -ārum, m. (Μητροπολῖται), *inhabitants of Metropolis*.

metrum -i, n. (μέτρον), *a measure*; esp. *poetical measure, metre*: Mart., Quint.

mětŭcŭlōsus -a -um (metus). (1) *full of fear, timid*: Pl. (2) *exciting fear, frightful*: Pl.

mětŭo -ŭěre -ŭi -ūtum (metus).

(1) intransit., *to fear, be afraid*: de sua vita, *for his life*, Cic. L.; ab Hannibale, *what H. might do*, Liv.; with dat.: senectae, *for his old age*, Verg.

(2) transit., *to fear*: deos, Pl., Ter.; insidias aliquo, Cic.; with infin.: metuit tangi, *he is afraid of being touched*, Hor.; Pl., Liv.; with clause, metuo ne . . ., *I fear that something will happen*: metuo ut . . ., *or* metuo ne non, *I fear that something will not happen*, Pl., Ter., Cic.

mětus -ūs, m. *fear, apprehension, dread*.

In gen.: in metu esse, Cic.; metum facere, *to cause fear*, Ov.; deponere metum, Cic.; solvere, Verg.; aliquem metū exonerare, Liv. With objective genit.: divum, Lucr.; existimationis, Cic. With ab: ab hoste, *of what the enemy may do*, Liv.

Esp., *reverence, awe*: laurus multos metu servata per annos, Verg.; Hor. Personified: Cic., Verg.

měus -a -um (voc. masc. sing. usually mī, but also, poet., meus; genit. pl. meum: Pl.), possessive adj. (me), *my, mine*.

(1) subjective, *belonging to me*: mei sunt ordines, mea discriptio, Cic.; with genit. in apposition: meum factum dictumve consulis, *my act or word as consul*, Liv.; meum est, *it is my business*, Hor.; with infin., *it is my duty to*: Cic.; meus hic est, *he is in my power*, Pl.; Nero meus, *my friend Nero*, Cic., voc.: mi germane, *my dear brother*, Ter.

(2) objective, *against me*: crimina mea, *charges against me*, Liv.; iniuria, Sall. N. as subst.: sing. **měum** -i, *my property*: Ter.; plur. **měa** -ōrum, n. *my possessions*: Cic.

M. pl. as subst. **měi** -ōrum, *my people*: Ter., Verg.

The cases of meus are frequently strengthened by the enclitic additions, -met, -pte: meopte, meāpte, meāmet, Pl.

Mēvānĭa -ae, f. *a town in Umbria* (now *Bevagna*).

Mezentĭus -i, m. *name of a tyrant of Caere* or *Agylla*.

mīca -ae, f. *a crumb, morsel, grain*: Lucr., Cat., Hor.

Mĭcipsa -ae, m. *son of Masinissa, king of Numidia*.

mĭco -are -ŭi, *to move rapidly to and fro, vibrate, flicker*.

LIT., in gen.: venae et arteriae micare non desinunt, Cic.; micat (equus) auribus, Verg.; corda timore micant, Ov.; esp., micare (digitis), *to play a game which involved holding out the fingers suddenly for another to guess their number* (cf. the Italian game of *alla mora*): quid enim sors est? Idem propemodum quod micare, Cic ; prov., of a thoroughly honourable man: dignus quicum in tenebris mices, Cic.
TRANSF., *to shine, glitter, sparkle*: ignibus aether, Verg.; micant gladii, Liv.; Hor., Ov.

Mĭdās (Mĭda) -ae, m. (Μίδας), *a king of Phrygia, who received from Bacchus the gift of turning to gold everything that he touched; as judge in a musical contest between Apollo and Pan he decided in favour of Pan, and Apollo punished him by changing his ears into those of an ass.*

migrātĭo -ōnis, f. (migro), *a removal, change of abode, migration*: Cic., Liv. TRANSF., verbi migrationes (sunt) in alienum multae, *metaphorical uses*, Cic.

migrātū, abl. as from migratus -ūs, m.; *see* migro.

migro -are.
(1) intransit., *to remove from one place to another, migrate.* LIT., etiam mures migrarunt, Cic.; a Tarquiniis, Liv.; Pl., Juv. TRANSF., a, *to depart*: de vita, ex vita, *to die*, Cic.; Pl., Hor.: b, *to change*: omnia migrant, *all things change*, Lucr.; in colorem marmoreum, Lucr.; in varias figuras, Ov.
(2) transit.: a, *to take from one place to another, transport*; in abl. of verbal noun: migratu difficilia, *hard to transport*, Liv.: b, *to transgress*: ius civile, Cic.

mīles -ĭtis, c. *a soldier.*
LIT., in gen., *a soldier*: scribere milites, *to enrol*, Sall.; ordinare, *to draw up in order*, Liv.; mercede conducere, Liv.; dimittere, Cic. L.; esp. (1) *a private soldier*: Cic., Sall., Liv. (2) *an infantryman*: Caes.
TRANSF., (1) miles, used collectively, *soldiery*, Verg., Liv., Ov. (2) fig., *a campaigner*: nova miles eram, Ov.; also *an attendant*: Ov. (3) *a piece on a draught-board*: Ov.

Mīlētus -i (Μίλητος). (1) m., myth., *father of Caunus and Byblis, mythical founder of Miletus.* (2) *a town in Asia Minor.*
¶ Hence adj. **Mīlēsĭus** -a -um, *Milesian*; m. pl. as subst., *Milesians*; also **Mīlētĭs** -ĭdis, f. (1) as subst., *daughter of Miletus=Byblis*: Ov. (2) as adj., *belonging to the town Miletus*: urbs, *Tomi, a colony of the Milesians*, Ov.

mīlĭtāris -e (miles), *of a soldier, of war, military*: tribuni, Cic.; signa, Caes.; disciplina, Liv.; aetas, *the legal period of military service, from the seventeenth to the forty-sixth year*, Liv. M. as subst. **mīlĭtāris** -is, *a soldier, military man*: Tac.
¶ Adv. **mīlĭtārĭtĕr**, *in a soldierly manner*: tecta sibi militariter aedificare, Liv.; Tac.

mīlĭtĭa -ae, f. (miles), *military service, warfare.*
LIT., munus militiae sustinere, Caes.; discere, Sall.; militiae vacatio, *exemption from military service*, Caes.; domi militiaeque, *at home and abroad, at peace and in war*, Cic.; Liv., Verg.
TRANSF., (1) *the military, soldiery*: cogere militiam, Liv.; Ov. (2) gen., *service*: Cic., Ov.

mīlĭtĭŏla -ae, f. (dim. of militia), *brief military service*: Suet.
mīlĭto -are (miles), *to serve as a soldier, be a soldier.* LIT., in exercitu alicuius, Cic.; sub signis alicuius, *under anyone's command*, Liv. TRANSF., *to serve*, esp. *under the banners of love*: militavi non sine gloria, Hor.; Pl., Ov.
mīlĭum -ii, n. (μελίνη), *millet*: Verg.
mīllĕ, numeral, *a thousand*, indecl. adj. and subst. Plur. **milia (millia)** -ium, *thousands*, subst.
LIT., equites mille (adj.), ap. Cic. L.; mille hominum (subst.), Cic.; plur.: viginti millibus peditum, quattuor equitum, Liv.; esp.: mille passuum, *a thousand paces, a Roman mile* (less by 142 yards than the English mile), Pl., Cic., Liv.
TRANSF., *innumerable, countless*: mille pro uno Caesones exstitisse, Liv.; temptat mille modis, Hor.; Verg.
millēsĭmus (-ensĭmus) -a -um (mille), *the thousandth*: pars, Cic. L.; n. as adv.: millesimum, *for the thousandth time*, Cic. L.
millĭārĭum (mīliārĭum) -i, n. *a mile-stone*: Cic.; aureum, *the central stone erected by Augustus in the Forum, from which distances were measured*: Tac. TRANSF., *a mile*: Suet.
millĭārĭus (mīliārĭus) -a -um (mille), *containing a thousand*: Plin. L., Suet.; *containing a thousand paces.*
milliēns (milliēs), adv. (mille), *a thousand times*. TRANSF., *innumerable times, countless times*: millies melius, *a thousand times better*, Cic.; Ter.
¹**Mĭlō (-ōn)** -ōnis, m. (Μίλων), *a celebrated athlete of Crotona.*
²**Mĭlō** -ōnis, m., T. Annius Milo Papianus, *enemy of Clodius, whom he killed in a fight on the Appian Way; on his trial for the murder he was defended by Cicero.*
¶ Hence adj. **Mĭlōnĭānus** -a -um, *relating to Milo*; f. as subst. **Mĭlōnĭāna** -ae (sc. oratio), *the speech of Cicero in defence of Milo.*
Miltĭădēs -is, m. (Μιλτιάδης), *the Athenian general who conquered the Persians at Marathon*, 490 B.C.
mīlŭīnus (milvīnus) -a -um (miluus), *of a kite*: Plin. TRANSF., *kite-like, rapacious*: Pl., Cic. L.
mīlŭus (milvus) -i, m. *a kite*: Pl., Cic., Hor. TRANSF., (1) *a fish, the gurnard*: Hor., Ov. (2) *a constellation, the kite*: Ov. (3) fig., of persons, *a kite*, i.e. *rapacious*: Pl.
mīma -ae, f. (mimus), *an actress, female mime*: Cic.
Mĭmallŏnĕs -um, f. pl. *Bacchantes.*
¶ Hence subst. **Mĭmallŏnĭs** -ĭdis, f. *a Bacchante*; adj. **Mĭmallŏnĕus** -a -um, *Bacchanalian.*
mīmĭcus -a -um (μιμικός), *farcical*: iocus Cic. Adv. **mīmĭcē**, *like a mime or buffoon*: Cat.
Mimnermus -i, m. (Μίμνερμος), *a Greek elegiac poet of Colophon, about* 560 B.C.
mīmŭla -ae, f. (dim. of mima), *a little actress*: Cic.
mīmus -i, m. (μῖμος). (1) *a mimic actor*: Cic., Ov. (2) *a mime, farce*: persona de mimo, Cic. TRANSF., *a farce*: Suet., Sen.
min'=mihine: Pers., *see* ego.
¹**mīna**, f. adj. *smooth, hairless*: Pl., Varr.

mĭna -ae, f. (μνᾶ). (1) *a Greek weight* = 100 *drachmae*: Plin. (2) *a Greek measure of metal, weighed out as money*; of silver: Pl., Cic.; of gold: Pl.

mĭnācĭae-ārum,f.(minax),*threats,menaces*:Pl.

mĭnācĭtĕr, adv. from minax; q.v.

mĭnae -ārum, f. (connected with ¹minor). LIT., *the battlements, parapets of a wall*: murorum, Verg. TRANSF., *threats, menaces*: minas iactare, Cic.; Pl., Liv., etc.; of animals: Ov., Verg.; of weather: Tib., Ov.

mĭnantĕr, adv. (¹minor), *threateningly*: Ov.

mĭnātĭo -ōnis, f. (¹minor), *a threatening, menace*: Pl.; plur.: Cic.

mĭnax -ācis, f. (¹minor). LIT., *projecting, overhanging*: scopulus, Verg.; Lucr. TRANSF., *threatening, full of threats*: homo, Cic.; vituli, Ov.; litterae, Cic. L.; fluvii, Verg.

¶ Adv. (with compar.) **mĭnācĭtĕr**, *threateningly*: Cic., Quint.

Mincĭus -i, m. *a tributary of the Po* (now *Mincio*).

mĭnĕo -ēre (connected with ¹minor), *to project, overhang, be suspended*: Lucr.

Minerva -ae, f. (formerly Menerva), *Minerva, daughter of Jupiter, goddess of wisdom, and patroness of all the arts and sciences, identified with the Greek Athene.*

TRANSF., (1) *wit, skill, art*, prov.: crassā Minervā, Hor.; invitā Minervā, *against the grain, without inspiration*, Cic.; sus Minervam (sc. docet), *when a foolish person begins to teach a wise one*, Cic. (2) *working in wool*: Verg., Ov.

Mĭnervĭum -i, n. (arx Minervae: Verg.), *a city and castle in southern Italy, near Otranto.*

mingo mingĕre minxi mictum, *to make water*: Hor.

mĭnĭānus -a -um (minium), *painted with vermilion*: Cic.

mĭnĭātŭlus -a -um (dim. of minatus), *coloured with red lead, painted vermilion*: Cic. L.

mĭnĭātus -a -um (minium), *coloured with red lead, painted vermilion*: Cic. L.

¶ Hence **mĭnĭo** -are, *to paint vermilion*: Plin.

mĭnĭmē, see parum.

mĭnĭmus, see parvus.

mĭnĭo -are (minium), verb from miniatus; q.v.

Mĭnĭo -ōnis, m. *a river in Etruria* (now *Mignone*).

mĭnister -tri, m. and **mĭnistra** -ae, f. (²minor), *a subordinate, servant, attendant, assistant.*

LIT., (1) *in a house*: Falerni, Cat.; cubiculi, Liv. (2) *in a temple, the servant of a god*: Martis, Cic.; Ov. (3) *in a public office*: ministri imperii tui, Cic. L.; Verg.

TRANSF., in gen., *supporter, aider, helper*: libidinis, Cic.; scelerum, Lucr.; ales minister fulminis, *Jupiter's eagle*, Hor.; ministro baculo, Ov.

mĭnistĕrĭum -i, n. (minister), *service, ministry, assistance, attendance, employment*: ministerio fungi, Liv.; triste ministerium, Verg.; Ov., Tac. TRANSF., in plur., *attendants, retinue*: Tac., Suet.

mĭnistra -ae, f., see minister.

mĭnistrātor -ōris, m. and **mĭnistrātrix** -īcis, f. (ministro), *a servant, attendant, assistant*: Cic., Sen., Suet.

mĭnistro -are (minister), *to serve, wait upon*; esp., *to wait at table.* LIT., servi ministrant, Cic.; with acc.: pocula, Cic.; cenam, Hor. TRANSF., (1) *to attend to, take care of, govern, direct*: navem velis, Verg.; iussa medicorum, Ov. (2) *to serve, supply, provide*: faces furiis Clodianis, Cic.; prolem, Tib.; furor arma ministrat, Verg.; vinum quod verba ministrat, Hor.

mĭnĭtābundus -a -um (minitor), *threatening, menacing*: Liv., Tac.

mĭnĭto -are (Pl.) and **mĭnĭtor** -ari, dep. (freq. of ¹minor), *to threaten*: alicui mortem, Cic.; huic orbi ferro ignique, Cic.; minitans per litteras se omnia quae conarentur prohibiturum, Cic.

mĭnĭum -i, n. (an Iberian word). (1) *native cinnabar*: Prop. (2) *red-lead*: Verg., Suet.

¹mĭnor -ari, dep. (connected with minae and mineo). LIT., *to jut out, project*: gemini minantur in caelum scopuli, Verg. TRANSF., *to threaten, menace*: alicui, Cic.; alicui crucem, Cic.; multa, Hor.; with abl.: ferro, Sall.; fig., of things: Cic., Verg., Hor.

²mĭnor -ōris, compar. of parvus; q.v.

Mĭnōs -ōis and -ōnis, acc. -ōem and -ōa, m. (Μίνως). (1) *a mythical king and lawgiver in Crete, son of Zeus; after his death, a judge in Tartarus.* (2) *Minos II, king of Crete, grandson of the preceding, husband of Pasiphaë, father of Ariadne, Phaedra, and Deucalion.*

¶ Hence subst. **Mĭnōis** -ĭdis, f. *a daughter of Minos, Ariadne*: Ov.; adj. **Mĭnōĭus** -a -um, *relating to Minos, Cretan*: virgo, Ariadne, Ov., adj. **Mĭnōus** -a -um, *relating to Minos*; poet. = *Cretan*: Thoas, *son of Ariadne*, Ov.; harenae, *shores of Crete*, Ov.

Mĭnōtaurus -i, m. (Μινώταυρος), *a monster, half-bull, half-man, the offspring of Pasiphaë and a bull, slain by Theseus.*

mintha -ae, f. (μίνθα), *mint*: Plin.

Minturnae -ārum, f. *town in Latium, on the borders of Campania.*

¶ Hence adj. **Minturnensis** -e, *of Minturnae.*

Mĭnŭcĭus -a -um, *name of a Roman gens*; esp. *of M. Minucius Rufus, magister equitum to the dictator Fabius Maximus Cunctator.*

mĭnŭme = minime; q.v.

mĭnŭmus = minimus; q.v.

mĭnŭo -ŭĕre -ŭi -ūtum, *to make smaller.*

LIT., (1) *to cut into pieces, chop up*: ligna, Ov.; Hor. (2) *to lessen, diminish*: sumptūs civitatum, Cic.; Hor., Ov.; intransit.: minuente aestu, *at the ebbing of the tide*, Caes.

TRANSF., *to lessen, diminish, lower, reduce, limit*: gloriam alicuius, Cic.; molestias vitae, Cic.; controversiam, Cic.; maiestatem P. R. per vim, Cic.; Pl., Caes., Liv.

¶ Hence partic. (with compar. and superl.) **mĭnūtus** -a -um, *small, little, minute*: litterae, Pl.; res, *trifles*, Cic.; philosophi, *petty, insignificant*, Cic.

¶ Adv. (with compar.) **mĭnūtē**, *in a small way, minutely*: Cic., Quint.

mĭnus, compar.; see parvus.

mĭnuscŭlus -a -um (dim. of compar. minor), *somewhat small*: Pl., Cic. L.

mĭnūtal -ālis, n. (minutus), *a dish of mince-meat*: Juv.

mĭnūtātim, adv. (minutus), *bit by bit, piecemeal, gradually*: discere, Lucr.; interrogare,
Cic.
mĭnūtĭa -ae, f. (minutus), *smallness, littleness*:
Sen.
mĭnūtus -a -um, partic. from minuo; q.v.
Mĭnÿas -ae, m. (Μινύος), *a mythical king of
Thessaly, ancestor of the Minyae.*
    ¶ Hence subst. Mĭnÿae -ārum, m. pl.
(Μινύαι), *the Argonauts, companions of Jason*;
Mĭnÿēĭăs -ădis, f. *daughter of Minyas*;
adj. Mĭnÿēĭus -a -um, *belonging to Minyas.*
mĭrābĭlis -e (miror), adj. (with compar.), *wonderful, marvellous, extraordinary, unusual*;
with dat.: mirabilis illi, Hor.; with quod
and indic.: Cic.; with indir. quest.: Cic.;
with acc. and infin.: Ter., Liv.; with abl.:
dictu, Cic., Verg., Liv.
    ¶ Adv. (with compar.) mĭrābĭlĭtĕr,
wonderfully, marvellously: laetari, Cic. L.;
mirabiliter moratus est, *is of an extraordinary
disposition*, Cic. L.
mĭrābundus -a -um (miror), *full of wonder,
wondering*: mirabundi quidnam esset, Liv.
mĭrācŭlum -i, n. (miror). (1) *a wonderful
thing, prodigy, miracle*: miracula philosophorum somniantium, Cic.; adiciunt miracula
huic pugnae, *wonders*, Liv. (2) *wonder,
surprise*: miraculum et questus, Tac.; Liv.
mĭrandus -a -um, gerundive from miror;
q.v.
mĭrātĭo -ōnis, f. (miror), *wonder, astonishment*:
Cic.
mĭrātor -ōris, m. (miror), *an admirer*: Hor.,
Ov.
mĭrātrix -īcis, f. adj. (miror), *wondering*: Luc.,
Juv.
mĭrē, adv. from mirus; q.v.
mĭrĭfĭcus -a -um (mirus/facio), *causing
wonder, wonderful, astonishing*: homo, Cic. L.;
turris mirificis operibus exstructa, Caes.;
convicium, voluptas, Cic.
    ¶ Adv. mĭrĭfĭcē, *wonderfully, extra-
ordinarily*: dolere, Cic.; loqui, Cat.
mirmillo (murmillo) -ōnis, m. *a kind of
gladiator, generally matched with a* retiarius:
Cic.
mĭror -ari, dep. (mirus). (1) *to wonder, be
astonished at.* With acc.: neglegentiam
hominis, Cic.; Pl., Verg., etc.; with acc. and
infin.: me ad accusandum descendere, Cic.;
with quod: mirari quod non rideret haruspex, Cic.; with indir. quest.: eius rei quae
causa esset miratus, Caes.; Cic.; with si:
miror si quemquam amicum habere potuit,
Cic.; with de: Cic. (2) *to admire, look on
with admiration*: puerorum formas et
corpora magno opere, Cic.; with genit. of
cause: Verg.
    ¶ Hence gerundive mĭrandus -a -um,
wonderful: Cic., Juv.
mĭrus -a -um, *wonderful, astonishing, extraordinary*: miris modis, *wondrously*, Pl., Ter.,
Lucr., Verg.; mirum in modum, Caes.;
mirum quam inimicus erat, *it is wonderful
how hostile*, i.e., *exceedingly hostile*, Cic. L.;
mirum quantum prŏfuit, Liv.; mirum est,
with acc. and infin., Cic.; mirum videtur,
with indir. quest., Cic.; quid mirum? *what
wonder?* Hor.
    ¶ Adv. mĭrē, *wonderfully*: favere, Cic. L.;
mire quam, *in a wonderful manner*, Cic. L.

miscellānĕa -ōrum, n. (miscellus), *a hash o
different meats, hotchpotch*: Juv.
miscellus -a -um (misceo), *mixed*: Cato., Sue
miscĕo miscēre miscŭi mixtum (cf. μίγνυμι
to mix, mingle.
    (1) *to mix* one thing with another. LIT.
mella Falerno, Hor.; Verg., Liv., etc
TRANSF., gravitatem modestiae, Cic.; fals
veris, Cic.; mixta metu spes, Liv.
    (2) *less closely, to associate, combine.* LIT.
to unite: sanguinem et genus cum aliquo
to marry, Liv.; se miscere viris, Verg.
corpus cum aliqua, Cic. TRANSF., sorten
cum rebus Romanis, Liv.
    (3) *to brew, mix up, prepare by mixing
LIT., mulsum, Cic.; pocula alicui, Ov
TRANSF., motūs animorum, Cic.; incendia
Verg.; certamina, Liv.
    (4) *to confuse, confound.* LIT., caelun
terramque, Verg.; Cic. TRANSF., mali
contionibus rempublicam, Cic.; domun
gemitu, Verg.
mĭsellus -a -um (dim. of miser), *miserable
wretched, little*: homo, Cic. L.; passer, Cat.
spes, Lucr.
Mīsēnus -i, m. *the trumpeter of Aeneas.*
    ¶ Hence subst. Mīsēnum -i, n.
promontory and town in Campania (nov
Punta di Miseno); adj. Mīsēnensis -e, o
Misenum.
mĭser -ĕra -ĕrum, adj. (with compar. miserior
superl. miserrimus -a -um), *miserable
wretched, unhappy, pitiable.*
    LIT., of persons: hic miser atque infelix
Cic.; miserrimum habere aliquem, *t
torment*, Cic.; o me miserum! Cic.; Verg
Hor., Ov., etc. TRANSF., of things. (1) *sa
wretched*: misera fortuna, Cic.; as paren
thetical exclamation: miserum! Verg. (2
pitiful, worthless: carmen, Verg.; Caes.
    ¶ Adv. (with compar.) mĭsĕrē. (1
sadly, miserably: vivere, Cic. (2) *violently
excessively*: amare, Ter.; cupis, Hor.
mĭsĕrābĭlis -e, adj. (with compar.) (miseror
(1) *sad, wretched*: aspectus, Cic.; with abl.
visū, Verg. (2) *mournful, plaintive*: vox, Cic.
elegi, Hor.
    ¶ Adv. mĭsĕrābĭlĭtĕr. (1) *miserably
pitiably*: emori, Cic. (2) *in a mournful c
plaintive manner*: epistula miserabilite
scripta, Cic. L.
mĭsĕrandus -a -um, gerundive from miseror
q.v.
mĭsĕrātĭo -ōnis, f. (miseror), *pity, compassion
cum quadam miseratione, Cic. TRANSF.,
pathetic speech or *tone*: uti miserationibus
Cic.; Quint.
mĭsĕrē, adv. from miser; q.v.
mĭsĕrĕor -ēre and mĭsĕrĕor -ēri, dep
(miser), *to pity, have compassion on, com
miserate*; with genit.: sociorum, Cic.
laborum tantorum, Verg.; Pl., Liv., Ov.
    Esp. impers.; act. mĭsĕrĕt and dep
mĭsĕrētur, *it excites pity, one pities*; wit
acc. of person feeling pity, genit. of th
occasion of pity: me miseret tui, Cic.; cave
te fratrum pro fratris salute obsecrantiur
misereatur, Cic.
mĭsĕresco -ĕre (misereo), *to pity, ha
compassion on, commiserate*; with genit.: regi
Verg.; impers.: me miserescit alicuius, *I hav
compassion on*, Pl., Ter.

mĭsĕrĭa -ae, f. (miser), *wretchedness, unhappiness, affliction, distress*: ubi virtus est, ibi esse miseria non potest, Cic.; in miseriis versari, Cic. L.; oneri miseriaeque esse, Sall. Personif., *daughter of Erebus and Nox*: Cic.

mĭsĕrĭcordĭa -ae, f. (misericors). (1) *pity, compassion, mercy*: populi, *on the part of the people*, Cic.; puerorum, *for boys*, Cic.; adhibere misericordiam, *to show*, Cic.; ad misericordiam inducere, Cic.; Caes., Liv. (2) *an appeal to pity*: Cic.

mĭsĕrĭcors -cordis (misereo/cor), *pitiful, compassionate*: in aliquem, Cic.; compar.: misericordior, Pl., Cic.

mĭsĕrĭtĕr, adv. (miser), *wretchedly, sadly*: Cat.

mĭsĕror -ari, dep. (miser). (1) *to bewail, lament, deplore*: fortunam, Cic.; casum, Sall. (2) *to pity, have compassion on*: aliquem, Sall., Liv., Verg.

¶ Hence gerundive **mĭsĕrandus** -a -um, *pitiable, lamentable*: Cic., Verg.

nissĭcĭus -a -um (mitto), *discharged from military service*: Suet.

nissĭlis -e (mitto), *that can be thrown, missile*: lapides, Liv.; ferrum, *a javelin*, Verg.; Hor. N. as subst., gen. plur. **missĭlĭa** -ium. (1) *missiles*: Liv., Verg. (2) missilia *or* res missiles, *gifts thrown among the people, donatives*, Suet.

nissĭo -ōnis, f. (mitto). (1) *a sending off, sending away*: legatorum, Cic.; litterarum, Cic. L. (2) *a letting go, releasing*: **a**, of a prisoner: Cic.: **b**, *a discharge from military service*: honesta, *honourable discharge*; gratiosa, *out of favour*, Liv.; Caes.: **c**, *permission given to gladiators to cease fighting*; hence, *quarter*: sine missione munus gladiatorium dare, *to exhibit gladiators who fought to the death*, Liv.: **d**, gen., *cessation, termination*: ludorum, Cic. L.

nissĭto -are (freq. of mitto), *to send repeatedly*: auxilia, Liv.; Sall.

missus -ūs, m. (mitto), *a letting go.* LIT., (1) *a sending*: missu Caesaris ventitare, *having been sent by Caesar*, Caes. (2) *a throwing, shooting*: pili, Liv. TRANSF., (2) *a shot, the distance shot*: missus bis mille sagittae, Lucr. (2) in races, *a course, heat*: Suet.

missus -a -um, partic. from mitto; q.v.

nĭtesco -ĕre (mitis), *to become mild or soft.* LIT., (1) of fruits, *to ripen, become ripe*: Cic., Ov. (2) of weather, *to become mild*: hiems, Liv.; frigora, Hor. TRANSF., (1) of abstr. things, *to be allayed, to subside*: seditio, Tac.; discordiae, Liv.; ira, Ov. (2) of persons or animals, *to become mild or tame*: ferae quaedam nunquam mitescunt, Liv.; Hor.

Mithrĭdātēs -is, m. (Μιθριδάτης), *name of several kings of Pontus*; esp. *of Mithridates VI* (135–63 B.C.), *who was conquered by Pompey.* Adj. **Mithrĭdātēus, Mithrĭdātĭcus** -a -um, *Mithridatic.*

mĭtĭgātĭo -ōnis, f. (mitigo), *an assuaging, appeasing*: Cic.

nĭtĭgo -are (mitis/ago), *to make mild or soft.* LIT., fruges, *to make ripe*, Cic.; cibum, *to make soft by cooking*, Cic.; agros, *to break up, loosen*, Cic. TRANSF., *to soothe, appease, pacify*: animum alicuius, Cic., Liv.; tristitiam et severitatem, Cic.; dolorem, Cic.; iras, Ov.; Tac.

mītis -e, adj. (with compar. and superl.), *mild, soft, ripe.* LIT., of fruits: poma, uva, Verg.; Ov.; of climate: caelo mitissimo, Liv.; of other natural objects and phenomena: Verg., Hor. TRANSF., (1) of character, *mild, gentle*: homo mitissimus atque lenissimus, Cic.; of animals: taurus, Ov.; animus, dolor, Cic.; aliquid mitiorem in partem interpretari, *put a lenient interpretation upon*, Cic. (2) of style, *mellow, mild*: mitis et compta oratio, Cic.

¶ N. acc. of compar. as compar. adv. **mĭtĭŭs**: Ov.

¶ Superl. adv. **mītissĭmē**: Caes.

mitra -ae, f. (μίτρα), *a head-dress, turban*; in general use among Asiatic nations, *but in Greece and Rome worn only by women and effeminate men*: Cic., Verg., Juv.

mitrātus -a -um (mitra), *wearing the mitra*: Prop.

mitto mittĕre mīsi missum, *to send, let go.*
(1) *to send, dispatch.* In gen.: filium ad propinquum suum, Cic.; legatos de deditione ad eum, Caes.; misi, qui hoc diceret, Cic.; Deiotarus legatos ad me misit, se esse venturum, *with the news that he was about to come*, Cic.; Curio misi, ut medico honos haberetur, *I sent word to Curius, asking*, Cic.; ad mortem, Cic. Sometimes *to escort*: animas sub Tartara, Verg. Esp., *to send as a gift, bestow*: munera, Hor.; funera Teucris, Verg.; salutem, *greetings*, Ov.; librum ad aliquem, *to dedicate*, Cic.
(2) *to let go, release.* LIT., **a**, *to throw, fling*: pila, Caes.; fulmina, Hor.; pueros in profluentem aquam, Liv.: **b**, *to throw off, shed*: luna mittit lucem in terras, Cic.; magna vis aquae caelo missa, Sall.; as medic. t. t., *to let blood*: Sen.; fig.: missus est sanguis invidiae sine dolore, Cic.: **c**, *to utter*: vocem, Caes., Cic., Liv.; sibila, Ov.: **d**, *to drop, release*: arma, Caes.; in the race-course, *to start the competitors*: quadrigas, Liv.; esp., *to dismiss, discharge, send away*; of soldiers: legiones missas fieri iubere, Cic.; of prisoners: mitti eum iubere, Liv. TRANSF., **a**, *to give up*: missos faciant honores, Cic.; mittere ac finire odium, Liv.; maestum timorem, Verg.; with infin.: Pl., Cic., Hor.: **b**, *to pass over, not to speak of* something: mitto illud dicere, Cic.; mitto de amissa parte exercitūs, Cic.

mĭtŭlus (**mȳtŭlus**, **mūtŭlus**) -i, m. (μιτύλος), *a species of edible mussel*: Hor.

mixtūra -ae, f. (misceo), *a mixing, mixture*: rerum, Lucr.; Quint.

mna=mina; q.v.

Mnēmŏnĭdĕs -um, f. pl. *the Muses, daughters of Mnemosyne*: Ov.

Mnēmŏsȳnē -ēs, f. (Μνημοσύνη), *Mnemosyne, mother of the Muses.*

mnēmŏsȳnum -i, n. (μνημόσυνον), *a souvenir, memorial*: Cat.

mōbĭlis -e, adj. (with compar. and superl.) (moveo), *movable, easy to move.* LIT., oculi, Cic.; hence, *active, rapid*: rivi, Hor.; venti, Ov. TRANSF., (1) *pliable, flexible*: mobilis aetas, Verg.; gens ad omnem auram spei mobilis, Liv. (2) *changeable, inconstant*: animus, Cic. L.; Galli sunt in capiendis consiliis mobiles, Caes.; Liv., Juv.

¶ Adv. (with compar.) **mōbĭlĭtĕr**, *with quick motion*. LIT., palpitare, Cic.; Lucr. TRANSF., ad bellum mobiliter excitari, *easily, quickly*, Caes.

mōbĭlĭtās -ātis, f. (mobilis), *movableness, mobility*. LIT., animal mobilitate celerrimā, Cic.; equitum, Caes.; linguae, *fluency*, Cic. TRANSF., *inconstancy, changeableness*: Cic., Tac.

mōbĭlĭtĕr, adv. from mobilis; q.v.

mōbĭlĭto -are (mobilis), *to set in motion*: Lucr.

mŏdĕrābĭlis -e (moderor), *moderate, restrained*: nihil moderabile suadere, Ov.

mŏdĕrāmen -ĭnis, n. (moderor), *a means of governing* or *guiding*. LIT., equorum, navis, Ov. TRANSF., rerum, *management, government*, Ov.

mŏdĕrantĕr, adv. from moderor; q.v.

mŏdĕrātē, adv. from moderor; q.v.

mŏdĕrātim, adv. (moderatus), *moderately, gradually*: Lucr.

mŏdĕrātĭo -ōnis, f. (moderor), *moderating, restraining*. LIT., effrenati populi, Cic.; mundi, Cic. TRANSF., *moderation, temperance, restraint*: temperantia et moderatio naturae tuae, Cic.; dicendi, *in speech*, Cic.

mŏdĕrātor -ōris, m. (moderor), *a governor, controller, manager*: tanti operis, Cic.; equorum, *a driver*, Ov.; arundinis, *a fisher*, Ov.

mŏdĕrātrix -īcis, f. (moderator), *she that governs* or *controls*: republica moderatrix omnium factorum, Cic.

mŏdĕrātus -a -um, partic. from moderor; q.v.

mŏdĕror -ari, dep. (and **mŏdĕro** -are, act.: Pl.) (from modus), *to set bounds to, keep within bounds; to regulate, moderate, restrain.* LIT., (I) with dat.: animo et orationi, Cic.; irae, Hor.; odio, Liv. (2) with acc.: gaudium, Tac.

TRANSF., *to control, govern, direct.* (I) with dat.: navi funiculo, Cic. (2) with acc.: equos, Caes.; habenas, Ov.; corpus, Cic.; cantūs numerosque, Cic.

¶ Hence, from pres. partic. moderans, adv. **mŏdĕrantĕr**, *with controlling force*: Lucr.

¶ Perf. partic. **mŏdĕrātus** -a -um, *restrained, controlled*; of persons: frugi homo et in omnibus vitae partibus moderatus ac temperans, Cic.; of things: convivium, otium, oratio, Cic.; ventus, Ov.

¶ Adv. (with compar. and superl.) **mŏdĕrātē**, *with restraint*: Caes., Cic., Liv.

mŏdestĭa -ae, f. (modestus), *moderation, freedom from excess*. Of weather: hiemis, *mildness*, Tac. Of behaviour and character, *restraint, propriety, orderliness*: neque modum neque modestiam victores habere, Sall.; in dicendo, Cic.; in milite modestiam et continentiam desiderare, *respect, obedience to authority*, Caes.

mŏdestus -a -um, adj. (with compar. and superl.) (modus), *moderate, keeping within bounds*; hence *orderly, restrained, unassuming*: mulier, Ter.; plebs, Cic.; adulescentuli modestissimi pudor, Cic.; videas dolere flagitiosis modestos, Cic.

¶ Adv. **mŏdestē**, *with moderation, with restraint*: Pl., Cic., Liv.

mŏdĭālis -e (modius), *containing a modius*: Pl.

mŏdĭcē, adv. from modicus; q.v.

mŏdĭcus -a -um (modus), *moderate, within bounds, limited*: convivia, potiones, no excessive, Cic.; fossa, *not very deep*, Liv. acervus, Hor.; of abstr. things: laus, Tac Of persons and character. (I) *temperate not extravagant*: severitas, Cic.; animu belli ingens, domi modicus, Sall.; modicu voluptatum, Tac. (2) *ordinary, undistin guished*: modicus originis, Tac.

¶ Adv. **mŏdĭcē**, *moderately*; hence (I to a limited extent*: modice locuples, *tolerabl well off*, Liv.; modice vinosus, Liv.; Cic. L (2) *temperately, with moderation, wit* restraint*: facere, Cic.; Liv.

mŏdĭfĭcātus -a -um (modus/facio), *measured* verba ab oratore modificata, Cic.

mŏdĭus -i, m. (genit. pl. modium: Cic. perhaps from modus), *a Roman corn measure* = 16 *sextarii, rather less than two gallons*: tritici, Cic. TRANSF., anulorum, Liv. pleno modio, *in full measure, abundantly* Cic. L.

mŏdŏ, adv. (mŏdō: Lucr.) (from modus), b* *measure, according to a limit*.

Hence (I) *only, merely, but, just.* In gen. semel modo, Pl.; quod dixerit *solere* modo non etiam *oportere*, Cic.; nemo eorum progredi modo extra agmen audeat, *so muc* as to go*, Caes.; ut ea modo exercitui satis superque foret, *that it alone was more thar enough for the army*, Sall. Esp.: a, colloq., ir commands, *only, just*: veniat modo, Cic. vide modo, *only see*, Cic.: b, in conditiona clauses, si modo, modo si, *or* modo alone with subj., *provided that, if only*: tu scis, s modo meminisit, me tibi dixisse, Cic.; quos valetudo modo bona sit, tenuitas ipsa delectat, *if the health be only good*, Cic.; mod* ne, *provided that . . . not*: tertia aderit, mod* ne Publius rogatus sit, Cic.: c, modo non, *all but, nearly*, Ter., Liv.: d, non modo . . sed (verum), *not only . . . but*: non mod* . . . sed (verum) etiam, *not only . . . but also* Cic.; non modo non . . . sed (verum ne . . . quidem, *not only not . . . but not even* Cic.; often with non modo for *not only not* Cic.

(2) of time. In gen.: a, present: adven* modo? *have you just come?* Ter.: b, pas* *lately*: modo hoc malum in rempublicam invasit, Cic.: c, future, *soon, directly*: Ter. Cic., Liv. Esp. in combination, modo . . modo, *sometimes . . . sometimes, now . . . now at one time . . . at another*: modo ait, mod* negat, Cic.; Ter., Liv.; so: modo . . . nunc Ov., Tac.; modo . . . interdum, Sall.; mod* . . . aliquando, Tac.; modo . . . tum (deinde postea), *first . . . afterwards*, Cic., etc.

mŏdŭlātē, adv. from modulor; q.v.

mŏdŭlātĭo -ōnis, f. (modulor), *a rhythmica measure*: Quint.

mŏdŭlātor -ōris, m. (modulor), *one wh* measures by rhythm, a musician*: Hor.

mŏdŭlor -ari, dep. (modulus), *to measure measure off, measure regularly*. In gen.: Plir Esp. of music. (I) *to measure rhythmicall* to modulate*: vocem, Cic.; virgines sonun vocis pulsu pedum modulantes, Liv. (2) *to sing to the accompaniment of* an instrument carmina avenā, Verg. (3) *to play* an instru ment: lyram, Tib.; perf. partic. in pass sense: Hor.

¶ Hence, from partic. modulatus, adv. **mŏdŭlātē**, *in time* (of music): *modulate* canentes tibiae, Cic.

mŏdŭlus -i, m. (dim. of modus), *a little measure*: metiri quendam suo modulo, Hor.

mŏdus -i, m. *a measure, standard of measurement.*

LIT., in gen.: Varr.; of *size as measured*: agri certus modus, Caes.; agrorum, Liv.; Cic. Esp. as musical t. t., *rhythm, measure, time*: vocum, Cic.; vertere modum, Hor.; modum dare remis Ov.; in plur., *strains, numbers*: flebilibus modis, Hor.; Liv., Ov.

TRANSF., (1) *limit, boundary*: modum imponere magistratui, Liv.; modum lugendi aliquando facere, *to make an end of bewailing*, Cic.; modum constituere, transire, Cic.; sine modo ac modestia, Sall. (2) *rule*: aliis modum pacis ac belli facere, Liv. (3) *manner, mode, way, method*: concludendi, Cic.; miris modis, *wondrously*, Pl., Ter., Lucr., Verg.; servorum modo, *after the manner of slaves*, Liv.; hostilem in modum, *in a hostile manner*, Cic.; mirum in modum, Caes.; quonam modo? Cic.; eius modi, *in that manner, of that kind*, Cic.; huius modi, Cic.

moecha -ae, f. (μοιχή), *an adulteress*: Cat., Hor.

moechisso -are (μοιχίζω), *to debauch*: Pl.

moechor -ari, dep. (moechus), *to commit adultery*: Hor.

moechus -i, m. (μοιχός), *an adulterer*: Ter., Hor., Juv.

moenĕra=munera; *see* **mūnus**.

moenĭa -ium, n. pl. (connected with munio), *the walls* or *fortifications of a city*. LIT., sub ipsis Numantiae moenibus, Cic. TRANSF., (1) in gen., *walls, ramparts, bulwarks*: mundi, theatri, Lucr.; caeli, navis, Ov.; alpes moenia Italiae, Liv. (2) *a city enclosed within walls*: Syracusarum moenia ac portus, Cic.; moenia triplici circumdata muro, Verg. (3) *a castle, dwelling*: Ditis, Verg.; Ov.

moenio=munio; q.v.

Moenus -i, m. *the river Main.*

moerus=murus; q.v.

Moesi -ōrum, m. pl. *a people between Thrace and the Danube*; hence subst. **Moesĭa** -ae, f. *the country of the Moesi*; adj. **Moesĭăcus** -a -um, *belonging to the Moesi.*

mŏla -ae, f. (molo), *a mill-stone.* Hence, gen. plur., *the mill* for grinding corn, olives, etc.: Pl., Ov.; so sing.: Juv. TRANSF., *grits, coarse meal* or *flour*, usually of spelt, which, mixed with salt, was sprinkled on victims before sacrifice: mola et vinum, Cic.; Verg.

mŏlāris -e (mola), *of a mill, to do with grinding*: Plin. M. as subst. **mŏlāris** -is. (1) *a mill-stone*: Verg., Ov., Tac.; poet., *a huge block of stone*: Verg. (2) (sc. dens), *a molar tooth, grinder*: Juv.

mōles -is, f. *a shapeless mass.*

LIT., in gen.: chaos, rudis indigestaque moles, Ov.; clipei, Verg.; ingenti mole Latinus, Verg. Esp. (1) *a mass of rock*: Caes., Ov. (2) *a massive construction; a dam, mole; a large building*: insanae substructionum moles, Cic.; regiae moles, Hor.; Caes., Verg. (3) moles belli, *large military machines*: refectis vineis aliāque mole belli, Liv.

TRANSF., (1) *a mass of men, large number*:

hostes maiorem molem haud facile sustinentes, Liv.; Verg., Tac. (2) *greatness, might, power*: tanti imperii, Liv.; Cic., Hor. (3) *trouble, difficulty*: maiore mole pugnare, Liv.

mŏlestē, adv. from molestus; q.v.

mŏlestĭa -ae, f. (molestus), *annoyance, troublesomeness.* In gen.: fasces habent molestiam, *are attended with annoyance*, Cic. L.; sine molestia tua, *without trouble to yourself*, Cic. L.; ex pernicie reipublicae molestiam trahere, *to be chagrined at*, Cic. L.; molestiam alicui aspergere, *to cause annoyance to*, Cic. L. Esp. of style, *affectation, stiffness*: Latine loquendi accurata et sine molestia diligens elegantia, Cic.

mŏlestus -a -um (moles), *burdensome, troublesome, annoying, irksome.* In gen.: labor, Cic.; adrogantia, Cic.; nisi molestum est, exsurge, Cic.; tunica, *a dress of inflammable materials put on condemned criminals and set alight*, Juv. Esp. of style, *affected, laboured*: veritas, Cic.; verba, Ov.

¶ Hence adv. (with compar. and superl.) **mŏlestē**. (1) *with annoyance*, moleste fero, *I take it badly, am annoyed*; with acc. and infin.: te de praedio aviae exerceri moleste fero, Cic. L.; foll. by si: Cic. L.; by quod: Cic. L. (2) *affectedly, in a laboured way*: Cat.

mōlīmen -ĭnis, n. (molior), *a great effort, exertion*: molimine vasto, *made by great effort*, Ov.; Lucr. TRANSF., *importance*: res suo ipsa molimine gravis, Liv.

mōlīmentum -i, n. (molior), *a great effort, exertion, endeavour*: sine magno commeatu atque molimento, Caes.; motam sede suā parvi molimenti adminiculis, Liv.

mōlĭor -iri, dep. (moles).

(1) transit., *to set in motion, stir, displace*: ancoras, *to weigh anchor*, Liv.; montes sede suā, Liv.; fulmina dextrā, *to hurl*, Verg.; arva ferro, *to work, till*, Lucr. Esp.: **a**, *to construct laboriously, build, erect*: muros, arcem, Verg.; classem, Verg.; atrium, Hor.; **b**, *to destroy laboriously, use force against*: portas, Liv. TRANSF., *to labour at anything*: nulla opera, Cic.; struere et moliri alicui aliquid calamitatis, *to contrive*, Cic.; alicui insidias, *to lay snares*, Cic.; morbos, Verg.; peregrinum regnum, *to strive after*, Liv.; fugam, Verg.; fidem, *to undermine credit*, Liv.

(2) intransit., *to toil, struggle, exert oneself*: in demoliendo signo permulti homines moliebantur, Cic.; agam per me ipse et moliar, Cic.; molientem hinc Hannibalem, *getting ready to leave*, Liv.

mōlītĭo -ōnis, f. (molior), *an effort, laborious undertaking*: rerum, Cic.; also of destruction: valli, *demolition*, Liv.

mōlītor -ōris, m. (molior), *a builder, contriver, author*: mundi Deus; navis, Ov.; caedis, Tac.

mōlītrix -īcis, f. (molior), *a female contriver*: Suet.

mollesco -ĕre (mollio), *to become soft*: Ov. TRANSF., *to become gentle* or *effeminate*: tum genus humanum primum mollescere coepit, Lucr.; Ov.

mollicellus -a -um (dim. of mollis), *dainty, little*: Cat.

mollĭcŭlus -a -um (dim. of mollis), *soft, tender, dainty*: Pl. TRANSF., *effeminate*: Cat.

mollĭo -ire (mollis), *to make pliable, soft, supple.*
LIT., lanam trahendo, *to spin*, Ov.; artūs oleo, Liv.; ceram pollice, Ov.; cibum vapore, Lucr.; frigoribus durescit humor, et idem mollitur tepefactus, Cic.; glebas, *to loosen, soften*, Ov.
TRANSF., (1) of a gradient, *to ease*: clivum anfractibus modicis, Caes.; Liv. (2) of growing things: fructus feros colendo, Verg. (3) of character and feeling, *to soften, make gentle*; in a bad sense, *to make effeminate*: poetae molliunt animos nostros, Cic.; feroces militum animos, Sall.; vocem, *make womanish*, Cic.; Hannibalem exsultantem patientiā suā molliebat, Cic. (4) of circumstances, *to make milder, render bearable*: poenam, Ov.

mollĭpēs -pědis (mollis/pes), *soft-footed*, i.e., *having a trailing walk* (Gr. ελλίπους): Cic. poet.

mollis -e, adj. (with compar. and superl.), *soft.*
LIT., physically *soft, tender, pliant, supple, flexible, yielding*: aquae natura, Lucr.; iuncus, acanthus, Verg.; crura, colla, Verg.; cervix, manus, Ov.; humus, Ov.; arcus, *unstrung*, Ov.; vina, *soft to the taste*, Verg.
TRANSF., (1) of weather, *mild*: aestas, Verg.; Zephyri, Ov. (2) of gradients, *easy*: fastigium, Caes.; clivus, Verg.; Liv., Tac. (3) of character, etc.: **a**, *gentle, sensitive, tender*: mollis animus ad accipiendam et ad deponendam offensionem, Cic.; homo mollissimo animo, Cic.: **b**, *effeminate, unmanly, weak*: disciplina, Cic.; corpus, Liv.; vita, Ov.: **c**, *easy, mild, pleasant*: mollem ac iucundam efficere senectutem, Cic.; oratio, Cic.; iussa, Verg.: **d**, *tender, moving*: verbis mollibus lenire aliquem, Hor.; illud mollissimum carmen, Cic.
¶ Adv. (with compar. and superl.) **mollĭtĕr**, *softly, easily, gently.* LIT., physically: quis membra movere mollius possit, Hor.; excudent spirantia mollius aera, Verg. TRANSF., (1) *mildly, gently, easily*: quod ferendum est molliter sapienti, Cic.; nimis molliter aegritudinem pati, Sall. (2) *weakly, effeminately*: delicate et molliter vivere, Cic.; Liv.

mollĭtĭa -ae, f. and **mollĭtĭēs** -ēi, f. (mollis), *softness.* LIT., physical *softness, flexibility, pliancy*: cervicum, Cic. TRANSF., of character, etc., *tenderness, mildness, sensibility*; in bad sense, *weakness, effeminacy*: animi, Caes., Cic.; naturae, Cic.; civitatum mores lapsi ad mollitiam, Cic.

mollĭtūdo -ĭnis, f. (mollis), *softness.* LIT., physical *softness, pliability*: adsimilis spongiis mollitudo, Cic. TRANSF., *tenderness, softness, sensibility*: humanitatis, Cic.

mŏlo -ĕre -ŭi -ĭtum (mola), *to grind in a mill*: cibaria molita, *meal*, Caes.

mŏlōcĭnārĭus -i, m. (μαλάχη), *one who dyes mallow-colour*: Pl.

Mŏlossi -ōrum, m. (Μολοσσοί), *the inhabitants of Molossia, a district of Epirus.*
¶ Hence adj. **Mŏlossus** -a -um, *Molossian*: pes, *a metrical foot, consisting of three long syllables*, Quint.; canis, Hor.; m. as subst. **Mŏlossus** -i, *a Molossian hound, in great request as a sporting dog*: Verg., Hor.; subst. **Mŏlossĭs** -ĭdis, f. *the country of the Molossi.*

mōly -ўos, n. (μῶλυ), *the herb moly, given by Mercury to Ulysses as a counter-charm against the enchantments of Circe*: Ov.

mōmen -ĭnis, n. (=movimen, from moveo), *movement, motion*: Lucr.; hence (1) *a moving mass*: e salso consurgere momine ponti, Lucr. (2) *momentum, impulse*: Lucr.

mōmentum -i, n. (=movimentum, from moveo).
(1) *movement, motion.* LIT., astra formā ipsā figurāque suā momenta sustentant, Cic.; Hor., Ov. TRANSF., **a**, *change, alteration*: momentum facere annonae, Liv.; Cic.: **b**, of time, *a turning-point, minute, moment*: parvo momento, Caes.; momento temporis, Liv.; momento horae, *in the short space of an hour*, Liv.; Cic.
(2) *a cause of motion, an impulse.* LIT., ut (arbores) levi momento impulsae occiderent, Liv. TRANSF., mental *impulse, influence*: parva momenta in spem metumque animum impellere, Liv.; Caes., Cic.; hence, *weight, importance*: esse maximi momenti et ponderis, Cic.; argumentorum momenta, *decisive proofs*, Cic.; iuvenis egregius maximum momentum rerum eius civitatis, *a man of commanding influence*, Liv.

Mōna -ae, f. (1) *the Isle of Man*: Caes. (2) *the Isle of Anglesey*: Tac.

mŏnaesēs -is, m. (Μοναίσης), *a Parthian king*: Hor.

mŏnēdŭla -ae, f. *a daw, jackdaw*: Cic., Ov.

mŏnĕo -ēre (connected with mens), *to remind, admonish, warn.*
In gen., with acc. of person: Terentiam de testamento, Cic.; aliquem de retinenda Sestii gratia, Cic.; with internal n. acc.: id ipsum quod me mones, Cic.; with acc. and infin., *to warn that* . . . : magis idoneum tempus te esse ullum umquam repertum, Cic.; with indir. quest.: monet quo statu sit res, Liv.; with ut and the subj., *to advise to* . . . : ut magnam infamiam fugiat, Cic.; so with subj. alone: eos hoc moneo desinant furere, Cic.; with ne and the subj.: ne id faceret, Cic.; with infin.: Sall., Verg., Tac.
Esp. (1) *to instruct, prompt, say with authority*: tu vatem, tu, diva, mone, Verg.; Liv. (2) *to admonish by punishment*: Tac.
¶ Hence n. pl. of partic. as subst. **mŏnĭta** -orum (1) *warnings*: Cic (2) *prophecies*: deorum, Cic.; Verg.

mŏnēris -is, f. (μονήρης), *a vessel having only one bank of oars*: Liv.

Mŏnēta -ae, f. (moneo). (1) *the mother of the Muses* (=Μνημοσύνη). (2) *a surname of Juno*; the Roman money was coined in the temple of Juno Moneta; hence moneta as: **a**, *the mint, the place where money was coined*: Cic. L.: **b**, *coined metal, money*: Ov.: **c**, *the die or stamp with which money was coined*: Mart. TRANSF., communi feriat carmen triviale monetā, Juv.

mŏnētālis -is, m. (moneta), *relating to the mint*; in jest, as subst., *one who asks for money*: Cic. L.

mŏnīle -is, n. *a necklace, a collar*: Cic., Verg., Ov.

mŏnīmentum = monumentum; q.v.

mŏnĭtĭo -ōnis, f. (moneo), *a reminding, warning*: Cic., Suet.

mŏnĭtor -ōris, m. (moneo), *one who reminds.* In gen.: officii, Sall. Esp. (1) *a prompter*:

a, *an orator's assistant*: Cic.: **b,** *a nomenclator, who reminds one of persons' names*: Cic. **(2)** *an adviser, instructor*: fatuus, Cic.; Hor.

mŏnĭtus -ūs, m. (moneo), *a reminding, warning, admonition.* In gen.: Ov. Esp., *an intimation of the will of the gods by oracles, augury, portents, omens,* etc.: monitus fortunae, Cic.

Mŏnoecus -i, m. (Μόνοικος, *he that dwells alone*), *surname of Hercules*: Monoeci Arx, *a promontory on the coast of Liguria* (now *Monaco*).

mŏnogrammos or **-us** -i, m. adj. (μονόγραμμος), of pictures consisting only of outlines, *sketched*: Epicurus monogrammos deos et nihil agentes commentus est, *incorporeal, shadowy*: Cic.

mŏnŏpŏdĭum -i, n. (μονοπόδιον), *a table with one foot*: Liv.

mŏnŏpōlĭum -i, n. (μονοπώλιον), *a monopoly, sole right of sale*: Suet.

mons montis, m. *a mountain.* LIT., mons impendens, Cic.; Caes., Verg., Ov., etc.; prov. of large promises followed by small performance: parturiunt montes, nascetur ridiculus mus, Hor. TRANSF., **(1)** *any large mass, great quantity*: mons aquarum, Verg.; maria montesque polliceri, *to make large promises,* Sall. **(2)** *a great rock*: Verg.

monstrātĭō -ōnis, f. (monstro), *a pointing out*: Ter.

monstrātor -ōris, m. (monstro), *a pointer-out*: hospitii, Tac. TRANSF., *an inventor*: aratri, Triptolemus, Verg.

monstro -are (monstrum), *to show, point out.* LIT., proceram palmam Deli monstrant, Cic.; Verg., Hor.

TRANSF., **(1)** *to point out, teach, inform*: tu istic si quid librarii mea manu non intellegent monstrabis, Cic. L.; Verg., Hor., Liv. **(2)** *to ordain, institute, appoint*: piacula, Verg. **(3)** *to inform against, denounce*: alii ab amicis monstrabantur, Tac.

monstrum -i, n. (moneo), *a significant supernatural event, a wonder, portent*: monstra deum, Verg.; Cic. TRANSF., **(1)** *of living beings*: monstrum horrendum, *Polyphemus,* Verg.; immanissimum ac foedissimum monstrum, *Clodius,* Cic.; ferarum, Verg. **(2)** *of things*: non mihi iam furtum, sed monstrum ac prodigium videbatur, Cic.; monstra nuntiare, Cic.

monstrŭōsus (**monstrōsus**: Luc.) -a -um (monstrum), *strange, wonderful, monstrous*: monstruosissima bestia, Cic.
¶ Adv. **monstrŭōsē,** *strangely, wonderfully*: Cic.

montānus -a -um (mons). **(1)** *of a mountain, found on mountains*: flumen, Verg.; Ligures, Liv. M. as subst. **montānus** -i, *a mountaineer*: Caes. **(2)** *mountainous*: Delmatia, Ov.; loca, Liv.; n. pl. as subst. **montāna** -ōrum, *mountainous country*: Liv.

montĭcŏla -ae, c. (mons/colo), *a dweller among mountains, highlander*: Ov.

montĭvăgus -a -um (mons/vagus), *wandering over the mountains*: cursus, Cic.; Lucr.

montŭōsus (**montōsus**: Verg.) -a -um (mons), *mountainous*: regio aspera et montuosa, Cic. N. pl. as subst. **montŭōsa** -ōrum, *mountainous country*: Plin.

mŏnŭmentum (**mŏnĭmentum**) -i, n. (moneo), *a memorial, monument.*

In gen.: monumenti causā, Cic.; laudis, clementiae, furtorum, Cic.

Esp. **(1)** *a commemorative building, a temple, gallery,* etc.: monumenta Africani, statues, Cic. **(2)** *written memorials, annals, memoirs*: monumenta rerum gestarum, Cic.; commendare aliquid monumentis, Cic.; Hor., Liv.

Mopsōpĭus -a -um (from Μοψοπία, *an ancient name of Attica*), *Attic, Athenian*: iuvenis, Triptolemus, Ov.; muri, urbs, *Athens,* Ov.

Mopsus -i, m. (Μόψος). **(1)** *the name of several soothsayers.* **(2)** *the name of a shepherd in Vergil.*

¹mŏra -ae, f. *delay.*

LIT., moram adferre, interponere, Cic.; sine morā, Cic. L.; moram creditoribus facere, *to put off the day of payment,* Cic.; trahere, moliri, Verg.; nec mora ulla est quin, Ter.; *a pause on a march*: Liv.; *a pause in speaking*: Cic.

TRANSF., **(1)** *space of time*: Ov., Liv. **(2)** *a hindrance*: Verg., Liv.

²mŏra -ae, f. (μόρα), *a division of the Spartan army*: Cic., Nep.

mŏrālis -e (from mos; a word formed by Cic.), *moral, ethical*: philosophiae pars, Cic.; Sen., Quint.

mŏrātor -ōris, m. (moror), *a delayer, retarder*: publici commodi, Liv.; esp. *an advocate who talked against time*: Cic.

¹mŏrātus, partic. from moror; q.v.

²mŏrātus -a -um (mos), *having certain manners* or *morals.* **(1)** *of persons*: bene, melius, optime moratus, Cic.; Pl., Liv. **(2)** fig., *of things credited with character*: male moratus venter, Ov.; Pl. **(3)** *of things, adapted to a character, in character, characteristic*: poema, Cic.; *recte morata fabula, in which the characters are well drawn,* Hor.

morbĭdus -a -um (morbus). **(1)** *sickly, diseased*: Varr., Plin. **(2)** *unwholesome, causing disease*: Lucr.

morbus -i, m. *disease, sickness.*

LIT., physical: mortifer, Cic.; in morbum cadere, incidere, Cic.; in morbo esse, *to be sick,* Cic.; morbo laborare, opprimi, Cic.; morbus ingravescit, *grows worse,* Cic.; ex morbo convalescere, *to get well,* Cic.; morbum simulare, Cic.

TRANSF., **(1)** mental disease: animi morbi sunt cupiditates immensae et inanes divitiarum gloriae, Cic.; Hor. **(2)** *distress*: Pl. **(3)** personif.: Verg.

mordax -ācis (mordeo), *biting, snappish.* LIT., canis, Pl. TRANSF., **(1)** *of physical qualities*: **a,** *stinging*: urtica, Ov.: **b,** *sharp*: ferrum, Hor.: **c,** *pungent*: fel, Ov. **(2)** *of character,* etc.: **a,** *biting, satirical*: Cynicus, Hor.; carmen, Ov.: **b,** *wearing, corroding*: sollicitudines, Hor.
¶ Compar. adv. **mordācĭus,** *more bitingly*: lima mordacius uti, Ov.

mordĕo mordēre mŏmordi morsum, *to bite.* LIT., canes mordent, Cic.; pabula dente, Ov.; ostrea, *to devour,* Juv.; Verg.

TRANSF., **(1)** *to bite into, cut into, take fast hold of*: fibula mordet vestem, Ov.; rura quae Liris quietā mordet aquā, Hor. **(2)** *to nip, bite, sting*: matutina parum cautos iam

frigora mordent, Hor.; Mart. (3) fig., *to vex,
sting, hurt, pain*: aliquem dictis, Ov.; valde
me momorderunt epistulae tuae, Cic. L.;
Hor.
mordĭcēs -um, m. pl. (mordeo), *bites*: Pl.
mordĭcus, adv. (mordeo), *with the teeth, by
biting.* LIT., auferre mordicus auriculam,
Cic.; Pl. TRANSF., tenere mordicus, *to keep
fast hold of*; perspicuitatem, Cic.
mōrē, adv. from morus; q.v.
mōrētum -i, n. *a rustic salad made of garlic,
parsley, vinegar, oil, etc.*: Ov.
mŏrĭbundus -a -um (morior). (1) *dying,
expiring*: iacentem moribundumque vidisti,
Cic.; pes, Lucr.; Pl., Liv. (2) *subject to death,
mortal*: membra, Verg. (3) *causing death,
deadly*: Cat.
mōrĭgĕror -ari, dep. (and **mōrĭgĕro** -are,
act.: Pl.) (mos/gero), *to comply with, gratify*:
voluptati aurium morigerari debet oratio,
Cic.; Ter.
mōrĭgĕrus -a -um (mos/gero), *compliant,
accommodating, obsequious*: Pl., Lucr.
Mŏrīni -ōrum, m. *a people in Gallia Belgica.*
mŏrĭor mori mortŭus sum mŏrĭtūrus, dep. *to
die.*
    LIT., ex vulnere, Liv.; ferro, Liv.; hoc
morbo, Cic.; fame, Cic.; frigore, Hor.;
amore, Ov.; in suo lectulo, Cic.
    TRANSF., of things, *to die away, wither
away, decay.* (1) of physical objects: segetes
moriuntur in herbis, Ov.; flammas et vidi
nullo concutiente mori, Ov. (2) of abstractions: suavissimi hominis memoria moritur,
Cic.; Pl., Ov., Liv.
    ¶ Hence partic. **mortŭus** -a -um, *dead*:
Pl., Cic., etc. TRANSF., (1) *decayed, extinct*:
Cic. (2) *half-dead*: Cic.
    ¶ M. as subst. **mortŭus** -i, *a corpse*: Pl.,
Cic.
mormyr -ȳris, f. (μορμύρος), *a sea-fish*: Ov.
mōrŏlŏgus -a -um (μωρολόγος), *talking like
a fool, foolish*: Pl.; subst. *a fool*: Pl.
¹mōror -ari, dep. (mora), *to delay.*
    (1) intransit., *to linger, loiter, tarry*: haud
multa moratus, Verg.; Caes., Cic., Hor.;
with infin.: alicui bellum inferre, Cic.; nihil
moror, foll. by quominus and subj., Liv.;
esp. *to stay, tarry in a place*: Brundisii,
Cic. L.; in provincia, Cic.; Hor.
    (2) transit., *to retard, detain, hinder*:
impetum sustinere atque morari, Caes.;
aliquem ab itinere, Liv.; esp.: **a**, *to detain
with a view to action*; of a judge dismissing a
person: C. Sempronium nihil moror, Liv.;
hence, nihil (*or* nil) morari, *to care nothing
for*: nil moror officium, Hor.: **b**, *to hold the
attention of*: novitate morandus spectator,
Hor.
²mōror -ari, dep. (μωρός), *to be foolish, to be
a fool*: Suet.
mōrōsē, adv. from morosus; q.v.
mōrōsĭtās -ātis, f. (morosus), *peevishness,
fretfulness, moroseness*: Cic.; *pedantry, fastidiousness in style*: Suet.
mōrōsus -a -um (mos), *peevish, morose, capricious, captious, fretful*: senes, Cic.; canities,
Hor. TRANSF., of things: morbus, *obstinate*,
Ov.
    Adv. **mōrōsē**, *peevishly, captiously*: Cic.
Morpheus (disyll.) -ĕos, m. (Μορφεύς), *god of
dreams.*

mors mortis, f. (morior), *death.*
    LIT., omnium rerum mors est extremum,
Cic.; mortem sibi consciscere, *to commit
suicide*, Caes., Cic.; obire, oppetere, Cic.;
alicui inferre, *to slay, kill*, Cic.; morti dare,
Hor.; plur., mortes, *deaths* of several
persons; clarae mortes pro patria oppetitae,
Cic.; of things, *destruction*: Lucr.
    TRANSF., (1) *a corpse*: Cic., Cat., Liv.
(2) *life-blood*: ensem multā morte recepit,
Verg. (3) *a cause of death* or *destruction*: mors
terrorque sociorum lictor Sextius, Cic.;
personif.: Cic., Verg.
morsus -ūs, m. (mordeo), *a bite, biting.*
    LIT., (1) serpentis, Cic.; morsu dividere
escas, Cic. (2) *eating*: mensarum, Verg.
    TRANSF., (1) *a seizing, laying hold of*, like
the bite of an anchor: Verg.; and meton.,
that which seizes: morsus uncus, *the fluke of
an anchor*, Verg.; roboris, *the cleft of a tree
holding fast a javelin*, Verg. (2) *a biting
taste, pungency*: Mart. (3) *corrosion*: Luc.
(4) *a carping* or *malicious attack with words*:
Hor. (5) *mental pain, sting, vexation*: doloris,
Cic.; curarum, Ov.
mortālis -e (mors), *subject to death, mortal.*
    LIT., omne animal esse mortale, Cic.;
mortalia saecla, Lucr.; m. as subst. **mortālis**
-is, *a mortal man, a man*; esp., plur., *mortals,
men*: Pl., Cic., Liv.
    TRANSF., (1) *transitory, temporary, perish-
able*: leges, inimicitiae, Cic. (2) *belonging
to mortal men, human, earthly*: condicio vitae,
Cic.; mucro, Verg.; n. pl. as subst. **mortālĭa**
-ium, *mortal affairs*, esp., *human sufferings*:
mentem mortalia tangunt, Verg.
mortālĭtās -ātis, f. (mortalis), *the being
subject to death.* LIT., Cic. TRANSF., (1)
death: mortalitatem explere, *to die*, Tac.
(2) *mankind*: Curt.
mortĭcĭnus -a -um (mors), *dead, carrion*:
Varr., Plin.; as a term of abuse: Pl.
mortĭfer or **mortĭfĕrus** -fĕra -fĕrum (mors/
fero), *causing death, fatal, deadly*: vulnus,
morbus, Cic.; bellum, Verg.
    Adv. **mortĭfĕrē**, *fatally*: Plin. L.
mortŭālĭa -ium, n. (mortuus), *funeral songs,
dirges*: Pl.
mortŭus -a -um, partic. from morior; q.v.
mōrŭlus -a -um (morum), *blackberry-
coloured*: Pl.
mōrum -i, n. (μῶρον, μόρον). (1) *a mulberry*:
Hor. (2) *a blackberry*: Verg., Ov.
¹mōrus -i, f. *a mulberry-tree*: Ov.
²mōrus -a -um (μωρός), *silly, foolish*: Pl.
mos mōris, m. *the will, humour, inclination*
of a person.
    In gen.: morem alicui gerere, *to comply
with a person's wishes, humour* him, Pl., Ter.,
Cic TRANSF., of things: caeli, Verg.
    Esp. (1) *custom, usage, wont*: de more suo
decedere, Cic.; more maiorum, Cic., Liv.;
sicut meus est mos, Hor.; with gerund: mos
est ita rogandi, Cic.; with infin.: magorum
mos est non humare corpora, Cic.; with acc.
and infin.: mos est Athenis laudari in
contione eos, Cic.; mos est (*or* moris est)
with ut and the subj.: mos est hominum ut
nolint eundem pluribus rebus excellere,
Cic.; Verg., Liv. TRANSF., of things, esp.
more (*or* in morem) with genit., *after the
manner of*: Verg., Hor. (2) *regular practice*

rule, law: mores viris ponere, Verg.; sine more, *without control*, Verg.; mos neque cultus erat, Verg. (3) in plur., *ways, conduct, character, morals*: suavissimi, iusti, feri, Cic.; totam vitam, naturam, moresque alicuius cognoscere, Cic.; describere hominum sermones moresque, Cic; Liv., Suet.

Mŏsa -ae, f. *a river in Gallia Belgica* (now *the Meuse*).

Mŏsella -ae, f. *a river in Gallia Belgica* (now *the Moselle*).

Mōsēs (Juv.) and **Mŏȳsēs** (Tac.) -is, m. *Moses*.

mōtĭo -ōnis, f. (moveo), *movement, motion*: corporum, Cic.; animi, Cic.

mōto -are (freq. of moveo), *to move about, move frequently*: lacertos, Ov.; zephyris motantibus, Verg.

¹**mōtus** -a -um, partic. from moveo; q.v.

²**mōtus** -ūs, m. (moveo), *a motion, movement*.

LIT., in gen.: navium, remorum, Caes.; natura omnia ciens motibus suis, Cic.; terrae, *an earthquake*, Cic., Lucr., Liv.; esp., *a motion of the body, movement, gesture*; of an orator: manuum motūs teneant illud decorum, Cic.; of actors and dancers: haud indecoros motūs more Tusco dare, Liv.; dare motus Cereri, *to lead dances*, Verg.; Hor.

TRANSF., (1) *motion of the mind*: **a**, of the senses: dulcem motum adferent, Cic.: **b**, of the mind, *mental activity*: motūs animorum duplices sunt, alteri cogitationis, alteri appetitūs, Cic.; Manto divino concita motu, *inspiration*, Ov.: **c**, of the passions, *emotion*: motūs animi nimii, Cic.; Verg. (2) *political movement*; *a rebellion, rising, riot*: omnes Catilinae motūs prohibere, Cic.; Caes., Hor., Liv.

mŏvĕo mŏvēre mōvi mōtum (connected with ἀμευσασθαι), *to move, set in motion, stir*.

LIT., of physical movement; in gen.: caelum, Cic.; reflex., se movere, and pass. in middle sense, moveri, *to move* (*oneself*): Liv., etc.; so intransit.: terra movit, Liv. Esp. (1) of dancing: Cic., Hor. (2) *to move away* from a place, *remove*: fundamenta loco, Cic.; se de Cumano, Cic.; as milit. t. t.; movere signa, movere castra, se movere, moveri, *or simply* movere, *to march away, change position*: castra ex eo loco, Caes. (3) *to dispossess* a person, *dislodge, expel*: hostem statu, Liv.; aliquem ex agro, Cic.; aliquem de senatu, Cic.; senatu, Sall.; e senatorio loco, Liv.

TRANSF., (1) *to move mentally, stir, influence, work upon*: movere ac moliri aliquid, Liv.; multa animo, Verg.; hence, *to begin*: bellum, Cic., Liv. (2) *to affect the feelings, move, stir, excite*: moveri memoriā amicitiae, Caes.; Roscii morte moveri, Cic.; specie, Verg.; Liv. (3) of a specific feeling or its expression, *to cause, produce, excite*: risum, Cic.; misericordiam, Cic.; with dat.: fletum populo, Cic.; Verg., Liv. (4) *to change, shake, shatter*: alicuius sententiam, Cic. L.; Liv.; fidem, Ov. (5) politically, *to arouse, excite, disturb*: quieta, Sall.; Cic.

mox, adv. (1) of future time, *soon, presently*: iussit mihi nuntiari mox se venturum, Cic.; Verg., Liv., etc.; with quam, *how soon*, Cic., Liv. (2) *then, thereupon*: mox rediit Cre-

monam reliquus populus, Tac.; mox... postremo, Liv.

Mŏȳsēs -is = Mōsēs; q.v.

mū, interj., *a murmur, tiny noise*: Enn., Pl.

mūcĭdus -a -um (mucus). (1) *snivelling*: Pl. (2) *mouldy, musty*: Juv.

Mūcĭus -a -um, *name of a Roman gens. Its most famous members were*: (1) C. Mucius Scaevola, *a Roman who came to Porsena's camp to kill him, and when caught, thrust his right hand into the fire, and received the name of Scaevola* (*left-handed*). (2) P. Mucius Scaevola, *friend of the Gracchi*. (3) Qu. Mucius Scaevola, *whose administration of the province of Asia* (121 B.C.) *was so upright that the Asiatics celebrated a festival in honour of him, called* Mūcĭa -ōrum, n. pl.

¶ Hence adj. **Mūcĭānus** -a -um, *relating to Mucius*: exitus, Cic.

mūcro -ōnis, m. *a sharp point or edge*. LIT., cultri, Juv.; esp., *a sword's point or edge*: Verg., Ov. TRANSF., (1) *a sword*: mucrones militum tremere, Cic.; Verg., Liv. (2) fig., *sharpness, point*: defensionis tuae, Cic. (3) *boundary*: Lucr.

mūcus -i, m. (μύξα; emungo), *the mucous matter of the nose*: Cat.

mūgil (**mūgĭlis**) -is, m. (μυξῖνος), *a fish*, perhaps *the mullet*: Plin., Juv.

mūgĭnor -ari, dep. *to loiter, trifle, dally*: dum tu muginaris, Cic. L.

mūgĭo -ire (cf. μυκᾶσθαι), *to bellow as an ox, low*.

LIT., of cattle: Liv.; partic. as subst., mugientes = *oxen*, Hor.

TRANSF., *to roar, bray, rumble, groan*: mugit tubae clangor, Verg.; sub pedibus mugire solum, Verg.; si mugiat Africis malus procellis, Hor.

mūgītus -ūs, m. (mugio), *the lowing, bellowing of cattle*: boum, Verg.; Ov. TRANSF., *a rumbling, groaning*: terrae, Cic.

mūla -ae, f. (mulus), *a female mule*: Cic., Juv., Suet.

mulcĕo mulcēre mulsi mulsum, *to stroke, touch lightly*. LIT., manu mulcens barbam, Ov.; virgā capillos, Ov.; Lucr., Verg. TRANSF., *to soothe, appease, charm*: aliquem fistulā, Hor.; dictis, Verg.; tigres, fluctus, iras, Verg.; vulnera, *to allay pain*, Ov.; Liv.

Mulcĭbĕr -ĕris and -ĕri, m. *a surname of Vulcan*: Cic., Ov.; meton., *fire*: Ov.

mulco -are, *to thrash, cudgel*. LIT., Pl., Ter., Cic., Liv. TRANSF., *to handle roughly*: Liv.

mulctra -ae, f. (mulgeo), *a milk-pail*: Verg.

mulctrārĭum -i, n. (mulgeo), *a milk-pail*: Verg.

mulctrum -i, n. (mulgeo), *a milk-pail*: Hor.

mulgĕo mulgēre mulsi, *to milk*: oves, Verg.; prov.: mulgere hircos, of an impossible undertaking, Verg.

mŭlĭĕbris -e (mulier), *of a woman, womanly, feminine*.

LIT., vox, Cic.; vestis, Nep.; certamen, *on account of a woman*, Liv.; Fortuna Muliebris, *revered in memory of the women who had appeased the anger of Coriolanus*, Liv.

TRANSF., *womanish, effeminate, unmanly*: sententia, Cic.; Hor.

¶ Adv. **mŭlĭĕbrĭtĕr**, *after the manner of a woman*; *effeminately, womanishly*: se lamentis muliebriter lacrimisque dedere, Cic.; Hor., Liv.

mŭlĭer -ĕris, f. (perhaps connected with mollis), *a woman*: Pl., Cic., etc.; also *a wife, matron*: virgo aut mulier, Cic.; Hor.

mŭlĭĕrārĭus -a -um (mulier), *womanish*: manus, *a troop of soldiers sent by a woman*, Cic.

mŭlĭercŭla -ae, f. (dim. of mulier), *a little woman*, used in pity or contempt: suas secum mulierculas in castra ducere, Cic.; Hor.

mŭlĭĕrōsĭtās -ātis, f. (mulierosus), *love of women*: Cic.

mŭlĭĕrōsus -a -um (mulier), *fond of women*: Pl., Cic.

mūlīnus -a -um (mulus), *of a mule, mulish*: Juv.

mūlĭo -ōnis, m. (mulus), *a mule-keeper, mule-driver*: Pl., Caes., Verg.

mūlĭōnĭus -a -um (mulio), *of a muleteer*: Cic.

mullŭlus -i, m. (dim. of mullus), *a little mullet*: Cic.

mullus -i, m. (μύλλος), *the red mullet*: Cic. L., Juv.

mulsus -a -um (mel), *honeyed*.
LIT., *mixed with honey, sweetened with honey*: Cato, Plin.; n. as subst. **mulsum** -i, *wine sweetened with honey, mead*: calix mulsi, Cic.; Pl., Liv.
TRANSF., *as sweet as honey*: dicta mulsa, Pl.; f. as subst. **mulsa** -ae, *my honey*: Pl.

multa -ae, f. (connected with mulco), *fine, mulct*; originally in cattle, later in money. LIT., multam alicui dicere, *to impose*, Cic.; multam petere, inrogare, *to propose*, Cic.; multam certare, *to contest*, Liv. TRANSF., *punishment, loss*: Pl., Cic. L., Liv.

multangŭlus -a -um (multus/angulus), *many-cornered*: Lucr.

multātīcĭus -a -um (multa), *relating to a fine*: pecunia, Liv.

multātĭo -ōnis, f. (multo), *a fining*: bonorum, Cic.

multēsĭmus -a -um (multus), *very small*: pars, Lucr.

multĭbĭbus -a -um (multus/bibo), *drinking much*: Pl.

multĭcăvus -a -um (multus/cavus), *having many holes, porous*: pumex, Ov.

multĭcĭa -ōrum, n. pl. (sc. vestimenta), *soft, finely woven garments*: Juv.

multĭfārĭam, adv. *on many sides, in many places*: Cic., Liv.

multĭfĭdus -a -um (multus/findo), *cloven into many parts*: faces, Ov. TRANSF., Ister, *having many branches*, Mart.

multĭformis -e (multus/forma), *having many shapes, multiform*: qualitates, Cic.; Sen.

multĭfŏrus -a -um (multus/foris), *having many openings, pierced with many holes*: multifori tibia buxi, Ov.

multĭgĕnĕris -e (multus/genus), *of many kinds*: Pl.

multĭgĕnus -a -um=multigeneris; q.v.: Lucr.

multĭiŭgus -a -um (Liv.) and **multĭiŭgis** -e (Cic. L.), adj. (multus/iugum), *yoked many together*. LIT., equi, Liv. TRANSF., *manifold, of many sorts*: litterae, Cic. L.

multĭlŏquax -ācis (multus/loquax), *talkative*: Pl.

multĭlŏquĭum -i, n. (multus/loquor), *talkativeness*: Pl.

multĭlŏquos -a -om (multus/loquor), *talkative*: Pl.

multĭmŏdīs, adv. (multis modis), *in many ways, variously*: Pl., Ter., Lucr.

multiplex -plĭcis (multus/plico), *having many folds*.
LIT., alvus est multiplex et tortuosa, Cic. TRANSF., (1) of material objects: **a**, *with many winds and turnings*: vitis serpens multiplici lapsu, Cic.; Ov.: **b**, *having many parts, manifold*: corona, Cic.; lorica, Verg. (2) in gen., *many times as large*: multiplex quam pro numero damnum est, Liv. (3) of abstr. things, *of many kinds, manifold*: multiplex ratio disputandi, Cic. (4) of persons, character, etc., *many-sided*: varius et multiplex et copiosus, Cic.; multiplices naturae, Cic.; ingenium, *versatile, changeable*, Cic.

multĭplĭcābĭlis -e (multiplico), *manifold*: Cic. poet.

multĭplĭcātĭo -onis, f. (multiplico), *multiplying*: Sen.

multĭplĭco -are (multiplex), *to increase many times, multiply*: aes alienum, Caes; domus multiplicata, *enlarged*, Cic.; flumina conlectis multiplicantur aquis, Ov.

multĭtūdo -inis, f. (multus), *a large number, multitude*. In gen.: navium, Caes.; litterarum, Cic.; multitudine freti, Liv. Esp., in concr. sense, *a large number of men, crowd, multitude*: tanta multitudo lapides ac tela iaciebat, Caes.; Cic., Liv.; also in a contemptuous sense, *the common people, mob*: famā et multitudinis iudicio moveri, Cic.

multĭvŏlus -a -um (multus/volo), *having many wishes or desires*: Cat.

multo -are (multa), *to punish*: aliquem morte, Cic.; exsilio, Liv.; vitia hominum damnis, ignominiis, vinculis, Cic.; Pl., Tac.; with dat.: Veneri esse multatum, *punished with a fine paid to Venus*, Cic.

multus -a -um; compar. **plūs** plūris; superl. **plūrĭmus** -a -um, *much, many*.
Posit. **multus**: sing., *much, great*; plur. *many, numerous*. In gen.: Cic., Verg., etc. M. pl. as subst.: multi, *many persons*, Cic.; also *the many, the common herd* (=oἱ πολλοί): unus de multis, Cic.; orator e multis, Cic. N. pl. as subst., multa, *many things*; ellipt.: ne multa, ne multis, *briefly, in brief*, Cic. Esp. (1) of time, *advanced*: ad multum diem, *till late in the day*, Cic.; multā nocte, *late at night*, Verg. (2) of discourse, *copious, diffuse, prolix*: ne in re nota multus et insolens sim, Cic. (3) in action, *busy, vigorous, zealous*: in eodem genere causarum multus, Cic. (4) in sing., of a large number, like the English *many a*: Hor., Verg.
N. acc. sing. as adv. **multum**, *much, greatly*: longe multumque superare, Cic.; multum mecum loquuntur, *often*, Cic.; multum iactatus in alto, Verg.; haud multum, Liv., Tac.
N. abl. sing., of measure, **multō**, *by much, by far*; with comparatives, superlatives, and words of similar force: multo pauciores, Cic.; multo maxima pars, Cic.; multo antepanere, Cic.; non multo post, *not long after*, Cic.
Compar. **plūs**. (1) in sing., n. only, *more*: plus posse, plus facere, Cic.; plus

pecuniae, Cic.; with quam: non plus quam semel, Cic.; with abl.: plus uno, plus aequo, Cic.; with numerals, often without abl. and without quam: plus ducentos passūs, Liv. Genit. of value **plūris**: pluris emere, vendere, *dearer, at a higher price*, Cic.; mea mihi conscientia pluris est quam omnium sermo, *is of more value to me*, Cic.; aliquem pluris aestimare, *to think more highly of*, Cic. (2) in plur., **plūrēs, plūră** (genit. plurium), *more numerous, several, many*: Caes., Cic., Liv., etc.; ellipt.: quid plura? *in short*, Cic. Superl. **plūrĭmus**, *most, very many*: plurimis verbis, Cic.; in sing., of a large number, like the English *full many a*; also of energy, insistence, etc., *strong*: Hor., Liv., Ov. N. as subst. **plūrĭmum** -i, *most*: Cic.; genit. of value **plūrĭmi**, *at the highest value or price*: Pl., Cic.

mŭlus -i, m. *a mule*: Pl., Cic., Tac.

Mulvĭus pons, *a bridge across the Tiber above Rome.*

Mummĭus -a -um, *name of a Roman gens; its most famous member was* L. Mummius Achaicus, *the destroyer of Corinth*, 146 B.C.

Munda -ae, f. *town in Hispania Baetica, where Julius Caesar defeated Pompey's son*, 45 B.C.

mundānus -i, m. (mundus), *a citizen of the world*: Cic.

mundĭtĭa -ae, f. and (not in Cic.) **mundĭtĭēs** -ēi, f. (mundus), *cleanness, neatness*. LIT., physical. (1) *cleanness*: Pl. (2) *neatness, spruceness, elegance*: non odiosa neque exquisita nimis, Cic.; Pl.; plur.: simplex munditiis, Hor.; Ov., Liv. TRANSF., of style or manners: *neatness, elegance*: Cic., Sall.

mundŭlus -a -um (dim. of mundus), *neat, spruce*: Pl.

¹**mundus** -a -um, *clean, neat, elegant*. LIT., supellex, Hor. TRANSF., (1) of manner of life, *elegant, refined*: homo, Cic.; cultus iusto mundior, *too elegant*, Liv. (2) of style, *neat, elegant*: verba, Ov.

¹**mundus** -i, m. (¹mundus). (1) *toilet-things, adornment*: muliebris, Liv. (2) *the universe, the world*. LIT., hic ornatus mundi, *harmony of the universe*, Cic.; mundi innumerabiles, Cic.; Lucr., Verg. TRANSF., *the inhabitants of the world, mankind*: quicumque mundo terminus obstitit, Hor.; fastos evolvere mundi, Hor.

mūnĕro -are (Pl., Cic.) and **mūnĕror** -ari, dep. (Cic., Hor.) (munus), *to give, present.* (1) *to give* a thing (acc.) *to* a person (dat.): natura aliud alii muneratur, Cic.; Pl. (2) *to present* a person (acc.) *with* a thing (abl.), Cic., Hor.

mūnĭa -iorum, n. pl., *duties, functions*; esp. *official duties, official business*: candidatorum, Cic.; Hor., Liv., Tac.

mūnĭceps -cĭpis, c. (munia/capio), *the citizen of a municipium*. LIT., municeps Cosanus, *of Cosa*, Cic. TRANSF., *a fellow-citizen, fellow-countryman*: meus, Cic.; municipes Iovis advexisse lagoenas, *country-men of Jupiter*, i.e. *Cretan*, Juv.

mūnĭcĭpālis -e (municipium), *belonging to a municipium, municipal*: homines, Cic., Tac.; sometimes in a contemptuous sense, *provincial*: eques, Juv.

mūnĭcĭpĭum -i, n. (municeps), *a town, borough*; esp. *a town in Italy, the inhabitants*

of which had the Roman citizenship, but were governed by their own magistrates and laws; a free town, municipal town: Caes., Cic., etc.

mūnĭfĭcē, adv. from munificus; q.v.

mūnĭfĭcentĭa -ae, f. (munificus), *generosity, bountifulness*: Sall., Liv.

mūnĭfĭco -are (munificus), *to present generously*: mortalis salute, Lucr.

mūnĭfĭcus -a -um (munus/facio), *generous, liberal*: in dando, Cic.; superl.: munificentissimus, Cic. TRANSF., *of wealth, splendid*: opes, Ov.

¶ Adv. **mūnĭfĭcē**, *generously*: Cic., Liv.

mūnīmen -ĭnis, n. (munio), *a protection, defence*: munimine cingere fossas, Ov.; ad imbres, *against the rains*, Verg.

mūnīmentum -i, n. (munio), *a fortification, defence, protection*. LIT., ut instar muri hae sepes munimenta praeberent, Caes.; tenere se munimentis, Tac.; Liv. TRANSF., *protection*: rati noctem sibi munimento fore, Sall.; Liv.

mūnĭo (moenĭo) -ire (cf. moenia), *to build, esp. to build a wall; also to surround with a wall, fortify.* LIT., locum, montem, Caes.; castra vallo fossāque, Caes.; Alpibus Italiam munierat natura, Cic.; domum praesidiis, Cic.; of roads, *to build*: viam, Cic., Liv.; iter, Nep. TRANSF., *to secure, defend, protect*: quae (herbescens viriditas) contra avium morsus munitur vallo aristarum, Cic.; munio me ad haec tempora, Cic.; sese ab insidiis, Liv.; munire alicui viam accusandi, *to prepare a way for*, Cic.

¶ Hence partic. (with compar. and superl.) **mūnītus** -a -um, *fortified, secured*: Caes., Cic., Lucr.

mūnītĭo -ōnis, f. (munio), *a fortifying, building up.* LIT., milites munitione prohibere, Caes.; esp. *a paving of roads*: ex viarum munitione quaestum facere, Cic.; munitio fluminum, *bridging over*, Tac. TRANSF., (1) concr., *a fortification*: urbem operibus munitionibusque saepire, Cic.; Liv., Tac. (2) fig., *a paving of the way*: Cic.

mūnīto -are (freq. of munio), *to pave, make passable*: viam, Cic.

mūnītor -ōris, m. (munio), *a builder of fortifications, a sapper, military engineer*: Verg., Liv., Tac.

mūnītus -a -um, partic. from munio; q.v.

mūnus (moenus) -ĕris, n. (cf. munia), *an office, function, employment, duty.* LIT., reipublicae, *a public office*, Cic.; fera moenera militiae, Lucr.; consulare munus sustinere, Cic.; belli munera inter se partiri, Liv.; Caes. TRANSF., (1) *a charge, tax*: imponere, remittere, Caes. (2) *an affectionate service, favour*: neque vero verbis auget suum munus, Cic. L.; totum muneris hoc tui est, Hor. (3) esp. *last services to the dead, funeral honours*: munere inani fungi, Verg.; Cat. (4) *a gift, present*: mittere alicui aliquid muneri, *to send or give as a present*, Caes.; munera Liberi, *wine*, Hor.; Cereris, *bread*, Ov.; opusculum maiorum vigiliarum munus, *the fruit of*, Cic. (5) *a public show, especially of gladiators, as given*, e.g., *by the aediles to*

the people: munus magnificum dare, praebere, Cic.; munus gladiatorium, Cic.
(6) *a public building* or *theatre erected by an
individual*: Ov.

mūnuscŭlum -i, n. (dim. of munus), *a small
gift, little present*: Cic. L., Verg., Juv.

Mŭnychĭa -ae, f. (Μουνυχία), *one of the ports
of Athens.* Adj. **Mŭnychĭus** -a -um=
Athenian: Ov.

¹mŭraena=murena; q.v.

²Mŭraena=Murena; q.v.

mūrālis -e (murus), *of a wall, mural*: pila
muralia, *used by those who defend a wall*,
Caes.; falces, *hooks* or *grappling-irons for
pulling down walls*, Caes.; corona, *the crown
given to the one who first scaled the wall of a
besieged city*, Liv.; corona, *the diadem of
Cybele, adorned with walls and towers*, Lucr.

Murcĭa -ae, f. *the goddess of sloth.*

¹mūrēna (mūraena) -ae, f. (μύραινα), *a sea-
fish; the murry* or *the lamprey*: Pl., Juv.

²Mūrēna -ae, m. (¹murena), *a cognomen in the
gens Licinia*; esp. of L. Licinius Murena,
defended by Cicero on a charge of bribery.

mūrex -icis, m. *the purple-fish, a shell-fish
from which the Tyrian dye was obtained.*
      LIT., Enn., Hor.; the shell in poets is
represented as the trumpet of Triton: Ov.;
it was also used to adorn grottoes: Ov.
      TRANSF., (1) *the purple dye itself*: Tyrioque
ardebat murice laena, Verg. (2) *a sharp
stone, projecting rock*, resembling the murex
in shape: acutus, Verg.

Murgantĭa -ae, f. (1) *a town in Samnium.*
(2) *a town in Sicily.* Adj. **Murgantīnus** -a
-um, *relating to Murgantia.*

mŭrĭa -ae, f. (cf. ἁλμυρίς), *brine, pickle*: Hor.

mŭrĭātĭcum -i, n. (muria), *a pickled fish*: Pl.

mŭrĭcĭdus -i, m. (mus/caedo), *a mouse-killer*;
i.e. *a coward*: Pl.

murmur -ŭris, n. *a murmur, humming,
roaring, rumbling, crashing.* (1) of men and
animals: populi, Liv.; of indistinct prayers:
placare deos precibus et murmure longo, Ov.;
the humming of bees: Verg.; *the roar of a lion*:
Mart. (2) of things; of the sea: Cic.; of the
wind: Verg.; of the sound of wind-instru-
ments: cornuum, Hor.; inflati buxi, Ov.

mǔrmŭrillum -i, n. (dim. of murmur), *a low
murmuring*: Pl.

murmŭro -are (murmur), *to murmur, make a
noise*; with acc.: flebile lingua murmurat
exanimis, Ov.; of things, *to roar*: mare
murmurans, Cic.

¹murra (myrrha) -ae, f. (μύρρα), *the myrrh-
tree*: Ov.; also *myrrh*: Verg., Ov.

²murra (myrrha) -ae, f. (μύρρα), *a mineral,
perhaps fluorspar, out of which costly vases
and goblets were made*: Plin.; hence, poet.,
the goblets themselves: Mart.

¹murrĕus (myrrheus) -a -um (¹murra).
(1) *perfumed with myrrh*: Hor. (2) *myrrh-
coloured*: Prop.

²murrĕus (myrrhĕus) -a -um (²murra), *made
of fluorspar*: pocula, Prop.; Sen.

¹murrĭnus (myrrhĭnus) -a -um (¹murra), *of
myrrh*: Pl.

²murrĭnus (myrrhĭnus) -a -um (²murra),
made of fluorspar: Plin.

mūrus (moerus) -i, m. *a wall*, esp. *a wall
round a city.*

LIT., urbis, Cic.; muro lapideo urbem
cingere, Cic.; muros ducere, Verg., Hor.;
also *the wall of a building*: Cic. L.; *a bank* or
dyke of earth: Caes.
      TRANSF., (1) *the rim* or *edge of a pot*: Juv.
(2) fig., *protection, defence*: lex Aelia et Fufia
propugnacula murique tranquillitatis, Cic.;
Graium murus Achilles, Ov.

¹mūs mūris, c. (μῦς), *a mouse* or *rat*: rusticus
or agrestis, *field-mouse*, Hor.; non solum
inquilini sed etiam mures migrarunt, Cic.;
under the name *mus* the Romans also
included the *marten, sable, ermine*, etc.

²Mūs Mūris, m. *the name of a family of the
gens Decia, two members of which*, P. Decius
Mus *and his son of the same name, devoted
themselves to death to gain victory for their
country.*

Mūsa -ae, f. (Μοῦσα), *a muse; a goddess of
music, literature, and the arts.* The Muses,
usually said to be the daughters of Zeus
and Mnemosyne, were nine in number,
namely, Clio, Euterpe, Thalia, Melpomene,
Terpsichore, Erato, Polyhymnia, Urania,
Calliope.
      TRANSF., (1) *song, poetry*: silvestris, Verg.;
pedestris, *poetry bordering on prose*, Hor.
(2) musae, *learning, studies*; agrestiores, Cic.
(3) *genius, wit*: Quint.

¹Mūsaeus -i, m. (Μουσαῖος), *a mythical Greek
poet.*

²mūsaeus -a -um (Musa), *poetical, musical*:
Lucr.

musca -ae, f. (μυῖα), *a fly*: Cic. TRANSF., *a
troublesome, inquisitive person*: Pl.

muscārĭus -a -um (musca), *relating to flies*:
Plin.; n. as subst. **muscārĭum** -i, *a fly-flap,
made of peacocks' feathers* or *an ox's* or *horse's
tail*: Mart.

muscĭpŭla -ae, f. and **muscĭpŭlum** -i, n.
(mus/capio), *a mouse-trap*: Phaedr., Sen.

muscōsus -a -um (muscus), *covered with
moss, mossy*: fontes, Verg.; compar.: nihil
muscosius, Cic. L.

muscŭlus -i, m. (dim. of mus), *a little mouse*:
Cic. TRANSF., (1) milit. t. t., *a shed, mantelet*:
Caes. (2) *sea-mussel*: Pl. (3) *a pilot-fish*:
Plin.

muscus -i, m. *moss*: Hor., Ov.

mūsēus -a -um=²musaeus; q.v.

mūsĭca -ae, f. and **mūsĭcē** -ēs, f., subst. from
musicus; q.v.

¹mūsĭcē -ēs, f.=musica; q.v.

²mūsĭcē, adv. from musicus; q.v.

mūsĭcus -a -um (μουσικός). (1) *belonging to
music, musical*: leges, *rules of music*, Cic.
(2) *belonging to poetry*: Ter.
      M. as subst. **mūsĭcus** -i, *a musician*: Cic.;
n. pl. **mūsĭca** -ōrum, *music*: Cic.; f. sing.
mūsĭca -ae and **mūsĭcē** -ēs (Quint.),
music, poetry, learned studies: Cic., Suet.
¶ Adv. **mūsĭcē**, *agreeably*: Pl.

mussĭto -are (freq. of musso). Intransit., *to
grumble inaudibly, to mutter to oneself*: Pl.,
Liv. Transit., *to keep quiet about* a thing: Pl.,
Ter.

musso -are. (1) *to murmer, mutter, whisper to
oneself*: mussantes inter se rogitabant, Liv.;
of bees, *to hum*: mussant oras et limina
circum, Verg. (2) *to keep quiet about* a thing:
Pl. (3) *to mutter only*; hence *to be at a loss*:
mussabat tacito medicina dolore, Lucr.;

mussat rex ipse Latinus, quos generos vocet, Verg.; with infin.: Verg.

mustācĕum -i, n. and **mustācĕus** -i, m. (mustum), *a must-cake, a laurel-cake, a sort of wedding-cake, mixed with must and baked on bay-leaves*: Cato, Juv.; prov.: laureolam in mustaceo quaerere, *to look for fame in trifles*, Cic. L.

nustēla (mustella) -ae, f. (dim. of mus), *a weasel*: Pl., Hor.

nustēlīnus (mustellīnus) -a -um (mustela), *of a weasel*: Ter.

nustus -a -um, *young, new, fresh*: agna, Cato; vinum, *must*, Cato.
N. as subst. **mustum** -i, *new wine, must*: Verg.; fig.: nova ista quasi de musto ac lacu fervida oratio, Cic.; meton.: ter centum musta videre, *vintages*, Ov.

Mūta -ae, f. (mutus), *a nymph, whom Jupiter made dumb because of her loquacity.*

nūtābĭlis -e (muto), *changeable, variable, inconstant*: ea forma reipublicae mutabilis est, Cic.; Verg., Liv.

nūtābĭlĭtās -ātis, f. (mutabilis), *changeableness*: mentis, Cic.

nūtātĭo -ōnis (muto). (**1**) *a changing, change, alteration*: facere mutationem alicuius rei, Cic.; Tac. (**2**) *a mutual change, exchange*: officiorum, Cic.; Ter.

nūtĭlo -are (mutilus), *to maim, mutilate, cut off*: naso auribusque mutilatis, Liv.; caudam colubrae, Ov. TRANSF., *to curtail, diminish*: exercitum, Cic.; Ter.

mūtĭlus -a -um, *maimed, mutilated.* LIT., esp. of animals which have lost one or both horns: alces mutilae sunt cornibus, Caes. TRANSF., sic mutilus minitaris, Hor.; mutila loqui, Cic.

Mŭtĭna -ae, f. *town in Cispadane Gaul (now Modena).*
¶ Hence adj. **Mŭtĭnensis** -e, *of Mutina.*

mūtĭo (muttĭo) -ire (from sound mu), *to mutter, mumble, murmur*: Pl., Ter.

mūtītĭo (muttītĭo) -ōnis, f. (mutio, muttio), *a muttering, mumbling*: Pl.

mūto -are.
(**1**) transit. *to move, shift*: ne quis invitus civitate mutetur, *should be removed from the state*, Cic.; Pl., Liv., Ov. Hence, *to change, alter.* LIT., physically: mutari alite, *to be changed into a bird*, Ov.; mutare iumenta, *to change horses*, Caes.; mutare calceos et vestimenta, mutare terram, *to go into another country*, Liv.; vellera luto, *to dye*, Verg. Esp. *to exchange, barter*: merces, Verg.; res inter se, Sall.; with abl., *to give or to get* one thing in exchange for another: Hor., Liv., Sall. TRANSF., of abstr. things: fidem, Pl., Ter.; consilium, Caes.; sententiam, voluntatem, Cic.
(**2**) intransit., *to change, alter*: Liv., Tac.

mūtŭātĭo -ōnis, f. (mutuor), *a borrowing*: Cic.

mūtŭē, adv. from mutuus; q.v.

mūtŭĭto -are (mutuor), *to wish to borrow*: Pl.

mūtŭor -ari, dep. (mutuus), *to borrow.* LIT., pecunias, Caes.; ab aliquo, Cic.; auxilia ad bellum, Hirt. TRANSF., orator subtilitatem ab Academicis mutuatur, Cic.; verbum a simili, *to speak metaphorically*, Cic.

mūtus -a -um, *unable to speak, inarticulate, dumb.* LIT., bestia, Cic.; Pl., Hor. TRANSF., (**1**) of things, *uttering no sound, mute, silent*:

imago, Cic.; artes quasi mutae, *the fine arts as opposed to rhetoric*, Cic. (**2**) of places, *still, quiet*: forum, Cic.; Pl. (**3**) of time: tempus mutum a litteris, *when nothing is written*, Cic. L.

mūtŭus -a -um (muto). (**1**) *interchanged, mutual, reciprocal*: nox omnia erroris mutui implevit, *on both sides*, Liv.; benevolentia, Cic.; mutuis animis amant amantur, Cat. N. as subst. **mūtŭum** -i, *reciprocity, equal return*: mutuum in amicitia, Cic.; pedibus per mutua nexis, *fastened on each other*, Verg.; inter se mutua vivunt, *by mutual exchange*, Lucr.; abl. as adv. **mūtŭō**, *mutually, reciprocally*: aestus maritimi mutuo accedentes et recedentes, Cic.; Suet.
(**2**) *borrowed, lent*: pecuniam dare mutuam, *to lend*, Cic.; sumere ab aliquo pecunias mutuas, *to borrow*, Cic. N. as subst. **mūtŭum** -i, *a loan*: Pl., Cic.

Mўcēnae -ārum, f. and **Mўcēnē** -ēs, f. (Μυκῆναι, Μυκήνη), *a city in Argolis, of which Agamemnon was king.*
¶ Hence adj. **Mўcēnaeus** -a -um and **Mўcēnensis** -e, *relating to Mycene* or *to Agamemnon*; m. pl. as subst. **Mўcēnenses** -ium, *inhabitants of Mycenae*; f. subst. **Mўcēnis** -idis=*Iphigenia*: Ov.

Mygdŏnĕs -um, m. (Μυγδόνες), *a Thracian people who afterwards settled in Phrygia.*
¶ Hence f. adj. **Mygdŏnĭs** -idis=*Lydian*: Ov.; adj. **Mygdŏnĭus** -a -um=*Phrygian*: Hor.

Myndus (-ŏs) -i, f. (Μύνδος), *a sea-town in Caria.*
¶ Hence **Myndĭi** -ōrum, m. *the inhabitants of Myndus.*

mўŏpăro -ōnis, m. (μυοπάρων), *a small piratical galley*: Cic.

mўrīcē -ēs, f. and **mўrīca** -ae, f. (μυρίκη), *the tamarisk*: Verg.

Myrmĭdŏnes -um, m. pl. (Μυρμιδόνες), *the Myrmidons, a people in Thessaly, under the rule of Achilles.*

Mўrōn -ōnis, m. (Μύρων), *a celebrated Greek sculptor, about* 430 B.C.

mўrŏpōla -ae, m. (μυροπώλης), *a seller of unguents*: Pl.

mўrŏpōlĭum -i, n. (μυροπώλιον), *a shop where unguents are sold*: Pl.

¹**myrrha**=¹murra; q.v.
²**myrrha**=²murra; q.v.
¹**myrrhĕus**=¹murreus; q.v.
²**myrrhĕus**=²murreus; q.v.
¹**myrrhĭnus**=¹murrinus; q.v.
²**myrrhĭnus**=²murrinus; q.v.

myrtētum (murtētum) -i, n. (myrtus), *a grove* or *thicket of myrtle-trees*: Pl., Sall., Verg.

myrtĕus (murtĕus) -a -um (myrtus), *of the myrtle*: Verg. TRANSF., *adorned with myrtle*: Tib.

myrtum -i, n. (μύρτον), *the myrtle-berry*: Verg.

myrtus -i and -us, f. (μύρτος), *the myrtle, myrtle-tree*: Hor.; also *a myrtle shaft*: Verg.

Myrtōus -a -um (Μυρτῷος): mare Myrtoum, *a part of the Aegean Sea between Crete, the Peloponnese, and Euboea.*

Mўsi -ōrum, m. pl. (Μύσοι), *the people of Mysia in Asia Minor.*
¶ Hence subst. **Mўsĭa** -ae, f. *their country*; adj. **Mўsus** -a -um, *Mysian.*

mystăgōgus -i, m. (μυσταγωγός), *a priest or attendant who showed sacred places to strangers*; *a cicerone*: Cic.

mystēria -ōrum, n. pl. (μυστήρια), *mysteries*; *secret rites in divine worship*; esp. *of the Eleusinian worship of Ceres*: Cic. Transf., *secrets, mysteries (of an art)*: mysteria rhetorum aperire, Cic.

mystēs or **mysta** -ae, m. (μύστης), *a priest at the mysteries*: Ov.

mystĭcus -a -um (μυστικός), *relating to the mysteries, secret, mystic*: Verg.

Mўtĭlēnae -ārum, f. and **Mўtĭlēnē** -ēs, f. (Μυτιλήνη), *capital of the island of Lesbos*. ¶ Hence adj. **Mўtĭlēnaeus** -a -um, *Mytilenean*.

N

N, n, the thirteenth letter of the Latin Alphabet, corresponds in sound to the Greek nu (*N, ν*). For the uses of N. as an abbreviation, see Table of Abbreviations.

Năbătaei -ōrum, m. (Ναβαταῖοι), *the Nabataeans in Arabia Petraea*. ¶ Hence adj. **Năbătaeus** -a -um, *Nabataean*, poet.=*Arabian, Eastern*; subst. **Năbătaea** -ae, f. (Ναβαταία), *their country, in Arabia Petraea*.

nablĭum -i, n. *a stringed instrument of uncertain form*; *a kind of harp* or *lyre*: Ov.

nae='ne; q.v.

naenĭa=nenia; q.v.

Naevĭus -a -um, *name of a Roman gens*; *its most notable member was* Cn. Naevius, *Roman dramatic and epic poet, of the third century* B.C. ¶ Hence adj. **Naevĭānus** -a -um, *Naevian*.

naevus -i, m. *a mole on the body*: Cic., Hor., Ov.

Nāĭăs -ădis and **Nāĭs** -ĭdis (-ĭdos); acc. plur. -ĭdas; f. (Ναϊάς, Ναΐς; *a swimmer*). Lit., *a water-nymph, Naiad*: Verg., Ov.; used attrib.: puellae Naiades, Verg. Transf., (1) *a nymph, hamadryad, Nereid*: Ov. (2) *water*: Tib. ¶ Hence adj. **Nāĭcus** -a -um, *belonging to the Naiads*.

nam, conj., generally used to explain or confirm a previous statement or command, and placed at the beginning of its clause.
(1) introducing an explanation, *for*: is pagus appellabatur Tigurinus; nam omnis civitas Helvetia in quattuor pagos divisa est, Caes.; sometimes as second word in clause: Hor. Hence: **a**, introducing a parenthesis: in insula quae est in Tiberino (nam opinor illud alteri flumini nomen esse) sermoni demus operam, Cic.: **b**, taking up the thought interrupted by a parenthesis: duplex inde Hannibali gaudium fuit (neque enim quidquam eorum, quae apud hostes agerentur, eum fallebat); nam et liberam Minucii temeritatem, Liv.: **c**, introducing examples to illustrate a previous general assertion, *for example*: vivo Catone minores natu multi uno tempore oratores floruerunt; nam et A. Albinus et litteratus et disertus fuit, Cic.: **d**, ellipt.: ... una domus erat, idem victus isque communis; nam quid ego de studiis dicam? Cic.

(2) used to add emphasis to a question nam quis te nostras iussit adire domum Verg. Often enclitic: quisnam? *who in th world?* Pl., Cic., Juv.; ubinam gentiu sumus? Cic.

Namnētes -um, m. *a people in Gallia Celtic near the modern Nantes*.

namquĕ, conj., a more emphatic form of na (q.v.), standing like it at the beginning of sentence or clause, though sometimes aft the first or second word: prodigium ex templo dedicationem secutum; namque l pidibus pluit, Liv.; Pl., Cic., Verg., etc.

nanciscor nancisci nactus and nanctus sun dep. *to light upon, obtain, meet*: anulun Ter.; turbidam tempestatem, Caes.; vit claviculis suis, quicquid est nacta, con plectitur, Cic.; spem, Cic., Liv.; morbun Nep.

Nantŭātes -ĭum, m. *a people in Gall Narbonensis*.

nānus -i, m. (νάννος, νᾶνος), *a dwarf*: Prop Juv., Suet.

Năpaeae -ārum, f. pl. (ναπαῖος), *dell-nymph* Verg.

nāpus -i, m. *a kind of turnip*: Plin., Mart.

Nār Nāris, m. *a river of Italy, that flows in the Tiber* (now *Nera*).

Narbo -ōnis, m. *town in southern Gaul* (no *Narbonne*). ¶ Hence adj. **Narbōnensis** -e, *of Narbo*

Narcissus -i, m. (Νάρκισσος), *Narcissus, son* Cephisus and Liriope, *a youth of remarkab beauty, who fell in love with his own reflectio in a fountain, and wasted away till he wa changed into the flower of the same nam* Verg., Ov.

nardus -i, f. and **nardum** -i, n. (νάρδος (1) *nard, a name given by the ancients* various aromatic plants: Plin. (2) *the unguen* or *balsam of nard*: Lucr., Hor., Tib.

nāris -is, f. *the nostril*; usually plur. **nāre** -ĭum, f. *the nostrils, nose*. Lit., fasciculum ad nares commover Cic.; Verg., Ov., Juv. Transf., *the nose*, as expressive of sagacit or of scorn or anger: homo naris obesae, *person of dull perception*, Hor.; hom emunctae naris, *a man of keen perceptio* Hor.; naribus uti, *to laugh at, mock at*, Hor ne sordida mappa nares corruget, *cause th guest to turn up his nose*, Hor.

Narnia -ae, f. *a town in Umbria on the N* (now *Narni*). ¶ Hence adj. **Narnĭensis** -e, *of Narnia*.

narrābĭlis -e (narro), *that can be narrated*: Ov

narrātĭo -ōnis, f. (narro), *a telling, relatin narrative*: rem narrare ita ut verisimil narratio sit, Cic.; Quint., Tac.

narrātĭuncŭla -ae, f. (dim. of narratio), *short narrative*: Quint., Plin. L.

narrātor -ōris, m. (narro), *a relater, narrato* Cic., Quint., Tac.

narrātus -ūs, m. (narro), *a narration, narr tive*: Ov.

narro -are (gnarus), *to make known*. Henc (1) *to relate, tell, narrate*: ego tibi ea narr quae tu melius scis quam ipse qui narro, Cic de mea sollicitudine, Cic. L.; male, ben narrare (de aliquo), *bring good* or *bad tiding* Cic. L.; with acc. and infin.: Cic. L.; wit indir. quest.: Ter., Cic. L. In passive, wi infin., usually with person or thing as subject, but sometimes impersonally; *he is said to . . .,* *it is told that . . .,* etc. (**2**) in gen., *to say, speak, tell*: narro tibi (a form of asseveration), *I assure you*, Cic. L.; with acc.: Ter.; with indir. quest.: Ter., Hor.

narthēcĭum -i, n. (*ναϱθήκιον*), *a case for keeping perfumes and medicines*: Cic.

narus=gnarus; q.v.

Nārycĭon -i, n. and **Nāryx** -rўcis, f. (*Νάϱυξ*), *a town of the Opuntian Locrians*. Adj. **Nārўcĭus** -a -um, *Narycian*: urbs, *Locri in Italy*, Ov.

nascor -i nātus (and gnatus) sum, dep. (connected with gigno), *to be born.*

    LIT., nasci patre certo, Cic.; so with ex: Cic., Liv.; with ab: Verg., Tac.; with de: Ov.; non nobis solum nati sumus, Cic.; post hominum genus natum, *since the beginning of the world*, Cic.; natus summo loco, *of a good family*, Cic.

    TRANSF., (**1**) of inanimate physical things, *to come into existence, arise, be produced*: nascitur ibi plumbum, Caes.; ab eo flumine collis nascebatur, Cic.; vulgo nascetur amomum, Verg. (**2**) of abstr. things, *to arise, spring up*: nulla tam detestabilis pestis est quae non homini ab homine nascatur, Cic.; Caes., Cat.

    ¶ Hence partic. **nātus** -a -um. As adj. (**1**) *born, fitted by nature*; with ad *or* in and the acc., or with dat.: Iudaei et Syrae nationes natae servituti, Cic.; poet. with infin.: animal natum tolerare labores, Ov. (**2**) *naturally constituted*: ita natus locus est, Liv.; pro re nata, *under present circumstances, as things are now*, Cic. (**3**) with annos, to express age: eques Romanus annos prope XC natus, *almost ninety years old*, Cic.

    As subst.: m. **nātus** -i, *a son*: Cic., Verg., etc.; f. **nāta** -ae, *a daughter*: Verg., etc.

Nāsĭca -ae, m. *name of a family of the Scipios*; esp. of P. Cornel. Scipio Nasica, *famous for his integrity*.

Nāso -ōnis, m. (nasus), *the cognomen of the poet P. Ovidius; see Ovidius.*

nassa -ae, f. *a narrow-necked basket for catching fish*: Plin. TRANSF., *a trap, net, snare*: ex hac naxa exire constitui, Cic. L.; Pl., Juv.

nassĭterna -ae, f. *a watering-pot*: Pl., Cato.

nasturcĭum -i, n. (nasus/torqueo), *a kind of cress*: Cic., Verg.

nāsus -i, m. *the nose.*

    LIT., nasus ita locatus est, ut quasi murus oculis interiectus esse videatur, Cic.

    TRANSF., (**1**) *the nose, as the seat of smell*: nasus illis nullus erat, Hor. (**2**) *the nose, as expressing sagacity, anger, scorn*, etc.: aliquem naso suspendere adunco, *to turn up the nose at, ridicule, mock*, Hor.; Mart., Pers. (**3**) *the nose, nozzle, spout of a vessel*: Juv.

nāsūtus -a -um (nasus), *having a large nose*: Hor. TRANSF., *acute, sagacious, satirical*: Mart.; compar.: Mart.

    ¶ Adv. **nāsūtē**, *satirically*: Phaedr.

nāta -ae, f., subst. from nascor; q.v.

nātālĭcĭus -a -um (natalis), *relating to birth,* and esp. *to the time of birth*: praedicta, *a horoscope*, Cic. N. pl. as subst. **nātālĭcĭa** -ōrum, *a birthday party*: Cic.

nātālis -e (natus), *of or relating to birth, natal*:

dies, Cic.; lux, Ov.; hora, Hor.; diem natalem suum agere, *celebrate*, Cic.

    M. as subst. **nātālis** -is (sc. dies), *a birthday*: Cic. L., Verg., Hor.; plur. **nātāles** -ĭum, m. *birth, origin*: Cornelius Fuscus, claris natalibus, *of illustrious family*, Tac.; Plin. L., Juv.

nătans -antis, partic. from nato; q.v.

nătātĭo -ōnis, f. (nato), *swimming*: Cic.

nătātor -ōris, m. (nato), *a swimmer*: Ov.

nātes, see natis.

nātĭo -ōnis, f. (nascor), *a being born, birth*; hence, personif.: Natio, *the goddess of birth*, Cic. TRANSF., (**1**) *a tribe, race, people*, esp. uncivilized: externae nationes et gentes, Cic.; Caes., Tac. (**2**) *a species, stock, class*: candidatorum, Cic.; Epicureorum, Cic.

nătis -is, f., usually plur. **nătes** -ĭum, f. *the rump, buttocks*: Hor., Juv.

nātīvus -a -um (nascor), *born, that which has come into existence by birth*: Anaximandri opinio est, nativos esse deos, Cic.; Lucr. TRANSF., (**1**) *native, natural, not artificial*: beluae nativis testis inhaerentes, Cic.; Lucr., Ov., Tac. (**2**) *inborn, innate*: Cic.

năto -are (freq. of no, nare), *to swim, float.*

    LIT., studiosissimus homo natandi, Cic. L.; in oceano, Cic.; natant aequore pisces, Ov.; natat uncta carina, *floats*, Verg.; poet., followed by acc.: caeca freta, Verg.

    TRANSF., (**1**) *to stream, flow*: qua se Tiberinus in altum dividit et campo liberiore natat, Ov. (**2**) *to swim with anything, be full of, overflow*; with abl.: natabant pavimenta vino, Cic.; omnia plenis rura natant fossis, Verg. (**3**) *of the eyes, to swim, to be glassy*: vinis oculique animique natabant, Ov.; Quint.

    ¶ Hence partic. **nătans** -antis; f. pl. as subst. natantes, *fishes*, Verg.

nātrix -icis, f. *a water-snake*: Cic.

nātū, abl. sing. as from natus, m. (nascor), *by birth*; used esp. to indicate age: magnus natu, grandis natu, *of considerable age*, Cic.; qui fuit maior natu quam Plautus et Naevius, *older*, Cic.; ex his omnibus natu minimus, *the youngest*, Cic.; Pl., Liv., etc.

nātūra -ae, f. (nascor). (**1**) *birth*: Cic.; naturā frater, adoptione filius, Liv.; Ter. (**2**) *nature, natural qualities*: **a**, of things: haec est natura propria animae et vis, Cic.; montis, Caes.; loci, Caes.; mollis aquae, Lucr.; Verg.: **b**, of men, *nature, natural disposition, character*: quae tua natura est, Cic.; versare suam naturam, Cic.; naturam expellas furcā, tamen usque recurret, Hor.: **c**, *the nature of things in general, the laws of nature, the order and constitution of the world*: quod rerum natura non patitur, Cic.; naturae satisfacere, *to pay the debt of nature, to die*, Cic.; naturae concedere, Sall.; in rerum natura fuisse, Cic.; de rerum natura, Lucr.: **d**, *an element, substance, essence*: ex duabus naturis conflata, Cic.

nātūrālis -e (natura), *natural.* (**1**) *produced by birth, natural*: pater, *own father* (opp. *adoptive father*), Cic.; filius, Liv. (**2**) *not artificial, natural*: societas, lex, Cic.; n. pl. as subst.: naturalia anteponantur non naturalibus, Cic. (**3**) *relating to nature*: quaestiones, Cic.

    ¶ Adv. **nātūrālĭtĕr**, *naturally, by nature, according to nature*: divinare, Cic.; Caes.

nātus -a -um, partic. from nascor; q.v.

nauarchus -i, m. (ναύαρχος), *a captain of a ship*: Cic., Tac.

nauci, *see* naucum.

nauclērĭcus -a -um (ναυκληρικός), *of the master of a ship*: Pl.

nauclērus -i, m. (ναύκληρος), *the master of a ship*: Pl.

naucum -i, n. *a trifle, something very small*; in genit. of value: non nauci habere, *to esteem lightly*, Cic.; Pl.

naufrăgĭum -i, n. (naufragus), *a shipwreck*. LIT., naufragium (naufragia) facere, *to suffer shipwreck*, Cic.; naufragio interire, Caes.; perire, Cic.; prov.: naufragia alicuius ex terra intueri, *to behold danger from a place of safety*, Cic.; tabula ex naufragio, *a plank from a shipwreck*, i.e. *a means of safety, way of deliverance*, Cic. L. TRANSF., (1) fig., *ruin, loss*: fortunarum, Cic. (2) *the remains of a wrecked ship, wreckage*; fig.: conligere naufragium reipublicae, Cic.

naufrăgus -a -um (navis/frango). (1) pass., *that suffers* or *has suffered shipwreck*: Marium Africā devictā expulsum et naufragum vidit, Cic.; corpora, Verg.; puppis, Ov.; fig.: patrimonio naufragus, Cic.; m. as subst., *a shipwrecked person*: Cic., Juv. (2) act., poet., *causing shipwreck*: mare, Hor.; unda, Tib.

naulum -i, n. (ναῦλον), *fare, passage-money*: Juv.

naumăchĭa -ae, f. (ναυμαχία). (1) *a naval battle exhibited as a spectacle*: Suet. (2) *the place in which the spectacle was exhibited*: Suet.

naumăchĭārĭus -a -um (naumachia), *of a mock sea-fight*: Plin.; m. as subst. **naumăchĭārĭus** -i, *one who fought in a mock sea-fight*: Juv.

Naupactus (-ŏs) -i, f. (Ναύπακτος), *a sea-port on the Gulf of Corinth* (now *Lepanto*). ¶ Hence adj. **Naupactĭus** -a -um, *of Naupactus*.

nausĕa -ae, f. (ναυσία), *sea-sickness*: navigavimus sine timore et nausea, Cic. L.; in gen., *sickness, nausea*: Hor., Sen.

nausĕo -are (nausea), *to be sea-sick*. LIT., Hor. TRANSF., (1) *to vomit, be sick*: quidlibet, modo ne nauseet, faciat, Cic. (2) *to cause disgust, nauseate*: ista effutientem nauseare, Cic.; Phaedr.

nausĕŏla -ae, f. (dim. of nausea), *a slight squeamishness*: Cic.

nauta and **nāvĭta** (poet.) -ae, m. (ναύτης), *a sailor, seaman, mariner*: Cic., Caes., Hor.

nautĭcus -a -um (ναυτικός), *of a sailor, nautical, naval*: verbum, Cic. L.; scientia atque usus nauticarum rerum, Caes.; m. as subst. **nautĭci** -ōrum, *sailors*: Liv.

nāvālis -e (navis), *of ships, naval, nautical*: bellum, pugna, Cic.; castra, *for the protection of ships when drawn upon shore*, Caes.; socii navales, *sailors* (chosen from the freedmen of the colonists and allies), Liv. N. as subst. **nāvāle** -is, *a station for ships*: Ov.; plur. **nāvālĭa** -ium. (1) *a dockyard*: Cic., Verg.; esp. *a place in Rome so called*: Liv. (2) *materials for ship-building*: Verg., Liv.

nāvĭcŭla -ae, f. (dim. of navis), *a little ship, boat*: Caes., Cic.

nāvĭcŭlārĭus -a -um (navicula), *relating to small ships*. F. as subst. **nāvĭcŭlārĭa** -ae (sc. res), *the business of a ship-owner*: navi culariam facere, Cic. M. as subst. **nāvĭcŭlārĭus** -i, *one who lets out ships, a ship-owner*: Cic.

nāvĭfrăgus -a -um (navis/frango), *causing shipwreck, ship-destroying*: Verg., Ov.

nāvĭgābĭlis -e (navigo), *navigable*: mare, Liv.; Tac.

nāvĭgātĭo -ōnis, f. (navigo), *a sailing, voyage*: primam navigationem (*chance of sailing*) ne omiseris, Cic. L.; Tac.

nāvĭger -gĕra -gĕrum (navis/gero), *ship-bearing, navigable*: mare, Lucr.

nāvĭgĭŏlum -i, n. (dim. of navigium), *a little ship, a bark*: ap. Cic. L.

nāvĭgĭum -i, n. (navigo), *a vessel, ship*: navigium facere, Cic.; Caes., Liv.

nāvĭgo -are (navis/ago). (1) intransit., *to sail, voyage*. LIT., ex Asia in Macedoniam, Cic.; Caes., Hor.; of ships: decrevimus, ut classis in Italiam navigaret, Cic.; Ov. TRANSF., **a**, *of a naval war, to proceed, go*: quam celeriter bell impetus navigavit, Cic.: **b**, *to swim*: Ov. (2) transit.: **a**, *to sail over, sail through, navigate*: terram, Cic.; aequor, Verg.: **b**, *to get* or *earn by navigation*: quae homines arant, navigant, aedificant, Sall.

nāvis -is, f. (acc. navem or -im; abl. nave or -i; cf. ναῦς), *a ship, vessel*. LIT., navis longa, *a man-of-war*, Caes.; oneraria, *a ship of burden, transport-ship*, Caes.; praetoria, *admiral's ship, flag-ship*, Liv.; tecta, *decked*, Liv.; aperta, *undecked*, Liv.; navis auri, *laden with gold*, Cic.; navem deducere in aquam, *to launch*, Liv.; subducere, *to beach*, Caes., Cic.; conscendere in navem, *to embark*, Cic.; prov.: navibus et quadrigis, *with all one's might*, Hor. TRANSF., (1) fig., *of the ship of state*, etc.: una navis bonorum omnium, Cic.; esse in eadem navi, *to be in the same boat*, Cic. (2) Navis Argolica, *or simply*, Navis, *the constellation Argo*, Cic. poet.

nāvĭta=nauta; q.v.

nāvĭtās (gnāvĭtās) -ātis, f. (navus), *energy, zeal*: Cic.

nāvĭtĕr, adv. from navus; q.v.

nāvo -are (navus), *to do anything zealously* or *energetically*: navare operam, Caes., Cic., Liv.; bellum, Tac.

nāvus (gnāvus) -a -um, *zealous, energetic*: homo navus et industrius, Cic. ¶ Adv. **nāvĭtĕr (gnāvĭtĕr)**. (1) *energetically*: Ter., Lucr., Liv. (2) *completely*: impudens, Cic. L.; Lucr.

Naxus (-ŏs) -i, f. (Νάξος), *an island of the Aegean Sea, the largest of the Cyclades*. ¶ Hence adj. **Naxĭus** -a -um, *Naxian*.

¹nē (nae), interj. (νή), *yes, verily, truly*; used before pronouns: ne illi multa saecula exspectanda fuerunt, Cic.; Pl., Liv.

²nē (formerly **nei**), the original Latin particle of negation. Adv., *not*. (1) *to negative a word* or *phrase*; rare in this sense, except in compounds such as nemo (=ne-homo), ne-scio, etc., and in ne ... quidem, *not even*: ne in oppidis quidem, Cic.; Verg., etc. (2) *to negative a clause*: **a**, in prohibitions; with the imperat.: ne timete, Liv.; Cic., Verg., etc.; with the subj.: ne te frustrere, Hor.; nobis nostras ne ademeris, Cic.; Hor., etc.: **b**, in wishes: ne id Iuppiter Opt. Max. sirit, Liv.; illud utinam ne vere scriberem, Cic.; ne vivam, si scio, *may I die if I know*, Cic.: **c**, in concessive and restrictive clauses: sint sane liberales ex sociorum fortunis, sint misericordes in furibus aerarii, ne illis sanguinem nostram largiantur, *only let them not lavish our blood*, Sall.: **d**, in purpose-clauses, ut ne, *that not*: quam plurimis de rebus ad me velim scribas, ut prorsus ne quid ignorem, Cic. L.; Pl.; so sometimes, qui ne, quo ne: **e**, in indirect command: moneo vos, ne refugiatis, Cic.

Conj., with subj., *lest, that not*. (**1**) in purpose-clauses: gallinae pennis fovent pullos, ne frigore laedantur, Cic.; ne multa dicam, *in short*, Cic. (**2**) after verbs of fearing: metuebat ne indicarent, Cic.; ne non, *that not*: timeo ne non impetrem, Cic.; Liv., etc. (**3**) after some verbs of causing and preventing: qui efficiant ne quid inter privatum ac magistratum differat, Cic.; Verg., Liv.

-nĕ (sometimes abbreviated to **n'**), interrog. enclitic particle. (**1**) in direct questions: **a**, without alternative: mitto alios; etiamne nobis expedit? Cic.; Verg., etc.; sometimes with positive or negative suggestion, usually without: **b**, with alternative: satisne ergo pudori consulat, si quis sine teste libidini pareat, an est aliquid per se ipsum flagitiosum? Cic.; Caes., Verg., etc.: **c**, sometimes affixed to another interrog.: quone malo mentem concussa? Hor.; Pl.

(**2**) in indirect questions: **a**, without alternative: ut videamus, satisne ista sit defectio, Cic.: **b**, with alternative: nescio gratulerne tibi an timeam, Cic.; also to introduce the alternative: ut in incerto fuerit, vicissent victine essent, Liv.

Nĕăpŏlĭs -pŏlis, acc. -pŏlim, f. (Νεάπολις). (**1**) *a part of Syracuse*. (**2**) *a sea-port in Campania* (now *Naples*).

nĕbŭla -ae, f. (cf. νεφέλη), *vapour, fog, mist*. LIT., matutina, Liv.; Lucr., Verg.; esp. of *cloud*: Verg., Hor.; *smoke*: Ov.

TRANSF., (**1**) of *dust*: pulveris, Lucr. (**2**) mentally: erroris, Juv. (**3**) of anything worthless: Pl., Ov.

nĕbŭlo -ōnis, m. (nebula), *a good-for-nothing fellow*: Ter.; Cic., Hor.

nĕbŭlōsus -a -um (nebula), *misty, foggy*: nebulosum et caliginosum caelum, Cic.

nĕc and **nĕquĕ**, negative particles.

Adv., *not*; an old sense, rare in class. Latin: qui nec procul aberat, Liv.; Verg.

Conj., *and not*: quia non viderunt nec sciunt, Cic.; neque unquam, *and never*, Cic.; sometimes with adversative force, *and yet not*: conscripsi epistulam noctu; nec ille ad me rediit, Cic. Sometimes to add a negative command or purpose-clause: ut ea praetermittam neque eos appellem, Cic.; Liv., etc. Often with other particles, etc.: neque vero, *and indeed not*, Cic.; nec tamen, *and yet not*, Cic.; nec enim, neque enim, *for ... not*, Cic.; neque non, nec non, necnon, *and also, and indeed*, Cic., Verg.; nec ... nec, neque ... neque, *neither ...*

nor; neque ... et, *not only not ... but also*; nec miror et gaudeo, Cic.; et ... neque, *not only ... but also not*, Cic.; nec ... quidem, *and not even*, Cic.; also nec alone sometimes stands for *not even*: Liv.

necdum (**neque dum**), adv. *and not yet*: Cic. L., Verg., Juv.

nĕcessārĭus -a -um (necesse), *necessary, unavoidable, inevitable*.

LIT., res, *necessity*, Caes.; omnia quae sint ad vivendum necessaria, Cic.; senatori necessarium est, nosse rempublicam, Cic.; iumentorum acervi necessarium cubile dabant, *the least possible, barest*, Liv.; tam necessario tempore, *pressing, urgent*, Caes. Abl. as adv. **nĕcessārĭō**, *necessarily, unavoidably*: Caes., Cic., etc. Adv. **nĕcessārĭē**, *necessarily, unavoidably*: Cic.

TRANSF., *closely connected* or *related*; esp. subst. **nĕcessārĭus** -i, m., **-a** -ae, f. *an intimate friend, connexion, relation*: meus familiaris ac necessarius, Cic.; Caes.

nĕcessĕ (old form **nĕcessum**), indecl. adj. n., found only in connexion with esse and habere; *necessary, unavoidable, inevitable, indispensable*: nihil fit, quod necesse non fuerit, Cic.; homini necesse est mori, Cic.; istum condemnetis necesse est, Cic.; eo minus habeo necesse scribere, Cic. L.

nĕcessĭtās -ātis, f. (necesse).

LIT., *inevitability, necessity*: necessitati parere, Cic.; necessitatem alicui adferre, Cic.; mors est necessitas naturae, Cic.; leti, Hor.; so: extrema, suprema, ultima necessitas, Sall., Tac.; plur.: necessitates, *requirements, necessary expenses*, Caes., Cic., Liv.; sing. sometimes in sense of *urgency*: Caes., Liv.

TRANSF., *intimate connexion, friendship, relationship*: si nostram necessitatem familiaritatemque violasset, Cic. L.; Caes.

nĕcessĭtūdo -inis, f. (necesse).

LIT., *necessity, inevitableness*: puto hanc esse necessitudinem, cui nullā vi resisti potest, Cic.; Tac., Sall.; sometimes *need, want*: Sall.

TRANSF., (**1**) *close connexion* or *relationship, intimate friendship*: liberorum necessitudo, Cic.; sunt mihi cum illo omnes amicitiae necessitudines, Cic. (**2**) plur., *intimate friends, near relations*: Tac., Suet.

nĕcessum = necesse; q.v.

necnĕ, *or not*. Generally in the second, or alternative, half of indirect questions: sintne dii necne, Cic.; Caes., Hor. More rarely in direct questions: sunt haec tua verba necne? Cic.

necnon (**neque non**), see nec.

nĕco -are (cf. νεκρός and nex), *to kill, slay, put to death*, usually by violent means: plebem fame, Cic.; aliquem igni, Caes.; aliquem ferro, Verg., Hor.

nĕcŏpĭnans -antis, *not expecting, unaware*: aliquem necopinantem liberare, Cic. L.; Lucr.

nĕcŏpīnātus (**nĕc ŏpīnātus**) -a -um, *unexpected*: bona, Cic.; Liv.; n. as subst.: ex necopinato, *unexpectedly*, Liv.; abl. as adv. **nĕcŏpīnātō**, *unexpectedly*: si necopinato quid evenerit, Cic.; Liv.

nĕcŏpīnus -a -um (opinor). (**1**) pass., *unexpected*: mors, Ov. (**2**) act., *not expecting, careless*: Phaedr., Ov.

nectar -ăris, n. (νέκταρ), *nectar, the drink of the gods.* LIT., Cic., Ov., etc. TRANSF., *of anything sweet or pleasant; honey*: Verg.; *milk*: Ov.; *wine*: Verg., Ov.

nectărĕus -a -um (νεκτάρεος), *of nectar.* LIT., aqua, Ov. TRANSF., *like nectar*: Mart.

necto nectĕre nexŭi and nexi nexum, *to tie, bind, connect, fasten together.*

    LIT., flores, Hor.; catenas, coronam, Hor.; comam myrto, Ov.; *of persons, to bind, fetter, enslave,* especially for debt: eo anno plebi Romanae velut aliud initium libertatis factum est, quod necti desierunt, Liv.; Cic.

    TRANSF., (1) *to affix, attach*: ex hoc genere causarum ex aeternitate pendentium fatum a Stoicis nectitur, Cic.; omnes virtutes inter se nexae et iugatae sunt, Cic. (2) *to put together, devise*: dolum, Liv.; causas inanes, Verg.; numeris verba, Ov.

nĕcŭbi, adv. *so that nowhere*: Caes., Liv. Luc.

nĕcunde, adv. *from nowhere*: Liv.

nēdum, conj. *not to say.*

    Hence (1) after (implied) negative, *much less, still less*; foll. by subj.: optimis temporibus nec P. Popillius nec Q. Metellus vim tribuniciam sustinere potuerunt, nedum his temporibus sine vestra sapientia salvi esse possimus, *much less could we at present,* Cic.; with ut and the subj.: ne voce quidem incommodi, nedum ut ulla vis fieret, Liv. (2) after (implied) affirmative, *much more*: adulationes etiam victis Macedonibus graves, nedum victoribus, Liv.

nĕfandus -a -um (ne/fari), *not to be spoken of*; hence *abominable*: scelus, Cic., Liv., etc.; n. as subst.: deos memores fandi atque nefandi, *of right and wrong,* Verg.

nĕfārius -a -um (nefas), *impious, abominable, execrable*: homo, Cic.; bellum, Cic.; Caes., Hor.; n. as subst., *an abominable action*: Liv.

    ¶ Adv. **nĕfārĭē**, *impiously*: Cic.

nĕfas, n. indecl., *that which is contrary to divine command; an impious deed, a sin, crime, abomination.*

    LIT., quicquid non licet, nefas putare debemus, Cic.; Mercurius quem Aegyptii nefas habent nominare, Cic.; per fas et nefas, *by fair means or foul,* Liv.; in omne nefas se parare, Ov.; with infin.: indicare in vulgus nefas (est), Cic.; sometimes used as an interjection, *monstrous! dreadful!*: heu nefas! Hor.

    TRANSF., *a horrible thing*: exstinxisse nefas laudabor (Helen, as the cause of the ruin of Troy), Verg.

nĕfastus -a -um (nefas), *forbidden, unholy.*

    LIT., in religious t. t.: dies nefasti, *on which no legal or public business could be transacted,* Liv.; Ov.

    TRANSF., (1) *unlucky, inauspicious*: ille et nefasto te posuit die, Hor.; ne qua terra sit nefasta victoriae suae, Liv. (2) *of action, forbidden, sinful*: quae augur iniusta, nefasta defixerit, Cic.; quid intactum nefasti liquimus? Hor.

nĕgātĭo -ōnis, f. (nego), *a denying*: negatio infitiatioque facti, Cic.

nĕgĭto -are (freq. of nego), *to deny frequently, persist in denying*: quam multos annos esse negitavisset, Cic.; Pl., Lucr.

neglectĭo -ōnis, f. (neglego), *neglect*: amicorum, Cic.

neglectus -ūs, m. (neglego), *a neglecting, neglect, disregard*: Ter.

neglĕgens -entis, partic. from neglego; q.v.

neglĕgentĭa -ae, f. (neglegens), *carelessnes, negligence*: in accusando, Cic.; with genit. deum, Liv.; sui, Tac.

neglĕgo -lĕgĕre -lexi -lectum (nec/lego), *neglect, disregard.* (1) of action omitted, *t omit, to fail to see to*: mandatum, Cic.; wit de: de Theopompo, summo homine, neglex mus, Cic.; with infin.: obire diem edict Cic. (2) of feeling, *to make light of, despise* periculum fortunarum et capitis sui, Cic. imperium alicuius, Caes. (3) of injuries, *overlook, pass over*: iniurias Aeduorun Caes.; Cic.

    ¶ Hence partic. (with compar.) **neglĕgen** -entis, *careless, indifferent, unconcerned* adulescentia, Liv.; in amicis deligendis, Cic. with genit.: amicorum, Cic.; Liv., Tac with ne and subj.: Hor.

    ¶ Adv. **neglĕgentĕr**, *carelessly, heedlessly* scribere, Cic.; Quint., Tac.; compar.: Cic.

nĕgo -are (ne/aio). (1) *to say no*: Diogenes ne Antipater negat, Cic.; with dat.: saepiu idem roganti, Cic.; Pl., Caes. (2) *to deny to assert that a thing is not so*: crimen, Cic. with acc. and infin.: Stoici negant, quicquam esse bonum nisi quod honestum sit, Cic. pass., with nom. and infin.: ibi vis fact (esse) negabitur, Cic.; non negare, foll. b quin.: negare non posse quin rectius s exercitum mitti, Liv. (3) *to deny a reques to refuse*: nunquam reo cuiquam tar praecise negavi, quam hic mihi, Cic.; of inanimate objects: poma negat regio, refus *to produce apples,* Ov.; with infin., *to refu to do*: Verg.

nĕgōtĭālis -e (negotium), *relating to business* Cic.

nĕgōtĭans -antis, m. partic. from negotio q.v.

nĕgōtĭātĭo -ōnis, f. (negotior), *banker business*: reliquiae negotiationis, Cic. L Liv.

nĕgōtĭātor -ōris, m. (negotior), *a busines man*; esp. *a banker*: Cic.

nĕgōtĭŏlum -i, n. (dim. of negotium), *a sma transaction, little business*: tua negotio Ephesi curae mihi fuerunt, Cic. L.

nĕgōtĭor -ari, dep. (negotium), *to carry o business*, esp. as *a banker*: Patris, *at Patr* Cic.; Sall.; also, in gen., *to trade*: Liv.

    ¶ Hence partic. **nĕgōtĭans** -antis; m. subst., *a business-man*: Cic. L., Suet.

nĕgōtĭōsus -a -um (negotium), *full of busines busy*: provincia, Cic.; homo, Sall.; die *working days,* Tac.

nĕgōtĭum -i, n. (nec/otium), *absence of leisur* Hence, *business, occupation, employment.*

    LIT., in gen.: Pl., Caes., Cic.; esp. *som single employment or commission*: negot privata, domestica, Cic.; negotium susciper transigere, Cic.; conficere, Caes.; negot forensia, Cic.; publica, Pl., Cic.; of a militar *task*: Caes.; of commerce: habere negot vetera in Sicilia, Cic.; Hor.; of househol *management*: negotium male gerere, Cic.

    TRANSF., (1) *pains, trouble*: neque es quidquam negoti (*any difficulty*) hanc su sarcinis adoriri, Caes.; negotium alic exhibere, *to cause trouble to a person,* Cic

Pl., Liv. (2) any *matter, thing*: Pl., Cic.; of a person: Cic.

Nēlēus -ēī and ĕŏs, m. (Νηλεύς), *a mythical king of Pylos, father of Nestor.*

¶ Hence adj. **Nēlēius** -a -um and **Nēlēus** -a -um, *of Neleus or Nestor*; subst. **Nēlīdēs** -ae, m. *a male descendant of Neleus; Nestor*: Ov.

Nĕmĕa -ae, f. (Νεμέα) and **Nĕmĕē** -ēs, f. (Νεμέη), *a valley in Argolis, where Hercules killed the Nemean lion, and founded the Nemean games.*

¶ Hence adj. **Nĕmĕaeus** -a -um, *Nemean*: leo, Ov.; subst. **Nĕmĕa** -ōrum, n. pl., *the Nemean games*: Liv.

Nĕmĕsis -is and -ios, f. (Νέμεσις), *the goddess of justice, who punished pride and arrogance.*

Nĕmetes -um, *a people in Gallia Belgica.*

nēmo -ĭnis, c.; acc. neminem, genit. nullius, dat nemini, abl. nullo (rarely nemine) (ne/hemo=homo), *no man, no one, nobody*: nemo omnium mortalium, Cic.; nemo unus, *not one person*, Cic., Liv., Tac.; nemo alius, *no one else*, Cic.; nemo est quin (with subj.), *there is no one who does not*, etc., Cic.; nemo non, *everyone*, Cic.; non nemo, *many a one*, Cic.; often with noun in apposition: nemo homo, Pl., Cic.; civis, Enn., Cic.

nĕmŏrālis -e (nemus), *of woods or groves*, sylvan: umbrae, antrum, Ov.

nĕmŏrensis -e (nemus), *belonging to a grove or wood*; esp. *of the grove of Diana at Aricia*: Ov.

nĕmŏrĭcultrix -īcis, f. (nemus/cultrix), *dwelling in the woods*: Phaedr.

nĕmŏrĭvăgus -a -um (nemus/vagus), *wandering in the woods*: Cat.

nĕmŏrōsus -a -um (nemus). (1) *woody, full of groves*: Zacynthos, Verg.; Ov. (2) *thickly leaved, full of foliage*: silvae, Ov.

nempe, conj. (nam/demonstr. suffix -pe), *forsooth, truly, certainly, to be sure*: nempe incomposito dixi pede currere versus Lucili, Hor.; ita dat tantam pecuniam Flacco, nempe idcirco dat, ut rata sit emptio, *of course*, Cic.

nĕmus -ŏris, n. (cf. νέμω), *a wood with glades and pasture land for cattle; a grove, forest*: agri et nemora, Cic.; Verg., Hor., Ov.

nēnia -ae, f. *a funeral song, dirge*: Cic., Hor., Suet. Transf., (1) *any mournful song*: Hor. (2) *an incantation*: Hor. (3) *a ditty, nursery song, lullaby*: Hor.

nĕo nēre nēvi nētum (νέω), *to spin*: stamina, fila, esp. *of the Parcae*, Ov. Transf., *to weave, interweave*: tunicam quam molli neverat auro, Verg.

Nĕoclēs -is and -i, m. (Νεοκλῆς), *father of Themistocles.*

¶ Hence **Nĕoclīdēs** -ae, m. *son of Neocles*, i.e., *Themistocles.*

nĕpa -ae, f. (1) *a scorpion*: Cic.; hence, *the constellation so called*: Cic. poet. (2) *a crab*: Pl.

Nĕphĕlē -ēs, f. (Νεφέλη), *wife of Athamas, mother of Phrixus and Helle.*

¶ Hence **Nĕphĕlēis** -ēidos, f. *a daughter of Nephele; Helle*: Ov.

nĕpos -ōtis, m. *a grandson.* Lit., Q. Pompeii ex filia nepos, Cic.; Pl., Tac. Transf., (1) *a brother's or sister's son, nephew*: Suet. (2) *a descendant*: Verg., Hor. (3) *a spendthrift, prodigal*: Cic.

¹Nĕpos -pōtis, m., C. Cornelius, *a Roman historian, friend of Atticus, Cicero, and Catullus.*

nĕpōtŭlus -i, m. (dim. of ¹nepos), *a little grandson*: Pl.

neptis -is, f. (¹nepos), *a grand-daughter*: Cic., Tac.; neptis Veneris, *Ino*, Ov.; neptes Cybeles, *the Muses*, Ov.

Neptūnus -i, m. *Neptune, god of the sea, brother of Jupiter, husband of Amphitrite, identified with the Greek Poseidon*; meton., *the sea*: Verg.

¶ Hence adj. **Neptūnius** -a -um, *Neptunian*: Troia, *built by Neptune*, Verg.; heros, *Theseus*, Ov.; subst. **Neptūninē** -ēs, f. *a grand-daughter of Neptune*: Cat.

nēquam, adj. indecl.; compar. **nēquior**, superl. **nēquissimus**, *worthless, good for nothing, bad*: quid est nequius effeminato viro? Cic.; liberti nequam et improbi, Cic.

¶ Adv. (with compar. and superl.) **nēquĭtĕr**, *worthlessly, badly*: Pl., Cic.

nēquāquam, adv. *by no means, not at all*: Pl., Caes., Cic., Hor.

nĕquĕ=nec; q.v.

nĕquĕdum=necdum; q.v.

nĕquĕo -ire -īvi and -ii -ĭtum (fut. nequibunt: Lucr.; imperf. nequibat: Sall.), *to be unable*: actam aetatem meminisse nequimus, Lucr.; cum Demosthenes rho dicere nequiret, Cic.; pass., with pass. infin.: quicquid sine sanguine civium ulcisci nequitur, iure factum sit, Sall.

nēquiquam (**nēquicquam**), adv. (1) *in vain, fruitlessly, to no purpose*: et sero et nequicquam pudet, Cic.; alicuius auxilium implorare, Caes.; Verg. (2) *without good reason*: Caes., Cat. (3) *with impunity*: Pl.

nēquĭtĕr, adv. from nequam; q.v.

nēquĭtīa -ae, f. and **nēquĭtiēs** -ēi, f. (nequam), *worthlessness, badness*: inertissimi homines nescio qua singulari nequitiā praediti, Cic.; esp. *extravagance, prodigality, wantonness*: uxor pauperis Ibyci, tandem nequitiae pone modum tuae, Hor.; Ov.

Nērēus -ĕos and -ĕi, m. (Νηρεύς), *a sea-god, son of Oceanus and Tethys; father, by Doris, of the Nereids*; meton., *the sea*: Tib., Ov.

¶ Hence subst. **Nērēis** -idis, f. *a daughter of Nereus, a Nereid*: Ov.; **Nērīnē** -ēs, f. *a Nereid*: Verg.; adj. **Nērēius** -a -um, *of Nereus*: genetrix, Thetis, *mother of Achilles*, Ov.; nepos, *Achilles*, Ov.

Nērĭtus (-ŏs) -i, m. (Νήριτος), *a small island near Ithaca.*

¶ Hence adj. **Nērĭtius** -a -um: ratis, *the ship of Ulysses*, Ov.; dux, *Ulysses*, Ov.

Nēro -ōnis, m. *a cognomen in the gens Claudia*; esp. of (1) C. Claudius Nero, *consul 207 B.C., who defeated Hasdrubal at the battle of the Metaurus.* (2) C. Claudius Nero, *the fifth Roman emperor* (A.D. 54–68).

¶ Hence adj. **Nĕrōnēus**, **Nĕrōnius**, and **Nĕrōniānus** -a -um, *Neronian.*

Nervii -ōrum, m. *a warlike people in the north of Gallia Belgica.*

nervōsus -a -um (nervus), adj. (with compar.), *sinewy, nervous, strong.* Lit., poples, Ov. Transf., *of style, vigorous*: quis Aristotele nervosior? Cic.

¶ Adv. (with compar.) **nervōsē**, *strongly,
vigorously*: nervosius dicere, Cic.
nervŭlus -i, m. (dim. of nervus), *nerve,
strength*; in plur.: nervulos adhibere, Cic. L.
nervus -i, m. (νεῦρον), *a sinew, tendon*; gen.
plur., nervi, *the sinews*.
   LIT., nervi a quibus artus continentur,
Cic.; Pl., Caes., Hor.
   TRANSF., (1) *the string of a musical instrument*: cantu vocum et nervorum et tibiarum
tota vicinitas personat, Cic. (2) *a bowstring*:
nervo aptare sagittas, Verg. (3) *the leather
with which shields are covered*: Tac. (4) *a strap
or thong with which the limbs are bound; bonds,
fetters*, and hence, *prison, imprisonment*: in
nervis teneri, Liv.; Pl., Ter. (5) fig., in plur.,
strength, vigour, effort: in quo omnes nervos
aetatis industriaeque meae contenderem,
Cic.; nervi belli pecunia, *money, the sinews
of war*, Cic.; nervi coniurationis, Liv.;
esp. of style, *vigour, energy*: nervi oratorii, Cic.
nescĭo -ire -īvi and -ĭi -ītum, *not to know, to be
ignorant of*.
   In gen.: de Oropo opinor, sed certum
nescio, *I do not certainly know*, Cic. L.; with
indir. quest.: nescis quanta cum expectatione sim te auditurus, Cic.; Ter., Ov.; with
acc. and infin.: Ter., Ov.
   Esp. (1) in phrases, nescio quis, quid, etc.,
I know not who or what, somebody *or* something: nescio quis loquitur, Pl.; oppidum
nescio quod, Cic.; nescio quid exsculpserunt,
Cic.; nescio quomodo, *I know not how,
somehow or other*, Cic. (2) *not to know* or
recognize a person or thing: non nescire
hiemem, Verg.; Pl. (3) *to be unable to do
anything, not to have learnt*: non tam
praeclarum est scire Latine quam turpe
nescire, Cic.; Stoici omnino irasci nesciunt,
Cic.; Verg., Hor.
nescĭus -a -um (nescio).
   (1) act.: **a**, *not knowing, ignorant, unaware*;
with genit.: nescia mens hominum fati
sortisque futurae, Verg.; non sum nescius,
ista inter Graecos dici, Cic.: **b**, *not knowing
how to do* anything, *unable*, with infin.: pueri
fari nescii, Hor.; cedere nescius, Hor.; Verg.,
Ov.
   (2) pass., *unknown*: nescia tributa, Tac.;
causa, Ov.
Nēsĭs -ĭdis, f. *an island in the Bay of Naples*
(now *Nisita*).
Nessus -i, m. (Νέσσος), *a centaur killed by
Hercules with a poisoned arrow*.
Nestōr -ōris, m. (Νέστωρ), *son of Neleus, king of
Pylos, the oldest and most experienced of the
Greek heroes before Troy*.
neu=neve; q.v.
neuter -tra -trum (ne/uter), *neither*.
   LIT., quid bonum sit, quid malum, quid
neutrum, Cic.; neutram in partem moveri,
Cic.; neuter consulum, Liv.
   TRANSF., (1) *of neither sex, neuter*: Cic.;
Ov. (2) in grammar: nomina neutra, *or*
simply, neutra, *neuter nouns*, Cic.
   ¶ Hence adv. **neutrō**, *in neither direction,
towards neither side*: neutro inclinatā spe,
Liv.; Tac.
neutĭquam (**ne ŭtĭquam**), adv. *by no means,
not at all*: monebas de Q. Cicerone ut eum
quidem neutiquam relinquerem, Cic.; Pl.,
Liv.

neutrŭbī, adv. (neuter/ubi), *in neither place*.
Pl.
nēvĕ or **neu**, adv. (ne/ve), *and not, or not, nor*
(esp. following ut or ne): rogo te, ne contra-
has, neve sinas, Cic.; cohortatus est, uti
suae pristinae virtutis memoriam retinerent,
neu perturbarentur animo, Caes.; sometimes after a plain subj.: hic ames dici pater
atque princeps, neu sinas Medos equitare
inultos, Hor.; sometimes repeated, *neither*
. . . *nor*: ut id neve in hoc, neve in alio
requiras, Cic.
nēvis nevult=nonvis nonvult, *see* nolo.
nex nĕcis, f. (cf. Gr. νέκρος, and neco), *death*,
usually *violent death, murder*: necem sibi
consciscere, *to commit suicide*, Cic.; vitae
necisque potestatem habere in aliquem,
Caes.; alicui necem inferre, Cic.; Caes., Verg.
   TRANSF., *the blood of the person slain*: manūs
nece Phrygiā imbutae, Ov.
nexĭlis -e (necto), *tied together, bound together,
plaited*: sinus, Ov.; Lucr.
nexum -i, n. (necto) and **nexus** -ūs, m. (q.v.),
*an arrangement between debtor and creditor,
by which the debtor pledged his liberty as
security for his debt*: propter unius libidinem, omnia nexa civium liberata, Cic.; se
nexu obligare, Cic.; Liv.
nexus -ūs, m. (necto), *a binding, tying together,
entwining, connecting*. LIT., atomorum, Cic.;
serpens, baculum qui nexibus ambit, Ov.
   TRANSF., (1) in gen., *restraint*: legis nexus,
Tac. (2)=nexum; q.v.
nī (**nei**) and **nīvĕ**, neg. adv. and conj. (1)
in the form quidni? *or* quid ni? *why not?*
Pl. (2) with subj.=ne: monent ni teneant
cursus, Verg. (3) with indic. *or* subj., *if not,
unless*: moriar ni puto, *I wish I may die if I
don't think*, Cic.; plures cecidissent ni nox
praelio intervenisset, Liv.; excidium minitans
ni causam suam dissociarent, Tac.; Verg.
nīcētērĭum -i, n. (νικητήριον), *the reward of
victory, prize*: Juv.
nīco nĭcĕre nĭci, *to beckon*: Pl.
Nīcomēdēs -is, n. (Νικομήδης), *a king of
Bithynia*.
Nīcŏpŏlĭs, acc. -im, f. (Νικόπολις), *name of
several cities founded by Augustus to commemorate his victory at Actium*.
nicto -are (nico), *to wink*: Pl. TRANSF., *of*
fire: Lucr.
nīdāmentum -i, n. (nidus), *the materials
for a nest*: Pl.
nīdĭfīco -are (nidus/facio), *to build a nest*:
Plin.
nīdor -ōris, m. (connected with κνῖσσα), *a
vapour, odour, reek*, esp. *arising from anything
burning*: ganearum, Cic.; Pl., Verg., etc.
nīdŭlus -i, m. (dim. of nidus), *a little nest*:
Ithaca illa in asperrimis saxulis tamquam
nidulus adfixa, Cic.
nīdus -i, m. *a nest*.
   LIT., effingere et constituere nidos, Cic.;
nidum tignis suspendit hirundo, Verg.; fig.:
me maiores pennas nido extendisse, Hor.
   TRANSF., (1) *the young birds in the nest,
nestlings*: nidi loquaces, Verg. (2) *any home,
dwelling*: celsae Acherontiae, Hor. (3) *a case,
bookcase*: Mart.
niger -gra -grum, adj. (with compar. and
superl.), *black, dark-coloured*.
   LIT., hederae, Verg.; silvae, Hor.; caelum

pice nigrius, Ov.; n. as subst. **nigrum** -i, *a black spot*: Ov.

TRANSF., (1) *making black, blackening*: Auster, Verg. (2) *relating to death*: ignes, *the funeral pyre*, Hor.; dies, *the day of death*, Prop. (3) *unlucky, unpropitious*: Hor., Prop. (4) of character, *black, wicked*: Cic., Hor.

nigrans -antis, partic. from nigro; q.v.

nigresco nigrescĕre nigrui (niger), *to become black, grow dark*: tenebris nigrescunt omnia circum, Verg.; Ov.

nigro -are (niger), *to be black*: Lucr.

¶ Hence partic. **nigrans** -antis, *black, dark*: Lucr., Verg.

nigror -ōris, m. (niger), *blackness*: mortis, Lucr.

nihil and contr. **nil** (from nihilum), n. indecl. *nothing*.

In gen., *nothing*: nihil agere, Cic.; with genit of subst. or n. adj.: nihil rerum humanarum, Cic.; nihil mali, Cic.; nihil est cur, quamobrem, quod, *there is no reason why*: nihil est cur gestias, Cic.; nihil ad rem, *it has nothing to do with the business*, Cic.; nil igitur mors est ad nos, Lucr.; nihil esse, *to be good for nothing*, Cic.; nihil non, *everything*: nihil mali non inest, Cic.; non nihil, *something*, Cic.; nihil nisi, *nothing but*, Cic.; nihil aliud nisi, *nothing else but*, Cic.; nihil agis quin ego audiam, *you do nothing that I do not hear of*, Cic.

Esp., as internal acc., or adv., *not at all, in nothing*: de fratre nihil ego te accusavi, Cic.; Thebani nihil moti sunt, Liv.; nihil valere, Cic.; nihil opus est, Ter., Cic.

nihildum, nihil dum, *nothing as yet*: Cic.

nihilominus, see nihilum.

nihilum (**nilum**, Lucr., Hor.) -i, n. (ne/hilum), *nothing*.

In gen.: ex nihilo oriatur, Cic.; ad nihilum venire, recĭdere, Cic.; nihili, genit. of price: facere, aestimare, *to think nothing of*, Cic.; pro nihilo putare, Cic.; de nihilo, *for nothing, without ground or reason*, Liv.; abl. of measure, with compar.,= *no*: nihilo benevolentior, Cic.; nihilo magis, Cic.; nihilominus= *no less, nevertheless, notwithstanding*: Ter., Caes., Cic.; nihilo aliter, Ter.

Esp. internal acc. as adv., *in no way, not at all*: Hor., Liv.

nil=nihil; q.v.

nilum=nihilum; q.v.

Nilus -i, m. (Νεῖλος), *the river Nile*. TRANSF., (1) *the god of the Nile*: Cic. (2) *a canal, aqueduct*: Cic.

¶ Hence adj. **Nilĭacus** -a -um, *belonging to the Nile*: fera, *a crocodile*, Mart.; modi, *Egyptian*, Ov.; **Nilōticus** -a -um, *of the Nile*; f. adj. **Nilōtis** -ĭdis.

nimbātus -a -um (nimbus), *trifling, frivolous*: Pl.

nimbĭfĕr -fĕra -fĕrum (nimbus/fero), *storm-bringing, stormy*: Ov.

nimbōsus -a -um (nimbus), *rainy, stormy*: Orion, Verg.; ventus, Ov.

nimbus -i, m. *a cloud*.

LIT., (1) *a black rain-cloud*: involvere diem nimbi, Verg.; Cic., Liv. (2) *a cloud, mist*: Verg.

TRANSF., (1) *a cloud, mass of anything*: fulvae harenae, Verg.; peditum, Verg.; ferreus, *of missiles*, Verg. (2) *a storm of rain, violent*

shower of rain: Cic., Verg.; fig.: hunc quidem nimbum cito transisse laetor, Cic.

nimirum, adv. (ni=ne/mirum), *undoubtedly, truly, certainly*: nimirum Themistocles est auctor adhibendus, Cic.; Verg., Liv. Often ironically, *doubtless, of course*: uni nimirum tibi recte semper erunt res, Hor.; Cic.

nimis, adv. (1) *very much*: Pl.; non nimis, *not particularly, not very much*: praesidium non nimis firmum, Cic.; Caes., Liv. (2) *too much, overmuch, excessively*: ne quid nimis, Ter.; Cic., etc.; with genit.: insidiarum, Cic.

nimium, see nimius.

nimius -a -um (nimis). (1) *very great, very much*: Pl. N. as subst. **nimium**, *much, a great deal*: Albi, ne doleas plus nimio, Hor.; esp. as internal acc., or adv.: heu nimium felix! Verg.; non nimium, *not particularly*, Cic.

(2) *excessive*: **a**, of quantity or degree, *too great*: celeritas, Cic.: **b**, of character, *intemperate, immoderate*: nimius in honoribus decernendis, Cic.; with genit.: imperii, Liv. N. as subst., *excess, too much*: nimium dixisse, Cic.; with genit.: nimium hostium, Liv.; as internal acc., or adv.: Cic., Verg.

ningo (**ninguo**) ningĕre ninxi (nix), *to snow*; usually impers.: ningit, *it snows*, Verg. TRANSF., ningunt floribus rosarum, Lucr.

ninguës -ium, f. pl. *snow*: Lucr.

Ninus -i, m. (Νίνος). (1) *king of Assyria, husband of Semiramis.* (2) *Nineveh, the capital of Assyria.*

Niŏbē -ēs, f. and **Niŏba** -ae, f. (Νιόβη), *daughter of Tantalus, wife of Amphion.*

¶ Hence adj. **Niŏbēus** -a -um, *of Niobe.*

Nireus -ĕi -ĕos; acc. Nirĕa, m. (Νιρεύς), *son of Charopus, the most beautiful of all the Greek heroes at the siege of Troy.*

nisi, conj. (nĭ/sī), *if not, unless.*

In gen., with indic. or subj., like si: nisi fallor, Cic.; quod nisi esset, certe postea non discessisset, Cic.

Esp. (1) after negatives and questions, *except*: hoc sentio, nisi in bonis, amicitiam non posse, Cic.; Labienus iuravit se, nisi victorem, in castra non reversurum, Cic.; often after nihil aliud, quid aliud, etc.: erat historia nihil aliud nisi annalium confectio, Cic. (2) nisi si, *except if*: nisi si qui ad me plura scripsit, Cic. (3) nisi quod, *except that*: praedia me valde delectant, nisi quod illum aere alieno obruerunt, Cic. L.; Pl., Tac. (4) nisi ut, *except on condition that*, Liv.

¹Nisus -i, m.

(1) *king of Megara, father of Scylla; changed into a bird after she cut off his purple hair.*

¶ Hence adj. **Nisaeus** -a -um, *of Nisus*: canes (of Scylla, the daughter of Phorcus, confused with Scylla, daughter of Nisus), Ov.; subst. **Niseis** -idis, f. *Scylla, daughter of Nisus*; adj. **Niseius** -a -um, *relating to Nisus*: virgo, *Scylla*, Ov.; f. adj. **Nisias** -ădis, *Megarian.*

(2) *the friend of Euryalus (in Vergil's Aeneid).*

²nisus (**nixus**) -ūs, m. (¹nitor), *a pressing, straining, effort*: stat gravis Entellus nisuque immotus eodem, *in the same firm posture*, Verg.; nisus per saxa, *ascent*, Sall.; *the* course of the stars: Cic.; *the pains of child-birth*: Verg., Ov.

¹nīsus -a -um, partic. from ¹nitor; q.v.

nītēdŭla -ae, f. *a small mouse, dormouse*: Cic.

nĭtĕo -ēre, *to shine, glitter, be bright.* LIT., luna nitet, Lucr.; Hor., Ov.; often of well-being, health, etc., *to glow, be sleek*: qui nitent unguentis, fulgent purpurā, Cic. TRANSF., not physically, *to flourish, shine*: vectigal in pace niteat, Cic.; illorum vides quam niteat oratio, Cic.

¶ Hence partic. **nĭtens** -entis, *shining, bright, glittering.* LIT., lacrimis oculos suffusa nitentes, Verg.; of animals: taurus, *sleek*, Verg.; of men, *bright, beautiful*: Cat.; of plants, *blooming*: nitentia culta, Verg. TRANSF., *brilliant*: oratio, Cic.

nĭtesco -ĕre (niteo), *to begin to shine, to be bright.* LIT., iuventus nudatos humeros oleo perfusa nitescit, Verg.; of animals, *to grow sleek, in good condition*: Plin. L. TRANSF., eloquentiae gloriā, Tac.

nĭtĭdē, adv. from nitidus; q.v.

nĭtĭdĭuscŭlus -a -um (dim. of compar. nitidior), *somewhat more brilliant*: Pl. Adv. **nĭtĭdĭuscŭlē**, *rather more brightly*: Pl.

nĭtĭdus -a -um (niteo), adj. (with compar. and superl.), *bright, brilliant, shining, glittering.* LIT., ebur, Ov.; of men and animals, *sleek, fat, in good condition*: vacca, Ov.; me pinguem et nitidum bene curatā cute vises, Hor.; of fields and plants, *flourishing, blooming, luxuriant*: campi, Cic.; fruges, Lucr. TRANSF., (1) in gen., *handsome, spruce, trim, elegant*: quos pexo capillo nitidos videtis, Cic.; ex nitido fit rusticus, Hor. (2) *refined, polished, cultivated*: nitidum quoddam genus verborum et laetum, Cic.; Quint., Juv.

¶ Adv. **nĭtĭdē**, *brightly, splendidly*: Pl.

Nitiobrīges -um, m. *a people in Aquitanian Gaul.*

¹nītor nīti nīsus *or* nixus sum, dep.

(1) *to rest, lean, support oneself.* LIT., with abl: stirpibus suis, Cic.; hastili, Cic.; baculo, Ov.; in hastam, Verg.; anguem pressit humi nitens, *standing firm*, Verg.: a, *to rest upon, depend upon*: in te nititur civitatis salus, Cic.: b, *to put one's trust in, lean upon*: consilio alicuius, Cic.; in nomine inani, Lucr.

(2) *to strive, exert oneself, make an effort.* LIT., of childbirth: Ov.; also of movement, *to press on, to climb, ascend*: gradibus, Verg.; in adversum, Verg.; per ardua, Liv. TRANSF., *to strain, strive, endeavour*: tantum, quantum potest, quisque nitatur, Cic.; pro libertate, Sall.; ad immortalitatem gloriae, Cic.; with infin.: Sall., Ov.

²nĭtor -ōris, m. (niteo), *brilliance, brightness, splendour.* LIT., diurnus, *daylight*, Ov.; argenti et auri, Ov.; often *glow of health, beauty*: urit me Glycerae nitor, Hor. TRANSF., (1) *splendour of birth*: Ov. (2) *elegance of style*: orationis, Cic.; nitor et cultus descriptionum, Tac.; Ov.

nitrum -i, n. (νίτρον), *natron, natural soda*: Plin.; used for washing: ap. Cic. L.

nĭvālis -e (nix), *of snow, snowy.* LIT., dies, Liv.; Othrys, *covered with snow*, Verg. TRANSF., (1) *snow-white*: equi candore nivali, Verg. (2) *cold*: Mart.

nĭvātus -a -um (nix), *cooled with snow, iced*: Suet.

¹nĭvĕ=ni; q.v.

²nĭvĕ=neve; q.v.

nĭvĕus -a -um (nix), *of snow, snowy.* LIT., agger, Verg.; mons, *covered with snow*, Cat. TRANSF., *white as snow, snowy*: lacerti, Verg.; lac, Verg.; Hor., Ov.

nĭvōsus -a -um (nix), *abounding in snow, snowy*: grando, Liv.; hiems, Liv.; Ov.

nix nĭvis, f. (cf. νίφα), *snow.* LIT., Cic., Verg.; often plur.: Hor., Liv. TRANSF., of hair: nives capitis, Hor.

nixor -ari, dep. (freq. of nitor). (1) *to lean upon*; with abl.: Lucr. (2) *to strive, strain*: Lucr., Verg.

¹nixus=²nisus; q.v.

²nixus, see ¹nitor.

no nāre nāvi (cf. νέω), *to swim.* LIT., Pl., Hor., etc.; prov.: nare sine cortice, *to be able to do without a guardian*, Hor.; of boats: Cat., Tib. TRANSF., (1) *to sail, flow, fly*: Verg., Cat. (2) of eyes, *to swim*: Lucr.

nōbĭlis -e (nosco), *known.*

LIT., *celebrated, renowned, well-known*: dies, Pl.; ex doctrina, Cic.; inimicitiae nobiles inter eos erant, Liv.; ut arcendis sceleribus exemplum nobile esset, Liv.; in a bad sense, *infamous, notorious*: nobilis clade Romanā Caudina pax, Liv.; scelere nobiles, Pl.

TRANSF., (1) of men, *noble, of noble birth*; esp. *belonging to a family which had held curule magistracies* (opp. novus *or* ignobilis): Cic.; nobili genere nati, Cic.; homo, Cic.; plur. as subst.: Liv. (2) of horses, *highly bred*: Ov., Juv. (3) of things, *fine*: tres nobilissimi fundi, Cic.

nōbĭlĭtās -ātis, f. (nobilis). LIT., *fame, celebrity*: Cic.; Liv. TRANSF., (1) *noble birth, nobility*: genere et nobilitate sui municipii facile primus, Cic.; Lucr., Ov. (2) meton., *the aristocrats, the nobility*: omnis nostra nobilitas interiit, Caes.; Liv.; plur.: Tac. (3) in gen., *excellence, worth*: signa summā nobilitate, Cic.; Ov., Tac.

¶ Adv. **nōbĭlĭtĕr**, *excellently, admirably*: Plin.

nōbĭlĭto -are (nobilis), *to make known, make famous, renowned*; in a good sense: poëtae post mortem nobilitari volunt, Cic.; in a bad sense, *to make notorious*: Phalaris, cuius est praeter ceteros nobilitata crudelitas, Cic.; Ter.

nŏcĕo -ēre, *to hurt, injure, harm*; with dat.: alteri, Cic.; and with internal acc.: nihil iis, Caes.; with clause as subject: nocet esse deum, Ov.; pass. impers.: ne quid eis noceatur, Cic.

¶ Hence partic. (with compar. and superl.) **nŏcens** -entis, *hurtful, injurious, noxious*: caules, Cic.; Hor.; esp. morally, *criminal, guilty, wicked*: homo, Cic.; as subst.: nocens, *a guilty person*, Cic., Ov., Liv.

nŏcīvus -a -um (noceo), *hurtful, injurious*: Phaedr.

noctĭfĕr -fĕri, m. (nox/fero), *the night-bringer*, i.e., *the Evening Star*: Cat.

noctĭlūca -ae, f. (nox/luceo), *something that shines by night*, i.e. *the moon*: Hor.

noctĭvăgus -a -um (nox/vagus), *wandering by night*: currus (of the moon), Verg.; Lucr.

noctū, abl. from nox; q.v.

noctŭa -ae, f. (nox), *the owl*: Pl., Verg.

noctŭābundus -a -um (noctu), *travelling by night*: tabellarius, Cic. L.

noctŭīnus -a -um (noctua), *of the owl*: Pl.

nocturnus -a -um (nox), *by night, nightly, nocturnal*: labores diurnos nocturnosque suscipere, Cic.; fur, Cic.; lupus, *preying by night*, Verg.; Bacchus, *worshipped at night*, Verg.

noctŭvĭgĭlus -a -um (noctu/vigilo), *night-waking*: Pl.

nŏcŭus -a -um (noceo), *hurtful, injurious*: Ov.

nōdo -are (nodus). (1) *to knot, tie in a knot*: crines in aurum, Verg.; collum laqueo nodatus amator, Ov. (2) *to make knotty*: Plin.

nōdōsus -a -um (nodus), *full of knots, knotty*. LIT., stipes, Ov.; lina, *nets*, Ov. TRANSF., Cicuta, *a usurer, cunning in ensnaring debtors*, Hor.

nōdus -i, m. *a knot*. LIT., Cic., Verg. TRANSF., (1) physical: **a**, *knot or knob on the joint of an animal*: crura sine nodis articulisque habere, Caes.: **b**, *a knot in the wood of plants*: Verg., Liv.: **c**, *a girdle*: Mart.; anni, *the equator*, Lucr.: **d**, *the knot into which the hair was sometimes collected*: Ov. (2) abstr.: **a**, *a tie, bond, connexion*: amicitiae, Cic.: **b**, *a bond, obligation*: exsolvere animos nodis religionum, Lucr.: **c**, *a knotty point, difficulty, entanglement, perplexity*: dum hic nodus expediatur, Cic.; Verg., Hor., Liv.

Nōla -ae, f. *a town in Campania* (now *Nola*). ¶ Hence adj. **Nōlānus** -a -um, *belonging to Nola*; plur. as subst. **Nōlāni** -ōrum, m. *the inhabitants of Nola*.

nōlo nolle nōlŭi (ne/volo), *to be unwilling, wish not to, refuse*. LIT., nolunt ubi velis, Ter.; with acc. of n. pron.: quae etiamsi nolunt, Cic.; with acc. and infin.: nolo enim eundem populum imperatorem esse et portitorem terrarum, Cic.; pluribus praesentibus eas res iactari nolebat, Caes.; with plain infin.: alienare nolui, Cic.; the imperat., noli, nolite, nolito, is frequently used with an infin. to form a periphrastic imperat.: noli putare, *don't imagine*, Cic.; Pl., Juv.; nollem, *I could wish not*: Carthaginem et Numantiam funditus sustulerunt; nollem Corinthum, Cic.; so: nollem factum, Ter.; with subj.: nolo accusator in iudicium potentiam adferat, Cic. TRANSF., *to wish evil, to be spiteful to*: alicui, Cic.

nŏmăs -ădis, c. (νομάς), *pasturing*; hence (1) plur.: nomades, *nomads, nations who lead a migratory, pastoral life*, Plin. (2) *a Numidian*: Verg., Prop.

nōmen -ĭnis, n. (connected with nosco), *a name*. LIT., in gen.: nomen est quod unicuique personae datur, quo suo quaeque proprio et certo vocabulo appellatur, Cic.; imponere nova rebus nomina, Cic.; appellare aliquem nomine, Cic.; cantus cui nomen neniae, Cic.; nomen dare, edere, profiteri, *to go for a soldier, enlist*, Liv. Esp. (1) *the gentile name of a Roman*, as e.g., Cornelius in P. Cornelius Scipio, though sometimes used for the praenomen (Publius) or the cognomen (Scipio): Cic. (2) in law: nomen alicuius

deferre, *to give information against, accuse*, Cic.; nomen recipere, *to receive an information*, Cic. (3) in business, of any name involved in a transaction; hence: certis nominibus, *on good security*, Cic.; nomina solvere, exsolvere, expedire, *to pay debts*, Cic.; nomina sua exigere, *to collect one's debts*, Cic.; nomen facere, *to set down a debt in the account-book*, Cic.; bonum nomen, *a good payer*, Cic.
TRANSF., (1) denoting the *person* or *community* that bears a name: nomina tanta, *such great ones*, Ov.; nomen Romanum, *the Roman power*, nomen Latinum, etc., Cic., Liv. (2) *fame, glory*: nomen habere, Cic.; Verg., Liv. (3) *name, cause, account, heading*: nomine meo, tuo, *in my name, on my behalf*, Cic.; nomine lucri, *for the sake of*, Cic.; hence also *ground, pretext*: nomen inductum fictae religionis, Cic.; Caes., Tac. (4) *the name* (as opposed to the thing): legionum, *the mere name*, Cic. L., Liv., Ov.

nōmenclātor -ōris, m. *a slave who told his master the names of the persons whom he met*: Cic.

Nōmentum -i, n. *a town fourteen miles north-east of Rome*. ¶ Hence adj. **Nōmentānus** -a -um, *of Nomentum*.

nōmĭnātim, adv. (nomino), *by name, expressly*: centuriones nominatim appellare, Caes.; de aliquo nominatim decernere, Cic.

nōmĭnātĭo -ōnis, f. (nomino), *a nomination to a public office*: Cic., Liv., Tac.

nōmĭnātus -a -um, partic. from nomino; q.v.

nōmĭnĭto -are (freq. of nomino), *to call regularly by name*: Lucr.

nōmĭno -are (nomen), *to name, give a name to*. LIT., (1) *to call*: amore quo amicitia est nominata, Cic. (2) *to mention, speak about*: Sulla quem honoris causā nomino, *whom I mention with the greatest respect*, Cic.; Caes. TRANSF., (1) *to make famous*: praedicari de se et nominari volunt omnes, Cic. (2) *to name, appoint, nominate to an office*: me augurem nominaverunt, Cic.; Liv. (3) *to denounce, give information against*: aliquem apud dictatorem, Liv.; Suet. ¶ Hence partic. **nōmĭnātus** -a -um, *well-known, noted, celebrated*: Cic.

nŏmisma -mătis, n. (νόμισμα), *a coin, a piece of money*: Hor., Mart.

nōn (old forms **noenum, noenu**; from ne/unum), adv. *not*. In gen.: non est ita, iudices, non est profecto, Cic.; non with negative following forms a weak affirmative, e.g.: non nihil, non nemo, non nullus, Cic.; non with negative preceding forms an emphatic affirmative: nihil non ad rationem dirigebat, Cic.; with superl., ironically: homo non aptissimus ad iocandum, Cic.; non quod, non quo, *not that, not because*: non quod sola ornent, sed quod excellant, Cic.; non nisi, *only*; non modum (solum), *not only*, Cic.; non ita, non tam, *not very, not particularly*: simulacra perampla, sed non ita antiqua, Cic.
Esp. (1) in questions=nonne?: non idem fecit? Pl. (2) in commands=ne: non petito, Ov.; Hor., Liv. (3) in answers, *no*: aut etiam aut non respondere, Cic. (4) negativing a noun: per medium, per non medium, Lucr.; Cic., Ov.

Nōnācris -is, f. (*Νώνακρις*), *a mountain and town in Arcadia.*
¶ Hence adj. **Nōnācrīnus** -a -um, *Arcadian*: virgo, Callisto, Ov.; **Nōnācrius** -a -um, *Arcadian*: heros, *Evander*, Ov.; subst. **Nōnācria** -ae, f.=*Atalanta*: Ov.

nōnae -ārum, f. (nonus), *the nones; the fifth day in all the months* (except March, May, July, and October, when it was the seventh); *so called from being the ninth day* (counting inclusively) *before the Ides.*

nōnāgēni -ae -a (nonaginta), *ninety each, ninety at a time*: Plin.

nōnāgēsimus (-ensimus) -a -um (nonaginta), *the ninetieth*: Cic.

nōnāgiēs (-iens), adv. (nonaginta), *ninety times*: Cic.

nōnāgintā, indecl. numer., *ninety*: Cic.

nōnānus -a -um (nona, sc. legio), *belonging to the ninth legion*: miles, Tac.; m. as subst.
nōnānus -i, *a soldier of the ninth legion*: Tac.

nondum, adv. *not yet*: Pl., Cic., Verg.

nongenti -ae -a, *nine hundred*: Cic.

nonnĕ, interrog. adv., asks a question to which an affirmative answer is expected. (1) in direct questions: nonne animadvertis? *do you not perceive?* Cic. (2) in indirect questions: quaero nonne id effecerit, Cic.

nonnēmo, nonnĭhil, *see* nemo, nihil.

nonnullus (**non nullus**) -a -um, *some*; in plur., *several*: nonnulla in re, Cic.; nonnulla pars militum, Caes.; non nullae cohortes, Caes.; m. as subst. **nonnulli**, *some*: Cic.

nonnumquam (**non numquam**), adv. *sometimes*: Caes., Cic.

nonnusquam, adv. *in some places*: Plin.

nōnus -a -um (novem), *the ninth*: Cic., Hor.; f. as subst. **nōna** -ae, *the ninth hour*, i.e., very roughly, three o'clock p.m.: Hor.

nōnusdēcimus -a -um, *nineteenth*: Tac.

Nōra -ōrum, m. (1) *a town in Sardinia.*
¶ Hence **Nōrenses** -ium, *the inhabitants of Nora.* (2) *a fort in Cappadocia.*

Norba -ae, f. *a town in Latium.*
¶ Hence adj. **Norbānus** -a -um, *of Norba.*

Nōrĭcum -i, n. *Noricum, a country between the Alps and the Danube.*
¶ Hence adj. **Nōrĭcus** -a -um, *Noric.*

norma -ae, f. (nosco), *a carpenter's square for measuring right angles*: Plin. TRANSF., any *rule, standard*: dirigere vitam ad certam rationis normam, Cic.; Hor., Plin. L.

nōs, plur. of ego; q.v.

Nortia -ae, f. *an Etruscan goddess of fate, worshipped at Volsinii.*

noscito -are (freq. of nosco), *to get to know.* Hence (1) *to observe, perceive*: Liv., Pl.; esp., *to investigate, explore*: aedes, vestigia, Pl. (2) *to recognize*: aliquem facie, Liv.; Pl., Tac.

nosco (old form **gnosco**; cf. *γιγνώσκω*) noscĕre nōvi nōtum (contracted forms: nosti, norim, noram, nosse), *to become acquainted with, get knowledge of*; hence in the perfect tenses, *to be acquainted with, to know.*
LIT., studeo cursos istos mutationum noscere, Cic.; quam (virtutem) tu ne de facie quidem nosti, Cic.; si Caesarem bene novi, Cic.; Pl., Liv., etc.
TRANSF., (1) *to inquire into, to investigate*: quae olim a praetoribus noscebantur, Tac.

(2) *to recognize*: ad res suas noscendas recipiendasque, Liv., Ter. (3) *to recognize, approve, acknowledge*: illam partem excusationis nec nosco, nec probo, Cic.; Caes.
¶ Hence partic. (with compar. and superl.) **nōtus** -a -um, *known*: res nota, Cic.; noti atque insignes latrones, Cic.; aliquid notum habere, *to know*, Cic.; m. pl. as subst.: noti, *friends, acquaintances*, Caes., Cic., Hor. Hence, *familiar, customary*: ulmus nota quae sedes fuerat columbis, Hor. Sometimes in bad sense, *notorious*: mulier, Cic.

noster -tra -trum (nos), *our, ours.* (1) subject.: provincia nostra, Caes.; Cic., etc. Esp., *a, on our side, one of us*: Furnius noster, *our friend* Furnius, Cic.; m. pl. as subst.: nostri, *our people*, Cic., etc.: b, *favourable to us*: nostra loca, Liv.; noster Mars, Verg. (2) object.: amor noster, *love for us*, Cic. L.; Liv.

nostrās -ātis, (noster), *of our country, native*: mirifice capior facetiis, maxime nostratibus, Cic. L.; philosophi, Cic.

nŏta -ae, f. (nosco), *a mark, token, note, sign.*
In gen.: signa et notae locorum, Cic.; Verg., Hor., Liv. TRANSF., *distinguishing mark, sign*: notae argumentorum, Cic.
Esp. (1) *marks in writing; letters, characters*: notae litterarum, Cic.; notae librariorum, *marks of punctuation*, Cic.; of secret writing, *cypher*: Verg.; poet., meton.: notae, *a writing, letter*, Ov. (2) *a distinguishing mark made on an object*: a, *a branded mark, brand*: barbarus compunctus notis Thraeciis, *tattooed*, Cic.; Verg. TRANSF., *disgrace, shame, ignominy*: quae nota domesticae turpitudinis non inusta vitae tuae est? Cic.: b, *a mark on a cask of wine* or *honey* (to mark the quality, vintage, etc.): Hor. TRANSF., *brand, sort, quality*: aliquem de meliore nota commendare, Cic. (3) *a critical mark in a book* (to express approval or disapproval): Cic. (4) polit. t. t., *the censor's mark of disgrace*, placed against a citizen's name: Cic., Liv.

nŏtābĭlis -e (noto), *remarkable, striking, noteworthy*: exitus, Cic. L.; compar.: Quint., Tac.
¶ Adv. **nŏtābĭlĭtĕr**, *remarkably*: Plin. L., Suet.; compar.: Tac.

nŏtārius -i, m. (nota), *a secretary* or *shorthand writer*: Quint., Plin. L.

nŏtātĭo -ōnis, f. (noto), *a marking.*
LIT., tabellarum, *a marking of the voting-tickets with different-coloured wax*, Cic. Esp. (1) *the stigma of the censor*: censoria, Cic. (2) *a choice*: iudicum, Cic.
TRANSF., *observing, noting, taking notice of*: naturae, Cic.

nŏtātus -a -um, partic. from noto; q.v.

nŏtesco nōtescĕre nōtŭi (1notus), *to become known*: Cat., Tac.

nŏthus -a -um (*νόθος*). LIT., (1) *of men illegitimate, bastard*: Verg. (2) *of animals, o mixed breed, hybrid, mongrel*: Verg. TRANSF., *not genuine, spurious*: Lucr., Cat.

nōtĭo -ōnis, f. (nosco). LIT., (1) *a making oneself acquainted*: Pl. (2) *an examination investigation*: pontificum, Cic.; Liv., Tac TRANSF., *an idea, notion, conception*: deorum Cic.; rerum, Cic.

nōtĭtĭa -ae, f. (1notus). (1) pass., *a bein*

known: hi propter notitiam sunt intromissi, Nep. TRANSF., *fame, celebrity*: Ov., Tac. (2) act., *knowledge, acquaintance*: notitia nova mulieris, Cic.; Caes., Liv.; hence, *an idea, notion, conception*: dei, Cic.; Lucr.

nŏtĭtĭēs -ēi, f.=notitia; q.v., Lucr.

nŏto -are (nota), *to mark.*

In gen.: tabellam cerā, Cic.; ungue genas, Ov. TRANSF., **a**, *to distinguish, mark out*: aliquem decore, Cic.; notat et designat oculis ad caedem unumquemque nostrum, Cic.: **b**, *to denote*: res nominibus, Cic.; aliquid verbis Latinis, Cic.: **c**, *to observe*: cantus avium, Cic.

Esp. (**1**) *to write*: Ov. (**2**) *to mark critically*: Ov. (**3**) polit. t. t., of the censor, *to place a mark against a Roman citizen's name*; *to censure publicly, reprimand*: quos censores furti et captarum pecuniarum nomine notaverunt, Cic. TRANSF., *to stigmatize*: Caes., Cic., Hor.

¶ Hence partic. (with superl.) **nŏtātus** -a -um, *marked out*: homo omnium scelerum libidinumque notis notatissimus, Cic.

nŏtōs=²notus; q.v.

¹**nōtus** -a -um, partic. from nosco; q.v.

²**nŏtus** (-ŏs) -i, m. (νότος), *the south wind.* LIT., Verg., etc. TRANSF., in gen., *wind*: Verg.

nŏvācŭla -ae, f. (novo), *a sharp knife* or *razor*: cotem novaculā praecīdere, Cic.; Liv., Mart.

nŏvālis -e, adj. (novus), *ploughed again* or *for the first time*: Varr.

¶ As subst. **nŏvālis** -is, f. and **nŏvāle** -is, n. (**1**) *fallow land*: Verg. (**2**) *a cultivated field*: Verg. (**3**) *crops*: Juv.

nŏvātrix -īcis, f. (novator), *she that renews*: rerum, Ov.

nŏvē, adv. from novus; q.v.

nŏvellus -a -um (dim. of novus), *new, young*: arbor, Cic.; Verg., Tib. TRANSF., *fresh, unfamiliar*: Liv., Ov.

nŏvem, indecl. numer., *nine*: Cic.; decem novem, *nineteen*, Caes.

November and **Nŏvembris** -bris, m. (novem), *relating to the ninth month of the Roman year, November*: Kalendae Novembres, Cic.; m. as subst., *November*: Mart.

nŏvendĕcim, **nŏvemdĕcim**, indecl. numer. (novem/decem), *nineteen*: Liv.

nŏvendĭālis -e (novem/dies), *of nine days.* Hence (**1**) *happening on the ninth day*: cena, *a funeral banquet*, Tac.; pulveres, *ashes of the dead* (as used in magic), Hor. (**2**) *lasting nine days*: feriae, *a nine days' festival on the occasion of any portent* (such as a shower of stones), Cic. L.; sacrum, *sacrificium*, Liv.

Nŏvensĭles dīvi (novus), *gods whose worship had been introduced from foreign countries* (opp. indigetes, *native*): Liv.

nŏvēni -ae -a (novem), *nine each, nine at a time*: Liv.; poet., *nine*: Ov.

nŏverca -ae, f. (novus), *a step-mother*: saeva, Verg.; gravis, Tac.; prov.: apud novercam queri, i.e., *in vain*, Pl.

nŏvercālis -e (noverca), *of* or *like a step-mother*: Juv., Tac.

Nŏvesĭum -i, n. *fort of the Ubii on the Rhine* (now *Neuss*).

nŏvīcĭus -a -um (novus), *new, fresh*: Pl. esp. *of persons who have not long been enslaved*: Pl., Ter.; m. pl. as subst. **nŏvīcii**: Syrum nescio

quem de grege noviciorum factum esse consulem, Cic.

nŏvĭēs (-ĭens), adv. numer. (novem), *nine times*: Verg.

Nŏvĭŏdūnum -i, n. (**1**) *a town of the Suessiones* (now *Soissons*). (**2**) *a town of the Aedui* (now *Nevers*). (**3**) *a town of the Bituriges, near Novan.*

nŏvĭtās -ātis, f. (novus), *newness.* In gen.: rei, Cic.; anni, Ov.; plur.: novitates=*new acquaintances*, Cic. Esp. (**1**) *the condition of a homo novus* (see novus), *newness of nobility*: Cic. L., Sall. (**2**) *novelty, unusualness, strangeness*: terror quem tibi rei novitas attulerit, Cic.; novitate exterritus ipsa, Lucr.; Caes., Sall., Ov.

nŏvo -are (novus), *to make new, renew.* LIT., transtra, Verg.; membra, *to revive*, Ov.; ager novatus, *a field reploughed*, Cic. TRANSF., (**1**) *to change, alter*: aliquid in legibus, Cic.; Verg., Ov.; esp.: novare res, *to alter the constitution of a state, make a revolution*, Liv., Tac. (**2**) *to invent* something *new*: verba, *invent new words*, Cic.; Verg., Ov.

nŏvus -a -um (cf. νέος), superl.: novissimus; q.v., *new, fresh, young* (opp. vetus).

In gen.: miles, *a recruit*, Liv.; luna, Caes.; lac, Verg., Cic., etc.

Esp. (**1**) in particular phrases: novus homo, *the first of a family to hold a curule office in Rome*, e.g., M. T. Cicero: Cic., Juv.; novae res, *political changes, a revolution*, Caes., Sall., Cic.; novae tabulae, *new account-books* (that is, *a cancellation of debts*), Cic.; novae tabernae, *certain money-changers' shops in the Forum which had been burnt down and rebuilt.* (**2**) *fresh, inexperienced*: equus, Cic.; novus delictis, *inexperienced in crime*, Tac. (**3**) *novel, unusual, extraordinary*: genus dicendi, Cic.; Caes., Verg., etc. **a** *another, a second*: Camillus, *a second Camillus*, Liv.; novus Hannibal, Cic.; also *revived, refreshed*: Verg., Ov.

¶ N. as subst. **nŏvum** -i, *a new thing, news, a novelty*: Pl., Cic.

Superl. **nŏvissimus** -a -um, *the latest, last.* LIT., in space: agmen, *the rear*, Caes.; m. pl. as subst.: Caes.; in time, *last*: Caes., Verg. TRANSF., *extreme, severest*: exempla, Tac.

¶ Hence adv. **nŏvē**; positive, *in a new* or *unusual manner*: Pl., Sen.; superl. **nŏvissimē**. (**1**) *lately, recently*: Sall. (**2**) *lastly, in the last place*: Liv., Sen.

nox noctis, f. (cf. νύξ), *night.*

LIT., nocte, *by night*, Cic. L., Liv., Juv.; de nocte, *by night*, Cic.; multā de nocte, *late at night*, Cic.; mediā nocte, *at midnight*, Cic.; noctes et dies urgeri, *night and day*, Cic.; eam noctem pervigilare, Cic.; personif.: Nox, *the goddess Night, sister of Erebus*, Cic., Verg.

TRANSF., (**1**) meton., *sleep*: Verg. (**2**) *the darkness of a storm*: Verg. (**3**) *death*: Verg., Hor. (**4**) *blindness*: Ov. (**5**) fig., *obscurity*: mei versus aliquantum noctis habebunt, Ov. (**6**) *gloom, peril*: haec reipublicae nox, Cic. (**7**) *ignorance*: Ov.

¶ Abl. form as adv. **noctū**, *by night*· Pl., Caes., Cic., Hor.

noxa -ae, f. (noceo), *harm, injury, damage*: sine ullius urbis noxa, Liv.; Ov. TRANSF., (**1**) *a* *fault, offence*: in noxa esse, Liv.; unius ob noxam, Verg.; Ov. (2) *punishment*: noxā liberari, Liv.

noxĭa -ae, f. (noxius), *a fault, offence, crime*: Pl., Caes., Cic.; alicui noxiae esse, *to be accounted a fault*, Liv.

noxĭōsus -a -um (noxia). (1) *hurtful*: Sen. (2) *guilty*: Sen.

noxĭus -a -um (noxa). (1) *noxius, hurtful, injurious*: tela, Ov.; Verg. (2) *culpable, guilty*: aliquem noxium iudicare, Liv.; with genit.: coniurationis, Tac.

nūbēcŭla -ae, f. (dim. of nubes), *a little cloud*: Plin. TRANSF., *a troubled expression*: frontis, Cic.

nūbes -is, f. (cf. nebula), *a cloud*.
    LIT., aer concretus in nubes cogitur, Cic.; Verg., etc.
    TRANSF., (1) *a cloud, a great number, dense mass of* anything: pulveris, Liv.; locustarum, Liv.; volucrum, Verg. (2) *a troubled expression, gloom*: deme supercilio nubem, Hor.; Ov. (3) *veil, concealment*: fraudibus obice nubem, Hor. (4) *an impending misfortune*: belli, Verg. (5) as emblem of something unsubstantial, *a phantom*: nubes et inania captare, Hor.

nūbĭfĕr -fĕra -fĕrum (nubes/fero), *cloud-bearing, cloud-bringing*: Ov.

nūbĭgĕna -ae, c. (nubes/gigno), *born of a cloud, produced from a cloud*: Stat.; esp. of the Centaurs, *offspring of Ixion and a cloud*: Ov.

nūbĭlis -e (nubo), *marriageable*: filia, Cic.; Verg., Ov.

nūbĭlus -a -um (nubes), *covered with clouds, cloudy, overcast*.
    LIT., annus, Tib. N. as subst., sing. **nūbĭlum**, *cloudy weather*: Plin. L., Suet.; plur. **nūbĭla** -ōrum, *clouds*: Verg., Hor.
    TRANSF., (1) act., *cloud-bringing*: Auster, Ov. (2) *dark*: via nubila taxo, Ov. (3) *unhappy, sad, gloomy*: toto nubila vultu, Ov.; nubila nascenti seu mihi Parca fuit, tempora, Ov.

nūbo nūbĕre nupsi nuptum (cf. nubes), *to cover, veil*; hence, of a bride, *to be married to, to marry anyone*: virgo nupsit ei cui Caecilia nupta fuerat, Cic.; nuptam esse cum aliquo, Cic. L.; nubere in familiam, *to marry into a family*, Cic.; aliquam nuptum conlocare, *to give in marriage*, Caes.
    ¶ Hence, f. of partic. **nupta**, *married*: filia, Cic.; subst. **nupta** -ae, f. *a bride*: Ter., Cat., Liv., etc.

Nūcĕrĭa -ae, f. *a town in Campania* (now *Nocera*).
    ¶ Hence adj. **Nūcĕrīnus** -a -um, *of Nuceria*.

nŭcĭfrangĭbŭlum -i, n. (nux/frango), *a nut-cracker* (in jest=*a tooth*): Pl.

nuclĕus -i, m. (dim. of nux), *the kernel of a nut*, or *a nut* itself, or *any nut-like fruit*: Pl.; also *the stone* or *uneatable kernel of fruits*: olivarum, Plin.

nūdĭus (nunc/dius=dies), *it is now the . . . day since*; always with the ordinal numerals: nudius tertius, *the day before yesterday*, Cic. L.; nudius tertius decimus, Cic.

nūdo -are (nudus), *to make naked, make bare, strip*.
    LIT., aliquem. Cic.; caput, Verg.

TRANSF., (1) physically: **a**, *to lay bare, uncover*: gladium, *to draw*, Liv.; viscera, Verg.: **b**, milit. t. t., *to lay bare, leave undefended*: murus nudatus defensoribus, Caes.; Verg., Liv.: **c**, *to strip, spoil, plunder*: spoliavit nudavitque omnia, Cic.; quem praeceps alea nudat, Hor.; Liv. (2) not physically: **a**, *to reveal, lay bare, expose*: vis ingenii scientiā iuris nudata, Cic.; animos, Liv.: **b**, *to divest, deprive of*: omnibus rebus tribuniciam potestatem, Caes.

nūdus -a -um, *naked, unclothed, bare*.
    LIT., nudo capite, *bare-headed*, Sall.; Caes., Cic., etc.
    TRANSF., (1) physically: **a**, *bare, empty, uncovered*: subsellia, Cic.: **b**, *defenceless*: Caes., Liv.: **c**, *deprived of*; with abl.: praesidio, Cic. L.; with genit.: loca nuda gignentium, Sall.; respublica nuda a magistratibus, Cic. (2) not physically: **a**, *unadorned, plain*: commentarii Caesaris, Cic.: **b**, *bare, mere, alone, only*: nuda ista si ponas, Cic.; hoc nudum relinquitur, Cic.

nūgae -ārum, f. pl. *trifles, nonsense, stuff, trumpery*. LIT., huncine hominem tantis delectatum esse nugis? Cic.; Pl.; applied to verses: nescio quid meditans nugarum, Hor. TRANSF., of persons, *foolish, trifling fellows*: amicos habet meras nugas, Cic.

nūgātor -ōris, m. (nugor), *a trifler, foolish fellow, humbug*: Pl., Cic., Liv.

nūgātōrĭus -a -um (nugator), *trifling, frivolous, futile*: mala nugatoriaque accusatio, Cic.; Pl.

nūgax -ācis (nugor), *trifling, frivolous*: ap. Cic. L.

nūgor -ari, dep. (nugae). (1) *to trifle, be frivolous, talk nonsense*: non inscite, Cic.; cum aliquo, Hor. (2) *to trick, cheat*: Pl.

nullus -a -um (ne/ullus), *no, none, not any*.
    LIT., nullā unā re, Cic.; nullo modo, nullo pacto, *by no means*, Cic.; nullo certo ordine neque imperio, Caes.; Verg., Liv., etc.
    TRANSF., (1) colloq., as a strong negative, *not at all*: Philotimus nullus venit, *no sign of*, Cic.; Pl. (2) as subst., esp. genit., nullius, and abl., nullo; *no one*: Cic., Verg. (3) *non-existent*: de mortuis loquor, qui nulli sunt, Cic.; hence, *ruined, of no account*: ecce me nullum senem, Pl.; nullus repente fui, Liv.

num, interrog. particle. (1) introducing a direct question, to which a negative answer is expected: Cic.; Hor., etc. Sometimes strengthened with -ne *or* -nam: deum ipsum numne vidisti? Cic.; Pl. Also with indef., quis, quid, quando: num quid vis? *is there anything else you want?* (a common form of leave-taking), Pl., Cic., Hor. (2) in indirect questions, *whether*: quaero num aliter ac nunc eveniunt evenirent? Cic.; Liv., etc.

Nŭma -ae, m., Pompilius, *the second king of Rome*.

Nŭmantĭa -ae, f. *a town in Hispania Tarraconensis, taken and destroyed by Scipio Africanus the younger*.
    ¶ Hence adj. **Nŭmantīnus** -a -um, *Numantine*.

numcŭbĭ, interrog. adv. *ever?*: Ter.

nŭmella -ae, f. *a shackle, fetter*: Pl.

nūmen -inis, n. (nuo), *a nodding with the head, a nod*. LIT., Lucr. TRANSF., as an expression of will, *command, consent*. In

gen.: ad numen mentis, Lucr. Esp., of a
deity, *the divine will, divine command*: deo
cuius numini parent omnia, Cic.; mundum
censent regi numine deorum, Cic.; numina,
divum, numinae fatorum, Verg. Hence, *the
might of a deity, majesty, divinity*: numen
Iunonis adora, Verg.; Cic., Liv.; of deities
themselves: magna numina, pia numina,
Verg.; of the Roman emperors: violatum
numen Augusti, Tac.

nŭmĕrābĭlis -e (numero), *that can be counted*:
Hor., Ov.

nŭmĕrātus -a -um, partic. from numero; q.v.

nŭmĕro -are (numerus), *to count*.
   LIT., singulos, Cic.; pecus, Verg.; aliquid
per digitos, *on the fingers*, Ov.; numera
senatum, *count the house* (to see if enough
members to transact business were present),
Cic. L. Esp. of money, *to count out money,
to pay*: militibus stipendium, Cic.; Caes., Liv.
   TRANSF., (1) *to count over* possessions,
i.e. *to own*: donec eris felix multos numerabis
amicos, Ov.; Juv. (2) *to reckon, consider*:
inter suos, Cic.; inter honestos homines,
Cic.; mortem in beneficii loco, Cic.;
Sulpicium accusatorem suum numerabat,
non competitorem, Cic.; sapientes cives,
qualem me et esse, et numerari volo, Cic.;
Liv., Ov., etc. (3) *to enumerate*: dies deficiat
si velim numerare quibus bonis male
evenerit, Cic.; Verg., Tac.
   ¶ Hence partic. **nŭmĕrātus** -a -um,
counted out; hence, *in hard cash, in ready
money*: dos, pecunia, Cic.; n. as subst.
nŭmĕrātum -i, *hard cash, money down*:
numerato solvere, Cic. L.; Liv., Hor.

nŭmĕrōsus -a -um (numerus). (1) *numerous*:
numerosissima civitas, *populous*, Tac. (2)
rhythmical, metrical, melodious: oratio, Cic.;
Horatius, Ov.
   ¶ Adv. **nŭmĕrōsē**. (1) *numerously*: Plin.
(2) *rhythmically*: circumscripte numeroseque dicere, Cic.

nŭmĕrus -i, m. (connected with *νέμω*), *a
measure.*
   Hence (1) *a number*. LIT., numerum
inire, *to count*, Caes. Esp.: **a**, *the total
number*: ad pristinum numerum duo augures
addidit, Cic.; haec enim sunt tria numero,
are three in number, Cic.; numero quadraginta,
forty in number, Sall.: **b**, *a (large) uncertain
number, a mass*: hominum, Cic.; innumerabilis frumenti numerus, *an enormous quantity*,
Cic.: **c**, *a division of the army, company,
detachment*: sparsi per provinciam numeri,
Tac. TRANSF., **a**, *a cipher*, i.e., *of no consequence*: nos numerus sumus, Hor.: **b**, in
plur., *calculations, mathematics*: Cic., Hor.:
c, *a category, class*: in deorum numero
referre, Cic.; Caes., Liv., etc.: **d**, *rank,
place, position, regard, consideration*: obtinere
aliquem numerum, Cic.; parentis numero
esse, Cic.; Caes., Hor.
   (2) *a portion, part of a whole*: elegans omni
numero poema, *in every respect*, Cic.; hence,
function: Ov. Esp. in music, *measure, metre,
number, time*: numeri ac modi, Cic.; numeri
graves, *heroic verse*, Ov.; impares, *elegiac*,
Ov.; extra numerum, *out of time*, Cic.
   ¶ Abl. sing. as adv. **nŭmĕrō**. (1) *just,
exactly, at the right time*: Pl. (2) *too quickly,
too soon*: Pl.

Nŭmĭda -ae, m. *a Numidian*; plur. **Nŭmĭdae**
-ārum, *the Numidians of North Africa.*
   ¶ Hence **Nŭmĭdĭa** -ae, f. *their country*;
adj. **Nŭmĭdĭcus** -a -um, *Numidian.*

Nŭmistro -ōnis, f. *a town in Lucania.*

Nŭmĭtor -ōris, m. *king of Alba, father of Ilia,
grandfather of Romulus and Remus.*

nummārĭus -a -um (nummus), *belonging to
money*: theca, Cic.; difficultas nummaria,
scarcity of money, Cic. TRANSF., *bribed with
money, venal*: iudex, Cic.

nummātus -a -um (nummus), *provided with
money, rich*: adulescens non minus bene
nummatus quam capillatus, Cic.; Hor.

nummŭlārĭus -i, m. (nummulus), *a money-
changer*: Mart., Suet.

nummŭlus -i, m. (dim. of nummus), *a little
piece of money*: nummulis acceptis ius ac fas
omne delere, *for a paltry sum*, Cic. L.

nummus -i, m.; genit. pl. usually nummum.
   In gen., *a piece of money, coin*: adulterini
nummi, *bad money*, Cic.; habere in nummis,
to have in cash, Cic.
   Esp., *the sesterce, a Roman coin* worth about
twopence: quinque millia nummum, Cic.;
Pl., Hor., etc. TRANSF., like the English
penny, to express a very small sum: ad
nummum convenit, *it comes right to a
farthing*, Cic. L.

numquam=nunquam; q.v.

nunc, adv. (cf. *νῦν*), *now, at present, at this
moment.*
   LIT., ut nunc est, *as things are now*, Cic. L.,
Hor.; nunc ipsum, *at this very moment*, Cic.;
qui nunc sunt, *the present generation*, Cic.;
Verg., Liv., etc.
   TRANSF., (1) of past or future time; *at
that time, already*: Caes., Cic., Hor., etc.;
nunc ... nunc, *now ... now, at one time ...
at another*, Liv. (2) *in these circumstances,
as it is*: Lucr., Cic.

nuncĭne=nuncne; *see* nunc.

nuncŭpātĭo -ōnis, f. (nuncupo), *a naming*;
esp. *the public pronouncing of a vow*: votorum,
Tac.

nuncŭpo -are (nomen/capio), *to name, call by
name*: aliquid nomine dei, Cic. Esp., *to
pronounce solemnly and openly*. (1) of state
vows: vota pro republica, Cic. (2) of
adoption: Tac. (3) of wills, *to nominate as
heir*: heredem, Tac.

nundĭnae -ārum, f. pl. (novem/dies; sc.
feriae), *market-day, held every ninth day*:
Cic. L.
   TRANSF., (1) *the market-place*: illi Capuam
nundinas rusticorum, horreum Campani
agri esse voluerunt, Cic.; Liv. (2) *traffic,
trade, business*: vectigalium flagitiosissimae
nundinae, Cic.

nundĭnālis -e (nundinae), *of the market*: Pl.

nundĭnātĭo -ōnis, f. (nundinor), *the holding
of a market, trafficking, trade, business*: fuit
nundinatio aliqua, Cic.

nundĭnor -ari, dep. (nundinae), *to transact
business, trade, traffic*. LIT., sedere nundi-
nantem, Liv. TRANSF., (1) *to buy*, esp.
corruptly: ab aliquo, Cic.; totum imperium
P. R., Cic. (2) *to be present in great numbers*
(as at a market): ubi ad focum angues
nundinari solent, Cic.

nundĭnum -i, n. (novem/dies; sc. tempus),
the market-time: trinum nundinum, *the*

interval between one market-day and the next but one (17–24 days): comitia in trinum nundinum indicere, Liv.; Cic.

nunquam (**numquam**), adv. (ne/unquam), never: Cic., etc.; numquam adhuc, numquam ante, numquam alias, Cic.; numquam non, always, Cic.; non numquam, sometimes, Cic. Also, as in colloq. English, for a strong negative, by no means: Pl., Verg.

nuntiātĭo -ōnis, f. (nuntio), relig. t. t., a declaration made by the augur about his observations: Cic.

nuntĭo -are (nuntius), to announce: vera, Cic.; victoriam, Liv.; domum, at home, Liv.; qui nuntiarent prope omnes naves adflictas esse, Caes.; oppugnata domus C. Caesaris per multas noctis horas nuntiabatur, Cic. With ut, or ne, and the subj., to give notice, command: paulo post ferunt nuntiatum Simonidi ut prodiret, Cic.; Liv., Tac. Abl. absol.: nuntiato, this being announced, news having come, Liv.

nuntĭus -a -um, announcing: nuntia littera venit, Ov.; with genit., bringing news of: Lucr., Ov.

M. as subst. **nuntĭus** -i. (1) a messenger, announcer: facere aliquem certiorem per nuntium, Cic.; Caes., Verg., etc. (2) a message, news: nuntium adferre, Cic.; esp., an official notice: nuntium uxori remittere, to send one's wife a letter of divorce, Cic. TRANSF., nuntium remittere virtuti, to renounce, Cic.

F. as subst. **nuntĭa** -ae, she that announces: historia nuntia veritatis, Cic.

N. as subst. **nuntĭum** -i, a message, news: Cat.

nūpĕr, adv. with superl. **nūperrĭmē** (for noviper, from novus), lately, not long ago: qui nuper Romae fuit, Cic.; Pl., Ter., Hor.; sometimes in comparatively recent times: nuper, id est, paucis ante saeculis, Cic.

nūpĕrus -a -um (nuper), recent: Pl.

nupta -ae, f. subst. from nubo; q.v.

nuptĭae -ārum, f. pl. (nubo), marriage, a wedding: nuptias facere, adornare, Pl.; Cornificia multarum nuptiarum, often married, Cic. L.; celebrare nuptias, Liv.

nuptĭālis -e (nuptiae), of marriage: ludi, Pl.; dona, Cic.; cena, Liv.

nuptus -a -um, partic. from nubo; q.v.

Nursĭa -ae, f. a town in the Sabine country (now Norcia).

¶ Hence adj. **Nursīnus** -a -um, belonging to Nursia.

nŭrus -ūs, f. (cf. νυός), a daughter-in-law: Ter., Cic., Verg., etc. TRANSF., a young married woman: Ov., Luc., Mart.

nusquam, adv. (ne/usquam), nowhere. LIT., nusquam alibi, Cic.; Pl., Verg., etc. TRANSF., (1) to no place: Pl., Liv. (2) in nothing, on no occasion: praestabo sumptum nusquam melius poni posse, Cic.; Verg., Liv. (3) to or for nothing: ut ad id omnia referri oporteat, ipsum autem nusquam, Cic.; Liv. (4) nusquam esse, not to exist, Pl., Cic., Hor.

nŭto -are (freq. of *nuo).

LIT., (1) to nod, keep nodding: Pl., Hor. (2) to sway, waver: ornus nutat, Verg.; nutant galeae, Liv.

TRANSF., to waver; in gen.: nutans acies, Tac.; nutante mundi ruinā, Luc.; in opinion:

etiam Democritus nutare videtur in natu deorum, Cic.; in fidelity: Galliae nutante Tac.

nūtrīcātus -ūs, m. (nutrico), a nursing: Pl.

nūtrīcĭus -i, m. (nutrix), a tutor, guardiar Caes.

nūtrīco -are and **nūtrīcor** -ari, dep. (nutrix to suckle, nourish. LIT., pueros, Pl. TRANSI to support, sustain: mundus omnia, sic membra et partes suas, nutricatur, Cic.; Pl.

nūtrīcŭla -ae, f. (dim. of nutrix), nurse, nanny Hor. TRANSF., Gallia nutricula seditiosorun Cic.

nūtrīmen -inis, n. (nutrio), nourishment: O

nūtrīmentum -i, n. (nutrio), nourishmen nutriment. TRANSF., (1) of fuel: ari(nutrimenta, Verg. (2) support, trainin(educata huius nutrimentis eloquentia, Cic.

nūtrĭo -ire (**nūtrĭor** -iri, dep.: Verg.), suckle, nourish, bring up. LIT., nutritus lac ferino, Ov. TRANSF., (1) physically: (plants: terra herbas nutrit, Ov.; of fire: ign foliis, Ov.; of bodies, in sickness, etc corpora, Liv. (2) not physically, to ma_ good, support, sustain: amorem, Ov.; me) rite nutrita, educated, Hor.; damnum natura Liv.

nūtrix -īcis, f. (nutrio), a nurse, foster-mothe LIT., ut paene cum lacte nutricis errore(suxisse videamur, Cic.; meton.: nutrices, t/ breasts, Cat. TRANSF., oratoris, Cic.; cur rum maxima nutrix nox, Ov.

nūtus -ūs, m. (*nuo), a nod. LIT., Verg., Ov esp. as an expression of will: signaque d(nutu, Ov.; Caes., Liv. TRANSF., (1) comman(will: deorum nutu, Cic.; auctoritate nutuq(deorum, Cic.; annuite nutum numenq(vestrum invictum Campanis, Liv.; saev nutu Iunonis eunt res, Verg. (2) gravitatio downward movement: Cic.

nux nŭcis, f. a nut. LIT., Pl., Verg., etc prov.: nux cassa, something entirely worthles Hor. TRANSF., (1) of similar fruit: castane: nuces, chestnuts, Verg. (2) a nut-tree, e.g. (almond-tree: Verg.

Nўctēlĭus -i, m. (Νυκτέλιος), belonging (Bacchus (because his mysteries were cele brated by night): Ov.

nympha -ae, f. and **nymphē** -ēs, f. (νύμφ(LIT., (1) a bride: Ov. (2) Nymphae, t(Nymphs, spirits believed to inhabit se(streams, woods, etc., Cic., Verg. TRANSI water: Prop.

Nymphaeum -i, n. (Νυμφαῖον), a promontor(and sea-port in Illyria.

Nÿsa (**Nyssa**) -ae, f. (Νύσα), a city whe Bacchus was said to have been brought up.

¶ Hence adj. **Nÿsaeus** -a -um, Nÿsea(f. adj. **Nÿsēïs** -idis, Nÿsean; **Nÿsēus** -(m.=Bacchus; f. adj. **Nÿsĭās** -ădis, of Bacchu(m. adj. **Nÿsĭgĕna** -ae, born in Nysa.

O

O, o, the fourteenth letter of the Latin Alphabe corresponding to the two Greek lette(Omicron and Omega (O, o, Ω, ω). For t(use of O. in abbreviations, see Table (Abbreviations.

ŏ! interj., *oh!* an exclamation of joy, astonishment, pain, etc. With voc., in addresses: o paterni generis oblite! Cic. With nom. or acc., calling attention to person or thing: o me miserum! Cic.; o fortunata mors! Cic. In wishes: o utinam, o si, *if only!* Verg., Hor., Ov. Sometimes as the second word of a phrase: spes o fidissima Teucrum! Ov.

Ŏărĭōn -ōnis, m. ('Ωαρίων)=Orion; q.v.

Ŏaxes -is, m. ('Ωαξις), *a river in Crete*: Verg.

ŏb, prep. with acc. (1) *in front of, before*: ignis qui est ob os effusus, Cic.; ob oculos versari, Cic.; Pl., Liv., etc. (2) *in return for*: ager oppositus est pignori ob decem minas, Ter.; Cic., Tac. (3) ob rem, *to the purpose, with advantage*: verum id frustra an ob rem faciam, in vestra manu situm est, Sall.; Pl., Ter. (4) *because of, on account of*; esp. with res, causa, n. of hic, is, etc.: Caes., Cic., Liv.; ob rem iudicandam pecuniam accipere, Cic.; ob iram, Verg., Liv.

ŏbaerātus -a -um, adj. (with compar.) (ob/aes), *in debt*: Liv.; m. as subst., esp. plur. **ŏbaerāti** -ōrum, *debtors*: Caes., Cic., Liv.

ŏbambŭlo -are, *to walk up and down, walk about near*; with dat.: muris, Liv.; with acc.: Aetnam, Ov.; with prep: ante vallum, Liv.; in herbis, Ov.

ŏbarmo -are, *to arm*: dextras securi, Hor.

ŏbăro -are, *to plough up*: Liv.

obba -ae, f. *a beaker, noggin*: Varr., Pers.

Obba -ae, f. *a town in Africa, near Carthage*.

ŏbbrūtesco -ĕre, *to become stupid* or *dull*: Lucr.

obc-, see occ-.

ŏbdo -dĕre -dĭdi -dĭtum, *to place before, put against*. LIT., pessulum ostio, *to bolt the door*, Ter.; fores, *to shut the door*, Ov. TRANSF., nullique malo latus obdit apertum, *presents an unprotected side*, Hor.

ŏbdormisco -dormiscĕre -dormīvi (dormio), *to go to sleep*: Pl., Cic., Suet.

ŏbdūco -dūcĕre -duxi -ductum. (1) *to draw over, draw in front*. LIT., fossam, Caes.; seram, Prop.; of persons, *to bring forward*: Curium competitorem, Cic. L. TRANSF., often with dat. of what one covers or blocks: labor quasi callum dolori, Cic. (2) *to cover*. LIT., trunci obducuntur libro aut cortice, Cic.; Verg., Ov. TRANSF., a, fig.: obducta cicatrix reipublicae, *a closed wound*, Cic.: b, *to swallow*: venenum, Cic.: c, *to wrinkle*: frontem, Hor.: d, *of time, to pass, spend*: diem posterum, Cic. L.

ŏbductĭo -ōnis, f. (obduco), *a covering, veiling*: capitis, Cic.

ŏbducto -are (freq. of obduco), *to bring as a rival*: Pl.

ŏbdūresco -ĕre, *to become hard, harden*. LIT., Prop. TRANSF., *to become hard-hearted*: miser obdurui, Pl.; animus ad dolorem, Cic. L.

ŏbdūro -are, *to be hard against*. TRANSF., *to stand out, hold out, persist*: destinatus obdura, Cat.; perfer et obdura, Ov.; impers.: obduretur hoc triduum, Cic. L.

ŏbēdĭens=oboediens; q.v.

ŏbēdio=oboedio; q.v.

ŏbēliscus -i, m. (ὀβελίσκος), *a pointed column, obelisk*: Plin.

ŏbĕo -ire -ivi and -ii -itum. (1) intransit., *to go to, go to meet, go*

against: ad omnes hostium conatus, *to oppose*, Liv.; in infera loca, Cic.; Lucr. Esp.: a, of the heavenly bodies, *to set*: in reliquis orientis aut obeuntis solis partibus, Cic.: b, *to die*: tecum vivere amem, tecum obeam libens, Hor. (2) transit., a, *to go to, over, traverse*: quantum flamma obire non potuisset, Cic.; provinciam, Cic.; clipeum obit pellis circumdata, Verg.; hence, *to go over, encompass*, by looking or speaking: Cic., Verg.: b, *to enter upon, engage in, apply oneself to* any undertaking; *to perform, execute*: negotium, Cic.; hereditatem, Cic.; bella, Liv.; pugnas, Verg.; vadimonium, *to discharge one's bail, to appear at the fixed time*, Cic.: c, with diem or mortem, *to die* (like obeo intransit.; see above): diem suum, Pl.; diem supremum, Nep.; mortem, Pl., Cic., Verg., Liv.; pass.: morte obitā, Lucr.

ŏbĕquĭto -are, *to ride up to*; with dat.: castris, Liv.

ŏberro -are, *to wander about*: tentoriis, Tac. TRANSF., chordā eādem, *to blunder over*, Hor.

ŏbēsĭtās -ātis, f. (obesus), *fatness, corpulence*: Suet.

ŏbēsus -a -um (ob/edo), *fat, plump*: turdus, Hor.; fauces, *swollen*, Verg. TRANSF., *coarse, unrefined*: iuvenis naris obesae, Hor.

ōbex -ĭcis, m. and f. (obicio). LIT., *bolt, bar, barrier, barricade*: fultosque emuniit obice postes, Verg.; viarum, Liv. TRANSF., *an obstacle, hindrance*: Plin.

obf-, see off-.

obg-, see ogg-.

ŏbhaerĕo -ēre, *to stick to, cleave to*: Suet.

ŏbhaeresco -haerescĕre -haesi -haesum, *to stick fast, adhere to*: Lucr., Suet.

ŏbiăcĕo -ēre, *to lie at, lie against*: saxa obiacentia pedibus, Liv.; Tac.

ōbĭcĭo -icere -iēci -iectum (ob/iacio), *to throw in the way*. LIT., se telis hostium, Cic.; corpus feris, Cic.; carros pro vallo, Caes.; offam Cerbero, Verg.; hastis prae se obiectis, Liv. TRANSF., a, *to expose*: consulem morti, Cic.; se in dimicationes, Cic. (2) *to inspire, cause, produce*: alicui errorem, Cic.; metum et dolorem, Cic.; obicitur animo metus, Cic.; hic aliud maius miseris obicitur, *presents itself*, Verg. (3) *to put before, hold before, as protection* or *obstacle*: Alpium vallum contra transgressionem Gallorum, *to oppose*, Cic.; nubem oculis, Ov. (4) *to bring up* anything as a reproach, *to throw in a person's teeth*: alicui furta, Cic.; Pl., Verg.; interfectos amicos, Tac.; with acc. and infin.: obicit mihi, me ad Baias fuisse, Cic. L.; with quod: non tibi obicio quod spoliasti, Cic.

¶ Hence partic. **obiectus** -a -um. (1) *lying near, opposite to*: insula obiecta Alexandriae, Caes. (2) *exposed to*: fortunae, Cic.; ad omnes casus, Cic. (3) *brought up against* a person; m. pl. as subst., *charges*: Cic., Quint.

obiectātĭo -ōnis, f. (obicio), *a reproach*: Caes.

obiecto -are (freq. of obicio), *to throw in the way, set against*. LIT. (of birds): caput fretis, *to dip, dive into*, Verg. TRANSF., (1) *to expose*: aliquem periculis, Sall.; se hostium telis, Liv.; caput periclis, Verg. (2) *to bring up* anything as a reproach, *to throw in a person's teeth*: alicui probrum, Cic.; with acc. and infin.: nobilitas obiectare Fabio fugisse eum Ap. Claudium conlegam, Liv.

¹**obiectus** -a -um, partic. from obicio; q.v.

²**obiectus** -ūs, m. (obicio), *a placing against, putting opposite*: insula portum efficit obiectu laterum, Verg.; Caes., Tac.

ŏbīrascor -irasci -īrātus sum, dep. *to grow angry at*; with dat.: fortunae, *with fortune*, Liv., Sen.

ŏbĭtĕr, adv. (ob), *on the way, in passing, on the journey*: Juv., Plin. TRANSF., *by the way, incidentally*: Juv., Plin.

ŏbĭtus -ūs, m. (obeo), *an approaching, going to*: Ter.; esp. of the heavenly bodies, *setting*: siderum, Cic. TRANSF., *death, downfall, destruction*: post obitum vel potius excessum Romuli, Cic.; Caes., Verg.

obiurgātĭo -ōnis, f. (ob/urgo), *a blaming, chiding, reproving*: Cic.

obiurgātor -ōris, m. (obiurgo), *a scolder, chider, reprover*: Cic., Sen.

obiurgātōrĭus -a -um (obiurgator), *reproachful, chiding*: epistula, Cic. L.

obiurgo -are, *to scold, chide, reprove, blame*. LIT., aliquem molli bracchio de Pompeii familiaritate, Cic. L.; meam verecundiam, Cic. L.; cum obiurgarer, quod nimiā laetitiā paene desiperem, Cic. L. TRANSF., *to chastise*: Pers., Suet.

oblanguesco -languescĕre -langui, *to become languid*: Cic.

oblātrātrix -īcis, f. (oblatro), *a railer*: Pl.

oblātro -are, *to bark at*; hence, *to rail at, scold*: Suet., Sen.

oblectāmen -inis, n. (oblecto), *a delight, pleasure*: Ov.

oblectāmentum -i, n. (oblecto), *a delight, amusement, pastime*: meae senectutis requies oblectamentumque, Cic.; rerum rusticarum, Cic., Liv.

oblectātĭo -ōnis, f. (oblecto), *a delighting, amusing*: animi, Cic.

oblecto -are (cf. delecto), *to attract, draw*. Hence (1) *to please, amuse*: cum eorum inventis scriptisque se oblectent, Cic.; se in hortis, Cic.; legentium animos fictis, Tac.; me cum aliqua re, Cic. (2) *to pass time pleasantly, while away* time: lacrimabile tempus studio, Ov.; senectutem, Cic.

oblēnĭo -ire (lenis), *to soothe*: Sen.

oblīdo -līdĕre -līsi -līsum (ob/laedo), *to crush*: collum digitulis duobus, *to throttle*, Cic.; oblisis faucibus, *strangled*, Tac.

oblĭgātĭo -ōnis, f. (obligo), *a bond, tie*: obligatio pecuniae, Cic.

oblĭgātus -a -um, partic. from obligo; q.v.

oblĭgo -are, *to bind, fasten to*. LIT., *to tie, bind up, bandage a wound*: vulnus, Cic.; medicum requirens a quo obligetur, Cic.; venas, Tac. TRANSF., (1) *to bind, oblige, make liable, put under a legal* or *religious obligation*: se nexu, Cic.; aliquem militiae sacramento, Cic.; foedere, Liv.; poet.: obligatam redde Iovi dapem, *that is due*, Hor.; praedia obligata, *mortgaged*, Cic. (2) *to make liable to punishment, make guilty*: populum scelere, Cic.; votis caput, Hor.; obligari fraude impiā, Cic. (3) *to put under a personal obligation*: aliquem sibi liberalitate, Cic. L.; Ov.

¶ Hence partic. **oblĭgātus** -a -um, *boun under an obligation*: obligatus ei nihil eran Cic. L.; compar.: Plin. L.

oblīmo -are (ob/limus), *to cover with slime* mud: agros, Cic.; sulcos, Verg. TRANSF rem patris, Hor.

oblīno -linĕre -lēvi -litum, *to smear, daub besmear*. LIT., obliti unguentis, Cic.; oblitu faciem suo cruore, Tac.; Ov. TRANSF., (1) *to stain, pollute, defile*: oblitu parricidio, Cic.; aliquem versibus atri Hor. (2) in perf. partic. oblitus -a -un *overloaded*: oblitus divitiis, Hor.

oblīquē, adv. from obliquus; q.v.

oblīquo -are (obliquus), *to make oblique, tur sideways, turn aside*: oculos, Ov.; Verg., Tac

oblīquus -a -um, *slanting, sideways, on one sid* LIT., partim obliquos, partim aversos partim etiam adversos stare vobis, Cic amnis cursibus obliquis fluens, Ov.; Liv N. as subst.: ab obliquo, *sideways, obliquel* Ov.; per obliquum, Hor. TRANSF., (1) of speech, *indirect, covert*: in sectatio, Tac.; oratio, *quoted speech*, Quin (2) *looking askance, envious*: invidia, Verg Hor.

¶ Adv. **oblīquē**, *sideways, aslant, obliquely* ferri, Cic.; Caes. TRANSF., *indirectl covertly, by implication*: Tac.

oblītesco -litescĕre -lĭtŭi (ob/latesco), *to hid conceal oneself*: a nostro aspectu, Cic., Sen.

oblittĕro -are (littera), *to cancel, blot out* nomina, *debts*, Tac. TRANSF., *to blot out o memory*: famam rei, Liv.; publici m beneficii memoriā privatam offensione oblitterarunt, Cic.

oblīvĭo -ōnis, f. (obliviscor), *forgetfulnes oblivion*. (1) pass.: laudem alicuius a oblivione atque a silentio vindicare, Cic dare aliquid oblivioni, Liv.; Hor. (2) act. in oblivionem negotii venire, *to forget*, Cic Tac.

oblīvĭōsus -a -um (oblivio). (1) *obliviou forgetful*: Cic. (2) *causing forgetfulnes* Massicum, Hor.

oblīviscor oblivisci oblītus sum, dep. (perhap connected with oblino), *to forget*. LIT., with genit.: temporum suorum Cic.; Verg., etc.; with acc. of thing: iniuria Cic.; Verg., etc.; with infin.: Ter., Ov with acc. and infin.: obliviscor Roscium — Cluvium viros esse primarios, Cic. Gerun dive and perf. partic. in pass. sense: Verg Hor. TRANSF., *to forget, lose sight of*: consue tudinis suae, Cic.; sui, *to forget onese* Cic., Verg.; poet., of things: sucos oblit priores, Verg.

oblīvĭum -i, n. (obliviscor), usually plu *oblivion, forgetfulness*: rerum, Lucr.; age oblivia laudis, *to forget*, Ov.; Verg., Tac.

oblongus -a -um, *oblong*: Tac.

oblŏquor -loqui -locutus sum, dep. *to spe against*. Hence (1) *to interrupt*: Pl. (2) answer back, contradict*; with dat.: Cic. L Liv. (3) *to abuse, chide*: Cat. (4) in musi *to accompany*: non avis obloquitur, Ov Verg.

obluctor -ari, dep. *to struggle against*: genib adversae harenae, Verg.; morti, Luc.

oblūdo -ĕre, *to play tricks on*: Pl.

obmōlĭor -iri, dep. *to build* or *pile against* (as a barrier or defence): nec in promptu erat quod obmolirentur, Liv.

obmurmŭro -are, *to roar against*; with dat.: precibus, Ov.

obmūtesco -mūtescĕre -mūtŭi, *to become dumb, become speechless.*

LIT., vocem mittenti non et linguam obmutuisse et manum obtorpuisse, Cic.; ego neque Antonium verbum facere patiar et ipse obmutescam, Cic.; Verg.

TRANSF., *to cease*: dolor animi obmutuit, Cic.

obnātus -a -um (*obnascor), *growing on*: obnata ripis salicta, *growing on the bank*, Liv.

obnītor -niti -nixus sum, dep. *to press against.*

LIT., taurus arboris obnixus trunco, Verg.; scutis corporibusque ipsis obnixi, Liv.; hence, *to take up a stand, maintain a firm position*: stant obnixa omnia contra, Verg.; Liv.

TRANSF., *to strive against, oppose*: consilio hostium, Tac.; Verg.

¶ Hence, from partic. obnixus, adv. **obnixē**, *firmly, vigorously*: Ter.

obnoxĭē, adv. from obnoxius; q.v.

obnoxĭōsus -a -um (obnoxius), *submissive, compliant*: Pl. Compar. adv. **obnoxĭōsĭus**, *more submissively*: Pl.

obnoxĭus -a -um (ob/noxa), *liable.* (1) *liable to punishment*: Pl., Liv. (2) *addicted to, guilty of*; with dat.: animus neque delicto neque lubidini obnoxius, Sall.; Ov. (3) *indebted, obliged, subject, obedient*: subiecti atque obnoxii vobis, Liv.; luna radiis fratris obnoxia, *dependent on*, Verg.; totam Graeciam beneficio libertatis obnoxiam Romanis, Liv. (4) *subject to, exposed to*: arbores quae frigoribus obnoxiae sunt, Liv.; terra bello, Ov.; urbs incendiis, Tac.

obnūbo -nūbĕre -nupsi -nuptum, *to cover*: comas amictu, Verg.; caput, ap. Cic., ap. Liv.

obnuntĭātĭo -ōnis, f. (obnuntio), in the language of augurs, *the announcement of an unfavourable omen*: Cic.

obnuntĭo -are, in the language of augurs, *to report an unfavourable omen*: consuli, Cic.

ŏboedĭentĭa -ae, f. (oboediens), *obedience, compliance*: Cic.

ŏboedĭo -ire (ob/audio). (1) *to give ear to, listen to*: alicui, Nep. (2) *to obey*; with dat.: praecepto, Cic.; magistratibus, Cic. TRANSF., tempori, Cic.

¶ Hence partic. (with compar. and superl.: Liv.) **ŏboedĭens** -entis, *obedient, compliant*; with dat.: nulli est naturae oboediens aut subiectus deus, Cic.; with dicto added: Liv.; with ad and the acc.: ad nova consilia, Liv. TRANSF., ventri, Sall.

¶ Adv. **ŏboedĭentĕr**, *obediently*: oboedienter imperata facere, Liv.; compar.: Liv.

ŏbŏlĕo -ēre, *to smell of anything, emit an odour*: Pl.

ŏbŏrĭor -ŏriri -ortus sum, dep. *to arise, appear.* LIT., lux, tenebrae, lacrimae, Liv.; Verg., etc. TRANSF., vide quanta lux liberalitatis et sapientiae tuae mihi apud te dicenti oboriatur, Cic.; bellum, indignatio, Liv.

obp-, *see* **opp-**.

obrēpo -rēpĕre -repsi -reptum, *to creep, to crawl up to.* LIT., Tib. TRANSF., *to steal upon, come on by surprise*; with dat.: senectus adulescentiae obrepit, Cic.; ad honores, Cic.; imagines obrepunt in animos dormientium, Cic.; with acc.: Pl., Sall.

obrepto -are (freq. of obripio), *to steal upon*: Pl.

obrētĭo -ire (ob/rete), *to catch in a net*: Lucr.

obrĭgesco -rĭgescĕre -rĭgŭi, *to become stiff*, esp. *to freeze*: nive pruināque, Cic. TRANSF., Sen.

obrōdo -ĕre, *to gnaw at*: Pl.

obrŏgo -are, *to amend* or *repeal a law by introducing another*: with dat.: Cic., Liv.

obrŭo -rŭĕre -rŭi -rŭtum; fut. partic. -rŭitūrus. Transit., *to cover over, to bury.* Intransit., *to fall, collapse*: Lucr.

LIT., sese harenā, Cic.; thesaurum, Cic.; obruere aliquem terrā; Verg., Liv.; esp. with water, *to swamp, drown*: submersas obrue puppes, Verg.; Ov.; hence: se vino, Cic.

TRANSF., (1) *to overwhelm, distress*: testem omnium risus obruit, *overwhelmed*, Cic.; obrui aere alieno, Cic.; obrutus criminibus, Cic.; Verg. (2) *to destroy, obliterate*: ut adversa quasi perpetuā oblivione obruamus, Cic.; Marius talis viri interitu sex suos obruit consulatūs, *obscured the fame of his six consulships*, Cic.; famam alicuius, Tac.

obrussa -ae, f. (ὄβρυζον), *the essaying of gold by fire.* LIT., Plin., Suet. TRANSF., Suet.; adhĭbenda tamquam obrussa ratio, *as a test*, Cic.; Sen.

obsaepĭo -saepire -saepsi -saeptum, *to fence in, enclose, block up, render inaccessible.* LIT., hostium agmina obsaepiunt iter Liv.; Tac. TRANSF., plebi iter ad curules magistratus, Liv.; Cic.

obsătŭro -are, *to stuff, choke*: Ter.

obscēnē, adv. from obscenus; q.v.

obscēnĭtās (**obscaenĭtās**) -atis, f. (obscenus), *impurity, indecency, obscenity*: verborum, Cic.; Suet.

obscēnus (**obscaenus**) -a -um, adj. (with compar. and superl.).

(1) *foul, repulsive, filthy.* LIT., volucres, *the Harpies*, Verg. TRANSF., *morally impure, indecent, obscene*: voluptates, Cic.; iocandi genus, Cic.; dicta, risus, Ov.

(2) *ill-omened, unpropitious*: volucres, owls, Verg.; Hor., Liv.

¶ Adv. (with compar.) **obscēnē** (**obscaenē**), *indecently*: Cic.

obscūrātĭo -ōnis, f. (obscuro), *a darkening*: solis, Cic. TRANSF., *disappearance*: Cic.

obscūrē, adv. from obscurus; q.v.

obscūrĭtās -ātis, f. (obscurus), *darkness, obscurity.*

LIT., latebrarum, Cic.; lucis, Liv.

TRANSF., (1) of language, *obscurity, unintelligibleness*: oratio quae lumen adhibere rebus debet, ea obscuritatem adfert, Cic.; verborum, Cic. (2) of condition, *obscurity, low birth*: Cic., Tac.

obscūro -are (obscurus), *to cover, darken, obscure.*

LIT., obscuratur luce solis lumen lucernae, Cic.; caelum nocte atque nubibus obscuratum, Sall.; Verg.; in gen., *to conceal*: Hor.

TRANSF., (1) *to veil, obscure, make unintelligible*: nihil dicendo, Cic. (2) *to hide, suppress*: fortuna res celebrat obscuratque, Sall.; eorum memoria obscurata est, Cic.

obscūrus -a -um, adj. (with compar.), *covered, dark, obscure*. Lit., lucus, Verg.; nox, Verg.; locus, Liv.; n. as subst., *darkness*: sub obscurum noctis, Verg.; of persons: ibant obscuri, *in the dark, darkling*, Verg. Transf., (1) of language, *obscure, unintelligible, indistinct*: Heraclitus obscurus, Cic.; brevis esse laboro, obscurus fio, Hor. (2) *unknown, obscure, not celebrated*: Pompeius humili atque obscuro loco natus, *of humble origin*, Cic.; n. as subst.: in obscuro vitam habere, Sall. (3) *gloomy*: Cic. (4) of character, *secret, reserved, close*: homo, Cic.; adversus alios, Tac.
¶ Hence adv. (with compar.) **obscūrē**. Lit., *darkly*: Cic. Transf., (1) *unintelligibly*: Quint. (2) *secretly*: Cic.

obsecrātĭo -ōnis, f. (obsecro), *an earnest entreaty, supplication*: obsecratione humili ac supplici uti, Cic. Esp., *a public prayer to the gods*: obsecratio a populo duumviris praeeuntibus facta, Liv.; Suet.

obsecro -are (ob/sacro), *to beseech earnestly, implore, entreat*: aliquem multis lacrimis, Cic.; obsecro te, ut id facias, Cic.; te hoc ut, Cic.; vostram fidem, Pl. Sometimes as a polite phrase, *pray, I beg*: Attica mea, obsecro te, quid agit? Cic.; Pl., Liv.

obsĕcundo -are, *to comply with, fall in with*: voluntatibus alicuius, Cic.; Ter., Liv.

obsēpĭo=obsaepio; q.v.

obsĕquēlla -ae, f. (obsequor), *compliance*: Pl., Sall.

obsĕquens -entis, partic. from obsequor; q.v.

obsĕquentĭa -ae, f. (obsequens), *complaisance*: Caes.

obsĕquĭōsus -a -um (obsequium), *compliant, yielding*: Pl.

obsĕquĭum -i, n. (obsequor), *compliance, complaisance, submission*. Lit., in populum Romanum, Liv.; obsequium erga aliquem exuere, Tac. Transf., (1) *indulgence*: ventris, *gluttony*, Hor. (2) of inanimate objects, *pliancy*: flectitur obsequio curvatus ab arbore ramus, Ov.

obsĕquor -sĕqui -sĕcūtus sum, dep. *to comply with, yield to, obey*. Lit., with dat., *obey*: tibi roganti, Cic.; neque, uti de M. Pompilio referrent, senatui obsequebantur, Liv. Transf., *to give in to* anything, *give oneself up to*: tempestati, Cic. L.; alicuius voluntati, Cic.
¶ Hence partic. **obsĕquens** -entis, *compliant, yielding, obedient*: patri, Ter., Cic. L.; of the gods, *favourable, gracious*: Pl.
¶ Adv. **obsĕquentĕr**, *compliantly, obediently*: haec facere, Liv.; Plin. L.

¹obsĕro -are, *to bolt, bar*: plebis aedificiis obseratis, Liv.; Ter. Transf., aures, Hor.

²obsĕro -sĕrĕre -sēvi -sĭtum. (1) *to sow* ground *thickly, cover* with seeds, etc. Lit., omnia arbustis, Lucr.; terram frugibus, Cic. Transf., esp. in partic. **obsĭtus** -a -um, *full of, covered with, beset by*: obsitus aevo, Verg.; vestis obsita squalore, Liv.; legati obsiti squalore et sordibus, Liv. (2) *to sow* seed *thickly*: frumentum, Pl. Transf., malos mores, Pl.

observans -antis, partic. from observo; q.v.

observantĭa -ae, f. (observans), *respect, attention*: observantia est, per quam aetate aut sapientiā, aut honore, aut aliquā dignitā antecedentes veremur et colimus, Cic.; i regem, Liv.

observātĭo -ōnis, f. (observo), *an observing, watching*. Lit., siderum, Cic.; Pl. Transf. *care, accuracy, circumspection*: summa era observatio in bello movendo, Cic.

observātor -ōris, m. (observo), *an observer, watcher*: Sen., Plin.

observĭto -are (freq. of observo), *to wato carefully*: motus stellarum, Cic.

observo -are, *to watch, observe, regar attend to*. Lit., occupationem alicuius, Cic.; tempu epistulae alicui reddendae, Cic. L.; hence, t *guard, keep*: greges, Ov. Transf., (1) of rules and arrangements *to keep, regard, observe*: leges, Cic.; prae ceptum, Caes. (2) of persons *to respect, pa regard to*: me ut alterum patrem, Cic. L. Verg.
¶ Hence partic. (with superl.) **observan** -antis, *attentive, respectful*: observantissimu mei homo, Cic. L.

obsĕs -sĭdis, c. (obsideo), *a hostage*. Lit. obsides accipere, dare, Caes.; Cic., Ov Transf., *a surety, security, pledge*; of persons seque eius rei obsidem fore pollicitus est *that he would be surety for that thing*, Nep. obsides dare, *to give security*, with acc. an infin., Cic.; of things: Cic., Liv.

obsessĭo -ōnis, f. (obsideo), *a blockade besetting*: viae, Cic.; Caes.

obsessor -ōris, m. (obsideo), *one who besets o haunts a place*: vivarum obsessor aquarun (of the water-snake), Ov.; esp., *one wh besieges* or *blockades*: curiae, Cic.; Luceriae Liv.

obsĭdĕo -sĭdēre -sēdi -sessum (ob/sedeo). (1) intransit., *to sit down near*: Pl., Ter. (2) transit. Lit., *to beset, haunt, frequent* aram, Pl.; esp., *to blockade, besiege*: omne aditus, Cic.; urbem, Caes., Liv.; hence, t *block, occupy, fill*: corporibus omnis obsidetu locus, Cic. Transf., *to block, watch over be on the look-out for*: totam Italiam, Cic. meum tempus, Cic.

obsĭdĭo -ōnis, f. (obsideo), *a blockade, siege* Lit., obsidione urbes capere, Cic.; obsidion solvere, eximere, *to raise the siege of* a place Liv.; Verg., Tac. Transf., *pressing danger* rempublicam liberare obsidione, Cic.

¹obsĭdĭum -i, n. (obsideo), *a blockade, siege besetting*. Lit., occupare obsidio Lace daemonis exercitum, Liv.; Tac. Transf *pressing danger*: Pl.

²obsĭdĭum -i, n. (obses), *the condition of hostage*: Tac.

obsīdo -sīdĕre -sēdi -sessum, *to blockad besiege, invest*: pontem, Sall.; milite campo Verg.; Liv.

obsignātor -ōris, m. (obsigno), *one who seal a sealer*: litterarum, Cic.; esp., *a witness to will*: testamenti, Cic. L.

obsigno -are, *to seal*. Lit., epistulam, Ci Esp., of a witness, *to sign and seal a document* Cic.; agere cum aliquo tabellis obsignatis, *t deal with anyone in strict form of law*, Ci Transf., *to stamp, impress*: formam verbi Lucr.

obsisto -sistĕre -stĭti -stĭtum, *to stand, place oneself before* or *in the way of*. LIT., alicui abeunti, Liv.; Pl. TRANSF., *to oppose, withstand, resist*: omnibus eius consiliis, Cic.; minis vatum, Lucr.; foll. by ne and the subj.: Cic., Nep.; by infin.: Tac.

obsĭtus -a -um, partic. from ²obsero; q.v.

obsŏlĕfīo -fieri -factus sum, *to become worn out*; hence, *to be degraded*: obsolefiebant dignitatis insignia, Cic.; Sen.

obsŏlesco -escĕre -ēvi -ētum, *to go out of use, decay, wear out*: oratio, Cic.; res per vetustatem, Cic.; laus, Tac.
¶ Hence partic. (with compar.) **obsŏlētus** -a -um, *worn out, decayed*. LIT., vestitu obsoletiore, Cic.; obsoletus Thessalonicam venisti, *dressed in old clothes*, Cic.; verba, *obsolete*, Cic. TRANSF., *threadbare, poor, ordinary*: crimina, Cic.; oratio, Cic.; gaudia, Liv.
¶ Compar. adv. **obsŏlētĭus**, *more shabbily*: Cic.

obsŏnātor -oris, m. (obsono), *a caterer*: Pl., Sen.

obsŏnĭum -i, n. (ὀψώνιον), *that which is eaten with bread*; e.g., *vegetables, fruit*, and esp. *fish*: Pl., Hor.

¹obsŏno -are and **obsōnor** -ari, dep. (ὀψωνέω), *to buy food, cater, provide a meal*: Pl., Ter. TRANSF., ambulando famem, *to buy the sauce of hunger*, Cic.

²obsŏno -are, *to interrupt by noise*: Pl.

obsorbĕo -ēre -ŭi, *to swallow, gulp down*: Pl., Hor.

obstetrix -īcis, f. (obsto), *a midwife*: Pl., Ter., Hor.

obstĭnātĭo -ōnis, f. (obstino), *resolution, persistence, firmness, obstinacy*: sententiae, Cic.; fidei, Tac.

obstĭno -are, *to persist in, be resolved on*; with acc.: Pl.; with infin.: obstinaverant animis aut vincere aut mori, Liv.; with ad: Tac.
¶ Hence partic. (with compar.; and superl.: Sen.) **obstĭnātus** -a -um, *resolved, persistent, firm, obstinate*: obstinatior voluntas, Cic.; obstinatior adversus lacrimas muliebres, Liv.; Tac.; with infin.: mori, Liv.
¶ Adv. **obstĭnātē**, *resolutely, persistently, obstinately*: negare, Caes.; Pl.; compar. and superl.: Suet.

obstĭpesco=obstupesco; q.v.

obstĭpus -a -um. (1) *leaning to one side* (opp. rectus): Lucr. (2) *bent back*: cervix (of a haughty person), Suet. (3) *bent* or *bowed down*: capite obstipo, Hor.

obsto -stare -stĭti -stātūrus. (1) *to stand at, before, against*: Pl. (2) *to stand in the way, to oppose, resist, hinder, obstruct*; with dat.: alicui, Pl.; meis commodis, Cic.; Verg.; vita cetera eorum huic sceleri obstat, *is inconsistent with*, Sall. With quin, quominus, ne and the subj.: quid obstat, quominus sit beatus? Cic.; ea ne impedirent tribuni, dictatoris obstitit metus, Liv.; with cur non: Ter.
¶ Hence n. pl. of pres. partic. as subst. **obstantĭa**, *hindrances, obstacles, impediments*: Tac.

obstrĕpo -strĕpĕre -strĕpŭi -strĕpĭtum. Intransit., *to make a noise, clamour at* or *against*: nihil sensere Poeni, obstrepente pluviā, Liv.; fontesque lymphis obstrepunt manantibus, Hor.; with dat.: obstrepunt portis,

Liv. Hence, *to disturb, interrupt by clamour*: sibi ipsi, Cic.; impers.: decemviro obstrepitur, Liv.; in gen., *to disturb, molest*: tibi litteris, Cic.
Transit., in pass. only. (1) *to be drowned by noise*: Cic. (2) *to be filled with noise*: Ov.

obstringo -stringĕre -strinxi -strictum, *to bind, bind up, tie fast*. LIT., ventos, Hor.; Pl. TRANSF., (1) *to put under an obligation*: civitatem iureiurando, *to bind by an oath*, Caes.; aliquem legibus, Cic.; beneficio obstrictus, Cic. (2) *to entangle, involve*: aliquem aere alieno, *in debt*, Cic.; se tot sceleribus, Cic.; se periurio, Liv.

obstructĭo -ōnis, f. (obstruo), *a hindrance, obstruction*: Cic.

obstrūdo=obtrudo; q.v.

obstrŭo -strŭĕre -struxi -structum, *to build against*.
LIT., pro diruto novum murum, Liv.; luminibus alicuius, *to block up the light, build before the windows*, Cic.; hence, *to block up, close*: portas, Caes.; aditus, Cic.; iter Poenis (*to the Carthaginians*) vel corporibus suis, Cic.
TRANSF., *to block, stop*: obstruere perfugia improborum, Cic.; viri deus obstruit aures, Verg.

obstŭpĕfăcĭo -făcĕre -fēci -factum, *to astound, stupefy, render senseless*; pass. **obstŭpĕfīo** -fīeri -factus sum, *to be astounded*: ipso miraculo audaciae obstupefecit hostes, Liv.; obstupefactis hominibus ipsā admiratione, Cic.

obstŭpesco (**obstĭpesco**) -stŭpescĕre -stŭpŭi, *to become senseless, to be astounded*: cum eorum aspectu obstipuisset bubulcua, Cic.; Verg.

obsum obesse obfŭi, *to be in the way, be against, be prejudicial to*; with dat.: obsunt auctoribus artes, Ov.; obest Clodii mors Miloni, Cic.; with infin.: nihil obest dicere, Cic.; Ov.

obsŭo -sŭĕre -sŭi -sūtum. (1) *to sew on*: caput, Ov. (2) *to sew up, close up*: spiritus oris obsuitur, Verg.

obsurdesco -descĕre -dŭi, *to become deaf.* LIT., hoc sonitu oppletae aures hominum obsurduerunt, Cic. TRANSF., *to turn a deaf ear*: Cic.

obtĕgo -tĕgĕre -texi -tectum, *to cover up.* Hence (1) *to protect*: se servorum et libertorum corporibus, Cic.; eam partem castrorum vineis, Caes. (2) *to conceal*: domus arboribus obtecta, Verg. TRANSF., *vitia multis virtutibus obtecta, Cic.
¶ Hence partic. **obtĕgens** -entis, *concealing*; with genit.: animus sui obtegens, Tac.

obtempĕrātĭo -ōnis, f. (obtempero), *compliance, obedience*: legibus, Cic.

obtempĕro -are, *to comply with, conform to, submit to*; with dat.: alicui, Cic.; imperio populi Romani, Caes.; with ad: ut ad verba nobis obediant, ad id, quod ex verbis intellegi possit, obtemperent, Cic.

obtendo -tendĕre -tendi -tentum.
(1) *to stretch before, spread before.* LIT., pro viro nebulam, Verg.; obtentā nocte, *under the shelter of night*, Verg.; Britannia Germaniae obtenditur, *lies opposite to*, Tac. TRANSF., *to forward as an excuse, plead,*

allege: matris preces, Tac.; valetudinem corporis, Tac.

(2) *to cover*, by interposing something, *to conceal*: diem nube atrā, Tac. TRANSF., quasi velis quibusdam obtenditur unius cuiusque natura, Cic.

¹**obtentus** -ūs, m. (obtendo), *a stretching* or *spreading before*. LIT., frondis, Verg. TRANSF., *a pretext, pretence, excuse*: tempora reipublicae obtentui sumpta, *taken as an excuse*, Tac.; sub eius obtentu cognominis, Liv.; Sall.

²**obtentus** -a -um, partic. from obtineo; q.v.

³**obtentus** -a -um, partic. from obtendo; q.v.

obtĕro -tĕrĕre -trīvi -trītum (syncop. pluperf. subj., obtrisset: Liv.), *to trample, crush*. LIT., obtriti sunt plures quam ferro necati, Liv. TRANSF., *to crush, destroy*: calumniam, Cic.; iura populi, Liv.

obtestātĭo -ōnis, f. (obtestor), *a solemn calling of gods to witness, an adjuring in the name of the gods*: obtestatio et consecratio legis, Cic.; tua obtestatio tibicinis, Cic. TRANSF., *an earnest entreaty*: Cic. L., Liv., Tac.

obtestor -ari, dep. *to call as witness*. LIT., deum hominumque fidem, Liv.; Cic., Tac. TRANSF., *to adjure, implore, entreat in the name of the gods*: per omnes deos te obtestor ut, Cic.; Verg.

obtexo -texĕre -texŭi, *to weave on, weave over*: Plin. TRANSF., *to cover*, caelumque obtexitur umbrā, Verg.

obtĭcĕo -ēre (ob/taceo), *to be silent*: Ter.

obtĭcesco -ticescĕre -ticŭi (obticeo), *to become quiet*: Pl., Hor., Ov.

obtĭnĕo -tinēre -tinŭi -tentum (ob/teneo).

(1) transit.: **a**, *to hold, possess, keep possession of*. LIT., suam quisque suam domum, Cic.; esp. milit. t. t.: vada custodiis, Cic.; citeriorem ripam armis, Liv.; Caes. TRANSF., **a**, *to hold, maintain*: principem locum, *to hold the chief place*, Caes.; auctoritatem, Cic.; hereditatem, Cic.; ius suum contra aliquem, Cic.; causam, *to carry one's point*, Cic.; esp., *to maintain an assertion*: duas contrarias sententias, Cic.: **b**, *to take hold of, grasp*. LIT., aures, Pl. TRANSF., ad obtinendam sapientiam, Cic.; Caes., Liv.

(2) intransit., *to hold, obtain, continue*: fama obtinuit, Liv.; pro vero obtinebat, Sall.

obtingo -tingĕre -tĭgi (ob/tango), *to fall to the lot of anyone, to happen, befall*: quod cuique obtigit, is quisque teneat, Cic.; cum tibi aquaria provincia sorte obtigisset, Cic.; si quid mihi obtigerit, *if anything should happen to me*, i.e. *if I should die*, Cic.; Pl., Ter.

obtorpesco -torpescĕre -torpŭi, *to become stiff, numb, insensible*: et linguam obmutuisse et manum obtorpuisse, Cic.; manus prae metu, Liv.; obtorpuerunt quodam modo animi, Liv.

obtorquĕo -torquēre -torsi -tortum, *to twist towards, to wrench, twist round* (usually found in perf. partic.): obtortā gulā in vincula abripi iussit, Cic.; Pl., Verg.

obtrectātĭo -ōnis, f. (obtrecto), *disparagement, detraction*: obtrectatio est aegritudo ex eo, quod alter quoque potiatur eo, quod ipse concupiverit, Cic.; laudis, Caes.; Liv.

obtrectātor -ōris, m. (obtrecto), *a detractor, disparager*: obtrectatores et invidi Scipionis Cic.; Quint.

obtrecto -are (ob/tracto), *to disparage, detract from*; with dat.: alicui, Cic.; gloriae alicuius Liv.; inter se, Nep.; with acc.: eius laudes Liv.; Tac.

obtrūdo (**obstrūdo**) -trūdĕre -trūsi -trūsum *to thrust upon*. Hence (1) *to gulp down, swallow down*: Pl. (2) *to force, obtrude* anything *upon*: virginem alicui, Ter.; Pl.

obtrunco -are, *to cut down*: gallum, Pl.; cervos Verg.; regem, Liv.

obtŭĕor -ēri, dep. and **obtŭor** -i, dep. *to look at, gaze at, behold*: Pl.

obtundo -tundĕre -tŭdi -tūsum and tunsum *to beat upon, thump*. LIT., os mihi, Pl.; also *to make dull by striking*: telum, Lucr. TRANSF., (1) *to make blunt, dull, weaken*: vocem, Lucr., Liv.; ingenia, Cic. (2) *to pound at, weary*: aures, Pl., Cic.; aliquem, Ter., Cic.

¶ Hence partic. (with compar.) **obtūsus** and **obtunsus** -a -um, *dull, blunt*. LIT., pugio, Tac.; Lucr., Verg. TRANSF., (1) *blurred, dulled*: neque tum stellis acies obtusa videtur, Verg. (2) of the intellect, *dulled, blunted*: animi obtusior acies, Cic.; Tac. (3) of feeling, *insensible*: pectora, Verg.

obturbo -are, *to disturb, put into confusion*. LIT., hostes, Tac. TRANSF., *to distract, harass*: obturbabatur militum vocibus, Tac.; me scriptio et litterae non leniunt sed obturbant, Cic. L.; solitudinem, Cic. L.

obturgesco -ĕre, *to swell up*: Lucr.

obtūro -are, *to stop up*. LIT., eas partes (corporis) obstructas et obturatas esse dicebat, Cic.; Pl. TRANSF., alicui aures, *to refuse to listen*, Hor.

obtūsus -a -um, partic. from obtundo; q.v.

obtūtus -ūs, m. (obtueor), *a looking at, gaze*: oculorum, Cic.; dum stupet obtutuque haeret defixus in uno, Verg. TRANSF., *contemplation*: Ov.

ŏbumbro -are, *to overshadow*. LIT., aethera telis, Verg.; Ov. TRANSF., (1) *to obscure, overcloud*: numquam obscura nomina, etsi aliquando obumbrentur, Tac. (2) *to conceal, protect, cover*: erroris sub imagine crimen, Ov.; Verg.

ŏbuncus -a -um, *bent inwards, hooked*: rostrum, Verg., Ov.

ŏbustus -a -um (ob/uro), *burnt, hardened in the fire*: sudes, Verg. TRANSF., gleba obusta (*pinched*) gelu, Ov.

obvallo -are, *to surround with a wall, wall round*. TRANSF., locus omni ratione obvallatus, Cic.

obvĕnĭo -vĕnire -vēni -ventum, *to come in the way of, to meet*. LIT., se in tempore pugnae obventurum, Liv. TRANSF., (1) *to occur, to happen*: vitium obvenit consuli, Liv. (2) *to fall to the lot of*: Syria Scipioni, Caes.; Liv.

obversor -ari, dep. *to move up and down before, appear before*. LIT., castris, Liv.; Appio in somnis eadem obversata species, *appeared*, Liv.; Plin. L., Tac. TRANSF., sed mihi ante oculos obversatur reipublicae dignitas, *hovers before my eyes*, Cic.; Lucr., Liv.

obversus -a -um, partic. from obverto; q.v.

obverto (**-vorto**) -vertĕre -verti -versum, *to turn towards, direct against*: signa in hostem, Liv.; proras pelago, Verg.; arcūs in aliquem, Ov. Middle, obverti, *to turn towards*: Ov.
¶ Hence partic. **obversus** -a -um, *turned towards*; m. pl. as subst. **obversi**, *opponents*: Tac.

obvĭam, adv. (ob/viam), *in the way, on the way*; hence, with dat., *towards, against, to meet* in a friendly or hostile manner.
LIT., obviam venire, Caes.; obviam alicui ire, prodire, procedere, Cic.; obviam alicui fieri, Cic.; Pl., Liv.
TRANSF., obviam ire. (**1**) *to oppose*: cupiditati hominum, Cic.; Liv. (**2**) *to help, remedy*: Tac.

obvĭgĭlātum -i, n. (ob/vigilo); obvigilato'st opus, *we must watch out*, Pl.

obvĭus -a -um (ob/viam), *in the way, meeting*.
LIT., obvium esse alicui, Cic., Sall.; dare se obvium alicui, *to meet*, Liv.; Verg.; obvias mihi litteras mittas, Cic. L.; esp. of hostility: infesta subit obvius hasta, Verg.; Cic., Sall.
TRANSF., (**1**) *exposed to*: furiis ventorum, Verg. (**2**) *ready at hand*: testes, Tac. (**3**) *affable, easy of access*: comitas, Tac.

obvolvo -volvĕre -volvi -volūtum, *to wrap up, cover all round*. LIT., capite obvoluto, *with head muffled up*, Pl., Cic., Liv. TRANSF., verbisque decoris obvolvas vitium, Hor.

occaeco -are (ob/caeco), *to make blind, to blind*.
LIT., occaecatus pulvere effuso hostis, Liv.
TRANSF., (**1**) *to darken, overcloud*: densa caligo occaecaverat diem, Liv. (**2**) *to conceal, make invisible*: semen, Cic. (**3**) *to make obscure, unintelligible*: obscura narratio totam occaecat orationem, Cic. (**4**) fig., *to blind, dull, benumb*: occaecatus cupiditate, Cic.; consilia, Liv.; artus, Verg.

occallesco -callescĕre -callŭi (ob/calleo), *to become thick-skinned, become hard*. LIT., Pl., Ov. TRANSF., *to become insensible, unfeeling*: Cic. L.

occăno -cănĕre -cănŭi (ob/cano), *to sound*: cornua, Tac.

occāsĭo -ōnis, f. (from occasum, supine of occĭdo), *a favourable moment, opportunity, occasion*: occasionem nancisci, Cic.; adripere, Liv.; amittere, Cic.; dimittere, Caes.; ut primum occasio data est, *as soon as an opportunity offered*, Cic.; per occasionem, ex occasione, *on a favourable opportunity*, Liv. With genit.: opprimendi, Cic.; criminandorum patrum occasiones, Liv. With ad: ad occupandam Asiam, Cic. With infin.: Pl., Ter. With ut: Pl., Quint.

occāsĭuncŭla -ae, f. (dim. of occasio), *a little chance*: Pl.

occāsus -ūs, m. (occido), *the setting of the heavenly bodies*. LIT., solis, Caes., Liv.; hence, *the west*: ab occasu, Verg.; Caes. TRANSF., *fall, destruction*: occasus interitusque reipublicae, Cic.; Troiae, Verg.

occătĭo -ōnis, f. (occo), *a harrowing*: Cic.

occātor -ōris, m. (occo), *a harrower*: Pl.

occēdo -cēdĕre -cessi -cessum (ob/cedo), *to go to, go towards, meet*: in conspectum alicuius, Pl.

occento -are (ob/canto). (**1**) *to sing to, sing a serenade to*: Pl. (**2**) *to sing a lampoon or pasquinade against*: old law ap. Cic.

occepto -are (occipio), *to begin*: Pl.

occĭdens -entis, m. (*see* ²occĭdo) (sc. sol), *the evening, the west*: Cic.

occĭdĭo -ōnis, f. (¹occĭdo), *complete slaughter, extermination, utter destruction*: occidione occidere, *to destroy utterly, slay to the last man*, Cic.; occidione occumbere, *to be slain to the last man*, Tac.; Liv.

¹occĭdo -cīdĕre -cīdi -cīsum (ob/caedo), *to strike down, beat to the ground*.
LIT., Ctesipho me pugnis occidit, Ter.; esp. *to kill, slay*: L. Virginius filiam suā manu occidit, Cic.; ipse fortissime pugnans occiditur, Caes.; Liv., Hor.
TRANSF., *to plague to death, torment*: rogando, legendo, Hor.; Pl.

²occĭdo -cīdĕre -cīdi -cāsum (ob/cado), *to fall, fall down*.
LIT., alia signa de caelo ad terram occidunt, Pl.; Liv. Esp. (**1**) of the heavenly bodies, *to set*: sol occidit, Liv.; Cat.; ab orto usque ad occidentem solem, *from the east to the west*, Liv. (**2**) *to die, perish*: in bello, Cic.; suā dextrā, *to die by one's own hand*, Verg.
TRANSF., *to perish, be ruined*: occidi, *I am lost*, Pl., Ter.; sin plane occidimus, Cic.; spes occidit, Hor.
¶ Hence pres. partic. **occĭdens** -entis, *setting*; m. as subst. (sc. sol), *the setting sun, the west*: Cic.
¶ Perf. partic. in act. sense, **occāsus** -a -um, *setting*: ante solem occasum, Pl.

occĭdŭus -a -um (²occĭdo), *setting*: dies, sol, Ov.; hence, *western, westerly*: Ov. TRANSF., *near death, sinking*: Ov.

occillo -are (occo), *to break up*: Pl.

occĭno -cĭnĕre -cĕcĭni and -cĭnŭi (ob/cano), *to sing inauspiciously*: si occinuerit avis, Liv.

occĭpĭo -cĭpĕre -cēpi -ceptum (ob/capio), *to begin*. (**1**) intransit.: a meridie nebula occepit, Liv.; Lucr., Tac. (**2**) transit.: quaestum, Ter.; magistratum, Liv., Tac.; with infin.: Pl., Liv., Tac.

occĭpĭtĭum -i, n. (ob/caput), *the back of the head, occiput*: Pl., Quint.

occĭput -ĭtis, n. (ob/caput), *the back of the head*: Pers.

occīsĭo -ōnis, f. (¹occĭdo), *a killing, slaughter*: parentis, Cic.

occīsor -ōris, m. (¹occĭdo), *a slayer, murderer*: Pl.

occīsus -a -um, partic. from ¹occĭdo; q.v., *unfortunate*: occisissimus sum omnium qui vivunt, Pl.

occlūdo -clūdĕre -clūsi -clūsum (ob/claudo), *to shut up, close up*. LIT., tabernas, Cic.; furax servus, cui nihil sit obsignatum nec occlusum, Cic.; Pl. TRANSF., *to restrain*: linguam, Pl.
¶ Hence partic. **occlūsus** -a -um, *shut up*; compar. and superl.: Pl.

occo -are, *to harrow*: Pl.; segetem, Hor.

occŭbo -are (ob/cubo), *to lie down*, esp. *to rest in the grave*: ad tumulum, quo maximus occubat Hector, Verg.; morte, Liv.

occulco -are (ob/calco), *to trample, tread down*: occulcare signa ordinesque (of elephants), Liv.

occŭlo -cŭlĕre -cŭlŭi -cultum, *to cover*, esp. for the purpose of hiding: virgulta multā terrā, Verg.; vulnera, Cic. L.; se silvā, Liv.

¶ Hence partic. (with compar. and superl.) **occultus** -a -um, *hidden, concealed, private*. LIT., occultissimus exitus, Liv.; Verg.; n. as subst., *concealment*: ex occulto, Ter., Sall., Liv. TRANSF., (1) of things: res, Lucr., Cic., Verg., Hor. N. as subst., *secrecy*; plur., *secrets*: Cic.; per occultum, Tac.; ex occulto, Cic., Liv., *secretly*. (2) of persons, *secret, close, reserved*: si me astutum et occultum lubet fingere, Cic. L.; Liv., Tac.
¶ Adv. (with compar. and superl.) **occultē**, *secretly, in secret*: latēre, Cic.; dicere, *obscurely*, Cic.; Caes., Liv., Ov.

occultātĭo -ōnis, f. (occulto), *a hiding, concealment*: occultatione se tutari, Cic.; Caes.

occultātor -ōris, m. (occulto), *a hider, concealer*: latronum, Cic.

occulto -are (freq. of occulo), *to hide, conceal*: se latebris, Cic.; Caes., Liv. TRANSF., flagitia, Cic.; Caes.

occultus -a -um, partic. from occulo; q.v.

occumbo -cumbĕre -cŭbŭi -cŭbĭtum, *to fall down, sink down*; esp., *to fall down in death*: mortem, *to die*, Cic., Liv.; morte, Liv.; morti, Verg.; so simply: occumbere, Cic. L., Ov.

occŭpātĭo -ōnis, f. (occupo), *a seizing, taking possession*. LIT., fori, Cic. TRANSF., (1) *a business, employment, occupation*: occupationes reipublicae, Caes.; maximis occupationibus impediri, Cic. (2) *an anticipation*: Cic.

occŭpo -are (ob/capio), *to take possession of, seize*, esp. so as to anticipate a rival.
LIT., totam Italiam suis praesidiis, Cic.; montem, Caes., Tac.; urbem, Verg., Liv.; aliquem amplexu, *to embrace*, Ov.; esp. *to fill, occupy* with anything: Tyrrhenum mare caementis, Hor.; aream fundamentis, Liv.; sometimes *to fall upon, attack*: aliquem gladio, Verg.; Ov.
TRANSF., (1) *to seize* an abstr. thing: regnum, Caes., Cic. (2) of abstr. subjects, *to seize, occupy, master*: pavor occupat animos, Liv.; mentes Siculorum occupat superstitio, Cic. (3) *to take up, employ, occupy*: Liv.; *to invest* money: pecuniam grandi faenore, Cic. (4) *to anticipate, get a start on*: occupat egressas quamlibet ante rates, Ov.; pericula, Tac. (5) *to do first*; with infin. as object: Pl., Hor., Liv.
¶ Hence partic. (with compar. and superl.) **occŭpātus** -a -um, *busy, engaged, occupied*: in apparando bello, Cic.; Caes., Liv.

occurro -currĕre -curri -cursum (ob/curro), *to run to meet, hasten to meet*.
LIT., often with dat.: Caesari venienti, Caes.; Hor., Liv.; esp., *to fall upon, attack*: duabus legionibus, Caes.
TRANSF., (1) of things, *to come in the way*: in asperis locis silex saepe impenetrabilis ferro occurrebat, Liv. (2) *to work against, oppose, counteract*: omnibus eius consiliis, Cic.; Tac. (3) *to meet* trouble, *cope with*: venienti morbo, Pers. (4) *to come into the thoughts, to present itself, occur*: animo, cogitationi, Cic.; in mentem, Cic., Liv., Tac.

occursātĭo -ōnis, f. (occurso), *a going to meet*; hence, *attention, officiousness*: facilis est illa occursatio et blanditia popularis, Cic.

occurso -are (freq. of occurro), *to run or go to meet*.

LIT., fugientibus, Tac.; esp., *to oppose* invidi, occursantes, factiosi, Sall.; occursa ocius gladio, Caes.
TRANSF., (1) *to forestall*: Plin. (2) *to occu* to the mind: Plin. L.

occursus -ūs, m. (occurro), *a meeting, falling in with*: vacuis occursu hominum vii Liv.; alicuius occursum vitare, *to avoi meeting with anyone*, Tac.

Ōcĕănus -i, m. (Ὠκεανός). (1) *the ocean, th sea which encompasses the earth*: Cic., Verg (2) personif., *the husband of Tethys an father of the Nymphs*.
¶ Hence **Ōcĕănītĭs** -ĭdis, f. *a daughter o Oceanus*: Verg.

ŏcellus -i, m. (dim. of oculus), *a little eye*: Pl. Cat., Ov.; as a term of endearment: ocell Italiae, villulae nostrae, Cic. L.

ōcĭmum -i, n. *basil*: Plin., Pers.

ōcĭor ōcĭus, compar. adj. (cf. ὠκύς), *swifter quicker*: ocior cervis, Hor.; Verg. Superl. ocissimus, Plin.
¶ Compar. adv. **ōcĭus**, *more swiftly* facere, Cic.; serius, ocius, sors exitura *sooner or later*, Hor.; sometimes = *swiftl* only: Caes., Verg. Posit.: ociter, Enn. superl.: ocissime, Pl., Sall.

Ocnus -i, m. (Ὄκνος), *the founder of Mantua*.

ocrĕa -ae, f. *a greave*: Verg., Liv.

ocrĕātus -a -um (ocrea), *wearing greaves* Hor.

Ocrĭcŭlum -i, n. *a town in Umbria, on th Tiber (now Otricoli)*.
¶ Hence adj. **Ocrĭcŭlānus** -a -um, *o Ocriculum*.

Octāvĭus -a -um, *name of a Roman gens*; esp of C. Octavius, the Emperor Augustus, calle C. Iulius Caesar Octavianus *after hi* adoption into the gens Iulia.
¶ Hence adj. **Octāvĭānus** a- -um, *Octavian*: bellum, *of Cn. Octavius with Cinna*, Cic.

octāvus -a -um (octo), *eighth*: ager effici cum octavo, *bears eight-fold*, Cic.; adv.: octavum, *for the eighth time*, Liv.; f. as subst octāva -ae (sc. hora), *the eighth hour*: Juv.

octāvusdĕcĭmus -a -um, *eighteenth*: Tac.

octĭēs (-ĭens), adv. (octo), *eight times*: Cic.

octingentēsĭmus -a -um (octingenti), *eight hundredth*: Cic.

octingenti -ae -a (octo/centum), *eight hundred* Cic., Liv.

octĭpēs -pĕdis (octo/pes), *having eight feet*: Prop., Ov.

octō, indecl. numer. (ὀκτώ), *eight*: Cic., etc.

Octōber -bris (octo), *belonging to the eighth month of the Roman year*, reckoning from March; *of October*: Idus, Kalendae, Cic.; m. as subst. (sc. mensis), *October*: Col.

octōdĕcim, indecl. numer. (octo/decem), *eighteen*: Liv.

octōgēnārĭus -a -um (octogeni), *consisting of eighty*: Plin. L.

octōgēni -ae -a (octo), *eighty each, eighty at a time*: Liv.

octōgēsĭmus -a -um (octoginta), *eightieth*: Cic., Juv.

octōgĭēs (-ĭens), adv. *eighty times*: Cic.

octōgintā, indecl. numer., *eighty*: Cic.

octōĭŭgis -e (octo/iugum), *yoked eight together*. TRANSF., octoiuges ad imperia obtinenda ire, *eight together*, Liv.

octōnārĭus -a -um (octoni), *consisting of eight together*: Quint.

octōni -ae -a (octo). (**1**) *eight each*: Pl., Caes. (**2**) *eight at a time, eight together*: Caes., Hor., Liv.

octŏphŏros -on (ὀκτώφορος), *borne by eight*: lecticā octophoro ferri, Cic. N. as subst. **octŏphŏrŏn** -i, *a litter carried by eight bearers*: Cic. L., Mart., Suet.

octŭplĭcātus -a -um (octuplus), *increased eight-fold*: Liv.

octŭplus -a -um (ὀκταπλοῦς), *eight-fold*: pars, Cic. N. as subst. **octuplum** -i, *an eight-fold penalty*: damnari octupli, Cic.

octussis -is, m. (octo/as), *a sum of eight asses*: Hor.

ŏcŭlātus -a -um (oculus). (**1**) *having eyes*: testis, Pl., Suet. (**2**) *catching the eye, conspicuous*: Pl.

ŏcŭlĕus -a -um (oculus), *sharp-sighted*: Argus, Pl.

ŏcŭlus -i, m. (connected with ὄσσομαι, ὄσσε), *the eye*.
LIT., oculos amittere, *to lose one's sight*, Cic.; esse in oculis, *to be visible*, Cic., Ov., Liv., etc.; ante oculos, Cic., Liv.; ante oculos ponere, *to set before one's eyes*, Cic.
TRANSF., (**1**) *the mind's eye*: Cic., etc. (**2**) *an ornament, treasure*: illos oculos orae maritimae (Corinth and Carthage) effodere, Cic. (**3**) *a bud* or *eye of a plant*: Verg.

ōdēum -i, n. (ᾠδεῖον), *a concert-hall*: Vitr., Suet.

ōdi ōdisse; fut. partic. ōsūrus. (**1**) *to hate, detest*: aliquem acerbe, Cic.; Ov., etc.; with infin.: Pl., Hor. (**2**) *to dislike, be displeased with*: Persicos apparatus, Hor.; Ov., Juv.

ŏdĭōsus -a -um (odium), adj. (with compar. and superl.), *hateful, odious, troublesome*: orator, Cic.; verbum, Cic.; Lucr., Ov., etc.
¶ Adv. **ŏdĭōsē**, *odiously, in a hateful manner*: Pl., Ter., Cic.

ŏdĭum -i, n. (odi), *hatred*: odium in omnes, Cic.; odium mulierum, *towards women*, Cic.; vestrum, *towards you*, Liv.; in odium alicuius inruere, *to become hated by anyone*, Cic.; odium est mihi cum aliquo, *I am at enmity with*, Cic.; odium saturare, placare, restinguere, Cic.; movere, exercere, Ov.; plur.: sibi conciliare odia, Caes.; Cic.; often *an object of hatred*: Antonius insigne odium omnium hominum, Cic.; esp. in dat.: alicui esse odio, *to be hated by*, Pl., Cic., Verg., etc.

ŏdor (older **ŏdōs**) -ōris, m. (ὄξω, ὀδμή), *a smell, odour*.
LIT., in gen.: Caes., Cic., Verg.; esp. (**1**) *an unpleasant smell, stench, stink*: camera inculto, tenebris, odore foeda, Sall. (**2**) *a sweet smell*: Hor.
TRANSF., (**1**) *a scent, suspicion, inkling, presentiment*: dictaturae, Cic.; suspicionis, Cic. (**2**) *perfume, incense*; plur., *perfumery, spices*: incendere odores, Pl., Cic.; Hor., Verg., etc.

ŏdōrātĭo -ōnis, f. (odoror), *a smelling, smell*: Cic.

¹ŏdōrātus -ūs, m. (odor). (**1**) *a smelling*: Cic. (**2**) *the sense of smell*: Cic.

²ŏdōrātus -a -um, partic. from odoro; q.v.

ŏdōrĭfĕr -fĕra -fĕrum (odor/fero). (**1**) *having a pleasant smell*: Prop. (**2**) *producing perfumes*: gens, Ov.

ŏdōro -are (odor), *to make odorous*: odorant aëra fumis, Ov.
¶ Hence partic. **ŏdōrātus** -a -um, *sweet-smelling*: cedrus, Verg.; capilli, Hor.; Ov.

ŏdōror -ari, dep. (odor), *to smell*.
LIT., *at* or *smell out*: Pl.; cibum, Hor.
TRANSF., (**1**) *to snuff at, nose* (as a dog); *to aim at, aspire to*: quos odorari hunc decemviratum suspicamini, Cic. (**2**) *to search into, track out, investigate*: quid sentiant, Cic. (**3**) *to get an inkling* or *smattering of*: philosophiam, Tac.

ŏdōrus -a -um (odor). (**1**) *sweet-smelling*: flos, Ov. (**2**) *keen-scented, tracking by smell*: odora canum vis, Verg.

ŏdōs=odor; q.v.

Odrўsae -ārum, m. pl. ('Οδρύσαι), *a people of Thrace*.
¶ Hence adj. **Odrўsĭus** -a -um, poet.= *Thracian.*

Ŏdyssēa -ae, f. ('Οδύσσεια), *the Odyssey, a poem by Homer, translated into Latin by Livius Andronicus*.

Oeāgrus or **Oeāger** -i, m. (Οἴαγρος), *a mythical king of Thrace, father of Orpheus*.
¶ Hence adj. **Oeāgrĭus** -a -um, poet.= *Thracian.*

Oebălus -i, m. (Οἴβαλος), *a king of Sparta, father of Tyndareus, grandfather of Helen*.
¶ Hence subst. **Oebālĭdēs** -ae, m. *a descendant of Oebalus*: puer, Hyacinthus, Ov.; plur.: Oebalidae, Castor and Pollux, Ov.; f. adj. **Oebālĭs** -ĭdis, *Spartan*: nympha, Helen, Ov.; matres, Sabine, as the Sabines were supposed to be descended from the Spartans, Ov.; adj. **Oebālĭus** -a -um, *Spartan* or *Sabine*; subst. **Oebālĭa** -ae, f. *Tarentum* (colonized from Sparta): Verg.

Oechālĭa -ae, f. (Οἰχαλία), *a town in Euboea*.
¶ Hence f. adj. **Oechālĭs** -ĭdis, *Oechalian.*

Oecleus -ĕi, m (Οἰκλεύς), *father of Amphiaraus*.
¶ Hence **Oeclīdēs** -ae, m. *son of Oecleus* =*Amphiaraus.*

oecŏnŏmĭa -ae, f. (οἰκονομία), as literary term, *arrangement, division*: Quint.

oecŏnŏmĭcus -a -um (οἰκονομικός). (**1**) *relating to domestic economy*; as subst., m., *the title of a book by Xenophon*: Cic. (**2**) *orderly, methodical*: Quint.

Oedĭpūs -pŏdis and -i, m. (Οἰδίπους), *king of Thebes, son of Laius and Jocasta. He was fated to kill his father and marry his mother; and he solved the riddle of the Sphinx*; prov.: Davus sum, non Oedipus, *I am no reader of riddles*, Ter.
¶ Hence adj. **Oedĭpŏdĭōnĭus** -a -um, *Oedipodean*: Ov.

Oeneūs -ĕi or -ĕos, m. (Οἰνεύς), *king of Aetolia* or *Calydon, father of Meleager, Tydeus, and Deianira*.
¶ Hence adj. **Oenēĭus** -a -um and **Oenēus** -a -um, *relating to Oeneus*: agri, Aetolia, Ov.; subst. **Oenīdēs** -ae, m. *son of Oeneus*; Meleager, or Diomedes, *son of Tydeus*: Ov.

Oenŏmāus -i, m. (Οἰνόμαος), *king in Elis, father of Hippodamia*.

Oenōnē -ēs, f. (Οἰνώνη), *a Phrygian nymph, loved and afterwards deserted by Paris*.

oenŏphŏrum -i, n. (οἰνοφόρον), *a basket* or *hamper for wine*: Hor., Juv.

Oenŏpĭa -ae, f. (*Οἰνοπία*), *the island afterwards called Aegina.*

¶ Hence adj. **Oenŏpĭus** -a -um, *Oenopian.*

oenŏpōlĭum i, n. (*οἰνοπωλεῖον*), *a wine-shop*: Pl.

Oenōtrĭa -ae, f. (*Οἰνωτρία*), *old name of the south-east part of Italy.*

¶ Hence adj. **Oenōtrĭus** -a -um and **Oenōtrus** -a -um, *Oenotrian*; meton., *Italian, Roman.*

oenus = unus; q.v.

oestrus -i, m. (*οἶστρος*), *the gad-fly, horse-fly*: Verg. TRANSF., *inspiration, frenzy*: Juv.

oesus = usus; q.v.

oesȳpum -i, n. (*οἴσυπος*), *the fat and dirt of unwashed wool*: Plin.; hence, *a - cosmetic prepared from it*: Ov.

Oeta -ae, f. and **Oetē** -ēs, f. (*Οἴτη*), *the mountain-chain between Thessaly and Macedonia, where Hercules burnt himself.*

¶ Hence adj. **Oetaeus** -a -um, *Oetean*: deus, Prop.; and simply: Oetaeus, *Hercules*, Ov.

ŏfella -ae, f. (dim. of offa), *a bit, morsel*: Juv.

offa -ae, f. *a ball* or *pellet of flour*: pultis, Cic.; Verg. TRANSF., *any mass* or *lump*: gummi in offas convolutum, Plin.; hence, *a swelling*: Juv.; *an abortion*: Juv.

offendo -fendĕre -fendi -fensum, *to strike, knock, dash against.*

(1) transit. LIT., aliquem cubito, Pl.; latus, Cic.; caput, scutum, Liv. TRANSF., **a**, *to hit upon, fall in with, come upon*: imparatum te, Cic. L.: **b**, *to shock, offend, displease*: aliquem, *or* alicuius animum, Cic.; Liv.; vitam, Lucr.

(2) intransit. LIT., *to knock against*; with dat., or in and abl.: dens solido, Hor.; Ov.; naves in redeundo (sc. terrae) offenderunt, *struck, ran aground*, Caes. TRANSF., **a**, *to stumble, make a mistake*: si quid offenderit, Cic.: **b**, *to give offence*; with dat.: Cic. L., Liv.: **c**, *to come to grief*: apud iudices, *to be condemned*, Cic.; Caes., Liv.: **d**, *to take offence*: Caes., Cic.

¶ Hence partic. (with compar.) **offensus** -a -um. (1) *injured, hurt*: offensus animus, Cic.; Ov. (2) *offensive*: civibus, Cic.

offensa -ae, f. (offendo), *a striking against, knocking against.* LIT., Plin. TRANSF., (1) *displeasure, offence*: magna in offensa sum apud Pompeium, Cic. L.; Ov. (2) *an injury*: offensas vindicet ense suas, Ov.

offensĭo -ōnis, f. (offendo), *a striking against, hitting against.*

LIT., pedis, *a stumbling*, Cic.

TRANSF., (1) *a misfortune, setback*: Caes., Cic.; esp. *an indisposition*: corporum, Cic. (2) *displeasure, disfavour, aversion*: effugere alicuius offensionem, Cic.; Tac. (3) plur., *offences against*: iudiciorum, Cic.

offensĭuncŭla -ae, f. (dim. of offensio). (1) *a slight displeasure*: Cic. L. (2) *a slight check*: Cic.

offenso -are (freq. of offendo). (1) *to strike, dash against*: capita, Liv.; Lucr. (2) TRANSF., *to stumble*: Quint.

¹**offensus** -a -um, partic. from offensus; q.v.

²**offensus** -ūs, m. (offendo), *a dashing against, a shock, collision*: Lucr. TRANSF., *offence, dislike*: Lucr.

offĕro offerre obtŭli oblātum (ob/fero), *to carry* or *bring to, place before, present, offer.*

LIT., aciem strictam venientibus, Verg.; os suum non modo ostendere, sed etiam offerre, Cic. Reflex., se offerre, and pass., offerri, *to present oneself, appear*: multis in difficillimis rebus praesens auxilium eius numinis oblatum est, Cic.; se hostibus offerre, Caes.; Verg., Liv.

TRANSF., (1) *to offer, expose*: nos periculis sine causa, Cic.; se morti, Caes.; se ad mortem pro patria, Cic.; vitam in discrimen, Cic. (2) *to bring forward, offer, proffer*: alicui operam suam, Liv.; foedus, Verg. (3) *to inflict, occasion*: alicui beneficium stuprum, mortem, Cic.; Ter.

offĕrūmenta -ae, f. (offero), *a present*: Pl.

offĭcīna -ae, f. (older form = **opificina**, from opifex), *a workshop, manufactory.* LIT., armorum, Caes.; Pl., Cic., Hor. TRANSF., falsorum commentariorum et chirographorum, Cic.; nequitiae, sapientiae, Cic.; Liv.

offĭcĭo -fĭcĕre -fēci -fectum (ob/facio), *to act against*; hence, *to get in the way of, impede, hinder.*

LIT., with dat.: alicui apricanti, *to stand between anyone and the sun*, Cic.; ipsa umbra terrae soli officiens, Cic.; Sall.; as transit. verb, in pass.: Lucr.

TRANSF., *to hinder, obstruct, injure*: meis commodis, Cic.; consiliis alicuius, Sall.; officiunt laetis frugibus herbae, Verg.; nomini, Liv.

offĭcĭōsus -a -um (officium), adj. (with compar. and superl.). (1) *obliging, courteous, attentive*: homo, Cic. L.; in aliquem, Cic.; Hor. (2) *dutiful*: dolor, Cic.; labores, Cic.

¶ Adv. (with compar. and superl.) **offĭcĭōsē**, *obligingly, courteously*: Cic., Plin. L.

offĭcĭum -i, n. (for opificium).

LIT., *dutiful* or *respectful action*: officium facere, Pl., Hor.; officio fungi, Cic.; officium praestare, Caes.; officio suo deesse, *to fail in one's duty*, Cic.; meorum officiorum conscientia, Cic.; esp. *of ceremonial action, attendance on some solemn occasion*: urbana officia alicui praestare, ap. Cic.; suprema in aliquem officia, *the last offices*, Tac.; officium triste, Ov.

TRANSF., (1) *sense of duty, respect, courtesy, deference*: homo summo officio praeditus, Cic.; Caes. (2) *submission, allegiance*: in officio continere, Cic.; Caes. (3) *official employment*: toti officio maritimo M. Bibulus praepositus, *over the whole naval service*, Caes.; confecto legationis officio, Caes.; so of things, *function*: corporis Lucr.; Ter.

offīgo -ĕre (ob/figo), *to fix in, fasten*: ita densos offigunt implicantque ramos, Liv.; Pl.

offirmo -are (ob/firmo), *to make firm, to fasten.* TRANSF., with reflex. pron., or intransit., *to be determined, persevere*: Pl., Ter.

¶ Hence partic. (with compar.) **offirmātus** -a -um, *firm, resolute*: Pl., Cic. L.

¶ Adv. **offirmātē**, *firmly, obstinately*: Suet.

offlecto -ere (ob/flecto), *to turn round*: Pl.

offōco -are (ob/fauces), *to choke*: Sen.

offrēnātus -a -um (ob/frenum), *curbed, restrained*: Pl.

offūcĭa -ae, f. (ob/fucus), *paint, rouge*: Pl. Transf., *deceit*: Pl.

offulgĕo -fulgēre -fulsi (ob/fulgeo), *to shine upon*: nova lux oculis offulsit, Verg.

offundo -fundĕre -fūdi -fūsum (ob/fundo), *to pour before*.

Lit., Pl.; esp. pass. as middle, offundi, *to be poured over, to be spread around*: nobis aër crassus offunditur, Cic.; hence, *to over-spread, to cover, conceal*: obscuratur et offunditur luce solis lumen lucernae, Cic.

Transf., (1) *to bring upon*: si quid tenebrarum offudit exsilium, Cic.; ne nimium terroris offundam, Liv.; omnium rerum terror oculis auribusque est offusus, Liv. (2) *to cover, overwhelm*: Cic.; pass.: offusus pavore, Tac.

oggannĭo -ire (ob/gannio), *to growl at*: Pl., Ter.

oggĕro -ĕre (ob/gero), *to proffer*: Pl.

Ŏgȳgēs -is and **Ŏgȳgus** -i, m. (᾿Ωγύγης), *mythical founder and king of Thebes*.

¶ Hence **Ŏgȳgĭus** -a -um, *Theban*: deus, Bacchus, Ov.

oh, interj. *oh! ah!*: Pl., Ter.

ŏhe, interj. *ho! hi!*: Pl., Hor., Mart.

oi, interj. *oh!* an exclamation of pain: Ter.

Olbĭa -ae, f. (᾿Ολβία), *name of several towns, esp. one on the east coast of Sardinia*.

¶ Hence adj. **Olbĭensis** -e, *Olbian*.

ŏlĕa -ae, f. (ἐλαία), *the olive, the fruit of the olive-tree*: Hor. Transf., *the olive-tree*: Cic., Verg., etc.

ŏlĕāgĭnus -a -um (olea), *of the olive-tree*: Verg.

ŏlĕārĭus -a -um (oleum), *of or for oil*: cella, Cic.; m. as subst., *an oil-seller*: Pl.

ŏlĕaster -tri, m. (olea), *the wild olive-tree*: Verg., Ov.

ŏlĕo -ēre (older **ŏlo** -ĕre) (cf. ὄζω, odor), *to emit an odour, smell*. Lit., bene, Cic. L.; with abl., *to smell of*: sulpure, Ov.; with acc.: nihil, Cic.; unguenta, Pl., Ter. Transf., *to smell of, to smack of*: nihil ex Academia, Cic.; malitiam, Cic.; Pl., Hor.

¶ Hence partic. **ŏlens** -entis, *smelling*. Lit., (1) *fragrant, sweet-smelling*: Verg., Ov. (2) *evil-smelling, stinking*: Verg., Hor. Transf., *musty*: Tac.

ŏlĕum -i, n. (ἔλαιον), *olive-oil, oil*. Lit., instillare oleum lumini, Cic.; prov.: oleum et operam perdere, *to lose time and trouble*, Pl. Transf., *effort, competition* (from the oil used in the palaestra by wrestlers): quoddam genus est verborum et laetum sed palaestrae magis et olei, Cic.

olfăcĭo -făcĕre -fēci -factum (oleo/facio), *to smell*. Lit., ea quae gustamus, Cic. Transf., *to scent out, detect*: nummum, Cic.; Ter.

olfacto -are (freq. of olfacio), *to smell at*: Pl.

ŏlĭdus -a -um (oleo), *smelling*: capra, *stinking*, Hor.; Suet.

ōlim, adv. (from ollus, old Latin for ille), *at that time*. (1) with cum or ubi, *then ... when ...*: Verg., etc. (2) *of the past, formerly, once upon a time, in times past*: qui mihi dixit olim, Cic.; Verg., Hor., etc. (3) *of the future, hereafter, one day*: non, si male nunc, et olim sic erit, Hor.; forsan et haec olim meminisse iuvabit, Verg.; Cic. L. (4) *with present, for a long time now*: Juv., Tac. (5) *at times, often*: ut pueris olim dant crustula blandi doctores, Hor.; Verg.

olit-, *see* holit-.

ŏlīva -ae, f. (ἐλαία), *an olive*: Pl., Hor. Transf., (1) *an olive-tree*: Cic., Verg., Hor. (2) *an olive-wreath*: Verg., Hor. (3) *a staff of olive-wood*: Verg., Ov.

ŏlīvētum -i, n. (oliva), *a place planted with olives, olive-grove*: Cic., Hor.

ŏlīvĭfĕr -fĕra -fĕrum (oliva/fero), *olive-bearing*: Verg., Ov.

ŏlīvum -i, n. (ἔλαιον), *olive-oil, oil*: Verg., etc. Transf., (1) *the palaestra* (cf. oleum): Hor. (2) *oil for anointing, unguent*: Cat.

olla -ae, f. (aulula), *a jar or pot*: Cic.

ollus, olle, obsolete form of ille -a -ud; q.v.

ŏlo=oleo; q.v.

ŏlor -ōris, m. *a swan*: Verg., Hor., etc.

ŏlōrīnus -a -um (olor), *of a swan*: Verg., Ov.

ŏlus, *see* holus.

Ŏlympĭa -ae, f. (᾿Ολυμπία), *a holy city and territory in Elis, where the Olympic games were held*.

¶ Hence adj. **Ŏlympĭăcus** -a -um, **Ŏlympĭcus** -a -um, **Ŏlympĭus** -a -um, *Olympian*; subst. **Ŏlympĭum** -i, n. *the temple of Jupiter Olympius*: Liv.; **Ŏlympĭa** -ōrum, n. *the Olympic games*: Cic.; **Ŏlympĭăs** -ădis, f. *an Olympiad or period of four years, elapsing between celebrations of the Olympic games; the first Olympiad is reckoned from 776 B.C.*; **Ŏlympĭŏnīcēs** -ae, m. (᾿Ολυμπιονίκης), *a victor at Olympia*: Cic.

¹**Ŏlympĭăs**, *see* Olympia.

²**Ŏlympĭăs** -ădis, f. (᾿Ολυμπιάς), *wife of Philip and mother of Alexander the Great*.

Ŏlympus -i, m. (῎Ολυμπος), *the name of several mountain ranges, esp. one on the borders of Macedonia and Thessaly, supposed to be the habitation of the gods*; poet.=*heaven*: Verg.

Ŏlynthus (-ŏs) -i f. (῎Ολυνθος), *town in Thrace, Chalcidice, on the borders of Macedonia*.

¶ Hence adj. **Ŏlynthĭus** -a -um, *Olynthian*.

ŏmāsum -i, n. *bullocks' tripe*. Transf., pingui tentus omaso, *with fat paunch*, Hor.

ōmĕn -inis, n. *an omen, sign, prognostication*.

Lit., hisce ominibus proficiscere, Cic.; i secundo omine, Hor.; omen avertere, *to avert an omen*, Cic.; accipere, *to accept*, Cic.

Transf., (1) *a good wish*, as a good omen: optima omina, Cic. (2) plur., *marriage ceremonies*: Verg. (3) *a solemn promise*: Ter.

ōmentum -i, n. *fat-skin, fat*: Pers.; sometimes *the caul, and hence the entrails, paunch*: Juv.

ōmĭnātor -oris, m. (ominor), *a diviner*: Pl.

ōmĭnor -ari, dep. (omen), *to presage, prophesy, predict*: malo alienae quam nostrae reipublicae ominari, Cic.; Hor.; with acc. and infin., or indir. quest.: Liv.

ōmĭnōsus -a -um (omen), *foreboding, ominous*: Plin. L.

ōmitto -mittĕre -mīsi -missum (ob/mitto), *to let go, let fall*. Lit., arma, Liv.; habenas, Tac. Transf., (1) *to let go, to give up, lay aside*: obsessionem, Caes.; timorem, Cic.; with infin., *to cease*: omittat urgere, Cic.; Pl., Hor., etc. (2) in speaking, *to leave out, omit*: ut haec omittam, Cic.; de reditu, Cic.; Liv. (3) *to disregard*: Caes., Liv.

¶ Hence partic. **ōmissus** -a -um, *negligent, remiss*: Ter.; compar.: Ter.

omnĭfĕr -fĕra -fĕrum (omnis/fero), *bearing everything, all-bearing*: Ov.

omnĭgĕnus -a -um; genit. plur., omnigenum: Verg. (omne/genus), *of all kinds*: Verg.

omnĭmŏdīs: Lucr. and **omnĭmŏdō**: Sen., adv. (omnis/modus), *in every case, in every way, wholly, entirely.*

omnīnō, adv. (omnis), *altogether, entirely, wholly.* (1) with positive force. In gen.: cum senatoriis muneribus aut omnino aut magna ex parte essem liberatus, Cic. Esp.: **a**, *in general*: de hominum genere aut omnino de animalibus loquor, Cic.: **b**, *in all*: quinque omnino fuerunt, Cic.: **c**, in concessive clauses, *certainly, admittedly*: pugnas omnino sed cum adversario facili, Cic.

(2) with a negative: **a**, with neg. first, usually in the sense *not altogether*: Cic., Verg., etc.; sometimes *not at all*: Cic., Hor.: **b**, with omnino first, *absolutely not, not at all*: Cic.

omnĭpărens -entis (omnis/parens), *all-producing*: terra, Verg.

omnĭpŏtens -entis (omnis/potens), *almighty, all-powerful*: Cat., Verg.

omnis -e, *all, every, whole.* (1) plur., *all* of a number: leges aliae omnes, Cic., etc.; m. as subst.: omnes, *all men*, Ter., Cic.; n. as subst., omnia, *all things, everything*: omnia facere, *to do whatever is possible*, Cic.; in eo sunt omnia, *everything depends upon that*, Cic.; per omnia, *in every respect*, Liv.; ante omnia, *especially*, Liv.; acc. as adv.: omnia, *in all respects*, Verg. (2) sing., *each, every* one out of a number: omni tempore, Caes.; omnis amans, *every lover*, Ov. (3) sing. or plur., *of all kinds*: holus omne, Hor.; omnibus precibus petere, Cic. (4) sing., *the whole* of one person or thing: Gallia omnis, Caes.; non omnis moriar, *not entirely*, Hor.; sanguinem suum omnem effundere, Cic.; n. as subst.: omne, *the universe*, Lucr.

omnĭtŭens -entis (omnis/tueor), *all-seeing*: Lucr.

omnĭvăgus -a -um (omnis/vagus), *wandering everywhere*: Cic.

omnĭvŏlus -a -um (omnis/volo), *all-wishing*: Cat.

Omphălē -ēs, f. ('Ομφάλη), *a queen of Lydia, whom Hercules served in woman's dress.*

ŏnăger and **ŏnăgrus** -i, m. *a wild ass*: Verg.

ŏnĕrārĭus -a -um (onus), *of* or *for freight, burden*, etc.: iumenta, *beasts of burden*, Liv.; navis oneraria, *a merchant* or *transport ship*, Caes., Liv.; also simply: oneraria, Cic. L.

ŏnĕro -are (onus), *to load, freight, burden.*

LIT., naves, Caes.; iumenta, Sall.; more generally, *to fill, weigh down*: aures lapillis, Ov.; ossa aggere terrae, Verg.; vina cadis, Verg.; mensas dapibus, Verg.; manūs iaculis, Verg.

TRANSF., (1) *to load, burden, oppress, overwhelm*: aliquem mendaciis, Cic.; aethera votis, Verg.; aliquem laudibus, Liv. (2) *to make more burdensome, to aggravate*: curas, Tac.; inopiam alicuius, Liv.

ŏnĕrōsus -a -um, adj. (with compar.) (onus), *heavy, burdensome.* LIT., praeda, Verg. TRANSF., *troublesome*: onerosior altera sors est, Ov.; Plin. L.

ŏnus -ĕris, n. *a load, burden, freight.*

LIT., merces atque onera, Cic.; Caes., Hor., etc.; more generally, *a weight*: tanti oneris turrim in muros conlocare, Caes.; Cic.

TRANSF., *a burden, trouble, charge*: oneri esse, *to be burdensome*, Sall., Liv.; plus oneris sustuli quam ferre me posse intellego, Cic. Esp., *a public burden, tax*: his temporibus hoc municipium maximis oneribus pressum, Cic.; haec omnia in dites a pauperibus inclinata onera, Liv.

ŏnustus -a -um (onus), *laden, loaded, freighted.* LIT., asellus onustus auro, Cic.; naves onustae frumento, Cic.; more generally, *full, filled*: onusti cibo et vino, Cic.; pharetra onusta telis, Tac.; with genit.: auri, Pl. TRANSF., pectus laetitiā, Pl.

ŏnyx -ychis (ὄνυξ), m. and f. *a kind of yellowish marble, onyx*, from which vessels and other articles were made: Plin., Mart. TRANSF., *a casket of onyx*: Hor., Mart.

ŏpācĭtās -ātis, f. (opacus), *shadiness*: arborum, Tac.

ŏpāco -are (opacus), *to shade, overshadow*: locum, Cic.; Verg.

ŏpācus -a -um. (1) *shaded, shady*: ripa, Cic.; Verg. (2) *dark, shadowy, obscure*: nox, Verg.; mater, the earth, Verg.; n. pl. as subst.: per opaca locorum, Verg.

ŏpella -ae, f. (dim. of opera), *a little labour, trouble, service*: Lucr., Hor.

ŏpĕra -ae, f. (¹opus), *trouble, pains, service, exertion.*

LIT., in gen.: laborem et operam in aliqua re consumere, Cic.; operam tribuere reipublicae, Cic.; operam dare, with dat., *to work hard at*, Pl., Ter., Cic., Ov.; est operae pretium, usually with infin., *it is worth while*, Cic., Liv., etc.; in abl.: operā meā, *thanks to me*, Cic.; Caes., etc. Esp., *a service, help*: Cn. Pompeius, qui est in operis eius societatis, *who is in the service of that company*, Cic.; operas alicui dare, Pl.

TRANSF., (1) *time for work*: deest mihi opera, Cic. L.; Liv. (2) *a day-labourer, workman*, gen. in plur.: operae fabrorum, Cic.; Hor., Liv., etc.; sometimes in a contemptuous sense, *mobsmen, gangsters*: Cic.; operae theatrales, *claqueurs*, Tac. (3) *work done*: Pl., Cic. L.

ŏpĕrārĭus -a -um (opera), *relating to work*: homo, *a day-labourer*, Cic. L. M. as subst. **ŏpĕrārĭus** -i, *a day-labourer, workman*; fig.: quidam operarii linguā celeri et exercitatā (of bad orators), Cic.; f. as subst. **ŏpĕrārĭa** -ae, *a work-woman*: Pl.

ŏpercŭlum -i, n. (operio), *a lid, cover*: Cic.; operculum dolii ferreum, Liv.

ŏpĕrīmentum -i, n. (operio), *a cover, covering*: Cic., Sall.

ŏpĕrĭo -pĕrīre -pĕrŭi -pertum (ob/pario), *to cover.*

LIT., capite operto esse, Cic.; terras umbrā nox, Verg.; reliquias malae pugnae, *to bury*, Tac.

TRANSF., (1) *to overwhelm*: iudicia operta dedecore, Cic.; contumeliis, Cic.; infamiā, Tac. (2) *to cover, conceal*: res opertae, Cic.; Ter., Tac. (3) *to close, shut up*: fores, Pl.; astium, Ter.; opertā lecticā latus est, Cic.

¶ Hence n. of partic. as subst. **ŏpertum** -i, *a secret place*, or *secret*: operta Apollinis, Cic.; telluris operta, Verg.; Liv.

ŏpĕror -ari, dep. (opus), *to work, labour, be busy, be occupied*; esp. in perf. partic. **ŏpĕrātus** -a -um, *engaged, busy* (which may be derived directly from opus): in cute curandā, Hor.; with dat. of the occupation: conubiis arvisque novis, Verg.; materiis caedendis, Tac.; esp., *to be engaged in worship*: sacris, Liv.; laetis in arvis, Verg.; with dat. of deity: deo, Tib.

ŏpĕrōsus -a -um, adj. (with compar.) (opera). (1) act., *laborious, painstaking, industrious*. LIT., senectus, Cic.; colonus, Ov.; of medicines, *active, powerful*: herba, Ov. (2) pass., *requiring much labour or trouble, toilsome, difficult*: artes, Cic.; moles mundi, Ov.; carmina, Hor.
¶ Adv. **ŏpĕrōsē**, *laboriously*: Cic., Ov.

ŏpertum -i, subst. from operio; q.v.

ŏpēs, *see* ops.

Ŏphĭūchus -i, m. ('Οφιοῦχος), *the snake-holder, a constellation*: Cic.

Ŏphĭūsa -ae, f. ("Οφίουσα), *old name of the island of Cyprus*.
¶ Hence **Ŏphĭūsĭus** -a -um, *Cyprian*: Ov.

ophthalmĭās -ae, m. (ὀφθαλμίας), *a fish*: Pl.

Ŏpĭcus -a -um, *Oscan*. TRANSF., *stupid, philistine*: Juv.

ŏpĭfĕr -fĕra -fĕrum (ops/fero), *helpful, rendering help*: deus (of Aesculapius), Ov.

ŏpĭfex -fĭcis, c. (opus/facio). (1) *a maker, framer, fabricator*: mundi, Cic.; verborum, Cic. (2) *a workman, artisan*: Cic.; opifices atque servitia, Sall.

ŏpĭfĭcīna=officina; q.v.

ŏpĭlĭo and **ūpĭlĭo** -ōnis, m. (for ovipilio, from ovis), *a shepherd*: Pl., Verg.

ŏpĭmĭtās -ātis, f. (opimus), *plentifulness*: Pl.

ŏpīmus -a -um, *rich, fruitful, fertile*.
LIT., ager, regio, Cic.; arva, Verg.; bos, Cic.; habitus corporis, Cic.
TRANSF., (1) *enriched, wealthy*: Hor.; with abl.: praedā, Cic. (2) *lucrative*: accusatio, Cic. (3) *sumptuous, abundant, copious*: praeda, Cic.; dapes, Verg.; esp.: spolia opima, *the spoils taken from the enemy's general when slain by the commander of the army himself*, Liv. (4) of speech, *overloaded*: genus dictionis, Cic.
¶ Adv. **ŏpīmē**, *richly, splendidly*: Pl.

ŏpīnābĭlis -e (opinor), *founded upon conjecture, conjectural*: Cic.

ŏpīnātĭo -ōnis, f. (opinor), *supposition, conjecture*: Cic.

ŏpīnātor -ōris, m. (opinor), *one who supposes or conjectures*: Cic.

¹ŏpīnātus -a -um, partic. from opinor; q.v.

²ŏpīnātus -ūs, m. (opinor), *a conjecture, supposition*: Lucr.

ŏpīnĭo -onis, f. (opinor), *opinion, conjecture, supposition*.
In gen., with subjective genit.: opinione vulgi, Cic.; with objective genit.: opinio eius diei, Cic.; with de: opinio de dis immortalibus, Cic.; adducere aliquem in eam opinionem ut, Cic.; magna nobis pueris opinio fuit, with acc. and infin., Cic.; ut opinio mea fert, *in my opinion*, Cic.; praeter opinionem, *contrary to expectation*, Nep.; celerius opinione, *quicker than was expected*, Caes.
Esp., *general impression, repute*: opinione nonnullā, quam de meis moribus habebat, Cic.; propter eximiam opinionem virtutis, Caes.; sometimes, *a bad name*: ingrati animi, Liv. Also *rumour, general report*: quae opinio erat edita in vulgus, Liv.; Caes.

ŏpīnĭōsus -a -um (opinio), *set in opinion*; superl.: Cic.

ŏpīnor -ari, dep. (**ŏpīno** -are: Pl.; from opinus), *to be of opinion, believe, suppose, conjecture*: sapiens nihil opinatur, Cic.; me in provinciam exiturum, Cic.; de vobis non secus ac de teterrimis hostibus opinatur, Cic.; often in parenthesis: ut opinor, *or* opinor, Pl., Cic., Hor.
¶ Hence partic. **ŏpīnātus** -a -um, in pass. sense, *conjectured, supposed, fancied*: bonum, Cic.

ŏpĭpărus -a -um (ops/paro), *splendid, rich, sumptuous*: Pl.
¶ Adv. **ŏpĭpărē**, *splendidly, sumptuously*: opipare apparatum convivium, Cic.; Pl.

ŏpisthŏgrăphus -a -um (ὀπισθόγραφος), *written on the back*: Plin. L.

ŏpĭtŭlor -ari, dep. (ops/tuli), *to help, aid*; with dat.: sentibus, Cic.; inopiae, Sall.; Liv.

ŏportet -tēre -tŭit, impers. *it behoves, it is proper, one should* or *ought to*.
Absol.: quidquid veto non licet, certe non oportet, Cic. With subj.: Cic., Hor., Liv.; with acc. and infin.: Pl., Ter., Cic.; with acc. and pass. infin.: hoc fieri et oportet et opus est, Cic.

oppēdo -ĕre, *to mock, insult*: Iudaeis, Hor.

oppĕrĭor -pĕriri -pertus (-pĕrītus: Pl.) sum, dep. (cf. experior), *to wait*. Intransit., *to wait*: ibidem, Cic. L.; Pl., Ter. Transit., *to await*: abi intro, ibi me opperire, Ter.; agmen, Liv.; Verg., etc.

oppĕto -ĕre -īvi and -ii -ītum (ob/peto), *to go to meet, encounter* (especially an evil): pestem, Pl.; esp.: mortem, *to die*, Cic., Liv.; so simply: oppetere, Verg.

oppĭdānus -a -um (oppidum), *of* or *belonging to a town* (except Rome, of which urbanus was used); sometimes in a contemptuous sense, *provincial, 'small-town'*: senex, Cic.; genus dicendi, Cic. M. pl. as subst. **oppĭdāni** -ōrum, *the inhabitants of a town*: Caes., Liv.

oppĭdātim, adv. (oppidum), *in the towns, by towns*: Suet.

oppĭdo, adv. *quite, very much, exceedingly* (colloq.): ridiculus, Cic.; Pl., Liv.; in answers, *certainly*: Pl.

oppĭdŭlum -i, n. (dim. of oppidum), *a little town*: Cic. L., Hor.

oppĭdum -i, n. (perhaps from ob and root of Gr. πέδον), *a town* (urbs being generally used for Rome): oppidum pervetus in Sicilia, Cic.; Verg., Liv., etc.
TRANSF., (1) *a fortified wood in Britain*: Caes. (2) of an *old man*: Pl.

oppignĕro -are (ob/pignero), *to pledge, pawn, give in pledge*: libellos pro vino, Cic.; Mart. TRANSF., filiam, Ter.

oppĭlo -are (ob/pilo). Transit., *to stop up, close up, block up*: scalas tabernae librariae, Cic. Intransit., *to pile up*: Lucr.

opplĕo -plēre -plēvi -plētum (ob/pleo), *to fill up, block*. LIT., nives omnia oppleverant, Liv.; Pl., Caes. TRANSF., nam vetus haec opinio Graeciam opplevit, Cic.; Pl.

oppōno -pōnĕre -pŏsŭi -pŏsĭtum (-postum: Lucr.) (ob/pono), *to put* or *place opposite* or *before*.
LIT., se venientibus in itinere, Caes.; oculis manŭs, Ov.; luna subiecta atque

opposita soli, Cic.; moles oppositae fluctibus, Cic.

TRANSF., (1) *to pledge against, mortgage for*: ager oppositus est pignori ob decem minas, Ter.; Pl., Cat. (2) *to set against, oppose, interpose*: auctoritatem suam, Cic.; esp. of arguments, *to allege as an objection*: alicui nomen, valetudinem alicuius, Cic.; with acc. and infin.: Cic. (3) *to set off against in the way of balance or comparison, to contrast*: nunc omni virtuti vitium contrario nomine opponitur, Cic.; Caes., etc.

¶ Hence partic. **oppŏsĭtus** -a -um, *standing against, opposite*: Buthrotum oppositum Corcyrae, Caes.; Cic., Ov.

opportūnē, adv. from opportunus; q.v.

opportūnĭtās -ātis, f. (opportunus), *convenience, fitness, appropriateness, suitableness*. LIT., loci, Caes. TRANSF., (1) *a fit time, opportunity*: temporis, Caes., Cic. (2) *an advantage*: opportunitate aliquā datā, Caes.; plur.: Cic.

opportūnus -a -um, adj. (with compar. and superl.) (ob/portus), *opportune, fit, suitable, convenient*.

LIT., of place: locus, Cic.; Caes., Liv.

TRANSF., (1) of time, *suitable, favourable*: tempus, Cic.; opportuni venerunt, Liv. (2) of things, *suitable, useful*; with dat.: ceterae res opportunae sunt singulae rebus fere singulis, Cic. (3) of persons, *suitable*: homines, Sall.; Ter., Liv. (4) *exposed, liable to*: huic eruptioni, Liv.; iniuriae, Sall.

¶ Adv. (with compar. and superl.) **opportūnē**, *seasonably, fitly, conveniently*: opportune adesse, Cic.; Caes., Liv.

oppŏsĭtĭo -ōnis, f. (oppono), *opposing, opposition*: Cic.

¹**oppŏsĭtus** -a -um, partic. from oppono; q.v.

²**oppŏsĭtus** -ūs, m. (oppono), *a placing against, opposing, interposition*: Cic.

oppressĭo -ōnis, f. (opprimo), *a pressing down, oppression*: Ter.; hence of *forcible suppression* or *seizure*: legum et libertatis, Cic.; curiae, Cic.

oppressiuncŭla -ae, f. (dim. of oppressio), *slight pressure*: Pl.

¹**oppressus** -ū, m. (opprimo), *a pressing down, pressure*: Lucr.

²**oppressus** -a -um, partic. from opprimo; q.v.

opprĭmo -prĭmĕre -pressi -pressum (ob/premo).

(1) *to press upon, press down*; often with destructive force, *to crush*. LIT., opprimi ruinā conclavis, Cic.; senem iniectu multae vestis, *to smother*, Tac.; of a flame, *to extinguish*: cum aquae multitudine vis flammae opprimitur, Cic. TRANSF., **a**, *to slur over* in pronunciation: litterae neque expressae neque oppressae, Cic.: **b**, in gen., *to weigh down, burden, crush, suppress*: Cic.; opprimi aere alieno, Cic.; somno, timore oppressus, Caes.; *perniciosam potentiam, to stamp out*, Cic.; nationem Allobrogum, Cic.; aliquem falso crimine, Liv.; dolorem, Cic.

(2) *to catch, take by surprise, surprise*. LIT., improvidos incautosque hostes, Liv.; Caes. TRANSF., numquam ille me opprimet consilio, Cic.; Antonium mors oppressit, Cic.; rostra, *to occupy*, Cic.; Liv.

opprobrāmentum -i, n. (opprobro), *a reproach, disgrace*: Pl.

opprobrĭum -i, n. (ob/probrum), *a reproach, scandal, disgrace*. LIT., maioris fugiens opprobria culpae, Hor. TRANSF., (1) *a verbal reproach, taunt*: morderi opprobriis falsis, Hor.; Ov. (2) *a cause of disgrace*: maiorum, Tac.; Ov., etc.

opprobro -are (ob/probrum), *to taunt, reproach*: Pl.

oppugnātĭo -ōnis, f. (oppugno). LIT., *an assault* on a town: oppidorum, Caes.; oppugnationem sustinere, Caes.; relinquere, Tac. TRANSF., any *attack*: iudicium sine oppugnatione, *without opposition*, Cic.

oppugnātor -ōris, m. (oppugno), *an assailant, one who attacks*: Tac. TRANSF., hostis et oppugnator patriae Antonius, Cic.

oppugno -are (ob/pugno), *to attack, assault*. LIT., oppidum, Cic.; castra, Caes.; urbem, Liv.; with play on pugnus, *to batter*: Pl. TRANSF., nos clandestinis consiliis, Cic.; Pl.

Ops ŏpis, f. (1) in nom. sing., as proper name, *the goddess of abundance, wife of Saturn, and mother of Jupiter*. (2) acc. sing. **ŏpem**, genit. **ŏpis**, abl. **ŏpe**, *might, power*, esp. *power to aid*: opem ab aliquo petere, Cic.; adferre, Ov.; omni ope atque operā enitar, Cic.; grates persolvere dignas non opis est nostrae, *is not in our power*, Verg. (3) plur. **ŏpēs**, *resources, means, wealth*, esp. military or political: opibus, armis, potentiā valere, Cic.; tantas opes prostravit, Cic.; Caes., Verg., etc.

ops-, see obs-.

optābĭlis -e (opto), *desirable, to be wished for*: mihi pax in primis fuit optabilis, Cic.; Ov.; compar.: Cic.

optātĭo -ōnis, f. (opto), *a wish*: alicui tres optationes dare, Cic.

optātō, adv. from opto; q.v.

optātus -a -um, partic. from opto; q.v.

optĭmātēs -ātis (optimus), *one of the best, aristocratic*: genus, Cic. M. pl. as subst. **optĭmātēs**, *the aristocratic party, the aristocrats*: Cic., Tac.

optĭmē, superl. of bene; q.v.

optĭmus (optŭmus) -a -um, superl. of bonus; q.v.

¹**optĭo** -ōnis, f. (opto), *choice, free choice, option*: utro frui malis optio sit tua, Cic.; si mihi optio daretur, utrum malim defendere, an, Cic.; Liv.

²**optĭo** -ōnis, m. *a helper, an assistant*: Pl., Tac.

optĭvus -a -um (opto), *chosen*: cognomen, Hor.

opto -are, *to choose, elect, select*. LIT., utrum vis, opta, dum licet, Pl.; locum tecto, Verg.; ut optet utrum malit an, Cic.; Liv. TRANSF., *to wish for, desire*: illam fortunam, Cic.; aliquid votis, Verg.; with infin.: Ter., Liv., Tac.; with acc. and infin.: Cic. Liv.; with ut and the subj.: optavit, ut in currum tolleretur, Cic.; Liv., Ov.; with subj. alone: crescat tua civibus opto urbs, Ov.; with acc. and dat., *to wish* a person something: alicui furorem et insaniam, Cic.; Liv.

¶ Hence partic. (with compar. and superl.) **optātus** -a -um, *wished for, desired, welcome*: rumores, Cic. L. N. as subst. **optātum** -i, *a wish*: optatum impetrare, Cic.; Ter., Ov.

¶ Abl. as adv. **optātō**, *according to one's wish*: Cic. L., Verg.

ŏpŭlens -entis, see opulentus.

ŏpŭlentĭa -ae, f. (opulens). (1) *wealth, riches, opulence*: Sall. (2) *the power, greatness of a state*: Sall., Verg., Tac.

ŏpŭlentĭtās -ātis, f. (opulentus), *riches, power*: Pl.

ŏpŭlento -are (opulentus), *to make opulent, enrich*: Hor.

ŏpŭlentus -a -um, also **ŏpŭlens** -entis, adj. (with compar. and superl.) (ops), *rich, wealthy, opulent*. LIT., civitas, Cic.; oppidum, Caes.; with abl.: Numidia agro virisque opulentior, Sall.; Verg.; with genit.: Ter., Hor. TRANSF., (1) *powerful, mighty*: reges, Sall.; factio, Liv. (2) *splendid, sumptuous*: res haud opulenta, Liv.; Pl. (3) *lucrative*: Liv.

¶ Adv. **ŏpŭlentē** and **ŏpŭlentĕr**, *richly, splendidly, sumptuously*: Sall.; compar.: ludos opulentius facere, Liv.

Ŏpuntĭŭs, see ²Opus.

¹ŏpus -ĕris, n. *a work, labour.*

LIT., in gen.: opera nostrarum artium, Cic.; opus quaerere, *to seek for work*, Cic.; res immensi operis, Liv.; Verg. Esp. (1) *work in the fields*: facere patrio rure opus, Ov. (2) *building*: lex operi faciundo, *a building-contract*, Cic. (3) milit. t. t.: naturâ et opere munitus, Caes.; Verg., Liv. (4) *literary*: Cic., Liv., Tac.

TRANSF., *work done, a finished work*. (1) in gen.: his immortalibus editis operibus, Liv.; Caes., etc. (2) *a building*: Cic., Liv., Verg. (3) milit. t. t., *works, lines, siege-engines*: operibus oppugnare urbem, Liv.; Mutinam operibus munitionibusque saepsit, Caes. (4) *a literary work* or *a work of art*: Silanionis opus (of a statue), Cic.; opus habeo in manibus, Cic.

A special use is found in the phrase **ŏpus est** (or **sunt**), *there is work for someone to do with something*; hence, *one needs, there is need, it is necessary*. (1) with abl. of the thing needed: opus est auctoritate tuâ, Cic.; Verg., Liv,. etc.; sometimes with abl. n. of perf. partic.: maturato opus est, *there is need of haste*, Liv., or of supine; scitu, Cic. (2) with genit.: quanti argenti opus fuit, Liv. (3) with acc.: Pl. (4) with nom.: dux nobis, et auctor opus est, Cic. L.; Liv. (5) with infin.: quid opus est adfirmare? Cic.; with pass. infin.: Liv.; with acc. and infin.: Cic. L., Liv. (6) with ut and subj.: Pl.

²Ŏpūs -puntis, f. ('Οποῦς), *a town in Locris.* Adj. **Ŏpuntĭŭs** -a -um, *Opuntian.*

ŏpuscŭlum -i, n. (dim. of ¹opus), *a little work*: Cic., Hor.

ōra -ae, f. (1) *an edge, border, rim, boundary*: oras pocula circum, Lucr.; regiones quarum nulla ora, Cic.; clipei, Verg. (2) *the coastline, coast*: Italiae, Cic. TRANSF., *the people of the coast*: Cic., Tac. (3) *a region, clime, country*: quâcumque in ora ac parte terrarum, Cic.; Acheruntis orae, *the lower world*, Lucr.; luminis orae, *the upper world*, Enn., Lucr., Verg. TRANSF., **a**, *the people of a district*: Liv.: **b**, oras belli, *great expanse*, Verg. (4) *a hawser, cable* reaching to shore: Liv., Quint.

ōrācŭlum (**ōrāclum**: Cat., Ov.) -i, n. (oro). LIT., *a solemn utterance, an oracle, divine response*: oraculum edere, Cic.; petere a

Dodona, Cic.; in gen., *a prophecy*: oracula fundere, Cic.; *a wise speech, oracular declaration*: physicorum, Cic. TRANSF., *the place where an oracle is given, an oracle*: illud oraculum Delphis, Cic.; fig.: domus iure consulti, oraculum civitatis, Cic.

ōrātĭo -ōnis, f. (oro), *speaking, speech, language.*

LIT., in gen.: quae (ferae) sunt rationis et orationis expertes, Cic.; also *style, language*: in hac est pura oratio, Ter.; orationem bonorum imitavi, Cic. Esp., *a set speech*: comparare ad id longam orationem, Cic.; habere orationem, *to deliver*, Ter., Caes., Cic.; in extrema oratione nostra, *at the end of our speech*, Cic.; Liv.

TRANSF., (1) *eloquence*: satis in eo fuit orationis, Cic. (2) *prose* (opp. to poetry): saepissime et in poematis et in oratione peccatur, Cic. (3) *an imperial message*: Tac., Suet.

ōrātĭuncŭla -ae, f. (dim. of oratio), *a little speech, short oration*: Cic., Quint.

ōrātor -ōris, m. (oro), *a speaker.* (1) *a spokesman, envoy*: Cic., Verg., Liv., etc. (2) *an orator*: Cic., etc.

ōrātōrĭus -a -um (orator), *of an orator, oratorical*: ingenium, Cic.; ornamenta, Cic. F. as subst. **ōrātōrĭa** -ae (sc. ars), *oratory*: Quint.

¶ Adv. **ōrātōrĭē**, *oratorically*: Cic.

ōrātrix -icis, f. (orator), *a female suppliant*: virgines oratrices pacis, Cic.; Pl.

ōrātū, abl. as from oratus -ūs, m. (oro), *by request*: oratu tuo, Cic.; Pl.

orbātor -ōris, m. (orbo), *one who deprives another of children or parents*: Ov.

orbĭcŭlātus -a -um (orbiculus), *circular, round*: Varr., Plin.

orbĭcŭlus -i, m. (dim. of orbis), *a little circle* or *disk*: Plin.

orbis -is, m. *a circle, ring, disk, anything round.*

LIT., torquere in orbem, Cic.; of troops: in orbem consistere, Caes.; of the heavens: orbis signifer, *the Zodiac*, Cic.; lacteus, *the Milky Way*, Cic.; of a star, *orbit*: Verg.; of a shield or wheel: Verg.; of the eye: Lucr., Verg.; of a serpent, *coils*: immensis orbibus angues incumbunt pelago, Verg.; Lucr. Esp.: orbis terrae, orbis terrarum, *the circle of the world, the world*, Cic., Verg., Liv.; hence, *country, land*: Eous, *the East*, Ov.; meton., *mankind*: orbis terrae iudicio ac testimonio comprobari, Cic.

TRANSF., (1) *rotation, round*: Cic. L., Liv. (2) of style, *rounding off, roundness*: verborum, Cic.

orbĭta -ae, f. (orbis), *a wheel-rut, mark of a wheel*: Cic., Verg. TRANSF., orbita veteris culpae, *bad example*, Juv.

orbĭtās -ātis, f. (orbus), *bereavement, loss of children or parents*: orbitates liberum, Cic.; Liv., etc. TRANSF., maximâ orbitate rei-publicae virorum talium, Cic. L.

orbo -are (orbus), *to bereave, to deprive of parents or children*: filio orbatus, Cic.; Ov. TRANSF., Italiam iuventute, Cic.

Orbōna -ae, f. (orbus), *the goddess invoked by bereaved parents*: Cic.

orbus -a -um (cf. Gr. ὀρφανός), *deprived of parents or children, bereft.*

LIT., orbus senex, Cic.; with abl.: liberis, Pl.; with genit.: Memnonis orba mei venio,

Ov.; subst. **orbus** -i, m. and **orba** -ae, f. *an orphan*: Ter., Liv.
   Transf., *deprived, destitute*; with abl.: rebus omnibus, Cic.; with genit.: luminis, Ov.

orca -ae, f. *a pot or jar with a large belly*: Hor., Pers.

Orcădĕs -um, f. pl. *islands near Scotland (now the Orkneys).*

orchăs -ădis, f. *a species of olive*: Verg.

orchestra -ae, f. (ὀρχήστρα), *the part of a Roman theatre reserved for the senators*; meton., *the senate*: Juv.

Orcīnus -a -um (Orcus), *relating to Orcus or the dead*: senatores, *those who became senators by the will of Caesar*, Suet.

Orcus -i, m. (connected with ἕρκος), *Orcus, the infernal regions*: Lucr., Verg., etc. Transf., (1) *the god of the lower world*: Cic., Verg., etc. (2) *death*: Lucr., Hor.

ordĕum=hordeum; q.v.

ordĭa prīma=primordia; *see* **primordium.**

ordĭnārĭus -a -um (ordo), *according to order, regular, ordinary*: consules, *elected in the regular manner* (opp. to suffecti), Liv.; ordinarii reipublicae usus, Liv.

ordĭnātim, adv. (ordinatus), *in good order, regularly, properly*: Caes.

ordĭnātĭo -ōnis, f. (ordino), *a setting in order, arrangement*: Plin. L.

ordĭnātus -a -um, partic. from ordino; q.v.

ordĭno -are (ordo), *to set in order.* Lit., physically: latius arbusta sulcis, Hor.; agmina, Hor.; aciem, Liv. Transf., (1) *to settle, arrange, appoint*: partes orationis, Cic.; aliter apud alios ordinatis magistratibus, Liv.; res publicas, Hor. (2) *to govern a people or country*: Plin. L., Suet.
   ¶ Hence partic. **ordĭnātus** -a -um, *in order, arranged, orderly*: disciplina, Liv.; Cic.; compar.: Sen.

ordĭor ordiri orsus sum, dep. (connected with ordo). Lit., *to begin a web, lay the warp*: Plin. Transf., in gen., *to begin, commence*: vitae quoddam initium, Cic. L.; esp., in speaking, *to begin*; with acc.: sermonem, Cic.; with infin.: de aliqua re disputare, Cic.; absol.: de aliquo paulo altius, Cic.; sic orsus Apollo, *began to speak*, Verg.
   ¶ Hence n. pl. of partic. as subst. **orsa** -orum, *beginnings, undertaking*: Verg., Liv.; esp. of speaking, *words uttered, speech*: Verg.

ordo -inis, m. (orior), *a series, line, row, order.*
   Lit., vitium, Cic., Verg.; *a row of seats in a theatre*: Cic.; *a row or bank of oars in a vessel*: Verg.; milit., *a line, rank, file*: ordines explicare, Liv.; ordine egredi, Sall.; Caes.; hence, *a company*: ordinem ducere, *to be a centurion*, Caes.; Cic., Liv.; ordines primi, *commanders*, Caes.; Liv.
   Transf., (1) politically and socially, *an order, rank, class*: senatorius, *or* amplissimus, *the senatorial body*, Cic.; equester, *the body of knights*, Cic.; Liv.; in gen., *a class, body of men*: publicanorum, Cic. (2) *order, arrangement*: nomina in ordinem referre, Cic.; res in ordinem adducere, *to put into order*, Cic.; Caes., Verg., Liv.
   In phrases: ordine, in ordinem, per ordinem, *in turn, in order*, Cic., Verg., etc.; ordine, *in due order, regularly, properly*, Cic.; ex ordine, *in regular succession*, Cic., Verg.;

extra ordinem, *in an unusual, irregular manner*: alicui provinciam decernere, Cic.; hence, *extraordinarily, very greatly*: Cic. L.

Ŏrĕăs -ădis, f. (Ὀρειάς), *a mountain-nymph, Oread*: Verg., Ov.

Ŏrestēs -ae and -is, m. (Ὀρέστης), *son of Agamemnon and Clytemnestra, who killed his mother to avenge the murder of his father.*
   ¶ Hence adj. **Ŏrestēus** -a -um, *Orestean.*

ŏrexis -is, f. (ὄρεξις), *desire, appetite*: Juv.

orgănĭcus -i, m. (ὀργανικός), *a musician*: Lucr.

orgănum -i, n. (ὄργανον), *an implement* or *instrument*: Plin.; esp., *a musical instrument*: Quint., Juv.

orgĭa -ōrum, n. pl. (ὄργια), (*nocturnal*) *festivals in honour of Bacchus*: Verg.; Ov.; hence, *any secret festival*; *mysteries*: Prop.; *orgies*: Juv.

ŏrĭchalcum -i, n. (ὀρείχαλκος), *yellow copper ore*; hence, *brass made from it*: Cic., Verg., etc.

ŏrĭcilla -ae, f. (=auricilla), *an ear-lap*: Cat.

Ŏrĭcŏs -i, m. and **Ŏrĭcum** -i, n. *a town on the coast of Epirus.*
   ¶ Hence adj. **Ŏrĭcĭus** -a -um, *Orician*; and subst. **Ŏrĭcĭni** -ōrum, m. *the inhabitants of Oricum.*

ŏrĭcŭla=auricula; q.v.

ŏrĭens -entis, m.=partic. from orior; q.v.

ŏrīgo -inis, f. (orior), *origin, source, beginning.* Lit., principii nulla est origo, Cic.; ab origine gentem corripiunt morbi, Verg.; Hor., etc. Transf., *an ancestor, founder of a race*: pater Aeneas Romanae stirpis origo, Verg.; Sall., Liv.

Ŏrīōn -ōnis, m. (Ὠρίων), *a mighty hunter, transformed into the constellation Orion.*

ŏrĭor ŏrīri ortus sum; fut. partic. ŏrĭtūrus (ŏrēris, ŏrītur in pres. indic.; sometimes ŏrērētur in imperf. subj.), dep. (cf. Gr. ὄρνυμι), *to rise.*
   Lit., (1) of persons: cum consul oriens de nocte silentio diceret dictatorem, Liv. (2) of the heavenly bodies: ortă luce, *in the morning*, Caes.; orto sole, Hor.
   Transf., in gen., *to arise, spring from, proceed from*: clamor, Caes.; ab his sermo, Cic.; caedes, Verg.; esp. (1) of persons, *to be born*: equestri loco ortus, Cic.; Caes. (2) of rivers, etc., *to rise*: Rhenus ex Lepontiis, Caes.; Liv., Tac.
   ¶ Hence partic. **ŏrĭens** -entis, *rising.* M. as subst. (1) *the rising sun*; personif., *the sun-god*: Verg. (2) *the east*: Cic., Verg. (3) *the morning*: Cic., Ov.

Ŏrīthyia (quadrisyll.) -ae, f. (Ὠρείθυια), *daughter of Erechtheus, the king of Athens, mother of Zethes and Calais by Boreas.*

ŏrĭundus -a -um (orior), *arising from, springing from*: ab ingenuis, Cic.; ex Etruscis, Liv.; Pl.

ornāmentum -i, n. (orno), *equipment, accoutrement, trappings, furniture.* Lit., certas copias et ornamenta vestra, Cic.; Pl.; often also *ornament, decoration, embellishment*: omnia ornamenta ex fano Herculis in oppidum contulit, Caes.; Cic.; *a badge of office*: Cic. Transf., *honour, ornament, distinction*: decus atque ornamentum senectutis, Cic.; Caes.; esp., *rhetorical ornament*: oratoria ornamenta dicendi, Cic.

ornātē, adv. from orno; q.v.

ornātrix -īcis, f. (ornator), *a female hairdresser, a tire-woman*: Ov., Suet.

ornātŭlus -a -um (dim. of ornatus), *rather elegant*: Pl.

¹ornātus -ūs, m. (orno). Lit., *dress, attire, equipment*: militaris, regalis, Cic.; Pl., Liv., Verg. Transf., *embellishment, ornament*: ornatum adferre orationi, Cic.

²ornātus -a -um, partic. from orno; q.v.

orno -are, *to equip, furnish, provide with necessaries, fit out*. Lit., aliquem armis, Verg.; decemviros apparitoribus, Cic.; classem, consules, Cic.; provinciam, *to provide, for the government of a province*, Cic.; Liv.; often also *to adorn, decorate, embellish*: domum suam, Cic.; cornua sertis, Verg. Transf., *to adorn, decorate, distinguish*: civitatem omnibus rebus, Caes.; hederā poetam, Verg.; esp. by praise: fuit ornandus in Manilia lege Pompeius, Cic.
¶ Hence partic. (with compar. and superl.) **ornātus** -a -um, *furnished, equipped, provided*. Lit., scutis telisque parati ornatique sunt, Cic.; Caes., Liv.; often *adorned, decorated, embellished*: Pl., Cic. Transf., ingenio bono, Pl.; artibus, Cic.; ornatissimus adulescens, Cic.
¶ Adv. **ornātē**, *ornately, splendidly, elegantly*: comparare convivium, Cic.; loqui, Cic.

ornus -i, f. *the mountain-ash*: Verg., Hor.

ōro -are ('os), *to speak*.
In gen.: talibus orabat Iuno, Verg.; Pl.
Esp. (1) *to speak as an orator*: vestra in nos promerita complecti orando, Cic.; ipse pro se oravit, *defended himself*, Liv. With acc., *to treat, argue, plead*: capitis causam, Cic.; litem, Cic. (2) *to beg, pray, entreat, beseech*; with acc. of the person entreated: Cic., Ov., Tac., etc.; oro te (parenthetic), *I pray*, Cic. L.; with acc. of the thing: auxilium ad bellum, Liv.; Ter., Tac.; with acc of pers. and acc. of thing: auxilia regem, Liv.; Cic. L., Verg. With ut or ne and the subj., or subj. alone: oro ut homines conserves; Pl., Caes., Verg. With infin.: Verg., Tac.

Ŏrōdēs -is and -i, m. *a king of the Parthians, who took Crassus prisoner*.

Ŏrontēs -is and -ae, m. (᾿Ορόντης), *the chief river of Syria*.
¶ Hence adj. **Ŏrontēus** -a -um, poet.= *Syrian*.

Orpheus -ei and -eos; acc. -ea and -ea, m. (᾿Ορφεύς), *a celebrated mythical minstrel of Thrace, husband of Eurydice*.
¶ Hence adj. **Orphēus** and **Orphĭcus** -a -um, *Orphic, of Orpheus*.

orphus -i, m. (ὀρφός), *a sea-fish, perhaps a sea-perch*: Ov.

orsa -ōrum, n. pl., from partic. of ordior; q.v.

¹orsus -ūs, m. (ordior), *a beginning, undertaking*: Cic. poet.; Verg.

²orsus -a -um, partic. from ordior; q.v.

orthŏgrăphĭa -ae, f. (ὀρθογραφία), *orthography*: Suet.

Ortōna -ae, f. *a town of the Frentani in Latium* (now *Ortona*).

¹ortus -ūs, m. (orior). (1) *a rising of the heavenly bodies*: solis et lunae reliquorumque siderum ortus, Cic.; Verg.; hence, *the east*: Ov., Ov. (2) *of persons, origin, birth*: primo ortu, Cic.; ortu Tusculanus, Cic.; ortum ducere ab Elide, Cic. (3) in

gen., *origin, source*: tribuniciae potestatis, Cic.; of plants: Lucr.; of a river: Ov.

²ortus -a -um, partic. from orior; q.v.

Ortÿgĭa -ae, f. and **Ortÿgĭē** -ēs, f. (᾿Ορτυγία). (1) *an island forming part of Syracuse*. (2) *the old name of the island of Delos*.
¶ Hence adj. **Ortÿgĭus** -a -um, *Ortygian*.

ŏryx -ÿgis, m. (ὄρυξ), *a species of wild goat or gazelle*: Juv.

ŏrÿza -ae, f. (ὄρυζα), *rice*: Hor.

¹ōs -ōris, n.
(1) *the mouth*. Lit., cadit frustum ex ore pulli, Cic.; Ov., etc. Transf., **a**, *mouth, opening*: portus, Cic.; dolii, Liv.; of a river, *source*: ora novem Timavi, Verg.: **b**, as the organ of speech, *voice, talk*: semper in ore habere, *to be always talking about*, Cic.; in ore vulgi esse, Cic.; uno ore, *unanimously*, Cic., Ter., Verg.; ruit profundo Pindarus ore, Hor.
(2) *the face, countenance*. Lit., in os adversum, Caes.; Cic., Verg., etc. Transf., **a**, *presence, sight*: in ore hominum, Cic.; Verg., Liv., etc.: **b**, *expression*; esp. with reference to modesty, or the lack of it: os durum! Cic.; Ter.; nostis os hominis, nostis audaciam, Cic.: **c**, *a mask*: Gorgonis, Cic.; Verg.

²ōs ossis, n. (cf. ὀστέον) *a bone*. Lit., dolorem cineri eius atque ossibus inussisti, Cic.; ossa legere, *to gather up the ashes of the bones after the burning of a corpse*, Cic.; Verg. Transf., (1) *heart, inmost being*: tum vero exarsit iuveni dolor ossibus ingens, Verg. (2) *of a meagre style*: ossa nudare, Cic.

oscen -ĭnis, m. (obs/cano), t. t. of augural language, *a bird from whose note auguries were taken* (e.g., the raven, owl, crow): Cic. L., Hor.

Osci -ōrum, *an ancient people of Italy*; adj. **Oscus** -a -um, *Oscan*.

oscillum -i, n. (dim. of ¹os), *a little mask*: Verg.

oscĭtātĭo -ōnis, f. (oscito), *opening of the mouth, gaping, yawning*: Mart.

oscĭto -are (¹os), *to open the mouth, gape, yawn*: Pl., Lucr.
¶ Hence partic. **oscĭtans** -antis, *yawning, sleepy, listless*: Ter., Cic.
¶ Adv. **oscĭtanter**, *listlessly*: Cic.

oscŭlābundus -a -um (osculor), *kissing*: Suet.

oscŭlātĭo -ōnis, f. (osculor), *a kissing*: Cic., Cat.

oscŭlor -ari, dep. (osculum), *to kiss*. Lit., consulem filium, Cic.; Pl. Transf., *to caress, make much of, make a pet of*: scientiam iuris tamquam filiolam osculari suam, Cic.

oscŭlum -i, n. (dim. of ¹os), *a little mouth*. Lit., oscula summa delibare, Verg.; Ov. Transf., *a kiss*: Cic. L., Verg., Ov., etc.

ōsŏr -ōris, m. (odi), *a hater*: Pl.

Ossa -ae, m. and f. (῎Οσσα), *a mountain range in Thessaly*. Adj. **Ossaeus** -a -um, *belonging to Ossa*.

ossĕus -a -um (²os), *bony*: Juv.

ossĭfrăgus -i, m. and **ossĭfrăga** -ae, f. (²os/frango), *the sea-eagle, osprey*: Lucr.

ostendo -tendĕre -tendi -tentum and -tensum (obs/tendo), *to hold out, show, display, expose to view*. Lit., manus, Pl.; os suum populo Romano, Cic.; equites sese ostendunt, *come in sight*, Caes.; supinatas Aquiloni glebas, Verg. TRANSF., *to show, reveal, present*: spem, metum, Cic.; salutis viam, Verg.; esp. by speech, *to make plain, declare*: nihil sibi gratius ostendit futurum esse, Cic.; quid sui consilii sit ostendit, Caes.

¶ Hence n. of partic. as subst. **ostentum** -i, *a prodigy, portent*: magnorum periculorum metus ex ostentis portenditur, Cic.; Suet.

ostentātio -ōnis, f. (ostento). (1) *a showing, revealing*: saevitiae, Liv. (2) *a showing off, parade, display*: ostentationis causa latius vagari, Caes.; ingenii, Cic. (3) *a deceitful show, pretence*: consul veritate, non ostentatione popularis, Cic.; Sen.

ostentātor -ōris, m. (ostento), *one who shows*; esp., *a boaster, vaunter, parader*: factorum, Liv.; Tac.

ostento -are (freq. of ostendo), *to hold out, present, offer.*

LIT., alicui iugula sua pro capite alicuius, Cic.; esp., *to show publicly, display, exhibit*: passum capillum, Caes.; equum armaque capta, Liv.; Verg.

TRANSF., *to show, reveal, present*: periculum capitis, Cic.; praemia, Sall.; minas, Liv. Esp. (1) *to show off, display*: triumphos suos, Sall.; tuam patientiam, Cic. (2) by speech, *to declare, make known*: prudentiam, Cic. L.; et simul ostentavi tibi me istis esse familiarem, Cic. L.

ostentŭi, dat. sing. as from ostentus, m. (ostendo), *for a show.* LIT., corpora abiecta ostentui, Tac.; esp., *merely for show*: illa deditionis signa ostentui credere, Sall. TRANSF., *as a sign, indication, proof*: ut Iugurthae scelerum ostentui essem, Sall.

ostentum -i, n., subst. from ostendo; q.v.

Ostĭa -ae, f. and **Ostĭa** -ōrum, n. (ostium), *the harbour and port of Rome, at the mouth of the Tiber* (now *Ostia Antica*).

¶ Hence adj. **Ostĭensis** -e, *relating to Ostia*: incommodum, *the destruction of the Roman fleet by the pirates*, Cic.; provincia, *the office of the quaestor, who superintended the aqueducts and the supply of corn to the city*, Cic.

ostiārium -i, n. (ostium), *a tax upon doors, a door-tax*: Caes.

ostiārĭus -i, m. (ostium), *a doorkeeper, porter*: Varr., Suet.

ostiātim, adv. (ostium), *from door to door*: compilare totum oppidum, Cic.; Quint.

ostĭum -i, n. ('os), *door*. LIT., ex actio ostiorum, *the door-tax*, Cic.; aperto ostio dormire, Cic.; Pl., Ter. TRANSF., in gen., *entrance*: portūs, Cic.; fluminis Cydni, *mouth*, Cic.; Oceani, *Straits of Gibraltar*, Cic.; Verg.

ostrĕa -ae, f. and **ostrĕum** -i, n. (ὄστρεον), *an oyster, mussel*: Cic., Hor., etc.

ostrĕātus -a -um (ostrea), *rough like an oyster-shell*: Pl.

ostrĕōsĭŏr -ōris, compar. adj. (ostrea), *richer in oysters*: Cat.

ostrĭfĕr -fĕra -fĕrum (ostrea/fero), *producing oysters*: Verg., Luc.

ostrīnus -a -um (ostrum), *purple*: colores, Prop.

ostrum -i, n. (ὄστρεον), *the purple dye prepared from a shell-fish*: vestes ostro perfusae, Verg. TRANSF., *stuff dyed with purple, a purple dress*: Verg., Hor.

ōsus -a -um, partic. from ōdi; q.v.

Ŏtho -ōnis, m. *a Roman* cognomen; esp. of (1) L. Roscius Otho, *author of a law giving special seats in the theatre to the knights*. (2) M. Salvius Otho, *a Roman emperor who succeeded Galba in* A.D. 69. Adj. **Ŏthōnĭānus** -a -um, *relating to Otho*.

Othrўădēs -ae, m. (᾽Οθρυάδης). (1) *son of Othrys=Panthus*: Verg. (2) *a Spartan, the sole survivor in a battle with the Argives*.

ōtĭŏlum -i, n. (dim. of otium), *a little leisure*: ap. Cic. L.

ōtĭor -ari, dep. (otium), *to be at leisure*: cum se Syracusas otiandi non negotiandi causā contulisset, Cic.; Hor.

ōtĭōsus -a -um, adj. (with compar. and superl.) (otium), *at leisure, without occupation.*

LIT., homo, Cic.; Pl., Ter.; esp., *free from public duties* or *occupied in literary work only*: numquam se minus otiosum esse quam cum otiosus, Cic.

TRANSF., (1) of persons, *calm, quiet*: Cic.; in a struggle, *indifferent, neutral*: Cic. (2) of things, *free, quiet, undisturbed*: provincia, Liv.; Caes., Cic.

¶ Hence adv. **ōtĭōsē**, *at leisure, without occupation*: Cic., Liv.; hence, *gently, quietly, easily*: Cic., Liv.

ōtĭum -i, n. *free time, leisure, ease.*

LIT., otium habere ad aliquid faciendum, Ter.; hebescere et languescere in otio, Cic.; otium Catulle tibi molestumst, Cat.; otium suum consumere in historia scribenda, Cic.; otium litteratum, Cic.; otia nostra, *my poetry*, Ov.

TRANSF., *peace, repose, quietness*: multitudo insolens belli diuturnitate otii, Caes.; otium domesticum, Cic.; otium divos rogat in patenti prensus Aegaeo, Hor.; ab hoste otium fuit, Liv.

ŏvans -antis, partic. as from ŏvo -are, *rejoicing, exulting*: ovans victoriā, Liv.; Verg. Esp., *celebrating the minor triumph, the ovatio*: ovantem in Capitolium ascendisse, Cic.; Liv. TRANSF., currūs ovantes, Prop.

ŏvātĭo -ōnis, f. (ovo), *an ovation, a kind of lesser triumph in which the victorious general proceeded to the Capitol on horseback or on foot*: Plin.

Ŏvĭdĭus -a, *name of a Roman gens*; esp. of P. Ovidius Naso, *the poet, who was born at Sulmo*, 43 B.C., *and died at Tomi*, A.D. 17.

ŏvīle -is, n. (ovis), *a sheepfold*: Verg.; also *a fold for goats*: Ov. TRANSF., *an enclosed place in the Campus Martius, used for voting*: Liv.

ŏvillus -a -um (ovis), *of sheep*: grex, Liv.

ŏvis -is, f. (ὄϊς), *a sheep*. LIT., pascere oves, Verg.; Cic., etc. TRANSF., (1) *wool*: Tib. (2) as a term of reproach, *simpleton, foolish fellow*: Pl.

ōvum -i, n. (ᾠόν), *an egg.*

LIT., ovum gignere, or parere, *to lay an egg*, Cic.; prov.: integram famem ad ovum adferre, *to the beginning of the meal* (as Roman dinners often began with eggs), Cic.; ab ovo usque ad mala, *from beginning to end*, Hor.; also of *the spawn* of fish: Cic.

TRANSF., *one of the seven egg-shaped balls by which the laps in circus races were counted*: ova curriculis numerandis, Liv.

P

P, p, the fifteenth letter of the Latin Alphabet, corresponds usually with the Greek pi (*Π, π*), sometimes with the Greek phi (*Φ, φ*). For the use of P. in abbreviations, see Table of Abbreviations.

păbŭlātĭo -ōnis, f. (pabulor), *procuring fodder, foraging*: pabulatione intercludi, Caes.

păbŭlātor -ōris, m. (pabulor), *a forager*: Caes., Liv.

păbŭlor -ari, dep. (pabulum), *to forage, seek fodder*: Caes., Liv., Tac.

păbŭlum -i, n. (cf. pasco), *food, nourishment.* LIT., of gods: pabula caelestia, *ambrosia*, Ov.; of men: dura, Lucr.; of animals, *fodder*: pabulum secare, convehere, Caes.; Sall., Verg., etc. TRANSF., amoris, Lucr.; studii atque doctrinae, Cic.

păcālis -e (pax), *of peace, peaceful*: laurus, Ov.

păcātus -a -um, partic. from paco; q.v.

Păchўnum -i, n. and **Păchўnus** (-ŏs) -i, f. (*Πάχυνος*), *the south-east promontory of Sicily* (now *Capo di Passaro*).

păcĭfĕr -fĕra -fĕrum (pax/fero), *peace-bringing*: oliva, Verg.; often used as an epithet of the gods, e.g., of Mercury: Ov.

păcĭfĭcātĭo -ōnis (pacifico), f. *a making of peace, pacification*: Cic. L.

păcĭfĭcātor -ōris (pacifico), m. *a peacemaker*: Cic. L., Liv.

păcĭfĭcātōrĭus -a -um (pacifico), *making peace, pacificatory*: legatio, Cic.

păcĭfĭco -are (pax/facio), *to make peace*: Sall., Liv.; hence, *to appease, pacify*: caelestes heros, Cat.

păcĭfĭcus -a -um (pax/facio), *peacemaking, pacific*: persona, Cic.

păcĭscor pacisci pactus sum, dep. (connected with pango), *to make a bargain* or *agreement, to covenant, contract.*

  (**1**) intransit.: cum illo, Pl.; paciscitur magnā mercede cum Celtiberorum principibus, ut copias inde abducant, Liv.; Hor., etc.

  (**2**) transit.: **a**, *to stipulate for, bargain for*: provinciam, Cic.; pretium, Cic.; ex qua domo pactus esset (feminam), *betrothed himself*, Liv.: **b**, with infin., *to bind oneself*: stipendium populo Romano dare, Liv.: **c**, *to give in exchange*: vitam pro laude, Verg.

  ¶ Hence perf. partic. in pass. sense **pactus** -a -um, *agreed upon, stipulated*: pretium, dies, Cic.; Hor., Liv. Esp., *betrothed*: Cic. L., Verg., Liv.; f. as subst.: Verg.

  ¶ N. as subst. **pactum** -i, *an agreement, covenant, treaty, pact*: manere in pacto, Cic.; stare pacto, Liv. In abl. **pactō,** *in* (some) *way*: alio pacto, *in another way*, Pl., Ter., Cic.; hoc pacto, Verg.

păco -are (pax), *to pacify, make peaceful*: omnem Galliam, Caes.; Amanum, Cic. L.; Verg.; poet., *to make fruitful*: incultae pacantur vomere silvae, Hor.

  ¶ Hence partic. (with compar. and superl.) **păcātus** -a -um, *made peaceful*; hence, *peaceful, quiet.* LIT., pacatae tranquillaeque civitates, Cic.; mare, Hor., Liv.; n. as subst. pacatum, *a peaceful country*: ex pacatis praedas agere, Sall. TRANSF.,

illorum oratio pacatior, Cic.; n. as subst.: Liv.

Păcŏrus -i, m. (*Πάκορος*), *son of Orodes, a king of Parthia.*

pactĭo -ōnis, f. (paciscor), *a bargain, contract, covenant, agreement, treaty.*
In gen.: facere pactionem de aliqua re, Cic.; arma per factionem dare, *to capitulate*, Liv.
  Esp. (**1**) *a contract between the farmers of the taxes of a province and its inhabitants*: pactiones conficere, Cic. L. (**2**) *a fraudulent* or *collusive agreement*: pactionis suspicio, Cic. (**3**) *a marriage-contract*: Pl., Liv.

Pactōlus -i, m. (*Πακτωλός*), *a river in Lydia, said to bring down golden sands.*
  ¶ Hence f. adj. **Pactōlis** -idis, *of Pactolus*: Nymphae, Ov.

pactor -ōris, m. (paciscor), *one who makes a contract* or *treaty, negotiator*: societatis, Cic.

pactum -i, n., subst. from paciscor; q.v.

pactus -a -um, partic. from paciscor; q.v.

Păcŭvĭus -i, m. *a Roman tragic poet, who was born in 220 B.C. and died about 132 B.C.*

Pădus -i, m. *the largest river in Italy* (now *the Po*).

Pădūsa -ae, f. *a canal running from the Po to Ravenna.*

paean -ānis, m. (*Παιάν*). (**1**) *the Healer, a surname of Apollo*: Cic.; hence adj. **paeānĭus** -a -um. (**2**) *a hymn, paean, originally addressed to Apollo only, but afterwards to other deities*: conclamant socii laetum paeana secuti, Verg.; Cic., Ov. (**3**)=paeon; q.v.

paedăgōgĭum -i, n. (*παιδαγωγεῖον*), *the place where boys of servile birth were trained as pages*: Plin. L.

paedăgōgus -i, m. (*παιδαγωγός*), *a slave who accompanied children to and from school and had charge of them at home*: Pl., Cic., etc. TRANSF., *any guide*: Sen., Suet.

paedor -ōris, m. *dirt, filth*: Lucr., Cic., Tac.

paelex (**pellex**) -lĭcis, f. (cf. *παλλακίς*), *a mistress, esp. of a married man; a concubine*: Cic.; barbara, *Medea*, Ov.; with genit. of the man's wife: Cic., Ov.

paelĭcātus -us, m. (paelex), *concubinage*: Cic.

Paelignĭ -ōrum, m. pl. *an Italian tribe.*
  ¶ Hence adj. **Paelignus** -a -um, *Pelignian*: anus, *a witch*, Hor.

paene, adv. *nearly, almost*: paene amicus, Cic.; Pl., Liv., etc.

paeninsŭla and **paenĕ insŭla** -ae, f. *a peninsula*: Cat., Liv.

paenĭtentĭa -ae, f. (paeniteo), *repentance, regret*: Liv., Tac.

paenĭtĕo -ēre (connected with poena). (**1**) *to repent, to regret, to be sorry*; only in infin., partic., and gerund: paenitens consilii, Sall.; Liv., Cic. (**2**) *to cause regret, make sorry, displease*; only in third person: me haec condicio, Pl. Usually as impers. verb, with acc. of pers. and genit. of thing: suae quemque fortunae paeniteat, Cic.; me paenitet consilii, Cic.; with genit. only: tamquam paeniteat laboris, Liv. With infin. as subject: non paenitet me vixisse, Cic.; ut fortiter fecisse paeniteat, Cic. With clause as subject: Quintum paenitet quod animum tuum offendit, Cic.; paenitet quod deduxisti, Liv. Absol.: paenitet et torqueor, Ov.

  ¶ Hence gerundive **paenĭtendus** -a -um,

regrettable, unsatisfactory; esp. with neg.: Liv., Suet.

paenŭla -ae, f. (φαινόλης), _a species of cloak, worn on a journey, or in wet, cold weather_: Cic., Hor., etc.; prov.: paenulam alicui scindere, _to press a guest to stay_, Cic. L.

paenŭlātus -a -um (paenula), _clothed in the_ paenula: Cic., Mart.

paeŏn -ōnis, m. (παιών), _a metrical foot, consisting of three short syllables and one long_: Cic., Quint

Paeŏnes -um, m. pl. (Παίονες), _the Paeonians, a people of Macedonia_; sing. **Paeŏn** -ŏnis, m. _a Paeonian_: Liv.

¶ Hence subst. **Paeŏnĭa** -ae, f. (Παιονία), _Paeonia, their country_; _a district of Macedonia, afterwards Emathia_; f. adj. **Paeŏnis**, _Paeonian_.

Paestum -i, n. _a town in Lucania, famous for its roses_ (now Pesto).

¶ Hence adj. **Paestānus** -a -um, _of Paestum_; m. pl. as subst. **Paestanī** -orum, _its inhabitants_.

paetŭlus -a -um (dim. of paetus), _having a slight cast in the eye_: Cic.

paetus -a -um, _having a cast in the eyes, squinting_: Hor., Ov.

pāgānus -a -um (pagus), _belonging to a village, rural_: focus, Ov. TRANSF., _rustic_: cultus, Plin. L.

¶ M. as subst. **pāgānus** -i, _a villager, countryman, yokel_: Cic., Tac., Juv.

Pāgăsa -ae, f. and **Pāgăsae** -ārum, f. pl. (Παγασαί), _a sea-port of Thessaly, where the ship Argo was built._

¶ Hence adj. **Pāgăsaeus** -a -um, _Pagasean_: puppis, carina, _the Argo_, Ov.; coniunx, Alcestis, _daughter of the Thessalian king Pelias_, Ov.; m. as subst. _Jason, leader of the Argonauts_: Ov.

pāgātim, adv. (pagus), _in villages, by villages_: Liv.

pāgella -ae, f. (dim. of pagina), _a little page_: Cic. L.

pāgĭna -ae, f. (pango), _a page_ of a letter, book, etc.: complere paginam, Cic.; Juv. TRANSF., _the contents of a page_: Cic. L., Mart.

pāgĭnŭla -ae, f. (dim. of pagina), _a little page_: Cic. L.

pāgus -i, m. (pango), _a village or country district_: Verg., Liv., Tac.; omnis civitas Helvetia in quattuor pagos divisa, _cantons_, Caes.; _the inhabitants of a village or canton_: pagus agat festum, Ov.; Caes.

pāla -ae, f. (pango). (1) _a spade_: Pl., Liv. (2) _the bezel of a ring_: Cic.

Pălaestīna -ae, f. and **Pălaestīnē** -ēs, f. (Παλαιστίνη), _Palestine._

¶ Hence adj. **Pălaestīnus** -a -um, _of Palestine_: aqua, _the Euphrates_, Ov.; m. pl. as subst. **Pălaestīni** -ōrum, _the inhabitants of Palestine_: Ov.

pălaestra -ae, f. (παλαίστρα), _a gymnasium or wrestling school._ LIT., Pl., Cic., Verg., etc. TRANSF., (1) _wrestling_: discere palaestram, Cic.; exercere, Verg.; Ov. (2) _training in rhetoric, etc., rhetorical exercises_: quasi quandam palaestram et extrema lineamenta orationi attulit, Cic.; eā palaestrā, Cic. L.

pălaestrĭcus -a -um (παλαιστρικός), _of the palaestra_: motus, Cic.; Pl., Quint. F. as subst. **palaestrĭca** -ae, _gymnastics_: Quint.

¶ Adv. **pălaestrĭcē**, _after the manner of the palaestra_: spatiari in xysto, Cic.

pălaestrīta -ae, m. (παλαιστρίτης), _the superintendent of a palaestra_: Cic., Mart.

pălam, adv. and prep.
Adv., _openly, publicly_: rem gerit, Cic.; Verg., etc.; palam agere et aperte dicere, Cic.; esse, ferre, facere: palam est res, Pl.; tum demum palam factum est, Liv.
Prep., with abl., _in the presence of_: te palam, Hor.; palam populo, Liv.

Pălātĭum -i, n. _the Palatine Hill in Rome, on which Augustus had his house._ Hence, in plur., _a palace_: Palatia fulgent, Ov.; Juv.

¶ Hence adj. **Pălātīnus** -a -um, _Palatine_: Apollo, _whose temple was on the Palatine_, Hor.; also _relating to the imperial palace, imperial_: Ov.

pălātum -i, n. and **pălātus** -i, m. _the roof of the mouth, the palate._
LIT., Verg., Ov.; esp. as _the organ of taste_: quae voluptas palato percipiatur, Cic.; Hor., Juv.
TRANSF., (1) _taste, critical judgment_: Epicurus dum palato quid sit optimum iudicat, Cic. (2) palatum caeli, _the vault of heaven_, Enn.

pălĕa -ae, f. (cf. Gr. παλύνω), _chaff_: Varr., Verg.

pălĕar -āris, n. _the dewlap of an ox_; gen. plur.: Verg., Ov.

Pălēs -is, f. _the tutelary goddess of herds and shepherds._

¶ Hence adj. **Pălīlis** -e, _belonging to Pales_: flamma, _a fire of straw, used in ceremonies at the feast of Pales_; n. pl. as subst. **Pălīlia** -ium, _the feast of Pales on the 21st of April._

Pălīci -ōrum, m. pl. (sing.: Palicus, Verg., Ov.), _twin sons of Jupiter by the nymph Thalia, worshipped as heroes in Sicily._

Pălīlis -e, _see_ Pales.

pălimpsestus -i, m. (παλίμψηστος), _parchment, from which old writing has been erased for the purpose of using the parchment again, a palimpsest_: Cic. L., Cat.

Pălinūrus -i, m. (Παλίνουρος). (1) _the pilot of Aeneas who fell into the sea off the coast of Lucania._ (2) _a promontory on the west coast of Lucania, named after him._

pălĭūrus -i, m. (παλίουρος), _a plant, Christ's thorn_: Verg.

palla -ae, f. _a long and wide outer garment._ LIT., _worn by Roman women_: Verg., Hor., etc.; also _by tragic actors_: Hor., Ov. TRANSF., _a curtain_: Sen.

pallăca -ae, f. (παλλακή), _a concubine_: Suet.

¹**Pallăs** -ădis and -ădos, f. (Παλλάς), _Athene, the Greek goddess of wisdom, identified with Minerva; she discovered the olive_: Palladis ales, _the owl_, Ov.; arbor, _the olive-tree_, Ov. TRANSF., (1) _the olive-tree_: Ov. (2) _olive-oil_: Ov. (3) _the image of Pallas, the Palladium_: Ov.

¶ Hence adj. **Pallădĭus** -a -um, _of Pallas_: rami, _olive-branches_, Verg.; latices oil, Ov.; arces, _Athens_, Ov.; n. as subst **Pallădĭum** -i, _an image of Pallas, esp. one in Troy, which fell from heaven_: Cic., Verg. Ov.

²**Pallăs** -antis, m. (Πάλλας). (1) _son of Pandion_ (2) _a king of Arcadia, the great-grandfather of Evander._ (3) _son of Evander._

[420]

¶ Hence adj. **Pallantēus** -a -um, *belonging to Pallas*; n. as subst. **Pallantēum** -i. (1) *a town in Arcadia.* (2) *a town in Italy, on the site of Rome*; also adj. **Pallantĭus** -a -um, *relating to Pallas*: heros, *Evander*, Ov.

palleo -ēre, *to be pale.* LIT., sudat, pallet, Cic.; Ov. TRANSF., (1) *to be yellow*: Mart. (2) *to be pale with fear* or *anxiety*: ambitione malā, Hor.; ad omnia fulgura, Juv.; with dat., *to fear for*: pueris, Hor.

¶ Hence partic. **pallens** -entis, *pale, wan*: umbrae Erebi, Verg.; Ov. TRANSF., (1) *pale* or *wan in colour, pale yellow, pale green*: violae, Verg.; hedera, Verg. (2) *making pale, causing paleness*: Ov., Mart. (3) *drooping, weak*: Tac.

pallesco pallescĕre pallŭi (palleo), *to grow pale, turn pale, lose colour.* LIT., nullā culpā, Hor.; with acc., *to turn pale at*: pontum, Hor. TRANSF., *to grow yellow*: pallescunt frondes, Ov.

pallĭātus -a -um (pallium), *clad in a pallium, i.e., as a Greek* (opp. togatus, *clad as a Roman*): Graeculus, Cic.

pallĭdŭlus -a -um (dim. of pallidus), *somewhat pale*: Cat., Juv.

pallĭdus -a -um, adj. (with compar.) (palleo), *pale, wan, pallid.* LIT., Verg., Hor., etc.; esp. with emotion: Ov. TRANSF., *causing paleness*: mors, Hor.; Prop.

palliŏlātus -a -um (palliolum), *wearing a cloak-cape* or *hood*: Suet.

palliŏlum -i, n. (dim of pallium). (1) *a little Greek cloak* or *mantle*: Pl., Mart., Juv. (2) *a hood*: Ov.

pallĭum -i, n. (1) *a coverlet*: Ov., etc. (2) *a Greek mantle*: Cic., Ov., etc.

pallor -ōris, m. (palleo), *paleness, pallor.* LIT., terrorem pallor consequitur, Cic.; Verg., Hor., etc.; esp. from emotion: amantium, Hor.; Pl., Ov. TRANSF., *fading*: Lucr., Ov.

palma -ae, f. (παλάμη). (1) *the palm of the hand.* LIT., Cic., Verg., etc. TRANSF., **a**, *the whole hand, the hand*: Pl., Cic., Verg.: **b**, *the blade of an oar*: Cat. (2) *the palm-tree.* LIT., Caes., Verg. TRANSF., **a**, *the fruit of the palm, a date*: Ov.: **b**, *a besom* or *broom made of palm-branches*: Hor., Mart.: **c**, *the palm-branch as a token of victory*: Liv.; hence, *victory, honour, glory*: plurimarum palmarum gladiator, Cic.; belli Punici, Liv.: **d**, *any branch, shoot, twig*: palma stipitis, Liv.

palmāris -e (palma), *deserving the palm* or *prize, excellent, admirable*: statua, Cic.; sententia, Cic.

palmārĭus -a -um, *of palms.* N. as subst. **palmārĭum** -i, n. (palma), *a masterpiece*: Ter.

palmātus -a -um (palma), *worked* or *embroidered with palm-branches*: tunica (worn by triumphing generals), Liv.; Mart.

palmĕs -ĭtis, m. (palma), *a young branch* or *shoot of a vine, a vine-sprout*: Verg., Ov. TRANSF., *any branch*: Luc.

palmētum -i, n. (palma), *a palm-grove*: Hor., Tac.

palmĭfĕr -fĕra -fĕrum (palma/fero), *abounding in palm-trees*: Prop., Ov.

palmōsus -a -um (palma), *full of palms*: Verg.

palmŭla -ae, f. (dim. of palma). (1) *the blade of an oar*: Verg. (2) *the fruit of the palm, a date*: Varr.

pālor -ari, dep. *to wander about, stray about.* LIT., agmen palatur per agros, Liv.; palantia sidera, Lucr.; Verg. TRANSF., *to stray*: Lucr., Ov.

palpātĭo -ōnis, f. (palpo), *a flattering*: Pl.

palpātŏr -ōris, m. (palpo), *a flatterer*: Pl.

palpēbra -ae, f. (palpo), *the eyelid*; gen. plur.: palpebrae, *the eyelids*, Lucr., Cic.

palpĭto -are (freq. of palpo), *to move quickly, tremble, throb*: cor palpitat, Cic.; esp. of persons in death-agony: Ov.

¹**palpo** -are and **palpor** -ari, dep. *to stroke* or *touch gently*: Ov. TRANSF., *to coax, flatter, wheedle*: Cic. L.; with dat.: Pl., Hor.; with acc.: quem munere palpat, Juv.

²**palpo** -ōnis, m. (¹palpo), *a flatterer*: Pers.

palpus -i, m. *the palm of the hand.* TRANSF., *flattery*: Pl.

pălūdāmentum -i, n. *the military cloak, a soldier's cloak*, esp., *a general's cloak*: Sall., Liv., Tac.

pălūdātus -a -um, *clad in the military cloak*, esp. *in a general's cloak*: Pansa noster paludatus profectus est, Cic.; Caes., Liv.

pălūdōsus -a -um (²palus), *marshy, boggy*: Prop., Ov.

pălumbēs -is, m. and f. *a wood-pigeon, ring-dove*: Verg., Hor.

¹**pālus** -i, m. (from root of pango), *a pale* or *stake*: aliquem ad palum adligare or deligare, Cic.; Ov.; esp., *a stake on which Roman recruits exercised their weapons*: aut quis non vidit vulnera pali? Juv.

²**pălus** -ūdis, f. *a swamp, marsh, bog, fen*: Cic.; Caes., Liv., etc.; tarda palus, *the Styx*, Verg.

păluster -tris -tre (²palus), *marshy, boggy, fenny*: limus paluster, Liv.; locus, Caes.; ranae, *living in marshes*, Hor. TRANSF., *filthy*: Pers.

Pamphylĭa -ae, f. (Παμφυλία), *a district in Asia Minor, between Cilicia and Lycia.* Adj. **Pamphylĭus** -a -um, *Pamphylian.*

pampĭnĕus -a -um (pampinus), *attached to* or *consisting of vine-tendrils*: hastae, *garlanded with vine-leaves*, Verg.; corona, *of vine-leaves*, Tac.

pampĭnus -i, m. and f. *a vine-tendril* or *vine-leaf*: uva vestita pampinis, Cic.; Pl., Verg., Hor.

Pān Pānos (acc. Pāna), m. (Πάν), *the god of flocks, woods, and shepherds*; plur. **Pānes**, *rural deities resembling Pan*: Ov.

pănăcēa -ae, f. and **pănăcēs** -is, n. (πανάκεια, πάνακες), *a fabulous plant, supposed to heal all diseases, panacea, heal-all*: Verg.

Pănaetĭus -i, m. (Παναίτιος), *a Stoic philosopher of Rhodes, teacher and friend of the younger Scipio Africanus.*

Pănaetōlĭum -i, n. (Παναιτώλιον), *the general assembly of Aetolia*: Liv. Adj. **Pănaetōlĭcus** -a -um, *of the whole of Aetolia*: concilium, Liv.

pānārĭum -i, n. (panis), *a bread-basket*: Plin. L.

Pănăthēnāĭcus -a -um (Παναθηναϊκός), *of the Athenian festival of the Panathenaea*; m. as subst. **Pănăthēnāĭcus** -i, *an oration of Isocrates delivered at the Panathenaea*: Cic.

Panchāĭa -ae, f. (Παγχαία), *a region of Arabia, famous for its frankincense.*

¶ Hence adj. **Panchāĭus** and **Panchaeus** -a -um, *Panchean.*

panchrestus (panchristus) -a -um (πάγ-χρηστος), *good* or *useful for everything*: medicamentum, *sovereign remedy*, i.e., *gold*, Cic.

pancrătĭcē, adv. *like one taking part in the* pancratium: Pl.

pancrătĭum (-ŏn) -i, n. (παγκράτιον), *a gymnastic contest, including both boxing and wrestling*: Prop., Plin.

Pandātărĭa (Pandātĕrĭa) -ae, f. *an island in the Tyrrhenian Sea, place of exile under the emperors.*

Pandīōn -ōnis, m. (Πανδίων), *a king of Athens, father of Procne and Philomela*: Pandionis populus, *the Athenians*, Lucr.; Pandione nata, *Procne* or *Philomela*, Ov.
¶ Hence adj. **Pandīŏnĭus** -a -um, *poet.= Athenian.*

¹**pando** -are (pandus), *to bend, bow, curve*: Plin., Quint.

²**pando** pandĕre pandi pansum and passum.
(1) *to stretch out, extend.* LIT., vela, Cic.; pennas ad solem, Verg.; racemi passi, *spread out to dry*, Verg.; crines passi, capillus passus, *dishevelled hair*, Caes.; passis manibus, *with outstretched hands*, Caes. TRANSF., vela orationis, Cic.; esp. with reflex: divina bona longe lateque se pandunt, Cic.
(2) *to throw open*; pass. as middle, *to open itself, open out.* LIT., ianuam, Pl.; moenia urbis, Verg.; panduntur inter ordines viae, Liv. TRANSF., *to lay open, reveal, disclose*: viam ad dominationem, Liv.; rerum naturam, Lucr.; res, Verg.; nomen, Ov.
¶ Hence partic. **passus** -a -um, *spread out to dry, dried*; n. as subst. **passum** -i, *wine made from dried grapes, raisin-wine*: Pl., Verg.

pandus -a -um, *bent, curved, crooked*: Verg., Ov.

pănēgўrĭcus -i, m. (πανηγυρικός), *an oration of Isocrates, celebrating the glories of Athens*: Cic.

Pangaeus -i, m. and poet. **Pangaea** -ōrum, n. pl. (τὸ Πάγγαιον), *a mountain range in Thrace and Macedonia.*

pango pangĕre panxi (for pepigi and pactum, see below), *to fasten, fix, drive in* (cf. πήγνυμι). LIT., clavum, Liv. TRANSF., *to compose, write*: versus de rerum natura, Lucr.; poëmata, Hor.; aliquid Sophocleum, Cic.
¶ In perf. forms only **pĕpĭgi** pactum, *to fix, settle, agree upon* (cf. paciscor): terminos, fines, Cic.; neque prima per artem temptamenta tui pepigi, Verg.; pacem, Liv.; with genit. of price: tanti pepigerat, Liv.; pretium quo pepigerant, Liv.; with ut and the subj.: ut vobis mitterem ad bellum auxilia pepigistis, Liv.; with infin.: obsides dare pepigerant, Liv.; esp. of a contract of marriage: haec mihi se pepigit, pater hanc tibi, *has betrothed*, Ov.

pănĭcĕus -a -um (panis), *of bread*: panicei milites, *the Baker Street Irregulars*, Pl.

pănĭcum -i, n. (panus), *a kind of wild millet*: Caes.

pānĭfĭcĭum -i, n. (panis/facio), *baking*: Varr. TRANSF., *cakes*: Suet.

pānis -is, m. (from root of pasco), *bread*: panis cibarius, *common bread*, Cic.; secundus, *black bread*, Hor.; plur., *loaves of bread*: ex hoc (genere radicis) effecti panes, Caes.

Pāniscus -i, m. (Πανίσκος), *a sylvan deity, a little Pan*: Cic.

pannĭcŭlus -i, m. (dim. of pannus), *a little garment*: bombycinus, Juv.

Pannŏnĭa -ae, f. *Pannonia, a district on the Danube, part of modern Hungary and Yugoslavia.* Adj. **Pannŏnĭcus** and **Pannōnĭus** -a -um.

pannōsus -a -um (pannus), *ragged, tattered*: Cic. L., Juv.

pannūcĕus (-ĭus) -a -um (pannus), *ragged*; hence, *wrinkled, shrivelled*: Pers.

pannus -i, m. *a piece of cloth.* (1) *a garment*: Hor., Juv. (2) sing. or plur., contemptuously, *a rag, rags*: Lucr., etc.

Pănomphaeus -i, m. (Πανομφαῖος), *the author of oracles, surname of Jupiter.*

Pănormus -i, f. and **Pănormum** -i, n. (Πάνορμος), *a town on the north coast of Sicily* (the modern *Palermo*).
¶ Hence adj. **Pănormītānus** -a -um, *of Panormus.*

pansa -ae (pando), *splay-footed, having broad feet*: Pl.

pansus -a -um, partic. from pando; q.v.

panthēra -ae, f. (πάνθηρα), *a panther*, perhaps also *a leopard*: Cic. L., Ov.

panthērinus -a -um (panthera), *like a panther*: Pl.

Panthūs -i, m. (Πάνθους), *a priest at Troy, father of Euphorbus.*
¶ Hence subst. **Panthŏïdēs** -ae, m. *a descendant of Panthus; Euphorbus*: Ov.; *Pythagoras* (who pretended that the soul of Euphorbus had passed into his): Hor.

pantĭcēs -um, m. pl. *bowels*: Pl.

pantŏmīmĭcus -a -um (pantomimus), *pantomimic*: Sen.

pantŏmīmus -i, m. (παντόμιμος) and **pantŏmīma** -ae, f. *a dancer, mime*: Sen., Suet.

păpae (παπαί), interj. *wonderful! indeed!*: Pl., Ter.

pāpăs -ae and -atis, m. (πάπας), *a tutor*: Juv.

păpāver -ĕris, n. *the poppy*: Verg., Liv., etc.

păpāvĕrĕus -a -um (papaver), *of the poppy*: comae, *the stamens of a poppy*, Ov.

Paphlăgō -ŏnis, m. (Παφλαγών), *a Paphlagonian.*
¶ Hence **Paphlăgŏnĭa** -ae, f. (Παφλαγονία), *a district in Asia Minor, between Pontus and Bithynia.*

Păphus (-ŏs) -i (Πάφος). (1) m. *son of Pygmalion, founder of the town Paphos.* (2) f. *Paphos, a town in Cyprus, sacred to Venus.*
¶ Hence adj. **Păphĭus** -a -um, *Paphian*: heros, *Pygmalion, father of Paphos*; myrtus *sacred to Venus*, Ov.

păpĭlĭo -ōnis, m. *a butterfly*: Ov.

păpilla -ae, f. *a nipple, teat*, used of both human beings and animals: Pl., Plin. L. TRANSF., *the breast*: Verg., etc.

Păpĭrĭus -a -um, *name of a Roman gens.*
¶ Hence adj. **Păpīrĭānus** -a -um, *Papirian.*

Păpĭus -a -um, *name of a Roman gens.*

pappo -are, *to eat*: Pl., Pers.

pappus -i, m. (πάππος), *an old man*: Varr. TRANSF., *the woolly seed of certain plants*: Lucr.

păpŭla -ae, f. *a pimple, pustule*: Verg.

păpўrĭfĕr -fĕra -fĕrum (papyrus/fero), *producing the papyrus*: Nilus, Ov.

păpȳrus -i, m. and f. and **păpȳrum** -i, n. (πάπυρος), *the plant papyrus*: Plin., Luc., Mart. TRANSF., (**1**) *a garment made from the plant*: Juv. (**2**) *paper made from it*: Cat., Mart., Juv.

păr păris, *equal, like, a match*.
In gen., *of persons or things, as adj*. or subst.: pari intervallo, Caes.; pares cum paribus facillime congregantur, Cic.; nube pari, Ov. As adj., with dat., *equal to*: est finitimus oratori poeta ac paene par, Cic.; also with cum: quaedam ex eis paria cum Crasso, Cic.; with inter se: inter se aequales et pares, Cic.; foll. by conj.: par atque, Cic.; par et, Cic. The point of resemblance is indicated by in and the abl.: ut sint pares in amore, Cic.; by abl.: libertate esse parem ceteris, Cic.; by ad: par ad virtutem, Liv.; by infin., poet.
Esp. (**1**) m. and f. as subst., *a companion*: Pl., Cic., Ov. (**2**) n. as subst.: **a**, *the like*: par pari respondere, Cic.; par impar ludere, *to play at odd and even*, Hor.: **b**, *a pair*: tria aut quattuor paria amicorum, Cic.; Hor., Ov.: **c**, *what is suitable, appropriate*: par est, or videtur, with infin., or acc. and infin., or ut and subj., Pl., Cic.
¶ Hence adv. **părĭter**. (**1**) *equally, alike*: caritate non pariter omnes egemus, Cic.; with cum: mecum pariter, Cic.; with ut: Pl.; with dat.: Liv. (**2**) *together, at the same time*: Caes., Verg., Liv., etc.; with cum: pariter cum luna crescere, Cic.

părābĭlis -e (paro), *easily procured, procurable*: divitiae, Cic.; Hor., etc.

părăbŏla -ae and **părăbŏlē** -ēs, f. (παραβολή), *a comparison*: Sen., Quint.

păraphrăsis -is, f. (παράφρασις), *a paraphrase*: Quint.

părārĭus -i, m. (paro), *an agent*: Sen.

părăsīta -ae, f. (parasitus), *a female toady, parasite*: Hor.

părăsītaster -tri, m. (parasitus), *a poor, contemptible parasite*: Ter.

părăsītătĭo -ōnis, f. (parasitus), *a playing the parasite*: Pl.

părăsītĭcus -a -um (parasitus), *like a parasite, parasitic*: Pl.

părăsītor -ari, dep. (parasitus), *to play the parasite*: Pl.

părăsītus -i, m. (παράσιτος, *eating with another*), *a guest*: Pl.; usually in bad sense, *a toady, parasite*: Pl., Cic., Hor.

părātē, adv. from paro; q.v.

părātĭo -ōnis, f. (paro), *a preparing for*: paratio regni, *a striving after sovereignty*, Sall.

păratrăgoedo -are (παρατραγῳδέω), *to talk pompously*: Pl.

¹părātus -a -um, partic. from paro; q.v.

²părātus -ūs, m. (paro), *preparation, fitting out, provision, equipment*: necessarius vitae cultus aut paratus, Cic.; Liv., Ov., Tac.

Parca -ae, f. *a goddess that allots his fate to each, goddess of fate*: Hor. Plur., Parcae, *the three Fates*, Clotho, Lachesis, and Atropos, Cic.

parcē, adv. from parcus; q.v.

parceprōmus -i, m. (parcus/promo), *a niggard*: Pl.

parcĭtās -ātis, f. (parcus), *sparingness*: Sen.

parco -parcĕre pĕperci (and parci) parsum, *to spare, to be sparing, to economize*.

LIT., tolerare posse parcendo, Caes.; with dat.: impensae, Liv.; sumptu, Cic. L.; with acc.: talenta natis parce tuis, Verg.
TRANSF., (**1**) *to spare, refrain from injuring*; with dat. of person or thing: aedificiis, Cic.; sibi, Caes., Verg., etc. (**2**) *to refrain from, keep oneself from*; with dat.: lamentis, Liv.; bello, metu, Verg.; with ab: ab incendiis, Liv.; with infin., *to forbear to*: Verg., Liv., etc.

parcus -a -um, adj. (with superl.) (parco), *sparing, frugal, thrifty, economical*. LIT., colonus, Cic.; with genit.: donandi, Hor. TRANSF., (**1**) of persons, *moderate, sparing*: in largienda civitate, Cic.; parcus deorum cultor, Hor. (**2**) of things, *scanty, small, meagre*: parco sale contingere, Verg.; lucerna, Prop.
¶ Hence adv. (with compar. and superl.) **parcē**, *sparingly, frugally, economically*: frumentum parce metiri, Caes.; Cic. TRANSF., *sparingly, moderately*: parcius dicere de laude alicuius, Cic.; parcius quatiunt fenestras, Hor.; Verg.

pardus -i, m. (πάρδος), *a panther*, perhaps also *a leopard*: Juv.

¹părens -entis, partic. from pareo; q.v.

²părens -entis, c. (pario), *a parent, father, mother*. LIT., quae caritas est inter natos et parentes, Cic.; alma parens Idaea deum, Hor.; Verg., etc.; *a grandfather*: Ov.; plur., *ancestors*: Verg. TRANSF., *author, cause, origin*: operum, Cic.; parens lyrae, *Mercury*, Hor.

părentālis -e (²parens), *parental, of parents* (or *ancestors*): umbra, Ov.; esp., *commemorating dead parents or other relatives*: dies, Ov.; n. pl. as subst. **părentālĭa** -ĭum, *a festival in honour of the dead*: Cic.

părento -are (²parens), *to celebrate the parentalia in honour of the dead, esp. of dead relatives*: Februario mense mortuis parentari voluerunt, Cic.; Lucr. TRANSF., *to bring an offering to the dead, i.e. to avenge the death of a person by that of another*: civibus Romanis, Caes.; parentandum regi sanguine coniuratorum esse, Liv.

părĕo -ēre (akin to paro), *to appear, become evident*.
LIT., caeli cui sidera parent, Verg.; esp. impers.: paret, legal formula, *it is proved*, Cic. TRANSF., *to obey, be obedient to*; in gen.: voluntati, legibus, Cic.; dicto, ducibus, Liv.; Caes.; esp. (**1**) *to yield, give way to*: necessitati, Cic.; promissis, *to perform one's promises*, Ov. (**2**) *to be subject to, to serve*: auctoritati senatūs, Cic.; Caes.
¶ Hence partic. (with compar.) **părens** -entis, *obedient*: parentiores exercitūs, Cic. M. pl. as subst., *subjects*: Sall.

părĭēs -ĕtis, m. *a wall, properly the wall of a house*: nullo modo posse iisdem parietibus tuto esse tecum, *within the same house*, Cic.; prov.: duo parietes de eādem fideliā dealbare, *to kill two birds with one stone*, ap. Cic. L.; Caes., Verg., Hor.

părĭĕtĭnae -ārum, f. pl. (paries), *old walls, ruined walls, ruins*: Cic. TRANSF., reipublicae, Cic.

Părīlia = Palilia (see Pales).

părĭlis -e (par), *similar, like, equal*: aetas, Ov.; Lucr.

pario — Parthaon

părĭo parĕre pĕpĕri partum; fut. partic., **părĭtūrus**, *to bring forth, to bear.*
LIT., quintum, *for the fifth time,* Cic.; of birds: ova, *to lay eggs,* Cic.; in gen., *to bring forth, produce*: fruges et reliqua quae terra pariat, Cic.
TRANSF., *to produce, occasion, create*: sibi salutem, Caes.; sibi laudem, Cic.; sibi letum, Verg.; gratiam, Liv.

Părĭs -ĭdis, m. (Πάρις), *a Trojan prince who carried away Helen from her husband Menelaus to Troy, and thus caused the Trojan war.*

Părīsĭi -ōrum, m. *a people in Gallia Celtica, whose capital was Lutetia (Parisiorum) (now Paris).*

părĭtĕr, adv. from par; q.v.

părĭto -are (freq. of paro), *to prepare, to get ready*: Pl.

¹parma -ae, f. (πάρμη), *a small round shield or buckler, used by light-armed troops and cavalry*: Liv.; poet., *any kind of shield*: Lucr., Verg.

²Parma -ae, f. *a town in Gallia Cispadana (now Parma).*
¶ Hence adj. **Parmensis** -e, *of Parma.*

parmātus -a -um (parma), *armed with the parma*: Liv.

parmŭla -ae, f. (dim. of parma), *a small round shield, buckler*: Hor.

Parnāsus (-ŏs) -i, m. (Παρνασός), *a mountain in Phocis, sacred to Apollo and the Muses.*
¶ Hence f. adj. **Parnāsis** -ĭdis, and adj. **Parnāsĭus** -a -um, *Parnassian, Delphian, relating to Apollo*: laurus, Verg.

păro -are. (1) *to set, put*: Pl. (2) *to prepare, make ready, provide, furnish.* With acc.: convivium, Cic.; bellum, Caes.; alicui necem, Liv.; with infin., *to prepare to do something*: publicas litteras Romam mittere parabam, Cic.; foll. by ut with the subj.: si ita naturā paratum esset, ut ea dormientes agerent, Cic.; absol., *to get ready*: Cic. L., Liv. (3) *to procure, get, obtain*: amicos, Cic.; exercitum, copias, Sall.; non modo pacem sed etiam societatem, Liv.; praesidium senectuti, Cic. Esp., *to procure with money, buy*: iumenta, Caes.; hortos, Cic. L.
¶ Hence partic. (with compar. and superl.) **părātus** -a -um, *prepared, ready.* In gen., of things: victoria, *easily won,* Liv.; parata in agendo et in respondendo celeritas, Cic.; omnia sibi esse ad bellum apta ac parata, Caes.; of persons: animo paratus, Caes.; ad omnia mulieris negotia paratus, Cic.; with dat.: vel bello vel paci, Cic.; acies parata neci, Verg.; with infin.: id quod parati sunt facere, Cic.; Caes.
Esp. (1) *provided, equipped*: adulescens et equitatu et peditatu et pecuniā paratus, Cic. (2) *skilled, well versed*: in agendo, Cic.
¶ Adv. **părātē,** *with preparation, readily*: ad dicendum venire magis audacter quam parate, Cic.

părŏcha -ae, f. (παροχή), *a supplying of necessaries*: Cic. L.

părŏchus -i, m. (πάροχος), *an officer, in Italy or in the provinces, who provided with necessaries ambassadors and magistrates when on a journey*: Cic. L., Hor. TRANSF., *a host*: Hor.

părŏpsis -ĭdis, f. (παροψίς), *a small dish, dessert-dish*: Juv., Suet.

Părŏs (-us) -i, f. (Πάρος), *an island in the Aegean Sea, famous for its white marble.*
¶ Hence adj. **Părĭus** -a -um (Πάριος), *Parian*: lapis, *Parian marble,* Verg.; iambi, *of Archilochus, who was born at Paros,* Verg.

parra -ae, f. *a bird of ill omen, perhaps the owl*: Hor.

Parrhăsĭa -ae, f. (Παρρασία), *a district in Arcadia.*
¶ Hence f. adj. **Parrhăsĭs** -ĭdis, f. *Arcadian*: ursa, *the Great Bear,* Ov.; as subst., *an Arcadian woman,* Callisto: Ov.; adj. **Parrhăsĭus** -a -um. (1) *Arcadian*: virgo, Callisto, Ov.; dea, Carmenta, Ov. (2) *relating to the Palatine Hill, imperial* (because the Arcadian Evander was said to have settled upon the Palatine): Mart.

¹Parrhăsĭus, see Parrhasia.

²Parrhăsĭus -i, m. (Παρράσιος), *a celebrated Greek painter of Ephesus, flourishing about 400 B.C.*

parrĭcīda -ae, c. (probably from pater/caedo), *a parricide, one who murders a parent or near relative.* LIT., parricida liberum, Virginius, Liv., Cic., Hor., etc. TRANSF., polit., *a murderer, assassin, traitor*: civium, Cic.; reipublicae, Cic.; of Caesar's murderers: Cic.

parrĭcīdĭum -i, n. (parricida). (1) *the murder of a parent or any near relative.* LIT., fratris, Liv.; patris et patrui, Cic. TRANSF., polit., *murder, assassination, treason*: patriae, *the betraying of one's country,* Cic.; of the murder of Caesar: Suet.

pars partis; acc. partim and partem; abl. parti and parte; f., *a part, portion, piece, share.*
LIT., urbis, Cic.; partes facere, *to divide,* Cic.; partem habere in aliqua re, *to have a share in,* Cic.; maxima pars hominum, Hor.; dimidia pars, ½, Caes.; tertia, ⅓, Caes.; partes duae, ⅔, Liv.; tres partes, ¾, Caes.
TRANSF., (1) *side, direction*: a sinistra parte, Caes.; in plur., *regions*: partes orientis, Cic. (2) *side, party*: nullius partis esse, *to be neutral,* Cic.; Caes., Sall., Tac. (3) *the part* or *role of an actor*: primas partes agere, Ter.; hence, in gen., usually plur., *part, office, function, duty*: tuum est hoc munus, tuae partes, Cic. L.; imperatoris, Cic. L.; Liv., etc.; sing.: Cic.
In phrases: pars . . . pars, *some . . . others,* Liv.; parte . . . parte, *partly . . . partly,* Ov.; pro parte, *or* pro sua, mea, etc., parte, *to the best of one's ability,* Cic. L., Ov.; also: pro virili parte, Cic., Liv., Ov.; magna ex parte, *to a great extent,* Cic.; omni (ex) parte, *altogether,* Cic., Liv.; magnam partem, *to a great extent,* Cic., Liv.; in eam partem, *in that direction,* Cic.; in utramque partem, *on both sides,* Cic.; in omnes partes, *altogether, completely,* Cic.; in partem venire alicuius rei, *to take a share in,* Cic.; multis partibus, *many times, much*: plures, Cic.
¶ Old acc. as adv. **partim.** (1) *partly*: Ter., Caes., Cic.; sometimes, *for the most part*: Pl. (2) used like a noun, *some*: partim ex illis dissipati iacent, Caes., Verg.

parsĭmōnĭa -ae, f. (parco), *thrift, parsimony*: Pl., Ter., Cic. TRANSF., of style: Cic.

Parthāŏn -ŏnis, m. (Παρθάων), *son of Agenor king of Calydon, father of Oeneus*: Parthaone natus, Oeneus, Ov.

[424]

parthĕnĭcē -ēs, f. (παϱθενιϰή), *a plant*: Cat.

Parthĕnŏpē -ēs, f. (Παϱθενόπη), *old name of the town Neapolis, from the siren Parthenope, who was said to have been buried there.* Adj. **Parthĕnŏpēïus** -a -um, *Parthenopean*: poet. = *Neapolitan*.

Parthi -ōrum, m. pl. (Πάϱθοι), *the Parthians, a Scythian people, famous for their archery.* ¶ Hence adj. **Parthĭcus** and **Parthus** -a -um, *Parthian*; subst. **Parthia** -ae, f. *their country, south-east of the Caspian.*

partĭceps -cĭpis (pars/capio), *sharing, participating in.* LIT., with genit.: animus rationis compos et particeps, Cic.; praedae ac praemiorum, Caes. As subst., *a partner, sharer, comrade*: huius belli ego particeps et socius et adiutor esse cogor, Cic. L.; alicui ad omne secretum, Tac. TRANSF., *cognizant*; with indir. quest.: Pl.

partĭcĭpĭālis -e (participium), *of the nature of a participle*: Quint.

partĭcĭpĭum -i, n. (particeps), *a participle*: Quint.

partĭcĭpo -are (particeps). (1) *to share with anyone*: laudes cum aliquo, Liv.; communicandumque inter omnes ius, Cic. (2) *with the person sharing as object, to cause to share*: Pl.; pass.: Lucr.

partĭcŭla -ae, f. (dim. of pars), *a small part, portion, particle*: caeli, Cic.; Hor., Quint.

artĭcŭlātim, adv. *piecemeal*: Varr., Sen.

artim, adv. *from pars*; q.v.

partĭo -ōnis, f. (pario), *a bringing forth*: Pl.

partĭo -ire and **partĭor** -iri, dep. (pars), *to share out, distribute, divide*: genus universum in species certas partietur ac dividet, Cic.; consules designati provincias inter se partiverant, Sall.; nonne aerarium cum eo partitus es? Cic.; Verg., Liv., etc. ¶ Perf. partic. in pass. sense **partītus** -a -um, *divided*: Caes., Liv., etc. ¶ Adv. **partītē**, *with proper divisions*: dicere, Cic.

artĭtĭo -ōnis, f. (partio), *a division, sharing, distribution*: Graecos partitionem quandam artium fecisse video, Cic.; aequabilis praedae partitio, Cic.; esp., *a logical or rhetorical division of a subject*: Cic., Quint.

artītus -a -um, partic. from partior; q.v.

arturĭo -ire (desider. of pario), *to desire to bring forth, have the pains of labour.* LIT., Ter., Ov.; prov.: parturiunt montes, nascetur ridiculus mus, Hor. TRANSF., *to be pregnant with anything, teem with, be full of.* (1) of physical products: nunc omnis parturit arbos, Verg.; Hor. (2) mentally: ut aliquando dolor P. R. pariat, quod iamdiu parturit! Cic.; ira minas, Ov.

partus -a -um, partic. from pario; q.v.

partus -ūs, m. (pario), *a bearing, bringing forth, a birth.* LIT., cum iam appropinquare partus putaretur, Cic.; Hor., Juv. TRANSF., (1) *the beginnings*: oratorum partus atque fontes, *beginnings*, Cic. (2) *young, offspring*: partum edere, Cic.; partus terrae, *the giants*, Hor.; Verg.

ărum, adv. (from same root as parvus), with compar. **mĭnŭs**, superl. **mĭnĭmē**.

Posit. **părum**, *too little, not enough* (opp. satis, nimium). With verbs, adverbs, adjectives: Pl., Caes., Cic., Hor., etc. As subst., *too little, not enough*: Cic.; with

genit., *too little of*: Cic.; parum est, *it is not enough that*; foll. by quod, Cic.; by acc. and infin., Liv.; parum habere, *to think too little, be dissatisfied with*; foll. by infin., Liv. Compar. **mĭnus**, *less*. (1) with verbs, adverbs, adjectives: Caes., etc. With quam: respondebo tibi minus fortasse vehementer, quam, etc., Cic.; with abl. of measure: puniendum certe nihilo minus, Cic. Esp. for *not, not at all*: nonnunquam ea quae praedicta sunt minus eveniunt, Cic.; sin minus, *but if not*, Cic. L.; minus minusque, *less and less*, Liv.; for quo minus, *see* quominus. (2) as subst., *less, a less amount*: Cic.; with genit.: minus militum periit, Liv.; Cic., etc. With quam, or abl. of comparison or of measure: cum paulo minus duobus milibus militum, Liv.; as internal acc., with posse: Cic.

Superl. **mĭnĭmē** (**mĭnŭmē**), *in the least degree, very little, least of all*: quod minime apparet et valet plurimum, Cic. With adjectives = *not at all, by no means*: homo minime ambitiosus, Cic.; Caes., Liv.; with genit.: minime gentium, Pl., Ter.; with quam, *as little as possible*: Cic. In replies, *by no means, not at all*: Pl., Ter., Cic.

părumpĕr, adv. *for a little while*: abduco parumper animum a molestiis, Cic.; Verg., etc.

Părus = Paros; q.v.

parvĭtās -ātis, f. (parvus), *littleness, smallness*: Cic.

parvŭlus -a -um (dim. of parvus), *very small, very little*: pecunia, Cic.; detrimentum, Caes.; res, Hor. Esp. of age, *young, little*: filius, Cic.; ab parvulis, *from childhood*, Caes.; Verg.

parvus -a -um, adj. (with compar. **mĭnor**, superl. **mĭnĭmus**).

Posit. **parvus** -a -um, *little, small.* LIT., of size, number, or extent: locus, Cic.; pisciculi, Cic.; cibus, Ov. TRANSF., (1) in gen., *slight, weak*: parvae murmura vocis, Ov. (2) of time, *short*: Caes., Cic., etc. (3) of age, *young*: a parvo, *from boyhood*, Cic.; Hor., etc. of value, *poor, insignificant*: pretio parvo vendere, Cic.; domus, Ov.; esp. in n. genit.: parvi facere, aestimare, ducere, *to hold cheap*, Pl., Cic., etc.; also abl.: parvo stat, Ov. N. as subst. **parvum** -i, *a little*: contentus parvo, Cic. L.

Compar. **mĭnor**, *smaller, less.* LIT., Hibernia minor quam Britannia, Caes. TRANSF., of time, *shorter*: Ov., Juv.; of age: minor natu, *younger*, Caes., Cic.; of value, *inferior*: virtute et honore, Hor.; capitis minor = capite deminutus, Hor.; minoris vendere, Cic.

Superl. **mĭnĭmus**, *smallest, least.* LIT., minima tela, Liv. TRANSF., minima licentia, Sall.; minimus natu, Cic., Sall.; prov.: minima de malis, *we must choose the least evil*, Cic. N. as adv. **mĭnĭmum**, *very little*: minimum valent, Cic.; Hor.

Rare superl. **parvissĭmus** -a -um: Varr., Lucr.

pasco pascĕre pāvi pastum (from root of panis). (1) transit., *to feed, lead to pasture.* LIT., sues, Cic.; Verg., Liv.; hence, gen., *to feed, keep, support*; of animals: ubi bestiae pastae

sunt, Cic.; of human beings: holusculis nos
soles pascere, Cic.; quot pascit servos, Juv.;
with place or pasture as subject: Verg., Hor.;
also, *to give as pasture*: asperrima (collium),
Verg.; pass. as middle, *to graze on*: frondibus,
Verg.; per herbas, Verg.; with acc.: silvas,
Verg. TRANSF., **a**, *to nourish, feed, make
grow*: aether sidera, Lucr.; Pergama flammas,
Ov.; of hair: barbam, Hor.; crinem, Verg.:
b, *to feast, gratify*: oculos in aliqua re, Cic.;
Verg.; pass. as middle, *to feast upon, delight
in*: Cic.

(2) intransit., of animals, *to graze, browse*:
pascentes capellae, Verg.; Pl.

pascŭus -a -um (pasco), *for pasture or grazing*:
ager, Cic. Lucr.; N. as subst. **pascŭum** -i,
a pasture; plur. **pascŭa** -ōrum, n. *pastures*:
Cic., Verg., Ov.

Pāsĭphăĕ -ēs, f. and **Pāsĭphăa** -ae, f.
(Πασιφάη), *daughter of Helios, sister of Circe,
mother of the Minotaur, Androgeus, Phaedra,
and Ariadne*. Adj. **Pāsĭphăēĭus** -a -um, *of
Pasiphaë*; subst. **Pāsĭphăēĭa** -ae, f.=
Phaedra: Ov.

Pāsĭthĕa -ae, f. and **Pāsĭthĕē** -ēs, f. (Πασιθέα,
Πασιθέη), *one of the three Graces*.

passer -ĕris, m. *a sparrow or other small bird*:
Cat., Cic.; as term of endearment: Pl.
TRANSF., (**1**) passer marinus, *an ostrich*, Pl.
(**2**) *a sea-fish, a plaice or flounder*: Ov.

passercŭlus -i, m. (dim. of passer), *a little
sparrow*: Cic.; as term of endearment: Pl.

passim, adv. (passus, from pando), *here and
there, up and down, far and wide*. LIT.,
fugere, Caes.; Numidae nullis ordinibus
passim consederant, Caes.; Cic., Verg., Liv.
TRANSF., *indiscriminately, promiscuously*:
scribimus indocti doctique poëmata passim,
Hor.

passīvus -a -um (patior), *passive*: Quint.

passum -i, n., subst. from pando; q.v.

¹passus -a -um, partic. from pando; q.v.

²passus -a -um, partic. from patior; q.v.

³passus -ūs, m. (pando), *a step, stride, pace*.
LIT., passūs perpauculi, Cic.; sequiturque
patrem non passibus aequis, Verg.; passibus
ambiguis Fortuna errat, Ov. TRANSF., (**1**) *a
footstep, track*: passu stare tenaci, Ov. (**2**) *the
pace*, a Roman measure of length, consisting
of five Roman feet: mille passus, *a mile*,
Cic., etc.

pastillus -i, m. *a lozenge used to give an agreeable smell to the breath*: Hor.

pastĭo -ōnis, f. (pasco), *pasturing, or a pasture*:
Cic.

pastor -ōris, m. (pasco), *a herd*; esp., *a
shepherd*: Cic.; pastorum domina, *Pales*,
Ov.; Verg., etc.

pastōrālis -e (pastor), *of a shepherd, pastoral*:
Cic., Verg., Liv., etc.

pastōrĭcĭus -a -um (pastor), *of shepherds*: Cic.

pastōrĭus -a -um (pastor), *of shepherds*: Ov.

¹pastus -a -um, partic. from pasco; q.v.

²pastus -ūs, m. (pasco), *pasture, feeding*. LIT.,
ad pastum accedunt, Cic.; Verg. TRANSF.,
fig., *food, sustenance*: animorum, Cic.

Pătăra -ae, f. (Πάταρα), *a city in Lycia, with a
celebrated oracle of Apollo*.
¶ Hence **Pătărĕüs** -ĕi and -ĕos, m. *a
surname of Apollo*; adj. **Pătăraeus** -a -um,
Patarean; subst. **Pătărāni** -ōrum, m. pl.,
the inhabitants of Patara.

Pătăvĭum -i, n. *a town in North Italy, birth-
place of the historian Livy* (now *Padua*).
Adj. **Pătăvīnus** -a -um, *Patavinian*.

pătĕfăcĭo -făcĕre -fēci -factum; pass.
pătĕfīo -fĭeri -factus sum (pateo/facio), *to
open, throw open, lay open*. LIT., aures
adsentatoribus, Cic.; sulcum aratro, Ov.; of
places, *to make accessible, to open up*: vias,
iter, Caes.; patefactum nostris legionibus
esse Pontum, Cic. TRANSF., *to bring to light,
disclose, reveal*: odium suum in me, Cic.;
with indir. quest.: Cic.

pătĕfactĭo -ōnis, f. (patefacio), *a throwing
open, disclosing*: rerum opertarum, Cic.

pătella -ae, f. (dim. of patera), *a dish, platter,
plate used for cooking and serving up food*:
Hor.; esp., *a dish in which offerings were
presented to the gods, a sacrificial dish*: Cic.,
Ov., Liv.

pătĕo -ēre (connected with πετάννυμι), *to be
open, stand open, lie open*.
LIT., semper propter necessarias utilitates
patent, Cic.; portae, Cic., Liv. Esp. (**1**) *to
be open, accessible*: aditus patuit, Cic.;
semitae, Caes. (**2**) *to lie open to, to be exposed
to*: vulneri, Liv.; Ov.; *to be revealed, dis-
closed, clear*: res patent, Cic. (**3**) *to stretch
out, extend*: Helvetiorum fines in longitudinem millia passuum CXL patebant, Cic.
TRANSF., (**1**) *to be open, accessible*: honores
alicui, Cic.; commoda plebi, Ov.; Verg
(**2**) *to be subject, liable to*: Cic., Liv. (**3**) *to
spread, extend*: in quo vitio latissime patet
avaritia, Cic.
¶ Hence partic. (with compar.) **pătens**
-entis. LIT., *open, unobstructed, accessible*:
caelum, Cic.; loca, Caes.; via, Liv. TRANSF.
(**1**) *exposed to*: domus patens cupiditati e
voluptatibus, Cic. (**2**) *evident*: Ov.
¶ Compar. adv. **pătentĭus**, *more openly*
Cic.

păter -tris, m. (πατήρ), *a father*.
LIT., aliquem patris loco colere, Cic.
plur.: patres, *parents*, Ov. Of animals, *sire*
Ov.
TRANSF., (**1**) pater familias, *or familiae
the head of a household*, Cic. (**2**) plur., patres
in gen. sense, *our fathers*; aetas patrum no
strorum, Cic.; also *forefathers*: Verg. (**3**) o
the gods: Lemnius, *Vulcan*, Cic.; Lenaeus
Bacchus, Verg.; Hor., Liv., etc. (**4**) *the titl
by which the senators were addressed*
patres, *or patres conscripti*, Cic. (**5**) pater
patriae, *father of his country*, a name give
to national heroes, Cic. (**6**) as a title c
respect towards an old man: Verg. (**7**) i
gen., *founder or head of any race, community
study*, etc.: Herodotus pater historiae, Cic.
Verg., etc.

pătĕra -ae, f. (pateo), *a shallow dish or sauce
from which a libation was poured*: Pl., Cic
Verg., etc.

Pătercŭlus -i, m., C. Velleius, *a Roma
historian under Augustus and Tiberius*.

păterfamĭlĭās, *see* pater.

păternus -a -um (pater), *of a father, paterna
Ter., Cic., Verg., etc. TRANSF., *of one
ancestors or of one's native country, nativ
flumen, Hor.; Ov., Prop.

pătesco pătescĕre pătŭi (pateo), *to be opene
lie open*. LIT., atria longa patescunt, Verg
deinde paulo latior patescit campus, *ope*

out, Liv.; Tac. TRANSF., (1) *to be revealed*: Danaum insidiae, Verg. (2) *to spread*: Liv.

pătĭbĭlis -e (patior). Pass., *endurable, bearable*: dolores, Cic. Act., *sensitive*: natura, Cic.

pătĭbŭlātus -a -um (patibulum), *pilloried*: Pl.

pătĭbŭlum -i, n. (pateo), *a pillory, a fork-shaped yoke, an instrument of punishment fastened to slaves and criminals*: Pl., Cic., Tac., etc.

pătĭens -entis, partic. from patior; q.v.

pătĭentĭa -ae, f. (patiens), *endurance*. LIT., physical: Cic.; with genit.: famis, frigoris, Cic. TRANSF., mental; in good sense, *resignation*: Cic., Hor.; in bad sense, *subjection, want of spirit*: Tac.

pătĭna -ae, f. (πατάνη), *a dish*: Pl., Cic. L., Hor.

pătĭnārĭus -a -um (patina), *in* or *of dishes*: Pl.

pătĭor păti passus sum, dep. (connected with πάσχω), *to suffer, undergo*.

LIT., physically: toleranter dolores, Cic.; gravissimum supplicium, Caes.; hiemem et aestatem, Sall.; Verg., etc.; of things: tunc patitur cultūs ager, Ov.

TRANSF., not physically, *to suffer, experience*: iniuriam, Cic.; novem saecula (of the crow), Ov.; multam repulsam, Ov.; esp., *to permit, allow*: ista, Cic.; with infin.: Verg., Hor.; with acc. and infin.: nullo se implicari negotio passus est, Cic.; Liv., etc.; with ut and the subj.: quod si in turpi reo patiendum non esset ut arbitrarentur, Cic.; in neg., foll. by quin: nullam patiebatur esse diem quin in foro diceret, Cic.; with adv.: facile, libenter, aequo animo, indigne pati, Cic.; with things as subjects: quantum patiebatur pudor, Cic.

¶ Hence partic. (with compar. and superl.) **pătĭens** -entis, *bearing, enduring, capable of enduring*. LIT., physically: Caes., etc.; with objective genit.: patiens laborum, Sall.; pulveris atque solis, Hor.; amnis navium patiens, *navigable*, Liv.; terra vomeris, Verg. TRANSF., mentally; *enduring, patient*: ut ne offendam tuas patientissimas aures, Cic.; animus, Ov.; in bad sense, *stubborn*: Prop.

¶ Adv. (with compar.) **pătĭentĕr**, *patiently*: ferre, Cic.; Hor., etc.

atrae -ārum, f. (Πάτραι), *a sea-port in Achaia* (now *Patras*). Adj. **Patrensis** -e, *of Patrae*.

atrātor -ōris, m. (patro), *an accomplisher, achiever*: necis, Tac.

atrĭa -ae, f. *fatherland, see* patrius.

atrĭcĭātus -ūs, m. *the rank of a patrician*: Suet.

atrĭcĭus -a -um (patres), *of the patres, patrician, noble*: familia, Cic.; gens: Juv. M. as subst., *a patrician*, and plur., patricii, *the Roman patricians* or *nobility*: Cic., Liv., Juv.; exire e patriciis, *to be adopted into a plebeian family*, Cic.

atrĭmōnĭum -i, n. (pater), *property inherited from a father, patrimony*: accipere duo lauta et copiosa patrimonia, Cic.; Juv. TRANSF., filio meo satis amplum patrimonium relinquam, memoriam nominis mei, Cic.

atrimus -a -um (pater), *having a father still living*: Cic., Liv., Tac.

atrisso -are (πατρίζω), *to resemble one's father*: Pl., Ter.

atrītus -a -um (pater), *inherited from one's*

father: patrita illa atque avita philosophia, Cic.

patrĭus -a -um (pater), *of* or *relating to a father, fatherly, paternal*. LIT., animus, Ter., Cic., Liv.; amor, Cic., Verg. TRANSF., (1) *hereditary*: res, *property inherited from one's father*, Cic.; mos, *ancestral*, Cic. (2) *native*: Cic., Verg.

¶ F. as subst. **patrĭa** -ae (sc. terra), *fatherland, native land*: aliquem restituere in patriam, Cic.; Verg., Ov., etc.

patro -are (pater), *to father*; hence *to accomplish, perform, execute, achieve*: promissa, Cic.; bellum, *to bring to an end*, Sall.; pacem, Liv.; iusiurandum, Liv.

patrōcĭnĭum -i, n. (patronus/cano).

LIT., *the services of a patron*: cuius patrocinio civitas plurimum utebatur, Sall.; esp., *defence in a court of law*: controversiarum patrocinia suscipere, Cic.

TRANSF., (1) patrocinia=*clients*, ap. Cic. L. (2) in gen., *defence, protection*: patrocinium voluptatis repudiare, Cic.; Liv.

patrōcĭnor -ari, dep. (patronus), *to protect, defend*: alicui, Ter., Tac.

Patroclus -i, m. (Πάτροκλος), *son of Menoetius, friend of Achilles, slain by Hector before Troy*.

patrōna -ae, f. (patronus), *a protectress, patroness*. LIT., esp., *the protectress of a freedman*: Plin. L. TRANSF., (1) of a goddess: Pl. (2) in gen., *protectress*: provocatio, patrona illa civitatis et vindex libertatis, Cic.

patrōnus -i, m. (pater), *a protector, defender*.

LIT., (1) *the patron* of clients, dependants, and ex-slaves: Pl., Cic. L., Liv., Tac. (2) *the patron of a body of clients; the patron at Rome of a foreign state* or *city*: Cic., Liv. (3) *a defender, advocate before a court of justice*: huic causae patronum exstiti, Cic.

TRANSF., in gen., *a defender, protector*: foederum, Cic.; Pl.

patrŭēlis -e (patruus), *descended from a father's brother*: frater patruelis, *cousin on the father's side*, Cic.; origo, Ov.; m. and f. as subst., *a cousin, son* or *daughter*, usually of a father's brother, sometimes of a father's sister: Cic.

¹**patrŭus** -i, m. (pater), *a father's brother, paternal uncle*. LIT., Cic., Hor. TRANSF., *a severe reprover*: Hor.

²**patrŭus** -a -um (¹patruus), *of an uncle*: Hor., Ov.; superl.: Pl.

pătŭlus -a -um (pateo), *open, standing open*. LIT., pina, Cic.; fenestrae, Ov.; nares, Verg. TRANSF., (1) *spreading, extended*: rami, Cic.; loca urbis, Tac.; Verg. (2) *open to all*: Hor.

paucĭlŏquĭum -i, n. (paucus/loquor), *a speaking but little*: Pl.

paucĭtās -ātis, f. (paucus), *fewness, scarcity, paucity*: oratorum, Cic.; militum, Caes.; Liv.

paucŭlus -a -um (dim. of paucus), *very small*; gen. in plur., *very few*: dies, Cic. L.; Pl., Ter.

paucus -a -um, oftener plur. **pauci** -ae -a, adj. (with compar. and superl.) (connected with paulus and Gr. παῦρος), *few, little*: pauco foramine (=paucis foraminibus), Hor.; paucis rebus, Cic.; pauciores viri, Cic.

¶ As subst., m. pl. **pauci** -ōrum, *a few*; esp. (1) (like οἱ ὀλίγοι), *the oligarchs*. (2) *the select few* (opp. populus): Cic.; n. pl. **pauca** -ōrum, *a few words*: ut in pauca conferam, Cic.; Verg., Liv.

paulātim (paullātim), adv. *gradually, little by little*: paulatim ab imo acclivis, Caes.; si paulatim haec consuetudo serpere ac prodire coeperit, Cic.; licentia crevit, Sall.

paulispĕr (paullispĕr), adv. *for a little while, for a short time*: partes alicuius suscipere, Cic.; foll. by dum: Cic.; by donec: Liv.; Caes., etc.

paulō (paullō), *see* paulus.

paulŭlo (paullŭlo), *see* paululus.

paulŭlus (paullŭlus) -a -um (dim. of paulus), *very little, very small*: pecunia, Pl.; via, Liv. N. as subst. **paulŭlum** -i, *a very little*: morae, Cic.; acc. as adv., *a little*: paululum respirare, Cic.; Caes.; **paulŭlo**, as abl. of price: Ter.; as abl. of measure, with compar.: paululo deterius, *a little worse*, ap. Cic. L.

¹**paulus (paullus)** -a -um (connected with paucus and Gr. παῦρος), *little, small*: sumptus, Ter. N. as subst. **paulum**, *a little*: paulum aliquid damni, Cic.; Hor., Liv.; acc. as adv., *a little*: commorari, Cic.; Caes.; **paulō**, as abl. of measure, esp. with compar.: paulo melior, *a little better*, Cic.; paulo ante, Lucr., Cic.; post paulo, Sall., Liv.

²**Paulus (Paullus)** -i, m. *the name of a family of the gens Aemilia, of which the most famous members were* (1) L. Aemilius Paulus, *who commanded, with C. Terentius Varro, at Cannae, in* 216 B.C., *and was there slain.* (2) L. Aemilius Paulus Macedonicus, *son of the preceding, the conqueror of Macedonia.*

pauper -ĕris (perhaps connected with paucus), adj. (with compar. and superl.), *poor, not wealthy.* (1) of persons: homo, Cic.; vir, Cic.; with genit.: argenti, Hor.; as subst.: pauper, *a poor man*, Ov. (2) of things, *poor, scanty, meagre*: domus, Verg.; Pl., Ov.

paupercŭlus -a -um (dim. of pauper), *poor*: Pl., Hor.

paupĕriēs -ēi, f. (pauper), *poverty*: Pl., Verg., Hor., Tac.

paupĕro -are (pauper), *to make poor*: Pl.; with abl., *to deprive of*: aliquem nuce, Hor.; Pl.

paupertās -ātis, f. (pauper), *poverty, humble circumstances* (opp. divitiae): infelix, Juv.; Cic., Hor., etc. TRANSF., of language: Quint.

pausa -ae, f. (παῦσις), *a cessation, end*: vitai, Lucr.; Pl.

pausia -ae, f. *a species of olive, which produced good oil*: Verg.

Pausiās -ae, acc. -an, m. (Παυσίας), *a Greek painter of Sicyon, contemporary with Apelles.* Adj. **Pausiācus** -a -um. *of Pausias*: tabella, Hor.

pausillŭlum = pauxillulum, *see* pauxillulus.

pauxillātim, adv. (pauxillus), *gradually, by degrees*: Pl.

pauxillispĕr, adv. (pauxillus), *gradually, by degrees*: Pl.

pauxillŭlus -a -um (dim. of pauxillus), *very little, very small*: Ter.; n. as subst. **pauxillŭlum** -i, *a very little*: Pl.

pauxillus -a -um (dim. of paucus), *small, little*: Pl., Lucr.; n. as subst. **pauxillum** -i, *a little*: Pl.

păvĕfactus -a -um (paveo/facio), *frightened, terrified*: Ov., Suet.

păvĕo păvēre păvi. (1) intransit., *to quake*

with fear, to panic: inde admiratione paventibus cunctis, Liv.; Ov., etc. (2) transit., *to quake at*: omnia Sall.; funera, Hor.; with infin.: Ov., Tac.,

păvesco -ĕre (paveo). (1) intransit., *to begin to quake, take fright*: omni strepitu, Sall. (2) transit., *to be alarmed by*: bellum, Tac.

păvĭdus -a -um (paveo), *trembling, quaking fearful.* LIT., of persons: matres, Verg. castris se pavidus tenebat, Liv.; with ne and the subj.: pavidi ne iam facta in urbem via esset, Liv.; with genit.: offensionum, Tac TRANSF., (1) of feelings: metus, Ov. (2 causing fear: Luc., Suet.

¶ Adv. **păvĭdē**, *fearfully, in a state o panic*: fugere, Liv.; Lucr.

păvīmento -are (pavimentum), *to pave* Cic. L.

păvīmentum -i, n. (pavio), *a pavement o tiles, brick, stone*, etc.: pavimentum facere Cic. L.; Caes., Hor.

păvĭo -ire (cf. παίω), *to beat*: terram, Cic. Lucr.

păvĭto -are (freq. of paveo). Intransit., *t tremble, quake with fear*: Verg.; *to shiver wit ague*: Ter. Transit., *to quake with fear at* Lucr.

pāvo -ōnis, m. (cf. Gr. ταῶς), *a peacock*: Lucr. Cic., Juv.

păvor -ōris, m. (paveo), *a trembling, quaking produced by fear or excitement*: Cic., Verg. alicui pavorem inicere, incutere, offundere *to cause fear*, Liv.; pavor aliquem capit foll. by ne and the subj., Liv.; plur.: pavore nocturni, Tac.

pax pācis, f. (root of paciscor), *peace.*

LIT., *a state of peace*, opp. to war: pacer conciliare, conficere, facere cum aliquo, *t make peace*, Cic.; pangere, componere, Liv. servare cum aliquo, *to keep*, Cic.; uti pace to be at peace, Cic.; turbare pacem, Tac. rumpere, Verg.; in pace, Cic.; bello a pace, Liv. Plur., paces, *conditions c proposals of peace*: bella atque paces, Sal Personif.: Pax, *the goddess of Peace*, Hor Ov., etc.

TRANSF., (1) in gen., *calm, serenity, quiel* flumen cum pace delabens, *quietly*, Hor semper in animo sapientis est placidissim pax, Cic. (2) in abl.: pace tuā dixerim, *wit your good leave*, Cic.; C. Claudi pace loqua Liv. (3) of the gods, *grace*: ab Iove ceterisqu dis pacem ac veniam peto, Cic.; Lucr Verg., Liv. (4) as interj.: pax! *peace!* Pl.

peccātum -i, subst. from pecco: q.v.

pecco -are, *to make a mistake, go wrong, e or sin.* With internal acc.: Empedocles mul alia peccat, Cic.; Pl., Ov. With erga: P with in and acc., *against*: Cic. L.; with and abl., *in relation to*: in matronā, Ho in servo necando, Cic.; with plain abl ingenuo amore, Hor.

¶ N. of partic. as subst. **peccātum** -i, *error, fault, sin*: confiteri, Cic.; luere, Verg Hor., etc.

pĕcŏrōsus -a -um (¹pecus), *rich in cattle*: Pro

pecten -inis, m. (pecto), *a comb.*

LIT., *for combing the hair*: deduce pectine crines, Ov.; Pl.

TRANSF., (1) *a weaver's comb*: Verg., O (2) *a rake*: Ov. (3) *the clasping of the han in trouble*: digiti inter se pectine iuncti, O

(4) *a quill,* with which the strings of the lyre were struck: Verg.; meton., *song*: alterno pectine, *in elegiac verse* (first a hexameter, then a pentameter), Ov. (5) *a shell-fish, the scallop*: Hor.

pectĭnātim, adv. (pecten), *in the form of a comb*: Pl.

pecto pectĕre pexi pexum (cf. πέκω), *to comb.* LIT., comas, Ov.; Verg., Hor., etc. TRANSF., (1) *to comb* or *card wool*: stuppam, Plin. (2) *to thrash, batter*: Pl.

¶ Hence partic. **pexus** -a -um, *with the nap on, woolly*: tunica, *new*, Hor.

pectus -ŏris, n. *the breast.* LIT., Cic., Verg., etc. TRANSF., (1) *the breast as the seat of the affections; the heart, soul*: toto pectore amare, *to love with the whole heart,* Cic.; forti pectore, *with courage,* Hor.; puro pectore, *with good conscience,* Hor.; Verg., Ov., etc. (2) *as the seat of reason, understanding, the mind*: toto pectore cogitare, Cic.; excidere pectore alicuius, *to be forgotten,* Ov.; Lucr., Verg., etc.

pecu, n.; nom. and acc. plur. pecŭa (connected with pecus), *sheep, flocks*: Pl., Liv. TRANSF., in plur., *pastures*: Cic.; *money*: Pl.

pĕcŭārĭus -a -um (pecu), *of sheep* or *cattle*: res, Pl., Cic. As subst. (1) m. *a breeder of cattle, grazier*: Cic. Plur.: pecuarii, *the farmers of the public pastures* (in the provinces), Liv. (2) n. pl. **pĕcŭārĭa** -ōrum, *herds of sheep* or *cattle*: Verg.

pĕcŭlātor -ōris, m. (peculor), *one who embezzles public money*: Cic.

pĕcŭlātus -ūs, m. (peculor), *the embezzlement of public money*: peculatum facere, Cic.; Pl., Liv.

pĕcŭlĭāris -e (peculium), *belonging to one's private property*: oves, Pl. TRANSF., *one's own, special, peculiar*: testis, Cic.; urbis vitia, Tac.; Liv.

¶ Adv. **pĕcŭlĭārĭtĕr,** *specially*: Plin., Quint.

pĕcŭlĭātus -a -um (peculium), *provided with property*: ap. Cic. L.

pĕcŭlĭo -are (peculium), *to give as private property.*

pĕcŭlĭŏlum -i, n. (dim. of peculium), *a nest egg*: Quint.

pĕcŭlĭōsus -a -um (peculium), *having private property*: Pl.

pĕcŭlĭum -i, n. (pecu), *small property, savings.* In gen., contemptuously: cupiditate peculii, Cic.; cura peculi, Hor. Esp., *property which members of a familia were allowed to regard as their own*; of the *savings of slaves*: Pl., Cic., Verg.; peculium castrense, *earned by the son on military service*; adventicium, *gained by inheritance from the mother.*

pĕcūnĭa -ae, f. (pecus), *property, wealth.* In gen.: pecuniam facere, *to gain property,* Cic.; Liv., Tac. Esp., *money, cash*: coacervare, conflare pecuniam, *to make money, to become rich,* Cic.; mutuam sumere ab aliquo, *to borrow,* Cic.; conlocatam habere, *to have on mortgage,* Cic.; plur., *sums of money*: Cic., Liv.

pĕcūnĭārĭus -a -um (pecunia), *of money, pecuniary*: res pecuniaria, Caes.; Cic., Tac.

pĕcūnĭōsus -a -um (pecunia), *wealthy, rich*: homo pecuniosissimus, Cic. TRANSF., *lucrative*: Mart.

pĕcus -ŏris, n. (cf. pecu), *cattle, a herd,*

flock (collect., while pecus -ŭdis=*a single head of cattle*). LIT., setigerum, *swine,* Ov.; lanigerum, *sheep,* Ov.; applied also to *bees*: Verg.; to *seals*: Hor. Esp., *a flock of sheep*: balatus pecorum, Ov. TRANSF., applied contemptuously to human beings: imitatorum servum pecus, *a servile herd,* Hor.; Cat., Juv.

²pĕcus -ŭdis, f. (cf. pecu), *a single head of cattle; a beast, animal.* LIT., quā pecude (sc. sue) nihil genuit natura fecundius, Cic.; squamigerum pecudes, *fishes,* Lucr.; pecudes et bestiae, *wild and domestic animals,* Cic. Esp., *a sheep*: pecus Helles, *the ram,* Ov.; Lucr., etc. TRANSF., applied contemptuously to a human being: stupor hominis, vel dicam pecudis? Cic.; Tac.

pĕdālis -e (pes), *a foot long* (or *wide*): Caes., Cic.

pĕdārĭus -a -um (pes), *of a foot.* TRANSF., senatores pedarii, *senators of inferior rank,* Tac.; so as subst. **pĕdārĭi** -ōrum, m.: Cic. L.

pĕdātus -a -um (pes): male pedatus, *ill set on his feet,* Suet.

pĕdes -ĭtis, m. (pes). As adj., *going on foot*: cum pedes iret, *on foot,* Verg.; pedes incedat, Liv. As subst., *a foot soldier*: Caes., Liv., etc.; collect, *infantry*: Liv.; equites pedites, *horse and foot,* i.e. *the whole people,* Cic., Hor., Liv.

pĕdester -tris -tre (pes), *on foot, pedestrian* (opp. equester). LIT., statua pedestris, Cic.; esp. as milit. t. t.: copiae, *infantry,* Caes.; scutum, *an infantry shield,* Liv.; acies, Liv., Tac.; sometimes, *on land* (opp. maritimus, navalis): iter, Caes.; pugna, Cic. TRANSF., (1) *of style, written in prose*: historiae, Hor. (2) *simple, ordinary, prosaic*: sermo, musa, Hor.

pĕdētemptim, adv. (pes/tempto), *by feeling one's way, gradually, carefully, cautiously*: timide et pedetemptim, Cic.; Pl., Ter., Liv.

pĕdĭca -ae, f. (pes). (1) *a fetter*: Pl. (2) *a trap, snare*: Verg., Ov., Liv.

pĕdĭcŭlōsus -a -um (pediculus), *lousy*: Mart.

pĕdĭcŭlus -i, m. (dim. of pedis), *a little louse*: Plin.

pĕdis -is, c. (pes), *a louse*: Pl.

pĕdĭsĕquus -i, m. and **pĕdĭsĕqua** -ae, f. (pes/sequor), *a follower, servant in attendance*; m. *a lackey, footman,* and f. *a waiting-woman.* LIT., Pl., Cic. L., etc. TRANSF., iuris scientiam eloquentiae tamquam ancillulam pedisequamque adiunxisti, Cic.

pĕdĭtastellus -i, m. (dim. from pedes), *a poor infantryman, footslogger*: Pl.

pĕdĭtātus -ūs, m. (pedes), *infantry*: Caes., Cic., etc.

pēdo pēdĕre pēpĕdi, *to break wind*: Hor.

¹pĕdum -i, n. *a shepherd's crook*: Verg.

²Pĕdum -i, n. *a town in Latium.* Adj. **Pĕdānus** -a -um, *of Pedum*; as subst., n. **Pĕdānum** -i, *an estate near Pedum*; m. pl. **Pĕdāni** -ōrum, *the inhabitants of Pedum.*

Pēgăsus (-ŏs) -i, m. (Πήγασος), *the winged horse which sprang from the blood of Medusa, and produced the fountain Hippocrene by a blow from his hoof.*

¶ Hence adj. **Pēgăsēius** and **Pēgăsēus** -a -um, *of Pegasus*; f. adj. **Pēgăsis** -ĭdis, *Pegasean*: undae, *fountains sacred to the Muses, Hippocrene, Aganippe*; as subst., sing., *a fountain-nymph*; plur.: Pegasides, *the Muses*, Ov.

pegma -ătis, n. (πῆγμα). (1) *a bookcase*: Cic. L. (2) *stage* or *scaffolding*: Sen., Juv., etc.

pĕiĕro and **periūro** -are (per/iuro), *to commit perjury, forswear oneself*: verbis conceptis, Cic.; Juv., etc.; with acc., *to swear falsely by*: Ov., Luc.; ius perieratum, *a false oath*, Hor.

pēiĕrātiuncŭla -ae, f. (dim. from peiiero= peiero), *a spot of perjury*: Pl.

pēiĕrōsus -a -um (peiiero=peiero), *perjured*: Pl.

pēior, compar. of malus; q.v.

pĕlăgĕ, see pelagus.

pĕlăgĭus -a -um (πελάγιος), *of the sea, marine*: conchae, Plin.; cursus, Phaedr.

Pĕlăgōnes -um, m. (Πελαγόνες), *the Pelagonians, a people in the north of Macedonia*. ¶ Hence **Pĕlăgōnĭa** -ae, f. *the country of the Pelagones*.

pĕlăgus -i, n. (πέλαγος), Greek plur.: pelage (πελάγη), Lucr.; *the open sea, the main*: Verg., etc.

pēlămȳs -ȳdis, f. (πηλαμύς), *the young tunny-fish*: Juv.

Pĕlasgi -ōrum, m. pl. (Πελασγοί), *the oldest inhabitants of Greece*, and hence, poet., *the Greeks*: Verg. ¶ Hence f. adj. **Pĕlasgĭăs** -ădis and **Pĕlasgĭs** -ĭdis and adj. **Pĕlasgus** -a -um, *Pelasgian, Greek*.

Pēleūs -ĕi and -ĕos, m. (Πηλεύς), *a mythical king of Thessaly, husband of Thetis, father of Achilles*. ¶ Hence **Pēlīdēs** -ae, m. *son of Peleus*. (1) *Achilles*. (2) *Neoptolemus, the son of Achilles*.

Pĕlĭās -ae, m. (Πελίας), *the king of Thessaly, who sent Jason to fetch the golden fleece*.

Pēlĭdēs, see Peleus.

Pēlĭon -i, n. (Πήλιον), *a lofty mountain range in Thessaly*. ¶ Hence adj. **Pēlĭăcus** and **Pēlĭus** -a -um, *of Pelion*: trabs, *the ship Argo* (the wood of which was cut from Mount Pelion), Prop.; f. adj. **Pēlĭăs** -ădis.

Pella -ae, f. and **Pellē** -ēs, f. (Πέλλα), *a city of Macedonia, birth-place of Alexander the Great*. ¶ Hence **Pellaeus** -a -um, *of Pella*: iuvenis, *Alexander*, Juv.; also *relating to Alexandria in Egypt*, and hence, *Egyptian*: Verg.

pellăcĭa -ae, f. (pellax), *an enticing, allurement*: Lucr.

pellax -ācis (pellicio), *deceitful, seductive*: Verg.

pellĕgo=perlego; q.v.

pellex=paelex; q.v.

pellĭcātus=pelicatus; q.v.

pellĭcĭo -lĭcĕre -lexi -lectum (per/lacio), *to entice, decoy, seduce*: mulierem ad se, Cic.; animum adulescentis, Cic.; populum in servitutem, Liv.; multo maiorem partem sententiarum suo lepore, *bring over to one's side*, Cic.; Tac., etc.

pellĭcŭla -ae, f. (dim. of pellis), *a little skin* or *hide*: haedina, Cic.; pelliculam curare, *to take care of one's skin*, Hor.

pellĭo -ōnis, m. (pellis), *a furrier*: Pl.

pellis -is, f. *a hide, skin*. LIT., caprina, Cic.; pelles pro velis tenuiter confectae, Caes.;

prov.: detrahere alicui pellem, *to disclose a person's faults*, Hor. TRANSF., (1) *dressed hide, leather, felt*: pes in pelle natat, Ov.; pellibus tecta tempora, Ov.; Hor. (2) milit., *huts covered with skins*: Caesar sub pellibus hiemare constituit, Caes.; Liv., Tac.

pellītus -a -um (pellis), *clothed in skins*: Sardi, Liv.; testes, *from Sardinia*, Cic.; oves pellitae, *covered with skins to protect the wool*, Hor.

pello pellĕre pĕpŭli pulsum. (1) *to strike, knock, beat*: terram pede, Hor.; humum pedibus, Cat.; fores, *to knock at the door*, Ter.; puer pulsus, *beaten*, Cic. (2) *to set in motion by pushing* or *striking*; *to impel, propel, move*. LIT., manu sagittam, Verg.; esp. in music: nervos in fidibus, Cic.; Ov. TRANSF., *to thrill, affect, impress*: species utilitatis pepulit eum, Cic.; Liv. (3) *to drive, drive away, dislodge*. LIT., cum viri boni lapidibus e foro pellerentur, Cic.; uti omnes ex Galliae finibus pellerentur, Caes.; aliquem possessionibus, Cic.; civitate, Cic.; regno, Hor.; in exsilium, Cic.; Verg. Liv.; esp. milit.: exercitum, Caes., Cic. TRANSF., maestitiam ex animis, *banish*, Cic.; curas vino, Hor.; Verg.

pellūcĕo=perluceo; q.v.

Pĕlŏponnēsus -i, f. (Πελοπόννησος), *the Peloponnesus*. ¶ Hence adj. **Pĕlŏponnensis** -e, **Pĕlŏponnēsĭăcus** and **Pĕlŏponnēsĭus** -a -um *Peloponnesian*.

Pĕlops -ŏpis, m. (Πέλοψ), *Pelops, son of Tantalus, father of Atreus and Thyestes grandfather of Agamemnon and Menelaus*. ¶ Hence f. adj. **Pĕlŏpēĭăs** -ădis and **Pĕlŏpēĭs** -ĭdis, *Peloponnesian*: Mycenae, Ov.; adj. **Pĕlŏpēus** and **Pĕlŏpēĭus** -a -um, *relating to Pelops* or *his descendants* virgo, *Iphigenia*, Ov.; arva, *Phrygia*, Ov. moenia, *Argos*, Verg.; subst. **Pĕlŏpĭdae** -ārum, m. pl., *descendants of Pelops*.

pĕlŏris -ĭdis, f. (πελωρίς), *an edible shell-fish, a clam*: Hor.

Pĕlōrus (-ŏs) -i, m. (Πέλωρος), *the north-east promontory of Sicily* (now *Punta del Faro*). ¶ Hence f. subst. **Pĕlōrĭăs** -ădis and **Pĕlōrĭs** -ĭdis, *the Pelorus district*.

pelta -ae, f. (πέλτη), *a small, light shield*: Verg. Liv., etc.

peltastēs or -a -ae, m. (πελταστής), *a soldier armed with the pelta*: Liv.

peltātus -a -um (pelta), *armed with the pelta*, Ov.

Pēlūsĭum -i, n. (Πηλούσιον), *a town in Egypt at the eastern mouth of the Nile*. ¶ Hence adj. **Pēlūsĭăcus** -a -um *Pelusian*.

pelvis -is, f. *a basin*: Juv.

pĕnārĭus -a -um (penus), *of* or *for provisions* cella, *a store-room*, Cic.

Pĕnātes -ĭum, m. pl., with or without di (penus), *the Penates, Latin deities of the household and family*: Cic., Verg., etc. TRANSF., *home, dwelling*: Penates relinquere Liv.; Cic., Verg.; poet., *the cells of bees*: Verg

pĕnātĭgĕr -gĕra -gĕrum (penates/gero), *carrying the Penates*: Ov.

pendĕo pendēre pĕpendi (cf. pendo), *to hang* (1) *to hang suspended*. LIT., ab umero Cic.; in, *or* ex arbore, Cic.; de collo, Ov.

with abl. alone: pendebit fistula pinu, Verg.
TRANSF., **a**, *to hang upon, depend on*: spes ex
fortuna, Cic.; in sententiis fama, Cic.; Liv.:
b, *to originate from*: hinc omnis pendet
Lucilius, Hor.: **c**, *to hang upon the lips of
anyone, listen attentively*: narrantis ab ore,
Verg., Ov.

(2) *to hang loose* or *free*. LIT., dum nubila
pendent, *hover*, Verg.; olor niveis pendebat
in aere pennis, *hung poised*, Ov.; fluidos
pendere lacertos, *to hang slack*, Ov. TRANSF.,
a, *to be suspended, discontinued*: pendent
opera interrupta, Verg.; of persons: nostro-
que in limine pendes, *hang about*, Verg.:
b, *to be in suspense, be uncertain, undecided*:
ne diutius pendeas, Cic., esp. with animi:
Ter., Cic.; of things, pendebat adhuc belli
fortuna, Ov.

pendo pendĕre pĕpendi pensum.

(1) transit., *to cause to hang down*; hence, *to
weigh*. LIT., pensas examinat herbas, Ov.; Cic.
Esp., *to pay* (since money was originally paid
by weight): Achaei ingentem pecuniam pen-
dunt L. Pisoni quotannis, Cic.; vectigal, Caes.;
Liv., Tac. TRANSF., **a**, *to weigh, consider,
judge*: res, non verba, Cic.: **b**, *to value,
esteem*; with genit.: magni, *at a high price*,
Pl., Lucr., Hor.: **c**, *to weigh, pay as
a penalty, suffer punishment*, Cic., Liv.;
maximas poenas pendo temeritatis meae,
Cic. L.; poenas capitis, Ov.

(2) intransit., *to weigh*: Lucr., Liv.

¶ Hence partic. **pensus** -a -um, *weighed*;
hence, *esteemed, valued, prized*; esp. in genit.
of n.: nihil pensi habere aliquid, *to put
no value upon, be indifferent about*, Sall., Tac.;
alicui nec quicquam pensi est, Sall.; illis nec
quid dicerent nec quid facerent quicquam
unquam pensi fuisse, *they cared nothing what
they did or said*, Liv.; Pl.

¶ N. as subst. **pensum** -i, *a portion of
wool weighed out to a spinner as a day's work*;
hence, *a day's work, task*: nocturna carpentes
pensa puellae, Verg.; mollia pensa, Verg.
TRANSF., in gen., *a task, duty, engagement*: me
ad meum munus pensumque revocabo, Cic.;
Pl.

pendŭlus -a -um (pendeo), *hanging, hanging
down*. LIT., collum, Ov.; Ov., Mart.
TRANSF., *in suspense, undecided*: spe pendulus,
Hor.

Pēnĕlŏpa -ae, f. and **Pēnĕlŏpē** -ēs, f.
(Πηνελόπεια, Πηνελόπη), *the wife of Ulysses,
mother of Telemachus, famous for her constancy.*

¶ Hence adj. **Pēnĕlŏpēus** -a -um, *of
Penelope.*

pĕnĕs, prep. with acc. (connected with
penitus), *in the possession of, in the power of*.
LIT., physically, *in the keeping of*: Cic., Caes.,
etc. TRANSF., *with, belonging to*: penes quem
est potestas, Cic.; penes se esse, *to be in one's
senses*, Hor.; penes quos laus fuit, Cic.; penes
Aetolos culpam belli esse, Liv.; me penes est
custodia mundi, Ov.; Tac.

pĕnĕtrābĭlis -e (penetro). (1) pass., *that can
be passed through, penetrable*: corpus nullo
penetrabile telo, Ov. (2) act., *penetrating,
piercing*: frigus, Verg.; fulmen, Ov.

pĕnĕtrālis -e (penetro). (1) *passing through,
penetrating*: frigus, ignis, Lucr.; compar.:
Lucr. (2) *inward, internal*: focus, Cic.;
tecta, Verg.

¶ N. as subst. sing. **pĕnĕtrāle** -ālis, gen.
plur. **pĕnĕtrālĭa** -ium, *inner chambers,
interior*. LIT., of a building: penetrale urbis,
Liv.; penetralia regum, Verg.; esp., *the
inmost shrine of a temple*: conditum in
penetrali fatale pignus, Liv.; Verg. TRANSF.,
(1) of a country: Tac. (2) fig., of a subject:
Quint., Tac.

pĕnĕtro -are (cf. penitus).

(1) transit.: **a**, *to set, place, put into*.
LIT., intra aedes penetravi pedem, Pl.
TRANSF., se in fugam, Pl.: **b**, *to pass through
or into, to penetrate*. LIT., Illyricos sinūs,
Verg.; Lucr. TRANSF., id Tiberii animum
altius penetravit, *sank deep into*, Tac.; Lucr.

(2) intransit., *to make one's way in, to
penetrate*. LIT., sub terras, Tac.; intra
vallum, Liv.; in urbem, Liv. TRANSF., nulla
res magis penetrat in animos, Cic.

Pēnēus -i, m. (Πηνειός), *the chief river of
Thessaly*; myth., as a river-god, *father of
Cyrene and Daphne.*

¶ Hence f. adj. **Pēnēĭs** -ĭdis and adj.
Pēnēĭus and **Pēnēus** -a -um, *of Peneus.*

pēnĭcillus -i, m. (dim. of peniculus), *a
painter's brush* or *pencil*: Cic. TRANSF., *style*:
Cic. L.

pēnĭcŭlus -i, m. (dim. of penis). (1) *a brush*:
Pl. (2) *a sponge*: Pl., Ter.

pēnis -is, m. (cf. πέος). (1) *a tail*: Cic. L.
(2) = membrum virile, Cic. L., Hor.

pĕnītē, adv. (penitus), *inwardly*: Cat.

¹pĕnĭtus -a -um, adj. *inward, internal*: Pl.;
superl.: Pl.

²pĕnĭtŭs, adv. *internally, inwardly.*

LIT., *in the inmost part, deep inside*:
argentum penitus abditum, Cic.; penitus
terrae defigitur arbos, Verg.; penitus suspiria
trahere, *from deep within*, Ov.; terrae penitus
iacentes, *widely*, Ov.

TRANSF., (1) *deeply*: inclusum penitus in
venis reipublicae, Cic.; ea penitus animis
vestris mandate, *impress deeply in your minds*,
Cic. (2) *through and through, thoroughly,
entirely, wholly*: diffidere reipublicae, Cic.;
perdere se ipsos, Cic.; perspicere, Cic.;
Verg., Hor. (3) with compar., *far*: Prop.

penna -ae, f. *a feather*. LIT., Pl., Ov.; *a feather
on an arrow*: Ov. TRANSF., (1) gen. in plur.,
wings (of birds or insects): aves pullos pennis
fovent, Cic.; Verg., etc. (2) *a flying, flight*:
Prop.

pennātus -a -um (penna), *feathered, winged*:
Lucr., Hor., Ov.

pennĭgĕr -gĕra -gĕrum (penna/gero), *feathered,
winged*: Cic.

pennĭpēs -pĕdis (penna/pes), *wing-footed*:
Cat.

pennĭpŏtens -entis (penna/potens), *able to fly,
winged*: Lucr.; plur. as subst. **pennĭpŏtentes**
-ium, *birds*: Lucr.

pennŭla -ae, f. (dim. of penna), *a little wing*:
Lucr.

pensĭlis -e (pendeo), *hanging, pendent*: Pl.;
uva, *hung up to dry*, Hor.

pensĭo -ōnis, f. (pendo), *a weighing out*; hence
paying, payment, day of payment: nihil
debetur ei, nisi ex tertia pensione, Cic.; Liv.;
rent: Suet.

pensĭto -are (freq. of penso), *to weigh carefully*.
LIT., *to weigh out*; hence, *to pay*: vectigalia,
Cic.; praedia quae pensitant, *are liable to*

taxes, Cic. Transf., *to weigh, ponder, consider*: imperatoria consilia, Liv.; Tac.

penso -are (freq. of pendo), *to weigh carefully.* Lit., aurum, Liv.; fig.: Romanos scriptores eādem trutinā, Hor. Transf., (1) *to weigh, estimate, to ponder, consider*: consilium, Liv.; amicos ex factis, Liv. (2) *to counterbalance, compensate, requite*: adversa secundis, Liv.; vulnus vulnere, Ov. (3) *to pay for, purchase with*: nece pudorem, Ov.

pensum -i, n. subst. from pendo; q.v.

pensus -a -um, partic. from pendo; q.v.

pentămĕter -tri, m. (πεντάμετρος), *a pentameter verse*: Quint.

Pentēlicus -a -um, *belonging to Mount Pentelicus, a mountain near Athens, celebrated for its marble quarries*: Hermae Pentelici, *made of Pentelic marble*, Cic.

Penthēus -ĕi and -ĕos (Πενθεύς), *king of Thebes, torn to pieces by his mother and her sisters in a Bacchic frenzy.*

¶ Hence subst. **Penthīdēs** -ae, m. *a descendant of Pentheus*: Ov.

pēnūria -ae, f. (cf. πεῖνα), *lack, want, esp. want of the necessaries of life, penury*: cibi, Lucr.; victūs, Hor.; sapientium civium bonorumque, Cic.; liberorum, Sall.; Liv.

pēnus -ūs and -i, c., **pēnum** -i, n., and **pĕnus** -ŏris, n. (connected with penitus), *provisions, store of food, victuals*: est enim omne, quo vescuntur homines, penus, Cic.; Verg., etc.

peplum -i, n. and **peplus** -i, m. (πέπλον, πέπλος), *the robe with which the statue of Athene at Athens was clad at the Panathenaea*: Cic.

per, prep. with acc.

(1) *of space, through, along, over*: equites per oram maritimam erant dispositi, Caes.; alterum iter per provinciam nostram multo facilius, Caes.; coronam auream per forum ferre, Cic.; per mare pauperiem fugiens, per saxa, per ignes, Hor.; Verg.; etc.; sometimes *before, in the presence of*: incedunt per ora vestra magnifici, Sall.; per manūs tradere, *to pass from hand to hand*, Caes., Liv.

(2) of time: **a**, *throughout, during*: ludi decem per dies facti sunt, Cic.: **b**, *in the course of, in a time of*: per somnum, *in sleep*, Verg.; quod fecisset per iram, Cic.

(3) *of the means or instrument by which anything is done, through*; so: **a**, *by means of*: per litteras, Cic.; per se (te, etc.), *by oneself, alone, without help*, Cic., Hor., Liv.: **b**, *with, by way of*: per ludum ac iocum, Cic.; per artem, Verg.; Liv., etc.: **c**, *under pretence of*: fraudare aliquem per tutelam aut societatem, Cic.; Caes., etc.

(4) *because of, on account of*: per avaritiam decipere, Cic.; per metum, *from fear*, Liv.; per duces stetisse ne vincerent, Liv. Esp.: **a**, with licet *or* possum: per me vel stertas licet, *as far as I am concerned*, Cic.; cum per valetudinem posses, venire tamen noluisti, Cic. L.: **b**, in entreaties, oaths, etc.=*by*: oro te per deos, Cic.; per deos atque homines, Cic. In this sense per is often separated from the noun which it governs: per ego te, fili, precor quaesoque, Liv.; per ego has lacrimas oro, Verg.

pēra -ae (πήρα), *a bag* or *wallet*: Mart.

pĕrabsurdus -a -um, *excessively absurd*: Cic.

pĕraccommŏdātus -a -um, *very convenient*: (in tmesis) per fore accommodatum, Cic. L.

pĕrācer -cris -cre, *very sharp*: iudicium, Cic. L.

pĕrăcerbus -a -um, *very sour, very harsh*: uva peracerba gustatu, Cic.; Plin. L.

pĕrăcesco -ācescĕre -ācŭi, *to become thoroughly sour.* Transf., ita mihi pectus peracuit, Pl

pĕractĭo -ōnis, f. (perago), *a finishing, completion*: peractio fabulae, Cic.

pĕrăcūtus -a -um, *very sharp.* Lit., falx Mart. Transf., (1) *very shrill, piercing*: vox Cic. (2) *sharp-witted, acute*: ad excogitandum Cic.

¶ Adv. **pĕrăcūtē**, *very sharply, very acutely*: queri, Cic.

pĕrădulescens -entis, *very young*: Cic.

pĕrădulescentŭlus -i, m. *a very young man* Nep.

pĕraequē, adv. *quite alike, quite equally*: Cic

pĕrăgĭto -are, *to drive about violently, harass* vehementius peragitati ab equitatu, Caes Transf., animos, Sen.

pĕrăgo -ăgĕre -ēgi -actum.

(1) *to pass through.* Lit., physically Theseus latus ense peregit, Ov. Transf., *a* of time: aestates, Hor.: **b**, in words, *to g through, go over, mention*: verbis auspicia Liv.; sententiam, Liv.; Hor.

(2) *to drive about, harass, disquiet.* Lit. agili freta remo, Ov.; agrum, *to till*, Ov Transf., totum Sempronium usque ed perago ut, ap. Cic. L.

(3) *to carry through, complete, finish accomplish*: navigationem, Cic.; inceptum Liv.; concilium, Caes.; fabulam vitae, Cic. as legal t. t., *to prosecute* a man till conviction reum, Liv.

pĕragrātĭo -ōnis, f. (peragro), *a wanderin through*: itinerum, Cic.

pĕragro -are (per/ager), *to wander through pass through, travel through.* Lit., omne provincias, Cic.; saltūs, Verg. Transf. omne immensum mente animoque, Lucr. onmes latebras suspicionum dicendo, Cic. also intransit.: per animos hominum, Cic.

pĕrămans -antis, *very loving*: homo peraman semper nostri fuit, Cic. L.

¶ Adv. **pĕrămantĕr**, *very lovingly* observare, Cic. L.

pĕrambŭlo -are, *to walk through, pass through traverse.* Lit., rura, Hor. Transf., frigu perambulat artus, Ov.; Hor.

pĕrămoenus -a -um, *very pleasant*: Tac.

pĕramplus -a -um, *very large*: Cic.

pĕrangustus -a -um, *very narrow, strait confined*: fretum, Cic.; aditus, Caes.; via Liv.

¶ Adv. **pĕrangustē**, *very narrowly*: Cic

pĕranno -are, *to live through a year*: Suet.

pĕrantīquus -a -um, *very old*: sacrarium, Cic

pĕrappŏsĭtus -a -um, *very suitable*: alicu Cic.

pĕrardŭus -a -um, *very difficult*: mihi ho perarduum est demonstrare, Cic.

pĕrargūtus -a -um, *very acute, witty*: Cic.

pĕrăro -are, *to plough through.* Transf., (1) *t furrow* the brow: rugis ora, Ov. (2) *to scratc letters on wax tablets, to write*: litteram, Ov. also *to write on*: Ov.

pĕrattentus -a -um, *very attentive*: perattento vestros animos habuimus, Cic.

¶ Adv. **pĕrattentē**, *very attentively*: aliquo audiri, Cic.

pĕraudĭendus -a -um, *needing to be heard all through*: Pl.

perbacchor -ari, dep. *to revel throughout*: multos dies, Cic.

perbĕātus -a -um, *very happy*: Cic.

perbellē, adv. *very prettily*: simulare, Cic. L.

pĕrbĕnē, adv. *very well*: loqui Latine, Cic.; Pl., Liv.

perbĕnĕvŏlus -a -um, *very well disposed*: alicui, Cic. L.

perbĕnignē, adv. *very kindly*: (in tmesis) per mihi benigne respondit, Cic.

perbĭbo -bĭbĕre -bĭbi, *to drink up, absorb*. LIT., lacrimas, Ov. TRANSF., *to imbibe, take in mentally*: rabiem, Ov.

perblandus -a -um, *very charming, very engaging*: successor, Cic. L.; Liv.

perbŏnus -a -um, *very good*: Pl., Cic.

perbrĕvis -e, *very short*: perbrevi tempore, *or simply* perbrevi, *in a very short time*, Cic.
¶ Adv. perbrĕvĭtĕr, *very shortly*: Cic.

perca -ae, f. (πέρκη), *a fish, the perch*: Ov.

percălĕfactus -a -um (per/calefacio), *thoroughly heated*: Lucr.

percălesco -cālescĕre -călŭi, *to become very warm*: Lucr., Ov.

percallesco -callescĕre -callŭi. (1) intransit., *to lose sensibility, become callous*: Cic. (2) transit., *to get a good knowledge of*: usum rerum, Cic.

percārus -a -um. (1)· *very dear, very costly*: Ter. (2) *very dear, much beloved*: Cic., Tac.

percautus -a -um, *very cautious*: Cic. L.

percĕlebro -are, *to speak of commonly*; pass., *to be much mentioned*: percelebrata sermonibus res est, Cic.

percĕlĕr -is -e, *very swift, very rapid*: interitus, Cic.
¶ Adv. percĕlĕrĭtĕr, *very rapidly*: auferre diploma, Cic. L.

percello -cellĕre -cŭli -culsum (per/*cello).
    (1) *to beat down, strike down, overturn, shatter*. LIT., aliquem, Verg.; quod duo fulmina domum meam per hos dies perculerint, Liv.; Pl. TRANSF., **a**, *to overthrow, ruin*: rempublicam, Tac.; Cic.: **b**, *to daunt, to unnerve*: hostes perculsi, Caes.; timore perculsa civitas, Cic.; quos pavor perculerat in silvas, *driven in terror to*, Liv.
    (2) *to strike, push*: aliquem genu, Liv.; cuspide, Ov. TRANSF., volucres perculsae corda tua vi, *smitten*, Lucr.

percenseo -censēre -censŭi, *to count through, count, reckon*. LIT., locos inveniendi, Cic.; gentes, Liv.; Tac.
    TRANSF., (1) *to survey, review*: captivos, Liv.; orationes, Liv. (2) *to travel through*: Thessaliam, Liv.; Ov.

perceptĭo -ōnis, f. (percipio), *a receiving, gathering together*. LIT., frugum fructuumque, Cic. TRANSF., *comprehension*: perceptiones animi, Cic.

perceptus -a -um, partic. from percipio; q.v.

percīdo -cīdĕre -cīdi -cīsum (per/caedo), *to beat, cut to pieces*: os alicui, Pl.

percĭo -cire -cīvi -citum and percĭĕo -cĭēre -cĭĕre, *to stir up, set in motion*: irai fax subdita percit, Lucr.; *to arouse by abuse*: Pl.
¶ Hence partic. percĭtus -a -um, *aroused, excited*: animo irato ac percito, Cic.; *also of character, excitable*: ingenium, Liv.; Sall.

percĭpĭo -cĭpĕre -cēpi -ceptum (per/capio), *to lay hold of, take possession of, seize*. LIT., Ov.; esp. *to collect, gather, harvest*: fructūs, Cic.
    TRANSF., (1) *of the senses, to feel, take in*: sensus percipit rem in se, Lucr.; orationem, Caes.; voluptatem, Cic.; sonum, Cic.; animus flammam, Verg.; Ov. (2) *with feeling as subject, to overtake, seize upon, thrill*: percipit me voluptas atque horror, Lucr.; Pl. (3) *to receive mentally*: **a**, *to learn*: omnium civium nomina perceperat, *he knew*, Cic.; with indir. quest.: Verg.: **b**, *to grasp, comprehend, understand*: aliquid animo, Cic.; Caes. (4) *of abstr. things, to gather, gain*: praemia, Caes.; Cic.
¶ Hence partic. perceptus -a -um; n. pl. as subst. percepta -ōrum, *principles, rules*: artis, Cic.

percĭtus -a -um, partic. from percio; q.v.

percīvĭlis -e, *very gracious*: Suet.

¹percōlo -are, *to strain, as through a sieve*: vinum, Cato.; umor per terras percolatur, *percolates*, Lucr.

²percŏlo -cŏlĕre -cŏlŭi -cultum. (1) *to adorn, decorate*: quae priores nondum comperta eloquentiā percoluere, Tac. (2) *to honour, reverence greatly*: patrem, Pl.; Tac. (3) *to complete*: Plin. L.

percōmis -e, *very friendly, courteous*: Cic.

percommŏdus -a -um, *very fit, appropriate*; with dat.: ipsis castris percommodum fuit, Liv.
¶ Adv. percommŏdē, *very conveniently, very appropriately*: percommode cadit quod, Cic.

percontātĭo (percunctātĭo) -ōnis, f. (percontor), *an inquiry, interrogation*: percontationem facere, Liv.; Caes., Cic.

percontātor (percunctātor) -ōris, m. (percontor), *an inquirer, asker of questions*: Pl., Hor.

percontor (percunctor) -ari, dep. (contus), *to sound with a pole*; hence, *to inquire, interrogate, question, investigate*: aliquem de aliqua re, Cic.; Liv.; ab *or* ex aliquo, Cic.; aliquem aliquid, Pl., Hor., Liv.; with indir. quest.: percontantes, quid praetor edixisset, ubi cenaret, quo denuntiasset, Cic.

percontŭmax -ācis, *very obstinate*: Ter.

percŏquo -cŏquĕre -coxi -coctum, *to cook thoroughly*. LIT.·. carnes, Plin. TRANSF., (1) *to heat thoroughly*: umorem, Lucr. (2) *to ripen*: uvas, Ov. (3) *to scorch, blacken*: nigra virum percocto saecla colore, Lucr.

percrēbresco -brescĕre -brŭi and percrēbesco -bescĕre -bŭi, *to become very frequent, become prevalent, get well known*: res percrebuit, Cic.; fama percrebruit, with acc. and infin., Caes.

percrĕpo -crĕpare -crĕpŭi -crĕpĭtum, *to resound, ring*: lucum illum percrepare mulierum vocibus, Cic.

percunctor percunctatio, etc.=percontor, percontatio, etc.; q.v.

percŭpĭdus -a -um, ·*very fond of*; with genit.: tui, Cic. L.

percŭpĭo -cŭpĕre, *to desire exceedingly*: Pl., Ter.

percŭrĭōsus -a -um, *very inquisitive*: Cic.

percūro -are, *to cure, heal thoroughly*: vixdum satis percurato vulnere, **Liv.** TRANSF., mentem, Sen.

percurro -currĕre -cŭcurri or -curri -cursum, *to run through.*
(1) intransit.: per temonem, Caes.; per omnes civitates oratio mea, Cic.
(2) transit., *to hasten through, travel through.* LIT., omnem agrum Picenum, Caes.; aristas, Ov.; Verg. TRANSF., **a**, in speaking, *to run over, mention in passing*: multas res oratione, Cic.; Verg., Tac.: **b**, *to run over in the mind* or *with the eye*: veloci percurrere oculo, Hor.; multa animo et cogitatione, multa etiam legendo, Cic.; Liv.: **c**, *to pass through* stages in a career: Suet., Plin. L.

percursātio -ōnis, f. (percurso), *a travelling through*: Italiae, Cic.

percursĭo -ōnis, f. (percurro), *a running through.* Hence (1) *a rapid consideration*: propter animi multarum rerum brevi tempore percursionem, Cic. (2) rhet. t. t., *a hasty passing over a subject*: huic (commorationi) contraria saepe percursio est, Cic.

percurso -are (freq. of percurro). (1) transit., *to ramble over* or *about*: ripas, Plin. (2) intransit., *to ramble, rove*: totis finibus nostris, Liv.

percussĭo -ōnis, f. (percutio), *a striking, beating.* LIT., capitis, Cic.; digitorum, *a snapping of the fingers*, Cic. TRANSF., *a beating time*, hence, *time, rhythm*: numerorum percussiones, Cic.

percussor -ōris, m. (percutio), *a striker*; esp. *a murderer, assassin*: Cic., Tac.

percussus -ūs, m. (percutio), *a beating, knocking, striking*: percussu crebro, Ov.; Sen.

percŭtĭo -cŭtĕre -cussi -cussum (per/quatio); perf. percusti, for percussisti, Hor.; instead of the pres. and imperf., ferio is generally used; *to strike hard.*
LIT., (1) *to strike through, pierce, transfix*: rostro navem, Liv.; venam, Sen. (2) *to strike down, cut down*: gladio, Cic.; esp. of beheading: securi percussus, Cic., Liv., Ov. (3) in gen., *to strike, beat*: aliquem lapide, Cic.; turres de caelo percussae, *struck by lightning*, Cic.; forem virgā, Liv.; lyram, Ov.; Lucr., Verg.; of money, *to stamp, coin*: Suet.
TRANSF., (1) mentally, *to strike, shock*: percussus calamitate, Cic.; atrocissimis litteris, Cic. L.; Verg. (2) colloq., *to deceive*: aliquem strategemate, Cic. L.; Pl. (3) fig., *to stamp*: Sen.

perdēcŏrus -a -um, *very comely*: Plin. L

perdēlīrus -a -um, *very silly, senseless*: Lucr.

perdifficilis -e, *very difficult*: navigatio, Cic. L.; quaestio, Cic.; superl.: Liv.
¶ Adv. **perdifficiliter**, *with great difficulty*: Cic.

perdignus -a -um, *very worthy*: tuā amicitiā, Cic. L.

perdīlĭgens -entis, *very diligent*: Cic. L.
¶ Adv. **perdīlĭgentĕr**, *very diligently*: Cic.

perdisco -discĕre -dĭdĭci, *to learn thoroughly*: dictata, Cic.; with infin.: hominis speciem pingere, Cic.

perdisertē, adv. *very eloquently*: Cic.

perdītē, adv. from perdo; q.v.

perdĭtor -ōris, m. (perdo), *a destroyer*: reipublicae, Cic.

perdĭtus -a -um, partic. from perdo; q.v.

perdĭū, adv. *for a very long time*: Cic.

perdĭuturnus -a -um, *lasting a very long time*: Cic.

perdīvěs -vĭtis, *very rich*: Cic.

perdix -dīcis, c. (πέρδιξ), *a partridge*: Plin. Mart.

perdo -dĕre -dĭdi -dĭtum (pres. subj. perdŭin -is -it -int, esp. in the execration: di te perduint! Pl., Ter., Cic.; in pass., gen., pereo perire), *to destroy, ruin, do away with.*
LIT., aliquem, Pl., Cic.; funditus civitatem Cic.; serpentem, *to kill*, Ov.
TRANSF., (1) *to ruin morally*: Cic., Hor (2) *to waste, squander*: operam, Cic.; tempus Cic.; oleum et operam, Cic. L.; Hor., Ov (3) *to lose*: liberos, Cic.; litem, *a law-suit* Cic.; vocem, Cic.; quod in alea perdiderat Cic.
¶ Hence partic. (with compar. and superl.) **perdĭtus** -a -um, of persons and things. (1) *wretched, miserable, ruined* valetudo, Cic.; res, Cic.; amor, Cat.; perditu luctu, *sunk in grief*, Cic. (2) *morally lost abandoned, profligate*: adulescens perditu ac dissolutus, Cic.; homo perditissimus, Cic iudicia, Cic.
¶ Adv. **perdĭtē**. (1) *desperately, immoderately*: filiam amare, Ter. (2) *in ar abandoned manner, very badly*: se gerere Cic. L.

perdŏcĕo -dŏcēre -dŏcŭi -doctum, *to teach o instruct thoroughly*: res difficilis ad perdo cendum, Cic.; aliquid mortales ore, Ov.; Pl. Lucr.
¶ Hence partic. **perdoctus** -a -um, *ver learned, very skilful*: Pl., Ter., Cic.
¶ Adv. **perdoctē**, *very learnedly, ver skilfully*: Pl.

perdŏlesco -dŏlescĕre -dŏlŭi (per/doleo), t *suffer violent pain or grief*: suam virtutem inrisui fore perdoluerunt, Caes.; Ter.

perdŏmo -dŏmare -dŏmŭi -dŏmĭtum, *to tam or subdue thoroughly*: tauros feroces, Ov. Latium, Liv.

perdūco -dūcĕre -duxi -ductum, *to lead through, bring along.*
LIT., aliquem Romam, Liv.; aliquem a Caesarem, Caes.; bovem ad stabula, Verg. esp. *to carry* or *construct buildings, aqueducts* etc., from one point to another: murum a lacu Lemano ad montem Iuram, Caes. viam a Bononia Arretium, Liv.
TRANSF., (1) *to bring to*: ad dignitatem Caes.; aliquem ad exitum, Cic. (2) *to brin over to one's opinion, induce to*: aliquem a suam sententiam, Cic. L.; Caes., Hor (3) *to continue, prolong*: res disputatione a mediam noctem perducitur, Caes.; Cic. L Liv. (4) *to spread over, smear over*: totun corpus ambrosiae odore, Verg.

perducto -are (freq. of perduco), *to lead to*: Pl

perductor -ōris, m. (perduco), *a guide*: Pl. *a pimp, pander*: Cic.

perdūdum, adv. *a long time ago*: Pl.

perdŭellĭo -ōnis, f. (perduellis), *a hostil attempt against the state, treason*: Cic., Liv.

perdŭellis -is, m. (per/duellum, archaic fo bellum). (1) *a public enemy*, esp. *one actuall carrying on hostilities*: Pl., Cic., Liv. (2) *private* or *personal enemy*: Pl.

perdŭim -is -it, etc., *see* perdo.

perdūro -are, *to last a long time, endure*: probitas longum perdurat in aevum, Ov.; Ter., Suet.

pĕrĕdo -esse -ēdi -ēsum, *to eat up, devour*. LIT., cibum, Pl. TRANSF., in gen., *to consume, destroy*: vellera morbo inluvieque peresa, Verg.; quos durus amor crudeli tabe peredit, Verg.; Hor.

pĕregrē, adv. (per/ager). (1) *in a foreign country, abroad*: habitare, Liv.; depugnare, Cic. TRANSF., animus est peregre, Hor. (2) *from abroad*: redire, Ter.; nuntiare, Liv. (3) *to a foreign country, abroad*: exire, Hor.; Pl.

pĕregrīnābundus -a -um (peregrinor), *travelling about*: Liv.

pĕregrīnātĭo -ōnis, f. (peregrinor), *a travelling or staying in foreign countries*: omne tempus in peregrinatione consumere, Cic. L.; of animals, *roaming*: Cic.

pĕregrīnātor -ōris, m. (peregrinor), *one who travels about*: Cic. L.

pĕregrīnĭtās -ātis, f. (peregrinus). (1) *the condition of a foreigner* or *alien*: Suet. (2) *foreign manners*: in urbem nostram infusa est peregrinitas, Cic.

pĕregrīnor -ari, dep. (peregrinus), *to stay or to travel in foreign countries*. LIT., totā Asiā, Cic.; in aliena civitate, Cic. TRANSF., (1) *to wander, ramble*: haec studia pernoctant nobiscum, peregrinantur, rusticantur, Cic.; in infinitatem omnem, Cic. (2) *to be strange, foreign*: philosophiam quae quidem peregrinari Romae videbatur, Cic.

pĕregrīnus -a -um (peregre), *foreign, of a foreigner, strange*. LIT., reges, Cic.; amores, *foreign sweethearts*, Ov.; terror, *caused by foreign enemies*, Liv.; as subst. **pĕregrīnus** -i, m. and **pĕregrīna** -ae, f. *a foreigner, stranger*: Cic.; esp. *a foreigner resident in Rome*: neque civis neque peregrinus, Cic. TRANSF., *strange to, inexperienced in*: in agendo, Cic.

ĕrēlĕgans -antis, *very elegant*: oratio, Cic.
¶ Adv. **pĕrēlĕgantĕr**, *very elegantly*: dicere, Cic.

ĕrēlŏquens -entis, *very eloquent*: Cic.

ĕremnĭa, n. pl. (per/amnis) (sc. auspicia), *the auspices taken on crossing a river* or *any running water*: Cic.

ĕremptus -a -um, partic. from perimo; q.v.

ĕrendĭē, adv. *the day after tomorrow*: scies igitur fortasse cras, summum perendie, Cic. L.; Pl.

ĕrendĭnus -a -um (perendie), *relating to the day after tomorrow*: perendinus dies, or simply, perendinus, *the day after tomorrow*, Pl., Caes., Cic.

ĕrennis -e (per/annus), *lasting or remaining throughout the year*. LIT., militia, Liv. TRANSF., *lasting, durable, perennial*: virtus, Cic.; cursus stellarum, Cic.; monumentum aere perennius, Hor. Esp. of water: aquae, Cic.; amnis, Liv., Ov.

ĕrennĭservus -i, m. (perennis), *a perpetual slave*: Pl.

ĕrennĭtās -ātis, f. (perennis), *duration, perpetuity*: fontium, Cic.; Pl.

ĕrenno -are (perennis), *to last many years, be durable*: arte perennat amor, Ov.

ĕrentĭcīda -ae, m. (pera/caedo), *a cutpurse* (alluding to parenticida): Pl.

pĕrĕo -ire -ii and -īvi -ĭtum, *to go through*; hence (often as pass. of perdo), *to go to waste, be lost, perish, pass away*. LIT., physically: pereunt victae sole tepente nives, Ov.; dolium lymphae pereuntis, *running away*, Hor.; urbes funditus, Hor.; of persons, *to perish, die*: foede, praeclare, Cic.; naufragio, Cic.; hominum manibus, Verg.; morbo, Hor. TRANSF., (1) *to pine away with love*: amore, Verg.; Cat., Hor.; with acc. of the beloved: Pl. (2) *to be ruined* or *lost*: fides, Pl., Cic.; virtus, Ov.; of persons, esp. with exaggeration: perii! *I am undone!* Pl., Ter.; peream si (nisi), a common form of imprecation, *may I die if* (not), Ov. (3) *to be lost, to be wasted, spent in vain*: ne oleum et opera philologiae nostrae perierit, Cic. L.; quia multis actiones et res peribant, Liv.; labor, Ov.

pĕrĕquĭto -are, *to ride through, ride round*. Intransit., per omnes partes, Caes.; Liv. Transit., *to ride round*: aciem, Liv.

pĕrerro -are, *to wander, ramble, stray through*: totum Latium, Liv.; forum, Hor.; pass.: pererrato ponto, Verg.; Ov. TRANSF., *to look over, scan*: luminibus tacitis, Verg.

pĕrērūdītus -a -um, *very learned*: Cic. L.

pĕrexĭgŭus -a -um, *very small, very little, very scanty*; of space: loci spatium, Caes.; of number, quantity, etc.: bona corporis, Cic.; argentum, Liv.; of time, *very short*: dies, Cic.
¶ Adv. **pĕrexĭgŭē**, *very scantily, very sparingly*: Cic. L.

perfabrĭco -are, *to over-reach*: Pl.

perfăcētus -a -um, *very witty, brilliant*: aliquid perfacetum dicere, Cic.
¶ Adv. **perfăcētē**, *very wittily*: perfacete dicta sunt, Cic.

perfăcĭlis -e. (1) *very easy*: erat perfacilis cognitu, Cic.; Caes. (2) *very courteous*: in audiendo, Cic.
¶ N. acc. as adv. **perfăcĭlĕ**, *very easily*: Cic.; *very readily*: Pl.

perfămĭlĭāris -e, *very intimate, familiar*: alicui, Cic. L.; m. as subst. *a very intimate friend*: meus, Cic.

perfectē, adv. from perficio; q.v.

perfectĭo -ōnis, f. (perficio). (1) *completion*: perfectio maximorum operum, Cic. (2) *perfection*: hanc perfectionem absolutionemque in oratore desiderans, Cic.

perfector -ōris, m. (perficio), *a perfecter, finisher*: Ter.; Cic.

perfectus -a -um, partic. from perficio; q.v.

perfĕrens -entis, partic. from perfero; q.v.

perfĕro -ferre -tŭli -lātum, *to carry through, bear to the end*. LIT., in gen.: onus, Hor.; lapis nec pertulit ictum, *did not bring the blow home*, Verg.; alveus fluminis non pertulit gravissimas naves, *did not admit of*, Liv.; reflex.: se perferre, *to betake oneself*, Verg. Esp. of news or messages, *to deliver, convey*: litteras ad aliquem, Cic.; alicui nuntium, Cic.; pass.: cum ad eum fama perlata esset, Liv.; absol., *to bring news*: equites pertulere consulem obsideri, Liv. TRANSF., (1) *to bring to an end, carry through, complete*: legem, Cic., Liv.; id quod suscepi, quoad potero, perferam, Cic.;

mandata, Tac. (2) *to bear, suffer, endure*: perfero et perpetior omnes, Cic.; omnes indignitates contumeliasque, Caes.; laborem, Verg.; with acc. and infin.: Prop., Tac.
¶ Hence partic. **perfĕrens** -entis, *enduring, patient*; as adj., with genit.: iniuriarum, Cic.
perfĭca -ae, f. adj. (perficio), *accomplishing, perfecting*: natura, Lucr.
perfĭcĭo -fĭcĕre -fēci -fectum (per/facio), *to bring to an end, complete, finish.*
 Lit., of physical productions: pontem, Caes.; candelabrum, Cic.; pocula, Verg.
 Transf., (1) of abstr. things, *to accomplish, achieve*: cogitata, Cic.; conata, Caes.; scelus, Cic.; comitia, Liv.; bellum, Liv.; munus, Verg.; so with clause as object, *to bring about, accomplish, effect*; foll. by ut *or* ne with subj., Caes., Cic., etc.; non perficio, foll. by quominus, Cic. (2) *to live through*: centum qui perficit annos, Hor. (3) *to make perfect, to perfect*: Achillem cithara, Ov.
 ¶ Hence partic. (with compar. and superl.) **perfectus** -a -um, *perfect, complete, finished*: homo, orator, Cic.; in dicendo, Cic.; in arte, Ov.; C. Memmius perfectus litteris, Cic.; of things: valvas perfectiores nullas ullo unquam tempore fuisse, Cic.; quod ego summum et perfectissimum iudicio, Cic.
 ¶ Adv. **perfectē**, *perfectly, completely*: Cic.
perfĭdēlis -e, *very faithful*: Cic. L.
perfĭdĭa -ae, f. (perfidus), *faithlessness, treachery, falsehood*: fraude et perfidiā aliquem fallere, Cic.; Caes., etc.
perfĭdĭōsus -a -um, adj. (with compar. and superl.) (perfidia), *faithless, treacherous*: Cic., Tac., etc.
 ¶ Adv. **perfĭdĭōsē**, *faithlessly, treacherously*: multa perfidiose facta, Cic.
perfĭdus -a -um (fides), *faithless, treacherous, false.* (1) of persons: amicus, Cic. (2) of inanimate objects: arma, verba, Ov.; perfidum ridens, Hor.
perfīgo -fīgĕre -fixi -fixum, *to pierce through, stab*: Lucr.
perflābĭlis -e (perflo), *that can be blown through*: Cic.
perflāgĭtĭōsus -a -um, *very shameful*: Cic.
perflo -are, *to blow through, blow over*: venti terras turbine perflant, Verg.; Lucr., Cic.
perfluctŭo -are, *to surge over*: Lucr.
perflŭo -flŭĕre -fluxi -fluxum, *to stream through, run away*: Lucr.; of a person not keeping a secret: Ter.
perfŏdĭo -fŏdĕre -fōdi -fossum. (1) *to dig through, pierce through*: parietes, Pl., Cic.; thorax perfossus, Verg. (2) *to excavate, make by digging*: fretum, Liv.
perfŏro -are. (1) *to pierce through*: navem, Cic.; operculum ferreum, Liv.; latus ense, Ov. (2) *to form by boring*: duo lumina ab animo ad oculos perforata, Cic.
perfortĭtĕr, adv. *very bravely*: Ter.
perfrĕquens -entis, *much visited, much frequented*: emporium, Liv.
perfrĭco -fricare -frĭcŭi -frĭcātum and -frictum, *to rub over.* Lit., caput sinistrā manu, Cic.; dentes, Ov. Transf., os, frontem, etc., *to obliterate every sign of shame* or *modesty, to put on a bold face*, Cic., Mart.
perfrīgĕfăcĭo -făcĕre, *to chill*: Pl.

perfrīgesco -frīgescĕre -frixi, *to catch a chill*: Juv.
perfrīgĭdus -a -um, *very cold*: tempestas, Cic.
perfringo -fringĕre -frēgi -fractum (per/frango), *to break through*; also *to break in pieces, shatter.*
 Lit., phalangem pilis, Caes.; portarum claustra, Lucr.; saxum, Cic.; naves perfregerant proras, Liv.
 Transf., of abstr. things, *to break through, break up*: decreta senatus, Cic.; conspirationem, Cic.
perfrŭor -frŭi -fructus sum, dep. (1) *to enjoy to the full*: laetitiā, Cic.; regali otio, Cic. L.; ad perfruendas voluptates, Cic. (2) *to execute completely*: mandatis patris, Ov.
perfŭga -ae, m. (perfugio), *a deserter*: Caes., Cic., Liv.
perfŭgĭo -fŭgĕre -fūgi -fŭgĭtum, *to flee away*; in gen., *to take refuge*: ad aliquem, Liv.; in fidem Aetolorum, Liv. Esp. *to desert to the enemy*: a Pompeio ad Caesarem, Caes.; Cic.
perfŭgĭum -i, n. (perfugio), *a place of refuge, shelter.* Lit., paludes, quo perfugio fuerant usi, Caes.; Cic. Transf., perfugium et praesidium salutis, Cic.; plur.: intercludere perfugia fortunae, Cic.
perfunctĭo -ōnis, f. (perfungor), *a performing, discharging*: honorum, Cic.
perfundo -fundĕre -fūdi -fūsum, *to pour over.*
 Lit., *to steep* in a fluid: aliquem aquā ferventi, Cic.; vivo flumine, Liv.; perfusus fletu, Liv.; liquidis odoribus, Hor.; ostro perfusae vestes, dyed, Verg.
 Transf., (1) *to steep in, fill with* anything: sol omnia luce, Lucr.; canitiem pulvere, Verg.; Lethaeo perfusa papavera somno, Verg. (2) *to fill with a feeling*: qui me horror perfudit! Cic. L.; sensus iucunditate quādam perfunditur, Cic.; timore, gaudio, Liv.
perfungor -fungi -functus sum, dep. *to perform fully, execute, discharge.*
 Lit., with abl.: reipublicae muneribus, Cic. Sometimes with the idea of enjoyment: epulis, Ov.; with acc.: Lucr.
 Transf., *to go through, endure*: molestiā, Cic. L.; periculis, Cic.; perf. partic. in pass. sense: memoria perfuncti periculi, Cic.
perfŭro -ĕre, *to rage furiously*: Verg.
¹**Pergămum** -i, n. and **Pergămus** -i, f (Πέργαμος -ον); also plur. **Pergăma** -ōrum, n. *the citadel of Troy* or *Troy*; hence adj **Pergămĕus** -a -um, *Trojan.*
²**Pergămum** -i, n. *a town in Mysia, on the river Caicus, capital of the kingdom o the Attalids*; hence adj. **Pergămēnus** -um, *of Pergamum.*
pergaudĕo -ēre, *to rejoice exceedingly*: Cic. L.
pergo pergĕre perrexi perrectum (per/rego) *to continue, proceed, go on with* anything.
 Lit., of physical action; with acc.: iter Sall., Liv., etc.; with infin.: ire, Cic., Liv absol.: in Macedoniam, Cic.; ad castra Caes.; Romam, Liv.
 Transf., with infin.: id agere perrexi, Cic perge quattuor mihi istas partes explicare Cic.; Lucr.; absol.: pergamus ad reliqua Cic.; esp. in speaking: Cic., Verg., Liv.
pergraecor -ari, dep. *to behave like an ou and-out Greek*: Pl.
pergrandis -e, *very large, very great.* (1) size: gemma, Cic. (2) of value: pecuni

summa, Cic. (3) of time: pergrandis natu, *very old*, Liv.

pergrăphĭcus -a -um, *very skilful*: Pl.

pergrātus -a -um, *very pleasant*: pergratum mihi feceris si, *you will give me great pleasure if*, Cic.

pergrăvis -e, *very weighty, very important*: oratio, Cic.; Ter.

¶ Adv. **pergrăvĭtĕr**, *very seriously*: aliquem reprehendere, Cic.

pergŭla -ae, f. (pergo), *a projection*; hence, *a balcony* or *outhouse used for various purposes*; *a shop, workshop*: Plin.; *a school*: Juv.; *a brothel*: Pl., Prop.

pĕrhĭbĕo -ēre -ŭi -ĭtum (per/habeo). (1) *to bring forward, cite*: quem Caecilius suo nomine perhiberet, Cic. L. (2) *to maintain, assert, hold*: ut Graii perhibent, *as the Greeks say*, Verg.; vatem hunc perhibebo optimum, Cic.; in pass.: montes, qui esse aurei perhibentur, Pl.

pĕrhĭlum, *a very little*: Lucr.

pĕrhŏnōrĭfĭcus -a -um. (1) *very honourable*: discessus, Cic. (2) *very respectful*: conlega in me perhonorificus, Cic. L.

¶ Adv. **pĕrhŏnōrĭfĭcē**, *very respectfully*: Cic.

pĕrhorresco -horrescĕre -horrŭi, *to begin to shudder* or *tremble*: aequor perhorruit, Ov. Esp. *to shudder with fear*; intransit.: recordatione consulatus vestri perhorrescere, Cic.; transit., *to shudder at*: tantam religionem, fugam virginum, Cic.; navita Bosporum, Hor.

pĕrhorrĭdus -a -um, *very dreadful*: silvae, Liv.

pĕrhūmānus -a -um, *very friendly, very civil*: epistula, Cic. L.

¶ Adv. **pĕrhūmānĭtĕr**, *very civilly, very kindly*: Cic. L.

Pĕrĭclēs -is, m. (Περικλῆς), *a famous Athenian statesman of the fifth century* B.C.

pĕrĭclītātĭo -ōnis, f. (periclitor), *trial, experiment*: Cic.

pĕrĭclĭtor -ari, dep. (periculum).

Intransit. (1) *to try, make a trial, venture*: periclitemur in exemplis, Cic.; Tac. (2) *to be in danger*: ut potius Gallorum vita quam legionariorum periclitaretur, Caes.; with abl., *to risk*: rebus suis, Liv.; with infin.: Plin., Quint.

Transit. (1) *to try, test, prove*: fortunam, Cic.; vires ingenii, Cic.; with indir. quest.: Caes. (2) *to endanger, risk*: non est salus periclitanda reipublicae, Cic.

pĕrĭcŭlōsus -a -um, adj. (with compar. and superl.) (periculum), *dangerous, perilous*: bellum, iter, vulnus, Cic.; annus, Liv.; with dat.: periculosae libertati opes, Liv.; Caes.; with in: in nosmet ipsos, Cic. L.

¶ Adv. **pĕrĭcŭlōsē**, *dangerously*: aegrotare, Cic. L.; superl.: Sen.

pĕrĭcŭlum (contr. **pĕrĭclum**) -i, n. (root of experior). (1) *a trial, proof, test, attempt*. In gen.: periculum facere, *to make a trial*, Caes.; ex aliis facere, Ter.; with genit.: fidei, Cic.; esp. *an attempt in authorship*: Cic. (2) *danger, peril, hazard*: salutem sociorum summum in periculum ac discrimen vocare, Cic.; capitis periculum adire, *danger of life*, Cic.; periculum obire, Hor., Liv.; periculum est, with ne and the subj., *there is danger that*, Cic., Liv.; periculo meo, *at my risk*,

Pl., Cic. (3) esp. *a trial, action, suit*: Cic.; hence, *a legal record* or *register*: pericula magistratuum, Cic.

pĕrĭdōnĕus -a -um, *very fit, suitable*: locus peridoneus castris, Caes.; with ad and acc.: Sall.

pĕrillustris -e. (1) *very plain, very evident*: Nep. (2) *very distinguished*: Cic. L.

pĕrimbēcillus -a -um, *very weak*: Cic. L.

pĕrĭmo (**pĕrĕmo**) -ĭmĕre -ēmi -emptum (per/emo), *to do away with, destroy, ruin, annihilate*.

LIT., sensu perempto, Cic.; Troia perempta, Verg.; corpus pallore et macie peremptum, Lucr. Esp. *to kill*: Lucr.; perf. partic. **pĕremptus** -a -um, *slain*: Verg., Ov.

TRANSF., *to thwart, frustrate*: reditum, consilium, Cic.; causam publicam, Cic.

pĕrincommŏdus -a -um, *very inconvenient*: Liv.

¶ Adv. **pĕrincommŏdē**, *very inconveniently*: accidit incommode, Cic. L.

pĕrindĕ, adv. *in like manner*. Absol.: Cic., Liv., etc. Foll. by ac, ut, or quam, *just as*: non perinde atque ego putaram, Cic. L.; Liv., Tac. Foll. by ac si, *just as if*: Caes., Cic., Liv.; so by quasi, or tamquam, Cic.

pĕrindignē, adv. *very indignantly*: Suet.

pĕrindulgens -entis, *very indulgent, very tender*: Cic.

pĕrinfāmis -e, *very infamous*: Suet.

pĕrinfirmus -a -um, *very weak*: Cic.

pĕringĕnĭōsus -a -um, *very clever*: Cic.

pĕrinīquus -a -um. (1) *very unfair*: Cic. (2) *very discontented, very unwilling*: periniquo animo pati, with acc. and infin., Cic. L.

pĕrinsignis -e, *very conspicuous, very remarkable*: Cic.

pĕrinvītus -a -um, *very unwilling*: Liv.

pĕrĭŏdus -i, m. (περίοδος), *a sentence, period*: Cic.

Pĕrĭpătētĭcus -a -um (Περιπατητικός), *Peripatetic; belonging to the Peripatetic* or *Aristotelian school of philosophy*; m. pl. as subst. **Pĕrĭpătētĭci** -ōrum, *Peripatetic philosophers*: Cic.

pĕrĭpetasma -ătis, n. (περιπέτασμα), *a curtain, hanging*: Cic.

pĕrīrātus -a -um, *very angry*: Pl., Cic. L.

pĕriscĕlis -ĭdis, f. (περισκελίς), *a garter* or *anklet*: Hor.

pĕristrōma -ătis, n. (περίστρωμα), *a curtain, coverlet, carpet, hanging*: Pl., Cic.

pĕristȳlium -i, n. (περιστύλιον), *a court with a colonnade round it*: Plin. L., Suet.

pĕristȳlum -i, n. (περίστυλον), *a peristyle, a colonnade round a building*: Cic., Suet.

pĕrītĭa -ae, f. (peritus), *knowledge derived from experience, skill*: Tac.; with genit.: locorum ac militiae, Sall.

pĕrītus -a -um, adj. (with compar. and superl.) (root of experior), *experienced, skilful, practised, expert*: absol.: peritissimi duces, Caes.; with genit.: rerum, Cic.; Caes., Liv., etc.; with abl.: quis iure peritior? Cic.; with ad: ad usum et disciplinam, Cic.; with infin.: cantare, Verg.

¶ Adv. (with compar. and superl.) **pĕrītē**, *skilfully, cleverly*: dicere, Cic.; peritissime venditare, Cic.

pĕriūcundus -a -um, *very pleasant, very delightful*: litterae, disputatio, Cic.

¶ Adv. **periūcundē**, *very pleasantly, very delightfully*: in aliqua re versari, Cic.

periūriōsus -a -um (periurus), *perjured*: Pl.

periūrium -i, n. (periurus), *false swearing, perjury*: Cic., Verg., etc.

periūro=peiero; q.v.

periūrus (pēiiĕrus: Pl.) -a -um, adj. (with compar. and superl.) (per/ius), *perjured*: periurus et mendax, Cic.; leno periurissimus, Cic.; m. as subst. *a perjured person*: Cic. TRANSF., in gen., *lying*: Pl.

perlābor -lābi -lapsus sum, *to glide through, glide along*: rotis summas levibus perlabitur undas, Verg.; Lucr.; with ad, *to glide to, penetrate to*: inde perlapsus ad nos et usque ad Oceanum Hercules, Cic.; Lucr., Verg.

perlaetus -a -um, *very joyful*: Liv.

perlātē, adv. *very widely, very extensively*: Cic.

perlectio -ōnis, f. (perlego), *a perusal*: Cic. L.

perlĕgo (pellĕgo) -lĕgĕre -lēgi -lectum. (1) *to survey thoroughly, scan*: omnia oculis, Verg.; Ov. (2) *to read through*: librum, Cic.; Pl., Caes.; senatum, *to call over the roll of senators*, Liv.

perlĕpĭdē, adv. *very pleasantly*: Pl.

perlĕvis -e, *very light, very slight*: perlevi momento, Cic.

¶ Adv. **perlĕvĭtĕr**, *very slightly*: pungit animi dolor, Cic.

perlībens (perlŭbens) -entis, partic. from perlibet; q.v.

perlībĕrālis -e, *well brought up, well-bred*: Ter.

¶ Adv. **perlībĕrālĭtĕr**, *very liberally*: Cic.

perlībet (perlŭbet) -ēre, *it is very pleasing*: Pl.

¶ Hence partic. **perlībens (perlŭbens)** -entis, *very willing*: Pl., Cic. L.

¶ Adv. **perlībentĕr (perlŭbentĕr)**, *very willingly*: Cic.

perlĭcĭo=pellicio; q.v.

perlīto -are, *to offer an auspicious sacrifice, to sacrifice with favourable omens*; with abl.: primis hostiis, Liv.; with dat.: saluti, Liv.

perlonginquus -a -um, *very long*: Pl.

perlongus -a -um. (1) *very long*: via, Cic. (2) *lasting a long time, tedious*: Pl.

¶ Adv. **perlongē**, *very far*: Ter.

perlŭbet, etc.=perlibet, etc.; q.v.

perlūcĕo (pellūcĕo) -lūcēre -luxi. (1) *to shine through, gleam through*. LIT., lux perlucens, Liv. TRANSF., *to shine through, be visible*: perlucet ex eis virtutibus, Cic. (2) *to be transparent*. LIT., aether, Cic.; amictus, Ov.; Juv. TRANSF., oratio, *is transparently clear*, Cic.

perlūcĭdŭlus -a -um (dim. of perlucidus), *transparent*: lapis, *pearl*, Cat.

perlūcĭdus (pellūcĭdus) -a -um (perluceo). (1) *shining, bright*: industris et perlucida stella, *bright*, Cic. (2) *transparent*: membrana, Cic.; Hor., Ov.

perluctŭōsus -a -um, *very mournful*: Cic. L.

perlŭo -lŭĕre -lŭi -lūtum, *to wash, bathe*: manūs undā, Ov.; pass., as middle, *to bathe*: in fluminibus perluuntur, Caes.; undā, Hor.

perlustro -are. (1) *to traverse, pass through*: agros, Liv. (2) *to survey, examine*: omnia oculis, Liv.; aliquid animo, Cic.

permădĕfăcĭo -ĕre, *to drench*: Pl.

permădesco -mădescĕre -mădŭi, *to grow effeminate*: Sen.

permagnus -a -um, *very great, very large*: numerus, Caes.; hereditas, Cic.; n. as subst.: permagnum aestimans, Cic.; permagni interest, Cic.

permānantĕr, adv. (permano), *by flowing through*: Lucr.

permānasco -ĕre, *to begin to trickle through*: Pl.

permănĕo -mănēre -mansi -mansum, *to remain, stay, abide*. LIT., Seleucus in maritima ora permanens, Liv.; Caes. TRANSF., (1) *to last, continue*: ut quam maxime permaneant diuturna corpora, Cic. Ov. (2) *to continue in an attitude, frame of mind*, etc.: in pristinā sententiā, Cic. L.; Liv.

permāno -are, *to flow through, to trickle through*.

LIT., in saxis ac speluncis permanat aquarum liquidus umor, Lucr.; succus in iecur, Cic.; with acc.: calor argentum, Lucr.

TRANSF., *to reach, penetrate, extend*: doctrina in civitatem, Cic.; ad aures alicuius, Cic.; Lucr., Caes.

permansĭo -ōnis, f. (permaneo), *a remaining, abiding*: in unā sententiā, Cic.

permărīnus -a -um, *going through the sea*: lares, *attending and guarding those who travel by sea*, Liv.

permātūresco -mātūrescĕre -mātūrŭi, *to become thoroughly ripe*: Ov.

permĕdĭocris -e, *very moderate*: Cic.

permĕdĭtātus -a -um, *well-prepared*: Pl.

permĕo -are, *to go through, pass through, traverse*. LIT., Tac.; with acc.: maria ac terras, Ov. TRANSF., intellegentia per omnia ea, Cic.

permētĭor -mētīri -mensus sum, dep. *to measure through, measure out*. LIT., soli magnitudinem, Cic. TRANSF., *to traverse*: aequor, Verg.; Lucr.

permingo -mingĕre -minxi, *to defile*: Hor.

permīrus -a -um, *very wonderful*: illud mihi permirum accidit, with acc. and infin., Cic.

permiscĕo -miscēre -miscŭi -mixtum, *to mix together, mingle thoroughly*.

LIT., naturam cum materia, Cic.; permixti cum suis fugientibus, Caes.; with abl.: Verg. with dat.: Liv., Verg.

TRANSF., (1) fructūs acerbitate permixtos Cic. (2) *to confuse, throw into confusion*: omnia iura divina et humana, Caes. Graeciam, Cic.; domum, Verg.

¶ Hence partic. **permixtus** -a -um, *mixed*: hence, *promiscuous*: Lucr.

¶ Adv. **permixtē**, *promiscuously*: Cic.

permissĭo -ōnis, f. (permitto). (1) *a yielding, surrender*: Liv. (2) *permission, leave*: me permissio mansionis tuae, Cic. L.

permissū, abl., *as from permissus, n.* (permitto), *by permission*: permissu legis Cic.; tuo, Cic.; Liv.

permĭtĭālis -e (permities), *destructive, annihilating*: Lucr.

permĭtĭēs -ei, f. *destruction, annihilation*: Pl. Liv.

permitto -mittĕre -mīsi -missum, *to let go through*.

LIT., equos permittunt in hostem, Liv esp. of weapons, *to let go, hurl*: saxum in hostem, Ov.

TRANSF., (1) *to let go, indulge*: tribunatur Liv. (2) *to give up, yield, surrender*: alicui potestatem, Cic.; consulibus rempublicam, Cic.; se in fidem ac potestatem populi, Caes. (3) *to relinquish, concede, sacrifice*: inimicitias patribus conscriptis, Cic.; permitto aliquid iracundiae tuae, *make some allowance for*, Cic. (4) *to allow, permit*; with dat. and infin.: Cic.; with dat. and ut and the subj.: Cic., Liv.; with acc. and infin.: ille meas errare boves permisit, Verg.

permixtē, adv. from permisceo; q.v.

permixtio -ōnis, f. (permisceo). (1) *a mixture*: Cic. (2) *confusion*: Sall.

permŏdestus -a -um, *very modest, very moderate*: Cic., Tac.

permŏdĭcus -a -um, *very moderate, small*: Suet.

permŏlestus -a -um, *very troublesome*: Cic. L.
¶ Adv. **permŏlestē**, *with much difficulty*: ferre (with acc. and infin.), Cic.

permollis -e, *very feeble*: Quint.

permŏlo -ĕre, *to grind thoroughly*. TRANSF., Hor.

permōtĭo -ōnis, f. (permoveo), *a movement, agitation*; esp. of the mind, *an emotion*: animi, Cic.

permŏvĕo -mŏvēre -mōvi -mōtum, *to move or stir up thoroughly*.
LIT., mare permotum, *agitated*, Lucr.
TRANSF., (1) *to move, excite, agitate* a person *mentally*: **a**, *to persuade, induce, influence*: conventum pollicitationibus, Caes.; nihil te curulis aedilitas permovit quominus ludos flagitio pollueres, Cic.; plebes dominandi studio permota, Sall.: **b**, *to stir, excite, affect*: mentem iudicum, Cic.; permotus metu, dolore, iracundiā, odio, Cic. L.; milites gravius permoti, Caes. (2) *to stir up, excite* a feeling: invidiam, misericordiam, metum et iras, Tac.

permulcĕo -mulcēre -mulsi -mulsum, *to stroke*. LIT., aliquem manu, Ov.; barbam alicuius, Liv. TRANSF., (1) *to charm*: sensum voluptate, Cic.; verbis aures, Hor. (2) *to soothe, soften*: animos, Lucr., Caes.; senectutem, Cic.; pectora dictis, Verg.; iram, Liv.; Tac.

permultus -a -um, sing., *very much*; plur., *very many*: colles, Caes.; viri, Cic. N. sing. as subst. **permultum** -i, *very much*; in acc.: permultum interest, Cic.; permultum ante, Cic. L.; in abl., with compar.: permulto clariora, *far brighter*, Cic.

permūnĭo -ire -īvi -ītum, *to fortify completely*, or *to finish fortifying*: quae munimenta incohaverat, permunit, Liv.; Tac.

permūtātĭo -ōnis, f. (permuto). (1) *a complete change*: magna permutatio rerum, Cic. (2) *an exchange, interchange*: captivorum, Liv.; mercium, Tac.; plur.: partim emptiones, partim permutationes, Cic.

permūto -are. (1) *to change completely*: ordinem, Lucr.; sententiam, Cic. (2) *to exchange, interchange*: nomina inter se, Pl.; captivos, Verg.; esp. *to exchange money*: ut cum quaestu populi pecunia permutaretur, Cic.

perna -ae, f. (πέρνα), *a ham*: Pl., Hor.

pernĕcessārĭus -a -um. (1) *very necessary*: tempus, Cic. L. (2) *very intimate*: homo intimus ac mihi pernecessarius, Cic.; m. as subst.: Cic. L.

pernĕcessē, indecl. adj. *very necessary*: Cic.

pernĕgo -are. (1) *to deny flatly, persist in denying*; with acc. and infin.: Cic.; de aliquo alicui, Tib. (2) *to persist in refusing*: Mart., Sen.

pernĭcĭābĭlis -e (pernicies), *deadly, destructive*: id perniciabile reo, Tac.

pernĭcĭēs -ēi, f. (old genit. pernicii, Cic.; old dat. pernicie, Liv.) (cf. neco), *destruction, disaster, ruin*: perniciem adferre vitae alicuius, Cic.; reipublicae moliens, Cic.; in nepotum perniciem, Hor.; Liv. TRANSF., *a dangerous person* or *thing*: pernicies provinciae Siciliae, Cic.

pernĭcĭōsus -a -um, adj. (with compar.; and superl.: Nep.) (pernicies), *destructive, ruinous*: exemplum, lex, Cic.; morbi, Cic.; scripta auctori suo, Ov.
¶ Adv. (with compar.) **pernĭcĭōsē**, *destructively, ruinously*: multa perniciose sciscuntur in populis, Cic.

pernĭcĭtās -ātis, f. (pernix), *swiftness, agility*: Cic., Liv., etc.

pernĭger -gra -grum, *quite black*: Pl.

pernĭmĭus -a -um, *far too much*: Ter.

pernix -nīcis, *swift, nimble, agile, active*: alae, Verg.; corpora, Liv.; with infin.: Hor.
¶ Adv. **pernĭcĭtĕr**, *swiftly, nimbly*: equo desilire, Liv.; Pl., Cat.

pernōbĭlis -e, *very famous*: epigramma Graecum, Cic.

pernocto -are (pernox), *to pass the night*: ad ostium carceris, Cic.; extra moenia, Liv. TRANSF., haec studia pernoctant nobiscum, Cic.

pernosco -noscĕre -nōvi -nōtum, *to investigate thoroughly, to become thoroughly acquainted with*: hominum mores ex corpore, oculis, vultu, Cic.; with indir. quest.: Ter.; in perf., *to know thoroughly*: Pl.

pernōtŭit -ŭisse (pernosco), *it has become well known*: Tac.

pernox -noctis, adj. *all-night*: luna pernox erat, Liv.; iacet pernox, Verg.

pernŭmĕro -are, *to count out, reckon up*: imperatam pecuniam, Liv.; Pl.

pēro -ōnis, m. *a boot of untanned hide*: Verg., Juv.

pĕrobscūrus -a -um, *very obscure*: quaestio, Cic.; fama, Liv.

pĕrŏdĭōsus -a -um, *very troublesome*: Cic. L.

pĕroffĭcĭōsē, adv. *very obligingly, very attentively*: qui me perofficiose observant, Cic. L.

pĕrŏlĕo -ēre, *to emit a strong smell*: Lucr.

pĕrōnātus -a -um (pero), *wearing boots of untanned leather*: Pers.

pĕropportūnus -a -um, *very opportune, very convenient*: deversorium, Cic.; Liv.
¶ Adv. **pĕropportūnē**, adv. *very opportunely, very conveniently*: Cic., Liv.

pĕroptātō, n. abl. as adv. (opto), *just as one would wish*: Cic.

pĕrŏpus, indecl. noun: peropus est, *it is very necessary*, Ter.

pĕrōrātĭo -ōnis, f. (peroro), *the conclusion of a speech, peroration*: Cic.

pĕrornātus -a -um, *very ornate*: Crassus in dicendo, Cic.

pĕrorno -are, *to adorn greatly*: senatum, Tac.

pĕrōro -are. (1) *to speak from beginning to end, to plead a cause throughout, explain* or *state thoroughly*: tantam causam, Cic. (2) *to*

conclude a speech, to wind up : quoniam satis
multa dixi est mihi perorandum, Cic.; also,
to close a case (of the last speaker at a trial):
Cic.; with an object, to conclude: totum hoc
crimen decumanum perorabo, Cic.; pass.:
res illā die non peroratur, Cic.

pĕrōsus -a -um (per/odi), hating, detesting;
with acc. obj.: decem virorum scelera, Liv.;
lucem, Verg.; plebs consulum nomen perosa
erat, hated, Liv.

perpāco -are, to pacify thoroughly: necdum
omnia in Graecia perpacata erant, Liv.

perparcē, adv. very sparingly: Ter.

perparvŭlus -a -um, very little: sigilla, Cic.

perparvus -a -um, very little: semina, Lucr.;
perparva et tenuis civitas, Cic.

perpastus -a -um (per/pasco), well fed: canis,
Phaedr.

perpaucŭli -ae -a, plur. adj. extremely few: Cic.

perpauci -ae -a, plur. adj. very few: Ter.,
Liv.; n. as subst.: perpauca dicere, Cic.;
Hor.

perpaulum (perpaullum) i, -n. a very little:
Cic.

perpauper -ĕris, very poor: Cic. L.

perpauxillum -i, n. a very little: Pl.

perpăvĕfăcio -făcĕre, to terrify: Pl.

perpello -pellĕre -pŭli -pulsum, to push hard,
drive along. TRANSF., to urge, compel,
constrain: animus hominem, Pl.; urbem eo
metu ad deditionem, Liv.; with ut or ne and
the subj.: Sall., Liv., Tac.

perpendĭcŭlum -i, n. (perpendo), a plumb-
line, plummet: ad perpendiculum columnas
exigere, Cic.; ad perpendiculum, in a straight
line, Caes.

perpendo -pendĕre -pendi -pensum, to weigh
carefully. TRANSF., to consider, examine,
investigate: aliquid ad disciplinae praecepta,
Cic.; perpenditur amicitia veritate, Cic.;
Suet.

perpĕram, adv. wrongly, falsely: iudicare,
facere, Cic.; Liv.

perpĕs -pĕtis (peto), continuous, unbroken:
noctem perpetem, throughout the night, Pl.

perpessĭo -ōnis, f. (perpetior), suffering, endurance: laborum, dolorum, Cic.

perpessū, abl. as from perpessus, m. (perpetior), in the enduring: Cic.

perpĕtĭor -pĕti -pessus, dep. (per/patior), to
bear to the end, endure: dolorem, Cic.; Hor.,
Ov.; with acc. and infin., to endure that: Pl.,
Verg., Ov.

perpĕtro -are (per/patro), to complete, accomplish, perform: caedem, sacrificium, bellum,
pacem, Liv.; with ut or ne and subj.: Tac.

perpĕtŭĭtās -ātis, f. (perpetuus), uninterrupted
succession, continuity: vitae, Cic.; dicendi,
Cic.; ad perpetuitatem, for ever, Cic.

¹perpĕtŭō, adv. from perpetuus; q.v.

²perpĕtŭo -are (perpetuus), to make continual,
continue, perpetuate: potestatem iudicum,
to maintain unbroken, Cic.; Pl.

perpĕtŭus -a -um (peto), continuous, uninterrupted. LIT., (1) of space: munitiones,
trabes, Caes.; agmen, Cic.; mensae, Verg.;
in perpetuum, continuously, Lucr. (2) of
time: ignis Vestae perpetuus ac sempiternus,
Cic.; quaestiones, with a standing body of
judges, Cic.; sopor, Hor.; in perpetuum, for
ever, Cic. TRANSF., universal, general: ius,
Cic.

¶ Abl. as adv. perpĕtŭō, uninterruptedly:
Cic., Ov., etc.

perplăcĕo -ēre, to please greatly: ea lex mihi
perplacet, Cic. L.; Pl.

perplexābĭlis -e (perplexor), intricate, obscure:
Pl.

¶ Adv. perplexābĭlĭter, perplexingly: Pl.

perplexor -ari, dep. (perplexus), to perplex: Pl.

perplexus -a -um, adj. (with compar.),
confused, intricate, entangled. LIT., iter,
Verg. TRANSF., obscure, ambiguous: sermones,
Liv.; perplexum Punico astu responsum,
Liv.

¶ Adv. perplexē and perplexim, confusedly, obscurely: indicare, Liv.; Ter.

perplĭcātus -a -um (per/plico), entangled,
involved: Lucr.

perplŭit -ĕre. LIT., (1) it rains through: Cato.
(2) in 3rd. pers. sing. and plur., to let the
rain through: perpluunt tigna, Pl.; Quint.
TRANSF., to run away like rain or to pour in
like rain: Pl.

perpŏlĭo -ire, to polish thoroughly: Plin
TRANSF., to polish, perfect, complete: illam
superiorem partem perpolire atque conficere,
Cic.

¶ Hence partic. perpŏlītus -a -um,
polished, accomplished, refined: perfecti in
dicendo et perpoliti homines, Cic.; vita
perpolita humanitate, Cic.

perpŏpŭlor -ari, dep. to lay waste, devastate
completely: Italiam, Liv.; perf. partic. ir
pass. sense: Liv.

perpŏtātĭo -ōnis, f. (perpoto), a continued
drinking, drinking-bout; plur.: intemperantissimae perpotationes, Cic.

perpŏto -are. (1) to continue drinking: totos
dies, Cic.; perpotant ad vesperum, Cic.; Pl
(2) to drink up: Lucr.

perprimo -primĕre -pressi -pressum (per,
premo), to press hard: cubilia, to lie upon
Hor.; Sen.

perprosper -ĕra -ĕrum, very favourable
valetudo, Suet.

perprūrisco -ĕre, to begin to itch all over: Pl.

perpugnax -ācis, very pugnacious: in dis
putando, Cic.

perpulcher -chra -chrum, very beautiful: Ter

perpurgo (perpūrĭgo: Pl.) -are, to mak
thoroughly clean. LIT., se quādam herbulā
Cic.; Pl. TRANSF., to explain thoroughly
to clear up: locum orationis, Cic.

perpŭsillus -a -um, very small, very little: Cic

perpŭto -are, to explain fully: Pl.

perquam, adv. very much, extremely: pel
quam breviter, Cic.; perquam pauci, Liv.

perquīro -quirĕre -quīsivi -quīsitum (per
quaero). (1) to inquire carefully for, to searc
for eagerly: vias, Caes.; vasa, Cic. (2) t
inquire carefully into: Cic.

¶ Hence, from partic. perquīsītus; com
par. adv. perquīsĭtius, more accurately
perquisitius et diligentius conscribere, Cic.

perrārus -a -um, very uncommon, very rare
Liv.

¶ Abl. as adv. perrāro, very rarely, ver
seldom: Cic., Hor.

perrĕcondĭtus -a -um, very abstruse: Cic.

perrēpo -rēpĕre -repsi -reptum, to crav
through, creep over: Tib.

perrepto -are (freq. of perrepo), to crawl abou
Pl.; with acc., to crawl through: Pl., Ter.

perrĭdĭcŭlus -a -um, *very laughable, very ridiculous*: Cic.
 ¶ Adv. **perrīdĭcŭlē**, *very laughably*: Cic.
errōgātĭo -ōnis, f. *the passing* of a law: Cic.
errōgo -are, *to ask in succession, to ask one after another*: sententias, Liv., Tac.
errumpo -rumpĕre -rūpi -ruptum.
 Intransit., *to break through, burst a way through*: per medios hostes, Caes.; per aciem, Liv.
 Transit., *to break through, burst through.* LIT., paludem, Caes.; cuneos hostium, Liv.; hence, *to shatter, burst*: rates, Caes.; limina, Verg. TRANSF., leges, Cic.
Persa or **Persē** -ae, f. (*Πέρση*), *a nymph, mother of Aeetes, Circe, and Hecate.*
 ¶ Hence f. adj. **Persēis** -ĭdis (*Περσηίς*), *Persean=magical*: herbae, Ov.
Persa, *see* Persae.
'ersae -ārum, m. pl. (*Πέρσαι*), *the Persians*; sing. **Persa** and **Persēs** -ae, m. *a Persian.*
 ¶ Hence subst. **Persĭa** -ae, f. *Persia.* **Persĭs** -ĭdis, f. (1) adj., *Persian*: Ov. (2) subst., *Persia.* Adj. **Persĭcus** -a -um, *Persian*; as subst., n. sing. **Persĭcum** -i, *a peach*: Plin., Mart.; n. pl. **Persĭca** -ōrum, *Persian history*: Cic.
ersaepĕ, adv. *very often*: Cic., Hor.
ersalsus -a -um, *very witty*: Cic.
 ¶ Adv. **persalsē**, *very wittily*: persalse et humaniter gratias mihi agit, Cic. L.
ersălūtātĭo -ōnis, f. (persaluto), *a general greeting*: Cic.
ersălūto -are, *to greet in succession, greet all round*: omnes, Cic.
ersanctē, adv. *very sacredly*: Ter., Suet.
ersăpĭens -entis, *very wise*: homo, Cic.
 ¶ Adv. **persăpĭentĕr**, *very wisely*: Cic.
erscĭentĕr, adv. (per/scio), *very discreetly*: Cic.
erscindo -scindĕre -scĭdi -scissum, *to tear to pieces*: omnia perscindente vento, Liv.
erscītus -a -um, *very clever*: Ter.; (in tmesis) per mihi scitum videtur, Cic.
erscrībo -scrībĕre -scripsi -scriptum, 'to *write down completely.*
 In gen.: rationes sunt perscriptae scite et litterate, Cic.; orationem, Cic.; res populi Romani, Liv.; de suis rebus ad Lollium, Cic. L.; with acc. and infin.: Caes.; with indir. quest.: Cic. L.
 Esp. (1) *to write in full, without abbreviation*: Hor. (2) *to note down officially, enter*: omnia iudicum dicta, interrogata, responsa, Cic.; in an account-book: falsum nomen, Cic. (3) *to make over* or *assign in writing*: illam pecuniam in aedem sacram reficiendam perscribere, Cic.; Ter., Liv.
erscriptĭo -ōnis, f. (perscribo). (1) *an entry, noting down*: Cic. (2) *a making over* or *assigning by a written document*: Cic. L.
erscriptor -ōris, m. (perscribo), *one who makes an entry*: Cic.
erscrūto -are (Pl.) and **perscrūtor** -ari, dep. *to search through, look through*: arculas muliebres, Cic. TRANSF., *to examine, investigate*: naturam rationemque criminum, Cic.
erseco -sĕcare -sĕcŭi -sectum, *to cut through.* TRANSF., (1) *to dissect*: rerum naturas, Cic. (2) *to cut away*: vitium, Liv.
ersector -ari, dep. (freq. of persequor), *to*

follow, pursue eagerly. LIT., accipitres persectantes, Lucr. TRANSF., *to investigate*: primordia, Lucr.; Pl.
persĕcūtĭo -ōnis, f. (persequor), *a prosecution*: Cic.
persĕdĕo (**persĭdĕo**) -sĕdĕre -sēdi -sessum, *to remain sitting*: in equo dies noctesque persedendo, Liv.
persegnis -e, *very sluggish, very languid*: proelium, Liv.
persĕnex -is, *very old*: Suet.
persentĭo -sentīre -sensi -sensum. (1) *to perceive distinctly*: eam tali peste teneri, Verg. (2) *to feel deeply*: pectore curas, Verg.
persentisco -ĕre. (1) *to begin to perceive distinctly*: Ter. (2) *to begin to feel deeply*: Lucr.
Persĕphŏnē -ēs, f. (*Περσεφόνη*), *the Greek name of Proserpina*; q.v.
persĕquor -sĕqui -sĕcūtus sum, dep. *to follow constantly, pursue to the end.*
 LIT., in gen.: vestigia alicuius, Cic.; Pl., Verg.; esp. (1) *to follow with hostile intent, pursue*: fugientes usque ad flumen, Caes.; Cic. (2) *to hunt out*: omnes solitudines, Cic. (3) *to overtake*: aliquem, Cic., Hor.
 TRANSF., (1) *to follow up, pursue* an abstr. thing: omnes vias, *to use every method*, Cic.; voluptates, *to strive after*, Cic.; ius suum, Cic.; artes, Cic. (2) *to follow, to imitate*: ironiam, Cic.; sectam et instituta alicuius, Cic.; Academiam veterem, Cic. (3) *to pursue hostilely, proceed against, punish, avenge*: civitatem bello, Caes.; iniurias, Cic.; mortem alicuius, Cic.; aliquem iudicio, *to prosecute*, Cic. (4) of actions, *to bring about, accomplish, perform, execute*: mea mandata, Cic. L.; incepta, Liv. (5) *to treat of verbally* or *in writing; set forth, expound, describe*: quae versibus persecutus est Ennius, Cic.; rationes, Lucr.
¹Persēs -ae and **Persēus** -ĕi, m. (*Πέρσης*), *the last king of Macedonia, defeated by the Roman general Aemilius Paulus* in 169 B.C.
 ¶ Hence adj. **Persĭcus** -a -um, *relating to Perseus.*
²Persēs -ae, m. *a Persian, see* Persae.
Persēus -ĕi and -ĕos, m. (*Περσεύς*), *son of Jupiter and Danaë, who killed Medusa, and rescued and married Andromeda.*
 ¶ Hence adj. **Persēus** and **Persēĭus** -a -um, *relating to Perseus.*
persĕvērans -antis, partic. from persevero; q.v.
persĕvērantĭa -ae, f. (persevero), *persistence*: Caes., Cic.
persĕvēro -are (perseverus), *to persist, persevere, continue*: in sua sententia, Cic.; impers. pass.: non est ab isto perseveratum, Cic.; with infin., *to continue to*: iniuriam facere, Cic.; also with infin. understood: una navis perseveravit, *continued on its course*, Caes.; so with acc. and infin., *to continue saying, insist that*: perseverabat se esse Orestem, Cic.; with n. acc.: id perseverare, Cic., Liv.
 ¶ Hence partic. **persĕvērans** -antis, *enduring, persistent*: Liv.
 ¶ Adv. (with compar.) **persĕvērantĕr**, *persistently*: bene coeptam rem tueri, Liv.
persĕvērus -a -um, *very strict*: imperium, Tac.

L.D.—15 *

Persĭa, *see* Persae.

Persĭcus, *see* Persae *and* Perses.

persīdo -sīdĕre -sēdi -sessum, *to sink in, settle down*: Lucr., Verg.

persigno -are, *to note down, record*: dona, Liv.

persimĭlis -e, *very like, very similar*; with genit.: istius, Cic.; with dat.: Hor.

persimplex -ĭcis, *very simple*: Tac.

persisto -ĕre, *to remain constant, persist*: in eadem impudentia, Liv.; with infin.: Cic., Tac.

Persĭus -i, m. (1) *an orator, contemporary of the Gracchi.* (2) A. Persius Flaccus, *a satirist in the reign of Nero.*

persolla -ae, f. (dim. of persona), *a little mask*; hence, as a term of reproach, *a little fright*: Pl.

persōlus -a -um, *quite alone*: Pl.

persolvo -solvĕre -solvi -sŏlūtum, *to unloose.* Hence (1) *to explain, expound*: Cic. L. (2) *to pay, pay off.* LIT., stipendium militibus, Cic. L.; eas alienum alienis nominibus suis copiis, *to pay the debts of others with one's own money*, Sall. TRANSF., *to pay*: grates, Verg.; meritam diis gratiam, Cic.; poenas, Cic., Verg.; also *to deal out*: poenae ab omnibus persolutae, Cic.

persōna -ae, f. *a mask*, esp. *as worn by actors in Greek and Roman drama.*

LIT., ut ex persona mihi ardere oculi hominis histrionis viderentur, Cic.; eripitur persona, manet res, Lucr.; Verg., etc.

TRANSF., (1) *role, part, character, person represented by an actor*: persona de mimo, Cic. (2) in gen., *the part which anyone plays*: accusatoris, Cic.; petitoris personam capere, Cic.; personam in republica tueri principis, *to act as a leading man in the state*, Cic.; alienam personam ferre, Liv. (3) *a personality, individuality, character*: huius Staieni persona, Cic.

persōnātus -a -um (persona), *clad in a mask, masked.* LIT., Roscius, Cic.; pater, Hor. TRANSF., *disguised, counterfeit*: quid est, cur ego personatus ambulem? Cic.; Sen., Mart.

persŏno -sŏnare -sŏnŭi -sŏnĭtum.

(1) intransit.: **a**, *to sound through, resound*: domus cantu personabat, Cic.; Hor.: **b**, *to make a penetrating noise, sound forth*: id totis personabat castris, Liv.; of persons, *to shout*: Tac.; *to perform upon a musical instrument*: cithara Iopas personat, Verg.

(2) transit.: **a**, *to fill with sound, cause to resound*: aequora conchā, Verg.; Cic. L., Hor.: **b**, *to proclaim loudly*: quas (res) isti in angulis personant, Cic.; with acc. and infin.: Cic.

perspecto -are (freq. of perspicio). (1) *to look at to the end*: certamen, Suet. (2) *to look all about*: aedes, Pl.

perspectus -a -um, partic. from perspicio; q.v.

perspĕcŭlor -ari, dep. *to investigate, explore thoroughly*: Suet.

perspergo -ĕre (per/spargo), *to sprinkle, moisten*: Tac. TRANSF., quo tamquam sale perspergatur omnis oratio, Cic.

perspĭcax -ācis (perspicio), *sharp-sighted, acute*: id quod acutum ac perspicax naturā est, Cic.; Ter.

perspĭcĭentĭa -ae, f. (perspicio), *a full awareness* or *knowledge*: veri, Cic.

perspĭcĭo -spĭcĕre -spexi -spectum (per/specio), *to see through, look through.*

LIT., ut prae densitate arborum perspici caelum vix posset, Liv.; Caes.; also more generally, *to look at attentively, survey, examine*: domum tuam, Cic.; Caes.; eas (epistulas) ego oportet perspiciam, *read through*, Cic. L.

TRANSF., *to regard mentally, observe, investigate, ascertain*: alicuius fidem, Cic.; animos regum, Cic.; with acc. and infin.: Cic. L.; with indir. quest.: ista veritas quae sit, non satis perspicio, Cic.

¶ Hence partic. (with superl.) **perspectus** -a -um, *ascertained, fully known*: virtus, Cic.; benevolentia perspectissima, Cic. L.

¶ Adv. **perspectē**, *with insight*: Pl.

perspĭcŭĭtās -ātis, f. (perspicuus), *clearness, brightness, transparency*: Plin. TRANSF., *clearness, perspicuity*: Cic., Quint.

perspĭcŭus -a -um (perspicio), *transparent, bright, clear.* LIT., aquae, Ov. TRANSF., *clear, evident*: utilitatis ratio aut perspicua nobis aut obscura, Cic.

¶ Adv. **perspĭcŭē**, *clearly, plainly*: plane et perspicue expedire aliquid, Cic.

persterno -sternĕre -strāvi -strātum, *to pave thoroughly*: viam silice, Liv.

pĕrstĭmŭlo -are, *to goad on violently*: Tac.

persto -stare -stĭti -stātum, *to stand firm, remain standing.* LIT., armati omnes diem totum perstant, Liv. TRANSF., (1) *to remain unchanged, to last, endure*: nihil est quod toto perstet in orbe, Ov. (2) *to stand firm, persist, persevere*: in incepto, Liv.; in sententiā, Caes., Liv.; talia perstabat memorans, Verg.; with infin.: Ov.

perstrĕpo -ĕre -ŭi, *to make a great noise*: Ter.

perstringo -stringĕre -strinxi -strictum.

(1) *to press tight, bind tight.* LIT., vitem, Cato. TRANSF., *to deaden, dull the senses*: aures, Hor.; horror ingens spectantes perstringit, Liv.

(2) *to graze.* LIT., portam aratro, Cic.; solum aratro, *to plough*, Cic.; femur, Verg. TRANSF., **a**, *to scold, blame, reproach*: voluntatem facetiis, Cic.; aliquem suspicione, Cic.; Tac.: **b**, *to touch upon*; in speaking: tantummodo perstringere unamquamque rem, Cic.

persŭādĕo -suādēre -suāsi -suāsum, *to persuade.*

(1) *to convince* of a fact; usually with dat. of pers. and the fact expressed either by acc. of n. pron., or by acc. and infin. clause: imprimis hoc volunt persuadere, non interire animas, Caes.; pass.: hoc ipsis Siculis ita persuasum est, Cic. Esp. with dat. of reflex., *to satisfy oneself, be convinced*: velim tibi ita persuadeas me tuis consiliis nullo loco defuturum, Cic. L.

(2) *to persuade, prevail upon* a person to do a thing; usually with dat. of pers. and with ut and the subj.: huic persuadet uti ad hostes transeat, Caes.; Pl., Cic., etc.; with infin.: Verg.

persuāsĭo -ōnis, f. (persuadeo). (1) *a convincing, persuasion*: Cic. (2) *a conviction, belief*: Quint., Suet.

persuāsū, abl. sing. as from persuasus, m. (persuadeo), *by persuasion*: huius persuasu, Cic.; Pl.

persubtīlis -e, *very fine*. Lit., Lucr. Transf., *very subtle*: oratio, Cic.

persulto -are (salto). (1) intransit., *to leap, gambol, skip about*: in agro, Liv.; Tac. (2) transit., *to range through*: captam Italiam, Tac.; Lucr.

pertaedet -taedēre -taesum est, *to cause weariness* or *disgust*; usually with acc. of person, genit. of thing: pertaesum est levitatis, Cic.; vos iniuriae pertaesum est, Sall.; with infin. as subject: Lucr.

pertĕgo -tĕgĕre -texi -tectum, *to cover over*: Pl.

pertempto -are, *to prove, test, try*.
Lit., pugionem utrumque, Tac.
Transf., (1) *to put to the test*: adulescentium animos, Liv.; Tac. (2) *to weigh, consider, to examine*: perspice rem et pertempta. (3) *to assail*: tremor corpora, Verg.

pertendo -tendĕre -tendi, *to stretch on*. (1) transit., *to continue, carry through*: hoc, Ter. (2) intransit., *to push on, proceed*: pars maxima Romam pertenderunt, Liv.; Ter., Prop.

pertĕnŭis -e, *very fine, very small*: Plin. Transf., *very slight*: spes salutis, Cic. L.; suspicio, Cic.

pertĕrebro -are, *to bore through*: columnam, Cic.

pertergĕo -tergēre -tersi -tersum, *to wipe over*. Lit., gausape mensam, Hor. Transf., *to brush*: Lucr.

perterrĕfăcio -făcĕre (perterreo/facio), *to frighten, terrify*: Ter.

perterrĕo -ēre, *to frighten, terrify*: maleficii conscientiā perterritus, Cic.; Ter., Caes.

perterricrĕpus -a -um (perterreo/crepo), *rattling terribly*: Lucr.

pertexo -texĕre -texŭi -textum, *to weave entirely*. Transf., *to complete, accomplish*: pertexe modo quod exorsus es, Cic.; Lucr.

pertica -ae, f. *a long pole* or *rod*: Ov., Plin.; esp. for measuring: Prop.

pertĭmĕfactus -a -um (pertimeo/facio), *thoroughly frightened*: ap. Cic. L.

pertĭmesco -tĭmescĕre -tĭmŭi (pertimeo), *to become very much afraid of*: de suis periculis, Cic.; with acc.: Caes., Cic.; with ne and subj.: Cic.

pertĭnācĭa -ae, f. (pertinax), *firmness, obstinacy, stubbornness*: hominum nimia pertinacia et adrogantia, Caes.; in pertinacia perstare, Liv.

pertĭnax -ācis, adj. (with compar. and superl.) (per/tenax), *having a firm hold, tenacious*: digito male pertinaci, Hor. Transf., (1) *tight-fisted, mean*: Pl. (2) *firm, persistent, stubborn, obstinate*: concertatio, Cic.; virtus, Liv.; in repugnando, Liv.
¶ Adv. (with compar. and superl.) **pertĭnācĭtĕr**, *firmly, obstinately*: fusos insequi, Liv.; Suet.

pertĭnĕo -tĭnēre -tĭnŭi (per/teneo), *to reach to, extend to*.
Lit., venae in omnes partes corporis pertinentes, Cic.; Belgae pertinent ad inferiorem partem fluminis Rheni, Caes.
Transf., (1) *to reach, extend*: eadem bonitas ad multitudinem pertinet, Cic.; Liv. (2) *to tend towards, to have as an object* or *result*: ea quae ad effeminandos animos

pertinent, Caes.; quorsum pertinet? Hor.; Cic. (3) *to relate to, belong to*: illa res ad officium meum pertinet, Cic.; esp. in phrase: quod pertinet ad . . . , *so far as . . . is concerned*, Cic., Caes., etc. (4) *to apply to, attach to, to fall upon*: ad quem suspicio maleficii pertineat, Cic.; Liv. (5) *to belong to*: regnum ad se, Cic.; Liv.

pertingo -ĕre (per/tango), *to stretch out, extend*: collis in immensum pertingens, Sall.

pertŏlĕro -are, *to endure to the end, bear completely*: Lucr.

pertorquĕo -ēre, *to twist, distort*: Lucr.

pertractātĭo -ōnis, f. (pertracto), *a thorough handling, detailed treatment*: rerum publicarum, Cic.

pertracto -are, *to lay hold of, handle, feel*.
Lit., barbatulos mullos exceptare de piscina et pertractare, Cic. Transf., *to treat, study, work upon*: philosophiam, Cic.; sensūs mentesque hominum, Cic.
¶ Hence, from partic. pertractātus, adv. **pertractātē**, *thoroughly*: Pl.

pertrăho -trăhĕre -traxi -tractum. (1) *to drag to a place, forcibly conduct*: aliquem in castra, Liv., Tac. (2) *to entice* or *allure to a place*: hostem ad insidiarum locum, Liv.

pertrecto=pertracto; q.v.

pertristis -e. (1) *very sorrowful*: Cic. poet. (2) *very austere*: quidam patruus, Cic.

pertŭmultŭōsē, adv. *in an agitated manner*: nuntiare, Cic. L.

pertundo -tundĕre -tŭdi -tūsum, *to bore through, perforate*: tigna, Lucr.; tunicam, Cat.
¶ Hence partic. **pertūsus** -a -um, *bored through, perforated*: dolium a fundo pertusum, Liv.; Lucr., Juv.

perturbātĭo -ōnis, f. (perturbo), *confusion, disorder*.
Lit., totius exercitūs, Caes.; caeli, *stormy weather*, Cic.
Transf., (1) *political disorder, disquiet, disturbance*: magnā rerum perturbatione impendente, Cic.; in plur.: Cic. (2) mental *confusion, disturbance*: animorum, Cic.; vitae, Cic.; Caes. (3) philosoph. t. t., *a passion, emotion*: perturbationes sunt genere quattuor, aegritudo, formido, libido, laetitia, Cic.

perturbātrix -īcis, f. (perturbo), *she that disturbs*: Cic.

perturbātus -a -um, partic. from perturbo; q.v.

perturbo -are, *to disturb thoroughly, throw into complete confusion*.
Lit., aciem, Sall.; ordines, Caes.
Transf., (1) politically, *to disturb, confuse*: condiciones factionesque bellicas periurio, Cic.; provinciam, Cic. (2) in mind, *to disquiet, alarm, upset*: de reipublicae salute perturbari, Cic.; perturbari animo, Caes.; clamore, Cic.
¶ Hence partic. (with compar.) **perturbātus** -a -um, *confused, disquieted, disturbed*: nunquam vidi hominem perturbatiorem metu, Cic. L.; tempora, Cic.; plebs, Liv.
¶ Adv. **perturbātē**, *confusedly, in a disorderly manner*: dicere, Cic.

perturpis -e, *very disgraceful*: Cic.

pertūsus -a -um, partic. from pertundo; q.v.

pĕrungo -ungĕre -unxi -unctum, *to anoint thoroughly, besmear*: corpora oleo, Cic.; Hor., Ov.

pĕrurbānus -a -um. (1) *very polite, refined,* or *witty*: Cic. (2) in a bad sense, *over-sophisticated*: Cic. L.

pĕrurgĕo -urgēre -ursi, *to urge strongly, earnestly press*: Suet.

pĕrūro -ūrĕre -ussi -ustum, *to burn thoroughly, to burn up.*
　Lit., agrum, Liv.; partic. perustus, *burnt*: sole, Prop.; solibus, Hor.
　Transf., (1) of passion, etc., *to consume, inflame*: perurimur aestu, Ov.; perustus inani gloriā, Cic. (2) *to gall, chafe*: subducant oneri colla perusta boves, Ov. (3) *to pinch, nip with cold*: terra perusta gelu, Ov.

Pĕrŭsĭa -ae, f. *one of the twelve allied Etruscan towns* (now *Perugia*).
　¶ Hence adj. **Pĕrŭsīnus** -a -um, *of Perusia*; m. pl. as subst., *its inhabitants.*

pĕrūtĭlis -e, *very useful*: Cic. L.

pervādo -vādĕre -vāsi -vāsum.
　(1) *to go through, come through, pass through.* Lit., incendium per agros pervasit, Cic.; per aequa et iniqua loca, Liv.; with acc.: Thessaliam, Liv.; Tac. Transf., *to spread, pervade*: opinio quae per animos gentium barbararum pervaserat, Cic.; with acc.: urbem atque forum, Liv.
　(2) *to attain, to reach, to arrive at.* Lit., in Italiam, Cic.; ad castra, Liv. Transf., locus nullus est quo non hominum libido pervaserit, Cic.; terror in totam aciem, Liv.

pervăgor -ari, dep. *to wander through, to rove about.*
　Lit., omnibus in locis, Caes.; with acc., *to wander through*: bello prope orbem terrarum, Liv.
　Transf., (1) *to be widely spread*: quod in exteris nationibus usque ad ultimas terras pervagatum est, Cic.; ne is honos nimium pervagetur, Cic. (2) *to pervade*: cupiditates, timores omnium mentes pervagantur, Cic.
　¶ Hence partic. (with compar. and superl.) **pervăgātus** -a -um. (1) *widespread, well known*: sermo, Cic.; pervagatissimus versus, Cic. (2) *common, general*: pars est pervagatior, Cic.

pervăgus -a -um, *wandering everywhere*: puer, Ov.

pervărĭē, adv. *very variously*: Cic.

pervasto -are, *to devastate, lay waste completely*: omnia ferro flammāque, Liv.; Tac.

pervĕho -vĕhĕre -vexi -vectum. (1) *to carry through, conduct through*: commeatūs, Liv.; pass. pervehi, as middle, *to travel, sail, pass through*: Caes.; with acc.: Oceanum, Tac. (2) *to carry, lead, conduct, bring to a place*: virgines Caere, Liv.; pass. pervehi, as middle, *to travel to*: in portum, Cic. L.; Chalcidem, Liv. Transf., ad exitūs, Cic.

pervello -vellĕre -velli, *to pluck, pull, twitch.* Lit., aurem, Phaedr.; Sen. Transf., (1) *to pain*: si te forte dolor aliquius pervellerit, Cic. (2) *to disparage*: ius civile, Cic. (3) *to stimulate*: stomachum, Hor.

pervĕnĭo -vĕnire -vēni -ventum, *to come through to, arrive at, reach.*
　Lit., Germani in fines Eburonum pervenerunt, Caes.; ad portam, Cic.
　Transf., (1) of persons, *to attain to, to arrive at* a state, position, etc.: in maximam invidiam, Cic.; in senatum, Cic.; ad suum, *to obtain one's own*, Cic.; ad primos comoedos,

to be ranked with, Cic. (2) of things, *to com* to; esp. *to come to one's knowledge or* in *one's possession*: pecunia ad Verrem perveni Cic.; res ad istius aures, Cic.; with acc. aures, Ov.

pervēnor -ari, dep. *to hunt through*: urben Pl.

perversĭtās -ātis, f. (perversus), *perversity* hominum, Cic. L.; opinionum, Cic.

perverto (pervorto) -vertĕre -verti -versun *to turn upside down, overturn, overthrow.*
　Lit., tecta, Cic.; Pl., Liv.
　Transf., (1) *to overthrow, undermin subvert, pervert*: amicitiam aut iustitian Cic.; omnia iura divina atque humana, Ci (2) in speech, *to trip up, put down*: nunqua (ille me) ullo artificio pervertet, Cic.
　¶ Hence partic. (with superl.) **perversu** -a -um, *crooked, awry, askew.* Lit., perversis simi oculi, *squinting dreadfully*, Cic.; Ov Transf., *distorted, perverse*: homo, sapienti mos, Cic.; Verg.
　¶ Adv. **perversē**, *awry, perversely* interpretari, Cic.; uti deorum beneficio, Cic.

pervespĕri, adv. *very late in the evening* Cic. L.

pervestīgātĭo -ōnis, f. (pervestigo), *a* *examination, investigation*: Cic.

pervestīgo -are, *to track out.* Lit., of hounds Cic. Transf., *to investigate, search into* pervestigare et cognoscere, Cic.; Liv.

pervĕtus -ĕris, *very old*: rex, Cic.; amiciti Cic. L.

pervĕtustus -a -um, *very old*: verba, Cic.

pervĭcācĭa -ae, f. (pervicax), *firmness, persistence*: in hostem, Tac.; in a bad sense *stubbornness, obstinacy*: mulierositas, pe vicacia, ligurritio, Cic.; pervicacia tua superbia, Cic.

pervĭcax -ācis (vinco), *firm, persistent*; wit genit.: recti, Tac.; in a bad sense, *stubbor* *obstinate*: Achilles, Hor.; with genit.: ira Tac.; adversus peritos, Tac.
　¶ Compar. adv. **pervĭcācĭus**, *more stu* *bornly*: Liv., Tac.

pervĭdĕo -vidēre -vīdi -vīsum.
　(1) *to look over, survey.* Lit., sol q pervidet omnia, Ov. Transf., cunctaqu mens oculis pervidet usa suis, Ov.; cum tu pervideas oculis mala lippus inunctis, Hor.
　(2) *to see through, discern, distinguish.* Lit ut neque . . . quae cuiusque stipitis palm sit pervideri possit, Liv. Transf., animi m firmitatem, Cic. L.; Liv.

pervĭgĕo -ēre, *to flourish, bloom continuall* opibus atque honoribus perviguere, Tac.

pervĭgil -ilis, *always watchful*: Ov., Juv.

pervĭgĭlātĭo -ōnis, f. (pervigilo), *a vigil, religious watching*: Cic.

pervĭgĭlĭum -i, n. *a keeping awake all nigh* Plin., Sen.; esp. *a religious watching, vigi* castra pervigilio neglecta, Liv.; pervigiliu celebrare, Tac.

pervĭgĭlo -are, *to remain awake all nigh* noctem, Cic.; Verg., Liv., etc.

pervīlis -e, *very cheap*: annona, Liv.

pervinco -vincĕre -vīci -victum, *to conqu completely.*
　Lit., pervicit Vardanes, Tac.
　Transf., (1) *to carry one's point*: pervic Cato, Cic. L. (2) *to surpass, outdo*: voc pervincunt sonum, Hor. (3) *to indu*

prevail upon: multis rationibus pervicerat Rhodios ut Romanam societatem retinerent, Liv. (**4**) *to achieve, effect*: pervicerunt remis ut tenerent terram, Liv. (**5**) *to prove, demonstrate*: aliquid dictis, Lucr.

pervĭus -a -um (per/via), *passable, accessible, having a road through.* LIT., pervius usus, tectorum inter se, Verg.; loca equo pervia, Ov.; transitiones, Cic.; n. as subst. pervium -i, *a passage*: Pl., Tac. TRANSF., *unobstructed, accessible*: nihil ambitioni pervium, Tac.; Pl.

pervīvo -ere, *to live on, survive*: Pl.

pervolgo=pervulgo; q.v.

pervŏlĭto -are (freq. of ¹pervolo), *to fly round, to flit about*; with acc.: volucres nemora, Lucr.; of light: omnia late loca, Verg.

¹pervŏlo -are. (**1**) *to fly through, fly round.* LIT., aedes, Verg.; iter aërium, Ov.; of light: mare ac terras, Lucr. TRANSF., *of any rapid motion*: LVI milia passuum cisiis, Cic.; totam urbem, Juv. (**2**) *to fly to* a place: in hanc sedem, Cic.

²pervŏlo -velle -vŏlŭi, *to wish greatly*; with infin., or acc. and infin.: pervelim scire, Cic.; Pl., Liv.

pervŏlūto -are (freq. of pervolvo), *to roll round*; esp. *to unroll, read* a book: libros, Cic.

pervŏlvo -volvĕre -volvi -vŏlūtum, *to roll about.* LIT., aliquem in luto, Ter. TRANSF., ut in iis locis pervolvatur animus, *may be engaged in*, Cic. Esp. *to unroll a book, to read*: Cat.

pervorsē, etc=perverse, etc.; *see* perverto.

pervulgo (pervolgo) -are. LIT., (**1**) *to publish, make publicly known*: res in vulgus pervulgata, Cic.; illas tabulas pervulgari atque edi P.R. imperavi, Cic. (**2**) *to make generally available*: praemia, Cic. (**3**) of a woman: se, *to prostitute herself*, Cic. TRANSF., *to frequent, haunt* a place: Lucr.

¶ Hence partic. **pervulgātus** -a -um. (**1**) *very usual, common*: consolatio, Cic. L. (**2**) *well known*: ista maledicta pervulgata in omnes, Cic.

pēs pĕdis, m. (πούς), *the foot* (used both of men and animals).

LIT., calcei apti ad pedem, Cic.; Verg., etc. Esp. in phrases, referring to the human foot, but often figuratively: (**1**) in gen.: pedem ferre, *to go*, Verg.; pedem referre, *to return*, Ov., etc.; pedem ponere, *to set foot, to go*; pedibus, *on foot*, also *by land*, Caes., Cic., Liv.; servus a pedibus, *an attendant, lackey*, Cic.; pede pulsare terram, *to dance*, Hor.; pedibus ire in sententiam alicuius, *to agree with, support someone's proposal*, Liv.; ne (quis) pedibus iret, *should vote*, Cic.; sub pedibus, *in one's power*, Verg.; sub pedibus esse, *to be thought little of*, Ov.; sub pede ponere, Hor.; ante pedes positum esse, *to be plain*, Cic.; circum pedes, *about one*, Cic.; pes secundus, felix, dexter, *happy or fortunate arrival*, Verg., Ov. (**2**) in milit. t. t.: pedibus merere, *to serve in the infantry*, Liv.; descendere ad pedes, *to dismount*, Liv.; pedem conferre, *to fight hand to hand*, Liv.

TRANSF., (**1**) *a foot* of a table, chair, etc.: Ov., etc. (**2**) of water: crepante lympha desilit pede, Hor.; Lucr., Verg. (**3**) pes (veli), *a rope* or *sheet, attached to the lower edge of a sail*; hence: pede aequo, *with fair wind*, Ov.;

facere pedem, *to veer out the sheet to catch a side wind*, Verg. (**4**) *a metrical foot*: Cic., Hor.; hence, *a measure, metre, species of verse*: Lesbius, Hor. (**5**) *a foot*, as a measure of length: pedem non egressi sumus, Cic.; Caes.

pessĭmus, pessime, *see* malus.

Pessĭnūs -untis, f. (Πεσσινοῦς, -οῦντος), *a town in Galatia, near Mount Dindymus, famous for its worship of Cybele.* Adj. **Pessĭnuntĭus** -a -um, *relating to Pessinus*.

pessŭlus -i, m. (πάσσαλος), *a bolt*: pessulum ostio obdere, Ter.; Pl.

pessum, adv. (old acc.), *to the ground, to the bottom, downwards*; esp. with ire and dare. LIT., ne pessum abeat ratis, Pl.; Lucr. TRANSF., (**1**) pessum ire, *to sink, be ruined, perish*, Pl., Tac. (**2**) pessum dare, *to destroy, ruin, put an end to*: Pl., Cic., Sall., Tac.

pestĭfĕr -fĕra -fĕrum (pestis/fero), *pestiferous, pestilential.* LIT., odor corporum, Liv. TRANSF., *destructive, injurious*: vipera, Cic.; civis, Cic.; Verg.

¶ Adv. **pestĭfĕrē**, *balefully, injuriously*: Cic.

pestĭlens -entis, adj. (with compar. and superl.) (pestis), *pestilential, unhealthy.* LIT., aedes, Cic.; annus pestilentissimus, Cic. TRANSF., *deadly, fatal, noxious*: homo pestilentior, Cic.; res, Cic.; Verg.

pestĭlentĭa -ae, f. (pestilens).

LIT., *a pestilential* or *unhealthy condition*: autumni, Caes.; agrorum genus propter pestilentiam vastum, Cic.

TRANSF., (**1**) *a plague, infectious disease*: pestilentia conflictati, Caes.; Cic., Liv. (**2**) *moral unwholesomeness*: Cat.

pestĭlĭtās -ātis, f.=pestilentia; q.v.: Lucr.

pestis -is, f. *a pest, pestilence, plague, infectious disease.*

LIT., pestem ab Aegypto avertere, Cic.; Verg., Liv.

TRANSF., (**1**) *destruction, ruin*: pestem in aliquem machinari, Cic.; Verg., Liv. (**2**) *an injurious thing* or *person, a pest, curse, bane*: illae inclusae in republica pestes, Cic.; Verg.

pĕtăsātus -a -um (petasus), *wearing the petasus* (q.v.); hence, *equipped for a journey*: Cic.

pĕtăsĭo (pĕtăso) -ōnis, m. (πετασών), *a fore-quarter of pork*: Varr., Mart.

pĕtăsuncŭlus -i, m. (dim. of petaso), *a little fore-quarter of pork*: Juv.

pĕtăsus -i, m. (πέτασος), *a broad-brimmed felt hat, used by travellers*: Pl.

pĕtaurum -i, n. (πέταυρον), *a spring-board used by acrobats*: Juv.

Pĕtēlĭa (Pĕtĭlĭa) -ae, f. *a town in the Bruttian territory, near modern Strongoli.*

¶ Hence adj. **Pĕtēlīnus** -a -um, *Petelian*.

pĕtesso (pĕtisso) -ĕre (freq. of peto), *to long for, strive after eagerly*: pugnam, Lucr.; laudem, Cic.

pĕtītĭo -ōnis, f. (peto). (**1**) *an attack, thrust, blow*: tuas petitiones effugi, Cic. TRANSF., *an attack in words*: novi omnes hominis petitiones rationesque dicendi, Cic. (**2**) *a requesting, application*: petitio indutiarum, Liv.; esp.: **a**, polit. t. t., *a standing for office, candidature*: consulatūs, Caes.; dare se petitioni, Cic. L.; Liv., Tac.: **b**, legal t. t., *a suit*: Cic., Quint.; also *a right of claim, right to bring an action*: cuius sit petitio, Cic.

pharetratus

pĕtītor -ōris, m. (peto), *one who strives after, a seeker*: famae, Luc.; esp. (1) polit. t. t., *a candidate*: Hor., Suet. (2) legal t. t., *a plaintiff in a civil or private suit*: Cic.

pĕtītūrio -ire (desider. of peto), *to desire to become a candidate*: video hominem valde petiturire, Cic. L.

pĕtītus -ūs, m. (peto), *an inclining towards*: Lucr.

pĕto -ĕre -īvi and -ii -ītum (cf. impetus, Gr. πέτομαι, πίπτω).

(1) *to make for, go to*: **a**, of places: Dyrrhachium, Cic.; loca calidiora, Cic.; caelum pennis, *to fly to*, Ov.; mons petit astra, *rears its head towards*, Ov.: **b**, of persons: ut te supplex peterem, Verg.; Ilionea petit dextrā, Verg.: **c**, with acc. of the route: alium cursum petere, Cic. L.

(2) *to make for, to attack, assail.* LIT., caput et collum, Cic.; aliquem telis, Liv.; Verg. TRANSF., *to attack, assail*: qui me epistulā petivit, Cic. L.; aliquem fraude, Liv.; Tac.

(3) *to seek, strive after, endeavour to obtain*: aliud domicilium, Caes.; sedes apibus statioque petenda, Verg.; praedam pedibus, Ov.; sapientiam, Cic.; mortem, Cic.; with infin.: Verg., Hor., Ov.

(4) *to ask for, beg, beseech, request, entreat*: alicuius vitam, Cic.; pacem a Romanis, Caes.; with ut or ne and the subj.: peto a te ut, etc., Cic.; with subj. alone: abs te peto, efficias ut, etc., Cic. TRANSF., of inanimate objects: quantum res petit, *demands*, Cic. Esp.: a, polit. t. t., *to stand for, canvass for*: consulatum, Cic.; Liv.: **b**, legal t. t., *to sue for*: hereditatis possessionem, Cic.: **c**, *to woo*: virginem petiere iuvenes, Liv.

(5) *to fetch, derive.* LIT., cibum e flamma, Ter.; aliquid ab impedimentis, Caes. TRANSF., gemitus alte de corde, Ov.; a litteris oblivionem, Cic. L.

pĕtorrĭtum (**pĕtōrĭtum**) -i, n. *an open, four-wheeled Gallic carriage*: Hor.

petra -ae, f. (πέτρα), *a stone, rock*: Plin.

Petrīnum -i, n. *an estate near Sinuessa in Campania.*

petrō -ōnis, m. (petra), *an old wether*: Pl.

Petrōnĭus i, m. *name of a Roman gens*; esp. of *a satirist under Nero, perhaps the Petronius Arbiter of Nero's court.*

pĕtŭlans -antis (peto), *impudent, pert, wanton*: homo, Cic.; genus dicendi, Cic.; sometimes *lascivious*: Cic.

¶ Adv. (with compar. and superl.) **pĕtŭlantĕr**, *impudently, pertly, petulantly*: petulanter vivere, Cic.; in aliquem invehi, Cic.

pĕtŭlantĭa -ae, f. (petulans), *impudence, pertness, wantonness*: Cic., Prop.

pĕtulcus -a -um (peto), *butting with the head*: agni, Lucr.; haedi, Verg.

pexātus -a -um (pexus), *wearing a garment with the nap on*, i.e. *a new garment*: Mart.

pexus -a -um, partic. from pecto; q.v.

Phaeāces -ācum, m. pl. (Φαίακες), *the Phaeacians, mythical inhabitants of the island of Scheria.* Sing., adj. and subst. **Phaeax** -ācis, m. *Phaeacian, a Phaeacian.*

¶ Hence subst. **Phaeācĭa** -ae, f. *the country of the Phaeacians*; adj. **Phaeācĭus** and **Phaeācus** -a -um, *Phaeacian*; subst.

Phaeācĭs -ĭdis, f. *a poem on the stay of Ulysses among the Phaeacians.*

Phaedō or **Phaedōn** -ōnis, m. (Φαίδων), *a disciple of Socrates and friend of Plato, who gave his name to a dialogue on the immortality of the soul.*

Phaedra -ae, f. (Φαίδρα) *daughter of Minos, wife of Theseus, and stepmother of Hippolytus.*

Phaedrus -i, m. (Φαίδρος). (1) *an Epicurean philosopher at Athens, teacher of Cicero.* (2) *a disciple of Socrates.* (3) *a freedman of Augustus, Thracian by birth, author of Latin fables.*

Phaestum -i, n. (Φαιστός), *a town on the south coast of Crete.*

¶ Hence subst. **Phaestĭăs** -ădis, f. *a female dweller in Phaestum.*

Phăĕthōn -ōntis, m. (Φαέθων), *the shining one.* (1) epithet of Helios, *the sun.* (2) *the son of Helios and Clymene, who was killed trying to drive the chariot of his father.*

¶ Hence adj. **Phăĕthontēus** -a -um, *relating to Phaethon*; subst. in plur. **Phăĕthontĭădes** -um, f. *the sisters of Phaethon, who were turned into poplars*; **Phăĕthūsa** -ae, f. (Φαέθουσα), *a sister of Phaethon.*

phăgĕr -gri, m. (φάγρος), *a fish*: Ov., Plin.

phălangae (**pălangae**) -ārum, f. pl. (φάλαγγες), *rollers on which heavy structures were moved*: Caes.

phălangītae -ārum, m. pl. (φαλαγγῖται), *soldiers belonging to a phalanx*: Liv.

Phălantus -i, m. (Φάλαντος), *a Spartan who emigrated to Italy and founded Tarentum*: regnata Laconi rura Phalanto, *the Tarentine territory*, Hor.

phălanx -angis, f. (φάλαγξ), *an array of soldiers in close order*: Verg., Juv. Esp. (1) *a division of a Greek army drawn up in battle array, a phalanx*: Nep. (2) *the Macedonian phalanx, a body of men drawn up in a close parallelogram, fifty abreast and sixteen deep.* (3) *Gauls and Germans drawn up in a similar parallelogram*: phalange factā, *in close formation*, Caes.

Phălărĭs -ĭdis, m. (Φαλαρίς), *a tyrant of Agrigentum, notorious for his cruelty.*

phălĕrae -ārum, f. pl. (τὰ φάλαρα), *metal bosses.* (1) *ornaments worn on the breast as a military decoration*: Cic., Liv., Verg. (2) *trappings on a horse's head and breast*: Liv., Verg.

phălĕrātus -a -um (phalerae), *wearing phalerae*: equi, Liv. TRANSF., *adorned*: Ter.

Phălērum -i, n. (Φαληρόν), *the oldest port of Athens.*

¶ Hence adj. **Phălērēus** -ĕi and -ĕos, m. *belonging to Phalerum*: Demetrius Phalereus, or simply, Phalereus, *regent of Athens* (about 300 B.C.); adj. **Phălērĭcus** -a -um, *belonging to Phalerum*; subst. **Phălērĭcus** -i, m. (sc. portus), *the harbour of Phalerum.*

Phănae -ārum, f. pl. (Φαναί), *a harbour and promontory in the south of Chios* (now *Cap Mastico*), *famous for its wine*; adj. **Phănaeus** -a -um, *Phanean*: rex Phanaeus, poet. for *Phanaean wine*, Verg.

phantasmă -ătis, n. (φάντασμα), *an apparition*: Plin. L.

phăretra -ae, f. (φαρέτρα), *a quiver*: Verg., Prop., etc.

phăretrātus -a -um (pharetra), *wearing a*

quiver: virgo, *Diana*, Ov.; puer, *Cupid*, Ov.; Verg., Hor.

pharmăceutrĭa -ae, f. (φαρμακευτρία), *a sorceress*: Verg.

phārmăcŏpōla (-ēs) -ae, m. (φαρμακοπώλης), *a seller of drugs, a quack*: Cic.

Pharsālus (-ŏs) -i, f. (Φάρσαλος), *a town in Thessaly, near which Pompeius was defeated by Caesar*, 48 B.C.
¶ Hence adj. **Pharsālĭcus** and **Pharsālĭus** -a -um, *Pharsalian.*

Phărus (-ŏs) -i, f., rarely m. (Φάρος), *an island off Alexandria, where Ptolemy Philadelphus built a lighthouse*; hence in gen. *a lighthouse*: Caes.
¶ Adj. **Phărĭus** -a -um, *of Pharus or Egyptian*: iuvenca, *Io*, Ov.; turba, *the priests of Isis*, Tib.; coniunx, *Cleopatra*, Mart.

Phăsēlis -idis, f. (Φασηλίς), *a town in Lycia.*
¶ Hence **Phăsēlītae** -ārum, m. pl. *the inhabitants of Phaselis.*

phăsēlus -i, m. and f. (φάσηλος), *an edible bean, the kidney-bean* or *French bean.* LIT., Verg. TRANSF., *a light bean-shaped boat*: Cic. L., Hor.

Phăsis -idis and -idos, m. (Φᾶσις), *a river in Colchis, flowing into the Black Sea.*
¶ Hence **Phăsis** -idis, f.; as adj., *Colchian*: volucres, *pheasants*, Mart.; also as subst., *the Colchian woman*= *Medea of Colchis*: Ov.; adj. **Phăsĭăcus** -a -um (Φασιακός), *Colchian*; adj. **Phăsĭānus**: Phasiana avis, *or* Phasiana, Plin., *or* Phasianus, Suet., *a pheasant*; f. adj. **Phăsĭās** -ădis (Φασιάς), *Colchian.*

phasma -ătis, n. (φάσμα), *a ghost, spectre*: Ter., Juv.

Phēgeūs -ĕi, m. (Φηγεύς), *the father of Alphesiboea.*
¶ Hence adj. **Phēgēīus** -a -um, *of Phegeus*; subst. **Phēgĭs** -ĭdis, f. *the daughter of Phegeus, Alphesiboea.*

phengītēs -ae, m. (φεγγίτης), *selenite* or *crystallized gypsum* (used for window panes): Suet.

Phĕrae- ārum, f. pl. (Φέραι), *a city in Thessaly, the residence of Admetus.*
¶ Hence adj. **Phĕraeus** -a -um, *Pherean* or *Thessalian*: vaccae, *of Admetus*, Ov.

Phĕreclēus -a -um, *of Phereclus, who built the ships in which Paris carried off Helen.*

Phĕrĕcȳdēs -is, m. (Φερεκύδης), (1) *a philosopher of Syros, teacher of Pythagoras.*
¶ Hence adj. **Phĕrĕcȳdēus** -a -um, *of Pherecydes.*
(2) *an Athenian chronicler*, fl. 480 B.C.

Phĕrētĭădēs -ae, m. *son of Pheres*= *Admetus.*

phĭăla -ae, f. (φιάλη), *a drinking-vessel*, broad at the bottom; *a bowl, saucer*: Juv., Mart.

Phīdĭās -ae, m. (Φειδίας), *a celebrated sculptor of Athens, contemporary of Pericles.*
¶ Hence adj. **Phīdĭacus** -a -um, *of Phidias.*

Phĭlaeni -ōrum (and -ōn), m. pl. (Φίλαινοι), *two Carthaginian brothers who submitted to be buried alive for the sake of their country*: arae Philaenon, *a town on the borders of Cyrene.*

phĭlēmă -atis, n. (φίλημα), *a kiss*: Lucr.

Phĭlippi -ōrum, m. pl. (Φίλιπποι), *a city in Macedonia, where Octavian and Antony defeated Brutus and Cassius.*
¶ Hence adj. **Phĭlippensis** -e and **Phĭlippēus** -a -um, *of Philippi.*

Phĭlippus -i, m. (Φίλιππος), *the name of several kings of Macedon, the most celebrated of whom was the father of Alexander the Great.* TRANSF., *name of a gold coin coined by Philip, worth* 20 *drachmae*: Pl., Hor.
¶ Hence adj. **Phĭlippēus** and **Phĭlippĭcus** -a -um, *relating to Philip*: orationes, *the speeches of Demosthenes against Philip*; f. as subst. **Phĭlippĭca** -ae and plur. **Phĭlippĭcae** -ārum, *the speeches of Demosthenes against Philip, and of Cicero against Antony*: Juv.

philitĭa or **phiditĭa** -orum, n. pl. (φιλίτια, φιδίτια), *the public meals of the Lacedaemonians*: Cic.

Phĭlo or **Phĭlōn** -ōnis, m. (Φίλων), *an academi philosopher, teacher of Cicero.*

Phĭloctētēs -ae, m. (Φιλοκτήτης), *son of Poeas, the companion of Hercules, who bequeathed to him his poisoned arrows; he joined in the expedition against Troy, but was left behind on the island of Lemnos, wounded by a snake; brought to Troy in the tenth year of the war and healed by Machaon; he slew Paris.*
¶ Adj. **Phĭloctētaeus** -a -um, *of Philoctetes.*

phĭlŏlŏgĭa -ae, f. (φιλολογία), *love of learning, study of literature*: Cic. L., Sen.

phĭlŏlŏgus -a -um (φιλόλογος), *learned, literary*; m. as subst. *a student of literature, a scholar*: Cic., Sen.

Phĭlŏmēla -ae, f. (Φιλομήλα), *the daughter of Pandion, king of Athens; turned into a nightingale.* TRANSF., *the nightingale*: Verg.

phĭlŏsŏphĭa -ae, f. (φιλοσοφία), *philosophy*: Cic., Sen. TRANSF., (1) *a philosophical subject*: Nep. (2) in plur.: philosophiae, *philosophical sects or systems*, Cic.

phĭlŏsŏphor -ari, dep. *to philosophize, to apply oneself to philosophy*: Pl., Cic.

phĭlŏsŏphus -a -um (φιλόσοφος), *philosophical*: scriptiones, Cic. As subst.; m., **phĭlŏsŏphus** -i, *a philosopher*: Cic.; f., **phĭlŏsŏpha** -ae, *a female philosopher*: Cic. L.

philtrum -i, n. (φίλτρον), *a love-potion, philtre*: Ov., Juv.

[1] **phĭlȳra** -ae, f. (φιλύρα), *the inner bark of the linden-tree, of which bands for chaplets were made*: Hor., Ov.

[2] **Phĭlȳra** -ae, f. (Φιλύρα), *a nymph, daughter of Oceanus, and mother of Chiron, changed into a linden-tree.*
¶ Hence adj. **Phĭlȳrēius** -a -um, *of Philyra*: heros, *Chiron*, Ov.; tecta, *of Chiron*, Ov.; subst. **Phĭlȳrīdēs** -ae, m. *son of Philyra*= *Chiron*: Ov.

phīmus -i, m. (φιμός), *a dice-box*: Hor.

Phīneūs -ĕi and -ĕos, m. (Φινεύς), *a king of Salmydessus in Thrace, who was deprived of sight and tormented by the Harpies for having put his sons to death on a false accusation.*
¶ Hence adj. **Phīnēius** and **Phīnēus** -a -um, *of Phineus*; subst. **Phīnīdēs** -ae, m. *a male descendant of Phineus.*

Phlĕgĕthōn -ontis, m. (φλεγέθων, *burning*), *a river in the infernal regions.*
¶ Hence f. adj. **Phlĕgĕthontĭs** -ĭdis, *of Phlegethon*: lympha, Ov.

Phlegra -ae, f. (Φλέγρα), *a district in Macedonia, afterwards called Pallene, where the gods were said to have killed the giants with lightning.*
¶ Hence adj. **Phlegraeus** -a -um, *of Phlegra*: campi, Ov. TRANSF., campus, *the field of Pharsalia*, Prop.

Phliūs -untis, f. (Φλιοῦς), *a city in the Pelo-ponnese, between Sicyon and Argos.*
¶ Hence adj. **Phliāsius** -a -um, *of Phlius.*
phōca -ae, f. and **phōcē** -ēs, f. (φώκη), *a seal, sea-calf*: Verg., Ov.
Phōcaea -ae, f. (Φώκαια), *a sea-port in Ionia, mother-city of Massilia.*
¶ Hence **Phōcaeensēs** -ium and **Phōcaei** -ōrum, m. pl. *the Phocaeans*; adj. **Phōcăïcus** -a -um, *Phocaean.*
Phōcis -idis, f. (Φωκίς), *Phocis, a district in the north of Greece, between Boeotia and Aetolia.*
¶ Hence adj. **Phōcăïcus** -a -um, *Phocian*; subst. **Phōcenses** -ium, m. pl. *the inhabitants of Phocis*; adj. **Phōcēus** -a -um, *Phocian*: iuvenis Phoceus, *or simply,* Phoceus, *the Phocian= Pylades, son of Strophius, king of Phocis,* Ov.; subst. **Phōcĭi** -ōrum, m. pl. *the Phocians.*
Phoebē -ēs, f. (Φοίβη). (**1**) *the sister of Phoebus, the Moon-goddess, Diana*; meton., *Night*: Ov. (**2**) *daughter of Leucippus.* (**3**) *daughter of Leda and sister of Helena.*
Phoebĭgĕna -ae, m. (Phoebus/gigno), *the son of Phoebus, Aesculapius*: Verg.
Phoebus -i, m. (Φοῖβος), *Apollo, the Sun-god.* Poet., *the sun*: fugat astra Phoebus, Hor.; sub utroque Phoebo, *in the east and west,* Ov.
¶ Hence subst. **Phoebăs** -ădis, f. (Φοιβάς), *a priestess of Phoebus, a prophetess*; adj. **Phoebēïus** and **Phoebēus** -a -um (Φοιβήϊος, Φοιβεῖος), *of Phoebus*: iuvenis, Aesculapius, Ov.; ales, *the raven,* Ov.; virgo, Daphne, Ov.
Phoenicē -ēs, f. (Φοινίκη), *a country on the Syrian coast, including the towns Tyre and Sidon.*
¶ Hence subst. **Phoenīces** -um, m. pl. (Φοίνικες), *the Phoenicians, famous for their skill in navigation and commerce, founders of several colonies, Carthage, Hippo, etc.*; subst. **Phoenissa** -ae, f. (Φοίνισσα), *a Phoenician woman*: exsul, Anna, *sister of Dido,* Ov.
phoenīcoptĕros -i, m. (φοινικόπτερος), *the flamingo*: Juv., Sen.
¹Phoenix -īcis, m. (Φοῖνιξ), *son of Amyntor, companion of Achilles at the Trojan war.*
²phoenix -īcis, m. (φοῖνιξ), *the phoenix, a fabulous bird of Arabia, said to live 500 years, and then to be burnt to death; from the ashes of the dying bird a new phoenix was said to spring.*
phōnascus -i, m. (φωνασκός), *a teacher of singing, etc.*: Quint., Suet.
Phorcus -i, m. (Φόρκος), *a sea-god, son of Neptune, father of Medusa.*
¶ Hence subst. **Phorcis** -ĭdos, f. *a daughter of Phorcus*: sorores Phorcides=Graeae, Ov.; subst. **Phorcȳnis** -idis and -idos, f. *the daughter of Phorcus, Medusa.*
Phōrōneūs -ĕi and -ĕos, m. (Φορωνεύς), *king of Argos, son of Inachus, brother of Io.*
¶ Hence subst. **Phōrōnis** -idis, f. *Io*: Ov.
Phrāātēs (Phrăhātēs) -ae, m. *name of several Parthian kings.*
phrăsis -is, f. (φράσις), *diction*: Quint.
phrĕnēsis -is, f. (φρενῖτις), *madness, frenzy*: Sen., Juv.
phrĕnētĭcus -a -um (φρενιτικός), *mad, frantic*: Cic.
Phrixus -i, m. (Φρίξος), *son of Athamas and Nephele, brother of Helle, with whom he fled to Colchis on a ram with a golden fleece.*

¶ Hence adj. **Phrixēus** -a -um, *of Phrixus*: stagna sororis Phrixeae, *the Hellespont,* Ov.
Phrȳgĕs -um, m. pl. (Φρύγες), *the Phrygians.*
¶ Hence subst. **Phrȳgĭa** -ae, f. *the country of Phrygia in Asia Minor*; adj. **Phrȳgĭus** -a -um (Φρύγιος), *Phrygian*; poet.=Trojan: maritus, Aeneas, Ov.; pastor, Paris, Verg.; mater, Cybele, Verg.; vestes, *embroidered,* Verg.; buxum, *the Phrygian flute,* Ov.; lapis, *Phrygian marble,* Ov.; adj. **Phryx** -ȳgis, *Phrygian or Trojan*: Verg., Ov.
phrȳgĭō -ōnis, m. *an embroiderer*: Pl.
¹Phryx -ȳgis, m. (Φρύξ), *a river in Lydia.*
²Phryx, *see* Phryges.
Phthĭa -ae, f. (Φθία), *a town in Thessaly, birth-place of Achilles.*
¶ Hence subst. **Phthĭăs** -ădis, f. (Φθιάς), *a woman of Phthia*; subst. **Phthĭōta** and **Phthĭōtēs** -ae, m. (Φθιώτης), *an inhabitant of Phthia*; subst. **Phthĭōtĭs** -idis, f. (Φθιῶτις), *Phthiotis, the district of Thessaly in which Phthia is*; adj. **Phthĭōtĭcus** (Φθιωτικός) and **Phthĭus** (Φθῖος), *belonging to Phthia*: rex, Peleus, Ov.
phthĭsis -is, f. (φθίσις), *consumption*: Sen., Juv.
phy, interj. *pish! tush!*: Ter.
phȳlăca -ae, f. (φυλακή), *a prison*: Pl.
Phȳlăcē -ēs, f. (Φυλακή), *a city in Thessaly, where Protesilaus reigned.*
¶ Hence f. adj. **Phȳlăcēïs** -ĭdis, *of Phylace*: matres, *Thessalian,* Ov.; adj. **Phȳlăcēïus** -a -um: coniunx, Laodamia, Ov.; subst. **Phȳlăcĭdēs** -ae, m. (Φυλακίδης), *a descendant of Phylacus; Protesilaus*: Ov.
phȳlăcista -ae, m. (φυλακιστής), *a gaoler*: Pl.
phȳlarchus -i, m. (φύλαρχος), *the head of a tribe, an emir*: Arabum, Cic. L.
Phyllis -idis and -idos, f. (Φυλλίς), *daughter of Sithon, changed into an almond-tree.*
Phyllēïs -ĭdis, f. and **Phyllēïus** -a -um, *of Phyllus (in Thessaly), Thessalian*: iuvenis, Caeneus, Ov.
physĭca -ae, f. and **physĭcē** -ēs, f. (φυσική), *physics, natural science*: Cic.
physĭcus -a -um (φυσικός), *relating to physics or natural philosophy, physical*: ratio, Cic. As subst. m. **physĭcus** -i, *a natural philosopher, scientist*: Cic.; n. pl. **physĭca** -ōrum, *natural philosophy, physics*: Cic.
¶ Adv. **physĭcē,** *in the manner of the natural philosophers*: dicere, Cic.
physĭognōmōn -ōnis, m. (φυσιογνώμων), *a physiognomist, one who judges men's characters by their features*: Cic.
physĭŏlŏgĭa -ae, f. (φυσιολογία), *natural philosophy, science*: Cic.
pĭābĭlis -e (pio), *expiable, that can be atoned for*: fulmen, Ov.
pĭăcŭlāris -e (piaculum), *atoning, expiating*: sacrificia. N. pl. as subst. **pĭăcŭlāria** -ium, *expiatory sacrifices*: Liv.; Pl.
pĭăcŭlum -i, n. (pio), *a means of expiating sin or appeasing a deity.* LIT., *an expiatory sacrifice*: porco feminā piaculum pati, Cic.; duc nigras pecudes, ea prima piacula sunto, *first victims,* Verg. TRANSF., (**1**) *punishment for sacrilege*: gravia piacula exigere, Liv. (**2**) *of a person as victim*: ut luendis periculis publicis piacula simus, Liv. (**3**) *any means of healing, remedy*: Hor. (**4**) *an act making expiation necessary, a sin, crime*: piaculum committere, Liv.; Tac.

pĭāmen -ĭnis, n. (pio), *a means of atonement or expiation*: Ov.

pīca -ae, f. *a jay* or *magpie*: Ov., Mart.

pĭcārĭa -ae, f. (pix), *a place where pitch is made, a pitch-hut*: Cic.

pĭcĕa -ae, f. (pix), *the spruce-fir*: Ov.

Pĭcēnum -i, n. *a district in central Italy on the Adriatic.*
¶ Hence adj. **Pīcens** -entis, *of Picenum*; m. pl. as subst. **Pīcentēs** -ĭum, *the people of Picenum*; adj. **Pĭcēnus** -a -um, *of Picenum.*

pĭcĕus -a -um (pix), *of pitch*: Luc. TRANSF., *pitch-black*: caligo, Verg.

pĭco -are (pix), *to smear with pitch* or *flavour with pitch*: Suet., Mart.

¹**pictor** -ōris, m. (pingo), *a painter*: Cic., Hor.

²**Pictor** -ōris, m. *a cognomen in the gens Fabia*; see Fabius.

pictūra -ae, f. (pingo), *painting.* LIT., *the art of painting*: ars ratioque picturae, Cic. TRANSF., (**1**) *a painting, picture*: Pl., Cic., Tac.; pictura textilis, *embroidery*, Cic.; of *mosaic work*: Verg. (**2**) *a word-picture, description*: Cic.

pictūrātus -a -um (pictura). (**1**) *painted*: Stat. (**2**) *embroidered*: vestes, Verg.

pictus -a -um, partic. from pingo; q.v.

¹**pīcus** -i, m. (**1**) *a woodpecker*: Ov. (**2**) *a griffin*: Pl.

²**Pīcus** -i, m. (Πῖκος), *an Italian deity, husband of Canens, father of Faunus; according to a later legend, changed by Circe into a woodpecker.*

pĭē, adv. from pius; q.v.

Pĭĕrus (-ŏs) -i, m. (Πίερος). Either *a king of Emathia, who gave his nine daughters the name of the nine Muses*; or *a Macedonian, father of the nine Muses.*
¶ Hence subst. **Pĭĕrĭs** -ĭdis or -ĭdos, f. (Πιερίς), *a Muse*; plur. **Pĭĕrĭdes**, *the Muses*; adj. **Pĭĕrĭus** -a -um, *Pierian*; hence *poetic*: via, *the study of poetry*, Ov.; modi, *poems*, Hor.; f. pl. as subst. **Pĭĕrĭae** -arum, *the Muses.*

pĭĕtās -ātis, f. (pius), *dutifulness, dutiful conduct.* LIT., (**1**) *towards the gods, piety*: est pietas iustitia adversus deos, Cic.; Lucr., Verg., etc. (**2**) *due compassion from the gods, respect for human qualities*: di, si qua est caelo pietas, Verg. (**3**) *dutifulness towards one's native country, patriotism*: erga patriam, Cic.; Liv. (**4**) *towards relatives, devotion*: quid est pietas nisi voluntas grata in parentes? Cic.; felix nati pietate, Verg.
TRANSF., in gen., *kindness*: Plin., Suet.

pĭger -gra -grum (piget), *sluggish, unwilling, lazy, slow.*
LIT., of persons and things: non sum piger, Hor.; serpens frigore pigra, Ov.; in labore militari, Cic.; gens pigerrima ad militaria opera, Liv.; with genit.: militiae, Hor.; with infin.: ferre laborem, Hor.
TRANSF., (**1**) *inactive, slow*: bellum, Liv.; campus, *unfruitful*, Hor.; palus, *sluggish, stagnant*, Ov. (**2**) *making slow, numbing*: brumae rigor, Lucr.; Cat., Tib.
¶ Adv. (with compar.) **pigrē**, *slowly, sluggishly*: Liv., Sen.

pĭget -gēre -gŭit -gĭtum est, impers., *it causes annoyance, it disgusts.*
LIT., with acc. of pers. and genit. of thing: me civitatis morum, Sall.; Ter.

With infin. or n. pron. as subject: illud quod piget, Pl.; referre piget, Liv. Absol.: oratione multitudo inducitur ad pigendum, Cic.
TRANSF., (**1**) *it causes regret*: illa me composuisse piget, Ov.; Ter. (**2**) *it causes shame*; with infin.: fateri pigebat, Liv.

pigmentārĭus -i, m. (pigmentum), *a seller of paints and unguents*: Cic. L.

pigmentum -i, n. (pingo), *a paint, colour, pigment.* LIT., aspersa temere pigmenta in tabula, Cic.; of cosmetics: Pl. TRANSF., of style, *ornament, decoration*: pigmenta Aristotelia, Cic.

pignĕrātor -ōris, m. (pigneror), *a mortgagee*: Cic.

pignĕro -are (pignus), *to give as a pledge, pawn, mortgage.* LIT., bona, Liv. TRANSF., cum velut obsidibus datis pigneratos haberent animos, Liv.

pignĕror -ari, dep. (pignus), *to take as a pledge.* Hence (**1**) *to claim as one's own*: Mars fortissimum quemque pignerari solet, Cic. (**2**) *to accept as a pledge of certainty*: quod des mihi pigneror omen, Ov.

pignus -nŏris and -nĕris, n. (connected with pango), *a pledge, pawn, security.*
LIT., se pignori opponere, Pl.; rem alicuius pignori accipere, Tac. Esp. (**1**) *security to enforce attendance of senators in the senate*: senatores pignoribus cogere, Cic.; Liv. (**2**) *a wager, bet, stake*: pignore certare cum aliquo, Verg., Pl.
TRANSF., *a pledge, token, assurance, proof*: voluntatis, Cic.; Liv., Tac. Esp. plur., *persons as pledges of love*: pignora coniugum ac liberorum, Liv.; communia pignora natos, Prop.; Ov., Tac.

pigrĭtĭa -ae, f. and **pigrĭtĭēs** -ēi, f. (piger), *sluggishness, indolence*: Cic.; ad sequendum, Liv.; Mart.

pigro -are (piger), *to be sluggish, lazy*: Lucr.

pigror -ari, dep. (piger), *to be sluggish, lazy*; with infin.: scribere ne pigrere, Cic. L.

¹**pīla** -ae, f. (pinso), *a mortar*: Ov.

²**pīla** -ae, f. (connected with pango), *a pillar*: nulla meos habeat pila libellos, *no bookstall, books being sold in Rome round pillars of buildings*, Hor.; saxea pila, *a pier* or *mole*, Verg.; pontis, *pier* of a bridge, Liv.

³**pīla** -ae, f. *a ball.* LIT., *a ball to play with*: pilā ludere, Hor.; Cic.; prov.: mea pila est, *I've won*, Pl. TRANSF., (**1**) *a game of ball*: quantum alii tribuunt alveolo, quantum pilae, Cic. (**2**) *a balloting-ball*: Prop. (**3**) *a crystal* or *amber ball to carry in the hand*: Prop.

pīlānus -i, m. (pilum)=triarius; q.v.

¹**pīlātus** -a -um (pilum), *armed with the pilum* or *javelin*: Verg.

²**Pīlātus**, see Pontius.

pīlentum -i, n. *a carriage, coach*, esp. used by Roman ladies: Verg., Hor., Liv.

pillĕātus (**pĭlĕātus**) -a -um (pilleus, q.v.), *wearing the felt cap*: fratres, *Castor and Pollux*, Cat.; coloni, Liv.; rex, Liv.

pillĕŏlus (**pĭlĕŏlus**) -i, m. (dim. of pilleus), *a little cap, skull-cap*: Hor.

pillĕus (**pĭlĕus**) -i, m. and **pīllĕum** -i, n. (πῖλος), *a felt cap, fitting close to the head, worn at feasts, especially the Saturnalia, and by slaves after manumission.* LIT., Pl., Liv.

TRANSF., servos ad pilleum vocare, *to summon the slaves to freedom*, Liv.

pĭlo -are (¹pilus), *to deprive of hair, make bald*: Mart.

pĭlōsus -a -um (¹pilus), *covered with hair, hairy*: genae, Cic.; Juv.

pīlum -i, n. (pinso). (1) *a pestle*: Plin. (2) *the heavy javelin of the Roman infantry*: mittere, Caes., Cic., Liv.

Pīlumnus -i, m. *husband of Danaë, father of Daunus, ancestor of Turnus.*

¹pĭlus -i, m. *a single hair*. LIT., munitae sunt palpebrae vallo pilorum, Cic. TRANSF., *a trifle* (usually with a neg.): ego ne pilo quidem minus me amabo, Cic. L.; non facit pili cohortem, Cat.

²pĭlus -i, m. (pilum), *a division of the* triarii *in the Roman army.* Esp. in phrase, primus pilus, *first division of* triarii: primi pili centurio, Caes.; aliquem ad primum pilum transducere, *to promote to be chief centurion*, Caes.; primum pilum ducere, *to be chief centurion*, Caes., Liv. TRANSF., of the officer himself: primus pilus, *the centurion of the first division, the chief centurion of the* triarii *and of the legion*, Caes.

Pimpla -ae, f. (Πίμπλα), *a place in Pieria, with a mountain and spring, sacred to the Muses.*

¶ Hence subst. **Pimplēïs (Piplēïs)** -ĭdis, f. *a Muse*: Hor.; adj. **Pimplēus** -a -um, *sacred to the Muses*: mons, Cat.; f. as subst. **Pimplēa** -ae, *a Muse*: Hor.

Pīnārĭus -a, *name of a Roman gens. The Pinarii and Potitii were the priests of Hercules at Rome.*

Pindărus -i, m. (Πίνδαρος), *a lyric poet of Thebes in Boeotia, contemporary with Aeschylus.* Adj. **Pindărĭcus** -a -um, *of Pindar, Pindaric.*

Pindus -i, m. (Πίνδος), *a mountain range between Thessaly and Epirus.*

pīnētum -i, n. (pinus), *a pine-wood*: Ov.

pīnĕus -a -um (pinus), *made of pine-wood or deal*: claustra, *the wooden horse of Troy*, Verg.; pineus ardor, *a fire of pine-wood*, Verg.

pingo pingĕre pinxi pictum, *to paint, to draw.* LIT., (1) *to paint a picture, represent pictorially*: ab Apelle pingi, Cic.; hominis speciem, Cic.; tabula picta, *a picture*, Cic.; Ov. (2) *to embroider*: toga picta, *the embroidered robe of the triumphing general*, Liv.; picti reges, *clad in embroidered garments*, Mart.; Cic., Verg. TRANSF., (1) *to stain, dye, colour*: frontem moris, Verg. (2) *to decorate, adorn*: bibliothecam, Cic. Hence, in speech or writing; *to embellish, depict eloquently*: Britanniam pingam coloribus tuis penicillo meo, Cic. L.

pinguesco -ĕre (pinguis), *to become fat or grow fertile*: sanguine pinguescere campos, Verg.

pinguis -e, adj. (with compar. and superl.) (cf. παχύς), *fat.*
LIT., (1) of men and animals, *fat*: Thebani, Cic.; pinguior agnus, Pl. N. as subst. pingue -is, *fatness, fat*: Verg. (2) of things, *fat, oily*: oleum, Verg.
TRANSF., (1) *rich, fertile*: sanguine pinguior campus, Hor.; hortus, Verg.; arae, *covered with fat of victims*, Verg. (2) *fertilizing*: Verg. (3) *besmeared*: crura luto, Juv. (4) *thick, dense*: caelum, Cic. (5) *heavy, stupid*: Cic.; ingenium, Ov. (6) *easy, quiet, undisturbed*: somnus, Ov.; otium, Plin. L.

pinguĭtūdō -ĭnis, f. (pinguis), *fatness.* TRANSF., of pronunciation, *broadness*: Quint.

pīnĭfĕr -fĕra -fĕrum (pinus/fero), *producing pines*: Verg.

pīnĭgĕr -gĕra -gĕrum (pinus/gero), *producing pines*: Ov.

¹pinna -ae, f. (another form of penna), *a feather*. LIT., Lucr., Cic., etc. TRANSF., (1) *a wing*: praepetibus pennis, Cic.; Verg., Hor.; prov.: alicui incidere pinnas, Cic. (2) *flight*: Ov. (3) *a feathered arrow*: Ov. (4) *a battlement along the top of a wall*: Caes.

²pinna (pīna) -ae, f. (πίννα), *a species of mussel*: Cic.

pinnātus -a -um (pinna), *feathered, winged*: Cic.

pinnĭgĕr -gĕra -gĕrum (pinna/gero), *having feathers, feathered, winged*: Lucr. TRANSF., piscis, *having fins*, Ov.

pinnĭrăpus -i, m. (pinna/rapio), *a crest-snatcher*, i.e. *a gladiator who fought against a Samnite having a peak to his helmet*: Juv.

pinnŭla -ae, f. (dim. of pinna), *a small feather or wing*: Pl.

pīnōtērēs -ae, m. (πινοτήρης), *the pinna-guard, a small crab found in the shell of the pinna.*

pinso pinsĕre; pinsi and pinsŭi; pinsum pinsĭtum and pistum (cf. πτίσσω), *to stamp, pound, crush*: Pl.

pīnus -i and -ūs, f. *a fir or pine or stone-pine.* LIT., Verg., Hor., Ov. TRANSF., *something made of pine-wood.* (1) *a ship*: Verg.; Hor., Ov. (2) *a pine-torch*: Verg. (3) *a garland of pine-leaves*: Ov. (4) *an oar*: Lucr.

pĭo -are (pius), *to seek to appease by an offering, to propitiate.* LIT., Silvanum lacte, Hor. TRANSF., (1) *to pay religious honours to, to venerate*: ossa, Verg.; Pl., Ov. (2) *to make good, atone for*: damna, Ov.; fulmen, *to avert the misfortune portended by lightning*, Ov.; nefas triste, Verg.; culpam morte, Verg.

pĭper pĭpĕris, n. (cf. πέπερι), *pepper*: Hor.

pīpĭlo -are (pipo), *to twitter, chirp*: Cat.

pīpo -are, *to chirp*: Varr.

pīpŭlus -i, m. and **pīpŭlum** -i, n. (pipo), *a chirping*; hence, *an outcry, upbraiding*: Pl.

Pīraeēūs and **Pīraeus** -i, m. *the Piraeus, a port of Athens, connected with the city by long walls.*

¶ Hence adj. **Pīraeus** -a -um, *of the Piraeus.*

pīrāta -ae, m. (πειρατής), *a pirate, corsair*: Cic., Luc.

pīrātĭcus -a -um (πειρατικός), *piratical*: myoparo, Cic. F. as subst. **pīrātĭca** -ae, *piracy*: piraticam facere, Cic.

Pīrēnē -ēs, f. (Πειρήνη), *a spring in Corinth, sacred to the Muses.*

¶ Hence f. adj. **Pīrēnĭs** -ĭdis (Πειρηνίς), *Pirenian*: Pirenis Ephyre, *Corinth*, Ov.

Pīrĭthŏus -i, m. (Πειρίθοος), *son of Ixion, king of the Lapithae, friend of Theseus, with whom he went down to the lower world to carry off Proserpina.*

pĭrum -i, n. *a pear*: Verg.

pĭrus -i, f. *a pear-tree*: Verg.

Pīsa -ae, f. (Πῖσα) and **Pīsae** -ārum, f. pl. *a town in Elis on the river Alpheus, where the Olympian games were held.*

¶ Hence adj. **Pīsaeus** -a -um, *Pisaean*: Arethusa, *because she came originally from*

Elis, Ov.; hasta, *of Oenomaus*, Ov. F. as subst. **Pisaea** -ae, *Hippodamia*: Ov.

Pīsae -ārum, f. *a town in Etruria* (now *Pisa*), *said to be a colony of Pisa in Elis.* ¶ Hence adj. **Pīsānus** -a -um, *Pisan*; m. pl. as subst. **Pisāni** -orum, *the inhabitants of Pisa.*

Pīsaurum -i, n. *a town in Umbria* (now *Pesaro*). ¶ Hence adj. **Pīsaurensis** -e, *Pisaurian.*

piscārius -a -um (piscis), *of fish*: forum, *the fish-market*, Pl.

piscātor -ōris, m. (piscor). (1) *a fisherman*: Pl., Cic. (2) *a fishmonger*: Ter.

piscātōrius -a -um (piscator), *of fishermen and fishing*: navis, *a fishing-smack*, Caes.; forum, *fish-market*, Liv.

piscātus -ūs, m. (piscor), *a fishing, catching of fish.* Lit., Pl. Transf., (1) *fish*: Pl., Cic. (2) fig., *a catch*: Pl.

piscĭcŭlus -i, m. (dim. of piscis), *a little fish*: Ter., Cic.

piscīna -ae, f. (piscis), *a tank for fish, fish-pond*: mullos exceptare de piscina, Cic.; Pl. Transf., (1) *a swimming-bath*: Plin. L., Suet. (2) *a reservoir*: Plin.

piscīnārius -a -um (piscina), *of fish-ponds*: Varr. M. as subst. **piscīnārius** -i, *one fond of fish-ponds*: Cic. L.

piscis -is, m. *a fish.* Lit., pisces capere, Cic.; Pl., Hor.; sing., used collectively: Ov. Transf., *the sign of the Zodiac so called*: pisces gemini, *or* gemelli, Ov.; piscis aquosus, Verg.

piscor -ari, dep. (piscis), *to fish*: ante hortulos alicuius, Cic.; Pl., Hor.

piscōsus -a -um (piscis), *abounding in fish*: amnes, Ov.; Verg.

piscŭlentus = piscosus; q.v.

Pisida -ae, m. (Πισίδης), *a Pisidian*; plur. Pisidae, *the Pisidians, inhabitants of Pisidia.* ¶ Hence **Pisidia** -ae, f. (Πισιδία), *a district in Asia Minor.*

Pīsistrătus -i, m. (Πεισίστρατος), *a tyrant of Athens, who died in* 527 B.C. ¶ Hence subst. **Pīsistrătĭdae** -ārum, m. pl. (Πεισιστρατίδαι), *the sons of Pisistratus.*

¹**pīso** -ōnis, m. (pinso), *a pestle*: Pl.

²**Pīso** -ōnis, m. *a surname in the* gens Calpurnia, *see* Calpurnius.

pistillum -i, n. (pinso), *a pestle*: Pl.

pistor -ōris, m. (pinso), *a grinder, miller*: Pl. Transf., (1) *a baker*: Cic., Mart. (2) Pistor, *surname of Jupiter*: Ov.

pistrilla -ae, f. (dim. of pistrina), *a small mortar* or *mill*: Ter.

pistrīna -ae, f. (pinso), *a bakehouse*: Plin.

pistrīnensis -e (pistrinum), *working a mill*: Suet.

pistrīnum -i, n. (pinso), *a mill* (usually worked by horses and asses, though sometimes by slaves as a punishment). Lit., homo pistrino dignus, Ter.; Pl., Cic. Transf., (1) *a bakery*: Pl., Sen., Suet. (2) in gen., *drudgery*: tibi mecum in eodem est pistrino vivendum, Cic.

pistris -is, f. and **pistrix** -trīcis, f. (πρῖστις), *any sea monster; a whale, shark, saw-fish.* Lit., Verg. Transf., (1) *the constellation of the Whale*: Cic. poet. (2) *a small, swift-sailing ship*: Liv. (3) *the name of a ship*: Verg.

pĭthēcĭum -i, n. (πιθήκιον), *a little ape*: Pl.

Pĭthēcūsa -ae, f. and plur. **Pĭthēcūsae** -ārum,

f. (Πιθηκοῦσα, Πιθηκοῦσαι), *an island* (*and a smaller island*) *in the Tyrrhenian Sea, near Cumae* (now *Ischia*).

Pittăcus (-ŏs) -i, m. (Πίττακος), *a tyrant of Mitylene, one of the Seven Wise Men of Greece.*

Pitthēus -ĕi and -ĕos, m. (Πιτθεύς), *king of Troezen, father of Aethra, who was the wife of Aegeus and mother of Theseus.* ¶ Hence subst. **Pitthēis** -idos, f. (Πιτθηΐς), *a daughter of Pittheus*, i.e. *Aethra*: Ov.; adj. **Pitthēius** and **Pitthēus** -a -um, *of Pittheus.*

pītŭīta -ae, f. (trisyll., poet.), *phlegm, rheum*: Cic., Hor., Sen.

pītŭītōsus -a -um (pituita), *full of phlegm*: homo, Cic.

pĭus -a -um (superl. piissimus, condemned by Cicero, but used later), *acting dutifully, dutiful.*
Lit., in gen.: pius Aeneas, Verg. Esp. (1) *towards the gods, holy, godly*: Pl., Cic., Ov. M. pl. as subst., *the good*; often of the dead: Cic., Verg. Of objects with religious associations, *holy*: luci, Hor. (2) *of the gods, compassionate*: Verg. (3) *towards one's country, patriotic*: bellum, Liv. (4) *towards relatives, devoted, affectionate*: in parentes, Cic.; adversus sororem, Liv.; Ov.
Transf., in gen., *honest, upright, kind*: pax, Cic.; n. as subst.: iustum piumque, *justice and equity*, Ov.; pium est, with infin.: Ov.

pix pĭcis, f. (cf. πίσσα), *pitch*: aliquid pice linere, Liv.; Caes., Verg., etc.

plācābĭlis -e, adj. (with compar.) (placo). (1) pass., *easy to appease, placable*: animi, Cic. L.; placabile ad iustas preces ingenium, Liv.; poet.: ara Dianae, Verg. (2) act., *appeasing*: Ter.

plācābĭlĭtās -ātis, f. (placabilis), *placability*: Cic.

plācāmen -ĭnis, n. (placo), *a means of appeasing*: plur.: placamina irae, Liv.

plācāmentum -i, n. (placo), *a means of appeasing*: Tac.

plācātē, adv. from placo; q.v.

plācātĭo -ōnis, f. (placo), *a soothing, appeasing*: deorum, Cic.

plācātus -a -um, partic. from placo; q.v.

plăcenta -ae, f. (cf. πλακοῦς), *a cake*: Hor., Juv.

Plăcentĭa -ae, f. *a town in Gallia Cispadana*, (now *Piacenza*). ¶ Hence adj. **Plăcentīnus** -a -um, *of Placentia.*

plăcĕo -ēre -ŭi and -ĭtus sum -ĭtum (cf. placo), *to please, be agreeable to, acceptable to.*
In gen., with dat.: velle placere alicui, Cic.; Hor., etc.: placere sibi, *to be pleased with oneself*, Cic.
Of actors, etc., *to please, to win applause*: admodum placere in tragoediis, Cic.
Esp. **placet**, *it pleases, it seems good, it is agreed*: si placet, Cic.; ut doctissimis placuit, Cic.; with ut: his placuit ut tu in Cumanum venires, Caes.; with infin.: nec mihi ipsi placebat diutius abesse, Cic.; Caes., Hor.; with acc. and infin.: placet Stoicis homines hominum causā esse generatos, Cic. As legal t. t., *to be resolved*: senatui placere ut, etc., Cic.; with acc. and infin.: Cic., Liv.
¶ Hence partic. **plăcĭtus** -a -um. (1) *pleasing, pleasant, agreeable*: amor, Verg.; Ov., etc. (2) *agreed upon*: locus, Sall. N. as subst. **plăcĭtum** -i, *that which pleases*

placidus   plausor

Verg. Hence, plur., *opinions, teaching*: placita
maiorum, Tac.
plăcĭdus -a -um, adj. (with compar. and
superl.) (placeo), *quiet, still, gentle*: reddere
aliquem placidum, Cic.; senectus, Cic.;
amnis, Ov.; placidior civitas, Liv.; placidis-
sima pax, Cic.
    ¶ Adv. (with compar.) **plăcĭdē**, *quietly,
gently*: ferre dolorem, Cic.; Caes., Liv.
plăcĭtus -a -um, partic. from placeo; q.v.
plāco -are (cf. placeo), *to soothe, calm, quiet.*
LIT., aequora tumida, Verg. TRANSF., *to
reconcile, appease*: animos, Cic.; aliquem
reipublicae, Cic.; homo sibi ipse placatus,
of a quiet mind, Cic.; Caes., Liv.
    ¶ Hence partic. (with compar. and superl.)
plăcātus -a -um, *soothed, appeased, pacified*:
placatiore eo et suā et regis spe invento, Liv.
Hence, *calm, gentle, quiet*: vita, Cic.; quies
placatissima, Cic.; mare, Verg.
    ¶ Adv. (with compar.), *calmly, composedly*:
omnia humana placate et moderate ferre,
Cic.
¹plāga -ae, f. (cf. plango, πληγή), *a blow, stroke,
stripe*. LIT., plagas accipere, Cic.; plagam
ferre, Verg.; also *a wound*: plagam infligere,
Cic. TRANSF., oratio parem plagam facit,
Cic.; levior est plaga ab amico, Cic. L.
²plăga -ae, f. (cf. πλακοῦς), *a flat surface.*
Hence, *a district, zone, tract, region*: aetheria,
the air, Verg.; ponti, Verg.; quattuor plagae,
the four zones, Verg.
³plăga -ae, f. *a net for hunting.* LIT., plagas
tendere, Cic.; in plagam cadere, Ov. TRANSF.,
a trap, snare: quas plagas ipsi contra se
Stoici texuerunt, Cic.; Antonium conieci in
Octaviani plagas, Cic.
plăgĭārĭus -i, m. *a kidnapper*: Cic.; hence, in
jest, *a literary thief, plagiarist*: Mart.
plăgĭgĕr -gěra -gěrum (plaga/gero), *stripe-
bearing*: Pl.
plăgĭgĕrŭlus -a -um (plaga/gerulus)=
plagiger, q.v.: Pl.
plăgĭpătĭda -ae, m. (plaga/patior), *a stripe-
bearer*: Pl.
plăgōsus -a -um (¹plaga), *fond of flogging*:
Orbilius, Hor.
plăgŭla -ae, f. (dim. of ³plaga), *a bed-curtain*:
Liv.
Planasĭa -ae, f. (Πλανασία), *an island south of
Elba* (now *Pianosa*), *a place of banishment
under the emperors.*
Plancĭus -a -um, *name of a Roman* gens; esp.
of Cn. Plancius, *whom Cicero defended when
tried for bribery.*
planctus -ūs, m. (plango), *a loud noise as of
beating*: Luc.; esp. *beating of the breast,
lamentation*: planctus et lamenta, Tac.
plānē, adv. from ¹planus; q.v.
plango plangěre planxi planctum (connected
with πλήσσω), *to beat, strike*, esp. *noisily.*
    LIT., in gen.: tympana palmis, Cat.; litora
planguntur fluctu, Ov.; esp. *to strike the
breast, head*, etc., as a sign of grief: pectora,
Ov.; femur, Ov.; lacertos, Ov.
    TRANSF. (cf. κόπτεσθαι), act. plangere and
passive as middle plangi, *to bewail*: planguntur matres, Ov.; agmina plangentia,
Verg.; with acc.: bovem, Tib.
plangor -ōris, m. (plango), *a striking* or *beating
accompanied by noise.* In gen.: Cat. Esp.

*beating of the head and breast in token of
grief*; *loud lamentation*: plangore et lamentatione complere forum, Cic.; plangorem dare,
Ov.
plānĭlŏquus -a -um (plane/loquor), *speaking
clearly*: Pl.
plānĭpēs -pĕdis, m. (planus/pes), *a mime who
played the part of slaves*, etc., *and wore no
shoes*: Juv.
plānĭtās -ātis, f. (planus), *plainness, distinctness*:
Tac.
plānĭtĭa -ae, f. and **plānĭtĭēs** -ēi, f. (planus),
a level surface, a plain: Cic., Liv., etc.
planta -ae, f. (**1**) *a green twig, cutting, graft*:
Cic., Verg.; also, in gen., *a plant*: Ov. (**2**) *the
sole of the foot* (with or without *pedis*): Verg.,
Ov., etc.
plantārĭa -ĭum, n. pl. (planta), *young trees,
slips*: Verg., Juv. TRANSF., *the hair*: Pers.
¹plānus -a -um, adj. (with compar. and superl.),
even, level, flat.
    LIT., locus, Cic.; aditus, Liv. N. as subst.
plānum -i, *a plain, level ground*: Sall., Liv.;
fig.: via vitae plana et stabilis, Cic.; de plano,
off-hand, easily, Lucr.
    TRANSF., *plain, clear, intelligible*: narratio,
Cic.; planum facere, *to explain*, Lucr., Cic.
    ¶ Hence adv. (with compar. and superl.)
plānē. (**1**) *distinctly, intelligibly*: loqui, Cic.;
planius dicere, Cic.; planissime explicare,
Cic. (**2**) *wholly, entirely, quite, thoroughly*:
plane eruditus, Cic.; carere, Hor. (**3**) in
answers, *certainly*: Pl., Ter.
²plānus -i, m. (πλάνος), *a vagabond, a charlatan*:
Cic.
Plătaeae -ārum, f. pl. (Πλαταιαί), *a town in
Boeotia, famed for a victory of the Greeks over
the Persians* (479 B.C.).
    ¶ Hence subst. **Plătaeenses** -ĭum, m. pl.
the inhabitants of Plataea.
plătălěa -ae, f. *a water-bird, the spoonbill*:
Cic.
plătănus -i, f. (πλάτανος), *the plane-tree*: Cic.,
Verg.; caelebs, *not used to train the vine on*
(like the elm), Hor.
plătěa -ae, f. (πλατεῖα), *a street*: Pl., Caes., Hor.,
etc.
Plăto (-ōn) -ōnis, m. (Πλάτων), *a celebrated
Greek philosopher, disciple of Socrates, founder
of the Academic philosophy.*
    ¶ Hence adj. **Plătōnĭcus** -a -um, *Platonic*;
m. pl. as subst. **Plătōnĭci** -ōrum, *the
Platonists*: Cic.
plaudo (**plōdo**) plauděre plausi plausum, *to
clap, strike, beat.*
    LIT., (**1**) with abl., *to make a clapping noise*:
alis, Verg.; pennis, Ov.; rostro, Ov. (**2**) with
acc., *to beat, clap*: pectora manu, Ov.; plausa
colla equorum, Verg.; pedibus choreas, *to
dance, stamping with the feet*, Verg.; plausis
alis, *struck together*, Ov. (**3**) absol., *to clap*:
manus in plaudendo consumere, Cic.;
impers.: huic ita plausum est ut, Cic.; in the
theatre: plaudite (said at the end of a piece),
Hor.
    TRANSF., *to show signs of approval,
applaud, to approve*: diis hominibusque
plaudentibus, Cic.; mihi ipse, Hor.
plausĭbĭlis -e (plaudo), *worthy of applause*:
Cic., Sen., Quint.
plausor -ōris, m. (plaudo), *an applauder at the
theatre*: Hor.

[452]

plaustrum (plostrum) -i, n. *a waggon, cart*: omnia ex locis publicis plaustris coacta, Cic.; Verg., etc. TRANSF., *Charles's Wain, the constellation of the Great Bear*: Ov.

plausus -ūs, m. (plaudo), *a clapping, a noise made by striking together*. LIT., plausum dare pennis, Verg. Esp. *the clapping of the hands in sign of approval*: Cic. TRANSF., *approbation, applause*: accipere plausum, Cic.

Plautius (Plōtius) -a -um, *name of a Roman gens*.
¶ Hence adj. **Plautiānus (Plōtiānus)** -a -um, *Plautian.*

Plautus -i, m., T. Maccius, *a celebrated Roman comic poet, born about 254 B.C.*
¶ Hence adj. **Plautinus** -a -um, *of Plautus*: Plautinus pater, *in a comedy of Plautus.*

plēbēcūla -ae, f. (dim. of plebs), *the common people, mob, rabble*: Cic. L., Hor.

plēbēius -a -um (plebs), *of the plebs or people* (opp. patricius), *plebeian*: familia, Cic.; ludi, *games in honour of the driving out of the kings or of the return of the plebeians from their secession to the Aventine Hill*, Liv.
TRANSF., *common, vulgar, low, mean, inferior*: sermo, *of the lower classes*, Cic. L.; purpura, Cic.

plēbēs -ēi and -i, f.=plebs; q.v.

plēbicŏla -ae, m. (plebs/colo), *a friend of the common people*: Cic., Liv.

plēbiscītum (or as two words, **plēbī scītum, plēbis scitum**) -i, n. (plebs/scisco), *a decree or ordinance of the people*: Pl., Cic., Liv.

plebs plēbis, f. (cf. πλῆθος), *the plebeians, the people* (opp. patricii, patres, senatus, while populus includes both these and the plebeians): consulem de plebe non accipiebat, Cic.
TRANSF., *the common people, the masses, the lower orders*: plebs et infima multitudo, Cic.; plebs eris, Hor.; plebs deorum, *the lower order of deities*, Ov.

¹**plecto**, *see* plexus.

²**plecto** -ĕre (cf. πλήσσω); usually pass., **plector** -i, *to be punished with blows*. LIT., tergo, Hor. TRANSF., *to be punished*: Cic., Hor., Ov.

plectrum -i, n. (πλῆκτρον), *a short stick with which the strings of a stringed instrument were struck; a quill*. LIT., Cic., Ov. TRANSF., (1) *the lyre*: Hor., Tib. (2) *lyric poetry*: Hor., Ov.

Plēias (Πληϊάς) -ādis, f. *a Pleiad*; usually plur. **Plēiădes** -ădum, f. *the Pleiads, the Seven Stars; according to the legend, the seven daughters of Atlas by Pleione* (Electra, Halcyone, Celaeno, Maia, Sterope, Taygete, Merope).

Plēiŏnē -ēs, f. (Πληϊόνη), *the wife of Atlas, mother of the Pleiads*: Pleiones nepos, *Mercury, son of Maia*, Ov.

plēnus -a -um, adj. (with compar. and superl.) (cf. compleo, expleo, etc.; Gr. πλέος), *full.*
LIT., in gen.; with genit.: argenti, Cic.; with abl.: plena domus ornamentis, Cic.; Liv.; absol.: plenissimis velis navigare, Cic.; calcari ad plenum, *fully, copiously*, Verg. Esp. (1) *plump, portly, stout*: homo, Cic.; velamina filo pleno, *thick*, Ov. (2) *pregnant*: Pl., Cic., Ov. (3) *filled, satisfied*: plenus eras minimo, Ov. (4) with genit. or abl. or absol., *well-stocked, rich*: exercitus plenissimus praedā, Cic.; urbes, Cic.; domus, Hor.; mensa, Verg.
TRANSF., (1) *full of, abounding in* something

abstract; with genit. or abl.: plenus timoris, Caes.; plenus expectatione, Cic.; laboris, Verg.; irae, Liv. (2) *full, of quantity and number; complete, entire*; in gen.: annus, Cic.; legio, Caes.; luna, Ov.; pleno gradu, *at quick step*, Liv.; esp.: **a**, *of age, mature*: Verg.: **b**, *of the voice, strong, loud*: vox, Cic.; pleniore voce, Cic.: **c**, *of style, full, copious*: Cic.
¶ Adv. (with compar. and superl.) **plēnē**, *fully, completely*: plene perfectae munitiones, Caes.; plene sapientes homines, Cic.

plērumquĕ, *see* plerusque.

plērus -a -um, old form of plerusque; q.v.

plērusquĕ -răquĕ -rumquĕ and plur. **plēriquĕ** -raequĕ -răquĕ, *very many, a large part, the most part.*
Sing.: iuventus pleraque, Sall.; Africa, Sall.; Liv. N. as subst., plerumque, *the greater part*: noctis, Sall.; Europae, Liv.; acc. as adv., *for the most part, mostly, generally, commonly*: Cic., Hor., etc.
Plur.: multi nihil prodesse philosophiam, plerique etiam obesse arbitrantur, Cic.; plerique Belgae, Caes.; in plerisque, *in most cases*, Cic.; with genit.: plerique Poenorum, Cic.; plerique ex factione, Sall.

plexus -a -um, partic. as from plecto (cf. πλέκω), *braided, plaited*: coronae, Lucr.; flores, Cat.

Plīăs=Pleias; q.v.

plīcātrix -īcis, f. (plico), *one who folds clothes, a bedmaker*: Pl.

plīco -are -ŭi and -āvi -ātum and ītum (cf. πλέκω), *to fold, fold together*: se in sua membra, Verg.; Lucr.

Plīnius -a -um, *name of a Roman gens. Its most famous members were* (1) C. Plinius Secundus (Maior, *the Elder), author of a Natural History in thirty-seven books, killed* A.D. 79, *at the eruption of Mount Vesuvius.* (2) C. Plinius Caecilius Secundus (Iunior, *the younger, nephew of* (1)), *author of letters and of a panegyric on Trajan.*

plōdo=plaudo; q.v.

plōrābilis -e (ploro), *deplorable, lamentable*: Pers.

plōrātor -ōris, m. (ploro), *a wailer, lamenter*: Mart.

plōrātus -ūs, m. (ploro), *a crying, weeping, lamenting*, usually plur.: Liv.

plōro -are. (1) intransit., *to lament, wail, cry aloud for grief*: plorando fessus sum, Cic. L.; iubeo te plorare (=οἰμώζειν λέγω σοι), *bad luck to you!* Hor. (2) transit., *to weep over, lament, deplore*: turpe commissum, Hor.; Juv.

plostellum -i, n. (dim. of plostrum), *a little waggon*: Hor.

plostrum=plaustrum; q.v.

ploxĕmum (ploxĭmum) -i, n. *a waggon-box*: Cat.

plŭit plŭĕre, plŭit or plūvit (cf. πλύνω), *it rains.* LIT., dum pluit, Verg.; Pl., Cic., etc.; with acc. or abl. of what falls: sanguinem pluisse, Cic.; lapides, lapidibus, Liv. TRANSF., fig., *a shower falls*: tantum glandis pluit, Verg.

plūma -ae, f. *the downy part of a feather or a small, soft feather*; plur.=*down.*
LIT., plumae versicolores columbarum, Cic.; in plumis delituisse Iovem, *to have been disguised as a bird*, Ov. Used to stuff

pillows, etc.; hence, meton.=*bolster, featherbed*: Juv. As an emblem of lightness, fickleness, etc.: plumā aut folio facilius moventur, Cic.

TRANSF., *the first down on the chin*: Hor.

plūmātĭlĕ -is, n. (pluma), *a garment embroidered with feathers*: Pl.

plūmātus -a -um (pluma), *covered with feathers*: Cic. poet.

plumbĕus -a -um (plumbum), *leaden, made of lead*. LIT., glans, Lucr.; Cic. L., Mart. TRANSF., *leaden*; hence (1) *poor, bad*: vina, Mart. (2) *dull, stupid*: plumbeus in physicis, Cic. (3) *heavy, oppressive*: ira, Pl.; auster, Hor.

plumbum -i, n. (akin to μόλυβδος), *lead*. LIT., plumbum album, *tin*, Lucr., Caes. TRANSF., (1) *a bullet*: Verg. (2) *a leaden pipe*: Hor.

plūmĕus -a -um (pluma), *downy, of fine feathers*: culcita, Cic.; torus, Ov. TRANSF., *as light as a feather*: Mart.

plūmĭpēs -pĕdis (pluma/pes), *feather-footed*: Cat.

plūmōsus -a -um (pluma), *feathered, downy*: Prop.

plŭo, *see* pluit.

plūrālis -e (plus), *plural*: Quint.

¶ Adv. **plūrālĭtĕr**, *in the plural*: Sen., Quint.

plūrĭfārĭam (plus), *on many sides, in many places*: Suet.

plūrĭmus, plurimum, *see* multus.

plūs, pluris, *see* multus.

pluscŭlus -a -um (dim. of plus), *somewhat more, rather more*: plusculā supellectile, Ter. N. as subst. **pluscŭlum** -i: causae in quibus plusculum negotii est, Cic.; acc. as adv.: Pl.

plŭtĕus -i, m. and **plŭtĕum** -i, n. *a shelter*.

LIT., as milit. t. t. (1) *a movable penthouse, shed* or *mantlet* (made of hurdles covered with hides to protect the besiegers of a town): Caes., Liv. (2) *a breastwork, battlement on a tower*: Caes., Liv.

TRANSF., (1) *the back of a bed* or *sofa*: Mart. (2) *the board on which a corpse is laid out*: Mart. (3) *a bookshelf, bookcase*: Juv. (4) *a couch*: Prop., Mart.

Plŭto (-ōn) -ōnis, m. (Πλούτων), *the king of the lower world, brother of Jupiter and Neptune, husband of Proserpina*.

¶ Hence adj. **Plŭtōnĭus** -a -um, *belonging to Pluto*: domus, *the grave*, Hor.

plŭvĭa -ae, f. subst. from adj. pluvius; q.v.

plŭvĭālis -e (pluvia), *relating to rain*: Auster, *bringing rain*, Verg.; aquae, *rain*, Ov.; fungi, *growing after rain*, Ov.

plŭvĭus -a -um (pluo), *of rain, rainy, rainbringing*: aquae, Cic.; Hyades, Verg.; venti, Hor.; Iuppiter, Tib.; arcus, *a rainbow*, Hor.

F. as subst. **plŭvĭa** -ae (sc. aqua), *rain*: Cic., Verg., etc.

pōcillum -i, n. (dim. of poculum), *a little drinking-cup*: pocillum mulsi facere, *to offer*, Liv.

pōcŭlum -i, n. (cf. potus, poto), *a drinking-cup, goblet*.

LIT., poculum impavide haurire, Liv.; poculum mortis exhaurire, Cic.; ducere, Hor.

TRANSF., *a drink, draught*: ad pocula venire, Verg.; amoris poculum, *a love-philtre*, Pl., Hor.; in tuis poculis, *over your cups*, Cic. Esp. *a poisonous draught*: Cic.

pŏdagra -ae, f. (ποδάγρα), *the gout in the feet*: podagrae doloribus cruciari, Cic.

pŏdagrōsus -a -um (podagra), *gouty*: Pl.

pōdex -icis, m. *the fundament, anus*: Hor.

pŏdĭum -i, n. (πόδιον), *a balcony*: Plin. L. Esp. *a balcony above the arena in the amphitheatre, where the emperor sat*: Juv., Suet.

Poeās (Paeās) -antis, m. (Ποίας), *the father of Philoctetes*: Poeante satus, *son of Poeas= Philoctetes*, Ov.

¶ Hence adj. **Poeantĭus** -a -um: proles =*Philoctetes*, Ov.; subst. **Poeantĭădēs** -ae, m. *son of Poeas=Philoctetes*: Ov.

pŏēma -ătis, n. (dat. and abl. pl.: poematīs, Cic.) (ποίημα), *a poem*: poema facere, componere, condere, Cic.; pangere, Hor.

pŏēmătĭum -i, n. (ποιημάτιον), *a short poem*: Plin. L.

poena -ae, f. (ποινή), *money paid as atonement, a fine*; hence, in gen., *punishment, penalty*.

LIT., poena dupli, octupli, Cic.; capitis, Caes.; mortis, Cic.; oculorum, *loss of eyesight*, Cic.; poenas iustas et debitas solvere, Cic.; dare, *to be punished*, Cic.; persolvere, Verg.; reddere, Liv.; poenas parentium a filiis expetere, *to visit the sins of the fathers on the children*, Cic.; poenas capere de aliquo, *to exact a penalty*, Liv.; poenam habere, *to be punished*, Liv.; poenā aliquem adficere, multare, Cic. Personif.: Poena, *the goddess of revenge* or *punishment*, Cic., Hor.

TRANSF., *loss, hardship*: Cic., Ov.

poenārĭus -a -um (poena), *penal*: Quint.

Poeni -ōrum, m. pl. *the Carthaginians* (originally colonists from Phoenicia): Liv. Considered treacherous by the Romans: Poeni foedifragi, Cic. Sing. **Poenus** -i, m. *a Carthaginian*; used for *Hannibal*: Cic., Liv.; collect.: Poenus advena, Cic.; Poenus uterque, *the Carthaginians in Africa and Spain*, Hor.

¶ Hence adj. **Poenus** -a -um, *Carthaginian*: navita, Hor.; leones, Verg.; adj. **Pūnĭcus, Poenĭcĕus** -a -um, *Phoenician, Punic, Carthaginian*: Punicum bellum, Cic.; fides=*faithlessness*, Sall.; so: ars, Liv.; Poeniceus color, *the Phoenician colour* (more technical than puniceus, q.v.), Lucr.

poenĭo=punio; q.v.

poenitet, *see* paenitet.

pŏēsis -is, acc. -in, f. (ποίησις), *poetry*: Cic., Hor.

pŏēta -ae, m. (ποιητής), *a maker*; in gen.: Pl.; esp. *a poet*: poeta comicus, tragicus, Cic.; Hor., etc.

pŏētĭcus -a -um (ποιητικός), *poetical*: verbum, Cic.; facultas, Cic.; Hor. F. as subst. **pŏētĭca** -ae (sc. ars) and **pŏētĭcē** -ēs (ποιητική, sc. τέχνη), *the art of poetry*: Cic., Hor., etc.

¶ Hence adv. **pŏētĭcē**, *poetically, after the manner of a poet*: ut poetice loquar, Cic.

pŏētrĭa -ae, f. (ποιήτρια), *a poetess*: Cic.

pol! interj. *by Pollux! truly! really!*: Pl., Ter., Hor.

Pŏlĕmo (-ōn) -ōnis, m. (Πολέμων), *a Greek philosopher at Athens, pupil of Xenocrates, teacher of Zeno and Arcesilaus*.

¶ Hence adj. **Pŏlĕmōnĕus** -a -um, *of Polemo*.

pŏlenta -ae, f. (perhaps connected with pollen), *pearl-barley, barley-groats*: Pl., Ov.

pŏlĭo -ire, *to polish, file, make smooth.* LIT., daedala signa, Lucr.; rogum asciā, ap. Cic.; esp. *to cover with white, to whiten*: columnas albo, Liv. TRANSF., *to adorn, embellish, to polish, finish*: orationem, Cic.; carmina, Ov. ¶ Hence partic. (with compar. and superl.) **pŏlītus** -a -um, *polished, refined, accomplished*: homo, Cic.; politior humanitas, Cic.; vir omni liberali doctrinā politissimus, Cic.; Lucr., Tac. ¶ Adv. (with compar.) **pŏlītē**, *in a polished manner, elegantly*: politius limare, Cic.

pŏlītĭa -ae, acc. -an, f. (πολιτεία), *the Republic* (title of a work by Plato): Cic.

pŏlītĭcus -a -um (πολιτικός), *relating to the state, political*: philosophi, Cic.

Pŏlītōrĭum -i, n. *a town in Latium.*

pŏlītus -a -um, partic. from polio; q.v.

pollen -ĭnis, n. and **pollis** -ĭnis, c. (cf. πάλη, palea), *fine flour, meal*: Ter.

pollens -entis, partic. from polleo; q.v.

¹**pollentĭa** -ae, f. (polleo), *power, might*, Pl. Personif., *the goddess of might*: Cic.

²**Pollentĭa** -ae, f. *a town in Liguria, famous for its wool* (now *Polenza*).

pollĕo -ēre, *to be strong, mighty, powerful, able*: qui in republica plurimum pollebant, *had the most power*, Cic.; ubi plurimum pollet oratio, Cic.; with abl.: formā, Prop.; Tac. ¶ Hence partic. **pollens** -entis, *powerful, mighty*: genus, Pl.; matrona, Ov.; herbae, Ov.; with abl.: viribus, Sall.; suis opibus, Lucr.

pollex -ĭcis, m. (1) *the thumb*: Aeginetis pollices praecīdere, Cic.; clavi ferrei digiti pollicis crassitudine, Caes.; verso pollice, *with a turn of the thumb* (down to show approval, up for disapproval), Juv.; Hor. (2) *the great toe*: Plin., Suet.

pollĭcĕor -cēri -cĭtus sum, dep. (pro/liceor), *to make an offer.* LIT., at a sale: Pl. TRANSF., *to offer, proffer, promise*: pecuniam, Cic.; senatui frumentum, Cic.; maria montesque, *to make boundless promises*, Sall.; sese itineris periculique ducem, Sall.; nihil ego tum de meis opibus pollicebar, Cic.; with pres. infin.: obsides dare, Caes.; Pl., Ter.; with acc. and fut. infin.: me tibi satisfacturum, Cic.; with adv.: liberaliter, Caes.; benigne, Liv. Esp. of an orator at the beginning of his speech, *to promise, declare*: docui quod primum pollicitus sum, Cic. ¶ Perf. partic. in pass. sense: pollicita fides, Ov.; n. as subst. **pollĭcĭtum** -i, *a promise*: Ov.

pollĭcĭtātĭo -ōnis, f. (pollicitor), *an offer, promise*: magnis praemiis pollicitationibusque polliceri, Caes.; Pl., Ter.

pollĭcĭtor -ari, dep. (freq. of polliceor), *to keep promising*: Pl., Ter., Sall.

pollĭnārĭus -a -um (pollen), *for fine flour*: cribrum, Pl.

pollinctor- ōris, m. (pollingo), *an undertaker*: Pl.

pollingo -lingĕre -linxi -linctum, *to lay out a corpse*: Pl.

Pollĭo (**Pōlĭo**) -ōnis, m., C. Asinius, *a Roman orator and writer of the Augustan age.*

pollis=pollen -inis; q.v.

pollūcĕo -lucēre -luxi -luctum, *to place upon the altar as a sacrifice, to offer*: decumam partem Herculi, Pl. Hence (1) *to put on the table as a dish*: Pl. (2) *to entertain*: Pl.

pollŭc -ŭĕre -ŭi -ūtum, *to befoul, defile, pollute.* LIT., ora cruore, Ov.; Verg., Tac. TRANSF., *to defile morally* or *ceremonially*; *to pollute, dishonour*: iura scelere, Cic.; caerimonias stupro, Cic.; sacra, Cic., Liv.; pacem, Verg. ¶ Hence partic. **pollūtus** -a -um, *defiled, polluted*; hence, *unchaste*: femina, Liv.; Tac.

Pollux -ūcis, m. (Πολυδεύκης), *the twin-brother of Castor, son of Tyndarus* (or *Jupiter*) *and Leda, renowned for his skill in boxing*: Cic., etc.; Pollux uterque, *Castor and Pollux*, Hor.

pŏlus -i, m. (πόλος), *the end of an axis, a pole.* LIT., polus gelidus, glacialis, *the north pole*, Ov.; australis, *the south pole*, Ov. TRANSF., sing. and plur., *the sky, the heavens*: Verg., Hor., Ov.

Pŏlўbĭus -i, m. (Πολύβιος), *a Greek historian, contemporary and friend of Scipio Aemilianus.*

Pŏlўhymnĭa -ae, f. (Πολύμνια), *one of the Muses.*

pŏlўpus -i, m. (πολύπους, Dor. πωλύπος), *the polypus, a marine animal*: Pl., Ov. TRANSF., *a polypus in the nose*: Hor.

pōmārĭus -a -um (pomum), *of fruit*: Cato. As subst., m. **pōmārĭus** -i, *a fruiterer*: Hor.; n. **pōmārĭum** -i, *a fruit-garden, orchard*: Cic., Hor., Ov.

pōmērĭdĭānus=postmeridianus; q.v.

pōmērĭum or **pomoerium** -i, n. (post/ moerus=murus), *a space left free from buildings on each side of the walls of a town, bounded by stones* (cippi *or* termini): pomerium intrare, transire, Cic.; Liv., Juv.

Pōmētĭa -ae, f. and **Pōmētĭi** -ōrum, m. pl. *an old town of the Volsci in Latium.* ¶ Hence adj. **Pōmētīnus** -a -um, *Pometine.*

pōmĭfĕr -fĕra -fĕrum (pomum/fero), *fruit-bearing*: Hor.

Pōmōna -ae, f. (pomum), *the goddess of fruit and fruit-trees.*

pōmōsus -a -um (pomum), *abounding in fruit*: Tib., Prop.

pompa -ae, f. (πομπή), *a solemn procession.* LIT., Cic., Verg., Liv.; pompam funeris ire, Ov.; of a wedding: pompam ducit, Ov.; of a triumph: Ov. TRANSF., (1) *a train, suite, retinue*: lictorum, Cic. L. (2) *display, parade, ostentation*: in dicendo, Cic.

Pompēii -ōrum, m. pl. *a town in the south of Campania, destroyed by an eruption of Vesuvius*, A.D. 79. ¶ Hence adj. **Pompēiānus** -a -um, *belonging to Pompeii*; m. pl. **Pompēiāni** -ōrum, *the inhabitants of Pompeii.*

Pompēius (trisyll.) or **Pompēius** -a -um, *name of a Roman gens. Its most famous members were*: Cn. Pompeius, *Pompey the Great* (106–48 B.C.), *triumvir with Caesar and Crassus, conqueror of Mithridates and the pirates, defeated by Caesar at Pharsalia and slain off Egypt; Sextus Pompeius Magnus, an opponent of Caesar, defeated at sea by Augustus; Pompeia, wife of P. Vatinius. As adj., Pompeian*: domus, Cic.; lex, *proposed by Cn. Pompey.* ¶ Hence adj. **Pompēiānus** -a -um, *belonging to Pompey*; m. pl. as subst. **Pompēiāni** -orum, *Pompey's troops* or *party.*

Pompĭlĭus -a -um, *name of a Roman gens*; esp. of Numa Pompilius, *second king of Rome, legendary founder of many religious*

rites. As adj., *Pompilian*: sanguis, *descendants of Numa Pompilius*, Hor.
pompĭlus -i, m. (πομπίλος), *the pilot-fish*: Ov.
Pompōnĭus -a -um, *the name of a Roman gens*; esp. of T. Pomponius Atticus, *friend of Cicero.*
Pomptīnus -a -um, *Pomptine* or *Pontine*: palus or paludes, *a marshy district in Latium, liable to flooding by the rivers Amasenus and Ufens, on the Appian road.* N. as subst. **Pomptīnum** -i, *the neighbourhood of the Pontine marsh.*
pōmum -i, n. *any kind of fruit*: Cic.; *a mulberry*: Ov.; plur.: poma, *fruit*, Verg., Hor. TRANSF., *a fruit-tree*: Verg., Plin. L.
pōmus -i, f. *a fruit-tree*: Tib.
pondĕro -are (pondus), *to weigh*. LIT., Pl., Prop. TRANSF., *to weigh mentally, to consider, ponder*: verborum delectum, Cic.; causas, Cic.
pondĕrōsus -a -um (pondus), *heavy, weighty*. LIT., Pl.; compar. and superl.: Plin. TRANSF., *weighty, significant*: epistula, Cic. L.
pondo (abl. of obs. pondus -i), *in weight*: corona libram pondo, *a pound in weight*, Liv.; Pl. As an indecl. subst., *a pound, pounds*: argenti pondo viginti milia, Caes.; auri quinque pondo, Cic.; Pl., Liv.
pondus -ĕris, n. (pendo), *a weight.*
  LIT., (1) *a weight used in a pair of scales*: paria pondera, Cic.; Liv. (2) abstr.: a, *the weight* of any body: magni ponderis saxa, Caes.; moveri gravitate et pondere, Cic.: b, usually plur., *balance, equilibrium*: tellus ponderibus librata suis, Ov.; Lucr.
  TRANSF., (1) *a heavy body, weight, burden, mass*: in terram feruntur omnia pondera, Cic.; auri pondus ingens, Liv. (2) fig., *an oppressive weight, burden*: pondera amara senectae, Ov.; Hor. (3) fig., *weight, authority, influence*: commendationem magnum apud te pondus habuisse, Cic. L.; id est maximi momenti et ponderis, Cic.; of words or thoughts: omnium verborum ponderibus est utendum, Cic.; Hor.
pōnĕ. (1) adv. *behind, at the back*: moveri et ante et pone, Cic.; Pl., Verg. (2) prep. with acc., *behind*: pone quos aut ante labantur, Cic.; Liv., Tac.
pōno pōnĕre pōsŭi (pōsīvi) pŏsĭtum and postum: Lucr. (po/sino), *to lay, put, place.*
  LIT., (1) *to put aside, lay down, discard*: arma, Caes., Liv.; libros de manibus, Cic. L.; velamina, Ov. (2) *to lay down, lay to rest*: artūs in litore, Verg.; somno positae, Verg.; positae det oscula frater, *laid out*, i.e. *dead*, Ov. (3) in gen., *to put* or *set* a person or thing in a place: in foro sellam, Cic.; coronam auream in Capitolio, Liv.; pone me pigris campis, Hor.; positi vernae circa Lares, Hor; pedem ponere, *to set foot*, Cic.; milit. t. t.. *to post, station*: Caes., Cic. (4) *to store, deposit, invest*: tabulas testamenti in aerario, Caes.; Cic., Liv.; of burial: corpus, Lucr.; Verg., Ov. (5) *to stake, wager*: pallium, Pl.; pocula, Verg. (6) *to put food* or *drink on the table, to serve, set before*: pavonem, Hor., Liv.; Ov. (7) of buildings, etc., *to found, set up*: templa, moenia, Verg.; Ov., Tac.
  TRANSF., (1) *to lay down, discard, give up*: vitam, Cic.; vitia, Cic.; dolorem, Cic.; moras, Verg.; curas, Liv. (2) *to settle, calm, smooth*:

comas, Ov.; tollere seu ponere vult freta, Hor.; intransit., of the winds, *to lull, abate*: Verg. (3) *to place, set*: ponere ante oculos, Cic.; te apud eum in gratiā, Cic. L.; in laude positus, Cic.; Liv. (4) *to lay out, invest, spend*: tempus in cogitatione, Cic.; totum diem in consideranda causa, Cic.; otia, Hor.; Liv. (5) *to stake*: omnem spem salutis in virtute, Cic.; Caes., Liv. (6) *to establish, ordain, appoint*: leges, Cic.; praemium, Cic.; Verg., Hor. Of persons, *to appoint*: alicui custodem, Caes.; aliquem custodem in frumento publico, Cic. (7) of an artist, *to represent, picture*: Orphea in medio silvasque sequentes, Verg.; ponere totum, *to present a whole*, Hor. (8) *to reckon, count*: mortem in malis, Cic.; aliquid in beneficii loco, Cic.; haud in magno discrimine ponere, *to attach no great importance to*, Liv.; with double acc., *to regard as*: aliquem principem, Cic. (9) *to lay down, assert, cite*: exemplum, Cic.; Liv.; nosmet ipsos commendatos esse nobis, Cic. (10) *to put forward* as a subject: quaestiunculam, Cic.; Juv.
  ¶ Hence partic. **pŏsĭtus** -a -um, *in place*; of snow, etc., *fallen*: posita, nix, Hor.; of places, *situated*: Roma in montibus posita, Cic.; Caes., Liv.
pons pontis, m. *a bridge.*
  LIT., pontem in flumine facere, Caes.; pontem facere in Tiberi, Liv.; pontem interscindere, *to cut down*, Cic.; vellere, Verg.; solvere, Tac.
  TRANSF., (1) *the gangway at the comitia, by which the voters passed into the saepta*: Cic. L., Ov. (2) *a gangway between a ship and the shore*: Verg., Liv. (3) *a drawbridge*: Verg. (4) *the deck of a ship*: Tac. (5) *a bridge between towers*: Verg.
pontĭcŭlus -i, m. (dim. of pons), *a little bridge*: Cic., Cat.
¹Pontĭcus -a -um, *see* Pontus.
²Pontĭcus -i, m. *a Roman poet, contemporary of Propertius and Ovid.*
pontĭfex -fĭcis, m. (pons/facio), *a pontiff, pontifex, Roman high priest*; plur.: pontifices, *a guild of priests at Rome, containing at first four, then eight, then fifteen members, the president of which was called* pontifex maximus, Caes., Cic.; pontifices minores, *a lower class of pontiffs, assistants to the guild* of pontifices, Cic., Liv.
pontĭfĭcālis -e (pontifex), *pontifical*: auctoritas, Cic.; Liv.
pontĭfĭcātus -ūs, m. (pontifex), *the office of pontiff, the pontificate*: Cic., Tac.
pontĭfĭcus -a -um (pontifex), *pontifical*: libri, Cic.; ius, Cic.
Pontĭus -a -um, *name of a Roman (originally Samnite) gens. Its most famous members were*: C. Pontius, *commander of the Samnites at the Caudine Forks*; L. Pontius Aquila, *one of the murderers of Caesar*; Pontius Pilatus, *procurator of Judea at the time of the crucifixion of Christ.*
ponto -ōnis, m. (pons), *a flat-bottomed boat, punt*: Caes.
¹pontus -i, n. (πόντος), *the sea*: aequora ponti, Lucr.; freta ponti, Verg.; ingens pontus, *a huge sea*, Verg.; *a wave of the sea*, Verg.
²Pontus -i, m. (Πόντος), *the Black Sea.* TRANSF., *the country on the shores of the Black Sea*;

esp. *a district of Asia Minor between Bithynia and Armenia, the realm of Mithridates, later a Roman province, Pontus.*

¶ Hence adj. **Pontĭcus** -a -um (Ποντικός), *belonging to Pontus, Pontic*: mare, *the Black Sea*, Liv.; serpens, *the dragon that guarded the golden fleece at Colchis*, Juv.

pŏpa -ae, m. *a junior priest or temple-servant, who slew the victims*: Cic., Prop., Suet.

pŏpănum -i, n. (πόπανον), *a sacrificial cake*: Juv.

pŏpellus -i, m. (dim. of populus), *the common people, rabble*: Hor.

pŏpīna -ae, f. (cf. πέπω, *to cook*), *a cook-shop, eating-house*: Pl., Cic. TRANSF., *the food sold at an eating-house*: Cic.

pŏpīno -ōnis, m. (popina), *a frequenter of eating-houses, glutton*: Hor.

poplĕs -ĭtis, m. *the ham, hough*. LIT., succidere poplitem, Verg.; femina poplitesque, Liv. TRANSF., *the knee*: duplicato poplite, *with bent knee*, Verg.; contento poplite, *with stiff knee*, Hor.

Poplĭcŏla=Publicola; q.v.

poppysma -ătis, n. (πόππυσμα), *a clucking of the tongue as a sign of approbation*: Juv.

pŏpŭlābĭlis -e (populor), *that can be laid waste, destructible*: Ov.

pŏpŭlābundus -a -um (populor), *laying waste, devastating*: Liv.

pŏpŭlāris -e, adj. (with compar.) (¹populus).
(1) *belonging to the same people or country, native*: flumina, Ov.; Ter., Hor. M. or f. as subst., *a fellow-countryman*: Solon popularis tuus, Cic. TRANSF., *an adherent, participator*: coniurationis, Sall.; Liv.
(2) *of the people, relating to the whole state, proceeding from the state*. In gen.: leges, Cic.; admiratio, Cic.; oratio, *to the people*, Cic.; aura, Hor. Esp.: **a**, *beloved by the people, popular*: Cic., Liv.: **b**, *of the people* (as opposed to the aristocracy), *popular, democratic*: popularis vir, Liv.; homo, Cic. M. pl. as subst. **pŏpŭlāres** -ium, *the popular party, the democrats*: Cic.

¶ Adv. **pŏpŭlārĭtĕr.** (1) *after the manner of the people, commonly, vulgarly*: loqui, scribere, Cic. (2) *in a popular manner, or, in a bad sense, like a demagogue*: agere, Cic.

pŏpŭlārĭtās -ātis, f. (popularis). (1) *fellow-citizenship*: Pl. (2) *an attempt to please the people, popular behaviour*: Tac.

pŏpŭlātĭo -ōnis, f. (populor), *a laying waste, devastating, plundering*: populatio agrorum ceterorum, Liv.; plur.: Veientes pleni iam populationum, *who had had their fill of plundering*, Liv.; hostem populationibus prohibere, Caes.

pŏpŭlātor -ōris, m. (populor), *a devastator, plunderer*: Liv.

pŏpŭlātrix -īcis, f. (populor), *a female devastator*: Mart.

pŏpŭlĕus -a -um (²populus), *of the poplar*: frondes, Verg.; Hor.

pŏpŭlĭfĕr -fĕra -fĕrum (²populus/fero), *producing poplars*: Ov.

pŏpulnus -a -um (²populus), *of poplar*: Pl.

Pŏpŭlōnĭa -ae, f. and **Pŏpŭlōnĭi** -ōrum, m. pl. *a town in Etruria*.

¶ Hence subst. **Pŏpŭlōnĭenses** -ĭum, m. pl. *the inhabitants of Populonia*.

pŏpŭlo -are and **pŏpŭlor** -ari, dep. (¹populus),

to lay waste, devastate, plunder. LIT., agros, Caes.; pass.: provinciae populatae, Cic.; litora, Verg. TRANSF., *to destroy, ruin, spoil, rob*: farris acervum curculio, Verg.; populatus hamus, *robbed of the bait*, Ov.

¹pŏpŭlus -i, m. (connected with πλῆθος, plenus), *a people, as forming a political community, a nation.*
LIT., populus Romanus, Cic.; populi liberi . . . reges, Cic.; reges et populi liberi, Sall.
TRANSF., (1) *a section of the community, the people*: **a**, opp. the senate: senatus populusque Romanus, Cic.; et patres in populi potestate fore, Liv.: **b**, opp. the plebs: non populi sed plebis iudicium esse, Liv. (2) in gen., *the people, the public*: malus poeta de populo, Cic.; coram populo, Hor. (3) *any crowd, host, multitude*: fratrum, Ov.; Liv. (4) *a district, canton*: frequens cultoribus alius populus, Liv.

²pŏpŭlus -i, f. *a poplar-tree*: Verg., Hor., Ov.

porca -ae, f. (porcus), *a sow*: Verg., Juv.

porcella -ae, f. (dim. of porcula), *a little sow*: Pl.

porcellus -i, m. (dim. of porculus), *a little pig*: Phaedr., Suet.

porcīnārĭus -i, m. (porcina), *a seller of pork*: Pl.

porcīnus -a -um, *of a swine or hog*: Pl. F. as subst. **porcīna** -ae (sc. caro), *pork*: Pl.

Porcĭus -a -um, *name of a Roman gens. Its most famous members were* (1) M. Porcius Cato (235-149 B.C.), *a famous censor, after whom Cicero named his work on old age.* (2) M. Porcius Cato (95-46 B.C.), *the Younger, also called Uticensis, from his suicide at Utica.* (3) Porcia, *sister of the younger Cato, wife of Domitius Ahenobarbus.* As adj., *Porcian*: lex, Cic.

porcŭla -ae, f. (dim. of porca), *a little sow*: Pl.

porcŭlus -i, m. (dim. of porcus), *a young pig, porker*: Pl.

porcus -i, m. *a pig, hog*: Pl., Cic.; porcus femina, *a sow*; used as a term of reproach: Epicuri de grege porcus, Hor.

porgo=porrigo; q.v.

porrectĭo -ōnis, f. (porrigo), *a stretching out, extension*: digitorum, Cic.

porrectus -a -um, partic. from porrigo; q.v.

porrĭcĭo -rĭcĕre -rectum, *to offer as sacrifice to the gods*: exta, Pl., Verg.; prov.: inter caesa et porrecta, *between the slaying and the offering of the victim—i.e. at the eleventh hour*, Cic. L.

¹porrĭgo -rĭgĕre -rexi -rectum (pro/rego), *to stretch out, reach out, extend.*
LIT., in gen.: manum, Pl.; membra, Cic.; hostem, *to lay low*, Liv.; middle, porrigi, *to be stretched out, to lie stretched out*: corpus porrigitur in novem iugera, Verg. Esp. (1) as milit. t. t., *to extend*: aciem, Sall.; Liv. (2) geograph. t. t.: scopulus frontem porrigit in aequor, Ov.; porrecta in dorso urbs, Liv.; Verg., Tac.
TRANSF., (1) se porrigere, *to extend, reach*: quo se tua porrigat ira, Ov. (2) syllabam, *to lengthen the quantity of a syllable*, Quint. (3) *to offer, grant*: praesidium clientibus, Cic.; Hor.

¶ Hence partic. (with compar.) **porrectus** -a -um, *stretched out, extended*. LIT., loca,

Caes.; porrectior acies, Tac. TRANSF., imperii maiestas, Hor.; mora, *long*, Ov.

²**porrigo** -gĭnis, f. (=prurigo), *scurf, dandruff*: Hor.

porro, adv. (*πόρρω*), *forward, further*.
LIT., in space; with verbs of motion: ire, Liv.; agere armentum, Liv.; Sall.; with verbs of rest, *at a distance*: inscius Aeneas quae sint ea flumina porro, Liv.
TRANSF., (1) in time, *far back, long ago*: Ov.; *in future*: Ter., Liv. (2) of succession, *again, in turn*: saepe audivi a maioribus natu, qui se porro pueros a sensibus audisse dicebant, Cic. (3) in an argument, *further, next*: sequitur porro, nihil deos ignorare, Cic.; Lucr.

porrus -i, m. and **porrum** -i, n. (*πράσον*), *a leek*: Hor., Juv.

Porsēna, Porsenna, Porsinna -ae, m. *a king of Etruria, who attacked Rome in order to bring back Tarquinius Superbus*: bona Porsinae regis veneunt, Liv.

porta -ae, f. (connected with *περάω, πορθμός*), *a gate*.
LIT., (1) *a city gate*, with or without urbis: Cic., Verg., etc. (2) *a gate of a camp*: porta decumana, Caes. (3) in gen., *any gate or door*: Verg., Ov.
TRANSF., portae iecoris, Cic.; quibus e portis occurri cuique deceret, *by what ways or means*, Lucr.

portātĭo -ōnis, f. (porto), *a carrying, conveying*: armorum, Sall.

portendo -tendĕre -tendi -tentum (pro/tendo), *to indicate, predict, presage*: magnitudinem imperii portendens prodigium, Liv.; with acc. and infin.: Cic.
¶ Hence n. of partic. as subst. **portentum** -i, *a prodigy, portent*: Cic., Verg. TRANSF., (1) *a wonderful story, extravagant tale*: poëtarum et pictorum, Cic.; Lucr. (2) *a monster, monstrosity*: hominum pecudumque portenta, Cic.; Lucr., Hor.; so of a human 'monster of depravity': portentum reipublicae (of Piso), Cic.; Juv.

portentĭfĭcus -a -um (portentum/facio), *supernatural, marvellous, miraculous*: venena, Ov.

portentōsus -a -um (portentum), *extraordinary, monstrous, unnatural*: Cic., Liv.

portentum -i, n. subst. from portendo; q.v.

porthmeus, acc. -ĕă, m. (*πορθμεύς*), *a ferryman*: Charon, Juv.

portĭcŭla -ae, f. (dim. of porticus), *a little gallery or portico*: Cic. L.

portĭcus -ūs, f. (porta), *a portico, colonnade, arcade, gallery*. LIT., cum paullulum inambulavisset in porticu, Cic.; Verg., etc. TRANSF., (1) *the Stoic school* (so named from *στοά, a porch*), *the Stoics*: clamat Zeno et tota illa porticus tumultuatur, Cic. (2) plur., milit. t. t., *galleries to protect the besiegers of a place*: Caes.

portĭo -ōnis, f. *a part, section, division*: vitae, faecis, Juv.; Liv.; pro portione, *in proportion, proportionally*, Cic., Liv.

portĭscŭlus -i, m. *a signal*, originally *a hammer giving the time to rowers*: Pl.

¹**portĭtor** -ōris, m. (portus), *a customs-officer, collector of harbour-dues*: Pl., Ter., Cic.

²**portĭtor** -ōris -m. (porto), *a carrier*; usually *a boatman, ferryman*: Charon, Verg.

porto -are, *to bear, carry, convey, bring*. LIT.,

onera, Caes.; omnia mecum porto mea, Cic.; Massilium in triumpho, Cic.; of persons: lectica portari, Cic.; with thing as subject: portans in corpore virus lolligo, Ov. TRANSF., sociis atque amicis auxilia portabant, Sall.; has spes cogitationesque secum portantes, Liv.; Ov.

portōrĭum i, n. (portus), *customs, harbour-dues, tax on imported and exported goods*: portorium vini instituere, Cic.; exigere, Cic.; Caes., Liv. TRANSF., *any toll, tax*: Cic. L.

portŭla -ae, f. (dim. of porta), *a little gate, postern*: Liv.

Portūnus -i, m. (portus), *the god of harbours* (identified with the Greek Palaemon).
¶ Hence **Portūnālĭa** -ium, n. pl. *the festival of Portunus, on the 17th of August*.

portŭōsus -a -um (portus), *having many harbours, abounding in ports*: superum mare, Cic.; compar.: portuosior, Sall.

portus -ūs, m. (connected with porta), *a harbour, port, haven*.
LIT., portus Caietae celeberrimus, Cic.; e portu solvere, Cic.; in portum pervehi, Cic.; as a place for levying duties: in portu operam dare, *to be a customs-officer*, Cic.; prov.: in portu navigare, *to be out of danger*, Ter. Poet., *the estuary of a river*: Ov.
TRANSF., *a place of refuge, haven*: nationum portus et refugium senatus, Cic.; se in philosophiae portum conferre, Cic.; Verg.

posca -ae, f. *vinegar and water mixed as a drink*: Pl., Plin.

posco poscĕre pŏposci, *to ask earnestly, request*.
LIT., in gen.: pugnam, Liv.; argentum, Cic.; audaciae partes sibi, Cic.; with ab: munus ab aliquo, Cic.; with double acc.: magistratum Sicyonium nummos poposcit, Cic.; Hor., Liv., etc.; absol.: poscimur, *we are called upon for a song*, Hor.; with ut and the subj.: Juv., Tac.; with acc. and infin.: Ov. Esp. (1) *to demand for punishment, require to be given up*: accusant ii, quos populus poscit, Cic.; Liv. (2) *to challenge to fight*: Turnum in proelia, Verg. (3) *to inquire*: causas, Verg. (4) *to ask or to offer a price*: Pl. (5) *to call upon a deity*: tua numina posco, Verg.
TRANSF., of things, *to demand, require*: quod res poscere videbatur, Caes.; Sall., Quint.

Pŏsīdōnĭus -i, m. (*Ποσειδώνιος*), *a Stoic philosopher, pupil of Panaetius and teacher of Cicero*.

pŏsĭtĭo -ōnis, f. (pono), *a placing, putting, posture*: corporis, mentis, Sen.; caeli, *situation, climate*, Tac.; Quint.

pŏsĭtŏr -ōris, m. (pono), *a founder, builder*: Ov.

pŏsĭtūra -ae, f. (pono), *a placing*. Hence (1) *a situation, posture*: Lucr. (2) *an ordering, formation*: Prop.

pŏsĭtus -ūs, m. (pono), *position, place, arrangement*: urbis, Ov.; regionis, Tac.; Ov.

possessĭo -ōnis, f. (possideo and possido).
LIT., *a getting possession* or *a possessing of* anything; *occupation, enjoyment*: fundi, Cic.; possessionem hereditatis alicui dare, eripere, Cic.; regni, Liv.; insulae, Tac.; fig.: prudentiae, doctrinaeque, Cic. TRANSF., *that which is possessed, a possession, property*:

paternae atque avitae possessiones, Cic.; Caes.

possessiŭncŭla -ae, f. (dim. of possessio), *a small property*: Cic. L.

possessor -ōris, m. (possideo), *a possessor, occupier*: locorum, Cic.; agrorum, Liv.; Hor. As legal t. t., *a defendant*: Quint.

possĭbĭlis -e (possum), *possible*: Quint.

possĭdĕo -sĭdēre -sēdi -sessum (sedeo), *to possess, have, hold.* LIT., ex edicto bona, Cic.; Caes., Liv. TRANSF., nomen, mores, Pl.; vim, Cic.

possĭdo -sĭdēre -sēdi -sessum (sido), *to take possession of, occupy.* LIT., bona sine testamento, Cic.; Lucr., Liv., Ov. TRANSF., totum hominem totamque eius praeturam, Cic.

possum posse pŏtŭi (potis/sum) (old forms possiem, potesse, etc., esp. in Pl.), *to be able, I* (*thou, he*, etc.) *can*.

In gen., of what is physically or morally possible, or permitted: potest fieri ut fallar, *I may be mistaken*, Cic.; fieri non potest ut non, *or* quin, *it cannot but be that*, Cic.; ut nihil ad te dem litterarum, facere non possum, *I cannot help writing to you*, Cic.; quantum potest, *or* ut potest, *as far as possible*, Pl., Cic. L.; with superl.: Caesari commendavi ut gravissime potui, *as strongly as I could*, Cic. L.

Esp., *to avail, have influence*; of persons: apud Sequanos plurimum, Caes.; omnia se posse censebat, Cic.; of things: plus potest apud te pecuniae cupiditas, Cic.

¶ Hence partic. (with compar. and superl.) **pŏtens** -entis, *able, powerful.* Hence (**1**) *capable*: regni, Liv.; neque iubendi neque vetandi, Tac.; Liv. (**2**) *mighty, influential*: **a**, in gen., of persons and societies: civis, civitas, Cic.; potentissimi reges, Cic.; with abl.: opibus, Ov.; Liv.,Tac.: **b**, with genit.: *master of*: potentes rerum suarum et urbis, Liv.; dum mei potens sum, *as long as I am my own master*, Liv.; Diva potens Cypri, *ruling over Cyprus*, Hor.; mentis, Ov.: **c**, of things, *powerful, efficacious*: nihil est potentius auro, Ov.; herba ad opem, Ov. (**3**) *in possession of*, having *obtained*; with genit.: pacis, Pl.; voti, Ov.

¶ Adv.(with compar.) **pŏtentĕr.** (**1**) *strongly, efficaciously*: Hor., Quint. (**2**) *according to one's power*: Hor.

post (older **postĕ**), adv. and prep., *behind, after*.

Adv. (**1**) of place, *behind, in the rear*: qui post erant, Cic.; Liv. (**2**) of time, *afterwards*: multis post annis, *many years afterwards*, Cic.; aliquanto post, multo post, Cic.; Caes., Verg. (**3**) *next, besides*: Pl.

Prep. with acc. (**1**) of place, *behind*: post nostra castra, Caes.; Verg., etc. (**2**) of time, *after*: post Brutum consulem, Cic.; foll. by quam: post diem tertium . . . quam dixerat, Cic. (**3**) of rank or preference, *next after*: neque erat Lydia post Chloen, Hor.; Sall.

postĕā, adv. (post), *thereafter, afterwards*: postea aliquanto, Cic.; Caes., Liv.; of succession: quid postea? *what then? what next?* Ter., Cic.

postĕāquam (or **postĕā quam**), conj. *after*; with indic.: posteaquam victoria constituta est, Cic.

postĕri, *see* posterus.

postĕrĭtās -ātis, f. (posterus), *future generations, posterity*: habere rationem posteritatis, Caes.; posteritati servire, Cic. TRANSF., *offspring*: Juv.

postĕrus (poster) -a -um, compar. **postĕrĭor** -us; superl. **postrēmus** and **postŭmus** -a -um (post).

Posit., *subsequent, following, next, future*: postero die, Cic.; credula postero (sc. diei), *trusting tomorrow*, Hor.; in posterum, *for the next day*, Caes., Liv.; *for the future*: Cic. M. pl. as subst. **postĕri** -ōrum, *posterity*: Cic., Tac.

Compar. **postĕrĭor** -us, *following after, next, later.* LIT., of space or time: posteriores cogitationes, *second thoughts*, Cic.; paulo aetate posterior, Cic., Ov. TRANSF., *inferior, worse*: nihil posterius, Cic.

Superl. **postrēmus** -a -um, *hindmost, last.* LIT., pagina, Cic.; acies, *the rear*, Sall.; Verg., etc. N. abl. as adv., postremo, *at last*: primum . . . deinde . . . postremo, Cic.; Hor., Caes.; n. acc.: postremum, *for the last time*, Cic.; ad postremum, *at last*, Pl., Liv. TRANSF., of rank or preference, *lowest, worst*: homines, Cic.

Superl. **postŭmus** -a -um, *the last, last-born* (esp. of children born after the father's will or death), *posthumous*: proles, Verg.

postfĕro -ferre, *to esteem less, consider of less account*: libertati plebis suas opes, Liv.

postgĕnĭti -ōrum, m. pl. (post/gigno), *posterity, descendants*: Hor.

posthăbĕo -ēre -ŭi -ĭtum, *to esteem less, make of less account*: omnibus rebus posthabitis, Cic.; posthabitā Samo, Verg.; with dat.: illorum mea seria ludo, Verg.

posthāc, adv. *hereafter, in future, afterwards*: Pl., Cic.

posthinc (or **post hinc**), *next*: Verg.

posthoc (or **post hoc**), *afterwards*: Hor.

postibi (or **post ibi**), *afterwards*: Pl.

posticulum -i, n. (dim. of posticum), *a little outhouse*: Pl.

postīcus -a -um (post), *hinder, back*: partes aedium, Liv.; Pl. N. as subst. **postīcum** -i, *a back-door*: Pl., Hor.

postĭdĕā, *afterwards*: Pl.

postĭlēna -ae, f. (post), *a crupper*: Pl.

postĭllā, adv. *after, afterwards*: Pl., Ter., Cat.

postis -is, m. *a door-post.* LIT., postem tenere (of a person who consecrated a temple), Cic.; Hor., Liv., etc. TRANSF. (usually plur.), *a door, doorway*: Verg., etc.

postlĭmĭnĭum -i, n. (post/limen), *the right to return home and resume one's rights*: ei esse postliminium, Cic.; usually abl.: postliminio, *by right of* postliminium, Cic.

postmĕrĭdĭānus (pōsmĕrĭdĭānus) -a -um (post/meridies), *of the afternoon, afternoon*: tempus, Cic.; Sen.

postmŏdŏ and **postmŏdum**, adv. *presently, soon*: Hor., Liv., etc.

postpartor -ōris, m. (post/pario), *an heir*: Pl.

postpōno -pōnĕre -pŏsŭi -pŏsĭtum, *to esteem less, consider of less account, put after*: omnia, Caes.; with dat.: scorto officium, Hor.

postprincĭpĭa -orum, n. pl. (post/principium), *a sequel*: Pl.

postpŭto -are, *to consider of less account*: Ter.

postquam (or **post quam**), conj. *after, when.* Usually with indic., esp. perf.: postquam Caesar pervenit, Caes.; with pluperf.: undecimo die, postquam a te discesseram, Cic. L.; Liv.; with imperf.: postquam ad id parum potentes erant, Liv.; Caes., Sall.; with historic pres. or historic infin.: postquam exui aequalitas, Tac.; Caes., Cic., Liv. With subj. in or. obliq.: Cic.

postrēmo, postrēmum, postrēmus -a -um, *see* posterus.

postrīdiē, adv. (posterus/dies), *the day after, on the next day*: primā luce postridie, Caes.; foll. by quam: postridie quam a vobis discessi, Cic. L.; with acc.: ludos, *the day after the games,* Cic. L.; with genit.: postridie eius diei, Caes.

postrīdŭo=postridie, q.v.: Pl.

postscaenĭum -i, n. (post/scaena), *the theatre behind the scenes*; fig.: postscaenia vitae, Lucr.

postscrībo -scrībĕre -scripsi -scriptum, *to write after*: Tac.

postŭlātĭo -ōnis, f. (postulo), *a claim, demand.* In gen.: ignoscendi, *for pardon,* Cic.; concedere postulationi eius, Cic. Esp. **(1)** *a complaint*: Pl., Ter. **(2)** as legal t. t., *an application to the praetor to allow a complaint* or *charge to be brought*: ap. Cic. L.

postŭlātor -oris, m. (postulo), *a plaintiff*: Suet.

postŭlātum -i, n. subst. from postulo; q.v.

postŭlātus -ūs, m. (postulo), *a legal complaint, accusation, suit*; in abl. sing.: Liv.

postŭlo -are (connected with posco), *to claim, demand, request.*

Lɪᴛ., in gen.; with acc.: auxilium, Caes.; quidvis ab amico, Cic. With ut, *or* ne, and the subj.: postulat abs te ut Romam rem reicias, Cic.; Liv., etc.; with subj. alone: Caes., Liv. With infin., or acc. and infin.: dicendo vincere non postulo, *I do not expect,* Cic.; hic postulat Romae se absolvi, Cic. With de: a senatu de foedere postulaverunt, Cic.; Caes. Esp. as legal t. t. **(1)** *to demand from the praetor a writ against someone*: Cic., Liv. **(2)** *to impeach, accuse*: aliquem de ambitu, Cic.; aliquem maiestatis, Tac.; Liv. Tʀᴀɴꜱꜰ., of things, *to demand, require*: cum tempus necessitasque postulat, Cic.; Caes.

¶ Hence n. of partic. as subst. **postŭlātum** -i, *a demand*; usually plur. **postŭlāta** -orum, *demands*: Caes., Cic.

postŭmus -a -um, superl. of posterus; q.v.

pōtātĭo -ōnis, f. (poto), *a drinking-bout*: hesterna ex potatione oscitante, Cic.; Pl.

pōtātor -ōris, m. (poto), *a drinker*: Pl.

pōtě, *see* potis.

pŏtens -entis, partic. from possum; q.v.

pŏtentātus -ūs, m. (potens), *political power, supremacy*: Caes., Cic., Liv.

pŏtentĕr, adv. from possum; q.v.

pŏtentĭa -ae, f. (potens), *power, might, ability.* In gen.: solis, Verg.; herbarum, *efficacy, potency,* Ov.; occulti fati, Juv. Esp. *political power*; esp. *unofficial* and *sinister*: erant in magnā potentiā qui consulebantur, Cic.; divitias potentia sequebatur, Sall.

pŏtērĭum -i, n. (ποτήριον), *a goblet*: Pl.

pŏtestās -ātis, f. (possum), *power.*

Lɪᴛ., in gen., *power to do something, power*

over something, control: habere potestatem vitae necisque in aliquem, Cic.; esse in potestate senatūs, Cic.; exisse ex potestate, *to have lost control of oneself,* Cic.; esse suae potestatis, Liv. Esp. *political power.* **(1)** *supremacy, dominion*: esse in alicuius ditione ac potestate, Cic.; Caes., Liv. **(2)** *the authority of a magistrate, official authority, office*: tribunicia, Caes.; praetoria, Cic.; dare alicui potestatem legati, Cic.; imperia et potestates, *military and civil commands,* Cic.; sometimes *an officer, a magistrate*: Cic., Verg.

Tʀᴀɴꜱꜰ., **(1)** *ability, opportunity, possibility, occasion*: data est potestas augendae dignitatis, Cic.; facere potestatem alicui, *to give an opportunity* or *permission to,* Caes., Liv.; potestas est, *it is possible,* with infin.: non fugis hinc praeceps dum praecipitare potestas, Verg. **(2)** *the properties* or *qualities* of a thing: plumbi, Lucr.; Verg.

pŏtin'=potisne. **(1)** with es, *can you?*: Ter. **(2)** sc. est, *can it be?*: Pl., Ter.

¹**pōtĭo** -ōnis, f. (poto), *a drinking.* Lɪᴛ., in media potione, Cic. Tʀᴀɴꜱꜰ., *a drink, a draught*: Cic. Esp. **(1)** *of medicine*: Pl. **(2)** *of poison*: Cic. **(3)** *a love-draught, philtre*: Hor.

²**pōtĭo,** -ire (potis), *to put in the power of*: aliquem servitutis, *to reduce to slavery,* Pl.

¹**pŏtĭor** -iri, dep. (potis) (pres. indic. pŏtītur: Verg.; imperf. subj. pŏtĕrēmur: Ov.). **(1)** *to get possession of, to obtain.* With acc.: sceptra, Lucr.; with abl.: urbe, Cic.; victoriā, Caes.; with genit.: regni, Cic. L.; vexilli, Liv. **(2)** *to possess, be master of.* With acc.: Pl., Ter.; with abl.: mari, Liv.; Cic., Ov.; with genit.: rerum, Cic.; Tac.

²**pŏtĭor,** *see* potis.

pŏtĭs, adj. with f. pŏtĭs, and n. pŏtĭs *or* pŏtĕ; compar. **pŏtĭor** -us; superl. **pŏtissĭmus** -a -um.

Posit. **pŏtĭs,** *able, capable*; usually in the phrase potis (or pote) est, *can, is able*: non potis est vis ulla tenere, Verg.; also in the sense *is possible*: Lucr., etc.

Compar. **pŏtĭor** -us, *preferable, better*: cives potiores quam peregrini, Cic.; potior patre, Cic.; mors servitute potior, Cic.; Caes., Hor., Liv. N. acc. as adv. **pŏtĭus,** *rather, more, preferably*: magnus (homo) vel potius summas, Cic.; potius quam, *rather than,* Caes., Cic., Liv.; foll. by ut and subj., or simply subj.: Cic., Liv.

Superl. **pŏtissĭmus** -a -um, *best of all, chief, principal*: quid potissimum sit, Cic.; Fabium potissimum auctorem habui, Liv. N. acc. as adv. **pŏtissĭmum,** *chiefly, above all*: Caes., Cic., Liv.

pōtĭto -are (freq. of poto), *to drink frequently, drink hard*: Pl.

pŏtĭus, *see* potis.

Potnĭae -ārum, f. pl. (Πότνιαι), *a place in Boeotia on the river Asopus, with well-known pastures.*

¶ Hence f. adj. **Potnĭăs** -ădis, *belonging to Potniae*: equae, Ov.; quadrigae, Verg.

pōto pōtare pōtāvi pōtātum and pōtum, *to drink.* Lɪᴛ., aquas, Ov.; absol.: huc veniunt potum iuvenci, Verg.; esp. *to drink heavily*: Cic., Sall., Liv.; impers. pass.: totos dies potabatur, Cic. Tʀᴀɴꜱꜰ., of things, *to absorb*: potantia vellera fucum, Hor.

⁋ Hence partic. **pŏtus** -a -um. (1) pass., *drunk, drunk up, drained*: sanguine poto, Cic.; poti faece tenus cadi, Hor. (2) act., *having drunk, drunken*: bene potus, Cic.; anus, Hor.

pŏtor -ōris, m. (poto), *a drinker*: aquae, Hor.; Rhodani, *a dweller by the Rhône*, Hor. Esp. *a tippler, drunkard*: Hor., Prop.

pŏtrix -īcis, f. (potor), *a female tippler*: Phaedr.

pŏtŭlentus (pōcŭlentus) -a -um (poto). (1) *drinkable, potable*; n. pl. as subst., *things that can be drunk*: esculenta et potulenta, Cic. (2) *drunk, intoxicated*: Suet.

¹**pŏtus**, partic. from poto; q.v.

²**pŏtus** -ūs, m. (poto), *a drinking, draught*: immoderatus, Cic.; Tac., etc.

prae, adv. and prep. (old locative).
Adv. *before, in front*: i prae, Pl., Ter. With ut *or* quam, *in comparison with*: Pl., Ter.
Prep., with abl., *before*. LIT., prae se pugionem tulit, Cic.; prae se armentum agens, Liv.; fig., prae se ferre, *to show, exhibit, betray*: scelus, Cic.; prae se iactare, Verg. TRANSF., (1) *in comparison with*: Atticos prae se agrestes putat, Cic.; prae nobis beatus, Cic.; Caes., Liv. (2) *on account of, because of*; usually with neg.: nec loqui prae maerore potuit, Cic.; prae clamore nulla adhortatio audita est, Liv.

praeăcŭo -ŭĕre, *to sharpen to a point*: Cato.
⁋ Hence partic. **praeăcūtus** -a -um, *sharpened to a point, pointed*: sudes, Sall.; stipites, Caes.; cuspis, Ov.

praealtus -a -um. (1) *very high*: rupes, Liv. (2) *very deep*: flumen, Liv.; Sall., Tac.

praebĕo -bēre -bŭi -bĭtum (=praehibeo, from prae/habeo), *to offer, hold out*.
LIT., crus alterum, Cic.; os ad contumeliam, Liv.; manūs verberibus, Ov.; aurum, *to present*, Pl.; sponsalia, Cic. L.
TRANSF., (1) *to provide, supply* abstr. things: opinionem timoris, Caes.; speciem horribilem, Caes.; spectaculum, Sall.; operam reipublicae, *to serve*, Liv. (2) with reflex., *to present* or *show oneself* in a certain character, *behave as, prove oneself*: misericordem se praebuit, Cic.; se virum, Cic.; in eos me severum, Cic.; without reflex.: Phormio strenuum hominem praebuit, Ter. (3) *to allow*: praebuit ipsa rapi, *allowed herself to be carried off*, Ov.

praebĭbo -bĭbĕre -bĭbi, *to drink before, to drink to*: ei cui venenum praebiberat, Cic.

praebĭtor -ōris, m. (praebeo), *a furnisher, supplier*: Cic.

praecălĭdus -a -um, *very hot*: Tac.

praecalvus -a -um, *very bald*: Suet.

praecantrix -īcis, f. (prae/cano), *a witch*: Pl.

praecānus -a -um, *prematurely grey*: Hor.

praecăvĕo -căvēre -cāvi -cautum. (1) intransit., *to take precautions, to be on one's guard*: providens et praecavens, Cic.; ab insidiis, Liv.; decemviris ab ira et impetu multitudinis, Liv.; with ne and the subj.: id ne accĭderet, sibi praecavendum existimabat, Caes. (2) transit., *to beware of, guard against beforehand*: illud, Pl.; peccata, quae difficillime praecaventur, Cic.

praecēdo -cēdĕre -cessi -cessum, *to go before, precede*.
LIT., (1) intransit.: praecedens consulis

filius, Liv.; cum equite, Liv. (2) transit.: classem, Liv.; agmen, Verg.
TRANSF., of time, *to go before, precede*: fama loquax praecessit ad aures tuas, Ov. Of rank, etc., *to surpass, excel*: reliquos Gallos virtute, Caes.; vestros honores rebus agendis, Liv.; with dat.: Pl.

praecello -ĕre (prae/*cello), *to surpass, excel*. Absol.: mobilitate, Lucr.; gravitate morum, Tac.; Liv. With acc.: aliquam fecunditate, Tac.; with dat.: genti, *to rule over*, Tac.
⁋ Hence partic. (with compar. (Plin.) and superl.) **praecellens** -entis, *excellent, admirable, distinguished, surpassing*: vir et animo et virtute praecellens, Cic.; vir omnibus rebus praecellentissimus, Cic.

praecelsus -a -um, *very high, very lofty*: rupes, Verg.

praecentĭo -ōnis, f. (praecino), *a musical prelude, a singing before a sacrifice*: Cic.

praeceps (old form praecĭpĕs) -cĭpĭtis (prae/caput), *headlong, headforemost*.
Adj. (1) of motion, *headlong, quick, hasty*. LIT., **a**, of persons: aliquem praecipitem deicere, Cic.; praeceps in terram datus, Liv.; praecipites se fugae mandabant, Caes.; praeceps amensque cucurri, Ov.; Hor., etc.: **b**, of other living things: columbae, Verg.: **c**, of other moving objects: praeceps amnis, Hor.; sol in occasum, Liv. TRANSF., of abstract nouns: profectio, Cic.; celeritas dicendi, Cic.; praeceps dies, *fast declining*, Liv.; praeceps aetas, Sall.: **b**, of character, *hasty, rash, blind*: mens, Cic.; homo in omnibus consiliis praeceps, Cic.; praeceps ingenio in iram, *inclined to*, Liv.; animus ad flagitia, Tac.
(2) of places, *steep, precipitous*. LIT., via, Cic.; locus, Caes.; saxa, Liv.; fig.: iter ad finitimum malum praeceps ac lubricum, Cic. TRANSF., *dangerous*: libertas, Liv.; lubricum genus orationis adulescenti non acriter intellegenti est saepe praeceps, Cic.; in tam praecipiti tempore, Ov.; Hor.
Subst. **praeceps** -cĭpĭtis, n. *a steep place, precipice*. LIT., turrim in praecipiti stantem, Verg.; in praeceps deferri, Liv. TRANSF., *danger*: prope totam rempublicam in praeceps dederat, Liv.; Hor., Ov.
Adv., *headlong*: praeceps trahere, dare, Tac.

praeceptĭo -ōnis, f. (praecipio). (1) *a preconception*: Cic. (2) *a precept*: Stoicorum, Cic. (3) *the right to receive in advance*: Plin. L.

praeceptĭvus -a -um (praecipio), *didactic*: Sen.

praeceptor -ōris, m. (praecipio), *a teacher, instructor, preceptor*: vivendi atque dicendi, Cic.

praeceptrix -trīcis, f. (praeceptor), *she that teaches*: quā (sapientiā) praeceptrice, Cic.

praeceptum -i, n. subst. from praecipio; q.v.

praecerpo -cerpĕre -cerpsi -cerptum (prae/carpo), *to pluck prematurely, gather before the time*. LIT., messes, Ov. TRANSF., *to intercept*: fructum officii tui, Cic.

praecīdo -cīdĕre -cīdi -cīsum (prae/caedo), *to cut short, cut off, lop, mutilate*.
LIT., alicui caput, Liv.; fistulas (aquae), Cic.; ancoras, *to cut the cables*, Cic.; canem, Liv.; cotem novaculā, Cic.

Transf., *to cut short*: amicitias magis decere diluere quam repente praecidere, Cic.; sibi reditum, Cic.; brevi praecidam, *I will express myself briefly*, Cic.
¶ Hence partic. **praecīsus** -a -um, *broken off*; of places, *steep, abrupt, precipitous*: saxa, Verg.; iter, Sall.; as rhet. t. t., *short, brief*: Quint.
¶ Adv. **praecīsē**. (1) *briefly, in few words*: id praecise dicitur, Cic. (2) *absolutely, decidedly*: negare, Cic.

praecinctus -a -um, partic. from praecingo; q.v.

praecingo -cingĕre -cinxi -cinctum, *to gird in front, surround with a girdle*. Lit., Pl.; esp. middle, praecingi, *to gird oneself*: praecingitur ense viator, Ov.; recte praecincti pueri, Hor.; altius ac nos praecincti, *girded higher, readier for rapid travel*, Hor.
Transf., *to face with*: fontem vallo, Prop.; Ov.

praecĭno -cĭnĕre -cĭnŭi -centum (prae/cano). (1) intransit.: **a**, *to sing* or *play before*: epulis magistratuum fides praecinunt, Cic.; praecinere sacrificiis, Liv.: **b**, *to sing an incantation*: Tib. (2) transit., *to prophesy, predict*: magnum aliquid deos populo Romano praecinere, Cic.; Tib.

praecĭpēs -is = praeceps; q.v.

praecĭpĭo -cĭpĕre -cēpi -ceptum (prae/capio), *to take before, receive in advance*.
Lit., aquam, Lucr.; pecuniam mutuam, Caes.; iter, *to get the start*, Liv.; si lac praeceperit aestus, *if the heat dries the milk beforehand*, Verg.; praecipitur seges, *ripens too fast*, Ov.
Transf., (1) mentally *to take beforehand, anticipate*: animo victoriam, Caes.; consilia hostium, *know beforehand*, Verg.; spe hostem, Verg.; spem, Liv. (2) *to instruct, advise, warn, admonish, teach*: hoc tibi praecipio, Cic.; alicui rationem tempestatum, Cic.; artem nandi, Ov.; illud potius praecipiendum fuit ut, Cic.; with subj. alone: Caes., Sall., Liv.; with infin.: temporibus parēre, Cic. Absol., *to be a teacher, to give instruction*: de eloquentia, Cic. Impers. pass.: ut erat praeceptum, Caes.
¶ Hence n. of partic. as subst. **praeceptum** -i, *a command, rule, injunction*: medicorum, philosophorum, rhetorum, Cic.; Latine loquendi, Cic.; praecepta dare, Cic., Verg.; observare, Caes.

praecĭpĭtantĕr, adv. from praecipito; q.v.
praecĭpĭtĭum -i, n. (praeceps), *a precipice*: Suet.

praecĭpĭto -are (praeceps).
(1) transit., *to cast down headlong*. Lit., se e Leucade, Cic.; sese in fossas, Caes.; Liv.; pass.: praecipitari, in middle sense, *to cast oneself down*, Sall., Liv.; poet.: lux praecipitatur aquis, *sinks beneath the waves*, Ov. Transf., **a**, *to cast down*: praecipitari ex altissimo dignitatis gradu, Cic.; rempublicam, Liv.; spem festinando, Ov.; pass. as middle: nox praecipitata, Ov.: **b**, *to rush along, press on with*: furor iraque mentem praecipitant, Verg.; moras omnes, Verg.; with infin.: dare tempus praecipitant curae, Verg.
(2) intransit., *to fall headlong, rush down*. Lit., Nilus praecipitat ex montibus, Cic.;

in fossam, Liv.; nox caelo, Verg. Transf., hiems iam praecipitaverat, Caes.; praecipitantem impellere, *to give a push to a falling man, to knock a man when he is down*, Cic.; praecipitare ad exitium, Cic. L.; respublica praecipitans, *hastening to its fall*, Cic.
¶ Hence adv., from pres. partic., **praecĭpĭtantĕr**, *headlong*: agere mannos, Lucr.

praecĭpŭē, adv. (praecipuus), *especially, chiefly, particularly, principally*: Cic.

praecĭpŭus -a -um (praecipio), *taken before*.
Hence (1) *peculiar, especial*: in communibus miseriis praecipuo quodam dolore angi, Liv. Esp. as legal t. t., *received beforehand*: Pl., Ter.; so n. as subst., of a legacy: Suet.
(2) *excellent, distinguished, extraordinary*: quos praecipuo semper honore Caesar habuit, Caes.; praecipuus toro (*distinguished by a seat of honour*) Aeneas, Verg.; praecipuus scientiâ rei militaris, Tac. N. as subst., sing.

praecĭpŭum -i, *pre-eminence, superiority*: homini praecipui a natura nihil datum esse, Cic.; plur. **praecĭpŭa** -ōrum = προηγμένα, *things* (in the Stoic philosophy) *that come next to the greatest good*: Cic.

praecīsus -a -um, partic. from praecido; q.v.

praeclārus -a -um, adj. (with compar.), *very bright, very clear*.
Lit., lux, Lucr.
Transf., (1) physically, *striking, beautiful*: vultus, Lucr.; urbs situ, Cic. (2) in gen., *remarkable, distinguished, excellent, admirable, famous*: indoles, Cic.; dies, Cic.; gens bello praeclara, Verg. (3) in a bad sense, *notorious*: sceleribus ferox atque praeclarus, Sall.
¶ Adv. (with superl.) **praeclārē**. (1) *very plainly, very clearly*: intellegere, Cic.; explicare, Cic. (2) *admirably, excellently*: gerere negotium, Cic.; meminisse, Cic.; expressing agreement, *very well*: Cic.

praeclūdo -clūdĕre -clūsi -clūsum (prae/claudo). Lit., *to close in front, shut up, shut against*: portas consuli, Caes.; Prop., Suet. Transf., *to close, make inaccessible*: speciem, Lucr.; sibi curiam, Cic.; maritimos cursus, Cic.; vocem alicui, *to stop a person's mouth*, Liv.

praeco -ōnis, m. *a public crier, herald* (in a court of justice, at public assemblies, at auctions): per praeconem vendere aliquid, *by auction*, Cic.; fundum subicere praeconi, *bring to the hammer*, Liv.
Transf., *a publisher, one who advertises*: tuae virtutis Homerum praeconem, Cic.

praecōgĭto -are, *to consider carefully beforehand*: multo ante facinus, Liv.; Quint.

praecognosco -cognoscere -cognĭtum, *to learn beforehand*: praecognito nostro adventu, ap. Cic. L.; Suet.

praecŏlo -cŏlĕre -cultum, *to cultivate before*; fig.: animi quasi ad virtutem praeculti, Tac.; nova et ancipitia, Tac.
¶ Hence partic. **praecultus** -a -um, *cultivated, adorned*: Stat., Quint.

praecompŏsĭtus -a -um (prae/compono), *composed beforehand, studied*: os, Ov.

praecōnĭus -a -um, *belonging to a praeco or crier*: quaestus, Cic.; Pl. N. as subst.
praecōnĭum -i, *the office of a public crier*: praeconium facere, Cic. L.
Transf., (1) *a publishing, making known*: tibi praeconium deferam, Cic.; praeconia

famae, Ov. (2) *a public laudation, com-mendation*: laborum, Cic.; formae, Ov.

praeconsūmo -sūmĕre -sumptum, *to use up beforehand*: Ov.

praecontrecto -are, *to handle beforehand*: Ov.

praecordĭa -ōrum, n. pl. (prae/cor), *the midriff, the diaphragm*. LIT., Cic., Juv. TRANSF., (1) *the stomach*: anulus in prae-cordiis piscis inventus, Cic.; quid veneni saevit in praecordiis, Hor. (2) *the breast, heart* (as the seat of feelings and passions): redit in praecordia virtus, Verg.; Hor., Juv.; praecordia mentis, Ov.

praecorrumpo -rumpĕre -ruptum, *to bribe beforehand*: me donis, Ov.

praecox -cŏcis and **praecŏquis** -e (prae/coquo), *ripe before the time, premature*. LIT., Plin. TRANSF., audacia, Sen.

praecultus -a -um, partic. from praecolo; q.v.

praecŭpĭdus -a -um, *very fond*: Suet.

praecurro -currĕre -cŭcurri and -curri -cursum, *to run before, go on ahead*. LIT., praecurrit ante omnes, Caes.; ad aliquem, Liv.; subst. **praecurrentia** -ium, n. *what goes before, antecedents*: Cic. TRANSF., (1) of abstr. things, *to go before*: eo fama iam praecurrerat de praelio Dyrrhachino, Caes.; Cic. (2) of time, *to precede*; with acc.: iudicium, Cic.; with dat.: ut certis rebus certa signa praecurrerent, Cic. (3) *to surpass*: celeritate, Caes.; with acc.: aliquem aetate, Cic.; with dat.: alicui studio, Cic.

praecursĭo -ōnis, f. (praecurro), *a going before*. Hence (1) *previous occurrence*: sine praecursione visorum, Cic. (2) *a skirmish*: Plin. L. (3) rhet. t. t., *preparation of the hearer*: Cic.

praecursor -ōris, m. (praecurro), *a forerunner*: Plin. Milit. t. t., *vanguard, advance-guard*: Liv. TRANSF., *a spy, scout*: in omni calumniā praecursorem habere, Cic.

praecursōrĭus -a -um (praecurro), *sent in advance*: Plin. L.

praecŭtio -cŭtĕre -cussi -cussum (prae/quatio), *to shake before, brandish before*: taedas, Ov.

praeda -ae, f. (connected with praehendo), *spoils of war, plunder, booty*. LIT., praedam facere, Caes.; militibus donare, Caes.; Cic., Liv. TRANSF., (1) of animals, *prey*: cervi luporum praeda rapacium, Hor. (2) in gen., *plunder, gain*: maximos quaestus praedasque facere, Cic.; Pl., Hor.

praedābundus -a -um (praedor), *plundering*: Sall., Liv.

praedamno -are, *to condemn before*: conlegam, Liv. TRANSF., spem, *to give up*, Liv.

praedātĭo -ōnis, f. (praedor), *a plundering, pillaging*: Tac.

praedātor -ōris, m. (praedor). LIT., *a plunderer, pillager, robber*: vexatores ac praedatores, Cic.; Sall. TRANSF., (1) *a hunter*: caprorum, Ov. (2) *a greedy person*: Tib.

praedātōrĭus -a -um (praedator), *plundering, pillaging, predatory*: naves, Pl., Liv.

praedātrix -īcis, f. (praedor), *a female plunderer*: Stat.

praedēlasso -are, *to weary beforehand*: Ov.

praedestĭno -are, *to appoint beforehand*: sibi similes triumphos, Liv.

praedĭātor -ōris, m. (praedium), *a buyer of landed estates*: Cic.

praedĭātōrĭus -a -um (praediator), *relating to the sale of land by auction*: ius, Cic.

praedĭcābĭlis -e (¹praedico), *praiseworthy*: Cic.

praedĭcātĭo -ōnis, f. (¹praedico). (1) *a making publicly known, proclamation*: temporis, Cic.; nefariae societatis, *relating to*, Cic. (2) *a praising, commending*: Pl., Cic. L., etc.

praedĭcātor -ōris, m. (¹praedico), *a praiser, commender, public eulogist*: Cic., Plin. L.

¹**praedĭco** -are, *to make publicly known, proclaim, publish*. LIT., of the praeco: dimidias venire partes, Cic.; Pl. TRANSF., (1) in gen., *to declare, say publicly, proclaim*: paucitatem nostrorum militum suis, Caes.; Cic.; with acc. and infin.: praedicantem contumeliam illam sibi a Cicerone impositam esse, Sall.; Caes. (2) *to praise, commend, eulogize, boast*: virtutem, Cic.; falsa de se, Cic.; Galli se omnes ab Dite patre prognatos praedicant, Caes.; verecundia in praedicando, Tac.

²**praedīco** -dīcĕre -dixi -dictum. (1) *to say beforehand*: illud tibi, Verg.; Ter. Hence, *to name beforehand*: loco praedicto, Liv.; praedicere diem, Tac. (2) *to predict, foretell, prophesy*: defectiones solis, Cic.; futura, Cic.; with acc. and infin.: nihil Antonium facturum (esse), Cic.; malum hoc, Verg. (3) *to warn, admonish, instruct, charge*: Pompeius suis praedixerat, ut Caesaris impetum exciperent, Caes.; Iunonem praedicere, ne id faceret, Cic.; Liv., Tac.

¶ Hence n. of partic. as subst. **praedictum.** (1) *a prophecy, prediction*: Cic.; Verg. (2) *an order, command*: Liv. (3) *a previous agreement, agreement*: Liv.

praedictĭo -ōnis, f. (²praedico). (1) *a prophesying, predicting*: Cic. (2) rhet. t. t., *a premising*: Quint.

praedictum -i, n. subst. from ²praedico; q.v.

praedĭŏlum -i, n. (dim. of praedium), *a small estate, little farm*: Cic., Plin. L.

praedisco -ĕre, *to learn before*: ea quae agenda sunt in foro, Cic.; Verg.

praedispŏsĭtus -a -um, *arranged at intervals beforehand*: nuntii, Liv.

praedĭtus -a -um (prae/do), *endowed, furnished, provided with*; with abl.: armis, Pl.; sensu, Lucr.; virtute, Cic.; crudelitate, Cic.

praedĭum -i, n. (praes), *a farm, landed estate*: rusticum, Cic.; praedium vendere, Cic.; Hor.

praedīvĕs -ĭtis, *very rich*: Liv., Ov., Tac.

praedo -ōnis, m. (praeda), *a robber, plunderer*: urbis, Cic.; maritimi, *pirates*, Nep.; Verg., etc.

praedŏcĕo -dŏcēre -doctum, *to teach before, instruct before*: praedocti ab duce, Sall.

praedŏmo -dŏmare -dŏmŭi, *to tame before*: Sen.

praedor -ari, dep. (praeda), *to plunder.* (1) intransit. LIT., praedatum exisse in agrum Latinum, Liv.; milites praedantes, Caes.; Cic. TRANSF., in gen., *to get gain*: in bonis alienis, Cic.; de aratorum bonis, Cic.; ex alterius inscitiā, Cic.

(2) transit., *to rob* or *carry off*. LIT., socios magis quam hostes, Cic.; ovem unam, Ov. TRANSF., amores alicuius, *one's sweetheart*, Ov.; singula de nobis anni praedantur, Hor.

praedūco -dūcĕre -duxi -ductum, *to lead forward, bring in front*: fossas viis, Caes.; murum, Caes.

praedulcis -e, *very sweet*. LIT., Plin. TRANSF., decus, Verg.

praedūrus -a -um, *very hard, very strong*. LIT., corium, Tac. TRANSF., (**1**) homo praedurus viribus, Verg. (**2**) *bold, harsh*: Quint.

praeēmĭnĕo -ēre, *to project*. LIT., Sall. TRANSF., *to excel*: ceteros peritiā legum, Tac.

praeĕo -ire -īvi and -ii -ĭtum, *to go before, precede*. LIT., Laevinus Romam praeivit, Liv.; Verg.; with dat.: Cic. TRANSF., (**1**) *to go over beforehand* verbally, *say in advance*; in gen.: ut vobis voce praeirent, quid iudicaretis, Cic.; esp. as relig. and legal t. t., *to dictate, go over a form of words*: praeire alicui, Cic.; verba praeire, Liv.; carmen, Liv.; sacramentum, Tac. (**2**) *to order, command*: omnia, ut decemviri praeierunt, facta, Liv.

praefātĭo -ōnis, f. (praefor), *a saying beforehand*. Hence (**1**) *a religious* or *legal form of words, formula*: donationis, Cic.; sacrorum, Liv. (**2**) *a preface, introduction*: Liv., Plin. L.

praefectūra -ae, f. (praefectus), *the office of superintendent* or *overseer*. LIT., urbis, Plin.; annonae, Tac.; vigilum, Tac. Esp. *a subordinate provincial command*: praefecturam petere, Cic. L.; Aegypti, Suet. TRANSF., (**1**) *an Italian town governed by a praefectus, a prefecture*: Caes., Cic. (**2**) *a district so governed*: Tac.

praefectus -a -um, partic. from praeficio; q.v.

praefĕro -ferre -tŭli -lātum. (**1**) *to bear before* or *in front*. LIT., ardentem facem, Cic.; fasces praetoribus, Cic. TRANSF., a, in gen.: clarissimum lumen praetulistis menti meae, Cic.: **b**, *to bring to light, show, display*: avaritiam, Cic.; haec eius diei praefertur opinio, Caes.: **c**, *to prefer*: aliquem sibi, Cic.; otium labori, Sall.; Gallorum quam Romanorum imperia, Caes.: **d**, *to anticipate*: diem triumphi, Liv. (**2**) *to carry by*; middle, praeferri=*to ride by*: praeter castra praelati, Liv.; Tac. TRANSF., middle or with reflex., *to surpass*: Caes.

praefĕrox ōcis, *very bold, impetuous*: legati, Liv.; Tac.

praeferrātus -a -um, *tipped with iron*: Pl., Plin.

praefervĭdus -a -um, *burning hot, very hot*. LIT., balneum, Tac. TRANSF., ira, Liv.

praefestīno -are. (**1**) *to hasten prematurely*: ne deficere praefestinarent, Liv.; Pl. (**2**) *to hasten by*: sinum, Tac.

praefĭca -ae, f. *the chief female mourner in a funeral procession*: Pl.

praefĭcĭo -fĭcĕre -fēci -fectum (prae/facio), *to set over, appoint as superintendent, overseer*, etc.: in eo statui fratrem, Cic.; usually with dat.: aliquem pecori, Cic.; bello gerendo, *or* bello, Cic.; legioni, Caes.; classi, Liv.; Verg., Tac. ¶ M. of partic. as subst. **praefectus** -i, *an overseer, superintendent*: his utitur quasi praefectis libidinum suarum, Cic.; totius Phrygiae, Nep. Esp. in Roman political life, *a civil* or *military officer* or *superintendent*:

annonae, Tac.; castrorum, *or* castris, Tac.; praefectus urbis, *or* urbi, *governor of the city* (*Rome*), *and commander of the five cohortes urbenae*, Liv.

praefīdens -entis, *over-confident*: sibi, Cic.

praefīgo -fīgĕre -fixi -fixum. (**1**) *to fix in front, fasten before*: ripa sudibus praefixis munita, Caes.; arma puppibus, Verg. (**2**) *to tip, point with*: iacula praefixa ferro, Liv.; Verg. (**3**) *to pierce through, transfix*: Tib.

praefīnĭo -ire, *to fix, prescribe, appoint beforehand*: successori diem, Cic.; sumptum funerum, Cic.; Lucr. ¶ Hence, from partic., adv. **praefīnīto**, *in the prescribed manner*: Ter.

praefiscĭnē (**praefiscĭnī**), adv. (fascinum), *without offence*: Pl.

praeflōro -are, *to deprive of blossom prematurely*; fig., *to diminish, lessen*: gloriam eius victoriae praefloratam apud Thermopylas esse, Liv.

praeflŭo -flŭĕre, *to flow past*: infimā valle, Liv.; Tac. With acc. of place: Tibur fertile, Hor.; Noricam provinciam, Tac.

praefōco -are (prae/faux), *to choke, suffocate*: viam animae, Ov.

praefŏdĭo -fŏdĕre -fōdi -fossum. (**1**) *to dig in front of*: portas, Verg. (**2**) *to bury previously*: aurum, Ov.

praefor -fāri -fātus sum, dep. *to speak before*. Hence (**1**) in gen., *to preface, to utter beforehand*: quae de deorum naturā praefati sumus, Cic. (**2**) of prayers, *to say beforehand*: maiores nostri omnibus rebus agendis quod bonum, faustum, felix sit, praefabantur, Cic.; carmen, Liv.; so with acc. of deity: divos, *to invoke*, Verg.

praefractus -a -um, partic. from praefingo; q.v.

praefrīgĭdus -a -um, *very cold*: Ov.

praefringo -fringere -frēgi -fractum (prae/frango), *to break off in front*: ligna, Lucr.; hastas, Liv., Caes. ¶ Hence partic. (with compar.) **praefractus** -a -um. (**1**) of style, *abrupt, disconnected*: Thucydides praefractior, Cic. (**2**) of character, *stern, severe, harsh*: Aristo Chius praefractus, ferreus, Cic. ¶ Adv. **praefractē**, *sternly, resolutely*: nimis praefracte vectigalia defendere, Cic.

praefulcĭo -fulcire -fulsi -fultum. (**1**) *to support, prop up*; fig.: illud praefulci atque praemuni ut, Cic. (**2**) *to use as a prop*: Pl.

praefulgĕo -fulgēre -fulsi. (**1**) *to gleam forth, shine forth*. LIT., equus praefulgens dentibus aureis, Verg. TRANSF., triumphali decore praefulgens, *conspicuous, distinguished*, Tac. (**2**) with dat., *to outshine*: Tac.

praegĕlĭdus -a -um, *very cold*: Alpes, Liv.

praegestĭo -ire, *to desire exceedingly*: praegestit animus videre, Cic.; Cat., Hor.

praegnans -antis (prae/root gna-, seen in gnascor), *pregnant*. LIT., Pl., Cic., Juv. TRANSF., *full of*: fusus stamine, Juv.; Pl.

praegrācĭlis -e, *very slim, lank*: Tac.

praegrandis -e, *huge, very great*: Plin., Pers.

praegrăvis -e, *very heavy*. LIT., onus, Ov. TRANSF., (**1**) *unwieldy, awkward*: praegravis corpore, Liv. (**2**) *stupefied*: Tac. (**3**) *wearisome*: Tac.

praegrăvo -are, *to press heavily upon, to weigh down*. LIT., praegravata telis scuta, Liv. TRANSF., (**1**) *to oppress, weigh down*: dantem et accipientem, Liv.; animum, Hor. (2) *to outweigh*: Hor., Suet.

praegrĕdĭor -grĕdi -gressus sum, dep. (prae/gradior). (1) *to go before, precede*: praegredientes amici, Cic.; with acc.: signa, agmen, Liv.; nuntios, famam, *outstrip*, Liv. (2) *to pass by, march by*: ea (castra), Liv.; Tac.

praegressĭo -ōnis, f. (praegredior), *a going before, precedence*: causae, Cic.

praegustātor -ōris, m. (praegusto), *one who tastes before, a taster*. LIT., Suet. TRANSF., libidinum tuarum, Cic.

praegusto -are, *to taste before*: cibos, Ov.; Liv., Juv.

praehĭbĕo -ēre (prae/habeo), *to offer, hold out, supply*: Pl.

praeiăcĕo, *to lie before*; with acc.: campus qui castra praeiacet, Tac.; with dat.: Plin.

praeiūdĭcātus -a -um, partic. from praeiudico; q.v.

praeiūdĭcĭum -i, n. *a previous judgment, a preliminary decision* or *examination* (for the sake of investigating facts for subsequent proceedings).
    LIT., de quo non *praeiudicium* sed plane *iudicium* iam pactum putatur, Cic.; apud eosdem iudices reus est factus, cum duobus iam praeiudiciis damnatus esset, Cic.
    TRANSF., (1) *a premature decision*: neminem praeiudicium tantae rei adferre, Liv. (2) *an example, precedent*: Pompeius vestri facti praeiudicio demotus, *by your example*, Caes.; Plin. L.

praeiūdĭco -are, *to decide beforehand, to give a preliminary judgment*. As legal t. t.: re semel atque iterum praeiudicata, Cic. In gen.: Cic.
    ¶ Hence partic. **praeiūdĭcātus** -a -um, *previously decided*: opinio praeiudicata, *a prejudice*, Cic.; Liv. N. as subst. **praeiūdĭcātum** -i, Cic., Liv.

praeiŭvo -iuvare -iūvi, *to assist before*: Tac.

praelābor -labi -lapsus sum, dep. *to glide past, before* or *along*: insula, in quam Germani nando praelabebantur, Tac.; with acc.: praelabi flumina rotis, Verg.

praelambo -ĕre, *to lick before, taste before*: Hor.

praelargus -a -um, *very abundant*: Pers.

praelĕgo -lĕgĕre -lēgi -lectum. (1) *to read out* as a teacher, *to lecture upon*: Quint., Suet. (2) *to sail past, coast along*: Campaniam, Tac.

praelĭgo -are. (1) *to bind in front*: sarmenta praeligantur cornibus boum, Liv. (2) *to bind up*: os obvolutum est folliculo et praeligatum, Cic. TRANSF., o praeligatum pectus! Pl.

praelongus -a -um, *very long*: gladius, Liv.

praelŏquor -loqui -locutus sum, dep. *to speak beforehand* or *speak first*: orationem, Pl.; Plin. L., Quint.

praelūcĕo -lūcēre -luxi, *to shine* or *carry a light before*. LIT., Pl., Suet.; Mart. TRANSF., (1) (amicitia) bonam spem praelucet in posterum, *sheds the kindly light of hope*, Cic. (2) *to outshine, surpass*; with dat.: nullus sinus Baiis praelucet, Hor.

praelūdo -ere, *to play beforehand*: Plin., Stat.

praelūsĭo -ōnis, f. (praeludo), *a prelude*: Plin. L.

praelustris -e, *very fine*: praelustri ab arce, Ov.

praemando -are, *to order beforehand*: Pl.
    ¶ Hence n. pl. of partic. as subst. **praemandāta** -ōrum, *a warrant of arrest*: Cic.

praemātūrus -a -um, *too early, premature*: cineres, Juv.; canities, Tac.
    ¶ Adv. **praemātūre**, *prematurely*: Pl.

praemĕdĭcātus -a -um, *protected by medicine* or *charms*: Ov.

praemĕdĭtātĭo -ōnis, f. (praemeditor), *a considering beforehand*: futurorum malorum, Cic.

praemĕdĭtor -ari, dep. *to practise* or *consider beforehand*: praemeditari quo animo accedam ad urbem, Cic. L.; with acc. and infin.: id praemeditari ferundum modice esse, Cic.; Tac.
    ¶ Hence perf. partic., in pass. sense **praemĕdĭtātus** -a -um, *considered beforehand*: mala, Cic.; Quint.

praemĕtŭo -ĕre, *to fear beforehand, be apprehensive*: suis, *for his men*, Caes.; with acc.: deserti coniugis iras, Verg.
    ¶ Hence partic. **praemĕtŭens** -entis, *fearing beforehand, apprehensive*; with genit.: Phaedr.
    ¶ Adv. **praemĕtŭentĕr**, *apprehensively, anxiously*: Lucr.

praemitto -mittĕre -mīsi -missum, *to send before, send on ahead*. LIT., legiones in Hispaniam, Caes.; edictum, Caes., Liv.; alicui odiosas litteras, Cic. L. TRANSF., haec favorabili oratione praemisit, Tac.

praemĭum -i, n. (prae/emo), *that which is taken first, the pick*.
    LIT., in war: pugnae, Verg.; Tac.; in the chase: leporem et gruem iucunda captat praemia, Hor.
    TRANSF., (1) *a gift, award*: honores et praemia, Caes.; vitai, Lucr.; fortunae, Cic. (2) *a reward, recompense*: praemia bene de republica meritorum, Cic.; alicui praemium dare pro aliqua re, Cic.; proponere, consequi, Caes.; augere, Tac. (3) *a notable exploit*: Verg.

praemŏlestĭa -ae, f. *trouble beforehand*: Cic.

praemŏlĭor -iri, dep. *to prepare beforehand*: res, Liv.

praemŏnĕo -ēre, *to warn, advise, admonish beforehand*. In gen.: me, ut magnopere caverem, praemonebat, Cic.; with acc. of the danger: conatūs hostium, Liv. Esp. *to foretell, presage*: de periculis, Cic.; Ilion arsurum, Ov.

praemŏnĭtus -ūs, m. (praemoneo), *a prediction, warning*: Ov.

praemonstrātor -ōris, m. (praemonstro), *a guide*: Ter.

praemonstro -are. (1) *to show in advance, point out the way*: Pl., Lucr. (2) *to prophesy, predict*: magnum aliquid populo Romano, Cic.

praemordĕo -mordēre -mordi -morsum, *to bite off*. LIT., Pl., Luc. TRANSF., *to pilfer*: aliquid ex aliquo, Juv.

praemŏrĭor -mŏri -mortŭus sum, dep. *to die prematurely*: Ov.
    ¶ Hence partic. **praemortŭus** -a -um, *prematurely dead*. LIT., membra, Ov. TRANSF., pudor, Liv.

praemūnĭo -ire, *to fortify in front*.
    LIT., aditūs duos magnis operibus, Caes.; Tac.

TRANSF., *to secure, make safe*: medicamentis, Suet.; quae praemuniuntur sermoni, *premised to meet objections*, Cic.
praemūnītĭo -ōnis, f. (praemunio), *a fortifying beforehand*; rhet. t. t., of an orator, *a preparation of the minds of his hearers*: Cic.
praenarro -are, *to relate beforehand*: Ter.
praenăto -are, *to swim before* or *past*: Verg.
Praeneste -is, n. (f. in Verg.), *a town in Latium, famous for its roses, its nuts, and for its temple and oracle of Fortuna* (now Palestrina).
¶ Hence adj. **Praenestīnus** -a -um, *Praeneste*: sortes, *the utterances of the oracle there*, Cic.
praenĭtĕo -ēre, *to outshine*; with dat.: cur tibi iunior praeniteat, Hor.
praenōmen -ĭnis, n. *the first name, the praenomen*; usually *that standing before the gentile name*, e.g. Marcus, in M. T. Cicero: Cic. L., Hor., Liv.; also of a *special title*: Suet.
praenosco -ĕre, *to get to know beforehand*: futura, Cic.; Ov.
praenōtĭo -ōnis, f. (praenosco), *a preconception, innate idea* (translation of πρόληψις): Cic.
praenūbĭlus -a -um, *very cloudy, very dark*: Ov.
praenuntĭo -are, *to announce beforehand, foretell, predict*: futura, Cic.
praenuntĭus -a -um, *foretelling*: verba, Ov. As subst. (m. f. and n.), *that which announces beforehand, a harbinger, sign, token, omen*: stellae calamitatum praenuntiae, Cic.; ales praenuntius lucis, *the cock*, Ov.; Lucr., Tac.
praeoccŭpātĭo -ōnis, f. (praeoccupo), *a taking possession of before*: locorum, Nep.
praeoccŭpo -are, *to take possession of before, seize before.*
LIT., iter, Caes.; loca, Liv.
TRANSF., (1) *to take possession of beforehand, to preoccupy*: animos timor praeoccupaverat, Caes.; Liv. (2) *to anticipate, to prevent*: ne adventu Caesaris praeoccuparetur, Caes.; with infin.: legem ipsi praeoccupaverant ferre, Liv.
praeŏlo -ĕre (oleo), *to give out a smell in advance*: Pl.
praeopto -are, *to choose before, to prefer*; with acc. and dat.: suas leges Romanae civitati, Liv.; otium urbanum militiae laboribus, Liv.; nemo non illos sibi, quam vos, dominos praeoptet, Liv.; with infin.: nudo corpore pugnare, Caes.; with ut: Pl.
praepando -ĕre, *to open wide in front, extend before*: Lucr., Verg.
praepărātĭo -ōnis, f. (praeparo), *preparation*: ad minuendum dolorem, Cic.
praepăro -are, *to make ready, prepare*: res necessarias ad vitam degendam, Cic.; naves, frumentum, Liv.; animos ad sapientiam, Cic.; aures (auditorum) praeparatae, Liv.; bene praeparatum pectus, Hor.; adv. phr.: ex praeparato, *by arrangement*, Liv.
praepēdīmentum -i, n. (praepedio), *a hindrance*: Pl.
praepĕdĭo -ire (prae/root ped).
LIT., *to entangle by the feet, shackle, fetter*: praepeditis Numidarum equis, Tac.; Pl.
TRANSF., *to hinder, impede, obstruct*: cum lassitudo ac vulnera fugam praepedissent, Liv.; singultu medios praepediente sonos,

Ov.; praepediri valetudine, *to be hindered by ill-health*, Tac.
praependĕo -ēre, intransit., *to hang before, hang in front*: Caes., Prop.
praepĕs -pĕtis (connected with peto; originally t. t. of augury), *quick in flight, rapidly flying, swift*: praepes avis, Enn.; m. and f. as subst., *a bird*: Ov.; esp. *a bird of good omen*: Liv.; praepetibus pennis se credere caelo, Verg.; praepes deus, *the winged god*—i.e., Cupid, Ov.
praepĭlātus -a -um, *having a ball* or *button in front* (of foils, etc): missilia, Liv.
praepinguis -e, *very fat, very rich*: solum, Verg.; Galba, Suet.; vox, *thick*, Quint.
praepollĕo -ēre. (1) *to be very powerful*: vir virtute praepollens, Liv. (2) *to surpass in power*: Tac.
praepondĕro -are, *to outweigh*; fig.: neque ea volunt praeponderari honestate, Cic.; without object, *to turn the scale*: Luc., Sen.
praepōno -pōnĕre -pŏsŭi -pŏsĭtum, *to put before, place before.*
LIT., in gen.: praeponens ultima primis, Hor. Esp., *to put over, set over as commander*, etc.: aliquem bello, provinciae, navibus, Cic.; militibus, Caes.
TRANSF., *to prefer*: salutem reipublicae vitae suae, Cic.
¶ Hence partic., used as subst., m. **praepŏsĭtus** -i, *a commander*: Cic., Tac.; n. **praepŏsĭtum** -i (translation of προηγμένον), *something to be preferred, something advantageous, but not* (in the Stoic philosophy) *absolutely good*, e.g. *riches*, etc.: Cic.
praeporto -are, *to carry before*: Lucr., Cat.
praepŏsĭtĭo -ōnis, f. (praepono), *a placing before.* Hence (1) as grammat. t. t., *a preposition*: Cic. (2) *a preferring, preference*: Cic.
praepŏsĭtus, partic. from praepono; q.v.
praepossum -posse -pŏtŭi, *to have the chief power*: Tac.
praepostĕrus -a -um, *having the last first, inverted, perverse.* LIT., ordo, Lucr.; verba, Cic. TRANSF., of persons: Sall., Cic.; of things: gratulatio, Cic.; consilia, Cic.
¶ Adv. **praepostĕrē**, *in a reversed order, perversely*: Cic., Plin. L.
praepŏtens -entis, *very powerful*: viri, Cic.; Carthago praepotens terrā marique, Cic.; with abl. instr.: praepotens armis Romanus, Liv.; with genit.: Iuppiter omnium rerum praepotens, *ruling over*, Cic.
praeprŏpĕrantĕr, adv. *very quickly, very hastily*: Lucr.
praeprŏpĕrus -a -um, *exceedingly quick, over-hasty, precipitate*: festinatio, Cic.; celeritas, Liv.; ingenium, Liv.
¶ Adv. **praeprŏpĕrē**, *very hastily, too quickly*: festinare, Liv.; Pl.
praepūtĭum -i, n. *the foreskin*: Juv.
praequam, see prae.
praequĕror -quĕri -questus sum, *to complain beforehand*: Ov.
praerădĭo -are, *to outshine*: Ov.
praerăpĭdus -a -um, *very rapid*: gurges, Liv.; Sen.
praerĭgesco -rĭgescĕre -rĭgŭi, *to grow very stiff*: Tac.
praerĭpĭo -rĭpĕre -rĭpŭi -reptum (prae/rapio). (1) *to snatch before somebody else*: oscula,

Lucr.; arma Minervae, Ov.; alicui laudem destinatam, Cic. (2) *to carry off before the time*: deorum beneficium festinatione, Cic. (3) *to anticipate, forestall*: hostium consilia, Cic.

praerōdo -rōdĕre -rōdi -rōsum, *to gnaw in front, to gnaw off, bite through*: Pl., Hor.

praerŏgātīvus -a -um (praerogo), *asked before others* (for vote, opinion, etc.): centuria, *voting first*, Cic.; omen praerogativum, *the indication given by the early voting*, Cic.

F. as subst. **praerŏgātīva** -ae, *the tribe or century to which the lot fell of voting first in the comitia*: Cic., Liv. TRANSF., (1) *the first century's vote*: Cic. (2) *a previous choice*: Liv. (3) *a sure sign, indication, presage*: triumphi, Cic.; voluntatis, Cic. N. pl. as subst.: Liv.

praerŏgo -are, *to ask before*: sententias, Suet.

praerumpo -rumpĕre -rūpi -ruptum, *to break off in front*: funes, Caes.; Ov.

¶ Hence partic. **praeruptus** -a -um, *broken off*. LIT., of places, *steep, precipitous*: saxa, Cic.; loca, Caes.; Verg., Hor. TRANSF., *headstrong, hasty*: iuvenis animo praeruptus, Tac.; dominatio, *ruthless*, Tac.

¹**praes** praedis, m. (praevideo), *a surety, one who stands bail*. LIT., praedem esse pro aliquo, Cic. L.; praedes dare, Cic. TRANSF., *the property of a security*: ne L. Plancus praedes tuos venderet, Cic.

²**praes**, adv. *at hand*: Pl.

praesaepes (praesaepis) -is, f. **praesaepe** -is, n. and **praesaepĭum** -i, n. (praesaepio), *an enclosure*. (1) *a crib, manger*: Ov.; certum praesaepe, contemptuously=*table*, Hor. (2) *a stall*: Verg., Juv. (3) *a hive*: praesaepibus arcent, Verg. (4) *a haunt, lodging, tavern*: in praesaepibus, Cic.; Pl.

praesaepĭo (-sēpĭo) -saepire -saepsi -saeptum, *to block up in front*: aditūs trabibus, Caes.

praesāgĭo -ire, and **praesāgĭor** -iri, dep. (Pl.), *to presage, forebode, have a presentiment of*: praesagire, id est, futura ante sentire, Cic.; de fine belli, Liv. TRANSF., *to foreshow, presage*: ap. Cic. L.

praesāgītĭo -ōnis, f. (praesagio), *a foreboding, presentiment*: Cic.

praesāgĭum -i, n. (praesagus). (1) *a presage, presentiment, foreboding*: malorum, Tac.; Ov. (2) *a prediction*: Tiberii de Servio Galbā, Tac.; Ov.

praesāgus -a -um. (1) *foreboding*: pectora, Ov.; with genit.: mens praesaga mali, Verg. (2) *predicting*: praesagi ignes fulminis, Verg.; verba, Ov.

praescĭo -scire, *to know beforehand*: Ter., Suet.

praescisco -ĕre, *to learn, find out beforehand*: praesciscere quam quisque eorum provinciam, quem hostem haberet volebat, Liv.; Verg.

praescĭus -a -um, *knowing beforehand, prescient*: corda, Verg.; with genit.: periculorum, Tac.

praescrībo -scrībĕre -scripsi -scriptum, *to write before, set before in writing*.

LIT., sibi nomen, Verg.; auctoritates praescriptae, *the names of senators contained in a decree of the senate*, Cic.

TRANSF., (1) *to put forward or use as a pretext*: Tac. (2) *to outline*: Tac. (3) *to dictate*: Tib. (4) in gen., *to prescribe, ordain,*

define, direct beforehand: iura civibus, Cic.; ne quid ageret, Cic. L.; quid fieri oporteret, Caes.

¶ Hence n. of partic. as subst. **praescriptum** -i, *something written down*. LIT., Sen. TRANSF., *a prescribed limit, regulation, rule*: legum, Cic.; intra praescriptum equitare, Hor.

praescriptĭo -ōnis, f. (praescribo), *a writing before*; hence, *a title, inscription, preamble, introduction*: legis, Cic.

TRANSF., (1) *a precept, rule, order*: rationis, Cic.; Tac. (2) *a pretext*: Caes., Tac.; as legal t. t., *an objection, demurrer*: Quint.

praescriptum -i, n. subst. from praescribo; q.v.

praesĕco -sĕcare -sĕcŭi -sectum, *to cut in front, cut short*: crines, Caes.; Ov.

praesegmĭna -um, n. pl. (praeseco), *clippings, parings*: Pl.

praesens -entis, partic. from praesum; q.v.

praesensĭo -ōnis, f. (praesentio). (1) *a presentiment, foreboding, premonition*: rerum futurarum, Cic. (2) *a preconception*: Cic.

praesentārĭus -a -um (praesens), *at hand, ready*: Pl.

praesentĭa -ae, f. (praesens), *presence*. LIT., alicuius, Cic., Verg.; animi, *presence of mind*, Caes., Cic. TRANSF., (1) of time: in praesentia, *for the present*, Caes., Cic. (2) *effect*: veri, Ov.

praesentĭo -sentire -sensi -sensum, *to feel or perceive beforehand, to have a presentiment of*: animo providere et praesentire, Caes.; futura, Cic.; dolos, Verg.

praesēpes, etc.=praesaepes, etc.; q.v.

praesēpĭo=praesaepio; q.v.

praesertim, adv. (prae/sero), *especially, chiefly*. In gen.: Caes., Cic., Hor. Esp.: praesertim cum, Caes., Cic., etc.; cum praesertim, Cic., Liv., etc.; praesertim si, Cic., Verg.

praesēs -sĭdis (praesideo), *sitting before* (i.e. *to protect, take care of*). Hence, *protecting*: locus, Pl.; dii, Tac.

As subst. (1) *a protector, protectress*: senatus reipublicae, Cic.; templorum, Cic., Liv. (2) *a chief, ruler, president*: praeses belli, *goddess of war* (of Minerva), Verg.; Liv.

praesĭdĕo -sĭdĕre -sēdi -sessum (prae/sedeo), *to sit before*. LIT., Suet. TRANSF., (1) *to watch over, protect, guard*: with dat.: huic imperio, Cic.; urbi, Cic.; foribus caeli (of Janus), Ov.; with acc.: Galliae litus, Tac.; Sall. (2) *to preside over, manage, direct, govern*; with dat.: rebus urbanis, Caes.; with acc.: exercitum, Tac.

¶ Hence partic. **praesĭdens** -entis, m. as subst., *a president, ruler*: Tac.

praesĭdĭārĭus -a -um (praesidium), *on guard*: milites, Liv.

praesĭdĭum -i, n. (praeses), *a sitting before*; hence *a protection, defence*.

LIT., alicui esse praesidio, Cic.; Hor., etc.; as milit. t. t., *guard, escort*: legiones quae praesidio impedimentis erant, Caes.; Cic.

TRANSF., (1) *that which defends, a defence, a protection, help*: classis praesidium provinciae, Cic.; Verg., Hor. Esp. as milit. t. t., *a garrison, guard*: locum praesidio tenere, Caes.; praesidia in urbes inducere, Cic.; oppido imponere, Liv. (2) *a place occupied by a garrison, a post*: cum legio praesidium occupavisset, Caes.; in praesidiis esse, Cic.; praesidium communire, Liv.; fig.: de praesidio et statione vitae decedere, Cic. (3) in gen., *help, assistance, support*: praesidio litterarum, Caes.; magnum sibi praesidium ad beatam vitam comparare, Cic.

praesignĭfĭco -are, *to show* or *announce beforehand*: hominibus futura, Cic.

praesignis -e (signum), *distinguished, remarkable above others*: Ov.

praesŏno -sŏnare -sŏnŭi, *to sound forth*: Ov.

praespargo -ĕre, *to scatter, strew before*: Lucr.

praestābĭlis -e, adj. (with compar.) (praesto), *distinguished, pre-eminent, remarkable*: res magnitudine praestabiles, Cic.; melius fuisse et praestabilius me civem in hac civitate nasci, Cic.; nullam dignitatem praestabiliorem, Cic. Also, in compar., *preferable*: Ter., Cic., Sall.

praestans -antis, partic. from ²praesto; q.v.

praestantĭa -ae, f. (praestans), *superiority, excellence*: si quam praestantiam virtutis, ingenii, fortunae consecuti sunt, Cic.; mentis, Cic.

praesterno -ĕre, *to strew, spread before*: Pl.

praestĕs -stĭtis (²praesto), *protecting*: Lares, Ov.

praestīgĭae -ārum, f. pl. (praestringo), *deception, illusion, juggling*: verborum, Cic.; Pl., Liv.

praestīgĭātor -ōris, m. (praestigiae), *a juggler*: Pl.

praestĭtŭo -stĭtŭĕre -stĭtŭi -stĭtūtum (statuo), *to prescribe, appoint beforehand*: tempus alicui, Cic.; diem operi, Cic.; Pl.

¹praestō, adv. (connected with ²praesto), *present, at hand, here, ready*: ipsum adeo praesto video, Ter.; quod adest praesto, Lucr. Esp. with esse, *to be at hand*, with the notion of *service* or *help*: quaestores consulibus ad ministeria belli praesto essent, Liv.; praesto esse virtutes ut ancillulas, Cic.; saluti tuae, Cic.

²praesto -stāre -stĭti -stĭtum (fut. partic. -stātūrus: Liv.) (1) (prae/sto), *to stand before*. LIT., Luc. TRANSF., *to be outstanding, be distinguished*: inter suos, Cic.; aliquā re, Cic.; with dat., *to surpass, excel*: virtute omnibus, Caes.; Cic., Liv.; with acc.: Liv. Praestat, impers., *it is better, it is preferable*; with infin.: Cic. L., Caes., Verg.; with quam: mori millies praestitit, quam haec pati, Cic. L. (2) transit. (praes/sto), *to become surety* or *guarantee for, answer for, be responsible for*. LIT., damnum emptori, Cic.; ego tibi a vi praestare nihil possum, Cic. L.; de me, Cic.; with acc. and infin.: nullos (praedones) fore quis praestare poterat? Cic. TRANSF., **a**, *to perform, execute, fulfil*: suum munus, Cic.; officium, Caes.; fidem alicui, *to keep one's word*, Cic., Liv.: **b**, *to show, manifest, exhibit*: benevolentiam, Cic. Esp. with se and acc. predicate, *to show oneself, behave oneself as*: se invictum, Ov.; praesta te eum, Cic. L.: **c**, *to offer, present*: terga hosti, Tac.; sententiam, *to give one's opinion*, Cic.

¶ Hence partic. (with compar. and superl.) **praestans** -antis, *excellent, distinguished, eminent*. Of persons: homo prudentiā

praestans Cic.; Aristoteles longe omnibus praestans et ingenio et diligentiā, Cic.; virginibus praestantior omnibus, Ov.; in illis artibus praestantissimus, Cic. Of things: praestanti et singulari fide, Cic.; praestanti corpore Nymphae, Verg.

praestōlor -ari, dep. (connected with ¹praesto), *to wait for, expect*; with dat.: tibi ad forum Aurelium, Cic.; with acc.: aliquem, Pl., Ter.; huius adventum ad Clupeam, Cic.

praestringo -stringĕre -strinxi -strictum, *to bind up, tie up in front*. LIT., faucem laqueo, Ov.; pollices nodo, Tac. TRANSF., *to make blunt* or *dull*: aciem oculorum, Pl., Liv.; fig.: aciem animi or mentis, Cic.; Tac.

praestrŭo -strŭĕre -struxi -structum. (1) *to build in front*; hence, *to block up, render impassable*: aditum montis, Ov. (2) *to build beforehand*; hence, *to prepare*: fraus fidem sibi in parvis praestruit, *gains itself credence in little things*, Liv.

praesŭl -sŭlis, c. (prae/salio), *one who jumps* or *dances before others, a dancer*: Cic.

praesultātor -ōris, m. (praesulto), *one who dances before others, a dancer*: Liv.

praesulto -are (prae/salto), *to leap* or *dance before*: hostium signis, Liv.

praesum -esse -fŭi, *to be before*; hence, *to be over, preside over*. LIT., with dat.: sacris, Cic.; navi faciendae, Cic.; provinciae, populo, Cic.; exercitui, Caes.; in Bruttiis, Liv. TRANSF., *to be the chief person, to take the lead*: temeritati T. Gracchi, Cic.; illi crudelitati, Cic.

¶ Hence partic. (with compar.) **praesens** -entis.

In gen., *present*, in space or in time; *here and now, at hand, now present*: quo praesente, *in whose presence*, Cic.; praesens tecum egi, *in person*, Cic. L.; Pl., Liv., etc.; compar.: Liv.; superl.: Quint. Phrases: praesenti tempore, Ov.; in praesenti (sc. tempore), Cic.; in praesens (tempus), *for the present time*, Cic., Hor.; in rem praesentem, Cic.

Esp. (1) *immediate, not delayed, ready*: pecunia, Pl., Cic.; poena, *immediately following the offence*, Cic.; decretum, *passed instantly*, Liv. (2) *immediately efficacious, effective, powerful*: auxilium, Cic.; compar.: memoria praesentior, *more vivid*, Liv.; with infin.: praesens imo tollere de gradu, Hor. (3) of character, *resolute, determined*: animus, Cic., Liv. (4) *aiding, propitious*: deus, Cic.

praesūmo -sūmĕre -sumpsi -sumptum, *to take beforehand*. LIT., remedia, Tac.; domi dapes, Ov. TRANSF., (1) *to enjoy beforehand, to anticipate*: fortunam principatūs, Tac. (2) *to represent to oneself beforehand*: spe praesumite bellum, Verg.; praesumptum habere, *to suppose, take for granted*, Tac.

¶ Hence partic. **praesumptus** -a -um, *taken for granted, presumed*: suspicio, *a preconceived suspicion*, Tac.

praesūtus -a -um (prae/suo), *sewn over in front*: praesuta foliis hasta, Ov.

praetempto -are, *to feel, try, test beforehand*. LIT., iter baculo, Ov. TRANSF., vires, Ov.

praetendo -tendĕre -tendi -tentum, *to stretch* or *hold out*.

LIT., hastas dextris, Verg.; ramum olivae manu, Verg.; saepem segeti, *to place before*,

Verg.; sermonem decreto, Liv. Hence praetendi, of places, *to lie before* or *in front*: praetentaque Syrtibus arva, Verg.; absol.: tenue praetentum litus, Liv.

TRANSF., *to hold out as a pretext, pretend*: hominis doctissimi nomen tuis immanibus et barbaris moribus, *allege in excuse for*, Cic.; coniugis taedas, Verg.; aliquid seditioni, Liv.

praetento = praetempto; q.v.

praetĕpesco -tĕpescĕre -tĕpŭi, *to glow before-hand*: si praetepuisset amor, Ov.

praeter (prae/suffix -ter; like inter, propter), adv. and prep.

Adv., *except*: nil praeter canna fuit, Ov.; Cic., Hor.; see also praeterquam.

Prep. with acc., *beyond*. LIT., *in space, past, by, beyond*: praeter castra Caesaris suas copias transduxit, Caes.; praeter oculos Lollii haec omnia ferebant, *before the eyes of*, Cic.; Lucr., Ov., etc. TRANSF., (1) *beyond, beside, contrary to*: praeter spem, Pl.; praeter modum, *beyond measure*, Cic.; praeter opinionem, Cic.; praeter naturam, Cic. (2) *beyond, more than*: praeter ceteros laborare, Cic.; Pl., Hor. (3) *except*: omnes praeter Hortensium, Cic.; nihil praeter suum negotium agere, Cic. (4) *besides, in addition to*: ut praeter se denos adduceret, Caes.; Liv.

praetĕrăgo -ĕre, *to drive past, drive by*: equum, Hor.

praeterbĭto -ĕre, *to go by*: Pl.

praeterduco -ĕre, *to lead past*: Pl.

praetĕrĕā. (1) *besides, beyond this, further*: Cic., Verg., etc. (2) *after this, hereafter*: Verg.

praetĕrĕo -ire -ivi and oftener -ii -itum, *to go by, pass by*.

LIT., with or without object: unda praeteriit, Ov.; hortos, Cic.; Verg., Hor. Of time: Ter., Ov., etc.

TRANSF., (1) *to escape the notice of, be unknown to*: non me praeterit, *I am not unaware*, Cic.; Liv. (2) *to pass by, pass over, omit*: nullum genus crudelitatis praeterire, Cic.; ut nulla fere pars orationis silentio praeteriretur, *was unapplauded*, Cic.; caedes praetereo, libidines praetereo, *I do not mention*, Cic.; praeterire non potui quin scriberem ad te, *I could not omit to*, Cic. L.; with infin.: Pl.; Philippus et Marcellus praetereuntur, *are passed over, get nothing*, Caes.; filium fratris (in a will), Cic. (3) *to surpass, outstrip*: iamque hos cursu, iam praeterit illos, Verg.; fig.: virtus tua alios praeterit, Ov.; praeterit modum, *transgresses*, Ov.

¶ Hence partic. **praetĕrĭtus** -a -um, *past, gone by*: tempus, Cic.; anni, Verg. N. pl. as subst. **praetĕrĭta** -orum, *the past*: Caes., Cic.

praetĕrĕquĭto -are, *to ride past, ride by*: Liv.

praeterfĕro -ferre, -tŭli -lātum, *to carry past*. Pass., praeterferri, *to be carried past, to pass*: Liv.

praeterflŭo -flŭĕre, *to flow past, flow by*. LIT., moenia: Liv. TRANSF., nec praeteritam (voluptatem) praeterfluere sinere, *vanish from the recollection*, Cic.

praetergrĕdĭor -grĕdi -gressus sum, dep. (praeter/gradior), *to pass by, go beyond*: castra, Cic. L.; primos suos, Sall.

praeterhāc, *beyond this, besides*: Pl.

praetĕrĭtus -a -um, partic. from praetereo; q.v.

praeterlābor -lābi -lapsus sum, dep. *to glide by, flow by*. LIT., with acc.: tumulum, Verg.; tellurem, Verg. TRANSF., *to slip away*: ante enim (definitio) praeterlabitur quam percepta est, Cic.

praetermĕo -are, *to pass by, go by*: Lucr.

praetermissĭo -ōnis, f. (praetermitto). (1) *a leaving out, omission*: sine ullius (formae) praetermissione, Cic. (2) *a passing over, neglecting*: aedilitatis, Cic.

praetermitto -mittĕre -mīsi -missum, *to let pass*. Hence (1) *to let go by*: diem, Cic. L.; occasiones, Caes. (2) *to neglect, omit*: gratulationem, Cic.; nihil praetermittere, foll. by quin, Cic. Ter. (3) in writing or speaking, *to pass over, omit*: quod dignum memoriā visum, praetermittendum non existimavimus, Caes.; verba, Cic.; tantam rem negligenter, Liv. (4) *to overlook, leave unpunished*: Liv.

praeternāvĭgo -are, *to sail past*: Suet.

praetĕro -ĕre, *to wear down*: Pl.

praeterquam or **praeter quam**, adv. (1) *more than, beyond*: Pl., Ter. (2) after neg., *except*: multitudo coalescere nulla re praeterquam legibus poterat, Liv.; Caes., Cic., Ov. (3) with quod, *apart from the fact that*: Cic., Liv.

praetervectĭo -ōnis, f. (praetervehor), *a passing place*: in praetervectione omnium, Cic.

praetervĕhor -vĕhi -vectus sum.

LIT., *to ride by, sail by, be carried past*: Cic.; with acc.: naves Apolloniam praetervectae, Caes.; classis praetervehens, Liv.

TRANSF., (1) of soldiers, *to march past*: Tac. (2) *to pass by*: locum cum silentio, Cic.; oratio aures vestras praetervecta est, Cic.

praetervŏlo -are, *to fly past*. LIT., quem praetervolat ales, Cic. TRANSF., *to slip by, escape*: praetervolat numerus, Cic.; occasionis opportunitas praetervolat, Liv.

praetexo -texĕre -texŭi -textum, *to weave before, form an edge, border, fringe*.

LIT., purpura saepe tuos fulgens praetexit amictus, Ov.

TRANSF., (1) *to fringe, border*: puppes praetexunt litora, Verg. (2) *to cover, conceal*: culpam nomine coniugi, Verg. (3) *to adorn*: Augusto praetextum nomine templum, Ov.; Cic. (4) *to put forward as a pretext*: cupiditatem triumphi, Cic.

¶ Hence partic. **praetextus** -a -um, *bordered*, esp. of the toga: toga purpurā praetexta, Liv.; toga praetexta, Cic. F. as subst. **praetexta** -ae, *a toga bordered with purple*, worn by the magistrates at Rome and in the Italian municipia and coloniae, and by free-born boys till they assumed the toga virilis: Liv. TRANSF. (sc. fabula), *a tragedy with Roman characters*: Hor.

¶ N. as subst. **praetextum** -i, *a pretence, pretext*: Tac.

praetextātus -a -um (praetexta, from praetexo), *wearing the toga praetexta*: Cic. Hence, of boys, *under age*: Cic., Juv. TRANSF., *veiled*; hence, *licentious*: mores, Juv.

praetextū, abl. sing. as from praetextus, m. (praetexo). (1) *outward appearance, consequence*: Tac. (2) *a pretext*: sub levi verborum praetextu, Liv.

praetĭmeo -ēre, *to fear beforehand*: Pl., Sen.
praetinctus -a -um (prae/tingo), *moistened beforehand*: Ov.
praetor -ōris, m. (for praeitor, from praeeo). LIT., *one who goes before*; hence, *a leader, chief.* Esp. (1) at Rome, *one of the praetors*, the Roman magistrates who helped the consuls by administering justice and by commanding armies, etc. Of these one, the praetor urbanus, judged disputes between Roman citizens; another, the praetor peregrinus, disputes between foreigners. The total number was raised by Sulla to eight, by Caesar to sixteen. The term praetor is also used for propraetor, a magistrate who, after he had been praetor, continued to govern a province or command an army: Cic., Liv. (2) used of other officers in Rome and Italy; of a *consul*, or *dictator*: Liv.; of one of the two chief magistrates at Capua: Cic. (3) outside Italy; the *leader of a league*: Liv.; a *Greek magistrate*: Liv.; *a* sufete *at Carthage*: Nep.
praetōriānus -a -um (praetorium), *belonging to the imperial body-guard, praetorian*: miles, Tac. M. plur. as subst. **praetōriāni** -ōrum, *the praetorian guard*: Tac.
praetōrĭus -a -um (praetor.)
Adj. (1) *relating to the praetor, praetorian*: **a,** of the praetor at Rome: comitia, *election of the praetor*, Liv.; ius, *administered by the praetor*, Cic.; potestas, *office of praetor*, Cic.: **b,** *of a propraetor in the provinces*: domus, Cic. (2) *relating to any general or commander*: navis, *the admiral's ship*, Liv.; imperium, *command of the fleet*, Cic.; porta, *the gate of the camp near the general's tent*, Caes.; cohors praetoria, *the general's body-guard*, Caes.; ironically: scortatorum praetoria cohors, Cic.
Subst. m. **praetōrĭus** -i, *an ex-praetor or man of praetorian rank*: Cic. L., Plin. L.
Subst. n. **praetōrĭum** -i (1) *the official residence of the praetor or propraetor in a province*: Cic.; hence, TRANSF., *a palace*: Juv. (2) *the headquarters in a Roman camp, where the general's tent was, and where the ara, the augurale, and the tribunal were, to which the soldiers were summoned to hear speeches from the general, the officers to hold councils of war*: fit celeriter concursus in praetorium, Caes.; praetorium mittere, dimittere, *to dismiss the council of war*, Liv.; poet., *the cell of the queen-bee*: Verg. TRANSF., *the imperial body-guard*: Tac.
praetorqueo -ēre, *to twist beforehand*: Pl.
praetrĕpĭdo -are, *to tremble exceedingly, to be hasty or impatient*: Cat.
praetrĕpĭdus -a -um, *anxious, restless*: Pers., Suet.
praetrunco -are, *to maim*: Pl.
praetūra -ae, f. (praetor), *the office of praetor at Rome*: praeturā se abdicare, Cic.; Tac.
praeumbro -are, *to overshadow*; fig., *to obscure*: Tac.
praeustus -a -um (prae/uro). (1) *burnt at the end or tip*: hasta praeusta, Liv.; stipites ab summo praeacuti et praeusti, Caes. (2) *frost-bitten*: Liv., Plin.
praevălĕo -vălēre -vălŭi *to be very strong or powerful, to be stronger than others, to prevail,*

to get the upper hand: praevalens populus, Liv.; praevalet pugnā equestri, Tac.
praevălĭdus -a -um, *very strong, very powerful.* LIT., physically: iuvenis, Liv.; Tac., Ov. TRANSF., (1) in influence, etc.: Blaesus, Tac.; urbs, Liv. (2) of things: terra, *too productive*, Verg.; vitia, Tac.
praevārĭcātĭo -ōnis, f. (praevaricor); of an advocate who has an understanding with the opposite party, *collusion*: Cic.
praevārĭcātor -ōris, m. (praevaricor), *an advocate who has a secret understanding with the opposite party, a double dealer*: praevaricator significat eum qui in contrariis causis quasi varie esse positus videatur, Cic.
praevārĭcor -ari, dep. (varico). LIT., *to walk crookedly*: Plin. TRANSF., of an advocate or accuser who has a secret understanding with the other side, *to be guilty of collusion*: Cic., Plin. L.
praevĕhor -vĕhi -vectus sum, *to ride or be carried before or past*: praevectus equo, *riding past*, Verg., Liv.; of missiles: Tac.; of a river: Tac.
praevēlox -ōcis, *very swift*: Plin., Quint.
praevĕnĭo -vĕnire -vēni -ventum, *to come before, anticipate, get the start of*: hostis breviore viā praeventurus erat, Liv.; with acc.: hostem, Liv.; morte praeventus, *overtaken by death*, Liv.; Ov.
praeverro -ĕre, *to sweep before*: veste vias, Ov.
praeverto **(praevorto)** -vertĕre -verti -versum, and **praevertor** -verti -versus sum. (1) of preference: **a,** act., *to put first, take first*: uxorem prae republica, Pl.; pietatem amori tuo, Pl.; Cic., Liv.: **b,** act. intransit. and pass. as middle, *to turn to first*: huic rei, Caes.; illuc praevertamur, Hor. (2) of early action; act. and pass. as middle, *to anticipate*: **a,** *to outstrip*: equo ventos, Verg.: **b,** *to forestall*: quorum usum opportunitas praevertit, Liv.; Pl., Ov.: **c,** *to surprise, preoccupy*: praevertere animos amore, Verg.
praevĭdĕo -vidēre -vīdi -vīsum, *to see before, foresee.* LIT., ictum venientem, Verg.; Ov. TRANSF., republica quam praevideo in summis periculis, Cic. L.; Tac.
praevĭtĭo -are, *to corrupt beforehand*: gurgitem, Ov.
praevĭus -a -um (prae/via), *going before, preceding*: Ov.
praevŏlo -are, *to fly before*: praevolantes grues, Cic.
pragmătĭcus -a -um (πραγματικός), *skilled in civil affairs, state business*, etc.: pragmatici homines, Cic. L. M. as subst. **pragmătĭcus** -i, *a person who supplied orators and advocates with materials for their speeches*: Cic.
prandĕo prandĕre prandi pransum (prandium), *to take lunch*: Pl., Cic. With acc., *to lunch upon*: holus, luscinias, Hor.
¶ Hence perf. partic. in act. sense **pransus** -a -um, *having lunched.* LIT., curatus et pransus (of soldiers), *ready for action, prepared for battle*, Liv.; pransus, potus, *having eaten and drunk well*, Cic.; pransus non avide, Hor. TRANSF., *well-fed*: Cic., Liv.
prandĭum -i, n. (conn. with πρώην), *a late breakfast or lunch*: prandium apparare, Pl.; (alicui) dare, Cic.; aliquem ad prandium invitare, Cic.

pransus -a -um, partic. from prandeo; q.v.

prăsĭnus -a -um (πράσινος), *leek-green*: Plin., Suet., Mart.

prātensis -e (pratum), *of a meadow, growing in a meadow*: fungus, Hor.

prātŭlum -i, n. (dim. of pratum), *a little meadow*: Cic.

prātum -i, n. *a meadow*. LIT., pratorum viriditas, Cic.; Verg. TRANSF., *meadow-grass*: Pl., Ov.

prāvē, adv. from pravus; q.v.

prāvĭtās -ātis, f. (pravus), *crookedness, irregularity, deformity*. LIT., membrorum, Cic.; oris, Cic. TRANSF., (1) *perversity*: Liv. (2) *depravity*: mentis, Cic.; Liv.

prāvus -a -um, adj. (with compar. and superl.), *crooked, irregular, deformed*. LIT., membra, Cic.; Lucr., Hor. TRANSF., (1) *perverse*: Cic., Hor. (2) *depraved, vicious*: Pl., Liv., Tac.
¶ Adv. **prāvē**. (1) *perversely, ill*: Cic., Hor. (2) *viciously*: Liv., Tac.

Praxĭtĕlēs -is and -i, m. (Πραξιτέλης), *a sculptor of Athens, famous for his statues of Aphrodite at Cnidus and of Eros at Thespiae.*
¶ Hence adj. **Praxĭtēlĭus** -a -um, *of Praxiteles.*

prĕcārĭus -a -um (precor), *begged for* or *obtained by entreaty.*
LIT., libertas, Liv.; orare precariam opem, Liv.; Tac. N. abl. as adv. **prĕcārĭo**, *by entreaty*: rogare, Cic.; Pl., Tac.
TRANSF., *uncertain, precarious*: forma, Ov.; imperium, Tac.

prĕcātĭo -ōnis, f. (precor), *a begging, request, prayer*: illa sollemnis comitiorum precatio, Cic.; Liv.

prĕces, *see* prex.

prĕcĭae -ārum, f. *a kind of vine*: Verg.

prĕcor -ari, dep. (prex), *to beg, entreat, request, pray, invoke.*
LIT., with acc. of thing and/or acc. of pers.: deos, Cic.; opem, Liv.; haec precatus sum, Cic.; with ab and abl. of pers.: Liv., Cic.; with ut *or* ne, or plain subj.: precor ab diis ut, Cic.; Hor., Liv., etc.; with acc. and infin.: Ov.; absol.: eum sororem dedisse Prusiae precanti atque oranti, Liv.; used also of things: dextra precans, Verg.
TRANSF., *to wish good* or *evil*: bene, Liv.; male, Cic.; vobis mala, Cic.; Hor.

prĕhendo prehendĕre prĕhendi prĕhensum and syncop., prendo prendĕre prendi prensum (prae/stem of χανδάνω), *to lay hold of, seize, grasp.*
LIT., aliquem manu, Cic.; of the soil: tellus prehendit stirpes, Cic. Esp. (1) *to catch, detain, in order to speak to*: Ter., Cic. L., Verg. (2) *to catch, detect, arrest*: in furto, Pl.; Cic., Liv. (3) *to seize violently, take hasty possession of*: Pharum, Caes.
TRANSF., (1) *to reach*: oras Italiae, Verg. (2) *to take in*, mentally or by the senses: Lucr., Cic.

prĕhenso and oftener **prenso** (freq. of prehendo) -are, *to lay hold of, clutch at.*
LIT., exeuntium manūs, Liv.; genua, Tac. TRANSF., *to canvass for votes*: patres, Liv.; absol.: prensat Galba, Tac.

prēlum -i, n. (premo). (1) *a wine-press* or *olive-press*: Verg. (2) *a clothes-press*: Mart.

prĕmo prĕmĕre pressi pressum, *to press.*
(1) in gen. LIT., ad pectora natos, Verg.;

vestigia alicuius, *to follow in anyone's footsteps*, Tac.; frena dente, *to champ*, Ov.; ore grana, Ov.; humum, *to lie on*, Ov. Sometimes *to make by pressing*: caseum, Verg.; lac, *to make cheese*, Verg. TRANSF., *to touch, hug, keep close to*: forum, Cic.; litus, Hor.; insulam premit amnis, *surrounds*, Ov.
(2) *to press hard, squeeze*. LIT., grave onere pressi, Caes.; Verg., Ov., etc. TRANSF., aere alieno, Caes.; formidine, Verg.; Cic.
(3) *to pursue closely, press upon.* LIT., hostes, Caes.; oppidum obsidione, Caes.; cervum ad retia, *to drive into the nets*, Verg. TRANSF., aliquem criminibus, Ov.; culpam poena comes, Hor.; Cic.
(4) *to suppress, cover, conceal.* LIT., canitiem galeā premimus, Verg.; ossa, *to bury*, Ov.; Hor. TRANSF., me pressit alta quies, Verg.; curam sub corde, Verg.
(5) *to press in.* LIT., dentes in vite, Ov.; presso vestigio, Cic. TRANSF., **a**, *to mark*: rem notā, Ov.: **b**, *to plant*: virgulta per agros, Verg.
(6) *to press down.* LIT., aulaeum, Hor. Sometimes *to make by pressing down*: sulcum, Verg. TRANSF., **a**, *to strike down*: armigerum, Verg.: **b**, *to disparage*, or *slander*: humana omnia, Cic.; superiores, Liv.
(7) *to press together, to close*: oculos, Verg.; collum laqueo, Hor.; quae dilatantur a nobis, Zeno sic premebat, Cic.
(8) *to check, curb.* LIT., equos currentes, *to check*, Verg.; umbram falce, Verg.; sanguinem, Tac. TRANSF., cursum, Cic.; vocem, Verg.; dicione populos, Verg.
¶ Hence partic. **pressus** -a -um, *subdued, measured*: Cic. Esp. of a writer or his style, *compressed, concise*: oratio, Cic.; orator, Cic.; Thucydides verbis pressus, Cic.
¶ Adv. (with compar.) **pressē**. (1) of pronunciation, *distinctly*: presse et aequabiliter et leniter, Cic. (2) of style, *briefly, concisely*: dicere, Cic. (3) *accurately, precisely*: pressius definire, Cic.

prendo=prehendo; q.v.

prensātĭo -ōnis, f. (prenso), *the canvassing for an office*: Cic. L.

prenso=prehenso; q.v.

pressē, adv. from premo; q.v.

pressĭo -ōnis, f. (premo), *leverage* or *means of leverage*: Caes.

presso -are (freq. of premo), *to press*: manu brachia, Hor.; ubera, *to milk*, Ov.

¹**pressus** -a -um, partic. from premo; q.v.

²**pressus** -ūs, m. (premo), *a pressing, pressure*: ponderum, Cic.

prestēr -ēris, m. (πρηστήρ). (1) *a fiery whirlwind* or *a waterspout*: Lucr. (2) *a kind of snake*: Plin., Luc.

prĕtĭōsus -a -um, adj. (with compar. and superl.) (pretium). (1) *costly, precious, of great value*: equus, Cic.; fulvo pretiosior aere, Ov.; res pretiosissimae, Cic., Hence *costly, dear*: Prop. (2) *extravagant, giving a high price for a thing*: emptor, Hor.
¶ Adv. **prĕtĭōsē**, *in a costly manner*: vasa pretiose caelata, Cic.

prĕtĭum -i, n. *worth, value, price.*
LIT., certum pretium constituere, *to fix the price*, Cic. L.; pretium habere, *to be worth something*, Cic.; esse in pretio, *to be prized*, Liv., Ov.; parvi pretii esse, Cic.

TRANSF., (1) operae pretium (with esse, *or* facere), *worth the trouble, worth while*: Cic., Liv., Juv. (2) *prize, reward*: pretium certaminis, Ov.; nullo satis digno morae pretio tempus terunt, Liv.; Verg.; for a crime, *punishment*: et peccare nefas, aut pretium est mori, Hor.; Juv. (3) *a ransom*: Liv. (4) *a bribe*: adduci pretio ad hominem condemnandum, Cic.; Hor.

prex prĕcis (sing. used only in dat., acc., and abl.; plur. more frequent) f. *a request, entreaty.*
LIT., preces adhibere, Cic.; prece humili, Cic.; omnibus precibus petere ut, Caes.; precibus flecti, Verg.; Liv. Esp. *prayer to a god*: Cic., Ov.
TRANSF., (1) *a curse, execration*: omnibus precibus detestari aliquem, Caes.; Hor., Ov. (2) *a kindly wish*: damus alternas accipimusque preces, Ov.

Priămus -i, m. (Πρίαμος), *the last king of Troy, husband of Hecuba, father of Paris, Hector, Cassandra*, etc.
¶ Hence f. subst. **Priămēïs** -ĭdis, *a daughter of Priam*; *Cassandra*: Ov.; m. subst. **Priămĭdēs** -ae, *a son of Priam*: Verg. Adj. **Priămēïus** -a -um, *belonging to Priam*: hospes, *Paris*, Ov.; coniux, *Hecuba*, Ov.

Priāpus -i, m. (Πρίαπος), *the god of gardens and vineyards*: Verg., Hor., Ov. Adj. **Priāpēïus** -a -um.

prīdem, adv. *long ago, long since*: iam pridem, Cic.; non ita pridem, *not very long ago*, Cic.; Lucr., Hor., etc.

pridĭē, adv. (dies), *on the day before.* With acc. or genit. of the day from which the reckoning is taken: pridie eum diem, Cic.; Liv.; pridie eius diei, Caes.; Tac. With quam: pridie quam Athenas veni, Cic. L.

prīmaevus -a -um (primus/aevum), *young, youthful*: Helenor, Verg.

prīmāni -ōrum, m. pl. (primus), *soldiers of the first legion*: Tac.

prīmārĭus -a -um (primus), *in the first rank, distinguished*: vir populi, Cic.; Pl.

prīmĭgĕnus -a -um (primus/geno=gigno), *original, primitive*: Lucr.

prīmĭpīlāris -is, m. (primipilus), *the centurion of the first maniple of the triarii, the chief centurion of a legion*: Sen., Tac.

prīmĭpīlus, *see* ²pilus.

prīmĭtĭae -ārum, f. (primus), *first-fruits.* LIT., Ov.; metallorum, *the minerals first taken out of a mine*, Tac. TRANSF., primitiae iuvenis miserae, Verg.

prīmĭtŭs, adv. *first, for the first time*: Lucr., Verg.

prīmō, adv. from primus; *see* prior.

prīmordĭum -i, n. (primus/ordior), *the first beginning, commencement, origin*: urbis, Liv. Plur.: primordia rerum, Cic.; Tac.; often of *atoms* in Lucr.

prīmōris -e, adj. (primus); nom. sing. not found; *first.*
(1) *foremost, at the tip*: primori in acie versari, Tac.; sumere aliquid digitulis primoribus, *with the tips of the fingers*, Pl.; aliquid primoribus labris attingere, *to treat superficially*, Cic. M. pl. as subst., primores, *the foremost*: cum primores caderent, Liv.
(2) *first in rank, most distinguished*: iuventus, Liv.; Cat., Tac. M. pl. as subst.,

primores, *the most illustrious*: civitatis, Liv.; Hor., etc.

prīmum, adv. from primus; *see* prior.

prīmus, *see* prior.

princeps -cĭpis, adj. (primus/capio), *first, foremost.* LIT., of place: princeps Horatius ibat, Liv.; Caes., Cic., Verg. TRANSF., (1) in time: princeps in proelium ibat, Liv.; Caes., Cic., Hor. (2) in rank: facile princeps, Cic.; Hor.
As subst., c., *leader.* In gen.: belli inferendi, Caes.; coniurationis, Cic.; Verg. Esp. (1) as polit. t. t.: princeps civitatis, Caes., Cic., Liv.; princeps senatūs, *the senator whose name stood first on the censor's list*, Liv.; princeps iuventutis, *a leader among the youth*, of the patricians, Liv., or of the knights, Cic.=*presumptive heir to the imperial throne*: Tac. Princeps, alone, as a title of the Roman emperor: Hor., Ov., Tac. (2) as milit. t. t., plur., principes; originally *the first rank in a Roman army, afterwards the second line, between the* hastati *and* triarii: Liv. In sing., princeps: **a**, *a maniple of the* principes: signum primi principis, Liv.; Cic.: **b**, *a centurion of the* principes: princeps prior, Caes.: **c**, *the centurionship of the* principes: Liv.

princĭpālis -e (princeps). (1) *first; in time, original*: Cic.; in rank, *chief*: Cic. (2) *of a prince*: Tac., Suet. (3) *of the chief place in a Roman camp* (principia): via, *the broad alley which passed through the centre of a Roman camp*, Liv.; porta, Liv.

princĭpātus -ūs, m. (princeps). (1) *the first place, pre-eminence*: tenere principatum sententiae, *to have the right to vote first*, Cic. Esp. *first rank in state* or *army*; *rule, dominion*: Cassio principatum dari, Cic.; principatum in civitate obtinere, Cic.; Caes., Tac. (2) *a beginning, origin*: Cic.

princĭpĭālis -e (principium), *original*; *of the beginning*, or *of the atoms*: Lucr.

princĭpĭum -i, n. (princeps).
(1) *a beginning, origin*, LIT., principium dicendi, Cic.; principio belli, Liv.; ducere principium ab, *to begin from*, Ov.; principio, *in the beginning, at first*, Cic., Lucr., Verg., etc.; a principio, Cic.; in principio, Cic. TRANSF., **a**, *a groundwork, foundation*: id est principium urbis, Cic.; plur., principia, *the elements, first principles*: iuris, Cic.: **b**, *the tribe* or *curia which voted first*: Faucia curia fuit principium, Liv.; also *the right to vote first*: Liv.: **c**, *the beginner, founder*: moris, Ov.
(2) plur. as milit. t. t. **princĭpĭa** -ōrum: **a**, *the front ranks*: Ter., Sall., Liv.: **b**, *the chief place in a camp, with the tents of the general and tribunes*; *the headquarters*: Nep., Liv., Tac.

prĭŏr prius, genit. -ōris, compar., and **prīmus** -a -um, superl. (connected with priscus), *former, first.*
Compar. **prĭŏr**, *fore, former.* (1) of place: pedes, Nep.; Caes., Cic. (2) of time: prioribus comitiis, Cic.; consul anni prioris, Liv.; priore aestate, *in the previous summer*, Cic. M. pl. as subst., priores -um, *ancestors*: Verg., Ov. (3) *of importance, higher*: res nulla prior potiorque visa est, Liv.; ut nemo haberetur prior, Liv.
N. acc. as adv. **prĭŭs**. (1) *before, previously*:

Cic., Liv., Verg. Esp. foll. by quam, or as one word, **priusquam**, *before*, conj.; usually with indic., or with subj. to denote a purpose of anticipation or prevention: Caes., Cic., Liv., etc. (2) *sooner, rather*: Caes., Cic., Liv. (3) *formerly, in former times*: Cat., Prop.

Superl. **primus** -a -um, *first, foremost*. (1) of place: Eburonum fines, Caes.; primus labris, *with the tips of the lips*, Cic. M. pl. as subst., primi, *the foremost*: Caes., Sall. (2) of time: primae litterae, Cic.; primis ab annis, Verg.; primā nocte, *in the first part of the night*, Caes.; with quisque, *the very first*: Cic., Liv. N. pl. as subst., prima, *the beginning*: Liv. N. sing. in phrases: a primo, *from the beginning*, Pl., Cic.; in primo, *at the beginning*, Cic., Liv. (3) of rank, station, etc., *first, most distinguished*: homines primi, Cic.; comitia prima (i.e., centuriata and tributa), Cic.; prima tenere, *to hold the first place*, Verg. Esp. partes primae, *or* simply, primae, *the leading part* (*on the stage*): primas agere, Ter., Cic.; dare, Cic. Phrases: ad prima, Verg.; in primis, *especially*, Cic.

N. acc. as adv. **primum**. (1) *at first*; esp. followed by deinde, tum, etc.: Caes., Cic., Hor., Liv. (2) *for the first time*: quo die primum convocati sumus, Cic.; Hor., Liv. (3) with ut, ubi, quam, simulae, *as soon as*: Cic.

N. abl. as adv. **primo**, *at first*: Cic., etc. Esp. followed by deinde, post, etc.: Caes., Cic., Liv.

priscus -a -um. (1) *ancient, antique*: priscis viris, Cic.; Tarquinius Priscus, *the first of his line*, Liv. Esp. *old-fashioned, venerable, belonging to the good old times*: priscam imitari severitatem, Cic.; Verg., Hor. (2) *former, previous*: Venus, Hor.; nomen, Ov.

¶ Adv. **priscē**, *in the old-fashioned way, sternly, severely*: agere, Cic.

pristinus -a -um (cf. priscus, primus), *former, previous, earlier*. In gen.: dignitas, Cic.; in pristinum statum redire, Caes.; Verg., Liv. Esp. (1) *just past, of yesterday*: diei pristini, Caes. (2) *old-fashioned*: Pl.

prius, see prior.

privatim, adv. (privatus). (1) *privately, as a private person, in private life*: privatim aliquid gerere, Cic.; Caes., etc. (2) *at home*: privatim se tenere, Liv.; Pl.

privatio -ōnis, f. (privo), *a freeing from*: doloris, Cic.

privatus -a -um, partic. from privo; q.v.

Privernum -i, n. *a town in Latium* (now *Piperno*).

¶ Hence adj. **Privernas** -ātis, *of Privernum*: Cic.

privigna -ae, f. (privignus), *a stepdaughter*: Cic. L.

privignus -i, m. (=privigenus; privus/gigno; *one begotten separately*), *a stepson*: Cic., Hor. In plur., *stepchildren*: Hor.

privilegium -i, n. (privus/lex), *a law relating to one person only, a special law, private law*: privilegium ferre, inrogare, Cic.

privo -are (privus). (1) in a bad sense, *to strip, deprive of*: aliquem vitā, Cic.; Lucr., Ov., etc. (2) in a good sense, *to free from*: aliquem dolore, Lucr., Cic.; Hor.

¶ Hence partic. **privatus** -a -um, as adj.,

private. LIT., (1) of things: privati et separati agri, Caes.; vita, Cic.; n. as subst.: in privato, *in private*, Liv.; in privatum vendere, *for private use*, Liv.; tributum ex privato conferre, *from one's private property*, Liv. (2) of persons: vir privatus, Cic., and m. as subst., privatus, *a private person*, Pl., Caes., Cic.; mulier, Hor. Esp. in imperial times, *not belonging to the royal family*: Tac. TRANSF., *ordinary*: carmina, Hor.

privus -a -um, *single, every*: in dies privos, Lucr. Used distributively, *one each*: bubus privis binisque tunicis donati, Liv. (2) *particular, special, one's own*: priva triremis, Hor.; Juv. (3) *deprived of*, with genit.: Sall.

¹**pro** (connected with πρό), adv. and prep.

Adv., only in phrases proquam, prout; q.v.

Prep., with abl. LIT., of space. (1) *before, in front of*: sedens pro aede, Cic.; Caesar pro castris suas copias produxit, Caes.; pro tribunali, *on the front of, on*, Cic.; Liv., etc. TRANSF., *for, on behalf of, in favour of*: hoc non modo non pro me, sed contra me est, Cic.; dimicare pro legibus, Cic. (2) *in place of, for*: ego ibo pro te, Pl.; pro consule, pro quaestore, Cic. (later as one word, proconsul, etc.). (3) *like, as good as*: pro damnato esse, *as good as condemned*, Cic.; se pro cive gerere, *to behave as a citizen*, Cic.; omnia pro infecto sint, Liv.; pro eo ac, ac si, quasi, *as if*, Cic. (4) *for, as a reward for*: pro meritis gratiam referre, Caes.; aliquem pro scelere ulcisci, Caes.; Cic., Liv., etc. (5) *in proportion to, according to, conformably with*: pro multitudine hominum, Caes.; pro caritate reipublicae, Cic.; agere pro viribus, Cic.; pro virili parte, *to the best of one's abilities*, Cic.; pro tempore et re, *as the time and circumstances demanded*, Caes.; pro mea parte, *for my part*, Cic.; pro se quisque, *each one according to his strength*, Cic.; ratā parte *or* pro ratā, *in proportion*, Caes.; pro eo quantum (or ut), *in proportion as*, Cic. (6) *by virtue of*: pro imperio, Ter., Liv.

²**pro!** (**proh!**), interj. *oh! ah!* With nom., voc., or acc.: pro dii immortales, Cic.; pro deum atque hominum fidem! Cic.; pro sancte Iuppiter, Cic.; Ter., Hor., etc.

proagorus -i, m. (προήγορος), *the chief magistrate in certain Sicilian cities*: Cic.

proavia -ae, f. *a great-grandmother*: Tac., Suet.

proavitus -a -um (proavus), *of a great-grandfather, ancestral*: regna, Ov.

proavus -i, m. *a great-grandfather*: Cic. TRANSF., *an ancestor, forefather*: Cic. L., Hor., Ov.

probabilis -e, adj. (with compar.) (probo). (1) *probable, credible, not impossible*: ratio, Cic.; mendacium, Liv. (2) *acceptable, worthy of approval, good*: probabilior populo orator, Cic.; vir ingenio sane probabili, Cic.; Liv.

Adv. (with compar.) **probabiliter**, *probably, credibly*: dicere, Cic.; probabilius accusare, Cic.; Liv.

probabilitas -ātis, f. (probabilis), *probability, credibility*: captiosa, Cic.

probatio -ōnis, f. (probo). (1) *a proving, trial, examination*: athletarum, Cic. (2) *an approving, approval*: Cic. (3) *proof, demonstration*: Quint.

prŏbātor -ōris, m. (probo), *one who approves, an approver*: facti, Cic.; Ov.

prŏbātus -a -um, partic. from probo; q.v.

prŏbē, adv. from probus; q.v.

prŏbĭtās -ātis, f. (probus), *honesty, uprightness*: Cic., Juv., Tac.

prŏbo -are (probus), *to make* or *find good*.
Hence (**1**) *to approve, pronounce good*: opera quae locassent, Liv.; domum tuam perspexi atque vehementer probavi, Cic. L.; consilium, Cic.; causam et hominem, Caes.; aliquem iudicem, Cic.
(**2**) *to judge by a certain standard*: amicitias utilitate, Ov.; Pl.
(**3**) *to recommend as good*: alicui libros oratorios, Cic. L.; se probare alicui, *to recommend oneself to someone*, Cic.; in pass.: probari alicui, *to appear worthy of approval*, Cic.
(**4**) *to show, prove, demonstrate*: crimen, causam, Cic.; with acc. and infin.: probare iudicibus Verrem pecunias cepisse, Cic.; Caes.
¶ Hence partic. (with compar. and superl.) **prŏbātus** -a -um. (**1**) *found good, approved*: ceterarum homines artium spectati et probati, Cic.; femina probatissima, Cic. (**2**) *acceptable*: ut nemo probatior primoribus patrum esset, Liv.; probatissimus alicui, Cic.

probrōsus -a -um (probrum), *shameful, disgraceful, infamous*: carmen, Tac.; Hor.; of persons: Tac., Suet.

probrum -i, n. (profero), *abuse, reproach*. LIT., alicui probrum obiectare, Cic.; probra iactare, ingerere, Liv.; Ov., Tac. TRANSF., (**1**) *ground for reproach, disgrace*, esp. in dat.: probro esse, Cic.; haberi, Sall. (**2**) *infamous conduct*: emergere ex paternis probris ac vitiis, Cic.; Pl., Ov., etc. Esp. *unchastity*: probri insimulasti pudicissimam feminam, Cic.

prŏbus -a -um, *good, excellent, fine*. (**1**) *good of its* (or *one's*) *kind*: argentum, Pl., Liv.; navigium, Cic. (**2**) *morally good, upright, virtuous, honourable*: filius, Cic.; Pl., Ter.
¶ Hence adv. **prŏbē**, *well, rightly, fitly, properly, excellently*: scire, nosse, meminisse, Cic.; de Servio probe dicis, Cic.; hoc probe stabilito et fixo, Cic.

Prŏca (Prŏcās) -ae, m. *an old king of Alba*.

prŏcācĭtās -ātis, f. (procax), *shamelessness, impudence*: Cic.

prŏcax -cācis (proco), *shameless, bold, impudent, importunate*. LIT., of persons: in lacessendo, Cic.; ingenio, Tac. TRANSF., of things: sermo, Sall.; scripta, Tac.; auster, *blustering*, Verg.
Adv. (with compar.) **prŏcācĭtĕr**, *shamelessly, impudently*: Liv., Tac.

prŏcēdo -cēdĕre -cessi -cessum, *to go forth.*
Hence (**1**) *to go ahead, to proceed*. LIT., ad forum, Pl. Esp. as milit. t. t., *to advance*: lente atque paulatim, Caes.; ad dimicandum, Liv.; of ships: quantum naves processissent, Caes. TRANSF., *to advance, progress*: magna pars operis Caesaris processerat, Caes.; in philosophiā, Cic.; in dando et credendo longius procedere, *to go too far*, Cic.; eo processit vecordiae ut, *he went to such a pitch of madness that*, Sall.; of time: dies procedens, Cic.; si (puer) aetate processerit, Cic.; multum diei processerat, Sall.

(**2**) *to come out*. LIT., e tabernaculo in solem, Cic.; alicui obviam procedere, *to go out to meet*, Cic.; in medium, Cic.; in contionem, Liv.; castris, Verg. TRANSF., of actions, etc., *to turn out in a certain way, to result*: si bene processit, Cic.; alicui bene, pulcherrime, Cic.; and absol., *to turn out well, to prosper*: si processit, Cic.; consilia alicui, Liv.; Pl., Tac.
(**3**) *to come on in succession*. LIT., Liv. TRANSF., stipendia, aera alicui procedunt, *mount up*, Liv.; of time: magni menses, Verg.

prŏcella -ae, f. (procello), *a storm, tempest, gale.*
LIT., nimbi, procellae, turbines, Cic.; Lucr., Verg., etc.
TRANSF., (**1**) *a sudden charge of cavalry, onset, wave*: primam procellam eruptionis sustinere non posse, Liv.; Tac. (**2**) in gen.: procellae insidiarum, Cic.; seditionum, Liv.; procellam temporis devitare, Cic.

prŏcello -ĕre (pro/cello), *to throw forward, cast down*: Pl.

prŏcellōsus -a -um (procella), *stormy, tempestuous*: Verg., Liv.

prŏcer -ĕris, m. *a chief*; usually plur. **prŏcĕres** -um, m. *chiefs, nobles, princes*: audiebam enim nostros proceres clamantes, Cic. L.; Verg., Liv.

prŏcērĭtās -ātis, f. (procerus), *height*. LIT., cameli adiuvantur proceritate collorum, *by the length of their necks*, Cic.; arborum, Cic. TRANSF., *length* (in rhythm and pronunciation): pedum, Cic.

prŏcērus -a -um, adj. (with compar. and superl.), *tall, long.*
LIT., collum, rostrum, Cic.; procerissima populus, Cic.; Verg., Liv., Tac.
TRANSF., (**1**) *upraised*: palmae, Cat. (**2**) in rhythm and pronunciation, *long*: procerior quidam numerus, Cic.
¶ Compar. adv. **prŏcērĭus**, *farther forward*: bracchium procerius proiectum, Cic.

prŏcessĭo -ōnis, f. (procedo), *a (military) advance*: Cic.

prŏcessus -ūs, m. (procedo), *a going forth, advance, progress*: gradus et quasi processus dicendi, Cic.; tantos progressus efficiebat ut, Cic.; Verg., Ov.

Prŏchўta -ae, f. and **Prŏchўtē** -ēs, f. (Προχύτη), *an island on the coast of Campania* (now *Procida*).

prŏcĭdo -cidĕre -cĭdi (pro/cado), *to fall down forwards, fall forward*; of persons: praeceps procidit ante proram, Liv.; of things: cupressus, Hor.

prŏcinctū, abl. as from procinctus, m. (procingo), *a being girded*. Hence, *a being equipped for battle, readiness for battle*: in procinctu ac castris habiti, Tac.; testamentum in procinctu facere, *on the battlefield*, Cic.

proclāmātor -ōris, m. (proclamo), *a bawler, vociferator* (of a bad advocate): Cic.

proclāmo -are, *to call out, cry out*; with acc. and infin.: se filiam iure caesam iudicare, Liv.; pro aliquo (contemptuously of an advocate), *to defend a person*, Liv.; Cic., Verg.

prŏclīno -are, *to bend over, incline forwards*: mare in litora, Ov.; adiuvare rem proclinatam, *tottering to its fall*, Caes.

prōclīvis -e and **prōclīvus** -a -um, adj. (with compar.) (pro/clivus), *inclined forwards.* LIT., *sloping downwards*: via proclivis, Liv.; n. as subst.: per proclive, *downwards*, Liv.; n. acc. as adv.: prōclīvĕ, *downwards*, Lucr., Cic. TRANSF., (**1**) *going downwards*: proclivi cursu et facili delabi, Cic. (**2**) *inclined to, ready to, prone to*: ad morbum, Cic.; ad comitatem, Cic. (**3**) *easy to do*: illa facilia, proclivia, iucunda, Cic.; alicui est proclive, with infin., Caes.; dictu proclive est, *it is easy to say*, Cic. N. acc. of compar. as adv., proclivius: labi verba, Cic.; Lucr.

prōclīvitās -ātis, f. (proclivis), *a slope.* TRANSF., *inclination, tendency, proneness*: ad morbos, Cic.

prōclīvus=proclivis; q.v.

Procnē (Prognē) -ēs, f. (Πρόκνη), *daughter of Pandion, sister of Philomela, and wife of Tereus; changed into a swallow.* TRANSF., *a swallow*: Verg.

prōco -are and **prōcor** -ari, dep. *to ask, demand*: Cic.

prōconsul (also **prō cōnsŭle**) -sŭlis, m. *a proconsul, one who serves as a consul* (esp. after having been a consul), in command of an army, or as governor of a province: Caes., Cic., Liv.

prōconsŭlāris -e (pronconsul), *of a proconsul, proconsular*: Liv., Tac.

prōconsŭlātus -ūs, m. (proconsul), *the office of proconsul*: Tac., Suet.

prōcrāstinātio -ōnis, f. (procrastino), *a putting off from day to day, procrastination*: Cic.

prōcrāstino -are (pro/crastinus), *to put off till tomorrow, defer*: rem, Cic.

prōcrĕātio -ōnis, f. (procero), *begetting, procreation*: Cic.

prōcrĕātor -ōris, m. (procreo), *a begetter*: procreatores=parents, Cic.; mundi, *creator*, Cic.

prōcrĕātrix -īcis, f. (procreator), *a mother.* TRANSF., *artium*, Cic.

prōcrĕo -are, *to beget.* LIT., *of living creatures*: de matre filios, Cic.; multiplices fetus, Cic. TRANSF., *to produce, cause, make*: inter arma civium (tribunatum) procreatum, Cic.

prōcresco -ĕre. (**1**) *to come forth, arise*: Lucr. (**2**) *to increase*: Lucr.

Procrustēs -ae, m. (Προκρούστης), *a robber in Attica, who tied his prisoners to a bed, stretching the limbs of those shorter than the bed, and mutilating those who were taller; killed by Theseus.*

prōcŭbo -are, *to lie stretched out, to lie along*: ubi saxea procubet umbra, Verg.

prōcūdo -cūdĕre -cūdi -cūsum, *to hammer out, to forge.* LIT., enses, Hor.; Lucr., Verg. TRANSF., linguam, *to form, train*, Cic.; ignem, *to produce*, Lucr.

prōcŭl, adv. (procello). LIT., *far; at, to, or from a distance*: non procul, sed hic, Cic.; procul hinc, Pl., Ter.; procul a terra abripi, Cic.; with abl. alone: procul coetu hominum, Liv.; urbe, Ov. TRANSF., *far, far away*: homines procul errant, Sall.; haud procul est quin, Liv.; procul ab omni metu, Cic.; procul dubio, *without doubt*, Liv.; of time: haud procul occasu solis, *not long before*, Liv.

prōculco -are (pro/calco), *to tread, trample*

down. LIT., is (aper) modo crescentes segetes proculcat in herba, Ov.; Liv. TRANSF., senatum, Tac.

Prōcŭlēius -i, m. *a Roman knight, friend of Augustus.*

prōcumbo -cumbĕre -cŭbŭi -cŭbĭtum. (**1**) *to lean* or *bend forward*: olli certamine summo procumbunt (of rowers), Verg.; tigna secundum naturam fluminis, Caes. (**2**) *to fall down, sink down.* LIT., of persons: procumbere alicui ad pedes, Caes.; ad genua alicuius, Liv.; vulneribus confectum procumbere, Caes.; of things: frumenta imbribus procubuerant, *were laid low*, Caes. TRANSF., *to sink, fall*: res procubuere meae, Ov.

prōcūrātio -ōnis, f. (procuro), *a taking care of, management, administration.* In gen., annonae, reipublicae, Cic.; mearum rerum, Cic. L. Esp. (**1**) *under the empire, the office of imperial procurator*: Tac. (**2**) *a religious act for the propitiation of an offended deity*: ut sue plena procuratio fieret, Cic.; Liv., Tac.

prōcūrātor -ōris, m. (procuro), *a manager, agent, factor.* In gen.: regni, *a viceroy*, Caes.; with genit. of person: procurator P. Quinctii, Cic. Esp. (**1**) *under the empire, an officer who collected imperial revenue and sometimes governed part of a province*: procurator Caesaris, Tac.; Iudaeae, Tac. (**2**) *a bailiff*: Cic.

procūrātrix -trīcis, f. (procurator), *she that governs*; fig.: sapientia totius hominis procuratrix, Cic.

prōcūro -are, *to take care of, look after.* In gen.: aliquem, Pl.; corpora, Verg. Esp. (**1**) *to manage, administer anyone's affairs*: alicuius negotia, Cic.; hereditatem, Cic. L. (**2**) *under the empire, to be a procurator*: Plin. L. (**3**) *to offer sacrifice in order to avert an evil omen*: monstra, Cic.; prodigia, Cic.

prōcurro -currĕre -curri and -cŭcurri -cursum, *to run forward.* LIT., of persons: ex castris, Caes.; ad repellendum hostem, Caes.; in vias, Liv.; Verg. TRANSF., of places, *to project, jut out, run forward*: infelix saxis in procurrentibus haesit, Verg.; terra procurrit in aequor, Ov.

prōcursātio -ōnis, f. (procurso), *a running forward, charge, skirmishing*: velitum, Liv.

prōcursātor -ōris, m. (procurso), *one who runs forward*; plur. as milit. t. t.: procursatores, *skirmishers*, Liv.

prōcurso -are, *to run forward, spring forward*; as milit. t. t., *to skirmish*: Liv.

prōcursus -ūs, m. (procurro), *a running forward*; esp. in military language, *an advance, charge*: procursu militum, Liv.

prōcurvus -a -um, *bent forward, curved forward*: falx, Verg.

¹**prŏcus** -i, m.=procer; q.v., Cic.

²**prŏcus** -i, m. (**1**) *a wooer, suitor*: Verg., Hor., etc. (**2**) *a canvasser*: impudentes proci, Cic.

Prŏcўōn -ōnis, (Προκύων), *a star which rises before the Dog-star*: Cic.

prōdĕambŭlo -are, *to walk about outside*: Ter.

prōdĕo -ire -ii -ĭtum. (**1**) *to advance, go forward.* LIT., longius, Caes.; Cic. L., Verg. TRANSF., **a**, *to project*: rupes prodit in aequor, Verg.: **b**, sumptu extra modum, *to exceed the mark*, Cic.

(2) *to come out, appear.* LIT., obviam mihi, Cic.; prodire ex portu, Caes.; in publicum, Cic. TRANSF., **a**, *to appear, show itself*: consuetudo prodire coepit, Cic.: **b**, *to turn out, appear as*: prodis ex iudice Dama turpis, Hor.

prŏdĭco -dīcĕre -dixi -dictum, *to fix for a later time, put off*: diem in Quirinalia, Cic.

prŏdictātor -ōris, m. *one who acts as dictator*: Liv.

prōdĭgē, adv. from prodigus; q.v.

prōdĭgentĭa -ae, f. (prodigo), *profusion, prodigality*: Tac.

prōdĭgĭālis -e (prodigium), *dealing in wonders*: Pl.

¶ Adv. **prōdĭgĭālĭtĕr**, *strangely, wonderfully*: Hor.

prōdĭgĭōsus -a -um (prodigium), *unnatural, strange, wonderful*: Ov., Tac.

prōdĭgĭum -i, n. *a prodigy, portent, ominous sign.*
LIT., multa prodigia eius vim declarant, Cic.; accipere in prodigium, Tac.; Verg.
TRANSF., (1) *an enormity, an unnatural thing*: prodigium videbatur civitatem frumentum improbare, suum probare, Cic. (2) *a monster*: prodigium triplex, Cerberus, Ov.; fatali portentum prodigiumque reipublicae (of Clodius), Cic.

prōdĭgo -ĭgĕre -ēgi -actum (pro/ago), *to drive forth*: sues, Varr. TRANSF., *to spend, waste*: aliena, Sall.; Suet., Tac.

prōdĭgus -a -um (prodigo), *prodigal, profuse, extravagant.*
LIT., Cic.; with genit.: aeris, Hor.; fig., with genit.: animae, *not sparing his own life*, Hor.; arcani, *revealing a secret*, Hor.; with in and the abl.: in honoribus decernendis nimius et tamquam prodigus, Cic.
TRANSF., *rich, abounding in*: locus prodigus herbae, Hor.

¶ Adv. **prōdĭgē**, *profusely*: Cic.

prōdĭtĭo -ōnis, f. (prodo), *a betraying, betrayal, treason*: amicitiarum proditiones et rerum publicarum, Cic.

prōdĭtor -ōris, m. (prodo), *a betrayer, traitor*: consulis, Cic.; risus latentis puellae proditor, Hor.; exercitus proditor disciplinae, Liv.

prōdo -dĕre -dĭdi -dĭtum.
(1) *to put forth, bring forth.* LIT., fumoso condita vina cado, Ov.; suspiria pectore, Ov. TRANSF., **a**, *to show*: crimen vultu, Ov.; exemplum, Liv.: **b**, *to proclaim as elected, to appoint*: flaminem, interregem, Cic.: **c**, *to publish*: decretum, Cic.; quae scriptores prodiderunt, Cic.
(2) *to forsake, to betray*: conscios, Cic.; classem praedonibus, Cic.; aliquem ad mortem, Verg.; utilitatem communem, Cic.; patriam, Cic.
(3) *to hand over, deliver, transmit*: sacra suis posteris, Cic.; esp. in writing: memoriae prodere, *to commit to writing*, Cic.; genus, Verg.

prōdŏcĕo -ēre, *to teach, inculcate*: Hor.

prodrŏmus -i, m. (πρόδρομος), *a forerunner*: Cic.

prōdūco -dūcĕre -duxi -ductum.
LIT., *to bring forward, bring out, extend*: unam navem longius, Caes.; equos, iumenta, Caes.; copias pro castris, Caes.; aliquem in contionem, Cic., Liv.; aliquem capite involuto ad necem, Cic.; aliquem funere,

Verg.; aliquem dolo in proelium, Nep.; ferrum incude, *to draw out*, Juv.
TRANSF., (1) *to bring forward*: **a**, into existence, *to produce*: nova (vocabula) quae genitor produxerit usus, Hor.: **b**, to maturity, *to bring up*: subolem, Hor.; of plants: arborem, Hor.: **c**, to knowledge, *to divulge, bring to light*: occulta ad patres crimina, Juv.: **d**, in gen., *to advance, promote*: aliquem ad dignitatem, Cic.; Liv. (2) in pronunciation, *to lengthen out, make long*: litteram, Cic.; syllabam, Ov. (3) in time: **a**, *to prolong, continue*: sermonem longius in multam noctem, Cic.; cenam, Hor.: **b**, *to put off, postpone*: rem in hiemem, Caes.; condicionibus hunc, quoad potest, producit, Cic.

¶ Hence partic. (with compar.) **prōductus** -a -um, *extended, lengthened, prolonged* in space or time: productiore cornu sinistro, Tac.; quinto productior actu fabula, Hor.; of syllables, *long* (in pronunciation): (syllaba) producta atque longa, Cic.

¶ N. pl. as subst. **prōducta** -ōrum (τὰ προηγμένα), *preferable things* (in the Stoic philosophy): Cic.

¶ Adv. **prōductē**, *in a lengthened manner, long* (of pronunciation): producte dici, Cic.

prōductĭo -ōnis, f. (produco), *an extending, lengthening*; of a syllable in pronunciation: Cic.; in time: temporis, *prolonging*, Cic.

prōductus -a -um, partic. from produco; q.v.

proelĭāris -e (proelium), *of battle*: Pl.

proelĭātor -ōris, m. (proelior), *a warrior, combatant*: Tac.

proelĭor -ari, dep. (proelium), *to give battle, fight.* LIT., ad Syracusas, Cic.; pedibus, Caes. TRANSF., vehementer proeliatus sum, *have striven*, Cic. L.

proelĭum -i, n. *a battle, fight.*
LIT., a physical combat: proelium committere Caes., Cic., Liv.; facere, Cic.; redintegrare, Caes.; inire, Liv.; proelio abstinere, Caes.; of animals, or winds: Verg.
TRANSF., (1) abstr., *strife*: proelia meā causā sustinere, Cic. L.; Ov. (2) plur.: proelia, *fighters, combatants*, Prop.

Proetus -i, m. (Προῖτος), *king of Tiryns, brother of Acrisius.*
¶ Hence subst. **Proetus** -ĭdis, f. *a daughter of Proetus*; plur., **Proetĭdes**, *the daughters of Proetus, who were punished with madness, and imagined themselves to be cows.*

prŏfāno -are (profanus), *to profane, desecrate*: sacra, Liv.; festum, Ov.

prŏfānus -a -um (pro/fanum), *lying before a temple, i.e. outside it*; hence, *not sacred, ordinary, common, profane.*
LIT., locus, Cic.; bubo, *of evil omen*, Ov.; vulgus, *uninitiated*, Hor.; procul este, profani, Verg. N. as subst.: Liv.
TRANSF., *impious*: verba, Ov.

prŏfectĭo -ōnis, f. (proficiscor), *a departure.* LIT., Caes., Cic. TRANSF., *source, origin*: pecuniae, Cic.

prŏfecto, adv. (pro/factus), *truly, really, indeed*: Cic., Hor., etc.

prŏfĕro -ferre -tŭli -lātum.
(1) *to bring forth* (from a place). LIT., nummos ex arca, Cic.; pecuniam alicui, *to offer*, Cic.; arma tormentaque ex oppido, Caes.; in conspectum liberos, Caes. TRANSF., **a**, of writings, *to publish, make known*:

orationem, Cic.: **b**, *to bring to light, reveal*: aliquid in medium, Cic.; in aspectum lucemque, Cic.; artem, Cic.: **c**, *to bring forward, produce, cite, mention*: testes, Cic.; nominatim multos, Cic.; exempla omnium nota, Cic.

(2) *to advance, bring forward*. LIT., signa, *to march on*, Liv.; inde castra, Liv.; digitum, Cic.; caput, Ov. TRANSF., *to impel*: Cic.

(3) *to enlarge, to extend*. LIT., aggerem, Caes.; fines agri publici paulatim, Liv.; fines officiorum paulo longius, Cic. TRANSF., in time, *to extend, lengthen*: beatam vitam usque ad rogum, Cic.; also *to put off, postpone*: diem auctionis, Cic.

professĭo -ōnis, f. (profiteor), *acknowledgment, declaration, profession*.

LIT., in gen.: bene dicendi, Cic. Esp. *public declaration of one's name, property, occupation*, etc.: haec pecunia ex eo genere est, ut professione non egeat, Cic.

TRANSF., (1) *a register of persons and their property*: Cic. (2) *an occupation, art, profession*: Suet.

professŏr -ōris, m. (profiteor), *an authority, an expert*: Quint.

professōrĭus -a -um (professor), *authoritative*: Tac.

prŏfessus -a -um, partic. from profiteor; q.v.

prŏfestus -a -um, *not kept as a festival, common*: dies, Pl., Hor., Liv.

prŏfĭcĭo -fĭcĕre -fēci -fectum (pro/facio). (1) of persons, *to make progress, advance, gain ground, get an advantage*: nihil in oppugnatione, Caes.; aliquid in philosophia, Cic. (2) of things, *to be of use, to assist, help*: nulla res tantum ad dicendum proficit, quantum scriptio, Cic.; of medical remedies: herbā proficiente nihil, Hor.; Liv., Ov.

prŏfĭciscor -ficisci -fectus sum (pro/facio), *to start forward, set out, depart*.

LIT., ex portu, Caes.; ad, *or* contra, hostem, Caes.; Puteolos, Cic.; cum exercitus parte frumentatum, Liv.

TRANSF., (1) *to proceed*: ad reliqua, Cic. (2) *to set out, begin*: a lege, Cic.; ab hoc initio, Caes. (3) *to arise from, spring from, originate from*: qui a Zenone profecti sunt, *Zeno's disciples*, Cic.; genus a Pallante profectum, Verg.

prŏfĭtĕor -fiteri -fessus sum, dep. (pro/fateor), *to acknowledge openly, confess, avow*.

LIT., in gen.: fateor atque etiam profiteor, Cic.; with acc. and infin.: profiteor me relaturum, Cic.; Caes. Esp. (1) *to profess or declare oneself anything*: se grammaticum, Cic. (2) with acc. of thing, *to profess any science, art*, etc.: philosophiam, Cic.; ius, Cic. (3) *to make a public statement, a return of property*, etc.: iugera, Cic.; frumentum, Liv.; indicium, Sall., Tac.; nomen, Cic.; absol.: profiteri, *to announce oneself as a candidate*, Sall.

TRANSF., *to offer, promise*: se adiutorem, Caes.; operam, Cic.; Hor., Ov.

prōflīgātor -ōris, m. (profligo), *a spendthrift*: Tac.

prōflīgo -are, *to strike to the ground*.

LIT., *to overthrow, overcome*: copias hostium, Cic.; classem hostium, Caes.

TRANSF., (1) *to ruin*: rempublicam, Cic.; rem, Liv. (2) *to lower, debase*: iudicia

senatoria, Cic. (3) *to bring almost to an end, nearly finish*: profligatum bellum et paene sublatum, Cic. L., Liv., Tac.

¶ Hence partic. (with superl.) **prōflīgātus** -a -um, *ruined, degraded*: tu omnium mortalium profligatissime, Cic.

prōflo -are, *to blow forth, breathe forth*: flammas, Ov.; fig.: toto proflabat pectore somnum, Verg.

prōflŭentĭa -ae, f. (profluo), *fluency*: Cic.

prōflŭo -flŭĕre -fluxi -fluxum, *to flow forth*. LIT., ex monte, Caes.; in mare, Cic.; Verg. TRANSF., *to proceed*: ab his fontibus profluxi ad hominum famam, Cic.; Tac.

¶ Hence partic. **prōflŭens** -entis, *flowing*. LIT., aqua, Cic.; f. as subst. (sc. aqua), *running water*: Cic. TRANSF., of style, *flowing, fluent*: genus sermonis, Cic.; Tac.

¶ Adv. **prōflŭentĕr**, *flowingly, easily*: Cic.

prōflŭvĭum -i, n. (profluo), *a flowing forth*: sanguinis, Lucr.

prōfor -fari -fātus sum, dep. *to say, speak, declare*: Lucr., Verg., Hor.

prōfŭgĭo -fŭgĕre -fūgi. (1) intransit., *to flee away, escape*: ex oppido, Caes.; domo, Pl., Cic., Liv.; Catilina ipse pertimuit, profugit, Cic. (2) transit., *to flee away from*: agros, Hor.

prōfŭgus -a -um (profugio), *flying, fleeing, fugitive*.

In gen.: populus, Tac.; domo, Liv.; e proelio, Tac.; poet.: Scythae, *wandering, migratory*, Hor.; of animals: taurus, Tac.; of things: currus, Ov.

Esp. of exiles: patriā profugus, Liv.; ex Peloponneso, Liv. M. as subst., *a fugitive, exile*: Ov.

prōfundo -fundĕre -fūdi -fūsum, *to pour forth, shed, cause to flow*.

LIT., sanguinem suum omnem, Cic.; vim lacrimarum, Cic.; lacrimas oculis, Verg. Reflex., se profundere, and pass. as middle, profundi, *to stream forth*: lacrimae se profuderunt, Cic.; Ov.

TRANSF., (1) *to stretch at full length*: somnus membra profudit, Lucr. (2) *to release, discharge, bring forth*: omnis multitudo sagittariorum se profudit, Caes.; of plants: quae (in vitibus) se nimium profuderunt, Cic.; ea quae frugibus atque bacis terrae fetu profunduntur, Cic.; clamorem, *to utter*, Cic.; omne odium in me, *to vent*, Cic. (3) *to spend, sacrifice, give up*: pro patria vitam, Cic.; in a bad sense, *to spend, lavish, squander*: pecuniam, Cic.; patrimonia, Cic.

¶ Hence partic. **prōfūsus** -a -um, *lavish, immoderate, extravagant*: hilaritas, Cic.; profusis sumptibus, Cic.; with genit.: alieni appetens, sui profusus, Sall.

¶ Adv. **prōfūsē**. (1) *in disorder*: profuse tendere in castra, Liv. (2) *lavishly, extravagantly*; compar.: profusius sumptui deditus erat, Sall.

prōfundus -a -um (fundus), *deep, profound*. LIT., mare, Cic.; Lucr., Verg., Hor. TRANSF., (1) *high*: caelum, Verg.; altitudo, Liv. (2) *deep, dense*: silvae, Lucr. (3) *boundless*: libidines, Cic.

¶ N. as subst. **profundum** -i, *depth, abyss*: spatium profundi, Lucr.; aquae, Cic.; absol., poet.= *the sea*: Verg.

prōfūsē, adv. from profundo; q.v.

prŏfūsus -a -um, partic. from profundo; q.v.

prŏgĕner -i, *a grand-daughter's husband*: Sen., Tac.

prŏgĕnĕro -are, *to engender, produce*: Hor.

prŏgĕnĭes -ēi, f. (gigno). (**1**) *descent, lineage*: Ter., Cic. (**2**) *progeny, offspring, descendants*: veteres, qui se deorum progeniem esse dicebant, Cic.; Verg., Liv., Ov.

prŏgĕnĭtor -ōris, m. (progigno), *the founder of a family, ancestor*: Ov.

prŏgigno -gignĕre -gĕnŭi -gĕnĭtum, *to engender, bring forth.* LIT., Cic., Verg., Ov. TRANSF., sensum acerbum, Lucr.

prognātus -a -um, *born, sprung from*: deo, Liv.; ex Cimbris, Caes.; ab Dite patre, Caes.; m. as subst., *a son*: Pl.; of plants: Cat.

Prognē=Procne; q.v.

prognostĭca -ōrum, n. (προγνωστικά), *signs of the weather*, a poem by Aratus, translated by Cicero: Cic.

prŏgrĕdĭor -grĕdi -gressus sum, dep. (pro/gradior).

(**1**) *to go forth, go out*: ex domo, Cic.

(**2**) *to go forwards, to advance.* LIT., regredi quam progredi mallent, Cic.; longius a castris, Caes.; Liv.; of ships: Caes. TRANSF., *to proceed, advance*: quatenus amor in amicitia progredi debeat, Cic.; in a speech: ad reliqua, Cic.; of time: paulum aetate progressus, *advanced in years*, Cic.

prŏgressĭo -ōnis, f. (progredior), *an advance.* In gen., *progress, increase*: progressionem facere ad virtutem, Cic. As rhet. t. t., *a gradual strengthening of expressions, a climax*: Cic.

prŏgressus -ūs, m. (progredior), *a going forwards, advance.* LIT., aliquem progressu arcere, Cic. TRANSF., *progress, increase*: aetatis, Cic.; tantos progressus habebat in Stoicis, *progress in the Stoical philosophy*, Cic.; progressūs facere in studiis, Cic.

proh!=pro! q.v.

prŏhĭbĕo -ēre (pro/habeo), *to hold back, hold in, check, restrain, hinder.*

In gen.: praedones a Sicilia, Cic.; aliquem a familiaritate, Cic.; vim hostium ab oppidis, Caes.; exercitum itinere, Caes.; conatūs alicuius, Cic.; with infin.: prohibeo aliquem exire domo, Cic.; with ne and the subj.: potuisti prohibere ne fieret, Cic.; neg., with quin and the subj.: nec, quin erumperet, prohiberi poterat, Liv.; with quominus: prohibuisse, quominus de te certum haberemus, Cic.

Esp. (**1**) *to hinder by words, forbid, prohibit*: lex recta imperans prohibensque, contraria, Cic. (**2**) *to preserve, defend, protect*: a quo periculo prohibete rempublicam, Cic.; Pl., Liv.

prŏhĭbĭtĭo -ōnis, f. (prohibeo), *a hindering, prohibition*: tollendi, Cic.

prŏĭcĭo -icere -iēci -iectum (iacio), *to throw forth.*

LIT., (**1**) *to fling forward*: effigiem, Tac.; clipeum prae se, Liv. Reflex., with se, or pass. as middle: se ex navi, Caes.; se ad pedes alicuius, Cic. (**2**) *to put forward, cause to project*: bracchium, Cic.; of buildings, pass., *to project*: tectum proiceretur, Cic. (**3**) *to fling out, throw away*: arma, Caes.; aliquem ab urbe, Ov.; Agrippam in insulam, Tac. TRANSF., (**1**) reflex., or pass., *to rush*

forward, plunge into: se in iudicium, Cic. (**2**) *to reject, abandon*: libertatem, Cic.; ab aliquo proici et prodi, Cic.; animas, Verg. (**3**) *to put off*: aliquem ultra quinquennium, Tac.

¶ Hence partic. **prŏiectus** -a -um. (**1**) *jutting forward, projecting*: urbs, Cic.; saxa, Verg. TRANSF., *prominent*: audacia, Cic. (**2**) *stretched out, prostrate, lying.* LIT., ad terram, Caes.; in antro, Verg. TRANSF., a, *abject, contemptible*: alga, Verg.; patientia, Tac.: b, *downcast*: vultus, Tac.: c, *addicted to*: ad audendum, Cic.

prŏiectĭcĭus -a -um (proicio), *exposed*: Pl.

prŏiectĭo -ōnis, f. (proicio), *a throwing forward, stretching out*: bracchii, Cic.

prŏiecto -are (freq. of proicio), *to reproach*: Pl.

prŏiectū, abl. as from proiectus, m. (proicio), *by a jutting out*: Lucr.

prŏiectus -a -um, partic. from proicio; q.v.

prŏin=proinde; q.v.

prŏindĕ and **prŏin** (the o and i sometimes scanned as one syllable), *consequently.* Hence (**1**) *in like manner*; foll. by ut or quam, *just as*: Liv., etc.; foll. by quasi, ac, or ac si, *just as if*: Caes., Cic. L., Liv., etc.; quam, tamquam: Cic. (**2**) *therefore, then, accordingly*; esp. used in phrases of exhortation, etc.: Cic., Verg., etc.

prŏlābor -lābi -lapsus sum.

(**1**) *to glide forward, slide forward, slip along.* LIT., (elephanti) clunibus subsistentes prolabebantur, Liv. TRANSF., in misericordiam animus, Liv.; verbum a cupiditate prolapsum, *slipped out*, Liv.; Cic.

(**2**) *to fall forward, fall down.* LIT., ex equo, Liv.; prolapsa Pergama, Verg. TRANSF., cupiditate, timore, Cic.; ita prolapsa est iuventus ut, Cic.; clade Romanum imperium, Liv.

prŏlapsĭo -ōnis, f. (prolabor), *a slipping, sliding*: Cic.

prŏlātĭo -ōnis, f. (profero). (**1**) *a bringing forward, mentioning*: exemplorum, Cic. (**2**) *an extension*: finium, Liv. (**3**) *a putting off, deferring*: iudicii, Cic.; Caes., Tac.

prŏlāto -are (freq. of profero). (**1**) *to extend, enlarge, lengthen*: agros, Tac.; vitam, Tac. (**2**) *to put off, delay, defer*: comitia, Liv.; malum, Cic.; Sall., Tac.

prŏlecto -are (freq. of prolicio), *to entice, allure*: egentes spe largitionis, Cic.; Pl., Ov.

prŏles -is, f. (alo), *offspring, descendants, posterity*: illa futurorum hominum, *future generations*, Cic.; Apollinea, Aesculapius, Ov.; Latonia, *Apollo and Diana*, Ov.; of animals: Verg.; of plants, *fruit*: Verg. Esp. *the youth* or *young men* of a race: equitum peditumque, Cic.

prŏlētārĭus -i, m. (proles), *by Servius' arrangement, a citizen of the lowest class who served the state only by being the father of children*: Cic., Liv. As adj.: Pl.

prŏlĭcĭo -licĕre -lixi (pro/lacio), *to lure forth, entice*: Ov., Tac.

prŏlixē, adv. from prolixus; q.v.

prŏlixus -a -um (pro/laxus), *widely extended, wide, broad, long.* LIT., barba, Verg.; Lucr., Ov. TRANSF., (**1**) *willing, obliging*: tua prolixa beneficaque natura, Cic. L.; compar.: Cic. L. (**2**) *of things, favourable*: cetera spero prolixa esse competitoribus, Cic. L.

❡ Adv. **prŏlixē**. LIT., *widespread*: Ter. TRANSF., *willingly*: Cic.

prŏlŏgus -i, m. (πρόλογος), *a prologue*: Ter. Also *the actor who speaks the prologue*: Ter.

prŏlŏquor -lŏqui -lŏcūtus sum, dep. *to speak out, say openly*: quod proloqui piget, Liv.; Pl., Prop.

prŏlūdo -lūdĕre -lūsi -lūsum, *to play before-hand, to prelude*. LIT., ad pugnam, Ov. TRANSF., ut ipsis sententiis, quibus pro-luserint, vel pugnare possint, Cic.; Juv.

prŏlŭo -lŭĕre -lŭi -lūtum. (1) *to wash away* or *off*: genus omne natantum litore in extremo fluctus proluit, Verg.; tempestas ex omnibus montibus nives proluit, Caes. (2) *to wash clean*: in vivo prolue rore manus, Ov.; leni praecordia mulso (of drinking), Hor.

prŏlūsĭo -ōnis, f. (proludo), *a prelude, pre-liminary exercise*: Cic.

prŏlŭvĭes -ēi, f. (proluo). (1) *an inundation*: Lucr. (2) *scourings, discharge*: ventris, Verg.

prŏmĕrĕo -ēre -ŭi -ĭtum and **prŏmĕrĕor** -ēri -ĭtus sum, dep. *to deserve*: reus levius punitus quam sit ille promeritus, Cic.; bene de multis, Cic.; plurima, Verg.; poenam, Ov.

❡ N. of partic. as subst. **prŏmĕrĭtum** -i, *deserts, merit*: vestra in nos universa prome-rita, Cic.; Lucr., Ov.

Prŏmētheūs -ĕi and -ĕos, m. (Προμηθεύς, *the Forethinker*), *son of Iapetus, brother of Epimetheus, and father of Deucalion. He stole fire from heaven and gave it to mankind; for which he was bound to a rock in the Caucasus, where a vulture devoured his liver.*

❡ Hence adj. **Prŏmēthēus** -a -um, *Promethean*: iuga, Prop.; rupes, *the Caucasus*, Mart. Subst. **Prŏmēthĭădes** -ae, m. *son of Prometheus; Deucalion.*

prŏmĭnĕo -ēre -ŭi, *to stand out, jut out, project*. LIT., collis prominens, Liv.; pro-minet in altum, Liv.; pectore nudo promi-nentes, Caes. TRANSF., (iustitia) foras tota promineat, Cic.; maxima pars (gloriae) in posteritatem prominet, *extends*, Liv.

❡ Hence partic. **prŏmĭnens** -entis, *jutting out, projecting*. N. as subst. **prŏmĭnens** -entis, *a projection*: in prominenti litoris, Tac.

prŏmiscŭē, adv. (promiscuus), *promiscuously, without distinction*: Caes.

prŏmiscŭo=promiscuus; q.v.: Liv. Adv. **prŏmiscē**=promiscue; q.v.: Cic., Liv.

prŏmiscŭus -a -um, *mixed, in common, in-discriminate, promiscuous.*

LIT., comitia plebi et patribus promiscua, Liv.; conubia, *between patricians and plebe-ians*, Liv.; divina atque humana promiscua habere, *to make no distinction between*, Sall.; in promiscuo esse, *to be common*, Liv. TRANSF., *commonplace, usual, general*: Tac.

prŏmissĭo -ōnis, f. (promitto), *a promise*: auxilii, Cic.

prŏmissor -ōris, m. (promitto), *a promiser*: Hor., Quint.

prŏmitto -mittĕre -mīsi -missum, *to let go forward, send forth.*

Hence (1) *to let grow*: capillum et barbam, Liv.

(2) *to promise, cause to expect, undertake*; with acc. of thing: donum, Pl.; donum Iovi

dicatum et promissum, Cic.; si Neptunus, quod Theseo promiserat, non fecisset, Cic.; with de and the abl.: Cic. L., Hor.; with acc. and fut. infin.: promitto tibi, si valebit, tegulam illum in Italia nullam relicturum, Cic.; with acc. of person: me ultorem, Verg.; promittere ad, *to accept an invitation*: ad fratrem promiserat, Cic.

❡ Hence partic. **prŏmissus** -a -um, *let grow, long, hanging down*: capillus, Caes.; caesaries, Liv.; barba, Verg., Liv.

❡ N. of partic. as subst. **prŏmissum** -i, *a promise*: promissum facere, *to make a promise*, Cic., Hor.; promissa servare, or promissis manere, *to keep promises*, Cic.; Verg., Liv.

prŏmo prŏmĕre prompsi promptum (pro/emo), *to bring forth, bring out, produce.*

LIT., medicamenta de narthecio, Cic.; aurum ex aerario, Cic.; vina dolio, Hor.; tela e pharetra, Ov.; vaginā pugionem, Tac.

TRANSF., *to bring forward, disclose, express*: animus eruditus, qui semper ex se aliquid promat, quod delectet, Cic.; argumenta, consilia, Cic.; plura adversus Cottam, Tac.

❡ Hence partic. (with compar. and superl.) **promptus** -a -um, *ready, at hand.*

LIT., sagittae, Ov.

TRANSF., (1) of persons, *prepared, resolute*: promptissimus homo, Cic.; with ad: ad vim promptus, Cic.; with in: in agendo, Cic.; with abl.: ingenio, linguā, Liv.; with dat.: veniae dandae, Liv. (2) *easy*: defensio, Cic.; Liv., Tac. (3) *visible, apparent, manifest*: aliud clausum in pectore, aliud promptum in lingua habere, Sall.; prompta et aperta, Cic.

❡ Adv. **promptē**, *promptly, quickly, read-ily*: Tac., Juv.

prŏmontŏrĭum -i, n. (promineo). (1) *a mountain ridge*: Liv. (2) *a promontory*: Cic., Liv., etc.

prŏmŏvĕo -mŏvēre -mŏvi -mōtum, *to move forwards, push onwards.*

LIT., saxa vectibus, Caes.; castra ad Carthaginem, Liv.; legiones, Caes. Esp. *to advance, to push on*: aggerem in urbem, Liv.; imperium, *to extend*, Ov.

TRANSF., (1) promovere arcana loco, *to bring to light*, Hor. (2) *to increase, improve*: doctrina vim promovet insitam, Hor. (3) *to postpone*: nuptias, Ter.

❡ N. pl. of partic. as subst. **prŏmōta** -ōrum (translation of the Greek προηγμένα), *preferable things, next after the absolute good*: Cic.

promptū, abl. as from promptus, m. (promo); only in the phrase in promptu, with these senses: (1) *in readiness*; with esse: Cic., Liv.; with habere: Cic. (2) *without difficulty*; with esse, *to be easy*: Sall., Ov. (3) *in evidence*; with esse, *to be clear, manifest*: Lucr., Cic.; in promptu ponere, *to make manifest*, Cic.; in promptu habere, Sall.

promptus -a -um, partic. from promo; q.v.

prŏmulgātĭo -ōnis, f. (promulgo), *a making publicly known, promulgation* (of a proposed law): Cic.

prŏmulgo -are, *to publish, promulgate. As legal t. t., to publish a proposed law*: leges, Cic., Liv.; promulgare de aliquo, Cic. In gen., *to make known*: proelia, Enn.; Cic.

promulsis — propendeo

prōmulsĭs -ĭdis, f. (pro/mulsum), *a dish taken as a relish before a meal* (*eggs, salt fish, radishes*, etc.): Cic. L.

prōmuntŭrĭum = promontorium; q.v.

prōmus -i, m. (promo), *a steward, butler*: Pl., Hor.

prōmūtŭus -a -um, *advanced, paid beforehand*: Caes.

prōnē, adv. from pronus; q.v.

prōnĕpōs -pōtis, m. *a great-grandson*: Cic., Ov.

prōneptis -is, f. *a great-granddaughter*: Pers.

prōnoea -ae, f. (πρόνοια), *providence*: Cic.

pronōmen -ĭnis, *a pronoun*: Varr., Quint.

prōnŭba -ae, f. (pro/nubo). (**1**) *a matron who attended on a bride at a Roman wedding.* (**2**) *epithet of Juno as the goddess who presided over marriage.* TRANSF., *of* Bellona, *as presiding over an unlucky marriage* (leading to war): Verg.; *so of the Furies*: Ov.

prōnuntĭātĭo -ōnis, f. (pronuntio). (**1**) *a public declaration*: Caes. Esp. *the decision of a judge, a judgment*: Cic. (**2**) in logic, *a proposition*: Cic. (**3**) in rhetoric, *delivery*: Cic., Quint.

prōnuntĭātor -ōris, m. (pronuntio), *a relater*: rerum gestarum, Cic.

prōnuntĭo -are, *to make publicly known, declare.*
    In gen.: pronuntiare quae gesta sunt, Caes.; iam capta castra, Caes.; pronuntiatur primā luce ituros, Caes.; te illo honore adfici pronuntiavit, Cic.; of an election result: pronuntiare aliquem praetorem, Liv.; praemia militi, *to promise*, Liv.
    Esp. (**1**) in the senate, *to announce a resolution and the name of its proposer*: Lentulus sententiam Calidii pronuntiaturum se negavit, Cic. (**2**) at a sale, *to make a statement as to defects*: cum in vendendo rem eam scisset et non pronuntiasset, Cic. (**3**) as rhet. t. t., *to declaim, recite, deliver*: summā voce versus multos uno spiritu, Cic.
    ¶ N. of partic. as subst. **prōnuntĭātum** -i, in logic, *a proposition*: Cic.

prōnŭrus -ūs, f. *a grandson's wife*: Ov.

prōnus -a -um, *inclined forward, stooping forward.*
    LIT., of persons: Lucagus pronus pendens in verbera, *leaning forward to the blow*, Verg.; volvitur in caput, Verg.; motu prono, Cic. Of things: amnis, *rushing down*, Verg.; Anxur fuit urbs prona in paludes, Liv.; via, *precipitous, steep*, Ov.; of heavenly bodies, *sinking, setting*: Orion, Hor. Of time, *hastening away*: menses, Hor.
    TRANSF., (**1**) *inclined towards*: ad luctum, Cic.; ad novas res, Tac.; in obsequium, Hor.; in hoc consilium, Liv. Also *well-disposed, favourable*: in aliquem, Tac. (**2**) *easy*: omnia virtuti prona, Sall., compar.: id pronius ad fidem est, *is more creditable*, Liv.
    ¶ Adv. **prōnē**, *on a slope*: Cic.

prŏoemĭor -ari, dep. (prooemium), *to make a preface*: Plin. L.

prŏoemĭum -i, n. (προοίμιον), *a preface, introduction, prelude*: Cic., Juv.

prōpāgātĭo -ōnis, f. (¹propago), *a spreading, propagation.* LIT., vitium, Cic. TRANSF., *extension, enlargement*: imperii nostri, Cic.; temporis, Cic.; vitae, Cic.; nominis, Cic.

prōpāgātor -ōris, m. (¹propago), *an extender, enlarger*: provinciae, Cic. L.

¹prōpāgo -are (pro/pango). LIT., *to spread, propagate* plants: Cato, Plin. TRANSF., *to extend, enlarge*: fines provinciae, Cic.; stirpem, Cic.; bellum, *to prolong*, Cic.; laudem alicuius ad sempiternam gloriam, Cic.; imperium consuli in annum, Liv.; Tac.

²prōpāgo -ĭnis, f. (cf. ¹propago). LIT., *a layer, slip* or *shoot*: Verg., Hor.; esp. of the vine: Cic. TRANSF., of men and animals, *offspring, race, posterity*: Romana, Verg.; catulorum, Lucr.; plur.: clarorum virorum propagines, *genealogies*, Nep.

prōpālam, adv. *publicly, in public*: dicere, Liv.; Cic., Tac.

prōpātŭlus -a -um, *open, uncovered*: in aperto ac propatulo loco, Cic.
    N. as subst. **prōpātŭlum** -i, *an open place, unroofed space*: in propatulo aedium, Liv. TRANSF., in propatulo, *publicly*, Sall.

prōpē, adv. and prep. (pro/suffix -pe). Compar. **prōpĭus**; superl. **proxĭmē**.
    Adv., *near*. (**1**) of space, *near*: volebam prope alicubi esse, Cic.; prope a Sicilia, Cic.; prope ad portas, Liv.; propius accedere, Cic.; proxime trans Padum, Caes. (**2**) of time, *near*: Pl., Ter., Liv. Hence, proxime, *a short time ago, just now*: quem proxime nominavi, Cic. (**3**) of other relations, *nearly*: annis prope quadraginta, Liv.; prope desperatis rebus, Cic.; prope adesse, *to be close at hand*, Cic.; prope erat ut pelleretur, *he was near being*, etc., Liv.; propius nihil est factum quam ut occideretur, Cic.; propius res aspice nostras, *more closely*, Verg.
    Prep. with acc. (**1**) of space, *near to*: prope me, Cic.; proxime hostem, *next to the enemy*, Caes. (**2**) of time, *near to, close on*: prope Kalendas Sext., Cic. (**3**) of approximation or similarity, *not far from, near to*: prope secessionem plebis res venit, Liv.; propius fidem est, *it deserves more credit*, Liv.; proxime morem Romanum, Liv.

prōpēdĭem, adv. *at an early date, very soon*: Pl., Cic., Liv.

prōpello -pellĕre -pŭli -pulsum, *to drive before one, drive forth, drive away.*
    LIT., hostes, Caes.; crates pro munitione obiectas, Caes.; corpus alicuius e scopulo in profundum, Ov.; navem in altum, Ov.; pecus extra portam, Liv.
    TRANSF., (**1**) *to drive away*: vitae periculum ab aliquo, Liv. (**2**) *to impel*: aliquem ad voluntariam mortem, Tac.

prōpĕmŏdŏ, adv. (prope/modus), *almost, nearly*: Pl., Liv.

prōpĕmŏdum, adv. (prope/modus), *almost, nearly*: Pl., Cic.

prōpendĕo -pendēre -pendi -pensum, *to hang down.* LIT., propendere illam boni lancem, Cic. TRANSF., bona propendent, *to preponderate*, Cic.; inclinatione voluntatis ad aliquem, *to be inclined to, favourable towards*, Cic.
    ¶ Hence partic. (with compar.) **prōpensus** -a -um. (**1**) *weighty*: Pl., Cic. (**2**) *tending towards*: ad veritatis similitudinem, Cic. (**3**) *inclined, disposed*: ad misericordiam, Cic.; in alteram partem, Cic.; esp. *favourably disposed*: Cic., Liv.

¶ Adv. **prōpensē**, *readily, willingly*; compar.: propensius, Liv.
prōpensĭo -ōnis, f. (propendeo), *inclination, propensity*: Cic.
prōpĕranter, adv. from propero; q.v.
prōpĕrantĭa -ae, f. (propero), *haste, rapidity*: Sall., Tac.
prōpĕrātĭo -ōnis, f. (propero), *haste*: Cic. L., Sall.
prōpĕrē, adv. from properus; q.v.
prōpĕro -are (properus).
    (1) intransit., *to hasten*: Romam, Cic.; in patriam, Caes.; ad aliquem, Caes.; alio, Sall.; with infin.: redire, Cic.; Caes., Hor.; also of things: properans aqua per agros, Hor.
    (2) transit., *to hasten something, to accelerate, complete quickly*: iter, Sall., Tac.; mortem, Verg.; opus, studium, Hor.
¶ Hence, from pres. partic., adv. (with compar.) **prōpĕrantĕr**, *hastily*: Lucr., Tac.; properantius, Sall., Ov.
¶ Past. partic. **prōpĕrātus** -a -um, *hasty*: Ov., Tac. N. as subst. **prōpĕrātum** -i, *haste*: Pl., Cic., Sall.; abl. as adv. **prōpĕrātō**, *in haste*: Tac.
Prōpertĭus -i, m., Sex. Aurelius, *a poet of the Augustan age, born in Umbria.*
prōpĕrus -a -um, *quick, rapid, hasty*: circumstant properi aurigae, Verg.; with genit.: Tac.; with infin.: Tac.
¶ Adv. **prōpĕrē**, Hor., Liv., etc.
prōpexus -a -um (pro/pecto), *combed forwards, hanging down*: propexa in pectore barba, Verg.; propexam ad pectora barbam, Ov.
prōpīnātĭo -ōnis, f. (propino), *a drinking to a person's health*: Sen.
prōpīno -are (προπίνω), *to drink to anyone*: propino hoc pulchro Critae, Cic.; Pl. TRANSF., *to give drink*: Mart.
prōpinquĭtās -ātis, f. (propinquus), *nearness*.
    (1) of place, *proximity*: loci, Cic.; hostium, Caes. (2) *friendship* or *relationship*: vinculis propinquitatis coniunctus, Cic.; Pl.
prōpinquo -are (propinquus).
    (1) intransit., *to come near, draw near, approach.* LIT., with dat.: scopulo, Verg.; ignis domui, Tac.; with acc.: campos, Tac. TRANSF., of time, *to draw near*: Parcarum dies et vis inimica propinquat, Verg.
    (2) transit., *to bring near, hasten on*: augurium, Verg.
prōpinquus -a -um (prope), *near*.
    (1) in space, *neighbouring*: provincia, Cic.; with dat.: propinquus cubiculo hortus, Liv.; with genit.: Liv. N. as subst.: in propinquo, *nearby*, Liv.
    (2) in time, *near*: reditus, Cic.; Liv., Tac.
    (3) in other relations: **a**, *similar*: quae propinqua videntur et finitima, Cic.: **b**, *nearly related, closely connected*; with dat.: tibi genere propinqui, Sall. M. and f. as subst., *a kinsman*: Caes., Cic., Hor.
¶ Adv. **prōpinquē**, *near, close by*: Pl.
prōpĭor -us, genit. -ōris, compar.: superl. **proxĭmus** -a -um (prope).
    Compar. **prōpĭor**, *nearer.* LIT., of place: portus, Verg.; pons, Caes.; with dat.: propior patriae, Ov. N. pl. as subst.: propriora, *the nearer regions*, Verg. TRANSF., (1) of time, *nearer, more recent*: epistula, Cic. L.; with dat.: propior leto, Ov. (2): **a**, of

relationship, *more closely connected*: societas, Cic.; quibus propior P. Quinctio nemo est, Cic.: **b**, *more closely affecting*: sua sibi propriora esse pericula quam mea, Cic.: **c**, *nearer in point of likeness, more similar*: sceleri propriora, Cic.; propius est vero, Ov.: **d**, *more suitable*: portus propior huic aetati, Cic.
    Superl. **proxĭmus (proxŭmus)** -a -um, *very near, nearest.* LIT., of place: oppidum, Caes.; vicinus, Cic.; with dat.: huic proximus locus, Cic.; with acc.: proximus quisque hostem, Liv.; with ab: dactylus proximus a postremo, Cic.; Liv., Ov. N. as subst., proximum -i, *the neighbourhood*: e proximo, Nep.; proxima Illyrici, Liv. TRANSF., (1) of time, *of the future, next, following*: nox, Caes.; annus, Cic.; of the past, *most recent*: quid proximā nocte egeris, Cic.; proximis superioribus diebus, Caes. N. abl. sing. as adv.: proximo, *very recently*, Cic. L. (2) of rank, preference, etc., *next*: proximus est huic dignitati ordo equester, Cic.; proximus post Lysandrum, Cic.; proximum est, with infin.: non nasci homini optimum est, proximum autem (*the next best thing*) quam primum mori, Cic.; proximum est, with ut and the subj., *the next thing is*, etc., Cic. (3) of resemblance, *most like*: proxima veris, Hor.; Cic., Verg. (4) of friendship or relationship, *nearest*: proximus cognatione, Cic.; Ter. M. pl. as subst. **proxĭmi** -ōrum, *near relations* or *close friends*: Cic.
prōpĭtĭo -are (propitius), *to soothe, propitiate, appease*: Venerem, Pl.; Tac.
prōpĭtĭus -a -um (prope), *favourable, gracious, propitious*: di, Pl., Cic.; of persons: Cic., Liv.; of things: Liv.
prōpĭus, compar. of prope; q.v.
prōpōla -ae, m. (προπώλης), *a retailer, huckster*: Pl., Cic.
prōpollŭo -ŭere, *to pollute worse*: Tac.
prōpōno -pōnĕre -pŏsŭi -pŏsĭtum, *to put forth, put on view, expose, display.*
    LIT., vexillum, Caes.; aliquid venale, *for sale*, Cic.; oculis or ante oculos, *before the eyes*, Cic.
    TRANSF., (1) *to publish, relate, tell*: rem gestam, Caes.; with indir. quest.: Caes., Cic. (2) *to propose, promise, offer as a reward or hold over as a threat*: praemia alicui, Cic.; poenam improbis, Cic.; Liv. (3) *to imagine, put before the mind*: sibi aliquem ad imitandum, Cic.; Liv. (4) *to propose to oneself, purpose, intend*: consecutus id, quod animo proposuerat, Caes.; with infin.: quibus propositum est contra omnes philosophos dicere, Cic.; with ut and subj.: Cic. (5) in logic, *to state the first premiss of a syllogism*: Cic.
    ¶ N. of partic. as subst. **prōpŏsĭtum** -i. (1) *a design, plan, purpose, intention*: propositum adsequi, *to accomplish a design*, Cic.; tenere, *to keep to a design*, Caes., Liv.; tenacem propositi, Hor. (2) *the subject* or *theme of a discourse*: ad propositum redeamus, Cic.; Liv. (3) *the first premiss of a syllogism*: Cic.
Prŏpontĭs -ĭdis and -ĭdos, f. (Προποντίς), *the Propontis* (now the *Sea of Marmora*).
    ¶ Hence adj. **Prŏpontĭăcus** -a -um, *of the Propontis.*

prōporrō, adv. *further, moreover,* or *altogether*: Lucr.

prōportĭo -ōnis, f. *proportion, analogy, similarity*: Cic., Quint.

prōpŏsĭtĭo -ōnis, f. (propono), *a setting before.* Hence (1) *a purpose*: vitae, Cic. (2) *the subject* or *theme of a discourse*: Cic. (3) in logic, *the first proposition of a syllogism*: Cic.

prōpŏsĭtum -i, n. subst. from propono; q.v.

prōpraetor -ōris, m. and **pro praetōre**. (1) *a praetor's deputy*: Caes., Sall., Liv. (2) *a Roman who, after having been praetor at Rome, was sent as governor to a province or given a military command*: Cic., Caes., Liv.

prŏprĭē, adv. from proprius; q.v.

prŏprĭĕtās -ātis, f. (proprius). (1) *a property, peculiarity*: rerum, Cic.; plur.: frugum proprietates, Liv. (2) *ownership*: Suet.

proprĭtim (proprius), *peculiarly, specially*: Lucr.

proprĭus -a -um, *one's own, special, particular, peculiar.*

Lit., opp. to communis *or* alienus: ista calamitas communis est utriusque nostrum, sed culpa mea propria est, Cic.; often with possess. pron.: proprius et suus, suus proprius, noster proprius, Cic.; proprii fines, Caes.; libri, Hor.; vires, Liv.

Transf., (1) *peculiar to a person* or *thing, characteristic of*: proprium est senectutis vitium, Cic.; fuit hoc proprium populi Romani longe a domo bellare, Cic.; libertatem propriam Romano generi, Cic.; nulla est in republica causa mea propria, *exclusively*, Cic. (2) *of words, peculiar*: discedebat a verbis propriis rerum ac suis, Cic. (3) *lasting, permanent*: munera, Hor.; illud de duobus consulibus perenne ac proprium manere potuisset, Cic.; Verg., etc.

¶ Hence adv. **prŏprĭē**. (1) *exclusively for oneself*: proprie parvā parte frui, Cic.; Hor. (2) *peculiarly, characteristically*: quod tu ipse tum amandus es, id est proprie tuum, Cic. (3) *in a proper sense*: cuius causam neque senatus publice neque ullus ordo proprie susceperat, Cic.; illud honestum quod proprie vereque dicitur, Cic.

proptĕr (prope), adv. and prep.

Adv., *near, hard by*: cum duo reges cum maximis copiis prope adsint, Cic.; Lucr., etc.

Prep. with acc. (sometimes put after acc.). Lit., of place, *near, hard by*: insulae propter Siciliam, Cic.; Verg., Tac., etc. Transf., *on account of, by reason of, because of*: metum, Cic.; frigora, Caes.; propter quos vivit, *whom he has to thank for his life*, Cic.; Liv., etc.

proptĕrĕā, adv. *on that account, therefore*: Pl., Cic. Often foll. by quia *or* quod: Cic.

prōpŭdĭōsus -a -um (propudium), *full of shame, infamous*: Pl.

prōpŭdĭum -i, n. (1) *a shameful action*: Pl. (2) *a wretch, villain, rascal*: propudium illud et portentum L. Antonius, Cic.; Pl.

prōpugnācŭlum -i, n. (propugno), *a fortification, rampart, fortress, defence.*

Lit., propugnaculum Siciliae, i.e. the fleet, Cic.; propugnacula imperii, Cic.; moenium, Tac.; Hor., Verg.

Transf., (1) *a bulwark, protection*: lex Aelia et Fufia propugnacula tranquillitatis,

---

Cic. (2) *grounds of defence*: firmissimo propugnaculo uti, Liv.

prōpugnātĭo -ōnis, f. (propugno), *a defence*: nostra propugnatio et defensio dignitatis tuae, Cic. L.

prōpugnātor -ōris, m. (propugno), *a defender.* Lit., duplici propugnatorum ordine defendi, Caes.; dimissio propugnatorum, Cic. Transf., *a defender*: patrimonii sui, Cic.

prōpugno -are. (1) *to skirmish in front*: Caes. (2) *to fight in defence.* Lit., uno tempore propugnare et munire, Caes.; e loco, Caes.; pro vallo, Liv.; pro suo partu (of animals), Cic. Transf., pro fama alicuius, Cic. Also transit., *to defend*: munimenta, Tac.

prōpulso -are (freq. of propello), *to drive back, repel, ward off.* Lit., hostem, Caes.; populum ab ingressione fori, Cic. Transf., frigus, famem, Cic.; suspicionem a se, Cic., Liv.

Prōpўlaea -ōrum, n. (τὰ προπύλαια), *the entrance to the Acropolis at Athens, built by Mnesicles*: Cic.

prō quaestōre, *a proquaestor; an ex-quaestor who helped to govern a Roman province*: Cic.

prōquam (or **pro quam**), conj., *in proportion as, according as*: Lucr.

prōra -ae, f. (πρῷρα), *the prow, bow of a ship.* Lit., Caes., Verg., etc. Transf., *a ship*: Verg., Ov.

prōrēpo -rēpĕre -repsi, *to creep forward, crawl forth*: Hor.

prōrēta -ae, m. (πρῳράτης), *the look-out man at the prow of a ship*: Pl.

prōreus -i, m. (πρῳρεύς)=proreta; q.v., Ov.

prōrĭpĭo -rĭpĕre -rĭpŭi -reptum (pro/rapio), *to snatch, tear, drag forth.* Lit., hominem, Cic.; se proripere, *to rush forward, hurry*: se in publicum, Liv.; se ex curia, Sall.; se portā foras, Caes.; quo proripis (sc. te)? Verg. Transf., libido non se proripiet, Cic.; Hor.

prōrĭto -are, *to provoke, incite*: Plin., Sen.

prōrŏgātĭo -ōnis, f. (prorogo). (1) *a prolongation of a term of office*: Liv. (2) *a deferring*: diei, Cic. L.

prōrŏgo -are. (1) *to prolong*: vitam, Pl.; imperium alicui, Cic.; provinciam, Cic.; Hor., Liv. (2) *to defer, put off*: dies ad solvendum, Cic.; Pl.

prorsum and **prorsŭs**, adv. (pro/versus), *forwards.* Lit., in space, *straight ahead*: Pl., Ter. Transf., (1) *utterly, absolutely, wholly*: ita prorsus existimo, Cic.; Pl., Ter.; non prorsus, nullo modo prorsus, *not at all*, Cic. (2) *in a word, to sum up*: Sall.

prorsus (**prōsus**) -a -um (pro/versus), *straightforward.* Of style, *in prose*: Quint.

prōrumpo -rumpĕre -rūpi -ruptum. (1) transit., *to cause to break forth; to thrust forth, send forth*: nubem atram, Verg.; mare proruptum, *the sea breaking in front*, Verg. Transf., prorupta audacia, *unbridled*, Cic. (2) intransit., *to burst forth, break forth.* Lit., per medios, Cic.; Verg., Tac. Transf., *to break out*: prorumpit pestis, Cic.; of persons: in scelera ut dedecora, Tac.

prōrŭo -rŭĕre -rŭi -rŭtum. (1) intransit.: **a**, *to rush forth*: qua proruebat, Caes.: **b**, *to fall down*: Tac. (2) transit., *to fling forward* or *down, cast to the ground, destroy*: munitiones, Caes.;

vallum, Liv.; Albam a fundamentis, Liv.; hostem profligare ac proruere, Tac.

prōsāpĭa -ae, f. *a family, race, stock* (an archaic word): Pl., Sall.; eorum, ut utamur veteri verbo, prosapiam, Cic.

proscaenĭum -i, n. (προσκήνιον), *the part of a theatre before the scenes, the stage*: Pl., Verg., Liv.

proscindo -scindĕre -scĭdi -scissum, *to tear in front, to rend.* LIT., ferro quercum, Luc. Esp., *to break up fallow land, plough up*: terram, Verg.; fig.: aequor, *to plough the waters*, Cat. TRANSF., *to censure, defame, satirize*: Ov.

proscrībo -scrībĕre -scripsi -scriptum. (1) *to make publicly known, publish*: legem, Cic.; Tac.; with acc. and infin., *to make it known that*: auctionem se facturum esse, Cic. L.; Suet. (2) *to offer publicly for sale* or *hire, advertise*: insulam, bona, fundum, Cic. (3) *to confiscate property*: possessiones, Cic.; Pompeium, *to confiscate P.'s estate*, Cic. (4) *to proscribe, outlaw* (by publishing the person's name in a list): aliquem, Cic.
¶ Hence m. pl. of partic. as subst. **proscripti** -ōrum, *the proscribed*: Sall.

proscriptio -ōnis, f. (proscribo). (1) *an advertisement of sale*: bonorum, Cic. (2) *a proscription, outlawry*: Cic.

proscriptŭrĭo -ire (desider. of proscribo), *to desire a proscription*: Cic. L.

prōsĕco -sĕcare -sĕcŭi -sectum, *to cut off in front, cut off.* Esp. (1) *to cut out the parts of a victim to be sacrificed*: exta, Liv. (2) *to plough up*: Plin. L.
¶ N. of partic. as subst. **prōsectum** -i, *part of a victim cut out to be offered to a god; the entrails*: Ov.

prōsēda -ae, f. (pro/sedeo), *a prostitute*: Liv.

prōsēmĭno -are, *to sow* or *scatter as seed.* LIT., vel in tegulis proseminare ostreas, Cic. TRANSF., *to disseminate, propagate*: Cic.

prōsĕquor -sĕqui -sĕcutus, dep. *to follow* or *accompany forth.*
LIT., (1) in a friendly sense, *to accompany, attend*, esp. *to 'see off'* a person going on a journey: aliquem usque ad agri fines, Cic.; prosequi exsequias, Ov.; of things: ventus prosequitur euntes, Verg. (2) in a hostile sense, *to attack, pursue*: hostem, Caes.; longius fugientes, Caes.; Liv.
TRANSF., (1) *to attend*: aliquem votis, ominibus, lacrimisque, Caes.; verbis honorificis, beneficiis, misericordiā, Cic.; eos honos, Cic.; Liv. (2) of a discourse, *to go on with, continue*: quod non longius prosequar, Cic. (3) *to imitate*: Cic.

Prōserpĭna -ae, f. (Περσεφόνη), *the daughter of Ceres and Jupiter, carried off by Pluto to be queen of the lower world.*

prōseucha -ae, f. (προσευχή), *a (Jewish) house of prayer, a conventicle*: Juv.

prōsĭlio -ire -ŭi (-ĭvi or -ii) (pro/salio), *to spring up, leap forth.* LIT., ex tabernaculo, Liv.; ab sede, Liv.; repente, Cic.; finibus suis, Verg.; of things: flumina prosiliunt, Ov. TRANSF., vaga prosiliet frenis natura remotis, Hor.; ad arma dicenda, Hor.

prōsŏcer -ĕri, m. *a wife's grandfather*: Ov., Plin. L.

prospecto -are (freq. of prospicio), *to look forward -look forth upon, survey.*

LIT., e puppi pontum, Ov.; euntem, Verg.; ex tectis fenestrisque, Liv. Of places, *to look towards*: villa quae subiectos sinūs prospectat, Tac.
TRANSF., *to look forward to, expect*: exsilium, Cic.; te quoque fata prospectant paria, *a like fate awaits*, Verg.

prospectus -ūs, m. (prospicio), *an outlook, view, prospect.*
LIT., unde longe ac late prospectus erat, Liv.; prospectum impedire, Caes.
TRANSF., (1) *sight, gaze*: aequora prospectu metior alta meo, Ov. (2) *a sight, a view*: Verg., Tac.

prospĕcŭlor -ari, dep. (1) intransit., *to look out to a distance*; hence, *to explore, reconnoitre*: Liv. (2) transit., *to look out for, wait for*: adventum imperatoris, Liv.

prosper (**prospĕrus**) -a -um (pro/spero), *according to one's hope*; hence, *fortunate, favourable, lucky, prosperous*: fortuna, Cic.; exitus, Cic.; successus, Liv.; with genit.: frugum, Hor. N. pl. as subst. **prospĕra** -ōrum, *prosperity, good fortune*: Luc., Tac.
¶ Adv. **prospĕrē**, *prosperously, fortunately, favourably*: procedere, Cic.; Liv., Tac.

prospĕrĭtās -ātis, f. (prosper), *prosperity, good fortune*: vitae, Cic.; plur.: improborum prosperitates, Cic.

prospĕro -are (prosper), *to make fortunate, to cause to succeed*: alicui victoriam, Liv.; Hor., Tac.

prospĕrus=prosper; q.v.

prospĭcĭentĭa -ae, f. (prospicio), *foresight, precaution*: Cic.

prospĭcĭo -spĭcĕre -spexi -spectum (pro/specio).
(1) intransit., *to look forward, look out.* LIT., ex castris in urbem, Caes.; multum, *to have a wide prospect*, Cic. L.; procul, Verg.; Caes., Hor.; *to be upon the watch*: Nep. TRANSF., *to take care, exercise foresight*; with dat.: consulite vobis, prospicite patriae, Cic.; with ut and the subj.: Cic.
(2) transit., *to see ahead, make out in the distance.* LIT., Italiam ab unda, Verg.; Hor., Liv. Of places, *to look towards*: domus prospicit agros, Hor.; Ov. TRANSF., **a**, *to foresee*: casus futuros, Cic.; Verg.: **b**, *to look out for, provide, procure*: ferramenta, Cic.; commeatus, Liv.

prosterno -sternĕre -strāvi -strātum, *to throw down in front, cast down.*
LIT., circa viam corpora humi, Liv.; se ad pedes alicuius, Cic.
TRANSF., (1) *to debase*: se, Cic. (2) *to overthrow, destroy, ruin*: omnia furore, Cic.; hostem, Cic.; virtutem, Cic.

prostĭtŭo -stĭtŭere -stĭtŭi -stĭtŭtum (pro/statuo), *to prostitute.* LIT., sese toto corpore, Cat.; Pl., Ov. TRANSF., vocem ingrato foro, Ov.

prosto -stare -stĭti, *to stand before.*
Hence (1) *to stand forward, project*: Lucr. (2) *to be exposed for sale*: liber prostat, Hor.; vox prostitit, Cic.; of persons, *to prostitute oneself*: Juv., Suet. TRANSF., illud amicitiae quondam venerabile nomen prostat, Hor.

prōsŭbĭgo -ĕre, *to dig up, root up*: terram, Verg.

prōsum prōdesse prōfŭi, *to be useful, do good, benefit*: illa quae prosunt aut quae nocent,

Cic.; with dat.: nec sibi nec alteri, Cic.; with ad: ad concordiam, Liv.; with infin. as subject: multum prodest ea quae metuuntur ipsa contemnere, Cic.; quid mihi fingere prodest? Ov.

Prōtăgŏrās -ae, m. (Πρωταγόρας), *a Greek sophist of Abdera, an older contemporary of Socrates.*

prōtĕgo -tĕgĕre -texi -tectum, *to cover over.*
LIT., (1) *to cover in front*: tabernacula protecta hederā, Caes.; aliquem scuto, Caes.; Verg. (2) *to furnish with a roof*: aedes, Cic.; Caes.
TRANSF., *to cover, protect*: iacentem, Cic.; regem, Liv.; Tac., etc.

prōtĕlo -are, *to drive off, put to flight*: Ter.

prōtēlum -i, n. *a team of draught-oxen.* TRANSF., *a series, succession*: Lucr.

prōtendo -tendĕre -tendi -tentum, *to stretch forward, stretch out*: bracchia in mare, Ov.; cervicem, Tac.; temo protentus in octo pedes, *eight feet long*, Verg.

prōtĕnŭs=protinus; q.v.

prōtĕro -tĕrĕre -trīvi -trītum, *to trample under foot, tread down.*
LIT., equitatus aversos proterere incipit, Caes.; frumentum, Liv.; Verg.
TRANSF., (1) *to overthrow, rout, defeat*: Poenos, Hor.; Cic. (2) *to drive away, push aside*: ver proterit aestas, Hor.

prōterrĕo -ēre, *to frighten away, scare away*: Themistoclem patriā pulsum atque proterritum, Cic.; aliquem verbis gravissimis, Cic.; Caes., Verg.

prōtervĭtās -ātis, f. (protervus), *boldness, impudence*: Cic. In a milder sense, *wantonness, pertness*: Hor.

prōtervus -a -um, *bold, impudent, shameless,* and in a milder sense, *wanton, pert.* LIT., animus, Pl.; homo, Cic.; iuvenes, Hor. TRANSF., of things, *violent, vehement*: venti, Hor.; stella canis, Ov.
¶ Adv. **prŏtervē**, *boldly, impudently*: Pl., Ter., Cic.; compar.: Ov.

Prōtĕsĭlāus -i, m. (Πρωτεσίλαος), *the husband of Laodamia, the first Greek to land near Troy in the Trojan war, and the first to be slain.* Adj. **Prōtĕsĭlāēus** -a -um, *of Protesilaus.*

Prōtĕus -ĕi and -ĕos, m. (Πρωτεύς), *a prophet and god of the sea, with the power of changing himself into different shapes*: Verg., etc.
TRANSF., *a changeable* or *crafty man*: Hor.

prŏthymē, adv. (προθύμως), *willingly*: Pl.

prŏthymĭa -ae, f. (προθυμία), *willingness*: Pl.

prōtĭnam, adv. *immediately, at once*: Pl., Ter.

prōtĭnŭs (**prōtĕnŭs**), adv. (tenus), *forward, further, further on.*
LIT., of place: ago capellas, Verg.; pergere, Cic., Liv.; of extent: cum protinus utraque tellus una foret, Verg.; Tac.
TRANSF., of time. (1) *continuously*: quem (morem) protinus urbes Albanae coluere sacrum, Verg. (2) *immediately*: protinus de via, Liv.; oratio protinus perficiens auditorem benevolum, Cic.

prōtollo -ĕre, *to put forth, stretch forward.* LIT., manum, Pl. TRANSF., *to lengthen, prolong*: Pl.

prōtrăho -trăhĕre -traxi -tractum, *to draw, drag forward*; esp. *to drag forth from a place.* LIT., aliquem hinc in convivium, Cic.; in medium, Verg.; Liv., Tac. TRANSF., (1) *to bring to light, reveal, make known*: auctorem

nefandi facinoris, Liv. (2) *to compel, force*: aliquem ad indicium, Liv.; ad paupertatem, Pl. (3) *to drag on in time, protract, defer*: Suet.

prōtrūdo -trūdĕre -trūsi -trūsum, *to push forward, thrust forth.* LIT., cylindrum, Cic.; Lucr., Hor. TRANSF., *to put off, defer*: comitia in Ianuarium mensem, Cic. L.

prōturbo -are, *to drive forward, drive away.* LIT., of persons: equites, Caes.; hostes telis missilibusque saxis, Liv.; Verg.; of things: pectore silvas, *to throw down*, Ov. TRANSF., mentally, *to overcome*: Tac.

prŏŭt, conj. (pro/ut), *just as, according as*: prout res postulat, Cic.; Liv.

prōvectus -a -um, partic. from proveho; q.v.

prōvĕho -vĕhĕre -vexi -vectum, *to carry forward.*
LIT., aër a tergo quasi provehit, Lucr.; Pl. Pass., provehi, in a middle sense, *to ride forward, drive, sail* (of persons in a ship or of the ship itself): Nasidius cum classe freto Siciliae provehitur, Caes.; Verg., Liv.
TRANSF., (1) *to carry on*: orationem, Cic.; vitam, Lucr. Pass., provehi, *to be carried away*: studio rerum rusticarum provectus sum, Cic.; longius in amicitia provehi, Cic.; quid ultra provehor? *why do I continue?* Verg. (2) *to advance, raise, promote*: aliquem ad summos honores, Liv.
¶ Hence partic. **prōvectus** -a -um, *advanced,* esp. *in age*: longius aetate provectus, Cic.; Tac.

prōvĕnĭo -vĕnire -vēni -ventum, *to come forth, come on.*
LIT., in scaenam, *to appear upon the stage*, Pl.; of corn, *to come up, shoot forth, grow*: frumentum propter siccitates angustius provenerat, Caes.
TRANSF., *to result, turn out, come about*: esp. *to turn out well, succeed*: ut initia belli provenissent, Tac.; carmina proveniunt animo deducta sereno, Ov.

prōventus -ūs, m. (provenio), *a coming forth, growing, product, crop.* LIT., proventu oneret sulcos, Verg. TRANSF., *result, issue*: pugnae, Caes.; secundi rerum proventūs, Caes.; esp., *fortunate result, success*: Liv.

prōverbĭum -i, n. (pro/verbum), *a proverb*: in proverbi consuetudinem venit, *has become a proverb*, Cic.; ut est in proverbio, *as is said in the proverb*, Cic.; quod est Graecis hominibus in proverbio, *is a proverb among*, Cic.; Liv.

prōvĭdens -entis, partic. from provideo; q.v.

prōvĭdentĭa -ae, f. (provideo). (1) *foresight, foreknowledge*: providentia est, per quam futurum aliquid videtur ante quam factum sit, Cic. (2) *forethought, providence,* esp. *divine*: deorum, Cic.

prōvĭdĕo -vĭdēre -vīdi -vīsum, *to look forward to, see at a distance.*
LIT., aliquem non providisse, Hor.; quid petatur provideri nequeat, Liv.; Pl., Ter.
TRANSF., (1) *to see beforehand, to foresee*: quod ego, priusquam loqui coepisti, sensi atque providi, Cic.; Caes.; with infin. quest.: Cic. (2) *to take precautions for* or *against something, to provide for, make preparation for*; with acc.: rem frumentariam, Caes.; consilia in posterum, Cic.; with de: de re frumentaria, Caes.; de Brundisio atque illa

ora, Cic. L.; with dat.: saluti hominum, Cic.; with ut *or* ne and the subj.: ne quid ei desit, Cic.; ut res quam rectissime agantur, Cic. L.; absol.: actum de te est, nisi provides, Cic. ¶ Hence partic. **prōvĭdens** -entis, *provident, prudent*: Cic.; compar.: quod est providentius, Cic.; superl.: Tac., Plin. L. ¶ Adv. **prōvĭdentĕr**, *providently, with forethought*: Sall.; superl.: providentissime constituere aliquid, Cic. ¶ N. abl. of perf. partic. as adv. **prōvīsō**, *with forethought*: Tac.

prōvĭdus -a -um (provideo). (**1**) *foreseeing*: rerum futurarum, Cic.; Hor., Liv., etc. (**2**) *providing, taking measures for*: natura provida utilitatum, Cic. (**3**) in gen., *cautious, prudent*: orator, Cic., Hor.

prōvincĭa -ae, f. *employment, charge, sphere of duty, office*: illam officiosam provinciam ut me in lectulo trucidaret, Cic.; quasi provincias atomis dare, Cic.; ultima Pompeio dabitur provincia Caesar, Luc. Esp. *the sphere of office assigned to a magistrate*: sortiri provincias (inter se), Liv.; *of the jurisdiction of the praetor urbanus and praetor peregrinus*: provincia urbana et peregrina, Liv.; *of a military command*: Sicinio Volsci, Aquilio Hernici (nam hi quoque in armis erant) provincia evenit, Cic.; *of a command at sea*: provincia classis, provincia maritima, Liv.; *of non-Roman magistrates*: Hannonis cis Iberum provincia erat, *had the command*, Liv. TRANSF., *a country outside Italy governed by a Roman magistrate, a province*. In gen.: primus annus provinciae erat, Cic.; alicui tradere provinciam, Cic. L.; administrare provinciam, Cic. L. Esp. *the first Roman province in Gaul* (now *Provence*): Caes.

prōvincĭālis -e, *of* or *relating to a province*: administratio, *government of a province*, Cic. L.; abstinentia, *moderation in governing*, Cic.; Tac. M. as subst., esp. plur. **prōvincĭāles** -ĭum, *inhabitants of the provinces, provincials*: Cic. L., Plin. L.

prōvīsĭo -ōnis, f. (provideo), *foresight*: animi, Cic.; esp. with the idea of *providing for* or *against something*; with genit.: temporis posteri, Cic.; vitiorum atque incommodorum, Cic.

prōvīso -ĕre, *to look out for, go to see*: Pl., Ter.

prōvīsō, adv. from provideo; q.v.

prōvīsor -ōris, m. (provideo). (**1**) *one who foresees* and *provides for* or *against something*; with genit.: utilium, Tac.; dominationum, Tac.

prōvīsū, abl. as from provisus (provideo), *by looking forward, by foreseeing*; esp. *by providing for* or *against something*; with genit.: rei frumentariae, Tac.; periculi, Tac.

prōvixisse, perf. infin. (pro/vivo), *to have lived on*: Tac.

prōvŏcātĭo -ōnis, f. (provoco), *a calling forth*. Hence, *a challenge*; esp. *an appeal to a higher court of law*: provocatio ad populum, Cic.; magistratus sine provocatione, *from whose decision there is no appeal*, Liv.

prōvŏcātor -ōris, m. (provoco), *one who challenges; a kind of gladiator*: Cic.

prōvŏco -are, *to call forth, call out*. In gen.: herum, Pl.; roseo ore diem (of Aurora), Ov. Esp. (**1**) *to excite, rouse, to provoke*: munificentiā nostrā provocemus plebem, Liv.; beneficio, iniuriīs, etc., Cic.; bellum, *to stir up*, Tac. (**2**) *to challenge to a contest*: me in aleam, Pl.; ad pugnam, Cic.; Verg., Liv. (**3**) as legal t. t., *to summon before a higher court, to appeal to a higher tribunal*: ad populum, Cic., Liv.; ab omni iudicio poenāque provocari licere, Cic.; fig.: provocare ad Catonem, i.e. *as an authority*, Cic. L.

prōvŏlo -are, *to fly forth*. TRANSF., of persons, *to rush forth, hasten forth*: subito, Caes.; ad primores, Liv.

prōvolvo -volvĕre -volvi -vŏlūtum, *to roll forward, roll along, roll over and over*. LIT., truncum, Verg.; congestas lapidum moles, Tac. Esp. with reflex., or pass. as middle, *to throw oneself down*: se alicui ad pedes, Liv.; provolvi ad genua alicuius, Liv. TRANSF., (**1**) multi fortunis provolvebantur, *were ruined*, Tac. (**2**) pass. as middle, *to abase oneself*: Tac.

prōvŏmo -ĕre, *to vomit forth*: Lucr.

proxĭme, superl. of prope; q.v.

proxĭmĭtās -ātis, f. (proximus), *nearness*. LIT., of place, *vicinity, proximity*: Ov. TRANSF., (**1**) *near relationship*: Ov. (**2**) *similarity*: Ov.

proxĭmus -a -um, superl. of propior; q.v.

prūdens -entis, adj. (with compar. and superl.) (contr. from providens), *foreseeing*. (**1**) *knowing, with intention, with one's eyes open*: quos prudens praetereo, Hor.; prudens et sciens sum profectus, Cic. (**2**) *versed, skilled, experienced, practised in*; with genit.: rei militaris, Nep.; rerum, Cic.; locorum, Liv.; with abl.: iure, Cic.; in iure, Cic.; with infin.: prudens dissipare, Hor. (**3**) *prudent, discreet, wise, judicious*: vir naturā peracutus et prudens, Cic.; ratio, Cic.; Ov., etc. ¶ Adv. **prūdentĕr**, *prudently, discreetly*: facere, Cic.; intellegere, Cic.; superl.: Cic.

prūdentĭa -ae, f. (prudens). (**1**) *foreseeing*: futurorum, Cic. (**2**) *knowledge of any subject*: iuris publici, Cic.; physicorum, Cic.; Juv. (**3**) *prudence, sagacity, discretion*: prudentia est rerum expetendarum fugiendarumque scientia, Cic.; prudentia cernitur in delectu bonorum et malorum, Cic.; Verg., etc.

prūīna -ae, f. *hoar-frost, rime*: Cic., etc. TRANSF., plur.: pruinae, *winter*, Verg.; *snow*: Verg.

prūīnōsus -a -um (pruina), *full of hoar-frost*: nox, Ov.

prūna -ae, f. *a live coal*: Verg., Hor.

prūnītĭus -a -um (prunus), *of plum-tree wood*: Ov.

prūnum -i, n. (prunus), *a plum*: Verg., Ov.

prūnus -i, f. (προύμνη), *a plum-tree*: Verg.

prūrīgo -inis, f. (prurio), *the itch*: Mart.

prūrĭo -ire, *to itch*: Juv., Mart., etc.

Prūsĭās (**Prūsĭa**) -ae, m. *king of Bithynia, who betrayed Hannibal to the Romans*.

prўtănēum -i, n. (πρυτανεῖον), *the town-hall in certain Greek cities where the prytanes assembled and where persons who had done distinguished service to the state were entertained*: Cic.

prўtănis -is, acc. -in, m. (πρύτανις), *a chief magistrate in certain of the Greek states*: Liv.

psallo psallĕre psalli (ψάλλω), *to play on* or *sing to a stringed instrument, especially the cithara*: psallere docta, Hor.; Sall., etc.

psaltērium -i, n. (ψαλτήριον), *a stringed instrument, the psaltery*: Cic., Verg., etc.

psaltēs -ae, m. (ψαλτής), *a player on the cithara*: Quint.

psaltrĭa -ae, f. (ψάλτρια), *a female player on, or singer to, the cithara*: Ter., Cic.

psĕcăs -ādis, f. (ψεκάς), *the female slave who anointed her mistress's hair*: Juv.

psēphisma -ātis, n. (ψήφισμα), *a decree of the people among the Greeks*: Cic., Plin. L.

Pseudŏcăto -ōnis, m. *a sham Cato*: Cic.

Pseudŏdămăsippus -i, m. *a sham Damasippus*: Cic.

Pseudŏlus -i, m. *The Liar* (title of a comedy by Plautus): Cic.

pseudŏmĕnos or **-us** -i, m. (ψευδόμενος), *a sophistical syllogism*: Cic.

pseudŏthўrum -i, n. (ψευδόθυρον), *a secret door*; fig.: per pseudothyrum revertantur (nummi), *in a secret way*, Cic.

psĭthĭus -a -um (ψίθιος), *psithian, name of a kind of Greek vine*: vitis, Verg.; f. as subst. **psĭthĭa** -ae (sc. vitis): Verg.

psittăcus -i, m. (ψίττακος), *a parrot*: loquax, Ov.

psychŏmantīum or **-ēum** -i, n. (ψυχομαντεῖον), *a place where necromancy is practised*: Cic.

-ptĕ, a suffix emphasizing pers. and possess. pron., esp. in the abl., *self, own*: suopte pondere, Cic.; suăpte manu, Cic.; Pl., Ter.

ptĭsăna -ae, f. (πτισάνη), *barley-groats*: Plin.

ptĭsănārĭum -i (ptisana), n. *a decoction of crushed barley or rice*: Hor.

Ptŏlemaeus -i, m. (Πτολεμαῖος), *name of a dynasty of Egyptian kings after the death of Alexander.*
 ¶ Hence adj. **Ptŏlĕmaeēus** and **Ptŏlĕmaeus** -a -um, *belonging to Ptolemy*; poet.=*Egyptian*; subst. **Ptŏlĕmăїs** -ĭdis, f. *name of several towns; one in Egypt, another in Phoenicia, another in Cyrene; also a name of Cleopatra.*

pūbens -entis (pubes), *arrived at puberty.*
 TRANSF., of plants, *in full growth, luxuriant*: Verg.

pūber -bĕris=²pubes; q.v.

pūbertās -ātis, f. (puber), *puberty, the age of maturity.* LIT., nondum pubertatem ingressus, Tac. TRANSF., *the signs of puberty, growth of hair*, etc.: Cic.; *virility*: Tac.

¹**pūbēs** -is, f. *the signs of puberty, the growth of hair*, etc. LIT., Caes. TRANSF., (1) *the pudenda*: Verg. (2) *the youth, adult male population*: omnis Italiae pubes, Verg.; Pl., Cic., etc.

²**pūbēs** and **pūbĕr** -ĕris, *arrived at the age of puberty, adult.*
 LIT., prope puberem aetatem, Liv.; Cic. M. pl. as subst. **pūbĕres** -um, *the men, the adult male population*: Caes., Sall., Tac.
 TRANSF., *downy*: folia, Verg.

pūbesco -bescĕre -būi (pubes), *to arrive at the age of puberty.*
 LIT., Hercules, cum primum pubesceret, Cic.; Verg., etc.
 TRANSF., (1) of plants, *to grow up, arrive at maturity*: quae terra gignit, maturata pubescunt, Cic. (2) *to be covered or clothed*: prata pubescunt variorum flore colorum, Ov.

publĭcānus -a -um (publicus), *relating to the farming of the public taxes*: Cic. Usually m. as subst. **publĭcānus** -i, *a farmer of the Roman taxes* (generally of the equestrian order): Cic., Liv.

publĭcātĭo -ōnis, f. (publico), *a confiscation*: bonorum, Cic.

publĭcē, adv. from publicus; q.v.

publĭcĭtŭs, adv. (publicus). (1) *at the public expense, in the public service*: Pl., Ter. (2) *publicly, before all the world*: Pl.

Publĭcĭus -a -um, *name of a Roman gens.*
 ¶ Hence adj. **Publĭcĭānus** -a -um, *Publician.*

publĭco -are (publicus). (1) *to appropriate to the public use, confiscate*: regnum, Caes.; privata, Cic. (2) *to make public, throw open, publish*: Tac., Suet. (3) *to prostitute*: corpus, Pl.

Publĭcŏla or **Poplĭcŏla** -ae, m. (populus/colo), *the people's friend; a surname of P. Valerius, the first consul of the Roman republic.*

publĭcus -a -um; also **poblĭcus** and **poplĭcus** (populus), *belonging to the people, public, in the name of the people, at the public expense.*
 LIT., res publica, or respublica, *the state*: sumptu publico, *at the cost of the state*, Cic.; bonum publicum, *the commonweal*, Liv.; causa, Cic., Liv.
 M. as subst. **publĭcus** -i, *a state official*: Pl., Caes. N. as subst. **publĭcum** -i. (1) *the property of the state, public territory*: Campanum, Cic. (2) *the public revenue, the treasury*: convivari de publico, *at the cost of the state*, Cic.; in publicum emere, Liv.; in publicum conferre frumenti quod inventum est, Cic. (3) *an open place, the open street*: prodire in publicum, Cic.; blandiores in publico quam in privato, Liv.; publico carere, *to remain at home*, Cic.; proponere in publicum, or in publico, *openly*, Liv., Cic. L.
 TRANSF., (1) *universal, general*: lux publica mundi, *the sun*, Ov.; publica cura iuvenum prodis, *general object of interest*, Hor. (2) *common, bad, ordinary*: structura carminis, Ov.
 ¶ Adv. **publĭcē**. (1) *for the people, publicly, at the public expense*: publice esse laudem, *it is an honour to the state*, Caes.; publice scribere, litteras mittere, Cic.; vesci, Liv. (2) *all together*: publice ire exsulatum, Liv.

Publĭlĭus -a -um, *name of a Roman gens.* As adj., *relating to the Publilian gens*: Liv.

Publĭus -i, m. *a Roman praenomen*, abbrev. P.

pŭdendus -a -um, gerundive from pudeo; q.v.

pŭdens -entis, partic. from pudeo; q.v.

pŭdĕo -ēre. (1) *to be ashamed*: Pl. (2) usually 3rd person, *to cause shame, fill with shame*; with acc. of the pers.: **a**, with n. pron., infin., or clause as subject: non te haec pudent? Ter.; pudet dicere, Cic.: **b**, impers., **pudet**, *without subject, but with* genit. of the thing causing shame: te huius templi pudet, Cic.; with genit. alone: pudet deorum hominumque, *it is a disgrace before God and men*, Liv.
 ¶ Hence gerundive **pŭdendus** -a -um, *of which one ought to be ashamed, shameful, disgraceful*: vulnera, Verg.; vita, Ov.; Cic.

¶ Partic. (with compar. and superl.) **pŭdens** -entis, *modest, shamefaced*: pudentes ac boni viri, Cic.; te videri pudentiorem fuisse, Cic.; femina pudentissima, Cic.; Hor.
¶ Adv. (with compar. and superl.) **pŭden-tĕr**, *modestly, bashfully*: Cic.; pudentissime hoc Cicero petierat, Cic.; Hor.

pŭdĭbundus -a -um (pudeo), *shamefaced, modest, bashful*: matrona, Hor.

pŭdīcē, adv. from pudicus; q.v.

pŭdīcĭtĭa -ae, f. (pudicus), *modesty, chastity, virtue*: Pl.; Cic., Liv.; personif. as a goddess: Liv.

pŭdīcus -a -um (pudeo), *modest, chaste, virtuous*. Lit., of persons: Cic., etc. Transf., of things: mores, preces, Ov.
¶ Adv. **pŭdīcē**, *modestly, chastely*: Pl., Ter., Cat.

pŭdor -ōris, m. (pudeo), *the feeling of shame, bashfulness, modesty, decency, honour*.
Lit., natura pudorque meus, *my natural modesty*, Cic.; paupertatis, *on account of poverty*, Hor.; famae, Cic.; pudor est, with infin., *I am ashamed*, Ov. Esp. *chastity, purity*: pudorem proicere, Ov.
Transf., *that which causes shame, a disgrace*: pudori esse, Liv.; Ov.

pŭella -ae, f. (puellus), *a girl, maiden*.
Lit., Cic., Verg., etc.; Danai puellae, *the Danaids*, Hor.
Transf., (**1**) *a young woman, young wife*; used of Penelope: Ov.; puella Phasias, Medea, Ov.; Cressa, Phaedra, Ov. (**2**) *a sweetheart*: Hor., Ov.

pŭellāris -e (puella), *of a girl* or *young woman, girlish, maidenly*: Ov., Tac.
Adv. **pŭellārĭtĕr**, *girlishly*: Plin. L.

pŭellŭla -ae, f. (dim. of puella), *a little girl*: Ter., Cat.

pŭellus -i, m. (dim. of puer, for puerulus), *a little boy*: Pl.

pŭer -i, m. *a child*.
Lit., of either sex, *a child*; plur., pueri=*children*: Cic., Hor., etc. Esp. *a male child, boy, lad*; used up to the age of about seventeen: puer sive iam adulescens, Cic.; a puero, a pueris, *from boyhood*, Cic.; ex pueris excedere, *to pass out of boyhood*, Cic. Sometimes=*son*: Latonae, Apollo, Hor.; Ledae pueri, Castor and Pollux, Hor.
Transf., (**1**) (like παῖς), *a serving-lad, servant, slave*: tuus, Cic.; pueri regii, *royal pages*, Liv. (**2**) *an unmarried man, a bachelor*: Ov. (**3**) colloq. form of address, *my boy*: Ter.

ŏuěra -ae, f. (puer), *a girl*: Varr., Suet.

ŏuěrīlis -e (puer), *youthful, boyish*. Lit., aetas, Cic.; Verg., Liv. Transf., *puerile, childish, silly*: consilium, Cic.
¶ Adv. **pŭěrīlĭtěr**. Lit., *boyishly, like a boy*: blandiri, Liv. Transf., *childishly, foolishly*: facere, Cic.; Pl., Tac.

ŏuěrītĭa (puertia: Hor.) -ae, f. (puer), *boyhood*: a pueritia, *from boyhood*, Cic.; Ter., Sall., etc.

ŏuerpěrĭum -i, n. (puerperus), *childbirth, labour*: Pl., Tac.

ŏuerpěrus -a -um (puer/pario), *relating to childbirth*: verba, *words supposed to assist labour*, Ov. F. as subst. **pŭerpěra** -ae, *a woman in labour*: Pl., Cat., Hor.

ŏuertĭa=pueritia; q.v.

pŭěrŭlus -i, m. (dim. of puer), *a little boy, a young slave*: Cic.

pūga (pȳga) -ae, f. (πυγή), *the rump, buttocks*: Hor.

pŭgil -ilis, m. (connected with pugnus), *a boxer, fighter with the* caestus: Ter., Cic., Ov.

pŭgĭlātĭo -ōnis, f. (pugil); *fighting with the* caestus; *boxing*: Cic.

pŭgĭlātus -ūs, m. (pugil), *fighting with the* caestus; *boxing*: Pl.

pŭgillāris -e (pugillus), *that can be grasped with the fist*: Juv. M. pl. as subst. **pŭgillāres** -ĭum, (sc. libelli), *writing-tablets*: Sen., Plin. L. So also n. pl. as subst. **pŭgillārĭa** -ĭum: Cat.

pŭgillus -i, m. (dim. of pugnus), *a handful*: Plin.

pŭgĭo -ōnis, m. (pungo), *a dagger, dirk, poniard*. Lit., cruentum pugionem tenens, Cic.; Tac. Transf., plumbeus pugio, *a weak argument*, Cic.

pūgĭuncŭlus -i, m. (dim. of pugio), *a little dagger*: Cic.

pugna -ae, f. (connected with pugnus), *a fight, a battle*.
Lit., res ad pugnam atque manūs vocabatur, Cic.; pugna equestris, *cavalry engagement*, Cic.; navalis, Cic.; pedestris, Verg.; pugnā decertare, Caes.; pugnam inire, Liv.
Transf., (**1**) *battle line, array*: pugnam mediam tueri, Liv. (**2**) in gen., *contest, contention*: doctissimorum hominum, Cic.; Pl.

pugnācĭtās -ātis, f. (pugnax), *desire of fighting, pugnacity*: Tac., Quint.

pugnācĭtěr, adv. from pugnax; q.v.

pugnācŭlum -i, n. (pugno), *a fortress*: Pl.

pugnātor -ōris, m. (pugno), *a fighter, combatant, soldier*: Liv., Suet.

pugnax -ācis (pugno), *fond of fighting, combative*. Lit., pugnax Minerva, Ov.; centurio, Cic. Transf., (**1**) of persons, *obstinate, contentious*: Cic. (**2**) of things: oratio pugnacior, Cic.; Plin. L., etc.
¶ Adv. **pugnācĭtěr**, *obstinately, contentiously*: certare cum aliquo, Cic.; pugnacissime defendere sententiam, Cic.

pugno -are (pugna), *to fight, combat, give battle*.
Lit., both of single combatants and of whole armies: cum hoste, Cic.; in hostem, Sall., Liv.; ex equo, Cic.; pro commodis patriae, Cic.; with acc.: pugnam, Pl., Cic., Liv.; proelia, Sall., Hor.; bella, Hor.; pugna summā contentione pugnata, Cic.; impers.: pugnatur uno tempore omnibus locis, Caes.; partic. as subst.: pugnantes, *the combatants*, Caes.
Transf., (**1**) in gen., *to struggle, to contend, fight*: pugnant Stoici cum Peripateticis, Cic.; with dat.: Verg., Cat.; with acc. and infin., *to maintain in dispute*: Cic.; of things: pugnat diu sententia secum, Ov. (**2**) *to strive, struggle, exert oneself*; followed by ut or ne or quominus with the subj.: illud pugna et enitere ut, Cic.; Liv., Ov.

pugnus -i, m. (cf. πύξ), *the fist*: pugnum facere, Cic.; aliquem pugnis concidere, Cic.; Pl., Hor., etc.

pulchellus -a -um (dim. of pulcher), *very pretty*: Bacchae, Cic. L.

¹**pulcher** -chra -chrum and **pulcer** -cra -crum, adj. (with compar. and superl.), *beautiful, fair, lovely.*
LIT., physically: puer, Cic.; quid aspectu pulchrius? Cic.; urbs pulcherrima, Caes.; Ter., Verg., Hor., etc.
TRANSF., morally, *excellent, admirable, fine*: exemplum, Caes.; facinus, Sall.; illis pulcherrimum fuit tantam vobis imperii gloriam tradere, Cic.; consilia, Verg.; Hor., etc.
¶ Adv. **pulchrē (pulcrē)**, *beautifully, finely, excellently*: dicere, Cic.; pulchre est mihi, *all's well with me*, Cic., Hor.; as an exclamation of approval, *bravo! well done!*: Ter., Hor.
²**Pulcher** -chri, m. *a Roman surname*, as of, e.g., P. Claudius Pulcher.
pulchritūdo -ĭnis, f. (¹pulcher), *beauty, excellence.* LIT., corporis, Cic., Liv. TRANSF., moral *excellence*: virtutis, Cic.; verborum, Quint.
pūlēium (pūlēgium) -i, n. *fleabane, pennyroyal*: Cic., Mart. TRANSF., ad cuius rutam puleio mihi tui sermonis utendum est, *sweetness*, Cic. L.
pūlex -ĭcis, m. *a flea*: Pl.
pullārius -i, m. (¹pullus), *the feeder of the sacred chickens*: Cic.
pullātus -a -um (²pullus), *clad in dirty* or *black garments*: Quint. Esp. of mourners: pullati proceres, Juv.
pullŭlo -are (¹pullus), *to shoot up, sprout out.* LIT., of plants: Verg.; poet.: tot pullulat atra columbis, *burgeons with*, Verg. TRANSF., quae (luxuria) incipiebat pullulare, *luxuriate*, Nep.
¹**pullus** -i, m. (root pu, whence puer), *a young animal.* LIT., in gen.: columbinus, Cic. L.; ranae, Hor. Esp. of chickens: Cic., Liv., Hor. TRANSF., of men. (1) as a term of endearment, *chicken, chick*: Pl., Hor. (2) pullus milvinus, *a young kite*, Cic. L.
²**pullus** -a -um (connected with πελλός), *dark-coloured, blackish, greyish-black*: capilli, Ov.; myrtus, *dark-green*, Hor.; esp.: pulla vestis, *a garment of undyed wool, worn as mourning*, Cic.; poet.: pulla stamina (of the threads of the Parcae), *sad, gloomy*, Ov. N. as subst. **pullum** -i, *a dark-coloured garment*: Liv., Ov.
pulmentārium -i, n. (pulmentum), *a relish, anything eaten with bread*: pulmentaria quaere sudando, *get an appetite by hard work*, Hor.; Pl.
pulmentum -i, n. (puls), *a relish*: Hor. In general, *food, victuals*: mullum in singula pulmenta minuere, *into small portions*, Hor.
pulmo -ōnis, m. (from πλεύμων = πνεύμων). (1) *the lung*; usually plur., pulmones, *the lungs*: Pl., Cic., Ov. (2) *the sea-lung*: Pl.
pulmōnĕus -a -um, *of the lungs, pulmonary*: Pl.
pulpa -ae, f. *flesh.* LIT., Mart. TRANSF., pulpa scelerata, *the flesh, as sign of sensuality*, Pers.
pulpāmentum -i, n. (pulpa), *flesh*, esp. *tit-bits*: mihi est pulpamentum fama, Cic.
pulpĭtum -i, n. *a platform*: Hor. Esp. for actors, *'the boards' of a theatre*: Hor., Juv.
puls pultis, f. (πόλτος), *a porridge of flour, pulse*, etc., *used at sacrifices and as food for the sacred chickens*: Cic., Juv.

pulsātĭo -ōnis, f. (pulso), *a knocking, striking, beating*: scutorum, Liv.; Pl., Cic.
pulso -are (freq. of pello), *to strike, beat, knock.* LIT., ostium, Pl.; pede libero tellurem, Hor.; pedibus spatium Olympi, Ov.; pulsare et verberare aliquem, Cic.; of using a lyre or bow: Verg. TRANSF., *to stir, move, affect*: dormientium animos externā et adventiciā visione pulsari, Cic.; pavor pulsans, Verg.
pulsus -ūs, m. (pello), *a beating, striking, blow, push.* LIT., remorum, Caes., Cic., Liv.; pedum, Verg.; lyrae, *a playing on the lyre*, Ov.; pulsum venarum attingere, *to feel the pulse*, Tac. TRANSF., *influence, impulse*: externus pulsus animos commovet, Cic.
pultātĭo -onis, f. (pulto), *a knocking*: Pl.
pultĭphăgus -i, m. (puls/φαγεῖν), *a porridge-eater*: Pl.
pulto -are (=pulso), *to knock, beat, strike*: ianuam, Pl.
pulvĕrĕus -a -um (pulvis). (1) *full of dust, dusty*: nubes, *dust-clouds*, Verg.; solum, Ov. (2) *raising dust*: palla (Boreae), Ov.
pulvĕrŭlentus -a -um (pulvis). (1) *full of dust, dusty.* LIT., via, Cic. L.; aestas, Verg. TRANSF., praemia militiae, Ov. (2) *raising dust*: Verg.
pulvillus -i, m. (dim. of pulvinus), *a little pillow*: Hor.
pulvīnar -āris, n. (pulvinus). (1) *a couch covered with cushions for the images of the gods at the Lectisternium* (q.v.): pulvinar suscipere, Liv.; dedicare, Cic.; ad omnia pulvinaria supplicatio decreta est, *at all the temples*, Cic. (2) *a state couch, for any distinguished person*: Ov., Juv.
pulvīnārĭum -i, n. (pulvinar), *an anchorage*: Pl.
pulvīnus -i, m. (1) *a pillow, cushion*: Pl., Cic., Sall. (2) *a seat of honour*: Juv., Suet.
pulvis -ĕris, m. (rarely f.), *dust, powder.*
LIT., multus erat in calceis pulvis, Cic.; pulvis eruditus, *the sand* or *dust in which mathematicians drew their diagrams*, Cic.; pulvis exiguus, *a handful of dust*, Hor.; pulvis hibernus, *dry winter*, Verg.; plur.: novendiales pulveres, *fresh ashes of the dead*, Hor.; prov.: sulcos in pulvere ducere, *to labour in vain*, Juv. Esp. *the dust of the circus* or *wrestling-place*: pulvis Olympicus, Hor.; domitant in pulvere currūs, Verg.
TRANSF., *a place of exercise, arena, scene of action*: doctrinam in solem atque pulverem produxit, Cic.; sine pulvere palmae, *prize without effort*, Hor.
pulviscŭlus -i, m. (dim. of pulvis), *fine dust*: Pl.
pūmex -ĭcis, m. (f. Cat.), *pumice-stone.* LIT., esp. as used for polishing marble, books, etc.: Cat., Hor., Ov. TRANSF., *any kind of soft, porous stone*: pumices cavi, Verg.; Ov.
pūmĭcĕus -a -um (pumex), *made of pumice-stone.* LIT., Ov. TRANSF., oculi, *dry*, Pl.
pūmĭco -are (pumex), *to polish with pumice-stone*: Cat., Mart.
pūmĭlio -ōnis, c. (pumilus), *a dwarf*: Lucr., Mart.
pūmĭlus -i, m. *a dwarf*: Stat., Suet.
punctim, adv. (pungo), *by stabbing, by thrusting* (opp. caesim): petere hostem, Liv.
punctum -i, n. subst. from pungo; q.v.

pungo pungĕre pŭpŭgi punctum, *to prick, puncture, stab.*
   LIT., neminem, Cic.; also *to make by piercing*: vulnus quod acu punctum videretur, Cic.
   TRANSF., (1) *to penetrate, enter*: corpus, Lucr. (2) *to touch, move*: sensum, Lucr. (3) *to prick off*; hence: puncto tempore, *in a moment*, Lucr. (4) *to sting, vex, annoy*: epistula illa ita me pupugit, ut somnum mihi ademerit, Cic. L.; Pl., Prop.
   ¶ N. of partic. as subst. **punctum** -i, *a prick.* LIT., *a little hole, small puncture*: Mart. TRANSF., (1) *a point, spot*: Plin. (2) in the comitia, *the point made on a tablet as a candidate was voted for*; hence *a vote*: quot in ea tribu puncta tuleris, Cic.; fig.: discedo Alcaeus puncto illius, Hor.; omne tulit punctum qui miscuit utile dulci, Hor. (3) *a mathematical point*: Cic. (4) *any small point in space*: quasi punctum terrae, Cic. (5) *a small portion of time, a moment*: temporis, Ter., Caes., Cic.; horae, Hor. (6) in discourse, *a short clause, section*: puncta argumentorum, Cic.
pūnĭcĕus -a -um (Punicus), *purple, red*: crocus, cruor, Ov.; Verg.
Pūnĭcus, Pūnĭcē, see Poeni.
pūnĭo (poenĭo) -īre and **pūnĭor** -īri, dep. (poena). (1) *to punish*: sontes, Cic.; aliquem supplicio, Cic.; peccatum, Cic.; Liv., Ov. (2) *to avenge*: dolorem, Cic.; necem, Cic.
pūnītor -ōris, m. (punio), *a punisher, avenger*: doloris, Cic.
pūpa -ae, f. (pupus), *a little girl*: Mart. TRANSF., *a doll*: Pers.
pūpilla -ae, f. (dim. of pupa). (1) *an orphan girl, ward, minor*: Cic. (2) (like Gr. κόρη), *the pupil of the eye*: Lucr.
pūpillāris -e (pupillus), *of an orphan* or *ward*: pecuniae, Liv.
pūpillus -i, m. (dim. of pupulus), *an orphan* or *ward*: Cic., Hor.
Pupinĭa -ae, f. (sc. regio), *the Pupinian country in Latium, a sterile tract of country*; also called Pupiniensis ager, Liv.
Pūpĭus -a -um, *name of a Roman gens.* As adj., lex Pupia, *a law proposed by Pupius.*
puppis -is, f. (acc. sing. puppim; abl. puppī, rarely puppĕ), *the poop* or *stern of a vessel.*
   LIT., navem convertere ad puppim, Cic. L.; ventus surgens a puppi, *from astern*, Verg.; fig.: sedebamus in puppi, *I sat at the helm of the state*, Cic.
   TRANSF., (1) *the whole ship*: Verg., Hor. (2) *the constellation of the Ship*: Cic.
pūpŭla -ae, f. (dim. of pupa), *the pupil of the eye.* LIT., Cic., Hor. TRANSF., *the whole eye*: Cic., Ov.
pūpŭlus -i, m. (dim. of pupus), *a little boy*: Cat.
pūpus -i, m. *a boy, child*: Varr. Used as a term of endearment: Suet.
pūrē, adv. from purus; q.v.
purgāmen -ĭnis, n. (purgo). (1) *filth, dirt, sweepings*: Vestae, *that which was annually swept from the temple of Vesta*, Ov. (2) *a means of purgation or expiation*: caedis, Ov.
purgāmentum -i, n. (purgo), *that which is cleaned out, sweepings, rubbish, filth*: urbis, Liv.; Tac.
purgātĭo -ōnis, f. (purgo), *a cleaning out,*

cleansing. LIT., alvi, *purging*, Cic. TRANSF., *excusing, justification*: Ter., Cic.
purgo -are (purigo, from purus).
   (1) *to clean, cleanse.* LIT., locum, *to clear*: Cic., Liv.; arva longis ligonibus, Ov.; with genit.: purgatum te illius morbi, *healed*, Hor. TRANSF., a, *to purge, cleanse*: pectora, Lucr.: b, *to excuse, defend, justify*: aliquem de luxuria, Cic.; civitatem facti dictique, Liv.; with acc. and infin., *to allege in defence*: Liv.: c, ceremonially, *to purify*: populos, Ov.
   (2) *to clear away, wash off.* LIT., bilem, Hor. TRANSF., esp. of accusations, etc.: crimina, Cic., Liv.; *malum facinus forti facinore*, Liv.; suspicionem, Liv.
pūrĭtĕr, adv. from purus; q.v.
purpŭra -ae, f. (πορφύρα), *the purple-fish.* LIT., Plin. TRANSF., (1) *purple dye, purple*: Verg., Hor. (2) *stuff dyed purple, purple cloth*: Cic., Verg., Ov. (3) '*the purple*', *high rank*, etc.: Lucr., Hor., Ov.
purpŭrātus -a -um (purpura), *clad in purple*: mulier, Pl.; Liv. M. as subst., *a man of high rank, a courtier*: purpuratis tuis ista minitare, Cic.; Liv.
purpŭrĕus -a -um (πορφύρεος).
   LIT., *purple-coloured*; and so of shades resembling purple, as *dark-red, dark-brown, dark-violet*: vestitus, Cic.; rubor, *blush*, Ov.; capillus, crinis, Verg.; mare, Cic.; flos rosae, Hor.
   TRANSF., (1) *clad in purple*: rex, Ov.; tyrannus, Hor. (2) in gen., *gleaming, bright, beautiful*: olores, Hor.; ver, Verg.
pūrus -a -um, adj. (with compar. and superl.), *clean, pure.*
   LIT., unda, Verg.; fons, Pl.; aëre purior ignis, Ov.; sol, Hor.; terra, *cleared of stones, stubble*, etc., Cic.; vestis, Verg. N. as subst., purum, *the clear sky*: Verg., Hor.
   TRANSF., (1) *without addition, simple, plain*: hasta, *without a head*, Prop.; argentum, *without reliefs*, Cic.; nardum, *unadulterated*, Tib. (2) morally, *upright, pure*: purus et integer, Cic.; with genit.: sceleris, Hor.; with abl.: vitio, Hor.; animam puram conservare, Cic. So of ceremonial: locus, *undefiled*, Liv.; familia, *free from mourning* (by completion of funeral rites), Cic. (3) of style, *pure, faultless*: oratio, Cic.; genus dicendi, Cic. (4) as legal t. t., *without conditions, absolute, unconditional*: iudicium, Cic. (5) in business, *clear (gain, profit)*: quid possit ad dominos puri ac reliqui pervenire, Cic.
   ¶ Hence adv. **pūrē** and poet. **pūrĭtĕr,** *purely, cleanly.*
   LIT., pure lauta corpora, Liv.; compar.: splendens Pario marmore purius, Hor.
   TRANSF., (1) *clearly, naturally, wholly*: pure apparere, Hor. (2) *uprightly, purely*: pure et eleganter acta vita, Cic.; si vitam puriter egi, Cat.; of ceremonial: pure et caste deos venerari, Cic. (3) of style, *purely, faultlessly*: pure et emendate loqui, Cic.
pūs pūris, n. *corrupt matter.* TRANSF., *bitterness, gall, venom*: Hor.
pŭsillus -a -um, dim. *very small, tiny, puny.* LIT., testis, Cic.; epistula, Cic. TRANSF., *petty, mean*: animus, Cic. L., Hor.; causa, Ov.

pŭsĭŏ -ōnis, m. *a little boy*: Cic., Juv.
pustŭla -ae, f. (pus), *a blister, pimple*: Sen., Mart.
pustŭlātus -a -um (pustula), *of metal, refined*: Suet., Mart.
pŭtă, imperat. from puto; q.v.
pŭtāmen -ĭnis, n. (puto), *a cutting, paring, shred, shell*: Cic.
pŭtātĭō -ōnis, f. (puto), *a pruning*: Cic.
pŭtātŏr -ōris, m. (puto), *a pruner*: Ov.
pŭtĕal -ālis, n. (puteus), *a stone curb round the mouth of a well*: Cic. L. TRANSF., *a similar enclosure round a sacred place*—e.g., the Puteal Libonis at Rome, where the usurers carried on business: Cic., Hor., Ov.
pŭtĕālis -e (puteus), *of a well*: undae, Ov.; lymphae, Lucr.
pŭtĕo -ēre, f. *to stink*: Cic.
Pŭtĕŏlī -ōrum, m. *a coast-town in Campania, with mineral springs, a favourite resort of the Romans* (now *Pozzuolo*).
  ¶ Hence adj. **Pŭtĕŏlānus** -a -um, *belonging to Puteoli*; m. pl. as subst. **Pŭtĕŏlāni** -ōrum, *the people of Puteoli*.
pŭter -tris -tre and **putris** -e (connected with puteo). LIT., *rotten, putrid*: poma, Ov.; fervent examina putri de bove, Ov. TRANSF., *loose, flabby, crumbling, friable*: gleba, Verg.; campus, Verg.; mammae, Hor.; oculi, *languishing,* Hor.
pŭtesco pūtescĕre pūtŭi (puteo), *to decay, become rotten*: Cic., Hor.
pŭtĕus -i, m. *a well, a pit*: Pl., Cic., Verg., Hor.
pūtĭdiuscŭlus -a -um (dim. of putidus), *somewhat affected, nauseous*: Cic.
pūtĭdus -a -um (puteo), *rotten, stinking, putrid.* LIT., caro, Cic. TRANSF., *foul, rotten*: femina, Hor.; compar.: cerebrum putidius, *more addled,* Hor. Esp. of style, *affected, in bad taste*: etiam Demosthenes, Cic.
  ¶ Hence adv. (with compar.) **pūtĭdē,** of discourse, *affectedly, disgustingly*: dicere, Cic.; putidius litteras exprimere, Cic.
pŭto -are (root pu, whence purus), *to cleanse, clear.*
  LIT., esp. of trees, *to lop, to prune*: vites, Verg.
  TRANSF., (1) *to clear up, settle*; esp. of accounts: rationes cum publicanis, Cic. L. Hence, *to weigh up, consider a matter*: illud, Cic.; multa, Verg. (2) *to reckon, estimate, value*; with genit. of value: magni putare honores, Cic.; with abl.: aliquid denariis quadringentis, Cic.; with pro and the abl.: aliquem pro nihilo, Cic.; with in and the abl.: in hominum numero putabat, Cic.; with acc. of predicate: se solum beatum, Cic. (3) *to consider, hold, believe, think*: recte, Pl. With acc. and infin.: noli putare me maluisse, Cic.; absol.: non putaram, Cic.; parenthetically: puto *or* ut puto, *I suppose,* Cic. L.; imperat., puta, used adverbially, *suppose, for example*: Hor., Sen.
pŭtor -ōris, m. (puteo), *a bad smell, stink* or perhaps *muddiness*: Lucr.
putrĕfăcĭo -făcĕre -fēci -factum (puter/facio). LIT., *to make rotten*; pass., *to become rotten, decay*: nudatum tectum patere imbribus putrefaciendum, Liv.; Lucr. TRANSF., *to make pliable, to soften*: ardentia saxa infuso aceto, Liv.; Lucr.

putresco -ĕre (puter), *to become rotten, to decay*: Hor.
putrĭdus -a -um (puter). LIT., *rotten, decayed*: dentes, Cic. TRANSF., *loose, flabby*: Cat.
pūtus -a -um (root pu, whence puto, purus), *pure, unmixed, unadulterated*; usually found in connexion with purus: Pl. Superl.: meae putissimae orationes, Cic. L.
pŭtus -i, m. (connected with puer), *a boy*: Verg.
pycta (-ēs) -ae, m. (πύκτης), *a boxer, pugilist*: Phaedr., Sen.
Pydna -ae, f. (Πύδνα), *a town in Macedonia, where Aemilius Paulus defeated Perseus, king of Macedonia,* 169 B.C.
  ¶ Hence **Pydnaei** -ōrum, m. pl. *the inhabitants of Pydna.*
pȳga=puga; q.v.
pȳgargus -i, m. (πύγαργος), *a species of antelope*: Juv.
Pygmaei -ōrum, m. (Πυγμαῖοι), *the Pygmies, a race of dwarfs supposed to inhabit Africa, and to engage in war with cranes.*
  ¶ Hence adj. **Pygmaeus** -a -um, *Pygmaean*: quae Pygmaeo sanguine gaudet avis, *the crane,* Ov.
Pygmălĭōn -ōnis, m. (Πυγμαλίων). (1) *grandson of Agenor, who fell in love with a beautiful statue which he had made; Venus at his prayer endowed it with life.* (2) *a king of Tyre, brother of Dido, whose husband he slew.*
Pylădēs -ae and -is, m. (Πυλάδης), *son of Strophius, and the faithful friend of Orestes*; prov. for *a faithful friend*: Ov.
  ¶ Hence adj. **Pylădēus** -a -um: amicitia i.e. *faithful, tender,* Cic.
Pylae -ārum, f. (πύλαι, gates), *a pass between mountains, defiles.* (1) Tauri, *separating Cappadocia from Cilicia,* Cic. (2)=*Thermopylae*: Liv.
  ¶ Hence adj. **Pylăĭcus** -a -um, *relating to Thermopylae*: conventus, *a congress held at Thermopylae,* Liv.
Pylus (-ŏs) -i, f. (Πύλος), *name of two cities in the Peloponnesus, one in Messenia, the residence of Neleus* (now *Palaio Navarino*); *the other in Triphylia, the residence of Nestor, hence called Nestorea*: Ov.
  ¶ Hence adj. **Pylĭus** -a -um, *of Pylos*; M. as subst. **Pylĭus** -i, *the Pylian,* i.e. *Nestor.*
pȳra -ae, f. (πυρά), *a funeral pyre*: Verg.
pȳrămĭs -ĭdis, f. (πυραμίς), *a pyramid*: Prop. Tac. TRANSF., *a cone*: Cic.
Pȳrămus -i, m. (Πύραμος). (1) *the lover of Thisbe.* (2) *a river in Cilicia.*
Pyrēnē -ēs, f. (Πυρήνη), *daughter of Bebryx, beloved by Hercules, buried in the mountain range called after her.*
  ¶ Hence adj. **Pyrēnaeus** -a -um, *belonging to Pyrene*: Pyrenaei Montes, *the Pyrenees, the mountains between Gaul and Spain.*
pȳrethrum -i, n. (πύρεθρον), *a plant, pellitory*: Ov.
Pyrgi -ōrum, m. (Πύργοι), *a town in Etruria.*
  ¶ Hence adj. **Pyrgensis** -e, *belonging to Pyrgi.*
pȳrōpus -i, m. (πυρωπός), *a kind of mixed metal bronze*: Lucr., Ov.
Pyrrha -ae and **Pyrrhē** -ēs, f. (Πύρρα), *daughter of Epimetheus, wife of Deucalion.* **Pyrrhĭā** -ădis, adj., *relating to the town of Pyrrha in Lesbos.*

pyrrhicha -ae and **pyrrhichē** -ēs, f. (πυρρίχη), *a dance in armour*: Plin., Suet.

Pyrrhō -ōnis, m. (Πύρρων), *a Greek philosopher of Elis, founder of the so-called Sceptical school, contemporary of Alexander the Great.* ¶ Hence **Pyrrhōnēi** -ōrum, m. pl. *the followers of Pyrrho.*

Pyrrhus -i, m. (Πύρρος). (1) *son of Achilles and Deidamia of Scyrus* (also called Neoptolemos), *founder of a monarchy in Epirus, killed at Delphi by Orestes.* (2) *a king of Epirus, enemy of the Romans.*

Pȳthăgŏrās -ae, m. (Πυθαγόρας), *Greek philosopher of Samos* (about 540 B.C.), *who afterwards settled in S. Italy, and founded the school named after him.* ¶ Hence adj. **Pȳthăgŏrēus** -a -um, *Pythagorean,* and subst. *a Pythagorean.*

Pȳtho -ūs, f. (Πυθώ), *the old name of Delphi.* ¶ Hence adj. **Pȳthĭcus, Pȳthĭus** -a -um, *Pythian, Delphic, relating to Apollo*: Cic., Liv. F. as subst. **Pȳthĭa** -ae, *the priestess who delivered the oracles at Delphi*; n. pl. as subst. **Pȳthĭa** -ōrum, (τὰ Πύθια), *the Pythian games, celebrated every fourth year near Delphi in honour of Apollo.*

Pȳthōn -ōnis, m. (Πύθων), *a great snake killed by Apollo near Delphi.*

pȳtisma -ātis, m. (πύτισμα), *the wine which is spit out* or *spurted through the lips* (in tasting): Juv.

pȳtisso -are (πυτίζω), *to spit out wine* (in tasting): Ter.

pyxĭs -ĭdis, f. (πυξίς), *a little box, casket, used for drugs,* etc.: veneni, Cic., Suet.

Q

Q, q, the sixteenth letter of the Latin Alphabet, only used before u and another vowel. Latin qu sometimes represents the Greek π; e.g. quinque πέντε, equus ἵππος, sequor ἕπω. For abbreviations in which Q. is used, *see* Table of Abbreviations.

quā, abl. f. of qui, used as adv. (1) relat., *by which way, on which side, where.* LIT., of place: ad omnes introitus qua adiri poterat, Cic.; ea . . . qua, Caes.; Verg. TRANSF., *whereby*: Caes., etc.; *as far as*: Cic., Liv.; qua . . . qua, *partly . . . partly, as well . . . as . . .*: qua dominus qua advocatus, Cic.; Liv. (2) interrog., *by what way? in what manner? how?*: illuc qua veniam? Cic.; Verg. (3) indef., *in any way, at all*: Verg.

quācumque (-cunque), adv. (often in tmesis), *by whatever way, wherever.* LIT., of place: quacumque iter fecit, Caes., Cic., Liv. TRANSF., *in whatever way*: Verg.

quādamtĕnŭs, adv. *to a certain point, so far*; found in tmesis: est quadam prodire tenus, Hor.

quadra -ae, f. *a square.* (1) *a square piece of bread used as a plate*: Verg. (2) *a dining-table*: alienā vivere quadrā, *to live at another person's table,* Juv. (3) *any square piece* or *morsel*: Hor., Mart.

quadrāgēni -ae -a, num. distrib. (quadraginta), *forty at a time, forty each*: Caes., Cic., Liv.

quadrāgēsĭmus (-gensĭmus) -a -um

(quadraginta), *fortieth.* F. as subst. **quadrāgēsĭma** -ae (sc. pars), *the fortieth part*; esp. *as a tax*: Tac.

quadrāgĭes (-iens), adv. (quadraginta), *forty times*: Cic., Liv.

quadrāginta, *forty*: Cic., etc.

quadrans -antis, m. (quadro), *a fourth part, quarter.* (1) heres ex quadrante, *heir to the fourth part of the property,* Suet. (2) *a coin, the fourth part of an* as: Liv., Juv.; esp. as *the price of a bath*: dum tu quadrante lavatum rex ibis, Hor. (3) *a liquid measure, quarter of a* sextarius: Mart.

quadrantal -ālis, n. *a liquid measure, containing* 8 congii: Pl.

quadrantārĭus -a -um (quadrans), *of a quarter.* (1) tabulae quadrantariae, *reduction of debts by a quarter in consequence of the* lex Valeria feneratoria, Cic. (2) *costing a quarter of an* as: mulier, Cic.

quadrātus -a -um, partic. from quadro; q.v.

quadrīdŭum (quatrīdŭum) -i, n. (quattuor, dies), *a space of four days*: quadriduo quo haec gesta sunt, Cic.; Pl., Liv.

quadriennĭum -i, n. (quattuor/annus), *a period of four years*: Cic.

quadrĭfārĭam, adv. (quattuor), *fourfold, in four parts*: Liv.

quadrĭfĭdus -a -um (quattuor/findo), *split into four portions*: Verg.

quadrīgae -ārum, f. (= quadriiugae; quattuor/iugum), *a team of four horses abreast,* esp. drawing a chariot; *a four-horse chariot.* LIT., alborum equorum, Liv.; curru quadrigarum vehi, Cic.; Verg.; etc. TRANSF., equis aut quadrigis poeticis, Cic.

quadrīgārĭus -a -um (quadrigae), *of a racing charioteer*: habitus, Suet. M. as subst., *a charioteer*: Suet.

quadrīgātus -a -um (quadriga), *stamped with the figure of a four-horse chariot*: Liv.

quadrĭgŭlae -ārum, f. (dim. of quadrigae), *a little team of four horses*: Cic.

quadriiŭgis -e (quattuor/iugum), *in a team of four*: equi, Verg.

quadriiŭgus -ā -um (quattuor/iugum), *in* or *with a team of four*: equi, Ov.; currus, Verg. M. pl. as subst. **quadriiŭgi** -ōrum, *a team of four horses*: Ov.

quadrĭlībris -e (quattuor/libra), *weighing four pounds*: Pl.

quadrĭmēstris -e (quattuor/mensis). (1) *four months old*: Varr. (2) *lasting four months*: Suet.

quadrĭmŭlus -a -um (dim. of quadrimus), *only four years old*: Pl.

quadrĭmus -a -um (quattuor), *four years old*: Cic. L., Hor., Liv.

quadrĭngēnārĭus -a -um (quadringeni), *of four hundred each*: Cic. L., Liv.

quadringēni -ae -a (quadringenti), *four hundred at a time, four hundred each*: Liv., Suet.

quadringentēsĭmus (-ensĭmus) -a -um (quadringenti), *the four hundredth*: Liv.

quadringenti -ae -a (quattuor/centum), *four hundred*: Cic.

quadringentĭēs (-iens), adv. (quadringenti), *four hundred times*: Cic.

quadrĭpertitus -a -um (quattuor/pars), *divided into four parts, fourfold*: distributio, Cic.; Tac.

quadrĭrēmis -e (quattuor/remus), *with four banks of oars*: navis, Liv.
  F. as subst. **quadrĭrēmis** -is, *a ship with four banks of oars, a quadrireme*: Caes., Cic., Liv.

quadrĭvĭum -i, n. (quattuor/via), *a place where four roads meet, a crossroads*: Cat., Juv.

quadro -are (quadrum).
  (1) transit., *to make square, to square.* TRANSF., *to join properly together, complete rhythmically*: quadrandae orationis industria, Cic.; acervum, Hor.
  (2) intransit., *to be square.* LIT., Verg., TRANSF., *to fit exactly, to suit*: omnia in istam quadrant, Cic. Esp., of accounts, *to agree*: quo modo sescenta eodem modo quadrarint, Cic.
  ¶ Hence partic. **quadrātus** -a -um, *squared, square*: saxum, Liv.; agmen, Cic., Liv., etc. N. as subst. **quadrātum** -i, *a square*: Cic., Hor.; as t. t. in astronomy, *quadrature*: Cic.

quadrum -i, n. *a square.* TRANSF., redigere omnes in quadrum numerumque sententias, *proper order*, Cic.

quadrŭpēdans -antis (quadrupes), *going on four feet, galloping*: Echetlus, *a Centaur*, Ov.; sonitus, *of a galloping horse*, Verg.; plur. as subst., *horses*: Verg.

quadrŭpēs -pĕdis (quattuor/pes), *four-footed, on four feet*: Ter., Ov. M. and f. as subst.

quadrŭpēs -pĕdis, *a four-footed animal, quadruped*: Cic., Verg., etc.

quadruplātor -ōris, m. (quadruplus), *a multiplier by four.* TRANSF., (1) *an exaggerator*: Sen. (2) *an informer*: Pl., Cic.

quadruplēx -plĭcis (quattuor/plico), *fourfold, quadruple*: Pl., Liv.

quadruplor -ari, dep. *to be an informer* (cf. quadruplator): Pl.

quadruplus -a -um (quattuor), *fourfold.* N. as subst. **quadruplum** -i, *four times the amount, four times as much*: iudicium dare in quadruplum, Cic.

quaerĭto -are (freq. of quaero). (1) *to seek eagerly*: Pl., Ter. (2) *to inquire eagerly about*: Pl., Ter.

quaero quaerĕre quaesii *or* quaesīvi quaesītum, *to seek, search for.*
  LIT., of persons and physical objects; sometimes with the further notion *to obtain, find, get*: suos, Caes.; portum, Caes.; viam, Lucr.; liberos ad necem, Cic.; argentum, Hor.; nummos, Cic.
  TRANSF., (1) *to seek* an abstr. thing: sibi honores, Cic.; gloriam bello, Cic.; fugam ex Italia, Cic.; omisso veteri consilio novum, Sall. With infin., *to seek to, wish to*: abrumpere lucem, Verg., Hor., Ov. (2) *to seek with longing, to miss, want*: Caesarem, Hor.; Cic. (3) of things, *to demand, require*: bellum dictatoriam maiestatem, Liv.; Cic., Ov. (4) *to seek to know, to ask, to inquire*: aliquid ex, de, ab aliquo, Caes., Cic., etc. With indir. quest.: Cic., Liv., etc. (5) *to investigate, inquire into*: rem, Ter., Cic.; de morte alicuius, Cic.; de servo in dominum, *to interrogate the slave (under torture) about his master*, Cic.
  ¶ Hence partic. **quaesītus** -a -um, *sought out*; so *unusual, select*; compar. and superl.:

Tac. In a bad sense, *far-fetched, affected* (of manner, etc.): Cic., Tac.
  ¶ N. as subst., sing. **quaesītum** -i, *question*: Ov.; plur. **quaesīta** -orum, *gains*: Verg., Ov.

quaesītĭo -ōnis, f. (quaero), *an interrogation (by torture)*: Tac.

quaesītor -ōris, m. (quaero), *an investigator, inquirer, esp. a judicial investigator*: Cic. of Minos: Verg.

quaesītum, subst. from quaero; q.v.

quaesītus -a -um, partic. from quaero; q.v.

quaeso -ĕre (another form of quaero) LIT., *to seek for*: Pl. TRANSF., *to beg, beseech, entreat.* With acc.: ventorum paces, Lucr. with ut *or* ne and the subj.: a vobis quaeso ut, Cic.; Liv. Absol., *I beg, I entreat*: tu quaeso, scribe, Cic. L.; Pl., Ter.

quaestĭcŭlus -i, m. (dim. of quaestus), *a small gain, slight profit*: Cic.

quaestĭo -ōnis, f. (quaero), *a seeking, searching*. LIT., Pl.
  TRANSF., *an inquiry, investigation*: tota fere quaestio tractata videtur, Cic.; in quaestionem vocare, *to investigate*, Cic.; Juv. Sometimes *a subject of inquiry*: Cic., Quint. Esp. *a judicial inquiry*, often with evidence taken from slaves under torture: hae quaestiones in senatu habitae, Cic.; quaestionem habere de viri morte, Cic.; quaestionem habere de servis in filium, Liv.; quaestionem inter sicarios exercere, *on a charge of assassination*, Cic.; quaestiones perpetuae, *standing courts of justice*, Cic.; extraordinariae Liv.

quaestĭuncŭla -ae, f. (dim. of quaestio), *a little question*: ponere alicui quaestiunculam, Cic. Quint.

quaestor -ōris, m. (for quaesitor, from quaero), *the quaestor*, in plur., *the quaestors, magistrates in Rome*: Cic., Liv., Tac., etc Of these, some tried criminal cases in the courts, or prosecuted at such trials; others were in charge of the state treasury; others accompanied consuls and praetors on military expeditions and to provincial commands, and acted as paymasters. The number of quaestors, originally two, was in the end raised to eighteen.

quaestōrĭus -a -um (quaestor), *belonging to a quaestor*: comitia, *for choice of a quaestor*, Cic.; officium, *duty of quaestor*, Cic.; scelus *committed by, or investigated by, a quaestor*, Cic.; porta, *a gate in the camp near the quaestor's tent*, Liv.
  N. as subst. **quaestōrĭum** -i. (1) (sc. tentorium), *the quaestor's tent in camp*: Liv. (2) (sc. aedificium), *the quaestor's dwelling in a province*: Cic. M. as subst. **quaestōrĭus** -i, *an ex-quaestor, one who had been quaestor*: Cic.

quaestŭōsus -a -um, adj. (with compar. and superl.) (quaestus). (1) *gainful, profitable* mercatura, Cic.; Liv. (2) *fond of gain*: homo Cic.; Pl. (3) *having gained much, rich*: Tac.

quaestūra -ae, f. (quaestor), *the office of quaestor, quaestorship*: Cic., Liv., Tac.

quaestus -ūs, m. (quaero), *a gaining, getting profit, gain, advantage.*
  LIT., quaestus ac lucrum unius agri unius anni, Cic.; quaestui deditum esse, *to be devoted to money-getting*, Sall.

qualibet — quantus

Transf., (1) *a source of profit*: quaestui
habere rempublicam, Cic. (2) *an occupation,
business*: quaestu iudiciario pasci, Cic.;
quaestum corpore facere, Pl., Liv., Tac.

quālĭbĕt (quālŭbĕt), adv. (f. abl. of quilibet).
Lit., *wherever you like, anywhere*: Pl., Tib.
Transf., *in any way you please*: Cat.

quālis -e, *of what sort, what kind of*.
(1) interrog., in direct and indirect
questions: qualis est istorum oratio? Cic.;
Pl., etc.
(2) relat., correlated to talis, (*such*) *as*.
With talis, *as*: qualem te praebuisti, talem te
impertias, Cic.; ut res non tales, quales ante
habitae sint, habendae videantur, Cic.
Without talis: bello, quale bellum nulla
barbaria gessit, *such a war as*, Cic.; qualis
exercet Diana choros, *like D. when she* . . . ,
Verg.
(3) indef., *having some quality or other*:
illa quae appellant qualia, Cic.
¶ Adv. **quālĭtĕr**, *as, just as*: Ov.

quāliscumquĕ (-cunquĕ) quālĕcumquĕ, adj.
(qualis). (1) relat., *of whatever kind, of
whatever sort*: homines qualescumque sunt,
Cic.; Liv., etc. (2) indef., *any, without
exception, any whatever*: sin qualemcumque
locum sequimur, Cic.

quālislĭbĕt quālĕlĭbĕt, *of what sort you will*:
formae litterarum vel aureae vel qualeslibet,
Cic.

quālĭtās -ātis, f. (qualis), *quality, property,
nature* (cf. Gr. ποιότης): Quint.

quālus -i, m. and **quālum -i**, n. *a wicker-
basket*: Verg., Hor.

quam, adv. *how, in what way*.
(1) interrog., in direct and indirect
questions; *to what extent? how much? how?*:
quam multis opus erit? Cic.; memoriā tenetis
quam valde admurmurarint, Cic. Elliptically:
mire quem, *to a surprising degree*, Cic. L.
(2) exclam.: quam multa, quam paucis!
Cic. L.; quam hoc non curo, Cic.
(3) relat.: **a**, *as*, correlated to tam (*or* sic):
tam consimilis est quam potest, Liv., Cic.;
with sic: Verg. Without tam: homo non, quam
isti sunt, gloriosus, Liv. Often with superl.
of adj. or adv.: quam maximā possum voce
dico, *with as loud a voice as possible*, Cic.;
quam celerrime potuit, Caes.; elliptically,
without possum: quam plurimo vendere,
as dear as possible, Cic.; quam primum, *as
soon as possible*, Caes., Cic., Verg.: **b**, with
comparatives or words implying comparison,
than, as: nihil est magis timendum quam,
Cic.; maior sum quam cui possit fortuna
nocere, Ov.; proelium atrocius quam pro
numero pugnantium editur, *fiercer than you
would expect from the number of the combatants*, Liv.; with a second comparative
following: longior quam latior, *more long
than wide*, Cic. Also with verbs implying a
comparison, such as malle, praestat: Caes.;
and with other parts of speech, such as aeque,
supra, ultra, secus, alius, aliter, alibi,
dissimilis, diversus. In phrases relating to
time, such as postero die, or postridie, quam:
Cic.; Liv.

quamdĭū or **quam dĭū**, adv. (1) interrog.,
how long?: Pl., Cic. (2) relat., *as long as, until*:
quamdiu potuit tacuit, Caes.; disces quamdiu
voles, Cic.

quamlĭbĕt (quamlŭbĕt), adv. *as much as you
please, ever so much*: manus quamlibet
infirmae, Ov.; Lucr.

quamobrem (quam ob rem), adv. (1)
interrog., in direct and indirect questions,
wherefore? why?: Pl., Caes., Cic. (2) relat. *on
which account, for which reason, wherefore,
why*: si res reperietur quam ob rem videantur,
Cic., Pl., etc.

quamquam (quanquam), conj. *although,
though*. Usually with indic., unless there is a
special reason for using subj.: medici
quamquam intellegunt saepe, tamen numquam aegris dicunt, Cic.; Hor., Liv., etc.
Elliptically, with adj. or partic.: omnia illa
quae sunt extra, quamquam expetenda,
summo bono continerentur, Cic.; Liv., etc.
Sometimes at the beginning of a sentence,
nevertheless, and yet: Cic., Verg.

quamvīs, adv. (quam/volo). (1) *as much as
you please, ever so much*: quamvis multos
nominatim proferre, Cic.; quamvis copiosē,
Cic. (2) as conj., *however much, although*,
with subj.: quamvis prudens sis, tamen,
Cic.; Verg.; with indic.: Verg., Liv., Ov.;
elliptically, with adj. or partic.: quamvis
iniqua passi, Cic.; Tac.

quānam, *by what way*: Liv.

quandō, adv., *when*. (1) interrog., in direct and
indirect questions, *when? at what time?*:
quando enim me ista curasse arbitramini?
Cic.; Hor., etc.; non intellegitur, quando
obrepat senectus. (2) indef., *at any time,
ever*: quaestio num quando amici novi
veteribus sint anteponendi, Cic.; also after
si, and ne: Cic., Liv., etc. (3) relat., *at the
time when*: tum quando legatos Tyrum
misimus, Cic.; Verg., etc. Sometimes
causal, *since, because*: Cic., Liv., etc.

quandōcumquĕ (-cunquĕ), adv. (in tmesis:
Hor.) (1) rel., *whenever, as often as*:
quandocumque trahunt invisa negotia Romam, Hor.: Liv., etc. (2) indef., *at some time
or other*: quandocumque mihi poenas dabis,
Ov.

quandōquĕ, adv. (1) relat., *whenever, as often
as*: Cic.; Hor., Liv. Sometimes causal,
since: Cic., Liv. (2) indef., *at some time or
other*: Cic. L., Tac.

quandōquĭdem, conj. *since, because*: Cic.,
Verg., Liv.

quantillus -a -um (dim. of quantulus), *how
little*; interrog., relat., and exclam.: Pl.

quanto, *see* quantus.

quantŏpĕrĕ (quanto ŏpĕrĕ), adv. (quantus/
opus), *with what great trouble, how much*.
(1) interrog., in indir. quest.: video quanto
se opere custodiant bestiae, Cic.; dici non
potest, quanto opere gaudeant, Cic. (2)
relat., *as much as*: Cic.

quantŭlus -a -um (dim. of quantus), *how
little, how small*. (1) interrog., in direct and
indirect questions: Lucr., Cic., Juv. (2)
exclam.: quantulus sol nobis videtur! Cic.
(3) relat.: Cic., Hor.

quantŭluscumquĕ -ācumquĕ -umcumquĕ,
however small: de hac mea, quantulacumque
est, facultate, Cic.; n. as subst.: quantulum-
cumque dicebamus, Cic.

quantum, *see* quantus.

quantus -a -um, *of what size, how great*.
(1) interrog., in direct and indirect

questions: aspice sim quantus, Ov.; Cic.,
etc. (2) exclam.: quantum instar in ipso!
Verg.; Cic., etc. (3) relat.: correlated to tantus,
(*as great*) *as*: cum tantis copiis quantas nemo
habuit, Nep.; Cic. Without tantus: ut
acciperent pecuniam quantam vellent, Cic.;
nox acta, quanta fuit, *as long as it lasted, the
whole long night*, Ov.; quantā maximā
celeritate potui, *with the greatest possible
speed*, Liv.; quantus quantus, *however great*,
Pl., Ter.

N. as subst. **quantum.** (1) interrog., *how
much?*: quantum dedit? Cic. (2) exclam.:
quantum mutatus ab illo Hectore, Verg.;
Cic. (3) relat.: quantum est ex Sicilia
frumenti, Cic.; quantum ego sentio, Cic.;
quantum in me est, *as far as in me lies*, Cic.;
in quantum, *in so far as*, Ov., Tac.; quantum
maxime accelerare poterat, Liv.

N. in genit. (or locative) of price, **quanti.**
(1) interrog., *at what price? how dear?*:
quanti emi potest? Pl.; cum scias, quanti
Tulliam faciam, *how highly I esteem*, Cic.
(2) exclam.: quanti est sapere! Ter. (3)
relat.: quanti locaverint, tantam pecuniam
solvendam, Cic.; quanti quanti, *at whatever price*, Cic.

N. in abl. of measure, **quanto.** (1)
interrog.: Cic. (2) exclam.: quanto sapien-
tius! *how much more wisely!* Cic. (3) relat.:
quanto diutius abest, magis cupio tanto, *the
longer he is away*, Ter.; Caes., Tac.

quantuscumquĕ -ācumquĕ -umcumquĕ, *how-
ever great*: bona, quantacumque erant, Cic.
N. as subst.: quantumcumque possum,
Cic.

quantuslĭbet -tālĭbet -tumlĭbet, *as great as
you will, however great*: ordo, Ov. N. acc.
like adv., *however much*: Liv.

quantusvīs -āvis -umvis (quantus/volo), *as
great as you please, however great*: quantasvis
magnas copias sustineri posse, Caes.;
portum satis amplum quantaevis classi, Liv.
N. acc. like adv., *however much*: ille catus,
quantumvis rusticus, Hor.; Cic.

quāpropter (1) interrog., *wherefore? why?*: Pl.,
Ter. (2) relat.; *on which account, wherefore*:
Pl., Ter., Cic.

quāquā, adv. *by whatever way*: Pl.

quārē or **quā rē**, adv. (qui/res). (1) interrog.,
how?: Pl., Ter.; *why?*: Cic., Hor. (2) relat.,
wherefore, on which account: Cic.

quartădĕcŭmāni -ōrum, m. (quartus decimus), *soldiers of the fourteenth legion*: Tac.

quartānus -a -um (quartus), *relating to the
fourth.*
   (1) *relating to the fourth day*: febris
quartana, Cic.; f. as subst. **quartāna**
(sc. febris) -ae, *a quartan fever*: Hor.
   (2) *relating to the fourth legion*; m. pl. as
subst. **quartāni** -ōrum, *the soldiers of the
fourth legion*: Tac.

quartārĭus -i, m. (quartus), *the fourth part
of a sextarius*: Liv.

quartus -a -um (quattuor), *the fourth*: pars,
Caes.; Cic., Verg.
   F. as subst. **quarta** -ae (sc. hora), *the
fourth hour*: Hor.
   N. acc. or abl. as adv. **quartum, quarto**,
for the fourth time: Cic., Liv., Ov.

quartusdĕcĭmus -a -um, *the fourteenth*: Cic.,
Tac.

quăsĭ, adv. *as if, just as.* (1) with indic., *just as*:
quasi poma ex arboribus, cruda si sunt, vix
evelluntur, Cic. (2) in hypothetical comparisons, *as if*: **a**, with subj.: sensu amisso fit
idem quasi natus non esset omnino, Cic.;
quid ego his testibus utor, quasi res dubia
aut obscura sit? Cic.; with added si: Pl.:
b, with partic.: hostes maximo clamore
insecuti quasi partā iam atque exploratā
victoriā, Caes.; Cic. (3) *as it were, a sort of*:
philosophia procreatrix quaedam et quasi
parens, Cic.; quasi in extremā paginā, Cic.
(4) with numerals, *about*: Pl., Ter., Cic.

quăsillus -i, m. and **quăsillum** -i, n. (dim. of
qualus), *a little basket*: Cic., Tib.

quassātĭo -ōnis, f. (quasso), *a shaking*: Liv.

quasso -are (freq. of quatio).
   (1) transit., *to shake violently.* LIT., in
gen.: caput, Pl., Verg.; hastam, Verg.; esp.,
to shatter, break in pieces: classis ventis
quassata, Verg.; naves quassatae, Liv.
TRANSF., rempublicam, Cic.
   (2) intransit., *to shake*: siliquā quassante,
Verg.; Pl.

quassus -a -um, partic. from quatio; q.v.

quătĕfăcĭo -făcĕre -fēci (quatio/facio), *to
shake, to weaken*: Cic. L.

quătĕnŭs, adv. *how far.* (1) interrog., in
indir. quest., *to what extent*: Cic. (2) relat.,
as far as: Liv. (3) *in so far as, since, seeing
that*: Hor., Ov., etc.

quătĕr, adv. (quattuor), *four times*: Verg., Ov.;
terque quaterque, *or* ter et quater, *again and
again, often*, Verg., Hor.

quătĕr dĕcĭens (-ies), *fourteen times*: Cic.

quăterni -ae -a, num. distrib. (quattuor), *four
at a time, four each*: quaternae centesimae,
interest at four per cent monthly, Cic.; Caes.,
Hor., Liv.

quătĭo quătĕre quassi quassum, *to shake.*
LIT., in gen.: alas, Verg.; caput, Ov.;
hastam, *to brandish*, Verg.; cymbala, Verg.;
risu populum, Hor. Esp., *to crash, shatter*:
muros arietibus, Liv.; Verg., Hor.; in partic.:
quassae naves, *leaky, shattered*, Liv.
   TRANSF., *to shake, agitate, trouble*:
aegritudine, Cic.; oppida bello, Verg.

quatrĭdŭum = quadriduum; q.v.

quattŭor, indecl. numer. adj. (cf. τέσσαρες
τέτταρες), *four*: Cic., Verg., etc.

quattŭordĕcim, indecl. numer. adj. (quattuor,
decem), *fourteen*: quattuordecim ordines, *or*
simply, quattuordecim, *the fourteen rows or
seats reserved in the circus for the knights
at Rome*, Cic.; Liv., etc.

quattŭorvĭrātus -ūs, m. (quattuorviri), *th
office of the quattuorviri*: ap. Cic. L.

quattŭorvĭri -ōrum, m. *a college of fou
magistrates*; e.g., in Rome, for the care of th
streets; in municipia and coloniae, *the chie
magistrates*: Cic.

-quĕ (cf. Gr. τε) an enclitic conj. always attache
to a word, *and*; if what is to be added consist
of more than one word, -que is normall
attached to the first word; but is sometime
postponed if the first word is a monosyllabl
or for metrical convenience in poetry.
   Alone, -que=*and, and also*, and *indeed*
used by all authors. Sometimes it introduce
an alternative, *or*: uxores habent den
duodenique inter se communes, Caes.
   Repeated, -que ... -que=*both ... and* ...

noctesque diesque, Cic.; quique Romae quique in exercitu erant, Liv.

In combination with other conjunctions: -que...et..., *both...and...*, Liv.; -que ...ac..., Verg., Liv.

quēis, quīs=quibus, *see* qui.

quēmadmŏdum (quem ad mŏdum), *in what manner, how.* (**1**) interrog., in direct and indirect questions: quemadmodum est adservatus? Cic.; Caes. (**2**) relat: ut quemadmodum vellent imperarent, Caes. Esp., corresponding with sic, ita, item, etc., *as, just as*: quemadmodum socius in societate habet partem, sic heres in hereditate habet partem, Cic.; Liv.

quĕo quīre quīvi and quiī quĭtum, *to be able.* With infin.: non queo reliqua scribere, Cic.; Verg., etc. With pass. infin., sometimes in pass. (cf. coepi): Pl., Ter., Lucr.

quercētum -i, n. (quercus), *an oak-wood*: Hor.

quercĕus -a -um (quercus), *oaken*: corōnae, *of oak leaves*, Tac.

quercus -ūs, f. *the oak*: Cic., Verg., etc. TRANSF., (**1**) *a crown of oak leaves for saving the life of a citizen in war*: Verg., Ov. (**2**) *acorns*: Juv.

uĕrēla (quĕrella) -ae, f. (queror), *a complaint, complaining.* LIT., epistula plena querelarum, Cic.; vestrum beneficium nonnullam habet querelam, *gives some occasion of complaint*, Cic.; Hor., Liv., etc. TRANSF., of *the plaintive sound of animals*: Lucr., Verg.; of *the noise of a flute*: Lucr.

uĕrībundus -a -um (queror), *complaining, plaintive*: vox, Cic.

uĕrĭmōnĭa -ae, f. (queror), *a complaining, complaint*: de tuis iniuriis, Cic.; Hor., Liv.

uĕrītor -ari, dep. (freq. of queror), *to complain excessively*: Tac.

uernĕus -a -um (quercus), *of the oak, oaken*: Suet.

uernus=querneus; q.v.: Verg., Ov.

uĕror quĕrī questus sum, dep. *to complain, lament, bewail.* LIT., with acc.: fatum, Caes.; iniurias, Cic.; Ov., etc. With de: de Milone, Cic. With acc. and infin.: se tum exstingui, Cic.; Liv., Ov., etc. TRANSF., *to make a plaintive sound*; of animals or birds: Verg., Hor.; of musical instruments: flebile nescio quid queritur lyra, Ov.

uerquētŭlānus -a -um (querquetum= quercetum), *of an oak-wood*: Querquetulanus mons, *old name of the Caelius mons at Rome*, Tac.

uĕrŭlus -a -um (queror), *complaining, querulous.* LIT., senex, Hor.; vox, Ov. TRANSF., *plaintive*: cicada, Verg.; tibia, Hor.

uestus -ūs, m. (queror), *a complaining, complaint, lament.* LIT., qui questus, qui maeror dignus inveniri in tanta calamitate potest, Cic.; Verg., Ov. TRANSF., of *the nightingale's song*: Verg.

ui, quae quŏd; pronoun.

(**1**) interrog. adj., in direct and indirect questions; *which? what? what kind of?*: qui cantus dulcior inveniri potest? Cic.; scribis te velle scire, qui sit reipublicae status, Cic.; tu te conlige, et qui sis considera, Cic.; considera, Cic.; Verg., Hor., etc.

(**2**) exclam., *what*: qui vir, et quantus! Cic.; qui strepitus circa comitum! Verg.

(**3**) indef.: qui, quae, and qua, quod; *any, some*: nisi qui deus subvenerit, Cic. Also after si, nisi, num: Caes., Cic., Liv.

(**4**) relat., *who, which, what, that.* In this sense, qui normally agrees in gender and number with its antecedent, but for case depends on its own verb: luna eam lucem, quam a sole accipit, mittit in terras, Cic. Often, as a 'connecting relative', it introduces a new sentence, *and this*: res loquitur ipsa; quae semper valet plurimum, Cic. In *gender*, it sometimes agrees with a complement in its own clause: agrum, quae postea sunt Mucia prata appellata, Liv. It is neuter when the relat. clause refers to the whole of the main clause: Lacedaemonii regem, quod numquam antea apud eos acciderat, necaverunt, Cic. In *number*, it is sometimes plural when the antecedent is a collective noun: equitatum praemittit qui videant, Cic. It is sometimes attracted into the *case* of its antecedent: illo augurio quo diximus, Cic.

The *mood* of the relat. clause is normally indic., whenever it makes a purely factual statement about a definite antecedent. But qui is foll. by the subj.: **a**, to express purpose, *in order that*: eripiunt aliis quod aliis largiantur, Cic.: **b**, to express cause, *because*: recte Socrates exsecrari eum solebat, qui primus utilitatem a natura seiunxisset, Cic.: **c**, to express tendency or result, after such words as is, talis, eiusmodi, aptus, idoneus, dignus: ego is sum qui nihil fecerim, *such a man as to*, Cic.: **d**, to express a general description, parallel to an adj.: mihi carus et illum qui pulchre nosset, Hor.: **e**, where the existence of the antecedent is denied or doubted; e.g. after nemo est qui: Cic., etc.

¶ Acc. n. sing. of qui relat. **quod**, like adv.: quod sciam, *as far as I know*, Pl., Cic., Liv.

¶ Abl. n. sing. of qui relat. **quō**, as abl. of measure. With comparatives: quo difficilius, hoc praeclarius, Cic. For its uses as abl. of instrument, *see* quo.

²quī (old abl. of ¹qui). (**1**) interrog., in direct and indirect questions, *in what manner? how?*: deum nisi sempiternum intellegere qui possumus? Cic.; Hor., Liv., etc. (**2**) exclam.: qui te di omnes perdant! Pl. (**3**) relat.: *wherewith, wherefrom*: in tanta paupertate decessit, ut qui efferretur, vix reliquerit, Nep.; Pl., Ter., Cic. (**4**) indef., *somehow*: Pl., Ter.

quĭă (**1**) interrog., in forms quiane and quianam; *why?*: Pl., Verg. (**2**) relat., *because*: Cic., Hor., etc. Often with ideo, idcirco, propterea, etc., as antecedent: quia mutari natura non potest, idcirco verae amicitiae sempiternae sunt, Cic.

quīcum (abl. of ¹qui/cum), *with whom, with which*: Cic.

quīcumquĕ (-cunquĕ) quaecumquĕ quodcumquĕ.

(**1**) relat., *whoever, whichever, whatever*: quicumque is est, Cic.; quācumque potui ratione, *in every possible way*, Cic.; ut quodcumque vellet, liceret facere, *anything that he chose*, Nep.; quodcumque hoc regni, *this kingdom, such as it is*, Verg. Sometimes quicumque=qualiscumque, *of whatever kind*:

quaecumque mens illa fuit, Gabinii fuit, Cic.
(2) indef., *any available*: quacumque ratione, *as best I can*, Cic.

quĭdam quaedam quoddam and subst. quiddam, *a certain person* or *thing* (known but not named).
LIT., quaedam vox, Cic.; quodam tempore, *at a certain time*, Cic.; subst.: quidam de conlegis nostris, Cic.; quiddam divinum, *something divine*, Cic.; with partitive genit.: quiddam mali, Cic. TRANSF., *a kind of, so to speak*: incredibilis quaedam magnitudo ingenii, Cic.

quĭdem, adv. *indeed, even*. Used to emphasize or to limit an assertion: non video causam, cur ita sit, hoc quidem tempore, *at least*, Cic.; doleo ac mirifice quidem, *and indeed, yes and*, Cic.; ille quidem hoc cupiens, *though so desiring*, Verg.; ... quidem ... sed = Gr. ... μέν ... δε, Quint. Esp. neg.: ne ... quidem, *not even* ..., Cic., Liv., etc.; also nec ... quidem, Cic., Liv.

quidnĭ? *why not?*: Cic.

quĭēs -ētis, f. *rest*.
LIT., in gen., *repose, quiet*: mors laborum ac miseriarum quies est, Cic.; quietem capere, *to enjoy*, Caes.; plur.: somno et quietibus ceteris, *kinds of rest*, Cic. Esp. (1) *rest at night, sleep*: ire ad quietem, Cic.; datur hora quieti, Verg. (2) *the sleep of death*: dura quies, Verg.; Prop. (3) *peace*: Sall.; *neutrality*: Tac. (4) of things, *calm*: Verg.
TRANSF., (1) *a dream*: Stat., Tac. (2) plur., *a resting-place, lair*: Lucr.

quĭesco -escĕre -ēvi -ētum (quies); syncop. forms: quierunt, quierim, quierant, quiessem, quiesse; *to rest, repose*.
LIT., in gen., *to rest from work*, etc.; of living beings: ipse dux (gruum) revolat, ut ipse quoque quiescat, Cic.; of things: prato gravia arma quiescunt, Verg.; quiescebant voces hominum canumque, Ov.; alta quierunt aequora, *were calm*, Verg.; ager qui multos annos quiescit, *lies fallow*, Cic. Esp. (1) *to lie down, to sleep*: cenatus quiescebat, Cic. (2) of the dead, *to rest in the grave*: placidā compostus pace quiescit, Verg. (3) *to be at peace*: urbs illa non potest quiescere, Cic.; Verg.; also *to be neutral*: quiescere in republica, Cic. L.
TRANSF., (1) *to cease from* an action; with infin.: Pl., Hor. (2) *to be free from*: civitas a suppliciis, Liv.

quĭētus -a -um (quies), adj. (with compar. and superl.), *resting*.
LIT., in gen.: quieto sedente rege ad Enipeum, Liv.; quietus aer, Verg.; sermo, calm, Cic. Esp. (1) *sleeping*: Tac. (2) *at peace, undisturbed, neutral*: quieta Gallia, Caes.; a seditione et a bello quietis rebus, Liv.; n. pl. as subst.: quieta movere, Sall.
TRANSF., of character, *quiet, peaceful, calm*: animus quietus et solutus, Cic.; quietus, imbellis, placido animo, Sall.; Caes., Verg.
¶ Adv. **quiētē**, *quietly, peaceably*: vivere, Cic.; apte et quiete ferre aliquid, Cic.

quīlĭbĕt quaelibet quodlibet and subst. quidlibet, *any you will, anyone, anything*: quaelibet minima res, *any smallest thing*, Cic.; quibuslibet temporibus, *at all times*,

Liv.; subst. quidlibet: impotens sperare, Hor.

quin (for quine, from qui/ne).
(1) in main clauses: **a**, in questions, *why not?* quin conscendimus equos? Liv.; Cic., Verg.: **b**, in commands, to encourage, *but come*: quin sic attendite, iudices, Cic.; Pl.: **c**, in statements, to add emphasis, *rather, nay rather, but indeed*: Pl., Ter.; quin potius, quin contra, Liv.; quin etiam, quin immo, Cic.; quin et, Hor.
(2) in subordinate clauses, with subjunctive: **a**, relat., *who not, that not*, after a neg. or virtual neg.; used unchanged in all genders and in various cases: nemo fuit quin illud viderit, Cic.; nulla est civitas quin, Caes.; nihil est quin, Cic.; numquam tam male est Siculis quin aliquid facete et commode dicant, *but that*, Cic.: **b**, with neg. verbs of refraining, hindering, etc., *but that, without*: nullum adhuc intermisi diem, quin aliquid ad te litterarum darem, Cic.; nihil abest quin sim miserrimus, Cic.; facere non possum quin, *I cannot help*, Cic.: **c**, after neg. verbs of doubting, ignorance, etc., *but that*: non dubitari debet quin fuerint ante Homerum poetae, Cic.; quis ignorat, quin tria Graecorum genera sint? *who does not know that?* Cic.; haud dubium est quin, Ter., Caes., etc.

quīnam quaenam quodnam, interrog. adj. *which, what?* In direct questions: sed quinam est ille epilogus? Cic. In indirect questions: quaesivit quasnam formosas virgines haberet, Cic.

Quinctĭus (Quintĭus) -a -um, *name of a Roman gens. Its most famous members were*: (1) L. Quinctius Cincinnatus, *summoned from the plough to be dictator*. (2) T. Quinctius Flamininus, *the conqueror of the Macedonian king Philip*.
¶ Hence adj. **Quinctĭānus** -a -um, *Quinctian*.

quincunx -cuncis (quinque/uncia), *five-twelfths of a whole*.
LIT., Hor., Cic.
TRANSF., *the form of the five spots on dice*. Hence applied to *a plantation in which rows of trees were so planted*: directi in quincuncem ordines, Cic.

quindĕciens (-ĭēs), adv. *fifteen times*: Cic., Mart.

quindĕcim, indecl. num. (quinque/decem) *fifteen*: Caes., Hor.

quindĕcimprīmi -ōrum, m. *the fifteen chief senators of a municipium*: Caes.

quindĕcimvir -i and **quindĕcimvĭri** -ōrum and -um, m. *a college of fifteen magistrates* esp.: quindecimviri sacris faciundis, *one of the three priestly colleges, in charge of the Sibylline books*, Tac.; separated: quindecim Diana preces virorum curet, Hor.

quindĕcimvĭrālis -e, *of the* quindecimviri: Tac.

quingēni -ae -a, num. (quingenti), *five hundred at a time, five hundred each*: Cic. L.

quingentēsĭmus (-ensĭmus) -a -um (quingenti), *the five hundredth*: Cic.

quingenti -ae -a, num. (quinque/centum) *five hundred*: Cic., Hor., etc.

quingentĭens (-ĭēs), adv. (quingenti), *five hundred times*: Cic.

quīni -ae -a, num. distrib. (quinque), *five at a time, five each*: Cic., Verg., etc.

quindēni or **quīni dēni** -ae -a, num. *fifteen at a time, fifteen each*: Liv.

quīnīvicēni -ae -a, num. *twenty-five each*: Liv.

quinquāgēni -ae -a, num. (quinquaginta), *fifty at a time, fifty each*: Cic., Mart.

quinquāgēsiens, *fifty times*: Pl.

quinquāgēsimus (-ensimus) -a -um (quinquaginta), *fiftieth*: Cic. F. as subst. **quinquāgēsima** -ae (sc. pars), *a fiftieth part*; as a tax: Cic.

quinquāgiēs (-iens), adv. *fifty times*: Plin.

quinquāginta, num. *fifty*: Pl., Cic., Verg.

quinquātrūs -uum, f. pl., and **quinquātria** -orum and -ium, n. pl. *a festival of Minerva*: maiores (celebrated on the 19th of March); minores, minusculae (on the 13th of June): Cic. L., Ov., Liv.

quinque, indecl. num., *five*: Cic.

quinquennālis -e (quinquennis). (1) *happening every five years, quinquennial*: celebritas ludorum, Cic. (2) *lasting for five years*: censura, Liv.

quinquennis -e (quinque/annus), *of five years, five years old*: vinum, Hor.; Ov., Liv.

quinquennium -i, n. (quinque/annus), *a period of five years*: ap. Cic.; Ov.

quinquepertītus (quinquepartītus) -a -um, *divided into five portions, fivefold*: Cic.

quinqueprimi -ōrum, m. *the five chief senators in a* municipium: Cic.

quinquerēmis -e (quinque/remus), *having five banks of oars*: navis, Liv. F. as subst. **quinquerēmis** -is (sc. navis), *a ship with five banks of oars, a quinquereme*: Cic., Liv.

quinquevir -i, and plur. **quinquevīri** -orum, m. *a commission of five men*, e.g. the agrarian commission for distributing the public land: Cic.; for repairing fortifications: Liv.; for helping the *tresviri* in the night-police: Liv.

quinquevīrātus -ūs, m. *the office of a* quinquevir: Cic.

quinquiēs (-iens), adv. *five times*: Cic.

quinquiplico -are, *to make fivefold*: Tac.

quintădĕcimāni -ōrum, m. *the soldiers of the fifteenth legion*: Tac.

quintānus -a -um (quintus), *of the fifth.* As subst., f. **quintāna** -ae (sc. via), *a road in a Roman camp which divided the fifth maniple and turma from the sixth*; used as a market: Liv. M. pl. **quintāni** -ōrum, *soldiers of the fifth legion*: Tac.

Quintīliānus (Quinct-) -i, m. *a Roman name*, esp. of M. Fabius Quintilianus, *born at Calagurris in Spain, head of a school of rhetoric at Rome.*

Quintīlis (Quinctīlis) -is, m. (with or without mensis), *the fifth month of the Roman year* (reckoning from March as the first), *afterwards called Iulius, in honour of Julius Caesar*: Cic. L., Suet.

quintus (quinctus) -a -um (quinque), *fifth*: Cic. N. acc. and abl.: quintum, quinto, *for the fifth time*, Liv.

Quintus, f. **Quinta**, *a common Roman praenomen*, the masculine usually abbreviated Q.

quintusdĕcimus -a -um, *fifteenth*: Cic., Liv.

quippĕ, conj. and adv. *certainly, indeed, by all means, to be sure.* In gen.: a te quidem apte et rotunde (dicta sunt), quippe habes enim a rhetoribus, Cic. Esp. (1) ironically, *of*

course, to be sure*: quippe homini erudito, Cic.; quippe vetor fatis, Verg. (2) in explanations; alone, or strengthened by etiam, or introducing a clause with qui *or* ubi: Cic., Verg., Liv., etc.

quippinī, adv. *why not?*: Pl.

Quirīnus -i, m. *the name of Romulus at his apotheosis*: populus Quirini, *the Romans*, Hor.; gemini Quirini, *Romulus and Remus*, Juv. The name Quirinus was also used of *Janus*: Suet.; *of Augustus*: Verg.; *of Antonius*: Prop.

¶ Hence adj. **Quirīnus** -a -um, *of Romulus*: collis, Ov.; adj. **Quirīnālis** -e, *of Romulus*: trabea, Verg.; collis, *the Quirinal Hill at Rome*, Cic.; n. pl. as subst. **Quirīnālia** -ium, *a festival in honour of Romulus, celebrated on the 17th of February*: Cic.

¹**Quirīs** -itis and pl. **Quirītes** -ium and -um, m. (Cures), *the inhabitants of the Sabine town Cures*: Verg., Liv. After the union of the Romans and Sabines the name *Quirites* was used of the citizens of Rome in their civil capacity. Hence the expressions *Populus Romanus Quiritium, Populus Romanus Quiritesque, Quirites Romani*: Liv. For a general to address his soldiers by the term *Quirites* was a reproach: Tac., Suet.

TRANSF., of the bees in a hive: Verg.

²**quiris** or **curis** (a Sabine word), *a spear*: Ov.

quirītātio -ōnis, f. (quirito), *a shriek, scream, cry of distress*: Liv.

quirītātus -ūs, m.=quiritatio; q.v.: Plin. L.

quirīto -are, *to utter a cry of distress, to shriek, scream, cry out*: vox quiritantium, Quint.

¹**quis** quid, pron.

(1) interrog., in direct and indirect questions, *who? what?* As subst.: quis clarior Themistocle? Cic.; quis tu? Cic.; considera quis quem fraudasse dicatur, Cic. As adj.: quis iam locus? Verg.; Cic., Liv.

Esp. n. nom. and acc. **quid?** *what?* Nominative: quid tum? *what follows?* Cic.; quid igitur est? *how stands it, then?* Cic.; with partitive genit., *how much? how many?*: quid pictarum tabularum? Cic.; to express surprise, quid! *what! how!*: quid! eundem nonne destituisti? Cic.; also to express transition to a fresh point: Cic. Accusative, *why? wherefore?*: sed quid argumentor? Cic.; quid ita? *why so? how so?* Cic.; quidni? *why not?* Cic.

(2) indef., *anyone, anybody, anything*: potest quis errare aliquando, Cic.; often after si, nisi, ne, num: Caes., Cic., Liv., etc.

²**quīs**=quibus; *see* qui.

quisnam quaenam quidnam, pron. interrog. *who? what?*: quisnam igitur tuebitur P. Scipionis memoriam mortui? Cic.; quisnam delator quibus indicibus quo teste probavit? Juv. Often joined with num: num quidnam novi (sc. accidit)? Cic. Sometimes separated, with nam placed first or afterwards: quid se nam facturum arbitratus est? Cic.; nam quis te nostras iussit adire domos? Verg.

quispiam quaepiam quodpiam, and subst. quidpiam *or* quippiam, *anyone, anything, someone, something*: quaepiam cohors, Caes.; si cuipiam pecuniam ademit, Cic. N. acc. as adv., *at all*: Pl., Cic.

quisquam quaequam quidquam *or* quicquam, *anybody, anyone, anything*; used chiefly in negative sentences, or in questions, etc.: estne quisquam qui? Cic.; nec quisquam, *and no one,* Verg.; with genit.: vestrum quisquam, Liv.

quisque quaequĕ quidquĕ, and adj. quodquĕ, *each, every, everyone, everybody, everything;* sometimes in sing. with a plur. verb. Rarely=uterque.

Chief uses: (1) with reflex.: quisque suos patimur manes, Verg.; pro se quisque nostrum debemus, Cic.; suo cuique iudicio est utendum, *everyone must use his own judgment,* Cic.; suum quisque flagitium aliis obiectantes, Tac. (2) in relat. clause: quod cuique obtigit, id quisque teneat, Cic.; abl. of measure with compar.: quo quisque est sollertior, hoc docet laboriosius, *the more . . . the more,* Cic. (3) in indir. quest. clause: quid quisque vitet, Hor.; Lucr., etc. (4) with superl.: doctissimus quisque, *all the most learned,* Cic.; optimum quidque rarissimum est, Cic.; Caes., Liv. (5) with numerals: **a,** with cardinal unus, *each one, every single one:* Caes., Cic.: **b,** with any ordinal: primo quoque tempore, *on the very first occasion,* Cic.; quinto quoque anno, *every five years,* Cic.

quisquĭlĭae -ārum, f. *rubbish, sweepings, refuse;* applied to persons: quisquiliae seditionis Clodianae, Cic.

quisquis quaequae quidquid (quicquid), and adj. quodquod, pron. (1) relat., *whoever, whichever, whatever:* quisquis ille est, *whoever he may be,* Pl.; auream quisquis mediocritatem diligit, Hor.; Cic.; with partitive genit.: deorum quisquis amicior Afris, Hor.; deorum quidquid regit terras, *all the gods who,* Cic.; acc. quidquid as adv., *however much:* Liv.; progredior, Liv. (2) indef., *anyone, anything, any:* Liv., Ter.

quīvīs quaevis quidvis, and adj. quodvis, pron., *whoever you will, whatever you will, anyone, anything:* quivis ut perspicere possit, Cic.; quidvis perpeti, Cic.; quodvis genus, Cic.; quivis unus, *anyone you please,* Cic.; Hor., etc.

quīviscumquĕ quaeviscumquĕ quodviscumquĕ, *whosoever or whatsoever.* Relat.: Mart. Indef.: Lucr.

¹quŏ, adv. of place (qui).
(1) *at what place, where;* in indir. quest.: Cic., Hor.
(2) *to what place, whither.*
LIT., **a,** interrog., in direct and indirect questions: quo, quo scelesti ruitis? Hor.; Cic.: **b,** relat.: ad partem provinciae venturum, quo te velle arbitrarer, Cic.; of persons: eos quo se contulit (=ad quos), Cic.; Caes., etc.: **c,** indef., *to any place, anywhither:* si quo erat prodeundum, Cic.; Caes., Liv., etc.
TRANSF., **a,** interrog., in direct and indirect questions, *how far? to what extent?:* scire quo amentiae progressi sitis, Liv.; also *to what end?:* quo tantam pecuniam? Cic.: **b,** relat., *to the end that, in order that:* Caes., Cic. L.

²quŏ (instrumental abl. of qui; q.v.). (1) *because,* introducing a reason: Cic. Often with non, and foll. by subj., introducing a rejected reason: non quo multa parum simili sint praedita forma, sed quod . . ., Lucr.; Cic. (2) *whereby,* introducing a result, or more often an intended result, a purpose,

with subj.: Caes., Cic., etc.; for quo minus see quominus.

quŏăd, adv. (usually monosyll. in verse), *how far,* in space or time.
(1) interrog.: videte nunc quoad feceri iter, Cic.; Ter. (2) relat.: **a,** in space, *as fa as:* Liv.: **b,** in time, *as long as:* quoad potui Cic.; also *until;* with indic.: quoad senatu dimissus est, Cic.; with subj.: quoad t videam, Cic.: **c,** in other relations, *as far as* quoad possunt ab homine cognosci, Cic. with partitive genit.: quoad eius facer possum, Cic.

quŏcircă, conj. *wherefore, on which account* Cic., Verg. In tmesis: quo, bone, circa, Ho

quŏcumquĕ, adv. *whithersoever:* Cic., Verg. Hor. In tmesis: num eam rationem, qu ea me cumque ducet, sequar; Cic.

quod (originally acc. n. of qui), relat. conj.
(1) introducing a clause which is subjec or object of a sentence; *the fact that, th point that:* praetereo quod illam sibi domun delegerat, Cic.; adde quod pubes tibi cresci omnis, Hor.; id quoque accesserat quod, Cic.
(2) introducing a clause in a more genera relation to a sentence: **a,** *as to the fact that whereas:* quod scribis, Cic. L.; Caes., etc. also with subj.: Cic., etc.: **b,** *because, on th ground that* (usually with indic., unless th author rejects the reason given, or puts i into the mouth of another): noctu ambulabat quod somnium capere non posset, Cic.; ti agam gratias, quod me vivere coegisti, Cic. bene facis, quod me adiuvas, Cic.: **c,** *why on which account;* esp.: quod agam, *there i reason for:* est magis quod gratuler, Cic. nihil est quod, Cic.; quid est quod? Cic. **d,** with a temporal clause, *since:* Pl., Cic. **e,** *as far as, to the extent that:* adiutabo quo potero, Ter.; Cic.
(3) introducing a fresh sentence, *and, bu now,* etc.; esp. foll. by si, nisi, utinam, cum etc.: Caes., Cic., Verg.

quŏdammŏdŏ, adv. *in a certain way, in certain measure:* Cic.

quŏiās=cuias; q.v.

quŏlĭbĕt, adv. *whithersoever you please:* Ov Liv.

quŏmĭnŭs (²quo/compar. adv. minus), *b which the less, so that not;* used with sub after verbs of hindering and preventing, suc as impedio, deterreo, obsto; also with st impers.: stetit per Trebonium quominus Cic.; Liv.

quŏmŏdŏ, adv. *in what manner, how.* (1 interrog., in direct and indirect questions Cic., Hor., etc. (2) exclam.: quomod mortem filii tulit! Cic. (3) relat., esp. corre sponding with sic, *or* ita: Cic., Liv.

quŏmŏdŏcumquĕ, adv. (1) relat., *in what ever way:* Cic. (2) indef., *somehow:* Pl.

quŏmŏdŏnam, adv. *how then?* Cic. L.

quŏnam, *whither then? whither pray?:* Cic. quonam haec omnia nisi ad suam pernicie pertinere? Caes.

quondam, adv. (=quomdam). (1) *at a certai time* in the past, *formerly, once:* Cic.; Ov etc. (2) *at some future time, sometime:* Verg Hor. (3) *at times, sometimes:* Cic., Verg Hor.

quŏnĭam, conj. (quom/iam), *since, seeing tha whereas, because:* Pl., Cic., Verg., etc.

quōpĭam, adv. *to any place at all*: Pl., Ter., Liv.

quōquam, adv. *to any place at all*: Pl., Lucr., Cic., etc.

quŏquĕ, adv., placed after the word which it emphasizes, *also, too*: tu quoque, Verg.; Cic., Hor., etc.

quōquō or **quŏ quō**, *whithersoever, to whatever place*: Pl., Ter., Cic.

quōquŏversŭs and **quōquŏvorsum** (**quō-quŏvorsum**), adv. *in every direction*: Caes., Cic.

quorsum (**quorsŭs**), adv. (=quo versus), *whither, to what place?* LIT., Ter. TRANSF., (1) quorsum haec pertinent? Cic. (2) *to what purpose? to what end?*: quorsum igitur haec disputo? Cic.

quŏt, adj. plur. indecl. *how many*. (1) interrog., in direct and indirect questions: quot sunt? Pl., Cic., etc. (2) exclam.: quot calamitates! Cic. (3) relat., in correlation with tot, *as many, so many*: quot homines, tot causae, Cic.; often without tot, esp. elliptically: quot annis, *every year*, Caes., Cic., Verg.

quŏtannis, *see* quot.

quotcumquĕ, *as many as, however many*: Cic.

quŏtēni -ae -a (quot), *how many each*: Cic.

quotidiānus (**cottīdĭānus**) -a -um (quotidie), *of every day, daily*. LIT., aspectus, Cic.; exercitatio, Caes.; vita, Cic.; abl. n. as adv.: quotidiano, *daily*, Cic. TRANSF., *everyday, common, ordinary*: verba, Cic. L.; Ter., Mart.

quŏtĭdĭe (**cŏtĭdĭe**, **cottĭdĭe**) adv. (quot/dies), *daily, every day*: Cic.

quŏtĭēs (**quŏtĭens**), adv. (quot), *how often*. (1) interrog.: Cic. (2) exclam.: Verg. (3) relat., in correlation with toties: Cic.; often without toties: quoties mihi potestas erit, non praetermittam, Cic.; ambigitur quoties, Hor.

quŏtĭescumquĕ (**-cunquĕ**), adv. *however often*: Cic.

quotquŏt, num. indecl. *however many, as many soever as*: Cic., Cat., Hor.

quŏtŭmus -a -um (quotus), *which in number?*: Pl.

quŏtus -a -um (quot), *which in number?* interrog. or exclam.: quotus erit iste denarius qui non sit ferendus? Cic.; hora quota est? *what o'clock is it?* Hor.; tu quotus esse velis rescribe, *how many guests you would like invited with you*, Hor.; quota pars, *how small a fraction*, Ov.; quotus quisque, *one in how many? how rare?*: quotus enim quisque disertus? Cic.

quŏtuscumquĕ (**-uscunquĕ**) -ăcumquĕ -umcumquĕ, *whatever in number*: pars quotacumque, *however small a fraction*, Tib.

quŏtusquisque, *see* quotus.

quŏŭsquĕ or **quō usquĕ**, adv. *until where?* Of place: Liv. Of time or degree, *how long? how far?*: quousque tandem abutere, Catilina, patientiā nostrā? Cic.

quōvīs, adv. *to any place at all*: Pl., Ter.

quum, more correctly **cum** (older quom), conj., *when*. (1) to introduce a temporal clause; *when, at a time when*. When such a clause is a pure indication of time, the indic. is used: qui non defendit iniuriam cum potest, iniuste facit, Cic.; cum haec scribebam, in expectatione erant omnia, Cic. L.; cum primum, *as soon as*, Cic. But when it describes the circumstances attending and affecting a past action, the imperf. and pluperf. subj. are common: cum cohortes ex acie procucurrissent, Numidae effugiebant, Caes.; Zenonem, cum Athenis essem, audiebam frequenter, Cic. (2) in an 'inverted' sentence, to introduce a temporal clause containing the main point of the sentence; here the indic. is used: nondum lucebat cum Ameriae scitum est, Cic.; vixdum satis patebat iter, cum perfugae ruunt, Liv. (3) in the sense of *whenever, as often as*, with indic.: cum ad aliquod oppidum venerat, in cubiculum deferebatur, Cic.; Caes., Liv. (4) in the temporal sense of *since, since the time when*, with indic.: multi anni sunt, cum Fabius in aere meo est, Cic. (5) with indic., to denote close correspondence between subordinate and main clauses, *in that*: cum tacent, clamant, *in being silent, they cry aloud*, Cic. (6) cum . . . tum . . . , *both . . . and . . . , not only . . . but also . . .* , Cic. (7) to introduce a cause, *since, as*, with subj.: cum vita sine amicis plena sit, Cic. (8) to introduce a concession, *although*: patrem meum, cum proscriptus non esset, iugulasti, Cic.

R

R, r, the seventeenth letter of the Latin Alphabet, corresponds with the Greek rho (ʼΡ, ǫ́). On account of the aspirate which always accompanies the Greek letter, we find it represented by rh in some words derived from that language. The letter r seems often to have replaced, or become an alternative to, an original s, when standing at the end of a word or between vowels; e.g. arbor, arbos; honor, honos; quaero, quaeso; naris, nasus. For abbreviations in which R. is used, see Table of Abbreviations.

răbĭdus -a -um (rabies), *raging, mad, savage*; of animals: canes, Lucr., Ov.; leones, Hor.; of persons: Cat.; of abstr. things: mores, Ov.; fames, Verg.

¶ Adv. **răbĭdē**, *madly, savagely, fiercely*: omnia appetere, Cic.

răbĭēs -ēi, f. (rabio), *madness, rage*.

LIT., of animals and men: contacto eo scelere velut iniectā rabie ad arma ituros, Liv.; Pl., Verg.

TRANSF., *raging, fury*: animi acerbitas quaedam et rabies, Cic.; ira et rabies Latinorum, Liv.; caeli marisque, Verg. Esp. of the inspired madness of the Sibyl: Verg.; of love: Ter., Lucr., Hor.

răbĭo răbĕre, *to be mad*: Varr., Sen.

răbĭōsŭlus -a -um (dim. of rabiosus), *somewhat furious*: Cic. L.

răbĭōsus -a -um (rabies), *raging, mad, savage*: canis, Hor.; vide ne fortitudo minime sit rabiosa, Cic.

¶ Adv. **răbĭōsē**, *madly, furiously*: Cic.

Răbĭrĭus -a -um, *name of a Roman gens. Its most famous members were*: (1) C. Rabirius Postumus, *accused of treason, and defended by Cicero*. (2) Rabirius, *a poet, contemporary of Vergil*.

Adj. **Răbĭrĭānus** -a -um, *relating to Rabirius.*

răbŭla -ae, m. (rabio), *a bawling advocate*: Cic., Quint.

răcēmĭfĕr -fĕra -fĕrum (racemus/fero), *bearing clusters*: uva, Ov.; capilli, Ov.

răcēmus -i, m. *a cluster*, esp. *of grapes*: uva lentis racemis, Verg.; Hor., Ov. TRANSF., *wine*: Ov.

Răcilius -a -um, *name of a Roman gens. Its most famous member was* L. Racilius, *a tribune of the people in the time of Cicero*; f. **Răcilĭa** -ae, *wife of the dictator* L. Q. Cincinnatus.

rădĭātus (radius), *provided with spokes* or *rays*: sol, Cic.; lumina, Ov.

rādĭcĭtŭs, adv. (radix), *with* or *by the root.* LIT., Plin. TRANSF., *roots and all, utterly*: extrahere cupiditatem, Cic.; Pl., Lucr.

rădīcŭla -ae, f. (dim. of radix), *a little root*: Cic.

rădio -are and **rădĭor** -ari, dep. (radius, *ray*), *to gleam, emit rays, radiate*: argenti radiabant lumine valvae, Ov. Esp. in partic. **rădĭans**, *gleaming*: luna, Verg.; Lucr., Ov.

rădĭus -i, m. *a staff, rod, stake.*
LIT., acuti atque alius per alium immissi radii, Liv. Esp. (**1**) *the spoke of a wheel*: Verg., Ov. (**2**) in mathematics: **a**, *a measuring-rod*: Cic., Verg.: **b**, *the radius* or *semidiameter of a circle*: Cic. (**3**) t. t. of weaving, *a shuttle*: Verg. (**4**) t. t. of botany, *a kind of long olive*: Verg.
TRANSF., *a ray, beam of light*: radii solis, Cic.; Pl., Lucr., Verg.

rădix -īcis, f. (perhaps connected with ῥίζα), *a root.*
LIT., *the root of a plant*: cortices et radices, Cic.; arbores ab radicibus subruere, Caes.; Verg. Sometimes *an edible root*: genus radicis quod appellatur chara, Caes.; *a radish*: Hor.
TRANSF., (**1**) *the root* or *lowest part of anything*, esp. *the foot of a mountain*: in radicibus Caucasi natus, Cic. (**2**) *foundation, basis, origin*: patientiae, Cic.; ex iisdem, quibus nos, radicibus natum, Cic.; Pompeius, eo robore vir iis radicibus, Cic.

rādo rādĕre rāsi rāsum, *to scrape, scratch, smooth.*
LIT., in gen.: tigna, Lucr.; lapides palmā, Hor.; esp. *to shave*: aliquem, Cic.; caput et supercilia, Cic.; caput, as a sign of slavery, Liv.; in pursuance of a vow: Juv.
TRANSF., (**1**) *to graze in passing*: litora, Verg.; terras, Hor. (**2**) *to erase*: nomen fastis, Tac. (**3**) *to hurt, offend*: Quint.

raeda -ae, f. (a Gallic word), *a travelling carriage with four wheels*: vehi in raeda, Cic.; Caes., Hor.

raedārius -i, m. (raeda), *the driver of a raeda; a coachman*: Cic.

Raeti (Rhaeti) -ōrum, m. *a people between the Inn and the Rhine.*
¶ Hence subst. **Raetĭa** -ae, f. *Raetia, their country*; adj. **Raetĭcus, Raetĭus, Raetus** -a -um, *Raetian.*

rallus -a -um (rarus), *thin, of fine texture*: Pl.

rāmāle -is, n. (ramus), usually plur. **rāmālĭa** -ium, *sticks, brushwood*: Ov., Tac.

rāmentum -i, n. (rado), usually plur. **rāmenta** -orum, *shavings, splinters, chips.* LIT., ferri,

Lucr. TRANSF., aurum cum ramento, *every halfpenny*, Pl.

rāmĕus -a -um (ramus), *of branches*: fragmenta, brushwood, Verg.

rāmex -ĭcis, m. (ramus). (**1**) *a rupture*: Plin., Juv. (**2**) plur.: ramices, *the blood-vessels of the lungs, the lungs*, Pl.

Ramnes -ium, m. and **Ramnenses** -ĭum, m. *one of the three tribes into which the early Roman citizens were divided by Romulus*: Liv. Hence *the name of one of the three centuries* of equites: Cic., Liv. Poet.=*nobles*: Hor.

rāmōsus -a -um (ramus), *full of boughs, branching, branchy.* LIT., arbor, Lucr.; Ov. TRANSF., hydra ramosa natis e caede colubris, *the hydra, from whose trunk, as from a tree, grew young serpents*, Ov.; Lucr., Verg.

rāmŭlus -i, m. (dim. of ramus), *a little branch, twig*: Cic.

rāmus -i, m. *a bough, branch, twig.*
LIT., in quibus non truncus, non rami, non folia, Cic.
TRANSF., (**1**) *a tree*: rami atque venatus alebat, Verg. (**2**) *a branch of a stag's antlers*: Caes. (**3**) plur., rami, *the arms of the Greek letter* Y, *regarded by the Pythagoreans as symbolical of the two paths of life*: Samii rami, Pers.

rāna -ae, f. *a frog.* LIT., Cic. L., Verg., Hor. TRANSF., rana marina, *a sea-fish, the frog-fish*: Cic.

rancens -entis, *stinking, putrid*: Lucr.

rancĭdŭlus -a -um (dim. of rancidus), *somewhat putrid*: Juv. TRANSF., *loathsome*: Pers.

rancĭdus -a -um (cf. rancens), *stinking, rank.* LIT., aper, Hor. TRANSF., *disgusting, offensive*; compar.: Juv.

rānuncŭlus -i, m. (dim. of rana), *a little frog, a tadpole*: Cic. In jest, used of the inhabitants of Ulubrae, which was near the Pontine marshes: Cic.

răpācĭda -ae, m. (rapax), *a robber*: Pl.

răpācĭtās -ātis, f. (rapax), *greediness, rapacity*: quis in rapacitate avarior? Cic.; Mart.

răpax -ācis (rapio), adj. (with compar.; and superl. in Plin.), *seizing, snatching, grasping greedy.*
LIT., lupus, Hor.; fluvius, Lucr.; ventus, Ov.; mors, Tib.; Orcus, Hor.
TRANSF., in gen., *grasping*: nihil est appetentius, similius sui, nec rapacius quam natura, Cic.

răpĭdē, adv. from rapidus; q.v.

răpĭdĭtās -ātis, f. (rapidus), *rapid flow, rapidity*: fluminis, Caes.

răpĭdus -a -um (rapio), *tearing, seizing, impetuous, swift.* LIT., of physical movement: ferae, equus, Ov.; sol, *fierce*, Verg.; amnis, Hor.; torrens, Verg. TRANSF., abstr.: oratio, Cic.; rapidus in consiliis, Liv.
¶ Adv. **răpĭdē**, *impetuously, rapidly.* LIT., rapide dilapsus fluvius, Cic. TRANSF., Cic.

răpīna -ae, f. (rapio). LIT., *robbery, plundering, pillage*; gen. in plur.: Cic., Hor., etc. TRANSF., *booty, plunder*: Verg.

răpĭo răpĕre răpŭi raptum (cf. ἁρπάζω), *to seize, snatch, tear away.*
LIT., (**1**) *to seize in order to keep, to snatch to oneself*: praedas, Verg.; bipennem dextrā, Verg.; corpus consulis, Liv.; virgines, Sall.,

Liv., Ov.; improvisa leti vis rapuit gentes, Hor. Also *to plunder* a place: Armeniam, Tac.; castra urbesque primo impetu, Liv. (2) *to hurry along* a person or thing in a particular direction: quo rapitis me? Pl.; aliquem hinc, Liv.; manipulos aliquot in primam aciem secum rapit, Verg.; reflex.: se rapere hinc ocius, *to hasten away*, Hor.; inde se ad urbem, id est ad caedem optimi cuiusque, Cic. Esp. *to hurry* a person off to punishment, etc.: in ius ad regem, Liv.; e carcere ad palum et ad necem, Cic. Transf., (1) *to seize, enjoy hastily, hasten along*: tecum solatia, Verg.; occasionem de die, Hor.; viam, Ov.; nuptias, Liv.; almum quae rapit hora diem, Hor.; animus cupidine caecus ad inceptum scelus rapiebat, Sall.; in a good sense: ad divinarum rerum cognitionem curā omni studioque rapi, Cic. (2) *to pervert, distort, lead astray*: ipsae res verba rapiunt, Cic.; rapi in invidiam, Cic.; commoda ad se, Cic.; Verg., Liv. ¶ N. of partic. as subst. **raptum** -i, *plunder*: Verg., Ov., Liv.

raptim, adv. (rapio), *violently, hastily, hurriedly*: haec scripsi raptim, Cic. L.; Verg., Liv., etc.

raptĭo -ōnis, f. (rapio), *a carrying off, abduction*: Ter.

rapto -are (freq. of rapio). Lit., physically, *to seize and carry away, hurry away*: huc illuc vexilla, Tac.; coniugem, Cic.; Hectora circa muros, Verg.; nubila caeli, Lucr. Also *to rob, plunder*: Tac. Transf., quid raptem in crimina divos, *accuse*, Prop.; me amor, *passion drives me on*, Pl.

raptor -ōris, m. (rapio), *a robber, plunderer.* Lit., Hor., Ov., Tac.; attrib.: lupi raptores, Verg. Transf., raptores alieni honoris, Ov.

raptus -ūs, m. (rapio). (1) *a tearing off, rending away*: Ov. (2) *a carrying off, abduction, rape*: Cic., Ov., Tac. (3) *plundering*: Tac.

răpŭlum -i, n. (dim. of rapum), *a little turnip*: Hor.

răpum -i, n. (cf. ῥάφη), *a turnip*: Varr.

rārē, adv. from rarus; q.v.

rārēfăcĭo -făcĕre -fēci -factum (rarus/facio), *to make thin, rarefy*: Lucr.

rāresco -ĕre (rarus). Lit., *to become thin, to lose density*: umor aquai ab aestu, Lucr.; tellus in aquas, Ov. Transf., (1) *to widen out*: ubi angusti rarescunt claustra Pelori, Verg.; paulatim rarescunt montes, Tac. (2) *to grow less*: sonitus, Prop.

rārĭtās -ātis, f. (rarus). (1) *want of density, thinness, looseness of texture, distance apart*: Cic. (2) *fewness, rarity*: dictorum, Cic.

rārus -a -um, adj. (with compar. and superl.), *loose, thin.* Lit., (1) *loose in texture, thin* (opp. densus): aer, Lucr.; retia, Verg.; cribrum, Ov.; rariores silvae, Tac. (2) *scattered, scanty, far apart*: vides habitari in terra raris et angustis in locis, Cic.; raris ac prope nullis portibus, Caes. As milit. t. t., *in loose order* (opp. confertus): ipsi ex silvis rari propugnabant, Caes.; ordines, Liv.; acies, Verg. Transf., (1) *rare, infrequent*: in omni arte optimum quidque rarissimum, Cic.; Oceanus raris navibus aditur, Tac.; nec Iliacos coetus nisi rarus adibat, *seldom*, Ov. (2)

extraordinary, distinguished: Cynthia rara meast, Prop.; rara quidem facie sed rarior arte canendi, Ov. ¶ As adv., abl. n. **rārō**; also **rārē**; *seldom, rarely*: Pl., Cic., Hor., Ov. Compar. **rārĭus**, Cic. L.

rāsĭlis -e (rado), *scraped, having a smooth surface, polished*: torno rasile buxum, Verg.

rastrum -i, n. (rado), plur., gen. rastri -ōrum, m. *an instrument for scraping; a toothed hoe, a rake, a mattock*: Verg., Ov.

rătĭo -ōnis, f. (reor), *a reckoning, account, computation, calculation.* Lit., in business; abstract or concrete: eius pecuniae, cuius ratio in aede Opis confecta est, Cic.; auri ratio constat, *comes right, is correct*, Cic.; rationem ducere, *or* habere, *to compute, calculate*, Cic.; rationem inire, Caes.; rationem referre, *give an account*, Cic.; plur.: rationes cum aliquo putare, Cic.; conferre, referre, subducere, Cic. Transf., (1) *consideration taken*, or *account rendered*, of any matter: alicuius rationem habere, Caes., Cic., Liv.; superis de rebus habenda nobis est ratio, Lucr.; rationem vitae suae reddere, Cic.; semper ita vivamus ut rationem reddendam nobis arbitremur, Cic.; cedo rationem carceris, quae diligentissime conficitur, Cic. (2) *any transaction, affair, business*: de tota illa ratione atque re Gallicana, Cic.; haec res non solum ex domestica est ratione, attingit etiam bellicam, Cic.; fori iudiciique rationem Messala suscepit, *public and legal business*, Cic.; rationes meas vestrae saluti anteposuissem, *my interests*, Cic. (3) *a reason, motive, ground*: rationem mei consilii accipite, Caes.; argumentis ac rationibus, Cic.; consilii causa ratioque, Cic.; non ratio est, *it is unreasonable*, Cic. As rhet. t. t., *ground or reason brought forward to support a proposition*: confirmare argumentis ac rationibus, Cic. (4) *a plan, scheme, system*: de summa caeli ratione deumque, Lucr.; meae vitae rationes ab ineunte aetate susceptae, Cic.; rationes belli gerendi, *principles*, Caes.; civitatis, Cic. Hence, *reasonableness, method, order, rule*: modo et ratione omnia facere, Cic.; Hor. (5) *a theory, doctrine, science, knowledge*: Epicuri ratio, *philosophical system*, Cic.; cum in eam rationem quisque loqueretur, Cic.; ratio tua coepit vociferari naturam rerum, Lucr. (6) *the faculty of mind which calculates and plans, the reason*: homo rationis particeps, Cic.; mens et ratio et consilium, Cic.; consilio et ratione, Cic.; ratione sagaci videndum, Lucr.

rătĭŏcĭnātĭo -ōnis, f. (ratiocinor). (1) *reasoning; deliberate consideration and conclusion*: Cic. (2) *a form of argument, syllogism*: Cic., Quint.

rătĭŏcĭnātīvus -a -um (ratiocinor), *argumentative, syllogistic*: Cic., Quint.

rătĭŏcĭnātor -ōris, m. (ratiocinor), *a calculator, accountant*: Cic. L.

rătĭŏcĭnor -ari, dep. (ratio). (1) *to compute, calculate*: Cic. (2) *to consider, deliberate*: Pl. (3) *to argue, infer, conclude*; with indir. quest., or with acc. and infin.: Cic.

rătĭŏnālis -e (ratio), *reasonable, rational*: Quint. ¶ Adv. **rătĭŏnālĭtĕr**, *reasonably*: Sen.

rătĭōnārĭum -i, n. (ratio), *a statistical account*: imperii, Suet.

rătis -is, f. Lit., *a raft*: Cic., Caes.; ratibus, quibus iunxerat flumen, resolutis, *pontoons*, Liv. Transf., *a ship, boat, vessel*: Verg.

rătĭuncŭla -ae, f. (dim. of ratio). (1) *a little reckoning, account*: Pl., Ter. (2) *a poor, insufficient reason*: huic incredibili sententiae ratiunculas suggerit, Cic. (3) *a petty syllogism*: concludunt ratiunculas Stoici, Cic.

rătus -a -um, partic. from reor; q.v.

raucīsŏnus -a -um (raucus/sonus), *hoarsely sounding*: Lucr., Cat.

raucus -a -um (connected with ravim), *hoarse*. Lit., (1) of men and animals: fauces, Lucr.; nos raucos saepe attentissime audiri video, Cic.; cornix, Lucr.; vox ranarum, Cic. Transf., of inanimate things, *harsh-sounding*: cornu, Pl.; murmur undae, Verg.; Hadria, Hor.

raudus (**rōdus**, **rūdus**) -ĕris, n. *a rough mass* or *lump*; esp. *a piece of copper used as a coin*: Liv.

rauduscŭlum -i, n. (dim. of raudus), *a small sum of money*: de raudusculo Numeriano, *the little debt of Numerius*, Cic.

Raurĭci -ōrum, m. *a Celtic people in Gaul, near modern Basle.*

Răvenna -ae, f. *a town in Gallia Cispadana, near the Adriatic, made a naval station by Augustus* (now *Ravenna*).
¶ Hence adj. **Răvennās** -ātis, m. *belonging to Ravenna.*

răvim, acc. sing. as from ravis, f. (cf. raucus), *hoarseness*: Pl.

răvĭo -ire (ravis), *to talk oneself hoarse*: Pl.

răvus -a -um, *tawny* or *greyish*: Hor., Cic.

rĕ- and (mainly before vowels and h) **rĕd-**, an insepar. particle, meaning sometimes *back*, as in recurro; sometimes *against*, as in reluctor; sometimes *again*, as in restituo.

rĕa, see reus.

rĕapsĕ, adv. (rē/eapse=ipsā), *indeed, in truth, really*: Pl., Cic.

Rĕātĕ -is, n. *an old town in the Sabine country* (now *Rieti*). Adj. **Rĕātīnus** -a -um, *Reatine*; m. pl. subst. **Rĕātĭni** -ōrum, *the people of Reate.*

rĕbellātĭo=rebellio; q.v.: Tac.

rĕbellātrix -icis, f. (rebello), *renewing war, rebellious*: Germania, Ov.

rĕbellĭo -ōnis, f. (rebello), *a renewal of war*, esp. *by a conquered people, a revolt*: rebellionem facere, Caes.; Liv., Tac.; plur.: Carthaginiensium rebelliones, Cic.

rĕbellis -e (rebello), *renewing a war, insurgent*. Lit., colonia, Tac.; Verg.; m. pl. as subst., *rebels*: Tac. Transf., amor, Ov.

rĕbellĭum=rebellio; q.v.: Liv.

rĕbello -are, *to renew a war, to revolt*. Lit., septies rebellare, Liv. Transf., *to renew any struggle, to fight back*: Ov., Sen.

rĕbīto -ĕre, *to go back, return*: Pl.

rĕbŏo -are. (1) *to echo, resound*: Verg. (2) *to make to resound*: Lucr.

rĕcalcitro -are (of a horse), *to kick back*; fig., *to deny access*: Hor.

rĕcălĕo -ēre, *to be warm again*: recalent nostro Tiberina fluenta sanguine, Verg.

rĕcălesco -ĕre, *to become warm again*. Lit., cum motu atque exercitatione recalescunt corpora, Cic. Transf., mens recalescit, Ov.

rĕcalfăcĭo -făcĕre -fēci -factum, *to make warm again*: Ov.

rĕcandesco -candescĕre -candŭi. (1) *to grow white*: recanduit unda, Ov. (2) *to become hot, to begin to glow*. Lit., (tellus) recanduit aestu, Ov. Transf., recanduit ira, Ov.

rĕcanto -are. (1) intransit., *to resound, echo*: Mart. (2) transit.: a, *to recall, recant*: recantata opprobria, Hor.: b, *to charm away*: curas, Ov.

rĕcēdo -cēdĕre -cessi -cessum, *to go back, draw back, recede, retreat, retire.*
Lit., physically. (1) of persons and animals: ex eo loco, Caes.; non modo e Gallia non discessisse, sed ne a Mutina quidem recessisse, Cic.; a stabulis apes, Verg. (2) of the movement of lifeless things: ut illae undae ad alios accedant, ab aliis autem recedant, Cic.; caput e cervice, *is severed*, Ov. (3) of the position of places; *to retire, stand back*: Anchisae domus recessit, Verg. Also of apparent movement, *to recede in the distance, disappear from view*: provehimur portu, terraeque urbesque recedunt, Verg.
Transf., (1) of men and animals, *to withdraw, retire*: anni recedentes, Hor.; ab officio, Cic.; ab armis, Cic.; a vita, Cic.; in otia, Hor. (2) of lifeless things: res ab usitata consuetudine recessit, Cic.; anni recedentes, Hor.; ira recessit, Ov.; in ventos vita, Verg.

rĕcello -ĕre, *to spring back, fly back*: cum (ferrea) manus gravi libramento recelleret ad solum, Liv.

rĕcens -entis (abl. sing., recenti, in poets sometimes recentē; genit. plur., recentium, in poets sometimes recentum), adj. (with compar. and superl.), *new, fresh, young, recent*.
Lit., caespites, Caes.; flores, Hor.; prata, Verg. Esp. of strength, *fresh, vigorous*; of soldiers: integri et recentes, Caes.; of horses: Liv.; of the mind: animus (consulis), Liv.
Transf., *fresh, in time, recent*. (1) of things: recenti re, recenti negotio, *while the business is still fresh*, Cic.; iniuriarum memoria, Caes.; victoria, Caes. (2) of persons: his recentibus viris, Cic.; m. pl. of compar. as subst.: recentiores, Cic. Esp. with abl. or prep., *to indicate point of departure*: Homerus, qui recens ab illorum aetate fuit, Cic.; cum e provincia recens esset, Cic.; recens a vulnere Dido, Verg.; praeturā, Tac.; Regini quidam eo venerunt, Romā sane recentes, *direct from Rome*, Cic.
¶ Adv. **rĕcens**, *lately, recently*, esp. with participles: sole recens orto, Verg.; recens ad Regillum lacum accepta clades, Liv.; Sall.; Tac.

rĕcensĕo -censēre -censŭi -censum, *to count again*; hence, *to review, muster, examine*. Lit., milit. t. t.: exercitum, legiones, Liv.; Verg., Liv.; polit. t. t., of the censor: equites, Liv.; poet., *to pass through*: signa (of the sun), Ov.
Transf., (1) *to go over in thought, review*: fataque fortunasque virum, Verg.; Liv., Ov. (2) *to go over in words, recount*: fortia facta, Ov.

rĕcensĭo -ōnis, f. (recenseo), *a reviewing, mustering, enumeration by the censor*: Cic.

rĕcensus -ūs, m. (recenseo), *a review, muster populi*, Suet.

rĕceptācŭlum -i, n. (recepto). (1) *a magazine, reservoir, receptacle*: cibi et potionis (of the stomach), Cic.; cloaca maxima receptaculum omnium purgamentorum urbis, Liv.; Tac. (2) *a place of refuge, shelter, retreat*: militum Catilinae, Cic.; receptaculum esse classibus nostris, Cic.; fugientibus, Liv.; Caes.

rĕceptĭo -ōnis, f. (recipio), *a receiving, reception*: Pl.

rĕcepto -are (freq. of recipio). (1) *to draw back*: hastam, Verg.; Saturni sese quo stella receptet, Verg. (2) *to receive back, take in*: Lucr. (3) *to receive frequently, harbour*: mercatores, Liv.

rĕceptor -ōris, m. (recipio), *one who receives or harbours, a harbourer*: praedarum, Tac.; ipse ille latronum occultator et receptor locus, Cic.

rĕceptrix -trīcis, f. (receptor), *a receiver*: furtorum, Cic.

rĕceptus -ūs, m. (recipio). (1) *a drawing back.* LIT., spiritus in receptu difficilis, Quint. TRANSF., *withdrawal, recantation*: nimis pertinacis sententiae, Liv.
(2) *a retiring, a retreat, return.* LIT., esp. milit. t. t., *a retreat, falling back*: ut expeditum ad suos receptum habeant, Caes.; Caesar receptui cani iussit, *ordered the signal of retreat*, Caes.; fig.: canere receptui a miseriis, Cic. TRANSF., *non tutissimus a malis consiliis receptus, Liv.; receptus ad Caesaris gratiam atque amicitiam, Caes. Of a *place of retreat*: Verg.

rĕcessim, adv. (recedo), *backwards*: Pl.

rĕcessus -ūs, m. (recedo), *a going back, receding, retreat.*
LIT., lunae accessus et recessus, Cic.; (aestuum maritimorum) accessus et recessus, *ebb and flow*, Cic.; recessum primis ultimi non dabant, *chance of retreating*, Caes.
TRANSF., (1) *withdrawal*: accessum ad res salutares, a pestiferis recessum, *disinclination for*, Cic.; ut metus recessum quendam animi et fugam efficiat, Cic. (2) *a place of retreat, quiet, retired place*: mihi solitudo et recessus provincia est, Cic.; Verg., Liv., etc.; fig.: in animis hominum tanti sunt recessus, *corners, intricacies*, Cic.

rĕcĭdīvus -a -um (recido), *returning, repeated*: nummus, Juv.; poet.: Pergama, *rebuilt*, Verg.

¹**rĕcĭdo** -cĭdĕre -ccĭdi -cāsūrus (re/cado), *to fall back.* LIT., recidunt omnia in terras, Cic.; Lucr., etc. TRANSF., (1) *to relapse, sink, fall*: in graviorem morbum, Liv.; in eandem fortunam, Cic.; cum ad eum potentatus omnis reccidisset, Cic. (2) *to recoil, fall back upon*: hunc casum ad ipsos recidere posse, Cic.; ut amentiae poena in ipsum eiusque familiam recidat, Cic. (3) *to fall back, descend, be reduced*: illa omnia ex laetitia ad lacrimas recciderunt, Cic.; ad nihilum, Cic.; quorsum recidat responsum tuum non magno opere laboro, Cic.; Liv.

²**rĕcĭdo** -cĭdĕre -cīdi -cīsum (re/caedo), *to cut back, lop away.* LIT., barbam falce, Ov.; caput, Ov.; ceras inanes, Verg. TRANSF., nationes, Cic.; ambitiosa ornamenta, Hor.; Tac.

rĕcingo -cingĕre -cinxi -cinctum, *to ungird, loosen*: tunicas, Ov.; pass. as middle: recingor anguem, Ov.

rĕcĭno -ĕre (re/cano), *to resound, echo.*

(1) intransit.: in vocibus nostrorum oratorum recinit quiddam et resonat urbanius, Cic.; parra recinens, *shrieking* (or perhaps *singing against*, i.e. *protesting*), Hor.
(2) transit., *to cause to resound*: cuius recinet iocosa nomen imago, Hor.; curvā lyrā Latonam, Hor.

rĕcĭpĭo -cĭpĕre -cēpi -ceptum (re/capio).
(1) *to hold back, retain*: sibi aliquid, Cic.; Pl.
(2) *to take back, draw back, fetch back.* LIT., ensem, Verg.; esp. as milit. t. t., *to draw back, cause to retreat*: milites defessos, Caes. Reflex., *se recipere, to withdraw, retire, retreat*: se ex hisce locis, Cic.; se ad nos, Cic.; esp. as milit. t. t.: se in castra, Caes., Liv. TRANSF., vocem ab acutissimo sono usque ad gravissimum sonum, Cic.; reflex.: se ad bonam frugem, Cic.; se ad reliquam cogitationem belli, Caes.
(3) *to take back, regain, recover.* LIT., obsides, Caes.; aliquem medio ex hoste, Verg.; Tarentum, Cic.; suas res amissas, Liv. TRANSF., *to recover*: antiquam frequentiam, Liv.; vitam herbis fortibus, Ov.; animos ex pavore, *to regain courage*, Liv.; mentem, Hor.
(4) *to receive, accept, take to oneself.* LIT., ferrum, gladium, *to receive the death-wound*, Cic.; necesse erat ab latere aperto tela recipi, Caes.; of animals: frenum, Hor.; of rivers: Mosa, parte quadam ex Rheno accepta, Caes. Esp. *to receive hospitably into a place, into friendship*, etc.: Xerxen, Cic.; aliquem libentissimo animo, Caes.; hos tutissimus portus recipiebat, Caes.; aliquem ad epulas, Cic.; in civitatem, Cic., Hor., Liv.; in fidem, Cic.; exercitum tectis ac sedibus suis, Cic.; aliquem domum suam, Cic.; senem sessum, Cic. Sometimes, like capio, *to take possession of, conquer*: oppidum, civitatem, Caes.; pecuniam ex novis vectigalibus, Cic. TRANSF., in gen., *to accept, admit, allow*: fabulas, *to believe*, Cic.; nec inconstantiam virtus recipit, *admits*, Cic.; causam Siculorum, *to take up*, Cic.; officium, Cic. Esp.: a, *to accept an obligation*; *to guarantee, promise, be responsible for*: pro Cassio et te, si quid me velitis recipere, recipiam, Cic.; ea quae tibi promitto ac recipio, Cic.; with acc. and fut. infin.: Caes., Cic. Hence n. of partic. as subst. **rĕceptum** -i, *an engagement, guarantee*: **b**, as legal t. t., of the praetor: recipere nomen, *to receive an accusation against anyone*, Cic.; recipere reum, Tac.

rĕcĭprŏco -are (reciprocus), *to move backwards, or to move backwards and forwards.*
(1) transit. LIT., animam, *to draw in and breathe out the air, to breathe*, Liv.; quinqueremem in adversum aestum reciprocari non posse, Liv. TRANSF., si quidem ista reciprocantur, *if the proposition is converted or reversed*, Cic.
(2) intransit.: fretum Euripi non septies die temporibus statis reciprocat, *ebbs and flows*, Liv.; Cic.

rĕcĭprŏcus -a -um, *returning, going backwards and forwards*: Plin.; mare, *ebbing*, Tac.

rĕcīsus -a -um, partic. from recīdo; q.v.

rĕcĭtātĭo -ōnis, f. (recito), *a reading aloud.*
(1) of documents in legal proceedings: Cic.
(2) of literary works: Tac., Plin. L.

rĕcĭtātor -ōris, m. (recito), *a reader aloud.* (**1**) of documents in legal proceedings: Cic. (**2**) of literary works, *a reciter*: Hor., Sen., Plin. L.

rĕcĭto -are, *to read aloud, read publicly.*
(**1**) officially: **a**, *to read a document*: litteras in senatu, in contione, Cic.; aliquid ex codice, Cic.; testimonium, Cic.: **b**, *to read out the name of a person*: testamento heredem aliquem, Cic.; aliquem praeterire in recitando senatu, *in reading the list of senators*, Cic.: **c**, *to read the words of an oath, to dictate*: Tac.
(**2**) *to read one's literary works before friends*: Hor., Ov., Plin. L.

reclāmātĭo -ōnis, f. (reclamo), *a crying out against, loud disapprobation*: Cic.

reclāmĭto -are (freq. of reclamo), *to cry out against loudly, violently contradict*; with dat.: Cic.

reclāmo -are. (**1**) *to cry out against, contradict loudly*. Lit., Cic., Hor., Liv.; with dat.: alicui, Plin. L.; orationi, Cic.; promissis, Cic.; with ne and the subj.: unā voce omnes iudices, ne is iuraret, reclamasse, Cic. Transf., quoniam ratio reclamat vera, Lucr. (**2**) *to reverberate, re-echo, resound*: scopulis reclamant aequora, Verg.

reclīnis -e (reclino), *leaning backwards, reclining*: Ov., Tac.

reclīno -are (re/*clino), *to bend back, cause to lean back*. Lit., se, Caes.; scuta, Verg.; partic., reclīnātus -a -um, *bent back, reclined*: Hor., Caes. Transf., nullum ab labore me reclinat otium, *releases me from labour*, Hor.

rĕclūdo -clūdĕre -clūsi -clūsum (re/claudo), *to unclose, to open.*
Lit., portas, Verg.; viam, Ov.; tellurem unco dente, *to turn over, cultivate*, Verg.; ensem, *to draw from the scabbard*, Verg.; pectus mucrone, *to pierce*, Verg.
Transf., ebrietas operta recludit, *reveals*, Hor.; fata, *to relax*, Hor.

rĕcōgĭto -are, *to think over again, reconsider*: de re, Cic.

rĕcognĭtĭo -ōnis, f. (recognosco), *a reviewing, inspection, examining*: agri Campani, Liv.; Cic.

rĕcognosco -noscĕre -nōvi -nĭtum. (**1**) *to recognize, to know again, to recall*: res, one's property, Liv.; illa reminiscendo, Cic.; recognosce mecum noctem illam, Cic. (**2**) *to review, inspect, examine, investigate*: decretum populi, Cic.; codicem, Cic.; dona populorum, Verg.; agros, Liv.

rĕcollĭgo=reconligo; q.v.

rĕcŏlo -cŏlĕre -cŏlŭi -cultum, *to cultivate again.*
Lit., desertam terram, Liv.; Ov. Also *to work again*: metalla intermissa, Liv.; *to revisit*: locum, Phaedr.
Transf., (**1**) *to practise again, resume*: artes, Cic.; studia, Cic. (**2**) *to set up again, rehabilitate, honour afresh*: imagines subversas, Tac.; dignitatem, Cic.; aliquem sacerdotiis, Tac. (**3**) *to reflect upon, to recall*: quae si tecum ipse recolis, Cic.; inclusas animas lustrabat studio recolens, Verg.

rĕcommĭniscor -i, dep. *to recollect*: Pl.

rĕcompōno -pōnĕre -pŏsĭtum, *to readjust, re-arrange*: comas, Ov.

rĕconcĭlĭātĭo -ōnis, f. (reconcilio), *a winning back, restoration, re-establishment*: concordiae, Cic.; gratiae, *reconciliation*, Cic.; also absol. in this sense: inridebatur haec illius reconciliatio, Cic.; Liv.

rĕconcĭlĭātor -ōris, m. (reconcilio), *a restorer*: pacis, Liv.

rĕconcĭlĭo -are, *to make good again, restore, repair*: diuturni laboris detrimentum sollertiā et virtute militum brevi reconciliatur, Caes.; existimationem iudiciorum, Cic.
Esp. *to restore good feeling* between persons; *with feeling as object*: concordiam, gratiam, Liv.; *with persons as object, to reunite, reconcile*: aliquem alicui, Cic.; inimicos in gratiam, Cic.

rĕconcinno -are, *to restore, renovate, repair*: pallam, Pl.; tribus locis aedifico, reliqua reconcinno, Cic.

rĕcondo -dĕre -dĭdi -dĭtum, *to put away, put back, store.*
Lit., gladium in vaginam, Cic.; prome reconditum Caecubum, Hor.; recondita alia (medicamenta), Liv.
Transf., (**1**) poet., *to thrust*, etc.: ensem in pulmone, Verg.; oculos, *to close again*, Ov. (**2**) mentally, *to store, hide*: mens alia recondit, e quibus memoria oritur, Cic.; Venerem interius, Verg.; Tac.; *to conceal*: voluptates, Tac.
¶ Hence partic. **rĕcondĭtus** -a -um, *put away, concealed*. Lit., locus, Cic.; n. pl.: occulta et recondita templi, *secret recesses*, Caes. Transf., (**1**) *abstruse, profound*: reconditae abstrusaeque res, Cic.; compar.: Cic. (**2**) of character, *reserved, mysterious*: naturā tristi ac reconditā fuit, Cic.

rĕconflo -are, *to rekindle*: Lucr.

rĕconlĭgo -legĕre -lēgi -lectum, *to collect again, gather together again*. Lit., sparsos ignes, Luc. Transf., se, *to regain courage*, Ov.; primos annos, *to become young again*, Ov.; animum alicuius, *to reconcile*, Cic. L.

rĕcŏquo -cŏquĕre -coxi -coctum, *to boil again, heat up again*. Lit., Peliam (*in order to make him young again*), Cic.; patrios enses, *to forge again*, Verg. Transf., recoctus scriba ex quinqueviro, *new-moulded*, Hor.

rĕcordātĭo -ōnis, f. (recordor), *a recollection, remembrance*: ultimi temporis recordatio, Cic.; plur.: recordationes fugio, Cic.; Plin. L., Tac.

rĕcordor -ari, dep. (re/cor).
(**1**) *to remember, recollect*; with genit.: flagitiorum suorum, Cic.; with acc.: maiorum diligentiam, Cic.; Caes., Verg., etc.; with acc. and infin.: hoc genus poenae saepe in improbos cives esse usurpatum, Cic.; Caes., Ov.; with indir. quest.: non recordor, unde ceciderim, Cic.; Caes.; with de: de ceteris, Cic.; absol.: si recordari volumus, Cic. (**2**) *to think of something in the future, to ponder over*: quae sum passura recordor, Ov.

recrĕo -are, *to create again*, or *restore to a sound condition, refresh, invigorate, revive.*
Lit., physically: sol lumen, Lucr.; vires, Lucr. Esp. reflex.: se recreare, and pass. as middle, recreari, *to revive, recover, be refreshed*: ex vulnere, Cic.; ex vulneribus, Liv.
Transf., in spirits, etc.: provinciam adflictam et perditam erigere atque recreare, Cic.;

adflictos animos, Cic.; recreare se ex magno timore, Cic.; civitas recreatur, Cic.

recrĕpo -are, *to echo, resound*: Cat. With acc.: Verg.

recresco -crescĕre -crēvi -crētum, *to grow again*: Lucr., Ov., Liv.

recrūdesco -crūdescĕre -crūdŭi, *to become raw again*. Of wounds, *to open afresh*: quae consanuisse videbantur, recrudescunt, Cic. Fig., *to break out again*: recrudescente Manliānā seditione, Liv.; Cic. L.

rectā, adv. from rectus; q.v.

rectē, adv. from rectus; q.v.

rectio -ōnis, f. (rego), *a ruling, direction*: rerum publicarum, Cic.

rector -ōris, m. (rego), *a ruler, governor, director, guide*. LIT., navis, *steersman*, Cic.; so in Verg. and Ov.; of a *driver* or *rider* of animals: Liv., Ov., Tac. TRANSF., rector et gubernator civitatis, Cic.; Olympi, *or* superum, *or* deum, *Jupiter*, Ov.; maris, *Neptune*, Ov.; animus incorruptus, rector humani generis, Sall.

rectrix -icis, f. (rector), *she that leads* or *guides*: Sen.

rectus -a -um, partic. from rego; q.v.

rĕcŭbo -are, *to lie back, to recline*: sub tegmine fagi, Verg.; Lucr., Cic.

rĕcumbo -cumbĕre -cŭbŭi, *to lie back, recline*.
LIT., of persons: in cubiculo, Cic.; in herba, Cic. Esp., *to recline at table*: in triclinio, Cic.; Hor.
TRANSF., *to sink down, fall down*: cervix in umeros, Verg.; pons, Cat.; unda, Hor.

rĕcŭpĕrātio -ōnis, f. (recupero), *a recovery*: libertatis, Cic.

rĕcŭpĕrātor (rĕcĭpĕrātor) -ōris, m. (re-cupero), *a recoverer*: urbis, Tac. Esp. as t. t.: recuperatores, *a board of arbiters appointed by the praetor to decide causes which required speedy settlement*, Cic.

rĕcŭpĕrātōrĭus -a -um (recuperator), *of the recuperatores* (q.v.): iudicium, Cic.

rĕcŭpĕro (rĕcĭpĕro) -are, *to get again, regain, recover*; of material things: villam suam ab aliquo, Cic.; urbem, Liv.; amissa, Caes.; rempublicam, Cic.; of persons: obsides, Caes.; si vos et me ipsum recuperaro, Cic. L.; of abstr. things: voluntatem, Cic.

rĕcŭro -are, *to restore, refresh*: Cat.

rĕcurro -currĕre -curri -cursum, *to run back, hasten back*.
LIT., of persons: ad aliquem, Cic.; ad redam, Cic.; in Tusculanum, Cic.; rure, Hor.
TRANSF., (1) of things: luna tum crescendo, tum defectionibus in initia recurrendo, Cic.; bruma recurrit iners, Hor.; naturam expellas furcā, tamen usque recurret, Hor. Esp. of the course of the sun and the year, *to roll round*: sol recurrens, Verg. (2) of persons, *to revert, return*: ad easdem deditionis condiciones, Caes.

rĕcurso -are (freq. of recurro), *to run back, hasten back, return*. LIT., Pl., Lucr. TRANSF., cura recursat, Verg.

rĕcursus -ūs, m. (recurro), *a return, coming back, retreat*: Verg., Ov., Liv.

rĕcurvo -are, *to bend* or *curve backwards*: colla equi, Ov.; aquas in caput, *make to flow back*, Ov.; undae recurvatae, *winding*, of the Maeander, Ov.

rĕcurvus -a -um, *bent* or *curved backwards*: cornu, Verg.; tectum, *labyrinth*, Ov.; aera, *hooks*, Ov.; nexus hederae, *winding*, Ov.

rĕcūsātio -ōnis, f. (recuso), *a refusal*: adimere alicui omnem recusationem, *possibility of refusing*, Cic.; Caes. Esp. as legal t. t., *a protest* or *a counter-plea*: Cic.

rĕcūso -are (re/causa), *to object to, protest against, refuse*.
LIT., in gen., with acc.: laborem, Caes.; molestias, Cic.; Verg.; with double acc.: populum Romanum disceptatorem, Cic.; with de and abl.: Caes., Cic. With infin.: non recusare mori, Caes., Cic., Liv., etc.; with ne and subj.: sententiam ne diceret recusavit, Cic.; Caes., Liv.; when a negative precedes, with quin *or* quominus and the subj.: non possumus quin alii a nobis dissentiant recusare, Cic.; non recusabo quominus omnes mea legant, Cic. Absol.: non recuso, non abnuo, Cic. Esp. as legal t. t., *to take exception, plead in defence*: quoniam satis recusavi, Cic.
TRANSF., with no person as subject: genua cursum recusant, Verg.; vincla leones, Verg.; Ov.

rĕcŭtio -cŭtĕre -cussi -cussum (re/quatio), *to strike back, cause to rebound*: Verg.

rĕcŭtītus -a -um (re/cutis), *circumcised*: Iudaei, Mart.

rēda -ae, f.=raeda; q.v.

rĕdambŭlo -are, *to walk back*: Pl.

rĕdămo -are, *to love in return*: Cic.

rĕdargŭo -gŭĕre -gŭi, *to refute, disprove, contradict*: redargue me, si mentior, Cic.; redarguere mendacium alicuius, Cic.; impro-borum prosperitates redarguunt vim omnem deorum, Cic; Verg.

rĕdauspĭco -are, *to take auspices for a return*; in jest=*to return*: Pl.

reddo -dĕre -dĭdi -dĭtum.
(1) *to give back, restore* something previously given or taken. LIT., obsides, captivos, Caes.; equos, Cic.; alicui pecuniam, Cic.; reflex.: se reddere convivio, *to return to*, Liv.; se terris, Verg.; pass., reddi, as middle: reddar tenebris, *I shall return to*, Verg. With abstr. obj.: alicui patriam, Liv.; ereptum honorem, Verg. TRANSF., **a**, in words, *to repeat, recite*: verba bene (of a parrot), Ov.; Cic., Hor., etc.: **b**, *to reproduce by imitation, to represent, reflect*: qui te nomine reddet Silvius Aeneas, Verg.; hominum facies, Lucr.
(2) *to give back* something *in return* for a thing previously given. In gen.: oscula, Ov.; beneficium, Cic.; pro vita hominis hominis vitam, Caes.; *to answer*: veras audire et reddere voces, Verg. Esp.: **a**, *to give back in another language*=*to translate, render, interpret*: cum ea quae legeram Graece, Latine redderem, Cic.; verbo verbum, Hor.: **b**, *to make, render, cause to be*, with double acc.: aliquem iratum, Cic.; itinera infesta, Caes.; aliquem avem, Ov.
(3) *to give* something *as due* or *expected*; *to pay up, deliver*: suum cuique, Cic. hono-rem, Cic.; caute vota, *to fulfil*, Verg.; responsa, Verg.; peccatis veniam, Hor.; rationem alicui, *to render an account*, Cic.; of the dying: eum spiritum, quem naturae debeo, patriae reddere, Cic.; vitam naturae, Cic.; of

sacrifice, *to offer*: liba deae, Ov.; of writing:
sed perge, Pomponi, de Caesare et redde
quae restant, Cic. As legal t. t., reddere
iudicium, *to grant a judicial inquiry*: in
aliquem, Caes.; reddere ius, *to administer
justice, pronounce sentence*: alicui petenti,
Caes.

rĕdemptĭo -ōnis, f. (redimo). (1) *a buying
up*: **a**, *bribing*: iudicii, *a corrupting by
bribery*, Cic.: **b**, *a farming of taxes*: Cic.
(2) *a ransoming, redemption*: captivorum,
Liv.

rĕdempto -are (freq. of redimo), *to ransom,
redeem*: captivos, Tac.

rĕdemptor -ōris, m. (redimo), *a buyer,
contractor, farmer* (of taxes): frumenti, Liv.;
caementa demittit redemptor, Hor.; Cic.

rĕdemptūra -ae, f. (redimo), *a contracting,
farming* (of taxes, etc.): redempturis auxisse
patrimonia, Liv.

rĕdĕo -ire -ii (-īvi) -ĭtum.
(1) *to go back, come back, return*. LIT., **a**,
of persons: e provincia, Cic.; a Caesare,
Cic.; Romam, Cic.; domum, Caes.; in
proelium, Liv.; ad suos, Caes.; victor ex
hac pugna redit, Liv.: **b**, of material things:
redeunt umerique manusque, Ov.; flumen
in eandem partem, ex qua venerat, redit,
Caes.; cum ad idem, unde profecta sunt,
astra redierint, Cic.; collis paulatim ad
planitiem redibat, *sloped down to*, Caes.;
redeunt iam gramina campis, Hor. TRANSF.,
in gen.: **a**, of persons: in pristinum statum,
Caes.; cum aliquo in gratiam, *to be reconciled
with*, Cic.; redire ad se, *to come to one's
senses*, Ter., Lucr., Liv.; redire ad se atque
ad mores suos, Cic.; ad sanitatem, Cic.: **b**, of
things: animus, Pl.; res in statum antiquum,
Liv.; forma prior rediit, Ov.; redit, *the
matter comes up again*, Cic. Esp., in speaking,
to return to a previous subject: sed de hoc
alias, nunc redeo ad augurem, Cic.; illuc
unde abii, Hor.; of the speech itself: Cic.
(2) of revenue, income, etc., *to come in*:
pecunia publica, quae ex metallis redibat,
Nep.; Mart.
(3) *to fall back upon, come to, be brought
to*: pilis omissis, ad gladios redierunt, Caes.;
Caesar ad duas legiones redierat, *was
reduced to*, Caes.; bona in tabulas publicas
redierunt, Cic.; summa imperii, summa
rerum redit ad aliquem, Caes.; mortuo
Tullo res (*government of the state*) ad patres
redierat, Liv.

rĕdhālo -are, *to breathe out again*: Lucr.

rĕdhĭbĕo -ēre -ŭi -ĭtum (re/habeo), *to take
back*, esp. of the buyer or seller of a damaged
article: mancipium, Cic., Pl.

rĕdĭgo -ĭgĕre -ēgi -actum (re/ago).
(1) *to drive back, bring back, lead back.*
LIT., in sua rura boves, Ov.; Lucr., Liv.
TRANSF., aliquem in concordiam, Pl.; rem
in pristinam belli rationem, Caes.; in
memoriam alicuius, *to a person's recollection*
(foll. by acc. and infin), Cic.
(2) of money, etc., *to draw in, call in,
collect*: quantam (pecuniam) ex bonis patriis
redegisset, Cic.; omnem pecuniam Idibus,
Hor.; magnam pecuniam in aerarium, Liv.;
in publicum redigere, *to confiscate*, Liv.
(3) *to bring* or *reduce to a specific state* or
condition. In gen.: Aeduos in servitutem,

Caes.; civitatem in dicionem potestatemque
populi Romani, Cic.; in ordinem, Liv.;
victoriam ad vanum et inritum, *to make
fruitless*, Liv.; aliquid ad certum, *to make
certain*, Liv.; eo ut, *to bring to such a point
that*, Liv.; with double acc.: quae facilia
ex difficillimis animi magnitudo redegerat,
had made difficulties easy*, Caes. Esp. *to
reduce in number, value*, etc.; *to lessen,
bring down*: ex hominum millibus LX vix
ad D, Caes.; nobilissima familia iam ad
paucos redacta, Cic.; vilem redigatur ad
assem, Hor.

rĕdĭmīcŭlum -i, n. (redimio), *a fillet, frontlet,
chaplet*: Cic., Verg., etc.; of *a fetter*: Pl.

rĕdĭmĭo -ire -ii -itum (imperf., redimibat:
Verg.), *to bind round, wreathe round, crown*:
sertis redimiri et rosā, Cic.; tempora vittā,
Verg.; silvis redimita loca, Cat.

rĕdĭmo -ĭmĕre -ēmi -emptum (re/emo).
(1) *to buy back, redeem*. LIT., domum, Cic.;
fundum, Cic.; captivos a servitute, Cic.;
aliquem pretio, Verg. TRANSF., *to ransom,
recover by payment*: se pecuniā a iudicibus,
Cic.; se a Gallis auro, Liv.
(2) *to buy up, contract for, farm, hire.*
LIT., vectigalia, Caes.; picarias, Cic.; opus,
Cic. TRANSF., *to buy*, i.e. *to procure, obtain
for a price*: pacem parte fructuum, Cic.;
pacem obsidibus, Caes.; omnium vitam
perditorum poenā, Cic.

rĕdintĕgro -are, *to restore, renew, repair*:
deminutas copias, Caes.; proelium, Caes.;
memoriam auditoris, Cic.; pacem, Liv.;
redintegravit luctum in castris consulum
adventus, Liv.

rĕdĭpiscor -i, dep. (re/apiscor), *to get back*:
Pl.

rĕdĭtĭo -ōnis, f. (redeo), *a going back, return*:
celeritas reditionis, Cic.; domum, Caes.

rĕdĭtus -ūs, m. (redeo).
(1) *a coming back, going back, return*. LIT.,
domum, Cic.; in urbem, Cic.; est hominibus
reditus in curiam, *they may return to*, Cic.;
intercludere alicuius reditum, Cic.; plur.:
sanguine quaerendi reditūs, Verg. TRANSF.,
ad rem, ad propositum, Cic.; in gratiam,
reconciliation, Cic.
(2) of money, etc., *returns, income, revenue*;
sing.: Nep.; plur.: reditūs metallorum, Liv.;
Ov.

rĕdĭvĭa=reduvia; q.v.

rĕdĭvīvus -a -um, *renewed, renovated*; applied
to old building materials used a second time:
lapis, Cic.; Cat.; n. as subst., sing. and pl.,
old building materials used again: Cic.

rĕdŏlĕo -ēre -ŭi, *to emit an odour, smell of
odour*. LIT., with abl.: redolere thymo,
smell of thyme, Verg.; Ov.; with acc.: vinum,
to smell of wine, Cic.; Ov. TRANSF., ita domus
ipsa fumabat, ut multa eius sermonis indicia
redolerent, Cic.; mihi quidem ex illius
orationibus redolere ipsae Athenae videntur,
Cic.; with acc.: doctrinam, Cic.; antiquitatem, Cic.

rĕdŏmĭtus -a -um, *tamed again, subdued
again*: Cic.

rĕdŏno -are. (1) *to give back*: te Quiritem
Hor. (2) *to give up*: graves iras et invisum
nepotem Marti redonabo, Hor.

rĕdūco -dūcĕre -duxi -ductum.

(1) *to draw backwards.* LIT., falces tormentis internis, Caes.; remos ad pectora, Ov.; auras naribus, *to draw in*, Lucr. TRANSF., socios a morte reduxi, *rescued*, Verg.; meque ipse reduco a contemplatu dimoveoque mali, *restrain*, Ov.

(2) *to bring back* (*home*), *to lead back*. LIT., aliquem domum, Cic.; aliquem de exsilio, Cic.; regem, Cic.; a pastu vitulos ad tecta, Verg.; poet.: solem, diem, noctem, Verg. Esp. of troops: legiones ex Britannia, Caes.; copias a munitionibus, Caes.; victorem exercitum Romam, Liv. TRANSF., aliquem in gratiam cum aliquo, Cic., Liv.; aliquem ad officium sanitatemque, Cic.; in memoriam, with indir. quest., Cic.; spem mentibus anxiis, Hor.; legem maiestatis, *to re-introduce*, Tac.

(3) *to bring to a certain state* or *condition*: (catulum) lambendo mater in artus fingit et in formam reducit (of the she-bear), Ov. ¶ Hence partic. **rĕductus** -a -um, *drawn back*; hence *withdrawn, retired*. LIT., of places, *remote, sequestered*: vallis, Verg. TRANSF., virtus est medium vitiorum et utrinque reductum, *distant from both extremes*, Hor.; applied to a painting, n. of compar.: reductiora, *the background*, Quint.; n. pl. reducta as subst. (sc. bona)=Stoic ἀποπροηγμένα: Cic.

rĕductĭo -ōnis, f. (reduco), *a bringing back*: regis Alexandrini, *restoration*, Cic. L.

rĕductor -ōris (reduco), *one who brings back*: plebis Romanae in urbem, Liv.

rĕduncus -a -um, *bent back, curved*: rostrum (aquilae), Ov.

rĕdundantĭa -ae, f. (redundo), *an overflowing*; of style, *redundancy*: Cic.

rĕdundo -are (re/unda), *to overflow, stream over.*
LIT., mare, lacus, Cic.; pituita, Cic.; perf. partic., redundatus, poet.=redundans, *overflowing*: aquae, Ov.
TRANSF., (1) *to overflow with*: Asia, quae eorum ipsorum sanguine redundat, Cic. (2) *to exist in abundance, be in excess*: multitudo, Cic., Tac.; ut neque in Antonio deesset hic ornatus orationis, neque in Crasso redundaret, Cic.; fig.: Asiatici oratores nimis redundantes, *copious, diffuse*, Cic. (3) with abl., *to abound in*: luctu victoria, Cic.; splendidissimorum hominum multitudine, Cic. (4) *to be left over, to overflow, to spread*: si quid redundabit de vestro frumentario quaestu, Cic.; nationes in provincias redundare poterant, Cic.; infamia ad amicos redundat, Cic.

rĕdŭvĭa (**rĕdĭvĭa**) -ae, f. *a hangnail, whitlow*; prov.: cum capiti mederi debeam, reduviam curo, *attend to a trifle*, Cic.

rĕdux -dŭcis (abl. rĕdŭcī or rĕdŭcĕ), adj. (reduco). (1) act., *bringing back, restoring*, epithet of Jupiter: Ov. (2) pass., *brought back, returned*: reduces socii, Verg.; me reducem esse voluistis, *brought me back from exile*, Cic.

rĕfectĭo -ōnis, f. (reficio), *a repairing, restoring*: Plin., Suet.

rĕfector -ōris, m. (reficio), *a repairer, restorer*: Suet.

rĕfello -fellĕre -felli (re/fallo), *to refute, disprove*: aliquem, Cic.; refellere et

redarguere mendacium alicuius, Cic.; dicta, Verg.; crimen ferro, Verg.

rĕfercĭo -fercire -fersi -fertum (re/farcio), *to stuff full, to cram.* LIT., cloacas corporibus civium, Cic.; Pl. TRANSF., complures aures istis sermonibus, Cic.; libros puerilibus fabulis Cic.; quae Crassus peranguste refersit in oratione sua, Cic.
¶ Hence partic. (with compar. and superl.) **rĕfertus** -a -um, *stuffed, crammed, filled*: aerarium refertius, Cic.; theatrum refertissimum, Cic.; with abl.: insula referta divitiis, Cic.; Caes., Liv.; with genit.: mare refertum praedonum, Cic.; with de: de nugis libri, Cic.

rĕfĕrĭo -ire, *to strike back, strike again.* LIT., Pl., Ter. TRANSF., *to reflect*: speculi referitur imagine Phoebus, Ov.

rĕfĕro rĕferre rettŭli rĕlatum (rēlatum, Lucr.).
(1) *to carry back, bring back.* LIT., candelabrum, Cic.; pecunias in templum, Caes.; aliquem in castra, Liv.; ad equestrem ordinem iudicia, Cic.; cum sanguine mixta vina, *to spit back*, Verg. Esp. referre pedem, or referre se, or pass., referri, as middle, *to return, to go back*: paulatim cedere ac pedem referre, Caes.; se iterum Romam, Cic.; classem relatam nuntio, Verg. TRANSF., of abstr. things: pro re certa falsam spem domum, Cic.; oculos animumque ad aliquem, Cic.; animum ad studia, Cic.; se ad philosophiam, Cic.; o mihi praeteritos referat si Iuppiter annos, Verg.; consilia in melius, *to restore*, Verg.
(2) *to bring again, restore, repeat*: caerimonias ex magno intervallo, Liv.; morem, Verg.; rem iudicatam, *to bring up again*, Cic. Esp. *to echo*: theatri natura ita resonans, ut usque Romam significationes vocesque referantur, Cic.; Hor., Ov. TRANSF., *to reproduce* by imitation, *to recall*: aliquem ore, Verg.; parentis speciem, Liv.
(3) *to say back, answer, return*: talia voce, Verg.; Cic.
(4) *to bring* something *as expected, to deliver.* LIT., of material objects: mercedem, Pl.; frumentum omne ad se referri iubet, Caes.; hanc ex faenore pecuniam populo, *deliver into the public treasury*, Cic.; octonis idibus aera, Hor.; *as a sacrifice*: sollemnia ludis, Verg. TRANSF., **a**, of abstr. things in gen.: salutem, Cic.; gratiam alicui, Pl., Cic.: **b**, *to bring back a message, report*, etc.: responsum, Cic.; rumores, Cic.; mandata, Caes.; with acc. and infin.: imminere Volscum bellum, Liv.; with indir. quest.: unde refert nobis victor quid possit oriri, Lucr.: **c**, *to bring* a matter *before an authority* (esp. by way of consultation), *to refer*: de signo Concordiae dedicando ad pontificum conlegium, Cic.; ad Apollinem, Cic.; esp., referre ad senatum, *to bring before the senate*; ad senatum de legibus abrogandis, Cic.; rem ad senatum, Liv.; with indir. quest.: Sall.: **d**, *to enter* in a record, etc., *register, put down*: iudicium in tabulas publicas, Cic.; aliquid in commentarium, in libellum, Cic.; aliquem in proscriptos, *in the list of proscribed*, Cic.; in numero deorum, Cic. Esp. of *accounts*: rationes, Cic.; pecuniam operi publico, *under the head of a public work*; aliquid in acceptum referre, or acceptum referre, *to*

enter as paid, Cic.: **e**, *to assign* to a cause: ad voluptatem omnia, Cic.; prospera ad fortunam, Tac.

rĕfert rēferre rētŭlit, impers. (res/fert), *it matters, it concerns, it makes a difference.* The *person* concerned is expressed by the abl. f. sing. of a possess. pron., such as meā, tuā, nostrā, vestrā; more rarely by ad: ad me, Pl.; or by genit.: faciendum aliquid, quod illorum magis quam suā retulisse videretur, Sall.; non ascripsi id quod tuā nihil referebat, Cic.; or by dat.: quid referat intra naturae fines viventi, iugera centum an mille aret? Hor. The *matter* of concern is seldom expressed by a nominative: studium atque voluptas, Lucr.; more often by an infin.: neque refert videre quid dicendum sit, Cic.; by an indir. quest. clause: quid refert, qua me ratione cogatis? Cic.; quid refert, utrum voluerim fieri, an gaudeam factum? Cic.; or by a conditional clause: Cic.; or by acc. and infin.: Cic. The *degree* of concern is expressed by an adv.: maxume, Pl.; or a n. acc.: quid refert? Cic.; nihil refert, Pl.; or by a genit. of value: permagni referre, Lucr.

rĕfertus -a -um, partic. from refercio; q.v.

rĕfervĕo -ēre, *to boil over*; fig.: refervens falsum crimen, Cic.

rĕfervesco -ĕre (referveo), *to boil up, bubble up*: sanguis refervescit, Cic.

rĕfĭcĭo -fĭcĕre -fēci -fectum (re/facio).

(1) *to make again, restore, repair.* LIT., of physical objects: pontem, naves, classem, Caes.; arma, Sall.; ea quae sunt omissa, Cic.; fana, aedes, Cic.; templa, Hor.; exercitum, *to make up* (in numbers), Liv. TRANSF., **a**, *to choose again*: tribunos, Cic.: **b**, *to re-establish, restore* a previous condition: salutem, Cic.; spem, Liv.: **c**, *to refresh, revive*: exercitum ex labore, Caes.; reficere se et curare, Cic.; fessum viā ac vigiliis militem, Liv.; me recreat et reficit Pompei consilium, *gives me strength*, Cic.

(2) *to get back again, receive, get*: plus mercedis ex fundo, Cic.; Liv.

rĕfīgo -fīgĕre -fixi -fixum, *to unfasten, demolish, remove.* LIT., tabulás, Cic.; signa templis, Hor. TRANSF., of laws, *to repeal, abrogate*: leges, Cic., Verg.

rĕfingo -ĕre, *to form anew*: cerea regna, Verg.

reflāgĭto -are, *to ask back, demand again*: Cat.

reflātū, abl. as from reflatus, m. (reflo), *by blowing against*: Plin. TRANSF., *by a contrary wind*: naves delatas Uticam reflatu hoc, Cic. L.

reflecto -flectĕre -flexi -flexum, *to turn back, bend back.*

(1) transit., LIT., cervicem, Ov.; oculos, Ov.; longos reflectitur ungues, *finds his nails bend into long talons*, Ov. TRANSF., *to turn back, divert*: animum, Cic.; mentes, Cic.; orsa in melius, Verg.

(2) intransit., *to yield, retreat*: morbi causa, Lucr.

reflo -are. (1) intransit., *to blow back, blow contrary*: etsi etesiae valde reflant, Cic. L. (2) transit., *to blow out, breathe out again*: Lucr.

reflŭo -flŭĕre -fluxi -fluxum. (1) *to flow back*: Ov. (2) *to overflow*: Nilus refluit campis, Verg.

reflŭus -a -um (refluo), *flowing back*: mare, Ov.

rĕfŏcillo -are, *to revive*: Plin. L.

rĕformātor -ōris, m. (reformo), *one who forms again, a reviver*: Plin. L.

rĕformīdātĭo -ōnis, f. (reformido), *excessive dread, fear, terror*: Cic.

rĕformīdo -are, *to dread, fear, be afraid of, shun, avoid.* LIT., of persons: aliquem, Cic.; bellum, Cic.; with infin.: refugit animus eaque dicere reformidat, Cic.; Liv.; with indir. quest.: nec, quid occurrat, reformidat, Cic.; absol.: vide, quam non reformidem, Cic. TRANSF., of things: ante (vites) reformidant ferrum, Verg.; lumina solem, Ov.

rĕformo -are, *to form again, mould anew*: Iolcus reformatus in annos primos, Ov.

rĕfŏvĕo -fŏvēre -fōvi -fōtum, *to warm again, cherish again, revive, restore, refresh.* LIT., corpus, Ov.; vires, Tac.; ignes tepidos, Ov. TRANSF., provincias internis certaminibus fessas, Tac.; Plin. L.

refractārĭŏlus -a -um (dim. of refractarius), *somewhat contentious, stubborn*: hoc iudiciale dicendi genus, Cic.

refractārĭus -a -um (refragor), *stubborn, contentious*: Sen.

refrāgor -ari, dep. (opp. to suffragor), *to oppose, withstand, thwart.* With dat.: petenti, Cic.; honori eius, Liv.; illa lex petitioni tuae refragrata est, *is opposed to*, Cic.

refrēno -are, *to rein back.* LIT., equos, Curt. TRANSF., *to hold back, restrain, curb*: fluvios, Lucr.; aquas, Ov.; fig.: animum, Cic.; iuventutem, Cic.; adulescentes a gloria, Cic.; Lucr., Hor.

refrīco -frĭcare -frĭcŭi -frĭcātum, *to rub again, scratch again.* LIT., vulnera, *to reopen*, Cic.; cicatricem, Cic. TRANSF., *to excite again, renew*: pulcherrimi facti memoriam, Cic.; tuis sceleribus reipublicae praeterita fata refricabis, Cic.; dolorem oratione, Cic.

refrīgĕrātĭo -ōnis, f. (refrigero), *a cooling, coolness*: me delectant et refrigeratio et vicissim aut sol aut ignis hibernus, Cic.

refrīgĕro -are, *to cool off.* LIT., ignem, Cic.; membra undā, Ov.; pass., refrigerari, as middle, *to cool oneself, grow cool*: umbris aquisve, Cic. TRANSF., *to cool, deprive of warmth*; hence, pass., *to grow cool* or *languid*: refrigerata accusatio, Cic.; sermone refrigerato, Cic.

refrīgesco -frīgescĕre -frixi, *to grow cold, cool down.* LIT., cor corpore cum toto refrixit, Ov.; Lucr. TRANSF., *to lose vigour; to flag, fail, grow stale*: illud crimen de nummis caluit re recenti, nunc in causa refrixit, Cic.; Romae a iudiciis forum, Cic.

refringo -fringĕre -frēgi -fractum (re/frango), *to break back, break up, break open.* LIT., claustra, Cic.; carcerem, Liv.; ramum, Verg. TRANSF., *to break, check*: vim fluminis, Caes.; vim fortunae, Liv.; Achivos, Hor.

rĕfŭgĭo -fŭgĕre -fūgi.

(1) intransit., *to flee back, run away, take to flight.* LIT., velocissime, Caes.; ad suos, Caes.; ex castris in montem, Caes.; Syracusas, Cic.; in silvam, Verg.; sol medio orbe, Verg.; vites a caulibus refugere

dicuntur, Cic. Transf., **a**, of places, *to recede from*: refugit ab litore templum, Verg.: **b**, *to shrink*: a consiliis fortibus, Cic.; Verg.: **c**, *to take refuge with, have recourse to*: ad legatos, Cic.

(2) transit., *to fly from, avoid, run away from.* Lit., impetum, Cic.; anguem, Verg. Transf., ministeria, Verg.; Hor., Ov.

rĕfŭgĭum -i, n. (refugio), *a place of refuge, a refuge*: silvae dedere refugium, Liv.; refugium populorum erat senatus, Cic.

rĕfŭgus -a -um (refugio), *fugitive, receding*: quidam in castra refugi, Tac.; m. pl. as subst.: refugi, *fugitives*, Tac. Transf., *receding, recoiling*: unda, Ov.

rĕfulgĕo -fulgēre -fulsi, *to gleam back, to shine brightly, to glitter.* Lit., arma refulgentia, Liv.; sol a liquidā aquā, Ov.; Verg. Transf., splendidaque a docto fama refulget avo, Prop.

rĕfundo -fundĕre -fūdi -fūsum, *to pour back, to make overflow.* Lit., vapores eādem, Cic.; aequor in aequor, Ov.; esp. in perf. partic.: refusus Oceanus, *ebbing and flowing*, Verg.; stagna refusa vadis, Verg. Transf., refunditur alga, Verg.

rĕfūtātĭo -ōnis, f. (refuto), *a refutation*: Cic., Quint.

rĕfūtātū, abl. as from refutatus, m. (refuto), *by refutation*: Lucr.

rĕfūto -are, *to drive back, press back.* Lit., nationes bello, Cic. Transf., *to check, repress*: clamorem, Cic.; cupiditatem, Cic.; virtutem aspernari ac refutare, Cic. Esp., *to refute, disprove*: sceleratorum periuria testimoniis, Cic.; fors dicta refutet! Verg.; tribunos oratione feroci, Liv.

rēgālĭŏlus -i, m. (dim. of regalis), *a small bird*, perhaps *the wren*: Suet.

rēgālis -e (rex), *of a king, royal, regal*: genus civitatis, *monarchical*, Cic.; nomen, Cic.; ornatus, Cic.; regalem animum in se esse, Liv.; carmen, *celebrating deeds of kings*, Ov.

¶ Adv. **rēgālĭtĕr**, *royally, regally*; in good sense: centum hostiis sacrificium regaliter Minervae conficere, Liv.; in bad sense, *despotically, tyrannically*: precibus minas regaliter addere, Ov.

rēgĕlo -are, *to thaw, warm*: Mart.

rēgĕro -gĕrĕre -gessi -gestum, *to carry back, bear back, throw back.* Lit., quo regesta e fossa terra foret, Liv.; tellurem, *to throw back again*, Ov. Transf., convicia, Hor.; culpam, Plin. L.; aliquid in commentarios, Quint.

rēgĭa, see regius.

rēgĭē, adv. from regius; q.v.

rēgĭfĭcus -a -um (rex/facio), *royal, princely, splendid*: luxus, Verg.

rēgigno -ĕre, *to bring forth again*: Lucr.

Rēgillus -i, m.

(1) *a town in the country of the Sabines, from which Appius Claudius came to Rome.*

¶ Hence adj. **Rēgillensis** -e and **Rēgillānus** -a -um, *belonging to Regillus.*

(2) *a lake in Latium, scene of a victory of the Romans over the Latins*, 496 B.C.

¶ Hence **Rēgillensis** -e, *surname of the Postumii, as the Roman commander was the dictator Postumius.*

(3) *a surname in the* gens Aemilia.

rĕgĭmen -ĭnis, n. (rego), *a directing, guiding, controlling.* Lit., equorum, Tac.; navis, Tac.; poet., *a rudder*: Ov. Transf., (1) *guidance, rule, government, direction*: totius magistratūs, Liv.; summae rei, Tac.; absol., *the government of a state*: Tac. (2) *a ruler, governor*: rerum, *of a state*, Liv.

rēgīna -ae, f. (rex), *a queen.* Lit., Pl.; of Cleopatra: Cic.; of Dido: Verg. Transf., (1) of goddesses: Pl., Cic., Verg. (2) *a king's daughter, a princess*; of Ariadne: Verg.; of Medea: Ov. (3) any *lady of rank*: Pl., Ter. (4) fig., *queen, mistress, sovereign*: haec una virtus (iustitia) omnium est domina et regina virtutum, Cic.; regina pecunia, Hor.

Rēgīnus, see Regium.

rēgĭo -ōnis, f. (rego).

(1) *a direction, line.* In gen.: nulla regione viarum, Lucr.; si qui tantulum de recta regione deflexerit, Cic.; haec eadem est nostra regio et via, Cic.; oppidi murus rectā regione, si nullus anfractus intercederet, MCC passus aberat, Caes.; rectā regione, *in a straight line*, Liv. Esp., *a boundary line, boundary*; usually plur.: res ea orbis terrae regionibus definiuntur, Cic.; fig.: esse regionibus officii continet, Cic.; in augurs' language, *the line of sight*: per lituum regionum facta descriptio, Cic. Phrase e regione, used as adv.: **a**, *in a straight line*: alterum e regione movetur, alterum declinat, Cic.; Lucr.: **b**, *opposite, over against*; with genit.: e regione solis, Cic.; with dat.: esse e regione nobis et contraria parte terrae, Cic.; Caes.

(2) *a space enclosed by lines*; hence *a region, country, territory, district.* Lit., regio aquilonia, australis, Cic.; locus in regione pestilenti saluber, Cic.; Caes., Verg., Liv. Esp.: **a**, *an administrative division, province, district*: principes regionum atque pagorum inter suos ius dicunt, Caes.; Cic., etc.: **b**, *a quarter, ward, in Rome*: Tac. Transf., *sphere, province, department*: bene dicere non habet definitam aliquam regionem, Cic.

rēgĭōnātim, adv. (regio), *according to districts*: tribūs describere, Liv.

Rēgĭum (Rhēgĭum) -i, n.

(1) *a town in Gallia Cispadana (now Reggio nell' Emilia).*

¶ Hence **Rēgĭenses** -ium, m. pl. *its inhabitants.*

(2) *a town in Calabria, opposite Messina in Sicily (now Reggio di Calabria).*

¶ Hence adj. **Rēgīnus** -a -um, *of Regium*; m. pl. as subst., *its inhabitants.*

rēgĭus -a -um (rex), *of a king, royal, regal.* Lit., anni, *the period of monarchy at Rome*, Cic.; ales, *the eagle*, Ov.; puer, Verg. Transf., *royal, splendid, magnificent*: moles, Hor.; Ov.

¶ F. as subst. **rēgĭa** -ae. (1) (sc. domus), *the royal dwelling, the palace.* In gen.: Cic., etc. Esp. a building in Rome on the Via Sacra, the palace of Numa, afterwards used by the Pontifex Maximus: Cic.; Ov. Transf., *the court, the royal family*: Liv.; Tac. (2) (=basilica), *a public hall*: Suet. (3) (sc. urbs), *a capital city*: Verg., Hor.

¶ Adv. **rēgĭē**, *royally*; in a good sense: Pl.; in a bad sense, *despotically, tyrannically*: crudeliter et regie fieri, Cic.; ea quae regie seu potius tyrannice statuit in aratores, Cic.

reglūtĭno -are, *to unglue, separate*: Cat.
regnātor -ōris, m. (regno), *a ruler, king*:
Olympi, *Jupiter*, Verg.; Asiae, Verg.; Tac.
regnātrix -trīcis, f. adj. (regno), *ruling*: domus,
Tac.
regno -are (regnum).
(1) intransit., *to exercise royal authority,
be a king, reign*. Lit., septem et triginta
regnavisse annos, Cic.; Verg.; impers. pass.:
post Tatii mortem ab sua parte non erat
regnatum, Liv. Transf., *to rule like a king*:
a, of gods and men, *to be master, have
absolute sway*; in a bad sense, *to be a tyrant*:
regnavit is quidem (Gracchus) paucos
menses, Cic.; Hor., Liv.: **b**, of things, *to
prevail, have the mastery*: ignis per alta
cacumina, Verg.; ardor edendi per viscera,
Ov.; ebrietas, Ov.
(2) transit., only in pass.: regnari, *to be
ruled by a king*: regnandam accipere Albam,
Verg.; terra regnata Lycurgo, Verg.; gentes
quae regnantur, Tac.
regnum -i, n. (rex).
(1) *royal power* or *authority, monarchy*.
Lit., superbi regni initium, Cic.; regnum
affectare, Liv. Transf., *supremacy, rule,
unrestrained power*: alicui regnum deferre,
Caes.; abuti ad omnia atomorum regno et
licentiā, Cic.; in a bad sense, in republican
times at Rome, *tyranny, despotism*: regnum
adpetere, Cic.; crimen regni, Ov.; regnum
iudiciorum, regnum forense, Cic.
(2) *a realm ruled by a king, a kingdom*.
Lit., fines regni, Caes.; Cic., etc. Transf.,
any possession, estate: in tuo regno, Cic.;
mea regna, Verg.
rĕgo rĕgĕre rexi rectum, *to guide, direct*.
Lit., equum, Liv.; regit beluam quocumque vult, Cic.; tela, Verg. Legal t. t.:
regere fines, *to mark out boundaries*, Cic.;
Tib.
Transf., (1) *to guide, direct*: errantem,
Caes.; motum mundi, Cic.; iuvenem, Cic.
L.; mores, Cic.; animum, Pl., Hor., Verg.
(2) as a ruler, *to direct, rule, govern, administer*:
rempublicam, Cic.; Massilienses summā
iustitiā, Cic.; imperio populos, Verg.;
Antium, Hor.
¶ Hence partic. **rectus** -a -um, *ruled*;
hence, as adj. (with compar. and superl.),
straight.
Lit., *in a straight line*. In gen., in any
direction, *straight*: rectis lineis, Cic.; recto
itinere ad Iberum contendere, Caes.; rectus
cursus hinc ad Africam, Liv.; recti oculi,
a straight, steadfast look, Cic.; abl. f. as adv.
rectā (sc. viā), *straight*: Pl., Caes., Hor.
Esp. vertically straight, *upright*: ita iacēre
talum, ut rectus adsistat, Cic.; saxa, *steep*,
Liv.
Transf., (1) *right, correct, proper*. In gen.:
rectum et iustum proelium, Liv.; quae sint
in artibus ac rationibus recta ac prava, Cic.;
n. as subst.: rectum pravumque, Cic.
Esp.: **a**, morally, *straightforward, honest,
upright*: consilia, Liv.; conscientia, Cic.;
praetor populi Romani rectissimus, Cic.
N. as subst., *right, virtue*: neque quidquam
nisi honestum et rectum alter ab altero
postulabit, Cic.; rectum est, *it is right*, with
acc. and infin., Cic.: **b**, *simple, natural,
plain, straightforward*: commentarii Caesaris,

Cic.; sermo, Cic.; figura, Prop. (2) as
grammat. t. t., casus rectus, the nom. (opp.
casus obliquus): Quint.
¶ Adv. (with compar. and superl.) **rectē**,
in a straight line. Lit., ferri, Cic. Transf.,
rightly, properly, well. In gen., *of conduct,
behaviour, health*, etc.: recte atque ordine
facere, iudicare, Cic.; recte et vere respondere, Cic.; recte factum, Caes.; apud matrem
recte est, *all is well*, Cic.; se alicui recte
committere, Caes. Esp. colloq., like English
perfectly, very good, it's all right, etc.: Pl.,
Ter., Hor.
regrĕdĭor -grĕdi -gressus sum (re/gradior),
to step back, go back. Lit., ut regredi quam
progredi mallent, Cic.; as milit. t. t., *to
retire, retreat*: Caes., Sall. Transf., in illum
annum, Cic.; Sall.
regressus -ūs, m. (regredior), *a going back,
return*. Lit., dare alicui regressum, Ov.;
plur.: conservare progressūs et regressūs,
Cic.; as milit. t. t., *a retreat*: Liv., Tac.
Transf., (1) *a return*: ab ira, Liv.; Tac.
(2) *refuge, recourse*: ad principem, Tac.
rēgŭla -ae, f. (rego), *a straight length*. Lit.,
a ruler: Cic.; *a plank*: Caes. Transf., *a rule,
pattern, model*: iuris, Cic.; regula ad quam
omnia iudicia rerum dirigentur, Cic.; Hor.,
Quint.
¹**rēgŭlus** -i, m. (dim. of rex). (1) *a petty king,
prince*: Sall., Liv., Tac. (2) *a king's son,
prince*: Sall., Liv.
²**Rēgŭlus**, *surname in the* gens Atilia, *esp. of
the consul* M. Atilius Regulus, *famous for
his return to captivity in the first Punic war*.
rēgusto -are, *to taste again or repeatedly*. Lit.,
Sen., Pers. Transf., crebro litteras alicuius,
to take pleasure in reading again, Cic. L.
rĕĭcĭo -icĕre -iēci -iectum; imper., reice,
dissyll.: Verg. (re/iacio), *to throw back*.
Lit., (1) *to throw behind*: scutum, Cic.;
amictum ex umeris, Verg.; togam ab umero,
Liv.; paenulam, *to throw back on the shoulders*
(to leave the hands free), Cic. (2) *to throw
away*: pila, Caes. (3) *to throw back at
someone*: telum in hostem, Caes.; of an echo:
Lucr. (4) with reflex., *to cast oneself back, to
sink back*: se in alicuius gremium, Lucr.; Ter.
(5) *to drive off* living beings: capellas a
flumine, Verg.; esp. as milit. t. t.: equitatum, Caes.; hostem ab Antiochea, Cic. L.
(6) as naut. t. t., of a storm, *to drive back,
cast up*: naves tempestate reiectae, Caes.;
reici austro ad Leucopetram, Cic.; Liv.
Transf., (1) *to throw off, fling aside*:
alicuius ferrum et audaciam in foro, Cic. L.;
hanc proscriptionem hoc iudicio a se aspernari, Cic.; esp., *to reject with scorn, disdain,
spurn*: bona diligere et reicere contraria,
Cic.; omnem istam disputationem, Cic.;
praedam, Hor. (2) as legal t. t., *to challenge
the* iudices, or jury: iudices, Cic.; recuperatores, Cic. (3) with ad, *to refer to*: aliquem
ad ipsam epistulam, Cic. L.; rem ad senatum,
Liv.; Caes. (4) *to put off*: totam rem in
mensem Ianuarium, Cic.
rĕiectānĕus -a -um (reicio), *to be rejected*;
n. pl. as subst. **rĕiectānĕa** -ōrum = the
Stoic ἀποπροηγμένα: Cic.
rĕiectĭo -ōnis, f. (reicio), *a throwing back*.
Lit., sanguinis, *a spitting of blood*, Plin.
Transf., in gen., *a rejection*: huius civitatis,

Cic.; esp., legal t. t., *the challenging of a
iudex or juror*: iudicum, Cic.

rēiecto -are (freq. of reicio), *to cast back,
throw back*: Lucr.

rĕlābor -lābi -lapsus sum, dep. *to slide, glide,
flow, fall back*. LIT., prenso rudente relabi,
Ov.; rivi montibus, Hor. TRANSF., nunc in
Aristippi furtim praecepta relabor, *slip back*,
Hor.

rĕlanguesco -languescĕre -langui, *to become
faint, faint away*. LIT., Ov. TRANSF., *to
slacken*: iis rebus relanguescere animos,
Caes.; taedio impetus regis, Liv.; indignatio,
Tac.

rĕlātio -ōnis, f. (refero), *a carrying back,
bringing back*. LIT., Quint. TRANSF., (1) as
legal t. t.: criminis, *a retorting of the accusation upon the accuser*, Cic. (2) as polit. t. t.,
a report, esp. one made by a magistrate to
the senate, etc.: Cic., Liv., Tac. (3) as
grammat. t. t., *a repetition*: Cic.

rĕlātor -ōris, m. (refero), *one who makes a
report*: ap. Cic. L.

rĕlātus -ūs, m. (refero), *a bringing before*.
(1) *a narrative, recital*: Tac. (2) *a report*:
Tac.

rĕlaxātio -ōnis, f. (relaxo), *a relaxation,
easing*: animi, Cic.; doloris, Cic.

rĕlaxo -are, *to loosen, widen, enlarge, relax*.
LIT., alvus tum astringitur, tum relaxatur,
Cic.; ora fontibus, Ov.; claustra, Ov.; vias
et caeca spiramenta, Verg.
TRANSF., *to ease, lighten, relax*: continua-
tionem verborum modo relaxet, Cic.; pater
nimis indulgens quidquid astrinxi relaxat,
loosens the reins which I drew tight, Cic.;
(risus) tristitiam ac severitatem mitigat et
relaxat, Cic.; animi cum se plane corporis
vinculis relaxaverint, *shall have freed themselves*, Cic. =*to slacken*: (dolor) levis dat
intervalla et relaxat, Cic. Pass. as middle:
insani cum relaxentur, *when they have a lucid
interval*, Cic.; act. intransit.: dolor relaxat,
eases, Cic.

rĕlēgātio -ōnis, f. (¹relego), *banishment; the
mildest form of exile from Rome, by which the
exile preserved his civil rights*: Cic., Liv.

¹rĕlēgo -are, *to send away*.
LIT., tauros procul atque in sola pascua,
Verg.; esp. as a punishment, *to remove*:
filium ab hominibus, Cic.; as legal t. t., *to
banish* (relegatio being the mildest form of
banishment): aliquem in exsilium, Liv.;
relegatus, non exsul dicor, Ov.; in insulam,
Tac.; in decem annos, Tac.
TRANSF., (1) *to put aside, reject*: Samnitium
dona, Cic.; Hor., Ov. (2) *to impute*: culpam,
Quint.

²rĕlĕgo -lĕgĕre -lēgi -lectum, *to gather up
again, to collect again*. LIT., filo relecto, Ov.
TRANSF., *to travel through again, sail along
again*: litora, Verg.; Hellespontiacas aquas,
Ov. (2) *to go over again*, in thought, speech,
etc.: scriptorem, Cic.; scripta, Ov.; suos
sermone labores, Hor.

rĕlentesco -ĕre, *to become languid, feeble
again*: amor, Ov.

rĕlĕvo -are.
(1) *to lift, raise up again*: e terra corpus,
Ov.
(2) *to make light again, to lighten*. LIT.,
epistulam graviorem perlectione, Cic. L.;

vimina favi, Ov.; relevari longā catenā, *to be
freed from*, Ov.
TRANSF., *to relieve, lighten, alleviate*:
communem casum misericordiā hominum,
Cic.; animum molestiis, Cic.; potius relevare
quam castigare, Cic.; relevari, *to be relieved*,
Cic., Ov.

rĕlictio -ōnis, f. (relinquo), *a leaving, deserting*:
reipublicae, Cic.

rĕlĭcŭos and **rĕlīcus**=reliquus; q.v.

rĕlĭgātio -ōnis, f. (religo), *a tying up*: vitium,
Cic.

rĕlĭgĭo (also in poets **rēlĭgĭo** or **rellĭgĭo**)
-ōnis, f. (relĕgo).
(1) as a quality of persons, *scrupulousness,
conscientious exactness*: **a**, primarily, *respect
for what is sacred, religious scruple, awe*:
tantā religione obstricta tota provincia est,
Cic.; perturbari religione et metu, Cic.; res
in religionem alicui venit, *is a matter of
conscience to*, Cic.; inclita iustitia religioque
Numae Pompilii, Liv.; ut velut numine
aliquo defensa castra oppugnare religio
fuerit, *scruples were felt about*, Liv. In a bad
sense, *superstition*: animos multiplex religio
et pleraque externa incessit, Liv.; tantum
religio potuit suadere malorum, Lucr.:
b, *strict observance of religious ceremonial*:
religio, id est cultus deorum, Cic.; religio
Cereris, *worship of Ceres*, Cic.; plur., religiones, *observances*: diligentissimus religionum
cultor, Liv.: **c**, in gen., *moral scruples, conscientiousness*: hac ego religione non sum ab
hoc conatu repulsus, Cic.; nulla in iudiciis
severitas, nulla religio, Cic.; in consilio
dando, Cic. L.; iurisiurandi, Caes., Cic.
(2) as a quality of gods and religious objects,
sanctity: deorum, Cic.; fani, sacrarii, Cic.;
loci, Verg. TRANSF., *an object of worship,
holy thing or place*: religio domestica (of a
statue), Cic.; a deorum religionibus demigrare, Cic.; quae religio aut quae machina
belli, Verg.

rĕlĭgĭōsus (poet. also **rēlĭgĭōsus** or **rellĭgĭōsus**) -a -um, adj. (with superl.) (religio).
(1) of persons, *scrupulous*: **a**, primarily, in
regard to religion: civitas, Liv.; in a bad
sense, *superstitious*: Ter.: **b**, *strict in religious
observance*: qui omnia, quae ad cultum deo-
rum pertinerent, diligenter retractarent sunt
dicti religiosi, Cic.: **c**, in gen., *conscientious*:
testis, Cic.; *holy, sacred*: templum sanctum
et religiosum, Cic.
(2) of actions, etc.: **a**, *required by religion*:
iura, Cic.: **b**, *involving religious difficulty*:
fructum religiosum erat consumere, Liv.
(3) of gods and religious objects, *holy,
sacred*: templum, Cic.; deorum limina, Verg.
¶ Adv. (with compar. and superl.)
rĕlĭgĭōsē. (1) *conscientiously, scrupulously*:
testimonium dicere, Cic. (2) *piously,
religiously*: deos colere, Liv.; religiosissime
templum colere, Cic.

rĕlĭgo -are, *to tie, fasten behind*. LIT., trabes
axibus, Caes.; aliquem ad currum, Cic.; cui
flavam religas comam? Hor. Esp. of mooring
ships: funiculum a puppi, Cic.; naves ad
terram, Caes.; religata in litore pinus, Ov.
TRANSF., quae (prudentia) si extrinsecus
religata pendeat, *connected with*, Cic.

rĕlīno -linĕre -lēvi -litum, *to unseal, open anything fastened by pitch*, etc.: Ter., Verg.

rĕlinquo -linquĕre -līqui -lictum, *to leave.*
(1) *to leave behind.* In gen.: aliquem in Gallia, Caes.; legatum castris praesidio, Caes.; fig.: aculeos in animo alicuius, Cic. Esp., at death, *to leave, bequeath*: alicui agrum, Pl.; heredem testamento reliquit hunc, Cic.; fig.: memoriam, Cic.; nomen, Hor.
(2) *to leave unchanged, allow to remain.* LIT., alicui ne paleas quidem ex omni fructu, Cic.; equitatus partem alicui, Caes.; relinquebatur una per Sequanos via, *there remained,* Caes. TRANSF., munitioni castrorum tempus relinqui volebat, Caes.; reipublicae laudem, Cic., Caes.; spes relinquitur, *remains,* Cic., Caes.; relinquitur with ut and the subj.: Cic., Caes. Also *to omit, leave out, pass over*: caedes relinquo, libidines praetereo, Cic. Esp. *to leave behind in a certain state*: aliquem insepultum, Cic.; rem integram, Cic.; sine imperio tantas copias, Caes.
(3) *to desert, abandon, forsake.* LIT., domum propinquosque, Caes.; equos, Caes.; signa, Liv.; urbem direptioni et incendiis, Cic.; relicta non bene parmula, Hor. TRANSF., relinquit aliquem animus, Caes.; ab omni honestate relictus, Cic.; rem et causam et utilitatem communem, Cic.; agrorum et armorum cultum, Cic.

rĕlĭquĭae (poet also **rēlĭquĭae** or **rellĭquĭae**) -ārum, f. pl. (relinquo), *remains, relics, remainder, remnant.*
LIT., coniurationis, Cic.; also with genit. of that which has spared or left: Danaum reliquias, *remnant left by the Greeks,* Verg.; Tac. Esp. (1) *fragments of food, remnants of a feast*: Pl.; fig.: vellem me ad cenam (*the murder of Caesar*) invitasses, reliquiarum nihil haberes (*not even Antony*), Cic. L. (2) *the remains of the dead*: humanorum corporum, Tac.; Marii, Cic.
TRANSF., vitae, Lucr.; pristinae fortunae reliquiae miserae, Cic.

rĕlĭquus (rĕlĭcus) -a -um (relinquo), *left behind, remaining, left.*
LIT., in gen.: spes, Cic.; reliquum facere, *to leave behind* a person or thing, Cic., Liv. Esp. (1) t. t. of business language, of a debt, *outstanding, remaining*: pecuniam reliquam ad diem solvere, Cic. (2) of time, *remaining, future*: gloria, Cic.; in reliquum tempus, Cic.
TRANSF., *the other, other than the part already specified*: reliqua pars exercitus, Caes.; reliqui omnes, *all the rest,* Cic.
¶ N. as subst. **rĕlĭquum** -i (and sometimes plur. **rĕlĭqua** -ōrum) *the rest, the remainder*: reliqua belli perficere, Liv.; reliquum est ut, foll. by subj., *it remains that,* Cic.; reliquum est, with infin., Sall.; in reliquum, *for the future,* Cic., Sall., Liv. Often in partitive genit.: nihil est reliqui, *nothing remains,* Cic.; nihil reliqui facere, *to leave nothing remaining,* Cic.

rellĭgĭo, rellĭgĭōsus, etc.=religio, etc.; q.v.
rellĭquĭae=reliquiae; q.v.
rĕlūcĕo -lūcēre -luxi, *to reflect a gleam, to glitter*: flamma, Verg., Liv.
rĕlūcesco -lūcescĕre -luxi (reluceo), *to become bright again, begin to shine again*: imago solis reluxit, Ov.; Tac.

rĕluctor -ari, dep. *to struggle against, resist*: vitulus, Verg.; dracones, Hor.
rĕmacresco -macrescĕre -macrui, *to grow thin*: Suet.
rĕmălĕdīco -ĕre, *to revile back*: Suet.
rĕmando -ĕre, *to chew again*: Plin.
rĕmănĕo -mănēre -mansi -mansum, *to remain behind, stay.* In gen.: Romae, Cic.; in exercitu, Cic.; ad urbem, Caes.; domi, Cic.; apud aliquem, Caes. Esp., *to remain, abide, continue*: animi remanent post mortem, Cic.; vestigia antiqui officii, Cic.; with predicative adj., *to remain in a certain condition*: pars integra remanebat, Cic.
rĕmāno -are, *to flow back*: Lucr.
rĕmansĭo -ōnis, f. (remaneo), *a remaining, continuing in one place*: Cic.
rĕmĕdĭum -i, n. (re/medeor), *a means of healing, a cure, remedy, medicine.* LIT., remedium quoddam habere, Cic.; remedio quodam uti, Cic.; remedio esse, Cic. TRANSF., incommodorum, Cic.; ad magnitudinem frigorum hoc sibi remedium comparare, Cic.; id remedium timori fuit, Liv.
rĕmĕo -are, *to go back, come back, return*: aër, Cic.; remeat victor, Verg.; with acc.: urbes, Verg.; aevum remeare peractum, *to live over again,* Hor.
rĕmētĭor -mētīri -mensus sum, dep. *to measure again, measure back* either physically or mentally: astra rite, Verg.; perf. partic. in pass. meaning: iter retro pari ratione remensum est, *has been traversed,* Lucr.; pelago remenso, Verg.
rēmex -mĭgis, m. (remus/ago), *a rower*: Pl., Cic., Hor.; sing. coll.=remiges, *crew*: Verg., Ov., Liv., Tac.
Rēmi (Rhēmi) -ōrum, m. *a people of N. Gaul,* near the modern *Rheims*: Caes., Luc., Tac.
rēmĭgātĭo -ōnis, f. (remigo), *a rowing*: Cic. L.
rēmĭgĭum -i, n. (remex), *rowing.* LIT., Pl., Verg. TRANSF., (1) *the oars*: Verg., etc.; also of the oar-like motion of wings: remigio alarum, Verg. (2) *the crew of rowers, oarsmen*: Liv.
rēmĭgo -are (remex), *to row*: Caes., Cic., Tac.
rēmĭgro -are, *to wander back, come back, return.* LIT., in domum suam, Cic.; Romam, Cic.; Caes., Lucr. TRANSF., ei ne integrum quidem erat, ut ad iustitiam remigraret, Cic.
rĕmĭniscor -i, dep. *to call to mind, recollect, remember*; absol.: de quaestoribus reminiscentem recordari, Cic.; with genit.: veteris incommodi populi Romani, Caes.; Ov.; with acc.: dulces Argos, Verg.; Ov.; with acc. and infin.: Lucr., Ov.; with indir. quest.: Liv.
rĕmiscĕo -miscēre -mixtum, *to mix up, mingle*: Lydis remixtum carmen tibiis, Hor.; Sen.
rĕmissē, adv. from remitto; q.v.
rĕmissĭo -ōnis, f. (remitto), *a returning, letting go back.*
LIT., obsidum captivorumque, Liv. Also, *a letting fall, lowering*: superciliorum, Cic.; vocis contentiones et remissiones, Cic.
TRANSF., (1) *breaking off, interrupting, ceasing*: morbi, Cic.; usūs, Cic. (2) *a remitting*: poenae, Cic.; tributi in triennium, Tac. (3) remissio animi: a, *relaxation, recreation*: Cic.: b, *quiet, inaction*: in acerbissima iniuria remissio animi ac dissolutio, Cic.

rĕmissus -a -um, partic. from remitto; q.v.

rĕmitto -mittĕre -mīsi -missum.

(1) *to send back* or *send again*: mulieres Romam, Cic. L.; obsides alicui, Caes.; litteras Caesari, Caes.; pila, intercepta, *to throw back*, Caes.; vocem nemora alta remittunt, *echo*, Verg.; chorda sonum, Hor. (2) *to let go back, relax.* LIT., habenas, Cic.; frena equo, Ov.; bracchia, Verg.; tunica remissa, Ov.; vincula, Ov.; calor mella liquefacta remittit, *loosens*, Verg.; vere remissus ager, *freed from ice and snow*, Ov. TRANSF., **a**, transit., *to cause to relax, to relieve, abate*: spes animos a certamine remisit, Liv.; cantus remittunt animum, Cic.; aliquid iracundiae, Cic.; aliquid laboris, Liv.; with infin., *to give up doing*: Ter., Sall., Hor.: **b**, intransit., *to ease off, abate*: cum remiserant dolores, Cic.; ventus remisit, Caes.; imbres, pestilentia, Liv. (3) *to give up, to yield.* LIT., umorem ex se, Verg. TRANSF., **a**, *to abandon* a feeling or idea: Lucr., Cic.: **b**, *to sacrifice, concede*, esp. when requested: provinciam remitto, exercitum depono, Cic.; with dat.: Gallis imperium, Caes.; inimicitias suas reipublicae, Liv.: **c**, *to forgive* an offence, or *remit* its punishment: alicui noxiam, Pl.; poenam, Liv.

¶ Hence partic. (with compar.) **rĕmissus** -a -um, *relaxed.* LIT., corporibus remissis, Cic.; arcus, Hor. TRANSF., (1) of weather, *mild*: ventus remissior, Caes.; frigora remissiora, Caes. (2) of character, style, etc.; in good sense, *mild, gentle*: Cic.; in bad sense, *negligent, remiss, inactive*: remissior in petendo, Cic.; Caes.

¶ Adv. (with compar.) **rĕmissē**, *gently, mildly*: remissius disputare, Cic.; Quint.

rĕmōlĭor -iri, dep. *to push back*: pondera terrae, Ov.; Sen.

rĕmollesco -ĕre, *to become soft again.* LIT., cera remollescit sole, Ov. TRANSF., (1) *to be moved by*: precibus, Ov. (2) *to become effeminate*: eā re ad laborem ferendum remollescere homines, Caes.

rĕmollĭo -ire, *to make soft again.* TRANSF., *to make effeminate, to weaken*: artus, Ov.

rĕmōra -ae, f. *a delay, hindrance*: Pl.

rĕmōrāmen -ĭnis, n. (remoror), *a delay*: Ov.

rĕmordĕo -mordĕre -morsum, *to bite again*; hence *to worry, disquiet, harass*: te cura remordet, Verg.; Lucr., Liv.

rĕmŏror -ari, dep. (1) intransit., *to remain behind, linger, loiter*: in Italia, Liv.; Lucr. (2) transit., *to delay, obstruct, hinder*: aliquem, Pl., Ov.; iter alicuius, Sall.; Ov., Cic. Perf. partic. in pass. sense: Pl., Ov.

rĕmōtē, adv. from removeo; q.v.

rĕmōtĭo -ōnis, f. (removeo), *a putting away, removing*: criminis, *repelling*, Cic.

rĕmōtus -a -um, partic. from removeo; q.v.

rĕmŏvĕo -mŏvēre -mōvi -mōtum, *to move back, withdraw, put away.*

LIT., pecora, Caes.; arbitros, Cic.; aliquid de medio, Cic.; aliquid ab oculis, Cic.; equos ex conspectu, Caes.

TRANSF., moram, Pl.; aliquem a republica, Caes., Liv.; aliquem senatu, Liv.; a negotiis publicis, Cic.

¶ Hence partic. (with compar. and superl.) **rĕmōtus** -a -um, *removed, withdrawn.*

LIT., *distant, far off, remote*: locus ab arbitris remotus, Cic.; loci remoti a mari, Cic.; Gades, Hor. TRANSF., *removed from, free from*: ab suspicione remotissimus, Cic.; a vulgari scientia remotiora, Cic.; ab inani laude remotus, Cic.; a vulgo, Hor. N. pl. as subst. **rĕmōta** -ōrum = the Stoic ἀποπροηγμένα, *things to be rejected*: Cic.

¶ Adv. (with compar.) **rĕmōtē**, *far off, at a distance*: aliae (stellae) propius a terris, aliae remotius eadem spatia conficiunt, Cic.

rĕmūgĭo -ire, *to bellow again, bellow back*: ad verba alicuius, Ov.; vox adsensu nemorum ingeminata remugit, Verg.; Hor.

rĕmulcĕo -mulcēre -mulsi, *to stroke back*: caudam, Verg.

rĕmulcum -i, n. (ῥυμουλκέω, for ῥυμὸν ἕλκω), *a tow-rope, towing cable*: navem remulco adducere, Caes.; Liv.

Rĕmŭlus -i, m. *a king in Alba*: Ov.

rĕmūnĕrātĭo -ōnis, f. (remuneror), *a recompense, repaying, return*: benevolentiae, Cic.

rĕmūnĕror -ari, dep. *to recompense, repay, reward*; with acc. of pers.: aliquem simillimo munere, Cic.; aliquem magno praemio, Caes.; Cat.; with acc. of thing: beneficia alicuius officiis, Cic.; absol.: in accipiendo remunerandoque, Cic.

rĕmurmŭro -are, *to murmur back*: nec fracta remurmurat unda, Verg.

¹**rēmus** -i, m. (cf. ἐρετμός), *an oar.*

LIT., navigium remis incitare, Caes.; Cic., Verg., etc. Prov., remis ventisque, *or* ventis remis, *by oars and sails, with all one's might*: res velis, ut aiunt, remisque fugienda, Cic.

TRANSF., (1) orationem dialecticorum remis propellere, Cic. (2) plur.: remi, *the hands and feet of a person swimming*, Ov. (3) plur., *the wings of a bird*: alarum remis, Ov.

²**Rēmus** -i, m. *the twin brother of Romulus, first king of Rome, killed by him in a quarrel at the foundation of the city.*

rĕnarro -are, *to relate again*: fata divum, Verg.; Ov.

rĕnascor -nasci -nātus sum, dep. *to be born again, arise, grow again.* LIT., de nilo, Lucr.; phoenix, Ov.; pinnae renascuntur, Cic. L. TRANSF., ab secunda origine velut ab stirpibus laetius feraciusque renata urbs, Liv.; bellum istuc renatum, Cic. L.; Hor.

rĕnāvĭgo -are, *to sail back*: Cic. L.

rĕnĕo -nēre, *to unspin, unravel*: dolent fila reneri, *that the destiny is reversed*, Ov.

rēnes -um, m. pl *the kidneys*: Pl., Cic., Hor.

rĕnĭdĕo -ēre, *to shine back, to glitter, be bright.*

LIT., pura nocturno renidet luna mari, Hor.; non ebur neque aureum mea renidet in domo lacunar, Hor.

TRANSF., *to beam with joy, to laugh, to smile*: homo renidens, Liv.; Ov., Tac.; with infin.: adiecisse praedam torquibus exiguis renidet, Hor.

rĕnĭdesco -ĕre (renideo), *to glitter*: Lucr.

rĕnītor -i, dep. *to oppose, withstand, resist*: Liv.

¹**rēno** -nare, *to swim back*: Hor.

²**rēno (rhēno)** -ōnis, m. *a garment made of fur*: Caes., Sall.

rĕnōdo -are. (1) *to tie back*: comam, Hor. (2) *to untie*: Val. Fl.

rĕnŏvāmen -ĭnis, n. (renovo), *a renewal, new condition*: Ov.

rĕnŏvātĭo -ōnis, f. (renovo), *a renewing, renewal, renovation.* LIT., mundi, Cic.; esp.: renovatio singulorum annorum, *compound interest*, Cic. TRANSF., renovatio timoris, Cic.; Liv.

rĕnŏvo -are, *to renew, renovate, restore, repair.* LIT., templum, Cic.; of land: agrum, arvum, either by ploughing or by leaving fallow, Ov.; of money: faenus in singulos annos, *to reckon compound interest*, Cic.; centesimae quotannis renovatae, Cic. TRANSF., (1) *to renew*: scelus suum illud pristinum, Cic.; bellum, Caes., Cic., Liv.; foedus, Liv.; ex morbo velut renovatus flos iuventae, Liv.; animos ad odium renovare, Cic. (2) *to repeat*: renovabo illud quod initio dixi, Cic. (3) *to refresh*: reficere et renovare rempublicam, Cic.; Liv.

rĕnŭmĕro -are, *to count over again*; hence *to pay back*: Pl., Ter.

rĕnuntĭātĭo -ōnis, f. (renuntio), *a formal report, public announcement*; with subjective genit.: eius, Cic.; with objective genit.: suffragiorum, Cic.

rĕnuntĭo -are.

(1) *to bring back word, report, announce.* In gen.: hoc mihi, Pl.; with acc. and infin.: Pl., Cic. L.; impers. pass.: renuntiatum est de obitu Tulliae filiae tuae, *I was informed*, Sulpicius ap. Cic. L. Esp. *to make an official announcement* or *declaration, to report*: aliquid ad senatum, Cic.; Caes., Liv.; of election results, *to declare* a candidate *elected*: L. Murenam consulem, Cic.; sacerdos Climachias renuntiatus est, Cic.

(2) *to disclaim, refuse, renounce*: amicitiam alicui, Liv.; hospitium alicui, Cic.; ne Stoicis renuntiaretur, Cic.

rĕnuntĭus -i, m. *one who brings back news*: Pl.

rĕnŭo -nŭĕre -nŭi, *to deny by a motion of the head, to refuse, deny, reject*: renuit negitatque Sabellus, Hor.; with dat.: huic decem millium crimini, *to deny*, Cic.; with acc.: nullum convivium, *to decline*, Cic.; Hor.

rĕnūto -are (freq. of renuo), *to refuse, decline*: Lucr.

rĕor rēri rătus sum, dep. *to reckon, think, be of opinion, suppose, judge*; with acc. and infin.: rentur eos esse, quales se ipsi velint, Cic.; rebantur enim fore ut, Cic.; Verg., etc.; with double acc.: alii rem incredibilem rati, Sall.; Verg.; absol., esp. in parenthesis: nam, reor, nullus posset esse iucundior, Cic.; ut reor, Cic.

¶ Hence partic., in pass. sense, **rătus** -a -um, *reckoned*; hence, *determined, fixed, settled*: rati astrorum ordines, Cic.; vita, Verg.; dicta, Ov.; ratum facere, *to ratify, confirm, make valid*, Cic.; ratum habere, ducere, *to consider valid*, Cic.; aliquid mihi ratum est, *I approve*, Cic.; pro rata parte, *or* simply pro rata, *according to a fixed proportion, in proportion*, Cic., Liv.

rĕpāgŭla -ōrum, n. pl. (re/pango), *the bars* or *bolts fastening a door.* LIT., convulsis repagulis, Cic.; Ov. TRANSF., omnia repagula pudoris officiique perfringere, *restraints, limits*, Cic.

rĕpandus -a -um, *bent backwards, turned up*: calceoli, Cic.

rĕpărābĭlis -e (reparo), *that can be repaired* or *restored*: damnum, Ov.; Sen.

rĕparco=reperco; q.v.

rĕpăro -are.

(1) *to prepare anew, repair, restore, renew, make good, get again*: perdere videbatur, quod reparare posset, Cic.; tribuniciam potestatem, Liv.; exercitum, Liv.; damna caelestia lunae, Hor.; cornua (of the moon), Ov.; vires, Ov.

(2) *to get in exchange, to purchase*: vina Syrā reparata merce, Hor.

rĕpastĭnātĭo -ōnis, f. (repastino), *a digging up again*: Cic.

rĕpastĭno -are, *to dig again, trench again*: Varr., Plin.

rĕpecto -pectĕre -pexum, *to comb back*: coma repexa, Ov.

rĕpello rĕpellĕre reppŭli, repulsum, *to drive back, drive away.* LIT., homines a templi aditu, Cic.; aliquem ex urbe, Cic.; hostes in silvas, Caes.; repagula, *to push back*, Ov.; amnes Oceani pede repellere, *to spurn* (of a star rising from the sea), Verg. TRANSF., *to banish, repel*: vim vi, Cic.; dolorem a se, Cic.; aliquem a spe, *to disappoint*, Caes.; criminationes, *to refute*, Cic.; conubia nostra, *to spurn*, Verg.; preces, Ov.

rĕpendo -pendĕre -pendi -pensum. LIT., *to weigh back again*: pensa, *to return an equal weight of*, Ov.; aurum pro capite, Cic.; miles auro repensus, *ransomed*, Hor. TRANSF., *to repay, requite*: gratiam, Ov.; si magna rependam, Verg.; pretium vitae, Prop.; damna formae ingenio, *make up for*, Ov.

rĕpens -entis, *sudden, unexpected.* LIT., adventus, Cic.; used like adv.: repens alia nuntiatur clades, Liv. TRANSF., *new, fresh, recent*: perfidia, Tac.

Adv. **rĕpentĕ**, *suddenly, unexpectedly*: Cic., Verg., etc.

rĕpenso -are (freq. of rependo), *to recompense, make up for*: Sen.

rĕpentinus -a -um (repens), *sudden, unlooked for, unexpected*: amor, Cic.; adventus, Caes.; venenum, *quick-working*, Tac.; ignoti homines et repentini, *upstarts*, Cic.

¶ N. abl. as adv. **rĕpentĭnō**, *suddenly, unexpectedly*: Pl., Caes., Cic.

rĕperco (rĕparco) -percĕre -persi or -pĕperci (re/parco), *to spare, be sparing with*, or *abstain from*: id, Lucr.; Pl.

rĕpercussus -ūs, m. (repercutio), *a rebounding, reverberation* (of sound, etc.); *echo, reflection*: quo plenior et gravior vox repercussu intumescat, Tac.; Plin. L.

rĕpercŭtĭo -cŭtĕre -cussi -cussum. LIT., *to strike back, drive back, cause to rebound* (of sound, etc.); esp. in perf. partic. **rĕpercussus**, *rebounding, reflected*: discus repercussus in aëra, Ov.; valles repercussae (clamoribus), Liv.; lumen aquae sole repercussum, Verg. TRANSF., *to refute, repel*: Quint., Plin.

rĕpĕrĭo rĕpĕrire, reppĕri, rĕpertum (re/pario), *to get again; to find, discover.* LIT., of persons and things: Pl., Caes., Cic., Verg. TRANSF., (1) *to find* an abstr. thing: sibi salutem, Caes.; nomen ex inventore, Cic.

(2) *to discover, ascertain, find out*: causas duas, Cic.; neque reperire poterat quanta esset, Caes.; Stoici inopes reperiuntur, *are found to be*, Cic.; improbus reperiebare, Cic.; with acc. and infin.: quem Tarentum venisse reperio, Liv.; Cic., etc.; in pass. with nom. and infin.: in Italiae partes Pythagoras venisse reperitur, Cic. (3) *to find out something new, discover, invent*: nihil novi, Cic.; vias sibi repperit usus, Verg.
¶ Hence partic. **rĕpertus -a -um**, *found, discovered*. N. as subst.: Graiorum obscura reperta, *discoveries*, Lucr.

rĕpertor -ōris, m. (reperio), *a discoverer, inventor*: doctrinarum, Lucr.; medicinae, Verg.

rĕpĕtentĭa -ae, f. (repeto), *recollection, remembrance*: nostri, *our consciousness*, Lucr.

rĕpĕtītĭo -ōnis, f. (repeto), *repetition*. In gen.: eiusdem verbi crebra repetitio, Cic. Esp. as a figure of speech = ἀναφορά, *the repetition of the same word at the beginning of several sentences*: Cic., Quint.

rĕpĕtītor -ōris, m. (repeto), *one who reclaims or demands back again*: nuptae ademptae Cic.

rĕpĕto -ĕre -īvi and **-ĭi -ītum**, *to seek again, make for again*.
LIT., of physical search or movement: urbem, Verg.; castra, Liv.; elephantos, *to go back and fetch*, Liv.; regem repetitum saepius cuspide, *attacked*, Liv.
TRANSF., (1) *to ask* or *demand back or again*: Gallum ab eodem repetit, Caes.; pecuniam, Cic.; promissa, Cic.; Salaminii Homerum repetunt, *claim as their countryman*, Cic.; repetita Proserpina, Verg. Esp.: **a**, res repetere, *to demand satisfaction of an enemy* (used of the Fetiales), Cic.: **b**, res repetere, *to claim back one's own property from a court*; hence, pecuniae repetundae, or, simply, repetundae, *money claimed back as having been extorted*, esp. *from provinces by their governors*: lex repetundarum pecuniarum, de pecuniis repetundis, *against extortion*, Cic. (2) *to return to, renew, begin again*: studia, Caes.; pugnam, Cic.; iter, Ov. With infin.: Lucr. (3) *to trace back from the beginning, to deduce*: populi originem, Cic.; aliquid alte, et a capite, Cic.; haec tam longe repetita principia, Cic.; omnem prima ab origine famam, Verg.; repetitis et enumeratis diebus, Caes. (4) *to go back over in mind, recollect, recall*: temporis illius memoriam, Cic.; memoriam ex annalibus, Liv.; noctem, Ov.; Verg.

rĕpĕtundae, see repeto.

rĕplĕo -plēre -plēvi -plētum.
(1) *to fill again, fill up*. LIT., exhaustas domos, Cic.; exercitum, Liv. TRANSF., quod voci deerat plangore replebam, Ov.
(2) *to make full, fill, satisfy*. LIT., delubra corporibus, Lucr.; corpora carne, Ov.; Verg., Liv. TRANSF., nemora gemitu, Lucr.; ut curantes eādem vi morbi repletos secum traherent, Liv.
¶ Hence partic. **rĕplētus -a -um**, *filled, full*; with abl. or genit.: Liv., etc.

rĕplĭcātĭo -ōnis, f. (replico), *a rolling again, folding round*: ut replicatione quādam mundi motum regat atque tueatur, Cic.

rĕplĭco -are, *to fold back, unroll*; hence *to turn*

over, review: memoriam temporum, Cic.; memoriam annalium, Cic.

rēpo rēpĕre repsi reptum (cf. ἕρπω), *to creep, crawl*. LIT., cochleae inter saxa repentes, Sall.; Lucr. TRANSF., of slow travellers: Hor.; of clouds: Lucr.; fig.: sermones repentes per humum, *an ordinary, prosaic style*, Hor.

rĕpōno -pōnĕre -pŏsŭi -pŏsĭtum; perf. partic. rĕpostus, poet. (re/pono).
(1) *to lay back*: cervicem, *to bend back*, Lucr.; Verg.
(2) *to put aside, to lay up in store, deposit*. LIT., pecuniam in thesauris, Liv.; arma, Caes.; tela, Ov.; faciemque deae vestemque, Verg.; falcem arbusta reponunt, *make unnecessary*, Verg.; tellure repostos, *buried, laid to rest*, Verg. TRANSF., **a**, *to place, cause to rest*: spem in virtute, Caes.; causam totam in iudicum humanitate, Cic.; Liv.: **b**, *to reckon, place*: sidera in numero deorum, Cic.: **c**, *to lay up, store, preserve*: manet alta mente repostum iudicium Paridis, Verg.
(3) *to put back in a previous position*. LIT., pileum capiti apte, Liv.; lapidem suo loco, Cic.; se in cubitum, *recline at table again*, Hor. TRANSF., nos in sceptra, *to restore*, Verg.; fabulam, *to act again*, Hor.
(4) *to replace by a substitute, put one in another's place*. LIT., ruptos vetustate pontes, Tac.; ligna super foco, Hor.; epulas, Verg. TRANSF., Aristophanem pro Eupoli, Cic. L.; ne tibi ego idem reponam, *do as much to you again*, Cic. L.

rĕporto -are, *to bring back, carry back*.
LIT., candelabrum secum in Syriam, Cic.; milites navibus in Siciliam, Caes. Esp. *to bring back home as victor*: nihil ex praeda domum, Cic.
TRANSF., *to bring back* abstr. things: alicui solatium aliquod, Cic.; victoriam, non pacem, domum, Liv. Esp. of reports, *to deliver*: adytis haec tristia dicta, Verg.

rĕposco -ĕre. (1) *to ask back again*: virginem, Pl.; alter a me Catilinam, alter Cethegum reposcebat, Cic.; with double acc.: aliquem simulacrum, Cic.; Parthos signa, Verg. (2) *to demand as a right, claim*: regem ad supplicium, Verg.; ab altero rationem vitae, Cic.; Liv.

rĕpŏsĭtōrĭum -i, n. (repono), *a tray, waiter, stand*: Plin., Sen.

rĕpostor -ōris, m. (repono), *a restorer*: templorum, Ov.

rĕpōtĭa -ōrum, n. (re/poto), *an after-party, a drinking on the day after an entertainment*: Hor.

rĕpraesentātĭo -ōnis, f. (repraesento). (1) *a vivid presentation, a lively description*: Plin., Quint. (2) *payment in cash*: Cic. L.

rĕpraesento -are (praesens), *to make present again, to bring back* before the eyes or mind's eye.
LIT., quod ipsum templum repraesentabat memoriam consulatus mei, Cic.; si repraesentari morte mea libertas civitatis posset, *brought about at once*, Cic.; virtutem moresque Catonis, *to reproduce*, Hor.
TRANSF., *to perform immediately, hasten*: se repraesentaturum id, Caes.; medicinam, *use directly*, Cic. L.; diem promissorum, Cic.

Esp. t. t. of commercial language, *to pay cash*: pecuniam, Cic. L.; Suet.

reprĕhendo -prĕhendĕre -prĕhendi -prĕhensum, and **reprendo** -prendĕre -prendi -prensum, *to catch, to hold again* or *hold back, to seize, hold fast, detain*.

LIT., aliquem pallio, Cic.; quosdam manu, Liv.; revocat virtus vel potius reprehendit manu, Cic.

TRANSF., (1) *to check, restrain*: Lucr., Cic. (2) *to blame, censure, reprove*: aliquem, Ter., Cic.; aliquem in eo quod, etc., Cic.; id in me reprehendis, Cic.; temeritatem militum, Caes. (3) as rhet. t. t., *to refute*: Cic.

reprĕhensĭo -ōnis, f. (reprehendo), *a holding back*. Hence, (1) *a stopping* or *check in speaking*: sine reprehensione, Cic. (2) *blame, censure*: culpae, Cic.; plur.: Cic., Quint. (3) as rhet. t. t., *a refutation*: Cic., Quint.

reprĕhenso -are (freq. of reprehendo), *to hold back eagerly, to hold fast*: singulos, Liv.

reprĕhensor -ōris, m. (reprehendo). (1) *a censurer, reprover*: Cic. (2) *an improver, reformer*: comitiorum, Cic.

repressor -ōris, m. (reprimo), *a restrainer*: caedis cottidianae, Cic.

reprĭmo -prĭmĕre -pressi -pressum (re/premo), *to hold back, restrain, hinder, repress*.

LIT., lacum Albanum, Cic.; dextram, Verg.; retro pedem, Verg.; (Mithridatem) repressum magna ex parte, non oppressum, Cic.

TRANSF., iracundiam, Ter.; furorem exsultantem, Cic.; animi incitationem atque alacritatem, Caes.; conatūs alicuius, Cic.; se, *to restrain oneself*, Cic.; concitatam multitudinem, Cic.

reprōmissĭo -ōnis, f. (repromitto), *a counter-promise*: Cic.

reprōmitto -mittĕre -mīsi -missum, *to make a counter-promise, to promise in return*: Pl., Cic.

repto -are (freq. of repo), *to creep, crawl*; esp. applied to slow walkers or travellers: Lucr., Hor.

repŭdĭātĭo -ōnis, f. (repudio), *a refusal, rejecting*: supplicum, Cic.

repŭdĭo -are (repudium), *to refuse, reject, disdain*. In gen.: gratiam populi, Caes.; cuius vota et preces a vestris mentibus repudiare debetis, Cic. Esp. of a married or betrothed wife, *to divorce, put away*: Pl., Ter., Suet.

repŭdĭum -i, n. *a putting away* a wife or betrothed, *a separation between married persons, divorce*: sponsae repudium renuntiare, Pl.; repudium dicere, Tac.

repŭĕrasco -ĕre, *to become a boy again, to frolic like a child*: Pl., Cic.

repugnantĭa -ae, f. (repugno). (1) *resistance, means of resistance*: natura hanc dedit repugnantiam apibus, Plin. (2) *incompatibility*: rerum, Cic.

repugno are, *to fight against, oppose, resist*.

LIT., nostri primo fortiter repugnare, Caes.; Verg., Liv.

TRANSF., (1) *to oppose, resist*: contra veritatem, Cic.; with dat.: fortunae, Cic.; non repugno, foll. by quominus and subj., Cic. (2) *to be naturally opposed* or *repugnant to, to be inconsistent with, incompatible with*: simulatio amicitiae repugnat maxime, Cic.;

haec inter se quam repugnent, plerique non vident, Cic.

¶ Hence partic. **rĕpugnans**, *contrary, opposed*; n. pl. as subst. **rĕpugnantĭa** -ium, *contradictions*: Cic., Quint.

¶ Adv. **rĕpugnantĕr**, *unwillingly*: Cic.

rĕpulsa -ae, f. (repello), *a repulse, rejection*. Esp. of a candidate for office: repulsa consulatūs, Cic.; aedilicia, Cic.; a populo repulsam ferre, Cic.; Caes., Hor. Also in gen., *a denial, refusal*: amor crescit dolore repulsae, Ov.

rĕpulsans -antis, partic. as from repulso -are (freq. of repello), *beating back*: colles verba repulsantes, *echoing*, Lucr.; vera repulsans pectus verba, Lucr.

rĕpulsū, abl. as from repulsus, m. (repello), *by striking back*; hence *by the reflection of light, echoing of sound*: Lucr.

rĕpulsus -a -um, partic. from repello; q.v.

rĕpungo -ĕre, *to prick again, goad again*; fig.: leviter illorum animos, Cic. L.

rĕpurgo -are, *to clean* or *clear again*. LIT., iter, Liv.; humum saxis, Ov.; caelum, Ov. TRANSF., *to clear away, purge away*: quicquid in Aenea fuerat mortale repurgat, Ov.

rĕpŭtātĭo -ōnis, f. (reputo), *a re-appraisal, reviewing consideration*: Tac.

rĕpŭto -are. (1) *to reckon back, count, compute*: ex hoc die superiores solis defectiones usque ad illam, Cic.; tempora, Tac. (2) *to think over, reconsider*: horum nihil umquam, Cic.; Ter., Sall., Tac.; with acc. and infin.: cum tibi nihil merito accidisse reputabis, Cic. L.; with indir. quest.: quid ille vellet, Cic.

rĕquĭēs -ētis, f. (voc., requies, Lucr.; acc., requietem and requiem, Cic.; abl., requiete, Cic. poet., requiē, Ov.), *rest, repose*: non labor meus, non requies, Cic.; curarum, Cic.; laborum, Verg.; animi et corporis, Cic.

rĕquĭesco -quĭescĕre -quĭēvi -quĭētum (syncop. perf. form, requierunt, Verg.; requiesse, Liv.); *to rest, repose*.

LIT., of persons: in sella, Cic.; sub umbra, Verg.; a muneribus reipublicae, Cic.; lecto, Prop. Esp. of the dead, *to rest in the grave*: in sepulcro requiescere mortuum, Cic.; Ov.

TRANSF., of things: vixdum requiesse aures a strepitu et tumultu hostili, Liv.; requiescit vitis in ulmo, *rests upon, is supported by*, Cic.; animus ex multis miseriis atque periculis requievit, Sall.; in spe huius, Cic.

¶ Hence pass. partic. **rĕquĭētus** -a -um, *rested, refreshed*: miles, Liv.; ager, *fallow*, Ov.

rĕquīrĭto -are (freq. of requiro), *to keep inquiring after*: Pl.

rĕquīro -quīrĕre -quīsii or -quīsīvi -quīsītum (re/quaero), *to ask* or *look for a missing person* or *thing*.

LIT., libros, Cic.; iuvenem, Ov.; portūs Velinos, Verg.

TRANSF., (1) *to demand, to desire, consider necessary*: virtus nullam voluptatem requirit, Cic.; in hoc bello virtutes multae requiruntur, Cic., Caes. (2) *to miss, feel the want of*: pristinum morem iudiciorum, Cic.; se vitamque, Lucr. (3) *to ask a question, inquire after* a thing: quae a me de Vatinio requiris, Cic.; quoniam nihil ex te hi requirunt, Cic.; causam, Ov.; with indir. quest.: illud quoque requirit, qua ratione fecerit, Cic.

rēs rĕi, f. (genit. also rēī and rēī, Lucr.), *a thing, object, matter, affair, circumstance.*
In gen.: divinae humanaeque res, Cic.; natura rerum, *the world, the universe, nature,* Lucr., Cic.; genit., rerum, used to strengthen a superl.: rerum pulcherrima, Roma, Verg.; sunt lacrimae rerum, Verg.; si res postulabit, *if the position requires it,* Cic.; homines nullā, re bonā digni, *good for nothing,* Cic.; pro re nata, *as it stands,* Cic. L.; pro re, *according to circumstances,* Liv., etc.; res populi Romani perscribere, *write the history of Rome,* Liv.
Esp., (1) emphatic, *the real thing, fact, truth, reality*: rem opinor spectari oportere, non verba, Cic.; hos deos non re, sed opinione esse, Cic.; quantum distet argumentatio ab re ipsa atque a veritate, Cic.; persona, manet res Lucr.; rē verā, *in truth,* Cic., Liv., etc. (2) *possessions, property, wealth*: rem facere, Cic. L., Hor.; augere, Cic.; plur.: privatae res, Cic. (3) *interest, advantage, benefit*: consulere suis rebus, Nep.; in rem suam convertere, Cic.; in rem (alicuius), *to one's advantage,* Pl., Ter., Liv.; so: ex re, Pl.; ab re, *against one's interests,* Pl., Liv. (4) *cause, ground, reason*; only in such phrases as eā re, ob eam rem, *on that account,* Cic.; qua re, quam ob rem, *wherefore.* (5) *a matter of business, an affair*: rem cum aliquo transigere, Cic.; de tota illa ratione atque re Gallicana, Cic. Hence res (alicui) est cum aliquo, *one has to do with*: tecum mihi res est, T. Rosci, quoniam, etc., Cic. (6) *a law-suit, cause, action*: utrum rem an litem dici oporteret, Cic.; Hor., Liv. (7) res publica *or* respublica, *the republic, state, commonwealth*: rem publicam sustinere, Cic.; e republica, *in the public interest,* Cic. So also res alone: unus homo nobis cunctando restituit rem, Enn.; res Romana, *the Roman state,* Liv.

rĕsacro=resecro; q.v.

rĕsaevĭo -ire, *to rage again*: Ov.

rĕsălūtātĭo -ōnis, f. (resaluto), *a greeting in return*: Suet.

rĕsălūto -are, *to salute again, return a greeting to*: aliquem, Cic.

rĕsānesco -sānescĕre -sānŭi, *to become sound again, to heal again*: Ov.

rĕsarcĭo -sarcire -sartum, *to patch again, mend, repair.* LIT., vestem, Ter.; tecta, Liv. TRANSF., *to repair, restore*: detrimentum, Caes.

rescindo -scindĕre -scĭdi -scissum, *to tear back, tear away again, cut away.*
LIT., vallum ac loricam falcibus, Caes.; pontem, Caes., Liv.; latebram teli, *to cut open,* Verg.; vulnus, *to open again,* Ov.; and fig.: luctus obductos, *to renew,* Ov.
TRANSF., (1) *to break open*: locum firmatum, Cic.; Lucr. (2) *to rescind, repeal, abrogate* a law, decree, etc.: acta M. Antonii, Cic.; res iudicatos, Cic.; Lucr., etc.

rescisco -sciscĕre -scīvi and -scii -scītum, *to find out, ascertain*: omnia, Ter.; Cic., etc.

rescrībo -scrībĕre -scripsi -scriptum.
(1) *to write again, rewrite*: Suet. Hence as milit. t. t.: **a,** *to enrol again*: ex eodem milite novas legiones, Liv.: **b,** *to transfer from one class of soldiers to another*: ad equum, *to transfer to the cavalry,* Caes. (2) *to write back, answer in writing.* In

gen.: ad aliquem, Cic. L.; alicui, Cic. L.; ad litteras, Cic. L.; Hor., Ov. Esp.: **a,** of the emperor, *to answer a petition or inquiry in writing*: Suet.; hence n. of partic. as subst., rescriptum -i, *an imperial rescript*: Tac.: **b,** in book-keeping, *to enter to the credit of an account, to pay, repay*: reliqua rescribamus, Cic.; Ter.; fig.: quod tu numquam rescribere (*pay again*) possis, Hor.

rĕsĕco -sĕcare -sĕcŭi -sectum, *to cut back, cut short.* LIT., linguam, Cic.; partem de tergore, Ov. TRANSF., libidinem, Cic.; spem longam, Hor.; ad vivum resecare, *to be painfully exact about,* Cic.

rĕsecro or **rĕsacro** -are (re/sacro). (1) *to implore again and again*: Pl. (2) *to free from a curse*: Nep.

rĕsēmĭno -are, *to produce again*: Ov.

rĕsĕquor -sĕqui -sĕcūtus sum, dep. *to follow again*: aliquem dictis, *to answer,* Ov.

rĕsĕro -are, *to unbolt, open.* LIT., limina, Verg.; fores ianuam, Ov. TRANSF., (1) *to open up*: Italiam exteris gentibus, Cic.; aures, Liv.; annum, Ov. (2) *to disclose, reveal*: augustae oracula mentis, Ov.

rĕservo -are. (1) *to lay up, keep back, reserve, keep*: hoc consilium ad extremum, Caes.; in aliud tempus, Caes.; praedam illis reservari, Caes.; Cic., Verg., etc. (2) in gen., *to save, preserve*: omnes, Cic.; Pallanta, Verg.; nihil ad similitudinem hominis, *nothing human,* Cic.

rĕsĕs -sĭdis (resideo), *sitting.* Hence (1) *staying, inactive*: reses in urbe plebs, Liv.; eum residem tempus terere, Liv.; Ov. (2) *calm, quiet*: animus, Verg.

rĕsĭdĕo -sĭdēre -sēdi -sessum (re/sedeo), *to remain sitting, to abide, stay.*
LIT., resideamus, *let us sit down,* Cic.; in equo, Ov.; in republica, Cic. TRANSF., in corpore nullum residere sensum, Cic.; resident spes in tua virtute, *depends upon,* Cic.; in nutu eorum auctoritas, Cic.

rĕsīdo -sīdĕre -sēdi, *to sit down, rest, settle.*
LIT., mediis aedibus, Verg.; Siculis arvis, Verg.; in villa, Cic.; in oppido aliquo, Cic. TRANSF., inanimate things. (1) *to sink down*: si montes resedissent, Cic.; maria in se ipsa residant, Verg. (2) *to sink, subside, abate*: mentes ab superiore bello, Caes.; cum tumor animi resedisset, Cic.; longiore certamine sensim residere Samnitium animos, Liv.; fig.: sex mihi surgat opus numeris, in quinque residat, *interchange hexameter and pentameter,* Ov.

rĕsĭdŭus -a -um (resideo), *remaining, left behind, outstanding*: odium, Cic.; simultas, Liv.; pecuniae, *arrears,* Cic. N. as subst. **rĕsĭdŭum** -i, *the remainder, residue*: Suet.

rĕsigno -are, *to unseal, open.*
LIT., litteras, Cic. L.; testamenta, Hor. TRANSF., (1) *to reveal*: venientia fata, Ov. (2) *to cancel, annul*: omnem tabularum fidem, Cic. (3) *to transfer from one account-book into another, to give back, resign*: cuncta, Hor.; quae dedit, Hor.

rĕsĭlĭo -sīlīre -sĭlŭi -sultum (re/salio), *to leap back, spring back.*
LIT., of persons: in gelidos lacus, Ov.; ad manipulos, Liv.; of inanimate things, *to spring back, rebound*: resilit grando a culmine tecti, Ov.; fig.: ubi scopulum offendis

eiusmodi, ut non modo ab hoc crimen resilire videas, Cic. Transf., *to contract, diminish*: in spatium breve, Ov.

rĕsīmus -a -um, *bent backwards, turned up*: nares, Ov.

rēsīna -ae, f. (ῥητίνη), *resin*: Plin., Mart.

rēsīnātus -a -um (resina), *resined.* (1) *flavoured with resin*: vinum, Mart. (2) *smeared with resin*: iuventus (to take hairs off the skin), Juv.

rĕsĭpĭo -sĭpĕre (re/sapio), *to have a smack, taste, flavour of anything.* Lit., Plin. Transf., Epicurus minime resipiens patriam, *with nothing of Athens about him*, Cic.

rĕsĭpisco -sĭpiscĕre -sĭpĭi, also -sĭpīvī; resīpui: Cic. L.; resipisset: Cic. (re/sapio), *to recover one's senses.* Lit., *to come to oneself again* (from fainting, etc.): Pl., Plin., Suet. Transf., *to become rational again, come to one's right mind*: Cic., Liv., etc.

rĕsisto -sistĕre -stĭti.

(1) *to stand again.* Lit., **a**, *to stay, continue*: ibi, Caes.; Romae, Cic.: **b**, *after motion, to stand still, halt*: Caes.; negabat se umquam cum Curione restitisse, *had stopped to talk*, Cic. L. Transf., **a**, *to stop short*; in speaking: sed ego in hoc resisto, *stop here*, Cic.; media in voce, Verg.: **b**, *to recover one's footing*: ubi lapsi resistamus, Cic.

(2) *to resist, oppose, withstand*; usually with dat. Lit., physically: of persons: iniuriis, Cic. L.; alicui pro republica, Cic.; esp. milit.: hostibus, Caes.; vi contra vim, Liv.; of things: quae nunc immotae perstant ventisque resistunt, Ov. Transf., morally: dolori fortiter, Cic.; lacrimis et precibus, Cic.; resistere et pugnare contra veritatem, Cic.; impers.: omnibus huis resistitur, Caes.; foll. by ne and the subj.: ne sibi statua poneretur, restitit, Nep.; foll. by quin and the subj.: vix deorum opibus, quin obruatur Romana res, resisti potest, Liv.; absol.: restitit et pervicit Cato, Cic.

rĕsolvo -solvĕre -solvi -sŏlūtum, *to unbind, untie, loosen, open.*

Lit., claustra, Lucr.; litteras, Liv.; vestes, Ov.; equos, *to unyoke*, Ov.; puella resoluta capillos, *with dishevelled hair*, Ov.; gleba se resolvit, *becomes loose*, Verg.; Cerberus immania terga resolvit fusus humi, *stretches out in sleep*, Verg.; ignis aurum resolvit, *melts*, Lucr.; nivem, Ov.; tenebras, *dissipates*, Verg.

Transf., (1) *to dispel, cancel, end*: curas, Verg.; litem lite, Hor.; iura pudoris, Verg. (2) *to relax, weaken*: ut iacui totis resoluta medullis, Ov. (3) *to release, free*: te piacula nulla resolvent, Hor. (4) *to unravel, reveal*: dolos tecti (Labyrinthi) ambagesque, Verg.; with indir. quest.: Lucr.

rĕsŏnābĭlis -e (resono), *resounding*: Echo, Ov.

rĕsŏno -are.

(1) intransit., *to sound back, give back an echo, resound, echo.* Lit., aedes plangoribus, Verg.; resonans theatrum, Cic.; ad nervos resonant in cantibus, Cic.; resonant avibus virgulta, Verg. With internal acc.: doces silvas resonare Amaryllida, Verg.; umbrae resonarent triste et acutum, Hor. Impers. pass.: in fidibus testudine resonatur, Cic.

Transf., gloria virtuti resonat, *is an echo of*, Cic. (2) transit., *to make resound*: lucos cantu, Verg.

rĕsŏnus -a -um (resono), *resounding, echoing*: voces, Ov.

rĕsorbĕo -ēre, *to swallow again, suck back*: saxa (of the sea), Verg.; Ov.

respecto -are (freq. of respicio), *to look often or eagerly back, look about.*

Lit., respectare ad tribunal, Liv.; with acc.: arcem Romanam, Liv.

Transf., *to have a regard for, give some thought to*: verum haec ita praetereamus, ut tamen intuentes et respectantes relinquamus, Cic.; with acc.: meum amorem, Cat.; si qua pios respectant numina, Verg.

respectus -ūs, m. (respicio), *a looking back, looking around one.*

Lit., sine respectu fugere, Liv.; incendiorum, *looking back upon*, Cic.; Verg. Meton., *a place of refuge, a retreat*: Cic., Liv.

Transf., *care, regard, respect, consideration*: Romanorum maxime respectus civitates movit, Liv.; sine respectu humanitatis, Liv.

respergo -spergĕre -spersi -spersum (re/spargo), *to sprinkle, splash.* Lit., manus sanguine, Cic.; aliquem cruore, Cic.; lumine terras (of the dawn), Lucr. Transf., servili probro repleri, Tac.

respersĭo -ōnis, f. (respergo), *a sprinkling*: pigmentorum, Cic.

respĭcĭo -spicĕre -spexi -spectum (re/specio), transit. and intransit., *to look behind, to look back.*

Lit., ad oppidum, Cic.; nusquam circumspiciens aut respiciens, Liv.; with acc., *to look back at* or *see behind one*: amicum, Verg.; quos ubi rex respexit, Liv.; angues a tergo, Verg.; tribunal, Liv.; Eurydicen suam, Ov.; with acc. and infin.: respiciunt atram in nimbo volitare favillam, Verg.

Transf., (1) *to look back upon, reflect upon*: spatium praeteriti temporis, Cic. (2) *to look to, provide for*: ut respiciam generum meum, Caes. (3) *to look to for help, etc., depend upon*: ad hunc summa imperii respiciebat, Caes. (4) *to look for something desired*: spem ab Romanis, Liv. (5) *to have a regard for, care for, consider*: rempublicam, Cic. L.; commoda populi, Cic.; Ter., Verg., etc.

respīrāmen -ĭnis, n. (respiro), *the windpipe*: Ov.

respīrātĭo -ōnis, f. (respiro). (1) *a taking breath, respiration.* Lit., Cic. Transf., *a pause in a speech while the speaker takes breath*: Cic. (2) *an exhalation*: aquarum, Cic.

respīrātus -ū, m. (respiro), *a taking breath*: Cic.

respīro -are.

(1) *to blow* or *breathe back, blow in a contrary direction*; of winds: Lucr., Cic.

(2) *to breathe again, to take breath.* Lit., animam, Cic.; ex ea pars redditur respirando, Cic. Transf., **a**, *to recover from fear, anxiety, etc.*: paulum a metu, Cic.; Verg., Liv.: **b**, of things, *to abate, decline*: cupiditas atque avaritia respiravit paulum, Cic.; oppugnatio respiravit, 'let up', *declined in violence*, Cic.; impers. pass.: ita respiratum est, Cic.

resplendĕo -ēre, *to glitter back, gleam again*: Verg.

respondĕo -spondēre -spondi -sponsum.

(1) intransit., *to match, correspond to, come up to, answer to*; with dat.: amori amore, Cic. L.; verba verbis respondeant, Cic.; tua virtus opinioni hominum respondet, Cic.; seges votis, Verg.; favor meritis, Hor. Of physical correspondence, *to lie opposite*: contra Gnosia tellus, Verg.; also *to resemble*: Lucr. Esp. as legal t. t., *to answer to one's name*, hence, *to appear, be present*: cum ad nomen nemo responderet, Liv.; Verrem non responsurum, Cic. TRANSF., pedes respondere non vocatos, Cic.

(2) transit., *to give an answer* (acc.) *to a person* or *thing* (dat.); *to answer, reply*. LIT., aliud tibi, Pl.; tibi de versibus plura, Cic.; nil mihi respondes? aut dic aut accipe calcem, Juv.; tibi non rescribam, sed respondeam, Sen.; orationi, epistulae, criminibus, etc., Cic.; with acc. and infin.: Pl., Caes., Cic. Esp. of lawyers, oracles, etc. *to give an official answer* or *opinion*: Cic., etc. TRANSF., of echoes: saxa respondent voci, Cic.; Ov.

¶ N. of partic. as subst. **responsum** -i, *an answer, reply*. In gen.: responsum dare alicui, Cic.; reddere, Cic., Liv.; auferre, obtain, Cic. Esp. (1) *the answer of an oracle* or *soothsayer*: haruspicum, Cic.; Sibyllae, Verg. (2) *the answer* or *opinion of a lawyer*: Cic.

responsĭo -ōnis, f. (respondeo), *a reply, answer*: responsionem elicere, Cic. Rhet. t. t.: sibi ipsi responsio, *a replying to one's own argument* (=ἀπόκρισις), Cic., Quint.

responsĭto -are (freq. of responso), *to keep giving an answer* or *opinion* (of legal advisers): Cic.

responso -are (freq. of respondeo), *to keep answering*. LIT., Pl. TRANSF., (1) *to re-echo*: lucus ripaeque responsant circa, Verg. (2) *to defy, withstand*; with dat.: cupidinibus, Hor.; cenis, Hor.

responsor -ōris, m. (respondeo), *one who answers*: Pl.

responsum -i, n. subst. from respondeo; q.v.

respublĭca, see res.

respŭo -spŭere -spŭi, *to spit back* or *out, to reject*.

LIT., reliquiae cibi, quas natura respuit, Cic.

TRANSF., *to reject, refuse, repel*: cum id dicat, quod omnium mentes aspernentur ac respuant, Cic.; defensionem, Cic.; poëtas, Hor.; condicionem, Caes.

restagno -are, *to overflow*. LIT., quas (paludes) restagnantes faciunt lacus, Liv.; restagnans mare, Ov. TRANSF., of places, *to be swamped*: late is locus restagnat, Caes.

restauro -are (cf. instauro), *to restore, rebuild*: aedem, Tac.

restĭcŭla -ae, f. (dim. of restis), *a thin rope* or *cord*: Cic.

restinctĭo -ōnis, f. (restinguo), *a slaking, quenching*: sitis, Cic.

restinguo -stinguĕre -stinxi -stinctum, *to put out again, extinguish, quench*.

LIT., ignem, Cic.; flammam, Lucr., Cic., Liv.

TRANSF., (1) *to slake, to quench*: sitim, Cic.; ardorem cupiditatum, Cic.; odium

alicuius, Cic. (2) *to extinguish, destroy*: studia, Cic.; animos hominum sensusque morte restingui, Cic.

restĭo -ōnis, m. (restis), *a rope-maker*: Suet. In jest, *one who is scourged with ropes*: Pl.

restĭpŭlātĭo -ōnis, f. (restipulor), *a counter-engagement*: Cic.

restĭpŭlor -ari, dep. *to obtain a promise in return*: Cic.

restis -is; acc. -im and -em; f. *a rope, cord*: Pl., Ter., Liv., etc.

restĭto -are (freq. of resto), *to remain behind, loiter, linger*: Pl., Ter., Liv.

restĭtrix -trīcis, f. (resisto), *she that remains behind*: Pl.

restĭtŭo -ŭĕre -ŭi -ūtum (re/statuo).

(1) *to put in its former place, replace, restore*. LIT., statuam, Cic.; Verg. TRANSF., *to reinstate, re-establish* a person, institution etc.: te in eundem locum, Cic.; Siciliam in antiquum statum, Cic. Esp. of restoring people to their rights, etc.: tribunos plebis in suam dignitatem, Caes.; Cic., Liv.

(2) *to put right again* what is amiss, *repair*: rem, aciem, proelium, Liv.; damna Romano bello accepta, Liv.

(3) *to give back, restore* a person or thing: bona iis, Caes.; captum victori, Liv.

restĭtūtĭo -ōnis, f. (restituo), *a restoration*: Capitolii, Suet.; pristinae fortunae, Suet.; damnatorum, *reinstatement*, Cic.

restĭtūtor -ōris, m. (restituo), *a restorer*: templorum, Liv.; salutis, Cic.

resto -stare -stĭti.

(1) *to make a stand against, resist, oppose, withstand*; with dat.: Lucr., Liv., etc.; absol.: ratio nulla est restandi, Lucr.

(2) *to stand still, stay behind, remain*. LIT., pugnandi causa nemo restitit, Caes.; Liv. TRANSF., *to be left over, survive*. Of persons, esp. *to remain alive*: restabam solus de viginti, Ov.; qui pauci admodum restant, Cic. Of material things: dona pelago et flammis restantia, *saved from*, Verg. Of abstract resources, possibilities, etc., *to remain available*: iam duo fata, Pl.; unam spem restare, Liv.; impers., restat, *it remains*, with ut and subj.: Cic., Hor.; or with infin.: Ter., Liv., Ov.

Esp. with reference to the future, *to await, be in store*: placet (vobis) socios sic tractari, quod restat, ut per haec tempora tractatos videtis, *for the future*, Cic.; hoc Latio restare canunt, with acc. and infin., Verg.

restringo -stringĕre -strinxi -strictum, *to bind back, bind tight*. LIT., restrictis lacertis, Hor. Of dogs, *to draw back* the teeth: Pl., Lucr. TRANSF., *to confine, restrict, restrain*: Tac., Plin. L.

¶ Hence partic. (with compar.) **restrictus** -a -um. LIT., *close, tight*: toga, Suet. TRANSF., (1) *stingy*: homo, Cic.; cum naturā semper ad largiendum ex alieno fuerim restrictior, Cic. (2) *strict, severe*: imperium, Tac.

¶ Adv. **restrictē**. (1) *sparingly*: tam restricte facere id, Cic. (2) *accurately, strictly*: praecipere, Cic.; observare, Cic.

rĕsulto -are (freq. of resilio), *to spring back, rebound*. LIT., corpora conflicta, Lucr.; tela resultant galeā, Verg. TRANSF., (1) of sound, *to echo*: imago vocis resultat, Verg.;

also of places, *to resound*: pulsati colles
clamore resultant, Verg. (2) of style, *to go
jerkily*: Quint., Plin. L.

rĕsŭmo -sūměre -sumpsi -sumptum, *to take
again, resume.* LIT., tabellas, Ov.; arma,
Tac. TRANSF., *to renew, repeat*: pugnam,
Tac.; vires, Ov.

rĕsŭpīno -are, *to throw* a person *on his back*: adsurgentem ibi regem umbone, Liv.; resupi-
nati Galli, *prostrate from intoxication*, Juv.

rĕsŭpīnus -a -um, *bent backwards, on one's
back.*
    LIT., resupinus haeret curru, Verg.;
resupinum aliquem fundere, *to lay low*, Ov.;
resupini natant, Ov.
    TRANSF., (1) *walking proudly, with the
nose high in the air*: Ov. (2) *lazy*: Quint.

rĕsurgo -surgere -surrexi -surrectum, *to rise
up again, appear again.*
    LIT., herba resurgens, Ov.; resurgam
(from bed), Ov.; arbor, urbs, Tac.
    TRANSF., regna Troiae, Verg.; amor, Verg.;
cum res Romana contra spem votaque eius
velut resurgeret, Liv.; legiones in ultionem,
Tac.

rĕsuscĭto -are, *to revive, resuscitate*: veterem
iram, Ov.

rĕsūtus -a -um, *ripped open*: Suet.

rĕtardātĭo -ōnis, f. (retardo), *a hindering*: Cic.

rĕtardo -are, *to slow down, retard, impede.*
LIT., aliquem in via, Cic.; motūs stellarum
retardantur, Cic.; Verg. TRANSF., celeritatem persequendi, Cic.; animos atque
impetūs, Cic.; aliquem a scribendo, Cic.; Ov.

rĕtaxo -are, *to censure*: Suet.

rētĕ -is, n. *a net.* LIT., both for fishes and for
animals: retia ponere cervis, Verg.; retia
tendere, Ov.; ex araneolis aliae quasi rete
texunt, Cic. TRANSF., amoris, Lucr.; Prop.

rĕtĕgo -tĕgĕre -texi -tectum, *to uncover, reveal,
lay bare, open.*
    LIT., thecam nummariam, Cic.; homo
retectus, *not covered by a shield*, Verg.
    TRANSF., (1) *to make visible, to illuminate*:
orbem radiis, Verg. (2) *to bring to light,
disclose*: arcanum consilium, Hor.; caecum
scelus, Verg.

rĕtempto -are, *to try* or *attempt again*: fila
lyrae, Ov.; viam leti, Ov. With infin.: Ov.

rĕtendo -tendĕre -tendi -tensum and -tentum,
to slacken, unbend: arcum, Ov.

rĕtentĭo -ōnis, f. (retineo), *a keeping back,
holding in.* LIT., aurigae, Cic. TRANSF., *a
withholding*: adsensionis, Cic.

¹rĕtento -are (freq. of retineo), *to hold firmly
back, hold fast.* LIT., agmen, Liv.; caelum a
terris, *to keep apart*, Lucr. TRANSF., *to
preserve, maintain*: sensūs hominum vitasque,
Cic. poet.

²rĕtento=retempto; q.v.

rĕtentus -a -um. (1) partic. from retendo;
q.v. (2) partic. from retineo; q.v.

rĕtexo -texĕre -texŭi -textum, *to unweave,
unravel.*
    LIT., quasi Penelope telam retexens, Cic.;
Ov.
    TRANSF., (1) *to undo, diminish*: dum luna
quater plenum tenuata retexuit orbem, Ov.
(2) *to reverse*: properata retexite fata, Ov.;
Verg. (3) *to dissolve, cancel, annul*: istius
praeturam, Cic.; orationem, *retract*, Cic.;
scriptorum quaeque, *to revise, correct*, Hor.

rētĭārĭus -i, m. (rete), *a fighter with a net,
a gladiator who had to try to entangle his
opponent*: Mart., Suet.

rĕtĭcentĭa -ae, f. (reticeo), *a keeping silent.*
In gen.: vestra virtus neque oblivione eorum
qui nunc sunt, neque reticentiā posterorum
sepulta esse poterit, Cic.; poena reticentiae,
for keeping silent, Cic. Esp. as rhet. t. t., *a
sudden pause* (Gr. ἀποσιώπησις): Cic., Quint.

rĕtĭcĕo -ēre (re/taceo). (1) intransit., *to keep
silence*: cum Sulpicius reticuisset, Cic.; de
iniuriis, Cic.; with dat., *to give no answer to*:
Liv., Tac. (2) transit., *to keep silent about*:
cogitationes suas, Cic.; quod ii, qui ea
patefacere possent, reticuissent, Cic. L.
Pass.: reticetur formula, Ov.

rētĭcŭlātus -a -um (reticulum), *net-like,
reticulated*: Varr., Plin.

rētĭcŭlum -i, n. (dim. of rete), *a little net.*
(1) *for catching fish*: Pl. (2) *a net-bag, bag of
net-work*: reticulum plenum rosae, Cic.;
reticulum panis, Hor. (3) *a hair-net*: Juv.

rētĭnācŭla -orum, n. pl. (retineo), *a rope,
cable*: Verg., Liv.

rĕtĭnens -entis, partic. from retineo; q.v.

rĕtĭnentĭa -ae, f. (retineo), *a retaining in the
memory, recollection*: Lucr.

rĕtĭnĕo -tĭnēre -tĭnŭi -tentum (re/teneo).
    (1) *to hold back, hold fast, detain.* LIT., of
persons: concilium dimittit, Liscum retinet,
Caes.; nisi iam profecti sunt, retinebis
homines, Cic.; of things: lacrimas, Ov.;
manus ab ore, Ov. TRANSF., *to keep back,
restrain*: moderari cursum atque in sua
potestate retinere, Cic.; retinere in officio,
Cic.; animos in fide, Liv.; gaudia, Ov.;
aegre sunt retenti, quin oppidum inrumpe-
rent, Caes.
    (2) *to keep, reserve, maintain.* LIT.,
armorum parte tertiā celatā atque in oppido
retentā, Caes. Esp. *to hold against opposition*:
oppidum, Caes. TRANSF., ut amicos ob-
servantiā, rem parsimoniā retineret, Cic.;
statum suum, Cic.; memoriam suae pristinae virtutis, Caes.; aliquid memoriā, Cic.;
Hor.
    ¶ Hence partic. **rĕtĭnens** -entis, as adj.
with genit., *tenacious*: sui iuris dignitatisque,
Cic.; Tac.

rĕtinnĭo -ire, *to resound, to ring again*: in
vocibus nostrorum oratorum retinnit et
resonat quiddam urbanius, Cic.

rĕtōno -are, *to thunder back, to resound*: Cat.

rĕtorquĕo -torquēre -torsi -tortum, *to twist
back, bend back.* LIT., oculos saepe ad hanc
urbem, Cic.; caput in sua terga, Ov.; bracchia
tergo, *to bind behind the back*, Hor. TRANSF.,
mentem, Verg.

rĕtorrĭdus -a -um, *parched up, dried up*: Varr.,
Plin.

retractātĭo -ōnis, f. (retracto). (1) *refusal,
denial*: sine ulla retractatione, Cic. (2)
reconsideration: Sen.

retracto (retrecto) -are.
    (1) *to handle again, undertake anew.* LIT.,
ferrum, Verg.; arma, Liv.; cruda vulnera,
to reopen old wounds, Ov. TRANSF., verba
desueta, Ov.; augere dolorem retractando,
Cic. L.; aliquid diligenter, *to reconsider*, Cic.
    (2) *to draw back, to refuse, be reluctant*:
Cic., Verg., Liv.; with acc., *to withdraw*:
dicta, Verg.

retractus -a -um, partic. from retraho; q.v.

retrăho -trăhĕre -trāxi -tractum, *to draw back, drag back.* LIT., manum, Cic.; Hannibalem in Africam, Cic.; se ab ictu, Ov.; aliquem ex fuga, Sall. TRANSF., (1) *to hold back, withdraw:* consules a foedere, Cic.; retrahere aliquid suspicio fuit, Liv.; se retraxit, ne pyxidem traderet, Cic. (2) *to draw on again, induce:* Treviros in arma, Tac.; in odium iudicis, Cic. ¶ Hence partic. (with compar.) **retractus** -a -um, *withdrawn;* hence *distant, remote:* retractior a mari murus, Liv.

retrĭbŭo -trĭbŭĕre -trĭbŭi -trĭbūtum, *to give again* or *give as due:* pro Siculo frumento acceptam pecuniam populo, Liv.; alicui fructum quem meruit, Cic.; Lucr.

retrō, adv. (from re and suff. -tro; cf. citro, ultro, intro), *backwards, back, behind.* LIT., redire, retro repetere, Liv.; retro respicere, Cic.; quod retro atque a tergo fieret, ne laboraret, Cic.; Verg., etc. TRANSF., (1) in time, *formerly, back:* et deinceps retro usque ad Romulum, Cic.; quodcunque retro est, Hor. (2) in other relations, *back, backwards:* Cic., Verg.

retrŏăgo -ăgĕre -ēgi -actum, *to drive back, lead back, reverse:* Plin., Quint.

retrorsum, adv. (retro/versum), *backwards, behind.* LIT., retrorsum vela dare, Hor. TRANSF., *in return, in reversed order:* deinde retrorsum vicissim, Cic.

retrūdo -trūdĕre -trūsum, *to push back, thrust back.* LIT., me invitum, Pl.; esp. in perf. partic. retrusus, *remote, obscure:* simulacra deorum iacent in tenebris ab isto retrusa atque abdita, Cic. TRANSF., voluntas abdita et retrusa, Cic.

rĕtundo rĕtundĕre rĕtŭdi (rettŭdi) rĕtūsum (rĕtunsum), *to hammer back, blunt, dull.* LIT., of pointed instruments: tela, Cic., Ov.; gladios, Cic.; stili mucronem, Cic. TRANSF., *to check* or *weaken:* impetum erumpentium, Liv.; linguas Aetolorum, Liv.; conlegam, Tac. ¶ Hence partic. **rĕtūsus (rĕtunsus)** -a -um, *dull, blunt.* LIT., ferrum, Verg.; Lucr., etc. TRANSF., *dull:* ingenium, Cic.

rĕus -i, m. and **rĕa** -ae, f. (res). (1) originally, *a party in a law-suit,* whether *plaintiff* or *defendant:* Pl., Cic. (2) in narrower sense, *a defendant.* LIT., reum facere aliquem, *to accuse,* Cic.; reum fieri, *to be accused,* Cic.; referre in reos (of the praetor), *to enter on the list of accused persons,* Cic. With genit.: rei capitalis, Cic.; capitis, Quint.; with de: Sextius qui est de vi reus, Cic. TRANSF., reus sine te criminis huius agor, *am accused,* Ov. (3) *bound for, answerable for,* with genit.: voti, *bound to fulfil my vow* (i.e., *having obtained the object of my wishes*), Verg.; suae partis tutandae, *answerable for,* Liv.

rĕvălesco -vălescĕre -vălŭi, *to become well again, be restored to health and strength.* LIT., ope qua revalescere possis, Ov. TRANSF., *to be restored, recover:* Laodicea revaluit propriis opibus, Tac.

rĕvĕho -vĕhĕre -vexi -vectum, *to carry back.* LIT., tela ad Graios, Ov.; praeda revecta,

brought back, Liv. Pass. as middle, revehi, *to drive back, ride back, sail back:* in castra, Liv.; Ithacam, Hor. TRANSF., ad superiorem aetatem revecti sumus (in discourse), *have gone back,* Cic.

rĕvello -vellĕre -velli -vulsum, *to tear, pull, pluck back* or *away.* LIT., tela de corpore, Cic.; caput a cervice, Verg.; saxum e monte, Ov.; morte ab aliquo revelli, *to be separated from,* Ov.; humum dente curvo, *to plough,* Ov. TRANSF., *to remove, banish:* consulatum ex omni memoria, Cic.

rĕvēlo -are, *to unveil, uncover, lay bare:* frontem, Tac.; os, Ov.; sacra, Ov.

rĕvĕnĭo -vĕnire -vēni -ventum, *to come back, return.* LIT., domum, Cic.; in urbem, Tac.; Pl. TRANSF., in gratiam, Pl.

rĕvērā, adv. from res; q.v.

rĕverbĕro -are, *to beat back, drive back:* Sen.

rĕvĕrendus -a -um, gerundive from revereor; q.v.

rĕvĕrens -entis, partic. from revereor; q.v.

rĕvĕrentĭa -ae, f. (revereor), *reverence, respect, fear, awe:* adversus homines, Cic.; legum, *for the laws:* Juv. Personif.: Ov.

rĕvĕrĕor -vĕrēri -vĕritus sum, dep. *to feel awe* or *respect, to revere, respect, fear:* adsentandi suspicionem, Cic.; multa adversa, Cic.; coetum virorum, Liv. ¶ Hence partic. **rĕvĕrens** -entis, *respectful, reverent:* erga patrem, Tac.; Plin. L. ¶ Adv. **rĕvĕrentĕr**, *reverently, respectfully:* Plin. L.; compar., reverentius, Tac.; superl., reverentissime, Suet., Plin. L. ¶ Gerundive **rĕvĕrendus** -a -um, *inspiring awe, venerable:* nox, Ov.; facies, Juv.

rĕverro (rĕvorro) -ĕre, *to sweep again:* Pl.

rĕversĭo (rĕvorsĭo) -ōnis, f. (reverto), *a turning back before the end of a journey* (reditus = *return after a journey completed*). LIT., reditu vel potius reversione, Cic.; consilium profectionis et reversionis meae, Cic.; sol binas in singulis annis reversiones ab extremo contrarias facit, Cic. TRANSF., *a return, recurrence:* tertianae febris et quartanae reversio, Cic.

rĕverto (rĕvorto) -vertĕre -verti, and in prose usually pass. in middle sense **rĕvertor (rĕvortor)** -verti -versus sum, *to turn back, return.* LIT., ex itinere, Cic.; ad aliquem, Caes.; Laodiceam, Cic.; cum victor a Mithridatico bello revertisset, Cic.; poet., of things: Tiberim reverti, Hor.; Lucr. TRANSF., *to return, come back:* ad sanitatem, *to a better frame of mind,* Caes.; Cic.; in gratiam cum aliquo, *to be reconciled with,* Liv.; poena reversura est in caput tuum, *doomed to fall,* Ov. Esp. in speaking, *to return, revert:* ad propositum revertar, Cic.; ad id, unde digressi sumus, revertamur, Cic.

rĕvĭdĕo -ēre, *to see again:* Pl.

rĕvincĭo -vincire -vinxi -vinctum, *to tie back, bind fast.* LIT., iuvenem manūs post terga revinctum, Verg.; trabes, Caes.; zona de poste revincta, Ov. TRANSF., mentem amore, Cat.

rĕvinco -vincĕre -vīci -victum, *to beat back, subdue.* LIT., catervae consiliis iuvenis revictae, Hor.; Lucr., Tac. TRANSF., *to refute:* aliquem, Cic., Tac.; crimina, Liv.

rĕvīresco -vīrescĕre -vīrŭi, *to grow green again.*
Lit., silvae, Ov.; arbor, Tac. Transf., *to grow strong, flourish again, revive*: senatum ad auctoritatis pristinae spem revirescere, Cic.; Tac.

rĕvīso -ĕre.
(1) intransit., *to pay a fresh visit, return.* Lit., ad stabulum, Lucr. Transf., furor revisit, *returns*, Lucr.
(2) transit., *to come to see again, revisit.* Lit., revise nos aliquando, Cic.; domos, Liv.; Verg. Transf., multos Fortuna, Verg.

rĕvīvisco -vīviscĕre -vixi, *to come to life again, revive.* Lit., Ter., Cic., Liv. Transf., reviviscere memoriam ac desiderium mei, Cic. L.

rĕvŏcābĭlis -e (revoco), *that can be revoked or called back*: Ov., Sen.

rĕvŏcāmen -inis, n. (revoco), *a calling back, recall*: Ov.

rĕvŏcātĭo -ōnis, f. (revoco), *a calling back.* Lit., a bello, Cic. Transf., revocatio ad contemplandas voluptates, Cic. In rhetoric, *a withdrawing, revocation*: verbi, Cic.

rĕvŏco -are, *to call again* or *back; to recall.*
Lit., in gen.: aliquem ex itinere, Cic.; qui me revocastis, *out of exile*, Cic.; qui non revocaturus esset, *not likely to invite back*, Cic.; with things as objects: oculos, Ov.; pedem, Verg.; gradum, Verg. Esp. (1) as milit. t. t., *to recall* troops, from leave, etc.: legiones ab opere, Caes.; Cic., Verg., Liv. (2) as polit. and legal t. t., *to summon again before a court of justice*, etc.: hominem revocat populus, Cic. (3) as theatrical t. t., *to encore*: cum saepius revocatus vocem obtudisset, Cic.; primos tres versus, Cic.; impers.: millies revocatum est, Cic.
Transf., (1) *to call back, bring back again, recover*: studia longo intervallo intermissa, *to take up again*, Cic.; se ad industriam, Cic.; se revocare, *to collect oneself*, Cic.; aliquem a tanto scelere, Cic.; omnia ad suam potestatem, Cic.; abi, quo blandae iuvenum te revocant preces, Hor. (2) *to apply to, refer to*: rem ad illam rationem coniecturamque revocabant, Cic. (3) *to recall, revoke*: facta, Ov.

rĕvŏlo -are, *to fly back*: dux gruum revolat, Cic.; revolat telum, Ov.

rĕvŏlūbĭlis -e (revolvo), *that can be rolled back*: pondus, Ov.; Prop.

rĕvolvo -volvĕre -volvi -vŏlūtum, *to roll backwards.*
Lit., in gen.: auster fluctūs, Tac.; usually with reflex., or pass. in middle sense: draco revolvens seso, Cic.; revolutus equo, *falling down from*, Verg.; ter revoluta toro est, Verg.; revoluta dies, *returning*, Verg. Esp., *to unroll* or *open a book*: Origines (a work of Cato's), Liv.; loca iam recitata, Hor.; Quint.
Transf., (1) act., *to go over again* (as in re-reading a book): iter omne, Verg.; visa, Ov.; dicta factaque secum, Tac. (2) esp. pass. in middle sense, *to roll back, come round again in due course*: omnia ad communes rerum atque generum summas revolventur, *will be brought back to*, Cic.; in speaking: ut ad illa elementa revolvar, Cic.; in veterem figuram, Verg.; ad dispensationem inopiae, Liv.

rĕvŏmo -vŏmĕre -vŏmŭi, *to vomit up, disgorge*: fluctūs, Verg.; Lucr., Ov.

rĕvorro = reverro; q.v.
rĕvorsio = reversio; q.v.
rĕvorto = reverto; q.v.
rēx rēgis, m. (rego), *ruler, king, prince.*
Lit., (1) at Rome. Of the original kings: Liv., etc. Later at Rome, of certain officials, such as rex sacrorum, rex sacrificiorum, Cic.; sacrificus, Liv.; sacrificulus, Liv., *a priest who performed the sacrifices which at first the kings performed.* Otherwise, under the republic, in a bad sense, *an unconstitutional ruler, despot, absolute monarch, tyrant*: rex populi Romani, i.e. *Caesar*, Cic.; decem reges aerarii, Cic.; Caes., Hor. (2) outside Rome: rex Deiotarus, Cic.; rex regum (of Agamemnon), Liv.; absol.: rex, of the Parthian king, Suet.; of the Persian king (like Gr. βασιλεύς), Nep.; regem deligere, creare, constituere, Cic.
Transf., (1) of gods: rex divum atque hominum, *or* deorum, *Jupiter*, Verg.; rex aquarum, *Neptune*, Ov.; rex Stygius, *Pluto*, Verg. (2) of a nation: populum late regem, Verg. (3) of royal persons, *a prince, member of the royal family*: reges excitos, *the king and queen*, Liv.; direptis bonis regum, Liv. (4) *a rich man*, esp. *a patron*: Pl., Hor. (5) in gen., *head, chief, leader*; of animals: rex apum, Verg.; of rivers: rex Eridanus, *chief stream in Italy*, Verg.

Rhădămanthus -i, m. (Ῥαδάμανθος), *son of Jupiter, brother of Minos, a judge in the lower world.*
Rhaeti = Raeti; q.v.
Rhamnes = Ramnes; q.v.
Rhamnūs -nuntis, f. (Ῥαμνοῦς), *a village of Attica, where the goddess Nemesis was worshipped.*
¶ Hence adj. **Rhamnūsĭus** -a -um: virgo, Cat., *or* simply, Rhamnusia, Ov., *Nemesis*; subst. **Rhamnūsis** -ĭdis, f. *Nemesis*: Ov.
rhapsōdĭa -ae, f. (ῥαψῳδία), *a rhapsody*: secunda, *the second book of the Iliad*, Nep.
¹**Rhēa** (**Rēa**) **Silvĭa**, *daughter of King Numitor of Alba, mother of Romulus and Remus by Mars.*
²**Rhĕa** -ae, f. (Ῥέα), *an old name of Cybele.*
rhēda = raeda; q.v.
rhēdārĭus = raedarius; q.v.
Rhēgĭum = Regium; q.v.
Rhēmi = Remi; q.v.
Rhēnus -i, m. *the Rhine*; in poets, meton., *the people dwelling on the Rhine.* Adj. **Rhēnānus** -a -um, *belonging to the Rhine.*
rhētor -ŏris, m. (ῥήτωρ). (1) *a teacher of rhetoric, a rhetorician*: Cic., Mart., Tac. (2) *an orator*: Nep.
rhētŏrĭcus -a -um (ῥητορικός), *of a rhetorician, rhetorical*: mos, ars, libri, doctores, Cic.
¶ As subst. **rhētŏrĭca** -ae *and* **rhētŏrĭcē** -ēs f. (ῥητορική), *the art of oratory*: Cic., Quint.; m. pl. **rhētŏrĭci** -orum, *teachers of rhetoric*: Cic.; *books on rhetoric*: Quint.; n. pl. **rhētŏrĭca** -ōrum, *a work on rhetoric*: Cic.
¶ Adv. **rhētŏrĭcē**, *rhetorically, oratorically*: Cic.
rhīnŏcĕrōs -ōtis, m. (ῥινόκερως), *a rhinoceros.* Lit., nasum rhinocerotis habere, Mart.; Plin., Suet. Transf., *a vessel made of the horn of the rhinoceros*: Juv.
rhō, n. indecl. (ῥῶ), *the Greek name of the letter R*: Cic.

Rhŏdănus -i, m. ('Ροδανός), *a river in Gaul* (now *the Rhône*): Rhodani potor, *a dweller on the banks of the Rhône*, Hor.

Rhŏdĭus, see Rhodus.

Rhŏdŏpē -ēs, f. ('Ροδόπη), *a mountain range in Thrace* (now *Despoto Dagh*).

¶ Hence adj. **Rhŏdŏpēĭus** -a -um, *Thracian*: vates, heros, Orpheus, Ov.

Rhŏdus (-ŏs) -i, f. ('Ρόδος), *Rhodes, an island off the south coast of Asia Minor, famous for its trade, its school of rhetoric, and its Colossus.*

¶ Hence adj. **Rhŏdĭus** -a -um, *Rhodian*; m. pl. as subst. **Rhŏdĭi** -ōrum, *the Rhodians*: Cic.; also adj. **Rhŏdĭensĭs** -e, *Rhodian*.

Rhoetēum ('Ροίτειον), *a promontory in the Troad.*

¶ Hence adj. **Rhoetēus** -a -um, *Rhoetean*; n. as subst. Rhoeteum -i, *the sea near Rhoeteum*: Ov.; poet.=*Trojan*: ductor, Aeneas, Verg.

Rhoetus (Rhoecus) -i, m. (1) *a giant*: Hor. (2) *a centaur*: Verg.

rhombus (-ŏs) -i, m. (ῥόμβος). (1) *a magician's circle*: Prop., Ov. (2) *the turbot*: Hor., etc.

rhomphaea (rumpĭa) -ae, f. *a long javelin*: Liv.

rhythmĭcus -i, m. (ῥυθμικός), *one who teaches the art of preserving rhythm in composition*: Cic., Quint.

rhythmus (-os) -i, m. (ῥυθμός), *rhythm, time, harmony*, either in music or speech: Quint.

rhŷtĭum -i, n. (ῥύτιον), *a drinking-horn*: Mart.

rīca -ae, f. *a veil*: Pl.

rīcĭnum -i, n. (rica), *a small veil* worn especially as an article of mourning: Cic.

rictus -ūs, m. and **rictum** -i, n. (ringor), sing. or plur., *the open mouth*; of man, esp. laughter: risu diducere rictum, Hor.; Cic., Ov.; of animals: rictūs Cerberei, Ov.

rīdĕo rīdēre rīsi rīsum.

(1) intransit., *to laugh*. LIT., in gen.: ridere convivae, cachinnare ipse Apronius, Cic.; in stomacho ridere, *to laugh grimly*, Cic.; with internal acc.: multum, Pl.; pass. impers.: ridetur, *there is laughter*, Hor. Esp., *to laugh* or *smile in a friendly manner*: cui non risere parentes, *upon whom*, Verg.; with internal acc.: dulce, Cat., Hor. TRANSF., *to look cheerful, look bright*: omnia nunc rident, Verg.; domus ridet argento, Hor.; with dat., *to smile for, to please*: ille terrarum mihi praeter omnes angulus ridet, Hor.

(2) transit., *to laugh at*, either pleasantly or otherwise: aliquem, Pl., Hor., Cic. L.; ioca tua, Cic. L.; periuria ridet amantum Iuppiter, Ov. Pass.: non sal sed natura ridetur, Cic.; Pyrrhi ridetur largitas a consule, Cic.

rīdĭbundus -a -um (rideo), *laughing*: Pl.

rīdĭcŭlārĭus -a -um (ridiculus), *laughable, droll*. N. pl. as subst. **rīdĭcŭlārĭa** -ōrum, *drolleries*: Pl.

rīdĭcŭlōsus -a -um (ridiculus), *laughable, droll*; superl.: Pl.

rīdĭcŭlus (rideo), *exciting laughter*. (1) in a good sense, *droll, humorous, funny*: cavillator facie magis quam facetiis ridiculus, Cic. L.; with infin.: (Porcius) ridiculus totas simul absorbere placentas, Hor. (2) in a bad sense, *laughable, absurd, ridiculous*: insania quae

ridicula aliis, Cic.; ridiculum poema, Hor.; ridiculum est, with infin., Cic.

¶ As subst., m. **rīdĭcŭlus** -i, *a joker, jester*: Pl., Ter.; n. **rīdĭcŭlum** -i, *a thing to laugh at, joke, jest*: ridiculi causa, Pl.; per ridiculum dicere, Cic.; plur.: sententiose ridicula dicere, Cic.

¶ Adv. **rīdĭcŭlē**. (1) in a good sense, *jokingly, humorously*: Cic. (2) in a bad sense, *ridiculously, absurdly*: homo ridicule insanus, Cic.

rĭgens -entis, p. adj. (from rigeo), *stiff, unbending*: aqua, *frozen*, Mart.

rĭgĕo -ēre (connected with frigeo), *to be stiff, to stiffen*.

LIT., esp. with cold: rigere frigore, Cic.; animalia gelu, Liv.; terga boum plumbo insuto ferroque rigebant, Verg.; lorica ex aere, Verg.; sine frondibus arbos, Ov.; cervix riget horrida, Ov.

TRANSF., of hair, *to stand on end*: gelido comae terrore rigebant, Ov.

rĭgesco rigescĕre rĭgŭi (rigeo), *to grow stiff*. LIT., esp. with cold: vestes rigescunt, Verg. TRANSF., of hair, *to stand on end*: metu capillos riguisse, Ov.

rĭgĭdus -a -um (rigeo), *stiff, unbending, rigid, hard*.

LIT., esp. from cold: tellurem Boreā rigidam movere, Verg.; artūs morte, Lucr.; crura, Cic.; cervix, Liv.; silex, Ov.; ensis, Verg.

TRANSF., (1) *making stiff*: frigus, mors, Lucr. (2) *stern, hard, inflexible*: innocentia, Liv.; vultus, mores, Ov.; censor, Ov.

¶ Adv. **rĭgĭdē**, *stiffly*. LIT., Sen. TRANSF., *severely*: Ov.

rĭgo -are.

(1) *to lead* or *conduct water*. LIT., aquam per agros, Liv. TRANSF., hinc motūs per membra rigantur, *flow*, Lucr.

(2) *to wet, moisten, bedew*. LIT., lucum fons perenni rigabat aquā, Liv.; ora lacrimis, fletibus, Verg., Ov. TRANSF., lux terras, Lucr.; Prop.

rĭgor -ōris, m. (rigeo), *stiffness, rigidity, hardness*. LIT., esp. of *rigidity* or *numbness produced by cold*: torpentibus rigore membra, Liv. In gen.: auri, Lucr.; ferri, Verg. TRANSF., *sternness, severity*: Ov.

rĭgŭus -a -um (rigo). (1) act., *watering, irrigating*: amnes, Verg. (2) pass., *well-watered, irrigated*: hortus, Ov.

rīma -ae, f. (connected with ringor), *a crack, cleft, fissure*: rimas agere, *to be cracked*, Cic. L., Ov.; explere, Cic.; naves rimis dehiscunt, *spring a leak*, Verg.; poet.: ignea rima micans, *the lightning*, Verg.

rīmor -ari, dep. (rima), *to cleave*.

LIT., terram rastris, Verg.

TRANSF., *to probe, pry into, search, examine*; physically: vultur viscera epulis, Verg.; haruspex pectora pullorum, Juv.; of abstr. things: secreta, Tac.; Cic.

rīmōsus -a -um (rima), *full of cracks, chinks, fissures*. LIT., cymba, Verg. TRANSF., quae rimosa bene deponuntur in aure, *that cannot keep a secret*, Hor.

ringor -i, dep. *to show the teeth*. TRANSF., *to snarl, growl, be angry*: Ter., Hor., Sen.

rīpa -ae, f. *the bank of a river*. LIT., ripa magni fluminis, Cic.; Verg., etc.; plur.:

ripae, of places along one bank of a river, Liv. TRANSF., *the shore of the sea*: Hor.

rīpŭla -ae, f. (dim. of ripa), *a little bank* (of a river): Cic. L.

riscus -i, m. (ῥίσκος), *a box, chest, trunk*: Ter.

rīsĭo -ōnis, f. (rideo), *laughing, laughter*: Pl.

rīsor -ōris, m. (rideo), *a laugher, mocker*: Hor.

rīsus -ūs, m. (rideo), *laughing, laughter*; in a bad sense, *jeering, ridicule*. LIT., risus consecutus est, non in te, sed in errorem tuum, Cic. L.; miros risus edere, Cic.; risum movere, commovere, excitare, *to cause laughter*, Cic.; risūs captare, *to try to raise a laugh*, Cic.; risum continere, *to check*, Cic.; risu cognoscere matrem, Verg. TRANSF., *an object of laughter*: deus omnibus risus erat, Ov.; Liv.

rītě, adv. (connected with ritus). LIT., as relig. t. t., *in due form, with proper ceremonies*: deos colere, Cic.; Verg., Liv., etc. TRANSF., (1) *properly, duly, fitly, rightly*: deum rite beatum dicere, Cic.; rebus rite paratis, Verg. (2) *fortunately, luckily*: propinquare augurium, Verg.; Hor. (3) *in the ordinary manner*: quorum plaustra vagas rite trahunt domos, Hor.; Verg.

rītus -ūs, m. *a religious custom, usage, ceremony, rite*. LIT., Cic., Liv., Verg. TRANSF., in gen., *a custom, usage*: ritus Cyclopum, Ov.; Liv. Esp. abl., ritu, with a genit., *after the manner of, as*: pecudum ritu, latronum ritu, Cic.; Hor., Liv., etc.

rīvālis -is, m. (rivus), *one who uses a brook in common with another*. TRANSF., *a rival in love, rival suitor*: Pl., Ov., etc.; prov.: se amare sine rivali, Cic., Hor.

rīvālĭtās -ātis, f. (rivalis), *rivalry* (in love): Cic.

rīvŭlus -i, m. (dim. of rivus), *a small brook, rivulet*; fig.: Cic.

rīvus -i, m. *a stream*. LIT., (1) of water: a fonte deductio, Cic.; rivos ducere, Ov.; Verg., etc. (2) of other fluids: lactis, Hor.; lacrimarum, Ov.; rivis currentia vina, Verg. TRANSF., *a stream, course*: fortunae, Hor.

rixa -ae, f. *a fight, quarrel, brawl*. LIT., rixa ac prope proelium fuit, Liv.; Cic., Hor., Juv. TRANSF., (1) *strife, contention*: Academiae nostrae cum Zenone magna rixa est, Cic. (2) *fighting between animals*: Ov.

rixor -ari, dep. (rixa), *to quarrel, brawl*. LIT., cum aliquo de amicula, Cic.; Lucr. TRANSF., *to contend, disagree*: Hor., Mart.

rōbīgĭnōsus -a -um (robigo), *rusty*. LIT., Pl. TRANSF., robiginosis dentibus cuncta rodit, *with envious teeth*, Mart.

rōbīgo (**rūbīgo**) -ĭnis, f. (robus=ruber), *rust*. LIT., on metal: scabra robigine pila, Verg.; ferrum robigine roditur, Ov. TRANSF., (1) physical; *blight* on plants, *mildew*: Verg.; *film* on the teeth: Ov. (2) *inaction*, mental *rust*: ingenium longā robigine laesum torpet, Ov.

¶ Personif. **Rōbīgo** (**Rūbīgo**) -ĭnis, f. [referred to by some authors as **Rōbīgus** (**Rūbīgus**) -i, m.], *the deity invoked by the Romans to preserve their grain from mildew*.

¶ Hence subst. **Rōbīgālĭa** -ĭum, n. *the festival of the deity Robigo, celebrated on the 25th of April*.

rōbŏrěus -a -um (robur), *oaken*: Ov.

rōbŏro -are (robur), *to strengthen, make firm*. LIT., artus, Lucr. TRANSF., pectora, Hor.; gravitatem (animi), Cic.

rōbur (**rōbus**, archaic) -ŏris, n. (connected with ῥώννυμι, ῥώμη), *hard wood*; esp., *oak, oak-wood*. LIT., quercus antiquo robore, Verg.; sapiens non est e saxo sculptus aut e robore dolatus, Cic.; Ov. TRANSF., (1) of things made of oak or other hard wood: in robore accumbunt, *on oaken benches*, Cic.; robur sacrum, *the Trojan horse*, Verg.; robur praefixum ferro, *a lance*, Verg. (2) *the underground dungeon in the prison of Servius Tullius at Rome*, also called the Tullianum: Lucr., Hor., Liv., Tac. (3) as a quality, *hardness, strength, firmness*: robora ferri, Lucr., Verg.; of human physical strength: neque his ipsis tantum umquam virium aut roboris fuit, Liv.; Cic., Verg.; of intellectual or moral strength: alter virtutis robore firmior quam aetatis, Cic.; robur incredibile animi, Cic.; Hor., Liv. (4) concr., *the pick, flower, pith of anything*: versaris in optimorum civium vel flore vel robore, Cic.; senatūs, Liv.; quod fuit roboris duobus proeliis interiit, Caes.; robora pubis, Verg.

rōbustus -a -um, adj. (with compar.) (robur), *of hard wood*, esp. *of oak, oaken*. LIT., stipites, Liv. TRANSF., physically or morally *strong, powerful, firm*: si esses usu atque aetate robustior, Cic.; animus, Cic.; respublica, Cic.

rōdo rōděre rōsi rōsum, *to gnaw, nibble at*. LIT., vivos ungues, Hor.; Cic., Ov. TRANSF., (1) *to eat away, corrode, consume*: ferrum (robigo), Ov. (2) *to disparage, backbite, slander*: absentem amicum, Hor.; absol.: in conviviis rodunt, Cic.

rŏgālis -e (rogus), *of the funeral pile*: Ov.

rŏgātĭo -ōnis, f. (rogo), *an asking*. (1) as polit. t. t., *a proposed law, a bill laid before the people*: Caecilia, *proposed by Caecilius*, Cic.; rogationem ad populum ferre, Caes.; ferre de, with abl., Cic., Liv.; perferre, Cic. L., Liv. (2) in gen., *a question*: Cic., Quint. (3) *a request, entreaty*: Cic.

rŏgātiuncŭla -ae, f. (dim. of rogatio). (1) *an unimportant proposal* or *bill*: Cic. (2) *a little question*: Cic.

rŏgātor -ōris, m. (rogo), *one who asks*. (1) *the proposer of a bill*: Cic. L. (2) *an officer who took the votes in the comitia, a polling-clerk*: Cic. (3) *a beggar*: Mart.

rŏgātū, abl. as from rogatus, m. (rogo), *at the request*: rogatu tuo, Cic.; eius rogatu, Cic.

rŏgĭtātĭo -ōnis, f. (rogito), *a proposed law*: Pl.

rŏgito -are (freq. of rogo), *to ask* or *inquire frequently* or *eagerly*: rogitantes alii alios Liv.; quid rei sint, rogitant, Liv.; multa super Priamo, Verg.; Pl., Ter.

rŏgo -are, *to ask, inquire, question*. LIT., in gen., with the person asked in the acc., and the question expressed by another acc., or by a phrase with de, or by an indir. quest. clause: quid me istud rogas? Cic. quae de te ipso rogaro, Cic.; rogatus de cybaea, quid responderit, Cic.; Pl., Ter. Hor., etc.

Esp. (1) as polit. t. t.: a, rogare aliquem

sententiam, *to ask a person his opinion*: quos priores sententiam rogabat, Cic.: **b**, rogare populum *or* legem, *to ask the people about a law*, hence, *to propose a law, introduce a bill*: Cic., Liv.: **c**, rogare (populum) magistratum, *to propose a magistrate to the choice of the people, offer a person for election*: ut consules roger praetor vel dictatorem dicat, Cic. **(2)** as milit. t. t.: rogare milites sacramento, *to administer an oath to the troops*, Caes.

TRANSF., *to ask a favour, entreat, request*; with the person asked usually in the acc. (rarely abl., after de *or* ab), and the favour expressed by another acc., or by clause with ut *or* ne and subj., or subj. alone: otium divos rogat, Hor.; id ut facias, te etiam atque etiam rogo, Cic. L.; Caesar consolatus rogat finem orandi faciat, Caes.

rŏgus -i, m. *a funeral pile*. LIT., rogum exstruere, Cic.; aliquem in rogum imponere, Cic. TRANSF., *destruction, death*: carmina diffugiunt rogos, Ov.; Prop.

Rōma -ae, f. *Rome*.

¶ Hence adj. **Rōmānus** -a -um, *Roman*: ludi, *the oldest games at Rome* (also called ludi magni), Cic.; Romano more, *straightforwardly, candidly*, Cic. L.; Romanum est, *it is the Roman custom*, foll. by acc. and infin., Liv. M. as subst., sing. and plur. *a Roman, the Romans*: Cic., Liv., etc.

Rŏmŭlus -i, m. *son of Ilia or Rhea Silvia and Mars, twin brother of Remus, the founder and first king of Rome, worshipped after his death under the name of Quirinus.*

¶ Hence adj. **Rŏmŭlĕus** -a -um, *of Romulus*: fera, *the she-wolf which suckled Romulus*, Juv.; adj. **Rŏmŭlus** -a -um, *belonging to Romulus*: ficus=Ruminalis, Ov.; Verg.; plur. subst. **Rŏmŭlĭdae** -ārum, poet., *the Romans*: Lucr., Verg.

rŏrārii -ōrum, m. pl. (ros), *a kind of light-armed troops, skirmishers*: Pl., Liv.

rŏrĭdus -a -um (ros), *bedewed*: Prop.

rŏrĭfĕr -fĕra -fĕrum (ros/fero), *dew-bringing*: Lucr.

rŏro -are (ros).

(1) intransit., *to cause dew, to drop or distil dew*. LIT., cum rorare Tithonia coniux coeperit, Ov. TRANSF., *to drip, drop, be moist*: pocula rorantia, Cic.; rorant pennae, Ov.; capilli rorantes, Ov.; rorabant sanguine vepres, Verg.

(2) transit., *to bedew, cover with dew.* LIT., roratae rosae, Ov. TRANSF., **a**, *to moisten, water*: ora lacrimis, Lucr.: **b**, *to drip, let fall in drops*: roratae aquae, Ov.

rōs rōris, m.

(1) *dew*. LIT., ros nocturnus, Caes.; Lucr., Verg., etc. TRANSF., poet., *moisture*: lympharum, Lucr.; rores pluvii, Hor.; stillare ex oculis rorem, Hor.; *of perfume*: Arabus, Ov.; Verg.

(2) ros marinus, or in one word rosmarinus, *rosemary*, Verg., Hor.; poet.: ros maris, Ov., or simply ros, Verg.

rŏsa -ae, f. (connected with ῥόδον), *a rose*. LIT., plena rosarum atria, Ov.; Cic., Hor., etc.

TRANSF., **(1)** sing. as collect.=*roses, a garland of roses*: reticulum plenum rosae, Cic.; in rosa, *crowned with roses*, Cic.; Hor.

(2) *a rose-tree*: Verg., Hor. **(3)** as a term of endearment: mea rosa, *my rosebud*, Pl.

rŏsārius -a -um (rosa), *made of roses*: Plin. N. as subst. **rŏsārĭum** -i, *a rose-garden*: Verg., Prop., Ov.

roscĭdus -a -um (ros), *bedewed, dewy*. LIT., mala, Verg.; dea, *Aurora*, Ov. TRANSF., **(1)** mella, *dripping like dew*, Verg. **(2)** *moistened, watered*: Hernica saxa rivis, Verg.

Roscĭus -a -um, *name of a Roman gens. Its most celebrated members were*:

(1) Sex. Roscius, *of Ameria, accused of the murder of his father, and defended by Cicero.*

(2) Q. Roscius, *of Lanuvium, a celebrated actor*; appellat., a Roscius=*a master in his art*; hence, adj. **Roscĭānus** -a -um, *Roscian*: imitatio, Cic.

(3) L. Roscius Otho, *friend of Cicero, tribune of the people, proposer of a lex Roscia.*

Rōsĕa (Rōsĭa) -ae, f. *a district in the Sabine country, famous for the rearing of horses.*

¶ Hence adj. **Rōsĕus (Rōsĭus)** -a -um, *Rosean.*

rŏsētum -i, n. (rosa), *a garden of roses*: Varr., Verg.

rŏsĕus -a -um (rosa). **(1)** *made of roses, full of roses*: strophium, Verg. **(2)** *rose-coloured, rosy*: dea, *Aurora*, Ov.; Phoebus, Verg.; os (of Venus), Verg.; Lucr., Cat.

rosmărīnus, *see* ros.

rostrātus -a -um (rostrum), *having a beak, beaked, curved*: navis, Cic.; corona, *a crown ornamented with small figures of the beaks of ships, given to the person who first boarded an enemy's ship*, Plin.; hence, poet., *of Agrippa*: cui tempora navali fulgent rostrata coronā, *with the crown of honour on his brow*, Verg.; columna rostrata, *the pillar adorned with ships' prows, erected in the forum to commemorate a naval victory*, Liv.

rostrum -i, n. (rodo), *that which gnaws*; in birds, *the beak*; in other animals, *the snout*. LIT., Cic., Liv., etc.; *of human beings*: Pl. TRANSF., *of things resembling a beak or snout*; esp. *the curved end of a ship's prow, a ship's beak* (used for ramming other ships): Caes., Verg., Liv., etc. Hence plur. **rostra** -ōrum, *the speaker's platform or tribune in the forum* (so called because ornamented with the prows of the ships taken from Antium in 338 B.C.): escendere in rostra, Cic., Liv.; descendere de rostris, Cic.

rŏta -ae, f. *a wheel*. LIT., in gen.: Lucr., Verg., Hor., etc. Esp. **(1)** *a wheel for torture* (Gr. τροχός): in rotam escendere, Cic.; used often of the wheel of Ixion: rota orbis Ixionii, Verg. **(2)** *a potter's wheel*: currente rotā cur urceus exit? Hor.; Tib., Sen.

TRANSF., **(1)** poet., *a chariot*: pedibusve rotāve, Ov.; plur.: rotae, Verg. **(2)** *the sun's orb*: Lucr. **(3)** Fortunae rota, *the wheel, the vicissitudes of fortune*, Cic. **(4)** poet.: imparibus vecta Thalia rotis, *in the unequal alternation of hexameter and pentameter, i.e. in elegiac verse*, Ov.

rŏto -are (rota), *to cause to turn round like a wheel, to whirl round, swing round*. LIT., ensem fulmineum, *to brandish*, Verg.; telum, Liv.; pass. as middle, rotari, *to revolve, to roll round*: circum caput igne rotato, Ov.; Verg. TRANSF., sermone rotato, *rounded*, Juv.

rŏtŭla -ae, f. (dim. of rota), *a little wheel*: Pl., Plin.

rotundē, adv. from rotundus; q.v.

rŏtundo -are (rotundus), *to round, make round*. Lit., Cic. Transf., *to make up a round sum of money*: mille talenta rotundentur, Hor.

rŏtundus -a -um, adj. (with compar.) (rota), *round, circular*; sometimes *spherical*. Lit., caelum, Hor.; nihil rotundius, Cic.; prov.: mutat quadrata rotundis, *turns everything upside down*, Hor.
    Transf., *rounded, perfect, complete, self-contained*: in se ipso totus teres atque rotundus, Hor.; esp. of style: verborum apta et quasi rotunda constructio, Cic.
    ¶ Hence adv. **rŏtundē**, of style, *elegantly, smoothly*: Cic.

rŭbĕfăcĭo -făcĕre -fēci -factum (rubeo/facio), *to redden, make red*: Ov.

rŭbellus -a -um (dim. of ruber), *reddish, somewhat red*: Plin., Mart.

rŭbĕo -ēre (*see* ruber), *to be red*: sanguine litus, Ov.; Verg., etc. Esp. *to be red with shame, blush*: Cic., Hor.
    ¶ Hence partic. **rŭbens** -entis, *red*: uva, Verg.; Lucr., Hor., etc. Esp. *red with shame, blushing*: Tib.

rŭber -bra -brum (cf. ἐρυθρός), *red, ruddy*. In gen.: sanguis, Hor.; aequor rubrum oceani, *reddened by the setting sun*, Verg. Esp.: Rubrum Mare, *the Red Sea, the Arabian and Persian Gulfs*, Cic., Verg., Liv.; Oceanus ruber, *the Indian Ocean*, Hor.

rŭbesco -bescĕre -bui (rubeo), *to grow red, become red*: mare rubescebat radiis, Verg.; Ov.

¹**rŭbēta** -ae, f. (rubus), *a species of toad found in bramble-bushes*: Prop., Juv.

²**rŭbēta** -ōrum, n. (rubus), *bramble-thickets*: Ov.

¹**rŭbĕus** (**rŏbĕus**) -a -um (ruber), *red, reddish*: Varr.

²**rŭbĕus** -a -um (rubus), *made of bramble*: virga, Verg.

Rŭbi -ōrum, m. *a town in Apulia* (now *Ruvo*).

Rŭbīco -ōnis, m. *a small river in Italy, south of Ravenna* (now *Pisatello*). *Before the time of Augustus this marked the boundary between Italia and Gallia Cisalpina, and its crossing by Caesar was an act of war against the senate.*

rŭbĭcundŭlus -a -um (dim. of rubicundus), *somewhat red* (for shame): Juv.

rŭbĭcundus -a -um (rubeo), *red, ruddy*: Priapus, *painted red*, Ov.; matrona, Ov.; Ceres, Verg.

rŭbĭdus -a -um (ruber), *red, reddish*: Pl.

rŭbīgo=robigo; q.v.

rŭbor -ōris, m. (rubeo), *redness*.
    Lit., in gen.: fucati medicamenta candoris et ruboris, Cic.; ille fusus et candore mixtus rubor, Cic.; Tyrii rubores, Verg.; saepe suum fervens oculis dabat ira ruborem, Ov. Esp. *reddening from shame, a blush*: Masinissae rubor suffusus, Liv.; Cic., Ov.
    Transf., (1) *bashfulness, modesty*: Cic., Liv. (2) *shame, disgrace*: censoris iudicium ruborem adfert, Cic.; rubori esse, *or* rubor esse, Liv.

rubrīca -ae, f. (ruber), sc. terra, *red earth*; esp. *red ochre*. Lit., Pl., Hor. Transf., *a law with its title* (or *rubric*) *written in red*: Pers., Quint.

rŭbus -i, m. *a bramble-bush*. Lit., Caes., Verg., etc. Transf., *a blackberry*: Prop.

ructo -are, and **ructor** -ari, dep. *to belch*: Pl., Cic., Juv.; with acc., *to belch out*: versūs, Hor.; Mart., Juv.

ructus -ūs, m. (connected with ructo), *a belching*: Pl., Cic. L.

rŭdens -entis (rudo), m. (f.: Pl.), *a rope, halyard, sheet*: rudentis explicatio, Cic.; stridor rudentum, Verg.

Rŭdiae -ārum, f. *a town in Calabria, birth-place of Ennius*.
    ¶ Hence adj. **Rŭdīnus** -a -um, *of Rudiae*: Rudinus homo, i.e. *Ennius*, Cic.

rŭdĭārĭus -i, m. (¹rudis), *a gladiator who had been presented with a* rudis, i.e. *one who has served his time, a discharged gladiator*: Suet.

rŭdĭmentum -i, n. (¹rudis), *the first trial or beginning in anything, an attempt, essay*. In gen.: primum regni puerilis, Liv.; esp. milit. t. t.: militare, Liv.; belli, Verg.; rudimentum adulescentiae ponere, *to 'pass out' as a soldier, complete basic training*, Liv.

¹**rŭdis** -e, *rough, raw, unwrought, uncultivated*. Lit., rudis campus, Verg.; rudis indigestaque moles, chaos, Ov.; lana, *unspun*, Ov.
    Transf., (1) *roughly made*: hasta, Verg.; Ov. (2) *untried, undisciplined*: agna, Mart. (3) *unrefined, ignorant, unskilled, awkward*: consilium, Pl.; forma quaedam ingenii admodum impolita et plane rudis, Cic.; rudis et integer discipulus, Cic.; rude carmen, Hor. With in and the abl. or the abl. alone: in disserendo, Cic.; arte, Ov. With ad and the acc.: rudis ad pedestria bella gens, Liv.; Ov. With genit.: Graecarum litterarum, Cic.

²**rŭdis** -is, f. *a small stick*. (1) *a ladle, scoop*, used for stirring and mixing: Plin. (2) *a staff used by soldiers and gladiators in fencing exercises, a foil*: Liv., Ov. A staff of this kind was given to a gladiator on his discharge from service: tam bonus gladiator rudem tam cito accepisti? Cic.; hence the phrase rude donari, *to be discharged*, Hor., Ov.

rŭdo rŭdĕre rŭdīvi rŭdītum, *to bellow, roar*; of lions: Verg.; of asses, *to bray*: Ov.; of men: Verg.; of inanimate things: prora rudens *creaking, rattling*, Verg.

¹**rūdus** (**rōdus**) -ĕris, n. (1) *broken fragments of stone used for plastering*, etc.: Plin. (2) *rubbish from ruined buildings*: Tac.

²**rūdus**=raudus; q.v.

Rufrae -ārum, f. *a town in Campania, on the borders of Samnium*.

rūfŭlus -a -um (dim. of rufus), *reddish, somewhat red*: Pl.

rūfus -a -um (connected with ruber), *red, ruddy*: Pl., Ter., Mart.

rūga -ae, f. *a wrinkle in the face*; as a sign of age: non rugae auctoritatem adripere possunt Cic.; rugis et instanti senectae, Hor.; of sadness: nunc ruga tristis abit, Ov.; of anger rugas coegit, Ov.; populum rugis supercilio que decepit, Cic.

rūgo -are (ruga), *to be wrinkled*: Pl.

rūgōsus -a -um (ruga), *full of wrinkles, wrinkled*: genae, Ov.; cortex pōpuli, Ov. pellis, Hor.

rŭīna -ae, f. (ruo), *a falling down, collapse*. Lit., in gen., *fall*: iumentorum sarcina rumque, Liv.; caeli, Verg. Esp. *the falling down of a building*: turris, Caes.; Cic.

ruinosus   rusticulus

ruinam dare, *to fall down*, Verg.; trahere,
Verg.
  Transf., (1) in gen., *fall, ruin, collapse,
catastrophe, destruction*: rerum, Lucr.; urbis,
Liv.; ruinae fortunarum tuarum, Cic.; ille
dies utramque ducet ruinam, Hor. (2) concr.,
the ruins of a building, debris; gen. in plur.:
ruinae templorum, Liv.; Ov. (3) of persons,
a destroyer, overthrower, bane: reipublicae,
Cic.
rŭīnōsus -a -um (ruina), *going to ruin*. Lit.,
aedes, Cic. Transf., *ruined, fallen*: domus,
Ov.
Rullus -i, m., P. Servilius, *tribune of the
people, against whom Cicero delivered three
speeches.*
rŭmex -icis, f. *sorrel*: Pl., Verg.
rŭmĭfĭco -are (rumor/facio), *to report*: Pl.
Rūmĭna -ae, f. *a Roman goddess, whose temple
stood near the fig-tree under which the she-
wolf had suckled Romulus and Remus.*
  ¶ Hence adj. Rūmĭnālis: ficus, Liv.
(also called Rūmĭna ficus), *the fig-tree above-
mentioned.*
rūmĭnātĭo -ōnis, f. (rumino), *a chewing the
cud.* Lit., Plin. Transf., *a turning over in
the mind, ruminating*: Cic. L.
rūmĭno -are (rumen, *the throat*), *to chew the
cud, ruminate, chew over again*: bos herbas,
Verg.
rūmor -ōris, m.
  (1) in the phrase: rumore secundo, *with
favouring shout*, Enn., Verg., Hor.
  (2) *a report, rumour, common talk, hearsay*:
rumores incerti, Caes.; rumor multa fingebat,
Caes.; rumor multa perfert, Cic.; rumor
vulgatur, increbrescit, Liv. The purport of
the rumour is rarely expressed by a genit.:
belli civilis, Tac.; more often by de and the
abl.: graves de te rumores, Cic.; Caes., Liv.;
also by acc. and infin.: Ter., Cic. L., etc.;
or by tamquam and clause: Tac.
  (3) *common* or *general opinion, popular
judgment*: rumorem quendam et plausum
popularem esse quaesitum, Cic.; adverso
rumore esse, Liv.; Hor., Tac.
rumpo rumpĕre rūpi ruptum, *to break,
shatter, burst open.*
  Lit., ilia, Cat.; vincula, Cic., Verg., etc.;
pontem, *to break down*, Liv.; frigore saxa
hiems, Verg.; pass.: inflatas rumpi vesiculas,
Cic.
  Transf., (1) fig. *to break* or *burst*: licentiā
audacium rumpebar, Cic. L.; unde tibi
reditum certo subtemine Parcae rupere,
cut off, Hor. (2) esp. as milit. t. t., *to break
through*: ordines, mediam aciem, Liv.; Verg.
(3) *to force open*: ferro per hostes viam, Liv.;
eo cuneo viam, Liv. (4) *to cause to break
forth*: fontem, Ov.; of sounds: questūs,
Verg.; often reflex., se rumpere, and pass.
as middle, rumpi, *to break forth*: tantus se
nubibus imber ruperat, Verg. (5) *to destroy,
violate, annul, make void*: foedera, Lucr.,
Cic.; ius gentium, Liv.; nuptias, Hor.; Verg.
(6) *to break off, interrupt*: visum, Cic.;
somnum, Verg.; silentia, Lucr., Verg., Ov.;
rumpe moras, Verg.
rūmuscŭlus -i, m. (dim. of rumor), *a trifling
rumour, idle talk, gossip*: imperitorum
hominum rumusculos aucupari, Cic.
rūna -ae, f. *a species of missile, a dart*: Cic.

runco -are, *to weed, thin out*: Varr., Plin., Pers.
rŭo rŭĕre rŭi rŭtum, but fut. partic. rŭĭtūrus,
to rush, to hasten.
  (1) intransit.: a, *to rush down, fall down,
collapse.* Lit., of persons: ruebant victores
victique, Verg.; of things: ruit alto a culmine
Troia, Verg.; de montibus amnes, Verg.;
Lucr., Liv., etc. Transf., *to fall, be ruined*:
ruere illam rempublicam, Cic.; ratio, Lucr.;
Liv.: b, *to rush along.* Lit., of persons: in
castra, ad urbem, Liv.; of things: venti
ruunt, Verg.; ruit oceano nox, *hastens over*,
Verg. Transf., of persons: ad interitum,
Cic.; ruere in agendo, in dicendo, *to be
precipitate*, Cic.; of things: omnia fatis in
peius, Verg.
  (2) transit.: a, *to hurl down*: cumulos
harenae, Verg.; immanem molem volvuntque
ruuntque, Verg.: b, *to cast up*: spumas salis
aere, Verg.; cinerem et confusa ossa focis,
Verg.; unde divitias aerisque ruam acervos,
Hor. As legal t. t., rūta et caesa, and, by
asyndeton, rūta caesa, *everything on an estate
dug up* (ruta), *and fallen down* (caesa);
minerals and timber: Cic.
rūpes -is, f. (rumpo), *a rock, cliff*: Caes., Liv.,
etc.
ruptor -ōris, m. (rumpo), *a breaker, violator*:
foederis, Liv.; pacis, Tac.
rūrĭcŏla -ae, adj. (rus/colo), *inhabiting* or
cultivating the country: boves, Ov.; deus,
Priapus, Ov. M. as subst. rūrĭcŏla -ae, *an
ox*: Ov.
rūrĭgĕna -ae, m. (rus/gigno), *one born in the
country, a rustic*: Ov.
rūro -are and rūror -ari, dep. (rus), *to live in
the country*: Pl., Varr.
rursŭs and rursum (also rūsum), adv. (contr.
from revorsus, revorsum, i.e. reversus,
reversum), *backward, back.*
  Lit., in space: Pl., Ter. Transf., (1) *on
the other hand, on the contrary, in return*:
capiunt voluptates, capiunt rusum miserias,
Pl.; reddere rursus, Hor. (2) *again, once
more, afresh*: Caes., Cic., etc.
rūs rūris, n. *the country* (in opposition to the
town), *lands, a country-seat, farm, estate.*
  Lit., habes rus amoenum, Cic.; acc., rus,
to the country, Pl., Ter.; locative, ruri (or
rurĕ), *in the country*: ruri vivere, Cic.; Liv.,
etc.; abl., rurĕ, *from the country*, Pl., Ter.
In plur.: Verg., Hor., etc.
  Transf., *rusticity*: manent vestigia ruris,
Hor.
ruscum -i, n. *butcher's broom*: Verg.
Rūsellae -ārum, f. pl., *a town of Etruria.*
  Adj. Rūsellānus -a -um, *belonging to
Rusellae.*
russus -a -um, *red, russet*: Cat., Lucr.
rustĭcānus -a -um (rusticus), *of* or *in the
country, rustic*: vita rusticana, Cic.; homines
rusticani, Cic.
rustĭcātĭo -ōnis, f. (rusticor), *a living in the
country*: Cic.
rustĭcē, adv. from rusticus; q.v.
rustĭcĭtās -ātis, f. (rusticus), *rustic manners,
rusticity*, in good or bad sense: Plin., Ov.
rustĭcor -ari, dep. (rusticus), *to live in the
country, to rusticate*: Cic.
rustĭcŭlus -a -um (dim. of rusticus), *somewhat
rustic*: Mart. M. as subst. rustĭcŭlus -i,
a countryman, rustic: Cic.

[527]

rustĭcus -a -um (rus), *of* or *belonging to the country, rural, rustic.* LIT., praedium, Cic.; vita, Cic.; homo, *a countryman,* Cic.; mus, Hor. TRANSF., *rustic, country-like.* In a good sense, *plain, simple, homely*: mores, Cic. In a bad sense, *clownish, countrified, awkward, boorish*: rustica vox et agrestis, Cic.; Verg. As subst., m. **rustĭcus** -i, *a countryman.* LIT., Cic., Hor., etc. TRANSF., *a boor, clown*: Pl., Verg., Ov.; f. **rustĭca** -ae, *a country-girl*: Ov.

¶ Adv. (with compar.) **rustĭcē**, *in a countrified manner*: loqui, Cic.; Hor.

¹**rūta** -ae, f. (ῥυτή), *the herb rue.* LIT., Cic. L.; plur.: Ov. TRANSF., *bitterness, unpleasantness*: Cic. L.

²**rūta caesa,** *see* ruo.

rŭtābŭlum -i, n. (ruo), *a fire-shovel*: Suet.

rūtātus -a -um (¹ruta), *flavoured with rue*: Mart.

Rŭtilius -a -um, *the name of a Roman gens. Its most famous member was P. Rutilius Rufus, an orator and historian, consul in the time of Marius.*

rŭtĭlo -are (rutilus). (1) intransit., *to shine with a reddish gleam*: arma rutilare vident, Verg. (2) transit., *to make red*: comae rutilatae, Liv.; Tac.

rŭtĭlus -a -um (connected with ruber), *red, golden, auburn*: capilli, Ov.; ignis, Verg.; cruor, Ov.; fulgor, Cic.

rutrum -i, n. (ruo), *a spade, shovel*: Liv., Ov.

rŭtŭla -ae, f. (dim. of ruta), *a little bit of rue*: Cic. L.

Rŭtŭli -ōrum, m. pl. *the Rutuli, an ancient people of Latium, whose capital was Ardea*; sing. **Rŭtŭlus** -i, m. *a Rutulian*: Verg.; Rutulus audax, *Turnus, king of the Rutuli,* Verg.

¶ Hence adj. **Rŭtŭlus** -a -um, *Rutulian*: rex, *Turnus,* Verg.

Rŭtŭpiae -ārum, f. *a town in Britain* (the modern *Richborough*).

¶ Hence adj. **Rŭtŭpīnus** -a -um, *belonging to Rutupiae.*

S

S, s, the eighteenth letter of the Latin Alphabet, corresponds in the middle of a word to the Greek sigma (Σ, σ, ς), at the beginning of a word to the Greek aspirate; e.g., sex=ἕξ, sal=ἅλς, serpo=ἕρπω. When standing between vowels it was occasionally interchanged with *r* (e.g. quaero, quaeso). At the end of a word it was often dropped by poets of the older period, e.g. vitā illā dignu' locoque, and in such conversational forms as ain, satin. By assimilation, the *s* of *dis* before *f* becomes *f*, as difficilis; it combines with gutturals to form *x* (e.g. rex=regs).

For abbreviations in which S. is used, see Table of Abbreviations.

Săba -ae, f. (Σάβη), *a town in Arabia Felix, famous for its perfumes.*

Hence adj. **Săbaeus** -a -um, *Sabaean, Arabian*; f. subst. **Săbaea** -ae (sc. terra), *the country of Sabaea, Arabia Felix*; m. pl. subst. **Săbaei** -ōrum, *the Sabaeans.*

Săbāzĭus -i, m. (Σαβάζιος), *a surname of Bacchus*: Cic.

¶ Hence **Săbāzĭa** -ōrum, n. pl. *a festival in honour of Bacchus.*

sabbăta -ōrum, n. pl. (σάββατα), *the Sabbath, the Jewish day of rest*: Plin., Suet.; tricesima sabbata, *a Jewish holiday, perhaps connected with the new moon,* Hor.

¶ Hence **sabbătārii** -ōrum, m. pl. *observers of the Sabbath, Jews*: Mart.

Săbelli -ōrum, m. (dim. of Sabini), *a poetic name of the Sabines*; sing. **Sabellus** -i, m. *the Sabine* (i.e. Horace, as owner of an estate in the Sabine country): Hor.

¶ Hence adj. **Săbellus, Săbellĭcus** -a -um, *Sabine.*

Săbīni -ōrum, m. pl. *an ancient people of Italy, northerly neighbours of the Latins.*

¶ Hence adj. **Săbīnus** -a -um, *Sabine*: Ov., etc. F. as subst. **Săbīna** -ae, *a Sabine woman*: Prop., Ov. N. as subst. **Săbīnum** -i (sc. vinum), *Sabine wine*: Hor.

Sabis -is, acc. -im, m. *a river in Gallia Belgica* (now the *Sambre*): Caes.

săbŭlo -ōnis, m. *gravel, sand*: Varr., Plin.

săbŭlōsus -a -um (sabulo), *sandy, gravelly*: Plin.

săbŭlum -i, n. *gravel, sand*: Varr., Plin.

săburra -ae, f. (sabulo), *sand used as ballast*: Verg., Liv.

săburro -are (saburra), *to load with ballast.* LIT., Plin. TRANSF., *to cram full* (with food): Pl.

saccĭpērĭum -i, n. (saccus/pera), *a pocket for a purse*: Pl.

sacco -are (saccus), *to strain* or *filter through a bag.* LIT., Plin., Mart., Sen. TRANSF., Lucr.

saccŭlus -i, m. (dim. of saccus), *a small bag,* esp. for money: Cat., Hor.

saccus -i, m. (σάκκος), *a sack, bag*: Cic. Esp. *a purse, money-bag*: Hor. Also *a filtering-bag*: Plin., Mart.

săcellum -i, n. (dim. of sacrum), *a small shrine* or *chapel*: Cic., Verg., etc.

săcer -cra -crum, *sacred, holy, consecrated.* LIT., (1) in favourable sense; with dat. and genit.: sacra Iovi quercus, Ov.; sacrum deae pecus, Liv.; illa insula eorum deorum sacra putatur, Liv. Absol.: sacra aedes, Cic.; vates, *sacred to Apollo,* Hor.; poet., of deities themselves: Vesta, Prop. In the names of certain places: sacer mons, *a hill three miles from Rome,* to which the Plebs seceded, Liv.; sacra via, *a street in Rome, leading from the Forum to the Capitol*; called also sacer clivus, Cic., Hor., Mart. (2) in unfavourable sense, *accursed, devoted to destruction*: eius caput Iovi (Stygio) sacrum esset, old law ap. Liv.; eum qui eorum cuiquam nocuerit sacrum sanciri, Liv.

TRANSF., (1) in favourable sense, *sacred*: sacro digna silentio, Hor.; amantes, Prop. (2) in unfavourable sense, *detestable, accursed, horrible*: is intestabilis et sacer esto, Hor.; auri sacra fames, Verg.

N. sing. as subst. **sacrum** -i, *a holy thing* or *place*: Pl., Hor. Esp. *a sacrifice* or *sacrificial victim*: Cic., Liv., etc. N. pl. as subst. **sacra** -orum, *holy things* or *places*: Cic., Verg., Ov. Esp. *sacred rites, worship*: sacra interire maiores noluerunt, Cic.; eisdem uti sacris, Cic.; sacra Cereris, Cic.; sacra facere Graeco Herculi, Liv.; sacra gentilicia, Liv. Poet.: sacra caelestia, *poems*, Ov.

săcerdōs -dōtis, c. (sacer), *a priest, priestess*: sacerdotes populi Romani, Cic.; in apposition: regina sacerdos, *Rhea, a vestal*, Verg.

săcerdōtālis -e (sacerdos), *priestly, sacerdotal*: Plin. L.

săcerdōtium -i, n. (sacerdos), *priesthood*: sacerdotium inire, Cic.; Caes., Liv.

sacrāmentum -i, n. (sacro), *that which binds* or *obliges a person.*

(**1**) legal t. t., *the money deposited with the* tresviri capitales *or* praetor *by the parties in a suit, which the defeated party lost*: de multae sacramento, Cic. Hence *any civil suit, legal process*: iusto sacramento contendere cum aliquo, Cic.

(**2**) milit. t. t., *the engagement entered into by newly enlisted soldiers, the military oath of allegiance* (originally *a preliminary engagement*, distinct from the formal iusiurandum): aliquem militiae sacramento obligare, Cic.; tenere, Caes.; milites sacramento adigere, Liv.; dicere sacramentum, Caes., or sacramento (abl.), Liv.; with dat. of person, *to swear allegiance to*: Liv., Tac. Hence *any oath* or *solemn promise*: perfidum sacramentum dicere, Hor.; Cic. L.

Sacrāni -ōrum, m. *a people in Latium.*

¶ Hence **Săcrānus** -a -um, *of the Sacrani*: acies, Verg.

sacrārium -i, n. (sacrum).

(**1**) *a place where sacred things are kept, the sacristy of a temple*: Cic., Liv.; Caere sacrarium populi Romani (as the Roman religious vessels, etc., were said to have once been taken to Caere), Liv. (**2**) *a place of worship, a chapel, shrine*: Bonae Deae, Cic.; Verg., Liv. Transf., scelerum, Cic.

sacrātus -a -um, partic. from sacro; q.v.

sacrĭcŏla -ae, c. (sacrum/colo), *a sacrificing priest* or *priestess*: Tac., Suet.

sacrĭfĕr -fĕra -fĕrum (sacra/fero), *carrying sacred things*: rates, Ov.

sacrĭfĭcālis -e (sacrificus), *of sacrifices*: Tac.

sacrĭfĭcātĭo -ōnis, f. (sacrifico), *a sacrificing*: Cic.

sacrĭfĭcium -i, n. (sacra/facio), *a sacrifice*: sacrificia publica ac privata, Caes.; facere sacrificium, Cic., Liv.

sacrĭfĭco -are (sacra/facio), *to offer sacrifice, to sacrifice*: in sacrificando, Cic.; with dat. of deity: Pl., Liv.; with acc. of victim: suem, Ov.; pecora, Liv.

sacrĭfĭcŭlus -i, m. (sacrificus), *a sacrificing priest*: Liv.; rex sacrificus, *the priest in Rome under the Republic who offered the sacrifices previously offered by the kings*: Liv.

sacrĭfĭcus -a -um (sacra/facio), *sacrificial, sacrificing*: ritus, Ov.; securis, Ov.; Ancus, Ov.

sacrĭlĕgium -i, n. (sacrilegus), *robbery of a temple, stealing of sacred things, sacrilege*: sacrilegium prohibere, Liv. Hence *profanation of religious rites*: Nep., Sen.

sacrĭlĕgus -a -um (sacra/lego), *stealing sacred things, sacrilegious.*

Lit., bellum, Cic.; manūs, Liv. M. as subst., *a temple-robber*: Pl.

Transf., in gen., *profaning sacred things, irreligious, impious*: linguae, Ov.; Cic., etc. M. and f. as subst., *an impious person*: Ter., Ov.

acro -are (sacer).

(**1**) *to dedicate to a god, consecrate.* Lit., in favourable sense: aurum, Cic.; aras, Verg.; in unfavourable sense, *to pronounce accursed*: caput, Liv. Transf., in favourable sense, *to devote, allot*: honorem alicui, Verg.; in unfavourable sense, *to doom*, Verg.

(**2**) *to make holy, make inviolable.* Lit., foedus, Liv.; lex sacrata, *a law, the violation of which was punished by a curse*, Cic.; sacrata Vesta, Ov. Transf., *to make imperishable, to immortalize*: aliquem Lesbio plectro, Hor.; vivit eloquentia Catonis sacrata scriptis omnis generis, Liv.; Ov.

¶ Hence partic. **sacrātus** -a -um, *holy, consecrated*: Verg., Ov.

sacrōsanctus -a -um (sacer/sancio), *consecrated with religious ceremonies*; hence, *holy, sacred, inviolable.* Lit., ut plebi sui magistratus essent sacrosancti, Liv.; possessiones, Cic.; potestas (of the tribune), Liv. Transf., *cherished*: alicuius memoria, Plin. L.

sacrum, see sacer.

saecŭlāris -e (saeculum), *relating to a* saeculum *or age*: ludi, *secular games* (celebrated at intervals of about 100 years), Suet.; carmen, *a hymn sung at the secular games*, Hor., Suet.

saecŭlum (poet. syncop. **saeclum**) -i, n.

(**1**) *the period of one human generation* (about 33⅓ years), *a generation.* Lit., multa saecula hominum, Cic.; Verg., Liv., etc. Transf., **a**, concr., *the people composing a generation*: Cic., Verg., etc. Hence plur., *successive generations* of people or animals, *races*: Lucr.: **b**, *the spirit of the age, the times*: ipse fortasse in huius saeculi errore versor, Cic.; mitescent saecula, Verg.

(**2**) in a wider sense, *the longest duration of a man's life, a hundred years, a century.* Lit., duobus prope saeculis ante, Cic.; Hor. Transf., *an indefinitely long time, an age*: saeclis effeta senectus, Verg.; Cic.

saepĕ, adv., comp. saepius, superl. saepissimē; *often, frequently*: Cic., Hor., etc.; bene saepe, Cic.; minime saepe, Caes.

¶ Hence **saepĕnŭmĕrō**, *repeatedly, again and again*: Caes., Cic., Sall.

saepes (**sēpes**) -is, f. *a hedge, fence*: Caes., Verg., etc.

saepimentum -i, n. (saepio), *a hedge* or *enclosure*: Cic.

Saepīnum -i, n. *a small town in Samnium.*

saepio saepire saepsi saeptum, *to surround with a hedge, to hedge in, to enclose.*

Lit., vepribus sepulcrum, Cic.; vallum arboribus, Liv.

Transf., (**1**) physically, in gen., *to shut in, to confine, to surround*: urbem moenibus, Cic.; se tectis, *to shut oneself up at home*, Verg.; natura oculos membranis vestivit et saepsit, Cic. (**2**) abstr.: locum cogitatione, Cic.; saeptus legibus, Cic.; Liv.

¶ N. of partic. as subst. **saeptum** -i, *a barrier, wall,* or *enclosure*: quibus saeptis beluas continebimus? Cic. Esp. in plur. **saepta** -ōrum, *the enclosure where the Romans voted at the comitia*: Cic.

saeta -ae, f. *a bristle, stiff hair.* Lit., saeta equina, *horsehair*, Cic.; of goats, cows, lions: Verg.; Lucr., etc. Transf., (**1**) of coarse, bristly, human hair: Verg., Ov., Juv.; (**2**) *part of an angler's line*: Ov., Mart.

Saetăbis -bis, f. *a town in Hispania Tarra-conensis, famous for its flax.* Adj. **Saetăbus** -a -um, *of Saetabis.*

saetĭgĕr -gĕra -gĕrum (saeta/gero), *having bristles, bristly*: sus, Lucr., Verg., Ov. M. as subst. **saetĭgĕr** -gĕri, *a boar*: Ov., Mart.

saetōsus -a -um (seta), *bristly*: aper, Verg.; frons, Hor.

saevē, adv. from saevus; q.v.

saevĭdĭcus -a -um (saevus/dico), *angrily spoken*: dicta, Ter.

saevĭo -ire -ii -ĭtum (saevus), *to rage, be fierce, be furious.*

LIT., of animals: saevit lupus, Ov.; anguis, Verg.; saevire coepisse (of elephants), Liv.; in pecudes, Ov.

TRANSF., of persons, *to be furious* or *take violent action*: saevit animis ignobile vulgus, Verg.; in obsides, Liv.; impers.: in ceteros saevitum esse, Liv. (2) of things, *to rage*: saevit ventus, Lucr.; pontus, Hor.; saevit venenum in praecordiis, Hor.; saevit amor ferri, Verg.

saevĭtĭa -ae, f. (saevus), *rage, ferocity.*
'LIT., of animals: canum, Plin.

TRANSF., (1) of persons: iudicis, Cic.; hostium, Sall.; creditorum, Tac.; in aliquem, Cic. (2) of things: undae, Cic.; annonae, Tac.

saevus -a -um, adj. (with compar. and superl.), *raging, fierce, furious, violent.*

LIT., of animals: leones, Lucr.; saevior leaena, Verg.

TRANSF., *fierce, cruel, savage.* (1) of persons: Aeneas saevus in armis, *terrible*, Verg.; poet. with infin.: quaelibet in quemvis opprobria fingere saevus, Hor. (2) of things: ventus, Cic. L., Liv.; scopulus, Verg.; verba, Hor.; hiems, Liv.

¶ Hence adv. (with compar. and superl.) **saevē**, *cruelly, barbarously, ferociously*: Hor., Luc., etc. Also **saevĭtĕr**: Pl.

sāga -ae, f. (sagus), *a prophetess, fortune-teller*: Cic., Hor., Ov.

săgācĭtās -ātis, f. (sagax), *keenness, acuteness.*
LIT., *keenness of the senses*; esp. *keenness of scent in dogs*: canum ad investigandum sagacitas narium, Cic. TRANSF., *mental acuteness, shrewdness*: hominis, Cic.

săgācĭtĕr, adv. from sagax; q.v.

Săgăris, acc. -im, abl. -i, m. and **Sangărĭus** -i, m. (Σαγγαριός), *a river in Phrygia and Bithynia, flowing into the Euxine* (now Sakaria).

¶ Hence f. adj. **Săgărītĭs** -ĭdis, and adj. **Sangărĭus** -a -um, *of Sagaris*: nympha, Ov.

săgātus -a -um (sagum), *clothed with a* sagum: Cic., Mart.

săgax -ācis (sagio), *keen, acute.*

LIT., *having keen senses*; esp. *keen-scented*: canes, Cic.; compar.: sagacior anser, Ov.

TRANSF., *mentally acute, shrewd, clever*: mens, Lucr., Cic.; superl.: sagacissimus ad suspicandum, Cic.; with infin.: sagax quondam ventura videre, Ov.; with genit.: utilium rerum, Hor.

¶ Hence adv. (with compar. and superl.) **săgācĭtĕr**, *keenly.* LIT., of the senses: Cic., Hor. TRANSF., of the mind, *acutely, shrewdly*: pervestigare, Cic.; Liv., etc.

săgīna -ae, f. (σάττω, to fill), *fattening, stuffing, cramming.* LIT., Pl., Cic. TRANSF., (1) *food, nourishment*: Tac., Juv. (2) *a fat animal*: Pl.

săgīno -are (sagina), *to fatten, feed up, cram.* LIT., porcum, Prop. TRANSF., *quae copia rerum omnium* (illos Gallos) saginaret, Liv.; sanguine reipublicae saginari, Cic.

săgĭo -ire, *to perceive quickly, feel keenly*: sagire sentire acute est, Cic.

săgitta -ae, f. *an arrow.* LIT., Cic., Verg., etc. TRANSF., *the Arrow, a constellation*: Cic. poet.

săgittārĭus -a -um (sagitta), *of an arrow*: Plin. M. as subst. **săgittārĭus** -i, *an archer.* LIT., sing., pl., and coll. sing. Caes., Cic., Tac. TRANSF., *the constellation Sagittarius*: Cic.

săgittĭfĕr -fĕra -fĕrum (sagitta/fero), *carrying arrows*: pharetra, Ov.; Geloni, Verg.

Săgittĭpŏtens -entis, m. (sagitta/potens), *the constellation Sagittarius*: Cic.

săgitto -are (sagitta), *to shoot arrows*: Pl.

sagmen -inis, n. *a bunch of sacred herbs plucked in the Capitol; carrying it the Roman fetiale became inviolable*: Liv.

săgŭlātus -a -um (sagulum), *wearing a* sagulum: Suet.

săgŭlum -i, n. (dim. of sagum), *a small military cloak*: Cic., Verg., etc.

săgum -i, n. (perhaps a Celtic word), *a mantle made of coarse wool, as worn by servants, by certain foreigners, and esp. by soldiers* (opp. toga): Caes., Hor., etc.; saga sumere ad saga ire, *to take up arms, prepare for war*, Cic.; in sagis esse, *to be in arms*, Cic.; saga ponere, *to lay down arms*, Liv.

Săguntum -i, n. and **Săguntus** (-ŏs) -i, f. *town on the coast of Spain, south of the Ebro, the besieging of which by Hannibal led to the outbreak of the second Punic war.*

¶ Hence adj. **Săguntīnus** -a -um, *Saguntine.* M. pl. as subst. **Săguntīni** -orum, *the people of Saguntum.*

săgus -a -um (perhaps connected with sagio) *prophetic, soothsaying*: aves, Stat.

Săis -is, f. (Σάις), *the old capital of Lower Egypt.*

¶ Hence subst. **Săītae** -ārum, m. pl. *the inhabitants of Sais.*

săl sălis, m. (cf. ἅλς), *salt.*

LIT., multi modii salis, Cic.; Verg., etc.

TRANSF., (1) *brine, sea-water, the salt sea*: campi salis, Verg.; Lucr., Ov. (2) sing. and plur., *wit*: sale et facetiis Caesar vicit omnes, Cic.; Hor., etc.

sălāco -ōnis, m. (σαλάκων), *a swaggerer, boaster, braggart*: Cic. L.

Sălămis -mīnis; acc. -mīna; f. (Σαλαμίς) (1) *an island and town in the Saronic Gulf over against Eleusis, scene of the great naval victory of the Greeks over the Persians* (now Koluri). (2) *a town in Cyprus, built by Teucer.*

¶ Hence adj. **Sălāmīnĭus** -a -um *relating to either Salamis*: m. pl. as subst. **Sălāmīnĭi** -ōrum, *the inhabitants of either Salamis.*

sălăpūtĭum -i, n. *a little man, manikin*: Cat.

sălārĭus -a -um (sal), *of salt*: annona, *yearly revenue from salt*, Liv.; Via Salaria, or simply Salaria, *a road beginning at the Porta Collina and leading into the Sabine country, the Salt Road*, so called because the Sabines used it for conveying their salt, Cic., Liv.

As subst., m. **sălārĭus** -i, *a dealer in salted fish*: Mart.; n. **sălārĭum** -i, *salt allowance, money given to soldiers for salt; hence any allowance, pay*: Tac., Suet., etc.

sălax -ācis (salio). LIT., of male animals, *lustful, lecherous*: aries, Ov. TRANSF., *exciting lust*: eruca, Ov.

sălebra -ae, f. (salio), *a jolting*; hence *a rough, uneven patch of road*. LIT., Hor., etc. TRANSF., of style, *roughness, ruggedness*: oratio haeret in salebra, Cic.

sălebrōsus -a -um (salebra), *rugged, rough*; of style: Quint., Sen.

Sălentini (Sallentīni) -ōrum, m. *a people at the south-eastern end of Italy*. Adj. **Sālentīnus** -a -um, *of the Salentini*.

Sălernum -i, n. *a maritime town in Campania, south-east of Naples* (now *Salerno*).

Sălĭāris, see Salii.

Sălĭātus -ūs, m. (Salii), *the office or dignity of a priest of Mars*, see Salii.

sălictum -i, n. (=salicetum, from salix), *a plantation of willows*: Cic., Verg., etc.

sălignus -a -um (salix), *made of willow-wood*: fustis, Hor., etc.

Sălĭi -ōrum, m. (salio, i.e., *the leapers, jumpers*), *a college of* 12 *priests of Mars Gradivus, instituted by Numa, who made solemn processions through Rome on the Kalends of March*: Cic., Verg., etc.

¶ Hence adj. **Sălĭāris** -e. LIT., *relating to the Salii*: carmen Numae, Hor. TRANSF., *splendid, magnificent* (from the sumptuous feasts that followed the procession of the Salii): epulari Saliarem in modum, Cic. L.; dapes, Hor.

sălillum -i, n. (dim. of salinum), *a little salt-cellar*: Cat.

sălinae -ārum, f. (sal), *salt-works, brine-pits*: Caes., Cic., Liv. Esp. *salt-works on the banks of the Tiber*, in full, salinae Romanae, Liv.

sălīnum -i, n. (sal), *a salt-cellar*: Pl., Hor., Liv.

sălĭo sălīre sălŭi (sălĭi, rare), saltum (cf. ἄλλομαι), *to spring, leap, jump bound*.

LIT., of living beings: de muro, Liv.; super vallum, Liv.; saliunt in gurgite ranae, Ov.; Verg. Esp. of sexual activity, *to leap*, as transit. verb: Lucr., Ov.

TRANSF., (1) physically, of things: salit grando, Verg.; sal *or* mica (salis) saliens, *sacrificial salt, which* (as a good omen) *leapt up when thrown into the fire*: farre pio et saliente micā, Hor.; pectora trepido salientia motu, Ov.; dulcis aquae saliens rivus, Verg. F. pl. of partic. as subst. **sălĭentēs** -ium (sc. aquae), *fountains*: Cic. L. (2) mentally: negotia, Hor.

săliunca -ae, f. *wild nard*: Verg.

săliva -ae, f. (connected with σίαλον), *spittle, saliva*. LIT., Cat. TRANSF., *appetite, taste*: Prop., Sen.

sălix -icis, f. *a willow*: Verg., etc.

Sallentīni=Salentini; q.v.

Sallustĭus -i, m. (1) C. Sallustius Crispus, of Amiternum, *the Roman historian Sallust, contemporary of Cicero*. (2) Sallustius Crispus, *great-nephew of the historian, friend of Augustus, famous for his great riches*.

¶ Hence adj. **Sallustĭānus** -a -um, *of Sallustius*.

salmăcĭdus -a -um (sal), *brackish*: Plin.

Salmăcis -ĭdis, f. (Σαλμακίς), *a fountain in Caria, fabled to make those who drank of it effeminate*. Personif., *the nymph of this fountain*: Ov.

Salmōneus -ĕos, m. (Σαλμωνεύς), *son of Aeolus, brother of Sisyphus; he imitated the thunder and lightning of Zeus, who on that account struck him with a thunderbolt, and hurled him down to Tartaras*.

¶ Hence **Salmōnĭs** -ĭdis, f. (Σαλμωνίς), *Tyro, the daughter of Salmoneus, mother of Neleus and Pelias by Neptune*.

Sălōnae -ārum, f. *a sea-port in Dalmatia*: Caes.

salpa -ae, f. *a kind of stock-fish*: Ov., Plin.

Salpīnātes -um, m. *a people of Etruria*: Liv.

salsāmentārĭus -i, m. (salsamentum), *a dealer in salt-fish*: Suet.

salsāmentum -i, n. (salsus). (1) *fish-pickle, brine*: Cic. (2) *salted or pickled fish*, gen. in plur.: Ter.

salsē, adv. from salsus; q.v.

salsūra -ae, f. (salsus), *a salting, pickling*. Hence *pickle*: Varr. TRANSF., meae animae salsura evenit, *I am in a bad humour*, Pl.

salsus -a -um (originally partic. from verb salo, *or* salio, *to salt*), *salted, salty*.

LIT., aequor, Lucr.; fluctus salsi, *the sea*, Verg.

TRANSF., *like salt, sharp, biting, witty, satirical*: inveni ridicula et salsa multa Graecorum, Cic.; male salsus, *with poor wit*, Hor.

¶ Hence adv. (with superl.) **salsē**, *wittily, humorously*: dicere, Cic.

saltātĭo -ōnis, f. (salto), *a dancing, dance*: Cic., etc.

saltātor -ōris, m. (salto), *a dancer*: Cic., Quint.

saltātōrĭus -a -um (saltator), *of or for dancing*: orbis, Cic.

saltātrix -trīcis, f. (saltator), *a female dancer, a dancing-girl*: Cic.

saltātus -ūs, m. (salto), *a dancing, dance*: Ov., Liv.

saltem, adv. *at least, at all events*. (1) affirmative, *at least, failing an* (expressed) *alternative*: eripe mihi hunc dolorem aut minue saltem, Cic.; nunc saltem ad illos calculos revertamur, Cic.; Hor., etc. (2) with the negatives non, neque, *not even, nor even*: Liv., Tac., etc. (3) interrog.: quis ego sum saltem, si non sum Sosia? Pl.

salto -are (freq. of salio), *to dance*, esp. *with pantomimic gestures*. LIT., ad tibicinis modos, Liv.; saltare in convivio, Cic. With acc., *to represent in pantomimic dancing*: Cyclopa, Hor.; carmina, poemata, *sing with gestures*, Ov. TRANSF., of orators: Hegesias saltat incidens particulas, *speaks jerkily*, Cic.

saltŭōsus -a -um (saltus), *wooded*: Sall., Liv., Tac.

¹**saltus** -ūs, m. (salio), *a spring, leap, bound*: saltu uti, Cic.; saltum dare, Ov.; Verg.

²**saltus** -ūs, m. (1) *a forest or mountain pasture*: saltibus in vacuis pascant, Verg.; de saltu agroque deicitur, Cic.; Lucr., etc. (2) *a pass through a mountain or forest, a dale, ravine, glade*: Thermopylarum, Liv.; saltus Pyrenaei, Caes.

sălūbris -e and **sălūber** -bris -bre, adj. (with compar. and superl.) (salus), *healthful, healthy, salubrious, wholesome*.

LIT., natura loci, Cic.; annus salubris, Cic.; somnus, Verg.; with dat.: Hor.

TRANSF., (1) in gen., *sound, serviceable, useful*: consilia, Cic.; quidquid est salsum aut salubre in oratione, Cic.; res salubrior, Liv.; sententia reipublicae saluberrima, Cic.

(2) *healthy, strong, vigorous*: corpora salu-
briora, Liv.; Tac.
¶ Hence adv. (with compar. and superl.:
Plin.) **sălūbrĭtĕr**, *healthfully, wholesomely.*
LIT., salubrius refrigerari, Cic. TRANSF.,
serviceably, advantageously: bellum trahere,
Liv.
sălūbrĭtās -ātis, f. (saluber).
(1) *wholesomeness*: loci, Cic.; tum salu-
britatis tum pestilentiae signa, Cic.
(2) *soundness, healthiness, health.* LIT.,
corporum, Tac.; Cic. TRANSF., omnis illa
salubritas Atticae dictionis et quasi sanitas,
Cic.
sălum -i, n. (σάλος), *the open sea*: propter vim
tempestatis stare ad ancoram in salo non
posse, Liv.; Cic.; poet., *the sea* generally:
altum, Hor.; Verg., etc. Sometimes *the
rolling of a ship at sea, motion of a ship*: salo
nauseāque confecti, Caes.
sălus -ūtis, f. (salvus), *health, soundness.*
LIT., physical: medicinā aliquem ad
salutem reducere, Cic.; Pl., Ov., etc.
Personif.: Salus, *a goddess with a temple on
the Quirinal*, Liv.
TRANSF., (1) in gen., *safety, welfare,
well-being*: utilitati salutique servire, Cic.;
spes salutis, Cic.; restitutio salutis meae,
my recall from exile, Cic.; salutem adferre
reipublicae, *to save*, Cic.; Verg., Liv. As
term of endearment: Pl. (2) *a means of
safety* or *deliverance*: nulla salus reipublicae
reperiri potest, Cic.; Pl., Verg. (3) *a wish
for a person's welfare* (spoken or written);
a salutation, greeting: salutem alicui dare,
nuntiare, Pl., Cic.; at the beginning of a
letter: salutem dicit (S.D.), *greets*, Pl.,
Cic. L.; elliptically: Anacharsis Hannoni
salutem (sc. dicit), Cic.; salutem dicere foro
et curiae, *to bid farewell to, renounce*, Cic.
sălūtāris -e (salus), *healthful.*
LIT., bringing physical health: ars, Hor.;
herba, Ov.; with dat.: Cic. N. pl. as subst.:
remedies, medicines: pro salutaribus mortifera
conscribere, Cic. As epithet of Jupiter
(cf. Σωτήρ): Cic.
TRANSF., in gen., *serviceable, wholesome,
advantageous*; of things and persons: ut
quae mala perniciosaque sunt, habeantur
pro bonis ac salutaribus, Cic.; tam beneficum,
tam salutarem, tam mansuetum civem
desiderant, Cic.; with dat.: consilium
salutare utrique, Cic.; oratio, Liv. Esp.:
salutaris littera—i.e. *the letter A*, abbreviation of absolvo (littera tristis, C=condemno),
Cic.
¶ Adv. **sălūtārĭtĕr**, *beneficially, advantageously*: uti armis, Cic.; se recipere,
ap. Cic. L.
sălūtātĭo -ōnis, f. (saluto), *a greeting, salutation.* In gen.: Cic., Liv. Esp. *a call,
ceremonial visit, waiting upon* a person: dare
se salutationi amicorum, Cic.; concr., *the
visitors*: ubi salutatio defluxit, Cic.
sălūtātor -ōris, m. (saluto), *a visitor, caller*:
Mart., Suet., Juv.
sălūtātrix -trīcis, f. adj. (salutator), *greeting,
saluting*: Mart. Esp. *paying a visit, calling*:
turba, Juv.
sălūtĭfĕr -fĕra -fĕrum (salus/fero), *health-
bringing*: puer, Aesculapius, Ov.; opem
salutiferam dare, Ov.

sălūtĭgĕrŭlus -a -um (salus/gero), *carrying
complimentary messages*: Pl.
sălūto -are (salus), *to wish well, to greet.*
LIT., *to greet* a person. In gen., at the
beginning or end of a meeting, or in a letter:
aliquem, Pl., Cic., Ov. Esp. (1) with double
acc., *to greet as, to name*: aliquem imperatorem, Tac.; Cic. L., etc. (2) *to call upon,
to pay court to, wait upon*: venit salutandi
causā, Cic. L.; Hor., etc.
TRANSF., *to pay respect to, reverence,
worship* a deity, place, etc.: deos, Pl.; Italiam,
Verg.; Cic.
salvē, adv. from salvus; q.v.; or imperat. from
salveo; q.v.
salvĕo -ēre (salvus), *to be well, be in good
health.* Used chiefly in the forms salve,
salvete, salveto, salvebis, salvere (iubeo), as
a greeting, *Good day! Good morning!* etc.
(1) in welcoming, or sending greeting to, a
person: *A.* salve, adulescens. *S.* et tu multum
salveto, adulescentula, Pl.; Dionysium velim
salvere iubeas, *greet Dionysius for me*, Cic. L.;
salvebis a meo Cicerone, *my son Cicero sends
you greeting*, Cic. L.; so of respects paid to a
deity, hail!: salve vera Iovis proles, Verg.;
Hor. (2) in bidding farewell: vale, salve,
Cic. L.; to the dead: salve aeternum mihi,
Verg.
salvus -a -um (connected with salus), *safe,
unhurt, well, sound.*
LIT., (1) of persons: salvus atque incolumis, Caes.; salvus revertor, Cic.; se salvo,
while he is alive, Cic.; Hor., etc. (2) of things:
navis, Pl.; clipeus, Cic. Esp. in abl. absol.,
saving, without infraction of: Cic.; salvo iure
nostrae veteris amicitiae, Cic.; salvo officio,
Cic.; Ov., etc.
TRANSF., in conversational formulae,
well off, all right: ne salvus sim, si, *may I die
if*, Cic. L.; salvus sis!=salve! Pl.; salva
res est, *it is all right*, Pl.
¶ Hence adv. **salvē**, *well, all right*; esp.:
satin salve? *is everything all right?* Pl., Ter.;
Liv.
Sămărobrīva -ae, f. *a town in Gallia Belgica*
(now *Amiens*): Caes., Cic. L.
sambūca -ae, f. (σαμβύκη), *a species of harp*: Pl.
sambūcina -ae, f. (sambuca/cano), *a female
harp-player*: Pl.
sambūcistrĭa -ae, f. (σαμβυκίστρια), *a female
harp-player*: Liv.
Sămē -ēs, f. (Σάμη), *older name of the island
Cephallenia* (now *Cefalonia*), *and its capital.*
Another form is **Sāmŏs** -i, f.
¶ Hence **Sămaei** -ōrum, m. pl. *the
inhabitants of Same.*
Samnĭum -i, n. *a mountainous region of central
Italy, between Campania and the Adriatic Sea.*
¶ Hence adj. **Samnis** -ītis, *Samnite*: Liv.
as subst., m. sing. **Samnis**, *a Samnite*
collectively, *the Samnites*: Liv.; also *a
gladiator armed with Samnite weapons*: Cic.
m. pl. **Samnītes** -ium, *the Samnites.* Also
adj. **Samnītĭcus** -a -um, *Samnite.*
¹**Sămŏs** (-us) -i, f. (Σάμος), *an island in the
Aegean Sea, off the coast of Asia Minor, the
birth-place of Pythagoras, famous for its
worship of Juno or Hera, and for its clay and
the vessels made from it.*
¶ Hence adj. **Sămĭus** -a -um, *Samian*:
vir, senex, Pythagoras, Ov.; as subst., m

sing. **Sămĭus** -i, *the Samian*, i.e. *Pythagoras*: Ov.; m. pl. **Sămĭi** -ōrum, *the inhabitants of Samos, Samians*: Cic.; n. pl. **Sămia** -ōrum (sc. vasa), *Samian ware*: Plin. Dim. adj. **Sămĭŏlus** -a -um, *Samian*: Pl.

²**Sămŏs**=Same; q.v.

Sămŏthrācē -ēs, f. and **Sămŏthrāca** -ae, f. and **Sămŏthrācĭa** -ae, f. *Samothrace, an island in the northern Aegean, opposite the mouth of the Hebrus, famous for the mystic rites of the Cabiri* (now *Samothraki.*)

¶ Hence subst. **Sămŏthrāces** -um, m. pl. *the inhabitants of Samothrace*: Ov.; adj. **Sămŏthrācĭus** -a -um, *Samothracian.*

sānābĭlis -e (sano), *that can be healed, curable.* Lit., physically: vulnus, Ov. Transf., of the mind: iracundi sanabiles, Cic.

sānātĭo -ōnis, f. (sano), *a healing, curing*: corporum, Cic.; malorum, Cic.

sancĭo sancire sanxi sanctum, and in Lucr. sancītum (connected with sacer), *to consecrate, hallow, make sacred* or *inviolable by a religious act.*

Lit., esp. of a law, league, etc., *to confirm, ratify, decree*: legem, Cic.; foedus sanguine alicuius, Liv.; alia moribus confirmarunt, sanxerunt autem alia legibus, Cic.; with ut or ne and subj.: Caes., Cic., Liv.; with acc. and infin.: Liv.

Transf., *to forbid on pain of punishment, provide against*: incestum supplicio, Cic.; Solon capite sanxit, si qui, *made it a capital offence*, Cic. L.

¶ Hence partic. (with compar. and superl.) **sanctus** -a -um, *consecrated, hallowed, holy, sacred, inviolable.* Lit., fana, Lucr.; tribuni, Cic.; officium, Cic.; fides, Liv.; libertas, Liv. Of deities: Lucr.; of the dead: Sall., Verg.; of Roman emperors: Ov.; of the senate: sanctissimum orbis terrae consilium, Cic.; vates, *the Sibyl*, Verg. Transf., *pure, virtuous, blameless*: nemo sanctior illo (viro), Cic.; vir in publicis religionibus sanctus, Cic.; sententia, Lucr.; mores, Juv.; coniux, chaste, Verg.

¶ Adv. (with compar. and superl.) **sanctē** *solemnly, conscientiously, scrupulously*: pie sancteque colere naturam, Cic.; se sanctissime gerere, Cic.; sanctissime observare promissa, Cic.

sanctĭmōnĭa -ae, f. (sanctus). (1) *sanctity, sacredness*: ad deorum religionem et sanctimoniam demigrasse, Cic. (2) *purity, chastity, virtue*: domum habere clausam pudori et sanctimoniae, Cic.

sanctĭo -ōnis, f. (sancio), *the article* or *clause in a law which defines the penalty*: legum sanctionem poenamque recitare, Cic.; Liv.

sanctĭtās -ātis, f. (sanctus). (1) *inviolability, sanctity*: tribunatūs, Cic.; templi insulaeque, Tac. (2) *purity, chastity*: matronarum, Cic.; Liv., Tac.

sanctĭtūdo -inis, f. (sanctus), *sanctity*: Cic.

sanctor -ōris, m. (sancio), *an enacter*: legum, Tac.

sanctus -a -um, partic. from sancio; q.v.

Sancus -i, m. *a Sabine deity, worshipped also at Rome.*

sandālĭārĭus -a -um (sandalium), *relating to sandals*: Apollo, *with a statue in the Street of the Sandal-makers*, Suet.

sandālĭgĕrŭlae -ārum, f. (sandalium/gero),

female slaves who carried their mistresses' sandals: Pl.

sandălĭum -i, n. (σανδάλιον), *a slipper, sandal*: Ter.

sandăpĭla -ae, f. *a kind of bier used for poor people*: Mart., Juv.

sandyx -dȳcis, f. (σάνδυξ), *vermilion* or *some similar colour*: Verg., Prop.

sānē, adv. from sanus; q.v.

Sangărĭus, *see* Sagaris.

sanguĭnans -antis (sanguis), *bloodthirsty*: eloquentia, Tac.

sanguĭnārĭus -a -um (sanguis), *of blood*; hence *bloodthirsty, savage*: iuventus, Cic. L.; Plin. L.

sanguĭnĕus -a -um (sanguis), *of blood, bloody.* Lit., imber, Cic.; guttae, Ov.; Mavors, Verg.; rixae, Hor.

Transf., *blood-red*: luna, Ov.; Verg., Liv.

sanguĭnŏlentus -a -um (sanguis), *stained with blood, bloody.* Lit., coniugis imago, Ov. Transf., (1) *wounding, injuring*: nulla exstat littera Nasonis sanguinolenta legi, Ov. (2) *blood-red*: color, Ov.

sanguis -inis, m. and old form **sanguen**, n. *blood.*

Lit., tauri sanguis, Cic.; sanguinem mittere, of doctors, *to bleed, let blood*, Cic. L.; sanguinem effundere, *to shed freely*, Cic. Sometimes *bloodshed*: odio civilis sanguinis, Cic.

Transf., (1) *blood-relationship, race, family*: magnam possidet religionem paternus maternusque sanguis, Cic.; Troiano a sanguine, Verg. (2) *a descendant, progeny*: reges, deorum sanguinem, Hor.; saevire in suum sanguinem, Liv.; Verg., Tac. (3) fig., *life-blood, strength, vigour*: amisimus sucum et sanguinem, Cic.; of orators: verum sanguinem deperdebat, Cic.; de sanguine aerarii detrahere, Cic.; reipublicae, Cic.; Verg.

sănĭēs -ēi, f. (connected with sanguis), *corrupted blood, bloody matter.* Lit., Lucr., Verg., etc. Transf., *venom, poison, slaver*: perfusus sanie atroque veneno, Verg.; sanies manat ore trilingui, Ov.; Hor.

sānĭtās -ātis, f. (sanus), *health, soundness.* Lit., physical: Pl., Cic., etc.

Transf., (1) mental; *reasonableness, good sense, sanity*: ad sanitatem se convertere, or redire, Cic.; Caes., Liv. (2) of style, *soundness* or *correctness, purity*: orationis, Cic.; Tac. (3) in gen.: victoriae, *genuineness*, Tac.

sanna -ae, f. (σάννας), *a mocking grimace*: Pers., Juv.

sannĭo -ōnis, m. (sanna), *one who makes grimaces, a buffoon*: Cic.

sāno -are (sanus), *to heal, cure, restore to health.* Lit., tumorem oculorum, Cic.; aliquem, Cic.; Ov., etc.

Transf., in gen., *to restore, repair*: mentem, Lucr.; incommodum commodis, Caes.; Cic.

Sanquālis (Sanguālis) -e (Sancus), *belonging to Sancus*: avis, *the bird sacred to Sancus, the osprey*, Liv.

Santŏnes -um, m. and **Santŏni** -ōrum, m. *a people in Aquitanian Gaul.*

¶ Hence adj. **Santŏnĭcus** -a -um, *belonging to the Santones.*

sānus -a -um, adj. (with compar. and superl.), *sound, healthy.*

LIT., physically: pars corporis, Cic.; aliquem sanum facere, Cic.; Hor., etc.

TRANSF., (1) in gen., *sound, uninjured*: respublica, Cic. L.; civitas, Liv. (2) *of sound mind, rational, sane*: homo, Cic.; vix sanae mentis, Liv.; mens sana in corpore sano, Juv. (3) of style, *sound, correct*: genus dicendi, Cic.; Plin. L.

¶ Hence adv. (with compar.) **sānē**. LIT., *rationally, sensibly*: non ego sanius bacchabor Edonis, Hor.; Pl. TRANSF., *really, indeed, to be sure*. In gen.: res sane difficilis, Cic.; sane vellem, *I could indeed wish*, Cic.; Pl., Hor., etc. Esp. (1) in answers, *surely, to be sure*: Pl., Ter., Cic. (2) in concessions, *admittedly, to be sure*: sint falsa sane, Cic. (3) with imperatives, *then, if you will*: age sane, Cic. (4) ironically: beneficium magnum sane! Phaedr. (5) sane quam, *how very much!* hence *exceedingly, extremely*; with verbs and adjectives: Cic.

săpa -ae, f. *must or new wine boiled down*: Varr., Ov.

săperda -ae, m. (σαπέρδης), *a salted fish from the Euxine*: Varr., Pers.

săpiens -entis, partic. from sapio; q.v.

săpientia -ae, f. (sapiens). In gen., *wisdom, good sense, discernment, prudence*: pro vestra sapientia, Cic.; Hor., etc. Esp. *proficiency in philosophy, in science, or in any department of knowledge*: princeps omnium virtutum illa sapientia, quam σοφίαν Graeci vocant, Cic.; sapientia, quae ars vivendi putanda est, Cic.; sapientia constituendae civitatis, Cic.; Lucr.

săpio sapĕre sapīvi *or* sapii, *to taste, have a flavour.*

LIT., physically. (1) *to taste*: Cato, Plin.; with acc., *to taste of*: mare ipsum, Sen.; Juv.; sometimes *to smell of*: crocum, Cic. (2) *to have taste, be able to taste*: nec sequitur ut, cui cor sapiat, ei non sapiat palatus, Cic.

TRANSF., mentally, *to discern, be sensible, be wise, think*: animus sibi per se, Lucr.; si sapis, Cat.; Cic., etc. With acc.: nullam rem, Pl.; nihil, Cic.; Hor.

¶ Hence partic. (with compar. and superl.) **săpiens** -entis, of persons and things, *wise, sensible, judicious*: rex aequus ac sapiens, Cic.; vera et sapiens animi magnitudo, Cic.; mores, Pl.; consilium, Ov. As subst. (1) *a sensible, judicious person*: insani sapiens nomen ferat, Hor. (2) *a wise man, a philosopher, a sage*: septem sapientes, The Seven Wise Men of Greece, Cic.; Hor., etc.

¶ Adv. (with compar. and superl.) **săpientĕr**, *wisely, discreetly, judiciously*: facere, Cic.; Pl., Ov., etc.

săpo -ōnis, m. (a Celtic word), *soap*: Plin.

săpor -ōris, m. (sapio), *taste.*

LIT., *the taste of a material thing*: qui non sapore capiatur, Cic.; dulcis, Cic., Hor.; salsus, Lucr.

TRANSF., (1) *sense of taste*: Lucr. (2) *taste in style or conduct*: vernaculus, Cic.; homo sine sapore, Cic. (3) *flavouring, juice*: gallae admiscere saporem, Verg.; Tib., Plin.

Sapphō -ūs; acc. Sapphō; f. (Σαπφώ), *a lyric poetess of Mytilene in Lesbos.*

¶ Hence adj. **Sapphĭcus** -a -um, *Sapphic.*

sarcĭna -ae, f. (sarcio), *a bundle, pack, portable luggage.* LIT., sing.: Pl., Hor.; plur.:

sarcinas conferre, Caes.; legionem sub sarcinis adoriri, Caes. TRANSF., (1) abstr., *a burden, load*: publica rerum, *burden of government*, Ov. (2) *of the womb*: Ov.

sarcĭnārĭus -a -um (sarcina), *of burdens or baggage*: iumenta, *beasts of burden*, Caes.

sarcĭnātor -ōris, m. (sarcio), *a patcher, mender, cobbler*: Pl.

sarcĭnātus -a -um (sarcina), *loaded, burdened*: Pl.

sarcĭnŭla -ae, f. (dim. of sarcina), *a little bundle*: Cat., Juv.

sarcĭo sarcire sarsi sartum, *to mend, patch, repair.* LIT., aedes, Pl.; lapsas ruinas generis (apum), Verg. TRANSF., *to make good, repair*: damna, Cic. L.; detrimentum, Caes.; iniuriam, Caes.; gratia male sarta, *not completely restored*, Hor.

¶ Hence partic. **sartus** -a -um, esp. in phrase, sartus et tectus, *or* sartus tectus, *in good condition*. LIT., of buildings, *in good repair*: aedem Castoris sartam tectam tradere, Cic.; omnia sarta tecta exigere, Cic.; Liv. TRANSF., *in good condition, well-preserved, safe*: M. Curium sartum et tectum, ut aiunt, ab omni incommodo conserves, Cic. L.; Pl.

sarcŏphăgus -a -um (σαρκοφάγος). LIT., *flesh-eating*: lapis, *a kind of stone used for coffins, which was believed to consume the body*, Plin. M. as subst. **sarcŏphăgus** -i, *a coffin, grave*: Juv.

sarcŭlum -i, n. (sarrio), *a light hoe*: Hor., Ov.

Sardēs (Sardīs) -ĭum, f. pl. (Σάρδεις), *Sardis, the old capital of Lydia on the Pactolus, residence of King Croesus.*

¶ Hence adj. **Sardĭānus** -a -um, *Sardian*; m. pl. as subst. **Sardĭāni** -ōrum, *the Sardians.*

Sardi -ōrum, m. (Σαρδώ=Sardinia), *the inhabitants of the island of Sardinia, the Sardinians; notorious for their perfidy*: Cic.

¶ Hence adj. **Sardus, Sardŏnĭus, Sardōus** (Σαρδῷος) -a -um, *Sardinian.* Subst. **Sardĭnĭa** -ae, f. *the island of Sardinia.*

¶ Hence adj. **Sardĭnĭensis** -e, *Sardinian.*

sardŏnyx -nychis, m. and f. (σαρδόνυξ), *a precious stone, the sardonyx*: Juv., Mart., Pers.

sargus -i, m. *an edible salt-water fish, the sargo*: Enn., Ov.

sărĭo=sarrio; q.v.

sărīsa -ae, f. (σάρισα), *the long Macedonian pike*: Liv., Ov.

sărĭsŏphŏrus -i, m. (σαρισοφόρος), *a Macedonian pikeman*: Liv.

Sarmăta -ae, m. (Σαρμάτης), *a Sarmatian*; plur. **Sarmătae** -arum, *the Sarmatians, a people living in what is now South Russia.*

¶ Hence subst. **Sarmătĭa** -ae, f. (Σαρματία), *Sarmatia, the country of the Sarmatae*; adj. **Sarmătĭcus** -a -um (Σαρματικός), *Sarmatic*: mare, *the Black Sea*, Ov.; adv. **Sarmătĭcē** loqui, Ov.; f. adj. **Sarmătĭs** -idis, *Sarmatian.*

sarmen -ĭnis, n.=sarmentum; q.v.: Pl.

sarmentum -i, n. *twigs, small branches, brushwood.* (1) green, esp. of the vine: Cic. (2) dry: fasces sarmentorum, *fascines*, Liv.; ligna et sarmenta circumdare, Cic.

Sarnus -i, m. *a river in Campania* (now *Sarno*).

Sarra (Săra) -ae, f. *the Hebrew Zor, old name of the city of Tyre.*
¶ Hence adj. **Sarrānus** -a -um, *Tyrian, Phoenician*: ostrum, Verg.
sarrācum -i, n.=serracum; q.v.
Sarrastes -um, m. *a people in Campania, living near the Sarnus.*
sarrĭo (sărĭo) -ire -ŭi and -īvi, *to hoe, to weed*: Pl., Varr.
sarrītor -ōris, m. (sarrio), *a hoer, weeder*: Varr.
sartāgo -ĭnis, f. *a frying-pan.* LIT., Plin., Juv. TRANSF., sartago loquendi, *medley, hotch-potch*, Pers.
sartor=sarritor; q.v.: Pl.
sartus -a -um, partic. from sarcio; q.v.
săt, sătăgĭto, sătăgo, *see* satis.
sătellĕs -ĭtis, c. *a guard, attendant*; plur. *escort, suite, train.*
        LIT., Cic., Liv., etc.
        TRANSF., (1) in gen., *a companion, attendant*: Aurorae, *Lucifer*, Cic.; Orci, *Charon,* Hor. (2) in a bad sense, *accomplice, abettor*: audaciae, Cic.; scelerum, Cic.
sătĭās -ātis, f. (satis), *a sufficiency, abundance*: cibi, Lucr.; frumenti, Sall. Sometimes *over-abundance, satiety*: quo de die epulatis iam vini satias esset, Liv.; amoris, Liv.; Ter.
Săticŭla -ae, f. *a town of Samnium.*
        ¶ Hence adj. **Săticŭlānus** -a -um, *Saticula*; subst. **Săticŭlus** -i, m. *an inhabitant of Saticula.*
sătĭĕtās -ātis, f. (satis), *a sufficiency, abundance*: ornandi, Pl. Sometimes (like satias), *over-abundance, satiety*: cibi, Cic.; amoris, Ter.; studiorum omnium satietas vitae facit satietatem, Cic.; Liv.
sătĭnĕ, sătĭn=satisne, *see* satis.
¹sătĭo -are (satis), *to satisfy, fill.*
        LIT., physically: satiati agni, Lucr.; desideria naturae, Cic.; sitim, Mart.; ignes odoribus, Ov.
        TRANSF., abstr. (1) *to satisfy, sate*: aviditatem legendi, Cic.; populum libertate, Cic.; Liv., etc. (2) *to overfill, to cloy, to satiate*: numerus agnoscitur, deinde satiat, Cic.; Tib., Tac.
²sătĭo -ōnis, f. (sero), *a sowing* or *planting*: Cic., Verg., Liv.; plur.: sationes, *sown fields*, Cic.
sătĭra, *see* satur.
sătĭs or **săt,** *enough.*
        (1) as indecl. adj. or subst., *enough, sufficient*: satis habeo, or sat habeo, Pl., Ter.; tantum quantum sat est, Cic.; satis superque, *enough and more than enough*, Cic., Liv., etc.; with genit.: ea amicitia non satis habet firmitatis, Cic.; nec sat rationis in armis, Verg.; as complement to infin.: satis erat respondere, Cic.; satis habeo, with infin.: Sall.; with quod: Liv.; satis est si, Pl., Liv., Hor.
        (2) as adv., *enough, sufficiently, fairly, quite.* With verbs: Cic., Verg., etc. With adj.: satis multa restant, Cic.; ipse satis ut in re trepida impavidus, Liv. With another adv.: sat diu, Cic.; satis honeste, Cic.; Caes., etc.
        Compar. **sătĭus,** *better, more advantageous*; esp. with infin., or acc. and infin.: mori satius esse, Cic.; mori me satius est, Ter.; Pl., Verg., Liv.
sătĭnĕ, sătĭn=satisne, introducing questions, esp. in phrase, satine salve? *see* salve.

¶ Hence **săt ăgĭto** or **sătăgĭto** -are, *to have enough to do, have one's hands full*: Pl.
¶ **sătĭs ăgo** or **săt ăgo** or **sătăgo** -ăgĕre. (1) *to satisfy* or *pay a creditor*: Pl. (2) *to have enough to do, have one's hands full*: Pl., Ter., Cic. L.
¶ **sătĭs do** dare dĕdi dătum, *to give bail* or *security*: Pl., Cic.; satis dato, *by bail, by security,* Cic. Similarly **sătĭs accĭpĭo** accipĕre, *to take bail* or *security*: Cic.
¶ **sătĭs făcĭo** or **sătisfăcĭo** făcĕre fēci factum, *to give satisfaction, satisfy, content.* In gen., usually with dat.: Cic. Esp. (1) *to satisfy,* i.e. *pay* a creditor: ipse Fufiis satisfacit, Cic.; Caes. (2) *to give satisfaction, make amends, make reparation*: alicui, Caes., Cic.; omnibus rationibus de iniuriis, Caes. (3) *to prove sufficiently*: alicui, with acc. and infin., Cic.
sătisdătĭo -ōnis, f. (satis/do), *a giving bail* or *security*: Cic. L.
sătisfactĭo -ōnis, f. (satis/facio), *amends, reparation, apology*: satisfactionem alicuius accipere, Cic., Caes.; recipere, Tac.
sătĭus, comp. of satis; q.v.
sător -ōris, m. (¹sero), *a sower, planter.* LIT., Lucr., Cic. TRANSF., *begetter, father, producer*: sator hominum atque deorum, i.e. *Jupiter*, Verg.; litis, Liv.; Pl.
satrăpēs -is; plur. satrapae -arum; m. (σατράπης, from a Persian word), *the governor of a Persian province, a satrap, viceroy*: Ter., Nep.
satrăpīa (satrăpēa) -ae, f. (σατραπεία), *a province governed by a satrap, satrapy*: Curt., Plin.
Satrĭcum -i, n. *a Latin town on the Appian Way, near Antium.*
        ¶ Hence **Satrĭcāni** -ōrum, m. *the inhabitants of Satricum*: Liv.
sătur -tŭra -tŭrum (satis), *full, sated.*
        LIT., pullus, Cic.; with abl., *full of*: Pl., Ov.; with genit.: Ter., Lucr., Hor.
        TRANSF., (1) of things or places, *rich*: Tarentum, Verg. (2) of colour, *full, rich*: color, Verg. (3) of rhetorical themes, *rich, copious*: nec satura ieiune (dicet), Cic.
        ¶ F. as subst. **sătŭra** -ae (sc. lanx). LIT., *a dish of various ingredients, a medley.* TRANSF., (1) in phrase, per saturam, *indiscriminately, confusedly*: quasi per saturam sententiis exquisitis, Sall. (2) **sătŭra** (or **sătĭra**), '*satire*', *a literary form loosely combining a variety of topics, claimed as a Roman invention*: satura quidem tota nostra est, Quint.; difficile est saturam non scribere, Juv.; Hor., Liv.
Sătŭrae palus, *a marsh in Latium.*
sătŭrēïa -ae, f.: Plin.; plur. **sătŭrēïa** -ōrum, n.: Ov., *the herb savory.*
Sătŭrēïānus -a -um, *belonging to a district of Apulia, hence poet.=Apulian*: Hor.
sătŭrĭtās -ātis, f. (satur). LIT., *satiety, repletion*: Pl. TRANSF., *abundance*: saturitas copiaque rerum omnium, Cic.
Sătŭrnālĭa, etc., *see* Saturnus.
Sătŭrnīnus -i, m. *a Roman surname*; esp. of L. Appuleius, *tribune of the plebs in* 102 B.C.
Sătŭrnus -i, m.
        (1) *the planet Saturn*: Hor.
        (2) *a mythical king of Latium, honoured as the god of agriculture and of civilization in general; identified with the* Κρόνος *of the*

Greeks and regarded as father of Jupiter:
Verg., Ov., etc.

¶ Hence adj. **Sāturnĭus** -a -um, *Saturn-
ian*: tellus, *or* arva, *Italy*, Verg.; gens, *the
Italians*, Ov.; numerus, *the Saturnian metre*,
Hor.; domitor maris, *Neptune*, *his son*, Verg.
As subst., m. **Sāturnĭus** -i, *Jupiter or Pluto*:
Ov.; f. **Sāturnĭa** -ae, *Juno*: Verg.; *also an
old town on the Capitoline Hill*: Verg.

¶ Adj. **Sāturnālĭa** -e, *belonging to Saturn*;
n. pl. as subst. **Sāturnālĭa** -ium and -iorum,
*a festival of Saturn beginning on the 17th of
December, at which there were public spectacles
and banquets, presents were exchanged, slaves
were waited upon by their masters.* The festival
lasted several days, the first of which was
called Saturnalia prima, the next Saturnalia
secunda, and the third Saturnalia tertia:
Cic. L., Liv.

¶ Hence adj. **Sāturnālĭcĭus** -a -um, *of
the Saturnalia*: Mart.

sătŭro -are (satur), *to satisfy, fill.*
LIT., physically: animalia ubertate mammarum, Cic.; Verg., Ov.; sola fimo, *to
manure*, Verg.
TRANSF., mentally: se sanguine civium,
Cic.; crudelitatem suam odiumque, Cic.;
homines saturati honoribus, Cic. Rarely,
to give more than enough, to make weary of:
me vitae, Pl.

¹**sătus** -a -um, partic. from ¹sero; q.v.

²**sătus** -ūs, m. (¹sero), *a sowing, planting.* LIT.,
Cic. TRANSF., (1) *metaphorical planting,
seed*: haec preparat animos ad satus accipien-
dos, Cic. (2) *begetting, origin*: Hercules Iovis
satu editus, Cic.; a primo satu, Cic.

sătўriscus -i, m. (σατυρίσκος), *a little satyr*: Cic.

sătўrus -i, m. (σάτυρος), *a satyr; a sylvan deity,
like an ape, with a horse's tail and two goat's
feet.* LIT., Cic., Hor., etc. TRANSF., *Greek
Satyric drama*, in which Satyrs formed the
chorus: Satyrorum scriptor, Hor.

saucĭātĭo -ōnis, f. (saucio), *a wounding*: Cic.

saucĭo -are (saucius), *to wound, hurt.* LIT.,
aliquem, Pl., Cic.; ungue genas, Ov.
TRANSF., (1) *to break up the ground* with the
plough: duram humum, Ov. (2) fig.: cor,
famam, Pl.

saucĭus -a -um, *wounded, injured, hurt.*
LIT., paucis sauciis, Caes.; Cic., Verg., etc.
TRANSF., (1) of things, *stricken, injured*:
malus saucius Africo, Hor.; glacies saucia
sole, Ov. (2) of persons, *stricken, distressed*:
gladiator ille, Cic.; animus eius, Cic. L.
Esp. *love-sick*: mens amore, Lucr.; regina
gravi saucia curā, Verg.; Ov.

Saurŏmătēs -ae, m. (Σαυρομάτης), *a Sarmatian, see* Sarmata.

sāvĭātĭo -onis, f. (savior), *a kissing*: Pl.

sāvĭŏlum -i, n. (dim. of savium), *a little kiss*:
Cat.

sāvĭor -ari, dep. (savium), *to kiss*: aliquem,
Cic.; Cat.

sāvĭum (suāvĭum) -i, n. (1) *a mouth ready
for kissing*: Pl. (2) *a kiss*: Atticae meis verbis
savium des volo, Cic. L.; Pl.

saxātĭlis -e (saxum), *frequenting rocks, to be
found among rocks*: Varr., Plin.

saxĕtum -i, n. (saxum), *a rocky place*: Cic.

saxĕus -a -um (saxum), *of rock, rocky, stony*:
scopulum, Ov.; umbra, *cast by a rock*, Verg.;
Niobe saxea facta, *turned to stone*, Ov.

saxĭfĭcus -a -um (saxum/facio), *turning into
stone, petrifying*: vultus Medusae, Ov.

saxĭfrăgus -a -um (saxum/frango), *stone-
breaking, stone-crushing*: Plin.

saxōsus -a -um (saxum), *full of rocks, rocky*:
valles, Verg. N. pl. as subst. **saxōsa** -ōrum,
rocky places: Plin., Quint.

saxŭlum -i, n. (dim. of saxum), *a little rock*:
Cic.

saxum -i, n. *a rock* or *large stone, a detached
fragment of rock.*
In gen.: saxo undique absciso rupes, Liv.;
saxa latentia, *reefs*, Verg.; saxum quadratum,
for building, Liv.; saxo lucum circumdedit
alto, i.e. *a stone wall*, Ov.
Esp. (1) Saxum sacrum, *the holy rock,
the place on the Aventine where Remus took
the auspices*, Cic. (2) *the Tarpeian rock*: Pl.,
Lucr., Cic. L.

scăbellum (scăbillum) -i, n. (dim. of scamnum). LIT., *a small stool, footstool*: Varr.
TRANSF., *a musical instrument played with
the foot, used to accompany dancing*: Cic.

scăber -bra -brum (scabo), *scabby, mangy*:
oves, Pl. Hence, in gen., *rough, scurfy*: unguis, Ov.; robigo, Verg.; scaber intonsusque
homo, Hor.

scăbĭēs -ēi, f. (scabo). LIT., *the scab, mange,
itch.* TRANSF., (1) *roughness*: Verg., Juv.
(2) *an itch, itching desire*: lucri, Hor.; Cic.

scăbĭōsus -a -um (scabies), *scabby, mangy*:
Pers. TRANSF., (1) *rough*: Plin. (2) *mouldy*:
Pers.

scăbo scăbĕre scābi (cf. σκάπτω), *to scratch, rub*:
caput, Hor.

Scaea porta -ae, f. and **Scaeae portae**
(Σκαιαὶ πύλαι), *the west gate of Troy.*

scaena (scēna) -ae, f. (σκηνή), *the boards of
the theatre, the stage, the scene, the theatre.*
LIT., de scaena decedere, *to go off the
stage*, Cic.; sphaeram in scaenam adferre,
Cic.; scaenis agitatus Orestes, *on the stage*,
i.e. *in the tragedies*, Verg.; Hor., Liv.
TRANSF., (1) of nature, *a background*: tum
silvis scaena coruscis, Verg. (2) *publicity,
the public eye, the world*: in scaena, id est, in
contione, Cic.; minus in scaena esse, *to be less
before the eyes of the world*, Cic.; scaenae
servire, Cic. L.; Hor. (3) *of schools of
rhetoric*: Tac. (4) *pretext, parade, outward
show*: scaenam ultro criminis parat, Tac.

scaenālis -e (scaena), *belonging to the theatre,
theatrical*: Lucr.

scaenĭcus -a -um (scaena), *of the stage, scenic,
theatrical*: ludi, Liv.; venustas, Cic. M. as
subst. **scaenĭcus** -i, *a stage-hero, an actor*:
Cic., Tac.

Scaevŏla -ae, m. (scaevus), *the left-handed,
a surname of the gens Mucia; see* Mucius.

scaevus -a -um (cf. σκαιός), *left, on the left.*
TRANSF., *awkward*: Sall.

¶ F. as subst. **scaeva** -ae, *an omen,
portent*: Pl.

scālae -ārum, f. pl. (scando), *a flight of stairs,
staircase, ladder*: se in scalas tabernae
librariae conicere, Cic.; scalas admovere
(muris, moenibus), *scaling-ladders*, Caes.
Liv.; muros scalis adgredi, Sall.; Verg.

Scaldis -is, m. *a river in Gallia Belgica* (now
the Scheldt): Caes.

scalmus -i, m. (σκαλμός), *a thole-pin, a rowlock*
navicula duorum scalmorum, *two-oared*, Cic

scalpellum -i, n. (dim. of scalprum), *a small surgical knife, lancet, scalpel*: Cic.

scalpo scalpĕre scalpsi scalptum (perhaps connected with γλάφω), *to carve, scrape, scratch.* LIT., apta manus est ad fingendum, ad scalpendum, Cic.; sepulcro querellam, Ov.; terram unguibus, Hor.; caput, Juv. TRANSF., *to tickle*: Pers.

scalprum -i, n. (scalpo), *a cutting instrument*; *a chisel*: Liv.; *a penknife*: Tac.

scalptor -ōris, m. (scalpo), *a cutter, engraver*: Plin.

scalptūra -ae, f. (scalpo), *a cutting, engraving.* LIT., gemmarum, Plin. TRANSF., *a figure engraved, an engraving*: Suet.

scalpurrio -ire (scalpo), *to scratch*: Pl.

Scămander -dri, m. (Σκάμανδρος), *a river at Troy, rising on Mount Ida and joining the Simois, also called Xanthus, on account of its red colour.*

scambus -a -um (σκαμβός), *bow-legged*: Suet.

scammōnĕa and **scammōnĭa** -ae, f. (σκαμμωνία), *the plant scammony*: Cic.

scamnum -i, n. (connected with σκήπτω), *a bench, stool*: cava sub tenerum scamna dare pedem, Ov.; ante focos scamnis considere longis, Ov.; Mart.

scando scandĕre scandi scansum, *to climb.* LIT., in aggerem, Liv.; in domos superas, Ov. With acc. object: superas, Ov.; malos, Cic.; muros, Verg., Liv.; Capitolium, Hor.
    TRANSF., *to mount, rise*: supra principem, Tac.; with acc.: scandit aeratas vitiosa naves cura, Hor.

scăpha -ae, f. (σκάφη), *a small boat, skiff*: Caes., Cic., Hor.

scăphĭum -i, n. (σκαφίον), *a pot, bowl*; esp. *a drinking-vessel*: Pl., Lucr., Cic.

Scăpŭla -ae, m. *a surname of the Cornelian gens*; adj. **Scăpŭlānus** -a -um, *belonging to Scapula*: horti, Cic. L.

scăpŭlae -ārum, f. pl. *the shoulder-blades*; in gen., *the shoulders, the back*: Pl., Sen.

scăpus -i, m. (*see* scamnum). (**1**) *the stalk of plants*: Plin. (**2**) *a weaver's beam*, or perhaps *a leash-rod*: Lucr.

scărĭfo -are (σκαριφάομαι), *to scratch up, scarify*: Plin., Mart.

scărus -i, m. (σκάρος), *a salt-water fish*; perhaps *the parrot-fish*: Hor.

scătebra -ae, f. (scateo), *a spouting up, bubbling up of water*: Verg.

scătĕo -ēre and (archaic) **scăto** -ĕre, *to gush, spout up, bubble out.* LIT., Lucr. TRANSF., *to teem, abound*, with liquid or other things; with abl.: arx scatens fontibus, Liv.; beluis pontus, Hor.; with genit.: terra ferarum, Lucr.; with acc.: Pl.

scăturrĭgo -gĭnis, f. (scaturrio), *a spring of bubbling water*; in plur.: scaturigines turbidae, Liv.

scăturrĭo -ire (scateo), *to gush, bubble.* TRANSF., Curio totus hoc scaturrit, *is full of* (love for this party), ap. Cic. L.

scaurus -a -um (σκαῦρος), *having projecting* or *swollen ankles*: Hor. As name, **Scaurus**, *a Roman surname in the gens Aemilia and gens Aurelia.*

scăzon -ontis, m. (σκάζων, *limping*), *an iambic trimeter with a spondee* or *trochee in the last foot*: Plin. L., Mart.

scĕlĕro -are (scelus), *to pollute, profane with guilt*: manūs, Verg.; Cat.
    ¶ Hence partic. (with compar. and superl.) **scĕlĕrātus** -a -um, *polluted, profaned by guilt.* LIT., terra, Verg.; limina Thracum, Ov.; esp.: Sceleratus Vicus, *the street on the Esquiline, where Tullia, the daughter of Servius Tullius, drove over the corpse of her father*, Liv.; Sceleratus Campus, *near the porta Collina, where unchaste Vestal virgins were buried alive*, Liv. TRANSF., (**1**) *impious, wicked, profane, infamous*: hasta sceleratior, Cic.; homo sceleratissimus, Cic.; insania, Verg.; coniuratio, Liv.; m. as subst.: Pl., Cic. (**2**) *wretched, tiresome, noxious*: frigus, Verg.; Pl.
    ¶ Adv. (with compar. and superl.) **scĕlĕrātē**, *impiously, wickedly*: facere, Cic.; dicere in aliquem, Cic.; sceleratissime machinari omnes insidias, Cic.

scĕlĕrōsus -a -um (scelus), *full of guilt, wicked, accursed*; often together with impius: facta, Lucr.; Ter.

scĕlestus -a -um (scelus). LIT., *wicked, accursed, infamous*: facinus, Cic.; sermo scelestior, Liv.; scelestissimum te arbitror, Pl. TRANSF., *unlucky, pernicious*: Pl.
    ¶ Adv. **scĕlestē**, *wickedly, impiously*: facere, Liv.; suspicari, Cic. L.; Pl.

scĕlus -ĕris, n. *a crime, evil deed, impious action.*
    LIT., scelus facere, admittere, committere, edere, concipere in se, suscipere, Cic.; scelus est (civem Romanum) verberare, Cic.; minister sceleris, Liv.; Tac., etc.
    TRANSF., (**1**) *misfortune, calamity*: Pl., Ter., Mart. (**2**) as a term of abuse, *scoundrel, rascal*: scelus viri, *a rogue of a man*, Pl.; Ter.

scēna=scaena; q.v.

scēnālis=scaenalis; q.v.

scēnĭcus=scaenicus; q.v.

Scepsis -is, f. (Σκῆψις), *a town in Mysia.*
    ¶ Hence adj. **Scepsĭus** -a -um, *of Scepsis*: Metrodorus, Cic.

sceptrĭfĕr -fĕra -fĕrum (sceptrum/fero), *sceptre-bearing*: Ov.

sceptrum -i, n. (σκῆπτρον), *a sceptre, royal wand* or *staff.* LIT., Cic., Verg., etc.; jestingly: paedagogorum, Mart. TRANSF., *dominion, kingdom, royal authority*: sceptra petit Evandri, Verg.; Lucr., Ov.

sceptūchus -i, m. (σκηπτοῦχος), *the wand-bearer, a high official in Eastern courts*: Tac.

schĕda and **scĭda** -ae, f. (σχίδη), *a strip of papyrus bark*: Plin. Hence *a leaf of paper*: ut scida ne qua depereat, Cic. L.; Mart., Quint.

schēma -ae, f. and -ătis, n. (σχῆμα), *shape, figure, form, fashion*: Pl., Suet.; of speech: Quint.

Schoeneūs -ĕi, m. (Σχοινεύς), *a king of Boeotia, father of Atalanta.*
    ¶ Hence adj. **Schoenēĭus** -a -um, *belonging to Schoeneus*: Schoeneia virgo, Atalanta, Ov.; subst. **Schoenēĭs** -ĭdis, f. *Atalanta*: Ov.

schoenŏbătēs -ae, m. (σχοινοβάτης), *a rope-walker, rope-dancer*: Juv.

schoenus -i, m. (σχοῖνος). (**1**) *an aromatic reed used by the Romans to flavour wine, and as an ingredient in an unguent*: Cato. (**2**) *a Persian measure of distance*: Plin.

schŏla -ae, f. (σχολή).

Lɪᴛ., *learned leisure; learned conversation, debate, dispute; a lecture, dissertation*: certae scholae sunt de exsilio, de interitu patriae, etc., Cic.; scholas Graecorum more habere, Cic.; vertes te ad alteram scholam, *matter*, Cic.

Tʀᴀɴsꜰ., (1) *a place where learned disputations are carried on, a school*: Cic., Quint., Plin. L. (2) *the disciples of a philosopher, a school, sect*: clamabant omnes philosophorum scholae, Cic.; Plin. L.

schŏlastĭcus -a -um (σχολαστικός), *of a school*; esp. *of a school of rhetoric, rhetorical*: controversiae, Quint.; Tac., Plin. L. As subst., n. pl. **schŏlastĭca** -ōrum, *rhetorical exercises*: Quint.; m. **schŏlastĭcus** -i, *a student* or *teacher of rhetoric*: Suet., Tac., etc.

scīda=scheda; q.v.

scĭens -entis, partic. from scio; q.v.

scĭentĭa -ae, f. (sciens), *a knowing, knowledge of, acquaintance with, skill in*. With subjective genit.: militum, Caes. With objective genit.: linguae Gallicae, Caes.; futurorum malorum, Cic.; iuris, Cic.; rei militaris, Cic. With in, or de: Cic., Plur.: tot artes, tantae scientiae, Cic.

scīlĭcĕt, adv. (contr. from scire licet, *one may know*), *evidently, certainly, of course*.

In gen. With acc. and infin.: Pl., Ter., Lucr., Sall. Usually as ordinary adv., to give emphasis: rogat et prece cogit, scilicet ut tibi se laudare et tradere cogar, *if you please*, Hor.; cur igitur eos manumisit? metuebat scilicet, *he was afraid, of course*, Cic.

Esp. (1) foll. by an adversative (tamen, sed tamen, or sed): nihil scilicet novi, ea tamen, quae te ipsum probaturum confidam, *to be sure*, Cic. (2) ironically, *of course, no doubt*: id populus curat scilicet, *much the people care about that!* Ter.; ego istius pecudis consilio scilicet aut praesidio uti volebam, Cic. (3) elliptically, esp. in answers: scilicet, *certainly*, Pl., Ter., Lucr. (4) explanatory, *namely*: Suet., Nep.

scilla (**squilla**) -ae, f. (σκίλλα). (1) *a sea-leek, squill*: Varr., Plin. (2) *a small lobster*, or perhaps *a crayfish* or *prawn*: Cic., Hor.

scin'=scisne, *see* scio.

scindo scindĕre scĭdi scissum (connected with σχίζω), *to cut, rend, tear asunder, split*.

Lɪᴛ., epistulam, Cic.; vestem de corpore, Prop.; lignum cuneis, Verg.; crines, Verg.; mater scissa comam, *with torn hair*, Verg.; prov.: paenulam alicui, *to tear off a person's travelling cloak*, i.e. *to urge him to stay*, Cic. L. With reflex., or pass. in middle sense, *to split up*: Verg., etc.

Tʀᴀɴsꜰ., *to part, divide, separate*: ne scindam ipse dolorem meum, Cic.; genus amborum scindit se sanguine ab uno, Verg.; in contraria studia scinditur vulgus, Verg.; verba fletu, *to interrupt*, Ov.

¶ Hence partic. **scissus** -a -um, *torn, rent*. Tʀᴀɴsꜰ., genus vocum, *harsh*, Cic.

scintilla -ae, f. *a spark*. Lɪᴛ., silici scintillam excudere, Verg.; Lucr., Liv., etc. Tʀᴀɴsꜰ., *a glimmer, faint trace*: ingenii, Cic.; belli, Cic. L.

scintillo -are (scintilla), *to sparkle, glitter*: scintillat oleum testā ardente, Verg.; Lucr., etc.

scintillŭla -ae, f. (dim. of scintilla), *a little spark*: virtutum quasi scintillulae, Cic.

scĭo scire scīvi or scii scītum (old fut., scibo Ter.; imperf., scibam: Cat.; syncop. perf. scisti: Ov.; infin., scisse: Cic.); *to understand, have knowledge of* (opp. nescio) Absol.: scio, in parenthesis, *I know*, Pl. quod sciam, *as far as I know*, Cic. With acc object.: litteras, Cic.; istarum rerum nihil Cic.; Hor., etc. With acc. and infin.: scio tibi ita placere, Cic.; scire tuum nihil est nisi te scire hoc sciat alter, Pers.; Hor., etc With indir. quest.: cum sciatis, quo quaeque res inclinet, Cic.; Hor., etc. With de and the abl.: cum is, qui de omnibus scierit, de Sulla se scire negavit, Cic. With infin., *to know how to*: vincere scis, Hannibal, Liv.; Cic. Hor. With adv.: scire Graece, Latine, *to understand Greek, Latin*.

¶ Hence partic. as adj. (with compar. and superl.) **scĭens** -entis. (1) *knowing, aware* hence like adv., *knowingly, intentionally*: u offenderet sciens neminem, Cic.; Pl., Ter (2) *knowing, understanding, versed in, acquainted with*; with genit.: belli, Sall. citharae, Hor.; scientissimus reipublicae gerendae, Cic.; with infin.: flectere equum sciens, Hor.; absol.: quis hoc homine scientior? Cic.

¶ Adv. (with compar. and superl.) **scientĕr**, *skilfully, expertly*: Caes., Cic.

¶ For **scītus** -a -um, *see* scisco.

¹scīpĭo -ōnis, m. (connected with sceptrum) *a staff, wand*: Pl., Cat.; eburneus, carried by *viri triumphales*, Liv.

²Scīpĭo -ōnis, m. (perhaps connected with σκήπτω), *a family of the gens Cornelia; see* Cornelius.

¶ Hence subst. **Scīpĭădēs** -ae, m. *one of the family of the Scipios, a Scipio*: Lucr., Verg.

Scīron -ōnis, m. (Σκίρων, Σκείρων). (1) *a noted robber on the coast between Megaris and Attica, killed by Theseus*. (2) *an Epicurean philosopher, contemporary of Cicero*.

scirpĕus (**sirpĕus**) -a -um (scirpus), *of rushes* simulacra (*see* Argei), Ov. F. as subst.

scirpĕa or **sirpĕa** -ae, *basket-work made of rushes* (to form the body of a waggon): Ov.

scirpĭcŭlus (**sirpĭcŭlus**) -a -um (scirpus), *o rushes*: Cato. M. and f. as subst. **scirpĭcŭlus** -i and **scirpĭcŭla** -ae, *a rush-basket*: Pl. Varr., Prop.

scirpus (**sirpus**) -i, m. *a rush, bulrush*; prov.: nodum in scirpo quaerere, *to find a difficulty where there is none*, Pl., Ter.

sciscĭtātor -ōris, m. (sciscitor), *an inquirer examiner*: Mart.

sciscĭtor -ari, dep. and **sciscĭto** -are: Pl. (freq. of scisco), *to inquire thoroughly, examine, ask, interrogate*. With acc. of thing inquired into: consulis voluntatem, Liv. ex eo eius sententiam, Cic.; Pl., Tac. With indir. quest.: sciscitari, uter Porsena esset, Liv.; Cic., etc.

scisco sciscĕre scīvi scītum (scio).

Lɪᴛ., (1) *to seek to find out, investigate, inquire*: Pl. (2) *to find out by inquiry*: Pl.

Tʀᴀɴsꜰ., as polit. t. t., *to approve by voting, vote, ordain, resolve*: quae sciasceret plebes, Cic.; Pl., Liv. With ut and the subj.: Athenienses sciverunt ut, Cic. Of an individual, *to vote for*: legem, Cic.

⁋ Hence partic. **scītus** -a -um. LIT., *knowing, shrewd, sensible, judicious*; mainly of persons: Pl., Ter., Liv.; with genit.: scitus vadorum, *acquainted with*, Ov.; lyrae, Ov.; also of things: sermo, Cic.; vetus illud Catonis admodum scitum est, *is a shrewd remark*, Cic. TRANSF., *pretty, fine*: Pl., Ter.

⁋ Adv. **scītē**, *skilfully*: loqui, Liv.; Pl., Cic.

⁋ N. of partic. as subst., *a decree, statute, ordinance.* In gen.: pontificis, Liv.; populi, Cic., Liv. Esp.: plebis, *or* plebi, *or* plebei scitum, *a decree of the people of Rome* (opp. senatūs consultum), Pl., Cic., Liv.

scissūra -ae, f. (scindo), *a splitting, separating, parting*: Sen., Plin.

scissus -a -um, partic. from scindo; q.v.

scītāmenta -ōrum, n. (scitus), *dainties, titbits*: Pl.

scītē, adv. from scisco; q.v.

scītor -ari, dep. (freq. of scio), *to seek to know, inquire, ask*: causas, Verg.; oracula, *to consult*, Verg.; with indir. quest.: quid veniat, scitatur, Ov.

scītū, abl. as from scitus, m. (scisco) *by* (with de, *about*) *a decree*, esp. *a decree of the Roman people*; cf. scitum (under scisco).

scītŭlus -a -um (dim. of scitus), *neat, pretty, elegant*: facies, Pl.

scītum -i, n. subst. from scisco; q.v.

scītus -a -um, partic. from scisco; q.v.

sciūrus -i, m. (σκίουρος), *a squirrel*: Plin., Mart.

scŏbis -is, f. (scabo), *that which is scratched or scraped off, filings, chips, shavings, sawdust*: Hor., Juv.

Scodra -ae, f. *a town in Illyria* (now *Shkodër*).

⁋ Hence **Scodrenses** -ium, m. *the inhabitants of Scodra.*

scomber -bri, m. (σκόμβρος), *a sea-fish, a mackerel*: Pl., Cat., etc.

scōpae -ārum, f. pl. *a besom or broom*, made of *a number of twigs* or *branches*: scopae viles, Hor.; Pl.; prov.: scopas dissolvere, *to untie a broom*, i.e. *throw anything into confusion*, Cic.

scŏpos -i, m. (σκοπός), *a mark set up to shoot at*: Suet.

scŏpŭlōsus -a -um (scopulus), *rocky, full of cliffs, craggy.* LIT., mare, Cic.; Luc. TRANSF., intellego quam scopuloso difficilique in loco verser, Cic.

scŏpŭlus -i, m. (σκόπελος), *a rock, crag, cliff*; esp. *a rock in the sea.*

LIT., ad scopulos adlidi, Caes.; adfligi, Cic.; poet., of a promontory: infames scopuli, Acroceraunia, Hor.; in comparisons: o scopulis undāque ferocior, Ov.

TRANSF., *danger, ruin*: ad scopulum ire, Lucr.; in hos scopulos incidere vitae, Cic.; of persons: vos geminae voragines scopulique reipublicae (of Piso and Gabinius), Cic.

scorpĭo -ōnis, m. and **scorpĭus** (-ŏs) -i, m. (σκορπίων), *a scorpion*: Liv., Pl., Ov. TRANSF., (1) *the Scorpion, as one of the signs of the Zodiac*: Cic., Ov. (2) *a military engine for throwing missiles*: Caes., Liv. (3) *a salt-water fish*, perhaps *the sculpin*: Ov., Plin.

scortātor -ōris, m. (scortor), *a fornicator*: Hor.

scortĕus -a -um (scortum), *of hides, leathern, made of leather*: Ov. F. as subst. **scortĕa** -ae (sc. vestis), *a leathern garment*: Mart.

scortillum -i, m. (dim. of scortum), *a little harlot*: Cat.

scortor -ari, dep. (scortum), *to whore, asssociate with harlots*: Pl., Ter.

scortum -i, n. LIT., *a skin, hide*: Varr. TRANSF., *a harlot, prostitute*: Cic., Hor., etc.

scrĕātor -ōris, m. (screo), *one who hawks or hems*: Pl.

scrĕātus -ūs, m. (screo), *a hawking, hemming*: Ter.

scrĕo -are, *to clear the throat, to hawk, hem*: Pl.

scrība -ae, m. (scribo), *a clerk, secretary*, or *notary in the service of the senate or magistrates*: scriba aedilicius, Cic.; Hor., etc.

scriblīta -ae, f. *a kind of pastry*: Pl., Mart.

scrībo scrībĕre scripsi scriptum (connected with γράφω), *to engrave with a sharp-pointed instrument, draw lines*; hence *to write.*

(1) of the physical action only, *to write, draw*: lineam, Cic.; litteram, Pl., Cic.; carmen, Prop.; pass.: mea manu scriptae litterae, Cic. Sometimes *to write on* a thing, with acc.: tabellas, Pl.; lapidem, Tib.

(2) with the additional idea of intellectual action, *to write letters, poems, books*, etc., *to compose.* In gen.: versūs, Lucr., Hor.; carmina, epistulam, litteras, Cic.; de republicā multa, Cic.; se ad scribendi studium contulit, Cic. Absol., *to write a letter*: alicui, Cic.; ad aliquem, Cic.; scriberem ad te de hoc plura, Cic. L. With acc. and infin.: scribitur nobis multitudinem convenisse, ap. Cic. L.; with indir. command: velim domum ad te scribas ut mihi tui libri pateant, Cic. L.; Scipioni scribendum, ne bellum remitteret, Liv.; with subj. alone: scribit Labieno, veniat, Caes. Sometimes *to write about* a subject, with acc.; pass.: scriberis Vario fortis, Hor. Esp.: **a**, polit. t. t., *to draw up* laws, etc.: leges, Cic.; senatūs consultum, Cic. L.; Liv.: **b**, legal: dicam scribere (alicui), *to bring an action* (*against*), Pl., Ter., Cic.; testamentum scribere, Cic. With double acc., *to appoint in writing*: aliquem heredem, Cic.: **c**, commercial t. t., *to order the payment* of money: nummos, Pl.; scribe decem a Nerio, Hor.: **d**, milit. t. t., *to enrol*: milites, legiones, Sall.; supplementum legionibus, Cic. L.; quinque milia colonorum Capuam, Liv.; fig.: scribe tui gregis hunc, *enrol him as one of your friends*, Hor.

⁋ N. of partic. as subst. **scriptum** -i, *something written or drawn.* (1) *a mark* or *line*: ludere duodecim scriptis, *to play a game like draughts*, Cic. (2) *a composition, piece of writing*: Latina scripta, Cic.; mandare scriptis, Cic.; Hor., etc. Esp. *a written decree, a law*: Cic.

scrīnium -i, n. *a case* or *box for books, papers*, etc.: Sall., Hor., Juv., etc.

scriptĭo -ōnis, f. (scribo). (1) *writing, the act of writing*: Cic. L. (2) *authorship, composition*: nulla res tantum ad dicendum proficit, quantum scriptio, Cic. (3) *the wording* of a document: Cic.

scriptĭto -are (freq. of scribo), *to write often*; esp. of letters, drafts of speeches, etc.: et haec et si quid aliud ad me scribas velim vel potius scriptites, Cic. L.; orationes multas, Cic.

scriptor -ōris, m. (scribo), *a writer.* (1) *a scribe, clerk, secretary*: Cic., Hor. (2) *a writer, author, composer*: rerum suarum domestici scriptores et nuntii, Cic.; scriptor rerum, *an* *historian*, Liv.; subtilis scriptor (Lysias), Cic.; Esp. as polit. t. t., *a draftsman of bills*: legis, Cic.; Quint.

scriptŭla -ōrum, n. (dim. of scriptum), *the lines on the board in the game of* duodecim scripta: Ov.

scriptum -i, n. subst. from scribo; q.v.

scriptūra -ae, f. (scribo), *a writing*.
 Lɪᴛ., esp. of literary composition: scriptura adsidua ac diligens, Cic.; scripturā aliquid persequi, Cic.; Liv., etc.
 Tʀᴀɴsꜰ., (1) *a piece of writing, composition*: Tac. (2) *a testamentary disposition*: deinde ex superiore et ex inferiore scriptura docendum id, quod quaeratur, Cic. (3) *a tax or rent paid on public pastures*: vectigal ex scripturā, Cic.; magistri scripturae, Cic.

scrīpŭlum (scrūpŭlum, scriptŭlum) -i, m. (scrupulus), *a small weight* or *measure*: argenti scripulum, Cic. L.; Plin., Mart.

scrŏbis -is, c. (1) *a ditch*: Pl., Cic., etc. (2) *a grave*: Mart., Tac.

scrōfa -ae, f. (γϱομφάς), *a breeding sow*: Varr., Juv.

scrōfĭpascus -i,m. (scrofa/pasco), *a keeper of pigs*: Pl.

scrūpĕus -a -um (scrupus), *of sharp stones, rugged, rough*: spelunca, Verg.

scrūpōsus -a -um (scrupus), *of sharp stones, rugged, rough*. Lɪᴛ., via, Pl. Tʀᴀɴsꜰ., ratio, Lucr.

scrūpŭlōsus -a -um (scrupulus). Lɪᴛ., *full of sharp stones, rough, rugged*: cotes, Cic. Tʀᴀɴsꜰ., *exact, accurate, scrupulous, precise*: Plin. L.
 ¶ Adv. **scrūpŭlōsē**, *accurately, exactly, scrupulously*: Quint.

scrūpŭlum=scripulum; q.v.

scrūpŭlus -i, m. (dim. of scrupus), *a small stone*. Tʀᴀɴsꜰ., *a worry, uneasiness, anxiety, doubt, scruple*: scrupulum alicui inicere, Ter., Cic.; scrupulus tenuissimus residet, Cic.; scrupulum ex animo evellere, Cic.

scrūpus -i, m. *a sharp stone*: Petr. Tʀᴀɴsꜰ., *a worry, anxiety*: Cic.

scrūta -ōrum, n. pl. (cf. γϱύτη), *frippery, trash*: Hor.

scrūtātor -ōris, m. (scrutor), *one who searches, an investigator*: Luc., Suet.

scrūtor -ari, dep. (scruta), *to turn over carefully, search through, investigate, examine, inspect*.
 Lɪᴛ., domos, naves, Cic.; non excutio te, non scrutor, Cic.; abdita loca, Sall.
 Tʀᴀɴsꜰ., *to examine thoroughly, hunt out*: reconditas litteras, Cic.; locos ex quibus argumenta eruamus, Cic.; arcanum, Hor.; mentes deum, Ov.; sua Caesarisque fata, Tac.

sculpo sculpĕre sculpsi sculptum (connected with scalpo; q.v.), *to carve, grave, cut, chisel*: ebur, Ov.; e saxo sculptus, Cic.

sculpōnĕae -ārum, f. pl. *wooden shoes, clogs*: Pl.

sculptĭlis -e (sculpo), *carved*: opus dentis Numidae, *work in ivory*, Ov.

sculptŏr -ōris, m. (sculpo), *a sculptor*: Plin., Plin. L.

sculptūra -ae, f. (sculpo). (1) *the work of carving, graving*, etc.: Quint. (2) esp. in plur., *works of plastic art*: Plin.

scurra -ae, m. (1) *a dandy, man-about-town*: scurrae locupletes, Cic.; Pl., Cat. (2) *a jester,*

buffoon, esp. in a rich man's service: Zeno Socratem scurram Atticum fuisse dicebat, Cic.; Pl., Hor., etc.

scurrīlis -e (scurra), *like a buffoon, mocking, jeering*: iocus, Cic.; dicacitas, Quint.
 ¶ Adv. **scurrīlĭtĕr**, *like a buffoon*: Plin. L.

scurrīlĭtās -ātis, f. (scurrilis), *buffoonery*: Quint., Tac.

scurror -ari, dep. (scurra), *to play the buffoon*: scurrantis speciem praebere, Hor.

scūtāle -is, n. (scutum), *the thong of a sling*: Liv.

scūtārĭus -i, m. (scutum), *a shield-maker*: Pl.

scūtātus -a -um (scutum), *armed with a shield*: cohortes, Caes.; Verg., Liv.

scŭtella -ae, f. (dim. of scutra), *a flat dish* or *saucer*: dulciculae potionis, Cic.

scŭtica -ae, f. *a whip*: Hor., Ov., Juv.

scūtĭgĕrŭlus -i, m. (scutum/gero), *a shield-bearer*: Pl.

scutra -ae, f. *a dish*: Pl.

¹**scŭtŭla** -ae, f. (dim. of scutra), *a little square-shaped dish*: Mart., Tac. Also *a patch on an eye*: Pl.

²**scŭtŭla** -ae, f. (σκυτάλη), *a roller, cylinder*. (1) *a roller for moving weights*: Caes. (2) *a cylinder round which Spartan dispatches were rolled*: Nep. (3) *a kind of snake*: Plin., Luc.

scŭtŭlātus -a -um (¹scutula), *lozenge- or diamond-shaped*: Plin. Of cloth, *checked*: Plin.; n. pl. as subst. **scŭtŭlāta** -ōrum (sc. vestimenta), *checked cloths, checks*: Juv.

scŭtŭlum -i, n. (dim. of scutum), *a little shield*: Cic.

scūtum -i, n. (cf. σκῦτος, *leather*), *a large quadrangular shield, made of wood covered with hides* (clipeus *a smaller oval shield of metal*).
 Lɪᴛ., pedestre, *of a foot-soldier*, Liv.; scutum abicere, Cic.; Verg., etc.
 Tʀᴀɴsꜰ., *defence*: scuto vobis magis quam gladio opus est, Liv.; Cic.

Scȳlăcēum (Scȳlăcĭum) -i, n. *a town in southern Italy* (now *Squillace*): navifragum, Verg.
 ¶ Hence adj. **Scȳlăcēus** -a -um, *of Scylaceum*: litora, Ov.

Scylla -ae, f. (Σκύλλα). (1) *a rock at the entrance to the straits between Sicily and Italy, opposite to Charybdis*. Personif., *daughter of Phorcus, changed by Circe into a monster, with dogs about the lower part of her body*. (2) *daughter of Nisus, king of Megara, who cut off her father's hair, on which his happiness depended, and was turned into the bird Ciris*.
 ¶ Hence adj. **Scyllaeus** -a -um (Σκυλλαῖος), *belonging to Scylla, esp. to Scylla* (1): Cic., Verg., etc.

scymnus -i, m. (σκύμνος), *a young animal, cub, whelp*: leonum, Lucr.

scȳphus -i, m. (σκύφος), *a drinking-cup, goblet*: inter scyphos, *over our wine, in our cups*, Cic., Verg., etc.

Scȳrus (-ŏs) -i, f. (Σκῦρος), *an island in the Aegean Sea, near Euboea, where Achilles was concealed by Lycomedes* (now *Skyros*).
 ¶ Hence f. adj. **Scȳrĭās** -ădis, *of Scyrus*: puella, *Deidamia, daughter of Lycomedes*, Ov.; and adj. **Scȳrĭus** -a -um, *of Scyrus*: membra, *of Pyrrhus* (son of Achilles and Deidamia), Ov.

scȳtăla -ae, f. and **scȳtălē** -ēs, f.=²scutula; q.v.

Scȳthēs (Scȳtha) -ae, m. (Σκύθης), *a Scythian*; plur. **Scȳthae** -arum, *the Scythians, a name for all the nomadic tribes to the north of the Black and Caspian seas.*

¶ Hence subst. **Scȳthĭa** -ae, f. (Σκυθία), *Scythia*; adj. **Scȳthĭcus** -a -um (Σκυθικός), *Scythian*: amnis, *the Tanais*, Hor.; f. subst. **Scȳthĭs** -ĭdis and **Scȳthissa** -ae, *a Scythian woman.*

¹sē=sed (set); q.v.

²sē or **sēsē**, acc. sing. and plur.; **sŭī**, genit.; **sĭbĭ**, dat.; **se** or **sese**, abl.; old form, sed for **se**; strengthened forms, sepse (=se ipse): Cic.; semet: Hor., Liv.; (cf. ἑ, σφε), reflexive pronoun of the third person.

(1) as reflexive proper, *himself, herself, itself, themselves.* The person referred to is usually the subject of the clause containing se: se ipsum amat, Cic.; sui conservandi causā profugerunt, Cic.; qui hoc sibi nomen adrogaverunt, Cic. But often, when se stands in a subordinate clause, it refers to the subject of the main sentence. Sometimes the reference is made clear by the context only: deforme est de se ipsum praedicare, Cic. Special phrases: apud se, *at one's house*, Pl., Cic.; *in one's senses*: Ter.; sibi velle, *to mean*, Liv.; secum=cum se.

(2) as reciprocal pronoun, esp. with inter, *each other*: ut inter· se contingant trabes, Caes.

Sēbēthos -i, m. *a river in Campania.*

¶ Hence f. adj. **Sēbēthĭs** -ĭdis, *of Sebethos*: nympha, Verg.

sēbum -i, n. *tallow, suet, fat, grease*: Pl., Plin.

sēcēdo -cēdĕre -cessi -cessum, *to go apart, go away, withdraw.*

LIT., secedant improbi, Cic.; in abditam partem aedium, Sall.; ad deliberandum, Liv.; polit. t. t., *to withdraw, secede*: plebs a patribus secessit, Sall.; in Sacrum Montem, Liv.

TRANSF., (1) mentally: Sen., Quint. (2) of things: tantum secessit ab imis terra, Ov.; Lucr., Cat.

sēcerno -cernĕre -crēvi -crētum, *to separate, part, sunder.*

LIT., nihil praedae in publicum, Liv.; se a bonis, Cic.; inermes ab armatis, Liv.; aliquem e grege imperatorem velut inaestimabilem, Liv.

TRANSF., (1) *to distinguish* in thought: blandum amicum a vero, Cic.; poet., with abl.: honestum turpi, Hor. (2) *to set aside, to reject*: frugalissimum quemque, Cic. L.

¶ Hence partic. (with compar.) **sēcrētus** -a -um, *set apart.* In gen., *separate, alone, special*: facultas, Lucr.; imperium, Liv.; Verg., etc. Esp. (1) of places, *retired, solitary*: colles, Tac.; secreta petere loca, Hor.; Ov. (2) *hidden, secret*: artes, Ov.; nec quicquam secretum alter ab altero habent, Liv.; Tac. (3) *deprived of*; with abl.: secreta cibo natura, Lucr.; with genit.: corpora secreta teporis, Lucr.

N. as subst. **sēcrētum** -i. (1) *retirement, solitude, a solitary place*: secreta Sibyllae, Verg.; abducere aliquem in secretum, Liv.; n. pl. of compar.: in secretiora Germaniae, Tac. (2) *a secret, mystery*: omnium secreta

rimari, Tac.; in secretis eius, *in his private papers*, Suet.; Ov.

¶ Abl. as adv. **sēcrētō**, *apart, separately*: consilia secreto ab aliis coquebant, Liv.; secreto hoc audi, tecum habeto, Cic. L.; Pl., Caes.

sēcespĭta -ae, f. (seco), *a sacrificial knife*: Suet.

sēcessĭo -ōnis, f. (secedo), *a going apart, withdrawal*: secessione factā, Liv.; secessiones subscriptorum, Cic.; milites vesperi secessionem faciunt, Caes. Esp. *a political withdrawal, secession*: plebis, Cic., Liv.; in Aventinum montem, Liv.; Sall.

sēcessus -ūs, m. (secedo), *a going apart, withdrawal.*

LIT., avium, *migration*, Plin. Esp. *withdrawal into solitude, retirement*: carmina secessum scribentis et otia quaerunt, Ov.; Quint., Tac.

TRANSF., *a place of retirement, a retreat, recess*: Verg., Sen., Suet.

sēclūdo -clūdĕre -clūsi -clūsum (claudo), *to shut off*; *to confine alone* or *to separate from another.* LIT., munitione flumen a monte, Caes.; carmina, antro seclusa, Verg.; Cic., Liv. TRANSF., supplicium a conspectu parentium ac liberum seclusum, Cic.; curas, *to banish*, Verg.

¶ Hence partic. **sēclūsus** -a -um, as adj., *secluded*: Verg.

sēcius, see secus.

sēco sēcare sēcŭi sectum, *to cut.*

LIT., in gen.: pabula, Caes.; unguis sectus, Hor.; Cic., Verg., etc. Esp. (1) medical t. t., *to cut, amputate, lance*: varices Mario, Cic.; Pl., Liv. (2) *to castrate*: Mart.

TRANSF., (1) *to wound, scratch, injure, hurt*: secuerunt corpora vepres, Verg.; si quem podagra secat, *torments*, Cat. (2) *to divide, cleave, part*: populos Allia, Verg.; sectus orbis, Hor.; of motion through: avis secat aethera pennis, Verg.; aequor puppe, Ov. (3) *to cut out, make by cutting*: viam, Verg. hence, fig.: spem, Verg. (4) *to lash in words, satirize*: urbem, Pers. (5) *to divide*: causas in plura genera, Cic.; hence, *to settle, decide*: lites, Hor.

sēcrētus -a -um, partic. from secerno; q.v.

secta -ae, f. (often associated with, and perhaps derived from, sequor), *a way, mode of life, procedure, plan.* In gen.: nos qui hanc sectam rationemque vitae secuti sumus, Cic. Esp. (1) *political school of thought, party*: sequi eius auctoritatem cuius sectam atque imperium secutus est, Cic.; Liv. (2) *a philosophical school*: philosophorum sectam secutus es, Cic.; Tac., Quint.

sectārĭus -a -um (seco), *cut, gelded*: Pl.

sectātor -ōris, m. (sector), *a follower, hanger-on*; plur., *a suite of attendants, train, retinue.* In gen.: lex Fabia quae est de numero sectatorum, Cic.; Tac. Esp. *a member of a philosophical school*: Tac., Suet.

sectĭlis -e (seco). (1) *cut*: ebur, Ov.; pavimenta, *made up of small pieces, mosaic*, Suet. (2) *that can be cut*: Mart., Juv.

sectĭo -ōnis, f. (seco), *a cutting.* LIT., Plin. TRANSF., *the buying up at auctions of state property (confiscated, taken in war, etc.)*: ad illud sectionis scelus accedere, Cic.; exercendis apud aerarium sectionibus famosus, Cic.; Tac. Concr., *property so auctioned*, *a lot*: sectionem eius oppidi universam Caesar vendidit, Caes.

¹**sector** -ōris, m. (seco), *a cutter.* Lit., collorum, *a cut-throat,* Cic.; Pl. Transf., *a buyer of state property*: bonorum, Cic.; Pompei, *of the property of Pompey,* Cic.

²**sector** -ari, dep. (freq. of sequor), *to follow eagerly* or *continually.*

Lit., (1) in a friendly way, *to accompany, attend*: aliquem totos dies, Cic.; esp. as a servant: ii servi ubi sunt? Chrysogonum sectantur, Cic.; Pl., Hor. (2) in a hostile manner, *to run after, harass, chase*: mulieres, Pl.; leporem, Hor.; apros, Verg.; Cic.

Transf., *to strive after, try to get* or *to find out*: praedam, Caes., Tac.; nomina, Hor.; virtutes, Tac.; with indir. quest.: Hor.

sectūra -ae, f. (seco), *a cutting.* Lit., Varr., Plin. Transf., *a place where something is cut* or *dug out*: aerariae secturae, *copper-mines,* Caes.

sĕcŭbĭtus -ūs, m. (secumbo), *a lying alone*: Cat., Ov.

sĕcŭbo -are -ŭi, *to lie alone, sleep by one's self.* Lit., Ov., Liv. Transf., *to live a solitary life*: Prop.

sĕcŭlāris=saecularis; q.v.

sĕcŭlum=saeculum; q.v.

sēcum=cum se; *see* ²*se.*

sĕcundāni -ōrum, m. (secundus), *soldiers of the second legion*: Liv., Tac.

sĕcundārĭus -a -um (secundus), *second-rate*: panis, Suet.; status de tribus secundarius, Cic.

sĕcundo -are (secundus), *to favour, assist, second*: di nostra incepta secundent, Verg.; secundante vento, Tac.; Ov.

sĕcundum, adv. and prep. (sequor).

Adv., *after, behind*: ite hac secundum, Pl. Prep. with acc., *following, after.* (1) in space: **a**, *close behind*: aram, Pl.: **b**, *along, by*: secundum flumen, Caes.; Cic. L. (2) in time: **a**, *just after*: secundum comitia, Cic.; secundum haec, *after this,* Liv.; Lucr., etc.: **b**, *during*: secundum quietem, *in the course of a dream,* Cic. (3) in other relations: **a**, *in addition to*: Caes., Cic.: **b**, of rank or preference, *after, next to*: secundum te, nihil mihi amicius est solitudine, Cic. L.; Pl., Liv.: **c**, *according to, in accordance with*: secundum naturam vivere, Cic.; Caes., Liv.: **d**, *in favour of, to the advantage of*: decernere secundum aliquem, Cic.; Liv., Tac.

sĕcundus -a -um, adj. (with compar. and superl.) (sequor), *following.*

(1) *going after, second.* Lit., in time: lumine secundo, *on the following day,* Enn.; vigilia, Caes.; mensa, *dessert,* Cic. L., Verg. Transf., of rank or preference: heres, *a person to inherit in case the first heir dies,* Cic.; partes secundae, *the second role,* Hor.; tu secundo Caesare regnes, Hor.; Liv. Esp. indicating inferiority: panis, *second-rate,* Hor.; nulli Campanorum secundus, Liv.

(2) *going the same way, attending.* Lit., esp. of wind or water, *following* (i.e., *favourable*): sĕcundo flumine, *with the stream, downstream,* Caes.; et ventum et aestum nactus secundum, Caes.; navem secundis ventis cursum tenentem, Cic.; superl.: vento secundissimo, Cic.; poet.: secunda vela dato, Ov.; curruque (dat.) volans dat lora secundo,

Verg. Transf., *supporting, favourable*: res secundae, *prosperity, success,* Cic., Verg., etc.; voluntas contionis, Cic.; secundo populo, *with the good-will of the people,* Cic.; secundo Marte, *with success in battle,* Verg.; superl.: leges secundissimae plebi, Liv.

¶ As subst. n. abl. sing. **sĕcundō**, *secondly*: Cic.; f. pl. **sĕcundae** -arum (sc. partes), *the second role*: secundas agere, Sen.; ferre, Hor.; Sen.; fuit M. Crassi quasi secundarum, *played second fiddle to Crassus,* Cic.; n. pl. **sĕcunda** -orum, *prosperity, success*: Ter., Hor., Liv., Tac.

sĕcūrē, adv. from securus; q.v.

sĕcūrĭcŭla -ae, f. (dim. of securis), *a little axe*: Pl.

sĕcūrĭfĕr -fĕra -fĕrum (securis/fero), *carrying an axe*: Ov.

sĕcūrĭgĕr -gĕra -gĕrum (securis/gero), *carrying an axe*: puellae, *the Amazons,* Ov.

sĕcūris -is; acc. -im or -em, abl. -i or -e; f. (seco), *an axe, hatchet.*

Lit., in gen.: Pl., Verg.; as a weapon of war, *a battle-axe*: Verg., Ov.; for killing victims at a sacrifice: Verg., Hor., Ov. Esp., for executing criminals, *the headsman's axe*: securi ferire, percutere, Cic.; saevus securi Torquatus (who had his own son beheaded), Verg.

Transf., (1) a mortal *wound, disaster*: graviorem infligere securim reipublicae, Cic. (2) (because secures, fasces, and virgae were carried by the lictors of the highest magistrates at Rome), *supreme power, Roman supremacy*: Gallia securibus subiecta, *completely subdued,* Caes.; Germania colla Romanae praebens animosa securi, Ov.

sĕcūrĭtās -ātis, f. (securus). Lit., *freedom from care.* In a good sense, *peace of mind, composure*: Cic., Liv., etc. In a bad sense, *carelessness, false confidence*: Quint., Tac. Transf., *freedom from danger, security*: Plin., Tac.

sĕcūrus -a -um, adj. (with compar.) (cura), *free from care.*

Lit., of persons, *unconcerned, fearless*: animus securus de aliqua re, Cic.; securior ab aliquo, Liv. With genit.: amorum, Verg.; famae, Ov. With indir. quest.: quid Tiridaten terreat, unice securus, Hor. Followed by ne and the subj.: ne quis etiam errore labatur vestrum quoque non sum securus, Liv. In a bad sense: reus, Quint.

Transf., of inanimate things. (1) *carefree, tranquil*: otia, Verg.; tempus, Quint.; Lucr.; etc. In a bad sense, *careless*: castrensis iurisdictio, Tac. (2) objectively, *safe, secure*: tempus, locus, Liv.; with genit.: sint tua vota licet secura repulsae, *safe against,* Ov. (3) *dispelling care*: latices, Verg.

¶ Hence adv. **sĕcūrē**. Lit., *without care, unconcernedly*: Plin. L., Suet. Transf., *safely*: Plin. L.

¹**sĕcus**, n. indecl., *sex*: virile et muliebre secus, Liv.; Pl., Tac.

²**sĕcŭs**, adv. (very rarely prep. with acc., in sense of secundum: Enn., Cato).

Posit., *otherwise, not so.* Lit., id secus est, Cic. Often foll. by atque (ac), *or quam, otherwise than, differently from*: Cic. With neg.: non secus, haud secus, *just so*; often foll. by atque (ac), *or* quam: Cic., Verg.,

Liv., Ov. Transf., *otherwise than one would wish*, i.e. *wrongly, badly*: secus existimare de aliquo, Cic.; scribere, Liv.; cadere, Tac.

Compar. **sĕquĭŭs** or **sētĭŭs**, *otherwise, not so*; esp. *less*. Lit., nihilo setius, *none the less*, Caes.; haud setius, non setius, Verg. Transf., *less well than one could wish, rather badly*: invitus quod sequius sit de meis civibus loquor, Liv.

sĕcūtor -ōris, m. (sequor), *a gladiator armed with a sword and shield who fought with a* retiarius: Juv., Suet.

sĕd (sē, sĕt), conj. (adv. only in compounds; prep. in old Latin=*without*).

(1) after a negative, to introduce the complementary positive, *but*: non cauponantes bellum sed belligerantes, Enn.; Pl., etc. Esp. in such phrases as non modo (non solum) . . . sed etiam (sed . . . quoque), *not only . . . but also*: non modo falsum illud esse, sed hoc verissimum, Cic.; negotiis non interfuit solum, sed praefuit, Cic.; Liv., Tac., etc.

(2) adversative in gen., *but, however*: vera dico, sed nequicquam, Pl. Often strengthened: sed tamen, Cic., Ov.; sed enim, *but in fact*, Pl., Cic., Verg.

(3) in transitions, esp. back to a main theme, *but however*: sed redeamus ad Hortensium, Cic.; ut peroravit (nam . . . peregerat), sed ut peroravit, Cic. Also in breaking off a discussion: sed haec hactenus, Cic.; Verg.

(4) in emphatic confirmation or amplification, *and indeed, and, what is more* (sometimes, in slang, *but*): scelus est, mihi crede, sed ingens, Mart.; Pl. Strengthened by etiam, or et: Cic. L.

sēdāmen -inis, n. (sedo), *a sedative*: Sen.

sēdātē, adv. from sedo; q.v.

sēdātĭo -ōnis, f. (sedo), *an allaying, soothing*, esp. of violent emotion: animi, Cic.; maerendi, Cic.; aegritudinis, Cic.

sēdātus -a -um, partic. from sedo; q.v.

sēdĕcĭm (sex/decem), *sixteen*: Pl., Caes., Liv.

sēdēcŭla -ae, f. (dim. of sedes), *a low seat or stool*: Cic. L.

sēdentārĭus -a -um (sedens), *sitting, sedentary*: sutores, Pl.

sĕdĕo sēdēre sēdi sessum, *to sit*.

Lit., of persons and animals. In gen.: cum tot summi oratores sedeant, Cic. With in and the abl.: in sella, in solio, in equo, Cic.; cornix sedet in humo, Ov. With abl. alone: carpento, sēde regiā sedet, Liv.; Verg., Ov. Esp. (1) of magistrates, etc., *to sit in council, sit in judgment*: Scaevolā in rostris sedente, Cic.; pro tribunali, Cic.; in tribunali, Cic.; Liv., etc. (2) with a suggestion of blame, *to, sit about, linger, be inactive*: consulibus sedentibus, Cic.; prov.: compressis manibus sedere, *to sit with folded hands*, Liv.; sedemus desides domi, Liv.; Verg. (3) milit. t. t., *to remain encamped, or to sit down before a place*: sedendo bellum gerere, Liv.; Verg.

Transf., of things. (1) *to be settled, stay fixed, lie still*: in liquido sederunt ossa cerebro, Ov.; clava sedet in ore viri, Ov.; of clothes: Quint.; of abstr. things: pallor in ore sedet, Ov. (2) of resolves, *to be firmly determined, to remain fixed*: idque pio sedet Aeneae, Verg.

sēdēs -is, f. (sedeo), *a seat*.

Lit., *a stool, chair, throne*: sedes honoris, sella curulis, Cic.; sedes ponere, Liv.; fig : priores sedes tenere, *the first rank*, Hor.

Transf., (1) *an abode, habitation, home*: sedes habere in Gallia, Caes.; eam sibi domum sedesque deligere, Cic.; sedes fundatur Veneri, *a temple*, Verg.; sceleratorum, *the infernal regions*, Cic.; Lucr., Liv. Of the dead, *the grave*: sedibus hunc refer ante suis et conde sepulcro, Verg. (2) of things, *place, seat, base, foundation*: suis sedibus convulsa Roma, Cic.; turrim convellimus altis sedibus, Verg.; montes moliri sede suā, Liv.

sĕdīle -is, n. (sedeo), *a seat*: Verg., Ov., etc. In plur., sĕdīlĭa, *seats* or *benches*; *in the theatre*: Hor.; in a ship, *benches for rowers*: Verg.

sēdĭtĭo -ōnis, f. (sed=*apart*/itio), *a going apart*; hence, *a civil* or *military revolt, insurrection, sedition, rising, mutiny*.

Lit., seditionem ac discordiam concitare, Cic.; conflare, Cic.; concire, Liv.; facere, Caes., Cic.; restinguere, Cic.

Transf., (1) between individuals, *a dissension, quarrel*: domestica (of brothers), Liv.; Ter., Ov. (2) between things: intestina corporis, Liv.; Pl.

sēdĭtĭōsus -a -um (seditio). Lit., *seditious, quarrelsome, turbulent*: civis, Cic.; oratio, Caes.; voces, Liv. Transf., *restless*: seditiosa ac tumultuosa vita, Cic.

¶ Adv. (with compar. and superl.) **sēdĭtĭōsē**, *seditiously*: Cic., Liv., Tac.

sēdo -are (connected with sedeo), *to settle, soothe, still, calm, allay*: flammam, Cic.; incendium, Liv.; pulverem, Phaedr. Transf., *to calm, assuage* any physical or mental disturbance: bellum, pugnam, invidiam, Cic.; rabiem, Hor.; contentionem, Liv.

¶ Hence partic. (with compar.) **sēdātus** -a -um, *calm, composed*: amnis, Cic., Hor.; animus, Cic. L.; cor, Verg.; sedato gradu abire, Liv.

¶ Adv. **sēdātē**, *calmly, tranquilly*: dolorem ferre, Cic.; Pl.

sēdūco -dūcĕre -duxi -ductum, *to take* or *lead apart*.

Lit., of persons: aliquem a debita peste, *to rescue from danger*, Cic.; singulos separatim, Liv.; Pl., Ov.

Transf., of things: vacuos ocellos, *to turn aside*, Prop.; vina paulum seducta, *put on one side*, Ov. Poet., *to separate, sever*: seducit terras unda duas, Ov.; mors animā seduxerit artus, Verg.

¶ Hence partic. **sēductus** -a -um, *remote, distant*: recessus gurgitis, Ov.; consilia seducta a plurium conscientiā, *withdrawn*, Liv.

sēductĭo -ōnis, f. (seduco), *a leading aside*: testium, Cic.

sēdŭlĭtās -ātis, f. (sedulus), *assiduity, zeal, application*: Cic.

sēdŭlus -a -um (perhaps from se/dolus). (1) *busy, diligent, assiduous*: homo, Cic.; apis, Tib., Ov. (2) in bad sense, *officious*: Hor., Prop., Ov.

¶ N. abl. as adv. **sēdŭlō**, *busily, zealously*: sedulo argumentari, Cic.; Pl., Ter. Hence, *purposely, designedly*: Pl., Ter., Liv.

sĕgĕs -ĕtis, f.
  LIT., originally *a cornfield*; hence *standing corn, a crop*: in proximas segetes, Caes.; laetae segetes, Verg.; iam seges est, ubi Troia fuit, Ov.; with genit.: seges farris est matura messi, Liv.
  TRANSF., (1) *field, ground, soil*, in gen.: fert casiam non culta seges, Tib.; ubi prima paretur arboribus seges, Verg. (2) fig., *ground, source, origin*: quid odisset Clodium Milos egetem ac materiem suae gloriae? Cic. (3) *any thickly packed mass*: seges clipeata virorum, Ov.; telorum, Verg. (4) *profit*: quae inde seges, Juv.; Ov.
Sĕgesta -ae, f. *a city on the north-west coast of Sicily.*
  ¶ Hence adj. **Sĕgestānus** -a -um, *of Segesta*; m. pl. as subst. **Sĕgestāni** -ōrum, *the inhabitants of Segesta*; also subst. **Sĕgestenses** -ĭum, m. pl., *the inhabitants of Segesta.*
sĕgestre -is, n. *a covering, wrapper* of straw or skins: Plin., Suet.
segmentātus -a -um (segmentum), *ornamented with purple or gold borders or patches*: cunae, Juv.
segmentum -i, n. (seco), *a piece cut off, cutting, shred*. LIT., Plin.; plur.: segmenta, *borders or patches of purple or gold sewn on women's dresses, gold or purple border*, Ov. TRANSF., *a zone or region of the earth*: Plin.
segnĭpēs -pĕdis (segnis/pes), *slow-footed*; of a horse: Juv.
segnis -e, adj. (with compar.), *slow, slothful, tardy, sluggish*. Absol., of persons: segniores castigat, Caes.; propter onus, Hor.; of things: obsidio, pugna, bellum, *sluggishly prosecuted*, Liv.; mors, *a lingering death*, Liv.; voluptas, Ov.; otium, Tac.; campus, *fallow*, Verg. With ad: segniores ad imperandum, Cic.; nec ad citharam segnis nec ad arcum, Ov.; Liv., Tac. With in and acc.: non in Venerem segnes, Verg.; with in and abl.: Suet. With genit.: laborum, Tac. With infin.: solvere nodum, Hor.; Ov.
  N. acc. as adv. **segnĕ**, and adv. **segnĭter** (with compar.), *slowly, sluggishly, slothfully*: Liv., etc.; nihilo segnius, Sall., Liv.
segnĭtĭa -ae, f. and **segnĭtĭēs** -ēi, f. (segnis), *sluggishness, slothfulness, slowness, tardiness*: Cic., Liv., etc.
Sĕgontĭăci -ōrum, m. *a people in the south of Britain*: Caes.
sēgrĕgo -are (grex), *to separate from the flock, segregate*. LIT., oves, Phaedr. TRANSF., in gen., *to separate, sever, remove*: aliquem a numero civium, Cic.; aliquem a se, Cic.; virtutem a summo bono, Cic.; Pl., Liv.
Sēiānus, see Seius.
sēiŭgātus -a -um, *disjointed, separated*: animi partem non ab actione corporis seiugatam, Cic.
sēiŭgis -is, m. (sex/iugum; sc. currus), *a chariot drawn by six horses*: Liv.
sēiunctim, adv. (seiungo), *separately*: Tib.
sēiunctĭo -ōnis, f. (seiungo), *a separation*: Cic., Quint.
sēiungo -iungĕre -iunxi -iunctum, *to separate, sever, disjoin.*
  LIT., Alpes Italiam a Gallia seiungunt, Nep.; se ab aliquo, Cic.; Lucr.

  TRANSF., se a libertate verborum, *to refrain from*, Cic.; bonum quod non possit ab honestate seiungi, Cic.; corpore seiunctus dolor absit, Lucr.
Sēius -i, m. *a Roman name.*
  ¶ Hence **Sēiānus** -a -um; as adj., *of Seius*: Varr.; as name, esp. of L. Aelius Seianus, *son of Seius Strabo, the* praefectus praetorii *of Tiberius*: Tac., Juv.
sēlectĭo -ōnis, f. (seligo), *a choosing out, selection*; si selectio nulla sit ab iis rebus, Cic.
Sēleucus -i, m. (Σέλευκος), *name of several kings of Syria, descended from* Seleucus Nicator, *a general of Alexander the Great.*
sēlibra -ae, f. (semi/libra), *half a pound*: Cato, Liv.
sēligo -lĭgĕre -lēgi -lectum (se/lego), *to choose, pick out, select*: exempla, Cic.; aliquem socium, Ov. Esp.: iudices selecti, *the judges appointed by the praetor in a criminal case*, Cic.
Sēlīnūs -nuntis, f. (Σελινοῦς). (1) *a sea-port in Sicily.* (2) *a town on the coast of Cilicia, afterwards called Trajanopolis.*
sella -ae, f. (= sedla, from sedeo), *a seat, chair, stool*: in sellā sedere, Cic.; Pl. Esp. (1) *a work-stool*: in foro sellam ponere, Cic. (2) *the chair of a teacher*: Cic. L. (3) *a magistrate's seat*; also called sella curulis: Caes., Cic., etc. (4) *a sedan-chair*; also called sella gestatoria: Juv., Mart., etc.
sellārĭus -a -um (sella), *relating to a seat or stool*. F. as subst. **sellārĭa** -ae, *a room furnished with seats, a sitting-room*: Plin., Suet.
sellisternĭa -orum, n. pl. (sella/sterno), *religious banquets in honour of goddesses, at which their images were placed on seats and food put before them*: Tac.
sellŭla -ae, f. (dim. of sella), *a little chair*: Tac.
sellŭlārĭus -a -um (sellula), *of a seat*: Gell. M. as subst. **sellŭlārĭus** -i, *a workman* (one that works seated): Liv.
sĕmĕl, numer. adv. *once, a single time.*
  LIT., semel atque iterum, *more than once*, Caes., Cic.; semel atque iterum ac saepius, Cic.; plus quam semel, Cic.; non semel sed saepe, Cic.
  TRANSF., (1) *for the first time, first*: semel ad Corfinium, iterum in Hispania, Caes.; Cic., Liv. (2) *once for all*: semel exorari soles, Cic.; aut vitam semel aut ignominiam finirent, Liv.; Verg., Ov. (3) indef., *once, ever, at any time*; esp. in subordinate clause, or with participle: interrupta semel cum sit repetentia nostri, Lucr.; qui semel verecundiae fines transierit, eum bene et naviter oportet esse impudentem, Cic.; incitato semel militi, Liv.
Sĕmĕla -ae, f. and **Sĕmĕlē** -ēs, f. (Σεμέλη), *daughter of Cadmus, mother of Bacchus by Jupiter*: Semeles puer, *Bacchus*, Hor.
  ¶ Hence adj. **Sĕmĕlēius** -a -um, *of Semele*: Semeleia proles, *Bacchus*, Hor.
sēmen -ĭnis, n. (cf. ¹sero), *what is sown or planted, seed.*
  LIT., of living creatures. (1) *seed* of men, animals, plants: semen manu spargere, Cic.; Lucr., Ov., etc. (2) *what has recently grown from seed, a seedling, scion, young shoot*, etc.; of plants: Verg.; *a child*: Ov.

TRANSF., (1) *a stock, the race*: Romanum, Cic.; regio semine orta, Liv. (2) of lifeless things, *elements*, e.g. of water, fire, stone, etc.: Lucr., Verg., Cic. (3) fig., *cause, origin*; of persons, *author, instigator*: stirps ac semen malorum omnium, Cic.; discordiarum, Liv.; Tac.

sēmentĭfĕr -fĕra -fĕrum (sementis/fero), *seed-bearing, fruitful*: Verg.

sēmentis -is; acc. -em and -im; f. (semen), *a sowing* or *planting*.
    LIT., sementes quam maximas facere, Caes.; prov.: ut sementem feceris, ita metes, Cic.
    TRANSF., plur.: sementes, *the young growing corn*, Ov.

sēmentīvus -a -um (sementis), *of seed* or *seed-time*: dies, Ov.

sēmestris (sēmenstris) -e (sex/mensis), *of six months, lasting six months*: regnum, Cic.; dux, Liv.; semestri digitos circumligat auro, *the ring of the tribunes, worn for six months*, Juv.

sēmēsus -a -um (semi/edo), *half-eaten, half-consumed*: praeda, ossa, Verg.; Hor., Ov.

sēmĭădăpertus -a -um (quinquesyll.), *half-open*: Ov.

sēmĭambustus -a -um (semi/amburo), *half-burnt*: Suet.

sēmĭănĭmis -e and **sēmĭănĭmus** -a -um (semi/anima; both found as quadrisyll. in verse), *half-alive, half-dead*: corpora semianima, Liv.; Lucr., Verg., etc.

sēmĭăpertus -a -um (semi/aperio), *half-open*: portarum fores, Liv.

sēmĭbarbărus -a -um, *semi-barbarous*: Suet.

sēmĭbos -bŏvis, m. adj., *half-ox*: vir, *the Minotaur*, Ov.

sēmĭcăper -pri, m. *half-goat*: Ov.

sēmĭcrĕmātus -a -um (semi/cremo), *half-burnt*: Ov.

sēmĭcrĕmus (semi/cremo), *half-burnt*: Ov.

sēmĭcrūdus -a -um. (1) *half-raw*: Suet. (2) *having half-digested*: Stat.

sēmĭcŭbĭtālis -e, *half a cubit long*: Liv.

sēmĭdĕus -a -um, *half-divine*: semideum genus, *the Nereids*, Ov. M. as subst., *a demigod*: Ov.

sēmĭdoctus -a -um (semi/doceo), *half-taught*: haec ut apud doctos et semidoctos ipse percurro, Cic.; Pl.

sēmĭermis (sēmermis) -e and **sēmĭermus (sēmermus)** -a -um (semi/arma): *half-armed, half-equipped*: Liv., Tac.

sēmĭēsus=semesus; q.v.

sēmĭfactus -a -um (semi/facio), *half-done, half-finished*: Tac.

sēmĭfĕr -fĕra -fĕrum (semi/ferus), *half-animal*. LIT., pectus Tritonis, Verg.; subst., of the centaurs: Ov. TRANSF., *half-wild, half-savage*: Verg.

sēmĭfultus -a -um (semi/fulcio), *half-propped*: Mart.

sēmĭgermānus -a -um, *half-German*: Liv.

sēmĭgraecus -a -um, *half-Greek*: Suet.

sēmĭgrăvis -e, *half-overcome*: vino, Liv.

sēmĭgro -are, *to go away, depart*: a patre, Cic.

sēmĭhĭans -antis (from semi/hio; trisyll.), *half-open*: labellum, Cat.

sēmĭhŏmo -hŏmĭnis, m. adj. (trisyll., poet.), *half-man*. LIT., Centauri, Ov. TRANSF., *half-wild*: Cacus, Verg.

sēmĭhōra -ae, f. *half an hour*: Cic.

sēmĭlăcer -cĕra -cĕrum, *half-mangled*: Ov.

sēmĭlautus -a -um (semi/lavo), *half-washed*: Cat.

sēmĭlīber -bĕra -bĕrum, *half-free*: Cic. L.

sēmĭlixa -ae, m. *half a sutler*; used as a term of reproach: Liv.

sēmĭmărīnus -a -um, *half in the sea*: corpora (Scyllarum), Lucr.

sēmĭmas -măris, m. (1) *half-male, hermaphrodite*: Ov., Liv. (2) *castrated*: oves, Ov.

sēmĭmortŭus -a -um, *half-dead*: Cat.

sēmĭnārĭum -i, n. *a plantation, nursery*. LIT., Cato. TRANSF., triumphorum, Cic.; senatūs, Liv.

sēmĭnātor -ōris, m. (semino), *a begetter, author*: qui est verus omnium seminator malorum, Cic.

sēmĭnex -nĕcis (not found in nom.), *half-dead*: Verg., Liv., Ov., Tac.

sēmĭnĭum -i, n. (semen). LIT., *a begetting*: Pl., Varr. TRANSF., *a race* or *breed*: Lucr.

sēmĭno -are (semen), *to sow* or *plant*: Col. Hence *to beget, produce*: Pl.; of plants: viscum, quod non sua seminat arbos, Verg.

sēmĭnūdus -a -um. (1) *half-naked*: Liv. (2) pedes prope seminudus, *nearly defenceless, without arms*, Liv.

sēmĭpāgānus -i, m. *half-rustic*: Pers.

sēmĭperfectus -a -um (semi/perficio), *half-finished*: Suet.

sēmĭpēs -pĕdis, m. *a half-foot*: Cato, Varr., Plin.

sēmĭplēnus -a -um, *half-full, half-manned*: naves, Cic.; stationes, Liv.

sēmĭpūtātus -a -um (semi/puto), *half-pruned*: vitis, Verg.

Sēmīrămis -is or -idis, f. (Σεμίραμις), *wife and successor of Ninus, king of Assyria*. Adj. **Sēmīrămĭus** -a -um.

sēmĭrāsus -a -um (semi/rado), *half-shaven, half-shorn*: Cat.

sēmĭrĕductus -a -um (semi/reduco), *half bent back*: Ov.

sēmĭrĕfectus -a -um (semi/reficio), *half-repaired*: Ov.

sēmĭrŭtus -a -um (semi/ruo), *half-ruined, half pulled down*: urbs, Liv.; castella, Tac. N. pl. as subst. **sēmĭrŭta** -ōrum, *half-demolished places*: Liv.

sēmis -issis, m. (semis/as), *the half of anything*. In gen.: Africae, Plin. Esp. (1) *half an as*: Cic. (2) as a rate of interest=6 *per cent per annum*: semissibus magna copia, *plenty of money to be had at 6 per cent*, Cic. (3) as a measure of land, *half a iuger*: Liv., Plin.

sēmĭsĕnex -senis, m. *an elderly man*: Pl.

sēmĭsĕpultus -a -um (semi/sepelio), *half-buried*: Ov.

sēmĭsomnus -a -um and **sēmĭsomnis** -e, *half-asleep, drowsy*: Pl., Cic. L., Liv., etc.

sēmĭsŭpīnus -a -um, *half-supine, half on the back*: Ov., Mart.

sēmĭta -ae, f. *a narrow way, footpath*.
    LIT., angustissimae semitae, Cic.; omnibus viis semitisque, Cic.; Caes., Verg., etc.
    TRANSF., pecuniam, quae viā visa est exire ab isto, eandem semitā revertisse, Cic.; fallentis vitae, Hor.; tranquillae vitae, Juv.

sēmĭtactus -a -um (semi/tango), *half-touched*: Mart.

sēmĭtālis -e (semita), *of the footpaths*: dei, Verg.

sēmĭtārĭus -a -um (semita), *of the footpaths*: Cat.

sēmĭtectus -a -um (semi/tego), *half-covered*: Sen.

sēmĭustŭlatus=semustulatus; q.v.

sēmĭustus (sēmustus) -a -um (semi/uro), *half-burnt*. Lit., Enceladi semustum fulmine corpus, Verg.; Tac. Transf., se populare incendium priore consulatu semiustum effugisse, Liv.

sēmĭvir -vĭri, m. adj., *half-man*.
    Lit., (1) *half-man, half-animal*: Chiron, *the centaur*, Ov.; bos, *the Minotaur*, Ov. (2) *a hermaphrodite*: Ov.
    Transf., (1) *castrated*: Juv. (2) *effeminate, unmanly*: Verg.

sēmĭvīvus -a -um, *half-dead, almost dead*. Lit., Cic. Transf., voces, *faint*, Cic.

sēmĭvōcālis -is, f. (sc. littera), *a semivowel* (i.e. one of seven, f, l, m, n, r, s, x): Quint.

Semnones -um, m. pl. *a people of northern Germany*: Tac.

sēmŏdĭus -i, m. (semi/modius), *a half-modius*: Mart., Juv.

sēmŏvĕo -mŏvēre -mōvi -mōtum, *to move away, set aside, separate*. Lit., qui voce praeconis a liberis semovebantur, Cic.; Ter. Transf., voluptatem, Cic.; Strato ab ea disciplina omnino semovendus est, Cic.; Lucr.
    ¶ Hence partic. sēmōtus -a -um, *removed, remote, distant*. Lit., locus a militibus semotus, Caes.; n. pl. as subst.: quae terris semota ridet, Hor. Transf., semota ab nostris rebus, Lucr.; arcana semotae dictionis, *exclusive, private*, Tac.

semper, adv. *always, at all times, on each occasion*; with verbs, adjectives, and adverbs: tu semper urges, Hor.; Pl., Cic., Verg., etc. Also with subst., almost as an adj.: heri semper lenitas, *the constant mildness*, Ter.; Hasdrubal pacis semper auctor, Liv.; Verg.

sempĭternus -a -um (semper), *continual, everlasting*: tempus, Cic.; ignes Vestae, Cic. Sometimes *lasting a long time* (but not for ever): gratiae, Pl.; amicitia, Cic. N. acc. as adv. sempĭternum, *for ever*: Pl.

Semprōnĭus -a -um, *name of a Roman gens*. *Its most famous members were the brothers Tiberius Sempronius Gracchus, and Gaius Sempronius Gracchus, tribunes of the people*. As adj., *Sempronian*: lex Cic.
    ¶ Hence adj. Semprōnĭānus -a -um: senatus consultum, *proposed by C. Sempronius Rufus*, Cic.; clades, *the defeat of the consul, C. Sempronius Atratinus*.

sēmuncia -ae, f. (semi/uncia), *half an uncia*, 1/24 *of an* as. (1) as a weight: auri, Cic., Liv. (2) in gen., as a fraction, 1/24: facit heredem ex deunce et semuncia Caecinam, Cic.; Pers.

sēmunciārĭus -a -um (semuncia), *relating to the fraction* 1/24: faenus, 1/24 *per cent monthly*, i.e. 1/2 *per cent per annum*, Liv.

sēmustŭlātus (sēmĭustŭlātus) -a -um (semi/ustulo), *half-burnt*: Cic.

Sēna -ae, f. *a town in Umbria on the Adriatic Sea, where Livius Salinator defeated Hasdrubal* (now *Senigallia*).
    ¶ Hence adj. Sēnensis -e, *of Sena*: proelium, Cic.

sēnācŭlum -i, n. (senatus), *an open space in the Forum, used for meetings of the Senate*: Liv.

sēnārĭŏlus -i, m. (dim. of senarius), *a trifling senarius*: Cic.

sēnārĭus -a -um (seni), *composed of six in a group*: senarius versus, and m. as subst. sēnārĭus -i, *a senarius, a verse of six feet* (generally iambic): Cic., Quint.

sĕnātor -ōris, m. (connected with senex). Lit., *a member of the Roman senate, a senator*: Caes., Cic., etc. Transf., outside Rome, *a member of any similar council*; among the Nervii: Caes.; the Rhodians: Cic.; the Macedonians: Liv.

sĕnātōrĭus -a -um (senator), *of a senator, senatorial*: ordo, Caes.; gradus, Cic.

sĕnātus -ūs (genit. occasionally -i), m. (senex), *a council of elders, the Senate*.
    Lit., at Rome: senatus populusque Romanus, Cic.; princeps senatūs, *the senator whose name stood at the head of the censor's list*, Liv.; in senatum venire, *to become a senator*, Cic.; de senatu movere, *to expel from the senate*, Cic.; senatum cogere, convocare, Cic.; vocare, Liv.; dimittere, Cic.; senatūs (senati) consultum, *a formal resolution of the senate*, Cic.
    Transf., (1) *any similar council* in other nations: Aeduorum, Caes.; Carthaginiensis, Liv. (2) in gen., *a council, meeting*: Pl.

Sĕnĕca -ae, m. *a family name of the Annaean gens; esp. of* (1) M. Annaeus Seneca, *a rhetorician from Corduba* (now *Cordova*), *in Spain*. (2) L. Annaeus Seneca, *his son, the Stoic philosopher and writer, tutor of Nero, who compelled him to commit suicide*.

sĕnecta, *see* ¹senectus.

¹sĕnectus -a -um (senex), *old, aged*: aetas, Pl., Lucr., Sall. F. as subst. sĕnecta -ae, *old age*: Lucr., Verg., etc.

²sĕnectus -ūtis, f. (senex), *old age*.
    Lit., vivere ad summam senectutem, Cic.; Verg., etc.
    Transf., (1) concr., *old men*: Cic., Juv. (2) *gloom, moroseness*: Hor. (3) *grey hair*: Verg. (4) *the slough of a serpent*: Plin. (5) of a thing, *age*: vini, Juv.; cariosa (tabellarum), Ov.

sĕnĕo -ēre (senex), *to be old*: Cat.

sĕnesco sĕnescĕre sĕnŭi (seneo), *to grow old*. Lit., tacitis senescimus annis, Ov.; senescens equus, Hor.; Cic., etc.
    Transf., (1) of persons, *to flag, lose power*: Hannibal famā et viribus, Liv.; Cic., Hor. (2) of things, *to wane, grow weak*: luna, hiems, laus, morbus, Cic.; Liv., etc.

sĕnex sĕnis (with compar. sĕnĭor, n. sĕnĭus, genit. sĕnĭōris); adj. and subst., *old, aged, an old person*.
    Adj. of persons: miles, Ov.; senem fieri, *to age*, Cic.; of animals: cervus, Ov.; of things: vis est senior, Cic.; senior, ut ita dicam, quam illa aetas ferebat, oratio, *maturer*, Cic.
    Subst. *an old* or *elderly man*: Pl., Cic., etc.; *woman*: Tib., Stat. Compar., esp. at Rome, *a man over 45 years old* (opp. iunior): (Servius Tullius) seniores a iunioribus divisit, Cic., Liv., etc.

sēni -ae -a (sex), *six at a time*, or *six each*: Caes., Verg., Liv., Ov.

sĕnīlis -e (senex), *of an old man, senile*: prudentia, Cic.; stultitia, Cic.; statua incurva, Cic.; animus, Liv.; amor, Ov.

¶ Adv. **sĕnīlĭtĕr**, *like an old man*: Quint.
sēnĭo -ōnis, m. (seni), *the number six upon dice*: Pers., Mart.
sĕnĭor, compar. of senex; q.v.
sĕnĭum -i, n. (senex), *old age*; esp. *the weakness of old age, decline, decay*.
　LIT., of persons: Tac., Suet.
　TRANSF., (1) of things: lentae velut tabis, Liv.; mundus se ipse consumptione et senio alebat sui, Cic. (2) *gloom, moroseness*: Hor. (3) *grief, chagrin, sadness*: tota civitas confecta senio, Cic.; Pl., Liv. (4) concr., *an old man*: Ter.
Sĕnŏnes -um, m. *two inter-related peoples, one in Gallia Lugdunensis, with chief town Agendicum (now Sens), the other in Gallia Cisalpina*: Caes., Liv.
sensĭbĭlis -e (sentio), *that can be perceived by the senses*: Sen.
sensĭcŭlus -i, m. (dim. of sensus), *a little sentence*: Quint.
sensĭfĕr -fĕra -fĕrum (sensus/fero), *producing sensation*: Lucr.
sensĭlis -e (sentio), *endowed with sensation, sensitive*: Lucr.
sensim, adv. (sentio), *perceptibly*; hence *just perceptibly, gradually, by degrees, slowly*: Pl., Cic., Liv., etc.
sensus -ūs, m. (sentio), *sense*.
　(1) physically; *sensation, feeling by the senses*; plur., *the senses*: voluptatis sensum capere, Cic.; sensus videndi, audiendi, Cic.; moriendi, *the sensation*, Cic.; so often in Lucr.
　(2) emotionally: **a**, *feeling*: amoris, amandi, diligendi, Cic.: **b**, *way of feeling, attitude*; esp.: communis sensus, *common humanity, fellow-feeling*, Cic., Hor., etc.
　(3) intellectually: **a**, *judgment, perception, understanding*: misero quod omnes eripit sensūs mihi, Cat.; Cic., Verg.: **b**, *way of thinking, attitude of mind*: Cic.: **c**, *the sense, meaning* of words, etc.: verbi, Ov.; testamenti, Hor.: **d**, concr., *a sentence*: Quint., Tac.
sententĭa -ae, f. (sentio), *a way of thinking, opinion, thought, meaning, purpose*.
　In gen.: sententiam fronte tegere, Cic.; in sententia manere, Cic.; ex sententia, *to one's mind*, Pl., Cic.; meā sententiā, *in my opinion*, Pl., Cic.; de sententia alicuius, *as someone wishes*, Pl., Cic., Liv.; prov.: quot homines tot sententiae, Ter., Cic.
　Esp., *an opinion formally expressed, a decision, a vote*: sententiam dicere, Cic.; dare, Liv.; in sententiam alicuius discedere, *to support a proposition*, Liv.; so: (pedibus) ire in sententiam, Liv.; rogare aliquem sententiam, Cic. L.; ex animi mei sententiā, *to the best of my knowledge and belief*, Cic.
　TRANSF., (1) *the meaning, signification, sense* of words, etc.: verborum, Lucr.; id habet hanc sententiam, Cic.; legis, Cic. (2) concr., *a thought expressed in words, a sentence, period*; esp., *a maxim, aphorism*: Cic., Hor., Quint.
sententĭŏla -ae, f. (dim. of sententia), *a short sentence, maxim, aphorism*: Cic., Quint.
sententĭōsus -a -um (sententia), *pithy, sententious*: Cic.
　¶ Adv. **sententĭōsē**, *sententiously*: dicere, Cic.

sentĭcētum -i, n. (sentis), *a thorn-brake*: Pl.
sentīna -ae, f. *bilge-water in the hold of a ship*.
　LIT., sentinae vitiis conflictari, Caes. In metaphor: sedebamus in puppi et clavum tenebamus; nunc autem vix est in sentinā locus, Cic. L.
　TRANSF., *rabble, dregs of the population*: reipublicae, Cic.; urbis, Cic.
Sentīnum -i, n. *a town in Umbria*.
　¶ Hence adj. **Sentīnās** -ātis, *belonging to Sentinum*.
sentĭo sentire sensi sensum, *to feel*.
　(1) physically: calorem et frigus, Lucr.; suavitatem cibi, Cic.; colorem, *to see*, Lucr.; pass.: posse prius ad angustias veniri quam sentirentur, Caes.; with acc. and infin., *to perceive* (by the senses) *that*: Pl., Lucr.
　(2) emotionally, *to experience, feel the force of*: **a**, with a feeling as object: voluptatem et dolorem, Cic.; gaudium victoriae, Liv.: **b**, more often, with an event or experience as object: quid ipse sensisset ad Avaricum, Caes.; tecum Philippos et celerem fugam sensi, Hor.; with acc. and infin.: fieri sentio et excrucior, *I feel it happening*, Cat. TRANSF., of things: ora senserat vastationem, Liv.; Verg., Hor.
　(3) intellectually: **a**, of the truth, *to realize, perceive*: id iam pridem sensi, Pl.; ex nocturno fremitu de profectione eorum senserunt, Caes.; with acc. and infin.: Pl., Cic., Hor., etc.; with Gr. construction: sensit medios delapsus in hostes, *realized that*, Verg.: **b**, of opinion, *to judge, think, suppose*: idem, Cic.; recte, Cic.; humiliter, Cic.; cum aliquo, Pl., Cic.; omnia praeclara atque egregia, Cic.; with acc. and infin.: Ter., Cic.; with double acc.: aliquem bonum civem, Cic.; as legal t. t., *to decide, to vote*: sentire lenissime, Cic. L.
　¶ N. pl. of partic. as subst. **sensa** -orum, *thoughts, sentiments*: Cic., Quint.
sentis -is, c. *a thorn-bush, briar*; usually plur.: rubi sentesque, Caes.; Lucr., Verg., etc.
sentisco -ĕre (sentio), *to begin to perceive, observe*: Lucr.
sentus -a -um, *neglected, rough*: loca, Verg.; Ter., Ov.
sĕorsum and poet. dissyll. **sorsum, sorsus** (se/verto), *apart, separately*: in custodiā habitus, Liv.; seorsum ab rege exercitum ductare, Sall.; abs te seorsum sentio, *I am of a different opinion*, Pl.; with abl. alone: seorsus corpore, *without a body*, Lucr.
sēpărābĭlis -e (separo), *separable*: Cic.
sēpărātim, adv. (separos), *apart, separately, differently*: nihil accidet ei separatim a reliquis civibus, Cic.; castra separatim habebant, Liv.; with ab: dii separatim ab universis singulos diligunt, Cic.
sēpărātĭo -ōnis, f. (separo), *a separation, severance*: distributio partium ac separatio, Cic.; Tac.
sēpăro -are (se), *to disjoin, sever, separate*.
　LIT., nec nos mare separat ingens, Ov.; senatoria subsellia a populari consessu, Cic.; Seston Abydena separat urbe fretum, Ov.
　TRANSF., *to consider or treat separately*: a perpetuis suis historiis bella ea, Cic.; Caes., Liv.
　¶ Hence partic. **sēpărātus** -a -um, *separate, apart, distinct*: volumen, Cic.; Caes., Hor., etc.

¶ Compar. adv. **sēpărātĭŭs**, *less closely*: Cic.

sĕpĕlĭbĭlis -e (sepelio), *that can be buried*; fig., *that can be concealed*: Pl.

sĕpēlĭo -pēlire -pēlīvi and pĕlĭi -pultum, *to bury.*
Lit., aliquem, Cic.; ossa, Ov.; Liv.
Transf., (1) *to put an end to, ruin, destroy*: patriam, Cic.; dolorem, Cic.; Lucr., Ov. (2) partic., sepultus, poet., *buried, sunk, immersed*: somno vinoque sepultus, Verg.; absol., *slumbering*: Verg., Hor.

sēpes=saepes; q.v.

sēpĭa -ae, f. (σηπία), *the cuttle-fish*: Pl., Cic. Transf., *its fluid, used as ink*: Pers.

sēpimentum=saepimentum; q.v.

sēpĭo=saepio; q.v.

sēpĭŏla -ae, f. (dim. of sepia), *a small cuttle-fish*: Pl.

Sēplāsĭa -ae, f. *a street in Capua, where unguents were sold.*

sēpōno -pōnĕre -pŏsŭi -pŏsĭtum, *to put on one side, place apart, reserve.*
Lit., aliquid ad fanum, Cic.; captivam pecuniam in aedificationem templi, Liv.; primitias magno Iovi, Ov.; de mille sagittis unam, Ov. Esp. *to put* a person *out of the way, banish*: aliquem in insulam, Tac.; Suet.
Transf., (1) *to reserve*: sibi ad eam rem tempus, Cic.; Tac. (2) *to distinguish, divide*: a ceteris dictionibus eam partem dicendi, Cic.; inurbanum lepido dicto, Hor. (3) *to put aside*: graves curas, *to banish*, Ov.

sēpŏsĭtus -a -um, p. adj. (from sepono). (1) *distant, remote*: fons, Prop. (2) *choice, select*: vestis, Tib.

seps sēpis, c. (σήψ). (1) *a species of venomous snake*: Pl., Luc. (2) *an insect*, perhaps the *wood-louse*: Plin.

sepsĕ=se ipse; *see* ipse.

septem, indecl. numer. (cf. ἑπτά), *seven*: Pl., Cic., etc. Absol.: septem (οἱ ἑπτά), *the Seven Wise Men of Greece*, Cic.

September -bris, adj. (septem), *belonging to September*: mensis September, *the seventh month of the Roman year* (reckoning from March), *September*: kalendae, nonae, idus (the 1st, 5th, 13th *of September*); horae, *the unhealthy time of September*, Hor.

septemdĕcim (septendĕcim), numer. *seventeen*: Cic., Liv.

septemflŭus -a -um (fluo), *having a sevenfold flood, with seven mouths*: Nilus, Ov.

septemgĕmĭnus -a -um, *sevenfold*: Nilus, *with seven mouths*, Cat.; Verg.

septempĕdālis -e, *seven feet high*: Pl.

septemplex -plĭcis (septem/plico), *seven-fold*: clipeus, *with seven layers of hide*, Verg.; Nilus, *with seven mouths*, Ov.

septemtrĭōnālis -e (septemtrio), *northern*: Plin. N. pl. as subst. **septemtrĭōnālia** -ium, *the northern regions*: Tac.

septemtrĭōnēs (septentrĭōnēs) -um, m. pl. *the seven plough-oxen.*
Hence (1) *the seven stars of either the Great Bear or the Little Bear constellation*: Pl., Cic., Ov. In sing., septemtrio -ōnis, *either of these constellations as a whole*: Cic. (2) in gen., *the north*; sing.: spectant in septemtrionem, Caes.; septemtrio a Macedonia obicitur, Liv.; in tmesis: septem subiecta trioni, Verg.; plur.: inflectens solcursum

tum ad meridiem, tum ad septemtriones, Cic.; Caes. (3) *the north wind*: Cic. L., Liv.

septemvir -vĭri, m.; plur. **septemvĭri** -ōrum, *a college* or *guild of seven persons.* (1) of the epulones, *see* epulo. (2) *a commission to divide public land*: Cic.

septemvĭrālis -e, *of* septemviri: auctoritas, Cic. M. pl. as subst. **septemvĭrāles** -ium= septemviri; q.v.

septemvĭrātus -ūs, m. *the office* or *dignity of a* septemvir: Cic., Plin. L.

septēnārĭus -a -um (septeni), *containing seven*: numerus, Plin. M. pl. as subst. **septēnārĭi** -orum (sc. versus), *verses containing seven feet, heptameters*: Cic.

septendĕcim=septemdecim; q.v.

septēni -ae, a (septem), *seven at a time* or *seven each*: duo fasces septenos habere libros, Liv.; septena fila lyrae, *the seven strings*, Ov. In sing.: gurgite septeno, of the Nile, Luc.

septentrio=septemtrio; *see* septemtriones.

septĭēs (septĭens), adv. (septem), *seven times*: Cic., Liv.

septĭmānus -a -um (septimus), *relating to the seventh*: nonae, *when falling on the seventh day of the month*, Varr. M. pl. as subst. **septĭmāni** -ōrum, *soldiers of the seventh legion*: Tac.

septĭmontĭālis -e, *of the festival of the seven hills, the* Septimontium: Suet.

septĭmus (septŭmus) -a -um (septem), *seventh*: Pl., Cic., Ov. N. acc. sing. as adv. **septĭmum**, *for the seventh time*: Cic.

septĭmus dĕcĭmus -a -um, *seventeenth*: Cic.

septingentēsĭmus (-ensĭmus) -a -um (septingenti), *seven hundredth*: Liv.

septingenti -ae -a (septem/centum), *seven hundred*: Cic., Caes., Liv.

septizōnĭum -i, n. (septem/zona), *a building in Rome*: Suet.

septŭāgēsĭmus (-ensĭmus) -a -um (septuaginta), *seventieth*: Cic., Liv.

septŭāginta, indecl. numer., *seventy*: Cic., Liv.

septŭennis -e (septem/annus), *of seven years, seven years old*: puer, Pl.

septum=saeptum; *see* saepis.

septunx -uncis, m. (septem/uncia), *seven-twelfths of the as, or of any unit*: auri, *seven ounces*, Liv.

sĕpulcrālis -e (sepulcrum), *of a tomb, sepulchral*: arae, Ov.; fax, *funeral torch*, Ov.

sĕpulcrētum -i, n. (sepulcrum), *a burial-place, cemetery*: Cat.

sĕpulcrum -i, n. (sepelio), *a place of burial, a grave, tomb.*
Lit., monumenta sepulcrorum, Cic.; onerare membra sepulcro, Verg. Also *the place where a corpse is burnt*: Ter., Verg. *A cenotaph*: Verg., Tac.
Transf., (1) *any place of destruction*: Enn. Cat. (2) plur., *the dead*: Cat., Ov. (3) comically: sepulcrum vetus, *of an old man*, Pl.

sĕpultūra -ae, f. (sepelio), *a burying, burial, interment*: sepultura aliquem adficere, *to bury*, Cic. Also *the burning of the body of the dead*: Tac.

Sēquăna -ae, m. *a river of Gaul* (now the *Seine*): Caes., Luc.

sĕquax -ācis (sequor), *following, attending.*
Lit., undae, fumus, Verg.; Latio dare terga sequaci, *pursuing*, Verg.; curae sequaces, *haunting*, Lucr.

TRANSF., naturas hominum varias moresque sequaces, *attendant*, Lucr.

sĕquester -tri or -tris, m. (**1**) *a depositary, a person in whose hands the matter in dispute is deposited till the dispute is settled*: Pl. (**2**) *a go-between* or *agent* (in cases of bribery): quo sequestre in illo iudice corrumpendo dicebatur esse usus, Cic. (**3**) *a mediator*: Sen., Luc.

sĕquestra -ae, f. (sequester), *a mediator*: pace sequestrā, Verg.

sĕquestrum -i, n. (sequester), *a deposit*: sequestro deponere, *by way of deposit*, Pl.

sĕquĭus=secius, compar. of secus; q.v.

sĕquor sĕqui sĕcūtus sum, dep. (connected with ἕπομαι), *to follow, accompany, attend.*

LIT., in gen., usually with acc.; of persons: qui ex urbe amicitiae causā Caesarem secuti, Caes.; vestigia alicuius, Ov.; Pl., Hor., etc.; of things: zonā bene te secutā, Hor.; neque arborum ulla te sequetur, Hor. Esp. *to follow in order to catch, to pursue*: hostes, Caes.; moechas, Hor.; feras, Ov.; *to follow a person to a place*: Formias, Cic.; secutae sunt nares vicinitatem oris, *have sought for*, Cic.

TRANSF., (**1**) of time or order, *to follow, ensue*: sequitur hunc annum nobilis clade Caudinā pax, Liv.; sequenti anno, Liv.; sequenti die, Liv.; sequitur clamor, Verg. (**2**) *to follow as a consequence, be the consequence of, be caused by*: moneo ne summa turpitudo sequatur, Cic.; gloria virtutem tamquam umbra sequatur, Cic. Hence, *to follow logically*: si hoc enuntiatum verum non est, sequitur, ut falsum sit, Cic. (**3**) of property, *to go to, fall to the share of*: urbes captae Aetolos sequerentur, Liv.; heredes monumentum ne sequeretur, Hor. (**4**) of things, *to follow easily, come of itself, yield*: ipse (ramus) facilis sequetur, Verg.; verba provisam rem, Hor.; Cic., Liv. (**5**) *to follow, conform to*, a leader, an order, plan, etc.: naturam ducem, Cic.; amicum, Cic.; auctoritatem, Caes., Cic. L.; rationem, leges, Cic. (**6**) *to strive after, aim at, seek to gain* an object: amicitiam fidemque populi Romani, Cic.; mercedes, Hor.; Caes., Liv., etc.

sĕra -ae, f. (²sero), *a movable bar* or *bolt for fastening doors*: centum postibus addere seras, Ov.

Sĕrāpĭs -pis and -pĭdis, m. (Σεράπις, Σαράπις), *a deity of the Egyptians, later worshipped in Greece and at Rome.*

sĕrēnĭtās -ātis, f. (serenus), *clear, bright, fair weather*. LIT., caeli, Liv. TRANSF., fortunae, Liv.

sĕrēno -are (serenus), *to make clear, serene, bright*. LIT., caelum, Verg. TRANSF., spem fronte, Verg.

sĕrēnus -a -um, *clear, bright, fair, serene.*

LIT., caelum, Lucr., Cic. L., Verg.; nox, Lucr., Cic., Verg.; pelagus, Verg.

TRANSF., aevum, Lucr.; frons, Cic.; animus, Ov.

N. as subst. **sĕrēnum** -i, *fair weather*: Liv., Luc., Pl.; soles et aperta serena, Verg.; Lucr.

Sĕrēs -um, m. (Σῆρες), *a people in eastern Asia, famous for their silken stuffs, the modern Chinese.*

¶ Hence adj. **Sērĭcus** -a -um, *Chinese*: pulvillus, *silken*, Hor.; Tac., etc. N. pl. as subst. **Sērĭca** -ōrum, *silken garments*: Prop.

sĕresco -ĕre (serenus), *to become dry*: Lucr.

Sergĭus -a -um, *name of a Roman gens*; esp. *of* L. Sergius Catilina, *the head of a conspiracy suppressed in the consulship of Cicero.*

¹**sēria** -ae, f. *a large jar for holding wine, oil,* etc.: Pl., Ter., Liv.

²**sēria**, see serius.

sērĭcātus -a -um (Seres), *clothed in silk*: Suet.

Sērĭcus, see Seres.

sĕrĭēs, acc. -em, abl. -e; genit. and dat. not found; f. (²sero), *a row, succession, chain, series.* LIT., iuvenum, *dancing hand in hand*, Tib. TRANSF., rerum, Cic.; innumerabilis annorum, Hor.; Ov. Esp., *a line of descent, lineage*: digne vir hac serie, Ov.; Prop.

sērĭŏla -ae, f. (dim. of ¹seria), *a small jar*: Pers.

Sērĭphus (-ŏs) -i, f. (Σέριφος), *an island in the Aegean Sea.* Adj. **Sērĭphĭus** -a -um, *Seriphian*; m. as subst. **Sērĭphĭus** -i, *a Seriphian.*

sērĭus -a -um, *serious, earnest* (used gen. of things, not persons): res, Pl., Cic.; with supine: verba seria dictu, Hor.

N. as subst. **sērĭum** -i, *earnest, seriousness*: Pl.; abl. **sērĭo** as adv., *in earnest, earnestly, seriously*: serio audire, Liv., Pl., Ter.; plur. **sēria** -orum, *serious things*: seria ac iocos celebrare, Liv.

sermo -ōnis, m. (²sero), *talk, conversation, discourse.*

LIT., in gen.: sermonem conferre cum aliquo, Cic.; esse in sermone omnium, *the subject of everyone's conversation*, Cic.; fit sermo inter eos, Cic.; Caes., Verg., etc. Esp. (**1**) *learned conversation, serious discussion*: sermonem cum aliquo habere de amicitia, Cic.; Hor. (**2**) *common talk, report, rumour*: vulgi; hominum, Cic.; Tac.

TRANSF., (**1**) *a subject of conversation*: Cataplus ille Puteolanus, sermo illius temporis, Cic. L.; Pl., Prop. (**2**) in writing or speaking, *a familiar, conversational style*, or *prose*: sermonis plenus orator, Cic.; scribere sermoni propiora, Hor.; hence, in Horace, of his *Letters* and *Satires* as opposed to his more ambitious poems. (**3**) *manner of speaking, language, style, expression, diction*: elegantia sermonis, Cic. L.; sermo rusticus, urbanus, Liv. (**4**) *language, dialect*: sermone debemus uti, qui natus est nobis, *our mother-tongue*, Cic.; quae philosophi Graeco sermone tractavissent, Cic.; patrii sermonis egestas, Lucr.

sermōcĭnātĭo -onis, f. (sermocinor), *a discussion, disputation*: Quint.

sermōcĭnor -ari, dep. (sermo), *to converse, talk, discuss.* In gen.: sermocinari cum isto diligenter, Cic. Esp., *to hold a learned discussion*: Suet.

sermuncŭlus -i, m. (dim. of sermo), *rumour, tittle-tattle*: urbani malevolorum sermunculi, Cic.; Plin. L.

¹**sĕro** sĕrĕre sēvi sătum, *to sow, set, plant.*

LIT., (**1**) of plants: oleam et vitem, Cic.; frumenta, Caes.; Verg. Also with land as object: iugera, Cic.; agrum, Ov. N. pl. of partic. as subst., sāta -ōrum, *standing corn, crops*: Verg., Ov. (**2**) of human beings, *to beget, engender, bring forth*; esp. in partic.,

sătus -a -um, *sprung, born*: non temere sati
et creati sumus, Cic.: with abl.: Anchisā
satus, *son of Anchises*, Verg.; satus Nereide,
son of Thetis, Ov.; satae Peliā, *daughters of
Pelias*, Ov.; also with de, and ab: Ov.
   Transf., *to produce, give rise to, spread*,
abstr. things: mores, Cic.; diuturnam
rempublicam, Cic.; rumores, Verg.; cum
patribus certamina, Liv.; discordias, Liv.;
crimina, Liv.

²**sĕro** sĕrĕre sĕrŭi sertum (cf. εἴρω), *to join
together, put in a row, connect.* Lit., only in
perf. partic., sertus; *see below.* Transf., fati
lege immobilis rerum humanarum ordo
seritur, Liv.; fabulam argumento, Liv.;
conloquia cum hoste, Liv.; multa inter sese
vario sermone serebant, Verg.
   ¶ Hence partic. **sertus** -a -um, *linked,
connected*: loricae, Nep.; sertas nardo
florente coronas, Luc. N. as subst. **sertum** -i,
usually plur. **serta** -orum, *a garland, wreath
of flowers*: sertis redimiri, Cic.; Verg., etc.
So also f. **serta** -ae, *a garland*: Prop.

serpens -entis, c. (serpo), *a creeping animal*;
hence, usually, *a snake, serpent.* Lit., Lucr.,
Cic., Verg., etc. Transf., *a constellation in
the northern hemisphere* (also called Draco
and Anguis): Ov.

serpentĭgĕna -ae, m. (serpens/gigno), *sprung
from a serpent*: Ov.

serpentĭpēs -pĕdis (serpens/pes), *snake-
footed*: Ov.

serpĕrastra -ōrum, n. *bandages* or *knee-splints
for straightening the crooked legs of children*:
Varr. In jest, of officers who keep their
soldiers in order: Cic. L.

serpillum = serpyllum; q.v.

serpo serpĕre serpsi serptum (ἕρπω), *to creep,
crawl.*
   Lit., of animals: quaedam bestiae
serpentes, quaedam gradientes, Cic.; serpere
per humum, Ov.
   Transf., (1) of the slow motion of material
things: vitis serpens multiplici lapsu et
erratico, Cic.; flamma per continua serpens,
Liv.; of a river: tectis in mare serpit aqua,
Ov. (2) of the slow progress of abstract
things; of prosaic poetry: serpit humi tutus,
Hor.; esp. of influences, rumours, etc.: si
paullatim haec consuetudo serpere ac
prodire coeperit, Cic.; serpit hic rumor,
foll. by acc. and infin., Cic.; Verg., Liv.

serpyllum (**serpillum, serpullum**) -i, n.
(ἕρπυλλον), *wild thyme*: Varr., Verg.

serra -ae, f. (perhaps = sec-ra, from seco),
a saw: Lucr., Cic., Verg., etc.

serrācum (**sarrācum**) -i, n. *a kind of waggon*:
Juv. Transf., *a constellation, the Wain*:
Juv.

serrātus -a -um (serra), *toothed like a saw,
serrated*: dentes, Plin. M. pl. as subst.
serrāti -ōrum (sc. nummi), *silver coins
notched on the edge, milled coins*: Tac.

serrŭla -ae, f. (dim. of serra), *a little saw*: Cic.

serta, *see* sero.

Sertōrius -i, m., Q., *a general of Marius who,
when Sulla gained the upper hand in Rome,
fled to Spain, and resisted there till he was
murdered by Perperna.* Adj. **Sertōriānus**
-a -um, *Sertorian.*

sertŭm, *see* sero.

sĕrum -i, n. *the watery part of curdled milk,*
whey: Verg., Ov. Transf., *the watery part*
or *serum of other things*: Plin.

sĕrus -a -um, adj. (with compar.).
   (1) *late*: gratulatio, Cic.; hora serior, Ov.;
serā nocte, Prop., Liv.; dies, Tac. Pre-
dicatively, *acting late*: serus abi, *go late
away*, Ov.; Hor.; with genit.: o seri studiorum! *late learned* (ὀψιμαθεῖς), Hor.
   (2) *too late*: Kalendae, Cic.; serum
auxilium post proelium, Liv.
   ¶ N. as subst. **sĕrum** -i, *a late hour*: rem
in serum trahere, *to retard*, Liv.; serum diei,
late in the day, evening, Liv. N. acc., sing.
and plur., **sĕrum** and **sĕrā**, as adv., *late*:
Verg.
   ¶ N. abl. sing. as adv. **sĕrō**. (1) *late*: Cic.
(2) *too late*: Pl., Cic., Liv.; prov.: sero
sapiunt (sc. Phryges), Cic. Compar. **sĕrius**
later: biduo serius, Cic.; serius ocius, *sooner
or later*, Hor. Superl. **sĕrissĭmē**: Caes.

serva -ae, f. *see* servus.

servābĭlis -e (servo), *that can be saved*: Ov.

servans -antis, partic. from servo; q.v.

servātor -ōris, m. (servo). (1) *a preserver,
saviour*: reipublicae, Cic.; salutis, Ov.; Liv.
(2) *a watcher*: Olympi, Luc.

servātrix - īcis, f. (servator), *she that preserves,
a preserver, saviour*: Ter., Cic., Ov.

servīlis -e (servus), *of a slave, slavish, servile*:
vestis, Cic.; tumultus, *a slaves' revolt*, Caes.;
servilem in modum, Caes.; servilis indoles,
Liv.
   ¶ Adv. **servīlĭtĕr**, adv. (servilis), *slavishly,
servilely*: ne quid serviliter muliebriterve
faciamus, Cic.; Tac.

Servīlius -a -um, *name of a Roman gens. Its
most celebrated members were* (1) C. Servilius
Ahala, *who as* magister equitum *under
Cincinnatus killed Maelius.* (2) P. Servilius
Rullus, *composer of the* lex Servilia, *concerning
the selling of the Italian public lands, against
which Cicero delivered his agrarian speeches.*

servĭo -ire (servus), *to be subject to* (with dat.).
to be a servant or *slave.*
   Lit., (1) in a household: alicui, Pl., Cic.,
etc.; apud aliquem, Pl., Cic., Liv.; with
internal acc.: servitutem, Pl., Cic., Liv.
(2) politically: rēgi, Cic.; Verg., Liv., Ov.
   Transf., (1) in gen., *to serve, help, comply
with, gratify*: alicui, Cic.; incertis rumoribus,
Caes.; tempori, Cic.; amori aliorum, Cic.;
iracundiae, Cic. (2) as legal t. t., of buildings
etc., *to be subject to certain rights other than
the owner's, to be mortgaged*, etc.: Cic.

servĭtĭum -i, n. (servus), *slavery, service,
servitude, subjection.*
   Lit., domestic and political: ducere aliquem in servitium, Liv.; civitatem a servitio
abstrahere, Cic.; servitio exire, Verg.
Transf., (1) animi imperio, corporis servitio
magis utimur, *the mind as master, the body as
slave*, Sall.; Verg., Tac. (2) concr., *slaves,
servants, a household of slaves*; used both sing.
and plur.: servitia concitare, Cic.; servitium
in scaenam immissum, Cic.; Pl., Liv.

servitrītĭus -a -um (servus/tero), *galled by
slavery*, as a term of abuse: Pl.

servĭtūdo -ĭnis, f. (servus), *slavery, servitude*:
Liv.

servĭtūs -ūtis, f. (servus), *the condition of a
slave; slavery, servitude.*
   Lit., domestic and political: diutina, Cic.;

perpetua, Caes.; muliebris, Liv.; aliquem in servitutem abducere, Cic.; addicere, Caes., Liv.; adserere, Liv.; anteponere mortem servituti, Cic.; servitute Graeciam liberare, Cic.

    Transf., (1) in gen., *subjection, obedience*: officii, Cic. (2) as legal t. t., of houses, lands, etc., *liability to certain burdens*, e.g., *a right of way*: fundo servitutem imponere, Cic. L. (3) concr., *slaves*: servitus crescit nova (of lovers), Hor.

Servius -a, *a Roman name, esp. in the Sulpician gens; see* Sulpicius.

servo -are, *to watch over, to keep.*

    Lit., (1) *to watch, observe.* Absol.: serva! look out! Pl., Hor. With object: uxor scelesta me omnibus servat modis ne, Pl.; iter alicuius, Caes.; sidera, *to observe*, Verg.; esp. of augurs: servare de caelo, Cic. (2) *to keep, protect, preserve, save*: populum, Cic.; aliquem liberā custodiā, Cic.; aliquem ex iudicio, Cic.; rem suam, Hor.; with double acc.: se integros castosque, Cic. Esp., *to keep for the future, lay up, reserve*: Caecuba centum clavibus, Hor.; se ad maiora, Liv.; eo me servavi, Cic.; with dat.: res iudicio voluntatique multitudinis, Cic.; vosmet rebus servate secundis, Verg.

    Transf., (1) *to keep, retain, observe* an abstr. thing: promissum, Pl., Cic.; fidem, Pl., Cic.; ordines, Caes.; amicitiam, Cic.; legem, Cic.; pacem cum aliquo, Cic.; amorem, Verg.; aequam mentem, Hor.; with ut *or* ne and the subj.: cum ita priores decemviri servassent, ut unus fasces haberet, Liv. (2) *to keep to, stay in* a place: limen, *stay at home*, Verg.; silvas et flumina, Verg.; atria, Hor.

    ¶ Hence partic. **servans** -antis as adj. (with superl.), *observing*: servantissimus aequi, Verg.

servŭla (servŏla) -ae, f. (dim. of serva), *a young female slave, servant-girl*: Cic. L.

servŭlus (servŏlus) -i, m. (dim. of servus), *a young slave*: Pl., Cic.

servus, adj., *serving*, and subst., *a slave.*

    Adj., servus -a -um, *serving, servile, subject.* Lit., homo, Pl.; capita, Liv.; Graeciae urbes, Liv. Transf., (1) in gen.: imitatores, servum pecus, Hor. (2) as legal t. t., of lands or buildings, *subject to rights other than those of the owners*: praedia serva, Cic.

    Subst., m. servus -i, *a slave, servant.* Lit., servi publici, *slaves of the state*, Cic.; Pl., etc. Transf., servi cupiditatum, Cic.; legum, Cic.; Plin. L. F. serva -ae, *a female slave*: Pl., Hor., Liv.

sēsămum (sīs-) -i, n. and **sēsăma** -ae, f. (σήσαμον, σησάμη), *sesame, an oily plant*: Pl., Plin.

sescēnāris -e (perhaps sesqui/annus), *a year and a half old*: bos, Liv.

sescēnārius -a -um (sesceni), *consisting of six hundred*: cohortes, Caes.

sescēni -ae -a (sescenti), *six hundred at a time* or *six hundred each*: Cic.

sescentēni=sesceni; q.v.: Suet.

sescentēsĭmus (-ensĭmus) -a -um (sescenti), *six hundredth*: Cic.

sescenti -ae -a (sex/centum), *six hundred*: Pl., Cic. Transf., to denote an indefinite round number, *countless*: epistulae, Cic.; Pl., Ter.

sescentĭēs (sescentĭens), adv. (sescenti), *six hundred times*: Cic. L., Plin. L.

sescentoplăgus -i, m. (sescenti/plaga), *one who receives innumerable stripes*: Pl.

sescuncĭa -ae, f. (sesqui/uncia), *one eighth of any unit*: Plin. As adj.: copulae sescunciae, *an inch and a half thick*, Pl.

sĕsĕlis -is, f. (σέσελις), *a plant, hartwort*: Cic.

Sĕsostris -is and **Sĕsōsĭs** -sĭdis, m. (Σέσωστρις), *a famous king of Egypt.*

sesqui, adv. (perhaps from semis/que), *one half more, half as much again*: sesqui maior, Cic.

sesquĭalter -altera -alterum, *one and a half*: Cic.

sesquĭhōra -ae, f. *an hour and a half*: Plin. L.

sesquĭlībra -ae, f. *a pound and a half*: Cato.

sesquĭmensis -is, m. *a month and a half*: Varr.

sesquĭmŏdĭus -i, m. *a peck and a half*: Cic.

sesquĭŏbŏlus -i, m. *an obolus and a half*: Plin.

sesquĭoctāvus -a -um, *containing ⅑ of a thing*: Cic.

sesquĭŏpus -ĕris, n. *the work of a day and a half*: Pl.

sesquĭpĕdālis -e, *a foot and a half long*: tigna, Caes. Hence *inordinately long*: dentes, Cat.; verba, Hor.

sesquĭpēs -pĕdis, m. *a foot and a half long, wide*, etc.: Pl.

sesquĭplāga -ae, f. *a blow and a half*: Tac.

sesquĭplex -plicis, *one and a half times as much*: Cic.

sesquĭtertĭus -a -um, *containing ⅓ of anything*: Cic.

sessĭbŭlum -i, n. (sedeo), *a seat, stool, chair*: Pl.

sessĭlis -e (sedeo), *fit for sitting*. (1) pass.: tergum (equi), Ov. (2) act., of plants, *low, dwarf*: lactuca, Mart., Plin.

sessĭo -ōnis, f. (sedeo). Lit., *sitting, the act of sitting*: status, incessio, sessio, Cic.; sessiones quaedam (*postures in sitting*) contra naturam sunt, Cic.; esp. (1) *a sitting idle, loitering*: Capitolina, Cic. L. (2) *a session for discussion*: post meridiana, Cic. Transf., *a place for sitting, seat*: Cic.

sessĭto -are (freq. of sedeo), *to sit much, sit often*: quam deam (Suadam) in Pericli labris scripsit Eupolis sessitavisse, Cic.

sessĭuncŭla -ae, f. (dim. of sessio), *a little company* or *assembly for conversation*: Cic.

sessor -ōris, m. (sedeo). Lit., *one who sits, a sitter*: Hor., Suet. Transf., *an inhabitant*: urbis, Nep.

sestertĭus -a -um (semis/tertius), *consisting of two and a half*; as adj., only with nummus and milia: nummo sestertio *or* sestertio nummo, *for a mere trifle*, Cic., Varr.

    M. as subst. **sestertĭus** -i; genit. plur. usually sestertium; *a sesterce, a silver coin*=¼ *denarius*=2½ *asses*; often written HS. Numbers of sesterces are expressed as follows. Below 2,000, by sestertii with cardinal num., e.g. centum sestertii. From 2,000 to 1,000,000, by milia sestertium or by sestertium without milia, treated as a n. noun, and so declined (=1,000 *sesterces*), with cardinal or distrib. num.: bis dena super sestertia nummum, 20,000 *sesterces*, Hor. From 1,000,000 upwards, by sestertium (as genit. pl. or declined; =here 100,000 *sesterces*) with numeral adv.: sestertium deciens, 1,000,000 *sesterces*, Cic.; sestertium ducenties, 20,000,000 *sesterces*, Liv.

Sestĭus -a -um, *name of a Roman gens. Its most famous members were* (1) L. Sestius, *tribune of the people, the author of a law enacting that one of the consuls should always be a plebeian.* (2) P. Sestius, *tribune of the people, who proposed the recall of Cicero from exile.*

¶ Hence adj. **Sestĭānus** -a -um, *Sestian.*

Sestus (Sestŏs) -i, f. (Σηστός), *a town on the Hellespont, home of Hero.* Adj. **Sestus** -a -um, *Sestian*: puella, *Hero*, Ov.

set=sed; q.v.

seta=saeta; q.v.

seu, *see* sive.

sĕvērĭtās -ātis, f. (severus), *gravity, seriousness, austerity, sternness*: censorum, censoria, Cic.; severitatem in filio adhibere, Cic.; imperii, Caes.

sĕvērĭtūdo -inis, f. (severus), *gravity, sternness*: Pl.

sĕvērus -a -um, adj. (with compar. and superl.), *grave, serious, strict, rigid, stern, austere.*

Of persons; in a good sense: Tubero vitā severus, Cic.; familia cum ad ceteras res tum ad iudicandum severissima, Cic. M. as subst.: Cat., Hor. In a bad sense, *hard, cruel*: Neptunus saevus severusque, Pl.; turba Eumenidum, Prop.; in aliquem, Cic., Liv.

Of things: frons, Pl., Ov.; iudicia, Cic.; Falernum (vinum), *harsh*, Hor.; amnis Cocyti, *grim*, Verg. N. pl. as subst.: Hor.

¶ Adv. (with compar. and superl.) **sĕvērē**, *seriously, gravely, austerely*: Caes., Cic.

Sĕvērus -i, m. *a Roman family name*, esp. of (1) Cornelius Severus, *epic poet in the time of Augustus, friend of Ovid.* (2) L. Septimius Severus, *emperor* A.D. 193–211. (3) Aurelius Alexander Severus, *emperor* A.D. 222–34.

Sĕvērus mons, *a mountain in the Sabine country, a branch of the Apennines.*

sĕvŏco -are, *to call aside, call away.* LIT., singulos, Caes.; plebem in Aventinum, Cic. TRANSF., *to withdraw, separate*: animum a voluptate, Cic.

sĕvum=sebum; q.v.

sex, indecl. numer. (ἕξ), *six*: Pl., Cic., etc.: sex septem, *six or seven*, Ter., Hor.

sexāgēnārĭus -a -um (sexageni), *containing sixty*; esp., *sixty years old*: Quint

sexāgēni -ae -a (sexaginta), *sixty at a time, or sixty each*: Cic., Liv.

sexāgēsĭmus (-ensĭmus) -a -um (sexaginta), *sixtieth*: Ter., Cic., Mart.

sexāgĭēs (sexāgĭēns), adv. (sexaginta), *sixty times*: Caes., Cic.

sexāginta, indecl. num. (sex), *sixty*: Pl., Cic., etc.

sexangŭlus -a -um, *hexagonal*: Ov., Plin.

sexcen-, *see* sescen-.

sexdĕcim=sedecim; q.v.

sexennis -e (sex/annus), *six years old*: Pl., Caes.

sexennĭum -i, n. (sexennis), *a period of six years*: Pl., Cic.

sexĭēs (sexĭens), adv. (sex), *six times*: Liv.

sexprīmi (or sex prīmi) -ōrum, m. *a board of six magistrates in a provincial town*: Cic.

sextādĕcĭmāni -ōrum, m. (sextusdecimus), *soldiers of the 16th legion*: Tac.

sextans -antis, m. (sex), *the sixth part of an* as, *or of any unit.* In gen., as a fraction: heredes in sextante, Cic. L. Esp. (1) as a coin, *two unciae*: Liv. (2) in weight, *the sixth part of a pound*: Ov., Plin. (3) in area, *a sixth of an acre*: Varr. (4) of liquid, *a sixth of a* sextarius: Mart.

sextārĭus -i, m. (sextus), *the sixth part.* Esp. in liquid measure, *the sixth part of a* congius (about a pint): Cic.

Sextīlis -e (sextus), *of the sixth month of the old Roman year* (reckoning from March): Hor., Liv. M. as subst. (sc. mensis), *the sixth month*, afterwards called *Augustus*: Cic.

sextŭla -ae, f. (sc. pars; from sextulus, dim. of sextus), *the sixth part of an uncia*, $\frac{1}{72}$ of *an* as: Varr.; as a fraction, $\frac{1}{72}$: Cic.

sextus -a -um (sex), *sixth*: Pl., Cic., etc. N. acc. as adv. **sextum**, *for the sixth time*: sextum consul, Cic.

sextusdĕcĭmus -a -um, *sixteenth*: Cic.

sexungŭla -ae, f. *six-claws*; nickname for a rapacious woman: Pl.

sexus -ūs, m. (connected with secus and seco), *sex*: hominum genus et in sexu consideratur, virile an muliebre sit, Cic.; Liv., etc.

sī, conj., *if, supposing that.* Often preceded by quod, quod si, *and if, but if*; foll. by modo, si modo, *if only*; si quis, *if anybody*; si non, si minus, nisi, *if not, unless.*

(1) with indic. verb (in any tense): **a**, indicating simply possibility: si falsum est, accingere contra, Lucr.; Cic., etc.: **b**, implying fact, esp. foll. by quidem: si quidem, *or* siquidem, *since, considering that*, Cic., etc.

(2) with subj. verb: **a**, with pres. subj., for a future condition which is possible but not likely: possis ignavus haberi ad cenam si intestatus eas, Juv.; Cic., etc.: **b**, with imperf. subj. for a present unfulfilled condition, pluperf. for a past unfulfilled: si id fecisses, melius famae consuluisses, Cic.; me truncus sustulerat nisi Faunus ictum dextra levasset, Hor.; emendaturus, si licuisset, eram, Ov.; **c**, to express a wish: si nunc foret illa iuventus! Verg.; esp. after o: o si solitae quicquam virtutis adesset, Verg.; o mihi praeteritos referat si Iuppiter annos, Verg.; Hor.: **d**, after perinde ac, etc., in comparisons: perinde existimans ac si usus esset, Caes.; Cic., etc.: **e**, with imperf. subj., of what often used to happen: chommoda dicebat si quando commoda vellet dicere, Cat.; Hor.: **f**, elliptically=*in the hope that, on the chance that, to see if*: pergit ad speluncam, si forte eo vestigia ferrent, Liv.; Cic., Caes., etc.: **g**, rarely, in indir. quest., *whether*: fatis incerta feror si Iuppiter unam esse velit urbem, Verg.

(3) elliptically, without verb; esp., si minus, *if not*, si non, si nihil aliud: Cic., Liv., etc.

sībĭla -orum, n. pl. (1) as adj., *hissing*: colla colubrae, Verg. (2) as subst., used by poets as plur. of sibilus (q.v.): calamorum sibila, Lucr.; serpens horrenda sibila misit, Ov.

sībĭlo -are (sibilus). (1) intransit., *to hiss, to whistle*: serpens, Verg.; anguis, Ov.; of red-hot iron in water: in tepida submersum sibilat unda, Ov. (2) transit., *to hiss at, hiss down*: aliquem, Cic. L., Hor.

sībĭlus -i, m. (poet. plur. sibila; q.v.), *a hissing, whistling.* In gen.: austri, Verg.; of persons, *whistling*: sibilo signum dare, Liv. Esp., *a contemptuous hissing*: sibilum metuis? Cic.; sibilis aliquem explodere, Cic.

Sĭbylla -ae, f. (Σίβυλλα), *a prophetess and priestess of Apollo, a Sibyl*; esp., *the Sibyl of Cumae, whom Aeneas consulted, and another who was said to have composed the Sibylline books, which were bought by Tarquin from an old woman, and kept in the Capitol, and consulted in time of danger*.
¶ Hence adj. **Sĭbyllīnus** -a -um, *of the Sibyl, Sibylline*: libri, Cic., Liv.; vaticinatio, Cic.; versus: Cic., Hor.

sīc (seic, sīce), *so, thus, in this way*.
In gen., with exact sense shown by general context, gesture, etc.: sive enim sic est, sive illo modo, Cic.; illa civitas popularis (sic enim appellant) in qua in populo sunt omnia, Cic.; Liv., etc. Sometimes with disparaging sense, *so so*: Pl. In the sense *just like that, without further ado*: sic armatus, *accoutred as he was*, Liv.; Cic. In affirmative answers, *just so, yes*: Ter., Cic., etc.
Esp. (1) introducing a description, quotation, etc., *like this, as follows*: ingressus est sic loqui Scipio, Cic.; sic velim existimes, te nihil gratius facere posse, Cic.; sic est vulgus; ex veritate pauca, ex opinione multa, existimant, Cic.; Verg., etc. (2) referring to a conditional or restrictive clause, *in that case, with this limitation*: recordatione amicitiae sic fruor, ut beate vixisse videar, Cic.; decreverunt, id sic ratum esset, si patres auctores fierent, Liv.; so in wishes: sic tua Cyrneas fugiant examina taxos, Verg. (3) in comparisons, *so*; gen. corresponding to ut: Atticum sic amo, ut alterum fratrem, Cic.; quemadmodum . . . sic, Cic.; sic . . . tanquam, Cic.; sic . . . quasi, Cic.; velut . . . sic, Liv.; ceu . . . sic, Verg. (4) leading up to consecutive clause, *so much, to such a degree*: Caecinam a puero semper sic dilexi ut non ullo cum homine coniunctius viverem, Caes.; Caes., etc.
¶ Hence interrog. **sīcĭnĕ (siccĭnĕ)? sīcīn'?** *is it thus that?*: Cat., etc.

sīca -ae, f. (seco), *a dagger, dirk, poniard*: maximus sicarum numerus et gladiorum, Cic.; Suet., etc.

Sīcāni -ōrum, m. pl. *an ancient people who migrated from Italy to Sicily*.
¶ Hence adj. **Sīcānus** and **Sīcānĭus** -a -um, *Sicanian*; poet.=*Sicilian*; subst. **Sīcānĭa** -ae, f. *Sicania=Sicily*; and f. adj. **Sīcānis** -ĭdis, *Sicanian, Sicilian*.

sīcārĭus -i, m. (sica), *an assassin, murderer*: Cic., Hor., etc. Esp.: accusare aliquem inter sicarios, *of murder*, Cic.

siccē, adv. from siccus; q.v.

siccĭnĕ (sīcĭnĕ), see sic.

siccĭtās -ātis, f. (siccus), *dryness*.
LIT., paludum, Caes.; Pl., Cic.; of weather, *drought*: Cic. L., Liv.
TRANSF., (1) of persons, *freedom from humours, firm health*: Cic. (2) of style, *plainness, simplicity, dryness*: orationis, Cic.

sicco -are (siccus), *to make dry, to dry*: paludes, Cic.; vellera, Verg.; herbas, Ov.; vulnera, *to stanch*, Verg.; calices, *to drain*, Hor.; ovis ubera, Verg.; ovem, Ov.

siccŏcŭlus -a -um (siccus/oculus), *with dry eyes*: Pl.

siccus -a -um, *dry*.
LIT., in gen.: harena, lignum, Verg.; oculi, *tearless*, Hor.; panis, Sen. Of weather: dies, Hor.; fervores, Ov.
TRANSF., (1) of the body, *free from humours, sound, firm, healthy*: corpora, Plin.; Pl., Cat. (2) *thirsting, thirsty*; sometimes *sober, temperate*: Pl., Cic., Verg., Hor. (3) of style, *plain, dry, simple*: oratio, Cic.; Tac.
¶ Hence adv. **siccē**, *dryly*; of style, *plainly*: Cic.

Sĭcĭlĭa -ae, f., see Siculi.

sĭcĭlīcŭla -ae, f. (dim. of sicilis), *a small sickle*: Pl.

sĭcĭlissĭto -are (Siculi), *to imitate Sicilian ways*: Pl.

sĭcĭlis -is, f. (sica), *a sickle*: Plin.

sīcĭnĕ (siccĭnĕ), see sic.

Sĭcŏris -is, m. *a tributary of the Hiberus in Spain (now Segre)*: Caes., Luc.

sīcŭbĭ, adv. *if anywhere*: Cic., Verg., etc.

Sĭcŭli -ōrum, m. *a people of Italy who migrated to Sicily, and gave the island its name*: Cic., etc.; sing. **Sĭcŭlus** -i, m. *a Sicilian*: Pl., Cic.; adj. **Sĭcŭlus** -a -um, *Sicilian*: tyrannus, *Phalaris*, Ov.
¶ Hence subst. **Sĭcĭlĭa** -ae, f. *Sicily*; adj. **Sĭcĭliensis**-e, and f. adj. **Sĭcĕlis** -ĭdis, *Sicilian*.

sīcundĕ, adv. *if from anywhere*: Cic. L., Liv.

sīcŭt and **sīcŭtī**, adv. *as, just as*.
In gen., with a verb: sicut sapiens poeta dixit, Cic.; sicut, sicuti . . . ita, Pl., Caes., Cic.; sicuti . . . sic, Caes.; without a verb: sicut apud nos, Cic.; viri in uxores, sicut in liberos, potestatem, Caes.
Esp. (1) to confirm the truth of something stated hypothetically, with esse, *as*: quamvis felix sit, sicuti est, Cic.; Caes., etc. (2) in a comparison, *as it were*: hic locus sicut aliquod fundamentum est huius constitutionis, Cic.; with verb in subj., *just as if*: sicuti foret lacessitus, Sall. (3) to add an example, *as for example*: quibus in causis omnibus, sicut in ipsā M. Curii, Cic. (4) to express a state or condition, *just as*: sicut eram, fugio, Ov.

Sĭcўōn -ōnis, f. (Σικυών), *a city in north-eastern Peloponnesus*.
¶ Hence adj. **Sĭcўōnĭus** -a -um, *Sicyonian*: calcei, Cic.; n. pl. as subst. **Sĭcўōnĭa** -ōrum, *a kind of soft shoes from Sicyon*: Lucr.; m. pl. as subst. **Sĭcўōnii** -orum, *the Sicyonians*: Cic.

sīdĕrĕus -a -um (sidus), *of the stars, starry*.
LIT., caelum, Ov.; ignes, *the stars*, Ov.; Canis, *the Dog-star*, Ov.; dea=Nox, Prop.
TRANSF., *heavenly*, or perhaps *gleaming, glittering*: clipeus, Verg.

Sĭdĭcīni -ōrum, m. *a people of Campania, whose chief town was Teanum*.
¶ Hence adj. **Sĭdĭcīnus** -a -um, *Sidicine*.

sīdo sīdĕre sīdi and sēdi sessum (cf. ἴζω), *to sit down, settle, alight*.
LIT., of living creatures: columbae super arbore sidunt, Verg.
TRANSF., of inanimate things. (1) *to sink down, settle*: orta ex lacu nebula campo quam montibus densior sederat, Liv.; Lucr., Ov., etc. (2) *to remain lying* or *fixed*: cum sederit glans, Liv.; as naut. t. t., *to stick fast, to be stranded*: ubi cymbae siderent, Liv.; Prop.

(3) *to vanish, disappear*: Prop. (4) of feelings, *to subside*: Tac.

Sīdōn -ōnis, f. (Σιδών), *an ancient city of Phoenicia.*

¶ Hence adj. **Sīdōnĭus** -a -um, *Phoenician, Sidonian*: amor, *of Jupiter for Europa*, Mart.; of purple: ostrum, Ov.; m. pl. as subst. **Sīdōnĭi** -ōrum, *the Sidonians*; also adj. **Sīdōnĭcus** -a -um, *Sidonian*; f. adj. **Sīdōnĭs** -ĭdis, *Sidonian, Tyrian*: concha, *Tyrian purple*, Ov.; tellus, *Phoenicia*, Ov.; as subst., *the Sidonian woman*: Europa, Ov.; Dido, Ov.; Anna, *sister of Dido*: Ov.

sīdus -ĕris, n. *a group of stars, constellation, or a single star, luminary.*

Lit., (1) strictly, *a constellation*; sing.: sidus Vergiliarum, Liv.; sidus aetherium, Ov.; plur.: illi sempiterni ignes, quae sidera et stellas vocatis, Cic.; Lucr., etc. (2) *a luminary, heavenly body*; esp. *a star*: Cic., Ov., etc. (3) more generally, *the time of year*: hiberno sidere, *in winter*, Verg.; mutato sidere, *at another season*, Verg. (4) *weather*: grave sidus et imber, Ov.; Minervae, *storm raised by Minerva*, Verg. (5) in astrology, *a star*, affecting human fortunes (cf. sideratio): haud secus quam pestifero sidere icti, Liv.; Cic., etc. (6) plur., in gen., *the heavens*: ad sidera missus, Juv.; ad sidera ferre, *to praise to the skies*, Verg.; esp. of exalted feeling or station: sublimi feriam sidera vertice, Hor.; Verg., Ov.

Transf., of any glorious or beautiful object; of eyes: geminum, sua lumina, sidus, Ov.; O sidus Fabiae, Maxime, gentis, *pride, glory*, Ov. As a term of endearment: Hor.

Sĭgambri=Sugambri; q.v.

Sīgēum -i, n. (Σίγειον), *a promontory and port in Troas, where was the grave of Achilles.*

¶ Hence adj. **Sīgēus, Sīgēĭus** -a -um, *Sigean.*

sĭgilla -ōrum, n. pl. (dim. of signum), *small figures, images*: patella in qua sigilla erant egregia, Cic.; *figures cut upon a signet-ring*: Cic.; hence *a seal*: Hor.

sĭgillātus -a -um (sigilla), *ornamented with small figures*: scyphi, Cic.

sigma -ătis, n. (σίγμα), *the Greek letter sigma*, and hence, *a semicircular dining-couch in the original shape of a capital sigma* (**C**): Mart.

signātor -ōris, m. (signo), *one who seals or signs a document.* Hence (1) *a witness to a will*: signatores falsi, *forgers of wills*, Sall. (2) *a witness to a marriage-contract*: Juv.

Signĭa -ae, f. *a city in Latium* (now *Segni*).

¶ Hence adj. **Signīnus** -a -um, *of Signia*; m. pl. as subst. **Signīni** -ōrum, *the inhabitants of Signia.*

signĭfĕr -fĕra -fĕrum (signum/fero), *bearing signs or figures, adorned with figures.* In gen.: puppis, Luc. Esp., *bearing stars, covered with constellations*: aether, Lucr.; orbis, *the Zodiac*, Cic.

¶ M. as subst. **signĭfĕr** -fĕri, *a standard-bearer.* Lit., as milit t. t.: Caes., Cic., etc. Transf., in gen., *a leader, head*: calamitosorum, Cic.; iuventutis, Cic.

significātĭo -ōnis, f. (significo), *an indication, sign, token, signal.*

In gen.: declarare aliquid significatione, Cic.; Caes.; with subjective genit.: litterarum, Cic.; with objective genit.: virtutis,

Cic.; with acc. and infin.: significatio fit non adesse constantiam, Cic.

Esp. (1) *a sign of assent, approbation*: omni significatione florere, Cic.; Caes. (2) *emphasis*: Cic. (3) *the meaning, signification of a word*: Cic., Quint.

significo -are (signum/facio), *to give a sign, to indicate, notify, show.*

In gen., with acc.: hoc mihi significasse et adnuisse visus est, Cic.; with acc. and infin.: omnes significabant ab eo se esse admodum delectatos, Cic.; Caes.; with indir. command: ut statim dimitterentur, Caes.; With indir. quest.: litterae neque unde neque quo die datae essent significabant, Cic.; with de and the abl.: de fuga, Caes.

Esp. (1) *to indicate what is to come, foreshow*: futura, Cic.; Ov., etc. (2) *to mean, signify*: uno verbo significari res duas, Cic.

¶ Hence partic. **significans** -antis, of style or delivery, *graphic, distinct, clear*: Quint.; compar.: Quint.

¶ Adv. **significantĕr**, *plainly, distinctly, clearly*: Quint.; compar.: acrius, apertius, significantius dignitatem alicuius defendere, Cic. L.

Signīnus, see Signia.

signo -are (signum), *to put a mark upon, mark, inscribe.*

Lit., in gen. (1) with acc. of the thing marked: humum pede certo, Hor.; silicem, Juv.; Verg., Ov. (2) with acc. of the mark made: summo vestigia pulvere, Verg.; caeli regionem in cortice signant, *cut in*, Verg.; nomina saxo, Ov. Esp. (1) *to mark with a seal, seal, seal up*: libellum, Cic. L.; volumina, Hor.; arcanas tabellas, Ov. (2) *to coin, stamp money*: argentum signatum, Cic.; Liv., Ov.

Transf., (1) *to impress, to indicate*: signatum memori pectore nomen habe, Ov.; ossa nomen (Caieta) signat, Verg. (2) *to observe, notice*: ora sono discordia, Verg.; Ov.

signum -i, n. *a sign, mark, token.*

In gen.: signa et notas locorum, Cic.; signum imprimere pecori, Verg.; with genit.: signa pedum sequi, *to follow the footsteps*, Ov.; signa doloris ostendere, Cic.

Esp. (1) as milit. t. t., *a standard, banner, ensign*: signa relinquere, *to desert*, Sall.; signa ferre, *to break up camp, march away*, Caes., Liv.; signa convelli iubere, *to give the signal for marching away*, Liv.; signa inferre, *to attack*, Caes., Cic., Liv.; signa conferre, either *to bring the standards together, to concentrate*, Caes., Liv.; or *to engage, to fight*: cum Alexandrinis, Cic.; Liv., etc. (2) milit. t. t., *a signal, order, command*: signum pugnae proponere, Liv.; signum tubā dare, Caes. (3) milit. t. t., *a watchword, password*: Tac., Suet. (4) *a signal for races to begin*: signum mittendis quadrigis dare, Liv. (5) *an indication of the future, a warning, symptom*: medici signa habent ex venis, Cic.; morborum, Verg. (6) *a physical representation of a person or thing, a figure, image, statue*: signum aëneum, marmoreum, Cic.; Lucr., Verg., etc. Esp. *a seal, signet*: Cic., Hor., etc. (7) *a group of stars, constellation*: Lucr., Cic.

sĭlānus -i, m. (Σιληνός, Doric Σιλανός), *a fountain*; originally one with water gushing from the mouth of a statue of Silenus; later, in gen., of water carried by pipes: Lucr.

Sĭlărus -i, m. *a river in Lucania* (now *the Sele*).

sĭlens, partic. from sileo; q.v.

sĭlentĭum -i, n. (sileo), *silence, stillness, quietness.*
  LIT., of persons: audire aliquid magno silentio, Cic.; silentium fieri iubere, Cic.; silentio praeterire, Cic.; silentium tenere, obtinere, Liv.; alta silentia rumpere, Verg.; Caes., etc. Esp. *ceremonial silence during the taking of auspices*: id silentium dicimus in auspiciis, quod omni vitio caret, Cic.
  TRANSF., (1) of nature, *stillness*: noctis, Caes., Lucr., Liv.; ruris, Ov. (2) *quiet, repose, inactivity*: iudiciorum ac fori, Cic. (3) *obscurity, ingloriousness*: vitam silentio transire, Sall.

Sĭlēnus -i, m. (Σιληνός), *the tutor and attendant of Bacchus, represented with a bald head, and riding on an ass, usually drunk.*

sĭlĕo -ēre -ŭi, *to be still, noiseless, silent.*
  LIT., of persons: ceteri de nobis silent, Cic. With acc., *to be silent about*: tu hoc silebis, Cic.; neque te silebo, Hor.; in pass.: res siletur, Cic.; n. pl. of gerundive as subst., silenda, *things to be silent about, secrets, mysteries*: Liv.
  TRANSF., (1) of nature: silet aer, Ov.; aequor, Verg.; nox, Verg.; late loca, Verg. (2) of abstr. things, *to be still, to rest, to be inactive*: leges inter arma, si quando ambitus sileat, Cic.; Tac. (3) fig., *to leave unsaid*: si chartae sileant quod bene feceris, Hor.
  ¶ Hence partic. **sĭlens** -entis, *silent, still*: nox, Verg., Liv., etc.; umbrae, *the dead*, Verg. Plur. as subst. **sĭlentēs**, *the dead*: Ov.; also *the Pythagoreans*: Ov.

sĭler -ĕris, n. *a species of willow, the brook-willow*: Verg.

sĭlesco -ĕre (sileo), *to become silent, grow still*: Verg., Ov., etc.

sĭlex -ĭcis, m. (rarely f.), *any hard stone, such as flint*, esp. as material for pavement.
  LIT., certo in loco silicem caedere, Cic.; vias in urbe silice sternere, Liv.; Juv., etc.
  TRANSF., (1) *a crag, rock, cliff*: acuta silex praecisis undique saxis, Verg.; Lucr. (2) of hardheartedness: dicam silices pectus habere tuum, Ov.

sĭlĭcernĭum -i, n. *a funeral feast*: Varr.; hence, as a term of abuse, applied to an infirm old man: Ter.

sĭlīgo -ĭnis, f. *a kind of very white wheat*: Cato, Varr., Plin. Hence *wheaten flour*: Juv.

sĭlĭqua -ae, f. *a husk, pod, shell*: Verg. TRANSF., in plur., *pulse*: Hor.

Sĭlĭus -a -um, *name of a Roman gens*; esp. of (1) A. Silius, *a friend of Cicero.* (2) P. Silius Nerva, *propraetor in Bithynia and Pontus,* 51 B.C. (3) C. Silius Italicus, *an epic poet of the first century* A.D., *author of an epic poem on the second Punic war in seventeen books.*
  ¶ Hence adj. **Sĭlĭānus** -a -um, *relating to Silius.*

sĭlō -ōnis, m. (silus), *a snub-nosed man*: Pl.

sĭlphĭum -i, n. (σίλφιον)=laserpicium; q.v.: Cato.

Sĭlŭres -um, acc. -as, *a British people living in South Wales.*

sĭlūrus -i, m. (σίλουρος), *a species of river-fish*, probably *the sheat-fish*: Juv.

sĭlus -a -um, *flat-nosed, snub-nosed, pug-nosed*: Cic.

silva (sĭlŭa, trisyll.: Hor.) -ae, f. (connected with ὕλη), *a wood, forest.*
  LIT., (1) strictly, *a wood*: silva densa, Cic.; silvarum dea, *Diana*, Ov.; Lucr., Verg., etc. (2) *a plantation, a grove, a park*: signa in silva disposita, Cic.; Hor. (3) any *quantity of shrubs* or *plants, bush*: Verg., etc. (4) poet., *a tree* or *trees*: Verg., Ov.
  TRANSF., (1) of physical objects, *a forest, a dense mass* or *quantity*: immanem aerato circumfert tegmine silvam, *a dense mass of spears*, Verg. (2) of abstr. things, *plenty, abundance*: virtutum et vitiorum, Cic.; esp., of materials for speaking and writing: silva rerum, Cic.; omnis ubertas et quasi silva dicendi, Cic.

Silvānus -i, m. (silva), *a Latin god of woods and forests*; plur., Silvani, *gods of the woodlands.*

silvātĭcus -a -um (silva). (1) *of woods* or *trees*: Cato, Varr. (2) of plants and animals, *wild*: Cato, Varr.

silvesco -ĕre (silva), of a vine, *to run wild, to run to wood*: Cic.

silvestris -e (silva), *belonging to woods*, or *covered with trees, wooded.*
  LIT., collis, Caes.; locus, Cic.; belua, Cic.; homines, Hor. N. pl. as subst., *woodlands*: Liv.
  TRANSF., (1) *growing wild, wild*: oliva, Ov.; Verg., Hor. (2) *rural, pastoral*: Musa, Verg.; Lucr.

Silvĭa, see Rhea.

silvĭcŏla -ae, m. and f. (silva/colo), *inhabiting woods*: Verg., Ov.

silvĭcultrix -trīcis, f. adj. (silva/colo), *inhabiting woods*: Cat.

silvifrăgus -a -um (silva/frango), *shattering the woods*: Lucr.

silvōsus -a -um (silva), *well wooded*: saltus, Liv.

sĭmĭa -ae, f. (simus), *an ape, monkey*: Cic., etc.; as a term of abuse: Pl., Plin. L.

sĭmĭlis -e; compar. similior, superl. simillimus (connected with simul), *like, resembling, similar*: Cic., Verg., etc. Most often with genit.: fratris, Cic.; non est veri simile ut occiderit, *it is not probable that*, Cic.; compar.: veri similius, Liv.; superl.: simillimum veri, Cic. Also with dat.: si similes Icilio tribunos haberet, Liv.; quid simile habet epistula aut iudicio aut contioni? Cic.; compar.: similius id vero fecit, Liv.; superl.: simillimus deo, Cic. With inter: homines inter se cum formâ tum moribus similes, Cic.; Ov.; foll. by ac, atque, et si, ut si, tamquam si: Caes., Cic.
  ¶ N. as subst. **sĭmĭle** -is, *a resemblance* or *comparison*: Cic., Quint.
  ¶ Adv. **sĭmĭlĭtĕr**, with compar. similius and superl. simillimē, *in like manner, similarly*; foll. by atque, ut si: Cic.

sĭmĭlĭtūdo -ĭnis, f. (similis), *likeness, resemblance.*
  In gen.: est inter ipsos similitudo, Cic.; est homini cum deo similitudo, Cic.; veri similitudo, *probability*, Cic. Sometimes *intended likeness, imitation*: Cic., Tac.
  Esp. (1) *a metaphor, simile*: Cic. (2) *uniformity of style, monotony*: Cic.

sĭmĭlo=simulo; q.v.

sĭmĭŏlus -i, m. (dim. of simius), *a little ape*, as a term of abuse: Cic. L.

sĭmītū, adv. (old form of simul), *together*: Pl.

sīmĭus -i, m. (simus; cf. simia), *an ape, monkey*: Mart.; as a term of abuse: Hor.

Sĭmŏis -mŏentis, m. (Σιμόεις), *a small stream in Troas, falling into the Scamander.*

Sĭmōnĭdes -is, m. (Σιμωνίδης), *a lyric poet of Ceos.* Adj. **Sĭmōnĭdēus** -a -um, *Simonidean.*

simplex -plicis; abl. sing. simplicī, in Lucr. simplicē; (root of semel/plico), *simple, single, uncompounded, unmixed.*

LIT., natura animantis, Cic.; res aperta et simplex, Cic.; aqua, *pure*, Ov.; simplici ordine urbem intrare, *in single file*, Liv.; plus vice simplici, *more than once*, Hor.

TRANSF., (1) *plain, not complicated*: causa, Cic.; genus mortis, *without torture*, Liv.; necessitudo, *unconditional*, Cic.; Hor. (2) morally *simple, straightforward, upright, guileless*: vir apertus ac simplex, Cic.; cogitationes, Tac.; Ov.; compar.: Hor.

¶ Adv. **simplĭcĭtĕr**, *plainly, simply*. LIT., Cic., Liv. TRANSF., (1) *simply, without art, artlessly*: loqui, Cic. (2) *frankly, candidly, honestly*: Plin. L.; compar. and superl.: Tac.

simplĭcĭtās -ātis, f. (simplex), *simplicity, simpleness*. LIT., Lucr. TRANSF., morally, *straightforwardness, guilelessness, honesty, candour*: puerilis, Liv.; sermo antiquae simplicitatis, Liv.; Ov., etc.

simplus -a -um (connected with simplex), *simple.* N. as subst. **simplum** -i, *the simple sum* or *number* (opp. double, etc.): Cic., Liv.

simpŭlum -i, n. *a ladle*; prov.: excitare fluctūs in simpulo, *to make a storm in a tea-cup, to make much ado about nothing*: Cic.

simpŭvĭum -i, n. *a sacrificial bowl*: Cic., Juv.

sĭmŭl, adv. (connected with similis), *at once, at the same time, together.* In gen.: cenare, Cic.; tres simul soles effulserunt, Liv.; excepto quod non simul esses, cetera laetus, Hor.; with cum: testamentum simul obsignavi cum Clodio, Cic.; with et, que, atque: simul inflatus exacerbatusque, Liv.; simul honoribus atque virtutibus, Liv.; with abl.: simul septemviris, Tac.; Ov., Hor.

In special phrases. (1) simul . . . simul, *not only . . . but at the same time, partly . . . partly . . .*: increpando simul temeritatem, simul ignaviam, Liv.; simul sui purgandi causā, simul ut, Caes. (2) simul atque (ac), simul ut, and sometimes simul alone, *as soon as*; esp. with perf. indic.: Caes., Cic., Verg., etc.

sĭmŭlācrum -i, n. (simulo), *an image, likeness, portrait, effigy.*

LIT., Helenae, deorum, Cic.; simulacra cerea, *dolls*, Ov.; belli simulacra cientes, *engaging in sham battles, on manœuvres*, Lucr.; also of *a reflection* in a mirror or in water: Lucr.

TRANSF., (1) *a shade, ghost*; of the dead: Lucr., Verg., Ov.; of *a figure in a dream*: vana (noctis), Ov. (2) as t. t. of the Epicurean philosophy, *a conception of an object in the mind*: Lucr. (3) in literature, *a character-picture*: Liv. (4) in gen., *an imitation, phantom, appearance* (opp. substance, reality): simulacra virtutis, Cic.; religionis, Cic.

sĭmŭlāmen -ĭnis, n. (simulo), *an imitation*: Ov.

sĭmŭlans -antis, partic. from simulo; q.v.

sĭmŭlātē, adv. from simulo; q.v.

sĭmŭlātĭo -ōnis, f. (simulo), *the assumed appearance of anything, pretence, feint, false show*: imitatio simulatioque virtutis, Cic. agere cum simulatione timoris, Cic.; Ter. Caes., Tac.

sĭmŭlātŏr -ōris, m. (simulo). (1) *an imitator* figurae, Ov. (2) *a pretender, counterfeiter, feigner*: segnitiae, Tac.; cuius rei line simulator ac dissimulator, Sall.; simulato in omni oratione, of Socrates, *a master in irony*, Cic.; Tac.

sĭmŭlo -are (similis), *to make like.*

Hence (1) *to cause* a person or thing *to resemble* another: corpora igni simulata Lucr.; Minerva simulata Mentori, Cic (2) *to make a copy of* a person or thing, *to represent* him or it: nimbos et non imitabili fulmen, Verg.; cupressum, Hor.; simulata Troia, *a counterfeit Troy*, Ov. (3) *to make oneself like* or *make oneself out to be* a person or thing, *to play the part of*: aegrum, Liv. anum, Ov.; aera Alexandri vultum simu lantia, Hor. (4) *to pretend* a thing is so, *put on an appearance of, simulate*, a feeling, action etc.: simulare gaudia vultu, Ov.; lacrimas Ov.; negotia, Sall.; pacem, Cic., Sall.; aliud agentes, aliud simulantes, Cic.; with acc. and infin.: se furere, Cic.

¶ Hence partic. **sĭmŭlans** -antis v compar., *imitating, imitative*: simulatio vocum ales, *the parrot*, Ov.

¶ Adv. from perf. partic. **sĭmŭlātē** *feignedly*: Cic.

sĭmultās -ātis, f. (simul), *a clash, rivalry jealousy, feud.* Sing.: simultatem deponere Cic. L.; Liv. Usually plur.: simultate exercere cum aliquo, Cic.; simultate dirimere, finire, Liv.

sĭmŭlus -a -um (dim. of simus), *somewhat snub-nosed*: Lucr.

sīmus -a -um (σιμός), *flat-nosed, snub-nosed* Verg.

sĭn, conj. *but if, if however.* (1) with preceding particle such as si, nisi, quando, dum si . . . sin aliter, Cic.; si . . . sin autem, Cic. si . . . sin minus, ellipt., *but if not*, Cic (2) without preceding particle; sometime strengthened by autem: Caes., Cic.

sĭnāpi -is, n. and **sĭnāpis** -is, f. (σίναπι) *mustard*: Pl., Plin.

sincērĭtās -ātis, f. (sincerus), *purity, soundness* LIT., olei, Plin. TRANSF., *integrity*: Sen. Phaedr.

sincērus -a -um, *pure, unmixed, whole, sound genuine.*

LIT., secernere fucata et simulata a sinceri atque veris, Cic.; membra, *intact*, Lucr.; vas Hor.

TRANSF., morally *uncorrupt, honourable sincere*: iudicium, Cic.; fides, Liv.; Minerva Ov.

¶ Hence adv. **sincērē**, *honestly, frankly sincerely*: pronuntiare, Caes.; Ter., Cat.

sincĭpĭtāmentum -i, n.=sinciput; q.v.: Pl.

sinciput -pĭtis, n. (semi/caput), *half a head* LIT., of the smoked chap of a pig: Juv., Pers TRANSF., *the brain*: Pl.

sindōn -ōnis, f. (σινδών), *fine cotton cloth muslin*: Mart.

sĭnĕ, prep. with abl., *without* (opp. cum) semper ille ante cum uxore, tum sine ea Cic.; sine dubio, Cic.; non sine gloriā, Hor.

sometimes after its case: vitiis nemo sine nascitur, Hor.

ingillātim, adv. (singillus=singulus), *singly, one by one*: Cic., Lucr., etc.

ingŭlāris -e (singulus), *alone, single, individual.* LIT., ubi aliquos singulares ex nave egredi conspexerant, Caes.; non est singulare nec solivagum genus hoc, Cic.; imperium, *absolute rule,* Cic. Esp. as grammat. t. t., *singular, belonging to the singular number*: Quint. TRANSF., *unique, extraordinary*; in a good sense: ingenio atque animo singulares, Cic.; Pompeii singularis eximiaque virtus, Cic.; in a bad sense: nequitia, Cic.
M. pl. as subst. **singŭlārēs** -ium, *troops specially employed,* perhaps *special guards*: Tac.
Adv. **singŭlārĭtĕr** (singlārĭtĕr: Lucr.). LIT., *singly*: Lucr.; *in the singular number*: Quint. TRANSF., *particularly, extraordinarily*: aliquem diligere, Cic.; Plin. L.

singŭlārĭus -a -um (singularis), *single*: catenae, Pl.

singŭli, *see* singulus.

singultim, adv. (singultus), *with sobs*: pauca loqui, *stammeringly,* Hor.

singultĭo -ire (singultus), *to gasp, hiccough.* LIT., Plin. TRANSF., *to throb*: Pers.

singulto -are (singultus). (**1**) intransit., *to gasp, hiccough, sob*: Quint.; of dying persons, *to rattle in the throat*: Verg. (**2**) transit., *to sob out, gasp out*: animam, Ov.

singultus -ūs, m. *a sobbing, gasping.* Of persons: singultuque pias interrumpente querellas, Ov.; multas lacrimas et fletum cum singultu videre potuisti, Cic.; Lucr., Hor. Of persons dying, *rattling in the throat*: Verg. Of similar sounds; *the croaking of a raven*: Plin.; *the gurgling of water*: Plin. L.

singŭlus -a -um, more freq. in plur. **singŭli** -ae -a (from root of semel). (**1**) *single, separate, one at a time, one alone*; sing.: singulum vestigium, Pl.; plur.: honestius universi quam singuli, Cic. (**2**) distributive, *one each*: binos in singulas civitates, Cic.; filiae singulos filios habentes, Liv.

sĭnister -tra -trum, adj. (with compar. sinisterior), *left, on the left hand.*
LIT., manus, Nep.; ripa, Hor.; cornu, Ter., Caes.
TRANSF., (**1**) *wrong, perverse*: mores, Verg.; Cat., Tac. (**2**) *unfavourable, adverse*: notus pecori sinister, Verg.; interpretatio, Tac. (**3**) as t. t. of augury: **a,** amongst the Romans, who, turning towards the south, had the east on the left, *favourable*: tonitrus, Ov.; Cic., Verg.: **b,** among the Greeks, who, turning towards the north, had the east on the right, *unfavourable*: omen, Ov.
¶ As subst., f. sing. **sĭnistra.** (**1**) (sc. manus), *the left hand*: Caes.; natae ad furta sinistrae, Ov. (**2**) (sc. pars), *the left side*: sub sinistra, Caes.; Pl., Cic. N. sing. **sĭnistrum** -i. (**1**) (sc. latus), *the left side*: Quint. (**2**) *evil*: Ov. M. pl. **sĭnistri** -orum, *the left wing*: Liv.
¶ Adv. **sĭnistrē,** *wrongly* or *unfavourably*: excipere, Hor.; rescribere, Tac.

sĭnistĕrĭtās -ātis, f. (sinister), *awkwardness*: Plin. L.

sĭnistrorsus (**sĭnistrorsum**), adv. (sinister/verto), *to the left*: Caes., Hor.

sĭno sĭnĕre sīvi sĭtum; syncop. perf., sisti; perf. subj., siris sirit siritis; pluperf. subj., sisset.
(**1**) *to place, put down, set down*; only used in this sense in the partic. situs; *see* below.
(**2**) *to let alone, leave.* LIT., neu propius tectis taxum sine, Verg. TRANSF., *to let, allow, permit.* In gen.: non feram, non patiar, non sinam, Cic.; id nos non sinemus, Ter.; with acc. obj. and infin.: vinum ad se importari omnino non sinunt, Caes.; nos transalpinas gentes oleam et vitem serere non sinimus, Cic.; in pass.: hic accusare eum moderate per senatūs auctoritatem non est situs, Cic.; with jussive subjunctive: sine pascat aretque, Hor.; Verg., Liv. Esp.: **a,** in conversation, sine, *well*: feriant sine litora fluctūs, Verg.; *or* sine, alone, *very well!* Pl.: **b,** ne di sinant (sirint), ne Iuppiter sirit, *God forbid!* Pl., Liv.
¶ Hence partic. **sĭtus** -a -um, *placed, laid down*; also *left, lying, situated.* LIT., lingua in ore sita est, Cic.; Philippopolis a Philippo sita, *founded, built,* Liv.; C. Marii sitae reliquiae apud Anienem, *buried,* Cic.; locus situs in media insula, Cic. TRANSF., (**1**) in gen., *placed*: voluptates in medio sitas esse dicunt, Cic. (**2**) situm esse in, with abl., *to rest upon, depend upon*: adsensio quae est in nostra potestate sita, Cic.; Pl., Sall., Tac.

Sĭnōpa -ae, f. and **Sĭnōpē** -ēs, f. (Σινώπη), *a town on the Black Sea, a colony from Miletus, birth-place of the cynic Diogenes.*
¶ Hence m. pl. of adj. as subst. **Sĭnōpenses** -ium, *the men of Sinope*: Liv., Tac. Adj. **Sĭnōpeūs** -a -um, *of Sinope*: Cynicus, Diogenes, Ov.

Sĭnŭessa -ae, f. *a town in Latium.* Adj. **Sĭnŭessānus** -a -um, *of Sinuessa.*

sĭnum, *see* ¹sinus.

sĭnŭo -are (²sinus), *to bend, curve, wind*: angues terga, Verg.; arcum, Ov.; muri introrsus sinuati, *bent inwards,* Tac.

sĭnŭōsus -a -um (²sinus), *full of windings, bendings, curves; sinuous.* LIT., vestis, Ov.; flexus (anguis), Verg. TRANSF., *roundabout, diffuse*: Quint.

¹sinus -i, m. and **sīnum** -i, n. *a large bowl*: Pl., Verg.

²sĭnus -ūs, m. *a bending, curve, fold.*
(**1**) in gen.: cedendo sinum in medio dedit, *formed a curve,* Liv.; of *the windings of a snake*: Cic.; poet., of *curls of hair*: Ov.; *a net*: Pl., Juv. Often *the belly of a sail swollen by the wind*: sinūs implere secundos, Verg.; pleno pandere vela sinu, Ov.
(**2**) *the hanging fold of the toga, the bosom, lap*: sinum implere floribus, Ov.; litteras in sinu ponere, Liv.; Verg., etc. Hence: **a,** *a purse*: Prop., Ov.: **b,** plur., *flowing robes*: indue regales sinus, Ov. TRANSF., *heart, bosom, lap,* denoting affection, secrecy, security, etc.: optatum negotium sibi in sinum delatum esse dicebat, Cic.; in sinu gaudere, *to rejoice in secret,* Cic.; in sinu gestare, *to hold dear,* Cic.; in sinu urbis sunt hostes, *in the heart,* Sall.
(**3**) *a fold in a coastline, a bay, gulf.* LIT., maritimus, Cic.; Caes., Verg., etc. TRANSF., *the land on a bay* or *gulf*: Liv., Tac.
(**4**) *a curve* or *dip in the earth, a hollow*: Liv.

sĭpărĭum -i, n. (connected with supparum).
(1) *a drop-scene at a theatre.* Lit., Cic., Juv.
Transf., *comedy.* (2) *a screen to exclude the
sun*: Quint.

sĭpho (sīfo) -ōnis, m. (σίφων). (1) *a siphon*:
Juv., etc. (2) *a fire-engine*: Plin. L.

Sĭpontum -i, n. (Σιπούς), *an important harbour
in Apulia.* Adj. Sĭpontīnus -a -um,
Sipontine.

Sĭpўlus -i, m. (Σίπυλος), *a mountain in Lydia,
where Niobe was turned into stone.*

sīquando or sī quando, *if ever*: Cic., Liv.

sīquĭdem or sī quĭdem, conj. *if indeed*;
sometimes *since, because*: Cic., etc.; *see* si.

sīremps and sīrempse (si/rem/ipsam), *like,
the same*: sirempse legem, Pl.; Sen.

Sīrēn -ēnis, f., usually plur. Sīrēnes -um, f.
(Σειρῆνες), *the Sirens, nymphs living off the
coast of Southern Italy, who by their song
lured mariners to destruction.* Transf.,
vitanda est improba Siren, desidia, Hor.

Sīrĭus -i, m.(σείριος), *the Dog-star, Sirius*: Verg.,
Tib. As adj.: sirius ardor, *of the Dog-star,*
Verg.

sirpĕ -is, n. (σίλφιον), *the plant asafoetida*
(cf. laser): Pl.

sīrus -i, m. (σειρός), *a pit* or *cellar for keeping
corn, a silo*: Plin.

sīs=(1) si vis; *see* ¹volo. (2) second sing. of
pres. subj. of sum; q.v. (3) dat. or abl.
plur. of suus; q.v.

Sīsenna -ae, m. (1) *L. Cornelius, a Roman
historian, contemporary of Cicero.* (2) *a
notorious slanderer in Rome in the time of
Horace.*

sisto sistĕre stĭti stătum (connected with sto).
(1) transit.: **a**, *to cause to stand, set, place*:
aciem in litore, Verg.; victima sistitur ante
aras, Ov.; esp. as legal t. t., *to produce, cause
to appear* in court; with reflex., or in pass.,
to appear in court: Cic., Liv., etc.; vadimonium sistere, *to appear on the appointed
day*, Cic., Nep.: **b**, *to stop, bring to a stand,
check.* Lit., legiones, Liv.; equos, Verg.;
pedem, gradum, Verg.; se, Liv.; iter, Tac.
Transf., querellas, lacrimas, Ov.; fugam,
Liv.: **c**, *to make firm, settle firmly, establish.*
Lit., effigiem, Tac. Transf., rem Romanam,
Verg.
(2) intransit.: **a**, *to place oneself, stand*:
Pl., Lucr., Verg.; esp., *to appear, present oneself in court*: Cic.: **b**, *to stand still, to halt*: ubi
sistere detur, Verg.: **c**, *to stand firm*: rempublicam sistere negat posse, Cic.; impers.
pass.: nec sisti posse, *and that no stand could
be made*, Liv.
¶ Hence partic. stătus -a -um, *fixed,
determined, regular*: locus, dies, Liv.;
sacrificium, Cic.; sacra, Ov.

sistrātus -a -um (sistrum), *furnished with a
sistrum*: Mart.

sistrum -i, n. (σεῖστρον), *a sort of rattle used in
the worship of Isis*: Verg., Ov., etc.

sĭsymbrĭum -i, n. (σισύμβριον), *an aromatic
herb sacred to Venus*; perhaps, *mint*: Ov.,
Plin.

Sĭsўphus -i, m. (Σίσυφος), *a son of Aeolus,
king of Corinth, a cunning robber; killed by
Theseus, and condemned in the lower world
to roll uphill a great stone which constantly
rolled back.*
¶ Hence adj. Sĭsўphĭus -a -um, *of*

Sisyphus: Ov. Subst. Sīsўphĭdēs -ae, m.
Ulysses, as a descendant of Sisyphus.

sĭtella -ae, f. (dim. of situla), *an urn, used fo
drawing lots*: Pl., Cic., Liv.

Sīthŏnĭi -orum, m. pl. *a Thracian tribe*; i
gen., *the Thracians.*
¶ Hence adj. Sīthŏnĭus -a -um an
Sīthōn -ōnis, *Sithonian, Thracian.* F. adj
Sīthŏnĭs -ĭdis, *Thracian*; as subst.,
Thracian woman.

sĭtĭcŭlōsus -a -um (sitis), *very dry, parched*
Apulia, Hor.

sĭtĭo -ire (sitis).
(1) intransit., *to thirst, be thirsty.* Lit.
Lucr., etc.; prov.: sitire mediis in undis, *t
starve in the midst of plenty*, Ov. Transf., o
plants, soil, etc., *to be dry, parched*: sitiun
agri, Cic.; tellus, Ov.
(2) transit., *to thirst for.* Lit., Tagum
Mart.; pass.: aquae sitiuntur, Ov. Transf.
to thirst after, eagerly desire: sanguinem, Cic.
honores, Cic.
¶ Hence partic. sĭtĭens -entis, *thirsting
thirsty.* Lit., Cic., Hor., etc. Transf., (1) o
plants and soil, *dry, parched*: Ov., Plin
(2) *eager, desirous*: virtutis, Cic.; Ov.
¶ Adv. sĭtĭentĕr, *thirstily, eagerly*: ex
petere, Cic.

sĭtis -is, f. thirst.
Lit., arentibus siti faucibus, Liv.; sitin
explere, Cic.; restinguere. Verg.; depellere
Cic.; Hor., Ov.
Transf., (1) of plants or soil, *dryness
drought*: deserta siti regio, Verg.; Tib
(2) *thirst, eager desire*: libertatis, Cic.
argenti, Hor.; Ov.

sĭtĭtor -ōris, m. (sitio), *a thirster*: aquae, *afte
water*, Mart.

sittўbus -i, m. *a strip of parchment on which th
title of a book was written*: Cic. L.

sĭtŭla -ae, f. (sĭtŭlus -i, m., Cato): *a jar fo
water*, or *for drawing lots*: Pl.

¹sĭtus -a -um, partic. from sino; q.v

²sĭtus -ūs, m. (sino).
(1) *layout, site, position, situation.* Lit.
urbis, Caes., Cic., Liv.; agri, Hor.; plur.
sitūs oppidorum, castrorum, Caes.; terrarum
Cic. Transf., **a**, *building structure*: monumentum regali situ pyramidum altius, Hor.
b, *a region of the earth, zone, quarter*: Plin.
(2) *a being left; neglect, want of cultivation
and consequent dirt, decay.* Lit., situ
durescere campum, Verg.; cessat terra situ,
Ov.; occupat arma situs, Tib.; canescunt
tecta situ, Ov. Transf., of the mind, *rusting,
dullness*: marcescere otio situque civitatem,
Liv.; senectus victa situ, Verg.

sīvĕ and sēu, conj. (si/ve).
(1) *or if*: si omnes declinabunt, sive aliae
declinabunt, Cic.; me, seu corpus spoliatum
lumine mavis, redde meis, Verg.
(2) in a disjunctive sense: **a**, sive (seu) . . .
(sive, seu), *whether . . . or*: Cimmeriis aspectum solis sive deus aliquis, sive natura
ademerat, sive loci situs, Cic.; sive casu,
sive consilio deorum, Caes.: **b**, with other
disjunct. particles: seu . . . aut, Verg.; -ne
. . . seu, Verg.; sive . . . an, Tac.: **c**, alone,
or: regis Philippi sive Persae, Cic.; Liv.,
Tac.

smăragdus -i, m. and f. (σμάραγδος), *a green
precious stone*, esp. *emerald*: Lucr., Ov., etc.

smăris -ĭdis, f. (σμαρίς), *a poor kind of sea-fish*: Ov., Plin.

smīlax -ăcis, f. (σμῖλαξ), *bindweed*: Plin. Personif.: Smilax, *a maiden changed into the plant of the same name*, Ov.

Smyrna (Zm-) -ae, f. (Σμύρνα), *a famous trading town in Asia Minor* (now *Izmir*). ¶ Hence adj. **Smyrnaeus** -a -um, *of Smyrna*.

sŏbŏles, sobolesco = suboles, subolesco; q.v.

sōbrĭĕtās -ātis, f. (sobrius), *moderation in drinking, sobriety*: Sen.

sōbrīna -ae, f. (sobrinus), *a female cousin on the mother's side*: Tac.

sōbrīnus -i, m. (for sororinus, from soror), *a male cousin on the mother's side*: Cic.

sōbrĭus -a -um (perhaps connected with ebrius), *sober, not intoxicated*. LIT., of persons: Cic., Hor., etc. TRANSF., (1) of things, *without wine*: lympha, Tib.; nox, Prop. (2) of persons, *moderate, frugal, continent*: homines plane frugi ac sobrii, Cic.; Ter., Hor. (3) *sober-minded, reasonable, sensible*: orator, homo, Cic.; Ter., Ov. ¶ Hence adv. **sōbrĭē**, *moderately, frugally, soberly*: vivere, Cic. TRANSF., *sensibly*: Pl.

soccātus -a -um (soccus), *wearing the soccus*: Sen.

soccŭlus -i, m. (dim. of soccus), *a little soccus*: Sen., Plin. L., etc.

soccus -i, m. *a light shoe* or *slipper in use among the Greeks*: Pl., Cic., Cat. Esp., *the low shoe worn by comic actors* (as the cothurnus by tragic): Ov.; hence, *comedy, comic style*: Hor.

sŏcer -ĕri, m. (connected with ἑκυρός), *a father-in-law*: Cic., Ov., etc.; plur.: soceri, *the father- and mother-in-law*, Verg., Ov.

sŏcĭa -ae, f., *see* socius.

sŏcĭābĭlis -e (socio), *easily united, compatible*: consortio inter reges, Liv.

sŏcĭālis -e (socius), *of partners*. (1) *of allies*: lex, Cic.; exercitus, Liv.; bellum, Juv. (2) *conjugal*: amor, Ov. (3) in gen., *sociable*: homo sociale animal, Sen. ¶ Adv. **sŏcĭālĭtĕr**, *sociably*: Hor.

sŏcĭennus -i, m. (socius), *a companion, comrade*: Pl.

sŏcĭĕtās -ātis, f. (socius), *partnership, companionship, fellowship, association*.

(1) political: *alliance, confederacy*: societatem belli facere, Caes.; Tac.

(2) commercial: societatem facere, Cic.; gerere, Cic.; iudicium societatis, *relating to partnership*, Cic.; esp. *a partnership of the publicani to farm taxes*: provinciarum, Caes.; Cic.

(3) in gen.: hominum inter ipsos, Cic.; vitae, beate vivendi, sceleris, Cic.; societatem coire, inire, conflare, Cic.

sŏcĭo -are (socius), *to unite, combine, associate*: vim rerum cum dicendi exercitatione, Cic.; vitae tuae periculum mecum, Cic.; omne genus hominum sociatum inter se, Cic.; nos urbe, domo socias, *givest us a share in*, Verg.; sociati parte laboris functus, Ov.

sŏcĭofraudus -i, m. (socius/fraudo), *one who cheats a comrade*: Pl.

sŏcĭus -a -um (connected with sequor), *sharing, accompanying*. (1) *acting together, allied*: socii Carthaginiensium populi, Liv.; classis socia, Ov.; Cic., Verg., etc. (2) of things, *joint, common*: consilia, Cic.; Ov.

¶ As subst., m. **socius** -i and f. **sŏcĭa** -ae, *a partner, companion, comrade, associate*.

(1) political, *an ally*: huic populo socii fuerunt, Cic.; Liv., etc.; esp. socii, *the Italians outside Latium in alliance with the Romans, the Allies*: Socii et Latini, Cic.; socii Latini nominis, *the Latin allies*, Liv.

(2) commercial, *a partner*: iudicium pro socio, *a judgment in a partnership suit*, Cic.; esp. socii, *an association of publicani for the purpose of farming the taxes*: Cic. (3) of relationship or marriage: socius sanguinis, *a brother*, Ov.; socius tori, *a husband*, Ov.; socia tori, *a wife*, Ov. (4) in gen.: socium ad malam rem quaerere, Pl.; socius regni, periculorum, belli, *an associate in*, Cic.

sŏcordĭa (**sēcordia**) -ae, f. (socors). (1) *folly, stupidity, weakness of intellect*: Suet. (2) *negligence, indolence, inactivity*: Liv., Tac.

sŏcors -cordis (se/cor). (1) *weak-minded, stupid, silly*: Cic., Liv., Tac. (2) *negligent, slothful, inactive*: Sall.; with genit., *careless about*: Ter., Tac. ¶ Compar. adv. **sŏcordĭus**, *too feebly*: ab Albanis socordius res acta, Liv.

Sōcrătēs -is, m. (Σωκράτης), *the famous Athenian philosopher, put to death in* 399 B.C. Adj. **Sōcrătĭcus** -a -um, *Socratic*: chartae, philosophy, Hor. M. pl. as subst. **Sōcrătĭci** -ōrum, *the followers of Socrates*.

socrus -ūs, f. (socer), *a mother-in-law*: Cic., Ov., etc.

sŏdālĭcĭum -i, n. (sodalis). LIT., *an association*; esp. *a secret society*: lex Licinia quae est de sodaliciis, Cic. TRANSF., in gen., *comradeship, intimacy*: Cat.

sŏdālĭcĭus -a -um (sodalis), *of companionship*: iure sodalicio, Ov.

sŏdālis -is, c. LIT., *a member of an association*. Esp. (1) *of a college of priests*: sibi in Lupercis sodalem esse, Cic.; sodales Augustales, Tac. (2) *of a secret society*: Pl., Cic. TRANSF., in gen., *a comrade, intimate companion, mate*. Of persons: Pl., Cic., etc. Of things, *a companion, attendant on*: sodalis hiemis (of the Hebrus), Hor.; poet. as adj.: sodalis Hebrus, Hor.

sŏdālĭtās -ātis, f. (sodalis). LIT., *an association*. Esp. (1) *a club for feasting*: Pl., Cic. (2) *a religious brotherhood*: quaedam sodalitas Lupercorum, Cic. (3) *a secret society*: Cic. TRANSF., in gen., *comradeship, intimacy*: officia sodalitatis familiaritatisque, Cic.

sŏdēs (for si audes), *if you please, with your leave* (colloq.): iube sodes nummos curari, Cic.; Pl., Hor.

sōl sōlis, m. *the sun*.

LIT., oriente sole, Caes.; solis occasu, Caes, Liv.; sol praecipitans, *inclining towards evening*, Cic.; supremo sole, *at evening*, Hor.; prov.: nondum omnium dierum sol occidit, *the sun has not yet set for ever*, Liv. Geograph. terms: oriens sol, ortus solis, *the east*; occidens sol, occasus solis, *the west*: Caes., Cic., etc.

TRANSF., (1) *the light, warmth, heat of the sun*: sol nimius, Ov.; ambulare in sole, Cic. Hence of work done in the sun: patiens pulveris atque solis, Hor.; cedat stilus gladio, umbra soli, Cic. (2) *a day*: tres soles erramus, Verg.; Lucr., etc. (3) *of distinguished persons*: P. Africanus sol alter, Cic.; solem Asiae

Brutum appellat, Hor. (4) personif., *the Sun-god, the Phoebus of the Greeks, father of Phaethon, Pasiphae, Circe*: Pl., Cic., etc.

sōlācĭŏlum -i, n. (dim. of solacium), *a small consolation*: Cat.

sōlācĭum -i, n. (solor), *a consolation, comfort, solace, relief*: servitutis, Cic.; solacium adferre, praebere, Cic.; absenti magna solacia dedisse, Cic.; id solacio est, Pl., Caes.; aves, solacia ruris, Ov.

sōlāmen -ĭnis, n. (solor), *a consolation, comfort*: Verg.

sōlāris -e (sol), *of the sun, solar*: lumen, Ov.

sōlārĭum -i, n. (sol). (**1**) *a sundial*: Pl., Varr. Hence *a place in the Forum, where a sundial stood*: non ad solarium versatus est, Cic. (**2**) *a balcony, terrace exposed to the sun*: Pl., Suet.

sōlāt-, see solac-.

sōlātor -ōris, m. (solor), *a consoler, comforter*: Tib., Stat.

soldūrĭi -ōrum, m. pl. (a Celtic word), *retainers, vassals*: Caes.

soldus＝solidus; q.v.

sŏlĕa -ae, f. (solum), *a leather sole strapped on the foot, a sandal.* Lit., soleas poscere (after dinner), Hor.; Pl., etc. Transf., (**1**) *a species of fetter*: ligneae, Cic. (**2**) *a kind of shoe for animals, not nailed, but tied on*: Cat., Suet. (**3**) *a fish, the sole*: Ov., Plin.

sŏlĕārĭus -i, m. (solea), *a sandal-maker*: Pl.

sŏlĕātus -a -um (solea), *wearing sandals*: Cic., Mart.

sōlennis, solennitas＝sollemnis, etc.; q.v.

sŏlĕo sŏlēre sŏlĭtus sum, *to be accustomed*: sic soleo, Ter.; ut solet, *as usual*, Cic.; with infin.: mentiri, Cic.; quā solitus sum uti, Cic.; Verg., etc.

¶ Hence partic. **sŏlĭtus** -a -um, *accustomed, wonted, habitual, usual*: solito matrum de more, Verg.; locus, Ov.; with dat.: Tac. N. as subst. **sŏlĭtum** -i, *that which is usual or customary*: praeter solitum, Verg., Hor. Esp. in. abl. with compar.: plus solito, Liv.; Ov.

sŏlers, solertia＝sollers, sollertia; q.v.

Sŏli -ōrum, m. (Σόλοι), *a town in Cilicia, a Greek colony, native place of the Stoic Chrysippus, of Menander, and of the astronomer Aratus.*

sŏlĭdē, adv. from solidus; q.v.

sŏlĭdĭtās -ātis, f. (solidus), *solidity*: nec dii habent ullam soliditatem nec eminentiam, Cic.

sŏlĭdo -are (solidus), *to make dense, firm, or solid*: area cretā solidanda, Verg.; muros, Tac.

sŏlĭdus (**soldus**) -a -um (cf. Gr. ὅλος), *dense, firm, solid.*

Lit., paries, Cic.; crateres auro solidi, Verg.; adamas, Verg.; superl.: Lucr., Ov. N. as subst. solidum -i, *firm ground, solid substance*, etc.: aliquem in solido locare, Verg.; Cic., Liv., etc.

Transf., (**1**) *whole, complete, entire*: partem solido demere de die, Hor., Verg., Liv. N. as subst., *the whole sum*: Cic. (**2**) *of abstr. things, firm, enduring, real*: fides, Pl.; laus, Cic.; utilitas, Cic.; libertas, Liv.

¶ Adv. **sŏlĭdē**, *firmly*: scire, *to know for certain*, Pl., Ter.

sōlĭfĕr -fĕra -fĕrum (sol/fero), *sun-bringing*: Sen.

sōlĭferrĕum -i, n. (sollus＝totus/ferrum *a javelin entirely of iron*: Liv.

sōlistĭmus -a -um (solus/sto), *full, complete* see tripudium.

sōlĭtārĭus -a -um (solus), *solitary, alone lonely*: solitarius homo atque in agro vitan agens, Cic.; quoniam solitaria non posse virtus ad ea pervenire, Cic.; Quint.

sōlĭtūdo -ĭnis, f. (solus). (**1**) *solitude, loneliness* loci, Cic.; in solitudine secum loqui, Cic. ubi solitudinem faciunt, pacem appellant Tac.; plur.: in animi doloribus solitudine captare, Cic.; Caes. (**2**) *a state of desertion deprivation, want*: liberorum, Cic.; Ter., Liv

sōlĭtus -a -um, partic. from soleo; q.v.

sōlĭum -i, n.

(**1**) *a chair of state, royal* or *official seat throne.* Lit., more patrio sedens in soli◦ consulentibus respondere, Cic.; regale, Liv. Verg., etc. Transf., *dominion, regal power* in paterno solio locare, Liv.; Lucr., Hor., Ov. Tac.

(**2**) *a bath-tub*: Lucr., Liv.

(**3**) *a stone coffin, sarcophagus*: Suet.

sōlĭvăgus -a -um (solus/vagus), *wandering alone.* Lit., bestiae, Cic. Transf., *solitary lonely, single*: cognitio, Cic.

sollemnis -e (sollus＝totus/annus), *yearly annual, recurring.*

Lit., sacra, Cato.; sacrificia, Cic.; Verg., Liv.

Transf., (**1**) *solemn, festive, religious* epulae, Cic., Tac.; ludi, Cic., Ov. (**2**) *usual customary, wonted*: lascivia militum, Liv. Verg., Hor.

¶ N. as subst. **sollemne** -is. (**1**) *a solemn feast, sacrifice, religious rite*: sollemne clavi figendi, Liv.; Verg., Tac. (**2**) *a custom* nostrum illud sollemne servemus, Cic. L.; inter cetera sollemnia, Liv.; Tac.

¶ Adv. **sollemnĭter**, *solemnly, religiously* omnia peragere, Liv.; *according to use custom*: Plin.

sollers -ertis, adj. (with compar. and superl.) (sollus＝totus/ars), *clever, skilful.* Lit., of persons: Ulysses, Ov.; quo quisque ol sollertior, Cic.; sollertissimus omnium, Sall.; with infin.: Hor., Ov.; with genit.: Musa lyrae sollers, Hor. Transf., of things: natura, Cic.; descriptio, Cic.; Verg., Liv., Ov.

¶ Adv. (with compar. and superl.) **sollerter**, *cleverly, skilfully*: Cic., Tac.

sollertĭa -ae, f. (sollers), *cleverness, skill, ingenuity*: Caes., Cic.; ingenii, Sall.; cogitandi, iudicandi, Cic.

sollĭcĭtātĭo -ōnis, f. (sollicito), *an inciting, instigation*: Cic.

sollĭcĭtē, adv. from sollicitus; q.v.

sollĭcĭto -are (sollicitus), *to move violently, disturb, shake, agitate.*

Lit., tellurem, *to plough*, Verg.; freta remis, Verg.; spicula, Verg.; stamina docto pollice, Ov.; mala copia aegrum stomachum, Hor.

Transf., *to rouse, vex, disquiet*: haec cura me sollicitat, Cic.; pacem, Liv.; Verg.; pass.: sollicitatus Iuppiter, Liv.; with infin.: Lucr., Ov. Esp. of bad influence, *to incite, instigate, tamper with*: civitates, Caes.; sollicitatus ab Arvernis pecuniā, Caes.; sollicitare, servos ad hospitem necandum, Cic.; dixit se sollicitatum esse, ut regnare vellet, Cic. L.; sollicitare iudicium donis, *seek to obtain by bribery*, Ov.

sollĭcĭtūdo -ĭnis, f. (sollicitus), *uneasiness, disquiet, anxiety, care*: cura et sollicitudo, Cic.; with objective genit.: nuptiarum, Ter.; in dat., *a cause of anxiety*: Pl., Ter.; plur.: sollicitudines domesticae, Cic.; Hor.

sollĭcĭtus -a -um (sollus=totus/cieo), *thoroughly* or *violently moved, disturbed, agitated, restless*.

LIT., motus, Lucr.; mare, Verg.; Ov.

TRANSF., (1) *mentally disturbed, anxious, uneasy, worried*: **a**, of persons, minds, communities: anxius animus aut sollicitas, Cic.; aliquem sollicitum habere, *to keep in a state of anxiety, to trouble*, Cic.; sollicitum esse de alicuius valetudine, Cic. L.; Aetolis sollicitus, Liv.; sollicitus propter difficultatem locorum, Liv.; meam vicem sollicitus, Liv.; sollicitus morte Tigelli, Hor.; with ne and the subj.: Cic., Liv.: **b**, of animals: canes, *watchful*, Liv., Ov.: **c**, of abstr. things: amor, Cic.; vita, Hor. (2) act., *disquieting, causing trouble*: opes, Hor.; cura, Ov.; Cic.

¶ Adv. **sollĭcĭtē**, *anxiously, carefully*: Sen., Plin. L.

sollĭferrĕum=soliferreum; q.v.

sollistĭmus=solistimus; q.v.

sollus -a -um (Oscan)=totus; q.v.

sōlo -are (solus), *to make solitary, make desert*: Sen.

sŏloecismus -i, m. (σολοικισμός), *a grammatical error, solecism*: Sen., Quint., Juv.

Sŏlōn -ōnis, m. (Σόλων), *one of the Seven Wise Men of Greece, a famous Athenian legislator, active about* 600 B.C.

sōlor -ari, dep. (1) *to comfort, console* a person: inopem, Hor.; Verg., Tac., etc. (2) *to assuage, soothe, relieve* a trouble or disturbance: famem, Verg.; laborem cantu, Verg.; aestum fluviis, Hor.; cladem, Tac.

solstĭtĭālis -e (solstitium), *of the summer solstice*.

LIT., dies, Cic.; nox, Ov.; orbis, *the tropic of Cancer*, Cic.; Lucr.

TRANSF., (1) *of summer* or *of the warmth of summer*: solstitiali tempore, Liv. (2) *of the sun, solar*: orbis, Liv.

solstĭtĭum -i, n. (sol/sisto), *the solstice*. LIT., Plin. Esp., *the summer solstice, the longest day*: Cic. TRANSF., *summer, summer-heat*: solstitium pecori defendite, Verg.; Hor., Ov., etc.

sŏlum -i, n. *the bottom* or *lowest part* of anything.

(1) in gen. LIT., fossae, Caes.; clivus ad solum exustus est, Liv.; astra tenent caeleste solum, *the floor of heaven*, Ov. TRANSF., *ground, foundation*: solum et quasi fundamentum oratoris, locutionem emendatam et Latinam, Cic.; Liv.

(2) *the sole* of a foot, or of a shoe: Pl., Lucr., Cic.

(3) *soil, ground, earth, land*. LIT., terrae, Lucr., Cat.; terrarum ultimarum, Cic.; solum exercere sub vomere, Verg. TRANSF., *country*: solum patriae, *the soil of one's native country*, Cic.; solum vertere, *to leave one's country, go into exile*, Cic., Liv.; solum natale, Ov.

Sŏluntīnus, *see* ²Solus.

¹**sōlus** -a -um, genit. sōlīus, dat. usually sōlī (connected with sollus), *alone, only, sole*. LIT., cum omnibus potius quam soli perire voluerunt, Cic.; per se solus, Liv.; solos novem menses, *only nine months*, Cic. TRANSF., of places, *solitary, uninhabited*: cum in locis solis maestus errares, Cic.; loca, Lucr.; Verg., etc.

¶ N. acc. as adv. **sōlum**, *alone, only, merely*. Affirmatively: unā de re solum est dissensio, Cic. Negatively: non solum . . . verum (sed) etiam, *not only . . . but also*, Cic., Hor., etc.; non solum . . . sed ne quidem, *not only not . . . but not even*, Cic.

²**Sōlūs** -untis, f. (Σολοῦς), *a town on the north coast of Sicily* near the modern *Bagheria*.

¶ Hence subst. **Sŏluntīnus** -i, m. *an inhabitant of Solus*: Cic.

sŏlūtē, adv. from solutus, *see* solvo.

sŏlūtĭlis -e (solvo), *easily coming to pieces*: Suet.

sŏlūtĭo -ōnis, f. (solvo). (1) *a loosening*: linguae, Cic. (2) *a paying, payment*: solutio rerum creditarum, Cic.; Caes., Liv. (3) *a solution, explanation*: Sen.

sŏlūtus -a -um, partic. from solvo; q.v.

solvo solvĕre solvi (poet. sŏlŭi, rare) sŏlūtum (se/luo), *to loosen*.

(1) *to untie, unbind, free, release* a person or thing. LIT., **a**, *to release from fetters*, etc.: aliquem, Cic., Verg., etc.; crines, capillos, Hor.; canem catenā, Phaedr.; equum senescentem, *to unyoke*, Hor.; epistulam, *to open*, Ov.; ora, Ov.; often of ships: naves, Caes., Liv.; classem, Liv.: **b**, *to release* a thing from *what holds it together; to dissolve, break up*: pontem, Tac.; Lucr.; pass.: solvuntur viscera, *putrefy*, Verg.; nives, Ov.; rigor auri solvitur aestu, Lucr. TRANSF., **a**, *to free from restrictions*: religione civitatem, Cic.; urbem obsidione, Liv.; formidine terras, Verg.; legibus solvi, *to be exempted from*, Cic., Liv.: **b**, *to break up, weaken*, or *bring to an end*: agmina diductis choris, Verg.; solvuntur frigore membra, Verg.; solvitur in somnos, Verg.; solvitur acris hiems, Hor.; homines solverat alta quies, Ov.

(2) *to loosen* what restricts. LIT., of physical bonds: zonam diu ligatam, Cat.; corollas de fronte, Prop.; catenas, Ov. Of untying a ship and setting sail: solvere funem, Verg.; retinacula, Ov.; absol.: naves ex portu solverunt, Caes. TRANSF., **a**, *to pay off, discharge* a debt: alicui pecuniam debitam, Cic.; Liv., etc.; solvendo non esse, *not to be up to paying*, i.e. *to be insolvent*, Cic.: **b**, *to pay* abstr. things *as due, to meet engagements*: vota, Cic., Ov.; exsequias, Liv.; iusta paterno funeri, Cic.; esp.: poenas, *a penalty*, Cic., Sall., etc.: **c**, *to throw off, break down* any restraining influence: luxuriā disciplinam militarem, Liv.; traditum a prioribus morem, Liv.; nodum amicitiae, Hor.; curam Lyaeo, Hor.; pudorem, Verg.; metum corde, Verg.: **d**, *to solve* a problem, *explain* a difficulty: carmina non intellecta, Ov.; iuris nodos et legum aenigmata, Juv.

¶ Hence partic. (with compar. and superl.) **sŏlūtus** -a -um, *loosened, unbound, free*. LIT., reus solutus causam dicis, testes vinctos attines, Pl.; Cic., Liv. Of soil, *loose*: Plin.

TRANSF., (1) *free from restrictions, independent*: solutus liberque animus, Cic.; soluta optio eligendi, Cic.; with ab: soluti a cupiditatibus, Cic.; ab omni imperio externo, Liv.; with abl. alone: ambitione, omni faenore, Hor.; with genit.: famuli operum soluti, Hor.; praedia, *unencumbered*, Cic. (2) in a bad sense, *unrestrained, unbridled, licentious*: libido solutior, Liv.; amores, Cic.; P. Clodi praetura, Cic. (3) *lax, lazy, negligent*: Cic., Liv. Tac. (4) of style: a, *fluent*: solutus atque expeditus ad dicendum, Cic.: b, *free from metrical restrictions, in prose*: oratio, verba, Cic.; verba soluta modis, Ov.
¶ Adv. (with compar.) **sŏlūtē**. LIT., *loosely*: Lucr. TRANSF., (1) *freely*: moveri, Cic. (2) *carelessly, negligently*: Cic.

somnĭātor -ōris, m. (somnio), *a dreamer*: Sen.
somnĭcŭlōsus -a -um (somnus), *sleepy, drowsy, sluggish*: senectus, Cic.; glires, Mart.
¶ Adv. **somnĭcŭlōsē**, *sleepily*: Pl.

somnĭfĕr -fĕra -fĕrum (somnus/fero), *sleep-bringing, sleep-causing*. LIT., virga (Mercurii), Ov. TRANSF., *narcotic, deadly*: venenum, Ov.; Luc.

somnĭo -are (somnium), *to dream*.
LIT., totas noctes, Cic.; de aliquo, Cic. With acc., *to dream of*: ovum, Cic.; with acc. and infin.: ovum pendēre ex fascia lecti, Cic.; Pl.
TRANSF., *to imagine foolishly*: portenta non disserentium philosophorum, sed somniantium, Cic.; with acc.: Pl., Cic.

somnĭum -i, n. (somnus), *a dream*. LIT., per somnia (*in a dream*) loqui, Cic.; Lucr., Verg., etc. TRANSF., *a fancy, day-dream*: *foolishness, nonsense*: Ter. Plur.: Cic., Hor., etc.

somnus -i, m. (for sopnus, from root of sopor and sopio), *sleep, slumber*.
LIT., Endymionis, Cic.; somnum capere non posse, *not to be able to sleep*, Cic.; somnum tenere, *to keep oneself from sleeping*, Cic.; petere, Ov.; invitare, Hor.; dare se somno, Cic.; in somnis (per somnum) aliquid videre, Pl., Cic., etc.; somnus altus, Hor.; aliquem ex somno excitare, Cic.
TRANSF., (1) *drowsiness, laziness, inactivity*: somno nati, Cic.; dediti somno, Sall. (2) with suitable adj., *the sleep of death*: longus, Hor. (3) *night*: libra die (=diei) somnique pares ubi fecerit horas, Verg. (4) personif.: Verg., Ov.

sŏnābĭlis -e (sono), *resounding*: sistrum, Ov.
sŏnĭpēs -pĕdis (sonus/pes), *sounding with the feet*. Usually m. as subst., *a horse*: Cat., Verg.
sŏnĭtus -ūs, m. (sono), *a sound, noise*: ventorum, Lucr.; verborum, Cic.; Olympi, *thunder*, Verg.

sŏnĭvĭus -a -um (sono), *sounding*, only used in augury in the phrase sonivium tripudium, *the noise of the food falling from the beaks of the sacred chickens*: Cic., *see* tripudium.

sŏno sŏnare sŏnŭi sŏnĭtum; pres. infin. sonēre: Lucr.; fut. partic. sŏnātūrus: Hor. (sonus).
LIT., *to sound, resound, make a noise*: sonuerunt tympana, Caes.; classica sonant, Verg.; sonare inani voce, *to produce an empty jingle of words*, Cic.; ripae sonant, *re-echo*, Verg.; silvae Aquilone, Hor. With acc. of the sound made: amnis rauca sonans, *sounding harshly*, Verg.; inconditis vocibus incohatum quiddam atque peregrinum

sonantes, Cic.; nec vox hominem sonat, *sounds human*, Verg.; furem sonuere iuvenci, i.e. *gave the alarm*, Prop.
TRANSF., (1) *to mean*: quid sonet haec vox, Cic. (2) *to sing of, to celebrate*: atavos et atavorum antiqua nomina, Verg.; bella, Ov.; pass.: lyrā sonari, Hor.

sŏnor -ōris, m. (sono), *a sound, noise, din*: sonorem dant silvae, Verg.; Lucr., Tac.
sŏnōrus -a -um (sonor), *sounding, resonant, ringing, loud*: cithara, Tib.; tempestas, Verg.

sons sontis (?sum), *guilty*: anima, Verg.; sanguis, Ov. As subst., esp. plur.: punire sontes, *the guilty*, Cic.; Liv., etc.
Sontĭātes -um, m. *a people in Gallia Aquitania*: Caes.

sontĭcus -a -um (sons), *important, critical*: morbus (*such a disease as excuses failure to appear in court*), Plin.; causa, *weighty, serious*, Tib.

sŏnus -i, m. *a noise, sound, din*. LIT., tubae, Caes.; ab acutissimo sono usque ad gravissimum sonum, *from the highest treble to the deepest bass*, Cic.; Verg., Liv., etc. TRANSF., *tone, character, style*: Cic., Quint.

sŏphĭa -ae, f. (σοφία), *wisdom*: Enn., Mart.
sŏphisma -ătis, n. (σόφισμα), *a sophism, fallacy*: Sen.
sŏphistes -ae, m. (σοφιστής), *a sophist*: Cic.
Sŏphoclēs -is and -i; voc. Sophocle; m. (Σοφοκλῆς), *the Greek tragic poet*.
¶ Hence adj. **Sŏphŏclēus** -a -um, *Sophoclean, of Sophocles*: Cic., Verg.
¹**sŏphŏs** (-ŭs) -i, m. (σοφός), *wise*: Phaedr. As subst., *a wise man*: Mart.
²**sŏphŏs** (σοφῶς), adv. *bravo! well done!* Mart.

sŏpĭo -ire.
(1) *to put to sleep, lull to sleep*. LIT., pervigilem draconem herbis, Ov.; esp. in perf. partic., sopitus, *lulled to sleep*: sopito corpore, Cic.; Lucr., Verg., Liv. Of the sleep of death: Lucr. TRANSF., of things, *to lull, quiet*: virtus sopita sit, Cic.; ignis sopitus, *slumbering under the ashes*, Verg.
(2) *to stun, render senseless*: impactus ita est saxo, ut sopiretur, Liv.

sŏpor -ōris, m. (connected with somnus), *deep sleep*.
LIT., sopor aliquem opprimit, Liv.; Lucr., Verg., etc. Sometimes *the sleep of death*: perpetuus sopor, Hor.; Pl., Lucr.
TRANSF., (1) *laziness, inactivity*: Tac., Mart. (2) *a sleeping draught*: patri soporem dare, Nep.

sŏpōrātus -a -um (sopor), *full of sleep*: hostes, Ov.; ramus vi soporatus Stygiā, Verg.
¶ Hence **sŏpōro** -are, *to put to sleep*: Plin.
sŏpōrĭfĕr -fĕra -fĕrum (sopor/fero), *causing deep sleep*: Verg., Ov.
sŏpōrus -a -um (sopor), *sleep-bringing*: Nox, Verg.

Sŏra -ae, f. *a town in Latium, on the right bank of the Liris (still called Sora)*.
¶ Hence adj. **Sŏrānus** -a -um, *belonging to Sora*.
Sŏractē -is, n. *a mountain in Etruria, on which stood a temple of Apollo (now Monte di S. Oreste)*.
Sŏrānus -a -um, *see* Sora.
sŏrācum -i, n. (σώρακος), *a pannier, hamper*: Pl.
sorbĕo -ēre -ŭi (cf. ῥοφέω), *to suck in, drink down, swallow*.

LIT., sanguinem, Pl.; Charybdis vastos sorbet in abruptum fluctus, Verg.; sorbent avidae praecordia flammae, Ov.
TRANSF., odia, *to swallow, put up with*, Cic. L.

sorbillo -are (sorbeo), *to sip*: Ter.
sorbilo, adv. (sorbeo), *by sipping*; hence, *drop by drop*: Pl.
sorbitio -ōnis, f. (sorbeo), *a draught, potion*: Pers.
sorbum -i, n. *the fruit of the* sorbus, *a service-berry*: Verg.
sorbus -i, f. *the service-tree*: Plin.
sordĕo -ēre (sordes), *to be dirty, be unwashed.* LIT., D. iam lavisti? Ph. num tibi sordere videor? Pl.; Sen. TRANSF., *to appear mean, vile,* worthless : cunctane prae campo sordent? Hor.; sordent tibi munera nostra, Verg.; with dat. : adeo se suis etiam sordere, Liv.
sordes -is, f. and often plur. **sordēs** -ium, *dirt, filth.*
LIT., sine sordibus ungues, Hor.; in sordibus aurium inhaerescere, Cic. Esp. *shabby* or *dirty garments, used by mourners and persons accused*: sordes lugubres, Cic.; Liv., Tac.
TRANSF., (1) *baseness* of rank or station: fortunae et vitae, Cic.; Liv., Tac.; apud sordem urbis et faecem, *the dregs of the people,* Cic. L. (2) *sordid conduct, meanness;* rarely in sing.: nulla in re familiari sordes, Cic.; gen. in plur.: mens oppleta sordibus, Cic.; Hor., Tac., Juv.
sordesco sordescĕre sordŭi (sordeo), *to become dirty*: Hor., Plin.
sordidātus -a -um (sordidus), *wearing shabby* or *dirty clothes*: Pl., Ter., Cic.; esp. of mourners: Cic., Liv.
sordidŭlus -a -um (dim. of sordidus), *somewhat dirty* or *mean*: servoli, Pl.; toga, Juv.
sordidus -a -um, adj. (with compar. and superl.) (sordeo), *dirty, filthy, shabby.*
LIT., amictus, Verg.; mappa, Hor.; Ov. Esp. *in shabby* or *dirty clothes, as a sign of mourning*: squalore sordidus, Cic.
TRANSF., (1) *poor, mean, base* in rank or condition: loco non humili solum sed etiam sordido natus, Liv.; rura, Verg.; Cic. (2) *mean* in conduct, *base, vile*: iste omnium turpissimus et sordidissimus, Cic.; cupido, Hor.; adulterium, Cic.
¶ Hence adv. **sordidē**. (1) *meanly, in a low station*: nasci, Tac. (2) TRANSF., a, *vulgarly, meanly*: dicere, Cic.: b, *sordidly, stingily*: Cic.
sordĭtūdo -ĭnis, f. (sordes), *dirt, filth*: Pl.
sŏrex -ĭcis, m. (cf. ὕραξ), *a shrew-mouse*: Ter., Varr.
sŏrĭcinus -a -um (sorex), *of a shrew-mouse*: Pl.
sŏrītēs -ae (dat. sŏrītī: Cic.), m. (σωρείτης), *a sorites, a conclusion reached by accumulation of arguments*: Cic.
sŏror, *a sister.*
LIT., Cic., Verg., etc.; plur.: sorores, *the Parcae*, Ov.; so: tres sorores, Cat., Hor.
TRANSF., (1) *a cousin*: Ov. (2) *a friend, playmate*: sorores meae, Verg. (3) of things alike or connected: per dexteram perque hanc sororem laevam, Pl.; Cat., Verg.
sŏrōrĭcīda -ae, m. (soror/caedo), *one who murders a sister*: Cic.
sŏrōrĭus -a -um (soror), *of* or *for a sister,*

sisterly: stupra, *incest*, Cic.; oscula, Ov.; Pl., Liv.
sors sortis (abl. sorti: Pl., Liv.), f. (from ¹sero, as fors from fero), *a lot.*
LIT., conicere sortes in hydriam, Cic.; sors mea exit, *comes out*, Cic.; omnium versatur urnā serius ocius sors exitura, Hor.; ut cuiusque sors exciderat, Liv.
TRANSF., (1) *a casting of lots*: res revocatur ad sortem, Cic.; alicui provincia sorte obvenit, Cic.; evenit, Liv. (2) *an oracular response, prophecy*: sors oraculi, Liv.; Cic., Verg. (3) *official duty* as allotted, esp. to a praetor: nunquam afuit nisi sorte, Cic.; sors urbana, peregrina, Liv. (4) with genit., *share, part*: in nullam sortem bonorum nato, Liv.; Ov. (5) *fate, fortune, destiny*: nescia mens hominum fati sortisque futurae, Verg.; inlacrimare sorti humanae, Liv.; Hor., Ov. (6) *money, capital out at interest*: sorte caret, usurā nec eā solidā contentus est, Cic. L.; Pl., Ter., Liv.
sortĭcŭla -ae, f. (dim. of sors), *a little lot* or *ticket*: Suet.
sortĭlĕgus -a -um (sors/lego), *prophetic, oracular*: Hor. M. as subst. **sortĭlĕgus** -i, *a soothsayer, fortune-teller*: Cic., Luc.
sortĭor -iri, dep.; and **sortio** -ire: Pl., Varr. (sors).
(1) intransit., *to cast lots*: Pl., Cic., Liv., Tac.
(2) transit., *to allot, cast lots for*; also *to obtain by lot.* LIT., provincias, Liv.; iudices, Cic.; Hor.; with clause as object: consules sortiti, uter dedicaret, Liv.; quasi sortiri, quid loquare, Cic. TRANSF., a, *to choose, select*: subolem, Verg.: b, *to share, divide*: laborem, Verg.: c, in gen., *to get, receive, obtain*: mediterranea Asiae, Liv.; amicum casu, Hor.; Ov.
¶ Hence partic. **sortītus** -a -um. (1) dep. sense, *having obtained* (by lot) or *cast lots for*: Cic., etc. (2) pass. sense, *gained by lot*: Cic. L., Prop. N. abl. sing. as adv. **sortītō**. LIT., *by lot*: Cic., Suet. TRANSF., *by fate*: Pl., Hor.
sortītio -ōnis, f. (sortior), *a casting lots, deciding by lot*: iudicum sortitio fit, Cic.; Pl.
sortītor -ōris, m. (sortior), *one who draws lots*: Sen.
¹**sortītus** -ūs, m. (sortior), *a casting of lots, deciding by lot*: Pl., Cic., Verg.
²**sortītus** -a -um, partic. from sortior; q.v.
sospĕs -ĭtis (connected with σῶς). (1) *safe, unhurt, uninjured*: sospites brevi in patriam ad parentes restituunt, Liv.; navis sospes ab ignibus, Hor.; Ov., etc. (2) *lucky, favourable*: diem hunc sospitem rebus meis agundis, Pl.
Sospĭta -ae, f. (sospes), *the Saviour*; an epithet of Juno: Cic., Ov.
sospĭtālis -e (sospes), *salutary*: Pl.
sospĭto -are (sospes), *to keep safe, preserve*: Romuli gentem, Cat.; suam progeniem, Liv.; Pl.
sōtēr -tēris; acc. -tēra; m. (σωτήρ), *a saviour*: Cic.
sōtērĭa -ōrum, n. pl. (σωτήρια), *presents given to celebrate a recovery from sickness*: Mart.
spādix -dīcis (σπάδιξ), *date-coloured, chestnut-coloured*: equi, Verg.
spādo -ōnis, m. (σπάδων), *a eunuch*: Liv., etc.
spargo spargĕre sparsi sparsum (connected with σπείρω).

(1) *to scatter, strew, sprinkle, pour forth, throw about.* Lɪᴛ., nummos populo, Cic.; nuces, flores, Verg.; per totam domum aquas, Hor.; semina humo, Ov. Tʀᴀɴsꜰ., **a,** *to scatter* abstract things, *spread, circulate*: animos in corpora humana, Cic.; arma (*war*) per agros, Liv.; voces in vulgum ambiguas, Verg.; Argolicas nomen per urbes Theseos, Ov.: **b,** *to send in various directions, distribute*: per vias speculatores, Liv.; also, *to disperse, scatter in flight*: spargere se in fugam, Liv.; of property, *to dissipate*: spargas tua prodigus, Hor.

(2) *to besprinkle* a person or thing with something. Lɪᴛ., humum foliis, Verg., aurora spargebat lumine terras, Verg.; debitā sparges lacrimā favillam vatis amici; Hor.; Lucr., Liv., etc. Tʀᴀɴsꜰ., litterae humanitatis sale sparsae, Cic.

¶ Hence partic. **sparsus** -a -um. **(1)** *spread out, scattered*: crines, *dishevelled*, Liv. **(2)** *speckled, spotted*: anguis maculis sparsus, Liv.; sparso ore, *with a freckled face*, Ter.

sparsĭo -ōnis, f. (spargo), *a sprinkling*, esp. of perfumes or presents in a theatre: Sen., Stat.

Sparta -ae, f. and poet. **Spartē** -ēs, f. (*Σπάρτη*), *Sparta, the capital of Laconia.*

¶ Hence adj. **Spartānus** -a -um, *Spartan*; m. as subst. **Spartanus** -i, *a Spartan*; adj. **Spartĭātĭcus** and **Spartĭcus** -a -um, *Spartan*; subst. **Spartĭātes** -ae, m. *a Spartan.*

Spartăcus -i, m. *a Thracian gladiator, leader in the gladiatorial war against the Romans,* 73–71 B.C.; *defeated by Crassus.*

spartum -i, n. (*σπάρτον*), *a plant, Spanish broom*, of which ropes, etc. were made: Varr., Liv.

spărŭlus -i, m. (dim. of sparus), *a kind of fish, a sea-bream*: Ov.

spărus -i, m. *a small spear* or *javelin with a curved blade*: Verg., Sall., Liv.

spătha -ae, f. (*σπάθη*). **(1)** *a wooden instrument for stirring* or *mixing, a spatula*: Plin. **(2)** *an instrument of similar shape used by weavers*: Sen. **(3)** *a broad two-edged sword without a point*: Tac.

spătĭor -ari, dep. (spatium), *to walk, walk about, take a walk, promenade.* Lɪᴛ., in xysto, Cic.; in siccā harenā, Verg.; Hor., Ov. Tʀᴀɴsꜰ., of things, *to spread out, expand*: alae spatiantes, Ov.; Plin., Sen.

spătĭōsus -a -um (spatium), *ample, wide, spacious, large.* Lɪᴛ., insula, Plin.; taurus, Ov. Fig., of time, *long*: nox, Ov.

¶ Hence adv. **spătĭōse.** **(1) a,** *widely, extensively*: Plin.: **b,** *greatly*: spatiosius increvit flumen, Ov. **(2)** fig., of time, *long*: Prop.

spătĭum -i, n. *space.*

Lɪᴛ., *space, extent, room.* In gen.: locus ac spatium, Lucr.; spatia locorum, Caes.; caeli spatium, Verg. Esp. **(1)** *distance between two points, interval*: paribus spatiis intermissae trabes, Caes.; Ov. **(2)** *dimensions, size, length*: oris et colli, Ov.; serpentis, Ov.; viae, Ov. **(3)** *a measured distance, tract, course*: eadem spatia quinque stellae conficiunt, Cic.; often *the course in a race*: spatia corripere, Verg.; quasi decurso spatio, Cic.; duobus spatiis tribusve factis, Cic.; fig.: decurrere spatium aetatis, Pl.; vitae, Ov. **(4)** *an open space, place for walking in, walk, promenade*: spatia silvestria, Cic.; locus planis porrectus spatiis, Hor.

Tʀᴀɴsꜰ., of time. In gen., *a space of time, period*: spatium praeteriti temporis, Cic.; diei, Caes.; spatio pugnae defatigati, Caes. Esp. **(1)** *sufficient time, leisure, opportunity*: nisi tempus et spatium datum sit, Cic.; si mihi aliquid spatii ad scribendum darent, Cic.; irae spatium dare, Liv.; Verg., etc. **(2)** *metrical time, measure, quantity*: Cic.

spĕcĭālis -e (species), *individual, particular, special*: Sen., Quint.

¶ Adv. **spĕcĭālĭtĕr,** *particularly*: Quint.

spĕcĭes -ēi; genit. and dat. plur. not found; f. (specio).

(1) act., *a seeing, view, look*: speciem aliquo vertere, Lucr.; invida praeclusit speciem natura videndi, Lucr.; doloris speciem ferre non possunt, Cic.

(2) pass., *sight, look.* Lɪᴛ., in gen., *shape, form, outward appearance*: speciem boni viri prae se ferre, Cic.; speciem ridentis praebere, Liv.; species urbis, Pl.; humana, Cic.; divina, Liv. Esp.: **a,** *beautiful form, beauty*: mulieris, Pl.; caeli, Cic.; triumpho maximam speciem captiva arma praebuere, Liv.: **b,** *outward show*, opp. reality: paucis ad speciem tabernaculis relictis, Caes.: **c,** *a vision, dream, phantom*: consuli visa species viri, Liv., Lucr., Ov.: **d,** *a representation, image, statue*: Cic. poet. Tʀᴀɴsꜰ., of mental showing: **a,** *appearance*, opp. reality, *pretext, pretence*: sub specie infidae pacis, Liv.; Cic.: **b,** *notion, idea*: eloquentiae, Cic.; Hor., Liv.: **c,** *a kind, species, division of a* genus: Cic., Quint.

spĕcillum -i, n. (specio), *a surgeon's probe*: Cic.

spĕcĭmen -inis, n. (specio), *a visible mark, token, example, model.* Lɪᴛ., creandi, Lucr.; ingenii, Cic.; specimen dare, Cic.; Verg., Liv.

Tʀᴀɴsꜰ., *a pattern, ideal*: prudentiae, Cic.; num dubitas quin specimen naturae capi debeat ex optima quaque natura? Cic.

spĕcĭo (spĭcĭo) spĕcĕre spexi (cf. *σκέπτομαι*), *to look at, behold, see*: Pl.

spĕcĭōsus -a -um (species), *beautiful, splendid, handsome.* Lɪᴛ., to the sight: mulier, Ov.; Hor. Tʀᴀɴsꜰ., to the mind, *imposing*: opes, Tac.; exemplum, Liv. In a bad sense, *plausible, specious*: causa, Cic. L.; titulus, Liv.; nomina, Ov.

¶ Hence adv. (with compar.) **spĕcĭōse,** *beautifully, splendidly, handsomely, showily*: speciosius instratus equus quam uxor vestita, Liv.

spectābĭlis -e (specto). **(1)** *visible*: corpus, Cic.; Ov. **(2)** *worth seeing, notable, remarkable*: heros, Ov.; victoria, Tac.

spectācŭlum (spectaclum: Prop.) -i, n. (specto), *a sight, show, spectacle.*

Lɪᴛ., in gen.: luctuosum, Cic.; rerum caelestium, Cic.; (alicui) spectaculum praebere, Cic., Liv., Ov.; spectaculo esse, Cic. L. Esp., *a spectacle in the theatre* or *circus*: apparatissimum, Cic.; gladiatorum, Liv.; circi, Liv.

Tʀᴀɴsꜰ., gen. plur., spectacula, *the seats in theatre* or *circus*: spectacula sunt tributim data, Cic.; Liv., etc.

spectāmen -inis, n. (specto), *a sign, token, proof*: Pl.

spectātĭo -ōnis, f. (specto), *a looking, watching, viewing.* In gen.: apparatūs, Cic.; animum spectatione levare, Cic. L. Esp. *inspection or testing of money*: Cic.

spectātor -ōris, m. (specto). (**1**) *a watcher, a spectator, observer*: quasi spectatores superarum rerum atque caelestium, Cic.; certaminis, Liv. Esp. *a spectator at the theatre* or *public games*: Pl., Cic. (**2**) *an inspector, examiner, critic*: formarum, Ter.; acrior virtutis spectator ac iudex, Liv.

spectātrix -trīcis, f. (spectator), *a female watcher, spectator, observer*: Pl., Ov.

spectātus -a -um, partic. from specto; q.v.

spectĭo -ōnis, f. (specio), *the right of certain magistrates to observe the auspices*: nos (augures) nuntiationem solum habemus, consules et reliqui magistratus etiam spectionem, Cic.

specto -are (freq. of specio), *to look at carefully, contemplate, observe, watch.*

LIT., in gen.: e terra alterius laborem, Lucr.; tota domus quae spectat in nos solos, Cic.; spectatumne huc venimus? Liv.; Pl., Ov., etc. Esp. (**1**) *to watch as a spectator, look on at*: fabulam, Pl.; ludos, Hor.; Megalesia, Cic. (**2**) *to look at for the purpose of examining* or *testing; to test, to examine*: spectatur in ignibus aurum, Ov.; Pl., Cic. (**3**) of places, *to look towards, face towards*: collis ad orientem solem spectabat, Caes.; spectare in Etruriam, Liv.; spectare inter occasum solis et septentriones, Caes.; with acc.: solem occidentem, Liv.

TRANSF., mentally. (**1**) *to consider, contemplate, observe*: audaciam meretricum, Ter.; Pl., Cic. Esp. *to look for*: quem locum probandae virtutis tuae spectas? Caes. (**2**) *to bear in mind, have a regard to, have in view*: magna, Cic.; fugam, Cic.; ad imperatorias laudes, Cic.; with ut and the subj.: spectavi semper ut possem, Cic. L.; with indir. quest.: Cic. L. (**3**) of things, *to tend to, incline to*: ad perniciem, Cic.; ad bene beateque vivendum, Cic.; quo igitur haec spectat oratio? Cic. (**4**) *to consider critically, to judge, test*: aliquem ex trunco corporis, Cic.; non ex singulis vocibus philosophi spectandi sunt, Cic.

¶ Hence partic. **spectātus** -a -um, *tried, proved, approved*; hence often *esteemed, respected*: homo, Cic.; castitas, Liv.; superl.: vir spectatissimus, Cic.

spectrum -i, n. (specio), *a spectre, apparition*: Cic.

¹**spĕcŭla** -ae, f. (specio), *a look-out, watch-tower.*

LIT., speculas per promunturia omnia ponere, Liv.; multo ante tamquam ex specula prospexi tempestatem futuram, Cic.; Verg., Liv.

TRANSF., (**1**) homines in speculis sunt, *are on the watch*, Cic. (**2**) *any lofty place*: Verg.

²**spĕcŭla** -ae, f. (dim. of spes), *a little hope, ray of hope*: qui aliquid ex eius sermone speculae degustarat, Cic.; Pl.

spĕcŭlābundus -a -um (speculor), *watching, on the watch*: Tac., Suet.

spĕcŭlāris -e (speculum). (**1**) *like a mirror*: Sen. (**2**) *transparent*: lapis, *a species of transparent stone*, perhaps *mica*, Plin.

¶ Hence **spĕcŭlāria** -iōrum, *window-panes*: Sen., Mart., etc.

spĕcŭlātor -ōris, m. (speculor) LIT., as milit.

t. t., a scout, spy: Caes., Cic., etc. TRANSF., in gen., *an observer, investigator*: naturae, Cic.; Prop.

spĕcŭlātōrĭus -a -um (speculator), *of a look-out* or *scout*: navigia, Caes.; naves, Liv. F. as subst.: speculatoria -ae, *a spy-boat*: Liv.

spĕcŭlātrix -īcis, f. (speculor), *a female observer, watcher*: Furiae sunt speculatrices et vindices facinorum et scelerum, Cic.

spĕcŭlor -ari, dep. (¹specula), *to look out, spy out, watch, observe.* unde sedens partes speculatur in omnes, Ov. With acc.: loca, Pl.; avem, Verg.; alicuius consilia, Sall.; Cic. With indir. quest.: quae fortuna esset, Liv.; Pl.

spĕcŭlum -i, n. (specio), *a mirror* (made of polished metal).

LIT., speculum suum consulere, Ov.; se speculo videre alterum, Hor.; Lucr., Cic., etc. TRANSF., (**1**) of water: lympharum, Phaedr. (**2**) in gen., *image, copy*: quae (parvos et bestias) putat esse specula naturae, Cic.; Lucr.

spĕcus -ūs, m., f., and n. (cf. σπέος). LIT., *a cave*, natural or artificial: horrendum, Verg.; Cic. L., Ov., etc. TRANSF., *a hole, hollow*: vulneris, Verg.

spēlaeum -i, n. (σπήλαιον), *a cave, grotto, den*: ferarum, Verg.

spēlunca -ae, f. (σπήλυγξ), *a cave, grotto, den*: Cic., Verg., etc.

spĕrābĭlis -e (spero), *that may be hoped for*: Pl.

Sperchēōs and **Sperchīus** -i, m. (Σπερχειός), *a river in Thessaly.*

¶ Hence f. adj. **Sperchēïs** -ēïdis, *of Spercheus*; subst. **Spĕrchĭōnĭdēs** -ae, m. *one who lives near the Spercheus.*

sperno spernĕre sprēvi sprētum. LIT., *to put away, remove*: Pl. TRANSF., *to reject, despise, scorn, spurn*: nos sprevit et pro nihilo putavit, Cic.; voluptatem, Hor.; Verg., etc.; poet. with infin.: nec partem solido demere de die spernit, Hor.

spēro -are (spes), *to look for, to expect.*

(**1**) most commonly, of good things, *to hope, hope for, promise oneself, flatter oneself*): bene, recte, Cic.; ut spero (in a parenthesis), Cic.; de otio nostro, Cic. L.; meliora, Cic. L.; omnia ex victoriā, Caes.; in pass.: sperata gloria, Cic. With acc. and fut. infin.: sperant se maximum fructum esse capturos, Cic.; Pl., etc.; more rarely with pres. or perf. infin.: spero ex hoc ipso non esse obscurum, Cic.; spero cum Crassipede nos confecisse, Cic. L.; with ut and subj.: Liv.

(**2**) of bad things, *to anticipate, forebode, fear*: id quod non spero, Cic.; tantum dolorem, Verg.; Cat., etc.

(**3**) *to believe in, trust in*: deos, Pl.

¶ Hence partic. **spērātus** -a -um, *hoped for*: Cic. F. as subst. **spērāta** -ae, one's *'intended', betrothed, bride*: Pl. N. pl. as subst. **spērāta** -ōrum, one's *hopes*: potiri speratis, *to realize one's hopes*, Liv.

spēs -ĕi, f. *expectation.*

(**1**) most commonly, of good things, *hope.* LIT., spes est exspectatio boni, Cic.; spes emptionis, Cic.; summae spei adulescentes, *of great promise*, Caes.; spes est in vobis, *rests in you*, Cic.; omnem spem salutis in virtute ponere, Caes.; spem fallere, eripere, adimere,

perdere, Cic.; praeter spem, Cic.; contra
spem, Liv. Foll. by acc. and infin., in such
phrases as: magna me spes tenet, Cic.; in
spem adducti, Cic.; magnam in spem venire,
Caes. Foll. by ut and subj., in similar
phrases : spem adferre, Cic.; spe agitari, Tac.
Esp. *prospects, expectations*, as an heir: Hor.,
Tac. Transf., **a**, personif.: Spes, *Hope as a
goddess*, with several temples in Rome, Cic.,
Ov., etc.: **b**, concr., *that which is hoped
for, hope*: spe potitur, *realizes his hope*, Ov.;
castra Achivom, vestras spes, uritis, Verg.;
of living creatures: spes gregis, Verg.; spes
nostra reliqua, Cicero, Cic. L.

(2) of bad things, *anticipation, fear, foreboding*: mala res, spes multo asperior, Sall.;
Cic., Liv.

sphaera -ae, f. (σφαῖρα), *a globe, sphere*. In gen.:
Cic. Esp. *an astronomical globe* or *sphere*: Cic.

sphaeristērĭum -i, n. (σφαιριστήριον), *a place
for playing ball*: Plin. L., Suet.

sphaerŏmăchĭa -ae, f. (σφαιρομαχία), *a kind of
boxing in which the combatants had iron balls
strapped to their hands*: Sen.

Sphinx Sphingis, f. (Σφίγξ), *the Sphinx, a
mythical monster at Thebes, who set riddles to
the passers-by, and destroyed them if they
could not answer*: Pl., Plin., etc.

spīca -ae, f. (**spīcum** -i, n.: Cic. poet.)
(from same root as spina). Lit., *a spike*;
hence, *an ear of corn*: ad spicam perducere
fruges, Cic.; Ov., etc. Transf., (1) *the
brightest star in the constellation Virgo*: Cic.
poet., Plin. (2) *the tuft* or *head of other plants
resembling the shape of an ear of corn*: Ov.

spīcĕus -a -um (spica), *consisting of ears of
corn*: corona, Tib.; serta, Ov.; messis, Verg.

spīcĭfĕr -fĕra -fĕrum (spica/fero), *wearing* or
carrying ears of corn: Sen., Mart.

spīcĭlĕgĭum -i, n. (spica/lego), *a gleaning*:
Varr.

spīco -are (spica), *to furnish with spikes* or
ears: Plin.

spīcŭlum -i, n. (dim. of spicum), *a sharp
point, sting*. Lit., of bees: Verg.; of the
scorpion: Ov.; *the point* of a spear, arrow,
javelin: Cic., Liv., Hor. Transf., *a spear,
javelin, dart*: Cic., Verg., Ov.

spīna -ae, f. (from same root as spica), *a thorn.*
Lit., Lucr., Verg., etc.

Transf., (1) *a thorn-bush*: Ov., Plin.
(2) of the *prickles* or *prickly bones* of animals
and fish: Cic., Verg., Ov. (3) *anxieties,
difficulties, subtleties, perplexities*: disserendi,
Cic.; spinas animo evellere, Hor.

spīnētum -i, n. (spina), *a thorn-hedge, thorn-
brake*: Verg., Plin.

spīnĕus -a -um (spina), *made of thorns, thorny*:
Ov.

spīnĭfĕr -fĕra -fĕrum (spina/fero), *thorn-
bearing*: Cic. poet.

spīnōsus -a -um (spina), *full of thorns, thorny,
prickly*. Lit., herbae, Ov. Transf., (1) of
style, *thorny, crabbed, obscure*: disserendi
genus, Cic.; compar.: Cic. (2) *full of cares,
anxious*: Cat.

spintēr -ēris, n. (σφιγκτήρ), *a bracelet*: Pl.

spīnus -i, m. (spina), *the blackthorn*: Verg.

spīra -ae, f. (σπεῖρα), *anything coiled, wreathed,
twisted; a coil* of a snake: Verg.; *the base of a
column*: Plin.; *a string for fastening a hat* or
cap under the chin: Juv.

spīrābĭlis -e (spiro). (1) pass., *that may be
breathed*: natura, cui nomen est aër, Cic.;
lumen caeli, Verg. (2) Act., *able to breathe*:
viscera, Plin.

spīrācŭlum -i, n. (spiro), *an air-hole*: Lucr.,
Verg., Plin.

spīrāmen -ĭnis, n. (spiro). (1) *an air-hole*:
Enn., Luc. (2) *a breath, puff*: Luc., Stat.

spīrāmentum -i, n. (spiro). Lit., *a breathing-
hole, air-hole*: Verg. Transf., *a breathing-
time, short pause, interval*: temporum, Tac.

spīrĭtus -ūs, m. (spiro), *breathing, breath,
breeze.*

Lit., spiritus Boreae, Verg.; unguenti,
exhalation, Lucr.; spiritum ducere, *to draw
breath*, Cic.; angustior, *short breath*, Cic.;
spiritum intercludere, Liv.; petitus imo
spiritus, *a sigh*, Hor.

Transf., (1) *the breath of life, life*: spiritum
auferre, Cic.; extremum spiritum effundere
in victoria, Cic.; dum spiritus hos regit artus,
Verg. (2) *divine* or *poetic inspiration*: poetam
quasi divino quoddam spiritu inflari, Cic.;
spiritum Graiae tenuem Camenae, Hor.;
Prop., Liv. (3) in gen., *spirit, disposition*, esp.
a high spirit, pride; sing. and plur.: fiducia
ac spiritus, Caes.; filia Hieronis, inflata
muliebri spiritu, Liv.; spiritūs tribunicii,
Cic.

spīro -are, *to breathe, blow.*

(1) intransit. Lit., zephyri spirant, Verg.;
freta spirantia, *surging*, Verg.; spirat e pectore
flamma, Verg.; graviter spirantis thymbrae,
heavy-scented, Hor. Esp. of living creatures,
to breathe, draw breath: dum spirare potero,
Cic.; Verg., etc. Transf., **a**, *to be alive*: ab
eo spirante defendi, Cic.; videtur Laelii
mens spirare in scriptis, Cic.; Hor.: **b**, *to
seem to live*, of works of art: spirantia signa,
Verg.: **c**, *to have poetic inspiration, to be
inspired*: quod spiro et placeo tuum est, Hor.
(2) transit. Lit., *to breathe out, exhale*:
Diomedis equi spirantes naribus ignem,
Lucr.; spirare ignem naribus, Verg.;
zephyros spirare secundos, Verg.; ambro-
siaeque comae divinum vertice odorem
spiravere, Verg. Transf., homo tribunatum
etiamnunc spirans, *inspired with the spirit of
a tribune*, Liv.; tragicum satis, *to have tragic
genius*, Hor.; Lucr., etc.

spissāmentum -i, n. (spisso), *a stopper, plug*:
Sen.

spissē, adv. from spissus; q.v.

spissesco -ĕre (spissus), *to become thick,
thicken*: Lucr.

spissīgrădus -a -um (spissus/gradior), *stepping
slowly*: Pl.

spissĭtūdo -ĭnis, f. (spissus), *closeness, density*:
Sen.

spisso -are (spissus), *to make thick, thicken*:
Ov., Plin.

spissus -a -um, *close, dense, thick.* Lit., corpus,
Lucr.; theatrum, *full*, Hor.; harena, Verg.;
nubes, Ov.; with abl.: corona spissa viris,
Verg. Transf., *slow, tardy, difficult*: spissum
opus et operosum, Cic. L.; Cic.; compar.:
Cic.

¶ Hence adv. **spissē**. Lit., *densely,
closely*: Plin. Transf., *slowly*: spisse atque
vix ad aliquem pervenire, Cic.

splēn splēnis, m. (σπλήν), *the spleen, milt*:
Plin., Pers.

splendĕo -ēre, *to shine, glitter, be bright.* Lit., splendet tremulo sub lumine pontus, Verg.; Pl., Lucr., etc. Transf., virtus splendet per sese semper, Cic.; Liv.

splendesco -ĕre (splendeo), *to become bright.* Lit., Verg. Transf., nihil est tam incultum, quod non splendescat oratione, Cic.

splendĭdus -a -um, adj. (with compar. and superl.) (splendeo), *shining, clear, bright, brilliant, splendid.*
Lit., lumina solis, Lucr.; fons splendidior vitro, Hor.; splendidissimus candor, Cic.
Transf., (1) of sound, *clear*: vox, Cic. (2) of rank, style, dignity, etc., *fine, brilliant, distinguished, outstanding*: oratio, Cic.; domus, Cat.; facta, Hor.; vir splendidissimus, Cic. (3) *showy, specious*: verba, Ov.; Cic.
¶ Hence adv. (with compar.) **splendĭdē**. Lit., *splendidly, magnificently*: ornare convivium, Cic. Transf., *finely, nobly*: acta aetas honeste ac splendide, Cic.; loqui, Cic.; splendide mendax, Hor.

splendor -ōris, m. (splendeo), *brilliance, brightness, lustre.*
Lit., flammae, Ov.; argenti, Hor.; Pl., Lucr., Cic.
Transf., (1) of sound, *clarity*: vocis, Cic. (2) of rank, style, dignity, etc., *brilliance, splendour, lustre, distinction*: animi et vitae, Cic.; imperii, Cic.; verborum Graecorum, Cic.

splēnĭātus -a -um (splenium), *plastered*: Mart.

splēnĭum -i, n. (σπλήνιον), *an adhesive plaster*: Mart., Plin.

Spōlētĭum -i, n. *a city of Umbria* (now *Spoleto*).
¶ Hence adj. **Spōlētīnus** -a -um, *of Spoletium.*

spŏlĭārĭum -i, n. (spolium), *the place in the amphitheatre where the slain gladiators were stripped of their arms and clothing*: Sen.

spŏlĭātĭo -ōnis, f. (spolio), *a plundering, stripping.* Lit., omnium rerum, Cic.; Liv. Transf., consulatūs, dignitatis, Cic.

spŏlĭātor -ōris, m. (spolio), *a plunderer*: monumentorum, Cic.; templorum, Liv.; Juv.

spŏlĭātrix -trīcis, f. (spoliator), *a female plunderer*: Venus, Cic.; Mart.

spŏlĭo -are (spolium), *to rob a man of his clothes, strip, despoil.*
Lit., aliquem vestitu, Cic.; corpus caesi hostis, Liv.
Transf., in gen., *to plunder, rob, despoil*: aliquem, Pl.; fana sociorum, Cic.; aliquem argento, dignitate, Cic.; Verg., Liv., etc.
¶ Hence partic. (with compar.) **spŏlĭātus** -a -um, *plundered*: Cic. L.

spŏlĭum -i, n., usually plur., *the skin* or *hide stripped from an animal.*
Lit., ferarum, Lucr.; leonis, Ov.
Transf., (1) *arms and clothing*, esp. *when stripped from an enemy*: spolia caesorum legere, Liv.; spolia ampla referre, Verg.; for spolia opima, see opimus. (2) *any booty* or *plunder taken from an enemy, spoils*: spolia classium, Cic.; Caes., Verg., Liv. (3) in gen., *any kind of plunder* or *booty*: aliorum spoliis nostras facultates augeamus, Cic.; sceleris, *the golden hair which Scylla robbed from her father*, Ov.

sponda -ae, f. *the frame of a bed* or *sofa, a*

bedstead: Ov. Hence *a bed*: Hor.; *a sofa*: Verg.; *a bier*: Mart.

spondālĭum (spondaulĭum) -i, n. *a sacrificial hymn, accompanied on the flute*: Cic.

spondĕo spondēre spŏpondi sponsum (perhaps connected with σπένδω), *to pledge oneself to a thing, promise solemnly, engage.*
Lit., (1) as polit. and legal t. t.: quis spopondisse me dicit? Cic.; spondere pacem, Liv.; with acc. and infin.: si spopondissemus urbem hanc relicturum populum Romanum, Liv. Esp. *to be a security, go bail* for a person: hic sponsum (supine) vocat, Hor.; pro multis, Cic.; Liv. (2) in gen., *to promise, vow*; with acc.: iis honores et praemia, Cic.; fidem, Ov.; quod de me tibi spondere possum, Cic.; with acc. and infin.: promitto, recipio, spondeo C. Caesarem talem semper fore civem qualis, Cic.; Verg., Liv.
Transf., of things: quod propediem futurum spondet et virtus et fortuna vestra, Liv.; Verg., Ov.
¶ Hence partic. as subst.: m. **sponsus** -i, *a betrothed man, bridegroom*: Cic., Hor.; f. **sponsa** -ae, *a betrothed woman, bride*: Pl., Ter., Cic. L., Hor.; n. **sponsum** -i, *a covenant*: sponsum negare, Hor.; Cic.

spondeus -i, m. (σπονδεῖος), *a spondee, a metrical foot consisting of two long syllables* (− −): Cic., Hor.

spondȳlus -i, m. (σφόνδυλος), *a kind of mussel*: Plin., Sen., Mart.

spongĭa (spongĕa) -ae, f. (σπογγιά), *a sponge.*
Lit., raritas quaedam et adsimilis spongiis mollitudo, Cic.; Lucr., etc.
Transf., (1) *an open-worked cuirass*: Liv. (2) *the roots of the asparagus*: Plin., Mart.

sponsa -ae, f. subst. from spondeo; q.v.

sponsālis -e (spondeo), *of betrothal*: Varr. N. pl. as subst. **sponsālĭa** -ium or -iōrum, *a betrothal*: sponsalia facere, Cic. L., Liv., Ov. Also *a betrothal feast*: Cic. L.

sponsĭo -ōnis, f. (spondeo), *a solemn promise, engagement, guarantee.*
In gen.: non foedere sed per sponsionem pax facta est, Liv.; Sall.
Esp., in civil process, *a solemn promise* or *engagement between two parties that the loser shall forfeit a certain sum, a kind of legal wager*: sponsionem facere, Cic.; Liv. Hence *a wager*, in gen.: Juv.

sponsor -ōris, m. (spondeo), *a surety, bail, guarantor*: Cic., Ov.

sponsū, abl. as from sponsus, m. (spondeo), *by an engagement*: Cic. L.

sponsus -i, m. and **sponsum** -i, n. subst. from spondeo; q.v.

spontĕ, abl., and **spontis**, genit., as from spons, f. (spondeo).
Abl. **spontĕ**. (1) of persons: **a**, *willingly, voluntarily, of one's own accord*: Italiam non sponte sequor, Verg.; usually with possessive adj. agreeing, sponte meā, tuā, etc., or with possessive genit.: sponte deorum, Luc.; Cic., Verg., Liv., etc.: **b**, *by oneself, unaided*: nec sua sponte sed eorum auxilio, Cic. L.; Pl., Caes. (2) of things: **a**, *by itself, automatically*: clamor sua sponte ortus, Liv.; Cic., Verg., etc.: **b**, *in itself, for its own sake, alone*: an est aliquid quod te sua sponte delectet? Cic.
Genit. **spontĭs**, in phrase: suae spontis, *one's own master*, Varr.

sporta -ae, f. (connected with σπυρίς), *a basket, hamper*: Cato, Plin., Mart.

sportella -ae, f. (dim. of sporta), *a little basket, fruit-basket*: Cic. L., Suet.

sportŭla -ae. f. (dim. of sporta). LIT., *a little basket*: Pl. TRANSF., *the dole which great men were accustomed to give to their clients, in the form of either food or money*: Juv., Mart., Suet. Hence, *any gift, present*: Plin. L.

sprētĭo -ōnis, f. (sperno), *contempt, disdain*: Liv.

sprētor -ōris, m. (sperno), *a despiser*: deorum, Ov.

spūma -ae, f. (spuo), *foam, froth, scum*: spumas agere, *to foam at the mouth*, Lucr., Cic.; Venus spumā procreata, *from the foam of the sea*, Cic.; spumas salis aere ruebant, Verg.; spuma caustica, *a soap used by the Germans and Gauls for dyeing their hair red*, Mart.

spūmātus -a -um (spuma), *covered with foam*: Cic. poet.

spūmesco -ĕre (spuma), *to begin to foam*: Ov.

spūmĕus -a -um (spuma), *foaming, frothy*: Verg., Ov.

spūmĭfĕr -fĕra -fĕrum (spuma/fero), *foam-bearing, foaming*: amnis, Ov.

spūmĭgĕr -gĕra -gĕrum (spuma/gero), *foaming*: Lucr.

spūmo -are (spuma), *to foam, froth*: spumans aper, Verg.; Lucr., Juv.

spūmōsus -a -um (spuma), *foaming, full of foam*. LIT., Cat., Ov., Verg. TRANSF., carmen, *frothy*, Pers.

spŭo spŭĕre spŭi spūtum (cf. πτύω), *to spit out*: terram, Verg.
  N. of partic. as subst. **spūtum** -i, *spittle*: Lucr., etc.

spurcē, adv. from spurcus; q.v.

spurcĭdĭcus -a -um (spurcus/dico), *talking obscenely*: Pl.

spurcĭfĭcus -a -um (spurcus/facio), *making filthy, polluting*: Pl.

spurcĭtĭa -ae, f. and **spurcĭtĭes** -ēi, f. (spurcus), *dirt, filth*. LIT., Lucr., Varr., Plin. TRANSF., of character: Lucr.

spurco -are (spurcus), *to make dirty, defile, pollute*: Pl.
  ¶ Hence partic. **spurcātus** -a -um, *foul*; superl.: helluo spurcatissimus, Cic.

spurcus -a -um, adj. (with compar. and superl.), *dirty, filthy, unclean, impure*. LIT., Lucr., Cat. TRANSF., of character and life: homo spurcissimus, Cic.; Hor., Mart.
  ¶ Hence adv. **spurcē**, *basely, impurely*: quin in illam miseram tam spurce, tam impie dixeris, Cic.

spūtātĭlĭcus -a -um (sputo), *abominable, detestable*: ap. Cic.

spūtātor -ōris, m. (sputo), *a spitter*: Pl.

spūto -are (freq. of spuo), *to spit, spit out*. LIT., cum atro mixtos sanguine dentes, Ov.; Pl. TRANSF., *to avert by spitting*: morbus, qui sputatur, Pl.

spūtum -i, n. subst. from spuo; q.v.

squālĕo -ēre, *to be rough, stiff*.
  LIT., squalentes conchae, Verg.; with abl.: tunica squalens auro, *stiff with*, Verg.
  TRANSF., (1) *to be overgrown or dirty from neglect*: squalent abductis arva colonis, Verg.; barba squalens, Verg.; coma squalens, Ov.; Tac. (2) *to wear mourning*: squalent munícipia, Cic.

squālĭdus -a -um (squaleo), *rough, stiff, scaly*. LIT., corpora, Lucr.
  TRANSF., (1) *rough from want of attention, squalid, dirty*: homo, Pl.; humus, Ov. (2) *in mourning*: reus, Ov.; Tac. (3) of style, *rough*; compar.: suā sponte squalidiora sunt, Cic.
  ¶ Hence adv. (with compar.) **squālĭdē**, *roughly, in a slovenly manner*: dicere, Cic.

squālor -ōris, m. (squaleo), *roughness, stiffness*. LIT., Lucr.
  TRANSF., (1) *dirt or roughness arising from neglect*: squaloris plenus ac pulveris, Cic.; obsita squalore vestis, Liv.; Pl., Tac. (2) *mourning*: squalor et maeror, Cic.; Liv., Tac. (3) of style, *roughness*: Quint.

squālus -i, m. *a kind of fish*: Ov., Plin.

squāma -ae, f. *a scale*. LIT., of a fish, serpent, etc.: Cic., Verg. TRANSF., (1) *scale armour*: Verg. (2) *a fish*: Juv.

squāmĕus -a -um (squama), *scaly*: Verg., Ov.

squāmĭfĕr -fĕra -fĕrum (squama/fero), *scale-bearing, scaly*: Sen.

squāmĭgĕr -gĕra -gĕrum (squama/gero), *scale-bearing, scaly*: Ov. M. pl. as subst. **squāmĭgĕri** -ōrum, *fishes*: Lucr., Plin.

squāmōsus -a -um (squama), *covered with scales, scaly*: Pl., Verg., Ov.

st! interj. *hush! hist!*: Pl., Cic. L.

Stābĭae -ārum, f. *a town in Campania, destroyed with Pompeii and Herculaneum by the eruption of Mount Vesuvius*.

stăbĭlīmen -ĭnis, n. (stabilio), *a stay, support*: Acc.

stăbĭlīmentum -i, n. (stabilio), *a stay, support*: Pl., Plin.

stăbĭlĭo -ire (stabilis), *to make firm*. LIT., stipites, Caes.; Lucr. TRANSF., *to make stable, to establish*: rempublicam, Cic.; Pl., Liv.

stăbĭlis -e, adj. (with compar.) (sto), *firm, steady, stable*. LIT., via, Cic.; solum, Liv.; stabilior Romanus erat, Liv. TRANSF., amici, matrimonium, oratio, Cic.; nihil est tam ad diuturnitatem memoriae stabile, Cic.; Hor., Ov., etc.
  ¶ Hence adv. **stăbĭlĭtĕr**, *firmly, durably*: compar.: Suet.

stăbĭlĭtās -ātis, f. (stabilis), *firmness, stability*. LIT., peditum in proeliis, Caes.; stirpes stabilitatem dant iis, quae sustinent, Cic. TRANSF., *durability, steadfastness*: amicitiae, Cic.; fortunae, Cic.

stăbĭlĭtor -ōris, m. (stabilio), *one who makes firm*: Sen.

stăbŭlārĭus -i, m. (stabulum), *a low innkeeper*: Sen.

stăbŭlo -are (stabulum). (1) transit., *to stable cattle*: Varr. Pass.: Ov. (2) intransit., *to have a stall*: centauri in foribus (Orci), Verg.

stăbŭlum -i, n. (sto), *standing-room, quarters*: stabula alta ferarum, Verg.; taurorum, apium, Verg. Also of human accommodation: pastorum, Cic.; esp. in disparaging sense, *a pothouse, haunt, brothel*: Pl., Cic., Mart., Plin. L. Hence as a term of abuse: stabulum flagitii, Pl.

stacta -ae, f. and **stactē** -ēs, f. (στακτή), *oil of myrrh*: Pl., Lucr., Plin.

stădĭum -i, n. (στάδιον). (1) *a stade, a Greek measure of length, nearly 607 ft.* (2) *a race-course*: qui stadium currit, Cic.

Stăgīra -ōrum, n. pl. (Στάγειρα), *a town in Macedonia, birth-place of Aristotle*.

¶ Hence subst. **Stăgīrītēs** -ae, m. (Σταγειρίτης), *the Stagirite*, i.e. *Aristotle.*

stagno -are (stagnum). (1) intransit. LIT., of water, *to form a pool, stagnate*: stagnans flumine Nilus, Verg. TRANSF., of places, *to be overflowed, lie under water*: orbis stagnat paludibus, Ov. (2) transit., *to overflow, inundate*: Tiberis plana urbis stagnaverat, Tac.; Ov.

stagnum -i, n. (connected with sto). LIT., *standing water, a pool, pond, marsh, swamp*: Liv., Verg., etc. TRANSF., *any narrow or enclosed stretch of water*: Phrixeae stagna sororis, *the Hellespont*, Ov.; stagnum navale, Tac.; Verg.

stălagmĭum -i, n. (σταλάγμιον), *an ear-drop, pendant*: Pl.

stāmen -inis, n. (connected with sto; cf. στήμων from ἵστημι), *the warp, which in the upright looms of the ancients was stretched in a vertical direction.* LIT., stamen secernit arundo, Ov.; Varr., Tib. TRANSF., (1) *the thread hanging from the distaff*: stamina ducere, *or* torquere, *to spin*, Ov.; esp. *the thread spun by the Parcae*, Ov.; hence: de nimio stamine queri, *of too long a life*, Juv. (2) *a thread of another kind*, e.g., *that by which Ariadne guided Theseus through the labyrinth*: Prop.; of a spider: Ov.; *the string* of a lyre: Ov. (3) *cloth woven of thread*; hence, *the fillet worn by priests*: Prop.

stāmĭnĕus -a -um (stamen), *full of threads*: Prop.

stannum -i, n. *an alloy of silver and lead*: Plin., Suet.

Stăta mater, f. *a goddess, perhaps Vesta*: Cic.

stătārĭus -a -um (sto), *standing firm, steady, stable, stationary*: miles, Liv.; orator, *calm*, Cic. ¶ As subst., f. **stătārĭa** -ae (sc. comoedia), *a quiet kind of comedy*: Ter.; m. pl. **stătārĭi** -ōrum, *the actors in the* comoedia stataria: Cic.

Statelli and **Statĭelli** -ōrum, m. *a people of Liguria.* ¶ Hence adj. **Statellās** -ātis, *belonging to the Statelli*: Liv.

stătēra -ae, f. (στατήρ), *a steelyard a balance*: aurificis, Cic.; Suet.

stătĭcŭlum -i, n. (statua), *a small statue*: Plin.

stătĭcŭlus -i, m. (sto), *a kind of slow dance*: Pl.

stătim, adv. (sto). LIT., *without yielding, firmly, steadfastly*: rem gerere, Pl. TRANSF., (1) *regularly*: Ter. (2) *on the spot, immediately, at once*: Pl., Caes., Cic., etc.; statim ut, *as soon as*, Cic.

stătĭo -ōnis, f. (sto), *a standing, standing still.* LIT., manere in statione, *to stand still*, Lucr.; Ov., Plin. TRANSF., *a place of abode or sojourn.* In gen.: pone recompositas in statione comas, *in place*, Ov.; Cic. L., Verg. Esp. (1) as milit. t. t.: **a**, *post, station*: in statione esse, Caes.; stationem relinquere, Verg.; Liv., etc.; fig.: de praesidio et statione vitae decedere, Cic.: **b**, *a picket*, esp. in plur.: stationes dispositas, Caes., Liv. (2) nautical t. t., *a roadstead, anchorage*: statio male fida carinis, Verg.; Caes., Liv.; fluctibus eiectum tutā statione recepi, Ov.

Stătĭus -i, m. (1) Caecilius Statius, *a Roman comic poet, born* 168 B.C. (2) P. Papinius Statius, *a poet of Domitian's time, author of the* Silvae, *a* Thebais, *and an unfinished* Achilleis.

stătīvus -a -um (sto), *standing still*: praesidium, Cic.; castra, *fixed quarters*, Liv., etc. N. pl. as subst. **stătīva** -ōrum (sc. castra): Liv., Tac.

¹stător -oris, m. (sto), *a magistrate's attendant*: Cic. L.

²Stător -ōris, m. (sisto), *the stayer of flight; a surname of Jupiter*: Cic., Liv., Ov.

stătŭa -ae, f. (status), *a statue, image.* LIT., simulacra deorum, statuae veterum hominum, Cic.; Pl., Hor., etc. TRANSF., of an impassive person, *an image*: Pl.

stătŭārĭus -a -um (statua), *of or relating to statues*: Plin. ¶ As subst., f. **stătŭārĭa** -ae (sc. ars), *the art of sculpture*: Plin.; m. **stătŭārĭus** -i, *a maker of statues; a statuary*: Quint.

stătūmen -inis, n. (statuo), *a stay, support, prop*: Plin. Plur., *the ribs of a ship*: Caes.

stătŭo -ŭere -ŭi -ūtum (status, from sto), *to cause to stand, put, place, set, set up.* LIT., aram et statuam, Pl.; tropaeum, Cic.; tabernacula, *to pitch*, Caes.; urbem, Verg.; captivos in medio, Liv. TRANSF., (1) *to establish, settle* a principle or point: exemplum, Pl., Cic.; modum, with dat., *a limit to*, Cic., Hor., Liv.; ius, iura, Cic., Liv.; pretium, diem, Liv. (2) *to give a ruling* or *make arrangements* affecting other persons: de aliquo, Caes., Sall., Tac.; de capite civis, Cic.; in aliquem aliquid gravius, Caes.; stipendium alicui de publico, Liv; with ut *or* ne and subj.: Caes., Cic., Liv., Ov. (3) *to decide* on a course of action for oneself; with infin.: Caes., Cic., Liv., etc. (4) *to decide* on a matter of fact, *come to a considered opinion*; with acc. and infin.: laudem statuo esse maximam, Cic.; Cat., Ov., etc.; with double acc.: voluptatem summum bonum statuens, Cic.

stătūra -ae, f. (sto), *stature, height size* of a person: homines tantulae staturae, *of such small stature*, Caes.; Pl., Cic.

¹stătus, partic. from sisto; q.v.

²stătus -ūs, m. (sto), *a standing, standing position, posture.* LIT., in gen.: status, incessus, sessio, Cic.; erectus, Cic. Milit. t. t., *a position*: statu movere hostem, Liv.; fig.: Cic. TRANSF., of abstr. things, *position, condition, state, mode of operation.* (1) in human affairs, private or political: restituere aliquem in pristinum statum, Cic.; omnes vitae status, Cic.; agnationibus familiarum distinguuntur status, Cic.; civitatis, Cic., etc.; reipublicae, Cic., etc. (2) in nature: mundi atque naturae, Cic.; caeli, Liv.; Lucr. (3) as rhet. t. t., *the answer to the action brought*: Cic. Also *the essential point*: Quint.

stĕga -ae f. (στέγη), *a ship's deck*: Pl.

stella -ae, f. (=sterula, connected with ἀστήρ), *a star.* LIT., Lucr., Cic., Verg., etc.; stella Saturni, stella Iovis, *the planet Saturn, planet Jupiter*, Cic.; stellae inerrantes, *fixed stars*, Cic.; vagae, *planets*, Cic.; stella comans, *a comet*, Ov. Poet., *a constellation* (cf. sidus): Verg., Ov.; also the sun: auget geminos stella serena polos, Ov.

Transf., *a figure in the form of a star*: Plin., Suet.

stellans -antis (stella), *starry, set with stars*. Lit., caelum, Lucr., Verg., Ov. Transf., *bright, shining, glittering*: gemma, Ov.

Stellātis campus or **ager**, *a fruitful district in Campania*.

¶ Hence adj. **Stellātīnus** -a -um, *Stellatian*.

stellātus -a -um (stella), *set with stars, starry*: Cepheus, *made into a star*, Cic.; Argus, *having many eyes*, Ov.; ensis, *bright, glittering*, Verg.

stellĭfĕr -fĕra -fĕrum (stella/fero), *star-bearing, starry*: stellifer cursus, Cic.

stellĭgĕr -gĕra -gĕrum (stella/gero), *star-bearing, starry*: Varr., Cic. poet.

stellĭo (stēlĭo) -ōnis, m. *a lizard with spots on its back*: Verg.

stemma -ătis, n. (στέμμα). Lit., *a garland, chaplet*: Plin., Sen. Transf., (1) *a genealogical tree*: Juv., etc. (2) *antiquity*: Mart.

stercŏrĕus -a -um (stercus), *filthy, foul*: miles, Pl.

stercŏro -are (stercus), *to dung, manure*: agrum, Cic.

stercus -ŏris, n. *dung, muck, manure*: Cic., Hor., etc.; as a term of reproach: stercus curiae, Cic.

stĕrilis -e (connected with Gr. στερεός, στερρός), *barren, unfruitful*.

Lit., of animals and plants: ager, Verg.; vacca, Verg.; Lucr.

Transf., (1) act., *making unfruitful*: robigo, Hor.; hiems, Mart. (2) *bare, empty*: corpora sonitu sterila (=sterilia), Lucr.; Pl., Juv. (3) in gen., *fruitless, vain*: amor, *unrequited*, Ov.; pax, Tac.; with genit.: virtutum, *unproductive of*, Tac.

stĕrilĭtās -ātis, f. (sterilis), *unfruitfulness, barrenness*. Lit., agrorum, Cic.; mulierum, Plin. Transf., fortunae, Plin.

sternax -ācis (sterno), *throwing to the ground*: equus, *throwing his rider*, Verg.

sterno sternĕre strāvi strātum (cf. στορέννυμι).

(1) *to stretch out, spread out*. Lit., corpora passim, Liv.; vellus in duro solo, Ov.; strata iacent passim sua quaque sub arbore poma, Verg.; reflex., se sternere, *to lie down*: se somno in litore, Verg.; pass. as middle: sterni passim ferarum ritu, Liv. Esp. *to throw down violently, strike to the ground, lay low*: caede viros, Verg.; ariete muros, Liv.; ingenti caede sterni, Liv.; Hor., Ov. Transf., *to overthrow*: adflictos se et stratos esse fatentur, Cic.

(2) *to strew, spread a thing* (with something else). Lit., with abl.: cubilia herbis, Lucr.; solum telis, Verg.; foliis nemus, Hor.; semitam saxo quadrato, Liv. Absol.: lectum, *to make, make up*, Pl., Cic.; equos, *to saddle*, Liv.; viam, *to pave*, Lucr. Transf., placidi straverunt aequora venti, *made smooth*, Verg.; odia militum, *to calm, allay*, Tac.

¶ Hence n. of partic. as subst. **strātum** -i, *a covering*. (1) *a bed-covering, coverlet, blanket*: Lucr., Ov.; hence *a bed*: molle stratum, Liv.; strato surgere, Verg. (2) *a horse-cloth, saddle-cloth, saddle*: Ov., Liv. (3) *a pavement*: strata viarum, Lucr.

sternūmentum -i, n. (sternuo), *a sneezing, sneeze*: Cic., Plin.

sternŭo -ŭĕre -ŭi (connected with πτάρνυμαι),

to sneeze. Lit., Plin.; with internal acc.: omen, Prop.; Cat. Transf., of a light, *to crackle, sputter*: Ov.

sternūtāmentum -i, n. (sternuo), *a sneezing, sneeze*: Sen.

sterquĭlĭnĭum -i, n. (stercus), *a dung-heap*: Pl., Ter., Varr.

Stertĭnĭus -ii, m. *a Stoic philosopher*: Hor.

sterto -ĕre, *to snore*: Pl., Lucr., Cic.

Sthĕnĕlus -i, m. (Σθένελος). (1) *one of the Epigoni, charioteer of Diomedes at Troy*. (2) *a king of Liguria, whose son Cycnus was changed into a swan*.

¶ Hence adj. **Sthĕnĕlēïus** -a -um, *Sthenelean*: proles, *Cycnus*, Ov.; f. adj. **Sthĕnĕlēïs** -ïdis, *Sthenelean*: volucris, *the swan*, Ov.

stĭbădĭum -i, n. (στιβάδιον), *a semicircular seat*: Mart., Plin. L.

stĭbĭum -i, n. (στίβι), *antimony*, used for dyeing the eyebrows and as an eye-salve: Plin.

stigma -ătis, n. (στίγμα). Lit., *a brand put upon slaves*: Sen., Juv., etc. Transf., (1) *infamy, stigma*: Mart., Suet. (2) *a cut inflicted by an unskilful barber*: Mart.

stigmătĭās -ae, m. (στιγματίας), *a branded slave*: Cic.

stilla -ae, f. (dim. of stiria), *a drop*: Cic., Mart.

stillĭcĭdĭum -i, n. (stilla/cado), *dripping* or *dropping moisture*: Lucr., Sen. Esp. *rain-water falling from the eaves of houses*: Cic.

stillo -are (stilla).

(1) intransit., *to drip, drop*. Of liquids, *to drip down*: de ilice stillabant mella, Ov.; Lucr. Of other things, *to drip with liquid*: saxa guttis, Lucr.; pugio stillans, *dripping with blood*, Cic.; Ov., Juv. (2) transit., *to drop, let drop*. Lit., ex oculis rorem, Hor., Ov. Transf., *to instil* feelings or ideas: tuae litterae, quae mihi quiddam quasi animulae stillarunt, Cic.; Juv.

stĭlus (not **stȳlus**) -i, m. (for stiglus; cf. στίζω, στίγμα).

(1) *a stake, pale*: Auct. B. Afr.

(2) *the pointed iron* or *bone instrument with which the Romans wrote on their waxen tablets*. Lit., Pl., Cic., Hor.; vertere stilum, *to turn the stilus, in order to erase with its blunt end*, Cic., Hor. Transf., **a**, *writing, composing, written composition*: Cic., Quint., Plin. L.: **b**, *mode of writing, speaking, style*: stilus exercitatus, *a practised pen*, Cic.; unus sonus est totius orationis et idem stilus, Cic.

stĭmŭlātĭo -ōnis, f. (stimulo), *a spurring on, stimulating*: Plin., Tac.

stĭmŭlātrix -īcis, f. (stimulator), *she that incites, a female stimulator*: Pl.

stĭmŭlĕus -a -um (stimulus), *relating to the goad*: supplicium, *punishment* (of slaves) *with the goad*, Pl.

stĭmŭlo -are (stimulus).

Lit., *to goad, prick*: Luc.

Transf., (1) *to disquiet, vex, annoy*: te conscientiae stimulant maleficiorum tuorum, Cic.; Pl., Cat., Liv. (2) *to incite, stir up, stimulate*: mentes, Lucr.; aliquem, Liv.; ad huius salutem defendendam stimulari, Cic.; ad arma, Liv.; ad iram, Tac. With infin.: Verg., Luc.

stĭmŭlus -i, m. and **stĭmŭlum**, n.: Pl. (for stig-mulus; cf. στίζω).

(1) milit. t. t., *a pointed stake to check the advance of troops*: Caes.

(2) *a goad, used for driving cattle, slaves,* etc. Lit., Pl., Tib., Ov. Transf., **a**, *a sting, torment*: doloris, Cic.; amoris, Liv.; Ov.: **b**, *a goad, spur, incentive*: gloriae, Cic.; alicui stimulos admovere, Cic.; Liv., etc.

stinguo -ĕre, *to extinguish* or *annihilate*: Lucr.

stīpātĭo -ōnis, f. (stipo), *a crowd of attendants, retinue*: Cic., Plin. L.

stīpātŏr -ōris, m. (stipo), *an attendant, follower*; plur., *a suite, train, retinue*: Cic., Sall., Hor.

stīpendĭārĭus -a -um (stipendium).

(1) *liable to taxes or tribute, tributary*: Aeduos sibi stipendiarios factos, Cic.; vectigal, *a yearly contribution*, Cic. M. pl. as subst. **stīpendĭārĭi** -ōrum, *tributaries*: socii stipendiariique populi Romani, Cic.; Caes., Liv.

(2) *of soldiers, serving for pay*: Liv.

stīpendĭum -i, n. (=stipipendium, from stips/pendo).

(1) *a tax, tribute, contribution*. Lit., stipendium imponere alicui, Caes.; pacisci annuum stipendium, Liv.; pendĕre, Caes., Liv., etc. Transf., *punishment*: quod me manet stipendium? Hor.; Cat.

(2) *the pay of a soldier*. Lit., stipendium numerare militibus, Cic.; dare, Liv.; persolvere, Cic. L.; flagitare, Caes.; stipendia merere, mereri, *to serve in the army*, Cic. Transf., **a**, *military service*: finis stipendiorum, Cic.; Sall., Liv., Tac.: **b**, *a year's service, campaign*: septem et viginti enumerare stipendia, Liv.; Pl., Tac.; fig.: tamquam emeritis stipendiis libidinis, ambitionis, Cic.

stīpĕs -ĭtis, m. *a log, stump, trunk of a tree.* In a rough state; poet., *a tree*: Ov.; *a branch*: Luc., Mart. Fashioned, *a post*: Caes.; *a club*: Ov. As a term of reproach, *blockhead*: Ter.

stīpo -are (connected with στέφω).

(1) *to press closely together, compress*: mella (of bees), Verg.; in arto stipatae naves, Liv.; Graeci stipati, quini in lectulis, saepe plures, Cic.

(2): **a**, *to crowd a place*: curia patribus stipata, Ov.; Plin. L.: **b**, *to press round a person, accompany, surround, attend*: senatum armatis, Cic. Transf., senectus stipata studiis iuventutis, Cic.

stips stĭpis, f. *a small coin, as a religious offering, gift*, or *fee*: stipem conferre, Liv.; Cic., Ov., Tac.

stīpŭla -ae, f. *a stalk, haulm*: Verg., Plin. Hence *stubble*: Verg., etc. Of a flute made of a reed, *a reed-pipe*: Verg.

stīpŭlātĭo -ōnis, f. (stipulor), *an agreement, covenant, stipulation*: Cic.

stīpŭlātĭuncŭla -ae, f. (dim. of stipulatio), *a trifling engagement* or *stipulation*: Cic.

stīpŭlātŏr -ōris, m. (stipulor), *one who demands a formal agreement*: Suet.

stīpŭlor -ari, dep. *to demand a formal agreement, to bargain, stipulate*: Pl., Varr., Cic.

stīrĭa -ae, f. *an icicle*: Verg., Plin., Mart.

stirpĭtŭs, adv. (stirps), *root and branch, thoroughly, entirely*: Cic.

stirps (**stirpes, stirpis**), stirpis, f. rarely m., *the stock* or *stem* of a tree or other plant, with the roots.

Lit., Cic., Verg., etc. Sometimes *a young*

shoot or *sprout*: Lucr. Also *a plant*: stirpes et herbae, Cic.; Luc., Tac.

Transf., (1) of men, *stock, source, origin*: divina, Verg.; ne Italicae quidem stirpis, Liv.; Herculis, Cic. Also concr., *offspring*: stirpem ex se relinquere, Liv. (2) *the root* of a race, city, etc., often with reference to wholesale destruction: Carthago ab stirpe interiit, *root and branch*, Sall.; Liv. (3) of abstr. things, *root, foundation, origin*: virtutis, stultitiae, superstitionis, Cic.

stīva -ae, f. *a plough-handle*: Verg.

stlātārĭus -a -um (from stlata, *a kind of ship*), *brought by sea, and therefore, costly*: Juv.

stlīs, archaic=lis; q.v.

stloppus -i, m. *the noise of a slap on the inflated cheeks*: Pers.

sto stāre stĕti stătum (cf ἵστημι, ἕστην), *to stand, stand still, remain standing.*

Lit., (1) of persons. In gen.: cum virgo staret, et Caecilia in sella sederet, Cic.; ad ianuam, Cic.; Verg., etc. Esp.: **a**, milit. t. t., *to stand, to be stationed*: ut quisque steterat, iacet, Pl.; pro portā, Liv.; Caes. Also *to stand firm*: stare in pugnā, Liv.; Caes.: **b**, in gen., *to stand fast, stay*: Cic., Hor. (2) of lifeless objects: **a**, *to stand up, stand firm*: domus, Cic.; statuae in rostris, Cic.; muri, Liv.; iam stabant Thebae, Ov.: **b**, of ships, *to lie at anchor*: stant litore puppes, Verg.; stare ad ancoram in salo Romana classis non poterat, Liv.: **c**, *to stand stiffly, be rigid*: obstipui, stĕteruntque comae, Verg.; with abl.: vides ut alta stet niva candidum Soracte, Hor.

Transf., in gen., *to stand*, of abstr. things: mentes rectae quae stare solebant, Enn.; pericula stant circum aliquem, Verg. Esp. (1) *to remain, be fixed*: stat sua cuique dies, Verg.; diu pugna neutro inclinata stetit, Liv.; (natura) tantā stat praedita culpā, Lucr.; omnis in Ascanio cari stat cura parentis, *rests upon*, Verg.; stat alicui sententia, with infin., *one is resolved to*, Liv., Ov.; so stat, alone: Cic. L., Verg. (2) *to stand firm, persist*: utinam respublica stetisset quo coeperat statu, Cic.; respublica stetit virtute tuā, Liv.; stas animo, Hor.; in fide stare, Cic.; in sententiā, Liv.; with abl.: suis stare iudiciis, *to stand by*, Cic. (3) of a play, *to succeed, hold the stage*: Hor. (4) with ab, cum, pro, *to stand by, be on the side of, support*: a senatu et a bonorum causā, Cic.; di cum Hannibale, Liv.; pro vobis adversus reges, Liv. (5) *to cost* (like English *stand*); with abl. of price, dat. of the party paying: centum talentis ea res Achaiis, Liv.; multo sanguine ac vulneribus ea Poenis victoria stetit, Liv.; Cic., Verg., etc. (6) stare per aliquem, *to happen through someone's fault, be due to someone*: per me stetisse ut credat, Ter.; a negative consequence is expressed by a clause with ne, quin, or quominus, e.g.: ne praestaremus per vos stetit, *it was your fault that we did not*, Liv.

Stōĭcus -a -um (Στωικός), *of the Stoic philosophy, Stoic*: schola, Cic. L.; libelli, Hor. As subst., m. **Stōĭcus** -i, *a Stoic philosopher, Stoic*: Cic., Hor.; n. pl. **Stōĭca** -ōrum, *the Stoic philosophy*: Cic.

¶ Hence adv. **Stōĭcē**, *like a Stoic, stoically*: Cic.

stŏla -ae, f. (στολή), *a long outer garment*; esp. *as worn by Roman matrons, and by musicians*: Cic., Hor., Ov. Transf., *a matron*: Plin., Stat.

stŏlātus -a -um (stola), *clad in a* stola: Suet. Transf., *matronly*: Mart.

stŏlĭdus -a -um, adj. (with compar. and superl.), *stupid, foolish, dull, obtuse*; of persons: o vatum stolidissime, Ov.; Lucr., Hor., etc.; of things: fiducia, superbia, Liv.; Cic., Ov.
¶ Hence adv. **stŏlĭdē**, *stupidly*: stolide laetus, stolide ferox, Liv.; Sall., Tac.

stŏmāchor -ari, dep. (stomachus), *to be angry, irritated, vexed*: stomachari coepit, Cic.; cum Metello, Cic.; iucundissimis tuis litteris, Cic.; quod de eādem re agam saepius, Cic. L.; se quid asperius dixeram, Cic.; with n. acc.: omnia, Cic. L.

stŏmāchōsus -a -um (stomachus), *peevish, irritable, cross*: Cic., Hor.; compar.: Cic. L.
¶ Hence compar. adv. **stŏmāchōsĭŭs**, *rather angrily*: rescripsi ei stomachosius, Cic. L.

stŏmāchus -i, m. (στόμαχος), *the gullet, the oesophagus.*
Lit., Cic.
Transf., (1) *the stomach*: stomachi calor, Cic.; stomachus aeger, Hor. (2) stomachus bonus, *a good digestion*; hence *good humour*, Mart., Quint. (3) *taste, liking*: ludi apparatissimi, sed non tui stomachi, Cic. L.; Plin. L. (4) *distaste, vexation, chagrin, anger*: stomachum facere, *or* movere, alicui, Cic.; epistula plena stomachi, Cic.; Hor.

stŏrĕa (**stŏrĭa**) -ae, f. (connected with στορέννυμι), *a rush mat*: Caes., Liv.

strābo -ōnis, m. (στραβών), *a squinter*: Cic., Hor. Hence, *an envious person*: Varr.

strāges -is, f. (sterno), *a throwing to the ground, overthrowing*, as a process; also, as a result, *debris*. In gen.: armorum, Liv.; aedificiorum et hominum, Tac.; stragem facere, Liv.; dare, Verg. Esp., *a slaughter, massacre, carnage*: confusae stragis acervus, Verg.; strages (plur.) facere, Cic.; edere, Cic., Verg.

strāgŭlus -a -um (sterno), *covering, serving as a cover, carpet*, etc.: vestis stragula, Cic., Hor., Liv. N. as subst. **strāgŭlum** -i, *a covering, rug, carpet, mattress*, etc.: textile, Cic.; Suet., Mart.

strāmen -ĭnis, n. (sterno), *straw, litter*: Verg., Ov., Plin.

strāmentum -i, n. (sterno), *straw, litter.*
Lit., casae, quae more Gallico stramentis erant tectae, Caes.; Verg., Hor., Liv. Transf., *a saddle, housing* (for mules): Caes.

strāmĭnĕus -a -um (stramen), *made of straw*: casa, Prop.; Quirites, *figures of straw thrown every year into the Tiber*, Ov.

strangŭlo -are, *to choke, strangle, throttle.*
Lit., aliquem, Cic. L.; strangulata laqueo, Tac.; Suet. Transf., *vocem*, Quint.; strangulat inclusus dolor, Ov.

strangūria -ae, f. (στραγγουρία), *a painful discharge of urine, strangury*: Cic., Plin.

strătēgēma -ătis, n. (στρατήγημα), *a piece of generalship, a stratagem.* Lit., Cic. Transf., strategemate hominem percussit, Cic. L.

strătēgus -i, m. (στρατηγός), *a general.* Lit., Pl. Transf., *the president* at a banquet: Pl.

strătĭōtĭcus -a -um (στρατιωτικός), *soldierly, soldierlike*: homo, Pl.

Strătŏnīcĕa -ae, f. (Στρατονίκεια), *a town in Caria.*
¶ Hence adj. **Strătŏnīcēus** -a -um and **Strătŏnīcensis** -e, *belonging to Stratonicea.*

strātum -i, n., subst. from sterno; q.v.

strātūra -ae, f. (sterno), *a paving, pavement*: Suet.

strēna -ae, f. Lit., *a favourable omen*: Pl. Transf., *a new year's gift* (Fr. étrennes): Suet.

strēnŭĭtās -ātis, f. (strenuus), *briskness*: Ov.

strēnŭo -are (strenuus), *to be brisk, prompt, active*: Pl.

strēnŭus -a -um, *brisk, prompt, active, vigorous.*
Lit., of persons: homo, Ter.; Cic.; fortis ac strenuus socius, Liv.; gens linguā strenua magis quam factis, Liv.; compar.: strenuior, Pl.; superl.: strenuissimus quisque ut occiderat in proelio, Sall. In a bad sense, *turbulent, restless*: Tac.
Transf., navis, *fast*, Ov.; inertia, *masterly inactivity*, Hor.
¶ Hence adv. **strēnŭē**, *briskly, promptly, actively*: arma capere, Cic.; Pl., Ter.

strĕpĭto -are (freq. of strepo), *to make much noise*; *to rustle, rattle, clatter*: Verg., Tib.

strĕpĭtus -ūs, m. (strepo), *a loud noise*; *a clattering, crashing, creaking, rumbling.* In gen.: rotarum, Caes.; fluminum, Cic.; valvarum, Hor.; inter strepitum tot bellorum, Liv.; plur.: strepitus nocturni, Liv. Of music: testudinis aureae dulcem strepitum, Hor.

strĕpo -ĕre -ŭi -ĭtum, *to make a loud noise*; *to clatter, creak, rattle, clash, rumble.*
(1) with the source of the noise as subject. Lit., mixti strepentium paventiumque clamores, Liv.; arma et scuta offensa quo levius streperent, *might make less noise*, Sall.; fluvii strepunt hibernā nive turgidi, Hor.; litui, Hor.; galea, Verg. With acc. of the noise made: haec cum (milites) streperent, *cried out*, Liv. Transf., intra arcem sententia Messalini strepebat, Tac.
(2) with places, etc., as subject, *to resound, ring* with noise: murmure campus, Verg.; aures clamoribus, Liv.

stria -ae, f. *a furrow, groove*: Varr.

strictim, adv. (stringo), *grazingly.* Hence (1) *close to the skin*: attondere, Pl. (2) *superficially, slightly, briefly, summarily*: aspicere, dicere, Cic.

strictūra -ae, f. (stringo), *a mass of iron*: Verg.

strictus -a -um, partic. from stringo; q.v.

strīdĕo strīdēre strīdi and **strīdo** strīdēre strīdi, *to make a harsh noise*; *to creak, grate, hiss*, etc.: of a metal: Lucr., Verg.; of a missile: Verg.; of the wind: Verg.; of the rope of a ship: Ov.; of a waggon: Verg.; of the sea: Verg.; of snakes: Tib., Verg.; of bees, *to hum*: Verg.

strīdor -ōris, m. (strido), *a creaking, grating, hissing, whistling cry* or *noise*; of the wind: Cic.; of the hinge of a door: Cic.; of a saw: Cic.; of elephants, *trumpeting*: Liv.; of a snake: Ov.; of a pig, *grunting*: Ov.; of asses, *braying*: Ov.; of bees, *humming*: Ov.; of men: tribuni plebis, Cic.

strīdŭlus -a -um (strido), *creaking, hissing, whistling, grating*: cornus (of a spear), Verg.; plaustra, Ov.; Sen.

strĭgĭlis -is (stringo), *a scraper used at the baths*: Pl., Cic., Hor., etc.

strĭgo -are. LIT., *to halt in ploughing*: Plin. TRANSF., in gen., *to check, stop*: Verg., Sen.

strĭgōsus -a -um (stringo), *lean, thin*. LIT., compar.: equi strigosiores, Liv. TRANSF., of an orator, *dry, meagre*: Cic.

stringo stringĕre strinxi strictum.

(1) *to draw tight together, to bind, tie*: tamquam laxaret elatum pedem ab stricto nodo, Liv.; stringebant magnos vincula parva pedes, Ov.; of cold: stricta matutino frigore vulnera, Liv.

(2) *to strip off, pluck, clip, prune*. LIT., folia ex arboribus, Caes.; frondes, Verg.; rubos, Liv.; esp., *to draw a weapon from its sheath, to unsheathe*: gladium, Caes., Verg., Liv.; ferrum, cultrum, Liv. TRANSF., stringatur iambus in hostes, Ov.

(3) *to graze, to touch lightly*. LIT., metas interiore rotā, Ov.; Verg., Prop. TRANSF., **a,** *to affect, injure*: nomen, Ov.; animum strinxit patriae pietatis imago, Verg.: **b,** in speech, *to touch upon*: Quint.

¶ Hence partic. (with compar.) **strictus** -a -um, *drawn together*. Hence (1) *close, tight*: nodus, Liv.; superl.: ianua strictissima, Ov. (2) of style, *brief, concise*: Quint. (3) *rigid, severe, strict*: Stat.

stringor -ōris, m. (stringo), *a shock from a touch, a twinge*: gelidai aquai, Lucr.

strix strĭgis, f. (στρίγξ), *a screech-owl*: Pl., Ov., etc.

strŏpha -ae, f. (στροφή), *a trick, device, artifice*: Sen., Mart., Plin. L.

strŏphĭārĭus -i, m. (strophium), *one who makes* or *sells strophia*: Pl.

strŏphĭum -i, n. (στρόφιον). (1) *a breast-band, stay, stomacher*: Pl., Cic., Cat. (2) *a head-band, a chaplet*: Verg.

Strŏphĭus -i, m. (Στρόφιος), *king of Phocis, father of Pylades*: Strophio natus, *Pylades*, Ov.

structĭlis -e (struo), *of building, used in building*: Mart.

structor -ōris, m. (struo). (1) *a builder, mason, carpenter*: Cic. L. (2) *a waiter, server, carver*: Mart., Juv.

structūra -ae, f. (struo), *a building, erecting, constructing*.

LIT., parietum, Caes. Also concr, *a building*: Plin.

TRANSF., of style, *arrangement, putting together*: verborum, Cic.; carminis, Ov.; Quint., Tac.

strŭēs -is, f. (struo), *a heap*: pontes et moles ex humanorum corporum strue facere, Liv.; lignorum, Liv.; Cic. L., Tac. Esp., *a heap of small sacrificial cakes*: Cato, Ov.

strŭix -īcis, f. (struo), *a heap*: Pl.

strūma -ae, f. (?struo), *a scrofulous tumour, struma*: Cic., Plin.

strūmōsus -a -um (struma), *afflicted with struma, scrofulous*: Juv.

strŭo strŭĕre struxi structum (connected with στορέννυμι, sterno), *to put together, put in order*.

LIT., (1) *to pile up*: ordinatim trabes, Caes.; arbores in pyram, Ov.; altaria donis, *to load with*, Verg., Hor. (2) *to build, erect, construct*: pyras, Verg.; domos, Hor.; Tac.; fornices, Liv. (3) *to arrange, dispose*: aciem, Verg., Liv., Caes.

TRANSF., (1) *to prepare* (something bad), *to devise, contrive*: alicui aliquid calamitatis, Cic.; periculosas libertati opes, Liv.; crimina et accusatores, Tac. (2) *to set in order, arrange*: rem domi, Pl.; compositi oratoris bene structa conlocatio, Cic.

strūthĕus (strūthĭus) -a -um (στρούθιος), *of a sparrow*: māla, *sparrow-apples, quinces*, Pl., Cato.

strūthĭŏcămēlus -i, m. (στρουθιοκάμηλος), *an ostrich*: Plin.

Strӯmō (-ōn) -mŏnis, m. (Στρυμών), *a river on the border of Thrace* (now *Struma*).

¶ Hence adj. **Strӯmŏnĭus** -a -um, *Strymonian*; poet. = *Thracian*: Ov.

stŭdĕo -ēre -ŭi (perhaps connected with σπεύδω, σπουδή, σπουδάζω), *to be eager, be earnest, take pains, strive after, be busy with*.

In gen., usually with dat.: praeturae, Cic.; novis rebus, *political change*, Caes., Cic.; laudi, Cic. With acc., esp. n.: id studere, ne super impunitatem etiam praemio sceleris frueretur, Liv.; id ut, Pl., Ter.; hoc unum, Hor. With infin., or acc. and infin.: studeo scire quid egeris, *I should like to know*, Cic.; Pl., Caes., etc.

Esp. (1) *to side with, support, favour*: Catilinae, Cic.; Ov., etc. (2) *to study* a subject: litteris, arti, Cic.; Quint., Tac.

stŭdĭōsus -a -um, adj. (with compar. and superl.) (studium), *eager, zealous, diligent, anxious, striving*.

In gen.: homo, Cic.; with genit.: venandi aut pilae, Cic.; dicendi, Cic.; studiosissimus homo natandi, Cic.; Hor., Ov.; with dat.: Pl.

Esp. (1) *favouring* a person or side, *partial, attached, devoted*; with genit.: studiosissimus existimationis meae, Cic. (2) *devoted to learning, studious*: cohors, Hor.; with genit.: litterarum, Cic.; m. pl. as subst., *students*: Cic.

¶ Hence adv. (with compar. and superl.) **stŭdĭōsē**, *eagerly, zealously, diligently*: qui haec caelestia vel studiosissime solet quaerere, Cic.; Ter., Ov., etc.

stŭdĭum -i, n. (studeo), *zeal, eagerness, application, fondness, enthusiasm, striving*.

In gen.: alacritate ac studio uti, Caes.; studio duci, Cic. With subjective genit.: amici, Cic.; with objective genit.: pugnae, Lucr.; pugnandi, Caes.; dicendi, Cic.; visendi, Verg. Plur.: Cic., Hor.

Esp. (1) *attachment to, zeal for, devotion to, goodwill towards* a person or cause: Diviciaci in populum Romanum, Caes.; studia Numidarum in Iugurtham accensa, Sall.; aliquid studio partium facere, Cic.; contraria studia, Verg. (2) *application to learning, study*; with genit.: doctrinae, Cic.; plur.: se studiis illis dedisse, Cic.; Hor.

stultē, adv. from stultus; q.v.

stultĭlŏquentĭa -ae, f. and **stultĭlŏquĭum** -i, n. (stultus/loquor), *foolish talk*: Pl.

stultĭlŏquus -a -um (stultus/loquor), *talking foolishly*: Pl.

stultĭtĭa -ae, f. (stultus), *foolishness, folly, silliness*: multorum stultitiam perpessum esse, Cic.; plur.: hominum ineptias ac stultitias non ferebat, Cic.; Caes., Hor., etc.

stultĭvĭdus -a -um (stultus/video), *seeing things in a foolish light*: Pl.

stultus

stultus -a -um, adj. (with compar. and superl.) (connected with stolidus), *foolish, silly, fatuous.* Lit., of persons: reddere, Pl., Cic., etc. M. as subst., *a simpleton, a fool*: Pl., Cic., etc. Transf., of things: loquacitas, Cic.; consilium stultissimum, Liv.; Ov., etc. ¶ Hence adv. (with compar. and superl.) **stultē**, *foolishly, sillily*: Pl., Cic., Liv.

stūpa=stuppa; q.v.

stŭpěfăcĭo -făcěre -fēci -factum, and pass. **stŭpěfīo** -fĭěri -factus sum (stupeo/facio), *to make senseless, benumb, stun*: privatos luctūs stupefecit publicus pavor, Liv.; stupefacti dicentum intuentur, Cic.; Verg., etc.

stŭpěo -ēre -ŭi, *to be stunned, struck senseless, astounded, amazed.*

Lit., of persons: cum semisomnus stuperet, Cic.; haec cum loqueris nos stupemus, Cic.; with abl. (*at* or *by*): carminibus, Hor.; Liv.; with in and abl.: in Turno, Verg.; Hor.; with ad: ad auditas voces, Ov.; Sen.; with acc.: donum exitiale Minervae, Verg.

Transf., of inanimate things, *to stand still, halt, cease*: stupuit Ixionis orbis, Ov.; stupente seditione, Liv.; stupuerunt verba palato, *died away*, Ov.

stŭpesco stŭpescĕre stŭpŭi (stupeo), *to become amazed, astounded*: Cic.

stŭpĭdĭtās -ātis, f. (stupidus), *dullness, senselessness*: Cic.

stŭpĭdus -a -um (stupeo). Lit., *senseless, stunned*: Pl., Cic. Transf., *stupid, dull*: stupidum esse Socratem dixit, Cic.; Mart., Juv.

stŭpor -ōris, m. (stupeo).

Lit., (1) *senselessness, insensibility*: sensūs, Cic.; in corpore, Cic. (2) *astonishment, amazement*: stupor patres defixit, Liv.

Transf., *dullness, stupidity*: Cic.

stuppa (**stūpa**) -ae, f. (στύππη), *tow, oakum*: Caes., Liv., etc.

stuppěus -a -um (stuppa), *made of tow*: vincula, Verg.; Ov.

stŭprātor -ōris, m. (stupro), *a ravisher, defiler*: Quint., Suet.

stŭpro -are (stuprum), *to ravish*: Pl., Cic., Liv. Also, in gen., *to defile, pollute*: pulvinar, Cic.

stŭprum -i, n. *disgrace, defilement*; esp. *ravishing, violation*: stuprum facere, inferre, Cic.; Pl., Liv., etc.

sturnus -i, m. *a starling*: Plin., Stat.

Stўgĭālis, Stygius; *see* Styx.

stўlŏbătēs -is and **stўlŏbăta** -ae, m. (στυλοβάτης), *the pedestal of a row of columns*: Varr.

stўlus, *see* stilus.

Stymphālus -i, m. and **Stymphālum** -i, n. (Στύμφαλος), *a lake with a river and town of the same name in Arcadia, haunt of mythical birds of prey with iron feathers, which were destroyed by Hercules.*

¶ Hence adj. **Stymphālĭcus** and **Stymphālĭus** -a -um, *Stymphalian*; and f. adj. **Stymphālis** -ĭdis, *Stymphalian.*

Styx, Stўgis and Stўgos; acc. Stўgem and Stўga; f. (Στύξ).

(1) *a river in Arcadia.*

(2) *a river in the infernal regions, by which the gods swore*; meton., *the lower world*: Verg.

¶ Hence adj. **Stўgĭālis** -e, *belonging to the Styx, Stygian*; and adj. **Stўgĭus** -a -um, *Stygian, infernal*: cymba (*or* carina), *the boat of Charon*, Verg.; Iuppiter, *or* pater, *or* rex,

sub

Pluto, Verg.; bubo, *dismal*, Ov.; vis, *fatal*, Verg.

sŭādēla -ae, f. (suadeo), *persuasion*: Pl. Personif.=Πειθώ, *the goddess of persuasion*: Hor.

sŭāděo suadēre suāsi suāsum, *to present in a pleasing manner*; hence *to recommend, advise.*

Lit., usually with dat. of person advised, the course advised being expressed by an acc., or an infin., or ut/ne with subj.: an C. Trebonio persuasi cui ne suadere quidem ausus essem? *to give advice*, Cic.; suadere pacem, legem, Cic.; quod ipse tibi suaseris, Cic.; mori, Cic.; ut decumbamus suadebo, Pl.; with subj. alone: se suadere, Pharnabazo id negotium daret, Nep. Sometimes, *to advise* a person *of a fact, to convince, persuade that*, with acc. and infin.: suadebant amici nullam esse rationem amittere eiusmodi occasionem, Cic.

Transf., of things: suadet enim vesana fames, Verg.; tantum religio potuit suadere malorum, Lucr.

sŭādus -a -um (suadeo), *persuasive*: Stat. F. as subst., personif. **Suāda** -ae, *Persuasion*: Enn., Cic.

sŭāsĭo -ōnis, f. (suadeo), *recommending, advice*: Sen. Esp. (1) polit. t. t., *the advocacy of a proposed law*: legis Serviliae, Cic. (2) as rhet. t. t., *eloquence of the persuasive kind*: Cic.

sŭāsor -ōris, m. (suadeo), *an adviser, recommender*: deditionis, Cic.; pacis, Ov. Esp., *one who advocates a proposed law*: legis, Liv.

sŭāsōrĭus -a -um (suadeo), *relating to persuasion*: Quint. F. as subst. **sŭāsōrĭa** -ae (sc. oratio), *persuasive discourse*: Quint.

sŭāsus -ūs, m. (suadeo), *an advising, persuading*: Ter.

sŭāvěŏlens -entis (suavis/oleo), *sweet-smelling*: Cat.

sŭāvĭdĭcus -a -um (suavis/dico), *sweetly speaking*: Lucr.

sŭāvĭlŏquens -entis (suavis/loquor), *sweetly speaking*: Enn., Lucr.

sŭāvĭlŏquentĭa -ae, f. (suaviloquens), *sweetness of speech*: Cic.

sŭāvĭŏlum=saviolum; q.v.

sŭāvĭor=savior; q.v.

sŭāvis -e, adj. (with compar. and superl.) (connected with ἡδύς), *sweet, pleasant, agreeable, delightful.*

Lit., to the senses: odor, Cic.; flores, Lucr. N. acc. like adv.: suave rubens, Verg.; Hor.

Transf., to the mind, of things or persons: homo, Ter.; litterae tuae, Cic. L.; Lucr., etc. ¶ Hence adv. (with superl.) **sŭāvĭtěr**, *sweetly, agreeably, pleasantly.* Lit., to the senses: quam suaviter voluptas sensibus blandiatur, Cic. Transf., to the mind: meminisse, Cic.; suavissime scriptae litterae, Cic. L.; Hor.

sŭāvĭtās -ātis, f. (suavis), *sweetness, pleasantness.* Lit., to the senses: cibi, odorum, coloris, Cic.; plur.: Cic. Transf., to the mind: vitae, hominis, Cic.; plur.: Cic.

sŭāvĭtūdo -ĭnis, f. (suavis), *sweetness, pleasantness*: Pl.

sŭāvĭum=savium; q.v.

sŭb, prep. with abl. and acc. (connected with ὑπό).

With abl. LIT., of place. (**1**) *underneath, under*: sub terra habitare, Cic.; sub pellibus hiemare, Cic.; vitam sub divo agere, Hor.; sub armis esse, *to be under arms*, Caes.; sub corona, sub hasta vendere, Cic.; sub hoc iugo dictator Aequos misit, Liv. (**2**) *nearly under, close under, at the bottom of, at the foot of*: sub monte consedit, Caes.; sub ipsis Numantiae moenibus, Cic.; Troiae sub moenibus altis, Verg.; sub oculis domini, Liv.; quo deinde sub ipso ecce volat, *just behind*, Verg. TRANSF., (**1**) of time, *at, near to*: sub luce, Hor., Ov., Liv.; sub adventu Romanorum, Liv. (**2**) *in the power of, under*: sub imperio alicuius, Caes.; sub regno alicuius, Cic.; sub rege, *under the rule of a king*, Cic., Hor.; sub iudice lis est, *before the judge*, Hor. (**3**) *under cover of*: sub nomine pacis bellum latet, Cic.; sub specie pacis, Liv. (**4**) *at, on*: Bacchi sub nomine risit, Ov.

With acc. LIT., of place. (**1**) *to* or *along the underside of; up under, down under, along under*: manum sub vestimenta deferre, Pl.; exercitum sub iugum mittere, Caes.; sub terras ire, Verg. (**2**) *to nearly under, close up to*: sub montem succedunt milites, Caes.; missi sub muros, Liv. TRANSF., (**1**) of time, *towards, just before*: Pompeius sub noctem naves solvit, Caes.; sub galli cantum, *about cockcrow*, Hor. (**2**) of time, *immediately after*: sub eas litteras statim recitatae sunt tuae, Cic. L.; Hor. (**3**) *into the power of, under*: sub legum potestatem cadere, Cic.; matrimonium vos sub legis superbissimae vincula conicitis, Liv.

sŭbabsurdus -a -um, *somewhat absurd*: Cic.

¶ Hence adv. **sŭbabsurdē**, *somewhat absurdly*: Cic.

sŭbaccūso -are, *to accuse* or *blame a little*: Cic.

sŭbactĭo -ōnis, f. (subigo), *a working up*; hence *preparation, discipline*: Cic.

sŭbadrŏgantĕr, adv. *somewhat arrogantly*: Cic.

sŭbaerātus -a -um, *having bronze underneath*: Pers.

sŭbagrestis -e, *somewhat rustic, somewhat boorish*: consilium, Cic.

sŭbālāris -e, *under the arms*: Nep.

sŭbalbus -a -um, *whitish*: Varr.

sŭbămārus -a -um, *somewhat bitter*: Cic.

sŭbăquĭlus -a -um, *somewhat dark-coloured, brownish*: Pl.

sŭbausculto -are, *to listen secretly*: Pl., Cic.

subbāsĭlĭcānus -i, m. (sub/basilica), *one who lounges about the basilicas*: Pl.

subbĭbo -bĭbĕre -bĭbi, *to drink a little*: Suet.

subblandĭor -iri, *to flatter, coax, caress a little*: Pl.

subc-, *see* succ-.

subdēbĭlis -e, *somewhat crippled*: Suet.

subdĭffĭcĭlis -e, *somewhat difficult*: quaestio, Cic.

subdĭffīdo -ĕre, *to be somewhat mistrustful*: Cic.

subdĭtīcĭus -a -um (subdo), *substituted, counterfeit*: Pl.

subdĭtīvus -a -um (subdo), *supposititious, substituted, counterfeit*: Pl., Cic.

subdo -dĕre -dĭdi -dĭtum.

(**1**) *to put, place, lay, set, under*. LIT., ignem, Cic., Liv.; with dat. of indir. object: manum oculo, Lucr.; subdita templo Appia,

lying under, or *near*, Ov. TRANSF., **a**, irae facem, Lucr.; alicui acriores ad studia dicendi faces, Cic.; ingenio stimulos, Ov.: **b**, *to subject, subdue*: ne feminae imperio subderentur, Tac.

(**2**) *in the place of another, substitute*: me in Hirtii locum, Cic. Esp., *to substitute falsely, counterfeit*: testamenta, Tac.; me subditum et paelice genitum appellant, Liv.

subdŏcĕo -ēre, *to teach as an assistant, to assist in teaching*: Cic. L.

subdŏlus -a -um, *concealing guile, secret, crafty*. LIT., of persons: homo, Pl.; adversus senem, Pl.; occultum ac subdolum, Tac. TRANSF., of things: oratio, Caes.; lingua, Ov.; Lucr., etc.

¶ Hence adv. **subdŏlē**, *slyly, craftily*: Cic.

subdŏmo -are, *to tame, subject*: Pl.

subdŭbĭto -are, *to doubt* or *hesitate a little*: subdubitare te, quā essem erga illum voluntate, Cic. L.

subdūco -dūcĕre -duxi -ductum.

(**1**) *to draw up from under, pull up, raise, remove*. LIT., in gen.: lapides ex turri, Caes.; tunicas usque ad inguen, Hor.; subduc cibum athletae, *take away*, Cic.; cataractam in tantum altitudinis, Liv. Esp.: **a**, naut. t. t., *to draw* or *haul up a ship on shore*: classem, Liv.; naves, Caes., Liv.: **b**, as milit. t. t., *to withdraw*: cohortes e dextro cornu, Liv.; copias in proximum collem, Caes.; Sall. TRANSF., in gen.: terra se pedibus, Lucr.; colles se, Verg.; Cic. Esp., of accounts, *to balance, cast up*: ratiunculam, Pl.; summam, Cic. L.; in gen.: subducere rationem, or rationes, *to take account of the situation*, Ter., Cic.

(**2**) *to take away stealthily, steal away*: viatica, Hor.; furto obsides, Liv.; de circulo se, Cic.; with dat.: pugnae Turnum, Verg.

subductĭo -ōnis, f. (subduco). (**1**) *the drawing up of a ship on dry land*: Caes. (**2**) *a reckoning, computing*: Cic.

subĕdo -esse -ēdi, *to eat from under, wear away*: scopulus, quem rauca subederat unda, Ov.

sŭbĕo -īre -ii *or* -īvi -ĭtum.

(**1**) *to go under, pass under*. LIT., in gen.: subit oras hasta per imas clipei, Verg.; with acc.: limina, Verg.; aquas, Ov.; tectum non subisse, Caes.; mucronem, *to run under*, Verg. Esp., as a bearer, *to go under* and *support*: ingenti subiere feretro, Verg.; asellus onus dorso gravius, Hor. TRANSF., *to undergo, submit to, take upon oneself*: quamvis carnificinam, Cic.; pro amico periculum aut invidiam, Cic.; Caes., Hor.

(**2**) *to come up from under, approach, advance, mount, climb*. LIT., in adveros montes, Liv.; in latebras, Ov.; ad urbem, Liv.; with dat.: muro, Verg.; with acc.: muros, Liv.; impositum saxis Anxur, Hor.; of things: ubi maxime montes Crotonenses Trasumenus subit, Liv.; Verg. TRANSF., in gen., *to come up, approach*: subeunt morbi tristisque senectus et labor, Verg.; with acc.: umbra terras, Ov.; lumina fessa sopor, Ov. Esp., *to come into*, or *come over, the mind*: subiit cari genitoris imago, Ov.; with dat.: subeunt mihi fastidia cunctarum, Ov.; subeant animo Latmia saxa tuo, Ov.; with acc.: horror animum subit, Tac.; mentem patriae subiit pietatis imago, Verg.; with acc. and infin.: cogitatio animum subiit indignum esse, etc., Liv.

(3) *to come on after, to follow*; sometimes *to come and support.* Lit., pone subit coniunx, Verg.; with dat.: primae legioni tertia, dexterae alae sinistra subiit, *came to help*, Liv.; with acc.: furcas subiere columnae, *replaced*, Ov. Transf., in quorum subiere locum fraudesque dolique, Ov.

¶ Hence partic. **sŭbĭtus** -a -um, as adj., *sudden.* (1) in act. sense, *coming suddenly, taking by surprise*: imbres, Lucr.; bellum, Caes.; Cic., etc. (2) pass., *suddenly done, hastily contrived, improvised* (cf. subitarius): consilia, Caes.; miles, Tac.; Liv.

¶ N. as subst. **sŭbĭtum** -i, *a sudden occurrence, emergency*: Pl.; Cic. L.; plur.: Liv., Tac.

¶ N. abl. sing. as adv. **sŭbĭtō**, *suddenly*: Cic., Verg., etc.

sūber -ĕris, n. *the cork-tree*; also *cork*: Verg.

subf-, *see* suff-.

subg-, *see* sugg-.

sŭbhorrĭdus -a -um, *somewhat rough*: Cic.

sŭbĭăcĕo -ēre -ŭi, *to lie under* or *close to*; usually with dat. Lit., Plin. Transf., *to be subject to, belong to, be connected with*: Quint.

sŭbĭcĭo -icĕre -iēci -iectum (sub/iacio).

(1) *to throw, place, set, under*; usually with dat. of what is above. Lit., ignem, Cic.; aliquid oculis, Cic.; cervices securi, Cic.; aedes colli, *to build under*, Liv.; castra urbi, *to pitch under the walls of*, Liv.; Caes., etc. Transf., **a**, *to submit* to a judge: res sensibus, sub sensūs, Cic.; Sullae libellum, Cic.; cogitationi aliquid, Cic.: **b**, *to subject* to an authority: Gallia securibus subiecta, Caes.; se alicui, se imperio alicuius, Cic.; gentes servitio, Liv.; fortunas innocentium fictis auditionibus, Caes.; aliquid praeconi, Liv., *or* voci praeconis, Cic., *or* sub praeconem, Cic., *to bring to the hammer, have sold by auction*: **c**, in thought, *to subordinate*: partes generibus, Cic.: **d**, in speech or writing, *to place after, append, subjoin, reply*: rationem, Cic.; pauca furenti, Verg.; Liv., etc.

(2) *to throw up from below, raise, lift.* Lit., corpora saltu in equos, Verg.; regem in equum, Liv.; tragulas inter carros, Caes. Transf., *to put into a mind, suggest*: aliquid, Ter.; subiciens quid dicerem, Cic.; consilia, Liv.; spem alicui, *to infuse*, Liv.

(3) *to substitute*: potiorem, Liv.; pro verbo proprio subicitur aliud, quod idem significet, Cic. Esp. *to insert by guile*: testamenta, *to counterfeit*, Cic.; testes, *to suborn*, Quint.

¶ Hence partic. **subiectus** -a -um. Lit., of places, *lying near, adjacent*: Heraclea, quae est subiecta Candaviae, Caes.; viae campus, Liv.; Cic., Verg. Transf., *subjected, subject*: nulli est naturae oboediens aut subiectus deus, Cic.; compar.: subiectior invidiae, Hor.

¶ Superl. adv. **subiectissĭmē**, *most submissively*: Caes.

subiectĭo -ōnis, f. (subicio). (1) *a laying under, placing under*: rerum sub aspectum paene subiectio, Cic. (2) *a counterfeiting, forging*: testamenti, Liv. (3) as rhet. t. t. (=ἀνθυπο-φορά), *the suggesting of an answer to one's own question*: Quint.

subiecto -are (freq. of subicio). (1) *to put under, apply from below*: lasso stimulos, Hor. (2) *to throw up from below*: saxa, Lucr.; Verg.

subiector -ōris, m. (subicio), *a forger, counterfeiter*: testamentorum, Cic.

sŭbīgo -ĭgĕre -ēgi -actum (sub/ago).

(1) *to drive under*; hence *to subject, constrain, subdue*; of animals: belua facilis ad subigendum, Cic.; of persons and communities: populos armis, Cic.; urbes atque nationes, Sall.; subacti bello, Liv. Also *to compel to do a thing*; with ad *or* in and the acc.: Volscos ad deditionem, Liv.; with infin.: Tarquinienses metu subegerat frumentum exercitui praebere, Liv.; Verg.; with ut and the subj.: ut relinquant patriam atque cives, Liv.; Pl.

(2) *to drive up from below.* Lit., sues in umbrosum locum, Varr.; naves ad castellum, Liv.; adverso flumine lembum remigio, *to row*, Verg.; ratem conto, *to push*, Verg. Esp. *to work the soil, break up, plough, cultivate*: terrai solum, Lucr.; glaebas, Cic.; Verg., Ov. Transf., *to work up, work on*: in cote secures, Verg. Hence *to train, discipline*: subacto ingenio, Cic.; subacti atque durati bellis, Liv.

sŭbimpŭdens -entis, *somewhat impudent*: Cic. L.

sŭbinānis -e, *somewhat vain*: Cic.

sŭbindĕ, adv. (1) *immediately afterwards*: Hor., Liv., etc. (2) *repeatedly, from time to time*: Mart., Plin. L.

sŭbinsulsus -a -um, *somewhat insipid*: Cic.

sŭbinvĭdĕo -ēre, *to envy somewhat*: subinvideo tibi, with acc. and infin., Cic.

¶ Partic. **sŭbinvīsus** -a -um, *somewhat hated*: Cic.

sŭbinvīto -are, *to invite mildly*; with ut and the subj.: Cic. L.

sŭbīrascor -īrasci -īrātus, dep. *to be a little angry*; with dat.: brevitati litterarum, Cic. L.; with quod: quod me non invitas, Cic. L.

sŭbĭtārĭus -a -um (subitus), *hastily contrived, improvised*: exercitus, milites, legiones, *gathered in haste*, Liv.; aedificia, Tac.

sŭbĭtō, adv. from subeo; q.v.

sŭbĭtus -a -um, p. adj. from subeo; q.v.

subiungo -iungere -iunxi -iunctum.

Lit., *to yoke beneath*: curru (dat.) tigres, Verg.

Transf., (1) *to join on, attach*: fundamenta rebus, Lucr.; puppis rostro Phrygios subiuncta leones, *having affixed to its beak*, Verg.; omnes artes oratori, Cic.; carmina percussis nervis, *to the strains of the lyre*, Ov. (2) *to subdue, subjugate*: urbes sub imperium, Cic.; mihi res, Hor.; Verg.

sublābor -lābi -lapsus sum, dep. (1) *to glide up*: annis sublapsa vetustas, Verg. (2) *to glide from beneath, slip away*: aedificia vetustate sublapsa, Plin. L.; retro sublapsa spes, Verg.

sublātē, adv. from tollo; q.v.; fig.: **a**, *loftily, sublimely*: dicere, Cic.: **b**, *proudly, haughtily*: de se sublatius dicere, Cic.

sublātĭo -ōnis, f. (tollo). (1) *a lifting up, elevation*: animi, Cic. (2) *an annulling*: Quint.

sublātus -a -um, partic. from tollo; q.v.

sublecto -are (lacto), *to flatter, wheedle*: Pl.

sublĕgo -lĕgĕre -lēgi -lectum. (1) *to gather from below, pick up*: Hor. (2) *to carry off* *secretly*: liberos parentibus, *to kidnap*, Pl. Transf., clam nostrum sermonem, *to eavesdrop*, Pl.; carmina, Verg. (3) *to choose in the place of another*: in demortuorum locum, Liv.; Tac.

sublestus -a -um, *slight, weak, trivial*: Pl.

sublēvātio -ōnis, f. (sublevo), *a relieving, lightening*: Cic.

sublēvo -are, *to raise from beneath, lift up, support.*
Lit., ab iis sublevatus murum ascendit, Caes.; aliquem stratum ad pedes, Cic. L.; Verg. Transf., (1) *to encourage* a person: aratores, Cic.; Caes. (2) *to lighten, alleviate* troubles: laborem, Caes.; res adversas, Cic.

sublīca -ae, f. *a pile, stake*: Caes., Liv. Esp. of the piles of a bridge: Caes.

sublīcius -a -um (sublica), *resting upon piles*: pons, *a wooden bridge across the Tiber, said to have been built by Ancus Martius*, Liv., Tac.

sublīgācŭlum -i, n. (subligo), *a cloth worn round the loins, a kilt*: Cic.

sublīgar -āris, n.=subligaculum; q.v.: Plin., Mart., Juv.

sublīgo -are, *to bind below, bind on*: clipeum sinistrae, Verg.

sublīmis -e (and archaic **sublīmus** -a -um: Lucr.), *high, raised, lifted up.*
Lit., ipsa Paphum sublimis abit, *went away on high*, Verg.; iret consul sublimis curru multiiugis equis, Liv.; sedens solio sublimis, Ov.; atrium, *lofty*, Hor.; columna, Ov. Transf., *sublime, elevated, lofty*: mens, Ov.; Hor. Esp. of style, *lofty, sublime*: carmina, Juv.; Hor.; so of authors: Aeschylus, Quint.; Lucretius, Ov.
¶ N. acc. sing. as adv. **sublīme**, *on high, aloft*: aer sublime fertur, Cic.; sublime elatus, Liv.; Lucr., Verg. Also compar. **sublīmius**: Ov., Quint.

sublīmĭtās -ātis, f. (sublimis), *loftiness, height.* Lit., Plin., Quint. Transf., *sublimity*: animi, Plin. Esp. of style: Quint., Plin. L.

sublīmus, see sublimis.

sublingio -ōnis, m. (sub/lingo), *a scullion*: Pl.

sublīno -līnĕre -lēvi -lĭtum. (1) *to smear below, to lay on colour as a ground*: Plin. (2) os alicui, *to smear by stealth*; hence *to cozen, cheat*: Pl.

sublūcĕo -ēre, *to gleam faintly, glimmer*: Verg., Ov.

sublŭo -lŭĕre -lūtum, *to wash below, bathe underneath*: Mart. Transf., of rivers, *to flow beneath*: hunc montem flumen subluebat, Caes.

sublustris -e, *gleaming faintly, glimmering*: nox, Hor., Liv., Verg.

subm-, see summ-.

subnascor -nasci -nātus sum, dep. *to grow up under, grow up out of* or *after*: Ov., Plin.

subnecto -nectĕre -nexŭi -nexum, *to bind, tie, bind on beneath.* Lit., antemnis totum subnectite velum, Ov.; aurea purpuream subnectit fibula vestem, Verg. Transf., Quint.

subnĕgo -are, *to deny a little, partly deny* or *refuse*: Cic.

subnĭger -gra -grum, *somewhat black, blackish*: Pl., Varr.

subnixus (subnīsus) -a -um (sub/nitor), *propped up on, supported by, resting upon*: usually with abl. Lit., circuli verticibus

subnixi, Cic.; solio subnixa resedit, Verg.; Pl. Transf., auxiliis, victoriā, Liv.; qui artis adrogantiā ita subnixi ambulant, Cic.; Tac.

subnŏto -are. (1) *to mark beneath, write underneath*: Plin. L. (2) *to notice secretly*: Mart.

subnūba -ae, f. (sub/nubo), *a rival*: lecti nostri, Ov.

subnūbĭlus -a -um, *somewhat cloudy*: nox, Caes.

sŭbo -are, *to be in heat*: Lucr., Hor., Plin.

sŭbobscēnus -a -um, *somewhat obscene*: Cic.

sŭbobscūrus -a -um, *somewhat obscure*: Cic.

sŭbŏdiōsus -a -um, *somewhat odious, rather unpleasant*: Cic. L.

sŭboffendo -ĕre, *to give some offence*: apud faecem populi, Cic. L.

sŭbŏlĕo -ēre, used only in 3rd pers., *to emit a smell*; hence, *to make itself felt*: subolet mihi, *I get it, I am on to it*, Pl.

sŭbŏlēs -is, f. (alo).
Lit., of plants, *a sprout, shoot, sucker*: Plin. Transf., of men and animals, *race, offspring, progeny*: iuventutis, Cic.; suboles imperatorum (Scipio), Liv.; deum, Verg.; haedus, suboles lascivi gregis, Hor.

sŭbŏlesco -ĕre, *to grow up*: Liv.

sŭbŏrĭor -ŏrīri, dep. *to arise after* or *in succession, to be duly supplied*: Lucr.

sŭborno -are. (1) *to furnish, equip, provide*: a natura subornatus, Cic.; Sen. (2) *to instigate secretly, suborn*: medicum indicem, Cic.; aliquem ad caedem regis, Liv.

sŭbortus -ūs, m. (suborior), *an arising after* or *in succession*: Lucr.

subp-, see supp-.

subrancĭdus -a -um, *somewhat putrid*: caro, Cic.

subraucus -a -um, *somewhat hoarse*: vox, Cic.

subrectus (surrectus), partic. from subrigo; q.v.

subrēmĭgo (surrēmĭgo) -are, *to row underneath*: Verg.

subrēpo (surrēpo) -rēpĕre -repsi, *to creep* or *crawl up to from below.* Lit., sub tabulas, Cic.; with acc.: moenia, Hor. Transf., somnus in oculos subrepit, Ov.; with dat.: quies ocellis, Ov.; subrepet iners aetas, Tib.

subreptīcius=surrepticius; q.v.

subrīdĕo (surrīdĕo) -rīdēre -rīsi -rīsum, *to smile*: Cic., Verg., etc.

subrīdĭcŭlē, adv. *somewhat laughably*: Cic.

subrĭgo (surrĭgo) -rĭgere -rexi -rectum (sub/rego; cf. surgo), transit. verb., *to raise, lift up*: aures, Verg.; se, Plin.; pass: subrecto mucrone, Liv.; turres subrectae, Plin.

subringor -i, dep. *to make a somewhat wry face, to be a little put out*: Cic. L.

subrĭpĭo=surripio; q.v.

subrŏgo (surrŏgo) -are, *to suggest that a person be chosen as substitute for another* (used of the magistrate presiding at the *comitia*; *sufficere* of the people choosing): in annum proximum decemviros alios, Cic.; conlegam in locum Bruti, Liv.; with double acc.: sibi Sp. Lucretium conlegam, Cic.

subrostrāni -ōrum, m. (sub/rostra), *loungers about the rostra, idlers*: ap. Cic. L.

subrŭbĕo -ēre, *to blush slightly, be rather red, reddish*: Ov.

subrŭbĭcundus -a -um, *somewhat red, reddish*: Plin., Sen.

subrūfus -a -um, *reddish*: Pl., Plin.

subrŭo -rŭĕre -rŭi -rŭtum, *to tear down below, undermine, overthrow.* Lit., arbores, Caes.; murum, Liv. Transf., *to destroy, undermine*: nostram libertatem, Liv.; Lucr., etc.

subrustĭcus -a -um, *somewhat clownish*: pudor, Cic.

subrŭtĭlus -a -um, *reddish*: color, Plin.

subscrībo -scrībĕre -scripsi -scriptum.
(1) *to write under, write beneath.* In gen.: statuis subscripsit reges esse exactos, Cic.; si quaeret Pater Urbium subscribi statuis, Hor. Esp. *to write at the foot of a document*: **a**, *to sign*: de supplicio ex more, Suet.: **b**, of the censor, *to write the ground of his censure beneath the name of the person censured*: istam causam, Cic.: **c**, of an accuser, *to attach details* (names of accusers, charges, etc.) *at the foot of an indictment*; hence, *to prosecute, accuse, help to accuse*: subscripsit quod is pecuniam accepisset, Cic.; Gabinium de ambitu reum fecit subscribente privigno, Cic. Hence, in gen., *to support, assent to*: odiis accusatorum, Liv.; irae Caesaris, Ov.
(2) *to note down, make a note of*: numerum aratorum, Cic.; Tac.

subscriptĭo -ōnis, f. (subscribo).
(1) *a writing beneath, subscription.* In gen.: Serapionis, Cic. L. Esp. *writing at the foot of a document*: **a**, *a signing, signature*: Suet.: **b**, of the censor, *the noting down of the offence censured*: subscriptiones censorum, Cic.: **c**, *the attaching of details at the foot of an indictment*, esp. *the name of the accuser, or joint-accuser*: Cic.
(2) *a record, register*: Cic.

subscriptor -ōris, m. (subscribo), *the signer of an indictment*; *an accuser* or *a joint-accuser*: Cic.

subsĕcīvus = subsicivus; q.v.

subsĕco -secare -sĕcŭi -sectum, *to cut away below*: ungues ferro, Ov.

subsellĭum -i, n. (sub/sella), *a bench below, seat on the floor.*
Lit., in the theatre: Pl., Cic., Suet.; in the senate-house: Cic.; in the market: Liv.; in the law-courts: Cic., Quint.
Transf., (1) *the occupants of a bench*: Mart. (2) *a law-court*: habitare in subselliis, Cic.

subsentĭo -sentire -sensi, *to notice secretly*: Ter.

subsĕquor -sĕqui -sĕcūtus sum, dep. *to follow, follow after.*
Lit., of persons: signa, Caes.; Liv., Ov., etc.
Transf., (1) of things: stella subsequitur, Cic.; hos motus subsequi debet gestus, Cic. (2) of persons, *to follow in opinion, comply with, imitate*: Platonem avunculum, Cic. (3) of persons, *to support a cause, feeling,* etc.: suo sermone humanitatem litterarum tuarum, Cic. L.

subservĭo -ire, *to be subject to, serve, comply with*; with dat.: Pl., Ter.

subsĭcīvus (**subsĕcīvus**) -a -um (sub/seco), *cut off and left over.*
Lit., t. t. of land-measuring; n. as subst., *a remainder* or *small patch of land*: Varr.
Transf., *extra, superfluous, spare*: tempora, Cic.; subsicivis operis, Cic.; Plin. L.

subsĭdĭārĭus -a -um (subsidium), *in reserve*: cohortes, Caes., Liv., Tac. M. pl. as subst. **subsĭdĭārĭi** -ōrum, *reserve troops*: Liv.

subsĭdĭum -i, n.

(1) as milit. t. t.: **a**, in concr. sense, *troops stationed in the rear, reserve troops, a reserve, auxiliary forces*: subsidia et secundam aciem adortus, Liv.; subsidium submittere, Caes. in subsidiis, Sall.: **b**, abstr., *military support, help, assistance*: subsidium ferre, Caes. subsidio proficisci, Caes.
(2) in gen., *aid, help, succour, support*: subsidium bellissimum existimo esse senectuti otium, Cic.; subsidio esse, *to be a help to*, Caes., Ov. In plur.: Caes., Cic., Tac.

subsīdo -sīdĕre -sēdi -sessum.
(1) *to crouch down, settle down, sink.* Of men and animals: adversus emissa tela a hoste, Liv.; elephanti clunibus subsidentes, Liv.; of females, *to submit to the male*: Lucr. Hor. Of things, *to sink down, subside*: subsidunt undae, Verg.; iussit subsidere valles, Ov.
(2) *to stay, remain, settle*: multitudo calonum in castris subsederant, Caes.; Cic. L. Verg.
(3) *to lie in wait, lurk in ambush*: in insidiis Liv.; in loco, Cic.; with acc.: Asiam devictam Verg.

subsignānus -a -um (sub/signum), *serving beneath the standard*: milites, *legionary soldiers kept as a reserve*, Tac.

subsigno -are. (1) *to write under, endorse*; with acc.: Cic. (2) *to enter on a list, to register*: praedia apud aerarium, Cic.

subsĭlĭo -silire -sĭlŭi (sub/salio), *to leap up, spring up*: Pl., Lucr., Prop.

subsisto -sistĕre -stĭti, *to stand.*
Lit., (1) *to make a stand*: Pl., Caes., Verg. of things: neque ancorae funesque subsistebant, Caes. Esp. *to make a stand against, withstand*; with acc.: feras, Liv.; Romanum nec acies subsistere ullae poterant, Liv with dat.: Hannibali atque eius armis, Liv (2) *to come to a stand, stop, halt*; of persons in itinere, Caes.; Liv., Verg.; of things substitit unda, Verg. (3) *to stay, remain*: ips Arimini, Caes.; Plin. L.
Transf., (1) *to withstand*: sumptui, a Cic. L. (2) *to stop, cease*: substitit clamo Ov. (3) *to remain, continue*: intra priore paupertatem, Tac.

subsortĭor -iri, dep. *to choose by lot as substitute*: iudices, *to choose fresh jurymen for those challenged by either party*, Ci Perf. partic. in pass. sense: Cic.

subsortĭtĭo -ōnis, f. (subsortior), *the choosing of a substitute by lot*: iudicum, Cic.

substantĭa -ae, f. (substo). (1) *substance, essence*: Quint. (2) *property, means, subsistence*: facultatum, Tac.

substerno -sternĕre -strāvi -strātum, *to strew* or *spread beneath, lay under*: Pl., verbena Ter.; gallinae nidos quam possunt molli sime substernunt, Cic. Transf., (1) of water pelage late substrata, Lucr.; Prop. (2) *to s out, provide, make available*: delicias, Lucr. Cic.

substĭtŭo -ŭĕre -ŭi -ūtum (sub/statuo). (1) *put next*; of troops: Auct. B. Afr. (2) *to p under, place before*: substituerat animo specie corporis, Liv.; funera fratrum oculis tu Ov. (3) *to put in the place of, to substitute*: locum eorum cives Romanos, Cic.; alique pro aliquo, Cic.; heredem, *to name a seco heir in case of the death of the first*, Suet.

ubsto -stare, *to stand firm*: Ter.

ubstringo -stringĕre -strinxi -strictum, *to draw together, tie, bind up.* LIT., crinem nodo, Tac.; aurem, *to bunch up the ear for listening,* Hor. TRANSF., *to check*: bilem, Juv.

¶ Hence partic. **substrictus** -a -um, *narrow, tight, contracted, small*: crura, Ov.

ubstructĭo -ōnis, f. (substruo), *that which is built below, a base, foundation*: Caes., Cic., Liv.

ubstrŭo -strŭĕre -struxi -structum, *to build beneath, lay a foundation*: Capitolium saxo quadrato substructum est, *built with a foundation of hewn stone*, Liv.; Pl.

ubsultim, adv. (subsilio), *by leaping*: Suet.

ubsulto -are (freq. of subsilio), *to spring up, leap up.* LIT., Pl. TRANSF., Quint.

ubsum -esse -fŭi.

(1) *to be near, be close at hand.* LIT., in space: mons, Caes.; templa mari subsunt, Ov. TRANSF., in time: noxi, Caes.; dies, Cic.

(2) *to be under.* LIT., nigra subest lingua palato, Verg.; Hor. TRANSF., **a**, *to be there, to exist*: subest nulla periculi suspicio, Cic.; tamquam spes subesset. Liv.: **b**, *to be subject*: Ov.

ubsūtus -a -um, *fringed, edged below*: vestis, Hor.

ubtēmen -minis, n. (contr. from subtexmen), *the weft* or *woof in weaving*: fert picturatas auri subtemine vestes, Verg.; Pl., Ov., etc.

ubtĕr (supter), adv. and prep. (sub).

Adv., *beneath, below, underneath*: omnia haec, quae supra et subter, Cic.; Lucr. (In composition subter means *under, beneath*, as in subterlabor, or *underhand, in secret*, as in subterduco.)

Prep., *beneath, below, underneath.* (1) with acc., *to* or *along the underside of*: cupiditatem subter praecordia locavit, Cic.; agere vias subter mare, Verg. (2) with abl.: subter litore, Cat.; Verg.

ubterdūco -dūcĕre -duxi, *to lead away secretly*: Pl.

ubterfŭgĭo -fŭgĕre -fūgi. (1) intransit., *to flee in secret*: Pl. (2) transit., *to evade, shun*: poenam, Cic.; Pl., Liv.

ubterlābor -lābi -lapsus sum, dep. (1) *to glide under, flow under*: fluctūs Sicanos, Verg. (2) *to slip away, escape*: Liv.

ubtĕro -tĕrĕre -trīvi -trītum, *to wear away underneath*: Pl., Plin.

ubterrānĕus -a -um (sub/terra), *underground, subterranean*: specus in fundo, Cic. L.; Juv., etc.

ubtervăcans -antis, *empty below*: Sen.

ubtexo -texĕre -texŭi -textum, *to weave beneath.* TRANSF., (1) *to draw together under*: patrio capiti (*the sun*) bibulas nubes, Ov. (2) *to cover, darken*: caelum fumo, Verg.; subtexunt nubila caelum, Lucr. (3) *to connect, join on*: lunam alutae, Juv.; in speech: subtexit deinde fabulae huic legatos in senatu interrogatos esse, Liv.

ubtīlis -e, adj., with compar. (for subtēlis; from tela), *finely woven.*

LIT., mitra, Cat.

TRANSF., (1) in gen., *slender, fine*: corpus, filum, Lucr. (2) of the senses, *discriminating*: palatum, Hor. (3) of the judgment, *discriminating, nice*: iudicium, Cic. L.; iudex,

Hor. (4) of style, *plain, simple, unadorned*: oratio, Cic.; subtilis scriptor atque elegans, Cic.

¶ Hence adv. (with compar. and superl.) **subtīlĭter.** (1) physically, *by fine links* or *passages*: Lucr. (2) of the judgment, *acutely, with discrimination*: iudicare, Cic.; Liv. (3) of style, *plainly, simply, without ornament*: dicere, Cic.; Quint.

subtīlĭtās -ātis, f. (subtilis). (1) physical *thinness, fineness, minuteness*: linearum, Plin. (2) of the judgment, *discrimination, acuteness*: sententiarum, sermonis, Cic.; Tac. (3) of style, *plainness, simplicity*: orationis, Cic.

subtĭmĕo -ēre, *to be a little afraid*: Cic.

subtrăho -trăhĕre -traxi -tractum. (1) *to draw up from beneath*: subtrahitur solum Oceani, Verg.; with dat.: subtractus Numida mortuo superincubanti Romano vivus, Liv. (2) *to draw away secretly, withdraw, remove, steal away.* LIT., hastatos ex acie, Liv.; me a curia, Cic. L.; with dat.: alicui cibum, Cic.; Pl. TRANSF., cui iudicio eum mors subtraxit, Liv.; aliquem irae militum, Tac.

subtristis -e, *rather sad*: Ter.

subturpĭcŭlus -a -um, *rather on the disgraceful side*: Cic. L.

subturpis -e, *rather disgraceful*: Cic.

subtŭs, adv. (sub), *beneath, below, underneath*: Pl., Liv.

subtūsus -a -um (sub/tundo), *somewhat bruised*: Tib.

sŭbūcŭla -ae, f. *a man's garment, a shirt*: Hor., Suet.

sŭbŭla -ae, f. (suo), *a shoemaker's awl*: Mart., Sen.

sŭbulcus -i, m. (sus), *a swineherd*: Varr., Mart.

Sŭbūra -ae, f. *a quarter of Rome, north-east of the Forum.* Adj. **Sŭbūrānus** -a -um, *belonging to the Subura.*

sŭburbānĭtās -ātis, f. (suburbanus), *nearness to the city*: Cic.

sŭburbānus -a -um, *near the city* (Rome), *suburban*: ager, gymnasium, Cic.; Hor., Tac.

¶ As subst., n. **sŭburbānum** -i (sc. praedium), *an estate near Rome, a suburban estate*: Cic.; m. pl. **sŭburbāni** -ōrum, *inhabitants of the towns near Rome*: Ov.

sŭburbĭum -i, n. (sub/urbs), *a suburb*: Cic.

sŭburgĕo -ēre, *to drive close to*: proram ad saxa, Verg.

sŭbūro -ūrĕre, *to burn a little, to singe*: Suet.

subvectĭo -ōnis, f. (subveho), *a carrying up, conveyance, transport*: frumenti, Liv.; plur.: ne ab re frumentaria duris subvectionibus laboraret, Caes.; Tac.

subvecto -are (freq. of subveho), *to carry up, convey, transport*: saxa umeris, Verg.; Pl., Tac.

subvectus -ūs, m. (subveho), *a carrying up*: Tac.

subvĕho -vĕhĕre -vexi -vectum, *to bring up, carry up, convey, transport*: frumentum flumine Arari, Caes.; subvecta utensilia ab Ostia, Tac.; commeatus ex Samnio, Liv.; pass.: ad arces subvehitur regina, Verg.

subvĕnĭo -vĕnire -vēni -ventum, *to come up to aid, to succour, relieve.* Absol.: Cic., Liv., etc. With dat.: circumvento filio subvenit, Caes.; patriae, Cic.; gravedini, Cic.; impers. pass.: reipublicae difficillimo tempore esse subventum, Cic.; Liv., etc.

subvento -are (freq. of subvenio), *to come to the help of* : Pl.

subvĕrĕor -ēri, dep. *to fear a little, be rather anxious* : Cic. L.

subversor -ōris, m. (subverto), *an overthrower* : suarum legum, Tac.

subverto (subvorto) -vertĕre -verti -versum, *to turn upside down, overthrow, overturn*. LIT., mensam, Suet.; montes, Sall.; Hor. TRANSF., *to ruin, destroy* : probitatem ceterasque artes bonas, Sall.; iura, Tac.

subvexus -a -um (sub/veho), *sloping upward* : Liv.

subvŏlo -are, *to fly up* : rectis lineis in caelestem locum, Cic.; Ov.

subvolvo -ĕre, *to roll up* : manibus saxa, Verg.

subvultŭrĭus -a -um, *somewhat vulture-like* : corpus, Pl.

succăvus (subcavus) -a -um, *hollow underneath* : Lucr.

succēdănĕus (succīdănĕus) -a -um (succedo), *taking another's place* : Pl.

succēdo -cēdĕre -cessi -cessum (sub/cedo).

  (**1**) *to go under*; usually with dat. LIT., tecto, Cic.; tumulo terrae, Verg. TRANSF., *to come under, submit to* : sub acumen stili, Cic.; oneri, Verg.

  (**2**) *to go from under, ascend, mount*. LIT., sub montem, Caes.; ad castra, sub vallum, in arduum, Liv.; with dat.: moenibus, Liv.; Verg. TRANSF., ad summum honorem, Lucr.; Verg.

  (**3**) *to come after* or *into the place of*; *to succeed, relieve*. LIT., of physical movement: in stationem, Caes.; in pugnam, Liv.; with dat.: ut integri et recentes defatigatis succederent, Caes. Of proximity, *to come next*: ad alteram partem succedunt Ubii, Caes. TRANSF., **a**, *to follow, succeed* in an office, etc.: in Pompei locum heres, Cic.; in paternas opes, Cic.; Caes., Liv.; with dat.: Cic.: **b**, in time, *to follow, succeed* : Caes., Ov.; with dat.: aetas aetati succedit, Cic.; Liv.; **c**, of things, *to turn out well, prosper, succeed* : hoc bene successit, Ter.; res nulla successerat, Caes. Absol.: succedit, *things go well*, si ex sententia successerit, Cic. L.; with dat.: coeptis succedebat, Liv.; pass.: nolle successum patribus, Liv.

succendo -cendĕre -cendi -censum (sub/ *cando), *to set on fire from below*. LIT., pontem, Liv.; aggerem, Caes.; Cic. TRANSF., *to kindle, inflame* ; of a blush : Luc.; of passion : Deucalion Pyrrhae succensus amore, Ov.; Prop., Juv.

succenseo=suscenseo; q.v.

¹**succentŭrĭo** -are, *to receive in a century as a substitute*; hence, *to put in the place of another, to substitute* : Ter.

²**succentŭrĭo** -ōnis, m. *an under-centurion* : Liv.

successĭo -ōnis, f. (succedo), *a succeeding*, or *taking the place of*, a person or thing; esp. *succession in an office* : in locum Antoni, ap. Cic. L.; Tac.

successor -ōris, m. (succedo), *a successor, follower* in office, possession : Cic., Liv. With genit.: studii, *heir to*, Ov.

successus -ūs, m. (succedo). (**1**) *an advance uphill, approach* : hostium, Caes.; equorum, Verg. (**2**) *success, happy issue* : successu exsultans, Verg.; prosperos successus dare orsis, Liv.; Ov., Tac.

succīdĭa -ae, f. (succīdo), *a flitch of baco* Varr. TRANSF., hortum ipsi agricolae succ diam alteram appellant, *their second flitc* Cic.

¹**succīdo** -cīdĕre -cīdi (sub/cado). (**1**) *to fa under* : Varr. (**2**) *to sink, flag, fail*: artŭ Lucr.; in mediis conatibus, Verg.; Pl.

²**succīdo** -cīdĕre -cīdi -cīsum (sub/caedo), *cut from under, cut down* : arbores, Caes succisis feminibus poplitibusque, Liv florem, Verg.

succīdŭus -a -um (succido), *sinking, failing* genu, Ov.

succinctus -a -um, partic. from succingo; q.v

succingo -cingĕre -cinxi -cinctum (sub/cingo *to gird below, gird up, tuck up the clothes* the girdle.

  LIT., esp. in pass., and in perf. partic. Scylla feris atram canibus succingitur alvum Ov.; pallā succincta, Verg.; Ov.

  TRANSF., (**1**) succincta comas pinus, *wi* bare trunk, Ov. (**2**) *to equip, arm*, esp. in per partic.: gladiis, Enn.; pharetrā, Verg.; cultr Liv. (**3**) in gen., *to surround, provide* : canibus, Cic.; Carthago succincta portibu Cic.; succinctus armis legionibusque, Liv.

  ¶ Hence partic. **succinctus** -a -um, adj., *concise, succinct* : Mart.

succingŭlum -i, n. (succingo), *a girdle* : Pl.

succĭno -ĕre, *to sing to, to accompany* : Pet TRANSF., in speech, *to chime in* : succin alter, Hor.

succlāmātĭo -ōnis, f. (succlamo), found onl in plur.; *shouting in reply* : Liv.

succlāmo -are, *to shout at* or *after anything call back* : haec Virginio vociferanti suc clamabat multitudo, Liv.; impers. pass. succlamatum est, Liv.; with acc. and infin. cum succlamasset nihil se mutare sententia Liv.

succollo -are (sub/collum), *to take upon th neck, to shoulder* : Suet.

succontŭmēliōsē (subcontumeliose), *some what insolently* : tractari, Cic.

succresco -crescĕre -crēvi, *to grow fro beneath, grow up, increase*.

  LIT., succrescit ab imo cortex, Ov.

  TRANSF., (**1**) in gen.: per seque vide succrescere vina, Ov.; Pl. (**2**) *to grow up t match* : non enim ille mediocris orato vestrae quasi succrescit aetati, Cic.; se gloria seniorum succrevisse, Liv.

succrispus=subcrispus; q.v.

succumbo -cumbĕre -cŭbŭi -cŭbĭtum (sub *cumbo, as decumbo, accumbo, etc.), *to l down under, fall down, sink down*.

  LIT., succumbens victima ferro, Cat omnes succubuisse oculos, *had sunk in slee* Ov.

  TRANSF., *to yield, give way, succum surrender*; with dat.: labori, Caes.; senectut Cic.; tempori, pugnae, Liv.; malis, Ov.

succurro -currĕre -curri -cursum (sub/curro

  (**1**) *to run beneath, go under*; usually wi dat. LIT., nequeat succurrere lunae corpu Lucr. TRANSF., **a**, *to undergo* : licet undiq omnes in me terrores impendeant, succurrar Cic.: **b**, *to come into the mind* (perhaps wi the notion *up from below*); *to occur* to one : quidque succurrit, libet scribere, Cic. L sed mihi succurrit numen non esse severur Ov.; Liv., etc.

(2) *to hasten to help, come to aid, succour,*
with dat. LIT., laborantibus, Caes., Cic.;
impers. pass.: si celeriter succurratur, Caes.
TRANSF., *to help, assist*: saluti fortunisque
communibus, Cic.; hic tantis malis haec
subsidia succurrebant, quominus omnis
deleretur exercitus, Caes.; Liv., etc.

succussio -ōnis, f. (succutio), *a shaking from
beneath, earthquake*: Sen.

succussus -ūs, m. (succutio), *a shaking*: Pac.
ap. Cic.

succūtio -cŭtĕre -cussi -cussum (sub/quatio),
to shake from beneath, fling aloft: Lucr.,
Mart., Juv.

sūcĭdus -a -um (sucus), *juicy, full of sap*: Pl.,
Mart., Juv.

sūcĭnum -i, n. (sucus), *amber*: Plin.

sūcĭnus -a -um (sucinum), *of amber*: gutta,
Mart.; Plin.

sūco -ōnis, m. *a sucker*; applied to a usurer:
ap. Cic. L.

Sucro -ōnis, m. *a river in Hispania Tarraconensis* (now *Xucar*); at its mouth was a
town of the same name.
¶ Hence adj. **Sucrōnensis** -e, *of or near
Sucro.*

¹**sŭcŭla** -ae, f. (dim. of sus), *a little sow*: Pl.
In plur.: Suculae, a wrong translation of
Gr. ὑάδες, *a constellation, the Hyades*: Cic.

²**sŭcula** -ae, *a winch, windlass, capstan*, Pl.

sūcus (succus) -i, m. (perhaps connected with
sugo), *juice, sap*.
LIT., stirpes ex terra succum trahunt, Cic.;
sucus is quo utimur, Cic.; sucus olivi, Ov.;
nectaris sucus ducere, *juice of nectar*, Hor.;
esp., in medicine, *a draught, potion*: amarus,
Ov.
TRANSF., (1) *flavour, taste*: piscis suco
ingratus, Ov.; Lucr., Hor. (2) *sap, vigour,
energy*: amisimus sucum et sanguinem, Cic.
Esp. of orators and speeches: orationis,
Pericli, Cic.

sūdārĭum -i, n. (sudo), *a handkerchief, towel*:
Cat., Mart., etc.

sūdātĭo -ōnis, f. (sudo), *a sweating*: Sen.

sūdātōrĭus -a -um (sudo), *of sweating,
producing perspiration*: unctio, Pl. N. as
subst. **sūdātōrĭum** -i, *a sweating-room,
sweating-bath*: Sen.

sūdātrix -trīcis, f. (sudator), *causing perspiration*: toga, Mart.

sŭdis -is, f. *a stake, pile*. LIT., ripa erat acutis
sudibus praefixis munita, Caes. TRANSF.,
a spike, point: Juv., etc.

sūdo -are.
(1) intransit., *to sweat, perspire*. LIT.,
puer sudavit et alsit, Hor.; Cic., etc. Esp.
miraculously: Cumis Apollo (i.e., *the statue
of Apollo*) sudavit, Cic.; Verg., Liv. TRANSF.,
a, *to drip with moisture*: scuta duo sanguine
sudasse, Liv.; cavae tepido sudant umore
lacunae, Verg.: **b,** *to drip from, distil*: balsama
odorato sudantia ligno, Verg. (3) fig., *to
make a great effort, work hard*: vides, sudare
me iamdudum laborantem, Cic. L., Lucr.,
etc.
(2) transit.: **a,** *to sweat out, to exude*:
durae quercūs sudabunt roscida mella, Verg.;
ubi tura balsamaque sudantur, Tac.: **b,** *to
soak with sweat*: vestes sudatae, Quint.

ūdor -ōris, m. *sweat, perspiration*.
LIT., sudor a capite et a fronte defluens,

Cic.; simulacrum multo sudore manavit,
Cic.; Verg., etc.
TRANSF., (1) *any kind of moisture*: veneni,
Ov.; maris, Lucr. (2) *great exertion, labour,
effort*: stilus ille tuus multi sudoris est, Cic.;
multo eius sudore ac labore sub populi
Romani imperium ditionemque cecīderunt,
Cic.; Verg., Liv.

sudŭculum -i, n. (sudor), *a whip, scourge*: Pl.

sūdus -a -um (se/udus), *dry, without moisture*:
Varr. Esp. of weather, *bright, cloudless*: ver,
Verg. N. as subst. **sudum** -i, *fine weather*:
Pl., Cic. L., Verg.

Suēbi (Suēvi) -ōrum, m. *a Germanic tribe.*

suēmus or **suēmus**, 1st pers. plur. as from
sueo (cf. suesco), *we are accustomed*: Lucr.

suesco suescĕre suēvi suētum (the u and e
commonly scan as one syllable).
(1) intransit., *to become accustomed*; with
dat.: militiae, Tac.; with infin.: mittere
suevit, Lucr.; with acc.: a te id, quod suesti
(syncop. perf.) peto, Cic. L.
(2) transit., *to accustom*: viros, Tac.
¶ Hence partic. **suētus** -a -um. (1) *accustomed to*; with dat.: latrociniis, Tac.; Verg.;
with infin.: Verg., Liv., etc. (2) *customary,
usual*: sueta apud paludes proelia, Tac.

Suessa -ae, f. (1) (Suessa Aurunca), *an old
town of the Aurunci, in Campania, birth-place
of the poet Lucilius* (now *Sessa*). (2) (Suessa
Pometia), *a town in Latium, a colony of Alba.*

Suessĭōnes -um, m. pl. *a Gallic people, near
the modern Soissons.*

Suētōnĭus -i, m., C. Suetonius Tranquillus,
*author of the Lives of the Caesars, a con-
temporary of the younger Pliny.*

suētus -a -um, partic. from suesco; q.v.

Suēvi=Suebi; q.v.

sūfes (suffes) -fētis, m. (from a Phoenician
word=*judge*), *the chief magistrate at Carthage*:
Liv.

suffarcĭno -are, *to stuff full, cram*: Pl., Ter.

suffĕro suffere (sub/fero), *to hold up, support*;
hence *to bear, endure, suffer*: plagas, Pl.;
vulnera, Lucr.; poenam sui sceleris, Cic.

suffertus -a -um (sub/farcio), *stuffed full,
crammed*: Suet.

suffes=sufes; q.v.

sufficĭo -ficĕre -fēci -fectum (sub/facio).
(1) transit.: **a,** *to put under*; hence, *to
imbue, stain, steep, suffuse*: lanam medicamentis, Cic.; angues ardentes oculos suffecti
sanguine, Verg.; also *to provide, supply*: ipsa
satis tellus sufficit umorem et gravidas fruges, Verg.; Danais animos viresque secundas
sufficit, Verg.; Lucr.: **b,** *to put in place of
another, to substitute*: aliam ex alia generando
suffice prolem, Verg.; polit. t. t., *to choose
as a substitute*: consul in sufficiendo conlega
occupatus, Cic.; conlegam suffici censori,
Liv.; esp.: consul suffectus, Liv.; of bees:
regem parvosque Quirites sufficiunt, Verg.
(2) intransit., *to be sufficient, be adequate,
suffice*; absol.: nec scribae sufficere, nec
tabulae nomina eorum capere poterant, Cic.;
Verg., Liv. With dat.: Volscis milites, Liv.;
Caes., Verg. With prepositions: quomodo
nos ad patiendum sufficiamus, Liv.; non
suffecturum ducem unum et exercitum unum
adversus quattuor populos, Liv.; nec locus
in tumulos nec sufficit arbor in ignes, Ov.
With infin., *to be in a position to, to be able*:

nec nos obniti contra nec tendere tantum
sufficimus, Verg.

suffīgo -fīgĕre -fīxi -fīxum (sub/figo), *to fix up,
to fasten*: aliquem cruci, Cic.; in cruce, Hor.;
Pl.

suffīmen=suffimentum; q.v.: Ov.

suffīmentum -i, n. (suffio), *incense*: Cic.

suffīo -ire (connected with θύω), *to fumigate,
perfume*. Lit., locum, Prop.; thymo, Verg.;
Lucr. Transf., *to warm*: Lucr.

sufflāmen -ĭnis, n. *a brake, drag, clog*. Lit.,
Juv. Transf., *a hindrance*: Juv.

sufflāmĭno -are (sufflamen), *to check by a
drag*: Suet.

sufflāvus -a -um (sub/flavus), *somewhat yellow*:
Suet.

sufflo -are (sub/flo).
   (1) intransit., *to blow*: Mart., Pers.
   (2) transit., *to blow up, puff up, inflate*.
Lit., buccas, Pl. Transf., se sufflavit uxori,
he has got into a temper with, Pl.

suffōco -are (sub/faux), *to strangle, choke,
suffocate*. Lit., patrem, Cic.; Lucr. Transf.,
urbem et Italiam fame, Cic. L.

suffŏdĭo -fŏdĕre -fōdi -fossum (sub/fodio), *to
pierce underneath, excavate, undermine*:
murum, Sall.; sacella, Cic.; equos, *to stab
from below*, Caes.

suffrāgātĭo -ōnis, f. (suffragor), *a voting in
favour of, support*: urbana, *of the city*;
militaris, *of the soldiers*, Cic.; consulatūs,
support in seeking the consulship, Cic.; plur.:
exstinctae (sunt) suffragationes, Cic.

suffrāgātor -ōris, m. (suffragor), *a voter in
favour of anyone*; *a political supporter*, or,
in gen., *supporter*: Pl., Cic., Plin. L.

suffrāgātōrius -a -um (suffragor), *relating to
the support of a candidate*: Q. Cic.

suffrāgĭum -i, n. (suffragor), *a voting tablet,
a vote*.
   Lit., polit. and judicial t. t.,: ferre suffragium, *to vote*, Cic.; inire suffragium, Liv.;
non prohiberi iure suffragii, Cic.; suffragia
legitima, Liv.; libera, Juv.
   Transf., (1) *the right to vote, franchise*:
alicui suffragium impertire, Liv.; sine
suffragio habere civitatem, Liv.; Cic. (2) in
gen., *judgment*; also *approval, support*: Cic.,
Hor.

suffrāgo -ĭnis, f. *the ham* or *hough on the hind
leg of a quadruped*: Plin.

suffrāgor -ari, dep. *to vote in favour*. Lit.,
suffragandi libido, Cic.; Liv. Transf., in
gen., *to favour, approve, support*: suffragante
fortunā, Cic. L.; with dat.: domus domino,
Cic.

suffringo -ĕre (sub/frango), *to break underneath*: talos alicui, Pl.; crura canibus, Cic.

suffŭgĭo -fŭgĕre -fūgi (sub/fugio). (1) *to flee,
get under cover*: in tecta, Liv. (2) *to fly from,
shun*: tactum, Lucr.; Suet.

suffŭgĭum -i, n. (suffugio), *a shelter, place of
refuge*. Lit., propinqua suffugia, Tac.; Ov.
Transf., *a refuge, remedy*: urgentium malorum suffugium, Tac.

suffulcĭo -fulcire -fulsi -fultum (sub/fulcio),
to support beneath, underprop: Pl., Lucr.

suffundo -fundĕre -fūdi -fūsum (sub/fundo).
   (1) *to pour over, spread through, suffuse*:
animum esse cordi suffusum sanguinem,
Cic.; of dropsy: intumuit suffusa venter ab
unda, *dropsy*, Ov.; of blushing: virgineum

ore ruborem, Ov.; rubor Masinissae suffusu
est, *M. blushed*, Liv.
   (2) *to steep, stain, cover* a thing (with fluids
etc.). Lit., suffundit lumina rore, Ov.
lacrimis oculos suffusa nitentes, Verg.; aethe
calore suffusus, Cic. Transf., animus null
in ceteros malevolentiā suffusus, Cic. L.
Lucr., Ov.

suffūror -ari (sub/furor), *to abstract secretly
steal*: Pl.

suffuscus -a -um (sub/fuscus), *brownish, dark
Tac.

Sŭgambri (Sўgambri, Sĭgambri) -ōrum, m
a Germanic tribe.

suggĕro -gĕrĕre -gessi -gestum (sub/gero), *t
bring up, supply, provide.*
   Lit., flammam costis aēni, Verg.; tel
mihi, Verg.; prodiga divitias alimentaqu
mitia tellus suggerit, Ov.; Pl., etc.
   Transf., (1) *to add, to attach*: verba qua
desunt, Cic.; huic incredibili sententia
ratiunculas, Cic.; Liv. (2) *to place next
Bruto statim Horatium, Liv.

suggestĭo -ōnis, f. (suggero), *a rhetorica
figure in which an orator answers his ow
question*: Quint.

suggestum -i, n. and **suggestus** -ūs, m
(suggero), *a raised place, height, elevatior
In gen.: Cato, Varr. Esp., *a platform fron
which an orator spoke to the people, soldier
etc.: illud suggestum ascendens, Cic.; i
suggestis consistere, Cic.; Caes., Liv., Tac.

suggrandis -e (sub/grandis), *somewhat large
Cic. L.

suggrĕdĭor -grĕdi -gressus sum, dep. (sub
gradior), *to go up to, approach*: Tac. Wit
acc., *to attack*: Tac., Sall.

sŭgillātĭo -ōnis, f. (sugillo), *a livid mark o
the skin, weal, bruise*. Lit., Pl. Transf.
a mocking, insulting: Liv., Plin.

sŭgillo -are, *to beat black and blue*. Lit., Plir
Transf., *to insult, affront*: aliquem, Liv.

sūgo sūgĕre sūxi suctum, *to suck*. Lit., Cic
Transf., cum lacte nutricis errorem, ĸ
imbibe, Cic.

sŭillus -a -um (sus), *of swine*: caro, Juv
caput, grex, Liv.

sulcātor -ōris, m. (sulco), *a plougher*: Luc
Stat.

sulco -are (sulcus), *to furrow, plough*. Lit
humum vomere, Ov. Transf., cutem rugi
to wrinkle, Ov.; harenam (of a snake), Ov.
esp. in sailing: vada carinā, Verg.; und
rate, Ov.

sulcus -i, m. (connected with ὁλκός), *a furro*
   Lit., sulcum imprimere, Cic.; Verg., Ov
   Transf., (1) *a ploughing*: Plin., Plin. l
(2) *any trench or ditch*: Verg., Ov. (3) *tł
track, path* of a moving body: Verg. (4)
wrinkle: Mart.

sulfur (sulpur) -ŭris, n. *sulphur*. Lit., Luc
Verg., Liv., etc. Transf., *lightning*: Pers
Luc.

sulfŭrātus -a -um (sulfur), *full of sulphu
containing sulphur*: Plin., Mart. N. pl. ĸ
subst. **sulfŭrāta** -ōrum. (1) *brimston
matches*: Mart. (2) *veins of sulphur*: Plin.

sulfŭrĕus -a -um (sulfur), *sulphurous*: aqu
Verg.; Ov., Plin.

Sulla (Sylla) -ae, m. *a name of a family in tł
gens Cornelia*; esp. of L. Cornelius Sull
the dictator, rival of Marius.

¶ Hence adj. **Sullānus** -a -um, *Sullan*; m. pl. as subst. **Sullāni** -ōrum, *the partisans of Sulla*; verb **Sullātŭrĭo** -īre, *to wish to imitate Sulla*: Cic.

Sulmo -ōnis, m. *a town in the country of the Paeligni, birth-place of Ovid* (now *Sulmona*).
¶ Hence adj. **Sulmōnensis** -e, *of Sulmo*.

Sulpĭcĭus -a -um, *name of a Roman* gens.
¶ Hence adj. **Sulpĭcĭānus** -a -um, *Sulpician*.

sulpur=sulfur; q.v.

sultis=si vultis; *see* volo.

sum esse, fŭi; fut. partic. fŭtūrus; fut. infin. often fŏre and imperf. subj. fŏrem for essem; pres. subj. fŭam for sim, poet. an irregular verb, from two different roots; cf. εἰμί and φύω.

(**1**) *to be, to exist, be living, be there, be so, happen*: adhuc sumus, Cic.; omnium qui sunt, qui fuerunt, qui futuri sunt, Cic.; non est periculum, Cic.; quid tibi est? *what is the matter with you?* Cic. Esp.: **a**, perf. fui, *to be over, be no more*: fuit, *he has lived*, Tib.; fuimus Troes, fuit Ilium, Verg.; Cic.: **b**, with relat., sunt qui, *there are some who*; with indic., when a definite known antecedent is meant: sunt qui audent, Cic.; with subj., indef.: sunt qui dicant, Cic.; sunt qui non habeant, est qui non curat habere, Hor.; est quod, *there is reason for, I* (*you*, etc.) *have reason to, cause to*: magis est quod gratuler, Cic.; nihil est quod (*or* cui), *there is no reason for*: nihil est, quod gestias, Cic.: **c**, est ut, with subj., *it is possible that, it may be that*: Cic.: **d**, with dat., *to be in one's possession*: est tibi, sitque, precor, natus, Ov.; cui nomen Arethusa est, Cic.; sibi cum illa nihil futurum, *that he would have nothing to do with her, Cic.

(**2**) as copulative verb, *to be so and so, with various kinds of complement*: **a**, with a noun, pronoun, or adj. in the same case as its subject: homo sum, Ter.; praeclara res est et sumus otiosi, Cic.: **b**, with noun or pronoun in various other cases; with genit. of price or value: frumentum fuit tanti, Cic.; of quality, description, or measurement: summi ut sint laboris, Cic.; esse with genit. can also mean *to belong to*: Gallia est Ariovisti, Caes.; *to be devoted to*: me Pompeii totum esse, Cic.; *to be the duty or nature of, to be characteristic of*: cuiusvis hominis est errare, Cic.; so with poss. pron.: est tuum videre, Cic.; esse with dat., *to be good for, or equal to*: non esse solvendo, *to be insolvent*, Cic.; with predicative dat., *to be, to prove*: impedimento esse alicui, Cic.; with abl. of quality or description: aegro corpore esse, *to be ill*, Cic.; simus eā mente, *so disposed*, Cic.: **c**, with adv.: sic est, Cic.; sit ita, Cic.; mihi pulchre est, Cic.; procul este, Liv., etc.: **d**, with preposition and noun or pronoun: esse ab, *to be on the side of*, Cic.; esse cum, *to be with, stay with, consort with*, Cic.; esse de, *to be about*: is liber, qui est de animo, Cic.; esse ad, *to be serviceable for*: res quae sunt ad incendia, Caes.

(**3**) as auxiliary verb, with participles and gerundives.
¶ Fut. partic. **fŭtūrus** -a -um, as adj., *future, about to be*: res., Cic.; tempus, Cic.; mors, Ov. N. as subst, **fŭtūrum** -i,

the future: futurum prospicere, Cic.; haud ignara futuri, Verg.; videre in futurum, Liv.

sūmen -inis, n. (=sugmen, from sugo), *a teat, breast*. LIT., Lucil. Esp., *the udder of a sow* (considered a delicacy by the Romans): Pl., Mart. TRANSF., *a sow*: Juv.

summa -ae, *see* summus.

Summānus -i, m. *an old Roman deity, to whom lightnings by night were ascribed*: Cic.
¶ Hence adj. **summānis** -e, *nightly*; perhaps once in Lucr.

summārĭum -i, n. (summa), *an epitome, summary*: Sen.

summās -ātis, m. and f. (summus), *of high birth, noble, illustrious*: Pl.

summātim, adv. (summa), *slightly, summarily, briefly*: quae longiorem orationem desiderant summatim perscribere, Cic. L.; Lucr., Liv.

summātus -ūs, m. (summus), *supremacy, chief authority*: Lucr.

summē, adv. from summus; q.v.

summergo -mergĕre -mersi -mersum, *to plunge under, to sink*: navem, Tac.; classem Argivum ponto, Verg.; often pass.: summersae beluae, *living under the water*, Cic.; summersus equus voraginibus, Cic.; ferrum summersum in unda, Ov.

summĕrus -a -um, *fairly pure*: Pl.

summĭnistro -are, *to help by supplying*. LIT., tela clam, Cic.; alicui pecuniam, Cic.; Caes. TRANSF., huic arti plurima adiumenta, Cic.

summissē (**submissē**), adv. from summitto; q.v.

summissĭo (**submissĭo**) -ōnis, f. (summitto), *a letting down, sinking, lowering*: contentio vocis et summissio, Cic.; orationis, Cic.

summissus (**submissus**) -a -um, partic. from summitto; q.v.

summitto (**submitto**) -mittĕre -mīsi -missum.

(**1**) *to let down, send under*. LIT., fasces, *to lower*, Liv.; alicui se ad pedes, *to fall at the feet of*, Liv.; caput in herba, Ov.; summisso vertice, Ov. TRANSF., **a**, with animum, *or* se, *to abase oneself, condescend, submit*: se in privatum fastigium, Liv.; animos amori, Verg.; Cic., etc.: **b**, *to subject, subordinate*: imperium Camillo, Liv.; citharae cannas, Ov.: **c**, *to moderate, lower*: vocem, Quint.; furorem, Verg.

(**2**) *to send up from below, to raise*. LIT., oculos, Ov.; esp.: **a**, *to cause to spring up*: tellus flores, Lucr.; non monstrum summisere Colchi maius, Hor.: **b**, *to rear, raise* (of farmers): tauros, vitulos, Verg. TRANSF., crinem, *to let grow*, Tac.; capillum, Plin. L.

(**3**) *to send as help*: subsidia alicui, Caes.; cohortes equitibus praesidio, Caes.

(**4**) *to send secretly*: Cic.
¶ Hence partic. (with compar.) **summissus** (**submissus**) -a -um. (**1**) *let down, lowered*. LIT., compar.: summissiores, *in a lower position*, Liv. TRANSF., **a**, of voice or speech, *quiet, mild, gentle*: vox, Cic.; oratio, Caes., Cic.; orator, Cic.: **b**, of character; in a good sense, *humble*: summissi petimus terram, Verg.; in a bad sense, *mean, abject*: ne quid humile, summissum faciamus, Cic. (**2**) *allowed to grow*: capillo summissiore, Suet.
¶ Adv. (with compar.) **summissē**. (**1**) of speech, *softly, calmly*: dicere, Cic.; Demosthenes summissius a primo, Cic. (**2**) of

character, *modestly, humbly*: supplicare, Cic.;
summissius nos geramus, Cic.; Ov., Tac.
¶ Also adv. **summissim**, *gently, softly*:
Suet.

Summoenĭum -i, n. (sub/moenia), *a place in
Rome, notorious for low company*. Adj.
Summoeniānus -a -um.

summŏlestus (submŏlestus) -a -um, *somewhat troublesome*: illud est mihi summolestum
quod parum properare Brutus videtur, Cic. L.
¶ Hence adv. **summŏleste (submŏlestē)**,
with some vexation: te non esse Romae
summoleste fero, Cic.

summŏnĕo (submŏnĕo) -ēre -ŭi, *to remind
secretly*: Ter., Suet.

summŏpĕre, adv. (or **summo opere**), *very
much, exceedingly*: Lucr., Cic., Liv.

summōrōsus (submōrōsus) -a -um, *somewhat
peevish*: Cic.

summŏvĕo (submŏvĕo) mŏvēre -mōvi
-mōtum.
(**1**) *to move up from below*: cohortes, Caes.
(**2**) *to move away, drive off, remove*. LIT.,
in gen., of persons and things: arbitros, Liv.;
strictis gladiis inertes, Liv.; populum aris,
Ov.; maris litora, Hor.; silva suis frondibus
Phoebeos summovet ictus, *keeps off*, Ov.;
summotis nubibus, Verg. Esp.: **a**, of the
lictor, *to clear a way* for a magistrate, *to keep
off, move back*: turbam, Liv.; impers. pass.:
summoveri iubet, Liv.; abl. absol.: summoto,
when a way had been cleared, Liv.: **b**, *to
banish, expel*: aliquem patriā, Ov. TRANSF.,
a, of persons, *to force away from, compel to
give up*: a bello Antiochum et Ptolemaeum
reges, Liv.; aliquem magnitudine poenae a
maleficio, Cic.: **b**, of abstr. things, *to
remove, banish*: tumultūs mentis et curas,
Hor.: **c**, pass. partic., summotus, *lying out
of the way, remote*: spelunca vasto summota
recessu, Verg.; Ov.

summūto (submūto) -are, *to exchange*: verba
pro verbis, Cic.

summŭla -ae, f. (dim. of summa), *a little sum*:
Sen.

summus -a -um, superl. of superus; q.v.

sūmo sūmĕre sumpsi sumptum (sub/emo),
to take.
LIT., in gen.: fustem, Pl.; legem in manūs,
Cic.; pecuniam mutuam, *to borrow*, Cic.;
cyathos, Hor. Esp. of clothes, etc., *to put on*:
calceos et vestimenta, Cic.
TRANSF., (**1**) in gen., *to take, choose, obtain*
a thing: sumpta navis est, Cic.; genus
signorum, *to buy*, Cic.; Hor. So of abstr.
things: frustra operam, Ter.; laborem,
Caes.; sibi studium philosophiae, with
infin.: Hor.; of time: tempus cibi, Liv.;
diem ad deliberandum, Caes. (**2**) *to exact* a
punishment: de aliquo supplicium, Cic.,
Liv.; poenas, Verg. (**3**) in an unfavourable
sense, *to take upon oneself*: sibi partes
imperatorias, Cic.; mihi non tantum sumo,
Cic.; sibi tantam adrogantiam, Caes. (**4**) *to
cite, to mention*: homines notos, Cic. (**5**) *to
take for granted, assume*: beatos esse deos
sumpsisti, Cic.; Lucr., Liv.

sumptĭo -ōnis, f. (sumo), *the premiss of a
syllogism*: Cic.

sumptŭārĭus -a -um (sumptus), *relating to
expense, sumptuary*: lex, Cic. L.; rationes,
Cic. L.

sumptŭōsus -a -um (sumptus). (**1**) of things,
costly, expensive: cenae, Cic.; compar.: ludi
sumptuosiores, Cic. L. (**2**) of persons, *lavish,
extravagant*: Pl., Ter., Cic.
¶ Hence adv. (with compar.) **sumptŭōsē**,
expensively, sumptuously: Cat., Cic., Plin. L.

sumptus -ūs, m. (sumo), *cost, expense*:
sumptui esse alicui, Pl., Cic. L.; sumptum
facere in rem, impendere, insumere, Cic.;
suo sumptu fungi officio, Cic.; plur.:
minuendi sunt sumptus, Cic.

sŭo sŭĕre sŭi sūtum, *to sew, stitch together, join
together*. LIT., tegimenta corporum vel
texta vel suta, Cic.; Verg. TRANSF., Ter.

sŭōmet and **sŭōpte**, *see* suus.

sŭŏvĕtaurīlĭa -ium, n. pl., sc. sacra (sus/ovis/
taurus), *a sacrifice of a pig, a sheep, and a bull*:
Liv., Tac.

sŭpellex -lectīlis, f. (super/lego), *household
furniture*. LIT., multa et lauta supellex, Cic.;
Pl., Hor., etc. TRANSF., in gen., *equipment*:
amicos parare, optimam vitae supellectilem,
Cic.; oratoria quasi supellex, Cic.; Pers.,
Quint.

¹**sŭper** -a -um, *see* superus.

²**sŭper**, adv. and prep. (cf. ὑπέρ).
Adv., *over, above*. LIT., in space: eo super
tigna bipedalia iniciunt, Caes.; Verg.
TRANSF., in other relations. (**1**) *besides,
beyond, moreover*: satis superque, *enough and
more than enough*, Cic., Hor.; super quam
quod, *besides the fact that*, Liv.; his accensi
super, Verg. (**2**) *remaining, left, over and
above*: quid super sanguinis (esse), Liv.;
Verg.
Prep. with abl. and acc. (**1**) with abl. LIT.,
of place, *over, above*: ensis super cervice
pendet, Hor.; Caes., Verg. TRANSF., **a**, of
time, *at*: nocte super media, Verg.: **b**, of
relation, *concerning, about*: hac super re
scribam ad te, Cic. L.; multa super Priamo
rogitans, Verg.; Liv.: **c**, *besides, beyond*: supe-
his, Hor. (**2**) with acc. LIT., of place: **a**, *over,
above, upon*: super aspidem adsidēre, Cic.;
aqua super montium iuga concreta erat, Liv.;
super templum circaque, Liv.: **b**, *beyond*:
super Numidiam Gaetulos accepimus, Sall.,
Hor., Verg. TRANSF., **a**, of time, *during*:
Plin. L.: **b**, *besides, beyond*: super cetero-
honores, Liv.; super cetera, Liv.; vulnu-
super vulnus, *wound on wound*, Liv.; Tac.
c, of superiority, *above, more than*: aetas e-
forma et super omnia Romanorum nome-
te ferociorem facit, *above all*, Liv.

sŭpĕrā, *see* supra.

sŭpĕrābĭlis -e (supero), *that can be surmounted*
LIT., murus, Liv. TRANSF., *conquerable*: n-
est per vim superabilis ulli, Ov.; null-
casibus superabilis Romani, Tac.

sŭpĕraddo -addĕre -addĭtum, *to add over an-
above, put on besides*: Verg., Prop.

sŭpĕrans -āntis, partic. from supero; q.v.

sŭpĕrātor -ōris, m. (supero), *one who over-
comes, a conqueror*: Ov.

sŭpĕrbē, adv. from superbus; q.v.

sŭpĕrbĭa -ae, f. (superbus), *pride*. (**1**) in
bad sense, *haughtiness, arrogance*: Pl., Cic
Verg. (**2**) in a good sense, *lofty spir-
honourable pride*: sume superbiam quaesita-
meritis, Hor.; Tac.

sŭpĕrbĭfĭcus -a -um (superbus/facio), *maki-
proud, making haughty*: Sen.

sŭperbĭo -ire (superbus). (1) of persons, *to be proud, be haughty, pride oneself*; with abl.: formā, Ov.; foll. by quod: Tac. (2) of things, *to be splendid, superb*: Prop., Plin.

sŭperbus -a -um, adj. (with compar. and superl.) (super), *haughty, exalted, proud*.

(1) in a bad sense, *arrogant, overbearing, puffed up*. Of persons: superbum se praebuit in fortuna, Cic. L.; superbiorem te pecunia facit, Cic. L.; as surname of the younger Tarquinius, last king of Rome: Cic.; with abl.: opibus, Verg.; pecuniā, Hor. Of things: oculi, Ov.; aures, Liv.; sceptra, Lucr.; victoria, virtus, Cic.; iudicium aurium superbissimum, *most fastidious*, Cic.

(2) in a good sense, *brilliant, magnificent, splendid*: triumphus, Hor.; populum late regem belloque superbum, Verg.

¶ Adv. (with compar. and superl.) **sŭperbē**, *haughtily, proudly*: superbe et crudeliter imperare, Caes.; preces superbissime repudiare, Cic.; Pl., Liv.

sŭpercĭlĭōsus -a -um (supercilium), *haughty, censorious*: Sen.

sŭpercĭlĭum -i, n. *an eyebrow*; plur., and sing. in collective sense, *the eyebrows*.

LIT., altero ad mentum depresso supercilio, Cic.; superciliorum aut remissio aut contractio, Cic.; capite et superciliis rasis, Cic.; Pl., Verg., etc.

TRANSF., (1) *nod, beck* (as expression of will): cuncta supercilio movere (of Jupiter), Hor. (2) *arrogance, censoriousness*: hunc Capuae Campano supercilio ac regio spiritu cum videremus, Cic.; supercilii severi matrona, Ov. (3) (like English *brow*), *a ridge, summit*: tramitis, Verg.; tumuli, Liv.

sŭpĕrēmĭnĕo -ēre, *to overtop*: omnes viros, Verg.; Ov.

ŭperfĭcĭēs -ēi, f. (super/facies), *the top, the surface*. In gen.: testudinum, Plin. Esp. as legal t. t., *something* (e.g., *a building*) *placed on the ground so as to become attached to it*: Cic.

ŭperfīo -fĭĕri, *to be left over*: Pl.

ŭperfixus -a -um, *fixed on the top*: Liv.

ŭperflŭo -flŭĕre, *to flow over, overflow*. LIT., of water: superfluentis Nili receptacula, Tac.; Plin. TRANSF., (1) of style: ut nos superfluentes iuvenili quādam dicendi impunitate et licentiā reprimeret, Cic., Quint., Tac. (2) in gen., *to be superfluous*: Sen.

ŭperflŭus -a -um (superfluo), *overflowing, superfluous*: Sen.

ŭperfundo -fundĕre -fūdi -fūsum, *to pour over, pour upon*.

LIT., (1) of fluids; esp. pass. in middle sense, *to overflow*: circus Tiberi superfuso irrigatus, Liv.; Ov., Plin. L. (2) in gen., *to spread about, throw about*: magnam vim telorum, Tac.; pass. as middle: hostes superfusi, *rushing in numbers*, Liv.

TRANSF., (1) superfudit se (regnum Macedoniae) in Asiam, *extended*, Liv. (2) with acc. of what is covered, *to spread over*: Tac.

ŭpergrĕdĭor -grĕdi -gressus sum, dep. (super/gradior), *to step over* or *beyond, overstep*; hence *to exceed, surpass*: aetatis suae feminas pulchritudine, Tac.

ŭpĕri, *see* superus.

ŭperiăcĭo -iacere -iēcti -iectum or -iactum, *to throw over, throw upon*.

LIT., membra superiecta cum tua veste fovet, Ov. Also, with abl., *to overtop*: scopulos superiacit undā pontus, Verg. TRANSF., *to exceed, go beyond*: fidem augendo, Liv.

sŭpĕrimmĭnĕo -ēre, *to overhang*: Verg.

sŭpĕrimpendens -entis (super/impendeo), *overhanging*: Cat.

sŭpĕrimpŏsĭtus -a -um (super/impono), *laid over, placed upon*: saxum ingens machinā, Liv.; Stat.

sŭpĕrincĭdens -entis, *falling on top*: Liv.

sŭpĕrincŭbans -antis, *lying over* or *upon*: superincubans Romanus, Liv.

sŭpĕrincumbo -cumbĕre -cŭbŭi, *to lie on, lie over*: Ov.

sŭpĕrinduco -dūcĕre -duxi -ductum, *to cover over*: Quint.

sŭpĕrindŭo -ŭĕre, *to put on over*: Suet.

sŭpĕringĕro -gĕrĕre -gestum, *to throw upon, heap upon*: Plin., Stat.

sŭpĕrinĭcĭo -inicere -iniēci -iniectum, *to throw upon*: raras frondes, Verg.; Ov., Plin.

sŭpĕrinsterno -sternĕre -strāvi, *to spread over, lay over*: tabulas, Verg.

sŭpĕrĭor -ōris, compar. of sŭpĕrus; q.v.

sŭperiūmentārĭus -i, m. *the chief groom, head of the drivers of beasts of burden*: Suet.

sŭperlātĭo -ōnis, f. (super/fero), rhet. t. t., *exaggeration, hyperbole*: veritatis, Cic.; Quint.

sŭperlātus -a -um (super/fero), *exaggerated, hyperbolical*: verba, Cic.; Quint.

sŭpernus -a -um (super), *above, upper, top*: Tusculum, *lying high*, Hor.; numen, *celestial*, Ov.

¶ Adv. **sŭpernē**, *above*, or *from above*: Hor., Liv.

sŭpĕro -are (super).

(1) intransit., *to go above, overtop, project*. LIT., superant capite et cervicibus altis, Verg. TRANSF., **a**, *to have the upper hand, prevail, conquer*: virtute facile, Caes.; per biduum equestri proelio, Caes.; superat sententia Sabini, Caes.; tantum superantibus malis, Liv.; totidem formā superante iuvencae, *of surpassing beauty*, Verg.: **b**, *to abound, be in abundance*: superante multitudine, Liv.; Pl., Verg.: **c**, *to remain, be over*: si quod superaret pecuniae retulisses, Cic.; Lucr.; esp. *to remain alive, to survive*: uter eorum vitā superavit, Caes.; superatne et vescitur aurā? Verg.: **d**, *to be too much, to exceed*: illis divitiae, Sall.; Cic.

(2) transit., *to rise above, surmount, overtop*. LIT., montes, Verg.; summas ripas fluminis, Caes.; turris superat fontis fastigium, Caes. Also *to go past*: promuntorium, Caes. TRANSF., in gen., *to surpass, excel, exceed*: aliquem doctrinā, Cic.; Pl., Verg., Ov. Esp. milit., *to overcome, conquer*: bello superatos esse Arvernos a Q. Fabio Maximo, Caes.; fig.: iniurias fortunae facile veterum philosophorum praeceptis, Cic.; casus omnes, Verg.

¶ Hence compar. of pres. partic. **sŭpĕrantĭŏr** -ōris, *more dominant*: Lucr.

sŭpĕrobrŭo -ŭĕre, *to overwhelm*: Prop.

sŭperpendens -entis, *overhanging*: saxa, Liv.

sŭperpōno -pōnĕre -pŏsŭi -pŏsĭtum, *to lay, place, put over*, or *upon*.

LIT., superpositum capiti decus, Liv.; Ov., Suet.

TRANSF., (**1**) *to put in authority*: in maritimam regionem superpositus, Liv. (**2**) *to prefer*: Sen. (**3**) *to postpone*: Quint.

sŭperscando -ĕre, *to climb over*: superscandens vigilum strata somno corpora, Liv.

sŭperscrībo -scrībĕre -scripsi -scriptum, *to write over*: Suet.

sŭpersĕdĕo -sĕdēre -sēdi -sessum, *to sit above, sit upon.*

LIT., with dat.: Suet.

TRANSF., (**1**) *to preside over*: Cato. (**2**) *to sit out* from a thing, *be above it*; *to forbear, refrain*; with abl.: labore, Cic. L.; proelio, Caes.; with infin.: loqui apud vos, Liv.; Tac.

sŭperstagno -are, *to spread out into a lake*: Tac.

sŭpersterno -sternĕre -strāvi -strātum, *to spread over* or *upon*: superstratis Gallorum cumulis, Liv.

sŭperstĕs -stĭtis (super/sto).

(**1**) *standing over* or *near*; *present, witnessing*: suis utrisque superstitibus praesentibus, old legal formula ap. Cic.; Pl.

(**2**) *surviving, living beyond* another; of persons or things; with dat.: ut sui sibi liberi superstites essent, Cic.; gloriae suae, Liv.; Pl., Ov., etc.; with genit.: aliquem non solum vitae, sed etiam dignitatis suae superstitem relinquere, Cic.; Liv., Tac., etc.

sŭperstĭtĭo -ōnis, f. (superstes), *unreasonable ideas*, esp. about religion; *superstition, fanaticism*: superstitiones aniles, Cic.; maiores nostri superstitionem a religione separaverunt, Cic.; victi superstitione animi, Liv.; una superstitio superis quae reddita divis, Verg.; quaenam illa superstitio, quod numen, interrogat, Tac.; exitialis, of Christianity, Tac.; so: prava, Plin. L.

sŭperstĭtĭōsus -a -um (superstitio). (**1**) act., *superstitious*: philosophi, Cic.; Liv. (**2**) pass., *an object of superstition, superstitiously believed in*; hence *prophetic*: Pl.

¶ Adv. **sŭperstĭtĭōsē.** (**1**) *superstitiously*: Cic. (**2**) *over-scrupulously*: Quint.

sŭperstĭto -are (superstes). (**1**) transit., *to preserve*: Enn. (**2**) intransit., *to be over, remain*: Pl.

sŭpersto -are, *to stand over* or *upon*: Verg., Liv.; with dat.: corporibus, Liv.; with acc.: Ov.

sŭperstrŭo -strŭĕre -struxi -structum, *to build upon*: Tac., Quint.

sŭpersum -esse -fui -fŭtūrus, *to be over and above*, either as remnant or as superfluity.

(**1**) as a remnant, *to be left, remain*; of persons or things: perexigua pars illius exercitus superest, Caes.; duae partes, quae mihi supersunt illustrandae, Cic.; et superesse videt de tot modo millibus unum, Ov. quod superest, *for the rest*, Lucr., Cic. L., Verg.; superest, foll. by infin., Liv., Ov. With dat.: **a**, *to be left over for*: Verg., Liv.; **b**, *to survive*: alicui, Liv.; pugnae, Liv.

(**2**) *to be plentiful, to abound*: vereor ne iam superesse mihi verba putes, quae dixeram defutura, Cic. L.; Ter., Verg., Liv. In a bad sense, *to be superfluous, be redundant*: ut neque absit quidquam neque supersit, Cic.

sŭpertĕgo -ĕre, *to cover over*; in tmesis: Tib.

sŭperurgĕo -ĕre, *to press from above*: Tac.

sŭpĕrus (rarely **sŭpĕr**) -a -um, adj. (with compar. **sŭpĕrĭor**, superl. **sŭprēmus** and **summus**).

Posit. **sŭpĕrus** -a -um, *situated above, upper, higher*. In gen.: res superae, Cic.; mare superum, *the upper sea*, i.e., *the Adriatic Sea*, Pl. Cic.; superis ab oris, *from the upper world*, Verg. M. pl. as subst. **sŭpĕri** -ōrum (**1**) *the gods above*: Verg., Hor., Ov. (**2**) *men on earth*: ad superos fleti, Verg. N. pl. as subst. **sŭpĕra** -orum. (**1**) *heights*: Verg. (**2**) *heavenly bodies*: Cic.

Compar. **sŭpĕrĭor** -ius, *higher, upper*. LIT., of place: pars collis, Caes.; domus, Cic.; ex loco superiore, Caes.; de loco superiore dicere, *from the tribunal* (as praetor), Cic. TRANSF., (**1**) of time, *earlier, former, past*; as applied to *older*: nox, *the night before last*, Cic.; omnes aetatis superioris Caes.; tempus, annus, Cic. (**2**) of rank, power, etc., *higher, greater*: superioris ordinis nonnulli, Caes.; milit. t. t.: discessit superior, *gained the advantage*, Nep.; with abl.: loco, fortunā, famā, Cic.; facilitate humanitate superior, Cic.

Superl. **sŭprēmus** -a -um. LIT., of place, *highest, uppermost*: montes, Verg.; Lucr. Hor. TRANSF., (**1**) in time or succession, *last, final*: sole supremo, *at the setting of the sun*, Hor.; Troiae supremum audire laborem Verg.; Ov.: esp. *of the end of life*: dies, *the day of death* (or *burial*), Cic., Liv. tempus, Hor.; honor, *last rites*, Verg.; Ov. Tac. (**2**) of degree, *highest, greatest*: supplicium, Cic.; Verg. (**3**) of rank, *highest*: Iuppiter supreme, Pl.

¶ N. sing. as subst. **sŭprēmum** -i, *the end*: ventum ad supremum est, Verg. Ac as adv., *for the last time*: Ov. N. pl. as subst **sŭprēma** -orum. (**1**) *death*: Plin., Ta. (**2**) *funeral rites*: Verg., Plin., Tac. (**3**) *a last will and testament*: Tac.

Used as another superl. **summus** -a -um (for submus), *highest, uppermost, at the top*. LIT., of place: summum iugum montis Caes.; summa urbs, *the highest part of the city*, Cic.; in summa sacra via, Cic.; per summa aequora, Verg. TRANSF., (**1**) of the voice, *highest, loudest*: vox summa, Hor., etc. (**2**) of time or succession, *last*: venit summa dies, Verg.; senectus, *extreme old age*, Cic Hor., etc. (**3**) of degree, rank, etc., *greatest, highest, most distinguished, most important*: summi viri, Pl., Cic.; poet. n. pl.: summum ducum Atrides, Ov.; summus erga vos amor Cic.; summo studio, Cic.; summa salus re publicae, Cic.; quo res summa loco, *how is it with the state?* Verg.

¶ F. as subst. **summa** -ae. (**1**) *what is the top; the highest place*; also *the main thing, most important point; a summary, the gist*: vobis summam ordinis consiliique concedur Cic.; ipsae summae rerum atque sententiae Cic.; summa belli, *supreme command*, Caes. rerum, *the highest power*, Cic.; imperii, Cae Cic. (**2**) *the sum total of an amount*: equitum magnum numerum ex omni summa separar Cic.; summarum summa, *the universe*, Lucr pecuniae, Cic.; vitae, Hor.

N. as subst. **summum** -i, *surface, to* Caes., Cic. Acc. as adv., *at most*: quattu aut summum quinque, Cic.; Liv.

¶ Adv. **summē**, *in the highest degree, extremely*: contendere, Cic.; Caes., Hor.

ŭpervăcănĕus -a -um (super/vaco), *superfluous, unnecessary*: opus, *done in leisure hours*, Cic.; timor, Sall.; oratio, Liv.

ŭpervăcŭus -a -um, *superfluous, unnecessary*: metus, Ov.; Hor., Liv.

ŭpervădo -ĕre, *to go over, surmount*: ruinas, Liv.; Sall.

ŭpervĕhor -vĕhi -vectus sum, *to ride* or *sail past*: promunturium Calabriae, Liv.

ŭpervĕnĭo -vĕnire -vēni -ventum. (1) with acc., *to come upon, rise above*: unda supervenit undam, Hor.; Ov. (2) *to arrive, come up*, esp. *unexpectedly*: legati superveniunt, Liv.; with dat.: huic laetitiae, Liv.; Verg., Hor.

ŭperventus -ūs, m. (supervenio), *a coming up, (unexpected) arrival*: Tac.

ŭpervīvo -ĕre, *to survive*; with dat.: Plin. L.

ŭpervŏlĭto -are, *to fly over*: sua tecta alis, Verg.; Tac.

ŭpervŏlo -are, *to fly over, fly above*: Verg.; with acc.: totum orbem, Ov.

ŭpīno -are (supinus), *to put face upwards, throw on the back*: Verg., Quint. Pass. in middle sense: nasum nidore supinor, Hor.

ŭpīnus -a -um (from sub; cf. Gr. ὕπτιος), *lying on the back, face-upwards*.

LIT., motus corporis pronus, obliquus, supinus, Cic.; manus supinas ad caelum tendere, *spread out with the palm upwards*, Verg.; Lucr., Liv., etc.

TRANSF., (1) of streams, *flowing up, returning*: nec redit in fontes unda supina suos, Ov. (2) of ground, *sloping upwards*: collis, Verg.; vallis, Liv.; Hor. (3) of character, *careless, negligent, lazy*: Cat., Quint., Juv.

ŭppaenĭtet -ēre, *to cause slight regret*: illum furoris, Cic. L.

ŭppalpor -ari, dep. *to caress, flatter a little*; with dat.: Pl.

ŭppar -păris (sub/par), *almost equal*: huic aetati suppares Alcibiades, Critias, Cic.

ŭppărăsĭtor -ari, dep. (sub/parasitor), *to flatter a little like a parasite*; with dat.: Pl.

ŭppărum -i, n. and **suppărus** -i, m. *a linen garment, usually worn by women*: Pl.

ŭppĕdĭtātĭo -ōnis, f. (suppedito), *an abundant provision*: bonorum, Cic.

ŭppĕdĭto -are.

(1) intransit., *to be at hand, be ready, suffice*: often with dat. of person: flumina suppeditant, Lucr.; cui si vita suppeditavisset, *had lasted long enough*, Cic.; ea quae suppeditent et ad cultum et ad victum, Cic.; Liv.

(2) transit., *to provide, supply, offer, give*: alicui frumentum, Cic.; cibos, Cic.; patria nobis praecepta, Lucr.; pass.: suppeditari aliquā re, *to be provided with*, Cic.

ŭppernātus -a -um (sub/perna), *lamed in the hip*. TRANSF., alnus suppernata securi, Cat.

ŭppĕtĭae -ārum, f. pl., used only in nom. and acc. (suppeto), *help, aid*: Pl., Suet. In acc., with verb of motion, *to come to help*: Pl.

ŭppĕtĭor -ari, dep. (suppetiae), *to come to help, assist*: mihi, Cic. L.

ŭppĕto -ĕre -īvi and -ii -ītum (sub/peto), *to be in store, be at hand*.

LIT., ne pabuli quidem satis magna copia suppetebat, Caes.; ut mihi ad remunerandum nihil suppetat praeter voluntatem, Cic.; si vita suppetet, *if I live so long*, Cic.; of materials for a speech: vererer ne mihi crimina non suppeterent, Cic.; Liv.

TRANSF., *to suffice, be enough for*: ut cotidianis sumptibus copiae suppetant, Cic.; Hor., Liv.

suppīlo -are, *to steal secretly, filch*: mihi pallam ex arcis, Pl. With personal object, *to rob, fleece*: Pl.

suppingo -pingĕre -pactum (sub/pango), *to fasten underneath*: Pl.

supplanto -are (sub/planta), *to throw down a person by tripping up his heels*: aliquem, Cic. TRANSF., Plin., Pers.

supplēmentum -i, n. (suppleo), *a filling up, completion*. (1) as a process: in supplementum classis, Liv. (2) concr., as milit. t. t., *a body of recruits, reinforcements*: supplementi cogendi, Caes.

supplĕo -plēre -plēvi -plētum, *to fill up, make complete*: summam, Lucr.; bibliothecam, Cic. L.; sanguine venas, Ov.; inania moenia, *to people*, Ov. Esp. milit. t. t.: legiones, Liv.; Verg., Tac.

supplex -plĭcis (sub/plico), *kneeling*; hence, *humbly entreating, supplicating, suppliant*.

LIT., of persons: supplex te ad pedes abiciebas, Cic.; Pl., Verg., etc.; with dat.: alicui, Pl., Cic., etc. M. as subst., *a suppliant*: Caes., Cic. With possess. pron.: vester est supplex, Cic.; Hor. With objective genit.: misericordiae vestrae, Cic.

TRANSF., of things: multis et supplicibus verbis, Cic.; Verg., Hor., etc.

¶ Adv. **supplĭcĭter**, *suppliantly, humbly*: respondere, Cic.; Caes., Verg., etc.

supplĭcātĭo -ōnis, f. (supplico), *a solemn public entreaty* or (more often) *thanksgiving; a religious festival* or *fast on account of public success* or *misfortune*: ad omnia pulvinaria supplicationem decernere, Cic.; prodigiorum averruncandorum causā supplicationes in biduum decernere, Liv.; Caes.

supplĭcĭter, adv. from supplex; q.v.

supplĭcĭum -i, n. (supplico), *a kneeling down, either in entreaty* or *to receive punishment*.

Hence (1) *a humble entreaty, supplication, prayer*: **a**, to the gods: precibus suppliciisque deos placare, Liv.; Pl., Sall.: **b**, to men: fatigati suppliciis regis, Sall.

(2) *punishment*; esp., *capital punishment*: sumere supplicium de aliquo, *to inflict punishment on*, Pl., Caes., Cic., etc.; ad ultimum supplicium progredi, Caes.; satis supplicii tulisse, Caes.; supplicia, haurire, Verg.; Hor., Tac.

supplĭco -are (supplex), *to kneel, beseech, entreat*: Pl., Cic., etc.; with dat.: alicui publice, Cic.; Caesari pro te, Cic. L. Esp. *to pray to the gods*: per hostias diis, Sall.; Pl., Liv.

supplōdo -plōdĕre -plōsi (sub/plaudo), *to stamp*: pedem, Cic.

supplōsĭo -ōnis, f. (supplodo), *a stamping*: pedis, Cic.

suppōno -pōnĕre -pŏsŭi (-pŏsīvi: Pl.) -pŏsĭtum (syncop. partic., suppostus: Verg.).

(1) *to put, place, lay under*; with dat. LIT., ova gallinis, Cic.; falcem maturis aristis,

Verg.; aliquem tumulo, *to bury*, Ov.; terrae dentes vipereos, *to sow*, Ov.; Hor. TRANSF., *to subject*: aethera ingenio suo, Ov.

(2) *to put next to, to add*: generi partes, Cic.

(3) *to put in the place of.* In gen.: aliquem in alicuius locum, Cic.; Pl. Esp. *to substitute that which is not genuine, to counterfeit, forge*: testamenta falsa, Cic.; Pl., Verg., Liv.

supporto -are (sub/porto), *to bring, carry, convey, up to*: frumentum, Caes.; omnia hinc in castra, Liv.

suppŏsītīcĭus -a -um (suppono), *put in the place of another, substituted*: Mart. Esp. *supposititious, spurious*: Pl.

suppŏsĭtĭo -ōnis, f. (suppono), *a substitution* of one for another: pueri, Pl.

suppŏsĭtrix -trīcis, f. (suppono), *she that substitutes*: puerorum, Pl.

suppostus, *see* suppono.

suppressĭo -ōnis, f. (supprimo), *embezzlement*: iudiciales (sc. pecuniae), Cic.

suppressus -a -um, partic. from supprimo; q.v.

supprĭmo -prīmĕre -pressi -pressum (sub/premo), *to press down, press under.*

LIT., navem, *to sink*, Liv.

TRANSF., (1) *to hold down, check, restrain*: hostem nostros insequentem, Caes; vocem, fugam, Ov.; impetum, iram, Liv. (2) *to keep back, suppress, conceal*: famam decreti, Liv.; pecuniam, nummos, *to embezzle*, Cic. ¶ Hence partic. **suppressus** -a -um, *checked, restrained*; as adj. (with compar.), of the voice, *low, subdued*: vox, Cic.; orator suppressior ut voce, sic etiam oratione, Cic.

supprōmus -i, m. (sub/promus), *an underbutler*: Pl.

suppŭdet -ēre (sub/pudet), *to cause some shame*; with acc. and genit.: eorum (librorum) me suppudet, Cic. L.

suppūrātĭo -ōnis, f. (suppuro), *a purulent ulcer, suppuration*: Plin., Sen. L.

suppūro -are (sub/pus), *to form matter, suppurate*: Cato, Plin.

suppus -a -um (sub), *head-downwards*: Lucr.

suppŭto -are (sub/puto). (1) *to prune beneath*: Cato. (2) *to count up, compute*: et sibi quid sit utile sollicitis supputat articulis, Ov.; Sen.

suprā, adv. and prep. (for superā, sc. parte; from superus).

Adv. (with compar. **sŭpĕrĭus**), *above, over, on the top.* LIT., of place: omnia haec, quae supra et subter, unum esse, Cic.; et mare quod supra teneant, quodque adluit infra, Verg.; toto vertice supra est, *is taller*, Verg. TRANSF., (1) of time, *before, previously*: pauca supra repetere, Sall.; hence, in writing, *above*: ut supra dixi, Cic.; uti supra demonstravimus, Caes. (2) of amount, degree, etc., *over, more, beyond*: supra adiecit Aeschrio, Cic.; ita accurate ut nihil possit supra, Cic.; supra deos lacessere, Hor. With quam, *more than*: rem supra feret quam fieri potest, Cic.; Sall.

Prep., with acc. LIT., of place, with verbs of rest or motion, *above, over*: fera salta supra venabula fertur, Verg.; supra subterque terram per dies quindecim pugnatum est, Liv.; of position at table: accumbere supra aliquem, Cic.; fig.: supra caput esse, *to be over a person's head, to be imminent*, Sall.,

Verg., Liv. TRANSF., (1) of time, *before* supra hanc memoriam, Caes.; Liv. (2) o amount, degree, etc., *more than, above beyond*: supra millia viginti, Liv.; supra modum, Liv.; supra vires, Hor.; Cic.

suprascando -ĕre, *to climb over, surmount* fines, Liv.

suprēmus, etc.; *see* superus.

sūra -ae, f. *the calf of the leg*: Pl., Verg., Ov.

surcŭlus -i, m. (dim. of surus). (1) *a youn* shoot, sprout, twig*: Verg.; surculum de fringere (as a sign of taking possession), Cic (2) *a slip, sucker*: Cic.

surdaster -tra -trum (surdus), *somewhat deaf* Cic.

surdĭtās -ātis, f. (surdus), *deafness*: Cic.

surdus -a -um, adj. (with compar.), *deaf.* LIT., Cic.; prov.: surdis canere, *to preac to deaf ears*, Verg.; haud surdis auribus dicta Liv.

TRANSF., (1) *deaf=not willing to hea insensible*: per numquam surdos in tua vot deos, Ov.; surdae ad omnia solacia aures Liv.; leges rem surdam, inexorabilem esse Liv. (2) *not heard, still, silent*: lyra, Prop. gratia, Ov. (3) of sounds, smells, etc. *indistinct, faint*: Pers., Plin., Quint.

surēna -ae, m. *a grand vizier, prime ministe among the Parthians*: Tac.

surgo surgĕre surrexi surrectum; syncop. per infin. surrexe: Hor. (sub/rego; cf. subrigo intransit. verb, *to rise, get up, stand up.*

LIT., in gen.: e lectulo, Cic.; de sellā, Cic. humo, Ov.; of orators: ad dicendum, Cic. often *to rise from bed* or *sleep*: Cic., Hor., Ov Of things: surgit dies, ventus, Verg.; so Hor.; ignis, Ov. Esp. of growing things o persons, *to spring up, arise*: surgens nova Carthaginis urbs, Verg.; surgens Iulus, Verg. Hor., etc.

TRANSF., animo sententia surgit, Verg discordia, Verg.; Ov., Tac., etc.

surpŭit, etc., forms from surripio; q.v.

surra-, *see* subra-.

surre-, *see* subre-.

surreptīcĭus (subreptīcĭus) -a -um (surripio *stolen.* LIT., puer, *kidnapped*, Pl. TRANSF *secret, surreptitious*: amor, Pl.

surri- *see* subri- (except surripio).

surrĭpĭo -rĭpĕre -rĭpŭi -reptum; syncop. form surpere: Lucr.; surpite: Hor.; surpuit: Pl surpuerat: Hor. (sub/rapio), *to take awa secretly; to steal, filch, pilfer.*

LIT., vasa ex privato sacro, Cic.; filium e custodia, Liv.; with dat.: me morti, Hor.; l Esp. of plagiarism: a Naevio vel sumpsis multa, si fateris, vel, si negas, surripuisti, Cic Sen.

TRANSF., virtus nec eripi nec surri potest, Cic.; Lucr., Ov.

surrŏgo=subrogo; q.v.

surru-, *see* subru-.

sursum (susum: Pl.; **sursus**: Lucr.), ad (sub/verto), *upwards, on high*; with ver of motion or rest: Ter., Cic., Lucr., et sursum deorsum, *up and down, backwar and forwards*, Cic.

sūs sŭis, c. (ὗς). (1) *a sow, swine, pig, hog*: C (2) *a kind of fish*: Ov.

suscensĕo -ēre -ŭi, *to be angry, bear a grudg* with dat.: alicui vehementer, Cic.; Pl., Te with n. acc.: illud vereor ne tibi illu suscensere aliquid suspicēre, Cic.; with propter and acc.: Ov.; with quia, or quod: Cic.; with acc. and infin.: Liv.

susceptĭo -ōnis, f. (suscipio), *an undertaking*: causae, Cic.

suscĭpĭo -cĭpĕre -cēpi -ceptum (subs=sub/capio), *to take up, catch up; to support or raise.*

LIT., in gen.: sol aeternam lampada mundi, Lucr.; dominam ruentem, Verg.; cruorem pateris, Verg. Esp., *to take up a new-born child from the ground, and so acknowledge it*: in lucem editi et suscepti sumus, Cic.; hence, filium, etc., suscepisse ex aliqua, *to have a child*: liberos ex filiā libertini suscepisse, Cic.; de te subolem, Verg.

TRANSF., (1) *to accept, receive* a person into a community or relationship: aliquem in civitatem, Cic.; discipulos, Quint. (2) *to take* a thing *upon oneself; to undertake, begin, take up*: bellum, negotium, Cic.; personam viri boni, Cic.; sacra peregrina, *to adopt*, Cic.; invidiam, Cic.; dolorem, Cic.; magnam molestiam, Cic.; morbos, Lucr.; rem, Liv. (3) *to maintain* a thing, *be ready to prove*: quae si suscipimus, Cic.; with acc. and infin.: Cic.

uscīto -are, *to stir up, make to rise.*

LIT., in gen.: terga aratro, Verg.; lintea, Ov.; Cat., Lucr. Esp. *to arouse from sleep*: somno, Pl.; e somno, Cic.

TRANSF., of persons, feelings, movements, etc., *to arouse, excite*: te ab tuis subsellis contra te testem suscitabo, Cic.; ignes sopitos, Verg.; viros in arma, Verg.; Romanum cum Saguntino bellum, Liv.

uspecto -are (freq. of suspicio). (1) *to keep looking up at, regard, gaze upon*: Ter. (2) *to look upon with suspicion, suspect*: aliquem, Tac.; with acc. and infin.: Tac.

suspectus -a -um, partic. from ¹suspicio; q.v.

²suspectus -ūs, m. (¹suspicio), *a looking upwards.* LIT., aetherium ad Olympum, Verg.; turris vasto suspectu, Verg. TRANSF., *looking up to; respect, esteem*: Ov.

uspendĭum -i, n. (suspendo), *a hanging of oneself*: suspendio perire, Cic.; Pl.; plur.: praebuit illa arbor misero suspendia collo, *has served for hanging*, Ov.

uspendo -pendĕre -pendi -pensum, *to hang up.*

LIT., in gen.: in litore vestes, Lucr.; Verg. Esp. (1) *to hang* a person: se, Pl.; aliquem in oleastro, Cic.; se de ficu, Cic.; Ov. (2) *to hang as an offering in a temple*: vestimenta deo maris, Hor.; Verg. (3) *to prop up, support*; with abl.: murum furculis, Liv.; Caes. (4) tellurem sulco tenui, *to plough up*, Verg.

TRANSF., (1) *to keep in suspense, leave undecided*: rem medio responso, Liv.; animos fictā gravitate, Ov.; in pass., *to hang upon, depend on*: Cic. L. (2) *to check, break off*: fletum, Ov.; spiritum, Quint. (3) naso suspendis adunco ignotos, *you sneer at*, Hor.

¶ Hence partic. **suspensus** -a -um, *hovering, hanging, suspended.*

LIT., of position or movement: saxis suspensam rupem, Verg.; suspenso gradu ire, Ter.; aquila suspensis demissa leniter alis, Liv.; Lucr., Cic.

TRANSF., (1) *hanging upon, dependent*: ex bono casu omnia suspensa sunt, Cic.; Liv.

(2) *ambiguous, uncertain, doubtful, in suspense*: animus, Cic.; aliquem suspensum tenere, Cic.; tot populos inter spem metumque suspensos animi habetis, Liv.; timor, Ov.; verba, Tac.

suspĭcax -ācis (suspicor). (1) act., *suspicious, suspecting*: animus, Tac.; Nep., Liv. (2) pass., *suspicious, suspected*: silentium, Tac.

¹suspĭcĭo -spĭcere -spexi -spectum (sub/specio).

(1) *to look from below, to look upwards.* LIT., in caelum, Cic. With acc.: caelum, Cic.; ramos, Ov. TRANSF., *to look up to; to esteem, respect*: viros, Cic.; eloquentiam, Cic.; Hor.

(2) *to look askance at, to suspect*: suspectus regi, et ipse eum suspiciens, novas res cupere, Sall.

¶ Hence partic. (with compar.) **suspectus** -a -um, *suspected*; of persons and things: aliquem suspectum habere, *to suspect*, Pl., Caes.; with dat.: meis civibus, Cic.; with de: cum filius patri suspectus esset de novercā, Cic.; with genit.: suspectus cupiditatis imperii, Liv.; with infin.: suspectus eius consilia fovisse, Tac.

²suspĭcĭo -ōnis, f. (1) *mistrust, suspicion*: in qua nulla subest suspicio, Cic.; suspicionem movere, Cic.; suspicio cadit in aliquem, Cic.; est suspicio, foll. by acc. and infin., Pl., Cic.; in suspicionem alicui venire, foll. by acc. and infin., Cic.; with genit.: suspicio stupri, Pl.; belli, Caes. (2) *a faint idea, imperfect conception*: deorum, Cic.

suspĭcĭōsus -a -um (²suspicio). (1) *feeling suspicion, suspecting, suspicious*: in aliquem, Cic.; Ter., Sen. (2) *exciting suspicion, suspicious*: crimen, Cic.; superl.: Cic.

¶ Hence adv. (with compar.) **suspĭcĭōsē**, *in a suspicious manner, suspiciously*: aliquid dicere, Cic.; suspiciosius dicere, Cic.

suspĭcor -ari, dep. (and **suspĭco** -are: Pl.).

(1) *to suspect*; with acc. of thing: res nefarias, Cic.; with acc. and infin.: ea quae fore suspicatus erat, Caes.; Pl., Ov., etc.; with acc. of person: Pl.

(2) *to conjecture, suppose, surmise*: licet aliquid etiam de Popilii ingenio suspicari, Cic.; quantum ex monumentis suspicari licet, Cic.; with indir. quest.: quid sibi impenderet coepit suspicari, Cic.; with acc. and infin.: quod valde suspicor fore, Ov.

suspīrātĭo -ōnis, f. (suspiro), *a deep breath, sigh*: Plin., Quint.

suspīrātus -ūs, m. (suspiro), *a deep breath, a sigh*: Ov.

suspīrĭtus -ūs, m. (suspiro), *a breathing deeply, a sigh*: Pl., Cic. L., Liv.

suspīrĭum -i, n. (suspiro), *a deep breath, a sigh*: Pl., Cic., etc.

suspīro -are (sub/spiro). (1) intransit., *to draw a deep breath, to sigh*: occulte, Cic. L.; Lucr., Hor.; in aliquo, *to sigh for, long for*, Ov. (2) transit., *to sigh for, long for*: amores, Tib.; Chloen, Hor.

susque dēque, adv. *up and down*; prov.: de Octavio susque deque (sc. fero, or habeo), *I do not trouble about O., one way or the other*, Cic.

sustentācŭlum -i, n. (sustento), *a prop, support*: Tac.

sustentātĭo -ōnis, f. (sustento), *forbearance*: habere aliquam moram et sustentationem, Cic.

sustento -are (freq. of sustineo), *to hold up, support, sustain.*
    Lit., multosque per annos sustentata ruet moles et machina mundi, Lucr.; fratrem ruentem dextrā, Verg.
    Transf., (1) in gen., *to sustain, support, strengthen*: rempublicam, Cic.; Troianas opes, Verg.; aciem, Tac. (2) *to sustain with food* or *money, maintain, support*: familiam, Ter.; se amicorum liberalitate, Cic.; aër spiritu ductus alit et sustentat animantes, Cic.; frumento plebem, Liv. (3) *to put off, hinder, delay*: rem, Cic. L.; hostem, *to check*, Tac.

sustĭnĕo -tĭnēre -tĭnŭi -tentum (subs=sub/teneo), *to hold up, support, sustain.*
    Lit., (1) onus, Pl.; aër volatūs alitum sustinet, Cic.; se a lapsu, *to keep oneself from falling*, Liv.; so, simply: se, Caes.; of trees: (arbores) sustineant poma, Ov. (2) *to hold back, check, restrain*: equum incitatum, Cic.; exercitum, Caes.; gradum, Ov.; Verg., etc.
    Transf., (1) *to sustain* a duty, or trouble: munus in republica, Cic.; sustines non parvam exspectationem, Cic.; labores, Cic.; vulnera, Caes.; certamen, Liv. With infin., *to endure to, have the heart to*: Liv., Ov.; with acc. and infin.: sustinebunt tales viri se tot senatoribus, tot populorum privatorumque litteris non credidisse, Cic.; Ov. (2) *to sustain with food*, etc.; *to support, maintain*: ager non amplius hominum quinque millia sustinere potest, Cic.; Verg., Liv. (3) *to put off, delay*: rem in noctem, Liv.; Caes. (4) *to check, restrain*: impetum hostis, Caes.; se a respondendo, Cic.; Liv.

sustollo -ĕre. (1) *to lift up, raise*: Pl., Cat., Lucr., Ov. (2) *to take away, remove, destroy*: filiam, Pl.

sŭsurrātor -ōris, m. (susurro), *a mutterer*: ap. Cic. L.

sŭsurro -are (susurrus), *to murmur, mutter, whisper*; of men: Ov.; of bees, *to hum*: Verg.; of water or wind: Verg.

¹sŭsurrus -i, m. *a murmuring, muttering, whispering, humming, buzzing*: Cic., Verg., Hor., etc.

²sŭsurrus -a -um (¹susurrus), *whispering, muttering*: lingua, Ov.

sūtēlae -arum, f. pl. (suo), *sewings together*; fig., *cunning tricks, artifices*: Pl.

sūtĭlis -e (suo), *stitched together, fastened together*: cymba, Verg.; Ov.

sūtor -ōris, m. (suo), *a shoemaker, cobbler*: Pl., Cic.; prov.: ne sutor supra crepidam (sc. iudicet), *let the cobbler stick to his last*, Plin.

sūtōrĭus -a -um (sutor), *of a shoemaker*: atramentum, *blacking*, Cic.

sūtrīnus -a -um (sutor), *of a shoemaker*: taberna, *cobbler's stall*, Tac.
    ¶ F. as subst. **sūtrīna** -ae. (1) (sc. ars), *a shoemaker's trade*: Varr. (2) (sc. taberna), *a shoemaker's shop*: Plin. N. as subst. **sūtrīnum** -i, *a shoemaker's trade*: Sen.

Sūtrĭum -i, n. *a town in Etruria* (now *Sutri*).
    ¶ Hence adj. **Sūtrīnus** -a -um, *of Sutrium*; m. pl. as subst. **Sūtrīni** -ōrum, *the inhabitants of Sutrium.*

sūtūra -ae, f. (suo), *a seam, suture*: Liv.

sŭus -a -um, reflexive possessive pronoun o 3rd person, *his, her, its, their* (*own*).
    (1) of simple possession; used of person and things; the owner being the grammatic subject of clause or main sentence, or to b understood from context: Caesar copiā suas divisit, Caes.; suus cuique erat locu definitus, Cic.; aliquem suum facere, *mak one's own*, Liv. With proprius: sua cuiqu laus propria debetur, Cic.; with the eth dat.: factus (consul) est bis, primum an tempus, iterum sibi suo tempore, Cic.; wi ipse: sua ipsam peremptam (esse) merced Liv.; strengthened by -pte or -met: Crassu suāpte interfectum manu, Cic.; cap suismet ipsi praesidiis, Liv.
    (2) in special senses: a, *proper, du suitable*: suum numerum habere, Cic.: favourable, propitious*: utebatur populo su Cic.: c, *independent, in one's own power*: poterit semper esse in disputando suus, Cic Pl.: d, rarely objective: iniuria sua, again himself*, Sall.
    ¶ As subst., *one's own people, propert* etc.: quem sui Caesarem salutabant, Cic ad suum pervenire, *to come into one's ow* Cic.

Sȳbăris -ris, f. (Σύβαρις), *a river and town* *Lucania, famous for luxury.*
    ¶ Hence subst. **Sȳbărīta** -ae. m. *Sybarite*; **Sȳbărītĭs** -ĭdis, f. *name of wanton poem*; adj. **Sȳbărītānus** -a -um a **Sȳbărītĭcus** -a -um, *of Sybaris.*

Sȳchaeus -i, m. *husband of Dido.*
    ¶ Hence adj. **Sȳchaeus** -a -um, *belongi to Sychaeus.*

sȳcŏphanta -ae, f. (συκοφάντης), *an inform trickster, deceiver*: Pl., Ter.

sȳcŏphantĭa -ae, f. (συκοφαντία), *craft, d ception*: Pl.

sȳcŏphantĭōsē, adv. (sycophanta), *roguish craftily*: Pl.

sȳcŏphantor -ari, dep. (συκοφαντέω), *to pl tricks, act craftily*: Pl.

Sȳēnē -ēs, f. (Συήνη), *a town in Upper Egy famous for its red granite* (now *Assouan*).
    ¶ Hence adj. **Sȳēnītēs** -ae, m. (Συηνίτη *of Syene.*

Sylla=Sulla; q.v.

syllăba -ae, f. (συλλαβή), *a syllable.* L syllaba brevis, longa, Cic.; Pl., Ov., e Transf., plur.: syllabae, *verses, poen* Mart.

syllăbātim, adv. (syllaba), *syllable by syllab* Cic.

syllŏgismus (or -os) -i, m. (συλλογισμός), *syllogism*: Sen., Quint.

syllŏgistĭcus -a -um (συλλογιστικός), *syllogist* Quint.

Sȳmaethus -i, m. (Σύμαιθος), *a river in easte Sicily.*
    ¶ Hence adj. **Sȳmaethēus** and **Sȳma thĭus** -a -um, *Symaethian*: flumina, Cic *fall into the Symaethus*, Verg.; heros, A son of the nymph of the Symaethus*, O f. adj. **Sȳmaethĭs** -ĭdis: nympha, *the nym of the river Symaethus.*

symbŏla -ae, f. (συμβολή), *a contribution money to a common feast*: Pl., Ter.

symbŏlus -i, m. and **symbŏlum** -i, (σύμβολος and -ον), *a sign, token, symbol*: Pl

symmētrĭa -ae, f. (συμμετρία), *symmetry*: P

ymphōnĭa -ae, f. (συμφωνία), *a concert, musical performance*: Cic., Hor., Liv.

ymphōnĭăcus -a -um (συμφωνιακός), *of* or *for a concert*: pueri, *singing boys*, Cic.

ymplegma -ătis, n. (σύμπλεγμα), *a group of wrestlers, closely embracing each other*: Plin., Mart.

yncĕrastum -i, n. (συγκεραστόν), *a dish of hotchpotch, hash*: Varr.

ӯnecdŏchē -ēs, f. (συνεκδοχή), *a figure of speech by which a part is put for the whole*, or *the cause for the result*; *synecdoche*: Quint.

ӯnedrus -i, m. (σύνεδρος), *a councillor* among the Macedonians: Liv.

Ӯnĕphēbi -ōrum, n. (συνέφηβοι), *The Young Companions* (a comedy by Statius Caecilius): Cic.

yngrăpha -ae, f. (συγγραφή), *a bond, promissory note, agreement to pay*: cedere alicui aliquid per syngrapham, Cic.; facere syngraphas cum aliquo, Cic.; ius dicere ex syngrapha, Cic.

yngrăphus -i, m. (σύγγραφος). (1) *a written contract*: Pl. (2) *a passport*: Pl.

ynl-, *see* syll-.

ӯnnăda -ōrum, n. pl. (τὰ Σύνναδα), *a small town in Phrygia, famous for its marble.*

¶ Hence adj. **Synnădensis** -e, *of Synnada.*

ӯnŏdūs -ontis, m. (συνόδους), *a fish,* perhaps *a kind of bream*: Ov.

ynthēsĭnus -a -um (συνθέσινος), *of a dressing-gown*: Suet.

ynthĕsis -is, f. (σύνθεσις, *a putting together*). (1) *a dinner-service, set of dishes*: Mart., Stat. (2) *a suit of clothes*: Mart. (3) *a light upper garment, dressing-gown*: Mart.

ӯphax -phācis, m. (Σύφαξ), *king of Numidia,* at the time of the second Punic war.

ӯrācūsae -ārum, f. pl. (Συρακοῦσαι), *the chief town of Sicily, a Corinthian colony, birth-place of Archimedes and Theocritus.*

¶ Hence adj. **Sӯrācūsānus, Sӯrācūsĭus, Sӯrācōsĭus** -a -um, *Syracusan.*

ӯrĭa -ae, f. (Συρία), *Syria, a country in Asia.*

¶ Hence adj. **Sӯrĭus, Sӯrus, Sӯrĭăcus** -a -um, *Syrian*; subst. **Sӯri** -ōrum, m. pl. (Σύροι), *the Syrians.*

ӯrma -mătis, n. (σύρμα), *a long, trailing robe, frequently worn by tragic actors*: Juv. TRANSF., *tragedy*: Mart., Juv.

ӯrŏphoenix -nīcis, m. (Συροφοίνιξ), *a Syrophoenician.*

ӯrŏs -i, f. (Σύρος), *an island in the Aegean Sea* (now *Sira*).

ӯrtis -is, f. (Σύρτις), *a sandbank, a quicksand*; esp. *one on the coast of Northern Africa, including Syrtis Major* (now *Sidra*)*, and Syrtis Minor* (now *Cabes*): Verg., Liv. TRANSF., *the coast opposite the Syrtis*: Hor.

¶ Hence adj. **Syrticus** -a -um, *of the Syrtis.*

T

, t, the nineteenth letter of the Latin Alphabet, corresponding with the Greek tau (Τ, τ). For the use of T. as an abbreviation, see Table of Abbreviations.

ăbānus -i, m. *a gad-fly, horse-fly*: Varr., Plin.

ăbella -ae, f. (dim. of tabula), *a small flat board* or *tablet.*

In gen.: liminis, *the threshold*, Cat.; *the tray* or *trough in which Romulus and Remus were exposed*: Ov.; parva, *a draught-board*, Ov.

Esp. (1) *a writing-tablet*: cerata, *covered with wax*, Cic.; Ov. Hence *a document, letter, record*, etc.: tabellas proferri iussimus, Cic.; tabellae quaestionis, Cic.; Pl., Liv., etc. (2) *a votive tablet hung up in a temple*: Hor., Ov. (3) *a voting-ticket, ballot*, as used at political elections and in law-courts: Caes., Cic., Prop.

tăbellārĭus -a -um (tabella).

(1) *of* or *relating to letters*: naves, *mail-boats*, Sen. M. as subst. **tăbellārĭus** -i, *a letter-carrier*: Cic., Liv.

(2) *relating to voting*: lex, Cic.; Plin. L.

tābĕo -ēre (tabum). (1) *to waste away, be consumed*: Lucr., Ov. (2) *to drip, run*: artūs sale (*sea-water*) tabentes, Verg.

tăberna -ae, f. *a booth, hut.* Hence (1) *a cottage, hovel*: pauperum tabernae, Hor. (2) *a stall, shop*: libraria, *a bookseller's shop*, Cic.; Hor., Liv., etc. (3) *an inn, tavern*: in tabernam devertere, Cic.; Pl., etc. (4) *an arcade*, or *block of seats, in the Circus*: Cic. (5) as a proper name: Tres Tabernae, *a place on the Appian Road.*

tăbernācŭlum -i, n. (taberna), *a hut, a tent*: tabernaculum in campo Martio sibi conlocare, Cic. Esp., in religious language, *a place outside the city chosen by the augurs for taking the auspices before the comitia*: capere tabernaculum, Cic., Liv.

tăbernārĭus -i, m. (taberna), *a shopkeeper*: Cic.

tăbernŭla -ae, f. (dim. of taberna), *a little shop, small tavern*: Suet.

tābēs -is, f. (cf. tabum), *wasting away, decay, melting.*

LIT., liquescentis nivis, Liv.; Cic., etc.

TRANSF., (1) *a disease, plague, pestilence*: tanta vis morbi, uti tabes, plerosque civium animos invaserat, Sall.; Liv. (2) *moral decay, demoralization*: Cic., Verg., etc. (3) *decayed matter, corruption*: sanguinis, Liv.; Lucr., etc.

tābesco tābescĕre tābŭi (tabeo), *to melt, waste away, be consumed.*

LIT., corpora calore, Ov.; Cic., Lucr.

TRANSF., *to pine, be spoiled, be ruined*: dolore, Cic.; nolite pati regnum Numidiae per scelus et sanguinem familiae nostrae tabescere, Sall.; Lucr., Hor., etc.

tābĭdŭlus -a -um (dim. of tabidus), *wasting, consuming*: mors, Verg.

tābĭdus -a -um (tabes). (1) pass., *melting, wasting, decaying, dissolving*: nix, Liv.; mens, Ov. (2) act., *consuming, causing to waste away*: lues, Verg.; venenum, Tac.; Ov.

tābĭfĭcus -a -um (tabes/facio), *melting, consuming, causing to waste away.* LIT., Lucr., Suet. TRANSF., mentis perturbationes, Cic.

tābŭla -ae, f. *a board, plank.*

In gen.: tabulam adripere de naufragio, Cic.

Esp. (1) *a writing-tablet*: Liv., etc. Hence *a document*; in plur., *a record, register*: tabulae publicae, Cic.; xii tabulae, *the Twelve Tables*, Cic.; of the censor's *lists*: Liv.; tabulae novae, *new account-books, by which old debts were cancelled*, Cic. (2) *a catalogue*, or *notice, of an auction*; hence *an auction*:

adest ad tabulam, *at the auction*, Cic. (3) *a gaming-board, draught-board*: Ov. (4) *a painted panel, a painting, picture*: tabula picta, *or*, simply, tabula, Cic.; Pl., etc.; prov.: manum de tabula, *hold! enough!* Cic. (5) *a votive tablet*: Hor. (6) *a map*: Cic. L.

tăbŭlārĭum -i, n. (tabula), *archives, records*: Cic., Verg., etc.

tăbŭlārĭus -i, m. (tabula), *a keeper of records*: Sen.

tăbŭlātĭo -ōnis, f. (tabula), *a flooring, planking, storey*: Caes.

tăbŭlātus -a -um (tabula), *floored, boarded*: Plin. L. N. as subst. **tăbŭlātum** -i, *a flooring, floor, storey*: Caes.; Verg., Liv. TRANSF., *a row* or *layer of vines*: Verg.

tābum -i, n. (sing. only; connected with τήκω). LIT., *corrupt moisture, matter*: terram tabo maculant; Verg.; Tac., etc. TRANSF., *a plague, pestilence*: corpora adfecta tabo, Liv.; Verg., Ov.

Tăburnus -i, m. *a range of mountains between Samnium and Campania.*

tăceo -ēre -ŭi -ĭtum, *to be silent, say nothing.*
(1) intransit. LIT., *not to speak*: an me taciturum tantis de rebus existimavistis? Cic.; Pl., Liv. etc. TRANSF., in gen. (=silere), *to be noiseless, still, quiet*: tacet omnis ager, Verg.; fig.: indoles illa Romana, Liv.; Ov.
(2) transit., *to be silent about* anything, *pass over in silence*: quod adhuc semper tacui, et tacendum putavi, Cic.; ut alios taceam, *to say nothing about others*, Ov.; pass.: aureus in medio Marte tacetur amor, Ov.; gerundive: dicenda tacenda locutus, Hor.

¶ Hence partic. **tăcĭtus** -a -um. (1) pass., *passed over in silence, unmentioned.* LIT., aliquid tacitum relinquere, Cic.; aliquid tacitum continere, Liv. TRANSF., **a**, *silently assumed, implied, tacit*: adsensio, Cic.: **b**, *secret, concealed*: iudicium, Cic.; vulnus, Verg.; Ov. (2) act.: **a**, of persons, *not speaking, silent, mute*: me tacito, *I being silent*, Cic.; hoc tacitus praeterire non possum, Cic.; often in the place of the adv.: tacita tecum loquitur patria, *silently*, Cic.; Pl., Hor., Liv.: **b**, of things, *still, quiet*: nox, Ov.; Verg., Hor.

¶ Adv. **tăcĭtē**, *silently, quietly*: Cic., Liv., etc.

tăcĭturnĭtās -ātis, f. (taciturnus), *silence, taciturnity*: opus est fide ac taciturnitate, Ter.; nosti hominis taciturnitatem, Cic.; Hor., etc.

tăcĭturnus -a -um, adj. (with compar.: Hor., and superl.: Pl.) (tacitus), *silent.* Of persons, *taciturn* (opp. loquax): homo, Cic.; ingenium statuā taciturnius, Hor. Of things, *still, quiet*: silentia, Lucr.; amnis, Hor.; Ov.

¹**tăcĭtus** -a -um, partic. from taceo; q.v.

²**Tăcĭtus** -i, m., Cornelius, *historian, friend of the younger Pliny, born between* A.D. *50 and 60.*

tactĭlis -e (tango), *that can be touched*: Lucr.

tactĭo -ōnis, f. (tango). (1) *a touching*: Pl. (2) *the sense of touch*: voluptates oculorum et tactionum, Cic.

tactus -ūs, m. (tango), *a touch, touching.*
LIT., chordae ad quemque tactum respondent, Cic.; Verg., etc.
TRANSF., (1) *influence, operation*: solis,

Cic. (2) *the sense of touch*: res sub tactum cadit, Cic.; Lucr.

taeda -ae, f. *pine-wood.*
LIT., Caes., Verg., Hor.
TRANSF., (1) *a board of pine*: Juv. (2) *torch* (*of pine-wood*): taedae ardentes, Cic. Esp. as used at weddings: taeda iugalis, Ov. meton.=*marriage*: Verg., Ov., etc.; also *an instrument of torture*: Lucr., Juv.

taedet taedēre taedŭit, and taesum est impers., *it causes weariness or boredom*; usually with acc. of pers. and genit. of thing: sunt homines quos libidinis infamiaeque sua neque pudeat neque taedeat, Cic.; Pl., etc. with infin. as subject: Ter., Verg.

taedĭfĕr -fĕra -fĕrum (taeda/fero), *torch-bearing*: dea, Ceres (*when searching for Pro*serpine), Ov.

taedĭum -i, n. (taedet), *disgust, weariness, boredom*: longinquae obsidionis, Liv.; taedi curarum fessus, Tac.; poet. in plur.: Verg., Ov.

Taenărus (-ŏs) -i, c. and **Taenărum** (-on) -i, n. (Ταίναρος and -ον), *a promontory an town in Laconia, with a temple of Neptun near which was supposed to be a way down t the underworld* (now *Cape Matapan*).

¶ Hence adj. **Taenărĭus** -a -um, *Taen arian*; poet. *Laconian, Spartan*: marit Helen, Ov.; fauces, *entrance into hell*, Verg porta, Ov.; valles, *the lower world*, Ov. f. adj. **Taenărĭs** -ĭdis, *Taenarian*; poet *Spartan, Laconian*: soror, Helena, Ov. m. subst. **Taenărĭdes** -ae, *a son of Taenarus a Spartan*: Ov.

taenĭa -ae, f.; abl. plur., contr. taenis: Verg (ταινία), *a fillet, head-band*: Enn., Verg.

taetĕr -tra -trum, adj. (with compar. an superl.), *foul, noisome, hideous, offensive.*
LIT., to the senses, esp. of smell: odo Cic.; tenebrae, Cic.; illud taeterrimum no modo aspectu, sed etiam auditu, Cic.; Lucr Verg., etc.
TRANSF., *hateful, hideous, disgracefu abominable*: homo, Cic. L.; sentent taeterrima, Cic.; libido, Hor.

¶ Hence adv. **taetrē**, *foully, hideousl offensively*: multa facere impure atque taetr Cic.; religionem impurissime taeterrimeq violasse, Cic.

tăgax -ācis (tango), *thievish, given to pilferin* Cic.

Tăges -is, m. *an Etruscan deity, grandson Jupiter, said to have taught the Etrusca soothsaying.*

Tăgus -i, m. *a river in Lusitania* (now *Tagus Tejo*), *celebrated for its golden sands.*

tālāris -e (talus), *of* or *stretching to the ankle* tunica, Cic.

¶ N. pl. as subst. **tālārĭa** -ĭum. (1) *win on the ankles, winged sandals*; assigned Mercury: Verg.; Perseus: Ov.; Minerv Cic. Prov.: talaria videamus, *let us think flight*, Cic. L. (2) *a long robe reaching to t ankles*: Ov.

tālārĭus -a -um (talus), *of dice*: ludus, Cic. Quint.

tălassĭo -ōnis or **tălassĭus** -i, m. *an ancie cry, uttered at Roman weddings*: Cat., Liv.

Tălăus -i, m. (Ταλαός), *one of the Argonau father of Adrastus*: Talai gener, Amphiara husband of Eriphyle, Ov.

tălĕa -ae, f. (talus), *a cutting, slip for planting*: Cato, Varr., Plin.; *a short stake* or *bar*: talea ferrea, *a bar of iron, used as money in Britain*, Caes.

tălentum -i, n. (τάλαντον). (**1**) *a (Greek) weight, which varied in different states, but was about half a hundredweight*: aurique eborisque talenta, Verg. (**2**) *a sum of money*, also varying in amount: Pl., Cic., etc.

tālĭo -ōnis, f. (talis), *retaliation*: Cic., Mart.

tālis -e, *of such a kind, such*.
  In gen.: Cic., Verg., Liv., etc. Often *such . . . as . . .*, or *such . . . that . . .*, when foll. by qualis, ut, atque, etc.: ut facillime, quales simus tales esse videamur, Cic.; tales esse ut laudemur, Cic.; talis qualem te esse video, Cic.
  Esp., *of such a distinguished, remarkable, special kind* (good or bad): tali dignitate praediti, Cic.; in tali tempore, Lucr.; tale facinus, Nep.

tālitrum -i, n. (talus), *a rap with the knuckles*: Suet.

talpa -ae, f. (m.: Verg.), *a mole*: Cic., Verg.

tālus -i, m. *the ankle, ankle-bone*.
  Lit., Ov., Plin., etc.
  Transf., (**1**) in gen., *the heel*: purpura usque ad talos demissa, Cic.; Hor., etc. (**2**) *a die* (made originally out of the ankle-bones of the hind feet of certain animals); these, as used among the Romans, had only four marked sides: talis ludere, Cic.; Pl., Hor.

tam, adv. (originally an accusative, like quam), *so, so far, to such a degree*. In gen., with adj., adv. or (rarely) verb: quid tu tam mane? Cic.; Pl., Lucr., etc. Often *so . . . as . . .*, or *so . . . that*, when foll. by quam, ut, atque, etc.: tam esse clemens tyrannus, quam rex importunus potest, Cic.; non essem tam inurbanus, uti ego gravarer, Cic.; quis est tam lynceus, qui nihil offendat? Cic.; quam magis . . . tam magis, *the more . . . the more*, Verg. Esp. non tam . . . quam . . ., *not so much . . . as . . .*: utinam non tam fratri pietatem quam patriae praestare voluisset, Cic.

tămărix -icis, f. *the tamarisk*: Luc.

Tămăsos -i, f. (Ταμασός), *a town in Cyprus*.
  ¶ Hence **Tămăsēus** -a -um, *belonging to Tamasos*: ager, Ov.

tamdĭū or **tam dĭū**, adv. *so long*: Pl., Cic. L. Often foll. by quamdiu, quoad, dum, quam, donec: tamdiu requiesco, quamdiu scribo, Cic. L.

tămĕn, conj. adversat. (tam), *however, yet, nevertheless, notwithstanding, for all that*: hi non sunt permolesti; sed tamen insident et urgent, Cic.; naturam expellas furcā, tamen usque recurret, Hor. Esp. resuming after a concessive clause introduced by quamquam, quamvis, si, etc.: quamquam abest a culpa, suspicione tamen non caret, Cic.; si Massilienses per delectos cives reguntur, inest tamen in ea condicione, etc., Cic.

Tămĕsis -is, m. and **Tămĕsa** -ae (Tac.), *a river in Britain* (now the Thames).

tămetsi, conj. (tam/etsi), *even if, although*; foll. by indic.: Cic.; by indic. or subj.: Pl., Ter.

tamquam (tanquam), adv. *so as, just as, like as*.
  In gen., in comparisons: quod video tibi

etiam novum accidisse tamquam mihi, Cic.; gloria virtutem tamquam umbra sequitur, Cic.; foll. by sic *or* ita, tamquam bona valetudo iucundior est, sic, etc., Cic. In Tac. often introducing a simple reason; e.g.: tamquam apud senem festinantes, *because he was an old man*.
  Esp. tamquam si, *just as if*, with subj.: tamquam si tua res agatur, Cic.; Pl., Liv. So with tamquam alone: tamquam clausa sit Asia, *as if*, Cic.; Liv., etc.

Tănăger -gri, m. *a river in Lucania*.

Tănagra -ae, f. (Τάναγρα), *a town in the east of Boeotia*. Adj. **Tănagraeus** -a -um, *of Tanagra*.

Tănăis -idis and -is, m. (Τάναϊς), *a river in Sarmatia* (now *the Don*).

Tănăquil -quīlis, f. *the wife of Tarquinius Priscus*.

tandem, adv. (tam/demonstr. suffix -dem), *at length, at last*.
  Lit., tandem vulneribus defessi pedem referre coeperunt, Caes.; Lucr., etc. Often strengthened by iam, *or* aliquando: Cic., Verg.
  Transf., in questions, *after all, pray, may I ask?*: quid tandem agebatis? Cic.; quod genus est tandem ostentationis et gloriae? Cic.; Pl., Hor., etc.

tango tangĕre tĕtĭgi tactum, *to touch*.
  Lit., physically. In gen.: terram genu, Cic.; aliquem cubito, Hor.; Lucr., etc. Esp. (**1**) of places: a, *to border on*: villa tangit viam, Cic.; Caes.: b, *to reach*: provinciam, Cic.; Verg., etc. (**2**) *to strike, push, hit*: chordas, Ov.; de caelo tactus, *struck by lightning*, Cic., Verg., Liv. (**3**) *to take* or *touch what one should not*; *to steal*, or *defile*: non teruncium de praeda, Cic. L.; virginem, Ter.; Liv. (**4**) *to sprinkle*: corpus aquā, Ov.; *to dye*: Juv. (**5**) of food and drink, *to touch, taste*: cibos dente, Hor.
  Transf., (**1**) of the feelings, *to touch, move, affect, impress*: minae Clodii modice me tangunt, Cic. L.; mentem mortalia tangunt, Verg.; Hor., Liv. (**2**) *to touch upon, mention*: ubi Aristoteles ista tetigit? Cic.; Ter. (**3**) *to undertake*: carmina, Ov. (**4**) *to cheat*: Pl.

Tantălus -i, m. (Τάνταλος), *a son of Jupiter, father of Pelops and Niobe. Having divulged heavenly secrets, he was punished in Hades by being placed near food and drink which drew back whenever he attempted to satisfy his everlasting hunger and thirst*.
  ¶ Hence adj. **Tantălĕus** -a -um, *of Tantalus*; m. subst. **Tantălĭdēs** -ae, *a son or descendant of Tantalus*; *Pelops*: Ov.; *Agamemnon*: Ov.; Tantalidae fratres, *Atreus and Thyestes*, Ov.; f. subst. **Tantălis** -idis, *a daughter or female descendant of Tantalus*; *Niobe, Hermione*: Ov.

tantillus -a -um (dim. of tantulus), *so little, so small*: Pl., Ter., Lucr. N. as subst. **tantillum** -i, *so small a thing, such a trifle*: Pl.

tantispĕr, adv. (tantus), *just so long*: Pl., Cic., Liv. Often foll. by dum: ut ibi esset tantisper, dum culeus compararetur, Cic.; Pl., Ter.

tantŏpĕrĕ or **tanto ŏpĕrĕ**, adv. *so greatly, so much*: discere, Cic.; Pl., etc.

tantŭlus -a -um (dim. of tantus), *so small, so little*: homines tantulae staturae, Caes.; Pl.,

Cic. N. as subst. **tantŭlum** -i, *so small a thing, such a trifle*: tantulo venierint, *at so small a price*, Cic.

tantum, *see* tantus.

tantummŏdo or **tantum modo**, adv. *only just*: ut tantummodo per stirpes alantur suas, Cic.; Caes., Hor.

tantus -a -um (tam), *of such a size, so great* (sometimes *so small*). Absol.: tot tantaque vitia, Cic.; tanta pecunia, Cic. With clause indicating size, amount, effect, etc.: (1) tantus ... quantus: nullam unquam vidi tantam (contionem), quanta nunc vestrum est, Cic. (2) tantus ... qui: nulla est tanta vis, quae non frangi possit, Cic. (3) tantus ... quam: Liv., Verg. (4) tantus ... ut: non fuit tantus homo in civitate, ut de eo potissimum conqueramur, Cic.; ceterarum provinciarum vectigalia tanta (*so small*) sunt, ut iis ad provincias tutandas vix contenti esse possimus, Cic.
    N. as subst. **tantum** -i, *so much*. In nom. and acc.: ut tantum nobis, quantum ipsi superesse posset, remitteret, Cic.; tantum religio potuit suadere malorum, Lucr.; Caes., etc. In genit. of price, or of value (commercial or moral) **tanti**, *for so much, worth so much*: hortos emit tanti, quanti Pythius voluit, Cic.; est mihi tanti, huius invidiae crimen subire, *it is worth my while*, Cic.; tanti non sit harena Tagi tu somno careas, Juv. In abl. of measure **tanto**, *by so much*; esp. before comparatives: tanto nos submissius geramus, Cic.; tanto ante, *so long before*, Cic.; with verbs expressing a comparison, as praestare: Ov. In phrase, in tantum, *so far, so much*: in tantum suam felicitatem virtutemque enituisse, Liv.
    N. acc. **tantum**, used like an adv. (1) *so much, so far*; with verbs: de quo tantum, quantum me amas, velim cogites, Cic.; with adj.: tantum magna, Hor. (2) *only*: nomen tantum virtutis usurpas, Cic.; Hor., Liv., etc.; tantum non, *all but*: Liv., Suet.; tantum quod, *only just*: Cic. L., Suet.; tantum quod hominem non nominat, *only that ... not*, Cic.; non tantum ... sed etiam, *not only ... but also*, Liv.

tantusdem tantădem tantundem, *just so much, just so great*: Pl., Liv. N. as subst. tantundem, *just so much, just that amount*: magistratibus tantundem detur in cellam, quantum semper datum est, Cic.; tantundemst, *it comes to the same thing*, Juv.; Pl., Liv., etc.; genit. of price: tantidem, *for just that price*, Pl., Ter., Cic.

tăpēta -ae, m. and **tăpēta** -orum, n. pl. and **tăpētia** -ium, n. pl. (τάπης), *drapery, tapestry*, as used for covering walls, floors, couches, etc.: Pl., Verg., Liv.

Tarbelli -ōrum, m. pl. *a people in Aquitania*.

tardē, adv. from tardus; q.v.

tardesco -ĕre (tardus), *to become slow*: Lucr., Tib.

tardigrădus -a -um (tardus/gradus), *slowly stepping*: Pac. ap. Cic.

tardĭpēs -pĕdis (tardus/pes), *slow-footed, limping*: deus, i.e., *Vulcan*, Cat.

tardĭtās -ātis, f. (tardus), *slowness, tardiness*.
    LIT., of persons: plerisque in rebus gerendis tarditas et procrastinatio odiosa est, Cic.; of things: pedum, Cic.; navium, Caes.;

esp., *slowness in speaking*: cursum contentiones magis requirunt, expositiones rerum tarditatem, Cic.
    TRANSF., *mental slowness, dullness, stupidity*: ingenii, Cic.

tardĭtūdo -ĭnis, f. (tardus), *slowness*: Pl.

tardiuscŭlus -a -um (tardus), *somewhat slow, tardy*: Ter.

tardo -are (tardus).
    (1) intransit., *to loiter, to be slow*: num quid putes reipublicae nomine tardandum esse nobis? Cic. L.
    (2) transit., *to make slow, slow down, to hinder, delay*: cursum, Cic.; with infin.: ut reliqui hoc timore propius adire tardarentur, Caes.; Hor., Ov.

tardus -a -um, adj. (with compar. and superl.), *slow, tardy*.
    LIT., (1) of living creatures: pecus, Cic.; homo, Cic.; in decedendo tardior, Cic.; tardior ad discedendum, Cic.; Verg., etc. (2) of things: tibicinis modi, Cic.; poena, Cic.; menses, Verg.; poet., *making slow*: podagra, Hor.
    TRANSF., (1) *slow of comprehension, dull, stupid*: nimis indociles quidam tardique sunt, Cic.; ingenium, Cic. (2) of speech or a speaker, *slow, measured, deliberate*: in utroque genere dicendi principia tarda sunt, Cic.
    ¶ Hence adv. (with compar. and superl.) **tardē**, *slowly*: Pl., Caes., Cic., Verg.

Tărentum -i, n. (Τάρας), *a wealthy town on the coast of Magna Graecia, famous for its purple dyes* (now *Taranto*).
    ¶ Hence adj. **Tărentīnus** -a -um, *Tarentine*; m. pl. as subst. **Tărentīni** -ōrum, *inhabitants of Tarentum*.

tarmĕs -ĭtis, m. *a wood-worm*: Pl.

Tarpēius -a -um, *name of a Roman family*, esp. *of* Sp. Tarpeius, *commander of the citadel at Rome, whose daughter Tarpeia was said to have admitted the Sabines into the citadel, and to have been crushed beneath their shields as her reward*. As adj., *Tarpeian*: lex, Cic.; mons Tarpeius, *the Tarpeian rock, a peak of the Capitoline Hill, from which criminals were thrown*.

Tarquinii -ōrum, m. pl. *an old town in Etruria, whence came the Tarquin family*.
    ¶ Hence adj. **Tarquĭnius** -a -um, *of Tarquinii*; the name of two kings of Rome, Tarquinius Priscus and Tarquinius Superbus; also adj. **Tarquĭniensis** -e, *of Tarquinii*.

Tarrăcīna -ae, f. and **Tarrăcīnae** -ārum, f. *a town in Latium*, formerly called *Anxur* (now *Terracina*).
    ¶ Hence adj. **Tarrăcīnensis** -e, *of Tarracina*.

Tarrăco -ōnis, f. *a town in Spain* (now *Tarragona*).
    ¶ Hence adj. **Tarrăcōnensis** -e, *of Tarraco*: Hispania Tarraconensis, *name of the north-east division of Spain*.

Tarsus -i, f. (Ταρσός), *the chief town of Cilicia*.
    ¶ Hence adj. **Tarsensis** -e, *of Tarsus*.

Tartărus (-ŏs) -i, m.; plur. **Tartără** -ōrum n. (Τάρταρος, plur., Τάρταρα), *the infernal regions*: Lucr., etc.
    ¶ Hence adj. **Tartăreus** -a -um, *Tartarean*: custos, *Cerberus*, Verg.; sorores, *the Furies*, Verg.

Tartessus (-ŏs) -i, f. (Ταϱτησσός), *a town in Hispania Baetica, on the Baetis.*
¶ Hence adj. **Tartessĭus** -a -um, *Tartessian*: litora, Ov.

Tarusātes -ium, m. pl. *a people of Aquitania.*

tăt! an exclamation of astonishment; *what!*: Pl.

tăta -ae, m. *daddy* (colloq. for *father*): Varr., Mart.

tătae = tat; q.v.

Tătĭus -i, m., Titus Tatius, *king of the Sabines, later co-regent with Romulus.* Adj. **Tătĭus** -a -um, *of Tatius.*

taurĕus -a -um (taurus), *of a bull*: terga, *ox-hides*, Verg.; meton., *a drum*: Ov. F. as subst. **taurĕa** -ae, *a whip of bull's hide*: Juv.

Tauri -ōrum, m. *a people of Scythian descent, living in the Crimea.* Adj. **Taurĭcus** -a -um, *Tauric.*

taurĭfĕr -fĕra -fĕrum (taurus/fero), *bull-bearing*: Luc.

taurĭformis -e (taurus/forma), *shaped like a bull*; of the river Aufidus: Hor.

Taurii ludi -ōrum, m. pl. *games celebrated in the Circus Flaminius at Rome in honour of the infernal deities*: Liv.

Taurīni -ōrum, m. pl. *a people in Gallia Cisalpina, with capital* Augusta Taurinorum (now *Turin*).
¶ Hence adj. **Taurīnus** -a -um, *of the Taurini.*

¹**taurīnus** -a -um (taurus), *of* or *like a bull*: tergum, Verg.; frons, Ov.; Lucr.

²**Taurīnus** -a -um, *see* Taurini.

Taurŏmĕnĭum (**Taurŏmĭnĭum**) -i, n. *a town on the east coast of Sicily* (now *Taormina*).
¶ Hence adj. **Taurŏmĕnĭtānus** -a -um.

¹**taurus** -i, m. (ταῦϱος), *a bull.*
LIT., Cic., Verg., etc.
TRANSF., (1) *the sign of the Zodiac so called*: Verg. (2) *the brazen bull of Phalaris*: Cic., Ov.

²**Taurus** -i, m. (Ταῦϱος), *a high mountain range in Asia Minor* (now *Allah Dag*). Tauri Pylae, *a narrow pass between Cappadocia and Cilicia*: Cic. L.

tax = tuxtax; q.v.

taxātio -ōnis, f. (taxo), *a rating, valuing, appraising*: eius rei taxationem facere, Cic.

taxillus -i, m. (talus), *a small die*: Cic.

taxo -are (freq. of tango), *to touch, to handle.* Hence (1) *to reproach, tax with a fault*: aliquem, Suet. (2) *to estimate, rate, appraise*: Sen., Suet.

taxus -i, f. *a yew-tree*: Caes., Verg., Ov.

¹**tē**, *see* tu.

²**-tĕ**, pronom. suffix added to tu, etc.

Tĕānum -i, n. (Τέανον). (1) Teanum Sidicinum, *a town in Campania* (now *Teano*). (2) Teanum Apulum *or* Apulorum, *a town in Apulia* (near the modern *Serracapriola*).
¶ Hence **Tĕānensēs** -ium, m. pl. *the inhabitants of Teanum.*

techna -ae, f. (τέχνη), *a cunning trick, artifice*: Pl., Ter.

tectē, adv. from tego; q.v.

tector -ōris, m. (tego), *a plasterer*: Varr., Cic.

tectŏrĭŏlum -i, n. (dim. of tectorium), *plaster* or *stucco work*: Cic. L.

tectōrĭus -a -um (tector), *used for covering.* In gen.: paniculum, *straw for thatching*, Pl.

Esp. *relating to the plastering* or *stuccoing of walls*: opus tectorium, Cic.; Plin.
N. as subst. **tectōrĭum** -i, *plaster, stucco, fresco painting*: concinnum, Cic. TRANSF., (1) *paste* put on the face: Juv. (2) in speech, *whitewash, flattery*: Pers.

Tectŏsāges -um, m. and **Tectŏsăgi** -ōrum, m. *a people in Gallia Narbonensis.*

tectum -i, n. subst. from tego; q.v.

tectus -a -um, partic. from tego; q.v.

Tĕgĕa -ae, f. (Τεγέα), *a city of Arcadia.*
¶ Hence adj. **Tĕgĕaeus** -a -um, *Tegean*, and poet. *Arcadian*: virgo, Callisto, *daughter of the Arcadian king* Lycaon, Ov.; aper, *the wild boar of Erymanthus*, Ov.; parens, Carmenta, *mother of Evander* (also called Tegeaea sacerdos), Ov.; domus, *of Evander*, Ov. M. as subst., *Pan*; f. as subst., *Atalanta*: Ov. Subst. **Tĕgĕātae** -arum, m. pl. *the inhabitants of Tegea.*

tĕgĕs -ĕtis, f. (tego), *a mat, rug, covering*: Varr., Juv.

tĕgĕtĭcŭla -ae, f. (dim. of teges), *a little mat* or *rug*: Mart.

tĕgillum -i, n. (dim. of tegulum), *a small hood* or *cowl*: Pl., Varr.

tĕgĭmen, tĕgŭmen, and **tegmen** -ĭnis, n. (tego), *a cover, covering*: mihi amictui est Scythicum tegumen, Cic.; Lucr., Liv., Verg.

tĕgĭmentum, tĕgŭmentum, and **tegmentum** -i, n. (tego), *a covering*: tegimenta corporum vel texta vel suta, Cic.; Caes., Liv., etc.

tegmen = tegimen; q.v.

tĕgo -gĕre texi tectum (cf. στέγω), *to cover.*
LIT., in gen.: amica corpus eius texit suo pallio, Cic.; casas stramentis, Caes.; Hor., etc. Esp. (1) *to bury, cover with earth*: ossa tegebat humus, Ov.; Mart. (2) *to conceal, hide*: ferae latibulis se tegunt, Cic.; Caes., etc. (3) *to cover so as to protect, to shield*: aliquem, Cic.; Hor., etc.
TRANSF., esp. (1) *to conceal*: aliquid mendacio, Cic.; Caes., etc. (2) *to protect*: legatos ab ira, Liv.; Cic., etc.
¶ Hence partic. as adj. (with compar. and superl.) **tectus** -a -um, *covered, concealed.*
LIT., naves, Liv.; scaphae, Caes. TRANSF., *concealing oneself, close, reserved, cautious*: tectior, cupiditas, Cic.; verba, Cic. L.; Verg.
¶ N. as subst. **tectum** -i. LIT., *a roof* or *ceiling*: Cic., Verg., Hor. TRANSF., *a shelter, abode, dwelling*: ager sine tecto, Cic.; aliquem tecto ac domo invitare, Cic.; inter annos XIV tectum non subire, *had not come under a roof*, Caes.; Triviae tecta, *her temple*, Verg.; Sibyllae, *grotto*, Verg.; doli tecti, *of the labyrinth*, Verg.
¶ Adv. (with compar.) **tectē**, *covertly*: Cic., Ov.

tĕgŭla -ae, f. (tego), *a roof-tile*: Cic. L., Ov., etc. In plur., tegulae, *a roof*: per tegulas demitti, Cic.; Pl., Liv.

tĕgŭmentum = tegimentum; q.v.

tĕgŭmen = tegimen; q.v.

tēla -ae, f. (for texla, from texo).
LIT., *that which is woven.* Hence *a web*: Penelope telam retexens, Cic.; Verg., etc.; *a spider's web*: Pl., Cat., Juv. Also *the warp*: Verg., Ov.
TRANSF., (1) *a loom*: Lucr., Ov. (2) fig., *a design*: Pl., Cic.

Telamon

Tělămōn -ōnis, m. (Τελαμών), *one of the Argonauts, father of Ajax and Teucer.* ¶ Hence adj. **Tělămōnĭus** -a -um, *Telamonian*; m. as subst., *Ajax*: Ov.; subst. **Tělămōnĭădēs** -ae, m. *a son of Telamon*, i.e., *Ajax*: Ov.

Tělĕgŏnus -i, m. (Τηλέγονος), *son of Circe and of Ulysses (whom he unintentionally killed); builder of Tusculum*: Telegoni moenia, *Tusculum*, Ov.

Tělĕmāchus -i, m. (Τηλέμαχος), *son of Penelope and Ulysses.*

Tělĕthūsa -ae, f. *mother of Iphis.*

Tellēna -ōrum, n. *a town in Latium.*

tellus -ūris, f. *the earth.*
LIT., either as *the world, the globe*, or as *earth, soil*: Cic., Verg., Hor., etc. TRANSF., poet. (1) *a land, district, country*: Gnosia, Verg.; Hor., Ov. (2) *land, possessions*: propria, Hor. Personif.: Tellus, *the Earth, as the all-nourishing goddess*, Cic., Hor., Liv.

Telmessus -i, f. (Τελμησσός), *an old town in Lycia on the borders of Caria.* ¶ Hence subst. **Telmesses** -ium, m. pl. *the inhabitants of Telmessus*; adj. **Telmessīcus** and **Telmessĭus** -a -um, *Telmessian.*

tēlum -i, n. *a missile; a dart, javelin, spear*, etc. LIT., volatile telum, Lucr.; arma atque tela militaria, Sall.; tela intendere, iacere, excipere, Cic.; Caes., Verg., Hor., Liv. TRANSF., (1) *any weapon; a dagger*, etc.: stare cum telo, Cic.; Hor., Ov.; hence of the caestus: Verg.; of the horns of a bull: Ov. (2) *a beam of light*: lucida tela diei, Lucr.; arbitrium est in sua tela Iovi, *his lightning*, Ov. (3) fig., *weapon, arrow, dart*: tela fortunae, Cic. L.; isto telo tutabimur plebem, Liv.; Ov.

tĕmĕrārĭus -a -um (temere). (1) *accidental, fortuitous, casual*: Pl. (2) *inconsiderate, thoughtless, rash*; of persons or things: homo, Caes.; consilium, Liv.; cupiditas, Cic.; bella, Ov.

tĕmĕrē, adv. *blindly, by chance, accidentally, casually, heedlessly, without cause* or *purpose.* In gen.: equo temere acto, Liv.; domus quae temere et nullo consilio administrator, Cic.; nihil temere, nihil imprudenter factum, Caes. Esp. with neg. (1) non temere est quod, *it is not for nothing that, it is not without importance* or *meaning*, Pl.; haud temere est visum, Verg. (2) non temere, *not lightly, not easily*: qui hoc non temere nisi libertis suis deferebant, Cic.; *not often*: Liv.

tĕmĕrĭtās -ātis, f. (temere). (1) *chance, accident*: temeritas et casus, non ratio nec consilium valet, Cic. (2) *rashness, heedlessness*, in thought or in action: temeritas cupiditasque militum, Caes.; numquam temeritas cum sapientia commiscetur, Cic.; Liv.

tĕmĕro -are (cf. temere), *to darken*; hence *to defile, dishonour*: templa, Verg.; thalamos, Ov.

Tĕmĕsē -ēs, f. and **Tempsa** -ae, f. *an old town in Bruttium, famous for its copper mines.* ¶ Hence adj. **Tĕmĕsaeus**, *of Temese*; also **Tempsānus** -a -um.

tēmētum -i, n. (cf. temulentus), *any intoxicating drink; wine*, etc.: Pl., Cic., Hor.

---

tempero

temno temnĕre tempsi temptum, *to despise, contemn*: praesentia, Lucr.; vulgaria, Hor.; Verg., Tac.

tēmō -ōnis, m. *a pole.* LIT., *the pole* or *beam of a waggon*: Verg.; of a plough: Verg., Caes., Ov., Juv. TRANSF., (1) *a waggon*: Juv. (2) *the constellation of Charles's Wain, the Great Bear*: Ov.

Tempē, n. pl., indecl. (τὰ Τέμπη,), *a valley in Thessaly, famous for its beauty, through which the river Peneus flowed.* TRANSF., *any beautiful valley*: Ov., Verg.

tempĕrāmentum -i, n. (tempero), *a right proportion of things mixed together.* LIT., eadem est materia, sed distat temperamento, Plin. TRANSF., in gen., *a middle way, mean, moderation*: inventum est temperamentum, quo tenuiores cum principibus aequari se putarent, Cic.; Tac.

tempĕrans -antis, partic. from tempero; q.v.

tempĕrantĭa -ae, f. (temperans), *temperance, moderation, self-control*: temperantia in praetermittendis voluptatibus cernitur, Cic.; Caes., Tac.

tempĕrātĭo -ōnis, f. (tempero). (1) *moderation, just proportion, proper mixture of ingredients*: caeli, caloris, corporum, civitatis, reipublicae, Cic. (2) *an organizing principle*: sol mens mundi et temperatio, Cic.

tempĕrātor -ōris, m. (tempero), *one who arranges* or *governs*: varietatis, Cic.; Mart.

tempĕrātus -a -um, partic. from tempero; q.v.

tempĕri temperius; *see* tempus.

tempĕrĭēs -ēi, f. (tempero). (1) *a proper mixture, tempering*: temperiem sumpsere umorque calorque, Ov.; Plin. L. (2) of climate, *mildness*: Hor., Plin. L.

tempĕro -are (tempus), *to set bounds, keep within limits.*
(1) intransit., *to observe proper limits, be moderate, control oneself.* In gen.: in multa, Liv. With dat.: **a**, *to control, use with moderation*: victoriae, Sall.; linguae, Liv.: **b**, *to spare*: hostibus superatis, Cic.; templis, Liv. With ab, or with plain abl., *to keep from, refrain from*: ab iniuriā, Caes.; a lacrimis, Verg.; Liv., Tac. With infin., or with ne and subj.: Pl. In neg., esp. with dat., foll. by quominus or quin and subj., *not to refrain from*: neque sibi temperaturos existimabat, quin in provinciam exirent, Caes.; Liv., Tac.
(2) transit., *to distribute* or *mix properly, to temper.* LIT., acuta cum gravibus, Cic.; esp., *to mix a drink, prepare*: poculum, Hor. TRANSF., **a**, *to mitigate*: amara lento risu, Hor.; Cic.: **b**, *to rule, regulate*: rempublicam legibus, Cic.; res hominum ac deorum, Hor. Verg., Ov.
¶ Hence partic. as adj. (with compar. and superl.) **tempĕrans** -antis, *moderate, temperate, continent, restrained*: homo temperantissimus, Cic.; temperantiores a cupidine imperii, Liv.; with genit.: Ter., Tac.
¶ Adv. (with compar.) **tempĕrantĕr** *temperately, moderately*: temperantius agere, Cic. L.; Tac.
¶ Perf. partic. as adj. (with compar. and superl.) **tempĕrātus** -a -um, *properly mixed, tempered, ordered, moderate.* LIT., esca, Cic.; loca temperatiora, Caes.; temperato usu Hor. TRANSF., *moderate, quiet, temperate*

mores, Cic.; homo temperatissimus, Cic.; oratio temperatior, Cic.; Hor., Liv.

¶ Adv. (with compar.) **tempĕrātē**, *moderately, temperately*: agere, Cic. L.; temperatius scribere, Cic. L.

tempestās -ātis, f. (tempus), *a space* or *period of time.*

(1) *a period, a season*: eā tempestate, *at that time*, Sall.; eādem tempestate, Cic.; multis ante tempestatibus, Liv.

(2) *weather.* In gen.: bona, certa, Cic.; clara, Verg.; turbulenta, Cic.; perfrigida, Cic.; tempestates, *kinds of weather*, Cic. L.; Lucr. Esp. *bad weather, storm, tempest*: immoderatae tempestates, Cic.; Caes., Verg., etc.

Transf., *a tempest, attack, fury*: invidiae, Cic.; querelarum, Cic.; telorum, Verg.; of persons: Siculorum tempestas (of Verres), Cic.; turbo ac tempestas pacis (of Clodius), Cic.

tempestīvĭtās -ātis, f. (tempestivus), *fit time, proper season*: sua cuique parti aetatis tempestivitas est data, Cic.

tempestīvus -a -um (tempus), *happening at the right time, opportune, seasonable, fit, appropriate.*

In gen.: nondum tempestivo ad navigandum mari, Cic.; oratio, Liv.; multa mihi ad mortem tempestiva fuere, *convenient opportunities*, Cic.

Esp. (1) *early*: cena, convivium, Cic.; Plin., Tac. (2) *ripe*: fructus, Cic.; pinus, Verg. Of persons, *ripe, mature*: puella tempestiva viro, Hor.; Ov.

¶ Adv. (with compar.) **tempestīvē**, *at the right time, seasonably*: caedi (of trees), Cic.; tempestivius in domum Pauli comissabere, Hor.

templum -i, n. (cf. τέμενος), *a section, a part cut off.*

Lit., (1) *a space in the sky* or *on the earth marked out by the augur for the purpose of taking auspices*: Liv. (2) *a consecrated piece of ground*, esp. *a sanctuary, asylum*: Liv.; of the curia, because consecrated by an augur: curia, templum publici consilii, Cic. (3) *a place dedicated to a particular deity, a shrine, temple*: Iovis, Cic.

Transf., (1) *any open space, quarter, region*: caeli templa, Enn., Lucr.; deus, cuius hoc templum est omne quod conspicis, Cic.; templa Parnassia, *Mount Parnassus*, Ov.; of the sea: loca Neptunia templaque turbulenta, Pl. (2) fig., *shrine, sanctuary*: templa mentis, Lucr. (3) *a rafter, crossŏeam*: Lucr., Vitr.

tempŏrālis -e (tempus), *temporary, lasting for a time*: laudes, Tac.; Sen.

tempŏrārius -a -um (tempus). (1) *temporary*: Plin. L., Sen. (2) *seasonable, adapted to time and circumstances*: Nep.

tempŏri, *see* tempus.

Tempsa, Tempsānus, *see* Temesa.

temptābundus -a -um (tempto), *trying, attempting*: Liv.

temptāmen -ĭnis, n. (tempto), *a trial, attempt*; found only in plur.: Ov.

temptāmentum -i, n. (tempto), *a trial, attempt, test, essay*: Verg., Ov., Tac.

temptātĭo -ōnis, f. (tempto). (1) *a trial, test*: Liv. (2) *an attack*: novae tentationes, *new attacks of disease*, Cic.

temptātor -ōris, m. (tempto), *an assailant*: Hor.

tempto -are, *to prove, try, test.*

Lit., of physical objects: in gen.: pectora manibus, Ov.; flumen pede, Cic.; venas, *to feel the pulse*, Quint.; Thetim ratibus, *to essay*, Verg. Esp. *to test by attack, to assail*: Achaiam, Caes.; castra, Liv.; of diseases: morbo temptari, Cic.; frigore corpus, Hor.

Transf., (1) in gen., *to test*: alicuius patientiam, Cic.; belli fortunam, Cic.; Liv. With indir. quest.: temptavi, quid in eo genere possem, Cic.; Pl., Verg. (2) *to attempt*: rem frustra, Caes.; quaestionem, Cic. With ut and the subj.: cum ille Romuli senatus temptaret, ut ipse gereret rempublicam, Cic. With infin.: irasci, Verg.; Liv., Ov. (3) *to work upon, tamper with, excite, disturb*: animos spe et metu, Cic.; iudicium pecuniā, *to try to bribe*, Cic.; animum precando, Verg.; Tac., etc.

tempŭs -ŏris, n. (cf. τέμενος, from τέμνω), *a division, section.*

(1) (in space; only of *the temples* of the head, usually plur. Lit., Lucr., Verg., etc. Transf., in gen., the head: Cat., Prop.

(2) in time; *a portion of time, period of time.* Lit., extremum tempus diei, Cic.; matutina tempora, *the morning hours*, Cic.; hibernum tempus anni, Cic.; certis temporibus, Cic.; praesens in tempus, Hor.; Lucr., etc. Also *time*, in gen.: fugit inreparabile tempus, Verg.; Cic., etc. Transf., a, *a fit time, occasion, opportunity*: tempus amittere, Cic.; tempus habere, Cic.; see also adverbial phrases, below. Esp. tempus est, with infin., *it is high time to*: tempus est dicere, Cic.; Verg., Liv.; with acc. and infin.: tempus est iam hinc abire me, Cic.; Verg.: b, *the state, condition of things*; freq. plur., *the times*: temporibus servire, Cic. Esp. *calamitous* or *dangerous circumstances*: nec miserae prodesse in tali tempore quibat, Lucr.; o saepe mecum tempus in ultimum deducte, Hor.; Cic.: c, *time in pronouncing a syllable, quantity*: Cic., Hor., Quint.: d, *time in grammar, tense of a verb*: Varr., Quint.

¶ As adv. **tempŏrĕ**, **tempŏrī**, and **tempĕrī** (with compar. tempĕrius), *at the right time, seasonably*: Pl., Cic., etc.

¶ Adverbial phrases: **ad tempŭs**, *at the right time*, or *for the occasion*: Cic., Liv.; **in tempŏrĕ**, *at the right moment*: Ter., Liv., Tac.; **ex tempŏrĕ**, *on the spur of the moment*, or *as the occasion demands*: Cic.; **pro tempŏrĕ**, *as the occasion demands*: Caes., Verg., etc.

tēmŭlentus -a -um (cf. temetum), *drunken, intoxicated, tipsy*: Cic., Liv., etc.

tĕnācĭtās -ātis, f. (tenax), *a firm holding, tenacity*: unguium tenacitate adripiunt, Cic. In relation to money, *stinginess*: Liv.

tĕnācĭtĕr, adv. from tenax; q.v.

tĕnax -ācis, adj. (with compar. and superl.) (teneo), *holding fast, griping, clinging, tenacious.*

Lit., forceps, Verg.; dens (of an anchor), Verg.; gramen, Hor.; complexus, Ov.; *holding fast to possessions, money*, etc., *sparing, frugal, stingy*: pater parcus et tenax, Cic.; with genit.: quaesiti tenax, Ov.

Transf., (1) in gen., *firm, steady*. In a

good sense, *resolute, steadfast*: longa tenaxque fides, Ov. Often with genit., *holding to*: propositi, Hor.; Verg., Juv. (2) in a bad sense, *obstinate*: equus, Liv.; ira, Ov.

¶ Adv. **tĕnācĭtĕr**, *firmly*. LIT., premere, Ov. TRANSF., *constantly, steadily*: miseros urgere, Ov.

Tenctĕri -ōrum, m. pl. *a Germanic people on the Rhine.*

tendĭcŭla -ae, f. (tendo). (1) *a stretcher* for clothes: Sen. (2) *a snare, trap*: aucupia verborum et litterarum tendiculae, Cic.

tendo tendĕre tĕtendi tentum and tensum (cf. τείνω), *to stretch, stretch out, extend, spread.*

(1) transit. LIT., plagas, Cic.; rete, Ter.; arcum, Verg.; praetorium, *to pitch*, Caes.; barbiton, *to string*, Hor. Esp. of the hands: tendebantque manūs, Verg.; Caes., Cic., Ov. Of persons, *to present*: parvum patri Iulum, Verg. TRANSF., *to direct, extend, present*: alicui insidias, *to lay snares for*, Cic., Sall.; iter ad naves, Verg.; spem amicis porrigere atque tendere, Cic.

(2) intransit. as milit. t. t., *to pitch one's tent, encamp*: Caes., Verg.; in iisdem castris, Liv.

(3) intransit. in gen., *to direct one's course to, tend, go, make for*. LIT., of persons: Venusiam, Cic. L.; ad aedes, Hor.; unde venis? et quo tendis? Hor.; Verg., Liv., etc. Of inanimate things: simulacra viis de rectis omnia tendunt, Lucr.; via tendit sub moenia, Verg. TRANSF., *to be inclined, tend in any direction, aim at, strive after*: ad reliqua alacri tendebamus animo, Cic.; sibi quisque tendentes, Tac.; foll. by infin., *to try, attempt*: manibus divellere nodos, Verg.; Liv., etc.; with ut and the subj.: ut delectum haberet, Liv.; with internal acc.: quid tendit? Cic.: **b**, *to strive, contend against*: contra, Verg., Liv.; with ne and the subj.: Liv.

tĕnebrae -ārum, f. pl. *darkness.*

LIT., in gen.: taetris tenebris, Cic.; obtenta densantur nocte tenebrae, Verg.; Lucr., etc. Esp. (1) *dark night, night*: quomodo redissem luce, non tenebris, Cic.; Liv., Ov. (2) *blindness*: tenebras et cladem lucis ademptae obicit, Ov.; Lucr. (3) *the darkness before the eyes in fainting*: tenebris nigrescunt omnia circum, Verg.; Pl., Ov. (4) *the darkness of death*: Pl., Prop.

TRANSF., (1) *a dark place*; of the lower world: Stygiae, Verg.; of a prison: clausi in tenebris, Sall.; of a hiding-place: cum illa coniuratio ex latebris atque ex tenebris erupisset, Cic. (2) *mental* or *social obscurity*: vestram familiam, obscuram e tenebris in lucem evocavit, Cic.; latent ista omnia crassis occultata et circumfusa tenebris, Cic.; qualibus in tenebris vitae quantisque periclis degitur hoc aevi quodcunquest! Lucr.

tĕnebrĭcōsus -a -um (tenebricus), *dark, gloomy, shrouded in darkness, obscure*. LIT., Cic., Cat. TRANSF., Cic.; superl.: illud tenebricosissimum tempus ineuntis aetatis tuae, Cic.

tĕnebrĭcus -a -um (tenebrae), *dark, gloomy*: Cic. poet.

tĕnebrōsus -a -um (tenebrae), *dark, gloomy*: palus, Verg.; Ov., etc.

Tĕnĕdus (-ŏs) -i, f. (Τένεδος), *an island in the Aegean Sea, near Troy* (still called *Tenedos*).

¶ Hence adj. **Tĕnĕdĭus** -a -um, *of Tenedos.*

tĕnellŭlus -a -um (dim. of tenellus), *sweet and tender, delicate, little*: Cat.

tĕnellus -a -um (dim. of tener), *tender, delicate*: Pl.

tĕnĕo tĕnēre tĕnŭi tentum (perhaps connected with tendo, τείνω), *to hold.*

Transit. (1) in gen. LIT., pyxidem in manu, Cic.; pateram dexterā manu, Cic.; cibum ore, Cic.; res oculis et manibus tenetur, *is visible and tangible*, Cic.; rem manu tenere, *to have at one's fingers' ends*, *to understand thoroughly*, Cic.; Verg., Ov., etc. TRANSF., **a**, *to hold in the mind, to understand, grasp, know*: quae et saepe audistis et tenetis animis, Cic.; Pl., Hor.: **b**, *to contain, comprise*; pass., teneri aliquā re, *to be contained in, to belong to*: si Asia hoc imperio non teneretur, Cic. (2) with the idea of retention, *to possess, own, keep*. LIT., multa hereditatibus, multa emptionibus tenebantur sine iniuria, Cic.; terras, Hor.; imperium, Caes.; rempublicam, Cic.; se iam tenet altera coniux, Ov. As milit. t. t., *to occupy, garrison*: locum praesidiis, montem, portum, Caes. TRANSF., *to hold fast in the mind*: memoriam alicuius, Cic.; memoriā tenere, *to remember*, foll. by acc. and infin., Cic.; absol., tenere, *to remember*: Verg., Hor.: **b**, *to catch, arrest*: teneo te, Cic.; teneri in manifesto peccato, Cic.: **c**, of passions, *to possess, master*: misericordia me tenet, Cic.; magna spes me tenet, with acc. and infin., Cic.: **d**, *to charm, amuse*: varias mentes carmine, Verg.; pueri ludis tenentur, oculi pictura tenentur, Cic.: **e**, *to hold fast, preserve, maintain*: auctoritatem, imperium in suos, Cic.; causam apud centum viros, *to gain*, Cic.; morem, Cic., Verg.; of a proposition: illud arte tenent accurateque defendunt, voluptatem esse summum bonum, Cic. (3) with the notion of perseverance in movement, *the 'tenor' of one's way*: cursum, Caes., Cic.; iter, Verg. With destination as object, *to reach*: cum navibus insulam, Tac.; Hesperiam, Ov.; Liv. TRANSF., per cursum rectum regnum, Cic. (4) with the notion of motion checked, *to hold fast, restrain, keep back*. LIT., se castris, Caes.; se oppido, Cic.; septimum iam diem Corcyrae teneri, *to be detained*, Cic.; manūs ab aliquo tenere, Ov.; Verg., Liv., etc. TRANSF., risum, dolorem, iracundiam, Cic.; lacrimas, Caes., Cic.; se ab accusando, *to refrain from*, Cic. L.; pass.: lege, foedere, promisso teneri, *to be bound*, Cic.

Intransit., *to keep on, persevere*. LIT., in a position or on a course: ab Sicilia classe ad Laurentem agrum, Liv.; medio tutissimus ibis, inter utrumque tene, Ov. TRANSF., *to persist, last, endure*: imber per totam noctem tenuit, Liv.; fama tenet, *the report holds*, with acc. and infin., Liv.; with ut, or ne, *to insist, stick to it, that*: Liv.

tĕner -ĕra -ĕrum, adj. (with compar. and superl.), *tender, delicate, soft.*

LIT., in gen.: corpus, Lucr.; arbores, Caes.; uva, Verg.; Hor., etc. Esp. *youthful, young*: a teneris, ut Graeci dicunt, unguiculis, *from childhood*, Cic.; Hor., etc.; as subst.: in teneris, *in childhood*, Verg.

TRANSF., *tender, soft, effeminate*: tenerum quiddam atque molle in animis, Cic.; mentes, Hor., Quint.; carmen, Ov. ¶ Hence adv. **tĕnĕrē**, *tenderly, delicately, softly*: Plin., Tac.

tĕnĕrasco -ĕre (tener), *to grow tender, weak, soft*: Lucr.

tĕnĕrĭtās -ātis, f. (tener), *tenderness, softness*: in primo ortu inest teneritas et mollities, Cic.

tĕnĕrĭtūdo=teneritas; q.v.: Varr., Suet.

tēnesmos -i, m. (τεινεσμός), *a straining at stool*: Nep.

tĕnŏr -ōris, m. (teneo), *course, continued movement*. LIT., unum labendi conservans usque tenorem, Lucr.; hasta servat tenorem, Verg.; Liv., Ov. TRANSF., *course, duration, career*: tenorem pugnae servabant, Liv.; fati, Ov.; vitae, Liv.; uno tenore, *in an uninterrupted course, uniformly*, Cic.

tensa -ae, f. *a car on which the images of the gods were carried at the Circensian games*: Cic., Liv., Suet.

tento, etc.; *see* tempto, etc.

tentīgo -inis, f. (tendo), *lecherousness*: Hor.

tentōrĭum -i, n. (tendo), *a tent*: Verg., Ov., etc.

tentus -a -um, partic. from tendo and teneo; q.v.

tĕnŭĭcŭlus -a -um (dim. of tenuis), *very poor, mean, slight*: apparatus, Cic. L.

tĕnŭis -e (sometimes dissyll.), adj. (with compar. and superl.), *thin, fine, slight, slender*. LIT., collum, Cic.; acus, Ov.; aqua, unda, Ov.; sulcus, Verg.; vestes, toga, Ov. TRANSF., (1) *refined, subtle*: argumentandi filum tenue, Cic.; oratio, orator, Cic.; distinctio, Cic.; Lucr., Hor. (2) *unimportant, little, slight*: oppidum, Cic.; praeda, Caes.; sermo, Cic.; gloria, Verg. (3) of persons: a, physically, *weak, feeble*: valetudo tenuissima, Caes.: b, mentally: animus, Caes.; spes, Cic.: c, of birth or position, *low, mean*: qui tenuioris ordinis essent, Cic.; tenues homines, Cic.; Hor., Liv. M. pl. of compar. as subst.: tenuiores, *persons of lower rank*, Cic. ¶ Hence adv. (with superl). **tĕnŭĭtĕr**, *thinly*. LIT., alutae tenuiter confectae, Caes. TRANSF., (1) *subtly, exactly*: disserere, Cic. (2) *moderately, not too well*: Ter. (3) *slightly*: tenuissime aestimare, Cic.

tĕnŭĭtās -ātis, f. (tenuis), *thinness, fineness*. LIT., animi, Cic. TRANSF., (1) *refinement, subtlety*: rerum et verborum, Cic. (2) *slightness, poverty*: aerarii, Cic.; hominis, Cic.; Caes.

tĕnŭo -are (tenuis), *to make thin, fine, slender, to attenuate*. LIT., adsiduo vomer tenuatur ab usu, Ov.; armenta macie, Verg.; vocis via est tenuata, Ov.; Hor., Tac. TRANSF., *to weaken, lessen, diminish*: iram, vires, Ov.; Hor.

¹**tĕnŭs** -ŏris, n. (root ten-, whence tendo), *a noose, gin, springe*: Pl.

²**tĕnŭs**, prep. with abl. and genit., always placed *after* its noun or pronoun (connected with teneo, tendo, τείνω), *up to, down to, as far as*. LIT., of place: a, with genit.: crurum tenus, Verg.; Corcyrae tenus, Liv.; Lucr.: b, with abl.: Tauro tenus regnare, Cic.; cadi faece tenus poti, Hor.

TRANSF., est quadam prodire tenus, si non datur ultra, *up to a certain point*, Hor.; vulneribus tenus, Liv.; verbo tenus, *in name, nominally*, Cic.; Tac.

Tĕŏs (Tĕus) -i, f. (Τέως), *a town on the coast of Ionia, birth-place of Anacreon*. ¶ Hence adj. **Tēĭus** -a -um, *Teian*; poet. =*Anacreontic*: Ov.

tĕpĕfăcĭo (tĕpĕfăcĭo: Cat.) -fēci -factum, *to make warm, to warm*: sol tepefaciat solum, Cic.; Verg., Hor., etc.

tĕpĕo -ēre, *to be lukewarm, tepid*. LIT., hiems tepet, Hor. Esp. in partic., tepens, *warm*: aurae, Verg. TRANSF., (1) *to be warm with love*: aliquo, *for someone*, Hor. (2) *to be only lukewarm in love*: seu tepet, sive amat, Ov.

tĕpesco tĕpescĕre tĕpŭi (tepeo), *to grow warm* (*not hot*). LIT., maria agitata ventis tepescunt, Cic.; Verg. TRANSF., of feelings, *to cool down*: Luc.

tĕpĭdus -a -um (tepeo), *lukewarm, tepid*. LIT., focus, Ov.; Lucr., Verg., etc. TRANSF., mens, Ov. ¶ Hence compar. adv. **tĕpĭdĭŭs**, *tepidly*: Plin. L.

tĕpor -ōris, m. (tepeo), *lukewarmness, moderate heat*. LIT., solis, Liv.; Lucr., Cic. TRANSF., in speech, *want of fire*: Tac.

tĕr, adv. (tres), *three times, thrice*. LIT., ter in anno, Cic.; ter centum, Verg.; Hor., etc. TRANSF., with indefinite sense: ter felix, Ov.; terque quaterque beati, Verg.

terdĕcĭēs (terdĕcĭens), adv. *thirteen times*: Cic., Juv.

tĕrĕbinthus -i, f. (τερέβινθος), *the terebinth-tree*: Verg., Plin.

tĕrebra -ae, f. (tero), *a gimlet, borer*: Cato, Plin.

tĕrebro -are (terebra), *to bore through, pierce, perforate*. LIT., latebras uteri, Verg.; Ov. TRANSF., *to coax, wheedle*: Pl.

tĕrēdo -ĭnis, f. (τερηδών), *a worm that gnaws wood*: Ov., Plin.

Tĕrentĭus -a -um, *the name of a Roman gens. Its most famous members were* (1) C. Terentius Varro, *consul* 216 B.C., *defeated by Hannibal at Cannae.* (2) M. Terentius Varro, *born* 116 B.C., *a celebrated grammarian, contemporary of Cicero.* (3) M. Terentius Afer, *freedman of P. Terentius Lucanus, the celebrated comic dramatist, contemporary of Laelius and Scipio Africanus.* (4) Terentia, *wife of Cicero.* As adj., *Terentian*: lex, *law proposed by the consuls Cassius and M. Terentius.* ¶ Hence also adj. **Tĕrentĭānus** -a -um, *Terentian*: exercitus, *of C. Terentius Varro*, Liv.; Chremes, *appearing in the comedies of Terence*, Cic.

Tĕrentus (-ŏs) and **Tărentus (-ŏs)** -i, f. *a place in the Campus Martius, where the ludi saeculares were held.* ¶ Hence adj. **Tĕrentīnus** -a -um.

tĕrĕs -rētis (tero), *rounded, polished, well-turned*. LIT., stipites, Caes.; lapillus, Ov.; Verg., etc. TRANSF., (1) of natural shape, *well-rounded, smooth*: 'cervices, Lucr.; surae, Hor.; Verg., Ov. (2) of taste, character, etc., *polished, refined elegant*: aures, oratio, Cic.; sapiens in se ipso totus teres atque rotundus, Hor.

Tēreus -ĕi and -ĕos, m. (Τηρεύς), *king of Thrace, husband of Procne, the sister of Philomela.*
¶ Hence subst. **Tēreïdēs** -ae, m. *the son of Tereus,* i.e. *Itys.*

tergĕmĭnus=trigeminus; q.v.

tergĕo -ēre and **tergo** -ĕre tersi tersum, *to wipe, scour, dry off, clean*: lumina lacrimantia manu, Ov.; spicula lucida tergent, *they burnish,* Verg.
¶ Hence partic. **tersus** -a -um. LIT., *clean, neat*: mulier, Pl.; plantae, Ov. TRANSF., *free from mistakes, neat*: iudicium, Quint.

tergīnum -i, n. (tergum), *a whip of leather, thong*: Pl.

tergĭversātĭo -ōnis, f. (tergiversor), *backwardness, reluctance, evasion*: mora et tergiversatio, Cic.

tergĭversor -ari, dep. (tergum/verto), *to turn the back*; hence, *to be backward and reluctant, shuffle, find excuses, evade*: quid taces? quid dissimulas? quid tergiversaris? Cic.; Liv.

tergo=tergeo; q.v.

tergum -i, n. *the back.*
LIT., as part of the body: Cic., etc. Esp. of turning the back in flight: terga vertere, Caes.; dare, Liv., Ov.; praebere terga fugae, Ov.; terga Parthorum dicam, *the flight,* Ov. Also in phrases, with prep.: a tergo, *in the rear,* Caes., Cic., Liv.; in tergo, Liv.
TRANSF., (1) *the back* of anything: castris ab tergo vallum obiectum, *from behind,* Liv.; of a ridge: Verg.; of the back of a scroll: Juv. (2) in gen., *a body*: centum terga suum, *a hundred swine,* Verg. (3) *a hide, skin*: taurinum, Verg.; meton., *a thing made out of hide*: duro intendere bracchia tergo, *boxing-gloves,* Verg.; so of *bags, shields,* etc.: Ov.

tergus -ŏris, n. (poet.; cf. tergum), *the back.* LIT., Prop. TRANSF., (1) *the body of an animal*: Ov. (2) *skin, hide, leather*: Verg.

termĕs -ĭtis, m. *a branch,* esp. of an olive-tree: olivae, Hor.

Termĭnālĭa -ĭum and -ĭōrum (Terminus), n. *the Festival of Terminus (god of boundaries), on the 23rd of February*: Cic. L., etc.

termĭnātĭo -ōnis, f. (termino), *a limiting, bounding.* Hence (1) *a determining*: versus inventus est terminatione aurium, Cic. (2) rhet. t. t., *the termination of a period*: ordo verborum alias aliā terminatione concluditur, Cic.

termĭno -are (terminus), *to bound, limit, set bounds to.*
LIT., finem loci quem oleae terminabant, Cic.; Lucr., Verg., Liv.
TRANSF., (1) in gen., *to limit, restrict*: sonos vocis paucis litterarum notis, Cic. (2) philosoph., *to define*: bona voluptate, mala dolore, Cic. (3) rhet. t. t., *to close, end*: sententiam, orationem, Cic.

termĭnus -i, m. (cf. τέρμα), *a boundary-mark, limit, boundary.*
LIT., nulli possessionum termini, Cic.; Hor., etc.
TRANSF., *a limit, end*: certos mihi fines terminosque constituam, extra quos egredi non possim, Cic.
Personif.: Terminus, *the god of boundaries,* Hor., Liv.

terni -ae -a (ter), *three in a group, three at a time,* or *three each*: Cic., Hor., etc. In sing.: terno consurgunt ordine remi, Verg.

tĕro tĕrĕre trīvi trītum (cf. τρίβω, τείρω), *to rub, wear away.*
LIT., in gen.: oculos, Ter.; (tempus) silices, Ov.; vestem, Hor.; calamo labellum, *to play the flute,* Verg. Esp. (1) *to rub for the sake of cleaning* or *polishing; to whet, to smoothe*: crura pumice, Ov.; radios rotis, Verg. (2) *to grind, thresh*: milia frumenti, Hor.; bacas, Verg.
TRANSF., *to use often, use up, spend*: se in opere longinquo, *to wear oneself out,* Liv. Esp. (1) of time: tempus, Cic., Liv.; aevum, Verg.; Pl., etc. (2) of language: verbum, Cic.
¶ Hence partic. as adj. (with compar.) **trītŭs** -a -um, *worn.* LIT., *much trodden, frequented*: iter, Cic.; Hor., Ov. TRANSF., (1) *practised*: aures, Cic. (2) of discourse, in common use, trite, well-known*: faciamus hoc proverbium tritius, Cic.

Terpsĭchŏrē -ēs, f. (Τερψιχορή), *the Muse of dancing*; hence=*muse, poetry*: Juv.

terra -ae, f.; genit. sing. terrai: Lucr. (cf. torreo), *that which is dry*; hence, *the earth.*
(1) *earth, land* (opp. to heavens, sea, air): terrae motus, *earthquake,* Cic.; terrā marique, *by land and sea,* Cic.; in terris, *on the earth,* Hor.; sub terras ire, *to visit the lower world,* Verg.
(2) *earth, ground, soil*: de terrā saxa tollere, Cic.; gleba terrae, Liv.; mihi terram inice, Verg.; terrae filius, *a son of the earth, an unknown person,* Cic. L.; gignuntur e terra, Cic.
(3) *a particular country, land, region*: terra Gallia, Caes.; abire in alias terras, Cic.; orbis terrarum, *the world,* Cic.; genit. plur. often partitive, with adv. of place: ubi terrarum sumus? *where in the world are we?* Cic.
Personif.: Terra, *the earth as a goddess,* Cic., Ov., etc.

terrēnus -a -um (terra), *earthen.* (1) *belonging to the earth, terrestrial*: bestiae, *land-animals,* Cic.; poet.: numina, *of the lower world,* Ov.; eques, *mortal,* Hor. (2) *made of earth, earthen*: tumulus, Caes.; agger, Verg. N. as subst. **terrēnum** -i, *land, ground*: herbidum, Liv.

tĕrreo terrēre terrŭi terrĭtum, *to frighten, terrify.* In gen.: aliquem, Cic., Liv., etc.; with ne and the subj.: Hor., Liv. Esp. (1) *to frighten away, scare away*: profugam per totum orbem, Ov.; Hor. (2) *to deter*: a repetendā libertate, Sall.; with quominus and the subj.: Caes.

terrestris -e, *of the earth, terrestrial* (opp. marinus, or caelestis): animantium genus terrestre, Cic.; terrestres navalesque pugnae, Cic.; res caelestes atque terrestres, Cic.; Capitolium terrestre domicilium Iovis, Cic.; Pl., Liv.

terreus -a -um (terra), *made of earth, earthly*: progenies, Verg.

terrĭbilis -e, adj. (with compar.) (terreo), *terrible, frightful, dreadful*: sonus, Liv.; mors est terribilis iis, Cic.; quam terribilis aspectu, Cic.; terribiles visu formae, Verg.; ipsi urbi terribilis erat, Liv.

terrĭcŭla -orum, n. pl. (terreo), *something that causes fright; a bogey*: Liv.

terrĭfĭco -are (terrificus), *to frighten, terrify*: Lucr., Verg.

terrĭfĭcus -a -um (terreo/facio), *causing terror, frightful, terrible*: Lucr., Verg., etc.

terrĭgĕna -ae, m. and f. (terra/gigno), *earthborn, sprung from the earth*: Lucr., Ov.

terrĭlŏquus -a -um (terreo/loquor), *terror-speaking*: Lucr.

terrĭto -are (freq. of terreo), *to frighten, intimidate, scare*: aliquem metu, Caes.; tribunicium domi bellum patres territat, Liv.; Pl., Verg.

terrĭtōrĭum -i, n. (terra), *the land belonging to a town, district, territory*: coloniae, Cic.

terror -ōris, m. (terreo), *fright, fear, terror, alarm, dread.*
LIT., minis et terrore commoveri, Cic.; adtulit terrorem hostibus, Caes.; facere terrorem et militibus et ipsi Appio, Liv.; incutere alicui terrorem, Liv.; tantus habet pectora terror, Verg.; with genit.: terror mortis, Cic.
TRANSF., *an object which causes terror*: terra repleta est trepido terrore, Lucr.; terrori alicui esse, Caes.; plur.: huius urbis terrores (Carthage and Numantia), Cic.; Romam tanti terrores erant adlati, Liv.; caelestes maritimique terrores, Liv.
Personif.: Terror, Ov.

tersus -a -um, partic. from tergeo; q.v.

tertĭādĕcĭmāni -ōrum, m. pl. (tertius decimus; sc. milites), *soldiers of the thirteenth legion*: Tac.

tertĭānus -a -um (tertius), *belonging to the third.*
(1) *of the third day*: febris, *tertian fever*, Cic.; f. as subst. **tertĭāna** -ae, *a tertian fever*: Plin.
(2) *belonging to the third legion*; m. pl. as subst. **tertĭāni** -ōrum, *soldiers of the third legion*: Tac.

tertĭus -a -um (cf. ter, tres), *third*: pars, Caes.; tertio quoque verbo, *at every third word*, Cic.; tertia regna, *the lower world*, Ov.; tertia Saturnalia, *the third day of the Saturnalia*, Cic.; ab Iove tertius Ajax, *of the third generation, great-grandson*, Ov.
¶ Acc. n. sing. as adv. **tertĭum**, *for the third time*: Cato, Cic., Liv.
¶ Abl. n. sing. as adv. **tertĭō**, (1) *for the third time*: tertio pecuniam dedit, Cic.; Ter., Liv. (2) *thirdly*: Caes.

tertĭusdĕcĭmus -a -um, *thirteenth*: Tac.

tĕruncĭus -i, m. (ter/uncia), *a fraction; three-twelfths.* Esp. (1) *a quarter of an as*: Varr. Hence *a very small sum*: ne teruncius quidem, *not a farthing*, Cic. (2) *the fourth part of an inheritance*: heres ex teruncio, *heir to one-fourth of a property*, Cic. L.

tervĕnēfĭcus -i, m. *an arch-poisoner*: Pl.

tesqua (tesca) -ōrum, n. pl. *wastes, deserts*: Hor.

tessella -ae, f. (dim. of tessera), *a small cube of stone used for pavements, playing dice, etc.*: Sen., Juv.

tessellātus -a -um (tessella), *set with small cubes*: pavimentum, *mosaic*, Suet.

tessĕra -ae, f. (perhaps connected with τέσσαρες), *a cube of wood, stone, or other substance, used for various purposes.*
(1) *a piece of mosaic paving*: Plin. (2) *a die*

for playing (with numbers on all six sides): tesseras iacere, Cic.; Ter., Liv., Ov. (3) *a square tablet on which the military watchword was written*; hence, *the watchword*: omnibus tesseram dare, Liv.; Verg. (4) *a token which entitled the holder to receive money or provisions*: Juv., Suet. (5) *tessera hospitalis, a token of hospitality* (a small die, which friends broke into two parts to aid subsequent recognition), Pl.

tessĕrārĭus -i, m. (tessera), *the officer who received from the general the ticket (tessera) on which the watchword was written, and communicated it to the army*: Tac.

tessĕrŭla -ae, f. (dim. of tessera). (1) *a little cube of stone for paving*: Lucil. ap. Cic. (2) *a little voting-ticket*: Varr. (3) *a ticket, for the distribution of food*: Pers.

testa -ae, f. (cf. torreo), *a piece of burnt clay.*
LIT., (1) *an earthen vessel; a pot, jug, urn*, etc.: vinum Graecā testā conditum, Hor.; Verg. (2) *a brick*, or *tile*: Cic. (3) *a potsherd*: Ov., Plin., etc. Esp. *the potsherd used in voting by the Greeks*: testarum suffragia, ostracism, Nep.
TRANSF., (1) *the shell of shell-fish*: Cic.; meton., *a shell-fish*: Hor. (2) poet., *a shell, covering*: lubrica testa, *ice*, Ov.

testāmentārĭus -a -um (testamentum), *relating to a will*: lex, Cic. M. as subst. **testāmentārĭus** -i, *a forger of wills*: Cic.

testāmentum -i, n. (testor), *a last will, a testament*: id testamento cavere, *to provide*, Cic.; testamentum conscribere, facere, Cic.; inritum facere, *to annul*, Cic.; obsignare, Caes.; resignare, Hor.

testātĭo -ōnis, f. (testor). (1) *a calling to witness*: ruptorum foederum, Liv. (2) *a bearing witness*: Quint.

testātor -ōris, m. (testor), *one that makes a will, a testator*: Suet.

testātus -a -um, partic. from testor; q.v.

testĭcŭlus -i, m. (dim. of ²testis); *a testicle*: Mart., Juv., Pers.

testĭfĭcātĭo -ōnis, f. (testificor), *a bearing witness, testifying.* LIT., hāc testificatione uti, Cic. TRANSF., *attestation, evidence, proof*: officiorum, Cic.

testĭfĭcor -ari, dep. (testis/facio), *to bear witness to, give evidence of.*
LIT., haec, Cic.; with acc. and infin., or indir. quest.: Cic., Ov.
TRANSF., (1) in gen., *to show, publish, bring to light*: sententiam, amorem, Cic. L.; Ov., Tac. (2) *to call to witness*: ap. Cic. L., Ov.
Perf. partic. sometimes in pass. sense: abs te testificata voluntas, Cic.; Ov.

testĭmōnĭum -i, n. (¹testis), *witness, evidence, testimony.*
LIT., testimonium in aliquem dicere, Cic.; Pl., Liv., etc.; *of a written attestation*: testimonium componere, obsignare, Cic.
TRANSF., in gen., *proof, evidence, indication*: dedisti iudicii tui testimonium, Cic.; Caes., Quint.

¹testis -is, c. *one who gives evidence, a witness.*
LIT., testis falsus, Cic.; testes dare in singulas res, Cic.; testes adhibere, citare, producere, Cic.; Pl., etc. Of things: Cic., Hor., etc.
TRANSF., *an eye-witness, spectator*: Cic., Ov., Juv.

²**testis** -is, m. *a testicle*: Pl., Hor.

testor -ari, dep. (¹testis).
(1) *to bear witness to, to give evidence of.* LIT., Ov., Quint. TRANSF., **a**, in gen., *to make known, publish, declare, assert*: utraeque vim testantur, Cic.; Ov.; also with acc. and infin., or indir. quest.: Cic. Sometimes as pass., *to be attested, declared*: testata est voce praeconis libertas Argivorum, Liv.: **b**, *to make a will*: Liv., Quint.
(2) *to call to witness*: omnes deos, Cic.; conscia sidera, Verg.; with acc. and infin.: Cic.
¶ Hence perf. partic. in passive sense (with compar.) **testātus** -a -um, *attested, proved, clear*: res, Cic.; Nep.

testū, abl. n., **testō**, abl. n., and **testum**, acc. n. (cf. testa), *an earthen pot*: Verg., Ov., etc.

testŭdĭnĕus -a -um (testudo). (1) *of a tortoise*: gradus, Pl. (2) *made of tortoise-shell*: lyra, Prop.; Juv.

testŭdo -inis, f. (testa), *a tortoise.*
LIT., Cic., Liv.
TRANSF., (1) *the shell of the tortoise, tortoise-shell*: varii testudine postes, Verg.; Cic., Ov. (2) *a curved string-instrument; the lyre, cithara*, etc.: Hor., Verg. (3) *an arch or vault*: Cic., Verg. (4) as milit. t. t.: **a**, *a shed to protect soldiers while attacking fortifications*: Caes.: **b**, *a formation with shields held over the soldiers' heads and interlocking*: Caes., Verg., etc.

testŭla -ae, f. (dim. of testa), *a potsherd*, esp. *as used at Athens for ostracism*: a Themistocle conlabefactus testulā illā, Nep.

tētĕr, *see* taeter.

Tēthys -thўos; acc. -thyn, f. (Τηθύς), *a marine goddess, wife of Oceanus, mother of the river-gods and sea-nymphs.*
TRANSF., *the sea*: Cat., Ov.

tetrachmum -i, n. (τετράχμον), *a Greek coin of four drachmae*: Liv.

tetrăcōlon -i, n. (τετράκωλον), *a period having four clauses*: Sen.

tetradrachmum (τετράδραχμον) = tetrachmum; q.v.: ap. Cic. L.

tetrāo -ōnis, m. (τετράων), *a bird; a guinea-fowl* or *black grouse* or *capercailzie*: Plin., Suet.

tetrarches -ae, m. (τετράρχης), *the ruler over one-fourth of a country, a tetrarch*: Cic., Hor., etc.

tetrarchĭa -ae, f. (τετραρχία), *the country governed by a tetrarch, a tetrarchy*: Cic.

Tetrica -ae, f. *a mountain in the Sabine country.*

tetrĭcus -a -um, *harsh, gloomy, severe, forbidding*: puella, Ov.; deae, *the Parcae*, Mart.; Liv.

tĕtŭli = tuli, *see* fero.

Teucer -cri, m. and **Teucrus** -i, m. (Τεῦκρος). (1) *son of Telamon, king of Salamis, and brother of Ajax*. (2) *son of Scamander, first king of Troy*; hence adj. **Teucrus** -a -um, *Teucrian*, poet. = *Trojan*; m. pl. as subst. **Teucri** -ōrum, *the Trojans*; subst. **Teucrĭa** -ae, f. *Troy.*

Teuthrās -thrantis, m. (Τεύθρας), *a king of Mysia, father of Thespius.*
¶ Hence adj. **Teuthrantēus** -a -um, *Mysian*; also adj. **Teuthrantĭus** -a -um, *of Teuthras*: turba, *the fifty sisters and daughters of Thespius*, Ov.

Teutŏni -ōrum, m. and **Teutŏnēs** -um, m. pl. *the Teutons, a Germanic people.*
¶ Hence adj. **Teutŏnĭcus** -a -um, *Teutonic* and poet. = *Germanic.*

texo texĕre texŭi textum, *to weave.*
LIT., of cloth: tegumenta corporum vei texta vel suta, Cic.
TRANSF., (1) *to twine together, intertwine, plait*: crates, Hor.; casas ex arundine, Liv.; flores, Ov.; Verg. (2) *to put together, construct, build*: basilicam in medio foro, Cic. L.; Verg. (3) *of speech or writing, to compose*: epistulas cotidianis verbis, Cic. L.; Ov.
¶ Hence n. of partic. as subst. **textum** -i, *woven cloth, a web.* LIT., Ov. TRANSF., (1) *any material plaited* or *put together; a fabric*: pinea texta carinae, Cat.; clipei, Verg., Lucr., Ov. (2) *of written composition, texture, style*: Quint.

textĭlis -e (texo), *woven, textile*: stragulum, Cic.; Lucr., Verg. Also *plaited*: Mart. N. as subst. **textĭle** -is, n. (sc. opus), *a woven fabric, a piece of cloth*: Cic., Liv.

textŏr -ōris, m. (texo), *a weaver*: Hor., etc.

textōrĭus -a -um (textor), *of weaving*: Sen.

textrīnum -i, n. (textor), *weaving*: Cic.

textrix -trīcis, f. (f. of textor), *a female weaver*: Tib., Mart.

textum -i, n. subst. from texo; q.v.

textūra -ae, f. (texo), *a web, texture.* Prop. TRANSF., *a putting together, construction*: Lucr., Luc.

textus -ūs, m. (texo), *a web; hence texture, structure*: Lucr. TRANSF., of speech or writing, *mode of putting together, connexion*: Quint.

thălămēgus -i, f. (θαλαμηγός), *a barge* or *gondola provided with cabins*: Suet.

thălămus -i, m. (θάλαμος).
LIT., *a room in the interior of a house*, esp. *a woman's bedroom*: Verg., Ov.
TRANSF., (1) in gen., *a place of abode, dwelling*: Eumenidum, Verg.; *of the cells of bees*: Verg. (2) *a marriage-bed*: Prop. Hence, meton., *marriage*: vita expers thalami, Verg.; thalamos in desere pactos, Verg.; Hor., Ov.

thalassĭcus -a -um (θαλασσικός), *sea-green*: Pl.

thalassĭnus -a -um (θαλάσσινος), *sea-green*: Lucr.

thălassĭo, thalassius, etc.; *see* talassio.

Thălīa -ae, f. (Θάλεια). (1) *the Muse of comic poetry.* (2) *one of the sea-nymphs.*

thallus -i, m. (θαλλός), *a green branch*: Verg.

Thapsus (-ŏs) -i, f. (Θάψος). (1) *a peninsula and town in Sicily.* (2) *a town in Africa where Caesar conquered the Pompeians.*

Thăsus (-ŏs) -i, f. (Θάσος), *an island in the Aegean Sea.* Adj. **Thăsĭus** -a -um, *Thasian.*

Thaumās -antis, m. (Θαύμας), *father of Iris.*
¶ Hence adj. **Thaumantēus** -a -um (of Thaumas): virgo, *Iris*, Ov.; **Thaumantĭās** -ădis, f. *daughter of Thaumas*, i.e., *Iris*; **Thaumantis** -idis, f. = Thaumantias.

thĕātrālis -e (theatrum), *of* or *for a theatre, theatrical*: consessus, Cic.; Tac.

thĕātrum -i, n. (θέατρον), *a theatre, a place for the performance of plays, games*, etc.
LIT., Cic., Verg., etc.
TRANSF., (1) *the people assembled in the theatre, the audience, 'house'*: theatra tota reclamant, Cic.; senatūs consultum frequentissimo theatro (populi) comprobatum,

Cic. (2) in gen., *a sphere, theatre* for any action: forum populi Romani quasi theatrum illius ingenii, Cic.

Thēbae -ārum, f. pl. (Θῆβαι), *Thebes; the name of several cities.* (1) *a city of Upper Egypt.* (2) *the chief city of Boeotia, founded by Cadmus, the birth-place of Pindar.* (3) *a town in Mysia, residence of Eetion, father-in-law of Hector, destroyed by Achilles.*

¶ Hence f. adj. **Thēbāis** -idis, *belonging to Thebes* (*in Egypt* or *in Boeotia* or *in Mysia*); f. pl. as subst., Thebaïdes, *women of Thebes*: Ov. Adj. **Thēbaeus** -a -um, *of Thebes in Egypt.* Adj. **Thēbānus** -a -um, *belonging to Thebes in Boeotia*: modi, *Pindaric*, Ov.; mater, *Agave*, Ov.; soror, *Antigone*, Ov.; semina, *the dragon's teeth sown by Cadmus*, Ov.; duces, *Eteocles and Polynices*, Prop. M. pl. as subst., Thebani, *the Thebans.* Subst. **Thēbāna** -ae, f. *a woman from Thebes in Mysia*; of Andromache, *daughter of Eetion*: Ov.

Thēbē -ēs, f. (Θήβη). (1)=Thebae; q.v. (2) *a nymph, beloved by the river-god Asopus.* (3) *the wife of the tyrant Alexander of Pherae.*

thēca -ae, f. (θήκη), *a case, sheath, envelope, covering*: vasa sine theca, Cic.

thēma -ătis, n. (θέμα). (1) *a theme, topic, subject*: Sen., Quint. (2) *the position of the heavenly bodies at the moment of a birth*: Suet.

Thĕmistoclēs -is and -i, m. (Θεμιστοκλῆς), *the general of the Athenians in the Persian war.*

¶ Hence adj. **Thĕmistoclēus** -a -um, *Themistoclean.*

Thĕocrĭtus -i, m. (Θεόκριτος), *Greek bucolic poet of the third century* B.C., *born at Syracuse.*

Thĕŏgŏnĭa -ae, f. (Θεογονία), *the Theogony, or Generation of the Gods, a poem by Hesiod*: Cic.

thĕŏlŏgus -i, m. (θεολόγος), *a theologian, one who treats of the origin and nature of the gods*: Cic.

Thĕŏphănēs -is, and -i, m. (Θεοφάνης), *a Greek historian, friend of Pompey.*

Thĕŏphrastus -i, m. (Θεόφραστος), *a Greek philosopher, pupil of Plato and Aristotle.*

Thēra -ae, f. (Θήρα), *an island in the Aegean Sea* (now *Thira*).

¶ Hence adj. **Thēraeus** -a -um, *Theraean.*

Thērāmĕnēs -ae, m. (Θηραμένης), *one of the thirty tyrants at Athens.*

Thĕrapnae -ārum, f. pl. (Θεράπναι), *a town of Laconia, the birth-place of Helen.*

¶ Hence adj. **Thĕrapnaeus** -a -um, *Therapnean*; poet., *Spartan*: marita, *Helen*, Ov.

Thērĭclēs -is, m. (Θηρικλῆς), *a celebrated maker of pottery and wooden vessels at Corinth.*

¶ Hence adj. **Thērĭclēus** or **Thērĭclīus** -a -um (Θηρίκλειος), *Thericlean*: pocula, Cic.

thermae -ārum, f. pl. (sc. aquae; from θερμός), *warm springs, warm baths*: Plin., etc. As proper name, **Thermae**, *a town with warm springs on the north coast of Sicily* (now *Termini*).

¶ Hence adj. **Thermĭtānus** -a -um, *of Thermae.*

Thermōdōn -ontis, m. (Θερμώδων), *a river in Pontus, on which the Amazons lived.*

¶ Hence adj. **Thermŏdontēus** (-tĭăcus) -a -um, *of Thermodon*; poet.=*Amazonian.*

thermŏpōlĭum -i, n. (θερμοπώλιον), *a place where warm drinks are sold*: Pl.

thermŏpōto -are, *to refresh with warm drinks*: Pl.

Thermŏpȳlae -ārum, f. (Θερμοπύλαι), *a pass between the sea and Mount Oeta, on the borders of Thessaly, where Leonidas and a small body of Spartans fell fighting against the Persian army in* 480 B.C.

thermŭlae -ārum, f. (dim. of thermae), *little warm baths*: Mart.

Thērŏdāmās -antis, m. (Θηροδάμας), *a Scythian king, who fed lions with human flesh.*

¶ Hence adj. **Thērŏdămantēus** -a -um, *of Therodamas.*

Thersītēs -ae, m. (Θερσίτης), *son of Agrius, one of the Greeks before Troy, notorious for his ugliness and scurrilous tongue.*

thēsaurārĭus -a -um (thesaurus), *of treasure*: Pl.

thēsaurus (old form **thēnsaurus**) -i, m. (θησαυρός).

(1) *a treasure, store, hoard.* LIT., thesaurum obruere, defodere, Cic.; Pl., etc. TRANSF., *a treasure* (of persons, etc.): Pl.

(2) *a treasury, store-house.* LIT., servata mella thesauris, Verg.; esp., *the treasury of a temple* or *state*: thesauros Proserpinae spoliare, Liv. TRANSF., thesaurus rerum omnium memoria, Cic.

Thēsēus -ĕi and -ĕos, m. (Θησεύς), *a king of Athens, son of Aegeus, husband of Ariadne and Phaedra, conqueror of the Minotaur.*

¶ Hence adj. **Thēsēus** -a -um, *of Theseus*: crimen, *the desertion of Ariadne*, Ov.; poet., *Athenian*: Prop.; adj. **Thēsēïus** -a -um, *of Theseus*: heros, *Hippolytus*, Ov.; subst. **Thēsīdēs** -ae, m. *a son of Theseus*; *Hippolytus*, Ov.; subst. **Thēsēïs** -idis, f. *a poem on Theseus*: Juv.

thĕsis -is, f. (θέσις), *a proposition, thesis*: Quint.

Thespĭae -ārum, f. pl. (Θεσπιαί), *a town in Boeotia, at the foot of Mount Helicon.*

¶ Hence f. adj. **Thespĭăs** -ădis (Θεσπιάς), *Thespian*: deae Thespiades, Ov., and, simply, Thespiades, Cic., *the Muses*; adj. **Thespĭus** -a -um, *of Thespiae*; subst. **Thespĭenses** -ium, m. pl. *the inhabitants of Thespiae.*

Thespis -idis, m. (Θέσπις), *the founder of the Greek drama, contemporary of Solon and Pisistratus.*

Thessălĭa -ae, f. (Θεσσαλία), *Thessaly, a region in the north of Greece.*

¶ Hence adj. **Thessălĭcus** -a -um, *Thessalian*: iuga (of Mount Pelion), Ov.; adj. **Thessălus** -a -um, *Thessalian*: tela (of Achilles), Hor.; ignes, *in the camp of Achilles*, Hor.; pinus, *the ship Argo*, Ov.; f. adj. **Thessălĭs** -idis, *Thessalian*: umbra, *of Protesilaus*, Prop.; as subst. *a Thessalian woman*: Luc.

Thessălŏnīca -ae, f. and **Thessălŏnīcē** -ēs, f. (Θεσσαλονίκη), *Thessalonica, a town in Macedonia* (now *Thessaloniki*).

¶ Hence subst. **Thessălŏnīcenses** -ium, m. pl. *the inhabitants of Thessalonica.*

Thestius -i, m. (Θέστιος), *a king of Aetolia, father of Leda and Althaea.*

¶ Hence subst. **Thestĭădēs** -ae, m. (Θεστιάδης), *a male descendant of Thestius*: respice Thestiaden, *Meleager* (*son of Althaea*), Ov.; **Thestĭăs** -ădis, f. *a daughter of Thestius*, i.e. *Althaea.*

Thestor -ŏris, m. (Θέστωρ), *father of the sooth-sayer Calchas.*
⁋ Hence subst. **Thestŏrĭdēs** -ae, m. (Θεστορίδης), *son of Thestor, i.e., Calchas.*
thēta, n. indecl. (θῆτα), *the Greek letter theta* (Θ, θ), *used by the Greeks on voting tickets as a symbol of condemnation, because beginning the word* θάνατος: Mart.
Thĕtis -idis or -idos, f. (Θέτις), *a sea-nymph, wife of Peleus, mother of Achilles.* Hence, poet., *the sea:* Verg.
thiăsus -i, m. (θίασος), *a Bacchic rout, a band of revellers:* Cat.
Thisbē -ēs, f. (Θίσβη). (1) *a beautiful Baby-lonian maiden, beloved by Pyramus.* (2) *a town in Boeotia;* hence adj. **Thisbēus** -a -um, *Thisbean=Babylonian.*
Thŏas -antis, m. (Θόας).
  (1) *a king of Lemnos, father of Hypsipyle.*
⁋ Hence subst. **Thŏantĭăs** -ādis, f. *a daughter of Thoas, i.e. Hypsipyle.*
  (2) *a king of the Tauric Chersonese, slain by Orestes.*
⁋ Hence adj. **Thŏantēus** -a -um, poet.= *Tauric.*
thŏlus -i, m. (θόλος), *a cupola, dome:* Verg., Ov.
thōrax -ācis, m. (θώραξ), *a breastplate, cuirass:* Liv., etc.
Thrācĭa -ae; also **Thrāca** -ae and **Thrācē** -ēs (Θρᾴκη); f. *the country of Thrace.*
⁋ Hence adj. **Thrācĭus** and **Thrēĭcĭus** -a -um, *Thracian:* sacerdos, *Orpheus,* Verg.; Samus, *Samothrace,* Verg.; f. adj. **Thrēssa** and **Thrēissa** -ae, *Thracian;* as subst., *a Thracian woman;* m. adj. **Thrāx** -ācis and **Thrēx** -ēcis, *Thracian;* as subst. (1) *a Thracian;* often in plur., Thraces -cum. (2) *a gladiator in Thracian armour.*
Thrāx, Thrēissa, etc., see Thracia.
thrŏnus -i, m. (θρόνος), *a lofty seat, throne:* Plin.
Thūcȳdĭdēs -is, m. (Θουκυδίδης), *the Athenian historian of the Peloponnesian war.*
⁋ Hence adj. **Thūcȳdĭdīus** -a -um, *Thucydidean.*
Thūlē (**Thȳlē**) -ēs, f. *an island in the extreme north of Europe, perhaps one of the Shetland Islands, perhaps Iceland:* Plin., Tac.
thunnus (thynnus) -i, m. (θύννος), *a tunny-fish:* Hor., Ov., Plin.
Thūrĭi -ōrum, m. pl. (Θούριοι) and **Thūrĭae** -ārum, f. *a town built on the site of the des-troyed Sybaris, on the Tarentine Gulf in southern Italy.*
⁋ Hence adj. **Thūrīnus** -a -um, *of Thurii.*
thūs, thūrārius, etc.=tus, turarius, etc.; q.v.
thȳa (θύα) and **thȳïa** (θυΐα) -ae, f. *the Greek name of the citrus-tree:* Plin.
Thȳestēs -ae and -is, m. (Θυέστης), *son of Pelops, brother of Atreus, who placed before him for food his own son.*
Thȳïăs (dissyll.= Θυιάς) and **Thȳăs** (Θυάς) -adis, f. *a Bacchante:* Verg.
Thȳlē=Thule; q.v.
¹**thymbra** -ae, f. (θύμβρα), *the herb savory:* Verg.
²**Thymbra** -ae and **Thymbrē** -ēs, f. (Θύμβρη), *a town in Troas, with a temple to Apollo.*
⁋ Hence adj. **Thymbraeus** -a -um, *Thym-braean; a surname of Apollo.*
thȳmum -i, n. (θύμον), *the herb thyme:* Verg., etc.
Thȳni -ōrum, m. pl. (Θυνοί), *a Thracian people, who emigrated to Bithynia.*

⁋ Hence subst. **Thȳnĭa** -ae, f. *Thynia, the northern part of Bithynia;* adj. **Thȳnĭăcus** and **Thȳnus** -a -um, *Thynian or Bithynian;* f. adj. **Thȳnĭăs** -ădis, *Thynian or Bithynian.*
thynnus=thunnus; q.v.
Thȳŏnē -ēs, f. (Θυώνη), *mother of Bacchus* (according to one legend), *identified by some with Semele.*
⁋ Hence **Thȳŏneus** -ei, m. *son of Thyone,* i.e. *Bacchus;* also **Thȳŏnĭānus** -i, m.; meton.=*wine:* Cat.
Thȳrē -ēs, f. (Θύρη), *a town in Argolis.*
⁋ Hence f. adj. **Thȳrĕātis** -idis (Θυρεᾶτις), *of Thyrea.*
Thyrĕum and **Thyrĭum** -i, n. *a town in Acarnania, near Leucas.*
⁋ Hence **Thyrĭenses** -ĭum, m. pl. *the inhabitants of Thyreum.*
thyrsĭgĕr -gĕra -gĕrum (thyrsus/gero), *bearing a thyrsus:* Sen.
thyrsus -i, m. (θύρσος), *the stalk or stem of a plant:* Plin. Esp. *a wand, twined round with ivy and vine-leaves, carried by Bacchus and his attendants:* Hor., Ov.; hence, fig., *a magic wand or goad:* Lucr., Ov.
tĭāra -ae, f. and **tĭāras** -ae, m. (τιάρα, τιάρας), *an oriental turban:* Verg., etc.
Tĭbĕris -bĕris, acc. -bĕrim, abl. -bĕri, m.; also poet. **Tībris** or **Thībris** -bridis, acc. -brin or -brim, m. *the river Tiber;* personif., *the river-god of the Tiber.*
⁋ Hence adj. **Tībĕrīnus** -a -um, *belonging to the river Tiber:* amnis, Liv.; flumen, Verg., *the river Tiber;* pater, *or* deus, *the river-god,* Verg.; m. as subst. **Tībĕrīnus** -i, *the river-god of the Tiber:* Cic., Verg.; f. adj. **Tībĕrīnis** -idis, *belonging to the river Tiber:* Tiberinides Nymphae, Ov.
Tĭbĕrĭus -i, m. *a common Roman praenomen,* abbreviated Ti. Esp., *the second emperor of Rome, Tiberius Claudius Nero Caesar.*
tĭbĭa -ae, f. *the shin-bone,* tibia: Phaedr., Plin. L.; meton., *a pipe, fife, flute, originally made of a hollow bone:* tibiis canere, Cic.; Hor., etc.
tĭbĭālis -e (tibia). (1) *relating to a shin;* n. as subst., *a legging:* Suet. (2) *relating to a flute:* Plin.
tĭbīcĕn -ĭnis, m. (tibia/cano). (1) *a flute-player,* piper: Pl., Hor., Cic. (2) *a pillar, prop:* Ov., Juv.
tĭbīcĭna -ae, f. (tibicen), *a female flute-player:* Pl., Hor., etc.
tĭbīcĭnĭum -i, n. (tibicen), *playing on the flute:* Cic.
Tībris=Tiberis; q.v.
Tĭbullus -i, m.; Albius, *a Roman elegiac poet, friend of Horace and Ovid.*
Tĭbŭr -bŭris, n. *an old town in Latium, on the Anio, a famous resort for rich Romans* (now Tivoli).
⁋ Hence adj. **Tĭburs** -burtis, *Tiburtine;* n. sing. as subst., *the Tiburtine district;* m. pl. subst. **Tĭburtes** -um, *the inhabitants of Tibur;* adj. **Tĭburtīnus** and **Tĭburnus** -a -um, *Tiburtine;* m. as subst. **Tĭburnus** -i, *the builder of Tibur.*
Tīcīnum -i, n. *a town in Cisalpine Gaul on the river Ticinus* (now Pavia).
Tīcīnus -i, m. *a river in Cisalpine Gaul* (now Ticino).
Tĭgellĭus -i, m. *name of two musicians at Rome,*

one a contemporary of Cicero, the other of Horace.

tĭgillum -i, n. (dim. of tignum), *a small beam*: Liv., etc.

tignārĭus -a -um (tignum), *concerned with beams*: faber, *a carpenter*, Cic.

tignum -i, n. (tego), *a beam of wood, a piece of timber*: Caes., Ov., etc.

Tigrānēs -is, m. (1) *a king of Armenia, son-in-law and ally of Mithridates, conquered by Lucullus.* (2) *his son.*

Tigrānŏcerta -ae, f., and -ōrum, n. pl. *the chief town of Armenia, founded by Tigranes.*

tigris -idis and -is, c.; acc. -idem and -im or -in, abl. -ide or -i, acc. plur., poet., -idas (τίγρις; in Persian=*an arrow*), *a tiger*. Lit., Verg., etc. Transf., *a tiger-skin*: Stat.

Tigris -idis and -is, m.; acc. -idem and -im, abl. -ide and -ĕ or -i, *the river Tigris.*

tĭlĭa -ae, f. *a linden* or *lime-tree*: Verg., Ov.

Tīmāgĕnēs -is, m. (Τιμαγένης), *a rhetorician of the time of Augustus.*

Tīmāvus -i, m. *a river in northern Italy, between Aquileia and Trieste* (now Timavo).

tĭmĕfactus -a -um (timeo/facio), *frightened, alarmed*: Lucr., Cic.

tĭmĕo -ēre -ŭi, *to be afraid, fear, dread*; with acc.: aliquem *or* aliquid, Cic., Hor., Ov., etc.; with ne, ne non, *or* ut and the subj.: timeo, ne non impetrem, Cic.; Caes., Hor., etc.; with infin., *to be afraid to*: nomen referre in tabulas, Cic.; Caes., Hor., etc.; with indir. quest.: quid possem, timebam, Cic.; Pl., Ter., Liv.; with dat., to express *fear for a person or thing*: sibi, Caes.; Verg., etc.; so with de: de republica, Cic.; with a and the abl., *to fear . . . from*: a quo quidem genere ego numquam timui, Cic.

¶ Hence partic. **tĭmens** -entis, *fearing, fearful*; as adj., with genit.: mortis, Lucr.; m. pl. as subst., *the fearful*: timentes confirmat, Caes.

tĭmĭdĭtās -ātis, f. (timidus), *fearfulness, timidity*: Cic.

tĭmĭdus -a -um, adj. (with compar. and superl.) (timeo), *fearful, timid, faint-hearted*: timidus ad mortem, Cic.; timidus in labore militari, Cic.; with genit.: timidus procellae, Hor.; foll. by the infin.: non timidus pro patria mori, Hor.

¶ Adv. (with compar. and superl.) **tĭmĭdē**, *timidly, fearfully*: Cic., Hor., etc.

tĭmŏr -ōris, m. (timeo), *fear, dread.*
Lit., definiunt timorem metum mali appropinquantis, Cic.; timorem deponite, Cic.; inicere timorem Parthis, Cic.; percelli timore, Cic.; foll. by ne and the subj.: Verg., Liv.; by acc. and infin.: Cic., Liv.
Transf., *an object exciting fear*: Cacus Aventinae timor atque infamia silvae, Hor., etc.
Personif., Timor, *son of Aether and Tellus*, Hor., Verg., Ov.

tinctĭlis -e (tingo), *in which something is dipped*: Ov.

tĭnĕa -ae, f. *a grub, larva, worm*: Verg., Hor., Ov.

tingo tingĕre tinxi tinctum (cf. τέγγω), *to wet, moisten.*
Lit., in gen.: tunica sanguine tincta, Cic.; Verg., etc. Esp., *to dye, colour*: Hor., Ov.

Transf., *to imbue, tinge, colour*: orator tinctus litteris, Cic.; Mart., Quint.

tinnīmentum -i, n. (tinnio), *a tinkling*: Pl.

tinnĭo -ire, *to ring, tinkle.* Lit., Enn., Pl., Varr. Transf., (1) *to talk* or *sing shrilly*: Pl., Suet. (2) *to make to chink*; hence *to pay money*: exspecto ecquid Dollabella tinniat, Cic. L.

tinnītus -ūs, m. (tinnio), *a ringing, tinkling, jingling*: Verg. Lit., Verg., Ov., etc. Transf., of language, *a jingle of words*: Tac.

tinnŭlus -a -um (tinnio), *ringing, tinkling, jingling*: Ov., etc.

tintinnābŭlum -i, n. (tintinno), *a bell*: Pl., Juv., etc.

tintinnācŭlus -a -um (tintinno), *ringing, jingling*: Pl.

tintinno (**tintĭno**) -are (tinnio), *to ring, jingle, tinkle*: Cat.

tīnus -i, f. *a shrub, the laurustinus*: Ov., Plin.

Tīphӯs -ȳos; acc. -phyn, voc. -phy, m. (Τῖφυς), *the helmsman of the Argo.*

tippŭla -ae, f. *a water-spider, water-fly*: Pl., Varr.

Tīrĕsĭās -ae, m. (Τειρεσίας), *a blind soothsayer of Thebes.*

Tīrĭdātēs -dātis, m. (Τιριδάτης), *name of several kings of Armenia.*

tīro -ōnis, m. *a young soldier, a recruit.* Lit., Caes., etc. Used like adj.: exercitus tiro, Cic. L., Liv. Transf., *a beginner, a learner*: in aliqua re, Cic.; Quint., etc.

tīrōcĭnĭum -i, n. (tiro), *the state of a recruit, rawness, inexperience.* Lit., iuvenis, Liv. Transf., (1) any *beginning, apprenticeship*: in L. Paulo accusando tirocinium ponere, Liv.; Quint., Suet. (2) in concrete sense, *a body of recruits*: Liv.

tīruncŭlus -i, m. (dim. of tiro), *a young beginner*: Sen., Juv., etc.

Tīryns -nthis or -nthos, f. (Τίρυνς), *an Argive town where Hercules was brought up.*

¶ Hence adj. **Tīrynthĭus** -a -um, *Tirynthian*; poet., *relating to Hercules*; so, simply **Tīrynthĭus** -i, m. *Hercules.*

Tīsĭphŏnē -ēs, f. (Τισιφόνη), *one of the Furies.*

¶ Hence adj. **Tīsĭphŏnēus** -a -um: tempora, Ov.

Tītan -tānis, m. (Τιτάν) and **Tītānus** -i, m.; usually plur. **Tītānes** -um and **Tītāni** -orum, *the sons of Uranus* (Heaven) *and Ge* (Earth), *who warred against Jupiter for supremacy in heaven, and were by him cast down into Tartarus; the name is also applied to some of their male relatives, esp. the Sun-god, son of Hyperion, and Prometheus.*

¶ Hence adj. **Tītānĭus** -a -um, *relating to the Titans*; f. as subst. **Tītānĭa** -ae, Latona: Ov.; Pyrrha: Ov.; Diana: Ov.; Circe: Ov.; adj. **Tītānĭăcus** -a -um, *Titanian*; f. adj. **Tītānis** -idis -idos, *Titanian*; also as subst., Circe: Ov.; Tethys: Ov.

Tīthōnus -i, m. (Τιθωνός), *the husband of Aurora, who obtained from his wife the gift of immortality, without perpetual youth, and was at last changed into a grasshopper.*

¶ Hence adj. **Tīthōnĭus** -a -um, *Tithonian*: Tithonia coniux, Aurora, Ov.

Tĭtĭes -ium, m. and **Tĭtĭenses** -ium, m. pl. *one of the three tribes* (Ramnes, Tities, and Luceres) *into which the Romans were at first divided, and out of which three centuries of* *knights are said to have been formed by Romulus.*

tĭtillātĭo -ōnis, f. (titillo), *a tickling*: Cic.

tĭtillo -are, *to tickle*. LIT., sensūs, Lucr., Cic. TRANSF., ne vos titillet gloria, Hor.; Sen.

tĭtīvillĭtĭum -i, n. *a trifle*: Pl.

tĭtŭbantĭa -ae, f. (titubo), *a wavering, staggering*: linguae, *stammering*, Suet.

tĭtŭbātĭo -ōnis, f. (titubo), *a staggering, reeling*: Sen. TRANSF., *uncertainty*: Cic.

tĭtŭbo -are, *to totter, stagger.* LIT., Silenus titubans annisque meroque, Ov.; vestigia titubata, *tottering*, Verg. TRANSF., (1) *to stammer*: lingua titubat, Ov. (2) *to falter, waver, hesitate*: si verbo titubarint (testes), Cic.; Pl., Hor., etc.
¶ Hence adv. from partic. **tĭtŭbantĕr**, *hesitatingly, uncertainly*: Cic.

tĭtŭlus -i, m. *an inscription, label, title.* LIT., titulum inscribere lamnae, Liv.; cum ingenti rerum a se gestarum titulo, Liv. Esp. (1) *a notice on a house that is to let*: sub titulum nostros misit avara lares, Ov. (2) *an epitaph*: sepulcri, Juv. TRANSF., (1) *a title of honour, honourable designation*: consulatūs, Cic.; Hor., Ov. (2) *glory, honour*: par titulo tantae gloriae fuit, Liv. (3) *a pretence, pretext*: quem titulum praetenderitis, Liv.; Plin. L.

Tĭtus -i, m. *a Roman praenomen*, abbreviated T. Esp. *of the emperor Titus Flavius Sabinus Vespasianus, son and successor of Vespasian.*

Tĭtyos -i, m. (Τιτυός), *son of Jupiter, punished for an insult to Latona by being stretched out in Tartarus, and having his liver devoured by vultures.*

Tĭtўrus -i, m. (Τίτυρος), *the name of a shepherd in Vergil's Eclogues*; poet., meton. (1) *the Eclogues of Vergil*: Ov. (2) *Vergil himself*: Prop.

Tmōlus and **Tīmōlus** -i, m. (Τμῶλος), *a mountain in Lydia, famous for its wine.*
¶ Hence adj. **Tmōlĭus** -a -um, *Tmolian*; m. adj. **Tmōlītēs** -ae, *dwelling on Mount Tmolus.*

tŏcŭlĭo -ōnis, m. (from τόκος, *interest*), *a usurer*: Cic. L.

tŏfīnus -a -um (tofus), *made of tufa*: Suet.

tŏfus (tōphus) -i, m. *tufa*: Verg., Ov., Plin.

tŏga -ae, f. (tego), *a covering*; esp., *the white woollen upper garment worn by the Romans in time of peace, when they appeared in public as citizens*; special kinds of the toga were: praetexta, *worn by magistrates and freeborn children*, Cic.; pura, *worn by young men on coming of age*, also called virilis, Cic.; candida, *worn by a candidate for office*, Cic. TRANSF., (1) *peace*: cedant arma togae, Cic. poet. (2) *Roman citizenship*: Hor. (3) *a prostitute* (because prostitutes also wore the *toga*): Tib.

tŏgātārĭus -ii, m. (toga), *an actor in the* Fabula togata (*see* togatus): Suet.

tŏgātŭlus -i, m. (dim. of togatus), *a little client*: Mart.

tŏgātus -a -um (toga), *wearing the toga*, i.e. as a Roman citizen, as opp. to a foreigner or a soldier: Cic., Liv.; gens, *the Roman people*, Verg.; turba, Juv.
¶ M. as subst. **tŏgātus** -i, *a Roman citizen*, esp. *a humble Roman, a client*: Juv. In plur., *Roman citizens*: Cic., Liv. F. as subst.

tŏgāta -ae. (1) (sc. fabula), *the national drama of the Romans, treating of Roman subjects*: Cic., etc. (2) *a prostitute* (as wearing the *toga*): Hor.

tŏgŭla -ae, f. (dim. of toga), *a little toga*: Cic., Mart.

tŏlĕrābĭlis -e, adj. (with compar. and superl.) (tolero). (1) pass., *that can be borne, bearable*: condicio, Cic.; Verg., Liv. (2) act., *tolerant, patient*: Ter. Compar. adv. **tŏlĕrābĭlĭtĕr**, *rather patiently*: aliquid tolerabilius ferre, Cic.

tŏlĕrantĭa -ae, f. (tolero), *a bearing, enduring*: rerum humanarum, Cic.; Tac., etc.

tŏlĕrātĭo -ōnis, f. (tolero), *a bearing, enduring*: dolorum, Cic.

tŏlĕro -are (connected with tollo), *to carry, to bear.* LIT., pondus, Plin. TRANSF., (1) of hardships, etc., *to endure, sustain*: hiemem, Cic.; inopiam, Sall.; Ov., etc.; with acc. and infin.: Sall.; with infin.: Tac. (2) *to support, keep up, maintain*: equitatum, Caes.; vitam, Caes., Verg.
¶ Hence pres. partic. **tŏlĕrans** -antis, *bearing, enduring*; as adj., with genit.: laborum, Tac. Adv. **tŏlĕrantĕr**, *patiently*: illa ferre, Cic.
¶ Perf. partic. **tŏlĕrātus** -a -um, *endurable*; compar.: Tac.

Tōlētum -i, n. *a town in Hispania Tarraconensis* (now *Toledo*).

tollēno -ōnis, m. (tollo). (1) *a machine for raising water, a swing-beam* or *swipe*: Plin. (2) *a machine for raising solid weights, a crane*: Pl., Liv.

tollo tollĕre sustŭli sublātum, *to take up.* (1) *to lift up, raise, elevate.* LIT., saxa de terra, Cic.; oculos, Cic.; aliquem in crucem, *to crucify*, Cic.; aliquem in currum, in equum, Cic.; Pl., Lucr., etc. Esp. as naut. t. t.: a, tollere ancoras, *to weigh anchor*, Caes., Liv.: b, *to have on board*: naves quae equites sustulerant, Caes.; Verg., Liv. TRANSF., a, *to raise, elevate*: laudes alicuius in astra, Cic.; clamorem, Cic.; animos, Pl., Ter., Sall., Liv.; aliquem honoribus, Hor.; aliquem laudibus, *to extol*, Cic.: b, of children, *to acknowledge as one's own*; hence, *to bring up a child*: Pl., Ter.; also *to get, have a child*: liberos ex Fadia, Cic.
(2) *to take up and away, to remove, carry off.* LIT., praedam, Caes.; frumentum de area, Cic.; solem mundo, Cic.; cibos, Hor. Esp.: a, *to purloin, steal*: omnes chlamydes, Hor.: b, *to destroy, get rid of*: aliquem de medio, Cic.; e medio, Liv.; Carthaginem, Cic.; Hor. TRANSF., *to remove, abolish*: amicitiam e mundo, Cic.; legem, Cic.; dictaturam funditus a republica, Cic.
¶ Used as perf. partic. pass. and as adj. (with compar.) **sublātus** -a -um, *aloft, proud, haughty*; with abl.: hāc victoriā, Caes.; rebus secundis, Verg.; absol.: leo fidens magis et sublatior ardet, Ov.

Tŏlōsa -ae, f. *a town in Gallia Narbonensis* (now *Toulouse*).
¶ Hence adj. **Tŏlōsānus** -a -um, *of Tolosa*; also **Tŏlōsās** -ātis, *Tolosan*; subst. **Tŏlōsātes** -ĭum, m. pl. *the inhabitants of Tolosa.*

Tŏlumnĭus -i, m. (1) *a king of the Veientines.* (2) *a soothsayer of the Rutuli.*

tŏlūtārĭus -a -um (tolutim), *trotting*: equus, Sen.

tŏlūtim, adv. (tollo), *trotting, on the trot*: Pl., Varr.

tŏmāculum (**tŏmaclum**) -i, n. (τομή), *a kind of sausage*: Juv., Mart.

tōmentum -i, n. *the stuffing of a pillow, mattress, cushion*, etc.: Varr., Plin.

Tŏmi -ōrum, m. pl. (Τόμοι) and **Tŏmis** -is, f. (Τόμις), *a town in Lower Moesia, on the Black Sea, Ovid's place of exile.*

¶ Hence subst. **Tŏmītae** -ārum, m. pl. *the inhabitants of Tomi*; adj. **Tŏmītānus** -a -um, *of Tomi.*

tŏmus -i, m. (τόμος), *a cutting, chip, shred*: Mart.

tondĕo tondēre tŏtondi tonsum, *to shave, shear, clip.*

(1) of hair, wool, etc.: barbam et capillum, Cic.; oves, Hor.; in pass.: eum tonderi et squalorem deponere coegerunt, Liv.; Verg., etc. TRANSF., *to fleece* a person: Pl., Prop.

(2) of grass, etc.: **a**, *to mow, reap, prune*: prata, Verg.; ilex tonsa bipennibus, Hor.; **b**, *to browse on, crop*: gramina, Lucr.; Verg.

tŏnitrus -ūs, m. and **tŏnitrŭum** -i, n. (tono), *thunder*: Cic., Lucr., Verg., etc.

tŏno -are -ŭi -ĭtum, *to thunder.*

LIT., caelum tonat fragore, Verg.; Iuppiter tonabat, Prop.; impers.: tonat, *it thunders*, Cic. Hence partic.: tonans, as a divine epithet, esp. of Jupiter: Ov., Mart.

TRANSF., (1) intransit., *to make a loud noise*: Pericles tonare dictus est, Cic.; Lucr., Verg. (2) transit., *to thunder forth*: verba foro, Prop.; Verg.

tonsa -ae, f. *an oar*: Lucr., Verg., etc.

tonsĭlis -e (tondeo). (1) *that can be shorn or cut*: Plin. (2) *shorn, clipped, cut*: Plin., Mart.

tonsillae -ārum, f. *the tonsils in the throat*: Cic.

tonsĭto -are (freq. of tondeo), *to shear or clip repeatedly*: Pl.

tonsor -ōris, m. (tondeo), *a hair-cutter, barber*: Cic., etc.

tonsōrĭus -a -um (tonsor), *of or for clipping*: culter, Cic.; Mart.

tonstrīcŭla -ae, f. (dim. of tonstrix), *a little female barber*: Cic.

tonstrīna -ae, f. (tondeo), *a barber's shop*: Pl., Plin.

tonstrix -īcis, f. (tonsor), *a female barber*: Pl., Mart.

tonsūra -ae, f. (tondeo), *a clipping, shearing, shaving*: capillorum, Ov.; Plin.

tonsus -ūs, m. (tondeo), *the mode of cutting or wearing the hair*: Pl.

tŏnus -i, m. (τόνος), *the tone* or *sound* of an instrument; applied to painting, *tone*: Pl.

tōphus, etc.=tofus, etc.; q.v.

tŏpĭārĭus -a -um, *of* or *relating to ornamental gardening*: Plin.

¶ M. as subst. **tŏpĭārĭus** -i, *a landscape gardener*: Cic. L., Plin. L. F. as subst. **tŏpĭārĭa** -ae, *the art of landscape gardening*: topiariam facere, Cic. L.

toppĕr, adv. *speedily, directly, forthwith*: Enn., etc.

tŏral -ālis, n. (torus), *the valance of a couch or sofa*: Hor.

torcŭlar -āris, n. (torqueo), *a wine* or *oil-press*: Plin. Also *an oil-cellar*: Plin.

torcŭlārĭus -e (torcular), *of a press*: Varr.

N. as subst. **torcŭlārĭum** -i, *a press*: Cato, Plin.

torcŭlus -a -um (torqueo), *of a press*: vasa, Cato. N. as subst. torculum -i, *a press*: Varr., Plin.

tŏreuma -ătis, n. (τόρευμα), *carved* or *embossed work*: Cic., Sall., Mart.

tormentum -i, n. (torqueo), *an instrument for twisting, winding, pressing.*

(1) in gen., *a windlass*: praesectis omnium mulierum crinibus tormenta effecerunt, Caes.

(2) *the rack*, or *any instrument of torture.* LIT., tormenta adhibere, Cic.; dare se in tormenta, Cic.; de servo in dominum ne tormentis quidem quaeri licet, Cic.; Caes. TRANSF., **a**, *suasion, pressure*: lene tormentum admovere ingenio, Hor.: **b**, *torture, torment*: tormenta suspicionis, Cic.; Hor., etc.

(3) *a military engine for discharging missiles*: ibi tormenta conlocavit, Caes.; Cic., Liv. Meton., *the missile so discharged*: telum tormentumve missum, Caes.

tormĭna -um, n. (torqueo), *the colic* or *gripes*: Cic.

tormĭnōsus -a -um (tormina), *suffering from the colic*: Cic.

torno -are (tornus), *to turn in a lathe, make round.* LIT., sphaeram, Cic. TRANSF., versūs male tornati, *badly turned, awkward*, Hor.

tornus -i, m. (τόρνος), *a lathe.* LIT., Verg., etc. TRANSF., angusto versūs includere torno, Prop.

Tŏrōnē -ēs, f. (Τορώνη), *a town of Chalcidice on the Aegean Sea* (now *Toron*).

¶ Hence adj. **Tŏrōnāïcus** -a -um, *of Torone.*

tŏrōsus -a -um (torus), *muscular, brawny*: colla boum, Ov.

torpēdo -ĭnis, f. (torpeo). (1) *torpor, lethargy, sluggishness, inertness*: Sall., Tac. (2) *a fish, the electric ray* or *torpedo*: Cic.

torpĕo -ēre, *to be sluggish, inert, numb.* LIT., physically: corpora rigentia gelu torpebant, Liv.; Verg., etc.

TRANSF., *to be inactive, continue inactive*: deum sic feriatum volumus cessatione torpere, Cic.; adeo torpentibus metu qui aderant, ut ne gemitus quidem exaudiretur, Liv.; si tua ne subitā consilia torpent, Liv.; Verg.

torpesco -pescĕre -pŭi (torpeo), *to become sluggish* or *numb*: ne per otium torpescerent manus aut animus, Sall.; torpuerat lingua metu, Ov.; Liv., Tac.

torpĭdus -a -um (torpeo), *numb, sluggish*: Liv.

torpor -ōris, m. (torpeo), *numbness, sluggishness.* LIT., Cic., etc. TRANSF., *mental dullness, inertness, inactivity*: sordes omnium ac torpor, Tac.

torquātus -a -um (torques), *wearing a twisted collar* or *necklace*: Allecto torquata colubris, *with a necklace of snakes*, Ov.; palumbus torquatus, *the ring-dove*, Mart.; esp. as the surname of T. Manlius, *who killed a gigantic Gaul in single combat, and took from him the necklace which he wore.*

torquĕo torquēre torsi tortum, *to twist, wind, wrench.*

In gen. LIT., cervices oculosque, Cic.; terra circum axem se torquet, Cic.; anguis tortus, Verg.; capillos ferro, *to curl*, Ov.; stamina digitis, *or* pollice, *to spin*, Ov. TRANSF., *to twist, turn, distort*: omnia ad commodum suae causae, Cic.; Verg.

Esp. (1) *to hurl violently, whirl*: iaculum in hostem, Verg.; hastas, Cic.; tela manu, Ov. (2) *to rack, torture, torment*. LIT., Pl., Cic., Suet. TRANSF., **a**, *to test*: aliquem mero, *to make a person drink in order to test him*, Hor.; torqueatur vita Sullae, *be accurately examined*, Cic.: **b**, *to torment, plague*: libidines te torquent, Cic.; exspectatione torqueor, Cic.; Hor.

¶ Hence partic. **tortus** -a -um, *twisted, crooked*: via, *the labyrinth*, Prop.; quercus, *an oak garland*, Verg.; vimen, *a bee-hive*, Ov. TRANSF., condiciones tortae, *intricate, perplexed*, Pl.

Adv. **tortē**, *crookedly, awry*: Lucr.

torquis (**torques**) -is, m. and f. (torqueo), *that which is twisted* or *curved*. (1) *a twisted collar* or *necklace*: torque detracto, Cic. (2) *a collar for draught oxen*: Verg. (3) *a ring, wreath, chaplet*: ornatae torquibus arae, Verg.; Plin.

torrĕo torrēre torrŭi tostum, *to burn, parch, dry up with heat* or *thirst*. LIT., aristas sole novo, Verg.; solis ardore torreri, Cic.; tosti crines, *singed*, Ov.; of fever: mihi torrentur febribus artus, Ov. TRANSF., of love: torret amor pectora, Ov.; Hor.

¶ Hence partic. as adj. **torrens** -entis (compar.: Juv.; superl.: Stat.). LIT., *burning, hot, parched*: miles sole torrens, Liv.; Verg. TRANSF., *rushing, seething*. (1) of water: Verg., etc. (2) of speech: oratio, Quint.; Juv. M. as subst. **torrens** -entis. LIT., *a torrent*: Cic., Verg., etc. TRANSF., of speech: Quint., Tac.

torresco -ĕre (torreo), *to become parched, be dried up*: Lucr.

torrĭdus -a -um (torreo), *parched, burnt, dry*.

LIT., campi siccitate torridi, Liv.; homo vegrandi macie torridus, Cic.; poet., in act. sense: aestas, *burning*, Verg.

TRANSF., *pinched, nipped with cold*: membra torrida gelu, Liv.

torris -is, m. (torreo), *a firebrand*: Verg.; Ov.

tortē, adv. from torqueo; q.v.

tortĭlis -e (torqueo), *twisted, twined*: aurum, *a golden chain*, Verg.; Ov., Plin.

torto -are (freq. of torqueo), *to torture, torment*: Lucr.

tortor -ōris, m. (torqueo). (1) *a torturer, tormentor*: Cic., Hor., etc. (2) *a wielder*: habenae, Luc.

tortŭōsus -a -um (²tortus), *full of turns and windings, tortuous*. LIT., alvus, Cic.; amnis, Liv. TRANSF., *intricate, involved*: genus disputandi, Cic.

¹**tortus** -a -um, partic. from torqueo; q.v.

²**tortus** -ūs, m. (torqueo), *a twisting, winding, curve*: serpens longos dat corpore tortūs, Verg.

tŏrŭlus -i, m. (dim. of torus), *a tuft*: Pl.

tŏrus -i, m. *any round swelling, a protuberance*. Hence (1) *a knot in a rope*: Plin. (2) *a fleshy part of the body, muscle*: tori lacertorum, Cic. poet.; colla tument toris, Ov. (3) *a bed, sofa, mattress, couch*: Verg., Ov.; *a marriage couch*: Verg., Ov.; *a bier*: toro componat, Ov. (4) *a mound* or *elevation of earth*: tori riparum,

Verg. (5) fig., *an ornament* (as if on a garland): Cic.

torvĭtās -ātis, f. (torvus), *savageness, wildness* (of appearance or character): vultūs, Tac.; Plin.

torvus -a -um (tero), *savage, gloomy, grim, fierce*; esp. of the eyes or the look: oculi, Ov.; lumine torvo, Verg.; torva tuens, *with grim look*, Verg.; taurus, Ov.; proelia, Cat.

tŏt, indecl. num. adj. *so many*: tot viri, Cic.; tot milia formosarum, Prop.; foll. by ut and the subj.: Cic.; with corresponding quot: Cic., etc.; with corresponding quoties: Cic.

tŏtĭdem, indecl. num. adj. *just as many*: totidem annos vixerunt, Cic.; Caes., Ov., etc.; with quot: totidem verbis, quot dixit, Cic.

tŏtĭens (**tŏtĭēs**), adv. (tot), *so often, so many times*: Cic., Verg., etc.; with corresponding quotiens, quotienscunque, *or* quot: Cic., Liv.

tōtus -a -um; genit. tōtīus, dat. usually tōti; *the whole, complete, entire*. In gen.: sex menses totos, Ter.; mons, Caes.; respublica, Cic.; totis viribus, Liv. Esp., of persons, *whole-hearted, absorbed*: in prece totus eram, Ov.; totus in Persea versus, Liv.; Caes., Hor. N. as subst. **tōtum** -i, *the whole*: Cic. L. In phrases: in toto, *on the whole*, Cic. L.; ex toto, Ov., etc.; in totum, Plin., etc.

toxĭcum -i, n. (τοξικόν), *poison for arrows*: Ov. In gen., *poison*: Pl., Hor., etc.

trăbālis -e (trabs). (1) *of* or *relating to beams of wood*: clavus, Cic., Hor. (2) *as strong* or *as large as a beam*: telum, Verg.

trăbĕa -ae, f. *a white robe with scarlet stripes and a purple seam*. (1) as worn by kings: Verg., Liv. (2) as worn by knights in solemn processions; hence, meton.=*the equestrian order*: Mart. (3) as worn by the augurs: Suet.

trăbĕātus -a -um (trabea), *clad in the* trabea: Quirinus, Ov.; Tac.

trabs trăbis, f. *a beam of wood*.

LIT., Caes., etc.

TRANSF., (1) *the trunk of a tree, a tree*: trabes acernae, Verg.; Ov. (2) *anything made out of beams*: **a**, *a ship*: Cypria, Hor.; Verg.: **b**, *a roof, house*: sub isdem trabibus, Hor.: **c**, *a table*: Mart.

Trăchās -chantis, f. *a town in Italy*=Tarracina.

Trăchīn -chīnis, f. (Τραχίν), *an old town in the Thessalian district of Phthiotis, residence of Ceyx, scene of the death of Hercules; afterwards called Heraclea*.

¶ Hence adj. **Trăchīnĭus** -a -um (Τραχίνιος), *Trachinian*: heros, *Ceyx*, Ov.; so, simply: Trachinius, Ov.; f. pl. as subst., Trachiniae, *The Trachinian Women, a tragedy by Sophocles*.

tractābĭlis -e (tracto), *that can be handled* or *wrought, manageable*.

LIT., tractabile omne necesse est esse, quod natum est, Cic.; non tractabile caelum, *stormy*, Verg.

TRANSF., *yielding, compliant, tractable*: virtus, Cic.; Verg., Ov.; compar.: nihil est eo (filio) tractabilius, Cic. L.

tractātĭo -ōnis, f. (tracto), *a handling, management*. LIT., beluarum, armorum, Cic. TRANSF., (1) *a treating of, handling*: philosophiae, Cic. (2) as rhet. t. t., *a particular use of a word*: Cic.

tractātor -ōris, m. (tracto), *a slave who rubbed a bather's limbs, a masseur*: Sen.

tractātrix -īcis, f. (tractator), *a masseuse*: Mart.

tractātus -ūs, m. (tracto), *a handling, working, management*. LIT., Plin. TRANSF., *treatment, management*: ipsarum artium tractatu delectari, Cic.; Quint., etc.

tractim, adv. (traho), *gradually, by degrees*: ire, Lucr.; susurrare, Verg.

tracto -are (freq. of traho).
    (1) *to drag along, haul, pull about*: tractata comis antistita, Ov.; persona, quae propter otium ac studium minime in iudiciis periculisque tractata est, Cic.; Lucr.
    (2) *to handle, manage*. LIT., of physical objects: manibus aliquid, Pl.; terram, Lucr.; vulnera, Cic.; gubernacula, *to steer*, Cic.; pecuniam publicam, *to manage the public finances*, Cic.; fila lyrae, Ov. TRANSF., **a**, in gen., *to treat, handle, manage*: causas amicorum, Cic.; bellum, *conduct a war*, Liv.; tractare condiciones, *to treat about terms*, Caes.; partes secundas, *to act, play*, Hor.; intransit.: de condicionibus, *to treat*, Nep.: **b**, *to treat, behave oneself towards a person*: aspere, Cic.; honorificentius, Cic.; Pl., Hor.

¹tractus -a -um, partic. from traho; q.v.

²tractus -ūs, m. (traho), *a dragging*.
    (1) abstr., as a process. LIT., tractu gementem ferre rotam, Verg.; Syrtes ab tractu nominatae. TRANSF., tractus orationis lenis et aequabilis, Cic.; tractus verborum, *drawling*, Cic.; belli, *extension*, Tac.
    (2) concr.: **a**, *a track, trail*: longos flammarum tractūs, Lucr.; Cic., Verg.: **b**, *extent, space occupied, position*: urbis, Cic.; castrorum, Liv.; hence, *a tract of country, district*: hoc tractu oppidi erat regia, Caes.; corruptus caeli tractus, Verg.

trādĭtĭo -ōnis, f. (trado). (1) *a giving up, surrender*: oppidorum, Liv. (2) *a giving over by means of words, an instruction, relation*: Quint., Tac.

trādĭtor -ōris, m. (trado), *a traitor*: Tac.

trādo (**transdo**: Caes.) -děre -dĭdi -dĭtum, *to hand over, give up, surrender*.
    LIT., of persons and material things.
(1) in gen.: alicui poculum, Cic.; equum comiti, Verg.; alicui testamentum legendum, Hor.; pecuniam regiam quaestoribus, Liv.; possessiones et res creditoribus, Caes. (2) for a particular purpose, for special treatment: alicui turrim tuendam, Caes.; alicui legionem, Caes.; alicui neptem Agrippinam, *in marriage*, Tac.; pueros magistris, *for instruction*, Cic. Esp.: **a**, *to hand over for detention or punishment*: aliquem in custodiam, Cic. L.; aliquem ad supplicium, Caes.; Pl.: **b**, *to give over to the enemy, deliver up, betray*: arma, Caes.; Cic., etc.
    TRANSF., (1) of abstr. things in gen.: alicui Galliae possessionem, Caes.; quae dicam trade memoriae, Cic. (2) *to hand down as any kind of inheritance to posterity*: inimicitias posteris, Cic.; haec consuetudo a maioribus tradita, Cic.; esp. *to hand down an account of an event, to report, relate*: qualia multa historia tradidit, Cic.; annales tradunt, foll. by acc. and infin., Liv.; so, tradunt, traditur, etc.; with acc. and infin.: Liv., Cic.; pers. pass., with nom. and infin.: Lycurgi temporibus Homerus etiam fuisse traditur, Cic. (3) *to communicate in teaching, to teach*: elementa loquendi, Cic.; virtutem hominibus,

Cic.; Caes. (4) with reflex., *to commit, surrender, devote* oneself: se totum alicui, Cic.; se quieti, Cic.; totos se voluptatibus, Cic.

trādūco (**transdūco**) -dūcĕre -duxi -ductum, *to carry over, lead over, bring over* or *across*.
    LIT., in gen.: hominum multitudinem trans Rhenum in Galliam, Caes.; Helvetios per fines Sequanorum, Caes.; Pl., Liv. Often with acc. of that over which a person or thing is brought: copias flumen, pontem, Caes. Esp. *to lead across* or *past in front of others*: traducti sub iugum et per hostium oculos, Liv.; often in the phrase traducere equum (of a knight when he passed muster at the censor's inspection): cum esset censor et in equitum censu C. Licinius Sacerdos prodisset ... iussit equum traducere, Cic.; Liv.
    TRANSF., (1) *to bring over, transpose, transfer*: Clodium ad plebem, Cic.; centuriones ex inferioribus ordinibus in superiores, Caes.; animos a severitate ad hilaritatem risumque, Cic.; aliquem a disputando ad dicendum, Cic.; aliquem ad suam sententiam, Cic. (2) of time, *to pass, spend, lead*: otiosam aetatem, Cic.; leniter aevum, Hor.; noctem his sermonibus, Liv. (3) *to show, display*: se Ulixem ancipitem, Juv. Esp. *to expose to ridicule, to 'show up'*: aliquem per ora hominum, Liv.; Juv., Mart.

trādūctĭo -ōnis, f. (traduco). (1) *a transferring*, esp. from one rank to another: hominis ad plebem, Cic.; also as rhet. t. t., *metonymy*: Cic. (2) of time, *passage* or *lapse of time*, Cic. (3) *disgrace, ridicule*: Sen.

trādūctor -ōris, m. (traduco), *a transferrer*: ad plebem (of Pompey, who let Clodius be transferred from a patrician to a plebeian family), Cic.

trādux -ūcis, m. (traduco), *a vine-layer, prepared for transplanting*: Plin., Tac.

trăgĭcŏcŏmoedĭa -ae, f. (τραγικοκωμῳδία), *tragi-comedy*: Pl.

trăgĭcus -a -um (τραγικός), *of tragedy, tragic*.
    LIT., poema, *tragedy*, Cic.; poeta, Cic.; actor, Liv.; Orestes, *appearing in a tragedy*, Cic.; m. as subst. **trăgĭcus** -i, *a tragic poet*: Cic., Quint.
    TRANSF., (1) *in tragic style, lofty, sublime*: orator, Cic.; Hor. (2) *of a tragic land, awful, fearful, horrible*: scelus, Liv.; Ov., Juv.
    ¶ Adv. **trăgĭcē**, *tragically, after the manner of tragedy*: Cic., Sen.

trăgoedĭa -ae, f. (τραγῳδία), *a tragedy*.
    LIT., tragoedias facere, Cic.; tragoediam agere, Cic.; Pl., Tac.
    TRANSF., (1) *a dramatic scene*: Appiae nomen quantas tragoedias excitat, Cic. (2) *pathetic* or *bombastic language*: istis tragoediis tuis perturbor, Cic. (3) *the art of tragedy*: Hor., Ov.

trăgoedus -i, m. (τραγῳδός), *a tragic actor, tragedian*: Pl., Cic., Hor.

trăgŭla -ae, f. (traho), *a species of javelin used by the Gauls and Spaniards*: Caes., Liv. TRANSF., tragulam inicere in aliquem, Pl.

trăgus -i, m. (τράγος). (1) *the smell under the arm-pits*: Mart. (2) *a kind of fish*: Ov.

trăhax -ācis (traho), *drawing to oneself*; hence, *greedy*: Pl.

trăhĕa -ae, f. (traho), *a sledge, drag*: Verg.

trăho trăhĕre traxi tractum, *to draw, drag*.

LIT., (1) in gen., *to trail, pull along*: vestem, Hor.; corpus fessum, Liv.; trahuntque siccas machinae carinas, Hor.; Verg., etc. Also of persons, *to bring along*: exercitum, Liv.; turbam prosequentium, Liv.; Verg. (2) *to drag, pull violently*: aliquem pedibus, Cic.; ad supplicium, Sall., Tac.; corpus tractum et laniatum, Cic.; aliquem a templo, Verg. Hence of plundering: praedam ex agris, Liv.; Cic., etc. (3) *to draw in, take up*: ex puteis aquam, Cic.; auras ore, Ov.; animam, *to breathe*, Liv.; of persons drinking, *to quaff*: pocula, Hor. (4) *to draw out*: ferrum e vulnere, Ov.; vocem imo a pectore, Verg.; of spinning: data pensa, Ov.; lanam mollire trahendo, Ov. Hence, in gen., *to lengthen*: Ov. (5) *to draw together, contract*: vultum, Ov.; vela, Verg.

TRANSF., (1) in gen., *to draw, attract*: trahit sua quemque voluptas, Verg.; quid est quod me in aliam partem trahere possit? Cic. L.; decus ad consulem, Liv.; crimen in se, Ov. (2) *to squander*: pecuniam, Sall. (3) *to take in* or *on, assume, derive*: squamam, Ov.; ruborem, Ov.; multum ex moribus (Sarmatarum) traxisse, Tac.; cognomen ex aliqua re, Cic.; maiorem ex pernicie et peste reipublicae molestiam, Cic.; consilium ex aliqua re, Sall. (4) *to prolong, lengthen, spin out*: comitia, Cic.; rem in serum, Liv.; noctem sermone, Verg.; vitam in tenebris, Verg.; of mental deliberation: Sall. (5) *to ascribe, refer, interpret*: aliquid in religionem, Liv.; fortuita ad culpam, Tac.

¶ Hence partic. as adj., of speech, *fluent, flowing*: oratio tracta et fluens, Cic. N. as subst., of things *pulled out fine*. (1) *a flock of wool when carded* or *combed out*: Tib. (2) *a long cake*: Cato.

traĭcio (*or* transĭcio: Caes.) -ĭcere -iēci -iectum (trans/iacio).

(1) *to throw* a thing (or person) *across* something; *to shoot across, convey over*. LIT., telum, Caes.; vexillum trans vallum, Liv.; membra super acervum levi pede, Ov.; malos antemnasque de nave in navem, Liv. Esp. *to transport* over the sea, a river, a mountain, etc.: legiones in Siciliam, Liv.; copias trans fluvium, Liv.; Marius traiectus in Africam, *having crossed*, Cic.; sese ex regia ad aliquem, Caes.; sese duabus navibus in Africam, Liv. Sometimes with the thing crossed also acc.: equitum magnam partem flumen, Caes.

(2) *to pass through* or *across* a thing (or person); *to cross, penetrate, pierce*: Trebiam navibus, Liv.; murum iaculo, Cic.; aliquem venabulo, Liv.; alicui femur tragulā, Caes.; pars magna equitum mediam traiecit aciem, Liv.

traiectĭo -ōnis, f. (traicio). (1) *a passing over, crossing over, passage*: stellarum, Cic. (2) *a transferring*: in alium, Cic. Esp. as rhet. t. t.: **a.** *the transposition of words*: verborum, Cic.; **b.** *hyperbole*: veritatis superlatio atque traiectio, Cic.

traiectus -ūs, m. (traicio), *a crossing over, passing over, passage*: fluminis, Liv.; commodissimus in Britanniam, Caes.

trālāt-=translāt-; q.v.

trālŏquor -loqui, dep. *to recount, relate*: Pl.

Tralles -ium, f. pl. *a town in western Asia Minor, near the modern Aydin*.

¶ Hence adj. **Trallĭānus** -a -um, *of Tralles*.

trālūcĕo=transluceo; q.v.

trāma -ae, f. *the woof* in weaving. LIT., Varr., Sen. TRANSF., trama figurae, *a lanky, lean person*, Pers.; tramae putidae, *trifles*, Pl.

trāmĕo=transmeo; q.v.

trāmes -itis, m. *a by-way, foot-path*. LIT., Apennini tramites, Cic.; transversis tramitibus transgredi, Liv. TRANSF., poet., *a way, course, path*: Lucr., Verg., etc.

trāmigro=transmigro; q.v.

trāmitto=transmitto; q.v.

trānăto (**transnăto**) -are, *to swim across*: Tac.; with acc. of place: Gangem, Cic.

trāno (**transno**) -are, *to swim over, swim across*. LIT., ad suos, Liv.; with acc. of place: flumen, Caes.; pass.: tranantur aquae, Ov.; Verg. TRANSF., with acc., in gen., *to pass through*: foramina, Lucr.; nubila, Verg.; genus igneum quod tranat omnia, *pervades*, Cic.

tranquillĭtās -ātis, f. (tranquillus), *quietness, calmness*. LIT., *a calm, freedom from wind, calm weather*: maris, Cic.; summā tranquillitate consecutā, Caes.; tanta subito malacia et tranquillitas exstitit, Caes.; Liv. TRANSF., *rest, peace*: summa tranquillitas pacis atque otii, Cic.; animi, Cic.; Liv., Tac.

tranquillo -are (tranquillus), *to calm*. LIT., mare oleo, Plin. TRANSF., animos, Cic.

tranquillus -a -um, adj. (with compar. and superl.), *quiet, calm, tranquil*. LIT., *calm*; esp., *free from wind*: mare, Cic., Liv.; serenitas, Liv. N. as subst. **tranquillum** -i, *a calm*: in tranquillo tempestatem adversam optare dementis est, Cic.; Liv. TRANSF., *peaceful, undisturbed, serene*: tranquilla et serena frons, Cic.; senectus, Hor.; tranquillum ab hostili metu agmen, Liv. N. as subst. **tranquillum** -i, *quiet*: rempublicam in tranquillum redigere, Liv.

¶ Adv. **tranquillē**, *quietly, calmly*: Pl., Cic.

trans, prep. with acc. *over, across, on* or *to the other side of*: trans Rhenum incolunt, Caes.; trans Alpes transfertur, Cic.; trans mare currunt, Hor.

transăbĕo -īre -ii, *to go through* or *past*: ensis transabiit costas, Verg.

transactor -ōris, m. (transigo), *a manager, accomplisher*: rerum huiuscemodi omnium transactor et administer, Cic.

transādīgo -ĭgĕre -ēgi -actum. (1) *to drive a thing through something else, to thrust through*: crudum ensem transadigit costas, Verg. (2) *to pierce, penetrate*: hasta horum unum transadigit costas, Verg.; Stat.

Transalpīnus -a -um, *beyond the Alps, transalpine*: Gallia, Caes.; bella, Cic.

transcendo (**transscendo**) -scendĕre -scendi -scensum (trans/scando), *to climb over, step over, pass over*. LIT., in hostium naves, Caes.; Liv. With acc.: muros, Liv.; Caucasum, Cic.; Caes. TRANSF., *to step over, transgress*: fines iuris, Lucr.; ordinem aetatis, Liv.

transcīdo -cīdĕre -cīdi -cīsum (trans/caedo), *to cut up*: Pl.

transcribo (**transscrībo**) -scrībĕre -scripsi -scriptum, *to copy, transcribe*. LIT., testamentum in alias tabulas, Cic. TRANSF., *to transfer, convey, assign*: nomina in socios, Liv.; alicui spatium vitae, Ov.; sceptra colonis, Ov.; matres urbi, Verg.

transcurro -currĕre -cŭcurri and -curri -cursum, *to run across* or *over, hasten over, hasten past.* LIT., ad forum, Ter.; per spatium, Lucr.; castra, Liv.; with acc.: caelum transcurrit nimbus, Verg. TRANSF., ad melius, Hor.; with acc.: suum cursum, Cic.; of time: Plin. L.

transcursus -ūs, m. (transcurro), *a running past, hastening through.* LIT., Liv., Sen. TRANSF., *a brief mention*: Plin.

transdo = trado; q.v.

transdūco = traduco; q.v.

transenna -ae, f. (**1**) *lattice-work, a grating*: Cic. (**2**) *a net for catching birds.* LIT., Pl. TRANSF., *a trap*: Pl.

transĕo -īre -iī -itum, *to go over, cross, pass over*; with or without object in acc.

LIT., (**1**) in gen.: in Helvetiorum fines, Caes.; Formias, Cic.; Euphratem, Cic.; pass.: Rhodanus transitur, Caes. (**2**) *to desert*: ad aliquem, Cic., Caes.; a patribus ad plebem, Liv. (**3**) *to outstrip, overtake*: equum cursu, Verg.

TRANSF., (**1**) *to be changed into, be transformed into*: in saxum, Ov. (**2**) *to make a transition, pass over*: transitum est ad honestatem dictorum et factorum, Cic.; ad partitionem, Cic.; in alicuius sententiam, Liv. (**3**) *to penetrate, pervade*: quaedam animalis intellegentia per omnia permanat et transit, Cic. (**4**) of time passing, *to go by*: transiit aetas quam cito! Tib.; dies legis transiit, Cic. (**5**) *to pass time, spend*: annum quiete et otio, Tac.; Sall. (**6**) *to pass beyond, to transgress*: fines verecundiae, Cic.; Ov. (**7**) *to surpass*: Luc. (**8**) *to pass over* a thing; i.e. *to omit, ignore* or *touch lightly on*: leviter transire et tantummodo perstringere unam quamque rem, Cic.; aliquid silentio, Cic. L.; Quint.

transfĕro transferre transtŭli translātum and trālātum, *to carry over* or *across; to transfer, transport, convey.*

LIT., (**1**) in gen.: Caesar paullo ultra eum locum castra transtulit, Caes.; aliquem trans Alpes, Cic.; o Venus, te Glycerae transfer in aedem, Hor. (**2**) in writing, *to copy*: litteras in libros, Cic.

TRANSF., (**1**) in gen., *to bring over, remove, transfer*: regnum ab sede Lavini, Verg.; omnia Argos, *to give the victory to Argos*, Verg.; in Celtiberiam bellum, Caes.; sermonem alio, *turn to another subject*, Cic. (**2**) *to put off, defer*: sese in proximum annum, Cic. (**3**) *to change*: Ov., Tac. (**4**) *to translate into another language*: istum ego locum totidem verbis a Dicaearcho transtuli, Cic. L.; Quint. (**5**) *to use* a word *figuratively* or *metaphorically*: verba, quae transferuntur, Cic.

transfīgo -fīgĕre -fixi -fixum. (**1**) *to pierce* a person *through, transfix*: puellam gladio, Liv.; transfixus hastā, Cic.; Caes. (**2**) *to thrust* a weapon *through*: hasta transfixa, Verg.; Luc.

transfĭgūro -are, *to transform, transfigure*: Sen., Suet., Plin., etc.

transfŏdĭo -fŏdĕre -fōdi -fossum, *to stab through, transfix*: alicui latus, Liv.; aliquem, Caes.; pass. partic. with acc. of respect: pectora duro transfossi ligno, Verg.

transformis -e (trans/forma), *changed, transformed*: Ov.

transformo -are, *to change, transform*: se in vultus aniles, Verg.; Quint.

transfŏro -are, *to pierce, thrust through*: Sen.

transfrēto -are (trans/fretum), *to cross the sea*: Suet.

transfŭga -ae, c. (transfugio), *a deserter.* LIT., specie transfugarum ad Flaccum venire, Liv.; Cic., Tac. TRANSF., transfuga divitum partes linquere gestio, Hor.; Plin.

transfŭgĭo -fūgĕre -fūgi -fūgĭtum, *to desert to the enemy.* LIT., Gabios, Romam, Liv.; quod in obsidione et fame servitia infida transfugerent, Liv.; Tac. TRANSF., ab adflicta amicitia transfugere et ad florentem aliam devolare, Cic.; Tac.

transfŭgĭum -i, n. (transfugio), *a going over to the enemy, deserting*: Liv., Tac.

transfundo -fundĕre -fūdi -fūsum, *to pour from one vessel into another.* LIT., Plin. TRANSF., *to transfer*: omnem amorem in hanc, Cic.; Tac.

transfūsĭo -ōnis, f. (transfundo), *a pouring out, pouring off.* LIT., Plin. TRANSF., *the migration of a people*: Cic.

transgrĕdĭor -grĕdi -gressus sum, dep. (trans/gradior), *to go across, pass over.*

LIT., in gen.: in Europam, Liv.; per montes, Liv.; with acc.: flumen, Caes.; Taurum, Cic. L.; esp. *to go over* to another side or party: in partes alicuius, Tac.

TRANSF., (**1**) *to pass on* to something fresh, in action or speech: tarde ad sacramentum, Tac. (**2**) *to pass beyond, exceed* a measure or time: Plin.

transgressĭo -ōnis, f. (transgredior), *a going over, passage*: ascensus et transgressio Gallorum (over the Alps), Cic. TRANSF., *a transposition of words*: verborum, Cic.

transgressus -ūs, m. (transgredior), *a going over, passage*: auspicium prosperi transgressus, Tac.; with objective genit.: amnis, Tac.

transĭgo -ĭgĕre -ēgi -actum (trans/ago), *to drive through.*

LIT., *to stab, pierce through*: se ipsum gladio, Tac.

TRANSF., (**1**) of time, *to pass, spend, lead*: tempus per ostentationem, Tac.; Sen., etc. (**2**) *to finish, complete, accomplish, transact*: negotium, Cic.; aliquid cum aliquo, Sall.; aliquid per aliquem, Cic.; Liv., Tac.; impers. pass.: si transactum est, *if it is done*, Cic. (**3**) *to settle* a difference or dispute, *come to an understanding*: cum aliquo HS. ducentis milibus, Cic.; transigite cum expeditionibus, *have done with*, Tac.

transĭlĭo (transsĭlĭo) -sĭlīre -sĭlŭi (trans/salio), *to spring over, leap across.*

LIT., de muro in navem, Liv.; with acc.: muros, Liv.; rates transiliunt vada, Hor.

TRANSF., ab illo consilio ad aliud, *to go over to*, Liv.; with acc.: rem, *to pass by, pass over*, Cic.; munera Liberi, *be immoderate with*, Hor.

transĭtans -antis, partic. as from trans to, *passing through*: Cic. L.

transĭtĭo -ōnis, f. (transeo), *a going across, passing over.*

LIT., imagines similitudine et transitione perceptae, Cic.; esp. *a going over from one party* or *side to another*: ad plebem transitiones, Cic.; sociorum, Liv.; **exercitus** transitionibus imminutus, Liv.

TRANSF., (1) *infection, contagion*: Ov. (2) concr., *a passage*: transitiones perviae Iani nominantur, Cic.

transĭtŏrĭus -a -um (transeo), *having a passage through*: domus, Suet.

transĭtus -ūs, m. (transeo), *a passing over* or *across, transit*.

LIT., transitus fossae, Cic.; transitum claudere, Liv.; in transitu capta urbs, *in passing*, Tac.; esp. *a passing over from one party* or *side to another*: facili transitu ad proximos et validiores, Tac.

TRANSF., (1) *a changing over, transition*: rerum, Tac. (2) of colours, *fading*: Ov., Plin.

translātīcĭus (trālātīcĭus) -a -um (transfero), *handed down as customary, prescriptive*: edictum, *received by a magistrat from his predecessor*, Cic.; hence, in gen., *common, usual*: Cic. L., Plin. L., etc.

translātĭo (trālātĭo) -ōnis, f. (transfero), *a transferring, handing over*. LIT., pecuniarum a iustis dominis ad alienos, Cic.; of plants, *grafting*: Varr., Plin.

TRANSF., criminis, Cic.; esp. (1) *a translation*: Quint. (2) *a metaphor, trope, figure*: Cic., Quint.

translātīvus -a -um (transfero), *transferable*: constitutio, Cic.

translātor -ōris, m. (transfero), *a transferrer*: quaesturae (of Verres), Cic.

translūcĕo (trālūcĕo) -ēre. (1) *to shine across*: Lucr. (2) *to shine through, be visible through*: Ov., Plin.

transmărīnus -a -um, *from beyond the sea, foreign, transmarine*: artes, Cic.; legationes, Liv.

transmĕo (trāmĕo) -mĕare, *to go over, across, through*: Plin., Tac.

transmigro -are, *to migrate, move from one place to another*: Veios, Liv.

transmissĭo -ōnis, f. (transmitto), *a passage*: ab eā urbe in Graeciam, Cic.

transmissus -ūs, m. (transmitto), *a passage*: pari spatio transmissus atque ex Gallia in Britanniam, Caes.

transmitto (trāmitto) -mittĕre -mīsi -missum.

(1) *to send across, send over, convey across, pass through, transmit*. LIT., equitatum celeriter, Caes.; classem in Euboeam ad urbem Oreum, Liv.; exercitum per fines, *to allow through*, Liv.; transmissum per viam tigillum, *passed across the road*, Liv. TRANSF., **a**, *to convey, make over, entrust*: bellum in Italiam, Liv.; huic hoc tantum bellum, Cic.; suum tempus temporibus amicorum, Cic.; Verg., etc.: **b**, of time, *to let pass*: Iunium mensem transmisimus, Tac.

(2) *to cross over, go across, pass through* or *over*. LIT., sin ante transmisisset, Cic.; ab Lilybaeo Uticam, Liv.; with acc. of what is crossed: tot maria, Cic.; Verg., Liv. TRANSF., **a**, *to leave unnoticed*: Scaurum silentio transmisit, Tac.: **b**, of time, *to spend*: Sen., etc.: **c**, *to go through, suffer*: Plin. L.

transmontāni -ōrum, m. pl. *dwellers beyond the mountains*: Liv.

transmŏvĕo -mŏvēre -mōvi -mōtum, *to remove* from one place to another. LIT., Syriā legiones, Tac. TRANSF., *to transfer*: Ter.

transmūto -are, *to change, transmute*: dextera laevis, Lucr.; incertos honores, Hor.

transnăto = tranato; q.v.

transnōmĭno -are, *to change the name of* a person or thing: Suet.

transpădānus -a -um, *beyond* (i.e. on the north side of) *the Po, transpadane*: colonia Caes.; clientes, Cic. M. as subst. **transpădānus** -i, *a person living on the north side of the Po*: Cat.; plur.: Cic.

transpectus -ūs, m. (transpicio), *a looking through, seeing through*: Lucr.

transpĭcĭo (transspĭcĭo) -spĭcĕre (trans/ specio), *to look through, see through*: Lucr.

transpōno -pōnĕre -pŏsŭi -pŏsĭtum, *to put over, remove, transfer*: Plin. L., Tac.

transportātĭo -ōnis, f. (transporto), *a removal*: Sen.

transporto -are, *to convey across, transport*: exercitum in Graeciam, Cic.; with another acc., of what is crossed: milites his navibus flumen transportat, Caes.

transrhēnānus -a -um (trans/Rhenus), *beyond* (i.e. on the east side of), *the Rhine*: Germani, Caes.

transtĭbĕrīnus -a -um (trans/Tiberis), *beyond the Tiber*. M. pl. as subst. **transtĭbĕrīni** -ōrum, *the people living beyond the Tiber*: Cic.

transtĭnĕo -ēre (teneo), *to go through, pass through*: Pl.

transtrum -i, n. (trans), *a cross-beam*; esp. *a thwart* or *bench in a ship on which rowers sat*, gen. plur.: Caes.

transulto (transsulto) -are (freq. of transilio), *to spring over* or *across*: Liv.

transūmo (transsūmo) -ĕre, *to adopt, assume*: Stat.

transŭo (transsŭo) -sŭĕre, *to sew through, stitch through*; hence *to pierce through*: exta transuta verubus, Ov.

transvectĭo (trāvectĭo) -ōnis, f. (transveho), *a carrying over* or *across* or *past*: Acherontis, Cic. Esp. *the riding of a Roman knight past the censor at the periodical muster*: Suet.

transvĕho (trāvĕho) -vĕhĕre -vexi -vectum, *to carry over* or *past, convey across, transport*. LIT., milites, Caes.; naves plaustris, Liv. Pass. in middle sense, transvehi, *to ride, sail, pass over* or *across*: in Africam, Sall.; Corcyram, Liv.; Tac. Esp. *to carry past others in a procession, to bear along in triumph*: arma spoliaque carpentis, Liv. Pass. in middle sense, of a knight, *to ride past the censor at a muster*: Liv., Suet.

TRANSF., of time, *to pass*: abiit iam et transvectum est tempus, Tac.

transverbĕro -are, *to pierce through, transfix, perforate*: bestiam venabulo, Cic. L.; pectus alicuius abiete, Verg.

transversārĭus -a -um (transversus), *lying across, transverse*: tigna, Caes.

transversus, trāversus and **transvorsus** -a -um, *transverse, oblique, athwart*.

LIT., fossa, Caes.; transverso ambulare foro, *across the forum*, Cic.; transverso itinere, *in an oblique direction*, Liv.; transversum digitum, *a finger's breadth*, Cic.

TRANSF., cuius in adulescentiam transversa incurrit misera reipublicae fortuna, *crossed, ran counter*, Cic.

N. as subst. **transversum** -i, *a cross-direction*: Plin. Esp. in phrases: de or ex

transverso, *sideways*, Pl.; de transverso, *unexpectedly*, Cic. L. N. pl. acc. used like adv.: venti transversa fremunt, Verg.

transvŏlĭto -are, *to fly across*: Lucr.

transvŏlo (trāvŏlo) -are, *to fly over or across*. LIT., of birds: Plin. TRANSF., (I) *to hasten over, hasten across*: Alpes, ap. Cic. L.; eques transvolat in alteram partem, Liv.; dum (vox) transvolat auras, *speeds through*, Lucr. (2) *to hasten past*: aridas quercus, Hor.; transvolat in medio posita, *passes by*, Hor.

trăpētus -i, m. **trăpētum** -i, n. and plur. **trăpētes** -um, m. (τραπέω, *to tread grapes*), *an oil-press*: Cato, Verg.

trăpezīta -ae, m. (τραπεζίτης), *a money-changer*: Pl.

Trăpĕzūs -untis, f. (Τραπεζοῦς), *a town in Pontus* (now *Trebizond*).

Trăsŭmēnus (also **Trasy-** and **Trasi-**; also with double **n**) -i, m. (with or without **lacus**), *the Trasimene lake, on the banks of which Hannibal conquered the Romans under Flaminius* (217 B.C.) (now *Lago di Perugia*).

trav- = transv-; q.v.

Trĕbĭa -ae, m. *a river in Cisalpine Gaul, where Hannibal conquered the Romans, 217 B.C.* (now *Trebbia*).

Trĕbŭla -ae, f. *name of three towns in Italy.*

trĕcēni -ae -a (tres/centum), *three hundred at a time* or *three hundred each*: Liv., Hor.

trĕcentēsĭmus -a -um (trecenti), *three-hundredth*: Cic.

trĕcenti -ae -a (tres/centum), *three hundred*: Cic., Verg., etc.

trĕcentiēs (trĕcentĭens), adv. (trecenti), *three hundred times*: Cat.

trĕchĕdipnum -i, n. (τρεχέδειπνος -ον, *hastening to dinner*), *a light garment worn by parasites at table*: Juv.

trĕdĕcim (tres/decem), *thirteen*: Liv.

trĕmēbundus -a -um (tremo), *trembling*: manus, Cic.; Lucr., Ov.

trĕmĕfăcĭo -făcĕre -fēci -factum (tremo/facio), *to cause to tremble*: Verg. Perf. partic. pass., tremefactus -a -um, *trembling*: Verg., Ov.

trĕmesco (trĕmisco) -ĕre (tremo), *to tremble, quake*; of things: tonitru tremescunt ardua terrarum et campi, Verg.; of persons: omnem tremescens ad strepitum, Ov. With acc., *to tremble at*: sonitum pedum vocemque, Verg.; with infin.: telum instare tremescit, Verg.

trĕmĭbundus = tremebundus; q.v.

trĕmisco = tremesco; q.v.

trĕmo -ĕre -ŭi (cf. τρέω, τρέμω), *to tremble, quake*; of things: tremit hasta, Verg.; of persons: toto pectore tremens, Cic.; corde et genibus, Hor.; with acc. of respect: tremis ossa pavore, Hor.; Lucr. With acc. object, *to tremble at, quake at*: offensam Iunonem, Ov.; te, Verg.; virgas ac secures dictatoris, Liv.

¶ Hence gerundive as adj. **trĕmendus** -a -um, *fearful, terrible, dread*: rex, Pluto, Verg.; Hor., Ov.

trĕmor -ōris, m. (tremo), *a trembling, quaking, tremor*. LIT., of the limbs: pallor et tremor et dentium crepitus, Liv.; of fire: tremor ignium clarus, Lucr.; of the earth: Verg.; plur.: Lucr., Ov. TRANSF., *an object which causes fear and trembling*: Mart.

trĕmŭlus -a -um (tremo), *trembling, quaking, quivering, tremulous*. LIT., of things: lumen, Verg.; mare, Ov.; of persons: accurrit ad me tremulus, Ter. TRANSF., *that causes trembling*: Prop.

trĕpĭdātĭo -ōnis. f. (trepido), *agitation, anxiety, alarm, trepidation*: Cic.; tantam trepidationem iniecit, Liv.; per trepidationem, Tac.

trĕpĭdē, adv. from trepidus; q.v.

trĕpĭdo -are (trepidus), *to be agitated, be busy and anxious, bustle about*.

LIT., of living beings: totis trepidatur castris, *the whole camp is in confusion*, Caes.; circa advenam, Liv.; ad arma, Liv.; inter fugae pugnaeque consilium, *to waver confusedly*. With acc., *to fear, be anxious about*: occursum amici, Juv.; with infin.: ne trepidate meas defendere naves, Verg.

TRANSF., of things: aqua per pronum trepidat rivum, Hor.; trepidant flammae, *flicker*, Hor.; with infin.: cuius octavum trepidavit (*has been hastening*) aetas claudere lustrum, Hor.

¶ Hence adv. from pres. partic. (with compar.) **trĕpĭdantĕr**, *anxiously, hurriedly*: omnia trepidantius timidiusque agere, Caes.

trĕpĭdus -a -um (cf. τρέω, τρέμω), *agitated, anxious, restless, disturbed*.

LIT., of living beings: trepida Dido, Verg.; civitas, Liv.; with genit.: rerum suarum, *on account of*, Liv.; Tac.

TRANSF., of things, actions, or situations: unda, Ov.; metus, Ov.; cursus, Verg.; in re trepida, in rebus trepidis, *in an emergency*, Liv.; Tac.

¶ Hence adv. **trĕpĭdē**, *in an agitated, anxious manner*: Liv., Suet.

trēs (archaic **treis** and **trīs**) trĭa, num. adj. (cf. τρεῖς, τρία), *three*: Pl., Cic., etc.

tressis -is, m. (tres/as), *three asses*: Varr., Pers.

tresvĭri = triumviri; q.v.

Trēvĕri (Trēvĭri) -ōrum, m. pl. *a powerful Germanic people, whose capital Augusta* or *Colonia Treverorum is now Trier*. Rarely in sing. **Trēvir** -vīri, *one of the Treveri*.

¶ Hence adj. **Trēvĕricus (Trēvĭricus)** -a -um, *of the Treveri*.

trĭangŭlus -a -um (tres/angulus), *three-cornered, triangular*. N. as subst. **triăngŭlum** -i, *a triangle*: Cic., Quint.

trĭāriī -ōrum, m. pl. (tres), *the oldest and most experienced Roman soldiers, who were drawn up in the third rank, behind the hastati and principes*: Liv. Hence prov.: res ad triarios rediit, *it's a critical situation*, Liv.

tribrăchys -ўos, m. (τρίβραχυς), *a metrical foot, consisting of three short syllables* (˘ ˘ ˘): Quint.

trĭbŭārĭus -a -um (tribus), *of or relating to a tribe*: Cic.

trĭbūlis -is, m. (tribus). (I) *one who belongs to the same tribe, a fellow-tribesman*: tribulis tuus, Cic.; Ter., Hor., Liv. (2) *one of the common people*: Mart.

trĭbŭlum -i, n. (tero), *a threshing machine*: Varr., Verg.

trĭbŭlus -i, m. *a thorny plant, the caltrop*: Verg.

trĭbūnăl -ālis, n. (tribunus), *the tribunal, a raised platform*; used for the direction of

meetings or the administration of justice: in tribunali Pompeii praetoris urbani sedentes, Cic.; Caes., Liv., etc. Also used by a general in the camp: Liv., Tac.
TRANSF., (1) the praetor's seat in the theatre: Suet. (2) *a monument erected in honour of the dead*: Tac. (3) *any mound, embankment of earth*: Plin.

trĭbūnātus -ūs, m. (tribunus), *the office* or *dignity of a tribune, tribuneship.* (1) *that of a tribune of the people*: Cic., Liv. (2) *that of a military tribune*: Cic., Liv.

trĭbūnīcĭus -a -um (tribunus), *of a tribune, tribunicial.* (1) *of a tribune of the people*: potestas, Cic.; m. as subst. **trĭbūnīcĭus** -i, *a person who has been tribune*: Cic., Liv. (2) *of a military tribune*: honos, Caes.

trĭbūnus -i, m. (tribus), *a tribune, an officer of one of the following kinds.* (1) tribunus Celerum, *commander of the Celeres* (q.v.) *under the kings*, Liv. (2) tribuni aerarii, *paymasters who assisted the quaestors, and who were afterwards made judges*, Cic. (3) tribuni militum, or militares, *military tribunes, officers of whom there were six to every legion; each of them commanded it for two months in the year*, Caes., Cic., etc. (4) tribuni militum consulari potestate, *military tribunes with consular power*, chosen to govern in the place of consuls, from 444 to 366 B.C., Liv. (5) tribuni plebis and (more frequently) simply tribuni, *the tribunes of the people, the magistrates who protected the plebeians*, Cic., Liv.

trĭbŭo -ŭĕre -ŭi -ūtum (tribus), *to divide out, allot, assign.*
LIT., rem universam in partes, Cic.; praemia alicui, Caes.; suum cuique, Cic.; Sall., etc.
TRANSF., (1) *to grant, give, show*: alicui misericordiam suam, Cic.; alicui magnam gratiam, Cic.; pacem terris, Ov.; Caes., etc. (2) *to allow, concede, yield*: valetudini aliquid, Cic.; mihi omnia, Cic.; Caes., etc. (3) *to ascribe, attribute*: id virtuti hostium, Caes.; Cic.

trĭbus -ūs, f. (from root of tres), *originally a third part of the Roman people.* Hence *a tribe, a division of the Roman people* (originally Ramnes, Tities, Luceres; eventually 35 in number): populum in tribus convocare, Cic.
TRANSF., *the lower classes, the mob*: Plin., Mart.

trĭbūtārĭus -a -um (tributum), *relating to tribute*: tabellae, Cic.

trĭbūtim, adv. (tribus), *according to tribes, tribe by tribe*: nummos dividere, Cic.

trĭbūtĭo -ōnis, f. (tribuo), *a distribution, dividing*: Cic.

trĭbūtum -i, n. (trĭbūtus -i, m.: Pl.) (tribuo), *a tax, fixed contribution, tribute*: tributum conferre, facere, pendĕre, Cic.; Caes., Liv., etc. TRANSF., *a gift, present* (esp. one considered as due): Ov., Stat., Juv.

trĭbūtus -a -um (tribus), *arranged according to tribes*: comitia, *in which the people voted by tribes*, Liv.

trīcae -ārum, f. (1) *trifles, trumpery, nonsense*: Pl., Mart. (2) *vexations, troubles, perplexities*: quomodo domesticas tricas (fert)? Cic. L.; Pl.

trīcēnārĭus -a -um (triceni), *containing the number thirty*: filius, *thirty years old*, Sen.

trīcēni -ae -a (triginta), *thirty at a time* or *thirty each*: Cic., Plin., Mart.

trīceps -cĭpĭtis (tres/caput), *three-headed*: Cic., Ov.

trīcēsĭmus (trīcensĭmus, trīgēsĭmus) -a -um (triginta), *thirtieth*: Cic., etc.

trĭchĭla -ae, f. *a summer-house, arbour*: Caes., Verg.

trīcĭēs (trīcĭens), adv. (triginta), *thirty times*: Cic.

trīclīnĭum -i, n. (τρικλίνιον), *a dining-couch, a couch on which the Romans reclined at meals*: Cic., Mart., etc. TRANSF., *a dining-room*: exornat ample et magnifice triclinium, Cic.

trīco -ōnis, m. (tricae), *a trickster*: Pl.

trīcor -ari, dep. (tricae), *to make difficulties, to shuffle, trifle*: cum aliquo, Cic. L.

trĭcorpor -pŏris (tres/corpus), *having three bodies*: forma tricorporis umbrae, *of Geryon*, Verg.

trĭcuspis -ĭdis (tres/cuspis), *having three points*: Ov.

trĭdens -entis (tres/dens), *having three teeth* or *prongs*: rostra, Verg. M. as subst. **trĭdens** -entis, *a trident, a three-pronged spear*: Juv., Plin.; as an attribute of Neptune: Verg., Ov.

trĭdentĭfĕr -fĕri, m. (tridens/fero), *the trident-bearer*, epithet of Neptune: Ov.

trĭdentĭgĕr -gĕri, m. (tridens/gero), *the trident-bearer*, epithet of Neptune: Ov.

trĭdŭum (trĭdŭom) -i, n. (tres/dies), *a space of three days*: cum tridui viam processisset, Caes.; triduo illum aut summum quadriduo periturum, Cic.

trĭennĭa -ium, n. pl. (tres/annus), *a festival celebrated every three years*: Ov.

trĭennĭum -i, n. (tres/annus), *a space of three years*: biennium aut triennium est cum nuntium remisisti, Cic.; multis locis Germaniae triennium vagati, Cic.; Pl., Caes.

trĭens -entis, m. (tres), *a third part, one-third.* In gen.: Cic. L.; of an inheritance: Suet. Esp. (1) *the third part of an* as: Hor. (2) *of a* sextarius: Prop.

trĭentābŭlum -i, n. (triens), *the equivalent in land for the third part of a sum of money*: Liv.

trĭērarchus -i, m. (τριήραρχος), *the commander of a trireme*: Cic., Tac.

trĭēris -e (τριήρης), *having three banks of oars.* Subst. **trĭēris** -is, f. *a trireme*: Nep.

trĭĕtērĭcus -a -um (τριετηρικός), *recurring every three years, triennial*: trieterica sacra, Ov.

trĭĕtēris -ĭdis, f. (τριετηρίς). (1) *a space of three years*: Mart. (2) *a triennial festival*: Cic.

trĭfārĭam, adv. *in three places, on three sides*: adoriri castra, munire, Liv.

trĭfaux -faucis (tres/faux), *having three throats, triple-throated*: latratus (Cerberi), Verg.

trĭfĭdus -a -um (tres/findo), *split in three parts, three-forked*: flamma (of lightning), Ov.

trĭfĭlis -e (tres/filum), *having three hairs*: Mart.

trĭformis -e (tres/forma), *three-formed, having three forms*: Chimaera, Hor.; dea, Hecate, Ov.; mundus (composed of air, sea, and earth), Ov.

trĭfūr -fūris, m. (tres/fur), *a three-fold thief, arch-thief*: Pl.

trĭfurcĭfĕr -fĕri, m. *an arch-rogue*: Pl.

trĭgĕmĭnus (**tergĕmĭnus**) -a -um, *of children, three born at a birth*: fratres, the Horatii and the Curiatii, Liv. In gen., *threefold, triple*: vir, *Geryon*, Hor.; canis, *Cerberus*, Ov.; tergemini honores, *the aedileship, praetorship, and consulship*, Hor.

trĭgintā, indecl. num. adj. (cf. τριάκοντα), *thirty*: Cic., etc.

trĭgon -ōnis, m. (τρίγων), *a ball for playing*: Hor., Mart.

trĭgōnālis -e (trigonum), *three-cornered*: pila (=trigon), Mart.

trĭlībris -e (tres/libra), *of three pounds' weight*: Hor.

trĭlinguis -e (tres/lingua), *having three tongues*: os (Cerberi), Hor.

trĭlix -īcis (tres/licium), *having three threads*: loricam consertam hamis auroque trilicem, Verg.

trĭmestris -e (tres/mensis), *of three months*: haedi, *three months old*, Varr.; Suet.

trĭmetrŏs (-us) -a -um (τρίμετρος), *containing three metra, i.e. three double feet*: Quint. M. as subst. **trimetrus** -i, *a trimeter*: Hor., Quint.

trĭmŏdĭa -ae, f. and **trĭmŏdĭum** -i, n. (tres/modius), *a vessel containing three modii*: Varr.

trĭmŭlus -a -um (dim. of trimus), *three years old*: Suet.

trĭmus -a -um (tres), *three years old*: equa, Hor.; Pl., Varr.

Trīnacrĭa -ae, f. (Τρινακρία), *the island of Sicily, so called from its triangular shape*.
 ¶ Hence adj. **Trīnacrĭus** -a -um, *Sicilian*; and f. adj. **Trīnacris** -īdis, *Sicilian*: Trinacris, alone=*Sicily*, Ov.

trīni -ae -a; also sing. **trīnus** -a -um (tres), *three at a time, three together*: trinae litterae, Cic.; trina castra, Caes., Liv.

Trinobantes -um, m. *a people in the east of Britain*.

trĭnoctĭālis -e (tres/nox), *of three nights*: Mart.

trĭnōdis -e (tres/nodus), *having three knots*: Ov.

trĭōbŏlus -i, m. (τριώβολος), *a coin of the value of three oboli*: Pl.

trĭōnēs -um, m. pl. *the ploughing oxen*; hence, *the constellations known as the Great Bear and Little Bear* (as the stars resembled the shape of a waggon and the oxen attached to it): Verg.

Trĭŏpās -ae, m. (Τριόπας), *a king of Thessaly, father of Erysichthon*.
 ¶ Hence subst. **Trĭŏpēïus** -i, m. *Erysichthon*: Ov.; and **Trĭŏpēïs** -īdis, f. *Mestra, daughter of Erysichthon*.

trĭparcus -a -um (ter/parcus), *very stingy*: Pl.

trĭpart-, *see* tripert-.

trĭpectŏrus -a -um (tres/pectus), *having three breasts*: Lucr.

trĭpĕdālis -e, *of three feet in measure*: parma, Liv.

trĭpertītus (**trĭpartītus**) -a -um, *divided into three parts, threefold, triple*: divisio, Cic.; Tac. N. abl. sing. as adv. **tripertīto** (**trĭpartīto**), *in three parts*: bona dividere, Cic.; Caes., Liv.

trĭpēs -pĕdis, *having three feet*: mulus, Liv.; Hor.

trĭplex -plĭcis (ter/plico), *threefold, triple*: acies, Caes.; Plato triplicem finxit animum, Cic.; aes, Verg., Hor.; deae, *the three Parcae*, Ov. As subst., m. pl. **triplĭcēs** -um (sc. codicilli), *a writing tablet with three leaves*:

Cic. L., Mart.; n. sing. **triplex** -plĭcis, *three times as much*: pediti in singulos centeni dati . . . triplex equiti, Liv.; Hor.

triplus -a -um, *threefold, triple*: pars, Cic.; Pl.

Triptŏlĕmus -i, m. (Τριπτόλεμος), *son of Celeus, king of Eleusis, the inventor of agriculture, and later a judge in the lower world*; prov.: Triptolemo dare fruges, *to carry coals to Newcastle*, Ov.

trĭpŭdĭo -are (tripudium), *to beat the ground with the feet, to dance*; esp. as a religious rite: Sen.; tripudiantes more suo (of the Spaniards), Liv.; fig.: tot in funeribus reipublicae exsultans ac tripudians, *dancing for joy*, Cic.

trĭpŭdĭum -i, n. (1) *a religious dance*: Salios per urbem ire canentes carmina cum tripudiis sollemnique saltatu, Liv.; so of a savage war dance: cantus (Gallorum) ineuntium proelium et ululatus et tripudia, Liv.; of other dances: Cat. (2) as t. t. of augury, *a favourable omen, when the sacred chickens ate so fast that the food fell out of their beaks*: Cic., Liv., Suet.

trĭpūs -pŏdis, m. (τρίπους), *a three-legged seat, tripod*: Verg., Hor. Esp. *the tripod of the Delphic priestess*: Cic., Verg., Ov.; hence, meton., *the Delphic oracle*: Ov.

trĭquetrus (tres/quattuor) -a -um, *three-cornered, triangular*: insula (of Britain), Caes.; also (because of the shape of Sicily), *Sicilian*: Lucr., Hor.

trĭrēmis -e (remus), *having three banks of oars*: naves, Caes. F. as subst. **trĭrēmis** -is, *a trireme*: Cic., Hor., Liv.

triscurria -ōrum, n. pl. (tres/scurra), *gross buffooneries*: Juv.

tristĭcŭlus -a -um (dim. of tristis), *somewhat sorrowful*: filiola, Cic. L.

tristĭfĭcus -a -um (tristis/facio), *causing sadness*: Cic. poet.

tristis -e, adj. (with compar. and superl.), *sad, sorrowful, gloomy, dismal, forbidding, harsh*; used either of passing moods or of fixed character. Of persons: tristis et conturbatus, Cic.; quos cum tristiores vidisset, Cic.; iudex, *severe*, Cic.; Erinys, Verg. Of actions, situations, places, etc.: natura, Cic.; tempora, Cic.; ira, Hor.; sors, Cic.; dicta, Ov.; ministerium, Verg.; triste et severum dicendi genus, Cic.; Tartara, *the gloomy underworld*, Verg. Of taste or smell, *harsh, bitter*: suci, Verg.; Lucr., Liv. N. as subst.: triste lupus stabulis, *a disastrous thing*, Verg.
 ¶ N. acc. **triste** (with compar. **tristĭus**), used like adv., *sadly, more sadly*: Cic., Hor., Prop.

tristĭtĭa -ae, f. and **tristĭtĭēs** -ei (tristis), *sadness, gloom, harshness*: in eadem tristitia permanere, Caes.; sermonis, Cic.; temporum, Cic. L.

trĭsulcus -a -um (tres/sulcus), *three-furrowed*; hence *three-pointed, three-pronged*: lingua (serpentis), Verg.; telum Iovis, *lightning*, Ov.

trĭtāvus -i, m. (tres/avus), *the father of the atavus or atava*: Pl. Transf., *any remote ancestor*: Varr.

trītĭcĕus (**trītĭcēïus**) -a -um (triticum), *of wheat, wheaten*: messis, Verg.; Ov.

trītĭcum -i, n. *wheat*: granum tritici, Cic.; Pl., Caes.

Trītōn -ōnis or -ōnos, m. (Τρίτων).
 (1) *Triton, son of Neptune, a god of the sea*,

represented with a horn made of a shell, which
he blew at the bidding of Neptune to calm the
waves.

(2) a lake in Africa, near the smaller Syrtis,
the supposed birth-place of several deities, esp.
of Minerva (Pallas).

¶ Hence adj. **Trītōnĭăcus** -a -um:
arundo, discovered by Minerva, Ov.; f. adj.
Trītōnĭs -ĭdis or -ĭdos, Tritonian: arx,
Athens, Ov.; pinus, the Argo, built at the
order of Minerva, Ov.; as subst., Minerva;
adj. **Trītōnĭus** -a -um, Tritonian; f. as subst.,
Minerva.

trītor -ōris, m. (tero), a rubber: Pl.

trītū, abl. as from tritus, m. (tero), by rubbing:
Cic.

trītūra -ae, f. (tero), a treading out of corn,
threshing: Varr., Verg.

trītus -a -um, partic. from tero; q.v.

triumphālis -e (triumphus), of or relating to
a triumph, triumphal: corona, of a triumphing
general, Liv.; provincia, the conquest of which
has earned a triumph, Cic.; porta, the gate
through which the triumphing general entered
Rome, Cic.; imagines, busts of ancestors who
had triumphed, Hor.

N. pl. as subst. **triumphālĭa** -ium,
the distinctions of a triumphing general: Tac.

triumpho -are (triumphus), to triumph, to
have a triumph.

LIT., de Numantinis, Cic.; ex Macedonia,
Cic.

TRANSF., (1) to triumph, gain a victory:
amor de vate triumphat, Ov. (2) to exult:
gaudio, Cic.; laetaris in omnium genitu et
triumphas, Cic.; Ter. (3) in pass., to be
triumphed over, be completely conquered: ne
triumpharetur Mithridates, Tac.; triumphati
Medi, Hor.; bos triumphatus, captured, Ov.

triumphus -i, m., old form **trĭumpus** -i, m.

LIT., a triumphal procession, a triumph,
granted by the senate to a general and his
army after an important victory; the general
entered Rome in a chariot with white horses,
and with a crown of laurel on his head, while
his soldiers and the spectators cried 'Io
triumphe!': alicui triumphum decernere,
Cic.; triumphum tertium deportare, Cic.;
triumphum agere, to triumph, with genit., or
de, or ex and abl., of the person or nation
triumphed over: Boiorum, Liv.; ex Aequis,
Liv.; Pharsalicae pugnae, Cic.; de Liguribus,
Liv.

TRANSF., any triumph, victory: ut repulsam
suam triumphum suum duxerint, Cic.

triumvir -viri, m. (tres/vir), a triumvir; usually
plur. **triumvĭri** (also **tresvĭri**) -orum or
-um, a board or commission of three, esp. for
any of the following purposes.

(1) coloniae deducendae, or agro dando,
commissioners for the formation of a colonia
and the division of land amongst the colonists:
cum triumvir coloniam deduxisset, Cic.
(2) triumviri capitales, superintendents of
prisons, who also saw to executions: Pl., Cic.,
Liv. (3) triumviri epulones, superintendents
of sacrificial feasts. (4) triumviri monetales,
the masters of the mint: Cic. (5) for repairing
or rebuilding temples: Liv. (6) chief magistrates in the municipia: Cic.

triumvĭrālis -e (triumvir), of a triumvir:
flagella (of the triumviri capitales), Hor.; Tac.

triumvĭrātus -ūs, m. (triumvir), the office of a
triumvir: in triumviratu (sc. agrario), Cic.; Liv.

trĭvĕnēfĭca -ae, f. (tres/venefica), an arch-
poisoner or sorceress: Pl.

Trivĭa, see trivius.

trĭvĭālis -e (trivium), of the crossroads; hence,
ordinary, 'common or garden', trivial: carmen,
Juv.

trĭvĭum -i, n. (tres/via), a place where three
roads meet, crossroads: Cic., Verg. TRANSF.,
an open street, public place: Cic., Hor., etc.

trĭvĭus -a -um (trivium), of three ways, of
crossroads; esp. of deities worshipped at
crossroads: dea, Prop., or virgo, Lucr.,
Diana or Hecate. F. as subst. **Trivĭa** -ae,
Diana or Hecate: Verg., etc.

Trōăs -ădis, see Tros.

trŏchaeus -i, m. (τροχαῖος). (1) a trochee, a
metrical foot (— ᴗ): Cic. (2)=tribrachys; q.v.

trŏchăĭcus -a -um (τροχαϊκός), trochaic: Quint.

trochlĕa -ae, f. a set of blocks and pulleys for
raising weights: Lucr., Quint.

trŏchus -i, m. (τροχός), a child's hoop: Hor.,
Ov., etc.

Trōes, see Tros.

Troezēn -zēnis, acc. -zēna, f. (Τροιζήν), an old
town in Argolis, residence of Pittheus, grandfather of Theseus.

¶ Hence adj. **Troezēnĭus** -a -um,
Troezenian.

Trōĭa, **Troianus**, see Tros.

Trōĭădes, see Tros.

Trōĭcus, see Tros.

Trōīlus (-ŏs) -i, m. (Τρώιλος), son of Priam,
taken prisoner and killed before Troy.

Trōĭŭgĕna -ae, c. (Troia/gigno), born in Troy,
Trojan: gentes, Lucr. As subst. (1) a
Trojan: Cat., Verg. (2) a Roman (as des-
cended from Aeneas): Juv.

trŏpaeum -i, n. (τρόπαιον), a trophy, a monument
of victory, originally consisting of arms taken
from the enemy and hung on the trunk of a
tree.

LIT., tropaeum statuere, or ponere, Cic.;
Verg., etc. TRANSF., (1) a victory: Sala-
minium, Cic.; Hor., Ov. (2) a memorial:
necessitudinis atque hospitii, Cic.; Prop.

Trŏphōnĭus -i, m. (Τροφώνιος), a brother of
Agamedes, with whom he built the Delphic
oracle; after his death he gave prophetic
answers to those who slept in his cave (near
Lebadia, in Boeotia).

¶ Hence adj. **Trŏphōnĭānus** -a -um.

trŏpis -is, f. (τρόπις), the lees of wine: Mart.

Trōs Trōis, m. (Τρώς), a king of Phyrygia, after
whom Troy was named.

¶ Hence **Trōĭă** or **Trōĭă** -ae, f. (Τροία),
the town of Troy, besieged and finally captured
by the Greeks; the name was also given to
a town built by Aeneas in the Laurentine
country: Liv.; to a town built by Helenus in
Epirus: Ov.; and to a Roman game played on
horseback: Verg.

Adj. **Trōus**, **Trōĭus**, **Trōĭcus**, **Trōianus**
-a -um, Trojan: iudex, i.e. Paris, Hor.; prov.:
equus Troianus, a hidden danger, Cic.
Subst. **Trōs** Trōis, m. a Trojan; plur.
Trōĕs -um, m. the Trojans. F. adj. and subst.
Trōăs -ădos, Trojan, a Trojan woman: Verg.

trŭcīdātĭo -ōnis, f. (trucido), a slaughtering,
massacre: civium, Cic.; non pugna sed
trucidatio velut pecorum, Liv.

trŭcīdo -are, *to cut to pieces, slaughter, massacre.* LIT., cives Romanos, Cic., Liv., etc. TRANSF., *to demolish, destroy, extinguish*: seu pisces, seu porrum, seu cepe, Hor.; ignem, Lucr.; ne faenore trucidetur, Cic.; Liv.

trŭcŭlentia -ae, f. (truculentus), *roughness, ferocity*: Tac.

trŭcŭlentus -a -um (trux), *rough, ferocious, savage, cruel.* LIT., of persons, actions, etc.: Pl., Cic., etc.; voces, Tac.; fetā truculentior ursā, Ov. TRANSF., of the sea, *wild, rough*: Cat.

¶ Hence compar. adv. **trŭcŭlentĭus**, *more ferociously*: quod truculentius se ferebat quam ceteri, Cic.; superl.: Quint.

trŭdis -is, f. *a pointed staff, stake*: Verg.

trŭdo trūdĕre trūsi trūsum, *to push, press, thrust.* LIT., apros in plagas, Hor.; adverso monte saxum, Lucr.; of buds: gemmas, Verg. TRANSF., *to press, urge, force*: ad mortem trudi, Cic.; truditur dies die, *one day presses hard on another*, Hor.; Ter., Tac.

trulla -ae, f. (dim. of trua, *a ladle*), *a ladle*, esp. *for transferring wine from the bowl to the cup*: Cic., Hor., etc. TRANSF., (1) *a pan for carrying live coals*: Liv. (2) *a washing-basin*: Juv.

trullĕum -i, n. *a basin, washing-basin*: Varr.

trunco -are (truncus), *to shorten by cutting off, maim, mutilate*: simulacra, statuas, Liv.; Ov. Tac.

truncus -a -um, *lopped, maimed, mutilated, cut short.*

LIT., pinus, *stripped*, Verg.; corpus, Liv.; truncae inhonesto vulnere nares, Verg.; frons (Acheloi amnis), *deprived of its horns*, Ov.; tela, *broken off*, Verg.; with genit.: animalia trunca pedum, *without feet*, Verg.

TRANSF., urbs trunca, sine senatu, sine plebe, sine magistratibus, Liv.

¶ M. as subst. **truncus** -i. (1) *a lopped tree, the stem* or *trunk of a tree*: trunci induti hostilibus armis, Verg.; Cic., Caes., etc. TRANSF., *the stem, main part*: ipso trunco (aegritudinis) everso, Cic. (2) *the trunk of the human body*: Lucr., Cic., Verg. TRANSF., as a term of reproach, *blockhead*: Cic.

trŭtĭna -ae, f. (τρυτάνη), *a balance, pair of scales*: ad ea probanda, quae non aurificis staterā, sed quādam populari trutinā examinatur, Cic.; Hor., Juv.

trŭtĭnor -ari, dep. (trutina), *to weigh*: Pers.

trux trŭcis (connected with tor-vus), *rough, savage, fierce, grim.* (1) of persons, their looks, etc.: tribunus plebis, Cic.; vultus, Hor., etc.; orator, Liv.; sententia, Liv. (2) of things, in gen.: classicum, Hor.; eurus, Ov.; pelagus, Hor.

tryblĭum -i, n. (τρύβλιον), *a dish*: Pl.

trȳgōnus -i and **trȳgon** -ŏnis, m. (τρυγών), *a fish, the sting-ray*: Pl., Plin.

tū, pron. of the 2nd person (usual declension: acc. te, genit. tŭi, dat. tĭbĭ, abl. te; plur. nom. vos, acc. vos, genit. vestrum and vestri, dat. vobis, abl. vobis) (cf. σύ, τύ), *thou, you.*

In gen.: Pl., Cic., etc. Often strengthened by -te: tute, Cic.; by -met: vosmet, Liv.; by -temet: tutemet, Lucr. Sing. frequently in the ethic dat.: ecce tibi exortus est Isocrates, Cic. Plur. sometimes associated with a singular name: vos, Romanus exercitus, Liv.; vos, o Calliope, *ye Muses*, Verg.

tŭātim, adv. (tuus), *in your own way, after your own fashion*: Pl.

tŭba -ae, f. (connected with tubus), *the straight war-trumpet of the Romans, used for giving military signals.*

LIT., tubae sonus, Caes.; cornua ac tubae, Liv.; tubā signum dandum, Caes.; used also in religious festivities, games, funeral processions: Hor., Verg., Ov.

TRANSF., belli civilis tubam quam illi appellant, Cic.; Mart.

¹**tūber** -ĕris, n. (tumeo), *a swelling, protuberance, hump.* LIT., cameli, Plin.; Ter. TRANSF., (1) plur.: tubera=*great mistakes* (opp. verrucae=*little slips*), Hor. (2) *a truffle*: Mart., Juv.

²**tūber** -ĕris. (1) m. *a kind of apple-tree*: Plin. (2) f. *the fruit of this tree*: Mart., Suet.

tŭbĭcen -inis, m. (tuba/cano), *a trumpeter*: Liv., Ov.

tŭbĭlustrĭum -i, n. (tuba/lustrum), *a feast of trumpets held on March 23rd and May 23rd*: Varr.; plur.: Ov.

tŭburcĭnor -ari, dep. *to eat greedily, to gobble*: Pl.

tŭbus -i, m. *a pipe, tube*: Plin.

tuccētum (or **tūcētum**) -i, n. *a kind of sausage*: Pers.

tŭdĭto -are (freq. of tudo=tundo), *to hammer on, strike often*: Lucr.

tŭĕor (or **tŭor**) tŭēri tŭĭtus and tŭtus sum, dep. and **tŭĕo** -ēre, *to look at, behold, regard.* In gen.: naturam, Cic.; poet. with n. pl. of adj. used adverbially: acerba, *to look severe*, Lucr.; Verg. Esp. *to look at with care*, or *for the purpose of protection, to keep, to guard.* LIT., castra, Caes.; fines suos ab excursionibus, Cic.; se ac suos, Liv. TRANSF., of abstr. things: concordiam, Cic.; dignitatem suam, Cic.; armis prudentiae causas tueri et defendere, Cic.

¶ Perf. partic. pass. of tueo as adj. (with compar. and superl.) **tūtus** -a -um. LIT., *watched over*; hence *safe, secure, out of danger*: perfugium, Cic.; tutiorem vitam hominum reddere, Cic.; medio tutissimus ibis, Ov.; tutus ab hostibus, Caes.; ab insidiis, Ov.; ad omnes casus, Caes.; Liv. TRANSF., *watchful, cautious*: consilia, Liv.; Hor. N. as subst. **tūtum** -i, *a safe place, safety*: esse in tuto, Ter., Cic. L., Liv. N. abl. as adv. **tūtō**, *safely*: Pl., Lucr., Caes. Adv. **tūtē**, *safely*: Pl. Compar. adv. **tūtĭus**: Caes., Sall.

tŭgŭrĭum -i, n. (tego), *a peasant's hut, cottage*: tugurium ut iam videatur esse illa villa, Cic.; Verg.

tŭĭtĭo -ōnis, f. (tueor), *a protecting, preserving*: sui, Cic.

Tullĭŏla -ae, f. (dim. of Tullia), *the pet name of Tullia, Cicero's daughter.*

Tullĭus -a -um, *the name of a Roman gens*; esp. of Servius Tullius, *the sixth king of Rome*; of M. Tullius Cicero, *the Roman orator and statesman*; and of *his daughter* Tullia, and brother, Q. Tullius Cicero.

¶ Hence adj. **Tullĭānus** -a -um, *Tullian*; n. as subst. **Tullĭānum** -i, *the underground part of a Roman state prison, said to have been built by Servius Tullius.*

tum, adv. of time.
LIT., *then, at that time*; the time referred

to being indicated by a clause or understood
from the context: Pl., Cic., etc.; cum . . .
tum, Cic.; ubi . . . tum, Ter.; postquam . . .
tum, Sall. Often strengthened by the addition
of demum: Liv.; of denique: Cic.; of vero:
Cic., etc.

TRANSF., (1) of temporal succession, *next,
then, thereupon*: in ripa ambulantes, tum
autem residentes, Cic.; often introducing
the words of a subsequent speaker: tum
Scipio, Cic.; Pl., Verg., etc. (2) of numeral
or logical succession, *then, afterwards, in the
next place*: gigni autem terram, aquam,
ignem, tum ex his omnia, Cic.; primum . . .
tum, Caes.; primum . . . deinde . . . tum . . .
tum, Cic. (3) as a conjunction: **a**, tum . . .
tum, *first . . . then*, or *at one time . . . at
another time*: Pl., Cic., etc.: **b**, cum . . . tum,
both . . . and especially; *not only . . . but also*:
Cic., Caes.

tŭmĕfăcĭo -făcĕre -fēci -factum (tumeo/facio),
to cause to swell. LIT., humum, Ov.; tume-
factus pontus, *swollen*, Ov. TRANSF., *to puff
up with pride*: Prop., Mart.

tŭmĕo -ēre, *to swell, be swollen, be puffed up.*
LIT., corpus omne veneno, Ov.; vere
tument terrae, Verg.

TRANSF., (1) *to swell with anger* or *excitement*: sapientis animus nunquam tumet,
Cic.; irā, Liv. (2) *to swell with pride*: laudis
amore, Hor. (3) in gen., *to be in a ferment*:
tument negotia, Cic. L. (4) of style, *to be
pompous, tumid*: Tac., Quint., Mart.

tŭmesco tŭmescĕre tŭmŭi (tumeo), *to begin to
swell*. LIT., tumescit mare, Verg.; Cic., Ov.
TRANSF., *to swell with anger* or *excitement*: ora
tumescunt, Ov.; tumescunt bella, Verg.

tŭmĭdus -a -um, adj. (with compar.: Liv.;
and superl.: Sen.) (tumeo), *swollen, puffed up,
tumid.*
LIT., membrum, Cic.; mare, Verg.
TRANSF., (1) *swollen with anger* or *excitement*: tumida ex ira tum corda residunt,
Verg. (2) *puffed up with pride*: tumidus
successu, Ov. (3) in style, *pompous, tumid,
bombastic*: sermones, Hor.; sermo tumidior,
Liv.
¶ Hence adv. **tŭmĭdē**, *pompously, bombastically*: Sen.

tŭmor -ōris, m. (tumeo), *a swelling, protuberance*. LIT., oculorum, Cic.; loci, Ov.
TRANSF., (1) *excitement of the mind*, esp. in
anger: animi, Cic.; tumor et ira deum, Verg.
(2) *pride*: intempestivos compesce tumores,
Ov.; Quint. (3) in gen., *ferment, commotion*:
rerum, Cic. L. (4) of style, *turgidity,
bombast*: Quint.

tŭmŭlo -are (tumulus), *to cover with a mound,
to bury*: Ov.

tŭmŭlōsus -a -um (tumulus), *full of mounds,
hilly*: Sall.

tŭmultŭārĭus -a -um (tumultus). LIT., of
troops, *hastily brought together, suddenly
levied*: miles, Liv. TRANSF., *done in a hurry
or on the spur of the moment, sudden, hasty,
improvised*: pugna (opp. iusta), Liv.; opus,
Quint.; dux, *chosen on the spur of the moment*,
Liv.; castra, Liv.

tŭmultŭātĭo -ōnis, f. (tumultuor), *a confusion,
bustle, tumult*: Liv.

tŭmultŭor -ari, dep. and **tŭmultŭo** -are
(tumultus), *to be confused, be in an uproar*:

Pl., Cic.; impers. pass.: in castris Romanorum praeter consuetudinem tumultuari
Caes.; Liv.

tŭmultŭōsus -a -um, adj. (with compar. and
superl.) (tumultus), *alarmed, disturbed,
confused*; also in more active sense, *disquieting, turbulent*: contio, Cic.; vita, Cic.;
mare, Hor.; quod tumultuosissimum pugnae
erat parumper sustinuit, Liv.; nuntius, Liv.;
in otio tumultuosi, *restless*, Liv.
¶ Hence adv. (with compar. and superl.)
tŭmultŭōsē, *confusedly, tumultuously*: tumultuose excepta est (res) clamoribus, Liv.;
ut hominem quam tumultuosissime adorian-
tur, Cic.

tŭmultus -ūs, m. (tumeo), *confusion, uproar,
bustle, tumult.*
LIT., (1) in gen.: tantum tumultum
inicere civitati, Cic.; tumultum praebere,
Liv.; sedare, Liv. (2) *the sudden breaking
out of war*, esp. *of civil war*; *insurrection,
rebellion*: Italicus, Cic.; servilis, Caes.;
Gallicus, Cic., Liv. (3) in the air, *storm*:
Iuppiter ruens tumultu, Hor.; Luc.
TRANSF., *mental disturbance, commotion,
excitement*: mentis, Hor.

tŭmŭlus -i, m. (tumeo), *a mound of earth,
hillock, hill*. In gen.: tumuli silvestres, Cic.;
Verg., Liv. Esp. *a sepulchral mound*: tumulus
Achillis, Cic.; inanis, *a cenotaph*, Cic.; Verg.,
Tac.

tunc, adv., of time (tum/-ce) used like tum; q.v.
LIT., *then, at that time*: Caes., Cic., etc.
Sometimes strengthened (like tum) by
demum, etc.: Sall., Liv., Ov.
TRANSF., (1) of temporal succession, *next,
then*: Cic., Liv. (2) of numeral or logical
succession, *in the next place*: Suet.

tundo tundĕre tŭtŭdi tunsum and tūsum, *to
beat, thump, strike repeatedly.*
LIT., in gen.: converso bacillo alicui oculos
vehementissime, Cic.; pectora manu, Ov.;
tunsae pectora palmis, Verg.; prov.: tundere
eandem incudem, *to harp on the same string*,
Cic. Esp. *to pound grain*, etc.: Verg., Plin.
TRANSF., *to deafen, importune*: aures, Pl.;
adsiduis hinc atque illinc vocibus heros
tunditur, Verg.; Pl.

tŭnĭca -ae, f. *a sleeved garment worn at Rome
by both men and women, a tunic*: Cic., Hor.,
etc. TRANSF., *a jacket, coating, covering*:
gemmae tenues rumpunt tunicas, Verg.;
Lucr., Cat.

tŭnĭcātus -a -um (tunica), *clothed in a tunic*:
Cic.; esp. of the poorer classes, who wore
only a tunic (without a toga over it): tunicatus
populus, Tac.; popellus, Hor.

tŭnĭcŭla -ae, f. (dim. of tunica), *a little tunic*:
Pl., Varr. TRANSF., *a little coating, a membrane*: oculorum, Plin.

tŭor = tueor; q.v.

turba -ae, f. (cf. τύρβη), *tumult, uproar, disturbance, commotion*, esp. *one caused by a crowd
of people.*
LIT., uxori turbas conciet, Pl.; quanta in
turba viveremus, Cic.; maximas in castris
effecisse turbas dicitur, Cic.
TRANSF., *a mob, swarm, throng, crowd.*
(1) of people: Cic., Liv., etc.; esp. contemptuously, *the mob*: admiratio vulgi atque
turbae, Cic. (2) of animals and things:
materiai, Lucr.; rerum, Ov.; pecorum, Liv.

turbāmentum -i, n. (turbo), *a means of disturbance*: Sall., Tac.
turbātĭo -ōnis, f. (¹turbo), *disturbance, disorder, confusion*: Liv.
turbātor -ōris, m. (¹turbo), *a disturber, troubler*: plebis, Liv.; Tac.
turbātus -a -um, partic. from turbo; q.v.
turbellae -ārum, f. (dim. of turba), *tumult, bustle, disorder*: Pl.
turbĕn -inis, n. = ²turbo; q.v.
turbĭdus -a -um, adj. (with compar. and superl.) (turba), *confused, disordered, unquiet, wild.*
  LIT., of physical objects: tempestas, Pl., Lucr., Caes.; aequora, Lucr.; aqua, Cic.; coma, Ov.; gurges caeno, Verg.
  TRANSF., (1) of persons, etc., *mentally disturbed, disordered* or *disorderly*: Aruns, Verg.; pectora turbidiora mari, Ov.; turbidum laetari, *with confused fear*, Hor.; sic turbidus infit, Verg.; milites, Tac. (2) of things, *unquiet, agitated*: res, Cic. N. as subst., *a troubled time, disquiet*: in turbido, Liv., Tac.
  ¶ Hence adv. **turbĭdē**, *confusedly, in disorder*: Cic., Tac.
turbĭnĕus -a -um (²turbo), *shaped like a top*: Ov.
¹turbo -are (turba), *to disturb, throw into disorder* or *confusion.*
  LIT., mare, aequora, Cic.; aciem, ordines, Liv.; turbatus capillos, *with disordered hair*, Ov. Sometimes without object, *to cause disorder*: ferae ita ruunt atque turbant ut, Cic.; (equites) modice primo impetu turbavere, Liv.; of water, *to trouble, make turbid*: pedibus manibusque lacus, Ov.
  TRANSF., *to upset, to disturb*: contiones, Liv.; delectum atque ordinem, Cic.; ne quid ille turbet, vide, Liv.; mentem dolore, Verg. Esp. *to cause a political disturbance, to unsettle*: Macer in Africa haud dubie turbans, Tac. Impers. pass.: si in Hispania turbatum esset, Cic.
  ¶ Hence partic. as adj. **turbātus** -a -um, *disturbed, perturbed, disordered.* LIT., mare, Liv. TRANSF., (1) *disquieted, restless, troubled*: voluntates populi, Cic. (2) *angered, exasperated*: Pallas, Verg.
  ¶ Adv. **turbātē**, *confusedly*: aguntur omnia raptim atque turbate, Caes.
²turbo -inis, m. (connected with turba), *a movement in a circle, an eddy, a whirling round.*
  LIT., of wind, smoke, missiles, etc.: caeli, Lucr.; quo turbine torqueat hastam, Verg.; Cic., etc.
  TRANSF., (1) fig., *a storm, commotion*: in turbinibus reipublicae, Cic.; mentis turbine agar, Ov.; tu procella patriae, turbo ac tempestas pacis atque otii, Cic. (2) *a child's top*: Verg., Tib. (3) *a reel*: Hor. (4) *a spindle*: Cat.
turbŭlentus -a -um, adj. (with compar. and superl.) (turba). (1) pass., *disturbed, confused, restless, stormy, boisterous.* LIT., tempestas, Cic.; concursio, Cic.; Pl. TRANSF., respublica, Cic. L.; animus, Cic. (2) act., *turbulent, causing disturbance*: civis, Cic.; consilia, Cic.; Caes., Tac.
  ¶ Hence adv. (with compar. and superl.) **turbŭlentē** and **turbŭlentĕr**, *in confusion, tumultuously*: nos nihil turbulenter, nihil

temere faciamus, Cic.; egit de Caepione turbulentius, Cic.
turda, see turdus.
Turdetāni -ōrum, m. pl. *a people in Hispania Baetica, near modern Seville.*
  ¶ Hence subst. **Turdetānĭa** -ae, f. *the country of the Turdetani.*
Turdŭli -ōrum, m. pl. *a people in Hispania Baetica.*
  ¶ Hence **Turdŭlus** -a -um, *Turdulian.*
turdus -i, m. and **turda** -ae, f. (1) *a thrush*: Hor., etc. (2) *a kind of fish*: Plin.
tūrĕus -a -um (tus), *of incense*: dona, Verg.
turgĕo turgēre tursi, *to swell up, be swollen.*
  LIT., frumenta turgent, Verg.; Ov., etc.
  TRANSF., of style, *to be pompous, turgid*: professus grandia turget, Hor.
turgesco -ĕre (turgeo), *to begin to swell, swell up.* LIT., semen turgescit in agris, Ov.
  TRANSF., (1) *to swell, be excited with passion*: sapientis animus nunquam turgescit, Cic. (2) of style, *to be pompous*: Quint.
turgĭdŭlus -a -um (dim. of turgidus), *swollen*: flendo turgiduli ocelli, Cat.
turgĭdus -a -um (turgeo), *swollen.* LIT., membrum, Cic.; Hor., etc. TRANSF., of style, *turgid, bombastic*: Hor.
tūrĭbŭlum -i, n. (tus), *a censer for burning incense*: Cic.
tūricrĕmus -a -um (tus/cremo), *burning incense*: arae, Lucr., Verg.
tūrĭfĕr -fĕra -fĕrum (tus/fero), *producing incense*: Indus, Ov.
tūrĭlĕgus -a -um (tus/lego), *collecting incense*: Ov.
turma -ae, f. (connected with turba). LIT., *a troop of cavalry containing thirty men, the tenth part of an* ala; *a squadron*: Caes., Cic. L., Hor. TRANSF., *any troop, throng*: equestrium (sc. statuarum), Cic.; Gallica (of the priests of Isis), Ov.
turmālis -e (turma), *of a troop* or *squadron.* LIT., m. pl. as subst., *the men of a squadron*: Liv. TRANSF., *of the equestrian order*: Stat.
turmātim, adv. (turma), *troop by troop, in troops*: Caes., Lucr., Liv.
Turnus -i, m. *a king of the Rutuli, killed by Aeneas.*
turpĭcŭlus -a -um (dim. of turpis), *somewhat ugly or deformed.* LIT., nasus, Cat. TRANSF., res turpiculae et quasi deformes, Cic.
turpĭfĭcātus -a -um (turpis/facio), *made foul, corrupted*: animus, Cic.
turpĭlucrĭcŭpĭdus -a -um (turpis/lucrum/cupidus) = αἰσχροκερδής, *greedy for foul gain*: Pl.
turpis -e, adj. (with compar. and superl.), *ugly, foul, unsightly, deformed.*
  LIT., physically: aspectus, Cic.; turpia membra fimo, Verg.; pes, Hor.
  TRANSF., morally *foul, disgraceful, shameful, base*: fuga, Cic.; quid turpius? Cic.; homo turpissimus, Cic.; turpe factu, Cic.; habere quaestui rempublicam turpe est, Cic.; Caes., Hor., etc. N. as subst. **turpĕ**, *a disgrace*: Cic., Ov.
  ¶ Hence adv. (with compar. and superl.) **turpĭtĕr**, *foully, in an ugly, unsightly manner.* LIT., claudicare, Ov.; desinere in piscem, Hor. TRANSF., *basely, dishonourably*: facere, Cic.; fugere, Caes.; turpius eicitur, quam non admittitur hospes, Ov.

turpĭtūdo -ĭnis, f. (turpis), *ugliness, un-
sightliness.* LIT., physical: Cic. TRANSF.,
moral *baseness, disgrace, infamy*: maximam
turpitudinem suscipere vitae cupiditate, Cic.;
Caes., Sall.; plur.: flagitiorum ac turpitudi-
num societas, Cic.

turpo -are (turpis), *to make ugly, befoul, defile.*
LIT., capillos sanguine, Verg.; Hor., Tac.
TRANSF., *to disgrace, dishonour*: ornamenta,
Cic.; castra urbanae seditionis contagione,
Liv.

turrĭgĕr -gĕra -gĕrum (turris/gero), *tower-
bearing*: urbes, Verg.; hence as epithet of
Cybele, who was represented with a crown
of towers: Cybele, Ov.; dea, *Cybele,* Ov.

turris -is, f. (τύρρις, τύρσις), *a tower.* In gen.:
Cic., Hor., etc. Esp. (**1**) *a tower with which
walls and camps were strengthened*: turris
latericia, Caes.; Cic., Verg. (**2**) *a tower of
wood for attacking towns*: Caes., Liv. (**3**) *a
tower full of armed soldiers* borne by
elephants, *a howdah*: Liv. (**4**) *a dove-cote*: Ov.

turrītus -a -um (turris), *turreted, furnished with
towers.* LIT., puppes, Verg.; moenia, Ov.;
turrita, as an epithet of Cybele, Ov. TRANSF.,
towering: scopuli, Verg.

turtur -ŭris, m. *a turtle-dove*: Pl., Verg., etc.

turtŭrilla -ae, f. (dim. of turtur), *a little
turtle-dove*: Sen.

tūs (thūs) tūris, n. (cf. θύος), *incense, frankincense*: tus incendere, Cic.; Verg., etc.

Tusci -orum, m. *the Tuscans, Etruscans, inhabitants of Etruria.*
    ¶ Hence adj. **Tuscus** -a -um, *Etruscan*:
amnis, *the Tiber*, Verg.; eques, *Maecenas*,
Verg.; vicus, *a street in Rome*, Liv.

¹tusculum -i, n. (dim. of tus), *a little incense*:
Pl.

²Tuscŭlum -i, n. *an old town in Latium*, near
Frascati.
    ¶ Hence adj. **Tuscŭlus** -a -um, *Tusculan*;
also **Tuscŭlānus** -a -um, *Tusculan*; m. pl.
as subst. **Tuscŭlāni** -ōrum, *the inhabitants
of Tusculum.*

tussĭo -ire (tussis), *to have a cough, to cough*:
male, Hor.; Pl.

tussis -is, acc. -im, f. *a cough*: Ter., Verg., etc.

tūtāmen -ĭnis, n. (tutor), *a defence, protection*:
Verg.

tūtāmentum -i, n. (tutor), *defence, protection*:
Liv.

tūtē, adv. from tutus; q.v.

tūtēla -ae, f. (tueor), *protection, guard, charge.*
    LIT., in gen.: tutelam ianuae gerere, Pl.;
cuius in tutela Athenas esse voluerunt, Cic.;
Liv. Esp. *of wards, etc., guardianship,
tutelage*: in alicuius tutelam venire, Cic.;
Hor.
    TRANSF., in concr. sensea. (**1**) act.,
protector, guardian: templi, Ov.; Hor. (**2**)
pass., *the person* or *thing protected*: virginum
primae puerique claris patribus orti, Deliae
tutela deae, Hor.; Prop., Ov.

tūtō, n. abl. of tutus; q.v.

¹tūtor -ōris, m. (tueor), *a watcher, a protector.*
In gen.: finium, Hor.; religionum, Cic.
Esp. *the guardian of a woman, a minor,* or
imbecile: aliquem tutorem instituere, Cic.;
Pl., Liv.; fig.: eloquentiae quasi tutores, Cic.

²tūtor -ari, dep.; also (esp. in pass.) **tūto** -are
(freq. of tueor), *to protect, preserve, watch,
keep.* LIT., domum, Pl.; oculos ab inferiore

parte, Cic.; urbem muris, Liv.; se adversus
iniusta arma, Liv. TRANSF., *to guard against*:
pericula, Sall.; inopiam, Caes.

tūtus -a -um, partic. from tueo; q.v.

tŭus -a -um, possess. pron. of the 2nd pers.
sing. (tu), *thy, thine, your.* (**1**) subjective: tua
bona, Cic.; m. pl. as subst.: tui, *your friends,
people, party*, Cic.; tuum est, *it is your duty,
it is for you to*, with infin., Pl., Ter. Sometimes *right, favourable for you*: tempore tuo
pugnasti, Liv.; Mart. (**2**) objective, *of, for,
towards you*: desiderio tuo, Ter.

tuxtax, *whack whack*, onomatop. imitation of
the sound of blows: Pl.

Tўăna -ōrum, n. pl. (Τύανα), *a town in Cappadocia, at the foot of Mount Taurus.*
    ¶ Hence adj. **Tўănēĭus** -a -um, *of Tyana.*

Tўdeūs -ĕi and -ĕos, m. (Τυδεύς), *son of
Oeneus, father of Diomedes.*
    ¶ Hence subst. **Tўdīdēs** -ae, m. (Τυδείδης),
the son of Tydeus, i.e. *Diomedes.*

tympănizo -are (τυμπανίζω), *to play the tambourine* or *kettle-drum*: Suet.

tympănotrība -ae, m. (τυμπανοτρίβης), *a
tambourine-player*: Pl.

tympănum (tўpănum) -i, n. (τύμπανον), *a
tambourine, kettle-drum* (esp. used by the
priests of Cybele). LIT., Verg., etc. TRANSF.,
a drum or *wheel for raising weights*: Lucr.,
Verg.

Tyndăreūs -ĕi and **Tyndărus** -i, m. (Τυνδα-
ρεός), *king of Sparta, husband of Leda; father
of Castor and Pollux, Helen and Clytemnestra.*
    ¶ Hence adj. **Tyndărĭus** -a -um; subst.
Tyndărĭdēs -ae, m. *a male descendant of
Tyndareus*: Tyndaridae, *Castor and Pollux,*
Cic.; **Tyndărĭs** -ĭdis, f. *a female descendant
of Tyndareus; Helen*: Verg., Ov.; *Clytemnestra*: Ov.

Tўphōeūs -ĕi and -ĕos, m. (Τυφωεύς), *a giant
who tried to force Jupiter from heaven, and
was buried beneath Etna.*
    ¶ Hence adj. **Tўphōĭus** -a -um and f. adj.
Tўphōĭs -ĭdis, *of Typhoeus*: Aetna, Ov.

Tўphōn -ōnis, m. (Τυφών), *another name for the
giant Typhoeus.*

tўpus -i, m. (τύπος), *a figure on a wall*: Cic. L.

tўrannĭcīda -ae, m. (tyrannus/caedo), *the
slayer of a tyrant, a tyrannicide*: Tac., etc.

tўrannĭcīdĭum -i, n. (tyrannus/caedo), *the
slaying of a tyrant*: Sen., Quint.

tўrannĭcus -a -um (τυραννικός), *tyrannical*:
leges, Cic.
    ¶ Adv. **tўrannĭcē**, *tyrannically, des-
potically*: ea quae regie seu potius tyrannice
statuit in aratores, Cic.

Tўrannĭo -ōnis, m. *a Greek grammarian and
geographer, contemporary of Cicero.*

tўrannis -ĭdis, f. (τυραννίς), *the supremacy of a
tyrant; despotism, tyranny*: vivit tyrannis,
tyrannus occidit, Cic.; tyrannidem delere,
Cic.; Ov., Juv., etc.

tўrannoctŏnus -i, m. (τυραννοκτόνος), *the slayer
of a tyrant*: Cic. L.

tўrannus -i, m. (τύραννος), *an absolute ruler,
prince, lord*: of Aeneas: Verg.; Phrygius,
Laomedon, Ov.; of Neptune, as ruler of the
sea: Ov. Esp., of one who usurps supreme
power and overthrows the constitution of his
state; *a usurper, despot, tyrant*: Cic., Liv.

Tўrās -ae, m. *a river in Sarmatia* (now the
Dniester).

tўrĭanthīna -ōrum, n. pl. (τυριάνθινος), *violet-coloured garments*: Mart.

Tўrĭus, *see* Tyrus.

tўrŏtărĭchos -i, m. (τυροτάριχος), *a dish of cheese and salt-fish*: Cic. L.

Tyrrhēni -ōrum, m. pl. *a Pelasgian people who migrated to Italy; from them sprang the Etruscans.*

¶ Hence subst. **Tyrrhēnĭa** -ae, f. *their country, Etruria*; adj. **Tyrrhēnus** -a -um, *Etruscan.*

Tyrrhēus -ĕi, m. *the shepherd of King Latinus.*

¶ Hence subst. **Tyrrhĭdae** -ārum, m. pl. *the sons of Tyrrheus, the herdsmen of King Latinus.*

Tўrus (-ŏs) -i, f. (Τύρος), *Tyre, a city of Phoenicia, famous for its purple.*

¶ Hence adj. **Tўrĭus** -a -um. (1) *Tyrian*: Ov., etc.; meton.=*purple*: vestes, Hor.; colores, Ov. (2) *of Thebes* (founded by the Phoenician Cadmus): Stat. (3) *of Carthage* (a Tyrian colony): urbs, *Carthage*, Verg. M. pl. as subst. **Tўrĭi** -ōrum, *the Tyrians or the Carthaginians.*

U

U, u, originally written V, v, the 20th letter of the Latin Alphabet, connected etymologically with the Greek upsilon (*Y, v*).

¹**ūber** -ĕris, n. (cf. οὖθαρ), *an udder, pap, teat, breast.* LIT., ubera praebere, Ov.; admovere, Verg.; Lucr., Tac., etc. TRANSF., *richness, abundance, fertility*: fertilis ubere campus, Verg.

²**ūber** -ĕris, adj. (with compar. and superl.) (connected with ¹uber), *rich, fertile, fruitful, abundant, copious.*

LIT., seges spicis uberibus, Cic.; uberior solito (of a river), *fuller than usual*, Ov.; arbor niveis uberrima pomis, Ov.; Hor., etc.

TRANSF., abstr., *rich, full of matter*: uberiores litterae, Cic.; quis uberior in dicendo Platone? Cic.; uberrima supplicationibus triumphisque provincia, Cic.; uberrimae artes, Cic.; Ov., Tac.

¶ Hence adv., in compar. **ūbĕrĭus** and superl. **ūberrĭmē**, *more and most abundantly, copiously.* LIT., provenit seges, Ov.; Cic. TRANSF., disputare, Cic.

ūbertas -ātis, f. (²uber), *fruitfulness, copiousness, abundance.* LIT., agrorum, frugum, Cic. TRANSF., in dicendo, Cic.; plur.: ubertates virtutis et copiae, Cic.

ūbertim, adv. (²uber), *abundantly, copiously*: fundere lacrimas, Cat.; Suet.

ūbī, *where.*

(1) interrog., in direct and indirect questions, *where?*: Pl., Cic., etc. Strengthened by nam: ubinam? Pl., Cic. With partitive genit.: terrarum, loci, etc.; quid ageres, ubi terrarum esses, Cic. L.; Pl., Liv.

(2) relat. LIT., *where*: omnes, qui tum eos agros, ubi hodie est haec urbs, incolebant, Cic.; ubi tyrannus est, ibi, etc., Cic.; ibi . . . ubi, Caes. TRANSF., *when, ubi ubi, wherever*: facile ubi ubi essent se conversuros aciem, Liv.; Pl., Ter. TRANSF., **a**, of time, *when, as soon as*: quem ubi vidi, equidem vim lacrimarum profudi, Cic.; ubi de eius

adventu Helvetii certiores facti sunt, legatos ad eum mittunt, Caes.; with primum: at hostes, ubi primum nostros equites conspexerunt, Caes.; Pl., Verg., etc.: **b**, of other relations, including personal relations, *wherein, whereby, with whom*, etc.: est, ubi id isto modo valeat, Cic.; Pl., Ter., etc.

ŭbĭcumquĕ (ŭbĭcunquĕ), adv. (1) relat., *wherever, wheresoever*: ubicumque erimus, Cic.; with partitive genit.: ubicumque gentium, terrarum, Cic. (2) indef., *everywhere*: malum est ubicumque, Hor.; Ov.

Ubĭi -ōrum, m. *a Germanic people living originally on the east bank of the Rhine, near Cologne.* Adj. **Ubĭus** -a -um, *Ubian.*

ŭbĭlĭbĕt, adv. *anywhere you please*: Sen.

ŭbīnam, strengthened form of ubi, interrog.; q.v.

ŭbīquĕ, adv. *everywhere*: omnes qui ubique sunt, *all in the world*, Cic.; Pl., Verg., etc.

ŭbīvis, *wherever you will, anywhere, everywhere*: Ter., Cic.

Ūcălĕgōn -ōnis, m. *name of a Trojan*: iam proximus ardet Ucalegon, Verg.

ūdus -a -um (contr. from uvidus), *wet, moist*: paludes, Ov.; oculi, *tearful*, Ov.; aleator, *drunken*, Mart.

Ūfens -tis, m. *a small river in Latium.*

¶ Hence adj. **Ūfentīnus** -a -um, *Ufentine.*

ulcĕro -are (ulcus), *to make sore, to ulcerate.* LIT., mantica cui lumbos onere ulceret, Hor.; nondum ulcerato Philoctetā morsu serpentis, Cic. TRANSF., iecur, *to wound the heart*, Hor.

ulcĕrōsus -a -um (ulcus), *full of sores, ulcerous.* LIT., facies, Tac. TRANSF., iecur, *wounded by love*, Hor.

ulciscor ulcisci ultus sum, dep. *to take vengeance.*

(1) *to take vengeance for, to avenge*: patrem, Cic.; se, Cic.; Ov. Sometimes in pass. sense: quidquid sine sanguine civium ulcisci nequitur, Sall.

(2) *to take vengeance on, to punish*: **a**, with acc. of person: aliquem, Pl., Cic., etc.: **b**, with acc. of thing: scelus, Cic.; iniurias, Caes., Cic., etc.

ulcus -ĕris, n. (cf. ἕλκος), *a sore, ulcer.* LIT., Lucr., Verg. TRANSF., ulcus (of love) enim vivescit et inveterascit alendo, Lucr.; quidquid horum attigeris, ulcus est, Cic.

ūlīgo -inis, f. (for uviligo, from uveo), *moisture, wetness of the earth*: uligines paludum, Tac.; Verg.

Ūlixēs -is or ei, m. Latin name for 'Οδυσσεύς; *Ulysses or Odysseus, son of Laertes, husband of Penelope, father of Telemachus; a king of Ithaca, famed for his cunning and for his wanderings after the siege of Troy.*

ullus -a -um; genit. usually ullīus, dat. ulli (contr. of unulus, from unus), *any*, used mainly in negative and hypothetical sentences.

(1) as adj.: sine ulla dubitatione, Cic.; neque ullam in partem disputo, *for or against*, Cic.; si ulla mea commendatio valuit, Cic. L.; Verg., etc.

(2) as subst., *anyone, anything*: nemo ullius nisi fugae memor, Liv.; Caes., Cic., etc.

ulmĕus -a -um (ulmus), *of elm, made of elm-wood*: Pl., Juv.

ulmitrība -ae, m. (ulmus/τρίβω, tero), *an*

elm-rubber; hence, *one often beaten with elm-rods*: Pl.

ulmus -i, f. *the elm*: Verg., Hor., etc.

ulna -ae, f. (cf. ὠλένη), *the elbow*. LIT., Plin. TRANSF., (1) *the arm*: ulnis aliquem tollere, Ov. (2) as a measure of length: **a**, *an ell*: Verg., Hor., Ov.: **b**, *as much as a man can span with both arms*, *a fathom*: Plin.

ulpĭcum -i, n. *a kind of leek*: Pl., Cato.

*****ultĕr** -tra -trum, compar. **ultĕrĭor**; superl. **ultĭmus**. Positive not found except in the adverbial forms ultra, ultro; q.v.

Compar. **ultĕrĭor** -ius, genit. -ōris, *on the other side, farther, beyond*. LIT., in space: Gallia, *Gaul on the north side of the Alps*, Cic.; equitatus, *placed farther off*, Caes.; tendebantque manus ripae ulterioris amore, Verg. TRANSF., in gen., *distant, more advanced, more remote*: ulteriora mirari, Tac.; ulteriora pudet docuisse, Ov.; quo quid ulterius privato timendum foret? Liv. N. acc. sing. used like adv.: Ov.

Superl. **ultĭmus** -a -um, *most distant, farthest, extreme, last*. LIT., in space: luna, quae ultima a caelo est, Cic., Liv., etc.; as subst.: recessum primi ultimis non dabant, Caes.; caelum, quod extremum atque ultimum mundi est, Cic.; ultima signant, *the goal*, Verg. Also with subst. to indicate *the farthest extremity* of a place: in ultimam provinciam, Cic. TRANSF., (1) in time or succession, *the most distant*; hence *original* or *last, final*: antiquitas, Cic.; principium, Cic.; dies, Ov.; lapis, *a gravestone*, Prop. Adv.: ad ultimum, *to the last*, Liv.; ultimum, *for the last time*, Liv. (2) in rank or degree: **a**, *highest, greatest*: natura, Cic.; supplicium, *capital punishment*, Caes.; n. as subst.: ultima audere, Liv.; ultimum bonorum, *the highest good*, Cic.; sceleratum, sed non, ad ultimum demens, Liv.: **b**, *meanest, lowest*: laus, Hor.; as subst.: cum ultimis militum, Liv.

ultĭo -ōnis, f. (ulciscor), *an avenging, punishing, revenge*: ultionem petere, Liv.; Tac.; with objective genit.: violatae per vim pudicitiae, Liv.

ultor -ōris, m. (ulciscor), *an avenger, punisher*: iniuriarum, Cic.; often in apposition to noun: tanti sanguinis ultor anulus, Juv.; as a surname of Mars: Ov., Tac.

ultrā, adv. and prep. (from *ulter; q.v.)

Adv., *beyond, on the far side, farther*. LIT., in space: Verg., etc. TRANSF., (1) in time: nec ultra bellum Latinum dilatum, Liv. (2) *beyond a certain limit, beyond, farther*: ultra neque curae neque gaudio locum esse, Sall.; estne aliquid ultra, quo progredi crudelitas possit? Cic.; foll. by quam: ultra quam satis est, Cic.; Liv., etc.

Prep. with acc., *beyond, on the far side of*. LIT., in space: ultra Silianum villam, Cic.; Caes., etc. TRANSF., (1) in time, *beyond*: ultra biennium, Tac.; Liv., Quint. (2) of number or measure, *beyond, more than*: modum, quem ultra progredi non oportet, Cic.; ultra vires, Verg.; Hor., etc.

ultrix -īcis, f. (ultor), *avenging*: Dirae, *the Furies*, Verg.

ultrŏ, adv. (from *ulter; q.v.), *to the far side, beyond*.

LIT., in space: Pl. Usually with citro, *up and down, on both sides*: ultro et citro cursare, Cic.

TRANSF., (1) *besides, moreover, and what is more*: ultroque iis sumptum intulit, Cic. (2) *of one's own accord, spontaneously, voluntarily, gratuitously*: ultro se offerre, Cic.; improbos ultro lacessere, Cic. Hence phrase: ultro tributa, *money spent by the state on public works*, Liv.

Ŭlubrae -ārum, *a place in Latium, near the Pontine Marshes*.

¶ Hence adj. **Ŭlubrānus** -a -um, *Ulubran*.

ŭlŭla -ae, f. (ululo), *an owl*: Verg.

ŭlŭlātus -ūs, m. (ululo), *a howling, wailing, shrieking, yelling*: ululatus nocturni, Liv.; of war-cries: Caes.; of mourning: Verg., Ov.

ŭlŭlo -are (connected with ὀλολύζω), *to howl, yell*. LIT., Tisiphone ululavit, Ov.; ululanti voce canere, Cic. Sometimes transit., *to howl to*; hence pass.: nocturnis Hecate triviis ululata per urbem, Verg. TRANSF., of places, *to resound with howling*: cavae plangoribus aedes femineis ululant, Verg.

ulva -ae, f. *sedge*: Verg.

umbella -ae, f. (dim. of umbra), *a parasol*: Juv.

umbĭlicus -i, m. (cf. ὀμφαλός), *the navel*.

LIT., Liv., Ov.

TRANSF., (1) *the middle, centre*: Siciliae, Cic.; terrarum, *Delphi*, Liv.; esp. *the end of the roller of a scroll*: Cat.; fig.: inceptos iambos ad umbilicum adducere, *bring to an end*, Hor. (2) *a kind of sea-snail*: Cic.

umbo -ōnis, m. (cf. ὀμφαλός), *a boss, a round projection*. (1) *the boss or centre of a shield*: summus clipei umbo, Verg.; hence, meton., *a shield*: salignae umbonum crates, Verg.; Liv., Juv. (2) *the elbow*: Mart. (3) *the full part or swelling of a garment*; meton., *a toga*: Pers.

umbra -ae, f. *a shade, shadow*.

LIT., arboris, Cic.; Verg., etc.; prov.: umbras timere, *to be frightened at shadows*, Cic.

TRANSF., (1) *a shady place*: tonsoris, *a barber's*, Hor. (2) *shade* in a painting: Cic. (3) *protection, shadow*: auxilii, Liv.; sub umbra Romanae amicitiae latēre, Cic. (4) *idleness, pleasant rest*: Veneris cessamus in umbra, Ov.; cedat umbra sōli, Cic. (5) *a phantom, ghost, shade*: Lucr., Verg., etc.; soli, Cic.; *appearance* (as opposed to reality), *shadow, semblance*: gloriae, Cic. (6) *an uninvited guest, brought by one who has been invited* (σκιά): Pl., Hor. (7) *a fish*, perhaps *the grayling*: Ov. (8) *a shadow, poor imitation*: civitatis, Cic.; foederis, Liv.

umbrāculum -i, n. (umbra). (1) *a shady place, arbour*: Verg.; hence *a quiet place* (as opp. to public life): doctrinam ex umbraculis eruditorum (*schools*) otioque in solem produxerat, Cic. (2) *a parasol*: Ov.

umbrātĭcŏla -ae, m. (umbra/colo), *a lounger in the shade*: Pl.

umbrātĭcus -a -um (umbra), *fond of the shade*: homo, *an idler*, Pl.

umbrātĭlis -e (umbra), *remaining in the shade*; *retired, contemplative*: vita, Cic.; oratio, Cic.

Umbri -ōrum, m. pl. *a people of central Italy*.

¶ Hence adj. **Umber** -bra -brum,

Umbrian; subst. **Umbrĭa** -ae, f. *Umbria, the country of the Umbri.*

umbrĭfĕr -fĕra -fĕrum (umbra/fero), *shady*: nemus, Verg.

umbro -are (umbra), *to cover, shade, overshadow*: umbrata tempora quercu, Verg.

umbrōsus -a -um (umbra), *shady*: ripa, Cic.; compar.: locus umbrosior, Cic.; cacumina, Verg.; salix, Ov.

ūmecto (**hūmecto**) -are (umectus), *to wet, moisten, water*: qua niger umectat flaventia culta Galesus, Verg.; vultum largo flumine, Verg.; Lucr.

ūmectus (**hūmectus**) -a -um (umeo), *moist*: Lucr.

ūmĕo (**hūmĕo**) -ēre (umor), *to be moist, wet*: Ov.; esp. in pres. partic. **ūmens** -entis, *moist*: umbra, Verg.; oculi, Ov.

ŭmĕrus (**hŭmĕrus**) -i, m. *the upper arm or shoulder*: sagittae pendebant ab umero, Ov.; Cic., Hor.; fig.: rempublicam umeris sustinere, Cic.

ūmesco (**hūmesco**) -ēre (umeo), *to become wet, grow moist*: Verg.

ūmĭdŭlus (**hūmĭdŭlus**) -a -um (dim. of umidus), *somewhat wet, moist*: Ov.

ūmĭdus (**hūmĭdus**) -a -um (umeo), *wet, moist, damp*: ligna, *unseasoned*, Cic.; mella, *liquid*, Verg.; nox, Verg. N. as subst. **ūmĭdum** -i, *a wet place*: Tac.

ūmor (**hūmor**) -ōris, m. (akin to ὑγρός), *moisture, fluid*: Bacchi, *wine*, Verg.; lacteus, *milk*, Lucr., Ov.; roscidus, *dew*, Cat.; circumfluus, *the sea*, Ov.; umor in genas labitur, *tears*, Hor.; plur.: umores marini, Cic.

umquam (**unquam**), adv. *at any time, ever* (used chiefly in negative, interrog., and conditional sentences): si numquam oritur, ne occidit quidem umquam, Cic.; haud umquam, Verg.; si quando umquam, Liv., Ov., etc.

ūnā, adv. from unus; q.v.

ūnănĭmus=unanimus; q.v.: Pl.

ūnănĭmĭtās -ātis, f. (unanimus), *concord, unanimity*: Liv.

ūnănĭmus -a -um (unus/animus), *of one mind, agreeing, unanimous*: sodales, Cat.; fratres, Verg.; Liv., etc.

uncĭa -ae, f. (unus), *the twelfth part of any whole.* In gen., *a twelfth*; e.g. of an inheritance: Caesar ex uncia, *heir to one-twelfth*, Cic. Esp. as a weight or measure, *an ounce, one-twelfth of a pound* (as, *or* libra): Pl., Juv.

unciārĭus -a -um (uncia), *of a twelfth part*: faenus, *one-twelfth of the capital yearly*, i.e., 8⅓ *per cent*, Liv., Tac.

unciātim, adv. (uncia), *by twelfths*. TRANSF., *little by little*: Ter.

uncīnātus -a -um (uncinus), *shaped like a hook, hooked*: uncinata corpora, Cic.

uncĭŏla -ae, f. (dim. of uncia), *a little twelfth part* (of an inheritance): Juv.

unctĭo -ōnis, f. (ungo), *an anointing*: Pl.; philosophum unctionis causā reliquerunt, *to wrestle in the palaestra*, Cic.

unctĭto -are (freq. of ungo), *to anoint, besmear*: Pl.

unctiuscŭlus -a -um (dim. of compar. of unctus), *somewhat unctuous*: Pl.

unctor -ōris, m. (ungo), *an anointer*: Pl., Cic. L.

unctūra -ae, f. (ungo), *the anointing of the dead*: Cic.

unctus -a -um, partic. from ungo; q.v.

¹**uncus** -i, m. (connected with ancus), *a hook*: uncus ferreus, Liv.; nec severus uncus abest, (*as typical of Necessitas*), Hor.; esp. *the hook with which the executioner dragged away the bodies of dead malefactors to throw them into the Tiber*: alicui uncum impingere, Cic.; Seianus ducitur unco spectandus, Juv.; Ov.

²**uncus** -a -um, *bent like a hook, hooked, curved*: manus, Verg.; aratrum, Verg.; hamus, Ov.

unda -ae, f. *water, esp. water in motion, a wave.* LIT., maris unda, Cic.; minax unda ponto recumbit, Hor.; Verg., etc.

　　TRANSF., (1) *any fluid*: Plin.; so of billowing smoke: Verg.; Lucr. (2) *a stream* of people: undae comitiorum, Cic.; unda salutantum, Verg. (3) *a surge* of abstr. things: curarum, Cat.; Hor.

undĕ, adv. (originally cunde), *whence, from where.*

　　(1) interrog., in direct and indirect questions, *whence?*: unde deiectus est Cinna? Cic.; unde domo? Verg.; non recordor unde ceciderim, Cic.; Caes., Liv., etc.

　　(2) relat. LIT., of place, *whence*: nec enim inde venit, unde mallem, Cic.; ut aliae eodem, unde erant profectae, referrentur, Caes.; Verg., etc. Repeated: unde unde, *from some place or other*, Hor. TRANSF., of other relations, including personal relations, *whence, how, from whom*: unde necesse est, inde initium sumatur, Cic.; qui cum necasset, unde ipse natus esset, Cic.; Liv., etc.; as legal t. t., unde petitur, *the accused person* or *defendant*: ego omnibus, unde petitur, hoc consilium dederim, Cic.

undĕcĭēs (**undĕcĭens**), adv. *eleven times*: Mart.

undĕcim (unus/decem), *eleven*: Cic. L., etc.

undĕcĭmus -a -um (unus/decimus), *eleventh*: legio, Liv.; annus, Verg.

undĕcumquĕ (**undĕcunquĕ**), adv. *from whatever place, whencesoever*: Quint., Plin. L.

undēni -ae -a, *eleven at a time* or *eleven each*: Musa per undenos emodulanda pedes, of elegiacs, Ov.; quater undenos implevisse Decembres, *forty-four years*, Hor.

undēnōnāginta (unus/de/nonaginta), *eighty-nine*: Liv.

undēoctōginta (unus/de/octoginta), *seventy-nine*: Hor.

undēquadrāginta (unus/de/quadraginta), *thirty-nine*: Cic.

undēquinquāgēsĭmus -a -um (undequinquaginta), *forty-ninth*: Cic.

undēquinquāginta (unus/de/quinquaginta), *forty-nine*: Liv.

undēsexāginta (unus/de/sexaginta), *fifty-nine*: Liv.

undētrīcēsĭmus -a -um (undetriginta), *twenty-ninth*: Liv.

undēvīcēsĭmus (undeviginti), *nineteenth*: Cic.

undēvīginti (unus/de/viginti), *nineteen*: Cic., Liv.

undĭquĕ, adv. (unde/que). (1) *from* or *on all sides, from everywhere, everywhere*: concurrere, Cic.; conligere, Cic.; Caes., Hor., etc. (2) *altogether, in every respect*: partes undique aequales, Cic.; undique religionem tolle, Cic.; Quint.

undĭsŏnus -a -um (unda/sono), *resounding with waves*: dei, *sea-gods*, Prop.

undo -are (unda). (1) intransit., *to rise in waves, surge, wave, undulate*: flammis inter tabulata volutus ad caelum undabat vortex, Verg.; fumus, Verg.; undantes habenae, *hanging loosely*, Verg. (2) transit., *to flood*: sanguine campos, Stat.

undōsus -a -um (unda), *full of waves, surging, billowy*: Verg.

ūnetvīcēsĭmāni -ōrum, m. (unetvicesimus), *soldiers of the twenty-first legion*: Tac.

ūnetvīcēsĭmus -a -um (unus/et/vicesimus), *twenty-first*: Tac.

ungo (unguo) ungĕre unxi unctum, *to anoint, besmear*: aliquem unguentis, Pl.; unctus est, accubuit, Cic.; of the anointing of a corpse: corpus, Ov.; of the dressing of food: caules oleo, Hor.; uncta carina, *pitched*, Enn., Verg. ¶ Hence partic. **unctus** -a -um, as adj., *besmeared, anointed, greasy*. LIT., manus, Hor.; taeda, *resinous*, Ov.; palaestra, *where one is anointed*, Ov.; Cic., etc. TRANSF., accedes siccus ad unctum, *to a rich and luxurious person*, Hor.; compar., unctior quaedam consuetudo loquendi, *rich, copious*, Cic. N. as subst. **unctum** -i, *a sumptuous repast*: Hor., Pers.

unguĕn -ĭnis, n. (unguo), *a fatty substance, an ointment*: Verg.

unguentārĭus -a -um (unguentum), *of salve or ointment*: taberna, Varr., Suet. As subst., m. **unguentārĭus** -i, *a dealer in unguents*: Cic., Hor.; f. **unguentārĭa** -ae. (1) *a female dealer in unguents*: Plin. (2) (sc. ars), *the art of preparing unguents*: Pl.; n. **unguentārĭum** -i, *money for unguents*: Plin. L.

unguentātus -a -um (unguentum), *anointed*: Pl., Cat.

unguentum -i, n. (ungo), *a salve, ointment, perfume*: Pl., Cic., Hor., etc.

unguĭcŭlus -i, m. (dim. of unguis), *a finger-nail (or toe-nail)*: integritas unguiculorum omnium, Cic.; Pl., Lucr.; prov.: qui mihi a teneris, ut Graeci dicunt, unguiculis (Gr. ἐξ ἁπαλῶν ὀνύχων) cognitus est, *from childhood*, Cic. L.

unguis -is, m. (cf. ὄνυξ), *a finger or toe-nail*; of animals, *a claw, hoof*: ungues ponere, Hor.; rodere, Hor.; prov.: ab imis unguibus usque ad verticem summum, *from top to toe*, Cic.; transversum unguem non discedere, *not to depart a hair's breadth from*, Cic. L.; de tenero ungui, *from childhood*, Hor.; ad (or in) unguem, *to a hair, nicely, perfectly*: ad unguem factus homo, Hor.; omnis in unguem secto via limite quadret, Verg.

ungŭla -ae, f. (unguis), *a hoof, claw, talon*. LIT., vestigium ungulae (equi), Cic.; Pl., Verg. TRANSF., *a horse*: ungula rapit currūs, Hor.

unguo = ungo; q.v.

ūnĭcŏlor -ōris (unus/color), *uniform in colour, of one colour*: torus, Ov.

ūnĭcornis -e (unus/cornu), *having one horn*: Plin.

ūnĭcus -a -um (unus), *one, only, sole*. LIT., filius, Cic.; Pl., Ter., etc. TRANSF., *singular, unparalleled, unique, alone in its kind*: liberalitas, Cic.; fides, Liv. ¶ Hence adv. **ūnĭcē**, *singly, especially, particularly*: diligere, Cic.; unice securus, Hor.

ūnĭformis -e (unus/forma), *having one form, simple*: Tac.

ūnĭgĕna -ae (unus/gigno). (1) *born at one birth, of the same race*: unigena Memnonis, Zephyrus, brother of Memnon, Cat. (2) *only-begotten, unique*: singularis hic mundus atque unigena, Cic.

ūnĭmănus -a -um (unus/manus), *having but one hand*: puer, Liv.

¹**ūnĭo** -ire (unus), *to unite*: Sen.

²**ūnĭo** -ōnis, m. (unus), *a single large pearl*: Sen., Plin., Mart.

ūnĭtās -ātis, f. (unus), *unity, oneness*: Sen., Plin.

ūnĭtĕr, adv. (unus), *in one, together*: aptus, Lucr.

ūnĭversālis -e (universus), *general, universal*: Quint., Plin. L.

ūnĭversĭtās -ātis, f. (universus), *the whole, the total*. LIT., generis humani, Cic.; rerum, the universe, Cic. TRANSF., alone, the universe, the world: Cic.

ūnĭversus (archaic, **ūnĭvorsus**) -a -um (unus/versus), *combined in one, whole, entire*: mundus, terra, provincia, Cic.; bellum, Liv.; Pl., etc.; plur. **ūnĭversi** -ae -a, *all together*: in illum universi tela coniciunt, Caes.; universi (homines), Cic. N. as subst. **ūnĭversum** -i, *the whole*; hence, *the whole world, the universe*: Cic. Adv. phrase: in universum, *in general, generally*, Liv., Tac. ¶ Hence adv. **ūnĭversē**, *generally, in general*: generatim atque universe loquar, Cic.

ūnŏcŭlus -i, m. (unus/oculus), *a one-eyed man*: Pl.

ūnus -a -um, genit. **ūnīus**, dat. **ūni**, *one*. LIT., (1) in gen.: divisit unum populum in duas partes, Cic.; foll. by alter: una ex parte . . . altera ex parte, Caes.; plur. (esp. with words used only in the plur.): unae decumae . . . alterae, Cic.; ad unum (unam) omnes, *all to a man*, Caes., Cic., Liv.; in unum, *into one place*: confluere, Cic.; Verg. (2) *only one, one alone*: Demosthenes unus eminet, Cic.; uni ex omnibus Sequani, Caes.; strengthened by the superl., or by omnium: summus vir unus omnis Graeciae, Cic.; iustissimus unus qui fuit, Verg. (3) *one, one and the same*: uno tempore, *at the same time*, Caes.; uno ore, Cic., Verg. TRANSF., indefinite, *a, an, one, someone, anyone*: sicut unus paterfamilias, Cic.; nemo unus, nullus unus, Cic.; ad unum aliquem confugere, Cic. ¶ Hence adv. **ūnā**, *in one, together*: qui una venerant, Cic.; with cum and the abl.: amores una cum praetexta ponere, Cic.; Caes., Verg., etc.

ūpĭlĭo (ōpĭlĭo) -ōnis, m. *a shepherd*: Verg.

ŭpŭpa -ae, f. *a hoopoe*: Varr.; also (with a play on the word), *a kind of hoe*: Pl.

Ūrănĭa -ae and **Ūrănĭē** -ēs, f. (Οὐρανία, Οὐρανίη, *the heavenly one*), *one of the nine Muses, the Muse of Astronomy*.

urbānĭtās -ātis, f. (urbanus), *city life, esp. life in Rome*. LIT., desiderium urbanitatis, Cic. L. TRANSF., *the city manner*. Hence (1) *politeness, urbanity, refinement of manner*: Cic.; plur.: deponendae tibi sunt urbanitates,

rusticus Romanus factus es, Cic. (2) *wit,
pleasantry*: Cic.; in a bad sense: Tac.
urbānus -a -um, adj. (with compar. and
superl.) (urbs), *of a city* (esp. Rome); *urban.*
    LIT., tribus, Cic.; praetor, Cic.; exercitus
(of Roman citizens), Liv.; suffragatio (of the
city population), Cic.; m. pl. as subst.
urbāni -ōrum, *the inhabitants of the city,
the townsfolk*: Cic., etc.
    TRANSF., *of the town, after the city fashion.*
Hence (1) *refined in manner, elegant*: homo,
a man of the world, Cic.; artes, Liv. (2) *witty,
pleasant, humorous*: homo urbanissimus, Cic.;
sales, Cic.; m. as subst., *a wit*: Hor.
    ¶ Hence adv. (with compar.) **urbānē.**
(1) *politely, civilly, courteously*: agere, Cic.
(2) *wittily, elegantly*: ridere Stoicos, Cic.;
Quint.
urbĭcăpus -i, m. (urbs/capio), *a taker of cities*:
Pl.
urbĭcus -a -um (urbs), *of* or *belonging to a city;
civic, urban*: Suet.
urbs -bis, f. *a walled town* or *city.*
    LIT., urbem condere, aedificare, Cic.;
capere, evertere, Cic.; urbem quam statuo
vestra est, Verg. Esp. *the city of Rome*: ad
urbem esse, *to be at* or *near Rome*, Cic., Caes.,
Sall.
    TRANSF., *the city=the dwellers in the city*:
urbs somno vinoque sepulta, Verg.
urcĕŏlus -i, m. (dim. of urceus), *a small jug*
or *pitcher*: Juv.
urceus -i, m. *a jug, pitcher*: Pl., Hor.
ūrēdo -ĭnis, f. (uro), *a blight upon plants*: Cic.
urgēo urgēre ursi, *to push, press, drive, urge.*
    LIT., hinc Palla instat et urget, Verg.;
naves in Syrtes urgere, Verg.; pass.:
legionem urgeri ab hoste, Caes.; Cic.
    TRANSF., (1) *to press upon, beset, oppress*:
urgens malum, Cic.; mortifero morbo
urgeor, Cic.; urget diem nox et dies noctem,
Hor.; pass., urgeri, with genit., *to be
pressed hard on account of something*: male
administratae provinciae alarumque criminum, Tac. (2) *to urge in speech, stress, press
hard upon*: interrogando, Cic.; Hor. (3) of
work, *to press on with, ply hard, follow up*:
opus, Tib.; propositum, Hor.; iter, Ov.; Cic.
ūrīna -ae, f. (cf. οὖρον), *urine*: Cic., etc.
ūrīnātor -ōris, m. (urinor), *a diver*: Liv.
ūrīno -are and **ūrīnor** -ari, dep. *to dive*: Cic.,
Varr.
urna -ae, f.
    LIT., *a jug, pitcher, urn* for liquids: Pl.,
Hor., etc.
    TRANSF., *a jar, pot.* (1) *for holding money*:
argenti, Hor. (2) *for the ashes of the dead*:
Ov. (3) *for throwing lots* or *votes* into:
nomina in urnam conicere, Liv.; educere ex
urna tres (iudices), Cic. Hence, of the urn of
fate, assigned to Jupiter and the Parcae:
omne capax movet urna nomen, Hor. (4) as
a measure of capacity, *half an amphora*: Plin.,
Pers., etc.
ūro ūrĕre ussi ustum (connected with εὔω), *to
burn.*
    LIT., in gen.: calore, Cic.; picem et
ceras, Ov.; odoratam nocturna in lumina
cedrum, Verg.; domos, Hor.; agros, Liv.
Esp. (1) as medical t. t., *to treat by burning,
to burn out*: in corpore si quid eiusmodi est
quod reliquo corpori noceat, id uri secarique

patimur, Cic. (2) as t. t. of painting, *to burn
in*: picta ustis coloribus puppis, Ov.
    TRANSF., (1) of physical processes com-
parable to burning: **a**, *to dry up, parch*:
fauces urit sitis, Hor.; Cic., Verg.: **b**, *to pinch,
chafe, gall*: calceus (pedem) urit, Hor.; lorica
lacertos, Prop.: **c**, *to pinch with cold*: ustus
ab adsiduo frigore Pontus, Ov.; Cic. (2) of
mental distress: **a**, *to consume with passion,*
and pass., *to be on fire, glow with passion*: me
tamen urit amor, Verg.; uritur infelix Dido,
Verg.; Hor.: **b**, *to disquiet, disturb, harass*: eos
bellum Romanum urebat, Liv.; Ov.
ursa -ae, f. (ursus), *a she-bear*: Ov. Meton.,
the constellations of the Great and Little Bear:
Ursa Maior, or Erymanthis, or Maenalis, or
Parrhasi, *the Great Bear*; Ursa Minor, or
Ursa Cynosuris, *the Little Bear*, Ov., Suet.
ursus -i, m. *a bear*: ursi informes, Verg.;
poscunt ursum, i.e. *a bear hunt in the circus,*
Hor.
urtīca -ae, f. (uro), *a nettle, stinging-nettle.*
    LIT., Hor., Plin. TRANSF., (1) *a sea-nettle*:
Plin. (2) *lustfulness, desire*: Juv.
ūrus -i, m. *a kind of wild ox*: Caes., Verg.
Usĭpĕtes -um and **Usĭpĭi** -ōrum, m. pl. *a
powerful Germanic tribe near the Tencteri, on
the Lippe and the Rhine.*
ūsĭtātus -a -um, adj. (with compar. and
superl.) (utor), *customary, usual, wonted*:
vocabula, Cic.; Caes.; facimus usitatius hoc
verbum, Cic.; utatur verbis quam usitatis-
simis, Cic.; usitatum est, foll. by acc. and
infin., *it is usual, customary*, Quint.
    ¶ Hence adv. **ūsĭtātē**, *in the usual manner*:
loqui, Cic.
uspĭam, adv. *anywhere, at any point*: Pl., Cic.
usquam, adv. (ubi/quam), *anywhere* (gen. used
in negative and conditional sentences).
    LIT., iste cui nullus esset usquam con-
sistendi locus, Cic.; with partitive genit.:
usquam gentium, Cic.; Verg., etc.
    TRANSF., (1) *at all, in any way*: Ter., Cic.
(2) *any whither, in any direction*: Pl., Hor.
usquĕ, adv. *at every point, through and through,
from . . . to, all the way, continuously.*
    LIT., of space: usque a mari supero
Romam proficisci, Cic.; usque ad castra
hostium accessit, Caes.; usque Romam, *as
far as Rome*, Cic.; usque quaque, *everywhere,*
Cic.
    TRANSF., (1) of time: usque a Romulo,
from the time of Romulus, Cic.; inde usque
repetens, Cic.; usque quaque, *always*, Cat.,
Cic.; usque eo se tenuit, Cic.; absol., *always,
constantly*: iuvat usque morari, Verg. (2) in
other relations: hoc malum usque ad bestias
perveniat, Cic.; Pl., Verg.
usquĕquāquĕ, *see* usque.
Ustīca -ae, f. *a valley in the Sabine country,
near Horace's estate.*
ustor -ōris, m. (uro), *a burner of corpses*: Cic.,
Cat., etc.
ustŭlo -are (dim. of uro), *to burn, scorch, singe*:
Cat.
¹ūsūcăpĭo or **ūsū căpĭo** -căpĕre -cēpi
-captum (usus/capio), *to acquire ownership
by length of use, obtain by prescription*: Cic.;
velut usucepisse Italiam, Liv.
²ūsūcăpĭo -ōnis, f. (usus/capio), *ownership
acquired by length of possession* or *use*:
usucapio fundi, Cic.

ūsūra -ae, f. (utor), *use, enjoyment.*
LIT., natura dedit usuram vitae, Cic.; unius horae, Cic. Esp., *the use of borrowed capital*: Cic.
TRANSF., *interest paid for money borrowed*: usura menstrua, Cic.; usurae gravissimae, Caes.; alicui usuram pendĕre, *to pay*, Cic. L.; fig.: terra numquam sine usura reddit quod accepit, Cic.; Liv.

ūsūrārĭus -a -um (usura). (1) *used, relating to use*: Pl. (2) *out at interest, paying interest*: Pl.

ūsurpātĭo -ōnis, f. (usurpo), *a using, use, making use*: doctrinae, Cic.; vocis, Liv.; itineris, *undertaking*, Liv.

ūsurpo -are (perhaps contr. from usu/rapio), *to make use of, to use, to bring into use.*
In gen.: genus poenae, Cic.; Liv., Tac.
Esp. (1) as legal t. t., *to take possession of, acquire*: amissam possessionem, Cic.; alienam possessionem, *to appropriate, usurp*, Liv. (2) *to grasp by the senses, to perceive, to notice*: aliquid sensibus, Lucr. (3) *to use a word, to mention*: nomen tantum virtutis usurpas, Cic.; hence *to call, name*: C. Laelius, is qui Sapiens usurpatur, Cic.; Lucr.

ūsus -ūs, m. (utor), *use, using, making use of, application, practice, exercise.*
LIT., in gen.: membrorum, Cic.; erat in tanta caligine maior usus aurium quam oculorum, Liv.; scientia atque usus rerum nauticarum, *theory and practice*, Caes.; usus magister est optimus, Cic. Esp. (1) *social intercourse, familiarity*: domesticus usus et consuetudo, Cic.; familiaris, Liv.; Ov. (2) as legal t. t., usus et fructus, usus fructusque, ususfructus, *the use and enjoyment of property not one's own*: usus fructus omnium bonorum, Cic.
TRANSF., (1) *practice, skill, practical experience*: militaris, Cic.; habere magnum in re militari, *or* in castris usum, Caes. (2) *utility, usefulness, profit*: magnos usus adfert ad navigia facienda, Cic.; Caes., Hor. Hence: usui esse, *or* ex usu esse, *to be useful, be of use*: Caes., Cic., Liv. (3) *need, want*: usum provinciae supplere, Cic. Hence phrases, usus est, usus venit, usus adest, *there is need of, occasion for*; absol.: si quando usus esset, Cic.; with abl.: si quid erit quod extra magistratus curatore usus sit, Cic.; ut equites Pompeianorum impetum, cum adesset usus, sustinere auderent, Caes.; si usus veniat, Caes.; also the phrase, usu venit, *it happens*: quid homini potest turpius usu venire? Cic.; Caes.

ūsusfructus, *see* usus.

ŭt *or* **ŭtī**, adv.
(1) with indic. verb: **a**, interrog., *how?* in direct (or poet., indirect) questions: ut valet? ut meminit nostri? Hor.; Pl., Liv.; aspice ut insignis Marcellus ingreditur, Verg.: **b**, exclam., *how!*: ut ille tum humilis, ut demissus erat! Cic.; Pl., Verg., etc.: **c**, relat., *as*; absol.: perge ut instituisti, Cic.; Caes., etc.; in a parenthesis: facilius est currentem, ut aiunt, incitare, Cic.; with verb omitted: vestemque relinquere ut anguis, Lucr.; Cic., Liv.; with corresponding sic, ita, item: omnia sic constitueram mihi agenda, ut tu admonebas, Cic.; ut optasti, ita est, Cic.; ut cum Titanis, ĭta cum Gigantibus, Cic.; with concessive force,

indeed ... *but*: Saguntini ut a proeliis quietem habuerant ... ita non nocte, non die umquam cessaverant ab opere, Liv.; ut quisque (with superl.), *in proportion as, the more* ... *the more*: ut quisque est vir optimus, ita difficillime esse alios improbos suspicatur, Cic.; Liv.; repeated: ut ut, *in whatever way*, Pl., Ter.: **d**, in oaths, protestations, etc.: ita vivam, ut maximos sumptus facio, Cic.: **e**, to introduce an explanation, *as, as being* (sometimes without verb): homo acutus ut Poenus, Cic.; aiunt hominem, ut erat furiosus, respondisse, Cic.; permulta alia conligit Chrysippus, ut est in omni historia curiosus, Cic.: **f**, temporal, *as, when*, esp. with the perf.: ut haec audivit, Cic.; Verg., Hor., Liv., etc.; strengthened by primum: ut primum loqui posse coepi, Cic.: **g**, temporal, *while, since*: ut Brundisio profectus es, nullae mihi abs te sunt redditae litterae, Cic. L.; Caes., Liv.: **h**, of place, *where*: Indos, litus ut tunditur undā, Cat.; Verg., Ov.
(2) with subjunctive verb: **a**, interrogative, *how*, in indirect questions: nescis ut res sit, Pl.; vides ut alta stet nive candidum Soracte, Hor.; Cic.: **b**, in wishes: ut illum di deaeque perdant! Ter.; Verg.: **c**, in concessions, *granted that*: Caes., Ov.: **d**, introducing a consequence, *so that*; often preceded by a demonstrative word (e.g. ita, tam, tantus, eo) or by a verb indicating causation: eo creverit, ut iam magnitudine laboret sua, Liv.; sol efficit ut omnia floreant, Cic.; Verg., etc.: **e**, explaining or defining, *namely that*: datur haec venia antiquitati, ut primordia urbium angustiora faciat, Liv.; vetus est lex amicitiae, ut ... , Cic.: **f**, to express a purpose, *that, in order that* (negat. ne *or* ut ne): idcirco omnes servi sumus, ut liberi esse possimus, Cic.; Romani ab aratro abduxerunt Cincinnatum, ut dictator esset, Cic.; Caes., Liv., etc.: **g**, in 'indirect command'; i.e. after verbs of commanding, persuading, asking, resolving, taking care, wishing, agreeing, etc.: equidem vellem, ut aliquando redires, Cic.; praecipitur ut nobis ipsis imperemus, Cic.; petunt atque orant ut, Caes.; postulant ut, Liv.; hortor ut, Cic.; suasit ut, Cic.; impellimur naturā ut, Cic.: **h**, after verbs of fearing (for ne non), *that not*: timeo ut sustineas, Cic.; Caes.

utcumquĕ (**utcunquĕ**), adv. (1) *in whatever manner, however*: utcumque se videri velet, Cic.; Pl., Verg., etc. (2) *whenever*: utcumque mecum eritis, Hor.; Liv.

ūtens -entis, partic. from utor; q.v.

ūtensĭlis -e (utor), *fit for use, useful*: Varr. N. pl. as subst. **ūtensĭlĭa** -ium, *useful things, utensils*: Liv., Tac.

¹ŭter ŭtris, m. (connected with uterus), *the skin of an animal used as a bag or bottle*: Aeolios Ithacis inclusimus utribus euros, Ov.; used (like a bladder) for crossing rivers: Caes., Liv.; fig., of conceit: tumidis infla sermonibus utrem, Hor.

²ŭter ŭtra ŭtrum; genit. ŭtrīus, dat. ŭtri. (1) interrog., *which of the two?* in direct and indirect questions: uter nostrum popularis est? tune an ego? Cic.; neque diiudicare posset, uter utri virtute anteferendus videretur, Caes.; plur., *which side? which of the two sets?* (2) relat., *the one (of two) which*:

utram vis, Pl.; Cic., etc. (3) indef., *one of the two, either of the two*: si uter velit, Cic.

ŭtercumquĕ (**-cunquĕ**) ŭtrăcumquĕ ŭtrumcumquĕ, *whichever of the two, whichever*: utercumque vicerit, Cic.

ŭterlĭbĕt ŭtrălĭbĕt ŭtrumlĭbĕt, *whichever of the two you please, either of the two*: utrumlibet elige, Cic.; Liv.

ŭterquĕ ŭtrăquĕ ŭtrumquĕ; genit. ŭtrĭusquĕ, dat. ŭtriquĕ, *each of two, both* (considered separately).

(1) sing.: uterque cum exercitu veniret, Caes.; sermones utriusque linguae, Cic.; uterque Poenus, *in Africa and in Europe*, Hor.; Phoebus, *the rising and the setting sun, morning and evening*, Ov.; uterque polus, *the North and South Pole*, Ov.; Oceanus, *the east and west*, Ov.; parens, *father and mother*, Ov.; in utramque partem, *on both sides, in both cases*, Cic. With partitive genit: uterque nostrum, Hor. With predicate in the plur.: uterque eorum ex castris exercitum educunt, Caes.; Tac., etc.

(2) plur.: **a**, usually, *each side, each set*: quoniam utrique Socratici et Platonici volumus esse, Cic.: **b**, sometimes of individuals, *each, both*: duae fuerunt Ariovisti uxores; utraeque in ea fuga perierunt, Caes.

ŭtĕrus -i, m. and **ŭtĕrum** -i, n. (cf. *οὖθαρ*), *the womb*; also in gen., *the belly*.

Lit., Pl., Cic., Hor., etc.

Transf., (1) *the cavities of the earth, out of which the first creatures are said to have been born*: Lucr. (2) *the inside*; of a ship: Tac.; of the Trojan horse: Verg.

ŭtervis ŭtrăvis ŭtrumvis; genit. ŭtrīusvis, dat. ŭtrīvis, *which of the two you will, either of the two*: utrumvis facere potes, Cic.; Ter., etc.

ŭtī=ut; q.v.

ūtĭbĭlis -e (utor), *that can be used, useful*: Pl.

Ŭtĭca -ae, f. *a town in Africa Propria, north of Carthage, where the senatorial party made their last stand against Caesar, and M. Porcius Cato the younger killed himself.*

¶ Hence adj. **Ŭtĭcensis** -e, *of Utica.*

ūtĭlis -e, adj. (with compar. and superl.) (utor), *useful, fit, profitable, serviceable, beneficial*; absol.: utiles et salutares res, Cic.; with ad and the acc.: homo ad eam rem utilis, Cic.; with in: res maxime in hoc tempus utilis, Liv.; with dat.: equi utiles bello, Ov.; non mihi est vita mea utilior, Cic.; with genit.: radix medendi utilis, Ov.; with infin.: tibia adesse choris erat utilis, Hor.; utile est, with infin.: numquam utile est peccare, Cic.; with acc. and infin.: eos utile est praeesse vobis, Liv.

¶ Hence adv. (with compar. and superl.) **ūtĭlĭtĕr**, *usefully, profitably*: utiliter a natura datum esse, Cic.; Hor., etc.

ūtĭlĭtās -ātis, f. (utilis), *usefulness, profit, advantage*: utilitas parta per amicum, Cic.; Pl., Hor.; plur.: utilitates ex amicitia maxime capientur, Cic.

ŭtĭnam, adv. *would that! oh that!*: utinam incumbat in causam! Cic.; utinam haberetis! Cic.; Hor., etc.; with quod: quod utinam minus vitae cupidi fuissemus! Cic.; with negat. utinam ne *or* utinam non, *would that . . . not!*: illud utinam ne vere scriberem! Cic. L.

ŭtĭquĕ, adv. *at any rate, certainly, at leas*: utique apud me sis, Cic.; commota est plebs, utique postquam . . . , Liv.

ūtor ūtī ūsus sum, dep. *to use, make use of, employ.*

Lit., of things; with abl.: sensibus, Lucr.; armis, Cic.; oratione, *to speak*, Cic.; male uti lege, *to make a bad use of the law*, Cic.; Caes., Hor., etc.; with acc.: cetera, Pl.; gerundive: huic omnia utenda ac possidenda tradiderat, Cic.

Transf., (1) *to be in possession of, possess, enjoy*: valetudine non bonā, Caes.; honore, Cic.; lacte et herbis, Ov. (2) of persons, *to associate with, be intimate with*: Trebonio multos annos utor, Cic.; Hor. (3) of persons, with a predicate, *to find*: facili me patre, Ter.; Cic., Hor.

¶ Hence partic. **ūtens** -entis, as adj. (with compar.), *possessing*: Cic.

utpŏtĕ, adv. *seeing that, inasmuch as*: utpote qui nihil contemnere solemus, Cic.; utpote lecti utrimque, Liv.; populus numerabilis, utpote parvus, Hor.

ūtrārĭus -i, m. ([1]uter), *one who carries water in skins, a water-carrier*: Liv.

ūtrĭcŭlārĭus -i, m. *a bagpiper*: Suet.

ŭtrimquĕ (**ŭtrinquĕ**), adv. (uterque), *from both sides, on both sides*: Cic., Hor., Liv., etc.

ŭtrō ([2]uter), adv. *to which of two places? to which side?*: Ov.

ŭtrŏbi (**ŭtrŭbi**), adv. ([2]uter), *at which of two places? where?*: Pl.

ŭtrŏbīquĕ (**ŭtrŭbīquĕ**), adv. *on each of two sides, on both sides*: sequitur ut eadem veritas utrobique sit, eademque lex, *with gods and men*, Cic.; Eumenes utrobique plus valebat, *both by land and sea*, Nep.; Hor., Liv.

ŭtrōlĭbĕt, adv. (uterlibet), *to either of two sides, to either side*: Quint.

ŭtrōquĕ, adv. (uterque), *to both sides, in both directions.* Lit., of place: utroque citius quam vellemus cursum confecimus, Cic.; Verg., Liv. Transf., *at each point, both ways*: si natura utroque adiuncta est, Cic.; Liv.

ŭtrŭbi, etc.=utrobi, etc.; q.v.

ŭtrum, adv. (n. of [2]uter), *whether*; used mainly in alternative questions.

(1) in direct questions: **a**, with a second clause: utrum ea vestra an nostra culpa est? Cic.; utrum cetera nomina in codicem accepti et expensi digesta habes annon? Cic.: **b**, without a second clause: utrum hoc bellum non est? Cic.

(2) in indirect questions: **a**, with a second clause: multum interest, utrum laus diminuatur an salus deseratur, Cic.; utrum illi sentiant, anne simulent, tu intelleges, Cic.; iam dudum ego erro, qui quaeram, utrum emeris necne, Cic.: **b**, without a second clause: hoc dicere audebis, utrum de te aratores, utrum denique Siculi universi bene existiment, ad rem id non pertinere, Cic.

ŭtŭt, adv. *however, see* ut.

ūva -ae, f. *a bunch of grapes.* Lit., uva colorem ducit, Verg.; Cic., etc.; meton., *the vine*: Verg. Transf., *a cluster similar to a bunch of grapes*; e.g. *a swarm of bees*: Verg., Plin.

ūvens -entis (partic. of *uveo), *moist, wet*: Petr.

ūvesco -ĕre (*uveo), *to become moist, be wet*: Lucr.; of persons drinking: Hor.

ūvĭdŭlus -a -um (dim. of uvidus), *moist, wet*: Cat.

ūvĭdus -a -um (*uveo), *moist, damp, wet.* LIT., vestimenta, Hor.; Menalcas, *wet with dew*, Verg.; Iuppiter uvidus austris, *rainy*, Verg. TRANSF., *drunken* or *having drunk*: Bacchus, Hor.; dicimus integro sicci mane die, dicimus uvidi, Hor.

uxor -ōris, f. *a wife, spouse.* LIT., uxor iusta, Cic.; duas uxores habere, Cic.; uxorem ducere, *to marry a wife*, Cic., etc.; uxori nuntium remittere, *to divorce a wife*, Cic. TRANSF., (1) of animals: olentis uxores mariti, *she-goats*, Hor. (2) *a man's cloak*: Mart.

uxorcŭla -ae, f. (dim. of uxor), *a little wife, wee wifie* (as a term of endearment): Pl.

uxōrĭus -a -um (uxor). (1) *of a wife*: res uxoria, Cic.; dos, Ov. (2) *too devoted to one's wife, uxorious*; of Aeneas, in relation to Dido: Verg.; amnis, *the Tiber, as the husband of Ilia*, Hor.

V

V, v, the twenty-first letter of the Latin Alphabet, corresponding partly to the Greek digamma (F). V frequently passes into u, e.g. solvo, solutum, navita, nauta; and between two vowels is often elided, e.g., deleverunt, delerunt; providens, prudens; ne volo, nolo. For the use of V. in abbreviations, see Table of Abbreviations.

văcātĭo -ōnis, f. (vaco), *a freedom, immunity, exemption from anything, a being without.* LIT., with genit.: vacatio militiae, Caes., Liv.; with ab: alicui dare vacationem a causis, Cic.; Liv. With subjective genit.: vacatio, adulescentiae, Cic. TRANSF., *money paid for exemption from military duties*: Tac.

vacca -ae, f. *a cow*: Cic., Verg., etc.

Vaccaei -ōrum, m. pl. *a people in Hispania Tarraconensis.*

vaccīnĭum -i, n. *the blueberry, whortle-berry*; or, according to some scholars, *the hyacinth*: Verg., Ov.

văcēfīo -fĭĕri (vacuus), *to be made empty*: Lucr.

văcerrōsus -a -um, *stupid*: Suet.

văcillātĭo -ōnis, f. (vacillo), *a rocking, reeling motion*: Suet., Quint.

văcillo (also **vaccillo**: Lucr.) -are, *to totter, reel, stagger, sway to and fro.* LIT., litterulae vacillantes, *written with unsteady hand*, Cic. L.; of persons: ex vino, Cic.; in utramque partem toto corpore, Cic.; Lucr. TRANSF., tota res vacillat et claudicat, Cic.; of persons: in aere alieno, *to be deep in debt*, Cic.; Lucr.

văcīvĭtās -ātis, f. (vacivus), *emptiness, want*: cibi, Pl.

văcīvus or **vŏcīvus** -a -um (vaco), *empty*: aedes, Pl.; with genit.: virium, *powerless*, Pl.; Ter.

¶ Adv. **văcīvē**, *idly, at leisure*: Phaedr.

văco -are, *to be empty, void.* LIT., in gen.: absol.: tota domus superior vacat, Cic.; with abl.: natura caelestis et terra vacat umore, Cic.; Verg., Liv., etc.

Esp., of property, *to be vacant, to have no master*: ut populus vacantia teneret, Tac.; Liv. TRANSF., (1) *to be free from* anything, *to be without*; with abl.: curā et negotio, Cic.; metu ac periculis, Liv.; with ab: ab opere, Caes.; ab omni concitatione animi semper, Cic.; of things: haec a custodiis classium loca maxime vacabant, Caes. (2) *to be free from work, be at leisure, have time*: scribes aliquid, si vacabis, Cic.; with dat., *to have time for, to have leisure for*: ego vero, inquam, philosophiae semper vaco, Cic.; Quint., Tac.; poet., with in and the acc.: in grande opus, Ov. (3) impers., vacat, *there is leisure (for), there is time (for)*; with infin.: hactenus indulsisse vacat, Verg.; dum vacat, Ov.

văcŭĕfăcĭo -făcĕre -fēci -factum (vacuus/facio), *to make empty*: morte superioris uxoris domum novis nuptiis, Cic.; adventu tuo ista subsellia vacuefacta sunt, Cic.

văcŭĭtās -ātis, f. (vacuus), *freedom, exemption, immunity, being without*; with genit.: doloris, Cic.; with ab: ab angoribus, Cic. Esp., *a vacancy in a public office*, e.g., the consulship: ap. Cic. L.

Văcūna -ae, f. *a goddess of the country*, esp. *among the Sabines.* Adj. **Văcūnālis** -e, *of Vacuna.*

văcŭo -are (vacuus), *to make void, to empty*: Lucr.

văcŭus -a -um, *empty, void, free from, exempt, without.* LIT., in gen.: castra, Caes.; theatrum, Hor.; viator, *empty-handed*, Juv.; with abl.: nihil igni vacuum, Cic.; with ab: ab his rebus, Cic.; vacuum oppidum ab defensoribus, Caes. N. as subst. **văcŭum** -i, *an empty place, vacuum*: per vacuum incurrere, Hor.; Lucr., Liv. Esp. *vacant, without a master*: praedia, Cic.; possessio regni, Caes.; venire in vacuum, Hor. TRANSF., (1) in gen., *free from something, without*; with abl.: animus sensibus et curis vacuus, Cic.; with ab: ab omni sumptu, Cic.; animus a talibus factis vacuus et integer, Cic.; with genit.: vacuus operum, Hor. (2) absol., *free, at leisure, exempt from work* or *duty*: quoniam vacui sumus, dicam, Cic.; animus, Cic.; mentes, Verg.; aures, Hor.; of time: cum vacui temporis nihil habebam, *leisure*, Cic.; dies, Cic.; nox, Liv. (3) with dat., *free for*: domus scelestis nuptiis, Sall.; Hor. (4) of women, *unmarried* or *widowed*: Ov., Tac. (5) *worthless, useless, vain*: vacua nomina, Tac.; Hor., Ov.

vădīmōnĭum -i, n. (¹vas), *bail, security, recognizance* (insuring appearance before a court of law): sine vadimonio disceditur, Cic.; vadimonium constituere, Cic.; vadimonium obire, *or* sistere, *or* ad vadimoniam venire, *to appear on bail*, Cic.; vadimonium deserere, *to forfeit recognizances*, Cic.

vādo -ĕre, *to go, hasten, rush*: vadimus haud dubiam in mortem, Verg.; ad aliquem postridie mane, Cic. L.; Tac., etc.

vădor -ari, dep. (¹vas), *to bind over by bail*: hominem in praesentia non vadatur, Cic.; tot vadibus accusator vadatus est reum, Liv.; responde re vadato, Hor.

vădōsus -a -um (vadum), *full of shallows, shallow*: mare, Caes.

vădum -i, n. *a shallow, shoal, ford* in a river or sea. Lit., exercitum vado transducere, Caes.; Verg., Liv., etc. Transf., (1) in gen., *water, river, sea*: Verg., Hor. (2) *the bottom of any stretch of water*: Hor., Ov., Plin. (3) fig., *shallows*, as typical either of *safety* or of *danger*: Pl., Ter., Cic.

vae interj. (cf. οὐαί), to express pain or anger, *alas! woe!*; absol.: Pl., Verg., Hor.; with dat.: vae victis, Liv., Ter.; with acc.: Pl.

văfer vafra vafrum, *artful, subtle, sly, crafty*: in disputando, Cic.; Hor., Ov.; superl.: somniorum vaferrimus interpres, Cic.

¶ Hence adv. **vafrē**, *artfully, craftily*: Cic.

vafrĭtia -ae, f. (vafer), *artfulness, slyness, subtlety, cunning*: Sen.

văgē, adv. from vagus; q.v.

văgīna -ae, f. *a sheath, scabbard*. Lit., gladius vaginā vacuus, Cic.; gladium e vagina educere, Cic.; Caes., Verg., etc. Transf., *any sheath, case*; esp. *the hull* or *husk of grain*: Cic.

văgĭo -ire, *to cry, whimper as a child*: repuerascere et in cunis vagire, Cic.; Ov., etc.

văgītus -ūs, m. (vagio), *the crying of young children*: dare vagitūs, Ov.; Verg.; of the *bleating* of kids: Ov.

¹văgor -ōris, m. (vagio)=vagitus: Enn., Lucr.

²văgor -ari, dep. (and **văgo** -are: Pl.) (vagus), *to wander, ramble, rove*.

Lit., in agris passim bestiarum more, Cic.; volucres huc illuc passim vagantes, Cic.; luna iisdem spatiis vagatur quibus sol, Cic.; of ships and sailors, *to cruise*: cum lembis circa Lesbum, Liv.; Verg., etc.

Transf., vagabitur tuum nomen longe atque late, *will be spread far and wide*, Cic.; animus vagatus errore, Cic.; vagabimur nostro instituto, *digress*, Cic.; Verg., Hor.

văgus -a -um, *wandering, roaming, roving*.

Lit., multitudo dispersa atque vaga, Cic.; matronae vagae per vias, Liv.; Hor.; of things: luna, Cic.; venti, Hor.

Transf., (1) *inconstant, fickle*: puella, Ov.; sententia, Cic. (2) *diffuse, aimless*: orationis genus, Cic.

¶ Hence adv. **văgē**, *dispersedly*: vage effusi per agros, Liv.

văh (**văhă**), interj. *ah! oh!*: Pl., Ter.

valdē, adv. (syncop. for valide, from validus; q.v.), *intensely, very much, greatly*. (1) with verbs: alicui adridere, Cic.; compar.: valdius oblectare, Hor.; superl.: Sen. (2) with adj. or adv.: valde magnus, Cic.; valde bene, Cic. (3) in replies, *certainly, very much so*: Pl.

vălēdīco -ĕre, *to say good-bye*: Sen.

vălens -entis, partic. from valeo; q.v.

vălentŭlus -a -um (dim. of valens), *strong*: Pl.

vălĕo -ēre, *to be strong*.

Lit., physically. (1) *to be vigorous, of good physique*: puer ille ut magnus es et multum valet, Pl.; alios velocitate ad cursum, alios viribus ad luctandum valere, Cic.; with infin.: valeo stare, Hor.; valet ima summis mutare deus, Hor. (2) *to be in good health, be well*: optime valeo, Cic.; bene, melius, Cic.; corpore, Cic.; a morbo, Pl.; absol.: valeo et salvus sum, Pl.; hence the phrase at the beginning of a letter: si vales, bene est (S. V. B. E.), Cic. L.; also with the addition: ego or ego quoque valeo (E. V. or E. Q. V.), Cic. L.

Transf., (1) politically, morally, etc., *to avail, have force, be strong, prevail*: multum equitatu, Caes.; plurimum proficere et valere, Cic.; longe plurimum valere ingenio, Cic.; of things: sine veritate nomen amicitiae valere non potest, Cic. Esp. with reference to a certain object, *to have force for, to be able to, to be strong enough for*: tu non solum ad neglegendas leges, verum etiam ad evertendas valuisti, Cic.; of things: illud perficiam, ut invidia mihi valeat ad gloriam, Cic.; with infin.: nec continere suos ab direptione castrorum valuit, Liv.; with in (*or* contra) and the acc., *to avail against*: in se, in Romanos, in ipsum, Cic.; definitio in omnes valet, *avails for all*, Cic.; hoc contra te, Cic. (2) *to be worth*: dum pro argenteis decem aureus unus valeret, Liv. (3) of words, *to mean, signify*: verbum, quod idem valeat, Cic. (4) as a farewell greeting: vale, or valeas, *adieu, farewell, good-bye*, Pl., Ter., Verg., etc.; esp. at the end of letters: vale, or bene vale, or cura ut valeas, Cic. L.; to the dead: Cat., Verg., Ov. So: valere iubere, *to bid farewell, say good-bye to*, Cic., etc. Hence as an expression of scorn, refusal, etc.: si talis est deus, valeat, *let me have nothing to do with him*, Cic.; quare valeant ista, *away with them!* Cic.; valeant puellae, Tib.; Hor.

¶ Hence partic. **vălens** -entis, as adj. (with compar. and superl.), *strong, powerful*.

Lit., physically. (1) *strong*: robusti et valentes satellites, Cic.; valentissimi homines, Cic.; valentes trunci, Verg. (2) *well, healthy*: medicus confirmat propediem te valentem fore, Cic.; Pl., Prop.

Transf., politically, morally, etc., *powerful, mighty*: civitas, Cic.; viribus cum valentiore pugnare, Cic.; valens dialecticus, Cic.; fraus valentior quam consilium meum, Cic.

¶ Adv. **vălentĕr**, *strongly, powerfully*; compar.: valentius spirare, Ov.

Vălĕrĭus -a -um, *name of a Roman gens*.

¶ Hence adj. **Vălĕrĭānus** -a -um, *of a Valerius*.

vălesco -ĕre (valeo), *to grow strong*. Lit., Lucr. Transf., superstitiones, Tac.

vălētūdĭnārĭus -a -um (valetudo), *sickly*: Varr. M. as subst., *an invalid*: Sen.

vălētūdo -ĭnis, f. (valeo), *state of health*.

Lit., physical: bona, Lucr., Cic.; incommoda, adversa, Cic.; infirmā atque aegrā valetudine usus, Cic.; Caes., Hor., etc. Esp. (1) in a bad sense, *ill-health, weakness*: oculorum, Cic. L.; adfectus valetudine, *ill*, Caes.; plur.: subsidia valetudinum, Cic. (2) in a good sense, *good health*: valetudinem amiseram, Cic.; Pl., Hor.

Transf., (1) *mental health*: quasi mala valetudo animi, Cic. (2) of style: Cic.

Valgĭus -a -um, *name of a Roman gens*.

valgus -a -um, *bow-legged*. Lit., Pl. Transf., suavia, *wry mouths*, Pl.

vălĭdus -a -um, adj. (with compar. and superl.) (valeo), *strong, powerful*.

Lit., physically. (1) *strong, stout, muscular*: homines, Pl.; tauri, Lucr.; vires, Verg.; as milit. t. t., of posts or stations, *strong*: valida urbs et potens, Cic.; valida urbs praesidiis, muris, Liv. (2) of medicines, *powerful, efficacious*: sucus, Ov.; Tac. (3) *healthy, well*:

si, ut spero, te validum videro, Cic. L.;
necdum ex morbo satis validus, Liv.

TRANSF., politically, morally, etc., *strong,
powerful, mighty, influential*: hostis validior,
Liv.; with abl.: ingenium sapientiā validum,
Sall.; Hor., Tac., etc.

¶ Hence adv. (with compar. and superl.)
vălĭdē (cf. valde), *strongly, powerfully,
mightily*: validissime favere alicui, ap. Cic. L.;
Pl. In answers, *certainly, to be sure*: Pl.

vallāris -e (vallum), *relating to the* vallum:
corona, *given to the soldier who first mounted
the fortifications of the hostile camp*, Liv.

valles (vallis) -is, f. *a vale, valley*. LIT., vicus
positus in valle, Caes.; Verg., Liv., etc.
TRANSF., *a hollow*: alarum, Cat.

vallo -are (vallum), *to fortify with a palisade*.
LIT., castra, Liv., Tac. TRANSF., *to fortify,
strengthen*: Catilina vallatus sicariis, Cic.;
sol radiis frontem vallatus, Ov.; Lucr.

vallum -i, n. (vallus), *a palisade made from
stakes and set up on a rampart*. LIT., oppidum
vallo et fossā cingere, Cic. L.; Caes., Verg.,
Liv. TRANSF., *a fortification, defence*: spica
munitur vallo aristarum, Cic.; Lucr.

vallus -i, m. *a post, stake.*
LIT., esp. (**1**) as a prop for vines: Verg.
(**2**) as part of a palisade: caedere, Liv.; Caes.;
collect. (like vallum), *a palisade, stockade*:
duplex vallus, Caes.
TRANSF., vallus pectinis, *a tooth of a comb*,
Ov.

valvae -ārum, f. pl. *folding-doors*: effractis
valvis (fani), Cic.; Caes., Hor., etc.

vănesco -ĕre (vanus), *to pass away, disappear*.
LIT., nubes, Ov.; Tac. TRANSF., amor, Ov.;
Tac.

Vangĭŏnes -um, m. pl. *a Germanic people on
the Rhine, near modern Worms.*

vānĭdĭcus -a -um (vanus/dico), *talking vainly,
lying*: Pl.

vānĭlŏquentĭa -ae, f. (vanus/loquor), *idle
talking, vaunting*: Pl., Liv., Tac.

vānĭlŏquus -a -um (vanus/loquor). (**1**) *lying*:
Pl. (**2**) *boasting, vaunting*: Liv.

vānĭtās -ātis, f. (vanus), *emptiness.* Hence (**1**)
worthlessness, unreality, untruth: opinionum,
Cic.; itineris, Liv. (**2**) *vanity, boasting,
ostentation*: Sall., Liv., Tac.

vānĭtūdo -inis, f. (vanus), *idle, lying talk*: Pl.

vannus -i, f. *a winnowing-fan*: vannus mystica
Iacchi (borne at the Bacchic festival), Verg.

vānus -a -um (connected with vaco), *empty,
void.*
LIT., arista, Verg.; imago, *shade, disembodied spirit*, Hor.; vanior acies hostium,
Liv.
TRANSF., (**1**) *vain, idle, worthless, meaning-
less, fruitless, groundless*: oratio, Cic.; spes,
Ov.; gaudia, Hor.; of missiles: ictus, Liv.
N. as subst., *that which is empty* or *vain*:
haustum ex vano, *from a false source*, Liv.;
vana tumens, *with empty show*, Verg.; with
genit.: vana rerum, Hor. (**2**) of persons, *vain,
ostentatious, boastful, unreliable, untrue*:
haruspex, Cic.; vanum se esse et perfidiosum
fateri, Cic.; vanus auctor est, *deserves no
credence*, Liv.

văpĭdus -a -um (connected with vapor),
spiritless, spoiled, flat: Pers.

¶ Hence adv. **văpĭdē**, *mouldily*: vapide
se habere, *to be feeling mouldy*, Aug. ap. Suet.

văpor (**văpōs**) -ōris, m. *vapour, steam*. LIT.,
aquarum, Cic.; Lucr., Hor. TRANSF., *warm
exhalation, warmth*: Lucr.; semen tepe-
factum vapore, Cic.; locus vaporis plenus,
Liv.

văpōrārĭum -i, n. (vapor), *a flue for conveying
steam*: Cic.

văpōro -are (vapor). (**1**) intransit., *to steam,
reek*: Plin.; fig.: Lucr. (**2**) transit., *to fill
with vapour, to heat, to warm*: laevum latus,
Hor.; templum ture, Verg.

vappa -ae, f. (connected with vapor), *spiritless,
flat wine*. LIT., Hor. TRANSF., *a good-for-
nothing, worthless fellow*: Hor.

văpŭlāris -e (vapulo), *well whipped*: Pl.

văpŭlo -are, *to be flogged, whipped, beaten.*
LIT., Lucr., Pl. TRANSF., (**1**) of troops, *to be
beaten*: ap. Cic. L. (**2**) in gen., *to be knocked
about*: Pl., Cic. L. (**3**) of things, *to be wasted*:
Pl., Sen.

vărĭantĭa -ae, f. (vario), *difference, variation*:
Lucr.

vărĭātĭo -ōnis, f. (vario), *difference, variation*:
Liv.

vărĭco -are (varicus), *to stand with feet apart,
to straddle*: Varr., Quint.

vărĭcōsus -a -um (varix), *having varicose
veins*: Pers., Juv.

vărĭcus -a -um (varus), *straddling*: Ov.

vărĭē, adv. from varius; q.v.

vărĭĕtās -ātis, f. (¹varius), *variety, difference,
diversity*: florum, pomorum, Cic.; multiplex
ratio disputandi rerumque varietas, Cic.; in
disputationibus, Cic.; plur.: varietates
temporum, Cic.

vărĭo -are (¹varius).
(**1**) transit., *to vary, diversify, variegate,
change, alter*. LIT., of material things: vocem,
Cic.; capillos, Ov.; (sol) variat ortum maculis,
Verg. TRANSF., of abstr. things: caloresque
frigoraque, Liv.; voluptatem, Cic.; quae de
Marcelli morte variant auctores, *relate
differently*, Liv.; variante fortunā eventum,
Liv.; cum timor atque ira in vicem sententias
variassent, Liv. In pass., variari, *to waver,
be divided, to vary*: variatis hominum
sententiis, Liv.
(**2**) intransit., *to be different, to vary.*
LIT., of material things: liventibus uva
racemis, Prop. TRANSF., lex nec causis nec
personis, Liv.; sic mei variant timores, Ov.;
dissidet et variat sententia, Ov.; quamquam
et opinionibus et monumentis litterarum
variarent, Liv.

¹vărĭus -a -um, *manifold.*
LIT., of colour, *diversified, variegated*:
columnae, Hor.; lynces, Verg.; caelum, Ov.;
Pl.
TRANSF., of the nature of things or persons,
various, manifold, changeable, diverse. (**1**) of
things: varium poema, varia oratio, varii
mores, varia fortuna, voluptas etiam varia
dici solet, Cic.; quales sint (dii) varium est,
different opinions are held, Cic.; fortunae varii
eventus, Caes. (**2**) of persons: varius et
multiplex et copiosus fuit, Cic.; esp. in bad
sense, *fickle, changeable*: animus, Sall.;
varium et mutabile semper femina, Verg.

¶ Hence adv. **vărĭē**, *diversely*. LIT., of
colour: Plin. TRANSF., in gen., *variously,
in different ways*: numerus varie diffusus,
Cic.; varie bellatum, *with varying success*, Liv.

²**Vărĭus** -a -um, *name of a Roman gens. Its most famous members were*: (**1**) Q. Varius Hybrida, of Sucro, in Spain, *tribune of the people*, 91 B.C., *author of a* lex de maiestate. (**2**) L. Varius, *a poet, the friend of Horace and Vergil.*

vărix -ĭcis, c. *a varicose vein*, esp. in the leg: Cic., Quint.

Varro -ōnis, m. *a surname in the gens* Terentia.
¶ Hence adj. **Varrōnĭānus** -a -um, *Varronian*: milites, *who served under C. Terentius Varro*, Liv.

¹**vārus** -a -um. LIT., *knock-kneed*: Pl., Hor. TRANSF., (**1**) *in gen., crooked, bent*: cornua, manus, Ov. (**2**) *diverse, different*: alterum (genus) huic varum, Hor.

²**Vărus** -i, m. *a surname used by several Roman families*; esp. of P. Quintilius Varus, *defeated and killed with his army by Arminius*, A.D. 9.
¶ Hence adj. **Vārĭānus** -a -um.

¹**văs** vădis, m. (vado), *a bail, surety*; used of persons: vades poscere, Cic.; vades deserere, Liv.; vas factus est alter (Damon) eius sistendi, Cic.

²**văs** vāsis, n.; plur. **vāsa** -ōrum, *a vessel, receptacle, utensil of any kind*: vas vinarium, Cic.; Pl., Lucr., etc. Esp. plur. as milit. t. t., *war materials, equipment*: vasa conligere, Cic.; vasa conclamare, *to give the signal for packing up*, Caes.

vāsārĭum -i, n. (²vas). (**1**) *an allowance given to the governor of a province for his outfit*: Cic. (**2**) *the hire of an oil-press*: Cato.

vascŭlārĭus -ii, m. (vasculum), *a maker of vessels*, esp. *in metal*: Cic.

vascŭlum -i, n. (dim. of ²vas), *a small vessel*: Pl., Cato., Juv.

vastātĭo -ōnis, f. (vasto), *a devastating, laying waste*: agri, Liv.; omnium, Cic.; plur.: depopulationes, vastationes, caedes, rapinae, Cic.

vastātor -ōris, m. (vasto), *a devastator, ravager*: Arcadiae (of a boar), Ov.; ferarum, Verg.

vastē, adv. from vastus; q.v.

vastīfĭcus -a -um (vastus/facio), *laying waste, devastating*: Cic. poet.

vastĭtās -ātis, f. (vastus), *a waste, emptiness, desolation.*
LIT., iudiciorum vastitas et fori, Cic.; Italiam totam ad exitium et vastitatem vocare, Cic.; Liv.
TRANSF., (**1**) *vastness, vast size*: Plin. (**2**) concr. in plur., vastitates, *devastators*: provinciarum vastitates, Cic.

vastĭtĭēs -ēi, f. (vastus), *devastation, destruction*: Pl.

vasto -are (vastus), *to empty, make empty.*
LIT., in gen.: forum, Cic.; Liv.; with abl.: cultoribus agros, Verg. Esp., *to lay waste, ravage, devastate*: agros, Caes., Cic.; omnia ferro ignique, Liv.; cultores, *to plunder*, Tac.
TRANSF., *to prey upon*: ita conscientia mentem excitam vastabat, Sall.

vastus -a -um, adj. (with compar. and superl.) (perhaps connected with vaco), *empty, waste, deserted, desolate.*
LIT., in gen.: loci coaedificati an vasti, Cic.; Liv., Tac. Esp., *laid waste, ravaged, devastated*: solum, Liv.; haec ego vasta dabo, *will ravage*, Verg.

TRANSF., (**1**) *vast, enormous*: vasta et immanis belua, Cic.; mare, Caes.; Verg., Liv.; animus, *insatiable*, Sall. (**2**) *rough, rude*: vastus homo atque foedus, Cic.; littera vastior, *rougher*, Cic.; Liv.
¶ Hence adv. (with compar.) **vastē**. (**1**) *widely, extensively*: vaste profundum, Lucr.; vastius insurgens, Ov. (**2**) *rudely, roughly*: loqui, Cic.

vātes -is (genit. pl. vatum *or* vatium), c. *a prophet, soothsayer, seer.*
LIT., Cicero quae nunc usu veniunt cecinit ut vates, Cic.; Verg., Liv., etc.
TRANSF., esp. from Vergil onwards, *a singer, bard, poet*: me quoque dicunt vatem pastores, Verg.; Hor.; cothurnatus, *a tragic poet*, Ov.; Maeonius, *Homer*, Ov.; Lesbia, *Sappho*, Ov.; vates Aeneidos, *Vergil*, Ov.

Vātĭcānus -a -um, *Vatican*: mons, collis, *the Vatican Hill on the west side of the Tiber*, Hor.; plur.: Vaticani colles, *the hill with its surroundings*, Cic.; ager Vaticanus, *the country round the Vatican, notorious for its bad soil, which produced poor wine*, Cic.

vātĭcĭnātĭo -ōnis, f. (vaticinor), *a soothsaying, prophesying*: earum litterarum vaticinationem falsam esse cupio, Cic.; plur.: sortes et vaticinationes, Caes.

vātĭcĭnātor -ōris, m. (vaticinor), *a soothsayer, prophet*: Ov.

vātĭcĭnĭum -i, n. (vates), *a prophecy*: Plin.

vātĭcĭnor -ari, dep. (vates/cano), *to prophesy.*
LIT., vaticinari furor vera solet, Cic., Liv.; with acc. and infin.: saevam laesi fore numinis iram, Ov.
TRANSF., (**1**) *to teach as a seer*: doctum quendam virum carminibus Graecis vaticinatum ferunt, Cic. (**2**) *to talk wildly, to rave*: sed ego fortasse vaticinor, Cic. (**3**) *to keep on about* an old subject: Pl.

vātĭcĭnus -a -um (vates), *soothsaying, prophetic*: Liv., Ov.

vătillum (**bătillum**) -i, n. *a chafing-dish or shovel*: Hor.

Vătīnĭus -a -um, *the name of a Roman gens*; esp. of P. Vatinius, *a dependent of Caesar, so bitterly attacked by Cicero that* odium Vatinianum *and* crimina Vatiniana *became proverbial.*

¹**-vĕ** (shortened form of vel), enclitic, *or, or perhaps*: duabus tribusve horis, Cic.; Caes., etc.; poet.: ve ... ve, Ov.; ve ... aut, Prop.; *either ... or.*

²**vē-** (**vae**), an inseparable particle, which either *negates or stresses a negation*; e.g. vecors, vesanus, vepallidus.

vēcordĭa (**vaecordĭa**) -ae, f. (vecors), *senselessness, folly, madness*: Ter., Ov., Sall.

vēcors (**vaecors**) -cordis (²ve/cor), *senseless, foolish, mad, insane*: mens, Cic.; impetus, Liv.; vecors de tribunali decurrit, Liv.; superl.: iste vecordissimus, Cic.

vectābĭlis -e (vecto), *that can be carried, portable*: Sen.

vectātĭo -ōnis, f. (vecto), *a riding, driving, sailing*, etc.: equi, Suet.; Sen.

vectĭgal -gālis, n. (vectigalis), *revenue.*
(**1**) public: a, *a state toll, a tax, impost, duty*: portoria reliquaque vectigalia, Caes.; vectigal pergrande imponere agro, Cic.; vectigalia pendĕre, *to pay*, Cic.: b, of money paid to magistrates: praetorium, Cic. L.

(2) private: *income, revenue*: ex meo tenui vectigali, Cic.; Hor., Plin. L.

vectīgālis -e (veho). (1) *relating to taxes*: pecunia, *paid in taxes*, Cic.; esp. *liable to taxes, tributary*: civitas, Cic.; Ubios sibi vectigales facere, Cic. (2) *bringing in private income*: equi, Cic.

vectio -ōnis, f. (veho), *a carrying, conveyance*: quadrupedum vectiones, Cic.

vectis -is, m. (veho). (1) for lifting or breaking, *a lever, crow-bar*: signum vectibus labefacere, Cic.; biremes impellere vectibus, Caes. (2) for securing, *a bar, bolt*: Cic., Verg.

Vectis -is or **Vecta** -ae, f. *the Isle of Wight.*

vecto -are (freq. of veho), *to carry, convey*: plaustris ornos, Verg.; fructus ex agris, Liv.; pass., *to ride* or *be driven*: equis, Ov.; carpentis per urbem, Liv.

vector -ōris, m. (veho). (1) act., *a carrier, bearer*: Ov. (2) pass., *one who is carried*; on a ship, *a passenger*: Cic., Verg.; on a horse, *a rider*: Prop., Ov.

vectōrius -a -um (vector), *for carrying*: navigia, *transports*, Caes.

vectūra -ae, f. (veho), *a conveying, carrying, transportation.* Lit., by ship, horse, or carriage: frumenti, Caes.; sine vecturae periculo, *of a sea-passage*, Cic. L.; Caes. Transf., *passage-money, fare*: Pl., Sen.

vĕgĕo -ēre, *to stir up, quicken, excite*: Enn., Lucr.

vĕgĕtus -a -um (vegeo), *lively, vigorous, fresh*: fessi cum recentibus ac vegetis pugnabant, Liv.; mens, Cic.; ingenium, Liv.

vĕgrandis -e, *small, diminutive*: farra, Ov.

vĕhĕmens (poet. also **vēmens**) -entis, adj. (with compar. and superl.), *violent, vehement, furious, impetuous.*

Lit., of living beings: nimis es vehemens feroxque naturā, Cic.; in agendo, Cic.; se vehementem praebere in aliquem, Cic.; lupus, Hor.

Transf., of inanimate or abstr. things: vehemens et pugnax exordium dicendi, Cic.; violentia vini, Lucr.; vehementius telum, Liv.; vehementior somnus, Liv.

¶ Hence adv. (with compar. and superl.) **vĕhĕmentĕr.** (1) *vehemently, violently*: se agere, Cic.; ingemuisse vehementius, Cic.; se vehementissime exercere in aliqua re, Caes. (2) *strongly, powerfully, forcibly, exceedingly*: hoc te vehementer etiam atque etiam rogo, Cic.; vehementer delectari, Cic.; vehementissime displicet, Cic.; Pl., Lucr.

vĕhĕmentia -ae, f. (vehemens). (1) *vehemence, violence, passion*: Plin. (2) *strength, power*: Plin.

vĕhĭcŭlum -i, n. (veho), *a vehicle, conveyance*, by land or by water: vehiculum frumento onustum, Liv.; Pl., Cic., Tac.

vĕho vĕhĕre vexi vectum, *to carry, convey.*

(1) act.; in gen.: reticulum umero, Hor.; taurus qui vexit Europam, Cic.; formica vehit ore cibum, Ov.; quod fugiens hora vexit, Hor. Esp.: **a**, by water: quos vehit unda, Ov.; **b**, on horseback or in a carriage: triumphantem (Camillum) albi vexerant equi, Liv.

(2) pass.: vehi, as middle, *to sail, ride, drive*, etc.: curru, Cic.; in navi, Cic.; in equo, Cic.; apes trans aethera vectae, Verg.; Ov., etc. So also in pres. partic.: vehens quadrigis, *riding*, Cic.

Vēii -ōrum, m. pl. *an old town in Etruria, for a long time the rival of Rome, but taken at last by Camillus.*

¶ Hence adj. **Vēiens** -entis, *Veientine*; m. pl. as subst. **Vēientes** -ium, *the Veientines*; also adj. **Vēientānus** -a -um and **Vēius** -a -um, *Veientine.*

Vēiŏvis (Vēdiŏvis) -is, m. (ve/Iuppiter), *an old Etruscan deity of the lower world.*

vĕl, conj. and adv. (imperat. of volo = *take what you will, the one or the other*).

Conj., *or*. (1) singly, *or*: oppidum vel urbem appellaverunt, Cic.; Pl., etc.; sometimes to correct a previous expression: ex hoc populo indomito vel potius immani, *or rather*, Cic. (2) doubled (sometimes repeated three or four times), *either . . . or*: cur non adsum vel spectator laudum tuarum vel particeps vel socius vel minister consiliorum? Cic.; quae vel ad usum vitae vel etiam ad ipsam rempublican conferre possumus, Cic.

Adv. (1) *even, actually*: per me vel stertas licet, Cic.; often with superl.: vel maxime, *especially*, Cic.; domus vel optima, Cic. (2) *for example*: raras tuas quidem, sed suaves accipio litteras; vel quas proxime acceperam, quam prudentes, Cic.; Ter.

Vēlabrum -i, n. *a district in Rome near the Palatine.*

vēlāmen -ĭnis, n. (velo), *a covering, garment*: Verg., Ov., Tac.

vēlāmentum -i, n. (velo), *a covering, veil*: Sen. Esp. plur., velamenta, *olive-branches wound round with wool, carried by suppliants*: ramos oleae ac velamenta alia supplicum porrigentes, Liv.; Ov., Tac.

vēlārĭum -i, n. (velum), *the awning over part of a theatre*: Juv.

vēlāti -ōrum, m. pl. (velo), milit. t. t., *the reserve, supernumary troops*; used always in the phrase: accensi velati, Cic.

vēlēs -ĭtis, m., usually plur., **vēlĭtēs**, *light-armed infantry, skirmishers*: Liv., Ov. Transf., scurra veles, Cic.

Vēlĭa -ae, f. (1) *a district on the Palatine Hill in Rome.* (2) *the Latin name of the Lucanian coastal town Elea* (Ἐλέα).

¶ Hence adj. **Vēlĭensis** -e and **Vēlīnus** -a -um, *Veline.*

vēlĭfĕr -fĕra -fĕrum (velum/fero), *carrying sail*: Prop., Ov.

vēlĭfĭcātĭo -ōnis, f. (velifico), *a sailing*: Cic. L.

vēlĭfĭco -are and dep. **vēlĭfĭcor** -ari (velum/facio), *to sail.*

Lit., Prop.; perf. partic. in pass. sense, velificatus -a -um, *sailed through*: Juv.

Transf., *to work for* an end: honori suo, Cic.

¹**Vēlīnus**, see Velia.

²**Vēlīnus** -i, m. *a river in the Sabine country.*

vēlĭtāris -e (veles), *of the velites* or *light-armed troops*: arma, Sall.; hastae, Liv.

vēlĭtātĭo -ōnis, f. (velitor), *skirmishing.* Transf., *wrangling, bickering*: Pl.

vēlĭtor -ari, dep. (veles), *to skirmish.* Transf., *to wrangle, dispute*: Pl.

Vēlĭtrae -ārum, f. pl. *a town of the Volsci in Latium* (now *Velletri*).

vēlĭvŏlans = velivolus; q.v.

vēlĭvŏlus -a -um (velum/volo), *flying with sails*; of ships: rates, Ov.; Lucr.; of the sea: Verg., Ov.

Vellēius -a -um, *the name of a Roman* gens; esp. of C. Velleius Paterculus, *a Roman historian under Augustus and Tiberius.*

vellĭcātĭo -ōnis, f. (vellico), *a twitting, taunting*: Sen.

vellĭco -are (vello), *to pluck, twitch.* Lit., Pl. Transf., *to taunt, criticize, rail at*: in circulis, Cic.; absentem, Hor.

vello vellĕre velli (vulsi, volsi) vulsum (volsum), *to pluck, pull, twitch.*

In gen.: alicui barbam, Hor.; latus digitis (to attract attention), Ov.; aurem, Verg. Esp., *to pluck off, pluck out*: spinas, Cic.; postes a cardine, Verg.; vallum, *to pull up the palisade,* Liv.; signa, *to take the standards out of the ground* in order *to march away,* Liv.; poma manu, *to pick,* Tib.

¶ Hence partic. **vulsus** -a -um, *plucked, beardless*: Pl., Prop., etc.

vellus -ĕris, n. *wool when shorn off, a fleece.* Lit., vellera trahere, *to spin,* Ov.; Lucr., Hor.

Transf., (1) *the whole skin with the wool,* either on or off the animal: Phrixea vellera, Ov.; poet., *any hide,* e.g., of a lion or stag, Ov. (2) *anything like wool* (in plur.): lanae vellera per caelum ferri, *fleecy clouds,* Verg.; Mart.

vēlo -are (velum), *to cover, veil, envelop.* Lit., capita amictu, Verg.; tempora myrto, Verg.; caput velatum filo, Liv.; Hor., etc. Transf., *to hide, veil*: odium fallacibus blanditiis, Tac.

vēlōcĭtās -ātis, f. (velox), *quickness, rapidity, velocity.* Lit., velocitas corporis celeritas vocatur, Cic.; Caes. Transf., mali, Tac.

vēlox -ōcis, adj. (with compar. and superl.) (*volo), *swift, rapid, quick, fleet.* Lit., pedites velocissimi, Caes.; cervi, Verg.; iaculum, Verg.; toxicum, *quick in operation,* Hor.; poet. like adv.: ille velox desilit in latices, Ov. Transf., animus, Hor.; nihil est animo velocius, Cic.; Tac., Quint.

¶ Hence adv. (with compar. and superl.) **vēlōcĭtĕr,** *quickly, rapidly, swiftly*: aliquid velociter auferre, Ov.; velocius pervolare in hanc sedem, Cic.; velocissime moveri, Cic.

¹vēlum -i, n.

(1) *a sail*: antemnis subnectere totum velum, Ov.; velo et remige portus intrat, Ov. More often plur.: vela dare, *to sail,* Cic., Verg., Hor., Liv.; vela facere, Cic., Verg.; contrahere, Cic. L.; fig.: dare vela ad id, unde aliquis status ostenditur, Cic.; pandere vela orationis, *to follow the current of one's speech,* Cic.; prov.: remis velisque, *with all one's might,* Cic.

²vēlum, *a covering, awning, curtain*: tabernacula carbaseis intenta velis, Cic.; velis amicti, non togis, *wrapped up like women,* Cic.; Lucr., Prop., etc.

vĕlŭt (**vĕlŭti**), adv. *as, even as, just as.*

(1) with indic.: velut in cantu et fidibus, sic ex corporis totius natura et figura varios modos ciere, Cic.; sometimes without following verb: velut hesterno die, Cic.; veluti pecora, Sall. Esp.: **a,** to introduce a simile: ac veluti magno in populo cum saepe coorta est seditio, sic, Verg.; Ov., etc.: **b,** to introduce an example, *as, as for instance*: in bestiis aquatilibus iis, quae gignuntur in terra, velut crocodili, Cic.

(2) with subjunctive, to introduce a hypothetical comparison, velut, *or* velut si, *as if, just as if, just as though*: absentis Ariovisti crudelitatem, velut si coram adesset, horrerent, Caes.; velut ea res nihil ad religionem pertinuisset, Liv.

vēmens=vehemens; q.v.

vēna -ae, f. *a blood-vessel, vein.* Lit., venae et arteriae a corde tractae, Cic.; Verg., Tac. Sometimes *an artery*; plur., *the pulse*: si cui venae sic moventur, is habet febrem, Cic.

Transf., (1) *a water-course*: venas et flumina fontis elicuere sui, Ov. (2) *a vein of metal*: aeris, argenti, auri, Cic.; venae peioris aevum, Ov. (3) *a vein* or *streak in wood or stone*: Plin. (4) *the inmost, vital part of anything*: periculum inclusum in venis et visceribus reipublicae, Cic. (5) *a vein of talent, disposition* or *natural inclination*: benigna ingenii vena, Hor.; Quint.

vēnābŭlum -i, n. (venor), *a hunting-spear*: aprum venabulo percutere, Cic. L.; Verg., Ov.

Vĕnăfrum -i, n. *a very old town of the Samnites in Campania, famous for its oil* (now *Venafro*).

¶ Hence adj. **Vĕnăfrānus** -a -um, *Venafran.*

vēnālĭcĭus -a -um (venalis), *relating to the sale of slaves*: Suet., Plin. M. as subst. **vēnālĭcĭus** -i, *a slave-dealer*: Cic.

vēnālis -e (venum), *on sale, to be sold.* Lit., horti, Cic.; Pl., Sall. M. as subst., venalis, *a slave put up for sale*: Pl., Cic.

Transf., *that can be bought with bribes, venal*: vox, Cic.; habere venalem in Sicilia iurisdictionem, Cic.; Prop., Liv.

vēnātĭcus -a -um (venatus), *of* or *for the chase*: canis, Pl.; Cic., Hor.

vēnātĭo -ōnis, f. (venor), *the chase, hunting.* Lit., aucupium atque venatio, Cic.; Caes. Transf., (1) *game*: venatio capta, Liv.; Plin. L. (2) *a beast hunt in the circus or amphitheatre*: ludorum venationumque apparatus, Cic.

vēnātor -ōris, m. (venor), *a hunter, sportsman*: Pl., Caes., etc.; fig.: physicus id est speculator venatorque naturae, Cic.

vēnātōrĭus -a -um (venator), *of* or *for the chase*: galea, Nep., Plin. L.

vēnātrix -īcis, f. (venator), *a huntress*: Ov., Verg.; attrib.: puella, Diana, Juv.

vēnātūra -ae, f. (venor), *hunting, the chase*: Pl.

vēnātus -ūs, m. (venor), *the chase, hunting*: labor in venatu, Cic.; Verg., Ov.

vendĭbĭlis -e (vendo), *on sale, saleable.* Lit., illa via Herculanea, Cic. Transf., *popular, acceptable*: oratio, Cic.; compar.: sint illa vendibiliora, Cic.

vendĭtātĭo -ōnis, f. (vendito), *a putting up for sale*; hence *a boasting, vaunting*: venditatio atque ostentatio, Cic.; sine venditatione, Cic.

vendĭtātor -ōris, m. (vendito), *a vaunter, boaster*: Tac.

vendĭtĭo -ōnis, f. (vendo), *a selling, sale*: bonorum, Cic.; plur.: quam ad diem proscriptiones venditionesque fiant, Cic.; Plin. L.

vendĭto -are (freq. of vendo), *to offer for sale repeatedly, try to sell.* Lit., Tusculanum, Cic. L.; Tac., etc.

Transf., (1) *to sell* (corruptly): decreta, Cic.; pacem pretio, Liv. (2) *to cry up, praise, advertise*: operam suam alicui, Liv.; se alicui, Cic.; se existimationi hominum, Cic.

vendĭtor -ōris, m. (vendo), *a seller, vendor*: Cic.

vendo -děre -dĭdi -dĭtum (contr. from venum/ do), *to put up for sale, to sell, vend.*

LIT., bona civium, Cic.; fanum pecuniā grandi, Cic.; male, *cheap*, Cic.; pluris, Pl., Cic.; ex empto aut vendito, Cic.

TRANSF., (1) *to sell, betray for money*: auro patriam, Verg.; se trecentis talentis regi, Cic. (2) *to cry up, recommend, advertise*: Ligarianam, Cic.; Hor., Prop.

The usual passive of vendo is veneo; q.v.

věnēfĭcĭum -i, n. (veneficus). (1) *a poisoning*: Cic., Liv., Tac. (2) *the preparation of drugs, magic, sorcery*: Cic., Ov.

věnēfĭcus -a -um (venenum/facio), *poisonous, magical*: artes, Plin.; verba, Ov.

¶ As subst., m. **věnēfĭcus** -i, *a poisoner, sorcerer, enchanter*: Cic., Hor., Ov.; f. **věnēfĭca** -ae, *a sorceress, a witch*: Pl., Hor.

věnēnārĭus -i, m. (venenum), *a poisoner*: Suet.

věnēnĭfěr -fěra -fěrum (venenum/fero), *poisonous*: Ov.

věnēno -are (venenum), *to poison, drug*: carnem, Cic.; odio obscuro, Hor.

¶ Hence partic. **věnēnātus** -a -um, *poisoned, poisonous, drugged, enchanted*: colubrae, Lucr.; telum, Cic.; virga, Ov.; fig.: iocus, Ov.

věnēnum -i, n. *a drug.*

(1) *poison.* LIT., venenum alicui dare, Cic.; veneno necare, Cic.; dare venenum in poculo, Cic.; Verg., Liv., etc. TRANSF., **a**, *ruin, destruction, bane*: discordia est venenum urbis, Liv.: **b**, *virulent speech*: pus atque venenum, Hor.; Ov.

(2) *a love-potion*: Pl., Cic., Hor., etc.

(3) *colouring matter, dye*: Assyrium, Verg.; Tarentinum, Hor.; *rouge*: Ov.

věnēo věnīre věni věnītum (venum/eo), *to go for sale, to be sold* (used as pass. of vendo): mancipia venibant, Cic.; venire sub corona a consule et praetore, Liv.; with abl. of price: auro, Hor.; with genit. of price: minoris, Cic.

věněrābĭlis -e (veneror), *venerable, reverend*: venerabilis vir miraculo litterarum, venerabilior divinitate, Liv.; of things: donum, Verg.; Hor., Tac.

věněrābundus -a -um (veneror), *reverent, respectful*: Liv., Suet.

věněrātĭo -ōnis, f. (veneror), *reverence, respect, veneration*: habet venerationem iustam quidquid excellit, Cic.; Tac.

věněrātor -ōris, m. (veneror), *a venerator, reverer*: domūs vestrae, Ov.

věněrěus, see venus.

věněror -ari, dep. (act. **věněro** -are: Pl.).

(1) *to ask reverently, beseech with awe*: nil horum veneror, Hor.; with ut *or* ne and subj.: Pl.

(2) *to revere, respect, worship, honour*: deos sancte, Cic.; Larem farre pio, Verg.; secundum deos nomen Romanum, Liv.; Augustum, Hor.; perf. partic. in pass. sense: Verg., Hor.

Věněti -ōrum, m. pl.

(1) *a people on the north-west coast of the Adriatic.*

¶ Hence subst. **Věnětĭa** -ae, f. *their country*; adj. **Věnětus** -a -um, *Venetian*, also *blue*: Juv., etc.

(2) *a people in Gallia Lugdunensis, near modern Vannes.*

¶ Hence subst. **Věnětĭa** -ae, f. *their country*; adj. **Věnětĭcus** -a -um.

věnĭa -ae, f. (connected with veneror), *grace, indulgence, favour.*

In gen.: dedi veniam homini impudenter petenti, Cic.; extremam hanc oro veniam, Verg.; Liv.

Esp., (1) *permission*: petere veniam legatis mittendis, Liv. Often in phrase, bonā (cum) veniā, *with your good leave*: bona venia vestra liceat, Liv.; Cic. (2) *pardon, forgiveness*: veniam impetrare errati, Cic.; dare veniam et impunitatem, Cic.; Caes., Liv., etc.

věnĭo věnīre věni ventum, *to come.*

LIT., of physical movement. (1) of persons: huc, Cic.; ad aliquem, Cic.; ad urbem, Cic.; sub aspectum, Cic.; domum ad aliquem, Cic.; sexto die Delum Athenis, Cic.; veniens hostis, Verg. With dat. of purpose: venire auxilio, subsidio, Caes.; with ad: ad cenam, Pl.; ad causam dicendam, Liv. Impers. pass.: ad quos ventum erat, Caes.; Cic. (2) of things: frumentum Tiberi venit, Liv.; dum tibi litterae meae veniant, Cic. L.; verbosa et grandis epistula venit a Capreis, Juv.

TRANSF., (1) of metaphorical movement in gen.: ut ad id aliquando, quod cupiebat, pulchro veniens in corpore virtus, Verg.; veniret, Cic.; venio ad recentiores litteras, Caes.; venire in mentem, *to come into one's head*, Cic. L.; in buccam, *to one's lips*, Cic. L. (2) *in course of time, to happen, come, arrive*: ubi ea dies quam constituerat venit, Caes.; venientis anni, *of the coming year*, Cic.; ventura bella, Verg.; nepotes venturi, Verg., Ov. (3) *to grow*: veniunt felicius uvae, Verg. (4) *to be derived from*: Bebrycia de gente, Verg.; fig., *to arise from*: maius commodum ex otio meo quam ex aliorum negotiis reipublicae venturum, Sall. (5) *to come to* or *fall into any state* or *condition*: in calamitatem, Cic.; in consuetudinem, Cic.; alicui in amicitiam, Caes.; Hor., Liv.

věnor -ari, dep. *to hunt.* LIT., ei qui venari solent, Cic.; leporem, Pl., Verg.; venatum ire, Verg. TRANSF., suffragia ventosae plebis, Hor.

věnōsus -a -um (vena), *full of veins, veiny*: Plin., Pers.

venter -tris, m. *the belly.*

LIT., (1) *the stomach*: fabā venter inflatur, Cic.; hence, fig., *gluttony*: ventrem fame domare, Liv.; ventri oboedire, Sall.; Hor.; Juv. (2) *the womb*: Juv.; meton., *the fetus, fruit of the womb*: Hor.

TRANSF., *a curve, protuberance*: cresceret in ventrem cucumis, Verg.

ventĭlo -are (ventus), *to wave, fan, brandish in the air.* LIT., ventilat aura comas, Ov.; Prop., etc. Esp. *to winnow grain*: Varr. TRANSF., *to fan the flames* of excitement, etc.: illius linguā, quasi flabello seditionis, illa tum est egentium contio ventilata, Cic.

ventĭo -ōnis, f. (venio), *a coming*: Pl.

ventĭto -are (freq. of venio), *to come often, resort*: domum, Cic. L.; in castra, Caes.

ventōsus -a -um (ventus), adj. (with compar. and superl.).

LIT., (1) *full of wind, windy*: folles, Verg.;
Germania ventosior, Tac.; ventosissima
regio, Liv. (2) *swift* or *light as the wind*: equi,
Ov.; Lucr.

TRANSF., (1) *windy, puffed up, vain*: gloria,
lingua, Verg. (2) *changeable, inconstant*:
plebs, Hor.; ingenium, Liv., Cic.

ventrĭcŭlus -i, m. (dim. of venter), *the belly*:
Juv.; cordis, *a ventricle*, Cic.

ventrĭōsus -a -um (venter), *pot-bellied*: Pl.

ventŭlus -i, m. (dim. of ventus), *a slight wind,
gentle breeze*: Pl., Ter.

ventus -i, m. *wind.*

LIT., ventus intermittitur, Caes.; cum
saevire ventus coepisset, Caes.; Lucr., Cic.,
etc.; prov.: in vento et aqua scribere, *to
labour in vain*, Cat.; profundere verba ventis,
Lucr.; dare verba in ventos, Ov.; dare verba
ventis, *not to keep one's word*, Ov.; ventis
tradere rem, *to consign to oblivion*, Hor.;
ferre videre sua gaudia ventos, Verg.

TRANSF., *the wind* as a sign of good or ill
success, popular favour, etc.: venti secundi,
Cic.; disturbance: omnes rumorum et
contionum ventos conligere, *rumours*, Cic.;
quicumque venti erunt, *whichever way the
wind blows*, Cic.; ventum popularem esse
quaesitum, Cic.; Hor., etc.

vĕnūcŭla (vennuncŭla) -ae, f. *a kind of
grape*: Hor.

vēnum and vēnō, acc. and dat. as from *venus,
n. *for sale*: venum or veno dare, Sall., Liv.,
Tac.; venum ire, *to be sold*, Sen.

venumdo (vēnundo) -dăre -dĕdi -dătum
(venum/do), *to offer for sale, to sell*; esp., of
captives: Tac., etc.

vĕnŭs -ĕris, f. *charm, loveliness, attractiveness.*

LIT., amoenitates omnium venerum atque
venustatum, Pl.; fabula nullius veneris,
Hor.

TRANSF., (1) as proper name, **Vĕnŭs**, *the
goddess of love, wife of Vulcan, mother of
Cupid*: Aeneadum genetrix hominum divumque voluptas alma Venus, Lucr.; Veneris
puer, *Cupid*, Ov.; Veneris filius, *Cupid*, Ov.,
or *Aeneas* (son of Anchises and Venus), Ov.;
mensis Veneris, *April*, Ov.; Verg., etc.
(2) *sexual love*: Verg., Liv., etc. (3) *a loved
one*: Lucr., Verg., Hor. (4) *the planet Venus*:
Cic. (5) *the Venus throw, the highest throw
of the dice*: Prop.

¶ Hence adj. **Vĕnĕrĕus (Vĕnĕrĭus)** -a
-um, *of Venus, relating to Venus*: Venerii servi,
and simply Venerii, *the slaves in the temple
of the Erycinian Venus*, Cic.; also *of sexual
love*: res Venereae, Cic.

Vĕnŭsia -ae, f. *an old town on the borders of
Lucania and Apulia* (now *Venosa*).

¶ Hence adj. **Vĕnŭsīnus** -a -um, *Venusine*,
esp. with reference to Horace, born at
Venusia.

vĕnustās -ātis, f. (venus), *loveliness, beauty,
charm, attractiveness*, Cic. TRANSF., of style, manner, etc.:
homo adfluens omni venustate, Cic., Pl.

vĕnustŭlus -a -um (dim. of venustus),
charming: Pl.

vĕnustus -a -um (venus), *charming, lovely,
graceful.* LIT., physically: gestus et motus
corporis, Cic.; Sirmio, Cat. TRANSF., of
style, manner, etc.: sermo, sententiae, Cic.;
Quint.

¶ Hence adv. **vĕnustē**, *charmingly*: Plin.
L., etc.

vēpallĭdus -a -um, *very pale*: Hor.

veprēcŭla -ae, f. (dim. of vepres), *a thorn-
bush*: Cic.

veprēs -is, m. (f., Lucr.), gen. plur. **vepres** -um,
a thorn-bush, briar-bush: sepulcrum saep-
tum undique et vestitum vepribus et dumetis,
Liv.; Verg., etc.

vēr vēris, n. (cf. ἔαρ), *spring.*

LIT., primo vere, *in the beginning of spring*,
Liv.; cum ver esse coeperat, Cic.; Verg., etc.

TRANSF., (1) *the spring-time of life*: aetatis,
Ov.; Cat. (2) *that which is brought by spring*:
Mart.; esp. ver sacrum, *an offering of the
firstlings*: ver sacrum vovere, Liv.

vērātrum -i, n. *hellebore*: Lucr., Plin.

vērax -ācis (verus), *speaking the truth, truthful*:
oraculum, Cic.; compar.: Herodotum cur
veraciorem ducam Ennio, Cic.; with infin.:
vosque veraces cecinisse Parcae, Hor.

verbēna -ae, f. and, more often, plur. **verbēnae**
-ārum, *sacred boughs of olive, laurel*, etc.,
carried by the *Fetiales* and by certain priests:
Cic., Liv., etc.

verbēnātus -a -um (verbenae), *crowned with
sacred boughs*: Suet.

verber -ĕris, n.; sing. only in genit. and abl.;
plur. **verbĕra** -ĕrum, *a lash.*

(1) concr., *a whip, scourge*; sing.: verber
tortus, Verg.; ictus verberis, Ov.; plur.:
iubet verbera adferri, Liv. TRANSF., *thong of a
sling* or *other missile weapon*: Verg.

(2) *a blow, stroke*; *a thrashing, flogging,
whipping*: sing.: trementes verbere ripae,
Hor.; plur.: castigare aliquem verberibus,
Cic.; verberibus lacerari, Liv. TRANSF.,
patruae verbera linguae, Hor.; contumeliarum
verbera, Cic.

verbĕrābĭlis -e (verbero), *deserving to be
flogged*; superl.: Pl.

verbĕrĕus -a -um (verber), *deserving to be
flogged*: Pl.

¹**verbĕro** -are (verber), *to beat, strike, flog,
thrash, scourge.*

LIT., aliquem pulsare et verberare, Cic.;
alicuius oculos virgis, Cic.; aethera alis,
Verg.; Mutinam tormentis, *to fire upon*, Cic.;
vineae grandine verberatae, *beaten down*,
Hor.

TRANSF., with words, *to attack, assail*:
orator istos verberabit, Cic.; Pl., Tac.

²**verbĕro** -ōnis, m. (verber), *one who deserves
a flogging, a rascal*: Pl., Ter., Cic. L.

verbōsus -a -um (verbum), *copious, diffuse,
wordy*: simulatio, Cic.; compar.: epistula
verbosior, Cic. L.

¶ Hence adv. **verbōsē**, *diffusely, verbosely*:
satis verbose, Cic.; compar.: haec ad te
scripsi verbosius, Cic. L.

verbum -i, n. (connected with εἴρω), *a word.*

In gen.: verbum nunquam in publico
facere, *never to speak in public*, Cic.; videtis
hoc uno verbo unde significari res duas, et
ex quo et a quo loco, Cic.; verbum voluptatis,
Cic.; ille dies nefastus erit, per quem tria
verba silentur, *when the praetor does not use
the formula*, Do, Dico, Addico, i.e., *does not
administer justice*, Ov.

In certain phrases: uno verbo, *in a word,
briefly*: ut uno verbo complectar, diligentia,
Cic.; ad verbum, e verbo, de verbo, pro

Vercellae

verbo, *word for word, literally, accurately*: fabellae Latinae ad verbum de Graecis expressae, Cic.; reddere verbum pro verbo, Cic.; verbi causā, *or* gratiā, *for example*: si quis, verbi causā, oriente Canicula ortus est, Cic.; meis (tuis, suis), verbis *in my*, etc., *name*: si uxori tuae meis verbis eris gratulatus, Cic. L.

Esp., (**1**) *mere words, mere talk* (opp. *reality*): existimatio, decus, infamia, verba sunt atque ineptiae, Cic.; in quibus (civitatibus) verbo sunt liberi omnes, *nominally*, Cic.; verba dare alicui, *to cheat, cozen, deceive*, Ter., Cic. L., Ov. (**2**) *an expression, saying*: quod verbum in pectus Iugurthae altius, quam quisquam ratus erat, descendit, Sall.; Pl., Ter. (**3**) *as grammat. t. t., a verb*: ut sententiae verbis finiantur, Cic.

Vercellae -ārum, f. pl. *a town in Gallia Cisalpina* (now *Vercelli*).

Vercingĕtŏrix -rīgis, m. *a Gallic chief in the time of Julius Caesar*.

vercŭlum -i, n. (dim. of ver), *little spring*, used as a term of endearment: Pl.

vērē, adv. from verus; q.v.

vĕrēcundĭa -ae, f. (verecundus), *modesty, feeling of shame, diffidence, bashfulness, shyness*: meam stultam verecundiam! Cic.; harum rerum commemoratione verecundia saepe impedivit utriusque nostrum, Cic.; with objective genit., *respect for, scruple about*: negandi, Cic.; deorum, Liv.; in dat., verecundiae est, with infin., *one is ashamed, one hesitates*: privati dictatorem poscere reum verecundiae non fuit, Liv.

vĕrēcundor -ari, dep. (verecundus), *to be bashful, ashamed, shy*: Pl., Cic.; with infin.: in publicum prodire, Cic.

vĕrēcundus -a -um (vereor), *bashful, modest, shy, diffident*; of persons: homo non nimis verecundus, Cic.; nec in faciendis verbis audax et in transferendis verecundus et parcus, Cic.; of things: vultus, Ov.; color, *a blush*, Hor.; oratio, Cic.; compar.: Cic.

¶ Hence adv. (with compar.) **vĕrēcundē**, *modestly, shyly, bashfully*: tum ille timide vel potius verecunde inquit, Cic.; Liv.

vĕrēdus -i, m. *a swift horse, hunter*: Mart.

vĕrēor -ēri -ĭtus sum, dep.

(**1**) *to be afraid or anxious, to fear*; with acc.: periculum, hostem, Caes.; bella Gallica, Cic.; Hor.; etc.; with dat., *or* de and abl., *to fear for*: Caes., Cic.; with infin.: quos interficere vereretur, Cic.; Caes., Hor., etc.; with ne (*that*), *or* ut, *or* ne non (*that not*): vereor ne turpe sit timere, Cic.; et tamen veremur ut hoc natura patiatur, Cic.; Hor., etc.

(**2**) *to have respect for, to revere*; with acc.: metuebant eum servi, verebantur liberi, Cic.; quem et amabat ut fratrem et ut maiorem fratrem verebatur, Cic.; Pl., Liv.

¶ Hence gerundive **vĕrendus** -a -um, as adj., *venerable, reverend*: maiestas, Ov.; patres, Ov.

Vergĭlĭus (Virgĭlĭus) -i, m., P. Vergilius Maro (70–19 B.C.), *the Roman poet; author of the Aeneid, the Georgics, and the Eclogues*.

Vergĭnĭus -a -um, *the name of a Roman gens*; esp. *of Verginia, the daughter of the centurion L. Verginius, who killed her in the market-place, to save her from the designs of the decemvir Appius Claudius*.

Verona

vergo vergĕre versi (connected with verto), *to turn*.

Intransit., *to bend, to be inclined*. LIT., omnibus eius (terrae) partibus in medium vergentibus, Cic.; Liv. TRANSF., *to be inclined, to verge*: nisi Bruti auxilium ad Italiam vergere quam ad Asiam maluissemus, Cic.; of time, *to draw to an end*: vergente auctumno, Tac.

Transit., *to bend, turn, incline*: Lucr., Ov.; pass. as middle: vergi, *to incline*, Lucr.

vergobrĕtus -i, m. *title of the highest magistrate of the Aedui*: Caes.

vērīdĭcus -a -um (verus/dico). (**1**) *truth-speaking, truthful*: vox, Cic.; veridica interpres deum, Liv. (**2**) *truly spoken, true*: Plin.

vērīlŏquĭum -i, n. (verus/loquor), a translation of ἐτυμολογία; *etymology*: Cic.

vērīsĭmĭlis -e (from verus (q.v.)/similis (q.v.)), *probable, likely*: Cic.

vērīsĭmĭlĭtūdo -ĭnis, f. (verisimilis), *probability*: Cic.

vērĭtās -ātis, f. (verus), *truth*.

LIT., (**1**) objectively, *the truth, the actual state or nature of things, reality*: veritatem patefacere, Cic.; in omni re vincit imitationem veritas, Cic.; imitari veritatem (of works of art), *to be true to nature*, Cic.; ex veritate, Sall. (**2**) subjectively, *truthfulness, the telling of the truth*: obsequium amicos, veritas odium parit, Ter.

TRANSF., in gen., *honesty*: in tuam fidem, veritatem confugit, Cic.; Ter.

vērĭverbĭum -i, n. (verus/verbum), *truthfulness*: Pl.

vermĕn -ĭnis, n. (verto), *a griping pain*: Lucr.

vermĭcŭlor -ari, dep. (vermiculus), *to be full of worms, to be worm-eaten*: Plin.

¶ Hence partic. **vermĭcŭlātus** -a -um, *vermiculated*: pavimentum, *inlaid so as to resemble worm-tracks*, Plin.

vermĭcŭlus -i, m. (dim. of vermis), *a little worm, grub*: Lucr., Plin.

vermis -is, m. (verto), *a worm*: Lucr., Plin.

verna -ae, c. *a slave born in the master's house.* LIT., Pl., Hor. TRANSF., *a native*: Mart.

vernācŭlus -a -um (verna), *of a slave born in the house*: Tac.; m. as subst. **vernācŭlus** -i, *a jester, buffoon*: Suet.

TRANSF., *native, domestic*: consilium, Pl.; crimen domesticum et vernaculum, Cic.

vernīlis -e (verna). (**1**) *slavish, mean, abject*: blanditiae, Tac. (**2**) *pert, froward*: verbum, Tac.

¶ Hence adv. **vernīlĭtĕr**, *like a slave*: fungi officiis, Hor.

vernīlĭtās -ātis, f. (vernilis). (**1**) *mean servility*: Sen. (**2**) *pertness*: Pl., Quint.

verno -are (ver), *to be spring-like, flourish, grow green*. LIT., vernat humus, Ov.; avis, Ov. TRANSF., dum vernat sanguis, *is lively*, Prop.

vernŭla -ae, c. (dim. of verna). (**1**) *a little slave born in the house*: Juv., etc. TRANSF., *native, indigenous*: Tac., Mart.

vernus -a -um (ver), *of spring, spring-like, vernal*: aequinoctium, Liv.; flores, Hor.; tempus, Cic., Lucr.

vērō, adv. from verus; q.v.

Vērōna -ae, f. *a town of northern Italy, birth-place of Catullus*.

¶ Hence adj. **Vērōnensis** -e, *of Verona*;

[636]

m. pl. as subst. **Vērōnenses** -ium, *the inhabitants of Verona.*
verpa -ae, f. *the penis*: Cat., Mart.
verpus -i, m. (verpa), *a circumcised man*: Cat., Juv.
¹verrēs -is, m. *a boar*: Hor. TRANSF., of a man: Pl.
²Verrēs -is, m., C. Cornelius, *praetor in Sicily, prosecuted by Cicero on charges of extortion, etc.*
¶ Hence adj. **Verrĭus** and **Verrīnus** -a -um, *of Verres*: ius (with a pun on ¹verres and on the double meaning of ius), Cic.
¹verrīnus -a -um (¹verres), *of a boar*: Plin.
²Verrīnus, see ²Verres.
verro verrĕre verri versum, *to drag, trail, sweep, pull*: versā pulvis inscribitur hastā, Verg.; maria ac terras ferre secum et verrere per auras, Verg.; on the threshing-floor, *to sweep together, collect together*: quidquid de Libycis verritur areis, Hor. Esp. *to sweep a place so as to clean it, to brush, scour*: aedes, Pl.; crinibus templa, Liv.; verrit humum pallā, Ov.; of animals swimming: aequora caudis, Verg.
verrūca -ae, f. *a wart*: Plin. TRANSF., *a small fault*: Hor.
verrunco -are (verto), *to turn out*, esp. as a relig. t. t., bene verruncare, *to turn out well, have a happy issue*: populo, Liv.
versābĭlis -e (verso), *movable, changeable*: Sen.
versābundus -a -um (verso), *whirling round, revolving*: turbo, Lucr.
versātĭlis -e (verso), *turning round, revolving.* LIT., templum caeli, Lucr.; Sen. TRANSF., *versatile*: ingenium, Liv.
versĭcŏlor -ōris (verto/color), *changing colour, of various colours, parti-coloured*: plumae, Cic.; vestimentum, Liv.; arma, Verg.
versĭcŭlus -i, m. (dim. of versus). (1) *a little line*: epistulae, Cic. L.; Hor. (2) disparagingly, *a poor little verse*: Cat., Verg.
versĭfĭcātĭo -ōnis, f. (versifico), *a making of verses, versification*: Quint.
versĭfĭcātor -ōris, m. (versifico), *a verse-maker, versifier*: Quint.
versĭfĭco -are (versus/facio), *to write verse, versify*: Quint.
versĭpellis (**vorsĭpellis** -e) (verto/pellis), *changing one's skin*; hence, *changing one's form.*
LIT., vorsipellem se facit (of Jupiter): Pl. TRANSF., *sly, subtle, crafty*: Pl.
verso (**vorso**) -are (freq. of verto), *to turn about often, turn hither and thither, twist round.*
LIT., massam forcipe, Verg.; lumina suprema, *cast a last look*, Ov.; manum, Ov.; levi teretem versare pollice fusum, Ov.; sortem urnā, *shake*, Hor.; exemplaria Graeca nocturnā versate manu, versate diurnā, *handle, study,* Hor. With reflex., and passive as middle, *to turn oneself round*: se in utramque partem, non sedutum, sed etiam corpore, Cic.; qui (orbes) versantur retro, Cic.
TRANSF., (1) *to bend, turn, ply*: mentem ad omnem malitiam et fraudem, Cic.; fors omnia versat, Verg.; verba, *to twist*, Cic. (2) *to work upon, influence, agitate*: muliebrem animum in omnes partes, Liv.; Cic.; odiis domos, Verg. (3) *to turn over in the mind,*

meditate upon: in animis secum unamquamque rem, Liv.; Verg., etc.
Pass. in special middle sense, *to be about, to hover, resort, stay.* LIT., domi, Pl.; cum aliquo, Cic.; in fundo, Cic.; intra vallum, Caes. TRANSF., of abstract relations: in malis, Ter.; alicui ante oculos dies noctesque, Cic. Esp., *to be engaged in, take part in, be employed in*: in sordida arte, Cic.; of things: iura civilia quae iam pridem in nostra familia versantur, Cic.
versōrĭa (**vorsōrĭa**) -ae, f. (verto), *a turning round*: versoriam capere, *to change course, turn,* Pl.
versum = ¹versus; q.v.
versūra -ae, f. (verto), *a turning, rotating.* Hence (1) *the borrowing of money to pay a debt*: versuram (ab aliquo) facere, Cic.; versurā solvere, Ter. (2) any *loan*: Cic., Nep.
¹versus (**vorsus**) and **versum** (**vorsum**), adv. *towards, in that direction.* (1) after another adv.: sursum versus, *upwards*, Cic. (2) after a preposition phrase indicating direction: ad se vorsum, Sall.; ad oceanum versus, Caes.; in forum versus, Cic. (3) (in form versus), after an accusative indicating direction: Romam versus, Cic.; Caes.
²versus (**vorsus**) -a -um, partic. from verro; q.v.; or from verto; q.v.
³versus (**vorsus**) -ūs, m. (verto), *a turning.* Hence (1) *the turning of a plough*; hence, *a furrow*: Plin. (2) *a row, line*: in versum distulit ulmos, Verg.; Liv. (3) in writing, *a line*, esp. of poetry: versūs Graeci, Latini, Cic.; facere versum, Cic.; Caes., Liv., etc.; *a step in a dance*: Pl.
versūtĭa -ae, f. (versutus), *a wile, stratagem*: Liv.
versūtĭlŏquus -a -um (versutus/loquor), *slyly speaking*: poet. ap. Cic.
versūtus -a -um, adj. (with compar. and superl.) (verto), *dexterous, adroit*; in bad sense, *cunning, crafty, sly*: acutus atque versutus animus, Cic.; versutissimus Lysander, Cic., Pl., Ov.
¶ Hence adv. **versūtē**, *adroitly, cunningly*: Cic.
vertebra -ae, f. (verto), *a joint*, esp., *a joint of the back, vertebra*: Plin., Sen.
vertex (**vortex**) -ĭcis, m. (verto).
(1) *that which turns, a whirl.* LIT., **a**, of water, *an eddy*: Verg., Liv., etc.: **b**, of wind or flame, *a whirlwind, gust*: Lucr., Verg., Liv. TRANSF., amoris, Cat.
(2) *the crown of the head.* LIT., ab imis unguibus usque ad verticem summum, Cic.; hence, in gen., *the head*: Cat., Verg., Ov. TRANSF., *the summit* of anything; *elevation*: Aetnae, Cic.; a vertice, *from above*, Verg.; Lucr., etc. (3) *the pole* of the heavens: Verg.
vertĭcōsus (**vortĭcōsus**) -a -um (vertex), *eddying*: mare, Sall.; amnis, Liv.
vertīgo -ĭnis, f. (verto), *a turning round, whirling round, revolution.* LIT., adsidua caeli, Ov. TRANSF., *giddiness, vertigo*: vertigo quaedam simul oculorum animique, Liv.
verto (**vorto**) vertĕre verti versum, *to turn, turn round*; often with a reflex.: vertere se, or in passive with middle sense, or alone as an intransitive verb, *to turn oneself.*
LIT., (1) in gen.: lumina, Verg.; stilum, Hor.; equos ad moenia, Verg.; reflex.: verti

me a Minturnis Arpinum versus, Cic.; pass.:
vertitur interea caelum, Verg. (2) *to turn up*;
in agriculture: terram aratro, Verg.; in
rowing: freta lacertis, Verg.; in drinking:
cadum, Hor. (3) as milit. t. t.: hostes, equites,
etc., in fugam, *to put to flight, rout*, Liv.;
Philippis versa acies retro, *the defeat at
Philippi*, Hor.; terga vertere, *to flee*, Caes.,
Liv.; with reflex: se, Caes.; intransit.:
versuros omnes in fugam extemplo ratus,
Liv. (4) of situation; esp. perf. partic. versus
-a -um, *turned, lying towards*: Epirus in
septentrionem versa, Liv.

TRANSF., (1) in gen., *to turn*: in nos vertite
iras, Liv.; pater totus in Persea versus, *devoted to*, Liv.; ex illa pecunia magnam
partem ad se, *to appropriate*, Cic.; intransit.:
verterat periculum in Romanos, Liv. (2) *to
interpret, construe, understand* in a certain
way, *to impute*: ne sibi vitio verterent, quod,
etc., Cic.; auspicia in bonum verterunt, Liv.
(3) *to alter, change*: natura cibos in corpora
viva, Lucr.; aliquid in lapidem, Ov.; terra
in aquam se vertit, Cic.; auster in Africum se,
Caes.; intransit.: fortuna iam verterat, Liv.;
middle: verso Marte, Liv. (4) *to translate*:
verterunt nostri poetae fabulas, Cic.; multa
de Graecis, Cic.; Platonem, Cic.; Pl., etc.
(5) *to change for another, exchange*: Pl., Hor.,
esp.: vertere solum, *to go into exile*, Cic.
(6) *to upset, to overthrow*: moenia ab imo,
Verg.; Callicratidas cum multa fecisset
egregie, vertit ad extremum omnia, *destroyed*,
Cic.; res Phrygias fundo, Verg. (7) pass. as
middle, of time: septima post Troiae
excidium iam vertitur aestas, *rolls round*,
Verg.; also act. intransit.: anno vertente, *in
the course of a year*, Cic. (8) pass. as middle,
to move in a certain sphere or *element, to
depend on, centre in*: in iure in quo causa illa
vertebatur paratissimus, Cic.; spes civitatis
in dictatore, Liv.

Vertumnus (Vortumnus) -i, m. (verto), *the
god of the changing year, and of all transactions
of sale*; near his statue the booksellers had
their shops.

vĕru -ūs, n. (1) *a spit*: Verg., Ov. (2) *a javelin*:
Verg., Tib.

vĕrŭīna -ae, f. (veru), *a small javelin*: Pl.

vērum, adv. from verus; q.v.

vērus -a -um, adj. (with compar. and superl.).

LIT., (1) objectively, *true, real, genuine*:
denarius, Cic.; timor, *well-grounded*, Cic.;
res verior, causa verissima, Cic.; Hor., etc.
(2) subjectively, *truthful, veracious*: vates, Ov.

TRANSF., *just, reasonable*: lex, Cic.; verum
est, with infin., or acc. and infin.: negat
verum esse adlici beneficio benevolentiam,
Cic.; Caes., etc.

¶ N. as subst. **vērum** -i. LIT., *the truth,
reality*: si rerum scire vis, Cic.; Pl., Hor.
Esp.: veri similis, *likely, probable*, Caes., Cic.,
Liv. TRANSF., *what is right, duty*: Hor., Sall.

¶ N. nom. as adv. **vērum**. LIT., *truly*:
Pl. TRANSF., *but, but yet, nevertheless, still*:
verum haec civitas isti praedoni ac piratae
Siciliensi Phaselis fuit, Cic.; non modo
(tantum, solum) . . . verum etiam, Cic.,
Hor., etc. Esp. (1) in passing to another
subject: verum praeterita omittamus, Cic.
(2) in breaking off a discourse: verum
quidem haec hactenus, Cic.; strengthened,

vēruntămen (vērumtămen), *but yet, notwithstanding, nevertheless*: consilium capit
primo stultum, verumtamen clemens, Cic.;
Pl.

¶ N. abl. as adv. **vērō**, *in truth, really,
indeed, in fact*.

LIT., ego vero cupio, te ad me venire,
I really wish, Cic. L. Often before affirmative
answers, *certainly, to be sure*: vero, mea
puella, Cic.; in negative answers: minime
vero, Cic.; Ter.

In addresses, invitations, demands: tu
vero me ascribe talem in numerum, *do
please*, Cic. In a climax, *even, indeed*: in
mediocribus vel studiis vel officiis, vel vero
etiam negotiis contemnendum, Cic.; Verg.
Sometimes ironically, *to be sure*: Cic., Verg.,
etc. In transitions in speech: nec vero tibi
de versibus respondebo, Cic.

TRANSF., as an adversative particle, *but
indeed, but in fact*; not first word in its clause:
illud vero plane non est ferendum, Cic.;
Caes., etc.

¶ Adv. (with compar. and superl.) **vērē**,
truly, really, rightly: nullum amans vere,
Cat.; verissime loqui, Cic.; Verg., Liv., etc.

vērūtum -i, n. (veru), *a javelin*: Caes., Liv.

vērūtus -a -um (veru), *armed with a javelin*:
Verg.

vervex -vēcis, m. *a wether*: Pl., Cic.; as a term
of abuse, *a sheep, dolt*: Pl., Juv.

vēsānĭa -ae, f. (vesanus), *madness, insanity*:
Hor.

vēsānĭens -entis (vesanus), *raging*: Cat.

vēsānus -a -um, *mad, insane*; of persons:
remex, Cic.; poeta, Hor.; of things, *furious,
wild*: fames, Verg.; impetus, Liv.

Vescĭa -ae, f. *a small town in Latium*.

¶ Hence adj. **Vescīnus** -a -um, *of Vescia*.

vescor -i, dep. (connected with esca), *to eat,
feed on*.

LIT., gen. with abl., rarely with acc.: dii
nec cibis nec potionibus vescuntur, Cic.;
lacte et ferinā carne, Sall.; humanis corporibus, Liv.; lauros, Tib.; absol.: vescentes sub
umbra, Liv.

TRANSF., *to use, enjoy*: vitalibus auris,
Lucr.; paratissimis voluptatibus, Cic.; aurā
aetheriā, *to breathe, live*, Verg.

vescus -a -um (connected with vescor).

(1) act., *consuming*: sal, Lucr.

(2) pass., *wasted, thin*: salicum frondes,
Verg.; farra, Ov.

vēsīca -ae, f. *the bladder*.

LIT., *the urinary bladder*: Cic., Hor.

TRANSF., (1) *anything made from a bladder*;
a purse, lantern, etc.: Ov., Mart., Varr. (2) of
style, *bombast, tumidity*: Mart.

vēsīcŭla -ae, f. (dim. of vesica), *a little
bladder*: Lucr., Cic.

Vĕsontĭo -ōnis, m. *a town in Gaul* (now
Besançon).

vespa -ae, f. *a wasp*: Varr., Plin.

Vespăsĭānus -i, m., T. Flavius Sabinus,
Roman emperor, A.D. 69–79.

vesper -ĕris or -ĕri, m. (cf. ἕσπερος), *evening*.

LIT., iam diei vesper erat, Sall.; primā
vesperis (sc. horā), Caes.; ante vesperum,
Cic.; sub vesperum, Caes.; primo vespere,
Caes., Cic. L.; abl. vespere and locat. vesperi,
in the evening, late: heri vesperi, Cic.; prov.:
quid vesper ferat, incertum est, Liv.; de

vesperi suo cenare, *to sup at one's own table*,
Pl.
   TRANSF., (**1**) *the west*: Verg., Ov. (**2**) *the
evening star*: Verg., Hor.

vespĕra -ae, f. (cf. ἑσπέρα), *evening*: ad vespe-
ram, *towards evening*, Cic.; primā vesperā,
Liv.; abl.: vesperā, *in the evening*, Plin.

vespĕrasco -ĕre (vespera), *to become evening*:
vesperascente iam die, *drawing towards
night*, Tac.

vespertĭlĭo -ōnis, m. (vesper), *a bat*: Plin.

vespertīnus -a -um (vesper), *of evening*. LIT.,
litterae, *received at evening*, Cic.; vespertinis
temporibus, Cic.; Hor. TRANSF., *western*:
regio, Hor.

vespĕrūgo -ĭnis, f. (vesper), *the evening star*:
Pl.

vespillo -ōnis, m. (vesper), *a corpse-bearer for
the poor, working at night*: Mart., Suet.

Vesta -ae, f. (connected with Ἑστία), *the
daughter of Saturn and Ops, goddess of the
hearth and domestic life*: ad Vestae (sc.
aedem), Hor.; a Vestae (sc. aede), Cic.
   ¶ Hence adj. **Vestālis** -e, *Vestal*: sacra,
the festival of Vesta, on the 9th of June, Ov.;
virgo Vestalis, and f. alone as subst. **Vestālis**
-is, *a Vestal virgin, one of the priestesses of
Vesta*, Cic., Liv., Ov.
   ¶ Hence again, adj. **Vestālis** -e, *of the
Vestal virgins*: oculi, *chaste*, Ov.

vester (voster) -tra -trum (vos), *your, yours*:
maiores vestri, Cic.; Pl., etc. Sometimes
objectively, *towards you, against you*: odio
vestro, Liv. M. as subst., *your master*: Pl.

vestībŭlum -i, n. *an entrance-court, court-yard*.
LIT., templi, Cic.; Verg., Ov., etc. TRANSF.,
(**1**) *any entrance to a place*: sepulcri, Cic.;
urbis, Liv.; in vestibulo Siciliae, Cic. (**2**) *a
beginning*: Cic.

vestĭgĭum -i, n. *a foot-step, track, foot-mark*.
LIT., vestigia in omnes ferentia partes,
Liv.; vestigium facere in foro, Cic.; vestigiis
aliquem sequi, Liv.; in suo vestigio mori,
to die in one's tracks, Liv.
   TRANSF., (**1**) *a trace, mark*: frons non
calamistri notata vestigiis, Cic.; in vestigiis
huius urbis, Cic.; fig.: vestigia sceleris,
avaritiae, Cic. (**2**) plur., *the foot*: Cic., Verg.
(**3**) abl., *with or without in or ex, at that
moment*: in illo vestigio temporis, Caes.;
repente e vestigio, Cic.

vestīgo -are (vestigium), *to track, trace*. LIT.,
feras, Sen. TRANSF., *to track down*: causas
rerum, Cic.; perfugas et fugitivos inquirendo,
Liv.

vestīmentum -i, n. (vestio), *clothing, a
garment*: Cic., Hor., etc.

Vestīni -ōrum, m. *a people of central Italy*.
   ¶ Hence adj. **Vestīnus** -a -um, *of the
Vestini*.

vestĭo -ire (vestis), *to dress, to clothe*.
   LIT., homines male vestiti, Cic.; animantes villis vestitae, Cic.; Verg. TRANSF.,
to cover, clothe, adorn: oculos membranis,
Cic.; campos lumine purpureo, Verg.; trabes
aggere, Caes.; se gramine, Verg.; fig.: inventa
oratione, Cic.

vestĭplĭca -ae, f. (vestis/plico), *a bedmaker,
laundress*: Pl.

vestis -is, f. (connected with ἐσθής), *a covering
or garment, clothing*.
   LIT., vestis lintea, Cic.; vestem mutare,

to put on other clothes, esp., *to put on mourning*, Liv., etc.
   TRANSF., (**1**) *a blanket, awning, carpet,
tapestry*: pretiosa vestis multa et lauta
supellex, Cic. (**2**) *the skin of a snake*: Lucr.
(**3**) *a spider's web*: Lucr.

vestispĭca -ae, f. (vestis/specio), *a mistress of
the robes, keeper of the wardrobe*: Pl.

vestītus -ūs, m. (vestio), *clothing, clothes, attire*.
   LIT., vestitus muliebris, Cic.; vestitum
mutare, *to go into mourning*, Cic.; ad suum
vestitum redire, *to go out of mourning*, Cic.
   TRANSF., *a covering*: riparum, Cic.; vestitus densissimi montium, Cic.; fig.: ea vestitu
illo orationis, quo consueverat, ornata non
erat, Cic.

Vĕsŭvĭus -i, m. *Vesuvius, the volcano in
Campania*.

vĕtĕrāmentārĭus -a -um (vetus), *of old things*:
sutor, *a cobbler*, Suet.

vĕtĕrānus -a -um (vetus), *old*: boves, Varr.;
hostis, Liv.; esp., of soldiers, *veteran*; plur.:
milites veterani; or m. alone as subst.:
veterani, *old soldiers, veterans*, Caes., Cic.,
Liv.; legio veterana, Cic.

vĕtĕrasco -ascĕre -āvi (vetus), *to grow old*:
Cic.

vĕtĕrātor -ōris, m. (vetus), *one who has grown
old in* or *become experienced in anything*: in
causis, Cic.; non sunt in disputando vafri,
non veteratores, non malitiosi, Cic. Absol.,
an old stager, old fox: Pl., Ter., Cic.

vĕtĕrātōrĭus -a -um (veterator), *cunning,
crafty*: Cic.
   ¶ Adv. **vĕtĕrātōrĭē**, *craftily*: dicere, Cic.

vĕtĕrīnus -a -um (perhaps contr. from
vehiterinus, from veho), *of draught*: bestia,
a beast of burden, Cato; equi, Lucr. N. and
f. pl. as subst. **vĕtĕrīnae** -ārum and
vĕtĕrīna -ōrum, *draught-animals*: Varr.,
Plin.

vĕternōsus -a -um, adj. (with superl). (veternus), *lethargic*: Cato, Plin. TRANSF., (**1**)
sleepy, dreamy: Ter. (**2**) *dull, without
energy*: animus, Sen.

vĕternus -i, m. (vetus), *age*; hence (**1**)
lethargy, sleepiness: Pl. (**2**) *inactivity, sloth*:
Verg., Hor.

vĕto (vŏto: Pl.) vĕtare vĕtŭi vĕtĭtum, *to
forbid, prohibit*.
   In gen.: vetant leges Iovis, Hor.; with acc.
and infin.: lex peregrinum vetat in murum
ascendere, Cic.; Verg., etc.; with infin.
alone: lex vetat delinquere, Cic.; with ut *or*
ne and the subj., or with subj. alone: edicto
vetuit ne quis se praeter Apellem pingeret,
Hor.; with acc. of the action prevented:
bella, Verg.; with person or action as subject
of the passive: vetitae legibus aleae, Hor.;
quippe vetor fatis, Verg. Esp., veto, *I forbid*,
spoken by interceding tribunes or other
magistrates, or by augurs.
   ¶ Hence n. of perf. partic. as subst.
vĕtĭtum -i. (**1**) *that which is forbidden*:
nitimur in vetitum semper cupimusque
negata, Ov. (**2**) *a prohibition*: quae contra
vetitum discordia? Verg.; iussa ac vetita, Cic.

vĕtŭlus -a -um (dim. of vetus), *little old, poor
little old*: equus, Cic.; filia, Cic.; Hor., etc.
M. as subst. **vĕtŭlus** -i, *an old man*: mi
vetule, *'old boy'*, Cic.; f. as subst. **vĕtŭla** -ae,
an old woman: Juv.

vĕtus -ĕris; abl. sing. usually -ĕre; superl. vĕterrĭmus -a -um (connected with ἔτος), *old, ancient, of long standing* (not new or young): senex, Pl.; navis, Caes.; amicus, amicitia, Cic.; with genit., *grown grey in, experienced in*: operis ac laboris, Tac.

¶ M. pl. as subst. **vĕtĕres** -um, *the ancients*: Ter., Cic. F. pl. **vĕtĕres** -um (sc. tabernae), *the old shops on the south side of the Roman Forum.* N. pl. **vĕtĕra** -um, *the remote past, antiquity*: illa vetera omittere, Cic.; Pl., etc.

vĕtustās -ātis, f. (vetustus). (1) *age*: vetustas possessionis, Cic.; verborum vetustas prisca, Cic.; aevi, Verg. (2) *antiquity, past time*: historia nuntia vetustatis, Cic.; Caes., Liv. (3) *long duration, length of time,* including future time: habitura vetustatem, *likely to last*, Cic.; de me nulla umquam obmutescet vetustas, *remote posterity*, Cic.; Lucr., Verg.

vĕtustus -a -um, adj. (with compar. and superl.) (vetus), *old, ancient.* In gen.: vinum, Pl.; hospitium, *of long standing*, Cic.; vetustissimus ex censoribus, Liv.; Verg., etc. Esp., *old-fashioned, antiquated*: vetustior et horridior ille, Cic.

vexāmen -inis, n. (vexo), *a shaking, upheaval*: mundi, Lucr.

vexātĭo -ōnis, f. (vexo), *a shaking, jolting, shock.* LIT., corporis, Cic.; Liv. TRANSF., *ill-treatment*: sociorum, Cic.; Liv.

vexātor -ōris, m. (vexo), *one who hustles, harasses, disturbs*: direptor et vexator urbis, Cic.

vexillārĭus -i, m. (vexillum). (1) *a standard-bearer*: Liv., Tac. (2) in plur. **vexillārĭi** -ōrum, under the empire, *veterans who had served sixteen years and were finishing their service in special battalions; a reserve corps*: Tac.

vexillātĭo -ōnis, f. (vexillum), *a detachment, corps*: Suet.

vexillum -i, n. (dim. of velum), *a standard, a flag.*

LIT., vexillum tollere, Cic.; esp., *the red flag displayed on the general's tent as the signal for battle*: vexillum proponere, Caes.

TRANSF., *the men who fought under one flag, a company, troop*; esp. of *detachments* on special service, of *reserves of veterans*, and of *auxiliary cavalry*: Liv., Tac.

vexo -are (freq. of veho), *to shake, toss, jostle.* LIT., venti vexant nubila, Ov.; rates, Verg.; Cic., Lucr., etc. TRANSF., *to harass, disquiet, molest, annoy*: agros, Caes.; hostes, Cic.; vexari difficultate viae, Liv.; sollicitudo vexat impios, Cic.

vĭa -ae, f. (old Lat., vea) (connected with veho), *a way.*

LIT., *a highway, road, street*: militaris, Liv.; strata viarum, Lucr., Verg.; declinare de via ad dexteram, Cic.; dare alicui viam per fundum, *to allow a passage through*, Cic. TRANSF., (1) concr., any *passage; the gullet*: Cic.; *the wind-pipe*: Ov.; *a cleft*: Verg.; *a stripe on clothing*: Tib. (2) abstr., *a course, march, journey*: de via languere, Cic.; unam tibi viam et perpetuam esse vellent, *wished that you should never return*, Cic.; viam flectere, Verg.; Ov., etc. (3) abstr., *means, way, method*: viam optimarum artium tradere, Cic.; ad gloriam, Cic.; per omnes

vias leti, Liv. Esp. *the right way*: viā dicere, *methodically, properly*: Cic.

vĭālis -e (via), *of the roads*: Lares, Pl.

vĭārĭus -a -um (via), *of roads*: lex, *for repairing roads*, ap. Cic. L.

vĭātĭcātus -a -um (viaticum), *provided with money for a journey*: Pl.

vĭātĭcus -a -um (via), *relating to a journey*: cena, *a farewell supper*, Pl. N. as subst. **vĭātĭcum** -i, *money for a journey*: viaticum congerere, Cic.; Pl., etc. TRANSF., *soldiers' savings*: Hor., Tac.; *prize-money of a soldier*: Hor.

vĭātor -ōris, m. (via). (1) *a traveller, wayfarer*: Cic., Verg., etc. (2) *an apparitor, a messenger attached to a magistrate's service*: Cic., Liv.

vībix -īcis, f. *a weal, mark of a blow*: Pl.

vibro -are.

(1) transit., *to cause to vibrate, move rapidly to and fro, brandish, shake*: vibrabant flamina vestes, Ov.; esp. of *weapons*: Cic.; poet., *to brandish and hurl* a weapon: spicula per auras, Ov.; fig.: truces iambos, Cat.; of hair, *to curl, frizzle*: crines vibrati, Verg.

(2) intransit., *to shake, tremble, quiver, vibrate*: tres vibrant linguae, Ov.; vibrat mare, *shimmers*, Cic.; gladius, Verg.; fig., of discourse: oratio incitata et vibrans, Cic.

vīburnum -i, n. *the wayfaring-tree*: Verg.

vīcānus -a -um (vicus), *dwelling in a village*: vicani haruspices, Enn.; Cic. M. pl. as subst. **vīcāni** -ōrum, *villagers*: Liv.

vĭcārĭus -a -um (vicis), *taking the place of a person* or *thing, substituted, vicarious*: operae nostrae vicaria fides amicorum supponitur, Cic.

M. as subst. **vĭcārĭus** -i, *one who takes another's place, a substitute*: Cic., Hor., Liv.; esp. *an under-servant, under-slave*: Cic., Hor.

vīcātim, adv. (vicus). (1) *from street to street*: servorum omnium vicatim celebratur totā urbe descriptio, Cic. (2) *in villages*: in montibus vicatim habitare, Liv.

vĭcĕ, vicem, see vicis.

vīcēnārĭus -a -um (viceni), *containing the number twenty*: Pl.

vīcēni -ae -a (viginti), *twenty at a time* or *twenty each*: Caes., Liv.

vĭces, see vicis.

vīcēsĭma, see vicesimus.

vīcēsĭmāni -ōrum, m. (vicesimus), *soldiers of the twentieth legion*: Tac.

vīcēsĭmārĭus -a -um (vicesimus), *relating to the* vicesima; q.v.: Liv.

vīcēsĭmus (**vīcensĭmus**) -a -um (viginti), *the twentieth*: dies vicesimus, Cic.; Pl., etc.

¶ F. as subst. **vīcēsĭma** (**vīcensĭma**) -ae, *the twentieth*, esp. (sc. pars), *the twentieth part as a toll* or *tax*: portorii, *export duty*, Cic.; also *a tax of five per cent on the value of manumitted slaves*: Cic. L., Liv.

vĭcĭa -ae, f. *a vetch*: Verg., Ov., etc.

vīcĭēs (**vīcĭens**), adv. (viginti), *twenty times*: Caes., Cic.; HS. vicies, 2,000,000 sesterces, Cic. L.

vīcīnālis -e (vicinus), *neighbouring, near*: ad vicinalem usum, *after the manner of neighbours*, Liv.

vīcīnĭa -ae, f. (vicinus), *neighbourhood, nearness, vicinity.*

LIT., in nostra vicinia, Cic.; Pl., Ter., Verg.

TRANSF., (1) *the neighbours*: Hispala ex

Aventino libertina non ignota viciniae, Liv.; funus laudet vicinia, Hor. (2) *likeness, similarity, affinity*: Quint.

vīcīnĭtās -ātis, f. (vicinus), *neighbourhood, vicinity, nearness.*

LIT., in ea vicinitate, Cic.; plur., *neighbourly connexions*: Cic.

TRANSF., (1) *the neighbours*: signum quod erat notum vicinitati, Cic. (2) *likeness, affinity*: Quint.

vīcīnus -a -um (vicus), *near, neighbouring.*

LIT., bellum, Liv.; with dat.: sedes vicina astris, Verg.; Thessalia quae est vicina Macedoniae, Liv. As subst., m. **vīcīnus** -i, and f. **vīcīna** -ae, *a neighbour*: vicini mei, Cic.; Verg., etc.; n. **vīcīnum** -i, *the neighbourhood, vicinity*: Plin.; plur.: sonitu plus quam vicina fatigat, Ov.

TRANSF., *similar, like*; with dat.: dialecticorum scientia vicina et finitima eloquentiae, Cic.; Liv.

vĭcis (genit.; nom. not found); acc. **vĭcem**, abl. **vĭcĕ**; plur., **vices, vĭcĭbus**, *change, interchange, alternation, vicissitude.*

LIT., in gen.: hāc vice sermonum, *interchange of discourse*, Verg.; vice humanarum fortunarum, Liv.; solvitur acris hiems gratā vice veris et Favoni, Hor. In adverbial phrases: per vices, *alternately*: clamare, Ov.; in vicem (invicem) and in vices, *alternately, reciprocally, by turns*: simul eramus invicem, Cic.; hi rursus in vicem anno post in armis sunt, Caes.; Verg., etc. Esp. (1) *requital, recompense, compensation, retaliation*: recito vicem officii praesentis, Cic.; redde vicem meritis, Ov.; Tac. (2) *the vicissitude of fate, fortune, lot, destiny*: tacite gementes tristem fortunae vicem, Phaedr.; convertere humanam vicem, Hor.; Cic., Liv.

TRANSF., *one's place, office, post, duty*: nulla est enim persona, quae ad vicem eius, qui e vita emigrarit, propius accedat, Cic.; fungar vice cotis, Hor.; vestramque meamque vicem explete, Tac. Adverbially, vicem, vice, in vicem, ad vicem, *in place of, instead of, like, as*: in qua re tuam vicem saepe doleo, *for you*, Cic. L.; Sardanapali vicem in suo lectulo mori, *like Sardanapalus*, Cic. L.; defatigatis invicem integri succedunt, Caes.

vĭcissātim=vicissim; q.v.: Pl.

vĭcissim, adv. (vicis), *in turn*: terra florere, deinde vicissim horrere potest, Cic.; considera nunc vicissim tuum factum, Cic.; Verg., etc.

vĭcissĭtūdo -inis, f. (vicis), *change, alteration, vicissitude*: imperitandi, Liv.; omnium rerum, Ter.; plur.: fortunae, Cic. L.

victĭma -ae, f. *an animal offered in sacrifice, a victim.* LIT., Caes., Verg., etc. TRANSF., se victimam reipublicae praebuisset (Decius), Cic.; victima nil miserantis Orci, Hor.

victĭmārĭus -i, m. (victima), *an assistant at a sacrifice*: Liv.

victĭto -are (freq. of vivo), *to live upon, feed upon*: ficis, Pl.; Ter.

victor -ōris, m. (vinco), *a conqueror, victor.*

LIT., absol.: parere victori, Liv.; in apposition, *as a conqueror, victorious*: victores Sequani, Caes.; victor exercitus, Cic.; victor currus, Ov.; with genit.: omnium gentium, Cic.; victor trium simul bellorum, Liv.; with abl.: bello civili victor, Cic.; Tac.

TRANSF., animus libidinis et divitiarum victor, Sall.

victōrĭa -ae, f. (victor), *victory, conquest.*

LIT., in war: victoriam reportare, Cic.; adipisci, Caes.; victoria Cannensis, Liv.; clarissima, Cic.; with de: victoria de Veientibus, Liv.; dare alicui victoriam, Liv.

TRANSF., in politics, law, etc.: Cic., Liv.

Personif.: Victoria, *goddess of Victory*, Pl., Cic., Ov.

victōrĭātus -i, m. (sc. nummus) (Victoria), *a silver coin stamped with a figure of Victory, worth half a denarius*: Cic., Liv.

victōrĭŏla -ae, f. (dim. of Victoria), *a small statue of Victory*: Cic.

victrix -trīcis, f. (vinco), *she that conquers*; in apposition, like adj., *victorious, conquering.*

LIT., Athenae, Cic.; litterae, *bringing news of victory*, Cic. L. TRANSF., mater victrix filiae, non libidinis, Cic.

victus -ūs, m. (vivo), *living.* Hence (1) *manner of life, way of living*: Persarum, Cic.; in omni vita atque victu excultus, Cic.; Caes., Hor. (2) *support, nourishment, food*: victum cotidianum in Prytaneo publice praebere, Cic.; plur.: persequi animantium ortus, victus, figuras, Cic.; Ov., etc.

vīcŭlus -i, m. (dim. of vicus), *a little village, a hamlet*: Cic., Liv.

vīcus -i, m. (connected with οἶκος).

(1) *a quarter* or *district of a town*, or *a street*: nullum in urbe vicum esse, Cic.; vicos plateasque inaedificat, Caes.; Liv., etc.

(2) *a village, hamlet*: Cic., Caes.

(3) *an estate, country-seat*: scribis te vicum venditurum, Cic. L., Hor.

vĭdēlĭcĕt, adv. (videre licet, *one can see*).

LIT., (1) *it is clear*; with acc. and infin.: Pl., Lucr. (2) as adv. *clearly, plainly, manifestly*: quae videlicet ille non ex agri consiturā, sed ex doctrinae indiciis interpretabatur, Cic. Often ironically, *forsooth, of course, to be sure*: homo videlicet timidus et permodestus (of Catiline), Cic.; Sall., etc.

TRANSF., *namely*: caste iubet lex adire ad deos, animo videlicet, Cic.

vĭdēn'=videsne? *see* video.

vĭdĕo vĭdēre vīdi vīsum (cf. εἶδον), *to see.*

(1) in gen. LIT., *to see with the eyes*: quam longe videmus? Cic.; aliquid, aliquem, Pl., Cic., etc.; with acc. and infin.: cum suos interfici viderent, Caes.; with ut and subj. (or indic.): vides ut alta stet nive candidum Soracte, Hor.; diem videre, *to live to see*, Cic. Sometimes of special intent, *to look at*: vide me, Pl.; Cic.; also *to go to see* a person: Cic. L.

TRANSF., not with the eyes: **a**, *to perceive* by other senses: mugire videbis sub pedibus terram, Verg.; Hor., etc.: **b**, with the mind, *to perceive, notice, observe, see*: aliquid in somnis, Cic.; plus in republica videre, *to have more political sense*, Cic. Sometimes of special intent, *to look into* a matter, *see to, see about, provide for*: alicui prandium, Cic. L.; with indir. quest.: videas si considere quid agas, Cic.; with ut *or* ne and the subj., *to see to it that*: videant consules ne quid respublica detrimenti capiat, Cic.

(2) special senses of passive (other than *to be seen*, simply): **a**, *to seem, appear, be thought*: ut imbelles timidique videamur,

Cic.; with infin.: ut beate vixisse videar, Cic.; ut exstinctae potius amicitiae quam oppressae esse videantur, Cic.; Verg., etc.; esp. in cautious expressions in official statements: maiores nostri voluerunt, quae iurati iudices cognovissent, ea non ut esse facta, set ut videri pronuntiarent, Cic.: **b**, with acc. and infin., *it appears*: non mihi videtur, ad beate vivendum satis posse virtutem, Cic.: **c**, videtur (alicui), *it seems good, seems right*: ubi visum est, Caes.; eam quoque, si videtur, correctionem explicabo, Cic.

¶ N. of perf. partic. as subst. **vīsum** -i, *a sight, appearance, vision*: visa somniorum, Cic.; Prop., Ov.

vĭdŭĭtās -ātis, f. (vĭduus), *want*: omnium copiarum, Pl. Esp. *widowhood*: Cic.

vĭdŭlus -i, m. (vieo), *a leather trunk*: Pl.

vĭdŭo -are (viduus), *to deprive of*; with abl. or genit.: urbem civibus, Verg.; arva numquam viduata pruinis, Verg.; Lucr. F. of perf. partic. **vĭdŭāta** -ae, *widowed*: Tac.

vĭdŭus -a -um, *deprived, bereaved, destitute*.
In gen., with genit. or abl. or a with abl.: pectus viduum amoris, Ov.; lacūs vidui a lumine Phoebi, Verg.; Hor.; *deprived of husband* or *wife, widowed*: Pl., Ov. Hence, f. as subst. **vidua** -ae. (1) *a widow*: Pl., Cic., Hor. (2) *an unmarried woman*: se rectius viduam et illum caelibem futurum fuisse, Liv.; Ov. TRANSF., of trees to which no vine is trained, or of unsupported vines: Cat., Hor.

Vĭenna -ae, f. *a town in Gallia Narbonensis. on the Rhône* (now *Vienne*).

vĭĕo -ēre, *to weave together*: Varr.
¶ Hence partic. **vĭētus** -a -um, *shrivelled, shrunken, withered*: senex, Ter.; Cic., etc.

vĭētor -ōris, m. (vieo), *a cooper*: Pl.

vĭgĕo -ēre, *to be vigorous, thrive, flourish*: animus in rerum cognitione viget, Cic.; viget memoria, Cic.; vigent studia rei militaris, Cic.; quem (Philonem) in Academia maxime vigere audio, Cic.; Lucr., Hor., Liv.

vĭgesco -ĕre (vigeo), *to become vigorous, begin to thrive*: Lucr., Cat., Tac.

vĭgēsĭmus=vicesimus; q.v.

vĭgil -ĭlis, *wakeful, watchful*.
LIT., canes, Hor.; ales, *the cock*, Ov. M. as subst., *a watchman*: Liv.; plur.: vigiles fanique custodes, Cic.
TRANSF., ignis, *ever-burning*, Verg.; cura, Ov.

vĭgĭlans -antis, partic. from vigilo; q.v.

vĭgĭlantĭa -ae, f. (vigilo), *watchfulness, vigilance*: Ter., Cic.

vĭgĭlax -ācis (vigilo), *watchful*: Subura, Prop.; curae, *disturbing*, Ov.

vĭgĭlĭa -ae, f. (vigil), *wakefulness, sleeplessness*.
LIT., patiens vigiliae, Sall.; plur.: Demosthenis vigiliae, Cic. Esp., *a watching for the security of a place, watch over a city, camp, etc.*: vigilias agere ad aedes sacras, Cic.; vestra tecta custodiis vigiliisque defendite, Cic.; Liv.
TRANSF., (1) *a watch, one of the four parts into which the Romans divided the night*: prima vigilia, Liv.; Caes. (2) *the watch, soldiers keeping watch, sentinels*: Caes., Liv.; esp. of the seven *cohortes vigilum*, serving as police, watchmen, and firemen: Tac. (3) *watchfulness, vigilance, care*: ut

vacuum metu populum Romanum nostrā vigiliā et prospicientiā redderemus, Cic.

vĭgĭlĭārĭum -i, n. (vigilia), *a watch-house*: Sen.

vĭgĭlo -are (vigil).
(1) act. and intransit., *to be awake, keep awake, watch*. LIT., ad multam noctem, Cic.; Hor., etc. TRANSF., of things: vigilantes curae, Cic.; lumina vigilantia, *the lights of a lighthouse*, Ov.; of persons, *to be vigilant, watchful, careful*: vigilabo pro vobis, Cic.; Hor.
(2) in pass., transit.: vigilata nox, *spent in watching*, Ov. So in gerundive, quae vigilanda viris, *to be watched over*, Verg.
¶ Hence partic. (with compar.) **vĭgĭlans** -antis, *watchful, vigilant*: oculi, Verg.; consul, Cic.; ut nemo vigilantior ad iudicium venisse videatur, Cic.
¶ Adv. (with compar. and superl.) **vĭgĭlantĕr**, *vigilantly*: se tueri, Cic.; enitar vigilantius, Cic.; vehementissime vigilantissimeque vexatus, Cic.

vĭgintĭ, indecl. num. adj. (connected with εἴκοσι), *twenty*: Cic., etc.

vĭgintĭvĭrātus -ūs, m. (vigintiviri), *the office of the* vigintiviri: Tac.

vĭgintĭvĭri -ōrum, m. pl. *a commission of twenty*; esp. *that appointed by Caesar for the division of lands in Campania*: Cic. L.

vĭgor -ōris, m. (vigeo), *vigour, force, energy*: aetatis, animi, Liv.; Verg., Hor.

vĭlĭco -are (vilicus), *to manage an estate as bailiff*: ut quasi dispensare rempublicam et in ea quodam modo vilicare possit, Cic.

vīlĭcus -a -um (villa), *of a country-seat*. As subst., m. **vīlĭcus** -i, *a bailiff, steward, overseer of an estate*: Cic., Hor., etc.; f. **vīlĭca** -ae, *a bailiff's wife*: Cat., Juv.

vīlis -e, adj. (with compar. and superl.), *cheap, worth little*.
LIT., servulus, Cic.; frumentum vilius, Cic.; res vilissimae, Cic.; Pl., etc.
TRANSF., in gen.: honor vilior fuisset, Cic.; pericula vilia habere, Sall.; Verg., etc.
¶ Adv. (with compar.) **vīlĭtĕr**, *cheaply*: Pl.

vīlĭtās -ātis, f. (vilis), *cheapness, low price*. LIT., annonae, Cic.; annus est in vilitate, *it is a cheap year*, Cic. TRANSF., *worthlessness, meanness*: Plin., Quint.

villa -ae, f. (perhaps connected with vicus), *a country-house, an estate, country seat, farm*. In gen.: qui ager neque villam habuit neque ex ulla parte fuit cultus, Cic.; Ter., Hor. Esp.: Villa Publica, *a public building in the Campus Martius, used for a census* or *levy, and to accommodate foreign ambassadors*, Cic. L., Liv.

villic-, see vilic-.

villōsus -a -um (villus), *shaggy, hairy*: leo, Verg., Ov.

villŭla -ae, f. (dim. of villa), *a small country-house, little farm*: Cic. L., Hor.

villum -i, n. (for vinulum, dim. of vinum), *a little sup of wine*: Ter.

villus -i, m. *shaggy hair*: animantium aliae villis vestitae, Cic.; tonsis villis, Verg.

vīmen -ĭnis, n. (vieo), *an osier, withe, twig*. LIT., scuta ex cortice facta aut viminibus intexti, Caes.; Verg., Ov. TRANSF., *a basket* or *vessel made of twigs*: Ov., Mart.

vīmentum=vimen; q.v.: Tac.

Vīmĭnālis collis, *one of the seven hills of Rome.*

vīmĭnĕus -a -um (vimen), *made of osiers, wicker*: tegumenta, Caes.; crates, Verg.

vin' = visne; *see* ¹volo.

vīnācĕus -a -um (vinum), *belonging to wine* or *a grape*: Cic. M. as subst. **vīnācĕus** -i, *a grape-stone*: Cato.

vīnālĭa -ium and -iorum, n. pl. (vinum), *the wine festivals, one held on the 23rd of April and the other on the 19th of August*: Ov.

vīnārĭus -a -um (vinum), *of* or *relating to wine*: vas, *a wine-cask*, Cic.; crimen, *relating to the duty on wine*, Cic. As subst., m. **vīnārĭus** -i, *a vintner*: Pl., Sall., Suet.; n. **vīnārĭum** -i, *a wine-jar, wine-flask*: Pl., Hor.

vincĭbĭlis -e (vinco), *that can be easily gained*: causa, Ter.

vincĭo vincire vinxi vinctum, *to bind, to tie round.*
    LIT., suras cothurno alte, Verg.; tempora floribus, Hor.; boves vincti cornua vittis, Ov.; esp., *to put in bonds, fetter*: manus laxe, Liv.; aliquem trinis catenis, Caes.; Pl., Cic.
    TRANSF., (1) *to surround, encompass*: loca praesidiis, Cic. L. (2) *to bind, restrain, confine, secure*: eius religioni te vinctum astrictumque dedamus, Cic.; si turpissime se illa pars animi geret, vinciatur, Cic.; membra orationis numeris, Cic.; linguas et ora, Ov.; somno vinctus, Liv., Ov., Tac.

vinco vincĕre vīci victum, *to conquer, overcome, defeat, subdue, vanquish.*
    LIT., (1) as milit. t. t.: ius esse belli ut qui vicissent iis quos vicissent quemadmodum vellent imperarent, Caes.; Pl., Cic., etc. (2) in any form of contest: iudicio (of the prosecutor), Cic.; at an auction: Othonem, *to outbid*, Cic.; in debate: vicit ea pars senatus, Sall.
    TRANSF., (1) in contests not between persons, *to master, get the mastery over*: non viribus ullis vincere posse ramum, Verg.; victus somno, Liv.; vincere noctem flammis (of lights), Verg.; multa saecula durando, *to outlast*, Verg.; aëra summum arboris iactu vincere, *to fly over*, Verg.; vincit ipsa rerum publicarum natura saepe rationem, Cic.; vinci a voluptate, Cic.; victus animi respexit, Verg. (2) *to surpass*: opinionem vicit omnium, Cic.; Hor. (3) *to prove successfully, win one's point*: vinco deinde bonum virum fuisse Oppianicum, Cic.

vincŭlum (vinclum) -i, n. (vincio), *a band, cord, chain.*
    LIT., in gen.: aptare vincula collo, Ov.; pennarum vincula, ceras, Ov., Cic.; Verg., etc. Esp. plur., vincula, *bonds, fetters*, and hence, meton., *imprisonment*: conicere aliquem in vincula, Caes.; rumpere alicuius vincula, Cic.; esse in vinculis et catenis, Liv.
    TRANSF., *any bond, fetter, chain*: ex corporum vinculis tamquam e carcere evolaverunt, Cic.; fidei, Liv.; vinculum ingens immodicae cupiditatis iniectum est, Liv.; vinculis propinquitatis coniunctus, Cic.; vinculum iugale, Verg.

Vindĕlĭci -ōrum, m. *a Germanic people, south of the Danube, with their capital at Augusta Vindelicorum* (now *Augsburg*).

vindēmĭa -ae, f. (vinum/demo), *the vintage.* LIT., Pl., Plin. L. TRANSF., *grapes, wine*: Verg.

vindēmĭātor -ōris, m. (vindemia), *a vintager,*

harvester of grapes. LIT., (quadrisyll.): Hor. TRANSF., (in the form vindēmĭtŏr), *a star in the constellation Virgo*: Ov.

vindēmĭŏla -ae, f. (dim. of vindemia), *a little vintage*: omnes meas vindemiolas reservo, perquisites, Cic.

vindex -ĭcis, c. (vindico).
    LIT., *one who lays claim to* or *protects, a claimant* or *protector*: aeris alieni, *a protector of creditors*, Cic.; iniuriae, *against wrong*, Liv.
    TRANSF., *an avenger, punisher*: coniurationis, Cic.; deae vindices scelerum; Cannarum, Juv.

vindĭcātĭo -ōnis, f. (vindico), *a defending, protecting,* or *avenging*: Cic.

vindĭcĭae -ārum, f. pl. (vindico).
    LIT., in law. (1) *things* or *persons claimed as property*: ni Appius vindicias ab libertate in servitutem dederit, *has adjudged a person to be a slave*, Liv. (2) *the making of such a claim*: iniustis vindiciis ac sacramentis petere aliquid, Cic.
    TRANSF., *protection*: Cic.

vindĭco -are (vim/dico).
    LIT., in law, *to claim* a person or thing as one's property *to lay legal claim to*: sponsam in libertatem, Liv.
    TRANSF., (1) in gen., *to lay claim to, arrogate, assume, appropriate*: Chii suum (Homerum) vindicant, Cic.; decus belli ad se, Liv.; partem aliquam sibi quisque vindicat, Cic.; Tac. (2) *to claim as free*; hence *to liberate, deliver* or *protect*: vindicare rem populi in libertatem, Cic.; te ab eo vindico et libero, Cic.; libertatem, Caes.; aliquem a verberibus, Cic. (3) *to avenge, punish, take vengeance on*: acerrime maleficia, Cic.; in cives militesque nostros, Cic.; iniurias, Liv.

vindicta -ae, f. (vindico).
    LIT., *the rod of freedom, the rod with which the praetor touched the slave who was to be manumitted*: si neque censu neque vindictā neque testamento liber factus est, Cic.; Pl., etc.
    TRANSF., (1) *deliverance*; with genit., *from a thing*: vindicta invisae huius vitae, Liv. (2) *vengeance, punishment*: Liv., Juv., Tac.

vīnĕa -ae, f. (vinum). LIT., *a vineyard*: Cic., Verg., etc. TRANSF., as milit. t. t., *a shed for sheltering besiegers, a mantlet, penthouse*: Caes., Cic.

vīnētum -i, n. (vinum), *a vineyard*: Cic., Verg., etc.

vīnĭtor -ōris, m. (vinum), *a vinedresser*: Cic., Verg.

vinnŭlus -a -um, *sweet, charming, pleasant*: Pl.

vīnŏlentĭa -ae, f. (vinolentus), *wine-drinking, intoxication*: Cic., Suet.

vīnŏlentus -a -um (vinum). (1) *mixed with wine*: medicamina, Cic. (2) *drunk with wine, intoxicated*: Ter., Cic.; m. pl. as subst., *drunkards*: Cic.

vīnosus -a -um, adj. (with compar. and superl.) (vinum), *full* or *fond of wine*: senex, Anacreon, Ov.; vinosior aetas, Ov.; Liv.

vīnum -i, n. (connected with οἶνος), *wine.*
    LIT., leve, Cic.; mutatum, *sour*, Cic.; vini plenus, Cic.; Verg., etc.; often in plur.
    TRANSF., (1) *the grape*: Pl. (2) *wine-drinking*: vino lustrisque confectus, Cic.; in vino ridere, Cic.; vino sepultus, Verg.

vĭŏla -ae, f. (cf. *ἴον*), *a violet* or *stock*. Lit., an tu me in viola putabas aut in rosa dicere? *on beds of violets or roses?* Cic.; Verg. Transf., *the colour of the violet, violet*: tinctus violā pallor amantium, Hor.

vĭŏlābĭlis -e (violo), *that can be injured*: numen, Verg.; cor, Ov.

vĭŏlārĭum -i, n. (viola), *a bed of violets*: Verg., Hor., Ov.

vĭŏlārĭus -i, m. (viola), *one who dyes violet*: Pl.

vĭŏlātĭo -ōnis, f. (violo), *an injury, violation, profanation*: templi, Liv.; Sen.

vĭŏlātor -ōris, m. (violo), *an injurer, violator, profaner*: templi, Ov.; gentium iuris, Liv.; Tac.

vĭŏlens -entis (vis), *vehement, violent, furious, impetuous*: Aufidus, Hor.
¶ Adv. **vĭŏlentĕr**, *violently, impetuously, vehemently*: aliquem accusare, Liv.

vĭŏlentĭa -ae, f. (violentus), *violence, vehemence, impetuosity*: hominis, Cic.; fortunae, Sall.; Lucr.

vĭŏlentus -a -um, adj. (with compar. and superl.) (vis), *violent, vehement, furious, impetuous*: homo, Cic.; ventus, Lucr.; violentissimae tempestates, Cic.; of style: Cic.; Eurus, Verg.; ingenium, imperium, Liv.

vĭŏlo -are (vis), *to treat with violence, violate, outrage, injure*. Lit., of places and things: urbem, Liv.; fines, Caes.; loca religiosa, Cic.; ebur sanguineo ostro, *to dye blood-red*, Verg.; of persons: hospites, Caes.; Liv. Transf., of abstr. things: ius, amicitiam, Cic.; foedera, Liv.

vīpĕra -ae, f. (perhaps for vivipera, from vivus/pario, *bearing its young alive*), *a viper*; also in gen., *a snake, serpent, adder*: Verg., Plin.; prov.: in sinu atque deliciis viperam illam venenatam et pestiferam habere, *to nourish a serpent in one's bosom*, Cic.; as a word of abuse, *viper*: Juv.

vīpĕrĕus -a -um (vipera). (1) *of a viper* or *a snake*: dentes, Ov.; anima, *poisonous breath*, Verg. (2) *having snakes*: monstrum, *snaky-haired Medusa*, Ov.; canis, *Cerberus*, Ov.; sorores, *the Furies*, Ov.

vīpĕrīnus -a -um (vipera), *of a viper* or *snake*: sanguis, Hor.; Plin.

vir viri, m. *a man, male person*. In gen.: de viro factus femina, Ov.; Cic., Verg., etc. Esp. (1) *a grown man* (opp. puer): Cic., Ov. (2) *a husband*: in viro suo Socrate, Cic.; of animals: vir gregis ipse caper, Verg. (3) emphatically *a man*, i.e. *a man of character* or *courage*, a 'he-man': tulit dolorem ut vir, Cic.; Liv., Hor.; meton., *virility*: Cat. (4) as milit. t. t., *a soldier, a man*, esp. *a foot-soldier*: equites virique, Liv. (5) *a single man, an individual*: vir virum legit, *each singles out his opponent*, Verg.; est ut viro vir latius ordinet arbusta sulcis, Hor.; Cic., Liv.

vĭrāgo -ĭnis, f. (virgo), *a man-like woman, female warrior, heroine*; of Pallas: bello metuenda virago, Ov.; Iuturna virago, Verg.

Virbĭus -i, m. *the name of Hippolytus after he was restored to life*; also *of his son*: Verg.

vīrectum (**vīrētum**) -i, n. (vireo), *greensward, turf*; plur.: virecta nemorum, *glades*, Verg.

vĭrĕo -ēre, *to be green*. Lit., arbores virent, Cic.; Verg., etc. Transf., *to be vigorous, healthy, fresh, youthful*: virebat integris sensibus, Liv.; Hor., Ov.
¶ Hence partic. **vĭrens** -entis, *green*; also *vigorous, fresh*: Hor., Ov.

vīres -ĭum, f. pl.; *see* vis.

vīresco -ĕre (vireo), *to grow green, become green*: iniussa virescunt gramina, Verg.

vīrētum = virectum; q.v.

virga -ae, f. *a green twig*.
Lit., turea, Verg.; viscata, *limed*, Ov. Esp., *a slip for planting*: Ov. As cut, *a rod*, for various purposes; *a rod for beating*: Pl., Juv.; esp. plur., virgae, *the rods of which the lictors' fasces were formed*: aliquem virgis caedere, Cic.; sing. collect., *the fasces*: Ov.; also *a broom*: Ov.; *a magic wand*, esp. of Mercury: Verg., Ov.
Transf., of things resembling a rod. (1) *a streak, stripe of colour, on clothes*: purpureis tingit sua corpora virgis, Ov. (2) *a branch* in a family tree: Juv.

virgātor -ōris, m. (virga), *one who beats with rods*: Pl.

virgātus -a -um (virga). (1) *made of twigs* or *osiers*: Cat. (2) *striped*: sagula, Verg.

virgētum -i, n. (virga), *an osier-bed, thicket of rods*: Cic.

virgĕus -a -um (virga), *made of twigs* or *rods*: flamma, *of burning twigs*, Verg.

virgĭdēmĭa -ae, f. (formed in jest from analogy with vindemia), *a rod-harvest*, i.e., *a good beating*: Pl.

Virgĭlĭus = Vergilius; q.v.

virgĭnālis -e (virgo), *of a virgin, maidenly*: habitus, vestitus, Cic.; Pl.

virgĭnārĭus = virginalis; q.v.

virgĭnĕus -a -um (virgo), *of a virgin, maidenly*: rubor, Verg.; forma, Ov.

virgĭnĭtās -ātis, f. (virgo), *virginity*: Cic., Verg., Ov.

virgo -ĭnis, f. *a maiden, virgin*.
Lit., Cic., etc.; Saturnia, *Vesta*, Ov.; Phoebea, *the laurel-tree into which Daphne was turned*, Ov.; in apposition: virgo dea, *Diana*, Ov.; virginis aequor, *the Hellespont*, Ov.; virgo vestalis, Cic.
Transf., (1) *the constellation Virgo*: Cic. poet. (2) Aqua Virgo, or simply Virgo, *a stream of water brought to Rome in an aqueduct by M. Agrippa*, Ov., Plin. (3) *a young married woman, young wife*: Verg.

virgŭla -ae, f. (dim. of virga), *a little twig, a little bough*. As cut, *a rod, staff*: virgulā stantem circumscribere, Cic.; esp.: virga divina, *a divining-rod*, Cic.; virga censoria, *a mark indicating that a passage is not genuine*, Quint.

virgultum -i, n. (virgula). (1) *a thicket, copse, brushwood*; gen. plur.: Caes., Cic., Liv., Ov. (2) *a slip for planting*: Lucr., Verg.

virguncŭla -ae, f. (dim. of virgo), *a young virgin, little girl*: Sen., Juv.

Vĭrĭāthus (**Vĭrĭātus**) -i, m. *a Lusitanian who commanded his countrymen in their war against the Romans* (149 B.C.).

vĭrĭdans -antis (viridis), *green*: laurus, Verg.; Lucr., etc.
¶ Hence verb **vĭrĭdor** -ari, *to become green*: Ov.

vĭrĭdārĭum -i, n. (viridis), *a pleasure-garden*: Cic.

vĭrĭdis -e (vireo), *green* (in all its shades), *grass-green, pea-green, sea-green.*
 LIT., ripa, Cic.; Venafrum, *rich in olive-trees,* Hor.; Mincius, Verg. N. pl. as subst. **vĭrĭdĭa** -ium, *green trees* or *herbs*: Sen., Plin. L.
 TRANSF., *fresh, young, blooming, vigorous*: iuventa, Juv.; Cic., etc.

vĭrĭdĭtās -ātis, f. (viridis), *greenness.* LIT., pratorum, Cic. TRANSF., *freshness, bloom*: senectus aufert viriditatem, Cic.

vĭrīlis -e (vir), *of a man, manly, male, virile.*
 LIT., (1) in relation to sex: stirps, Liv.; secus, *male sex,* Pl., Sall.; vox, Ov.; in grammar, *masculine*: Varr. (2) in age, *adult*: aetas, Hor.; toga, *assumed by the Roman youths in their fifteenth* or *sixteenth year,* Cic., Liv.
 TRANSF., *like a man,* i.e. *manly, courageous, spirited*: animus, Cic.; ingenium, Sall. Hence phrase, pars virilis, *a man's part,* i.e. *one's proper share, duty*: est aliqua pars mea virilis, Cic.; pro virili parte, *to the utmost of one's ability,* Cic., Liv., Tac.
 ¶ Hence adv. **vĭrīlĭtĕr**, *manfully, courageously, vigorously*: Cic., Ov.

vĭrīlĭtās -ātis, f. (virilis), *manhood, virility*: Plin., Tac., Quint.

vĭrīpŏtens -entis (vires/potens), *mighty* (epithet of Jupiter): Pl.

vĭrītim, adv. (vir), *man by man, individually*: agros viritim dividere civibus, Cic.; viritim commonefacere beneficii sui, Sall.; Hor.

vĭrōsus -a -um (virus), *stinking, fetid*: castorea, Verg.

virtus -ūtis, f. (vir), *manliness, manly excellence.*
 In gen., *excellence, capacity, worth, goodness, virtue.* LIT., in human beings: animi, corporis, Cic. TRANSF., in animals, inanimate, or abstract things: equi, Cic.; herbarum, Ov.; oratoriae virtutes, Cic.
 Esp. (1) *moral excellence, virtue*: honesta in virtute ponuntur, Cic. (2) *valour, bravery, courage*: Caes., Liv., etc.; plur.: virtutes, *deeds of bravery,* Tac. (3) personif., *Virtue*: Pl., Cic., Liv.

vĭrus -i, n. (1) *a slimy liquid, slime*: Verg., Plin. (2) *poison,* esp. of snakes, *venom*: Lucr., Verg.; fig.: aliquis apud quem evomat virus acerbitatis suae, Cic. (3) *a harsh, bitter taste* or *smell*: taetrum, of salt water, Lucr.

vis, acc. vim, abl. vi; plur. **vīres** -ium, f. *force, power, strength.*
 LIT., physical; sing.: celeritas et vis equorum, Cic.; fluminis, Caes.; plur.: vires nervique, sanguis viresque, Cic.; Caes., Hor., etc. Esp. *hostile force, violence*: per vim, Caes.; alicui vim adferre, Cic.; fit via Verg.; vi ac virtute evadendum esse, Liv.
 TRANSF., (1) sing., *a large number, quantity*: hominum, Pl., Liv.; magna vis auri argentique, Cic. (2) plur., as milit. t. t., *troops, forces*: satis virium ad certamen, Liv.; Verg., Ov. (3) sing. and plur., *intellectual* or *moral strength, might, power, influence*: vis illa divina et virtus orationis, Cic. (4) sing., of things, *force, nature, meaning, essence*: in quo est omnis vis amicitiae, Cic.; verbi, nominis, Cic.

viscātus -a -um (viscum), *smeared with birdlime*: virga, Ov.

visce̅rātio -ōnis, f. (viscera), *a public distribution of meat*: Cic., Liv.

viscum -i, n. and **viscus** -i, m. (cf. ἰξός). (1) *mistletoe*: Verg., Plin. (2) *bird-lime* (made from mistletoe berries): Pl., Cic., Verg.

viscus -ĕris, usually plur. **viscĕra** -um, n. *the flesh of a body*; also *the internal organs, entrails, viscera.*
 LIT., e visceribus sanguis exeat, Cic.; haerentia viscere tela, Ov.; Lucr., etc.
 TRANSF., (1) plur., *the womb*: Ov.; hence *a child* or *children*: diripiunt avidae viscera nostra ferae, Ov. (2) plur., *the inmost part* or *heart* of anything: viscera montis, Verg.; reipublicae, Cic.; aerarii, Cic.

visendus -a -um, gerundive from viso; q.v.

visĭo -ōnis, f. (video), *a seeing, view.* LIT., eamque esse dei visionem, ut similitudine cernatur, Cic. TRANSF., (1) *an appearance*: adventicia, Cic. (2) *a notion, idea*: doloris, Cic.; veri et falsi, Cic.

visĭto -are (freq. of viso). (1) *to see often*: Pl. (2) *to visit*: aliquem, Cic., Suet.

viso vīsĕre visi vīsum (freq. of video), *to look at carefully, contemplate.*
 LIT., agros, Liv.; visendi causā venire, Cic.; Pl., Verg., Tac.
 TRANSF., (1) *to come to see, go to see, look into, see after*: aedem Minervae, Pl.; with indir. quest.: Pl., Ter., etc. (2) *to go to see, visit, call upon*; with acc.: domum alicuius, Cic. L.; Hor.; with ad: Ter., Lucr., Ov.
 ¶ Hence gerundive **visendus** -a -um as adj., *worth seeing, notable*: ornatus, Cic.; n. pl. as subst. **visenda** -ōrum, *things worth seeing*: Liv.

visum -i, n. subst. from video; q.v.

visus -ūs, m. (video), *seeing, sight.*
 LIT., oculorum, Lucr.; visu nocere, Cic.; obire omnia visu, Verg.; plur.: visūs effugiet tuos, Ov.
 TRANSF., *what is seen, a sight, appearance*: hoc visu laetus, Liv.; Verg., Ov.

vīta -ae, f. (vivo), *life.*
 LIT., as a state or period: in vita esse, *to be alive,* Cic.; vitam amittere, Cic.; vitam profundere pro aliquo, Cic.; vitam miserrimam degere, Cic.; vitam alicui adimere, auferre, Cic.; in vita, *during my life,* Cic.; vitae summa brevis, Hor.; Verg., etc.
 TRANSF., (1) *life, way of living*: rustica, Cic.; communis, Cic., Liv., etc. (2) *a career*: Nep., Tac. (3) *my life,* as a term of endearment: mea vita, Cic. L.; Pl., Ter., Prop. (4) *a soul, shade in the lower world*: tenues sine corpore vitae, Verg.

vītābĭlis -e (vito), *that may* or *ought to be shunned*: Ov.

vītābundus -a -um (vito), *trying to avoid, avoiding, shunning*: vitabundus erumpit, Sall.; with acc.: vitabundus castra hostium, Liv.

vītālis -e (vita). (1) *of life, vital*: vis, Cic.; vitalia saecla, *generations of living men,* Lucr.; viae, *the windpipe,* Ov. N. pl. as subst. **vītālĭa** -ium, *vital parts*: Sen., Plin. (2) *living, surviving*: Pl., Hor.
 ¶ Adv. **vītālĭtĕr**, *vitally*: Lucr.

vītātĭo -ōnis, f. (vito), *an avoiding, shunning*: oculorum, lucis, urbis, fori, Cic.; doloris, Cic.

Vĭtellĭus -a -um, *the name of a Roman gens.* Esp. of Aulus Vitellius, *the Roman emperor who succeeded Otho* (A.D. 69), *notorious for gluttony and idleness.*

¶ Hence adj. **Vĭtellĭus** and **Vĭtellĭānus** -a -um, *Vitellian.*

vĭtellus -i, m. (dim. of vitulus). (**1**) *a little calf,* as a term of endearment: Pl. (**2**) *the yolk of an egg:* Cic., Hor.

vītĕus -a -um (vitis), *of a vine:* pocula, *wine,* Verg.

vĭtĭātĭo -ōnis, f. (vitio), *a defiling, ravishing:* Sen.

vĭtĭātor -ōris, m. (vitio), *a violator, ravisher:* Sen.

vītĭcŭla -ae, f. (dim. of vitis), *a little vine:* Cic.

vītĭfer -fĕra -fĕrum (vitis/fero), *vine-bearing:* Plin., Mart.

vītĭgĕnus -a -um (vitis/gigno), *produced from the vine:* liquor, Lucr.

vĭtĭo -are (vitium), *to injure, damage, corrupt, spoil, mar.*
 LIT., vitiatus aper, *high,* Hor.; omnem salibus amaris, Ov. Esp., *to debauch:* Ter., Ov., etc.
 TRANSF., *to forge, falsify:* senatūs consulta, Liv.; comitiorum et contionum significationes, Cic.

vĭtĭōsĭtās -ātis, f. (vitiosus), *viciousness, corruption:* Cic.

vĭtĭōsus -a -um, adj. (with compar. and superl.) (vitium), *faulty, defective, corrupt, bad.*
 LIT., physically: Varr.; vitiosas partes (*unsound limbs*) reipublicae exsecare, sanare, Cic.
 TRANSF., (**1**) in gen., *defective, faulty, wrong:* suffragium, Cic.; lex, Cic.; vitiosissimus orator, Cic.; consul, dictator, *elected informally,* Cic., Liv. (**2**) *morally faulty, corrupt, wicked:* vitiosa et flagitiosa vita, Cic.; progeniem vitiosiorem, Hor.
 ¶ Hence adv. **vitiōsē**, *faultily, defectively, perversely, wrongly:* vitiose se habere, Cic.

vītis -is, f. *a vine.* LIT., Cic., Verg., etc.
 TRANSF., *the centurion's staff, made of a vine-branch:* Ov., Tac.; meton., *the post of centurion:* Juv.

vītĭsător -ōris, m. (vitis/sator), *one who plants vines:* Verg.

vĭtĭum -i, n. *a fault, defect, blemish, imperfection.*
 LIT., physical: corporis, Cic.; si nihil est in parietibus aut in tecto vitii, Cic.; aeris, Verg.; ignis vitium metallis excoquit, Ov.
 TRANSF., (**1**) in gen., *fault, imperfection, defect:* vitio civitatis, non suo, *through the fault,* Cic.; vitia in dicente acutius quam recta videre, Cic.; Caes., etc. (**2**) *a moral fault, crime, vice:* vitium fugere, Hor.; nullum ob totius vitae non dicam vitium, sed erratum, Cic.; in vitio esse, Cic. Esp. *the debauching* of a woman: vitium per vim offerre, Ter.; Pl., Ov. (**3**) as relig. t. t., *a defect in auguries* or *auspices:* tabernaculum vitio (*against the auguries*) captum, Cic.

vīto -are, *to avoid, shun.*
 LIT., tela, Caes.; fugā mortem, Caes.; hastas, Ov.; aspectum, oculos hominum, Cic.
 TRANSF., with acc.: stultitiam, Cic.; suspiciones, Caes.; with ne and the subj.: vitandum est oratori utrumque, ne aut scurrilis iocus sit aut mimicus, Cic.; with the infin.: tangere vitet scripta, Hor.

vĭtrĕus -a -um (vitrum), *made of glass.*
 LIT., hostis, *a glass draughtsman,* Ov. N. pl. as subst., *glassware:* Stat., Mart.

TRANSF., *like glass, glassy, transparent, glittering:* unda, Verg.; ros, Ov.; Circe, Hor.; fama, *glittering* (or *brittle*), Hor.

vītrĭcus -i, m. *a stepfather:* Cic., Ov., Tac.

vitrum -i, n. (**1**) *glass:* merces in chartis et linteis et vitro delatae, Cic.; Lucr., etc. (**2**) *woad, a plant producing a blue dye:* Caes.

Vitrŭvĭus -i, m., M. Vitruvius Pollio, *of Verona,* author of De Architectura Libri X, *composed probably about* 14 B.C.

vitta -ae, f. (connected with vieo), *a ribbon, band, fillet,* esp. worn round the head of sacrificial victims, of priests and priestesses: Verg.; also bound round altars: Verg., Ov.; and round the branches carried by suppliants: Verg., Hor., Ov.

vittātus -a -um (vitta), *bound with a fillet:* capilli, Ov.

vītŭla -ae, f. (vitulus), *a calf, heifer:* Verg., etc.

vītŭlīnus -a -um (vitulus), *of a calf:* caruncula, Cic.; assum, *roast veal,* Cic. L. F. as subst. **vītŭlīna** -ae, *veal:* Pl., Nep.

vītŭlor -ari, dep. *to celebrate a festival, be joyful:* Pl.

vītŭlus -i, m. *a bull-calf.* LIT., Cic., Verg., etc. TRANSF., of the young of other animals, e.g. of a horse: Verg.; vitulus marinus, *or,* simply, vitulus, *a sea-calf,* Plin., Juv., Suet.

vĭtŭpĕrābĭlis -e (vitupero), *blamable:* Cic.

vĭtŭpĕrātĭo -ōnis, f. (vitupero), *a blaming, scolding, censure:* in vituperationem venire, adduci, cadere, Cic.; meton., *that which is blamable, blameworthy conduct:* Cic.

vĭtŭpĕrātor -ōris, m. (vitupero), *a blamer, vituperator:* philosophiae, Cic.

vĭtŭpĕro -are (vitium/paro). (**1**) relig. t. t., *to spoil an omen:* Pl. (**2**) *to blame, scold, censure, vituperate:* consilium, Cic.; aliquem, Cic.

vīvācĭtās -ātis, f. (vivax), *hold on life:* Plin.

vīvārĭum -i, n. (vivus), *a place where living animals are kept, a park, warren, preserve, fish-pond,* etc.: excipiant senes, quos in vivaria mittant, Hor.; Plin., Juv.

vīvātus -a -um (vivus), *quickened, vivid:* Lucr.

vīvax -ācis, adj. (with compar.) (vivo), *long-lived, tenacious of life,* and in gen., *lasting, enduring:* phoenix, Ov.; oliva, Verg.; gratia, Hor. TRANSF., *brisk, lively, vigorous:* sulfura, *readily inflammable,* Ov.; discipuli, Quint.

vīvesco (**vīvisco**), vīvescĕre vixi (vivo), *to begin to live:* Plin. TRANSF., *to grow lively:* Lucr.

vīvĭdus -a -um (vivo), *full of life, animated.* LIT., gemma, Ov. TRANSF., (**1**) of pictures and statues, *life-like, true to life:* signa, Prop. (**2**) in gen., *lively, vigorous:* vis animi, Lucr.; senectus, Tac.; virtus, Verg.

vīvĭrādix -īcis, f. (vivus/radix), *a cutting which has a root, a layer:* Cic.

vīvisco=vivesco; q.v.

vīvo vīvĕre vixi victum (cf. βιόω), *to live, be alive.*
 LIT., of persons and animals. In gen.: ad summam senectutem, Cic.; annum, Ov.; with cognate acc.: vitam tutiorem, Cic.; si vivo, *or* si vivam, *if I live* (in threats), Ter.; ita vivam, *as true as I live,* Cic.; perf.: vixisse, *to have had one's life, be finished,* Pl., Cic. Esp. (**1**) *to live well, to enjoy life:* vivamus, mea Lesbia, Cat.; quando vivemus? *have leisure,* Cic. L.; vive, vivite, in saying goodbye, *farewell,* Hor., Verg. (**2**) *to live on,*

survive: Cic., Liv. (3) with reference to what supports life, *to live on* anything: de suo, Pl.; lacte atque pecore, Caes.; parcius, Hor. (4) with adj. as predicate, *to live as*, i.e. *to be*: miserrimus, Cic.; molesta, Cat. (5) with reference to place or circumstances, *to live, dwell*: Syracusis, Cic.; cum timore, Cic.; in litteris, Cic.; in paupertate, Cic.; cum aliquo valde familiariter, Cic.

TRANSF., of inanimate or abstract things: cinis, Ov.; vulnus, Verg.; auctoritas, Cic.; scripta, Ov.

vīvus (vivos) -a -um (vivo), *alive, living.*

LIT., of persons and animals: aliquem vivum capere, Liv.; patrem et filium vivos comburere, Cic.; vivus vidensque, Ter., Cic.

TRANSF., vox, *of a living person*, Cic.; vivos ducent de marmore vultus, *lifelike*, Verg.; arundo, *living*, Ov.; flumen, *running water*, Verg., Liv.; lucerna, *burning*, Hor.; ros, *fresh*, Ov.; sulfur, *natural*, Liv.

¶ N. as subst. **vīvum** -i, *that which is alive, the flesh with life and feeling*: calor ad vivum adveniens, Liv.; neque id ad vivum reseco, *cut to the quick*, i.e., *take too seriously, in too literal a sense*, Cic.

vix, adv. (connected with vis *or* vinco), *with difficulty, with effort, scarcely.*

In gen.: vix et aegre, Pl.; vix teneor quin accurram, Cic. L.; Caes., etc.

Esp. of time, *only just*: vix tandem legi litteras, Cic. L.; vix erat hoc plane imperatum, cum illum spoliatum stipatumque lictoribus videres, Cic.; vix inopina quies laxaverat artus, et, Verg.; vix proram attigerat, rumpit Saturnia funem, Verg.

Strengthened by dum, gen., in one word, **vixdum**, *hardly yet*: vixdum coetu nostro dimisso, Cic.; Ter., Liv., Tac.

vŏcābŭlum -i, n. (voco), *a name, appellation*: res suum nomen et proprium vocabulum non habet, Cic.; cui (oppido) nomen inditum e vocabulo ipsius, Tac.; Hor. As grammat. t. t., *a noun substantive*: Varr., Quint.

vŏcālis -e (vox), *uttering sounds, vocal, speaking, singing*: Orpheus, Hor.; ne quem vocalem praeterisse videamur, *anyone with a good voice*, Cic.; carmen, Ov.

¶ F. as subst. **vŏcālis** -is (sc. littera), *a vowel*: Cic., Quint.

vŏcāmen -ĭnis n. (voco), *a name, appellation*: Lucr.

vŏcātĭo -ōnis, f. (voco). (1) *a summoning before a court of law*: Varr. (2) *an invitation to dinner*: Cat.

vŏcātor -ōris, m. (voco), *an inviter*: Plin., Mart., etc.

vŏcātus -ūs, m. (voco). (1) *a calling, summoning, invocation*: Cic.; plur.: vocatūs mei, Verg. (2) *an invitation*: Suet.

vōcĭfĕrātĭo -ōnis, f. (vociferor), *a loud calling, shouting*: Cic., Quint.

vōcĭfĕror -ari, dep. (vōcĭfĕro -are, act.: Varr.), (vox/fero), *to cry aloud, shout, vociferate.*
LIT., of persons: palam, Cic.; talia, Verg.; de superbia patrum, Liv.; with acc. and infin.: quod vociferabare decem milia talentum Gabinio esse promissa, Cic.; Liv.; with indir. quest.: Liv. TRANSF., of things: Lucr.

vŏcĭto -are (freq. of voco). (1) *to be accustomed*

to name: has Graeci stellas Hyadas vocitare suerunt, Cic.; Lucr., Tac. (2) *to shout loudly* or *often*: Tac.

vŏco -are (vox), *to call, summon.*

LIT., in gen.: Dumnorigem ad se, Caes.; aliquem in contionem, Cic.; patres, Verg.; ad bellum, Liv. Esp. (1) *to call upon, invoke*: deos, Verg., Hor. (2) *to summon before a court of law*: aliquem in ius, Cic.; Liv. (3) *to invite*: ad cenam, Cic.; Pl., Ter. (4) *to call, name, designate*: ego vocor Lyconides, Pl.; patrioque vocat de nomine mensem, Ov.; Hor., etc.

TRANSF., (1) fig., *to call, urge*: in spem, ad vitam, Cic. L.; Verg., etc. (2) *to bring, put, place in any state* or *condition*: ne me apud milites in invidiam voces, Cic.; ad calculos amicitiam, Cic.; in dubium, *to call in question*, Cic.; Ov., Tac.

vōcŭla -ae, f. (dim. of vox), *a low, weak voice*: Cic. L.; Prop. TRANSF., (1) *a low tone in singing* or *speaking*: falsae voculae, Cic. (2) contemptuously, *a little, petty speech*: incurrere in voculas malevolorum, Cic. L.

vŏlaema pĭra, n. pl. *a kind of large pear*: Verg.

Vŏlăterrae -ārum, f. *an old town in Etruria* (now *Volterra*).

¶ Hence adj. **Vŏlăterrānus** -a -um, *of Volaterrae*; m. pl. as subst. **Vŏlăterrāni** -ōrum, *the inhabitants of Volaterrae.*

vŏlātĭcus -a -um (²volo), *having wings, winged, flying*: Pl. TRANSF., *fleeting, flighty, inconstant*: Academia, Cic. L.; illius furentes ac volatici impetus, Cic.

vŏlātĭlis -e (²volo), *having wings, winged, flying*: bestiae, Cic.; puer, Cupid, Ov. TRANSF., (1) *swift, rapid*: ferrum, Verg. (2) *fleeting, transitory*: aetas, Ov.; Sen.

vŏlātus -ūs, m. (²volo), *a flying, flight*: Cic.

Volcae -ārum, f. pl. *a people in Gallia Narbonensis.*

Volcānus (Vulcānus) -i, m. *Vulcan, the god of fire, son of Jupiter and Juno, husband of Venus, who made the weapons, thunder-bolts, etc., of the gods*: Cic., Hor., etc. TRANSF., *fire*: Volcanum navibus efflant, Ov.; Verg.

¶ Hence adj. **Volcānĭus** -a -um and **Volcānālis** -e, *belonging to Vulcan*; n. pl. as subst. **Volcānālia** -ium, *the annual festival of Vulcan, on the 23rd of August.*

vŏlens -entis, partic. from ¹volo; q.v.

volgo, volgus = vulgo, vulgus; q.v.

vŏlĭto -are (freq. of ²volo), *to fly about, fly to and fro, flit, flutter.*

LIT., aves volitare, Cic.; hic aliae (stellae) volitant, Cic.; umbrae inter vivos, Lucr.; of persons, *to rush around, hasten about*: cum gladiis toto foro, Cic.

TRANSF., homo volitans gloriae cupiditate, Cic.; cum illa coniuratio palam volitaret, Cic.

volnĕro = vulnero; q.v.

¹vŏlo velle vŏlŭi (contr., vin = visne, sis = si vis, sultis = si vultis) (cf. βούλομαι), *to be willing, to wish.*

In gen.: faciam, quod vultis, Cic.; usually with infin.: volui id quidem efficere, Cic.; volo scire, velim scire, *I should like to know*, Cic.; with acc. and infin.: iudicem me esse, non doctorem volo, Cic.; Hor., etc. Sometimes with ut and the subj.: volo, uti respondeas, Cic.; Pl., Ter.; or with the subj. alone: visne hoc primum videamus? Cic.

Esp. (1) in parenthesis with si, often in contr. forms: sis, sultis: refer animum, sis, ad veritatem, *please*, Cic. (2) with acc. of person, *to want for something*: centuriones trium cohortium me velle postridie, Cic.; num quid me vis? Pl., Ter. (3) with dat. of person, *to wish well* or *ill to*: Pl., Ter. (4) esp. with dat. of reflex., *to mean, signify*: quid ergo illae sibi statuae equestres inauratae volunt? Cic.; Verg. (5) *to express a wish with authority, to will, ordain*: maiores de singulis magistratibus bis vos sententiam ferre voluerunt, Cic.; Liv. (6) *to suppose, maintain*: vultis omnia evenire fato, Cic.; Liv. (7) foll. by quam, *to prefer*: malae rei se quam nullius, duces esse volunt, Liv.; Cic., Ov.

¶ Hence partic. **vŏlens** -entis. (1) *willing, voluntary*: Sall., Verg. (2) *favourable, inclined to*: Liv., Sall.; dis volentibus, *by the help of the gods*, Sall.; volentia alicui, *favourable tidings* or *events*, Sall.

¹vŏlo -are, *to fly*. Lit., Lucr., Cic., etc.; f. pl. of partic. as subst., volantes -ium, *flying creatures, birds*: Verg. Transf., *to move rapidly, rush*: currus, Verg.; fulmina, Lucr.; aetas, Cic.; fama, Verg.

vŏlōnēs -um, m. pl. *volunteers*, i.e. *the slaves who were bought at the public expense to serve as soldiers after the battle of Cannae, each of them being asked* 'velletne militare': Liv.

Volsci -ōrum, m. pl. *a people in Latium, on the banks of the Liris.* Adj. **Volscus** -a -um, *Volscian*.

volsella -ae, f. (vello), *a pair of tweezers* or *pincers*: Mart.

Volsĭnii (Vulsĭnii) -ōrum, m. pl. *a town in Etruria* (now *Bolsena*).

¶ Hence adj. **Volsĭnĭensis** -e, *Volsinian*.

volsus -a -um, partic. from vello; q.v.

Voltĭnĭus -a -um, *Voltinian*: tribus, *a Roman tribe*.

¶ Hence subst. **Voltĭnĭenses** -ĭum, m. pl. *citizens of the Voltinian tribe*.

Voltumna -ae, f. *the goddess of the twelve allied Etruscan states*.

voltur=vultur; q.v.

Volturnus=Vulturnus; q.v.

voltus=vultus; q.v.

vŏlūbĭlis -e (volvo), *rolling, revolving, turning round, twisting round*.

Lit., buxum, *a top*, Verg.; caelum, Cic.; amnis, Hor.

Transf., (1) *changeable, inconstant*: fortuna, Cic. (2) of discourse, *rapid, fluent*: Appii Claudii volubilis erat oratio, Cic.

¶ Hence adv. **vŏlūbĭlĭtĕr**, *fluently*: funditur numerose et volubiliter oratio, Cic.

vŏlūbĭlĭtās -ātis, f. (volubilis), *revolving motion, revolution*.

Lit., mundi, Cic.

Transf., (1) *mutability, inconstancy*: fortunae, Cic. (2) *flow of words, fluency*: verborum, linguae, Cic.; Quint. (3) *roundness*: capitis, Ov.

vŏlŭcer vŏlucris vŏlucre (²volo), *flying, winged*.

Lit., angues, Cic.; deus, or puer, *Cupid*, Ov.; bestiae volucres, *birds*, Cic. F. as subst. **vŏlucris** -is (sc. avis), *a bird* or *flying insect*: Lucr., Cic., Verg., etc.

Transf., (1) *fleet, rapid, swift*: lumen,

Lucr.; fumi, Verg.; sagitta, Verg.; nuntius, Cic.; fig.: nihil est tam volucre quam maledictum, Cic. (2) *fleeting, transitory*: fortuna, Cic.; Hor., Tac.

vŏlūmen -ĭnis, n. (volvo), *anything rolled*.

(1) *a book, roll, scroll*: volumen plenum querelae, Cic.; plur.: volumina selectarum epistularum, Cic.; Hor., etc. Esp. *a part of a larger work*: Cic., Nep.; mutatae ter quinque volumina formae, *the fifteen books of the Metamorphoses*, Ov.

(2) *a roll, wreath, whirl, fold*: anguis sinuat immensa volumine terga, Verg.; Ov.

vŏluntārĭus -a -um (voluntas), *voluntary*. (1) subject., *doing something of one's own accord*: procurator, Cic.; auxilia sociorum, Cic.; milites, *volunteers*, Caes.; m. pl. as subst. **vŏluntārii** -ōrum, *volunteers*: Caes., Liv. (2) object., *done of one's own free will*: mors, *suicide*, Cic.; deditio, Liv.

vŏluntās -ātis, f. (¹volo), *will, wish, inclination*.

Lit., in gen.: me conformo ad eius voluntatem, Cic.; sit pro ratione voluntas, Juv.; Lucr., etc.; voluntate, *of one's own free will*: meā voluntate concedam, *willingly*, Cic.; similarly with prepositions, such as *ad* and *ex*: Cic. Esp. *goodwill*: confisus municipiorum voluntatibus, Caes.; mutua voluntas, Cic. L.

Transf., (1) *a last will, testament*: testamenta et voluntas mortuorum, Cic. (2) *meaning, sense, signification*: Quint.

vŏlup, adv. (connected with voluptas), *agreeably, delightfully, pleasantly*: Pl., Ter.

vŏluptābĭlis -e (voluptas), *giving pleasure, pleasant*: Pl.

vŏluptārĭus -a -um (voluptas), *relating to pleasure, esp., to sensual pleasure*.

(1) *pleasant, causing pleasure*: possessiones, Cic. L.; Pl. (2) *concerned with pleasure*: disputationes, Cic. (3) *devoted to pleasure, sensual*; of the Epicureans as opp. to the Stoics: homo (of Epicurus), Cic.

vŏluptās -ātis, f. (volup), *pleasure, delight, enjoyment*.

Lit., hominum divumque, Cic.; voluptate capi, Cic.; alicui voluptati esse, Cic.; voluptatibus frui, Cic.; voluptates corporis, *sensual pleasures*, Cic.

Transf., (1) plur.: voluptates, *public shows*, Cic., Tac. (2) of persons, as a term of endearment: care puer, mea sera et sola voluptas, Verg.; Pl.

vŏluptŭōsus -a -um (voluptas), *full of pleasure, delightful*: Quint., Plin. L.

vŏlūtābrum -i, n. (voluto), *a place where pigs roll, slough*: Verg.

vŏlūtābundus -a -um (voluto), *rolling, wallowing*: in voluptatibus, Cic.

vŏlūtātĭo -ōnis, f. (voluto), *a rolling about, wallowing*: Cic. Transf., *disquiet*: animi, Sen.; rerum humanarum, Sen.

vŏlūto -are (freq. of volvo), *to roll round, tumble about*.

Lit., se in pulvere, Plin.; ne fluxa habenā volutetur in iactu glans, Liv.; in luto, Cic.; partic.: volutans, in middle sense, *rolling about*, Verg.

Transf., in gen.: vocem per atria, Verg.; vocem volutant litora, Verg.; pass. as middle: volutari in omni genere flagitiorum, Cic. Esp. (1) *to turn over in the mind, revolve, consider*:

condiciones cum amicis, Liv.; nihil umquam nisi sempiternum et divinum animo, Cic.; Pl., Verg. (2) *to busy, occupy*: animum saepe tacitis cogitationibus, Liv.; in veteribus scriptis studiose et multum volutatum esse, Cic.

volva (vulva) -ae, f. (volvo). (1) *any covering, husk, shell*: Plin. (2) *the womb*; esp., *a sow's womb, a favourite delicacy among the Romans*: Hor.

volvo volvĕre volvi vŏlūtum, *to roll, wind, turn round, twist round.*

    LIT., in gen.: oculos huc illuc, Verg.; rivers: saxa glareosa, Liv.; of the wind: ignem ad fastigia summa, Verg.; Lucr., etc. Often pass., volvi, as middle, *to roll*: curru, *from a chariot*, Verg.; humi, Verg.; volvuntur stellarum cursus sempiterni, Cic.; of tears: lacrimae volvuntur inanes, Verg. Esp., *to unroll a book, to read*: libros Catonis, Cic. Meton.: orbem, *to form a circle* (of men), Liv.

    TRANSF., (1) of time, *to make, roll round*: pronos volvere menses (of the moon-goddess), Hor.; tot casūs, *to experience, go through*, Verg.; pass. in middle sense: ut idem in singulos annos orbis volveretur, Liv.; volvendis mensibus, Verg.; so in present partic.: volventibus annis, *in the course of the years*, Verg. (2) *to turn over in the mind, entertain thoughts of*: ingentes iam diu iras eum in pectore volvere, Liv.; bellum in animo, Liv.; multa secum, Sall.; sub pectore sortes, Verg.; veterum monumenta virorum, Verg.

vōmer (vōmis) -ĕris, m. *a ploughshare*: Cic., Verg., etc.

vŏmĭca -ae, f. *an ulcer, sore, boil.* LIT., Pl., Cic. TRANSF., *a plague, curse*: Liv.

vōmis -ĕris, m. = vomer; q.v.

vŏmĭtĭo -ōnis, f. (vomo), *a vomiting, throwing up*: vomitione alvos curare, Cic.

vŏmĭto -are (freq. of vomo), *to vomit much*: Sen., Suet.

vŏmĭtor -ōris, m. (vomo), *one who vomits*: Sen.

vŏmĭtus -ūs, m. (vomo), *a vomiting.* LIT., Pl., etc. TRANSF., as term of abuse: Pl.

vŏmo -ĕre -ŭi -ĭtum (connected with ἐμέω), *to vomit*; as transit. verb. *to vomit forth, throw up.* LIT., Pl., Cic. TRANSF., vitam, Lucr.; animam, flammas, Verg.

vŏrāgo -inis, f. (voro), *a pit, chasm, abyss.*

    LIT., in the earth: Liv.; in water: summersus equus voraginibus, Cic.; Verg., Liv. TRANSF., gurges et vorago patrimonii, Cic.; Liv.

vŏrax -ācis (voro), *gluttonous, voracious*: Charybdis, Cic.; compar.: ignis voracior, Ov.

vŏro -are (connected with βιβρώσκω and βορά), *to eat greedily, swallow up.*

    LIT., Pl., Cic.

    TRANSF., (1) in gen., *to consume, devour*: Charybdis vorat carinas, Ov.; illam (= navem) rapidus vorat aequore vortex, Verg. (2) *to hasten over, attend to eagerly, devour*: litteras, literature, Cic.; viam, Cat.

vors-, *see* vers-.

vort-, *see* ver-.

vōs, *you*, plur. of tu; q.v.

vōtīvus -a -um (votum), *of or relating to a vow, votive, vowed*: ludi, Cic.; iuvenca, Hor.

vōtum -i, n. (voveo), *a vow.*

    LIT., *a solemn* (*conditional*) *promise to the gods*: vota nuncupare, suscipere, concipere, Cic.; solvere, reddere, Cic.; exsequi, Verg.

    TRANSF., (1) *that which has been vowed, a votive offering*: spolia hostium, Vulcano votum, Liv.; votis incendimus aras, Verg. (2) in gen., *a prayer, wish, desire*: hoc erat in votis, *this was what I wished*, Hor.; voti potens, *having gained his wish*, Ov.; Cic., Liv.

vŏvĕo vŏvēre vōvi vōtum, *to vow, promise* (*conditionally*) *to a god.*

    LIT., decumam Herculi, Cic.; aedem, Liv.; with acc. and fut. infin.: vovisse dicitur uvam se deo daturum, Cic.

    TRANSF., *to pray for, to wish*: elige, quid voveas, Ov.; Hor.

vox vōcis, f. (connected with voco), *a voice, cry, call.*

    LIT., vocis contentio et remissio, Cic.; vocem attenuare, Cic.; magna voce dicere, Cic.; rustica vox et agrestis quosdam delectat, *pronunciation*, Cic.; in omni verbo posuit acutam vocem, *accent*, Cic.; Latina voce, *language*, Cic. Of animals: boum, Verg.

    TRANSF., (1) of things, *sound, tone*: sonus et vox omnis, Lucr.; septem discrimina vocum, *the lyre with its seven strings*, Verg. (2) *a thing said with the voice, a saying, utterance*: haec te vox non perculit? Cic.; carpi nostrorum militum vocibus, Caes.; consulum voci atque imperio non oboedire, Cic.; nescit vox missa reverti, Hor.; voces Marsae, *formula, magic incantation*, Hor.

Vulcānus = Volcanus; q.v.

vulgāris (volgāris) -e (vulgus), *common, ordinary, usual*: hominum consuetudo, Cic.; opinio, Cic. N. pl. as subst. **vulgāria** -ium, *ordinary things*: anteponantur rara vulgaribus, Cic.

    ¶ Adv. **vulgārĭtĕr**, *in the ordinary way*: Cic. L.

vulgātus -a -um, partic. from ¹vulgo; q.v.

vulgīvăgus -a -um (vulgus/vagus), *wandering, vagrant*: Lucr.

¹vulgo (volgo) -are (vulgus), *to make common, make generally accessible, spread, publish*: cum consulatum vulgari viderent, Liv.; munus vulgatum ab civibus esse in socios, Liv.; vulgare famam interfecti regis, Liv.; dolorem verbis, *to impart*, Verg.; carmina, *to publish*, Tac.

    ¶ Hence partic. as adj. (with compar. and superl.) **vulgātus** -a -um, *common*; esp. *commonly known*: vulgatior fama est, with acc. and infin., Liv.

²vulgō (volgō) = abl. of vulgus; q.v.

vulgus (volgus) -i, n. (acc. sometimes m.). (1) *the people, the multitude, the public*: non est consilium in vulgo, non ratio, Cic.; Verg., Liv. (2) *a mass, crowd*: vulgus incautum ovium, Hor.; patronorum, Cic. (3) contemptuously, *the rabble, the crowd, the mob*: sapientis iudicium a iudicio vulgi discrepat, Cic.; odi profanum vulgus, Hor.; Verg., Liv.

    ¶ Abl. as adv. **vulgō**, *commonly, generally, before the public, in public, openly*: vulgo totis castris testamenta obsignabantur, Caes.; vulgo nascetur amomum, Verg.

vulnĕrātĭo (volnĕrātĭo) -ōnis, f. (vulnero), *wounding, a wound*: maior haec est vitae, famae, salutis suae vulneratio, Cic.

vulnĕro (volnĕro) -are (vulnus), *to wound, injure.* LIT., physically: aliquem, Cic.; corpus, Cic.; Caes., Liv. TRANSF., eos nondum voce vulnero, Cic.; Verg., Liv.

vulnĭfĭcus (volnĭfĭcus) -a -um (vulnus/facio), *inflicting wounds*: telum, Ov.; chalybs, Verg.

vulnus (volnus) -ĕris, n. *a wound.*

LIT., physical. (**1**) of injuries to living beings: vulnus inferre, Caes.; infligere, Cic.; vulnus accipere, excipere, Cic.; mori ex vulnere, Liv. Sometimes of the instrument giving the wound: haesit sub gutture vulnus, Verg. (**2**) of injuries to things: falcis, Ov.; ornus vulneribus evicta, Verg.

TRANSF., vulnera reipublicae imponere, Cic.; poet., *wounds to the feelings,* esp. from love: vulnus alit venis, Verg.; Lucr.

vulpēcŭla (volpēcula) -ae, f. (dim. of vulpes), *a little fox*: Cic.

vulpēs (volpēs) -is, f. *a fox*: Hor.; prov.: vulpes iungere, of something impossible, Verg.; often also as an emblem of cunning, slyness: animi sub vulpe latentes, Hor.

vulsus -a -um, partic. from vello; q.v.

vultĭcŭlus -i, m. (dim. of vultus), *look, aspect*: non te Bruti nostri vulticulus ab ista oratione deterret? Cic.

vultŭōsus -a -um (vultus), *grimacing, full of airs, affected*: Cic., Quint.

vultur (voltur) -ŭris, m. *a vulture*: Verg., Liv. TRANSF., applied to *a rapacious man*: Sen.

vultŭrīnus (voltŭrīnus) -a -um (vultur), *of or akin to a vulture*: Plin., Mart.

vultŭrĭus (voltŭrĭus) -i, m. *a vulture.* LIT., Lucr., Liv., etc. TRANSF., (**1**) *a rapacious man*: Pl., Cic. (**2**) *an unlucky throw at dice*: Pl.

Vulturnum (Volturnum) -i, n. *a town in Campania on the river Volturnus* (now *Castel Volturno*).

Vulturnus (Volturnus) -i, m. *a river in Campania* (now *Volturno*).

vultus (voltus) -ūs, m. *the expression of the face, countenance, look, aspect.*

LIT., hilaris atque laetus, Cic.; acer, aestus, Hor.; plur.: vultus ficti simulatique, Cic.; vultus instantis tyranni, *threatening frown,* Hor.

TRANSF., (**1**) *the face*: cadere in vultūs, Ov. (**2**) *the look, appearance* of anything: salis (of the sea), Verg.; naturae, Ov.

X

X, x, the twenty-first letter of the Latin alphabet, corresponds with the Greek Ξ, ξ. It arises out of the combination of c and s (dico, dixi), g and s (lego, lexi), h and s (traho, traxi), q and s (coquo, coxi).

xĕnium -i, n. (ξένιον), *a present given to a guest*: Plin. L., Mart. TRANSF., in gen., *a gift, present*: Plin. L.

Xĕnŏphōn -ontis, m. (Ξενοφῶν), *an Athenian historian and general, pupil of Socrates.*

¶ Hence. adj **Xĕnŏphontēus (-tīus)** -a -um, *of Xenophon.*

xērampĕlĭnae -ārum, f. pl. (ξηραμπέλιναι), *dark-red garments*: Juv.

Xerxēs -is, m. (Ξέρξης), *the king of the Persians who invaded Greece and was defeated at Salamis.*

xĭphĭas -ae, m. (ξιφίας), *a sword-fish*: Plin., Ov.

xystĭci -orum, m. pl. (ξυστικός), *athletes*: Suet.

xystus -i, m. and **xystum** -i, n. (ξυστός), *an open colonnade, a walk planted with trees, promenade*: Cic., Plin. L., etc.

Y

Y, y, a letter borrowed from the Greek in order to represent the Greek upsilon (Y).

Z

Z, z, an old Latin letter, in classical times used only to represent the Greek zeta (Z, ζ).

Zăma -ae, f. (Ζάμα), *a town in Numidia, scene of the victory of Scipio over Hannibal* (201 B.C.).

zāmĭa -ae, f. (ζημία), *damage, injury, loss*: Pl.

Zanclē -ēs, f. (Ζάγκλη), *old name of the town Messana* (now *Messina*) *in Sicily, so called from its sickle-like form.*

¶ Hence adj. **Zanclaeus** and **Zanclēïus** -a -um, *of Zancle.*

zēlŏtypus -a -um (ζηλότυπος), *jealous*: Juv., Quint., Mart.

Zēno (-ōn) -ōnis, m. (Ζήνων). (**1**) *a Greek philosopher of Citium in Cyprus, founder of the Stoic school.* (**2**) *a Greek philosopher of the Eleatic school, teacher of Pericles.* (**3**) *a later Greek philosopher of the Epicurean school, teacher of Cicero and Atticus.*

zĕphўrus -i, m. (ζέφυρος), *a warm west wind, zephyr*: Verg., Hor., Ov.; poet., in gen., *wind*: Verg.

Zeuxĭs -idis, m. (Ζεῦξις), *a celebrated Greek painter.*

zm-, see sm-.

zōdĭăcus -i, m. (ζωδιακός), *the zodiac*: Cic. poet.

Zōïlus -i, m. (Ζωίλος), *a severe critic of Homer; hence, in gen., any petty critic*: Ov.

zōna -ae, f. (ζώνη), *a girdle.*

LIT., (**1**) *a maiden's girdle*: Cat. (**2**) *a money-belt*: Liv.

TRANSF., (**1**) *the constellation called Orion's Belt*: Ov. (**2**) zonae, *terrestrial zones,* Verg., Ov.

zōnārĭus -a -um (zona), *of a girdle*: Pl. M. as subst. **zōnārĭus** -i, *a girdle-maker*: Cic.

zōnŭla -ae, f. (dim. of zona), *a little girdle*: Cat.

zōthēca -ae, f. (ζωθήκη), *a private room*: Plin. L.

zōthēcŭla -ae, f. (dim. of zotheca), *a little private room*: Plin. L.

ENGLISH-LATIN DICTIONARY

A

A, an, indef. art.: often not translated: a certain, *quidam.* Distributively: twice a year, *bis in singulis annis.*

abaft, aft, adv. *a puppi, a tergo.*

abandon. (1) of persons, *hominem (de)relinquĕre;* = to forsake, to 'leave in the lurch', *hominem deserĕre, destituĕre.* (2) of things, *rem relinquĕre, omittĕre, ab re desistĕre.*

abandoned, = wicked, *perditus, nefarius;* see also WICKED.

abandonment, *(de)relictio;* or use infin., e.g. *deserĕre amicum,* the — of a friend.

abase, *frangĕre* (e.g. *animum, audaciam*), *comprimĕre, coercĕre.*

abasement, *demissio, deminutio.*

abash, *(hominem) percellĕre, perturbare.*

abate, v. (1) transit. *imminuĕre, remittĕre.* (2) intransit. *cadĕre, imminui, decrescĕre;* of passion, *defervescĕre.*

abatement, *remissio, deminutio:* — in taxation, *vectigalium deminutio.*

abbey, *abbatia* (= cloister: eccl.); in Class. Lat. *templum.*

abbot, *abbas (-ātis:* eccl.); nearest equivalent in Class. Lat. *pontifex.*

abbreviate, *imminuĕre, (de)curtare, praecidĕre, circumcidĕre, contrahĕre.*

abbreviation, = shortening, *compendium, contractio* (e.g. *orationis*): mark of —, *sigla (-orum,* plur.: legal t. t.).

abdicate, *magistratu, dictaturā,* etc., *se abdicare; magistratum,* etc., *eiurare.*

abdication, *abdicatio, eiuratio.*

abdomen, *abdomen.*

abduction, *raptus (-ūs), raptio.*

abed, *in lecto:* to lie —, *(in lecto) cubare.*

aberration, *error.*

abet, *(hominem) adiuvare:* to — in a crime, *sceleris participem* or *socium esse.*

abettor, *socius, adiutor;* see also ACCOMPLICE.

abeyance. (1) to be in —, *iacere, in dubio esse, intermitti.* (2) to leave in —, *rem integram relinquĕre.*

abhor, *abhorrēre ab, abominari, detestari, odisse, odio habēre.*

abhorrence, *detestatio, odium.*

abhorrent. (1) = inconsistent with, *abhorrens, alienus, contrarius.* (2) see HATEFUL.

abide. (1) = linger in, *(com)morari, manēre.* (2) = last, *durare.* (3) to abide by, *stare (in re* or *re).*

abiding, *diuturnus, stabilis, mansurus.*

ability: in gen., *potestas, vires, facultas;* = mental strength, *ingenium:* according to one's —, *pro sua parte, pro parte virili.*

abject, *abiectus, contemptus, humilis.*

abjure, *abiurare, eiurare, recusare.*

ablative, *(casus) ablativus* (gram.).

able, adj.: in gen., *potens* (with genit.): = mentally strong, *ingeniosus:* to be —, *posse, valēre* (esp. of physical strength).

able-bodied, *firmus, robustus, validus.*

ablution, *lavatio, ablutio.*

abnegation, *animi moderatio, temperantia.*

abnormal, *novus, inusitatus, mirus, incredibilis, singularis.*

aboard: to go —, *(in navem* or *navem) conscendĕre;* to be —, *in nave esse;* to put —, *in navem imponĕre;* to have —, *vehĕre.*

abode. (1) = sojourn, *habitatio.* (2) see HOUSE.

abolish, *abolēre, tollĕre, subvertĕre, delēre, exstinguĕre.*

abolition, *dissolutio:* — of debts, *tabulae novae (-arum,* plur.).

abominable, *detestabilis, immanis, nefarius* (= wicked).

abominate, *odisse, detestari.*

aborigines, *indigenae, aborigines.*

abortion, *abortio, abortus (-ūs):* to cause an —, *partum abigĕre, abortum facĕre.*

abortive. LIT., of premature birth, *abortivus.* TRANSF., = unsuccessful, *inritus.*

abound. (1) = to be plentiful, *abundare, superesse.* (2) to — in, *re abundare, adfluĕre, circumfluĕre.*

about. (1) adv. of time or number, *fere, ferme, circiter:* he is — to go, *iturus est.* (2) prep. of place, *circa, circum;* of time, *circa;* of respect, = concerning, *de* with abl.

above. (1) adv. of place, *supra:* from above, *desuper, superne;* the above-mentioned, *quod supra scriptum est.* (2) prep.: a, of place, *super,* with acc. or abl.; *supra,* with acc.: b, of degree, *super, supra,* with acc.

above-board, adj. *legitimus.*

abreast, *pariter:* two horses yoked —, *equi biiugi* or *biiuges.*

abridge; see ABBREVIATE.

abroad, adv. (1) = out of doors: *foras,* with verbs of motion; *foris,* with verbs of rest. (2) = in a foreign land, *peregre;* nations —, *gentes externae* or *exterae;* to go —, *peregre proficisci;* to travel —, *peregrinari.* (3) to spread — = publish, *divulgare.*

abrogate, *abrogare, rescindere.*

abrupt. LIT., = steep, *abruptus, arduus, praeruptus.* TRANSF., (1) of speech, *abruptus,* (2) = sudden, *subitus, repentinus, improvisus.*

abruptly, *abrupte, praerupte, subito, de improviso, repente.*

abscess, *vomica, abscessus (-ūs:* Cels.).

abscond, *delitescĕre, latēre, occultari.*

absence, *absentia:* — abroad, *peregrinatio;* in my —, *me absente;* leave of —, *commeatus (-ūs).*

absent, adj. *absens:* to be —, *abesse.*

absent, v.: to — oneself, *se removēre, non comparēre.*

absolute, *absolutus, simplex:* — power (polit.), *dominatio, imperium singulare;* an — ruler, *dominus populi.*

absolutely, *plane, prorsus, omnino;* opp. to relatively, *per se, simpliciter.*

absolve, *(ab)solvĕre;* see also ACQUIT.

absorb. LIT., *(com)bibĕre, absorbēre, (ex)haurire.* TRANSF., *absorbēre, tenēre:* absorbed in a thing, *totus in re.*

abstain, (se) re abstinēre.

abstinence, abstinentia, continentia, modestia, moderatio, temperantia: days of —, = fast days, ieiunium.

abstinent, abstinens, sobrius, moderatus, temperatus.

abstract, subst. epitome (-es), or epitoma.

abstract, adj. = removed from the sphere of the senses, quod nullo sensu percipi potest; an — idea, notio nulli sensui subiecta; an — discussion, disputatio paulo abstrusior.

abstract, v. abstrahĕre, sevocare; for the sense to steal, see STEAL.

abstracted, = lost in thought, omnium rerum (or sui) oblītus.

abstraction, = forgetfulness, oblivio.

abstruse, abstrusus, obscurus, reconditus.

abstruseness, obscuritas.

absurd, absurdus, ineptus, inscitus, ridiculus.

absurdity. (1) as a quality, insulsitas, ineptia. (2) = an absurd thing, ineptia.

absurdly, absurde, inepte, inscite, ridicule.

abundance, (rerum) abundantia, adfluentia, ubertas, copia.

abundant, largus, amplus.

abundantly, abunde, abundanter, large, cumulate.

abuse, subst. (1) = the wrong use of a thing, usus (-ūs) perversus; or use verb abuti. (2) = abusive language, convicium, maledictum. (3) = a bad custom, mos pravus, mos perversus.

abuse, v. transit. (1) = to misuse, (re) abuti. (2) = to speak abusively to, (homini) maledicĕre.

abusive, maledicus, maledicens, contumeliosus.

abusively, maledice, contumeliose.

abut, v.: to — on a thing, rei adiacēre, rem attingĕre.

abyss. LIT., profundum, gurges (-itis: esp. containing water), barathrum, vorago. TRANSF., gurges, vorago.

academic, scholasticus (mainly of the study of rhetoric: Quint., Tac.): an — (i.e. theoretical) question, render by phrase such as res ad cognitionem modo pertinens.

academy. (1) the Academy at Athens, Academia. (2) = a school, ludus, schola.

accede; see AGREE.

accelerate, accelerare; see also HASTEN.

accent, in pronunciation: vox, sonus (-ūs), tenor.

accept, accipĕre, recipĕre: to — an office, munus suscipĕre; to — an invitation to dinner, promittĕre ad cenam.

acceptable, iucundus, acceptus, gratus.

acceptance. (1) acceptio. (2) = approbation, comprobatio.

acceptation, = significance, significatio.

access. (1) = approach, aditus (-ūs), accessus (-ūs): I have —, mihi est aditus; there is — to me, ad me est aditus. (2) as medic. t., = the periodical return of a fever, impetus, tentatio, accessio (Cels.).

accessary, subst. = accomplice, conscius, (culpae) socius.

accessible, facilis.

accession. (1) = increase, accessio. (2) accession to the throne, initium regni.

accessory, adj. = additional; use verb accedo.

accident, casus (-ūs).

accidental, fortuitus.

accidentally, forte, casu, fortuito.

acclaim, acclamation, clamor, acclamatio (but in Cic. always of disapproval).

acclaim, acclamare (but in Cic. only of disapproval).

accommodate, accommodare.

accommodating, obsequens, facilis: to be — to, (homini) morem gerĕre, morigerari.

accommodation. (1) = adjustment of differences, reconciliatio, compositio; see AGREEMENT. (2) = quarters, place of reception, hospitium.

accompaniment. (1) comitatus (-ūs). (2) in music, adiunctio fidium voci; or use verb: to sing to a flute —, ad tibiam canĕre.

accompany. (1) = to go with: in gen., (hominem) comitari; as a mark of respect, prosequi, deducĕre, reducĕre; in a crowd, stipare; accompanied by, cum (with abl.). (2) in music = to play an accompaniment for another, (homini) concinĕre.

accomplice, socius, sceleris conscius, adfinis, satelles.

accomplish, conficĕre, perficĕre, absolvere, peragĕre, exsequi.

accomplished, (per)politus, elegans, doctus, humanus, eruditus.

accomplishment. (1) = fulfilment, confectio, perfectio, absolutio; or use verb. (2) = an acquired skill, ars.

accord, subst. (1) as musical term; see HARMONY. (2) of one's own — = without compulsion or influence, sponte (suā), voluntate (suā); beyond expectation, gratuitously, ultro.

accord, v. transit. (1) = grant; q.v. (2) = agree; q.v.

accordance: in — with, ex, de, pro with abl.; secundum, ad with acc.; according to circumstances, ad tempus, pro re; in — with my wishes, ut volui.

according to; see ACCORDANCE.

accordingly, ergo, itaque, quae cum ita sint.

accost, appellare, compellare, adoriri.

accouchement, partus (-ūs).

account, subst. (1) = reckoning, ratio: to take into —, rationem habēre rei (genit.); — books, tabulae (-arum, plur.), codex; to put a thing down to a person's —, rem (homini) expensam ferre; the —s balance, ratio constat. (2) to be of —, magni or maximi haberi; to be of no —, nullo numero esse. (3) = pretext, reason: on my —, meā de causā, meo nomine; on no —, minime, nullo modo; on — of anything, propter rem, ob rem. (4) = narrative, memoria, narratio: give an — of, rem narrare.

account, v. (1) = to think, consider, habēre, aestimare, ducĕre. (2) to — for, rationem de re reddĕre.

accountable; see RESPONSIBLE.

accountant, scriba.

accoutre; see EQUIP.

accredit: to — an ambassador, legatum facĕre, legatum publica auctoritate mittĕre.

accretion, accessio, incrementum, cumulus.

accumulate, (co)acervare, (ac)cumulare, congerĕre, exaggerare.

accumulation, cumulus, acervus, congestus (-ūs).

accuracy. (1) = care taken, cura, diligentia. (2) = truth, veritas.

accurate. (1) of persons, = careful, pains-taking, *diligens, religiosus.* (2) of things, *verus* (in accordance with fact), *accuratus* (executed with care).

accusation, as legal t. t. *accusatio, criminatio, crimen*: a false —, *insimulatio, calumnia.* In gen., *incusatio*; also the words cited above.

accusative, as gram. t. t. *accusativus (casus).*

accuse, legal t. t. (*hominem rei*, genit., or *de re*) *accusare, postulare, compellare, citare, reum facĕre, arguĕre, insimulare* (often falsely); *nomen hominis de re deferre.*

accused, subst. and adj. *reus.*

accuser: on a criminal charge, *accusator*; in a civil suit, *petitor*; = an informer, *index, delator*; or use verb.

accustom, (*hominem*) *adsuefacĕre* (*re, rei* dat., *ad rem*, or with infin.): to — oneself, to grow accustomed, *adsuescĕre, consuescĕre,* with *ad* or dat. or infin; to be accustomed, *solēre.*

accustomed, *adsuetus, solitus.*

ace, in cards. Use terms from dice; the side of the die marked 1, *canis* (= the dog-throw, i.e. worst); the best throw, the — of trumps, *Venus* (*-eris*), (*iactus*) *basilicus.*

acerbity, *acerbitas.*

ache, subst. *dolor.*

ache, v. *dolēre.*

achieve. (1) = to finish, *facĕre, conficĕre, efficĕre, perficĕre.* (2) = to gain, reach, *adsequi, consequi.*

achievement. (1) = the doing of anything, *confectio.* (2) = a deed, *facinus* (*-ŏris*, n.; but more usual in bad sense); *res gesta*; or use verb.

acid, adj. (1) = sharp to the taste, *acidus, acerbus, acer.* (2) in temper, *acer, acerbus, morosus.*

acknowledge. (1) = to accept as one's own, *agnoscĕre*: to — a child, *suscipĕre, tollĕre* (the father raised a new-born child from the ground). (2) = to admit, *fatēri, confitēri.* (3) = to give thanks for, *gratias agĕre*: to — a payment, (*in*) *acceptum referre* (i.e. to place to the credit side of an account-book); to — a letter, *rescribĕre* with dat. or *ad.*

acknowledged, *cognitus, probatus, spectatus.*

acknowledgment. (1) = confession, *confessio*; or use verb. (2) = thanks, *gratiae.*

acme, *fastigium*: to reach the — of glory, *summam gloriam adsequi.*

acorn, *glans.*

acquaint; see INFORM.

acquaintance. (1) = knowledge: of a thing, *scientia*; of a person, *usus* (*-ūs*), *familiaritas, consuetudo cum homine.* (2) = a person slightly known, *amicus, familiaris, noti* (used as subst. only in plur.).

acquainted, *notus, cognitus*: — with a person, *familiaris*; — with a thing, *rei* (genit.) *peritus, gnarus, sciens; in re versatus.*

acquiesce, (*in*) *re acquiescĕre, rem aequo animo cr patienter ferre, re contentus esse.*

acquiescence, *adsensus* (*-ūs*); see ASSENT.

acquire, *adquirĕre, adipisci*; see also GAIN.

acquirement, acquisition. (1) = anything gained; see GAIN. (2) = acquired skill or knowledge, *ars, scientia*: a man of many —s, *vir perpolitus, multis artibus eruditus.* (3) the process of —, *comparatio, adeptio.*

acquisitive, *lucri studiosus.*

acquit, (*rei*, genit., or *de re*) *absolvĕre*; (*re*) *liberare, purgare.*

acquittal, *absolutio, liberatio.*

acrid, *acer, acerbus, mordax.*

acridity, *acerbitas.*

acrimonious, *mordax, acerbus, amarus, aculeatus.*

acrimony, *acerbitas.*

across. (1) adv.: use compound verb with *trans-*. (2) prep.: = to the other side of, *trans, per,* with acc.; = on the other side of, *trans*; of a bridge, across a river, *in flumine.*

act, subst. (1) of a play, *actus* (*-ūs*). (2) of Parliament, *lex.* (3) = thing done, *factum*: in plur., *res gestae, gesta* (*-orum*, plur.) or *acta* (*-orum*, plur.: esp. of public life); caught in the —, *manifestus*; it is the — of a wise man to, *sapientis est,* with infin.

act, v. (1) intransit. = to do, behave (esp. with adv.), *agĕre, facĕre, se gerĕre*; of drugs, *efficax esse*; on the stage, see below. (2) transit., to — a part on the stage, *in scena esse*; to — the chief part, *primas partes agĕre*; to — a play, *fabulam agĕre*; fig., to — a part in ordinary life, *personam sustinēre* or *partes agere.*

action. (1) = the doing of anything, *actio.* (2) = a deed, thing done, *factum*; see ACT. (3) = battle, *pugna, proelium.* (4) = part of a play, *actio.* (5) = gesticulation, *actio, gestus* (*-ūs*). (6) = legal proceedings, *lis, actio*; in a Greek court, *dica*; to bring an —, *litem* or *actionem intendĕre, dicam scribĕre, diem dicĕre, lege agĕre.*

actionable, (*res*) *cuius actio est.*

active. (1) = quick, *celer, acer, promptus, alacer, agilis.* (2) = industrious, *impiger, (g)navus, industrius, strenuus.*

actively, *impigre, industrie, (g)naviter, strenue.*

activity. (1) = quickness, *celeritas, agilitas.* (2) = industry, *industria, (g)navitas.*

actor. (1) in gen. = one who acts, *qui agit* or *facit, actor.* (2) on the stage, *histrio, actor*: comic —, *comoedus*; tragic —, *tragoedus.*

actress. Only men acted in 'straight plays' in classical times; perhaps use *mima.*

actual, *verus.*

actually, *vere, re verā.*

actuate, *movēre, excitare, impellĕre.*

acumen, *ingenii acies* or *acumen.*

acute. (1) of pain, *acutus, acer, gravis, vehemens acerbus.* (2) of intellect, *acutus, subtilis, acer, perspicax, sagax.* (3) see ANGLE.

acutely. (1) of feeling, *acute.* (2) of intellect, *acriter, subtiliter.*

acuteness, *ingenii acies* or *acumen, subtilitas.*

adage, *proverbium.*

adamant, subst. *adamas* (*-antis*).

adamantine, adj. *adamantinus, adamanteus.*

adapt, *accommodare, aptare.*

adaptation, *accommodatio.*

adapted, *aptus* or *idoneus* (*ad rem* or *rei*, dat.).

add, *addĕre, adicĕre, adiungĕre*: to — up, *summam facĕre, computare.*

adder, *vipera, coluber.*

addict, v.: to — oneself, *se dare, dedĕre,* or *tradĕre; se ad studium rei conferre.*

addicted, adj. *rei* (dat.) *deditus.*

addition. (1) = an adding to, *adiectio, accessio,* or use verb. (2) = a thing added, *additamentum, appendix.* (3) in arith. *additio* (Quint).

additional, *novus, addĭtus, adiectus.*

addled: an — egg, *ovum abortivum* (Mart.), *ovum inritum, zephyrium* (Plin.).

address, subst. (1) = a speech delivered in public, *contio, oratio.* (2) the — of a letter, *inscriptio.* (3) = place, *locus.* (4) = tact, adroitness, *dexteritas, sollertia.*

address, v. transit. (1) to — oneself, i.e. to apply oneself to anything, *se rei* (dat.) *dedĕre, tradĕre, ad* or *in rem incumbĕre.* (2) = to speak to, *hominem adloqui, adfari, appellare, compellare;* to — a letter to, *homini epistulam inscribĕre;* to — a meeting, *verba facĕre apud populum.*

adduce, *adducĕre, producĕre, proferre.*

adept, *callidus, peritus.*

adequate, (*rei,* dat., or *ad rem*) *aptus, idoneus, accommodatus;* or use adv. *satis.*

adequately, *apte, satis.*

adhere. LIT., (*in*)*haerēre.* TRANSF., (*in*)*haerēre;* also, of adhering to persons, *studēre, deditum esse;* of adhering to principles, etc., *in re stare, manēre.*

adherence, adhesion, express by verb.

adherent, *socius, fautor, cliens.*

adhesive, *tenax.*

adieu! *vale!* plur. *valete:* to bid —, *hominem valēre iubēre.*

adjacent, *contiguus, vicinus, finitimus:* to be —, *adiacēre;* to be — to, *tangĕre, attingĕre,* with acc.

adjective, *nomen adiectivum* (gram.).

adjoin; see ADJACENT.

adjourn, *ampliare, rem differre, proferre.*

adjournment, *dilatio.*

adjudge, *addicĕre, adiudicare.*

adjudicate; see JUDGE.

adjunct; see ADDITION.

adjure, = to entreat, *obsecrare, obtestari.*

adjust. (1) see ARRANGE. (2) see ADAPT.

adjustment, *accommodatio.*

adjutant, *optio* (*-ōnis*).

administer, *rem administrare, procurare:* to — an oath to, *hominem* (*ad*) *ius iurandum adigere;* to — medicine, *medicinam dare, adhibere;* to — justice, *ius· dicĕre* or *reddĕre;* to — the government, *rempublicam gubernare* or *administrare.*

administration. (1) as the act of administering, *administratio, procuratio.* (2) as a body of ministers, *ei qui reipublicae praesunt;* see also GOVERNMENT.

admirable, (*ad*)*mirabilis;* see also EXCELLENT.

admirably, *admirabiliter, mirum in modum, praeclare.*

admiral, *praefectus classis:* to appoint as —, *praeficĕre classi;* to be an —, *classi praeesse.*

admiration, *admiratio.*

admire, (*ad*)*mirari:* to be —d, *admirationi esse.*

admissible, *aequus;* or use verb.

admission. (1) = leave to enter, *aditus* (*-ūs*), *accessus* (*-ūs*); or use verb. (2) = confession, *confessio;* in argument, *concessio.*

admit. (1) = to allow to enter, *admittĕre, recipĕre; adeundi copiam* or *potestatem facĕre.* (2) in argument, to concede, *concedĕre, dare.* (3) = to confess, *fatēri, confitēri.* (4) to admit of, allow, leave possible, *habēre, recipĕre, pati;* or use *possum.*

admonish, *monēre, admonēre, commonēre.*

admonition, (*ad*)*monitio.*

ado: with much —, *vix, aegre;* see also FUSS.

Prov.: to make much — about nothing, *arcem facĕre e cloaca* (Cic.).

adolescence, *adulescentia.*

adolescent, subst. *adulescens.*

adopt. LIT., as legal t. t. *adoptare:* in gen. = to choose, accept, *asciscĕre, adsumĕre, accipĕre, recipĕre:* to — a resolution, *constituĕre, consilium inire;* to — an opinion, *ad sententiam accedĕre.*

adoption, *adoptio.*

adoptive, *adoptivus.*

adorable, *sanctus, venerandus.*

adoration, *cultus* (*-ūs*), *veneratio.*

adore, v. transit.: = to worship, *venerari, colĕre:* in gen. = to love, to admire, *colĕre, diligĕre, amare.*

adorn, (*ex*)*ornare, decorare.*

adornment, *ornatus* (*-ūs*), *exornatio.*

adrift, to be. LIT., *fluctibus* or *vento iactari.* TRANSF., in mind, (*animo*) *vagari.*

adroit, *callidus, sollers, dexter.*

adroitly, *callide, dextere.*

adroitness, *dexteritas.*

adulation, *adulatio, adsentatio, blanditia.*

adult, *adultus, pubes.*

adulterate, *adulterare, corrumpĕre, vitiare.*

adulterer, *adulter, moechus* (Hor.).

adulteress, *adultera* (Hor.), *moecha* (Hor.).

adulterous, *adulter* (Hor.).

adultery, *adulterium,* sometimes *stuprum:* to commit —, *adulterare,* or use phrase.

adults, subst. *puberes* (plur. only).

adumbrate, *adumbrare.*

adumbration, *adumbratio.*

advance, subst. = a forward movement (lit. and fig.), *progressus* (*-ūs*).

advance, v. (1) intransit. = to go forward. LIT., *progredi, procedĕre;* in riding, sailing, etc., *provehi.* TRANSF., *procedĕre, progredi, proficĕre:* to become advanced in years, *aetate provehi.* (2) transit. = to carry forward. LIT., *promovēre.* TRANSF., **a** = to promote, *provehĕre, adiuvare, augēre:* to — anyone's interests, *homini consulĕre:* **b** = to pay in advance, *in antecessum dare* (Sen.).

advance-guard, *primum agmen.*

advancement, *gradus* (*-ūs*) *amplior;* or use verb.

advantage, *commodum, lucrum, fructus* (*-ūs*), *emolumentum, utilitas, bonum* (esp. in plur. *bona,* — s): — of a position, *loci opportunitas;* it is to my —, *ex meā re est;* to be of —, *expedire, prodesse, utile, ex usu* or *usui esse.*

advantageous, *quaestuosus, utilis, fructuosus, opportunus.*

advantageously, *utiliter.*

advent, *adventus* (*-ūs*).

adventitious, adj. *adventicius, externus.*

adventure, subst. (1) of active type = exploit, *facinus* (*-oris,* n.), *inceptum.* (2) of passive type, *casus* (*-ūs*).

adventure, v. *audēre, tentare, experiri, periclitari.*

adventurer, use phrase, according to context.

adventurous, *audax.*

adventurously, *audacter.*

adverb, *adverbium* (gram.).

adversary, *adversarius;* see ENEMY.

adverse, *adversus, contrarius, infensus.*

adversely, *contra, secus.*

adversity, *res adversae, miseria, calamitas.*

advert to, = refer to, (*rem*) *attingere, perstringĕre.*

advertise. (1) = to inform; q.v. (2) = to make publicly known, *praedicare, pronuntiare*. (3) to announce that a thing is for sale, *rem proscribĕre, rem (venalem) inscribĕre*.

advertisement, = notice of sale, *proscriptio*.

advice, *consilium*: by my —, *me auctore*.

advise, v. transit. (1) = to give advice to, *homini suadere, consilium dare, auctorem esse, consiliari* (Hor.). (2) = to inform; q.v.

advisedly, *consulto, consulte, considerate, de industriā*.

adviser, *suasor, consiliarius, auctor*.

advocate, subst.: as legal t. t., *patronus*; contemptuous, *causidicus*; in gen., *suasor, auctor*.

advocate, v. transit. *suadēre*.

adze, *ascia*.

aerial, *aĕrius, aetherius*.

afar, *procul, longe*.

affability, *comitas, facilitas*.

affable, *adfabilis, comis*.

affably, *comiter*.

affair, *res, negotium*; sometimes *ratio*.

affect, v. transit. (1) = to influence, *adficĕre, tangĕre, (com)movēre*. (2) = to be fond of, *diligĕre, amare*. (3) to make a show of, *simulare, imitari*.

affectation, *simulatio, imitatio, ostentatio*.

affected, of attitudes, etc., *quaesitus, simulatus*; of style, *putidus, molestus*

affectedly, *putide, moleste*.

affection. (1) = a state of a thing influenced from without, esp. of a mind, *(animi) adfectio, adfectus (-ūs)*. (2) = a friendly sentiment, *amor, caritas, studium*: dutiful —, *pietas*.

affectionate, *amans* (e.g. *uxoris*): dutifully —, *pius*.

affectionately, *amanter, pie*.

affiance, subst. (1) = trust, *fiducia, fides*. (2) = marriage contract, *sponsalia (-ium*, plur. : Sen.).

affiance, v. transit. = betroth, *(de)spondeo*.

affidavit, *testimonium per tabulas datum* (Quint.).

affinity. (1) = relationship, *propinquitas, necessitudo, consanguinitas* (by blood), *cognatio* (on the side of the father or the mother), *agnatio* (on the side of the father), *adfinitas* (by marriage). (2) in gen. = close connexion, similarity, *cognatio, coniunctio*.

affirm, *adfirmare, confirmare*.

affirmation, *adfirmatio*.

affirmative, use verb.

affix, *adfigĕre, adligare, adnectĕre*.

afflict, *adflictare, vexare, dolore adficĕre*.

affliction, *aegritudo, dolor, maestitia, miseria, molestia*.

affluence, = wealth, *divitiae, opes, copia*.

affluent, = wealthy, *dives*.

afford. (1) = to supply, *praestare, praebēre, sufficĕre, suppeditare*. (2) can —, = be rich enough to buy; use phrase.

affray, = disturbance, breach of the peace, *rixa, pugna, tumultus (-ūs)*.

affright; see FRIGHTEN.

affront, subst. *contumelia*.

affront, v. transit. = to insult, *contumeliā adficĕre*.

affronting, adj. *contumeliosus*.

afield, *in agros* (with verbs of motion), *in agris* (with verbs of rest).

afloat: to be —, *navigare, navi vehi*.

afoot, *pedibus* (e.g. *pedibus ire*).

aforesaid, *quem* (or *quod*) *supra scripsi* or *commemoravi*.

afraid, *timidus, pavidus, trepidus, terrĭtus*: to be — (of), *(hominem, rem) timēre, metuĕre, reformidare, pavēre*.

afresh; see AGAIN.

after. (1) prep. : **a**, of place, *post*, with acc. : **b**, of time, *post*, with acc.; sometimes *ab* or *ex*, with abl. : **c**, of rank = coming after, inferior to, *secundum*, with acc.; or use adj. *secundus ab*, with abl. : **d**, of conformity, according to, *ad*, with acc. (e.g. *ad normam* = after a set rule). (2) conj. *postquam* or *postea quam* (usually with perf. or historic present indic.); *cum, ubi*; often rendered by perf. part. (3) adv., after, *post, postea, dein(de), inde*; = after this, *posthac*; when the interval between the events is defined, use *post* or *postea* with abl. of measure, or *post* (prep.) with acc., e.g. *paulo post, biduo post, paucis postea mensibus, aliquot post menses*.

afternoon, subst. *postmeridianum tempus*: in the —, *post meridiem*.

afternoon, adj. *postmeridianus*.

again. (1) when an event is repeated, in gen., *rursus, rursum, denuo*; = a second time, *iterum*; — and —, *iterum atque iterum, iterum ac saepius, identidem*; never —, *numquam postea* (or *posthac*); often render by compound verb with *re-*, e.g. to rise —, *resurgĕre*. (2) of addition in gen. = further, moreover, *porro, autem*: as large —, *altero tanto maior*.

against, of physical movement or of opposition in gen., *contra, adversus, in*, with acc. : — expectation, *praeter* or *contra opinionem*; — the stream, *adverso flumine*; — my will, *me invito*; for and —, *in utramque partem*.

age, subst. (1) = time of life, *aetas*, poet. *aevum*; of the same —, *aequalis*; twenty years of age, *viginti annos natus*. (2) an age = a period of time, *aetas, saeculum*; these are also used of the people living at a particular period. (3) = old age; of persons, *senectūs (-utis)*; of things, *vetustas*.

aged, = old, *aetate provectus*; poet. *grandaevus, longaevus*: an — man, *senex (-is)*.

agency. (1) = action; q.v. (2) = instrumentality, *opera*. (3) the work of an agent, *procuratio*.

agent, = one who transacts business for another, *procurator*.

aggrandize, *amplificare, augēre*.

aggrandizement, *amplificatio*; or use verb.

aggravate. (1) properly = to make worse, *(ad)-gravare, exulcerare*. (2) colloq. = to annoy, *vexare, exasperare, lacessĕre*.

aggregate, *summa*.

aggression, *impetus (-ūs), incursio, incursus (-ūs), iniuria*; often use *ultro* with verb.

aggressive, *hostilis, infensus*.

aggressor, the, *qui ultro* (or *prior*) *oppugnat, qui iniuriam facit*.

aggrieve; see GRIEVE.

aghast, *stupefactus, (ex)terrĭtus, perturbatus*: to stand —, *stupēre, obstupescĕre*.

agile, *agilis, velox, pernix*.

agility, *agilitas, pernicitas, velocitas*.

agitate. (1) = to move to and fro, to shake, *agitare, quatĕre, vibrare, (com)movēre, (con)-turbare*. (2) mentally, to disturb, excite, percutĕre, perturbare, sollicitare, commovĕre, percellĕre. (3) = to discuss, (rem or de re) agĕre; (rem) agitare, disputare, disserĕre.

agitated, sollicitus, trepidus.

agitation. (1) physical, agitatio, iactatio. (2) mental, animi motus, commotio, concitatio.

agitator, polit. t. t. turbator plebis or vulgi.

ago, abhinc, followed by acc. (rarely abl.): long —, (iam) pridem, iam dudum.

agonize, (ex)cruciare, torquēre.

agony, aegritudo, dolor.

agrarian, agrarius.

agree. (1) = to be of one mind, concinĕre, consentire, congruĕre: not to —, dissentire; it is agreed by all, constat inter omnes. (2) to — upon, arrange, settle, componĕre, constituĕre, pacisci; it is agreed upon by us, convenit inter nos.

agreeable, = pleasant. (1) of things, acceptus, gratus, dulcis, suavis. (2) of persons, commodus, lepidus.

agreement. (1) = harmony, consensus (-ūs), concordia, unanimitas, constantia. (2) = an arrangement, compact, pactum, pactio, conventum.

agricultural, rusticus.

agriculture, agri cultura (or as one word, agricultura); agri cultio (or as one word); or agrorum cultus (-ūs); res (plur.) rusticae.

agriculturist, agricola.

aground, to run, sidĕre.

ague, febris.

ah! aha! interj. a, ah, aha.

ahead, use compound verb with prae- or pro-.

aid, subst. = help, auxilium, adiumentum, subsidium, opem (nom. ops not used).

aid, v. transit. (hominem) adiuvare, (homini) subvenire, succurrĕre, opem ferre.

ailing, aeger; see SICK.

aim, subst. finis, propositum, consilium; or use verb meaning 'aim at'.

aim, v. LIT., to take —, telum conlineare, telum dirigĕre or intendĕre; to — at, telo petĕre. TRANSF., to — at (any objective or result), rem (animo) intendĕre, adfectare, petĕre, quaerĕre, rem (or ad rem) spectare, rei (dat.) studēre, id agĕre ut . . .

air, subst. LIT., aër (the atmosphere near the earth), aether (the pure upper air), aura (air in motion, breeze), anima (usually = breath): in the open —, sub Iove, sub divo. TRANSF., (1) = look, manner, vultus (-ūs), aspectus (-ūs), species: to give oneself —s, iactare. (2) = a tune, modus, numeri (-orum, plur.).

air, v. ventilare.

airy, aerius.

Aix, Aquae Sextiae.

akin. (1) = related, consanguineus, propinquus, agnatus (on the father's side), cognatus (on the father's or the mother's). (2) = similar, connected, finitimus, propinquus, vicinus.

alabaster, alabastrites (-ae, m.: Plin.): an — box, alabaster.

alack! = alas; q.v.

alacrity, alacritas, pernicitas.

alarm, subst. (1) = loud noise, clamor, strepitus (-ūs). (2) = disturbance, turba, tumultus (-ūs). (3) = fear, terror, trepidatio, pavor.

alarm, v. transit. conturbare, (per)terrēre.

alas! heu! eheu! vae! ei!

alcove, zotheca (Plin.).

alder, alnus, f.; adj. alneus.

alderman, use title of an appropriate magistrate, according to context.

ale, cerevisia (a Gallic word).

ale-house, caupona.

alert, vigil, alacer, promptus.

alias, nomen alienum: to assume an —, nomen sibi fingĕre.

alien, adj. (1) = foreign, peregrinus, externus. (2) incompatible, adverse, alienus, aversus.

alien, subst. peregrinus, advena, alienigena.

alienate, v. transit. (1) as legal t. t. (ab)alienare. (2) = to estrange, (ab)alienare, avertere.

alienation. (1) as legal t. t., abalienatio. (2) = estrangement, alienatio.

alight, v. descendĕre.

alike, adj. par, similis.

alike, adv. pariter, similiter, aeque, eodem modo.

alive, vivus: to be —, in vita or in vivis esse, vivĕre; see LIFE.

all, = every single, omnis; = the whole, totus; — together, cunctus, universus; — men without exception, nemo non; — the best men, optimus quisque; not at —, minime; in —, in summa, omnino (e.g. there were five in —, quinque omnino erant); it is — up with, — over with, actum est de, with abl.; it is — one, nihil interest; — but, tantum (or modo) non (Liv.); — right, salve; are you — right? satin salve?

allay, lenire, sedare, mitigare.

allegation, adfirmatio; see also ACCUSATION.

allege, = assert; q.v.; to — by way of excuse, praetendĕre.

allegiance, fides: to swear — to, in verba hominis iurare; to keep in one's —, in officio retinēre.

allegory, allegoria (Quint.), continua translatio.

alleviate, (ad)levare; see also ALLAY.

alleviation, levatio, mitigatio, levamen(tum).

alley, angiportus (-ūs).

alliance, societas, foedus (-eris): matrimonial —, matrimonium.

allot. LIT., = assign by lot, sortiri; in gen. = to distribute, grant, distribuĕre, assignare, addicĕre, adiudicare.

allotment. (1) = act of allotting, assignatio. (2) an allotment of land, ager assignatus, possessio.

allow. (1) = permit, (hominem) sinĕre, pati (homini) permittĕre, concedĕre: I am allowed licet mihi; not to — oneself to, non committere ut . . . (2) = admit, acknowledge concedĕre, confiteri. (3) = to grant; q.v.

allowable, concessus, licitus, or use indecl. subst. fas.

allowance. (1) = indulgence, indulgentia: to make — for, ignoscĕre, condonare. (2) = an amount allowed, of food, diaria, demensum.

alloy, subst.: without —, sincerus, purus.

alloy, v. transit. = to spoil, corrumpĕre, vitiare

allude to, = to refer to, significare, designare attingere.

allure, v. transit. adlicĕre, inlicĕre, adlectare invitare, inescare.

allurement, invitamentum, blandimentum blanditia, inlecebra.

alluring, blandus.

allusion, significatio, mentio, or use verb.

ally, subst. socius: relating to an —, socialis.

ally, v. (1) = to make an alliance, foedus facĕre (or ferire), societatem inire. (2) = join together as allies, sociare.

almanack, *fasti* (*-orum,* plur.), *ephemeris* (*-ĭdis*).

almighty, *omnipotens.*

almond, *amygdala* (Plin.), *amygdalum* (Ov.).

almond-tree, *amygdala* (Plin.)

almost, *prope, paene;* more loosely = more or less, about, *fere, ferme;* it — happens, *haud multum abest quin fiat.*

alms, *stips* (*-is,* f.: nom. not used).

aloe, *aloë* (*-es*).

aloft, *sublime, alte;* often to be rendered by *sublimis* as adj.

alone, adj. *solus, unus;* sometimes *sine arbitris, remotis arbitris* (= without witness).

alone, adv. = only; q.v.

along. (1) adv. *porro, protinus.* (2) prep. *secundum, praeter,* with acc.: — with, *una cum.*

aloof, *procul*: to stand — from, *se ab homine* (or *re*) *removēre.*

aloud, *clare, clarā voce, magnā voce;* see also LOUD.

alphabet, *litterarum nomina et contextus* (*-ūs*: Quint.); see also LETTER.

alphabetical, *in litteras digestus.*

already, *iam.*

also, *etiam, praeterea* (= besides), *insuper* (= moreover), *quoque* (always after the word to which it refers), *necnon* (= moreover, joins sentences), *item, itidem* (= again, likewise). When something fresh is added about a person or thing already mentioned (esp. by way of contrast), *idem* is often used.

altar. LIT., in gen, *ara; altaria,* plur.= a high altar. TRANSF., in metaphor, *ara.*

alter, v. (1) transit. *mutare, commutare, immutare,* (*con*)*vertĕre; novare* (= to give a new form); *emendare, corrigĕre* (= to put right); *variare* (= to change often); *invertĕre* (= to turn upside down); *corrumpĕre* (= to falsify or spoil). (2) intransit., use passive of above verbs.

alterable, *mutabilis.*

alteration, (*com*)*mutatio* : a sudden (or violent) —, *conversio;* —s in the weather, *caeli varietas;* — of fortune, *fortunae vicissitudines.*

altercation, *altercatio, iurgium, rixa.*

alternate, v. (1) transit. *alternare, variare;* to — rest and labour, *otium labore variare* (Plin.). (2) intransit. *variari, variare.*

alternate, adj. *alternus.*

alternately, *invicem.*

alternation, *vicissitudo.*

alternative, adj. and subst., express by phrase: there is no — left except . . ., *nihil restat nisi ut* . . .; there is no — to peace or war, *inter pacem et bellum nihil est medium.*

although, *quamquam* (normally with the indic., as indicating a fact; sometimes introducing a complete sentence); *etsi* or *tametsi* (with indic. for fact, subj. for supposition); *quamvis* (= however much; normally with subj., as indicating an imaginary concession; sometimes without verb); *licet* (= granted that, with subj.); *ut* (with subj.); *cum* (with subj.).

altitude, *altitudo.*

altogether, = wholly, *omnino.*

alum, *alumen* (Plin.).

always, *semper, numquam non*: the best is — the last, *optimum quidque est ultimum.*

amalgamate, (*com*)*miscēre.*

amalgamation, *coniunctio, mixtura;* or use verb.

amanuensis, *librarius, servus a manu.*

amass, (*co*)*acervare, aggerare, accumulare;* see also ACCUMULATE.

amatory, *amatorius;* see also LOVE.

amaze, *obstupefacĕre.*

amazed, (*ob*)*stupefactus, stupidus* : to be —, *stupēre,* (*ob*)*stupescĕre.*

amazement, *stupor.*

amazing, *mirus, admirabilis.*

amazingly, *admirabiliter, mirum in modum.*

amazon. LIT., *Amazon.* TRANSF., *virago.*

ambassador, *legatus* (as a deputy in state affairs); *orator* (as a deputy to deliver a specific verbal message).

amber, *sucinum, electrum* (Plin.).

ambiguity, *ambiguitas;* or use *ambages,* plur. (= a riddle); or adj. or verb.

ambiguous, *anceps, ambiguus, dubius.*

ambiguously, *ambigue.*

ambition, *gloria;* or use phrase, such as *laudis studium, contentio honorum.*

ambitious, *gloriae* (or *laudis*) *adpetens, cupidus,* etc.; *ambitiosus* is used more often of the process of courting favour than of the spirit of ambition.

amble, *lente procedĕre.*

ambrosia, *ambrosia.*

ambrosial, *ambrosius.*

ambush, *insidiae,* plur. (= the place and the troops).

ameliorate, (*rem* or *hominem*) *meliorem facĕre, corrigĕre, emendare.*

amen! *fiat! esto!*

amenable, (*dicto*) *oboediens* (with dat.).

amend. (1) *emendare, corrigĕre.* (2) intransit. *melior fieri*: to — in health, *convalescĕre.*

amendment, *correctio, emendatio.*

amends, *satisfactio, expiatio*: to make — for, *rem expiare, satisfacĕre.*

amenity, *amoenitas.*

amethyst, *amethystus* (Plin.).

amiability, *suavitas.*

amiable, *suavis, amabilis.*

amiably, *suaviter.*

amicable; see FRIENDLY.

amidst, *inter,* with acc.; see also AMONG.

Amiens, *Samarobriva.*

amiss, *male, perperam, prave*: to take —, (*rem*) *aegre* (or *moleste*) *ferre, in malam partem accipĕre.*

ammunition: in gen., *instrumenta* (*-orum,* plur.) or *apparatus* (*-ūs*) *belli, arma* (*-orum*); see also BULLET.

amnesty, use *venia* or *ignoscĕre*: to proclaim a general —, *omnium factorum dictorumque veniam et oblivionem in perpetuum sancire.*

among, *inter,* with acc.; sometimes *in,* with abl., or *apud,* with acc.

amorous, in good sense, *amans;* in bad sense, *libidinosus.*

amount, *summa;* sometimes rendered by adj. indicating size.

amount to, v. *efficĕre*: what does it — to? *quae summa est?* it —s to the same thing, *idem* or *par est, nihil interest.*

amphibious, express by phrase.

amphitheatre, *amphitheatrum.*

ample, *amplus.*

amplify, *amplificare.*

amplitude, *amplitudo.*

amply, *ample, abunde.*

amputate, *praecīdĕre, amputare.*

amputation, use a verb.

amuse, *delectare, oblectare.*

amusement, *delectatio, oblectatio, oblectamentum*: for —'s sake, *animi causā.*

amusing, *facetus, festivus.*

anachronism, use phrase, e.g. *tempora miscere, invertĕre.*

analogy, *similitudo*; the Gr. ἀναλογία is translated by Cicero *comparatio proportioque.*

analogous, *similis.*

analyse, *explicare, expedire, quasi in membra discerpĕre.*

analysis, *explicatio, enodatio.*

anapaest, *anapaestus pes.*

anarchical, *legibus carens.*

anarchy: in gen. *licentia*; as a political condition, use phrase, e.g. *civitas in qua libido multitudinis pro legibus est.*

anathema; see CURSE.

anatomy, anatomical, etc., use phrase referring to the structure of the body (*compages, conformatio corporis*), or to the process of dissection (*incīdĕre*).

ancestor. (1) sing. = the founder of a family, *auctor generis* or *gentis* (or, poet., *sanguinis*). (2) plur. = ancestors in gen., *maiores*; poet., *avi, patres.*

ancestral, *avitus, proavitus.*

ancestry, *origo, genus.*

anchor, subst. *ancora*: to cast —, *ancoram iacĕre*; the — holds, *ancora subsistit*; to lie at —, *consistĕre in ancoris* or *ad ancoras*; to raise (or weigh) —, *ancoram tollĕre* or *solvĕre.*

anchor, v. *navem ad ancoras deligare*: to be —ed, *ad ancoram consistĕre.*

anchorage, *statio.*

ancient, *antiquus* (usually of what no longer exists); *vetus, vetustus* (= of long standing, old but still existing); *priscus* (= old-fashioned); *pristinus* (= former, earlier); *inveteratus* (= grown old), *obsoletus* (= obsolete): the —s, *veteres, antiqui*, sometimes *antiquitas.*

and, *et* (most general word); *-que* (enclitic, connecting two related words or clauses); *atque, ac* (*ac* not before words beginning with vowel or h; these two connect with emphasis, = 'and also'); *autem* (as a formula of transition between clauses, esp. in continuing an argument or story).

'And' may often be suppressed in the Latin: (1) between clauses, either by simple asyndeton or by a change of construction which makes one clause subordinate to another (e.g. using *cum* or a participle): *urbe relicta in villam se recepit* = he left the city and retired to his country-seat. (2) between single words by asyndeton, esp. between three or more words in a list, e.g. *patria a laboribus, consiliis, periculis meis servata est*; the alternative treatment of such lists is usually to insert *et* between all the items.

And so, *itaque*; and yet, *tamen*; and not, *et non* (to negative a single word); *neque* or *nec* (to negative a whole clause); and no one, *nec quisquam*; and never, *nec unquam.*

anecdote, *fabula, fabella, narratiuncula.*

anew, *denuo, de* or *ab integre*; see also AGAIN.

anger, subst. *ira, iracundia, indignatio, bilis, stomachus.*

anger, v. transit. *lacessĕre, inritare*; *iram, bilem*, etc., *homini movere.*

angle, *angulus.*

angle, v. *piscari, hamo pisces capĕre, harundine pisces captare.*

angler, *piscator.*

angrily, *iracunde.*

angry, adj. *iratus*; often —, prone to anger, *iracundus*; to be (or become) —, *irasci, suscensĕre, stomachari*, with dat.

anguish, *cruciatus* (-*ūs*), *tormentum, dolor, angor.*

angular, *angulatus.*

animadvert, *animadvertĕre* (= to notice, to censure, or to punish).

animal, subst. (1) = any living creature, *animal, animans.* (2) = a living but not human creature, *bestia*; *pecus* (-*udis*, f.: usually a domestic —); *belua* (a large —); *fera* (a wild —).

animal, adj. *animalis*; or use genit. of *animal, animans, corpus*, etc.

animate, v. transit. LIT., = to give life to, *animare.* TRANSF., = to make lively, *excitare, incitare.*

animate, adj. *animalis, animatus.*

animated, adj. LIT., *animatus, animans, animalis.* TRANSF., = lively, *vegetus, alacer.*

animation, = vigour, *alacritas, vigor.*

animosity, *odium, invidia, simultas.*

ankle, ankle-bone, *talus.*

anklet, *periscelis* (-*idis*, f.).

annals, *annales* (-*ium*, plur.).

annex, v. transit. (1) = add, (*ad*)*iungere, addĕre.* (2) = conquer, *sibi subicĕre, in dicionem suam redigĕre.*

annexation, use verb.

annihilate, *delēre, exstinguĕre.*

annihilation, *exstinctio, interitus* (-*ūs*), *excidium.*

anniversary, *festus dies anniversarius.*

annotate, *adnotare* (Plin.).

annotation, *adnotatio.*

announce, (*re*)*nuntiare, praedicare.*

announcement, use verb.

announcer, *praeco.*

annoy, *lacessĕre, inritare, vexare*; *homini molestiam adferre.*

annoyance, *molestia, vexatio, cruciatus* (-*ūs*): a source of —, *in commodum.*

annual, *annuus, anniversarius* (= taking place every year).

annually, *quotannis.*

annuity, *annua pecunia.*

annul, *tollĕre, delere, abrogare, abolēre, (dis)solvĕre.*

anodyne, use phrase, e.g. *dolorem levare.*

anoint, v. (*in*)*unguĕre.*

anointing, subst. *unctio.*

anomaly, *anōmalia* (Varro); usually to be rendered by adj.; see IRREGULAR.

anon, adv. *brevi* (*tempore*), *mox*: ever and —, *interdum.*

anonymous, *sine nomine*: — poems, *carmina incertis auctoribus vulgata* (Tac.).

another, pron. and adj. *alius*; often repeated in a different case, to indicate either diversity (e.g. *alius aliud dicit*, one says one thing, another says another), or reciprocal action (e.g. *alius alium timet*, they fear one another). *Alter* (= a second) is used when there are only two persons or things involved, or when it is not suggested that there are more: *alter alterum timet*, they both fear each other; *Verres, alter Orcus*, another Orcus, a second Orcus.

Reciprocal action can also be expressed by *inter se* (e.g. *inter se timent*, they fear each other).

At — time, *alias*; in — place, *alibi*; to — place, *alio*; —'s, *alienus*.

answer, subst.: in gen., *responsum*: — to a charge, *de ensio, excusatio*; a written —, *rescriptum*; — of an oracle, *oraculum, sors*.

answer, v. (1) to give an —: in gen., (*rem homini*) *respondēre*; by letter, *rescribēre*; to a charge, *se defendēre, excusare*; of an oracle, *responsum dare*. (2) to — for, *rem praestare*; see SURETY. (3) — to = to correspond to, *rei respondere*; see AGREE. (4) = succeed; q.v.

answerable, adj. = accountable; use phrase, e.g. *homini de re rationem reddere*.

ant, *formica*.

antagonist, *adversarius*; in a law-court, often *iste*.

antagonistic, *contrarius, adversus, infensus*.

antecedent, adj. *antecedens, prior*.

antecedents, subst. *antecedentia (-ium)*, neut. plur.

antechamber, *vestibulum, atriolum*.

antelope; see DEER.

anterior, *antecedens, prior*.

anthem, *cantus (-ūs), carmen*.

anthropoid, *homini similis*.

anthropomorphism, use phrase, e.g. *deos tamquam humano corpore fingere*.

anticipate. (1) = to act first or prematurely, to forestall a person or thing, *occupare, praecipēre, praevertēre, antevertēre*. (2) = to expect, *exspectare, credēre*.

anticipation. (1) = early or premature action; use a verb; see ANTICIPATE. (2) = expectation, *exspectatio, spes, timor*.

antics, *ludi, ioca (-orum, plur.)*.

antidote, *remedium*; cf. the phrase, *veneficiis remedia invenire* (Cic.).

antipathy. (1) of things, *rerum discordia, repugnantia*. (2) of persons, *odium*.

antipodes. LIT., *antipodes (-um, plur.)*. TRANSF., = the opposite, render by adj. *adversus, contrarius*.

antiquary, antiquarian, *rerum antiquarum studiosus*.

antiquated, *obsoletus, priscus*.

antique, *antiquus*.

antiquity, *antiquitas, vetustas*.

antithesis. (1) as rhet. t. t. *contentio*. (2) = the opposite, *contrarium*.

antler, *cornu*.

anvil, *incus (-ūdis, f.)*.

anxiety, *anxietas, cura, sollicitudo, trepidatio, pavor*.

anxious, *anxius, sollicitus, trepidus*: to be —, *laborare*.

anxiously, *anxie, sollicite*.

any, *ullus* (= any at all; used after a negative; in questions; after a verb of denying, forbidding or preventing; sometimes after *si*, and in comparisons such as 'greater than any . . .'); *quisquam* (substantival, but used like *ullus* in apposition to words denoting persons or collective words referring to persons); *qui, qua* (rarely *quae*), *quod* (used

after *si, nisi, ne, num*); *ecqui?* (= is there any who? used in impassioned questions); *quivis* (= any you please; positive, opposed to *certus* or *quidam*); *quilibet* (like *quivis*, but suggesting a less deliberate choice).

anybody, anyone, pron: use the various words given above for 'any', as appropriate in their substantival forms, i.e. *quisquam* (= anyone at all); *quis* (after *si, nisi, num, ne, cum, quo, quanto*); *ecquis* (in impassioned questions); *quivis, quilibet* (= anyone you please); see also SOMEBODY.

anywhere. (1) = at any place, *usquam* (= — at all; cf. *quisquam*); *ubivis* (= — you please; cf. *quivis*). (2) = to any place, *quoquam* (cf. *quisquam*); *quolibet* (cf. *quilibet*).

apace, *celeriter*.

apart, *seorsum*; more often to be rendered by the adj. *diversus* (= in different directions), or by compound verbs with *dis-* and *se-* (e.g. *distare, separare*).

apartment; see ROOM.

apathetic, *hebes, lentus*.

apathy, *stupor, lentitudo*.

ape, *simia, simius*.

ape, v. transit. *imitari*; see IMITATE.

Apennines, the, *Apenninus (mons)*.

aperture; see OPENING.

apex, *apex, cacumen*.

aphorism, *sententia, dictum, elogium*.

apiary, *alvearium, mellarium* (Varro).

apiece, use distrib. num. (e.g. *deni* = ten —).

apologist, *defensor*.

apologize, v. intransit. *excusare*.

apology. (1) = defence, *defensio*. (2) = excuse, *excusatio*.

apologue, *apologus, fabula*.

apophthegm, *elogium, sententia, dictum*.

apostrophe, as rhet. t. t. *apostrophe*.

apostrophize; see ADDRESS.

apothecary, *medicus*.

appal, (*ex*)*terrēre*; see FRIGHTEN.

apparatus, *apparatus (-ūs)*.

apparel, *vestis, vestimentum*.

apparent. (1) = evident, *manifestus, apertus*: to make —, *patefacēre*; to be —, *apparēre*; it is —, *liquet*. (2) opp. to real, *fictus, simulatus*; or use *species* or *videor*.

apparently, *ut videtur, in speciem*.

apparition. (1) = appearing, *adventus (-ūs)*. (2) = spectre, *simulacrum, species*.

appeal, subst. (1) as legal t. t. *appellatio, provocatio*. (2) = entreaty, *obtestatio, obsecratio, preces*.

appeal, v. intransit. (1) as legal t. t.: to a magistrate, on any matter, *hominem* (esp. *tribunum*) *appellare*; to the people, on a matter of life and death, *ad populum provocare*. (2) — to = entreat, *obtestari, obsecrare*. (3) — to = please, *homini placere*.

appealing, *supplex*.

appear. (1) = become visible, be evident, *apparēre, conspici* (= to be seen), *exsistere*: to — in public, *in publicum prodire*. (2) = to be present, put in an appearance, *comparēre, adesse*: to — in court, *in iudicium venire*. (3) = to seem, *videri*.

appearance. (1) = arrival, *adventus (-ūs)*; or use verb. (2) = looks, *aspectus, species, facies, habitus (-ūs)*. (3) = semblance, *species*: to put on an — of, *rem simulare*.

appeasable, *placabilis*.
appease. (1) of men and gods, *placare*. (2) of anger, hunger, etc., *sedare*.
appeasement, *placatio*.
appellant, *appellator*; see APPEAL, v.
append, *addĕre*, *adiungĕre*.
appendage, *appendix*, *accessio*; or use verb.
appertain; see BELONG.
appetite: in gen., *appetentia*, *appetitio*, *appetitus* (*-ūs*); = desire for food, hunger, *fames*.
applaud, *homini* (*ap*)*plaudĕre*; see also PRAISE.
applause, *plausus* (*-ūs*); see also PRAISE.
apple, *malum*: — tree, *malus*, f.
apple-cart, to upset the, prov., *plaustrum percellĕre* (Pl.).
appliance, *apparatus* (*-ūs*), *instrumentum*.
application. (1) = request, *petitio*. (2) = putting to, use verb. (3) — of the mind, *animi intentio*, *diligentia*.
apply, v. (1) transit.: **a** = put on, bring to bear, esp. of instruments, (*rem rei*) *adhibere*, *admovēre*: **b**, apply oneself = set oneself to a pursuit or task, *se ad rem conferre*, *applicare*; *rei* (dat.) *incumbĕre*. (2) intransit., to apply to: **a** = refer to, *pertinere ad*, with acc.: **b** = approach a person, for help, etc., *ad hominem confugĕre*, *hominem adire* or *convenire*.
appoint, of persons, times, etc., *constituĕre*, *destinare*, *dicĕre*; of persons, to — as, *creare*, *facere*; to = to command over, *praeponere*, *praeficere*, with acc. and dat.
appointment. (1) as an action, *creatio*; or use verb. (2) = an office, *munus* (*-eris*); sometimes *magistratus* (*-ūs*). (3) = agreement to meet, *constitutum*; or use verb.
apportion, *dividĕre*, *dispertire*, *distribuĕre*, *dispensare*, *adsignare*.
apposite, *aptus*, *accommodatus*.
appraise, = to fix the value of, *aestimare*; see also VALUE.
appreciate, *aestimare*; see also VALUE.
appreciative, *aequus*.
apprehend. (1) = seize, arrest, *comprehendĕre*. (2) = to grasp mentally, *comprehendĕre*, *complecti* (*animo* or *mente*), *intellegĕre*. (3) = fear; q.v.
apprehension. (1) = arrest, *comprehensio*. (2) = mental grasp, *intellegentia*. (3) = fear, *timor*; see FEAR.
apprehensive; see TIMID.
apprentice, subst., use phrase, such as *homini* (e.g. *sutori*) *addictus*.
apprentice, v. transit. *addicĕre*.
approach, subst. *adventus* (*-ūs*), *aditus* (*-ūs*), *accessus* (*-ūs*), *appropinquatio*.
approach, v. transit. and intransit. LIT., of physical movement, *accedĕre* (*ad*), *appropinquare* (with *ad* or dat.), *adventare*. TRANSF., (1) of time, *appetĕre*, *appropinquare*. (2) = to approximate, *accedĕre* (*ad*).
approbation; see APPROVAL.
appropriate, adj. *idoneus*, *aptus*, *accommodatus*, *congruens*.
appropriate, v. transit. = take for oneself, (*ad*)*sumĕre*, *sibi adrogare*, *sibi vindicare*.
appropriately, *apte*, *accommodate*, *convenienter*.
approve (of) = think good, *probare*, *approbare*, *comprobare*.
approval, *approbatio*, *comprobatio*: I obtain

your — for a thing, *rem tibi probo*; with your —, *te auctore*, *pace tuā*.
approved, *probatus*, *spectatus*.
approximate, adj. *propinquus*; see NEAR.
approximate, v.; see APPROACH.
April, *Aprilis* (*mensis*).
apron, *subligaculum*.
apt. (1) = appropriate; q.v. (2) = prone, *pronus*, *propensus*: — to learn, *docilis*.
aptitude, *habilitas*.
aptly, *apte*.
aquatic, *aquatilis*.
aqueduct, *aquae ductus* (*-ūs*); also *aqua* alone, when a name is to be added.
aquiline, *aduncus*.
arable; see PLOUGH.
arbiter, *arbiter*, *disceptator*.
arbitrarily, = capriciously, *libidinose*.
arbitrary, adj. (1) = capricious, *libidinosus*. (2) of power = absolute, *infinitus*, or use *dominari* or *dominatio*.
arbitrate, v. *disceptare*, *diiudicare*.
arbitration, *arbitrium*.
arbour, *umbraculum*.
arc, *arcus* (*-ūs*).
arcade, *porticus* (*-ūs*).
arch, subst. *arcus* (*-ūs*), *fornix*.
arch, adj. *petulans*, *lascivus*, *improbus*, *malus*.
arch, v. transit. *arcuare* (Plin. L.); see also CURVE.
arch-, as prefix, render by the adj. *summus*, *praecipuus* or *primarius*, agreeing with subst.
archaeology, *rerum antiquarum scientia*.
archaic, *antiquus*; to sound —, *antiquitatem redolēre*.
archaism, *verbum obsoletum*.
archer, *sagittarius*.
archery, render by verb (e.g. *sagittis petĕre*).
archipelago, use phrase, perhaps Vergil's *freta consita terris*.
architect, *architectus*.
architecture, *architectura*.
archives, *tabulae* (or *tabellae*) *publicae*.
arctic, *septentrionalis*, *arctous*; see NORTHERN.
ardent, *ardens*, *fervens*, *acer*.
ardently, *acriter*, *ardenter*, *vehementer*.
ardour, *ardor*, *fervor*, *studium*.
arduous, *arduus*, *difficilis*.
area, *area*, *superficies*.
arena, *harena* (lit. and fig.)
argue. (1) = to discuss or dispute, *de re disserĕre*, *disputare*. (2) = to approach a conclusion by argument, *argumentari*, *conligĕre*.
argument. (1) = dispute, *disputatio*. (2) = subject, or line of reasoning, *argumentum*.
arid, *aridus*, *siccus*.
aright, *recte*, *bene*; see also RIGHT.
arise. LIT., *surgĕre* (in prose usually of persons), *oriri* (usually of heavenly bodies). TRANSF., = to come into existence, *oriri*, *cooriri*, *exoriri*, *exsistĕre*; see also RISE.
aristocracy. (1) = aristocrats, *primores*, *optimates* (*-um* or *-ium*, = the aristocratic party, opp. *populares*); *patricii* (opp. *plebeii*); *nobiles* (= magistrates and relatives of magistrates): a supporter of the —, *nobilitatis fautor*. (2) = a form of government, *optimatium dominatus* (*-ūs*); or use phrase, e.g. *ubi penes optimates est respublica*.
aristocrat, aristocratic; see ARISTOCRACY.
arithmetic, *arithmetica* (*-orum*, plur.).
arithmetical, *arithmeticus*.

arithmetician, use phrase.

ark, = chest, *arca.*

arm, subst. LIT., of the human body, *bracchium* (strictly the forearm); *lacertus* (strictly the upper arm); arms = embrace, *complexus (-ūs), manūs* (plur.); to sit with arms folded (and do nothing), *compressis manibus sedere.* TRANSF., (1) anything shaped like an arm, e.g. an 'arm' of the sea, *bracchium, cornu.* (2) the arm of the law, *magistratuum potestas.*

arm, v. (1) transit. *armare,* lit. and fig. (2) intransit. *armari, arma capĕre.*

arm-chair, *sella.*

armed, *armatus.*

armistice, *induciae (-arum,* plur.).

armour, *arma (-orum,* plur.), *armatura;* armour-bearer, *armiger.*

armourer, *faber armorum.*

armoury, *armamentarium.*

arm-pit, *ala.*

arms, *arma (-orum,* plur.: defensive, or for close combat); *tela* (plur.: offensive, of all kinds); without —, *inermis;* to raise the cry 'to arms', *ad arma conclamare;* to take up —, *arma capĕre* or *sumĕre;* to lay down —, *arma (de)ponĕre;* to be under —, *in armis esse;* to bear — against, *arma ferre contra hominem.*

army, *exercitus (-ūs):* — in marching array, *agmen;* — in battle-array, *acies.*

aromatic, *odorus, odoratus.*

around. (1) adv. *circa, circum.* (2) prep. *circa, circum,* with acc.

arouse. LIT., *(e somno) excitare, suscitare.* TRANSF., *excitare, erigĕre, (com)movēre.*

arraign; see ACCUSE.

arrange. (1) of physical objects, *ordinare, componĕre, disponĕre, digerĕre;* of troops in particular, *instruĕre.* (2) of abstr. matters, *constituĕre, componĕre.*

arrangement, *ordo, ratio, conlocatio, compositio, dispositio;* or use verb.

arrant, render by superl., or *summus.*

array: of battle —, *acies;* = dress, *vestis.*

array, v. transit.; see ARRANGE; = to dress, *vestire.*

arrears, *pecuniae residuae.*

arrest. (1) = put under —, *comprehendĕre, deprehendĕre, in custodiam dare.* (2) = stop; q.v.

arrival, *adventus (-ūs), accessus (-ūs).*

arrive, *advenire, pervenire, adventare;* by ship or on horseback, *advehi, pervehi.*

arrogance, *adrogantia, superbia.*

arrogant, *adrogans, insolens, superbus.*

arrogantly, *adroganter, superbe.*

arrogate, v. transit. *sibi adrogare, (ad)sumĕre.*

arrow, *sagitta.*

arsenal, *armamentarium:* naval —, *navalia (-ium,* plur.).

arsis, *sublatio* (Quint.).

art, *ars* (the most general word; often opp. to *natura* or *ingenium*); *artificium* (= the practice of an —, or workmanship); *peritia* (= acquired skill): the fine —s, *artes ingenuae, liberales, humanae, elegantes* (or use compar. of one of these adjectives); a work of —, *artis opus (-eris,* n.), *opus arte factum.*

artful, *callidus, versutus, vafer, astutus.*

artfully, *astute, callide.*

artfulness, *astutia, calliditas, dolus.*

artichoke, *cinara* (Col.).

article, subst. (1) in gen. = a thing, object,

res. (2) = a clause or item in a law or agreement, *caput, condicio.*

article, v. transit.; see APPRENTICE.

articulate, adj. *clarus.*

articulate, v. transit. *dicĕre, articulare* (Lucr.).

articulation, = pronunciation, *appellatio.*

artificer, *artifex, opifex.*

artificial, *artificiosus.*

artificially, *arte, manu, opere* (opp. to *naturā*).

artillery, *tormenta (-orum,* plur., including the *ballista, catapulta,* and the *scorpio*).

artisan, *opifex, faber.*

artist, *artifex;* or *poeta, pictor,* etc.

artistic, *artifex.*

artistically, *artificiose, summa arte.*

artless, *simplex;* of speech or writing, *incomptus, inconditus, incompositus.*

artlessly, *simpliciter, sine arte.*

artlessness, *simplicitas.*

as, adv. and conj. (1) temporal = while, when; see WHILE. With single nouns, often not translated, e.g. *Cicero consul,* Cicero as consul; *Cato senex,* Cato as an old man. (2) causal = because, since, *cum, quod, quia, quoniam, quippe qui.* (3) concessive: e.g. strong as he was, he could not, *cum, quamquam,* etc. (4) comparative: as . . . (so) . . ., *(sic)ut . . . (ita)* . . .; as . . . as . . ., *tam . . . quam . . .;* such . . . as . . ., *talis . . . qualis . . .;* as great as . . ., *tantus . . . quantus . . .;* as many as . . ., *tot . . . quot . . .;* as often as . . ., *totiens . . . quotiens;* as quickly as possible, *quam celerrime;* as soon as, *simul ac;* the same as, *idem ac, atque, qui.* (5) in other phrases: as far as, *tenus* (prep.), *usque* (adv. = all the way), *quatenus, quoad, quod, quantum* (conjunctions); as if, as though, *quasi, ut si, tamquam (si), velut (si);* as follows, *ita;* as to, as regards, *quod ad . . . attinet,* or *ab* (in respect of), or *de* (concerning); to consider as, *habere,* with acc. or *pro* and abl.

ascend, *scandĕre, ascendĕre:* to — the throne, *regnum accipĕre* or *suscipere, rex fieri.*

ascendant, ascendency, render by adj. *superior* or *summus:* to be in the —, *praevalēre, praestare.*

ascent, *ascensus (-ūs).*

ascertain, *explorare, cognoscĕre, comperire, discĕre.*

ascetic, render by phrase (e.g. *cibo abstinere*).

ascribe, *ascribĕre, adiudicare, attribuĕre, adsignare, conferre.*

ash (tree), *fraxinus;* adj. *fraxineus;* mountain-ash, *ornus.*

ashamed, *pudore adfectus:* I am — of, *pudet me* (acc.), with genit. or infin.; I am rather —, *suppudet me.*

ashes, *cinis (-ĕris):* glowing —, embers, *favilla;* to lie in sackcloth and —, *sordidatum* or *atratum esse.*

ashore. (1) of rest, *in litore:* — and afloat, *terrā marique.* (2) of motion, *in litus* or *terram:* to put men —, *exponĕre.*

aside, *seorsum:* to go —, *secedĕre;* to call —, *sevocare;* to lay —, *seponĕre.*

ask. (1) to — a person a question, *hominem rogare, interrogare; ex* (or *ab*) *homine quaerĕre;* to — a person's opinion or advice, *hominem consulĕre.* (2) to — a person for, or to do, a thing, *hominem rogare, ab homine petĕre, hominem* or *ab homine poscĕre, rem,* or *ut. . . .*

askance: to look — at, *limis oculis adspicĕre.*
aslant, *oblique, ex transverso.*
asleep, *dormiens, in somno, per somnum.*
asp, *aspis (-ĭdis).*
aspect, = appearance, looks, *aspectus (-ūs), forma, facies, species*: of places, to have a certain —, *spectare,* with *ad* and acc.
asperity, *asperitas, acerbitas.*
asperse, *infamiā* or *suspicione aspergere, calumniari.*
aspersion, *calumnia, opprobrium.*
asphalt, *bitumen.*
aspirate, subst. *aspiratio.*
aspirate, v. *aspirare* (Quint.).
aspire: to — to, *ad rem aspirare, contendere, rem adfectare.*
aspiration, *appetitio, adfectatio*; or use verb.
ass, *asinus* (also used contemptuously of persons): a little —, *asellus*; a she-ass, *asina.*
assail. LIT., *oppugnare, adoriri, adgredi.* TRANSF., *oppugnare, adoriri, appetĕre*; — with words, *invehi in,* with acc.
assailant, *qui oppugnat.*
assassin, *sicarius, percussor.*
assassinate, *(insidiis) interficĕre.*
assassination, *caedes*: to accuse of —, *accusare inter sicarios.*
assault, subst.: in gen., *impetus (-ūs), incursus (-ūs), oppugnatio*: as legal t. t., *vis*: to commit an —, *vim (et manūs) inferre.*
assault, v. transit.; see ASSAIL.
assay, subst. *obrussa.*
ass-driver, *asinarius.*
assemble, v. (1) transit. *convocare, in unum locum cogĕre* or *contrahĕre* or *compellĕre.* (2) intransit. *convenire, coire.*
assembly, *coetus (-ūs), conventus (-ūs)* (general terms); *concilium* (for hearing speakers and making decisions); *consilium* (for deliberation); *contio* (for hearing speakers only).
assent, subst. *adsensio, adsensus (-ūs).*
assent, v. intransit.: to — to, *(homini) adsentire, adsentiri* (dep.), *adnuĕre* (often with acc. of the thing proposed); to — regularly, *adsentari* (dep.).
assert. (1) = to state, *dicĕre, adfirmare, confirmare*; to keep —ing, *dictitare.* (2) = to maintain, to — a right, *ius retinĕre, obtinēre*; to — the freedom of, *in libertatem vindicare.*
assertion (1) = a statement, *adfirmatio.* (2) = maintenance, *defensio, vindicatio.*
assess, *aestimare.*
assessment, *aestimatio, census (-ūs).*
assessor. (1) = one who assesses, *censor.* (2) = a judge's assistant, *adsessor.*
assets, *bona (-orum,* plur).
assiduity, *adsiduitas, sedulitas.*
assiduous, *adsiduus, sedulus, industrius, diligens.*
assiduously, *adsidue, sedulo, industrie, diligenter.*
assign, *rem homini adsignare, (at)tribuĕre.*
assignation, = appointment, *constitutum*: to keep an —, *ad constitutum venire.*
assimilate. (1) = to make like, *rem cum re (ad)aequare, rem rei similem facĕre.* (2) = to digest, *concoquĕre.*
assimilation, use verb.
assist, *(hominem) (ad)iuvare, (homini) opem* or *auxilium ferre, auxiliari, opitulari, subvenire.*
assistance, *opem* (nom. sing. not used), *auxilium, adiumentum.*

assistant, *adiutor, adiutrix.*
associate, subst. *socius, sodalis*: an — in crime, *conscius.*
associate. v. (1) transit. *(con)iungĕre, (con)sociare, congregare.* (2) intransit., use the above verbs in the pass., or with a reflex.: to — with a person, *homine uti.*
association, *societas, sodalitas, conlegium, sodalicium.*
assort, *digerĕre.*
assortment, use phrase, e.g. *res* or *merces conlectae, digestae.*
assuage, *mitigare, lenire, sedare, levare.*
assume. (1) = take to oneself, *rem sibi adrogare, (ad)sumĕre, occupare, suscipĕre.* (2) = to take for granted, *ponĕre, sumĕre.*
assumption. (1) = a taking, use verb. (2) = a taking for granted, *sumptio*; or use verb.
assurance. (1) = a strong assertion, *confirmatio.* (2) = confidence, *fiducia.*
assure. (1) to assert confidently to a person, *homini (pro certo) adfirmare, confirmare.* (2) = to secure; q.v.
assured. (1) of things, *certus, exploratus.* (2) of persons, to be (or feel) —, *credĕre, confidĕre, pro certo habēre.*
assuredly, *profecto, certe.*
astern, *in* or *a puppi.*
asthma, *dyspnoea* (Plin.).
asthmatic, *asthmaticus* (Plin.).
astonish, *obstupefacĕre.*
astonished, *attonitus*: to be —, *obstupescĕre, stupēre, rem admirari.*
astonishing, *mirabilis, mirus.*
astonishingly, *mire, mirum in modum, mirabiliter.*
astonishment, *stupor, (ad)miratio.*
astound; see ASTONISH.
astray, use adj. *vagus,* or verb such as *errare, vagari, palari.*
astringency, *adstrictio* (Plin.).
astringent, *adstrictorius* (Plin.).
astrologer, *astrologus, mathematicus, Chaldaeus.*
astrology, *astrologia.*
astronomy, treat as astrology; q.v.
astute, *astutus, callidus.*
asunder, *seorsum*; often rendered by compound verb with *dis-* or *se-* (e.g. *discurrĕre, sevocare).*
asylum; see REFUGE.
at. (1) of place, *ad, apud,* with acc; sometimes *in* with abl. The locative of proper names is used to indicate 'at', e.g. *Romae, Brundisii, Gadibus*; also *domi* = at home. (2) of time, usually rendered by abl. case, e.g. *prima luce,* at daybreak; sometimes by *ad* with acc., e.g. *ad meridiem,* at midday; at dinner, *inter cenam*; at present, *nunc, in praesentia*; at once, *statim*; at first, *primo, primum*; at last, *postremo, tandem.* (3) 'at' in expressions indicating price or value is rendered by genit. or abl. case.
atheist, *qui deum esse negat.*
athlete, *athleta.*
athwart; see ACROSS.
Atlantic, *mare Atlanticum, Oceanus.*
atmosphere, *aër, caelum.*
atmospheric, use the genit. *aëris* or *caeli*; see AIR.
atom, *atomus*; Lucr. uses a number of special words and phrases for 'atoms', esp. *primordia rerum.*

atomic power, render by phrase such as *vis ex materia fissili conflata.*

atone: to — for a thing, *rem (ab)luĕre, (ex)piare.*

atonement, *piaculum.*

atrabilious, *melancholicus.*

atrocious, *nefandus, nefarius, atrox, immanis.*

atrociously, *nefarie.*

atrocity. (1) as a quality = atrociousness, *immanitas, atrocitas.* (2) = an atrocious deed, *res atrox, nefas.*

atrophy, *tabes (-is, f.).*

attach. LIT., = to fasten one thing to another, *adfigĕre, adligare.* TRANSF., = to associate mentally, bring together in friendship, etc., *adiungere, applicare.*

attached, adj. LIT., *aptus.* TRANSF., = fond, *studiosus.*

attachment, *studium, amor, caritas.*

attack, subst. *impetus (-ūs), oppugnatio, incursus (-ūs), concursus (-ūs), petitio.*

attack, v. transit. LIT., *oppugnare, adoriri, adgredi, petĕre; impetum facĕre, signa inferre in hostem.* TRANSF., *oppugnare, adoriri, appetĕre:* — with words, *insectari, invehi in,* with acc.; to be —ed by a disease, *morbo corripi.*

attacker, *oppugnator.*

attain, *adsequi, consequi.*

attainable, render by verb.

attainment. (1) = the getting of anything, *adeptio, comparatio.* (2) = an acquired skill, *ars;* plur., attainments, *doctrina, eruditio.*

attempt, subst. *conatus (-ūs), conata* (neut. plur.), *inceptum.*

attempt, v. *conari, temptare.*

attend. (1) of physical presence: **a,** to — (upon) a person; as an escort, friend, etc., *hominem comitari, prosequi, deducĕre* (esp. to his home), *(ad)sectari, homini apparēre;* as a servant, *homini famulari, ministrare:* **b,** to — (at) a gathering, etc., *rei* (dat.) *adesse, interesse, rem frequentare.* (2) of mental application = to pay attention. In gen., to — to an undertaking, pursuit, etc., *rei* (dat.) *(in)servire, operam dare, rem curare.* More particularly, to — to what is going on, be attentive, *rem animadvertĕre, ad rem animum attendĕre, hoc agĕre;* not to —, *aliud agĕre.*

attendance, of friends or dependents, *apparitio, adsectatio;* of large numbers, *frequentia;* of servants, *ministerium.*

attendant. (1) = escort, *(ad)sectator, apparitor, stipator.* (2) = servant, *servus, minister, famulus.*

attention. (1) = alertness, concentration; *animus attentus, animi intentio.* (2) = an attentive action, *officium.*

attentive. (1) = paying attention, concentrating, alert, *attentus, intentus, erectus.* (2) = helpful, kind, *officiosus, observans.*

attentively, *attente, intente.*

attenuate, v. transit. *attenuare, extenuare.*

attenuation, *extenuatio* (Sen.).

attest. (1) = vouch for, certify, *(rem) testari, testificari, testimonio confirmare.* (2) = to call to witness, put on oath, *(hominem) testari, testem facĕre.*

attestation. (1) = giving evidence, *testificatio.* (2) = a piece of evidence, *testimonium.*

attire, subst. *vestis, vestitus.*

attire, v. transit.; see DRESS.

attitude. (1) physical, *(corporis) habitus (-ūs), status (-ūs).* (2) mental, *animus.*

attract, *attrahĕre, ad se trahĕre, adlicĕre.*

attraction. (1) = physical effect, use phrase such as *vis attrahendi.* (2) = charm, *inlecebrae* (plur.). (3) = pleasant object, *oblectamentum.*

attractive, *iucundus, suavis blandus.*

attribute, subst. (1) = natural quality, use phrase with *natura* or *proprius.* (2) as grammat. t. t. *attributio, attributum.*

attribute, v. transit. *rem homini (at)tribuĕre, adsignare.*

attrition, render by verb *terĕre.*

attune, use phrase with *concinĕre* or *consonus.*

auburn, *fulvus.*

auction, *auctio:* to hold an —, *auctionem facĕre, auctionari;* to sell by —, *auctione vendĕre;* to sell by public —, *sub hastā vendĕre;* to bid at an —, *licĕri;* to be knocked down at an — to, *homini addici.*

auctioneer, *magister auctionis,* or use *praeco* (strictly = the crier of bids, etc.).

audacious, *audax, protervus, confidens.*

audacity, *audacia, protervitas.*

audible, express by phrase.

audience. (1) = the receiving and hearing of anyone, *admissio, aditus (-ūs):* to grant an — of the senate, *senatum dare.* (2) = a group of hearers, *auditores, audientes, corona* (esp. of a crowd round a public speaker); a large —, *(magna) audientium frequentia.*

audit, v. transit. *rationes dispungĕre.*

augment, v. transit. *rem (ad)augere, amplificare; rem rei addĕre.*

augmentation, *amplificatio, accessio.*

Augsburg, *Augusta Vindelicorum.*

augur, subst. *augur.*

augur, v. transit. = foretell, *praedicĕre, vaticinari, augurari.*

augury. (1) = prediction, *augurium.* (2) = a thing predicted, omen, *augurium, omen.*

August, *(mensis) Sextilis;* later, in honour of Augustus, *(mensis) Augustus.*

august, adj. *augustus, inlustris, magnificus.*

aunt, *amita* (= a father's sister); *matertera* (= a mother's sister).

auriferous, *aurifer.*

auspices, *auspicium.*

auspicious, *felix prosper, secundus, faustus.*

auspiciously, *feliciter, fauste, prospere.*

austere, *austerus, severus, tristis.*

austerely, *austere, severe.*

austerity, *austeritas, severitas.*

authentic, *certus, verus.*

authentically, *certo auctore.*

authenticity, *fides, auctoritas.*

author. (1) = originator, *auctor, inventor.* (2) = the writer of a book, *scriptor.*

authoritative, adj. (1) in a good sense, *gravis.* (2) in a bad sense, *imperiosus, adrogans.*

authority. (1) abstr.: in gen., *auctoritas, gravitas:* lawfully constituted —, *potestas, imperium.* (2) pers.: an — for a statement, or action, *auctor;* the authorities, *magistratūs, potestates.*

authorize, *auctor esse, potestatem facĕre, permittere (homini)* with *ut* or infin.

autocracy, *imperium singulare.*

autocrat, *dominus.*

autograph, use phrase with *manu* and *scribĕre.*

autumn, *autumnus*: in — time, *autumnali tempore.*

autumnal, *autumnalis.*

Autun, *Augustodunum.*

auxiliary, subst., usually plur.: auxiliaries, *auxilia, (milites) auxiliares.*

auxiliary, adj. *auxiliaris, auxiliarius.*

avail. (1) = to be of use, *valēre, (homini) prodesse.* **(2)** to — oneself of = to use, *re uti.*

avarice, *avaritia.*

avaricious, *avarus.*

avaunt! *abi! apage!*

avenge, *vindicare, ulcisci:* to — oneself on, *hominem (pro re) ulcisci.*

avenger, *ultor, vindex.*

avenue, a shady walk, *xystus.*

aver; see AFFIRM, ASSERT.

averse, *aversus, alienus* (both with *ab* or dat.).

avert, *avertĕre, amovĕre, prohibēre.*

aversion, *odium, fuga, animus, aversus.*

aviary, *aviarium* (Varro).

avoid, *vitare, (de)fugĕre, declinare, aversari.*

avow, *fatēri, profitēri, confitēri.*

avowal, *confessio.*

avowed, *apertus.*

avowedly, *aperte.*

await, v. transit. *exspectare, manēre, opperiri.*

awake, adj. *vigilans:* to be —, *vigilare;* to be — all night, *pervigilare.*

awake, v. **(1)** transit. *(e somno) excitare, (ex)suscitare.* **(2)** intransit. *expergisci, excitari.*

award, subst. *arbitrium, addictio.*

award, v. *rem homini addicĕre, adiudicare;* see also GIVE.

aware, *gnarus* (with genit.): to be —, *sentire, scire, novisse.*

away, *procul;* often rendered by compound verb with *ab-:* — with you! *abi! apage!*

awe, subst. *formido, reverentia, veneratio:* to stand in — of, *(re)verēri.*

awe, v. transit. *terrēre; formidinem,* etc., *inicere.*

awful, = awe-inspiring, terrible, *dirus, formidolosus, terribilis.*

awhile, *aliquamdiu, paulisper, parumper.*

awkward, *agrestis, rusticus, rudis, inscitus.*

awkwardly, *inscite, rustice.*

awkwardness, *rusticitas, inscitia.*

awl, *subula* (Mart.).

awning, *velum.*

awry. (1) adj. *obliquus, perversus.* **(2)** adv. *oblique, perverse.*

axe, *securis, dolabra.*

axis, axle, *axis.*

ay, aye, adv. *ita, ita est, recte, certe, vero, sane;* often rendered by repetition of verb, e.g. Will he come? —! *venietne? veniet:* I say —, *aio.*

azure, *caeruleus.*

B

baa, subst. *balatus (-ūs).*

baa, v. intransit. *balare.*

babble, v. *blaterare, garrire.*

babbler, *garrulus.*

babe, baby, *infans.*

baboon; see APE.

bacchanal, f. subst. *baccha.*

bachelor, *caelebs.*

back, subst. *tergum, dorsum:* on one's —, *supinus* (adj.); to hit in the —, *(hominem) aversum caedĕre;* behind one's —, *clam* (adv.); to break the — of (*fig.*), *profligare.*

back, v. **(1)** transit.: **a** = to make to go backwards, *retro movēre:* **b** = to support, *homini favere.* **(2)** intransit. = to go —, *se recipĕre, recedĕre.* **(3)** phrase: to — water, *remos or remis inhibēre, navem retro inhibēre.*

back, backwards, adv. *retro, retrorsum;* often rendered by compound verb with *re-.*

backbite, v. transit. *(hominem) rodĕre, (homini) absenti maledicĕre.*

bacon, *lardum.*

bad. (1) in a physical sense, *malus:* — weather, *tempestas mala, adversa, foeda* (= foul); a — road, *via iniqua;* — money, *nummi adulterini;* in — health, *aeger;* to go —, *corrumpi.* **(2)** in a moral sense, *malus, pravus* (lit. = crooked), *turpis* (lit. = ugly, foul), *improbus, perversus, nequam.*

badge, *signum, insigne, nota.*

badger, *meles (-is,* f.: Plin.).

badly, *male, prave, turpiter, improbe.*

badness, *pravitas, turpitas, nequitia.*

baffle, v. transit. *eludĕre, ad inritum redigĕre.*

bag, *saccus, culeus.*

baggage, *sarcinae (-arum,* plur.), *impedimenta (-orum,* plur.), *vasa (-orum,* plur.).

bail, subst. **(1)** = the security given, *vadimonium.* **(2)** = the person giving security, *vas (vadis), sponsor.*

bail, v. = to give bail, *spondēre.*

bailiff. (1) on an estate, *procurator, vilicus.* **(2)** an officer of a court of justice, *apparitor.*

bait, subst. *esca.*

bait, v. transit. **(1)** = to put bait on (a hook), *escam (hamo) imponĕre.* **(2)** = to feed horses, *cibum praebēre.* **(3)** = to worry, tease, *vexare, lacessĕre.*

bake, *coquĕre, torrēre.*

baker, *pistor;* f. *pistrix.*

bakery, *pistrinum, pistrina* (Varr.).

balance, subst. **(1)** = scales, *trutina, libra, lanx* (= the pan of the scales). **(2)** = balanced state, use verb *libro:* to lose one's —, *labi.* **(3)** = the remainder, use adj. *reliquus.*

balance, v. LIT., *aequis ponderibus librare.* TRANSF., *compensare:* the accounts —, *ratio constat.*

balcony, *maenianum.*

bald, adj. LIT., *glaber, calvus.* TRANSF., of language, *incultus, impolitus, aridus.*

baldness, *calvitium.*

bale, subst. *fascis.*

bale (out), v. transit. *egerĕre, exhaurire.*

baleful, *perniciosus, exitiosus.*

balk, subst. **(1)** = a beam, *tignum, trabs.* **(2)** = a ridge, *limes (-itis).*

balk, v. transit. *frustrari, eludĕre.*

ball. (1) = a round object; in gen., *globus:* a — to play with, *pila;* to play —, *pilā ludĕre;* a football (or any ball with air in it), *follis;* = a bullet, q.v. **(2)** = a dance, *saltatio.*

ballad, *carmen.*

ballast, *saburra.*

ballet, *pantomimus* (Plin.): — dancer, *pantomimus,* m. (Suet.), *pantomima,* f. (Sen.).

ballot, *suffragium, tabella.*

balm. LIT., *balsamum.* TRANSF., *solatium.*
balmy. LIT., *balsaminus.* TRANSF., *suavis.*
Baltic Sea, *mare Suevicum.*
balustrade, *cancelli (-orum,* plur.).
bamboo, *harundo Indica* (Plin.).
ban; see FORBID.
band, subst. (1) = a thing that binds or is
  bound on, *fascia, ligamen, ligamentum* (Tac.).
  (2) = a company, association, *manus, turba,
  grex, caterva.*
band (together), v.; see COMBINE.
bandage; see BAND and BIND.
band-box, *capsula* (Cat., Sen.).
bandit, *latro.*
bandy, v. in the phrase: to — words with, *cum
  homine altercari.*
bandy, bandy-legged, *loripes.*
bane. LIT., *venenum, virus (-i).* TRANSF.,
  pernicies, pestis.
baneful, *perniciosus, exitiosus.*
bang, subst. *crepitus (-ūs), sonitus (-ūs).*
bang, v.; see STRIKE.
banish, v. LIT., *homini aquā et igni interdicĕre;
  hominem (in exsilium) eicĕre, (ex)pellĕre,
  exterminare, relegare, deportare.* TRANSF.,
  exterminare, eicĕre, (ex)pellĕre, amovēre.
banishment, *interdictio aquae et ignis, relegatio, deportatio, exsilium.*
bank, subst. (1) of earth, *agger, torus* (Verg.).
  (2) of a river, or lake, *ripa.* (3) a — of oars,
  transtrum. (4) where money is deposited,
  exchanged, etc., *argentaria (taberna* or *mensa),
  mensa publica.*
bank, v. *pecuniam* (or other suitable object)
  apud argentarios conlocare.
banker, *argentarius.*
bank-rate, *nummus.*
bankrupt, *decoctor:* to become —, *(rationes)
  conturbare, decoquĕre;* to be —, *non esse
  solvendo.*
bankruptcy; see BANKRUPT: a national —,
  tabulae (-arum, plur.) *novae.*
banner, *vexillum.*
bannock, *placenta (avenacea).*
banquet, *epulae (-arum,* plur.), *convivium, cena.*
banter, subst. *cavillatio, ludibrium.*
banter, v. *cavillari, iocari.*
bar, subst. (1) = a long piece of any solid substance: *asser* (of wood, Tac.), *later* (of metal,
  Plin.). (2) = a bolt, *claustrum, obex, repagula
  (-orum,* plur.), *sera.* (3) as legal t. t., sometimes *forum:* to practise at the —, *causas
  agere, dicere, orare;* coll. = advocates, *patroni.*
bar, v. transit. (1) to bolt, *occludĕre, obserare.*
  (2) = to hinder, *impedire, prohibēre.*
bar, barring; see EXCEPT.
barbarian, *barbarus.*
barbaric, barbarous. (1) = foreign, strange,
  outlandish, *barbarus, barbaricus* (Verg.).
  (2) = savage, cruel, *barbarus, ferus, immanis, saevus, crudelis.*
barbarity, *immanitas, barbaria.*
barbarously, *barbare, saeve, crudeliter.*
barbed, *hamatus.*
barber, *tonsor:* a —'s shop, *tonstrina.*
bard, *vates.*
Barcelona, *Barcino.*
bare, adj. (1) in gen., *nudus.* (2) = mere, *merus.*
bare, v. transit. *nudare, aperire.*
barefaced, *impudens.*
barefoot, *pedibus nudis.*
barely, *vix, aegre.*

bargain, subst. *pactio, pactum:* to get a —,
  bene emĕre.
bargain, v. *(cum homine) pacisci,* with acc. of
  thing bargained for, or *ut* clause.
barge, *linter.*
bark, subst. (1) of trees, *cortex, liber.* (2) of
  dogs, *latratus (-ūs).*
bark, v. *latrare.*
barley, *hordeum.*
barn, *horreum.*
baron; see NOBLE.
barracks, *castra (-orum,* plur.).
barrel, *cupa, seria, dolium, orca.*
barren, *sterilis, infecundus.*
barrenness, *sterilitas.*
barricade, subst. *munimentum:* a — of felled
  trees, *concaedes* (Tac.).
barricade, v. transit. *inaedificare, praesepire,
  intersepire, obstruĕre, oppilare.*
barrier, *septum, cancelli (-orum,* plur.), *claustra
  (-orum,* plur.).
barrister; see ADVOCATE.
barrow, *ferculum.*
barter, subst. *(per)mutatio mercium.*
barter, v. *merces mutare, rem re mutare, rem
  pro re pacisci.*
base, subst. *basis, fundamentum, radix.*
base, adj. (1) in gen., *turpis.* (2) — coin,
  nummi (-orum, plur.), *adulterini.* (3) — born,
  ignobilis, humili loco natus.
basely, *turpiter.*
baseness, *turpitudo.*
bashful, *pudens, pudicus, verecundus.*
bashfully, *verecunde.*
bashfulness, *pudor, verecundia.*
basin, (for washing) *pelvis* (Juv.), *trulla* (Juv.).
basis; see BASE.
bask, *apricari.*
basket, *corbis, qualus, qualum, sporta, calathus.*
bas-relief, *toreuma.*
bass, adj. (in music), *gravis.*
bastard, *nothus.*
bat, subst. (1) the flying creature, *vespertilio.*
  (2) for games, *clava.*
batch, *numerus.*
Bath, *Aquae Sulis.*
bath, subst. *balineum, balneum, balneae (-arum,*
  plur.), *balnearia (-orum,* plur.), *lavatio:* hot or
  mineral —s, *thermae (-arum,* plur.).
bath, bathe, v. (1) transit. *lavare, abluĕre,
  perfundere.* (2) intransit. *lavari, perlui.*
bath-tub, *alveus.*
battalion, *cohors.*
batter, *pulsare, percutĕre, verberare;* see BEAT:
  to — down, *perfringĕre.*
battering-ram, *aries.*
battery. (1) = assault, *vis.* (2) = a collection
  of artillery, *tormenta (-orum,* plur.).
battle, *proelium, pugna:* a pitched —, *proelium
  iustum.*
battle-array, *acies* (opp. to *agmen* = line of
  march).
battle-axe, *bipennis* (Hor., Verg.), *securis* (Hor.,
  Verg.).
battle-cry, *clamor.*
battle-field, *locus pugnae;* sometimes *acies.*
battlement, *pinna.*
bawl, *vociferari, clamitare.*
bay, subst. (1) the tree, *laurea, laurus.* (2) of
  the sea, *sinus.* (3) at —, *hostibus oppositus.*
bay, adj. *spadix, badius.*
bay, v. *latrare.*

be, *esse*; often also *existĕre, exstare, versari* (esp. with reference to occupation or surroundings), (*se*) *habēre* with adv. (describing condition).

beach, *litus*.

beacon (**1**) = lighthouse, *pharus*. (**2**) = fire, *ignis*.

bead, *baca*.

beak, *rostrum*.

beaker, *poculum*.

beam, subst. (**1**) of wood, *tignum, trabs*; adj. *trabalis*. (**2**) of light, *radius, iubar*. (**3**) of a balance, *scapus* (Vitr.).

beam, v. (*ad*)*fulgēre*.

bean, *faba*; kidney bean, *phaselus*.

bear, subst. (**1**) the animal, *ursus, ursa*. (**2**) the constellation, *arctos, septentriones*: the Great —, *ursa maior*; the Little —, *ursa minor*.

bear, v. (**1**) = to carry, *ferre, gestare, portare*. (**2**) = to endure, undergo, (*per*)*ferre, pati, sustinēre, tolerare*. (**3**) = to have, to entertain (feelings, etc.), *gerĕre*. (**4**) = to produce, bring forth, *parĕre*: of the earth, trees, etc., *ferre*.

beard, subst. *barba*.

beard, v.; see DEFY.

bearer, = a porter, *baiulus*: of letters, *tabellarius*.

beast, *bestia* (esp. wild), *belua* (esp. large), *pecus* (*-udis*, f., *per* tame), *fera* (a wild —), *iumentum* (a — of burden); as a term of contempt, *belua, bestia*.

beastliness, *spurcitia*.

beastly, *spurcus, immundus*.

beat, subst., in music, *ictus* (*-ūs*: Hor.).

beat, v. (**1**) transit.: **a** = to strike, *ferire, caedĕre, percutĕre, pulsare, verberare*; to be beaten, *vapulare*; to beat down, (*pro*)*sternĕre*: **b** = to overcome, *vincĕre, superare*. (**2**) intransit. *palpitare, salire*.

beating, subst. *ictus* (*-ūs*), *verbera* (*-um*, plur.).

beau, *homo bellus* or *elegans*.

beautiful, *pulcher, speciosus, formosus* (esp. in form), *venustus* (= elegant), *bellus* (= fine), *amoenus* (of landscapes, etc.).

beautifully, *pulchre, venuste, belle, eleganter*.

beautify, (*ex*)*ornare*.

beauty, *pulchritudo, species, forma, venustas, amoenitas* (of places).

beaver, *castor* (Juv.), *fiber* (Plin.).

becalmed, *ventis destitutus*.

because, *quod, quia, quoniam, cum* (with subj.), *quandoquidem*; often also rendered by *ut qui, quippe qui*, by a participle, or by abl. abs.: — of, *propter, ob* with acc.

beck, = a nod, *nutus* (*-ūs*).

beckon, (*homini*) *digito innuĕre*.

become, v. (**1**) intransit. *fĭeri, evadĕre, nasci, oriri, exsistĕre*; often rendered by the inceptive verbs, as: to — warm, *calescĕre*; to — rich, *ditescĕre*; what will — of me? *quid mihi* (or *me*) *fĭet*? (**2**) transit. = to suit, (*hominem*) *decĕre*, (*ad hominem*) *convenire*.

bed. (**1**) for sleeping on, *lectus*: to make a —, *lectum sternĕre*; to go to —, *cubitum ire*; a little —, *lectulus*. (**2**) in a garden, *area* (Plin.). (**3**) of a river, *alveus*.

bed-chamber, bedroom, *cubiculum*.

bed-clothes, bedding, *stragulum, lodix* (Juv.).

bedaub, (*ob*)*linĕre, perungĕre*.

bedeck, (*ex*)*ornare*.

bedew, *inrorare*.

bedizen, (*ex*)*ornare*.

bee, *apis*: — hive, *alvus, alveus, alvearium*; a swarm of —s, *examen apium*.

beech, *fagus*, f.; of —, adj. *fageus* (Plin.), *faginus* (Verg., Ov.), *fagineus* (Ov.).

beef, (*caro*) *bubula* (Plin.).

beer, *cer(e)visia* (Plin.).

beetle, subst. *scarabaeus* (Plin.).

beetle, v. *prominēre, imminēre*.

befall, *accidĕre, contingĕre, evenire*.

befit, (*ad hominem* or *rem*) *convenire, aptum esse, idoneum esse*; (*hominem*) *decēre*.

befool, *infatuare, decipĕre*.

before. (**1**) adv., in space, *prae*, or render by compound verb with *prae-*; in time, *prius, ante*: the year —, *superior annus*; the — mentioned, *qui supra dictus est*. (**2**) prep.: **a**, in space = in the presence of, *coram* with abl., *apud* with acc.; in advance of, *prae* with abl.; in front of, *ante* with acc., *pro* with abl.: **b**, in time, *ante* with acc.: — my consulship, *ante me consulem*: **c**, of preference, *ante* with acc. (**3**) conj. *ante quam* or *antequam, prius quam* or *priusquam*.

beforehand, *antea*, or render by compound verb with *prae-*.

befoul, *inquinare, foedare* (Verg.).

befriend, (*hominem*) *adiuvare*, (*homini*) *favēre*.

beg. (**1**) = to be a beggar, *mendicare, stipem petĕre*. (**2**) = to ask earnestly, (*hominem*) *precari, orare, rogare, flagitare*, (*ab homine*) *petĕre*.

beget, *gignĕre, generare, procreare*.

beggar, subst. *mendicus*.

beggar, v. transit. *ad inopiam redigĕre*.

beggarly, *miser, vilis*.

beggary, *egestas, paupertas, mendicitas*.

begin, *incipĕre* (in perfect, use *coepisse*, etc.), *ordiri, inchoare, initium facĕre, instituĕre*; often render by inceptive verb (or imperfect tense). Prov.: well begun is half done, *dimidium facti qui coepit habet* (Hor.).

beginning, *initium, principium, primordium, inceptio, inceptum*: — of a speech, *exordium*; the —s of a science, *elementa, rudimenta, incunabula* (all neut. plur.). Often rendered by another part of speech, e.g. *vere novo, ineunte vere* = in the — of spring; *primo vespere*, at the — of the evening; from — to end, *ab ovo usque ad māla*.

beginner = novice, *tiro*.

begone! *abi! apage te!*

begrudge, *rem homini invidēre*.

beguile, *decipĕre, fallĕre*.

behalf: on — of, *pro*, with abl.; on my —, *mea causa*.

behave, *se gerĕre*: well behaved, *bene moratus*.

behaviour, *mores* (*-um*, plur.).

behead: in gen. *detruncare, obtruncare*; in execution, *securi ferire*.

behind. (**1**) adv. *pone, post, retro, a tergo*: to attack a person —, *hominem aversum adgredi*. (**2**) prep. *pone, post*, with acc.

behold, v. transit. *adspicĕre, conspicĕre, intueri, contemplari, spectare*.

behold! interj. *en! ecce!*

beholden, = indebted, *homini obnoxius*.

behoof; see BEHALF.

behove: it behoves, *decet, convenit, oportet*.

being, *natura*: a human —, *homo*; often rendered by verb *esse*.

belated, *serus*.

belch   big

belch, subst. *ructus (-ūs).*
belch, v. *(e)ructare.*
beldam, = an old woman, *anicula.*
beleaguer, *obsidēre.*
belfry, *turris.*
belie. (1) = to tell lies about, misrepresent, *criminari, calumniari.* (2) = to refute, *refellēre, refutare.*
belief, *fides (fidem homini habēre,* to believe a person; *fidem facere,* to inspire belief); *opinio* (= view or conviction; of anything, *rei* or *de re); persuasio.*
believe. (1) to — a person (or other source of information), *homini credēre, fidem habēre, fidem tribuēre.* (2) to — an assertion, or that a thing is so; *credēre* with acc., or acc. and infin.; also *putare, arbitrari, opinari, reri, existimare, censēre, sentire:* I firmly —, *mihi persuasum est, persuasum habeo;* to — in God, *credēre deum esse;* — me (used parenthetically), *mihi crede, crede mihi;* I — (used parenthetically), *credo, opinor, puto.*
believer, *qui credit.*
bell, *tintinnabulum;* sometimes *aes.*
bellow, subst. *mugitus (-ūs).*
bellow, v. *mugire.*
bellows, *follis.*
belly, *venter, alvus, abdōmen, uterus* (strictly = the womb).
belong, *esse,* with genit. or possess. adj.; *(ad rem* or *hominem) attinēre, pertinēre.*
below (1) adv. *subter, infra.* (2) prep. *infra* with acc., *subter* gen. with acc., *sub (sub rem ire, sub re esse);* see UNDER.
belt, *cingulum, zona, balteus* (esp. a sword-belt).
bemoan, *deplorare.*
bench, *scamnum, subsellium:* a work-bench, *mensa;* for rowers, *transtrum.*
bend. (1) transit. *(in)flectēre, inclinare.* (2) intransit., use same verbs in pass., or with reflex.
bending, *flexus (-ūs), flexio, inclinatio.*
beneath; see BELOW.
benediction; see BLESS.
benefactor, express by verb.
beneficence, *beneficentia, liberalitas.*
beneficent, *liberalis, beneficus.*
beneficial, *utilis, salutaris.*
benefit, subst. *beneficium.*
benefit, v. (1) transit. *(homini) prodesse, (hominem) (ad)iuvare.* (2) intransit. *proficēre.*
benevolence, *benevolentia.*
benevolent, *benevolus.*
benighted. LIT., *nocte oppressus.* TRANSF., see IGNORANT.
benign, *benignus (erga hominem).*
benignity, *benignitas.*
bent, subst. *animi inclinatio, voluntas, ingenium.*
bent, adj. LIT., *curvus.* TRANSF., — on a thing, *rei* (genit.) *studiosus, cupidus.*
benumb, use phrase with adj. *torpidus* or verbs *obtorpescēre, torpēre.*
bequeath, *rem homini legare.*
bequest, *legatum.*
bereave, *orbare.*
bereaved, *orbus.*
bereavement, *orbitas.*
berry, *baca, bacula, acinus.*
Besançon, *Vesontio.*
beseech, *(hominem) orare, implorare, obtestari.*
beseem; see BECOME.

beset, of places, *obsidēre;* more generally, *urgēre, premēre, circumvenire,* with acc.; *instare* with dat.: a —ting sin, *vitium maximum.*
beside, prep. (1) = near, *prope, iuxta,* with acc. (2) = except, *praeter.* (3) = away from: — the point, *nihil ad rem;* — oneself, *sui impotens;* to be — oneself with joy, *laetitiā efferri* or *elatum esse.*
besides, *praeter* with acc., prep.; *praeter quam,* adv.; *praeter quam quod,* conj. (= — the fact that). As adv. = in addition, *praeterea, ultro, ad hoc.*
besiege, *obsidēre, circumsedēre.*
besieger, *obsessor, obsidens, qui obsidet.*
besmear, *(ob)linēre.*
bespatter, *adspergēre, conspergēre, (com)-maculare.*
bespeak, *imperare.*
best, *optimus;* see GOOD: to the — of one's ability, *pro virili parte;* to have the — of it, *superiorem esse* or *discedere.*
bestir: to — oneself, *se (com)movēre, incitare, excitare.*
bestow, *(at)tribuēre, conferre, impertire, largiri;* see also GIVE.
bet, subst. *pignus (-oris).*
bet, v. *pignore contendere* (Cat.) or *certare* (Verg.).
betake: to — oneself, *se conferre.*
betimes, *mature.*
betoken, *significare.*
betray. (1) = to disclose, reveal, *prodēre, aperire, detegēre.* (2) = to hand over to an enemy, *prodēre, tradēre.*
betrayal, *proditio;* often expressed by verb.
betrayer, *proditor.*
betroth, *(de)spondēre.*
betrothal, *sponsalia (-ium* or *-iorum,* plur.).
better, adj. *melior, potior* (= preferable): is —, *melius* or *satius est, praestat;* I am — (in health), *melius me habeo;* I am getting —, *convalesco.*
better, adv. *melius.*
better, v. transit. *meliorem facĕre, corrigĕre, emendare.*
between, *inter* with acc.
beverage, *potio, potus (-ūs).*
bevy, *grex.*
bewail, *deplorare, deflēre, (con)queri.*
beware, *cavēre:* — of the dog, *cave canem* or *a cane;* — of going, *cave (ne) eas.*
bewilder, *(con)turbare, dubium facĕre.*
bewitch. LIT., *fascinare.* TRANSF., see CHARM.
beyond. (1) adv. *ultra, supra.* (2) prep.; lit. *trans* with acc.; lit. and fig., *ultra, extra, supra, praeter,* with acc.
bias, subst. *inclinatio* or *propensio animi.*
bias, v. transit. *inclinare (animum).*
Bible, *biblia (-orum,* plur.: eccl.); *(divina) scriptura* (eccl.). In some senses, Homer was the Greek and Roman 'Bible'.
bibulous, *bibulus* (Verg.).
bid, subst. (at a sale), *licitatio.*
bid, v. transit. (1) = to command, *iubēre, imperare.* (2) = to invite, *invitare.* (3) at a sale, *licēri.*
bidding. (1) see COMMAND. (2) at a sale, *licitatio.*
bide, *manēre.*
bier, *feretrum* (Verg.), *sandapila* (Juv.).
big, *magnus, grandis, vastus.*

bile, *bilis.*

bilge-water, *sentina.*

bilious, *biliosus* (Cels.).

bill. (1) of a bird, *rostrum.* (2) = a proposed law, *rogatio*: to bring forward a —, *rogationem* or *legem ferre*; to adopt a —, *accipĕre*; to reject a —, *antiquare*; to carry a —, *perferre.* (3) financial, *syngrapha.*

billet, subst. = a letter, *epistula.*

billet, v. transit.: to — troops, *milites per domos disponĕre.*

billow, *fluctus (-ūs).*

billowy, *fluctuosus.*

bind, v. transit. LIT., by tying, (ad)*ligare*, *obligare, vincire*, (ad)*stringĕre*; to — back, *religare, restringĕre*; to — together, *conligare, constringĕre.* TRANSF., to engage, oblige, make liable, *obligare, adstringĕre*: to — an apprentice, (*hominem homini*) *addicĕre*; to — over, *vadari.*

bindweed, *convolvulus* (Plin.).

biographer, *qui res gestas narrat, scribit.*

biography, *vita* (Tac.).

biped, *bipes.*

birch, *betula* (Plin.).

bird, *avis, volucris, ales*: a — cage, *cavea*; — catcher, *auceps*; — lime, *viscum.* Prov.: —s of a feather . . ., *pares cum paribus facillime congregantur* (Cic.); to kill two —s with one stone, *de eadem fidelia duo parietes dealbare* (Cic.).

birth, *ortus (-ūs)*: of noble —, *nobili genere* or *loco natus.*

birthday, *dies natalis.*

biscuit, *panis.*

bishop: *episcopus* (eccl.).

bit. (1) of a horse, *frenum.* (2) = piece, *frustum.*

bitch, *canis (femina).*

bite, subst. *morsus (-us).*

bite, v. *mordēre.*

biting, *mordens, mordax, acidus.*

bitter, *amarus, acerbus, acidus, asper.*

bitterly, *amare, aspere, acerbe.*

bitterness, *acerbitas, asperitas.*

bitumen, *bitumen* (Tac.).

bivouac, subst. *excubiae.*

bivouac. v. *in armis excubare.*

black, *ater* (strictly, dead —), *niger* (strictly, glossy —). Black clothes, mourning, *pulla vestis*: dressed in —, *sordidatus, pullatus, atratus.* A — man, negro, *Aethiops.*

blackberry, *rubus.*

blackbird, *merula.*

blacken, v. (1) transit. = to make black, *nigrum facĕre.* (2) intransit. = to grow black, *nigrescĕre* (Verg., Ov.).

blacklead, *plumbum nigrum* (Plin.).

Black Sea, *Pontus Euxinus.*

blacksmith, *faber (ferrarius).*

bladder, *vesica.*

blade. (1) of grass, *herba.* (2) of an oar, *palma.* (3) of a knife, *lamina.*

blame, subst. *culpa, reprehensio, vituperatio.*

blame, v. transit. *reprehendĕre, culpare, vituperare.*

blameless, *innocens, integer, sanctus.*

blamelessness, *innocentia, integritas, sanctitas.*

bland, *blandus, lenis, mitis.*

blandishment, *blanditia, blandimentum, adulatio.*

blandly, *blande.*

blank, *vacuus.*

blanket, *lodix* (Juv.).

blast, subst. *flamen, flatus (-ūs), flabra (-orum, plur., Verg.), adflatus (-ūs).*

blast, v. (1) transit.: to — a trail, perhaps *semitam aperire.* (2) transit.; see BLIGHT.

blaze, subst. *flamma.*

blaze, v. intransit. *ardēre*, (con)*flagrare.*

bleach, *candidum facĕre* or *reddĕre.*

bleak; see COLD.

blear-eyed, *lippus*: to be —, *lippire.*

bleat, subst. *balatus (-ūs).*

bleat, v. *balare.*

bleed. v. (1) intransit. *sanguinem dare, effundĕre.* (2) transit.: to — a person (as an old-fashioned cure), *homini sanguinem mittĕre.*

bleeding, adj., of wounds, *crudus* (Ov.).

blemish, subst. *vitium, mendum, macula, labes.*

blemish, v. transit. (com)*maculare.*

blend, (com)*miscēre.*

bless. (1) = to invoke a blessing on; use phrase, such as *hominem bonis ominibus prosequi.* (2) = to make prosperous, *beare, fortunare, secundare* (Verg.).

blessed, *beatus, fortunatus.*

blessedness, *felicitas.*

blight, subst. *robīgo, lues* (Verg.).

blight, v. transit. *robigine adficĕre*; fig. of hopes etc., *frustrari.*

blind, adj. *caecus* (lit. and fig.), *oculis captus*: — of one eye, *altero oculo captus, luscus.*

blind, v. transit. (oc)*caecare, oculis privare, caecum reddĕre.* Prov.: the — leading the —, *qui sibi semitam non sapiunt, alteri monstrant viam* (Enn.).

blindly = rashly, *temere.*

blindfold, *oculis opertis.*

blindness, *caecitas.*

blink, *connivēre, nictare.*

bliss, *felicitas.*

blister, *pustula.*

blithe, *laetus, hilaris.*

bloated, *turgidus, tumidus.*

block, subst. *stipes, truncus, caudex.*

block, v. transit. *claudĕre, occludĕre, opplēre, obstruere, obsaepire.*

blockade, subst. *obsessio, obsidio.*

blockade, v. transit. *obsĭdēre, obsīdĕre, circumvallare.*

blockhead, use words given under BLOCK (subst.).

blood. LIT., *sanguis, cruor* (= gore, blood shed): in cold —, *consulte, consulto.* TRANSF., = birth, race, *sanguis, genus.*

bloodless, *exsanguis* (= lacking blood), *incruentus* (= without bloodshed).

blood-red, *cruentus* (Verg.), *sanguineus* (Verg.).

blood-relation, *consanguineus.*

bloodshed, *caedes*; sometimes *sanguis* or *cruor.*

bloodshot, *sanguine suffusus.*

blood-stained, *cruentus.*

blood-thirsty, *sanguinarius.*

bloody, *cruentus* (= blood-stained), *sanguineus* (= consisting of blood).

bloom, subst. *flos*: to be in —, *florēre.*

bloom, v. *florēre, vigēre*: to begin to —, *florescĕre.*

blooming, adj. *florens, floridus, nitidus.*

blossom; see BLOOM.

blot, subst., on paper, *litura*; in gen. (lit. and fig.), *macula, labes.*

blot, v. transit. (lit. and fig.), (com)*maculare* : to — out, *delēre, exstinguĕre.*
blow, subst. (lit. and fig.), *ictus (-ūs), plaga, verbera (-um,* plur.); *calamitas* (fig. only).
blow, v. *flare* (transit. or intransit.): to — into, *inflare*; to — on, *adflare.*
blowing, subst. *flatus (-ūs).*
bludgeon, *fustis.*
blue, *caeruleus*: black and —, *lividus.*
blunder, subst. *error, erratum, mendum.*
blunder, v. *errare.*
blunt, adj. LIT., *hebes.* TRANSF., (1) = dull, *hebes, obtusus.* (2) = rude, *agrestis, rusticus.*
blunt, v. transit. (lit. and fig.), *hebetare, obtundĕre.*
bluntly, of speech, *libere, liberius.*
blush, subst. *rubor.*
blush, v. *erubescĕre, rubēre.*
bluster, subst. *declamatio.*
bluster, v. intransit. *declamare, declamitare.*
boar, *verres*: a wild —, *aper.*
board, subst. (1) = a plank, *tabula.* (2) = food, *victus (-ūs), alimentum.* (3) = a body of officials, *conlegium.*
board, v. (1) transit.: **a,** to — up, — over, *contabulare*: **b,** to — a person, *homini victum dare*: **c,** to — a ship, *navem conscendĕre.* (2) intransit.: to — with anyone, *apud hominem habitare.*
boast, *gloriari, se iactare*: to — of, *re gloriari, rem iactare.*
boaster, *iactator, homo gloriosus.*
boasting, subst. *gloriatio, iactatio.*
boastful, *gloriosus.*
boastfully, *gloriose.*
boat, *linter, scapha, navicula.*
boatman, *nauta.*
bodily, *corporeus.*
body, *corpus (-ŏris),* in most senses of the English word): a little —, *corpusculum*; a — of men, *manus, numerus, grex*; as a —, *universi.*
bodyguard, *stipatores, satellites, cohors praetoria*: to belong to the king's —, *a latere regis esse.*
bog, *palūs (-ūdis).*
boggy, *uliginosus, paluster.*
bogy, *terricula (-orum,* plur.).
boil, subst. *vomica.*
boil, v. (1) transit. *coquĕre*: to — down, *decoquĕre.* (2) intransit. *fervēre, (ef)-fervescĕre, (ex)aestuare.*
boiler, *vas, vasis,* n.; in a bath, *caldarium.*
boisterous, *turbidus*; of weather, *turbulentus, procellosus.*
bold, *audax, confidens, ferox, animosus*; put a — face on things, *animosus atque fortis appare* (Hor.).
boldly, *audacter, confidenter, ferociter, animose.*
boldness, *audacia, confidentia.*
bole, *truncus, stirps.*
Bologna, *Bononia.*
bolster, *cervical, culcita, pulvinus.*
bolt, subst. (1) = a fastening, *obex (-icis), sera, pessulus, claustrum.* (2) = a weapon, *telum.*
bolt, v. transit. *claudĕre, occludĕre, obserare.*
bombard, *verberare.*
bombast, (*verborum*) *tumor, inflata oratio, ampullae (-arum,* plur.: Hor.).
bombastic, *inflatus.*
bond. (1) = a tie, *vinculum, ligamentum, compes (-pĕdis), catena.* (2) = a legal document, *chirographum, syngrapha.*

bondage, *servitus (-utis), servitium.*
bone, *os (-ossis,* n.).
bony, *osseus* (Juv.).
book, *liber* (the most general word); *volumen* (in roll form); *codex* (in modern book form); account-books, *tabulae (-arum,* plur.).
bookbinder, *glutinator.*
bookcase, *pegma (-atis,* n.).
bookseller, *bibliopola.*
boon, *beneficium, bonum.*
boorish, *agrestis, inurbanus, rusticus.*
boorishly, *rustice, inurbane.*
boot, *calceus*: an army —, *caliga.*
bootless, *inutilis, inritus.*
bootlessly, *frustra.*
booty, *praeda, spolia.*
boozy, *ebriosus.*
Bordeaux, *Burdigala.*
border, subst. *margo (-inis)*; of a stream, *ripa*; of a country, *finis.*
border, v.: to — on, *adiacēre, attingĕre*; see also ADJOIN.
bore, subst. = a boring person, *homo importunus* or *odiosus.*
bore, v. transit. (1) = to perforate, *perforare, terebrare.* (2) = to weary, (*hominem*) *obtundĕre, defatigare, vexare*; (*homini*) *taedium movere*: I am bored, *taedet me.*
boredom, *taedium.*
born: to be —, *nasci.*
borrow, *mutuari, mutuum sumĕre.*
borrowed, *mutuus, alienus.*
bosom, subst. (lit. and fig.), *sinus (-ūs), pectus (-ŏris), gremium.*
boss, *umbo, bulla.*
botany, (*ars*) *herbaria* (Plin.).
both, *ambo*; often also use *uterque* (=each of two): both … and …, *et … et …, cum … tum …* .
bother, subst. *molestia, incommodum.*
bother, v.; see ANNOY: to — to do a thing, *curare facere.*
bottle, *lagena, ampulla*: — of hay, *manipulus.*
bottom. (1) Of anything, *fundus, solum*; often use adj. *infimus* or *imus* agreeing with the thing itself (e.g. *imum mare,* the — of the sea): to get to the — of, *rem perspicĕre* or *penitus intellegere.* (2) of a person, *clunes (-ium,* plur.), *nates (-ium,* plur.), *pyga.*
boudoir, *gynaecium.*
bough, *ramus.*
Boulogne, *Gesoriacum.*
bounce, *resilire.*
bound, subst. (1) = a limit. LIT., see BOUNDARY. TRANSF., *finis, modus, terminus*: to keep within —s, *intra fines se coercēre.* (2) = a jump, *saltus (-ūs).*
bound, v. (1) = to limit, (*de*)*finire, terminare.* (2) = to jump, *salire.*
boundary, *finis, terminus, confinium.*
boundless, *infinitus, immensus.*
bounty. (1) as a quality, *largitas, liberalitas, munificentia.* (2) = a reward, *praemium.*
bountiful, *largus, liberalis.* Lady Bountiful, render by reference to the 'horn of plenty' or 'horn of Amalthea', *cornu copiae* or *cornu Amaltheae.*
bountifully, *large, liberaliter.*
Bourges, *Avaricum.*
bout, *certamen*: a drinking —, *comissatio.*
bow, subst. (1) the weapon, *arcus (-ūs)*; prov.: to draw a — at a venture, *mittere lineam* (Pl.).

(2) of a ship, *prora*. (3) = a movement of the body, *corporis inclinatio*; often to be rendered by *salutatio*.

bow, v. (1) in gen., *flectĕre, demittĕre, inclinare*. (2) to — to a person, *hominem salutare*; fig., *obsequi, obtemperare*, with dat.

bowman, *sagittarius*.

bowstring, *nervus* (Verg.).

bowels, *viscera* (*-um*, plur.: lit. and fig.); *alvus*.

bower, *umbraculum* (Verg.).

bowl, subst. *crater* (Verg.), *cratera, patera*.

bowl, v. transit. *volvĕre*.

box, subst. (1) = a (wooden) receptacle, *arca, capsa, cista, pyxis*. (2) the shrub, *buxus*; adj. *buxeus*. (3) = a blow, slap, *alapa* (Juv.), *colaphus* (Pl.).

box, v. intransit. *pugnis certare*.

boxer, *pugil*.

boy, *puer*.

boyhood, *aetas puerilis, pueritia*: from —, *a puero, a pueris*.

boyish, *puerilis*.

boyishly, *pueriliter*.

brace, subst. (1) = a strap, *fascia, vinculum*. (2) = a stay (rigid), *fibula*. (3) = a pair, *par*.

brace, v. transit. LIT., physically, (*ad*)*ligare*. TRANSF., mentally, (*con*)*firmare*.

bracelet, *armilla*.

brackish, *amarus* (Verg.).

brag; see BOAST.

braid, subst. *limbus* (Verg.): a — of hair, *gradus* (Quint.).

braid, v. transit. *texĕre, nectĕre*.

brain, *cerebrum*.

bramble, *rubus, vepris*.

bran, *furfur* (Plin.).

branch, subst. *ramus* (in most senses of the English word).

branch, v. intransit. *dividi*.

brand, subst. (1) = a firebrand, *torris, fax*. (2) = a mark, *nota*.

brand, v. transit. *notam* (*homini*) *inurĕre, notare*.

brandish, *vibrare, iactare*.

brass, *orichalcum*.

bravado, *iactatio*.

brave, *fortis, audax, strenuus, animosus*.

bravely, *fortiter, strenue*.

bravery, *fortitudo*.

bravo! *euge! factum bene! macte!*

brawl, subst. *rixa, iurgium*.

brawl, v. intransit. *rixari*.

brawny, *robustus, lacertosus*.

bray, v. (1) transit. = to pound, *contundĕre*. (2) intransit. *rudĕre*.

brazen, *a*(*h*)*eneus, a*(*h*)*enus* (Lucr.), *aereus* (Verg.); strictly, these refer to bronze. TRANSF., = shameless, *impudens*: a — face, *os durum* or *durissimum*.

breach, subst., express by verb. LIT., in walls, etc.: to make a —, *perfringĕre discutĕre*. TRANSF., a — of treaty, *foedus ruptum* or *violatum*: to commit a — of duty, *officium neglegĕre* or *deserĕre, ab officio discedĕre*.

bread. LIT., *panis*. TRANSF., daily —, subsistence, *victus* (*-ūs*).

breadth, *latitudo*.

break, subst. = a gap, *intervallum*: — of day, *prima lux, diluculum*.

break, v. (1) transit. LIT., *frangĕre, confringĕre, rumpĕre*: to — in pieces, *comminuĕre*; to — off, *defringĕre*; to — open, *refringĕre*.

TRANSF., **a** = to weaken, subdue, *domare, frangere, infringere*: **b**, to interrupt, put an end to: to — a treaty, *foedus violare*; — a promise, *fidem fallĕre*; to — silence, *silentium rumpĕre*; to — off meetings, relationships, etc., *dirimĕre, dirumpĕre, interrumpĕre*; to — up a camp, *castra movēre*. (2) intransit. LIT., *frangi, confringi, rumpi*: the clouds —, *nubes discutiuntur*; to — in, *inrumpĕre*; — out, *erumpere*; — up, *dissolvi*. TRANSF., day —s, *inlucescit*; to — down, see FAIL; to — out, of disturbances, *exoriri, exardescĕre, gliscĕre*; to — with a person, *dissidĕre ab homine*.

breaker, *fluctus* (*-ūs*).

breakfast, subst. *ientaculum* (on rising), *prandium* (about noon).

breakfast, v. intransit. *ientare* (Suet.), *prandēre*.

breakwater, *moles*.

breast, subst. *pectus* (*-ŏris*, n.: lit. and fig.), *animus* (fig.): the —s, *mammae* (*-arum*, plur.).

breast, v. transit. *obniti*, with dat.

breastbone, *os pectoris* (Cels.).

breast-plate, *lorica, thorax*.

breastwork, *pluteus, lorica*.

breath, *spiritus* (*-ūs*), *anima*: to take —, *animam recipere* (Ter.); to hold one's —, *animam continere*; to put out of —, *exanimare*.

breathe, *spirare, spiritum ducĕre*: to — again, *respirare*; to — upon, *adflare*; to — out, *exhalare*.

breathless, *exanimatus, exanimis*.

breeches, *bracae*: wearing —, *bracatus*.

breed, subst. *genus*.

breed, v. (1) transit. *gignĕre, generare, parĕre, procreare*: to — or rear animals, *alĕre*. (2) intransit. *nasci*.

breeding; see EDUCATION.

breeze, *aura*.

Brescia, *Brixia*.

brevity, *brevitas*.

brew, *coquĕre*: to be brewing, of trouble, *imminēre, impendēre*.

briar; see BRIER.

bribe, subst. *pretium*.

bribe, v. transit. (*pretio, pecuniā*, etc.) *corrumpĕre*: to try to —, *pretio, pecuniā*, etc., *temptare*; able to be bribed, *venalis*.

briber, *corruptor, largitor* (on a large scale).

bribery, *largitio* (on a large scale); or use verb.

brick, *later*; of —, adj., *latericius*.

bridal, adj. *nuptialis*: — bed, *lectus genialis*; — veil, *flammeum* (Juv.).

bride, bridegroom: engaged, *sponsa, sponsus*; (just) married, (*nova*) *nupta*, (*novus*) *maritus*.

bridge, *pons*: a little —, *ponticulus*; to make a —, *pontem facĕre in fluvio*; to break down a —, *pontem interrumpĕre, interscindĕre*.

bridle, *frenum*.

bridle, v. transit. (*in*)*frenare* (lit. and fig.); see also RESTRAIN.

brief, subst., of a barrister; use *causa*.

brief, adj. *brevis*: in —, *ne longus sim*.

briefly, *breviter, paucis* (*verbis*), *strictim*.

brier, briar, *vepris, dumus, frutex*.

brigade, *legio*; see also TROOP.

brigand, *latro*.

bright. (1) = shining, *clarus, lucidus, splendidus, candidus, fulgens*; of weather, *serenus*: to be —, *clarēre*; to grow —, *clarescĕre*; (2) = clever, *argutus, acutus*.

brighten, v. (1) transit. *inlustrare, inluminare.* (2) intransit. *clarescĕre.*

brightly, *lucide, clare, splendide, candide.*

brightness, *candor, splendor, nitor, fulgor*; of weather, *serenitas.*

brilliant (lit. and fig.), *splendidus, inlustris, luculentus, praeclarus.*

brim, *ora, margo, labrum.*

brimstone, *sulfur.*

Brindisi, *Brundisium.*

brine, *muria, salsamentum.*

bring, v. transit. LIT., by carrying, (*ad*)*ferre*, (*ad*)*portare*; by leading, pulling, etc. (*ad*)*ducĕre*: to — back, *referre, reducĕre*; to — together, *cogĕre.* TRANSF., to — about, *efficĕre* (*ut*); to — before the senate, *rem ad senatum referre*; to — forward, *in medium proferre*; to — in, yield, *reddĕre*; to — on, induce, *adferre, inferre, importare*; to — over, *in partes suas trahĕre, traducĕre*; to — to a certain state, *adducĕre, redigĕre*; to — to an end, *ad finem perducĕre*; to — up, *educare.*

brink, *margo, ripa*: on the — of death, *moriturus.*

brisk, *alacer, vegetus.*

briskness, *alacritas.*

bristle, subst. *saeta.*

bristle, v. intransit. *horrēre.*

bristly, *saetosus.*

brittle, *fragilis.*

brittleness, *fragilitas* (Plin.).

broach, lit. and fig., *aperire*; fig. *rem divulgare.*

broad, *latus, amplus*: — day, *clarus* or *multus dies.*

broadly, *late.*

brogue = a kind of shoe, *pero*; = uncouth speech, *sermo rusticus.*

broil, subst. *rixa.*

broil, v. transit. *torrēre.*

broker, *interpres.*

bronze, subst. *aes.*

bronze, adj. *a(h)eneus, a(h)enus* (Lucr.), *aereus* (Verg.).

brooch, *fibula.*

brood, subst. *fetus* (-*ūs*).

brood, v. *incubare* (lit. and fig.); see also PONDER.

brook, subst. *rivus, rivulus.*

brook, = to tolerate, *ferre, tolerare.*

broom. (1) the plant, *genista.* (2) = a besom, *scopae* (-*arum*, plur.).

broth, *ius* (*iuris*).

brothel, *ganea, lupanar, lustra* (-*orum*, plur.).

brother, *frater*; a full —, (*frater*) *germanus.*

brotherhood. LIT., *germanitas.* TRANSF., = an association, *societas sodalitas.*

brotherly, *fraternus.*

brow. (1) = eyebrow, *supercilium.* (2) = forehead, *frons.* (3) of a hill, *summus collis.*

brown, *fuscus* (dark), *fulvus* (yellowish), *spadix* (chestnut).

browse, to — upon, (*at*)*tondēre* (Verg.).

bruise, v. *contundĕre.*

bruit, v. transit. (*di*)*vulgare.*

brush, subst. *penicillus, peniculus* (Pl.).

brush, v. transit. *verrĕre*, (*de*)*tergēre*: to — aside, *excutĕre.*

brush-wood, *virgultum, sarmentum* (both usually plur.).

brutal, brutish, *ferus, inhumanus, immanis.*

brutality, *immanitas.*

brutally, *inhumane, immaniter*: to behave —, *saevire.*

brute; see BEAST; as a term of abuse, *pecus, belua.*

bubble, subst. *bulla* (Ov.).

bubble, v. intransit. *bullare* (Cato).

buccaneer, *pirata, praedo.*

bucket, *situla* (Pl.), *hama* (Juv.).

buckle, *fibula.*

buckler, *scutum, clipeus, parma.*

bud, subst. *gemma, germen* (Verg.).

bud, v. *gemmare, gemmas agĕre.*

budge, *loco cedĕre.*

buff, *luteus.*

buffalo, *bos.*

buffet, = a blow, *alapa, colaphus.*

buffoon, *sannio, scurra, balatro* (Hor.).

buffoonery, *scurrilitas* (Quint.).

bug, *cimex* (-*icis*).

bugbear; see BOGY.

bugle, *bucina.*

build, v. transit. *aedificare*, (*ex*)*struĕre, construĕre, condĕre.*

builder, *aedificator, structor.*

building, subst. (1) = the process, *aedificatio, exstructio.* (2) = the thing built, *aedificium.*

bulb, *bulbus* (Plin.).

bulk, *magnitudo, amplitudo, moles.*

bulky, *amplus, ingens.*

bull, *taurus.*

bullock, *iuvencus.*

bullet, *glans.*

bullion, *aurum, argentum.*

bully, rendered by adj., such as *procax* or *importunus.*

bulrush, *iuncus, scirpus.*

bulwark, *propugnaculum* (lit. and fig.).

bump, subst. (1) = a swelling, *tumor, tuber.* (2) = a bang, knock, *ictus* (-*ūs*).

bump, v.: to — into, *offendĕre.*

bumper; see CUP.

bunch, of fruit, *racemus, uva*; see also BUNDLE.

bundle, *fascis, fasciculus, manipulus, sarcina.*

bung, *obturamentum* (Plin.).

bungling; see AWKWARD.

buoyancy. LIT., *levitas.* TRANSF., *hilaritas.*

buoyant. LIT., *lēvis.* TRANSF., *hilaris.*

burden, subst. *onus* (-*eris*): beast of —, *iumentum.*

burden, v. transit. *onerare, opprimĕre.*

burdensome, *gravis, molestus.*

bureau, *scrinium.*

burgess, burgher, *municeps, civis.*

burglar, *fur.*

burglary, *furtum*: to commit a —, *parietes perfodĕre.*

burn, subst. (1) = the result of —ing, *ambustum* (Plin.). (2) = a stream; q.v.

burn, v. (1) transit.: to start —ing, set on fire, *incendĕre*; to — up, *comburĕre*, (*con*)*cremare.* (2) intransit. = to blaze (lit. and fig.), *ardēre, flagrare*; to — (or be —t) down, *deflagrare*; or use pass. of the transit. verbs.

burnish, *polire.*

burrow, *cuniculus* (Plin.).

burst, v. transit. (*di*)*rumpĕre*; see also BREAK.

burial, *sepultura, humatio.*

burial-ground, *sepulturae locus, sepulcrum.*

bury, *humare, sepelire.*

bush, *frutex, dumus.*

bushy, *fruticosus.*

bushel, *medimnus.*

busily, *sedulo, industrie.*

business, *res, negotium*: it is my —, *meum est.*

business-man, *negotiator.*
buskin, *cothurnus.*
bust, *effigies.*
bustle, subst. *festinatio, trepidatio.*
bustle, v. intransit. *festinare, trepidare.*
busy, *occupatus, negotiosus.*
busy-body, *ardelio* (Phaedr., Mart.).
but. (1) = except, *praeter,* with acc.; after neg. or in a question, often *nisi:* all but, *tantum non.* (2) = only, *modo, tantum solum.* (3) = adversat. conj., *sed* (most common, used in correction or transition); *verum* (= but in fact); *at* (in strong opposition); *atqui* (= and yet, yes but); *tamen* (= however, nevertheless); *autem, vero* (as second word in clause, mildly adversative = on the other hand); but, you may say, *at(enim)*; but if, *sin* or *quodsi;* not only . . . but also . . ., *non modo* (or *solum*) . . . *sed etiam* . . .; in strong contrasts, 'but' is often omitted by asyndeton.
butcher, *lanius.*
butcher, v. transit., of animals, *caedĕre, iugulare;* of persons, *trucidare.*
butchery, *caedes.*
butler, *cellarius* (Pl.), *promus* (Pl.).
butt, subst. = an object of ridicule, *ludibrium.*
butt, v. *arietare* (Verg.), *cornu petĕre.*
butter, *butyrum* (Plin.).
butterfly, *papilio.*
buttocks, *clunes* (-ium, plur.), *nates* (-ium, plur.), *pyga.*
buttress, subst. *anteris* (Vitr.).
buttress, v. transit. *fulcire.*
buxom, adj. *hilaris.*
buy, v. transit. (*co*)*emĕre, mercari.*
buyer, *emptor.*
by. (1) of place, *ad, apud, iuxta, prope,* with acc.: to go —, *praeterire;* to stand —, *adesse.* (2) of time: — night, *noctu, nocte;* — moonlight, *ad lunam.* (3) of means or manner, *per* with acc.: — stealth, *furtim;* — chance, *forte;* — heart, *memoriter.* (4) of agency, *ab* (*homine*). (5) of measure, with compar. or superl., express by abl. (6) in adjuration, *per* with acc. (7) of distribution: one by one, *singuli, singillatim.*
by-way, *trames* (-itis), *semita, deverticulum.*
by-word: to become a —, *contemptui* or *ludibrio esse.*

C

cab; see CARRIAGE.
cabal, = a plot, *coniuratio;* = a body of plotters, *coniurati.*
cabbage, n. *brassica, caulis* (strictly = a stalk).
cabin, *casa, tugurium.*
cabinet. (1) = a room, *conclave.* (2) = a cupboard, desk, etc., *armarium;* repository of precious things, *thesaurus, scrinium.* (3) = a government, ministry, *penes quos summa rerum est.*
cable, *ancorale, funis ancorarius.*
cackle, *strepĕre.*
cadaverous, *exsanguis* (= bloodless).
cadence, *numerus:* to have a rhythmical —, *numerose cadĕre.*
cadet, *tiro.*
Cadiz, *Gades* (-ium, plur.).
cage, *cavea.*

cairn, *lapidum acervus.*
cajole, (*homini*) *blandiri.*
cajolery, *blanditiae* (-arum, plur.).
cake, subst. *placenta.*
cake, v. intransit. = to stick together, *concrescĕre.*
calamity, *calamitas, clades.*
calamitous, *calamitosus, luctuosus.*
calculate, *computare.*
calculated, *ad rem accommodatus, aptus, idoneus.*
calculation, *ratio:* to make a strict —, *rem ad calculos vocare.*
caldron, *a(h)enum* (Verg.), *cortina* (Plin.).
calendar, *fasti* (-orum, plur.).
calf, *vitulus, vitula:* of a —, *vitulinus;* the — of the leg, *sura.*
call, subst. (1) = a cry, *vox.* (2) = a visit, *salutatio.*
call, v. (1) = to cry out, *clamare.* (2) = to name, *vocare, dicĕre, nominare, appellare.* (3) = to summon, (*ad*)*vocare;* to — aside, *sevocare;* to — away, *avocare;* to — back, *revocare;* to — out, *evocare;* to — together, *convocare.* (4) to — for = to demand, (*de*)*poscĕre, flagitare.* (5) to — on = to visit, *salutare, visĕre.*
caller, = visitor, *salutator;* in plur., —s, often *salutatio.*
calling, = vocation, office, *munus* (-ĕris, n.).
callous, LIT., *callosus.* TRANSF., *durus.*
callow, = unfledged, *implumis* (Hor.).
calm, subst. *quies, tranquillitas, otium, pax:* — at sea, *malacia.*
calm, adj. *quietus, tranquillus, placidus, sedatus.*
calm, v. transit. *sedare, lenire, tranquillare.*
calmly, *tranquille, placide, sedate, aequo animo.*
calumniate, *calumniari, criminari.*
calumniator, *obtrectator.*
calumny, *criminatio, calumnia.*
Cambridge, *Cantabrigia* (late Latin); adj., of —, *Cantabrigiensis.*
camel, *camelus.*
camp, *castra* (-orum, plur.): to pitch a —, *castra ponĕre;* to break up (or strike) —, *castra movēre.*
campaign, *stipendium.*
can, subst.; see JUG.
can, v. *posse;* see also ABLE.
canal, *fossa.*
cancel, *delēre, tollĕre, inducĕre.*
candid, *candidus, liber, apertus sincerus, verus, simplex.*
candidate, *candidatus:* to be a — for, *petĕre.*
candidly, *candide, libere, aperte, sincere.*
candour, *libertas, candor.*
candle, *candela:* to work by — light, *lucubrare.* Prov.: to burn the — at both ends, *Herculi quaestum conterĕre* (Pl.).
candlestick, *candelabrum.*
cane, subst. = in gen., *harundo, calamus;* of —, *harundineus;* for walking, *baculum;* for correction, *ferula.*
cane, v. transit. (*ferulā*) *verberare.*
canine, *caninus.*
canister; see BOX.
canker, v. transit. *corrumpĕre.*
cankerworm, *eruca* (Plin.).
cannon, *tormentum.*
cannot, *nequire;* see also CAN and ABLE.
canoe, *cymba;* see also BOAT.
canon, = a rule, *lex, regula, norma.*

canopy, *aulaeum.*

cant, subst., i.e. phrases repeated monotonously, *cantilena.*

Canterbury, *Durovernum.*

canton, *pagus.*

canvas, in a sail, *carbasus* (Verg.), *velum.*

canvass, = to ask votes from, *ambire.*

canvassing, lawful, *ambitio*; unlawful, *ambitus (-ūs).*

cap, *pileus, galerus* (Verg.).

capability, *facultas.*

capable, *(ad rem) aptus, idoneus*; *(rei,* genit.) *capax* (Tac.); often rendered by *posse.*

capacious, *capax, amplus.*

caparison, *phalerae (-arum,* plur.).

caper, *exsultare.*

capital, subst. (1) = chief city, *caput*; or *use-urbs* with adj. (2) of a pillar, *capitulum* (Vitr.). (3) = sum of money, *sors, caput.*

capital, adj., of crime or punishment, *capitalis*; for more general senses, see EXCELLENT, etc.

capitulate; see SURRENDER.

caprice, *libido, levitas.*

capricious, *inconstans, levis.*

captain, in gen., *princeps, dux*; in the army, perhaps *centurio*: — of a ship, *navarchus, praefectus navis, magister.*

captious, *morosus, difficilis.*

captivate, *capĕre, delenire, permulcēre.*

captive, *captus, captivus.*

captivity, *captivitas.*

capture, *capĕre, comprehendĕre.*

car, *carrus, cisium, plaustrum, vehiculum*; see also CARRIAGE.

caravan, *comitatus (-ūs).*

carbuncle, *carbunculus* (Plin.).

carcase, *cadaver.*

card, subst. *charta*: to play at —s; see DICE.

card, v. transit. *pectĕre.*

cardinal; see CHIEF.

care, subst. (1) = attention, caution, *cura, diligentia.* (2) = anxiety, *cura, sollicitudo*: free from —, *securus.* (3) = management, *cura, curatio.*

care, v. to — for, — about, *curare*; not to — about, *nil morari.*

career, *curriculum, cursus (-ūs).*

careful, *diligens, accuratus, attentus.*

carefully, *diligenter, accurate.*

careless, *neglegens.*

carelessness, *imprudentia, neglegentia, incuria.*

caress, subst. *complexus.*

caress, v. *(homini) blandiri, (hominem) permulcēre.*

caressing, *blandus.*

cargo, *onus (-ĕris),* n.

caricature, v. transit. *vultum in peius fingĕre* (Hor.).

carnage, *caedes, strages.*

carnal, render by genit. *corporis.*

carnival, *feriae (-arum,* plur.); perhaps *Saturnalia (-ium,* plur.).

carousal, *comissatio, potatio.*

carouse, v. *comissari, potare.*

carp, subst. *cyprinus* (Plin.).

carp, v.: to — at, *carpĕre, vellicare, calumniari.*

carpenter, *faber (tignarius).*

carpet, *tapeta (-ae), tapeta (-orum,* plur.), *tapetia (-ium,* plur.).

carriage. (1) = the act of carrying, *gestura.* (2) = bearing, mien, *habitus.* (3) = a vehicle in gen., *vehiculum*: a four-wheeled

travelling —, *raeda, petorritum*; a ladies' —, *carpentum, pilentum.*

carrier, *gerulus*: letter —, *tabellarius.*

carrion, *cadaver.*

carry. LIT., *ferre, portare, vehĕre*; as a possession, or for use, *gerĕre*: to — across, *transportare*; to — back, *referre, reportare*; to — off, *auferre*; to — out, *efferre, exportare.* TRANSF., to — a bill, *legem perferre*; to — a city (by storming it), *urbem expugnare, vi capĕre*; to — on (= practise, administer), *exercēre, gerĕre*; to — out (= perform), *conficĕre, exsequi.*

cart, *plaustrum.*

Cartagena, *Carthago Nova.*

carve, *caelare, scalpĕre, sculpĕre*: to — meat, *scindĕre, secare.*

carver, artistic, *caelator, sculptor*: a — of meat, *carptor* (Juv.).

carving, *caelatura, scalptura, sculptura.*

cascade, *aquae ex alto desilientes.*

case. (1) = a receptacle, *theca, involucrum.* (2) in grammar, *casus (-ūs).* (3) judicial, *causa.* (4) = chance, set of circumstances, *res, casus*; often expressed by verb.

casement, *fenestra.*

cash, subst. = ready money, *pecunia praesens* or *numerata.*

cash, v. transit. *praesenti pecuniā solvĕre.*

cashier, subst., express by phrase.

cashier, v. transit. = to discharge, *exauctorare.*

cask, *dolium, cupa.*

casket, *arcula, capsula* (Cat.), *cistula* (Pl.).

casque, *galea, cassis.*

cast, subst. = a throw, *iactus.*

cast, v. transit. LIT., = to throw, *iacĕre, conicĕre, iactare, mittĕre*: to — down, *deicĕre*; to — off, *deponĕre, exuĕre*; to — out, *eicĕre, expellĕre.* TRANSF., to — blame, *culpam conicĕre, conferre, in hominem*; to — in metal, *fundĕre*; to be — in a suit, *causā cadĕre*; to be — down, *adfligi*; to — up (of accounts), *computare, subducĕre.*

castaway, *perditus, profligatus*: — by shipwreck, *naufragus.*

castigate; see PUNISH.

castle, *castellum*: to build —s in the air, *somnia sibi fingĕre, vigilantem somniare.*

castrate, *exsecare.*

casual, *fortuitus, forte oblatus.*

casually, *forte, casu, fortuito.*

cat, *feles* (or *felis*).

catacomb, *puticuli (-orum,* plur.: Varro).

catalogue, *index* (Quint.).

catapult, *catapulta.*

cataract. (1) in the eye, *glaucoma* (Plin.). (2) see CASCADE.

catarrh, *gravedo, pituita.*

catastrophe; see DISASTER.

catch, *capĕre, excipĕre, deprehendĕre, comprehendĕre*: to — up, by following, *adsequi, consequi*; to — a disease, *in morbum cadĕre*; to — fire, *ignem concipere, comprehendere*; prov.: to — a Tartar, *lupum auribus tenēre.*

categorical, *simplex, definitus.*

category, *genus (-ĕris), numerus.*

cater, *obsonare.*

caterpillar, *eruca* (Plin.).

cattle, *boves*; collect., *pecus (-oris)*; a single head of —, *pecus (-udis).*

caul, *omentum* (Cels.).

cauldron; see CALDRON.

cause, subst. *causa* (in nearly all senses of the English word); sometimes *materia* (= occasion, ground), *res* (= case, affair).

cause, v. transit. *facĕre, efficĕre* (both often with *ut* clause); *movĕre, excitare, exhibēre, dare.*

causeway, *agger.*

caustic, *mordax, acerbus.*

cauterize, *adurēre.*

caution, subst. = carefulness, *cautio, cura, prudentia.*

caution, v. transit. *monēre.*

cautious, *providus, prudens, cautus.*

cautiously, *prudenter, caute.*

cavalcade, *comitatus (-ūs).*

cavalier, = horseman, *eques.*

cavalierly, *adroganter, insolenter.*

cavalry, *equitatus, equites (-um,* plur.), *copiae equestres* : to serve in the —, *equo merēre.*

cave, *caverna, specus, spelunca, antrum.*

cavity; see HOLE.

cavil; see CARP.

caw, *crocire* (Pl.).

cease, *desinĕre* (absol., or with infin.); *desistĕre* (= leave off, fail to finish; with abl., or *de,* or *ab,* or infin.).

ceaseless, *perpetuus, adsiduus.*

ceaselessly, *perpetuo, adsidue.*

cedar, *cedrus.*

cede, *concedĕre.*

ceiling, in gen., *tectum;* panelled, *lacunar;* vaulted, *camera.*

celebrate, *celebrare.*

celebrated, *celeber, clarus, inlustris, nobilis.*

celebration, *celebratio.*

celebrity, *gloria, laus, claritas;* = a celebrated person, *vir insignis.*

celerity, *celeritas.*

celestial, *caelestis, divinus.*

celibacy, *caelibatus (-ūs:* Sen.).

cell, *cella, cubiculum.*

cellar, in gen., use *cella:* a wine —, *apotheca.*

cement, subst. *gluten* (= glue), *ferrumen* (Plin.).

cement, v. transit., lit. and fig. *conglutinare.*

cemetery, *sepulcra (-orum,* plur.).

censer, *turibulum.*

censor, *censor.*

censorious, *severus.*

censure, subst. *reprehensio, vituperatio.*

censure, v. transit. *reprehendĕre, vituperare.*

census, *census (-ūs):* to take a —, *censēre.*

cent, = a small coin, *teruncius;* for percentages, see PERCENTAGE.

centaur, *centaurus.*

centre, subst. *media pars;* the — of anything is usually expressed by *medius,* agreeing as adj. with the thing itself (e.g. *media urbs,* the — of the city): the — of government, *sedes imperii.*

centre, v., to — in, see DEPEND.

centurion, *centurio.*

century, *centum anni, saeculum.*

ceremonial, ceremony, *ritus (-ūs), caerimonia.*

ceremonious, *sollemnis.*

certain, *certus* (in all senses of the English word); *stabilis, fidus* (= trustworthy); *status* (= settled); *exploratus* (of things of which one feels sure): a — person (who could be named if necessary), *quidam;* to know for —, *certo scire.*

certainly, *certo, haud dubie;* in answers,

profecto, sane; = admittedly, *certe, quidem, sane.*

certainty, certitude, express by adj. *certus.*

certify, *confirmare.*

cerulean, *caeruleus.*

cessation, *intermissio.*

chafe. v. (1) transit. *calefacĕre.* (2) intransit. *stomachari, aestuare.*

chaff, *palea.*

chagrin, *aegritudo, stomachus, dolor.*

chain, subst. *catena, vinculum;* fig. = a connected series, *series;* of mountains, *montes continui* (Hor.).

chain, v. transit. *vincire, catenas homini inicĕre.*

chair, *sella, sedile, cathedra.*

chairman, *qui conventui praeest.*

chalice, *calix.*

chalk, *creta.*

challenge, (*ad pugnam) provocare.*

chamber, *cubiculum.*

chamberlain, *cubicularius.*

chamber-pot, *matula, matella.*

champ, *mandĕre.*

champion, *propugnator, defensor.*

chance, subst. *casus (-ūs), fors:* by —, *forte, casu;* game of —, *alea.*

Chance (personif.), *Fortuna.*

chance, v. (1) transit., see RISK. (2) intransit. *accidĕre;* see also HAPPEN.

chandler, *candelarum propola.*

change, subst. *(com)mutatio, permutatio, immutatio, vicissitudo.*

change. v. (1) transit. *(com)mutare, immutare:* to — completely, *convertĕre (in);* to — the subject, *sermonem alio transferre;* to — money, *permutare;* see also EXCHANGE. (2) intransit. *(com)mutari.*

changeable, *mutabilis, inconstans, varius.*

changeableness, *mutabilitas, varietas.*

changeling, *puer subditus.*

channel, *fossa, canalis, fretum.*

chant, subst. *cantus (-ūs), carmen.*

chant, v. *canĕre, cantare.*

chaos, *chaos,* only in nom., acc., and abl. sing.; in gen. = confusion, *confusio, perturbatio.*

chaotic, *confusus, perturbatus.*

chapel, *aedicula, sacellum.*

chapter, of a book, *caput.*

character. (1) = a symbol in writing, a letter, *littera.* (2) = the disposition or nature of a person, *natura, ingenium, animus, mores (-um,* plur.), *indoles* (esp. of moral —): good —, *virtus;* strength of —, *constantia.* (3) = the natural quality of anything, *ingenium, proprietas.* (4) = role, part played (on the stage or in life), *persona, partes (-ium,* plur.). (5) = reputation, *opinio, fama, existimatio:* to give a servant a —, *commendare.*

characteristic, subst. *proprietas;* see also CHARACTERISTIC, adj.

characteristic, adj. *proprius:* it is — of a person to . . ., *hominis est facere.*

characteristically, *proprie, more suo.*

characterize, *notare, designare.*

charcoal, *carbo.*

charge, subst. (1) = price, *pretium.* (2) = command, commission, *mandatum.* (3) = care of, duty of looking after, *cura, custodia, tutela;* to take — of, *curare.* (4) = accusation, *accusatio, crimen.* (5) = attack, *impetus (-ūs), incursus (-ūs).*

charge, v. (**1**) to fix a price, *pretium facĕre, constituĕre.* (**2**) to — a thing to a person's account, *rem homini imputare.* (**3**) to — a person with a duty, *rem homini committĕre, mandare.* (**4**) = accuse, *accusare, arguĕre, insimulare.* (**5**) = to attack, (*in hominem*) *invadĕre* or *impetum facĕre* or *incurrĕre.*

chargeable, with a fault, *culpae adfinis* or *obnoxius.*

charger. (**1**) = dish, *lanx.* (**2**) = horse, *equus.*

chariot, *currus (-ūs):* a two-horsed —, *bigae (-arum,* plur.); four-horsed —, *quadrigae (-arum,* plur.).

charioteer, *auriga.*

charitable, *benignus, liberalis, beneficus.*

charitably, *benigne, liberaliter.*

charity, as a sentiment, *benignitas;* as conduct, *beneficentia, liberalitas.* Prov.: — begins at home, *tunica propior pallio* (Pl.).

charlatan, *ostentator.*

Charles, *Carolus* (post-class.).

charm, subst. (**1**) = a magic formula, *carmen.* (**2**) = an amulet, *fascinum.* (**3**) = an attraction, or attractive quality, *blandimentum, dulcedo, lepor, venustas.*

charm, v. transit.: by magic, *fascinare;* see also DELIGHT.

charmer. (**1**) = magician, *magus.* (**2**) = charming person, *deliciae (-arum,* plur.).

charming, *suavis, venustus, lepidus;* of country, *amoenus.*

chart, *tabula.*

chary, *parcus.*

chase, subst. *venatio, venatus (-ūs).*

chase, v. transit. (**1**) *venari;* see PURSUE. (**2**) = to engrave, *caelare.*

chasm, *hiatus (-ūs), specus (-ūs).*

chaste, *castus, pudicus.*

chastise, *castigare;* see also PUNISH.

chastisement, *castigatio, animadversio.*

chastity, *castitas, pudicitia.*

chat, subst. *sermo.*

chat, v. *fabulari, garrire.*

chatter, *garrulitas.*

chattering, *garrulus, loquax.*

cheap, *vilis:* to buy —, *bene emere.*

cheapen, *pretium (rei) minuĕre;* for fig. sense, see DISPARAGE.

cheat, subst. (**1**) = a deception, *fraus, fallacia, dolus.* (**2**) = a deceiver, *circumscriptor, fraudator, fraus* (Pl., Ter.).

cheat, v. *fallĕre, decipĕre, circumvenire, fraudare.*

check, subst. *impedimentum, mora.*

check, v. *continēre, impedire, reprimĕre.*

checkmate, v. *ad incitas redigĕre* (Pl.).

cheek, *gena;* when puffed out, *bucca.*

cheer, subst. (**1**) = a shout, *clamor.* (**2**) to be of good —, *bono animo esse.*

cheer, v. (**1**) = to shout, *clamare.* (**2**) = to gladden, *exhilarare, erigĕre.*

cheerful, *hilaris, laetus.*

cheerfully, *hilare, laete.*

cheering, subst. *favor.*

cheerless, *tristis, maestus, inlaetabilis* (Verg.).

cheese, *caseus.*

cheque, *perscriptio.*

chequered, *varius.*

cherish, *forēre, colĕre, observare, tuēri.*

cherry, *cerasus* (Prop., Ov.).

chess, *lusus latrunculorum.*

chest. (**1**) = part of the body, *pectus (-oris),* n. (**2**) = a receptacle, *arca, cista, armarium.*

Chester, *Deva.*

chestnut, *castanea* (Verg., Plin.).

chew, *mandĕre.*

chicanery, *dolus, calumnia.*

chicken, *pullus (gallinaceus).*

chide, *obiurgare, increpare.*

chiding, *obiurgatio.*

chief, subst. *caput, princeps, dux.*

chief, adj. *primus, praecipuus.*

chiefly, *praecipue.*

chieftain, *regulus.*

child, male, *filius;* female, *filia:* a small —, *infans;* children (of either sex = young people), *pueri;* children (with reference to their parents), *liberi.*

child-birth, *partus (-ūs).*

childhood, *pueritia, aetas puerilis.*

childish, *puerilis.*

childishly, *pueriliter.*

childless, *(liberis) orbus.*

chill, subst. *horror.*

chill, adj. *frigidus.*

chill, v. transit. *refrigerare.*

chime, subst. *concentus (-ūs).*

chime, v. *concinĕre.*

chimera, *commentum.*

chimerical, *commenticius, inanis, vanus.*

chin, *mentum.*

china, use *murra,* and adj. *murrinus.*

chine, *tergum.*

chink, *rima.*

chip, *assula* (Pl., Cat.). Prov.: a — of the old block, render by phrase such as *filius patri similis* or the verb *patrissare* (Pl., Ter.).

chirp, *pipilare* (Cat.).

chisel, subst. *scalprum, caelum.*

chivalrous, *magnanimus.*

chivalry, as an institution, *ordo equester, res equestris;* as a spirit, perhaps *magnanimitas.*

choice, *delectus (-ūs), electio;* = freedom to choose, *optio.*

choice, adj. *electus, eximius.*

choir, *chorus.*

choke, v. transit. *suffocare, animam intercludĕre.*

choler; see ANGER.

choose, v. *eligĕre, deligĕre.*

chop, *abscidĕre, praecidĕre.*

chord, *nervus.*

choric: a — ode, *canticum.*

chorister, *puer symphoniacus.*

chorus, *chorus.*

Christ, *Christus.*

Christendom, *civitas* or *respublica Christiana.*

Christian, *Christianus* (subst. and adj.).

chronic, *longinquus, diuturnus.*

chronicle, subst. *annales (-ium,* plur.).

chronicle, v. transit. *in annales referre.*

chronicler, *annalium scriptor.*

chronology, *temporum* (or *rerum*) *ordo* (or *ratio*).

church, *ecclesia* (eccl.).

churl, *homo agrestis, rusticus, inurbanus.*

churlish, *agrestis, rusticus, inurbanus.*

cider, *vinum ex malis confectum.*

cimetar, *acinaces* (Hor.).

cinder, *cinis.*

cipher, subst. (**1**) = a secret writing, *notae (-arum,* plur.). (**2**) = a nobody, *numerus.*

cipher, v. intransit. *computare.*

circle, *orbis, circulus;* = a group of people, *corona;* family —, *familia.*

circuit, *circuitus (-ūs), orbis, circulus.*

circular, *rotundus.*
circulate, v. transit. *circumagĕre, dispergĕre;* of news, rumours, etc., *divulgare.*
circulation, render by verb; to be in —, *in manibus esse.*
circumference; see CIRCLE and CIRCUIT.
circumlocution, *circumitio verborum, circumlocutio* (Quint.).
circumnavigate, *circumvehi (navi* or *classe).*
circumscribe, *circumscribĕre, definire.*
circumspect, *cautus, providus, prudens.*
circumspection, *cautio, prudentia, circumspectio.*
circumstance, *res,* sometimes *tempus:* according to —s, *pro re (natā);* in these —s, *quae cum ita sint.*
circumstantial, of accounts, etc., *accuratus.*
circumvallation, *circummunitio.*
circumvent, *circumvenire, circumscribĕre.*
cistern, *cisterna* (Tac.), *lacus, puteus.*
citadel, *arx.*
cite, v. (1) = to quote, *proferre, memorare.* (2) to — before a court, *citare, in ius vocare.*
citizen, *civis.*
citizenship, *civitas.*
city, *urbs.*
civic, *civilis, civicus.*
civil. (1) = civic, *civilis, civicus:* — war, *bellum civile, intestinum, domesticum.* (2) = polite, *urbanus.*
civilization, *humanus cultus (-ūs), humanitas.*
civilize, *expolire;* or use phrase with *humanus* or *humanitas.*
civilized, *humanus.*
civilly, *urbane.*
clad, *vestitus.*
claim, subst. *postulatio.*
claim, v. transit. *postulare, vindicare, adserĕre:* to — back, *repetĕre.*
claimant (at law), *petitor.*
clammy, *lentus.*
clamorous, *clamosus* (Juv.); see also NOISY.
clamour, subst. *vociferatio, clamor.*
clamour, v. *(con)clamare, vociferari:* to — for, *flagitare.*
clan, *gens, tribus (-ūs).*
clandestine, *clandestinus, furtivus.*
clandestinely, *clam, furtim.*
clang, subst. *clangor, sonus (-ūs), sonitus (-ūs).*
clang, v. *strepĕre, (re)sonare.*
clank, subst. *crepitus (-ūs), strepitus (-ūs).*
clank, v. *crepare, crepitare.*
clap, subst.: of the hands, *plausus (-ūs);* = of wings, *alarum crepitus (-ūs);* of thunder, *tonitrus (-ūs).*
clap, v.: with the hands, *(manibus) plaudĕre.*
clarify, *deliquare* (Varro).
clash, subst. (1) = collision, *concursus (-ūs).* (2) = loud noise, *crepitus (-ūs), strepitus (-ūs).*
clash, v. (1) to — together, *concrepare.* (2) = to disagree, *inter se (re)pugnare, dissidĕre, discrepare.*
clasp, subst. (1) = a fastener, *fibula.* (2) see EMBRACE, GRASP.
clasp, v. transit. (1) see FASTEN. (2) see EMBRACE.
class: in gen., *genus (-eris);* political or social, *classis, ordo.*
classic, adj., as a vague term of praise, *optimus, praecipuus, eximius.*
classical, from the Roman point of view, *Graecus.*
classify, *in genera describĕre.*

clatter, subst. *crepitus (-ūs), strepitus (-ūs).*
clatter, v. intransit. *crepare, strepĕre.*
clause, *pars, membrum, caput.*
claw, *unguis:* of a crab, *bracchium* (Plin.).
clay, *argilla.*
clean, adj. *purus, mundus;* a — sweep, *everriculum.*
clean, adv. = quite, *prorsus.*
clean, v. transit. *purgare.*
cleanliness, *munditia, mundities.*
clear, adj. *clarus* (in most senses of the English word); of weather, etc., *serenus, lucidus;* of style, *lucidus, candidus, apertus;* = unobstructed, *apertus;* = evident, intelligible, *planus, manifestus:* it is —, *apparet, liquet.*
clear, v. (1) transit. LIT., = to make — and unobstructed, *expedire:* to — away obstacles, etc., *amovēre, detergēre.* TRANSF., to — up a matter, *expedire, explicare, enodare.* (2) intransit.: it (i.e. the weather) is clearing up, *disserenat.*
clearly, *clare, distincte, perspicue, plane, manifeste, lucide, aperte.*
clearness, *claritas;* (of weather) *serenitas.*
cleave. (1) transit. = to split, *(dif)findĕre, scindĕre.* (2) intransit. = to stick, *(ad)haerēre.*
cleaver, *culter.*
cleft, *rima.*
clemency, *clementia, mansuetudo.*
clement, *clemens, mansuetus, indulgens, lenis.*
clench: to — the fist, *digitos comprimĕre.*
clergyman, clerical, *clericus* (eccl.).
clerk, *scriba.*
clever, *sollers, callidus, astutus, catus.*
cleverly, *sollerter, callide, astute.*
cleverness, *sollertia, calliditas.*
client, *cliens* (= both dependent in gen. and client of a lawyer); *consultor* (of a lawyer); in the courts, a lawyer refers to his client as *hic.*
cliff, *scopulus, cautes.*
climate, *caelum.*
climax, *gradatio.*
climb, subst. *ascensus (-ūs).*
climb, v. *scandĕre, ascendĕre, escendĕre, eniti.*
cling, *(ad)haerēre* with dat., *amplecti* with acc.
clink, subst. *tinnitus (-ūs).*
clink, v. *tinnire.*
clip, *tondēre, praecidĕre, circumcidĕre, resecare.*
cloak, subst. *amiculum, pallium;* for journeys or bad weather, *lacerna, paenula:* a soldier's —, *sagum.*
cloak, v. transit. in fig. sense, *dissimulare, tegĕre.*
clock, *horologium:* a water- —, *clepsydra.*
clod, *glaeba.*
clog, subst. (1) = a hindrance, *impedimentum.* (2) = a wooden shoe, *sculponea* (Pl.).
clog, v. = to hinder, *impedire.*
cloister, = colonnade, *porticus (-ūs).*
close, subst. (1) = end, *finis, exitus.* (2) see ENCLOSURE.
close, adj. (1) = reserved, *taciturnus, tectus, occultus.* (2) = niggardly, *parcus.* (3) = near, *propinquus, vicinus, finitimus:* a — friend, *familiaris.* (4) = closely packed, *densus, spissus, confertus, artus:* to fight at — quarters, *comminus pugnare.*
close, adv. *prope, iuxta:* — to, *prope, iuxta,* with acc.
close. v. (1) transit.: **a** = to shut, *claudĕre, occludĕre:* **b** = to finish, *finire, conficĕre,*

(2) intransit.: **a** = to be shut, *claudi*: **b** = to come to an end, *finiri*: **c**, to — with any-one (to fight), *manum conserĕre*.

closely, *arte, dense*: — resembling, *simillimus*.

closeness, = nearness, *propinquitas, vicinitas*.

closet, *cubiculum*.

clot, subst.: — of blood, *sanguis concretus*.

clot, v. *concrescĕre*.

cloth, *textum, textile*.

clothe, v. transit. *vestire, amicire*: — oneself, *induĕre sibi vestem*.

clothes, clothing, *vestis, vestitus (-ūs), vesti-menta (-orum*, plur.).

cloud, subst. LIT., *nubes*: a storm- —, *nimbus*. TRANSF., *nimbus*.

cloud, v. transit. *obscurare*.

cloudless, *serenus*.

cloudy, *nubilus*.

clown, = countryman, *homo rusticus, agrestis*; see also BUFFOON.

clownish, *rusticus, agrestis*.

cloy, *satiare, saturare*.

club, subst. (1) = cudgel, *clava, fustis*. (2) = association, *circulus, sodalitas*.

club, v.; see ASSOCIATE.

clubfooted, *scaurus* (Hor.).

cluck, *singultire* (Col.), *glocire* (Col.).

clue. LIT., of thread, *glomus (-eris), filum*. TRANSF., = an indication, *indicium*.

clump, *globus*.

clumsy, *inhabilis, ineptus, inscitus*.

clumsily, *inepte, inscite, laeve* (Hor.).

clumsiness, *inscitia*.

cluster, = bunch, *racemus, uva* (esp. of grapes), *corymbus* (esp. of ivy-berries). All these words are poetical.

clutch, *comprehendĕre, adripĕre*.

coach; see CARRIAGE.

coachman, *raedarius, auriga*.

coagulate, v. *coire, concrescĕre*.

coal, *carbo*: a live —, *pruna* (Verg., Hor.). Prov.: to carry —s to Newcastle, *in silvam ligna ferre* (Hor.).

coalesce, *coalescĕre, coire*.

coalition, *coniunctio, consociatio*.

coarse. LIT., *crassus*. TRANSF., of behaviour, etc., *inhumanus, incultus, inurbanus*.

coarsely. LIT., *crasse*. TRANSF., *inculte*.

coarseness. LIT., *crassitudo*. TRANSF., *in-humanitas, mores inculti*.

coast, subst. *litus (-ŏris), ora*: on the —, *maritimus*.

coast, v. *oram legĕre, praetervehi*.

coat. (1) = an article of clothing, *toga, tunica*. (2) = hide, *vellus (-ĕris), pellis*.

coax, *(homini) blandiri, (hominem) permulcēre*.

cobble, *(re)sarcire*.

cobbler, *sutor*. Prov.: let the — stick to his last, *sutor ne supra crepidam* (Plin.).

Coblenz, *Confluentes (-ium*, plur.).

cock, *gallus (gallinaceus)*.

cock-a-hoop: to be —, *exsultare*.

code, use *lex*, or plur. *leges*.

codify, *digerere*.

coequal, *aequalis*.

coerce, *coĕrcēre, cohibēre, cogĕre*.

coercion, *coercitio, vis*.

coffer, *cista, arca*.

coffin, *arca, capulus*.

cog, of a wheel, *dens*.

cogency, *pondus, vis*.

cogent, *firmus, validus, gravis*.

cogitate, *cogitare*.

cogitation, *cogitatio*.

cognition, cognizance, *cognitio*.

cognizant, *conscius*.

cohabit, *consuescĕre*.

coheir, *coheres*.

cohere, *cohaerēre* (lit. and fig.).

coherent, *cohaerens, contextus, congruens*.

cohort, *cohors*.

coin, *nummus*: good —, *nummi boni*; bad —, *nummi adulterini*.

coin, v. transit. *cudĕre, signare*.

coinage, *res nummaria*.

coincide, *competĕre, congruĕre*; often rendered by *idem* (e.g. *idem esse, eodem tempore fieri*).

coincidence, *concursatio*; often = chance; q.v.

coition, *coitus (-ūs), concubitus (-ūs)*.

Colchester, *Camulodunum*.

cold, subst. *frigus (-ŏris), algor*: a — in the head, *gravedo*; to be left in the —, *algēre* (Juv.).

cold, *frigidus, gelidus*: to be —, *frigēre, algēre*; in — blood, *consulto*.

coldly, *frigide, gelide*.

collapse, v. *conlabi, concidĕre, corruĕre*.

collar, subst. ornamental, *monile, torques*; for prisoners, etc., *boia* (Pl.), *collare* (Pl.).

collar, v. transit. *(com)prehendĕre*.

collar-bone, *iugulum* (Cels.).

collate, v. transit. *conferre*.

collation. (1) = comparison, *conlatio*. (2) = a meal, *cena*.

colleague, *conlega*.

collect, v. (1) transit. *conligĕre, comportare, con-quirĕre, congerĕre*: — oneself, *se conligĕre*; to — money, taxes, etc., *exigĕre*. (2) intransit. *convenire, coire*.

collection, of money, *conlatio*; of anything heaped together, *congeries*; often rendered by verb.

college, *conlegium, societas, sodalitas*.

collide, *confligĕre*.

collision, *concursus, concursio*.

collocation, *conlocatio*.

colloquy, *conloquium*.

colloquial, adj.: — speech, *sermo humilis*.

collusion, *conlusio, praevaricatio*.

Cologne, *Colonia Agrippina*.

colonel, *tribunus militum, praefectus*.

colony, *colonia*.

colonist, *colonus*.

colonial, *colonicus*; or express by genit. of *colonia*.

colonnade, *porticus (-ūs)*.

colossal, *vastus, ingens, immanis*.

colour, subst. (1) as a quality of bodies, *color*: of the same —, *concolor*; of a different —, *discolor*. (2) = colouring matter, paint, *pigmentum*. (3) = pretext, *species, praetextus*. (4) plur. = standards, *signum, vexillum*.

colour, v. (1) transit. *colorare, tingĕre, inficĕre*. (2) intransit.; see BLUSH.

colt, *eculeus*.

column. (1) = a pillar, *columna*. (2) as milit. t. t., *agmen*: in two —s, *bipartito*; in three —s, *tripartito*.

comb, *pecten*; of a cock, *crista* (Juv.).

comb, v. transit. *(de)pectĕre*.

combat, subst. *pugna, certamen*.

combat, v.; see FIGHT.

combination, *(con)iunctio, societas*: in —, *coniuncti -ae -a*.

combine, v. transit. *(con)iungĕre, consociare, miscēre.*

come, *venire* (lit. and fig.), *pervenire, advenire, accedĕre*: to — often, *ventitare, locum frequentare;* —l *agĕ!;* to — about, *fieri, evenire;* to — across, *invenire;* to — back, *revenire, redire;* to — by, see OBTAIN; to — down, *descendĕre;* to — near, *appropinquare;* to — off (from a contest) *discedĕre;* to — on, *procedĕre, pergĕre;* to — out, *exire, egredi;* to — to oneself, *ad se redire;* to — to light, *in lucem proferri;* to — to help, *subvenire;* to — together, *convenire;* to — up, *succedĕre;* to — upon, *invenire.*

comedy, *comoedia.*

comeliness, *venustas, decor, pulchritudo.*

comely, *bellus, venustus, pulcher.*

comet, *cometes (-ae).*

comfort, subst. (1) = consolation, *solatium, consolatio.* (2) = comfortableness, *commoda (-orum,* plur.).

comfort, v. *(con)solari, adlevare.*

comfortable, *commodus:* to make oneself —, *genio indulgēre* (Pl.).

comforter, *consolator.*

comic, comical. (1) = belonging to comedy, *comicus.* (2) = ridiculous, *ridiculus, facetus.*

comically, *ridicule, facete.*

coming, subst. *adventus (-ūs).*

command, subst. (1) = the right to give orders, *imperium:* the supreme —, *summa imperii;* to be in —, *imperare, praeesse.* (2) = an order given, *imperium, iussum, mandatum;* of the senate, *decretum.* (3) = self- —, *continentia, temperantia.*

command, v. (1) = to be in —, *imperare, praeesse,* with dat.; *ducĕre,* with acc.: to — oneself, *sibi imperare.* (2) = to give a particular order, *(hominem) iubēre (facĕre), (homini) imperare* or *praecipĕre (ut faciat).* (3) = to dominate by position, *imminēre, despectare* (Verg.).

commander, *dux, imperator, praefectus.*

commemorate, *celebrare.*

commemoration, *celebratio.*

commence, *incipĕre;* see also BEGIN.

commend. (1) = to commit, entrust, *commendare, committĕre, credĕre.* (2) = to praise, recommend, *laudare, commendare, probare.*

commendable, *laudabilis.*

commendably, *laudabiliter.*

commendation, *commendatio, laus.*

commendatory, *commendaticius.*

comment, subst.: spoken, *dictum;* written, *adnotatio* (Plin. L.).

comment, v. = to express an opinion, *sententiam dicĕre, censēre.*

commentary, *commentarius, commentarium.*

commentator, *interpres, explanator.*

commerce, *commercium, negotia (-orum,* plur.), *mercatura.*

commercial, use phrase with *commercium:* — interests, *negotia (-orum,* plur.); a — traveller, *institor.*

commingle, *(com)miscēre;* see MINGLE.

commiserate, *(com)miserari;* see PITY.

commissariat, *res frumentaria, commeatus (-ūs).*

commissary, *procurator.*

commission, subst. (1) = an allotted task, *mandatum:* to execute a —, *mandatum exsequi.* (2) = a position of trust (e.g. in the army), *munus (-ĕris).*

commission, v. *mandare;* see also CHARGE.

commit. (1) = to entrust, *mandare, commendare, committĕre, credĕre.* (2) = to do, perpetrate, *facĕre, committĕre (in se) admittĕre, patrare:* to — a fault, *peccare, errare;* to — murder, *occidĕre.* (3) = to oblige, engage, *obligare, obstringĕre.*

committee, *consilium;* — of two, *duumviri;* — of three, *triumviri;* etc.

commodious, *commodus, opportunus, aptus.*

commodiously, *commode, opportune, apte.*

commodity, = an article, *res, merx.*

common, subst. = — land, *ager publicus.*

common, adj. (1) = belonging to several or all people, *communis:* this is — to you and me, *hoc mihi tecum commune est;* the phrase, *communis sensus (-ūs)* is used by Hor. for 'common decency', by Lucr. for 'common experience'; in —, *communiter.* (2) = belonging to the people or state, *publicus.* (3) = commonplace, vulgar, ordinary, *vulgaris, quotidianus:* the — people, *plebs;* a — soldier, *gregarius miles.*

commonly, = usually, *fere, ferme, plerumque.*

commonplace, subst. *locus communis.*

commonplace, adj. *vulgaris.*

commonwealth, *respublica, civitas.*

commotion, *tumultus (-ūs), motus (-ūs), agitatio, turba.*

commune, *(cum homine) conloqui.*

communicate, *communicare;* see also SHARE, TELL.

communication, *communicatio;* with a person, *commercium, usus (-ūs), consuetudo.*

communicative, = talkative, *loquax.*

communion. (1) in gen. = fellowship, intercourse, *commercium, societas, consuetudo, coniunctio.* (2) as eccl. t. t. *communio, eucharistia, cena Domini.*

community. (1) = COMMUNION. (2) = state, society, *civitas, respublica, commune.*

commute; see EXCHANGE.

compact, subst. *pactio, pactum, conventus:* according to —, *ex pacto;* to form a —, *pacisci (cum homine).*

compact, adj. *densus, crassus, confertus, solidus, pressus.*

compactly, *confertim.*

companion, *comes, socius, sodalis:* boon —, *combibo, compotor* (f. *compotrix*).

companionable, *adfabilis, facilis.*

companionship, *sodalitas, societas.*

company. (1) = a trading association, *societas.* (2) as milit. t. t., *manipulus.* (3) of actors, *histrionum grex* or *familia.* (4) = any kind of association, *coetus (-ūs), grex.*

compare, *comparare, componĕre, conferre, aequiperare.*

comparable, *comparabilis;* or express by verb.

comparative, *comparativus;* more often rendered by compar. of adj.

comparison, *comparatio, conlatio:* in — with, *prae, ad.*

compass, subst. (1) = extent, *ambitus (-ūs), circuitus (-ūs).* (2) a pair of compasses, *circinus.* (3) a mariner's —; the stars make the best classical equivalent.

compass, v. (1) see ENCOMPASS. (2) see ACCOMPLISH.

compassion, *misericordia.*

compassionate, *misericors.*

compatible, *congruens, conveniens.*

compatriot, *civis.*
compel, *cogĕre, compellĕre, subigĕre, adigĕre.*
compendious, *brevis.*
compendium, *epitome* or *epitoma.*
compensate: to — for, *compensare, rependĕre* (poet.).
compensation, *compensatio.*
compete, (*cum homine*) *contendĕre, certare*: to — for an office, *petĕre.*
competent, adj.; see ABLE: to be —, *competĕre.*
competition, *contentio, certamen, certatio.*
competitor, *competitor.*
compile, *componĕre.*
complacent, = self-satisfied, *qui sibi placet.*
complain, (*con*)*queri* (*de re* or *rem*).
complaint. (1) *questus* (-*ūs*), *querimonia, querela.* (2) = illness, *morbus.*
complaisance, *obsequium, obsequentia, indulgentia.*
complaisant, *comis, indulgens, facilis, obsequens, obsequiosus* (Pl.): to be — to, *morem homini gerĕre.*
complement, *complementum;* when a fixed number of men is the sense, use phrase such as *numerum complēre.*
complete, adj. *absolutus, perfectus, iustus, integer, plenus.*
complete, v. *complēre, explēre, supplēre, absolvĕre, conficĕre.*
completely, *omnino, prorsus, plane.*
completion, *confectio, absolutio, finis.*
complex, *multiplex.*
complexion, *color.*
compliance, *obsequium.*
complicate, *impedire.*
complicated, *involutus, impeditus.*
complication, *implicatio.*
compliment, *laus:* to pay —s, (*con*)*laudare;* to send one's —s to, *salutare, valēre iubēre.*
complimentary, *honorificus.*
comply, v.: to — with, (*homini* or *rei*) *obsequi,* (*con*)*cedĕre, parēre, morem gerĕre.*
components, *partes* (-*ium,* plur.), *elementa* (-*orum,* plur.).
compose. (1) = to make up, constitute, *componĕre, efficĕre:* to be —d of, (*ex rē* or *rē*) *consistĕre, constare.* (2) of literary composition, *componĕre, scribĕre, condĕre, pangĕre.*
composed, = calm, *tranquillus.*
composer, *scriptor.*
composition. (1) the act, *compositio;* literary, *scriptio, scriptura.* (2) the product of literary —, *scriptio, scriptum.*
composure, *tranquillitas, aequus animus.*
compound, adj. *compositus, multiplex.*
compound, v. = mix, *miscēre, confundĕre.*
comprehend. (1) = to contain, *continēre, complecti.* (2) = to understand, (*mente*) *comprehendĕre, complecti; intellegĕre, perspicĕre.*
comprehension, *comprehensio, intellegentia;* often rendered by verb.
comprehensive, *late patens.*
compress, *comprimĕre, condensare, concludĕre, coartare.*
compression, of style, *compressio;* otherwise render by verb.
compromise, subst.; render by verb.
compromise, v. (1) = to settle a matter in dispute, *rem componĕre, compromittĕre* (= to agree to abide by the decision of an arbitrator). (2) = to entangle, embarrass, *impedire:*

without compromising one's loyalty, *salvā fide.*
compulsion, *vis, necessitas:* under —, *coactus -a -um.*
compunction, *paenitentia:* I feel —, *paenitet me.*
compute, *computare;* see also RECKON.
comrade: in gen., *socius, comes, sodalis;* = a fellow-soldier, *contubernalis, commilito.*
comradeship, *sodalitas, contubernium* (Tac.).
concave, (*con*)*cavus.*
conceal, *celare* (often with double acc.), *occulĕre, occultare,* (*re*)*condĕre, abdĕre* (= to put out of sight).
concede, (*con*)*cedĕre, permittĕre.*
conceit, conceited, render by the phrase *sibi placēre.*
conceive. (1) physically, *concipĕre.* (2) mentally, *concipĕre,* (*ex*)*cogitare, intellegĕre, comprehendĕre.*
concentrate. (1) = to bring together, *conligĕre, contrahĕre, in unum conferre.* (2) to — on, attend completely to, (*animum*) *attendĕre, hoc* (or *id*) *agĕre.*
conception. (1) physical, *conceptio, conceptus* (-*ūs*). (2) mental, *notio, opinio.*
concern, subst. (1) = an affair, *res, negotium.* (2) = anxiety, *cura, anxietas, sollicitudo.*
concern, v.: to — a person, *ad hominem pertinēre, attinēre;* often also rendered by the impersonal verbs *interest* and *refert;* to be —ed in, *versari* (*in re*), *adfinem esse* (*rei,* genit. or dat.); to be —ed about, *curare.*
concerning, = about, *de* with abl.
concert, subst. *symphonia, concentus* (-*ūs*): in —, *consensu.*
concert, v.: to — measures, *consilia conferre.*
concession, *concessio;* or render by verb.
conciliate, *conciliare.*
conciliation, *conciliatio.*
conciliatory, *pacificus, blandus.*
concise, *brevis, pressus, concisus, adstrictus.*
concisely, *adstricte, breviter.*
conciseness, *brevitas.*
conclave; see ASSEMBLY.
conclude. (1) = to finish, *finire, conficĕre, concludĕre.* (2) = to draw a conclusion, *concludĕre, conligĕre.*
conclusion, *finis, conclusio.*
conclusive, *gravis, certus.*
concoct. LIT., *miscēre.* TRANSF., *fingĕre, excogitare, conflare.*
concoction, *potus* (-*ūs*).
concord, *concordia, consensus* (-*ūs*).
concordant, *concors.*
concourse, *concursus* (-*ūs*), *concursio, frequentia.*
concrete, = solid, *solidus.*
concubinage, *concubinatus* (-*ūs*).
concubine, *concubina, paelex.*
concupiscence, *libido.*
concur, *consentire, congruĕre, concinĕre.*
concurrence, *consensio, consensus* (-*ūs*).
concurrently, *una, simul.*
condemn, *damnare, condemnare* (judicially or otherwise); for milder senses of the word, see BLAME, DISAPPROVE.
condemnation, *damnatio, condemnatio.*
condemnatory, *damnatorius* (rare).
condense, v. (1) transit. *densare, spissare.* (2) intransit. *concrescĕre.*
condensed, adj., physically, *densus, spissus, concretus;* of style, *pressus, densus.*

condescend, *se submittĕre, descendere.*
condescending, *comis, facilis.*
condescension, *comitas, facilitas.*
condign, = due, *debitus, meritus.*
condiment, *condimentum.*
condition. (1) = state, *condicio, status* (-*ūs*), *sors, res* (esp. plur.): in good —, *sartus tectus.* (2) = stipulation, *condicio, pactum, lex:* on — that, *eā condicione ut.*
conditional, express by subst. *condicio.*
conditioned, adj. *adfectus:* well, ill —, *bene, male moratus.*
condole, *casum hominis dolēre.*
conduce, *conducĕre (ad rem).*
conducive, *utilis,* with dat. or *ad.*
conduct, subst. (1) = behaviour, *vita, mores* (-*um,* plur.); or express by phrase. (2) = management, *administratio.*
conduct, v. (1) = to lead, (*de*)*ducĕre, perducĕre.* (2) = manage, *gerĕre, administrare:* — oneself, *se gerĕre.*
conductor, *dux.*
conduit, *canalis.*
cone, *conus, meta.*
confectionery, *crustum* (Verg., Hor.).
confederacy, *foedus* (-*ĕris,* n.), *societas.*
confederates, *socii, foederati.*
confer. (1) = to give, *conferre, tribuĕre;* see also GIVE. (2) = to talk with, *conloqui, consultare.*
conference, *conloquium.*
confess, *fateri, confiteri.*
confession, *confessio.*
confidant, *conscius* (f. *conscia*).
confide. (1) = to entrust, *committĕre, mandare, credĕre.* (2) to — in, (*con*)*fidĕre,* with abl. or dat.
confidence, *fides, fiducia, confidentia* (= esp. self —).
confident, (*con*)*fidens.*
confidential (1) = trustworthy, *fidus, fidelis.* (2) see SECRET.
confidently, (*con*)*fidenter.*
confiding, adj. *credulus.*
confine, subst. *finis, terminus, confinium.*
confine, v. *includĕre, coercēre, cohibēre, continēre:* to be —d (in childbed), *parēre;* to be —d to bed, in gen., *lecto tenēri.*
confined, adj. *artus:* a — space, *artum.*
confinement, *inclusio;* = imprisonment, *custodia;* = childbirth, *partus* (-*ūs*).
confirm, (*con*)*firmare;* = to ratify (laws, etc.), *sancire, ratum facĕre.*
confiscate, *publicare.*
confiscation, *publicatio.*
conflagration, *incendium, ignis.*
conflict, subst. *certamen, pugna;* of opinions, *dissensio.*
conflict, v. (1) = to fight, *pugnare, certare, contendĕre.* (2) = to differ, *dissentire, discrepare, repugnare.*
confluence, = a meeting of rivers, *confluens* or plur. *confluentes.*
conform: to — to, *obsequi, obtemperare, inservire* (all with dat.).
conformable, *accommodatus, congruens, consentaneus.*
conformation, *conformatio, forma, figura.*
conformity, *convenientia:* in — with, *ex, secundum.*
confound. (1) = confuse, *confundĕre,* (*per*)*miscēre.* (2) = to astonish, *obstupefacĕre.* (3) = to frustrate, *ad inritum redigĕre, frustrari.*

confraternity, *societas, sodalitas.*
confront, v. (*homini*) *obviam ire* or *se opponĕre.*
confuse, *confundĕre,* (*per*)*miscēre,* (*per*)*turbare.*
confused, *confusus, perplexus.*
confusedly, *confuse, perplexe.*
confusion, *confusio, perturbatio, trepidatio.*
confute, *refellĕre, redarguĕre, confutare, refutare.*
congeal. (1) transit. *congelare* (Varro, Mart.). (2) intransit. *congelare* (Ov.), *concrescĕre.*
congenial, *gratus, concors.*
congeries, *congeries.*
congratulate, (*homini rem* or *de re*) *gratulari.*
congratulation, *gratulatio.*
congregate, v. intransit. *congregari, convenire, coire, confluĕre.*
congregation, *conventus* (-*ūs*), *coetus* (-*ūs*).
congress, *conventus* (-*ūs*), *concilium.*
congruity, *convenientia;* see also CONFORM.
conjecture, subst. *coniectura, opinio.*
conjecture, v. *augurari, conicĕre, coniectare, coniecturam facĕre* (or *capĕre*).
conjectural, express by verb or subst.
conjugal, adj. *coniugalis* (Tac.).
conjugate, as grammat. t. t. *declinare.*
conjugation, as grammat. t. t., *declinatio.*
conjunction, as grammat. t. t., *coniunctio.*
conjure, v. (1) transit. = to entreat, *obtestari, obsecrare:* to — up, (*mortuorum*) *animas elicĕre.* (2) intransit. = to perform conjuring tricks, *praestigiis uti.*
conjurer, *magus, praestigiator* (Pl.).
connect, *adligare,* (*con*)*iungĕre, connectĕre.*
connexion, *coniunctio;* between persons, *societas, necessitudo;* by marriage, *adfinitas;* = a person connected by marriage, *adfinis.*
connive: to — at, *in re connivēre, rem dissimulare, rei* (dat.) *indulgēre.*
connivance, *indulgentia.*
connoisseur, render by *iudex* or *existimator* (with adj.).
conquer, (*de*)*vincĕre, superare.*
conqueror, *victor.*
conquest, *victoria.*
consanguinity, *consanguinitas* (rare); often rendered by *sanguis.*
conscience, *conscientia* (= good or bad —; often qualified by adj. or objective genit.): a good —, *recta conscientia, mens sibi conscia recti* (Verg.); to have a good —, *nullius culpae sibi conscium esse, nil conscire sibi* (Hor.).
conscientious, *religiosus, sanctus.*
conscientiously, *religiose, sancte;* or use phrase with *fides.*
conscientiousness, *religio, sanctitas, fides.*
conscious. (1) = with feeling, render by *sentio* or *sensus.* (2) — of, = aware of, *gnarus, conscius.*
consciously, render by adj. *prudens.*
consciousness, *sensus* (-*ūs*).
conscript; see RECRUIT.
conscription, *delectus* (-*ūs*).
consecrate, *consecrare, dedicare.*
consecrated, *sacer.*
consecration, *consecratio, dedicatio.*
consecutive, *continens, continuus.*
consecutively, *continenter.*
consent, subst. *consensus* (-*ūs*): without your —, *te invito.*
consent, v.: to — to, *velle.*
consequence. (1) = result, *consecutio;* more often *exitus* (-*ūs*), *eventus* (-*ūs*): the — was

that, *ex quo factum est ut*; in — of, *ex, propter*.
(2) = importance, *auctoritas, momentum, pondus (-ĕris,* n.); it is of —, *interest, refert*.
consequent, in logic, *consequens*.
consequently, *itaque, ergo, igitur*.
conserve, *(con)servāre*; of fruit, etc., *condīre*.
conservative, as polit. t. t., express by phrase, e.g. *qui nihil in republica immutari vult*.
consider. (1) = to think about, contemplate mentally, *considerare, expendĕre, deliberare, intueri, contemplari*. (2) = to take into account, have a proper regard for, *respicĕre, consulĕre* with dat. (3) to hold a particular view: to — that, *arbitrari* or *ducĕre*, with acc. and infin.; = to regard as, *ducĕre, habēre, existimare*.
considerable, *magnus, gravis*: a — amount, *aliquantum*.
considerably, *aliquantum*.
considerate, *humanus, officiosus. benignus*.
considerateness, *humanitas, benignitas*.
consideration. (1) = thought, *consideratio, deliberatio, contemplatio, consilium*; often rendered by verb. (2) = regard for a person or thing, *ratio, respectus (-ūs)*. (3) see IMPORTANCE.
considering, use *ut*: pretty calm, considering the critical situation, *satis ut in re trepida impavidus* (Liv.).
consign, *committĕre, credĕre, mandare*.
consist, = to be made up of, *consistĕre* or *constare (re, in re, ex re)*; *contineri (re)*.
consistency, = constancy, *constantia*.
consistent. (1) — with, *consentaneus, congruens, conveniens*. (2) = unchanging, *constans*.
consistently, *constanter*.
consolation, *solatium, consolatio*.
console, *(hominem) (con)solari, (homini) solatio esse*.
consoler, *consolator*.
consonant, subst., as grammat. t. t., *consonans* (Quint.).
consonant, adj. *consentaneus, congruens, conveniens*.
consort, subst. *comes, socius* (f. *socia*); = husband or wife, *maritus, marita; coniunx*.
consort, v.: to — with, *homine familiariter uti, homini socium esse*.
conspicuous, *conspicuus, clarus, manifestus, insignis*.
conspicuously, *clare, manifeste*.
conspiracy, *coniuratio*.
conspirator, *coniuratus*.
conspire, *coniurare, conspirare*.
constable, *lictor*.
constancy. (1) = steadiness, *constantia, firmitas*. (2) = fidelity, *fides, fidelitas*.
constant. (1) = unchanging, steadfast, *constans, firmus, stabilis*. (2) incessant, *continuus, perpetuus*. (3) = faithful, *fidelis, fidus*.
constantly. (1) = steadfastly, *constanter*. (2) = incessantly, *semper, perpetuo*.
constellation, *sidus (-ĕris,* n.), *signum*.
consternation, *pavor, terror*.
constipation, *alvus adstricta* (Cels.).
constituent, *pars, elementum*.
constitute, v. transit. (1) = to form, make up, *componĕre, efficĕre*. (2) = to establish, arrange, *statuĕre, constituĕre, designare*. (3) = to appoint, *creare, facĕre*.

constitution. (1) physical, *corporis constitutio, adfectio, habitus (-ūs)*. (2) of a state, *civitatis* (or *reipublicae) status (-ūs)* or *forma*; sometimes *respublica* alone.
constitutional. (1) = natural, *innatus, insitus*. (2) = according to law, *legitimus*.
constitutionally (1) = naturally, *naturā*. (2) = legally, *legitime, e republica*.
constrain, *cogĕre, compellĕre, necessitatem imponĕre*.
constraint, *vis*: under —, *invitus -a -um*.
construct, *facĕre, fabricari*; see also BUILD, MAKE.
construction. (1) as an act, *fabricatio, aedificatio, constructio*. (2) = form, plan, *structura, figura, forma*. (3) = interpretation, *interpretatio*: to put a good, bad — on, *rem in bonam, malam partem accipĕre*.
construe, *interpretari, accipĕre*.
consul, *consul*: an ex- —, *vir consularis*.
consulship, *consulatus (-ūs)*.
consult. (1) = to take counsel together, *consultare, deliberare*. (2) to — a person, *hominem consulĕre*; to — the senate, *ad senatum referre*; to — a book, *librum adire*. (3) to — a person's interests, *homini consulĕre*.
consume, *consumĕre, conficĕre, absumĕre*.
consummate, adj. *summus, absolutus, perfectus*.
consummate, v. *consummare, absolvĕre, cumulare, perficĕre, conficĕre*.
consummately, *summe, absolute, perfecte*.
consummation, *absolutio, perfectio*.
consumption, = act of consuming, *consumptio, confectio*.
contact, *(con)tactus (-ūs)*: to make — with a person, *cum homine congredi*.
contagion, *contagio*.
contagious, render by phrase.
contain, *capĕre, habēre, continēre, comprehendĕre*: to — oneself, *se continēre, se cohibēre*.
contaminate, *contaminare, inquinare, polluĕre*.
contamination, *macula, labes*.
contemplate, *contemplari, intueri*.
contemplation, *contemplatio*.
contemplative, *in contemplatione (rerum) versatus*.
contemporaneous, *quod eodem tempore est* (or *fit*).
contemporary, adj. and subst. *aequalis*.
contempt, *contemptus (-ūs), fastidium*.
contemptible, *contemnendus, contemptus, abiectus, turpis*.
contend. (1) = to struggle, *contendĕre, (de)certare, decernĕre, pugnare*. (2) = to maintain in argument, *contendĕre, confirmare, adfirmare*.
content, contentment, subst. *animus contentus* or *aequus*.
content, adj. *contentus*: — with a thing, *re contentus*; he was — to say, *satis habuit dicĕre*.
content, v. transit. *homini satisfacĕre*: to — oneself with saying, *satis habēre dicĕre*.
contentedly, *aequo animo*; or use adj. *contentus*.
contention; see STRIFE, QUARREL, ARGUMENT.
contentious, *pugnax*.
contents, *quod in libro continetur*.
conterminous, *confinis*.
contest, subst. *certatio, certamen, contentio, pugna*.

contest, v. *contendĕre*; see also CONTEND.
context, *argumentum* or *ratio verborum*.
contiguity, *vicinitas, propinquitas.*
contiguous, *confinis, continens.*
continence, *continentia, temperantia, castitas, castimonia.*
continent, subst. *continens.*
continent, adj. *continens, castus.*
continental, express by phrase with *continens.*
continently, *continenter, temperanter, caste.*
contingency, *casus (-ūs).*
contingent, subst. *quantum militum quaeque civitas mittĕre debet*; sometimes *auxilia (-orum,* plur.).
contingent, adj. *fortuitus, forte oblatus.*
continual, *continuus, perpetuus, adsiduus.*
continually, *continenter, adsidue, perpetuo.*
continuance, continuation, *perpetuitas, adsiduitas, continuatio, diuturnitas.*
continue. v. (1) transit. = to carry on, *extendĕre, prorogare, producĕre, continuare, persequi*: to — after an interruption, *renovare.* (2) intransit.: **a** = to persevere, *persistĕre, pergĕre, perseverare*: **b** = to last, remain, *durare, (per)manĕre, stare.*
continuity, *continuatio, perpetuitas.*
contort, *depravare, detorquĕre, distorquĕre.*
contortion, *distortio, depravatio.*
contour, *forma, figura, lineamenta (-orum,* plur.).
contraband, *merces vetitae.*
contract, subst. *pactum, conventio, condicio, conductio, locatio, redemptio.*
contract, v. (1) = to draw in, *contrahĕre, adducĕre.* (2) = to form, bring about, incur, *contrahĕre.* (3) to — for, make a — about, *contrahĕre, locare* (= to give a — for), *conducĕre* or *redimĕre* (= to take a — for). (4) intransit. = to become smaller, *se contrahĕre, minui.*
contracted, *contractus, angustus, brevis.*
contraction, = the act of contracting, *contractio.*
contractor, *conductor, redemptor.*
contradict. (1) = to speak against, *(homini) obloqui, contradicere.* (2) = to be incompatible, *(inter se) repugnare, (ab re) discrepare.*
contradiction. (1) in speech, render by phrase. (2) = incompatibility, *repugnantia, discrepantia, diversitas* (Tac.).
contradictory, *contrarius, repugnans, diversus.*
contrary, subst.: on the —, *contra, ex contrario*; in answers (= no, on the —), *immo.*
contrary, adj., *adversus, contrarius*: a — wind, *ventus adversus.*
contrary to, *contra, praeter,* with acc.
contrast, subst. *diversitas, varietas, dissimilitudo, discrepantia.*
contrast, v. (1) transit. *comparare, conferre.* (2) intransit. *discrepare.*
contravene, *violare, frangĕre.*
contribute, v. (1) = to give, with others, *contribuĕre, conferre.* (2) = to help, *prodesse, adiuvare.*
contribution, express by verb.
contributor, *conlator*; or express by verb.
contrite, adj.; see PENITENT.
contrition, *paenitentia.*
contrivance. (1) = the act of contriving, *inventio, excogitatio.* (2) = a thing contrived, *machina, inventum* (Ter.).

contrive, *excogitare, invenire, fingĕre, machinari*: to — so that, *facĕre* or *efficĕre ut.*
control, subst. *potestas, imperium, dicio, regimen* (Tac.): self —, *moderatio, temperantia.*
control, v. transit. *moderari, temperare, cohibĕre, coercēre, continēre.*
controversial, = disputed, *controversus.*
controversy, *controversia, altercatio, disceptatio, contentio.*
controvert, *refellĕre, refutare.*
contumacious, *contumax, pertinax.*
contumaciously, *contumaciter, pertinaciter.*
contumacy, *pertinacia, contumacia.*
contumelious, *contumeliosus, probrosus.*
contumeliously, *contumeliose.*
contumely, *contumelia.*
convalescent, use verb *convalescĕre.*
convene, *convocare.*
convenience, *commoditas, commoda (-orum,* plur.), *opportunitas.*
convenient, *commodus, opportunus, habilis, accommodatus, idoneus.*
conveniently, *commode, opportune, accommodate.*
convention. (1) = assembly, *conventus (-ūs).* (2) = agreement, *foedus (-ĕris,* n.), *pactio, pactum.* (3) = custom, *mos.*
conventional, *translaticius, usu receptus.*
converge, *coire, in unum vergere.*
conversant, *in re versatus* or *exercitatus, rei* (genit.) *peritus.*
conversation, *sermo, conloquium*: to be the subject of —, *in ore* (or *in sermone) omnium esse.*
converse, v. *(cum homine) conloqui, sermonem conferre.*
conversion, *(com)mutatio, conversio*: religious —, express by phrase with *sentire (de deis)* or *sententia.*
convert, v. transit. *(com)mutare, convertĕre*: to — to an opinion, *ad sententiam traducĕre.*
convex, *convexus.*
convey. (1) see CARRY. (2) as legal t. t., *transcribere, abalienare.*
conveyance. (1) see CARRIAGE. (2) as legal t. t. *abalienatio*; or express by verb.
convict, v. *damnare, condemnare, convincĕre.*
conviction. (1) the act of convicting, *damnatio.* (2) = belief, opinion, *opinio, sententia.*
convince, *persuadēre (de re)*: I am —d, *mihi persuasi, persuasum habeo, mihi persuasum est.*
convincing, *ad persuadendum accommodatus; gravis.*
convivial, *hilaris.*
conviviality, *hilaritas.*
convoke, *convocare.*
convoy, subst. *praesidium, custodia*; for ships in —, use phrase such as *navibus longis (naves) onerarias protegĕre.*
convoy, v. transit. *deducĕre, comitari.*
convulse, *agitare, percutĕre, (com)movēre*: — the state, *civitatem quassare, labefactare, concutĕre.*
convulsion, *motus, turba*; as medical t. t., *convulsio* (Plin.).
convulsive, *spasticus* (Plin.).
cony, *cuniculus.*
cook, subst. *coquus.*
cook, v. *coquĕre.*
cool, subst. *frigus (-oris* n.).
cool, adj. LIT., *frigidus.* TRANSF., of temperament or behaviour, *lentus* (= phlegmatic),

impavidus (= undismayed), *impudens* (= impudent).

cool, v. (**1**) transit., lit. and fig., *refrigerare*. (**2**) intransit., lit. and fig., *refrigerari, defervescĕre*.

coolness, render by adj.

coolly. LIT., *frigide*. TRANSF., *lente*; see also COOL, adj.

coop, *cavea*.

cooper, *vietor* (Pl.).

co-operate, *unā agĕre*: to — with, (*hominem*) *adiuvare*.

co-operation, *opera, auxilium*.

cope, v.: to — with a person, *homini resistĕre*; able to —, *par*.

coping, *fastigium*.

coping-stone: to put the — on, *cumulum* (*rei*, dat.) *adferre* or *addĕre*.

copious, *copiosus, abundans, largus*.

copiously, *copiose, abundanter, large*.

copiousness, *copia, abundantia*.

copper, subst. *aes*: a — vessel, *a(h)enum*.

copper, adj. *a(h)enus*.

coppice, copse, *silva*.

copulation, *concubitus* (-*ūs*), *coitus* (-*ūs*).

copy, subst. *exemplum, exemplar*.

copy, v. transit. *imitari, exprimĕre*; in writing: to — out, *transcribĕre, describĕre*.

coquet, express by verb *pellicĕre*.

coral, *curalium*.

cord, subst. *restis, funis*.

cord, v. *constringĕre*.

cordial, *benignus, comis*.

cordiality, *benignitas, comitas*.

cordially, *benigne, comiter, amice*.

cordon, *corona*; in hunting, *indago*.

Cordova, *Corduba*.

core, *nucleus, granum*.

Corfu, *Corcyra*.

cork, subst. *cortex*.

cork, v. *obturare*.

corn (the grain), *frumentum* (sing. = grain, plur. = standing corn): the price of —, *annona*; a — field, *seges*.

corn (on the foot), *clavus* (Plin.).

corner, *angulus*.

cornet. (**1**) the musical instrument, *cornu, buccina*. (**2**) as milit. t. t. *vexillarius, signifer*.

cornice, *corona* (Vitr.).

coronation, express by phrase with *diadema*; see CROWN.

coroner, express by phrase, e.g. *magistratus qui de mortuis inquirit*.

corporal, subst. *decurio*.

corporal and **corporeal**, adj. *corporeus*, or express by genit. of *corpus*: — punishment, *verbera* (-*um*, plur.).

corporation, *sodalitas* (religious), *municipium, conlegium*.

corps, *manus* (-*ūs*, f.).

corpse, *cadaver*.

corpulence, *obesitas* (Suet.).

corpulent, *obēsus, pinguis*.

correct, adj. (**1**) of conduct, *honestus, rectus*. (**2**) of style, *emendatus, rectus, purus*. (**3**) = true, *verus*.

correct, v. *corrigere, emendare*; = to punish, *punire, castigare, animadvertĕre*.

correction, *correctio, emendatio*; = punishment, *poena, castigatio, animadversio*.

correctly, *recte, honeste, pure, vere*.

correctness, express by adj.

correspond, v. (**1**) = to agree, *respondĕre, congruĕre, convenire* (with dat.). (**2**) to — by letter, *litteras dare et accipĕre*.

correspondence. (**1**) = agreement, *congruentia, convenientia*. (**2**) = letters, *litterae, epistulae, epistularum commercium*.

correspondent, render by phrase.

corresponding, *par*.

corroborate, *confirmare, comprobare*.

corroboration, *confirmatio*.

corrode, *rodĕre* (Ov.).

corrupt, adj. (**1**) in gen. = depraved, *corruptus, impurus, pravus*. (**2**) = venal, *venalis*.

corrupt, v. *corrumpĕre, depravare, vitiare*.

corrupter, *corruptor*.

corruptible, = venal, *venalis*.

corruption, *corruptio, depravatio, corruptela*.

corruptly, *corrupte, impure, prave*.

corsair, *pirata*.

corslet, *thorax, lorica*.

cortège, *comitatus* (-*ūs*).

coruscation, *fulgor, splendor*.

cosmetic, *fucus*.

cost, subst. *pretium, sumptus* (-*ūs*), *impensa, impendium*; — of living, *annona*.

cost, v. (con)*stare, vēnire* (with abl. or sometimes genit. of price).

costliness, *caritas*.

costly, *carus, pretiosus*.

costume, *vestitus* (-*ūs*), *habitus* (-*ūs*).

cot, *lectulus*.

cottage, *casa, tugurium*.

cottager, *rusticus*.

cotton, *gossypion* (-*ium*: Plin.).

couch, subst. *lectus, lectulus, cubile*.

couch, v. (**1**) transit.: **a**, to — a weapon, *intendĕre*: **b** = to express in words, *dicĕre* or *scribĕre* (**2**) intransit. *cubare, latēre, delitescĕre*.

cough, subst. *tussis*.

cough, v. *tussire*.

council, *concilium, consilium* (smaller and more select than *concilium*): a — of war, *consilium, praetorium*.

councillor, *senator, decurio*.

counsel, subst. = advice, *consilium, auctoritas*.

counsel, v.; see ADVISE.

count, subst. *comes* (late Latin).

count, v. (**1**) = to number, reckon up, (*e*)*numerare, percensēre, computare*. (**2**) = to consider, hold, *habēre, ducĕre*. (**3**) to — upon: to — upon a person's loyalty, etc., *homini confidĕre*; to — upon a thing happening, *rem exploratam habēre*.

countenance, subst. (**1**) = face, *vultus, os* (*oris*). (**2**) = favour, *favor*.

countenance, v. (**1**) = approve, *approbare*. (**2**) = allow, *permittĕre*.

counter, subst. (**1**) for counting with, *calculus*. (**2**) in a shop, *mensa*.

counter, adv.: — to, *contra*; to run — to, *adversari*.

counteract, *resistĕre*.

counter-balance, (*ex*)*aequare, compensare*.

counterfeit, adj. *falsus*: — coin, *nummus adulterinus*.

counterfeit, v. *simulare*.

counterpane, *lodix* (Juv.).

counterpart, *res simillima*.

countless, *innumerabilis, innumerus*.

country. (**1**) opp. to town, *rus*: in the —, *ruri*; to live in the —, *rusticari*. (**2**) = one's native land, *patria.* (3) = a tract of land, *agri* (*-orum,* plur.), *fines* (*-ium,* plur.); region, *terra, regio;* of what —? *cuias?*

country-house, *villa.*

countryman, (*homo*) *rusticus:* fellow- —, *civis, popularis.*

country-town, *municipium, oppidum.*

couple, *par, bini -ae -a:* a married —, *coniuges* (Cat.).

couple, v. transit. (*con*)*iungĕre, copulare.*

courage, *audacia, constantia, fortitudo, virtus* (*-ūtis,* f.), *animus;* to take —, *animum capĕre* or *recipĕre.*

courageous, *fortis, audax, strenuus, animosus.*

courageously, *fortiter, audacter, strenue.*

courier, *nuntius, tabellarius.*

course, subst. *cursus* (*-ūs*): — of life, career, *vitae curriculum;* a steady, uninterrupted —, *tenor;* a — of action deliberately adopted, a plan, *ratio, consilium;* in the — of a few days, *intra paucos dies;* of —, *scilicet, sane;* a — at dinner, *ferculum.*

course, v. *venari.*

court, subst. (1) = an enclosed space, *area.* (2) a royal —, *aula, regia.* (3) a — of justice; as a place, *forum, basilica;* as a body or authority, *iudicium, ius* (*iuris*).

court, v. transit. (1) = to seek a person's favour (esp. a lady's), *petere, colere.* (2) = to seek to obtain a thing, *quaerĕre, captare.*

courteous, *comis, urbanus, adfabilis.*

courteously, *comiter, urbane.*

courtesy, *urbanitas, comitas.*

courtier, *purpuratus, aulicus* (Tac.).

courtship, *amor* or express by verb.

cousin, (*con*)*sobrinus* (f. *-a;* strictly on the mother's side); *patruelis* (only on the father's side).

cove, *sinus* (*-ūs*).

covenant, subst. *pactio, pactum, conventio.*

covenant, v. *pacisci.*

cover, subst. (1) = lid, *operimentum.* (2) = shelter, *perfugium:* under — of, *re tectus.* (3) = pretence, *species.*

cover, v. transit. (1) to — over, — up, (*con*)*tegĕre, obtegĕre, operire, velare.* (2) = to protect, *protegĕre, defendĕre.*

covering, *tegmen.*

coverlet, *stragulum.*

covert, subst. = thicket, *dumetum.*

covert, adj.: see SECRET.

covet, *adpetĕre, concupiscĕre.*

covetous, *avarus, avidus, adpetens.*

covetously, *avare, avide, adpetenter.*

covetousness, *avaritia, aviditas.*

cow, subst. *vacca.*

cow, v. transit. *domare.*

coward, *homo ignavus, timidus.*

cowardice, cowardliness, *ignavia, timiditas.*

cowardly, *ignavus, timidus.*

cower, express by phrase.

cowherd, *armentarius.*

cowl, *cucullus* (Juv.).

coy, *verecundus.*

coyness, *verecundia.*

cozen; see CHEAT.

crab, *cancer.*

crabbed. (1) in temper, *acerbus, difficilis, morosus.* (2) of style, etc., *implicatus, impeditus.*

crack, subst. (1) = noise, *crepitus* (*-ūs*), *fragor.* (2) = fissure, *rima.*

crack, v. (1) transit. *frangĕre, findĕre, rumpĕre:* to — a joke, *iocari;* to — a whip, *flagello insonare.* (2) intransit.: **a** = to break open, *dissilire, dehiscĕre, rimas agĕre:* **b** = to make a noise, *crepare.*

cradle, *cunae* (*-arum,* plur.), *cunabula* (*-orum,* plur.): from the —, = from childhood, *a puero, a teneris unguiculis.*

craft. (1) = cunning, *dolus, astutia.* (2) = skill or trade, *ars, artificium.* (3) = boat, *cymba, scapha.*

craftily, *astute, callide, versute, dolose.*

craftsman, *artifex, opifex.*

crafty, *astutus, callidus, versutus, dolosus.*

crag, *scopulus, rupes.*

cram, *farcire, refercire, confercire, stipare.*

cramp, subst. (1) in the muscles, *tetanus,* (Plin.). (2) of metal, *fibula, uncus.*

cramp, v.; see CONFINE.

crane, subst. (1) the bird, *grus,* (2) the machine, *trochlea, tolleno.*

crane, v.: to — the neck, *cervicem protendĕre.*

crank, of a machine, *uncus.*

cranny, *rima.*

crash, subst. *fragor, strepitus* (*-ūs*).

crash, v. *strepĕre.*

crater, *crater* (Plin.).

crave; see BEG, NEED.

craving, *desiderium.*

crawl, *repĕre, serpĕre.*

crazy. (1) = physically decrepit, *decrepitus, imbecillus.* (2) = mentally deranged, *cerritus* (Pl., Hor.).

creak, v. *stridĕre, crepare.*

creaking, subst. *stridor, crepitus* (*-ūs*).

crease, subst. *ruga.*

crease, v. *rugare.*

create. LIT., = to bring into existence, *creare, gignĕre, generare, facĕre.* TRANSF., (1) = to give rise to, occasion, cause, *creare, praebĕre, facĕre, efficĕre.* (2) = to appoint, *creare, facĕre.*

creation; use *initium* (= beginning), or *creatio* (= appointment), or render by verb.

creative, render by verb.

creator, *creator, fabricator, auctor.*

creature, *animal.*

credibility, *fides, auctoritas.*

credible, *credibilis.*

credit, subst. (1) = belief, *fides:* to give — to, *fidem habere,* with dat. (2) as commercial t. t. *fides.* (3) = authority, esteem, *gratia, auctoritas, existimatio.*

credit, v. transit. (1) = to believe, *credĕre.* (2) to — a thing to a person, *rem acceptam homini referre.*

creditable, *honestus, honorificus.*

creditably, *honeste.*

creditor, *creditor.*

credulity, *credulitas* (Ov., Tac.); or express by phrase.

credulous, *credulus.*

creek, *sinus* (*-ūs*), *aestuarium.*

creep; see CRAWL.

crescent-shaped, *lunatus* (Verg.).

crest, *crista, iuba.*

crested, *cristatus, iubatus.*

crestfallen, *demissus.*

crevice; see CRACK.

crew. (1) on a ship, *nautae* (*-arum,* plur.). (2) in gen. = gang, *grex.*

crib, = manger, *praesepe* (Ov.).

---

crier, *praeco.*

crime, *delictum, maleficium, facinus (-inoris =* a daring bad deed), *flagitium* (= scandalous conduct).

criminal, *scelestus, sceleratus, nefarius.*

criminally, *nefarie.*

crimson, *coccineus.*

cringe, v. : to — to, *adulari.*

cringing, *abiectus.*

cripple, subst., use *homo* with adj.; see CRIPPLED.

cripple, v. LIT., *claudum* etc. *facĕre.* TRANSF., *debilitare, frangĕre, infringĕre.*

crippled, (lit. and fig.) *claudus, mancus, debilis.*

crisis, *discrimen, tempus (-oris,* n.).

crisp. (1) = curled, *crispus.* (2) = brittle, *fragilis.*

criterion, *norma, obrussa.*

critic, *iudex, criticus, existimator.*

critical, adj. (1) = discriminating, *elegans.* (2) = belonging to a crisis, *anceps, dubius :* a — moment, *tempus (-oris,* n.), *occasio.*

criticism, *iudicium.*

criticize. (1) = to judge, *iudicare.* (2) = to find fault with, *reprehendĕre, culpare.*

croak, subst. *vox, querela.*

croak, v. *crocire* (Pl.), *queri.*

crock, *olla.*

crockery, *fictilia (-ium,* plur.).

crocodile, *crocodilus :* — tears, *lacrimulae.*

crocus, *crocus.*

crone, *vetula, anus (-ūs), anicula.*

crook, subst., a shepherd's, *pedum* (Verg.).

crook, v.; see CURVE.

crooked, (lit. and fig.) *pravus.*

crookedly, *prave.*

crookedness, *pravitas.*

crop, subst. (1) of corn, etc., *messis, fruges (-um,* plur.). (2) of birds, *ingluvies.*

crop, v. (1) of animals = to browse on, *(at)tondĕre.* (2) in gen. = to cut off, cut short, *praecidĕre, amputare.*

cross, subst., the instrument of punishment, *crux.*

cross, adj. (1) = transverse, *transversus, obliquus.* (2) = annoyed, bad-tempered, *difficilis, morosus.*

cross, v. transit. (1) = to go across, *transire, transgredi, (se) traicĕre.* (2) = to oppose a person, *homini obsistĕre, adversari.* (3) to — a person's mind (of thoughts, etc.), *homini subire.* (4) to — out, *delēre.*

cross-examine, *interrogare.*

cross-purposes, express by adj. *contrarius.*

crossing, subst., as an action, *transitus (-ūs).*

crouch, *se demittĕre.*

crow, subst. *cornix.*

crow, v. LIT., of cocks, etc., *canĕre.* TRANSF., = to boast, *gloriari.*

crowd, subst. *turba, vulgus, frequentia, multitudo.*

crowd, v. (1) transit. *(co)artare, stipare, cogĕre.* (2) intransit. *concurrĕre, confluĕre, congregari.*

crowing, subst., of a cock, *cantus (-ūs).*

crown, subst. (1) = any wreath or garland, *corona.* (2) = a king's — (lit.), *insigne regium, diadema (-ătis,* n.). (3) = a king's power, sovereignty, *regnum :* to assume the —, *regnum accipĕre.* (4) the — of the head, *vertex.* (5) = crowning glory, consummation, *cumulus.*

crown, v. transit. *coronare :* — a king, *diadema regi imponĕre.*

crucible, *catinus* (Plin.).

crucifixion, *crucis supplicium;* or render by phrase.

crucify, *cruci adfigĕre, in crucem tollĕre.*

crude. (1) = raw or unripe, *crudus.* (2) = rough, unfinished, *informis, incultus, rudis.*

crudely, *inculte.*

crudity, render by adj.

cruel, *crudelis, saevus, atrox.*

cruelly, *crudeliter, atrociter.*

cruelty, *crudelitas, saevitia.*

cruise, subst. *navigatio.*

cruise, v. *(per)vagari, circumvectari, navigare.*

crumb, = a small piece, *mica.*

crumble. v. (1) transit. *friare, comminuĕre, conterĕre.* (2) intransit., render by pass. of transit. verbs.

crumple, *(cor)rugare.*

crupper, *postilena* (Pl.).

crush, subst.; see CROWD.

crush, v. LIT., *opprimĕre, contundĕre, conterĕre, conculcare* (by treading). TRANSF., *adfligĕre, opprimĕre, obruĕre, frangĕre.*

crust, *crusta.*

crutch, *baculum.*

cry, subst. *clamor, adclamatio, vociferatio;* of distress, *ploratus (-ūs), eiulatus (-ūs);* of children, *vagitus (-ūs).*

cry, v. *clamare, conclamare, exclamare, adclamare, clamitare;* in distress, *plorare, eiulare;* of children, *vagire.*

crystal, subst. *crystallus.*

crystal, adj. *crystallinus.*

cub, *catulus.*

cube, *tessera, cubus* (Vitr.).

cubic, *cubicus* (Vitr.).

cubit, *cubitum.*

cuckoo, *cuculus.*

cucumber, *cucŭmis.*

cud: to chew the —, *ruminare, remandĕre* (Plin.).

cudgel, subst. *baculum, fustis.*

cudgel, v. *mulcare; fusti ferire, percutĕre, verberare.*

cue, = hint, *signum, indicium:* to give a — to, *homini innuĕre.*

cuff, subst. (1) = blow, *alapa, colaphus.* (2) = sleeve, *manica extrema.*

cuff, v. *colaphum,* etc., *infligĕre.*

cuirass, *thorax, lorica.*

culinary, *coquinarius* (Plin.).

culminate, render by phrase; see CULMINATION.

culmination, *fastigium.*

culpable, *culpandus.*

culprit; see CRIMINAL.

cultivate, *(ex)colĕre, exercēre, studēre* (with dat. = to apply oneself to).

cultivation, **culture**, *cultus (-ūs), cultura* (lit. and fig.); = liberal ideas, knowledge of literature, etc., *humanitas, litterae (-arum,* plur.).

cultivator, *cultor.*

cumber, *impedire (prae)gravare, onerare.*

cumbersome, **cumbrous**, *inhabilis, gravis, incommodus.*

cumbrously, *incommode.*

cunning, subst. *calliditas, astutia, dolus.*

cunning, adj. *callidus, astutus, versutus, dolosus.*

cunningly, *callide, astute, versute.*

cup, *poculum, scyphus, calix*: in one's —s, *in poculis, inter scyphos.*

cup-bearer, *minister* or *servus.*

cupboard, *armarium.*

cupidity, *cupiditas, avaritia.*

cupola, *tholus* (Verg.).

curator, *curator, custos.*

curb, subst. (lit. and fig.), *frenum.*

curb, v. transit. *frenare, coercēre, comprimēre, cohibēre.*

curd, *lac concretum.*

curdle, v. (1) transit. *coagulare* (Plin.). (2) intransit. *concrescēre* (Verg.).

cure, subst. *medicina, sanatio.*

cure, v. transit. (1) = to heal, remedy, *sanare mederi.* (2) = to preserve, *condire.*

curiosity, express by phrase, such as *noscendi studium.*

curious. (1) = inquisitive, *curiosus;* or render by phrase. (2) = strange, *insolitus, novus, singularis, mirus.* (3) = careful, *diligens;* of — workmanship, *daedalus* (Verg.).

curl, subst. *cincinnus, cirrus* (Varro).

curl, v. transit. *crispare* (Plin.).

curling-irons, *calamister.*

curly, *crispus* (Pl.).

currants, *uvae passae.*

currency, *nummi* (-*orum,* plur.).

current, subst., in a river, *flumen*: with the —, *secundo flumine;* against the —, *adverso flumine;* at sea, *aestus.*

current, adj. (1) = this, *hic* (e.g. the — year, *hic annus*). (2) = common, *usitatus, vulgaris:* to be —, *valēre.*

currently, *vulgo.*

curry, v.: to — leather, *subigere* (Cato); to — favour, *blandiri.*

currycomb, *strigilis* (Col.).

curse, subst. (1) of malign speech, *exsecratio, imprecatio.* (2) = a malign influence, *pernicies, pestis.*

curse, v. transit. *exsecrari, detestari.*

cursorily, *breviter, strictim, summatim.*

cursory, express by adv.; see CURSORILY.

curt, *brevis, abruptus.*

curtly, *breviter, praecise.*

curtail, (*co*)*artare,* (*im*)*minuēre.*

curtain, *velum, aulaeum;* in a theatre, *aulaeum, siparium.*

curve, subst. *flexus* (-*ūs*), *sinus* (-*ūs*).

curve, v. transit. (*in*)*curvare,* (*in*)*flectēre.*

cushion, *pulvinus, pulvinar.*

custody, *custodia, carcer, vincula* (-*orum,* plur.).

custom, *consuetudo, mos, institutum, usus* (-*ūs*): it is a —, *moris est.*

customary, *usitatus, tritus, vulgaris, cottidianus, translaticius, solitus.*

custom-duty, *vectigal, portorium.*

customer, *emptor.*

cut, subst.; see BLOW, WOUND; a short —, *via compendiaria.*

cut, v. LIT., *secare, caedēre:* to — corn, etc., (*de*)*metēre;* to — the throat, *iugulare;* to — away, *abscindēre;* to — down, *succīdēre;* to — off, *praecīdēre;* to — out, *exsecare;* to — up, *scindēre, concīdēre.* TRANSF., to — off = intercept, *interclūdēre;* to — off = destroy, *absūmēre, exstinguēre;* to — short, *praecīdēre, amputare;* to — up (troops in battle), *trucidare.*

cutlery, *cultri* (-*orum,* plur.).

cutter, *navis actuaria.*

cut-throat, *sicarius.*

cutting, subst., of a plant, *talea* (Cato).

cutting, adj., of speech, *mordax.*

cuttlefish, *sepia, lolligo.*

cycle, *orbis, circulus.*

cylinder, *cylindrus.*

cymbal, *cymbalum.*

cynic, *cynicus.*

cynical, *mordax.*

cypress, *cupressus.*

D

dabble, v. transit. *adspergēre:* to — in a thing, *rem leviter attingēre.*

dad, daddy, *tata* (Varro).

daffodil, *narcissus* (Ov.).

dagger, *pugio, sica.*

daily, adj. = of the daytime, *diurnus;* = of every day, *cottidianus.*

daily, adv. *cottidie;* with comparatives, etc., *in dies.*

dainties, *cuppedia* (-*orum,* plur.), *scitamenta* (-*orum,* pl.).

daintiness. (1) = fussiness, *cuppedia.* (2) = elegance, grace, *venustas.*

dainty. (1) = particular, *fastidiosus.* (2) = elegant, *elegans, delicatus, lautus.*

dairy, render by phrase.

dale, *vallis.*

dalliance, *lascivia, ludus, lusus* (Ov.).

dally. (1) = to linger, *morari.* (2) = to sport amorously, *lascivire, ludere* (Pl., Ov.).

dam, subst. (1) = mother, *mater.* (2) = pier, breakwater, *moles, agger.*

dam, v. transit. *obstruēre, coercēre.*

damage, subst. *damnum, detrimentum, incommodum, noxa.*

damage, v. transit. *laedēre* (with acc.), *nocēre, obesse* (with dat.).

dame, *matrona, domina.*

damn, *damnare, condemnare.*

damp, subst. *umor.*

damp, adj. *umidus, udus* (Hor.).

damp, v. transit. LIT., *umectare.* TRANSF., to — spirits, etc., *comprimēre, restinguēre.*

damsel, *puella, virgo.*

dance, subst. *saltatio, saltatus, chorea* (Verg.).

dance, v. *saltare.*

dancer, *saltator* (f. *saltatrix*).

dandle, *manibus agitare.*

dandy, *homo elegans* (Sen.).

danger, *periculum, discrimen.*

dangerous, *periculosus, anceps, infestus, lubricus.*

dangerously, *periculose.*

dangle, (*de*)*pendēre.*

dank, *umidus.*

Danube, *Danubius.*

dapper, *nitidus.*

dappled, *maculosus.*

dare, *audēre;* = to challenge, *provocare.*

daring, subst. *audacia.*

daring, adj. *audax.*

dark, subst.: to be in the — about, *rem ignorare;* see also DARKNESS.

dark, adj. LIT., (1) opp. to light, *obscurus, caliginosus, opacus.* (2) in colour, *fuscus, niger, pullus.* TRANSF., (1) = mysterious, obscure, *obscurus, incertus.* (**2**) = gloomy, bad, *tenebricosus, atrox.*

darken, v. transit. (lit. and fig.), *obscurare, occaecare, tenebras offundĕre* (with dat.).

darkling, *obscurus* (Verg.).

darkly, *obscure.*

darkness, *obscuritas, tenebrae* (-*arum*, plur.), *caligo.*

darling, subst. *deliciae* (-*arum*, plur.), *vita, mel* (Pl.), *melculum* (Pl.).

darling, adj. *suavissimus, mellitus* (Cat.).

darn, *sarcire.*

darnel, *lolium.*

dart, subst. *telum, iaculum.*

dart, v. (**1**) = to throw —s, *iaculari, tela (e)mittĕre.* (**2**) = to dash, rush, *provolare, se conicĕre, ferri.*

dash, subst. (**1**) = a rush, *impetus* (-*ūs*). (**2**) = a small amount, *non nihil.*

dash, v. (**1**) transit.: to — one thing against another, *adfligere, offendĕre, impingĕre*; to — down, *proruĕre*; to — out, *elidĕre*; to — a person's hopes, *spem ad inritum redigĕre.* (**2**) intransit.; see DART.

dastardly, *ignavus.*

data, *concessa* (-*orum*, plur.).

date, subst. (**1**) the fruit, *palmula* (Varro). (**2**) = a particular time, *dies, tempus*: out of —, *obsoletus.*

date, v. (**1**) transit.: to — a letter, *diem in epistula ascribĕre*; to — an event, *rem tempori adsignare* or (*at*)*tribuĕre.* (**2**) intransit., *incipĕre, originem habēre.*

dative, (*casus*) *dativus* (Quint.).

daub, (*ob*)*linĕre,* (*per*)*ungĕre.*

daughter, *filia*: a little —, *filiola*; — -in-law, *nurus* (-*ūs*).

daunt; see FRIGHTEN.

dauntless, *impavidus.*

dawdle, *cessare.*

dawdler, *cessator.*

dawn, subst. *diluculum, prima lux, aurora* (poet.): it is —, *lucescit.*

dawn, v. (*in*)*lucescĕre.*

day, *dies*: before —, *ante lucem*; at break of —, *primā luce*; by —, *interdiu*; — breaks, *lucescit*; late in the —, *multo die*; good —, *salve* (*salvete*); a lucky —, *dies albus* or *candidus*; an unlucky —, *dies ater*; the — star, *lucifer*; for the —, *in diem*; a period of two —s, *biduum*; of three —s, *triduum*; to—, *hodie*; every other —, *tertio quoque die, alternis diebus*; from — to —, *in dies*; — after —, *diem de die*; every —, see DAILY; on the — before, *pridie*; of the — before, *hesternus*; on the — after, *postridie* (*eius diei*); in our —, *nostrā memoria* or *aetate, nostro tempore, nostris temporibus*; to pass one's —s, *vitam degĕre*; the —time, *tempus diurnum*; the other —, *nuper.*

day-break; see DAWN and DAY.

dazzle, *perstringĕre, caecare*: to be —d, *stupēre.*

dead, LIT., *mortuus, exanimis, exanimus*; the —, as existing in the underworld, *inferi* (-*orum*, plur.). TRANSF., = dull, *languidus*: at — of night, *nocte intempestā.*

deaden, *hebetare, obtundĕre, enervare, debilitare, frangĕre.*

deadly, *mortifer, exitialis, perniciosus.*

deadness, *stupor, torpor.*

deaf, *surdus, auribus captus.*

deafen, *exsurdare* (Plin.), *obtundĕre.*

deafness, *surditas.*

deal, subst. (**1**) of timber, use adj. *abiegnus.* (**2**) = a quantity, *aliquantum.* (**3**) = a distribution, apportioning, *distributio, partitio*; or render by verb; a new — (= drastic measures for economic reform), perhaps *tabulae novae.*

deal, v.: to — out, *dividĕre, distribuĕre, dispertire*; to — with; see TREAT.

dealer, *mercator, negotiator*: a retail —, *institor, caupo, propola.*

dealing, *commercium, negotium, usus* (-*ūs*): to have —s with, *cum homine rationem* or *commercium habēre*; upright —, *fides*; double —, *fraus.*

dear, (**1**) = expensive, *carus, pretiosus.* (**2**) = beloved, *carus.*

dearly, = at a high price, *care, magno pretio.*

dearness, *caritas.*

dearth, *inopia, caritas, penuria.*

death, *mors, letum, obitus* (-*ūs*), *nex* (violent): day of —, *dies supremus.*

death-bed, use adj. *moriens* or *moribundus.*

debar, *excludĕre, prohibēre.*

debase, *corrumpĕre, vitiare.*

debasement, *ignominia.*

debate, subst. *disceptatio, controversia, disputatio.*

debate, v. *disceptare, disputare.*

debauch, subst. *comissatio.*

debauch, v.: in gen. *corrumpĕre, depravare, vitiare*: to — a woman, (*con*)*stuprare.*

debauchee, *ganeo.*

debaucher, *corruptor,* (*con*)*stuprator.*

debauchery, *stuprum.*

debenture, *syngrapha* (= a bond).

debility, *infirmitas, imbecillitas, debilitas.*

debt, *aes alienum*: to get into —, *aes alienum contrahĕre*; to be in —, *in aere alieno esse, obaeratum esse*; a general cancellation of —s, *tabulae novae.*

debtor, *debitor, obaeratus.*

debit, v.: to — a thing to a person, *homini rem expensam ferre.*

decade, *decem anni.*

decamp, *discedĕre.*

decant, *diffundĕre.*

decanter, *lagena.*

decapitate; see BEHEAD.

decay, *tabes, defectio virium.*

decay, v. *marcescĕre, senescĕre, tabescĕre.*

decease, *obitus* (-*ūs*); see DEATH.

deceit, *fallacia, fraus, dolus.*

deceitful, *fallax, dolosus, fraudulentus.*

deceitfully, *fallaciter, dolose.*

deceive, *decipĕre, fallĕre, circumvenire, fraudare.*

deceiver, *fraudator.*

December, (*mensis*) *December.*

decency, *honestas, decentia, decorum.*

decent, *honestus, decens, decōrus.*

decently, *honeste, decenter, decōre.*

deception, *fraus, dolus, fallacia.*

decide, (**1**) = to settle a thing, *rem statuĕre, constituĕre, decernĕre, diiudicare.* (**2**) to — to do, *constituĕre, statuĕre,* with infin. or *ut.*

decided, (**1**) of things = fixed, *certus.* (**2**) of persons = resolute, *stabilis, constans, firmus.*

decidedly, *firme, firmiter, constanter*; in answers, *vero, plane, sane.*

deciduous, *deciduus* (Plin.).

decimate. Lit., *decimare* (Tac.), *decimum quemque ad supplicium legĕre.* Transf., see DESTROY.

decipher, *explanare, interpretari, explicare.*

decision. (1) = a settlement, thing decided, *arbitrium, decretum, sententia, diiudicatio.* (2) of character, *constantia, firmitas.* (3) = outcome, *eventus.*

decisive, render by phrase.

deck, subst. *pons* (Tac.).

deck, v. (1) see ADORN. (2) a decked ship, *navis constrata.*

declaim, *pronuntiare, declamare.*

declamation, *declamatio, pronuntiatio.*

declamatory, *declamatorius.*

declaration, *declaratio, professio, praedicatio*: — of war, *belli denuntiatio.*

declare, *declarare, profiteri, praedicare, pronuntiare, confirmare*: to — war, *bellum denuntiare* or *indicĕre*; to — for a person, *ab* or *cum homine stare.*

declension, *declinatio* (Quint.).

decline, subst. *deminutio.*

decline, v. (1) transit. = to refuse, *recusare, renuĕre*: to — battle, *pugnam detrectare*; as grammat. t. t., *declinare* (Quint.). (2) intransit. = to fail, *deficĕre, (de)minui, decrescĕre, senescĕre.*

declivity, *declivitas, clivus.*

decoction, *decoctum* (Plin.).

decompose. (1) transit. *(dis)solvĕre, resolvĕre.* (2) intransit. *dissolvi, tabescĕre, putrescĕre.*

decomposition, *(dis)solutio, tabes.*

decorate, *(ex)ornare, decorare.*

decoration, *ornatus (-ūs), ornamentum.*

decorous, *decorus.*

decorously, *decore.*

decorum, *decorum*; see also DECENCY.

decoy, subst. *inlex.*

decoy, v. *inlicĕre, adlicĕre, inescare.*

decrease, subst. *deminutio, imminutio.*

decrease, v. (1) transit. *(de)minuĕre, imminuĕre, extenuare.* (2) intransit. *decrescĕre*; or use pass. of transit. verbs.

decree, subst. *decretum, edictum*: of the senate, *senatusconsultum*; of the people, *plebiscitum.*

decree, v. *decernĕre, edicĕre, sciscĕre, iubere, sancire*; impers. *placet*, with *ut* or acc. and infin.

decrepit, *decrepitus.*

decrepitude, *senectus, aetas decrepita.*

decry, *vituperare, obtrectare.*

dedicate, *(de)dicare, consecrare.*

deduce. (1) = to derive, *(de)ducĕre.* (2) = to infer, *conligĕre, concludĕre.*

deduct, *detrahĕre, deducĕre.*

deduction. (1) = decrease, *deductio, deminutio.* (2) = inference, render by verb.

deed. (1) = an action, *factum, res gesta, facinus* (usually bold and bad). (2) a document, *tabula, syngrapha.*

deep, subst. = the — sea, *altum, pontus* (poet.).

deep, adj. Lit. *altus, profundus*: ten feet —, *decem pedes altus.* Transf., of sounds, *gravis*; of thoughts, etc., *altus*: — in thought, *in cogitatione defixus*; of feelings and qualities, *summus, gravis.*

deepen, *altiorem facĕre*; = to increase, *augēre.*

deeply, *alte, penitus, graviter* (of feeling).

deer, *cervus* (f. *cerva*).

deface, *deformare, foedare.*

defame, *calumniari, obtrectare.*

default. (1) = error, *culpa, peccatum, delictum.* (2) = lack, *defectio, inopia.* (3) as legal t. t., to let judgment go by —, *vadimonium deserĕre, ad vadimonium non venire.*

defeat, subst. *clades*; of a candidate for election, *repulsa.*

defeat, v.; see CONQUER, BAFFLE.

defect, *labes (-is),* f., *vitium, mendum.*

defective, *imperfectus, mendosus, mancus, vitiosus*: to be —, *deficĕre, deesse.*

defectively, *mendose, imperfecte, vitiose.*

defection, *defectio.*

defend, *defendĕre, tueri, tutari, pro homine propugnare*; in a law-court, *hominis causam dicere.*

defendant, *reus.*

defence, *defensio, tutela, praesidium*; in a law-court, *defensio, patrocinium.*

defenceless, *inermis.*

defensive, express by phrase with *defendĕre*: — weapons, *arma (-orum,* plur.).

defer. (1) = to postpone, *differre, proferre, procrastinare, prolatare.* (2) to — to, *(homini) cedĕre, obsequi, morem gerĕre.*

deference, *observantia, obsequium.*

deferential, *submissus, observans.*

deferentially, *submisse.*

defiance, *provocatio*: in — of, *contra* (with acc.).

deficiency, *defectio, inopia, penuria.*

deficient, see DEFECTIVE.

defile, subst. *angustiae (-arum,* plur.), *fauces (-ium,* plur.), *saltus (-ūs).*

defile, v. *contaminare, maculare, inquinare, spurcare, foedare, violare, polluĕre.*

defilement, *macula, labes.*

define, *(de)finire, circumscribĕre.*

definite, *certus, constitutus, status, definitus.*

definitely, *certe, certo, definite.*

definition, *(de)finitio.*

deflect, v. (1) transit. *deflectĕre.* (2) intransit. *declinare, errare.*

deform, *deformare, in peius vertĕre.*

deformed, *distortus, deformatus.*

deformity, *deformitas, pravitas.*

defraud, *(de)fraudare, circumscribĕre, circumvenire.*

defrauder, *fraudator.*

defray, *suppeditare, solvĕre.*

defunct, *mortuus.*

defy, = to challenge, *provocare.*

degenerate, adj. *degener*, or render by phrase, such as *peior avis* (Hor.).

degenerate, v. intransit. *degenerare, depravari, peior fieri.*

degradation, *ignominia, dedecus (-ŏris,* n.).

degrade, Lit., *defendĕre*, to lower in rank or position, *in ordinem cogĕre* (of soldiers), *ex loco movere.* Transf., see DISGRACE.

degrading, *indignus, indecorus.*

degree. (1) = amount, extent, *gradus (-ūs)*: to some —, *aliquantum*; to such a —, *eo* with genit.; by —s, *gradatim, sensim.* (2) = rank, station, *gradus, ordo.*

deification, *consecratio* (Tac.).

deified, *consecratus*; of the Roman emperors after death, *divus.*

deify, *consecrare, inter deos* or *in deorum numerum referre.*

deign, *dignari* or *velle*, with infin.

deism, *deum esse putare.*

---

deist, *qui deum esse putat.*
deity, *deus, numen.*
dejected, *maestus, perculsus, adflictus*: to be —, *in maerore esse* or *iacēre.*
dejectedly, *maeste.*
dejection, *aegrimonia, maestitia, tristitia, maeror.*
delay, subst. *mora, cunctatio, cessatio.*
delay, v. (1) transit. = to retard, *(re)morari, detinēre, tardare, retinēre, (homini) moram facēre.* (2) intransit. *(com)morari, cunctari, cessare.*
delectation, *delectatio, oblectatio.*
delegate, subst. *legatus.*
delegate v. transit. (1) = to depute a person, *legare, adlegare.* (2) = to commit to a person, *rem homini committēre, mandare, delegare.*
deleterious, *noxius.*
deliberate, adj. *consideratus, cogitatus, lentus, prudens.*
deliberate, v. *deliberare, consulēre, consultare, considerare.*
deliberately, *cogitate, considerate, lente, prudenter, consulto.*
deliberation, *deliberatio, consultatio*; see also SLOWNESS.
deliberative, *deliberativus*: a — body, consilium.
delicacy. (1) of taste, style, etc., *elegantia, subtilitas*; = humane feeling, tact, *humanitas.* (2) of health, *imbecillitas, infirmitas.* (3) of flavour, *suavitas*; see also DAINTIES.
delicate. (1) = tender, *tener, mollis, delicatus.* (2) in taste, style, etc., *elegans, subtilis*; = tactful, *humanus.* (3) in health, *imbecillus, infirmus.* (4) of tasks, = requiring care, *difficilis*; or express by phrase.
delicately, *molliter, delicate, eleganter, subtiliter.*
delicious, *suavis, dulcis.*
deliciously, *suaviter.*
delight, subst. *delectatio, voluptas.*
delight, v. (1) transit. *delectare, oblectare.* (2) intransit.: to — in, *(rē) gaudēre, delectari, oblectari.*
delightful, *iucundus, suavis, acceptus, gratus.*
delightfully, *iucunde, suaviter, grate.*
delightfulness, *suavitas, iucunditas.*
delineate, (lit. and fig.) *describēre, depingēre, adumbrare.*
delineation, *adumbratio, descriptio.*
delinquency, *delictum, scelus (-ēris, n.).*
delinquent, *homo maleficus.*
delirious, *delirus.*
delirium, *delirium* (Cels.), *furor.*
deliver. (1) see FREE. (2) = to hand over, *prodēre, dedēre, tradēre.* (3) = to utter, *pronuntiare*; see also SPEAK. (4) in childbirth, to be delivered, *partum edēre.*
deliverance, *liberatio, salus (-ūtis).*
deliverer, *liberator, vindex.*
delivery, of an orator or actor, *actio, elocutio, dictio.*
dell, *vallis.*
delude, *delūdēre*; see also DECEIVE.
deluge, subst. LIT., *eluvio, diluvium* (Verg.). TRANSF., *vis magna.*
deluge, v. transit. *inundare.* TRANSF., to be deluged with, *(re)cumulari.*
delusion. (1) = deception, *fraus, dolus, fallacia.* (2) = error. *error.*
delusive, *falsus, fallax vanus.*

delve, *fodere.*
demagogue, *plebicola, plebis dux*: to play the —, *populariter agēre.*
demand, subst. *postulatio, flagitatio.*
demand, v. *poscēre, postulare, flagitare.*
demarcation, in the phrase, a line of —, *terminus, finis, confinium.*
demean, v., to — oneself: (1) = to conduct oneself, *se gerēre.* (2) = to lower oneself, *descendēre, se demittēre.*
demeanour, *mores (-um,* plur.), *habitus (-ūs).*
demerit, *culpa*; see also BLAME, FAULT.
demigod, *heros.*
demise, subst. *obitus (-ūs).*
demise, v.; see BEQUEATH.
democracy, *reipublicae forma popularis, civitas in quā omnia per populum administrantur*; or use phrase such as *penes omnes est respublica.*
democrat, *plebicola, popularium fautor.*
democratic, *popularis.*
demolish, *demoliri, diruēre, evertēre.*
demolition, *demolitio, eversio.*
demon, *daemon* (eccl.).
demonstrable, demonstrative, render by phrases.
demonstrate, *demonstrare, docēre, (con)firmare, probare.*
demonstration. (1) = pointing out, proof, *demonstratio.* (2) = display, *ostentatio.*
demoralization, *mores corrupti.*
demoralize. (1) = to corrupt, *mores corrumpēre*, or *depravare.* (2) = to unnerve, *percellēre.*
demur. (1) as legal t. t. = to object to, *exceptionem facēre.* (2) = to hesitate, *dubitare, haesitare.*
demure, *verecundus.*
demurrer, as legal t. t. *exceptio.*
den, *specus (-ūs), latibulum, lustra (-orum,* plur.); fig.: a — of vice, *stabulum.*
denial, *negatio, repudiatio.*
denizen, *incola.*
denominate, *(de)nominare.*
denote, *designare, indicare, significare.*
denotation, *significatio.*
denounce. (1) in gen. = to speak against, *increpare, vituperare.* (2) before a court, *accusare, nomen deferre.*
denouncer, *accusator, index, delator.*
dense, *densus, confertus, creber, crassus.* TRANSF., = stupid, *stolidus.*
densely, *dense, confertim.*
density, *densitas*; see also STUPIDITY.
dent, subst. *nota, vestigium.*
dentist, *medicus.*
denunciation, *delatio, accusatio.*
deny. (1) = to say that ... not, *negare, infitias ire.* (2) = to disown, *infitiari, renuēre.* (3) = to refuse to give, *negare.* (4) to — oneself a thing, *ab re temperare.*
depart, *abire, abscedēre, discedēre, excedēre, digredi, (de)migrare.*
department. (1) = office, *munus (-ēris,* n.), *provincia.* (2) = branch, division, *pars, genus (-ēris,* n.).
departure, *abitus (-ūs), discessus (-ūs).*
depend. (1) = to be dependent on, *pendēre ex re (homine), in re (or homine) positum* or *situm esse, in manu hominis esse, in potestate hominis verti.* (2) = to rely on, *homini (con)fidēre*: — upon it, *mihi crede.*

L.D.—23   [689]

dependence, *clientela*; = reliance, *fiducia*.

dependency, *provincia*.

dependent, subst. *ciiens*.

dependent, adj. *obnoxius*; or render by verb.

depict, (lit. and fig.) *depingĕre, effingĕre, describĕre*.

deplorable, *flebilis, miserabilis*.

deplore, *deplorare, deflēre*.

deploy, *explicare, dilatare*.

deponent, subst. as legal t. t. *testis, index*.

depopulate, (*de*)*populari*; better rendered by phrase, such as *civibus nudare*.

deport. (1) = to remove from a country, *deportare*. (2) to — oneself, *se gerĕre*.

deportment, *gestus (-ūs), habitus (-ūs), mores (-um*, plur.).

depose. (1) = to remove from office, *loco movēre, abrogare homini magistratum*. (2) as a witness, *testari, testificari*.

deposit, subst. *depositum*; see also PLEDGE.

deposit, v. (1) = to lay down, (*de*)*ponĕre*. (2) = to put away safely, *deponĕre*.

deposition. (1) = removal from office, render by verb. (2) = evidence, *testimonium*.

depository, *apotheca, receptaculum*.

depravation, *depravatio, corruptio*.

deprave, *depravare, corrumpĕre, vitiare*.

depravity, *pravitas (morum), mores depravati* or *corrupti*.

deprecate, *deprecari*: to — as a bad omen, *abominari*.

deprecation, *deprecatio*.

depreciate, = to disparage, *elevare, detrahĕre* (with *de* and abl.), *obtrectare* (with dat.).

depreciation, *obtrectatio*.

depredation, *direptio, expilatio, latrocinium*.

depress. LIT., physically, *premĕre, deprimĕre*. TRANSF., mentally, *animum frangĕre, infringĕre, adfligĕre*.

depression, = low spirits, *tristitia, maeror*; or render by *animus* with pass. partic.

deprivation, *privatio, spoliatio, ademptio*.

deprive, (*hominem re*) *privare*, (*de*)*spoliare, orbare*; (*rem homini*) *adimĕre, eripĕre*.

deprived, *orbus (re)*: — of a natural faculty, *captus* (with abl.).

depth, *altitudo*; of feeling, etc., express by adj. *summus* or *gravis*. Prov.: to be out of one's —, *in alieno foro litigare* (Mart.).

deputation, *legatio, legati (-orum*, plur.).

depute, (*ad*)*legare*.

deputy, *legatus, vicarius*.

derange, *perturbare, conturbare*.

deranged, = insane, *demens insanus*.

derangement. (1) = confusion, *perturbatio*. (2) = insanity, *dementia, insania*.

deride, *deridēre, inridēre*.

derider, *inrisor*.

derision, *inrisio*.

derivation, as grammat. t. t., *declinatio*; otherwise render by verb

derive, (*de*)*ducĕre, trahĕre*

derogate, v.: to — from, *derogare, detrahere* (with *de* and abl., or dat.).

derogatory, render by verb.

descend. (1) = to come down, *descendĕre*. (2) = to stoop, lower oneself, *descendĕre*. (3) of property. to — to, *pervenire ad hominem*.

descendant, *prognatus*; plur. *progenies, posteri*.

descended from, *ortus* or *oriundus ab*.

descent. (1) = downward movement, *descensus (-ūs)*; or use the verb. (2) = downward slope, *declivitas, locus declivis*. (3) = origin, *origo, genus (-ĕris, n.), progenies*. (4) = attack, *inruptio, incursio, escensio*.

describe. (1) in words, *describĕre, verbis exsequi, depingĕre, explicare, exponĕre, enarrare*. (2) = to draw, *describĕre*: to — a circle, *circumscribĕre*.

description, *descriptio*, (*e*)*narratio, expositio*.

desecrate, *profanare, polluĕre, violare*; formally, *exaugurare* (opp. *inaugurare*)

desecration, *violatio*; or express by phrase, such as *polluta sacra (-orum*, plur.).

desert, subst. *dignitas, meritum*.

desert, subst. = wilderness, *solitudo, vastitas*; or use subst. with *desertus*.

desert, adj. *desertus, solus, vastus*.

desert, v. (1) = to abandon, *deserĕre*, (*de*)*relinquĕre, destituĕre*. (2) = to become a deserter, *signa deserere* or *relinquĕre, ad hostem transfugĕre*.

deserter, *desertor, transfuga*.

desertion, (*de*)*relictio*; by a soldier, *transitio ad hostem*.

deserve, (*rem*) (*com*)*merēre*, (*com*)*merēri*; *dignum esse (re*): to — well, *bene merēri*.

deservedly, *merito, pro meritis, iure*.

deserving, (*re*) *dignus*.

design, subst. (1) = outline, form, *descriptio, lineamenta (-orum*, plur.), *forma*. (2) = purpose, *consilium*: by —, *consulto*.

design, v. (1) = to delineate, *designare, describĕre*. (2) = to intend, *in animo habēre, cogitare, proponĕre*.

designate, *designare, notare, nominare*.

designation, *designatio*; see also NAME.

designedly, *consulto, de industria*.

designing, *callidus, astutus, vafer*.

desirable, *optabilis*.

desire, subst. *appetitio, appetitus (-ūs), appetentia, cupiditas, cupido, desiderium*.

desire, v. *appetĕre, expetĕre, cupĕre, concupiscĕre, desiderare, avēre, optare*.

desirous, *rei* (genit.) *appetens, cupidus, avidus, studiosus*.

desist, *desistĕre, absistĕre*.

desk, *mensa, scrinium*.

desolate, adj. (1) = waste, *vastus, desertus*; (2) = bereaved, *orbus, solus*.

desolate, v. *vastare, populari*.

despair, subst. *desperatio*.

despair, v. *desperare, spem abicere*.

despairing; see DESPERATE.

despatch, *litterae (-arum*, plur.), *epistula*; see also SENDING and HASTE.

despatch, v. (1) = to send, *mittĕre*: to — on public business, *legare*. (2) = to complete, finish, *conficĕre, perficĕre, absolvĕre*; with haste, *maturare, accelerare*. (3) = to kill, finish off, *interficĕre, interimĕre*.

desperado, *homo desperatus* or *perditus*.

desperate. (1) = hopeless, *desperatus exspes*. (2) = dangerous *periculosus*.

desperately, *desperanter*; sometimes rendered by superl. (e.g. — wicked, *sceleratissimus*): to be — in love, *amare perdite* (Ter., Cat.), *misere* (Pl.).

desperation, *desperatio*.

despicable, *contemptus*.

despise, *contemnĕre, contemptui habēre, despicĕre, aspernari, spernĕre*.

despite, *odium, malitia*: ın — of, *contra, adversus* (with acc.).

despond, v. *desperare, se animo demittĕre, animum demittĕre.*

despondency, *animus demissus.*

despot, *tyrannus, dominus.*

despotic, *imperiosus, superbus, tyrannicus.*

despotically, *superbe, tyrannice.*

despotism, *dominatus (-ūs), tyrannis, dominatio, regnum.*

dessert, *mensa secundia.*

destination, = end of journey, express by phrase with *locus.*

destine, *destinare, constituĕre.*

destined, *destinatus*; = fated, *fatalis,* sometimes *natus.*

destiny, *fatum, sors.*

destitute, *inops, egens*: — of anything, *rĕ inops, destitutus, privatus,* or use *sine* with abl.

destitution, *inopia, egestas.*

destroy, *perdĕre, destruĕre, diruĕre, evertĕre, exscindĕre, delēre, exstinguĕre, subvertĕre* (esp. of institutions: Sall., Tac.): to — oneself, *mortem sibi consciscĕre.*

destroyer, *perditor, exstinctor.*

destructible, *fragilis*; or render by verb.

destructibility, *fragilitas.*

destruction, *eversio, excidium, exstinctio, pernicies.*

destructive, *perniciosus, exitiōsus, funestus.*

destructively, *perniciose.*

desuetude, *desuetudo*: to fall into —, *obsolescĕre.*

desultory, *inconstans, lĕvis.*

detach. Lit., = to break off, *defringĕre, avellĕre.* ,Transf., in gen. = to separate, *separare, seiungĕre, disiungĕre.*

detachment, = a body of troops, *manus (-ūs), delecti (milites).*'

detail, subst. in plur., details, *singula (-orum), singulae res*: to go into —, *de singulis agĕre.*

detail, v. *(singula), explicare, exsequi.*.

detain, *tenēre, retinēre.*

detect, *(rem) invenire, reperire, patefacĕre; (hominem in re) deprehendĕre.*

detection, express by verb.

detention, *retentio*; = custody, *custodia.*

deter, *deterrēre, absterrēre.*,

deteriorate. (1) transit. *(rem* or *hominem) deteriorem facĕre, depravare, corrumpĕre.* (2) intransit. *deteriorem fieri, corrumpi.*

deterioration, *deterior condicio* or *status (-ūs).*

determination. (1) = settlement, *arbitrium, iudicium.* (2) = intention, *institutum, consilium.* (3) = decision of character, *constantia, firmitas animi.*

determine. (1) = settle, *decernĕre, statuĕre, constituĕre, diiudicare.* (2) = decide to do, *statuĕre, constituĕre, decernĕre,* with infin.

determined. (1) = with one's mind made up, *certus.* (2) in gen. = resolute, *constans, firmus.*

detest, *odisse, detestari.*

detestable, *detestabilis, odiosus.*

detestably, *odiose.*

detestation, *odium.*

dethrone, *regno expellĕre.*

detract, v.: to — from, *detrahĕre, derogare* (with *de* and abl.); *obtrectare* (with dat.).

detraction, *obtrectatio.*

detriment, *damnum, detrimentum, incommodum.*

detrimental, *perniciosus, iniquus*: to be —, *detrimento esse.*

devastate, *(per)vastare; devastare, (de)populari, perpopulari.*

devastation. (1) as an act, *vastatio, (de)populatio.* (2) as a state, *vastitas.*

develop, v. (1) transit.: **a** = to explain, *explicare, evolvĕre, explanare*: **b** = to bring out, unfold, *educare, excolĕre, alĕre.* (2) intransit. *crescĕre, adolescĕre, augēri.*

development. (1) verbal, *explicatio, explanatio.* (2) = growth, progress, *auctus (-ūs), progressus (-ūs).*

deviate, *declinare, degredi, decedĕre, discedĕre, aberrare.*

deviation, *declinatio, digressio.*

device. (1) = emblem, *insigne*; as an inscription, *inscriptio.* (2) = plan, *machina, dolus.*

devil, *diabŏlus* (eccl.): go to the —! *abi in malam crucem.* Prov.: talk of the —, *lupus in fabula* (or *in sermone*); — take the hindmost, *occupat extremum scabies* (Hor.).

devilish, *nefandus.*

devious, *devius, vagus.*

devise. (1) = to think of, *excogitare, invenire, fingĕre, machinari.* (2) see BEQUEATH.

devoid, of a thing, *re vacuus, liber.*

devolve, v. (1) transit. *deferre, permittere, mandare.* (2) intransit. *(per)venire, permitti,* etc.

devote. (1) = to dedicate, *devovēre, consecrare, (de)dicare.* (2) to give anything completely, *dedĕre, conferre*: to — oneself, *se dedĕre* or *conferre* or *applicare*; *operam dare, incumbere, inservire.*

devoted, *deditus, studiosus.*

devotedly, *studiose.*

devotion. (1) = act of dedication, *devotio, dedicatio.* (2) = zeal, *studium.* (3) plur., devotions; see PRAYERS.

devour, *(de)vorare, comedĕre, consumĕre.*

devouring, *edax.*

devout, *pius* (erga deos), *venerabundus.*

devoutly, *pie, sancte.*

dew, *ros*: — falls, *rorat* (Varro).

dewy, *roscidus* (Verg.).

dewlap, *palearia (-ium,* plur.).

dexterity, *dexteritas, sollertia, calliditas.*

dexterous, *dexter, sollers, callidus.*

dexterously, *dext(e)re, sollerter, scienter.*

diadem, *diadema (-atis,* n.), *insigne (regium).*

diagonal, *diagonalis* (Vitr.).

diagram, *descriptio, forma.*

dial, *solarium.*

dialect, *lingua, dialectos* (Suet.): to speak in the Doric —, *Dorice loqui.*

dialectics, *dialectica (-ae), dialectica (-orum,* plur.).

dialogue. (1) philosophical, *dialogus.* (2) in plays, *diverbium.* (3) = conversation, *sermo, conloquium.*

diamond, *adamas* (Plin.): —-shaped, *scutulatus* (Plin.).

diaphragm, *praecordia (-ium,* plur.).

diarrhoea, *alvi profluvium* (Cels.).

diary, *commentarii diurni* (Suet.).

dice, die, *talus, tessera*: to play at —, *talis* or *tesseris ludĕre, aleā ludĕre*; a — box, *fritillus* (Juv.).

dicer, *aleator.*

dictate, v. (1) = to read to one who writes down, *dictare.* (2) see ORDER.

dictation, = orders, *arbitrium, praescriptum*; see also ORDER.

dictator, *dictator.*

dictatorial. (1) = of an actual dictator, *dictatorius.* (2) in gen., *imperiosus.*

dictatorship, *dictatura.*

diction, *dicendi* or *scribendi genus (-ĕris), dictio, sermo.*

die, v. LIT., *mori,* (*mortem*) *obir⌐,* (*vitā*) *decedĕre,* (*mortem*) *occumbĕre,* (*mortem*) *oppe-tĕre.* TRANSF., of wind, to — away, *cadĕre*; of abstr. things, to — out, *emori.*

diet, *victus (-ūs), diaeta.*

differ, *discrepare, dissidēre, dissentire, differre.*

difference, *varietas, diversitas*: — of opinion, *discrepantia, dissensio.*

different, *alius, discrepans, diversus, dissimilis, varius*: — people do — things, *alii alia faciunt.*

differently, *aliter, diverse, varie.*

difficult, *difficilis, arduus, impeditus.*

difficulty, *difficultas*: a source of —, *impedi-mentum*; to be in difficulties, *laborare*; with —, *vix, aegre, difficulter*; without —, *nullo negotio.*

diffidence, *verecundia, diffidentia.*

diffident, *verecundus, diffidens.*

diffidently, *verecunde, diffidenter.*

diffuse, v. (1) transit. *diffundĕre.* (2) intransit. *diffundi, permeare, fluĕre.*

diffuse, adj. *verbosus, fusus.*

diffusely, *verbose, fuse.*

dig, *fodĕre*: to — up, — out, *effodĕre, eruĕre.*

digger, *fossor* (poet.).

digest, subst., as legal t. t., *digesta (-orum,* plur.).

digest, v. *concoquĕre.*

digestion, *concoctio* (Plin.).

digestible, *facilis ad concoquendum.*

dignified, *gravis, augustus.*

dignify, *honestare, honorare.*

dignity. (1) of rank, *dignitas, amplitudo.* (2) of air or character, *honestas, gravitas, auctoritas, maiestas, dignitas.*

digress, *digredi, aberrare.*

digression, *digressio.*

dike. (1) = an earthwork, *moles, agger.* (2) = a ditch, *fossa.*

dilapidated, *ruinosus, obsoletus* (Hor.).

dilapidation, *ruina.*

dilate. (1) = to extend, *dilatare.* (2) to — upon, *de re latius dicĕre.*

dilatoriness, *cunctatio, tarditas, mora.*

dilatory, *tardus, lentus.*

dilemma, as logic. t. t. *complexio*; in gen.: the horns of a —, *res in angustias deductae.*

diligence, *diligentia, industria adsiduitas.*

diligent, *diligens, industrius, adsiduus.*

diligently, *diligenter, industrie, adsidue.*

dilute, *aquā* (*per*)*miscēre, diluĕre.*

dim, adj. *obscurus, hebes*: to grow —, *hebescĕre.*

dim, v. transit. *obscurare, hebetare.*

dimension, *modus.*

diminish, v. (1) transit. (*im*)*minuĕre, de-minuĕre.* (2) intransit. (*im*)*minui, deminui.*

diminutive; see SMALL.

dimness, *obscuritas.*

dimple, *gelasinus* (Mart.).

din, subst. *strepitus (-ūs)*: to make a —, *strepĕre, strepitum edĕre.*

din, v.: to — a thing into a person, *hominis aures obtundĕre.*

dine, *prandēre, cenare.*

dingy, *fuscus, sordidus.*

dining-room, *triclinium.*

dinner, *prandium* (morning), *cena* (evening).

dint, subst. (1) = a mark, *nota, vestigium.* (2) by — of, *per,* or use instrumental abl.

dint, v. *signare, imprimĕre.*

dip, subst., render by verb.

dip, v. (1) transit. *tingĕre, mergĕre.* (2) intransit.: **a** = to plunge in, *tingi, mergi*: **b,** in gen. = to sink, *vergĕre*: **c,** to — into a book, *librum attingĕre.*

diploma, *diploma (-ătis,* n.: Suet.).

diplomacy. LIT., express by phrase with *legatus* or *legatio.* TRANSF., = skill in dealing with people, *astutia.*

diplomat, *legatus.*

diplomatic, adj. = tactful, clever, *astutus, callidus.*

dire, *dirus, atrox.*

direct, adj. *rectus.*

direct, v. (1) physically = to turn, aim, *dirigĕre, intendĕre.* (2) = to regulate, manage, *dirigĕre, regĕre, gubernare, administrare, procurare.* (3) see ORDER. (4) = to show the way, (*homini*) *viam monstrare.* (5) to — a letter, (*homini*) *epistulam inscribĕre.*

direction. (1) = course, *cursus (-ūs), via, regio*: in both —s, *utroque*; in every —, *quoquo-versus*; in which —? *quo? quorsum?* in different —s, *diversi*; in the — of Rome, *Romam versus.* (2) = management, *cura, regimen, administratio, moderatio, gubernatio, pro-curatio.* (3) see ORDER.

directly. (1) = in a straight course, *rectā.* (2) = immediately, *statim, confestim.*

directness, of speech, *simplicitas.*

director, *magister, praeses, curator, procurator, praefectus.*

dirge, *nenia.*

dirt, *caenum, sordes, inluvies, limus* (= mud).

dirtily, *spurce.*

dirty, adj. LIT., *spurcus, sordidus immundus*: to be —, *sordēre.* TRANSF., *sordidus, turpis.*

dirty, v. transit. *inquinare, polluĕre* (Verg., Tac.).

disable, *enervare, debilitare.*

disabuse, (*homini*) *errorem demĕre* or *eripĕre.*

disadvantage, *incommodum, iniquitas.*

disadvantageous, *incommodus, iniquus.*

disadvantageously, *incommode, inique.*

disaffected, (*ab*)*alienatus, aversus*; or use phrase, *animo alienato* or *averso.*

disaffection, *alienatio, animus alienus* or *aversus.*

disagree, *discrepare, dissentire, dissidēre*; of food, *non facile concoqui, stomacho gravem esse.*

disagreeable, *ingratus, gravis, molestus, in-iucundus.*

disagreeably, *ingrate, graviter, moleste.*

disagreement, *discrepantia, dissensio, dissi-dium.*

disallow, *vetare.*

disappear, LIT., = to vanish, *e conspectu* (or *ex oculis*) *abire, evanescĕre.* TRANSF., in gen. = to be destroyed, *exstingui, tolli.*

disappearance, render by verb.

disappoint, *frustrari, spem fallĕre, spe depellĕr, deicĕre.*

disappointment, render by phrase with *spes*: a feeling of —, sometimes *dolor.*

disapproval, *improbatio.*

disapprove, *improbare, condemnare.*

disarm, (*hominem*) *armis exuĕre, arma* (*homini*) *adimĕre.*

disarrange, (*con*)*turbare, perturbare, confundĕre.*

disarrangement, *perturbatio.*

disaster, *clades, calamitas, incommodum, offensio.*

disastrous, *calamitosus, funestus, perniciosus.*

disastrously, *calamitose, funeste, perniciose.*

disavow, *diffiteri, infitiari, infitias ire, abnuĕre.*

disavowal, *infitiatio.*

disband, *exauctorare, missos* (plur.) *facĕre, dimittĕre.*

disbelief, use verb.

disbelieve, *non credĕre.*

disburden, *exonerare, liberare, expedire.*

disburse; see PAY.

disc, *orbis.*

discern, (*dis*)*cernĕre, dispicĕre.*

discerning, *intellegens, perspicax, sagax, subtilis, prudens.*

discernment, = insight, *intellegentia, prudentia, iudicium, subtilitas.*

discharge, subst. (1) from service, (*di*)*missio.* (2) = shooting, *emissio, coniectio, coniectus* (*-ūs*). (3) = performance, express by verb.

discharge, v. (1) from service: as a soldier, *missum facĕre, dimittĕre, exauctorare;* as a gladiator, *rude donare.* (2) = to shoot, let fly, (*e*)*mittĕre, conicĕre.* (3) = to perform: to — a duty, *munus obire, munere* (*per*)*fungi.*

disciple, *discipulus, auditor.*

discipline, subst. *disciplina:* sense of —, *modestia;* want of —, *licentia.*

discipline, v. *instituĕre, exercĕre.*

disclaim, *repudiare;* see also DISAVOW.

disclose, *detegĕre, retegĕre,* (*in medium*) *proferre, indicare, aperire, patefacĕre.*

disclosure, *patefactio, indicium.*

discolour, *decolorare* (Suet.); or render by phrase.

discomfit, *profligare, adfligĕre.*

discomfiture, *clades, incommodum.*

discomfort, *incommodum.*

disconcert, *percellere, perturbare.*

disconsolate, *maestus.*

discontent, *molestia, taedium.*

discontented, render by phrase with *contentus.*

discontinue, *interrumpĕre, intermittĕre* (temporarily), *omittĕre, dirimĕre* (for good).

discord. (1) in music, express by adj. *dissonus* or verb *discrepo.* (2) = disagreement, *dissensio, dissidium, discordia.*

discordant. (1) in music, *dissonus, absonus.* (2) = disagreeing, *discors, discrepans, dissonus.*

discount, subst. *deductio, decessio:* to pay without —, *solidum solvĕre.*

discountenance, *improbare, condemnare.*

discourage, *animum frangĕre, infringĕre, adfligĕre;* to — from, *deterrere* (with *ab, de,* or *ne* clause), *dissuadēre.*

discouragement, *animi infractio.*

discourse, subst. (1) = conversation, *sermo, conlocutio, conloquium.* (2) = a set speech, *oratio, contio.*

discourse. (1) to — with, converse, *confabulari, conloqui.* (2) = to make a speech, *orationem facĕre* or *habēre, contionari.*

discourteous, *inurbanus, inlepidus.*

discourteously, *inurbane, inlepide.*

discourtesy, *inurbanitas.*

discover, v. (1) = to find, *invenire, reperire,*

comperire; of facts, *cognoscĕre,* with acc. and infin. (2) see DISCLOSE.

discoverer, *inventor.*

discovery, *inventio, investigatio;* = a thing discovered, *inventum.*

discredit, subst. = disgrace, *dedecus* (*-ŏris,* n.), *ignominia, probrum, infamia.*

discredit, v. *fidem* (*hominis* or *homini*) *imminuĕre* or *abrogare* or *derogare.*

discreditable, *inhonestus, turpis.*

discreet, *prudens, cautus, consideratus.*

discreetly, *prudenter, caute, considerate.*

discretion, *prudentia, iudicium:* at one's —, *suo arbitrio.*

discriminate, *diiudicare, discernĕre, distinguĕre, internoscĕre.*

discrimination, as an act, *distinctio, discrimen;* as a quality; see DISCERNMENT.

discursive, *varius, vagus.*

discuss, *disceptare, disputare, disserĕre, agitare.*

discussion, *disceptatio, disputatio.*

disdain, subst. *fastidium, contemptio.*

disdain, v. *spernĕre, fastidire, aspernari, despicĕre, dedignari* (Verg., Tac.).

disdainful, *fastidiosus.*

disease, *morbus.*

diseased, *aeger, aegrotus.*

disembark, v. (1) transit. *exponĕre.* (2) intransit. *egredi.*

disembarkation, *egressus* (*-ūs*).

disembarrass, *expedire, liberare, exonerare.*

disenchant; see DISABUSE.

disengage, *solvĕre, liberare, expedire, avocare.*

disengaged, *otiosus, vacuus.*

disentangle, *expedire, explicare, exsolvĕre.*

disfavour, *invidia, offensa.*

disfigure, *deformare.*

disfranchise, (*homini*) *civitatem adimĕre,* (*hominem*) *suffragio privare.*

disfranchisement, render by verb.

disgorge. LIT., (*e*)*vomĕre.* TRANSF., = to give up, *reddĕre.*

disgrace, *dedecus* (*-oris,* n.), *turpitudo, infamia, ignominia.*

disgrace, v. *dedecorare, dehonestare, dedecori esse* (with dat.).

disgraceful, *turpis, inhonestus, flagitiosus, probrosus.*

disgracefully, *turpiter, inhoneste, flagitiose.*

disguise, subst. LIT., in dress, *vestis mutata;* for the face, = mask, *persona.* TRANSF., *species, simulacrum, simulatio, persona.*

disguise, v. LIT., *alienā veste occultare.* TRANSF., *rem dissimulare, occultare.*

disgust, subst. *fastidium, taedium, satietas, stomachus, nausea.*

disgust, v. *fastidium, taedium,* etc., *movere* (*homini*).

disgusting, *foedus, taeter, molestus.*

disgustingly, *foede, moleste.*

dish, subst. *patina, patella, lanx.*

dish, v.: to — up, *adponĕre.*

dishearten, *animum frangĕre,* or *infringĕre:* to be —ed, *animum* (or *se animo*) *demittĕre.*

dishonest, *malus, improbus, fraudulentus.*

dishonestly, *male, improbe, fraudulenter.*

dishonesty, *improbitas, fraus.*

dishonour, subst. in gen.; see DISGRACE: — done to a woman, *stuprum.*

dishonour, v. in gen.; see DISGRACE: to — a woman, *stuprare.*

dishonourable, *inhonestus.*

disinclination, *declinatio* (rare), *animus aversus*.
disinclined, *aversus*: to be —, *nolo*.
disingenuous, *parum candidus*; see also DECEITFUL.
disinherit, *exheredare*, *exheredem facĕre*.
disinherited, *exheres*.
disintegrate, v. transit. *dissolvĕre*.
disinter, *effodĕre*, *eruĕre*.
disinterested, render by phrase, such as *suae utilitatis immemor*.
disinterestedness, *abstinentia*.
disjoin, *disiungĕre*, *seiungĕre*.
disjointed, *incompositus*.
disjointedly, *incomposite*.
disk, *orbis*.
dislike, subst. *odium*, *fastidium*.
dislike, v. *fastidire*, *abhorrēre* (with *ab*); or use phrase, e.g. *haud multum amare*.
dislocate, *extorquēre*, *luxare* (Plin., Sen.).
dislocation, *luxus* (-*ūs*: Cato).
dislodge, (*de*)*pellĕre*, *expellĕre*, *summovēre*, *deicĕre*.
disloyal, *improbus*, *infidus*, *infidelis*.
disloyalty, *infidelitas*.
dismal, *maestus*, *luctuosus*, *tristis*, *miser*.
dismally, *maeste*, *misere*.
dismantle, *nudare*, *diruĕre*; see also DEMOLISH.
dismast, *malo privare*.
dismay, *consternatio*, *pavor*, *terror*.
dismay, v. *consternare*, *pavefacĕre*, (*per*)*terrere*, *percellĕre*.
dismember, *discerpĕre*.
dismiss, *dimittĕre*, *missum facĕre*, *ablegare*; see also DISCHARGE.
dismissal, *dimissio*; see also DISCHARGE.
dismount, *ex equo* (or *equis*) *desilire*.
disobedience, *contumacia*; or express by phrase.
disobedient; see DISOBEY.
disobey, use *non*, *male* or *parum* with a verb meaning 'obey'; sometimes render by *neglegĕre*.
disoblige, *offendĕre*.
disorder, subst. *confusio*, *turba*, (*per*)*turbatio*; = disease, *morbus*.
disorder, v. (*con*)*turbare*, *perturbare*, *miscĕre*, *confundĕre*.
disordered, = sick, *aeger*.
disorderly. (1) = confused, *confusus*, (*con*)-*turbatus*, *perplexus*, *incompositus*, *turbidus*, *inordinatus*. (2) = insubordinate, turbulent, *turbidus*, *turbulentus*.
disorganization, disorganize; see DISORDER.
disown, *repudiare*, *infitiari*.
disparage, *detrectare*, *extenuare*, *elevare*, *obtrectare* (with dat.).
disparagement, *obtrectatio*.
disparaging, render by verb.
disparity, *dissimilitudo*, *differentia*.
dispassionate, *placidus*, *placatus*, *tranquillus*.
dispatch; see DESPATCH.
dispel, *discutĕre*, *dissipare*, *dispellĕre*.
dispense. (1) = to distribute, *distribuĕre*, *dividĕre*. (2) = to — with, (*di*)*mittĕre* (= get rid of), *re carēre* (= be without).
dispersal, dispersion, *dissipatio*, *diffugium* (Tac.).
disperse. v. (1) transit. *dissipare*, *dispergĕre*, *dispellĕre*. (2) intransit. *dilabi*, *diffugĕre*; or use pass. of transit. verbs.
dispirited; see DESPONDENT.
displace, *loco* (*suo*) *movēre*.

display, subst. *ostentatio*.
display, v. *ostentare*, *ostendĕre*, *prae se ferre*, *exhibēre*: to — oneself = to appear, *apparēre*.
displease, *displicēre* (*homini*), *offendĕre* (*hominem*).
displeasure, *offensio*, *offensa*, *indignatio*.
disposal, = the power to use a thing as one wishes, *arbitrium*: at the — of anyone, *penes hominem*, *in potestate hominis*.
dispose. (1) = to arrange, settle, *ordinare*, *statuĕre*, *constituĕre*. (2) = to incline, *inclinare*. (3) to — of; see SELL, USE, and RID.
disposed, *inclinatus*, *propensus*, *proclivis*, *pronus*.
disposition. (1) = arrangement, *conlocatio*, *ordinatio*, *dispositio*. (2) = natural character, *ingenium*, *indoles*, *natura*.
dispossess, *possessione depellĕre*, *deturbare*.
disproportion, *inaequalitas* (Quint.), *dissimilitudo*.
disproportionate, *inaequalis*, *impar*.
disprove, *refellĕre*, *redarguĕre*.
dispute, subst. *controversia*, *disceptatio*, *concertatio*, *altercatio*, *rixa*.
dispute, v. *ambigĕre*, *disputare*, *disceptare*, *rem in controversiam vocare* or *adducĕre*; = to quarrel, *concertare*, *altercari*, *rixari*.
disqualify. (1) as legal t. t., *excipĕre*. (2) in gen. = to hinder, *impedire*, *prohibēre*.
disquiet, render by phrase.
disquieted, *inquietus*, *sollicitus*.
disquisition; see SPEECH or TREATISE.
disregard, subst. *neglegentia*, *incuria*.
disregard, v. *neglegĕre*, *omittĕre*, *parvi facĕre*.
disregardful, *neglegens*, *immemor*.
disreputable, *infamis*.
disrepute, *infamia*.
disrespect, *insolentia*
disrespectful, *insolens*.
dissatisfaction, *molestia*, *offensa*, *offensio*.
dissatisfied, *male* (or *parum*) *contentus*: I am —, *paenitet me* (with genit. of cause).
dissatisfy, *displicēre* (with dat.).
dissect, *persecare*.
dissemble, *dissimulare*.
dissembler, *dissimulator*.
disseminate, *spargĕre*, *dispergĕre*, *serĕre*, *disseminare*.
dissemination, use verb.
dissension, *discordia*; see DISCORD.
dissent, subst. *dissensio*.
dissent, v. *dissentire*, *dissidēre*.
disservice, *incommodum*, *detrimentum*.
dissimilar, *dissimilis*, *dispar*.
dissimulation, *dissimulatio*.
dissipate, *dissipare*; see also DISPERSE.
dissipated, *dissolutus*, *luxuriosus*.
dissipation, *luxuria*, *licentia*.
dissolve, v. (1) transit. *liquefacĕre*, (*dis*)*solvĕre*. (2) intransit. *liquescĕre*, (*dis*)*solvi*.
dissolute; see DISSIPATED.
dissolution, *dissolutio*.
dissoluteness, *licentia*.
dissonant, *dissonus*, *absŏnus*.
dissuade, (*homini*) *dissuadēre*, (*hominem*) *dehortari*, *deterrēre*.
dissuasion, *dissuasio*.
dissyllabic, *disyllăbus* (Quint.).
distaff, *colus*, f.: on the — side, *materno genere* (Sall.).
distance, subst. *spatium*, *intervallum*, *longinquitas*: at a —, *procul*, *longe*; from a —, *eminus*, *ex longinquo*.

distance, v. *superare*; see also SURPASS.

distant, *remotus, longinquus*: to be —, *distare, abesse.*

distaste, *fastidium.*

distasteful, *molestus, iniucundus, ingratus.*

distemper, *morbus, lues* (poet.).

distend, *distendĕre* (poet.): to — the cheeks, *inflare buccas* (Pl., Hor.).

distil, v. (1) transit. = to pour out by drops, *stillare.* (2) intransit. = to drip, *stillare.*

distinct. (1) = separate, *distinctus, separatus, disiunctus.* (2) = clear, *distinctus, clarus, perspicuus.*

distinction. (1) between things, *discrimen, distinctio.* (2) honourable —, *honor, dignitas, decus*; a mark of —, *insigne.*

distinctive, *proprius.*

distinctively, *proprie.*

distinctly, *distincte, clare, perspicue.*

distinguish. (1) between things, *distinguĕre, secernĕre, diiudicare, internoscĕre.* (2) see HONOUR: to — oneself, *clarescĕre* (Lucr., Tac.).

distinguished, *insignis (prae)clarus, nobilis, egregius*: to be —, *eminēre.*

distort, *detorquēre, distorquēre.*

distorted, *pravus*; or use partic.

distortion, as an act, *distortio*; as a state, *pravitas.*

distract. (1) = to make inattentive, *distringĕre, distrahĕre, distinēre, avocare* (Sen.). (2) = to agitate, *(con)turbare, perturbare.*

distracted, distraught, *(con)turbatus, perturbatus, amens, vecors.*

distraction, render by verb; see also AGITATION, FRENZY.

distrain, v.: to — upon, *(hominis) bona vendĕre.*

distress, subst. *miseria, aerumna, labor*; financial —, *angustiae (-arum,* plur.).

distress, v. *angĕre, vexare, sollicitare, adflictare, cruciare.*

distressed, *sollicitus, anxius, adflictus, miser*: to be —, *laborare.*

distressing, *gravis, acerbus.*

distribute, *distribuĕre, partiri, dispertire, dividĕre.*

distribution, *partitio, distributio*; or render by verb.

district, *ager, regio, terra.*

distrust, subst. *diffidentia.*

distrust, v. *diffidĕre* (with dat.).

distrustful, *suspiciosus, diffidens.*

disturb, *(con)turbare, perturbare, commovēre.*

disturbance, *turba, turbatio, tumultus (-ūs), motus (-ūs).*

disturber, *turbator.*

disunion, = discord, *dissensio, dissidium, discordia.*

disunite, *seiungĕre, secernĕre, disiungĕre, dissociare.*

disused, *desuetus.*

ditch, *fossa.*

ditcher, *fossor* (poet.).

dithyrambic, *dithyrambicus.*

ditty, *nenia, carmen.*

diurnal, *diurnus.*

dive, v. LIT., into a liquid, *urinari, se (de)mergĕre, se submergĕre.* TRANSF., to — into a subject, *rem explorare, investigare.*

diver, person, *urinator*; bird, *mergus* (poet.).

diverge, *decedere, declinare, discedĕre, digredi*; of roads, *in diversas partes ferre.*

divergence, *declinatio.*

diverse, *alius, diversus, dispar, impar, dissimilis.*

diversely, *aliter, diverse, dissimiliter.*

diversify, *variare, distinguĕre.*

diversion. (1) = a turning aside, *derivatio, deductio.* (2) = a distracting, *avocatio.* (3) = a recreation, *oblectatio, oblectamentum.*

diversity, *diversitas, discrepantia.*

divert. (1) = to turn aside, *avertĕre, derivare, deducĕre.* (2) see DISTRACT. (3) = to amuse, *delectare, oblectare.*

diverting, *iocosus.*

divest, *nudare, spoliare, privare*: to — oneself of a thing (lit. and fig.), *exuĕre, detegĕre.*

divide. (1) transit. *dividĕre, partiri, dispertire, distribuĕre*; see also SEPARATE. (2) intransit. LIT., *dividi, discedĕre.* TRANSF., = to vote, *in sententiam (pedibus) ire,* or *discedĕre.*

divination, *divinatio, vaticinatio, auguratio*: the substance or result of —, *vaticinium, oraculum.*

divine, adj. *divinus, caelestis*: by — providence or inspiration, *divinitus.*

divine, v. *divinare, vaticinari, augurari, hariolari, praesentire, praesagire, coniectare.*

divinely, *divine, divinitus.*

diviner, *haruspex, hariolus.*

divinity, *divinitas, numen.*

divisible, *dividuus.*

division. (1) as an act, *partitio, divisio.* (2) = a part, *pars*; of an army, *legio.* (3) for voting, *discessio.*

divorce, subst. *divortium, discidium* (= separation), *repudium* (= putting away).

divorce, v., of the man, *divortium facĕre cum uxore, repudium remittĕre uxori, uxorem repudiare*; of the woman, *divortium facĕre cum marito.*

divulge, *(di)vulgare, (in medium) proferre, declarare, aperire, patefacĕre.*

dizziness, *vertigo*: causing — (of a window), *caligans* (Juv.).

dizzy, *vertiginosus*: a — height, *immensa.*

Dnieper, *Borysthenes.*

do, *facĕre, efficĕre, agĕre, gerĕre*: how do you —? *quid agis?* I have nothing to — with him, *nihil mihi cum illo est*; that will —, *iam satis est*; he is done for, *de eo actum est*; prov., no sooner said than done, *dictum factum*; to — away with; see ABOLISH, KILL; to — without; see DISPENSE.

docile, *docilis.*

docility, *docilitas.*

dock, subst. (1) for ships, *navale,* or plur. *navalia.* (2) in the — (= on trial), *reus.*

dock, v.; see CURTAIL.

doctor, subst. *medicus.*

doctor, v. *curare.*

doctrine, *dogma (-ătis,* n.), *disciplina.*

document, *litterae (-arum,* plur.), *instrumentum, tabula, diploma (-atis,* n.).

dodge, subst.; see TRICK.

dodge, v. = to get away from, *eludĕre.*

doe, *cerva.*

doer, *actor, auctor*; or render by verb.

doff, *exuĕre.*

dog, subst. *canis*: a young —, *catulus*; of a —, *caninus.* Prov.: — won't eat —, *canis caninam non est* (Varro).

dog, v. *indagare, investigare.*

dogged, *pervicax, pertinax, improbus* (poet.).

doggedly, *pertinaciter.*

doggedness, *pervicacia, pertinacia.*
doggerel, *versūs inculti* (plur.).
dogma, *dogma, placitum* (Tac.): it is a — of the Stoics that all sins are alike, *placet Stoicis omnia peccata esse paria.*
dogmatic, perhaps *adrogans.*
doing; see ACTION.
dole, subst. *stips*; or render by *diaria* (*-orum*, plur. = daily ration) or by *sportula* (= client's allowance: Juv.).
dole, v., to — out; see DISTRIBUTE.
doleful, *tristis, flebilis, maestus.*
dolefully, *flebiliter, maeste.*
dolefulness, *tristitia, maeror.*
doll, *pupa* (Pers.).
dolphin, *delphinus.*
dolt, *stipes, caudex* (*codex*), *baro.*
doltish, *rusticus, stolidus.*
domain. (1) = a kingdom, *regnum.* (2) = any estate, *possessio.*
dome, *tholus* (poet.).
domestic, subst.; see SERVANT.
domestic, adj. (1) = of the home or family, *domesticus, familiaris, privatus*: — animals, *animalia quae nobiscum degunt* (Plin.). (2) opp. to foreign, *intestinus, domesticus.*
domesticate; see TAME.
domicile, *domicilium, domus.*
dominant, render by verb.
dominate, *dominari, regnare.*
domination, *dominatio, dominatus* (*-ūs*); see also DOMINION.
domineer, *dominari, regie se gerēre.*
domineering, *imperiosus, superbus.*
dominion. (1) = power, rule, *potestas, ius* (*iuris*), *imperium, dicio*; of a Roman emperor, *principatus* (*-ūs*: Tac.); of a king, *regnum*; of a tyrant, *dominatio, dominatus* (*-ūs*), *tyrannis.* (2) = realm, *regnum.*
Don, *Tanais.*
donation, *donum*; see also GIFT.
doom, subst. *fatum, sors.*
doom, v. *condemnare, damnare*; see also CONDEMN, DESTINE.
doomsday, *dies extremi iudicii* (eccl.).
door, *ostium, ianua, fores* (*-um*, plur.), *valvae* (*-arum*, plur.): a back —, *posticum*; out of —s. *foras* (of going out), *foris* (of being out); from — to —, *ostiatim.*
doorkeeper, *ianitor* (f. *ianitrix*).
doorpost, *postis.*
dormant: to lie —, *iacēre.*
dormitory, *cubiculum.*
dormouse, *glis.*
dose, subst. *potio, medicamentum.*
dose, v. *medicamentum dare.*
dot, *punctum.*
dotage, *senium.*
dotard, *senex, delirus.*
dote, v. (1) = to drivel, ramble, *delirare.* (2) to — upon, *deamare, deperire.*
double, adj. *duplex* (= twofold), *duplus* (= twice as much), *geminus* (= twin, making a pair), *bipartitus* (= in two parts), *anceps* (= two-headed, doubtful): at the—, *pleno gradu.*
double, v. (1) = to make twice as great, *duplicare.* (2) = to sail round, *flectēre, circumvehi.*
double-dyed. LIT., *bis tinctus.* TRANSF., use superl. (e.g. a —villain, *homo sceleratissimus*).
double-faced; see DECEITFUL.
doublet, *tunica.*

double-tongued, adj. *bilinguis* (lit. and fig.; poet.).
doubly, *bis, dupliciter.*
doubt, subst. *dubitatio, scrupulus*: without —, *sine dubio, haud dubie*; to throw — upon, (rem) *in dubium vocare.*
doubt, v. *dubitare, animi pendēre*: I do not — that, *non dubito quin.*
doubtful, adj. (1) = doubting, *dubius, incertus.* (2) = open to doubt, *dubius, incertus, anceps, ambiguus.*
doubtfully, *dubitanter* (= doubtingly), *dubie* (= not for certain), *ambigue.*
doubtless, *sine dubio.*
dough, *farina.*
doughty, *fortis, strenuus.*
dove, *columba, columbus* (Hor.), *palumbes* (= ring-dove; poet.).
dove-cot, *columbarium* (Varro).
Dover, *Portus Dubris.*
dovetail, subst. *securicula* (Vitr.), *subscus* (*-ūdis*: Vitr.).
dovetail, v. LIT., render by subst. TRANSF., *inter se cohaerēre.*
dower, dowry, *dos.*
dowerless, *indotatus* (Hor.).
down, subst. (1) of feathers, soft hair, etc., *pluma, lanugo.* (2) = a hill, *collis, clivus.*
down, adv. and prep.: — from, *de* with abl.; — stream, *secundo flumine*; 'down' is often rendered by a compound verb with *de-*; see also DOWNWARDS.
downcast, *demissus, tristis, maestus.*
downfall, (*oc*)*casus* (*-ūs*), *ruina.*
downpour, *imber.*
downright, adj. (1) = complete, *merus, summus*; or express by adv. (2) = straightforward, *simplex.*
downright, adv. *plane, prorsus, omnino.*
downtrodden, *adflictus.*
downwards, *desuper, deorsum*: sloping —, *declivis*; see also DOWN.
downy, *plumeus.*
doze, v. *dormitare.*
dozing, *somniculosus, semisomnus.*
dozen, *duodecim.*
drab, *ravus*; see BROWN.
drag, subst. = brake, *sufflamen* (Juv.).
drag, v. (lit. and fig.), *trahēre*: to — away, *abstrahēre*; to — down, *detrahēre*; to — out, *extrahēre*; see also DRAW and PROTRACT.
dragon, *draco, serpens; anguis* (the constellation).
drain, subst. *fossa, incile* (Cato), *cloaca.*
drain, v. (1) of fields, etc., *siccare.* (2) of drink, (*ex*)*haurire, ducere* (Hor.).
drake, *anas mas*; see DUCK.
dram, *potiuncula* (Suet.).
drama, *fabula.*
dramatic, *scaenicus.*
dramatize, *ad scaenam componēre* (Quint.).
draper, express by phrase, such as *qui pannos vendit.*
drapery, as a business, express by phrase, such as *pannorum mercatura*; see also CURTAIN and CLOTHING.
draught. (1) = a drink, *haustus* (*-ūs*), *potio.* (2) of air, *spiritus* (*-ūs*), *aura.*
draw. v. (1) transit. LIT., *trahēre, ducēre*; of fluids, *haurire*; to — a sword, *gladium* (*de*)*stringēre*; to — lots, *sortes ducēre*; to — aside, *seducēre*; to — off, *detrahēre, deducēre*;

to — out, *extrahĕre, educĕre*; to — tight, *adducĕre, adstringĕre*. TRANSF., **a**, to make lines, etc., by drawing, *ducĕre*: **b**, to portray by drawing, *describĕre, (de)pingĕre*: **c** = to induce, *movēre* (e.g. *risum*, laughter): **d**, logically: to — a conclusion, *concludĕre*: **e**, to — up (a document), *scribĕre, conscipĕre*: **f**, to — up (troops) *instruĕre*.. (2) intransit.: **a**, to — near; see APPROACH : **b**, to — back, *recedĕre, se recipĕre*.

draw-bridge, *pons, ponticulus*.

drawer. (1) of water, *aquarius* (Juv.). (2) a chest of drawers, *armarium*. (3) plur., —s, as worn, *feminalia (-ium*, plur.)

drawing, *pictura*.

drawl, render by phrase, with *lentus* or *lente*.

dray, *carrus, plaustrum*.

dread; see FEAR.

dream, subst. *somnium*: in a —, *in somno, in somnis, in quiete*.

dream, v. *somniare, dormitare*: to — of, *vidēre in somnis*.

dreamy, *somniculosus*.

dreary, *tristis, miser, luctuosus, maestus*.

drearily, *misere, maeste*.

dregs, *faex*; used offensively of people, *faex, sentina*.

drench, *madefacĕre, perfundĕre*.

dress, subst. *vestis, vestitus (-ūs), ornatus (-ūs), habitus (-ūs)*.

dress, v. (1) = to clothe, *vestire*; see also CLOTHE. (2) = to prepare food, *coquĕre*. (3) = to attend to wounds, *curare*.

dressed, *vestitus*: — in black, *sordidatus*; — in white, *albatus*.

dressing, as medic. t. t. *fomentum* (Hor.), *cataplasma* (Plin.).

drift, subst. = tendency or aim, *consilium, ratio*: what is the — of the speech? *quo spectat oratio?* what is your —? *quid vis?*

drift, v. *ferri, fluitare*.

drill, subst. (1) for boring, *terebra*. (2) of soldiers, *exercitatio*.

drill, v. (1) = to bore, *perforare, terebrare*. (2) = to train or exercise, *exercēre, exercitare*.

drily, (of style) *sicce, ieiune, exiliter, frigide*.

drink, subst. *potio, potus (-ūs)*: to die of —, *perire potando* (Pl.).

drink, v. *bibĕre, potare, haurire* (= drink up), *sorbēre* (= suck in): to — to a person's health, *homini propinare*.

drinker, *potor, potator* (habitual): a fellow —, drinking companion, *combibo, compotor*.

drinking; see DRINK (subst.).

drinking-bout, *potatio, comissatio*.

drip, *stillare*.

dripping, subst. *stillicidium*.

drive, subst. (in a carriage, etc.), *gestatio*.

drive, v. (1) transit. LIT., *agĕre, pellĕre, agitare*: to — away, *abigĕre, fugare*; to — back, *repellĕre*; to — forward, *propellĕre* (e.g. *navem*); to — down, *depellĕre*; to — out, *expellĕre, exturbare*; to — together, *cogĕre, compellĕre*. TRANSF., = to force, *cogĕre, compellĕre*. (2) intransit.: **a**, in a carriage, etc., *(in)vehi, gestari* (Sen., Juv.): **b**, of involuntary movement in gen., *ferri*: **c**, to — at, *petĕre*.

drivel, subst.; see NONSENSE.

drivel, v. *delirare, ineptire*.

driver, of a vehicle, *raedarius, auriga*; of animals, *agitator*.

drizzle, v. *leniter pluĕre*.

droll, *lepidus, iocularis, ridiculus, facetus*.

drollery, *iocus, facetiae (-arum*, plur.).

drolly, *lepide, ridicule, facete*.

dromedary, *(camelus) dromas*.

drone, *fucus* (Verg.).

droning, *bombus* (Varro).

droop, v. (1) transit. *demittĕre*. (2) intransit.: **a** = to hang down, *(de)pendēre*: **b** = to wither, *languēre, languescĕre, flaccescĕre*: **c** = to fail, *concidĕre, cadĕre*.

drop, subst. *gutta, stilla*.

drop, v. (1) transit. LIT., = to let fall, *demittĕre, deicĕre*. TRANSF., = to give up, *omittĕre, demittĕre*. (2) intransit.: **a** = to fall in drops, *(de)stillare*: **b** = to fall to the ground, *delabi, decidĕre, excidĕre*: **c**, to — on = take by surprise, *opprimĕre*.

dropsical, *hydropicus* (Hor.).

dropsy, *aqua intercus, hydrops* (Hor.).

dross. LIT., *scoria* (Plin.). TRANSF., = refuse, *faex, sentina, quisquiliae (-arum*, plur.).

drought, *siccitas*.

drove, *grex, armentum*.

drover, *pecuarius, armentarius*.

drown. LIT. (*in aquam*) *summergĕre, aquā suffocare*. TRANSF., with noise, *obstrepĕre*.

drowsy, *somniculosus, semisomnus, oscitans* (= yawning).

drudge, subst. *servus, mediastinus*.

drudge, v. *servire*.

drudgery, *opera servilis*; sometimes *sudor*.

drug, subst. *medicamentum*; poisonous —, *venenum*.

drug, v., render by phrase with *medicamentum*.

drum, *tympanum*: to beat the —, *tympanum pulsare*.

drunk, *ebrius, temulentus*.

drunkenness, as a state, *ebrietas*; as a habit, *ebriositas, vinolentia*.

drunkard, *homo ebriosus, vinolentus*.

dry, adj. LIT., *siccus, aridus* (= withered, parched), *sitiens* (= thirsty), *torridus*. TRANSF., *exilis, frigidus, ieiunus, aridus, austerus*.

dry, v. (1) transit. *siccare*: to — tears, *abstergēre lacrimas*. (2) intransit. *siccari, arescĕre*.

dryness. LIT., *siccitas*. TRANSF., *ieiunitas, exilitas, siccitas*.

dry-nurse, *nutrix assa*.

dubious; see DOUBTFUL.

duck, subst. *anas*; duck (or colloq. ducks) as a term of endearment, *corculum* (Pl.); see also DARLING.

duck, v. (1) under water, *(sub)mergĕre, demergĕre in aquam*. (2) to — the head, *caput demittĕre*.

duckling, *anaticula*.

ductile, *ductilis* (Plin.).

dudgeon, *ira, stomachus*: in high —, *iratus*.

due, subst. in gen. *ius* (*iuris*), *debitum*; dues = money due, *vectigal*; harbour —, *portorium*.

due, adj. (1) = owed, *debitus*: to be —, *debēri*; to pay money before it is —, *pecuniam repraesentare*. (2) more generally, *meritus, iustus idoneus, dignus*.

duel, *certamen*; or render more exactly by phrase.

dulcimer, *sambuca* (Pl., Pers.).

dull, adj. (1) of colours, *hebes, obscurus*. (2) of cutting edges, *obtusus, hebes*. (3) of weather, = cloudy, *(sub)nubilus*. (4) of the mind = stupid, *tardus, hebes, obtusus*. (5) = uninteresting, *aridus, ieiunus, frigidus, insulsus*.

dull, v. *hebetare, obscurare, obtundĕre.*
dully, *languide, tarde, frigide.*
dulness, of mind, (*ingenii*) *tarditas, stupor*; other senses should be rendered by a phrase.
dumb, *mutus, elinguis*: to become —, *obmutescĕre*; to be —, i.e. silent, *tacēre.*
dumbfounder, *obstupefacĕre.*
dumbness, express by adj. or verb.
dun, adj. *fuscus, suffuscus.*
dun, v. = to demand, *flagitare, exposcĕre.*
dunce, *stipes, blennus* (Pl.).
dung, *stercus (-ŏris), fimus.*
dungeon, *carcer, robur.*
dunghill, *sterquilinium* (Pl.), *fimetum* (Plin.).
dupe, subst. *homo credulus.*
dupe, v. *lactare* (Pl.); see also DECEIVE.
duplicate; see COPY.
duplicity, *fallacia, fraus*; see DECEIT.
durable, *firmus, solidus, stabilis, perpetuus.*
durability, *firmitas, stabilitas.*
durably, *firme, solide, stabiliter.*
duration, *temporis spatium*: long —, *diuturnitas*; short —, *brevitas.*
during, *per* with acc. (= throughout); *in* with abl. (of time within which); *inter* with acc. (e.g. *inter cenam* = — dinner); often rendered by abl. absol. (e.g. — the reign of Augustus, *Augusto imperatore*).
dusk, *crepusculum* (Pl., Ov.): it grows —, *advesperascit.*
dusky, *fuscus*; see DARK.
dust, subst. *pulvis*: to raise —, *pulverem movēre* or *excitare*; to lay the —, *pulverem sedare*; to throw — in a person's eyes, *tenebras homini offundere.*
dust, v. *detergĕre.*
duster; see BRUSH.
dusty, *pulverulentus.*
dutiful, duteous, *pius, officiosus.*
dutifully, *pie, officiosē.*
dutifulness, *pietas, oboedientia.*
duty, (1) one's —, *officium, munus*; sense of —, *pietas, religio, fides*; it is my —, *meum est or debeo.* (2) = tax, *vectigal.*
dwarf, *nanus* (Juv.), *pumilio* (Sen.).
dwarfish, *pusillus.*
dwell, *habitare, (in)colĕre, domicilium habēre*; to — upon a subject, *in re commorari, rem longius prosequi.*
dweller, *incola.*
dwelling, *domicilium, sedes, domus.*
dwindle, *(de)minui, decrescĕre, extenuari.*
dye, subst. *fucus* (of a red colour: Hor.); generally to be rendered by verb, e.g. *tingo.*
dye, v. *tingĕre, inficĕre, colorare.*
dyer, *infector.*
dynasty, use phrase with *domus* (e.g. *domus Flavia*).
dyspepsia, *cruditas.*
dyspeptic, *crudus.*

E

each. (1) of two, *uterque*; from (or on) — side, *utrimque*; in — direction, *utroque*. (2) of three or more, *unusquisque, quisque, omnis*; one —, two —, etc., use distrib. adj.; — other, *inter se, alius alium.*
eager. (1) for anything, *rei* (genit.) *cupidus,*
avidus, studiosus, adpetens. (2) in gen. = keen, *acer, fervidus.*
eagerly, *cupide, studiose, acriter.*
eagerness, *cupiditas, aviditas, studium, adpetentia, ardor, impetus (-ūs).*
eagle, *aquila.*
ear. (1) as part of the body, *auris*; sometimes *auricula*: to be over head and —s in debt, *aere alieno demersum esse.* (2) of corn, *spica, arista.*
early, adj. *matutinus* (= in the morning), *novus* (= fresh, just begun), *maturus* (= in good time), *tempestivus* (also = in good time, esp. of banquets), *praematurus* (= too early).
early, adv. *mane* (in the morning), *mature, tempestive* (= in good time), *praemature* (= too early).
earn, *merēre* and *merēri*: to — one's living, *victum quaerere* (or *quaeritare*).
earnest, subst, *arrhabo* or *arrha* (Pl., Plin.).
earnest, adj. *enixus, intentus, gravis, serius*: in —, *serio.*
earnestly, *acriter, intente, impense, magnopere.*
earnestness, *studium, contentio.*
earnings, *quaestus (-ūs), lucrum.*
earrings, *inaures (-ium,* plur.).
earth. (1) = soil, *terra, solum.* (2) = the globe, *terra, orbis (terrarum), tellus (-uris*; poet.).
earth-born, *terrigena* (Lucr., Ov.).
earthen, *terrenus.*
earthenware, as adj., *fictilis*; as subst., *fictilia (-ium,* plur.).
earthly, *terrestris*; as opposed to heavenly, *humanus*: — life, *haec vita.*
earthquake, *terrae motus (-ūs).*
earthwork, *agger.*
earth-worm, *vermis.*
ease, subst. (1) = rest, *tranquillitas, quies, otium, pax*: to be at —, *quiescĕre*; at — (mentally), *tranquillo animo.* (2) = readiness, *facilitas.*
ease, v. *exonerare, laxare, (ad)levare, expedire.*
easily. (1) = without difficulty, *facile, nullo negotio.* (2) = tranquilly, *tranquille, quiete, placide.*
easiness, *facilitas,* esp. of temper, for which also *indulgentia*; — of belief, *credulitas.*
east, subst. *oriens, orientis (solis) terrae* or *partes.*
eastern, easterly, express by genit. *orientis,* or by phrase, such as *ad orientem versus.*
easy. (1) = not difficult, *facilis, expeditus, proclivis.* (2) = tranquil, *tranquilus, quietus, otiosus, placidus.* (3) of temper, *facilis, indulgens, remissus.*
eat, *edĕre, comedĕre, (re) vesci, manducare* (= to chew), *vorare* (= to swallow), *gustare* (= to taste): to — away, *rodĕre* (Ov.).
eatable, *esculentus, edulis* (Hor.).
eatables; see FOOD.
eating-house, *popina.*
eaves, *suggrunae (-arum,* plur.: Vitr.).
eaves-dropper, *auceps* (Pl.).
ebb, subst. *aestūs decessus (-ūs),* or *recessus (-ūs)*: at the —, *minuente aestu.*
ebb, v. *recedĕre, cadĕre.*
ebony, *hebenus* (Verg.).
ebriety, *ebrietas, temulentia*; see DRUNK.
Ebro, *Hiberus.*
ebullition. LIT., use *effervescĕre.* TRANSF., of passions, *impetus (-ūs), aestus (-ūs).*

eccentric, *inusitatus, novus, mirus.*
echo, subst. *imago vocis.*
echo, v. LIT., = to give an —, *voci respondēre, vocem reddĕre, remittĕre, referre, resonare.* TRANSF., = to imitate, repeat, *adsentari, exprimĕre.*
éclat, *gloria.*
eclipse, subst. *defectio, defectus (-ūs).*
eclipse, v. transit. *obscurare* (lit. and fig.): to be —d, of sun or moon, *obscurari, deficĕre, laborare.*
economical, *frugi, attentus, diligens, parcus.*
economically, *diligenter, parce.*
economy. (1) = household management, *rei familiaris administratio;* political —, *rei publicae administratio.* (2) = frugality, *parsimonia.*
ecstasy. (1) = frenzy, *insania, furor.* (2) = bliss, *elatio, voluptaria.*
ecstatic, *fanaticus, furens, insanus.*
eddy, *vertex.*
edge. (1) a cutting —, *acies;* with the — of the sword, *caesim.* (2) = margin, *margo, ora, fimbriae (-arum,* plur.); often rendered by adj. *extremus.*
edible, *esculentus, edulis* (Hor.).
edict, *edictum, decretum, consultum, iussum.*
edify, *docēre.*
edit, *librum edĕre.*
edition, *editio* (Quint.).
educate, *instituĕre, erudire, educare.*
education, *educatio, disciplina, doctrina, eruditio:* a man of good —, *homo liberaliter educatus.*
educator, *magister, praeceptor, educator* (Tac.).
eel, *anguilla* (Pl., Juv.).
efface, *delēre, abolēre, exstinguĕre.*
effect, subst. (1) = consequence, *effectus (-ūs), eventus (-ūs), consecutio.* (2) = influence, *vis, effectus (-ūs):* to have great —, *multum valēre;* without —, *frustra, nequioquam.* (3) = purpose, gist: to this —, *use huiusmodi,* with subst. (4) in —, *revera, reapse.* (5) effects = property, *res, bona (-orum,* plur.).
effect, v. *facĕre, efficĕre, conficĕre.*
effective, effectual, as philosoph. t. t. *efficiens;* in gen. *efficax.*
effectively, *efficienter, efficaciter* (Quint.); sometimes *graviter* (= weightily).
effeminacy, *mollitia, mollities, vita delicata.*
effeminate, *mollis, effeminatus, delicatus, muliebris.*
effeminately, *molliter, effeminate, muliebriter.*
effervesce, *effervescĕre.*
effervescence, render by verb.
effete, *effetus, obsoletus.*
efficiency, efficacy, *efficientia, vis.*
efficient, *habilis;* see also EFFECTIVE.
effigy, *effigies, imago, simulacrum.*
efflux, *effluvium.*
effort, *opera, labor, contentio, conatus (-ūs):* to make an —, *operam dare, contendĕre, (e)niti.*
effrontery, *impudentia, os (impudens).*
effulgence, *splendor, fulgor.*
egg, subst. *ovum:* a fresh —, *ovum recens;* to lay —s, *ova parĕre, gignĕre;* yoke of —, *vitellus;* white of —, *album* or *albumen ovi* (Plin., Cels.). Prov.: teach your grandmother to suck —s, *sus Minervam, ut aiunt, docet.*
egg, v., to — on; see INCITE.
egg-shell, *ovi putamen* (Plin.).
egoism, egotism, *sui ostentatio, sui amor.*

egoist, egotist, *qui sibi soli studet* (or *consulit*).
egregious (in good or bad sense), *insignis, singularis, praeclarus.*
egress, *egressus (-ūs), exitus (-ūs).*
eider-down, render by phrase such as *plumae (anatum) mollissimae.*
eight, adj. *octo:* — each, *octoni;* — times, *octies.*
eighteen, *duodeviginti:* — times, *decies octies*
eighteenth, *duodevicesimus.*
eighth, *octavus:* an —, *octava pars.*
eightieth, *octogesimus.*
eighty, *octoginta:* — each, *octogeni;* — times, *octogies.*
either, *alteruter;* = which ever you like, *utervis, uterlibet;* if either . . ., *si uter . . .;* either . . . or, *aut . . . aut* (where one must be true, and both cannot be), *vel . . . vel* (used more freely); not . . . either . . . or, *neque (nec) . . . neque (nec).*
ejaculate, *vocem emittĕre.*
ejaculation, *vox.*
eject, *eicĕre, extrudĕre, expellĕre;* from a property, *deicĕre.*
ejection, *expulsio, eiectio, deiectio.*
eke, v.: to — out, *rei* (dat.) *parcĕre.*
elaborate, adj. *elaboratus, exquisitus, accuratus.*
elaborate, v. *elaborare, expolire.*
elaborately, *exquisite, accurate.*
elaboration, *diligentia;* or render by verb.
elapse, of time (= to pass between events), *intercedĕre, interesse, praeterire.*
elastic, fig.; see HOPEFUL.
elated, *elatus:* to become —, *efferri.*
elation, *animus elatus;* = joy, *gaudium.*
Elbe, *Albis.*
elbow, *cubitum.*
elder, *maior* (natu).
elderly, *aetate provectus.*
elect, adj. *designatus.*
elect, v. *creare, legĕre, eligĕre, deligĕre, designare;* as a colleague, *cooptare:* — into a premature vacancy, *sufficĕre.*
election. (1) the act of choice, *electio, suffragia (-orum,* plur.: = the votes). (2) as an occasion, *comitia (-orum,* plur.): to hold an —, *comitia habēre;* day of —, *dies comitialis.*
electioneering, subst. *ambitio.*
electioneering, adj. *candidatorius.*
elective, *suffragiis creatus.*
elector, *qui ius suffragii habet;* as polit. t. t., *elector* (late Latin).
elegance, *elegantia, urbanitas, venustas, munditia.*
elegant, *elegans, venustus, bellus, lautus, nitidus, comptus, mundus, urbanus.*
elegantly, *eleganter, venuste, belle, nitide, urbane.*
elegy, *elegia, elegi (-orum,* plur.).
element. (1) as scientific t. t. *elementum;* in plur., *principia rerum, primordia rerum.* (2) in gen. = a part, *membrum, pars.* (3) in plur. = the first principles of a subject, *elementa (-orum), principia (-orum), rudimenta (-orum).* (4) to be in one's —, *re familiariter uti;* to be out of one's —, *in re peregrinum ac hospitem esse.*
elementary, *primus;* or render by phrase.
elephant, *elephantus, elephas.*
elevate. LIT., *(at)tollĕre, extollĕre, levare.* TRANSF., *tollĕre, evehĕre, efferre.*
elevated. LIT., of places, *editus, altus, (ex)celsus, praecelsus.* TRANSF., *elatus, (ex)celsus.*

elevation. (1) = a raising, *elatio*; or render by verb. (2) of mind or character, *magnanimitas elatio, altitudo.* (3) = rising ground, *locus editus* or *superior.*

eleven, *undecim* : — each, *undēni*; — times, *undecies.*

eleventh, *undecimus.*

elf; see FAIRY.

elicit, *elicĕre, evocare eblandiri* (by coaxing), *extorquēre* (by force).

eligibility, of things, *opportunitas*; of persons, express by adj. *dignus.*

eligible, *opportunus, idoneus, dignus.*

elk, *alces.*

ell, *ulna, cubitum.*

elm, *ulmus* (Verg.); of an —, *ulmeus* (Pl.).

elocution, *pronuntiatio.*

elongate; see LENGTHEN.

elope, express by phrase, such as *clam fugĕre.*

elopement, *fuga.*

eloquence, *eloquentia, facultas* or *vis* or *copia dicendi, facundia* (Hor., Tac.).

eloquent, *eloquens, dicendi peritus, facundus, disertus* (= fluent).

eloquently, *copiose, facunde, diserte.*

else, adj. *alius.*

else, adv. (1) = besides, *praeterea.* (2) = otherwise, *aliter, alioqui(n).*

elsewhere, *alibi.*

elucidate; see EXPLAIN.

elude, *eludĕre, (e)vitare, declinare.*

elusive, *fallax.*

Elysium, *Elysium* (Verg.); see also PARADISE.

Elysian, *Elysius* (Verg.)

emaciate, *attenuare, macerare.*

emaciated, *macer.*

emaciation, *macies.*

emanate, *emanare, fluĕre, effundi.*

emancipate, *liberare*; of slaves, *manumittĕre.*

emancipation, *liberatio*; — of slaves, *manumissio.*

emancipator, *liberator.*

embalm, *condire.*

embank, *molem opponĕre fluctibus.*

embankment, *agger, moles.*

embark, v. (1) transit. *imponĕre in navem.* (2) intransit. *conscendĕre (navem)*; fig.: to — upon a course, *rationem inire.*

embarrass. (1) = to confuse, *(con)turbare.* (2) = to hinder, *(hominem) impedire, (homini) obstare* or *officĕre.*

embarrassed, *impeditus.*

embarrassing, *difficilis, dubius.*

embarrassment, *implicatio, scrupulus* : financial —, *angustiae (-arum,* plur.*), res angusta domi* (Juv.).

embassy, *legatio, legati (-orum,* plur.).

embattled, *instructus.*

embellish, *(ex)ornare, decorare.*

embellishment, *decus (-oris,* n.*), ornamentum.*

embers, *cinis, favilla.*

embezzle, *avertĕre, intervertĕre, intercipĕre, supprimĕre.*

embezzlement, *peculatus (-ūs), suppressio.*

embezzler, *pecuniae aversor, interceptor.*

embitter, *exacerbare.*

embittered, *uniquus, inimicus.*

emblem, *insigne, signum, simulacrum.*

embodiment, *simulacrum, effigies.*

embody: to — troops, *milites conscribĕre*; in gen. = to include, *includĕre.*

embolden, *confirmare*; or use phrase.

emboss, use *caelare.*

embrace, subst. *amplexus (-ūs), complexus (-ūs).*

embrace, v. LIT., *amplecti, amplexari, complecti.* TRANSF., (1) = to contain, *comprehendĕre, complecti.* (2) to — an opportunity, *occasionem capere* or *adripĕre.* (3) to — an opinion, *in sententiam transire, sententiae adsentiri.*

embrocation, *fomentum* (Cels.).

embroider, *(acu) pingĕre* (poet.): to — figures on a fabric, or some second material into it, *intexĕre* (poet.).

embroidery, *ars acu pingendi* : a piece of —, *pictura* (Lucr.), *opus acu pictum.*

embroil, *conturbare*: to — in a matter, *rē implicare.*

embryo, *partus (-ūs).*

emend, *emendare, corrigĕre.*

emendation, *emendatio*; or render by verb.

emerald, *smaragdus* (Lucr., Ov.).

emerge, *emergĕre, exsistĕre.*

emergency, *casus (-ūs), discrimen, tempus.*

emigrant, render by verb.

emigrate, *(e)migrare, demigrare.*

emigration, *(e)migratio.*

eminence. (1) = high ground, *locus editus, clivus, tumulus.* (2) = distinction, *praestantia, fastigium, amplissimus gradus (-ūs).*

eminent, *insignis, (prae)clarus, nobilis, egregius, eximius.*

eminently, *egregie, eximie, praecipue, imprimis, prae ceteris*; sometimes adequately rendered by a superlative.

emissary, *legatus, emissarius.*

emit, *(e)mittĕre, iacĕre.*

emolument, *emolumentum, lucrum, quaestus (-ūs).*

emotion, *animi motus (-ūs),* or *adfectus (-ūs),* or *commotio* or *concitatio.*

emperor, *imperator, princeps.*

emphasis, *vis, emphasis* (Quint.): to have —, *vim habēre, multum valēre.*

emphasize, render by phrase, such as *vehementius dicere.*

emphatic, *gravis, vehemens*; emphatic repetition (as rhet. t. t.), *concursio.*

emphatically, *graviter, vehementer.*

empire, *imperium, principatus (-ūs), regnum.*

empirical, adj. *in usu tantum et experimentis positus* (Cels.): an — physician, *empiricus.*

employ, *(re) uti*; *(rem) usurpare, exercēre* : to — for a particular purpose, *rem* (or *hominem*) *ad rem adhibēre, in re conlocare*; pass., of persons, to be —ed, *detinēri, versari, occupatum esse.*

employment. (1) as an act, *usus (-ūs), usurpatio.* (2) = business, *res, negotium.*

emporium, *emporium.*

empower, *homini rei* (genit.) *potestatem facĕre.*

emptiness, *inanitas.*

empty, adj. LIT., *inanis, vacuus, cassus* (poet.). TRANSF., *inanis, vanus, cassus.*

empty, v. *vacuefacĕre, exinanire, exonerare* (= to unload), *exhaurire* (= to drain).

empyrean, *caelum.*

emulate, *aemulari.*

emulation, *aemulatio.*

emulator, *aemulator, aemulus.*

emulous, *aemulus.*

emulously, *certatim.*

enable, *homini rei* (genit.) *facultatem facĕre.*

enact, *(legem) sancire, sciscĕre, iubēre;* more generally, *statuĕre, constituĕre:* to get (a law) enacted, *perferre.*

enactment, = law, *sanctio, lex, plebiscitum, senatusconsultum.*

enamoured; see LOVE.

encamp, v. *castra ponĕre, considĕre.*

enchant. LIT., *(ef)fascinare.* TRANSF., *capĕre, permulcēre, delectare.*

enchantment. LIT., see CHARM. TRANSF., *delectatio, blandimentum, inlecebra.*

enchantress, *venefica.*

encircle, *circumplecti, cingĕre, circumdare.*

enclose, *includĕre, cingĕre, saepire, continēre.*

enclosure, = enclosed place, *saeptum, saepimentum.*

encomium, *laus, laudatio.*

encompass; see ENCIRCLE.

encore, v. transit. *revocare.*

encounter, subst. *congressus (-ūs), concursio:* a hostile —, *concursus (-ūs).*

encounter, v. (1) of one person (or party) meeting another (with or without hostility), *concurrĕre, congredi, obviam fieri* (or *ire*): to — by chance, *incidĕre, offendĕre.* (2) = to face unwelcome things, *obire, oppetĕre* (esp. of death).

encourage, *(ad)hortari, cohortari, confirmare, excitare, erigĕre, animum (homini) addĕre.*

encouragement, *confirmatio, (ad)hortatio, cohortatio, hortamen(tum).*

encroach, v.: in gen. to — on, *occupare, invadĕre;* to — on rights, *ius imminuĕre.*

encroachment, *iniuria.*

encumber, *onerare, praegravare, impedire.*

encumbrance, *onus (-ĕris,* n.), *impedimentum.*

end, subst. (1) = termination, *finis, exitus (-ūs), clausula* (= the conclusion of anything written), *caput* (= top or extremity of a physical object); often also rendered by the adj. *extremus* (e.g. *in extrema oratione,* at the — of the speech). Phrases: in the —, *tandem, denique;* to bring to an —, put an — to, see END, v.; the war has come to an —, *debellatum est.* (2) = aim or object, *finis, consilium, propositum:* to what —? *quo?*

end, v. (1) transit. *finire, conficĕre, terminare, ad finem adducĕre* or *perducĕre:* to — a meeting, or contest, *dirimĕre.* (2) intransit. *finem* or *exitum habere, desinere,* or use pass. of transit. verbs: to — well (badly), *bene (male) evenire.*

endanger, *in periculum,* or *in discrimen, adducĕre* or *vocare, periclitari.*

endear, *devincire.*

endearments, *blanditiae (-arum,* plur.).

endeavour, subst. *conatus (-ūs), nisus (-ūs), contentio.*

endeavour, v. *conari, (e)niti, contendĕre.*

ending; see END, subst.

endless, *infinitus, perpetuus, aeternus, sempiternus.*

endlessly, *sine fine, perpetuo.*

endorse; see ALLOW, SANCTION.

endow. (1) to — a daughter, *dotem filiae dare.* (2) in gen. *hominem,* etc., *re donare, instruĕre, ornare, locupletare.*

endowed, *(re) ornatus, praeditus, instructus.*

endue; see ENDOW.

endurance, *patientia, perpessio, tolerantia.*

endure. (1) = to bear, *(per)ferre, sustinēre, tolerare, pati, perpeti.* (2) = to last, *(per)manere, durare.*

endurable, *tolerabilis, patibilis.*

enduring, *perpetuus, perennis.*

enemy, *hostis* (public), *inimicus* (personal or private), *adversarius* (= any kind of opponent): of (or like) an —, *hostilis.*

energetic, *acer, strenuus, impiger, vehemens.*

energetically, *acriter, strenue, impigre, vehementer.*

energy, *vis, vigor, virtus (-ūtis), impetus (-ūs), contentio.*

enervate, *enervare, debilitare, (e)mollire, frangĕre.*

enervation, *debilitatio, languor.*

enfeeble; see ENERVATE.

enforce. (1) to — an argument, *confirmare.* (2) in gen. *exsequi.*

enfranchise, *in civitatem adscribĕre, adsciscĕre, accipĕre, recipĕre; civitate donare.*

enfranchisement, *civitas,* or *civitatis donatio.*

engage. (1) = to bind, make liable, *obligare, obstringĕre.* (2) = to hire, *conducĕre.* (3) = to — a person in conversation, *sermonem cum homine incipĕre, instituĕre, conferre.* (4) = to promise, undertake, *spondĕre, promittĕre, recipĕre.* (5) = to join battle with, *cum homine confligĕre, congredi.* (6) = to — in a business, *in rem ingredi, rem obire, suscipĕre.*

engaged. (1) = busy, *occupatus.* (2) — to be married, *sponsus, pactus.*

engagement. (1) = a promise, *sponsio, stipulatio, pactum, pactio, promissum:* to keep an —, *fidem servare;* an — to marry, *pactio nuptialis.* (2) = a promise to meet, appointment, *constitutum.* (3) = any piece of business, *occupatio, negotium.* (4) = a battle, *pugna, proelium.*

engaging, *blandus, suavis.*

engagingly, *suaviter.*

engender, *gignĕre, generare;* see also CAUSE, PRODUCE.

engine, *machina, machinatio, machinamentum.*

engineer, *machinator:* a military —, sapper, *faber.*

England, *Anglia;* but the more classical *Britannia* (= Britain) will often serve.

English, *Anglus, Anglicus,* or (more class.) *Britannus, Britannicus.*

engrave, *scalpĕre, incīdĕre, insculpĕre.*

engraving, *scalptura* (Plin., Suet.).

engraver, *scalptor* (Plin.).

engross. (1) = to buy up, *coëmĕre.* (2) = to occupy exclusively, *occupare, tenēre.*

engulf, *absorbēre, (de)vorare, (ex)haurire.*

enhance, *augēre, amplificare, (ex)ornare, exaggerare.*

enhancement, *accessio, amplificatio.*

enigma *aenigma (-ătis,* n.), *ambages (-um,* plur.).

enigmatic, *obscurus, perplexus, ambiguus.*

enigmatically, *ambigue, per ambages, perplexe.*

enjoin; see COMMAND.

enjoy. (1) = to have and take pleasure in, *rē frui, gaudēre; voluptatem capĕre* or *percipĕre ex re;* to — oneself, *se oblectare.* (2) = to have, simply, *re uti, rem habēre:* he —ed a good education, *liberaliter educatus est.*

enjoyment *fructus (-ūs), usus (-ūs), gaudium, voluptas.*

enkindle, *accendĕre, incendĕre, inflammare.*

enlarge. (1) = to make larger, *amplificare, dilatare, augēre, laxare.* (2) to — upon, *pluribus (verbis) disputare.*
enlargement, *amplificatio, incrementum*; often to be rendered by verb.
enlighten. LIT., *inlustrare, inluminare.* TRANSF., *docēre, erudire.*
enlightenment, *humanitas.*
enlist, v. (1) transit., of troops, *milites (con)-scribēre, comparare, sacramento adigēre* or *obligare*; in gen. = to win over, *conciliare.* (2) intransit. *nomen dare* or *profitēri, sacramentum dicēre.*
enlistment, render by verb.
enliven, *excitare, exhilarare.*
enmity, *inimicitia, odium, simultas.*
ennoble, LIT., *nobilium ordini adscribēre.* TRANSF., in gen., *ornare, honestare, inlustrare.*
ennui, *taedium.*
enormity. (1) as a quality, *immanitas.* (2) = a monstrous action, *scelus* (-eris, n.), *flagitium, facinus* (-oris, n.).
enormous, *ingens, immanis, immensus.*
enormously, *praeter modum,* or render by superl. of adj. (e.g. — high, *altissimus*).
enough, *sat, satis, adfatim*: more than —, *nimis, abunde, satis superque*; not —, *parum*; but —! *sed haec hactenus.*
enquire, see INQUIRE.
enquiry, see INQUIRY.
enrage, *irritare, exasperare, inflammare.*
enrapture, *oblectare, capēre.*
enrich, *locupletare, locupletem facēre, ditare, divitiis ornare.*
enroll, (ad)scribēre; see also ENLIST.
enshrine, *dedicare consecrare.*
ensign (1) = a banner, *signum (militare), vexillum.* (2) = a banner-bearer, *signifer, aquilifer, vexillarius.*
enslave, (hominem) in servitutem redigēre, or servitute adficēre; (homini) servitutem iniungēre.
enslaved. LIT., use *servus.* TRANSF., *addictus, emancipatus.*
ensnare, (lit. and fig.) *capēre, inretire, inlicēre.*
entail. LIT., express by phrase. TRANSF., *adferre, inferre*; see also CAUSE.
entangle, (lit. and fig.) *impedire, implicare, inretire.*
entanglement, *implicatio.*
enter. LIT., = to go in or into, *intrare, introire, inire, ingredi*: to — in a vehicle, or on horseback, *invehi.* TRANSF., (1) = — into, or upon, any undertaking, *ingredi, inire, suscipēre, incipere*: to — public life, *ad rempublicam accedēre*; to — an alliance, *societatem facēre.* (2) to — into a book, *referre.*
enterprise, *inceptum, opus* (-ĕris, n.), *facinus* (-ŏris, n.: usually bold and bad).
enterprising, *promptus, acer, strenuus, audax.*
entertain. (1) = to have, *habēre.* (2) = to amuse, *delectare, oblectare.* (3) = to receive hospitably, *hospitio accipēre, excipēre.*
entertainer, *hospes.*
entertaining; see AMUSING.
entertainment. (1) = hospitality, *hospitium*; (2) = banquet, *epulae* (-arum, plur.), *convivium.* (3) see AMUSEMENT.
enthusiasm, *studium, fervor, ardor, alacritas*; sometimes *furor.*

enthusiast, *homo fanaticus*; or render by phrase.
enthusiastic, *fanaticus, ardens, fervidus, calidus vehemens.*
enthusiastically, *ardenter, acriter, vehementer.*
entice, *adlicēre, adlectare, inlicēre, pellicēre.*
enticement, *inlecebrae, esca.*
enticing, *blandus, inlecebrosus* (Pl.).
enticingly, *blande, inlecebrose* (Pl.).
entire, *totus, integer, solidus.*
entirely, *omnino, plane, prorsus, penitus.*
entirety, render by *totus.*
entitle. (1) = to name, *inscribēre, appellare, nominare.* (2) = to give a title to, *ius* or *potestatem aliquid faciendi dare.*
entomb, *humare, condēre.*
entrails, *intestina* (-orum, plur.), *viscera* (-um, plur.), *exta* (-orum, plur.).
entrance, subst. (1) as an act, *ingressio, introitus* (-ūs). (2) = place of —, *aditus* (-ūs), *introitus* (-ūs), *ostium*; see also DOOR.
entrap; see ENSNARE.
entreat, *precari, rogare, orare, obsecrare*: to — successfully, *exorare.*
entrench, *vallo* or *fossā* or *operibus (com)-munire, vallare.*
entrenchment, *vallum, munitio, munimentum, opera* (-um, plur.).
entrust, *(con)credēre, committēre, permittēre, mandare, commendare.*
entry; see ENTRANCE; in accounts, *nomen* (e.g. *nomen in tabulas referre,* to make an —).
entwine, *(in)nectēre, implicare, redimire* (all these are poet.); *circumplicare* (Cic.).
enumerate, *(di)numerare, enumerare.*
enunciate, *edicēre, indicare, pronuntiare, enuntiare.*
enunciation, *enuntiatio.*
envelope, subst. *involucrum.*
envelope, v. *involvēre, obducēre, circumfundēre.*
envenom. LIT., *venenare, veneno imbuēre.* TRANSF., *exasperare, exacerbare.*
enviable, *fortunatus, beatus*; or render by phrase.
envious, *invidus, lividus*: an — disposition, *invidentia.*
environ, *circumdare, circumplecti.*
environs, render by phrase with *loca* and *circum.*
envoy, *legatus*; see AMBASSADOR.
envy, subst. *invidia, livor, malevolentia.*
envy, v. (rem homini) *invidēre.*
ephemeral, *unius diei, caducus, brevis.*
epic, adj. *epicus, herōicus*: an —, or — poem, *epos* (in nom. and acc. sing. only).
Epicurean. LIT., adj. and subst. *Epicurēus.* TRANSF., in gen. = hedonist, hedonistic, *voluptarius.*
epidemic, *morbus, pestilentia, lues.*
epigram, *epigramma* (-ătis, n.).
epigrammatic, *salsus.*
epilepsy, *morbus comitialis* (Sen.).
epilogue, *epilŏgus.*
episcopacy, *episcopatus* (-ūs: eccl.).
episode, *embolium, excursus* (-ūs).
epistle, *epistula, litterae* (-arum, plur.).
epitaph, *titulus, elogium.*
epithalamium, *epithalamium* (Quint.), *carmen nuptiale.*
epithet, *epitheton* (Quint.).

epitome, *epitome, summarium* (Sen.).
epitomize; see ABRIDGE.
epoch, *tempus* (-ŏris, n.), *aetas, saeculum.*
equable, *aequus, aequabilis, constans, stabilis.*
equability, *aequus animus, aequabilitas.*
equably, *aequo animo, aequabiliter.*
equal, subst. *par, compar* (Pl.).
equal, adj. *aequus, aequalis, par, parilis* (poet.), *compar:* to divide into twelve — parts, *in duodecim partes aequaliter dividĕre;* to be — to doing anything, *sufficĕre.*
equal, v. *(ad)aequare, aequiparare.*
equality, *aequalitas, aequabilitas.*
equalize, *(ex)aequare, adaequare.*
equally, *aeque, aequaliter, pariter.*
equanimity, *aequus animus, aequitas animi, aequa mens* (Hor.).
equator, *circulus aequinoctialis* (Varro).
equestrian, subst. *eques* (-ĭtis).
equestrian, adj. *equester* or *equestris.*
equidistant, to be, *pari intervallo inter se distare.*
equilateral, *aequis lateribus.*
equilibrium, *aequilibrium* (Sen.): to hold in —, *librare.*
equinox, *aequinoctium.*
equinoctial, *aequinoctialis* (Plin.).
equip, *armare, instruĕre, ornare.*
equipment, *arma* (-orum, plur.), *armamenta* (-orum, plur., esp. of ships), *armatura, instrumenta* (-orum, plur.).
equipoise; see EQUILIBRIUM.
equitable, adj. *aequus, iustus, meritus.*
equity, *aequitas, aequum, iustitia.*
equivalent: to be — to anything, *pro re valēre;* see also EQUAL.
equivocal, *ambiguus, anceps, dubius.*
equivocation, *ambiguitas, amphibolia.*
equivocate, *tergiversari.*
era, *tempus;* see also AGE.
eradicate, *exstirpare, evellĕre, eruĕre, exstinguĕre, excīdĕre, eradĕre, tollĕre.*
eradication, *exstinctio,* or render by verb.
erase, *delēre, inducĕre.*
erasure, *litura.*
ere, *priusquam, antequam;* see also BEFORE.
erect, adj. *(e)rectus.*
erect, v. (1) = to set upright, *erigĕre, tollĕre.* (2) = to build, *aedificare, exstruĕre, excitare.*
erection. (1) as an act, *aedificatio, exstructio.* (2) = a building, *aedificium.*
erotic, *amatorius.*
err, *errare, vagari, in errore versari; falli* (= to be mistaken); *peccare* or *delinquĕre* (= to go wrong, sin).
errand, *mandatum:* an —-boy, *nuntius, tabellarius.*
erratic, *vagus, inconstans, erraticus* (rare).
erroneous, *falsus.*
erroneously, *falso, perperam.*
error, *error, erratum, peccatum* (= a sin).
erst, *quondam, olim.*
erudite, *litteratus, doctus, eruditus.*
erudition, *doctrina, eruditio.*
eruption, *eruptio.*
escape, subst. *fuga, effugium.*
escape, v. (1) transit. *rem (hominem) (ef)fugĕre, subterfugĕre; elabi, evadĕre* (with *ex* and abl.); of facts, etc.: to — one's observation or memory, *fugĕre, praeterire, fallĕre.* (2) intransit. *(ef)fugĕre, elabi, evadĕre.*

escarpment, *vallum.*
escheat, subst. *hereditas caduca* (Leg.).
eschew, *vitare;* see also AVOID.
escort, *comitatus* (-ūs): under a person's —, *homine comitante.*
escort, v. *comitari, deducĕre, prosequi.*
esculent, *esculentus.*
esoteric, *arcanus, occultus.*
especial, *praecipuus;* sometimes *maximus, summus.*
especially, *praesertim, praecipue, maxime, in primis (imprimis), summe.*
esplanade, *ambulatio.*
espouse; see BETROTH and MARRY.
esquire, *armiger* (late Latin).
essay, subst. (1) = an attempt, *conatus* (-ūs). (2) = a treatise, *libellus.*
essay, v. *conari.*
essayist, *scriptor.*
essence, *natura, vis:* it is the — of affection, *amicitiae (proprium) est.*
essential, *verus, proprius.*
essentially, *reapse, vere, necessario.*
establish. (1) = to set up, *statuĕre, instituĕre, constituĕre.* (2) = to make strong, *confirmare, stabilire.* (3) = to prove, *probare, vincĕre.*
establishment. (1) = act of —, *constitutio, confirmatio.* (2) = household, *familia.*
estate. (1) = condition, *status* (-ūs), *habitus* (-ūs), *condicio, fortuna, sors.* (2) = property, *res, fundus, praedium, ager, villa, possessio.*
esteem, subst. *opinio, existimatio.*
esteem, v. (1) = to think, *aestimare, existimare, putare.* (2) = to respect, *diligĕre, verēri, magni facĕre.*
estimable, *laudatus, bonus, optimus, honestus, gravis, probus.*
estimate, subst. (1) in terms of money, *aestimatio.* (2) in gen. = judgment, *iudicium.*
estimate, v. = to value, *aestimare, censēre.*
estimation; see ESTEEM.
estrange, *(ab)alienare.*
estrangement, *alienatio, discidium.*
estuary, *aestuarium.*
eternal, *aeternus, sempiternus, immortalis, perpetuus.*
eternally, *in aeternum, perpetuo, semper.*
eternity, *aeternitas:* for all —, *in aeternum, in perpetuum, in omne tempus.*
ether, *aether.*
ethereal, *aetherius.*
ethical, *moralis* (invented by Cicero); or use phrase with *mores* or *officia.*
ethics, *philosophia quae est de vita et moribus, philosophia moralis, ethice* (Quint.).
etiquette, *mos, usus* (-ūs).
etymology, *etymologia, explicatio verborum, nominum interpretatio.*
eucharist, *eucharistia* (eccl.).
eulogist, *laudator.*
eulogize, *(con)laudare.*
eulogy, *laudatio, laus.*
eunuch, *eunūchus, spado.*
euphemism, euphemistic, render by phrase, such as *mitiorem in partem vertere dicendo.*
euphony, *sonus* (-ūs) *dulcis* or *suavis.*
evacuate, *locum vacuefacĕre* or *(de)relinquĕre; loco (ex loco), discedĕre, excedĕre, egredi:* to — by withdrawing troops, *milites deducĕre.*
evade, *(ef)fugĕre, subterfugere;* see also ESCAPE: to — the point, *tergiversari.*
evangelist, *evangelista* (eccl.).

evaporate, evaporation, express by phrases, such as *in vaporem vertĕre, verti*.
evasion, *latebra, ambages (-um,* plur.*), tergiversatio*.
evasive, *ambiguus*.
evasively, *ambigue*.
eve, subst.: on the — of, render by *instare* or *sub* (with acc.); see also EVENING.
even, adj. *aequus, planus*; of temper, *aequus, aequabilis*; of numbers, *par*.
even, adv. *etiam, vel, adeo*: not —, *ne* . . . *quidem*; — if, *etsi, etiamsi*.
evening, subst. *vesper (-ĕris,* or *-ĕri), tempus vespertinum*: in the —, *vesperi*; good —! *salve*; the — of life, *vita occidens*.
evening, adj. *vespertinus*: the — star, *Hesperus, Vesper*.
evenly, *aequaliter, aequabiliter, pariter*.
evenness, *aequalitas* (Sen.): — of temper, *aequus animus*.
event. (1) = result, *eventus (-ūs), exitus (-ūs)*. (2) = occurrence, *res (gesta), factum, casus (-ūs)*: at all —s, *certe, saltem*; in the — of, use *si*.
eventful, *memorabilis*: that — day, *ille dies*.
ever, adv. (1) = always, *semper, perpetuo*. (2) = at any time, *umquam (unquam), quando* (after *num* and *si*): for —, *in aeternum, in perpetuum*.
everlasting; see ETERNAL.
every, *quisque, omnis*: — one, each separately, *unusquisque*; one in — ten, *decimus quisque*; —body, *omnes (-ium,* plur.*)*, sometimes *nemo non,* or *nemo est quin*; — day, *cottidie* (see also DAILY); —thing, *omnia (-ium,* plur.*)*; — -where, *ubique, passim*; from — side, *undique*.
evict, *(ex)pellĕre, depellĕre, detrudĕre, deturbare*.
eviction, *evictio* (Leg.); or render by verb.
evidence, subst. (1) as legal t. t. *testimonium, indicium*. (2) in gen., *argumentum*.
evident, *manifestus, apertus, evidens, perspicuus*: it is —, *apparet, liquet* (with acc. and infin.).
evidently, *aperte, manifeste, perspicue, evidenter*.
evil, subst. *malum, incommodum*.
evil, adj. *malus, pravus, improbus*.
evil-doer, *(homo) maleficus*.
evil-speaking, *maledicus*.
evince, *ostendĕre, probare, praestare*.
evoke, *evocare, elicĕre, excitare*.
evolve, *evolvĕre, explicare*.
evolution. (1) of soldiers, *decursus (-ūs)*. (2) in nature, use phrase, such as *rerum progressio*.
ewe, *ovis femina*: — lamb, *agna*.
ewer, *urceus, hydria, urna*.
exacerbate; see EMBITTER.
exact, *exactus, subtilis, diligens*.
exact, v. *rem ab homine exigĕre, rem homini imperare*.
exacting, *rapax*.
exaction, *exactio*.
exactitude, exactness, *subtilitas, diligentia*.
exactly, *diligenter, accurate, subtiliter*.
exaggerate, *augēre, in maius extollĕre*.
exaggeration, *superlatio, traiectio*: I dislike idle —, *nihil auctum ex vano velim* (Liv.).
exalt, *augēre, amplificare, evehĕre, efferre, (ex)tollĕre*.

exaltation, (1) of feeling, *elatio*. (2) in rank, use phrase such as *dignitatis accessio*.
exalted, *altus, (ex)celsus, elatus*.
examination, *investigatio, inquisitio*.
examine, *investigare, inquīrĕre, inspicĕre, (per)scrutari*.
example, *exemplum, exemplar, documentum*: to set an —, *exemplum praebēre*; for —, *verbi causā, exempli gratia, vel*.
exasperate, *inritare, exacerbare, exasperare*.
exasperation, *ira*.
excavate, *(ex)cavare, effodĕre*.
excavation, *cavum*.
exceed, *excedĕre, egredi*.
excel, *excellĕre, praestare* (both with dat.); *(ex)superare* (with acc.).
excellence, *excellentia, praestantia*.
excellent, *excellens, praestans, egregius, optimus, praeclarus, praecipuus*.
excellently, *excellenter, egregie, optime, praecipue*.
except, prep. *praeter* (with acc.); sometimes *extra* (with acc.); often rendered by past partic. of *excipĕre* in abl. absol. (e.g. except you, *te excepto*); *nisi* after a neg. (e.g. *nisi in te nullam spem habeo*).
except, v. *excipĕre, eximĕre*.
excepted, *eximius*.
exception, *exceptio*; all without —, *omnes ad unum*.
exceptional, adj. *rarus*.
exceptionally, *praeter modum*.
excess. (1) in quantity, *nimium*. (2) in conduct, *intemperantia, licentia, luxuria*.
excessive, *nimius, immodicus, immoderatus*.
excessively, *nimis, immodice, immoderate, praeter modum*.
exchange, subst. *permutatio*; of money, *collybus*.
exchange, v. *(per)mutare*: to — letters, *litteras dare et accipĕre*.
exchequer, *aerarium, fiscus*.
excitable, *inritabilis, fervidus*.
excite. (1) of persons, *excitare, concitare, (com)movēre, incendĕre*. (2) of feelings, disturbances, etc., *(com)movēre, excitare, concitare, conflare*.
excited, *trepidus*.
excitement, *concitatio, commotio, perturbatio*.
exclaim, *(ex)clamare, vociferari, conclamare* (of more than one person).
exclamation, *exclamatio, vox*.
exclude, *excludĕre, prohibēre, eximĕre, arcēre*.
exclusion, *exclusio* (Ter.), or render by verb.
exclusive. (1) = in choice of acquaintance, render by phrase such as *parum adfabilis, rari aditūs est*. (2) of properties = belonging to one only, *proprius*.
excrement, *excrementum* (Plin.), *stercus (-ŏris)*.
excrescence, *tuber* (Ter., Plin.).
excruciating, *acerbissimus*: — pain, *dolor summus* or *maximus*.
exculpate, *excusare, (ex)purgare*.
exculpation, *purgatio*.
excursion, *iter (-ĭneris)*: to make an —, *excurrĕre*.
excusable, *excusabilis* (Ov.); or render by verb *excuso*.
excuse, subst. *excusatio*; see also PRETEXT.
excuse, v. (1) = to make excuses for, *excusare, (ex)purgare*. (2) = to pardon, *(homini) ignoscĕre, veniam dare*.

execrable; see ABOMINABLE.

execrate, *exsecrari, detestari, abominari*; see CURSE.

execute. (1) = to carry out, *exsequi, persequi, efficěre, perficěre*. (2) = to punish by death, *supplicium (de homine) suměre; hominem necare, securi ferire.*

execution. (1) = carrying out, *effectio*; or render by verb. (2) = capital punishment, *supplicium*. (3) — on goods, *bonorum venditio, emptio*. (4) = slaughter in gen., *strages, caedes.*

executioner, *carnifex.*

executive, use phrase with *administrare.*

exegesis, *explanatio, interpretatio.*

exemplary, adj.; see EXCELLENT.

exempt, adj. *immunis, liber, solutus, vacuus.*

exempt, v. *excipěre, eximěre, immunem facěre, liberare, solvěre.*

exemption, *immunitas, vacatio, vacuitas.*

exercise, subst. *exercitatio*; = a literary task, *thema (-atis*: Quint.).

exercise, v. transit. (1) = to carry on, *exercēre, facěre, efficěre, fungi* (with abl.). (2) = to work, train, *exercēre.*

exert, v. *contenděre, intenděre*: to — oneself, *niti, eniti, conari*; see also USE, EMPLOY, EXERCISE.

exertion, *contentio, intentio, conatus (-ūs).*

Exeter, *Isca Dumnoniorum.*

exhale, *(ex)halare.*

exhalation, *exhalatio.*

exhaust, *exhaurire* (lit. and fig.); in gen. = to wear out, *absuměre, consuměre, conficěre, fatigare.*

exhausted, *effetus, confectus, defessus, fatigatus.*

exhaustion; see FATIGUE.

exhibit, v. LIT., *proponěre, exponěre, exhibēre.* TRANSF., in gen. = to manifest, *praestare, praebēre.*

exhibition, = show, *spectaculum, ludi (-orum,* plur.).

exhilarate, *(ex)hilarare, hilarem facěre.*

exhilaration, *hilaritas.*

exhort, *(ad)hortari*; see ENCOURAGE.

exigence, *necessitas, angustiae (-arum,* plur.).

exile, subst. (1) = banishment, *exsilium, relegatio*: in —, adj. *extorris*; to be in —, *exsulare*. (2) = person banished, *exsul, profugus* (poet.).

exile, v. transit. *eicěre, exterminare, relegare, (ex)pellěre*; see also BANISH.

exist, *esse, exsistěre, exstare.*

existence, use *esse.*

exit. (1) = a going out, *exitus (-ūs), egressus (-ūs).* (2) = way out, *exitus (-ūs), effugium, ostium.*

exonerate, *(culpā) liberare.*

exorbitant, *immodicus.*

exorbitantly, *immodice.*

exordium, *exordium, prooemium.*

exoteric, Cic. uses the Greek word ἐξωτερικός, Gellius the Latin form *exotericus.*

exotic, *peregrinus, externus.*

expand, v. transit. *(ex)panděre, extenděre, laxare, dilatare.*

expanse, *spatium.*

expatiate, *pluribus (verbis) disputare.*

expatriate; see BANISH.

expect, *exspectare, sperare* (usually of good things).

expectant, *adrectus, suspensus.*

expectation, *exspectatio, spes, opinio.*

expectorate, *exscreare, exspuěre.*

expectoration, *exscreatio* (Plin.).

expediency, *utilitas.*

expedient, subst. *machina, ratio, consilium.*

expedient, adj. *commodus, utilis*: it is —, *expedit.*

expedite, *expedire, maturare.*

expedition. (1) = speed, *celeritas*. (2) military, *expeditio.*

expeditious, *celer, promptus, maturus.*

expeditiously, *celeriter, prompte, mature.*

expel, *(ex)pellěre, eicěre, exigěre.*

expend, *expenděre, impenděre, erogare* (of public money).

expense, *impensa, impendium, dispendium* (poet.), *sumptus (-ūs,* esp. excessive).

expensive, *sumptuosus, carus, pretiosus.*

expensively, *sumptuose, pretiose.*

expenditure, of public money, *erogatio*; in gen., see EXPENSE.

experience, subst. *(rerum) usus (-ūs), experientia, peritia* (including knowledge or skill gained by —): I speak from —, *expertus dico.*

experience, v. *experiri, pati, (usu) cognoscěre*: I — a thing, *res mihi usu venit.*

experienced, *(rerum) peritus, exercitatus, versatus in rebus.*

experiment, *experimentum, periculum*: an unfortunate —, *res infeliciter temptata.*

experimental, render by phrase.

expert, *sciens, callidus*; see also EXPERIENCED.

expertness, expertise, *calliditas, sollertia.*

expiate, *luěre, expiare*: *poenas sceleris dare, penděre, dependěre, solvěre.*

expiation, *expiatio, poena, piaculum, luella* (Lucr.).

expiatory, *piacularis.*

expiration. (1) physical, *exspiratio*. (2) = end, q.v.: at the — of the year, *anno exeunte*; after the — of the year, *anno exacto.*

expire. LIT., = to breathe one's last, *exspirare, animam edere.* TRANSF., of time = to end, *exire.*

explain, *exponěre, expedire, explanare, explicare, interpretari, enodare.*

explanation, *explicatio, explanatio, interpretatio, enodatio.*

explanatory, render by verb.

explicit, *apertus, definitus.*

explicitly, *plane, diserte, definite.*

explode. (1) transit. = to discredit (a theory), *exploděre, refellěre, confutare, refutare*. (2) intransit. = to burst, *dirumpi.*

export, *exportare.*

exportation, *exportatio.*

exports, *merces (quae exportantur).*

expose. (1) in gen. *exponěre*. (2) to — to (danger, etc.), *obicěre, offerre*. (3) = to show up, unmask, *detegěre, coarguěre*. (4) of parts of the body, *(de)nudare.*

exposition, *expositio*; see also EXPLANATION.

exposure, render by verb.

expound; see EXPLAIN.

express, (in words) *expriměre, significare, declarare, demonstrare*: to — oneself, *loqui, dicěre.*

expression. (1) = a thing said, *verbum, sententia, vocabulum, dictum, vox*. (2) of the features, *vultus (-ūs)*: void of —, *languens, languidus.*

expressive, of movements, *argutus*; of style, *significans* (Quint.); often expressed by *vis.*

expressively, *significanter* (Quint.).

expressiveness, *vis*; of movements, *argutiae* (-*arum*, plur.).

expulsion, *exactio, expulsio.*

expunge, *delēre, inducēre, oblitterare.*

expurgate, *(ex)purgare.*

exquisite, *exquisitus, conquisitus, venustus.*

exquisitely, *exquisite, venuste.*

extant: to be —, *exstare.*

extemporary, *subitus, extemporalis* (Quint.): to speak —, *ex tempore dicēre.*

extend, v. (1) transit. *extendēre, distendēre, augēre, propagare, amplificare, dilatare.* (2) intransit. *patēre, extendi, distendi*: to — to, *pertinēre ad.*

extension, = the act of extending, *porrectio* (e.g. *digitorum*), *productio, prolatio, propagatio.*

extensive, *magnus, amplus, latus.*

extensively, *late.*

extent, *ambitus* (-*ūs*), *spatium*: to this —, *hactenus*; to a certain —, *aliqua ex parte*; of what —? *quantus?*

extenuate, *levare, mitigare, minuēre.*

extenuation, *imminutio* (Quint.); or express by verb.

exterior, subst. *facies, forma, species.*

exterior, adj.; see EXTERNAL.

exterminate, *ad unum interficēre, interimēre, eradicare, exstirpare.*

extermination, *internecio, occidio.*

external, *externus, exter(us), exterior, extraneus.*

externally, *extrinsecus.*

extinct, *exstinctus, obsoletus.*

extinction, *exstinctio.*

extinguish, *exstinguēre, restinguēre.*

extirpate, *exstirpare, eradicare, excīdere.*

extol, *laudibus (ef)ferre, (con)laudare.*

extort, as an actionable offence, *exprimēre, extorquēre.*

extortion, *res repetundae*; otherwise render by verb.

extortionate, *rapax, avarus.*

extra, adv. *praeterea.*

extract, subst., render by verb.

extract, v. (1) in gen. *extrahēre, evellēre, exprimēre.* (2) from a book, *excerpēre.*

extraction. (1) as an act, *evulsio.* (2) = origin, *origo, genus* (-*eris*, n.).

extraneous; see EXTERNAL.

extraordinarily, *extra ordinem, praeter morem* or *consuetudinem* or *modum, mire, mirifice.*

extraordinary, *extraordinarius* (= specially arranged), *inusitatus, insolitus, novus, inauditus, mirus.*

extravagance. (1) in expenditure, express by *sumptus* (-*ūs*), with adj. (2) in gen. = excess, *intemperantia, immoderatio.*

extravagant. (1) = lavish, *prodigus, effusus, sumptuosus.* (2) in gen. = excessive, *nimius, immoderatus, immodicus, intemperans.*

extravagantly. (1) = lavishly, *prodige, effuse, sumptuose.* (2) in gen. = excessively, *immoderate, immodice, intemperanter.*

extreme, subst.; see EXTREMITY.

extreme, adj. *extremus, ultimus, summus.*

extremely, *summe*; often rendered by superl. (e.g. — good, *optimus*).

extremity. (1) physical: **a** = top, *cacumen, vertex, fastigium*: **b**, in gen. = farthest part, *extremitas*; or render by adj. *extremus.* (2) =

extreme degree, render by adj. *extremus* or *summus.*

extricate, *expedire, (ex)solvēre, liberare.*

extrude, v. transit. *extrudēre, expellēre, eicēre.*

exuberance, *ubertas, luxuria.*

exuberant, *luxuriosus, laetus*: to be —, *exuberare.*

exuberantly, *uberrime.*

exude, *(ex)sudare* (Verg.), *manare.*

exult, *exsultare, gestire, laetitiā efferri, laetari, gloriari.*

exultant, *laetus.*

exultation, *laetatio, exsultatio* (Tac.).

eye, subst. *oculus, lumen* (poet.), *ocellus* (poet.): before one's —s, *ante oculos, in conspectu*; blear——d, *lippus*; — in trees, etc., *oculus, gemma*; of a needle, *foramen.*

eye, v. *adspicēre, contemplari, intuēri*: to — askance, *oculis limis adspicēre.*

eye-ball, *pupula, pupilla* (Lucr.).

eyebrow, *supercilium.*

eye-lid, *palpebra* (usually plur.).

eyesight, *acies.*

eyesore, express by phrase such as *res horrida aspectu.*

eye-witness, *arbiter.*

F

fable, *fabula* (esp. with adj. such as *ficta* or *commenticia*).

fabled, **fabulous**, *fabulosus, fictus, commenticius, falsus.*

fabric, built, *aedificium*; woven, *textum, textile*; in gen., and fig., *compages.*

fabricate, *fabricari, texēre.*

fabrication. (1) = making, *fabricatio.* (2) = falsehood, *commentum, mendacium.*

fabricator, *auctor.*

face, subst. *facies, vultus* (-*ūs*: with ref. to the expression), *os* (-*oris*: properly = the mouth): — to —, *coram*; to make —s, *os distorquēre* (Ter.); to set one's — against, *adversari*; in the — of, see FACING.

face, v. (1) = to be opposite, *(a)spectare.* (2) = to encounter, confront, *obire* (with acc.); *obviam ire*, or *se opponēre* or *offerre* (with dat.). (3) to — about, *signa convertēre.*

facetious, *iocosus, iocularis, lepidus, facetus.*

facetiously, *iocose, lepide, facete.*

facetiousness, *facetiae* (-*arum*, plur.).

facial, *quod ad faciem pertinet.*

facilitate, *(rem) faciliorem reddere.*

facility, *facilitas.*

facing, *contra, adversus.*

facsimile, of a document, *descriptio imagoque tabularum* (Cic.).

fact, *res, factum*: in —, *reapse, etenim, sane, profecto.*

faction, *factio, pars.*

factious, *factiosus, partium studiosus, turbulentus, seditiosus.*

factiously, *per factionem, seditiose.*

factiousness, *factio, studium partium.*

factitious, adj.; see FALSE.

factor, *(negotiorum) (pro)curator.*

factory, *fabrica, officina*: — hands, *operae.*

faculty, *vis, facultas.*

fade, *pallescēre* (Ov.).

faded

faded; see PALE.
fading, = transient, *caducus, fluxus, fragilis.*
Faenza, *Faventia.*
fagot, *fascis, sarmenta* (*-orum,* plur.).
fail, subst.: without —, *certo, omnino.*
fail, v. (1) intransit.: **a** = to give out, prove inadequate, *deficĕre* (grow short), *deesse* (be short): **b** = not to succeed, *concidĕre, cadĕre, offendĕre;* see also BANKRUPT. (2) transit. *deficĕre, deserĕre, destituĕre* (with acc.); *deesse* (with dat.).
failing, *error, peccatum, vitium.*
failure, *defectio* (e.g. *virium*); or use verb.
fain: I would — do, *velim facĕre, libens faciam.*
faint, subst.: in a —, *intermortuus.*
faint, adj. *languidus, confectus, defussus:* to damn with — praise, *laudare maligne.*
faint, v. *conlabi,* (*animo*) *linqui* (Ov., Suet.).
faint-hearted, *timidus.*
faintly, *languide.*
faintness, *languor.*
fair, subst. *mercatus* (*-ūs*), *nundinae* (*-arum,* plur.).
fair, adj. (1) = beautiful, *pulcher, venustus, formosus.* (2) of weather, *serenus:* — weather, *sudum.* (3) = favourable, *secundus, idoneus.* (4) opp. to dark, *candidus.* (5) morally, *aequus, iustus.* (6) = moderately good, *mediocris.*
fairly. (1) = justly, *aeque, iuste.* (2) = moderately, *mediocriter.*
fairness. (1) = beauty, *pulchritudo, forma, venustas.* (2) = justice, *iustitia, aequitas.*
fairy, *nympha;* of the streams, *Naias, Nais;* of the woods, *Dryas* (usually plur. *Dryades*), *Fauni* (*-orum,* plur.).
faith. (1) = fidelity, *fides, fidelitas, pietas:* in good —, *ex fide bona.* (2) = belief, *opinio, persuasio, fides:* to have — in, (*homini*) *credĕre, confidĕre.*
faithful, *fidelis, fidus.*
faithfully, *fideliter.*
faithfulness, *fidelitas, fides, constantia.*
faithless, *perfidus, perfidiosus, infidelis, infidus.*
faithlessly, *perfide, perfidiose, infideliter.*
faithlessness, *perfidia, infidelitas.*
falchion; see SWORD.
fall, subst. LIT., *casus* (*-ūs*), *lapsus* (*-ūs*). TRANSF., (1) = ruin, *ruina, excidium casus* (*-ūs*). (2) = lessening, *deminutio.* (3) = autumn, *autumnus.*
fall, v. (1) to — down, *cadĕre, decidĕre, delabi, ruĕre;* to — apart, *dilabi;* to — at a person's feet, *se ad pedes hominis proicĕre;* to — back, *recidĕre;* to — forward, *procidĕre, prolabi;* to — foul of, *incurrĕre;* to — in, *incidĕre;* to — off, *delabi;* to — out, *excidĕre.* (2) to — dead, *cadĕre, concidĕre, occidĕre, perire.* (3) fig. = to perish, be ruined, *cadĕre, occidĕre,* (*cor*)*ruĕre.* (4) of a city, *expugnari, capi.* (5) = to sink, fall; of the wind, *cadĕre, concidĕre;* of the voice, *cadĕre.* (6) in price, *cadĕre.* (7) to — away = to desert, *desciscĕre;* = to lose flesh, *corpus amittĕre.* (8) to — back = to retreat, *pedem referre.* (9) to — back on, *recurrĕre* or *confugĕre ad.* (10) to — in with, *incidĕre, offendĕre.* (11) to — in love with, (*ad*)*amare.* (12) to — upon = attack, *invadĕre, incurrĕre.* (13) to — out = to happen, *cadĕre, evenire;* = to disagree, *dissentire, dissidĕre.*

fare

fallacious, *fallax, vanus, falsus.*
fallaciously, *fallaciter, falso.*
fallacy, *vitium, captio.*
fallible, *errori obnoxius.*
fallow: the field lies —, *ager cessat, quiescit, cultu vacat;* — ground, *novalis* (Verg.).
false, *falsus* (opp. *verus*); *fictus, commenticius* (= made up), *subditus* (= forged), *simulatus* (= pretended), *fucatus, fucosus* (= under — colours), *fallax* (= deceptive), *mendax* (= lying); *perfidus* (= treacherous): a — oath *periurium;* to play —, *deesse.*
falsehood, *mendacium, commentum, falsum.*
falsely, *falso, perperam:* to swear —, *peierare.*
falsification, use verb.
falsify, *vitiare, corrumpĕre, interpolare.*
falsity, use adj.
falter, *haesitare, haerēre, titubare.*
falteringly, *titubanter.*
fame, *laus, gloria, claritas, fama.*
famous, (*prae*)*clarus, inlustris, celeber.*
familiar. (1) = well known, *familiaris, notus.* (2) = acquainted, (*rei,* genit.) *sciens, gnarus, peritus:* to become —, *adsuescĕre.*
familiarly, *familiariter.*
familiarity, *familiaritas, consuetudo.*
family, subst. *familia* (originally = a household; also used as a part of the *gens* or Roman clan); *domus* (*-ūs*); *gens* (= clan); *genus* (more general; = race, stock); *cognatio, stirps, propinqui* (*-orum,* plur.); of good —, *nobilis, honesto loco natus.*
family, adj. *familiaris, domesticus; gentilis, gentilicius* (= belonging to a *gens*), *privatus* (opp. to *publicus*).
famine, *fames, cibi inopia.*
famish, v. (1) transit. *fame enecare, conficĕre.* (2) intransit. *fame enecari, confici, perire.*
fan, subst. (1) for winnowing, *vannus* (Verg.). (2) for fanning oneself, *flabellum.*
fan, v. *ventilare.*
fanatical, *fanaticus.*
fancied, *opinabilis, opinatus.*
fanciful = imaginative; render by phrase.
fancy, subst. (1) as a faculty, *inventio, cogitatio.* (2) = an idea, notion, *opinio:* a mere —, *somnium* (Ter.). (3) = liking, preference, *libido.*
fancy, v. (1) = to imagine, *fingĕre.* (2) = to think (on slight grounds), *opinari, putare, haud scire an, nescire an.*
fang, *dens.*
fanged, *dentatus* (Ov.).
far. (1) in space, *procul, longe:* from — off, *e longinquo, eminus* (opp. *comminus*); farther, *longius, ultra;* as — as, *tenus* (prep.), *quatenus* (adv.), *usque* (adv. = all the way); — and wide, *longe lateque.* (2) in degree: — better (best), *longe* or *multo melior* (*optimus*); — from it, *minime;* so —, thus —, *hactenus;* so — from staying he ran away, *tantum aberat ut maneret ut aufugeret,* or *adeo non mansit ut aufugeret,* or *non modo non mansit sed ultro aufugit;* to go too —, *modum excedĕre;* as — as, *quantum, quod* (e.g. *quod ad me attinet*).
farce, *mimus.*
farcical, *mimicus, ridiculus.*
farcically, *mimice, ridicule.*
fare, subst. (1) = food, *cibus, victus* (*-ūs*): poor —, *tenuis victus;* good —, *lautus victus.*

[707]

(2) = money paid for journey, *vectura* (Pl., Sen.), *naulum* (Juv.).

fare, v. *se habēre*, with adv.

farewell! interj. *ave! avete! vale! valete!* : to bid —, *valēre iubēre*.

far-fetched, *longe repetitus, arcessitus*.

farm, subst. *fundus, praedium, ager*.

farm, v. (1) = to till, *arare, colēre*. (2) = to hire (taxes, etc.), *redimēre, conducēre*. (3) to — out = let out on contract, *(e)locare*.

farmer. (1) on a farm, *agricola, arator, colonus*. (2) see CONTRACTOR, HIRER : a — of revenues, *publicanus*.

farming. (1) on a farm, *aratio, agricultura* (or as two words), *agrorum cultus (-ūs), res rusticae*. (2) = hiring, *redemptio, conductio*.

farrago, *farrago* (Juv.).

farrier, render by phrase, such as *qui equis soleas ferreas suppingit*.

farrow, subst. *fetus (-ūs)*.

farrow, v. *parēre, fetum edēre*.

farthing, (as a very small coin) *quadrans, teruncius* : I do not care a — for, *haud flocci facio*.

fascinate, *fascinare* (Verg.); see also CHARM.

fascination. LIT., *fascinum, fascinatio* (Plin.). TRANSF., *blanditia, dulcedo*.

fashion, subst. (1) = custom, way, *mos, consuetudo, ritus (-ūs)* : after the — of men, *hominum ritu*. (2) = style of dress, *habitus (-ūs), ornatus (-ūs)*. (3) = the prevailing —, what is fashionable, *saeculum* (Tac.) ; out of —, *obsoletus*.

fashion, v. *fabricari, (ef)fingēre*; see also MAKE.

fashionable, *elegans, quod moris est*.

fashionably, *de more, eleganter*.

fast, subst. *ieiunium*.

fast, adj. (1) = quick, *celer, citus, velox, pernix, rapidus*. (2) = fixed, firm, *firmus, stabilis* : to hold —, *tenēre, retinēre*; to stick —, *adhaerēre*; to make —, *firmare, stabilire*.

fast, adv. (1) = quickly, *celeriter, rapide*. (2) = firmly, *firme, firmiter*.

fast, v. *ieiunium servare*.

fasten, *(ad)figēre, (ad)ligare, deligare, adnectēre* : to — together, *configēre, connectēre*; see also TIE, BIND.

fastening, *vinculum, compages, claustra (-orum,* plur.), *repagula (-orum,* plur.).

fastidious, adj. *fastidiosus, delicatus, elegans*.

fastidiously, *fastidiose, delicate, eleganter*.

fat, subst. *adeps, sebum* (Pl.) : to live on the — of the land, *delicatissimis cibis uti*.

fat, adj. *pinguis, obesus, nitidus* (= sleek), *saginatus* (= fattened).

fatal, *perniciosus, funestus, exitialis, exitiosus*.

fatalism, fatalist, use phrase with *fatum* (e.g. *omnia fato fieri credēre*).

fatality. (1) = power of fate, *fatum*. (2) = accident, *casus (-ūs)*.

fate, *fatum, necessitas, sors*. Personif., *Fortuna*; the Fates, *Parcae*.

fated, *fatalis*.

father, subst. *pater, parens, genitor* (poet.).

father, v. : to — upon, *ascribēre, tribuēre*.

father-in-law, *socer*.

fatherless, *orbus*.

fatherly, *paternus*.

fathom, subst. *ulna* (Plin.).

fathom, v. *explorare*.

fatigue, subst. *(de)fatigatio, lassitudo*.

fatigue, v. *(de)fatigare, (de)lassare* (poet.).

fatigued, *(de)fatigatus, (de)fessus, lassus* (poet.).

fatness, *obesitas* (Suet.), *pinguitudo* (Plin.).

fatten. (1) transit. *saginare, farcire* (Cato). (2) intransit. *pinguescēre*.

fatuity, *fatuitas, ineptia*.

fatuous, *fatuus, ineptus*.

fatuously, *inepte, insulse*.

fault, *culpa, vitium, peccatum, delictum, menda, noxa* : at —, *in culpā*; to find — with, *culpare, accusare, reprehendēre*.

faultily, *mendose, vitiose*.

faultless, *integer, innocens, emendatus*.

faultlessly, *integre, innocenter, emendate*.

faulty, *mendosus, vitiosus*.

favour, subst. (1) = a position of —, *gratia*. (2) = a disposition to —, goodwill, *favor, studium, benevolentia*. (3) = an act of —, *beneficium* : to do a —, *(homini) gratum facēre* or *gratificari*.

favour, v. *(homini) favēre, studēre, suffragari*. Prov. : fortune —s the brave, *fortuna fortes adiuvat*.

favourable, *propitius* (of the gods), *commodus, prosperus, idoneus, secundus*.

favourably, *benigne, commode, prospere*.

favourer, *fautor* (f. *fautrix*).

favourite, subst. *deliciae (-arum,* plur.).

favourite, adj. *carus, gratiosus, gratus, acceptus*.

favouritism, use phrase, such as *praecipuus favor*.

fawn, *hinnuleus* (Hor.).

fawn, v. : to — upon, *adulari*.

fawning, subst. *adulatio*.

fealty, *fides, fidelitas* : to swear — to, *in nomen* (or *verba*) *hominis iurare*.

fear, subst. *metus (-ūs), timor, pavor, terror, formīdo* : for —, *propter metum, prae metu* (usually with neg.).

fear, v. *metuēre, timēre, verēri* (of awe or reverence), *extimescēre, pertimescēre*.

fearful. (1) = afraid, *timidus, trepidus, pavidus*. (2) = dreadful, *dirus, horribilis, terribilis, formidolosus*.

fearfully. (1) = with fear, *timide, pavide*. (2) = causing fear, *dire, trepide, formidolose*.

fearless, *fidens, impavidus, intrepidus*; or render by phrase.

fearlessly, *sine metu, sine timore, fidenter, impavide*.

fearlessness, *fidentia, audacia*.

feasible, *quod fieri potest*.

feast, subst. (1) = feast-day, *dies festus*. (2) = banquet, *convivium, epulum, epulae (-arum,* plur.), *daps*.

feast, v. (1) transit. *pascēre*. (2) intransit. *epulari, convivari, vesci, pasci*.

feat, *facinus (-ŏris,* n.), *factum, res gestae* (plur.).

feather, subst. *penna (pinna), pluma* (= down). Prov. : birds of a feather . . . , *pares cum paribus facillime congregantur* (Cic.).

feather, v. : to — one's nest, *res suas augēre, sibi consulēre* or *providēre*.

feathery, *plumeus* (Plin.), *plumosus* (Plin.).

feature, (1) of the face, *lineamentum* : the —s, *vultus (-ūs)*. (2) = peculiarity, *proprietas*; or render by adj. *proprius*.

February, *(mensis) Februarius*.

fecund, *fecundus*.

fecundate, *fecundare* (Verg.).

fecundity, *fecunditas, fertilitas*.

federal, *foederatus, foedere sociatus*.

fee, subst. *merces.*

fee, v. *mercedem dare.*

feeble, *imbecillus, tenuis, infirmus, invalidus, languidus, debilis;* of sight, etc., *hebes.*

feebleness, *imbecillitas, debilitas, infirmitas, languor.*

feebly, *infirme, languide.*

feed, v. (1) transit. *pascĕre, alĕre* (with acc.); *cibum dare* or *praebēre* (with dat.). (2) intransit. *vesci, (de)pasci;* see also EAT, GRAZE.

feel. (1) = to touch, handle, *temptare, tangĕre.* (2) = to experience through the senses, *sentire.* (3) to — an emotion, *laetitiam,* etc., *capĕre, percipĕre, sentire* (usually in strong sense, = feel the force of); *laetitiā,* etc., *adfici;* often rendered by particular verbs, e.g. to — joy, *laetari;* — pain, *dolēre.* (4) with a complement: a, of persons: to — hot, glad, etc., render by particular verbs (e.g. *calēre, laetari),* or phrases suggested by (1) and (2) above: b, of things, *esse (tactu)* (e.g. *asper tactu esse,* to feel rough).

feeler, *crinis* (Plin.), *corniculum* (Plin.).

feeling, subst. (1) through the senses, *sensus* (-*ūs*), *tactus* (-*ūs*). (2) = emotion, state of mind, *animus, animi motus* (-*ūs*) or *adfectus* (-*ūs*), *sensus* (-*ūs*); kindly —, *humanitas;* — for truth, *veritatis studium;* — for the beautiful, *elegantia.*

feeling, adj. *humanus, misericors.*

feign, *fingĕre, simulare.*

feigned, *fictus, simulatus.*

feignedly, *ficte, simulate.*

feint, *simulatio.*

felicitate, *(homini) gratulari.*

felicitation, *gratulatio.*

felicitous. (1) = happy, *felix, beatus.* (2) of style, *venustus.*

felicitously. (1) = happily, *beate.* (2) of style, *venuste, apte.*

felicity. (1) = happiness, *vita beata.* (2) of style, *venustas.*

fell, subst. *collis, clivus.*

fell, adj. *dirus, saevus.*

fell, v. of timber, *caedĕre, excidĕre.* (2) in gen. = to knock down, *(con)sternĕre.*

fellow. (1) = associate, *socius, comes, sodalis.* (2) = equal, *par.* (3) = person, *homo.*

fellow-citizen, fellow-countryman, *civis, municeps.*

fellow-feeling, *consensio;* or render by *societas* with genit. of the feeling concerned.

fellow-heir, *coheres.*

fellow-pupil, *condiscipulus.*

fellow-servant, *conservus* (f. *conserva*).

fellow-soldier, *commilito.*

fellowship, *societas, sodalitas, communitas;* a corporation, guild, *conlegium.*

felon; see CRIMINAL.

felt, *coactum.*

female, subst. *femina, mulier.*

female, adj. *muliebris, femineus* (poet.).

feminine, *muliebris, femineus* (poet.); as grammat. t. t. *femininus* (Varro, Quint.).

fen, *palus* (-*ūdis,* f.), *uligo.*

fence, subst. *saepes, saepimentum;* prov.: to sit on the —, *duabus sellis sedēre* (quoted by Sen.).

fence, v. (1) = to enclose, *saepire, saepto circumdare.* (2) = to fight with swords, *batuĕre* (Suet.).

fencer, *gladiator* (nearest equivalent).

fencing, *ars gladiatoria:* a — master, *lanista.*

fenny, *uliginosus, paluster.*

ferment, subst. LIT., *fermentum* (Plin.). TRANSF., *tumor, fervor, aestus* (-*ūs*).

ferment, v. *fervēre.*

fern, *filix* (poet.).

ferocious, *ferus, saevus, atrox, trux, truculentus.*

ferocity, *saevitia, atrocitas.*

ferret, subst. *viverra* (Plin.).

ferret, v.: to — out, *rimari.*

ferrugineous, *errugineus* (Pl., Verg.), *ferratus* (of water: Sen.).

ferry, subst. *traiectus* (-*ūs*): — -boat, *scapha, cymba;* — -man, *portitor.*

ferry, v. *traicĕre, transmittĕre.*

fertile, *ferax, fecundus, fertilis, opimus, uber, fetus.*

fertility, *fertilitas, ubertas, fecunditas.*

fervent, fervid, *fervidus, fervens, ardens.*

fervently, *ardenter, ferventer.*

fervour, *ardor, fervor.*

festival, *dies festus, feriae* (-*arum,* plur.), *sollemne.*

festive, *hilaris, festus, festivus* (Pl.).

festivity. (1) see FESTIVAL. (2) = mirth, *festivitas, hilaritas.*

festoon, subst. *serta* (-*orum,* plur.).

fetch, *adferre, advehĕre, apportare, adducĕre, arcessĕre* (= to send for), *advehĕre;* of a sigh or breath, *petĕre, ducĕre.*

fetid, *teter, foetidus, gravis.*

fetidness, *foetor.*

fetter, subst. (lit. and fig.) *compes, catena, vinculum.*

fetter, v. LIT., *vincula, catenas, compedes (homini) inicĕre.* TRANSF., *impedire.*

feud, *simultas; inimicitia.*

fever, *febris:* a slight —, *febricula;* to be in a — (of excitement, etc.), *trepidare, aestuare.*

feverish. LIT., *febriculosus* (Gell.). TRANSF., *commotus, trepidus:* — excitement, *summa trepidatio.*

few, *pauci, rari:* very —, *perpauci;* how —! *quam pauci!* (plur.), *quotus quisque!* (sing.).

fiat; see COMMAND.

fib, *mendaciunculum* (once in Cic.).

fibre, *fibra.*

fibrous, *fibratus* (Plin.); or use subst.

fickle, *inconstans, varius, lĕvis, mutabilis, mobilis.*

fickleness, *inconstantia, levitas, mutabilitas, mobilitas.*

fictile, *fictilis.*

fiction, *res ficta, fabula, commentum.*

fictitious, *commenticius, fictus.*

fiddle, *fides* (-*ium,* plur.).

fiddler, *fidicen.*

fidelity, *fidelitas, fides, constantia.*

fidget, v. intransit. *trepidare, satagĕre* (Quint.), *quiescĕre non posse.*

fidgety, *inquietus.*

fie! *phy* (Ter.), *pro.*

field. (1) = a piece of land, *ager, arvum* (arable land), *seges* (= a cornfield), *pratum* (= meadow), *campus* (= plain). (2) milit.: — of battle, *acies;* in the —, *militiae* (opp. *domi*); to take the — against, *arma ferre adversus* (*hominem*). (3) fig. = scope, sphere, *campus, locus, area;* often to be rendered by a particular subst., e.g. *historia*, — of history.

field-day, *dies quo milites lustrantur*, or *exercentur*.

fiend, *diabolus* (eccl.).

fiendish, *nefandus, immanis, atrox.*

fierce, *ferox, ferus, saevus, atrox, trux, truculentus, immanis.*

fiercely, *ferociter, saeve, atrociter.*

fierceness, *ferocitas, atrocitas, saevitia.*

fiery. Lit., *igneus, flammeus.* Transf., *ardens, fervens, fervidus, ferox.*

Fiesole, *Faesulae (-arum*, plur.).

fife, *tibia.*

fifer, *tibicen.*

fifteen, *quindecim* : — each, *quini deni* ; — times, *quindecie(n)s.*

fifteenth, *quintus decimus.*

fifth, *quintus.*

fiftieth, *quinquagesimus.*

fifty, *quinquaginta* : — each, *quinquageni.*

fig. (1) the tree, *ficus.* (2) the fruit, *ficus* : dried —, *Carica, Cauneae (-arum*, plur.). (3) not to care a — for, *non flocci facĕre.*

fight, subst. *pugna, certamen*; with fists, *pugilatio.*

fight, v. *(de)pugnare, dimicare, proeliari, digladiari, bellare, (con)certare* : to — a battle, *proelium committĕre.*

fighter, *pugnator, proeliator.*

figment; see FICTION.

figurative, *translatus.*

figuratively, *per translationem.*

figure, subst. (1) = form, shape, *figura, forma, species, facies, schema (-atis*, n.), *conformatio.* (2) concr. = an image or representation, *signum, figura, imago*; written or drawn, *descriptio.* (3) a — of speech, *conformatio, figura* (Quint.), *schema* (Quint.).

figure, v. *fingĕre*; see also IMAGINE.

figured, *sigillatus, caelatus.*

filament, *fibra, filum.*

file, subst. (1) the tool: for metal, *lima*; for wood, *scobina* (Varro). (2) milit. t. t., *ordo* : the rank and —, *milites.*

file, v. *limare, polire.*

filings, *scobis* (Hor., Juv.).

filial, *pius (erga parentes).*

filially, *pie.*

fill, subst. one's —; render by adv. *satis* or adj. *satur.*

fill, v. Lit., = to make full, — up, *implēre, complēre, replēre, supplēre, opplēre* (= — so as to block up). Transf., (1) with feelings, *laetitiam*, etc., *homini inicĕre* or *incutĕre*; rarely *hominem laetitiā implēre* or *complēre.* (2) of offices, *fungi*, with abl.

fillet, *fascia, redimiculum, vitta* (round the head as an ornament), *infula* (relig. t. t.).

filly, *equula* (Varro).

film. (1) = thin skin, *membrana.* (2) = dimness, darkness, *caligo, nubes.*

filter, subst. *colum* (Verg.).

filter, v. transit. *(per)colare* (Plin.), *liquare* (Hor.).

filth. Lit., see DIRT. Transf., *impuritas, foeditas, obscenitas.*

filthily, *foede, impure.*

filthiness; see FILTH.

filthy. Lit., see DIRTY. Transf., *impurus, obscenus.*

fin, *pinna* (Plin.).

final, *ultimus, extremus.*

finally, *ad extremum, denique, postremo.*

finance, finances, domestic, *res familiaris* or *nummaria* or *pecuniaria*; of a state, *vectigalia (-ium*, plur.), *aerarium, fiscus.*

financial, render by phrase, such as *ad aerarium pertinens.*

find, v. *invenire, reperire*; *offendĕre* (= to come upon) : to — by experience, *experiri*; to — out (facts), *cognoscĕre, invenire*; he found admirers, *non deerant qui eum admirarentur*; to — fault, *vituperare, culpare*; to — favour, *gratiam conciliare.*

finder, *inventor, repertor* (Verg., Tac.).

fine, subst. *multa.*

fine, adj. (1) in gen., as term of commendation, *praeclarus, pulcher, bellus, elegans* : the — arts, *artes liberales.* (2) = thin, *tenuis, subtilis.* (3) = pure, *purus.* (4) of weather, *serenus, sudus.* Phrase, in —, *denique.*

fine, v. *multare.*

finely, (1) *praeclare, belle, eleganter.* (2) *tenuiter, subtiliter.*

fineness. (1) *elegantia.* (2) = thinness, *tenuitas, subtilitas.* (3) of weather, *serenitas.*

finery, *munditia, apparatus (-ūs), lautitia.*

finesse, *artificium.*

finger, subst. *digitus*: fore—, *digitus index* (Hor.); little —, *digitus minimus* (Hor.); to snap the —s, *digitos* (or *digitis) concrepare*; not to swerve a —'s breadth, *digitum (transversum) non discedĕre*; not to lift a —, *ne manum quidem vertĕre.*

finger, v. *tangĕre, attrectare.*

finger-tips, *extremi digiti.*

finical, *putidus.*

finically, *putide.*

fining, subst. *multatio.*

finish, subst. *absolutio, perfectio, lima* (= polish, lit. = file).

finish, v. (1) = to complete, *conficĕre, consummare, absolvĕre, peragĕre, perficĕre.* (2) = to put an end to, *finire, terminare.*

finished, adj. *limatus* (= polished), *absolutus, perfectus.*

finisher, *confector.*

finishing, *ultimus, extremus.*

finite, *finitus, circumscriptus.*

finitely, *finite.*

fir, *abies* (= silver fir: Verg.); *pinus* (strictly = pine: poet.).

fire, subst. Lit., *ignis, flamma, incendium* (= conflagration): to be on —, *ardēre, flagrare*; to set on —, *incendĕre, inflammare*; prov. : to be between two —s, *hac urget lupus, hac canis angit* (Hor.). Transf., (1) = ardour, (*animi) vis, vigor, impetus (-ūs), ardor, fervor*: to be on —, *ardēre, flagrare*; to lack — (of speakers), *languēre, frigēre.* (2) of missiles, *telorum coniectus (-us).*

fire, v. (1) transit. *incendĕre, inflammare.* (2) intransit., fig. : to — up, *exardescĕre.*

fire-brand, *fax* (lit. and fig.), *torris* (Verg.).

fire-brigade, *vigiles (adversus incendia instituti)* (Suet.).

fire-engine, *sipho(n)* (Plin.).

fire-place, fire-side, *caminus, focus.*

fire-wood, *lignum* (usually plur.).

firm, *firmus, stabilis, solidus, immobilis, constans* (fig. only).

firmly, *firmiter, firme, solide, constanter.*

firmness, *firmitas, firmitudo, stabilitas* : — of mind, *obstinatio, constantia, perseverantia.*

first, adj. *primus, prior* (of two); sometimes *princeps.*

first, adv. *primum, primo.*

first-born, *natu maximus, natu maior* (of two).

first-fruits, *primitiae (-arum,* plur.: Ov., Tac.).

firstling, *primus genitus.*

fiscal, *fiscalis* (Leg.).

fish, subst. *piscis;* coll., *piscatus (-ūs);* of —, adj., *piscarius* (Pl.).

fish, v. Lit., *piscari.* Transf., (1) to — out, *expiscari.* (2) to — for, *captare, aucupari.*

fishbone, *spina piscis.*

fisherman, *piscator.*

fishery, *cetarium* (Hor.).

fishhook, *hamus* (Hor.).

fishing, *piscatus (-ūs:* Pl.); of — , adj., *piscatorius.*

fishing-line, *linum* (Ov.).

fishing-net, *rete, iaculum* (= a casting-net: Pl., Ov.).

fishing-rod, *harundo* (Ov.).

fishing-smack, *horia* (Pl.).

fishmonger, *cetarius.*

fissure, *rima.*

fist, *pugnus.*

fisticuffs, *pugilatio.*

fistula, *fistula* (Cels.).

fit, subst. (of a disease, passion, etc.), *impetus (-ūs).*

fit, fitted, adj. *aptus, idoneus, commodus, opportunus, habilis, accommodatus.*

fit, v. (1) transit. *aptare, accommodare:* to — out, *(ex)ornare, instruĕre.* (2) intransit. *convenire* (with *ad* and acc.); *aptum, idoneum,* etc., *esse.*

fitly, *apte, commode, opportune.*

fitness, *habilitas, opportunitas, convenientia.*

five, *quinque:* — each, *quini;* a period of — years, *lustrum, quinquennium;* lasting — years (or coming every — years), *quinquennalis;* — years old, *quinquennis;* — times, *quinquie(n)s.*

fifth, *quintus.*

fives, use *pila* (e.g. *pilis ludĕre*).

fix, v. *(ad)figĕre:* to — in, *infigĕre;* to — down, *defigĕre;* see also Establish, Appoint.

fixed, *certus.*

flabby, flaccid, *marcidus, fluidus, flaccus* (Varro).

flag, subst. *signum, vexillum:* — ship, *navis praetoria.*

flag, v. *languescĕre, frigĕre* (of conversation, etc.), *refrigescĕre* (of preparations, etc.).

flagitious, *flagitiosus, nefarius, foedus.*

flagon, *lagēna.*

flagrant, *impudens, manifestus.*

flagrantly, *impudenter, manifeste.*

flail, *pertica* (Plin.), *fustis* (Col.).

flake, of snow, use plur. *nives.*

flambeau, *fax, taeda.*

flame, subst. *flamma* (lit. and fig.).

flame, v. *ardēre, flagrare.*

flame-coloured, *flammeus* (Plin.), *rutilus.*

flaming, *flammeus.*

flank, *latus (-ĕris,* n.).

flap, subst. *lacinia* (Pl.).

flap, v.: to — the wings, *alis plaudĕre* (Verg.); in gen., *fluitare* (Ov., Tac.).

flare, v. *flagrare.*

flash, subst. *fulgor:* — of lightning, *fulgur.*

flash, v. *fulgēre, splendēre:* the eyes —, *oculi scintillant* (Pl.).

flask, *ampulla.*

flat. (1) = level, *planus, aequus, pronus* (= lying —): to lay —, *sternĕre;* the — of the hand, *palma.* (2) of wine, *vapidus* (Hor.). (3) of jokes, etc., *insulsus, frigidus.*

flatly, *plane.*

flatter, *(hominem) adulari, (homini) adsentari* or *blandiri.*

flatterer, *adsentator.*

flattering, *blandus.*

flatteringly, *adsentatorie.*

flattery, *adulatio, adsentatio, blanditia, blandimentum.*

flatulence, *inflatio.*

flaunt, v. transit. *iactare, ostentare.*

flavour, subst. *sapor, sucus* (poet.).

flavour, v. *condire.*

flaw, *vitium, mendum.*

flawless, *emendatus.*

flax, *linum* (Verg.), *carbasus* (Plin.).

flaxen. (1) = of flax, *lineus* (Plin.). (2) = of colour, *flavus* (poet.).

flay, *pellem detrahĕre corpori.*

flea, *pulex* (Pl.).

fledged, *plumatus* (poet.).

flee, *(ef)fugĕre* (transit. and intransit.); *fugam petĕre, capessĕre,* etc.: to — in different directions, *diffugĕre;* to — for refuge to, *confugĕre ad.*

fleece, subst. *vellus (-ĕris,* n.: poet.).

fleece, v. Lit., *tondēre.* Transf., = to rob, *expilare, spoliare.*

fleecy, *laniger* (Verg.).

fleet, subst. *classis.*

fleet, adj. *velox, celer, volucer* (poet.), *pernix.*

fleeting, *fugax, caducus, fluxus.*

fleetness, *velocitas, pernicitas.*

flesh, *caro* (often = meat), *viscera (-um,* plur.), *corpus (-ŏris,* n.).

fleshy, *carnosus* (Plin.).

flexibility, *facilitas;* or render by adj.

flexible, *flexibilis, lentus, facilis.*

flicker, *trepidare, micare, coruscare* (poet.).

flight. (1) = fleeing, *effugium, fuga:* to put to —, *fugare.* (2) = flying, *lapsus (-ūs), volatus (-ūs).* (3) of stairs, *scalae (-arum,* plur.).

flightiness, *mobilitas, levitas.*

flighty, *mutabilis, mobilis, levis, inconstans.*

flimsiness, Lit., *tenuitas.* Transf., *inanitas.*

flimsy. Lit., *(nimis) tenuis.* Transf., *inanis.*

flinch, *refugĕre.*

fling, *iacĕre, conicĕre, iaculari* (Verg., Tac.): to — away, *abicĕre, proicĕre;* to — a thing at a person, *hominem re petĕre.*

flint, *silex.*

flippancy, *petulantia.*

flippant, *petulans.*

flirt, v., perhaps *osculari,* or *subblandiri* (with dat.: Pl.).

flirtation, perhaps *osculatio.*

flit, *volitare.*

flitch, *succidia.*

float, *innare, (in)matare* (Verg.), *fluitare;* in the air, *pendēre, volitare.*

flock, subst. Lit., *grex, pecus (-ŏris,* n.). Transf., of persons, *caterva, multitudo.*

flock, v. *adfluĕre, confluĕre:* to — together, *concurrĕre, convolare.*

flog, *verberare:* to be flogged, *vapulare.*

flogging, *verbera (-um,* plur.), *verberatio.*

flood. subst. Lit., (1) = deluge, *eluvio, diluvium* (Verg.). (2) = tide, *aestūs accessus (-ūs).*

Transf., *vis magna, flumen* (poet., and of words in Cic.).

flood, v. transit. *inundare*. Transf., to be flooded (out) with, *(re) cumulari*.

flood-gate, *cataracta* or *cataractes* (Plin.).

floor, *solum, pavimentum* (of stone), *contabulatio, contignatio* (both of wood, = a storey).

flop, v. colloq., *frigēre, cadēre*.

floral, *floreus* (poet.).

Florence, *Florentia*.

florid. Lit., in colour, *rubicundus*. Transf., *floridus*.

flounce, subst. *instita* (Hor.), *segmenta (-orum,* plur.: Ov., Juv.).

flounced, *segmentatus* (Juv.).

flounder. Lit., *volutari, fluitare*. Transf., *titubare*.

flour, *farina* (Plin.).

flourish, subst., in style, *calamister*.

flourish, v. (1) intransit. *florēre, vigēre*: to begin to —, *florescēre*. (2) transit. *vibrare*; see also BRANDISH.

flourishing, *florens, opulentus*.

flout, *ludificari, cavillari, deridēre, inridēre*.

flow, subst. Lit., *fluxio, lapsus (-us)*; of the tide, *accessus (-ūs)*. Transf., of words, *volubilitas, copia (verborum)*.

flow, v. *fluēre* (to — freely), *labi* (to glide along), *manare* (to ooze): to — apart, *diffluēre*; — back, *refluēre* (poet.); — between, *interfluēre*; — down, *defluēre*; — into, *influēre*; — past, *praeterfluēre*; — together, *confluēre*.

flower, subst. Lit., *flos, flosculus* (dim.). Transf., (1) = best part, *flos, robur*. (2) a — of speech, *flos, flosculus*.

flower, v. (lit. and fig.), *florēre, (ef)florescēre*.

flowery, *floreus* (poet.), *floridus* (lit. and fig.).

flowing. Lit., *fluens, manans*. Transf., of speech, *fluens, volubilis, fusus*.

fluctuate, *fluctuare* or *fluctuari, pendēre (animi) iactari*.

fluctuation, *fluctuatio*.

fluency, *facundia, volubilitas*.

fluent, *volubilis, disertus, (pro)fluens*.

fluently, *volubiliter*.

fluid, subst. *liquor, humor*.

fluid, adj. *liquidus, fluidus* (poet.).

fluke, of an anchor, *dens* (Verg.).

flurry; see EXCITE, HURRY.

flush, subst. *rubor*.

flush, v. *rubescēre* (poet.).

fluster, *agitare, commovēre, sollicitare*.

flute, *tibia, harundo* (Ov.).

flute-player, *tibicen*.

fluted, *striatus* (Vitr.).

flutter, subst. *trepidatio*.

flutter, v. *trepidare, volitare*.

flux; see FLOW.

fly, subst. *musca*.

fly, v. *volare, volitare*: to — away, *avolare*; to — in, *involare*; to — out, *evolare*; to — to, *advolare*; to — up, *subvolare*; see also FLEE.

flying, *volatilis, volucer*: — hair, *crines passi*.

foal, subst. *eculeus, pullus equi, pullus equinus*.

foal, v. *parēre*.

foam, subst. *spuma*.

foam, v. *spumare, (ex)aestuare*.

foamy, *spumans, spumeus, spumifer, spumosus* (all poet.).

fodder, *pabulum*.

foe, *hostis* (public), *inimicus* (private).

fog, *nebula, caligo*.

foggy, *nebulosus, caliginosus*.

foible, *vitium*.

foil, subst. (1) a fencer's —, *rudis*. (2) of metal, *lamina, brattea* (poet.).

foil, v. *ad inritum redigēre, eludēre*.

foist, *supponēre, subdēre*.

fold, subst. (1) in fabric, etc., *sinus (-ūs)*. (2) for animals, *ovile* (for sheep: poet.), *stabulum* (for cattle).

fold, v. *(com)plicare*: with —ed hands, *compressis manibus*.

folding-doors, *valvae (-arum,* plur.), *fores (-um,* plur.).

foliage, *frons*, or plur. *frondes*; *folia (-orum,* plur.).

folk; see PEOPLE.

follow. Lit., *(con)sequi, insequi, subsequi* (closely), *prosequi, persequi* (to the end), *(con)sectari* (eagerly), *comitari* (= to accompany). Transf., (1) to — as a leader, teacher, etc., *sequi*. (2) in time, *sequi*: to — after, succeed, *succedēre* (with dat.), *excipēre* (with acc.). (3) = to conform to, *(con)sequi, subsequi*: to — one's own judgment, *suo ingenio uti*. (4) to — out, — up, an abstract thing, *exsequi*. (5) logically, *sequi*: what —s? *quid igitur?* it does not — that, if . . ., *non, si . . ., idcirco*.

follower, *(ad)sector*: —s of Socrates, *Socratici* (and so with many other names).

following, subst. *secta*.

following, *(in)sequens, proximus, posterus*: on the — day, *postero die, postridie (eius diei)*.

folly, *stultitia, fatuitas, insipientia, ineptia*.

foment. Lit., *fovēre*. Transf., *sollicitare, excitare*.

fomentation, *fomentum* (Cels.).

fomenter (of trouble), *fax, instimulator*.

fond. (1) = loving, *amans, studiosus, cupidus* (with genit.); *amicus* (with dat.). (2) = foolish, *stultus*.

fondle, *(per)mulcēre, amplexari*.

fondly. (1) = lovingly, *amanter*. (2) = foolishly, *stulte*.

fondness. (1) = love, *studium, amor, caritas*. (2) = folly, *stultitia*.

food, *cibus, esca, victus (-ūs), alimentum*: to take —, *cibum capēre*; to digest —, *cibum conficēre* or *concoquēre*; a —-shop, *popina*; of animals, *pabulum, pastus (-ūs)*.

fool, subst. *homo stultus, fatuus*, or *ineptus*; *sannio* (one who plays the — on purpose): to play the —, *nugari, ineptire, desipēre*.

fool, v. *(e)ludēre, ludificare* or *ludificari*.

foolery, *ineptiae (-arum,* plur.), *nugae (-arum,* plur.).

foolhardy, *temerarius*; see also RASH.

foolish, *stultus, fatuus, ineptus, insulsus*.

foolishly, *stulte, inepte, insulse*.

foot, subst. Lit., of the body, *pes*: on — (adj.), *pedes, pedester*; to serve on —, *pedibus merēri* or *stipendia facēre*. Transf., (1) the — of a piece of furniture, *pes*. (2) = the lowest part of anything, *radix*: usually rendered by the adj. *infimus* or *imus* (e.g. *infimus mons* = the — of the mountain). (3) as a measure, *pes*: a — in size, *pedalis*; a — and a half in size, *sesquipedalis*; two — in size, *bipedalis*. (4) a metrical — *pes*.

foot, v.; see TREAD, DANCE.

footing, *ratio, status (-ūs)*: on an equal —, *ex aequo*.

footman, *pedisequus, servus a pedibus*.

footpad, *latro*.
foot-path, *semita, callis*.
foot-print, *vestigium*.
foot-soldier, *pedes*.
footstool, *scamnum* (Ov., Mart.), *scabillum* (Varro).
for, prep. (1) = on behalf of, instead of, *pro* (with abl.). (2) = as: I take you — a good man, *te pro bono homine habeo*, or *te bonum hominem esse puto*; left — dead, *pro occiso relictus*. (3) in return —, *pro*, with abl.; where things are bought and sold for money, use genit. or abl. of price (e.g. *quanti emisti? viginti assibus*). (4) = by reason of, because of, *propter, ob*, with acc.; in negative sentences, *prae*, with abl. (5) of time: **a** = to last for, for the purposes of, *in* with acc.: — the next day, *in posterum diem*; — the present, *in praesens tempus*; to live — the day, *in diem vivĕre*: **b** = during, render by acc. or by *per*, with acc. (6) expressing purpose, or tendency, render by dat. or by *ad*, with acc. (7) = according to, in proportion to, considering, *pro*, with abl.; sometimes *ut* (e.g. a wise man, for these days, *homo sapiens, ut in illa aetate*). (8) of advantage or disadvantage (e.g. good for, bad for), render by dat. (9) after substantives = towards (e.g. love for), render by objective genit. or by *erga, adversus*, with acc. (10) = in spite of, use participle or concessive clause.
for, conj. *nam(que), etenim, quippe* (all usually at beginning of clause); *enim* (second word in clause); see also BECAUSE.
forage, subst. *pabulum*.
forage, v. *pabulari, frumentari*.
forager, *pabulator, frumentator*.
foraging, subst. *pabulatio, frumentatio*.
forbear, = to refrain, *parcĕre, supersedĕre, temperare*, (*se*) *abstinĕre, se continĕre*.
forbearance, *abstinentia, continentia, patientia*.
forbid, *vetare, interdicĕre*: it is forbidden, *vetitum est, non licet*.
force, subst. (1) in gen. *vis, impetus* (*-ūs*), *momentum, manus* (sing. or plur.): to be in —, *valēre*. (2) milit., forces, *copiae* (*-arum*, plur.).
force, v.: to — a way in, through, out, *in-, per-, e-rumpere*; to — out, *exprimĕre, extorquēre*; see also COMPEL
forced. (1) of language, *arcessitus*. (2) milit. t. t.: a — march, *magnum iter*.
forcemeat, *insicia* (Varro).
forcible. (1) = done by force, *per vim factus*. (2) = strong (esp. of language), *validus, nervosus, gravis, vehemens*.
forcibly, *vi, per vim, valide, nervose, graviter, vehementer*.
ford, subst. *vadum*.
ford, v. *vado transire*.
forearm, subst. *bracchium*.
forearm, v.; see WARN, PREPARE: to be —ed, *praecavēre*.
forebode. (1) = to forewarn about, *portendĕre, praesagire*. (2) = to have a presentiment of, *praesagire, praesentire, augurari*.
foreboding, subst. *praesensio*.
forecast, v. *praevidēre, prospicĕre*.
forefather, *avus, abavus, atavus, proăvus*; —s, *maiores* (*-um*, plur.).
forefinger, *digitus index*.
forego, *dimittere*, (*con*)*cedĕre*.
forehead, *frons* (*-ntis*).

foreign. LIT., *peregrinus, externus, adventicius*. TRANSF., = different, incompatible, *abhorrens, alienus*.
foreigner, *peregrinus, alienigena, advena, hospes*.
foreknow, *praenoscĕre*.
foreknowledge, render by verb.
foreland, *promontorium*.
foreman, *procurator*.
foremost, *primus, princeps*.
forenoon, *dies antemeridianus*.
forensic, *forensis*.
forerunner, *praenuntius*.
foresee, *praevidēre, providēre, prospicĕre*.
foresight, *providentia, provisio, prospicientia*.
forest, *silva*; sometimes *saltus* (*-ūs*: = wooded pasture).
forestall, *praevenire*; see also ANTICIPATE.
foretell, *praedicĕre*.
forethought, *providentia*.
forewarn, *praemonēre*.
forfeit, subst. *poena, multa*.
forfeit, v. (*rem*) *amittĕre*, (*re*) *multari*.
forge, subst. *fornax, officina*.
forge, v. LIT., in metal, *procudĕre, fabricare* or *fabricari*. TRANSF., (1) = to make or fashion abstract things, *fabricare* or *fabricari, fingĕre, conflare*. (2) = to counterfeit; of documents, *subicĕre, supponĕre*; of money, *adulterinos nummos facĕre* or *cudĕre*.
forged, of money, *adulterinus*.
forger, (of wills, etc.) *subiector, testamentarius*.
forgery, (of documents) *subiectio*.
forget, *oblivisci, dediscĕre*: to be forgotten, *e memoriā excidĕre*.
forgetful, *obliviosus, immemor*.
forgetfulness, *oblivio, oblivium* (poet., esp. in plur.); as a personal characteristic, *immemor ingenium*.
forgive, (*rem homini*) *ignoscĕre* or *condonare*; (*rei*, genit., *homini*) *veniam dare*.
forgiveness, *venia*.
forgiving, *facilis, clemens, exorabilis*.
fork, (for hay-making, etc.) *furca, furcilla*.
forked, *bifurcus*.
forlorn, *relictus, destitutus*.
form, subst. (1) = shape, *figura, forma, facies*; sometimes *species* or *genus*, in the sense of type, kind. (2) = of words, procedure, etc.; see FORMULA; in proper —, *rite*; for —'s sake, *dicis causā*. (3) = bench, *scamnum* (Ov., Mart.).
form, v. (1) = to shape, make, (*ef*)*fingĕre, figurare*, (*con*)*formare, fabricari, facĕre, efficĕre*; to — a plan, *consilium inire* or *capĕre*. (2) milit. t. t.: to — (up) troops, *instruĕre, ordinare*.
formal, *formalis* (Suet.).
formally, *rite* (= in due form).
formality, *ritus* (*-ūs*).
formation, *conformatio, forma*.
former, *prior, pristinus* (= ancient), *superior* (= immediately preceding): the —, the latter, *hic . . . ille, is . . . ille . . . hic*.
formerly, *antea, olim, quondam*.
formidable, *metuendus, timendus, formidandus, terribilis, formidolosus, gravis*.
formidably, *formidolose*.
formless, *informis, rudis*.
formula, *formula, carmen, verba* (*-orum*, plur.).
fornication, *stuprum*.
forsake, (*de*)*relinquĕre, deserĕre, destituĕre*.

forsooth! *scilicet, sane, nempe, quippe.*

forswear. (1) = to deny on oath; see ABJURE. (2) = to swear falsely, *periurare.*

fort, *arx, castellum, castrum.*

forth. (1) of place, *foras;* often rendered by compound verb with *e-* or *ex-* or *pro-.* (2) of time, *inde.* (3) and so —, *et cetera.*

forthcoming, express by fut. indic. or fut. partic. or the phrase *in eo esse ut.*

forthwith, *extemplo, statim, confestim, protinus.*

fortification, *munitio, munimentum.*

fortify, (*com*)*munire, praemunire, emunire, circummunire.*

fortitude, *fortitudo, virtus (-ūtis,* f.).

fortuitous, *fortuitus, forte oblatus.*

fortuitously, *forte, fortuito, casu.*

fortunate, *felix, fortunatus, beatus, secundus* (= favourable).

fortunately, *feliciter, fortunate.*

fortune. (1) *fortuna, fors, casus (-ūs);* personif.: the goddess of —, *Fortuna.* (2) = wealth, *divitiae (-arum,* plur.), *res (familiaris), census (-ūs), opes (-um,* plur.), *bona (-orum,* plur.), *fortunae (-arum,* plur.).

fortune-teller, *sortilegus, hariolus:* a female —, *saga.*

forty, *quadraginta:* — each, *quadrageni;* — times, *quadragie(n)s.*

forum, *forum:* of the —, *forensis.*

forward, adj. (1) = early, *praecox.* (2) = pert, *protervus.*

forward, forwards, adv. *porro, ante:* backwards and —, *ultro citro(que);* to go —, *pergĕre;* often rendered by compound verb with *pro-.*

forward, v. (1) of letters, etc., *perferendum curare.* (2) = to help, promote, *adiuvare.*

fosse, *fossa.*

foster, *nutrire, alĕre.*

foster-brother, *conlacteus.*

foster-child, *alumnus,* f. *alumna.*

foster-father, *nutricius.*

foster-mother, *nutrix.*

foster-sister, *conlactea* (Juv.).

foul, *foedus, putidus, turpis, obscenus, immundus:* — play, *dolus malus.*

foully, *foede, turpiter, nefarie.*

foulness, *foeditas.*

found. (1) of cities, etc., *condĕre, fundare, constituĕre.* (2) = to cast in metal, *fundĕre.*

foundation, *fundamenta (-orum,* plur.), *sedes* (mainly poet.): from the —s, *funditus.*

founder, subst. *conditor, auctor.*

founder, v. *submergi, deperire.*

foundling, *infans expositicius* (Pl.).

fount, or **fountain.** LIT., *fons, caput.* TRANSF., *fons, principium, origo.*

four, *quattuor:* — each, *quaterni;* — times, *quater;* — years old, *quadrimus;* a period of — years, *quadriennium;* going on — feet, *quadrupes;* —fold, *quadruplex;* — times as much, *quadruplum.*

fourteen, *quattuordecim:* — each, *quaterni deni;* — times, *quater decies.*

fourteenth, *quartus decimus.*

fourth, *quartus:* for the — time, *quartum;* in the — place, *quarto;* a — part = a quarter, *quadrans.*

fowl, subst. (1) = any bird, *avis, volucris, ales.* (2) = a hen, *gallina.*

fowl, v. *aucupari.*

fowler, *auceps.*

fowling, *aucupium.*

fox, *vulpes:* a little —, *vulpecula;* of a —, *vulpinus.* TRANSF., a sly old —, *veterator.*

fraction, *pars.*

fractious, *morosus, difficilis.*

fractiousness, *morositas.*

fracture, subst. as medic. t. t. *fractura* (Cels.).

fracture, v. *frangĕre.*

fragile, *fragilis.*

fragility, *fragilitas.*

fragment, *fragmentum, fragmen* (poet.).

fragrance, *odor suavis.*

fragrant, *suavis; suaveolens* (poet.), *odorifer* (poet.), *odoratus* (poet.), *odorosus* (poet.).

frail, adj. *infirmus, imbecillus, debilis, fragilis.*

frailty, *infirmitas, imbecillitas, fragilitas.*

frame, subst. (1) = structure, *compages;* of the body, *corpus (-ŏris).* (2) the — of a picture, window, etc., *forma* (Plin.). (3) — of mind, *animus.*

frame, v. (1) of physical things, *fingĕre, fabricare* or *fabricari.* (2) = to draw up in words, *concipĕre, componĕre.*

framework, *compages, contignatio.*

France, *Gallia.*

French, *Gallicus:* a —man, *Gallus.*

franchise, *civitas, ius (iuris,* n.).

frank, *candidus, apertus, simplex, liber.*

frankincense, *tus (turis,* n.).

frankly, *candide, aperte, simpliciter.*

frankness, *simplicitas, libertas* (Ov., Quint.).

frantic, *insanus, fanaticus, amens.*

frantically, *insane.*

fraternal, *fraternus.*

fraternally, *fraterne.*

fraternity. (1) = the relation between brothers, *germanitas, fraternitas* (Tac.). (2) = society, *sodalitas, sodalicium.*

fratricide. (1) as an act, *parricidium fraternum.* (2) as a person, *fratricida.*

fraud, *fraus, dolus (malus), fallacia, circumscriptio.*

fraudulent, *fraudulentus, dolosus.*

fraudulently, *fraudulenter, dolo malo, dolose.*

fraught, *refertus, repletus.*

fray, *pugna;* see also FIGHT.

freak: a — of fancy, *libido.*

freckle, *lenticula* (Cels.), *lentigo* (Plin.).

freckled, adj. *lentiginosus* (Val. Max.).

free, adj. (1) in gen. = unrestricted, *liber, solutus:* of one's own — will, *sua voluntate, sua sponte;* — from a thing, (*a*) *rē liber, solutus, vacuus, rei* (genit.) *expers;* — from taxes, *immunis;* — from guilt, *innocens;* — from danger, *tutus;* — from care, *securus;* to be — from, (*re*) *carēre.* (2) of space = open, unoccupied, *patens, apertus.* (3) = without cost, *gratuitus.* (4) = generous, *largus, munificus, liberalis.*

free, v. in gen., *liberare, eximĕre, solvĕre, expedire;* of slaves, *liberare, manumittĕre.*

freebooter, *latro, praedo.*

free-born, *ingenuus.*

freedman, in relation to the former master, *libertus* (f. *liberta*); as a member of a special class in society, *libertinus* (f. *libertina*).

freedom. (1) in gen. *libertas, licentia:* — of choice, *arbitrium.* (2) — from a particular burden, *vacatio, immunitas;* — from punishment, *impunitas.* (3) in bad sense = — abused, excessive —, licence, *licentia.*

freehold, *praedium liberum* or *immune.*

freeholder, *qui praedium liberum habet,* or simply *possessor.*

freely. (1) = without restriction, *libere, solute.* **(2)** = generously, *large, munifice, liberaliter.*

freeman, *homo liber.*

free-speech, *sermo liber* or *liberior.*

free-thinking; see SCEPTICAL.

free-will, *voluntas:* to have —, *sponte suā agĕre.*

freeze. (1) v. transit. *glaciare* (Hor.), *(con)gelare* (poet.). **(2)** intransit. *conglaciare, congelare* (Varro, Mart.); impers., it is freezing, *gelat* (Plin.).

freight, *onus (-ĕris,* n.).

freight, v. *onerare.*

freighted, *onustus.*

French, *Gallicus.*

Frenchman, *Gallus.*

frenzied, *furens, insanus, vesanus, amens.*

frenzy, *furor, insania, amentia.*

frequency, *frequentia, crebritas.*

frequent, adj. *frequens, creber.*

frequent, v. *celebrare, frequentare, in loco versari.*

frequented, *frequens, celeber;* of a road, *tritus.*

frequently, *frequenter, crebro, saepe;* often rendered by adj. *frequens.*

fresh. (1) = new, *recens, novus.* **(2)** = as good as new, refreshed, untired, *recens, integer, vegetus.* **(3)** = cold, *frigidus.*

freshen. (1) transit. = to invigorate, *recreare, reficĕre.* **(2)** intransit., of wind, *increbrescĕre.*

freshness, *viriditas.*

fret. (1) transit.: **a** = to chafe, wear away, *atterĕre*: **b** = to distress, *sollicitare, vexare, angĕre, macerare.* **(2)** intransit. *angi, dolĕre, macerari.*

fretful, *morosus, stomachosus.*

fretfully, *morose, stomachose.*

fretfulness, *morositas, stomachus.*

friable, *puter* or *putris* (poet.).

fricassee, *sartago* (Pers.).

friction, *tritus (-ūs).*

friend, *amicus* (f. *amica*), *sodalis, familiaris:* a great —, *amicissimus.*

friendless, *sine amicis, amicorum expers* or *inops.*

friendliness, *comitas, humanitas, benignitas, adfabilitas.*

friendly, *amicus, benevolus, humanus, benignus, comis.*

friendship, *amicitia, familiaritas.*

frieze. (1) in architecture, *zoophorus* (Vitr.). **(2)** the cloth, *gausape* or *gausapum* (Hor., Ov.).

fright, *terror, pavor;* see also FEAR.

frighten, *(ex)terrēre, terrorem homini inicĕre* or *incutĕre.*

frightful, *terribilis, horribilis, horridus, formidolosus.*

frightfully, *terribilem in modum, formidolose.*

frigid, *frigidus* (lit. and fig.).

frill, *segmenta (-orum,* plur.: Ov., Juv.).

fringe, *fimbriae (-arum,* plur.), *limbus* (Ov.).

frisk, *salire, lascivire.*

friskiness, *lascivia.*

frisky, *lascivus* (poet.).

frith, *fretum, aestuarium.*

fritter, subst. *laganum* (Hor.).

fritter, v.: to — away, *(con)terĕre, dissipare.*

frivolity, *nugae (-arum,* plur.), *levitas.*

frivolous, *levis, inanis, frivolus, nugax.*

fro: to and —, *huc (et) illuc, ultro citro(que).*

frock; see GOWN.

frog, *rana:* a small —, *ranunculus.*

frogman, (i.e. one engaged on military operations under water) *urinator.*

frolic, *ludus, lascivia.*

frolic, v. *ludĕre, lascivire.*

frolicsome, *lascivus, ludibundus, iocosus.*

from. (1) in space, *a, ab, ex* (= out of), *de* (= down from), all these with abl.; sometimes rendered by abl. alone (e.g. *domo, rure, Romā*), or by a special adv. (e.g. *hinc* = from here, *inde* = from there). **(2)** in time, *a, ab,* with abl.: from morning to night, *a mane ad noctem;* from boyhood, *a puero, a parvo.* **(3)** of cause, source, origin, *a, ab, ex, de* (all with abl.); *propter* (with acc.); sometimes rendered by abl. alone; when denoting position in a list, *a, ab* (e.g. *quartus ab Arcesila,* = the fourth from Arcesilas). **(4)** of material, made from = made of, *de* or *ex* (with abl.). **(5)** of separation, difference, change, *a, ab, de, ex* (with abl.); with some verbs denoting removal, from is expressed by dat. (e.g. *adimere, eripĕre*).

front, subst. *frons (-ntis,* f.), *pars prior:* in — of, *pro* with abl.; to attack in —, *hostes adversos adgredi.*

front, adj. *prior, anticus* (opp. to *posticus*).

front, v. **(1)** = to look towards, *aspectare.* **(2)** = to oppose, *adversari.*

frontage, *frons.*

frontier, *finis, terminus, confinium.*

fronting, *adversus, oppositus.*

frontlet, *frontalia (-ium,* plur.).

frost, *gelu, pruina;* = frosty weather, in gen. *frigus (-ŏris,* n.).

frost-bitten, *praeustus.*

frosty, *frigidus* (lit. and fig.).

froth, subst. *spuma.*

froth, v. *spumare.*

frothy, *spumosus, spumeus, spumifer* (all poet.).

froward, *contumax, pertinax, difficilis.*

frowardly, *contumaciter, pertinaciter.*

frowardness, *contumacia, pertinacia, pervicacia.*

frown, subst. *frontis contractio.*

frown, v. *frontem contrahĕre* or *adducĕre.*

frowsy, *sordidus, immundus.*

frozen, *rigidus* (poet.): to be —, *rigēre.*

fructify; see FERTILIZE.

frugal, *parcus, frugi* (indecl.).

frugality, *parsimonia, frugalitas, diligentia.*

frugally, *parce, frugaliter, diligens.*

fruit. LIT., the —s of the earth, *fructus (-ūs), frux* and plur. *fruges* (esp. of grain), *fetus (-ūs), pomum* (esp. = the fruit of trees), *baca* (= a berry); to bear —, *fructum ferre* or *reddĕre.* TRANSF., of any result, *fructus (-ūs), frux, effectus (-ūs).*

fruitful, *frugifer, fecundus, fertilis, uber, fructuosus.*

fruitfully, *fecunde; utiliter* (= profitably).

fruitfulness, *fecunditas, fertilitas, ubertas.*

fruition, *fructus (-ūs).*

fruitless, adj. *inutilis, sterilis, cassus, inritus.*

fruitlessly, *incassum, frustra, nequicquam, re infectā.*

fruit-tree, *pomum* (Cato, Verg.).

frustrate, *ad vanum* or *ad inritum redigĕre;* less often *frustrari.*

frustration, express by adv. *frustra* or adj. *vanus* or *inritus.*

fry, subst. (1) of fish, *examen* (Plin.). (2) contemptuously, of people, perhaps *plebecula* or *homunculi* (-*orum*, plur.).

fry, v. *frigĕre* (Hor.).

frying-pan, *sartago* (Juv.); prov.: out of the — into the fire, *de fumo in flammam* (Ammianus Marcellinus, 4th cent. A.D.).

fuel, *ligna* (-*orum*, plur.); prov.: to add — to the flames, *oleum addĕre camino* (Hor.).

fugitive, subst. *fugitivus, profugus.*

fugitive, adj. *fugax, fugitivus.*

fulfil, *explēre, implēre, exsequi, efficĕre, conficĕre, peragĕre.*

fulfilment, *confectio*; or render by verb.

full, adj. (1) = filled, *plenus, repletus, refertus* (all with genit. or abl.): — of food, *satur*; — of people, crowded, *frequens.* (2) = complete, *plenus, integer, iustus, solidus*; of a writer or speaker, *copiosus.*

full, v., of cloth, *durare.*

full-blown. LIT., of flowers, *apertus.* TRANSF., *superbus, tumidus.*

fuller, n. *fullo* (Pl.).

full-grown, *adultus, pubes (puber).*

fulling, subst. *fullonica* (Pl.).

fully, *plene*; in speech or writing, *copiose, abundanter.*

fulminate, *fulminare* (poet.), *intonare, minas iactare.*

fulmination, *minae* (-*arum*, plur.).

fulsome, *putidus*: — flattery, *nimia adulatio.*

fulsomely, *putide.*

fumble; see FEEL.

fume, subst. *vapor, halitus* (-*ūs*).

fume, v. *(ex)aestuare.*

fumigate, *suffire* (poet.).

fun, *iocus, ludus.*

function, *munus* (-*ĕris*, n.), *officium, pars.*

fund. LIT., = money, *pecunia.* TRANSF., *copia.*

fundament, *anus.*

fundamental, *primus, principalis.*

fundamentally, *penitus.*

fundamentals, *elementa* (-*orum*), *principia* (-*orum*).

funeral, subst. *funus* (-*ĕris*, n.), *exsequiae* (-*arum*, plur.), *(funebria) iusta* (-*orum*, plur.).

funeral, adj. *funebris*: — pile, *rogus, pyra*; — procession, *pompa funebris.*

funereal, *funebris, lugubris.*

fungous, *fungosus* (Plin.).

fungus, *fungus* (Plin.).

funnel, *infundibulum* (Cato).

funnily, *ridicule.*

funny, *ridiculus, iocularis.*

fur, *pellis.*

furbish, *interpolare, expolire.*

furious, *rabidus, furens, furiosus, furibundus.*

furiously, *rabide, vehementer.*

furl, *(vela) contrahĕre.*

furlong, *stadium.*

furlough, *commeatus* (-*ūs*): on —, *in commeatu.*

furnace, *fornax.*

furnish. (1) = to provide or equip, *(re)(ad)ornare, instruĕre.* (2) = to supply, give, *suppeditare, praebēre.*

furnished, *(re)instructus, praeditus.*

furniture, of a house, *supellex*; more generally *apparatus* (-*ūs*).

furrier, *pellio.*

furrow, subst. *sulcus.*

furrow, v. *sulcare* (poet.).

further, adj. *ulterior.*

further, adv. *ulterius, amplius, praeterea, porro.*

further, v. *(ad)iuvare* (with acc.); *servire* or *consulĕre* (with dat.).

furtherance, *auxilium.*

furtherer, *adiutor.*

furthest, *ultimus.*

furtive, *furtivus.*

furtively, *furtim, furtive.*

fury, *furor, rabies*; mythol., *Furia, Erinnys* (poet.).

furze, *ulex* (Plin.).

fuse, *liquefacĕre, fundĕre.*

fuss, subst. *trepidatio, tumultus* (-*ūs*).

fuss, v. *trepidare, satagĕre* (Quint.).

fussy, perhaps *curiosus.*

fustian, *gausape* or *gausapum* (Hor., Ov.).

fusty; see MOULDY.

futile, *futilis, inanis, vanus.*

futility, *futilitas.*

future, subst. *futura* (-*orum*, plur.): in —, for the —, *in futurum, in posterum, in reliquum.*

future, adj. *futurus, posterus.*

futurity, *tempus futurum* or *posterum.*

G

gabble, *garrire, blaterare.*

gable, *fastigium.*

gad, *vagari.*

gadfly, *asilus* (Verg.), *tabanus* (Varro).

gag, subst. use phrase, e.g. *linteum in os iniectum.*

gag, v. *os homini obvolvĕre et praeligare* (Cic.).

gage, *pignus* (-*ŏris*, n.); see also PLEDGE.

gaiety, *hilaritas, laetitia, festivitas.*

gaily, *hilare, laete, festive.*

gain, subst. *lucrum* (opp. *damnum*), *quaestus* (-*ūs*; = profit), *commodum* (= advantage), *emolumentum* (opp. *detrimentum*), *compendium* (= savings), *praeda* (= booty), *praemium* (= a prize).

gain, v. *lucrari, lucri facĕre, consequi, capĕre*: to — a victory, *victoriam reportare*, or *vincĕre*; the enemy has —ed the day, *hostis vicit* or *victor evasit*; to — a prize, *praemium auferre*; to — favour with, *gratiam inire apud*, or *cum*; to — over, *conciliare.*

gainful, *quaestuosus, lucrosus.*

gainsay; see CONTRADICT.

gait, *incessus* (-*ūs*).

gaiters, *ocreae* (-*arum*, plur.; = greaves).

gala; see FESTIVAL.

galaxy, *orbis lacteus, via lactea* (Ov.).

gale, *ventus, aura* (= breeze).

gall, subst. *fel, bilis.*

gall, v. LIT., = to chafe, *terĕre.* TRANSF., = to annoy, *mordēre, urĕre.*

gallant, subst., render by *iuvenis*, with adj.; = paramour, *amator.*

gallant, adj. (1) = brave, *fortis, animosus.* (2) = attentive to females, *officiosus.*

gallantly, = bravely, *fortiter, animose.*

gallantry. (1) = bravery, *virtus* (-*ūtis*, f.), *fortitudo.* (2) *amores* (-*um*, plur.).

gallery, *porticus* (-*ūs* = an open — with pillars): a picture —, *pinacotheca* (Plin.); an underground —, *cuniculus.*

galley, *navis longa, biremis, triremis.*

galling, *mordax* (Hor.).

gallipot, *aulula* (or *ollula*).

gallon, *congius.*

gallop, subst. *gradus (-ūs), citatus:* at a —, *equo admisso* or *(con)citato.*

gallop, v. *equo admisso vehi* or *currĕre.*

gallows, *crux* (crucifixion and strangling were the Roman equivalents to hanging; see also HANG).

gamble, v. *aleā ludĕre.*

gambler, *aleator.*

gambling, *alea.*

gambol, subst. *lusus (-ūs).*

gambol, v. *ludĕre, lascivire.*

game, subst. (1) as played, *ludus, lusio, ludicrum:* a — of chance, *alea.* (2) as hunted, *ferae (-arum,* plur.); on table, *(caro) ferina* (Verg.), *venatio.*

game, adj.; see SPIRITED.

game, v.; see GAMBLE.

gamesome, *ludibundus.*

gamester, gaming; see GAMBLE.

gaming-table, *alveus* (Suet.).

gammon, *perna.*

gammon, interj. = nonsense! *gerrae!* (Pl.).

gander, *anser (mas* or *masculus).*

gang, *grex, caterva;* in a sinister sense, *sodalicium, operae (-arum,* plur.).

gangrene, *gangraena* (Cels.).

gangway, *forus.*

gaol, *carcer;* sometimes *vincula (-orum,* plur.).

gaoler, *(carceris) custos.*

gap, *lacuna, hiatus (-ūs).*

gape, *(in)hiare, (de)hiscĕre.*

garbage, *purgamentum, quisquiliae.*

garble, = to falsify, *corrumpĕre, vitiare.*

Garda, Lake, *Benacus (lacus).*

garden, subst. *hortus:* a small —, *hortulus;* pleasure- —s, *horti (-orum,* plur.).

garden, v. *in horto fodĕre, hortum colĕre.*

gardener, *topiarius* (= an ornamental —); otherwise render by phrase, e.g. *qui hortum colit.*

gardening, *hortorum cultus (-ūs).*

garden-stuff, *olus (-ĕris,* n.).

gargle, *gargarizare* (Cels.).

garish, = bright, *clarus, splendidus.*

garland, *corona, sertum* (usually plur.).

garlic, *alium.*

garment, *vestimentum;* see CLOTHES.

garner, subst. *horreum.*

garner, v. *condĕre.*

garnish, *(ex)ornare, instruĕre, decorare.*

Garonne (river), *Garumna.*

garret, *cenaculum.*

garrison, subst. *praesidium.*

garrison, v. *(urbi) praesidium imponĕre, (in urbe) praesidium conlocare, (urbem) praesidio firmare.*

garrulity, *garrulitas* (Ov.), *loquacitas.*

garrulous, *garrulus, loquax, verbosus.*

garrulously, *loquaciter.*

garter, *periscĕlis* (Hor.); in plur. only, *genualia (-ium:* Ov.).

gas, render by *spiritus (-ūs)* or *vapor.*

gasconade, *iactatio, ostentatio.*

gash, subst. *vulnus (-ĕris,* n.).

gash, v. *vulnerare, caesim percutĕre.*

gasp, subst. *anhelitus, singultus (-ūs).*

gasp, v. *anhelare, singultare* (Verg.).

gasping, adj. *anhelus* (Verg).

gastric, *ad stomachum pertinens.*

gate, of a house, *ianua, ostium;* of a city, *porta.*

gate-keeper, *ianitor.*

gate-post, *postis.*

gather, v. (1) transit. *legĕre, conligĕre, congregare, conferre:* to — fruit, or flowers, *legĕre, carpere.* TRANSF., = to conjecture, *conicĕre, conligĕre.* (2) intransit.: **a** = to assemble, *convenire, congregari:* **b**, of a sore, *suppurare.*

gathering, subst. (1) as an act, *conlectio.* (2) = an assembly, *coetus (-ūs), concilium.* (3) = a sore, *suppuratio* (Cels.).

gaudy, subst.; see FEAST.

gaudy, adj. *fucatus, magnificus.*

gauge, v. *metiri;* see also MEASURE.

gaunt, *macer.*

gauntlet, in plur., *manicae (-arum):* to run the —, *per militum ordines currentum virgis caedi.*

gauze, *vestis Coa* (Plin.).

gay. (1) of spirits, *hilaris, laetus festivus.* (2) of colour, etc., *splendidus, nitidus.*

gaze, subst. *obtutus (-ūs), conspectus (-ūs).*

gaze, v.: to — at, *intuĕri, contuĕri, contemplari.*

gazelle, *dorcas* (Mart., Plin.).

gazette, *acta (diurna) (-orum,* plur.).

gear, *ornatus (-ūs), supellex, apparatus (-ūs).*

geld, *castrare* (Pl.).

gelding, *canterius* (Varro).

gem, *gemma.*

gender, *genus (-ĕris,* n.).

genealogical, *de origine scriptus, ad originem pertinens.*

genealogy, render by *origo* or *stirps.*

general, subst. *dux, imperator* (= commander-in-chief); a lieutenant- — (subordinate commander), *legatus,* sometimes *dux;* the —'s tent, *praetorium.*

general, adj. *generalis* (= relating to the *genus:* Quint.); *communis* (= common to all); *publicus* (= belonging to the whole people or state), *vulgaris* (= common, ordinary); often rendered by genit. plur. *omnium* or *omnium rerum* (e.g. the — good, *omnium salus*): in —, *ad summam, in universum, universe, generatim* (opp. *singillatim*), *communiter.*

generality, = most people, *vulgus (-i,* n.), *plerique.*

generalize, *de omnibus (rebus),* or *generatim,* or *universe, loqui.*

generally. (1) = in general; see GENERAL. (2) = usually, *fere, ferme, vulgo, plerumque.*

generalship, *ductus (-ūs):* under the — of Caesar, *Caesare duce.*

generate, *gignĕre, generare, procreare, parĕre;* see also CAUSE.

generation. (1) the act, *procreatio.* (2) = age, *saeculum, aetas:* the present —, *huius aetatis homines.*

generative, *genitalis* (poet.): — organs, *genitalia (-ium,* plur.: Cels.).

generator, *procreator, generator.*

generosity, *benignitas, liberalitas, beneficentia.*

generous. (1) = of noble birth, *generosus, nobilis.* (2) = of noble (esp. liberal) disposition, *generosus, magnificus, benignus, liberalis.*

generously, *benigne, liberaliter, large.*

genesis; see ORIGIN.

Geneva, Lake of, *Lemannus (lacus).*

genial, *comis, benignus, genialis* (poet.).

geniality, *comitas.*

genially, *comiter.*

genitive, *(casus) genitivus* (Quint.).

genius. (1) in the special Roman sense, a person's — or attendant spirit, *genius*. (2) = high natural ability, render by *ingenium* or *indoles*, qualified by adj. such as *praeclarus*: a —, = a man of —, *homo ingeniosus, homo praeclaro ingenio (praeditus)*, or simply *ingenium*.

genteel, *elegans, urbanus*.

genteelly, *eleganter, urbane*.

gentility, *elegantia, urbanitas*.

gentle. (1) = well-born, *generosus, ingenuus, nobilis*. (2) = mild, *lenis, mitis, clemens, mansuetus, placidus*.

gentleman. (1) by birth, *homo generosus, ingenuus, nobilis; homo honeste* or *nobili loco natus*. (2) in behaviour and disposition, *homo liberalis* or *generosus*.

gentlemanly, *liberalis, ingenuus, generosus, honestus*.

gentleness, *clementia, mansuetudo, lenitas*.

gentlewoman; see LADY.

gently, = mildly, softly, *leniter, mansuete, mite, molliter, placide*.

gentry, *nobilitas, nobiles* (-*ium*, plur.).

genuflexion; see KNEEL.

genuine, *sincerus, merus, germanus*.

genuinely, *reapse, sincere, vere*.

genuineness, render by phrase with adj.

geography, *geographia, terrarum* or *regionum descriptio*.

geometer, geometrician, *geometres* (-*ae*).

geometrical, *geometricus*.

geometry, *geometria*.

George, *Georgius* (late Latin).

germ, *germen, semen*.

german, *germanus, cognatus*.

German, *Germanus, Germanicus*.

germane, *adfinis*.

Germany, *Germania*.

germinate, *germinare* (Plin.).

germination, *germinatio* (Plin.).

gestation, *partūs gerendi tempus* (Plin.).

gesticulate, *se iactare, gestum facĕre* or *agĕre*.

gesticulation, *iactatio, gestus* (-*ūs*), *motus* (-*ūs*).

gesture, *gestus* (-*ūs*), *motus* (-*ūs*).

get, v. (1) transit. *capĕre, adipisci, nancisci, (com)parare, consequi*: to — by asking, *impetrare*; to — back, *recipĕre*; to — the better of, *superare, vincĕre*; to — anything done, *rem faciendam curare*; to — hold of, *prehendĕre*. (2) intransit., to — = to become, *fieri*; to — along, *procedĕre*; to — at, *attingĕre*; to — away, *effugĕre, abire*; colloq., to — away with (i.e. not be punished for) an offence, *impune ferre*; to — back, *redire*; to — down, *descendĕre*; to — in, *introire*; to — out, *egredi, exire, emergĕre*; to — to, *pervenire ad*; to — up, *surgĕre*.

ghastliness, *pallor*; see also HORROR.

ghastly, *exsanguis, pallidus, cadaverosus* (Ter.), *luridus* (Hor., Ov.); see also TERRIBLE.

ghost, *manes* (-*ium*, plur.), *lemures* (-*um*: Hor.), *larva* (Pl.), *umbra* (poet.): the Holy —, *Spiritus Sanctus* (eccl.); to give up the —, *exspirare, animam efflare* or *edere*.

ghoul, *larva* (Pl.).

giant, use phrase, such as *vir maior quam pro humano habitu*; in mythol., one of the —s, *gigas*.

gibbet; see GALLOWS.

gibe, subst. *cavillatio*.

gibe, v. *cavillari.*

giddiness, *vertigo* (lit. and fig.), *levitas* (fig.), *temeritas* (fig.).

giddy. LIT., *vertiginosus* (Plin.). TRANSF., *lĕvis, inconstans*.

gift, *donum, munus* (poet.): natural —s, *natura et ingenium*.

gifted: a — man, *vir summi ingenii*.

gig, *cisium*.

gigantic; see GIANT.

giggle, *cachinnare*, qualified by adv., such as *summisse*.

gild, *inaurare*.

gills, *branchiae* (-*arum*, plur.: Plin.).

gimlet, *terebra* (Plin.).

gin, = a trap, *laqueus, pedica*.

gingerly, *pedetemptim, sensim*.

gipsy, no class. equivalent; perhaps use *Cingarus* (f. *Cingara*).

giraffe, *camēlŏpardālis* (Plin.).

gird. LIT., *(suc)cingĕre, accingĕre*: to — oneself, *(suc)cingi* or *accingi* (e.g. *gladio, ferro*); to — on, *accingĕre*. TRANSF., to — oneself, *se accingĕre* or *accingi*.

girder, *trabs*.

girdle, *zona* (poet.), *cingulum* (poet.), *balteus* (= belt).

girl, *puella, virgo*.

girlhood, *aetas puellaris*: she did it in her —, *puella fecit*.

girlish, *puellaris* (Ov.), *virginalis*.

girth. (1) = distance round, *ambitus, circuitus, complexus* (all -*ūs*). (2) of a horse, *cingula* (Ov.). (3) of a bed, *fascia*.

gist, *summa, index*.

give, *dare, praebĕre, tribuĕre, largiri, donare*: to — an account, *rationem reddĕre*; to — an audience, *sui potestatem facĕre, colloquendi copiam facĕre*; to — an opportunity, *copiam facĕre*; to — back, *reddĕre*; to — forth, *edĕre*; to — in, see YIELD; to — out (= to announce publicly), *praedicare*; (= to fail), *deficĕre*; to — up, transit., *amittĕre, dimittĕre, deponĕre, dedĕre* (= to surrender), *tradĕre* (= to hand over), *prodĕre* (= to betray); to — up, intransit. (= to cease), *desistĕre*; to — up hope of, *desperare* (*rem*); to — way, *cedĕre* (see also YIELD); to — way to an emotion, *luctui*, etc., *indulgĕre*.

giver, *qui donum dat; dator* (Verg.).

gizzard, *ingluvies* (Verg.), *guttur* (Ov.).

glad, *laetus, hilaris* or *hilarus*.

gladden, *(ex)hilarare*.

glade, *silva, saltus* (-*ūs*).

gladiator, *gladiator*: a trainer of —s, *lanista*.

gladiatorial, *gladiatorius*: to give a — show, *gladiatores dare*.

gladly, *laete, libenter*.

gladness, *laetitia, hilaritas*.

glance, subst. *aspectus* (-*ūs*).

glance, v. (1) = to look, *aspicĕre*. (2) to — at = to touch lightly upon, (*rem*) *attingĕre, perstringĕre, strictim dicĕre*.

gland, *glans* (Cels.).

glare, subst. (1) of bright light, *fulgor*. (2) = a fierce look, *oculi torvi* (poet.); see also GLARE, v.

glare, v. (1) of bright light, *fulgēre*. (2) = to look fiercely, *intentis* or *torvis* (poet.) *oculi intueri, torva tueri* (Verg.).

glass, subst. *vitrum*: a looking —, *speculum*.

glass, adj. or **glassy,** *vitreus* (poet.); prov.: those who live in —-houses should not throw

stones, perhaps *loripedem rectus derideat* (Juv.).
gleam, subst. *fulgor*: — of hope, *spēcula*.
gleam, v. *fulgēre*.
glean, *spicilegium* (Varro) *facĕre*.
gleaning, subst. *spicilegium* (Varro).
glee, *hilaritas, laetitia, gaudium*.
gleeful, *hilaris, laetus*.
glen, (*con*)*vallis*.
glib, *loquax, garrulus, volubilis*.
glibly, *loquaciter, volubiliter*.
glibness, *loquacitas, garrulitas, volubilitas*.
glide, (*pro*)*labi*.
glimmer, *sublucēre*.
glimmering, adj. *sublustris*.
glimpse; see SIGHT.
glisten; see GLITTER, v.
glitter, subst. *fulgor*.
glitter, v. *fulgēre, nitēre, lucēre, candēre* (poet.).
glittering, *lucidus, nitidus, coruscus* (poet.), *candidus* (= glittering white).
gloat: to — over, *aspectu* (*rei, hominis*, etc.) *se delectare*.
globe, *globus, sphaera*: the — (= the earth), *orbis terrarum* or *terrae*.
globular, *globosus*.
gloom. LIT., *obscuritas, caligo, tenebrae* (*-arum*, plur.). TRANSF., *caligo, tenebrae* (*-arum*, plur.), *tristitia, maeror, maestitia*.
gloomily, *maeste*.
gloomy. LIT., = dark, *obscurus, tenebrosus* (poet.), *caliginosus*. TRANSF., = sad, *tristis, maestus*.
glorify, *laudare, celebrare, laudibus ornare* or *efferre* or *tollĕre*.
glorious, (*prae*)*clarus, amplus, inlustris, gloriosus* (often = vainglorious).
gloriously, *gloriose*, (*prae*)*clare, ample*.
glory, subst. *gloria, honor* (*honos*), *decus* (*-ŏris*, n.), *laus*.
glory, v. (*re*) *gloriari*.
glorying, subst. *gloriatio*.
gloss, subst. (**1**) = shine, *nitor*. (**2**) = an explanation, *interpretatio*.
gloss, v.: to — over, *extenuare*.
glossary, *glossarium* (Gell.).
glossy, *nitidus*.
Gloucester, *Glevum*.
glove, *manicae* (*-arum*, plur. = long sleeves).
glow, subst. *ardor, fervor*.
glow, v. *ardēre, ardescĕre* (poet.), *flagrare*.
glow-worm, *cicindēla* (Plin.), *lampyris* (Plin.).
glue, subst. *gluten* (Lucr., Verg.).
glue, v. *glutinare* (Plin.).
glut, subst. *satias, satietas*: a — in the market, render by *vilitas annonae*.
glut, v. *satiare, saturare, explēre*.
glutinous, *lentus, glutinosus* (Cels.).
glutton, *helluo*.
gluttonous, *edax, vorax, gulosus* (Juv., Sen.).
gluttony, *gula, edacitas*.
gnarled: see KNOTTY.
gnash: to — the teeth, (*dentibus*) (*in*)*frendĕre*.
gnashing, *stridor dentium* (Cels.).
gnat, *culex* (poet.).
gnaw, (*ad*)*rodĕre*: to — to pieces, *corrodĕre*.
gnawing, *mordax* (Hor.).
gnome. (**1**) see MAXIM. (**2**) see FAIRY.
go, v. (**1**) absol., of physical movement; *ire, meare* (poet.), *vadĕre* (esp. = to — fast or violently), *gradi* (= to step), *proficisci* (= to set out), *abire* or *discedĕre* (= to depart).

(**2**) qualified : with an adj., to — so and so (= to become), *fieri*; with an adv., to — well, badly, etc., *bene, male*, etc., *cedĕre*; to — astray, *errare*; to — away, *abire, discedĕre*; to — back, *redire, reverti*; to — before, *anteire*; to — beyond, *excedĕre*; to — by (= to pass), *praeterire*; to — by (= to follow, observe), *sequi*; to — down, *descendĕre*; to — forth, *exire, prodire*; to — forward (lit. and fig.), *procedĕre*; to — in, *inire, intrare, ingredi*; to — off (lit. and fig.), *abire*; to — on (= to proceed, continue), *pergĕre*; to — on (= to happen), *fieri, agi*; to — on well, *succedĕre*; to — on board, (*navem*) *conscendĕre*; to — out, *exire, egredi* (of a fire, *exstingui*); to — over, *transire, transgredi*; to — round, *circumire*; to — to and fro, *commeare*; to — under, *subire*; to — up, *ascendĕre*; to — without (a thing), *carēre* (*re*); to let —, *dimittĕre, omittĕre*.
goad, subst. *stimulus*: to kick against a —, *adversum stimulum calcare*.
goad, v. *stimulare, incitare*.
goal, *meta* (poet.), *calx*.
goat, m. *caper* (Verg.), *hircus* (Verg.); f., *capra, capella*.
goatherd, *caprarius* (Col.).
gobble, (*de*)*vorare, obsorbēre* (Pl., Hor.).
go-between, *conciliator, interpres*, f., *internuntius*.
goblet, *poculum, scyphus*; see also CUP.
goblin, *larva*.
god, *deus, divus* (mainly poet.), *numen* (*divinum*); plur., the —s, *di* (*dii*), *divi, numina, caelestes, superi* (poet.); —s of the household, *lares, penates*; by the —s, *per deos*; so help me —, *ita me deus* (*ad*)*iuvet* or *amet*; — willing, *dis volentibus* (Sall.); — forbid! *quod di omen avertant! ne di sinant! di meliora!*
goddess, *dea, diva* (mainly poet.).
godhead, *numen*.
godless, *impius*.
godlike, *divinus*.
godliness, *pietas* (*erga deos*).
godly, *pius* (*erga deos*).
godsend, *res quasi divinitus oblata*.
gold, *aurum*.
gold-dust, *ballux* (Plin.).
golden, *aureus*.
gold-leaf, *auri lamina* (Plin.), or *bractea* (poet.).
gold-mine, *aurifodina* (Plin.).
goldsmith, *aurifex*.
good, subst.: in gen. *bonum, salus* (*-utis*, f.), *utilitas*: to do —, *prodesse* (*homini, rei*); the highest —, *summum bonum*. In plur. = property, possessions, *bona* (*-orum*, plur.); = wares, merchandise, *merx*; colloq., of a person, a bad bit of —s, *mala merx* (Pl.).
good, adj.: in gen. = good of its kind, *bonus, probus*; = morally, *bonus, probus, honestus*; = kind, *bonus, benignus*; = useful, *utilis*; = suitable, convenient, *opportunus, commodus*; = wholesome, health-giving, *saluber, salutaris*. In phrases: a — many, *plerique, aliquot, complures*; a — while, *aliquantum temporis*; — fortune, *res secundae* (plur.); — health, *bona valetudo*; — day! *salve!*; my — friend, *o bone*; to make —, *sarcire, restituĕre*.
good! interj. *euge!* or *eugepae!* (Pl., Ter.), *bene habet, praeclare*.
good-breeding, *humanitas, comitas*.
goodbye, *vale, ave* (plur. *valete, avete*).

good-fellowship, *comitas, iucunditas.*
good-for-nothing, *nequam.*
good-humour, *comitas, facilitas.*
good-humoured, *comis, facilis, benignus.*
good-looking, *pulcher, venustus.*
goodly; see GOOD, GOOD-LOOKING, or LARGE.
good-nature, *facilitas, comitas, humanitas, benignitas.*
good-natured, *facilis, comis, humanus, benignus.*
goodness: in gen., of what is good in its kind, *bonitas:* moral —, *probitas, virtus (-ūtis,* f.); = kindness, *benignitas, bonitas.*
good-tempered, *mitis, lenis.*
goose, *anser.*
gore, subst. *cruor.*
gore, v. *(cornibus) transfigēre, confodēre.*
gorge, subst. (1) = throat, *gula, guttur, fauces (-ium,* plur.). (2) = a narrow pass, *angustiae (-arum,* plur.), *fauces (-ium,* plur.).
gorge, v. transit. *(ex)satiare, (ex)saturare:* to — oneself, *exsatiari, se ingurgitare.*
gorgeous, *splendidus, magnificus, lautus, speciosus.*
gorgeously, *splendide, magnifice, laute.*
gorgeousness, *splendor, magnificentia.*
gormandize, *helluari.*
gormandizer, *helluo.*
gory, *cruentus, cruentatus.*
gospel, *evangelium* (eccl.).
gossamer, *aranea* (Lucr.).
gossip, subst. (1) = idle talk, *sermo, rumor.* (2) = a talkative person, *homo garrulus, homo loquax.* (3) = friend, *familiaris.*
gossip, v. *sermonem conferre, rumores spargēre, garrire.*
gouge, v. *(scalpro) eximēre* or *eruēre.*
gourd, *cucurbita* (Plin.).
gout, *articulorum dolor, arthritis* (Vitr.): — in the hands, *chiragra* (Cels.); — in the feet, *podagra;* to suffer from —, *(ex) pedibus laborare.*
gouty, adj. *arthriticus.*
govern. (1) politically: to — a state, a province, etc., *rempublicam, provinciam gubernare, administrare, gerēre, curare, tractare, temperare.* (2) in gen. = to restrain, guide, *rei* (dat.) *moderari, rem temperare, regēre, coercēre.*
government. (1) = the business of governing, *administratio, gubernatio, procuratio, cura.* (2) = supreme power, *imperium, regnum, dicio.* (3) = holders of supreme power, *ii qui reipublicae praesunt, penes quos est reipublica.*
governor. (1) in gen. *gubernator, rector.* (2) with delegated and limited powers, *praefectus, propraetor, proconsul, legatus.*
governorship, *praefectura.*
gown, man's, *toga;* woman's, *stola, palla.*
grace, subst. (1) = favour, goodwill, *gratia, favor:* by the — of god, *dei beneficio, deo favente;* to get into a person's good —s, *gratiam hominis inire* or *conciliare;* with a good, bad —, *cum bonā, malā gratiā* (Ter.). (2) = gracefulness, charm, *lepos (lepor), venustas, elegantia.* (3) myth., in plur., the Graces, *Gratiae (-arum).*
grace, v. *honestare, (ad)ornare, decorare.*
graceful, *venustus, decorus, elegans, lepidus.*
gracefully, *venuste, decore, eleganter, lepide.*
graceless, *improbus, nequam.*
gracious, *propitius* (esp. of gods); see also KIND.

grade, *gradus (-ūs).*
gradual; see GRADUALLY.
gradually, *paullatim, gradatim, sensim.*
graft, subst. *surculus.*
graft, v. *inserēre* (poet.).
grain. (1) = particle, *granum, mica* (Lucr., Hor.). (2) = corn, *frumentum.*
graminivorous, *(animal) quod herbis pascitur.*
grammar. (1) as a science, *grammatica (-orum,* plur.). (2) = a book on —, *liber grammaticus.*
grammarian, *grammaticus.*
grammatical, *grammaticus* (Quint.).
granary, *horreum, granaria (-orum,* plur.).
grand, *grandis, magnificus, amplus.*
granddaughter, *neptis.*
grandee, *homo nobilis;* in plur., *nobiles (-ium), proceres (-um).*
grandeur, *amplitudo, maiestas, magnificentia;* of language, *granditas.*
grandfather, *avus.*
grandiloquence, *oratio tumida.*
grandiloquent, *grandiloquus.*
grandmother, *avia.*
grandson, *nepos.*
grange, = country-house, *villa.*
granite, use *lapis* or *saxum.*
grant, subst. (1) = gift, *donum.* (2) = the act of granting, *concessio.*
grant, v. (1) = to bestow, *permittere, concedēre;* see also GIVE. (2) = to admit, *concedēre, dare:* —ed that, *ut* with subj.; granted, *esto.*
grape, *acinus* or *acinum* (Plin.): a bunch of —s, *uva, racemus* (poet.).
graphic, *expressus:* to give a — description, *rem tanquam sub oculos subicēre.*
grapple: to — with, LIT., *cum homine,* etc., *luctari.* TRANSF., *obviam ire* (with dat.).
grappling-iron, *ferrea manus (-ūs), harpago.*
grasp, subst. LIT., physical, *complexus (-ūs);* often *manūs (-uum,* plur.). TRANSF., mental, *captus (-ūs);* or render by verb.
grasp, v. LIT., physically, *(ap)prehendēre, comprehendēre, prensare.* TRANSF., mentally, *intellegēre; animo* (or *mente* or *cogitatione) comprehendēre* or *complecti;* see COMPREHEND; to — at (lit. and fig.), *captare, adfectare, appetēre.*
grasping, *avarus, appetens.*
grass, *gramen, herba.*
grasshopper, *gryllus* or *grillus* (Plin.).
grassy, *gramineus, herbidus, herbosus* (poet.).
grate, subst. *focus, caminus.*
grate, v. (1) = to rub, *(con)terēre.* (2) = make a grating noise, *stridēre;* see ANNOY.
grateful. (1) = thankful, *gratus.* (2) = pleasant, *gratus, acceptus, iucundus.*
gratefully, *grate, grato animo.*
gratification. (1) = the act of gratifying, *expletio, delectatio.* (2) = pleasure, *voluptas, oblectamentum.*
gratify, *(homini) gratificari, morem gerere;* see also PLEASE.
gratifying, *gratus.*
grating, subst. (1) = an arrangement of bars, *cancelli (-orum,* plur.), *clatri* or *clathri (-orum,* plur.: Hor.). (2) = a harsh noise, *stridor.*
gratis, *gratiis* or *gratis, gratuito.*
gratitude, *gratus animus.*
gratuitous, *gratuitus.*
gratuitously, *gratiis* or *gratis, gratuito.*

gratuity; see ALMS, GIFT.

grave, subst. LIT., = place of burial, *sepulcrum*; = place of cremation, *bustum*: to carry to the —, *sepelire, funus hominis prosequi*. TRANSF., = the state of death, *mors, inferi (-orum,* plur.).

grave, adj. *gravis, serius, tristis, severus*.

grave, v.; see ENGRAVE.

gravel, *glarea*.

gravity. LIT., physical, *gravitas, pondus (-eris,* n.). TRANSF., = seriousness, *gravitas, tristitia, severitas*.

gravy, *ius (iuris,* n.), *sucus*.

gray; see GREY.

graze. (1) of the feeding of animals; transit. *pascĕre*; intransit. *pasci*. (2) = to touch in passing, *radĕre* (poet.), *stringĕre* (poet.).

grazier, *pecuarius*.

grazing, subst. *pascua (-orum,* plur.).

grazing, adj., of land, *pascuus*.

grease, subst. *adeps, lardum* or *laridum*.

grease, v. *ung(u)ĕre; adipe,* etc., *inlinĕre* or *oblinĕre*.

greasy, *unctus* (= rubbed with grease), *pinguis* (= fat).

great, adj. (1) without qualification, great. LIT., of size, *magnus, grandis, amplus, vastus, ingens*. TRANSF., **a**, of persons, cities, etc., *magnus, amplus, clarus, inlustris, grandis* (poet.); as plur. subst., the great, *nobiles (-ium):* **b**, with descriptive words, often rendered by superl. of adj., e.g. a — friend, *amicissimus:* **c**, with abstract nouns, *magnus, summus, impensus*. (2) qualified: greater, *maior;* greatest, *maximus;* as — as, *tantus quantus;* how —, *quantus;* so —, *tantus;* too —, *nimius*.

greatcoat, use a word meaning 'cloak', e.g. *pallium, lacerna, paenula*.

great-grandfather, *proavus*.

great-grandmother, *proavia* (Suet.).

great-grandson, *pronepos*.

greatly, adv. *magnopere, valde, vehementer*.

greatness, *magnitudo, amplitudo, gravitas*.

greaves, *ocreae*.

Greece, *Graecia*.

greed, *avaritia, aviditas, cupiditas*.

greedily, *avare, avide, cupide*.

greedy, *avarus, avidus, cupidus*.

Greek, adj. and subst. *Graecus, Graius* (poet., or with heroic associations), *Graeculus* (disparaging).

green, subst. (1) = greenness, *viriditas, color viridis*. (2) = a grassy space, *campus*.

green, adj. (1) in colour, *viridis, virens* (of living things), *prasinus* (Plin.): to be —, *virēre;* to become —, *virescĕre*. (2) = fresh, *viridis, recens, crudus* (= unripe).

greenhorn, *tiro*.

greenness, *viriditas*.

greens, *holus (-eris,* n.).

greet, *salutare, (homini) salutem dicĕre, (hominem) salvēre iubēre;* of several persons, *consalutare*.

greeting, *(con)salutatio, salus (-utis,* f.).

gregarious, *qui congregari solent*.

Gregory, *Gregorius* (late Latin).

grey, *canus* (= hoary), *caesius* (= ·grey-blue, esp. of eyes), *glaucus* (= grey-blue: Verg.).

greybeard, *senex*.

greyness, *canities*.

gridiron, *craticula* (Mart.).

grief, *dolor, aegritudo, maeror* (= grief as

exhibited, sadness), *luctus (-ūs;* esp. of mourning), *aegritudo, cura, sollicitudo*.

grievance, *iniuria* (= wrong done); *querimonia, querel(l)a* (= complaint).

grieve, v. (1) transit. *(hominem) dolore,* etc., *adficĕre; (homini) dolorem,* etc., *adferre* or *facĕre; (ex)cruciare, angĕre*. (2) intransit. *dolēre, maerēre, lugēre; dolore,* etc., *adfici; hominem rei* (genit.) *piget*.

grievous, *acerbus, gravis, molestus*.

grievously, *acerbe, moleste, graviter*.

grievousness, *acerbitas, molestia, gravitas*.

griffin, *gryps* (Verg.).

grill, v. *torrēre;* see also ROAST.

grim, *torvus* (poet.), *trux* (poet.), *saevus*.

grimace, subst. *os distortum:* to make —s, *os (dis)torquēre*.

grimness, *saevitia, torvitas* (Plin., Tac.).

grimy; see DIRTY.

grin, subst. use *rictus (-ūs)*.

grin, v. intransit., use *ridēre*.

grind, v. LIT., *molĕre:* to — the teeth, *dentibus frendĕre*. TRANSF., = to oppress, *opprimĕre, vexare*.

grinder, (of teeth) *dens genuinus*.

grindstone, *cos*.

grip, subst., use *manus (-ūs,* f.).

grip, v.; see SEIZE.

gripes, griping pains, *tormina (-um,* plur.: Plin.): subject to —, *torminosus*.

grisly, *foedus, teter, horrendus*.

grist, *farina*.

gristle, *cartilago* (Plin.).

gristly, *cartilagineus* (Plin.).

grit, subst., of barley, *ptisăna* (Cels.); of sand, *harena;* of gravel, *glarea*.

groan, subst. *gemitus (-ūs)*.

groan, v. *gemĕre, gemitūs ēdĕre:* to — over, *ingemo,* with dat. (poet.).

groceries, *condimenta (-orum,* plur.).

groin, *inguen*.

groom, subst. *agaso, equiso* (Varro): — of the chamber, *cubicularius*.

groom, v. *curare*.

groove, *canalis*.

grope, *praetemptare* (poet.).

gropingly, *pedetemptim*.

gross, subst. = 144; express by numeral.

gross, adj. LIT., = thick, *crassus, densus, pinguis*. TRANSF., (1) = great, too great, *magnus, nimius, incredibilis*. (2) = disgraceful, *turpis, foedus, indecōrus*.

grossly. (1) = much, too much, *graviter, nimium*. (2) = indecently, *turpiter, foede, indecore*.

grossness. (1) = greatness, (excessive) amount or degree, *(nimia) magnitudo*. (2) = indecency, *turpitudo*.

grot, grotto, *antrum* (poet.).

grotesque, *immanis, mirus;* sometimes *ridiculus*.

ground. subst. LIT., (1) = earth, soil, *humus* (f.), *solum, terra:* on the —, *humi*. (2) as milit. t. t. = place, position, *locus*. TRANSF., = reason, basis, *causa, ratio:* on the — that, *quod* (with subj.); to gain —, *proficĕre;* of a rumour, *percrebescĕre*.

ground, v. (1) transit. = to teach, *docēre*. (2) intransit., of a ship, *sidĕre*.

groundless, *vanus, futilis, fictus, falsus*.

groundlessly, *temere, ex vano, falso*.

groundlessness, *vanitas*.

groundwork. LIT., of a building, *substructio,*

fundamentum. Transf., of abstract things, *fundamentum, principium.*
group, subst. *caterva, globus, circulus.*
group, v. *disponĕre.*
grouping, *dispositio.*
grove, *lucus, nemus (-ŏris,* n.), *silva.*
grovel, *humi iacēre, humi serpĕre.*
grovelling, *abiectus, humilis, sordidus, submissus, servilis.*
grow. (1) intransit. *crescĕre, augeri:* to — up, *adolescĕre, pubescĕre;* with complement = to become, *fieri,* or use inceptive verb. (2) transit. *alĕre, colĕre:* to — a beard, *barbam promittĕre.*
grower, *cultor.*
growl, subst. *fremitus (-ūs).*
growl, v. *fremĕre.*
grown, grown-up, *adultus, pubes, grandis.*
growth, *auctus (-ūs), incrementum.*
grub, subst. *vermiculus.*
grub, v.: to — up, *eruĕre.*
grudge, subst. *simultas, invidia, inimicitia.*
grudge, v. *(rem homini) invidēre.*
gruel, *cremor* (Pl., Ov.), *ptisana* (Varro, Plin.).
gruff, *asper.*
gruffly, *aspere.*
gruffness, *asperitas* (Lucr., Tac.).
grumble, *murmurare, mussare, fremĕre.*
grunt, subst. *grunnitus (-ūs).*
grunt, v. *grunnire* (Varro, Juv.).
Guadalquivir (river), *Baetis.*
guarantee, subst. (1) as a thing, *fides, sponsio, vadimonium* (= recognizance). (2) = guarantor, *vas, praes, sponsor, obses* (= hostage).
guarantee, v. *praestare, fidem homini dare* or *interponĕre, pro homine intercedĕre.*
guard, subst. (1) = protection, watch, *custodia, praesidium, tutela, excubiae (-arum,* plur.): to keep or mount —, as milit. t. t., *excubare, excubias* or *custodias* or *vigilias agĕre, in statione esse;* at night, *vigilare;* in gen., to be on one's —, *(prae)cavēre;* off one's —, *incautus, imprudens.* (2) = the persons on —, *custodes (-um,* plur.), *custodia, praesidium, excubiae (-arum,* plur.: Tac.).
guard, v. *custodire, tuēri, praesidēre* with dat.; see also PROTECT.
guarded, *cautus, circumspectus.*
guardedly, *caute.*
guardian: in gen., *custos, defensor, praeses, propugnator;* of a ward, *tutor.*
guardianship: in gen., *custodia, praesidium, fides, tutela;* of a ward, *tutela.*
guerdon, *praemium, merces (-ēdis,* f.).
guess, subst. *coniectura.*
guess, v. *conicĕre, divinare, augurari, opinari, suspicari.*
guest, in a house, m. *hospes (-ĭtis,* f. *hospita;* at a party, *conviva:* an uninvited —, *umbra;* to receive as —, *hospitio excipĕre.*
guidance, *ductus (-ūs), consilium;* often render by *dux* or *auctor* (e.g. *te duce,* under your —).
guide, subst. Lit., *dux.* Transf., *dux, auctor.*
guide, v. Lit., *ducĕre.* Transf., *regĕre, gubernare, moderari.*
guild, *collegium.*
guildhall, *curia;* in a Greek city, *prytaneum.*
guile, *dolus, astutia.*
guileful, *dolosus, astutus.*
guileless, *simplex, apertus, candidus.*
guilelessly, *simpliciter.*
guilelessness, *simplicitas.*

guilt, *vitium, culpa, noxia.*
guiltily, *scelerate*
guiltless, adj. *innocens, insons, innoxius:* to be —, *extra culpam esse.*
guilty, *noxius, sons, sceleratus, nocens.*
guise, *habitus (-ūs), species.*
gulf, *sinus (-ūs* = a bay), *gurges* (= an abyss).
gull, subst. perhaps use *gavia* (= seamew: Plin.).
gull, v.; see CHEAT.
gullet, *gula, guttur.*
gullible, *credulus.*
gully, *alveus.*
gulp, subst. *haustus (-ūs).*
gulp, v. *haurire, obsorbēre, gluttire* (Pl., Juv.).
gum, subst. (1) of the mouth, *gingiva* (Cat., Juv.); of trees, etc., *gummi* (Plin.).
gum, v. *glutinare* (Plin.).
gummy, *gummosus* (Plin.).
gun, use *tormentum* (= engine for hurling stones, etc.).
gurgle, *murmurare, susurrare* (poet.).
gush, v.: to — forth, — out, *effundi, profundi, scatēre* (Lucr.).
gust, *flabra (-orum,* plur.); or render by phrase, such as *venti impetus (-ūs).*
gusty, *turbidus, procellosus.*
gut, subst. *intestinum* (often in plur.).
gut, v. = to empty, *exinanire.*
gutter, *canalis, cloaca.*
guttural, of sounds, *gravis.*
guzzle, *(per)potare;* see also GULP.
guzzler, *potor, homo ebriosus.*
gymnasium, *gymnasium, palaestra.*
gymnastic, *gymnicus, palaestricus* (Quint.).
gymnastics, *palaestra.*
gypsum, *gypsum* (Plin.).

H

ha! ha!
haberdashery, *panni (-orum,* plur.).
habiliment, *vestimentum;* see also DRESS.
habit. (1) = custom, *consuetudo, mos, usus (-ūs).* (2) = state, constitution, *habitus (-ūs).* (3) see DRESS.
habitable, *habitabilis.*
habitat, habitation, *domicilium, sedes (-is), tectum, domus.*
habitual, *inveteratus, usitatus.*
habitually, *de* or *ex more.*
habituate, *consuefacĕre, adsuefacĕre.*
hack, subst. = a horse, *caballus.*
hack, v. *caedĕre:* to — in pieces, *concīdĕre.*
hackneyed, *tritus.*
haft, *manubrium.*
hag, *anus (-ūs), anicula.*
haggard, *morbo* or *maerore* or *macie confectus.*
haggle, *de pretio ambigĕre;* see also QUIBBLE, QUARREL.
hail, subst. *grando.*
hail, v. (1) it —s (i.e. hail falls), *grandinat* (Sen.). (2) = to greet, *salutare, appellare.*
hail, interj. *salve!* plur. *salvete!*
hair. Lit., (1) a single hair, *pilus, capillus, saeta* (= a bristle). (2) coll., use plur. of the above or *crinis* (sing. or plur.), *comae (-arum,* plur.), *caesaries* (= flowing), *villus* (sing. or plur. = the thick hair of beasts): downy —, *lanugo;*

to cut —, *pilos recīdĕre, tondĕre.*
Transf., not to deviate by a —'s breadth,
non transversum, ut aiunt, digitum discedere.

hair-cloth, *cilicium.*

hairdresser, *tonsor, cinerarius* (Cat.), *ciniflo*
(Hor.).

hairpin, *crinale* (Ov.).

hairsplitting, *disserendi spinae (-arum,* plur.),
minuta subtilitas.

hairy, *pilosus, crinītus* (Verg.), *capillatus,
comatus* (Cat., Suet.).

halcyon, subst. *alcedo* (Pl.), *(h)alcyon* (Verg.).

halcyon, adj. *serenus:* — days, *dies sereni et
tranquilli, alcedonia (-orum,* plur.: Pl.),
(h)alcyonei dies (Varro).

hale, adj. *sanus, validus, robustus.*

hale, v. *rapĕre, trahĕre.*

half, subst. *dimidium, dimidia pars, semis* (esp.
in connexion with money or land): — as
much again, *dimidio plus.*

half, adj. *dimidius, dimidiatus.*

half, adv. usually rendered by prefix *semi-*; see
below.

half-asleep, *semisomnus, semisomnis, semiso-
pitus.*

half-brother, *eodem patre* or *eadem matre
natus.*

half-burnt, *semiustus.*

half-dead, *semianimus, semianimis.*

half-eaten, *semesus* (poet.).

half-hour, *semihora.*

half-moon, *luna dimidiata.*

half-open, *semiapertus.*

half-pound, *selibra.*

half-yearly, *semestris.*

hall, *atrium*; for public purposes, *forum,
conciliabulum, curia.*

hallo! heus! ohe! (Pl., Hor.).

halloo, subst. *clamor.*

halloo, v. *clamare, vociferari.*

hallow, *consecrare, dedicare, inaugurare.*

hallowed, *sacer, sanctus.*

hallucination, n. *error, somnium* (esp. in plur.).

halm, *calamus.*

halo, *corona.*

halt, subst. render by verb.

halt, adj. *claudus.*

halt, v. (**1**) = to limp, *claudicare.* (**2**) = to
stop, *consistĕre.* (**3**) = to hesitate, *dubitare,
haerĕre, haesitare.*

halter, for a horse, *capistrum* (Verg.); for
strangling, *laqueus.*

halve, *aequas partes* or *ex aequo dividĕre.*

halved, *dimidiatus.*

halves! interj. *in commune!* (Sen.).

ham, (**1**) = the back of the knee, *poples (-ĭtis,*
m.). (**2**) salted, smoked, etc., *perna.*

hamlet, *vicus, viculus.*

hammer, subst. *malleus* (Pl.).

hammer, v. *malleo (con)tundĕre.*

hamper, subst. *corbis*; see also BASKET.

hamper, v. *implicare, impedire.*

hamstring, v. *poplitem succidĕre.*

hand, subst. Lit., as part of the body, *manus
(-ūs,* f.), *palma* (strictly = the palm): the right
—, *(manus) dextra* or *dextera*; the left —,
(manus) sinistra or *laeva*; to give a person
one's —, *homini dextram porrigĕre*; to shake
—s, *dextras (inter se) iungĕre*; to raise one's
—s (in surprise), *manūs tollĕre*; to pass from
— to —, *per manūs tradĕre*; to hold in the —,
manu tenēre. Transf., (**1**) = handwriting;

q.v. (**2**) = a workman, *opera* (usually plur.);
colloq. : an old —, *veterator.* (**3**) in phrases, to
indicate physical contact, availability, etc.: to
be at —, *praesto esse, adesse*; (ready) to —, *ad
manum*; in —, on —, *in manibus*; — to —
(in fighting), *comminus*; to lay (violent) —s
on a person, *(vim et) manūs homini inferre*;
to take in —, *suscipĕre, in manūs sumĕre*; to
be in a person's —(s), i.e. power, *in manu*
or *in manibus* or *in potestate hominis (positum)
esse, apud hominem esse, penes hominem esse.*
(**4**) on the one —, on the other, *et . . . et . . .*;
to give an idea of contrast, use *quidem* (not
first word) in first clause, and *sed* or *autem*
(not first word) in second clause; but contrast in Latin is often expressed without a
preposition, by asyndeton.

hand, v. *dare, tradĕre, porrigĕre:* to — down,
tradĕre, prodĕre; to — round, *circumferre.*

hand-bill, *libellus.*

handcuffs, *manicae (-arum,* plur.).

handful. Lit., *manipulus* (Verg.), *pugillus* (Cato,
Plin.). Transf., render by *pauci* (plur.) or
parvus; = a nuisance, render by adj. *gravis*
or *molestus.*

handicraft, *artificium.*

handiwork, *opus (-ĕris,* n.), *opificium.*

handkerchief, *sudarium* (Cat.).

handle, subst. Lit., *manubrium, capulus* (esp.
of a sword), *ansa* (of a cup, etc.). Transf.,
sometimes *ansa*; see also OPPORTUNITY.

handle, v. *tractare, contrectare, pertractare.*

handling, *tractatio.*

handsome. Lit., *formosus, venustus, bellus,
speciosus, pulcher.* Transf., *liberalis.*

handsomely, *praeclare, ample, liberaliter.*

handsomeness, *pulchritudo, venustas.*

handwriting, *manus (-ūs,* f.), *chirographum.*

handy, *habilis, promptus.*

hang, v. (**1**) intransit. *pendēre:* to — on (i.e.
stay close), *haerēre*; to — over, *imminēre*;
to — back, *cessare.* (**2**) transit. *suspendĕre:* to
— the head, *caput demittĕre.*

hangdog, subst. *verbero, furcifer.*

hanger; see SWORD.

hanger-on, *adsecla.*

hanging, subst. (as a means of death), *sus-
pendium.*

hangman, *carnifex.*

hanker: to — after, *desiderare*; see also DESIRE.

haphazard, adv. *temere.*

hapless, *miser, infelix*; see also UNLUCKY.

haply, *fortasse, forsitan*: if —, *si forte.*

happen, *fieri, accidĕre, contingĕre, evenire, usū
venire.*

happily, *beate, feliciter.*

happiness, *vita beata, beate vivĕre, felicitas.*

happy. (**1**) of persons, circumstances, etc.,
beatus, felix, fortunatus. (**2**) of language,
aptus.

harangue, subst. *contio:* to deliver a —,
contionari.

harass, *vexare, sollicitare, exagitare, exercēre.*

harbinger, *praenuntius, antecursor.*

harbour, subst. Lit., *portus (-ūs):* — dues,
portorium; full of —s, *portuosus.* Transf.,
portus (-ūs), refugium, perfugium.

harbour, v. (*hospitio) excipĕre.*

hard, adj. (**1**) to the touch, *durus, rigidus.* (**2**)
= unfeeling, *durus.* (**3**) of times and circumstances, *durus, asper, acerbus, iniquus,
indignus.* (**4**) = difficult, *difficilis, arduus.*

hard, adv. *summā vi, enixe*: to be — pressed, *premi*.

harden, v. (1) transit. *durum facĕre* or *reddĕre, durare* (poet.). (2) intransit. *obdurescĕre* (lit. and fig.).

hard-hearted, *durus, ferreus*.

hardihood, *audacia*.

hardiness, *robur (-ŏris)*; see also STRENGTH.

hardly. (1) = scarcely, *vix, aegre*. (2) = cruelly; q.v.

hardness. LIT., *duritia* (or *durities*). TRANSF., = severity, *iniquitas, crudelitas, saevitia*.

hardship, *labor, incommodum, molestia, aerumna*; with the further notion of injustice, *iniuria*.

hardware, *ferramenta (-orum,* plur.: Varro).

hardy, *durus, robustus*.

hare, *lepus (lepŏris,* m.).

hare-brained, *temerarius*.

hare-lip, *labrum fissum* (Cels.).

hark! interj. *heus!*

harlequin, *sannio*.

harlot, *scortum, meretrix*.

harm, subst. *damnum, detrimentum*.

harm, v. *nocēre* (with dat.), *laedĕre* (with acc.).

harmful, *nocens, noxius*.

harmless, *innocens, innoxius* (poet.), *innocuus* (poet.).

harmlessness, *innocentia*.

harmonious. LIT., of sounds, *concors, consonus* (Ov.), *canorus*. TRANSF., *concors, congruens, consentiens, conveniens*.

harmoniously, *concorditer, congruenter, convenienter*.

harmonize, v. (1) transit. LIT., *concordes facĕre* or *reddĕre*. TRANSF., *componĕre, (re)conciliare*. (2) intransit. *concinĕre, consentire*.

harmony. LIT., of sounds, *concentus (-ūs)*, *concordia*: science of —, *harmonice* or *harmonica* (Vitr.). TRANSF., of feeling, etc., *consensus (-ūs), consensio, concordia, convenientia*.

harness, subst. *ornamenta equi, arma equestria*.

harness, v. *(equum) ornare*.

harp, subst. *lyra*.

harp, v. LIT., *psallĕre*. TRANSF., to — on, *vaticinari* (Pl.); to — on the same old string, *cantilenam eandem canĕre* (Ter.), *eandem incudem tundĕre* (Cic.).

harper, harpist, m. *fidicen, psaltes (-ae:* Quint.); f. *fidicina, psaltria*.

harpy, *harpyia* (Verg.).

harrow, subst. *(h)irpex* (Cato), *crates* (Verg.).

harrow, v. LIT., *occare* (Hor.). TRANSF., to — the feelings, *(ex)cruciare, torquēre*.

harrowing, *terribilis, atrox*.

harry, *vexare, torquēre, cruciare*.

harsh. (1) in sound, *raucus, absonus, asper*. (2) in taste, *acer, acerbus asper*. (3) — in temper, *asper, acerbus severus, morosus, durus*.

harshly, *aspere, acerbe, severe*; see also CRUELLY.

harshness, *asperitas, severitas, acerbitas*.

hart, *cervus*.

harvest, subst. *messis*.

harvester, *messor*.

hash, *minutal* (Juv.).

hasp; see LOCK, BOLT.

hassock, *pulvinus* (= cushion).

haste, subst. *festinatio, properatio, properantia*

(Sall., Tac.), *celeritas, trepidatio* (= nervous haste).

haste, hasten, v. (1) intransit. *properare, contendĕre, festinare, maturare*. (2) transit. *accelerare, maturare, properare, praecipitare*.

hastily, *propere, properanter, raptim*.

hastiness, of temper, *iracundia, stomachus*.

hasty. (1) = hurried, *(prae)properus, citus, citatus, praeceps*. (2) = irritable, *iracundus, stomachosus, pronus in iram*.

hat, *petăsus* (broad-brimmed): to take the — off (as a mark of respect), *caput nudare*.

hatch, v. LIT., *(ex ovis) excludĕre*. TRANSF., = to concoct, *moliri, machinari, (con)coquĕre*.

hatches, *claustra (-orum,* plur.).

hatchet, *securis, ascia, dolabra*.

hate, hatred, *odium, invidia, inimicitia*: to conceive a —, *odium suscipĕre (in hominem)*; to incur —, *in odium venire*.

hate, v. *odisse*: to be —d by a person, *odio homini esse*.

hateful, *odiosus, invisus*.

hatefully, *odiose*.

haughtily, *superbe, insolenter, adroganter*.

haughtiness, *superbia, insolentia, contumacia, adrogantia, fastidium, fastus (-ūs*; mostly poet.).

haughty, *superbus, insŏlens, contumax, adrogans*.

haul, v. *trahĕre, ducĕre*.

haulm; see STALK.

haunch, *clunis*.

haunt, subst. *latebrae (-arum,* plur.), *latibulum, lustra (-orum,* plur.).

haunt, v. (1) = to keep going to, *frequentare, (con)celebrare*. (2) of spirits, cares, etc., *agitare, insectari, sollicitare, vexare*.

haunted, use phrase, such as *larvis infestus*.

have, *habēre, tenēre, esse* (with property as subject, e.g. *res est mihi*): to — with one, — on one, *secum habēre* or *portare* or *gestare, esse cum re* (e.g. *cum telo*); to — a thing done, *curare rem gerendam*; to — to do, *debēre facĕre*, or express by gerund or gerundive.

haven, *portus (-ūs)*; see also HARBOUR.

havoc, *vastatio, strages*.

hawk, subst. *accipiter (-tris,* m.).

hawk, v. = to sell, *venditare*.

hawk-eyed, adj. *lyncēus*.

hay, *faenum*.

hay-cock, hay-stack, hay-rick, *faeni acervus*.

hay-cutter, *faenisex*.

hay-fork, *furca*.

hazard, subst. *fors, casus (-ūs), periculum* (= risk, danger), *alea* (lit. = gambling).

hazard, v.; see DARE or ENDANGER.

hazardous, *periculosus, anceps, dubius, lubricus*.

hazardously, *periculose*.

haze, *nebula, caligo*; see also FOG.

hazel, subst. *corylus*.

hazel-nut, *nux avellana* (Plin.).

hazy, *nebulosus*.

he, is often expressed by the form of the verb, (e.g. *amat* = he loves). Otherwise render by *hic, ille, is, iste*, or sometimes by *homo*. He himself, *ipse*.

he-, (prefixed to the names of animals) is rendered by the adj. *mas* or by a special form of the noun (e.g. *ursus* = he-bear; *ursa* = she-bear).

head

Hebrew

head, subst. Lit., of the body, *caput, vertex* (esp. = the top of the head): the back of the —, *occipitium* (Pl., Quint.); of meeting or colliding, — on, *frontibus adversis.* Transf., (1) of any other physical object, *caput*; or render by adj. *summus.* (2) = understanding or memory, *mens, animus, ingenium, iudicium*: to come into a person's —, *homini in mentem venire*; to have a thing in one's —, *rem memoriā tenēre*; to put their —s together, *consilia inter se communicare.* (3) = any person, an individual, *caput.* (4) = chief person, leader, *caput, princeps, dux.* (5) = chief point, chief place, *caput*: to be at the —, *praeesse*; to put at the —, *praeficĕre.* (6) = any point, a heading, *caput.*

head-, adj. *primus, primarius, princeps, praecipuus.*

head, v. *ducĕre, ducem* or *auctorem esse, praeesse.*

head-ache, *capitis dolor* (Cels.).

head-band, *infula, vita, redimiculum.*

head-dress, *mitra.*

header; see DIVE.

headland, *promontorium.*

headless, *capite praeciso.*

headlong, *praeceps.*

headpiece, *cassis* (of metal), *galea* (of leather).

headquarters, *praetorium, principia* (-*orum,* plur.).

headship, *locus princeps* or *primus, principatus* (-*ūs*).

headstrong, *pertinax, contumax, pervicax, temerarius.*

head-wind, *ventus adversus.*

heady, = intoxicating, *fervidus* (Hor.).

heal, v. (1) transit. *sanare, medēri* (*homini*), *curare* (= to take care of a person, nurse). (2) intransit. *consanescĕre, sanum fieri, coire* (of wounds: Ov.).

healing, subst. *sanatio.*

healing, adj. *saluber, salutaris.*

health, *sanitas, valetudo* (*bona valetudo* = good health), *salus* (-*utis,* f.): to be in —, *valēre*; to drink to a person's —, *propinare homini.*

healthful, *saluber, salutaris.*

healthily, *salubriter.*

healthy, *sanus, salvus, validus, saluber* (of places).

heap, subst. *acervus, strues, cumulus, agger.*

heap, v. Lit., *cumulare, coacervare, aggerare* (Verg.), *congerĕre.* Transf., of abstract things, *congerĕre, ingerĕre.*

hear. Lit., *audire, exaudire* (= to catch, or overhear), *auscultare* (= to listen to), *auribus percipĕre.* Transf., (1) = to find out, learn, *cognoscĕre, accipĕre.* (2) to — a cause, *causam cognoscĕre.* (3) to — from a person, *litteras ab homine accipĕre.*

hearer, *auditor.*

hear-hear! *euge* (Pl., Ter.), *bene, optime!*

hearing, subst. (1) as a sense, *auditus* (-*ūs*). (2) as a process, *auditio.* (3) a — (= an audience), *audientia*; in my —, *me audiente.* (4) a judicial —, *cognitio*; see also TRIAL.

hearken, *auscultare*; see also HEAR.

hearsay, *rumor, auditio.*

hearse, render by *vehiculum.*

heart. Lit., the physical organ, *cor* (*cordis,* n.). Transf., (1) = the innermost part, esp. of a country, *interiora* (n. plur.), or render by

adj. *intimus.* (2) = the seat of feeling, etc., *animus, mens, pectus* (-*ŏris,* pl.), *praecordia* (-*orum,* plur.: Verg., Hor.): from the —, *ex animo*; I have a thing at —, *res mihi curae* or *cordi est.* (3) = courage, *animus*: to be of good —, *bono animo esse.* (4) = memory: to know by —, *memoriā tenēre*; to learn by —, *ediscĕre.* (5) dear —, as term of endearment, *cor* (Pl.), *corculum* (Pl.), (*mea*) *vita.*

heart-break, *angor, dolor.*

heart-breaking, heart-rending, *miserabilis, maestus, acerbus, flebilis.*

heart-broken, *animo fractus* or *adflictus.*

heartfelt, *verus.*

heartily, *summo studio.*

heartiness, *studium, alacritas.*

heartless, *durus, crudelis, ferreus, immitis, inhumanus, saevus.*

heartlessly, *crudeliter, saeve, inhumane.*

heartlessness, *crudelitas, inhumanitas, saevitia.*

heart-sick, *animo aeger.*

heart-whole, *integer* (Hor.).

hearty, *verus* (= true, genuine), *alacer* (= brisk, cheerful), *benignus* (= cordial, kind).

hearth, *focus.*

heat, subst. Lit., *calor, ardor* (= burning —), *fervor* (= boiling —), *aestus* (-*ūs* = glowing —, feverish —). Transf., (1) of passion, etc., *ardor, fervor, aestus*; see also ANGER. (2) = a course in a race, *missus* (-*us*: Suet.).

heat, v. transit. Lit., *calefacĕre, fervefacĕre* (esp. in past. part.). Transf., *accendĕre, incendĕre, inflammare.*

heath. (1) as a plant, *erīce* (-*es,* f.: Plin.). (2) = a place overgrown with heath, use phrase, such as *loca inculta.*

heathen, adj. *paganus* (eccl.).

heave, v. (1) transit. (*at*)*tollĕre, extollĕre*: to — a sigh, *gemitum dare,* or *ēdĕre* or *ducĕre.* (2) intransit. *aestuare, fluctuare, tumescĕre.*

heaven. (1) = the sky, *caelum, polus* (poet.): to be in the seventh —, *in caelo esse.* (2) = heavenly powers, gods, *di* (*dii, dei*), *superi* (poet.): the will of —, *numen divinum* or *deorum*; for —'s sake! *per deos immortales! pro deum fidem! pro deum atque hominum fidem*; — forbid, *di meliora.*

heaven-born, heavenly, *caelestis, divinus*: heavenly bodies, *caelestia* (-*ium,* n. plur.).

heavenward, *in* or *ad caelum.*

heavily, *graviter,* sometimes *magnopere* (= much).

heaviness. Lit., *gravitas, pondus* (-*eris,* n.). Transf., (1) of the atmosphere, *crassitudo.* (2) = depression, sadness, *tristitia, maeror, maestitia.*

heavy. Lit., of physical weight, *gravis* (opp. *levis*), *ponderosus* (Pl., Varro). Transf., (1) of other physical qualities: of food (= indigestible), *gravis, difficilis ad concoquendum*; of air (= oppressive), *crassus*; of soil, *spissus*; of rain (= plentiful), *magnus.* (2) of abstract qualities: **a** = oppressive, troublesome, *gravis, molestus, difficilis*: **b** = downcast, sad, *tristis, adflictus, maestus*: **c,** of speech, style, etc., *frigidus.*

heavy-armed: the — troops, *gravior armatus* (-*ūs*).

Hebrew, adj. *Hebraeus* or *Hebraicus* (both eccl.).

[725]

hecatomb, *hecatombe* (Varro).
hectic, *febriculosus* (Cat.).
hector, *se iactare.*
hectoring, *gloriosus.*
hedge, subst. *saepes, saepimentum.*
hedge, v. *saepire.*
hedgehog, *ericius* (Varro), *erinaceus* (Plin.), *echinus* (Hor.).
heed, subst.: to take —, *cavēre, curare.*
heed, v. transit. *curare, observare;* = to obey, *parēre* or *obedire* (with dat.).
heedful, *cautus, circumspectus.*
heedless, *neglegens, incautus, temerarius.*
heedlessly, *neglegenter, incaute, temere.*
heedlessness, *neglegentia, temeritas.*
heel, subst. *calx:* to be at a person's —s, *hominis vestigiis instare;* to fall head over —s, *ire praecipitem (per caputque pedesque).*
heel, v., of a ship, *in latus labi* or *inclinari.*
heft, *manubrium.*
heifer, *iuvenca.*
height. LIT., *altitudo proceritas* (= tallness). TRANSF., **(1)** abstr. = high degree, *altitudo,* or render by adj. *summus* (e.g. — of glory, *summa gloria).* **(2)** a — = a high place, *locus editus, locus superior, altitudines* (-um, plur.).
heighten. LIT., render by compar. *altior.* TRANSF., = to make more of, *augēre, amplificare, exaggerare.*
heinous, *foedus, detestabilis, nefarius, nefandus, immanis, atrox.*
heinously, *foede, nefarie, atrociter.*
heinousness, *atrocitas.*
heir, *heres:* sole —, *heres ex asse;* — to half an estate, *heres ex dimidia parte;* to appoint a person one's —, *hominem heredem (testamento) scribēre* or *facēre.*
heiress, *heres,* f.
heirloom, *res hereditaria.*
heirship, *hereditas.*
Helen, *Helena.*
hell, *inferi* (-orum, plur.), *Tartarus* (-os), or n. plur. *Tartara; Gehenna, Infernus* (eccl. terms).
hellebore, *(h)elleborus* (Pl., Verg.), *veratrum* (Lucr., Plin.).
Hellenic, *Graecus.*
hellhound, *furia, Erinnys.*
hellish, *infernus, nefandus, immanis.*
helm, *gubernaculum* (lit. and fig.), *clavus* (strictly = the tiller).
helmet, *cassis* (of metal), *galea* (originally of leather).
helmsman, *gubernator.*
help, subst. *auxilium, subsidium, ops* (only *opis, opem, ope* in use), *adiumentum* (= a means of aid), *salus* (-ūtis = rescue).
help, v. **(1)** = to assist, *(hominem) (ad)iuvare, (homini) subvenire, succurrere:* so — me God, *ita me di ament.* **(2)** = to serve out food, *dare, porrigēre, dividēre.* **(3)** = to prevent: I can't — saying, *facēre non possum quin dicam.*
helper, *adiutor;* f. *adiutrix.*
helpful, *utilis.*
helping, *auxiliaris, auxiliarius* (esp. of auxiliary troops).
helpless, *inermis, inops.*
helplessness, *inopia.*
helpmeet, *socius, consors.*
helter-skelter, render by adj. *praeceps.*
hem, subst. *limbus, instita.*
hem, v. **(1)** = to sew, *suēre.* **(2)** to — in,

circumsedēre, obsidēre, circumvallare (with entrenchments).
hemisphere, *hemisphaerium* (Varro).
hemorrhage, *haemorrhagia* (Plin.).
hemp, *cannabis* (Varro, Pers.).
hempen, *cannabinus* (Varro).
hen. (1) the domestic fowl, *gallina.* **(2)** = a female bird in gen., *femina.*
hence. (1) of place, *hinc;* as interj., *apage, procul.* **(2)** of time, render by abl. (e.g. *paucis diebus,* a few days —), or *post* (e.g. *post paucos dies).* **(3)** = for this reason, *hinc, ita, quamobrem.*
henceforth, henceforward, *posthac.*
hen-coop, *cavea.*
hen-house, *gallinarium* (Plin.).
Henry, *Henricus* (late Latin).
her, pron.; see SHE; as pronom. adj. often not expressed in Latin; when expressed, it is represented by *eius, illius, huius,* or (especially if the owner is the subject of the sentence) by *suus.*
herald, subst. **(1)** as an official, *caduceator, fetialis, praeco.* **(2)** in gen. = forerunner, *praenuntius.*
herald, v. *nuntiare.*
herb, *herba, olus* (oleris, n.).
herbage, *herba* or plur. *herbae.*
herbalist, *herbarius* (Plin.).
herculean, *fortissimus.*
herd, subst. LIT., *grex;* of large cattle, *armentum;* of a —, *gregalis, gregarius;* in —s, *gregatim.* TRANSF., of people, *grex, multitudo, caterva:* the common —, *vulgus* (-i, n.).
herd, v. intransit. *congregari.*
herdsman, *pastor;* of large cattle, *armentarius* (Varro, Verg.).
here, = at this place, *hic:* to be —, *adesse;* = hither, *huc;* from — (hence), *hinc;* only — and there, *rarus* (adv. *raro);* they fought only — and there, *rari proeliabantur.*
hereafter, *posthac, aliquando.*
hereditary, *hereditarius, paternus.*
herein, *in hac re.*
heresy, *haeresis* (eccl.); or render by phrase such as *a ceteris dissentire.*
heretic, heretical, *haereticus* (eccl.).
hereupon, *hic.*
heritage, = an inherited estate, *heredium, hereditas, patrimonium.*
hermaphrodite, *androgynus, semimas.*
hermetically, *arte clausus.*
hermit, *homo solitarius, eremīta* (eccl.), *anachoreta* (eccl.).
hero. (1) = demigod, *heros.* **(2)** = brave man, *vir fortis* or *fortissimus, dux fortissimus.* **(3)** = the principal person; in a poem, *de quo (fabula) scripta est;* in a play, *persona prima, qui primas partes agit.*
heroic. (1) *heroicus* (e.g. the — age, *tempora heroica).* **(2)** = brave, valiant, *fortis, fortis et invictus:* a — action, *praeclarum atque divinum factum.*
heroically, *fortiter.*
heroine. (1) = demi-goddess, *heroina* (poet.), *herois* (poet.). **(2)** = brave woman, *femina fortissima.* **(3)** the — of a story, *de qua (fabula) scripta est.*
heroism, *eximia virtus* (-ūtis), *animus fortis et invictus, animi magnitudo.*
heron, *ardea* (Verg.).
hers; see HER.

herself, reflex., *se* (*ipsam*); otherwise *ipsa*.
hesitate, *dubitare, cunctari, haerēre, haesitare.*
hesitation, *dubitatio, haesitatio, cunctatio.*
heterogeneous, *diversus, dissimilis.*
heterogeneousness, *natura diversa.*
hew, *caedēre, concīdĕre, dolare.*
hewn, hewn stone, *saxum quadratum.*
hexameter, *hexameter* (or *-trus*).
hey, interj. *eia! age!*
heyday, *flos aetatis.*
hiatus, *hiatus* (*-ūs*).
hibernate, = to sleep through the winter, *per hiemem dormire* or *quiescĕre.*
hiccough, hiccup, *singultus* (*-ūs*).
hidden, *occultus, absconditus*: to lie —, *latēre.*
hide, subst. *corium, vellus* (*-ĕris*, n.: poet.), *pellis.*
hide, v. (1) transit. *abdĕre, abscondĕre, celare, occulĕre, occultare*; of feelings, etc., *dissimulare.* (2) intransit., render by verbs given above, with reflex.
hideous, *foedus, turpis, deformis*; see also UGLY.
hideously, *foede.*
hideousness, *foeditas, deformitas.*
hiding-place, *latibulum, latebra* (gen. plur.).
higgledy-piggledy, *confuse.*
high, adj. LIT., *altus* (fifty feet —, *quinquaginta pedes altus*), (*ex*)*celsus*, (*in altum*) *editus, procērus* (= tall), *sublimis* (= raised aloft). TRANSF., (1) in degree, rank, etc., *amplus, summus.* (2) in money: a — price, *pretium magnum*; to buy at a — price, *magno* or *pretio impenso emĕre*; to set a — value on, *magni aestimare.* (2) of sound, *acutus.* (4) of meat = bad, *rancidus, puter* (*putris*).
high, adv. *alte*: to aim —, *magnas res* (*ad*)*petĕre.*
high-born, *generosus, nobili loco ortus.*
high-bred, *generosus.*
high-day, *dies festus.*
high-flown, *tumidus*: to use — words, *ampullari.*
high-handed, *superbus, imperiosus.*
highlander, *homo montanus.*
highlands, *loca montuosa* (*-orum*, plur.).
highly: to value —, *magni aestimare*; very —, *permagni.*
high-mettled, *acer.*
high-minded, *magnanimus, generosus.*
high-mindedness, *magnanimitas.*
highness, *altitudo.*
high-priced, *carus.*
high-priest, Pontifex Maximus.
high-spirited, *generosus, ferox, fortis, animosus.*
high-treason, *maiestas, perduellio.*
high-water, high-tide, *plurimus aestūs accessus* (*-ūs*).
highway, *via.*
highwayman, *latro, grassator.*
hilarity, *hilaritas, laetitia.*
hill, *collis, tumulus*: up —, *adverso colle.*
hillock, *tumulus.*
hilly, *montuosus, clivosus* (Verg., Ov.).
hilt, *capulus.*
him; see HE.
himself, reflex., *se* (*ipsum*); otherwise render by *ipse.*
hind, subst. (1) = female stag, *cerva.* (2) = servant, *verna, servus.* (3) = peasant, *rusticus, agrestis.*
hind, adj. *aversus, posterior.*

hinder, *impedire, prohibēre, retardare, impedimento esse* (with dat.), *obstare* (with dat.), *officĕre* (with dat.).
hindmost, *postremus, ultimus, novissimus* (esp. of troops).
hindrance, *impedimentum.*
hinge, subst. *cardo* (lit. and fig.: poet.).
hinge, v.: to — on a thing, *in re contineri* or *versari.*
hint, subst. *significatio.*
hint, v.: to — at, *significare, subicĕre.*
hip, *coxendix* (Pl., Suet.).
hire, subst. *merces.*
hire, v. *conducĕre.*
hired, *conductus, mercenarius.*
hireling, *mercenarius.*
hirer, *conductor.*
his, often not expressed in Latin; when expressed, it is represented by *eius, illius, huius*, or (esp. if the owner is the subject of the sentence) by *suus.*
hiss, hissing, subst. *sibilus* (plur. *sibila*).
hiss, v. *sibilare, stridēre* or *stridĕre* (poet.): to — an actor off the stage, *histrionem exsibilare* or *explodĕre.*
hist! interj. *st!*
historian, *rerum* (*gestarum* or *antiquarum*) *scriptor*; *historicus.*
historic, historical: the — style of writing, *genus historicum*; — truth or accuracy, *historiae fides*; — writings, *libri ad historiam pertinentes.*
history, *historia, rerum gestarum memoria, res* (*gestae*), *annales*: ancient —, *antiquitatis memoria.*
histrionic, *scaenicus*: the — art, *ars ludicra.*
hit, subst. *plaga, ictus* (*-ūs*): 'a —!' *hoc habet* (= 'he has caught it').
hit, v. LIT., *ferire, tundĕre, percutĕre*: to be — by lightning, *de caelo tangi.* TRANSF., (1) to — it off = to agree, *convenire.* (2) to — upon, *offendĕre, incidĕre* (with *in* and acc., or dat.). (3) to be hard —, *adfligi.* (4) prov.: you have — the nail on the head, *rem acu tetigisti* (Pl.).
hitch, subst. *impedimentum* (= hindrance), *mora* (= delay), *scrupulus* (= mental difficulty).
hitch, v. (*ad*)*iungĕre, adnectĕre.*
hither, adj. *citerior.*
hither, adv. *huc*: — and thither, *huc illuc, ultro* (*et*) *citro.*
hitherto, *adhuc, hactenus.*
hive, *alvearium, alveus* (Plin.), *alvus* (Varro, Plin.).
ho! interj. *heus!*
hoar, *canus.*
hoard, subst. *copia, acervus.*
hoard, v. *conligĕre, conquirĕre, coacervare.*
hoar-frost, *pruina.*
hoarse, *raucus*: a little —, *subraucus.*
hoarsely, *raucā voce.*
hoarseness, *rauca vox.*
hoary, *canus, incanus* (poet.).
hoax, *ludificatio.*
hoax, v. *ludificari, inludĕre.*
hobble, *claudicare.*
hobby, *studium.*
hobby-horse. LIT., *harundo* (Hor.). TRANSF., to ride one's —, *ineptiis suis plaudĕre.*
hobgoblin, *larva.*
hobnob: to — with, (*homine*) *familiariter uti.*

hock, *poples.*

hodge-podge, *farrāgo* (Juv.).

hoe, subst. *sarculum* (Hor.), *marra* (Plin.).

hoe, v. *sarire* (Pl., Varro).

hog, *sus, porcus.*

hoggish. Lit., *suillus.* Transf., see FOUL, GLUTTONOUS.

hogshead, *dolium.*

hoist, *sublevare, tollēre*: to — sails, *vela dare.*

hold, subst. (1) = grasp, *manus (-ūs)*: to take —, (*ap)prehendēre, comprehendēre*; to have a — over, (*hominem*) *devinctum* or *obligatum habēre.* (2) of a ship, *caverna.*

hold, v. (1) = to have, occupy, keep, possess, *tenēre, retinēre, obtinēre, possidēre, habēre, gestare* (on the person): to — an office, *gerēre* (e.g. *praeturam*). (2) = to contain, *capēre, continēre.* (3) = to keep against attack, *retinēre, defendēre.* (4) = to conduct, *agēre, habēre* (e.g. *comitia,* an election). (5) to — an opinion, to — that, *censēre, ducēre, sentire*; see also CONSIDER. (6) = to check, *cohibēre*: to — one's tongue, *tacēre.* (7) to — back, intransit. *cunctari.* (8) to — forth; transit. *porrigēre*; intransit., = to discourse, *contionari.* (9) to — good, *convenire.* (10) to — in, *inhibēre, cohibēre.* (11) to — on one's course, *cursum tenēre.* (12) to — out (= to endure) *durare, sustinēre, perferre.* (13) to — with, (*cum homine*) *consentire, convenire.*

holder. (1) personal: a — of land, *possessor.* (2) applied to things, *retinaculum, capulus* (= handle).

holdfast, *fibula.*

holding, subst. *possessio.*

hole, *cavum, foramen, rima* (= a chink), *lacuna* (= a pit, a cavity): to bore a —, *pertundēre, perforare*; see also HOVEL.

holiday, *dies festus, feriae (-arum,* plur.).

holily, *sancte.*

holiness, *sanctitas, religio.*

Holland, *Batavia.*

hollow, subst. (1) see HOLE: the — of the hand, *manus cava,* (2) = valley, *convallis, valles (vallis).*

hollow, adj. Lit., (*con)cavus* = hollowed out, *exesus* (Verg.). Transf., (1) = deep in sound, *fuscus, raucus.* (2) = insincere, false, *vanus, simulatus, fucatus.*

hollow, v. (*ex)cavare.*

holm-oak, *ilex* (poet.).

holy, *sacer, sanctus, sacrosanctus* (e.g. of tombs, oaths), *augustus* (= august, venerable): The Holy Ghost, *Spiritus Sanctus* (eccl.).

homage, *cultus (-ūs), observantia, verecundia*: to do —, *colēre, observare, salutare.*

home, subst. *domus, domicilium*: at —, *domi, inter suos*; at my —, *domi meae*; at — and abroad, *domi militiaeque*; to stay at —, *publico carēre, in publicum non prodire, domi sedēre*; he is at —, *est intus*; from —, *domo*; —wards, to one's —, *domum.*

home, adj. *domesticus, familiaris.*

home, adv.: to strike —, *ferrum adigēre*; to come — to a person, *homini in pectus alte descendēre.*

home-bred, *domesticus, intestinus, vernaculus.*

homeless, *domo profugus, domo carens.*

homeliness, *simplicitas.*

homely, *simplex, rudis, rusticus.*

home-made, *domesticus.*

homesickness, *suorum desiderium.*

homewards, *domum.*

homicidal; see MURDEROUS.

homicide. (1) = murder, *caedes.* (2) = murderer, *homicida.*

homily, *oratio.*

homogeneity, *natura similis.*

homogeneous, *eiusdem generis, eodem genere.*

honest, *probus, sincerus, simplex, candidus, frugi.*

honestly, *sincere, simpliciter, candide.*

honesty, *probitas, sinceritas, fides, simplicitas*: to show —, *fidem adhibēre.*

honey, *mel*; as a term of endearment, *mel* (or *melculum*) *meum* (Pl.), *deliciae meae, voluptas mea.*

honeycomb, *favus.*

honeyed, honied, *mellitus, suavis, dulcis.*

honour, subst. (1) = official distinction, *dignitas, honos (honor)*: the highest —, *amplissimus dignitatis gradus.* (2) = moral integrity, honourableness, *honestas, fides*: sense of —, *pudor.* (3) = reputation, *fama, existimatio.* (4) of a woman = chastity, *pudor, pudicitia.* (5) an — to = a glory or credit to, *decus.* (6) in plur.: —s paid, esp. last —s, *iusta, suprema* (Tac.).

honour, v. *colēre, honorare, decorare, celebrare.*

honourable. (1) = much honoured, *honoratus, amplus.* (2) = bringing honour, *honestus, honorificus.*

honourably. (1) = creditably, virtuously, *honeste.* (2) = in a manner conferring honour, *honorifice.*

hood, *cucullus* (Juv.).

hoodwink, *ludificari, fallēre, inludere.*

hoof, *ungula.*

hook, subst. *hamus, uncus* (= a large iron —): by — or by crook, *quocunque modo.*

hook, v. *hamo capēre.*

hooked, *aduncus, hamatus.*

hoop, *circulus* (Suet.): a child's —, *trochus* (Hor., Ov.).

hoopoe, *upupa* (Varro, Plin.), *epops* (Verg., Ov.).

hoot, hooting, subst. (1) of owls, *cantus (-ūs), carmen.* (2) of persons, *vociferatio.*

hoot, v. (1) of owls, *canēre* (Verg.). (2) of persons, *vociferari, obstrepēre*: to — off the stage, *explodēre.*

hop, v. *salire.*

hope, subst. *spes*: a gleam of —, *spēcula*; to entertain a —, *spem habēre, sperare*; to have no —, *desperare.*

hope, v. *sperare* (usually with acc. object = to — for, or with acc. and infin. = to — that): I — for the best, *recte spero* (Ter.).

hopeful. (1) = full of hope, express by *spes* or *spero.* (2) = exciting hope, *bonae spei* (Tac.).

hopefully, *cum magna spe.*

hopeless. (1) = having no hope, *spe carens, exspes* (Hor.). (2) = about which (or whom) one can have no hope, *desperatus.*

hopelessly, *sine spe, desperanter* (rare).

hopelessness, *desperatio* (as a mental state), *res desperatae* (as a state of affairs).

horde, *grex, caterva.*

horizon. Lit., *orbis finiens, circulus finiens* (Sen.). Transf., = the sky in gen., *caelum, prospectus* (= view).

horizontal, *aequus, libratus.*

horizontally, *ad libram.*

horn. (1) as a substance, *cornu.* (2) the —s of the moon, *cornua lunae.* (3) as a drinking-cup, *poculum.* (4) as a musical instrument, *cornu, buccina, tuba*: to blow the —, *cornu* or *buccinam inflare.*

horned, *corniger* (poet.), *cornutus* (Varro).

hornet, *crabro* (Verg.).

horn-pipe, *saltatio.*

horny, *corneus.*

horoscope, *horoscopus* (Pers.), *genesis* (Suet.): to cast a —, *sidera natalicia notare.*

horrible, horrid, *horrendus* (poet.), *horribilis, nefarius, nefandus, foedus, atrox.*

horribleness, *foeditas.*

horribly, *foede.*

horrify, *(ex)terrēre, obstupefacĕre, horrificare* (poet.).

horror, *horror, timor, pavor*: a —, = a monster, *monstrum.*

horse. (1) the animal, *equus (ecus)*, f. *equa*: an ordinary —, a hack, *caballus*; a Gallic —, *mannus*; a gelding, *canterius*; prov.: to spur the willing —, *addĕre calcaria sponte currenti* (Plin. L.). (2) = cavalry, *equites (-um,* plur.), *equitatus (-ūs).*

horseback: to ride on —, *in equo vehi, equitare*; to fight on —, *ex equo pugnare.*

horsebreaker, *equorum domitor.*

horse-cloth, *stratum.*

horse-flesh. (1) as meat, *caro equina.* (2) living = horses, *equi.*

horse-fly, *tabanus* (Varro, Plin.).

horse-hair, *pilus equinus.*

horse-laugh, *cachinnus.*

horseman, *eques.*

horsemanship, *equitandi ars.*

horse-race, *curriculum equorum; cursus (-ūs) equorum* or *equester; equorum certamen.*

horse-shoe, *solea.*

horse-soldier, *eques.*

horse-whip; see WHIP.

hortatory, *monens, hortans.*

horticulture, *hortorum cultura* or *cultus (-ūs).*

hose; see STOCKINGS.

hospitable, *hospitalis, liberalis.*

hospitably, *hospitaliter, liberaliter, comiter.*

hospital, *valetudinarium* (Cels.).

hospitality, *hospitium, hospitalitas.*

host. (1) = one who entertains, *hospes*; at a feast, *convivator*; at an inn, *caupo.* (2) = a multitude, *multitudo.* (3) = an army, *exercitus (-ūs).*

hostage, *obses.*

hostel(ry), *caupona.*

hostess, *hospita.*

hostile, *hostilis* (of a public enemy), *hosticus* (also of a public enemy: poet), *inimicus, infestus, infensus.*

hostilely, *hostiliter, inimice, infeste, infense.*

hostility, *animus inimicus* or *infestus, inimicitia, odium*; in plur., *hostilities, hostilia (-ium,* n. plur.), *bellum*: to commence —, *bellum facĕre.*

hot. LIT., *calidus, fervidus, fervens* (= boiling, seething), *candens* (= white —), *aestuosus, ardens.* TRANSF., *calidus, fervidus, fervens, acer.* To be —, *calēre, fervēre, candēre, aestuare*; to become —, *calescere, fervescĕre*; to make —, *calefacĕre, fervefacĕre.*

hotbed, (fig.) *semen.*

hotel, *deversorium, caupona, hospitium.*

hotheaded, *fervidus, temerarius, imprudens.*

hotly, *ardenter, acriter.*

hound, subst. *canis (venaticus)*: to keep a pack of —s, *canes alĕre ad venandum.*

hound, v.: to — on, *instigare, urgēre, stimulare, incitare.*

hour, *hora*: half an —, *semihora*; what — is it? *quota hora est?*; in his last —, *eo ipso die, quo e vita excessit*; leisure —s, *tempus otiosum, tempus subsicivum*; from — to —, *in horas.*

hourly, *singulis horis.*

house, subst. *domus* (= the building, and also those who inhabit it, the family), *aedes, aedificium, domicilium, tectum, villa* (= country —), *insula* (= a — let out in flats), *familia* (= family, household), *gens* or *genus* (= race or clan): at my —, *apud me, domi meae*; to keep —, *rem domesticam administrare* or *curare.*

house, v. (1) = to receive visitors, *hospitio* or *domo excipĕre.* (2) = to store, *condĕre.*

housebreaker, *fur.*

household, subst. *domus, familia.*

household, adj. *domesticus*: — gods, *lares (-um,* plur.), *penates (-ium,* plur.).

householder, *paterfamilias.*

house-keeper, *promus* (Pl., Hor.).

house-keeping, *cura rei domesticae.*

house-maid, *ancilla.*

house-wife, *materfamilias, hera.*

hovel, *tugurium, gurgustium.*

hover, *(circum)volitare, imminēre.*

how. (1) interrog. (in direct and indirect questions), *quomodo? quemadmodum? qui? ut? quo pacto?*: how are you? how do you do? *ut vales?* With adj. or adv. *quam?*: how great? *quantus?*; how small? *quantulus?*; how many? *quot?*; how often? *quotie(n)s?*; how dear? *quanti?*; how much greater? *quanto maior?* (2) in exclamations, *ut, quam.* With adj. or adv. *quam; quantus, quantulus,* etc. (see (1) above) are also used in exclamations. Sometimes 'how' may be rendered by an exclamatory accusative: how blind I was, that I could not foresee that! = *me caecum, qui haec ante non viderim!*; how treacherous are the hopes of men! *o fallacem hominum spem!*

howbeit, *(at)tamen.*

however. (1) adv. *quamvis, quamlibet, quantumvis utcunque*: — great, *quantuscunque, quantus quantus*; — many, *quotquot*; — often, *quotienscunque.* (2) conj. *sed, autem, (at)tamen, nihilominus.*

howl, howling, subst. *ululatus (-ūs), eiulatus (-ūs), eiulatio.*

howl, v. *ululare, fremĕre, eiulare.*

hubbub, *tumultus (-ūs), turba.*

huckster, *caupo, institor.*

huddled together, *conferti.*

hue, *color*: to raise a — and cry, *furem conclamare.*

huff, *stomachus, (irae) impetus (-ūs)*: to be in a —, *irasci, moleste ferre, stomachari.*

hug, subst. *complexus (-ūs).*

hug, v. *amplecti, amplexari, complecti*: to — the shore, *litus premĕre* (Hor.) or *legĕre.*

huge, *immanis, vastus, immensus, ingens.*

hugeness, *magnitudo, moles.*

hulk, (= the body of a ship) *alveus navis.*

hull, of a nut, *cortex, folliculus* (Varro); of a ship; see HULK.

hum, subst. *fremitus (-ūs), murmur, susurrus, stridor, bombus* (Lucr., Cat.).

hum, v. *fremĕre, strepĕre, susurrare* (poet.), *murmurare, murmur edĕre;* = to sing softly, *secum canĕre* or *cantare.*

human, *humanus;* often rendered by the genit. plur. *hominum;* = mortal, *mortalis;* — feelings (in gen.), *humanitas;* human life, *res (humanae);* human being, *homo.*

humane, *misericors, clemens;* sometimes *humanus.*

humanely, *clementer, humane.*

humanity. (1) = the peculiar nature of man, *humanitas, natura* or *condicio humana.* (2) = mankind, the human race, *humanum* or *hominum genus (-ĕris), gens humana.* (3) = kindly feeling, *humanitas, clementia, misericordia.* (4) humanities, *artes liberales* (plur.), *humanitas.*

humanize, *humanum reddĕre, excolĕre.*

humanly, *humano modo* (= after the manner of men): — possible, *quod ut in rebus humanis fieri potest.*

humble, adj. (1) = mean, obscure, *humilis, obscurus:* of — origin, *humili loco natus.* (2) = modest, unassuming, *summissus, modestus, moderatus, verecundus.*

humble, v. *infringĕre, comprimĕre (audaciam hominis):* to — oneself, *se* or *animum summittĕre, summisse se gerĕre.*

humbly, *summisse, modeste, moderate:* to request —, *supplicibus verbis orare.*

humbug, subst. *gerrae* (Pl.), *nugae, tricae* (all *-arum,* plur.); of a person, *nebulo.*

humbug, v. *ludificari, (homini) verba dare, circumvenire, inludĕre.*

humdrum, *iners, tardus, segnis* (= sluggish).

humid, *humidus.*

humidity, *humor.*

humiliating, render by phrase with *dedecus (-ŏris).*

humiliation, *dedecus (-ŏris, n.);* see DISGRACE.

humility, *animus submissus, demissus, modestia.*

humorist, *homo iocosus, lepidus, facetus, festivus.*

humorous, of situations, etc., *ridiculus;* of persons, see HUMORIST.

humour. (1) = fluid, *humor.* (2) = temper, temperament, disposition, *ingenium, natura, animus, animi habitus (-ūs):* in a good —, *hilaris, comis;* in a bad —, *difficilis, morosus;* to be in a bad —, *sibi displicēre;* what sort of — are you in? *quid tibi animi est?* (3) = fancy, caprice, *voluptas, libido:* I am in the — to do, *libet mihi facĕre.* (4) = sense of fun, turn for joking, *lepos in iocando, festivitas, facetiae (-arum,* plur.).

humour, v. *(homini) gratificari, obsequi, indulgēre, morem gerĕre, morigerari.*

hump, *gibbus* (Juv.), *gibba* (Suet.).

humpbacked, *gibber* (Varro, Suet.).

hunch; see HUMP.

hundred, adj. *centum:* a — at a time, *centeni -ae -a;* a — times, *centie(n)s;* — years, *centum anni,* or sometimes *saeculum.*

hundred-fold, *centuplex* (Pl.).

hundred-handed, *centimanus* (poet.).

hundred-headed, *centiceps* (Hor.).

hundredweight, *centumpondium* (Pl.).

hunger, subst. *fames* (lit. and fig.); = starvation, *inedia:* — is the best sauce, *cibi condimentum fames.*

hunger, v. *esurire:* to — after, *sitire, (rei,* genit.) *avidum esse.*

hungrily, *avide.*

hungry, *esuriens, ieiunus, famelicus* (Pl., Ter., Juv.).

hunt, v. *venari, consectari.*

hunt, hunting, subst. *venatio, venatus (-ūs).*

hunter, huntsman, *venator.*

hunting-spear, *venabulum.*

huntress, *venatrix* (poet.).

hurdle, *crates.*

hurl, *iacĕre, iaculari, conicĕre.*

hurling, subst. *coniectus (-ūs).*

hurly-burly, *tumultus (-ūs);* see TUMULT, NOISE.

hurrah! *io!* (Pl., Hor.) *euax!* (Pl.).

hurricane, *tempestas, turbo, procella.*

hurried, *citatus, citus, praeceps.*

hurriedly, *festinanter, propere, cursim, raptim.*

hurry, subst. *festinatio, trepidatio.*

hurry, v. (1) transit. *accelerare, incitare, rapĕre* (= to rush off), *urgēre* (= to push ahead), *maturare* (= to — on a process). (2) intransit. *festinare, properare, maturare, contendĕre:* to — about, *discurrĕre* (in different directions), *trepidare, cursare.*

hurt, subst. *vulnus (-ĕris,* n.); see also INJURY.

hurt, adj. (1) physically, *saucius.* (2) in the feelings, *offensus.*

hurt, v. (1) transit. *laedĕre* (with acc.), *nocēre* (with dat.): to — a person's feelings, *hominem offendĕre;* to be — at a thing, *rem aegre ferre.* (2) impers.: it — s, *dolet* (Pl.).

hurtful, *nocens, noxius, molestus.*

husband, subst. *maritus, vir, coniunx.*

husband, v. *(rei,* dat.) *parcĕre.*

husbandman, *agricola, colonus, arator* (= ploughman).

husbandry, *res rustica,* or plur. *res rusticae, agricultura.* In gen. sense, see THRIFT.

hush, interj. *st!, tace,* plur. *tacēte.*

hush, v. *comprimĕre;* see also SUPPRESS.

husk, *folliculus* (Varro).

husky, *fuscus, (sub)raucus;* see also HOARSE.

hustings, *suggestus (-ūs:* = platform), *comitium* (= place of election).

hustle, v. *offendĕre, pulsare.*

hut, *casa, tugurium.*

hutch, *cavea* (= cage).

huzza, = hurrah; q.v.

hyacinth, perhaps *hyacinthus* or *hyacinthos* (Verg.).

Hyades, *Hyades (-um,* plur.), *suculae (-arum,* plur.).

hymeneal, *nuptialis.*

hymn, subst. *carmen, hymnus* (eccl.); a — in honour of Apollo, *paean.*

hymn, v. *canĕre, cantare, celebrare.*

hyperbole, *hyperbole* or *hyperbola, veritatis superlatio.*

hyperbolical, *superlatus.*

hypercritical, *nimium severus.*

hypochondria, *atra* (or *nigra) bilis.*

hypochondriacal, *melancholicus.*

hypocrisy, *(dis)simulatio, fraus.*

hypocrite, *(dis)simulator.*

hypocritical, *simulatus, fictus.*

hypocritically, *simulate, ficte.*

hypothesis, *opinio, sententia* (= opinion); *ratio, condicio* (= condition); *coniectura* (= conjecture): on this —, *hoc posito.*

hypothetical, *opinabilis.*

hysteria, = undue excitement, *animi perturbatio, concitatio.*

I

I, is often not expressed in Latin, when indicated by the termination of a verb. When for the sake of emphasis or contrast it is expressed, it is represented by *ego, ego ipse*, or *egomet*: I for my part, *equidem*. The first person plur. is sometimes used for the first sing., esp. in poetry.

iambic, subst. *iambus*.

iambic, adj. *iambeus* (Hor.).

ice, *glacies, gelu*.

icicle, *stiria* (Verg.).

icy, *glacialis* (Verg.), *gelidus, frigidus*.

idea. (1) = a notion, conception of some person or thing, *notio, notitia, informatio, imago, forma*: to form an — of a thing, *rem animo concipĕre, cogitatione fingĕre*; innate —s, *notiones animo insitae*; vague —s, *intellegentiae adumbratae*. (2) more generally = thought, *cogitatio, opinio, sententia*: to have noble —s, *egregia* (n. plur.) *sentire*. (3) = purpose, intention, *consilium, sententia, institutum*: what is the — of this? *quorsum hoc spectat?* (4) as philosoph. t. t., the Platonic —, *species*.

ideal, subst. (1) = the idea of something in its perfect state, *exemplar, specimen*, (*expleta et*) *perfecta forma, eximia species*: the — of an orator, *imago perfecti oratoris*. (2) = a purpose, aim; see PURPOSE: to have lofty —s, *ad excelsa spectare*.

ideal, adj. (1) = perfect in its kind, *perfectus, optimus, summus, omnibus numeris absolutus*: — perfection, *absolutio et perfectio*. (2) = existing only in the mind, *commenticius*.

idealist, = one who seeks perfection in life, *qui ad altissimum quidque spectat*.

idealize, = to (mis)take the real for the perfect, *meliorem in partem accipĕre* or *interpretari, pro perfecto habēre*: one who —s the past, *laudator temporis acti* (Hor.).

ideally (not really), *cogitatione non re*.

identical, *idem, unus et idem*: to be —, *nihil differre*.

identify. (1) = to consider to be the same, *eundem* (*idem*) *esse putare*. (2) = to recognize, *agnoscĕre*.

identity. (1) = sameness, render by *idem*. (2) to establish a person's —, = to find out who he is, *cognoscĕre quis sit*.

ides, *idūs* (-*uum*, f. plur.).

idiocy, *fatuitas*.

idiom, *propria loquendi ratio*.

idiomatic, *proprius*.

idiot, *homo fatuus*.

idiotic, *fatuus*.

idle, adj. (1) = inactive, unemployed, *otiosus, vacuus, ignavus, piger, segnis, deses, feriatus* (= on holiday). (2) = useless, *inutilis, vanus, inritus, inanis*; see also USELESS.

idle, v. *cessare, nihil agĕre*.

idleness. (1) = inactivity, *cessatio, otium*. (2) = laziness, *ignavia, segnitia, pigritia, desidia*.

idler, *homo deses, cessator*.

idly. (1) = inactively, *segniter*. (2) = in vain, uselessly, *frustra, inaniter, incassum*.

idol, LIT., *idolum* (eccl.). TRANSF., *amores* (-*um*, plur.), *deliciae* (-*arum*, plur.).

idolator, *deorum fictorum cultor*.

idolatrous, *idololatricus* (eccl.), *fictos deos colens*.

idolatry, *deorum fictorum* (or *simulacrorum*) *cultus* (-*ūs*): to practise —, *colĕre deos fictos*.

idolize, (*tamquam deum*) *colĕre*.

idyl, render by *bucolica* (-*orum*, n. plur. = pastoral poetry: Ov.).

idyllic, render by phrase, e.g.: an — picture of leisured life, *pulcherrima quaedam vitae umbratilis descriptio*.

if: the ordinary equivalent is *si*, which, if it introduces a clause, has an indicative verb in that clause so long as the condition is 'open' (i.e. when nothing is implied about the fulfilment or non-fulfilment of the condition). *Si* is followed by the subjunctive when the condition is unlikely to be fulfilled or already unfulfilled; the present subj. being used of what *may* happen, the imperf. of what *might be* so but is not, the pluperf. of what *might have been* so but was not (the imperf. sometimes of what might have been so often or for a long time). And —, *quodsi*; but —, *sin*; — indeed, *si quidem, siquidem*; — only, *si modo* (or *dum modo* with subj.); — perhaps, *si forte*; even —, *etsi, etiamsi*; as —, *quasi, tamquam* (see also AS) — . . ., or —, *si . . ., sive*; — not (= always unless), *nisi*; — not (= only — not, or even — not), *si non, si minus*; — not (elliptically = otherwise), *sin minus*; — anyone, *si quis*; — someone, *si aliquis*; — ever, *si quando*.

Conditions can also be represented by a participle (e.g. I should never have thought of it, — you had not reminded me, *non mihi, nisi admonito, in mentem venisset*); or by a jussive clause (e.g. even if you drive out nature with a pitchfork, she will still keep coming back, *naturam expellas furca, tamen usque recurret*).

ignite, v. (1) transit. = to set on fire, *accendĕre, incendĕre*. (2) intransit. *exardescĕre, accendi, incendi, ignem* or *flammam concipĕre*.

igneous, *igneus*.

ignition, render by verb.

ignoble. (1) by descent, *ignobilis humilis, obscuro loco natus*. (2) in character, *humilis, inliberalis, inhonestus, abiectus, turpis*.

ignobly, *humiliter, inhoneste, turpiter*.

ignominious, *turpis*.

ignominiously, *turpiter, cum ignominia*.

ignominy, *ignominia, infamia, dedecus* (-*ŏris*), *turpitudo*.

ignorance, *inscientia, inscitia, imprudentia, ignoratio, ignorantia*: to confess one's —, *confiteri se ignorare*.

ignorant, *inscius, ignarus, imprudens, imperitus* (= inexperienced), *indoctus* (= untaught), *rudis*; to be — of, *nescire, ignorare*.

ignorantly, *inscienter, inscite, imprudenter, imperite, indocte*; or render by adj.

ignore, *praeterire, neglegĕre*.

ill, subst. *malum*.

ill, adj. (1) = sick, unwell, *aeger, aegrotus*: to be —, *aegrotare, morbo adfectum esse* or *laborare*; to fall —, *morbo corripi, in morbum incidĕre*; to be — in bed, *cubare*. (2) = evil, *malus*; — fame, *infamia*.

ill, adv. *male, prave*: to take a thing —, *rem aegre* or *moleste ferre*.

ill-advised, *inconsultus, temerarius*; see also RASH.

ill-affected, *aversus, inimicus, infestus.*
ill-bred, *agrestis, inhumanus, inurbanus.*
ill-breeding, *inhumanitas.*
ill-disposed, *malevolus.*
ill-fated, *infelix, miser*; see also UNHAPPY.
ill-favoured; see UGLY.
ill-gotten, *male partus.*
ill-health, *valetudo infirma.*
ill-mannered; see ILL-BRED.
ill-matched, *impar.*
ill-natured, *malevolus, morosus, difficilis, malignus.*
ill-omened, *dirus, tristis, obscenus* (poet.).
ill-starred, *infelix.*
ill-temper, *acerbitas, stomachus, morositas, iracundia.*
ill-will, *malevolentia.*
illegal, *quod contra leges fit.*
illegally, *contra leges.*
illegible, *quod legi non potest.*
illegitimate. (1) of actions, *non legitimus.* (2) of persons, *nothus.*
illegitimately, *non legitime, contra leges.*
illiberal, *inliberalis, sordidus, avarus, malignus.*
illiberality, *inliberalitas, avaritia, malignitas.*
illicit, *inlicitus* (Tac.), *vetitus* (Verg.); see also ILLEGAL.
illimitable, *infinitus.*
illiterate, *inliteratus, indoctus, ineruditus.*
illness, *morbus, aegrotatio, valetudo infirma or adversa.*
illogical, *absurdus, parum consentaneus*; of persons, *disserendi imperitus.*
illogically, *nulla ratione, contra artem disserendi.*
illume, illumine, illuminate. (1) = to throw light on, *conlustrare, inlustrare, inluminare.* (2) = to enlighten the mind, *docēre, erudire.* (3) = to adorn with pictures, *varie pingēre, coloribus distinguēre.*
illumination, render by verb.
illusion, *error, somnium, opinio falsa or vana.*
illusive, illusory, *vanus, falsus.*
illustrate. (1) to — a book, *librum picturis ornare.* (2) = to explain, *inlustrare*; see also EXPLAIN.
illustration. (1) in a book, *pictura, tabula.* (2) = example, *exemplum.*
illustrious, (*prae*)*clarus, amplus* (esp. in superl.), *splendidus, inlustris, insignis, egregius, eximius.*
image. (1) in visible form, *imago, simulacrum, effigies.* (2) mental, a conception, *imago, species*; see also IDEA.
imagery, render by phrase, such as *imagines ante oculos proponēre.*
imaginable, *quod cogitari potest.*
imaginary, *opinabilis, commenticius, imaginarius, fictus, falsus, inanis.*
imagination, *cogitatio*: a vivid —, *cogitatio uberrima, vis ingenii*; creatures of the —, *res cogitatione fictae.*
imaginative, *aptus ad excogitandum, ingeniosus.*
imagine, *animo concipēre, cogitatione fingēre, excogitare, comminisci*; = to think, *putare, opinari.*
imbecile, *fatuus, stultus*; see also FOOLISH.
imbecility, *imbecillitas animi or ingenii, fatuitas* (rare), *stultitia.*
imbibe, *bibere, combibēre, imbibēre*; *se re imbuēre, re inficī*: to — errors with one's mother's milk, *errores cum lacte nutricis sugēre* (Cic.).

imbrue, *imbuēre, madefacēre*: — with blood, *cruentare.*
imbue, *inficēre, imbuēre, tingēre.*
imitable, *imitabilis, quod imitari possumus.*
imitate: in gen., *imitari*; = to portray, produce a copy of, *exprimēre, effingēre*; = to emulate, endeavour to equal, *aemulari,* (*per*)*sequi.*
imitation. (1) = the act of imitating, *imitatio, aemulatio*; or render by verb. (2) = a copy, *effigies, imago, simulacrum.*
imitator, *imitator,* f. *imitatrix; aemulus, aemulator.*
immaculate, *purus, sanctus, castus, integer.*
immaculately, *pure, sancte, caste.*
immanent, (*in re*) *inhaerens.*
immaterial. (1) = not consisting of matter, *sine corpore, expers corporis.* (2) = unimportant, *nullius momenti, nullo momento, lēvis.*
immature, *immaturus, crudus.*
immeasurable, *immensus, infinitus, vastus, ingens.*
immediate. (1) = without the intervention of another, *proximus.* (2) = without delay, *praesens.*
immediately. (1) = with none intervening: to apply — to a person, *ipsum adire*; — before, *sub* with acc.; — after, *sub* with acc.; — after (in time or rank), *secundum.* (2) = at once, *statim, protinus, confestim, extemplo.*
immemorial: from time —, *ex omni memoria aetatum* (Cic.); it is an — custom, *consuetudo ab antiquis temporibus inveteravit.*
immense, *ingens, vastus, immensus, infinitus.*
immensely, *in immensum*; = very much, *maxime, valae.*
immensity, *immensitas.*
immerge, (*im*)*mergēre, submergēre.*
immersion, render by verb.
immigrate, (*im*)*migrare.*
immigrant, *advena.*
immigration, *adventus* (-*ūs*); or render by verb.
imminent, *praesens*: to be in — danger, *in summo periculo esse*; to be — (of trouble, etc.), *instare, imminēre, impendēre.*
immobility, render by movēre.
immoderate, *immodicus, immodestus, immoderatus, nimius, intemperans.*
immoderately, *immoderate, immodeste, immodice, intemperanter, extra modum, praeter modum.*
immoderation, *intemperantia*: — in speaking, *immoderatio verborum.*
immodest, *impudicus, inverecundus, impudens.*
immodestly, *impudenter.*
immodesty, *impudicitia.*
immolate, *immolare.*
immolation, *immolatio.*
immoral, *pravus, male moratus, perditus, inhonestus, vitiosus, turpis, corruptus*; see also WICKED.
immorality, *mores mali or corrupti or perditi*; *turpitudo, vitia* (-*orum,* plur.).
immorally, *inhoneste, turpiter, flagitiose, perdite, prave.*
immortal, *immortalis* (of gods, the soul and things, e.g. glory); *aeternus, sempiternus* (of things): the — Homer, *Homerus, vir divinus*; to have — life, *vitā sempiternā frui*; the —s (i.e. the gods), *di immortales.*

immortality, *immortalitas, aeternitas*; = immortal glory, *immortalis* or *sempiterna gloria*.

immortalize, *immortali gloriā adficĕre, immortali gloriae commendare*.

immovable, *immobilis, immotus, stabilis*: to be — (lit.), *loco suo non posse moveri*.

immune, *immunis*; see also FREE.

immunity, *vacatio, immunitas* (e.g. *tributorum*); see also FREEDOM.

immure, *includĕre*; see also SHUT.

immutability, *immutabilitas, constantia, stabilitas*.

immutable, *immutabilis, constans, stabilis*.

immutably, *constanter*; or render by phrase.

impair, *(im)minuĕre, comminuĕre, debilitare, frangĕre, infringĕre*.

impale, *(hastā* or *palo) transfigĕre*.

impalpable, *quod tangi non potest*.

impart, *impertire, communicare, dare, tribuĕre, donare*.

impartial, *aequus, aequabilis, integer, incorruptus*: to be —, *neutri parti favēre*.

impartiality, *aequitas, aequabilitas*.

impartially, *ex aequo et bono, integre, incorrupte*.

impassable, *invius, insuperabilis, impeditus*.

impassioned, *concitatus, fervidus, ardens, vehemens*.

impassive, *lentus*.

impassivity, *lentitudo, lentus animus*.

impatience, *impatientia morae, festinatio*.

impatient, *impatiens morae, ardens, vehemens, acer, avidus*: to be — at a thing, *(rem) aegre* or *moleste ferre*; to be — to do, *gestire facĕre*.

impatiently, *ardenter, acriter, vehementer, avide*.

impeach, *accusare*; see also ACCUSE.

impeacher, *accusator*.

impeachment, *accusatio*.

impede, *impedire*; see also HINDER.

impediment, *impedimentum*: an — in speech, *haesitantia linguae*; to have an —, *linguā haesitare, balbutire* (Hor.).

impel, *impellĕre, urgēre, incitare*.

impend, *impendēre, imminēre*.

impenetrable, *impenetrabilis* (Plin.), *impervius* (Tac.), *impeditus*; see also IMPASSABLE.

impenitent, *obstinatus, offirmatus*.

imperative. (1) as grammat. t. t., *imperativus* (adj.). (2) = commanding, render by *impero*. (3) = necessary; q.v.

imperfect. (1) as grammat. t. t. *imperfectus* (adj.). (2) = unfinished, *imperfectus, rudis, incohatus* (3) = faulty, *vitiosus, mendosus*.

imperfection, *vitium, mendum, culpa*, or render by adj. (e.g. the — of human nature, *natura hominum imperfecta et mendosa*).

imperfectly, = faultily, *vitiose, mendose, male*.

imperial, render by a genit., e.g. *imperatoris, principis, Caesaris, imperii*; adjectives occur in late authors, such as *principalis* and *imperatorius* in Suet.

imperil, *in discrimen adducĕre*.

imperious, *imperiosus, superbus, adrogans*.

imperiously, *superbe, adroganter*.

imperishable, *immortalis, aeternus*; see also ETERNAL, IMMORTAL.

impersonal, grammat. t. t. *impersonalis*.

impersonate: to — a person, *partes hominis agĕre, hominem imitari*.

impertinence, *insolentia*.

impertinent. (1) = rude, *insolens*. (2) = not to the point, *quod nihil ad rem est*.

impertinently, *insolenter*.

imperturbable, *stabilis, constans, firmus, gravis, immobilis*.

imperturbably, *constanter, firme, graviter, tranquille*.

impervious; see IMPENETRABLE.

impetuosity, *violentia, vis, incitatio, impetus (-ūs)*.

impetuous. (1) of things, *violentus, rapidus, vehemens*. (2) of persons, *vehemens, violentus, acer, fervidus, rapidus*.

impetuously, *violenter, vehementer, acriter*.

impetus, *impetus (-ūs), vis*.

impiety, *impietas (erga deos), nefas, scelus (-ĕris)*.

impious, *impius (erga deos), nefarius, scelerosus, scelestus*.

impiously, *impie, nefarie*.

impinge, *incidĕre, impingi*.

implacability, *odium implacabile* or *inexorabile*.

implacable, *implacabilis, inexorabilis*.

implacably, *atrociter, saeve*.

implant, *inserĕre, ingenerare, ingignĕre*.

implead, *in ius vocare*.

implement, *instrumentum*: an iron —, *ferramentum*.

implicate, *implicare, admiscēre, inligare*.

implicated, *implicatus, conscius* (with genit.), *adfinis* (with dat.).

implication; see IMPLY.

implicit. (1) = implied, *tacitus, quod intellegitur (quamquam non dictum)*. (2) = complete, absolute, *totus, summus*: to have — faith in a person, *homini summam fidem adhibēre, totum se homini committĕre*.

implicitly. (1) = by implication, *tacite*. (2) see ALTOGETHER.

implore, *implorare, rogare, orare* (all these with acc. of person and/or acc. of thing); *obsecrare, exposcĕre* (both with acc. of person or acc. of thing); *obtestari* (with acc. of person).

imply. (1) of persons = to mean, to make clear without actually saying, *significare*. (2) of things = to involve, *(in se) habēre*: to be implied in a thing, *in re inesse*.

impolite, *inurbanus, rusticus, agrestis, inhumanus, inlepidus*.

impolitely, *inurbane, rustice, inhumane*.

impoliteness, *rusticitas, inhumanitas*.

impolitic, *imprudens, inconsultus*.

import, subst. (1) in plur. = imported goods, *res quae importantur*. (2) = meaning, *vis, significatio*.

import, v. (1) = to bring into a country, *invehĕre, importare*. (2) = to signify, *significare, valēre*.

importance. (1) of things, *momentum, pondus (-ĕris), vis*: to be of no —, *nullius momenti esse*. (2) of persons = influence, high position, *amplitudo, dignitas, auctoritas*.

important, *gravis, magnus*: to be —, *magni momenti esse, multum valēre, magnam vim habēre*; to deem a thing more — (most —), *antiquius (antiquissimum) habēre*.

import-duty, *portorium*.

importunate, *molestus, improbus*; see also TROUBLESOME.

importune, *fatigare*: to — a person for a thing, *rem hominem* (or *ab homine*) *flagitare*.

importunity, *flagitatio*.

impose, *imponĕre, iniungĕre*: to — upon; see
CHEAT.

imposing, *speciosus, magnificus.*

imposition. (1) = the act of imposing, express
by *imponĕre*. (2) = a deceit, deception,
fallacia, fraus.

impossibility; see IMPOSSIBLE.

impossible, *quod fieri non potest*: it is quite
—, *nullo modo fieri potest.*

impost, *vectigal, tributum.*

impostor, *fraudator.*

imposture, *fraus, fallacia.*

impotence, *imbecillitas, infirmitas.*

impotent, *invalidus, infirmus, imbecillus, impotens.*

impound, = to confiscate, *publicare.*

impoverish, *in egestatem redigĕre, exhaurire.*

impoverishment, *egestas, inopia, paupertas.*

impracticable, = impossible, *quod fieri non
potest.*

imprecate, (*im*)*precari, exsecrari*; see also
CURSE.

imprecation, *preces* (*-um*, plur.), *exsecratio*; see
also CURSE.

impregnable, *inexpugnabilis.*

impregnate. (1) = to make pregnant, *gravidam* or *praegnantem facĕre.* TRANSF., = to
render prolific, *fecundare* (Verg.), *fertilem
reddĕre.* (2) in gen. = to fill, imbue, infuse,
(*rem homini* or *rei*, dat.) *inicĕre, incutĕre,
adferre, addĕre.*

impregnation, render by verb.

impress. LIT., *imprimĕre.* TRANSF., (1) = to —
a thing upon a person's mind, *imprimĕre,
inculcare.* (2) = to make an impression on,
to affect, (*com*)*movēre animum.*

impression. LIT., *impressio*; = a copy,
exemplum, imago expressa; = footstep,
vestigium. TRANSF., = an effect on the mind,
animi motus (*-ūs*): to make an —, *animum
(com)movēre*; an — of a person, *memoria*; —,
= thought, idea, *opinio*; to be under an —,
= to think, *putare, opinari.*

impressive, *gravis, vehemens.*

impressively, *graviter, vehementer.*

impressiveness, *gravitas.*

imprint, subst.; see IMPRESSION.

imprint, v. *imprimĕre*; see also IMPRESS.

imprison. LIT., *in custodiam* or *carcerem* or
vincula conicĕre. TRANSF., *includĕre.*

imprisonment, *custodia, carcer, vincula*
(*-orum*, plur.).

improbability; see IMPROBABLE.

improbable, *non verisimilis.*

impromptu, *ex tempore.*

improper, *indecōrus, indignus*: to be —,
dedecēre or *non decēre, indignum esse.*

improperly, *indecore, perperam, indigne.*

impropriety, *quod indecorum est.*

improve, v. (1) transit. *meliorem facĕre, emendare, corrigĕre, excolĕre.* (2) intransit.
meliorem fieri, proficĕre (= to make progress),
convalescĕre (= to — in health).

improvement, *correctio, emendatio*; or render
by *melior* and *fieri.*

improvidence, *imprudentia.*

improvident, *improvidus, incautus, imprudens.*

improvidently, *improvide, imprudenter.*

improvise, render by phrase with *ex tempore.*

improvised, *subitarius.*

imprudence, *imprudentia, temeritas* (= rashness).

imprudent, *temerarius, inconsultus.*

imprudently, *temere, inconsulte, imprudenter.*

impudence, *impudentia, os impudens* (or
durum or *ferreum*).

impudent, *impudens, procax, improbus, confidens.*

impudently, *impudenter.*

impugn, *impugnare, oppugnare, improbare.*

impulse. (1) physical, *impulsio, impulsus* (*-ūs*);
or render by verb. (2) mental, *impetus* (*-ūs*),
impulsus (*-ūs*), *impulsio, stimulus*; at a person's
—, *homine auctore, hominis impulsu*; of one's
own —, *sua sponte.*

impulsive, *vehemens, acer.*

impunity, *impunitas*: with —, *impune.*

impure, *impurus, obscenus, contaminatus,
inquinatus, foedus, spurcus, turpis, incestus*
(esp. = unchaste).

impurely, *impure, obscene, foede, spurce,
turpiter.*

impurity, *impuritas, obscenitas, turpitudo,
incestus* (*-ūs* = unchastity).

imputation. (1) = the act of imputing,
render by verb. (2) = charge, *crimen, culpa,
accusatio.*

impute, *adsignare, ascribĕre, attribuĕre, conferre* (esp. with *culpam* as object), *imputare*
(Tac. and poet.).

in. (1) of place : render by locative, if available
(e.g. in Rome, *Romae*; in the house, *domi*; in
the country, *ruri* or *rure*); otherwise by *in*
with abl. (e.g. *in Italia*) or by plain abl. (e.g.
eo loco, hac regione, his terris). Sometimes,
when in = into, use *in* with acc. (2) of
time: render by abl., or by *in* and abl. (esp.
with reference to the circumstances of the
moment, e.g.: in such a time of crisis, *in tali
tempore*). Sometimes 'in the course of' is rendered by *de* with abl., e.g.: in the night-time,
de nocte. In some contexts the word 'in'
disappears, e.g.: I did it in my boyhood, *puer
feci.* (3) of other relations: in a certain
situation, render by *in* with abl.; in a certain
manner, plain abl.; in a certain state or
mood, *per* with acc. (e.g.: in sleep, *per somnum*; in anger, *per iram*); in respect of, plain
abl. (sometimes *in* with acc.); in the case of,
in with abl.; in the hands of, *penes* with acc.;
in the writings of, *apud* with acc.; to have a
friend in Cicero, *Ciceronem amicum habēre*;
you do right in saying, *recte facis cum dicis.*

inability, *imbecillitas, infirmitas, inopia* (=
want of means); otherwise render by *non
posse.*

inaccessible. (1) of places, *inaccessus* (Verg.,
Tac.). (2) of persons, difficult to see, *rari
aditūs.*

inaccuracy. (1) of a person, *indiligentia.* (2)
of a thing (e.g. a report), render by adj. *falsus.*

inaccurate. (1) of a person, *indiligens.* (2) of
reports, etc., *falsus.*

inaction, inactivity, *otium, quies, cessatio*;
with the further idea of laziness, *desidia,
inertia, ignavia.*

inactive, *quietus, iners, deses, ignavus, segnis.*

inadequate, *impar*; or render by phrase with
satis.

inadequately, *parum, haud satis.*

inadmissible, *inlicitus* (Tac.); or render by
phrase.

inadvertence, *imprudentia.*

inadvertent, *imprudens.*

inadvertently, *imprudenter, casu, temere.*
inalienable, *quod abalienari non potest.*
inane, *inanis.*
inanimate, *inanimus, inanimatus.*
inanition, *inanitas.*
inapplicable, to be, *non valēre.*
inapposite; see INAPPROPRIATE.
inappreciable, *minimus.*
inappropriate, *non idoneus.*
inaptitude, *inutilitas* (= uselessness); see also
INABILITY.
inarticulate, *parum distinctus.*
inasmuch as, *quandoquidem.*
inattention, *animus non attentus, neglegentia,
incuria, indiligentia, inscitia.*
inattentive, *non attentus, neglegens:* to be —,
aliud agĕre.
inaudible, *quod audiri non potest.*
inaugural, *aditialis* (Plin.); or render by verb
auspicari.
inaugurate, *inaugurare, dedicare, consecrare;*
see also BEGIN.
inauguration, *dedicatio, consecratio.*
inauspicious, *infelix, infaustus* (poet.), *nefastus.*
inauspiciously, *infeliciter, malis ominibus.*
incalculable, *immensus, ingens.*
incandescent, *candens.*
incantation, *carmen, cantio.*
incapability, *inscitia;* or render by phrase
with *non posse.*
incapable, *inhabilis;* or render by phrase with
non posse.
incapacitate, *inutilem reddĕre.*
incapacity, *inscitia.*
incarcerate, incarceration; see IMPRISON
and IMPRISONMENT.
incarnate, *incarnatus* (eccl.); *specie humana* or
corpore indutus.
incarnation, *incarnatio* (eccl.).
incautious, *incautus, inconsultus, temerarius.*
incautiously, *incaute, inconsulte, temere.*
incendiary, *incendiarius* (Tac.), *incendiorum
auctor.*
incense, subst. *tus* (*turis*); of —, adj. *tureus*
(poet.).
incense, v. *accendĕre, incendĕre;* see also EXAS-
PERATE.
incentive, *stimulus, incitamentum, inritamentum, invitamentum, inlecebra.*
inception, *initium.*
inceptive, *incipiens.*
incessant, *perpetuus, adsiduus, continuus;* see
also CONTINUOUS.
incessantly, *perpetuo, adsidue, continenter.*
incest, *incestus* (-ūs), *incestum.*
incestuous, *incestus.*
inch, as a lineal measure, *uncia* (Plin.): not to
yield an —, not to depart an —, (*ab re*) *non
transversum digitum discedĕre;* — by —,
paullatim, sensim.
inchoate, *incohatus.*
incident, *casus* (-ūs), *res.*
incidental, *fortuitus, forte oblātus.*
incidentally, *casū, forte, fortuito, obiter* (Plin.,
Juv.).
incipient, render by phrase, with *initium* or
incipio.
incision, *incisura* (Plin.); to make an —; see
CUT.
incisive, *mordax* (Hor.).
incisively, *praecise.*
incisors, *dentes qui secant* (Cels.).

incite, *instigare, incitare, excitare, stimulare,
incendĕre, impellĕre.*
incitement; see INCENTIVE.
incivility, *inurbanitas, rusticitas, inhumanitas.*
inclemency. (1) of persons, *severitas, crudelitas, saevitia.* (2) of the weather, *asperitas*
(Tac., Ov.); or render by adj.
inclement. (1) of persons, *severus, crvdelis,
saevus.* (2) of weather, *gravis, asper.*
inclination. (1) physical, *inclinatio;* = slope,
fastigium, clivus. (2) mental, = disposition,
propensity, *inclinatio, voluntas, studium:* to
have an — for a thing, *ad rem propensum,
proclivem, pronum esse, rei* (dat.) *studēre,
rei* (genit.) *esse studiosum, rei* (genit.) *studio
teneri;* to be guided by one's own —, *studiis
suis obsequi.*
incline, v. (1) transit. *inclinare.* (2) intransit.
inclinari, (se) inclinare (with *ad* or *in* and acc.);
propendēre (with *in* and acc.).
inclined, *inclinatus, propensus, proclivis, pronus*
(all with *ad* and acc.): I am — to think, *haud
scio an;* see also INCLINATION.
inclose; see ENCLOSE.
include, *comprehendĕre, complecti, continēre,
adnumerare, adscribĕre:* to — among the
accused, *in reos referre;* without including
you, *te excepto;* to be —d in that number, *in
eo numero esse* or *haberi.*
included, render by verb, or sometimes by
cum or *in:* there were 300 soldiers, the
prisoners —, *milites erant trecenti cum captivis.*
incognito, *incognitus, ignoratus, alieno* or
dissimulato nomine.
incoherent, *interruptus, dissipatus;* or render
by verb *cohaereo.*
incoherently, *interrupte:* to speak —, *haud
cohaerentia dicĕre.*
incombustible, *qui ignibus non absumitur.*
income, *vectigal* (public or private —),
reditus (-ūs = returns), *fructus* (-ūs = produce), *pecunia, quaestus* (-ūs); to make an —,
quaestum facĕre; he has an — to live on,
habet unde vivat.
incommode, *incommodum* or *molestum esse.*
incommodious, *incommodus, molestus;* see
also INCONVENIENT.
incomparable, *incomparabilis* (Plin.); *unicus,
divinus, singularis, eximius, egregius.*
incomparably, *unice, eximie, egregie.*
incompatibility, *repugnantia, diversitas.*
incompatible, *alienus* (with *ab* and abl.);
contrarius, repugnans (with dat.): to be —
with, *abhorrēre* (with *ab* and abl.), *repugnare*
(with dat., or, of two persons or things,
inter se).
incompetence, *inscitia;* see INABILITY.
incompetent. (1) legally: to be —, *ius* or
potestatem non habēre. (2) in gen., *inscitus,
inhabilis, inutilis;* see also FOOLISH, INCAPABLE.
incompetently, *inscite.*
incomplete, *imperfectus, incohatus.*
incompletely, *imperfecte.*
incomprehensible, *quod comprehendi* or
intellegi non potest.
incompressible, *quod comprimi non potest.*
inconceivable, *quod* (*mente* or *cogitatione*)
comprehendi non potest; sometimes =
incredible, incredibilis.
inconceivably, *incredibiliter, mirum in modum.*
inconclusive, (*argumentum*) *quo nihil efficitur.*
incongruity, *repugnantia.*

incongruous

incongruously, *non apte,*.
inconsequent, adj. see INCOHERENT.
inconsiderable, *lēvis, tenuis, exiguus, parvus.*
inconsiderate. (1) in gen. = unthinking, *inconsideratus, inconsultus, incautus.* (2) = without thought for others, express by phrase, such as *sibi tantum consulēre, aliorum commoda non respicēre.*
inconsiderately, *inconsiderate, incaute, nullo consilio, nulla ratione, temere.*
inconsistency, *inconstantia, mutabilitas, repugnantia.*
inconsistent, *inconstans:* — with, *alienus, contrarius, absonus, repugnans*; see also INCOMPATIBLE.
inconsistently, *inconstanter.*
inconsolable, *inconsolabilis* (poet.), *qui nullo solacio levari potest.*
inconspicuous, *obscurus, parum insignis.*
inconstancy, *inconstantia, levitas, varietas, mutabilitas* (mentis)*, mobilitas.*
inconstant, *inconstans, varius, lēvis, mutabilis, mobilis.*
incontestable, *quod refutari non potest.*
incontinence, *incontinentia, intemperantia.*
incontinent, *incontinens, intemperans.*
incontinently, *incontinenter*; = immediately, *statim.*
incontrovertible, *quod refutari non potest.*
inconvenience, *incommodum, incommoditas* (Ter.): to cause — to a person, *homini negotium exhibēre* or *facessēre.*
inconvenient, *inopportunus, incommodus.*
inconveniently, *incommode*: very —, *perincommode.*
incorporate; see UNITE, or ESTABLISH.
incorrect. (1) = mistaken, false, *falsus, perversus, mendosus*: the account is —, *ratio non convenit* or *non constat.* (2) = morally wrong, *improbus, iniustus.*
incorrectly, *perperam, falso, mendose.*
incorrigible, *perditus, qui corrigi non potest.*
incorrupt, incorruptible, *incorruptus, integer, sanctus, innocens.*
incorruptibility, *integritas, sanctitas, innocentia.*
incorruptibly, *incorrupte, integre, sancte.*
increase, subst. *incrementum, auctus* (-ūs)*, accretio, accessio.*
increase, v. (1) transit. *augēre, amplificare, multiplicare, dilatare.* (2) intransit. *crescēre, augēri, gliscēre,* (in)*crebrescēre.*
incredible, *incredibilis.*
incredibly, *incredibiliter, incredibilem in modum.*
incredulous, *incredulus* (Hor.).
increment, *incrementum*; see also INCREASE.
incriminate, *suspectum reddēre:* to — oneself, *se scelere adligare.*
incubate, *incubare* (Plin.).
inculcate, *inculcare,* (in *animo*) *insculpēre*; sometimes render by *docēre.*
incumbent: it is — upon me to do, *meum est facēre, debeo facēre, oportet me facēre, faciendum est mihi.*
incur, *incurrēre* (in *rem*), (rem) *suscipēre* or *contrahēre:* to — disgrace, *dedecus in se admittēre.*
incurable, *insanabilis, immedicabilis* (Ov.); *desperatus* (= despaired of).

incursion, *incursio*; see also ATTACK.
indebted. (1) = owing money, *obaeratus:* to be —, *in aere alieno esse*; to be heavily —, *aere alieno obrutum esse.* (2) in gen. = obliged, *obnoxius, obligatus:* to be — to a person for a thing, *rem homini acceptam referre.*
indecency, *turpitudo, obscenitas.*
indecent, *indecōrus, obscenus, turpis.*
indecently, *indecore, turpiter, obscene.*
indecision, *dubitatio, haesitatio, inconstantia.*
indecisive, *dubius, anceps.*
indecisively (of fighting), *aequo marte.*
indeclinable, *indeclinabilis* (grammat. t. t.).
indecorous, *indecōrus*; see also INDECENT.
indeed. (1) emphatic; *vere, profecto, sane:* but —, *enimvero*; and —, *atque adeo*; yes —, *vero*; then —, *tum vero.* (2) concessive, *quidem* (often preceded by a pronoun), *scilicet.* (3) interrogative, *ain tu? itane est?* (4) ironical, *scilicet, nimirum, videlicet, sane.*
indefatigable, *adsiduus* (= constantly active)*, impiger, indefessus* (poet.).
indefatigably, *adsidue, impigre.*
indefeasible, *in perpetuum ratus.*
indefensible, *quod defendi non potest.*
indefinable, *quod* (verbis) *definiri non potest:* an — element of danger, *nescio quid periculi.*
indefinite, *incertus, dubius, anceps, ambiguus:* for an — period, *in incertum*; as grammat. t. t., the — pronoun, *pronomen infinitum* or *indefinitum.*
indelible, *indelibilis* (Ov.)*, quod delēri non potest*; sometimes can be rendered simply by *sempiternus, perpetuus.*
indelicate, *inurbanus, impudicus, impurus*; see also INDECENT.
indemnify, *damnum* (homini) *restituēre* or *sarcire*; see also COMPENSATE.
indemnity; see INDEMNIFY: an act of —, *lex oblivionis* (Nep.).
indenture, *pactum.*
independence, *libertas.*
independent, *liber, solutus, sui iuris, sui potens*; = exempt from taxes, etc., *immunis:* to be —, *sui iuris* or *suae potestatis* or *in sua potestate esse*; to live in an — fashion, *ad suum arbitrium vivēre.*
independently, *libere.*
indescribable, *inenarrabilis, incredibilis, singularis*; sometimes rendered by *nescio quis* (e.g. that wonderful and — thing, *illud nescio quid praeclarum*).
indescribably, *inenarrabiliter, singulariter, mirum in modum.*
indestructible, *quod everti non potest,* or *perennis, perpetuus* (= lasting).
indeterminate, *incertus*; see also INDEFINITE.
index. (1) in gen. = any kind of indication, *index.* (2) = the hand that points to the hour of the day, use *gnomon* (Plin.), or *horarum index.* (3) = a table of contents, *index* (Quint.).
India, *India.*
Indian, subst. *Indus*; adj. *Indicus.*
indicate, *indicare, significare, arguēre* (poet.): to — in advance, *praenuntiare, portendēre.*
indication, *indicium, index, argumentum, vestigium, significatio, signum.*
indicative. (1) in gen. render by subst. *indicium* or verb *indico.* (2) as grammat. t. t., the — mood, *modus indicativus.*
indict, = to accuse, *accusare, nomen deferre*; see also ACCUSE, ACTION.

[736]

indictable, *accusabilis, quod lege animadverten-dum est.*
indictment: bill of —, *libellus* (Juv.), *crimen, accusatio*; see also ACCUSATION.
indifference, = neglect, heedlessness, *negle-gentia, incuria*; = calmness, *aequus animus, aequitas animi, securitas*; = coldness, apathy, *lentitudo*; towards a person, *animus alienatus ab homine.*
indifferent. (1) of persons = negligent, *neglegens, remissus, dissolutus*; = calm, *securus,* or render by phrase *aequo animo*; = cold, apathetic, *lentus*; towards a person, *durus, alienatus* (*ab homine*): to be — about a thing, *rem nil morari, neglegĕre, nihili facĕre*; to become —, *obdurescĕre.* (2) = neither good nor bad, *nec bonus nec malus*; *indifferens* (attempted by Cicero as a trans-lation of the Greek ἀδιάφορος), *mediocris*; see also IMPARTIAL.
indifferently. (1) of persons = with in-difference, *dissoluto* or *remisso animo, negle-genter, lente, aequo animo.* (2) = middlingly, *mediocriter.* (3) = without distinction, *pro-miscue.* See also IMPARTIALLY.
indigence, *inopia, egestas, mendicitas.*
indigent, *inops, egens, mendicus.*
indigenous, *vernaculus*; applied to persons, *indigĕna,* or render by phrase, such as *in illa terra natus*; see also NATIVE.
indigestible, *difficilis ad concoquendum, gravis.*
indigestion, *cruditas.*
indignant, *indignans,indignabundus,(sub)iratus*: to be —, *indignari, stomachari.*
indignantly, express by adj. or partic.; see INDIGNANT.
indignation, *indignatio, indignitas* (= sense of wrong), *stomachus, ira.*
indignity, *ignominia, indignitas, contumelia*; see also INSULT.
indirect. (1) physically, *non rectus, devius.* (2) abstract = through a third party, render by phrase. (3) of speech, *obliquus* (Tac.). (4) as grammat. t. t. *obliquus* (e.g. *oratio obliqua*: Quint.).
indirectly, *oblique* (Tac.), *per circumitionem.*
indirectness, in speech, *circumitio.*
indiscoverable, *quod inveniri non potest.*
indiscreet, *inconsultus*; see also INCONSIDERATE, IMPRUDENT.
indiscretion, see IMPRUDENCE.
indiscriminate, *promiscuus.*
indiscriminately, *promiscue, sine ullo dis-crimine, passim* (Hor.), *temere.*
indispensable, *necessarius.*
indispose, *alienare, abstrahĕre, avocare.*
indisposed. (1) = not well, *aegrotus, infirmā valetudine.* (2) = unwilling, disinclined, *aversus, alienus*; or render by *nolle.*
indisposition. (1) = minor sickness, *commo-tiuncula.* (2) = unwillingness, *animus aversus* or *invitus* or *alienus.*
indisputable, *certus, manifestus, haud dubius.*
indisputably, *sine ulla controversia, certe, haud dubie.*
indissoluble, *indissolubilis*; or render simply by *aeternus.*
indistinct. (1) to the senses, *parum clarus, obtusus* (of the voice: Quint.). (2) to the understanding, *obscurus, perplexus.*
indistinctly, *parum clare, obscure, perplexe, confuse.*

indistinguishable, *quod discerni non potest.*
indite, *scribĕre*; see also WRITE.
individual, subst. *homo*: people as —s, *singuli*; see also MAN, PERSON.
individual, adj. *proprius, singularis, singuli* (*-ae -a,* plur.).
individuality, *propria natura, proprium in-genium.*
individually, *singillatim, viritim, in singulos.*
indivisible, *individuus, quod dividi non potest*: small — bodies, *corpuscula individua.*
indocile, *indocilis.*
indocility, *ingenium indocile.*
indoctrinate, *erudire, docĕre, instituĕre.*
indolence, *ignavia, inertia, desidia, segnities.*
indolent, *ignavus, iners, deses, segnis, piger.*
indolently, *ignave, segniter.*
indomitable, *invictus, indomitus.*
indoor, adj. *umbratilis.*
indoors, adv. *domi, intus.*
indorse; see ENDORSE.
indubitable, *haud dubius, certus.*
induce, (*hominem*) *inducĕre, adducĕre, impellĕre, inlicĕre* (*ad* or *in rem,* or with *ut* clause); (*homini*) *persuadēre* (*ut*).
inducement, *incitamentum, inlecebra, causa, praemium.*
induct, *inaugurare.*
induction, in logic, *inductio* (Quint.).
indulge. v. (1) transit.: **a** = to give way to a person, *homini indulgēre, morem gerĕre*: **b** = to give way to passions, etc., *rei* (dat.) *indulgēre, se dedĕre, (in)servire.* (2) intransit. *nimis sibi indulgēre.*
indulgence, *indulgentia, benignitas, venia* (= the overlooking of faults).
indulgent, *indulgens, benignus, remissus, facilis.*
indulgently, *indulgenter, benigne.*
industrious, *industrius, (g)navus, acer, sedulus, adsiduus, strenuus, diligens.*
industriously, *industrie, (g)naviter, acriter, adsidue, strenue, diligenter.*
industry, *industria, adsiduitas, sedulitas, dili-gentia.*
indwelling, *qui intus est, insitus, innatus.*
inebriate, v. *ebrium facĕre.*
inebriated, *ebrius, temulentus.*
inebriation, *ebrietas*; see also DRUNKENNESS.
ineffable, *quod verbis exprimi non potest, inauditus*; = too horrible to utter, *infandus*; = incredible, *incredibilis*; = unheard of, *inauditus.*
ineffably, *supra quam enarrari potest, in-credibiliter.*
ineffective, ineffectual, inefficient, of things, *invalidus, inritus, inutilis*; of persons, *inutilis, inritus* (Verg., Tac.): to be —, *effectu carēre.*
ineffectively, ineffectually, *frustra, nequic-quam, incassum.*
inelegance, render by phrase, such as *sine elegantia.*
inelegant, *invenustus, inelegans, inconcinnus, inlepidus, inurbanus.*
inelegantly, *ineleganter, inlepide* (Pl., Hor.), *inurbane.*
ineligible, = unsuitable, *inopportunus*; other senses must be rendered by phrases (see ELIGIBLE).
inept, *ineptus*; see also ABSURD.
inequality, *inaequalitas, dissimilitudo.*
inequitable, *iniquus, iniustus.*

inequitably, *inique, iniuste.*
inert, *iners, tardus, segnis.*
inertly, *tarde, signiter.*
inertness, *inertia;* see also INDOLENCE.
inestimable, *inaestimabilis, singularis, unicus.*
inestimably, *singulariter, unice.*
inevitable, *necessarius, haud dubius, inevitabilis* (Ov., Tac.).
inevitably, *necessario.*
inexact, *haud accuratus* (of things), *indiligens* (of persons).
inexactness, *indiligentia:* — of expression, *verba non accurata.*
inexcusable, *quod nihil excusationis habet.*
inexhaustible, *quod exhauriri non potest, infinitus.*
inexorable, *inexorabilis;* or render by *rigidus, severus, durus.*
inexpediency, *inutilitas,* or render by adj.
inexpedient, *inutilis, inopportunus.*
inexperience, *imperitia, inscitia, inscientia, insolentia.*
inexperienced, inexpert, *imperitus, ignarus* (with genit.), *rudis.*
inexpiable, *inexpiabilis.*
inexplicable, *inexplicabilis.*
inexplicably, *nescio quo modo.*
inexpressible, *inauditus, inenarrabilis;* see also INEFFABLE.
inexpugnable, *inexpugnabilis;* see also IMPREGNABLE.
inextinguishable, *inexstinctus* (Ov.); *quod exstingui non potest.*
inextricable, *inexplicabilis, inextricabilis* (Verg., of the Labyrinth).
infallibility, render by adj. *certus.*
infallible, *certus, haud dubius;* of a person, *qui errare non potest:* to be —, *omni errore carēre.*
infallibly, *certo.*
infamous, *infamis, turpis, flagitiosus.*
infamously, *turpiter, flagitiose;* or render by phrase with *infamia.*
infamy, *infamia, dedecus, ignominia, probrum.*
infancy, *infantia* (Tac.), *pueritia;* often to be rendered by phrase with *infans.*
infant, subst. *infans.*
infant, adj. *infans, puerilis.*
infanticide, *infantium caedes.*
infantine, *puerilis.*
infantry, *pedites* (-*um,* plur.), *peditatus* (-*ūs*).
infatuate, *infatuare* (= to make a fool of), *occaecare* (= to blind), *pellicēre* (= to inveigle).
infatuated, *amens, demens.*
infatuation, *amentia, dementia, furor.*
infect. LIT., express by means of subst. *contagio* (= infection). TRANSF., *vitiis inficēre, contaminare.*
infection, *contagio, contagium* (poet.), *contactus* (-*ūs*).
infectious, render by subst. *contagio:* an — disease, *pestilentia.*
infecundity, *sterilitas.*
infelicitous, *infelix;* see also UNHAPPY.
infelicity, *infelicitas, malum;* see also UNHAPPINESS.
infer, *concludĕre, conligĕre, inferre* (as logical t.t.).
inference. (1) as a logical process, *argumentatio, coniectura.* (2) = conclusion drawn, *conclusio, coniectura;* a futile little —, *conclusiuncula.*
inferior, subst. render by adj.

inferior, adj. *inferior, deterior, minor, impar.*
infernal. LIT., *infernus:* the — regions, *inferi* (-*orum,* plur.), *Orcus* (poet.). TRANSF., = diabolical, *nefandus, nefarius.*
infertile, *sterilis.*
infertility, *sterilitas.*
infest, *infestum reddĕre* or *habēre.*
infested, *infestus.*
infidelity. (1) in gen. = unfaithfulness, *infidelitas, perfidia.* (2) = adultery; q.v.
infinite, *infinitus, immensus.*
infinitely. LIT., *infinite, ad* or *in infinitum* (Plin.). TRANSF., colloq. = very much, *incredibiliter, sane quam.*
infinitesimal, *minimus,* (*per*)*exiguus.*
infinity, *infinitas.*
infirm, *infirmus, imbecillus, invalidus, debilis.*
infirmary; see HOSPITAL.
infirmity. (1) = weakness, debility, *infirmitas, imbecillitas, debilitas.* (2) = a failing, *vitium;* of health, *morbus.*
inflame, = to excite, *inflammare, accendĕre, incendĕre:* to be —d, *inflammari, ardēre, flagrare.*
inflammable, *facilis ad exardescendum, quod celeriter accenditur.*
inflammation, *inflammatio* (Cels.).
inflammatory, (of speech, etc.) *seditiosus, turbulentus.*
inflate. LIT., = to blow into, fill with air, *inflare, sufflare* (Pl., Plin.). TRANSF., = to puff up, (*animum*) *inflare, tumefacĕre* (poet.).
inflated, *inflatus, tumidus, turgidus.*
inflation. LIT., *inflatio.* TRANSF., render by verb or adj.
inflect, as grammat. t. t. *declinare* (Quint.).
inflection, as grammat. t. t., *declinatio* (Varro), *flexura* (Varro), *flexus* (-*ūs:* Quint.).
inflexibility, *obstinatio, pertinacia.*
inflexible, *rigidus, obstinatus, pertinax.*
inflexibly, *obstinate, pertinaciter.*
inflict, (*rem homini*) *adferre, inferre, infligĕre, imponĕre, iniungĕre;* (*re hominem*) *adficĕre:* to — punishment on a person, *poenam de homine capĕre* or *sumĕre, hominem poena adficĕre, hominem punire;* see also PUNISH.
infliction. (1) as a process, render by verb. (2) = trouble inflicted, *malum, incommodum.*
inflorescence, *flos.*
influence, subst., in gen., *vis, pondus* (-*eris*), *momentum:* divine —, *adflatus* (-*ūs*) *divinus, instinctu divino* (abl. sing. only); personal —, *auctoritas* (= prestige), *opes* (-*um,* plur.), *potentia* (= unofficial power), *gratia* (= interest);* to have (personal) —, (*opibus, gratiā, auctoritate*) *valēre, pollēre, posse* (with a person, *apud hominem*);* to have no —, *nihil posse;* to exercise a beneficial —, *prodesse* (with dat.);* to have an injurious or prejudicial —, *nocēre.*
influence, v. *movēre, impellēre.*
influential, *potens, gravis* (= weighty), *gratiosus.*
influx, render by *influĕre* (e.g.: the — of the Gauls into Italy, *influentes in Italiam Gallorum copias*).
inform. (1) = to give form or shape to, (*ef*)*fingĕre,* (*con*)*formare, informare.* (2) = to give information to a person, (*rem homini*) *nuntiare;* (*hominem de re*) *certiorem facĕre,* or *docēre.* (3) to — against a person, *hominis nomen deferre.*

informal, informally, render by phrase, such as *haud sollemni more*; see also INFORMALITY.

informality, at auspices, etc., *vitium*; otherwise render by phrase.

informant, *auctor*, or render by verb.

information. (1) = news, intelligence, *nuntius*: to receive —, *nuntium accipĕre, certiorem fieri, docēri.* **(2)** = knowledge, *scientia, doctrina*; see also KNOWLEDGE. **(3)** = accusation, *delatio, indicium.*

informer, *delator* ('Tac.), *index.*

infraction; see INFRINGEMENT.

infrequency, *raritas.*

infrequent, *rarus*; see also RARE.

infringe, *rumpĕre, frangĕre, violare.*

infringement, *immunitio, violatio*; or render by verb.

infuriate, *efferare, exasperare*; see also ENRAGE.

infuriated, *furens*; see also ENRAGED.

infuse. LIT., *infundĕre.* TRANSF., *inicĕre, incutĕre.*

infusion. LIT., *infusio* (Plin.); = the fluid in which a thing is steeped, *dilutum* (Plin.). TRANSF., render by verb.

ingathering, = collecting of fruits, *perceptio (frugum).*

ingenerate, *generare, gignĕre, parĕre.*

ingenious, *subtilis, sollers, callidus, artificiosus*; or render by phrase with *ingenium.*

ingeniously, *subtiliter, sollerter, callide, artificiose.*

ingenuity, *subtilitas, ars, sollertia, acies ingenii.*

ingenuous, *ingenuus, apertus, simplex, liber.*

ingenuously, *ingenue, aperte, simpliciter, libere.*

ingenuousness, *ingenuitas, libertas.*

ingle-nook, *focus.*

inglorious, *inglorius, inhonestus, turpis.*

ingloriously, *sine gloria, inhoneste, turpiter.*

ingot, *later.*

ingraft, *inserĕre.*

ingrained, *insitus, inveteratus.*

ingrate, subst. *homo ingratus.*

ingratiate, to — oneself = to commend oneself, *(hominis) favorem sibi conciliare, gratiam inire ab homine*; to — oneself with the people, *auram popularem captare, gratiam populi quaerĕre.*

ingratitude, *animus ingratus.*

ingredient, *pars, membrum*; or render by relative clause.

ingress, *ingressus (-ūs).*

ingulf; see ENGULF.

inhabit, *(locum) incolĕre* (usually of a community); *(in loco) habitare* (usually of an individual); *locum tenēre*: densely —ed, *frequens.*

inhabitable, *habitabilis.*

inhabitant, *incola, habitator; homo,* esp. in the plur. *homines*: —s of a town, *cives (-ium,* plur.), *municipes (-um,* plur.).

inhale, *spiritu (spirando) ducĕre, spiritu haurire.*

inharmonious, *discors, absonus, dissonus.*

inhere, *inesse, inhaerēre.*

inherent, *insitus, innatus, proprius.*

inherently, *natura, per se.*

inherit, = to be heir, *heredem esse (homini)*; transit.: to — a thing, *rem hereditate accipĕre*; to — everything, *heredem ex asse esse* (Quint.); see also HEIR.

inheritance, *hereditas* (= right of —, and the — itself).

inherited, *hereditarius, patrius, paternus.*

inhibit, *interdicĕre*; see also FORBID.

inhibition, *interdictum*; see also PROHIBITION.

inhospitable, *inhospitalis* (Hor.), *inhospitus* (poet.).

inhospitality, *inhospitalitas* (Cic.: rare).

inhuman, *inhumanus, immanis, crudelis.*

inhumanity, *inhumanitas, immanitas, crudelitas.*

inhumanly, *inhumane, crudeliter.*

inimical, *inimicus*; see also HOSTILE.

inimitable, *haud imitabilis, inimitabilis* (Quint.); or render by phrase, such as *quod nulla ars (or nemo) consequi potest imitando.*

iniquitous, *iniustus, iniquus, improbus.*

iniquitously, *iniuste, inique, improbe.*

iniquity, *iniustitia, iniquitas, improbitas*; see also WICKED.

initial, subst. *prima littera nominis.*

initial, adj. *primus.*

initiate. (1) to — a person: into a religion, etc., *initiare*; in gen., *imbuĕre, instituĕre.* **(2)** to — a thing = to begin, *coepisse, incipĕre*; see also BEGIN.

initiation, render by verb.

initiative: to take the —, *occupare, priorem* (or *primum*) *facĕre.*

inject, *infundĕre.*

injudicious, *inconsultus, inconsideratus, temerarius*; see also IMPRUDENT.

injudiciously, *inconsulte, inconsiderate, temere.*

injunction; see COMMAND.

injure, *(hominem) laedĕre, violare* (= to knock about); *(homini) nocēre, damnum inferre* or *adferre*: to — a cause, *obesse* (with dat.).

injurer, *qui iniuriam facit.*

injurious, *noxius, damnosus, gravis, malus, adversus, iniquus.*

injuriously, *male.*

injury. (1) = harm, *detrimentum, incommodum, damnum, malum, vulnus (-ĕris* = physical wound). **(2)** = wrong, *iniuria.*

injustice. (1) as a quality, *iniustitia.* **(2)** = an unjust act, *iniuria.*

ink, *atramentum.*

inkling, *odor*: I have an —, *subolet mihi* (Pl.).

inland, *mediterraneus.*

inlay, *inserĕre, variare, distinguĕre.*

inlet, of the sea, *aestuarium.*

inly, *penitus.*

inmate, = lodger, *deversor, inquilinus*; see also INHABITANT.

inmost, innermost, *intimus*: — heart, — being, *viscera (-um,* plur.), *intimum pectus* (Cat.), *medulla.*

inn, *deversorium, hospitium, caupona.*

innate, *innatus, insitus, ingeneratus, proprius, nativus.*

inner, *interior, intestinus* (opp. *externus,* foreign); *domesticus* (opp. *foris,* abroad, out of doors); sometimes = of the mind (rather than the body), *animi.*

innkeeper, *caupo.*

innocence, *innocentia*; = moral purity, *integritas*; = simplicity, *simplicitas*; = chastity, *castitas*: to prove one's —, *se purgare.*

innocent, *innocens, insons, culpā vacuus* or *carens, extra culpam*; = morally pure, in gen., *integer, sanctus*; = chaste, *castus.*

innocently. (1) = without guilt, *integre, caste.* (2) = without intention, *imprudens* (adj.).

innocuous, *innocuus.*

innocuously, *innocue* (Suet.), *sine fraude.*

innovate, *(res) novare, mutare.*

innovation, render by verb *novare* or *mutare*: political —s, *res novae* (plur.).

innovator, render by verb.

innumerable, *innumerabilis, innumerus* (poet.).

inobservant, *neglegens.*

inoculate. (1) in gardening, *inoculare* (Col.). (2) as medic. t. t. *variolas inserere* has been suggested.

inodorous, *sine odore, odore carens.*

inoffensive, adj. *innocens.*

inopportune, *inopportunus*; see also INCONVENIENT.

inordinate, *immoderatus, immodicus, nimius.*

inordinately, *praeter modum, immoderate, immodice, nimis, nimium.*

inorganic, render by phrase, referring to life *(vita)* or growth *(crescere).*

inquest, *quaestio*: to hold an —, *de morte (hominis) quaerere.*

inquire. (1) in gen. = to ask questions, *quaerere, exquirere, sciscitari, percontari, rogare, interrogare.* (2) systematically, esp. judicially, = to hold an inquiry, *(de re) quaerere, (in rem) inquirere, cognoscere, quaestionem habere.*

inquiry. (1) in gen. = the asking of questions, *percontatio, interrogatio*; or render by verb. (2) systematic, esp. a judicial —, *quaestio, inquisitio, cognitio*: to hold an —, see INQUIRE; to preside at an —, *quaestioni praeesse.*

inquisition; see INQUIRY.

inquisitive, *audiendi cupidus, curiosus.*

inquisitively, *curiose.*

inquisitiveness, *cupiditas* or *studium audiendi* or *cognoscendi, curiositas* (Cic. L.).

inquisitor, *quaesitor.*

inroad, *incursio, incursus (-ūs), inruptio*: to make an —, *incurrere, incursionem facere.*

insalubrious, *insalubris, gravis*; see also UNHEALTHY, UNWHOLESOME.

insane, *insanus* (lit. and fig.), *mente captus, amens* (= distracted), *demens* (= permanently deranged), *furiosus* (= raving), *vecors.* Most of these words are used of abstract things as well as of persons.

insanely, *insane, dementer, furiose.*

insanity, *insania, furor* (= raving madness), *amentia* (usually temporary), *dementia, vecordia.*

insatiable, *insatiabilis, inexplebilis, insaturabilis* (rare).

inscribe, *inscribere, ascribere, consignare.*

inscription, *inscriptio, index, titulus, epigramma (-ătis, n.), carmen* (in verse).

inscrutability, *obscuritas*, or render by adj.

inscrutable, *obscurus, occultus, tectus.*

insect, *insectum* (Plin.), *bestiola* (= a small animal).

insecure, *instabilis, incertus, lubricus*; or render by neg. with *tutus, munitus*, or *firmus*; = beset by enemies, *infestus.*

insecurely, render by neg. with *tuto* or *firme.*

insecurity, render by adj.

insensate; see INSANE, or INSENSIBLE.

insensibility. LIT., *torpor.* TRANSF., *animus durus, lentitudo.*

insensible. LIT., *sensūs expers*: to be —, *sensu*

carere. TRANSF., *durus, lentus*: to become —, *obdurescere.*

insensibly, *sensim, paulatim.*

inseparable, render by phrase, positive such as *perpetuo comitari*, or negative such as *seiungi non posse.*

insert, *inserere, includere, intericere, ponere* (esp. of periods of time, but also in speaking or writing), *addere, adscribere* (in writing), *infigere* (of physical objects = to fasten in).

insertion, *interpositio*; usually to be rendered by verb.

inside, subst. *pars interior.*

inside, adv. *intus*; with verbs of motion, *intro.*

inside, prep. *in* with abl., *intra* with acc.

insidious, *insidiosus, fallax, dolosus, fraudulentus.*

insidiously, *insidiose, per insidias, fallaciter, dolose, fraudulenter.*

insidiousness, *fallacia, dolus, fraus.*

insight, = knowledge, understanding of facts, *cognitio, intellegentia, perspicientia*; as a personal quality = intelligence, *iudicium, consilium, ingenium subtile* or *acutum.*

insignia, *fasces (-ium,* plur.), *insignia (-ium,* plur.).

insignificance, *exiguitas*; or render by adj.

insignificant, = small, *parvus, exiguus, minutus*; = unimportant, *lēvis, nullius momenti, nullus.*

insincere, *falsus, simulatus, fucosus, fucatus, fallax, dolosus.*

insincerely, *falso, fallaciter, simulate, dolose.*

insincerity, *fucus, fallacia, dolus, simulatio.*

insinuate. (1) to — oneself = to work oneself into favour, *se insinuare, adrepere, inrepere.* (2) = to suggest, hint, *significare*; see also HINT.

insinuating, *blandus.*

insinuation, *significatio.*

insipid. LIT., *elutus* (Hor.): to be —, *nil sapere* (Juv.). TRANSF., *insulsus, ineptus, frigidus.*

insipidity, render by adj.

insipidly, *insulse, inepte, frigide.*

insist, = to state positively, *confirmare, declarare, dictitare*; = to demand, *instare, (ef)flagitare, (ex)poscere.*

insnare; see ENSNARE.

insolence, *insolentia, contumacia, impudentia, adrogantia, superbia.*

insolent, *insolens, contumax, impudens, adrogans, superbus.*

insolently, *insolenter, contumaciter, audacter, impudenter, adroganter, superbe.*

insoluble. LIT., *quod liquefieri non potest.* TRANSF., *inexplicabilis*; or render by phrase.

insolvency; see INSOLVENT.

insolvent, to be, *non esse solvendo.*

insomuch, . . . that, *sic, ita*, or *adeo*, followed by *ut.*

inspect, *inspicere, introspicere, perspicere, intueri, contemplari*; see also EXAMINE.

inspection. (1) = the art of looking; render by verb. (2) = watch, guardianship, *cura, custodia, tutela.*

inspector, *custos, curator, praefectus.*

inspectorship, *cura, praefectura.*

inspiration. (1) = breathing in, *spiritus (-ūs).* (2) divine —, *divinus adflatus (-ūs), divino instinctu* (abl. sing. only); by divine —, *divinitus.* (3) = suggestion, in gen., *monitus (-ūs), consilium*; see also SUGGESTION.

inspire. (1) = to put feelings into the mind, in gen., (*homini virtutem*, etc.) *inicĕre, incutĕre*; (*hominem*) *excitare, incitare, incendĕre, inflammare.* (2) supernaturally; see INSPIRED.

inspired, *divino spiritu inflatus* or *tactus* or *instinctus* (Quint.); in a disparaging sense = frenzied, *fanaticus.*

inspirit, *animum* (*homini*) *addĕre*; see ENCOURAGE.

instability, *inconstantia*; or render by adj.

install, *inaugurare*; see also INAUGURATE.

instalment, *pensio, pars, portio.*

instance, subst. (1) = urgent request, *preces* (-*um*, plur.); often render by abl. absol., e.g.: at their —, *his petentibus,* or *his auctoribus.* (2) = example, *exemplum, specimen*: for —, *verbi causā* or *gratiā, ut, velut, vel.*

instance, v. *dicĕre, referre*; see also MENTION.

instant, subst. *punctum temporis, momentum temporis* or *horae*: at the very —, (*in*) *tempore ipso.*

instant, adj. (1) = urgent, *vehemens, intentus, acer, impensus.* (2) = imminent, immediate, *praesens.*

instantaneous, *subitus, praesens.*

instantaneously, *momento temporis, e vectigio*; see also INSTANTLY.

instantly, = immediately, *statim, confestim, protinus, extemplo, continuo, e vestigio*; = urgently, *intente, acriter, vehementer, impense.*

instead, adv. *potius, magis.*

instead of, prep. (1) with subst., *prō* with abl., (*in*) *loco* with genit., *in locum* with genit. (= to take the place), *vicem* with genit. (following its subst.). (2) with verbal subst. in -*ing* (e.g. — of fighting, he sleeps), *non . . . sed* (*non pugnat sed dormit*); or render with *posse* or *debēre* (*cum possit,* or *debeat, pugnare, dormit*); to heighten the contrast, *non modo non . . . sed etiam* (*non modo non pugnat, sed etiam dormit*); or *adeo non . . . ut,* or *tantum abest ut . . . ut.*

instep, *pes superior.*

instigate, *instigare, sollicitare, incitare, impellĕre, stimulare, suadēre.*

instigation, *stimulus*: at your —, *te auctore, impulsu tuo.*

instigator, *auctor, concitator, impulsor, suasor.*

instil. LIT., *instillare.* TRANSF., *instillare* (Hor.); see also INSPIRE.

instinct, subst. *natura*: — for = natural appetite for, *appetitus* (-*ūs*).

instinct, adj.: — with a thing, *re imbutus.*

instinctive, *naturalis*; or render by phrase.

instinctively, *naturā, naturā duce, naturaliter.*

institute, subst. and **institution.** (1) = foundation, act of instituting, *initium*; or render by verb, e.g.: after the —of the state, *post civitatem institutam,* or *civitate institutā.* (2) = custom, *institutum, lex, mos.* (3) = a corporation, *collegium, sodalitas.*

institute, v. *condĕre* (= to found, of cities, etc.), *instituĕre, constituĕre, statuĕre, conciliare* (of peace, harmony, etc.); sometimes simply *facĕre, efficĕre.*

instruct. (1) = to teach, *erudire* (*hominem in re*), *docēre* (*hominem rem*), *instituĕre* or *informare* (*hominem ad rem*). (2) = to order, (*homini*) *praescribĕre, mandare, praecipĕre*; see also ORDER.

instruction. (1) = the process of teaching,

institutio, eruditio, disciplina, doctrina. (2) = direction, *praeceptum, praescriptum, mandatum.*

instructive, render by *utilis.*

instructor, *magister, praeceptor.*

instrument. (1) = tool, *instrumentum, vas, machina* (= a contrivance): iron or steel —s, *ferramenta* (-*orum,* plur.); a stringed (musical) —, *fides* (-*ium,* plur.). (2) legal (= a deed) *instrumentum, tabula, litterae* (-*arum,* plur.).

instrumental. (1) = contributing to a purpose, *utilis, aptus*: I am — in preventing, *per me stat quominus,* with subj. (2) = relating to musical instruments: — music, *cantus nervorum et tibiarum*; — and vocal music, *vocum et fidium cantus* (-*ūs*).

instrumentality, *opera, ministerium,* or render by *per* with acc. or abl. absol. (e.g. *per te, te auctore*).

insubordinate, *seditiosus, turbulentus*; or render by neg. with *parēre* or *oboedire.*

insubordination, *immodestia* (Tac.), *seditio* (= mutiny).

insufferable, *intolerabilis, intolerandus.*

insufficiency, *inopia, imbecillitas* (= weakness); or render by phrase.

insufficient, *haud sufficiens, impar* (= unequal); or render by *parum* or *haud satis.*

insufficiently, *parum, haud satis.*

insular, render by *insula* (e.g.: through our — position, *eo ipso quod insulam incolimus*).

insult, subst. *contumelia, probrum.*

insult, v. (*homini*) *contumeliam imponĕre,* (*homini*) *insultare* (= to exult over).

insulting, *contumeliosus, probrosus, maledicus.*

insultingly, *contumeliose, maledice.*

insuperable, *in(ex)superabilis* (of mountains, etc.); of persons = invincible, *invictus*; otherwise render by phrase, such as *quod superari non potest.*

insupportable; see INTOLERABLE.

insurance, render by phrase, such as *fides de damno resarciendo interposita.*

insure, (*de damno,* etc.) *cavēre.*

insurgent, subst. and adj. *rebellis* (Verg., Tac.).

insurrection, *rebellio, seditio, motus* (-*ūs*), *tumultus* (-*ūs*).

insurrectionary, *seditiosus.*

insusceptible; see INSENSIBLE.

intact, *intactus, integer, salvus, incolumis* (= unharmed).

intangible, *intactilis* (Lucr.); or render by phrase with *tangĕre.*

integral, *necessarius.*

integrity, *integritas, probitas, innocentia, sanctitas.*

integument, *tegumentum*; see also COVER, COVERING.

intellect, *mens, ingenium, intellegentia*: acuteness of —, *ingenii acumen* or *acies, subtilitas, sagacitas.*

intellectual, render by genit. of *mens,* etc.

intelligence. (1) see INTELLECT. (2) = news, *nuntius.*

intelligencer, *nuntius.*

intelligent. (1) = having some understanding, *mente praeditus, mentis compos, intellegens.* (2) = having a good intelligence, *sapiens, prudens, ingenio acuto* (or *subtili*) *praeditus*: to be —, *sapĕre, intellegentiā valere.*

intelligently, *intellegenter, sapienter, prudenter, acute.*

intelligible, *quod facile intellegi potest, planus, perspicuus* (= clear).
intelligibly, *perspicue, plane.*
intemperance, *intemperantia, immoderatio, impotentia;* in drink, *ebrietas.*
intemperate, *intemperans, impotens, immodicus, immoderatus:* — in drink, *ebriosus.*
intemperately, *intemperanter, immodice, immoderate.*
intend. (1) with infin. as object: I — to do, *facĕre in animo habeo, mihi est in animo, certum mihi est, propositum mihi est, cogito, destino, intendo;* sometimes simply *facturus sum.* **(2)** with subst. or pronoun as object, *cogitare, intendĕre.*
intense. (1) of physical conditions, *magnus, acer, summus, nimius, impensus.* **(2)** of mental attitudes, *acer, intentus, ardens.*
intensely, *valde, magnopĕre, acriter, summe.*
intensify, *maiorem reddĕre, amplificare, augēre;* see also INCREASE.
intensity, *vis, gravitas.*
intensive, as grammat. t. t. *intentivus.*
intent, subst.; see INTENTION.
intent, *intentus, attentus, erectus:* to be — upon, *animum (in rem) intendĕre, (rei,* dat.) *incumbĕre* or *studĕre* or *operam dare.*
intention, *consilium, propositum, institutum:* my — is, *id sequor, ut;* with the — of, *eo consilio ut;* see also INTEND.
intentional, render by phrase.
intentionally, *consulto, de industria, dedita opera.*
inter, *sepelire, humare.*
intercalary, *intercalaris, intercalarius.*
intercalate, *intercalare.*
intercede, *(de)precari;* see also ENTREAT, BEG.
intercession, *deprecatio* (usually to avert some evil); often to be rendered by the verb *deprecari* or the subst. *deprecator* (=intercessor).
intercessor, *deprecator.*
intercept. (1) = to seize in transit. (e.g. a letter), *intercipĕre, excipĕre.* **(2)** in gen. = to cut off, *intercludĕre.*
interchange, subst. *permutatio, vicissitudo.*
interchange, v. *(com)mutare, permutare;* see also EXCHANGE.
interchangeable, *quae inter se (com)mutari possunt.*
interchangeably, *invicem.*
intercommunication, (of rooms, etc.) *commeatus (-ūs).*
intercourse. (1) in gen. = dealings, relations, *usus (-ūs), commercium* (esp. commercial), *consuetudo, convictus (-ūs* = social —, lit. living together), *congressus (-ūs).* **(2)** sexual, *concubitus (-ūs), consuetudo, coitus (-ūs:* Ov.).
interdict, subst. *interdictum.*
interdict, v. *interdicĕre.*
interest, subst. **(1)** = attention, *studium, exspectatio* (in relation to the future); see also INTERESTED. **(2)** = advantage, *bonum, utilitas, usus (-ūs), commoda (-orum,* plur.), *rationes (-um,* plur.), *causa:* in a person's —, *ex usu hominis;* in the public —, *e republicā;* against the public —, *contra rempublicam;* it is in my —, *e re mea est, interest mea, rēfert mea, expedit mihi;* your —s are affected, *tua res agitur* (Hor.); to consult a person's —s, *homini* (or *hominis rationibus) consulĕre;* to oppose a person's —s, *contra rem hominis venire.*

(3) = influence, *gratia.* **(4)** — on money, *faenus (-oris), usura* (often in plur.); compound —, *anatocismus;* simple —, *perpetuum faenus;* monthly —, *usura menstrua;* an exorbitant rate of —, *faenus iniquissimum;* — at 1% per month (= 12% per annum), *centesimae (-arum,* f. plur.); to lend out money on —, *faenerari, pecuniam dare faenore* or *faenori, ponĕre in faenore nummos* (Hor.); the act of lending money on —, *faeneratio;* in metaphor, to repay kindness with —, *beneficium cum usuris* (or *cumulate) reddĕre.*
interest, v. **(1)** = to excite interest, hold the attention, *tenēre;* sometimes *iucundum esse, delectare, placēre.* **(2)** to — a person in some other person or thing, *homini rem* (or *hominem) commendare;* reflex.: to — oneself in a person or thing, *studēre, operam dare* (with dat.).
interested. (1) = attentive, keen, *attentus, erectus:* — in, *rei* (genit.) *studiosus.* **(2)** = concerned, with something at stake, render by phrase; see INTEREST, subst. (2).
interesting, render by phrase, e.g.: an — book, *liber qui tenere legentem potest;* sometimes = pleasant, *iucundus;* see also INTEREST, v.
interfere, *intervenire, se interponĕre, se immiscēre, se offerre* (with dat. of person or thing); = to hinder, *(hominem) interpellare, prohibēre, impedire;* see also HINDER.
interference, *intercessio* (of the tribunes' veto); otherwise render by verb.
interim, *temporis intervallum:* in, or during, the —, *interim;* as adj. an — decree, *edictum ad tempus propositum.*
interior, subst. *pars interior.*
interior, adj. *interior, internus;* see also INNER, INTERNAL.
interjacent, *interiacens, interiectus.*
interject, *interponĕre, intericĕre.*
interjection, *interiectio* (Quint.).
interlace, *implicare;* see also ENTWINE.
interlard; see MIX.
interline, *interscribĕre* (Plin.).
interlocutor, render by verb; see CONVERSE, TALK.
interlude, *embolium.*
intermarriage, *connubium.*
intermarry, *inter se matrimonio coniungi.*
intermeddle, see INTERFERE.
intermediate, *medius.*
interment, *sepultura, humatio.*
interminable, *infinitus.*
interminably, *infinite, sine fine.*
intermingle, *(inter)miscēre;* see also MINGLE, MIX.
intermission, *intermissio;* or render by verb.
intermit, *intermittĕre;* see also CEASE, INTERRUPT.
intermittent, as medic. t. t. *febris intermittens* (Cels.).
intermittently, *aliquando, nonnumquam, interdum.*
internal; see INNER.
internally, *intus, penitus.*
international: — law, *ius (iuris,* n.) *gentium.*
internecine, *internecivus.*
internuncio, *internuntius.*
interpellation, *interpellatio.*
interpolate. (1) = to insert, *addĕre, inserĕre.* **(2)** = to falsify, *corrumpĕre, interpolare.*
interpolation, render by verb.

interpose. (1) = to place between, *interponĕre, intericĕre.* (2) = to intervene, *se interponĕre;* see also INTERFERE, INTERRUPT.

interposition. (1) = a placing between, *interiectus (-ūs), interventus (-ūs), interpositu* (abl. sing. only); or render by abl. absol. (e.g.: *mari interiecto* = by the — of the sea. (2) = mediation, intervention, *interventus (-ūs:* Plin. L.): by divine —, *divinitus;* see also INTERPOSE, INTERVENE.

interpret. (1) from one language into another, *interpretari;* see also TRANSLATE. (2) = to explain, or make out the meaning of, *interpretari, conicĕre, explanare:* to — favourably (unfavourably), *in bonam (malam) partem interpretari* or *accipĕre.*

interpretation, *interpretatio, explanatio, coniectio* (of dreams only), *enarratio* (Quint.): to put a good or bad — upon; see also INTERPRET (2).

interpreter, *interpres, coniector* (of dreams).

interregnum, *interregnum.*

interrex, *interrex.*

interrogate, *(inter)rogare, quaerĕre, exquirĕre;* see also ASK, INQUIRE.

interrogation, *percontatio, quaestio* (often under torture), *interrogatio* (Quint.).

interrogative, in gen., render by verb; as grammat. t. t., *interrogativus.*

interrogator, *qui interrogat.*

interrogatory, render by verb.

interrupt. (1) to — a speaker or speech, *(orationem) interrumpĕre, (hominem) interpellare, interfari, (homini) obloqui* (Pl.), *(homini) obstrepĕre* (= to shout down); = to break off a conversation, *sermonem dirimĕre* or *incidĕre.* (2) in gen. = to break into or break off any process, *(rem) interrumpĕre, interpellare, intermittĕre, (rei,* dat.) *intervenire.*

interruptedly, *interrupte.*

interruption. (1) in speaking, *interpellatio, interfatio.* (2) in gen. = pause, interval, *intermissio, intercapedo, intervallum.*

intersect, *secare, scindĕre.*

intersection, = the figure X, produced by two lines intersecting, *decussatio* (Vitr.), *decussis* (Vitr., Plin.); to form this figure, *decussare* (Cic.).

intersperse, *(im)miscĕre;* see also MIX.

interstice, *rima, foramen.*

intertwine; see ENTWINE.

interval, (in space or time) *intervallum, spatium (interiectum):* to leave an —, *spatium relinquĕre* or *intermittĕre;* in the —, *interim;* at —s, *aliquando, nonnumquam, interdum.*

intervene. (1) = to be between, *interiacĕre, intercedĕre.* (2) = to come between (lit. and fig.), *intercedĕre, intervenire, supervenire, se interponĕre* (all with dat.).

intervention, *interventus (-ūs).*

interview, subst. *congressio, congressus (-ūs), conloqium:* to ask for an —, *conloquium petĕre.*

interview, v. *congredi (cum homine).*

interweave, *intexĕre;* see also ENTWINE.

intestate, *intestatus;* also as adv., *intestato.*

intestine, adj. *intestinus;* see INTERNAL.

intestine(s), subst. *intestinum* (usually plur.), *ilia, viscera, exta* (all plur.).

intimacy, *familiaritas, familiaris* or *domesticus usus (-ūs), amicitia, consuetudo, necessitudo.*

intimate, adj. *familiaris, intimus, coniunctus:*

to have an — knowledge of a thing, *rem penitus perspectam cognitamque habēre;* an — friend, *familiaris, intimus;* to be on — terms with a person, *homine familiariter uti.*

intimate, v. *significare, indicare;* in a threatening manner, *denuntiare;* see also INFORM, SAY.

intimately, *familiariter, intime, coniuncte, penitus.*

intimation, *significatio, nuntius, denuntiatio.*

intimidate, *(de)terrēre;* or render by subst. = fear *(timorem, metum,* etc.), a verb such as *inicĕre* or *incutĕre,* and dat. of person. See also FRIGHTEN, TERRIFY.

intimidated, adj. *timefactus.*

intimidation, = threats, *minae (-arum,* plur.); or render by verb.

into, *in* with acc. in all senses.

intolerable, *intolerabilis, intolerandus:* almos —, *vix tolerabilis, vix ferendus;* — conduct, *intolerantia.*

intolerably, *intoleranter:* it is — cold, *intolerabile est frigus.*

intolerance, *superbia, adrogantia, acerbitas;* or render by phrase.

intolerant, = unable to bear, *intolerans;* = harsh, uncharitable, *immitis, difficilis, acerbus, inhumanus, superbus.*

intone, *voce praeire* (= to lead, to sound the first note): to — prayers, *preces canĕre.*

intoxicate, *ebrium reddĕre, inebriare* (Sen.).

intoxicated, *ebrius, temulentus.*

intoxicating, render by verb.

intoxication, *ebrietas.*

intractable, *indocilis, difficilis.*

intractability, render by adj.

intransitive, *intransitivus* (grammat. t. t.).

intrepid, *intrepidus, impavidus;* see also FEARLESS.

intrepidity, *animus intrepidus* or *impavidus; fortitudo;* see also COURAGE.

intricacy, *contortio.*

intricate, *contortus, implicatus, perplexus, tortuosus, impeditus.*

intrigue, subst. (1) = a plot, *dolus, fallacia, clandestinum consilium, artificia (-orum,* plur.). (2) = an amour, *adulterium.*

intrigue, v. (1) = to plot, *dolis, fallaciā,* etc., *contendĕre;* see also PLOT, CONSPIRE. (2) see INTEREST, FASCINATE.

intriguer, render by phrase with *dolus* or *fallacia.*

intrinsic, = real, *versus, in re ipsa positus.*

intrinsically, *per se, vere.*

introduce. (1) = to bring in: of persons, *introducĕre, inducĕre* (in speaking or writing); of things, including abstract things, *introducĕre, inducĕre, invehĕre:* to — many changes, *multa mutare* or *novare.* (2) of persons, to make one known to another, *introducĕre, commendare.*

introduction. (1) = a bringing in, *introductio, inductio, invectio.* (2) an — to a book, etc., *prooemium, exordium, praefatio;* to say by way of —, *praefari.* (3) an — of one person to another, render by verb; a letter of —, *litterae commendaticiae* (plur.).

introductory: to make — remarks, *praefari.*

introspection, *ipsum se inspicĕre.*

intrude, *se interponĕre* or *offerre (homini).*

intrusion, *importunitas;* see also INTRUDE, INTERFERE.

intrusive, *molestus, importunus.*

intrusively, *moleste.*

intrust; see ENTRUST.

intuition, *cognitio, perceptio, comprehensio;* as a quality = keen perception, *ingenii* or *mentis acumen* or *acies;* = preconception, *anticipatio.*

intuitive, intuitively, render by phrase contrasting natural perception with experience, e.g. *ingenii vi non usu cognoscere.*

inundation, *eluvio, diluvium* (Verg., Plin. L.)

inure, *adsuefacĕre;* see ACCUSTOM.

inurn, *in urnam condĕre.*

inutility, *inutilitas* (Lucr.).

invade, *invadĕre* (with *in* and acc. in Cic.), *bellum inferre* (with dat.), *incurrĕre, incursionem* or *inruptionem facĕre;* see also ATTACK, ASSAIL.

invader, *hostis.*

invalid, subst. *aeger, aegrotus, valetudinarius* (Sen.); of a soldier, *causarius.*

invalid, adj. *inritus, infirmus, nugatorius, vitiosus.*

invalidate, *inritum facĕre, tollĕre, infirmare, labefactare, rescindĕre;* see also ABROGATE, ABOLISH.

invasion, *incursio, inruptio.*

invective, *convicium, probrum, invectio* (rare); sometimes rendered by *verba* (*-orum,* plur.) with adj., e.g. *acerba, aculeata.*

inveigh against, *invehi* (with *in* and acc.), *insectari, incessĕre, increpare.*

inveigle; see MISLEAD, SEDUCE.

invent, *invenire, reperire, excogitare, comminisci.*

invention. (1) as an act or faculty, *inventio, excogitatio,* or render by verb (e.g. *hamis repertis,* by the — of hooks). (2) = a thing invented, *inventum* (esp. plur.), *reperta* (*-orum,* plur.: Lucr.). (3) = a falsehood, *commentum, fabula, mendacium.*

inventive, *habilis ad excogitandum:* the — faculty, *inventio, excogitatio.*

inventor, *inventor* (with f. *inventrix*), *repertor* (poet.), *auctor, architectus.*

inventory, *tabula, index* (Quint.).

inverse, *inversus, conversus.*

inversion, *conversio.*

invert, (*con*)*vertĕre, invertĕre:* to — the order of words, *ultima primis praeponĕre* (Hor.).

invest. (1) to — a person with an office, *magistratum homini dare, mandare, deferre.* (2) to — a person or thing with a quality, *rem homini* or *rei* (dat.), *addĕre, impertire; re* (*ex*)*ornare;* see also IMPART, GIVE. (3) to — money, (*in re*) *pecuniam conlocare, occupare, ponĕre* (Hor.). (4) = to besiege, *circumsedĕre, obsidĕre, vallo* or *fossā cingĕre* or *circumdare, obsidione claudĕre.*

investment, render by verb; see INVEST.

investigate, *exquirĕre, indagare,* (*per*)*scrutari, investigare;* by judicial process, *quaerĕre, cognoscĕre.*

investigation, *investigatio, indagatio, inquisitio* (all these three used with *veri* by Cic.): a judicial —, *quaestio, cognitio;* see also INQUIRY.

investigator, *investigator, indagator* (with f. *indagatrix*).

investiture; see INSTALLATION.

inveteracy, *inveteratio.*

inveterate, *inveteratus, penitus defixus* or *insitus:* to become —, *inveterascĕre.*

inveterately, *penitus.*

invidious, = causing ill-will, *invidiosus.*

invidiously, *invidiose.*

invidiousness, *invidia.*

invigorate, *corroborare,* (*con*)*firmare:* to — again, reinvigorate, *reficĕre.*

invigorating, *aptus ad corpus* (etc.) *reficiendum.*

invigoration, render by verb.

invincible, *invictus, in*(*ex*)*superabilis;* or render by phrase with *posse* and *vincĕre* or *superare.*

inviolability, *sanctitas;* or render by adj.

inviolable, *inviolabilis* (Verg., Tac.), *inviolatus* = sacred, holy, *sanctus, sacrosanctus.*

inviolably, *inviolate.*

inviolate, *integer; inviolatus, intactus;* see also INTACT, SAFE.

invisible, *caecus;* or render by phrase with *posse* and *cernĕre:* to be —, *sub oculos non cadĕre, non comparēre.*

invitation, *invitatio:* at your —, *invitatus* (or *vocatus*) *a te, invitatu tuo;* to accept an —, *promittĕre.*

invite. LIT., *invitare* (*hominem ad rem*), *vocare* (*hominem ad rem*): to — oneself to dinner with a person, *condicĕre homini ad cenam.* TRANSF., = to allure, *adlectare, invitare;* see also ALLURE.

inviting, *blandus, gratus, amoenus.*

invitingly, *blande, grate, amoene.*

invocation, of help, *imploratio;* of witnesses, *testatio.*

invoice, *libellus.*

invoke, *invocare, implorare:* to — as a witness, *testari, invocare testem.*

involuntarily, *non sponte* (*suā*); or render by adj. *invitus.*

involuntary, *invitus, coactus, non voluntarius.*

involution, *implicatio.*

involve. (1) = to wrap up, envelop, *involvĕre.* (2) = to implicate, associate a person in a thing, *hominem re implicare* or *adligare, ad rem admiscēre:* to be —d in a thing, *in re versari;* to be —d in debt, *aere alieno laborare.* (3) = to imply, comprise, *continēre, habēre:* to be —d, *inesse* (*in re* or *rei,* dat.).

invulnerable, *invulnerabilis* (Sen.): to be —, *vulnerari non posse.*

inward, *interior;* see also INNER.

inwardly, *introrsus* or *introrsum, intus, intrinsecus.*

inweave, *intexĕre.*

inwrought, *intextus.*

irascibility, *iracundia, cerebrum* (Hor.).

irascible, *iracundus, in iram praeceps, stomachosus, cerebrosus* (Hor.).

ire; see ANGER.

Ireland, *Hibernia.*

iris, the flower, *iris* (Plin.).

irk: it —s, *piget, taedet* (with acc. of person; he distasteful thing is rendered by an infin. or genit. of subst.); *molestum est* (with dat. o person).

irksome, *gravis, molestus, operosus, odiosus.*

irksomeness, *taedium, molestia.*

iron, subst. (1) the metal, *ferrum:* of —, made of —, *ferreus;* tipped with —, *ferratus;* —-mines, —-works, *ferrariae* (*-arum,* plur.). (2) plur., —s = fetters, *vincula, compedes:* in —s, *ferratus,* adj. (Pl.).

iron, adj. *ferreus* (lit. and fig.): — tools, *ferramenta* (*-orum,* plur.).

ironical, render by phrase, e.g. *verbum per*

ironiam dictum; in the description of persons, adapt the phrase of Cic., *in omni oratione simulatorem, quem εἴρωνα Graeci nominarunt, Socratem accepimus.*

ironically, *per ironiam.*

ironmongery, *ferramenta* (-orum, plur.).

irony, *ironia* (= the Greek εἰρωνεία: Cic.), *dissimulatio.*

irradiate, *inlustrare, conlustrare.*

irrational, *absurdus, rationis expers, brutus* (esp. of animals), *insanus* (= mad), *stultus* (= stupid), *caecus* (= blind).

irrationally, *absurde.*

irreclaimable, *quod emendari non potest.*

irreconcilable. (1) of persons, anger, etc., *implacabilis, inexorabilis.* (2) of propositions, (*res*) *inter se repugnantes, contrariae*; see also INCONSISTENT.

irrecoverable, adj. *inreparabilis* (Verg., Sen.).

irrefragable, *certus, firmus*; or render by phrase such as (*argumentum*) *quod refelli non potest.*

irrefutable; see IRREFRAGABLE.

irregular, *enormis* (= shapeless: Tac., Quint.); *incompositus* (= rough: Verg., Hor., Quint.); *inusitatus* (= unusual); *inaequabilis, inaequalis* (= not uniform); as grammat. t. t., *anomalus*; of procedure at elections, *vitiosus*; of troops, *tumultuarius.*

irregularity, *enormitas* (= shapelessness: Quint.); as grammat. t. t., *anomalia*; of conduct, *licentia*; at an election, *vitium.*

irregularly, *exormiter, incomposite, praeter morem*; at an election, *vitio.*

irrelevant, *alienus:* it is —, *nihil ad rem pertinet.*

irreligion, *impietas erga deos, deorum neglegentia.*

irreligious, *impius erga deos:* an — man, *contemptor religionis.*

irreligiously, *impie.*

irremediable; see INCURABLE.

irremovable, *immobilis, immutabilis.*

irreparable, *inreparabilis* (Verg., Sen.): an — loss, *damnum quod nullo modo resarciri potest.*

irreprehensible; see BLAMELESS.

irreproachable; see BLAMELESS.

irresistible, *invictus, in*(*ex*)*superabilis*; or render by phrase, e.g. *cui nullā vi resisti potest.*

irresistibly, *ita ut nullo modo resisti possit.*

irresolute, *dubius, incertus, varius, infirmus:* to be —, *dubitare, haesitare.*

irresolutely, *dubitanter*; or render by adj.

irresolution, *dubitatio, haesitantia, cunctatio*; or render by *animus* with adj.

irrespective of, *sine ullo discrimine*, with genit.

irresponsible, render by phrase with *rationem reddĕre* (= to give an account).

irretrievable; see IRRECOVERABLE.

irreverence, *impietas erga deos, nulla rerum divinarum reverentia.*

irreverent, *inverecundus, impius erga deos.*

irreverently, *impie.*

irrevocable, *inrevocabilis.*

irrigate, *inrigare.*

irrigation, *inrigatio, inductio aquarum.*

irritable, *inritabilis, stomachosus, iracundus.*

irritably, *stomachose.*

irritate. (1) physically, e.g.: to — a wound, *inflammare* (Plin.). (2) mentally, *inritare, iram* (*homini*) *movēre.*

irritation, = annoyance, *stomachus*; see also ANGER.

irruption, *inruptio, incursio.*

isinglass, *ichthyocolla* (Plin.).

island, *insula.*

islander, *insulanus, insulae incŏla.*

isle; see ISLAND.

islet, *parva insula.*

isolate, *secernĕre, seiungĕre, separare*; see also SEPARATE.

isolated, *remotus, solus.*

isolation, *solitudo.*

isosceles, *isosceles* (late Latin).

issue, subst. (1) = outcome, result, *exitus* (-ūs), *eventus* (-ūs): a happy —, *successus* (-ūs). (2) = subject, *res, causa*: the point at —, *res de quā agitur.* (3) = offspring, *liberi* (-orum, plur.), *progenies, stirps, proles* (poet.), *suboles* (poet.); male —, *stirps virilis*; to leave —, *stirpem relinquĕre.* (4), as medic. t. t. = discharge, *profluvium* (Lucr.), *fluxio* (Plin.).

issue, v. (1) transit. = to give out: **a,** of orders, etc., *edĕre, proponĕre, pronuntiare*: to — a decree, *edicĕre*: **b,** of stores, rations, etc., *dispensare, distribuĕre.* (2) intransit. = to come out: **a,** of physical movement: to — forth, *exire, egredi, evadĕre, erumpĕre*: **b** = to end up, turn out, *evadĕre, exire, evenire* (of things only).

isthmus, *isthmus* or *isthmos.*

it: often not expressed in Latin, esp. as the subject of a verb. Otherwise to be rendered by pronoun, e.g. *hic, haec, hoc,* or *is, ea, id,* or *ille, illa, illud.*

Italian, *Italicus, Italus.*

Italy, *Italia.*

itch, subst. (1) as a disease, *scabies* (Cels.). (2) as a sensation, *prurigo* (Mart.), *prurītus, -ūs* (Plin.).

itch, v. LIT., *prurire* (Juv.), *formicare* (Plin.). TRANSF., *prurire* (Pl., Mart.): to — to do a thing, *gestire facĕre.*

item, subst., in a list, *pars, res*; or render by *singula* (-orum, n. plur.), = the separate —s.

iterate, *iterare.*

itinerant, *circumforaneus.*

itinerary, *itineris descriptio.*

ivory, subst. *ebor.*

ivory, adj. *eburneus.*

ivy, *hedera* (poet.): — -mantled, *hederā obsitus.*

J

jabber, v. *blaterare, garrire, strepĕre, crepare.*

jabbering, subst. *clamor, strepitus* (-ūs).

jack, = a tool for various purposes, render by *machina* or *instrumentum:* a — of all trades, *qui se ad omnia aptum esse putat.*

jackanapes, *sannio.*

jackass, *asinus* (lit. and fig.).

jackdaw, *graculus* (Phaedr., Mart.).

jacket, *tunica.*

jade. (1) = a poor horse, *caballus.* (2) of a woman, *mulier importuna, puella proterva.*

jaded, *fatigatus,* (*de*)*fessus*; see also WEARY.

jagged, *serratus* (Plin. = with teeth like those of a saw): — rocks, *saxa aspera* or *praerupta.*

jail, *carcer*; see also GAOL, PRISON.

jailbird, *furcifer.*

jam, subst. *fructūs condīti* (plur.).
jam, v. *comprimĕre.*
jamb, *postis.*
James, *Iacobus* (late Latin).
janitor, *ianitor* (f. *ianitrix*: Pl.); *ostiarius* (Varro).
January, *Ianuarius* (*mensis*).
jar, subst. (1) = a vessel, *olla* (originally *aula*); *cadus* (esp. for wine: poet.); *dolium* (= cask); *seria* (large); *urceus* (Pl., Hor.); *urna* (esp. for the ashes of the dead); *amphora* (large, with two handles: Hor.). (2) on the —, of a door, *semiapertus.* (3) = quarrel, *rixa, iurgium.*
jar, v. = to be discordant, lit. or fig., *discrepare, dissonum* or *absonum* or *discordem esse.*
jargon, perhaps *sermo barbarus.*
jarring, = discordant, *dissonus, absonus, discors.*
jasper, subst. *iaspis* (Verg.).
jasper, adj. *iaspideus* (Plin.).
jaundice, n. *morbus regius* or *arquatus* (Cels.).
jaundiced. Lit., *arquatus* (Lucr.). Transf., *lividus, invidus.*
jaunt, n. *iter, excursio* (Plin.): to take a —, *excurrĕre* (Plin.).
javelin, *pilum, iaculum*: to come within — - range, *ad teli coniectum venire*; to throw a —, *iaculari.*
jaw, *mala, maxilla* (Cels.); in metaphor, the —s (of death, etc.), *fauces* (-*ium*, plur.).
jealous, *invidus, lividus*: to be — of a person, *homini aemulari* or *invidēre.*
jealousy, *invidia, aemulatio.*
jeer, jeering, subst. *cavillatio, ludibrium, inrisio.*
jeer, v. *cavillari*: to — at, *cavillari, inridēre, deridēre, in ludibrium vertĕre.*
jeering, render by verb, or by phrase such as *cum irrisione, per ludibrium.*
jejune, *ieiunus, aridus, exilis.*
jejunely, *ieiune.*
jejuneness, *ieiunitas, siccitas.*
jeopardize, *in periculum* or *discrimen vocare* or *adducĕre*; see also ENDANGER.
jeopardy; see DANGER.
jerk, subst. *motus* (-*ūs*) *subitus, impetus* (-*ūs*).
jerk, v. intransit. *salire.*
jerkin, *tunica.*
jerkiness, in style, *salebra.*
jerky, of style, *salebrosus* (Quint.).
Jerusalem, *Hierosolyma* (-*orum*, n. pl.).
jest, subst. *iocus, ridiculum*: in —, *ioco* (opp. *serio*), *per iocum.*
jest, v. *iocari, ioco uti, ioca agĕre, ioculari, cavillari.*
jester, *scurra.*
jet. (1) the mineral, *gagates* (Plin.): — -black, *niger* or *nigerrimus.* (2) a — of water, *aqua saliens* or *exsiliens.*
jetsam, *res naufragio eiectae* (plur.).
jetty, *moles.*
Jew, *Iudaeus.*
jewel, *gemma*; see also GEM.
jewelled, *gemmeus, gemmatus.*
jeweller, *qui gemmas vendit* or *sculpit.*
Jewish, *Iudaicus, Iudaeus* (Plin.).
jig; see DANCE.
jilt, *repudiare.*
jingle, *tinnire.*
jingling, subst. *tinnītus* (-*ūs*: Verg., Sen.).
job, = a piece of work, *opus* (-*ĕris*, n.): a put-up —, *fraus.*

jobber, = a stockjobber, *argentarius.*
jockey, *agaso* (= groom).
jockey, v. *circumvenire*; see also CHEAT.
jocose, jocular, *iocosus, iocularis, ridiculus, facetus.*
jocosely, *iocose, ioculariter* (Plin.), *per iocum, facete.*
jocoseness, jocularity, *iocus, facetiae* (-*arum*, plur.), *hilaritas.*
jog, subst. *impulsus* (-*ūs*); or render by verb.
jog, v. (1) transit. *fodicare* (lit. and fig.), *impellere.* (2) intransit.: to — on, — along, *lente progredi.*
John, *Ioannes* (late Latin).
join. v. (1) = to bring together, bring one to another, connect (lit. and fig.), (*con*)*iungĕre, conectĕre, copulare*: to — closely together, *conligare, conglutinare*; to — in a row, without a break, *continuare*; to — battle, *proelium* or *pugnam committĕre.* (2) physically = to be connected with, (*con*)*iungi, adiungi, conecti.* (3) of persons = to come up to, meet, (*homini*) *occurrĕre, supervenire.* (4) of persons: to — an association, (*cum homine*) *se coniungĕre,* or *societatem inire* or *coire.* (5) to — in, take part in, (*rei,* dat.) *interesse,* (*rei,* genit.) *participem esse.*
joiner, *faber.*
joint, subst. (1) in an animal or human body, *commissura, articulus, artūs* (-*uum,* plur.), *vertebra* (Sen.), *nodus.* (2) in a plant, *nodus, geniculum* (Plin.). (3) in a manufactured thing, *coagmentum, compages, compactura, iunctura* (Verg.).
joint, adj. *communis*; see also COMMON.
jointed, *geniculatus.*
joint-heir, *coheres.*
jointly, *coniuncte, coniunctim, una, communiter.*
joint-stock company, *societas.*
jointure, *annua* (-*orum,* plur.: Plin. L.).
joist, *tignum transversum* or *transversarium.*
joke; see JEST.
joker, *homo ridiculus.*
joking apart, *extra iocum, remoto ioco.*
jollity, *hilaritas, lascivia.*
jolly, *hilaris, lascivus* (poet.).
jolt, v. (1) to — a person or thing, *iactare, concutĕre, quassare.* (2) to — against, *offendĕre.*
jolting, subst. *iactatio, quassatio*; or render by verb.
jostle, *fodicare*; see also JOLT.
jot, subst.: not a —, *nihil, minime*; not to deviate a —, *non transversum unguem discedĕre*; not a — less, *ne pilo quidem minime*; not to care a — for, *non flocci facĕre.*
jot, v.: to — down, *adnotare* or *scribĕre.*
journal. (1) = diary, *ephemĕris.* (2) = newspaper, *acta diurna* (-*orum,* plur.).
journalist, render by phrase, such as *actorum diurnorum scriptor.*
journey, subst. *iter, cursus* (-*ūs*), *via*: a day's —, *iter unius diei*; to be on a —, *in itinere esse*; to undertake a —, *iter facĕre*; a — abroad, *peregrinatio*; a — by sea, *navigatio.*
journey, v. *iter facĕre*: to — abroad, *peregrinari*; see also TRAVEL, MARCH.
journeyman, *opifex.*
Jove, *Iuppiter*: by —! *mehercle!*
jovial, *hilaris, lascivus.*
joviality, *hilaritas, lascivia.*
jovially, *hilare, lascive.*

joy. (**1**) as a feeling, *gaudium, laetitia,* (esp. = exuberant —): to feel —, *gaudēre, laetari*; to jump for —, be beside oneself with —, *laetitiā* or *gaudio exsultare, efferri*; a transport of —, *effusa laetitia*; shouts of —, *clamores laetantium.* (**2**) in concrete sense, = a source of — (esp. in plur.), *gaudium, voluptas.*

joy, v. *gaudēre, laetari, exsultare.*

joyful, *laetus, hilaris, laetabilis, laetificus* (= making glad: Lucr.).

joyfully, *laete, libenter, hilare*; often to be rendered by adj. *laetus* or *libens.*

joyfulness; see JOY.

joyous; see JOYFUL.

jubilant, *laetitiā* or *gaudio exsultans* or *triumphans*; see also EXULT.

jubilee, *festi dies* (plur.).

judge, subst. (**1**) in court, *iudex* (general term, often applied to the jurors rather than the presiding judge): the presiding —, *quaesitor, praetor* (*urbanus,* for cases between Romans, *peregrinus,* between foreigners); a — deciding according to equity, *arbiter*; for special, e.g. very urgent, cases, *recuperator.* (**2**) in gen., *iudex, aestimator, existimator*; see also CRITIC.

judge, v. (**1**) in court, *iudicare, indicium exercēre, ius dicēre.* (**2**) in gen., *iudicare, existimare, censēre*: to — between, *diiudicare.*

judgment. (**1**) in court, *iudicium*: a — according to equity, decision of an arbitrator, *arbitrium*; to pronounce —, *ius dicĕre*; a — seat, *tribunal.* (**2**) in gen.: **a** = a considered opinion, *iudicium, sententia*: in my —, *meo iudicio, me iudice, quantum ego iudico, meā sententiā*: **b**, as a faculty = discernment, *iudicium, consilium.*

judicature, *iurisdictio.*

judicial, = concerned with courts of law, *iudicialis, forensis*: a — decree, *edictum*; a — injunction (pending trial), *interdictum*; a — investigation, *iudicium*; — organization, *ratio iudiciorum.*

judicially, *iure, lege*: to proceed —, *lege agĕre.*

judicious, *sagax, sapiens, prudens, subtilis.*

judiciously, *sagaciter, sapienter, prudenter, subtiliter.*

judiciousness, *sagacitas, prudentia, sapientia, consilium.*

jug, *urceus* (Pl., Hor.): a little —, *urceolus* (Juv.); see also JAR.

juggle, *praestigias agĕre.*

juggler, *praestigiator,* and f. *praestigiatrix* (Pl.).

juggling, subst. LIT., *praestigiae* (*-arum,* plur.). TRANSF., = trickery, *dolus, fraus, astutiae* (*-arum,* plur.).

juice, *sucus, melligo uvae.*

juicy, *suci plenus, sucosus* (Plin.).

jujube. (**1**) the tree, *zizyphus* (Col.). (**2**) the fruit, *zizyphum* (Pl'n.).

July, *Quinctilis* (*mensis*); after Julius Caesar, *Iulius* (*mensis*).

jumble, subst. *congeries* (Ov.), *turba*; of the contents of a book, *farrago* (Juv.), *sartago* (Pers.): a nasty —, — of filth, *conluvies, conluvio.*

jumble, v. (*per*)*miscēre.*

jump, subst. *saltus* (*-ūs*).

jump, v. *salire*: to — for joy, *exsultare gaudio*; to — in, *insilire*; to — over, *transilire*; to — out, or up, *exsilire.*

junction, (*con*)*iunctio.*

juncture, *tempus, tempestas.*

June, (*mensis*) *Iunius.*

jungle, render by phrase describing vegetation, e.g. *loca virgultis obsita* (plur.).

junior, *iunior,* (*natu*) *minor.*

juniper, *iuniperus* (Verg.).

juridical, *iuridicialis*; see also JUDICIAL.

jurisconsult, *iuris* or *iure peritus, iuris* or *iure consultus.*

jurisdiction, *iurisdictio.*

jurisprudence, *iuris prudentia.*

jurist; see JURISCONSULT.

juror, *iudex.*

jury, *iudices* (*-um,* plur.).

just, adj. *iustus, aequus* (= fair, impartial), *meritus* (= deserved).

just, adv. (**1**) of time, *commodum*: — now (= at this moment), *in praesentiā*; — lately, *modo, nuperrime, recens*; having — arrived, *recens*; — as, *cum maxime*; — before night, *sub noctem*; — thirty days, *triginta dies ipsi.* (**2**) in gen., of degree, quantity, etc. = exactly, *admodum*; often rendered by *ipse,* esp. with numerals (e.g.: = eleven legions, *ipsae undecim legiones*). In comparisons: — as, *ita* (or *sic*) *ut, tamquam, perinde ac*; — as great, *tantusdem*; — as much, *tantundem*; — as many, *todidem*; see also AS. In replies, — so, *ita, ita vero, admodum* (Pl., Ter.). (**3**) in gen. = only, *modo, solum, tantum.*

justice, as a quality or virtue, *iustitia*; = equity, impartiality, *aequitas*; = one's rights, just treatment, *ius* (*iuris,* n.): — requires that, etc., *aequum est* (with acc. and infin.); in —, *iure.*

justiciary; see JUDGE.

justifiable, *iustus, legitimus.*

justifiably, *recte, iure.*

justification, *purgatio, excusatio*; or render by verb.

justify, *purgare* (= to — completely); *excusare* (= to excuse, show reason for defects in a person or thing).

justly, *iustē, iurē, legitime, merito.*

jut: to — out, *exstare, eminēre, prominēre*; of geographical features, *excurrēre.*

juvenile, *puerilis, iuvenilis.*

juxtaposition, render by verb, such as *ponēre.*

K

kale, *crambe.*

keel, *carina.*

keen. (**1**) physically (e.g. of winter, or a cutting edge), *acer.* (**2**) of feeling = poignant, *acerbus, acer.* (**3**) of perception = acute, penetrating, *acutus, subtilis, perspicax, sagax.* (**4**) = zealous, enthusiastic, *acer, studiosus, alacer.*

keenly. (**1**) = poignantly, bitterly, *acerbe, acriter.* (**2**) = with penetration, *acute, acriter, subtiliter, sagaciter.* (**3**) = enthusiastically, *studiose, summo studio.*

keenness. (**1**) = poignancy, *acerbitas.* (**2**) = penetration, acute perception, *subtilitas, sagacitas, perspicacitas*; of vision or looks, *acies.* (**3**) = enthusiasm, *studium, alacritas.*

keep, subst. *arx.*

keep, v. (1) transit. LIT., *(con)servare, adservare, custodire, tenēre, continēre, habēre*: to — to oneself, *sibi habēre*; of goods = to store up, *condĕre*; of animals = to support, maintain, *alĕre*; to — in, *includĕre, continēre*; to — apart, *distinēre*; to — back, *retinēre, cohibēre* (= to restrain); to — off, *arcēre, defendĕre, propulsare.* TRANSF., **a,** of abstract things = to observe, maintain, *(ob)servare, retinēre*: to — faith, *fidem servare* or *praestare*; to — watch, *custodias agĕre*; to — a secret, *rem celare* or *reticēre* or *occultam tenēre*: **b,** to — accounts, *tabulas conficĕre*: **c,** to — one's bed, *iacēre, cubare*: **d,** to — a person in a certain state, *habēre* (with adverbial phrase or participle). (2) intransit.: **a** = to remain (in a place or condition), *(re)manēre*: to — silent, *tacēre, reticēre*: **b** = not to get spoilt, *durare* or render by negative phrase: **c,** to — on doing a thing, *pergĕre* (with infin.), *perseverare.*

keeper, *custos, curator.*

keeping, subst. *custodia, tutela*: to be in —, *convenire, congruĕre*; see also AGREE.

keepsake, *donum.*

keg, *dolium*; see also CASK, JAR.

ken, *conspectus (-ūs).*

kennel. (1) for dogs, *stabulum canis* or *canum.* (2) = gutter, drain, *cloaca.*

Kent, *Cantium.*

kerb, *crepido.*

kerchief, *sudarium*; see also HANDKERCHIEF.

kernel. LIT., of fruits, *nucleus* (Plin.). TRANSF., = best or most essential part of anything, *medulla, flos, robur.*

kettle, *cortina* (Pl., Cato), *lebes* (Verg., Ov.), *a(h)enum* (Verg., Ov.).

kettle-drum, *tympanum.*

key. LIT., *clavis.* TRANSF., the (military) — to a position, *ianua, claustra (-orum,* plur.).

kick, subst. *calcitratus (-ūs*: Plin.), *pedis* or *calcis ictus (-ūs)*: take a —, *accipe calcem* (Juv.).

kick, v. *calcitrare* (Plin.), *calces remittĕre, (rem* or *hominem) calce petĕre*: to — back, *recalcitrare* (Hor.); prov.: to — against the pricks, *advorsum stimulum calcare* (Ter.).

kid, *haedus, haedulus* (Juv.).

kidnap; see STEAL.

kidney, *renes (renum,* plur.).

kidney-bean, *phaselus* (Verg.).

kill, *interficĕre* (general term); *caedĕre* (= to — by beating, stabbing, etc.); *occīdĕre* (= to cut down, esp. in battle); *conficĕre* (= despatch, make an end of); *necare* (= to put to a violent death); *enecare* (stronger than *necare*: Pl.); *interimĕre, e medio tollĕre* (= do away with, remove from the scene); *trucidare* (= to butcher, massacre); *iugulare* (= to cut the throat of); *obtruncare* (= to cut down, esp. in battle); *percutĕre* (esp. of an executioner); *leto dare* (= to put to death, an archaic phrase: Verg., Juv.): to — oneself, *mortem sibi consciscĕre, manūs sibi adferre, se interimĕre*; to — time, *horas fallĕre* (poet.); to — the fatted calf, *saginam caedĕre* (Pl.).

kiln, *fornax.*

kin; see KINDRED.

kind, subst. *genus (-ĕris,* n.); *modus* (esp. in genit., e.g. *eiusdem modi*): of such a —, *talis*; in logic, *species, forma*; by —s, according to its —, *generatim*; a — of (to qualify metaphors, etc.), render by *quasi* or by

quidam agreeing with subst.; every — of, *omnis* or plur. *omnes.*

kind, adj. *benignus, beneficus* (in action), *benevolus* (in disposition), *facilis, humanus*; = friendly, *amicus, comis*; = indulgent, *indulgens*; = gentle, mild, *clemens*; of gods = favourably disposed, *propitius*: you are too —, *benigne, recte*; a — action, *beneficium, officium.*

kindle, v. (1) transit. LIT., *accendĕre, incendĕre, inflammare*: to — from below, *succendĕre, ignem subdĕre* (with dat.). TRANSF., of passions, etc., *accendĕre, incendĕre, inflammare, conflare, excitare, incitare.* (2) intransit. *(ex)ardescĕre.*

kindly, adj.; see KIND, adj.

kindly, adv. *benigne, comiter, clementer, indulgenter, amice, humane.*

kindness. (1) as a quality, *bonitas, benignitas, benevolentia, comitas, humanitas, clementia, indulgentia.* (2) = an act of —, *beneficium, officium*; see also FAVOUR.

kindred, subst. (1) abstr., *consanguinitas, cognatio, necessitudo.* (2) = relatives, *consanguinei, cognati, necessarii (-orum,* plur.); see also RELATIVES.

king, *rex*: a petty —, *regulus*; to be —, *regem esse, regnum obtinēre, regnare*; to make oneself —, *regnum occupare*; as happy as a —, render by *rex* (= a specially fortunate person: Pl., Hor.).

kingcraft, *ars regendi.*

kingdom, *regnum.*

kingfisher, n. *(h)alcedo* (Pl.), *(h)alcyon* (Verg.).

kingly, *regius, regalis.*

kingship, *regia potestas, regnum.*

kinsman; see RELATIVE.

kiss, subst. *osculum, suavium, basium* (Cat., Juv.).

kiss, v. *osculari, suaviari, basiare* (Cat., Mart.): — Attica for me, *Atticae meae meis verbis suavium des* (Cic. L.).

kissing, subst. *osculatio, basiatio* (Cat.).

kitchen, *culina.*

kitchen-garden, *hortus olitorius* (Leg.).

kitten, render by *catulus* (= the young of any animal) with a reference to *feles* (= cat).

knapsack, *mantica, sarcina.*

knave, *homo nequam* or *sceleratus*; more colloquially, *scelestus* (Pl., Ter.), *furcifer* (Pl.), *veterator.*

knavery, *nequitia, malitia, fraus, dolus.*

knavish, *nequam, malitiosus, fraudulentus.*

knavishly, *malitiose, fraudulenter.*

knead, *depsĕre* (Cato), *subigĕre.*

knee, *genu.*

knee-deep, *genus tenus, genibus tenus.*

knee-pan, *patella* (Cels.).

kneel, *genibus niti*: to — down, *genu terram tangĕre.*

knife, *culter*: a small —, *cultellus* (Hor.).

knight, *eques.*

knighthood, *ordo equester* (= the whole order); *dignitas equestrius, locus equester* (= the rank).

knightly, *equester*; = worthy of a knight, *equite dignus.*

knit, *acubus texĕre*: to — the brow, *frontem contrahĕre* or *adducĕre.*

knob, n. *bulla* (of a door, etc.); *nodus* (in plants: Verg.).

knobbed, knobbly, *nodosus* (Ov.).

knock, v. *pulsare:* to — against, *offendĕre* (e.g. *pedem in saxum*); to — at a door, *fores* or *ostium pulsare·* to — down, *sternĕre*; to — out (teeth, etc.), *elidĕre*; to — up = to arouse, *suscitare*; = to tire, *conficere, (de)fatigare*; —ed up = tired, exhausted, *(de)fessus.*

knocking, subst. *pulsatio.*

knock-kneed, *varus* (Hor.).

knot, subst. LIT., in anything flexible, also in wood, *nodus.* TRANSF., (I) = a tie, *nodus, vinculum.* (2) = a group of people, *circulus.*

knot, v. *nodare* (Verg., Ov.), *nectĕre*; see also TIE.

knotty, LIT., *nodosus.* TRANSF., *difficilis, spinosus*: a — point, *nodus.*

know. (I) to — facts, *scire, cognitum* or *compertum habēre*; to — for certain, *certo* or *certe scire*; to — very well, *probe scire, non ignorare, non esse ignarum* or *nescium*; to — how to, *scire,* with infin.; to get to —, *(cog)noscĕre*; let me —, *certiorem me fac*; as far as I —, *quantum scio, quod sciam*; not to —, *nescire, ignorare*; I don't — what to say, *non* (or *nihil*) *habeo quod dicam.* (2) = to be acquainted with, *novisse* (perf. of *noscĕre*): not to —, *ignorare.* (3) to — again = to recognize, *agnoscĕre, cognoscĕre, noscitare.*

knowing, adj. (I) = conscious, aware, *sciens, prudens.* (2) = clever, *callidus, versutus, astutus.*

knowingly, *consulto, de industriā*; often rendered as adj. by *sciens* or *prudens.*

knowledge, subjectively, as the state of knowing, *scientia, notitia, cognitio, prudentia*; objectively, as something imparted and acquired, *doctrina, disciplina*: to bring a thing to a person's —, *hominem de re docēre* or *certiorem facĕre*; to have no — of, *ignorare*; without the — of a person, *clam homine, imprudente homine.*

known, *notus*: to make —, *declarare.*

knuckle, subst. *articulus (digiti).*

knuckle, v. *obtemperare, se summittĕre* (with dat.).

L

label, *scheda (scida)* = a strip of papyrus bark, leaf of paper; *tessera* = a square piece of stone or wood; *pittacium* (Petr.).

laborious, *laboriosus, operosus*: to be —, *magni laboris esse.*

laboriously, *laboriose, operose.*

labour, subst.: in gen., *labor, opus (-eris,* n.*), opera, occupatio, moles* (poet., but also in Liv. and Tac.): learned —s, *studia*; — by night, *lucubratio*; to lose one's —, *operam (et oleum) perdĕre*; in childbirth, *partus (-ūs), nisus* or *nixus (-us:* Verg., Ov.); to be in —, *parturire.*

labour, v. (I) = to work, toil, exert oneself, *laborare, opus facĕre, niti, contendĕre*: to — at, over, on a thing, *rem* or *in re elaborare, rei* (dat.) *operam dare, in rem incumbĕre.* (2) = to be distressed, *laborare* (with abl.). (3) to — under a delusion, *decipi, falli.* (4) to — in childbirth, *parturire.*

laboured, *adfectatus* (Quint), *nimis exquisitus.*

labourer, *operarius, opera.*

labyrinth, *labyrinthus.*

labyrinthine, *labyrinthēus* (Cat.); fig., of

difficulties etc., *perplexus, impeditus, inextricabilis* (Verg.).

lace, subst.: render by phrase, such as *texta (-orum,* plur.*) reticulata*: a shoe- —, *li(n)gula* (= shoe-latchet: Juv.).

lacerate, *lacerare, laniare.*

laceration, *laceratio, laniatus (-ūs).*

lachrymose, *lacrimabundus, lacrimosus* (poet.).

lack, subst. *inopia, penuria, egestas.*

lack, v. *(re) carēre, (rĕ* or *rei,* genit.) *egēre* or *indigēre.*

lackey, *pedisequus.*

lack-lustre, adj. *decolor.*

laconic. LIT., = Spartan, *Laconicus.* TRANSF., = brief, concise, *brevis, adstrictus.*

laconically, *breviter, adstricte.*

lad, *puer.*

ladder, *scalae (-arum,* plur.*)*: a rung of a —, *scalarum gradus (-ūs).*

lade, = to load, *onerare.* ·

laden, *onustus, oneratus, gravis*: — with debt, *aere alieno obrutus.*

lading, subst. *onus (-ēris,* n.*).*

ladle, subst. *trulla, cyathus* (for wine: Pl., Hor.), *cocleare* (Mart.).

ladle, v. *haurire.*

lady, in gen., *femina, mulier*: a married —, or — of quality, *matrona*; the — of the house, mistress, *domina, hera, materfamilias.*

lady-like, *liberalis, honestus, quod matronā dignum est.*

ladyship, *domina.*

lady's-maid, *famula, ornatrix* (Ov.).

lag, *cessare, morari, cunctari.*

laggard, *cessator, cunctator*; or render by adj. *ignavus.*

lagoon, *lacus (-ūs), lacuna* (Lucr.).

laic, lay, adj. *laicus* (eccl.).

lair, *latibulum, cubile.*

laird, *dominus, possessor.*

lamb, *agnus* and f. *agna*: of a —, *agninus*; as meat, *(caro) agnina* (Pl., Hor.).

lambent, render by verb *lambēre.*

lambkin, *agnellus* (Pl.).

lame, adj. *claudus*; in gen. = feeble, *debilis*: to be —, *claudum esse, claudicare* (also used metaphorically); a — excuse, *excusatio vana.*

lame, v. *claudum reddĕre.*

lameness, *claudicatio.*

lament, lamentation, *lamentum* (usually in plur.), *lamentatio* (= the act of lamenting), *comploratio, ploratus (-ūs), fletus (-ūs* = weeping*); querimonia, querela* (= complaint).

lament, v. *lamentari, deflēre, (de)plorare, complorare.*

lamentable, = to be lamented, or lamenting, *lamentabilis, flebilis, miserandus, miserabilis.*

lamentably, *miserandum in modum, miserabiliter, flebiliter.*

lamented, of dead persons in gen., *flebilis* (poet.); of dead and deified Roman emperors, use *divus.*

lamp, *lucerna, lychnus.*

lamp-black, *fuligo.*

lampoon, subst., use adj. *famosus,* with subst. *carmen* (Hor.) or *libellus* (Suet.).

lamp-stand, *lychnuchus.*

lance, subst. *lancea, hasta, sarisa*; fig.: to break a — with a person, *cum homine certare, contendĕre.*

lance, v. *incidĕre.*

lancet, *scalpellum.*

land, subst. (1) opp. to sea, *terra*, *tellūs* (*-ūris*, f.: poet.); by — and sea, *terrā marique*. (2) — as possessed, cultivated, etc., *ager*, *solum*, *terra*. (3) = a particular country or region, *terra*, *regio*, *ager*, *fines* (*-ium*, plur.): one's native —, *patria*; of what —? *cuias?* of our —, *nostras*.

land, adj. *terrestris*, *terrenus*: a — battle, *pugna pedestris*.

land, v. (1) transit. (*in terram*) *exponĕre*. (2) intransit. (*ex nave*) *egredi*.

landed, adj.: — property, *agrum*, *possessio* (usually in plur.); a — proprietor, *agrorum possessor*.

landing, subst. *egressus* (*-ūs*), *litoris appulsus* (*-ūs*): to make a —, *navi exire*; a hostile —, prelude to raid or invasion, *escensio*.

landlord, *agrorum possessor* (= proprietor), *caupo* (= innkeeper).

landmark, *lapis*, *terminus*.

landscape. (1) = actual country, *regio*, *terra*. (2) in painting, use phrase such as *regio in tabulā picta*.

landslide, *terrae lapsus* (*-ūs*).

lane, = narrow street, *angiportum* or *angiportus* (*-ūs*); a country —, *semita*.

language. (1) in gen. = speech, *oratio*. (2) the — of a people, tongue, *lingua*, *sermo*. (3) = diction, style, manner of speaking, *oratio*, *sermo*, *dictio*: the — of common everyday life, *sermo cotidianus*. (4) = things said, *verba* or *dicta* (*-orum*, plur.).

languid, *languidus*, *languens*, *remissus*, *lassus*: to be —, *languēre*.

languidly, *languide*.

languish, *languēre*, *languescĕre*, *tabescĕre*; to — in prison, *in carcere vitam miserrimam trahĕre*; to — in slavery, *servitute premi*.

languor, *languor*.

lank, lanky, *prolixus*; see also TALL, LONG, LEAN.

lantern, *lanterna*.

lap, subst. (1) a person's —, *gremium* (= bosom), *sinus* (*-ūs* = a fold of the gown). (2) on a racecourse, *spatium*.

lap, v. LIT. = to lick, lick up, *lambĕre*, *ligur(r)ire*, *lingĕre*. TRANSF., of water = to touch, wash, *lambĕre* (Hor.).

lap-dog, *catellus*.

lapidary, *scalptor* (Plin.).

lappet, *lacinia*.

lapse, subst. (1) = an error, backsliding, *lapsus* (*-ūs*), *error*, *peccatum*. (2) of time = flight, expiry, *fuga* (Hor.): after the — of a year, *interiecto anno*.

lapse, v. (1) = to go wrong, *errare*, *peccare*. (2) of property, *reverti*.

larboard, adj. *laevus*; see also LEFT.

larceny, *furtum*; to commit —, *furtum facĕre*.

lard, *adeps*, *lar(i)dum*.

larder, *cella penaria*, *carnarium* (for meat: Pl.).

large, *magnus*, *grandis*, *amplus*.

large-hearted, in gen. *magnanimus*; esp. = generous, kind, *largus*, *liberalis*, *benignus*, *benevolus*.

largely, = to a great extent, *magnam partem*, *magna ex parte*.

largeness, *magnitudo*, *amplitudo*; — of mind, *magnanimitas*.

largess, *largitio*, *congiarium*.

lark, *alauda* (Plin.).

larynx, *guttur*.

lascivious, *impurus*, *impudicus*, *libidinosus*, *lascivus* (rather = playful).

lasciviously, *impudice*.

lasciviousness, *impudicitia*, *libido*.

lash, subst. (1) = a whip, *flagrum*, *flagellum*, *lorum* (usually in plur.), *flagellum*, *scutica* (Hor., Ov.). (2) = a blow (lit. and fig.), *verber*.

lash, v. (1) = to whip, *flagellare*, *verberare*. (2) = to tie, bind, (*ad*)*nectĕre*, (*ad*)*ligare*.

lashing, subst. *verberatio*.

lassitude, *lassitudo*, *languor*.

last, subst.: a shoemaker's —, *forma*; prov.: let the cobbler stick to his —, *ne sutor supra crepidam* (Plin.).

last, adj. (1) = final, — in a series, *ultimus*, *extremus*, *postremus*, *novissimus*: to breathe one's —, *animam efflare*. (2) = most recent, *proximus*; in the — twenty years, *his viginti annis*; at —, *tandem*, *postremum*; see also LASTLY.

last, v. *durare*, (*per*)*manēre*.

lasting, *stabilis*, *diutinus*, *diuturnus*, *perennis*, *mansurus* (poet.).

lastly, *postremo*, *ad postremum*, *ad extremum*, *denique*, *novissime* (Quint.).

latch, *pessulus* (= bolt).

latchet, *corrigia*.

late, adj. (1) = coming —, *serus*. (2) = recent, *recens*; —r, *recentior*, *inferior*. (3) the — = the dead, *demortuus*; of an emperor, *divus*.

late, adv. = too —, *sero*: far too —, *admodum sero*; rather —, *serius*; two days too —, *biduo serius*; too — for, *serius* (*quam*); prov.: better — than never, *potius sero quam numquam*; — at night, *multa nocte*.

lately, of late, *nuper*, *recens*, *modo*.

lateness, render by adj.

latent, render by participle meaning 'hidden', e.g. *occultus*, *abditus*, *absconditus*.

lateral, render by phrase *a latere*.

lath, render by *asser* (= pole, post).

lathe, *tornus* (Verg., Plin.): to work at the —, *tornare*.

lather, *spuma*.

Latin, adj. *Latinus*: the — tongue, *lingua Latina*, *sermo Latinus*; to translate into —, *Latine reddĕre*; to know —, *Latine scire*; to speak (in) —, *Latine loqui*.

latinity, *latinitas*.

latitude, = freedom, *libertas*, *licentia* (esp. in speech); see also FREEDOM, FREELY.

latter, *posterior*: the former . . . the —, *hic . . . ille* (sometimes in reverse order).

lattice, *cancelli* (*-orum*, plur.).

laud, subst. *laus*.

laud, v. *laudare*, *extollĕre*; see also PRAISE.

laudable, *laudabilis*, *laudatus*, *laude dignus*.

laudably, *laudabiliter*.

laudatory, *honorificus*.

laugh, laughing, laughter, *risus* (*-ūs*), *cachinnus* (= a loud laugh), *cachinnatio* (= loud laughter): to be a — stock, *ludibrio* or *inrisui esse*, to raise a —, *risum movēre*; to try to raise a —, *risum captare*.

laugh, v. (1) intransit. *ridēre*, *risum edĕre* or *tollĕre*: to — loudly, *cachinnare*. (2) to — at, transit. (*dē*)*ridēre*, *inridēre*.

laughable, *ridiculus*.

laughter; see LAUGH.

launch, v. (1) to — a ship, *deducĕre*. (2) = to hurl, *immittĕre*, (*con*)*torquēre*. (3) intransit., to — out. LIT., *in aequor efferri.* TRANSF., = to enter upon a subject, esp. by way of digression, *exspatiari* (Quint.).

laundress, render by *vestiplica* (= a clothes-folder: Pl.).

laurel. LIT., *laurus* (*-i* and *-ūs*), *laurea*; adj., of —, *laureus*: decked with —, *laureatus.* TRANSF., *laurus, laurea*; see also GLORY.

laurelled, *laureatus.*

lava, render by phrase, such as *massa ardens, saxa liquefacta* (*-orum*, plur.).

lave, *lavare*; see also WASH.

laver, *aqualis* (Pl.), *labrum.*

lavish, adj. *prodigus, profusus, in largitione effusus*: a — giver, *largitor.*

lavish, v. *profundĕre, effundĕre, largiri.*

lavishly, *large, prodige, effuse.*

lavishness, *effusio, largitas, munificentia*; see also LIBERALITY.

law, *lex* (= statute —), *ius* (more general), *fas* (= divine —); sometimes *norma* or *regula* (= rule, standard): to carry a —, *legem perferre*; to be bound by a —, *lege teneri*; the spirit of a —, *legis voluntas* or *sententia*; to go to — with a person, *lege agere cum homine.*

law-breaker, *legis violator.*

lawful, *legitimus*: it is —, *licet.*

lawfully, *legitime, lege, per leges, salvis legibus.*

lawgiver; see LEGISLATOR.

lawless, *audax, effrenatus.*

lawlessly, *effrenate, licenter, contra legem.*

lawlessness, *(effrenata) licentia.*

lawn. (1) = fine linen, *sindon* (Mart.). (2) of grass, *pratum, pratulum* or *herba* (= grass).

lawsuit, *lis, controversia.*

lawyer, *iurisconsultus, iurisperitus* (both are also found as pairs of words, or with *iure* instead of *iuris*).

lax, *(dis)solutus, remissus, laxus, neglegens.*

laxity, laxness, *neglegentia*; or render by phrase.

laxly, *(dis)solute, remisse, laxe, neglegenter.*

lay, subst.; see SONG.

lay, v. (1) = to place, *ponĕre, (con)locare*: to — foundations, *fundamenta iacĕre.* (2) with abstract object: to — an ambush, *insidiari, insidias conlocare* or *facĕre*; to — siege, *obsidĕre.* (3) to — eggs, *(ova) parĕre.*
    With adv., prep., etc.: to — aside, *(de)ponĕre*; to — before, *proponĕre*; to — down an office, *magistratu se abdicare*; to — down arms, *ab armis discedĕre*; — down a proposition, *confirmare, statuĕre*, see also STATE; to — out money, see SPEND; to — up, *condĕre, reponĕre*, see also STORE; to — upon, *imponĕre*; to — hands upon a person, *manūs - homini inferre*; to — waste, *vastare.*

layer. (1) in building, etc., *corium* (Cato), *tabulatum* (Verg.). (2) of a plant, *propago.*

lazar, n.; see LEPER.

lazily, *pigre, ignave, segniter.*

laziness, *ignavia, segnitia, segnities, pigritia.*

lazy, *piger, ignavus, segnis, iners.*

lead, subst. *plumbum*; of —, adj. *plumbeus.*

lead, subst. = leadership; q.v.

lead, v. (1) = to conduct, *ducĕre*: to — out, *educĕre*; to — past, *traducĕre*; to — back, *reducĕre.* (2) to — the way = go first, *(homini) praeire.* (3) = to command (an army), *ducĕre (exercitum), praeesse (exercitui).* (4) = to induce, *adducĕre (hominem) per-*

suadēre (homini). (5) = to pass, spend, *agĕre.* (6) of roads: to — in · a certain direction (without object), *ferre, ducĕre* (Verg.).

leaden, *plumbeus.*

leader, *dux, ductor, auctōr, princeps.*

leadership, *ductus* (*-ūs*): under my —, *me duce.*

leading, *princeps, primarius, summus*; see also CHIEF.

leaf. (1) of a tree, *folium, frons.* (2) of a book, *scheda* (or *scida*), *pagina, charta.* (3) of metal, etc., *bractea, lamina.*

leafless, *foliis carens* or *nudatus.*

leafy, *frondosus, frondeus, frondifer* (all poet.).

league, subst. *foedus* (*-eris*, n. = treaty), *pactum* (= agreement), *societas* (= alliance or union).

league, v. *foedus inire (cum homine).*

leak. subst. *rima*: to spring a —, *rimam agĕre.*

leak, v.: to — away, *perfluĕre.*

leaky, *rimosus* (Verg.), *rimarum plenus.*

lean, adj. *macer, exilis*; *strigosus* (of horses, etc.); see also THIN.

lean, v. LIT., *(se) inclinare*: to — upon, *(rē) (in)niti.* TRANSF., see INCLINE.

leanness, *macies.*

leap, subst. *saltus* (*-ūs*).

leap, v. *salire*: to — down, *desilire*; — forward, *prosilire*; — on, *insilire*; — for joy, *gestire, exsultare.*

leaping, *saltus* (*-ūs*).

leap-year, *annus bisextus.*

learn. (1) as from a teacher, *discĕre, ediscĕre* (by heart), *memoriae mandare* (= to commit to memory), *perdiscĕre* (thoroughly); word for word, *ad verbum ediscĕre*; — in addition, *addiscĕre.* (2) in gen. = to get to know, *discĕre, cognoscĕre, certiorem fieri.*

learned, *doctus, eruditus, litteratus.*

learnedly, *docte, erudite, litterate.*

learner, *discipulus.*

learning, *doctrina, eruditio.*

lease, subst. *conductio.*

lease, v. *conducĕre* (= take a — of), *locare* (= give a — of).

leash, *lorum, copula* (Ov.).

least, adj. *minimus*; see also LITTLE.

least, adv. *minime*: at —, *saltem, certe, (at)tamen*; not in the —, *nihil omnino, ne minimum quidem.*

leather, *corium* (Sall.), *aluta* (tanned); adj. of —, leathern, *scorteus* (Ov.).

leave, subst. (1) = permission, *permissio, licentia*: to give —, *potestatem facĕre*; with your —, *pace tuā, bonā tuā veniā*; I have —, *mihi licet*; give me — to clear myself, *sine me expurgem.* (2) to take — of, *valēre iubēre.* (3) — of absence, *commeatus* (*-ūs*).

leave, v. (1) = to desert, abandon, *relinquĕre, deserĕre, destituĕre.* (2) to — property, *relinquĕre, legare*; see also BEQUEATH. (3) = to depart, *excedĕre, discedĕre, proficisci, digredi.*
    With adv.: to — off, *(rem) ponĕre, (rē) desistĕre, (facĕre) desistĕre, (facĕre) desinĕre*; to — out, *omittĕre, praetermittĕre.*

leaven, subst. *fermentum* (Tac.).

leaven, v. *fermentare* (Plin.).

leavings, *reliquiae* (*-arum*, plur.).

lecture, subst. *schola, acroasis.*

lecture, v.; see REPROVE.

lecture-room, *schola, auditorium* (Quint., Tac.).

ledge: — of rock, *dorsum.*

ledger, *codex accepti et expensi.*

leech, *hirudo, sanguisuga* (Plin.); see also DOCTOR.

leek, *porrum* and *porrus* (Hor., Juv.).

leer, perhaps *oculis limis intueri.*

leering, *limus* (Pl., Ov., Quint.).

lees, *faex.*

left, = remaining, *reliquus:* to be —, *restare;* see also LEAVE.

left, (opp. right) *sinister, laevus:* the — hand, *sinistra;* on the —, *a sinistrā, ad laevam.*

left-handed, render by phrase, e.g. *qui manu sinistra pro dextrā utitur.*

leg, *crus* (*cruris*, n.): — of a table, *pes mensae.*

legacy, *legātum:* to make (or leave) a —, *legare.*

legal, *legitimus,* or render by phrase, e.g. *quod ex lege* or *legibus* or *secundum leges fit.*

legalize: to — an action, *ferre* or *sancire ut aliquid fiat.*

legally, *legitime, lege.*

legate, *legatus, nuntius.*

legation, *legatio.*

legend. (1) on coins, etc., *inscriptio, titulus.* (2) = a myth, fable, *fabula.*

legendary, *commenticius, fictus, fabulosus.*

legerdemain, *praestigiae* (-*arum*, plur.).

leggings, *ocreae* (-*arum*, plur.: Verg.).

legible, *quod facile legi potest.*

legion, *legio.*

legionary, *legionarius.*

legislate, *leges facĕre, constituĕre, condĕre, scribĕre;* see also LAW.

legislation, render by verb.

legislator, render by verb.

leisure, *otium:* to be at —, *otiosum esse, otium habēre, otiari, vacare, cessare;* at —, *otiosus, vacuus;* not at —, *occupatus;* hours of —, *tempus otiosum.*

leisurely, *lentus;* see also SLOW; as adv. *otiose.*

lend. LIT., *mutuum dare, commodare:* to — at interest, *fenerari, fenori dare.* TRANSF., = to give, *dare, praebēre.*

length, *longitudo;* sometimes *proceritas;* in time, *longinquitas, diuturnitas:* at —, (= at last) *tandem, denique, tum demum;* (= fully) *copiose, fuse.*

lengthen, v. *longiorem facĕre:* — in time = to prolong, *producĕre, prorogare.*

length-wise, *in longitudinem.*

lengthy, adj.: — in words, *verbosus, longus.*

leniency, *clementia, lenitas.*

lenient, *mitis, clemens, lenis.*

leniently, *clementer.*

lentil, *lens* (Verg.).

leonine, *leoninus* (Varro).

leper, render by phrase.

leprosy, *lepra* (usually plur.: Plin.).

Lerida, *Ilerda.*

less, adj. *minor.*

less, adv. *minus;* see also LITTLE: much —, *nedum.*

lessee, *conductor.*

lessen, (*de*)*minuĕre, imminuĕre.*

lessening, *deminutio, imminutio.*

lesson. (1) of regular teaching: to give —s, *docēre;* to take —s from a teacher, *audire magistrum.* (2) a —, = a warning or example, *documentum.*

lest, conj. *ne* with subj.

let. (1) in gen. = to allow, *sinĕre, pati, concedĕre* (with dat.), *permittĕre* (with dat.).

(2) in special senses and phrases; in commands: — us go, *eamus;* to — alone, (*rem*) *omittere,* (*a re, ab homine*) *abstinēre;* to — down, *demittĕre;* to — fly, *emittĕre;* to — go, (*di*)*mittĕre, missum facĕre;* to — in, *admittĕre;* to — off, *absolvĕre;* to — slip, *amittere, omittere;* to — a person know, *homini dicĕre, hominem docēre* or *certiorem facĕre.* (3) = lease; q.v.

lethal, *mortifer, exitialis, funestus.*

lethargic, *torpidus:* a — person, *lethargicus* (Hor.).

lethargy, *lethargus* (Hor.), *torpor* (Tac.), *veternus* (Pl.).

letter. (1) of the alphabet, *littera:* to the —, *ad verbum, ad praescriptum, ad litteram* (Quint.). (2) = an epistle, *litterae* (-*arum*, plur.), *epistula:* by —, *litteris, per litteras;* to write a — to a person, *epistulam* (or *litteras*) *ad hominem dare, scribĕre, mittĕre.*

letter-carrier, *tabellarius.*

lettered, *litteratus.*

letters, = learning, *doctrina, eruditio, litterae* (-*arum*, plur.): a man of —, *homo doctus, eruditus, litteratus.*

lettuce, *lactuca* (Hor.).

levee, *salutatio.*

level, subst. = — ground, *planities,* sometimes *aequum:* to put on a —, (*ex*)*aequare;* to be on a —, render by *aequus* or *par.*

level, adj. *aequus, planus.*

level, v. (1) = to make even, (*ex*)*aequare.* (2) = to bring to the ground, *solo aequare, complanare, sternĕre.* (3) to — a weapon, *librare.*

lever, *vectis.*

leveret, *lepusculus.*

levity, of character, *inconstantia, lĕvitas;* = jesting, *iocus, iocatio.*

levy, subst. *dilectus* (-*ūs*): to make or hold a —, *dilectum habēre* or *agĕre;* see also ENLIST.

levy, v. (1) to — soldiers, *milites* (*con*)*scribĕre.* (2) to — tribute, *tributum imponĕre* or *imperare, vectigal exigĕre.*

lewd, *impudicus, incestus, impurus.*

lewdly, *inceste, impure.*

lewdness, *incestum, libido.*

liable, *obnoxius.*

liar, (*homo*) *mendax.*

libation, *libamentum, libamen:* to make a —, *libare.*

libel, *libellus famosus, carmen famosum* (if in verse).

libellous, *famosus, probrosus.*

liberal, *liberalis, largus, munificus, benignus, beneficus:* too —, *prodigus, profusus;* the — arts, *artes liberales, artes ingenuae.*

liberality, *liberalitas, munificentia, largitas;* of thought, etc., *animus ingenuus, liberalis.*

liberally, *liberaliter, large, munifice, benigne:* to give —, *largiri.*

liberate, *liberare:* to — a slave, *manumittĕre.*

liberation, *liberatio;* = of a slave. *manumissio.*

liberator, *liberator.*

libertine, *homo dissolutus, ganeo.*

libertinism, *licentia morum, mores dissoluti.*

liberty, *libertas:* excessive —, *licentia;* at —, *liber;* you are at — to do it, *facĕre tibi licet* or *integrum est.*

librarian, *bibliothecarius* (late Latin).

library, *bibliotheca.*

libration, *libratio* (Vitr.).

licence, subst. (1) = permission, *copia, potestas.* (2) = liberty, *licentia* (often in bad sense).

license, v. *potestatem dare.*

licentious, *dissolutus, impudicus, libidinosus.*

licentiously, *per licentiam, dissolute, impudice.*

licentiousness, *libido, impudicitia, vita dissoluta.*

lick, *lingĕre* (Pl., Cat.), *lambĕre*: to — up, *ligur(r)ire* (Hor.).

lickerish, *fastidiosus, delicatŭs.*

licorice, *glycyrrhiza* (Plin.).

lid, *operculum, operimentum* (Plin.).

lie, subst. *mendacium*: to tell a —, *mentiri, mendacium dicĕre*; give a person the —, *mendacii hominem coarguĕre.*

lie, v. = to tell a lie, *mentiri.*

lie, v. = to be situated. LIT., *iacēre, cubare* (in bed, etc.), *situm esse, positum esse.* TRANSF., as far as —s in me, *quantum est in me*; to — in this (= to consist in this), *hac re contineri, in hac re situm esse* or *versari.*
With prep., etc.: to — between, *interiacēre*; to — down, *procumbĕre, decumbĕre*; to — hid, *latēre*; to — in (of childbirth), *parturire*; to — in wait, *insidiari*; to — still, *quiescĕre.*

lief: I had as —, *malim.*

lieu: in — of, *pro, loco, vice.*

lieutenant, in gen. of any deputy, *legatus*; in the army, perhaps *centurio* (infantry), *praefectus* (cavalry).

life. (1) = the being alive, *vita, anima*: to have —, *vivĕre, in vitā esse*; to come to —, *nasci, in lucem edi*; to put an end to one's —, *mortem sibi consciscĕre*; to take away —, *vitam (homini) adimĕre*; to restore to —, *ad vitam revocare, e mortuis excitare*; to come to — again, *reviviscĕre*; to venture one's —, *capitis periculum adire*; to cost a person his —, *morte stare*; to try a person for his —, *de capite quaerĕre*; to flee for one's —, *fugā salutem petĕre*; if I could without losing my —, *si salvo capite potuissem*; to depart this —, *diem obire supremum*; the necessaries of —, *victus (-ūs)*; time of —, *aetas*; early —, *iniens aetas*; the prime of —, *flos aetatis, integra aetas.* (2) = way of living, considered socially, morally, etc., *vita.* (3) = career, *cursus (-ūs)* or *curriculum vitae* (in respect of duration); otherwise *vita*; a — as written about = biography, *vita, vitae descriptio.* (4) fig. = liveliness, *vis, vigor, alacritas*; in oratory, *sucus*, comb. *sucus et sanguis*: full of —, *vividus, vegetus, alacer*; to put — into, *animum facĕre* or *addĕre.* (5) the —, = the reality, render by *ipse.*

life-guards, (*milites*) *praetoriani* (= the imperial bodyguard).

lifeless. LIT., *exanimis, exanimus* (= deprived of life); *inanimus* (= never having life). TRANSF., of style, *frigidus, exilis, exsanguis* (Tac.), *aridus, ieiunus.*

lifelessly, *frigide.*

life-time, *aetas, aevum* (poet.): in my —, *me vivo.*

lift, subst., render by verb.

lift, v. (*at*)*tollĕre, extollĕre,* (*sub*)*levare*: to — upright, *erigĕre.*

ligament, ligature, *ligamentum* (Tac.), *ligamen* (Prop., Ov.).

light, subst. (1) = brightness, means of seeing, *lumen, lux*: to give —, *lucem edĕre* or

fundĕre; to see the — of day, *in lucem edi, nasci*; to bring to —, *in lucem proferre, patefacĕre, detegĕre*; to stand in a person's —, *hominis luminibus officĕre*; fig.: to stand in one's own —, *utilitati suae* or *commodis suis male consulĕre*; to place in an odious —, *in invidiam adducĕre*; to see in a false —, (*rem*) *fallaci iudicio vidēre.* (2) = what gives light, *lumen, lucerna* (= a lamp), *candela* (= a taper or torch of wax, tallow, etc.), *cereus* (= a wax taper or torch): to light a —, *lumen, lucernam, candelam accendĕre*; to write or work by lamp- —, *ad lucernam scribĕre, lucubrare.*

light, adj. (1) opp. to dark, *clarus, inlustris, lucidus* (poet.), *candidus* (in colour). (2) opp. to heavy, *lĕvis* (lit. and fig.): — soil, *solum tenue*; —-armed troops, *milites levis armaturae, milites expediti*; —-hearted, *hilaris, curis vacuus*; —-minded, *lĕvis, vanus.*

light, v. (1) = to set light to, *accendĕre.* (2) = to illuminate, *inlustrare, conlustrare.* In phrase: to — upon, *incidĕre, offendĕre.*

lighten. (1) = to make less heavy, *exonerare.* (2) = to cause lightning, *fulgurare, fulgĕre.* (3) = to light; q.v.

lighthouse, *pharus* (Plin.).

lightly, *leviter* (lit. and fig.), *temere*: to make — of, *parvi facĕre* or *pendĕre* (= without consideration); — clad, *expeditus, nudus.*

lightness, *lĕvitas* (lit and fig.).

lightning, *fulmen, fulgur*: struck by —, *fulmine ictus, de caelo tactus.*

lightsome, *hilaris.*

like, adj. = similar, *similis* (with genit. or dat.), *consimilis* (usually with dat.), *par* (= matching, equal; with dat.); *instar* (indecl. n. subst. with genit.); — each other, *similes inter se*; to make —, *ad similitudinem rei fingĕre*; that is — him, *hoc dignum est illo, hoc ille habet.*

like, adv. *similiter, instar* (indecl. n. subst., with genit.), *modo* (with genit.), *ritu* (with genit., used only of living beings); see also AS.

like, v. *amare, diligĕre, carum habēre, delectari* (*rē* or *ab homine*): I — this, *hoc mihi placet* or *cordi est*; I — to do it, *iuvat me facĕre, libet mihi facĕre*; just as you —, *arbitratu tuo.*

likelihood, *veri similitudo, probabilitas.*

likely, *veri similis, probabilis*: it is — that, *veri simile est,* with acc. and infin.

like-minded, *concors.*

liken, *comparare*; see also COMPARE.

likeness. (1) = resemblance, *similitudo* or render by adj. (2) = portrait, *effigies, imago.*

likewise, *item, itidem* or render by *idem.*

liking, *amor* (= affection), *voluptas* (= pleasure), *libido* (= caprice): to one's —, *gratus, acceptus, iucundus.*

lily, *lilium* (Verg.).

limb, *membrum, artus (-uum,* plur.).

limber, *flexibilis, mollis, lentus.*

lime, subst. (1) the mineral = limestone, *calx*: quick- —, *calx viva* (Vitr.). (2) bird —, *viscum.* (3) the tree, *tilia* (Verg.).

lime, v. = to smear with bird- —, *visco illinĕre.*

lime-burner, *calcarius* (Cato).

lime-kiln, (*fornax*) *calcaria* (Cato).

limed, *viscatus* (Varro).

lime-tree, *tilia* (Verg.).

limit, subst. *terminus, finis, limes, modus, circumscriptio.*

limit, v. *finire, terminare, circumscribĕre.*
limitation, *determinatio, circumscriptio*; = exception, *exceptio.*
limited, *parvus, angustus, brevis*: a — monarchy, *condiciones regiae potestati impositae.*
limitless, *immensus, infinitus.*
limn; see PAINT.
limp, subst., render by verb.
limp, adj. *languidus.*
limp, v. *claudicare, claudum esse* (= to be lame); see also LAME.
limpet, *lepas* (Pl.).
limpid, *limpidus* (Cat.), *pellucidus, liquidus* (poet.).
limpness, *languor.*
Lincoln, *Lindum.*
linden-tree, *tilia* (Verg.).
line. (1) in geometry, etc., *linea, regio*: in a straight —, *e regione, rectā lineā, ad lineam*; to draw a —, *lineam ducĕre* or *scribĕre.* (2) a boundary —, *finis, modus, regio.* (3) literary; in poetry, *versus (-ūs), versiculus*; in letters: to write a few —s in reply, *pauca rescribĕre.* (4) as milit. t. t.: — of battle, *acies*; — of march, *agmen*; the front- —, *prima acies, hastati* (-orum, plur.), *principia* (-iorum, plur.); the second —, *principes* (-um, plur.); the third —, *triarii* (-orum, plur.); to draw up the army in three —s, *aciem triplicem instruĕre*; in plur., lines (= entrenchments, etc.), *munitiones* (-um, plur.), *munimenta* (-orum, plur.), *vallum, agger.* (5) = a cord, thin rope, *funis, funiculus, linea*: a carpenter's —, *amussis* (Varro), *linea*; a fishing —, *linea* (Mart.); a plumb —, *perpendiculum.* (6) genealogical: in the father's —, *a patre.*
line, v. fig.: to — streets with troops, etc., *complēre, saepire.*
lineage, *stirps, genus (-eris, n.), origo, progenies.*
lineaments, *lineamenta* (-orum, plur.); see also FEATURE.
linear, *linearis* (Plin.).
linen, the material, *linum*: — cloth, *lintea vestis, linteum* (Pl.); adj., of —, *linteus.*
linger, *cessare, morari, cunctari.*
lingerer, *cunctator, cessator.*
lingering, subst. *mora, cunctatio, cessatio.*
lingering, adj. *tardus, lentus, cunctabundus* (only of people); see also SLOW.
linguist, render by phrase, such as *homo multarum linguarum sciens.*
liniment, *unguentum.*
link, subst. (1) = torch, *fax, taeda, funale.* (2) = bond, *vinculum, necessitudo.* (3) of a chain, *annulus* (Mart.).
link, v. *connectĕre, (con)iungĕre*; see also UNITE.
lint, *linamentum* (Cels.).
lintel, *limen superum.*
lion, *leo*; adj., of a —, *leoninus.*
lion-hearted, *magnanimus.*
lioness, *leaena* (poet.).
lip, *labrum, labia* (Pl., Ter.): a little, or dainty, —, *labellum*; the upper —, *labrum superius*; the lower —, *labrum inferius*; fig., with reference to speech, *os.*
lip-salve, *unguentum.*
lip-service; see FLATTERY.
liquefy, *liquefacĕre.*
liquid, subst. *liquor, umor, latex.*
liquid, adj. *liquidus*: to become —, *liquescĕre, liquefieri*; to make —, *liquefacĕre.*
liquidate; see PAY.

liquor; see LIQUID.
Lisbon, *Olisipo.*
lisp, *balbutire* (= to stammer).
lisping, *blaesus* (Ov., Juv.).
list, *tabula, libellus, index* (Quint.): to write out a — of things, *res perscribĕre.*
list, v.; see WISH, DESIRE, PLEASE.
listen; see HEAR.
listener, *auscultator*; or render by verb.
listless, *socors, deses, languidus, piger, oscitans.*
listlessly, *languide, oscitanter.*
listlessness, *languor, socordia, desidia.*
lists, *campus, spatium*; fig.: to enter the — against a person, *cum homine contendĕre.*
litany, *litania* (eccl.), or *preces (-um,* plur. = prayers).
literal: to employ a word in its — sense, *verbum proprie dicĕre*; the — sense, *propria vis.*
literally, *ad verbum*: to translate —, *ad verbum transferre, verbum pro verbo reddĕre.*
literary, *litteratus, litterarum studiosus*: — tastes, *studia (-orum,* plur.) *litterarum.*
literature, *litterae (-arum,* plur.), *litterarum monumenta (-orum,* plur.): a smattering of —, *litterulae (-arum,* plur.: Hor.).
lithe, *mollis, flexibilis.*
litigant, render by verb.
litigate, *litigare, rem lite persequi.*
litigation, *lis.*
litigious, *litigiosus.*
litter, subst. (1) the vehicle, *lectīca*: a small —, *lecticula.* (2) = brood, *fetura, fetus (-ūs), suboles.* (3) of straw, *stramentum.*
litter, v. = to bring forth young, *parĕre, fetum edĕre.*
little, a little, used as subst., *paulum* (positive word), *parum* (= too little; a modified negative), *nonnihil*: just a —, *paululum, aliquantulum*; a — better, *paulo melior*; a — before, *sub* (with acc.); a — sad, *subtristis*; — by —, *sensim, gradatim*; he said —, *pauca dixit.*
little, adj. *parvus, parvulus, exiguus, pusillus*; often rendered by diminutive of subst., such as *munusculum* (= a — present): — ones = children, *pueri, liberi* (with reference to parentage); so —, *tantulus*; how —, *quantulus*; for a — while, *parumper, paulisper.*
little, adv. *paulum, parum, nonnihil, aliquantulum.*
littleness, *parvitas, exiguitas.*
liturgy, *liturgia* (eccl.).
live, adj. = living; q.v.
live, v. *esse, in vitā esse, spirare, vivĕre* (esp. of more than mere physical existence): as I — ! *ita vivam!*; to — for self, *sibi vivĕre*; to — on anything, *re vivĕre* or *vesci*; to — well (i.e. luxuriously), *laute vivĕre*; to — at or in a place, *locum incolĕre, locum* or *in loco habitare*; see also DWELL.
livelihood, *victus (-ūs).*
liveliness, *alacritas.*
livelong, *totus.*
lively, *alacer, vegetus, vehemens*: to feel a — joy, *valde* or *vehementer gaudēre*; to form a — idea of anything, *rem tanquam praesentem contemplari.*
liver, *iecur.*
livery, *vestis (quam famuli gerunt).*
livery-stables, *stabulum (mercenarium).*
livid, *lividus*: a — colour, *livor*; to be —, *livēre* (all these words commonest in poets).

living, adj. *vivus.*

lizard, *lacerta* (poet.), *lacertus, stellio* (Plin.).

lo! *en, ecce.*

load, subst. *onus* (*-ěris*, n.): a cart- —, *vehes* (Plin.); a — on the mind, *tristitia, molestia, animi dolor* or *aegritudo.*

load, v. (1) in gen. *onerare, onus* (*homini*) *imponere*: to — with reproaches; see REPROACH. (2) of firearms, *arma parare, instruěre.*

loaded, *onustus, oneratus.*

loaf, *panis.*

loam, *lutum.*

loamy, *cretosus* (= of chalk or clay: Cato, Ov.).

loan, *mutuum, res commodata*; of money, *pecunia mutua* or *credita, argentum mutuum* (Pl.).

loath, *invitus*: I am —, *piget me, nolo.*

loathe, v. *fastidire, odisse, aspernari* (*a re* or *ab homine*), *abhorrěre.*

loathing, *fastidium, odium.*

loathsome, *teter, foedus.*

loathsomeness, *foeditas.*

lobby, *vestibulum.*

lobster, *cancer* (= crab).

local, render by a genitive, such as *loci, regionis*: — difficulties, *locorum difficultates.*

locality, *locus* or *loci natura* or *situs* (*-ūs*).

loch, *lacus* (*-ūs*).

lock, subst. (1) on a door, *claustra* (*-orum,* plur.). (2) on a river, *piscina* (Plin.). (3) of hair; see HAIR; of wool, *floccus* (Varro).

lock, v. *obserěre, occluděre*: to — out, *claustro foras excluděre*; to — up = confine, *concluděre.*

locker, *armarium.*

lock-jaw, *tetanus* (Plin.).

locomotion, *motus* (*-ūs*).

locust, *locusta* (Plin.).

lodge, subst. *casa* (= a cottage).

lodge, v. (1) intransit.: **a** = to stay temporarily at a place, *deversari, devertěre*: **b** = to stick, *haerěre.* (2) transit.: **a** = to put up as a lodger, *hospitio excipěre, tecto recipěre*: **b** = to drive home a weapon, *adigěre.*

lodger, *deversor, inquilinus.*

lodgings, *deversorium* (or dim. *deversoriolum*), *deverticulum, meritoria* (*-orum,* plur.).

loft, *cenaculum*: hay—, *faenilia* (*-ium,* plur.: Verg., Ov.).

loftily, *alte, excelse, sublime* (lit.), *elate* (fig.); = proudly, *superbe.*

loftiness. LIT., *altitudo.* TRANSF., *altitudo, elatio, excelsitas.*

lofty. LIT., *altus, praealtus,* (*ex*)*celsus, editus* (of places), *sublimis* (= aloft, mostly poet.). TRANSF., (*ex*)*celsus, elatus, sublimis*; of speech, *grandis.*

log, *lignum, tignum* (= beam), *stipes* (= trunk of tree).

loggerhead: to be at —s; see QUARREL.

logic, *logica* (*-orum,* plur.), *dialectica* (*-ae,* f. sing. or *-orum,* n. plur.); *disserendi ratio.*

logical, *logicus, dialecticus* (= connected with logic): — questions, *dialectica* (*-orum,* plur.); a — consequence, *consequens*; — precision, *disserendi subtilitas*; — subtleties, *disserendi spinae* (*-arum,* plur.).

logically, *dialectice*; often simply *ratione.*

logician, *dialecticus.*

loin, *lumbus.*

Loire, *Liger.*

loiter, *cessare*; see LINGER.

loll, *recumběre, recubare.*

London, *Londinium.*

lone, lonely, lonesome, *solus, solitarius, avius, reductus* (of situation: poet.).

loneliness, *solitudo.*

long, adj. (1) of extension in space, *longus, procērus* (= tall): very —, *praelongus*; — hair, *capillus promissus*; six feet —, *longus pedes sex* or *in longitudinem sex pedum*; a foot —, *pedalis, pedem longus*; a — way, *longe, procul.* (2) of extension in time, *longus, longinquus, diuturnus, diutinus*: for a — time, *diu*; a — time ago, *iam pridem.*

long, adv. of time, *diu*: — ago, *iam pridem*; how —? *quamdiu?*; so —, *tam diu*; — after, *multo post.*

long, v. *avēre, cupěre, gestire, desiderare* (= to regret, miss); see also DESIRE.

longer, adv. of time, *diutius, longius, amplius*: no —, *non iam* (having now ceased), *non diutius*; how much —? *quousque?*

longing, *desiderium, appetitus* (*-ūs*), *appetitio, aviditas, cupido.*

longingly, *cupide, avide.*

long-suffering; see PATIENT.

look, subst. (1) as an action, *aspectus* (*-ūs*), *conspectus* (*-ūs*), *obtutus* (*-ūs* = gaze): to cast, or direct, a — at, *aspectum* or *oculos convertěre* (*in rem*), *aspicěre.* (2) = expression of face, *vultus* (*-ūs*). (3) = appearance, in gen. *species, facies.*

look, v. (1) of using the eyes: to —, or — at, *aspicěre, intueri, contemplari, spectare*; to — about, *circumspicěre*; to — back, *respicěre*; to — down, *despicěre*; fig.: to — down upon, *despicěre*; to — for, see SEEK; to — out, *prospicěre, prospectare*; fig.: to — to (= to heed, attend to), *respicěre, respectare, consulěre* (with dat.); to — up, *suspicěre.* (2) of position: to — in a certain direction, *spectare.* (3) = to have a certain appearance, to seem, *videri, speciem praebēre.*

looking-glass, *speculum.*

look-out, render by verb.

loom, subst. *tela* (poet.).

loom, v. render by phrase, such as, *in conspectum e longinquo dari.*

loop, subst. *laqueus* (= noose).

loop, v.; see TIE.

loophole, *foramen* (= hole), *fenestra.*

loose, adj. (1) = slack, *laxus, fluxus, remissus*: with one's hair —, *passis crinibus.* (2) of soil, *rarus* (3) = not firmly fixed, *mobilis* (Plin.). (4) = at liberty, (*carcere,* etc.) *liberatus, solutus.* (5) of morals, (*dis*)*solutus effrenatus, remissus.*

loose, v. (*re*)*laxare, remittěre,* (*re*)*solvěre*; see also UNTIE.

loosely, *laxe,* (*dis*)*solute.*

loosen; see LOOSE, v.

lop: to — off, *amputare, praeciděre.*

lopsided; see UNEVEN.

loquacious, *loquax, garrulus* (poet.), *verbosus.*

loquaciously, *loquaciter.*

loquacity, *loquacitas, garrulitas* (Ov., Quint.).

lord, *dominus.*

lordly, = proud, *superbus, adrogans*; see also PROUD.

lordship, *imperium, dominatus* (*-ūs*).

lore, *eruditio, doctrina.*

lorn, *solus, desertus*; see also LONELY, FORLORN.

lose. LIT., physically, *amittĕre, perdĕre* (wilfully or destructively), *iacturam facĕre* (with genit.). TRANSF., (1) to — an abstract thing, *amittĕre, perdĕre*; to — a battle, *vinci*; to — a chance, *occasionem amittĕre*; to — colour, *pallescĕre*; to — heart, *animo cadĕre* or *deficĕre*; to — one's labour, *nihil agĕre*; to — sight of, *e conspectu amittĕre*; to — one's way, *errare.* (2) = to be deprived of, *privari, orbari* (with abl.): to — troops in battle, *amittĕre, desiderare*; to — the use of an eye, *altero oculo capi.*

losing, subst. *amissio.*

loss, *damnum, detrimentum, iactura*: to make good a —, *damnum resarcire*; the — of a battle, *pugna adversa*; I am at a —, *dubius sum, haereo, dubito.*

lost, to be, *perire*: all is —, *actum est de summa re*; — in thought, *in cogitatione defixus.*

lot, *sors*: casting of —s, *sortitio, sortitus (-ūs)*; by —, *sorte, sortito*; to decide by —, *sortiri*; more generally = fortune, *sors, fortuna*: it falls to my —, *mihi contingit*; colloq.: a bad — (of a person), *mala merx* (Pl.).

loth; see LOATH.

lottery, *sors, sortitio, alea* (= game of dice).

loud, *clarus* (= clear), *magnus* (= strong).

loudly, *magna voce.*

loudness, *magnitudo, vocis*; or render by adj.

lounge, v. *nihil agĕre, desidĕre.*

lounger, *homo deses.*

louse, *pediculus* (Plin.).

lousy, *pediculosus* (Mart.).

lout, *homo rusticus* or *agrestis.*

loutish, *rusticus, agrestis.*

love, subst. *amor, caritas* (= affection), *pietas, studium* (= enthusiasm): a — affair, *amor*; the god of —, *Cupido, Amor*; the goddess of —, *Venus*; my —! *mea voluptas! meum cor! deliciae meae!*

love, v. *amare* (with passion), *diligĕre, carum habĕre, studĕre* (with dat.) *amore prosequi* or *amplecti*: to — dearly, *ex animo* or *toto pectore, amare*; to — passionately, *deperire* (poet.).

loved, *carus, acceptus, gratus.*

loveliness, *venustas, amoenitas.*

lovely, *bellus, venustus, amabilis, amoenus* (of things, esp. scenery).

lover, *amator, amans*, and f. *amatrix*: a — of literature, *litterarum studiosus.*

loving, adj. *amans, studiosus.*

loving-kindness, *misericordia.*

lovingly, *amanter.*

low, adj. (1) of position or stature, *humilis, demissus.* (2) of voice, *gravis, submissus.* (3) of price, *vilis*: to buy at a — price, *parvo emĕre* (4) of character or standing, *humilis, ignobilis, obscurus, tenuis, abiectus, turpis.* (5) of spirits, *tristis, maestus.*

low, adv. *humiliter* (Plin. L.), *demisse* (Ov.): to speak —, *submisse*, or *submissā voce, dicĕre.*

low, v., of cattle, *mugire.*

low-born, *obscuro* (or *humili*) *loco natus.*

lower, adj. *inferior*: the — regions = underworld, *inferi (-orum,* plur.).

lower, v. *demittĕre*: to — the voice, *vocem submittĕre*; to — oneself = condescend, *se submittĕre, descendĕre.*

lowering, adj.; see DARK, THREATENING.

lowest, *infimus, imus*; see also LOW.

lowing, of cattle, *mugitus (-ūs).*

lowlands, *loca plana.*

lowliness. (1) of rank, *humilitas, obscuritas.* (2) as a virtue, *modestia*; see also HUMILITY.

lowly. (1) of rank, *humilis, obscurus.* (2) = unassuming, *modestus.*

lowness. (1) of position or stature. *humilitas.* (2) of birth, etc., *humilitas, ignobilitas, obscuritas.* (3) of price, *vilitas.*

low-spirited, *animo demisso, adflictus, maestus, tristis*; see also SAD.

loyal, *fidelis, fidus.*

loyally, *fideliter.*

loyalty, *fides, fidelitas.*

lozenge, *pastillus* (Hor.).

lubricate, *ung(u)ĕre.*

lucid. LIT., = bright, *(pel)lucidus.* TRANSF., *dilucidus, lucidus* (Hor., Quint.), *perspicuus.*

lucidity, *perspicuitas.*

lucidly, *(di)lucide, perspicue.*

Lucifer. (1) = the morning star, *Lucifer, Phosphorus* (Mart.), *Eous* (Verg.). (2) = Satan, *Lucifer* (eccl.).

luck, *fortuna, fors, casus (-ūs)*: good —, *fortuna secunda, res secundae, felicitas*; bad —, *adversa fortuna, res adversae*; good — to it! *bene vertat!*; to try one's —, *fortunam tentare*; to trust to —, *fortunae se committĕre.*

luckily, *feliciter, fauste, prospere.*

lucky, *felix, fortunatus, faustus.*

lucrative, *quaestuosus, lucrosus* (Ov.).

lucre, *lucrum, quaestus (-ūs).*

lucubration, *lucubratio.*

ludicrous, *ridiculus*; see also RIDICULOUS, ABSURD.

ludicrously, *ridicule.*

lug, *trahĕre.*

luggage, *impedimenta (-orum,* plur.); *vasa (-orum,* plur.); *sarcinae (-arum,* plur. = knapsacks); all these refer particularly to military baggage.

lugubrious, *lugubris, flebilis, maestus, tristis*; see also SAD.

lukewarm. LIT., *tepidus.* TRANSF., = unenthusiastic, *languidus, frigidus, lentus, remissus.*

lukewarmly, *languide, frigide, lente, remisse.*

lukewarmness. LIT., *tepor.* TRANSF., *languor.*

lull, subst., render by verb.

lull, v. (1) transit. *sedare* (e.g. *ventos, insolentiam*): to — to sleep, *sopire, somnum suadĕre* (poet.). (2) intransit.: the wind —s, *venti vis cadit, venti sedantur.*

lullaby, *cantus (-ūs)*: to sing a —, *lallare* (Pers.).

lumber, *scruta (-orum,* plur.: Hor.).

luminary. LIT., = a heavenly body, *sidus (-eris,* n.). TRANSF., of a distinguished person, *lumen.*

luminous. LIT., *lucidus, inlustris.* TRANSF., see LUCID.

lump, *massa* (poet.), *glaeba* (*gleba*).

lumpy, *crassus, glebosus* (Plin.).

lunar, *lunaris.*

lunatic; see MAD, MADMAN.

lunch, subst. *prandium.*

lunch, v. *prandĕre.*

lung, *pulmo*: —s, *pulmones, latera.*

lunge; see STAB.

lupine, *lupinus, lupinum* (Cato).

lurch, subst.; see ROLL: to leave in the —, *deserĕre, destituĕre.*

lurch, v.; see ROLL.

lure. Lit., *inlex* (Pl.). Transf., *inlex* (Pl.), *inlecebra, esca.*
lure, v. *adlicĕre, inlicĕre, pellicĕre.*
lurid, *obscurus, caliginosus* (*luridus* = pale yellow, ghastly).
lurk, *latēre, latitare, delitescĕre.*
luscious, (*prae*)*dulcis.*
lusciousness, *dulcedo.*
lust, subst. *libido, cupiditas.*
lust, v.: to — after, *concupiscĕre.*
lustful, *libidinosus, impudicus.*
lustily, *valide.*
lustiness, *vigor, robur.*
lustral, *lustralis.*
lustration, *lustratio.*
lustre. (1) = brightness, *nitor, splendor*: to throw — on, *inlustrare.* (2) = a space of five years, *lustrum.*
lustrous, *inlustris, splendidus, clarus*; see also BRIGHT.
lusty, *validus, vegetus.*
lute, *lyra* (poet.), *fides* (*-ium*, f. plur.), *cithara* (poet.).
luxuriant, *laetus, luxuriosus*: to be —, *luxuriare.*
luxuriate, *luxuriare.*
luxurious, *luxuriosus, mollis, delicatus, lautus.*
luxuriously, *luxuriose, delicate, molliter.*
luxury, *luxus* (*-ūs*), *luxuria* or *luxuries, lautitia, apparatus* (*-ūs*).
lye, *lixivia* (Plin.).
lynx, *lynx* (poet.).
lynx-eyed, *lynceus.*
Lyons, *Lugdunum.*
lyre; see LUTE.
lyric, lyrical, *melicus, lyricus* (Hor., Ov.): — poems, *lyrica* (*-orum*, plur.: Plin. L.); — poets, *lyrici* (*-orum*, plur.: Quint.).

M

Maas or **Meuse,** *Mosa.*
mace, *fasces* (*-ium*, plur.).
mace-bearer, *lictor.*
Macedonia, *Macedonia*: a —n, *Macedo*; —n, adj. *Macedonius, Macedonicus.*
macerate, *macerare* (Plin.).
machination, *machina, dolus.*
machine, *machina, machinatio, machinamentum*; sometimes *compages* (= framework).
machinery; see MACHINE.
mackerel, *scomber* (Pl., Cat.).
mad, lit and fig. *insanus, vecors, vesanus, furiosus, demens, mente captus, rabidus* (poet.), *phreneticus*: to be —, *furĕre* (= to rave), *insanire.*
madcap, *homo* or *iuvenis ingenio praeceps.*
madden, (*homini*) *furorem incutĕre, mentem alienare*; fig., with anger, *exacerbare, exasperare.*
madder, *rubia* (Plin.).
madly, *insane, furiose, dementer.*
madman, *homo insanus,* etc.; see MAD.
madness, lit. and fig. *insania, amentia, dementia, vecordia, furor, rabies.*
magazine. (1) = a store, *horreum, receptaculum, armamentarium* (for arms). (2) = a paper; see JOURNAL.
maggot, *vermis, vermiculus.*
maggoty, *verminosus* (Plin.).

magi, *magi* (*-orum,* plur.).
magic, subst. *ars magica, magice* (Plin.).
magic, adj. Lit., *magicus* (poet.). Transf., render by *mirabilis* or *mirus* (e.g. a — power, *mira quaedam vis*).
magician, *magus* (Ov.).
magisterial, *ad magistratum pertinens.*
magistracy, *magistratus* (*-ūs*).
magistrate, *magistratus* (*-ūs*).
magnanimity, *magnanimitas* (rare), *magnitudo animi, magnus animus*; see also GENEROSITY.
magnanimous, *magnanimus*; see also GENEROUS.
magnet, (*lapis*) *magnes.*
magnetic. Lit., render by subst. Transf., see ATTRACTIVE.
magnificence, *magnificentia, splendor, apparatus* (*-ūs*); *lautitia* (of good living).
magnificent, *magnificus, splendidus, praeclarus, amplus; lautus* (of banquets); *sumptuosus* (= expensive).
magnificently, *magnifice, splendide, praeclare, ample.*
magnify, *augēre, amplificare, exaggerare, in maius extollĕre; in maius accipĕre* (= to take a thing more seriously than one need).
magniloquence, *magniloquentia.*
magniloquent, *magniloquus.*
magnitude, *magnitudo, amplitudo, spatium* (= extent): to discover the — of a thing, *cognoscĕre quanta res sit.*
magpie, *pica* (Ov.).
maid. (1) = a virgin, *virgo.* (2) in gen. = a girl, *puella.* (3) = a servant-girl, *ancilla, famula.*
maiden, maidenly, *virgineus* (poet.), *virginalis.*
maidenhood, *virginitas.*
maid-servant, *ancilla, famula.*
mail. (1) = armour, render by *arma* (*-orum,* plur.) or by mentioning items of armour, e.g. *lorica* (= breastplate). (2) = letters, *litterae* (*-arum,* plur.).
mailed, *loricatus.*
maim, *mutilare, truncare*; see also INJURE.
maimed, *mancus, truncus* (poet.).
main, subst. = sea, *pelagus* (poet.), *altum.*
main, adj. *primus, praecipuus, princeps*: the — point, *caput, res* (*summa*); his — object is, *id potissimum spectat* or *sequitur*; see also CHIEF.
mainland, *terra* (*continens*).
mainly, *praecipue, potissimum.*
main-sail, *velum.*
maintain. (1) = to preserve, uphold, *sustinēre, sustentare,* (*con*)*servare, tueri*; esp. against opposition, *tenēre, retinēre, obtinēre.* (2) = to keep in the necessaries of life, *sustinēre, sustentare, alĕre.* (3) to — in argument, *contendĕre, confirmare, adfirmare.*
maintainer, (*con*)*servator, adsertor* (= champion: Ov., Tac.), *vindex* (= champion); or render by verb.
maintenance, in gen. *conservatio, salūs*; or render by verb; = livelihood, *victus* (*-ūs*).
maize, *far.*
majestic, *augustus, sanctus* (= venerable), *magnificus* (= grand).
majestically, *auguste.*
majesty, *maiestas, dignitas, amplitudo*: divine —, *numen*; his —, *rex*; her —, *regina.*
major, subst. (1) in the army, perhaps *tribunus militum.* (2) in law = a person of

age to manage his own concerns; render by phrase such as *sui iuris* or *suae potestatis*.

major, adj. = greater, *maior*; in logic: the — premise, *propositio*.

major-domo, *dispensator, vilicus.*

majority. (1) = the greater number, *maior pars, maior numerus, plures* (= more people), *plurimi* (= most); *plerique* (= a large number): Servius took care that the — did not prevail, *Servius curavit ne plurimum plurimi valerent*; to secure a — of votes, *vincĕre.* **(2)** = full age; see MAJOR, subst. **(2).**

make, subst. *figura, forma, conformatio.*

make. (1) = to form, construct, create, *facĕre, efficĕre, fabricari, aedificare, creare*: to — completely, *conficĕre*; to — amends, *satisfacĕre*; to — a bed, *lectum sternĕre*; to — haste, *maturare, properare*; to — progress, *proficĕre*; to — a speech, *orationem habēre*; to — war, *bellum inferre*; to — one's way, *iter facĕre, pervenire.* **(2)** = to give a certain quality to, e.g.: to — a man good, *hominem bonum facere* or *reddere*; to — level, *aequare*; to — fast, *vincire, constringĕre*; to — good, *reparare, resarcire.* **(3)** = to appoint, e.g.: to — a man consul, *hominem consulem facere, creare, instituĕre, efficĕre.* **(4)** in valuing: to — much or little of a thing, *rem magni,* or *parvi, facĕre.* **(5)** = to cause, compel, *facere* or *efficere* (with *ut* and subj.); *cogĕre* (with infin.): to — a person laugh, *risum homini movēre.* **(6)** = to reach, in certain phrases, e.g.: to — a harbour, *portum capĕre.* **(7)** in arithmetic = to form, come to, *efficĕre, esse.* **(8)** with prep. or adv.: to — away with, *interficĕre, tollĕre*; to — for, *petĕre*; to — up a total, *efficĕre, explēre*; to — up a story, *fingĕre, comminisci*; to — way, *cedĕre.*

maker, *fabricator*; or render by verb.

makeshift, adj. *subitarius.*

maladministration, *prava rerum administratio.*

malady; see ILLNESS.

malapert, *petulans, procax*; see also SAUCY.

malapropos, adv. *intempestive.*

malaria, render by phrase, such as *caelum grave et pestilens.*

malcontent, *homo rerum novarum cupidus.*

male, adj. *virilis* (only of man), *mas, masculus*: the — sex, *virilis sexus (-ūs).*

malediction, *exsecratio, dirae (-arum,* plur.); see also CURSE.

malefactor, *homo maleficus* or *sceleratus.*

maleficent, *maleficus.*

malevolent, *malevolus*; see also MALICIOUS.

malformation, *quod informe est.*

malice, *malignitas, invidia, malevolentia, malitia* (= roguery).

malicious, *malevolus, malignus* (poet.), *invidus.*

malign, v.; see SLANDER.

malignant; see MALICIOUS.

maligner, *obtrectator.*

malignity, *malevolentia*; of a disease, *vis morbi.*

mallard, *anas mas* or *masculus.*

malleable, *ductilis* (Plin.), *lentus, mollis.*

mallet, *fistuca* (for ramming), *malleus* (Plin.).

mallow, *malva* (Hor.), *malache* (Plin.).

malpractice, v.; see MISDEED.

malt, render by phrase, such as *hordeum aquā perfusum et sole tostum.*

Malta, *Melita.*

maltreat, *male tractare, vexare*; see also INJURE.

maltreatment; see INJURY.

malversation, *peculatus (-ūs).*

mama, *mamma* (Varro).

mammal, *animal.*

mammon, *divitiae (-arum,* plur.); see also RICHES.

man. LIT., *homo* (= human being, with all the implications of humanity); *vir* (= 'he-man', opposed to woman or child); men, plur., often *mortales* (esp. in the historians): all men, *homines, genus humanum*; many men, *multi*; all to a —, *omnes ad unum*; — by —, *viritim*; no —, *nemo*; there are men who, *sunt qui*; a — of the world, *homo urbanus.* TRANSF., a — in the game of draughts, *calculus*; a — in chess, *latro* (Ov.), *latrunculus* (Suet.); a merchant- —, *navis mercatoria*; a — -of-war, *navis longa.*

man, v. transit. = to furnish with men, *complēre*: to be sufficiently —ned (of a ship), *suum numerum habēre.*

manacle, subst. *manica* (poet.), *compes, catena.*

manacle v. *vincire.*

manage, *tractare, regĕre, administrare, gerĕre, (pro)curare, dispensare, moderari.*

manageable, *habilis, tractabilis, docilis, facilis.*

management, *administratio, tractatio, cura* (care, e.g. of a family), *(pro)curatio, dispensatio, moderatio.*

manager, *administrator, (pro)curator, dispensator, moderator, praefectus.*

mandate, *imperatum, iussum, mandatum.*

mandible, *maxilla.*

mandrake, mandragora, *mandrăgoras* (Plin.).

mane, *iuba*: with a —, *iubatus.*

manful, *virilis, fortis.*

manfully, *viriliter.*

mange, manginess, *scabies* (Cato, Verg.).

manger, *praesaepe* or *praesaepis* (Cato, Ov.).

mangle, v. *(di)laniare, lacerare.*

mangled, *truncus, lacer.*

mangy, *scaber* (Pl., Cato).

manhood, *pubertas* (Plin.), *aetas constans, firmata, corroborata* or *adulta*: to reach —, *togam virilem sumĕre.*

mania, *insania.*

maniac, *homo insanus*; see also MAD.

manifest, adj. *apertus, manifestus, perspicuus, evidens, notus, cognitus*: it is —, *patet, apparet, manifestum est.*

manifest, v. *aperire, patefacĕre, manifestum facĕre, (in medium) proferre, declarare, ostendĕre.*

manifestation, *declaratio, demonstratio, indicium.*

manifestly, *aperte, manifesto, sine dubio, perspicue, evidenter, palam* (= openly), *scilicet.*

manifesto, *edictum.*

manifold, *multiplex, varius.*

maniple, *manipulus.*

manipulate, *tractare*; see also HANDLE.

manipulation, *tractatio.*

mankind, *homines (-um,* plur.), *genus humanum.*

manliness, *virtus (-ūtis), animus virilis* or *fortis*; see also COURAGE.

manly, *virilis, fortis*; see also BRAVE.

manner, *ratio, modus, via*: in this —, *hoc modo, hac ratione, sic*; one's usual — (= custom), *consuetudo, mos, institutum, ritus (-ūs)*; = sort, kind, *genus*: — of writing, *oratio, sermo*; in the — of, *modo, in modum, ad modum, ritu, more*, with genit. or adj. (e.g.: in the — of slaves, *servilem in modum*).

mannerism, *ratio* (e.g.: a new — in speaking, *nova ratio loquendi*), or render by adj. *putidus* (= affected).

mannerly, adj. *urbanus*; see also POLITE.

manners, *mores* (-*um*, plur.): a person of good —, *homo bene moratus* or *modestus* or *urbanus*.

mannikin, *homuncio, homunculus, humullus*.

manœuvre. (**1**) milit. t. t., *decursus* (-*ūs*), *decursio* (Suet.). (**2**) = trick, stratagem, *artificium, dolus*.

manœuvre, v. (*in armis*) *decurrěre, evagari*.

manor, *fundus, praedium*.

mansion, *aedes* (-*ium*, plur.), *domus*; see also HOUSE.

manservant, *servus, famulus*.

manslaughter, *hominis caedes, homicidium* (Quint., Tac.).

mantelet, *vinea, pluteus, testudo*.

mantel-piece, *mensa, abacus, tabula*.

mantle, *amiculum, palla* (for women), *pallium, palliolum* (small: Pl., Juv., etc.), *lacerna* (for journeys or bad weather), *chlamys* (of Greek type), *paenula* (for travelling), *sagum* (= soldier's —), *paludamentum* (= general's —).

manual, subst. *libellus*.

manual, adj. render by *manū*: to get a bare living by — labour, *manuum mercede inopiam tolerare* (Sall.).

manufactory, *officina*.

manufacture, subst. *fabrica*.

manufacture, v. *fabricari* or *fabricare*; see also MAKE.

manufacturer, *opifex, artifex, fabricator*.

manumission, *manumissio*.

manumit, *manu mittěre*, or as one word, *manumittěre*.

manure, *stercus* (-*ŏris*), *fimus*.

manure, v. *stercorare*.

manuscript, *chirographum*.

many, *multi*; often rendered by *creber* or *frequens* (= — together): an assembly of — people, *magna frequentia* (*hominum*); a good —, *complures, plerique*; very —, *permulti, plurimi*; — -sided, or — times as great, *multiplex*; — a time, *saepe, saepenumero*; as — as, *tot . . . quot*; just as —, *totidem*; as — times as, *totiens . . . quotiens*; prov.: — men, — minds, *quot homines, tot sententiae* (Ter.); of — meanings, *ambiguus*.

many-coloured, *variis coloribus distinctus, multicolor* (Plin.).

map, *tabula*.

map, v. *terrarum situs pingěre*: to — out, *designare, describěre*.

maple, *acer* (Plin.): of —, *acernus* (poet.).

mar, *foedare, deformare, corrumpěre*; see also SPOIL.

marauder, *praedator, direptor*.

marauding, *praedatorius, praedabundus*.

marble, subst. *marmor*.

marble, adj. *marmoreus*.

March, (*mensis*) *Martius*.

march, subst. *iter*: a regular day's —, *iustum iter*; two days' — or journey, *bidui iter*; *castra* (-*orum*, plur.) was also used in counting marches, since the Romans would pitch camp every night, hence, e.g., after five

days' —, *quintis castris*; to make forced —es, *magnis itineribus contenděre*; troops on the —, *agmen*; — off, beginning of —, *profectio*; the signal for beginning the —, *profectionis signum*; on the —, *in itinere, iter faciens*.

march, v. (**1**) intransit. *iter facěre, inceděre*: to — off, *proficisci*; to — fast, *contenděre*; to — faster, *iter accelerare*; to — without interruption, *iter continuare*; to — behind, — in the rear, *agmen clauděre, cogěre*. (**2**) transit. *ducěre*: to — back, *reducěre*; — across, *tra(ns)ducěre*; see also LEAD.

marches, *fines* (-*ium*, plur.), *confinium*; see also BOUNDARY.

mare, *equa* (Verg., Hor.).

margin, *margo*.

marginal, *in margine scriptus* or *positus*.

marine, adj. = belonging to the sea, *marinus, ad mare pertinens*.

mariner, *nauta*.

marines, subst. *classiarii, classici milites, classica legio*.

maritime, adj. *maritimus*: to be a — power, *classe* (*classibus*) *multum valēre*.

marjoram, *amarācus* (Plin.).

mark, subst. (**1**) = what identifies or indicates, *nota, signum, indicium, vestigium* (= trace): it is the — of a wise man to do so, *est sapientis facěre*; to make one's —, *clarum fieri*. (**2**) = a thing aimed at, *scopus* (Suet.).

mark, v. (*de*)*signare, notare*; = to take notice of, *observare, animadvertěre*: to — out, lit. *metiri, metari*; fig. *designare, (de)notare*.

marked, *inlustris, insignis*.

marker, *index*.

market. (**1**) the place, *macellum* (for provisions), *forum* (general term): the cattle —, *forum boarium*; the vegetable —, *forum olitorium*. (**2**) the business, *mercatus* (-*ūs*), *nundinae* (-*arum*, plur.).

market, v. *obsonare* (Pl., Ter.), *nundinari*.

marketable, *venalis*.

market-day, *nundinae* (-*arum*, plur.).

market-garden, *hortus*.

market-place, *forum*.

marksman, render by *sagittarius* or *iaculator*.

marl, *marga* (Plin.).

marriage, *coniugium, matrimonium, nuptiae* (-*arum*, plur.), *conubium*: lawful —, *matrimonium iustum* or *legitimum, nuptiae iustae et legitimae*; a — festival, wedding, *nuptiae*; to arrange a —, *nuptias conciliare*; to demand in —, *sibi* (*in matrimonium*) *petěre*; to be united to a person in —, *in matrimonio habēre*; to give one's daughter in —, *filiam in matrimonium dare* or *nuptum dare, filiam* (*in matrimonium*) *conlocare*.

marriageable, *nubilis, adultus* (= grown up).

marriage-contract, *pactio nuptialis*.

marriage-settlement, *dos*.

marrow, *medulla* (lit. and fig.).

marry, v. (**1**) = to perform a marriage ceremony, render by phrase, such as *conubium sancire, matrimonio iungěre*. (**2**) = to give in marriage; see MARRIAGE. (**3**) = to take a person as husband or wife, *matrimonio se* (*con*)*iungěre cum viro* or *femina in matrimonium accipěre* or *recipěre*; of a man: to — a woman, *ducěre* (*in matrimonium*); of a woman: to — a man, *nuběre* (with dat.); of a couple: to — each other, *matrimonio* or *nuptiis* (*con*)*iungi*; to be married, to be a married man, *uxorem duxisse*;

to be a married woman, *nuptam esse viro.*
(4) as intransit. v. = to get married; of a man, *uxorem ducĕre* (*in matrimonium*); of a woman, *nubĕre viro*; of a woman: to — out of her station, *enubĕre*; to — beneath her, *denubĕre* (Tac., Ov.).

marry! interj. *medius fidius, mehercle.*

Marseilles, *Massilia.*

marsh, *palus* (*-udis,* f.).

marshal, subst. *dux.*

marshal, v. *instruĕre, disponĕre.*

marshy, *paluster, uliginosus* (= swampy: Varro).

mart; see MARKET.

martial, *militaris, bellicosus*: — law, *ius* (state of war), or plur. *iura belli, lex belli.*

martyr, subst. *martyr* (eccl.): to become a — for a cause, *pro re mortem occumbĕre.*

martyrdom, *martyrium* (eccl.).

marvel, subst. *miraculum, portentum.*

marvellous, (*per*)*mirus,* (*ad*)*mirandus, mirificus,* (*ad*)*mirabilis.*

marvellously, *mirum in modum, mire, mirifice,* (*ad*)*mirabiliter.*

masculine, *virilis, masculus.*

mash, subst. *farrago* (Varro, Verg.).

mash, v. (*con*)*tundĕre,* (*con*)*terĕre.*

mask, subst. LIT., *persōna* (esp. on the stage), *larva* (= an ugly —: Hor.). TRANSF., *persona, species, simulatio, integumentum*: to assume a —, *personam induĕre* or *suscipĕre*; to wear a —, (*alienam*) *personam ferre* or *gerĕre, simulare*; wearing a —, *personatus*; under the — of friendship, *per simulationem amicitiae.*

mask, v.: to — oneself, *personam induĕre* or *suscipĕre*; to — another person, *homini, personam imponĕre*; to — a feeling, design, etc., *tegĕre, occultare, dissimulare.*

mason, *structor, faber* (= carpenter, smith, etc.).

masonry, *structura* (Vitr.).

masquerade, render by phrase with adj. *personatus* (= wearing a mask).

Mass, as a religious service, *missa* (eccl.).

mass, *massa* (Verg.), *moles* (whole): a great —, *magna copia* or *vis*; in the —, *per saturam* (Sall.); a — of people, *multitudo, vulgus.*

mass, v.: to — together, (*ac*)*cumulare*; see also COLLECT.

massive, *solidus* (= dense), *magnus* (= great), *gravis* (= heavy).

massiveness, *gravitas*; or render by adj.

massacre, subst. *caedes, strages, trucidatio, internecio.*

massacre, v. *caedĕre, trucidare, trucidando occidĕre, stragem ēdĕre* or *facĕre.*

masseur, *tractator* (Sen.).

masseuse, *tractatrix* (Mart.).

mast. **(1)** on ships, *malus.* **(2)** = acorns, etc. *glans.*

master, subst. **(1)** = owner, person in authority, *dominus*; of a house, *dominus, pater familias* (or in one word, *paterfam-*), *herus* (esp. in relation to the slaves): of any property, *possessor*: to become —, *potiri* (with genit. or abl.); to be —, *imperare, praeesse* (with dat.); to play the —, *dominari.* **(2)** = overseer, manager, *magister*: — of the feast, *arbiter bibendi.* **(3)** a school- —, *magister.* **(4)** fig. in relation to oneself: one's own —, *sui potens, sui iuris.* **(5)** = an expert,

---

artifex, antistes, homo rei peritus or *in re perfectus* (*et absolutus*).

master, v. **(1)** = to subdue, *domare, vincĕre, superare*: to — oneself, or one's passions, *continĕre et coercĕre se ipsum, cupiditates coercĕre, continĕre, regĕre.* **(2)** to — a subject = to understand, *intellegĕre,* (*per*)*discĕre, comprehendĕre, consequi, cognitum habĕre.*

master-builder, *architectus.*

masterful, *superbus, imperiosus, adrogans.*

masterly, *artificiosus* (of persons and things), *artifex* (of persons), *palmaris* (of things); or render by phrase with *ars* or *artificium.*

master-piece, *opus summo artificio factum.*

mastery, = victory, *victoria.*

mastic, mastich, *mastiche* (Plin.).

masticate, *manducare, mandĕre.*

mastication, use verb.

mastiff, perhaps *canis Molossus* (Hor.).

mat, subst. *storea* or *storia, teges* (Varro, Juv.).

mat, v.: to — together, *implicare.*

match, subst. **(1)** for getting a light, *sulphurata* (*-orum,* plur.: Mart.). **(2)** = one's equal (in a contest, etc.); render by adj. *par* (with dat.): no — for, *impar.* **(3)** = a contest, *certamen.* **(4)** = a marriage, *condicio, nuptiae* (*-arum,* plur.).

match, v. **(1)** = to be comparable to, *parem esse, aequare*: to — together, *comparare.* **(2)** in a contest: **a** = to bring together as opponents, *componĕre, conferre*: **b,** to — oneself with = to contend with, *congredi, certare* (*cum homine*).

matchless, *singularis, incomparabilis* (Plin.), *unicus, praestans* (or in superl. *praestantissimus*), *egregius*; see also EXCELLENT.

match-maker, (*nuptiarum*) *conciliator* (or f. *-trix*).

mate, subst. *socius* (= companion), *coniunx* (= husband or wife).

mate, v. **(1)** in chess, *ad incitas redigĕre* (Pl.). **(2)** = to be united, *coniungi.*

material, subst. *materies* or *materia, copia rerum*: warlike —, *apparatus* (*-ūs*) *belli*; in speech, discussion, etc., *silva.*

material, adj. **(1)** = consisting of matter, *corporeus.* **(2)** = not trivial; see IMPORTANT.

materialism, render by phrase, such as *opinio eorum qui nihil in naturā esse statuunt nisi corpora.*

materially, *multum, magnopere*; see also MUCH.

maternal, *maternus.*

maternity, render by phrase with *mater* or *maternus.*

mathematical, *mathematicus* (Vitr., Plin.): — calculation, *mathematicorum ratio*; of — certainty, *certissimus.*

mathematician, *mathematicus.*

mathematics, *mathematica* (Sen.).

matin, adj. *matutinus.*

matricide, *matricidium* (= the crime); *matricida* (= the person).

matrimonial, adj.; see CONJUGAL.

matrimony, *matrimonium*; see also MARRIAGE.

matron, = a married woman, *matrona.*

matronly, *matronalis.*

matter, subst. **(1)** = physical substance, *corpus, res corporeae, ea quae cerni tangique possunt.* **(2)** in discussion or writing: — available, *materies* or *materia, silva, copia rerum*; — chosen, subject- —, the — in hand, *res, propositum, institutum*; that has nothing to do with the —, *hoc nihil est ad rem*; but let us return to the — in hand (after a digression), *sed ad propositum (revertamus)*; to cut the — short, *ut paucis dicam*. (3) = affair, in gen., *res, causa*: how do —s stand? *quo loco res est? ut res se habet?*; the — is settled, *iudicata res est*; a business- —, *negotium*; domestic —s, *res domestica* or *familiaris*; money —s, *res nummaria* or *pecuniaria*. (4) = trouble: what's the —? *quid (rei) est?* (5) = pus, *pūs (pūris*: Cels.).

it matters, *interest, refert*: it — to me, *meā interest* or *refert*; it — to him, *eius interest* or *refert*; it — a great deal, *magnopere* (adv.) or *multum* (n. acc.) or *magni* (n. genit of value) *interest* or *refert*.

matting; see MAT.

mattock, *dolabra*.

mattress; see BED.

mature, *maturus, adultus*.

mature, v. LIT., (1) transit. *maturare, coquěre*. (2) intransit. *maturescěre*. TRANSF., *parare, efficěre*; see also PREPARE.

maturity, *maturitas*: to come to —, *maturescěre*.

matutinal, *matutinus*.

maudlin; see DRUNKEN, SILLY.

maul, *mulcare*; see also INJURE.

maunder, *nugari, delirare*.

mausoleum, *mausoleum* (Suet.); see also TOMB.

maw, *ingluvies* (Verg.), *venter*; see also STOMACH.

mawkish, *putidus*.

mawkishly, *putide*.

maxim, in gen. *praeceptum, regula* (= rule, standard), *lex* (= law): a philosophical — (= tenet, dogma), *praeceptum, dogma (-atis*, n.), *institutum, sententia*.

maximum, *quod maximum est*.

May, *(mensis) Maius*.

may, v. (1) I may do = I have the power to do, *possum facěre*. (2) I may do = I have permission, am allowed to do, *licet mihi facěre*. (3) I may do = perhaps I will do, render by *fortasse* or by *forsitan* with subjunctive. (4) in order that I may do, *ut faciam*. (5) may I die! *moriar*. (6) I fear that he may die, *timeo ne moriatur*.

May-day, *Kalendae Maiae*.

mayor, *urbis praefectus* (Suet.).

mayoralty, *urbis praefectura*.

maze, *labyrinthus* (Plin.).

mazy, *inexplicabilis* (Plin.), *inextricabilis* (Verg.).

mead, as a drink, *mulsum*.

mead, meadow, *pratum*: a small —, *pratulum*; adj. of the —, *pratensis* (Hor.).

meagre. (1) = thin, poor, *macer, ieiunus, exilis*. (2) = scanty, *exiguus*.

meagrely, *ieiune, exiliter*.

meagreness, *ieiunitas, exilitas*.

meal. (1) = flour, *farina*. (2) of food, in gen. *cibus; epulae (-arum*, plur.: = banquet): a light early —, *ientaculum*; a morning —, *prandium*; the main — of the day, *cena*. To take a —, *eděre, cibum capěre, pranděre, cenare*.

mean, subst. *modus, mediocritas*: there is no — between peace and war, *inter pacem et bellum medium nihil est*.

mean, adj. (1) = central, midmost, *medius*. (2) = low in rank, *humilis, ignobilis, obscurus*. (3) = morally low, *inliberalis, abiectus*,

sordidus, turpis, foedus: a little bit —, *subturpiculus*.

mean, v. (1) = to intend, *in animo habēre, cogitare, velle*: to — well by a person, *homini bene velle* or *favēre*. (2) = to signify, indicate, have a certain force (esp. of words and speakers), *significare, sibi velle, valēre* (of words only). (3) = to refer to, allude to, a person or thing, *significare, dicěre, intellegěre*.

meander, render by phrase, such as *flexuoso cursu fluěre*.

meaning. (1) see PURPOSE, AIM. (2) = signification, *significatio, vis* (= force), *sententia, sensus (-ūs*: Hor., Quint.), *notio* (= idea, conception); often to be rendered by verb.

meanly, *inliberaliter, abiecte, sordide, turpiter*; — born, *humili loco natus*.

meanness. (1) moral, *inliberalitas, animus abiectus, sordes* (plur.). (2) of rank, *humilitas, obscuritas*.

means. (1) = instrument or method, way or chance of doing a thing, *via, ratio, consilium, facultas*: by this —, *ita*; to try all —, *omnia experiri, nihil inexpertum omittěre*; to endeavour by all —, *omni ope atque operā eniti*; by fair —, *recte*; by foul —, *foede, turpiter*; by all —, *omnino*; by no —, *haudquaquam, nequaquam, minime, nullo modo*; by — of, render by instrumental abl. or by *per* with acc. (2) = resources, *res familiaris, fortuna, opes (-um*, plur.): I have — to live, *habeo unde vivam*; limited private —, *res angusta domi* (Juv.), *tenuis fortuna*; out of your own —, *tuis opibus, privato sumptu*.

meantime, in the, *interea, interim*.

measurable, *quod metiri possumus*.

measure, subst. (1) = standard of measurement, *mensura, modus*: weights and —s, *mensurae et pondera* (Plin.); in full —, *pleno modio, cumulate*; according to the — of, *pro* with abl.; beyond —, *praeter* or *extra modum, immodice, immoderate, nimis*; in some —, *aliquatenus, aliqua ex parte*. (2) = steps taken, course of action, *ratio, consilium*: —s, *rationem inire, consilium capěre, consulěre, providěre*; to have recourse to extreme —s, *ad extrema consilia descenděre*. (3) in music, *modi, numeri (-orum*, plur.); see also METRE.

measure, v. (1) transit. *(di)metiri, permetiri*: to — out (= mark out, lay out), *metari*. (2) intransit. *esse*, with genit. of measure.

measured, *mensus*; see also MODERATE.

measureless, *immensus, infinitus*.

measurement, *mensio* or *mensura* (= the act), *mensura* (= the standard used).

measurer, *mensor* (Hor., Ov.).

measuring-rod, *decempěda* (10 ft. long).

meat. (1) in gen. = food, *cibus*; see also FOOD. (2) = flesh, *caro*: a small piece of —, *caruncula*.

mechanic, *faber, opifex*.

mechanical, *machinalis* (Plin.), *mechanicus* (Gell.): a — contrivance, *machina, machinatio*.

mechanism, *machina, machinatio*.

medallion, *clipeus* or *clipeum* (in the form of a shield).

meddle, *se interponěre, (rem) attingěre*; see also INTERFERE.

meddler, *ardelio* (Phaedr., Mart.), *homo importunus*.

mediate, adj. opp. to immediate: causes, *causae adiuvantes*.

mediate, v. (1) intransit. *se interponĕre*; see also RECONCILE. **(2)** transit.: to — a peace, *pacem conciliare.*

mediation, render by *deprecator* (e.g.: by my —, *me deprecatore*).

mediator, *deprecator, arbiter, conciliator* (with genit. = one who brings about an arrangement).

medical, *medicus* (Verg., Plin.), *medicinus* (Varro): a — man, *medicus.*

medicinal, *medicatus* (Sen.), *saluber, salutaris.*

medicine. (1) = a remedy, *medicina, medicamen, medicamentum, remedium.* **(2)** = medical science, *medicina, ars medendi*: to practise —, *medicinam exercēre.*

medicine-box, *narthecium, pyxis.*

mediocre, *mediocris.*

mediocrity, *mediocritas.*

meditate, *cogitare, meditari, commentari*; see also THINK and INTEND.

meditation, *cogitatio, commentatio, meditatio.*

meditative, *in cogitatione defixus.*

Mediterranean Sea, *Mare Internum, mare nostrum.*

medium; see MEAN and MEANS.

medlar, *mespilum* (Plin.): — -tree, *mespilus* (Plin.).

medley, *farrago* (Juv.); in an offensive sense, *conluvies, conluvio*: a literary —, *satura.*

meed, *praemium*; see also REWARD.

meek, *demissus, modestus, verecundus.*

meekly, *modeste, verecunde.*

meekness, *animus demissus, modestia, verecundia.*

meet, adj.; see FIT, PROPER.

meet, v. (1) transit. LIT., of one person falling in with another, *homini obviam fieri* or *esse, in hominem incidĕre, hominem offendĕre* or *nancisci* or *convenire, cum homine congredi*: to go to — a person, *homini obviam ire* or *venire, homini occurrĕre, hominem convenire*; to send one person to — another, *hominem homini obviam mittĕre.* TRANSF., **a** = to encounter, face (e.g. to — danger), *periculo obviam ire, se offerre, se opponĕre, se committĕre*; to — death, *mortem obire* or *oppetĕre* or *occumbĕre*: **b,** to — a person half way, — his wishes; see COMPLY. **(2)** intransit.: to — together. LIT., of persons, *inter se congredi* or *convenire* or *concurrĕre, coire*; *confluĕre* (in large numbers), *concurrĕre, convolare* (in haste); of troops: to — in battle, *(inter se) congredi, signa inter se conferre, cum infestis signis concurrĕre.* TRANSF., of things, *coire* (poet.).

meeting, *congressio, concursus (-ūs), concursio*; = an assembly, *conventus (-ūs), coetus (-ūs)*: a crowded —, *celeber conventus, celebritas, frequentia*; a — of the people, *comitia* (-orum, plur.).

melancholic, adj. = hypochondriacal, *melancholicus* (μελαγχολικός).

melancholy, subst. **(1)** = hypochondria, *atra bilis*; Cic. also uses the Greek μελαγχολία. **(2)** = sorrow, sadness, *tristitia, maestitia.*

melancholy, adj. *tristis, maestus.*

mêlée, *pugna, proelium*; see also BATTLE.

mellow, adj. LIT., *maturus, mitis* (poet.): of wine, *lenis* (Ter.), *mollis* (Verg.). TRANSF., of style, etc., *maturus, mitis.*

mellow, v. (1) transit. *coquĕre.* **(2)** intransit. *maturescĕre.*

melodious, *canorus, numerosus* (= measured, rhythmical).

melodiously, *numerose.*

melodiousness, render by adj.

melodramatic, perhaps *mirificus.*

melody, *melos* (poet.), *cantus (-ūs).*

melon, *melo* (Plin.).

melt, v. (1) transit. LIT., *liquidum facĕre, liquefacĕre, dissolvĕre.* TRANSF., = to move to tenderness, *ad misericordiam vocare* or *adducere.* **(2)** intransit. LIT., to — away, *liquescĕre, liquefieri, dissolvi, tabescĕre, dilabi* (= to break up). TRANSF., = relent; q.v.

melting, *mollis, delicatus.*

member. (1) of the body, *membrum*; see also LIMB. **(2)** of a sentence or speech, *pars, membrum, articulus, incisio, incisum.* **(3)** of a community or society: of a nation, *civis*; of the senate, *senator*; of a race, *gentilis*; of a corporation, *sodalis.*

membrane, *membrana.*

memento, *monumentum.*

memoirs, *historiae (-arum,* plur.), *commentarii (-orum,* plur.).

memorable, *memorabilis, memoriā dignus, memorandus* (poet.).

memorandum, *libellus*: a — -book, *adversaria (-orum,* plur.).

memorial, *monumentum*: a written —, *libellus.*

memory, *memoria, recordatio* (= recollection): to keep in —, *memoriā tenēre* or *custodire*; to the — of, *ad memoriam (hominis)*; from —, *ex memoria, memoriter* (= with good —); to commit to —, *memoriae mandare, ediscĕre*; in the — of man, *post hominum memoriam*; to have a good —, *memorem esse, memoriā valēre*; to have a bad —, *memoriā vacillare*; to escape one's —, *excidĕre e memoriā* or *ex animo.*

menace, menacing; see THREATEN, THREAT, THREATENING.

menagerie, render by phrase, such as *ferae saeptis inclusae.*

mend, v. (1) transit. LIT., *reficĕre, reparare, reconcinnare, (re)sarcire.* TRANSF., *emendare, corrigĕre*: to — one's pace, *gradum addĕre.* **(2)** intransit. LIT., *(ex morbo) convalescĕre.* TRANSF., in gen. = to improve, *meliorem fieri.*

mendacious, *mendax.*

mendaciously, *falso, per mendacium.*

mendacity, *mendacium*; see also LIE.

mendicancy, mendicity, *mendicitas, egestas.*

mendicant, *mendicus.*

menial, subst.; see SERVANT.

menial, adj. *servilis*; see also MEAN.

menstrual, *menstruus* (Plin.).

mensuration, *ars metiendi.*

mental, render by the genit. *animi, ingenii, mentis*: to possess outstanding — gifts, *multum ingenio valēre, praestantissimo ingenio praeditum esse.*

mentality, = mind; q.v.

mentally, *mente, animo, cogitatione.*

mention, subst. *mentio, commemoratio* (= reminder or recital): to make —, *mentionem facĕre.*

mention, v. *mentionem facĕre (rei,* genit., or *de re), commemorare (rem)*: to — accidentally, or in passing, *(casu) in mentionem rei incidĕre*; to — by name, *nominare*; not to —, to omit, *omittĕre*; above- —ed, render by *supra* with *commemorare* or *dicĕre.*

mentor; see ADVISER.
mephitic, *foetidus.*
mercantile, render by the genit. *mercatoris* or *mercatorum* (= of the merchants), or by *commercium, mercatura* (e.g. *mercaturas facĕre* = to be engaged in — transactions); see also COMMERCIAL.
mercenary, subst. *miles mercenarius* or *conducticius.*
mercenary, adj. *mercenarius* (= paid), *conductus* (= hired), *venalis* (= readily bribed).
mercer, perhaps *linteo* (= linen-weaver: Pl.).
merchandise, = goods, *merx, res venales.*
merchant, *mercator, negotiator.*
merchantman, merchant-ship, *navis mercatoria* (Pl.) or *oneraria.*
merciful, *misericors, clemens, mansuetus, lenis.*
mercifully, *clementer, mansuete.*
merciless, *immisericors, inexorabilis, immitis, inclemens, inhumanus, crudelis, durus, ferreus.*
mercilessly, *inclementer, inhumane, crudeliter.*
mercilessness, *inclementia* (Verg.), *inhumanitas, crudelitas.*
mercurial, *mobilis, lĕvis.*
mercury, (1) the god, *Mercurius.* (2) the planet, *stella Mercurii, Mercurius.* (3) the metal, *argentum vivum* (Plin.).
mercy, *misericordia, clementia, mansuetudo, venia* (= pardon): at a person's —, *in manu hominis, obnoxius homini.*
mere, subst. *lacus* (-ūs); see also LAKE.
mere, adj. *merus, solus, unus;* often rendered by *ipse* (e.g.: by the — sight, *ipso aspectu*).
merely, *tantum, modo, solum;* see also ONLY.
meretricious, *fucatus.*
merge; see DIP or MINGLE.
Merida, *Emerita Augusta.*
meridian, *circulus meridianus* (Sen.); see also HEIGHT, SUMMIT.
meridian, adj. *meridianus.*
merit, subst. *meritum, dignitas, virtus:* according to —, *pro* or *ex, merito, pro dignitate.*
merit, v.; see DESERVE.
merited, *meritus, debitus.*
meritorious, *laude dignus, laudabilis:* to act in a — manner towards a person, *bene merēre de homine.*
meritoriously, *bene, optime.*
merle, *merula.*
merrily, *hilariter, festive.*
merriment, *hilaritas, festivitas.*
merry, *hilarus, hilaris, festivus;* see also GAY.
merry-andrew, *sannio.*
mesh, *macula.*
mess, subst. (1) = food. (2) = a common meal, *convivium.* (3) = dirt, *squalor, conluvio.* (4) = confusion, *turba, perturbatio* or *confusio rerum.*
message, *nuntius, mandatum.*
messenger, *nuntius* (and f. *nuntia*), *tabellarius* (= letter-carrier).
Messiah, *Messias* (eccl.).
messmate, *conviva, sodalis.*
metal, *metallum* (poet.); it is more usual to specify a particular metal, e.g. *ferrum, aes.*
metallic, *metallicus* (Plin.).
metamorphose, *mutare, transformare;* see also TRANSFORM.
metamorphosis, *metamorphosis* (only as title of Ovid's poem: Quint.); otherwise use verb.
metaphor, *translatio, verba translata.*

metaphorical, *translatus.*
metaphorically, *per translationem, translatis verbis:* to use a word —, *verbum transferre.*
metaphysics, render by *philosophia.*
mete; see MEASURE.
metempsychosis, render by phrase, such as *animarum ab aliis post mortem ad alios transitio.*
meteor, *fax (caelestis).*
meteorite, render by phrase, such as *lapis qui caelo decidit.*
method, *ratio, via, modus, ars.*
methodical, render by phrase with *ratio* or *via.*
methodically, *ratione et viā.*
metonymy, *immutatio, metonymia* (or written as Greek, μετωνυμία).
metope, *metopa* (Vitr.).
metre, *numerus, metrum* (Quint.).
metrical, *numerosus, metricus* (Quint.).
metropolis, *caput;* see also CAPITAL.
mettle, *animus, audacia, ferocitas.*
mettlesome, *animosus, audax, ferox.*
Meuse; see MAAS.
mews; see STABLE.
miasma, *noxius terrae halitus* (-ūs: Plin.).
mica, *phengītes (lapis)* (Plin.).
microscopic, adj. = very small, *minimus, exiguus.*
midday, subst. *meridies, tempus meridianum.*
midday, adj. *meridianus.*
midden, *sterquilinium* (Cato, Varro).
middle, subst. *medium;* more often rendered by *medius* as adj. agreeing with a subst., e.g.: the — of the road, *media via;* to seize a person by the —, *hominem medium adripĕre.*
middle, adj. *medius:* the — way, *mediocritas.*
middling, *mediocris.*
midland, adj. *mediterraneus.*
midnight, subst. *media nox.*
midriff, *praecordia* (-iorum, plur.).
midst, subst. render by adj. *medius:* in the — of the enemy, *inter hostes;* in the — of the march, *in ipso itinere.*
midsummer, *media* or *summa aestas.*
midway, render by adj. *medius.*
midwife, *obstetrix.*
midwinter, *bruma.*
mien, *habitus* (-ūs), *vultus* (-ūs: = expression of face).
might, subst. = strength, *vis, robur, nervi* (-orum, plur.): with all one's —, *summā vi, summā ope, omnibus viribus atque opibus, omnibus opibus ac nervis.*
might, v.; see also MAY.
mightily, adv. *magnopere, valde, summā vi, vehementer.*
mighty, *potens, validus;* see also POWERFUL, STRONG.
migrate, *abire, discedĕre, proficisci, migrare; e terrā excedĕre, solum mutare* or *vertĕre* (= to leave one's own country, esp. of an exile).
migration, *profectio.*
migratory, render by verb: a — bird, *advena volucris* (Varro).
Milan, *Mediolanum.*
milch, adj.; see MILK.
mild, adj. (1) physically, *lenis, mitis* (of fruit: Verg.; of climate: Liv.), *tepidus* (= warm: poet.): to make —, *mitigare, lenire;* to grow — (of fruit, etc.), *mitescĕre; lēvis* (= light, e.g. punishment, opp. *gravis*). (2) of action

and character, *mitis, clemens, indulgens, mansuetus*: a — punishment, *poena levis.*

mildew, *robigo* or *rubigo* (Verg.), *mucor* (Plin.), *situs (-ūs:* Sen.).

mildly, *leniter, clementer, mansuete.*

mildness, of character, *lenitas, mansuetudo, clementia*; often better rendered by adj.

mile: a Roman —, *mille,* plur. *milia (passuum).*

milestone, *miliarium, lapis.*

militant, render by verb, e.g. *pugnare*: the church —, *ecclesia militans* (eccl.).

military, adj. *militaris, bellicus*: — age, *aetas militaris*; men of — age, *iuventūs (-ūtis,* f.); — service, *militia*; — preparations, or stores, *apparatus (-ūs) belli*; — skill, *rei militaris peritia*; the — oath, *sacramentum.*

militate: to — against a thing, *contra rem facĕre, rei* (dat.), *obstare* or *adversari.*

militia, perhaps *cives ad hostem propulsandum armati.*

milk, subst. *lac*: new —, *lac recens*; curdled —, *lac concretum*; prov.: to drink in with one's mother's —, *cum lacte nutricis sugĕre*; fig.: the — of human kindness, *benignitas.*

milk, v. *mulgēre* (Verg.).

milk-pail, *mulctra* (Verg.), *mulctrum* (Hor.).

milk-white, milky, *lacteus*: the — Way, *lacteus orbis, via lactea* (Ov.).

mill, *mola* (esp. in plur. = the machine: Pl., Juv.), *pistrinum* (= the building); adj., belonging to the —, *molaris* (Plin.).

milled, of coins, *serratus* (Tac.).

miller, *pistor* (Pl.).

millet, *milium* (Verg.).

mill-hopper, *infundibulum* (Vitr.).

million, *decies centena mil(l)ia*: two, three —s, *vicies, tricies centena mil(l)ia.*

millionaire; see RICH.

mill-stone, *mola* (Pl.), *molaris* (poet.).

milt, = spleen, *lien* (Pl.).

mimic, v. *imitari*; see also IMITATE.

mimicry, *imitatio.*

minaret, *turris.*

mince, v. transit. (**1**) lit. *concidĕre, consecare.* (**2**) fig. *extenuare*: not to — matters, *sine fuco a fallaciis dicĕre.*

mince, mincemeat, subst. LIT., *minutal* (Juv.). TRANSF., to make — of, *concīdĕre, trucidare, fartem facĕre (ex hostibus*: Pl.).

mincing, *putidus.*

mind, subst. (**1**) as a faculty, *animus* (esp. as the seat of feeling and will), *mens* (esp. as intellect, reason), *ingenium* (= intellect or character): to show presence of —, *praesenti animo uti*; to be in one's right —, *sanae mentis esse, mentis compotem esse*; to be out of one's —, *insanire, mente captum esse, mente alienatā esse*; weakness of —, *ingenii infirmitas* or *imbecillitas*; I call a thing to —, *mihi venit in mentem rei* (genit.); to have it in — to (= to intend), *cogitare, in animo habēre*; to bear in —, *meminisse, memoriā tenēre* or *comprehendĕre* or *custodire*; to call to —, *recordari, in memoriam reducĕre*; to make up one's —, *statuĕre, constituĕre.* (**2**) as a particular way of thinking or feeling, *sensus (-ūs), sententia*: to be of one —, *eadem sentire, consentire*; I have a — to, *libet mihi.*

mind, v. (**1**) = to attend to, *animum (ad rem) advertĕre* or *attendĕre,* (*rem) animadvertĕre* or *attendĕre, curare, agĕre*: — your own

business, *tuum negotium age, res tuas cura*; mind you come, *cura* or *fac (ut) venias.* (**2**) = to resent, object to, (*rem) aegre* or *moleste ferre*: I do not — going, *ire volo, non recuso quin* (or *quominus), eam.*

mindful, *memor, haud immemor* (with genit.): to be —, *meminisse* (with genit.), *respicere* or *respectare* (with acc. = have a regard for).

mine, subst. (**1**) = a source of minerals, *metallum*: a gold —, *aurifodina* (Plin.). (**2**) milit. t. t., *cuniculus.* (**3**) fig. = a rich store, *fons uberrimus, thesaurus.*

mine, possess. pron. *meus.*

mine, v. (**1**) = to dig for minerals, render by *(ef)fodĕre.* (**2**) milit. t. t., *cuniculos agĕre.*

miner, *metallicus* (Plin.).

mineral, subst. *metallum* (poet.).

mineral, adj. *metallicus* (Plin.); or render by phrase.

mingle; see MIX.

miniature, render by *tabella* or *pictura.*

minimum, *minimum, pars minima.*

minion, *minister, servus, cliens.*

minister, subst. (**1**) = servant, *minister, servus.* (**2**) a — of state, render by phrase, such as *principis socius et administer omnium consiliorum* (Sall.), or *ille penes quem est cura administrandae reipublicae.*

minister, v. (**1**) to — an occasion, *occasionem dare* or *praebēre.* (**2**) to — to, (*rei,* dat.), *conducĕre, prodesse.*

ministration; see SERVICE, OFFICE.

ministry. (**1**) = service, function, *ministerium.* (**2**) political, *qui rempublicam administrant.*

minor, subst. *filius* (f. *filia) familias*: no longer a —, *sui iuris.*

minor, adj.; see LITTLE, SMALL; the — premise, as logic. t. t., *adsumptio.*

minority. (**1**) as a time of life, *aetas nondum adulta.* (**2**) = the smaller number, *pars* or *numerus minor.*

minotaur, *minotaurus* (Verg.).

minstrel, *citharoedus*; see also SINGER, MUSICIAN.

minstrelsy, *cantus (-ūs)*; of sounds in unison, *concentus (-ūs).*

mint, subst. (**1**) the plant, *ment(h)a* (Ov.). (**2**) the place where money is coined, *monēta.*

mint, v. see COIN.

minuet; see DANCE.

minus, prep. *sine* with abl.

minute, subst. = moment, *punctum* or *momentum temporis.*

minute, adj. (**1**) = very small, *exiguus, pusillus, perparvus, minutus.* (**2**) = exact, *subtilis, diligens, minutus, accuratus.*

minutely, *subtiliter, minute* (Quint.), *accurate, diligenter.*

minute, v. *in tabulas referre, litteris consignare.*

minuteness, render by adj.

minutes, plur. subst. *libellus, commentarii (-orum,* plur.), *acta (-orum,* plur.); see also NOTE.

minutiae, *singula (-orum,* plur.); see also DETAIL, PARTICULAR.

minx, render by phrase, such as *lasciva puella.*

miracle, *res mira, miraculum.*

miraculous, *mirus, mirificus, mirandus, mirabilis*: by — interposition, *divinitus*; in a — manner, *mirum in modum, mirandum in modum, mirabiliter.*

mire, *lutum*; see also MUD.

mirror, *speculum*.

mirth, *hilaritas, laetitia, gaudium, risus (-ūs =* laughter).

mirthful, *hilaris (hilarus), laetus.*

mirthfully, *hilare, laete.*

miry, *luteus, lutulentus*; see also MUDDY.

misadventure, *casus (-ūs), incommodum*; see also MISFORTUNE.

misanthrope, render by phrase, such as *qui genus humanum* or *hominum universum genus odit.*

misanthropy, *animus hominibus inimicus.*

misapplication, *usus (-ūs) perversus.*

misapply, *(re) abuti* or *perverse uti.*

misapprehend; see MISUNDERSTAND.

misbecome, *(res hominem) dedecet.*

misbehave, *male* or *indecōre se gerĕre.*

miscalculate, *male computare*; in gen. = to make a mistake, *errare, falli, decipi.*

miscalculation, *error.*

miscarriage, = an untimely birth, *abortus (-ūs), abortio*; a — of justice, *iudicium perversum.*

miscarry. (1) = to have a miscarriage, *abortum facĕre* (Plin.). (2) in gen. = to fail, *cadĕre, parum* or *secus procedĕre.*

miscellaneous, *varius, diversus, promiscuus.*

miscellany, as a literary form, *satura.*

mischance; see MISFORTUNE.

mischief. (1) = damage, *malum, incommodum, damnum.* (2) = wrongdoing, *maleficium.*

mischief-maker, *mali auctor.*

mischievous. (1) = harmful, *noxius, perniciosus, maleficus.* (2) = playful, saucy, *lascivus* (poet.).

mischievously, *perniciose.*

mischievousness. (1) = injuriousness, render by adj. *noxius* or verb *nocēre.* (2) = playfulness, *lascivia.*

misconceive, *perperam accipĕre.*

misconception, *opinio falsa, error.*

misconduct, *delictum, peccatum.*

misconstrue; see MISINTERPRET.

miscreant, *(homo) scelestus* or *sceleratus*; sometimes *scelus (-eris,* n.: Pl., Ter.).

misdeed, *facinus (-ŏris,* n.), *scelus (-ĕris,* n.), *maleficium, malefactum, delictum, peccatum.*

misdemeanour, *delictum.*

misdirect. (1) to — a letter, *epistulam perperam inscribĕre.* (2) = to misuse, *abuti, perperam uti.*

misemploy, *abuti.*

miser, *homo avarus.*

miserable, *miser, misellus, miserabilis, miserandus, infelix* (= unhappy), *adflictus* or *aerumnosus* (= much distressed): to lead a — life, *in miseriā esse* or *versari*; sometimes expressed by a diminutive (e.g.: a — little mortal, *homunculus).*

miserably, *misere, miserabiliter.*

miserliness, *avaritia, sordes (-ium,* plur.).

miserly, *avarus, tenax, malignus* (Pl., Hor.).

misery, *miseria, aerumna, angor, maeror, maestitia, tristitia* (= sorrow).

misformed, *deformis, distortus.*

misfortune, *fortuna adversa, res adversae* (plur.), *malum, calamitas, incommodum*: he had the — to, *accĭdit ei ut.*

misgive, render by *diffidĕre* (= to distrust) or by *malum praesagire* (= to have a presentiment of trouble).

misgiving, *metus (-ūs), timor, sollicitudo, praesagium* (Ov., Tac.).

misgovern, *male regĕre* or *administrare.*

misguide, *in errorem inducĕre*; see also MISLEAD.

mishap; see MISFORTUNE.

misinform, *falsa docēre.*

misinterpret, *male* or *perperam interpretari.*

misinterpretation, render by verb.

misjudge, *male iudicare.*

mislay; see LOSE.

mislead, *decipĕre, fallĕre, in errorem inducĕre.*

misleading, render by verb.

mismanage; see MISGOVERN.

misogynist, render by phrase, such as *qui mulieres odit.*

misplace, *(in) alieno loco conlocare*; misplaced, fig., can be rendered by *male* or *perperam,* e.g.: with —d humour, *male salsus* (Hor.).

misprint, *mendum.*

mispronounce, *male pronuntiare.*

misquote, render by phrase, such as *verba auctoris vitiose proferre.*

misrepresent, *calumniari, depravare.*

misrule; see MISGOVERN.

miss, subst., render by verb.

miss. (1) = to feel the loss of what was once enjoyed, *desiderare, requirĕre, desiderio* (with genit.) *movēri.* (2) = to fail to meet or find, *(de)errare (a via, ab homine).* (3) = to fail to strike, *destinatum non ferire* (Curt.). (4) = to — out, to omit, *amittĕre, omittĕre, praetermittĕre*; see also OMIT.

misshapen, *deformis, distortus.*

missile, subst. *telum, (telum) missile; iaculum* or *pilum* (= javelin); *hasta* (= spear).

missile, adj. *missilis.*

missing, to be, *desiderari, deesse.*

mission, = sending out, *missio*; = delegation, *legatio.*

missive; see LETTER.

misspell, *mendose scribĕre.*

misspend, *perdĕre*; see also WASTE, SQUANDER.

misstatement, *quod falsum est*: a deliberate —, *mendacium.*

mist, *nebula*; fig. *caligo.*

mistake, subst. *error, erratum, lapsus (-ūs), peccatum*: in — for, *pro* (with abl.); to make a —, *errare, peccare, labi*; to see one's —, *errorem suum agnoscĕre*; a — in writing, *mendum*; to correct a — in writing, *mendum tollĕre*; full of written —s, *mendosus.*

mistake, v. *ignorare, parum intellegĕre*: you — me for another, *alium esse putas.*

mistaken, to be, *errare, labi, in errore versari, falli*: if I am not —, *nisi fallor, nisi (animus) me fallit*; I may be —, *potest fieri ut fallar.*

mistakenly, *per errorem, perperam.*

mistress. (1) = a female owner or manager, *domina*: the — of a house, *materfamilias* (or as two words), *hera* (with reference to the servants), fig. of abstract things, *dominatrix, gubernatrix.* (2) a school- —, *praeceptrix, magistra.* (3) = a sweetheart, *amica, puella, domina, hera* (all poet.). (4) = a kept woman, *amica, concubina, paelex.*

misty, *nebulosus, caliginosus*; fig. *obscurus.*

misunderstand, *perperam,* or *non recte, intellegĕre*; see also MISINTERPRET.

misunderstanding. (1) about facts = mistake, *error.* (2) between persons, *offensio, dissensio, dissidium.*

misuse, subst. *usus (-ūs) perversus*.

misuse, v. *abuti* or *male uti* (with abl.).

mitigate, *lenire, mitigare, mitiorem facĕre, mollire, levare*.

mitigation, *mitigatio, levatio, levamentum*.

mitre, *mitra* (eccl.).

mitten; see GLOVE.

mix, v. (1) transit.: to — one person or thing with another, *rem re* (or *cum re*) *miscēre* or *admiscēre* or *temperare*; to — in, *immiscēre*; to — together, *commiscēre*; to — up = to involve, implicate, *admiscēre, implicare*; to — up = to confuse, *confundĕre, permiscēre*. (2) intransit., use passive of verbs given above: to — with people, *se cum hominibus (con)iungĕre, inter homines versari*.

mixed, *(per)mixtus, promiscuus*.

mixture. (1) = the act of mixing, *mixtura* (Lucr., Quint.), *temperatio* (esp. in proper proportions). (2) = blend, compound, *permixtio*: a — of good and evil, *bona mixta malis*; of food, *farrago* (Juv.); of filth, *conluvio, conluvies*.

mnemonics, *ars memoriae*.

moan, subst. *gemitus (-ūs)*.

moan, v. *gemĕre*.

moat, *fossa*.

mob, *turba, multitudo*; in a disparaging social sense, *vulgus, plebs, sentina reipublicae, faex populi*.

mob, v.; see SURROUND.

mobile, *mobilis*; see also FICKLE.

mobility. LIT., *mobilitas, agilitas*. TRANSF., = fickleness, *mobilitas, levitas, ingenium mobile*; see also FICKLENESS.

mock, adj. *simulatus, fictus, falsus*.

mock, v. *deridēre, inridēre, inludĕre, ludibrio habēre, ludificari, cavillari*; see also DISAPPOINT, FRUSTRATE.

mocker, *derisor, inrisor, cavillator*.

mockery, *inrisio, inrisus (-ūs), cavillatio, ludibrium, ludificatio*.

mockingly, *per ludibrium*.

mode, *ratio, modus, via*: customary —, *mos, consuetudo*; — of dress, *habitus (-ūs)*.

model, subst. *exemplar, exemplum, proplasma* (Plin.).

model, adj. *optimus*.

model, v. = to shape, *fingĕre, formare*.

Modena, *Mutina*.

moderate, adj. (1) = restrained, *moderatus, modicus, modestus, temperatus*: to be —, *modum servare*. (2) = middling, not great, *modicus, mediocris*.

moderate, v. *moderari* or *temperare* (with dat.), *coercēre* (with acc.), *modum imponĕre* or *adhibēre* (with dat.).

moderately. (1) = with restraint, *moderate, modeste, modice, temperate*. (2) = not greatly, *modice, mediocriter*.

moderation, *modus, moderatio, modestia, continentia* (= self-control), *temperantia, abstinentia*.

modern, *recens, novus, huius aetatis*; sometimes simply *hic*: the — generation, *homines qui nunc sunt* or *vivunt*.

modest. (1) = with a sense of shame, *pudens, verecundus, modestus, demissus*. (2) = moderate, slight, *mediocris, modicus*.

modestly, *prudenter, verecunde, modeste*.

modesty, *pudor, verecundia, modestia*.

modicum, *paulum, paululum*.

modification: with this —, that, *ita . . . ut*.

modify, *(im)mutare*; see also CHANGE.

modulate, *modulari*.

modulation, *flexio, flexus (-ūs*: Quint.).

moiety; see HALF.

moist, *humidus*.

moisten, *conspergĕre* (= to sprinkle), *rigare* (= water), *humectare* (poet.).

moisture, *humor*.

molar, subst. *dens genuinus*.

mole. (1) = mound, *moles, agger*. (2) the animal, *talpa*. (3) = a mark on the body, *naevus*.

molecule; see PARTICLE.

mole-hill, n. perhaps *talpae grumus*; prov.: to make mountains out of —s, render by phrase, such as *mala in maius accipĕre* or *extollĕre*.

molest, *sollicitare, vexare*.

molestation, *vexatio*; or render by verb.

mollify, *mollire, mitigare, lenire*.

molten, *liquefactus*; see also MELT.

moment. (1) of time, *punctum* or *momentum temporis*; in a — = immediately, *statim, e vestigio, confestim*; for the —, *in praesens*; at the —, *hoc tempore, in praesentiā*; at the — when, *cum maxime*. (2) = importance; of great —, *magni momenti*; see also IMPORTANCE.

momentary, *brevissimus*.

momentous, adj. *magni momenti*; see IMPORTANT.

momentousness; see IMPORTANCE.

momentum, (in mechanics) *momentum, impulsus (-ūs), impetus (-ūs), vis*.

monarch, *rex* (= king), *princeps* (= chief, used as a title by the emperors), *dominus* (= any absolute —), *tyrannus* (esp. unconstitutional or oppressive): to be the —, *regnare, dominari*.

monarchical, *regius*: a — form of government, *genus reipublicae regium*; see also MONARCHY.

monarchy. (1) as a form of government, *imperium singulare, potestas regia, tyrannis, dominatus (-ūs), regnum*. (2) = the state so governed, *regnum, civitas quae ab uno regitur, respublica in quā penes unum est summa omnium rerum*.

monastery, *monasterium* (eccl.), *coenobium* (eccl.).

monetary, *pecuniarius, nummarius, argentarius*.

money, *pecunia, argentum* (poet.), *aes* (esp. = copper —, or in the phrase *aes alienum*, = borrowed —); much —, *pecunia magna* or *grandis*; ready —, *pecunia praesens* or *numerata*; a piece of —, *nummus*; good —, *nummi probi*; bad —, *nummi adulterini*.

money-bag; see PURSE.

money-broker, *argentarius*.

moneyed, *dives, pecuniosus*; see also RICH.

money-making, subst. *quaestus (-ūs)*.

moneyless, *inops*; see also POOR.

mongrel, *hibrida* (Hor.).

monition, *monitio* (= the act), *monitum* (= the warning given).

monitor, *(ad)monitor*.

monk, *monăchus* (eccl.).

monkey, *simia*.

monody, use Greek μονῳδία.

monograph, *libellus*; see also BOOK.

monologue, render by phrase.

monomania, *insania*.

monopolize   mote

monopolize, render by phrase.
monopoly, *monopolium* (Suet.); or render by
  phrase.
monosyllable, *monosyllabon* (Quint.).
monotheist, *qui unum modo deum esse credit.*
monotone, use Greek μονοτονία.
monotonous, *canorus* or render by phrase with
  idem and *semper*: to harp —ly on a theme,
  cantare (Pl.).
monsoon, *ventus qui* (*certo tempore*) *flare
  consuevit.*
monster, *monstrum, portentum, belua* (lit. =
  beast).
monstrous, *immanis, monstruosus, portentosus*:
  monstrous! (as comment on an action), *o
  facinus indignum!*
monstrously, *monstruose, praeter naturam.*
month, *mensis* (*-is*, m.).
monthly, adj. *menstruus.*
monthly, adv. *singulis mensibus, in singulos
  menses.*
monument, *monumentum.*
monumental, adj. LIT., render by subst.
  TRANSF., = great, important, *gravis, magni
  momenti.*
mood, of mind, *animus*; as grammat. t. t.,
  modus.
moody, *morosus.*
moon, *luna.*
moonlight, subst. *lunae lumen.*
moonlight, adj.: a — night, *nox lunâ inlustris.*
moor, subst. **moorland,** render by phrase,
  such as *loca* (*-orum,* plur.) *fruticetis obsita.*
moor, v. *religare, deligare.*
moor-hen, *fulica* (poet.).
moorings, use verb.
moot, v.; see SUGGEST, ARGUE.
moot point: it is a —, *incertum* or *dubium est,
  adhuc sub iudice lis est* (Hor.).
mop, subst. *peniculus* (Pl.).
mop, v. *detergêre* (Pl.).
mope, *tristem* or *maestum esse.*
moping, *tristis, maestus*; see also SAD.
moral, subst. = teaching of a story, render by
  phrase, such as *res ad quam fabula spectat.*
moral, adj. (**1**) = relating to morals, *moralis*:
  — teaching, *morum praecepta* (*-orum,* Pl.);
  the — standard, *recti pravique discrimen*;
  — philosophy, *ethice* (Quint.); — corruption,
  mores corrupti. (**2**) = morally correct,
  upright, *honestus, probus, bene moratus,
  sanctus*; see also UPRIGHT. (**3**) it is a —
  certainty, *verisimillimum est* with acc. and
  infin.
morale, = state of mind or spirits, *animus.*
moralist, *qui de moribus praecipit.*
morality, *mores* (*-um,* plur.).
moralize, *de moribus praecipêre.*
morally, *honeste, probe, sancte.*
morals, *mores* (*-um,* plur.).
morass, *palûs* (*-ûdis,* f.).
morbid, LIT., *aeger, morbidus* (Varro, Lucr.):
  a — condition of body, *aegrotatio.* TRANSF.,
  aeger, aegrotus: a — condition of mind,
  aegritudo.
more, subst. = a greater amount, *plus.*
more, adj. (**1**) sing., *plus* or *amplius* with
  genit. (e.g.: — money, *plus pecuniae*). (**2**) plur.,
  plures; many —, *multo plures* (= a far larger
  number), *multi alii* (= many besides);
  see also MORE, adv.
more, adv., often rendered by compar. of adj.

or adv.; otherwise by *magis* (= to a greater
  degree), *potius* (= rather, for preference),
  amplius (= to a larger extent, or in addition),
  ultra: — than, in gen., *magis quam, potius
  quam*; — than, followed by cardinal number,
  amplius (without *quam*), or *plus* (with or
  without *quam*), or *supra* (with acc.); — than
  once (= several times), *semel ac saepius*;
  — than human, — than a king (i.e. in a
  different category), *plus quam*; — than all,
  maxime omnium; no — than (= just as much,
  or little, as), *non magis quam*; no — (= no
  longer), *non iam*; nay, —, *immo*; the — ...
  the more — ..., *quo* (with compar.), *eo*
  (with compar.).
moreover, *praeterea, ultro, ad hoc* (Sall.).
moribund, *moribundus.*
morn, morning, subst. *tempus matutinum*:
  before —, *lucem*; the first light of —, *prima
  lux, diluculum*; in the —, *mane, matutino
  tempore*; early in the —, *multo mane, bene
  mane, primâ luce, ubi primum inluxit*; this —,
  hodie mane; on the following —, *postridie
  mane*; good —! *salve!*
morning, adj. *matutinus.*
morning-star, *Lucifer.*
morose, *morosus, tristis, acerbus, difficilis.*
morosely, *morose, acerbe.*
moroseness, *morositas, acerbitas.*
morrow. (**1**) = the day that followed, *posterus*
  (or *insequens*) *dies*; on the —, *postero die,
  postridie.* (**2**) = the day that is to follow,
  tomorrow, *crastinus dies*; adv., on the —,
  to- —, *cras.*
morsel, *offa, mica* (poet.), *pars exigua*; see also
  PARTICLE.
mortal, adj. (**1**) = subject to death, *mortalis.*
  (**2**) = deadly. LIT., *mortifer*; see also FATAL.
  TRANSF., of enemies, hatred, etc., *capitalis.*
mortality. (**1**) = our mortal state, *condicio
  mortalis, mortalitas.* (**2**) = number of deaths,
  render by verb.
mortally. LIT., render by adj., e.g.: to be —
  wounded, *mortiferum vulnus accipêre.* TRANSF.,
  misere, nimium, vehementer.
mortar. (**1**) for pounding and mixing, *pila*
  (Plin.), *mortarium* (Plin.). (**2**) for binding
  together, *arenatum* (Plin.).
mortgage, subst. *pignus* (*-ôris,* n.).
mortgage, v. *pignori dare, obligare.*
mortification. (**1**) as medic. t. t., *gangraena*
  (Cels.). (**2**) fig. *offensio, dolor*; see also
  VEXATION.
mortify, v. (**1**) intransit. as medic. t. t.,
  putrescêre. (**2**) fig. *offendêre, vexare.*
mortifying, = vexatious, *molestus, gravis.*
mosaic, subst. *pavimentum* or *opus tessellatum*
  (Suet.).
mosaic, adj. *tessellatus* (Suet.).
mosquito, *culex* (Hor.).
moss, *muscus* (Hor., Ov.).
mossy, *muscosus, musco circumlitus* (Hor.).
most, adj., in sing., *plurimum* with genit. of
  subst.; in plur., *plurimi, plerique*: for the —
  part, *plerumque* (of frequency), *maximam
  partem* (of extent); at the —, *summum.*
most, adv., often rendered by use of superl. of
  adj. or adv.; otherwise *maxime, plurimum.*
mostly, *fere, plerumque* (of frequency);
  maximam partem (of extent).
mote, *corpusculum*; see also PARTICLE; the
  biblical saying about the — in thy brother's

[767]

eye and the beam in thine own is similar to Horace's *qui ne tuberibus propriis offendat amicum postulat, ignoscet verrucis illius.*

moth, *blatta* (Verg.).

mother. LIT., *mater, genetrix* (poet.). TRANSF., in metaphors, *mater, parens, procreatrix*; of a —, adj., *maternus.*

mother-country, *patria.*

mother-in-law, *socrus (-ūs).*

motherless, *matre orbus* or *carens.*

motherly, *maternus.*

mother-tongue, *patrius sermo.*

motion, subst. **(1)** = movement, *motus (-ūs), motio, agitatio* (= rapid —): to be in —, *movēri, agitari*; to set in —, *movēre, impellēre.* **(2)** = a proposal, *sententia* (esp. in the senate), *rogatio* (= a — for a law or decree): to bring forward a —, *rogationem* or *legem (re)ferre.*

motion, v. = to make a gesture, *adnuěre, significare.*

motionless, *immotus, immobilis.*

motive, *causa, ratio*: to act from a —, *ratione adductus facěre*; often to be rendered by *ob* (= on account of), *quod* (= because), *cur* (= why).

motley, *varius, versicolor.*

mottled, *maculosus.*

motto, *sententia, dictum, praeceptum.*

mould, subst. **(1)** = shape, *forma.* **(2)** = soil, *terra*; see also EARTH.

mould, v. *formare, (ef)fingěre.*

moulder, *putrescěre.*

mouldering, *puter* (poet.).

mouldiness, *mucor* (Col.), *situs (-ūs).*

mouldy, *mucidus* (Juv.): to be —, *mucēre* (Cato); colloq.: to feel —, *vapide se habēre* (Suet.).

moult, *plumas ponēre.*

mound, *tumulus, agger.*

mount, subst.; see HORSE.

mount, v. **(1)** intransit.; see RISE; = to get on horseback, *conscendēre (equum).* **(2)** transit.: **a** = to ascend, *scandēre, ascendēre, conscendēre, escendēre*: to — a horse, *conscendēre equum* or *ascendēre in equum*: **b** = to furnish with horses, *milites equis imponēre*: —ed, *equo vectus*: **c**, to — guard, *in statione esse, vigilias* or *custodias agěre.*

mountain, *mons*: of a —, *montanus*; full of —s, *montuosus*; roaming the —s, *montivagus*; the top of a —, *summus mons*; the foot of a —, *infimus mons.*

mountaineer, *(homo) montanus.*

mountainous, *montuosus, montanus.*

mountebank, *circulator, plănus.*

mourn, v. **(1)** transit. *maerēre, lugēre.* **(2)** intransit. *maerēre, lugēre, squalēre* (= to wear mourning and neglect one's outward appearance); also *esse* or *iacēre in luctu* or *in maerore.*

mournful. (1) = causing sorrow, *luctuosus, tristis, acerbus.* **(2)** = showing sorrow, *tristis, maestus, lugubris, flebilis, lamentabilis.*

mournfully, *maeste, flebiliter*; more often rendered by adj.

mourning, subst. **(1)** = sorrow, *maeror, maestitia, dolor.* **(2)** = outward signs of sorrow, *luctus (-ūs), vestis lugubris, squalor, sordes (-ium,* plur.): in —, adj. *sordidatus.*

mouse, *mus (muris)*: a little —, *musculus.*

mouse-hole, *cavum muris.*

mouse-trap, *muscipula* (Lucil., Sen.).

moustache, render by the phrase *labrum superius non radēre,* not to shave the upper lip (Caes.).

mouth. (1) of living beings, *os (oris,* n.): with open —, *hians*; to be in everyone's —, *in ore omnium esse, per ora omnium ferri.* **(2)** — of a river, etc., *os (oris,* n.), *ostium.*

mouthpiece, = spokesman, *orator.*

movable, *mobilis, agilis*: — property, *res quae moveri possunt.*

move. (1) transit. LIT., *(com)movēre*: to — rapidly, *agitare*; to — round, *versare, circumagēre*; prov.: to — heaven and earth, *caelum ac terras miscēre.* TRANSF., **a** = to work upon a person's feelings, *(animum) (com)movēre, flectěre*: to — to action, *impellēre*: **b**, to — that a thing be done, *(re)ferre, censēre*; see also SUGGEST. **(2)** intransit. *movēri, se movēre, ferri, se ferre, labi* (gently): to — forward, *progredi*; to — off, *proficisci*; to — to a new home, *migrare.*

movement, n. *motus (-ūs)*: to observe the enemy's —s, *quae ab hostibus agantur cognoscēre*; see also MOTION.

mow, *demetěre, secare*; see also CUT.

mower, *faenisex* (Varro).

much, subst. *multum* or *multa.*

much, adj. *multus* (agreeing with subst. or often in n. sing. with genit. of sing. subst., e.g.: — time, *multum temporis*); sometimes *magnus* (= great): to have — (of a thing), *abundare (re)*; too —, adj. *nimius.*

much, adv. *multum, valde*: very —, *magnopere, plurimum*; with compar. or superl. (e.g. — greater, — the smallest), *multo*; too —, adv. *nimium, nimis*; — less, *nedum, ne dicam.*

muck; see DIRT.

muck-heap, *sterquilinium* (Cato, Varro).

mucous, *mucosus* (Cels.).

mucus, *mucus* (Cat.).

mud, *lutum, caenum.*

muddle, subst. *turba, confusio.*

muddle, v. *confunděre, (per)miscēre, turbare*: to — through, *temere* or *nulla ratione rem gerěre.*

muddy, *lutulentus, luteus* (poet.); of fluids, *turbidus.*

muffin; see CAKE.

muffle, *velare, obvolvěre.*

muffler: wearing a —, *capite obvoluto.*

mug; see CUP.

muggy, *humidus* (= damp), *densus* (= thick), *calidus* (= warm).

mulberry, *morum* (Hor., Plin.): — -tree, *morus* (Ov., Plin.).

mulct, *multare.*

mule, *mulus.*

mull: —ed wine, *vinum fervidum.*

mullet, *mullus, mugil(is)* (Plin., Juv.).

multifarious, *multiplex, varius.*

multifariously, *varie, multis modis.*

multiform, *multiformis.*

multiplication, *multiplicatio* (Sen.).

multiply, *multiplicare*; see also INCREASE.

multitude. (1) = a large number of things or persons, *(rerum* or *hominum) multitudo, vis,* or render by *multus.* **(2)** the —, in a contemptuous sense, *vulgus, multitudo.*

multitudinous, *creber, frequens, multus.*

mumble, v.; see MUTTER.

mummer; see ACTOR.

mummy, *homo mortuus arte medicatus* (Tac.).
munch, *manducare.*
mundane, perhaps *quotidianus* (= of everyday life).
municipal, *municipalis.*
municipality, *municipium.*
munificence, *munificentia, largitas, liberalitas*; see also GENEROSITY.
munificent, *munificus, liberalis*; see also GENEROUS.
munificently, *munifice, large, liberaliter.*
muniment, *munimentum.*
munition, *belli instrumenta* (-orum, plur.) or *apparatus* (-ūs).
mural, *muralis.*
murder, subst. *caedes, occisio, homicidium* (Quint., Tac.), *nex* (passive in sense = violent death): the — of a near relative, *parricidium*; to accuse of —, *inter sicarios accusare.*
murder, v. *necare, caedĕre, occidĕre, interficĕre, de* or *e medio tollĕre.*
murderer, *homicīda, sicarius, percussor*: the — of a father or near relative, *parricīda*; of a brother, *fratricīda*; of a mother, *matricīda*; but the — of a particular person is often best indicated by a relative clause (e.g. *qui illum necavit*).
murderous, *sanguinarius, cruentus* (poet.).
murk; see DARK.
murmur, subst. (1) = any low sound, *murmur, susurrus, fremitus* (-ūs). (2) = complaint, *querela*; see also COMPLAINT.
murmur, v. (1) = to make a low noise, *murmurare, fremĕre, mussare, susurrare* (poet.). (2) = to complain, *fremĕre, queri*; see also COMPLAIN.
murmuring, *susurrus* (Ov.).
muscle, in anatomy, *musculus* (Cels.), *torus*; —s, in general sense = physical strength, *lacerti* (-orum, plur.), *nervi* (-orum, plur.).
muscular, *lacertosus*; see also STRONG.
muse, *Musa, Camena* (Hor.).
museum, *musēum* (Varro, Suet.).
mushroom, *fungus* (poet.), *boletus* (Pl., Juv.).
music. (1) as an art, *ars musica, musica, musicē* (=μουσική), *musica* (-orum, n. plur.). (2) = a particular piece of —: as composed, *modi* (-orum, plur.); as played or sung, *modi, cantus* (-ūs); vocal —, *vocum cantus*; instrumental — (strings), *fidium* or *nervorum cantus*; instrumental — (wind), *tibiarum cantus*; by several performers, *concentus* (-ūs), *symphonia.*
musical. (1) = concerned with music, *musicus, melicus* (Lucr.), *symphoniacus.* (2) = understanding music, render by phrase, such as *artis musicae peritus.* (3) = melodious, *canorus, numerosus.*
musician, *musicus*; or refer to the player of a particular instrument, such as *fidicen* or *tibicen.*
musket; see GUN.
muslin, *sindon* (Mart.).
must, subst. *mustum.*
must, v. (1) representing absolute *necessity* (e.g. arising out of a law of nature); render by gerundive (pers. or impers.), e.g.: all — die, *omnibus moriendum est*; or by *necesse est*, with infin. or subj. (rarely introduced by *ut*), e.g.: man — die, *homini necesse est*

mori (Cic.). (2) representing moral obligation or duty; render by gerundive; or by *debēre*, with infin.; or by *oportet*, with acc. and infin., or with subj. clause; or sometimes by possess. pron., e.g.: I — (= it is my duty), *meum est*, with infin.; or simply by the constructions of direct command (imperat., *ne* with perf. subj., etc.). (3) representing conditional necessity: **a,** of what one — do, if a certain purpose is to be achieved, render by gerundive, or by *opus est* (with infin. or abl.): **b,** of what — logically be so, if some condition is fulfilled, *necesse est* or *debēre* (often in Lucr.). (4) representing (alleged) inward necessity: I — = I cannot help, *facĕre non possum quin*; but often rendered by simple indic., e.g.: I — confess, *confiteor, fateor*; I — regret, *doleo*; this one thing I — say, *unum illud dico.*
mustard, *sinapi* (Plin.).
muster, subst.; see ASSEMBLY.
muster, v. (1) transit. *recensēre*; in gen. sense = to assemble, *convocare*; fig.: to — up courage, *animum sumere* or *erigĕre.* (2) intransit. = to assemble, *congregari, coire, convenire, adesse.*
musty, *mucidus* (of bread and wine: Juv., Mart.); in gen. perhaps *obsoletus*; see also OLD.
mutability, *mutabilitas*; see also CHANGE.
mutable, *mutabilis, inconstans, mobilis*; see CHANGEABLE.
mute, adj. *mutus.*
mutilate, *mutilare* (gen. of minor injuries), *truncare* (more serious).
mutilated, *mutilus, mutilatus, truncus* (poet.), *truncatus, debilis* (= infirm), *curtus* (= docked).
mutilation, render by verb.
mutiny, subst. *seditio, motus* (-ūs).
mutiny, v. *seditionem facĕre.*
mutineer, *homo seditiosus.*
mutinous, *seditiosus.*
mutinously, *seditiose.*
mutter, *mussare, mussitare, muttire* (Pl., Ter.), *murmurare.*
muttering, subst. *murmur, muttitio* (Pl.).
mutton, render by *caro* (*ovilla*).
mutual, *mutuus.*
mutually, *mutuo, invicem.*
muzzle, = fastening for the mouth, *fiscella* (Plin.).
my, *meus* (only used for the sake of emphasis or clarity); sometimes *noster*: I have seen — brother, *fratrem vidi*; I am — own master, *meus sum, mei iuris sum*; it is — business, — duty, *meum est*; I, for — part, *quod ad me attinet, ego quidem.*
myriad, = ten thousand, *decem millia*; = an indefinitely large number, *sescenti.*
myrmidon, *satelles, adsecula.*
myrrh, *murra* (or *myrrha*: Verg., Ov.); of —, *murrinus* (Pl.); anointed with —, *murreus* (Hor.).
myrtle, *myrtus* (Hor., Verg.); of —, adj., *myrteus* (Verg.); a — berry, *myrtum* (Verg.); a — grove, *myrtetum* (Pl., Sall., Verg.).
myself; see SELF.
mysterious, *occultus, secretus, arcanus* (Hor.); see also SECRET.
mystery. (1) in the specifically religious sense, *mysteria* (-orum, plur.); to initiate into,

to celebrate or perform, the mysteries, *mysteria facĕre*. (2) in gen., *res occulta*.

mystic, adj. (1) = belonging to religious mysteries, *mysticus*. (2) in gen.; see STRANGE.

mystification, *ambages* (*-um*, plur.).

mystify, *tenebras homini* (or *animo hominis*) *offundere*.

myth, *fabula*.

mythical *fabulosus* (Hor., Tac.).

mythology, *fabulae* (*-arum*, plur.), *historia abularis* (Suet.).

N

nag, subst. *caballus*; see also HORSE.

nag, v. (colloq.) *increpitare*, *conviciari*.

naiad, *naias* (Verg.).

nail, subst. (1) on the fingers and toes, *unguis*: to cut the —s, *ungues recīdere* or *resecare*; to bite one's —s, *ungues rodere*. (2) for hammering, *clavus*: to drive a —, *clavum* (*de*)*figere*; fig.: you have hit the — on the head, *(rem) acu tetigisti*.

nail, v. (*clavis*) *adfigere* or *configere*.

naive, *simplex*.

naked, *nudus* (lit. and fig.): half- —, *seminudus*; to strip —, *nudare*.

nakedly, *aperte*.

nakedness, *nudatum*, or *nudum, corpus*; fig., of style, *ieiunitas, exilitas, siccitas*.

name, subst. LIT., *nomen, vocabulum, cognomen* (= the family name): my — is Balbus, *est mihi nomen Balbus* (or *Balbo*; dat. often in Liv.); to bear a —, *nomen ferre* or *habēre*; by — (i.e. with the —(s) mentioned), *nominatim*. A distinguished Roman had three personal names: *praenomen* (of the individual, e.g. *Publius*); *nomen* (of the *gens*, e.g. *Cornelius*); *cognomen* (of the *familia*, e.g. *Scipio*); sometimes as a special distinction he had an *agnomen* or second *cognomen* (e.g. *Africanus*). TRANSF., (1) good — = reputation, *nomen, fama, existimatio*. (2) = mere name, opp. to reality, *nomen*: in — , *verbo*. (3) = authority, warrant: tell him in my —, in the — of the senate, *dic ei meis verbis, senatūs verbis*.

name, v. (1) = to give a name to, *nominare, appellare, dicĕre nuncupare*; (*homini* or *rei*) *nomen dare*, (*im*)*ponĕre*. (2) = to mention by —, *nominare*. (3) = to appoint; q.v.

nameless, *nominis expers*: a certain person who shall be —, *homo quidam*.

namely, often rendered by simple apposition, otherwise by relative clause or by *dico* (= I mean, I refer to).

namesake, *homo eodem nomine appellatus*.

nap, subst. (1) = sleep, *somnus* (*brevis*). (2) of cloth, *villi* (*-orum*, plur.: Verg.).

nap, v.; see SLEEP; fig.: Homer is caught —ping, *dormitat Homerus* (Hor.).

nape, of the neck, *cervix*.

napkin, *mappa* (Hor., Juv.), *mantele* (Verg.).

Naples, *Neapolis*.

Narbonne, *Narbo*.

narcissus, *narcissus* (Plin.).

narcotic, render by phrase, with verb *sopire* or subst. *somnus*.

nard, *nardus* (Plin.).

narrate, (*e*)*narrare, referre, memorare*; see also TELL, RELATE.

narration, *narratio, expositio*.

narrative, subst. *narratio, historia, fabula*.

narrative, adj., render by verb, *narrare*.

narrator, *narrator*.

narrow, adj. LIT., *angustus, artus* (= tightened, confined), *contractus* (= narrowed). TRANSF., *angustus, pusillus*; to have a — escape, *vix* or *aegre periculum effugĕre*.

narrow, v. (1) transit.: to — down, *coartare, contrahĕre*. (2) intransit., use pass. of above verbs.

narrowly. (1) = scarcely, *aegre, vix*. (2) = closely, carefully, *accurate, diligenter*.

narrowness, *angustiae* (*-arum*, plur.); fig.:—of mind, *animus angustus* or *pusillus*.

narrows, *angustiae* (*-arum*, plur.), *fauces* (*-ium*, plur.).

nasal, *narium* (genit. of *nares* = nose).

nascent, *nascens*.

nastiness. (1) = unpleasantness, *amaritudo, gravitas*. (2) = foulness, *foeditas*.

nasty. (1) = disagreeable, *amarus, gravis*. (2) = foul, *foedus, spurcus, taeter, immundus*.

natal, *natalis, natalicius*.

nation, *populus, gens* (= people, stock), *civitas* (= body of citizens), *respublica* (= state), *natio* (= tribe, not highly civilized).

national, render by genit. of word for 'nation', with or without addition of *proprius* (= peculiar to): the — cause, *respublica*; in the — interest, *e republica*.

nationality, render by word for 'nation'; of what —? *cuias?*

native, subst. *indigena*: a — of Rome, *homo Romae natus* or (*a*) *Roma oriundus*.

native, adj. *indigĕna*: — land, *patria*; — language, *patrius sermo*; see also NATURAL.

nativity, in gen. render by *nasci*; in astrology, *thema* (*-ătis*, n.: Suet.), *genesis* (Suet.).

natural, *naturalis* (= coming from, or conforming to, nature); *nativus* (= —, not artificial; also native, inborn); *innatus* (= inborn), *insitus* (= inborn); *simplex* (= unaffected), *candidus* (= unaffected); of rock, *vivus* (Verg.); quite — (i.e. not surprising), *minime mirus*; — ability or disposition, *indoles, ingenium, natura*; — death, *mors necessaria*; — science or philosophy, *physica, naturae investigatio*; — products, *ea quae gignuntur*.

naturalist, render by phrase with (*rerum*) *natura*.

naturalize: to — a person, *homini civitatem dare*; to — an animal or plant, *importare*.

naturally, *secundum naturam, naturaliter*; *sponte* (= without compulsion); *simpliciter* (= unaffectedly).

nature, in gen. *natura*: the realm of —, *rerum natura*; the — of a person (or thing), *natura, ingenium, indoles*; sometimes *rus* (*ruris* = countryside); by —, according to —, *naturā, naturaliter, secundum naturam*; of —, natural law, *lex naturae* or *naturalis*; the phenomena and working principles of —, *naturae species ratioque* (Lucr.); sometimes, in the sense of 'character', to be rendered by *talis* or *eiusmodi* (= of that —), and *qualis?* (= of what —?).

naught, *nihil*: to set at —, *parvi facĕre, neglegere*.

naughtiness, *improbitas, petulantia, malitia.*
naughty, *improbus, petulans, malus.*
nausea, *nausea, fastidium* (= disgust).
nauseous; see LOATHSOME, DISGUSTING.
nautical, naval, adj. *navalis* (e.g. *pugna*), *nauticus* (= of ships or sailors), *maritimus* (= belonging to the sea).
nave, of a wheel, *modiolus* (Plin.).
navel, *umbilicus.*
navigable, *navigabilis, navium patiens.*
navigate, *navigare.*
navigation, *navigatio* (= voyage); otherwise render by phrase *res nauticae* (plur.) or by verb *navigare.*
navigator, *nauta;* see SAILOR.
navy, *classis, copiae navales, naves* (= ships).
nay, as answer to a question (= no), *non;* introducing a correction, — rather . . . (= no indeed . . .), *immo* (*vero*); introducing an amplification (= and what is more), *atque adeo.*
neap-tide, render by phrase, such as *aestūs minimus accessus* (*-ūs*).
near, adj. *propinquus:* —er, *propior;* —est, *proximus; vicinus* (= neighbouring); — relationship, *necessitudo.*
near, adv. *prope, iuxta, propter.*
near, prep. *ad, prope, propter, iuxta,* with acc.
nearly, *prope, paene* (= all but), *fere* or *ferme* (= pretty well): — related, *genere propinquus.*
nearness, *propinquitas* (of place or relationship).
nearsighted, render by phrase, such as *non longe prospicĕre posse.*
neat. (1) = clean and tidy, *nitidus, mundus, comptus, elegans, concinnus.* (2) = undiluted, *merus* (poet.).
neat-cattle, *armenta* (*-orum,* plur.).
neat-herd, *armentarius* (Lucr., Verg.).
neatly, *nitide, compte, eleganter, concinne.*
neatness, *elegantia, munditia, concinnitas.*
nebulous, *nebulosus.*
necessaries, *res necessariae* (plur.): — of life, use phrase, such as *ea quae sunt ad vivendum necessaria* or *quae ad vitam opus sunt.*
necessarily, *necessarie, necessario;* often to be rendered by *necesse est* (e.g.: he must — fear many, *necesse est multos timeat*).
necessary, adj. *necessarius:* this is —, *hoc est necessarium, opus est hoc* (nom. or abl.), *usus est hoc* (abl.); it is — to go, *opus est ire, necesse est ire* (or *eamus*), *eundum est.*
necessitate, *cogĕre;* see also COMPEL.
necessity. (1) = what must be, *necessitas, necessitudo* (rare), *res necessaria:* there is a — for, *opus est* (with nom. or abl.), *usus est* (with genit.); to perceive the — of a thing, *vidēre necessarium esse.* (2) = want, *necessitas, egestas;* a time of —, *tempus* (*-ŏris,* n.).
neck. LIT., of a living being, *collum, cervix* (before Aug. period almost always used in the plur., *cervices*), *gula* (= throat), *fauces* (*-ium,* plur.: = throat). TRANSF., of other things, *collum* (of a poppy: Verg.; of a bottle: Cato, Phaedr.).
neck-cloth, *focale* (Hor., Quint.).
necklace, *monile, torques* (*torquis*).
necromancer, render by phrase, such as *qui animas mortuorum excitat.*
nectar, *nectar.*
need, subst. *necessitas:* there is — of, *opus est*

(with nom. or abl.), *usus est* (with abl.); there is — to, *opus est* (with infin.) or *necesse est* (with infin.) or use gerundive.
need, v. *requirĕre, egēre* (with genit. or abl.): to be —ed; see NEED, subst.; —s must; see MUST.
needful, *necessarius.*
neediness, *egestas, indigentia, inopia;* see also POVERTY.
needle, *acus* (*-ūs*).
needless; see UNNECESSARY.
needlework, render by phrase, such as *opus acu factum.*
needy, *egens, indigens, inops.*
nefarious, *nefarius;* see also ABOMINABLE, WICKED.
negation, *negatio, infitiatio.*
negative, adj., of words, *negans.*
neglect, subst. and **negligence,** *neglegentia, indiligentia, incuria.*
neglect, v. *neglegere, intermittĕre, praetermittĕre, omittĕre, relinquĕre, deserĕre:* to — one's duty, *officio* (dat.) *deesse.*
neglectful, negligent, adj. *neglegens, indiligens, remissus;* see also CARELESS.
negotiate, *agĕre* or *conloqui* (*cum homine de re*): with object, to — a peace (i.e. arrange it), *pacem componĕre* or *conciliare.*
negotiation, = conference, parley, *conloquium;* more often expressed by verb, e.g.: —s are in progress, *agitur* (*de re*).
negotiator, *legatus, orator, internuntius, conciliator* (e.g. *pacis*).
negro, *Aethiops.*
neigh, *hinnire, hinnitum edĕre.*
neighing, *hinnitus* (*-ūs*).
neighbour. LIT., *vicinus* (with f. *vicina*); plur. —s, *vicini, finitimi, vicinia.* TRANSF., = fellow man, *alter* (sing. = another), *ceteri* (plur. = others); or render by repetition of *homo* (e.g.: a man should help his —, *homo homini succurrere debet*).
neighbourhood, *vicinia, vicinitas.*
neighbouring, *vicinus, propinquus, finitimus, confinis, proximus.*
neighbourly, render by phrase, such as *ut decet vicinum.*
neither, pron. neuter: in — direction, *neutro.*
neither, conj. *nec* (or *neque*): —, nor, *nec* (or *neque*), *nec* (or *neque*); in commands, wishes, etc., neither is *neve* (or *neu*) and neither, nor is usually *ne, neve* (or *neu*).
nephew, *filius fratris* or *sororis.*
nepotism, render by phrase, such as *nimius in suos favor.*
nereid, *Nereis.*
nerve, LIT., no equivalent. TRANSF., of vigour, etc., *nervi* (*-orum,* plur.; lit. = sinews).
nervous. (1) = vigorous, *nervosus.* (2) see TIMID.
nervously; see TIMIDLY.
nervousness, *timiditas, trepidatio.*
nest, *nidus:* a little —, *nidulus.*
nestle, *in gremio esse* or *haerēre.*
nestling, *pullus:* —s, *nidi* (*-orum,* plur.: Verg.).
net, subst. *rete, plăga* (usually plur.), *everriculum* (= a drag- —: Varro), *funda* (Verg.), *casses* (*-ium,* plur., for hunting: poet.).
net, v.; see CATCH.
nettle, *urtica.*
nettled, adj. *offensus, subiratus.*
network, *reticulum.*

neuter, as grammat. t. t., *neuter, neutralis* (or *nullius*).

neutral, *medius, neutrius partis:* to remain —, *medium se gerěre, neutri parti se adiungěre, quiescěre.*

neutrality, render by adj. or verb.

neutralize; see COUNTERBALANCE.

never, *nunquam, non umquam:* and —, *nec unquam;* as a strong general negation, *minime, minime vero, minime gentium.*

nevertheless, *nihilominus, nihilo setius, (at)-tamen;* see also HOWEVER.

new, *novus* (of what did not exist before); *recens* (of what has only recently come into existence), *novellus;* — to a person = unaccustomed, *insolitus.*

new-born, *recens natus* (Pl.).

new-comer, *advena.*

new-fangled, new-fashioned, *mirus* (= strange), *novus* (= new), *inauditus* (= unheard of).

newly, *nuper, modo, recens* (adv.): — arrived, *recens* (adj.); — enslaved, *novicius.*

newness, *novitas, insolentia* (= strangeness) (of what is uncommon).

news, *res, nuntius:* what —? *quid novi?;* — reached Rome, *Romam nuntiatum est.*

newspaper, *acta* (-*orum,* n. plur.) with adj. *diurna* (Tac.) or *publica* (Tac.) or *urbana* (Cic.).

newt, *lacertus, lacerta* (= lizard).

next, adj. *proximus:* in the — year, *proximus* or *insequens annus;* the — day, *posterus dies;* on the — day, *postero die* or *postridie.*

next, adv. *deinceps, deinde, postea* (= afterwards).

next, prep.; see NEAR.

nib, = point of a pen, *acumen.*

nibble, *(ad)roděre, gustare* (= to taste).

nice. (1) = pleasant, *suavis, dulcis.* (2) = fastidious, *delicatus.* (3) = penetrating, discerning, *accuratus, diligens, subtilis, exquisitus.*

nicely. (1) = well, *bene, probe.* (2) = with discernment, *accurate, diligenter, subtiliter.*

nicety. (1) = fastidiousness, *fastidium.* (2) = precision, *subtilitas;* to a —, *ad unguem* (Hor.).

niche, *aedicula* (for statues).

nick: in the — of time, *in ipso articulo (temporis), opportunissime.*

nickname, render by phrase, such as *nomen per ludibrium datum.*

niece, *fratris* or *sororis filia.*

niggardly; see MISERLY.

night, *nox, tenebrae* (-*arum,* plur. = darkness): till —, *in noctem;* by —, *nocte, noctu, de nocte;* early in the —, *concubiā nocte;* in the dead of —, *intempestā nocte;* — and day, *noctes et dies;* of the —, *nocturnus;* lasting all —, *pernox.*

nightfall: at —, *sub noctem.*

nightingale, *luscinia* (Hor.), *Philomela* (Verg.).

nightlight; see LAMP.

nightly, adj. *nocturnus.*

nightmare, *insomnium* (Tac., Verg.), *suppressio nocturna* (Plin.).

nightshade, *solanum* (Plin.).

Nile, *Nilus.*

nimble, *agilis;* see also QUICK, SWIFT.

nine, *novem:* — times, *novie(n)s;* — each, *noveni.*

nineteen, *undeviginti:* — each, *undeviceni.*

nineteenth, *undevicesimus, nonus decimus.*

ninety, *nonaginta:* — each, *nonageni.*

ninth, *nonus.*

nip, v. *vellicare* (Pl.); with cold, *urěre.*

nipple, *papilla* (Plin.).

nitre; see SALTPETRE.

no, adj. *nullus* (with subst. agreeing or in partitive genit.), *non ullus, nemo* (with personal subst. in apposition), *nihil* with partitive genit. (e.g.: — news, *nihil novi,* — trouble, *nihil negoti).* Often 'no' with an abstract subst. can be rendered as 'not' or 'nothing' with a verb, e.g.: to have — feeling, *nihil sentire.* By — means, *minime, haudquaquam nequaquam.* And —, *nec ullus.*

no, adv. (1) in answers, *non, minime (vero);* introducing a correction, = — but, nay rather, *immo (vero):* to answer yes or —, *aut etiam aut non respondēre;* to say —, *negare;* to say — to a thing, *rem abnuěre* or *recusare.* (2) with comparatives adj. or adv. *non, nihilo.*

nobility. (1) of birth, *nobilitas, genus nobile.* (2) = the nobles; see NOBLE, subst. (3) of character, use adj. with *animus.*

noble, subst. *unus e nobilibus, homo nobilis* or *generosus;* in plur. the nobles, *nobiles, proceres.*

noble, adj. (1) by birth, *nobilis, generosus, nobili* or *inlustri loco natus.* (2) morally, *ingenuus, praeclarus, honestus, liberalis.*

nobly. (1) — born; see NOBLE. (2) in a noble spirit, *ingenue, praeclare, honeste.*

nobody, *nemo:* and —, *nec quisquam;* in commands, etc., *ne quis* (and —, *neve quis*) with subj.; a —, *terrae filius.*

nocturnal, *nocturnus.*

nod, subst. *nutus* (-*ūs*).

nod, v. *nutare* (Pl., Hor.): to — assent, *adnuěre;* = to doze, *dormitare* (Hor.).

noise, subst. *sonitus* (-*ūs*); *strepitus* (-*ūs*; = loud —, din); *fremitus* (-*ūs*; = a roaring —); *crepitus* (-*ūs*; = clattering or creaking); *stridor* (= a loud, harsh —); *fragor* (= the — of breaking); *murmur* (= murmur or roar): to make a —, *strepěre, freměre, (con)crepare;* or use *facěre* with subst.

noise, v.: to — abroad; see PUBLISH.

noiseless, *tacitus.*

noiselessly, *tacite, (cum) silentio.*

noisily, *cum strepitu.*

noisy: a — meeting, *contio tumultuosa;* but often to be rendered by subst. or verb; see NOISE.

noisome, *foedus, taeter.*

nomadic, *vagus.*

nomads, *nomades* (Plin.), *vagae gentes.*

nomenclature, render by phrase with *nomen* or *nominare.*

nominal and **nominally,** *nomine, verbo.*

nominate, *nominare, dicěre, facěre, designare, creare;* see also APPOINT.

nomination, *nominatio, designatio* (Tac., Suet.).

nominative, *casus* (-*ūs*) *nominativus* or *rectus* (Quint.).

nominee, render by verb *nominare.*

nonagenarian, *homo nonaginta annos natus.*

nonchalant, nonchalantly, use the phrase *aequo animo.*

nonentity, *nihil;* = an obscure person, *terrae filius.*

nonsense, *ineptiae (-arum,* plur.), *nugae (-arum,* plur.), *somnia (-orum,* plur.); as interj., nonsense! *gerrae!* (Pl.), *fabulae!* (Ter.): to talk —, *garrire.*

nonsensical, *absurdus, ineptus;* see also FOOLISH.

none, *nemo, nullus;* see also NO, NOBODY.

nook, *angulus* (Hor.).

noon, *meridies:* of —, adj. *meridianus.*

noose, *laqueus.*

nor, *nec* or *neque;* in commands, etc., *neve* or *neu* (sometimes *nec* or *neque*).

normal; see REGULAR.

north, subst. *septentrio* (or plur. *septentriones*), *aquilo, Boreas* (poet.).

north or **northern** or **northerly,** *septentrionalis* (Varro), *aquilonaris:* — wind, *aquilo, Boreas* (poet.).

north-east, adj. *inter septentriones et orientem spectans:* the — wind, *aquilo.*

north pole, n. *polus glacialis* (Ov.), *polus* (Ov.), *arctos* (Ov.).

North Sea, *Oceanus Germanicus.*

northwards, *(ad) septentrionem versus.*

north-west, adj. *inter septentriones et occasum solis spectans:* — wind, *Caurus* (or *Corus*).

nose, *nasus, nares (-ium,* plur. = nostrils): with a large —, *nasutus* (Hor.); to blow the —, *se emungĕre* (Suet.), *emungi* (Juv.); to turn up the — at anyone (from contempt), *hominem naso adunco suspendĕre* (Hor.).

nosegay, *fasciculus.*

nostrils, *naris* (usually plur.).

nostrum, *medicamentum.*

not, *non, haud* (esp. before adv. and adj.): — at all, *nullus* (colloq., agreeing with subject), *minime, nullo modo, haudquaquam, nequaquam, neutiquam;* — enough, *parum, minus;* not even . . . , not . . . either, *ne . . . quidem* (with the emphatic word(s) placed between *ne* and *quidem*); — one (= — even one), *ne unus quidem;* — so very, *non ita, haud ita;* — to say . . . , *ne dicam . . . .* Do —: = nor, *nec* or *neque;* = instead of, and — rather, *et non, ac non, non.* Do —: in questions, do — you see? *nonne vides? non vides?;* in commands, do — come, *noli venire, ne veneris, cave (ne) venias, ne venias* (colloq.), *ne veni* (poet.), *parce* or *fuge venire* (poet.). That —: to fear that . . . —, *timēre ne non* or *ut;* to say that . . . —, *negare;* in order that . . . —, *ne* with subj.

notable; see REMARKABLE.

notary, *scriba.*

notation, *notatio* (= the act of marking); see also WRITING.

notch, v. *incidĕre.*

note, subst. (1) in music, *sonus, vox.* (2) a —, as made in a — -book, *adnotatio* (Plin. L.). (3) = letter, *epistula, codicilli (-orum,* plur.).

note, v. (1) = to make a —, *adnotare* (Plin. L.); see also WRITE. (2) see NOTICE.

note-book, *adversaria (-orum,* plur.), *commentarius.*

noted; see FAMOUS.

note-of-hand, as commercial t. t. *chirographum* (Suet.).

nothing, *nihil (nil), nulla res, nihilum* (in certain cases): — of the kind, *nihil tale;* — new, *nihil novi;* out of — comes —, *de nihilo nihil fit;* worth —, *nihili;* good for —,

nequam; — but, *nihil aliud nisi.* And —, *nec quidquam.* That . . . nothing: in commands, etc., *ne quid;* in statements, he said that —, *negavit quicquam.*

notice, subst. (1) = — taken, the act of noticing, *animadversio, notatio;* more often rendered by verb. (2) = — given, announcement, warning, *promulgatio, denuntiatio;* or render by verb. (3) concr., a —, as a visible object, *proscriptio, titulus.*

notice, v. *animadvertĕre.*

noticeable; see REMARKABLE.

notification, *promulgatio, denuntiatio.*

notify, *(rem homini) (de)nuntiare;* see also INFORM.

notion, *notio, suspicio;* see also CONCEPTION, IDEA.

notoriety, *fama* (in gen.), *infamia* (in bad sense).

notorious. (1) in gen., *notus, manifestus, clarus, insignis, nobilis.* (2) in a bad sense, *notus, infamis, nobilis* (Pl., Ter.).

notwithstanding. (1) as adv. *nihilominus* (or in two words, *nihilo minus*), *tamen, attamen.* (2) as prep. = in spite of; see SPITE.

nought; see NOTHING.

noun, *nomen* (Quint.).

nourish, (lit. and fig.) *alĕre, nutrire.*

nourishing, render by phrase, such as *in quo multum alimenti est.*

nourishment, *alimentum, cibus.*

novel, subst. *fabula.*

novel, adj. *novus;* see also NEW, UNCOMMON.

novelist, *qui fabulas componit.*

novelty. (1) = newness, *novitas, insolentia.* (2) = a new thing, *res nova.*

November, *(mensis) Novembris* or *November.*

novice, *novicius* (strictly = a new slave), *tiro* (strictly = a new soldier); often rendered by adj. *rudis;* see also INEXPERIENCED.

novitiate, *tirocinium.*

now. (1) as adv. of time, *nunc* (opp. *tunc;* at this moment, at the time present to the writer); *iam* (= at this, or that, very time, already; it can be used of the past); *hoc tempore, in praesentiā, in praesenti, hodie* (= today): just —, *nunc ipsum* (= at this very moment), *modo* (= a moment ago); now . . . now . . . , *modo . . . modo . . . ;* for a long time —, *iamdudum, iampridem, iam diu;* — and then, *interdum, aliquando, nonnunquam;* from —, *iam inde, ab hoc tempore.* (2) as a particle of transition, *autem, vero, quidem, equidem, sed.*

nowadays, *nunc, hodie, hodierno tempore.*

nowhere, *nusquam.*

nude, *nudus;* see also NAKED.

nudge, *fodicare* (Hor.), *fodĕre* (Ter.).

nugatory, *nugatorius;* see also VAIN.

nugget, *glaeba.*

nuisance, render by adj. *molestus* or *gravis.*

null, *vanus, inritus, inanis, nullus.*

nullify, *ad inritum redigĕre.*

nullity, *vanitas, inanitas;* or render by adj.

numb, adj. *torpens:* to be —, *torpēre;* to grow —, *torpescĕre.*

numb, v. render by phrase, such as *torpore adficĕre.*

number, subst. *numerus* (in most senses of the Eng.): a large—, *multitudo, copia,* or render by adj. such as *multus, frequens, creber;* to find out the — of the enemy, *cognoscĕre quot sint hostes.*

number, v. (*di*)*numerare, numerum inire*: to —
among the gods, *referre in numerum deorum.*
numbering, subst.: a — of the people, *census*
(-*ūs*).
numbering, partic. = amounting to, *ad* with
acc.
numberless, *innumerus, innumerabilis.*
numbness, *torpor.*
numerical, render by subst. *numerus* (=
number).
numerous, plur. *multi, plurimi, frequentes*
(= crowded), *crebri* (= crowded); sing.: a —
assembly, *multitudo, frequentia.*
nun, *monacha* (eccl.), *nonna* (eccl.).
nuptial, *nuptialis, genialis* (esp. with *lectus*):
a — song, *epithalamium* (Quint.), *hymenaeus*
(Pl., Ov.).
nuptials, subst. *nuptiae* (-*arum,* plur.), *hymenaeus* (or in plur.: Verg.).
nurse, subst. *nutrix* (= a children's —, with
dim. *nutricula*); fig. in metaphors, *altrix*:
a — for the sick, render by phrase with
curare or *adsidēre.*
nurse, v. *nutrire, gestare* (= to carry in the
arms: Ter.), *fovēre* (= to fondle: Verg.):
to — the sick, *curare* (*hominem*), *adsidēre*
(*homini*).
nursery. (1) for children, render by phrase.
(2) for plants, *seminarium.*
nursling, *alumnus.*
nurture, *educatio*; see also EDUCATION.
nut, *nux*; in metaphor: you have only one more
— to crack, but a hard one, *unus tibi restat
nodus, sed Herculaneus* (Sen.).
nutriment, nutrition; see FOOD.
nutshell. LIT., *putamen.* TRANSF., to put the
thing in a —, *ne multa* (*dicam*).
nymph, *nympha*: a water- —, *Naias* or *Nais*
(poet.); a mountain- —, *Oreas* (Verg.);
a wood- —, *Dryas* or *Hamadryas* (Verg.);
a sea- —, *Nereis* (poet.).

O

o! oh! interj. *o!, oh!* (Pl., Ter.), *pro!* or *proh!*
(expressing surprise or indignation), *heu!*
(expressing pain): — that (in wishes), *utinam,
o si* (poet.); —, but, *atqui.*
oak, *quercus* (-*ūs*), *aesculus* (= the winter or
Italian —: Verg., Hor.), *ilex* (= the holm- —:
poet.); adj., of —, oaken, *quernus* (poet.),
aesculeus (poet.), *ilignus* (poet.); the wood of
the —, *robur*; an — -wood, — -forest,
quercetum (Hor.), *aesculetum* (Hor.).
oak-apple, *galla* (Plin.).
oakum, *stuppa*; adj., made of —, *stuppeus*
(poet.).
oar, *remus, tonsa* (poet.), *palma* (poet.).
oaten, *avenaceus* (Plin.).
oath, *iusiurandum, sacramentum* (military); the
form or wording of an —, *verba* (-*orum,* plur.):
a false —, *periurium*; to bind by an —,
iureiurando obstringĕre; to take the —
according to the usual form, *verbis conceptis
iurare*; to swear a military — of allegiance,
sacramentum dicĕre.
oats, *avena.*
obdurate, adj.; see OBSTINATE.

obedience, *oboedientia, obtemperatio, obsequium.*
obedient, *oboediens, dicto audiens, obtemperans,
obsequens* (all with dat.); often to be rendered
by verb.
obediently, *oboedienter.*
obeisance; see BOW.
obelisk, *obeliscus* (Plin.).
obese; see FAT.
obey, (*homini, legibus,* etc.), *parēre, oboedire,
obtemperare, obsequi*; (*homini*) *auscultare,
dicto audientem esse.*
obituary: the nearest Roman equivalent to
our — notice was perhaps the funeral oration,
laudatio.
object, subst. (1) in gen. = thing, esp. one
apparent to the senses, *res.* (2) an — of . . . ,
= that to which a particular thing is done;
this is rendered by the predicative dat.
(e.g.: to be an — of hatred, *odio esse*), or by
certain abstract nouns used in a concrete
sense (e.g. *amor* or *amores* = an — of love),
or by the passive of a suitable verb (e.g.
amari = to be an — of love). (3) purpose,
aim, *consilium, propositum, finis*; often
rendered by verb, e.g. my —, *quod volo* or
peto or *sequor, quod specto, id ad quod specto*;
with the — of, *eo consilio ut*; to make anything one's —, *rem sibi proponĕre.*
object, v. (1) = to feel annoyance, *gravari,
moleste ferre.* (2) = to make objections,
contra dicĕre recusare, repugnare: to — to
doing a thing, *recusare facĕre, nolle facĕre*;
but you will —, *at* (*enim*); but someone may
—, *sed fortasse quispiam dixerit.*
objection, *quod contra dicitur, contradictio*
(Quint., Tac.): I have no —, *non recuso, non
repugno, nihil impedio, per me licet.*
objectionable; see BAD.
objective, subst. *locus qui petitur*; see also
OBJECT, DESTINATION.
objective, adj. *externus* (= outside the self);
or render by *in rebus* or *in rerum naturā.*
objector, *qui contra dicit.*
objurgate, *obiurgare.*
oblation; see OFFERING.
obligation, usually to be rendered by verb;
sometimes *officium* (= duty), *religio* (= sense
of —): I am under an — to do, *debeo* or *meum
est facĕre*; to be under an — to a person,
homini gratiam debere; adj., under —,
obnoxious; see also OBLIGE.
obligatory; see OBLIGE and COMPULSORY.
oblige. (1) = to constrain, compel, *cogĕre.*
(2) = to put under an obligation, (*hominem
homini*) *obligare* or *obstringĕre*, (*hominem*)
devincire. (3) = to do a favour to a person,
homini gratum facĕre, commodare.
obliging, *humanus, comis, facilis, officiosus.*
obligingly, *comiter, officiose.*
obligingness, *humanitas, comitas, facilitas.*
oblique. LIT., *obliquus* (= slanting). TRANSF.,
obliquus (Tac.), or render by phrase, e.g. *per
ambages*; as grammat. t. t., — cases, *casūs
obliqui* (Varro); — narrative, *oratio obliqua*
(Quint.).
obliquely. LIT., *oblique, in obliquum.* TRANSF.,
oblique (Tac.) or *per ambages.*
obliquity, *obliquitas* (Plin.): moral —, *pravitas,
iniquitas.*
obliterate, *delēre, abolēre*; see also ERASE,
DESTROY.

oblivion — odiously

oblivion, *oblivio, oblivium* (poet.).
oblivious, *immemor, obliviosus*.
oblong, *oblongus* (Plin.).
obloquy, *odium* (= hatred); *opprobrium, vituperatio, maledictum* (= abuse).
obnoxious. (1) = subject, liable, *obnoxius*. **(2)** = objectionable, *noxius, invisus*.
obscene, *obscenus, inquinatus, foedus, turpis*.
obscenely, *obscene, turpiter*.
obscenity, *obscenitas, turpitudo*.
obscure. LIT., *obscurus*; see also DARK. TRANSF., **(1)** = not easily understood, *obscurus, caecus, involutus* (= involved), *reconditus* (= abstruse), *ambiguus* (= of uncertain meaning), *perplexus* (= puzzling), *incertus* (= vague): rather —, *subobscurus*. **(2)** = undistinguished, *obscurus, humilis*.
obscure, v. *obscurare* (lit. and fig.), *tenebras offundere* or *obducere* (with dat.).
obscurely, *perplexe, ambigue, per ambages*: — born, *obscuro loco natus*.
obscurity. LIT., *obscuritas, tenebrae (-arum, plur.)*; see also DARKNESS. TRANSF., **(1)** of style, etc., *obscuritas, oratio involuta, perplexa*, etc. **(2)** of birth, *obscuritas, humilitas*.
obsequies; see FUNERAL.
obsequious, *(nimis) obsequens*: an — friend, *adsentator*.
obsequiousness, *obsequentia*.
observance, *mos* (= habit), *ritus (-ūs*; = usage), *conservatio* (= maintenance): religious —, *cultus (-ūs) deorum*.
observant, *attentus* (= attentive): — of, *diligens*, with genit.
observation. (1) = the act of observing, *observatio, animadversio, notatio*: power of —, *ingenii acumen* or *acies, sagacitas*. **(2)** = remark, *dictum*; see also REMARK.
observatory, *specula*.
observe. (1) = to watch, notice, *observare, animadvertere, spectare, contemplari, considerare*: to — the flight of birds (as an omen), *auspicari*; to — the sky, in gen. for any omen, *de caelo servare*. **(2)** = to keep to, maintain, *(ob)servare, conservare*. **(3)** see REMARK.
observer, *spectator* (with f. *spectatrix*), *speculator* (with f. *speculatrix*), *animadversor*: an acute —, *homo acutus, sagax*.
obsolete, *obsoletus*; sometimes rendered by phrase, e.g.: — words, *verba ab usu cotidiani sermonis iam diu intermissa* (Cic.); to become —, *obsolescere*.
obstacle, *impedimentum, obex* (= a barrier); often to be rendered by verb.
obstinate, *pertinax, pervicax, obstinatus, offirmatus*: an — illness, *morbus longinquus* (= long).
obstinately, *pertinaciter, pervicaciter, obstinate, obstinato animo*.
obstinacy, *pertinacia, pervicacia, obstinatio, animus obstinatus*.
obstreperous, *tumultuosus*.
obstruct, *obstruere, obsaepire, obstare* (with dat.), *officere* (with dat.); see also HINDER, OPPOSE.
obstruction, *impedimentum, obstructio*; see also OBSTACLE.
obstructive, render by verb.
obstructor, *intercessor*.
obtain, v. (1) transit. *adipisci* (after effort), *consequi* (after effort), *nancisci* (esp. by

chance), *potiri* (with genit. or abl.): to — in addition, *adquirere*; to — by asking, *impetrare, exorare*; to — favour, *gratiam sibi conciliare*; to — the support of (at elections, etc.), *ferre*; to — an audience, *ad conloquium admitti*. **(2)** intransit.; see PREVAIL.
obtaining, subst. *adeptio*; or render by verb.
obtrude, *ingerere, inculcare*.
obtuse, *hebes, obtusus, retusus*.
obviate, *(rei,* dat.) *occurrere* or *obviam ire, (rem) praecavere*.
obvious, *apertus, manifestus, perspicuus*.
obviously, *aperte, manifesto, perspicue*.
occasion, subst. **(1)** = time, *tempus*: for the —, *ad tempus*; on that —, *tum*. **(2)** = suitable time, opportunity, *occasio*: to give — for criticism, *ansam reprehensionis* (or *ad reprehendendum) dare*; to rise to the —, *occasione uti*; to fail to rise to the —, *occasioni deesse*.
occasion, v. *auctorem esse rei* (genit.), *creare* (= to give rise to), *movēre* (= to excite, e.g. laughter, *risum*); or render by subst. with *dare*; see also OCCASION, subst.
occasional; see OCCASIONALLY.
occasionally, *raro* (= seldom); *interdum, aliquando* (= sometimes); *occasione datā, per occasionem* (= as opportunity arises).
occident; see WEST.
occiput, *occipitium* (Plin.), or render by phrase, such as *aversa pars capitis*.
occult, *occultus*; see also ABSTRUSE, OBSCURE.
occupancy, *possessio*.
occupation. (1) = taking, *occupatio*. **(2)** = business pursuit, *occupatio, negotium, quaestus (-ūs*; profitable).
occupy. (1) = to take possession of, *capere, occupare*: to — beforehand, *praeoccupare*. **(2)** = to hold, *habēre, tenēre, obtinēre, possidēre*. **(3)** = to engage the time or attention of, *occupare, tenēre, detinēre*; pass.: to be occupied with a matter, *in re versari*.
occur. (1) = to come into one's mind, render by *in mentem homini venit* (with the matter as subject, or else in genit.), *subit (animum), succurrit, occurrit, incidit (in mentem)*. **(2)** of passages in books, *reperiri* (= to be found), *esse in oratione, apud scriptorem*, etc. **(3)** = to happen, *fieri, incidere, accidere*.
occurrence, *casus (-ūs), res (gesta)*.
ocean, *oceanus*.
ochre, *ochra* (Plin.).
octagon, *octogonum* (Vitr.).
octagonal, *octogonos* (Vitr.).
octave, *diapāson* (Vitr.).
October, *(mensis) October*.
octogenarian, *homo octoginta annos natus*.
ocular, render by *oculus*; see EYE.
oculist, *ocularius medicus* (Cels.); or render by phrase.
odd. (1) = not even, *impar*. **(2)** = remaining, left over: — moments, *tempora subsiciva*. **(3)** see STRANGE, EXTRAORDINARY.
oddity, oddness; see STRANGENESS.
odds, *pignus (-ŏris,* n.: = wager, stake): to be at —, to — to disagree, *dissentire, dissidēre*.
ode, *carmen*; see also SONG, POEM.
Oder, river, *Viadua*.
odious, *odiosus, invisus, invidiosus* (= exciting bad feeling): to be — to a person, *homini esse odio* or *in odio*.
odiously, *odiose*.

[775]

odiousness, *foeditas* (= foulness).

odium, *invidia*: causing —, *invidiosus*.

odoriferous, odorous, *suaveolens, odorus, odorifer, odoratus* (all poet.).

odour, *odor*; fig.; see REPUTE.

Odyssey, *Odyssēa*.

of, usually rendered by the genitive; sometimes by a subst. in apposition to another subst. (e.g.: the city of Rome, *urbs Roma*); of = composed of, is rendered by *ex* (poet. *de*) or special adj. (e.g.: a basin of marble, *labrum ex* (*de*) *marmore factum, labrum marmoreum*); of = about, concerning, *de* with abl.

off, adv. often rendered by compound verbs in *ab-* (*au-*), *de-*, *ex-*: far —, *longe* or *procul*; to be far —, *longe abesse*; to be well —, *abundare*.

off, prep. (**1**) = detached from, not on, *extra* (with acc.; = outside, away from), *e* or *ex* (= out of); — duty, *otiosus*. (**2**) = detached from, but near to, perhaps *contra* (= opposite): an island lying — Alexandria, *insula obiecta Alexandreae* (dat.: Caes.).

offal; see REFUSE, subst.

offence. (**1**) = displeasure, *offensio, offensa*: to give —, *offendĕre*; to take —, *offendi.* (**2**) = a fault, *peccatum, delictum, noxa.*

offend. (**1**) = to hurt, displease, *offendĕre, laedĕre*: to be —ed, *aegre* or *moleste ferre*; to have in it something which —s, *habēre aliquid offensionis.* (**2**) = to commit an offence, *peccare.*

offender, *peccans* (Nep., Sen.); or render by verb (e.g. *qui deliquit*).

offensive. (**1**) = giving offence, *odiosus molestus, gravis, foedus*; or render by verb. (**2**) opp. to defensive, render by phrase *bellum inferre* or by *occupare* (= to anticipate) or by *ultro* (= without provocation).

offensively, *odiose.*

offensiveness, render by adj.

offer, subst. *condicio* (also — an — of marriage); or render by verb.

offer, v. (**1**) transit. *offerre, profiteri* (esp. help, services, etc.), *praebēre, porrigĕre* (= to hold out): to — violence to a person, *vim homini adferre*; to — battle to the enemy, *copiam pugnandi hostibus facĕre*; to — sacrifice, *sacrificare, sacra* or *sacrificium facĕre.* (**2**) intransit. = to present itself, *offerri, dari, incidĕre.*

offering, *donum*; see also SACRIFICE.

office. (**1**) = any duty or function, *munus* (*-eris*, n.), *officium, partes* (*-ium*, plur.). (**2**) = official position, *magistratus* (*-ūs*: = magistracy), *honor, provincia.* (**3**) a good —, = a kindness, *beneficium, officium.* (**4**) = place of business, *tabularium* (= record-office).

officer, official, subst., in gen. *praefectus*: an army —, perhaps *tribunus militum* or *centurio*; a naval —, *classis praefectus*; a (high) state —, *magistratus* (*-ūs*); a minor —, *minister.*

official, adj. *publicus* (= of the state).

officially, *publice.*

officiate *munere* or *officio fungi*: at a religious ceremony, *operari, sacrificare.*

officious, *molestus, sedulus* (poet.).

officiously, *moleste.*

officiousness, *sedulitas* (Hor.); or render by phrase, such as *nimium studium.*

offing, (*mare*) *altum.*

offscourings, *purgamenta* (*-orum*, plur.).

offspring, *progenies, stirps, proles* (poet.), *liberi* (*-orum*, plur.: = children).

oft, often, *saepe, saepenumero, crebro* (= repeatedly); sometimes rendered by the adj. *creber* or *frequens* (e.g.: he was — in Rome, *erat Romae frequens*) or by frequentative verbs (e.g.: to read —, *lectitare*): how —? *quotie(n)s?*; so —, *totie(n)s.*

ogle, *oculis limis intueri* or *adspicĕre* (Pl., Quint.).

ogre, *larva* (Pl.).

oh! see O !

oil, subst. *oleum*; of or for —, adj. *olearius.*

oil, v. *oleo ungĕre* or *perfundĕre.*

oil-seller, *olearius* (Pl.).

oily, *oleaceus* (Plin.), *oleosus* (Plin.).

ointment, *unguentum*: — for the eyes, *collyrium* (Hor.).

old. (**1**) in gen. = of long standing, not new, *vetus, vetustus, inveteratus*: — and worn out, *obsoletus*; an — soldier, *veteranus* (*miles*). (**2**) = of living beings = having lived long, *grandis* (*natu*), *senex, grandaevus* (poet.), *vetulus* (with a touch of pity or contempt): an — man, *senex, vetulus*; as a jovial form of address, — man ! — boy ! *mi vetule*; an — woman, *anus, anicula, vetula*; to grow —, *senescĕre*; to be eight years —, *octo annorum esse, octo annos natum esse, octo annos habēre.* (**3**) = no longer existing: of — times (often = good old), *antiquus, priscus, pristinus*; in the — days, *olim, quondam.*

old age, *senectus* (*-ūtis*): the grief or feebleness of — —, *senium.*

old-fashioned, *obsoletus, antiquus, priscus.*

olden, *priscus*; see OLD.

older, *grandior, maior* (*natu*).

oldest, *natu maximus.*

oligarchy, *paucorum potentia* or *dominatio, respublica quae paucorum potestate regitur.*

olive, (tree or fruit) *oliva, olea*: the wild — -tree, *oleastris* (Verg., Ov.); an — grove, *olivetum*; of the —, adj. *oleaginus* (Verg.).

Olympiad, *Olympias* (*-iadis*).

Olympic, adj. *Olympicus*: the — games, *Olympia* (*-orum*, plur.).

omelet, *laganum* (Hor.).

omen, *omen, auspicium.*

ominous, ominously, render by phrase such as *omen infaustum* or *triste* (= a bad omen).

omission, *praetermissio*; or render by verb.

omit, *omittĕre, praetermittĕre, praeterire, transire, intermittĕre* (for a time).

omnipotent, *omnipotens* (poet.).

omnipresent, render by phrase, such as *ubique praesens.*

omniscient, render by phrase, such as *omnia providēre et animadvertere.*

on, adv. *porro*; often rendered by compound verb in *pro-*: to go —, *pergĕre, procedĕre*; right — = all the way, *usque.*

on, prep. (**1**) of place, *in* with abl. (e.g.: on horseback, *in equo*); sometimes abl. alone (e.g.: on foot, *pedibus*; on land and sea, *terrā marique*). On a certain side = in a certain direction, is rendered by *a* (*ab*) with abl. (e.g.: on the front, *a fronte*); sometimes by abl. alone (e.g.: on the right, *dextrā*); on all sides, *undique.* See also ON TO. (**2**) of time: **a,** of time when, abl. alone (e.g.: on the fourth day, *quarto die*): **b** = immediately after, *e (ex)* with abl., or abl. absol. **(3)** of other relations: on = about, concerning, *de* with abl.; on account of, *propter* or *ob*, with acc.; on condition that, *ea lege ut*; to be on a person's side, *stare* or *facĕre cum homine*; on hand, *in manibus*; of playing on a musical instrument, abl. alone.

on to, prep. *in* with acc.

once. (1) as numeral, *semel*: — for all, *semel*; — more; see AGAIN; — or twice, *semel et iterum*; more than —, *semel ac saepius, non semel*; not (even) —, *ne semel quidem.* **(2)** = at one period, *aliquando* (past, pres., or fut.), *olim* (past, rarely fut.), *quondam* (past only). **(3)** in phrase, at —: **a** = at the same time, *simul, uno tempore*: **b** = immediately, *statim, ilico, continuo*: **c**, all at —; see SUDDENLY.

one. (1) as a numeral, in gen., *unus -a -um*: — of, *unus* with genit. or with *e (ex)* and abl.; — only, *unus, unicus*; — of two, *alter*; — or the other of two, *alteruter*; each — (of two), *uterque*; each — (of more than two), *(unus) quisque*; — at a time, — by —, *singuli (-orum, plur.)* or adv. *singillatim*; — or two, *unus vel (or aut) alter*; not (even) —, *ne unus quidem*; more than —, *non unus, plus uno, plus quam unus*; — and all, *omnes, cuncti, universi* (plur.). **(2)** — and the same, stressing identity, *idem*; it is all — to me, *nihil meā interest.* **(3)** indef. = a person, any individual, *homo,* or rendered by verb in first pers. plur. or in second sing. (esp. subj.), or by impers. verb or impers. pass. (e.g.: — sees, *videmus*; — can, *possis*; — may, *licet*; — lives, *vivitur*: — who, *is qui*; — . . . (but) another, *alius . . . alius*; — another (of reciprocal action, feeling, etc.), render by *inter* with acc. of plur. pron. *(inter nos,* etc.) or by *alius* (or *alter*) used in different cases *(alius alium amat)*; — day, *aliquando*; at — time . . . at another time, *modo . . . modo.*

one-eyed, *luscus, altero oculo captus.*

onerous, *gravis.*

oneself, in apposition with subject, *ipse*; as reflexive, *se* (or other pronoun, according to the person used).

one-sided, *inaequalis, iniquus, impar.*

onion, *caepa* or *caepe* (poet.).

only, adj. *unus, unicus, solus, singularis.*

only, adv. *solum, tantum, dumtaxat, modo* (esp. after *si* and *dum,* and with imperatives); sometimes *non nisi* or *nihil nisi*: not — . . . but also, *non solum* (or *modo*) . . . *sed* (or *verum*) *etiam*; not — not . . . but not even . . . , *non modo (non)* . . . *sed ne . . . quidem.*

onset, onslaught, *impetus (-ūs), incursio, incursus (-ūs.).*

onward; see ON, adv.

onyx, *onyx* (Plin.).

ooze, subst. *uligo* (Verg., Tac.).

ooze, v. *manare, sudare* (poet.).

oozy, *uliginosus* (Varro, Plin.).

opal, *opalus* (Plin.).

opaque, render by phrase, such as *haud pellucidus.*

open, adj. LIT., **(1)** = not closed, *(ad)apertus, patens* (= wide —), *patulus*; *hians* (= wide —, yawning); half- —, *semiapertus*; to stand —, *patēre.* **(2)** = exposed, not shut in, *apertus, patens, propatulus*; an — space, *propatulum*; in the — air, *sub divo, sub Iove* (poet.). TRANSF., **(1)** = accessible: to lie —,

be —, *patēre* (with dat.). **(2)** = manifest, *apertus, manifestus, clarus.* **(3)** = candid, *apertus, simplex, candidus.* **(4)** of questions = undecided, *integer*: it is an — question, *ambigitur, adhuc sub iudice lis est* (Hor.).

open, v. **(1)** transit. LIT., *aperire, patefacĕre, reserare* (poet.), *recludĕre* (poet.), *pandĕre* (poet.). In particular phrases: to — a book, *librum (e)volvere, volumen explicare*; to — a letter, *epistulam aperire, resignare, solvĕre*; to — one's mouth, *hiscĕre*; to — a vein, *venam incidĕre.* TRANSF., **a**, to — formally (of places of worship, etc.), *inaugurare, consecrare, dedicare*; less formally, to — a school, shop (i.e. begin business there), *ludum, tabernam aperire*: **b**, of abstract things = to disclose, *aperire, patefacere*; see also EXPLAIN and BEGIN. **(2)** intransit. *aperiri, se aperire, patefieri, pandi* (poet.), *discedĕre* (of. heaven, the earth, etc.), *dehiscĕre* (= to gape —): to — again (of wounds), *recrudescĕre*; to — out (e.g. of a plain), *patescĕre.*

opening. (1) as an act, render by verb. **(2)** = aperture, *foramen, fenestra.* **(3)** the — of a church, etc., *consecratio, dedicatio.* **(4)** = opportunity, *occasio, opportunitas, ansa.* **(5)** = beginning, *initium, exordium.*

openly, *apertē, palam, manifesto.*

openness, *animus simplex* or *candidus.*

opera, render by *fabula.*

operate. (1) transit.; see USE. **(2)** intransit., in gen., *vim* or *effectum habēre*; in war, *rem agĕre* or *gerĕre*; in surgery, *secare* (= to cut), *scalpellum admovēre* (Cels.).

operation. (1) = the act of doing, *effectio.* **(2)** = an act done or to be done, *res (gesta* or *gerenda)*: a business —, *negotium*; in war, to draw up a plan of —s, *rei gerendae ordinem componĕre, totius belli rationem describĕre*; in surgery, render by verb; see OPERATE.

operative, adj. *efficax.*

ophthalmia, *oculorum inflammatio* (Cels.), *lippitudo* (Cels.).

opiate, *medicamentum somnificum* (Plin.).

opine, *opinari, arbitrari*; see also THINK.

opinion, *opinio*: a considered —, *iudicium, sententia* (esp. when officially expressed); general or public —, *(hominum* or *omnium) opinio* or *existimatio* (esp. with objective genit.); a rooted —, *opinio confirmata* or *inveterata*; an erroneous —, *opinio falsa, opinionis error*; to hold as one's —, *opinari, sentire*; to give as one's —, *censēre*; in my —, *ut mea fert opinio, meā sententiā, meo iudicio, me iudice, ut mihi quidem videtur*; I express my —freely, *sententiam meam aperio*; to give a legal —, *(de iure) respondēre.*

opinionated, render by phrase, such as *opinione sua nimium fretus.*

opium, *opium* or *opion* (Plin.).

opponent, *adversarius*; in a lawcourt: my —, *iste.*

opportune, *opportunus, commodus* (= convenient), *idoneus* (= suitable).

opportunely, *(per)opportune, commode.*

opportuneness, *opportunitas, commoditas.*

opportunity, *occasio, facultas, copia, potestas*: to give an —, *(rei,* genit., *homini) occasionem dare* or *praebēre, facultatem dare, potestatem* or *copiam facere*; given the —, *per occasionem, occasione datā* or *oblatā*; to meet with an —, *occasionem nancisci*; to seize an —, *occasionem* *adripĕre*; to avail oneself of an —, *occasione uti*; to lose an —, *occasioni deesse, occasionem amittĕre, praetermittĕre, dimittĕre*.

oppose. (1) = to set up a person or thing against another, *opponĕre, obicĕre*. (2) = to resist, counter, fight against, (*homini* or *rei*, dat.) *adversari, repugnare, resistĕre, obsistĕre, obstare*.

opposed, *adversus, adversarius, contrarius* (with dat.).

opposite adj. LIT., of physical position, *adversus, oppositus, contrarius*: — to (or —), as prep., *contra* (with acc.), *e regione* (with genit. or dat.). TRANSF., *adversarius, contrarius*.

opposition. (1) = the act of opposing, render by verb. (2) = difference, *repugnantia, discrepantia*. (3) = a body of opponents, *factio adversa* or *adversaria*.

oppress, *premĕre, opprimĕre, vexare, adfligĕre*.

oppression, *vexatio, iniuria*.

oppressive, *molestus, gravis, iniquus* (= unjust).

oppressively, *moleste, graviter, inique*.

oppressor, *tyrannus*; or render by verb.

opprobrious, *probrosus, turpis*.

opprobrium, *dedecus, opprobrium*.

optative, adj.: the — mood, *modus optativus* (grammat. t. t.).

optical, adj.: an — illusion, *mendacium oculorum*.

optics, *optice* (*-es*, f.: Vitr.).

option, *optio*; see also CHOICE.

optional, render by phrase, such as *optionem dare, potestatem facere, permittĕre*.

opulence, *opulentia* (Sall.); see also RICHES, WEALTH.

opulent, *opulentus*; see also RICH.

or. (1) in statements, commands, etc., to mark a sharp or important distinction, *aut*; less strong (= — perhaps, — if you like), *vel, -ve*: — at least, *aut certe, vel certe*; — else, — otherwise, *aut, vel*; — rather, *vel* (*potius*); in an alternative conditional clause, whether . . . or . . . , *sive* (or *seu*) . . . *sive* (or *seu*); either . . . or, *aut* . . . *aut* (i.e. definitely one of two things, and not both), *vel* . . . *vel* (less strong); with a negative, not . . . or, *neque* (or *nec*) . . . *neque* (or *nec*). (2) in alternative questions, *an*, more rarely *anne* or *ne*; or not, in alternative direct questions, *an non* (*annon*); in alternative indirect questions, *necne*.

oracle, *oraculum, sors, responsum* (*oraculi* or *sortium*): to consult an —, *oraculum consulĕre*; to ask an — for an answer, *oraculum petĕre* (*a deo, a Dodona*, etc.); to give an — or oracular response, *oraculum dare* or *edĕre, responsum dare, respondĕre*.

oracular; see ORACLE.

oral, render by verb *dicĕre* or *loqui* (= to speak) or by adj. *praesens* (= present).

Orange (the city), *Arausio*.

oration, *oratio, contio* (to a popular meeting): to deliver an —, *orationem* (or *contionem*) *habēre*.

orator, *orator*.

oratorical, *oratorius*.

oratory, *doctrina dicendi, vis dicendi, ars oratoria* (Quint.), *rhetorica*; sometimes *eloquentia* (= eloquence).

orb, *globus, sphaera, orbis*.

orbit, *orbis, circulus, ambitus* (*-ūs*).

orchard, *pomarium*.

orchestra. (1) = part of a theatre, *orchestra* (occupied in fact by any senators present in the audience: Juv., Suet.). (2) = a band of musicians, *symphonia, symphoniaci* (*-orum*, plur.).

orchid, *orchis* (Plin.).

ordain. (1) see DECREE, APPOINT, INSTITUTE. (2) to — as deacon or priest, *in sacerdotum numerum recipĕre, ordinare* (eccl.).

ordeal; see DANGER, TRIAL.

order. (1) = methodical arrangement, *ordo*: alphabetical —, *litterarum ordo*; chronological —, *temporum ordo*; to arrange in —, *ordinare, disponĕre, digerĕre*; in —, *ordine, ex ordine, per ordinem*; out of — (= in an exceptional way), *extra ordinem*; good — (= restraint, regular behaviour, etc.), *ordo, modus, modestia, disciplina*; to keep a person in —, *hominem disciplinā coercēre, in officio continēre*. (2) = class, rank, group, *ordo* (e.g. *senatorius, equestris*); = fraternity, *conlegium* (= corporation); in architecture, *genus* (*-eris*, n.: Vitr.). (3) = a command, *iussum, mandatum, imperatum* (military), *edictum* (= decree): by — of the consul, *consulis iussu* (abl.); without —s from the consul, *iniussu consulis*; to give —s; see ORDER, v. (4) in phrase, in — that, introducing a final clause; render by *ut* with subj. (neg. *nē*), by a relative with subj., by *ad* with acc. of gerund or gerundive, by *causā* after genit. of gerund or gerundive or (after verb of motion) by supine in *-um*.

order, v. (1) = to arrange, *ordinare, componĕre, digerĕre, disponĕre*. (2) = to command, *iubēre, imperare, edicĕre*. (3) = to command that something be produced, to demand, *imperare* (with acc.).

orderly, subst. *minister*.

orderly, adj. (1) = well-arranged, *compositus, dispositus*. (2) = well-behaved, *modestus* (= unassuming).

ordinal, adj.: an — number, *numerus ordinalis* (Gram.).

ordinance, *edictum*; see also DECREE, EDICT, RULE.

ordinarily, *ferme, fere, plerumque*.

ordinary, adj. (1) (= usual), *usitatus, cotidianus* or *quotidianus, communis, translaticius*. (2) = mediocre, *mediocris, vulgaris*.

ordination, *ordinatio* (eccl.).

ordnance; see ARTILLERY.

ordure, *stercus* (*-ŏris*, n.).

ore, *aes*.

oread, *oreas* (poet.).

organ, in gen.; see INSTRUMENT, MEANS: —s of the body, *corporis partes* or *membra*; the internal —s, *exta* (*-orum*, plur.); as a musical instrument, *organum* (Suet.).

organic, adj.: an — body, *animans, animal*; — disease, *vitium corporis*.

organism, *corporis compages*.

organization, *descriptio, temperatio*; or render by verb; political —, *reipublicae forma*.

organize, *ordinare, constituĕre, componĕre, describĕre, temperare, apparare*.

orgies; see REVELRY.

Orient, Oriental; see EAST, EASTERN.

orifice, *foramen, fenestra*.

origin. (1) in gen. = source, beginning, *origo, principium, initium, ortus* (*-ūs*), *fons*. (2) of persons = birth, descent, *origo*: of lowly —, *humili loco* or *genere natus*.

original, subst. = pattern, model, *exemplum*, *exemplar*.

original, adj. (1) = primary, *primus, principalis*; sometimes *antiquus, pristinus, priscus* (= ancient). (2) = one's own, *proprius* or (*sui*) *ipsius*; sometimes *novus* (= new).

originality, render by phrase such as *proprietas ingenii*.

originally, = at first, *primum, primo, initio, principio*.

originate. v. (1) transit.; see CREATE, PRODUCE, BEGIN. (2) intransit.: to — from a thing, *ab re* (*ex*)*oriri* or *proficisci, ex re fieri*.

originator, *auctor*.

orisons, *prĕces* (*-um*, plur.).

Orleans, *Cenabum*.

ornament, subst. *ornamentum, decus* (poet.): fig. an — of the state, *lumen* (or *decus*) *civitatis*.

ornament, v. (*ex*)*ornare, decorare*; see also ADORN.

ornamental, render by verb.

ornate, (*per*)*ornatus*: an — style, *genus orationis pictum et expolitum*.

ornately, *ornate*.

ornithology, render by reference to *aves* (*-ium*, plur. = birds).

orphan, *orbus* (subst. and adj.): to make an —, *orbare* (*parentibus*).

orthodox, *orthodoxus* (eccl.).

orthography, *recte scribendi scientia* or *ratio, orthographia* (Suet., Quint.).

oscillate. LIT., *agitari*. TRANSF., see DOUBT, HESITATE.

oscillation. LIT., *agitatio*. TRANSF., of the mind, *dubitatio*.

osier, subst. *vimen*.

osier, adj. *vimineus*.

osprey, *ossifragus* (Lucr., Plin.).

ossify, *in os mutari*.

ostensible, *simulatus, fictus* (= feigned).

ostensibly, *speciē* (abl.), *per speciem*.

ostentation, *iactatio, ostentatio, venditatio*.

ostentatious, *gloriosus, iactans*.

ostentatiously, *gloriose*.

ostler, *agaso*.

ostracism. LIT., at Athens, *testarum suffragia* (*-orum*, plur.: Nep.). TRANSF., in gen., render by *expellĕre*.

ostrich, *struthiocamelus* (Plin.).

other. (1) as adj. = different, *alius, diversus*. (2) as adj. and pron., *alius*: the — (of two individuals), *alter*; the —s (of two groups), *alteri* (plur.); the —s (= all the —s), *ceteri, reliqui*, sometimes *alii*; —s (= one's neighbours or fellow-creatures), *ceteri* (plur.), *alter* (sing.); — people's, belonging to another, adj., *alienus*; on the — hand, *contra, ex contrario, autem*.

otherwise. (1) = differently, *aliter, secus*. (2) = in other respects, *alioqui(n), cetera* (n. plur.), *ceteroqui(n)*. (3) = if not, else, *aliter, alioqui(n), si minus*.

otter, *lutra* or *lytra* (Plin.).

ottoman, *lectus*; see also COUCH.

ought, pron.; in statements, after neg., *hilum*; after *si, ne, nisi, num*, render by *quid*.

ought, v. render by gerund or gerundive (e.g. *virtus colenda est*, virtue — to be practised; *parendum est mihi*, I — to obey);

or by *debēre* (of any kind of obligation), with the agent as subject, and the action indicated by an infin.; or by *oportet* (impers.), with the agent in the acc. and the action indicated by infin. or subj.: — to have done, — to have been, etc., is expressed by past tense of *esse* with gerund(ive) or of *debēre* or *oportet* with pres. infin. (e.g.: I — to have gone, *ire debui*); see also MUST.

ounce, *uncia*: half- —, *semuncia*.

our, ours, *noster*: — people, *nostri* (*-orum*, plur.); of — country, *nostras*; —, = just mentioned, under discussion, *hic*.

ourselves; see WE, SELF.

ousel, *merula*.

out, adv. *foras* (of going out from inside), *foris* (of being or staying out), *extra*; often rendered by compound verbs in *e-* or *ex-*: — you go, *exi*.

out of, prep. (1) = away from, to the outside of, *e* or *ex* with abl., *extra* with acc., *de* with abl.: — doors, *foras*. (2) = outside, on the outside of, *extra* with acc.: — range, *extra teli iactum*. Fig.: to be — one's mind, *sui* or *mentis non compotem esse, alienatā mente esse*; to be — one's mind for joy, *laetitia ex(s)ultare, efferri*; — one's mind from anger, *prae iracundia non esse apud se*; — one's mind from fright, *metu exanimatum esse*. (3) = arising from, because of, *propter* with acc., *per* with acc., *a* or *ab* with abl., *e* or *ex* with abl.; often rendered by a participle with the abl., e.g.: — fear, *metu coactus*; — shame, *pudore adductus*.

outbid, *licitatione vincĕre*.

outbreak. (1) = act of breaking out, *eruptio*. (2) = beginning, *initium, principium*. (3) = a disturbance, *seditio*.

outcast, *exsul, extorris, profugus*.

outcry, *clamor, vociferatio, voces* (*-um*, plur.), *convicium*; expressing disapproval, *acclamatio, convicium*.

outdo, *superare, vincĕre*.

outer, *exterior*; see also OUTSIDE, OUTWARD.

outflank, *circumire, circumvenire*.

outgrow, render by phrase; e.g.: to — one's strength, *corpore maiorem quam pro viribus fieri*.

outhouse, *tugurium*.

outlandish, *peregrinus, barbarus*.

outlast, *diutius durare*, with *quam* or abl.

outlaw, subst. *proscriptus*.

outlaw, v. (*hominem*) *proscribĕre*, (*homini*) *aquā et igni interdicĕre*.

outlawry, *proscriptio, aquae et ignis interdictio*.

outlay, *sumptus* (*-ūs*), *impensa*.

outlet, *exitus* (*-ūs*), *egressus* (*-ūs*: Tac.), *effluvium* (Plin., Tac.), *emissarium*; see also MOUTH.

outline, subst. (*extrema*) *lineamenta* (*-orum*, plur.); as represented, in a sketch, etc., *adumbratio*.

outline, v. *describĕre, adumbrare*.

outlive, (*homini*) *superesse* or *superstitem esse*.

outlook. (1) of physical situation, render by *spectare ad* (= to look towards). (2) = prospects, *spes*. (3) = mental attitude, *animus*.

outlying, *longinquus*.

outnumber, *numero* or *multitudine superare, plures esse quam*.

outpost, *statio*.

outrage, subst. *iniuria, contumelia, indignitas, flagitium.*

outrage, v. *violare, vexare, iniuriā adficĕre.*

outrageous, *immanis, contumeliosus, immoderatus, indignus.*

outrageously, *indigne, immoderate.*

outride, *equitando superare.*

outrider, *praecursor*; or render by phrase.

outright. (1) = at once, *statim, ilico.* (2) = completely, *plane, prorsus, omnino.*

outrun, *cursu superare* or *vincĕre.*

outset, *initium*; see also BEGINNING.

outside, subst. = surface, *superficies* (Plin.); = outward appearance, *species*: on the —, *extrinsecus*; at the — (= at most), *summum.*

outside, adj. *exter* or *exterus, externus*; see also OUTER.

outside, adv. *extra, extrinsecus, foris* (with verbs of rest), *foras* (with verbs of motion).

outskirts; see SUBURB.

outspoken; see FRANK.

outspread, *patulus, passus.*

outstanding, *reliquus*; see also DEBT.

outstrip, (*cursu*) *superare* or *vincĕre, praevertĕre* (poet.).

outvote, *suffragiis vincĕre.*

outward, adj. *exter* or *exterus, externus*; — show, *species.*

outward, outwardly, adv. *extra, extrinsecus.*

outweigh, *praeponderare* (lit. and fig.; rare), *vincĕre, superare, potiorem* or *antiquiorem esse.*

outwit, *circumvenire*; see also DECEIVE.

outworks, *munimenta exteriora* (n. plur.).

oval, adj. *ovatus* (Plin.).

ovation, *ovatio* (= a Roman lesser triumph); fig.: to receive an —, *magnis clamoribus excipi.*

oven, *furnus* (Pl., Hor.).

over, adv. *super, insuper, supra*: to be — (= to remain), *superesse, superare*; — and done with, *confectus, peractus*; it is all — with us, *actum est de nobis*; — and — again, *identidem, etiam atque etiam*; —much, *praeter modum*; often rendered by compar., e.g. — timid, *timidior.*

over, prep. (1) = across, to (or on) the far side of, *super* or *trans*, with acc., *per* with acc. (of motion across); to make a bridge — a river, *pontem in flumine facĕre.* (2) = above, on top of, *super* or *supra*, with acc. (3) = more than, *super* with acc., *amplius* (with numerals), *plus quam.*

overawe, (*de*)*terrēre.*

overbalance, *praeponderare*; see also OUTWEIGH.

overbearing, *adrogans, insolens, superbus.*

overboard: to throw a thing —, *rei* (genit.) *iacturam facĕre*; to fall —, *in mare excidĕre.*

overcast, (of the sky) *nubilus* (Tib., Plin.).

overcharge, in money, *nimium exigĕre, nimio vendĕre*; see also OVERLOAD.

overcoat, *amiculum*; see also CLOAK.

overcome, (*de*)*vincĕre, superare.*

overdo: to — a thing, *nimium laborem in rem conferre, modum excedĕre in re.*

overdone, (*nimis*) *elaboratus.*

overdraw: to — an account, *aes alienum contrahĕre* or *conflare* (= to incur debt).

overdressed, render by phrase, such as *nimis splendide ornatus.*

overdrive, (*de*)*fatigare.*

overdue, *debitus*; see also OWING.

overeat, *nimis edĕre, helluari.*

overfill, *supra modum implēre.*

overflow, subst.; see FLOOD.

overflow, v. *redundare* (lit. and fig.), *effundi*: to — on to, *inundare*, with acc.

overgrown. (1) = covered over with foliage, etc., *obsitus.* (2) see HUGE, ENORMOUS.

overhang, *imminēre, impendēre.*

overhastily, *praepropere.*

overhasty, *praeproperus, praeceps.*

overhaul; see EXAMINE, INSPECT; also OVERTAKE.

overhead, adv. *supra, insuper*: from —, *desuper.*

overhear, *excipĕre, subauscultare, exaudire.*

overheat: to — oneself, *sudare* (= to perspire).

overjoyed, *laetitiā exsultans.*

overland, adv. *terrā* (opp. *mari*).

overlap, *imminēre, impendēre* (with dat. = to overhang).

overlay, = to spread over, *inducĕre, illinĕre* (poet.): to — with gold, *inaurare.*

overload, *nimis* or *nimio pondere onerare.*

overloaded, *nimis oneratus*: — with business, *negotiis obrutus.*

overlong, *praelongus, nimis longus.*

overlook. (1) = to watch or examine, (*ob*)*servare, inspicĕre, intuēri.* (2) = to command a view over, *prospicĕre* (Plin.), *intuēri* (Plin. L.). (3) = to pardon, (*rem homini*) *ignoscĕre* or *condonare*, (*rei*, genit., *homini*) *veniam dare*, (*in re*) *connivēre.* (4) = to miss, fail to notice, *praeterire, omittĕre, praetermittĕre.*

overmuch, adv. *nimis, nimium.*

overnight, adv. *vesperi* (= in the evening).

overplus; see SURPLUS.

overpower, *opprimĕre, superare, vincĕre, debellare.*

overpowering; see OVERWHELMING.

overrate, *nimis magni facĕre.*

overreach, *circumvenire, circumscribĕre*; see also CHEAT.

overripe, render by phrase, such as *qui iam maturitatem excessit.*

overrule, *vincĕre*; of providence, etc., *gubernare.*

overrun. (1) = to roam (destructively) over, (*per*)*vagari.*

overscrupulous, render by compar., such as *diligentior, religiosior.*

oversee, (*pro*)*curare.*

overseer, *custos*, (*pro*)*curator.*

overshadow, *obumbrare* (poet.), *inumbrare* (poet.), *officĕre* (with dat.).

oversight. (1) = failure to remember or notice, *error, erratum, incuria.* (2) = superintendence, *curatio, procuratio, cura.*

oversleep, *diutius dormire.*

overspread, *obducĕre, inducĕre.*

overstate; see EXAGGERATE.

overstrain, *nimis contendĕre.*

overt, *apertus, manifestus.*

overtake. (1) = to catch up with, *adsequi, consequi.* (2) = to surprise, *opprimĕre, deprehendĕre, supervenire* (with dat.).

overtask, render by phrase, such as *nimium facĕre cogĕre.*

overtax, render by phrase, such as *iniquis oneribus premĕre.*

overthrow, subst. *clades, ruina, excidium.*

overthrow, v. LIT., = to throw down, *deicĕre, adfligĕre, diruĕre.* TRANSF., = to destroy, shatter, suppress, *adfligĕre, evertĕre, subvertĕre, profligare, opprimĕre, perdĕre.*

overtop, *eminĕre, exstare* (both intransit., = to stand out); *superare, supereminĕre* (both transit. but poet.).

overture. (1) diplomatic, *condicio*: to make —s, *condiciones ferre, agere cum homine, hominem sollicitare* (for sinister purposes). (2) musical, *exordium* (= beginning, prelude).

overturn, *evertĕre, subvertĕre*; see also OVERTHROW.

overweening, *superbus, insolens.*

overwhelm, *obruĕre, opprimĕre, demergĕre, (sub)mergĕre.*

overwhelming, adj., render by verb.

overwork, subst. *labor immoderatus* or *nimius.*

overwrought, of persons = strained, *nimis intentus.*

overzealous, *nimis studiosus.*

owe, v. transit. *debēre (rem homini)*: to — much money, *aere alieno laborare* or *obrutum esse.*

owing; see DUE.

owing to, prep. *propter, ob, per,* with acc.: — you = thanks to you, *beneficio tuo, operā tuā*; it was — you that . . . not, *per te stetit quominus.*

owl, *ulula, noctua, strix, bubo* (all poet.): of an —, adj., *noctuinus* (Pl.).

own, in gen.: one's —, *proprius, suus*; my —, *meus*; your —, *tuus, vester*; his —, their —, *suus* if the owner is the subject of the clause or sentence, otherwise usually *ipsius, ipsorum*; emphatically: one's — private or special, *peculiaris*; of one's — household or country, *domesticus.*

own, v. (1) = to confess, *fatēri, confitēri*; see also CONFESS. (2) = possess, *habēre, tenēre, possidēre*; see also POSSESS.

owner, *possessor, dominus*: to be the — of a thing, *rem possidēre.*

ownership, *dominium.*

ox, *bos*; of oxen, adj., *bubulus*; a driver of oxen, *bubulcus.*

oxherd, *armentarius* (Verg.).

oyster, *ostrea, ostreum* (poet.).

oyster-bed, *ostrearium* (Plin.).

oyster-shell, *ostreae testa.*

P

pabulum, *pabulum*; see also FOOD.

pace, subst. (1) = a step, *gradus (-ūs), passus (-ūs), gressus (-ūs*: poet.). (2) as a measure = 5 Roman feet, *passus (-ūs)*. (3) = speed, in gen., *velocitas*; of walking or marching, *gradus (-ūs)*: at a smart or quick —, *pleno* or *citato gradu*; to quicken or mend one's —, *gradum addĕre.*

pace, v. (1) transit.: **a** = to go along, render by intransit. verb with *per* and acc.: **b** = to measure by pacing, *passibus metiri.* (2) intransit. *gradi, incedĕre, ambulare, spatiari*; see also MARCH, WALK.

pacific, *pacificus, pacifer* (poet.); or render by *pacis* = of peace.

pacification, *pacificatio, compositio, pax.*

pacificator, *pacificator, pacis auctor, pacis reconciliator.*

pacify, *placare* (of individuals), *pacare* (of countries and peoples), *sedare* (usually of abstract things), *lenire, componĕre* (= to reconcile).

pack, subst. (1) = bundle, *sarcina, sarcinula* (Juv.). (2) = crowd, *turba, grex.* (3) a — of dogs, *canes (-um,* plur.).

pack, v. (1) to — tightly, *stipare, co(artare).* (2) to — up, of luggage, etc., *conligĕre, componĕre.* (3) to — a jury, a meeting, etc., render by phrase, such as *suos inter iudices introducĕre.*

packet, *fasciculus.*

pack-horse, *equus clitellarius.*

pack-saddle, *clitellae (-arum,* plur.).

pack-thread, *linea.*

pact, *pactio, pactum, foedus (-eris,* n.).

pad; see CUSHION.

paddle, subst. *remus*; see also OAR.

paddle, v.: to — a boat, *lintrem remo impellĕre.*

padlock, render by *claustra (-orum,* plur.).

Padua, *Patavium.*

paean, *paean* (poet.).

pagan, *paganus* (eccl.).

page, (1) a — -boy, *puer*; a — at court, *puer regius.* (2) of a book, *pagina.*

pageant, *spectaculum* (= show), *pompa* (= procession).

pagoda, *templum* or *aedes* (= temple).

pail, *hama* (Plin. L., Juv.), *situla* (Pl.).

pain, subst. *dolor* (in gen. of body and mind): violent —, *cruciatus (-ūs*; of body and mind); to cause —, *dolorem facĕre*; to feel —, *dolēre, dolore adfici.*

pain, v. transit. *dolore adficĕre, cruciare, angĕre*; pass.: to be —ed (= to be grieved), *dolēre, rem aegre ferre.*

painful, *gravis, acerbus, molestus*: it is — to remember, *piget recordari.*

painfully, *graviter, acerbe, dolenter, summo* or *magno cum dolore.*

painless, *sine dolore, doloris expers.*

painlessness, *indolentia,* or render by phrase.

pains, = exertion, *opera, labor, studium, negotium*: to take — over a thing, *rei* (dat.) *operam dare, in re operam consumĕre, in re elaborare, contendĕre, (e)niti.*

painstaking, *operosus, sedulus, laboriosus.*

paint, subst. *pigmentum, fucus* (esp. = red —).

paint, v. (1) as an artist, *pingĕre*: to — a person (i.e. his portrait), *pingĕre, depingĕre* (Nep., Prop.). (2) = to colour, *inficĕre, inducĕre* (Plin.), *fucare* (Verg., Hor., Tac.): to — in different colours, *coloribus distinguĕre*; to — with cosmetics, *pingĕre* (Pl.), *fucare* (Ov., Quint.).

paint-brush, *penicillus.*

painter, *pictor*: a house- —, *qui (parietes,* etc.) *colore inducit.*

painting, (1) as an art, *pictura, ars pingendi.* (2) as a work of art, *tabula (picta), pictura.*

pair, subst. *par*: of horses or oxen, *iugum*; often rendered by *bini* (plur. = two at a time), sometimes by *uterque* (= each) or *ambo* (plur. = both).

pair, v. (1) transit. *(con)iungĕre.* (2) intransit. *(con)iungi, coire* (Lucr., Ov.; = to cohabit).

palace, *domus (-ūs) regia* or simply *regia*; *aedes (-ium,* plur.) *regiae*; *palatium* only in poetry and late prose.

palatable, *iucundi saporis* (= of pleasant taste), *iucundus, suavis, dulcis.*

palatal, *palatilis* (Gram.).

palate, *palatum*: a keen —, *subtile palatum* (Hor.); he has a keen —, *sapit ei palatum* (Cic.).

palatial, *regius.*

palaver, *nugae* (*-arum*, plur.); see also NON-SENSE.

pale, subst. (1) = a stake, *palus, vallus, sudis.* (2) = a hedge, fence, boundary, *saepes, limes* (Tac.).

pale, adj. *pallidus, luridus, albus* (= white), *decolor* (= discoloured; poet.): to be —, *pallēre*; to grow —, *exalbescēre.*

pale, v.; see PALE, adj.

paleness, *pallor.*

Palermo, *Panormus.*

palfrey, *equus* or *caballus.*

palimpsest, *palimpsestus.*

palinode, *palinodia* (better written as Greek παλινῳδία).

palisade, *vallum, vallus*: surround with a —, *vallo munire* or *cingēre* or *circumdare, vallare.*

pall, subst., in gen. = cloak, *pallium*; as a covering over the dead, render by *tegumentum* or *involucrum feretri.*

pall, v. *fastidium movere*; or render by *taedet.*

pallet, = a small bed, *lectulus, grabatus.*

palliasse, *stramentum* (Verg., Hor.).

palliate, *excusare, extenuare*; see also EXCUSE.

palliation, render by verb.

pallid; see PALE.

pallor, *pallor.*

palm, subst. (1) of the hand, *palma.* (2) the tree, *palma*; also used of a palm-branch worn in token of victory: adorned with —, *palmatus.*

palm, v.: to — off, *imponēre, supponēre*; to — off lies on a person, *centones homini sarcire.*

palmary, *palmaris.*

palmer; see PILGRIM.

palmistry, either use χειρομαντεία in Greek characters, or phrase such as *ars eorum qui manuum lineamenta perscrutantur.*

palmy, *florens* (= flourishing), *optimus* (= best).

palpable. (1) = tangible, *tractabilis, quod tangi* (or *sentiri*) *potest.* (2) in gen. = obvious, evident, *manifestus, evidens, apertus.*

palpably, *manifesto, aperte.*

palpitate, *palpitare, micare.*

palpitation, *palpitatio* (Plin.).

palsy; see PARALYSIS.

paltry, *vilis, minutus, pusillus.*

pamper, (*homini*) *nimis indulgēre.*

pamphlet, *libellus.*

pamphleteer, *libellorum scriptor*

pan, *patina*: a small —, *patella*; a frying- —, *sartago* (Plin., Juv.).

panacea, *panchrestum medicamentum*; as a plant = heal-all, *panacea* (Verg.).

pancake, *laganum* (Hor.), *placenta* (Hor.).

pander, subst. *leno.*

pander, v. *lenocinari* (lit. and fig.); see also FLATTER, INDULGE.

pane, of glass; render by *vitrum* (= glass) or by phrase such as *vitreum quadratum* (= glass square).

panegyric, *laudatio, laus, laudes.*

panegyrist, *laudator* (with f., *laudatrix*), *praedicator.*

panel, of a door, *tympanum* (Vitr.): a panelled ceiling, *lacunar, laquearia* (*-ium*, plur.: Verg.,

Sen.); fig.: a — of experts, advisers, etc., *consilium.*

pang, *dolor, doloris stimulus.*

panic, subst. *pavor, terror.*

panic, v. *pavēre.*

panic-stricken, *pavidus.*

pannier, *clitellae* (*-arum*, plur.).

panoply; see ARMOUR.

panorama; see PROSPECT, VIEW.

pant, v. LIT., to — for breath, *anhelare.* TRANSF., to — for, *sitire, concupiscēre.*

pantaloon, *sannio, scurra, mimus.*

pantheism render by phrase, such as *deum in universā rerum naturā situm esse credēre.*

panther, *panthēra.*

panting, subst. *anhelitus* (*-ūs*).

pantomime, *mimus.*

pantry, *cella penaria.*

pap. (1) = of the breast, *papilla* (Plin.), *mamilla* (Juv.); see also BREAST. (2) = soft food for infants, *puls.*

papa, *pater*; see also FATHER.

papacy, *papatus* (eccl.).

papal, *papalis* (eccl.).

paper, subst. (1) as material for writing on, *charta*: a piece or sheet of —, *chartula, scida* (*scheda*): — made of papyrus, *papyrus* (Mart., Juv.). (2) already written on: a — for reading, *charta, scriptum, libellus*; public —s, *tabulae publicae*; a news—, *acta* (*diurna*).

paper, adj. *chartaceus* (Leg.).

papyrus, *papyrus* or *papyrum* (Plin., Mart.).

par: on a — with, *aequus, aequalis, par*, with dat.

parable, *parabola* (Quint.); sometimes rendered by *similitudo* (= analogy, simile) or *translatio* (= metaphor).

parabolical, parabolically, *per similitudinem.*

parade, subst. (1) milit. t. t., *decursus* (*-ūs*), *decursio* (Suet.). (2) = show, *ostentatio, apparatus* (*-ūs*); see also SHOW, DISPLAY.

parade, v. (1) transit. = to display, *ostentare.* (2) intransit., of troops, *decurrēre.*

paradigm, *paradigma* (*-atis*, n.; grammat. t. t.).

paradise, *paradisus* (eccl.), *sedes beatorum* or *piorum.*

paradox, in sing., render by phrase, such as *quod est admirabile contraque opinionem omnium*; in plur., *admirabilia* (*-ium*, n. plur. as philosoph. t. t.).

paradoxical; see PARADOX.

paragon, *specimen*; see also PATTERN.

paragraph, *caput* (= section).

parallel, subst.; see MATCH or COMPARISON.

parallel, adj. LIT., geometrically, *parallelos* or *parallelus* (Vitr.): — to, *e regione*, with genit. or dat. TRANSF., = similar, corresponding, *par*, (*con*)*similis, congruens.*

parallel, v.; see MATCH or COMPARE.

paralyse, fig. = weaken, *debilitare, enervare, adfligēre.*

paralysed. LIT., *membris* (or *pede, manu*, etc.) *captus* or *debilis.* TRANSF., *debilis, torpens, torpidus*: to be —, *torpēre*; to become —, (*ob*)*torpescēre.*

paralysis. LIT., *paralysis* (Plin.); or render by phrase, such as *nervorum remissio.* TRANSF., *debilitas, torpedo* (Sall., Tac.).

paralytic, *paralyticus* (Plin.).

paramount, *summus, antiquissimus*; see also CHIEF, SUPREME.

paramour, male, *adulter*; female, *paelex* (*pellex*).
parapet, *pluteus, lorica.*
paraphernalia, *apparatus* (*-ūs*).
paraphrase, subst. *interpretatio, paraphrasis* (Quint.).
paraphrase, v. *interpretari, explicare, circuitu verborum ostendĕre* (Quint.).
parasite, *parasitus* (and f. *parasita*; = a person who dines out at one's expense); *adsecula* (= a hanger-on in general).
parasitic, *parasiticus* (Pl.).
parasol, *umbella* (Juv.), *umbraculum* (Tib., 'Ov.).
parboiled, *semicoctus* (Plin.).
parcel. (1) = package, *fascis* (Verg., Tac.), *fasciculus,* (2) see PART, PORTION.
parcel out, v. *partiri, dividĕre, distribuĕre.*
parch, *torrēre,* (*ex*)*urĕre.*
parched, *aridus, torridus.*
parchment, *membrana.*
pardon, subst. *venia* (*rei,* genit.).
pardon, v.: to — a person for doing a thing, *homini rem ignoscĕre* or *condonare* or *concedĕre, homini veniam rei* (genit.) *dare.*
pardonable, *excusabilis* (Ov.); or render by verb.
pare, (*re*)*secare, subsecare* (Ov.).
parings, *praesegmina* (*-um,* plur.: Pl., Plin.).
parent, *parens.*
parentage, *stirps, genus* (*-ĕris,* n.).
parental, render by the genit. *parentum,* e.g.: — love, *parentum amor.*
parenthesis, *interpositio, interclusio* (cf. *quam nos interpositionem vel interclusionem dicimus, Graeci παρένθεσιν vocant, dum continuationi sermonis medius sensus intervenit,* Quint.).
parenthetical, adj.: a — remark, *verba* (*orationi*) *interposita.*
parhelion, *parelion* (Sen.); or render by phrase, such as *sol alter* or *imago solis.*
pariah, fig., render by phrase, such as *unus e faece populi.*
Paris, *Lutetia.*
parish, *paroecia* or *parochia* (eccl.).
parity; see EQUALITY.
park, subst. *vivarium* (= preserve: Plin.), *horti* (*-orum,* plur. = pleasure-gardens), *viridarium* (= garden planted with trees).
parley, subst. *conloquium, sermo.*
parley, v. *conloqui, sermones* or *consilia conferre, agĕre, disceptare.*
parliament, render by *senatus* (*-ūs*): an act of —, *senatūs consultum;* house of —, *curia;* member of —, *senator.*
parliamentary, *senatorius, quod ad senatum pertinet.*
parlour; see ROOM.
parochial, *parochialis* (eccl.).
parody, subst. *ridicula imitatio;* or perhaps introduce the Greek παρῳδία.
parole, *fides* (*data*).
paroxysm. LIT., *febris accessio* (Cels.) or *accessus* (*-ūs*). TRANSF., *vis, impetus* (*-ūs*).
parricidal; see MURDEROUS.
parricide. (1) as a person, *parricida, patris sui interfector.* (2) as an act, *parricidium.*
parrot, *psittacus* (Ov., Plin.).
parry, v. transit. = to check, ward off, *repellĕre, propulsare, defendĕre, arcēre.*
parse, render by phrase, such as *quae sint singula verba explicare.*

parsimonious, *parcus, sordidus, tenax, restrictus, malignus* (Pl., Hor.).
parsimoniously, *parce, sordide* (Suet., Plin. L.), *restricte, maligne.*
parsimony, *parsimonia* (in favourable sense), *tenacitas, malignitas;* see also MEANNESS.
parsley, *apium* (Hor., Plin.).
parsnip, *pastinaca* (Plin.).
parson, render by *sacerdos.*
part, subst. (1) a — of anything, in gen. *pars, membrum;* the middle, farthest, lowest, highest — of a thing is rendered by adj. such as *medius, extremus, infimus, summus,* agreeing with the thing concerned (e.g.: the central — of a line of battle, *acies media;* the highest — of a mountain, *mons summus*): in two, three —s, *bifariam, trifariam* or *bipartito, tripartito;* for the most —, *maximam partem, fere, plerumque;* in —; see PARTLY. (2) = share, concern, function: I for my —, *equidem, ego pro mea parte;* to do one's —, *officio* or *munere fungi;* it is the — of a king to do this, *regis est hoc facĕre;* to take — in a thing, *rei* (genit.) *partem capĕre* or *participem esse; rei* (dat.) *interesse* or *se immiscēre; rem attingĕre;* to have no — in a thing, *rei* (genit.) *expertem esse.* (3) = side, cause, *partes* (*-ium,* plur.): to take a person's —, *homini adesse, favēre, in partes hominis transire;* to take one person's — against another, *stare cum altero adversus alterum.* (4) — in a play, role, *partes* (*-ium,* plur.), *persona:* to play the chief —, *primas* (*partes*) *agĕre.* (5) = sense, interpretation: to take in good (bad) —, *in bonam* (*malam*) *partem accipĕre.* (6) = region, *locus, regio.* (7) = agency: on his —, *by* him, *ab illo.* (8) —s = talents, ability, *ingenium.*
part, v. (1) transit. *separare, dividĕre, partiri, dissociare.* (2) intransit. *digredi, discedĕre.*
partake, in gen.: to — of, *participem esse rei* (genit.); of food, *gustare,* and see also EAT.
partaker, *particeps, socius* (*rei,* genit.), *adfinis* (adj. with *rei* genit. or dat.).
parterre, render by phrase, such as *area floribus consita.*
partial. (1) = affecting only a part, render by *partim* or by phrase, such as *aliqua ex parte.* (2) = favouring a person, group, etc., *studiosus* or *cupidus* (with genit.); *iniquus* (= unfair).
partiality, *studium, cupiditas, iniquitas* (= gross unfairness).
partially. (1) see PARTLY. (2) *per studium, inique* (= unfairly).
participate, (*rei,* genit.) *esse participem, socium, adfinem, consortem;* (*rei,* dat.) *interesse.*
participation, *societas.*
participator, *particeps, socius, adfinis, concors.*
participle, *participium* (Quint.).
particle. (1) = a small piece, *particula, frustum* (esp. of food), *mica* (poet.). (2) as grammat. t. t., *particula* (Gell.).
particoloured, *versicolor, varius.*
particular, adj. (1) = individual, peculiar, *proprius, separatus.* (2) = special, outstanding, *singularis, praecipuus;* a — friend, *familiaris.* (3) = exacting, fastidious, fussy, *elegans, delicatus.*
particularity, render by adj.
particularize, *nominare* (= to name), *enumerare* (= to enumerate).

particularly = especially, very much, *vehementer, magnopére, praesertim, praecipue, maxime, imprimis, impense* (= eagerly).

particulars, subst. *singula* (*-orum,* n. plur.) or *singulae res* (plur.).

parting, subst. *digressus* (*-ūs*), *digressio, discessus* (*-ūs*).

partisan. (1) as a person, *fautor, homo studiosus* (with genit.). (2) as a weapon, *bipennis* (Verg.).

partisanship, *studium, favor.*

partition. (1) = the act of dividing, *partitio.* (2) = a barrier between rooms, etc., *paries.*

partitive, *partitivus* (Gram.).

partly, *partim, parte,* (*aliqua*) *ex parte.*

partner. (1) in gen., *socius, particeps, consors.* (2) in marriage, *coniunx*; see also HUSBAND, WIFE.

partnership, *consortio, societas*: to enter into — with a person, *cum homine societatem inire, hominem sibi sociam adiungére.*

partridge, *perdix* (Varro, Mart.).

parturition, *partus* (*-ūs*).

party. (1) = a number of persons with a common aim, *partes* (*-ium,* plur.), *factio* (esp. political), *secta* (of philosophers or other learned men): to belong to anyone's —, *hominis partes* or *sectam sequi, cum homine facére* or *stare*; not to belong to any — -, *nullius partis esse*; to split up into two parties, *in duas partes discedére* (Sall.). (2) = any small band, *manus*; see also BAND, COMPANY. (3) = a social gathering, *convivium.*

party-spirit, *studium* (*partium*).

party-strife, *certamen partium* or *factionum.*

party-wall, *paries.*

parvenu, *novus homo.*

paschal, *paschalis* (eccl.).

pasha, *satrapes* (Ter., Nep.).

pasquinade, *libellus famosus*; if a poem, *carmen famosum.*

pass, subst. (1) geographical, *angustiae* (*-arum,* plur.), *saltus* (*-ūs*), *fauces* (*-ium,* plur.). (2) abstr.: matters have come to such a — that . . . , *eo ventum est ut,* with subj.; see also CONDITION.

pass, v. (1) of going past a point or from one point to another: **a,** transit. *transgredi, transire, praetervehi, praetergredi, egredi, excedére* (fig.); see also SURPASS, EXCEED: **b,** intransit., *ire, transire, praeterire*; fig. of property: to — into a person's possession, *ad hominem pervenire*: **c,** to — over, transit. *praeterire, transire, omittére, praetermittére* (also = to let pass): **d,** to — away; see PERISH: **e,** to — off (of pains, etc.), *abire, decedére.* (2) of time: **a,** transit., of persons, *agére, degére, transigére* (Tac.), (*tra*)*ducére, consumére*; with the idea of waste, (*con*)*terére*: **b,** intransit., of the time itself, *transire, abire, praeterire, cedére, labi* (poet.). (3) to — a law (of the legislative body), *legem sancire* or simply *iubére*; to get a law —ed (of the person initiating legislation), *legem perferre.* (4) = to convey in a certain direction, *tradére, porrigére, traicére*: to — one thing through, or into, another, *inserére, immittére.* (5) in relation to a test or standard: **a,** transit., to —, = to approve, accept as adequate, (*ap*)*probare*: to — oneself off as a friend, *amicum se ferre* or *profiteri*: **b,** intransit. = to be approved, (*ap*)*probari, satisfacére* (with

dat.): to — for a friend, *amicum* or *pro amico haberi.* (6) to come to —; see HAPPEN.

passable. (1) of places, *pervius, transitu facilis.* (2) = tolerable, *tolerabilis, mediocris.*

passably, *tolerabiliter, mediocriter.*

passage. (1) = the act of passing, *transitus* (*-ūs*), *transitio, transgressio, transgressus* (*-ūs*: Sall., Tac.), *tra*(*ns*)*missio, tra*(*ns*)*missus,* (*-ūs*), *traiectio, traiectus* (*-ūs*): — across a river, *transitus* or *transvectio fluminis*; to grant a — to a person, *transitum* or *iter* (*per agros,* etc.), *homini dare.* (2) = way, road, *iter, via.* (3) a — in a book, *locus, caput* (= chapter).

passenger, *viator* (on foot), *vector* (on horseback, on a ship, etc.).

passing, in the phrase, in —, *praeteriens* (partic.), *obiter* (Plin., Juv.), *in transitu* (Tac.).

passion. (1) = the act of suffering, *perpessio, toleratio* (with genit.): the — of Christ, *passio* (eccl.). (2) = emotion, *animi impetus* (*-ūs*), *motus* (*-ūs*), *commotio, permotio, concitatio, perturbatio* (as philosoph. t. t.); often to be rendered by a verb with *animus,* e.g.: to arouse —, *animum* (*com*)*movére.* (3) = uncontrolled or undesirable emotion, *libido, cupiditas*: to overcome one's —s, *cupiditates coercére* or *cohibére.* (4) = anger, *ira, iracundia*: to fly into a —, *exardescére.* (5) = extreme fondness, *studium.*

passionate, adj. (1) = eager, ardent, *cupidus, concitatus, vehemens, ardens, flagrans, fervidus, impotens* (= wild, uncontrolled). (2) = hottempered, *iracundus, cerebrosus.*

passionately. (1) = eagerly, ardently, *cupide, vehementer, effuse.* (2) = angrily, *iracunde.*

passionateness, *animi ardor, furor* (= extreme —); = hot temper, *iracundia.*

passionless, render by phrase, such as *cupiditatis expers, omni animi perturbatione vacuus.*

passive. (1) in gen., render by verb, such as *pati* or *tolerare*: to remain —, *quiescére.* (2) as gramm. t. t., *passivus* (Gram.).

passively. (1) in gen., *aequo animo, patienter.* (2) as gramm. t. t., *passive* (Gram.).

passiveness, *patientia*; see also PATIENCE.

Passover, *Pascha* (eccl.).

passport, *syngraphus* (Pl.) or render by phrase, such as *facultas eundi data.*

password, *tessera.*

past, subst. *praeteritum tempus*; also rendered by the n. plur. of *praeteritus* (Cic.) and by the n. sing. after the prepositions *de* and *ex* (Liv.) and *in* (Suet.).

past, adj. (1) = gone by, *praeteritus, ante actus.* (2) = immediately preceding, *prior, superior, proximus.*

past, adv., render by compound verbs beginning with *praeter-, trans-,* or *tra-*; e.g.: to go —, *praeterire.*

past, prep.: of motion = to the far side of, *praeter,* with acc. (= past the front of), *trans,* with acc. (= across); of situation, = on the far side of, *ultra* or *trans,* with acc.

paste, subst., render by *farina* (= flour: Plin.) or *gluten* (= glue: Lucr.).

paste, v. *glutinare* (Plin.).

pastime, *ludus* (= game), *oblectamentum, oblectatio.*

pastor; see SHEPHERD; as eccl. term, *pastor.*

pastoral, = of shepherds, *pastoralis, pastoricius*; in a wider sense, *agrestis, rusticus*: — poetry, *bucolica* (*-orum,* n. plur.: Ov.).

pastry, *crustum* (Verg., Hor.), *crustulum* (Hor.).
pastry-cook, *crustulareus* (Sen.); see also BAKER.
pasture, subst. *pascuum* (esp. plur.), *ager pascuus* (= — land): common — land, *ager compascuus*; to drive to —, *pastum agĕre.*
pasture, v. (1) transit. *pascĕre.* (2) intransit. *pabulari* (= to graze), *pasci* (= to feed).
pat, subst., render by phrase, such as *plaga lĕvis.*
pat, adv. *in tempore, opportune, commodum.*
pat, v. *permulcēre* (= to caress).
patch, *pannus* (Hor.).
patch, v. *(re)sarcire, rei* (dat.) *pannum adsuĕre* (Hor.).
patchwork, *cento.*
patent, subst., use *diploma* (-*atis*, n.).
patent, adj. = open, plain, *manifestus, apertus, clarus.*
paternal, *paternus, patrius:* a — disposition, *animus paternus (in hominem).*
path. (1) in gen. = a way. LIT., *via, iter.* TRANSF., *via;* a — of life, *via vitae* or *vivendi.* (2) = a narrow or rough road, *semita, trames.*
pathetic, *flebilis, maestus, tristis;* see also SAD.
pathetically, *flebiliter, maeste.*
pathless, *invius.*
pathologist, *medicus.*
pathos, *maestitia, tristitia.*
pathway; see PATH.
patience, *patientia, tolerantia* (usually with genit., e.g. *tolerantia doloris), perseverantia* (= persistence in a labour, quest, etc.), *aequus animus* or *aequitas animi* (= calmness, resignation).
patient, subst. *aeger, aegrotus.*
patient, adj. *patiens, tolerans* (with genit. of what is endured: Tac.).
patiently, *patienter, toleranter, tolerabiliter, aequo animo* (= calmly, with resignation).
patois, *dialectos* (Suet.).
patriarch, *patriarcha* (eccl.).
patriarchal, *patriarchalis* (eccl.); see also OLD.
patrician, subst. and adj. *patricius.*
patrimony, *patrimonium.*
patriot, *reipublicae amicus, civis bonus:* to be a —, *amare patriam, bene de republica sentire.*
patriotic, *patriae* or *reipublicae amans;* on — grounds, *reipublicae causā.*
patriotically, *pro patria.*
patriotism, *patriae amor* or *caritas, pietas erga patriam, reipublicae studium:* if — is a crime, *si scelestum est amare patriam* (Cic.).
patristic, *patrum* or *quod ad patres pertinet* (eccl.).
patrol, subst. *circitores* or *circuitores* (-*um*, plur.: Vegetius, 4th cent. A.D.).
patrol, v. transit. = to go round examining, *circumire, lustrare.*
patron. (1) at Rome, in relation to a 'client', *patronus.* (2) in gen. = a protector, guardian, *patronus, praeses, cultor, tutela* (poet.).
patronage, = the relation at Rome between patron and client, *patrocinium* (from the patron's side), *clientela* (from the client's); more generally, *praesidium.*
patroness, *patrona.*
patronize, *favēre* (with dat.); or render by phrase, such as *auctoritate, sustentare.*
patronymic, *patronymicum nomen* (Gram.).
patten, *sculponea* (usually plur.: Pl.).

patter, subst. *crepitus* (-*ūs*).
patter, v. *crepare, crepitare, crepitum dare.*
pattern, *exemplum, exemplar, specimen, documentum.*
paucity, *paucitas,* or render by adj.
paunch, *abdomen, venter.*
pauper; see POOR.
pause, subst. *mora* (= delay), *respiratio* (= a — for breath), *intervallum, intermissio, intercapēdo, pausa* (Pl., Lucr.).
pause, v. *interquiescĕre* (= to — from time to time), *intermittĕre, subsistĕre, morari, moram facĕre.*
pave, (*viam*) *sternĕre* or *munire.*
pavement, *pavimentum, via strata* (= paved road).
Pavia, *Ticinum.*
paving, *stratura* (Suet.).
paving-stone, *saxum quadratum.*
pavilion, *papilio* (late Latin); see also TENT.
paw, subst. *pes* (= foot), *ungula* (= claw).
paw, v. (*solum,* etc.) *pedibus ferire.*
pawn, subst. *pignus* (-*ĕris* or -*ŏris,* n.); see also PLEDGE; at chess, *latrunculus* (Suet.), *latro* (Ov.).
pawn, v. *pignerare, oppignerare, pignori dare* or *opponĕre.*
pawnbroker, *pignerator.*
pay, subst. *stipendium* (esp. of soldiers), *merces.*
pay, v. (1) transit. LIT., of money, (*per*)*solvĕre, exsolvĕre, dissolvĕre, pendĕre, dependĕre, numerare, repraesentare* (in ready cash). TRANSF., to — attention, see ATTENTION; to — honour to a person, *honorem homini habēre;* to — a penalty, *poenam dare* or *luĕre;* to — one's respects to a person, *hominem salutare.* (2) intransit. = to be profitable, *prodesse, lucro esse, quaestuosum* or *fructuosum esse.*
payable, render by verb.
pay-day, *dies,* with or without explanatory phrase.
paymaster, in gen., *dispensator* (Juv.), or render by phrase; in the army, *tribunus aerarius.*
payment, *solutio, repraesentatio* (in ready cash).
pea, *pisum* (Plin.), *cicer* (= chick-pea: Hor.).
peace, subst. *pax, otium, concordia* (= agreement): in —, *in pace;* terms of —, *pacis condiciones* (-*um,* plur.); to bind over to keep the —, *pecuniā de vi cavēre.*
peace! interj. *tace, tacete! pax!*
peaceable, *placidus, placabilis.*
peaceably, *placide.*
peaceful, *pacatus, placidus, quietus, tranquillus.*
peacefully, *placide, quiete, tranquille, cum* (*bonā*) *pace.*
peacefulness, *tranquillitas.*
peace-offering, *piaculum, placamen, placamentum* (Tac.).
peach, (*malum*) *persicum* (Plin.).
peacock, *pavo.*
peak, *cacumen, apex, fastigium* (fig.); often rendered by the adj. *summus.*
peal, subst.: — of laughter, *cachinnus;* — of applause, *plausus* (-*ūs*); — of thunder, *tonitrus* (-*ūs*).
peal, v. *sonare;* see also RING.
pear, *pirum* (Verg.).
pearl, *margarita.*
pear-tree, *pirus* (Verg.).
peasant, *rusticus, agrestis, homo rusticanus, paganus.*
peasantry; see PEASANT.

pease; see PEA.

pebble, *calculus, lapillus* (Ov.).

peccadillo, *(leve) delictum*; see also FAULT.

peccant, *peccans*.

peck, subst., as a measure, render by *modius*.

peck, v. *vellicare*.

pectoral, *pectoralis* (Cels.).

peculation, *peculatus (-ūs)*.

peculiar. (1) = belonging to one individual or one class only, *proprius, peculiaris*. (2) = remarkable, outstanding, *singularis, praecipuus, mirus*.

peculiarity, *proprietas*; or render by adj. *proprius*.

peculiarly, *praesertim, imprimis (in primis), mirum in modum, mire*.

pecuniary, *pecuniarius*; or render by subst. *pecunia*.

pedagogue, *paedagogus* (= the slave who accompanied a child to school); in gen. = schoolmaster, *magister*.

pedant, *homo nimis diligens*; sometimes simply *homo molestus* or *ineptus*.

pedantic, *nimis diligens*; sometimes simply *molestus* or *ineptus*.

pedantry, *ineptiae (-arum,* plur.), *molestia*.

pedestal, *basis, stylobates* (Varro).

pedestrian, subst. *pedes (-itis)*.

pedestrian, adj. *pedester*: to make a — tour, *iter pedibus facēre*.

pedigree, *stemma (-atis,* n.: Sen., Juv.); see also GENEALOGY.

pedlar, *institor*.

peel, subst. *cutis* (Plin.), *corium* (Plin.), *tunica* (Plin.).

peel, v. (1) transit. *cutem*, etc., *detrahēre*: to — a tree, *corticare arborem* (Plin.). (2) intransit. *cutem (de)ponēre*.

peep, subst. *aspectus (-ūs), conspectus (-ūs)*: at — of day, *diluculo, primā luce*.

peep, v. *(strictim) prospicēre, inspicēre*; see also LOOK; *enitēre, emicare* (= to shine), *apparēre, conspici, conspicuum esse* (= to be seen, the latter two esp. of objects that are very conspicuous).

peer, subst. (1) = an equal, *par*. (2) = a noble, *unus e patriciis* or *nobilibus*: house of —s, *senatus (-ūs)*.

peer, v.: to — into, *rimari, scrutari*.

peerage: to raise a person to the —, *hominem ad amplissimum gradum producēre*.

peerless, *unicus, singularis*.

peevish, *stomachosus, morosus, difficilis, iracundus*.

peevishly, *stomachose, morose, iracunde*.

peevishness, *stomachus, morositas, difficultas, iracundia*.

peg, *clavus* (= nail): a wooden —, *cultellus ligneus* (Vitr.).

peg, v.; see FASTEN.

pelf, *lucrum*.

pelisse, *pallium*.

pell-mell, *effuse, confuse, passim*.

pellucid, *pellucidus*; see also TRANSPARENT.

pelt, v. (1) transit., render by *iacēre, conicēre*, etc.; see also THROW. (2) intransit., e.g. of rain, *ferri, descendēre*: —ing rain, *magnus* or *maximus imber*.

pen, subst. (1) for writing, *calamus, stilus*. (2) = fold, *saeptum*.

pen, v. (1) = to write, *scribēre, litteris mandare*. (2) = to fold, *saeptis includēre*.

penal, *poenalis* (Leg.); or render by subst. or verb.

penalty, *poena, damnum, multa, supplicium*: to exact a —, *poenam (re)petēre*; to pay the —, *poenas dare* or *(ex)pendēre*.

penance, *piaculum, poena, satisfactio* (eccl.).

pence; see PENNY.

pencil, for drawing, *penicillus*; for writing, *stilus*; see also PEN.

pendant, *stalagmium* (Pl.).

pending, adj., in law: the matter is still —, *adhuc sub iudice lis est*.

pending, prep. (1) = during, *per* with acc. (2) = until, render by *dum* with subj.

pendulous, *pendulus* (Hor., Ov.).

penetrable, *penetrabilis* (Ov.), *pervius*.

penetrate. (1) transit. *pervadēre, penetrare* (poet.). (2) intransit. *penetrare, permanare, pervadēre, pervenire, (se) insinuare*; mentally, *descendēre*.

penetrating, adj. LIT., physically, of cold, etc., *penetralis* (Lucr.), *penetrabilis* (poet.), *acutus, acer*. TRANSF., mentally, *sagax, perspicax, subtilis*.

penetration, *acies, acumen*.

peninsula, *paeninsula*.

penitence, *paenitentia*.

penitent, render by the impersonal verb *paenitet*.

penitentiary, = prison, *carcer*.

pen-knife; see KNIFE.

penman, *scriptor*.

penmanship, *ars scribendi*.

penny, *as, nummus (sestertius)*: not a — (will I give, etc.), *ne nummum quidem*; to the last — (or farthing), *ad nummum, ad assem*.

pension, *annua (-orum,* n. plur.: Plin. L.).

pensive, *in cogitatione, defixus*; see also THOUGHTFUL.

pentagon, *pentagon(i)um* (late Latin).

pentameter, *(versus) pentameter* (Quint.).

Pentecost, *pentecoste* (eccl.).

penthouse, milit. t. t., *vinea*.

penultimate, *paenultimus* (Aul. Gell.).

penurious, *parcus, sordidus, avarus, tenax*.

penuriously, *sordide, avare, parce*.

penuriousness, *sordes (-is,* f.: usually in plur.), *tenacitas*; see also MEANNESS, PARSIMONY.

penury, *inopia, egestas*; see also POVERTY.

peony, *paeonia* (Plin.).

people. subst. (1) as plur. = persons, *homines, mortales*; often rendered without subst. by a plur. adj. (e.g.: our —, *nostri*) or by 3rd pers. plur. of verb (e.g.: — say, *ferunt*): young —, *pueri* (= children), *adulescentes*. (2) = a community, *populus*; adj., of the —, *publicus*; in the name of the —, *publice*. (3) = race, tribe, *gens, natio, nomen*. (4) the common —, *plebs, vulgus, multitudo*; more contemptuously, *plebecula, popellus* (Hor.); a man of the —, *homo plebeius, homo de plebe*.

people, v. = to fill with people, *frequentare, complēre*.

peopled; see POPULOUS.

pepper, *piper* (Hor., Ov.).

peradventure; see PERHAPS.

perambulate, *perambulare* (Pl., Hor.), *peragrare, pervagari, (per)lustrare, percurrēre* (quickly).

perambulation, *lustratio, peragratio*.

perceivable; see PERCEPTIBLE.

perceive. (1) with the senses, *sentire, percipĕre*; or render by particular verbs, such as *vidēre, cernĕre* (= to see), *audire* (= to hear). (2) with the understanding, *sentire, percipĕre, intellegĕre, animadvertĕre, cognoscĕre, vidēre.*

percentage, *pars, portio*; to render particular percentages, in rates of interest, etc., use *centesima* (*pars*), which is 1% monthly (12% per annum).

perceptible, *manifestus* (= clear); or render by phrase, such as *quod percipere possis, quod percipi potest.*

perceptibly, *ita ut percipi possit.*

perception. LIT., render by verb. TRANSF., = discernment, *iudicium, animi* (or *mentis* or *ingenii*) *acies* or *acumen, sagacitas.*

perceptive, *sagax*; or render by verb.

perch, subst. (1) as a measure, *pertica* (Plin.). (2) the fish, *perca* (Ov., Plin.).

perch, v. *insidĕre* (= to settle on), *insīdēre* (= to sit on).

perchance; see PERHAPS.

percolate, *permanare.*

percolation, *percolatio* (Vitr.); or render by verb.

percussion, *ictus* (-*ūs*; = blow).

perdition, *exitium, interitus* (-*ūs*), *pernicies.*

peremptorily, in requests, *adroganter*; in refusals, *praecise.*

peremptory, *adrogans.*

perennial, *perennis, iugis* (esp. of water).

perfect, adj. *plenus, absolutus, perfectus, absolutus et perfectus, integer* (= complete, sound, intact), *merus* (= thorough, nothing but . . .), *verus* or *germanus* (= real, genuine).

perfect, v. *perficĕre, absolvĕre, ad summum perducĕre, cumulare.*

perfection, *absolutio, perfectio, integritas* (= soundness): to attain —, *ad perfectionem pervenire.*

perfectly, *plene, absolute, perfecte, plane* (= wholly); often rendered by superl. of adj.

perfidious, *perfidus, perfidiosus.*

perfidiously, *perfidiose, perfide* (Sen.).

perfidy, *perfidia.*

perforate, *perforare,* (*per*)*terebrare* (= to bore through).

perforce, *vi, per vim, necessario*; or render by adj. *invitus* (= unwilling) or partic. *coactus* (= forced).

perform. (1) in gen., (*rē*) (*per*)*fungi,* (*rem*) *exsequi, perficĕre, conficĕre, peragĕre, obire* or *praestare* (both with such objects as *officium* or *munus*). (2) on the stage = to play a part, *partes agĕre, in scaenā esse.*

performance. (1) = the act of performing, (*per*)*functio, confectio, exsecutio* (Tac.). (2) a — on the stage: dramatic, *fabula*; musical, *concentus* (-*ūs*), *symphonia.*

performer. (1) in gen., *auctor, confector*; or render by verb. (2) on the stage: dramatic, *actor, histrio* (see also ACTOR); musical, *acroama* (-*atis*, n.).

perfume, subst. *odor* (*odos*), *unguentum.*

perfume, v. *odorare* (Ov.), *odore adficĕre*: to — by burning incense, etc., *suffire.*

perfumer, = a seller of perfumes, *myropola* (Pl.), *unguentarius.*

perfunctory, *neglegens*; see also CARELESS.

perhaps, *perchance, peradventure, fortasse, forsitan* (usually with subj.), *forsan* (poet.), *fors* (Verg.); sometimes *haud scio an* (with

subj.): if —, unless —, lest —, *si forte, nisi forte, ne forte.*

peril; see DANGER, RISK.

perilous; see DANGEROUS.

period. (1) = a portion of time, *tempus, tempestas* (formal, somewhat archaic), *aetas* (often = — of life), *spatium temporis* (= space of time). (2) = end, *finis, terminus.* (3) as rhet. or grammat. t. t., *periodus* (Quint.), in Cic. (*verborum* or *orationis*) *circuitus* (-*ūs*) or *comprehensio* or *complexio* or *continuatio*; a well-rounded —, *orbis verborum*; the structure of the —, (*verborum*) *compositio.*

periodical, subst.; see JOURNAL.

periodical, adj. = recurring at stated intervals, *sollemnis.*

periodically, *certis* (or *statis*) *temporibus.*

peripatetic, as philosoph. t. t., *peripateticus.*

periphery, *perimetros* (Vitr.).

periphrasis; see PARAPHRASE.

perish, *perire, interire, occidĕre, exstingui, absumi.*

perishable, *fragilis, caducus, fluxus* (= unstable); or render by phrase with verb.

perishableness, *fragilitas.*

peristyle, *peristylum.*

periwinkle, the plant, *vinca pervinca* (Plin.).

perjure, *periurare* (or *peierare*), *periurium facĕre.*

perjured, *periurus.*

perjury, *periurium.*

perky, *protervus*; see also SAUCY.

permanence, *perennitas, stabilitas.*

permanent, *perennis, stabilis.*

permanently, *perpetuo.*

permeable, *penetrabilis* (poet.).

permissible, *licitus* (Verg.): it is —, *licet.*

permission, *permissio* (very rare), *facultas, potestas, copia, venia*: with your —, *concessu* (or *permissu*) *tuo, pace tuā*; without your —, *te invito*; I give you —, *tibi permitto* or *concedo, tibi potestatem* or *copiam facio*, or *sino, tibi per me licet.*

permissive, render by verb.

permit, subst.; see PERMISSION.

permit, v. (*hominem*) *sinĕre* (with infin.); (*homini*) *permittĕre* or *concedĕre* (both with either infin. or *ut* clause); (*homini*) *potestatem, copiam*, etc., *facĕre* (with genit.); see also ALLOW.

permutation, (*per*)*mutatio.*

pernicious, *perniciosus, exitiosus, exitialis, exitiabilis, funestus, damnosus* (= ruinous), *noxius* (= injurious).

perniciously, *perniciose, exitiose, funeste.*

peroration, *peroratio, epilogus, conclusio*: to make a —, *perorare.*

perpendicular, *directus.*

perpendicularly, *ad lineam, recta lineā.*

perpetrate, *committĕre* or *in se admittĕre*; see also COMMIT.

perpetration, render by verb.

perpetrator, *auctor*; or render by relative clause, such as *qui illud facinus in se admisit.*

perpetual, *sempiternus, perennis, adsiduus* (= incessant), *perpetuus* (= continuous).

perpetually, *adsidue, perpetuo.*

perpetuate, render by adj.

perpetuity, *perpetuitas* (= continuity); see also ETERNITY.

perplex, *distrahĕre, sollicitare, dubitationem* (*homini*) *adferre.*

perplexed, *dubius, inops consilii.*
perplexing, *difficilis, perplexus, impeditus, dubius.*
perplexity, *dubitatio;* see also DOUBT.
perquisite, *peculium* (= small savings, esp. a slave's); or render by phrase such as *pecuniae* (*-arum,* plur.) *extraordinariae.*
persecute, *insectari, vexare.*
persecution, *insectatio, vexatio.*
persecutor, *vexator, insectator.*
perseverance, *perseverantia, constantia, pertinacia, pervicacia.*
persevere, (*in re*) *perseverare, constare, perstare, persistĕre,* (*per*)*manēre, pergĕre* (= to press on).
persevering, *perseverans, constans, pertinax, pervicax, tenax* (with genit.: Hor.).
perseveringly, *perseveranter, constanter, pertinaciter* (Suet.).
persist; see PERSEVERE.
persistence, *permansio* (*in re*); see also PERSEVERANCE.
person. (1) = a human being, *homo, caput, mortalis* (esp. plur.); in person, *ipse, praesens, coram.* (2) of physical as opposed to mental and other qualities, *corpus* (= body), *species* (= outward appearance), *forma* (= shape, esp. beautiful). (3) as grammat. t. t. *persona* (e.g. *tertia:* Quint.).
personage, personality, *persona* (= character borne, part played in the world); *hominis natura, ingenium* (= disposition).
personal. (1) in gen., *privatus, proprius;* more often render by pronouns, such as *ipse, ego, tu, se:* to make a — appearance, *ipse* or *praesens* or *coram adesse;* — appearance (= looks), *corporis habitus* (*-ūs*). (2) as grammat. t. t., a — verb, *verbum personale* (Gram.).
personality; see PERSONAGE; in plur. = offensive personal remarks, *maledicta* (*-orum,* plur.).
personally; see PERSONAL: I —, *equidem;* I know him —, *eum de facie novi.*
personalty, (*bona*) *sua.*
personate, = to impersonate a person, *hominis partes agĕre* or *personam gerĕre, tueri* or *sustinere.*
personification, *prosopopoeia* (Quint.), *personarum fictio* or *confictio.*
personify, (*rem*) *tanquam hominem loquentem inducĕre,* (*rei,* dat.) *orationem* (*at*)*tribuĕre,* (*rem*) *humanā specie induĕre.*
personnel, render by *homines* (= persons), *milites* (= soldiers), etc.
perspective, *scaenographia* (= theatrical drawing: Vitr.), an artist's treatment of —, *ea ars pictoria quā efficit ut quaedam eminēre in opere, quaedam recessisse credamus* (Quint.).
perspicacious, *perspicax, sagax, acutus.*
perspicaciously, *perspicaciter.*
perspicacity, *perspicacitas, acies* or *acumen ingenii.*
perspicuity, *perspicuitas.*
perspicuous, (*di*)*lucidus, clarus, inlustris, perspicuus, apertus.*
perspicuously, (*di*)*lucide, clare, perspicue, aperte.*
perspiration, *sudor.*
perspire, *sudare, sudorem emittere* (Plin.).
persuade, *persuadēre* (when convincing a person of a fact, with *homini* and acc. of neut.

pron. or acc. and infin. clause; when inducing a person to act, with *homini* and *ut* clause); *adducĕre* (*hominem,* usually with *ut* clause); *inducĕre* (*hominem,* with *in* or *ad* and acc. of noun or *ut* clause): to allow oneself to be —d, *persuadēri sibi pati;* to try to —, *suadēre.*
persuasion, *persuasio:* by my —, *persuasu meo.*
persuasive, persuasively, persuasiveness, render by verb, e.g.: a — speech, *oratio ad persuadendum accommodata.*
pert, *protervus, procax.*
pertain, (*ad rem, ad hominem*) *pertinēre, attinēre:* —ing to, *proprius* (with genit. or dat.).
pertinacious, *pertinax, obstinatus pervicax.*
pertinaciously, *pertinaciter, obstinate.*
pertinacity, *pertinacia, obstinatio.*
pertly, *proterve.*
pertness, *protervitas, procacitas*
perturbation, *perturbatio;* see also AGITATION, DISTURBANCE.
Perugia, *Perusia.*
peruke, *capillamentum* (Suet.).
perusal, n. *lectio, perlectio* (*pell-*).
peruse, (*per*)*legĕre, evolvĕre.*
pervade, LIT., *permanare.* TRANSF., *permanare, perfundĕre, invadĕre.*
perverse, *perversus, pravus.*
perversely, *perverse, perperam, prave.*
perversion, *corruptio, depravatio.*
perversity, *perversitas, pravitas.*
pervert, v. *depravare, corrumpĕre, deflectĕre, detorquēre.*
pervious, *pervius.*
pest. LIT., see PESTILENCE. TRANSF., of a troublesome person or thing, *pestis, pernicies, lues.*
pester, *sollicitare, vexare;* see also TROUBLE, ANNOY.
pestilence, *pestilentia, pestis lues* (poet.), *morbus.*
pestilential, *pestilens, foedus.*
pestle, *pilum* (Cato), *pistillum* (Plin.).
pet, subst. *deliciae* (*-arum,* plur.), *amores* (*-um,* plur.); see also FAVOURITE.
pet, v. *petĕre, fovēre, in deliciis habēre.*
petard, in the phrase, he is hoist with his own —, perhaps *in suos laqueos ipse incidit* or *qua via alios captavit ipse captus est* (adapted from Ter.).
Peter, *Petrus* (late Latin).
peter out, *evanescere.*
petition, subst. (1) in gen.; see PRAYER, REQUEST. (2) a formal —, *libellus;* to sign a — (along with others), *libellum subscribĕre;* to grant a person's —, *homini petenti satisfacĕre, adnuĕre.*
petition, v. *petĕre, rogare, implorare.*
petitioner, *qui rogat, qui libellum adfert.*
petrify, LIT., *in lapidem* (*con*)*vertĕre:* to be petrified, *lapidescĕre* (Plin., rare). TRANSF., *obstupefacĕre:* to be petrified (with astonishment, etc.), *obstupescĕre, obtorpescĕre, stupēre, attonitum esse.*
petticoat, perhaps *tunica;* the Romans had no real equivalent: — government, *imperium uxorium* or *muliebre.*
pettifogger, *leguleius, rabula.*
pettifogging; see PALTRY.
pettish; see PEEVISH.

petty, *minutus, tenuis*; see also LITTLE, TRIFLING, PALTRY.

petulance, *petulantia, protervitas.*

petulant, *petulans, protervus.*

pewter, no equivalent; render as another metal or alloy.

phaeton; see CARRIAGE.

phantom, *simulacrum, imago*; see also GHOST.

Pharisee, *Pharisaeus* (eccl.); see also HYPOCRITE.

pharmacy, *(ars) medicamentaria* (Plin.).

phase, *status (-ūs), ratio*: different —s, *vices* (plur.).

pheasant, *(avis) Phasiana* (Plin.), *Phasianus* (Suet.).

phenomenon. (1) in gen. = an occurrence evident to the senses, *res* (e.g. in the phrase *rerum cognoscěre causas*). **(2)** = a remarkable (and significant) occurrence, *res mira* or *nova, ostentum, prodigium, portentum, miraculum.*

phial; see BOTTLE.

philanthropic, *hominibus* (or *generi humano*) *amicus, humanus.*

philanthropy, *benevolentia, humanitas.*

Philip, *Philippus.*

Philippic, = one of Demosthenes' speeches against Philip or one of Cicero's against Antony, *(oratio) Philippica.*

Philistine. LIT., *Philistinus* (eccl). TRANSF., *homo humanitatis expers.*

philological, *grammaticus.*

philologist, *grammaticus, philologus* (less precise than the English word).

philology, *grammatica (-ae,* f. sing.; also *-orum,* n. plur.), *philologia.*

philosopher, *philosophus* (and f. *philosopha), sapiens.*

philosophical, *philosophus;* = wise, *sapiens:* — writings, *libri qui sunt de philosophiā;* — subjects, *ea quae in philosophiā tractantur;* — precepts, *philosophiae* or *philosophorum praecepta* (-orum, plur.); it is not a common, but a — term, *non est vulgi verbum, sed philosophorum.*

philosophically, *philosophorum more, sapienter;* more generally = calmly, *aequo animo.*

philosophize, *philosophari;* more generally, *ratiocinari, disputare.*

philosophy, *philosophia.*

philtre, *philtrum* (Ov., Juv.), *amatorium medicamentum* (Suet.) or *amatorium* alone (Sen., Quint.).

phlegm. LIT., *pituita.* TRANSF., = coolness, insensitivity, *patientia, ingenii tarditas* or *lentitudo.*

phlegmatic, *tardus, patiens, lentus.*

phlegmatically, *patienter, lente, aequo animo.*

phoenix, *phoenix.*

phonetic, phonetically; render by phrase, such as *sonum verbi ipsum litteris expriměre.*

phosphorescent, phosphorescence, render by subst. *lux* or verb *lucēre.*

photograph, subst., render by *pictura* or *imago.*

phrase, subst. *locutio;* sometimes *verbum.*

phrase, v.; see EXPRESS, SAY.

phraseology, *locutio, dicendi genus (-ěris,* n.).

phthisical, *phthisicus* (Plin.).

phthisis, *phthisis* (Cels.).

physic, subst.; see MEDICINE.

physic, v.; see CURE.

physical. (1) = natural, corporeal; render by

the genit. *naturae* or *corporis:* — defects, *vitia corporis;* — strength, *vires (corporis).* **(2)** referring to the science of physics, *physicus.*

physically, in gen., *naturā;* = in the manner of the physicist, *physice.*

physician; see DOCTOR.

physics, *physica (-orum,* n. plur.).

physiognomist, *physiognomon* or render by phrase, such as *qui se profitetur hominum mores naturasque ex corpore, oculis, vultu, fronte pernoscěre* (Cic.).

physiognomy, *oris habitus (-ūs)* or *lineamenta (-orum,* n. plur.).

physiology, *physiologia* (wider than the English term, covering all natural science).

Piacenza, *Placentia.*

piano, render as some other instrument, using e.g. *lyra* or *cithara.*

pick, subst. **(1)** = a — axe, *dolabra.* **(2)** = the best part, *flos, robur.*

pick, v. LIT., physically = to pluck, gather, *legěre, carpěre, conligěre:* to — up, *tollěre;* to — out, *eligěre.* TRANSF., see CHOOSE.

picked, *delectus, electus, selectus.*

picket, *statio, custodia:* to post —s, *stationes disponěre.*

pickle, subst. *salsura* (Varro), *muria* (Hor.).

pickle, v. *muriā condire* (Plin.).

picnic, *convivium;* for more descriptive phrases, see Lucr. II, 29–33.

pick-pocket, *sector zonarius* (Pl.), *fur* (= thief).

pictorial, pictorially, render by phrase, such as *per tabulas.*

picture, subst. *tabula (picta), pictura, imago (picta):* a word —, *pictura,* or render by phrase, such as *rem verbis expriměre* or *depingěre.*

picture, v.: to — to oneself = to imagine, *animo* or *cogitatione fingěre, cogitatione depingěre, ante oculos proponěre;* = to recall vividly, *memoriam (rei,* genit.) *repraesentare.*

picture-frame, *forma (in quā includitur pictura).*

picture-gallery, *pinacotheca* (Plin.).

picturesque, *amoenus, venustus.*

picturesqueness; see BEAUTY.

pie, *crustum* (Verg., Hor.); see PASTRY.

piebald, *bicolor* (Verg.).

piece. (1) = a part, a bit, *pars, fragmentum* (poet. *fragmen* = a — broken off), *segmentum* (= a — cut off: Plin.), *frustum* (esp. of food), *mica* (= a crumb; poet.), *membrum:* a — of cloth, *pannus;* a piece of a thing is often represented by a subst. denoting the thing itself, or a diminutive, e.g.: a — of land, *agellus,* a — of meat, *caruncula;* to break into —s, *confringěre, comminuěre;* to tear to —s, *discerpěre, carpěre, dilacerare;* to fall to —s, *dilabi, (dis)solvi.* **(2)** a — of money, a coin, *nummus.* **(3)** = an artistic or literary production; render according to sense, e.g. *pictura* (= a painting), *carmen* (= a song), *fabula* (= a play).

piecemeal, *membratim, minutatim.*

piece together, v. *consuěre* (Pl.), *fabricari.*

pied, *maculosus, versicolor.*

pier. (1) = the support of a bridge or similar structure, *pila, moles.* **(2)** = a mole, breakwater, etc., *moles, agger.*

pierce, *pungěre:* to — through, *perforare, perfoděre, confoděre, transfigěre.*

piercing, adj. (**1**) of sounds, *acer, acutus*; see also SHRILL. (**2**) of the mind, *acutus, acer, sagax, perspicax.*

piety, *pietas* (*erga deum* or *deos*), *religio* (= religious feeling), *sanctitas* (= holiness of life).

pig, *porcus, sus*: a small —, *porcellus* (Phaedr., Suet.).

pigeon, *columba, columbus* (= a male —: Pl., Hor.), *palumbes* (= a wood —: Verg., Hor.); a — cote, *columbarium* (Varro).

piggery, *hara.*

piggish, *suillus, porcīnus* (Pl.).

pig-headed; see OBSTINATE.

pigment; see PAINT.

pigmy; see PYGMY.

pigsty, *hara.*

pike. (**1**) the weapon, *hasta, sarissa.* (**2**) the fish, *lupus* (Hor., Mart.).

pilaster, *parastata* (Vitr.).

pile, subst. (**1**) = a mass, heap, *strues, congeries, cumulus, acervus.* (**2**) a funeral —, *rogus, pyra* (Verg.). (**3**) = any large edifice, *moles.* (**4**) a — driven into the ground, *sublica, sudis*; a bridge built on —s, *pons sublicius.*

pile, v. (*co*)*acervare, cumulare, congerĕre, exstruĕre.*

pilfer, *surripĕre, furari*; see also STEAL.

pilferer, *fur.*

pilgrim, render as traveller, by *viator* or *peregrinator.*

pilgrimage, render as travel, by *iter* or *peregrinatio sacra.*

pill, *pilula* (Plin.); fig.: a hard — to swallow, *res difficilis ad concoquendum.*

pillage, subst. *rapina, direptio, compilatio, expilatio, depopulatio* (= laying waste).

pillage, v. *diripĕre* (*de*)*populari* (= to lay waste), *compilare, expilare, spoliare, praedari.*

pillager, *praedator, direptor, expilator, populator.*

pillar. LIT., *columna, pila.* TRANSF., = support, stay, *columen.*

pillared, *columnatus* (Varro), *columnis instructus.*

pillory, render as fetter or chain, e.g. by *numella* (Pl.).

pillow, subst. *pulvinus, cervical* (Suet., Juv.).

pillow, v. (*suf*)*fulcire*; see also SUPPORT.

pilot, subst. *gubernator.*

pilot, v. *gubernare* (lit. and fig.).

pimp, n. *lēno.*

pimple, *pustula* (Sen., Mart.).

pimply, *pustulosus* (Cels.).

pin, subst. *acus* (*-ūs*; = needle).

pin, v. (*ad*)*figĕre*; fig.: to — down (to an admission, etc.), (*ad* or *in rem*) *compellĕre.*

pincers, *forceps* (Verg., Ov.).

pinch, subst. LIT., *aculeus* (= sting), *morsus* (*-ūs*; = bite). TRANSF., in the phrase, at a —, *coactus* (= compelled).

pinch, v. (**1**) = to nip, *urĕre, vellicare* (Quint.). (**2**) = to stint, inconvenience, confine, *coartare, urgēre*: to — oneself, *fraudare se victu suo.*

pinching, adj. of poverty, *angustus* (Hor., Juv.); or render by *extremus, summus*, etc.

pine, subst. *pinus* (poet.): of —, adj. *pineus* (poet.).

pine, v. *tabescĕre,* (*con*)*senescĕre, confici*: to — for a thing, *rem desiderare.*

pining, subst. *tabes.*

pinion, subst. of a bird, *penna* (poet.); see also WING.

pinion, v. (*re*)*vincire,* (*homini*) *vincula, catenas,* etc., *inicĕre.*

pink, *puniceus* (poet.).

pin-money, *peculium* (= small savings, esp. of slaves).

pinnace, (*navis*) *actuaria, lembus.*

pinnacle, *fastigium* (lit. and fig.).

pint, perhaps *sextarius*: half a —, *hemina* (= half of a *sextarius*: Pl.).

pioneer, *praecursor, explorator*; or render by phrase with *primus.*

pious, *pius* (*erga deos, patriam, parentes*, etc.), *religiosus* (= scrupulous, conscientious), *sanctus* (= saintly).

piously, *pie, sancte, religiose.*

pip, in fruit, *acinus, granum.*

pipe, subst. (**1**) = a tube for carrying liquids, *tubus* (Plin.), *tubulus, canalis, fistula.* (**2**) = a musical instrument, *fistula, tibia, calamus* (= a reed- —: poet.), *avena* (= an oaten —: Verg.).

pipe, v. = to play on a pipe, *fistulā* or *tibiā canĕre* or *cantare*; colloq., to — down, *conticescĕre.*

piper, *fistulator, tibicen.*

pipkin, *olla* (old form *aula*).

piquancy, *sal, vis.*

piquant, LIT., to the taste, *acer.* TRANSF., = stimulating, interesting, humorous, *salsus, facetus.*

pique, subst. *offensio, ira.*

pique, v. *vexare, sollicitare*; see also VEX, ANNOY: to — oneself, (*de re*) *se iactare, sibi placēre.*

piracy, *latrocinium* (*maritimum*).

pirate, *praedo* (*maritimus*), *pirata.*

piratical, *piraticus, praedatorius.*

piscatory, *piscatorius.*

pistol, render as bow, by *arcus* (*-ūs*).

pit, subst. in gen., *fovea, puteus* (Verg.), *fossa* (= a ditch), *fodina, specus*; in the theatre, *cavea* (= the whole auditorium; to indicate the seats of the lower classes, add the adj. *media* or *summa* or *ultima*).

pit against, v. (*hominem homini*) *opponĕre,* (*hominem cum homine*) *committĕre.*

pit-a-pat: to go —, *palpitare.*

pitch, subst. (**1**) the substance, *pix*; made of —, or —-black, adj. *piceus* (poet.). (**2**) = degree, *fastigium, gradus* (*-ūs*): to such a — of madness, *eo amentiae*; the highest — of a thing can be rendered by using the adj. *extremus* or *summus.* (**3**) in music, *sonus, vox*: at the highest — of the voice, *voce summa*; a high —, *vox acuta*; a low —, *vox gravis.* (**4**) = slope, *fastigium.*

pitch, v. (**1**) of tents, camp, etc., *ponĕre, statuĕre, constituĕre, conlocare, tendĕre.* (**2**) = to throw, *iacĕre, conicĕre.* (**3**) = to smear with —, *picare* (Cat., Suet.). (**4**) intransit.: to — upon, (*in rem, in hominem*) *incidĕre, incurrĕre.*

pitcher, *urceus* (Pl., Hor.).

pitchfork, *furca.*

piteous, pitiable, *miser, miserabilis, miserandus, flebilis,* (*e*)*lamentabilis.*

piteously, *misĕre, miserabiliter, flebiliter, miserandum in modum.*

pitfall, *fovea.*

pith, *medulla* (lit. and fig.).

pithy. LIT., *medullosus* (Cels.). TRANSF., *sententiosus* (= full of meaning), *nervosus* (= vigorous), *densus* (= condensed: Quint.).

pitiful. (1) = full of pity, *clemens, misericors*. (2) see PITEOUS. (3) = mean, *abiectus, sordidus, vilis, humilis, contemptus*; see CONTEMPTIBLE.

pitifully. (1) = with pity, *clementer*. (2) see PITEOUSLY. (3) = meanly, *abiecte, sordide, humiliter*.

pitifulness. (1) = disposition to pity, *clementia, misericordia*. (2) see PITEOUSNESS. (3) = meanness, *humilitas*.

pitiless, *immisericors, inexorabilis, durus, ferreus, inhumanus, crudelis*.

pitilessly, *immisericorditer, inhumane, crudeliter*.

pitilessness, *crudelitas, inhumanitas, saevitia*.

pitman; see MINER.

pittance, *mercedula* (= poor pay), *stips, pecunia exigua*.

pity, subst. *misericordia, miseratio:* to excite —, *misericordiam* (*homini*) *commovēre;* it is a — that, (*per*)*incommode accidit ut;* deserving —, *miserandus, miseratione dignus;* see also PITIFUL.

pity, v. *misereri* (*hominis*), *miserari* (*hominem*); or use the impers. *miseret* (e.g.: I — him, *miseret me eius*).

pivot, *cnodax* (Vitr., rare); or render by *cardo* (= hinge).

placability, *placabilitas*.

placable, *exorabilis, placabilis*.

placard, *libellus, titulus*.

place, subst. (1) = position, site, spot, *locus* (also = — in a book), *regio* (= district): open —, *area, spatium;* at, to, from this —, *hic, huc, hinc;* at, to, from that —, *ibi, eo, inde;* at, to, from the same —, *ibidem, eodem, indidem;* at, to, from another —, *alibi, alio, aliunde;* in no —, *nusquam*. (2) = proper or appointed position, *locus, sedes, statio:* in — of, (*in*) *loco* with genit., or *pro* with abl.; to rise from one's —, *exsurgēre*. (3) = occasion, opportunity, *locus*. (4) = situation, office, *munus* (-*ĕris*, n.), *officium;* of a state official, *magistratus* (-*ūs*): to appoint a man to another's —, *hominem in locum alius sufficēre;* it is not my — to do so, *non est meum* or *non me decet, facĕre*. (5) in enumeration: in the first —, *primo, primum;* in the next —, *deinceps*. (6) to take —, to happen, *fieri, accidĕre*.

place, v. *ponĕre,* (*con*)*locare, statuĕre* (= to — upright): to — oneself, *consistĕre;* to — here and there, *disponĕre;* to — near, *apponĕre;* to — over (i.e. put in command), *praeponĕre, praeficĕre;* to — round, *circumdare, circumiacēre;* to — under, *supponĕre;* to — upon, *imponĕre, superponĕre;* to — before; see PREFER.

placid, *placidus, quietus, tranquillus*.

plagiarism, *furtum*.

plagiarist, render by phrase, such as *qui aliorum scrinia compilat* (Hor.), or *scriptor qui aliena furatur*.

plagiarize, *furari* (*rem ab homine*).

plague, subst. LIT., *pestis, pestilentia;* see also PESTILENCE. TRANSF., *pestis, pernicies, lues, malum:* the — take you! *in malam crucem!;* what the — is it? *quid, malum, est?;* to be a — to a person, *homini molestum esse;* see also PLAGUE, V.

plague, v. *vexare, sollicitare, exercēre, exagitare,* (*homini*) *molestum esse, molestiam exhibēre*.

plain, subst. *campus, planities, planum, aequor* (= any level surface, not only of the sea); of the —, adj. *campestris*.

plain, adj. (1) = clear to the senses or understanding, *clarus, planus, perspicuus, evidens, manifestus*. (2) = candid, unreserved, *simplex, candidus, sincerus, apertus, liber*. (3) = unadorned, *simplex, inornatus;* of style, *subtilis, pressus, tenuis, attenuatus*. (4) = not beautiful, *invenustus* (Cat.).

plainly. (1) = clearly, *clare, plane, perspicue, evidenter, manifesto*. (2) = candidly, *simpliciter, candide, sincere, aperte, libere*. (3) = without ornament, *simpliciter*.

plainness. (1) = clearness, *evidentia, perspicuitas*. (2) = candour, *simplicitas*. (3) = lack of ornament, *simplicitas*. (4) = lack of beauty; see UGLINESS.

plaint; see COMPLAINT.

plaintiff, *petitor*.

plaintive, *miserabilis, flebilis, lamentabilis, queribundus, querulus* (poet.).

plaintively, *miserabiliter, flebiliter*.

plaintiveness, render by adj.

plait, subst. (1) = a fold, *sinus* (-*ūs*), *ruga*. (2) = a braid of hair, *gradus* (-*ūs:* Quint., Suet.).

plait, v. *plicare, intexĕre*.

plan, subst. (1) a — as drawn, a map, diagram, *descriptio*. (2) abstr. = layout, scheme of arrangement, *forma, figura, conformatio*. (3) a — of action, *consilium, cogitatio, propositum, institutum, ratio;* to conceive, or form, a —, *consilium capĕre* or *inire*.

plan, v. (1) = to design, mark in outline, *designare, describĕre*. (2) = to form a — of action, (*ex*)*cogitare, intendĕre, consilium capĕre* or *inire*.

plane, subst. (1) = a flat surface, *planum, libramentum*. (2) the tool, *runcina* (Plin.). (3) the tree, *platanus*.

plane, v. *runcinare* (Varro).

planet, *stella errans* or *vaga, sidus* (-*ĕris*, n.) *errans*.

plank, *tabula, axis:* to nail —s, *coaxare* (Vitr.); to cover with —s, *contabulare*.

planking, *contabulatio, coaxatio;* or render by plur. of PLANK.

plant, subst. *herba, planta* (Ov., Juv.); in plur., —s, *sata* (-*orum;* = things sown: Verg., Ov.).

plant, v. (1) = to put in as a plant, *serĕre, ponĕre* (Verg., Hor.). (2) = to fill or cover with plants, *conserĕre, obserĕre*. (3) in gen. = to put in position, *ponĕre, statuĕre* (= to set up), *constituĕre, infigĕre* (e.g. *signum,* a standard). (4) to — a colony, *coloniam deducĕre*.

plantain, *plantago* (Plin.).

plantation, *plantarium* (= nursery garden: Plin.), *seminarium* (= nursery garden), *arbustum* (esp. of trees round which vines were planted), *quercetum* (= oak-grove: Hor.), *pinetum* (= pine-grove: Ov.), *locus arboribus consĭtus* (gen. term).

planter, *sator, qui serit:* —s of a colony, *coloni*.

planting, subst. as an act, *satio, satus* (-*ūs*), *consitio, consitura*.

plash, subst. *murmur, sonus, sonitus* (-*ūs*).

plash, v. *murmurare*.

plaster, subst. (**1**) as used in building, *gypsum* (Plin.), *arenatum* (Plin.), *tectorium*: a bit of — work, *tectoriolum.* (**2**) in medicine, *emplastrum* (Cels.).

plaster, v. *gypsare* (Col.), *gypso*, etc., *inlinĕre* or *obducĕre.*

plasterer, *tector.*

plastic, adj. *plasticus* (Vitr.).

plate, subst. (**1**) = a thin layer of metal, *lam(i)na, bractea* (poet.). (**2**) = wrought metal, esp. for use at table, *argentum* (= silver —), *vasa* (*-orum*, plur.), *argentea* or *aurea.* (**3**) = a platter, *catillus* (Hor.), *patella* (Hor.).

plate, v.: to — with silver, *argento inducĕre.*

platform, *suggestus* (*-ūs*) or *suggestum* (*-i*), *tribunal*: the — chiefly used for public speaking at Rome was called *rostra* (*-orum*, plur.).

Platonic, *Platonicus*: the — philosophy, *Academia*; a — philosopher or Platonist, *Academicus, Platonicus.*

platter, *catillus* (Hor.), *patella* (Hor.).

plaudit, *plausus* (*-ūs*); see also APPLAUSE.

plausibility, *verisimilitudo, probabilitas*; in bad sense, *simulatio, species.*

plausible, = probable, *veri similis* (or as one word *verisimilis*), *probabilis*; in bad sense, *fucatus, fucosus, speciosus.*

plausibly, = reasonably, with probability, *probabiliter*; in bad sense, *in speciem, simulate.*

play, subst. (**1**) = amusement, *ludus, lusus* (*-ūs*), *lusio*: child's — (of something easily done), *ludus.* (**2**) at the theatre, *fabula* (dim. *fabella*), *ludus scaenicus*: a comic —, *comoedia*; a tragic —, *tragoedia.* (**3**) = scope, free action, *campus, area*: to give free — to a person or thing, *dare ludum* (with dat.: Pl., Hor.). (**4**) = movement, *motus* (*-ūs*), *gestus* (*-ūs*), *argutiae* (*-arum* plur.). (**5**) fair —, *aequum* (*et*) *bonum, condicio aequa.*

play, v. (**1**) on a musical instrument, *modulari* (poet.), *canĕre*, both with abl. of the instrument played (e.g. on a stringed instrument, *fidibus*): to — on a stringed instrument, *psallĕre.* (**2**) = to amuse oneself, *ludĕre* (with abl. of what one —s with or at), *lascivire*: to — together, — with, *conludĕre* (Hor.). (**3**) to — a part, *partes agĕre, personam ferre, gerĕre, sustinĕre.* (**4**) to — the fool, *ineptire* (Ter., Cat.), *desipĕre.* (**5**) to — a trick on a person, *hominem ludificare* or *ludificari, homini imponĕre.* (**6**) to — into the hands of an opponent, *praevaricari.*

play-bill, *libellus.*

player. (**1**) on a musical instrument: on strings, *fidicen* (with f. *fidicina*: Pl., Ter.), *psaltes* (Quint., with f. *psaltria*), *citharista* (with f. *citharistria*: Ter.); on a wind instrument, *tibicen* (with f. *tibicina*). (**2**) see GAMBLER. (**3**) on the stage, *histrio, actor*; see also ACTOR.

playfellow, playmate, *conlusor.*

playful, *lascivus* (poet.), *iocosus.*

playfully, *iocose.*

playfulness, *lascivia.*

playground, *area* (Hor.).

playhouse; see THEATRE.

plaything, *ludibrium* (= what lies at the mercy of some person or thing); otherwise render by phrase, such as *id quod pueris in lusum offertur.*

playwriter, playwright, *fabularum scriptor.*

plea. (**1**) at law, *petitio, exceptio* (= an objection made by the defendant against the plaintiff's statements), *defensio* (= defence). (**2**) = excuse, *excusatio.*

plead. (**1**) at law = to conduct a case, *causam agĕre, dicĕre, orare*: to — often, *actitare.* (**2**) to — as an excuse, *causari, obtendĕre* (Tac., Plin. L.). (**3**) = to beg, entreat, *orare, obsecrare, implorare.*

pleader, *orator, causidicus* (usually contemptuous).

pleasant, pleasing, *acceptus, gratus, iucundus, suavis, dulcis*; of places, *amoenus*; of manner, *comis, urbanus.*

pleasantly, *iucunde, suaviter, commode*; in manner, = affably, *comiter, urbane.*

pleasantness, *iucunditas, dulcedo, suavitas, commoditas*; of places, *amoenitas*; of manner, *comitas, urbanitas.*

pleasantry, *facetiae* (*-arum*, plur.), *lepos, festivitas, iocus* (= joke).

please, v. (**1**) = to give pleasure to, (*homini*) *placĕre*, (*hominem*) *delectare*, (*homini*) *gratum* or *cordi esse*, (*homini*) *adridĕre*; often rendered by the impers. *libet*, with dat. of person pleased, and n. pron. or infin. as subject: to be —d with oneself, *sibi placĕre.* (**2**) = to see fit, be disposed, *velle*; if you —, *si placet, si libet, si* (*tibi*) *videtur, nisi molestum est*; more colloq., please! *sis* (= *si vis*: Ter.), *amabo.*

pleasing, adj.; see PLEASANT.

pleasure. (**1**) = enjoyment, delight, *voluptas, delectatio, delectamentum* (rare), *oblectamentum, gaudium, laetitia, iucunditas*: sensual —s, (*corporis*) *voluptates*; fond of —, *voluptarius*; to derive — from a thing, *re delectari, voluptatem ex re capĕre*; to give a person —, *gratum homini facĕre.* (**2**) = liking, inclination, choice, *arbitrium, libido*; or render by verb, such as *velle* or *placĕre.*

pleasure-grounds, *horti* (*-orum*, plur.).

plebeian, *homo plebeius, homo de plebe*: the —s, *plebeii, plebs*; the order of the —s, *ordo plebeius, plebs.*

plebeian, adj. *plebeius* (opp. *patricius*).

pledge, subst. *pignus* (*-ēris* or *-ŏris*), *cautio, arrabo* (Pl., Ter.).

pledge, v. (*op*)*pignerare, obligare*: to — one's word, *fidem interponĕre* or *obligare, spondĕre, promittĕre, recipĕre.*

plenary; see FULL, COMPLETE.

plenipotentiary, render by *legatus* (= ambassador).

plenitude; see FULL.

plenteous, plentiful, *uber, abundans, copiosus, largus.*

plentifully, *uberius, uberrime* (not in posit.), *abunde, abundanter, copiose, large, cumulate, effuse.*

plenty, *ubertas, copia, abundantia, adfluentia*; sometimes *satis* (= enough) with genit.: to have — of a thing, *rē abundare.*

pleonasm, render by phrase, such as *nimia copia verborum.*

pleurisy, *pleuritis* (Vitr.).

pliable, pliant, *lentus, flexibilis* (lit. and fig.), *mollis* (lit. and fig.).

pliancy, pliability, *lentitia* (Plin.), *lentor* (Plin.), *mollitia* (lit. and fig.).

plight, subst.; see CONDITION, STATE.

---

plight, v.; see PLEDGE.

plinth, *plinthus* or *plinthis* (Vitr.).

plod, *repĕre* (Hor.); or render by phrase, such as *tarde progredi*.

plot, subst. (1) of ground, *agellus, area.* (2) = a scheme, conspiracy, *coniuratio, consensio, conspiratio.* (3) of a story, play, etc., *argumentum fabulae.*

plot, v. (1) intransit. = to conspire, *coniurare, consentire, conspirare.* (2) transit. *machinari;* see also PLAN, DEVISE.

plotter; see CONSPIRATOR.

plough, subst. *aratrum:* a —man, —boy, *arator, bubulcus;* a —share, *vomer;* a — handle, *stiva* (Verg.).

plough, v. *arare* (absol. and with acc.): to — in, *inarare* (Varro); to — up, *exarare, proscindĕre* (Lucr., Verg.); to — round, *circumarare.*

ploughing, subst. *aratio.*

pluck, subst. = courage, *animus, virtus* (-*ūtis*).

pluck, v. *vellĕre* (= to tear up or away): to — out, *evellĕre;* to — flowers, *flores carpĕre, decerpĕre;* to — up courage, *animum recipĕre.*

plug, *operculum* (= lid), *obturamentum* (Plin.).

plum, *prunum* (Verg., Ov.).

plumage, render as feathers, by *plumae* or *pennae* (*pinnae*).

plumber, *artifex plumbarius* (Vitr.).

plumb-line, plummet, *linea, perpendiculum.*

plume, subst. *pluma, penna* (*pinna*).

plume, v.: to — oneself, *sibi placēre;* to — oneself on a thing, *rem iactare, rē superbire.*

plump, *pinguis.*

plumpness, *pinguitudo* (Cato, Varro).

plum-tree, *prunus* (Verg.).

plumy, *plumis obductus, plumatus* (poet.), *plumosus* (Prop.), *pennatus* (poet.).

plunder, subst. *praeda, rapina* (= act of plundering): to live by —, (*ex*) *rapto vivĕre.*

plunder, v. *praedari* (transit. or intransit.), *praedam facĕre, diripĕre, compilare, expilare,* (*de*)*spoliare:* to — completely, *exinanire, everrĕre, extergĕre.*

plunderer, *direptor, spoliator, praedator, expilator.*

plunge, v. (1) transit. LIT., *mergĕre* (*in rem* or *in re*), *demergĕre, submergĕre, immergĕre;* see also THRUST. TRANSF., = to bring into a situation, *adducĕre, detrudĕre.* (2) intransit. LIT., *se mergĕre, immergĕre,* etc. TRANSF., = to commit oneself fully (to a way of living, etc.), *se mergĕre, se ingurgitare.*

pluperfect, *tempus praeteritum plus quam perfectum* (Gram.).

plural, adj. *pluralis* (Quint.); in the —, *pluraliter* (Quint.).

plurality, render by *plures* (= more) or *multitudo* (= a number).

ply, v. *exercēre.*

Po, the river, *Padus.*

poach, v. render by phrase, such as *furtim feras intercipĕre.*

poacher, *fur* (= thief).

pocket, subst. *sinus* (-*ūs*), since the ancients had no —s in their garments, but used the folds in the toga; or render by *sacculus* (= small bag: Juv.) or *crumena* (= purse: Pl., Hor.).

pocket, v. = to take dishonestly, *intercipĕre, avertĕre.*

pocket-book, *pugillares* (-*ium*, plur.: Plin.).

pocket-handkerchief, *sudarium* (Cat., Suet.).

pocket-knife, *culter.*

pocket-money, *peculium.*

pod, *siliqua* (Verg., Plin.).

poem, *carmen* (esp. a lyric, epic, or dramatic —), *pŏēma* (-*ătis,* n.): to write a —, *carmen* or *poema facĕre, scribĕre, condĕre.*

poesy; see POETRY.

poet, *pŏēta, carminum auctor* or *scriptor* or *conditor, vates* (= bard; poet.).

poetaster (as term of contempt), *pŏēta malus;* or render by reference to some poet disparaged by the classical writers, such as *Maevius* or *Bavius.*

poetess, *poetria.*

poetical, *poeticus.*

poetically, *poetice, poetarum more.*

poetry, *poetice* or *poetica, poesis:* a piece of —; see POEM.

poignant, *acer;* see also KEEN.

point, subst. (1) = sharp end, *acumen, cuspis, spiculum, cacumen, mucro.* (2) as geograph. t. t., *promontorium.* (3) = place, spot, *locus:* highest —, *vertex, culmen, apex* (fig.), *fastigium* (fig.); the highest — of the mountain, *summus mons.* (4) of time: on the — of doing a thing, render by *in eo est, ut,* with subj. or by fut. partic.; on the — of death, *moribundus.* (5) = an item, topic, esp. a topic under consideration: the — at issue, *res, caput;* to the —, *ad rem;* the — in dispute, *quaestio;* an important —, *res magni momenti;* the most important —, *res maximi momenti, res gravissima.* (6) see DEGREE, PITCH.

point, v. (1) = to make sharp, (*prae*)*acuĕre.* (2) to — out, indicate, (*digito*) *monstrare, indicare.*

point-blank, render by adj. *directus:* to refuse —, *praecise* or *prorsus negare.*

pointed, adj. LIT., (*prae*)*acutus.* TRANSF., = witty, significant, *salsus, aculeatus.*

pointedly, *salse.*

pointer. (1) = an indication, *index, indicium.* (2) the dog, *canis* (*venaticus*).

pointless, *insulsus, frigidus, ineptus, inanis.*

poise, v. *librare.*

poison, subst. *venenum, virus* (Verg., Plin.), *toxicum* (Pl., Hor.); sometimes *medicamentum.*

poison, v. (1) = to render poisonous, *venenare, veneno imbuĕre.* (2) to kill (or attack) with —, *veneno* (*hominem*) *necare, venenum* (*homini*) *dare;* to — oneself, *veneno sibi mortem consciscĕre;* fig.: to — the minds of the young, render by phrase, such as *animos adulescentium malis libidinibus inficĕre.*

poisoner, *veneficus* (with f. *venefica*).

poisoning, subst. *veneficium.*

poisonous, *venenatus, veneno imbutus* or *infectus* or *tinctus.*

poke, v.: to — a person, *hominem fodĕre* or *fodicare* (Hor.); to — the fire, *ignem excitare;* to — about, *rimari, perscrutari.*

poker, render by *ferramentum* (= any iron tool).

polar, *septentrionalis* (*septemt*-: = northern).

pole. (1) = long rod, *contus* (Verg., Tac.), *pertica* (Ov., Plin.), *longurius, asser.* (2) of the earth, *axis, cardo* (Ov.), *polus* (Ov.): the south —, *axis meridianus;* the north —, *axis septentrionalis* (*septemt*-); also simply *axis.*

poleaxe; see AXE.

polecat, *feles.*

L.D.—26*

polemical, render by verb *disputare* or subst. *disputatio* or *controversia.*

polemics, *disputationes* (*-um,* plur.), *controversiae* (*-arum,* plur.).

police: the work of the — can be described generally by some such phrase as *publicae* or *urbanae securitatis cura*; the magistrates responsible for such work in Rome were the aediles (*aediles, -ium,* plur.); for —men, — constables, use *vigiles* (*-um,* plur.; strictly = night —: Suet.).

policy. (1) = view or aim in politics, *ratio rei publicae gerendae, consilia* (*-orum,* plur.); or render by the verb *sentire* (*de republica*). (2) in gen. = prudence, *prudentia, consilium.*

polish, subst. = the state of having been polished, *nitor* (lit. and fig.).

polish, v. *polire, perpolire, expolire* (all both lit and fig.); *limare* (fig. only; lit. = to file).

polished, *nitidus, mundus, elegans*; or render by past. partic. such as *limatus* or (*per*)*politus*; see also POLITE.

polite, *urbanus, comis, humanus.*

politely, *urbane, comiter, humane, humaniter.*

politeness, *urbanitas, comitas, humanitas.*

politic, *prudens, sagax, astutus, circumspectus, providus.*

political, *civilis, publicus, politicus* (= relating to — science); often rendered by *reipublicae* (genit. sing.): — change, *res* (*rerum,* plur.) *novae*; a — discussion, *sermo de republicā habitus*; — questions, *res civiles*; — opinions, see POLICY; — science, *ratio civilis, reipublicae gerendae ratio.*

politician, *vir rerum civilium* (or *reipublicae*) *peritus.*

politics, *civilis ratio, respublica*; to take up —, *ad rempublicam accedere, rem publicam attingere*; to be engaged in —, *in republica versari*; to take no part in —, *reipublicae deesse*; what are his —? *quid de republica sentit?*

polity, *reipublicae forma.*

poll, subst. (1) see HEAD. (2) = voting, *suffragium, comitia* (*-orum,* plur.; = the assembly for elections).

poll, v. (1) = to lop, (*am*)*putare, praecidere.* (2) see VOTE.

pollard, render by partic., such as *amputatus.*

polling; see POLL, subst.

polling-booth, *saeptum, ovile.*

poll-tax, *exactio capitum*: to impose a —, *tributum in singula capita imponere.*

pollute, *polluere, inquinare, contaminare, foedare, maculare.*

pollution. (1) the act, render by verb. (2) = filth, *conluvio, impuritas.*

poltroon; see COWARD.

polygamy, render by phrases, such as *plures uxores habere* (of a man), *pluribus nuptam esse* (of a woman).

polyglot, *pluribus linguis scriptus.*

polygonal, *polygonius* (Vitr.), *multangulus* (Lucr.).

polypus, *polypus* (as animal, Plin.; and as tumour, Cels.).

polytheism, *multorum deorum cultus* (*-ūs*).

polytheist, *qui multos deos colit.*

pomade, pomatum, *capillare* (Mart.), *unguentum.*

pomegranate, *mālum granatum* or *Punicum* (Col.).

pommel, subst.; see SADDLE.

pommel, v.; see BEAT.

pomp, *apparatus* (*-ūs*); of literary or rhetorical style, *pompa, tumor* (Sen., Quint.).

pompous, *magnificus* (Ter.), *gloriosus*; of style, *tumidus* (Quint., Plin. L.).

pompously, *magnifice, gloriose.*

pompousness, pomposity, *magnificentia*; see also POMP.

pond, *stagnum, piscina, lacus* (*-ūs*), *lacuna* (poet.).

ponder, *considerare, ponderare, secum reputare,* (*in*) *animo volutare.*

ponderous, *ponderosus, gravis.*

poniard, *pugio, sica.*

pontiff, *pontifex.*

pontoon, render by *pons* (= bridge or gangway) or by *ponto* (= ferry-boat).

pony, *mannus* (Lucr., Hor.), *mannulus* (Plin.).

pool; see POND.

poop, *puppis.*

poor. (1) = not rich, *pauper* (= poor but not destitute), *pauperculus, perpauper* (= very poor; rare), *tenuis, inops* (= destitute: Hor., Ov.), *egens* (= destitute), *mendicus* (= poverty-stricken); a — man, subst. *pauper, egens.* (2) = of quality = inferior, *mediocris, tenuis*; of language, *exilis, ieiunus, inops*; of soil, *macer, exilis, ieiunus.* (3) = wretched, pitiable, *miser, infelix, miserandus*: — little, *misellus.*

poorly, adj.: to be —, *aegrotare, infirma valetudine esse.*

poorly, adv. *tenuiter, mediocriter, misere.*

pop, v. *crepare*: to — out, *evadere, exsilire.*

pope, *pontifex, papa* (both eccl.).

poplar, *pōpulus* (poet.): of the —, adj. *pōpuleus* (poet.).

poppy, n. *papaver* (*-ĕris,* n.).

populace, *multitudo, plebs*: the dregs of the —, *populi faex* or *sentina*; see also PEOPLE.

popular. (1) = belonging to the people, *popularis*: the — party, *populares* (*-ium,* plur.). (2) = liked, in favour, *popularis* (rare) *gratiosus, populo* (or *in vulgus*) *gratus* or *acceptus*: to be —, *gratiā multum valēre, in gratiā esse* (*apud hominem*); to become —, *gratiam inire* (*ab homine* or *apud hominem*). (3) of style, etc., render by phrase, such as *ad commune iudicium accommodatus.*

popularity, *gratia, populi favor* or *studium*: the breath of — or of popular favour, *popularis aura* (poet.).

populate; see PEOPLE, v.

population, *civium* or *incolarum numerus, cives* (*-ium,* plur. = citizens), *incolae* (*-arum,* plur. = inhabitants); see also PEOPLE.

populous, *frequens, celeber.*

populousness, *hominum* (or *civium*), *frequentia* or *celebritas* or *multitudo.*

porch, *vestibulum.*

porcupine, *hystrix* (Plin.).

pore, subst. *foramen.*

pore, v.: to — over a thing, (*totum*) *se abdere rē* or *in re.*

pork, *porcina* (Pl.): a — seller, *porcinarius* (Pl.).

porker, *porcus.*

porosity, *raritas.*

porous, *rarus.*

porphyry, *porphyrites* (Plin.).

porpoise, *porculus marinus* (Plin.).

porridge, *puls.*

porringer, *catillus* (Hor.), *patella.*

port. (1) = harbour, *portus (-ūs)*. (2) see GAIT.

portable, *quod portari potest.*

portcullis, *cataracta.*

portend, *portendĕre, significare, denuntiare.*

portent, *portentum, ostentum, prodigium, monstrum, signum, omen.*

portentous, *portentosus, monstr(u)osus.*

portentously, *monstr(u)ose.*

porter. (1) = keeper of a gate, *ianitor* (with f. *ianitrix*: Pl.), *ostiarius* (Varro, Suet.). (2) = one who carries burdens, *baiulus.*

portfolio, *scrinium* (Hor., Ov.).

porthole, *fenestra.*

portico, *porticus (-ūs).*

portion, *pars, portio*; see also PART, SHARE: a marriage —, *dos.*

portly, *pinguis, corpulentus* (Pl., Quint.).

portmanteau, *vidulus* (Pl.), *mantica* (Cat., Hor.).

portrait, *imago (picta).*

portray, *depingĕre* (in words or colours); *expingĕre* (in words only).

position. (1) physical = place, site, *locus, situs (-ūs), sedes, status (-ūs), positura* (Lucr.). (2) abstr. = state, situation, *locus, status (-ūs), condicio*; for a person's — (= rank, standing, etc.), the foregoing words are used, and also *gradus (-ūs).*

positive, = certain, *certus*: a — statement, *adfirmatio*; to make a — statement, *confirmare, adfirmare*; as grammat. t. t., *positivus* (Gram.).

positively, *adfirmate* (with verbs of assertion), *certe, certo* (with verbs of knowing).

positiveness, = positive assertion, *adfirmatio.*

possess. LIT., = to have a thing, *possidēre, habēre, tenēre*; or render by *esse*, with the possession as subject and possessor in the dat., e.g.: I — a book, *est mihi liber*. TRANSF., (1) to — a quality, render by *esse* with adj. or with genit. or abl. of quality. (2) of feelings, etc., to overcome, overwhelm a person, *invadĕre, occupare, capĕre, incedĕre.*

possession. (1) = the state of possessing, *possessio*; to have —, *possidēre*; to take —, *occupare, capĕre, (rē* or *rei*, genit.) *potiri.* (2) = property, *possessio, res, bona (-orum,* plur.).

possessive. (1) in gen., render by phrase, such as *tenax suorum.* (2) as grammat. t. t., *possessivus* (Gram.).

possessor, *possessor, dominus.*

possibility, usually rendered by *posse* (e.g.: there is no — of his coming, *fieri non potest ut veniat*); sometimes by *potestas, facultas, copia* (= opportunity).

possible, render by the verb *posse*: it is — for me to live, *vivĕre possum*; it is — that, *fieri potest, ut*, with subj. Sometimes instead of *posse* the impersonal expressions *licet* (= it is allowed), *fas est* (= it is lawful), or *est ut* (with subj.) may be used. As . . . as — is usually rendered by *quam* followed by superl. adj. or adv., with or without *posse* (e.g.: as quickly as —, *quam celerrime*); sometimes by *ut*, followed by superl. adv. and *posse* (e.g.: I did it as carefully as —, *feci ut diligentissime potui*); as great as —, can be translated by *quantus maximus*, with *posse*; as soon as —, *quam primum, primo quoque tempore*; all —, every —, *omnis.*

possibly, render by *posse* (e.g.: it may — be that, *fieri potest ut*), see also PERHAPS.

post, subst. (1) = something set upright in the ground, *palus* (= a stake), *cippus* (esp. gravestone: Hor.): a door - —, *postis.* (2) milit. t. t., *statio, praesidium.* (3) = office, *locus, munus (-ĕris,* n.); of a magistrate, *magistratus (-ūs).* (4) = an arrangement for the conveyance of letters, *tabellarii (-orum,* plur. = letter-carriers): to send through the —, *per tabellarios mittĕre.*

post, v. (1) to — up a notice, etc., in public, *proponĕre.* (2) = to station troops, *(dis)-ponĕre, (con)locare, constituĕre.* (3) to — a letter, *litteras* (or *epistulam) tabellario dare.*

postage, *vecturae pretium.*

posterior, subst. *nates (-ium,* plur.: Pl., Juv.), *clunes (-ium,* plur.), *pyga* (Hor.).

posterior, adj. *posterior.*

posterity, *posteritas, posteri (-orum,* plur.), *minores (-um,* plur.; poet.).

postern, *posticum.*

posthaste, *quam celerrime.*

posthumous; of a son, *post patrem mortuum natus*; of a book, perhaps *post auctorem mortuum editus.*

postillion; see RIDER, GROOM.

postman, *tabellarius* (= private letter-carrier).

postpone, *differre, proferre, prorogare, reicĕre.*

postscript, render by phrase, such as *res epistulae subiecta.*

postulate, subst. *sumptio.*

posture. (1) of body, *status, habitus, gestus* (all *-ūs).* (2) of affairs, *status (-ūs), res, condicio, ratio*; see also POSITION, STATE.

pot, *olla.*

potbellied, *ventriosus* (Pl.).

potent; see POWERFUL, EFFICACIOUS.

potentate, *res, tyrannus, princeps.*

potential, *potentialis* (Gram.); see also POSSIBLE.

potherbs, *holus (-ĕris,* n.).

pothook, *uncus.*

pothouse, *caupona.*

potion, *potio*; see also PHILTRE.

potsherd, *testa* (Ov., Plin.).

pottage, *ius (iuris,* n.).

potter, subst. *figulus* (Varro, Juv.): a —'s wheel, *rota figularis* (Pl.); a —'s workshop, *figlina* (Plin.).

potter, v. (colloq): render by phrase such as *in opusculis versari.*

pottery. (1) the art, *figlina* (Varro). (2) = pots, etc., *fictilia (-ium,* n.).

pouch, *sacculus* (Cat., Juv.), *saccus.*

poulterer, *qui altiles vendit.*

poultice, *emplastrum* (Cato, Cels.); *malagma, -ătis,* n. (= an emollient —: Cels.).

poultry, *aves cohortales* (plur.: Col.), *altiles (-ium,* plur. = fattened —: Hor.).

poultry-yard, *cohors* (Ov.).

pounce: to — upon, *involare*; see also SEIZE.

pound, subst. (1) as a measure of weight, *libra*; the old abl. sing. *pondo* is sometimes added after *libra* and occasionally used alone with a numeral, *libra* being understood (e.g.: five —s of gold, *auri quinque pondo).* (2) = an enclosure, *saeptum (publicum).*

pound, v. *(con)tundĕre, (con)terĕre.*

pour, v. (1) transit. *fundĕre*: to — forth, *profundĕre*; to — in, *infundĕre*; to — out, *effundĕre.* (2) intransit. *fundi, fluĕre, ferri.*

pouring, adj. (of rain), *effusus.*

pout, *labellum extendĕre* (Juv.).

poverty. (1) of means, *paupertas, angustiae rei familiaris* (= narrow means), *tenuitas, egestas* (= destitution), *inopia* (= destitution), *mendicitas* (= beggary). (2) = of quality = inferiority, inadequacy, *egestas, inopia;* of style, *ieiunitas, exilitas.*

powder, subst. *pulvis.*

powder, v. (1) = to reduce to —, *in pulverem conterĕre.* (2) = to sprinkle with —, *pulvere conspergĕre.*

power. (1) = force, vigour (physical or otherwise), *vis* (and plur. *vires,* esp. of physical —), *robur, lacerti* (-*orum,* physical), *nervi* (-*orum,* plur.), *potentia;* military —, *opes* (-*um,* plur.); with all one's —, *summā* (or *omni*) *ope.* (2) = authority: absolute —, *dominatio, singulare imperium;* royal —, *regnum;* = sovereignty (esp. of one people over another), *dicio;* — in gen. (esp. natural or properly conferred), *imperium, potestas, ius* (*iuris,* n.); unofficial —, *potentia;* in the — of a person, *penes hominem, in potestate* or *manu* or *dicione hominis;* to have the — to do a thing, *posse;* to have great —, *multum posse* or *valēre.*

powerful. (1) physically, *validus, valens, robustus, lacertosus.* (2) in influence, etc., *potens, valens, validus.* (3) of speech, *gravis, nervosus, validus* (Quint.).

powerfully, *graviter, vehementer, valde.*

powerless, *invalidus, impotens, infirmus, imbecillus:* to be —, *nihil posse.*

powerlessness, *imbecillitas, infirmitas.*

practicability, *facultas, potestas;* or render by the verb *posse.*

practicable, *quod fieri* or *effici potest, facilis* (= easy, opp. *difficilis*).

practical, of a person, (*rerum*) *usu peritus, ipso usu perdoctus:* — knowledge, *usus* (-*ūs*); to have a — knowledge of a thing, *rem usu cognitam habēre, usu didicisse, rei* (genit.) *usum habēre.*

practically, = by experience, (*ex*) *usu;* see also NEARLY, ALMOST.

practice. (1) = exercise, experience, *usus* (-*ūs*), *exercitatio, tractatio, facultas* (opp. to *ars* = theory: Cic.). (2) = custom, *mos, consuetudo.* (3) = deed, line of conduct, *facinus* (-*oris,* n.), *factum.*

practise. (1) = to do, exercise, engage in, *facĕre, exercēre, factitare, tractare.* (2) = to do a thing by way of preparation, rehearse, *meditari.*

practitioner, = doctor, *medicus.*

praetor, *praetor.*

praetorian, *praetorius, praetorianus* (Tac.).

praetorship, *praetura.*

pragmatical, = meddlesome, *molestus, qui res alienas tractat.*

prairie, *campus.*

praise, subst. *laus, laudatio* (= a laudatory oration), *praedicatio* (= the act of praising, esp. in public), *praeconium;* to damn with faint —, *maligne laudare.*

praise, v. *laudare, conlaudare,* (*homini*) *laudem tribuĕre,* or *impertire,* (*hominem*) *laude adficĕre, laudibus efferre, praedicare.*

praiseworthily, *laudabiliter.*

praiseworthy, *laudabilis, laude dignus, laudandus, laudatus, praedicabilis.*

prance, *exsilire, exsultare.*

prank, *iocus.*

prate, prattle, *garrire, blaterare* (Hor.).

pray, *precari, rogare, orare, obsecrare* (all of these often with acc. of deity or person —ed to; what is —ed for is rendered by another acc. or an *ut* clause); *supplicare* (with dat. of deity or person); to — against, — that a thing may not happen, *deprecari.*

prayer, *preces* (-*um,* plur.; also abl. sing. *prece*), *precatio, imploratio, votum* (= a prayer involving a conditional promise, a vow).

prayerful, *supplex.*

praying, subst. *precatio, preces* (-*um,* plur.), *supplicatio* (humble): a day of — and thanksgiving, *supplicatio et gratulatio;* to appoint —, *supplicationem decernĕre.*

preach, *docēre, orationem* or *contionem habēre;* in eccl. Latin, *contionari* or *praedicare.*

preacher, *praedicator* (eccl.): a — to deaf ears (as a semi-proverbial phrase), *monitor non exauditus.*

preamble, *exordium.*

precarious, *incertus, dubius.*

precaution: to take —s, *providēre, praecavēre.*

precede, (in space or time) *anteire, antegredi, antecedĕre, praeire* (in space; also of one speaker dictating to another), *praegredi* (in space).

precedence, *prior locus:* to take — of a person, *homini antecedĕre;* to let anyone have —, *homini cedĕre.*

precedent, *exemplum.*

preceding, *prior, superior;* of one immediately before, *proximus.*

precept, *praeceptum, praescriptum, mandatum, lex.*

preceptor, *magister, praeceptor.*

precincts, *termini* (-*orum,* plur.), *fines* (-*ium,* plur.).

precious, *magni pretii, splendidus, egregius, eximius:* a — stone, *gemma.*

precipice, *locus praeceps.*

precipitancy, precipitation, *temeritas.*

precipitate, adj. *temerarius, praeceps, inconsultus.*

precipitate, v. *praecipitare, deicĕre, deturbare:* to — oneself, *sese praecipitare, praecipitari, se inferre, inferri.*

precipitately, *temere.*

precipitous, *praeceps, praeruptus.*

precise. (1) of things, *definitus, accuratus, subtilis.* (2) of persons, *diligens, elegans.*

precisely, *subtiliter;* see also JUST.

precision, *subtilitas, elegantia;* of persons, perhaps *diligentia.*

precocious, *praecox* (Sen., Quint.).

preconceived, *praeiudicatus.*

preconception, *praeiudicata opinio.*

preconcerted, *ex composito factus.*

precursor, *praecursor, praenuntius* (with f. *praenuntia*).

predatory, *praedatorius, praedabundus.*

predecessor, in an office, *decessor* (Tac.); or render by adj. *proximus.*

predestination, *praedestinatio* (eccl.).

predetermine, *praefinire, praestituĕre.*

predicament, *difficultas, angustiae* (-*arum,* plur.).

predicate, subst. *attributio, attributum.*

predicate, v. *praedicare, dicĕre.*
predict, *praedicĕre, vaticinari.*
prediction, *praedictio, praedictum, vaticinatio.*
predilection, *studium;* see also AFFECTION.
predispose, *(animum) inclinare.*
predisposed, *propensus, proclivis.*
predisposition, *(animi) proclivitas, (voluntatis) inclinatio, studium.*
predominance, *potentia, principatus (-ūs);* see also POWER, SUPREMACY.
predominant. (1) *potens, praepollens;* see also POWERFUL. (2) = more numerous, *plures.*
predominate. (1) *(prae)pollēre, superare, vincĕre.* (2) = to be more numerous, *plures esse.*
preeminence, *praestantia, excellentia, eminentia.*
preeminent, *praestans, praestabilis, excellens, praecipuus, egregius, insignis.*
preeminently, *praecipue;* see also ESPECIALLY.
preexist, *antea exstare* or *esse.*
preexistence, render by verb.
preface, subst. *prooemium, praefatio.*
preface, v. (= to say by way of —), *praefari.*
prefatory: to make a few — remarks, *pauca praefari.*
prefect, *praefectus.*
prefecture, *praefectura.*
prefer. (1) to — a charge against a person, *nomen hominis deferre;* see also ACCUSE. (2) = to put one person or thing before another, *anteponĕre, praeponĕre, anteferre, praeferre, praeoptare* (all these with acc. and dat. as in English); with infin. as object, *malle, praeoptare.*
preferable, *potior, melior.*
preferably, *potius.*
preference, *praepositio;* or render by verb PREFER.
preferment, *honor* (= office).
prefix, v. *praeponĕre, praescribĕre* (in writing).
pregnancy, *graviditas.*
pregnant, LIT., *praegnans, gravida (ex viro):* to be —, *gravidam* or *praegnantem esse, ventrem ferre, partum ferre* or *gestare.* TRANSF., of physical objects, *gravidus* (poet.); of language, *pressus* (= concise); of events, *magni* or *maximi momenti.*
prehensile, *ad prehendendum aptus* or *habilis.*
prejudge, *praeiudicare.*
prejudice, subst. (1) = a premature judgment, *opinio praeiudicata:* a deep-rooted —, *opinio confirmata* or *inveterata;* an absurd —, *opinio prava* or *perversa;* a — against a person, *invidia.* (2) = damage, *detrimentum;* without —, *sine fraude.*
prejudice, v.: to — the jury against a person, *hominem iudicibus suspectum reddĕre, iudices ab homine alienare;* to be —d about a matter, *rem praeiudicatam habēre;* to come with no —s, *nihil praeiudicati adferre.*
prejudicial, *noxius, nocens, damnosus.*
prelate, *episcopus* (eccl.).
preliminary, adj.: a — inquiry, *praeiudicium;* — remarks, *praefatio;* — sparring, *prolusio.*
prelude, subst. LIT., *prooemium.* TRANSF., *prolusio, praelusio atque praecursio* (Plin. L.).
premature, *immaturus, praematurus* (Juv., Tac.), *praeproperus, acerbus.*
prematurely, *ante tempus, praemature* (Pl.).
premeditate, *praemeditari, cogitare;* see also PURPOSE, ON.

premeditation, *praemeditatio;* see also PURPOSE.
premier, = prime minister, perhaps *vir penes quem est summa reipublicae.*
premise, premises. (1) in logic, —, *principia (-orum,* plur.): the minor —, *adsumptio;* the major —, *propositio.* (2) — = a building, *aedificium, domus;* see also HOUSE, BUILDING.
premise, v. *praefari, ponĕre.*
premiss; see PREMISE, (1).
premium, *praemium.*
premonition, *monitio, monitum.*
premonitory, *quod praemonet.*
preoccupation. LIT., *praeoccupatio.* TRANSF., *animus rei* (dat.) *deditus;* see also PREOCCUPY.
preoccupy. LIT., = to seize beforehand, *(prae)occupare.* TRANSF., to be preoccupied about a thing, *totum in re versari.*
preparation. (1) = the act of preparing, *praeparatio, apparatio, apparatus (-ūs), praemeditatio* (= premeditation), *meditatio* (= the preparing of a lesson, etc.), *commentatio* (= the thinking over anything, e.g. a play, a speech). (2) a — as made, a measure taken in advance: to make —s, *parare.*
preparatory, render by verb.
prepare, *(ap)parare, praeparare, comparare, instruĕre:* to — for war, *bellum (ap)parare;* to — a speech, lesson, etc., *meditari, commentari;* to — oneself, *se (com)parare (ad rem).*
preponderance, preponderate; see PREDOMINANCE, PREDOMINATE.
prepossess, = to win over, *delenire, permulcēre.*
prepossessing; see AGREEABLE, CHARMING.
prepossession, *sententia praeiudicata;* see also PREJUDICE.
preposterous, *praeposterus;* see also ABSURD, PERVERSE.
prerogative; see RIGHT.
presage, subst. *praesagium* (Ov., Tac.), *augurium.*
presage, v. (1) = to foreshow, *portendĕre, significare.* (2) = to forebode, *praesagire, augurari.*
prescient, *praesciens* (poet.).
prescribe, *praescribĕre.*
prescriptive: — right, perhaps *ius ex usu factum.*
presence. LIT., *praesentia:* frequent —, *adsiduitas;* in my —, *coram me* (abl.), *me praesente.* TRANSF., — of mind, *praesens animus.*
present, subst. *donum, munus.*
present, adj. (1) physically —, *praesens:* to be —, *adesse* (with dat.); to be — and take part in what goes on, *interesse* (with dat.). (2) of time, *praesens,* but more often *hic* (= this); sometimes *hodiernus;* at —, *nunc, hoc tempore, hodie;* for the —, *in praesentia, in praesens (tempus), ad praesens* (Tac.). (3) as grammat. t. t., *praesens* (Gram.).
present, v. (1) = to bring forward, *offerre, obicĕre, praebēre* (all with acc. and dat. as in English): to — oneself (or itself), *occurrĕre, obvenire, dari* (of opportunities, etc.). (2) = to give, *donare, munerari* (both with either direct and indirect object like English 'present to,' or with acc. of recipient and abl. of gift, like English 'present with'); *dare (rem homini).* (3) = to introduce, *introducĕre, inducĕre.*

presentation (as an act), *donatio*; or render by verb.

presentiment, *praesagitio, augurium, praesagium* (Ov., Tac.): to have a —, *praesagire.*

presently, = soon, *mox, brevi.*

preservation. (1) as an act, *conservatio, tuitio*; or render by verb. (2) = safety, *salūs (-ūtis).*

preserve, subst. (= jam, etc.), *fructus (-ūs), condĭtus.*

preserve, v. (1) = to keep safe, *(con)servare, tueri* (= to watch over), *sustinēre* (= to uphold, support; so also *sustentare*). (2) = to conserve, *condire.*

preserver, *(con)servator* (with f. *servatrix*).

preside, *praesidēre, praeesse* (with dat.).

presidency, *praefectura*; or render by verb.

president, *praefectus*; or render by verb.

press, subst. *prelum* (used also in modern Latin for printing —), *torcular* (for wine, oil, etc.: Plin.).

press, v. (1) transit. LIT., of physical pressure, *premĕre, comprimĕre*: to — in, *imprimĕre*; to — out, *exprimĕre*; to — into shape, *premĕre* (Verg., Hor.). TRANSF., = to urge, harry, *premĕre, urgēre, instare* (with dat.). (2) intransit.: to — on, — forward, *pergĕre, instare, contendĕre.*

press-gang, render by phrase, such as *qui nautas vi comparant.*

pressing, adj.; see IMPORTANT, URGENT.

pressure. LIT., *pressus (-ūs), vis, pondus (-eris,* n.), *impressio, nisus (-ūs).* TRANSF., render by verb.

prestige, *nomen, gloria, fama.*

presume. (1) = to take liberties; render by *sibi adrogare* or *sibi sumĕre*, with object (= to take upon oneself); with infin. (= to dare), *audēre.* (2) = to assume, suppose, *sumĕre, credĕre.*

presumption. (1) = presumptuousness, *adrogantia.* (2) = supposition, *coniectura, opinio*; or render by verb.

presumptive, render by verb.

presumptuous, *adrogans.*

presumptuously, *adroganter.*

presumptuousness, *adrogantia.*

pretence, *simulatio, species*: under — of, *simulatione, per simulationem, per speciem, per causam,* with genit.; without the least —, *sine fuco ac fallaciis.*

pretend, *simulare, fingĕre*: to — that a thing is not so, *dissimulare.*

pretended, *simulatus, fictus.*

pretender, in gen. *simulator*: one who claims the throne, *qui regnum sibi adrogat* or *adfectat.*

pretension. (1) = a claim, *postulatio.* (2) = display, *ostentatio.*

preterite, *praeteritum (tempus)* (Gram.).

preternaturally, *praeter naturam, mirabili quodam modo.*

pretext, *praescriptio, titulus, causa, simulatio, species, praetextum* (Tac.), *obtentus (-ūs*: Tac.): to use as a —, *praetendĕre, obtendĕre* (Tac., Plin. L.), *praescribĕre* (Tac.); see also PRETENCE.

prettily, *belle, concinne, lepide, venuste* (Quint., Plin. L.).

prettiness, *concinnitas, venustas.*

pretty, adj. *bellus, pulcher, pulchellus, concinnus, lepidus, venustus.*

pretty, adv. *satis, admodum.*

prevail. (1) = to be prevalent, *esse, obtinēre*: to begin to —, *increbrescĕre.* (2) = to win, *vincĕre, superare, superiorem esse.* (3) to — upon (a person) = to persuade, *(homini) persuadēre, (hominem) adducĕre, (ab homine) impetrare*; to — upon by entreaty, *exorare.*

prevalent, (of beliefs, etc.) *(per)vulgatus.*

prevaricate, *tergiversari.*

prevarication, *tergiversatio.*

prevent, *prohibēre*: to try to —, *obstare* (with dat.), *impedire.*

prevention, *prohibitio*; or render by verb.

preventive, render by verb.

previous; see PRECEDING.

prey, subst. *praeda*: a beast of —, *fera.*

prey, v. LIT., *praedari.* TRANSF., *animum,* etc., *(ex)edĕre, consumĕre.*

price, subst. *pretium:* — of corn (and cost of living in gen.), *annona*; at a high —, *magni (pretii)*; at a low —, *parvi (pretii)*; at what —? *quanti?*; what is the — of this? *quanto hoc constat?*; the — has fallen, *pretium iacet*; the — is rising, *pretium augetur*; high —s, *caritas annonae.*

price, v. = to set a — on a thing, *(rei, dat.) pretium, constituĕre,* or *statuĕre.*

priceless, *inaestimabilis, pretiosissimus.*

prick, subst. *punctum* (Mart.); or render by verb.

prick, v. *pungĕre, stimulare* (esp. with a goad or spur): to — up one's ears, *aures erigĕre* or *adrigĕre.*

prickle, *aculeus, spina.*

prickly, *aculeatus, spinosus, spinifer* (poet.).

pride. (1) = haughtiness, *superbia, insolentia, spiritus (-ūs*; often in plur.), *contumacia* (= obstinacy), *adrogantia* (= arrogance), *fastidium* (= scorn, disdain), *fastus (-ūs)*; = scorn, disdain; poet.). (2) = source of —, *decus* (Hor., Cat.).

priest, *sacerdos, flamen* (of one particular god, e.g. *flamen Dialis*): high —, *antistes, pontifex maximus.*

priestcraft, *ratio* or *artes sacerdotum.*

priestess, *sacerdos*: a chief —, *antistes, antistita.*

priesthood, *sacerdotium.*

priestly, render by genit. *sacerdotis* or *sacerdotum.*

priestridden, *sacerdotibus subiectus.*

prig, render by phrase, such as *qui nimiam virtutis speciem prae se fert.*

prim, *(nimis) diligens.*

primal, primeval; see ANCIENT, FIRST.

primarily, *initio, primo* (= at first), *praecipue* (= chiefly).

primary, *primus, principalis*: the — meaning of a word, *naturalis* or *principalis verbi significatio* (Quint.); = chief, *praecipuus.*

prime, subst. (1) = the best period of life, *integra aetas*: to be in one's —, *vigēre, florēre.* (2) = the best part of anything, *flos, robur.* (3) see MORNING.

prime, adj. (1) = first, *primus.* (2) = excellent, *eximius, optimus.*

prime-minister, *vir penes quem summa rerum est.*

primitive, *priscus, antiquus*; see also PRIMARY.

prince. (1) = a king's son, *filius regis, regulus.* (2) = king, *rex, regulus* (= petty king).

princess, *mulier regii generis, filia regis.*

principal, subst. (1) = head of a school, *magister*. (2) = capital, opp. to interest, *caput, sors, nummi (-orum,* plur.).
principal, *primus, princeps, principalis, praecipuus* (= chief).
principality, render by phrase, such as *terra principis imperio subiecta*.
principally, *maxime, praecipue, imprimis, maximam partem* (= for the most part).
principle. (1) = beginning, element, *principium, elementum, primordium*. (2) = rule, esp. for conduct, *institutum, institutio, ratio, decretum, consilium, regula, praeceptum* (as transmitted by a teacher), *disciplina* (= set of —s), *iudicium* (= considered opinion): on —, *ratione, animi quodam iudicio*; a man of —, *homo constans or gravis*; to remain true to one's —s, *sibi constare*; want of —, *levitas*; a man without —s, *homo levis* or *inconstans*.
print, subst. = an imprint, *nota impressa*; a foot —, *vestigium*.
print, v. (1) in gen., *imprimĕre*. (2) to — a book, *librum typis describĕre, exscribĕre, exprimĕre* (modern Latin).
printing-press, *prelum* (with or without the adj. *typographicum*; modern Latin).
prior, adj. *prior*; see also EARLY, BEFORE, PRECEDING.
prism, *prisma (-ătis,* n.; late Latin).
prison, *carcer, ergastulum* (= a private — for debtors or slaves), *vincula (-orum,* plur. = chains), *custodia* (strictly = confinement, imprisonment): to put in —, *in carcerem* (or *vincula* or *catenas*) *conicĕre*; to keep in —, *in custodiā habēre*.
prisoner: a — of war, *captivus* (with f. *captiva*: Ov.); in gen., *(homo) captus, homo comprehensus*; = a person on trial, render by *reus* (= the accused).
pristine, *pristinus, priscus, antiquus.*
prithee! *quaeso, cedo.*
privacy, *solitudo.*
private. (1) = of the individual, *privatus* (opp. *publicus*), *proprius* (opp. *communis*), *domesticus* or *familiaris* (both = of one's own family or household); — affairs, *res privata* or *domestica*; — life, *vita privata*, sometimes *otium* (in contrast with political activity); a — enemy, *inimicus*. (2) = secret, not for general knowledge, *arcanus, secretus* (Quint.). (3) a — soldier, *miles gregarius, manipularis.*
privateer, *navis praedatoria.*
privately, *clam, secreto, occulte, remotis arbitris* (= without witnesses), *privatim* (= in a private capacity).
privation. (1) = act of depriving, *privatio, ademptio* (Tac.). (2) = state of want, *inopia, egestas.*
privative, as grammat. t. t., *privativus* (Gram.).
privet, *ligustrum* (Verg., Ov.).
privilege, *ius (iuris,* n.), *praecipuum, beneficium*; in neg. sense = exemption, *immunitas.*
privileged, render by phrase, such as *iure praecipuo praeditus*; in neg. sense = exempt, *immunis.*
privy, subst. *latrina* (Pl., Suet.), *forica* (Juv.).
privy, adj. (1) see PRIVATE; privy-council, render by phrase, such as *consilium regis*. (2) — to a thing, *conscius rei* (genit.).
privy-purse, *fiscus* (Tac., Suet.).
prize, subst. (1) = reward, *praemium, palma*

(poet.): to offer a —, *praemium (pro)ponĕre.* (2) = booty, prey, *praeda.*
prize, v. *magni aestimare* or *facĕre.*
prize-fighter, *pugil* (= boxer).
pro and con, *in utramque partem.*
probability, *veri similitudo* (or as one word *verisim-*); *probabilitas* (of guesses, etc.).
probable, *veri similis* (or as one word, *verisim-*); *probabilis* (only of guesses, etc.).
probably, *probabiliter*: — he did so, *veri simile est eum fecisse.*
probation, *probatio*: a time of —, render by phrase, such as *tempus ad hominem experiendum, constitutum.*
probationer, *tiro*; see also NOVICE.
probe, subst. *specillum* (Cels.).
probe, v. *scrutari, rimari.*
probity, *probitas.*
problem, *quaestio.*
problematical, *dubius, incertus.*
proboscis, *proboscis* (Varro, Plin.).
proceed. (1) = to go ahead, *pergĕre, procedĕre, progredi*. (2) to — from, = to arise from, *proficisci, emanare, oriri*. (3) = to act, *agĕre, facĕre*. (4) to — against a person, in the courts, *litem homini intendĕre.*
proceeding, proceedings. (1) in gen. = transactions, *acta (-orum,* plur.). (2) legal, *lis, actio.*
proceeds, *reditus (-ūs), fructus (-ūs).*
process. (1) = method of proceeding, *ratio*. (2) at law, *lis, actio*. (3) in — of time, *tempore* (Ov.).
procession, *pompa.*
proclaim, *declarare, pronuntiare, praedicare, edicĕre* (by decree), *promulgare* (= to publish laws, etc.).
proclamation. (1) = the act of proclaiming, *pronuntiatio, declaratio, praedicatio*. (2) = the thing proclaimed, *edictum.*
proclivity, *proclivitas.*
proconsul, *pro consule* (also, but less often, *proconsul*).
proconsular, *proconsularis* (Tac.).
procrastinate, *differre, procrastinare.*
procrastination, *procrastinatio*; see also DELAY.
procreate, *procreare.*
procreation, *procreatio.*
procure, *(com)parare, conciliare* (= to collect together), *quaerĕre*: to — in addition, *adquirĕre*; see also OBTAIN.
procurer, *leno.*
procuring, subst. = obtaining, *comparatio, conciliatio.*
prodigal, subst. *nepos.*
prodigal, adj. *prodigus, profusus, effusus.*
prodigality, *effusio, prodigentia* (Tac.).
prodigious, *ingens, immanis.*
prodigy, *prodigium, portentum, miraculum.*
produce, subst. *fructus (-ūs)*: the — of the earth, *fructus (-ūs)*, or render by phrase, such as *ea quae terra gignit* or *parit, ea quae gignuntur e terrā, id quod agri efferunt.*
produce, v. (1) = to bring forward, *proferre, exhibēre, producĕre*. (2) = to bring into existence, *(pro)creare, gignĕre, parĕre, generare*; of the earth, *(ef)ferre, (ef)fundĕre* (abundantly). (3) = to cause, bring about, *facĕre, efficĕre.*
product. (1) in gen., *opus (-eris,* n.). (2) in arithmetic, *summa quae ex multiplicatione effecta est* (Col.).

production, *opus* (*-ĕris* = work): an artistic —, *artificium.*
productive, in gen., *ferax, uber*; see also FRUITFUL: — of, *rei* (genit.) *efficiens.*
productiveness, *ubertas.*
proem, *prooemium.*
profanation, *violatio, nefas.*
profane, adj. (1) = not sacred, *profanus.* (2) = impious, *impius.*
profane, v. *violare, polluĕre, profanare* (poet.).
profanely, *impie.*
profanity, *impietas.*
profess, *profitĕri.*
professed, *manifestus, apertus*; or render by verb.
professedly, *ex professo* (Sen.); or render by verb.
profession. (1) = declaration, *professio.* (2) = employment, *munus* (*-ĕris,* n.), *ars.*
professor, *professor* (Quint., Suet., Plin. L.).
proffer, v. *promittĕre*; see also OFFER.
proficiency, *scientia, peritia* (Tac.).
proficient, *peritus, sciens.*
profile, render by phrase, such as *faciei latus alterum:* a — portrait, *imago obliqua* (Plin.); in plur. also *catagrapha* (*-orum:* Plin.).
profit, subst. *lucrum, quaestus* (*-ūs*)*, fructus* (*-ūs*)*, reditus* (*-ūs*)*, emolumentum, compendium* (= — acquired by saving).
profit, v. (1) = to be of service, *prodesse* (with dat.), *proficĕre* (*ad rem*)*, conducĕre* (with dat. or *ad*). (2) = to gain advantage, *proficĕre, utilitatem* (*ex re*) *capĕre, lucrum* (*ex re*) *facĕre.*
profitable, *utilis, fructuosus, frugifer, quaestuosus* (in material sense).
profitably, *utiliter.*
profitless, *inutilis, vanus.*
profligacy, *nequitia, flagitium, mores* (*-um,* plur.) *perditi.*
profligate, subst. *homo perditus* or *profligatus.*
profligate, adj. *perditus, flagitiosus, nequam, profligatus.*
profligately, *perdite, nequiter.*
profound, *altus* (lit. and fig.).
profoundly, *penitus* (= completely); *abscondite* (= abstrusely).
profundity, *altitudo* (lit. and fig.).
profuse, *effusus, profusus*; see also EXTRAVAGANT.
profusion, *largitas, effusio.*
progenitor, *parens.*
progeny, *progenies*; see also OFFSPRING.
prognostic, *signum:* to be a — of, (*rem*) *praenuntiare.*
prognosticate; see FOREBODE.
programme, *libellus.*
progress, subst. (1) = journey, *iter.* (2) = advance, improvement, *progressus* (*-ūs*)*, progressio, processus* (*-ūs*): to make much (little) —, *multum* (*parum*) *proficĕre.*
progress, v. *progredi, proficĕre.*
progression, *progressus* (*-ūs*).
progressive, render by verb.
prohibit, *vetare, interdicĕre.*
prohibition, *interdictum.*
project, subst. *consilium, inceptum, propositum.*
project, v. *prominēre, eminēre, exstare, proici.*
projectile, (*telum*) *missile.*
projector, *auctor.*
proletariat, *proletarii* (*-orum,* plur.).

prolific; see FRUITFUL.
prolix, *longus, verbosus, multus* (of persons only).
prolixity, render by adj.
prologue, *prologus* (Ter., Quint.).
prolong, (*pro*)*ducĕre, prorogare, propagare, extendĕre, continuare, trahĕre* (= to drag out, make too long).
prolongation, *productio, prorogatio, propagatio.*
prolonged, *longus, diuturnus.*
promenade, *ambulatio* (= both the act and the place).
prominence. LIT., *eminentia.* TRANSF., = prestige, importance, *dignitas, auctoritas*; see also PROMINENT.
prominent. LIT., = projecting, *prominens*; or render by verb, such as *prominēre, eminēre, exstare.* TRANSF., = distinguished, *excellens, praestans, egregius, praeclarus, inlustris*; or render by verb, such as *excellĕre, praestare.*
promiscuous, *promiscuus.*
promiscuously, *promiscue, temere.*
promise, subst. (1) a — made in words, *promissum, fides:* to keep a —, *promissum facĕre* or *praestare, fidem servare*; to break a —, *fidem violare* or *frangĕre.* (2) = shown, prospective merit, *spes.*
promise, v. (1) = to make a — in words, *promittĕre, polliceri, profiteri, fidem dare*; to — a thing to a person, *rem homini promittĕre* or *polliceri*; to — to do so, *se facturum esse promittĕre,* etc.; to — often, *pollicitari* (Pl.). (2) = to show —, look like doing well, *bonam spem ostendĕre.*
promising, subst. as an action, *promissio, pollicitatio.*
promising, adj. *bonae* or *optimae spei* (genit.).
promissory, adj.: a — note, *chirographum* (Suet.).
promontory, *promontorium:* a small —, *lingua, li*(*n*)*gula.*
promote. (1) = to raise a person to a higher position, *provehĕre, producĕre, promovēre* (Plin. L.). (2) = to further, assist a cause, etc., *rem* (*ad*)*iuvare* or *amplificare* or *augēre*; *rei* (dat.) *consulĕre* or *prodesse.*
promoter, *auctor, adiutor, fautor.*
promotion. (1) = rise to a higher position, render by verb; = the higher position itself, *amplior honoris gradus* (*-ūs*)*, dignitatis accessio.* (2) = furthering, *amplificatio.*
prompt, *promptus.*
prompt, v. = to suggest a thing to a person, *rem homini subicĕre*; see also INDUCE, IMPEL.
prompter, *qui rem homini subicit.*
promptitude, *celeritas.*
promptly, *cito*; see also QUICKLY.
promptness, *celeritas.*
promulgate, *promulgare.*
promulgation, *promulgatio.*
prone. (1) = face-downwards, *pronus.* (2) = liable, inclined, (*ad rem*) *pronus, proclivis, propensus.*
proneness, *proclivitas*; or render by adj.
prong, *dens.*
pronoun, *pronomen* (Quint.).
pronounce. (1) = to articulate, speak, *enuntiare, exprimĕre, dicĕre.* (2) = to announce, to utter formally, *pronuntiare, declarare:* to — sentence, *sententiam dicĕre* or *pronuntiare.*

pronunciation, *appellatio, locutio*; sometimes simply *vox* or *(vocis) sonus.*

proof, subst. (1) = the act of proving, *probatio, demonstratio, argumentatio*: the — of it is difficult, *difficile est probatu.* (2) the means of proving, conclusive evidence or argument, *argumentum, signum, indicium, documentum, testimonium*: to be a —, *argumento* or *documento esse* (predicative dat.); to bring forward a —, *argumentum adferre.* (3) = trial, *experimentum, temptamentum* (poet.); to put to the —, *experiri, temptare.*

proof, adj. : — against a thing, *invictus ab re* or *adversus rem.*

prop, subst. Lɪᴛ., *adminiculum, pedamentum* (for vines: Varro), *statumen* (Plin.). Tʀᴀɴsꜰ., *adminiculum, firmamentum, columen, praesidium.*

prop, v. *fulcire*: to be —ped up by a thing, *(re) niti*; see also sᴜᴘᴘᴏʀᴛ.

propaganda, render the general idea by a phrase, such as *vulgus ad quidlibet credendum per libellos adducĕre.*

propagate. Lɪᴛ., to — plants by layers, *propagare*; — by grafting, *inserĕre*; of living creatures, *gignĕre, procreare.* Tʀᴀɴsꜰ., = to spread, *vulgare, serĕre.*

propagation. Lɪᴛ., of plants, *propagatio.* Tʀᴀɴsꜰ., render by verb.

propel, *propellĕre, impellĕre.*

propensity, *proclivitas* or *animus (ad rem) proclivis* or *pronus* or *propensus.*

proper. (1) = peculiar, characteristic, *proprius.* (2) = true, genuine, *verus, germanus.* (3) = becoming, right, *decōrus, honestus*: it is —, *decet.* (4) = suitable, *aptus, idoneus, rectus.* (5) as grammat. t. t. *proprius* (Gram.).

properly. (1) = in the strict sense, truly, *proprie, vere.* (2) = correctly, suitably, *apte, recte.*

property. (1) = a peculiarity, characteristic, *proprietas,* or render by adj. *proprius.* (2) = what one owns, *bona (-orum,* plur.), *fortuna* (esp. in plur.), *res* (sing. or plur.), *possessiones (-um,* plur.), *census (-ūs)*; private —, *res familiaris*; inherited —, *patrimonium*; petty — (= small savings, etc.), *peculium*; movable —, *res (rerum,* plur.) *moventes* or *quae moveri possunt*; the — of a person is often represented by the n. sing. or plur. of a possess. pron. (e.g. *mea*).

property-tax, *tributum ex censu conlatum.*

prophecy. (1) the act, *praedictio* (e.g. *rerum futurarum), vaticinatio.* (2) that which is prophesied, *praedictum, vaticinium* (Plin.).

prophesy, *praedicĕre, praenuntiare, vaticinari, augurari.*

prophet, *vates, vaticinator* (Ov.).

prophetess, *vates, fatiloqua.*

prophetic, *divinus, fatidicus, vaticinus.*

prophetically, *divinitus,* or render by phrase, such as *caelesti quodam instinctu mentis, instinctu divino adflatuque.*

propinquity; see ɴᴇᴀʀɴᴇss.

propitiate, *placare, propitiare* (Pl., Tac.).

propitiation, *placatio*: a means of —, *piaculum, placamentum* (Tac.).

propitious, *propitius, faustus* (of thing only).

propitiously, *fauste*; or render by adj.

proportion, subst. = portion, *pars, portio*; = relationship, *ratio, commensus (-ūs)*: Vitr.):

in —, *pro portione, pro ratā parte*; in — to, *pro,* with abl., or render by clauses, e.g.: one's happiness is in — to one's virtue, *quo quisque melior est, eo beatior,* or *ut quisque est vir optimus, ita idem beatissimus.*

proportion, v. *accommodare (ad rem).*

proportional, proportionate; see ᴘʀᴏᴘᴏʀ-ᴛɪᴏɴ.

proposal, *condicio, sententia, consilium* (= advice): to make a —, *condicionem ferre*; a — for a law or decree, *rogatio.*

propose. (1) = to bring forward for consideration, *ponĕre*: to — a law, *legem ferre* or *rogare, rogationem*; to — marriage to a lady, perhaps *feminam in matrimonium petĕre.* (2) = to intend, *cogitare, in animo habēre.*

proposer, of a law, *legis* (or *rogationis) lator,* in gen., *auctor.*

proposition. (1) see ᴘʀᴏᴘᴏsᴀʟ. (2) in logic, *pronuntiatum, propositio* (Quint.), *thesis* (Quint.).

proprietor, *possessor, dominus.*

proprietorship, *dominium, possessio.*

propriety, *convenientia, decōrum, honestas.*

prorogation, *prorogatio.*

prorogue, *(rem homini) prorogare.*

prosaic, *ieiunus, frigidus.*

proscribe, *proscribĕre.*

proscription, *proscriptio.*

prose, *(soluta) oratio.*

prosecute. (1) = to carry out, *persequi, exsequi, perficĕre.* (2) = to bring an action against a person, *hominem reum facĕre, iudicio persequi, accusare*; *hominis nomen deferre, homini litem* or *actionem intendĕre*: a —d person, *reus.*

prosecution. (1) = carrying out, *exsecutio* (Tac.); or render by verb. (2) at law, *accusatio, delatio, actio, lis.*

prosecutor, *accusator.*

proselyte, *discipulus.*

proselytize, *(hominem) discipulum facĕre.*

prosody, *versuum lex et modificatio* (Sen.).

prospect. Lɪᴛ., = view, *prospectus (-ūs)*; of places, to command a —, *prospicĕre* (Hor., Ov.), *prospectare* (Tac.). Tʀᴀɴsꜰ., = hope, *spes.*

prospective, *futurus*; see also ꜰᴜᴛᴜʀᴇ.

prospectively, *in futurum.*

prospectus, *libellus, titulus.*

prosper. (1) transit. *fortunare, secundare* (poet.). (2) intransit. *florēre, vigēre, prosperā* or *secundā fortunā uti.*

prosperity, *res (rerum,* plur.) *secundae* or *prosperae* or *florentes, prosperitas.*

prosperous, *secundus, prosper(us), florens.*

prosperously, *bene, prospere, fortunate.*

prostitute, subst. *meretrix, scortum.*

prostitute, v. Lɪᴛ., *(corpus) vulgare, publicare* (Pl.); to — oneself, *prostare* (Juv., Suet.). Tʀᴀɴsꜰ., *(re) abuti.*

prostitution, *vita meretricia, quaestus (-ūs) meretricius.*

prostrate, adj., render by verb.

prostrate, v. Lɪᴛ., = to throw down, *(pro)sternĕre*: to — oneself before a person, *ad pedes hominis procumbĕre* or *se proicĕre* or *prosternĕre.* Tʀᴀɴsꜰ., = to break the spirit of a person, render helpless, *animum adfligĕre, percellĕre, frangĕre, debilitare*: to be —d by grief, *in maerore iacēre.*

prostration, render by verb.

protect, *tuēri, tutari, defendĕre;* (*pro*)*tegĕre, munire* (= to fortify), *custodire* (= to guard), (*homini*) *praesidio esse:* to — a person's interests, *homini cavēre, consulĕre.*

protection, *tutela, praesidium, fides, custodia:* to take under one's —, *in fidem recipĕre;* State —, *fides publica.*

protective, render by verb.

protector, *defensor, propugnator, custos, tutor* (Hor.).

protest, subst. *recusatio:* a tribune's official —, *intercessio.*

protest, v. (1) = to state positively, *adseverare, adfirmare, confirmare.* (2) to — against a thing, *recusare, intercedĕre* (with dat., esp. of the tribunes).

protocol, *tabulae* (-*arum,* plur.), *commentarii* (-*orum,* plur.).

prototype, *exemplum, exemplar.*

protract, (*pro*)*ducĕre, prorogare, trahĕre.*

protrude. (1) transit. *protrudĕre.* (2) intransit. *protrudi, prominēre.*

protuberance, *tuber* (Plin.), *gibber* (Plin.).

protuberant; see PROJECTING.

proud, *superbus, adrogans, fastidiosus* (= disdainful): — of a thing, *re elatus;* to be — of a thing, *rē elatum esse, gloriari, superbire* (Ov.).

proudly, *superbe, adroganter.*

prove, v. (1) = to show clearly, *probare, ostendĕre, declarare, docēre:* to — a thing to a person's satisfaction, *rem homini probare.* (2) to — oneself, = to show oneself in a certain light, *se praestare* or *praebēre* or *exhibēre.* (3) intransit. = to turn out, *fieri, evadĕre, evenire* (of things only), *exire;* of persons, sometimes render as — oneself (see (2) above).

proven: not —, *non liquet.*

provender, *pabulum;* see also FOOD, FODDER.

proverb, *proverbium, verbum* (Pl., Ter.): according to the —, *ut aiunt.*

proverbial, proverbially, render by phrase, such as *proverbii loco* (= as a proverb), *in proverbium* (or *proverbii consuetudinem*) *venire* (= to pass into a proverb).

provide. (1) = to supply, furnish, (*rem homini*) (*com*)*parare, praebēre, suppeditare;* (*hominem re*) *instruĕre, ornare.* (2) to — for = to make provision for, *consulĕre* or *providĕre,* with dat. (3) to — against (*pro*)-*vidēre, praecavēre* (*ne quid fiat*). (4) to require, order (as a law does), *iubēre.*

provided that, conj. *dum, dummodo, modo, eā lege* (or *condicione*) *ut* (all with subj.).

provided with, adj. (*re*) *instructus, ornatus, praeditus.*

providence, *providentia:* divine —, *divina* or *deorum providentia* (*providentia* alone in Quint. and Sen.).

provident, *providus, diligens* (= careful).

providentially, *divinitus.*

providently, *diligenter,* or render by adj.

province. (1) = duty, *provincia, officium.* (2) = district, *regio* (in gen.), *provincia.*

provincial. (1) = belonging to a province, *provincialis.* (2) = countrified, unsophisticated, *rusticus, agrestis, inurbanus.*

provision, subst. = stipulation, *condicio, cautio:* to make —; see PROVIDE.

provision, v.: to — a town, *oppidum cibo* or *rebus necessariis instruĕre.*

provisional, provisionally, render by the phrase, *ad* or *in tempus.*

provisions, *cibus, cibaria* (-*orum,* plur.), *alimentum, victus* (-*ūs*): — for an army, *commeatus* (-*ūs*), *res frumentaria, frumentum.*

proviso; see PROVIDE.

provocation, provocative, render by verb; without —, *ultro.*

provoke. (1) = to call forth, (*com*)*movēre, ciēre.* (2) = to make angry, *inritare, lacessĕre.* (3) to — to anything, *incitare, concitare, impellĕre.*

provoking, *molestus.*

provost, *praeses, praefectus.*

prow, *prora.*

prowess, *virtus* (-*ūtis*); see also VALOUR.

prowl, *vagari, peragrare:* to — for plunder, *praedari.*

proximate, *proximus:* — causes, *antecedentia* (-*ium,* n. plur.).

proximity; see NEARNESS.

proxy, = deputy, *procurator, vicarius:* by —, *per procuratorem.*

prudence, *prudentia, cautio, circumspectio;* want of —, *imprudentia.*

prudent, *prudens, cautus, circumspectus, consideratus, providus.*

prudently, *caute, considerate.*

prudish, *rusticus, severus, tetricus.*

prune. LIT., of trees, (*am*)*putare, recīdĕre* (Cato), *pampinare* (of vines: Varro). TRANSF., *amputare, recīdĕre.*

pruner, of trees, *putator* (Varro, Ov.).

pruning, subst. *putatio.*

pruning-hook, *falx.*

prurience, *libido, prurigo* (Mart.).

prurient, *libidinosus.*

pry, *rimari, investigare, scrutari.*

psalm, *psalmus* (eccl.).

psalmist, *psalmista* (eccl.).

psalter, *psalterium* (eccl.).

psaltery, *psalterium* (eccl.).

pshaw! *phy!* (Ter.).

psychical, render by phrase with *anima* (= soul); the main subject matter of — research is described in Lucr. I, 112–135.

psychology, psychological, psychologist, render by phrases, such as *naturam mentis investigare.*

puberty, *aetas puber, pubertas.*

public, subst. *homines* (-*um,* plur.), *populus* (= the people), *vulgus:* the reading —, render by phrase with *legĕre.*

public. (1) = not private, not secret, *publicus, communis:* in —; see PUBLICLY; to show oneself in —, *in publicum prodire;* never to appear in —, *publico carēre* or *se abstinēre;* a —-house, *caupona, deversorium.* (2) = of the State, *publicus, forensis:* — life, *respublica, forum;* the — interest, *respublica;* at the — expense, *sumptu publico, publice;* in a — capacity, *publice;* — opinion, *vulgi opinio.*

publican. (1) = farmer of the public taxes, *publicanus.* (2) = inn-keeper, *caupo.*

publication. (1) in gen. = a making known, *praedicatio.* (2) of a book, *editio libri* (Plin.); = a book, *liber.*

publicity, *celebritas, lux* (= the light of day).

publicly, = in public, *aperte, palam, coram omnibus, in propatulo, in publico, foris.*

publish. (1) in gen., (*di*)*vulgare, praedicare,*

patefacĕre, proferre, efferre, ēdĕre. (2) of
books, *proferre, ēdĕre.*
publisher, of a book, *qui librum edendum
curat.*
pudding, *placenta* (= cake: Hor., Juv.).
puddle, *stagnum.*
puerile, *puerilis, ineptus.*
puff, subst., render by verb.
puff, v. (1) = to blow hard, pant, *anhelare.*
(2) to — out = to inflate, *inflare.* (3) pass.:
to be —ed up, *elatum* or *inflatum esse,
tumēre* (poet.).
pugilism, *pugilatus (-ūs:* Pl.), *pugilatio.*
pugilist, *pugil.*
pug-nosed, *simus* (Verg., Plin.).
pull, subst. *tractus (-ūs:* Sall., Verg.); or render
by verb.
pull, v. (1) = to twitch, tweak, *vellĕre* (e.g.:
to — the ear, *aurem:* Verg., Hor.), *vellicare*
(Pl., Quint.). (2) forcibly = to drag,
trahĕre: to — away, *avellĕre;* to — back,
retrahĕre, revellĕre; to — down = to demolish, *demoliri, disicĕre, diruĕre, destruĕre,
evertĕre;* to — out, *(e)vellĕre, eripĕre.*
pullet, *pullus (gallinaceus).*
pulley, *trochlea* (Vitr.).
pullulate, *pullulare* (Verg.).
pulmonary, *pulmoneus* (Pl.); or render by
phrase.
pulp, *caro* (Plin., of fruits).
pulpit, render by *suggestus (-ūs).*
pulsate, *palpitare, agitari, moveri.*
pulse. (1) of the blood, *venarum pulsus (-ūs:*
Plin.). (2) the vegetable, *legumen.*
pulverize, *in pulverem redigĕre.*
pumice, *pumex* (poet.): of —, adj. *pumiceus*
(Ov.); to smooth with —, *pumicare* (Mart.,
Cat.).
pump, subst. (1) for raising water, *antlia*
(Mart.); perhaps *tympanum* (Lucr., Verg.).
(2) = a slipper, *solea, crepida, soccus.*
pump, v. LIT., *exhaurire* (= to pump out a
liquid, or — a thing dry), *egerĕre* (= to — out
a liquid). TRANSF., to — a person for
information, *expiscari (rem ab homine).*
pumpkin, *pepo* (Plin.).
pun, subst. *facetiae (-arum,* plur.), *logos* (or *-ūs*).
pun, v. *iocari.*
punch, subst. (1) the drink, *calidum* (Pl.);
a — bowl, *cratera.* (2) see BLOW.
punch, v. *obtundĕre* (Pl.); to — a hole through,
pertundĕre (Pl., Lucr.).
punctilio, perhaps *diligentia* (= carefulness);
in matters of religion, *religio.*
punctilious, *diligens* (= careful); in religious
matters, *religiosus.*
punctiliously, *diligenter, accurate.*
punctual, in gen., *diligens* (= exact, careful):
to be — in keeping an appointment, *ad
tempus advenire.*
punctuality, *diligentia* (= carefulness, in gen.).
punctually, *diligenter, ad tempus* (= at the
appointed time).
punctuate, *distinguĕre, interpungĕre* (Sen.).
punctuation, *distinctio, interpunctio:* a —
mark, *interpunctum.*
puncture, subst. *punctum* (Plin.).
puncture, v. *(com)pungĕre.*
pungent, *acer, acutus.*
pungently, *acriter, acute.*
punish: to — a person, *hominem punire,
multare, ulcisci, castigare, in hominem*

*animadvertĕre, hominem poenā adficĕre,
ab homine poenam* (or *poenas) persequi* or
(re)petĕre; to — with exile, a fine, imprisonment, *exilio, pecuniā, vinculis multare;* to —
an offence, *ulcisci, exsequi* (with acc.); to
be —ed, *puniri, plecti, poenas dare* or *(ex-)
pendĕre* or *(per)solvĕre.*
punishable, *poenā dignus;* or render by verb.
punisher, *vindex, ultor;* or render by verb.
punishment. (1) as an act, *castigatio, animadversio.* (2) the — inflicted, *poena, supplicium*
(esp. = capital —), *noxa* (Liv.), *multa:* to be
liable to a —, *poenā tenēri;* to undergo —,
poenam subire; to award or decide on a —,
poenam constituĕre; see also PUNISH.
puny, *pusillus, exiguus:* a — fellow, *homunculus,
homuncio.*
pupil. (1) of the eye, *pupula, pupilla* (Lucr.).
(2) at a school, *alumnus* (with f. *alumna*),
discipulus (with f. *discipula*).
puppet, *pupa* (= a doll: Varro, Pers.).
puppy, *catulus, catellus.*
purchasable, *venalis.*
purchase, subst. (1) as an act, *emptio.*
(2) = thing bought, *merx* (= merchandise),
quod emptum est.
purchase, v. *(co)emĕre, mercari.*
purchaser, *emptor.*
pure. (1) physically = untainted, unmixed,
purus, integer, sincerus, merus (esp. of wine:
Pl., Ov.). (2) in gen. = sheer, unalloyed,
'pure and simple', *merus, sincerus.* (3) of
language, *purus, emendatus.* (4) in a moral or
religious sense, *purus, integer, sanctus, castus,
emendatus.*
purely. (1) = wholly, *prorsus, plane.* (2) =
correctly, of language, *pure, emendate, integre.*
(3) in a moral or religious sense, *pure, puriter*
(Cat.), *integre, caste.*
purgation, *purgatio, lustratio.*
purgative, subst. *medicina quae alvum movet*
or *purgat.*
purgatory, *purgatorium* (eccl.).
purge, subst. (1) medical; see PURGATIVE.
(2) political, perhaps *proscriptio.*
purge, v. in medicine, *alvum purgare* or
movēre; in gen., see PURIFY.
purification, *purgatio:* a ceremonial —,
lustratio; the festival of —, *Februa (-orum,*
n. plur.; on Feb. 15th).
purify, *(re)purgare, expurgare, purum facĕre*
(in gen.); *purificare* (Plin.); *lustrare* (with
religious ceremonial), *emendare* (= to —
from faults).
purist, (in language) *homo in scribendo* (or
dicendo) diligentior.
puritan, *homo severior* or *tetricus.*
puritanism, *(nimia) severitas, rigida innocentia*
(a phrase used by Livy of Cato the censor).
purity. (1) moral or religious, *castimonia,
castitas* (esp. = chastity), *integritas, sanctimonia, sanctitas.* (2) of language, *integritas,
sinceritas.*
purl, v. *murmurare, susurrare* (poet.).
purloin, *avertĕre, surripĕre, furari.*
purple, subst. *purpura* (Verg.), *ostrum* (Verg.),
conchylium, color purpureus.
purple, adj. *purpureus, conchyliatus.*
purport, subst.; see MEANING, OBJECT.
purport, v.; see MEAN.
purpose, subst. *propositum, consilium, institutum, sententia, animus, mens, voluntas:* for

the — of doing something, *eo consilio ut*, with subj., or render by *ut* alone, with subj. or by *ad* with gerund(ive); on —, *consulto, de industriā, dedittā operā, consilio*; without —, *temere*; to no —, *frustra, nequiquam*; to the —, *ad rem, apposite*.

purpose, v. *statuěre, cogitare, in animo habēre*; see also INTEND.

purposeless, *vanus, inanis, inritus, cassus, inutilis*.

purposely, = on purpose; see PURPOSE.

purr, v. *murmurare*.

purse, *marsupium* (Pl.), *zona* (Hor.), *crumena* (Pl., Hor.), *arca* (strictly = money-box; also = money).

purse-proud, *pecuniā superbus* (Hor.).

pursuance (in — of) and **pursuant** (to), render by *ex*, with abl., or *secundum*, with acc.

pursue, *sequi, persequi, prosequi, consectari, insequi, insectari, (homini) insistĕre, (homini) instare*.

pursuing, *sequax* (Lucr., Verg.).

pursuit. (1) the act of pursuing, physically; render by verb. (2) = eager search for anything, *consectatio, studium*. (3) = an occupation that one follows, *negotium, occupatio, artificium*.

purveyor, *obsonator* (Pl., Sen.); or render by *providēre*.

pus, *pus* (Cels.).

push, subst. *(im)pulsus (-ūs), impetus (-ūs)*.

push, v. (1) = to impel, move along, *(im)pellěre, (pro)trudĕre, urgēre*: to — forward, *propellěre*; to — back, *repellěre*; to — down, *depellěre*. (2) intransit.: to — on, *contendĕre, instare, pergĕre*.

pushing, adj. *protervus, petulans, confidens*.

pusillanimity, *timiditas; animus timidus, abiectus, humilis, infractus*.

pusillanimous, *timidus, abiectus, humilis, (in)fractus*.

pusillanimously, *timide, abiecte, humiliter, animo abiecto*.

pustule, *pustula* (Cels.).

put. LIT., physically = to place, *ponĕre, (con)locare*: to — away (safely), *condĕre, abděre*; to — aside, *seponĕre*; to — back, *reponĕre, recondĕre*; to — down, *deponĕre, demittĕre*; to — forward, *porrigĕre, extendĕre*; to — one thing into another, *imponĕre, immittĕre, inserĕre*; to — on, in gen., *imponĕre, superponĕre*; to — on, of clothes, *induĕre, sumĕre*; to — off, of clothes, *exuĕre, (dē)ponĕre*; to — out, *exserĕre, eicĕre, extrudĕre, expellĕre*; to — one thing to another, *apponĕre, applicare*; to — together, *conligĕre, conferre, componĕre*; to — under, *subicĕre, supponĕre, subdĕre*; to — up (= to erect), *erigĕre, statuĕre*. TRANSF., to — a question, *quaestionem (pro)ponĕre*; to — a value on, *aestimare*; to — down (= to suppress), *tollĕre, comprimĕre*; to — forward (as a candidate, etc.) *producĕre*, (as an argument, etc.) *adferre*; to — in (with a ship), *appellĕre*; to — in order, *ordinare*; to — in writing, *perscribĕre*; to — off (= to postpone), *differre, prorogare*; to — out (a fire), *exstinguĕre*; to — out to sea, *(navem) solvĕre*; to — out of the way, *de medio tollĕre*; to — (a person) over (something or somebody), *(hominem) praeficere*, with dat.; to — to death, *interficĕre, leto dare*; to — to flight, *in fugam dare, fugare*; to — under

(= to subject), *subicĕre*; to — up (a person as guest), *hospitio accipĕre*; to — up with (a person as host), *(ad hominem) devertĕre* or *deverti*; to — up with (= to tolerate), *ferre, tolerare, devorare*.

putative, *falsus* or render by phrase, such as *qui dicitur esse*.

putrefy, *putescĕre*: to cause to —, *putrefacĕre*.

putrid, *putridus, putidus, puter* (or *putris*: Verg., Hor.).

putty, render by *gluten* (= glue: Lucr.).

puzzle, *quaestio* (= a question), *aenigma* (= a riddle), *nodus* (= a knotty point).

puzzle, v. *dubium facĕre, animum distrahĕre, impedire*: to be —d, *dubitare, haerēre, haesitare*.

puzzling, *difficilis, ambiguus, obscurus, perplexus*.

Pygmy, *pygmaeus* (= one of the Pygmies, Plin., etc.); in gen. = dwarf, *nanus* (Juv.), *pumilio* (Sen., Mart.), *pumilus* (Stat., Suet.),

pyramid, *pyramis*.

pyramidal, render by phrase, such as *in pyramidis formam factus*.

pyre, *rogus, pyra* (Verg.).

Pyrenees, *Pyrenaei montes, Pyrenaeum, Pyrene*.

pyrites, *pyrites* (Plin.).

pyrrhic, subst., — = the metrical foot, *(pes) pyrrhichius* (Quint.).

pyrrhic, adj., a — victory, render by phrase, such as *victoria, ut aiunt, Pyrrhi regis modo incassum relata*.

pyx, *pyxis*.

Q

quack, subst. = an itinerant seller of medicine, *pharmacopola circumforaneus*: a — philosopher, *circulator* (Sen.); to play the —, *circulari* (Sen.).

quadrangle, = courtyard, *area*.

quadrangular, *quadrangulus* (Plin.).

quadripartite, *quadripartitus*.

quadruped, *quadrupes*.

quadruple, *quadruplex*.

quaff, v. *perpotare* (Lucr.), *ducĕre, haurire*.

quag(mire), *palus (-udis)*.

quail, subst. (the bird), *coturnix* (Lucr., Plin.).

quail, v. *animo deficĕre* or *cadĕre, pavēre*.

quaint. (1) in a good sense, *lepidus, facetus, concinnus*. (2) = odd, *insolitus, novus, mirus*.

quake, *tremĕre, contremiscĕre, pavēre*.

qualification. (1) = right, *ius (iuris*, n.); or render by adj. (2) = limitation, condition, *exceptio, condicio*.

qualified, *(ad rem) idoneus, accommodatus, aptus, (rē) dignus*.

qualify, v. (1) transit.: **a** = to make fit, *aptum* or *idoneum reddĕre, instituĕre* (= to train): **b** = to modify, restrict, *extenuare, circumscribĕre, deminuĕre*. (2) intransit. = be (or be held) suitable, *aptum* or *idoneum esse* (or *haberi*).

quality. (1) = nature, character, *natura, ingenium, indoles, qualitas* (as philosoph. t. t. only, a word coined by Cic. to represent the Greek ποιότης): of what —? *qualis*?; of such a —, *talis*; a good —, *virtus (-ūtis*); a bad —, *vitium*. (2) = kind, sort, *genus (-ēris*, n.); of wine, *nota*. (3) = high birth or rank, render by adj. (e.g.: a lady of —, *generosa femina*).

qualm, *fastidium* (= a feeling of disgust), *nausea* (= vomiting), *nauseola* (= slight squeamishness): a — of conscience, render by *conscientia* (*mala*).

quantity. (1) = number, *numerus, quantitas* (Plin., Quint.): a certain —, *aliquot* (in apposition to a plur. subst.), *aliquantum* (with partitive genit. of sing. subst.); a large —, *multitudo, copia, vis, pondus* (-*eris*, n.; = weight); in what —? (= how many?) *quot?*; in such — (= so many), *tot.* (2) = shortness or length of syllables in scansion, *mensura, quantitas* (Gram.).

quarrel, subst. *iurgium, altercatio, rixa* (with violence; = brawl).

quarrel, v. *iurgare, altercari, rixari*.

quarrelsome, *litigiosus, pugnax*; or render by phrase.

quarry, subst. (1) a stone —, *lapicidinae* (-*arum*, plur.), *lautumiae* (-*arum*, plur.). (2) = prey, *praeda*.

quarry, v. *caedĕre, excidĕre*.

quart, (as a measure) *duo sextarii*.

quartan, adj. *quartanus*: a — ague, (*febris*) *quartana*.

quarter. (1) = a fourth part, *quarta pars, quadrans* (of certain measures only). (2) = region, district, *vicus* (in a town), *regio, pars, plaga* (poet.). (3) = mercy, *venia*: to grant a person —, *homini parcĕre*; see also QUARTERS.

quarter, v. *quadrifariam dividĕre* or *dispertire*: to — a man (as a punishment), *in quattuor partes distrahĕre* (Sen.). (2) to — troops, *milites per hospitia disponĕre*.

quarter-day, *dies constitutus* or *dictus* or *certus*.

quarter-deck, *puppis* (Verg.).

quartering, render by verb.

quarterly, *trimestris* (Varro, Suet.): money to be paid —, *pecunia tertio quoque mense solvenda*.

quarters, *hospitium, habitatio, tectum* (= roof, shelter), *deversorium* (= lodgings), *mansio* (Plin., Suet.): winter — (for troops), *hiberna* (-*orum*, n. plur.); summer —, *aestiva* (-*orum*, n. plur.); at close —, *comminus*; to come to close —, *manum conserĕre*.

quash, *rescindĕre, infirmare, inritum facĕre*.

quaver; see TREMBLE.

quay, *margo* (Varro), *crepido*.

queen, *regina*: — bee, *rex apium* (Verg.).

queenly, render by phrase, such as *reginae similis*.

queer, *novus, insolitus, mirus*; = absurd, *ridiculus*.

quell, *opprimĕre, comprimĕre, compescĕre* (poet.), *sedare* (= to settle, calm).

quench, (lit. and fig.) *exstinguĕre, restinguĕre*.

querulous, *queribundus, querulus* (poet.); or render by the verb (*con*)*queri*.

query; see QUESTION.

quest; see SEEK, SEARCH.

question, subst. (1) = an inquiry, a thing asked, *quaestio, rogatio* (rarer), *interrogatum*: to put a —, *quaestionem* (*pro*)*ponĕre*; to decide a —, *quaestionem solvĕre*; it is a difficult —, *magna quaestio est*. But the word is often best rendered by a verb, as in the following examples: to ask —s, (*inter*)*rogare*; the — now is, *nunc id quaeritur* (or *agitur*); he failed to answer my —, *mihi*

quaerenti nihil respondit. (2) = doubt, dispute, *controversia, dubium*: without —, *sine controversiā, sine dubio, procul dubio*; there is no — that he did it (or of his having done it), *haud dubium est quin fecerit.* (3) = matter (in dispute), *res*.

question, v. (1) = to ask (a person) questions, (*hominem*) (*inter*)*rogare, percontari*; (*ex* or *ab* or *de homine*) *quaerĕre* or *exquirĕre*. (2) = to doubt, *dubitare.* (3) = to express doubt (on a point), (*rem*) *in dubium* (or *incertum*) *vocare*.

questionable, *incertus, ambiguus, anceps, dubius*.

questioning, subst. (*inter*)*rogatio, percontatio, quaestio*.

quibble, subst. *captio, cavillatio* (Quint.).

quibble, v. *cavillari*.

quibbler, *cavillator* (Sen.).

quibbling, adj. *captiosus*.

quick, subst., in the phrase, to cut to the —, *ad vivum resecare*.

quick, adj. (1) see ALIVE. (2) see FAST, SPEEDY. (3) of disposition = prompt, active, *promptus, alacer, expeditus.* (4) = — witted, *acutus, astutus, sagax, catus, perspicax*.

quicken. (1) = to make alive, *animare.* (2) = to make go fast, *incitare, accelerare, maturare.* (3) in gen. = to stimulate, *incitare, excitare, stimulare, incendĕre*.

quicklime, *calx viva* (Vitr.).

quickly, *cito, celeriter, velociter, mature, mox* (= soon).

quickness. (1) physical, *velocitas*; see also SPEED. (2) of intellect, *ingenii acumen* or *acies, sagacitas*.

quicksand, *syrtis* (Verg.).

quicksilver, *argentum vivum* (Plin.).

quick-tempered, *iracundus, stomachosus, cerebrosus* (Hor.).

quick-witted; see QUICK.

quiescent, render by verb, *quiescĕre*.

quiet, subst. *quies, requies, tranquillitas, pax, otium* (= leisure), *silentium* (= silence).

quiet, adj. *quietus, tranquillus, pacatus, sedatus* (= settled, calm), *placidus* (= placid, undisturbed), *otiosus* (= at leisure), *taciturnus* (= not talking): to be —, *quiescĕre, silēre* (= to make no noise), *tacēre* (= not to talk).

quiet, quieten, v. *tranquillum* or *quietum reddĕre, tranquillare* (fig.), *pacare* (= to pacify), *sedare* (= to settle, calm).

quietly, *quiete, tranquille, placide, placate* (= calmly), *otiose* (= in leisurely fashion), *silentio* (= in silence), *tacite* (= silently).

quietness; see QUIET, subst.

quill. (1) the feather, *penna.* (2) of porcupines, etc., *spina.* (3) for striking the strings of an instrument, *plectrum, pecten* (Verg.).

quilt, *stragulum*.

quinquennial, *quinquennalis* (= done once in every five years).

quinsy, *angina* (Pl., Plin.), *synanche* (Cels.).

quintessence, *quinta pars* (Hor.), *flos*.

quip, *dictum*.

quire (of paper), *scapus* (Plin.).

quirk, *captiuncula, calumnia*.

quit, *decedĕre* (*de loco*); see also LEAVE, DESERT.

quite. (1) = completely, *admodum, prorsus, plane, omnino, penitus, funditus*: to be of — a different opinion, *longe aliter sentire*: often rendered by negative (*non, haud, neque,* etc.) with adj. or adv. of opposite meaning, e.g. — certain, *haud dubius*. (2) = fairly, moderately, *satis*.

quiver, subst. *pharĕtra* (poet.): wearing a —, *pharetratus* (poet.).

quiver, v. *tremĕre, micare, trepidare* (poet.).

quivering, adj. *tremulus* (poet.).

quoit, *discus*.

quota, *(rata) pars*.

quotation. (1) = act of quoting, *prolatio, commemoratio*. (2) = passage quoted, *locus adlatus*.

quote, *adferre, proferre, (com)memorare* (= to mention).

quoth, he or she, *inquit, ait*.

quotidian, *cot(t)idianus*.

R

rabbit, *cuniculus* (Varro, Mart.).

rabble, *multitudo, turba, plebecula, conluvio*.

rabid, *rabidus* (poet.); see also MAD.

rabidly, *rabide*.

race, subst. (1) = family, stock, people, *genus* (-*ĕris*, n.); *gens* (usually smaller), *stirps* (= lineage), *progenies* (= descent or progeny), *prosapia* (archaic), *semen* (lit. = seed), *proles* (= progeny; poet.), *nomen* (lit. = name), *propago* (poet.). (2) = a contest of speed, *cursus* (-*ūs*), *certamen, curriculum*.

race, v. (*cursu*) *certare* or *contendĕre*.

race-course, *curriculum, stadium, circus*.

race-horse, *equus, celes* (Plin.).

racer, = runner, *cursor*.

raciness, *succus, sapor*.

rack. (1) = manger, *faliscae* (-*arum*, plur.: Cat.). (2) the instrument of torture, *eculeus, tormentum, quaestio* (= examination under torture).

rack, v. = to torment. LIT., *torquĕre, (ex)cruciare*. TRANSF., *torquĕre, (ex)cruciare, vexare*.

racket, = noise, *strepitus* (-*ūs*).

racy, *salsus*.

radiance, *fulgor, claritas, candor, splendor, nitor*.

radiant, = bright, *clarus, candidus, splendidus, nitens, nitidus, fulgens*.

radiate, *fulgĕre, radiare* (poet.).

radiation, *radiatio* (Plin.).

radical, subst., render by adj.; see RADICAL, adj. (4).

radical, adj. (1) = original, innate, *insitus, innatus*. (2) as grammat. t. t., a — word, *verbum nativum, primigenium, primitivum* (Gram.). (3) = complete, entire, *totus*. (4) in politics, *novarum rerum cupidus* or *studiosus*.

radically, *radicitus, funditus, penitus, prorsus, omnino*; see also ALTOGETHER.

radish, *raphanus* (Plin.), *radix* (Hor.).

radius, *radius*.

raffle, subst. and verb, render by the word *alea* (= gambling), or the phrase *aleā ludĕre* (= to gamble).

raft, *ratis*.

rafter, *canterius* (Vitr.), *tignum, trabs*.

rag, *pannus*.

ragamuffin, *homo pannosus*.

rage, subst. *rabies, furor* (= frenzy), *saevitia,*

ira (= anger): — for a thing = eager longing, *cupido, studium, aviditas*.

rage, v. *furĕre, saevire*.

raging, *furens, furibundus, saevus, rabidus* (poet.).

ragged, of people, *pannosus* (Cic.), *pannis obsitus* (Ter.); of clothes, *lacer*.

rail, subst. = bar, *tignum transversum*.

rail, v. (1) to — off, (*con*)*saepire*. (2) to — at = to abuse, (*homini*) *maledicĕre, conviciari,* (*hominem*) *maledictis* or *conviciis consectari*.

railing, subst. *saepimentum, saepes* (= hedge, fence).

raillery, *iocus, cavillatio*.

raiment, *vestis, vestitus* (-*ūs*), *vestimenta* (-*orum*, plur.).

rain, subst. *pluvia, imber*: a sudden shower of —, *imber repente effusus*; the — continues, *imber tenet* (Liv.).

rain, v.: it —s, *pluit*.

rainbow, *arcus* (-*ūs*) *pluvius* (Hor.); also *arcus* (-*ūs*) alone.

rain-cloud, *nimbus*.

rainy, *pluvius, pluvialis* (poet.), *aquosus* (poet.), *imbrifer* (poet.).

raise. (1) = to lift up, (*ex*)*tollĕre, (e)levare, sublevare, erigĕre*. (2) see ERECT, BUILD. (3) = to increase, *augĕre*: to — a price, *pretium efferre* (Varro). (4) = to promote, elevate, *producĕre, provehĕre, efferre*. (5) = to arouse, to stir up, (*animum*, etc.) *excitare, erigĕre, tollere, recreare*. (6) = to get together, *conligĕre, comparare, conscribĕre*. (7) to — a siege, *oppidum obsidione liberare*.

raisin, *acinus passus* (Plin.), *racemus passus* (Verg.).

rake, subst. (1) the agricultural implement, *rastellus* (Varro, Suet.), *pecten* (Ov.). (2) = a prodigal, roué, *ganeo, nepos, vappa* (Cat., Hor.), *homo dissolutus* or *perditus*.

rake, v. *radĕre, pectine verrĕre* (Ov.).

rakish, *perditus, profligatus, dissolutus*.

rally, v. (1) transit.: a, to — troops, *aciem* or *ordines restituĕre, milites in ordinem revocare*: b, = to banter, *ludĕre, inridēre*. (2) intransit. = to recover, *se conligĕre, se reficĕre, convalescĕre* (from illness).

ram, subst. *aries* (= both the animal and a battering —).

ram, v. *fistucā adigĕre, fistucare* (Cato, Plin.).

ramble, subst. = a walk, *ambulatio*: to go for a —, *ire ambulatum*.

ramble, v. LIT., *errare, vagari, ambulare* (= to walk about). TRANSF., = to digress, *aberrare, vagari, exspatiari* (Quint.).

rambler, *erro* (= vagrant: Hor., Ov.).

rambling, *vagus* (lit. and fig.).

ramification, render by *pars*.

ramify, (*in partes*) *dividi*; see also EXTEND.

rammer, *fistuca*.

rampant, *ferox, superbus* (= proud): to be —, *superbire*; in heraldry, *erectus* or *adrectus*.

rampart, LIT., *vallum, agger*. TRANSF., *vallum, propugnaculum, praesidium*.

rancid, *rancidus* (Hor.).

rancorous, *malevolus, malignus, invidus, infestus*.

rancorously, *maligne, infeste*.

rancour, *odium* (*occultum*), *invidia, malevolentia*.

random, *in casu positus, fortuitus*, or render by adv.: at —, *temere*.

range, subst. (**1**) = a row, *ordo, series*: a — of mountains, *montes* (*-ium,* plur.) *perpetui.* (**2**) of a missile, (*teli*) *coniectus* (*-ūs*), or *iactus* (*-ūs*: Verg.). (**3**) in gen., = class, *genus* (*-eris,* n.); if the idea of variety within the class is to be stressed, render by subst. *varietas* or adj. *varius.*

rank, subst. (**1**) = a row of soldiers, *ordo*: to keep one's —s, *ordinem servare*; to break —s, *ordine egredi*; fig.: the —s of a party, *partes* (*-ium,* plur.). (**2**) = degree, station, *ordo, gradus* (*-ūs*), *locus* (esp. of birth): high —, *dignitas, fastigium, summus locus.*

rank, adj. (**1**) of plant growth, *luxuriosus.* (**2**) of smell, *foetidus, graveolens* (Verg.). (**3**) = great, extreme, *magnus, maximus, summus.*

rank, v. = to place in a particular class, *numerare, habēre.*

rankle, v.: to — in the mind, (*hominem*) *mordēre, pungēre, stimulare.*

ransack. (**1**) = to plunder, *diripēre, expilare, spoliare.* (**2**) = to search thoroughly, *rimari,* (*per*)*scrutari.*

ransom, subst. (**1**) = the money paid, *pretium, pecunia.* (**2**) = the arrangement, *redemptio.*

ransom, v. *redimēre.*

rant, subst. *sermo tumidus, ampullae* (*-arum,* plur.; Hor.).

rant, v. *declamare, ampullari* (Hor.).

ranter, *orator tumidus.*

rap, subst., with the knuckles, *talitrum* (Suet.); at a door, *pulsatio.*

rap, v. *pulsare* (esp. at a door); — over the knuckles, see REBUKE, CENSURE.

rapacious, *rapax, avidus.*

rapacity, *rapacitas, aviditas.*

rape, subst. *raptus* (*-ūs*); to commit —, (*mulierem*) *rapēre,* (*mulieri*) *vim* or *stuprum* or *vitium offerre.*

rapid, subst. *vertex, gurges.*

rapid, adj. *rapidus, celer, velox, citus.*

rapidity, *rapiditas, celeritas, velocitas.*

rapidly, *rapide, cito, celeriter.*

rapier, *gladius* (= sword).

rapine, *rapina.*

rapture, (*summa*) *voluptas, exsultatio*; see also HAPPINESS.

rapturous; see HAPPY.

rare. (**1**) = uncommon, *rarus, inusitatus.* (**2**) = thin, *rarus, tenuis.* (**3**) = exceptional, *singularis, eximius.*

rarefaction, render by adj., e.g. the — of the atmosphere, *aer extenuatus.*

rarefy, *extenuare.*

rarely, *raro.*

rarity. (**1**) = fewness, *raritas, paucitas.* (**2**) = a rare thing, *res rara* or use the proverbial expressions *alba avis, rara avis.*

rascal, *homo scelestus* or *nequam, scelus* (*-eris,* n.: Pl., Ter.), *furcifer, verbero.*

rascality, *scelus* (*-ĕris,* n.).

rascally, *scelestus, nequam.*

rase, = to level with the ground, *solo aequare* or *adaequare.*

rash, subst. *eruptio(nes)* (Plin.).

rash, adj. *praeceps, inconsultus, inconsideratus, temerarius.*

rashly, *inconsulte, inconsiderate, temere.*

rashness, *temeritas.*

rasp, subst. *scobina* (Plin.).

raspberry: a — bush, *rubus Idaeus* (Plin.).

rat, *mus*; a — trap, *muscipula* (Sen.).

rate, subst. (**1**) = price, *pretium*: to buy at a high or low —, *magno* or *parvo emēre*; — of interest, *usura, fenus* (*-ŏris,* n.); — of exchange, *collybus.* (**2**) = tax, *vectigal, tributum.* (**3**) = manner, condition, *modus*: at any —, *certe, utique.* (**4**) see SPEED.

rate, v. (**1**) = to value, *aestimare.* (**2**) = to scold, *increpare, obiurgare.*

rather. (**1**) = in preference, *potius, citius, libentius, prius*: I would —, *malo* (with infin); or —, *vel potius*; nay, —, *immo* (*vero*). (**2**) = somewhat, *aliquantum*; with a comparative, *paulo, aliquanto*; sometimes rendered by a compound verb in *sub-*.

ratification, *sanctio,* or render by verb.

ratify, *sancire, ratum facēre, confirmare.*

ratio; see PROPORTION.

ratiocination, *ratiocinatio*; see also REASONING.

ration, *demensum* (Ter.), *cibaria* (*-orum,* plur.), *diaria* (*-orum,* plur.).

rational. (**1**) = possessing reason, *ratione praeditus, rationis particeps.* (**2**) = agreeable to reason, (*rationi*) *consentaneus*: to act —ly, *prudenter* or *considerate agěre.*

rationalism, rationalist, render by the phrase *eorum opinio qui hominum ratione omnia comprehendi censent* (Cic.).

rationality, *ratio.*

rationally, *ratione*; see also RATIONAL.

rattle, subst. (**1**) = a noise, *crepitus* (*-ūs*), *strepitus* (*-ūs*), *sonitus* (*-ūs*). (**2**) a child's —, *crepitaculum* (Mart., Quint.), *crepitacillum* (Lucr.).

rattle, v. (**1**) transit. *insonare* with abl. (**2**) intransit. *crepare, crepitum dare, strepěre, sonare.*

ravage, (*per*)*vastare,* (*de*)*populari.*

ravaging, subst. *vastatio, populatio.*

rave, *furěre, insanire, bacchari*; colloq. = to talk wildly, *delirare, vaticinari, hariolari.*

raven, *corvus.*

ravening, ravenous, *rapax, vorax, edax, famelicus* (= famished: Pl., Ter., Juv.).

ravenousness, *rapacitas.*

ravine, *fauces* (*-ium,* plur.).

raving, *furens, furibundus, insanus.*

ravish. (**1**) in gen. = to carry off, *rapěre, abstrahěre, abducěre.* (**2**) = to debauch, (*con*)*stuprare.* (**3**) see DELIGHT.

ravisher, *raptor* (poet.), *stuprator* (Quint., Suet.).

ravishing; see DELIGHTFUL.

raw. (**1**) = uncooked, *crudus, incoctus* (Pl.). (**2**) of wounds, *crudus* (Ov., Plin. L.). (**3**) of materials = unworked, undressed, *crudus* (Verg.), *rudis* (Verg., Ov., Plin.), *infectus.* (**4**) = untrained, inexperienced, *rudis, imperitus*: a — recruit, *tiro.* (**5**) of weather, *frigidus* (= cold), *humidus* (= damp).

raw-boned, *strigosus.*

ray. (**1**) of light, *radius, iubar* (poet.); fig.: a — of hope, *specula.* (**2**) the fish, *raia* (Plin.).

raze; see RASE.

razor, *novacula.*

reach, subst. (**1**) = grasp, capacity, *captus* (*-ūs*), or render by verb; of a weapon = range, *coniectus* (*-ūs*), *iactus* (*-ūs*: Verg.). (**2**) = tract, region, *tractus* (*-ūs*), *regio.*

reach, v. (**1**) see EXTEND, STRETCH. (**2**) = to touch, get to, (*rem, locum*) *tangěre, contingěre,* *attingĕre, adipisci*; of land, etc., *capĕre*; (*ad rem, ad locum*) (*per*)*venire, accedĕre*; of reports, etc.: to — a person's ears, *ad hominem deferri.* (3) = to pass, hand over, *porrigĕre, praebĕre.*

react: to — upon = to affect, *adficĕre*; to — to = to take in a certain way, (*rem*) *ferre* or *accipĕre,* (*adversus rem*) *se gerĕre,* with adv.

reaction; see REACT and REACTIONARY.

reactionary, render by phrase, such as *rem* (*publicam*) *ad pristinum statum revocare velle.*

read, *legĕre* (with acc. of either matter or author), *evolvĕre* (= to unroll and —); to — through, *perlegĕre*; to — quickly through, *percurrĕre*; to — often, *lectitare*; to — aloud, *recitare*; to — the stars, *astra cognoscĕre*; well- —, adj., of a person, *litteratus*; fairly well- —, *litteris tinctus.*

readable, *iucundus legenti.*

readily, = willingly, *prompte* (Tac.), *prompto* or *parato animo, libenter, facile.*

readiness, *animus promptus* or *paratus, facilitas*: — of speech, *volubilitas linguae, lingua prompta*; in —, *paratus, expeditus, in promptu.*

reader, *legens, qui legit, lector* (= a regular or professional —), *recitator, anagnostes.*

reading, *lectio*: a complete —, *perlectio*; a — aloud, *recitatio*; a — in an author (= a version of the text), *lectio* (late Latin).

reading-desk, perhaps *pulpitum* (Hor.).

ready, *paratus* (*ad rem,* or with infin.), *promptus, expeditus*: — money, *pecunia praesens* or *numerata*; to make —, (*com*)*parare, instruĕre*; to be — (for use), *praesto esse*; to be — (= willing) to do a thing, *velle.*

real. (1) = genuine, true, not fictitious, *verus, sincerus, solidus, germanus*; a — scholar, *vere doctus*; sometimes rendered by *ipse* (e.g.: the — man, *homo ipse*). (2) in law: — estate, *fundus praedium, res* (*rerum,* plur.) *soli* (Sen., Plin. L.).

realism, realistic, render by the phrase *veritatem imitari.*

reality, *res* (*vera*), *veritas*: in —, see REALLY.

realization. (1) = completion, effect, *effectus* (-ūs). (2) = comprehension; render by verb.

realize. (1) = to carry into effect, *facĕre, efficĕre, perficĕre, ad effectum adducĕre.* (2) = to grasp mentally, *intellegĕre, comprehendĕre, sentire, animo* (or *mente*) *concipĕre.* (3) = to get in one's money, *pecuniam redigĕre.*

really. (1) = in reality, *re, re ipsa, re vera, vere, profecto.* (2) in questions: is it — so? *itane est?*; —? *ain tu?*

realm, *civitas* (= citizen body), *respublica* (= state), *regnum* (= kingdom).

reanimate, = to encourage, *animum erigĕre.*

reap. LIT., (*de*)*metĕre, messem facĕre*; prov.: as you sow, so you will —, *ut sementem feceris, ita metes*; to — where we have not sown, *alienos agros demetĕre, sub arbore quam alius consevit legĕre fructum* (Liv.). TRANSF., in gen. = to gain, *fructum* (*ex re*) *capĕre, percipĕre.*

reaper, *messor.*

reaping-hook, *falx.*

reappear, *redire* (= to return), *rursus apparēre.*

rear, subst., of a marching formation, *agmen extremum* or *novissimum*; of a fighting

formation, *acies novissima* or *extrema*: to form the —guard, *agmen claudĕre* or *cogĕre*; to attack the enemy in the —, *hostes aversos* or *hostes a tergo adgredi.*

rear, v. (1) see RAISE, LIFT. (2) = to rear, *alĕre, edŭcare.* (3) intransit., of horses, *tollĕre se adrectum* (Verg.).

reason, subst. (1) = cause, *causa, ratio* (= intelligible cause, grounds): to quote as a —, *causam adferre*; for valid —s, *iustis de causis*; for this (or that) —, *ideo, idcirco*; for this —, namely that, etc., *propterea quod*; by — of, *propter* (*rem*), *ob* (*rem*), *ex* (*re*); there is no — why, etc., *non est* (or *nihil est*) *quod* or *cur,* with subj.; for what —? *cur? quid? quare? quamobrem?*; for no —, without —, *temere.* (2) as a faculty, *ratio, mens, consilium*: to lose one's —, *rationem amittĕre*; to recover one's —, *resipiscĕre, ad sanitatem reverti, ad bonam frugem se recipĕre.*

reason, v. *ratiocinari, reputare*: to — with another person, (*de re*) *ad hominem disceptare,* (*rem*) *cum homine disputare,* (*de re*) *cum homine disserĕre.*

reasonable. (1) of persons, *rationis particeps* (= rational), *prudens* (= sensible). (2) = fair, according to reason, (*rationi*) *consentaneus, aequus, iustus, par, modicus* (= moderate, in price, etc.).

reasonableness. (1) = rationality, *ratio.* (2) = fairness, moderation, *aequitas, moderatio.*

reasonably. (1) = rationally, *ratione.* (2) = adequately, *satis.*

reasoner, *disputator.*

reasoning, *ratio, ratiocinatio*; see also REASON.

reassemble, *reducĕre in unum*; or render as assemble again; see ASSEMBLE (transit. and intransit.) and AGAIN.

reassert, *iterare* (= to repeat), *restituĕre* (= to restore).

reassume, *recipĕre, resumĕre.*

reassure, (*animum*) *confirmare, recreare, erigĕre.*

rebel, subst. *homo seditiosus, hostis patriae*; or render by relative clause.

rebel, adj.; see REBELLIOUS.

rebel, v. *seditionem* (*com*)*movēre* or *concitare*; *rebellare, rebellionem facĕre* (both these of conquered peoples), *deficĕre* or *desciscĕre* (*a rege, a republica*).

rebellion, *seditio, defectio, motus* (-ūs), *tumultus* (-ūs), *rebellio* (of a conquered people).

rebellious, *seditiosus, turbulentus, novarum rerum cupidus* or *studiosus, rebellis* (of conquered peoples: Verg., Tac.).

rebelliously, *seditiose, turbulente*(*r*).

rebellow, *reboare* (Verg.), *remugire* (Verg.).

rebound, subst., render by verb.

rebound, v. *repelli* (= to be driven back), *resilire, resultare* (poet.).

rebuff, subst. *repulsa.*

rebuff, v. *repellĕre, reicĕre.*

rebuild, *restituĕre, reficĕre*; or render as build again.

rebuke, subst. *reprehensio, vituperatio, obiurgatio, convicium, castigatio.*

rebuke, v. *reprehendĕre, vituperare, obiurgare,* (*verbis*) *castigare, increpare, increpitare.*

rebuker, *castigator, obiurgator.*

rebut, *redarguĕre, repellĕre, refellĕre.*

recall, subst. *revocatio*; or render by verb.

recall, v. (1) physically, *revocare, reducĕre, reverti iubēre.* (2) to — to mind, *recordari, in memoriam revocare, redigĕre, reducĕre,* (rem memoriā or memoriam rei, genit.) *repetĕre.*
recant, *recantare* (Hor.), *retractare* (Verg.), *revocare* (Sen.).
recantation, *receptus* (-ūs); or render by verb.
recapitulate, *enumerare, commemorare, referre* (= to relate).
recapitulation, *enumeratio, conlectio.*
recapture, v. *recipĕre.*
recast. LIT., *recoquĕre* (Verg.), *reficĕre.* TRANSF., *reficĕre, renovare.*
recede, *recedĕre, retro cedĕre.*
receipt. (1) = the act of receiving, *acceptio* or render by verb (e.g.: after the — of the money, *pecuniā acceptā*): to acknowledge the — of, *testari se accepisse.* (2) on the credit side of a ledger, a —, *acceptum*; to enter as a —, *acceptum referre.* (3) = a document acknowledging that something has been received, *apocha, acceptilatio* (Leg.). (4) see RECIPE.
receive. (1) in gen. = to take, accept, *capĕre, accipĕre, excipĕre, percipĕre, recipĕre, ferre.* (2) to — a person into one's house, *hominem hospitio accipĕre* or *excipĕre, ad se (domum) recipĕre.* (3) to — a person into a community, *hominem (in civitatem,* etc.) *asciscĕre, ascribĕre, admittĕre, adsumĕre, adgregare.* (4) = to take anything said or done in a certain manner, *accipĕre, interpretari*; to take a thing well, *in bonam partem accipĕre, aequi bonique facĕre*; to take ill, *in malam partem accipĕre, aegre* or *moleste ferre.* (5) with abstr. subst. as object, often to be rendered by passive verb; e.g.: to — a good education, *liberaliter educari.*
receiver, *receptor* (with f. *receptrix*; both esp. in bad sense, of thieves, etc.).
recent, *recens, novus.*
recently, *nuper, recens.*
receptacle, *receptaculum, cella* (= store-room), *horreum* (= granary, barn), *apotheca* (esp. for wine), *armarium* (= cupboard).
reception, *acceptio, hospitium* (in a house); or render by verb, e.g.: to meet with a good —, *benigne excipi.*
receptive, *docilis* (= teachable).
receptiveness, receptivity, *docilitas* (= teachableness).
recess. (1) = retired place, *recessus* (-ūs), *latibulum, penetrale* (usually plur. and mostly poet.). (2) = holidays, *feriae* (-arum, plur.).
recipe, = instructions for the preparation of medicine or food, *compositio* (Sen.).
recipient; see RECEIVE and RECEIVER.
reciprocal, *mutuus.*
reciprocally, *mutuo, invicem.*
reciprocate, *inter se dare.*
reciprocity, *vicissitudo*; or render by verb.
recital, *enumeratio, narratio, commemoratio.*
recitation, *recitatio.*
recite. (1) = to say aloud, *pronuntiare, recitare.* (2) = to narrate, *enumerare, (com)memorare, dicĕre, (e)narrare, referre, exponĕre.*
reciter, *recitator.*
reckless, *neglegens, temerarius, inconsideratus, incautus, imprudens*: — of, *neglegens* with genit.
recklessly, *neglegenter, temere, imprudenter, inconsiderate.*

recklessness, *imprudentia, neglegentia, temeritas.*
reckon. (1) = to count, calculate, *computare, (e)numerare.* (2) see CONSIDER. (3) to — on, *confidĕre,* with dat.
reckoning, subst. *ratio, computatio* (Sen.): to make a —, *rationem inire* or *subducĕre.*
reclaim, v. (1) = to ask back, *repetĕre, reposcĕre.* (2) = to reform a person, *corrigĕre, emendare, ad virtutem revocare.*
recline, v. (1) transit. *reclinare.* (2) intransit. *se reclinare, recumbĕre, iacēre* (= to lie).
recluse, *homo solitarius.*
recognition, render by verb.
recognizance, *sponsio, vadimonium.*
recognize. (1) = to know again, *agnoscĕre, cognoscĕre, noscitare.* (2) = to acknowledge, *noscĕre, (com)probare* (= to approve), *accipĕre* (= to receive): to — a child officially as one's own, *tollĕre, suscipĕre.*
recoil, *resilire* (lit. and fig.), *resultare* (poet.), *recellĕre*: to — in horror, *refugĕre.*
recollect, *(com)meminisse, reminisci, recordari, memoriā repetĕre, memoriam (hominis, rei) repetĕre* or *revocare* or *renovare.*
recollection, *memoria, recordatio.*
recommence, v. (1) transit. *redintegrare, de integro instaurare, renovare.* (2) intransit. *renasci, renovari.*
recommend, *commendare, probare, suffragari* (with dat.): to — a course of action, *suadēre (homini) ut,* with subj.
recommendation, *commendatio, laudatio, suffragatio* (esp. by voting in favour): a letter of —, *litterae* (-arum, plur.) *commendaticiae.*
recommendatory, *commendaticius.*
recompense, subst. *remuneratio, praemium, merces.*
recompense, v. *remunerari.*
reconcile. (1) of persons (and deities) = to make friendly, *placare, (in gratiam) reconciliare, componĕre (aversos amicos:* Hor.); *(hominem cum homine) in gratiam reducĕre* or *restituĕre*: to become —d, *(cum homine) in gratiam redire* or *reverti.* (2) = to make congruous, *accommodare.* (3) to — oneself to = to submit to, *patienter* or *aequo animo ferre, rei* (dat.) *se submittĕre.*
reconciliation, *reconciliatio concordiae* or *gratiae*; or render by verb.
recondite, *reconditus, exquisitus.*
reconnaissance, render by verb; see RECONNOITRE.
reconnoitre, *explorare, (pro)speculari, situm* or *naturam loci cognoscere*: a —ing vessel, *navigium speculatorium, speculatoria.*
reconquer, *recipĕre, recuperare (recip-).*
reconsider, *denuo, rursus* or *iterum considerare, reputare,* etc.; see also CONSIDER.
record, records, subst. (1) sing., in gen., *tabulae* (-arum, plur.), *historia, monumentum.* (2) in plur., more specifically, the —s, *fasti* (-orum); *annales* (-ium, plur.; = yearly —s, chronicles); *acta* (-orum, plur.) *urbana* or *diurna* (= —s of public proceedings). (3) in sport = a recorded time, distance, etc.; render by periphrasis, e.g.: he broke all —s as a runner, *tam celeriter quam nemo antea currebat.*
record, v. *perscribĕre, in tabulas referre, litteris* or *memoriae mandare.*
recorder, as a law officer, *quaesitor.*

record-office, *tabularium.*

recount, *referre, (e)narrare, (com)memorare.*

recourse: to have — to a person or thing, *confugĕre, se conferre, se applicare* (all with *ad* and acc.); to have — to something low = to stoop to, *descendere* (*ad rem*).

recover, v. (1) transit. *recuperare (recip-), recipĕre, reparare*: to — one's debts, *nomina sua exigĕre*; to — oneself, *se conligĕre*; to — one's reason, *resipiscĕre*; to — one's health, *convalescĕre* (*e morbo*). (2) intransit. *refici, recreari, respirare* (lit. = to breathe again), *emergĕre* (= to extricate oneself); see also (1) transit. above.

recoverable, *reparabilis* (Ov., Sen.); or render by verb.

recovery. (1) of goods, etc., *recuperatio (recip-)*. (2) in health, *salus (-utis)* or *sanitas restituta, valetudo confirmata.* (3) in law, *evictio* (leg.).

recreant. (1) = apostate, *apostata* (eccl.). (2) see COWARD, COWARDLY.

recreate. (1) = to create anew, *renovare, recreare* (Lucr.); see also RENEW. (2) = to amuse, refresh, *recreare.*

recreation, *requies* (= rest), (*animi*) *remissio, relaxatio, oblectatio.*

recrimination, (*mutua*) *accusatio* (Tac.).

recruit, subst. *tiro*: the —s, collect. *delectus (-ūs), supplementum*; an army of —s, *exercitus (-ūs) tiro.*

recruit, v. (1) in gen., of strength, etc., *recreare, reficĕre.* (2) milit.: of existing bodies = to fill up, *supplēre, explēre*; of new formations or of individuals = to enrol, *conscribĕre, delectum habēre*: a —ing officer, *conquisitor.*

recruiting, subst. *conquisitio, delectus (-ūs).*

rectification, *correctio, emendatio.*

rectify, *corrigĕre, emendare.*

rectilineal, (*di*)*rectus.*

rectitude, *probitas, integritas, honestas.*

rector, of a college, parish, etc.; render by *rector.*

recumbent, (*re*)*supinus* (= on one's back), *recubans, reclinatus.*

red, *ruber, rubens* (poet.); *rubicundus, rubidus* (Pl.), *sanguineus* (= blood- —); of the hair, *rufus* (Pl., Ter.), *rutilus* (Ov., Tac.): reddish, rather —, *rufulus* (Pl.), *puniceus* (poet.); to be —, *rubēre*; the — Sea, *Sinus Arabicus.*

redden, v. (1) transit. *rubefacĕre* (poet.). (2) intransit. *rubescĕre* (poet.).

redeem, *redimĕre* (= to buy back), *liberare* (= to set free): to — a pledge, *repignerare* (Leg.).

redeemer, = a liberator in gen., *liberator, vindex*; in Christian thought, *redemptor* (eccl.).

redemption, in gen. = a buying back, *redemptio*; = a deliverance, *liberatio*; in Christian thought, *redemptio* (eccl.).

red-hot, *candens, fervens.*

red-lead, *minium* (Verg., Plin.).

redness, *rubor.*

redolent, *redolens* (with acc.).

redouble, *ingeminare* (Verg., Ov.), *congeminare* (Verg.).

redoubt, *castellum, propugnaculum.*

redound, *redundare*; sometimes render by predicative dat., e.g.: it —s to my credit, *est mihi honori.*

redress, subst. *satisfactio*; or render by verb.

redress, v. *restituĕre, compensare, sarcire.*

reduce. (1) = to bring to any condition, *redigĕre, revocare* (both with *ad* or *in* and acc.): — to order, *in integrum reducĕre* (civil affairs, etc.); to — to ashes, *incendio delēre*; to be —d to, *redire,* with *ad* and acc. (2) = to diminish, (*im*)*minuĕre, deminuĕre.* (3) = to conquer, *vincĕre, expugnare* (of a stronghold).

reduction, = diminution, *deminutio*; of strongholds, *expugnatio*; otherwise render by verb.

redundancy, of style, *redundantia.*

redundant, *supervacaneus.*

re-echo, v. (1) transit. *referre.* (2) intransit. *resonare, resultare* (Verg., Tac.).

reed, *harundo, calamus, canna* (Ov.).

reedy, *harundineus* (Verg.).

reef, subst. *dorsum* (Verg.); or render as rocks, by *scopuli, saxa.*

reef, v.: to — one's sails, *contrahĕre vela* (Hor.).

reek, *fumare.*

reel, subst. = a dance, *saltatio.*

reel, v. *titubare, vacillare.*

re-elect, *reficĕre.*

re-establish, *restituĕre.*

re-establishment, *restitutio.*

refectory, *cenaculum.*

refer. (1) to — a matter (or a person) to an authority, standard, etc., (*rem ad senatum,* etc.) *referre* or *deferre,* (*rem, hominem, ad senatum,* etc.) *reicĕre*: to — all things to the standard of art, *omnia ad artem revocare.* (2) = to assign, attribute, impute, *referre* (*ad rem*), *delegare* or *ascribĕre* or *attribuĕre* (all with dat.). (3) to — to = to mention, *perstringĕre, mentionem facĕre* (with genit.). (4) to — to = to mean, to be speaking of, *dicĕre* (with acc.), *spectare* (with *ad* or plain acc.).

referable, render by verb.

referee, *arbiter.*

reference, = regard, respect, *ratio*; otherwise render by verbs: with — to (a matter), *quod attinet ad* (*rem*).

refill, *replēre.*

refine. LIT., of liquids, *liquare* (Hor.); of metals, *purgare* (Plin.). TRANSF., (*ex*)*polire, excolēre.*

refined, adj. (*ex*)*politus, urbanus, humanus, liberalis, elegans*; of the senses or intellect, *subtilis*: — torture, *exquisitum supplicium.*

refinement, of manners, etc., *urbanitas, humanitas, elegantia*; of intellect, etc., *subtilitas.*

reflect, v. (1) transit. LIT., of light, *repercutĕre* (Verg., Plin. L.), *remittĕre* (Sen.), *regerĕre* (Plin.), *reddĕre* (poet.). TRANSF., **a** = to represent or show, *ostendĕre*: the mind is —ed in the face, *imago mentis est vultus*: **b** = to confer, bring, *adferre*: this —s credit on you, *hoc tibi est honori.* (2) intransit.: **a,** to — = to think, about anything, (*rem*) *considerare, reputare, cogitare, commentari*: **b,** to — upon = to blame, *culpare, reprehendĕre, vituperare.*

reflection. (1) = the reflecting of light, *repercussus (-ūs*: Plin.). (2) = image reflected, *imago.* (3) = consideration, thought, *cogitatio, consideratio, deliberatio, ratio, consilium*: without —, *nullo consilio, nulla ratione, temere.* (4) = blame, *reprehensio, vituperatio.*

reflective; see THOUGHTFUL.

reflux, *recessus (-ūs).*

reform, subst., or **reformation,** *correctio, emendatio.*
reform, v. LIT., = to put back into formation, esp. of troops, *restituĕre, reficĕre.* TRANSF., (**1**) transit. = to amend, *corrigĕre, emendare.* (**2**) intransit. = to get better, *se corrigĕre.*
reformer, *corrector, emendator* (with f. *emendatrix*).
refract, *infringĕre.*
refractoriness, *contumacia.*
refractory, *contumax.*
refrain, subst. *carmen.*
refrain, v. (*se*) *abstinēre, se continēre,* (*sibi* or *animis*) *temperare* (all commonly with *ab* and abl.): I cannot — from saying, *facĕre non possum quin dicam.*
refresh, *recreare, reficĕre:* to — oneself with meat and drink, *cibo ac potione corpus firmare.*
refreshing, *iucundus;* or render by verb.
refreshment. (**1**) abstr., *refectio* (Quint.). (**2**) = food, *cibus.*
refrigerate, = to cool, *refrigerare.*
refuge, *perfugium, refugium, asylum, receptaculum, portus* (*-ūs;* lit. = harbour): to seek — at a place, *ad locum confugĕre* or *perfugĕre.*
refugee, *fugitivus* (= a runaway slave, or a deserter), *exsul* (= exile).
refulgent, *splendidus;* see also BRIGHT.
refund, *reddĕre, dissolvĕre.*
refusal, *recusatio, repudiatio* (= rejection).
refuse, subst. *purgamentum, faex* (= dregs, also fig.), *quisquiliae* (*-arum,* plur.; = sweepings, usually fig.), *sentina* (= bilge-water; also fig.).
refuse, v. (**1**) to — a thing = refuse to give it, (*rem*) (*de*)*negare.* (**2**) to — a thing = refuse to accept it, (*rem*) *recusare, respuĕre, repudiare;* to — battle, *pugnam detrectare.* (**3**) to — to do a thing, *nolle* (with infin.), *recusare* (with infin. or ne and subj.; when negatived, with *quominus* or *quin*).
refutation, *refutatio, dissolutio* (of charges, etc.); or render by verb.
refute, (**1**) to — a person, (*hominem*) *refellĕre, redarguĕre, refutare, convincĕre, revincĕre.* (**2**) to — a thing, e.g. a charge, (*crimen*) *refellĕre, redarguĕre, refutare, confutare, convincĕre, revincĕre, diluĕre, dissolvĕre.*
regain, *recipĕre, reciperare.*
regal; see ROYAL.
regale; see ENTERTAIN: to — oneself; see FEAST.
regalia, *ornatus* (*-ūs*), *regius, insignia* (*-ium,* plur.), *regia.*
regard, subst. (**1**) = consideration, *respectus* (*-ūs*), *ratio, cura:* to have — for; see REGARD, v. (**2**) = esteem, *studium, amor* (= love): Cicero sends his —s, *Cicero tibi salutem plurimam dicit.* (**3**) = respect, reference; see REFERENCE.
regard, v. (**1**) = to look at, *observare, intueri.* (**2**) = to bear in mind, have a care for, *respicĕre, spectare, rationem habēre* (with genit.): not to —, *neglegĕre.* (**3**) = to consider, *ducĕre, habēre.* (**4**) = to concern, relate to, *attinēre, pertinēre, spectare* (all with *ad* and acc.).
regardless, *neglegens, incuriosus* (Suet., Tac.).
regardlessly, *neglegenter, incuriose.*
regency, *regni administratio* or *procuratio, interregnum.*

regeneration, *regeneratio* (eccl.).
regent, *procurator regni, interrex.*
Reggio, *Rhegium.*
regicide. (**1**) = murder of a king, *regis caedes.* (**2**) = murderer of a king, *regis interfector* or *occisor* (Pl.).
regiment, *legio* (of infantry), *turma equitum* (of cavalry).
region, *regio, tractus* (*-ūs*), *locus, plaga* (poet.), *ora* (= shore), *pars* (= part, district).
register, *liber, tabulae* (*-arum,* plur.), *album:* to enter in a —, *in tabulas* or *album referre.*
register, v. *perscribĕre, in album* or *tabulas referre.*
registrar, *tabularius* (Sen.).
registration, render by verb.
regret, subst. *dolor* (= grief), *desiderium* (= longing), *paenitentia* (= repentance).
regret, v. (**1**) in gen. = to grieve about, *dolēre.* (**2**) = to feel the loss of, *desiderare, requirĕre.* (**3**) = to repent of an action, render by the impers. verb *paenitet;* e.g.: I — having done it, *paenitet me fecisse.*
regrettable, *paenitendus.*
regular. (**1**) = correct, according to rule or procedure, *ordinarius, iustus, legitimus, rectus, status:* — troops, *milites legionarii.* (**2**) = constant, undeviating, even, *certus, constans, aequabilis.*
regularity, *ordo, constantia, aequabilitas.*
regularly. (**1**) = correctly, in due order, *ordine, ordinatim, iuste, legitime, recte.* (**2**) = constantly, evenly, *constanter, aequabiliter.*
regulate, *ordinare, componĕre, dirigĕre, moderari, administrare.*
regulation. (**1**) as an act, *administratio.* (**2**) = an order, *iussum, praeceptum, institutum, lex, edictum* (= edict).
rehabilitate, *restituĕre.*
rehearsal, *meditatio* (= previous study).
rehearse, *praeludĕre* (Plin.), *meditari* (= to practise); of the producer, *fabulam docēre.*
reign, subst., of a king, *regnum;* of an emperor, *imperium, principatus* (*-ūs:* Tac.): in the — of King Deiotarus, *Deiotaro regnante* or *rege;* see also RULE.
reign, v. *regnare* (as a king), *imperare* (as an emperor: Tac., Suet.); see also RULE, GOVERN.
reimburse, (*rem homini*) *reddĕre;* see also REPAY.
rein, subst. *habena, frenum, lorum:* to pull in the —s, *habenas adducĕre* (lit. and fig.); to loosen the —s, *habenas permittĕre, frenos dare* (lit. and fig.).
rein, v. *frenare* (lit. and fig.).
reinforce, (*con*)*firmare, augēre* (= to increase).
reinforcement, *supplementum, novae copiae* (*-arum,* plur.: = new forces), *subsidium* (= reserve; sing. or plur.).
reins, *renes* (*-um,* plur.).
reinstate, *restituĕre.*
reinvigorate, *reficĕre.*
reiterate, *iterare;* see also REPEAT.
reject, *reicĕre, repudiare, respuĕre* (= to spit out), *spernĕre, aspernari:* to — a bill, *legem antiquare;* to — prayers, *preces aversari.*
rejection, *reiectio, repudiatio, repulsa* (of a candidate).
rejoice. (**1**) intransit.: to — (at a thing), (*re*) *gaudēre, laetari,* (*ex re*) *laetitiam percipĕre;*

to — wildly, *exsultare, gestire*. (**2**) intransit. *laetificare, exhilarare, delectare, laetitiā adficĕre*.

rejoicing, *gaudium, laetitia*.

rejoin. (**1**) see RETURN. (**2**) see ANSWER.

relapse, subst., render by verb.

relapse, v. *recidĕre, relabi* (Hor.).

relate, v. (**1**) = to tell in detail, *(e)narrare, (com)memorare, referre, tradĕre* (= to hand down); see also TELL. (**2**) to — to = to concern, (*ad rem, hominem*) *spectare, pertinēre, attinēre*.

related. (**1**) by birth or marriage, *propinquus, cognatus, consanguineus, adfinis* (by marriage): more nearly —, *propior*; most nearly —, *proximus*. (**2**) in gen. = connected, *finitimus, cognatus, propinquus, coniunctus*: closely —, *arte connexus*.

relation. (**1**) abstr. = connexion, *ratio*; in — to, *ad* with acc., *pro* with abl. (= in proportion to), *erga* with acc. (of persons); see also RELATIONSHIP: to have business —s with a person, *cum homine rem* or *negotium contrahĕre*; hospitable —s, *hospitium*; friendly —s, *familiaritas, necessitudo, amicitia*. (**2**) = a relative, *propinquus* (with f. *propinqua*), *cognatus* (with f. *cognata*), *adfinis* (by marriage). (**3**) see NARRATIVE.

relationship. (**1**) between persons, *propinquitas, cognatio, agnatio* (on the father's side), *adfinitas* (by marriage), *germanitas* (of brothers and sisters), *consanguinitas* (by blood). (**2**) in gen., *cognatio, coniunctio*.

relative, subst.; see RELATION (**2**).

relative, adj. opp. to absolute; render by *spectare ad* (= to relate to) or *comparare* (= to compare) or negatively (e.g. *non simpliciter, non per se*).

relax, v. (**1**) transit. (*re*)*laxare, remittĕre*. (**2**) intransit. (*re*)*languescĕre, animum remittĕre, relaxari, se relaxare*.

relaxation, (*animi*) *relaxatio, remissio, oblectatio* (= amusement).

relay, subst. = a supply of horses for successive use, *equi recentes* or *per viam dispositi*.

release, subst. *liberatio, missio*.

release, v. *liberare*, (*ex*)*solvĕre, laxare*: to — a prisoner or soldier, *missum facĕre*; to — a slave, *manu mittĕre*; to — from a service, *exauctorare*.

relent, *molliri, iram remittĕre*.

relentless, *immisericors, inexorabilis, saevus, durus, crudelis*.

relentlessly, *saeve, crudeliter*.

relevant, to be, *ad rem spectare* or *attinēre*.

reliance, *fides, fiducia*; see also CONFIDENCE.

relic, relics, *reliquiae* (-*arum*, plur.; = remains).

relict, *vidua*; see also WIDOW.

relief. (**1**) = alleviation, (*ad*)*levatio, sublevatio, levamen*(*tum*), *adlevamentum, remedium* (= remedy), *laxamentum, delenimentum*. (**2**) = aid, *auxilium, subsidium*. (**3**) in art, as t. t. *eminentia, asperitas* (Vitr.): to engrave in —, *caelare*; an engraver in —, *caelator*; a bas-—, *caelamen* (Ov.).

relieve. (**1**) = to lighten, ease, *levare, adlevare, sublevare, laxare, exonerare*. (**2**) = to aid; see AID, HELP. (**3**) = to take another's place, (*hominem*) *excipĕre*, (*homini*) *succedĕre*.

religion, *religio* (primarily = religious feeling), *cultus* (-*ūs*) *deorum*; see also RELIGIOUS.

religious, of persons, *erga* (or *adversus*) *deos, pius, sanctus, religiosus*: — scruple, — feeling, *religio*; — observances, *ritūs* (-*uum*, plur.), *religiones* (-*um*, plur.), *caerimoniae* (-*arum*, plur.), *res* (*rerum*, plur.) *divinae, sacra* (-*orum*, plur.).

religiously, *pie, sancte, religiose*.

relinquish, *relinquĕre*; see also ABANDON.

relish, subst. (**1**) = flavour, *sapor*. (**2**) = something tasty, *promulsis, condimentum*. (**3**) = liking, fondness, *studium*.

relish, v.; see ENJOY.

reluctance, with —, *coactus, invitus*.

reluctant, *invitus, coactus*: to be —, *nolle*.

rely, (*con*)*fidĕre* (usually with dat.), *fidem habēre* (with dat.), *niti* (with abl.): —ing upon, *fretus* (with abl.), *nixus* or *nisus* (with abl.).

remain. (**1**) in gen. = to stay, endure, (*per*)*manēre, remanēre, durare* (= to last), *stare* (= to stand), *exstare* (= to — extant), *morari* (= to linger), *se tenēre* (= to confine oneself in a place): to — unchanged in a thing, *in re perseverare*. (**2**) = to be left over, *restare, superare, superesse*: it only —s that, *restat ut*, with subj.

remainder, *residuum, reliquum, quod restat*.

remaining, adj. *reliquus, residuus, superstes* (= surviving).

remains, *reliquiae* (-*arum*, plur.).

remand, subst. *comperendinatio, comperendinatus* (-*ūs*), *ampliatio* (Sen.).

remand, v. (**1**) = to send back, *remittĕre*. (**2**) as legal t. t. (*reum*) *ampliare, comperendinare*.

remark, subst. = a saying, *dictum*: that — of Plato's, *illud Platonis*; I must first make a few introductory —s, *pauca ante dicenda sunt*.

remark, v. (**1**) see OBSERVE, PERCEIVE. (**2**) = to say, *dicĕre*.

remarkable, *singularis, insignis, notabilis, memorabilis; conspicuus* (= striking), *mirus* (= wonderful), *memoriā dignus* (= worth mentioning).

remarkably, *insigniter, singulariter, mire* (= wonderfully); often rendered by superl. of adj. or by adj. with *per-* (e.g.: — small, *perparvus*).

remedial, *salutaris*.

remedy. (**1**) medical, *remedium, medicina, medicamen*(*tum*): to apply a — for a complaint, *morbo medicinam adhibēre*. (**2**) in gen., for any evil, *remedium, medicina, medicamentum, medicamen* (poet.).

remember, (*com*)*meminisse, reminisci, recordari, memoriā tenēre* or *custodire* (= to keep in mind), *memoriā* (or *memoriam rei*, genit.) *repetĕre* (= to recall): as far as I can —, *ut mea memoria est, quantum memini, nisi animus* (or *memoria*) *me fallit*; — me to Cicero, *Ciceronem meis verbis saluta*.

remembrance, *memoria, recordatio*.

remind, (*ad*)*monēre, commonēre, commonefacĕre*.

reminiscence. (**1**) abstr., *recordatio*. (**2**) —s, written up as a book, perhaps *commentarii* (-*orum*, plur.).

remiss, *neglegens*.

remission, *remissio, venia* (= pardon).

remissness, *neglegentia*.

remit. (**1**) = to send back, *remittĕre*. (**2**) = o send (of money, etc.), *mittĕre*. (**3**) = to

excuse, let off (debts, etc.), (*pecunias*, etc.)
remittĕre or *condonare*, (*delicti*, etc.) *gratiam
facĕre*.
remittance, render by *pecunia*.
remnant; see REMAINDER.
remonstrance, *reclamatio*, (*ad*)*monitio*.
remonstrate, *reclamare, reclamitare* (with dat.).
remorse, *conscientia mala, paenitentia* (= penitence): to feel —, *conscientiā mordĕri* or
cruciari or *angi*, or render by the impers.
paenitet.
remorseless, *immisericors*; see also PITILESS.
remote. LIT., physically, *remotus, amotus,
semotus, disiunctus, longinquus*. TRANSF.,
remotus, disiunctus, alienus.
remotely, *vix* (= hardly).
remoteness, *longinquitas*.
remount, *equum iterum conscendĕre*.
removal. (1) in gen., *amotio, depulsio* (=
averting); *relegatio* or *amandatio* (= the
sending away of a person). (2) to a new
home, *migratio, demigratio, profectio* (=
starting).
remove, subst. = degree, step, *gradus* (-ūs).
remove, v. (1) transit. *removēre, amovēre,
submovēre* (esp. of people), *emovēre, semovēre,
tollere, auferre, transferre* (= to — elsewhere),
amoliri (= to — with difficulty); = to carry
away, *avehĕre, asportare*; = to lead away,
abducĕre; = to drive away, *depellĕre, propulsare*; = to send out of the way, *ablegare,
relegare, amandare*. (2) intransit. —, in gen., *se
movēre, discedĕre, abire*; = to change one's
place of residence, *migrare, emigrare, trans-
migrare, demigrare, commigrare* (in a body).
remunerate, *remunerari*; see also RECOMPENSE,
REWARD.
remuneration, *remuneratio, praemium*; see
also REWARD.
rend, (*dis*)*scindĕre*, (*di*)*rumpĕre, divellĕre* (= to
pull in pieces).
render. (1) = to give back or give as due,
reddĕre, referre, tribuĕre; to — an account,
rationem reddĕre; to — thanks, *gratias agĕre*.
(2) = to make, cause to be, *facĕre, efficĕre,
reddĕre*. (3) see TRANSLATE.
rendering, render by verb; see also TRANS-
LATION.
rendezvous, perhaps *locus ad conveniendum
constitutus*; the general idea of a — is expressed in Verg. Aen. II. 716, *hanc ex
diverso sedem veniemus in unam*.
rending, *discidium, laceratio*.
renegade, *transfuga, apostata* (eccl.).
renew. (1) = to make new or as new, (*re*)-
novare, reficĕre, reconcinnare. (2) = to begin
afresh, to repeat, *renovare, instaurare* (*de
integro*), *integrare, redintegrare, repetĕre,
iterare*: to — the war (of a conquered people),
rebellare, rebellionem facĕre.
renewable, render by verb.
renewal, *renovatio, instauratio*.
renounce, (*rem*) *renuntiare, se* (*re*) *abdicare*,
(*rem*) *reicĕre* or *repudiare* or *eiurare* (Tac.):
to — a project, *incepto* or *conatu desistĕre*; to
— one's right, *de iure suo decedĕre*.
renovate; see RENEW.
renovation; see RENEWAL.
renown, *fama, gloria, laus, nomen*.
renowned, *clarus, inlustris*; see also FAMOUS.
rent, subst. (1) = a tear, *scissura* (Sen.); or
render by verb. (2) = proceeds, money paid

for the use of land, etc., *reditus* (-ūs), *vectigal,
merces* (-*ēdis*): the — of a house, *merces
habitationis*.
rent, v. (1) = to let out, *locare*. (2) = to hire,
conducĕre.
rental; see RENT (2).
renunciation, *abdicatio, repudiatio, reiectio*; or
render by verb.
reopen, *iterum, aperire*.
repair, subst.: in good —, *sartus tectus*; in
bad —, *ruinosus, obsoletus*; see also REPAIR, v.
repair, v. (1) transit. *reficĕre, reparare,
(re)sarcire, restituĕre, reconcinnare*; with abstr.
subst. as object, *resarcire*. (2) = to make
one's way, *se conferre*; see also GO.
reparation, *satisfactio*.
repartee, render by phrase, such as *responsum
haud infacetum*: skill in —, *celeritas in
respondendo*.
repast; see MEAL.
repay, *reddĕre, referre, reponĕre, solvĕre*: to — in
the same coin, *par pari respondĕre*; see also
PAY.
repayment, *solutio*; or render by verb.
repeal, subst. *abrogatio, derogatio, obrogatio*;
see also REPEAL, v.
repeal, v. *rescindĕre, tollĕre, abrogare, derogare*
(partly), *obrogare* (with dat.; = to substitute
one law for another).
repeat. (1) = to do again, *iterare, redintegrare*.
(2) = to say again (or again and again),
iterare, decantare (monotonously), *ingeminare*
(poet.): to — in the same words, *iisdem
verbis reddĕre*.
repeatedly, *identidem, iterum atque iterum,
saepenumero, etiam atque etiam*.
repel, *repellĕre, propulsare, reicĕre, fugare* (= to
put to flight): to — an accusation, *culpam a
se amovēre, crimen dissolvĕre* or *diluĕre*.
repent, render by the impers. *paenitet*; e.g.:
I — of having done that, *paenitet me id
fecisse*; I — of the crime, *paenitet me sceleris*;
to — a little, render by *subpaenitet*.
repentance, *paenitentia*.
repentant, *paenitens*; or render by finite verb.
repertory, *thesaurus*.
repetition, *iteratio, repetitio* (Quint.), *gemina-
tio*; as rhet. t. t.: the — of the same word at
the beginning of sentences, *repetitio*; at the
end of sentences, *conversio*.
repine: to — at, (*con*)*queri*.
repining, *querela* (= complaint).
replace. (1) = to put back, *reponĕre, restituĕre*.
(2) to — one person or thing by another,
substituĕre.
replenish, *replēre, supplēre*.
replete; see FULL.
repletion, *satietas*.
reply, subst. *responsum, responsio* (esp. = a
refutation).
reply, v. *respondēre*: to — by letter, *rescribĕre*.
report, subst. (1) official, *relatio, renuntiatio*.
(2) = rumour, *fama, rumor, auditio, sermo*:
a — spreads, *fama* (or *rumor*) *serpit, manat,
increbrescit*; a — is prevalent, *fama* (or *rumor*)
viget, obtinet; to spread a —, *famam* (or
rumorem) *spargĕre, dissipare*. (3) = a loud
noise, *fragor, crepitus* (-ūs).
report, v. (re)*nuntiare, referre, adferre, deferre*
(esp. = to authorities): it is —ed, *ferunt,
tradunt, traditur, dicitur*.
repose, subst. (*re*)*quies, otium*; see also REST.

repose, v. (1) transit. *(re)ponĕre.* (2) intransit. *quiescĕre.*

repository, *thesaurus, receptaculum.*

reprehend, *reprehendĕre;* see also REBUKE.

reprehensible, *culpā dignus, reprehendendus, vituperabilis, vituperandus.*

represent. (1) = to portray, *exprimĕre, (ef)fingĕre, simulare* (poet.), *(de)pingere* (in painting or speech), *adumbrare* (= to sketch, lit. and fig.), *imitari, repraesentare* (Quint., Plin. L.): to — something exactly or to the life, *veritatem imitari, ad verum exprimĕre;* to — vividly, *ante oculos ponĕre;* to — a person as doing something (in a play, etc.), *hominem facĕre,* with partic. or infin. (2) = to state, point out, *(homini) dicĕre* or *ostendĕre, (hominem) docĕre* or *monĕre.* (3) = to play the part of some other person, *hominis personam gerĕre* or *partes agĕre;* or render by the prep. *pro* (with abl.), or the phrase *in loco* (with genit.) = instead of.

representation. (1) = the act of portraying, *repraesentatio* (Quint.); or render by verb. (2) = that which portrays, an image, likeness, *imago, effigies.* In other senses, render by verbs.

representative, *vicarius, procurator* (= agent, manager).

repress, *opprimĕre, comprimĕre, cohibĕre.*

reprieve, subst., render by phrase, such as *dilatio suplicii.*

reprieve, v., render by phrase, such as *supplicium differre.*

reprimand, subst. *reprehensio, vituperatio, animadversio, convicium.*

reprimand, v. *reprehendĕre, vituperare, animadvertĕre.*

reprisals, *talio:* to make —s, *vim vi repellĕre, par pari respondĕre.*

reproach, subst. (1) the act of —ing, *exprobratio, obiectatio.* (2) = the words used, *probrum, convicium, contumelia, opprobrium* (Hor.). (3) = a disgrace, scandal, *opprobrium* (Hor.), *probrum.*

reproach, v. *increpitare, obiurgare, incusare:* to — a person for a thing, *rem homini exprobrare* or *obicĕre* or *obiectare.*

reproachful, *obiurgatorius;* or render by verb.

reprobate, subst., render by *homo,* with adj.; see REPROBATE, adj.

reprobate, adj. *perditus, profligatus, nequam, sceleratus.*

reprobation; see CONDEMNATION.

reproduce, *regignĕre* (Lucr.); or render by phrase, such as *denuo generare* or *ferre.*

reproduction, reproductive, render by verb.

reproof, *vituperatio, culpa, castigatio, reprehensio, obiurgatio, animadversio, exprobatio.*

reprove, *vituperare, reprehendĕre;* see also REPROACH, v.

reprover, *reprehensor, obiurgator, castigator.*

reptile, *bestia serpens, animans repens* (Lucr.).

republic, *respublica, civitas* (= state, simply): a —, as opp. to other forms of government, *respublica* (or *civitas*) *libera* or *popularis.*

republican, subst. *vir popularis, vir liberae reipublicae studiosus;* L. Iunius Brutus, who expelled Tarquinius, may sometimes stand as the type of ardent —.

republican, adj. *popularis;* or render by the genit. *reipublicae liberae.*

republish, render by phrase, such as *(librum) denuo edĕre.*

repudiate; see REJECT.

repudiation, *repudiatio;* of a son, *abdicatio filii* (= disowning, disinheriting: Quint.); of a wife, *divortium, repudium;* see also REJECTION.

repugnance, *repugnantia* (= incompatibility), *odium* (= hatred): to feel —, *abhorrēre.*

repugnant, *repugnans, diversus, aversus, alienus* (with *ab*): to be —, *repugnare,* with dat.

repulse, subst., of a candidate, *repulsa;* otherwise render by verb.

repulse, v. *repellĕre, propulsare, reicĕre.*

repulsive, *odiosus, foedus;* see also DISGUSTING.

repurchase, *redimĕre.*

reputable, *honestus;* see also RESPECTABLE.

reputation, good or bad, *fama, opinio:* good —, *existimatio, gloria, laus, nomen, honor;* bad —, *mala fama, infamia.*

repute; see REPUTATION: to be in good —, *bene audire;* to be in bad —, *mala audire, infamiā flagrare.*

reputed, *qui (quae, quod) dicitur, fertur.*

request, subst. *preces (-um,* plur.), *rogatio, postulatio* (= urgent —, demand): at my —, *rogatu* or *oratu meo, me rogante, a me rogatus;* what is your —? *quid petis?;* to grant a —, *precibus obsequi.*

request, v. *(hominem) precari, orare, rogare, obsecrare, implorare; (ab homine) petĕre; postulare* (= to — urgently, demand).

requiem, *missa defunctorum* (= Mass for the dead; eccl.).

require. (1) = to demand, *poscĕre, postulare, exigĕre, imperare (rem homini).* (2) = to need, call for, *(rē) egĕre, (rem) requirĕre, desiderare, postulare* (without object); often rendered by *opus esse* (e.g.: I — a sword, *opus est mihi gladio*); sometimes by a genit. only (e.g.: it —s much hard work to do so, *multi laboris est facĕre*).

requirement, *postulatio;* or render by verb.

requisite, subst. *res necessaria, (id) quod opus est.*

requisite, adj. *necessarius;* or render by verb; see REQUIRE.

requisition, *postulatio;* or render by *imperare* (with acc. of thing demanded, dat. of person called upon).

requital, render by verb.

requite, *compensare, rependĕre* (poet.).

rescind, *rescindĕre, abrogare, tollĕre;* see also REPEAL.

rescript, *responsum:* an imperial —, *rescriptum* (Tac.), *codicilli (-orum,* plur.: Suet.).

rescue, subst. *liberatio;* or render by verb.

rescue, v. *liberare, exsolvĕre, servare, eripĕre, salutem (homini) adferre:* to — one's country from slavery, *patriam in libertatem vindicare.*

research, *eruditio* (= learning), *investigatio* (= inquiry).

resemblance, *similitudo:* bearing a —, *similis;* bearing a close —, *simillimus.*

resemble, *similem esse* (with genit. or dat.), *accedĕre (ad rem, ad hominem), (rem, hominem) attingĕre.*

resent, *aegre* or *moleste ferre, in malam partem accipĕre.*

resentful, *iracundus.*

resentment, *ira, stomachus.*

reservation, = qualification, *exceptio:* with this —, that, *hac lege* or *hac condicione ut,* with subj.

reserve, subst. **(1)** = store, *copia.* **(2)** milit. t. t., —s, the —, *subsidia (-orum,* plur.), *subsidiarii (-orum,* plur.); in —, adj. *subsidiarius.* **(3)** in manner, *taciturnitas* (= habitual silence), *verecundia:* without —, *aperte, simpliciter.*

reserve, *(re)servare, retinēre* (= to keep back), *reponěre* (= to store up).

reserved, *reconditus, taciturnus* (= habitually silent), *verecundus, occultus, tectus* (= secretive).

reservoir, *lacus (-ūs), castellum* (= the — of an aqueduct: Plin.), *cisterna* (underground: Plin.), *piscina* (= a pond: Plin.), *(aquae) receptaculum* (Vitr.).

reside, v. Lit., *habitare (locum, in loco, apud hominem):* to begin to —, to settle, *considēre.* Transf., of abstr. things, *(in re) residēre, versari, constare, inesse.*

residence. **(1)** the act of residing, *habitatio, mansio, commoratio:* — in the country, *rusticatio.* **(2)** = place of —, *domus, domicilium, sedes.*

resident, subst. *habitator, incola* (sometimes = a foreign —).

resident, adj., render by verbs.

residue, *quod residuum* or *reliquum est.*

resign. **(1)** = to lay down an office: at the appointed time, *abire* with abl. *(magistratu), decedere* with *de* and abl., *deponěre* with acc.; prematurely, *se abdicare* with abl., sometimes *deponěre.* **(2)** in gen. = to give up, *(con)cedĕre, deponĕre, remittĕre:* to — oneself, *animum submittĕre.*

resignation. **(1)** = the act of giving up, *abdicatio.* **(2)** = a resigned attitude, *animus submissus* or *aequus:* to bear with —, *aequo animo* or *moderate ferre.*

resin, *resina* (Plin.).

resinous, *resinaceus* or *resinosus* (Plin.).

resist, *resistĕre, obsistĕre, restare, obstare, repugnare, adversari* (all with dat.).

resistance, render by verb.

resistless, *cui nullo modo resisti potest.*

resolute, *fortis, firmus, constans, obstinatus, offirmatus.*

resolutely, *fortiter, firme, firmiter, constanter, obstinate.*

resolution. **(1)** = separation into parts, *(dis)solutio, dissipatio.* **(2)** = determination, as a quality, *constantia, firmitudo, obstinatio.* **(3)** = a particular purpose, *sententia, consilium, propositum.* **(4)** the — of a deliberative body, *sententia, decretum, scitum.*

resolve, subst.; see REVOLUTION.

resolve, v. **(1)** = to break down into parts, *dissolvĕre, dissipare;* fig., of problems = to solve, *(dis)solvĕre.* **(2)** = in gen., to determine, *statuĕre, constituĕre, decernĕre, destinare;* or render by the impers. *certum est* (e.g.: I have —d, *certum est mihi*). **(3)** of a deliberative body, *censēre, sciscĕre, iubēre;* or render by the impers. *placet.*

resolved, *certus* (with genit. or infin.: Verg., Tac.); or render by verb.

resonant, *resonans.*

resort, subst. **(1)** = place, *locus.* **(2)** = recourse; render by verb.

resort, v. **(1)** to — to a place, *locum celebrare, frequentare; ad locum ventitare, commeare.* **(2)** to — to = to have recourse to, *(re) uti, (ad rem, ad hominem) confugere, decurrēre* or *descendĕre.*

---

resound, *resonare, personare.*

resource, resources. **(1)** = help, support, *auxilium, subsidium, adiumentum.* **(2)** = means (abstr. or concr.) to an end, *facultates (-um,* plur.). **(3)** more specifically = wealth or power, *opes (-um,* plur.), *bona (-orum,* plur. = goods), *pecunia* (= money).

respect, subst. **(1)** = esteem, *observantia, reverentia, honor.* **(2)** respects, in the phrase: to pay one's —s to, *salutare (hominem).* **(3)** = regard, relationship: in all —s, *omnino, ab* (or *ex) omni parte, in omnes partes;* in that —, *in eam partem;* in — of, *ad* or *in* with acc., *de* or *ab* with abl., or sometimes plain abl.

respect, v. **(1)** = to think highly of, *observare, suspicĕre, (re)vereri, colĕre, magni aestimare.* **(2)** = to concern; see CONCERN or RELATE.

respectability, *honestas.*

respectable, *honestus, venerabilis.*

respectably, *honeste, bene.*

respectful, *observans, verecundus.*

respectfully, *verecunde, reverenter* (Plin.).

respecting, *de* with abl.

respective, *proprius, suus* (often with *quisque;* e.g.: each has his — duties, *sua cuique sunt officia).*

respiration, *respiratio, respiratus (-ūs), spiritus (-ūs).*

respiratory, *qui (quae, quod) ad respiratum pertinet.*

respite; see REPRIEVE.

resplendent, *splendidus;* see also BRIGHT.

respond, response; see ANSWER.

respondent, as legal t. t., *reus.*

responsibility, responsible, often rendered by the phrase *rationem reddĕre* (= to give an account), e.g.: to be — for a thing, *rationem rei* (genit.) *reddĕre debēre;* to hold a person —, *rationem ab homine reposcĕre;* to make oneself — for a thing, *rem praestare* or *in se recipĕre* or *promittĕre.*

responsive, perhaps *apertus* (= open), *facilis* (= tractable), *comis* (= affable).

rest, subst. **(1)** = repose, quiet, *(re)quies, otium, pax* (poet.), *tranquillitas.* **(2)** see PROP. **(3)** = remainder, *reliquum, residuum, quod restat:* the — of, followed by a subst., is often expressed by *reliquus* or *residuus* or *ceteri* (usually plur.), agreeing with the subst. (e.g.: the — of the troops, *ceteri milites).*

rest, v. **(1)** transit. = to place, *ponĕre* (lit. and fig.). **(2)** intransit. Lit., = to repose, *(re)quiescĕre, adquiescĕre, conquiescĕre, cessare* (= to do nothing), *otiari* (= to be at leisure), *quietem capĕre:* to — upon, *(re) (in)niti.* Transf., it —s with a person, *in homine situm* or *positum est, penes hominem est.*

resting-place, *cubile, deversorium* (= inn, also fig.); or render by phrase, such as *locus ad quietem aptus.*

restitution, render by verb.

restive, perhaps *ferox.*

restless, *inquietus, sollicitus* (= anxious), *turbidus, turbulentus, tumultuosus* (of the sea, etc.).

restlessness, *inquies (-ētis:* Plin.), *motus (-ūs;* = movement).

restoration, *refectio* (Suet.); or render by verb.

restorative, subst. *medicina.*

restore. **(1)** = to give back, *reddĕre, referre.*

(2) = to reinstate, replace, *restituĕre, redintegrare, referre, reficĕre, reconciliare*: to — a king, *regem reducĕre* or *restituĕre*; to — a person to health, *sanare, sanum facĕre, sanitatem homini restituĕre*.

restorer, *restitutor, reconciliator* (e.g. *pacis*).

restrain, *coercēre, tenēre, retinēre, continēre, cohibēre, inhibēre, moderari, reprimĕre, comprimĕre, supprimĕre,* (*re*)*frenare* (= to bridle).

restraint. (1) = the act of restraining, *moderatio*. (2) = due bounds, reasonable limits, *modus, moderatio*. (3) = a check, hindrance, *impedimentum, repagula* (*-orum,* plur.); see also RESTRICTION.

restrict, *coercēre, circumscribĕre,* (*de*)*finire*; see also RESTRAIN.

restriction, *modus, finis, angustiae* (*-arum,* plur.).

restrictive; render by verb; see RESTRICT.

result, subst. *exitus* (*-ūs*)*, eventus* (*-ūs*)*, effectus* (*-ūs*)*, consequentia, fructus* (*-ūs;* esp. = the — of work): the — is that, *evenit ut,* with subj.; without —, *nequiquam, re infecta*.

result, v. intransit. *fieri, evenire, evadĕre, consequi* (= to follow as a —), *oriri,* (*ex re*) *manare*.

resume, *repetere, recolere*; see also RECOMMENCE.

resumption, render by verb.

resurrection, *resurrectio* (eccl.).

resuscitate, *resuscitare* (poet.), *ab inferis excitare*; see also REVIVE.

retail, *divendĕre*.

retailer, *caupo*.

retain, *tenēre, retinēre, obtinēre* (*con*)*servare*.

retainer. (1) = an attendant, *cliens, adsector, famulus, satelles*. (2) = a retaining fee, *arrhabo* (Pl., Ter.).

retake, *reciperare, recipĕre*.

retaliate, *par pari respondēre*; more generally *ulcisci* (= to take vengeance).

retaliation, render by *ultio* (= revenge).

retard, (*re*)*morari,* (*re*)*tardare, moram facĕre* or *adferre* (with dat.).

retch, v. *nauseare*.

retire, v. (1) physically = to go back or away, *abire,* (*re*)*cedĕre, concedĕre, excedĕre, decedĕre, secedĕre* (= to go apart or aside); as milit. t. t., *pedem referre, se recipĕre, decedĕre*. (2) = to withdraw from an activity: in gen., *se removēre* (*a negotiis,* etc.), *recedĕre*; see also RESIGN.

retired, adj. *secretus, remotus, reductus* (poet.), *solitarius*: a — life, *vita umbratilis*; a — spot, *recessus* (*-ūs*).

retirement. (1) as an act, *recessus* (*-ūs*) or render by verb. (2) as a state, *solitudo, otium, vita a rebus publicis remota, vita privata ac quieta*.

retiring, adj. *verecundus*; see also MODEST.

retort; see REPLY.

retrace, *repetĕre*: to — one's steps, *pedem referre*.

retract, *renuntiare*.

retreat, subst. (1) = the act of —ing, *reditus* (*-ūs*)*, recessus* (*-ūs*)*, regressus* (*-ūs*)*, recursus* (*-ūs*)*, receptus* (*-ūs;* of soldiers, etc.), *fuga* (= flight): to sound the —, (*signum*) *receptui canĕre*. (2) = place of refuge; see REFUGE.

retreat, v. *se recipĕre, pedem* or *gradum referre, fugĕre* (= to flee); of a commander, *castra referre, exercitum* (or *copias*) *reducĕre*.

retrench, *sumptūs minuĕre, circumcidĕre, contrahĕre*.

retrenchment, render by verb.

retribution, retributive, render by *poena* (= punishment).

retrieve; see RECOVER.

retrograde, of actual backward movement, render by phrase with *retro*; in the sense of change for the worse, render by phrase such as *res in deteriorem partem mutare*.

retrogression, *recessus* (*-ūs*)*, regressus* (*-ūs*).

retrospect, *respectus* (*-ūs;* = looking back), (*praeteritorum*) *memoria*.

retrospective, retrospectively, render by *retro* (= backwards in time) or by reference to *praeterita* (*-orum,* n. plur. = the past).

return, subst. (1) = a journey back, *reditus* (*-ūs*)*, regressus* (*-ūs*)*, reditio* (rare). (2) = a giving back, *remuneratio;* or render by verb. (3) = an official declaration, *renuntiatio, professio*: to make a —, *renuntiare, profiteri*.

return, v. (1) transit., *reddĕre, referre, restituĕre, remittĕre*: to — thanks, *gratias agĕre*; to — a kindness, *gratiam referre*; to — like for like, *par pari referre, paria paribus respondere*; — good for evil, *maleficia benefactis remunerari*; to — a man as consul, *hominem consulem renuntiare*. (2) intransit., *redire* (= to go back), *reverti* (= to turn back), *revenire* (rare), *remeare, remigrare, recurrĕre* (= to hasten back), *repetĕre* (with acc. = to return to), *se referre*.

returned, adj. *redux*.

reunite. LIT., render by phrase, such as *iterum coniungĕre*; see also UNITE. TRANSF., *reconciliare*; see also RECONCILE.

reunion, *reconciliatio* (= reconciliation); see also ASSEMBLY.

reveal, *patefacĕre, manifestum reddĕre, aperire, in medium* (or *lucem*) *proferre, evulgare, divulgare*; see also BETRAY, PUBLISH.

revel, subst., and **revelry,** *comissatio, bacchatio, orgia* (*-orum,* plur.: Juv.).

revel, v. LIT., *comissari,* (*per*)*bacchari*. TRANSF., *luxuriare, exsultare*.

revelation, *patefactio,* or render by verb; the book of —, *Apocalypsis* (eccl.).

reveller, *comissator*.

revenge, subst. *ultio, vindicta, vindicatio, ulciscendi cupiditas, poena* (= punishment).

revenge, v. to avenge, *ulcisci, vindicare, poenas rei* (genit.) *expetĕre*: to — oneself on a person, *hominem ulcisci* (*pro re*)*, in hominem vindicare, poenas ab homine expetĕre*.

revengeful, *ulciscendi cupidus*.

revenue, *vectigal, reditus* (*-ūs*).

reverberate, = to resound, *resonare*: —ing, *repercussus*.

reverberation, *repercussus* (*-ūs*: Plin. L., Tac.).

revere, reverence, v. (*re*)*vereri, venerari, observare, colĕre*.

reverence, subst. *reverentia, veneratio, verecundia, observantia*: religious —, *religio* or *pietas erga deos*.

reverend, *venerabilis, reverendus* (eccl.).

reverent, *verecundus*; in the religious sense, *religiosus, venerabundus, pius*.

reverently, *verecunde, religiose*.

reverie, *cogitatio* (= thought): lost in a —, *in cogitatione defixus, nescioquid meditans* (Hor.).

reverse, subst. (1) = a change to the opposite, *conversio,* (*com*)*mutatio, vicissitudo*. (2) = the opposite, *contrarium.* **(3)** = defeat, *clades*; see also DEFEAT. **(4)** = hind part, *pars aversa.*

reverse, v. *invertĕre, (com)mutare, convertĕre*; see also CHANGE.

reversible, render by verb.

reversion, as legal t. t. *hereditas.*

revert, *redire, revolvi.*

review, subst.; in gen., *recognitio*; of troops, *recensio, lustratio* (with religious rites); or render by verb.

review, v., in gen., *inspicĕre, contemplari, considerare, percensēre, recognoscĕre*: to — troops, *percensēre, recensēre, inspicĕre, lustrare* (with religious rites); to — a book, perhaps *de libro iudicium exprimĕre.*

reviewer, render by verb.

revile, *conviciari, insectari, maledicĕre (homini), maledicta in hominem dicĕre* or *conferre.*

reviler, *conviciator.*

reviling, subst. *maledictio, insectatio, probrum, convicium.*

revise, *retractare*; see also REVIEW, CORRECT.

revision, *limae labor* (lit. = work with the file: Hor.), *emendatio.*

revisit, *revisĕre.*

revive, v. **(1)** transit. *recreare, excitare, ad vitam revocare*; of abstr. things, *redintegrare.* **(2)** intransit. *revirescĕre, recreari, respirare, renasci* (lit. = to be reborn).

revocable, *revocabilis* (Ov., Sen.); or render by verb.

revocation, *revocatio, abrogatio, rescissio.*

revoke, *inritum facĕre, abrogare, rescindĕre, renuntiare.*

revolt, subst. *defectio, seditio, tumultus (-ūs), motus (-ūs)*; of a conquered people, *rebellio.*

revolt, v. **(1)** transit. = to disgust, *offendĕre.* **(2)** intransit. *deficĕre, desciscĕre, seditionem (com)movēre*; of a conquered people, *rebellare, rebellionem facĕre.*

revolting, adj. = disgusting, *taeter* (tet-), *nefandus, foedus, turpis.*

revolution. **(1)** = turning round, *conversio, orbis, ambitus (-ūs).* **(2)** a political —, *res* (*rerum,* plur.) *novae, reipublicae conversio* or *commutatio.*

revolutionary, subst. *homo turbulentus, seditiosus, novarum rerum studiosus* or *cupidus.*

revolutionary, adj. *seditiosus, turbulentus*: to hold — views, *novis rebus studēre, contra rempublicam sentire.*

revolutionize, *novare, commutare.*

revolve. **(1)** = to turn round, intransit., *se (re)volvĕre* or *(re)volvi. se circumagĕre* or *circumagi, circumverti, converti.* **(2)** = to ponder, transit., *(rem) reputare, considerare, animo volvĕre* or *volutare* or *versare.*

revulsion; see DISGUST.

reward, subst. *praemium* (honourable), *merces* (= pay), *pretium* (= price), *fructus (-ūs*; = fruit, esp. of labour): to offer a —, *praemium (pro)ponĕre.*

reward, v. *remunerari, compensare, praemio (hominem) adficĕre, praemium (homini) dare* or *tribuĕre* or *persolvĕre.*

rewrite, *iterum scribĕre.*

rhapsody, perhaps *oratio grandiloqua.*

rhetoric, *rhetorica, rhetorice* (Quint.), *ars dicendi, bene dicendi scientia* (Quint.): teachers of —, *rhetorici* or *rhetorici doctores*; a treatise on —, *ars rhetorica* or *rhetorica*

(-orum, n. plur.); to teach —, *dicendi praecepta tradĕre.*

rhetorical, *rhetoricus, oratorius.*

rhetorically, *rhetorice.*

rheum, *gravedo, humor.*

rheumatism, *dolor artuum.*

Rhine, river, *Rhenus.*

rhinoceros, *rhinoceros* (Plin.).

Rhône, river, *Rhodanus.*

rhubarb, *radix pontica* (Cels.).

rhyme, subst., no equivalent in classical Latin; render by phrase, such as *extremorum verborum similis sonitus (-ūs).*

rhythm, *numerus, modus, rhythmus* (Quint.).

rhythmical, *numerosus.*

rhythmically, *numerose, modulate.*

rib, *costa* (poet.); of a ship, *statumen.*

ribald, *obscenus.*

ribaldry, *sermo obscenus, obscenitas.*

riband, ribbon, *redimiculum, taenia* (Verg.) *vitta* (Hor.).

Ribchester, *Bremetennacum.*

rice, *oryza* (Hor.).

rich. **(1)** = possessing wealth, *dives, locuples, copiosus, opulentus* (esp. of places), *pecuniosus, bene nummatus, beatus* or *fortunatus* (= fortunate, wealthy): very —, *perdives, praedives*; to grow —, *ditescĕre* (Lucr., Hor.). **(2)** = costly, sumptuous, *opimus, pretiosus, lautus, opulentus* (Pl.). **(3)** in gen. = copious, fertile (lit. and fig.), *copiosus, abundans, uber, ferax*: to be — in anything, *rē abundare.*

Richard, *Ricardus* (late Latin).

riches, *divitiae (-arum,* plur.), *opes (-um,* plur.), *fortunae (-arum,* plur.), *facultates (-um,* plur.), *copia* (also plur.), *pecunia* (= money), *gaza* (= treasure).

richly, *copiose, abundanter, ample, pretiose* (= expensively), *laute* (= sumptuously).

richness, *abundantia, ubertas*; see also ABUNDANCE, SPLENDOUR.

rick, *meta* (Col.).

rid. **(1)** v. = to free from, *liberare (re)*; see also FREE. **(2)** in the phrase, to get — of or to — oneself of, *(rem) deponĕre, dimittĕre*; to have got — of, *(re) solutum, vacuum esse.*

riddance, *liberatio.*

riddle, subst. **(1)** = an enigma, *aenigma (-ătis,* n.), *ambages (-um,* plur.; = ambiguity in speech or action).

riddled, = pierced through and through, e.g. with wounds, *confossus.*

ride, v. **(1)** on a horse, *equitare, (equo) vehi*: to — across, *transvehi, adequitare*; to — back, *revehi*; to — between, *interequitare*; to — by, *praetervehi*; to — off, *avehi*; to — round, *circumvehi, circumequitare*; to — through, *perequitare*; to — up to, *adequitare.* **(2)** in a vehicle: to — in a chariot, *ire curru*; to — at anchor, *in ancoris consistĕre.*

rider, *eques, vector* (poet.): a good —, *homo equitandi peritus.*

ridge, *iugum, montis dorsum.*

ridicule, subst. *ridiculum.*

ridicule, v. *inridēre, deridēre, (in)ludĕre*: to be —d, *ludibrio esse.*

ridiculous, *ridiculus, deridiculus, perridiculus.*

ridiculously, *(per)ridicule*: rather —, *subridicule.*

ridiculousness, render by adj.

riding, *equitatio* (Plin.), *equitatus (-ūs*: Plin.); or render by verb.

rife, of reports, etc., render by past tenses of *percrebescĕre* (= to become prevalent).

rifle, subst.; see GUN.

rifle, v.; see PLUNDER.

rift, *rima.*

rig, subst. *habitus (-ūs).*

rig, v. *armare, ornare.*

rigging, *armamenta (-orum,* plur.), *rudentes (-um,* plur.).

right, subst. (1) = — hand; see RIGHT, adj. (1). (2) moral —, *fas, ius.* (3) a —, as created or recognized by law, *ius, iusta (-orum,* n. plur.): with perfect —, *optimo iure.*

right, adj. (1) opp. to left, *dexter:* the — hand, (*manus*) *dextra;* on the — hand, *dextrā;* to the —, *dextrorsus;* fig.: a little — hand man, *dextella.* (2) in geometry: at — angles, *ad pares angulos.* (3) morally, *rectus, iustus, aequus, verus:* it is —, *fas est.* (4) = suitable, proper (of correct answers to questions, effective means to ends, etc.), *rectus, verus:* at the — time, *ad tempus;* you are —, *ita est ut dicis;* if I am —, *nisi fallor;* it is all —, *bene habet.*

right, rightly, adv. *recte, vere, iuste* (= righteously), *rite* (= duly), *iure* (= justifiably), *merito* (= deservedly), *bene* (= well): and quite — too, *et recte* (*quidem*), *et iure* (*quidem*), *et merito* (*quidem*), *neque* (*id*) *iniuria, neque* (*id*) *immerito;* it serves me —, *iure plector.*

righteous, *bonus, probus, sanctus, aequus, iustus.*

righteously, *bene, probe, sancte, iuste.*

righteousness, *probitas, sanctitas, pietas.*

rightful, *legitimus, iustus.*

rightfully, *legitime, iuste, iure.*

rigid. LIT., *rigidus, durus.* TRANSF., *rigidus, durus, severus.*

rigidity, *rigor* (poet. and Tac.).

rigidly. LIT., *rigide* (Sen.), *dure* (Hor.). TRANSF., *rigide* (Ov.), *severe.*

rigour, *severitas, duritia* (Ter., Tac.).

rill, *rivus, rivulus.*

rim, *ora.*

rime, *pruina.*

Rimini, *Ariminum.*

rind, *cortex* (of trees), *liber* (= inner bark); see also SKIN.

ring, subst. *circulus* (Verg.), *orbis:* a finger —, *anulus;* ear - —s, *inaures (-ium);* a — of people, *corona.*

ring, v. = to make a ringing noise, *tinnire;* of the ears, *tintinare* (Cat.); in gen. = to resound, *resonare, personare:* to — at a door, render as knock; see KNOCK.

ring-dove, *columba, palumbes.*

ringing, subst. *tinnitus (-ūs:* poet. and Sen.).

ringing, adj. *tinnulus* (Cat., Ov.), *canorus.*

ringleader, *auctor, princeps, caput, dux, signifer.*

ringlet, *cincinnus, cirrus* (Juv.).

rinse, *eluĕre, conluĕre* (Cato, Plin.).

riot, subst. (1) = disorder, *turba, motus (-ūs), tumultus (-ūs).* (2) = extravagant conduct, in gen., *comissatio, bacchatio, luxuria.*

riot, v. (1) to be disorderly, render by subst., with *movēre* or *concitare.* (2) = to revel, *comissari, bacchari, luxuriare.*

rioter, *homo turbulentus.*

riotous, adj. (1) = disorderly, *turbulentus.* (2) = extravagant, wild, in gen., *luxuriosus, comissabundus:* — living, *luxuria.*

riotously, *turbulente.*

rip, *scindĕre, divellĕre;* see also TEAR, CUT.

ripe, *maturus, tempestivus* (lit. and fig.); *coctus, maturatus.*

ripen, v. (1) transit. *maturare, coquĕre* (Verg.). (2) intransit. *maturari, maturescĕre, ad maturitatem pervenire.*

ripeness, *maturitas* (lit. and fig.).

ripple, subst., perhaps *unda.*

ripple, v., perhaps *susurrare* (Verg.).

rise, subst. (1) = origin, beginning, *ortus (-ūs):* to give — to, *parĕre, efficĕre.* (2) = increase, *incrementum:* a — in prices, *annona carior.* (3) a — in dignity, etc., *ascensus (-ūs).* (4) = rising ground, *clivus, collis.*

rise, v. (1) = to get up, (*ex*)*surgĕre, consurgĕre* (esp. of a number of people), *adsurgĕre* (*homini,* as a mark of honour to a person), *se erigĕre, se levare:* to — again, *resurgĕre* (poet.); of the sun, stars, etc., *oriri.* (2) = to originate, start, (*co*)*oriri, surgere, nasci.* (3) = to increase, *increbescĕre, crescĕre;* of prices, *augĕri, crescĕre, ingravescĕre.* (4) to — in dignity, in the world, etc., *crescĕre* (*ad opes,* etc.), *emergĕre, ascendĕre.* (5) = to rebel, *consurgĕre, cooriri* (Tac.); see also REBEL; to — again, *resurgĕre* (eccl.).

risible, risibility, render by the verb *ridēre.*

rising, subst. (1) = act of rising, *ortus (-ūs).* (2) see REBELLION.

rising, adj.: — ground, *clivus, collis;* slightly — ground, *collis paullulum ex planitie editus.*

risk, subst. *periculum* (= danger), *discrimen, alea* (= hazard): at my own —, *meo periculo.*

risk, v. (*rem*) *in discrimen offerre, in periculum adducĕre* or *vocare.*

rite, ritual, subst. *ritus (-ūs):* with due —s, *rite;* see also CEREMONY.

ritual, adj., render by subst.

ritualist, render by phrase, such as *homo de sacris* (*rite faciendis*) *diligentissimus.*

rival, subst. *aemulus* (with f. *aemula*), *competitor* (esp. for polit. office; f. *competitrix*); in love, *rivalis.*

rival, adj. *aemulus:* a — candidate, *competitor* (with f. *competitrix*).

rival, v. *aemulari, certare* (*cum homine*).

rivalry, *aemulatio, certamen;* in love, *rivalitas.*

river, subst. *flumen, fluvius, amnis, rivus* (= rivulet), *torrens* (= torrent).

river, adj. *fluviatilis, fluvialis* (poet.), *flumineus* (Ov.).

river-bed, *alveus.*

rivet, *clavus* (= nail).

road, *via, iter, semita* (= path): on the —, *in itinere, obiter* (Juv., Plin.), *inter viam;* lying off the —, *devius;* to pave a —, *viam sternĕre, munire.*

roadstead, *statio* (Verg.).

roadster, — a hack, *caballus* (Hor.), *mannus* (Hor.).

roam, *palari, vagari, errare.*

roaming, *vagus, errabundus.*

roar, subst. *fremitus (-ūs), mugitus (-ūs).*

roar, v. *mugire* (esp. of cattle), *rudĕre* (poet.), *fremĕre, vociferari* (of persons only).

roast, v. *torrēre, frigĕre* (Pl., Hor.).

roast, roasted, adj. *assus:* — meat, *assum, caro assa;* — veal, *assum vitulinum.*

rob. (1) to — a person or place, (*hominem,* etc., *re*) (*ex*)*spoliare, despoliare, fraudare* (by trickery); (*templum,* etc.) *compilare, expilare;*

(*rem homini*) *adiměre, eripěre*. (2) without object, *latrocinari*.

robber, *praedo* (= a plunderer, on land or sea), *latro* (= bandit, highwayman), *pirata* (= pirate), *fur* (= thief), *ereptor*: a band of —s, *latrocinium*.

robbery, *latrocinium, spoliatio, rapina*.

robe, subst.; in gen., *vestis, vestimentum*: a woman's —, *palla, stola*; a — of state, *trabea*.

robe, v. *vestire*.

robust, *robustus, validus*; see also STRONG.

Rochester, *Durobrivae*.

rock, subst. *saxum, rupes, scopulus* (= crag, cliff), *cautes* (= a sharp —).

rock, v. (1) transit. *agitare, quatěre, motare* (poet.). (2) intransit. *agitari, nutare, vacillare*.

rocky, *scopulosus, saxosus* (Verg.), *saxeus*.

rod, *virga, ferula* (= cane), *decempěda* (for measuring).

roe. (1) of fish, *ova* (*-orum*, plur.). (2) = female deer, *caprea*.

roebuck, *capreolus* (Verg.).

rogue, (*homo*) *nequam* or *scelestus* or *malitiosus, veterator*, (*tri*)*furcifer* (Com.).

roguery, *fraus, dolus, malitia, nequitia*.

roguish, *nequam, scelestus, malitiosus*; less seriously, *protervus, lascivus*.

roguishly, *nequiter, sceleste*; less seriously, *proterve*.

role, *partes* (*-ium*, plur.), *persona*.

roll, subst. (1) made of something rolled up, esp. paper, *volumen*. (2) of names = list, *album* (Tac., Suet.). (3) of bread, render by *panis*.

roll, v. (1) transit. *volvěre, devolvěre* (down), *evolvěre* (out or away), *provolvěre* (forward; poet.), *subvolvěre* (up: Verg.), *volutare, versare* (over and over). (2) intransit. *volvi, volutari*: tears — down one's cheeks, *lacrimae per genas manant*.

roll-call: to answer a —, *ad nomina respondēre*.

roller, *cylindrus* (Verg.), *phalangae* (*-arum*, plur.; put under ships).

rolling, adj. *volubilis*.

Roman, *Romanus*: a — citizen, *civis Romanus, Quiris*; — literature, *litterae* (*-arum*, plur.) *Latinae*.

romance, subst. *fabula*.

romance, v. *fabulari*.

romantic, *fictus* or *commenticius* (= imaginary); *mirus* or *novus* (= strange).

Rome, *Roma*; as a nation, *populus Romanus*.

romp; see PLAY.

roof, subst. *tectum, culmen*: to receive under one's —, *hospitio excipěre*.

roof, v. (*tecto*) *tegěre*.

roofless, *hypaethrus* (Vitr.).

room. (1) = available space, *locus, spatium*: to make —, *locum dare*. (2) = apartment, *conclave, cubiculum* (= bed—), *cella* (= store— or garret), *cenaculum* (= upper — or garret); *cenatio* (= dining—: Plin. L., Juv.).

roominess, *laxitas*.

roomy, *laxus, spatiosus* (Ov., Quint.).

roost, subst. *pertica* (Col.).

roost, v. *stabulari* (Varro).

root, subst. LIT., *radix, stirps*; by the —s, *radicitus* (Varro, etc.). TRANSF., = basis, origin, *radix, stirps, fons*.

root, v. LIT., to — or to become —ed = to take —, *radicari* (Col.), *radices capěre*

(Cato) or *agěre*. TRANSF., of customs, etc.: to become —ed = to take —, *radices agěre, insiděre, inhaerescěre, inveterascěre*: to be —ed, *inhaerěre*; —ed, *inveteratus*, (*penitus*) *defixus*; for — up, see UPROOT.

rope, *funis, restis* (thinner), *funiculus* (= a cord), *rudens* (= part of a ship's rigging), *retinacula* (*-orum*, plur. = hawsers).

rosary, = garden of roses, *rosarium* (Verg.), *rosetum* (Verg.).

rose, *rosa*.

rosemary, *ros marinus* (Hor.).

rosin, *resina* (Plin.).

rosy, *roseus* (Verg.).

rot, subst. (1) = decay, *tabes*. (2) colloq.; see NONSENSE.

rot, v. *putescěre, putrescěre* (Hor.), *tabescěre*.

rotate, *se volvěre, volvi, circumagi*; see also REVOLVE.

rotation, *ambitus* (*-ūs*), *circuitus* (*-ūs*): in —, *ordine*.

rotatory, *versatilis* (Lucr., Plin.).

rotten, *putrefactus, putridus*: to make —, *putrefacěre*.

rotundity, *figura rotunda, rotunditas* (Plin.).

roué, *vappa* (Cat., Hor.).

rouge, subst. *fucus*.

rouge, v. *fucare*.

rough. LIT., *asper, horridus* (= bristly), *hirsutus* (= shaggy). TRANSF., (1) of weather, *horridus, turbidus, atrox*. (2) of manner, etc., *asper, horridus, turbidus, atrox, incomptus, incultus, hirtus* (Hor.), *hirsutus* (Ov.): a — outline, *adumbratio*.

roughen, (*ex*)*asperare* (lit. and fig.).

roughly, = harshly, *aspere, dure, duriter*; to indicate —, i.e., in outline, *adumbrare*.

roughness. LIT., *asperitas*. TRANSF., of manners, etc., *asperitas*; of style, *salebra, squalor* (Quint.).

round, subst. (1) *orbis*; see also RING, CIRCLE. (2) in fighting, render by *congressus* (*-ūs*).

round, adj. *rotundus, globosus, orbiculatus* (Varro, Plin.).

round, adv. and prep. *circum, circa*.

round, v. (1) = to make —, *rotundare, tornare, conglobare*. (2) = to sail —, *flectěre*. (3) to — off, = complete, *concluděre, absolvěre*.

roundabout, *devius*: a — way, *ambages* (*-um*, plur.), *circuitus* (*-ūs*).

rounded, *teres* (lit. and fig.).

roundelay; see SONG.

roundly, *plane, praecise*.

rouse, *excitare*.

rout, subst. (1) = flight, *fuga*. (2) = confusion, mob, *turba, tumultus* (*-ūs*).

rout, v. *fugare, dissipare, funděre*: to — out, *eruěre*.

route; see WAY, ROAD, JOURNEY.

routine, subst. *usus* (*-ūs*), *ordo*.

rove; see WANDER.

rover, = pirate, *pirata, praedo*.

row, subst. (1) = line, *ordo, versus* (*-ūs*): first, second, etc., — of seats, *sedilia prima, secunda*, etc.; in a —, (*ex*) *ordine, in ordinem*. (2) = quarrel, *rixa*; see also QUARREL. (3) see NOISE.

row, v. *remigare*; transit., to — a boat, *lintrem remis propellěre*; intransit., to — hard, *remis contenděre*.

royal. (1) = belonging to a king, *regius*, or render by genit. of *rex*. (2) = kingly,

worthy of a king, *regalis*. (3) in the special
sense of being a king, render by *rex*; e.g.:
he murdered his — master, *regem dominum
interfecit*.
royalist, *qui regis partibus studet.*
royally, *regie, regaliter, regio more.*
royalty, *regnum, regia maiestas* or *dignitas* or
potestas.
rub, *terĕre, conterĕre*: to — at, *atterĕre* (poet.); to
— down, *(de)fricare* (poet.); to — out, *delēre.*
rubbish, *rudus,* (-*eris,* n. = rubble: Tac.),
quisquiliae (-*arum,* plur.); see also NONSENSE.
rubble, *rudus* (-*eris,* n.: Tac.).
rubric, *rubrica* (eccl.).
ruby, subst. *carbunculus* (Plin.).
ruby, adj., of colour, *purpureus* (poet.).
rudder, *gubernaculum, clavus* (strictly = tiller).
ruddy, *rubicundus* (poet.).
rude. (1) = unfinished, *rudis, inconditus,
horridus.* (2) = ill-mannered, *asper, importunus, procax, inhumanus, petulans, insolens.*
rudely. (1) = without finish, *incondite,
horride.* (2) with bad manners, *procaciter,
petulanter, insolenter.*
rudeness, *inhumanitas, importunitas, petulantia,
insolentia.*
rudimentary, *incohatus.*
rudiments, *elementa* (-*orum,* plur.); see also
ELEMENTS.
rue, *ruta.*
rue; see REGRET, REPENT.
rueful; see SORROWFUL.
ruff; see COLLAR.
ruffian, *latro* (= bandit), *sicarius* (= assassin),
homo nefarius, etc.
ruffianly, *nefarius, nequam, sceleratus, facinorosus.*
ruffle, v. LIT., *agitare*: to be —d, *inhorrescĕre*
(poet.). TRANSF., see EXCITE, IRRITATE.
rug, *stragulum.*
rugged, *asper, horridus, praeruptus* (of ground);
see also ROUGH, UNEVEN.
ruin, subst. (1) = downfall, collapse (lit. and
fig.), *ruina, interitus* (-*ūs*), *exitium, pernicies.*
(2) concr., *parietinae* (-*arum,* plur.; e.g.
Corinthi), *ruinae* (-*arum,* plur.; = debris).
ruin, v. *perdĕre, pessum dare, adfligĕre, conficĕre* (= to wear out), *prosternĕre, profligare.*
ruinous, *exitiosus*: — expenditure, *sumptus*
(-*ūs*) *effusus*; = in ruins, *ruinosus.*
rule, subst. (1) as physical object = ruler,
regula: a ten-foot —, *decempeda.* (2) =
regulation, precept, *lex, praeceptum, praescriptum, praescriptio*; to lay down as a —,
praecipĕre, praescribĕre. (3) = standard,
criterion, *regula, norma.* (4) = régime,
government, *imperium, regnum* (of a king),
dominatio, dominatus (-*ūs*), *regimen* (Tac.).
rule, v. *regnare* (as king; without object),
dominari (in *hominibus*), (*homines*) *regĕre* or
temperare or *moderari,* (*hominibus*) *praeesse*
or *imperare*; fig.: to — one's passions, etc.,
temperare, with dat.; see also RULING.
ruler. (1) = one who rules, *rector, moderator,
dominator, dominus, rex* (= king). (2) see
RULE, subst.
rumble, subst. *murmur.*
rumble, v. (*in*)*sonare, murmurare.*
ruminant, adj. *ruminalis* (Plin.).
ruminate. LIT., *ruminare* (Plin., Verg., Ov.),
remandĕre (Plin.). TRANSF., see MEDITATE.
rumination, *ruminatio* (lit. and fig.).

rummage, *perscrutari.*
rumour, subst. *rumor, fama, sermo* (= talk),
opinio (= opinion), *auditio* (= hearsay).
rumour, v.: it is —ed, *fertur, ferunt, fama est.*
rump, *clunes* (-*ium,* plur.: Hor.), *nates* (-*ium,*
plur.: poet.), *pyga* (Hor.).
rumpled, of hair, *incomptus.*
run, subst. *cursus* (-*ūs*) *citatus.*
run, v., in gen., *currĕre, cursu ferri*; of fluids = to
flow, *fluĕre*; to — a race, *cursu certare,
certatim currĕre*; to — about, *cursare,
cursitare*; to — across, *transcurrĕre*; to —
after, *sequi*; to — aground, of a ship, *sidĕre*;
to — away (*au*)*fugĕre*; in a battle, *terga
(hosti) dare, se in fugam dare*; to — back,
recurrĕre; to — down, *decurrĕre*; see also
DISPARAGE; to — forward, *procurrĕre, se
proripĕre*; to — into, *incurrĕre, incĭdĕre*;
to — out, *excurrĕre*; of time, *exire*; to —
over = to drive over, *obterĕre equos,* etc., *per
hominem agĕre*; = to pass quickly over in
speech, etc., *percurrĕre, perstringĕre*: to —
through, *percurrĕre*; to — up to, *occurrĕre.*
runaway, *fugitivus.*
runner, *cursor.*
running, adj., of water, *vivus* (Verg.).
rupture, subst. LIT., *hernia* (Cels.), *ramex*
(Cels.). TRANSF., *dissensio, discordia, dissidium.*
rupture, v. *frangĕre, confringĕre, rumpĕre.*
rural, *rusticus, rusticanus, agrestis.*
ruse, *dolus.*
rush, subst. (1) = the plant, *iuncus* (Pl., Ov.),
scirpus (Pl., Ter.): of —es, adj., *iunceus* (Ov.),
scirpeus (Ov.); full of —es, *iuncosus* (Ov.);
a — basket, *scirpiculus* or *-a* (Pl., Prop.).
(2) = a running, a dash, *impetus* (-*ūs*),
concursus (-*ūs*; of many together).
rush, v. *ruĕre, ferri, currĕre*: to — away,
avolare; to — forward, *se proripĕre*; to — in,
inruĕre, inferri; to — out, *evolare, (se) erumpĕre*; see also RUN, v.
russet, *fulvus* (poet.).
rust; subst. *robigo* (in metal and corn; also
fig.: Pl., Verg., Ov.); *ferrugo* (= — of iron:
Plin.); *aerugo* (= — of copper).
rust, v. LIT., render by phrase, such as
*robiginem trahĕre, robigine obduci, robigine
infestari* (all in Plin.); transit. *robiginem
obducĕre* (with dat.: Plin.). TRANSF., *torpescĕre*
(Sall., Tac.).
rustic, *rusticus, rusticanus, agrestis.*
rusticate, v. intransit. *rusticari, rure habitare.*
rustle, subst. *crepitus* (-*ūs*), *sonus.*
rustle, v. *crepare* (poet.), *crepitare* (poet.).
rusty, *robiginosus* (Pl.); or render by subst. or
verb.
rut, *orbita.*
ruth; see PITY.
rye, *secale* (Plin.).

S

Sabbath, *sabbata* (-*orum,* plur.: Hor., Plin.).
sable, adj. *niger, ater*; see also BLACK.
sabre, *gladius, ensis* (poet.), *acinaces* (Hor.).
sacerdotal, *sacerdotalis* (Suet.); or render by
phrase.
sack, subst. (1) = a bag, *saccus, culeus.* (2) the
— of a city, *direptio.*
sack, v. *diripĕre, spoliare.*
sackbut, *bucina.*

sackcloth: in — and ashes, *sordidatus*.
sacker, *direptor*.
sacrament, *sacramentum* (eccl.).
sacred, *sacer, sanctus, sacrosanctus, religiosus, augustus*: to declare —, *sancire*.
sacredly, *sancte, religiose*.
sacredness, *sanctitas, religio*.
sacrifice, subst. LIT., *sacrificium, sacra (-orum,* n. plur.), *res divina*; = the victim, *victima, hostia*: human —, render by the phrase *homines immolare*. TRANSF., = voluntary loss of anything, *iactura*.
sacrifice, v. LIT., *sacrificare; sacrificium* or *sacra* or *rem divinam facĕre; immolare*, usually with acc. object; *caedĕre* (= to slaughter). TRANSF., = to give up, *iacturam rei* (genit.) *facĕre*: to — one's life for one's country, *vitam pro patria profundĕre*; in gen. = to give up one thing for another, *rem rei* (dat.) *condonare* or *posthabĕre*.
sacrificer, render by verb.
sacrificial, *sacrificus* (Ov.); or render by subst. or verb.
sacrilege, *sacrilegium*.
sacrilegious, *sacrilegus*.
sacristan, *aedituus*.
sacristy, *sacrarium*.
sad. (1) of persons = sorrowful, *maestus, tristis*. (2) of things = causing sadness, *gravis, acerbus, tristis, luctuosus*.
sadden, *contristare* (ap. Cic. L.), *maestitiā, dolore,* etc., *adficĕre*.
saddle, subst. *ephippium*.
saddle. v. LIT., *(equum) sternĕre*. TRANSF., to — a person with a thing, *rem homini imponĕre*.
saddle-bags, n. *hippoperae (-arum,* plur.: Sen.).
sadly, render by adj.
sadness, *maestitia, tristitia, dolor* (= pain of mind or body), *maeror, aegritudo, aegrimonia*.
safe, subst. *armarium, arca*.
safe, adj. (1) = in no danger, protected, *tutus*; feeling —, *securus*. (2) = — and sound, now out of danger, *incolumis, salvus, sospes* (poet.). (3) = reliable, *fidus*.
safe-conduct, *fides (publica)*.
safeguard, *propugnaculum, munimentum*.
safely, *tuto*; or render by adj.
safety, *salūs (-utis,* f.), *incolumitas*; in —, *tuto,* or render by adj.; —*pin, fibula*.
saffron, subst. *crocus* (poet.).
saffron, adj. *croceus* (Verg.).
sagacious, *sagax, prudens, perspicax*.
sagaciously, *sagaciter, prudenter*.
sagacity, *sagacitas, prudentia, perspicacitas*.
sage, subst. (1) the plant, *salvia* (Plin.). (2) = a wise man, *sapiens*.
sage, adj. *sapiens*; see also WISE.
sail, subst. *velum*: to set —, *vela dare, (navem) solvĕre*; to furl one's —s, *vela contrahĕre*.
sail, v. *navigare, velificari* (poet.); or render by pass. of *veho* and its compounds; e.g.: to — past, *praetervehi*; to — out, *enavigare*.
sailing, subst. *navigatio*.
sailor, *nauta, navita* (poet.).
saint, *(vir) sanctus, (femina) sancta* (eccl.).
saintly, *sanctus*.
sake: for the — of, *causā, gratiā* (e.g.: for my —, *meā causā*; for his —, *illius causā*); *ergo* (following a genit.; archaic), *pro* (with abl.), *ob* or *propter* (both with acc.; = on account of).

salaam, v. *corpus humi prosternĕre*.
salable, *vendibilis* (Hor.).
salad, *acetaria (-orum,* plur.: Plin.).
salamander, *salamandra* (Plin.).
salary, *merces, salarium* (Plin., Tac., Juv.).
sale, *venditio* (in gen.), *hasta* (= auction): to offer for —, *venum dare*; for —, adj., *venalis*.
salesman, *venditor*.
salient, *praecipuus*; see also PRINCIPAL.
saline, *salsus*.
Salisbury, *Sorbiodunum*.
saliva, *saliva* (Cat., Sen., Juv.).
sallow, *pallidus, luridus* (poet.).
sally, subst. *eruptio*. For the other sense, see JEST.
sally, v. *erumpĕre, eruptionem facĕre*.
salmon, *salmo* (Plin.).
saloon, *atrium, exedra*.
salt, subst. *sal*.
salt, adj. *salsus*.
salt, v. *sale condire*.
salt-cellar, *salinum* (Hor.).
salt-mine, salt-works, *salinae (-arum,* plur.).
saltness, *salsitudo* (Vitr.); or render by adj.
salubrious, *saluber* or *salubris*.
salubriously, *salubriter*.
salubriousness, *salubritas*.
salutary, *salutaris, utilis*.
salutation, *salutatio; salūs (-utis,* f., esp. in phrase *salutem dicĕre)*.
salute, *salutare, consalutare* (of several people at once).
salvation, *salūs (-utis,* f.).
salve, *unguentum*; for the eyes, *collyrium* (Hor.).
salver; see DISH.
Sambre, river, *Sabis*.
same, *idem, eadem, ĭdem*: one and the —, *unus (et idem)*; the — as, *idem qui,* more rarely *idem ac* (or *atque*); in the — place, *ibidem*; to the — place, *eodem*; from the — place, *indidem*; at the — time, *simul, eodem tempore*; it is all the — to me, *meā nihil interest*.
sameness, render by *idem*.
sample, *exemplum, specimen, documentum*.
sanatory, *saluber* or *salubris, salutaris*.
sanctification, *sanctificatio* (eccl.).
sanctify, *(con)secrare, dedicare, sanctificare* (eccl.).
sanctimonious, render by phrase, such as *sanctimoniae speciem prae se ferre*.
sanction, subst. *confirmatio, auctoritas*: with (or without) the — of a person, *hominis iussu (iniussu)*.
sanction, v. *confirmare, sancire, ratum facĕre, ratum esse iubĕre*; see also ALLOW.
sanctity, *sanctitas, sanctimonia, sanctitudo* (rare), *caerimonia, religio*.
sanctuary. (1) = a holy place, *templum, delubrum, fanum*. (2) = a refuge, *asylum, receptaculum*.
sand, *harena, sabulum* (Plin.), *saburra* (for ballast).
sandal, *crepida, solea*; wearing —s, *crepidatus, soleatus*.
sand-pit, *harenaria*.
sandstone, *tofus* (Vitr., Plin.).
sandy, *harenosus* (Verg., Plin.), *sabulosus* (Plin.).
sane, *sanus, animi* or *mentis compos*.
sangfroid, *aequus animus*.
sanguinary. (1) = bloody, *atrox, cruentus,*

sanguineus (poet.). (2) = bloodthirsty, *sanguinarius.*

sanguine; see HOPEFUL.

sanity, *mens sana.*

Saône, river, *Araris.*

sap, subst. *sucus.*

sap, v. LIT., *cuniculos agĕre;* transit., *subruĕre, suffodĕre* (Tac.). TRANSF., *corrumpĕre, haurire;* see also UNDERMINE.

sapient, *sapiens.*

sapless, *aridus.*

sapling, *arbor novella.*

sapper, *munitor.*

sapphire, *sapp(h)irus* (Plin.).

Saragossa, *Caesaraugusta.*

sarcasm, *facetiae* (-*arum*, plur.), *asperiores* or *acerbae.*

sarcastic, *acerbus.*

sarcastically, *acerbe.*

sarcophagus, *sarcophagus* (Juv.).

sardine, *sarda* (Plin.).

sardonyx, *sardonyx* (Plin.).

sash, *zona* (poet.).

Satan, *Satanas* (eccl.).

satanic; see DEVILISH.

satchel, *loculus* (Hor.), *pera* (Phaedr., Mart.), *sacculus* (poet.).

satellite, *satelles.*

satiate, (*ex*)*satiare, explēre, saturare.*

satiety, *satietas, satias.*

satin, render as silk; q.v.

satire. (1) the specifically Roman form, *satura* or *satira.* (2) in gen., render by *carmen* or *libellus* with adj.; see SATIRICAL.

satirical, *famosus, probrosus* (Hor., Tac.), *acerbus.*

satirist, *satirarum scriptor;* more generally, *derisor* (= mocker: Pl., Hor., Quint.).

satirize, *perstringĕre, lacessĕre, insectari,* with abl. of instrument, e.g. *famoso carmine.*

satisfaction, *satisfactio* (= amends), *expletio* (= fulfilment), *voluptas* (= pleasure).

satisfactorily, *bene, ex sententia.*

satisfactory, *idoneus* (= suitable).

satisfy. (1) = to give satisfaction to, content a person, *homini satisfacĕre* or *placēre:* to be satisfied, *satis habēre;* satisfied with a thing, *re contentus.* (2) to — by proof, to make a person sure, *homini satisfacĕre* or *persuadēre;* I am satisfied that, *mihi persuasum est,* with acc. and infin. (3) to supply a want, *explēre.*

satrap, *satrapes* (Ter., Nep.).

saturate; see SOAK.

satyr, *satyrus.*

sauce, *ius* (*iuris,* n.), *condimentum.*

saucepan, *cacabus* (Varro, Col.).

saucer, *patella.*

saucily, *petulanter, proterve, procaciter.*

sauciness, *protervitas, procacitas.*

saucy, *petulans, protervus, procax.*

saunter, *ambulare, vagari, repĕre* (Hor.).

sausage, *tomaculum* (Juv.), *farcimen* (Varro): smoked —, *hillae* (-*arum,* plur.: Hor.).

savage, subst., render by *homo* with adj.

savage, adj. *ferus, indomitus* (= untamed), *efferatus* (= wild), *immanis* (= monstrous), *saevus, trux, atrox* (= cruel).

savagely, *saeve, atrociter.*

savageness, *feritas, immanitas, saevitia, atrocitas.*

savant, *vir doctus* or *litteratus.*

save, prep. and conj.; see EXCEPT.

save, v. (1) = to preserve, (*con*)*servare, tuēri:* God — you, *salve, ave, salvēre te iubeo* (at meeting), *salve et vale* (at parting). (2) = to rescue, *liberare, eripĕre* (*ex periculo*), *servare.* (3) to — up, not to use, *reservare, parcere* (with dat.).

saving, subst. *conservatio* (= preservation), *compendium* (= economy).

saving, adj. *parcus.*

savings, *peculium.*

saviour, (*con*)*servator* (with f. *servatrix*), *liberator;* of Christ, *Salvator* (eccl.).

savory, *thymbra* (Verg.).

savour, subst. *sapor.*

savour, v. *sapĕre* (= to have a taste), *redolēre* (= to smell of).

savoury, adj. *conditus.*

saw. (1) = saying, *dictum, verbum, proverbium.* (2) the tool, *serra:* a small —, *serrula.*

saw, v. (1) transit. *serrā secare.* (2) intransit. *serram ducĕre* (Varro).

sawdust, *scobis* (Hor., Juv.).

sawing, subst. *serratura.*

say, *dicĕre, loqui, narrare, fari* (poet.): to — positively, *adfirmare, confirmare, adseverare;* to — that not, *negare;* it is said that, they — that, *dicunt, tradunt, ferunt,* with acc. and infin. (the passive of these verbs is also used, but personally rather than impersonally; e.g.: it is said that they are good, *dicuntur esse boni*). Parenthetically, in quoted speech, 'said I', etc. is rendered by the defective verbs *inquam* and *aio; inquam* is also often used (= I say, I repeat), after emphatic repetitions.

saying, subst. (1) = the act of saying, *dictio.* (2) = a thing said, *dictum, verbum:* that well-known — of Plato's, *illud Platonis;* as the — is, *ut aiunt.*

scab, (the disease) *scabies* (Verg., Juv.).

scabbard, *vagina.*

scabby, *scaber* (Pl., Cato).

scaffold; see EXECUTION.

scaffolding, *machina, pegma* (Sen., Juv.).

scald, render by phrase, such as *aquā ferventi perfundĕre.*

scale, subst. (1) of a fish, *squama.* (2) of a balance, *lanx:* a pair of —s, *libra, trutina.* (3) = gradation, *gradus* (-*ūs*): on the — of, *instar,* with genit.; on a larger, smaller —, *maior, minor.* (4) in music, *diagramma* (-*ătis,* n.: Vitr.).

scale, v. (1) = to remove the —s of a fish, *desquamare* (Pl.). (2) = to climb (esp with ladders), (*scalis*) *ascendĕre, conscendĕre.*

scaling-ladder, *scalae* (-*arum,* plur.).

scallop, (the fish) *pecten* (Hor.).

scalp, *cutis capitis.*

scalpel, *scalpellum.*

scaly, *squameus, squamosus, squamifer, squamiger* (all poet.).

scamp; see KNAVE.

scamper; see HURRY.

scan, v. (1) in gen. = to examine, *inspicĕre,* (*per*)*scrutari, contemplari, considerare.* (2) metrically, *metiri.*

scandal. (1) see DISGRACE. (2) see SLANDER.

scandalize, *offendĕre;* see also SHOCK.

scandalous, *mali* or *pessimi exempli, probrosus, turpis;* see also DISGRACEFUL.

scansion, render by verb.

scant, scanty, *angustus, exiguus, parvus, tenuis.*
scantily, *anguste, exigue.*
scantiness, *angustiae (-arum, plur.), exiguitas.*
scar, *cicatrix.*
scarce, *rarus.*
scarcely, *vix, aegre.*
scarcity, *paucitas, raritas, inopia, penuria, caritas* (= high price).
scare, *terrēre;* see also TERRIFY.
scarecrow, *formido* (Hor.).
scarf, *fascia.*
scarlet, subst. *coccum* (Verg., Hor.).
scarlet, adj. *coccineus* or *coccinus* (Mart., Juv.).
scathe, subst.; see HARM.
scathe, v. = to harm, *laedĕre, nocēre* (with dat.).
scatheless, *salvus, incolumis.*
scathing (of words), *aculeatus, acerbus, mordax* (Ov.).
scatter, v. (1) transit. = to throw about, *spargĕre, serĕre* (= to sow, of seeds); = to drive hither and thither, disperse, *dispergĕre, dissipare, disicĕre, fundĕre* (esp. of beaten troops). (2) intransit. *dispergi, dissipari, dilabi, diffugĕre.*
scene. (1) of a play = stage, *scaena:* to appear on the —, *in scaenam prodire;* the place before the —, *proscaenium.* (2) in gen. = place, *locus:* to come upon the —, *intervenire.* (3) = spectacle, *prospectus (-ūs), spectaculum.*
scenery. (1) in a theatre, *scaena, apparatus (-ūs) scaenae.* (2) natural —, *loca (-orum,* plur.); beautiful coastal —, *orarum ac litorum amoenitates (-um,* plur.).
scent, subst. (1) = sense of smell, *odoratus (-ūs):* keen —, in dogs, *narium sagacitas;* keen-scented, *sagax, odorus* (Verg.). (2) = odour, *odor,* fig.: to get — of, *olfacĕre;* to put on the wrong —, *in errorem inducĕre.* (3) = perfume, *unguentum.*
scent, v. (1) to detect by —, *odorari.* (2) = to perfume, *odorare* (Ov.), *odoribus perfundĕre.*
scent-bottle, *arcula* (= box for scents).
scented, adj. *odoratus* (poet.).
sceptic, sceptical, scepticism, render by the verb *dubitare* or by a phrase such as *omnia in quaestionem vocare.*
sceptre, *sceptrum.*
schedule, *libellus, tabula.*
scheme, subst. *consilium, ratio:* to form a —, *rationem inire;* see also PLAN.
scheme, v.; see above, and PLAN.
schism, *schisma (-ătis,* n.: eccl.).
scholar. (1) = a pupil, *discipulus.* (2) = a man of learning, *vir doctus* or *litteratus* or *eruditus:* a great —, *vir doctissimus.*
scholarly, *doctus, litteratus, eruditus.*
scholarship, = learning, *litterae (-arum,* plur.), *doctrina, eruditio.*
school, subst. LIT., *ludus (litterarum)* (elementary), *schola* (more advanced). TRANSF., (1) = the followers of a certain teacher, *schola, secta.* (2) fig., of influences, etc., *officina;* e.g.: his house was considered a — of eloquence, *domus eius officina eloquentiae habita est.*
school, v. *docēre;* see also TEACH, TRAIN.
school-fellow, *condiscipulus.*
schooling, subst. *disciplina, institutio.*
schoolmaster, *magister.*
schoolmistress, *magistra.*

science. (1) = knowledge in gen., *scientia.* (2) = systematic knowledge in a particular field, *ars, doctrina, disciplina.* (3) in particular: natural —, *physica* or *physice, physiologia, rerum naturae scientia, investigatio naturae.*
scientific, *physicus* (= concerned with natural science), or render by phrase (see SCIENCE): — principles, *artis praecepta;* — inquiries, *quaestiones naturales.*
scientifically, *physice* (= in the manner of a scientist), *ratione* (= systematically).
scientist, *physicus.*
scimitar, *acinaces* (Hor.), *ensis falcatus* (Ov.).
scintillate, *scintillare;* see also SPARKLE.
scintillation, *scintilla* (= spark).
sciolism, sciolist, render by adj. *semidoctus.*
scion. LIT., of plants, *surculus.* TRANSF., of persons, *progenies.*
scissors, *forfices (-um,* plur.: Mart.), *forficulae (-arum,* plur.: Plin.).
scoff, v.: to — at, *inridēre, inludēre, in ludibrium vertēre, ludibrio habēre;* to be —ed at, *ludibrio esse.*
scoffer, *inrisor; derisor* (Hor.).
scoffing, subst. *inrisio, inrisus (-ūs), inlusio.*
scold, subst. (= a —ing female), *oblatratrix* (Pl.).
scold, v. *obiurgare, increpare, conviciari.*
scolding, subst. *obiurgatio, convicium.*
scoop, subst.; see LADLE.
scoop, v.: to — out = hollow out, *(ex)cavare.*
scope, = free play, *campus, locus, area.*
scorch, *amburēre, adurēre, torrēre.*
scorched, *torridus.*
scorching; see HOT.
score, subst. (1) = account, *ratio, nomen;* on the — of friendship, *amicitiae nomine.* (2) = total, *summa.* (3) = 20, *viginti.*
score, v. (1) = to mark, *notare, signare.* (2) to — a thing up against a person, or in his favour, *rem homini imputare* (Ov., Tac.). (3) = to obtain, render by verb suggested by context; e.g.: to — a success, *rem bene gerĕre;* to — a victory or a point, *(per)vincĕre.*
scorn, subst. *contemptus (-ūs), contemptio, fastidium.*
scorn, v. *contemnĕre, fastidire, spernĕre, aspernari.*
scorner, *contemptor.*
scornful, *fastidiosus.*
scornfully, *fastidiose, contemptim.*
scorpion, *scorpio* (Pl., Ov.); *nepa.*
scot, = a contribution, *symbola* (Pl., Ter.); in law: — and lot, *vectigal;* — free, *immunis.*
Scotland, *Caledonia.*
Scottish, *Caledonius.*
scoundrel, *homo nefarius, nequam,* etc.; see also RASCAL.
scour, *(de)tergēre, (ex)purgare* (= to cleanse); fig.: to — the land, *agrum,* etc., *pervagari, percurrēre.*
scourge, subst. LIT., = whip, *flagrum, flagellum, lora (-orum,* plur.). TRANSF., *pestis;* see also PLAGUE.
scourge, v. *virgis* or *verberibus caedĕre, verberare.*
scourging, subst. *verbera (-um,* plur.).
scout, subst. *explorator, speculator.*
scout, v. *explorare, speculari.*
scowl, subst. *contractio frontis, vultus (-ūs) trux* or *truculentus.*
scowl, v. *frontem contrahĕre, corrugare.*
scraggy, *strigosus;* see also THIN.

scramble, v.: to — for, *diripĕre* (Quint., Suet.); to — up, *scandĕre, escendĕre.*
scrap, *frustum, fragmentum.*
scrape, subst. *angustiae (-arum,* plur.), *difficultas.*
scrape, v. *radĕre:* to — off, *abradĕre;* to — together, *corradĕre* (Pl., Lucr.).
scraper, (for the flesh) *strigil* or *strigilis.*
scratch, v. *scabĕre* (Hor.), *scalpĕre* (Hor., Juv.), *radĕre:* to — out, *delēre.*
scrawl, subst. and verb, render by phrase such as *neglegenter scribĕre;* see also SCRIBBLE.
scream, subst. *vociferatio, ululatus (-ūs).*
scream, v. *clamitare, vociferari, ululare.*
screech, v. *ululare;* — -owl, *ulula* (Verg.).
screeching, subst. *ululatus (-ūs).*
screen, *umbraculum* (= anything that gives shade).
screen, v. *(pro)tĕgere, tuēri, defendĕre.*
screw, subst., render by *clavus* (= nail).
scribble, v. *(rem) chartis inlinĕre* (Hor.); or render by phrase such as *neglegenter scribĕre.*
scribe, *scriba, librarius.*
scrip; see PURSE, WALLET.
scripture, *(sancta) scriptura* (eccl.).
scrivener, *scriba;* see also NOTARY.
scrofula, *struma* (Cels.).
scrofulous, *strumosus* (Col.).
scroll, *volumen.*
scrub, *(de)tergĕre.*
scruple, = hesitation or difficulty, *dubitatio, haesitatio, cunctatio, religio, scrupulus:* to allay a person's —, *scrupulum ex animo evellĕre.*
scruple, v. *dubitare;* or render by phrase with *religio* (e.g. *rem religioni habēre, religio est, religio obstat ne,* etc.).
scrupulous, *religiosus, accuratus, diligens.*
scrupulously, *religiose, accurate, diligenter;* sometimes rendered by superl., e.g.: — clean, *mundissimus.*
scrutinize, *(per)scrutari;* see also EXAMINE.
scrutiny, *(per)scrutatio.*
scuffle, *rixa, turba.*
scull, subst. = oar, *remus.*
scull, v. *remigare.*
sculler, *remex.*
scullery, *culina* (= kitchen).
scullion; see SLAVE.
sculptor, *sculptor* (Plin.), or render by phrase.
sculpture, subst. **(1)** the art, *ars fingendi, sculptura* (Quint.). **(2)** = a work by a sculptor, *signum* (= statue), or render by *opus (ĕris,* n. = work), or *marmor* (= marble).
sculpture, v. *sculpĕre.*
scum. LIT., *spuma* (poet.); of metals, *scoria* (Plin.). TRANSF., *faex* or *sentina (reipublicae,* etc.).
scurf, *furfur* (Plin.), *porrigo* (Hor.).
scurfy, *porriginosus* (Plin.).
scurrility, *contumelia, scurrilitas* (Quint.).
scurrilous, *contumeliosus, probrosus, scurrilis.*
scurrilously, *contumeliose, scurriliter* (Plin.).
scurvy, adj. (of knaves, etc.), *humilis, ignobilis, nequam.*
scutcheon, *insigne* (or in plur.).
scuttle, subst. *cista* (= box).
scuttle, v. render by phrase such as *navem perforare.*
scythe, *falx.*
sea, subst. *mare, pelagus (-i,* n. = the open —: poet.), *aequor* (poet., Sall., Tac.), *pontus*

(poet.), *oceanus* (= the ocean), *altum* (= 'the deep'), *salum* (= the high —): by land and —, *terra marique;* on or near the —, adj., *maritimus;* beyond the —, *transmarinus;* to be at —, lit. *navigare,* fig. *fluctuare.* Names of particular —s: the Mediterranean —, *mare nostrum;* the Adriatic —, *mare superum;* the Tyrrhenian —, *mare inferum;* the Black —, *Pontus (Euxinus);* the Red —, *sinus Arabicus;* the Dead —, *(lacus) Asphaltites* (Plin.).
sea, adj. *marinus, maritimus, aequoreus* (poet.).
sea-calf, *phoca* (Verg.).
sea-coast, *ora (maritima).*
seafaring, *maritimus.*
sea-fight, *pugna navalis.*
sea-girt, *circumfluus* (Lucan).
sea-green, *thalassinus* (Lucr.), *thalassicus* (Pl.).
sea-gull, *gavia* (Plin.).
seal, subst. **(1)** on a letter, etc., *signum.* **(2)** the animal, *phoca* (Verg.).
seal, v. *(con)signare, obsignare.*
sealing-wax, *cera.*
seam, *sutura.*
seaman, *nauta.*
seamanship, *ars navigandi.*
sear, adj. *aridus* (= dry), *serus* (= late).
sear, v. *(ad)urĕre.*
search, subst. *indagatio, investigatio, inquisitio, exploratio;* often rendered by verb.
search, v. **(1)** to — a place, *investigare, perscrutari, explorare.* **(2)** to — a person, *excutĕre.* **(3)** to — for, *quaerĕre, exquirĕre, petĕre, indagare;* see also SEEK.
seasick, to be, *nauseare:* feeling —, adj., *nauseabundus* (Sen.).
seasickness, *nausea.*
season, subst., of the year, *tempus, tempestas* (Lucr.), *hora* (Hor.): the succession of the four —s, *commutationes (-um,* plur.), *temporum quadripartitae;* in due —, *tempore, ad tempus;* for a —, *in tempus;* see also OCCASION, OPPORTUNITY.
season, v. **(1)** = to flavour, *condire.* **(2)** = to harden, *durare.*
seasonable, *tempestivus, opportunus.*
seasonably, *tempore, ad tempus, tempestive, opportune.*
seasoning, *condimentum* (= the material), *conditio* (= the act).
seat, subst. **(1)** to sit on, *sedes, sella, sedile* (poet.), *cathedra* (= chair; poet.): a bench, row of —s, *subsellium;* to take a —, *sedēre.* **(2)** = abode, home, dwelling, *domicilium, sedes.*
seat, v. *ponĕre, conlocare;* to — oneself or be seated, see SIT.
sea-water, *aqua marina* (Plin.).
seaweed, *alga.*
secede, *abire, decedĕre, secedĕre.*
seceder, render by verb.
secession, *secessio.*
seclude, *secludĕre, segregare, removēre.*
secluded, *secretus* (poet. and Tac.), *seclusus* (Verg.); see also LONELY.
seclusion, *solitudo:* a life of —, *vita umbratilis* (Sen.).
second, subst. **(1)** in a fight, render by verb. **(2)** = a very short space of time, *momentum (temporis).*
second, adj. *secundus, alter:* a — father (= equivalent to another one), *alter parens;* — thoughts, *posteriores cogitationes;* — to,

secundus or *alter ab*, with abl.; for the — time, *iterum*; in the first place, in the —, *primum, deinde.*

second, v. = to support, *adesse, auxilio esse, subvenire, suffragari* (all with dat.); *(ad)iuvare*: to — a motion, *in sententiam dicĕre.*

secondary, *secundarius, inferior, minoris momenti.*

seconder, *suasor, auctor.*

second-hand, render by phrase, such as *usu trĭtus.*

secondly, *secundo, deinde.*

second-rate, *inferior.*

second-sight, *praesagitio.*

secrecy, *secretum.*

secret, subst. *res occulta* or *arcana, arcana* (*-orum,* n. plur.): in —, *clam.*

secret, adj. *occultus, arcanus, secretus, abditus, absconditus, tectus*; = underhand, furtive, *clandestinus, furtivus*: to keep a thing —, *celare, occultare*; to be kept — (of things), *latēre, clam esse.*

secretary, *scriba, servus a manu* (Suet.).

secretaryship, *scribae munus* (*-ĕris,* n.).

secrete, *celare, occultare, abdĕre, abscondĕre*; see also HIDE.

secretly, *clam, in occulto, occulte, furtim* (= furtively).

sect, *secta, schola, disciplina, familia.*

sectary, sectarian, render by phrase, such as *homo sectae studiosus.*

section, *pars, portio.*

secular, = temporal, worldly, *saecularis* (eccl.), *profanus.*

secularize, *exaugurare, profanum facĕre.*

secure, (1) = carefree, *securus, incautus.* (2) = (objectively) safe, *tutus*; see also SAFE.

secure, v. (1) = to make safe, *tutum reddĕre, munire, confirmare* (= to strengthen). (2) = to tie up; see FASTEN. (3) = to arrest, *comprehendĕre.*

securely, = safely, *tuto.*

security. (1) = safety, *salūs* (*-utis,* f.), *incolumitas.* (2) = pledge, *pignus* (*-ĕris,* n.), *cautio, vadimonium* (= bail): to give —, *satis dare, cavēre.*

sedan, *lectica.*

sedate, *sedatus, placidus, gravis.*

sedately, *sedate, placide, graviter.*

sedateness, *gravitas.*

sedative, = a calming medicine, *medicina quae dolorem compescit.*

sedentary, *sedentarius* (Col.), or render by phrase with *sedēre.*

sedge, *ulva* (Verg.).

sediment, *faex* (Hor., Lucr.), *sedimentum* (Plin.).

sedition, *seditio, motus* (*-ūs*).

seditious, *seditiosus, turbulentus.*

seditiously, *seditiose.*

seduce, in gen. = to lead astray, *a rectā viā abducĕre, corrumpĕre, sollicitare* (= to tamper with), *in errorem inducĕre*; esp. to — a woman, *stuprum cum femina facĕre* or *feminae* (dat.) *inferre.*

seducer, *corruptor, corruptela* (Pl., Ter.); or render by verb.

seduction, *corruptela, stuprum.*

seductive, render as pleasing, pleasant; or else by verb.

sedulity, *sedulitas, adsiduitas, industria, diligentia.*

sedulous, *sedulus, adsiduus, industrius, diligens.*

sedulously, *sedulo, adsidue, industrie, diligenter.*

see, subst. *sedes* (eccl.).

see, v. LIT., with the eyes, *vidēre, cernĕre* (= to — clearly), *conspicari* or *conspicĕre* (= to catch sight of), *adspicĕre* (= to look at), *spectare* or *intueri* (= to watch, gaze at); to go to —, *visĕre, visitare.* TRANSF., with the mind. (1) = to understand, perceive, *vidēre, intellegĕre.* (2) to — to a thing = make provision for it, *rem providēre* or *prospicĕre, rei* (dat.) *consulĕre.*

seed, *semen*: to run to —, *in semen exire* (Plin.); fig., see OFFSPRING, LINE.

seed-plot, *seminarium* (lit. and fig.).

seed-time, *sationis tempus, sementis.*

seedling, *arbor novella.*

seeing that; see SINCE.

seek, *quaerĕre, exquirĕre, (ex)petĕre, indagare, adfectare* (esp. with abstract object): to — to do = to endeavour, *conari, tendĕre,* with infin.

seeker, *indagator* or render by verb.

seeking, subst; see SEARCH.

seem, *vidēri* (mostly used personally): to — good, *videri.*

seeming, subst. *species.*

seeming, adj. *fictus, speciosus, falsus.*

seemingly, *in speciem, ut videtur.*

seemliness, *decorum.*

seemly, *decorus, honestus, decens* (Hor., Ov.): it is —, *decet, convenit.*

seer, *vates.*

seethe, v. (1) transit. *fervefacĕre, coquĕre.* (2) intransit. *fervēre, aestuare* (poet.).

segment, *segmentum* (Plin.).

segregate, *segregare, seponĕre, semovēre, seiungĕre.*

segregation, *seiunctio*; or render by verb.

seignior, *dominus.*

Seine, river, *Sequana.*

seize, *(ap)prehendĕre, comprehendĕre, rapĕre, adripĕre, corripĕre*; of abstract things, places, etc., *occupare, invadĕre* (used also of passions, etc., seizing people); to be —d by illness, *morbo adfici*; to — an opportunity, *occasionem adripĕre.*

seizure, *comprehensio*; = a bout of illness, *tentatio.*

seldom, *raro.*

select, adj. *(e)lectus, delectus, selectus, exquisitus* (of very careful choice).

select, v. *legĕre, eligĕre, deligĕre*; see also CHOOSE.

selection, *electio, delectus* (*-ūs*); = things chosen, *res selectae*: a — of passages, *ecloga* (Varro).

self. (1) emphatic, *ipse*; or render by personal pronoun, with or without a suffix such as *-te* or *-met.* (2) reflexive; third person, *se* or *sese*; other persons rendered by ordinary personal pronoun with *ipse* or with suffix *-te* or *-met.* (3) in special phrases: by one—, *solus*; beside one—, *mente captus*; in it—, *per se*; a second —, *alter idem.*

self-confidence, *fiducia sui.*

self-confident, *confidens.*

self-control, *imperium sui, moderatio, continentia, modestia, temperantia*: to exercise —, *sibi imperare, se continēre.*

self-denial, *animi moderatio, temperantia*; or render by phrase, such as *nihil sibi indulgĕre.*

self-destruction; see SUICIDE.

self-evident, *manifestus, apertus, (quasi) ante oculos positus*: this is —, *hoc sua sponte apparet.*

self-indulgence, *intemperantia.*

self-indulgent, *impotens sui, effrenatus, intemperans.*

self-love, *amor sui.*

self-preservation, *corporis sui tutela.*

self-satisfied, to be, *sibi placēre.*

self-seeking, *cupiditas.*

selfish, to be, *sibi (soli) consulĕre* or *(in)servire.*

selfishness; see SELFISH.

self-taught, *domo doctus* (Pl.).

self-willed, *pertinax, pervicax* (Hor., Tac.); see also OBSTINATE.

sell, *vendĕre, divendĕre* (in lots), *venundare* or *venum dare* (esp. of slaves): to try to —, *venditare*; to be sold, *vēnire.*

seller, *venditor, institor, propola.*

selling, subst. *venditio*; see also SALE.

semblance, *species, imago*; see APPEARANCE.

semicircle, *hemicyclium* (Vitr.).

seminary; see SCHOOL.

senate, *senatus (-ūs).*

senate-house, *curia.*

senator, *senator.*

senatorial, *senatorius.*

send, *mittĕre*: to — a person on a mission, *legare*; to — across, *transmittĕre*; to — away, *ablegare, amandare, relegare, dimittĕre*; to — back, *remittĕre*; to — for, *arcessĕre, accire*; to — forth, *emittĕre*; to — forward, *praemittĕre*; to — in, *immittĕre, intromittĕre*; to — round, *circummittĕre*; to — word to a person, *hominem certiorem facĕre.*

senior, = older, *(natu) grandior* or *maior*: to be — to a person, *homini aetate anteire, antecedĕre.*

seniority, render by adj.

sensation. (1) = feeling or the capacity for feeling, *sensus (-ūs)*: a — of pain, *dolor*; a — of joy, *gaudium*; to have no —, *omni sensu carēre, nihil sentire.* (2) = an excitement, perhaps *(animi) commotio*: to create a —, *admirationem movēre.*

sensational, *mirificus, mirus, admirabilis.*

sensationally, *mire, mirifice.*

sense. (1) = sensation, feeling, *sensus (-ūs)*: the —s, *sensūs* (plur.); the — of sight, *sensus videndi, visus (-ūs)*; — of hearing, *sensus audiendi, auditus (-ūs)*; — of taste, *gustatus (-ūs)*; — of smell, *odoratus (-ūs)*; the world of —, *res (rerum,* plur.) *externae* or *sensibus subiectae.* (2) = understanding, intelligence, good —, *iudicium, prudentia, mens*; out of one's —s, *mente captus*; in one's —s, *mentis compos.* (3) = meaning (of a word), *vis, significatio, sententia*; to ascribe a — to a word, *verbo notionem subicĕre.*

senseless. (1) = unconscious, *(omni) sensu carens.* (2) = foolish, *rationis expers.*

sensible. (1) = able to be perceived by the senses, *manifestus, perspicuus, evidens*; or render by phrase, such as *sensibus percipi, sub sensus cadĕre.* (2) = intelligent, judicious, *prudens.*

sensibly. (1) = in a manner evident to the senses, *ita ut sentiri possit.* (2) = intelligently, *prudenter.*

sensitive. (1) = capable of sensation, *patibilis, sensilis* (Lucr.). (2) emotionally, *mollis.*

sensitiveness, sensibility. (1) physical, render by phrase with *sensus* or *sentire.* (2) emotional, *mollitia (animi, naturae).*

sensitive-plant, *aeschynomene* (Plin.).

sensual, *libidinosus.*

sensuality, *libido, voluptas corporis.*

sentence, subst. (1) = a proposition, something said, *sententia, enuntiatio, enuntiatum, sensus (-ūs)*: Quint., Tac.). (2) = a judicial decision, *iudicium, decretum, sententia*: to pronounce —, *sententiam ferre* or *pronuntiare*; see also SENTENCE, v.

sentence, v. *damnare, condemnare, multare* (with abl. of punishment).

sententious, adj. *verbosus* (= prolix), *sententiosus* (= pithy), *opinionibus inflatus* (= conceited).

sententiously, *verbose* (= verbosely), *sententiose* (= pithily).

sentient; see SENSITIVE.

sentiment. (1) = opinion, *sententia, opinio, iudicium*; —s, plur., *sensa (-orum,* n. plur.: rare); to hold (or entertain) —s, *sentire.* (2) = feeling, *sensus (-ūs), animus.*

sentimental, *mollis, effeminatus.*

sentimentality, *mollitia (animi)*

sentinel, sentry, *excubitor, vigil*; —s, plur., *stationes, vigiliae, excubiae*; to be on — duty, *stationes* or *custodias* or *vigilias agĕre, in statione esse*; to place —s, *stationes disponĕre*; to make the round of the —s, *vigilias circumire* (Sall.).

separable, *separabilis, dividuus*; or render by verb.

separate, adj. *separatus, secretus, disiunctus*; sometimes *proprius* (= peculiar, individual).

separate, v. *separare, seiungĕre, disiungĕre, secernĕre, discernĕre, dividĕre*: we are —d by a great distance, *magno locorum intervallo disiuncti sumus.*

separately, *separatim*; sometimes *viritim* (= man by man) or *singuli* (adj. = as individuals, one by one).

separation, *separatio, disiunctio.*

September, *(mensis) September.*

septennial, *qui (quae, quod) septimo quoque anno fit.*

sepulchral, *sepulcralis* (Ov.), *feralis* (poet.).

sepulchre, *sepulcrum.*

sepulture, *sepultura.*

sequel, *eventus (-ūs), exitus (-ūs)*; or render by the verb *sequi.*

sequence, *ordo, series.*

seraph, *seraphus* (eccl.).

serenade, subst., render by phrase, such as *concentus (-ūs) ante fores dominae factus.*

serene, *serenus, tranquillus.*

serf, *servus.*

serfdom, *servitūs (-utis, f.).*

serious, of persons, *gravis, severus, austerus, tristis* (= sad); of things, *serius, gravis, magni momenti* (= important).

seriously, *serio, graviter severe.*

seriousness, *gravitas, severitas, tristitia.*

sermon, render by *contio* or *oratio.*

serpent, *serpens, anguis.*

serried, *densus, confertus.*

servant, *servus, famulus, minister, administer, puer* (= serving boy), *ancilla* (= serving maid).

serve. (1) = to do service to, *servire, deservire, prodesse, praesto esse, commodare* (all with dat.). (2) = to wait at table, *famulari, ministrare*: to — up food or drink at table, *apponĕre, ministrare*. (3) to — as a soldier, (*stipendia*) *merēre, stipendia facĕre, militare*; to — out one's time, (*stipendia*) *emerēre*. (4) to — as (or for) something (e.g. as an example), *esse* with either predicative dat. or *pro* and abl. (5) to — out (things to people, in gen.), *ministrare* (*res hominibus*); see also DISTRIBUTE.

service. (1) in gen. = the process of working for some person or thing, *opera, ministerium*: to do a person good —, *bene homini servire, bene de homine mereri*. (2) = a particular helpful action, *officium, opera*; in plur., sometimes *merita* (*in hominem*). (3) — in the army, etc., *militia, stipendia* (-orum, plur.; lit. = pay).

serviceable, *utilis opportunus, aptus* (*rei*, dat. or *ad rem*).

servile. LIT., *servilis*. TRANSF., *humilis, abiectus*.

servility, *adulatio*; see also MEANNESS.

servitude, *servitūs* (-utis, f.), *servitium*: to free from —, *in libertatem vindicare, servitute eximĕre*.

session, *conventus* (-ūs): during a Parliamentary —, *cum senatus habetur*.

set, subst. (1) see COMPANY, COLLECTION. (2) = a young plant, *propago*.

set, adj. *status, constitutus, praescriptus*: a — speech, *oratio*; of — purpose, *consulto*.

set, v. (1) transit. = to place, *ponĕre, statuĕre, constituĕre, sistĕre, con*(*locare*): to — about, *incipĕre, suscipĕre*; to — (one person or thing) against another, *opponĕre*; to — apart, *secernĕre, seponĕre*; to — aside, see REJECT; to — forth, *exponĕre, expromĕre*; to — free, *liberare*; to — on, see INCITE; to — on fire, *incendĕre, accendĕre*; to — in gold (of jewels), *auro includĕre* (Lucr.); to — over, *praeficĕre*; to — sail, *vela dare*; to — up, *statuĕre, constituĕre*. (2) intransit., of the sun, etc., *occidĕre*: to — out, *proficisci*.

settee, *lectus, lectulus*.

setting, subst., of the sun, etc., *occasus* (-ūs)

settle, v. (1) transit.: **a,** to — people in a place, *conlocare, constituĕre*: **b,** to — a (disputed) matter, *statuĕre, constituĕre, definire, componĕre, conficĕre*; to — accounts, *rationes putare* or *conficĕre*; to — a debt, *solvĕre, expedire*. (2) intransit. (*con*)*sidĕre, consistĕre, se conlocare*; see also SINK and ALIGHT.

settlement, *constitutio, compositio, pactum* (= agreement): the — of a daughter, *filiae conlocatio*; the — of a colony, *coloniae deductio*.

settler, *advena, colonus*.

seven, *septem*: — at a time, — each, *septeni*; — times, *septie*(*n*)*s*.

seven hundred, *septingenti*.

seventeen, *septemdecim* (*septen*-): — at a time, — each, *septeni deni*; — times, *septie*(*n*)*s decie*(*n*)*s*.

seventeenth, *septimus decimus*.

seventh, *septimus*.

seventieth, *septuagesimus*.

seventy, *septuaginta*: — at a time, — each, *septuageni*; — times, *septuagie*(*n*)*s*.

sever, *dividĕre, dirimĕre, separare, secernĕre, disiungĕre*.

several. (1) = some, *nonnulli*, (*com*)*plures*,

aliquot. (2) = respective, *suus* (with *quisque*), *proprius*.

severally, *singillatim*; or render by adj. *singuli*.

severe, *severus, austerus, durus, acerbus, gravis*.

severely, *severe, rigide, austere, dure, duriter, acerbe*: — wounded, *graviter ictus*.

severity, *severitas, gravitas, acerbitas*.

Severn, river, *Sabrina*.

Seville, *Hispalis*.

sew, *suĕre*.

sewer, *cloaca*.

sex, *sexus* (-ūs): male —, *virilis sexus*; female —, *muliebris sexus*.

sexagenarian, *sexagenarius* (Quint.).

sexton, *aedituus*.

sexual, in gen., render by phrase with *sexus*: — intercourse, *concubitus* (-ūs), *coitus* (-ūs: Ov., Suet.).

shabbily. LIT., *obsolete*. TRANSF., *sordide*.

shabbiness. LIT., render by adj. TRANSF., *sordes* (-ium, plur.).

shabby. LIT., *obsoletus, pannosus* (of persons). TRANSF., *sordidus, turpis*: slightly —, *subturpiculus*.

shackle, v. *vinculis, catenis*, etc., *constringĕre* or *vincire*.

shackles, *vincula, catenae, compedes* (-um): — for the feet, *pedicae* (Pl.); for the hands, *manicae* (poet.).

shade, subst. (1) = lack of light, *umbra*: living in —, *umbratilis*; a lover of —, *umbraticola* (Pl.). (2) = disembodied spirit, *umbra* (poet.), *simulacrum* (poet.); in plur., the —s, *manes* (-ium).

shade, v. *opacare*, (*in*)*umbrare* (poet.); see also DARKEN.

shadow, *umbra* (lit. and also fig., as in such expressions as 'a — of his former self').

shadowy, = unsubstantial, *vanus, inanis*.

shady. LIT., *umbrosus, opacus, umbrifer* (poet.). TRANSF., colloq., = disreputable, *infamis*.

shaft. (1) = arrow, *sagitta*. (2) = handle, *hastile*. (3) in architecture, *truncus* (Vitr.), *scapus* (Vitr.). (4) the — of a carriage, *temo*. (5) the — of a mine, *puteus* (Plin.).

shake, v. (1) transit. *quatĕre, concutĕre, tremefacĕre, labefactare, agitare, vibrare*: to — often (or violently), *quassare*; to — hands, *iungĕre dextras*; to — off, *excutĕre*. (2) intransit. *quassari, agitari, tremĕre*.

shaking, subst. *quassatio* (in act. sense), *tremor* (in pass. sense).

shallow, subst. *vadum*.

shallow, adj. LIT., *humilis, vadosus* (= full of —s). TRANSF., *levis*.

sham, subst. *fallacia, dolus, fraus*.

sham, adj. *fictus, falsus, simulatus*: a — fight, *simulacrum pugnae*.

sham, v. *simulare*.

shambles, *laniena* (= a butcher's shop); *strages* (= massacre).

shame, subst. (1) = modesty, sense of —, *pudor, verecundia, rubor*: to lose all sense of —, *pudorem exuĕre*; to feel —, render by the impersonal *pudet*. (2) = disgrace, as a state, *ignominia, infamia, dedecus* (-ōris, n.). (3) = a disgrace, a source of —, *dedecus* (-oris, n.), *probrum, flagitium*; —! *pro pudor! o indignum facinus!*

shame, v. *pudorem* (or *ruborem*) *incutĕre* or *adferre*.

shamefaced, *verecundus*.
shameful, *turpis, foedus, ignominiosus, probrosus, inhonestus, flagitiosus.*
shamefully, *turpiter, foede, inhoneste, flagitiose.*
shamefulness, *turpitudo, ignominia.*
shameless, *impudens, inverecundus*: a — expression of face, *os impudens* or *durum*.
shamelessly, *impudenter.*
shamelessness, *impudentia.*
shank, subst. *crus (cruris, n.).*
shape, subst. *forma, figura, species.*
shape, v. *(con)formare, figurare, fingere.*
shapeless, *informis.*
shapeliness; see BEAUTY.
shapely, *formosus.*
share, subst. (1) = part, portion, *pars, portio, sors*: without a — in, *exsors, expers (rei,* genit.). (2) of a plough, *vomer.*
share, v. *partiri, communicare, sortiri* (Verg.).
sharer, *particeps, socius, consors.*
shark, *pistrix* (Verg.).
sharp. LIT., *acutus.* TRANSF., (1) to the taste or feelings = severe, bitter, *acer, acerbus*; of language, *asper, mordax* (Hor.). (2) of sense or perception = acute, keen, *acer, acutus, subtilis* (of taste or judgment), *sagax.*
sharpen, *(ex)acuere* (lit. and fig.).
sharper, *veterator, fraudator, praestigiator* (Pl., Sen.).
sharply, *acriter, acute, aspere* (= harshly), *acerbe* (= bitterly).
sharpness, *asperitas* (= harshness), *acerbitas* (= bitterness); of intellect, *(ingenii) acumen, perspicacitas, subtilitas*; in other senses, render by adj.
shatter, *frangere, confringere, discutere, elidere, quassare.*
shave, *(caput,* etc.) *(ab)radere, tondere*; to get —d, *tonderi.*
shavings, *scobis* (Hor., Juv.).
shawl; see MANTLE.
she, as a pronoun, is expressed, when emphatic, by *illa, ea, ista, haec*; as an adjective, is expressed by feminine forms of words, e.g.: a — -wolf, *lupa.*
sheaf, *merges* (Verg.).
shear, *tondere.*
shearing, subst. *tonsura* (Ov., Plin.).
shears, *forfex* (Mart.).
sheath, *vagina.*
sheathe, *in vaginam recondere.*
shed, subst. *tugurium, taberna*; milit. t. ι., *pluteus, vinea.*
shed, v. *(dif)fundere, effundere, profundere*: to — tears, *lacrimas effundere, lacrimare.*
shedding, subst. *effusio*: — of tears, *fletus (-ūs).*
sheep, *ovis, bidens* (Verg.).
sheep-fold, *ovile* (Verg., Ov.).
sheepish, *insulsus.*
sheer. (1) = steep, *abruptus, praeruptus.* (2) = pure, utter, nothing but; *germanus, merus, purus putus* (Pl.).
sheet. (1) on a bed, *lodix* (= blanket: Juv.). (2) of paper, *scheda, plagula* (Plin.). (3) of metal, *lamina.* (4) of a sail, *pes* (Verg.).
sheet-anchor, *ancora.*
shelf, *pluteus* (Juv.); of rocks, *dorsum* (Verg.).
shell, subst. (1) of fish, *testa, concha.* (2) of nuts, etc., *putamen, cortex.*
shell-fish, *concha, conchylium.*
shelter, subst. *perfugium, asylum, receptaculum*; under — of, *tectus*, with abl.

shelter, v. (1) transit. *(pro)tegere, defendere, tutari, in tutelam recipere.* (2) intransit. *latere.*
shelving, *declivis, proclivis.*
shepherd, *pastor, upilio* (Verg.): of a —, adj., *pastoralis, pastoricius.*
sheriff, render by *praetor* or *aedilis.*
shew; see SHOW.
shield, subst. LIT., *scutum, clipeus, parma, pelta, ancile* (esp. — which fell from heaven): a — -bearer, *armiger.* TRANSF., see PROTECTION.
shield, v. *(scuto) defendere* or *(pro)tegere*: to — from danger, *a periculo defendere*; see also PROTECT.
shift, subst. = resource, expedient, *ratio, consilium, dolus* (= trick), *remedium* (= cure for troubles): everyone made — for himself, *sibi quisque consulebat.*
shift, v. = to change, *(per)mutare*; see also CHANGE.
shifty, *versutus, varius.*
shin, *crus (cruris* n.), *tibia* (= — bone: Phaedr., Plin. L.).
shine, *(con)lucere, fulgere, splendere, nitere, micare* (= to glitter): to — forth, *elucere, effulgere*; to — upon *adfulgere.*
ship, subst. *navis, navigium* (of smaller vessels): a war —, *navis longa*; a flag —, *navis praetoria*; a merchant —, *navis oneraria*; a light, fast —, *(navis) actuaria*; of a —, adj., *navalis, nauticus*; a little —, *navicula*; the captain of a —, *navarchus.*
ship, v. *in navem (naves) imponere.*
shipper, ship-owner, *navicularius.*
shipping, *naves (-ium* plur.), *navigia (-orum,* plur.).
shipwreck, *naufragium* (lit. and fig.): to suffer —wreck, *naufragium facere*; —ed, adj., *naufragus.*
shire, *ager.*
shirt, *subucula* (Hor., Suet.), *tunica.*
shiver, v. (1) transit.; see SHATTER. (2) intransit. *horrere*; sometimes *tremere* (= to tremble), *algere* (= to be cold).
shoal. (1) = a shallow, *vadum.* (2) = a large number of fish, render by *vis.*
shock, subst. (1) physical, esp. in battle, *impetus (-ūs), concursus (-ūs)*: at the first —, *ad primum impetum.* (2) mental: of surprise, *stupor, miraculum*; of displeasure, disgust, etc., *offensio.*
shock, v. *commovere, perturbare, offendere* (= to disgust).
shocking, *indignus, turpis, odiosus, atrox* (of cruelty, etc.).
shoe, subst. *calceus, calceamentum, solea* (= slipper); a heavy —, *caliga*; —s that fit, *calcei apti ad pedem*; the — pinches, *calceus urit* (Hor.).
shoe, v. *calceare.*
shoe-maker, *sutor.*
shoot, subst. *surculus, planta, virga, propago* (= layer).
shoot, v. (1) transit., of missiles, *iaculari, (e)mittere, iacere, conicere*: to — at (a person or thing), *telo, sagittā,* etc., *petere*; to — = to hit, *telo,* etc., *ferire.* (2) intransit. *volare*; see also DASH, DART.
shooting-star; see METEOR.
shop, *taberna*: a work—, *officina*; a book —, *taberna, libraria*; a barber's —, *tonstrina* (Pl., Plin.); to keep a —, *tabernam exercere* (Suet.).

shopkeeper, *tabernarii* (*-orum,* plur. only).
shore, subst. *litus* (*-ŏris,* n.), *ora, acta.*
shore up, v. *fulcire.*
short, *brevis:* — of stature, *humilis, exiguus;* a
— cut, *via compendiaria;* in —, *denique, ad
summam, ne multa;* cut it —, *verbo dicas;*
a — memory, *memoria hebes;* the —est day,
dies brumalis, bruma; to fall — of, *non
attingĕre.*
shortcoming, *delictum.*
shorten, *praecidĕre, breviorem facĕre* or *reddĕre:*
to — a syllable, *syllabam corripĕre* (Quint.).
shortening, subst., of a syllable, *contractio.*
short-hand, *notae* (*-arum,* plur.: Sen., Suet.).
short-lived, *brevis, fluxus.*
shortly. (1) = in few words, briefly, *breviter,
summatim, strictim, compresse, paucis verbis.*
(2) = in a short time, *brevi, propediem, mox:*
— before (or after), *brevi* (or *haud multo*)
ante (or *post*).
shortness, *brevitas, exiguitas.*
short-sighted. LIT., *lusciosus* or *luscitiosus* (Pl.).
TRANSF., *improvidus.*
shot. (1) = the act of shooting, or range of a
shot, *teli iactus* (*-ūs*), or *coniectus* (*-ūs*), or
ictus (*-ūs*). (2) = the missile, (*telum*) *missile,
glans* (= bullet); to fire a —, *telum emittĕre.*
should, of obligation, render by gerund or
gerundive, or by *debēre* with infin.; otherwise
render by subjunctive.
shoulder, subst. *humerus:* — -blades, *scapulae*
(*-arum,* plur. only: Pl., Ov.).
shoulder, v. *in humeros tollĕre.*
shout, shouting, subst. *clamor, vociferatio,
acclamatio, conclamatio:* to raise a —,
clamorem tollĕre.
shout, v. (*con*)*clamare, vociferari:* to keep —ing,
clamitare.
shove, v. *trudĕre, impellĕre.*
shovel, subst. *pala, batillum* (Plin.).
show, subst. (1) = an exhibition, spectacle,
spectaculum, munus (*-eris,* n.), *ludi* (= games).
(2) = display, *ostentatio, apparatus* (*-ūs*).
(3) = appearance without reality, *species:* to
make a — of something, *speciem rei* (genit.)
praebēre or *prae se ferre, rem simulare;* under
a — of friendship, *per simulationem amicitiae.*
show, v. (1) = to point out, (*de*)*monstrare,
commonstrare.* (2) = to display, exhibit,
ostendĕre, ostentare, exhibēre: to — oneself
(in a certain light), *se* (with adj., etc.) *praebēre* or *praestare;* to — off, transit., *ostentare,*
intransit., *se iactare.* (3) = to make clear a
fact, to prove, *monstrare, ostendĕre, docēre,
probare.*
shower, subst. *imber, pluvia:* a sudden —,
imbres repente effusi; fig., *imber* (poet.), *vis.*
shower, v. *effundĕre.*
showery, render by phrase with *imber.*
showy, *speciosus, magnificus.*
shred, subst. *frustum* (= a scrap).
shred, v. *minutatim secare* or *scindĕre.*
shrew, *oblatratrix* (Pl.), *mulier importuna.*
shrewd, *acutus, prudens, astutus, perspicax,
sagax.*
shrewdly, *acute, prudenter, astute, sagaciter.*
shrewdness, (*ingenii*) *acumen* or *acies, prudentia, sagacitas.*
shriek, subst. *ululatus* (*-ūs*), *clamor.*
shriek, v. *ululare, clamare.*
shrift; see CONFESSION.
shrill, *acutus, argutus.*

shrilly, *acute.*
shrimp, fig., see DWARF.
shrine, *aedicula, delubrum, sacellum, sacrarium.*
shrink. (1) transit. *contrahĕre.* (2) intransit. *se
contrahĕre;* to — from a thing, *ab re refugĕre,
abhorrēre;* *rem declinare, detrectare.*
shrinking, subst. *contractus* (*-ūs:* Varro); see
also FEAR, DREAD.
shrive; see CONFESS and ABSOLVE.
shrivel, render by adj. *rugosus* or *vietus*
(= shrivelled).
shroud, subst., render by phrase, such as
mortui vestimentum.
shroud, v. *involvĕre, velare, tegĕre.*
shrub, *frutex* (poet.), *arbuscula* (Varro).
shrubbery, *arbustum.*
shudder, shuddering, subst. *horror, tremor.*
shudder, v. *horrēre, tremĕre:* to begin to —,
horrescĕre.
shuffle. (1) transit. = to mix, (*com*)*miscēre.*
(2) intransit. *claudicare* (= to limp), *tergiversari* (= to be evasive).
shuffling, subst. *tergiversatio.*
shun, (*de*)*fugĕre, vitare, declinare.*
shunning, subst. *fuga, declinatio, vitatio.*
shut, *claudĕre, operire:* to — in, *includĕre,
coercēre;* to — out, *excludĕre.*
shutter, *foricula* (Varro), *valvae* (*-arum,* plur.:
Vitr.).
shuttle, *radius* (poet.).
shy, adj. *timidus, verecundus* (= modest): to
be — of a thing; see SHRINK.
shy, v., of a horse, *consternari, terrēri, saltum in
contraria facĕre* (Ov.).
shyly, *timide, verecunde.*
shyness, *timor, verecundia, pudor.*
sibilant, *sibilans.*
sibyl, *sibylla.*
sibylline, *sibyllinus.*
Sicily, *Sicilia.*
sick, *aeger* (in body or mind), *aegrotus:* a —
man, *aeger, aegrotus;* to be —, = to be ill,
aegrotare, infirma valetudine esse; = to
vomit, *vomĕre, vomitare* (i.e. often: Sen.,
Suet.); to be — all over something, *con-
vomĕre;* to feel —, *nauseare.* TRANSF., of
boredom or disgust, render by the impersonal
taedet.
sicken. (1) transit.; see DISGUST. (2) intransit.
in morbum incidĕre.
sickle, *falx.*
sickly, *infirmus;* see also ILL, WEAK.
sickness. (1) = vomiting, nausea, *vomitus*
(*-ūs:* Pl., Sen.), *nausea* (esp. at sea). (2) in
gen. = illness, *morbus, aegrotatio,* (*infirma*)
valetudo.
side, subst. LIT., a physical —, *latus* (*-ĕris,* n.),
pars (= part), *regio* (= district): at the —, *ab
latere;* on this —, *hinc;* on this — of, *citra* (or
cis, with acc.); on that —, *illinc;* on (or from)
all —s, *undique;* on (or from) both —s,
utrinque. TRANSF., = faction, *pars* (esp. in
plur.); to be on a person's —, *ab homine stare*
or *facĕre;* of descent, on the mother's —,
materno genere (Sall.).
side, adj. *obliquus, transversus.*
side, v.: to — with a person, *ab homine stare* or
facĕre, homini favēre or *studēre, hominis
studiosum esse.*
sideboard, *abacus.*
sidelong, *obliquus, transversus, limus* (Pl., Ter.,
Ov.).

sidereal, render by genit. plur., *siderum.*

sideways, *oblique, per obliqua;* or render by *obliquus* as adj.

siege, *oppugnatio* (= attack), *obsidio* (= blockade, investment).

sieve, *cribrum.*

sift. LIT., *cribrare* (Col.), *cribro secernĕre.* TRANSF., *investigare, (per)scrutari, explorare.*

sigh, subst. *suspirium.*

sigh, v. *suspirare, suspiria ducĕre:* to — for, fig., *desiderare.*

sighing, subst. *suspiratus (-ūs).*

sight, subst. (1) as faculty or action, *visus (-ūs), aspectus (-ūs):* good —, *acies (oculorum), oculi acres* or *acuti;* to lose one's —, *oculos amittĕre, oculis capi;* to know (a person) by —, *de facie nosse;* at first —, *primo aspectu;* to catch — of, *conspicĕre, conspicari.* (2) = view, range of —, *conspectus (-ūs).* (3) = a thing seen, *species* (= an appearance), *facies;* to be a —, *spectaculo esse;* what a disgusting —! *o rem visu foedam!*

sight, v. *conspicari, conspicĕre.*

sign, subst. *signum, indicium, vestigium* (= footmark), *nota* (= mark), *insigne* (= badge), *nutus (-ūs:* = nod), *symbolus* (= a token: Pl.): a — of the future, *omen, ostentum, portentum;* a good —, *omen faustum;* a bad —, *omen sinistrum.*

sign, v. (1) to — a document, *(con)signare, subscribĕre* (Suet.). (2) see SIGNAL.

signal, subst. *signum:* the — for battle (on the trumpet), *classicum;* to give a —, *signum dare, canĕre* (on the trumpet).

signal, adj. *insignis, maximus, egregius.*

signal, v. *significare, signum dare.*

signalize, *insignire* (Tac.), *insignem reddĕre* or *facĕre.*

signally, *insigniter, insignite, egregie.*

signature, *subscriptio* (Suet.), *nomen (subscriptum).*

signet, *signum* (= seal).

significance, signification, *significatio, vis;* see also MEANING.

significant; see EXPRESSIVE.

signify, *significare;* of words, *valĕre;* see also MEAN, ANNOUNCE, PORTEND, MATTER.

Silchester, *Calleva Atrebatum.*

silence, subst. *silentium, taciturnitas* (= absence of speech): to pass over in —, *silentio praeterire;* to keep —, *tacĕre, silēre;* see also SILENT.

silence, v. *in silentium redigĕre, comprimĕre, confutare;* see also CHECK.

silent, *silens, tacitus* (= not speaking), *taciturnus* (= habitually not speaking), *mutus* (= speechless, dumb): to be —, *silēre* (= to make no noise), *tacēre* (= not to speak); to be — about a thing, *rem tacēre;* to become —, *conticescĕre;* be —! *quin taces!*

silently, *tacite, silentio.*

silk, *bombyx* (Plin.) or *vestis serica.*

silken, *sericus* (poet. and Tac.), *bombycinus* (Plin.).

silk-worm, *bombyx* (Plin.).

silky; see SMOOTH.

sill, of a door, *limen inferum* (Pl.).

silliness, *stultitia, fatuitas, insulsitas, infacetiae (-arum,* plur.: Cat.).

silly, *stultus, fatuus, infacetus, ineptus, insulsus.*

silt, subst. *limus.*

silver, subst. *argentum:* wrought —, *argentum factum;* adorned with —, *argentatus.*

silver, silvery, adj. *argenteus:* — mine, *argenti metalla (-orum,* plur.); — -foil, — -leaf, *bractea argentea* (Plin.); — -mine, *argenti fodina* (or as one word: Plin.), *argentarium metallum* (Plin.); — -plate, *argentum (factum), vasa (-orum,* plur.) *argentea.*

silver, v. *argento inducĕre.*

similar, *similis* (with genit. or dat.), *par* (with dat.).

similarity, *similitudo.*

similarly, *similiter, pariter.*

simile, *similitudo, translatio.*

similitude, *similitudo.*

simmer, *fervescĕre, lente fervēre.*

simony, *simonia* (eccl.).

simper, v. *subridēre, inepte ridēre.*

simple: in gen., *simplex;* also *sincerus* (= guileless), *inconditus* (= artless), *ineptus* or *insulsus* (= silly), *merus* or *germanus* (= sheer).

simples, *herbae (medicinales).*

simpleton, *homo stultus, fatuus, ineptus;* see also FOOL.

simplicity: in gen., *simplicitas, natura simplex;* also *stultitia* (= folly), *innocentia* (= guilelessness).

simplify, *simplicem reddĕre.*

simply, *simpliciter;* see also ONLY.

simulate, *simulare.*

simulation, *simulatio.*

simultaneous, render by adv. or phrase.

simultaneously, *eodem tempore, simul, una.*

sin, subst. *peccatum, delictum, nefas:* to commit a —, *peccare, delinquĕre.*

sin, v. *peccare, delinquĕre.*

since, adv. *postea, abhinc* (e.g. he died two years —, *abhinc annos duos* (or *annis duobus) mortuus est);* long —, *iamdudum, iampridem.*

since, prep. *e, ex, a, ab, post:* — the foundation of the city, *post urbem conditam;* — that time, *ex eo tempore;* — childhood, *a pueritiā, a puero.*

since, conj. (1) of time, *cum* (with indic.), *postquam, ex quo (tempore).* (2) causal, *cum* (with subj.), *quandoquidem, quia, quoniam* (all these with indic.): — in fact, *siquidem* (with indic.). Since may also be rendered by the relative *qui* (or *ut qui,* or *utpote qui),* with the subj.

sincere, *sincerus, simplex, candidus* (Hor.), *verus.*

sincerely, *sincere, vere, ex animo, simpliciter:* yours —, in letters, *vale (valete).*

sincerity, *animus sincerus, candor* (Ov.), *veritas, simplicitas.*

sinecure, render by phrase, such as *munus omni labore vacuum.*

sinew, *nervus.*

sinewy, *nervosus.*

sinful, *impius, improbus, pravus, malus.*

sinfully, *impie, prave.*

sinfulness, *impietas, pravitas.*

sing, *canĕre, cantare, modulari:* to — often, *cantitare;* to leave off —ing, *decantare.*

singe, *amburĕre, adurĕre.*

singer, *cantor* (with f. *cantrix:* Pl.), *cantator* (Mart.).

singing, subst. *cantus (-ūs), concentus (-ūs:* of voices in harmony).

single, adj. *unus, solus, unicus, singularis;* of a

man, = unmarried, *caelebs*; in — combat, *comminus*; not a — one, *ne unus quidem*.

single, v.: to — out, *eligĕre*; see also CHOOSE.

singly, *singillatim, viritim* (= man by man, esp. of distributing things); often rendered by adj. *singuli* (= one by one).

singular. (**1**) as opp. to plural, *singularis*: the — number, *numerus singularis* (Quint.); in the —, *singulariter* (Quint.). (**2**) = outstanding, unparalleled, *singularis, unicus, egregius, eximius, maximus* (= very great). (**3**) = strange, *mirus, mirificus, mirabilis, novus, inusitatus, insolens.*

singularity, render by adj.

singularly, *singulariter, unice, egregie, eximie, maxime, mire, mirifice, mirabiliter.*

sinister, *sinister* (= left-handed); also = wrong or unfavourable, in Verg. and Tac.); *infaustus* (= unlucky: Verg., Tac.); *pravus* (= wrong).

sink, v. (**1**) transit. *(sub)mergĕre, demergĕre, immergĕre, deprimĕre.* (**2**) intransit. *(con)-sīdĕre, desīdĕre, submergi, demergi, immergi*: to — in ruins, *conlabi, corruĕre*; to — in a swoon, *conlabi* (Verg.); fig., of prices, courage, etc., *cadĕre*; to — into the mind, *in animum penetrare* or *descendĕre.*

sinless, *integer, sanctus.*

sinner, *peccans* (Nep., Sen.), *peccator* (eccl.); or render by verb.

sinuous, *sinuosus* (Verg.).

sip, subst., render by verb.

sip, v. (*primis labris*) *degustare, sorbillare* (Ter.).

sir, in addresses, *bone vir, vir optime.*

sire; see FATHER.

Siren, *Siren.*

sirocco, *auster.*

sister, *soror, germana*: a father's —, *amita*; a mother's —, *matertera*; of a —, *sororius.*

sisterhood, *sorores* (-*um*, plur.), *sororum societas* (eccl.).

sit, v. (**1**) transit.: to — a horse, *in equo haerēre*; see also PLACE, SETTLE. (**2**) intransit.: in gen. = to be in a sitting position, *sedēre*; to — down, *consīdĕre, adsīdĕre*; to — near, *adsīdĕre* (with dat.); to — at table, *accumbĕre, discumbĕre*; of a court, *habēri* (with abstract subject, e.g. *conventus*), *sedēre* (of the magistrates); to — up, *vigilare* (= to stay awake), *lucubrare* (= to work late); of fowls, (*ovis*) *incubare* (Plin.); as milit. t. t., to — down before a place, *oppidum circumsedēre*; see also BESIEGE.

site, *situs* (-*ūs*).

sitting, subst. *sessio, consessus* (-*ūs*, of a court, etc.).

situated, *situs, positus, conlocatus*; to be — near, *adiacere* (with dat.).

situation. (**1**) = position, *situs* (-*ūs*), *locus, positus* (-*ūs*: Sall., Tac., Ov.); an advantageous —, *opportunitas loci.* (**2**) = state of affairs, (*rerum*) *status* (-*ūs*). - (**3**) = office, *munus* (-*eris*, n.).

six, *sex*: — at a time, *or* — each, *seni*; — times, *sexie(n)s.*

sixteen, *sedecim*: — at a time, *or* — each, *seni deni*; — times, *sedecie(n)s.*

sixteenth, *sextus decimus.*

sixth, *sextus*: for the — time, *sextum.*

sixtieth, *sexagesimus.*

sixty, *sexaginta*: — at a time, *or* — each, *sexageni*; — times, *sexagie(n)s.*

size. (**1**) = greatness, bulk, *magnitudo,*

amplitudo: small —, *parvitas*; to discover the — of the fleet, *cognoscĕre quanta sit classis*; of the same — as, *instar*, with genit.; of great —, *magnus.* (**2**) = glue, *gluten* (Verg., Lucr.).

skate, render by phrase, such as *solea ferrata.*

skeleton, *ossa* (-*ium*, n.), *ossium compages*; he is a mere —, *vix ossibus haeret* (Verg.).

sketch, subst. *adumbratio, descriptio.*

sketch, v. *describĕre, designare, adumbrare* (esp. fig.).

skewer, *veru* (= spit: Varro, Verg.).

skiff, *scapha, cymba, navicula, lintriculus.*

skilful, *sollers, peritus, dexter, sciens, callidus, habilis* (= handy), *exercitatus* (= practised).

skilfully, *sollerter, perite, callide, scienter, habiliter.*

skill, *sollertia, peritia, scientia, ars, artificium, calliditas.*

skim, v. LIT., *despumare* (Verg.), *spumam eximĕre.* TRANSF., to — over a thing, *perstringĕre, percurrĕre, transcurrĕre.*

skin, subst. *cutis, pellis, membrana* (esp. thin), *corium* (= hide).

skin, v. *deglubĕre* (Varro), *pellem* or *corium detrahĕre*; to — over, *cicatricem* (*ob*)*ducĕre.*

skin-deep, *lĕvis.*

skinny; see THIN.

skip, v. LIT., *salire* (= to leap); to — for joy, *exsultare.* TRANSF., = to pass over, *transilire, praeterire.*

skipper, *navis magister*; see also CAPTAIN.

skirmish, subst. *proelium lĕve*; fig., in words, *velitatio* (Pl.).

skirmish, v. *proeliis parvulis cum hoste contendĕre, velitari* (Pl.).

skirmisher, *veles.*

skirt, subst. = border, *limbus* (Verg., Ov.).

skirt, v. *tangĕre*; to — the coast, *oram legĕre.*

skittish, *protervus, lascivus* (mainly poet.); to be —, *lascivire.*

skittishly, *proterve.*

skittishness, *protervitas, lascivia.*

skulk, *latēre, delitescĕre.*

skull, *caput, calvaria* (Cels.).

sky, *caelum*: a clear —, *caelum serenum*; under the open —, *sub divo.*

skylark, *alauda* (Plin.).

skylight, *fenestra.*

slack. (**1**) of things = loose, *laxus, fluxus, remissus.* (**2**) of persons = careless, idle, *remissus, segnis, piger, neglegens.*

slacken, v. (**1**) transit. (*re*)*laxare, remittĕre.* (**2**) intransit. *laxari, remitti.*

slackly, *laxe* (= loosely), *segniter, neglegenter.*

slackness, *remissio, neglegentia* (= carelessness), *pigritia* (= laziness).

slake, v.: to — thirst, *sitim restinguĕre, exstinguĕre, explēre, depellĕre*; to — lime, *calcem macerare* (Vitr.).

slander, subst. *calumnia, (falsa) criminatio, falsum crimen, maledictio, maledictum, obtrectatio.*

slander, v. *calumniari, criminari, obtrectare* (with dat.), *maledicĕre* (with dat.).

slanderer, *obtrectator.*

slanderous, *maledicus, famosus* (Hor., Tac.).

slanderously, *falso, maledice, per calumniam.*

slang, perhaps render by adapting the phrase of Cic., *maledictum ex trivio adripere* (= to pick up an abusive expression from the gutter).

slanting, *obliquus, transversus.*
slap, subst. *alapa* (Juv.).
slap, v. *manu ferire.*
slash, subst.; see CUT, WOUND.
slash, v. *caedĕre, incidĕre.*
slate, render by *tabula* (= writing tablet), or by *tegula* (= tile).
slattern, render by phrase, such as *mulier sordida.*
slaughter, subst. *caedes, occidio, strages*: a general —, *internecio, occidio, trucidatio.*
slaughter, v. *caedĕre, concidĕre, trucidare, mactare* (esp. in sacrifice).
slaughterer, *lanius.*
slaughterhouse, *laniena.*
slave, subst. *servus, ancilla* (= female —), *verna* (= a home-born —: Pl., Hor., Mart.), *famulus* (= household —), *mancipium* (considered as a purchase): the —s of a household, *familia*; a body of —s, *servitium* (also in plur.); to sell as a —, *sub coronā vendĕre*; a fellow —, *conservus*; of a —, adj., *servilis*; to be a —, *servire*; fig., to be a — to a thing, *rei* (dat.) *oboedire, (in)servire.*
slave (away), v. = to toil, *laborare, sudare.*
slave-dealer, *venalicius, mango.*
slavery, *servitus* (-*ūtis,* f.), *servitium, famulatus* (-*ūs*).
slave-trade, *venditio* (= selling) or *emptio* (= buying) *servorum.*
slavish, *servilis, vernilis* (Tac.).
slavishly, *serviliter, verniliter* (Hor.).
slaver, subst. *saliva.*
slay, *interficĕre, occidĕre, interimĕre, conficĕre, necare, trucidare* (= to butcher).
slayer, *interfector, occisor* (Pl.), *percussor* : — of a man, *homicida*; — of a parent or close relative, *parricida.*
sledge, *trahea* (Verg.).
sledge-hammer, *malleus.*
sleek, *lēvis* (= smooth), *nitidus* (= shining): to be —, *nitēre.*
sleep, subst. *somnus, sopor* (poet.: strictly = heavy —), *quies*: deep —, *somnus artus*; to be overcome by —, *somno capi* or *opprimi*; in one's —, *dormiens*; want of —, *vigilia*; I haven't had a wink of —, *somnum oculis meis non vidi.*
sleep, v. *dormire, quiescĕre*: to try to —, *somno* (or *quieti*) *se tradĕre*; to — soundly, *arte* or *graviter dormire*; to be unable to —, *somnum capĕre non posse.*
sleepily, *somniculose.*
sleepiness, *veternus* (esp. in old people: Pl.), *somni cupido* (Sall.).
sleepless, *insomnis* (Verg., Tac.), *exsomnis* (Verg.), *vigilans.*
sleeplessness, *insomnia, vigilia, vigilantia.*
sleepy, *semisomnus* (or -*somnis*), *somniculosus, somno gravis.*
sleet, render by phrase, such as *nix grandine mixta.*
sleeve, *manicae* (-*arum,* plur.).
sleight of hand, *praestigiae* (-*arum,* plur.).
slender, *tenuis* (lit. and fig.), *gracilis, exilis.*
slenderly, *tenuiter.*
slenderness, *tenuitas, gracilitas.*
slice of bread, *(panis) frustum.*
slice, v. *concidĕre, secare.*
slide, v. *labi.*
slight, adj. *lēvis, tenuis, exiguus, parvus*: not in the —est, *minime.*

slight, v. *neglegĕre, parvi facĕre, contemnĕre.*
slim, *exilis*; see also SLENDER.
slime, *limus, virus* (Verg.).
slimy, *limosus* (Verg., Ov.).
sling, subst. (1) the weapon, *funda.* (2) — for the arm, *fascia, mitella* (Cels.); to have the arm in a —, *bracchium fascia involutum habēre.*
sling, v. *(fundā) mittĕre, torquēre.*
slink, v.: to — away, *sese subducĕre.*
slip, subst. (1) = the act of slipping. LIT., *lapsus* (-*ūs*). TRANSF., *culpa* (= fault), *error* (= mistake); or render by verb. Prov.: there's many a — 'twixt the cup and the lip, *inter os et offam* (Cato). (2) of a plant, *surculus*; see also SHOOT.
slip, v. *labi, titubare* (= to stagger: poet.): to — away, *aufugĕre, se subducĕre, elabi, dilabi* (in various directions); to let —, *amittĕre, omittĕre*; to — from the memory, *de memoria excidĕre.*
slipper, *crepida, solea* (Pl., Hor.).
slippery, *lubricus*; colloq., a — customer, *anguilla* (Pl.).
slit, subst. *rima* (= an opening or leak), *scissura* (Plin.).
slit, v. *incidĕre* (= to cut into), *findĕre* (= to cleave), *scindĕre* (= to tear).
sloe, *prunum silvestre* (Plin.): the —-tree, *prunus, silvestris* (Col.).
slogan, *dictum, praeceptum.*
sloop; see SHIP.
slope, subst. *clivus, fastigium*: an upward —, *acclivitas*; a downward —, *declivitas.*
slope, v. *vergĕre.*
sloping, (upwards) *acclivis*; (downwards) *declivis, proclivis, pronus, fastigatus.*
sloth, *inertia, segnitia, segnities, desidia, ignavia, socordia, pigritia.*
slothful, *iners, segnis, deses, desidiosus, ignavus, socors, piger.*
slothfully, *segniter, ignave.*
slough, *palūs* (-*ūdis*); see also MUD: the — of a snake, *vernatio* (Plin.), *exuviae* (-*arum,* plur.: Verg.).
slovenliness, *sordes* (-*ium,* plur.; = filth), *neglegentia.*
slovenly, *sordidus, discinctus, neglegens.*
slow, *tardus, lentus, segnis, piger, serus* (= late).
slowly, *tarde, lente, segniter, sensim* (= gradually).
slowness, *tarditas, segnitas, pigritia.*
slug, *limax* (Pl.).
sluggard, *homo ignavus.*
sluggish, *segnis, piger, ignavus.*
sluggishly, *segniter, ignave.*
sluggishness, *pigritia, ignavia, inertia.*
sluice, *emissarium.*
slumber; see SLEEP.
slur, subst. *macula, nota*; see also DISGRACE.
slur over, v. *extenuare.*
slut, *mulier sordida.*
sly, *vafer, subdolus, astutus, versutus.*
slyly, *vafre, subdole, astute, versute.*
slyness, *dolus, astutia.*
smack, subst. (1) = flavour, taste, *sapor, gustus* (-*ūs*). (2) = a blow, *alapa* (Juv.). (3) = a small ship, *lenunculus*: a fishing- —, *horia* (Pl.).
smack, v.: to — of a thing, *rem sapĕre, (red)-olēre.*

small, *parvus, parvulus, exiguus, minutus, brevis* (= short), *tenuis* (= thin), *angustus* (= narrow): a — mind, *animus pusillus*; so —, *tantulus*; how — *quantulus*; however —, *quantuluscunque*.

smallness, *parvitas, exiguitas, tenuitas, brevitas* (= shortness).

smart, subst. *dolor, morsus* (*-ūs*), *cruciatus* (*-ūs*).

smart, v. = to feel pain, *dolēre*; to — for a thing, *plecti*; see also PUNISH.

smart, adj. (1) = sharp, painful, *acer, acerbus, gravis.* (2) = active, *acer, alacer.* (3) = witty, *salsus.* (4) = elegant, fine, *lautus, mundus, nitidus, ornatus*; rather —, *ornatulus* (Pl.).

smartness. (1) = activity, briskness, *alacritas.* (2) = elegance, *munditia*; or render by adj.

smattering, render by phrase, such as *lēvis scientia*: having a — of Greek, *litterulis Graecis imbutus* (Hor.); having a — of philosophy, *philosophiam odoratus* (Tac.).

smear, v. (*in*)*linĕre, oblinĕre.*

smell, subst. *odoratus* (*-ūs*; = the sense), *odoratio* (= the act), *odor* (= the result): a bad —, *foetor*; to have a bad —, *male olēre*; a — of burning, *nidor.*

smell, v. (1) = to perceive a —, *olfacĕre*; fig., to — out, *olfacĕre, odorari.* (2) = to give off a smell, (*red*)*olēre* (with acc. of what a thing —s of).

smelt, *fundĕre* (Plin.), *coquĕre* (Plin.).

smile, subst. *risus* (*-ūs*): with a —, *subridens.*

smile, v. (*sub*)*ridēre, renidēre*: to — at, *adridēre* (with dat.).

smirk, *risus* (*-ūs*).

smite, v. *ferire* (with perfect, supine, etc., from *percutĕre*): fig., to be smitten with love, *amore flagrare, ardēre* (with acc. of the loved one: poet.).

smith, *faber*: a blacksmith, *faber ferrarius.*

smithy, *officina, fabrica.*

smoke, subst. *fumus.*

smoke, v. (1) = to emit —, *fumare.* (2) to — out, fumigate, *suffire* (poet.).

smoky, *fumosus.*

smooth, adj. *lēvis, teres, lenis*; of style, *lenis*; of manner, *comis, blandus*; of temper, *aequus, aequabilis.*

smooth, v. *lēvare, lēvigare* (Varro), *limare* (with file).

smoothly, *leniter.*

smoothness, *lēvitas, lenitas, aequabilitas.*

smother. LIT., *suffocare, animam interclūdĕre.* TRANSF., *opprimĕre, comprimĕre.*

smoulder, v. *fumare.*

smuggle, render by phrase, such as *furtim importare* or *invehĕre.*

smuts, *fuligo.*

smutty, = smoky, *fumosus.*

snack, *cenula, ientaculum* (Pl., Mart.).

snaffle, *frenum.*

snail, *cochlea* (or *coclea*).

snake, *anguis, serpens, vipera* (poet.).

snaky, *vipereus* (Ov.), *anguineus* (Ov.).

snap, subst. *crepitus* (*-ūs*; = any sharp noise), *fragor* (= a noise of breaking).

snap, v. (1) transit. = to break, *frangĕre, praefringĕre,* (*prae*)*rumpĕre*: to — the fingers, *digitis concrepare*; to — up, *adripĕre, corripĕre.* (2) intransit. = to get broken suddenly, *dissilire* (poet.), *frangi, rumpi.*

snappish, *morosus, difficilis, mordax* (Hor.).

snare, subst. (lit and fig.), *laqueus, plaga, insidiae* (*-arum*: strictly = ambush).

snare, v. (lit. and fig.), *inlaqueare* (Hor.).

snarl, subst. *gannitus* (*-ūs*: Lucr., Mart.).

snarl, v. (*og*)*gannire* (poet.), (*sub*)*ringi.*

snatch, *rapĕre, corripĕre*: to — at, *captare*; to — away, *eripĕre, abstrahĕre, avellĕre*; to — secretly, *surripĕre.*

sneak, = to go stealthily, creep, (*cor*)*repĕre*; to — in (lit. and fig.), *inrepĕre*; to — away, (*furtim*) *se subducĕre*; to have a —ing fear, *subtimēre.*

sneer, subst. *rhonchus* (Mart.).

sneer, v.: to — at, *deridēre, inridēre, naso adunco suspendĕre* (Hor.).

sneeze, *sternuĕre* (Plin.).

sneezing, *sternumentum, sternutamentum* (Sen.).

sniff: to — at, *odorari.*

snip, *circumcidĕre, amputare.*

snob, snobbery, snobbish, render by phrase, such as *iactare genus* (= to boast of one's ancestry), or *generosiores admirari*; see also Hor. Sat. I. 6, 1-6, where Maecenas is described as no snob.

snore, *stertĕre.*

snort, v. *fremĕre.*

snorting, subst. *fremitus* (*-ūs*).

snout, *rostrum.*

snow, subst. *nix* (and in plur., *nives* = — lying on the ground, — drifts).

snow, v.: it —s, *ningit* or *ninguit* (Verg.).

snowy, *nivosus, niveus* (poet.; also = — white).

snub; see REBUKE.

snub-nosed, *silus, simus* (Verg.).

snuff, subst., of a candle, *fungus* (Verg.).

snuff, v.: to — a candle, render by phrase, such as *candelae fungum demĕre*; to — out, *ex*(*s*)*tinguĕre*; to — up, *naribus haurire.*

snug; see COMFORTABLE.

so. (1) as adv. = in this way, thus, *sic, ita, hoc modo*: is it so? *itane est?* it is so, *ita est, sic habet, ita se res habet*; and so on, *et cetera*; =, to such an extent, *sic, ita, adeo, tam*; so . . . as, *tam . . . quam*; so that (final), *ut* with subjunc. (neg. *ne*); so that (consec.), (*ita adeo,* etc.) *ut* with subjunc. (neg. *ut non*); so that (restrictive, = on condition that), *ita . . . ut* (with subjunc.); so great, *tantus*; so small, *tantulus*; so many, *tot*; so many times, *totie*(*n*)*s*; so much, *tantum*; so far, *eo* (*usque*) = all that way, *hactenus* = hitherto; so far as I can, *quantum ego possum*; so far as I am concerned, *quantum ad me attinet*; so far from being asleep, I am reading, *tantum abest ut dormiam ut legam,* or *adeo non dormio ut legam,* or *non modo non dormio sed etiam lego*; so long as (= provided that), *dum* (*modo*), with subjunc. (2) as conj. = accordingly, and so, *itaque, ergo, igitur*; in asseverations, *ita* (e.g. so help me God, *ita me di ament*).

soak, *madefacĕre*: to — up, *bibĕre*; to — through, *permanare.*

soap, *sapo* (Plin.).

soar, *sublime ferri, subvolare, se tollĕre* (lit. and fig.).

sob, subst. *singultus* (*-ūs*).

sob, v. *singultare* (Quint.); or render by subst.

sober. LIT., *sobrius.* TRANSF., *sobrius, temperans, temperatus, modestus, moderatus, severus* (= grave).

soberly, *sobrie, temperate, modeste, moderate.*

sobriety. Lit., *sobrietas* (Sen.). Transf., *temperantia, moderatio, modestia.*
so-called, *quem (quam, quod) dicunt.*
sociability, *comitas, facilitas.*
sociable, *comis, facilis, socialis* (Sen.).
sociably, *socialiter* (Hor.).
social, *communis* (= common to all), *civilis* (= common to all the citizens of a state), *congregabilis* (= gregarious): — life, *vitae societas, vita communis*; — sense (= tact), *sensus (-ūs) communis.*
socialism, socialist, render by phrase, such as *bona communicare, bona communia habēre* (= to share goods).
society. (1) in the widest sense = human beings in association, *homines (-um,* plur.), *hominum coetus (-ūs), conventus (-ūs), congressus (-ūs)*: life in —, *communis vita, vitae societas.* (2) = a limited association of persons for a common end, *societas, sodalitas, conlegium* (= guild, corporation), *factio* (political, often sinister). (3) the —, or company, of an individual, *convictus (-ūs), consuetudo*: to admit a person into one's —, *hominem socium admittĕre.*
sock; see STOCKING.
socket, *cavum* (= hollow, cavity).
sod, *caespes.*
soda, *nitrum* (Plin.).
sodden, *madidus.*
sofa, *lectus, lectulus, grabatus.*
soft, *mollis, lenis, tener, mitis*; fig. = effeminate, *mollis, effeminatus.*
soften, v. (1) transit. *(e)mollire, mitigare, lenire.* (2) intransit. *molliri, mollescĕre* (poet.), *mitescĕre.*
softly, *molliter, leniter.*
softness, *mollitia* or *mollities.*
soil, subst. *solum, terra, humus.*
soil, v. transit. *inquinare, polluĕre, maculare*; see also DEFILE.
sojourn, subst. *commoratio, mansio*: — abroad, *peregrinatio.*
sojourn, v. *(com)morari, manēre*: to — abroad, *peregrinari.*
sojourner, *hospes* (= guest), *peregrinus* or *advena* (= foreigner, alien), *inquilinus* (= tenant).
solace, subst. *solatium, consolatio.*
solace, v. *(con)solari, (homini) solatium praebēre,* or *dare* or *adferre.*
solar, *solaris* (Ov.); or render by genit. *solis* (= of the sun).
solder, subst. *ferrumen* (Plin.).
solder, v. *devincire, (con)ferruminare* (Plin.), *(im)plumbare* (Vitr., Plin.).
soldier, *miles*: a private —, *miles (gregarius), gregarius, manipularis*; a fellow —, *commilito*; foot —, *pedes*; horse —, *eques*; to serve as a —, *stipendia merēre* or *merēri.*
soldierly, *militaris, rei militaris peritus, militarius* (Pl.): in a — manner, *militariter.*
soldiery, *milites (-um,* plur.), or as collect. sing. *miles.*
sole, subst. (1) of the foot or of a shoe, *solum*; of the foot only, *planta* (poet. and Sen.). (2) the fish, *solea* (Ov., Plin.).
sole, adj. *solus, unus, unicus*: — command, *singulare imperium.*
solecism, *soloecismus* (Sen., Quint., Juv.); see also IMPROPRIETY.
solely, *solum, tantum*; or render by adj. *solus.*

solemn. (1) in connexion with religion, *sollemnis, sanctus, religiosus.* (2) in gen. = serious, *serius, severus, tristis, gravis.*
solemnity; see GRAVITY, SERIOUSNESS.
solemnization, *celebratio.*
solemnize, *celebrare.*
solemnly, *sollemniter* (in connexion with religion), *sancte, graviter.*
solicit. (1) = to ask for, court, *petĕre, poscĕre, flagitare, captare.* (2) = to incite, tamper with persons, *sollicitare.*
solicitation, *preces (-um,* plur.), *flagitatio*: at your —, *impulsu tuo.*
solicitor, *advocatus*; see also ADVOCATE.
solicitous, *sollicitus, anxius*; see also ANXIOUS.
solicitously, *sollicite, anxie.*
solicitude, *sollicitudo, cura, anxietas.*
solid, subst. *solidum.*
solid, adj. *solidus, stabilis, firmus*: — food, *cibus firmus* (Varro); — ground, *solidum.*
solidity, *soliditas.*
solidly, *firme, firmiter.*
soliloquy, soliloquize, render by the phrase *secum loqui* (= to talk to oneself).
solitary: in gen. *solus*; of living things, *solitarius, solivagus*; of places, *desertus, devius* (= off the beaten track). See also SOLE.
solitude, *solitudo* (as both state and lonely place).
solo, *canticum.*
solstice: the summer —, *solstitium* (with adj. *solstitialis*); the winter —, *bruma* (with adj. *brumalis*).
solubility, soluble, render by verb *(dis)solvĕre.*
solution. (1) = act of dissolving *(dis)solutio.* (2) = liquid after solution, *dilutum* (Plin.). (3) of problems, etc., *explicatio, solutio* (Sen.).
solve, *(dis)solvĕre, enodare, expedire, explicare.*
solvent, render by verb *(dis)solvĕre*: to be — (= able to pay), *solvendo esse.*
some, somebody, someone. (1) in gen. *aliquis -quid,* pron., and *aliqui -qua -quod,* adj. (= — unspecified); *aliquid* is often used with a partitive genit. of subst. or adj. (e.g. — dignity, *aliquid dignitatis*; — bitterness, *aliquid amari*); *quispiam* (rarer); *quis, quid,* pron., and *qui, qua, quod,* adj. (indef., usually after *si, nisi, ne* or *num*); *nescioquis,* pron., and *nescioqui,* adj. (= — or other; casual or disparaging); *quidam, quaedam quoddam,* and subst. *quiddam* (= certain, known but not further described; but in plur. sometimes indefinite); *nonnullus* (esp. in plur. = — few); *aliquot* (plur., indecl.; = a certain number of); *complures (-ium,* plur.; = several). (2) some, with numerals, = about, *circiter, fere, ad* with acc. (3) some, disparagingly, = no more than, a mere, 'some old', *unus.* (4) distributively: — ... others, *alii ... alii*; — say one thing, others another, *alii aliud dicunt.* (5) in other phrases: there are — who, *sunt qui* (with subjunc., unless the antecedent is identified); to — degree, *aliquantum*; to — small extent, *aliquantulum*; at — time, *aliquando*; for — time, *aliquamdiu*; — few times, *aliquotie(n)s*; by — way, *aliqua*; from — place, *alicunde*; to — place, *aliquo.*
somehow, *nescio quomodo, nescio quo pacto.*
somersault, *saltus (-ūs*; = leap).
something, *aliquid, nonnihil*; see also SOME.
sometimes, *aliquando, nonnunquam* (= fairly

often), *subinde, interdum* (= now and then); distributively, sometimes ... sometimes ..., *modo ... modo, alias ... alias, interdum ... interdum.*

somewhat, *aliquantum, aliquantulum, nonnihil.*

somewhere, *alicubi.*

somewhither, *aliquo.*

somnambulist, *qui dormiens ambulat.*

somnolent; see SLEEPY.

son, *filius, natus* (poet.): a little —, *filiolus;* foster- —, *alumnus;* a — -in-law, *gener;* a step- —, *privignus;* —s and daughters, *liberi.*

song, *carmen, cantus (-ūs), canticum;* prov., the old sweet —! *cantilenam eandem canis* (Ter.).

songster, render by verb.

sonorous, *canorus, clarus.*

sonorously, *canore, clare.*

soon, *mox, brevi* (*tempore*), *cito, iam, propediem, mature* (= promptly): — after, *post paullo, non ita multo post;* too —, *ante tempus;* as — as possible, *quam primum, primo quōque tempore;* as — as, *simul ac* or *atque, ubi primum.*

sooner. (1) = more early, *maturius:* prov., no — said than done, *dictum factum* (Ter.). (2) = for preference, rather, *potius, libentius:* I had —er, *mallem.*

soot, *fuligo.*

sooth, = truth, *verum, veritas:* in —, *vere, certe.*

soothe, *mulcēre, lenire, placare, sedare, levare, mitigare, tranquillare.*

soothing, of speech, etc., *blandus.*

soothsayer, *haruspex, hariolus, auspex, vates.*

soothsaying, subst. *haruspicina, auspicium.*

sooty, *fuligine oblĭtus.*

sop, *frustum, offa* (*panis*).

sophism, sophistry, *captio, sophisma* (Sen.).

sophist, in the Greek professional sense, *sophistes;* in gen., *homo captiosus.*

sophistical, *captiosus.*

soporific, adj. *soporifer, soporus, somnifer* (all poet.).

sorcerer, *veneficus.*

sorceress, *venefica, maga, saga.*

sorcery, *ars magica.*

sordid, *sordidus, abiectus, inliberalis, humilis.*

sordidly, *sordide, abiecte, inliberaliter.*

sordidness, *sordes, inliberalitas.*

sore, subst. *ulcus (-eris,* n.).

sore, adj. (1) = painful, *gravis, acer, acerbus, molestus.* (2) = hurt, render by verb *dolēre:* fig., to be — about a thing, *rem graviter ferre.*

sorely, *graviter.*

sorrel, subst. *lapathum* or *lapathus* (Hor.).

sorrel, adj. *spadix* (Verg.).

sorrow, subst. *dolor, aegritudo, maeror, maestitia, tristitia, paenitentia* (= regret), *desiderium* (= longing), *luctus (-ūs,* esp. of bereavement): to my great —, *cum magno meo dolore.*

sorrow, v. *dolēre, maerēre, dolore adfici, lugēre* (= to mourn).

sorrowful, *tristis, maestus, lugubris, dolore* (or *luctu* or *maerore*) *adflictus.*

sorrowfully, *maeste;* see also SADLY.

sorry; see SAD, SORROWFUL; to be —, = to regret having done a thing, is rendered by the impersonal *paenitet;* to be — for, = to pity, by *misereri* (with genit.), *miserari,* or the impersonal *miseret;* I'm — it happened, *nollem factum* (Ter.).

sort, subst. (1) = kind, *genus:* of what —? *qualis? cuiusmodi?;* of that —, *talis, eiusmodi;* a — of (= as it were a, what one might call a), *quidam,* agreeing with subst.; he is not the — of man to, *non is est qui* with subjunc. (2) = rank, *ordo.* (3) = manner, *modus, ratio.*

sort, v. *digerēre.*

sortie, *excursio, eruptio:* to make a —, *erumpēre.*

so-so, *mediocriter.*

sot, *potator* (Pl.), *homo ebriosus.*

sottish, *ebriosus.*

soul. (1) = the vital principle, associated with the body in life, and perhaps quitting it at death, *anima.* (2) = the rational principle in man, *animus,* rarely *anima.* (3) = the emotional faculty, *animus, pectus (-oris,* n.): with all one's —, *ex animo, toto pectore.* (4) = a single person, *caput, homo, anima* (Verg., Tac.): not a —, *nemo, ne unus quidem.*

sound, subst. (1) = noise, *sonus, sonitus (-ūs), strepitus (-ūs).* (2) see STRAIT.

sound, adj. (1) = healthy, whole, *sanus, integer, validus:* safe and —, *incolumis, salvus, sospes;* to be — in health, *bonā* or *integra valetudine uti, bene valēre.* (2) = deep, of sleep, *altus, artus.* (3) of knowledge, etc., *altus, accuratus.* (4) of arguments, *gravis.*

sound, v. (1) = to make a noise, *sonare;* to — a trumpet, *tubam inflare;* to — to arms, *ad arma conclamare;* to — the battle call, *bellicum canēre;* to — the retreat, *receptui canēre;* to — a person's praises, *hominem laudare* or *laudibus ferre.* (2) = to test, try, *temptare, percontari* (= to question).

soundly. (1) of sleep, *arte.* (2) of beating, etc., *male, pessime, graviter.*

soundness, *sanitas, integritas;* of arguments, *gravitas.*

soup, *ius (iuris,* n.).

sour, adj. LIT., *acerbus, amarus, acidus* (poet.): very —, *peracerbus;* to turn —, *acescēre* (Hor.). TRANSF., *acerbus, amarus, morosus.*

sour, v. *exacerbare.*

source, *fons, caput, origo, principium, stirps:* to have its — in a thing, *ex re nasci, manare, proficisci.*

sourness, *acerbitas, amaritudo, morositas* (= peevishness).

south, subst. *meridies, regio australis* or *meridiana:* facing —, *ad meridiem versus* or *spectans.*

south, southerly, southern, adj. *meridianus, australis:* the — wind, *auster.*

south-east: to face —, *inter meridiem et solis ortum spectare;* the — wind, *euronotus* (Plin.), *vulturnus* (Plin.).

southernwood, *abrotonum* or *abrotonus* (Hor.).

southwards, *in* or *ad meridiem.*

south-west: to face —, *inter occasum solis et meridiem spectare;* the — wind, *Africus* (Verg., Plin.).

sovereign, subst. *rex, dominus, princeps, tyrannus* (arbitrary or despotic).

sovereign, adj. = one's own master, *sui iuris:* a — remedy, *remedium efficacissimum.*

sovereignty, *summa rerum* or *imperii,* (*summum*) *imperium, dominatio, dominatus (-ūs), regnum, tyrannis* (arbitrary or despotic).

sow, subst. *sus.*

sow, v. *serēre, semen spargēre:* prov., as you —, so shall you reap, *ut sementem feceris, ita metes.*

sower, *sator.*

sowing, subst. *satio, satus (-ūs), sementis.*

space, *spatium, locus*: a — of time, *spatium (temporis)*; a — between, = interval, gap, *intervallum.*

spacious, *amplus.*

spaciousness, *amplitudo, laxitas.*

spade, *pala.*

Spain, *Hispania.*

span, subst., as a measure, *palmus* (Plin.): the — of life, *vitae summa* (Hor.); the — of the arch was 20 ft., *arcus viginti pedes latus erat.*

span, v.; see MEASURE; of bridges, render by *iungěre.*

spangled, *distinctus.*

spaniel, render by *canis.*

Spanish, *Hispanus, Hispanicus, Hispaniensis.*

spank, v. *nates pulsare* (Juv.).

spar, subst. (1) mineral, *lapis specularis* (Plin.). (2) of timber, *asser, longurius.*

spar, v. *pugnis certare.*

spare, adj.; see THIN.

spare, v. *parcěre* (with dat.).

sparing, *parcus.*

sparingly, *parce.*

spark, *scintilla, igniculus* (esp. fig.): a — of hope, *spēcula.*

sparkle, v. *scintillare* (poet.), *fulgēre, nitēre.*

sparrow, *passer* (Cat.).

spasm, *spasmus* (Plin.), *spasma (-ătis,* n. : Plin.).

spasmodically, render by phrase, such as *haud uno tenore.*

spatter, *spargěre, aspergěre.*

spawn, subst. *(piscium) ova (-orum,* plur.).

spawn, v. *ova gigněre.*

speak, *dicěre* (= to express ideas, or make a speech), *loqui* (= to articulate or converse), *fari, verba facěre*: to — Greek, *Graecā linguā uti, Graece loqui*; to — against a person, = to oppose in speech, *contra hominem dicěre*; = to accuse, *in hominem dicěre or invehi*; to — out, *eloqui*; to — to, *(hominem) adfari, appellare, adloqui*; to — together, *conloqui.*

speaker, *orator* (= orator), *is qui dicit* (= one who happens to be speaking).

speaking, adj. of a likeness, *verus, expressus.*

spear, subst. *hasta*; see also LANCE.

spear, v. *hastā transfigěre.*

special, *praecipuus, eximius, egregius, proprius, peculiaris* (= one's own —).

specialist, *homo* (rei, genit.) *peritus.*

speciality, *quod proprium est* (with dat.).

specially, *praecipue, eximie, egregie, imprimis (in primis), maxime, prae ceteris, praesertim, valde.*

specie, *aurum* (or *argentum) signatum.*

species, *genus (-ěris,* n.), *species.*

specific, subst.; see REMEDY.

specific, adj. (1) = peculiar, *proprius, peculiaris.* (2) = explicit, definite, *disertus.*

specifically, *diserte.*

specify, *denotare*; of a number of items, *enumerare.*

specimen, *specimen, documentum, exemplum.*

specious, *speciosus.*

speck, *macula.*

speckled, *maculis distinctus, maculatus, maculosus.*

spectacle, *spectaculum.*

spectator, at a show, *spectator*; otherwise render by the verb *spectare.*

spectre; see GHOST.

speculate. (1) = to consider, ponder, wonder, *cogitare, quaerěre, inquirěre.* (2) see GUESS. (3) in business, *quaestui servire.*

speculation. (1) = thought, *cogitatio*: scientific —, *rerum contemplatio*; philosophical —, *philosophia.* (2) = guess, *coniectura.* (3) in business, *negotium, mercatura.*

speculative, = conjectural, *coniecturalis*: — philosophy, *philosophia contemplativa* (Sen.).

speech. (1) the faculty, *oratio.* (2) = a particular —, *oratio*; a short —, *oratiuncula*; a — before a meeting of the people, *contio*; to deliver a —, *orationem* or *contionem habēre, contionari.*

speechless; see DUMB.

speed, subst. *celeritas, velocitas*; = haste, *properatio, festinatio.*

speed, v. (1) transit. = to accelerate, *maturare*; = to make prosperous, *fortunare.* (2) intransit. = to hasten, *properare, festinare*; see also SUCCEED.

speedily, *cito, celeriter, velociter, propere, festinanter.*

speedy, *citus, celer, velox.*

spell, subst. *carmen.*

spell, v. render by *scribere* (= write).

spellbound, *defixus, stupens, stupefactus.*

spend. (1) of money, *insuměre (in rem), erogare* (esp. of public money). (2) of time, *agěre, degěre, consuměre, (con)terěre* (= to waste): to — the night, *pernoctare.* (3) = to exhaust, *conficěre, consuměre*: to — itself; see ABATE.

spendthrift, *nepos, homo prodigus.*

spew, *(e)voměre.*

sphere. (1) geometrical, *sphaera, globus.* (2) = field of activity, *provincia.*

spherical, *globosus.*

sphinx, *sphinx.*

spice, *condimentum* (lit. and fig.).

spicy, *condītus*; fig. *salsus.*

spider, *aranea* (poet. and Sen.): a small —, *araneola.*

spider's-web, *aranea* (poet.).

spike, *clavus, cuspis.*

spikenard, *nardus* (Plin.).

spill, *effunděre.*

spin, v. (1) transit.: to — thread, *nēre* (poet.); to — round, *versare, circumagěre, in orbem agěre*; to — out, = to prolong, *ducěre.* (2) intransit. render by passive verb.

spindle, *fusus* (poet.).

spine, *spina* (Verg.).

spinner, render by verb.

spinster, *virgo, innupta* (poet.).

spiral, subst. *coclea* (Cels., Col.).

spiral, adj. *tortuosus.*

spire, *turris.*

spirit. (1) = vital principle, *anima*; see also SOUL. (2) = character, disposition, *animus, ingenium, indoles, natura*: the — of the age, *temporum* or *huius aetatis ratio* or *mores (-um,* plur.). (3) = energy, animation, courage, *animus, spiritus (-ūs), vis, ferocia, vigor*: a man of —, *homo ferox*; with —, *ferociter.* (4) = disembodied —, *anima, manes (-ium,* plur.). (5) = intention, real meaning (opp. to letter), *consilium, sententia, voluntas* (Quint.). (6) in Christian doctrine, the Holy Spirit, *Spiritus (-ūs) Sanctus* or *Sacer* (eccl.). **(7)** = strong drink, render as WINE.

spirited, *animosus, generosus, ferox, acer.*

spiritedly, *animose, ferociter, acriter.*

spiritless, *ignavus.*

spiritual. **(1)** in gen. = of the spirit, render by genit., such as *animi* or *ingenii.* **(2)** = incorporeal, *corporis expers.* **(3)** opp. to secular, *sacer, ecclesiasticus* (eccl.).

spiritualism, spiritualist, render by phrase, such as *credĕre inter mortuos ac vivos commercium esse.*

spirituality, *animus rerum divinarum studiosus.*

spit, subst. *veru* (Verg.).

spit, v. *spuĕre* (Plin.): to — back, — out, *respuĕre*; to — upon, *consputare.*

spite, subst. *malignitas, malevolentia, livor, invidia, odium*: in — of, render by abl. abs. (e.g.: in — of your unwillingness, *te invito*), or by concessive clause (with *cum, quamvis,* etc.).

spite, v.; see VEX, ANNOY.

spiteful, *malignus, malevolus, lividus.*

spitefully, *maligne.*

spittle; see SALIVA.

splash, v. transit. *aspergĕre.*

spleen. LIT., *lien* (Pl.), *splen* (Pl.). TRANSF., *stomachus, invidia, odium.*

splendid, *splendidus, magnificus, egregius, (prae)clarus.*

splendidly, *splendide, magnifice, (prae)clare.*

splendour, *splendor, magnificentia, apparatus, -ūs* (= pomp).

splenetic. LIT., *lienosus* (Pl.). TRANSF., *stomachosus, malevolus, malignus.*

splice, *(con)iungĕre, connectĕre, inter se texĕre.*

splint, *canalis* (Cels.), *ferulae* (Cels.).

splinter, *ossis fragmentum* (of bone); *assula* (Pl., Cat.) or *ligni fragmentum* (of wood).

split, subst. *fissura* (Plin.), *scissura* (Plin.), *rima* (= crack).

split, v. **(1)** transit. *(dif)findĕre, scindĕre.* **(2)** intransit. *(dif)findi, dissilire* (= to leap apart: poet.).

spoil, subst. *praeda*: the —s of war, *spolia (-orum,* plur.); —s taken from the person of an enemy, *exuviae (-arum,* plur.).

spoil, v. **(1)** = to plunder, *(ex)spoliare.* **(2)** = to injure, mar, *corrumpĕre, perdĕre, vitiare.* **(3)** = to over-indulge a person, *homini nimis indulgĕre* or *morigerari.*

spoiler, *spoliator.*

spoiling, spoliation, *spoliatio.*

spoke, *radius* (Verg., Ov.).

Spoleto, *Spoletum.*

spondee, *spondēus.*

sponge, subst. *spongia* (Plin.).

sponge, v. = to cadge, *parasitari* (Pl.).

sponger, *parasitus.*

spongy, *spongiosus* (Plin.).

sponsor, *sponsor* (eccl.); fig., of measures, etc., *auctor.*

spontaneity, render by *sponte* or *ultro.*

spontaneous, *voluntarius, spontaneus* (Sen.).

spontaneously, *(sua) sponte, ultro.*

spoon, *cocleare* (Mart.).

sport, subst. **(1)** = play, *ludus, lusus (-ūs).* **(2)** = hunting, *venatio.* **(3)** = mockery, *ludibrium, inriso.*

sport, v. *ludĕre, lascivire.*

sportive, adj. *lascivus* (poet.), *iocosus, festivus.*

sportively, *per iocum, iocose.*

sportiveness, *lascivia, iocus.*

sportsman, *venator.*

spot, subst. **(1)** = mark, stain (lit. and fig.), *macula, nota.* **(2)** = place, *locus.*

spot, v. LIT., *notare, maculis* or *notis distinguĕre, maculare.* TRANSF., *maculare, inquinare.*

spotless. LIT., *sine maculis.* TRANSF., *purus, sanctus, integer.*

spotted, *maculosus, maculis distinctus.*

spouse, *coniunx;* also *maritus* (= the husband), *uxor* (= the wife).

spout, subst. *os.*

spout, v. LIT., *exsilire.* TRANSF., *declamare.*

sprain, *intorquĕre, convellĕre* (Col.).

sprawl, render by phrase, such as *humi prostratum iacēre.*

spray, subst. **(1)** liquid, *aspergo* (poet.). **(2)** on a tree, *virgula.*

spread, v. **(1)** transit. *(ex)pandĕre* (= to lay open), *explicare* (= to unfold), *extendĕre* (= to stretch out), *spargĕre* (= to scatter), *(di)vulgare* (= to publish, broadcast), *dilatare* (= to stretch out). **(2)** intransit., of physical objects, *(ex)pandi, extendi,* etc. (see above); of abstract things, *percrebescĕre, increbescĕre, (di)vulgari, manare.*

spreading, adj. *patulus* (Verg.).

sprig, *surculus, virgula.*

sprightliness, *alacritas* (= briskness), *facetiae (-arum* = pleasantries).

sprightly, *alacer* (= brisk), *facetus* or *salsus* (= humorous).

spring, subst. **(1)** = fountain, *fons, scaturigo* (rare). **(2)** = origin, in gen., *fons, origo, principium, causa.* **(3)** the season, *ver, tempus vernum*: at the beginning of —, *primo* or *ineunte vere;* of —, adj. *vernus;* the — of life, *iniens aetas.*

spring, v. LIT. = to leap, *salire;* to — forth, *exsilire;* to — down, *desilire;* to — forward, *prosilire.* TRANSF., to — up, — from *(ex* or *ab re,* etc.), *nasci, (ex)oriri, proficisci;* to — up, of plants, *crescĕre;* of winds, *surgĕre* (Verg.); to — a leak, *rimas agĕre* (Ov.).

spring-tide, *aestus (-ūs) maximus.*

sprinkle, *spargĕre, aspergĕre, conspergĕre:* to — on, *inspergĕre.*

sprite, *faunus* (= faun) or *nympha* (= nymph).

sprout, subst. *surculus.*

sprout, v. *pullulare* (Verg.), *germinare* (Plin.).

spruce, adj. *comptus, bellus, concinnus, nitidus, elegans.*

sprucely, *belle, ornate, nitide, eleganter.*

sprung from *(a gente,* etc.) *ortus* or (more remotely) *oriundus.*

spur, subst. *calcar* (lit. and fig.).

spur, v.: to — a horse, *equo calcaria subdĕre, equum calcaribus concitare* or *stimulare;* fig., to — on; see INCITE.

spurious, *adulterinus, falsus.*

spurn, *fastidire, aspernari, repudiare*: to — with the foot; see KICK.

spurt, subst. *nisus (-ūs);* see also EFFORT.

spy, subst. *explorator, speculator, emissarius.*

spy, v. *explorare, speculari.*

squabble, subst. *rixa, altercatio, iurgium.*

squabble, v. *rixari.*

squadron, of cavalry, *(equitum) turma* or *ala*: of ships, *classis.*

squalid, *sordidus, spurcus.*

squalidly, *sordide.*

squall, subst. (1) of wind, *procella*. (2) by an infant, *vagitus (-ūs)*.

squall, v. *vagire*.

squalor, *sordes* (often plur.).

squander, *profundĕre, effundĕre, perdĕre, dissipare*.

squanderer, *nepos*.

square, subst. *quadratum* (= a — figure), *quadra* (= a — piece: poet.), *forum* (= a market- —).

square, adj. *quadratus*.

square, v. = to make square, *quadrare*: intransit., to — with, *quadrare* (*in rem*); of accounts, transit. *subducĕre*, intransit. *quadrare*.

squash, v. *conterĕre, contundĕre*.

squat, adj. *habitu corporis brevis atque obesus* (Suet.).

squat, v. *subsidĕre, considĕre*.

squatter, *inquilinus*: —'s rights, render by *usu capĕre* (= to obtain a prescriptive right to).

squeak, subst. *stridor*.

squeak, v. *stridĕre* (poet.).

squeamish, *fastidiosus, delicatus*.

squeamishness, *fastidium*.

squeeze, subst. *compressio*.

squeeze, v. *premĕre, comprimĕre*: to — out, *exprimĕre*.

squint, v. *limis* or *perversis oculis esse, strabonem esse*: a person who —s, *strabo*.

squire, *armiger* (late Latin).

squirrel, *sciurus* (Plin.).

squirt, v. (1) transit. *eicĕre*. (2) intransit. *emicare, exsilire*.

stab, subst. *ictus (-ūs* = a blow), *vulnus (-eris*, n. = a wound).

stab, v. *confodĕre, (sicā, pugione*, etc.) *ferire*.

stability, *stabilitas, firmitas, constantia*.

stable, subst. *stabulum*: prov., to lock the — door after the horse is stolen, *clipeum post vulnera sumĕre* (Ov.).

stable, adj. *stabilis, firmus, constans*.

stable, v. *stabulare* (Varro).

stack, subst. *cumulus, acervus, strues*.

stack, v. *cumulare*.

staff. (1) = a stick, *baculum, bacillum, scipio* (carried before officials): an augur's —, *lituus, baculum*; a herald's —, *caduceus*. (2) = a body of assistants: military, *legati (-orum*, plur.); a — appointment, *legatio*; civil, *adiutores (-um*, plur.), *ministri (-orum*, plur.).

stag, *cervus*.

stage. (1) of a theatre, *proscaenium, scaena, pulpitum* (Hor.): of the —, *scaenicus*; to go on the —, *in scaenam prodire*. (2) = degree, *gradus (-ūs)*.

stagger, v. (1) transit. = to shock, *commovēre, percellĕre, obstupefacĕre*. (2) intransit. *titubare, vacillare*.

stagnant, *stagnans* (Plin.), *piger, lentus*.

stagnate. LIT., *stagnare* (Verg.). TRANSF., perhaps *hebescĕre, languēre*.

staid; see SOBER.

stain, subst. (lit. and fig.), *macula, labes, nota*.

stain, v. LIT., see DYE, DIRTY. TRANSF., *maculare, foedare, polluĕre, inquinare*.

stainless, *purus, integer, intemeratus* (Verg., Ov., Tac.).

stair, *gradus (-ūs)*: a —case, *scalae (-arum*, plur.); I live up three flights of —s, *scalis habito tribus* (Mart.).

stake, subst. (1) = a post, *palus, stipes, sudes*.

(2) = pledge, *pignus (-oris*, n.): fig., to be at —, *agi, in discrimen adduci, in discrimine esse*; my honour is at —, *fama agitur mea*.

stake, v. *(de)ponĕre* (Verg.).

stale, adj. *vetus, obsoletus*.

stalk, subst. *culmus, caulis* (Cato, Verg.), *calamus* (Verg.).

stalk, v. (1) = to strut, *incedĕre*. (2) = to follow carefully, render by phrase.

stall, subst. (1) for cattle, *stabulum* (Verg.). (2) = a little shop, *taberna*.

stall, v. *stabulare* (Varro).

stallion, *(equus) admissarius* (Plin.).

stamen, *stamen* (Plin.).

stammer, subst. *haesitantia, haesitatio linguae*.

stammer, v. *balbutire, linguā haesitare*.

stammering, adj. *balbus*.

stamp, subst. (1) = impression, *nota, signum, imago (impressa)*: fig., persons of that —, *eiusmodi homines*. (2) of the foot, *pedis supplosio*.

stamp, v. (1) = to mark, *signare, notare, signum* or *notam imprimĕre*: to — money, *nummos signare* or *cudĕre* (Ter.). (2) with the foot, *pedem supplodĕre*: to — underfoot, *conculcare*.

stanch; see STAUNCH.

stand, subst. (1) = a place for standing, *locus, statio*. (2) = a place for standing things on, *abacus* (= sideboard, etc.). (3) = the act of standing, *mora*: to come to a —, *consistĕre, subsistĕre*; to make a — against, *resistĕre* (with dat.).

stand, v. (1) = to be upright, *stare, consistĕre*: to — aloof, *abstare* (Hor.); to — aside, *recedĕre*; to — by a person, *homini adesse*; to — by one's word, *in fide stare, fidem servare*; to — fast, *consistĕre, subsistĕre, restare, perstare*; to — for an office, *petĕre*; not to — on ceremony, render by phrase, such as *cum homine amicissime agĕre*; to — in need of, *egēre, indigēre* (with abl. or genit.); to stand in a person's way, *homini obstare*; to — on end, of hair, *stare* (Verg., Ov.); to — out, *eminēre, exstare*; to — out to sea, *vela dare*; to — round, *circumstare*; to — up, *surgĕre*; to — up for a person = to rise at his approach, *homini adsurgĕre*; = to defend, *defendĕre*. (2) = to set upright, place, *statuĕre, constituĕre, sistĕre* (mainly poet.). (3) = to tolerate, *tolerare, perferre, pati, perpeti, sustinēre*.

standard. (1) = flag, *vexillum, signum, aquila* (= the eagle of the legion). (2) = measure, *regula, norma*.

standard-bearer, *vexillarius, signifer, aquilifer*.

standing, subst. *condicio, gradus (-ūs), locus, ordo*: of long —, *vetus*.

standstill: to be at a —, *haerēre*.

stanza, render by phrase, such as *versuum series*.

staple, subst. (1) = market, *emporium* (Plin.). (2) see HOOK.

staple, adj.; see REGULAR, PECULIAR.

star. LIT., *stella, astrum, sidus (-eris*, n.; strictly = a constellation): the — under which one is born, *sidus natalicium*. TRANSF., = a distinguished person, *lumen*.

starboard, render by phrase, such as *latus navis dextrum*.

starch, *amylum* (Plin.).

stare, subst. *obtutus (-ūs)*.

[838]

stare, v.: to — at, *spectare, intueri*; to stand —ing, in astonishment, *stupēre*.

stark, *rigidus*: — naked, render by phrase such as *omni veste exutus*.

starlight, starry, adj. *sideribus inlustris* (Tac.), *stellans* (poet.), *stellifer* (rare), *astris distinctus et ornatus*.

starling, *sturnus* (Plin.).

start, subst. (1) = a sudden movement, *saltus* (-*ūs*: = jump): by fits and —s, *haud uno tenore*. (2) = a beginning, *initium, principium, exordium*. (3) = a setting out, *profectio*: to get (or have) the — of a person, *hominem antecedēre, occupare* (Ov.).

start, v. (1) transit. *instituēre, adgredi, incipēre, initium* (*rei*, genit.) *facēre*; of game, *excire, excitare*. (2) intransit.: **a** = to jump, move suddenly, *expavescēre*; to — up, *exsilire*: **b** = to begin, *incipēre, (ex)ordiri, initium facēre*: **c** = to set out, *proficisci*.

starting-place, *carceres* (-*um*, plur.; originally of races).

startle; see FRIGHTEN.

startling, *terribilis, formidolosus* = strange, wonderful, *mirus*.

starve, v. (1) transit. *fame* or *inediā necare*: to — oneself to death, *inediā vitam finire*. (2) intransit. *fame* (or *inediā*) *confici, consumi, perire, interire*.

state, subst. (1) = condition, *status* (-*ūs*), *condicio, locus, fortuna*. (2) = polity, *respublica* (= commonwealth), *civitas* (= body of citizens), *regnum* (= kingdom): of —, adj., *publicus, civilis*; affairs of —, *respublica, negotia* (-*orum*, plur.), *publica*. (3) = grandeur, *apparatus* (-*ūs*), *magnificentia*.

state, adj. *publicus*.

state, v. *narrare, praedicare, profiteri, adfirmare, confirmare, adseverare, dicēre*.

stateliness, render by adj.

stately, *lautus, magnificus*.

statesman, *vir reipublicae peritus* (or *peritissimus*, for a good, clever or consummate —).

statesmanship, *ars reipublicae regendae, ratio* or *scientia civilis*.

station, subst.; see POSITION, RANK.

station, v.; see PLACE, SET.

stationary, *immobilis, immotus*: a — camp, (*castra*) *stativa* (-*orum*, plur.).

stationery; see PAPER.

statistics, render by *census* (-*ūs*) or *numerus* (= number).

statuary; see SCULPTOR, SCULPTURE.

statue, *signum, statua* (of a man), *simulacrum, effigies*.

stature, *statura*.

statutable, *legitimus*.

statute, *lex*.

staunch, adj. *firmus, certus, fidus*.

staunch, v. (*sanguinem*) *sistēre* or *cohibēre* (Cels.).

stay, subst. (1) = a prop, support, *adminiculum* (lit. and fig.). (2) = a sojourn, abiding, *mansio, commoratio*.

stay, v. (1) transit.: **a** = to prop, *fulcire*: **b** = to stop, arrest, (*de*)*morari, detinēre, cohibēre*; see also CHECK. (2) intransit. = to abide, tarry, (*com*)*morari, manēre*: to — with a person, *apud hominem manēre, commorari*, or *in hospitio esse*.

stays, render by *strophium*.

stead: in — of, *pro*, with abl.; *loco* or *in vicem*, with genit; see also INSTEAD.

steadfast, steady, *stabilis, firmus, constans, fidus*.

steadily, *firme, firmiter, constanter*.

steadiness, steadfastness, *stabilitas, firmitas, constantia*: want of —, *inconstantia*.

steak: see MEAT.

steal, v. (1) transit., to — property, *furari, surripēre, subducēre, avertēre, intercipēre*. (2) intransit. = to go quietly or stealthily, *subrepēre*: to — in, *inrepēre*; to — away, *se subducēre* or, of a number, *dilabi*.

stealing, subst. *furtum*.

stealth: by —, *furtim, clam*.

stealthily; see STEALTH.

stealthy, *furtivus, clandestinus, occultus, tectus*.

steam, subst. (*aquae*) *vapor, nīdor* (from anything cooked), *fumus* (= smoke).

steam, v. *vaporare* (Plin.).

steam-engine, render by phrase, such as *machina vi vaporis impulsa*.

steed, *equus*.

steel, subst. *chalybs* (Verg.); = sword, *ferrum*.

steel, v.: to — oneself, fig., *obdurescēre*.

steep, subst. *locus praeceps*.

steep, adj. *praeruptus, praeceps, arduus*.

steep, v. *madefacēre, imbuēre* (lit. and fig.): to — oneself in crime, *in flagitia se ingurgitare*.

steepness, render by adj.

steeple, *turris* (= tower).

steeplechase; see RACE.

steer, subst. *iuvencus* (Verg.).

steer, v. *gubernare, regēre*: fig., to — clear of a thing, *rem vitare, rē abstinēre*.

steerage, *puppis*: — passengers, *qui in puppi vehuntur*.

steering, subst. *gubernatio*.

steersman, *gubernator, rector*.

stem, subst. (1) of a tree, *stirps, truncus*. (2) of a plant, *caulis, calamus*. (3) = race, *progenies, stirps, prosapia, familia, genus* (-*ēris*, n.).

stem, v. = to check, *cohibēre, sistēre, coercēre, reprimēre*; see also RESIST.

stench, *foetor, putor* (Lucr.).

step, subst. (1) = a stair, *gradus* (-*ūs*). (2) = a pace, *gradus* (-*ūs*), *passus* (-*ūs*), *gressus* (-*ūs*: poet.): to take a —, *gradum facēre*; at a quick —, *pleno gradu*; with measured —, *presso gradu*; to quicken one's —, *gradum addēre*; — by —, *gradatim, pedetentim*. (3) = a plan, measure, *ratio, consilium*.

step, v. *gradi*: to — across, *transgredi*; to — in, *ingredi*; to — forwards, *progredi*.

step-brother, *filius vitrici* (on the father's side), *filius novercae* (on the mother's).

step-daughter, *privigna*.

step-father, *vitricus*.

step-mother, *noverca*.

step-sister, *filia vitrici* or *novercae*.

step-son, *privignus*.

Stephen, *Stephanus* (late Latin).

stereotyped, *tritus, translaticius*.

sterile, *sterilis* (lit. and fig.).

sterility, *sterilitas*.

sterling, *verus, bonus*.

stern, subst. *puppis*.

stern, adj. *durus, severus, austerus*.

sternly, *severe, dure* (Ter., Hor.), *duriter* (Ter., Lucr.).

sternness, *severitas*.

stew, v. (*igne lento*) *coquēre*.

steward, *procurator, dispensator* (Juv., Suet.), *administrator*; of a farm or estate, *vilicus.*
stewardship, *cura, procuratio, administratio.*
stick, subst. *baculum, bacillum* (smaller), *virga* (= rod), *clava* or *fustis* (= cudgel).
stick, v. (1) transit. *figĕre, adfigĕre*: to — in, *infigĕre.* (2) intransit. LIT., *haerēre, adhaerēre, adhaerescĕre.* TRANSF., a = to adhere (to a thing), *(in re) manēre, (rei,* dat.) *adhaerescĕre*: b = to get stuck, *haerēre, haesitare, dubitare.*
sticking-plaster, *emplastrum* (Cato, Plin.).
stickler, render by adj. *diligens* (= careful), with genit.
sticky, *tenax, lentus* (poet.).
stiff. LIT., *rigidus, durus*: to be — (esp. with cold), *rigēre.* TRANSF., = unbending, awkward, *rigidus, difficilis.*
stiffen, v. (1) transit. *rigidum facĕre.* (2) intransit. *rigescĕre* (Verg.).
stiffly, *rigide, dure, duriter.*
stiff-necked, *obstinatus*; see also OBSTINATE.
stiffness, *rigor* (poet.).
stifle. LIT., *suffocare, spiritum intercludĕre.* TRANSF., *reprimĕre, opprimĕre, exstinguĕre.*
stigma, *nota.*
stigmatize, *notare, notam inurĕre* (with dat.).
still, adj. *tranquillus, quietus, placidus, immotus.*
still, adv. (1) of time, *adhuc, etiam, etiamnunc* (or *etiamnum*, or either as two separate words; = even now), *etiamtum* (= even then). (2) with compar., *etiam, adhuc* (rare). (3) see NEVERTHELESS.
still, v. *sedare, placare.*
stilling, subst. *sedatio.*
stillness, *silentium, tranquillitas, quies.*
stilts, *grallae* (-*arum,* plur.: Varro): one who walks on —, *grallator* (Pl., Varro).
stimulant, *vinum* (= wine).
stimulate, *stimulare, excitare, incitare, inritare.*
stimulus, *stimulus, incitamentum, inritamentum* (mostly in plur.), *calcar* (= spur).
sting, subst. *acumen, aculeus* (lit. and fig.).
sting, v. *pungĕre* (lit. and fig.), *aculeos infigĕre.*
stingily, *parce, sordide, maligne.*
stinginess, *parsimonia, tenacitas, malignitas, sordes* (usually plur.).
stinging, *mordax* (Hor., Ov.), *acerbus, aculeatus.*
stingy, *parcus, sordidus, tenax, malignus* (Pl., Hor.).
stink, *foetor, putor* (Lucr.), *taeter odor.*
stint, subst. *inopia*; see also NEED.
stint, v. *parce dare, parcĕre* (with dat.).
stipend; see SALARY.
stipendiary, *mercenarius, stipendiarius.*
stipulate, *stipulari, (de)pacisci.*
stipulation, *stipulatio, pactum, condicio*: a small —, *stipulatiuncula.*
stir, subst. *motus* (-*ūs*), *tumultus* (-*ūs*), *turba.*
stir, v. (1) transit., *(com)movēre, exagitare.* (2) intransit., *se movēre, moveri, progredi*; see also GO, ADVANCE.
stitch, subst. (1) of a needle, render by verb. (2) in the side, *lateris dolor.*
stitch, v. *(con)suĕre.*
stock, subst. (1) of a tree, *truncus, stirps.* (2) = origin, family, *genus, stirps.* (3) = store, quantity, *copia, vis.* (4) — in trade, equipment, *instrumenta* (-*orum,* plur.).
stock, adj.; see COMMON, TRITE.
stock, v. = to furnish, equip, *instruĕre, ornare, replēre* (fully).

stockade, *vallum.*
stocking, *tibiale* (Suet.).
stock-still, *immotus.*
stoic, subst. and adj. *stoicus.*
stoical, *ferreus, durus, rigidus, austerus.*
stoically, *austere, stoice.*
stoicism, *stoicorum ratio* or *doctrina.*
stomach, subst. LIT., *stomachus.* TRANSF., = appetite, liking, *stomachus*; a high —; see ARROGANCE, PRIDE.
stomach, v. *concoquĕre.*
stomacher, *strophium.*
stone, subst. (1) in gen., *lapis, saxum* (large): a — quarry, *lapidicina* (usually plur.); a —'s throw, *lapidis iactus* (-*ūs*); adj. —, of —, *lapideus*; prov., to run into a — wall, *incurrĕre amentem in columnas*; to squeeze blood from a —, *aquam a pumice postulare* (Pl.); to kill two birds with one —, *de eadem fidelia duo parietes dealbare* (ap. Cic. L.). (2) in the human body, *calculus* (Cels.). (3) in fruit, *nucleus* (Plin.); see also KERNEL. (4) precious —, *gemma.*
stone, v. *lapides in hominem conicere*: to — to death, *lapidibus cooperire.*
stony, = of stone, *lapideus, saxeus*: = full of stones, *lapidosus* (Ov.), *saxosus* (Verg.).
stony-hearted, *durus, ferreus.*
stool, *scabellum* (Varro).
stoop, v. LIT., *caput* (or *se*) *inclinare, demittĕre, submittĕre.* TRANSF., *descendĕre*; see also CONDESCEND.
stooping, adj. *pronus, inclinatus.*
stop, subst. (1) = sojourn, stay, *mansio.* (2) = pause, *intermissio, pausa* (Lucr.). (3) as punctuation, *interpunctum.* (4) to put a — to; see STOP, v.
stop, v. (1) transit. *sistĕre, prohibēre, inhibēre, coercēre, comprimĕre*: to — up, *obturare, occludĕre.* (2) intransit.: a = to halt, *(con)sistĕre, subsistĕre*: b = to stay, *manēre, (com)morari*: c = to cease, refrain, *desinĕre, omittĕre.*
stoppage, *mora, obstructio, impedimentum.*
stopper, *obturamentum* (Plin.).
store, subst. *copia, vis, abundantia* (= plenty): to have a — of a thing, *rē abundare.*
store, v. *coacervare, reponĕre, condĕre.*
store-house, *horreum* (esp. for grain), *thesaurus, apotheca.*
storeman, *cellarius* (Pl.).
store-room, *cella*; see also STORE-HOUSE.
storey, *tabulatio, tabulatum.*
stork, *ciconia.*
storm, subst. *tempestas, procella*: prov., a — in a teacup, *(excitare) fluctus in simpulo.*
storm, v. (1) transit. = to take by assault, *expugnare, vi capĕre*; to try to —, *oppugnare.* (2) intransit. *furĕre, saevire*: to — at a person, *hominem insectari.*
storm-cloud, *nimbus.*
stormily, *turbide, turbulente, tumultuose.*
storming, subst. *expugnatio.*
stormy, *turbulentus, turbidus, procellosus, tumultuosus.*
story, (1) = a tale, *fabula, res, narratio, narratiuncula*: to tell a —, *narrare*; there is a —, the — goes, *ferunt.* (2) = a falsehood, *mendacium*: to tell stories = to lie, *mentiri.* (3) see STOREY.
story-teller, *narrator*; = liar, render by adj. *mendax.*

stout. (**1**) = fat, *obesus* (Verg., Hor.), *pinguis*. (**2**) = thick, *crassus, densus*. (**3**) = strong, *validus, robustus*. (**4**) = brave, *fortis*.

stoutly, *fortiter, acriter, valide, robuste*.

stoutness; see CORPULENCE.

stove, *focus, caminus*.

stow; see STORE.

straddle, *varicare* (Quint.).

straddling, adj. *varicus* (Ov.).

straggle, *vagari, deerrare, palari*.

straight, adj. (*di*)*rectus*; = upright, *erectus*.

straight, adv. *rectā, recto itinere*.

straighten, *corrigĕre*.

straightforward, *simplex, apertus*.

straightway; see IMMEDIATELY.

strain, subst. (**1**) = exertion, *intentio, contentio*. (**2**) of music, etc., *modus*; see also TUNE, SONG. (**3**) = manner, *modus*: in this —, *ita, sic* (= thus).

strain, v. (**1**) transit., (*in*)*tendĕre, contendĕre*; = to sprain; see SPRAIN; = to filter; see FILTER. (**2**) intransit., *niti, contendĕre*.

strained, of language; see FAR-FETCHED.

strait, subst. (**1**) = narrow sea, *fretum*: the —s of Messina, *fretum Siciliense*; the —s of Gibraltar, *fretum Gaditanum* (Plin.). (**2**) = any narrow passage, *angustiae* (*-arum*, plur.). (**3**) fig., sing. or plur. = difficulty, *angustiae* (*-arum*, plur.), *res angusta, inopia* (= want).

strait, *artus, angustus* (= bound up).

straiten, *in angustias adducĕre*.

strand, subst. *litus* (*-oris*, n.), *ripa, acta*.

strand, v. *navem vadis* (or *litoribus*) *inlidĕre* or *impingĕre*.

strange, adj. (**1**) = foreign, *peregrinus, externus, exterus, extraneus, adventicius* (= coming from abroad). (**2**) — to something, = unversed in it, in (or *ab*) *re alienus, in re* (or *rei*, genit.) *rudis, rei* (genit.) *ignarus*. (**3**) = unusual, *insolitus, inusitatus, novus, mirus, mirabilis*: — to relate, *mirabile dictu*. (**4**) = not belonging to one, *alienus*.

strangely, *mirum in modum, mirabiliter, inusitate*.

strangeness, *novitas, insolentia*; or render by adj.

stranger, *hospes, advena, peregrinus, externus* (in plur. only); see also STRANGE.

strangle, *strangulare, laqueo interimĕre, gulam laqueo frangĕre*.

strap, subst. *lorum*.

strap, v. *loris* (*con*)*stringĕre* or *vincire*.

stratagem, *ars, dolus, consilium, astus* (*-ūs*: Pl., Verg., Tac.), *insidiae* (*-arum*, plur.).

strategist, *dux prudens* or *peritus*.

strategy, *ars belli gerendi*.

stratum; see LAYER.

straw, *stramentum*: of —, adj. *stramineus* (Prop., Ov.).

strawberry, *fragum* (used in plur. only: Verg., Ov.).

stray, adj. *errabundus*.

stray, v. (*ab*)*errare, vagari, palari*.

streak, subst. *linea, nota* (= mark).

streak, v. *lineis*, or *variis coloribus, distinguĕre*.

stream, subst. *flumen, rivus*: up —, *adverso flumine*; down —, *secundo flumine*.

stream, v. *fluĕre, effundi*.

streamer, *vexillum*.

street, *via, vicus, platea, angiportus* (*-ūs*; = a narrow street or alley): in the —s, *in publico*.

strength, *vires* (*-ium*, plur.), *robur, nervi* (*-orum*), *opes* (= resources), *firmitas* or *firmitudo* (= stability, firmness): — of mind, *robur animi*.

strengthen. (**1**) transit., (*con*)*firmare*, (*con*)-*roborare, stabilire*. (**2**) intransit., render by pass. of transit. verbs.

strengthening, subst. *confirmatio*.

strenuous, *strenuus, impiger, acer*, (*g*)*navus*.

strenuously, *strenue, impigre, acriter*.

strenuousness, (*g*)*navitas, studium*.

stress, *momentum, vis, pondus* (*-ĕris*, n.): — of weather, *tempestas, vis tempestatis*; see also EMPHASIS and PRESSURE.

stretch, subst. (**1**) = effort, *contentio, intentio, nisus* (*-ūs*): at a —, *uno tenore*. (**2**) = expanse, *tractus* (*-us*), *spatium*.

stretch, v. (**1**) transit., (*ex*)*tendĕre, contendĕre, intendĕre*: to — forth, or out, *porrigĕre, protendĕre* (Verg., Tac.); to — out in front, *obtendĕre* (Verg.). (**2**) intransit., render by pass. of transit. verbs; see also EXTEND.

stretcher; see LITTER.

strew, *sternĕre, spargĕre*.

strict. (**1**) = careful, exact, *diligens, religiosus, accuratus* (of things only): the — letter of the law, *summum ius* (*iuris*, n.). (**2**) = severe, rigorous, *severus, rigidus, austerus*.

strictly. (**1**) = carefully, *accurate*. (**2**) severely, *severe, rigide, austere*.

strictness. (**1**) = carefulness, *accuratio, diligentia*. (**2**) = severity, *severitas, rigor* (Ov., Tac.).

stricture, *animadversio, reprehensio, vituperatio*.

stride, subst. *ingens gradus* (*-ūs*).

strife, *certatio, certamen, contentio, controversia* (= dispute), *rixa* (= quarrel).

strike, v. (**1**) transit. *ferire, percutĕre, pulsare, caedĕre*: to — a flag or sail, *demittĕre*; to — a coin, *cudĕre* (Pl., Ter.); to — a bargain, *pacisci*; to be struck by lightning, *fulmine* or *de caelo, tangi*; to — a person mentally, *percutĕre, percellĕre*; to — one thing against another, *rem rei* (dat.) *infligĕre* or *inlidĕre* (Verg., Hor.); to — down, *adfligĕre*; to — out, *elidĕre, delēre* (= to erase); to — together, *conlidĕre*. (**2**) intransit.: to — against, *offendĕre, incurrere, inlidi* (Verg.); to — in; see INTERVENE.

striking; see REMARKABLE.

string, subst. *linum, linea, filum, funiculus, resticula*: a shoe- —, *corrigia*; a bow- —, *nervus* (Verg.); the — of a musical intrument, *chorda, nervus, fides* (usually plur.).

string, v.: to — an instrument, *nervos aptare*, with dat.; to — together; see BIND.

stringent; see SEVERE.

strip, subst.: of paper, *scidula chartae*; of cloth, *lacinia*.

strip, v. (**1**) transit. *spoliare*, (*de*)*nudare, exuĕre* (all with acc. of person, abl. of clothes, etc.); *vestem detrahĕre* (with dat.). (**2**) intransit. *vestem exuĕre* or *deponĕre*.

stripe; see STREAK and STROKE.

stripling, *adulescens, adulescentulus*.

strive. (**1**) in gen. = to make an effort, (*e*)*niti, coniti, contendĕre, operam dare, conari, studēre*. (**2**) to — after a thing, *ad* (or *in*) *rem* (*co*)*niti* or *contendĕre, rem adfectare, rei* (dat.), *studēre*. (**3**) to — against, *obniti, resistĕre* (with dat.). (**4**) to — with others, in competition, *contendĕre*, (*de*)*certare*.

striving, subst. *nisus (-ūs), certatio, contentio*: — after, *appetitio, contentio* (with genit.).

stroke. (**1**) = blow, *ictus (-ūs), verber, plaga.* (**2**) in writing, etc., *linea* (Plin.). (**3**) a — of lightning, *fulmen.* (**4**) a — of fortune, *eventus (-ūs).* (**5**) a — of policy = stratagem, *ars, artificium.*

stroke, v. (*per*)*mulcēre, demulcēre.*

stroll, subst. *ambulatio*: a short —, *ambulatiuncula.*

stroll, v. *ambulare, spatiari, reptare* (Pl., Lucr., Hor.).

strong, adj. *valens, validus, firmus, robustus, fortis, lacertosus* (= muscular): of flavours, etc., *acer*; of winds or currents, *vehemens*; of arguments, *gravis, firmus*; a — memory, *memoria tenax*; a — position, *locus munitus*; to be —, in gen. *valēre*; in resources, influence, etc., *pollēre.*

strongly, *valide, valde, firmiter, fortiter, vehementer.*

stronghold, *arx.*

structure. (**1**) abstract, *ratio, forma, conformatio, structura.* (**2**) material, *aedificium, opus (-ĕris, n.), moles, compages.*

struggle, subst. *certamen, luctatio.*

struggle, v. *luctari, niti, contendĕre*: to — out, *eniti*; see also STRIVE.

strumpet, *scortum, meretrix.*

strut, (*superbe*) *incedĕre.*

stubble, *stipulae (-arum,* plur.: poet.).

stubborn, *pertinax, pervicax, obstinatus, contumax.*

stubbornly, *pertinaciter, pervicaciter, obstinate, contumaciter, obstinato animo.*

stubbornness, *pertinacia, pervicacia, contumacia, obstinatio, obstinatus animus.*

stucco; see PLASTER.

stud, *bulla, fibula* (= clasp): of horses, *equi (-orum,* plur.), *equaria* (Varro).

studded, *distinctus.*

student, render by phrase, such as *homo doctrinae studiosus*; see also SCHOLAR.

studied, *meditatus, commentatus, exquisitus.*

studious, *litterarum studiosus, in studiis litterarum versatus.*

studiously, *summo studio, studiose.*

study, subst. (**1**) = application, *studium, meditatio, commentatio*: the — of something, *cognitio* (with genit.). (**2**) = learned —, *studium* (esp. in plur.), *litterae (-arum,* plur.). (**3**) see ROOM.

study, v. (**1**) in gen. = to pay attention to a thing, *rei* (dat.), *studēre, incumbēre* or *operam dare.* (**2**) = to inquire systematically into a subject, *rem cognoscĕre, in rem inquirere.* (**3**) of literary studies, *litteris studēre, in litteris versari*: to — late at night, *lucubrare.*

stuff, subst. (**1**) in gen. = matter, *materia, materies.* (**2**) = gear, *impedimenta (-orum), supellex.* (**3**) = fabric, *textile, tela*: a piece of —, *pannus.* (**4**) — and nonsense, *nugae (-arum,* plur.), *gerrae (-arum,* plur.: Pl.).

stuff, v. *farcire, refercire, saginare, replēre*; see also FILL.

stuffing, *fartum* (in food: Plin.), *tomentum* (for cushions: Varro, Tac.).

stultify, render by phrase, such as *ad vanum* or *ad inritum* or *ad ineptias redigĕre.*

stumble, *offendĕre*: to — upon, *incidĕre in,* with acc.

stumbling, subst. *offensio, offensatio* (Sen.).

stumbling-block, *offensio* (eccl.); or render by phrase such as *offensionem habēre* (= to cause stumbling).

stump, *stipes (-ĭtis), truncus.*

stun. LIT., *sopire* or render by phrase, such as *sensu privare.* TRANSF., (*ob*)*stupefacĕre, perturbare, percellĕre*: to be —ned, *stupēre, torpēre.*

stunt, v., render by phrase, such as *incrementum impedire.*

stupefaction, *stupor, torpor* (Sen., Tac.).

stupefy; see STUN.

stupendous, *ingens, immanis*; see also WONDERFUL.

stupid, *stupidus, stolidus, hebes, obtusus, stultus.*

stupidity, *stupiditas, stupor, stultitia.*

stupidly, *stolide, stulte.*

stupor, *stupor, torpor.*

sturdy; see STRONG, FIRM, CONFIDENT.

sturgeon, *acipenser.*

stutter, v. *balbutire*; see also STAMMER.

sty, *hara, suile* (Col.).

style, subst. (**1**) in gen. *genus (-ĕris,* n.), *ratio, modus, mos* (= custom): — of dress, *habitus (-ūs).* (**2**) of language, *dicendi* or *scribendi genus, orationis* or *sermonis genus, oratio, sermo, elocutio.*

style, v. *appellare*; see also NAME.

stylish, *speciosus, elegans, nitidus, lautus, magnificus.*

stylishly, *speciose, eleganter, magnifice.*

suave, *suavis, urbanus, blandus.*

suavity, *suavitas, urbanitas.*

subaltern, perhaps *subcenturio* or *optio* (Tac.).

subdivide, render by phrase, such as *iterum dividĕre*; see also DIVIDE.

subdivision, *pars.*

subdue, *in imperium* or *dicionem redigĕre, subiungĕre, subigĕre, domare.*

subject, subst. (**1**) of a person, *civis*; or render by the verb *parēre* (= to obey). (**2**) = a matter, *res, quaestio, argumentum.* (**3**) as grammat. t. t., *subiectum* (Gram.).

subject, adj. *subiectus, obnoxius* (with dat.): to be — to a person, *in dicione hominis esse.*

subject, v. *subicĕre, obnoxium reddĕre* (with dat.).

subject-matter, *materia, res.*

subjection, *servitus (-ūtis), officium, patientia* (Tac.).

subjective, render by personal pronouns or by *opinio* (= — view, as opp. to *res* = objective fact).

subjectivity, render by phrase, such as *quod in opinione constat.*

subjoin, *subiungĕre, subicĕre, supponĕre.*

subjugate, (*per*)*domare, subigĕre, subiungĕre, in dicionem suam redigĕre.*

subjunctive, adj.: the — mood, *modus subiunctivus* (Gram.).

sublime, *elatus, excelsus, grandis, sublimis* (Quint.).

sublimely, *elate, excelse.*

sublimity, *elatio, excelsitas, sublimitas* (Quint.).

sublunary, *infra lunam positus*; see also EARTHLY.

submarine, render by phrase, such as *quod sub mari* (*positum*) *est.*

submerge, *submergĕre.*

submersion, render by verb.

submission, *obsequium, officium*; see also SUBJECTION.

submissive, *oboediens, obnoxius, submissus.*
submit, v. (**1**) transit. = to lay a thing before
an authority, *referre (ad senatum,* etc.).
(**2**) intransit. *se* or *animum submittĕre, (con)-*
cedĕre, obtemperare, parere (all with dat.): to
— to, = to endure, *perferre.*
subordinate, subst. *minister.*
subordinate, adj. *inferior, subiectus* (with
dat.).
subordinate, v. *subicĕre, posthabēre.*
subordination, = obedience, *obsequium,*
disciplina.
suborn, *subornare, subicĕre.*
subpœna, *denuntiatio testimonii.*
subscribe. (**1**) = to write underneath, *sub-*
scribĕre. (**2**) to — to, = to agree to, *adsentiri,*
subscribĕre, with dat. (**3**) = to contribute,
conferre.
subscriber, = one who writes under, *sub-*
scriptor; otherwise render by verb.
subscription, = that which is written under,
subscriptio; = contribution, *conlatio, conlecta.*
subsequent, *(in)sequens, posterior.*
subsequently, *postea.*
subserve, *(in)servire, obtemperare, obsequi*; see
also SERVE, ASSIST.
subservience, *obtemperatio, obsequium.*
subservient, *obsequens*; see also SUBMISSIVE.
subside, *residĕre, considĕre, remittĕre, cadĕre.*
subsidiary, *subsidiarius.*
subsidy, *subsidium, vectigal, tributum* (= tax).
subsist, *esse, constare*: to — on a thing, *re*
vivĕre or *vesci.*
subsistence, *victus (-ūs), alimenta (-orum,*
plur.).
substance, *natura, corpus (-ŏris,* n.), *res*; =
property, *res, bona (-orum,* plur.).
substantial, *verus* (= real), *firmus, solidus*
(= firm, solid), *gravis* (= considerable,
important), *amplus* (= large, grand).
substantially, *firmiter* (= solidly), *magna ex*
parte (= to a great extent).
substantiate; see PROVE, ESTABLISH.
substantive, as grammat. t. t., *nomen* (Gram.).
substitute, subst. *vicarius*: as a — for, *pro*
(with abl.).
substitute, v. *supponĕre, subdĕre, substituĕre,*
sufficĕre (esp. of the replacing of magistrates).
substitution, render by verb.
substructure, *substructio.*
subterfuge, *deverticulum, latebra, tergiversatio.*
subterranean, *subterraneus.*
subtle. LIT., = thin, fine, *tenuis, subtilis* (Lucr.,
Plin.). TRANSF., *subtilis, argutus, acutus*; see
also CLEVER, CUNNING.
subtlety. LIT., = fineness, *tenuitas.* TRANSF.,
ingenii acies or *acumen, subtilitas, argutiae*
(-arum, plur.).
subtly, *subtiliter, argute, acute.*
subtract, *deducĕre.*
subtraction, render by *deducĕre.*
suburb, *suburbium* (rare).
suburban, *suburbanus.*
subvert, *subvertĕre, evertĕre.*
subversion, *eversio*; see also OVERTHROW.
succeed, v. (**1**) transit. = to come after, *(sub)-*
sequi, excipĕre (with acc.), *succedĕre* (with dat.
or *in locum* with genit.): to — to the throne,
regnum excipĕre. (**2**) intransit. = to do well,
have success; of persons, *rem bene* or
prospere gerĕre, florēre (= to prosper, in gen.);
or render by the impersonal *succedit (homini);*

of things, *succedĕre, bene* (or *prospere)*
procedĕre or *evenire.*
success, *res* (rerum, plur.) *prosperae* or
secundae, felicitas, prosperitas, successus (-ūs):
without —, *frustra, re infectā.*
successful; of persons, *felix, fortunatus*; of
things, *prosper, secundus, felix.*
successfully, *feliciter, prospere, bene.*
succession; of one individual following
another, *successio*; of a continuous series,
continuatio, series: in —, *ex ordine.*
successive, *continuus.*
successively, *(ex) ordine, in ordinem, deinceps.*
successor, *successor.*
succinct, *brevis.*
succinctly, *brevi, breviter.*
succour, subst. *auxilium, subsidium.*
succour, v. *subvenire, auxiliari, succurrĕre,*
with dat.
succulent, *sucosus* (Plin.), *suci* (or *succi) plenus.*
succumb, *succumbĕre.*
such, adj. *talis*; often also rendered by *huius*
modi (= of this kind) or *eius modi* (= of that
kind): such . . . as, *talis . . . qualis*; such
that, such as to, *talis ut,* with subj., sometimes
is qui, with subj.; such a, foll. by adj., *tam*
(so also where Eng. noun is represented by
Latin adj.; e.g. — a fool, *tam stultus);* — a
large, *tantus*; — a small, *tantulus*; — is your
courtesy (as a parenthetic clause), *quae tua*
est humanitas; to — a degree, *adeo*; in — a
way, *tali modo, ita, sic.*
suck, subst. *suctus (-ūs*: Varro, Plin.): to give
—, *mammam praebēre, ad ubera admittĕre* (of
animals).
suck, v. *sugĕre, bibĕre* (= to drink): to — up,
— out, *exsorbēre.*
sucker, *surculus, planta.*
suckle, v.; see SUCK.
suckling, *(infans) lactens.*
suction, *suctus (-ūs*: Varro, Plin.).
sudatory, adj. *sudatorius* (Pl.).
sudden, *subitus, repens, repentinus, inopinatus,*
necopinatus.
suddenly, *subito, repente, (ex)inopinato, (de)-*
improviso, repentino.
suddenness, render by adj.
sue. (**1**) to — for, = to entreat, *rogare, orare,*
postulare, (ex)poscĕre, (ef)flagitare. (**2**) to —
a person at law, *hominem in ius vocare,*
hominem iudicio persequi, litem homini inten-
dĕre or *inferre.*
suet, *sebum* (Pl.).
suffer. (**1**) with object = to endure, *pati, perpeti,*
(per)ferre, tolerare, sustinēre, accipĕre, subire:
to — loss, *damno adfici, detrimentum* (or
damnum) accipĕre or *facĕre*; to — shipwreck,
naufragium facĕre; to — a disgrace, *dedecus*
(in se) admittĕre. (**2**) without object, = to be
in pain, *dolorem,* etc. *ferre*; *dolore,* etc. *adfici*;
aegrotare (= to be ill); of abstract things, =
to be impaired, *minui*: to — from, *laborare*
(with abl.); to — for, = be punished for,
poenas dare (with genit.). (**3**) = to permit,
allow, *pati, sinĕre, permittĕre* (with dat.).
sufferance, *patientia, toleratio, perpessio*: on
—, *precarius,* adj.
sufferer, *aeger, aegrotus*; otherwise render by
verb.
suffering, *dolor* (= pain), *miseria* (= misery);
see also PAIN.
suffice, *sufficĕre, suppetĕre, suppeditare, satis esse.*

sufficiency, *quod satis est.*
sufficient, render by the adv. *satis.*
suffocate, *suffocare;* see also STRANGLE, STIFLE.
suffrage, *suffragium.*
suffuse, *suffundĕre.*
sugar, *saccharum* or *saccharon* (Plin.).
suggest, (*rem homini*) *subicĕre* : to — that a thing be done, *auctorem esse* or *suadēre ut,* with subjunc.
suggestion, *admonitio, monitum, consilium* : at my —, *me auctore, meo admonitu.*
suggestive, render by verb.
suicide, *mors voluntaria* : to commit —, *vim* or *manus sibi inferre, sibi mortem consciscĕre.*
suit, subst. (1) at law, *actio, lis, causa.* (2) of clothes, *vestis, vestitus (-ūs).* (3) see PETITION. (4) see COURTSHIP.
suit, v. (1) = to adapt, *accommodare, componĕre.* (2) = to fit, be suitable, *convenire, congruĕre, cadĕre* (with *in* and acc.): it —s, = it becomes, *decet;* = it is expedient, *expedit.* (3) see PLEASE.
suitable, *idoneus, aptus, accommodatus, opportunus, consentaneus, conveniens, congruens, dignus* (= worthy), *decens* or *decorus* (= becoming).
suitableness, *opportunitas;* or render by adj.
suitably, *idonee, apte, accommodate, digne, opportune.*
suite. (1) = retinue, *comitatus (-ūs), comites (-um,* plur.). (2) a — of rooms, *conclavia (-ium,* plur.); see also ROOM.
suitor, = wooer, *procus* (poet.); see also CANDIDATE and PETITIONER.
sulkily, sullenly, *morose.*
sulkiness, sullenness, *morositas.*
sulky, sullen, *morosus, tristis, tetricus.*
sully, *maculare, inquinare, contaminare.*
sulphur, *sulfur* (or *sulpur*): dipped in —, *sulfuratus* (Plin., Mart.).
sulphurous, *sulpureus* (Verg., Plin.).
sultan; see KING.
sultriness, *aestus (-ūs).*
sultry, *aestuosus.*
sum, subst. *summa* : a — of money, *pecunia;* for a large —, *magni* or *magno.*
sum up, v. *computare, subducĕre, rationem inire* : to — up in words, *breviter repetĕre.*
summarily, = briefly, *breviter, summatim;* = quickly, *sine mora, statim, confestim.*
summary, subst. *epitoma* or *epitome, summarium* (Sen.).
summary, adj. (1) = brief, *brevis.* (2) = quick, sudden, *subitus, repentinus;* see also IMMEDIATE and HASTY.
summer, *aestas* : of —, adj. *aestivus;* at the beginning of —, *ineunte aestate;* at the height of —, *summā aestate;* at the end of —, *extremā aestate.*
summer-house; see ARBOUR.
summit. LIT. (1) *cacumen, culmen, vertex* : often rendered by the adj. *summus* (e.g. the — of the mountain, *summus mons*). TRANSF., *culmen, fastigium;* or render by *summus.*
summon, in gen. (*ad*)*vocare, arcessĕre, accire, citare* : to — a number of people, *convocare;* to — before a court, (*hominem*) *appellare, in ius vocare,* (*homini*) *diem dicĕre;* to — to surrender, *invitare ad deditionem;* to — up one's courage, *animum conligĕre.*
summoner, *viator.*
summons: at the — of a person, *hominis*

arcessitu or *accitu;* otherwise render by verb.
sumptuary, adj. *sumptuarius.*
sumptuous, *sumptuosus, lautus;* see also COSTLY, MAGNIFICENT.
sumptuously, *sumptuose, opipare.*
sumptuousness, *apparatus (-ūs), lautitia, luxus (-ūs);* or render by adj.
sun, subst. *sol* : the rising —, *sol oriens;* the setting —, *sol occidens.*
sun, v. : to — oneself, *apricari.*
sunbeam, *radius solis.*
sunburnt, *adustus.*
Sunday, *dies dominica* (eccl.).
sunder, *separare, disiungĕre;* see also SEPARATE.
sundial, *solarium.*
sundry, *diversus, varius.*
sunlight, (*solis*) *lux.*
sunny, *apricus.*
sunrise, *solis ortus (-ūs)* : from — to sunset, *ab orto usque ad occidentem solem.*
sunset, *solis occasus (-ūs).*
sunshine, *sol.*
sup, *cenare.*
superabound, *superare, superesse.*
superabundance, *abundantia.*
superannuate, v. *rude donari* (Hor.; originally of gladiators).
superannuated, *emeritus* (poet.), *rude donatus* (Hor.; originally of gladiators).
superb, *magnificus, lautus, splendidus.*
superbly, *magnifice, laute, splendide.*
supercilious, *superbus, fastidiosus, insolens.*
superciliousness, *fastus (-ūs), superbia, insolentia.*
supererogation, render by the adv. *sponte* (= of one's own accord).
superficial. LIT., *exterior, externus.* TRANSF., = shallow, *levis.*
superficially, *strictim, lĕviter* : — educated, *litterulis imbutus* (Hor.).
superficies, *superficies* (Plin.); see also SURFACE.
superfine, (= of very fine texture) *tenuissimus, persubtilis.*
superfluity, *quod supervacaneum est, quod superest.*
superfluous, adj. *supervacaneus, supervacuus* : to be —, *superesse.*
superfluously, *ex supervacuo.*
superhuman, *divinus, maior quam pro homine* : a — task, *opus quod ultra hominis vires est;* of — size, *humanā specie amplior.*
superintend, (*pro*)*curare, administrare, praeesse* (with dat.).
superintendence, *cura,* (*pro*)*curatio, administratio.*
superintendent, *praefectus,* (*pro*)*curator.*
superior, *superior, praestantior, melior* (= better): to be —, *praestare, superare;* relying on — numbers, *multitudine fretus.*
superiority, *prior locus;* or render by the adj. *superior.*
superlative: in gen. *optimus, eximius, egregius, singularis, excellens;* as grammat. t. t., *superlativus* (gram.).
supernal, *superus, caelestis.*
supernatural, *divinus, caelestis;* or render by phrase, such as *ultra quod rerum natura patitur* : by — agency, *divinitus.*
supernumerary, adj. in gen., render by phrase such as *praeter iustum numerum;* of

soldiers, as adj., *ascriptivus* (Pl.); as subst. in plur., supernumeraries, *accensi (-orum)*.

superscription, *inscriptio.*

supersede, *in locum* (with genit.) *substitui, succedĕre* (with dat.).

superstition, *superstitio.*

superstitious, *superstitiosus, superstitione imbutus* (of persons only).

superstitiously, *superstitiose.*

superstructure; see BUILDING.

supervene, *supervenire*; see also FOLLOW, SUCCEED.

supervise, *(pro)curare*; see also SUPERINTEND.

supervision, *(pro)curatio*; see also SUPERINTENDENCE.

supine, subst. *supinum* (gram.).

supine, adj. LIT., = on the back, *supinus.* TRANSF., *lentus, iners, neglegens, supinus* (Quint., Juv.).

supinely, *lente, neglegenter.*

supineness, *socordia, neglegentia, inertia.*

supper, *cena.*

supplant, render by phrase, such as *in alterius locum inrepĕre.*

supple, *mollis, flexibilis, lentus.*

supplement, *supplementum* (esp. milit.), *incrementum.*

suppliant, subst. and adj. *supplex.*

supplicate, *supplicare, obsecrare, obtestari.*

supplication, *obsecratio, obtestatio.*

supply, subst., and plur. **supplies**, in gen. *copia* (sing. and plur.), *facultas* (sing. and plur.): milit. —, *commeatus (-ūs)*; — of corn, *frumentum, res frumentaria*; a sufficient —, *satis.*

supply, v. (1) = to fill a gap, make good a loss, *supplēre.* (2) = to provide, (*rem homini*) *suppeditare, ministrare.*

support, subst. (1) = prop, stay (lit. and fig.), *firmamentum*; see also PROP. (2) = maintenance, *alimentum, victus (-ūs)*. (3) = help, *subsidium, adiumentum, auxilium, favor.*

support, v. (1) = to hold up, *sustinēre, ferre, fulcire*; see also PROP. (2) = to bear, endure, (*per*)*ferre, tolerare.* (3) = to maintain, keep, *alĕre, sustinēre, sustentare.* (4) = to help, *adesse, suffragari*, with dat.; *adiuvare*, with acc.

supporter, *adiutor, suffragator, fautor*; see also HELPER, PARTISAN.

suppose, (1) = to lay down, assume, *ponĕre, sumĕre, facĕre* (esp. imperat.). (2) = to believe, think, *credĕre, existimari, putare, opinari*; see also BELIEVE, IMAGINE, THINK.

supposing that, *fac* with acc. and infin., or *ut* with subjunc.

supposition, *opinio, coniectura.*

supposititious, *subditus, subditivus, subditicius* (Pl.).

suppress, *supprimĕre, reprimĕre, comprimĕre, exstinguĕre* (= to put down, destroy).

suppression, render by verb.

suppurate, *suppurare* (Plin.).

suppuration, *suppuratio* (Plin.).

supremacy, *principatus (-ūs), dominatus (-ūs), dominatio, regnum* (= kingship), *imperium* (= supreme power).

supreme, *supremus, summus*: the — power, *imperium.*

supremely, *unice, praecipue, maxime.*

sure, *certus* (= certain), *tutus* (= safe), *securus* (= free from apprehension), *firmus* (= trust-

worthy), *fidelis* (= faithful): I am —, *pro certo habeo, certo scio*; I have made — of this (as being a fact), *hoc compertum* or *cognitum* or *exploratum habeo*; make — that something is done, *fac* or *cura*, with *ut* and subjunc.; to be —, *certe, profecto, scilicet* (often ironical).

surely. (1) in statements, *certe, nimirum, profecto, scilicet* (often ironical), *saltem* (= at least). (2) in questions: —, introducing a question to which a positive answer is expected, *nonne*; — not, *num.*

surety, *vas, praes, sponsor* (of a person), *vadimonium* (= money given as bail).

surf; see FOAM, WAVE.

surface, *superficies* (Plin.), or render by adj. *summus* (e.g. the — of the water, *summa aqua*): to come to the —, *emergĕre.*

surfeit, subst. *satietas.*

surfeit, v. LIT., to — oneself, *se ingurgitare.* TRANSF., = to fill up, to give enough and more to, *satiare, saturare, explēre.*

surge, subst. *fluctus (-ūs).*

surge, *fluctuare* (= to toss about): to — forward, *proruĕre.*

surgeon, *medicus, chirurgus* (Cels.).

surgery, *chirurgia* (Cels.).

surliness, *morositas, difficultas, asperitas.*

surly, *morosus, difficilis, asper.*

surmise, subst. *coniectura.*

surmise, v. *suspicari, augurari, coniecturam facĕre* or *capĕre.*

surmount, *transcendĕre, (ex)superare.*

surmountable, *(ex)superabilis.*

surname, *cognomen, cognomentum* (Pl., Tac.).

surpass, *vincĕre* or *(ex)superare* (with acc.), *antecellĕre, excellĕre, praestare* (with dat.).

surplice, *vestis (sacerdotalis).*

surplus, subst. *residuum, reliquum, quod superest.*

surplus, adj.; see EXTRA.

surprise, subst. (1) as a feeling, *(ad)miratio.* (2) = anything unexpected, render by adj.; see SURPRISING, UNEXPECTED. (3) in particular = a sudden attack, *subita incursio, adventus (-ūs) hostium repentinus.*

surprise, v. (1) = to astonish, *admirationem (homini) movēre*: to be —d, *(ad)mirari.* (2) = to take by —, attack suddenly, *opprimĕre, imprudentem* or *necopinantem* or *ex improviso adoriri.*

surprising, *mirus, mirabilis*; see also WONDERFUL.

surrender, subst. *deditio, traditio, cessio* (legal t. t.).

surrender, v. (1) transit. *dedĕre, tradĕre, (con)cedĕre.* (2) intransit. *se dedĕre.*

surreptitious, *furtivus, clandestinus.*

surreptitiously, *furtive, furtim, clam.*

surrogate, *vicarius.*

surround, *cingĕre, circumdare, circumvenire, circumcludĕre, circumfundĕre, circumvallare* (milit. t. t. = to invest).

surrounding, adj., of places, *circumiectus.*

survey, subst. *contemplatio, observatio, conspectus (-ūs)*; of land, *mensura* (Plin. L.).

survey, v. (1) = to look at, inspect, *spectare, contemplari, considerare, intuēri, contuēri, perlustrare.* (2) = to measure land, *agrum metiri, mensuram agĕre* (Plin. L.).

surveyor, (of land) *decempedator, metator.*

survival, render by verb.

survive, *superesse, superare, superstitem esse.*

surviving, *superstes.*

survivor, *superstes.*

susceptibility, *mollitia* or *mollities.*

susceptible. (**1**) = impressionable, *mollis.* (**2**) see CAPABLE, LIABLE, PRONE.

suspect, adj. *suspectus.*

suspect, v. *suspicari, suspicionem habēre*; = to think, fancy, *putare*; to be —ed; see SUSPICION.

suspend. (**1**) = to hang up, *suspendēre.* (**2**) = to break off, defer, *intermittēre, differre.* (**3**) to — from office, *loco (hominem) movēre, magistratum (homini) abrogare.*

suspense, *dubitatio*: in —, adj. *suspensus*; to be in —, *suspenso animo exspectare, dubitare, in dubio esse.*

suspension, *dilatio* (= delay): — of hostilities, *induttiae* (-*arum*, plur.).

suspicion, *suspicio*: to incur —, *in suspicionem cadēre* or *venire.*

suspicious, (= either causing suspicion or ready to suspect), *suspiciosus, suspicax.*

suspiciously. (**1**) = so as to excite suspicion, *suspiciose.* (**2**) = with suspicion, render by subst. or adj.

sustain, (= to uphold or to endure) *sustinēre, sustentare*; more passively = to have happen to one, *accipēre.*

sustenance, *alimentum, victus* (-*ūs*).

sutler, *lixa* (Sall.).

swaddling-bands, *fasciae* (-*arum*, plur.: Pl.), *incunabula* (-*orum*, plur.: Pl.).

swagger, *gloriari, se iactare.*

swain, *agrestis, rusticus, colonus.*

swallow, subst. *hirundo.*

swallow, v. (*ab*)*sorbēre,* (*de*)*vorare.*

swamp, subst. *palūs* (-*ūdis*).

swamp, v. (*de*)*mergēre, immergēre, opprimēre* (= to overwhelm).

swampy, *paluster, paludosus* (poet.).

swan, *cygnus, olor* (poet.); of a —, adj. *cygneus*: a — song, *vox cygnea.*

sward; see GRASS.

swarm, subst. (**1**) of bees, *examen.* (**2**) of people, etc.; see CROWD.

swarm, v. *congregari*: to — out, *effundi*; to — up; see CLIMB.

swarthy, *fuscus, adustus, furvus* (poet.).

sway, subst. *imperium, dominatio, dominium, dicio.*

sway, v. (**1**) transit.: **a** = to move from side to side, *agitare, motare* (poet.): **b,** see GOVERN and INFLUENCE. (**2**) intransit. *vacillare, nutare.*

swear, (*iusiurandum*) *iurare, iureiurando adfirmare*: to — falsely, *falsum iurare, peierare* or *periurare*; to — by Jupiter, (*per*) *Iovem iurare*; to — allegiance to a person, *in nomen hominis iurare* (Suet.).

sweat, subst. *sudor.*

sweat, v. *sudare.*

sweep, subst. (**1**) = a sweeper, render by verb. (**2**) = a wide expanse, *ambitus* (-*ūs*), *spatium, circuitus* (*ūs* = circuit or circumference).

sweep, v. *verrēre*: to — along, *verrēre* (poet.).

sweepings, *quisquiliae* (-*arum*, plur.).

sweet, *dulcis, suavis, iucundus* (= pleasant).

sweeten, *dulcem reddēre* or *facēre.*

sweetheart, *deliciae* (-*arum*, plur.), *amores* (-*um,* plur.).

sweetly, *dulciter, suaviter, iucunde.*

sweetness, *dulcedo, dulcitudo, suavitas, iucunditas* (= pleasantness).

swell, subst., at sea; see WAVE.

swell, v. (**1**) transit. *tumefacēre* (poet.), *inflare, augēre* (= to increase). (**2**) intransit. *tumēre, tumescēre, turgēre* (poet.), *turgescēre, crescēre* (= to grow).

swelling, subst. *tumor, struma* (= scrofulous —), *tuber* (Ter., Hor., Plin.).

swerve, subst. *declinatio.*

swerve, v. *declinare.*

swift, subst. *apūs* (*apodis*: Plin.).

swift, adj. *citus, velox, celer, pernix.*

swiftly, *cito, celeriter, perniciter.*

swiftness, *celeritas, velocitas, pernicitas.*

swill, subst. *conluvies* or *conluvio.*

swill, v. *potare, ingurgitare*: to — oneself, *ingurgitare se.*

swim, v. *nare, natare*: to — across, *tranare*; to — down, *denatare* (Hor.); to — to, *adnare.*

swimmer, *natator* (Ov.).

swimming, subst. *natatio.*

swindle, subst. *fraus.*

swindle, v. *fraudare, circumvenire*; see also CHEAT.

swindler, *fraudator.*

swine, *sus, porcus*; adj., of —, *suillus*: a herd of —, *grex suillus.*

swineherd, *subulcus* (Varro), *suarius* (Plin.).

swing, v. (**1**) transit. *agitare, vibrare, iactare.* (**2**) intransit. render by pass. of above verbs.

switch, subst. *virga, virgula.*

switch, v.; see ALTER, CHANGE.

Switzerland, *Helvetia.*

swoon, subst., render by verb.

swoon, v. *animo linqui* (Sen.): to fall in a —, *conlabi.*

swoop, subst. *impetus* (-*ūs*).

swoop, v. *impetum facēre, incurrēre.*

sword, *gladius, ensis* (poet.), *ferrum* (esp. in general or abstract sense): with fire and —, *ferro et igni*; to have a — at one's side, *gladio succinctum esse*; to draw the —, *gladium* (*de*)*stringēre* or (*e vaginā*) *educēre*; to sheathe the —, *gladium in vaginam recondēre*; to put to the —, *interficēre.*

swordfish, *xiphias* (Ov.).

sycophancy, *sycophantia* (Pl.), *adsentatio, adulatio.*

sycophant, *sycophanta* (Pl., Ter.), *adsentator, adulator.*

syllable, *syllaba.*

syllogism, *ratiocinatio, syllogismus* (Sen., Quint.).

syllogistic, *ratiocinativus, syllogisticus* (Quint.).

sylvan, *silvestris.*

symbol, *symbolum* or *symbolus* (Pl.), *signum, imago*; see also SIGN.

symbolic, render by subst. or verb.

symbolize; see REPRESENT.

symmetrical, *concinnus, par, aequalis, congruens.*

symmetrically, *pariter, aequaliter*; in style, *concinnitas.*

symmetry, *convenientia, congruentia* (Plin. L., Suet.), *aequalitas, symmetria* (Plin.).

sympathetic, *concors* (= agreeable, harmonious), *humanus* (= kind), *misericors* (= compassionate).

sympathize, *congruēre, consentire, eadem sentire, miserēri* (with genit. = to pity).

sympathy. (1) in gen. = harmony, agreement, *consensus* (*-ūs*), *concordia*. (2) = understanding and fellow-feeling, *humanitas* or render by phrase, such as *societas doloris* (*laetitiae*, etc.), *animus dolore* (*laetitiā*, etc.) *alterius adfectus*.

symphony, *symphonia, concentus* (*-ūs*).

symptom, (*morbi*) *nota* or *indicium* or *signum*.

synagogue, *synagoga* (eccl.).

synchronism, *aequalitas temporum*.

syncope; see FAINT.

syndicate, *societas*; see also COMPANY.

synod, *synodus* (eccl.).

synonym, *vocabulum idem significans* or *declarans*.

synonymous, *idem significans* or *declarans*.

synopsis, *epitome* or *epitoma, breviarium* (Suet., Tac.), *summarium* (Sen.), *synopsis* (legal writers).

syntax, *syntaxis* (gram.) or render by phrase, such as *verborum constructio*.

syntactical, render by subst.

Syracuse, *Syracusae* (*-arum*, plur.).

syringe, *sipho* (Suet.).

syrup, render by phrase, such as *potio dulcis*.

system, *formula, ratio, disciplina, artificium, instituta* or *praecepta* (*-orum*, plur. = rules).

systematic, *accuratus, artificiosus, compositus, perpetuis praeceptis ordinatus* (Liv.).

systematically, *ordine, accurate, artificiose, composite*.

systematize, *ad rationem* or *ad artem redigere* or *revocare*.

T

tabernacle, *tabernaculum*.

table. (1) = a board, flat surface, *tabula, mensa*; see also TABLET. (2) = an article of furniture, *mensa, monopodium* (= μονοπόδιον, a — with only one foot), *orbis* (= a round —: Mart., Juv.), *quadra* (= a square —: Juv.): to set or lay the —, *mensam* (*ap*)*ponere*; to sit down at —, *accubare*; to rise or get up from —, *surgere a mensā* or *cenā*; at —, *inter cenam, inter epulas*; to wait at —, *ad mensam consistere*. (3) = meal, fare, *cena, victus* (*-ūs*), *epulae* (*-arum*, plur.). (4) = list, *index*.

table-cloth, render by *linteum*, or phrase.

table-napkin, *mappa* (Hor., Juv.).

tablet, *tabula, tabella, album, cera* (covered with wax), *aes* (of bronze), *pugillares* (*-ium*, plur.: Plin.), *codicilli* (*-orum*, plur.: Plin.).

table-talk, *sermo* (*familiaris*).

tabular, render by phrase, such as *per indices expositus*.

tacit, *tacitus*.

tacitly, *tacite*.

taciturn, *taciturnus*.

taciturnity, *taciturnitas*.

tack, subst. = a small nail, *clavulus* (Varro): in sailing, to try a different —, *mutare velificationem*.

tack, v. in sailing, *reciprocare*; see also NAIL and SEW.

tackle, subst. *instrumenta* (*-orum*, plur.), *armamenta* (*-orum*, plur.), *arma* (*-orum*, plur.).

tackle, v. *tractare*; with hostile intent, *congredi, obviam ire*.

tact, *dexteritas, communis sensus* (*-ūs*).

tactful, *dexter*.

tactfully, *dextere* or *dextre*.

tactician, (*vir*) *rei militaris peritus*.

tactics, *res militaris, belli ratio*.

tactless, *ineptus, insulsus, infacetus, molestus*.

tactlessness, *ineptiae* (*-arum*, plur.).

Tadcaster, *Calcaria*.

tadpole, *ranunculus*.

taffeta, render by phrase, such as *pannus sericus*.

tail, *cauda*: to wag the —, *caudam movēre*.

tailor, *textor*.

taint, subst. *contagio, contagium* (poet.), *vitium* (= fault, blemish).

taint, v. *imbuere, inficere, contaminare, inquinare, corrumpere*.

take. (1) in gen. = to get hold of a person or thing, *capere, sumere, tollere* (= to lift, pick up), *accipere* (= to accept, receive), *rapere* (= to seize), *adripere* (= to snatch up), *occupare* (= to take before somebody else does), (*com*)*prehendere* (= to grasp): to — by storm, *expugnare*; to — fire, *ignem comprehendere*; prov.: devil — the hindmost, *occupet extremum scabies* (Hor.). (2) to — away, *auferre, demere, adimere, surripere, eripere*. (3) to — down, *demere, detrahere* (= to drag down); in writing, *litteris mandare*; see also WRITE. (4) to — in, *recipere, accipere*; mentally, *concipere, percipere, comprehendere*; see also DECEIVE. (5) to — on, *suscipere*; see also UNDERTAKE, TACKLE. (6) to — out, *eximere, promere*. (7) to — up, *sumere, tollere, suscipere*: to — up arms, *arma capere* or *sumere*; = to occupy, in space, *occupare*; = to occupy, of time, *consumere*. (8) with various abstract nouns: to — advantage of a thing, *re uti*; to — care, *cavēre*; to — offence, *offendi*; to — pains, *operam dare*; to — part, *interesse*; to — a person's part, *homini favēre, cum homine facere*; to — place, *fieri*; see also under the nouns concerned. (9) = to move from one place to another: by carrying, *ferre*; by leading, *ducere*. (10) = to endure, put up with, *accipere*, esp. with *in bonam* (or *malam*) *partem*; *ferre*, esp. with adv. (11) = to — for, — it that, etc.; see CONSIDER, SUPPOSE. (12) intransit., to — to a thing or place, *se conferre ad*, with acc. (13) intransit., to — after; see RESEMBLE.

taking, subst. *acceptio, occupatio, expugnatio* (of a city); or render by verb.

tale, *narratio, fabula, historia*: a short —, *fabella, narratiuncula* (Quint., Plin. L.).

tale-bearer, *delator* (= informer: Juv., Tac.), *sycophanta* (Pl., Ter.).

talent. (1) = a weight or coin, *talentum*. (2) = faculty, ability, *ingenium, indoles, (ingenii) facultas*.

talented, *ingeniosus, eximii ingenii*: to be —, *ingenio abundare* or *valēre*.

talisman, *amuletum* (Plin.).

talk, subst. *sermo, conloquium*: common —, *fama*; petty —, *sermunculus*.

talk, v. (*con*)*loqui, sermocinari, (con)fabulari* (Pl.), *sermonem conferre*: to — nonsense, *garrire, blaterare* (Hor.); to — to a person, *hominem adloqui, adfari, admonēre*.

talkative, *loquax, garrulus* (poet.).

talkatively, *loquaciter*.

talkativeness, *loquacitas*.

tall, *longus, procerus, (ex)celsus*.

tallness, *proceritas, statura procera*.

tallow, *sebum* (Pl.).

tally, v. *convenire*; see also FIT, SUIT.

Talmud, *Talmudum* (late Latin).

talon, *unguis, ungula.*

tamarisk, *tamarix* (Lucr.).

tambourine, *tympanum.*

tame, adj. LIT., *cicur* (by nature, of animals), *mansuetus, placidus, mitis*: to grow —, *mansuefieri, mitescĕre, mansuescĕre* (poet.). TRANSF., *demissus, abiectus, ignavus lentus, languidus, ieiunus*; of language, *frigidus.*

tame, v. *mansuefacĕre, mansuetum facĕre* or *reddĕre, domare, frangĕre, frenare* (= to bridle), *coercĕre* (= to restrain, repress).

tamely, *demisse, abiecte, ignave, ieiune, frigide.*

tameness, render by adj. or verb.

tamer, *domitor,* with *domitrix* (Verg., Ov.).

taming, *domitus* (-*ūs*).

tamper; see MEDDLE; to — with = to tempt, *temptare, sollicitare.*

tan, v.: to — skins, *conficĕre*; of the sun, *colorare.*

tangent, render by phrase, such as *linea circulum contingens.*

tangible, *tractabilis,* or render by phrase with *tangi* and *posse.*

Tangier, *Tinge* or *Tingi.*

tangle, subst. *implicatio, nodus.*

tangle, *implicare*; see also ENTANGLE.

tank, *lacus* (-*ūs*).

tanner, *coriarius* (Plin.).

tantalize; see TEASE.

tantamount; see EQUIVALENT, SAME.

tap, subst. (**1**) = a light blow, *plaga lĕvis.* (**2**) of a cask, *obturamentum* (Plin.).

tap, v. *lĕviter ferire*: to — a cask, *relinĕre* (Ter.).

tape; see RIBBON.

taper, subst., *cereus, funalis.*

taper, v., render by *fastigium* (= slope) or *fastigatus* (= sloping).

tapestry, *pictura acu facta, stragulum pictum, velum* (= curtain).

taphouse, *taberna.*

tapis: to bring on the —, *in medium proferre.*

tar, *pix liquida* (Plin.).

Taranto, *Tarentum.*

tardily, *tarde, lente.*

tardiness, *tarditas.*

tardy, *tardus, lentus.*

tare; see WEED.

target: a — to shoot at, *scopos* (Suet.); see also SHIELD.

tariff, *formula.*

tarnish, *inquinare*; intransit., of metals, *inquinari*: to — one's honour, *nomini* or *decori officĕre.*

tarpaulin, render by phrase, such as *linteum pice munitum.*

Tarragona, *Tarraco.*

tarry, (*com*)*morari, cunctari, cessare, dubitare* (= to hesitate): without —ing, *sine morā, propere, festinanter.*

tart, subst. *scriblita* (Pl.), *crustulum* (Hor.).

tart, adj. *acerbus, amarus, acidus* (Verg., Hor., Sen.); see also SOUR.

tartly, *acerbe.*

tartness, *acerbitas.*

task, subst. *pensum* (lit. of women spinning wool), *opus* (-*ĕris*, n. = work), *negotium* (= business): to take to —; see REBUKE, CENSURE.

task, v. *pensum* (*homini*) *dare* or *imponĕre.*

task-master, *operis exactor.*

tassel, *fimbriae* (-*arum,* plur.; = fringe).

taste, subst. LIT., (**1**) = the sense of —, *gustatus* (-*ūs*), *palatum.* (**2**) = flavour of things tasted, *sapor, gustatus* (-*ūs*): a sweet —, *dulcedo.* (**3**) = a small quantity that is tasted, *gustus* (-*ūs*: Tac., Mart., Juv.). TRANSF., (**1**) = discernment, critical — in any field, *iudicium, intellegentia, palatum*; good —, *elegantia, iudicium elegans* or *subtile*; lack of —, *insulsitas.* (**2**) = a liking, preference, *gustatus* (-*ūs*), *studium.*

taste, v. (**1**) transit. (*de*)*gustare,* (*de*)*libare, gustu explorare* (Tac.): to — again, *regustare*; to — beforehand, *praegustare* (poet.). (**2**) intransit. *sapĕre*: to — like —, of, (*rem*) *sapĕre*; to — pleasant, *iucunde sapĕre.*

tasteful, = showing good taste or judgment, *elegans, politus, scitus, concinnus.*

tastefully, *polite, eleganter, scite.*

tasteless, LIT., *insulsus, sine sapore.* TRANSF., *inelegans, insulsus, infacetus.*

tastelessly, *ineleganter, insulse, infacete.*

tastelessness, *insulsitas.*

tatter, *pannus*; see also RAG.

tattered, *pannosus.*

tattle, v. *garrire.*

tattler, *homo garrulus.*

tattoo, v. *notis compungĕre.*

taunt, subst. *probrum, contumelia, convicium, opprobrium* (Hor., Ov.).

taunt, v. (*rem homini*) *obicĕre.*

taunting, *contumeliosus.*

tauntingly, *contumeliose.*

tautology, render by phrase such as *ĭdem bis dicĕre.*

tavern, *caupona, taberna.*

tavern-keeper, *caupo.*

tawdry, *fucosus*; see also VULGAR.

tawny, *fulvus* (poet.).

tax, subst., and **taxation,** *vectigal, tributum, stipendium, exactio*: to collect a —, *vectigal* (etc.) *exercēre* or *exigĕre*; to pay a —, *vectigal* (etc.) *pendĕre*; exempt from taxation, *immunis* (*tributorum*).

tax, v. (**1**) = to impose a tax, *vectigal, tributum,* etc., (*homini*) *imponĕre.* (**2**) to — a person with a thing (= to accuse), *hominem rei* (genit.) *incusare, insimulare, accusare* (more formally).

taxable, *vectigalis, stipendiarius.*

tax-collector, tax-gatherer, (*vectigalium*) *exactor.*

teach, (*hominem rem* or *facĕre*) (*e*)*docēre*; (*hominem re*) *instituĕre, instruĕre, imbuĕre, erudire*; (*homini rem* or *facĕre*) *praecipĕre*: to — thoroughly, *perdocēre*; to — as an assistant, *subdocēre*; to — the opposite of a thing, — not to do it, *dedocēre.*

teachable, *docilis, qui* (*quae*) *docēri potest.*

teachableness, *docilitas.*

teacher, *doctor, magister* (with f. *magistra*), *praeceptor* (with f. *praeceptrix*), *professor* (esp. of rhetoric: Quint.).

teaching, subst. *doctrina, disciplina, eruditio, institutio, praecepta* (-*orum,* plur.).

teacup, prov.: to make a storm in a —, *excitare fluctūs in simpulo.*

team, *iugum* (= a pair of horses or oxen), *protelum* (of oxen: Cato); of athletes, *manus* (-*ūs*).

tear, subst. *lacrima, fletus (-ūs* = weeping): a crocodile —, *lacrimula*; a flood of —s, *vis lacrimarum*; with —s in one's eyes, *lacrimis obortis*; to shed —s, *lacrimas effundĕre* or *profundĕre, lacrimare, flēre* (= to weep); to move a person to —s, *fletum homini movēre.*

tear, v. (1) transit. *(di)scindĕre, (di)laniare, (di)lacerare, (di)vellĕre, distrahĕre* (= to pull apart): to — away, *abscindĕre, avellĕre*; to — down, *rescindĕre, revellĕre*; to — out, *evellĕre, convellĕre*; fig., to be torn by conflicting emotions, etc., *distrahi*; to — a person to pieces (by malicious talk), *differre* (Prop., Tac.). (2) intransit.; see HURRY, RUSH.

tearful, *lacrimans, lacrimosus* (poet.), *flebilis, lacrimabundus.*

tearfully, *multis cum lacrimis, magno cum fletu.*

tearing, subst., or **tear,** subst. *scissura* (Sen., Plin.); see also RENT.

tearless, *sine lacrimis*; of eyes, *siccus.*

tease, *fatigare, vexare, obtundĕre.*

teasel, *dipsacus* or *dipsacos* (Plin.).

teat, *mamma, mamilla* (Juv.).

technical: a — term, *verbum artis proprium, vocabulum opificibus usitatum.*

technicality; see TECHNICAL.

technology, *ars, artificium.*

tedious, *lentus, longus, longinquus* (= longlasting), *molestus* (= tiresome).

tediously, *moleste, lente, cum taedio.*

tediousness, *molestia.*

teem, *scatēre*; see also ABOUND.

teeming; see FRUITFUL.

teethe, v. *dentire* (Plin.).

tell. (1) = to relate, give information, (*rem homini*) *(e)narrare, referre, (com)memorare, dicĕre, enumerare* (= to recount); (*hominem*) *docēre* (= to teach, inform). (2) = to command, (*hominem*) *iubēre*, (*homini*) *imperare.* (3) = to count, *numerare.* (4) intransit. = to have effect, *valēre.*

temerity, *temeritas.*

temper, subst. (1) = proportion, tempering of physical ingredients, *temperatio.* (2) = disposition of mind, *ingenium, animus*: to be in a good —, *iucunde esse*; bad —, *ira, iracundia, stomachus*; to be in a bad —, *sibi displicēre, stomachari.*

temper, v. *temperare, miscēre, lenire* (= to soften).

temperament; see TEMPER, DISPOSITION.

temperance, *temperantia, continentia, moderatio, modestia.*

temperate, *temperans, temperatus, continens, moderatus, modestus, sobrius, frugi.*

temperately, *temperate, continenter, moderate, modeste, sobrie, frugaliter.*

temperateness, *temperantia*: of climate, *temperies* (Hor.).

temperature, with reference to heat and cold, render by *calor* and *frigus*: moderate —, *temperies* (Hor.).

tempest, *tempestas, procella*: a — arises, *tempestas* (or *procella*), (*co*)*oritur.*

tempestuous, *procellosus, turbidus, turbulentus, violentus, vehemens.*

tempestuously, *turbide, turbulente, violenter, vehementer.*

tempestuousness, *violentia.*

temple. (1) of a god, *aedes* (*sacra*), *templum, fanum, delubrum*: a small —, *aedicula*; in poetry sometimes the name of a god stands

for his —. (2) of the head, *tempus (-oris,* n.: poet.).

temporal, = pertaining to this life, *humanus*: — welfare, *huius vitae felicitas*; as opposed to 'spiritual' or 'sacred', *profanus* (opp. *sacer*); as grammat. t. t., the — augment, *augmentum temporale.*

temporarily, temporary, render by the phrase *ad* or *in tempus* (= for the time being).

temporize, *temporibus servire*; see also DELAY.

tempt, (*at*)*temptare, sollicitare, inducĕre, invitare, inlicĕre.*

temptation. (1) as an act done, *sollicitatio.* (2) as a danger encountered, *inlecebra, temptatio* (eccl.).

tempter, *sollicitator* (Sen.), *temptator* (eccl.).

ten, *decem*: — each, — at a time, *deni*; — times, *decie(n)s*; containing —, *denarius*; the number —, *decussis* (Vitr.); a board of —, *decemviri* (plur.).

tenable, render by phrase, such as *quod tenēri potest.*

tenacious, *tenax, pertinax, retinens* (with genit.).

tenaciously, *tenaciter.*

tenacity, *tenacitas, pertinacia.*

tenancy, render by phrase with *condicio* (= terms).

tenant, *conductor, inquilinus, incola, habitator.*

tenantry, use plur. of TENANT, or sometimes *clientes* (*-um*, plur.).

tend. (1) transit. *colĕre, curare.* (2) intransit. *pertinēre, spectare, tendĕre.*

tendency, *inclinatio, proclivitas*; often rendered by adj., such as *pronus* or *propensus* (= inclined).

tender, adj. *tener, mollis, delicatus, amans* (= affectionate), *indulgens* (= kind, fond).

tender, v. *deferre*; see also OFFER.

tenderly, *molliter, indulgenter.*

tenderness. (1) = softness, *mollitia* or *mollities.* (2) = kindness, affection, *indulgentia, amor.*

tendon, *nervus.*

tendril, *clavicula, pampinus.*

tenement; see HOUSE.

tenet, *praeceptum, decretum, institutum, placitum* (Tac., Sen.).

tennis, render by *pila* (= a game of ball).

tenor, tenour. (1) = unbroken course, *tenor.* (2) = drift, purport, *exemplum, sententia*; see also MEANING.

tense, subst. *tempus (-oris,* n.: gram.).

tense, adj. *intentus, attentus.*

tension, *intentio.*

tent, *tabernaculum, contubernium, tentorium* (poet.): a general's —, *praetorium.*

tentacle, *corniculum* (Plin.), *bracchium* (Plin.), *flagellum* (Ov.).

tentative, render by phrase with *experiri* or *temptare.*

tenterhooks; see SUSPENSE.

tenth, *decimus.*

tenuity, *raritas*; see also THINNESS.

tenure, render by *possessio* or *possidēre.*

tepid, *tepidus* (poet.), *tepens* (poet.): to become —, *tepescĕre*; to be —, *tepēre* (poet.); to make —, *tepefacĕre.*

tepidity, *tepor.*

tergiversation, *tergiversatio.*

term, subst. (1) see LIMIT, BOUNDARY. (2) = a limited time, *spatium* (*temporis*), *dies.*

(3) = word, *verbum, vocabulum.* (4) = condition, *condicio, lex*: to be on good —s with a person, *homine familiariter uti.*

term, v.; see CALL, NAME.

termagant, render by phrase, such as *mulier iurgiis addicta.*

terminal, adj., render by phrase, such as *quod certis diebus fit.*

terminate. (1) transit.; see END. (2) intransit. *finiri, terminari*; see also END.

termination, *finis, exitus (-ūs), clausula.*

terminology, *(propria) artis vocabula (-orum,* plur.).

terrace, render by *solarium* (Pl., Suet.) or *ambulatio* (= a place for walking).

terrestrial, *terrestris, terrenus, humanus* (= human).

terrible, *terribilis, terrificus* (poet.), *horribilis, horrendus* (poet.), *atrox, immanis, dirus.*

terribly, *terribilem in modum, atrociter.*

terrific; see DREADFUL, TERRIBLE.

terrify, *(per)terrēre*; see also FRIGHTEN.

territorial, render by subst.; see TERRITORY.

territory, *fines* (lit. = boundaries), *ager, regio, terra, tractus (-ūs)*: the — round a town, *territorium*; the — of a people is often represented by the name of the people, e.g. the — of the Sabines, *Sabini (-orum,* plur.).

terror, *terror, formido, metus (-ūs), pavor, timor.*

terse, *pressus, brevis, angustus, densus* (Quint.), *strictus* (Quint.).

tersely, *presse, breviter, anguste, paucis verbis.*

terseness, *brevitas,* or render by phrase, such as *oratio pressa.*

tertian, *(febris) tertiana.*

tessellated, *tessellatus* (Suet.).

test, subst.; see TRIAL, EXAMINATION.

test, v. *temptare, experiri, periclitari, explorare, spectare.*

testaceous, *testaceus* (Plin.).

testament. (1) (= will), *testamentum.* (2) in the Bible: the New —, *Testamentum Novum* (eccl.), the Old —, *Testamentum Vetus* (eccl.).

testamentary, *testamento institutus, testamentarius.*

testator, *testator* (leg.), or *is qui testamentum facit.*

testatrix, *testatrix* (leg.).

testify, *testari, testificari, testimonio confirmare, declarare* (= to show, in gen.).

testifying, subst. *testificatio.*

testimonial, perhaps render by *litterae commendaticiae* (= letters of recommendation).

testimony, *testimonium.*

testy, *morosus.*

tether; see TIE.

tetrameter, *tetrametrus* (very late).

tetrarch, *tetrarcha.*

tetrarchy, *tetrarchia.*

text, *oratio, verba (-orum,* plur.), *locus* (= passage).

textile, subst. *textile, textum* (Ov.).

textile, adj. *textilis.*

textual, render by phrase, such as *quod ad verba scriptoris pertinet.*

texture, *textura* (poet.), *textus (-ūs*: poet.).

Thames, *Tamesis* or *Tamesa.*

than, after a comparative is usually rendered by the conjunction *quam* (rarely *ac, atque*), or by the abl. case (e.g. virtue is more

excellent than gold, *virtus est praestantior quam aurum* or *praestantior auro*). But before a numeral *amplius, plus, minus* and *longius* are often used alone, with the force of *amplius quam, plus quam,* etc. (e.g. more than two hundred soldiers, *amplius ducenti milites*).

thane, *dominus.*

thank, v. = to express thanks, *gratias* or *grates (homini pro re* or *ob rem) agĕre,* also *gratias* or *grates persolvĕre, reddĕre, tribuĕre*; = to feel gratitude, *gratiam (homini) habēre*; = to show gratitude (by acts, etc.), *gratiam referre*:—you! (in accepting), and No,—you! (in declining) are both rendered by *benigne (dicis)*; to have to — (i.e. to be indebted to) a person for a thing, *rem homini acceptam referre*; — heaven, *est dis gratia* (Ter.).

thankful, *gratus.*

thankfully, *grate, grato animo.*

thankfulness, *animus gratus.*

thankless, adj. *ingratus* (= both ungrateful and bringing no thanks).

thanklessly, *ingrate.*

thanks, as subst. *gratia* or plur. *gratiae* (esp. with *agĕre), grates*: to return or express —; see THANK, v.; — to you, *propter te, tuā operā, beneficio tuo.*

thanksgiving, *gratiarum actio*: a public —, *supplicatio, supplicium.*

thankworthy, *laudabilis, gratiā* or *laude dignus, gratus.*

that, demonstr. pron. *ille, illa, illud,* or *is, ea, id,* or *iste, ista, istud*: and — (too), amplifying a previous statement, is rendered by *et is* or *isque* or *atque is* (is agreeing with the subst. that is to be further described, e.g. in a house, and — a small one, *in domo, et ea parva,* or being made neuter if no particular subst. is concerned, e.g. he replied, and — at length, *respondit idque multis verbis*); —famous, — great, *ille, illa, illud*; — of yours, — near you, *iste, ista, istud* (often also used contemptuously); those, followed by a relative clause or a participle, is rendered by *ii* (or *ei) qui,* or *illi qui* (e.g. those who die, or those dying, *ii qui moriuntur*); where the English avoids repetition of a substantive by means of the phrase — of (or those of), the Latin either repeats the subst. or understands it, e.g. does the moon shine by its own light or by — of the sun? *utrum luna suo lumine an solis (lumine) utitur?* The neuter of *is* is used in the internal acc. in some phrases, e.g. of — age, *id aetatis*; at — time, *id temporis.*

that, relat. pron. *qui, quae, quod*; see also WHICH, WHO.

that, conj. (1) in 'indirect statement'; clauses beginning with —, when dependent on verbs of learning, thinking, knowing, saying, etc., are rendered by the acc. and infin. (e.g. I say — you are wrong, *dico te errare*); to say — not, *negare,* with acc. and infin.; but in negative or interrogative sentences 'to doubt —' is *dubitare quin,* with subj. (2) in 'indirect command'; clauses beginning with —, when dependent on verbs of commanding, asking, advising, etc., are rendered by *ut* (negative *ne*) with subj.; but *iubēre* (= to command —) and *vetare* (= to forbid, or command — not) are followed by acc. and infin., and so are other such verbs occasionally, esp. in poetry.

(3) after verbs of fearing, — (= lest) is rendered by *ne* followed by subj.; — not, by *ne non* or *ut*; e.g. I fear — you may (or will) make a mistake, *timeo ne erres*. (4) in final clauses, —, or in order —, or so —, followed by English subjunctive, is rendered by *ut* (negative *ne*, sometimes *ut ne*) followed by subj.; sometimes also by a relative clause with subj.; — the more . . . (with compar. adj. or adv. in final clause), *quo magis, quo maior*, etc.; and — not, *neve* or *neu*. (5) in consecutive clauses, —, or so —, followed by English indicative is rendered by *ut* (negative *ut non*) followed by subj. (6) other restrictive or explanatory clauses, beginning with —, are rendered by various constructions; e.g. to wish —, *velle, optare*, etc., followed by acc. and infin., or *ut* and subj., or plain subj.; to wonder —, *mirari*, followed by acc. and infin. or *quod* or (more hypothetically) *si* (so also to rejoice —, *gaudēre* or *laetari*); it is necessary —, *necesse est*, with acc. and infin. or subj.; it is possible —, *fieri potest ut*; it is inevitable —, *non potest fieri quin*; on condition —, *ea condicione ut* or *ita ut*; granted —, *ut* or *licet*, with subj.; the fact —, *quod*, with indic.; not —, *non quod* or *non quo*, with subj. (7) in main clauses, O —, expressing a wish, is rendered by *o si* or *utinam*, with subj. (8) exclamations, beginning with —, are rendered by the acc. and infin. (sometimes with *-ne* attached to the first word); e.g. alas! — you should have got into so much trouble on my account! *me miserum! te in tantas aerumnas propter me incidisse!*

thatch, *stramentum.*

thatched: a — cottage, *casa stramento tecta* or *casa straminea* (Ov.).

thaw, subst., render by verb.

thaw, v. (1) transit. (*dis*)*solvĕre, liquefacĕre.* (2) intransit. (*dis*)*solvi, liquefiĕri, liquescĕre, tabescĕre.*

the, no regular equivalent in Latin; sometimes rendered by the demonstr. pron. *is, ea, id,* esp. as part of the antecedent of a relative clause; — famous, *ille, illa, illud;* —, preceding a comparative (e.g. more, better, more happily) is rendered by *eo* (or *tanto*) if demonstrative, by *quo* (or *quanto*) if relative, e.g. — more people have, — more they want, *homines quo plura habent, eo ampliora cupiunt;* but sometimes in such sentences superlatives are used, with *ut* and *ita,* e.g. — better a man is, — harder he finds it to suspect wickedness in others, *ut quisque est vir optimus, ita difficillime alios improbos suspicatur.*

theatre, *theatrum, scaena* (= stage), *spectaculum* (= show).

theatrical, *scaenicus, theatralis;* or render by the genit. *histrionum* (= of actors), e.g. — gestures, *histrionum gestūs.*

theatrically, *more histrionum.*

theft, *furtum.*

their, theirs, *suus,* if reflexive (= — own); otherwise *eorum* or *illorum* (if the owners are female, *earum* or *illarum*).

them, render by the oblique cases of the plur. of *is, ea, id* or of *ille, illa, illud;* but — is often not rendered, when the context makes it clear who is intended.

theme, *res, propositio, propositum, id quod propositum est, quaestio, id quod quaerimus, institutum, argumentum.*

themselves, *se* or *sese;* see also SELF.

then. (1) as adv. of time: at that time, *tum, tunc, eo tempore, id temporis;* thereupon, *tum, deinde, inde;* — and there, *ilico.* (2) of logical connexion = therefore, *ergo, igitur.*

thence, *inde, illinc, istinc, abhinc* (= from where you are).

thenceforth, adv. *inde, ex eo tempore.*

theocracy, render by phrase such as *regnum deorum.*

theogony, render by phrase such as *origines* (-*um,* plur.) *deorum.*

theologian, *theologus.*

theological, *theologicus* (eccl.); see also THEOLOGY.

theology, *theologia* (eccl.); otherwise render by phrase, such as *sententiae* (-*arum,* plur.) *de deorum natura habitae.*

theorem, *theorema* (Gell.).

theoretical, render by phrase, such as *quod in cognitione versatur:* — knowledge, *ratio* or *doctrina;* to possess — knowledge of a thing, *rem ratione cognitam habēre.*

theoretically, render by subst.; see THEORY.

theorist, render by phrase, such as *qui res ratione (non usu) cognitas habet.*

theory, *ratio, doctrina, ars, scientia:* to combine — and practice, *doctrinam ad usum adiungĕre.*

therapeutic, therapeutics; see HEALING.

there, = at that place, *ibi, illic, istic* (= where you are): to be —, *adesse;* to stand —, *adstare;* — is, *est;* — are, *sunt;* = to that place, *eo, illuc;* see also THITHER.

thereabouts, *prope* (= near), *ferme* or *fere* (= nearly).

thereafter, thereupon, *inde, deinde, subinde, exinde, postea* (= afterwards, more generally).

therefore, *igitur, ergo, itaque* (= and so), *ideo* or *idcirco* or *propterea* (= for that reason), *proin(de)* (esp. introducing a command), *eo* (esp. with comparatives), *quare* or *quamobrem* or *quapropter* (= wherefore).

therein, *in eo, in ea re.*

thesis; see THEME.

they, often not rendered in Latin, when the subject of the verb is easily supplied; when emphatic, it is rendered by the nom. plur. of *is, ea, id* or of *ille, illa, illud.*

thick. (1) = stout, having thickness, of solid objects, *crassus, pinguis* (= fat), *callosus* (Hor.). (2) = closely packed, dense, *densus, artus, spissus* (poet.), *confertus, concretus, creber, frequens* (= numerous). (3) of the voice, *obtusus* (Quint.). (4) in the — of, render by *medius,* e.g. in the — of the fight, *in media pugna.*

thicken, v. (1) transit. *densare, spissare* (Ov., Plin.). (2) intransit. render by pass. of transit. verbs or by *concrescĕre* (= to curdle) or *spissescĕre* (Lucr.).

thicket, *dumetum, fruticetum* (Hor.), *locus sentibus obsitus.*

thickly, *confertim, crebro, frequenter, spisse* (Plin.).

thickness, *crassitudo, crebritas, frequentia.*

thick-set, *robustus, compactus* (Plin., Suet.); see also STOUT.

thick-skinned

thick-skinned, *durus*: to become —, *ob-durescĕre, occallescĕre*.
thief, *fur*; in a candle, *fungus* (Verg.).
thieve, *furari*; see also STEAL.
thievish, *furax, tagax*.
thievishly, *furaciter*.
thigh, *femur*.
thin, adj. (1) = slim, *tenuis, gracilis, exilis, macer, subtilis* (Lucr.). (2) = rare, not dense, *tenuis, rarus*.
thin, v. *attenuare, extenuare*; of trees, *conlucare* (Cato, Col.), *interlucare* (Plin.).
thine, *tuus*.
thing. (1) in gen., *res, negotium* (= business, affair); very often rendered simply by the neuter of an adj. or pron. (e.g. all —s, every—, *omnia*). (2) —s, plur., in the particular sense of clothes, *vestis, vestitus (-ūs)*; of personal effects, property, luggage, *res* (plur.), *supellex, vasa (-orum*, plur.).
think. (1) in gen. = to have ideas, to reflect, *cogitare*. (2) to think a particular thought, to believe, suppose, *opinari, credĕre, putare, arbitrari* (= to hold a well-considered opinion), *reri* (= to reckon, calculate), *iudicare* (= to judge), *censēre* (= to hold and express an opinion), *sentire* (= to hold views, more generally, esp. with adv. or neuter adj.). (3) to — over, — about, *(rem) reputare, versare* (poet.), *agitare, (rem* or *de re) cogitare.* (4) to — to do, — of doing, *cogitare, meditari*; see also INTEND.
thinker, in gen., render by verb; a speculative or philosophical —, *philosophus*.
thinly, *tenuiter, graciliter, rare*.
thinness, *tenuitas, gracilitas, raritas* (= looseness of texture), *macies* (= leanness); — of voice or style, *exilitas*.
third, *tertius*: for the — time, *tertium*, or *tertio*; a —, *tertia pars, triens*.
thirdly, *tertio*.
thirst, subst. *sitis* (lit. and fig.): to slake one's —, *sitim explēre* or *sedare*.
thirst, v. *sitire*.
thirstily, *sitienter*.
thirsty, *sitiens, siccus* (= dry): to become —, *sitim conligĕre*.
thirteen, *tredecim, decem et tres*: — each, or — at a time, *terni deni*; *terdecie(n)s*.
thirteenth, *tertius decimus*.
thirtieth, *trigesimus* or *trice(n)simus*.
thirty, *triginta*: — each, or — at a time, *triceni*; — times, *tricie(n)s*.
this, demonstr. pron. *hic, haec, hoc*, sometimes *hicce, haecce, hocce*: — way and that, *huc (et) illuc*; on — side, adv., *citra*; on — side of, prep., *cis, citra*; of — year, *hornus* (Hor.); of — kind, *huiusmodi*.
thistle, *carduus* (Verg.).
thither, *eo, illuc, istuc* (= to where you are): hither and —, *huc (et) illuc, huc atque illuc*.
thole-pin, *scalmus*.
thong, *lorum*; see also STRAP.
thorn, *sentis, spina* (Lucr., Verg., Tac.): fig., a — in one's side, *stimulus*.
thorn-brake, thorn-hedge, *vepres (-um*, plur.), *dumetum, spinetum* (Verg.), *senticetum* (Pl.).
thorn-bush, *vepres, dumus, sentis*.
thorny. LIT., *spinosus, spineus* (poet.), *sentus* (poet.). TRANSF., *arduus, difficilis, impeditus*.
thorough; see COMPLETE.
thoroughbred, *generosus*.

threateningly

thoroughfare, abstr. = a going through, *transitus (-ūs)*; concr. = a road through, *iter (pervium), via (pervia)*.
thoroughly, *penitus, prorsus, omnino, plane, funditus*; see also COMPLETELY.
thou, pron., often not rendered in Latin, when the context makes the personal reference clear; otherwise represented by *tu* or (more emphatic) *tute* or *tutemet*.
though; see ALTHOUGH.
thought, *cogitatio* (= — as faculty, process or particular idea), *mens* (= —s, general or particular), *cogitatum* (= a reflection, idea), *memoria* (= memory), *sententia* (= opinion), *mens, animus* (= mind), *opinio* (= supposition or conjecture), *consilium* (= view, plan), *coniectura* (= conjecture); often also —s may be rendered by a phrase, such as *quae mente concipimus, quae (animo) cogitamus, sentimus, versamus*: to be deep in —, *in cogitatione defixum esse*.
thoughtful, *in cogitatione defixus* (= lost in thought), *prudens* (= wise, sensible), *providus* (= farsighted).
thoughtfully, *prudenter*.
thoughtfulness; see THOUGHT.
thoughtless, *inconsultus, neglegens, imprudens, temerarius* (= rash).
thoughtlessly, *inconsulte, neglegenter, imprudenter, temere*.
thoughtlessness, *neglegentia, temeritas* (= rashness).
thousand. LIT., as an exact number, one — is usually rendered by means of *mille* as an indeclinable adj. (or subst.), two or more —(s) by *milia* (or *millia*) as a declinable subst.; a — times, *millie(n)s*. TRANSF., as an indefinitely large number, a — is represented by *mille* or by *sescenti* (lit. = 600), a — times by *millie(n)s*.
thousandth, *mille(n)simus*.
Thrace, *Thracia*.
thraldom, *servitūs (-ūtis)*; see also SLAVERY, SERVITUDE.
thrash: to — (or thresh) corn, *terĕre* (Varro), *deterĕre* (Col.), *excutĕre* (Varro); in gen.; see BEAT, FLOG.
thrashing, threshing, *tritura* (Verg.).
thrashing-floor, threshing-floor, *area*.
thrashing-machine, *tribulum* (Verg.).
thread, subst. LIT., *filum* (poet.), *linea, linum, licium* (poet.), *subtemen* (poet.), *stamen* (poet.); prov.: to hang by a —, *filo pendēre* (Ov.). TRANSF., of a speech, etc., *filum, argumentum*.
thread, v. *inserĕre*: to — a needle, *filum per acum conicere* (Cels.); to — one's way, *se insinuare*.
threadbare, *obsoletus, tritus* (lit. and fig.).
threat, *minae (-arum*, plur.), *(com)minatio, denuntiatio*.
threaten. LIT., to — a person with a thing, *rem homini minitari, (com)minari, denuntiare, intentare*; to — to do a thing, — that one will, *minari*, etc., *se facturum esse*. TRANSF., (1) of wars, etc. = to impend, *(im)minēre, impendēre, instare, ingruĕre* (poet. and Tac.). (2) to —, i.e. to seem likely to do a thing, render by *videri* with fut. infin. or by fut. partic. with *esse*.
threatening, *minax, minitabundus*; = impending, near at hand, *instans, imminens*.
threateningly, *minaciter*.

[852]

three, *tres*: — :imes, *ter*; — each, or — at a time, *trini* or *terni* (also used for —, with subst. of plural form, e.g. — camps, *trina castra*); in — parts, adj. *tripertitus* or *tripartitus*; into — parts, *trifarium, tripertito* or *tripartito*; in — forms or shapes, adj. *triformis* (poet.); a period of — days, *triduum*; a period of — years, *triennium*; — years old, *trimus* (Pl., Hor.).

threefold, *triplus, triplex.*

three-footed, *tripes* (Hor.).

three-headed, *triceps.*

three hundred, *trecenti*: — each, or — at a time, *treceni*; — times, *trecentie(n)s* (Cat.).

three hundredth, *trecente(n)simus.*

three-pronged, *tridens* (poet.), *tricuspis* (Ov.).

three-tongued, *trilinguis* (Hor.).

thresh; see THRASH.

threshold, *limen* (lit. and fig.).

thrice, *ter*: twice or —, *bis terque.*

thrift, *frugalitas, parsimonia.*

thriftily, *frugaliter, parce.*

thrifty, *frugi, parcus.*

thrill, subst. of pleasure, *voluptas, gaudium, laetitia*; of fear, *horror.*

thrill, v. (1) transit. *commovēre*: to be —ed, i.e. overjoyed, *laetitiā efferri, exsultare.* (2) intransit., of sounds, *resonare.*

thrilling, = exciting, *mirificus, mirus*; or render by verb.

thrive, *vigēre, virēre, florēre.*

throat, *fauces* (-*ium*, plur.), *iugulum, guttur*: to cut the — of, *iugulare.*

throb, subst. *palpitatio* (Plin.); or render by verb.

throb, v. *salire, palpitare, micare.*

throe, *dolor.*

throne. LIT., as a seat, (*regale*) *solium, sedes* (or *sella*) *regia.* TRANSF., = royal power, *regnum, imperium*: to be on the —, *regem esse, regnare*; to seize the —, *regnum occupare*; to succeed to the —, *regnum excipēre*; to succeed one's father on the —, *patri in regnum succedēre*; to call to the —, *ad regnum accire*; to drive from the —, *regno expellēre* or *spoliare*; to restore to the —, *in regnum restituēre.*

throng, subst. *multitudo, celebritas, frequentia*; see also CROWD.

throng, v. *celebrare, stipare, frequentare*; see also CROWD.

throstle, *turdus* (Hor.).

throttle, subst. *gurgulio.*

throttle, v. *suffocare, animam* or *spiritum intercludēre.*

through, prep. (1) of place or time, *per*, with acc. (2) as denoting instrument or means, *per* with acc. or simple abl. (3) = on account of, *propter*, or *ob*, with acc.

through, adv., render by compound verb with *trans-* or *per-* (e.g. to go —, *transire*; to read —, *perlegēre*): — and —, *penitus, prorsus, omnino.*

throughout; see THROUGH.

throw, throwing, subst. *iactus* (-*ūs*), *coniectus* (-*ūs*): a —, at dice, *alea.*

throw, v. *iacēre, conicēre, mittere* (esp. of weapons): to — a thing at a person, *re hominem petēre*; to — a javelin, *iaculari*; to — about, *iactare, spargēre* (= to sprinkle); to — across, *traicēre*; to — away, *abicēre*; to — back, *reicēre*; to — down, *deicēre, praecipitare, deturbare, proruēre, adfligēre*;

to — forward, *proicēre*; to — in, *inicēre, immittēre*; to — in the way, *obicēre*; to — on, *inicēre*; to — oneself at a person's feet, *homini ad pedes se proicēre*; to — oneself into, (*rei*, dat.) *se dedēre, studēre, incumbēre*; to — off, *excutēre*; to — open, *patefacēre*; to — out, *eicēre*; to — up, *subicēre.*

thrower, *iaculator* (Hor.).

thrum, in weaving, *licium* (Verg.).

thrust, subst. *petitio, ictus* (-*ūs* = blow); see also ATTACK, PUSH.

thrust, v. *trudēre*; see also PUSH, DRIVE.

thumb, (*digitus*) *pollex.*

thump, subst. *colaphus* (Pl., Quint.).

thump, v. (*con*)*tundēre.*

thunder, subst. *tonitrus* (-*ūs*), *fragor* (= a crashing noise); in gen. = any noise, clamour, *sonitus* (-*ūs*).

thunder, v. (*in*)*tonare* (impers. and also of persons, transit. and intransit.).

thunder-bolt, *fulmen*: struck by a —, *de caelo tactus.*

thunder-storm, *tonitrua et fulmina, tempestas cum tonitribus.*

thunder-struck, *attonitus, obstupefactus.*

thus, *ita, sic*; see also SO.

thwart, subst. *transtrum.*

thwart, v.; see HINDER, PREVENT.

thy, *tuus.*

thyme, *thymum* (poet.).

tiara, *tiara* (poet.).

Tiber, river, *Tiberis.*

ticket, *tessera* (Suet.).

tickle, *titillare.*

tickling, subst. *titillatio.*

ticklish. LIT., render by phrase, such as *titillationis minime patiens.* TRANSF., = hard to handle, awkward, *lubricus, difficilis.*

tidal, render by phrase, such as *quod ad aestum pertinet*: — wave, *unda* (*aestu facta*).

tide, (*marinus* or *maritimus*) *aestus* (-*ūs*): the ebb and flow of the —s, *marinorum aestuum accessus et recessus* (both -*ūs*); to come in, of the —, *accedēre, se incitare* (*ex alto*); to go out, *recedēre, minuēre*; the turn of the —, *commutatio aestūs.*

tidily, *munde* (Pl.).

tidiness, *munditia.*

tidings, *nuntius*; see also NEWS.

tidy, *mundus*; see also NEAT.

tie, subst. LIT., *vinculum, nodus.* TRANSF., of friendship, etc., *vinculum, nodus, coniunctio, necessitudo.*

tie, v.; see BIND: to — a knot, *nodum facēre.*

tier, *ordo*; see also ROW.

tiger, *tigris* (poet.).

tight, *strictus, a(d)strictus, angustus, artus*: a — rope, *funis contentus* (Hor.).

tighten, v. *stringēre, a(d)stringēre, intendēre, contendēre, adducēre.*

tightly, tightness, render by adj. or verb.

tile, *tegula, testa*: a pan —, *imbrex.*

till, subst., for money, *arca.*

till, prep. (*usque*) *ad*, with acc.: — now, *hactenus*; — when? *quo usque? quem ad finem?* then and not — then, *tum demum*; — late at night, *ad multam noctem*; — daylight, *ad lucem.*

till, conj. *dum, donec, quoad* (all with indic., unless purpose or expectation is implied, when the subj. is used); not . . . —, is sometimes rendered by *non prius* (or *ante*) *quam.*

till, v. *colĕre, arare* (= to plough).

tillage, *cultus (-ŭs), cultura.*

tiller. (1) the person, *agricola, (agri)cultor.* (2) the thing, *(gubernaculi) clavus* (Verg.).

tilt, v. (1) transit. *(in)vertĕre.* (2) intransit. *(hastis) ex equis pugnare.*

timber, *materia* or *materies*: to get —, *materiari.*

time, subst. (1) in gen. *tempus (-ŏris,* n.), *dies* (= day, appointed —; sometimes more generally), *aevum* (poet.), *tempestas* (archaic), *spatium* (= space of —), *intervallum* (= interval), *saeculum* (= generation, age, the —s), *otium* (= leisure), *occasio* (= opportunity): — of life, *aetas;* to spend —, *tempus ducĕre, degĕre;* to waste —, *tempus terĕre, perdĕre;* for a —, *ad* or *in tempus;* for all —, *in omne tempus;* at the right —, on —, *ad tempus, (in) tempore, tempori, temperi, tempestive, mature, opportune;* in our —, *nostrā memoriā;* in ancient —s, *antiquis temporibus, antiquitus;* from the — when, *ex quo (tempore);* at —s, from — to —, *interdum, nonnunquam;* in the mean—, *interea, interim;* at the same —, *simul, eodem tempore;* at another —, *alias;* once upon a —, *olim;* it is (high) — to go, *tempus (maximum) est ut eamus.* (2) — of day, *hora.* (3) — in music, *tempus, numerus;* to beat —, *manu intervalla signare;* in —, *numerose, ad numerum;* out of —, *extra numerum.* (4) in multiplication or repetition, three, four —s, etc., render by the numeral adverbs, *ter, quater,* etc.

time, v., render by phrase, such as *tempus observare.*

timely, adj. *maturus, tempestivus, opportunus.*

timely, adv. *ad tempus, mature, tempestive, opportune.*

timepiece; see CLOCK.

time-server, *adulator, adsentator* (= flatterer); or render by adj. such as *levis, inconstans* (= fickle).

timid, *timidus, pavidus, trepidus, verecundus* (= bashful), *ignavus* (= cowardly).

timidity, *timiditas, verecundia* (= shyness); see also FEAR.

timidly, *timide, pavide.*

timorous; see TIMID.

tin, *plumbum album, stannum* (Plin.).

tincture, *color.*

tinder, *fomes* (Verg., Luc.).

tinge, *color.*

tinge, v. *imbuĕre, colorare, inficĕre, tingĕre.*

tingle; see ITCH.

tinker, render by phrase, such as *a(h)enorum refector.*

tinkle, v. *tinnire.*

tinkling, subst. *tinnitus (-ŭs:* poet.).

tinkling, adj. *tinnulus* (poet.).

tinsel, = metal leaf, *bractea* (poet.).

tip, subst. *cacumen, apex* (poet.); often rendered by the adj. *extremus* (e.g. the —s of the fingers, *extremi digiti).*

tip, v. (1) of weapons = to head, point, *praefigĕre.* (2) to — up, — over, *(in)vertĕre, inclinare.*

tipple, *(per)potare.*

tippler, *potator* (Pl.), *potor* (Hor., Prop.).

tippling, subst. *(per)potatio.*

tipsily, render by adj.

tipsy, *temulentus, ebrius.*

tiptoe, on, *suspenso gradu*: to rise on —, *in*

digitos erigi (Quint.); see also EXPECTATION, SUSPENSE.

tire, v. (1) transit. *(de)fatigare.* (2) intransit. *(de)fatigari.*

tired, *(de)fessus, fatigatus, lassus* (poet.): to be — of, render by the impers. *taedet,* e.g. I am — of saying, *taedet me dicĕre;* I am — of words, *taedet me verborum.*

tiresome, tiring, *importunus, molestus, laboriosus* (of things only).

tiro, *tiro, rudis et tiro.*

tissue, LIT., see TEXTURE. TRANSF., the thing is a — of falsehoods, *tota res e mendaciis constat.*

tit-bits, *cuppedia (-orum,* plur.), *scitamenta (-orum,* plur.).

tit for tat, render by the phrase *paria paribus respondēre* (= to return like for like).

tithe, *decuma, decima pars.*

title, *titulus, inscriptio* or *index* (= — of a book), *nomen* or *appellatio* (= name), *praescriptio* (= heading, preamble), *vindiciae (-arum,* plur.; = right): to give a book a —, *inscribĕre librum;* to give any person a —, *hominem appellare* with acc. of the title (e.g. *regem*).

title, *minima pars.*

titled, *nobilis.*

titter, v.; see LAUGH.

tittle-tattle, *sermunculus;* see CHATTER, GOSSIP.

titular, render by *nomine,* opp. to *re.*

Tivoli, *Tibur.*

to. (1) — is most commonly rendered by the Latin dative case, in one of its various uses; e.g. with verbs, such as to give, say, show, recommend — a person, *homini dare, dicĕre, ostendĕre, suadēre;* or with adjectives, such as equal, similar, agreeable, useful — a person, *homini aequus, similis, gratus, utilis.* (2) motion —, is rendered by *ad* with acc. (except that the acc. of *domus* and *rus* and of the names of towns or small islands is generally used without *ad* in this sense). *Ad* is also used of several relations analogous to motion towards, such as reference — or tendency —; e.g. death is nothing — us, *nil mors est ad nos;* — the purpose, *ad rem;* — extreme old age, *ad summam senectutem;* — a man, *ad unum;* to be beaten — death, *ad necem caedi.* (3) *in,* with acc., is used of motion —, as well as of motion into; also of analogous relations; e.g. — a late hour, *in multum diei;* — that effect, *in eam sententiam.* (4) —, = towards, of personal relationships, is rendered by dat., or by *erga* with acc., or by *in* with acc. (sometimes abl.). (5) —, = in comparison with, is rendered by *prae,* with abl. (6) —, before a verb, forming the English infinitive, is rendered in various ways; as subject or object of a verb, by the Latin infin. (e.g. — err is human, *humanum est errare;* I want — go, *volo ire);* often by oblique cases of the gerund (e.g. a desire — live, *studium vivendi);* expressing a purpose, by a final clause (usually with *ut* and subj.); in indirect command, usually by *ut* and subj. (except with *iubēre* and *vetare);* worthy —, *dignus qui,* with subj.; about —, followed by verb, is rendered by a future partic. (7) — and fro, *huc (et) illuc, huc atque illuc.*

toad, *bufo* (Verg.).

toadstool, *fungus* (Pl., Hor.).

toady; see FLATTER.

toast, v. = to scorch, *torrēre, frigēre* (Pl., Hor.); = to drink to a person's health, *homini propinare.*
today, subst. *hodiernus dies*: of —. adj., *hodiernus.*
today, adv. *hodie.*
toe, *(pedis) digitus.*
together, *unā, simul, coniunctim* or *communiter* (= jointly): all —, *omnes ad unum, cuncti, universi* (opp. *singuli*).
toil, subst. *labor, opera*; for —s = nets, see NET.
toil, v. *(e)laborare, sudare.*
toilet, *cultus (-ūs), ornatus (-ūs).*
toilsome, *laboriosus, operosus.*
token, *signum*; see also SIGN.
Toledo, *Toletum.*
tolerable. LIT., of what can be tolerated, *tolerabilis, tolerandus, patibilis.* TRANSF., = middling, *tolerabilis, mediocris, modicus.*
tolerably, *tolerabiliter, mediocriter, modice, satis* (= sufficiently).
tolerance, toleration, *tolerantia* or *toleratio* (= bearing of anything), *indulgentia, lenitas, facilitas* (= kindness, indulgence); see also TOLERATE.
tolerate, *tolerare, (aequo animo) ferre*; in religious matters, render by phrase, such as *aliena sacra permittēre*: to — a thing being done, *rem fieri pati, sinēre, permittēre.*
toll, subst. *vectigal, portorium.*
toll, v., render by *sonare.*
toll-collector, *exactor (portorii), portitor.*
tomb, *sepulcrum, tumulus* (lit. = mound).
tomb-stone, *lapis* (Tib.), *cippus* (Hor.), *monumentum.*
tome, *liber*; see also BOOK.
tomorrow, subst. *crastinus dies*: of —, adj. *crastinus.*
tomorrow, adv. *cras*: on the day after —, *perendie.*
ton, tun, as a vessel, *seria, dolium*; as a measure of liquids, perhaps render by *culleus* (= 115 gallons), the largest Roman liquid measure.
tone, *sonus, sonitus (-ūs), vox*; fig., see CHARACTER, MANNER.
tongs, *forceps* (Verg., Ov.).
tongue, *lingua* (in all senses of the English word), *ligula* (= neck of land), *examen* (of a balance: Verg.), *sermo* (= language).
tonic, *medicina.*
tonnage, expressed by numbers of *amphorae*, e.g. *navis plus quam trecentarum amphorarum* (1 *amphora* = about 1/40 of a ton).
tonsils, *tonsillae (-arum,* plur.).
too. (1) = also, *etiam, quoque, praeterea.* (2) = excessively; with adj. or adv., render by *nimis* or *nimium* or by the comparative of the adj. or adv. concerned: — stupid to know, *stultior quam qui sciat*; — small for the number of people, *minor quam pro numero hominum*; — much, *nimis* or *nimium*; — little, *parum*; — late, adj. *serus,* adv. *sero* or *serius.*
tool: an iron —, *ferramentum*; —s, plur., *instrumentum*; = a person, used as a —, *minister.*
tooth, *dens*: false teeth, *dentes empti* (Mart.)
toothache, *dolor dentium* (Cels.): to have —, *laborare (ex) dentibus.*
toothed, *dentatus* (Plin.).
toothless, *edentulus* (Pl.).

toothpick, *dentiscalpium* (Mart.).
toothpowder, *dentifricium* (Plin.).
toothsome, *dulcis.*
top, subst. (1) = summit, *cacumen, culmen*; or render by adj. *summus* (e.g. the — of the mountain, *summus mons*). (2) a child's —, *turbo* (Verg.).
top, adj. *summus.*
top, v. *(ex)superare.*
topaz, *topazos* (Plin.), *chrysolithos* (Ov., Plin.).
toper, *potator* (Pl.), *potor* (Hor.).
topic, *res.*
topical, perhaps *hodiernus* (= of today) or *hic* (= this present).
topography, *locorum descriptio.*
topsy-turvy: to turn everything —, *omnia turbare et miscēre.*
torch, *fax, taeda.*
torment, subst. *cruciatus (-ūs), tormentum* (usually plur.); see also TORTURE.
torment, v. *(ex)cruciare, torquēre, angēre, vexare, sollicitare, agitare.*
tormentor, *vexator*; or render by verb.
tornado, *turbo, tempestas.*
torpid, *torpens* (= numb), *lentus* or *iners* (= sluggish, inactive).
torpor, *torpor.*
torrent, *torrens.*
torrid, *torridus.*
tortoise, *testudo.*
tortoise-shell, *testudinis putamen* (Plin.), *testudinis testa* (Varro).
torture, subst. LIT., of pain deliberately inflicted, *tormentum* (usually plur.), *cruciatus (-ūs), carnificina.* TRANSF., *cruciatus (-ūs), tormentum, dolor, angor*; see also PAIN.
torture, v. *(ex)cruciare, (ex)torquēre*: to have a person —d, *homini tormenta admovēre, de homine tormentis quaerēre.*
torturer, *tortor, carnifex* (= executioner).
toss, tossing, subst. *iactus (-ūs), iactatio.*
toss, v. *iactare.*
total, subst. *summa, universitas.*
total, adj. *totus, cunctus, universus, omnis.*
totality; see TOTAL, subst.
totally, *omnino, plane, prorsus, funditus, penitus*; or render by adj. *totus.*
totter, v. *labare, vacillare, titubare, nutare.*
touch, subst. *(con)tactus (-ūs), tactio*: the finishing —, *manus ultima* or *extrema.*
touch, v. LIT., of physical contact, *tangēre, attingēre, contingēre* (all three also = to border upon, of countries, etc.): to — at, *navem appellere ad,* with acc. TRANSF., = to influence, affect, *tangēre, attingēre, (com)-movēre*; = to relate to, *pertinēre ad,* with acc.: to — (briefly) (up)on a subject, *rem (leviter, breviter* or *strictim) tangēre, attingēre, perstringēre.*
touching, render by phrase with *animum movēre* or *tangēre.*
touching, prep. *de,* with abl.; see also CONCERNING.
touchstone, *coticula* (Plin.); fig. *obrussa* (= test).
touchy, *mollis ad accipiendam offensionem* (Cic.), *inritabilis, iracundus.*
tough, *lentus, durus.*
toughness, *duritia.*
tour, *iter, peregrinatio, lustratio*: to make a — of, *peragrare, circumire, lustrare.*
tourist; see TRAVELLER.

tournament, render by phrase, such as *certamen equitum.*

tow, subst. *stuppa*: of —, adj. *stuppeus* (Verg., Ov.).

tow, v. *trahĕre.*

toward, towards, prep. (**1**) of physical movement, *adversus* with acc.; *versus* (adv., used after plain acc. of place-name, or after phrase with *in* or *ad* and acc.); *in* or *ad* alone with acc. (rare); *obviam*, with dat. (= so as to meet a person). (**2**) of time = near to, *ad* or *sub*, with acc. (**3**) of personal relations, *adversus, erga, in,* all with acc.; *contra* (= against); sometimes rendered simply by objective genit.

towel, *mantele* (Verg.).

tower, subst. *turris*: a — of strength, fig., *arx* or *praesidium.*

tower, v. *eminēre, exstare*: to — over, *imminēre,* with dat.

towering, *arduus*: fig., in a — rage, *iracundiā elatus, iratissimus.*

town, *urbs, oppidum, municipium* (esp. = a free — in Italy); of a —, adj., *urbanus.*

town-hall, *curia.*

townsman, *civis, oppidanus.*

towrope, *remulcum.*

toy; see PLAYTHING, PLAY.

trace, subst. (**1**) = track, indication, *vestigium, indicium, significatio.* (**2**) see STRAP.

trace, v. (**1**) = to draw, mark out, *designare, describĕre, adumbrare.* (**2**) = to follow up, track, find by indications, *(in)vestigare, odorari, indagare.*

tracing, subst. *investigatio, indagatio.*

track, subst.; see PATH and TRACE: to die in one's —s, *in suo vestigio mori.*

track, v.; see TRACE.

tracker, *investigator, indagator* (with f. *indagatrix*).

trackless, *avius, invius.*

tract, (**1**) (= region), *tractus (-ūs), regio.* (**2**) = treatise, *libellus.*

tractable, *tractabilis, docilis, facilis, flexibilis.*

tractableness, *docilitas, facilitas;* or render by adj.

trade, subst. (**1**) = commerce. in gen. *mercatura commercium, mercatus (-ūs*); often disparaging). (**2**) = a person's chosen occupation, *ars, artificium.*

trade, v. *mercaturam* or (of several) *mercaturas facĕre, (com)mercari, negotiari.*

trader, *mercator;* see also MERCHANT.

tradesman, *caupo.*

tradition, *memoria, litterae (-arum,* plur.; documentary), *fama* (oral): there is a —, — tells us, *tradunt, memoriae traditum* (or *proditum) est.*

traditional, render by phrase, such as (*a maioribus*), *posteris traditus* or *proditus.*

traduce; see SLANDER.

traducer, *obtrectator.*

traffic, (**1**) see COMMERCE and TRADE. (**2**) of people and vehicles, render by verb, such as *commeare* (= to pass to and fro).

tragedian, (**1**) = writer of tragedies, *tragicus.* (**2**) = tragic actor, *tragoedus, tragicus actor.*

tragedy, *tragoedia*: to perform a —, *tragoediam agĕre*; fig. *casus (-ūs).*

tragic, *tragicus, tristis* (= sad), *luctuosus* (= mournful), *miserabilis* (= wretched), *atrox* (= frightful).

tragically, *tragice, miserabiliter, atrociter.*

tragicomedy, *tragicomoedia* (Pl.).

train, subst. (**1**) a robe with a —, *syrma* (Juv.). (**2**) = procession, *pompa.* (**3**) in gen. = series, *ordo, series.*

train, v. (**1**) = to educate, *(e)docēre, instituĕre.* (**2**) = to exercise, drill, *exercēre*: thoroughly —ed, *exercitatus.*

trainer, in gen. *exercitor* (Pl.), *magister;* of horses, *equorum domitor;* of gladiators, *lanista.*

training, *disciplina, exercitatio.*

trait, *nota, proprietas, proprium;* sometimes render by genit. and *est* (e.g. = it is the — of a wise man, *sapientis est*).

traitor, *proditor* or perhaps *civis impius* (= disloyal citizen).

traitorous; see TREACHEROUS.

trammel; see HINDER and HINDRANCE.

tramp; see WALK, MARCH.

trample, v., or — upon, lit. and fig. *calcare, conculcare, proculcare, proterĕre, obterĕre.*

trance, render by phrase, such as *animus a corpore abstractus* (Cic.).

tranquil, *tranquillus, placidus, quietus.*

tranquillity, *tranquillitas, otium, quies.*

tranquillize, *tranquillare, placare, pacare, sedare.*

transact, *gerĕre, agĕre, transigĕre, conficĕre.*

transaction, *res, negotium.*

transcend, *(ex)superare, excellĕre* (with dat.); see also SURPASS.

transcendent, *praestans, singularis, eximius, egregius.*

transcendental, render by phrase, such as *quod sensu percipi non potest.*

transcribe, *transcribĕre;* see also COPY.

transcript, *exemplum, exemplar.*

transfer, subst. *translatio* (= the act of —ring), *mancipium* (of property).

transfer, v. *transferre, traducĕre, transmittĕre, traicĕre, transfundĕre* (freely, wholesale).

transferable, render by verb.

transference, *translatio.*

transfiguration, *transfiguratio* (eccl.).

transfigure, *(com)mutare, transfigurare* (eccl.).

transfix, *transfigĕre, traicĕre, confodĕre.*

transform, *(con)vertĕre, (com)mutare.*

transformation, render by verb.

transfuse, *transfundĕre.*

transfusion, render by verb.

transgress, (**1**) transit. *transcendĕre, violare.* (**2**) intransit. *ab officio discedĕre, delinquĕre, peccare.*

transgression, *delictum, peccatum;* see also CRIME, FAULT.

transgressor, render by verb; see also CRIMINAL, OFFENDER.

transient, adj. *brevis, fugax, caducus, instabilis, fluxus, incertus.*

transit, *transitus (-ūs);* see also PASSAGE.

transition, *transitio, transitus (-ūs), transgressio.*

transitive, *transitivus* (gram.).

transitory; see TRANSIENT.

translate. (**1**) to render into another language, *(con)vertĕre, transferre* (Quint.), *reddĕre, interpretari*: to — from Greek into Latin, *e Graeco in Latinum (con)vertĕre, Latine reddĕre;* to — literally, or word for word, *verbum e verbo exprimĕre, verbum pro verbo reddĕre.* (**2**) = to remove to another sphere; see PROMOTE, TRANSFER.

translation. (1) as an action, *translatio, interpretatio.* (2) = a work translated, *liber conversus* or *translatus.*
translator, *interpres.*
translucent, *perlucidus*; see also TRANSPARENT.
transmarine, *transmarinus.*
transmigration: — of souls, render by phrase, such as *animarum in nova corpora quasi migratio.*
transmission, render by verb.
transmit, *transmittĕre, tradĕre* (= to hand over, hand down).
transmute; see CHANGE.
transom, *tignum transversum* or *transversarium.*
transparency, *perspicuitas*; or render by adj.
transparent. LIT., *perlucidus (pellucidus), perspicuus* (Ov.): to be —, *perlucēre, lucem transmittĕre.* TRANSF., *perlucidus, evidens, manifestus*; see also CLEAR.
transparently, *manifesto.*
transpire. LIT., *exhalari, emanare.* TRANSF., (1) of secrets, etc., *(di)vulgari, pervulgari, efferri (foras* or *in vulgas), percrebrescĕre.* (2) of events; see HAPPEN.
transplant, (lit. and fig.) *transferre, traducĕre* (of peoples).
transplantation, *translatio.*
transport, subst. (1) as an action, render by verb. (2) as a ship, *navigium vectorium, navis oneraria.* (3) as a state of mind, of rage, *(nimia) iracundia*; of delight, *laetitia effusa* or *gestiens.*
transport, v. LIT., *transportare, transferre, transmittĕre, traicĕre, transvehĕre*; for banishment, *relegare.* TRANSF., to be —ed: with rage, *iracundiā exardescĕre*; with delight, *gaudio* or *laetitiā efferri* or *exsultare* or *gestire.*
transportation; see BANISHMENT.
transpose, *traicĕre.*
transposition, *traiectio.*
transubstantiation, *transubstantiatio* (eccl.).
transverse, *transversus, transversarius* (= lying across, of beams, etc.).
transversely, *ex transverso* (Pl.); or render by adj.
trap, subst. (1) for catching creatures, *laqueus*; see also SNARE, NET: a mouse —, *muscipulum* or *muscipula* (Phaedr.). (2) colloq. —s = belongings: pack your —, *conlige sarcinulas* (Juv.).
trap, v. *inretire*; see also ENSNARE.
Trapani, *Drepanum* or *Drepana (-orum,* plur.).
trappings, *ornamentum, ornatus (-ūs), insignia (-ium,* plur.); of horses, *phalerae (-arum,* plur.).
trash. (1) = rubbish, *quisquiliae (-arum,* plur.), *scruta (-orum,* plur.: Hor.). (2) = nonsense, *nugae (-arum,* plur.), *gerrae (-arum,* plur.: Pl.).
trashy, *vilis.*
travail, subst.; see CHILDBIRTH, LABOUR.
travail, v. *parturire.*
travel, subst. *iter, peregrinatio* (abroad).
travel, v. *iter facĕre, peregrinari* (abroad), *proficisci* (= to set out): to — through, *obire, circumire, peragrare, (per)lustrare.*
traveller, *viator, vector* (= passenger), *peregrinator* (= one who travels or resides abroad).
traverse, *obire, peragrare, (per)lustrare.*
travesty; see PARODY.
tray, *ferculum.*

treacherous, *perfidus, perfidiosus, infidelis, infidus, fallax.*
treacherously, *perfidiose.*
treachery, *perfidia, fraus, infidelitas* (= faithlessness), *proditio* (= betrayal).
tread, subst. *(in)gressus (-ūs), gradus (-ūs), vestigium.*
tread, v. *ingredi, incedĕre, insistĕre*; see also WALK: fig., to — in one's father's footsteps, *vestigiis* (or *vestigia) patris ingredi*; to — upon; see TRAMPLE.
treason. (1) in gen. *perfidia, proditio.* (2) as a crime, high —, *maiestas, perduellio*: to commit —, *maiestatem minuĕre* or *laedĕre.*
treasonable, render by subst.
treasure, subst. *thesaurus, gaza, opes (-um,* plur.), *divitiae (-arum,* plur. = riches), *copia* (= quantity, store); fig., of persons, *deliciae (-arum,* plur.), *amores (-um,* plur.).
treasure, v.; see VALUE: to — up, *(re)condĕre, reponĕre.*
treasure-house, *thesaurus.*
treasurer, *praefectus aerarii* (Plin.).
treasury, *aerarium, fiscus.*
treat, subst. *delectatio* (= delight); or render by verb.
treat, v. (1) = to discuss a subject, *rem tractare, persequi; de re disputare* or *disserĕre.* (2) to —, = to a patient or complaint, *curare.* (3) to —, = to entertain, *invitare.* (4) = to behave towards a person (or thing), with adv. or adverbial phrase, *habēre, tractare.* (5) to — with, = to negotiate, *agĕre (cum homine).*
treatise, *liber* (= book), *libellus.*
treatment, *tractatio, curatio*: kind —, *comitas, humanitas*; cruel, unkind —, *saevitia*; often to be rendered by verb.
treaty, *pactio, pactum, foedus (-ĕris,* n.), *conventio, conventum*: according to the —, *ex pacto, ex convento, ex conventu*; to conclude a —, *foedus,* etc., *facĕre, icĕre, ferire, pangĕre*; to break a —, *foedus violare, rumpĕre.*
Trebizond, *Trapezūs (-ūntis).*
treble, adj. (1) see THREE, TRIPLE. (2) of voices, *acutus.*
treble, v. *(rem) triplicem facĕre.*
tree, *arbor*: a genealogical —, *stemma (-ătis,* n.: Sen., Juv.).
trefoil, *trifolium* (Plin.).
trellis; see LATTICE.
tremble, *tremĕre, contremiscĕre, micare* (= to flicker, quiver): to — at, *(rem, hominem) tremĕre, contremiscĕre, extimescĕre*; to cause to —, *tremefacĕre* (poet.).
trembling, subst. *tremor.*
trembling, adj. *tremebundus, tremulus* (poet.).
tremendous, = frightening, *terribilis*; = huge, *ingens, immanis.*
tremendously, *valde, vehementer, magnopere, maxime.*
tremulous; see TREMBLING, adj.
trench, subst. *fossa*; see also DITCH.
trench, v. *fossam fodĕre* or *facĕre*: to — upon; see ENCROACH.
trencher; see PLATE.
trepan, subst. *modiolus* (Cels.).
trepidation, *trepidatio.*
Trent, *Tridentum.*
trespass, subst. *delictum, peccatum*; otherwise render by verb.
trespass, v. *in alienum fundum ingredi*; fig., see TRANSGRESS.

trespasser, *qui in alienum fundum ingreditur.*

tress; see HAIR.

trial. (1) = the act of trying or proving, *temptatio, experimentum, experientia, periculum*: to make —, *periculum facĕre, experiri.* (2) = attempt, *conatus (-ūs).* (3) in court, *iudicium, quaestio*: to bring to —, *in iudicium adducĕre* or *vocare.*

triangle, *triangulum.*

triangular, *triangulus, triquetrus.*

tribal, render by genit. of subst.; see TRIBE.

tribe, at Rome, *tribus (-ūs)*: by —s, *tributim*; of a—, *tribuarius*; a fellow —sman, *tribulis*; in gen., of uncivilized peoples, *natio, gens.*

tribulation, *miseria, incommodum, aerumna.*

tribunal. (1) = judgement-seat, *tribunal.* (2) = law court, *iudicium*; fig., of critics, etc., *arbitrium.*

tribune. (1) at Rome: a military —, *tribunus militum* or *militaris*; of the people, *tribunus plebis.* (2) = platform, *suggestum.*

tribuneship, *tribunatus (-ūs).*

tributary, subst., render by the verb *influĕre* (= to flow in).

tributary, adj. *vectigalis, stipendiarius.*

tribute, *tributum, vectigal, stipendium.*

trick, subst. *dolus, fraus, machina, techna* (Pl., Ter.).

trick, v.; see DECEIVE.

trickery, *fallacia, astutia* (both also in plur.); see also TRICK.

tricky, adj. *versutus, argutus* (Hor.).

trickle, v. *manare, rorare, stillare.*

trident, *tridens* (Verg., Ov.).

tried, *spectatus, cognitus, probatus, expertus.*

triennial, *trietericus* (Ov.).

Trier, *Augusta Treverorum.*

Trieste, *Tergeste.*

trifle, subst. *res parvula,* or *minuta,* or *parvi momenti, titivillitium* (Pl.).; —s, *nugae (-arum,* plur.): to buy for a —, *parvo* or *vili emĕre.*

trifle, v. *nugari, ludĕre, ineptire* (Ter., Cat.).

trifler, *nugator.*

trifling, subst. *ludus, iocus, ineptiae (-arum,* plur.).

trifling, adj. *lēvis, minutus, nugatorius.*

trill, *fritinnire* (of birds: Varro).

trim, adj.; see NEAT.

trim, v. (1) = to put in order, *concinnare* (Pl.); of the hair, *comĕre.* (2) = to prune, *(am)putare.* (3) in politics, *temporibus (in)servire.*

trimeter, *trimetrus* (Hor., Quint.).

trimmer, render by verb; see TRIM, v. (3).

trimming, subst. *fimbriae (-arum,* plur.; = border, fringe).

Trinity, *trinitas* (eccl.).

trinket: a woman's —s, *mundus*; an infant's —s (= amulets), *crepundia (-orum,* plur.).

trio, = three together, *tres, tria*; in music, *concentus (-ūs) trium vocum.*

trip, subst. (1) see STUMBLE, ERROR. (2) see JOURNEY, EXCURSION.

trip, v. (1) transit.: to — up, *supplantare.* (2) intransit. = to stumble, *offendĕre*: to — along, *leviter ire.*

tripartite, *tripertitus* or *tripartitus.*

tripe, *omasum* (bullock's: Hor.).

triple, *triplex.*

tripod, *tripūs (-podis).*

trireme, *(navis) triremis.*

trisyllable, *trisyllabum verbum* (Varro).

trite, *tritus, pervulgatus*: — topics, *loci communes.*

triumph, subst. (1) a Roman —al procession, *triumphus*: to celebrate a — over a people, *triumphare* or *triumphum agere de* (with abl.). (2) in gen. = a success, *victoria,* rarely *triumphus.* (3) = great rejoicing, *exsultatio*: shouts of —, *exsultantium clamores.*

triumph, v. (1) = to celebrate a —, *triumphare, triumphum agĕre.* (2) = to exult, *exsultare,* sometimes *triumphare.* (3) to — over, = to conquer, *superare, vincĕre.*

triumphal, *triumphalis*: a — procession, *triumphus.*

triumphant. (1) = victorious, *victor.* (2) = in high spirits, *elatus, exsultans.*

triumvirate, *triumviratus (-ūs).*

trivial, *lēvis*; see also TRIFLING.

triviality, render by adj.

trochaic, *trochaicus* (Quint.).

trochee, *trochaeus.*

Trojan, subst. *Tros*; adj. *Troianus.*

troop, subst. *caterva, grex, manus (-ūs), globus, turma* (of horsemen): —s, *copiae, milites*; many —s, *magnae copiae, multi milites.*

troop, v. *confluĕre.*

trooper, *eques.*

trope, *verbum translatum, translatio, tropus* (Quint.).

trophy, *tropaeum*; see also MEMORIAL.

tropic, in astronomy, render by *circulus* or *orbis*: the —s, = very hot countries, *regiones torridae.*

tropical, = very hot, *aestuosus*; see also TROPIC.

trot, subst. *gradus (-ūs) citatus* or *tolutilis* (Varro): at a —, *tolutim* (Pl., Varro).

trot, v.; see TROT, subst.

troth, *fides*: to plight —, *fidem dare.*

troubadour; see SINGER, MUSICIAN.

trouble, subst. (1) = disturbance, adversity, mishap, *molestia, incommodum, calamitas, labor, aerumna, malum, fortuna adversa, res* (plur.) *adversae.* (2) = of mind, *sollicitudo, anxietas*; see also GRIEF, SORROW. (3) — taken, pains, tiresome effort, *opera, negotium, labor, sudor.* (4) = political commotion, *tumultus (-ūs).*

trouble, v. (1) transit. *vexare, agitare, sollicitare, fatigare, (con)turbare* (= to confuse), *perturbare, (hominem) sollicitum habēre, sollicitudine* or *aegritudine adficĕre, (homini) molestiam exhibēre*: may I — you to hand me that book? *da mihi, quaeso, istunc librum.* (2) intransit. or reflex: to — (oneself), *laborare*; to — about a thing, *rem curare, rei* (dat.) *operam dare*; not to — about a thing, *rem neglegĕre.*

troubler, *turbator*; or render by verb.

troublesome, *molestus, gravis, incommodus, iniquus, laboriosus* (= laborious).

trough, *alveus.*

troupe, of actors, *histrionum familia, grex, caterva.*

trousers, *brac(c)ae (-arum,* plur.).

truant, subst.; render by phrase.

truant, adj. *fugitivus.*

truce, *indutiae (-arum,* plur.).

truck; see BARROW.

truckle, *(homini) morem gerĕre, obtemperare.*

trudge; see WALK.

true. (1) = in accordance with fact, *verus,*

verax (= truthful): it is —, in parenthesis, as an admission, *quidem*; as — as I live, supporting a statement, *ita vivam ut*, with indic.; as an answer; see YES. (2) = genuine, real, *verus, sincerus, germanus*. (3) = loyal, *fidus, fidelis*.

true-hearted, *fidelis, simplex.*

truffle, *tuber* (Plin., Juv.).

truly, *vere, profecto* (= certainly), *sane, certe*; see also REALLY.

trumpery; see TRASH, TRIFLE.

trumpet, subst. *tuba* (usually straight); *bucina, lituus, cornu* (curved): a — call, *classicum* (also used of the — itself); to sound the — for retreat, *(signum) receptui canĕre.*

trumpet, v., of an elephant, perhaps *stridĕre*; transit.: to — abroad, *celebrare, praedicare.*

trumpeter, *tubicen, bucinator.*

trumpeting, subst., of an elephant, *stridor.*

trump up, *fingĕre*; see also INVENT.

truncheon, *scipio, fustis* (= cudgel).

trundle, *volvĕre.*

trunk. (1) of a tree, *truncus, stirps.* (2) of the body, *truncus* (often *corpus* can be used). (3) = box, chest, *arca, vidulus* (Pl.). (4) of an elephant, *manus (-ūs), proboscis.*

truss, = bandage, *fascia*: a — of hay, *fascis.*

trust, subst. (1) = confidence, *fiducia, fides.* (2) anything entrusted, *mandatum, creditum, depositum.*

trust, v. (1) = to feel, or place, confidence, *(homini,* etc.) *(con)fidĕre, credĕre, fidem habēre*: not to —, *diffidĕre.* (2) transit. = to entrust, *(con)credĕre, committĕre, mandare, commendare.*

trustee, *custos, administrator, procurator.*

trustworthiness, *constantia, fides.*

trustworthy, *certus, firmus, constans, fidus, fidelis, locuples.*

truth, as a quality, *veritas*: the —, in a particular case, = the fact(s), *verum, vera* (= n. sing. or plur. of *verus*), sometimes *veritas*; in accordance with —, *ex veritate* (Sall.); in —, *enimvero*; see also TRULY.

truthful, *verus, verax, veridicus.*

truthfulness, *veritas, veritatis studium* or *amor.*

try, subst. = *conatus (-ūs).*

try, v. (1) = to make trial of, *temptare, experiri, periclitari, explorare, spectare* (= to examine critically), *periculum rei* (genit.) *facĕre.* (2) = to attempt, *conari, temptare, eniti.* (3) in court, to — a case, *iudicare, cognoscĕre, quaerĕre, iudicium exercēre.*

trying, adj. *molestus, gravis, incommodus.*

tryst, render by phrase with *constituĕre* (= to arrange, 'make a date').

tub, *dolium, labrum.*

tube, *tubus* (Plin.).

tuber, *tuber* (Plin.).

tubercle, *tuberculum* (Cels.).

tuberous, *tuberosus* (Varro).

tuck, v.: to — up, *succingĕre* (poet.); see also FOLD.

tuff-stone, *tophus* or *tofus* (Verg., Ov., Plin.).

tuft, of hair, *crinis*; of wool, *floccus* (Varro) of feathers, *crista.*

tufted, *cristatus.*

tug, subst., render by verb.

tug, v. *trahĕre.*

tuition; see INSTRUCTION.

tumble, subst. *casus (-us), ruina.*

tumble, v. (1) transit. = to disarrange, *(per)turbare, miscēre.* (2) intransit.; see FALL.

tumbledown, adj. *obsoletus* (Hor.).

tumbler. (1) = acrobat, *petaurista* (Varro). (2) = glass, *poculum.*

tumid, *tumidus, inflatus, turgidus.*

tumour, *tumor, tuber* (Ter., Plin.), *struma* (= scrofulous —).

tumult, *tumultus (-ūs), seditio, motus (-ūs), concitatio, turba.*

tumultuous, *tumultuosus, turbulentus, turbidus, concitatus.*

tumultuously, *tumultuose, turbulente.*

tumulus, *tumulus.*

tun; see TON.

tune, subst. = air, *cantus (-ūs), carmen, modi (-orum,* plur.), *numeri (-orum,* plur.): to keep in —, *concentum servare*; out of —, *absonus*; to be out of —, *discrepare.*

tune, v.: to — a stringed instrument, *fides ita contendĕre nervis ut concentum servare possint* (Cic.).

tuneful, *canorus.*

tunic, *tunica.*

tunnel, subst. *cuniculus.*

tunnel, v. *cuniculum facĕre.*

tunny, *thynnus* or *thunnus* (Plin.).

turban, *mitra.*

turbid, *turbidus.*

turbot, *rhombus* (Hor.).

turbulence, = disturbance, *tumultus (-ūs)*; of character, render by adj.

turbulent, *turbulentus, seditiosus, turbidus.*

tureen, *patina.*

turf, *caespes, herba* (= grass).

turgid, *tumidus*; see also TUMID.

Turin, *Augusta Taurinorum.*

turmoil, *turba*; see also TUMULT.

turn, turning, subst. (1) = a turning movement, *conversio.* (2) = a change of direction, physically, *flexus (-ūs), anfractus (-ūs).* (3) = a change in the course of events, *vicissitudo, commutatio*: to take a different —, *aliter cadĕre*; to take a — for the better (worse), *in melius (peius) mutari.* (4) see CAST, FORM, MANNER, DISPOSITION. (5) of alternation or succession, sometimes *sors* (= lot): by —s, = alternately, *alternis, invicem.* (6) a good —, *officium.* (7) a — of speech, *conformatio verborum, genus dicendi.*

turn, v. (1) transit. *(con)vertĕre* (in most senses of the English word), *advertĕre* (= to turn towards), *versare, torquēre* (= to twist), *flectĕre* (= to bend), *inclinare*: to — aside, *deflectĕre*; to — away, *avertĕre*; to — back, *reflectĕre* (poet.); to — one's back, *tergum vertĕre*; to — over, in a book, *librum evolvĕre*; to — round, *circumagĕre, rotare, volvĕre* (= to roll), *contorquēre*; to — upside down, *evertĕre, subvertĕre* (Tac., Sall. and poet.); to — on the lathe, *tornare*; fig., to — one's attention to, *animum advertĕre, animadvertĕre*; to — one person against another, *hominis animum ab homine alienare*; to — away, = to dismiss, *dimittĕre*; to — down, = to reject, *repudiare*; to — out, = to eject, *exigĕre, expellĕre, evertĕre*; to — over a new leaf, *mores emendare*; to —, = to change, *convertĕre, (com)mutare*; see also CHANGE. (2) intransit., render by transit. verbs in passive, or with reflexive object, e.g. *(con)verti, se (con)vertĕre*: fig., to — against a

person, *ab homine desciscĕre* or *alienari*; to —
aside, *deverti*; to — back, *reverti*; to — in,
=̂ to go to bed, *cubitum ire*; to — out, = to
issue, end up, *evenire, evadĕre, cadĕre*; see
also BECOME; to — up, *incidĕre*; to —, = to
alter, be changed, (*com*)*mutari, converti*; see
also CHANGE; to — king's evidence, *indicium
profiteri* (Sall.).

turncoat, render by phrase, such as *qui
sententiam* or *consilium mutat*.

turnip, *rapum* (Plin.).

turnkey, *ianitor* or *custos carceris*.

turpentine, *resina terebinthina* (Cels.).

turpitude, *turpitudo, dedecus* (*-oris*, n.).

turret, *turris, turricula* (Vitr.).

turtle, turtle-dove, *turtur* (Verg.).

Tuscany, *Etruria*.

tush, *phy* (Ter.).

tusk, *dens*.

tutelage, *tutela*; see also PROTECTION.

tutelary : the — god of a place, *deus praeses
loci, deus qui loco praesidet, deus cuius tutelae*
or *cuius in tutelā locus est*.

tutor, *magister, praeceptor, nutricius*.

twang, subst. *crepitus* (*-ūs*), *sonus, sonitus* (*-ūs*).

twang, v. *crepare, crepitare, sonare*.

tweak, *vellĕre, vellicare*.

tweezers, *volsella* (Pl.).

twelfth, *duodecimus*.

twelve, *duodecim*; — each, or — at a time,
duodeni; — times, *duodecie(n)s*.

twelve hundred, *mille et ducenti* : — each,
— at a time, *milleni et duceni*.

twelvemonth, *annus*.

twentieth, *vicesimus*.

twenty, *viginti* : — each, or — at a time,
viceni; — times, *vicie(n)s*.

twice, *bis* : — as much, *bis tantum*; — as great,
altero tanto maior.

twig, *surculus, ramulus, virgula*.

twilight ; in the evening, *crepusculum* (Pl.,
Ov.); in the morning, *diluculum*.

twin, subst. and adj. *geminus*.

twine, subst.; see STRING.

twine, v. (1) transit. *circumplicare, implicare,
intorquēre*. (2) intransit. : to — round a thing,
rem complecti, circumplecti; or render by
pass. of transit. verbs.

twinge, *dolor, cruciatus* (*-ūs*), *stringor* (Lucr.).

twinkle, *micare, fulgēre, coruscare* (Verg.),
scintillare (poet.).

twinkling, subst. *fulgor* (= brightness,
glitter): in the — of an eye, *temporis puncto*.

twirl, *versare*; see also SPIN.

twist, v. (1) transit. (*in*)*torquēre*, (*in*)*flectĕre,
nectĕre, texĕre* (= to weave). (2) intransit.,
render by transit. verb in pass., or with
reflexive object; see also TWINE.

twit, to — a person with a thing, *rem homini
obicĕre*.

twitch, v. *vellĕre, vellicare*.

two, *duo* : — each, or — at a time, *bini* (also
used for — with a subst. that is plural in
form; e.g. — camps, *bina castra*); a period
of — days, *biduum*; a period of — years,
biennium; — years old, lasting — years,
bimus; — months old, lasting — months,
bimestris; — feet long (or broad), *bipedalis*;
in — parts, adj. *bipartitus*, adv. *bipartito*.

two-coloured, *bicolor* (poet.).

two-edged, *bipennis* (poet.).

twofold, *duplex*.

two-footed, *bipes* (Verg.).

two-headed, *biceps, anceps* (Ov.).

two hundred, *ducenti* : — each, — at a time,
duceni; — times, *ducentie(n)s*.

type. (1) = model, *exemplar, exemplum*.
(2) = form, character, class, *forma, figura,
genus* (*-eris*, n.). (3) = symbol, *significatio*
(eccl.), *imago* (eccl.). (4) = letters, *litterarum formae*.

typical, *typicus* (eccl.): that was thoroughly
— of Caesar, *habebat hoc omnino Caesar*.

typify; see REPRESENT.

typographical, typography; see PRINT.

tyrannical, adj. *tyrannicus, superbus, saevus,
crudelis*.

tyrannically, *tyrannice, superbe, regie*.

tyrannicide. (1) the act, *tyrannicidium* (Sen.,
Quint.); or render by phrase. (2) the person,
tyrannoctonus, tyrannicida (Sen., Tac.),
tyranni interfector.

tyrannize, *dominari*.

tyranny, *dominatio, dominatus* (*-ūs*), *tyrannis*
(*-idis* = usurped power), sometimes *regnum*;
or render by phrase, such as *saevitia reg-
nantium*.

tyrant, *tyrannus* (= a usurper or despot, but
not necessarily unjust or harsh), *dominus*
(= despot); to cover all the implications of
the English word, add adj., such as *superbus,
saevus, crudelis*.

tyro; see TIRO.

U

ubiquity, ubiquitous, render by phrase, such
as *omnibus locis praesens*.

udder, *uber*.

uglily, *turpiter*.

ugliness, *deformitas, foeditas*.

ugly, *deformis, turpis, foedus*.

ulcer, *vomica, ulcus* (*-eris*, n.).

ulcerate, *suppurare* (Plin.): to cause to —,
ulcerare.

ulcerous, *ulcerosus* (Tac.).

ulterior, *ulterior*; see also FURTHER.

ultimate, *extremus, ultimus*; see also FURTHER,
LAST.

ultimately, *ad extremum, ad ultimum, postremo*;
see also LAST, END.

ultimatum, perhaps *extrema condicio*.

ultra, render by a superlative adj. or by phrase
such as *praeter* or *ultra modum*.

ultramarine, subst. *color caeruleus*.

umbrage. (1) see SHADE. (2) see OFFENCE.

umbrageous; see SHADY.

umbrella, *umbella* (= parasol: Mart., Juv.),
umbraculum (= parasol: Tib., Ov.).

umpire, *arbiter, disceptator* (with f. *discepta-
trix*).

un-, as a negative prefix, has its nearest Latin
equivalent in the prefix *in-*, but this is not
found attached to all Latin adjectives and
adverbs. Some English words in un- are
best rendered by the single Latin words
suggested below, others by a phrase consisting of a negative (such as *non, haud,
parum, minime*) and some Latin equivalent
for the corresponding positive word in
English (e.g. unsown = not sown, *non satus*).

unabashed, = undaunted, *constans, firmus, intrepidus;* = shameless, *impudens.*

unabated, *integer* (= whole).

unable, render by phrase, with *non posse* or *nequire.*

unaccented, render by phrase, such as *(syllaba) sine accentu* (Quint.) *enuntiata.*

unacceptable, *ingratus, iniucundus.*

unaccompanied, *solus, incomitatus* (Ov.), *sine comitatu;* see also ALONE; of the voice, *sine symphonia* (Plin.).

unaccomplished, *imperfectus, infectus.*

unaccountable, *inexplicabilis, inenodabilis.*

unaccustomed. (1) largely of persons, = unused to, *insuetus* (with genit. or dat.), *insolitus (ad rem), insolens* (with genit. or *in* and abl.), *inexpertus (ad rem).* (2) largely of things = not in ordinary use, unusual, *insuetus, insolitus, insolens, inusitatus.*

unacquainted, *ignarus, imperitus, inscius* (all with genit.).

unadorned, *inornatus, incomptus, simplex.*

unadulterated, *sincerus, merus, integer, incorruptus.*

unadvisable, *inutilis* (= useless), *temerarius* or *inconsultus* (= rash).

unadvised, *inconsideratus, imprudens, temerarius, inconsultus.*

unadvisedly, *inconsiderate, imprudenter, temere, inconsulte, sine consilio.*

unaffected. (1) = simple, *simplex, candidus, inadfectatus* (of speech: Quint.). (2) = not moved, *immotus, constans:* to remain —, *non adfici.*

unaffectedly, *simpliciter, sine fuco ac fallaciis.*

unaffrighted, unafraid, *impavidus, intrepidus, interritus* (Verg., Ov., Tac.).

unaided, *sine ope, sine auxilio, nullius auxilio fretus.*

unalleviated, *non mitigatus;* see also ALLEVIATE.

unallotted, *non sorte datus.*

unallowable, *inlicitus.*

unalloyed, *purus, sincerus, merus.*

unalterable, *immutabilis.*

unaltered, *immutatus* (rare in this sense), *integer.*

unambiguous, *certus, clarus.*

unambitious, *modestus* or render by phrase, such as *nullos honores adfectare.*

unamiable, *morosus, difficilis.*

unanimity, *unanimitas, consensio, consensus (-ūs), concordia.*

unanimous, *unanimus, concors.*

unanimously, *omnium iudicio* or *sententiis* or *consensu, uno consensu, una voce, uno ore:* they decide —, *ad unum omnes decernunt;* to be elected —, *omnium suffragiis creari.*

unanswerable, render by phrase, such as *non posse revinci* or *refutari.*

unanswered: to leave —, *non respondēre,* or (of a letter) *non rescribēre* (with dat.).

unappalled; see UNAFRAID.

unappeased, *non satiatus, implacatus* (poet.).

unapproachable; of places, *invius* or *avius;* of persons, *rari aditūs.*

unarmed, *inermis, nudus.*

unasked, *(suā) sponte, ultro.*

unassailed, *integer, tutus.*

unassuming, *modestus, modicus.*

unattainable, render by phrase, such as *quod attingi non potest.*

unattempted: to leave nothing —, *nihil inexpertum omittĕre, omnia experiri.*

unattended, *incomitatus* (poet.), *sine comitibus.*

unauthenticated, *sine auctore editus.*

unauthorized, *inlicitus* (Tac.), *inconcessus* (Verg., Ov., Quint.).

unavailable, render by phrase, such as *haud in medium prolatus.*

unavailing, *inritus, futilis, vanus.*

unavenged, *inultus.*

unavoidable, *inevitabilis* (Ov., Tac.); or render by phrase, such as *quod evitari non potest.*

unavowed; see SECRET.

unaware, *inscius, nescius, ignarus;* see also UNAWARE, adv.

unaware, unawares, adv. *(de) improviso, (ex) insperato, (ex) inopinato, (ex) necopinato;* often rendered by adj. agreeing with the person taken by surprise, e.g. *imprudens, inopinans, inopinatus, necopinans.*

unawed; see UNAFRAID.

unbar, *reserare.*

unbearable, adj.; see INTOLERABLE.

unbeaten, *invictus.*

unbecoming, *indecorus, indignus, turpis.*

unbecomingly, *indecore, turpiter.*

unbefriended, adj. *auxilio* or *amicis carens.*

unbelief, render by phrase, with *non credĕre;* in a religious context, perhaps *impietas.*

unbeliever, *qui non credit.*

unbelieving, *incredulus* (Hor.).

unbeloved, *nemini carus.*

unbend, *remittĕre, (re)laxare.*

unbending, *rigidus, durus.*

unbewailed, *infletus, indefletus, indeploratus* (all poet.).

unbiassed, *integer;* or render by phrase, such as *neutro inclinatus.*

unbidden, *invocatus, iniussus* (Hor.); or render by the adv. *ultro* or *(suā) sponte.*

unbind, *(dis)solvĕre, laxare.*

unblamable; see BLAMELESS.

unblemished, adj. *purus, integer, in(con)taminatus, innocens* (= innocent), *castus* (= chaste, pure).

unbloody, *incruentus.*

unblushing, *impudens:* — effrontery, *os durissimum.*

unborn, *nondum natus.*

unborrowed; see ORIGINAL, GENUINE.

unbosom: to — oneself, *se patefacĕre, (rem) confitēri.*

unbought, *non emptus, inemptus* (Verg., Hor., Tac.).

unbound, of hair, *passus, solutus;* see also LOOSE.

unbounded, *infinitus, immensus;* see also IMMODERATE.

unbribed, *incorruptus, integer.*

unbridled, LIT., *infrenatus, effrenatus, infrenis* or *infrenus* (both Verg.). TRANSF., *effrenatus, effusus.*

unbroken: in gen. *integer, sincerus;* of duration in time, *perpetuus;* of horses, *intractatus, indomitus.*

unbrotherly, *parum fraternus.*

unbuckle, *diffibulare* (Stat.), *refibulare* (Mart.); see also UNFASTEN, UNTIE.

unburden, *(re) exonerare, liberare, levare, solvĕre.*

unburied, *inhumatus, insepultus.*

unburnt, *inconsumptus* (Ov.).

unbutton, *diloricare, discingĕre* (= ungirdle).

uncalled, *invocatus*: — for; see UNNECESSARY.

uncancelled; see CANCEL.

uncared for, *neglectus.*

unceasing, *perpetuus, continuus, adsiduus*; see also INCESSANT.

unceremonious, *simplex* (= natural), *inurbanus* (= rude).

unceremoniously, *simpliciter, inurbane.*

uncertain, *incertus, ambiguus, dubius* (= doubtful), *anceps* (= undecided): to be —, *incertum* or *dubium* or *in incerto* or *in dubio esse, dubitare, haerēre, haesitare, animi* or *animo pendēre.*

uncertainly, render by adj.

uncertainty, *dubitatio, dubium*; or render by adj.

unchain, *e vinculis eximēre, vincula solvēre*; see also LOOSE.

unchangeable, *immutabilis, certus, stabilis, constans.*

unchangeableness, *immutabilitas, constantia.*

unchangeably, *constanter.*

unchanged, *immutatus* (rare in this sense), *integer*; sometimes *idem* (= same).

uncharitable, *durus, inhumanus, iniquus, malignus* (poet.), *inhumaniter.*

uncharitableness, *inhumanitas.*

uncharitably, *inhumaniter, maligne.*

unchaste, *incestus, impudicus, libidinosus* (= lustful), *obscaenus* (= obscene, foul).

unchastity, *incestum, impudicitia* (Pl., Tac.), *libido.*

unchecked, *liber*; see also UNRESTRAINED.

uncivil; see RUDE.

uncivilized, *ferus, immansuetus, immanis, barbarus, incultus*; or render by phrase, such as *omnis cultūs et humanitatis expers.*

unclasp, *refibulare* (Mart.); see also LOOSE.

uncle, *patruus* (= a father's brother), *avunculus* (= a mother's brother): great- —, *patruus* or *avunculus magnus.*

unclean, *impurus, inquinatus*; see also DIRTY, FOUL.

unclouded, *serenus, tranquillus.*

uncoil, *evolvēre, explicare.*

uncoiling, subst. *explicatio.*

uncoined, *infectus.*

uncombed, *impexus* (poet.), *horridus, incomptus.*

uncomfortable. (1) = causing discomfort, *molestus, incommodus, gravis.* (2) = feeling discomfort: I am —, *male me habeo, male est mihi.*

uncomfortableness, *molestia.*

uncomfortably, *incommode.*

uncommanded; see UNBIDDEN.

uncommon, *rarus, insolitus, inusitatus, egregius, singularis.*

uncommonly, *plus* or *magis solito, praeter solitum* (poet.), *eximie* (= exceptionally): — well, *egregie.*

uncommunicative; see RESERVED, SILENT.

uncomplaining, *patiens.*

uncompleted, *imperfectus.*

uncompounded, *simplex.*

uncompromising: to give an — refusal, *praecise negare*; see also UNCONDITIONAL.

unconcerned, *securus, neglegens, incuriosus* (Tac.).

unconditional, *simplex, purus.*

unconditionally, *simpliciter, sine ulla pactione* (Sall.).

unconfined, *liber.*

uncongenial; see UNPLEASANT.

unconnected: of style, *disiunctus, dissolutus, inconditus.*

unconquerable; see INVINCIBLE.

unconquered, *invictus.*

unconscionable; see UNREASONABLE.

unconscious. (1) = insensible, (*omni*) *sensu carens.* (2) = ignorant, *inscius, ignarus*: I am not —, *non sum inscius, non me fugit, non me praeterit, non ignoro.*

unconsciousness, render by adj. or verb; see UNCONSCIOUS.

unconsecrated, *profanus.*

unconsidered, *neglectus.*

unconstitutional, *non legitimus.*

unconstitutionally, *contra legem, contra rempublicam.*

unconstrained, *liber.*

unconsumed, *inconsumptus* (Ov.).

uncontaminated, *in*(*con*)*taminatus.*

uncontested, render by phrase, such as *sine certamine.*

uncontrollable, *impotens.*

uncontrolled, *liber, effrenatus*: — sovereignty, *dominatus* (-ūs).

unconvinced, *ad credendum non adductus.*

uncooked, *crudus, incoctus* (Pl.).

uncork, *relinēre* (= to remove the pitch with which a jar was sealed: Ter.); or perhaps *obturamentum extrahēre.*

uncorrupt, *incorruptus, purus.*

uncourteous; see RUDE.

uncouth, *rudis, incultus, agrestis, rusticus, inconditus, inhumanus.*

uncouthness, *inhumanitas.*

uncover, *detegēre, retegēre, reclūdēre, aperire, nudare.*

unction, *unctio*: extreme —, *unctio extrema* (eccl.); to speak with —, perhaps *speciosius dicēre.*

unctuous, *pinguis* (Verg.), *nitidus* (poet.); of speech, perhaps *speciosus.*

uncultivated, of soil, *incultus, vastus* (= waste); of manners, etc., *inhumanus, rudis, agrestis, indoctus* (Pl., Hor.).

uncurbed; see UNBRIDLED.

uncut, *intonsus* (of hair or of trees: poet.); *incaeduus* (of trees: Ov.); *integer* (= whole).

undamaged, *inviolatus, integer* (= whole).

undaunted, *impavidus, intrepidus, interritus* (poet. and Tac.).

undecayed, *incorruptus.*

undeceive, *errorem* (*homini*) *eripēre.*

undecided. (1) of persons, *incertus, dubius, ambiguus* (Tac.). (2) of things, *incertus, dubius, integer, ambiguus, anceps* (esp. of the issue of a conflict): the case is still —, *adhuc sub iudice lis est* (Hor.).

undecked, of a ship, *apertus*: an — ship, *aperta navis* or *aphractus*; in gen., see UNADORNED.

undefended, *indefensus, nudus* (= exposed to attack).

undefiled, *incorruptus, purus.*

undefined, *infinitus.*

undeniable, *evidens, haud dubius.*

undeniably, *certe, sine dubio, procul dubio.*

under, prep. (1) in space: *sub* (to be —, *sub* with abl.; to go —, or go along —, *sub* with acc.); *subter* (used like *sub*); *infra* (with acc.); close —, = at the foot of, near, *sub*, with abl.

(2) in rank or merit: *sub* (e.g. *sub rege esse, sub regem cadĕre*), *infra* (with acc.); under Teucer's leadership, *Teucro duce*; often rendered by the adj. *inferior*. (3) in size or number: *infra* or *intra* (with acc.); otherwise render by *minor* or *minus* (= less), with abl. of comparison or *quam* or in the sense 'less than' (see under THAN); to be — age, *impubem esse, haud sui iuris est*. (4) of conditions, circumstances, etc., — which things are done: — this condition, *hac condicione*; — these circumstances, *quae cum ita sint*; — a pretence of, *specie, per speciem, sub specie, per simulationem*, with genit.; — sail, *passis velis*.

under-butler, *suppromus* (Pl.).

under-current. LIT., of water, *flumen*, etc., *subterfluens* (Plin.) or *subterlabens* (Verg.). TRANSF., render by the adj. *intimus* (= innermost, of thoughts, etc.) or by the verb *latēre* (= to lie hidden).

under-garment, *subucula* (Varro, Hor.).

underdone, *semicoctus* (Plin.).

underestimate, *minoris facĕre* or *aestimare*.

undergo, *subire, sustinēre, pati, perpeti, (per)ferre, tolerare*: to — punishment, *poenas dare* or *(de)pendĕre*.

underground, adj. *subterraneus*: an — passage, *cuniculus*.

underground, adv.: to be —, *sub terris* or *terrā esse*; to go —, *sub terras* or *terram ire*.

undergrowth, *virgulta (-orum*, plur.).

underhand, *clandestinus, insidiosus*; see also SECRET: by — means, *insidiose*.

underlie. LIT., *(sub re) iacēre*. TRANSF., of hidden meanings, etc., render by *latēre, celari* or *tacite significari*.

underline, perhaps *notare*.

underling, *(ad)minister, satelles, adsecula*.

undermaster, *hypodidascalus*.

undermine. LIT., *suffodĕre, (cuniculo* or *cuniculis) subruĕre*. TRANSF., *subruĕre, evertĕre* (= to overthrow), *labefactare* (= to cause to fall).

undermost, *infimus, imus*; see also LOW.

underneath, prep.; see UNDER.

underneath, adv. *infra, subter, subtus*.

under-officer, perhaps *optio* (Tac.) or *succenturio*.

underpin, *substruĕre, (suf)fulcire* (Pl., Lucr.); see also SUPPORT.

underrate, *minoris facere* or *aestimare*.

undersell, *minoris (quam ceteri) vendĕre*.

understand. (1) = to comprehend, grasp with the intellect, *intellegĕre*; *(animo* or *mente) comprehendĕre* or *amplecti* or *complecti* or *percipĕre*: to — a thing thoroughly, *rem cognitam habēre*; I don't — you, *nescio quid velis*. (2) to — one thing as meaning another = to interpret it, take it in a certain sense, *intellegĕre* (with acc. of thing and acc. of accepted meaning), *interpretari*; see also MEAN. (3) = to be informed, get information (not necessarily true), *intellegĕre, accipĕre, audire, certiorem fieri*: to give to —, *(homini) dicĕre, (hominem) certiorem facĕre*.

understanding. (1) as a faculty, *mens, ingenium*; see also INTELLECT. (2) see AGREEMENT.

undertake, *suscipĕre, (in se) recipĕre* (= to become responsible for), *adgredi, incipĕre* (= to begin), *moliri* (of laborious under-

takings), *conari* (= to try), *audēre* (= to dare), *promittĕre* (= to promise); as a business proposition, *rem faciendam conducĕre*.

undertaker, (of funerals) *libitinarius* (Sen.), *pollinctor* (Pl.), *vespillo* (Mart., Suet.).

undertaking, subst. (1) as an action, *inceptio*. (2) = work undertaken, *inceptum, coeptum, res suscepta*.

undervalue, *minoris facĕre* or *aestimare, contemnĕre* (= to despise).

underwood; see UNDERGROWTH.

underwriter, perhaps *consponsor* (= a joint surety).

undeserved, *immeritus, indignus* (poet. in this sense), *iniustus* (= unjust).

undeservedly, *immerito, indigne*.

undeserving, *indignus, immerens* (poet.), *immeritus* (poet.).

undesigned, *fortuitus*.

undesigning, *simplex, candidus*.

undesirable; see BAD, WORTHLESS.

undetected, *secretus*; see also SECRET.

undeveloped, *immaturus, nondum adultus*.

undigested, *crudus* (Juv.), *imperfectus* (Juv.).

undiminished, *inlibatus, indelibatus* (Ov.), *integer* (= whole).

undiscerning, *hebes*; see also STUPID.

undisciplined, *inexercitatus, inconditus*.

undiscovered, *inrepertus* (Hor.).

undisguised, *apertus*.

undisguisedly, *palam*.

undistinguished, *mediocris, inglorius, ignobilis*.

undisturbed, *otiosus* (= at leisure), *tutus* (= safe); or render by verb.

undivided, *indivisus* (Varro), *totus, integer*.

undo, of knots, etc., *(dis)solvĕre, resolvĕre, expedire*. (2) see RUIN.

undone. (1) = not done, *infectus*: what is done cannot be —, *factum infectum fieri non potest*; to leave —, *omittĕre*. (2) = ruined, *perditus*: we are —, *periimus, actum est de nobis*.

undoubted, *certus, haud dubius, haud ambiguus*.

undoubtedly, *haud dubie, sine dubio, scilicet*.

undress, subst. and adj., render by *discinctus* (= ungirt, partly dressed: poet.).

undress, v. (1) transit.: to — a person, *hominem veste exuĕre* or *spoliare* or *nudare, homini vestem detrahĕre*. (2) intransit. *vestem exuĕre* or *(de)ponĕre*: a room for —ing, *apodyterium*.

undressed. (1) = naked, *nudus*. (2) = not worked at, unprocessed, *crudus* (Varro, Plin., Col.), *rudis* (poet.).

undue, *nimius, immodicus*.

undulate, *fluctuare, vacillare, aestuare, undare* (poet.).

undulating, *sinuosus* (= winding: poet.).

unduly, *nimis, nimium*.

undutiful, *impius, officii immemor*.

undying; see IMMORTAL.

unearth, *detegĕre, effodĕre*.

unearthly, render by phrase, such as *non* (or *plus quam*) *humanus* or *mortalis*.

uneasily, render by adj.

uneasiness, *sollicitudo, (animi) perturbatio*; see also ANXIETY.

uneasy, in mind, *anxius, sollicitus, trepidus*: to be —, *aestuare*.

unedifying, *frigidus, insulsus*.

uneducated, *indoctus, ineruditus, rudis*.

unembarrassed, *expeditus, liber*; see also FREE.

unemployed, *otiosus, vacuus*; or render by phrase such as *expers laborum, nullis occupationibus implicatus* (Cic.).

unencumbered, *liber, expeditus.*

unendowed, *indotatus.*

unenlightened, *indoctus, rudis, humanitatis expers.*

unenterprising, *iners, socors, piger.*

unenviable, *miser, tristis*; see also PITIFUL.

unequal. (1) = not equal, simply, *impar, dispar, inaequalis* (Hor., Tac.), *dissimilis* (= dissimilar). (2) = inferior, *impar, inferior.*

unequalled, *summus, singularis*; or render by phrase, such as *tantus quantus nemo antea.*

unequally, *inaequaliter, impariter* (Hor.).

unerring, *certus.*

unessential, *adventicius.*

uneven, *iniquus, inaequabilis, inaequalis, impar, asper* (= rough).

unevenly, *inaequaliter.*

unevenness, *iniquitas, asperitas* (= roughness).

unexamined, *inexploratus.*

unexampled, *unicus, singularis, novus, inauditus* (= unheard of); or render by phrase, such as *talis qualis nemo antea.*

unexceptionable, *locuples* (of witnesses, etc.), *probus, bonus*; see also GOOD.

unexecuted, *infectus, imperfectus* : to leave —, *omittěre.*

unexercised, *inexercitatus.*

unexhausted, *indefessus* (= unwearied : Verg., Ov., Tac.), *inexhaustus* (Verg., Tac.), *integer* (= not used up, whole), *recens* (= fresh).

unexpected, *inexspectatus, insperatus, necopinatus, improvisus.*

unexpectedly, *(ex) insperato, (ex) improviso, praeter spem, praeter opinionem*; often rendered by adj. agreeing with the person surprised, e.g. *imprudens* or *necopinans*; see also UNAWARE, UNAWARES.

unexplored, *inexploratus.*

unextinguishable, *inexstinctus* (poet.).

unfading, *immortalis* (= immortal); or render by phrase, such as *semper florens.*

unfailing, *perennis* or *perpetuus* (= perpetual), *certus* (= sure).

unfair, *iniquus, iniustus, immeritus* (= not deserved).

unfairly, *inique, iniuste, iniuriā.*

unfairness, *iniquitas, iniuria.*

unfaithful, *infidelis, infidus, perfidus, perfidiosus* : to be —, *fidem fallěre.*

unfaithfully, *infideliter.*

unfaithfulness, *infidelitas, perfidia, mala fides.*

unfamiliar; see UNACCUSTOMED.

unfashionable, render by phrase, such as *quod contra consuetudinem fit.*

unfasten, *(re)solvěre, (re)laxare, refigěre* (of what is nailed fast).

unfathomable, *immensus, infinitus.*

unfavourable, *iniquus, adversus, aversus, alienus*; of omens, *malus, tristis, funestus, infaustus* (poet. and Tac.), *sinister* (Verg., Tac.).

unfavourableness, *iniquitas*; or render by adj.

unfavourably, *male*; or render by adj.

unfeathered, *implumis* (Verg.).

unfed, *impastus* (Verg.).

unfeeling, *durus, lentus, ferreus, inhumanus* : to become —, *obdurescěre.*

unfeelingly, *inhumane, inhumaniter.*

unfeigned, *verus, sincerus, simplex.*

unfeignedly, *vere, sincere, ex animo.*

unfeminine; see UNWOMANLY.

unfilial, *impius (erga parentes).*

unfinished, *imperfectus*; = rough, rude, *rudis, impolitus.*

unfit, adj. *inutilis, incommodus, indignus* (= unworthy).

unfit, v. *inutilem redděre.*

unfitness, *inutilitas.*

unfitting; see IMPROPER.

unfix, *refigěre.*

unfixed, *mobilis.*

unfledged, *implumis* (Verg.).

unfold, v. (1) transit. *explicare, aperire, expanděre* (Lucr.), *explanare* (in words only). (2) intransit., render by pass. of transit. verbs.

unforced, render by adv. *ultro* or *sponte* (*sua*).

unforeseen, *improvisus.*

unforgiving, *implacabilis, inexorabilis.*

unforgotten, render by negative phrase with *oblivisci* (= to forget) or *oblivio* (= oblivion) or by positive phrase with *memoria* (= memory).

unformed, *informis* (= shapeless), *imperfectus* or *nondum perfectus* (= not finished); of language, *inconditus.*

unfortified, *immunitus.*

unfortunate; see UNLUCKY.

unfounded, *vanus, fictus, falsus.*

unfrequented, *avius, devius, desertus.*

unfriendliness, *inimicitia, simultas.*

unfriendly, *inimicus, iniquus, alienus.*

unfruitful, *sterilis, infecundus* (Sall., Verg.); see also BARREN.

unfruitfulness, *sterilitas, infecunditas* (Tac.).

unfulfilled, *inritus, vanus* : to remain —, *exitum* (or *eventum*) *nullum habēre.*

unfurl, of sails, *panděre, explicare* (Pl.).

unfurnished, *imparatus* : an — house, *domus nuda atque inanis.*

ungainly, *inhabilis*; see also AWKWARD.

ungenerous, *inliberalis, sordidus* : — conduct, *inliberalitas.*

ungenerously, *inliberaliter.*

ungenteel, *ignobilis, inhonestus.*

ungentle; see UNKIND, ROUGH.

ungentlemanly, *inliberalis, indecorus.*

ungirt, *discinctus* (Hor.).

ungodly; see IMPIOUS.

ungovernable, *indomitus* (= untamed), *effrenatus* (= unbridled), *impotens* (= without self-control).

ungraceful, *invenustus, inelegans.*

ungracious, *iniquus, morosus, asper.*

ungraciously, *iniquo animo, morose, aspere.*

ungrateful, *ingratus, beneficii* (or *beneficiorum*) *immemor.*

ungrudging; see LIBERAL.

unguarded. (1) = not guarded, *incustoditus* (Ov., Tac.), *indefensus.* (2) = imprudent, *incautus, imprudens.*

unguardedly, *incaute, temere.*

unguent, *unguentum.*

unhallowed, *profanus.*

unhappily, *misere, infeliciter* (Ter.); see also SADLY.

unhappiness, *miseria, aerumna, aegrimonia*; see also SORROW.

unhappy, *infelix, infortunatus, miser, aerumnosus, adflictus;* see also SAD.

unharmed, *salvus, incolumis, inviolatus.*

unharness, *disiungĕre, solvĕre.*

unhatched, *nondum (ex ovo) exclusus.*

unhealthiness. (1) = poor health, (*mala*) *valetudo, imbecillitas corporis.* (2) = unwholesomeness, *gravita..*

unhealthy. (1) = liable to ill-health, *valetudine adfectus, ad aegrotandum proclivis, infirmae valetudinis, infirmus, imbecillus.* (2) = unwholesome, *pestilens, gravis.*

unheard, *inauditus:* to punish a person —, *hominem indictā causā* or *inauditum* or *absentem condemnare;* —of, *inauditus, novus.*

unheeded, *neglectus.*

unheroic, *ignavus;* see also COWARDLY.

unhesitating, *strenuus, confidens.*

unhesitatingly, *strenue, confidenter.*

unhewn, *rudis.*

unhindered, *liber, expeditus.*

unhinged, in mind, *mente captus.*

unhistorical, *commenticius, fictus.*

unholy, *profanus;* see also IMPIOUS.

unhonoured, *inhonoratus.*

unhook, *refigĕre, refibulare* (= to unbuckle: Mart.).

unhoped for, *insperatus.*

unhurt, *integer, incolumis, salvus, intactus, inviolatus.*

unicorn, *monoceros (-ōtis:* Plin.).

uniform, subst., render by *arma* (-*orum*, plur.) or by phrase, such as *vestitus (-ūs) militaris.*

uniform, adj. *constans, aequabilis, aequalis;* or render by phrase such as *unius generis* or if movement is involved by *tenor* (= uninterrupted course).

uniformity, *aequabilitas, aequalitas, constantia.*

uniformly, *constanter, aequabiliter, aequaliter, uno tenore.*

unimaginable, render by phrase, such as *supra quam quod cogitari potest.*

unimpaired, *integer, intactus, inviolatus.*

unimpassioned, *lentus, integer;* or render by phrase, such as *omni cupiditate carens, sine irā et studio.*

unimpeachable, *locuples* (of witnesses, etc.), *sanctus* (morally).

unimportant, *lĕvis, nullius momenti.*

uninformed, *indoctus.*

uninhabitable, *inhabitabilis.*

uninhabited, *desertus;* or render by phrase, such as *cultoribus vacuus.*

uninitiated LIT., *profanus* (Hor.). TRANSF., *ignarus, imperitus.*

uninjured, *incolumis, integer, salvus, inviolatus.*

uninspired, render by phrase, such as *divino spiritu* (or *adflatu*) *haud instinctus.*

uninstructed, *indoctus, rudis.*

unintelligible, *obscurus.*

unintelligibly, *obscure* (Quint.).

unintentional, unintentionally, render by adv., such as *forte, non sponte* or by adj. agreeing with the agent, such as *imprudens, insciens.*

uninteresting, *ieiunus, frigidus.*

unintermitting, *continuus, adsiduus.*

uninterred, *inhumatus, insepultus.*

uninterrupted, *continens, continuus, adsiduus, perpetuus, perennis:* an — course, *tenor.*

uninterruptedly, *continenter, uno tenore, perpetuo.*

uninured; see UNACCUSTOMED.

uninvestigated, *inexploratus.*

uninvited, *invocatus.*

uninviting, *iniucundus.*

union. (1) = the act of uniting, (*con*)*iunctio, consociatio, congregatio.* (2) = agreement, *consensio, consensus* (-*ūs*), *concordia;* see also AGREEMENT. (3) = united body, *societas, sodalitas, concilium;* see also SOCIETY. (4) see MARRIAGE.

unique, *unicus, singularis.*

unison, (in music) *concordia vocum.*

unit, *monas* (-*ădis*: late Latin); otherwise render by adj. *singuli* (= one at a time).

unite, v. (1) transit. (*con*)*iungĕre, copulare, congregare* (= to collect into a flock), (*con*)*sociare* (as partners), *miscēre* (= to mix, lit. and fig.); see also JOIN. (2) intransit. *coire, consentire* (= to agree); or render by pass. of transit. verbs: to — in partnership, *societatum* (*cum homine*) *inire;* see also JOIN, AGREE.

united, *coniunctus, consociatus, socius.*

unity, render by *unus* (= one): e.g. there was — of opinion among them all, *sententia inter omnes una erat;* see also UNION.

universal, *universus, communis* (= belonging to all), *omnium* (= of all); see also GENERAL.

universality, *communitas* (= fellowship); or render by adj.

universally, *universe, in universum:* — beloved, *ab omnibus dilectus.*

universe, *mundus, mundi* or *rerum universitas, rerum natura.*

university, *academia* (late Latin).

unjust, *iniustus, iniquus, iniurius, iniuriosus.*

unjustifiable, render by phrase, with *excusare* (= to excuse); see also UNJUST.

unjustly, *iniuste, inique, iniuriose, contra ius, iniuriā.*

unkempt, *neglectus, incomptus.*

unkind, *inhumanus, severus.*

unkindly, *inhumane, severe.*

unkindness, *inhumanitas, severitas.*

unknowing, *inscius, insciens, ignarus.*

unknown, *ignotus, incognitus, incompertus* (rare), *inexploratus* (= unexplored), *obscurus* (= obscure): a person — to me, *nescio quis.*

unlace; see UNTIE, LOOSEN.

unlamented, *infletus* (Verg.), *indefletus* (Ov.), *indeploratus* (Ov.).

unlatch, *reserare;* see also OPEN.

unlawful, adj. *non legitimus, vetitus, inlicitus* (Sen., Tac.): it is —, *nefas est, non licet.*

unlawfully, *contra legem* or *leges.*

unlearn, *dediscĕre.*

unlearned, *indoctus, inliteratus, ineruditus* (rare), *litterarum expers* or *imperitus.*

unlearnedly, *indocte.*

unleavened, *sine fermento* (Cels., Vulgate).

unless, *nisi* (contracted *ni*): — by any chance, *nisi forte.*

unlettered; see UNLEARNED.

unlike, *dissimilis, dispar, diversus.*

unlikely; see IMPROBABLE.

unlimited, *infinitus, immensus.*

unload. (1) = to free from a burden (lit. or fig.), *exonerare, onere liberare* or *levare.* (2) = to put down or empty out a burden, *deponĕre, exponere.*

unlock, *recludĕre, reserare.*

unlooked-for, *inexspectatus, insperatus*; see also UNEXPECTED.

unloose, *solvĕre.*

unlovely, *inamabilis* (poet.), *inamoenus* (Ov.).

unluckily, *infeliciter, secus.*

unlucky, *infelix*; see also UNFAVOURABLE, UNHAPPY.

unman, *enervare, debilitare, percellĕre.*

unmanageable; see UNGOVERNABLE.

unmanly, *viro indignus, effeminatus* (= effeminate), *mollis* (= soft).

unmannerly, *male moratus, inurbanus*; see also RUDE.

unmarried, *caelebs.*

unmask. LIT., *personam (homini) detrahĕre* or *eripĕre.* TRANSF., *detegĕre, aperire, patefacĕre.*

unmatched, *unicus, singularis.*

unmeaning, *inanis.*

unmelodious, *raucus, parum canorus.*

unmentioned: to remain —, *omitti, praetermitti*; to leave —, *omittĕre, praetermittĕre.*

unmerciful, *immisericors, inclemens, inexorabilis, immitis.*

unmercifully, *immisericorditer* (Ter.), *inclementer.*

unmindful, *immemor, incuriosus* (Tac.).

unmingled; see UNMIXED.

unmistakable; see CLEAR, CERTAIN.

unmitigated, often to be rendered by the superl. of an adj., e.g. a war of — cruelty, *bellum atrocissimum*; see also COMPLETE, ABSOLUTE.

unmixed, *merus, simplex.*

unmolested, *incolumis, inviolatus.*

unmoor, *solvĕre.*

unmoved, *immotus*: to be or remain —, *non (com)movēri.*

unmutilated, *integer, salvus.*

unnatural. (1) = outside the ordinary course of nature, *monstruosus, portentosus*; of character, *immanis*; of persons ignoring the natural rights of parents, etc., *impius*; of crimes, *nefarius.* (2) see AFFECTED.

unnaturally, *contra naturam, praeter naturam.*

unnavigable, *innavigabilis.*

unnecessarily, *cum non opus est, ex supervacuo, praeter necessitatem*; sometimes rendered by compar. of adj. or adv. (e.g. — long, *longior*) or by *nimis* or *nimium* (= too).

unnecessary, *non necessarius, quod non opus est, supervacaneus, supervacuus, vanus* (= idle, e.g. *metus*): it is — to mention them, *eos non est necesse* (or *non opus est* or *nihil attinet*) *nominare.*

unnerve; see UNMAN.

unnoticed: to leave —, *praetermittĕre, praeterire (silentio), neglegĕre*; to go —, *fallĕre, latēre.*

unnumbered, *innumerabilis, innumerus* (poet. and Tac.).

unobserved; see UNNOTICED.

unoccupied. (1) of persons, *otiosus, vacuus*; see also UNEMPLOYED. (2) of ground, *apertus, purus.*

unoffending, *innocens, immerens* (poet.).

unopened; see OPEN, v.

unorganized, *inconditus.*

unorthodox, render by phrase, such as *a ceteris (de rebus divinis) dissentire.*

unostentatious; see MODEST.

unpack; see UNLOAD.

unpaid, (of money or debts) *non solutus,*

residuus; of the creditor, *cui non satisfactum est.*

unpalatable, *amarus* (= bitter).

unparalleled, *unicus, singularis*; see also UNEQUALLED.

unpardonable, render by phrase, such as *quod excusari non potest.*

unpatriotic, *patriae immemor*: an — citizen, *malus civis.*

unperceived; see UNNOTICED.

unphilosophical, *philosophiae expers.*

unpitied, *immiserabilis*; otherwise render by verb.

unpitying, *immisericors, immitis, inexorabilis.*

unpleasant, *molestus, ingratus, iniucundus, odiosus, incommodus*; see also DISAGREEABLE.

unpleasantly, *iniucunde, odiose, incommode.*

unpleasantness, *incommodum, molestia.*

unploughed, *inaratus* (Verg., Hor.).

unpoetic, render by phrase, such as *a poetarum ratione alienus.*

unpolished, *impolitus* (lit. and fig.), *rudis.*

unpolluted, *impollutus* (Tac.), *intemeratus* (poet. and Tac.), *integer.*

unpopular, *invidiosus, ingratus, offensus, invisus*: to be (very) —, *in (magnā) invidiā esse*; to become —, *in invidiam venire*; to make —, *in invidiam adducĕre.*

unpopularity, *invidia, offensio.*

unpractised, *inexercitatus, rudis.*

unprecedented, *novus, inauditus.*

unprejudiced, *integer*; see also UNBIASSED.

unpremeditated, *subitus*; or render by the phrase *ex tempore* (= on the spur of the moment).

unprepared, *imparatus.*

unprepossessing; see UNPLEASANT, UNLOVELY.

unpretending; see MODEST.

unprincipled, *improbus, nequam.*

unproductive, *infecundus* (Sall., Verg.), *sterilis.*

unprofitable: to be —, *nullum fructum adferre, nil prodesse.*

unprofitably, *mutiliter, frustra, incassum, nequiquam.*

unpromising; see PROMISE.

unpronounceable, *ineffabilis* (Plin.); or render by phrase with *enuntiare* (= to pronounce).

unpropitious; see UNFAVOURABLE.

unprotected, *indefensus, non custoditus.*

unproved, *argumentis non (con)firmatus.*

unprovided, *imparatus*; see also PROVIDE.

unprovoked, *inlacessitus* (Tac.), *non lacessitus*; or render by *ultro* (= of one's own accord).

unpublished, *nondum editus.*

unpunished, *impunitus, inultus*; or render by adv. *impune*, e.g. to go — for a thing, *rem impune ferre.*

unpurchased, *inemptus* (poet. and Tac.), *non emptus.*

unqualified. (1) see UNSUITABLE. (2) see UNCONDITIONAL. (3) = very great (of approval, success, etc.), *summus, maximus.*

unquenchable, *inexstinctus* (Ov.).

unquestionable, *certus, haud dubius*: it is — that, *dubitari non potest quin*, with subj.

unquestionably, *sine dubio, procul dubio, scilicet.*

unravel. LIT., *retexĕre.* TRANSF., *explicare, enodare, evolvĕre, dissolvĕre.*

unread, *non lectus*: an — man, *homo litterarum expers.*

unreasonable, *absurdus* (= irrational), *iniquus*

(= unfair): it is — that, *non* (or *nulla*) *ratio est*, with acc. and infin.

unreasonably, *absurde, inique* (= unfairly).

unrefined, *crudus, rudis*; of manners; see RUDE.

unregarded, *neglectus*.

unrelenting, *immitis, inexorabilis*; see also UNMERCIFUL.

unremitting, *continuus, adsiduus*.

unrepentant, render by phrase, such as *quem non paenitet*.

unreproved, *incastigatus* (Hor.), *non reprehensus*.

unrequested, *ultro oblatus* (= freely offered).

unrequited, *inultus* (= unavenged).

unresented, adj. *inultus, impunitus*.

unreserved. (1) = open, frank, *liber, apertus, simplex*; see also FRANK. (2) see UNCONDITIONAL.

unreservedly, *absolute, sine ulla exceptione*.

unrest; see RESTLESSNESS.

unrestrained, *effrenatus, effusus, indomitus, impotens*.

unrevenged, *inultus*.

unrewarded, *sine praemio, inhonoratus*.

unrighteous, *improbus, iniustus, iniquus, impius* (= undutiful).

unrighteously, *improbe, inuste, inique, impie*.

unrighteousness, *improbitas, impietas*.

unripe, *immaturus, crudus*.

unripeness, *immaturitas* (Suet.).

unrivalled, *eximius, unicus, singularis, praestantissimus*; or render by relative clause, e.g. *tantus quantus nemo antea fuit*.

unroll, *evolvēre, explicare*.

unroof; see UNCOVER.

unruffled, *tranquillus, immotus*.

unruliness, *effrenatio, impotentia, ferocitas*.

unruly, *effrenatus, impotens, ferox, turbidus, turbulentus*.

unsafe, *infestus, intutus* (Tac.), *periculosus* (= dangerous), *lubricus* (lit. = slippery), *incertus* (= uncertain).

unsaid, *indictus*.

unsaleable, *invendibilis* (Pl.).

unsalted, *sale non condītus*.

unsaluted, *insalutatus* (Verg.).

unsatisfactorily, *male, minus bene, secus* (esp. of results).

unsatisfactory, *non idoneus* (= unsuitable), *paenitendus* (usually with a neg.), sometimes *malus*.

unsatisfied, render by phrase, such as *cui non satisfactum est*.

unsavoury; see UNPALATABLE.

unsay; see RECANT.

unscrew, render by *solvēre*.

unseal, *resignare*.

unsearchable, *inexplicabilis, inexploratus*; or render by verb.

unseasonable, *intempestivus, incommodus, importunus, immaturus* (lit. = unripe).

unseasonably, *intempestive, incommode*.

unseasoned, of food, *non condītus*; of wood, *viridis, humidus*.

unseemly; see INDECOROUS.

unseen, *invisus*.

unselfish, *suae utilitatis immemor, omni carens cupiditate, gratuitus* (= done without hope of reward), *liberalis* (= generous).

unselfishly, *gratuito, liberaliter*.

unselfishness, *abstinentia, continentia*; or render by adj.

unserviceable, *inutilis*.

unsettle, *labefacĕre, (com)movēre, (per)turbare, (hominem* etc.) *dubium facĕre*.

unsettled. (1) in gen., *inconstans, varius, mobilis, mutabilis, incertus, vagus*. (2) see UNPAID.

unshackled, *liber, solutus*.

unshaken, *immotus, inlabefactus* (Ov.), *inconcussus* (Luc.).

unshaved, *intonsus*.

unsheathe, *(de)stringĕre, e vaginā educĕre*.

unship, *exponĕre*.

unshod, *pedibus nudis*.

unshorn, *intonsus*.

unsightly; see UGLY.

unsisterly, *quod sororis non est*.

unskilful, unskilled, *inscitus, imperitus, rudis, ignarus* (= ignorant), *inexercitatus* (= unpractised).

unskilfully, *inscite, imperite*.

unskilfulness, *imperitia, inscitia* (Tac.).

unslaked: of lime, *vivus* (Vitr.); of thirst, *non expletus*.

unsociable, *insociabilis, difficilis*.

unsoiled; see UNBLEMISHED.

unsolicited; see UNASKED.

unsophisticated, *simplex*.

unsorted, *incompositus, inordinatus*.

unsound. (1) of material things, *puter, putris* (= rotten), *vitiosus* (Pl.). (2) abstract, *vitiosus, infirmus, vanus, pravus*: of — mind, *insanus*.

unsoundness, of mind, *insanitas*; in gen., *infirmitas, pravitas*.

unsown, *non satus*.

unsparing. (1) = cruel, *inclemens*; see also CRUEL, UNMERCIFUL. (2) see LIBERAL.

unsparingly. (1) = cruelly, *inclementer, crudeliter*. (2) = liberally, *large, profuse*.

unspeakable, *infandus, inenarrabilis*.

unspoiled, *incorruptus, integer*.

unstable, unsteady, *mobilis, levis, inconstans, instabilis, incertus*.

unstained, *purus, in(con)taminatus, integer, intemeratus* (poet. and Tac.).

unsteadily, render by adj.

unsteadiness, *mobilitas, levitas, inconstantia*.

unstring: to — a bow, *arcum retendĕre* (Ov.).

unstrung: of the nerves, etc., *fractus, debilitatus*.

unstudied, (of style) *simplex*.

unsubdued, *indomitus*.

unsuccessful, *infelix, infaustus* (Tac.), *improsper* (Tac.): to be —, *rem* (or *negotium*) *male gerere*.

unsuccessfully, *infeliciter, improspere* (Tac.).

unsuitable, unsuited, *incommodus (alienus)*.

unsuitableness, *incommoditas*.

unsuitably, *incommode*.

unsuspected, *non suspectus, in quem nulla suspicio cadit*.

unsuspecting, unsuspicious, *incautus, minime suspicax*.

untainted, *incorruptus, non infectus, integer*.

untamed, *indomitus, ferus*.

untasted, *ingustatus* (Hor.).

untaught, *indoctus*.

unteachable, *indocilis*.

untenable, render by verb, e.g. *tenēre* (= to hold), *defendĕre* (= to defend).

unterrified, *interritus* (poet. and Tac.), *impavidus*.

unthankful; see UNGRATEFUL.
unthinking; see THOUGHTLESS.
untie, (*dis*)*solvĕre, laxare.*
until, prep. *ad* or *in* with acc.
until, conj. *dum, donec, quoad*; see also TILL.
untilled, *incultus, inaratus* (= unploughed: Verg., Hor.).
untimely, *immaturus, intempestivus, incommodus*: an — death, *mors immatura* or *acerba* (Verg.).
untiring, *adsiduus, indefessus* (poet. and Tac.).
unto; see TO.
untold. (1) *nulli* or *non dictus.* (2) see COUNTLESS, INNUMERABLE.
untouched, *intactus, integer*; = uninfluenced, *immotus.*
untoward, *adversus*; see also UNFAVOURABLE.
untranslatable, *quod verbis reddi non potest.*
untried, *inexpertus, intemptatus* (poet. and Tac.).
untrodden, of paths, etc., *non tritus.*
untroubled, *tranquillus, placidus, quietus*; = carefree, *securus.*
untrue, *falsus.*
untruly, *falso.*
untruth, *falsum, mendacium.*
unturned: to leave no stone —, render by general phrase, such as *nihil non adhibēre.*
untwine, **untwist**, (*re*)*solvĕre, retexĕre.*
unused. (1) see UNACCUSTOMED. (2) = not yet used, *recens, novus, integer*; see also FRESH.
unusual, *inusitatus, insuetus, insolĭtus, insolens*: in an — manner, *inusitate.*
unutterable, *infandus, inenarrabilis.*
unutterably, *supra quam quod enuntiari potest.*
unvanquished, *invictus.*
unvarnished. LIT., *fuco non inlitus.* TRANSF., *simplex, nudus, sine fuco* (*ac fallaciis*); see also PLAIN.
unvarying; see UNCHANGED, IMMUTABLE.
unveil, (lit. and fig.) *detegĕre, aperire, patefacĕre, (de)nudare.*
unversed, *rudis, imperitus.*
unviolated, *inviolatus.*
unwalled, *muris non circumdatus, sine muris, immunitus* (= unfortified).
unwarily, *incaute, imprudenter.*
unwariness, *imprudentia.*
unwarlike, adj. *imbellis.*
unwarrantable, *iniquus, iniustus*; see also UNJUST.
unwary, *incautus, imprudens.*
unwashed, *inlotus* (Pl., Verg.).
unwatched, *incustoditus* (Ov., Tac.).
unwavering; see FIRM.
unwearied, *indefessus* (poet. and Tac.), *integer* (= still fresh), *adsiduus, sedulus.*
unweave, *retexĕre.*
unwelcome, *ingratus, iniucundus.*
unwell, *aeger, invalidus, infirmus.*
unwholesome, *pestilens, gravis, insalubris* (Plin.).
unwieldy, *inhabilis*; see also CLUMSY.
unwilling, *invitus*: to be —, *nolle.*
unwillingly, render by adj. *invitus* (= unwilling).
unwillingness, render by adj., or verb *nolle.*
unwind, *retexĕre, explicare.*
unwise, *insipiens, stultus.*
unwisely, *insipienter, stulte.*
unwitting, *inscius, insciens.*

unwomanly, *quod non mulieris est.*
unwonted; see UNUSUAL.
unworthily, *indigne.*
unworthiness, *indignitas.*
unworthy, *indignus.*
unwounded, *invulneratus, sine vulnere, integer.*
unwrap, *evolvĕre, explicare.*
unwritten, *non scriptus.*
unwrought, *rudis, infectus.*
unyielding; see INFLEXIBLE.
unyoke, *disiungĕre.*
up, prep.: — the river, *adverso flumine*; — the mountain, *in adversum montem.*
up, adv. *sursum*; as an exclamation, *age!*: — to, *usque ad* (with acc.), *tenus* (with abl. or genit. plur. and placed after its subst. or pronoun); from one's youth —, *a puero*; to burn —, *comburĕre*; to dig —, *effodĕre, eruĕre*; to dry —, *excrescĕre*; to give —, *tradĕre*; to go —, *ascendĕre*; to stay — (at night), *vigilare.*
upbraid, *reprehendĕre, obiurgare, increpare, exprobrare.*
upbraiding, *obiurgatio, exprobratio, convicium.*
uphill, adj. *adclivis, arduus.*
uphill, adv. *adverso colle, adversus collem.*
uphold, *sustinēre, sustentare, fulcire* (= to prop).
upholsterer, render by phrase, such as *qui* (*domum*, etc.) *instruit* or (*ex*)*ornat.*
upland, adj. *editus*; see MOUNTAINOUS.
upon, prep. (1) in space: *super* (with acc., more rarely abl.); *in* (to go —, *in* with acc.; to be —, *in* with abl.); — a side, or — a person's side, *a* or *ab*, with abl. (2) in time = directly after: *e* or *ex* (with abl.), *sub* (with acc.); or render by abl. absol. or temporal clause. (3) in other relations: — this condition, *hac condicione*; — this subject, *de hac re*, more rarely *super hac re*; see also ON.
upper, *superus, superior*: to get the — hand, *superare, vincĕre*; the — storeys of a house, *pars superior aedium.*
uppermost, *summus, supremus*, or *princeps* (in rank or dignity).
uppish, *adrogans, superbus.*
upright. LIT., = vertical, (*e*)*rectus.* TRANSF., morally, *probus, honestus, ĭnteger, iustus, gravis.*
uprightly, *recte, probe, honeste, integre.*
uprightness, *probitas, integritas, honestas.*
uproar, *tumultus* (-*ūs*); see also NOISE.
uproarious, *tumultuosus.*
uproot, *radicitus tollĕre, extrahĕre, evellĕre.*
upset, adj. *adflictus, perculsus.*
upset, v. *evertĕre, subvertĕre.*
upshot, *exitus* (-*ūs*), *eventus* (-*ūs*).
upside-down: to turn —, *omnia turbare et miscēre.*
upstart, *novus homo.*
upwards, *sursum* (*versus*); see also MORE.
urbane, *urbanus.*
urbanity, *urbanitas*; see also POLITENESS.
urchin. (1) see HEDGEHOG. (2) human, *pusio, puer.*
urge, v. LIT., physically, *impellĕre, incitare, urgēre.* TRANSF., by words, moral pressure, etc., *impellĕre, urgēre, incitare, stimulare, (homini) stimulos admovēre, (homini) instare*: to — a course upon a person, *rem* (or *ut* clause) *homini suadēre.*

urgency, *gravitas, necessitas.*
urgent; of matters, *necessarius, gravis, magni momenti;* of persons, *vehemens,* or render by verb: at my — request, *orante me atque obsecrante.*
urgently, *vehementer, magnopere.*
urine, *urina, lotium* (Suet.).
urn, *urna.*
usage, *mos, consuetudo:* it is an accepted —, *more* or *usu receptum est;* see also CUSTOM.
use, subst. (1) = the act of using, *usus (-ūs), usurpatio, usura:* to make — of, *(re) uti;* to come into —, *in usum venire;* to go out of —, *exolescĕre.* (2) = usefulness, *utilitas, usus (-ūs):* to be of great —, *maxime prodesse, utilissimum* or *magno usui esse.*
use, v. (1) = to make use of, *uti* (with abl.), *abuti* (with abl.; = to use fully), *usurpare* (with acc.), *adhibĕre* (= to apply, bring to bear): to — wrongly, *abuti.* (2) = to treat, *tractare.* (3) to — up, *consumĕre.*
used; see ACCUSTOMED.
useful, *utilis, aptus, idoneus, accommodatus, commodus:* to be —, *utilem esse, usui esse, prodesse.*
usefully, *utiliter, apte, commode.*
usefulness, *utilitas, usus (-ūs), commoditas.*
useless, *inūtilis, vanus, inanis, inritus:* to be —, *nihil prodesse.*
uselessly, *inutiliter* (only after negative), *frustra, incassum, nequiquam.*
usher, subst. (1) = under-teacher, *hypo-didascalus.* (2) = any subordinate official, perhaps *apparitor.*
usher, v.: to — in. LIT., *introducĕre.* TRANSF., see BEGIN.
usual, *usitatus, solitus, consuetus, tritus* (of language = commonplace), *more* or *usu receptus* (= customary): as is —, *ut fit;* more than —, *plus* (or *magis) solito.*
usually, *ferme, fere, plerumque:* as — happens, *ut fit, ut fieri solet.*
usucaption, *usucapio.*
usufruct, *usus (-ūs) et fructus (-ūs),* or *usus fructus.*
usurer, *faenerator, toculio.*
usurp, in gen. *(rem) sibi adsumĕre, (rem* or *in rem) invadĕre:* to — the throne, *regnum occupare.*
usurpation, render by verb.
usurper, render by verb.
usury, *faeneratio, usura:* to practise —, *faenerari.*
utensils, *vasa (-orum), utensilia (-ium), supellex, instrumentum.*
uterine, *uterinus* (leg.).
utilitarian, render by phrase, such as *qui ex utilitate omnia aestimat.*
utility; see USEFULNESS.
utmost, *extremus, ultimus, summus:* to do one's —, *summis viribus contendĕre, omni ope atque operā eniti.*
utter, adj., render by *totus* (= whole); see also UTMOST.
utter, v. *dicĕre, pronuntiare, effari, emittĕre:* not to — a word, *verbum nullum facĕre.*
utterance, *dictum* (= a saying), *pronuntiatio* (= delivery).
utterly, *omnino, penitus, funditus.*
uxorious, *uxorius* (Verg., Tac.); or render by phrase.

V

vacancy. (1) = empty space, *vacuum, inane, inanitas* (= emptiness). (2) = an unoccupied post or place in a community, render by *vacuus:* chosen to fill a —, *suffectus.* (3) — of mind, *stupiditas.*
vacant, in gen. *vacuus:* to be —, *vacuum esse, vacare;* of persons = without intelligence, *stupidus.*
vacate, in gen. *vacuefacĕre:* to — an office, *se magistratu abdicare, magistratum eiurare* (Tac.).
vacation, *feriae (-arum,* plur.).
vacillate, *vacillare.*
vacillating, *dubius, incertus, ambiguus.*
vacillation, *dubitatio;* see also DOUBT, HESITATION.
vacuity; see VACANCY or EMPTINESS.
vagabond, vagrant, subst. *erro* (Hor., Ov.), *grassator.*
vagabond, vagrant, adj. *vagus.*
vagary, *ineptiae (-arum,* plur. = silliness); see also WHIM.
vague, *incertus, dubius, ambiguus, anceps, vagus.*
vaguely, *incerte, dubie, ambigue.*
vagueness, render by adj.
vain. (1) = empty, worthless, *inanis, vanus, lēvis.* (2) = fruitless, *vanus, inritus;* see also VAINLY. (3) = self-satisfied, vainglorious, *vanus, gloriosus* (= boastful): to be —, *sibi placēre.*
vainglorious, *vaniloquus, gloriosus.*
vainglory, *ostentatio, gloria.*
vainly, in vain, *frustra* (with special reference to the disappointed agent), *nequiquam* (with special reference to the end not achieved), *incassum* (or *in cassum), inaniter* (= idly): to labour in vain, *(oleum et) operam perdĕre.*
vale; see VALLEY.
valediction, valedictory; see FAREWELL.
Valencia, *Valentia.*
valentine, render by phrase, such as *epistula amatoria.*
valet, *cubicularius.*
valetudinarian, subst. and adj. *valetudinarius* (Varro, Sen.); or render by phrase, such as *suae valetudinis (nimis) studiosus.*
valiant, valorous, *fortis, animosus, strenuus, acer;* see also BRAVE.
valiantly, *fortiter, animose, strenue, acriter.*
valid. (1) of arguments, reasons, etc., *firmus, gravis, iustus, certus, legitimus.* (2) of laws, *ratus:* to be —, *ratum esse, valēre;* to make —, *ratum facĕre, ratum esse iubēre.*
validity, (of reasons, etc.) *gravitas, pondus (-ĕris,* n.); otherwise render by adj.
valise, *vidulus* (Pl.), *mantica* (Cat., Hor.).
valley, *(con)vallis.*
valorous; see VALIANT.
valour, *virtūs (-ūtis,* f.), *fortitudo;* see also BRAVERY.
valuable, *pretiosus, magni pretii;* see also USEFUL, GOOD.
valuation, *aestimatio.*
value, subst. *aestimatio* (= estimated worth), *pretium* (lit. = price): to be of great —, *magni esse, multum prodesse;* see also VALUE, v. and VALUABLE.

value, v. (1) = to set a certain value on a person or thing, *aestimare, facĕre, ducĕre, pendĕre, putare* (all with genit. or abl. of the assessment): to be highly —d, *magni fieri;* to — one thing above another; see PREFER. (2) = to set a high value on, *magni facĕre, diligĕre, multum tribuĕre* (with dat.).

valueless; see WORTHLESS.

valuer, *aestimator.*

valve, *epistomium* (Sen.).

vampire. (1) as a mythical blood-sucking creature, render by *lamia* (Hor.) or *larva* (Pl.) = ghost, or perhaps by *Harpyiae* (*-arum;* = the Harpies). (2) as a species of bat, *vespertilio.*

van. (1) of an army, *primum agmen* (on the march), *prima acies* (in battle). (2) as a vehicle; see CARRIAGE, CART.

vane; see WEATHERCOCK.

vanish, v.intr. (*e*)*vanescĕre, dilabi* (= to glide away in different directions).

vanity. (1) = emptiness, *inanitas, vanitas.* (2) = empty pride, self-satisfaction, *vanitas, gloria, ostentatio.*

vanquish, (*de*)*vincĕre, superare, domare* (= to subdue).

vanquisher, *victor* (with f. *victrix*), *domitor* (= subduer).

vapid, *vapidus* (Pers.), *ieiunus, insulsus.*

vapour, *vapor, halitus* (*-ūs*: poet.), *nebula, exhalatio.*

variable, *varius, mobilis, mutabilis, inconstans;* see also CHANGEABLE.

variableness, *mobilitas, mutabilitas;* see also CHANGE, VARIATION.

variance, = disagreement, *discordia, dissensio, discrepantia:* to be at — with, (*ab homine*) *dissidĕre, discordare, discrepare;* of several, to be at — among themselves, use the verbs given above, with *inter se.*

variation, *varietas, variatio, vicissitudo, commutatio;* see also CHANGE.

varicose, *varicosus* (Pers., Juv.): a — vein, *varix.*

varied; see VARIOUS.

variegated, *varius, versicolor.*

variety, *varietas, diversitas, vicissitudo:* a — of things, *res multae* or *variae.*

various, *varius, diversus, multiplex* (= manifold); or render by *alius* (e.g. — opinions are held, *alii alia censent*).

variously, *varie, diverse.*

varlet; see SERVANT or RASCAL.

varnish, subst. LIT., *atramentum* (Plin.). TRANSF., = disguise, specious appearance, *color, fucus, species.*

varnish, v. LIT., *atramento inlinĕre.* TRANSF., see CONCEAL, DISGUISE.

vary, v. (1) transit. *variare, mutare;* see also CHANGE. (2) intransit., use pass. of transit. verbs; see also CHANGE.

vase, *vas, urceus* (Pl., Hor.), *urceolus* (Juv.).

vassal, *cliens.*

vassalage, *clientela.*

vast, *vastus, amplus, magnus, ingens, immanis, immensus;* see also GREAT.

vastly, *magnopere, maxime, incredibiliter, valde.*

vastness, *amplitudo, magnitudo, immensitas.*

vat, *cupa, dolium.*

vaticinate; see FORETELL.

vault, subst. (1) = arched roof, *fornix, camera, concameratio* (Vitr.). (2) = a —ed chamber,

fornix, camera: a — underground, *hypogĕum;* see also TOMB.

vault, v. (1) in building, *confornicare* (Vitr.), *concamerare* (Plin.). (2) = to leap, *salire;* see also LEAP.

vaulted, *fornicatus.*

vaunt; see BOAST.

veal, (*caro*) *vitulina* (Pl.): roast —, *assum vitulinum.*

veer, *se vertĕre, verti;* see also TURN.

vegetable, subst., in gen. *planta:* an edible —, *holus* (*-eris,* n.); — garden, *hortus holitorius;* — gardener, *holitor;* — market, *forum holitorium.*

vegetable, adj.; render by phrase, such as *qui* (*quae, quod*) *ad plantas pertinet:* the — kingdom, *ea quae terra gignit, arbores stirpesque.*

vegetate, v. LIT., see GROW. TRANSF., *hebescĕre.*

vegetation, *herbae, plantae* (*-arum,* plur.).

vehemence, *vis, incitatio, contentio, impetus* (*-ūs*), *violentia* (= violence), *aestus* (*-ūs*) or *fervor* or *ardor* (= heat of passion, etc.), *studium* (= eagerness).

vehement, *vehemens, incitatus, acer, violentus* (= violent), *fervens* or *fervidus* or *ardens* (= passionate).

vehemently, *vehementer, incitate, acriter, contente, animose, ardenter.*

vehicle. (1) = a means of transport, *vehiculum;* see also CARRIAGE, WAGGON. (2) in gen.; see MEANS.

veil, subst. LIT., *rica* (Pl.): a bridal- —, *flammeum* (Plin.), *flammeolum* (Juv.). TRANSF., = cover, disguise, *involucrum, integumentum.*

veil, v. *velare, tegĕre* (lit. and fig.).

vein, *vena, arteria* (= artery).

vellum, *membrana* (Hor.).

velocity, *velocitas;* see also SWIFTNESS.

velvet; see SILK.

velvety; see SMOOTH.

venal, *venalis, nummarius.*

venality, *animus venalis.*

vend, *vendĕre.*

vender, *venditor.*

vendible, *vendibilis.*

veneer, v., render by phrase, such as *sectilibus laminis operire.*

venerable, *venerabilis;* see also REVEREND.

venerate, *colĕre, observare, admirari, venerari.*

veneration, *cultus* (*-ūs*), *veneratio.*

venereal, *venereus.*

vengeance, *ultio, vindicta:* the taking of —, *vindicatio;* to take —, *ulcisci, vindicare;* see also REVENGE.

venial, *veniā dignus.*

venison, (*caro*) *ferina* (Sall., Verg.).

venom, subst. *venenum virus;* see also POISON.

venomous, *venenifer* (Ov.), *venenatus* (lit. and fig.: Ov.); see also POISONOUS.

venous, *venosus* (Plin.).

vent, subst. LIT., *foramen, spiramentum* (Verg.), *spiramen* (Luc.), *spiraculum* (Lucr., Verg.), *emissarium.* TRANSF., to find —, *erumpĕre;* to give —, see VENT, v.

vent, v.: to — one's anger, etc. on a person, *stomachum,* etc., *in hominem erumpĕre, effundĕre, evomĕre.*

vent-hole; see VENT, subst.

ventilate, **vice**

ventilate. LIT., *ventilare* (= to fan): to — a room, *ventum* (*in cubiculum*, etc.), *immittĕre*. TRANSF., *in medium proferre*.
ventilation, render by verb.
ventilator; see VENT, subst.
ventricle, *ventriculus*.
ventriloquist, *ventriloquus* (eccl.); otherwise render by phrase, such as *qui sonos alienos suā voce imitatur*.
venture, subst. *periculum* (= risk), *alea* (= hazard), *facinus* (-*ŏris*, n.; = bold act): at a —, *temere*.
venture, v. (1) = to dare, *audēre*, *periclitari*; prov., nothing —, nothing win, *fortes fortuna adiuvat*. (2) = to endanger, expose to risk, *periclitari*.
venturesome, venturous, *audax*, *temerarius* (= rash).
venturesomely, venturously, *audacter*, *temere*.
venturousness, *audacia*, *temeritas*.
veracious, *verus*, *verax*, *veridicus*, *veritatis amans*.
veracity, *veritas*.
veranda, *subdialia* (-*ium*; plur. = open galleries: Plin.), *podium* (= balcony: Plin.), *porticus* (-*ūs*, f. = colonnade).
verb, *verbum* (grammat. t. t.).
verbal, render by *verbum* or *vox*: to give a — translation, *verbum pro verbo reddĕre*.
verbally, = in direct conversation, render by *conloquium* (= conversation) or *praesens* (= present) or *coram* (= face to face); see also VERBATIM.
verbatim, *ad verbum*, *totidem verbis*.
verbiage, *verba* (-*orum*, plur.).
verbose, *verbosus*.
verbosely, *verbose*.
verboseness, verbosity, *copia* or *ubertas verborum*, *profluentia loquendi*.
verdant, *viridis*, *viridans* (Lucr., Verg.).
verdict, *sententia*, *iudicium*: to pronounce a —, *iudicare*, *sententiam dicĕre* or *pronuntiare*.
verdigris, *aerugo* (Plin.).
verdure, *viriditas*.
verge, subst. LIT. = brink, *margo*, *ora*. TRANSF., render by fut. partic. (e.g. on the — of falling, *casurus*) or by *instare* (= to impend) or by *prope* (= nearly).
verge, v. *vergĕre*, *inclinare*, *appropinquare* (= to — on, to approach).
verger, *apparitor*, *lictor*.
verification, *confirmatio*; see also PROOF.
verify, *confirmare*, *probare*.
verily, *profecto*, *sane*, *certe*.
verisimilitude, *verisimilitudo* (also as two words, *veri similitudo*).
veritable, *verus*; see also TRUE, GENUINE.
verity; see TRUTH.
vermilion, subst. *minium* (Prop.).
vermilion, adj. *minianus*, *miniaceus* (Vitr.); see also RED.
vermin, render by phrase, such as *bestiolae molestae* (-*arum*, plur.); more generally, *pestis*.
vernacular: — tongue, *sermo patrius*, *sermo noster*, *lingua nostra*, *verba* (-*orum*, plur.) *nostratia*.
versatile, *versatilis*, *agilis*, *varius et multiplex*.
versatility, *facilitas*, *ingenium facile*, *agilitas*.
verse. (1) = a single line of poetry, *versus* (-*ūs*), *versiculus*. (2) = poetry, *versūs* (plur.), *poēsis*: a piece of —, poem, *poema*, *carmen*.

versed, (*in re*) *versatus* or *exercitatus*, (*rei*, genit.) *peritus*: thoroughly —, (*in re*) *perfectus*.
versification, *versificatio* (Quint.), *versuum ratio*.
versify, *versūs* (or *carmina*) *facĕre*, *scribĕre*, *condĕre*, *pangĕre*.
version, *liber* (*scriptoris*) *conversus*.
vertebra, *vertebra* (Plin.).
vertex, *vertex* or render by *summus*; see also SUMMIT.
vertical, (*di*)*rectus*: a — line, *linea*, *perpendiculum*.
vertically, *recte*, *directo*, *ad lineam*, *ad perpendiculum*.
vertiginous, *vertiginosus* (Plin.).
vertigo, *vertigo*.
very, adj. *ipse*; see also TRUE, REAL.
very, adv., with adj. or adv. is most often rendered by a superlative (e.g. — good, *optimus*; — well, *optime*); sometimes by special forms with the prefix *per*- (e.g. — few, *perpauci*). Other words and phrases used in this sense are: *maxime*, *summe*, *admodum*, *perquam*, *valde*. Not (so) —, before adj. or adv., *non ita*, *haud ita* (e.g. not so — many, *non ita multi*; not — long after, *haud ita multo post*); — much, with verbs, is rendered by *magnopere*, *maxime*, *summe*, *admodum*, *valde*, *impense*.
vesicle, *vesica* (Plin.).
vesper, = the evening star, *Hesperus*, *Vesper* (Verg., Hor.).
vessel. (1) in gen. = any receptacle, *vas*: a blood —, *arteria vena*. (2) = ship, *navis*.
vest, subst. *subucula* (Hor.).
vest, v.; see CLOTHE or INVEST.
vestal: a — virgin, *virgo vestalis*; in gen., see PURE, CHASTE.
vested, render by *ius* (*iuris*, n. = right).
vestibule, *vestibulum*.
vestige, *vestigium*, *indicium* (= indication).
vestry, *sacrarium*.
vesture; see GARMENT.
vetch, *vicia* (Verg.).
veteran, subst. and adj. *veteranus*; in gen. = old, *vetus*; = an old hand, in any sphere, *veterator*.
veterinary, *veterinarius* (Col.).
veto, subst. *intercessio* (of the tribunes).
veto, v. *intercedĕre* (with dat.; of the tribunes); see also FORBID.
vex, *vexare*, *sollicitare*, *offendĕre*, *pungĕre*, *mordēre*: to be —ed at, *aegre* or *moleste ferre*, or render by the impers. *piget*; see also ANNOY.
vexation, (*animi*) *aegritudo*, *indignatio*, *stomachus*, *molestia*, *offensio*.
vexatious, *molestus*, *gravis*, *odiosus*.
vexatiously, *graviter*.
viaduct, *pons*.
vial; see BOTTLE.
viands, *cibus*.
viaticum, *viaticum*.
vibrate, v., transit. and intransit., *vibrare*; see also SHAKE.
vibration, *motus* (-*ūs*); or render by verb.
vicar, *vicarius* (eccl.).
vicarious, *vicarius*.
vicariously, render by *loco*, with genit. (= in place of), or *pro*, with abl.
vice, *vitiositas*, *vitium*, *turpitudo*, *flagitium* (= a vicious act), *libido*.

[871]

vice; render by *vicarius* (= substitute, deputy).

Vicenza, *Vicentia.*

vicious, *vitiosus, turpis, flagitiosus, pravus, perditus, vitiis contaminatus* or *inquinatus*: a — disposition, *animus libidini deditus*; fig., a — circle, can sometimes be rendered by the phrase *versurā solvĕre* (lit. = to pay debts by means of further borrowing).

viciously, *turpiter, flagitiose, perdite.*

viciousness, *vitiositas*; see also VICE.

vicissitude, *vicissitudo, varietas, vices* (plur.): the —s of fortune, *fortunae vicissitudo, varia fortuna, varia vitae ratio.*

victim, *victima, hostia, piaculum* (Verg.): fig., to be the — of, (*rē* or *ab homine*) *adfligi* or *vexari*; see also VICTIMIZE.

victimize; see CHEAT, OPPRESS.

victor, *victor* (with f. *victrix*); see also CONQUEROR.

victorious, *victor,* m., with f. *victrix; superior;* or render by verb *vincĕre* or *superare.*

victoriously, render by adj. or v.; see VICTORIOUS.

victory, *victoria, triumphus* (lit. = a triumphal procession), *tropaeum* (poet.: lit. = a trophy): to gain a —, *vincĕre, superare, victoriam consequi* or *adipisci, victoriā potiri.*

victual, (*exercitui,* etc.) *rem frumentariam providĕre, frumentum* (com)*parare.*

victualler, *caupo.*

victuals, *cibus, cibaria* (-*orum,* plur.).

vie: to — with, (*cum homine*) *certare* or *contendĕre*; (*hominem* or *homini*) *aemulari.*

Vienna, *Vindobona.*

Vienne, *Vienna.*

view, subst. (**1**) = vision or field of vision, *aspectus* (-*ūs*), *conspectus* (-*ūs*), *prospectus* (-*ūs*), *acies*: a — down, *despectus* (-*ūs*); to be in —, *in conspectu esse*; to come into —, *in conspectum venire* or *cadĕre*. (**2**) mental —, point of —, = judgment, opinion, *sententia, iudicium*: in my —, *meo iudicio, me iudice, ut mihi (quidem) videtur*; to hold —s, *sentire* (esp. with adv. or n. acc. of adj.).

view, v. *adspicĕre, intueri, contemplari*; see also INSPECT, SEE.

vigil, in gen. = watch, wakefulness, *vigilia, pervigilatio, vigilantia*; in connexion with religion, *vigiliae* (-*arum,* plur.), *pervigilium.*

vigilance, *vigilantia, custodia, cura, diligentia.*

vigilant, *vigil* (poet.), *vigilans, intentus, providus, diligens.*

vigilantly, *vigilanter, intente, diligenter.*

vigorous, *strenuus, impiger, acer, vegetus, virilis, vividus, fortis.*

vigorously, *fortiter, acriter, strenue, impigre.*

vigour, (physical and mental) *vis, nervi* (-*orum,* plur.), *lacerti* (-*orum,* plur.), *vigor* (poet. and late prose).

vile, *vilis, abiectus, nequam, turpis, detestabilis, sordidus, foedus.*

vilely, *abiecte, nequiter, turpiter, sordide, foede.*

vileness, *turpitudo, nequitia, foeditas.*

vilify; see SLANDER.

villa, *villa* (properly = a country-house).

village, *pagus, vicus*; adj., of a —, *paganus, vicanus.*

villager, *paganus, vicanus, rusticus, agrestis.*

villain. (**1**) see VILLEIN. (**2**) = scoundrel, *homo scelestus, sceleratus,* etc.; see also VILLAINOUS; colloq., *verbero,* or use words

denoting 'villainy', such as *scelus* (-*ĕris,* n.) or *flagitium.*

villainous, *scelestus, sceleratus, nefarius, nequam, flagitiosus, facinorosus.*

villainy. (**1**) as a disposition, *improbitas, pravitas, nequitia*; see also WICKEDNESS. (**2**) as act, *scelus* (-*ĕris,* n.), *facinus* (-*ŏris,* n.), *flagitium.*

villein, *villanus* (late Latin).

vindicate. (**1**) = to maintain, *tenēre, obtinēre, defendĕre, propugnare* (*pro re, pro homine*; = to fight for): to — one's liberty, *se in libertatem vindicare.* (**2**) = to justify, *probare, purgare.*

vindication, *vindicta, defensio, propugnatio.*

vindicator, *vindex, defensor, propugnator.*

vindictive, *ulciscendi cupidus*: a — spirit, *ulciscendi* or *ultionis cupiditas.*

vindictively, render by adj.

vine, *vitis*: a small —, *viticula*; a wild —, (*vitis*) *labrusca* (Verg.); the tendril of a —, *clavicula*; the leaf of a —, *pampinus.*

vine-dresser, *vinitor, vitis cultor.*

vinegar, *acetum.*

vineyard, *vinea, vinetum*: a — planted with trees, *arbustum* (Verg., Hor.).

vinous, *vinosus* (Plin.).

vintage, *vindemia* (Pl., Varro).

vintager, *vindemiator* (Hor.).

vintner, *vinarius* (Pl., Sall.).

violable, *violabilis* (Ov.); or render by verb.

violate, *violare, rumpĕre.*

violation, *violatio*; often rendered by verb: in — of the law, *contra leges*; without — of the law, *salvis legibus*; see also RAPE.

violator, *violator, ruptor.*

violence, *violentia, vis, saevitia, manus* (-*ūs*); sing. or plur.; = physical force), *impotentia* (= lack of restraint), *gravitas* (of weather, etc.): to do — to, *violare, vim adferre* (with dat.).

violent, *violentus, saevus, vehemens, impotens* (= lacking self-restraint), *gravis* (of illness, weather, etc.): — death, *nex.*

violently, *vi, per vim, violenter, vehementer, graviter.*

violet, subst. *viola, ion* (Plin.): a bed of —s, *violarium* (poet.); the colour, *viola* (Hor.).

violet, adj. *ianthinus* (Plin.).

violin, render by *fides* (-*ium,* plur.; = strings).

viper, *vipera, aspis*; of a —, adj. *vipereus* (poet.), *viperinus* (Hor.); fig., as a term of reproach, *vipera, excetra.*

virago. LIT., = female warrior, *virago* (poet.) or *mulier* or *virgo bellicosa.* TRANSF., of any aggressive female, *mulier importuna.*

virgin, subst. *virgo.*

virgin, adj. LIT., *virginalis, virgineus* (poet.). TRANSF., *intactus.*

virginity, *virginitas.*

virile, *virilis*; see also MANLY.

virility, *virilitas* (Plin., Tac.); see also MANHOOD.

virtual, virtually, render by phrase, such as *re non verbo.*

virtue. (**1**) moral —, goodness, *virtūs* (-*ūtis,* f.), *probitas, honestas, honestum, rectum*; of chastity in particular, *pudicitia, sanctimonia, sanctitas.* (**2**) = the goodness of anything in its kind, *virtūs, bonitas.* (**3**) = efficacy, *virtūs, vis*; often render by verb, e.g. *posse, valēre, prodesse.*

(4) by (or in) — of, *per* (with acc.), *ex* (with abl.), *pro* (with abl.).

virtuoso, render by the adj. *peritus* (= skilled).

virtuous, *virtute praeditus* or *ornatus, frugi, integer* (= blameless); of chastity in particular, *honestus, probus, pudicus, castus.*

virtuously, *cum virtute, honeste.*

virulence, in gen. *vis*; of diseases, etc., *gravitas*; of hostility, etc., *acerbitas, virus,* n.

virulent, *gravis, acerbus*; see also BITTER.

virulently, *graviter, acerbe.*

visage; see FACE.

viscera, *viscera (-um), exta (-orum).*

viscous, *lentus* (Verg.), *tenax* (Verg.).

visible, *aspectabilis, conspicuus* (= clear to be seen), *manifestus* (= plain): to be —, *apparēre, in conspectu esse*; our whole — world, *haec omnia quae videmus.*

visibly, *manifesto*, or render by phrase, such as *quod cernere possis*; see also CLEARLY, EVIDENTLY.

vision. **(1)** = the faculty of sight, *visus (-ūs), aspectus (-ūs), sensus (-ūs) oculorum* or *videndi.* **(2)** = a thing seen, *visus (-ūs), visum, visio, species.* **(3)** = an apparition, phantom, *simulacrum* (poet.), *imago.*

visionary. **(1)** of things, opp. to real, *inanis, fictus, vanus.* **(2)** of character, *fanaticus* (= enthusiastic, frenzied), or render by phrase, such as *cogitationi deditus.*

visit, subst. *salutatio* (= a ceremonial call), *mansio* or *commoratio* (= a stay): to pay a —, *visēre.*

visit, v. **(1)** = to go to see, *(in)visēre, visitare, adire, salutare* (= to call upon), *intervisēre* (= to drop in on occasionally), *frequentare* (= to — regularly, e.g. as a pupil at a school), *obire* or *circumire* (= to go round). **(2)** = to punish, *animadvertēre, punire.*

visitation; see PUNISHMENT.

visitor, *salutator* (Juv., Suet.), *hospes* (= guest), *advena* (= newcomer, foreigner).

visor, *buccula* (= cheek-piece).

vista, *prospectus (-ūs)*; see also VIEW.

visual, render by the genit. *oculorum* (= of the eyes).

vital, *vitalis* (= belonging to life): the — principle, *anima*; see also IMPORTANT, ESSENTIAL.

vitality, *vis (vitalis)*; see also LIFE.

vitally, *vitaliter* (Lucr.); see also ESSENTIALLY.

vitiate. **(1)** = to pervert, *depravare, vitiare, corrumpēre.* **(2)** = to invalidate, *inritum reddēre.*

vitiation. **(1)** *corruptio, depravatio.* **(2)** see INVALIDATION.

vitreous, *vitreus* (poet.).

vituperate, *vituperare, reprehendēre*; see also ABUSE, SCOLD.

vituperation, *vituperatio, reprehensio.*

vituperative; see ABUSIVE.

vivacious, *vividus, vegetus, alacer, acer.*

vivaciously, *acriter.*

vivacity, *alacritas, vigor* (poet.).

vivid; see LIVELY.

vixen, *vulpes*; used of women, perhaps *canis* (Pl., Hor.).

vizier, *surena* (Tac.).

vocabulary, *index verborum* (= list of words), *copia verborum* (= stock or flow of words).

vocal, *vocalis*: — and instrumental music, *vocum nervorumque cantus.*

vocation, *officium, partes (-ium,* plur.), *munus (-ĕris,* n.).

vocative, *casus (-ūs) vocativus* (grammat. t. t.).

vociferate, *vociferari, clamare.*

vociferation, *vociferatio, clamor.*

vociferous, vociferously, *magno (cum) clamore.*

vogue, *mos.*

voice, subst. LIT., *vox, vocis sonus*; sometimes *cantus (-ūs*; = song): a high —, *vox acuta* (opp. *vox gravis*); in a loud —, at the top of one's —, *clarā* or *magnā voce*; to raise the —, *attollēre sonum*; to lower the —, *submittēre vocem.* TRANSF., = expressed opinion, 'say', *vox, sententia*; of a number of people, *consensus (-ūs).*

voice, v.; see UTTER, EXPRESS.

void, subst. *inanitas, inane, vacuum.*

void, adj. **(1)** = empty, *inanis, vacuus*: — of, *vacuus* (with abl.), *expers* or *inops* (with genit.); to be — of, *(re) carēre*; see also EMPTY. **(2)** = invalid, *inritus, vanus.*

void, v.; see VACATE.

volatile, *volaticus, lēvis, mobilis.*

volatility, *lēvitas, mobilitas (ingenii* or *animi),* or render by adj. with *animus* or *ingenium.*

volcanic, volcano, render by phrase, such as *mons e cuius vertice ignes erumpunt* or *mons flammas eructans*; or by reference to some specific volcano, such as Mt. Etna.

volition, *voluntas.*

volley. LIT., of missiles, *tela (-orum,* plur.) *coniecta.* TRANSF., of words, etc., *tempestas, flumen.*

volubility, *linguae solutio, volubilitas.*

voluble, *volubilis*; see also FLUENT.

volume. (1) = book or division of book, *liber, volumen.* **(2)** = size, *magnitudo, amplitudo.* **(3)** = abundance, quantity, *copia.*

voluminous, *copiosus, magnus, amplus.*

voluntarily, *ultro, (meā, suā,* etc.) *voluntate* or *sponte.*

voluntary, *voluntarius, volens, non coactus, non invitus*; or render by adv. *(mea,* etc.).

volunteer, subst. *voluntarius (miles).*

volunteer, v. *operam suam profiteri, rem ultro suscipēre.*

voluptuary, *homo voluptarius* or *luxuriosus.*

voluptuous, *voluptarius, luxuriosus, libidinosus, mollis, delicatus.*

voluptuousness, *voluptas, libido, luxuria.*

vomit, subst. *vomitio, vomitus (-ūs:* Plin.).

vomit, v. *(e)vomēre*: to — often, *vomitare* (Sen., Suet.).

voracious, *edax, (cibi) avidus, vorax.*

voraciously, *avide.*

voracity, *edacitas, (cibi) aviditas.*

vortex, *vertex, turbo.*

votary, *cultor* (poet.); or render by verb, such as *consecrare, dedēre, tradēre* (= to devote).

vote, subst. *suffragium, punctum, sententia* (= deliberative —), motion, free expression of opinion): to obtain a —, *punctum ferre*; the right to a —, *suffragium, ius suffragii.*

vote, v. *suffragium ferre* or *inire, sententiam ferre, censēre*: to — in favour of a motion, *in sententiam pedibus ire*; to — for a law, *legem sciscēre*; to support by —ing, *suffragari* (with dat.; also = to support, in gen.); the right to —, *suffragium, ius suffragii.*

voter, *suffragator* (= one who votes in favour of anyone), *qui suffragium fert* (= one who gives a vote), *qui suffragium habet* (= one who has the right of voting).

voting-tablet, *tabella, suffragium.*

votive, *votivus.*

vouch, v. : to — for, = to take responsibility for a thing, *rem praestare* or *in se recipĕre*; more generally, = to assert, warrant, *adseverare, testari, testificari, adfirmare, confirmare, adiurare.*

voucher; see WITNESS or WARRANT.

vouchsafe, *concedĕre.*

vow, subst. *votum, devotio, sponsio, promissum* or *fides* (= promise).

vow, v.: to — a thing to a deity, *rem deo (de)vovĕre*; in gen. = to undertake, promise, *(de)spondĕre, promittĕre.*

vowel, *littera vocalis.*

voyage, subst. *navigatio, cursus (-ūs).*

voyage, v. *navigare;* see also SAIL, TRAVEL.

voyager, *peregrinator* (= a traveller), *vector* (= a passenger).

vulgar, *vulgaris, usitatus, plebeius* (= peculiar to the *plebs,* plebeian), *inliberalis* or *sordidus* (= mean, low).

vulgarism, *sermo vulgaris.*

vulgarity, render by adj.

vulgarly, *vulgo;* see also VULGAR.

vulnerable, *qui (quae, quod) vulnerari potest.*

vulpine, *vulpinus* (Plin.).

vulture, *vultur, vulturius.*

W

wabble, *vacillare.*

wabbling, *vacillatio* (Quint., Suet.).

wad; see STUFF.

wade: to — through a river, *vado flumen transire.*

waft, *ferre,* perhaps with acc. of *sublimis* (= aloft) agreeing with object.

wag, subst. *ioculator, homo festivus* or *iocosus.*

wag, v. *movēre, quassare.*

wage: to — war, *bellum gerĕre (cum hostibus* or *contra hostes).*

wager, subst. *sponsio, pignus (-oris:* poet.).

wager, v. *sponsionem facĕre, pignore certare* (Verg.).

wages, *merces, stipendium.*

waggery, *festivitas, ioca (-orum,* plur.).

waggish, *facetus, iocosus.*

waggle; see WAG.

waggon, *plaustrum, vehiculum, carrus.*

waggoner, render by phrase, such as *plaustri agitator.*

wagtail, *motacilla* (Plin.).

waif, render by phrase, such as *infans destitutus.*

wail, *plorare, plangĕre* (poet.).

wailing, subst. *ploratus (-ūs).*

wain, *plaustrum* (also used of Charles's —, the constellation, by Ovid).

wainscot, *paries* (= party-wall).

waist, render by *corpus (-ŏris,* n.) *medium,* or by *medius* agreeing with the person concerned (e.g. he seized Servius round the —, *Servium corripuit medium).*

waistcoat, render by *subucula* (Hor.).

wait, subst. *mora* (= delay) or render by verb: to lie in — for, *aucupari* (with acc.), *insidiari*

or *insidias (com)parare* or *conlocare* (with dat.).

wait, v. *manēre:* to — for, *opperiri, exspectare, praestolari;* to — to see how things will turn out, *exspectare quo res evasura sit;* to — on, at table, *ministrare (homini);* to — on, = to visit formally, *salutare.*

waiter, *famulus, minister, puer.*

waiting, subst. (1) = delay, etc., *mora, exspectatio, mansio, commoratio.* (2) at table, *ministerium.* (3) = the paying of a call, *salutatio.*

waive, *(rem) concedĕre, (de re) decedĕre.*

wake, subst.; see WATCH: in the — of, *post* or *pone* (with acc.).

wake, v. (1) transit. *(e somno), expergefacĕre, excitare, (ex)suscitare.* (2) intransit. *expergisci,* or use pass. of transit. verbs.

wakeful, *vigil, exsomnis* (Verg.), *insomnis* (poet.).

wakefulness, *insomnia, vigilantia, vigilia.*

walk, subst. (1) a — as taken, *ambulatio;* a short —, *ambulatiuncula;* to go for a —, *ire ambulatum.* (2) = manner of —ing, gait, *incessus (-ūs), ingressus (-ūs).* (3) = a place for —ing, *ambulatio, ambulatiuncula, ambulacrum* (Pl.). (4) fig., a — of life; see CAREER, PURSUIT.

walk, v. *pedibus ire, ambulare, gradi* or *ingredi* (= to step), *incēdere* (esp. majestically): to — about, — up and down, *obambulare, inambulare, spatiari.*

walker, *pedes* (adj.; = on foot), *ambulator* (with f. *ambulatrix;* = a stroller: Cato, Mart.); or render by verb.

walking, subst.; see WALK, subst.

wall, subst.; in gen., *murus, moenia (-ium,* plur. = the —s of a town), *maceria* (round gardens, etc.), *paries* (= party —, partition): the ruins of the old —s, *parietinae (-arum,* plur.); to build a —, *murum aedificare, exstruĕre, (per)ducĕre* (emphasizing length); prov., backs to the —, *res ad triarios rediit* (i.e. we are down on our last reserves).

wall, v. *muro cingĕre* or *circumdare, munire* (= to fortify).

wallet, *saccus, pera* (Mart.), *crumena* (Pl., Hor.).

wallow, *volutari.*

walnut, *iuglans* (= the fruit or the tree).

wan, *pallidus* (poet.), *exsanguis* (poet.).

wand, *virga, virgula.*

wander, *vagari, palari, errare:* to — away, *deerrare, aberrare;* to — through, *pererrare* (poet.), *pervagari;* to — in mind, *delirare.*

wanderer, *erro* (poet.), *peregrinator* (= one who travels abroad).

wandering, subst. *error, erratio.*

wandering, adj. *errabundus, vagus.*

wane, v. *decrescĕre, senescĕre* (of the moon, and fig. of life), *minui.*

want, subst. *penuria, inopia, egestas* (= destitution), *desiderium* (= — as felt, esp. of what is lost), *defectio, angustiae (-arum,* plur.); sometimes rendered by a negative word, e.g. — of self control, *intemperantia,* — of energy, *inertia:* to be in —; see WANT, v.; in —, adj. *inops, egenus, egens.*

want, v. (1) = to be in — of, *egēre* (with genit. or abl.), *indigēre* (with genit. or abl.), *requirĕre* (with acc.), *desiderare* (with acc.; esp. = to feel the — of what is lost); or render by *opus est,* with dat. of person and abl. (or nom.) of what is —ed; without obj., = to live in —, be needy, *egēre, inopiā adfici* or *laborare*. (2) = to wish for, wish to have or do, *velle, avēre*; see also WISH.

wanting, = defective, *vitiosus*; sometimes rendered by a negative word, e.g. — in foresight, *improvidus*: to be, or be found —, *deesse, deficēre*.

wanton, subst. *meretrix, scortum.*

wanton, adj. *lascivus* (poet.), *petulans, protervus, impudicus, lībidinosus*: — injuries, *iniuriae ultro factae.*

wanton, v. *lascivire.*

wantonly, *petulanter, proterve*; = without provocation, *ultro.*

wantonness, *lascivia, petulantia, protervitas.*

war, subst. *bellum*; sometimes *arma (-orum,* plur.; = arms) or *militia* (= warfare): — on land, *bellum terrestre*; — at sea, *bellum navale*; foreign —, *bellum externum*; civil —, *bellum intestinum, domesticum, civile*; a — of extermination, *bellum internecinum*; in war, *bello, belli tempore*; in — and in peace, *pace belloque, domi bellique* or *belloque, domi militiaeque*; to cause —, *bellum movēre* or *excitare* or *ciēre*; to declare —, *bellum indicēre (hostibus,* dat.); to make — upon, *bellum inferre (hostibus,* dat.); to wage, or carry on, a —, *bellum gerēre (cum hostibus* or *contra hostes).*

war, v. *bellare, bellum gerēre, belligerare.*

warble, *canēre*; see also SING.

war-cry, *clamor (bellicus), ululatus (-ūs;* of Gauls), *baritus (-ūs;* of Germans: Tac.): to raise the —, *clamorem tollēre.*

ward, subst. (1) = a quarter of a town, *regio, vicus.* (2) = custody, *custodia*; see also CUSTODY. (3) = a minor, *pupillus* (f. *pupilla).*

ward, v.: to — off, *arcēre, propulsare, defendēre, avertēre*; to — off by prayers, *deprecari.*

warden, warder, *custos.*

wardrobe, *vestiarium* (Plin.); sometimes rendered by *vestis* or *vestimenta (-orum,* plur.) = clothing: mistress of the —, *vestispica* (Pl.).

ware, wares. (1) *merx*; see also GOODS, MERCHANDISE. (2) see POTTERY.

warehouse, *horreum, apotheca, receptaculum mercium.*

warfare, *militia,* sometimes *Mars*; see also WAR, subst.

war-horse, *equus militaris* or *bellator* (Tac.); or simply *equus.*

wariness, *prudentia, cautio, circumspectio.*

warlike, *militaris, bellicus, bellicosus, ferox, belliger* (Ov.).

warm, *calidus* (lit. and fig.): very —, *fervens* (lit. and fig.); luke-—, *tepidus* (poet.); — water, *cal(i)da* (Cato, Tac.); to be —, *calēre*; to become —, *calescēre, calefieri.*

warm, v. *calefacēre, tepefacēre* (= to make slightly warm).

warmly, *ferventer*; see also VEHEMENTLY.

warmth, *calor* (lit. and fig.); great —, *fervor* (lit. and fig.); slight —, *tepor.*

warn, *(ad)monēre* (when pointing out a fact, with acc. and infin.; when suggesting a course of action, with *ut* clause): to — in advance, *praemonēre.*

warning, subst. *(ad)monitio, monitus (-ūs), (ad)monitum, exemplum* or *documentum* (= an object-lesson): to serve as a —, *exemplo* or *documento* (dat.) *esse.*

warp, subst., in weaving, *stamen* (Varro, Ov.).

warp, v. LIT., of timber, intransit. *pandari* (Vitr.). TRANSF., *depravare, torquēre*; see also DISTORT.

warrant, subst. (1) abstract = authority, *auctoritas, potestas*; or render by *auctor* (e.g. under the — of Caesar, *Caesare auctore).* (2) = written authorization, *mandatum, diploma (-ătis,* n.: Tac.).

warrant, v. *(con)firmare, praestare* (= to make oneself responsible for), *promittēre* (= to promise): I (or I'll) — you, *meherc(u)le, medius fidius*; see also PROMISE, UNDERTAKE.

warrantable, render by verb; see ALLOW.

warranty, *satisdatio*; see also GUARANTEE.

warren, *leporarium* (Varro).

warrior, *miles* (= soldier), *homo* or *vir militaris, bellator.*

wart, *verruca* (Plin.): covered with —s, *verrucosus* (Pers.).

wary, *providus, prudens, circumspectus* (Quint.), *cautus.*

wash, subst. (1) = the act of washing, *lavatio*; or render by verb. (2) = a colour-—, *fucus* (esp. of red colour).

wash, v. (1) transit. *lavare*: to — out, — away, *abluēre* (Tac.), *eluēre* (poet.). (2) intransit. *lavari.*

wash-basin, *aqualis* (Pl.).

wash-tub, *labrum.*

wasp, *vespa* (Varro).

waspish, *acerbus*; see also IRRITABLE.

waste, subst. (1) = unprofitable expenditure, *effusio, sumptus (-ūs) effusus, dispendium* (poet.), *iactura* (lit. = throwing away), *damnum* (= loss). (2) = waste land, *vastitas, solitudo, loca (-orum) vasta.* (3) = discarded material, *ramenta (-orum*: Lucr., Plin.), *scobis* (= sawdust, etc.: Hor., Juv.).

waste, adj. *vastus, incultus, desertus*: to lay —, *vastare, (de)populari, perpopulari.*

waste, v. (1) transit. = to use or spend unprofitably, *consumēre, conficēre, dissipare, perdēre, profundēre, dispendi facēre* (Lucr.): to — time, *tempus perdēre* or *terēre*. (2) intransit.: to — away, *(con)tabescēre, consumi, confici.*

wasteful, *profusus, effusus, prodigus.*

wastefully, *profuse, effuse, prodige.*

wastefulness, *profusio, effusio*; see also WASTE, subst.

watch, subst. (1) = the act of keeping awake and watching, *excubiae (-arum,* plur.), *vigilia*: to keep —, *vigilare, vigilias agēre,* (2) concrete, the —, = those keeping —, *vigilia, statio, excubiae* (Tac.); see also WATCHMAN. (3) = a quarter of a night, *vigilia.* (4) = a timepiece, *horologium.*

watch, v. (1) transit. = to observe, *(ob)servare, spectare, tuēri* (poet.): to — for, *ex(s)pectare, opperiri, insidiari* (with dat.); to — over, *custodire, tuēri, observare.* (2) intransit. = to stay awake, *vigilare, excubare.*

watchful, *vigil* (poet.), *vigilans.*

watchfully, *vigilanter.*

watchfulness, *vigilantia, vigilia*; see also CARE.

watchman, *vigil, excubitor, custos.*

watchtower, *specula.*

watchword, *tessera, signum.*

water, subst. *aqua* (the plur is used of a large quantity, also of medicinal springs); *liquor* *latex, lympha, unda* (all poetic): running —, *aqua viva, flumen vivum*; fresh —, *aqua dulcis*; salt- —, *aqua salsa*; sea- —, *aqua marina*; rain- —, *(aqua) pluvia, aqua caelestis*; to go for, fetch —, *ire, aquari* (esp. as milit. t. t.); of the —, = aquatic, *aquatilis, aquaticus* (Ov.); concerned with —, *aquarius*; by land and —, *terrā marique*; to travel by —, *navigare*; prov., still —s run deep, *altissima quaeque flumina minimo sono labuntur* (Curt.); —, = urine, *urina*; —, of a diamond, *splendor*.

water, v. *(in)rigare, conspergĕre* (= to sprinkle): to make a person's mouth —, *salivam homini movēre*.

water-carrier, *aquator, aquarius* (Juv.; also, as a sign of the Zodiac, in Hor.).

water-clock, *clepsydra*.

water-closet, *latrina* (Pl., Suet.).

water-fall, render by phrase, such as *aqua ex edito desiliens* (Plin.).

water-fowl, *avis aquatica* (Plin.).

watering, subst. = fetching of water, *aquatio*.

watering-place. (1) for getting ordinary water, *aquatio*. (2) for bathing, etc., *aquae (-arum,* plur.) or render by adj. *maritimus* (= of or at the seaside).

water-jug, *hydria, urceus* (Hor.).

waterman; see SAILOR, BOATMAN.

waterproof, render by phrase, such as *aquae vi resistens*.

watersnake, *hydrus* (Verg.).

waterspout, *prester* (Lucr., Plin.), *typhon* (Plin.).

waterworks, *aquae*, or *aquarum, ductus (-ūs)*.

watery, *aquatilis* (Plin.), *aquosus* (= abounding in water).

wattle, subst. (1) = hurdle, *cratis*. (2) of a cock, *palea* (Varro).

wattle, v. *contexĕre*; see also WEAVE.

wave, subst. *fluctus (-ūs), unda* (poet.).

wave, v. (1) transit. *agitare, iactare, vibrare, rotare* (poet.). (2) intransit. *fluctuare, undare* (poet.).

waver, *fluctuare, dubitare, vacillare, labare*.

wavering, subst. *animus incertus* or *dubius, dubitatio, fluctuatio*.

wavering, adj. *incertus, dubius*.

wax, subst. *cera*: a — candle, — light, *cereus*.

wax, v. (1) transit. = to cover with wax, *(in)cerare* (poet.). (2) intransit. = to grow, *crescĕre*; see also GROW.

waxen, *cereus*.

way. (1) abstract: **a** = journey, *via, cursus (-ūs), iter*: — up to, access, *aditus (-ūs)*; on the —, *in itinere, obiter* (Plin., Juv.); to get under — (of a ship), *ancoram solvĕre*: **b**, in gen. = manner, *modus, ratio, via*; in this —, *sic, ita, hoc modo*: **c** = custom, *mos, institutum*: **d**, —s and means; see RESOURCES: **e**, to get one's own —, *pervincĕre*. (2) concrete = road, track, *via*: — up to, approach, *aditus (-ūs)*; a quick —, short cut, *via compendiaria*; a bye- —, narrow —, *trames, deverticulum, semita, callis* (esp. through hills or woods), *angiportus (-ūs)* or *angiportum* (= a narrow street); a place where two —s meet, *bivium*; where three, *trivium*; in the —, adj. *obvius*; out of the —, *devius, avius, remotus, reconditus* or *exquisitus* (fig.); to get out of the —, *de via decedĕre*; the milky —, *orbis lacteus*.

wayfarer, *viator*.

waylay, *(homini) insidiari* or *insidias facĕre*.

wayside, render by phrase, such as *ad viam*.

wayward; see WILFUL.

we, is often sufficiently indicated by the form of the Latin verb (e.g. *amamus* = we love); when emphatic, render by *nos*: — ourselves, *nos ipsi, nosmet ipsi*.

weak, *infirmus, debilis, imbecillus, invalidus, languidus* (= faint), *confectus* (= worn out), *hebes* (= dull, faint), *tenuis* (of health or character), *exiguus* (= scanty), *exilis* (= meagre), *lēvis* (of character, arguments, etc.).

weaken, v. transit. *debilitare, enervare, infirmare, attenuare, extenuare, (com)minuĕre* (= to lessen), *frangĕre* (lit. = to break), *obtundĕre* (= to make dull), *labefactare* (= to shake).

weakening, subst. *debilitatio, infractio, deminutio*; or render by verb.

weakly, adj. *invalidus*; see also WEAK.

weakly, adv. *infirme*; or render by adj.

weakness, *imbecillitas, infirmitas, debilitas, virium defectio, languor, lēvitas* (of arguments, etc.), *vitium* (= fault).

weal. (1) see WELFARE: the public —, *respublica*. (2) = a mark on the body, *vibex* (Pl.).

wealth, *divitiae (-arum,* plur.), *opes (-um,* plur.), *copia* (esp. with genit., = — of), *opulentia*.

wealthy, *dives, locuples, pecuniosus, opulentus, opulens*.

wean. LIT., *(infantem) lacte depellĕre* (Hor.), *a matre prohibēre*. TRANSF., *dedocēre* (= to teach not to do).

weapon, *arma (-orum,* plur.; defensive), *telum* (offensive).

wear, subst. *usus (-ūs)*.

wear, v. (1) transit.: **a**, to — away, — out, *(con)terĕre, atterĕre* (Sall.), *exedĕre*: **b** = to have on the body, *gerĕre, gestare, (re) indutum esse*; —ing the toga, *togatus*; —ing shoes, *calceatus*. (2) intransit. = to last, *durare*: to — out, *(usu) (con)teri*, etc.; to — off, *evanescĕre*.

weariness, *(de)fatigatio, lassitudo, taedium* (= disgust).

wearisome, *laboriosus, molestus, operosus*.

weary, adj. *(de)fatigatus, (de)fessus, languidus, lassus* (poet.).

weary, v. (1) transit. *(de)fatigare, lassare* (poet.), *obtundĕre* (= to bore). (2) intransit. *defetisci*; or render by pass. of transit. verbs or by the impersonal *taedet*.

weasel, *mustela* (Pl., Hor.).

weather, subst. *caelum, caeli status (-ūs), tempestas*: fine —, *tempestas serena* or *serenum* alone as n. subst.; dry —, *siccitas*.

weather, v.: to — a cape, *promontorium circumvehi*; to — a storm, *vim tempestatis perferre*.

weather-wise, render by phrase, such as *caeli mutationum peritus*.

weave, *(con)texĕre*: to — one thing into another, *intexĕre*.

weaver, *textor* (poet.).

web, *tela, textum* (poet.), *textura* (poet.).

web-footed, render by phrase, such as *aves quibus pedes ad nandum accommodati sunt*.

wed; see MARRY.

wedding; see MARRIAGE: — day, *dies nuptiarum*; to fix the — day, *diem nuptiis dicĕre*.

wedge, subst. *cuneus*: — shaped, *cuneatus*; in — formation, *cuneatim*.

wedge, v.: to — together; see CROWD.

wedlock, *matrimonium*; see also MARRIAGE.

weed, subst. (1) = a useless plant, *herba inutilis*. (2) see CLOTHES, DRESS; in widows' —s, *viduarum more vestita*.

weed, v. (e)*runcare* (poet.).

week, *septem dierum spatium, septem dies*.

week-days, render by *dies profesti* (opp. *dies fasti*).

weekly, render by phrase; see WEEK.

ween; see THINK.

weep, *lacrimare, lacrimas fundĕre, flēre, (de)plorare, lamentari*: to — for, — over, *inlacrimare, (de)plorare, (de)flēre, lamentari*.

weeping, subst. *fletus (-ūs), lacrimae (-arum*, plur. = tears), *ploratus (-ūs), lamentatio, lamenta (-orum*, plur.).

weevil, *curculio* (Pl., Verg.).

weigh, v. (1) transit. = to find the weight of, (ex)*pendĕre, perpendĕre, pensare, pensitare, examinare, ponderare*; fig., of mentally —ing ideas, use the above verbs or *considerare, reputare*; see also CONSIDER. (2) to — down, *opprimĕre, gravare* (lit. and fig.). (3) intransit. = to have a certain weight, render by phrases, e.g. to — much, *magni ponderis esse*; see also WEIGHT.

weight. LIT., *pondus (-eris*, n.), *gravitas, momentum*; = a heavy object used in a machine, *libramentum*: in —, *pondo*. TRANSF., of moral worth, etc., render by words given above or *auctoritas*: to attach great — to a thing, *rem magni aestimare*; to have great — (with a person), *multum valēre (apud hominem)*; to have no —, *nihil valēre*.

weighty, *gravis* (lit. and fig.).

weir, *moles, agger*.

welcome, subst. *salutatio*; or render by adj. or verb.

welcome, adj. *acceptus, gratus, commodus, exoptatus*.

welcome! interj. *salve*.

welcome, v. *salutare, salvēre iubēre*: to — to one's home, (*hospitio*) *accipĕre* or *excipĕre*.

weld, (con)*ferruminare* (Plin.).

welfare, *salūs (-ūtis*, f.), *commodum, utilitas*: to try to promote a person's —, *hominis commodis (or simply homini) consulĕre*.

welkin; see SKY.

well, subst. *puteus*.

well, adj. *salvus, sanus, integer, valens*: to be —, (*bene*) *valēre, bene (se) habēre*; to get —, *convalescĕre*; not to be —, *male se habēre*.

well, adv. *bene, recte* (= rightly), *belle* (colloq.), *probe* (colloq.): very —, *optime, praeclare*; it is —, *bene est, bene habet*; to do oneself —, *bene sibi facĕre* (Pl.); to take a thing —, *rem in bonam partem accipĕre*; prov., to let — alone, *quieta non movēre, quod bene cessit relinquĕre* (Sen.).

well, v.: to — up, *scatēre* (poet.); see also SPRING.

well-affected; see WELL DISPOSED.

well-being, *salūs (-ūtis*, f.).

well-born, *nobilis*; see also NOBLE.

well-bred, *comis, urbanus*; see also POLITE.

well-disposed, *benevolus (in* or *erga hominem)*.

well-earned, *meritus*.

well-fed, *corpore amplo, pinquis, opimus, obesus* (poet.).

well-informed, *doctus, eruditus*; see also LEARNED.

well-known, (*omnibus*) *notus, celebratus, pervulgatus*.

well-meaning, *benevolus, amicus*.

well-spent: a — life, *vita bene acta*.

well-trained, *exercitatus*.

well-versed, (*in re*) *versatus*, (*rei*, genit.) *peritus*.

well-wisher, *homo (hominis) studiosus* or *qui (hominem) salvum vult*.

welter, subst. *congeries*.

welter, v. *volutari*.

Weser, river, *Visurgis*.

west, subst. *regio ad occidentem vergens, occidens, solis occasus (-ūs)*: to face the —, *ad occidentem (solem) spectare*.

west, adj. *occidentalis* (Plin.), *occiduus* (Ov.); or render by phrase, such as *ad occidentem*; the — wind, *Zephyrus* (poet.), *Favonius*.

westerly, = from the west, *ab occidente*; see also WEST, adj.

western; see WEST, adj.

westward, westwards, *ad occasum, ad occidentem*.

wet, subst.; see RAIN.

wet, adj. *umidus, madidus, udus* (poet.), *uvidus* (poet.): to be —, *madēre, umēre* (poet.).

wet, v. *madefacĕre, umectare* (poet.), (in)*rigare*.

wether, *vervex*.

wetness, *umor*.

wet-nurse, *nutrix*.

wettish, *umidulus* (Ov.).

whale, *balaena* (Pl., Ov.), *cetus* or *cetos* (Pl., Verg., Plin.).

wharf, *navale, crepido*.

what. (1) interrog.: as pronoun, *quid? quidnam?*; as adj. *qui, quae, quod*, sometimes *quis*, esp. of male persons: of — sort? *qualis?* of — size? *quantus?* (2) relative = that which, (*id*) *quod*, (*ea*) *quae*. (3) exclamatory, as adj. *qui, quae, quod*; sometimes *qualis*.

whatever, whatsoever. (1) as universal relative: pronoun *quidquid* or *quodcunque*, adj. *quisquis* or *quicunque*; in — way, *quocunque modo*; in — place, *ubicunque, quacunque*; to — place, *quocunque*. (2) any —, as an indefinite adj. or pronoun, *quisquis, quicunque, quivis*; in a negative (or virtually negative) sentence, *quisquam*.

wheat, *triticum*: winter —, *siligo* (Cato, Varro); of —, *triticeus* (Verg., Ov.); a — field, *ager tritico consitus*.

wheaten, *triticeus* (Verg., Ov.).

wheedle, (e)*blandiri*.

wheel, subst. *rota, tympanum* (in water-mills, etc.: Lucr., Verg.), *orbis* (poet.).

wheel, v. (1) = to turn round: transit., *convertere, circumagĕre*; intransit., as milit. t. t., *signa convertĕre*. (2) = to push forward on wheels, *propulsare*.

wheel-rut, *orbita*.

wheelwright, render by phrase, such as *qui rotas facit*.

wheeze, *anhelare*; see also PANT.

whelm; see OVERWHELM.

whelp, *catulus, scymnus* (Lucr.).

when. (1) interrog., in direct and indirect questions, *quando*. (2) relative; *cum* (usually with indic. when referring to present or future action, subj. when referring to past); *ut* or *ubi* (with indic.); *quando* (with indic., often with causal force); —, = after, can be rendered by *postquam* (with indic.); — is often also rendered by abl. absol. or other participial clause.

whence, interrog. and relat. *unde*.

whencesoever, *undecumque* (Quint., Plin. L.).

whenever, whensoever, *quandocumque, utcumque, quoties, quotiescumque*; also rendered by *cum*, with indic. (usually perf. or pluperf.).

where. (1) interrog., in direct and indirect questions, *ubi*: — from, *unde*; — to, *quo*; — in the world? *ubi(nam) gentium?* (2) relat. *ubi, qua*.

whereas, *quoniam, quod, quando, cum*; see also BECAUSE, SINCE.

whereby, render by the relative, *qui, quae, quod*.

wherefore. (1) interrog. *cur?* see also WHY. (2) relat. *quare, quamobrem, quapropter, quocirca, proinde* (esp. introducing a command).

wherein, *in quo, in quibus, ubi*.

whereof, render by genit. of relat., or prep. (such as *de* or *ex*) and relat.

whereupon, render by relat. phrase or clause, such as *quo facto*.

wherever, *ubicumque, quacumque*.

wherry; see BOAT.

whet, *(ex)acuĕre* (lit. and fig.).

whether, pron. (archaic), = which of the two, *uter*.

whether, conj. (1) interrog., in single indirect questions, e.g. I asked — this was true; *num, -ne* (attached to first word of clause), *utrum* (rare), *an* (esp. after *dubito* and *haud scio*). The mood in the interrog. clause is subj. Occasionally *si*, with subj. is used elliptically in the sense 'to see —', 'to find out —'; e.g. they made an attempt to see — Ardea could be taken at the first rush, *tentata res est, si primo impetu capi Ardea posset*. (2) interrog., in disjunctive indirect questions, e.g. I asked — this report was true or false; — ... or, is here represented by *utrum* ... *an, -ne* ... *an*, ... *an*; — ... or not, is *utrum* ... *necne, -ne* ... *necne*, ... *necne*. The mood in the interrog. clauses is subj. (3) in disjunctive conditional sentences, when a thing is so in either of two conditions, e.g. — this is true or false, I shall go; — ... or, is here represented by *sive* (or *seu*) ... *sive* (or *seu*). The mood in the alternative clauses is indic. or subj. according to the ordinary rules for conditional sentences.

whetstone, *cos*.

whey, *serum* (Verg., Ov.).

which. (1) interrog., in direct and indirect questions, *quis* — of the two, *uter*; — in the series or order, *quotus*. (2) relat. *qui, quae, quod*.

whiff, *halitus* (*-ūs*; = breath).

while, subst. *tempus* (*-ŏris*, n.), *spatium, mora*: a little —, *breve spatium*; in a little —, *brevi, mox*; for a little —, *parumper, paulisper*; a little — after, *paulo post*.

while or **whilst**, *dum* (with pres. indic. in the sense 'within the time when', but in the sense 'throughout the time when' with various tenses of indic. according to context); *donec* (less common); *quoad* (rare in this sense); sometimes *cum* (= when; see WHEN); often rendered by present partic. (e.g. — weeping, *lacrimans*) or by *inter* with acc. of gerund.

while, v.: to — away the time, *tempus fallĕre* (Ov.); see also PASS.

whim, *libido*.

whimper; see WHINE.

whimsical, *lĕvis* (= fickle).

whine, v. *vagire* (esp. of children).

whining, subst. *vagitus* (*-ūs*: poet.).

whinny, *hinnire* (Lucr., Quint.).

whip, subst. *lora* (*-orum*, plur.), *flagrum, flagellum, scutica* (poet.).

whip, v. *verberare*.

whirl, v. (1) transit. *(con)torquĕre, rotare* (poet.). (2) intransit.; render by pass. of transit. verbs.

whirling, subst. *vertigo* (Ov., Sen.); or render by verb.

whirlpool, *vertex, vorago, gurges*.

whirlwind, *turbo, vertex*.

whirr, subst. *stridor*.

whirr, v. *stridĕre* or *stridēre* (poet.).

whisk; see SWEEP, SNATCH.

whiskers, render by phrase, such as *genae pilosae* or *hirsutae*.

whisper, subst. *susurrus* (Ov.).

whisper, v. *susurrare* (poet.), *insusurrare*: to — a thing into a person's ear, *rem homini in aurem insusurrare*.

whisperer, *susurrator* (ap. Cic. L.).

whist, subst.; render by *alea* (= dice).

whist, or **whisht**, interj. *st! tace, tacete*.

whistle, subst. (1) as a sound, *sibilus*. (2) as an instrument; see PIPE.

whistle, v. *sibilare*.

whit: not a —, *ne minimum quidem, minime*; with a comparative, *nihilo, ne pilo quidem*.

white, subst., of an egg or of the eye, *album* (Cels.); see also WHITENESS.

white, adj. *albus* (= dead —, opp. *ater*), *candidus* (= shining —, opp. *niger*), *canus* (= hoary), *niveus* (= white as snow): to be —, *albēre, albicare* (poet.), *canēre* (poet); to be — hot, *candēre*.

white-lead, *cerussa* (Plin.).

whiten, v. (1) transit. *dealbare, candefacĕre* (Pl.). (2) intransit. *albescĕre, candescĕre* (poet.).

whiteness, *albitudo* (Pl.), *candor*.

whitewash, subst. *albarium* (Vitr.).

whitewash, v. *dealbare*.

whither. (1) interrog. *quo? quonam? quorsum?* (2) relat. *quo*.

whithersoever, *quoquo, quocunque*.

whitlow, *paronychium* or *paronychia* (Plin.).

Whitsuntide, *Pentecoste* (eccl.).

whiz, subst. *stridor*.

whiz, v. *stridĕre* or *stridēre* (poet.).

whizzing, *stridulus* (poet.).

who. (1) interrog., in direct and indirect questions, *quis, quid*: —, out of two, *uter, utra, utrum*. (2) relat., *qui, quae, quod*.

whoever, *quicunque* (with indic.), *quisquis* (with indic.); see also WHATEVER.

whole, subst.: the — of a thing, *tota res*; absol., the —, *summa, universitas totum, solidum*; on the —, *in toto, plerumque, ferme, fere*.

whole, adj. (1) opp. to part, *totus, omnis, cunctus, universus, solidus*. (2) = unimpaired, unhurt, *integer, sanus, sincerus*.

wholesale, render by phrase, such as *mercatura magna*: a — dealer, — merchant, *negotiator, mercator*.

wholesome, *saluber, salutaris, utilis.*
wholesomeness, *salubritas, utilitas.*
wholly, *omnino, prorsus;* often also rendered by *totus,* adj., agreeing with the subject of the sentence; see also ALTOGETHER.
whoop, subst. *clamor, ululatus (-ūs).*
whore, *scortum, meretrix.*
whose, *cuius,* plur. *quorum, quarum, quorum.*
why, interrog., in direct and indirect questions, *cur, quid, quare, quam ob rem (quamobrem), quapropter* (Pl., Ter.): — should . . . , *cur* or *quid est quod,* both with subj.; —, as a rhetorical question, *quid enim?;* — not, *cur non, quin* (with indic., esp. in calls for action), *quidni* (with subj.).
why, interj. *immo, enimvero.*
wick, *ellychnium* (Plin.), *filum* (Juv.).
wicked, *improbus, malus, nefarius, scelestus, sceleratus, scelerosus, pravus, perditus* (= abandoned), *nequam* (= worthless).
wickedly, *improbe, male, nefarie, sceleste, scelerate, prave, nequiter.*
wickedness, *improbitas, scelus (-ĕris,* n.), *malitia, pravitas, nequitia.*
wicker, *vimineus, craticius* (Vitr.): — work, *crates* (usually plur.).
wide, *latus, laxus, amplus, patens, spatiosus* (poet.).
widely, *late.*
widen, v. (1) transit. *amplificare, dilatare, laxare.* (2) intransit. *patescĕre;* or use pass. of transit. verbs.
widespread, *longe lateque diffusus.*
widow, *vidua.*
widowed, *viduus, orbus.*
widower, *vir viduus.*
widowhood, *viduitas, orbitas.*
width, *latitudo, amplitudo, laxitas.*
wield, *tractare, uti* (with abl.).
wife, *uxor, coniunx, marita* (poet.): to take a —, *uxorem ducĕre.*
wig, *capillamentum* (Suet.), *galerum* (Juv., Suet.).
Wight, Isle of, *Vectis.*
wild, adj. *ferus, agrestis* (lit. = of the field), *indomitus* (= untamed), *incultus* or *rudis* (= unworked or uncivilized), *vastus* (= desolate), *ferox* (= daring, untameable), *saevus* (= cruel, brutal), *insanus* or *amens* (= mad), *lascivus* (= playful): a — beast, *fera.*
wilderness, wilds, *loca (-orum,* plur.) *deserta, solitudo, vastitas.*
wildly, *ferociter, saeve, insane.*
wildness, *feritas, ferocia;* or render by adj.
wile, *ars, dolus;* see also TRICK.
wilful, *contumax, pertinax, pervicax, obstinatus, libidinosus.*
wilfully, (1) = obstinately, stubbornly, *contumaciter, pervicaciter.* (2) = deliberately, *consulto, consilio, de industriā, dedita operā;* or render by adj. *sciens* or *prudens.*
wilfulness, *contumacia, pertinacia, pervicacia, libido.*
will, subst. (1) = volition or purpose, *voluntas, animus, consilium, propositum* (= chosen purpose), *arbitrium* (= decision), *libido* (= fancy, caprice), *studium* (= keenness): against one's —, *invitus,* adj. (2) = testament, *testamentum:* to make a —, *testamentum facĕre;* to make a — in favour of a person, *hominem heredem suum testamento facĕre;* without making a —, *intestato* (abl. n. sing.: Cic.), *intestatus* (agreeing with subject: Juv.).

will, v. (1) as a sign of the future tense, render by the Latin future. (2) = to be willing, wish, *velle, avēre, cupĕre.* (3) = to leave property by one's will, *legare, relinquĕre.*
William, *Gulielmus* (late Latin).
willing, adj. *libens, volens, paratus, promptus.*
willingly, *libenter;* often rendered by adj. *libens,* agreeing with the subject.
willingness, *voluntas, studium, animus libens* or *promptus.*
willow, *salix* (Lucr., Verg.).
wily, *vafer, astutus, versutus;* see also CUNNING, adj.
win, v. (1) transit.; see GET, GAIN. (2) intransit. *vincĕre, superare, victoriam adipisci* or *parĕre.*
Winchester, *Venta Belgarum.*
wind, subst. (1) in gen. *ventus, aura, flatus (-ūs:* mostly poet.), *flamen* (poet.): a favourable, unfavourable —, *ventus secundus, adversus;* the — rises, *ventus increbrescit* or *cooritur;* the — sinks, *ventus cessat, cadit;* to run before the —, *vento se dare.* (2) = flatulence, *inflatio.*
wind, v. (1) = to blow into a wind instrument, *inflare;* see also BLOW, PLAY. (2) = to turn, twist, *volvĕre, torquĕre, sinuare* (poet.): to — one's way in, *(se) insinuare.*
windfall, render by phrase, such as *lucrum insperatum* or *quod imprudenti contingit.*
winding, subst. *sinus (-ūs), flexus (-ūs).*
winding, adj. *flexuosus, tortuosus.*
windlass, *ergata* (Vitr.).
windmill, *mola venti* (leg.).
window, *fenestra.*
window-shutters, *luminaria (-ium,* plur.).
windpipe, *aspera arteria.*
windward, *ad ventum conversus.*
windy, *ventosus.*
wine, *vinum:* sour —, *vappa* (Hor.); — not diluted with water, *merum;* the — god, *Bacchus* (poet. = wine).
wine-bibber, *homo vinosus.*
wine-cellar, *apotheca.*
wine-merchant, *vinarius* (Pl., Sall.).
wing, subst. LIT., *ala, pennae (-arum,* plur.; lit. = feathers). TRANSF., — of an army, *cornu, ala;* on the —, adj., *alarius.*
wing, v.: to — one's way, *volare;* see also FLY.
winged, *alatus, aliger, pennatus* (all poet.), *pinniger* (Cic.).
wink, subst. *nictatio* (Plin.).
wink, v. *conivēre, nictare* (Pl., Lucr.): to — at a thing, in re *conivēre.*
winner, *victor.*
winning, adj. *venustus* (= lovely), *suavis* (= sweet), *blandus* (= persuasive), *comis* (= courteous).
winnow, *ventilare* (Varro), *evannĕre* (Varro).
winnowing-fan, *ventilabrum* (Col.), *vannus* (Verg.).
winter, subst. *hiems, tempus hibernum* or *hiemale, bruma* (lit. = the shortest day): a hard —, *hiems gravis* or *acris;* a mild —, *hiems mitis.*
winter, adj. *hiemalis, hibernus, brumalis* (poet.).
winter, v. *hiemare, hibernare, hiberna agĕre* (of troops).
winter-quarters, *(castra, -orum,* plur.) *hiberna.*
wintry; see WINTER, adj., and COLD.
wipe, *(abs)tergēre, detergēre, extergēre* (Pl.): to — out (fig.), *abolēre, delēre.*
wire, render by *filum* or *filum ferreum.*

wisdom, *sapientia* (esp. theoretical), *prudentia* (practical), *consilium, ratio.*

wise, subst.; see MANNER, WAY.

wise, adj. *sapiens, prudens* (= sensible, prudent), *peritus* (= experienced): to be —, *sapère.*

wiseacre, render by phrase, such as *qui se sapientem esse iactat.*

wisely, *sapienter, prudenter.*

wish, subst. *optatio* (= the act of —ing), *optatum* (= the thing —ed for), *desiderium* (= desire, longing), *voluntas* (= will), *votum* (= prayer): according to one's —, *ex sententiā*; against my —es, *me invito.*

wish, v. *velle, cupère, (ex)optare*: not to —, *nolle*; to — more, prefer, *malle*; to — for something had and lost, *desiderare*; to — a person joy, *homini gratulari.*

wisp: a — of a girl, *iuncea puella* (Ter.).

wistful, wistfully, wistfulness, render by phrase with *desiderium* (= yearning, longing, esp. for what is lost).

wit. (1) as a quality, *ingenium, (ingenii) acumen, dicacitas* (= power of repartee), *facetiae (-arum,* plur.; = witticisms), *sal* (= pungency), *lepos* (= charm): with one's —s about one, *sanus*; out of one's —s, *insanus.* **(2)** as a person, *(homo) ridiculus* (Pl.) or *facetus*; see also WITTY.

wit, v.: to —, = namely, *videlicet, scilicet, dico* (= I mean).

witch, *venefica, saga.*

witchcraft, *veneficium, ars magica* (poet.), *magice* (Plin.); see also MAGIC.

with, prep. **(1)** of accompaniment, co-operation, agreement, etc. (esp. in relation to persons), *cum,* with abl.: e.g. he went — her (— me, — you), *cum eā iit (mecum, tecum)*; — a person (= at his house), *apud hominem*; colloq. I'm — you (= I follow, I understand), *istic sum.* **(2)** of action done — a certain instrument, abl. alone: e.g. he killed them — a sword, *gladio eos necavit.* **(3)** of the manner in which an action is done, or of the circumstances or results attending it, *cum,* with abl.; but the abl. alone is often used when the subst. concerned is qualified by an adj. or demonstrative: e.g. he did it — care, *cum curā fecit*; he did it — the greatest care, *summā curā fecit.* **(4)** = in consequence of, plain abl., or *ex* with abl., or *propter* with acc.; see also CONSEQUENCE, ACCOUNT. **(5)** in other miscellaneous phrases: to become angry — a person, *homini irasci*; to carry weight — a person (i.e. in his judgment), *apud hominem multum valère*; to begin — a subject, *a re exordiri*; — pleasure, *libenter*; — all one's heart, *ex animo.*

withal, *simul.*

withdraw, v. **(1)** transit. *avertère, avocare, revocare, removère, detrahère, abstrahère, abducère, deducère, subducère.* **(2)** intransit. *(re)cedère, discedère, se recipère, se removère*: to — from office, *magistratu se abdicare.*

wither, v. **(1)** transit. *urère* (= to scorch, parch), *corrumpère*; see also DESTROY. **(2)** intransit. *marcescère, marcère, (ex)arescère* (Suet.).

withered, *marcidus.*

withhold, *retinère, supprimère, comprimère, recusare* (= to refuse).

within, prep. **(1)** of space, *intra* or *inter* (with acc.); *in* (with abl.; = in); *cis* or *citra* (with acc.; = on the near side of). **(2)** of time, render by plain abl. (Cic., Caes.) or by *intra* with acc. (Liv.): — human memory, *post hominum memoriam.* **(3)** of other relations, *intra,* with acc. (e.g. — the law, *intra legem*): to be (or come) — a little of, render by the phrase *haud multum abest quin,* with subj.

within, adv. *intus, intro* (with verbs of motion = to the inside).

without, prep. **(1)** in gen., *sine,* with abl.; *extra,* with acc. (mainly of place; = outside): to be (or go) — a thing, *re carere*; being — a thing, *re carens, rei* (genit.) *expers.* Very often the idea is expressed by a negative word or phrase, e.g. — any trouble, *nullo negotio*; — resistance, *nullo repugnante*; — result, *re infecta, nequicquam*; — the orders of, *iniussu (hominis)*; or by a specific positive word, such as *nudus* (= — clothes), *integer* (= — harm). **(2)** followed by verbal noun in -ing (e.g. — coming); render in one of the following ways: **a,** by a partic. or adj. with a negative or in a negative form (e.g. — knowing, *inscius* or *imprudens*; — hearing the case, *causā incognitā*; — sending out scouts, *inexplorato*; — making a will, *intestato*): **b,** by *neque* (= and not): or, by *ita . . . ut non* (= in such a way that . . . not), e.g. playful — being naughty, *ita lascivus ut nihil peccet*: **d,** after a previous negative, by *quin* and subj. (e.g. I never see — wondering, *numquam video quin mirer*).

without, adv. *extra, extrinsecus, foris* (= out of doors).

withstand, *resistère, obsistère, obstare* (with dat.).

withy, *vimen.*

witless; see FOOLISH, SENSELESS.

witness, subst. **(1)** = a person who gives evidence, *testis*: to call or appeal to a person as a —, *testari, antestari*; to be a —, appear as a —, *testari, testimonium dicère, testem exsistère*; a reliable —, *testis locuples.* **(2)** = evidence; q.v. **(3)** = a party present, *arbiter, spectator* (= onlooker): in the presence of (before) many —es, *multis audientibus, coram multis.*

witness, v. **(1)** = to give evidence, *testari, testimonium dicère, testificari.* **(2)** = to see, *vidère, spectare*; see also SEE.

witticism, *dictum, facetiae (-arum,* plur. only); see also WIT.

wittily, *facete, lepide.*

witty, *dicax, facetus, lepidus, salsus.*

wizard, *veneficus, magus* (Hor.).

wizened, *retorridus* (Phaedr.), *rugosus* (= wrinkled: poet.).

woad, *vitrum.*

wobble; see WABBLE.

woe, *dolor, mala (-orum,* plur.), *res* (plur.) *adversae, luctus (-ūs)*; see also SORROW; as interj. *vae (mihi!), pro dolor!*

woeful; see SAD, SORROWFUL.

wolf, *lupus, lupa*; of a —, adj. *lupinus.*

wolfish, *saevus.*

woman, *femina* (opp. *vir*), *mulier* (esp. a grown —): a young —, *puella, virgo*; an old —, *anus (-ūs)*; a little —, *muliercula*; a little old —, *vetula*; in gen. = the female sex, —kind, *sexus (-ūs) muliebris, mulieres (-um,* plur.).

womanish, *muliebris, mollis, effeminatus*; see also EFFEMINATE.

womanly, *muliebris.*

womb, *alvus, uterus.*

wonder, subst. (**1**) as a feeling, *(ad)miratio, stupor* (stronger); see also ASTONISHMENT. (**2**) = a wonderful thing, *miraculum, res mira, mirum*: and no —, *nec mirum, neque id mirum.*

wonder, v. *(ad)mirari*: to — at, *(ad)mirari,* with acc.; I — that, *miror* with acc. and infin.; I — whether, why, what, etc., *scire velim (miror* and *demiror* are so used only when an element of actual surprise is present, e.g. I — why on earth he did that).

wonderful, *mirus, mirificus, (ad)mirabilis, (ad)mirandus*: very —, *permirus.*

wonderfully, *mire, mirifice, (ad)mirabiliter.*

wont, subst. *mos, consuetudo*; see also CUSTOM.

wont, adj. *(ad)suetus*: to be —, *solēre, consuevisse.*

woo, *ambire, (in matrimonium) petĕre.*

wood. (**1**) as a substance, *lignum, materia (materies)*: a piece of —, *lignum*; of —, adj., *ligneus*; to get — (esp. for an army), *lignari*; the getting of —, *lignatio.* (**2**) = a collection of trees, *silva, nemus (-ŏris,* n.), *lucus* (= grove), *saltus (-ūs)*; = wooded upland pasture.

wooden, *ligneus.*

woodland, *silvae (-arum,* plur.,) *nemora (-um,* plur.), *saltus (-ūs).*

wood-louse, *oniscus* (Plin.).

woodman, *lignator* (esp. for an army).

wood-nymph, *(hama)dryas* (poet.).

wood-pecker, *picus* (Plin.).

wood-pigeon, *palumbes* (poet.).

woody, wooded, *silvestris, silvosus, nemorosus* (poet.).

wooer, *procus* (poet.).

woof, *subtemen* (poet.), *trama* (Varro, Sen.).

wool, *lana.*

woollen, woolly, *laneus.*

word, subst. (**1**) = a part of speech, *verbum, vocabulum* (= name; as grammat. t. t. = noun), *nomen* (= name), *dictum* (= saying), *vox* (= utterance): — for —, *verbum pro verbo, ad verbum*; in a — (i.e. briefly), *breviter, ut paucis dicam, paucis, quid multa? ne multa.* (**2**) = information, in such phrases as to send —, bring —; see TELL, REPORT, WRITE. (**3**) = — of honour, promise, *fides*: to keep one's —, *fidem servare*; to break one's —, *fidem fallĕre* or *violare.*

word, v.; see EXPRESS.

wordy, *verbosus.*

work, subst. *opus (-ĕris,* n.; = a particular piece of —, sometimes a finished —), *factum* (= deed), *pensum* (= allotted task), *liber, libellus* (= a literary —), *opera* or *labor* (= effort made over —): a small —, *opusculum*; a — of art, *artificium, ars* (poet.); — done by candlelight, *lucubratio*; — done in leisure hours, *operae (-arum,* plur.) *subsicivae*; the —s (in machinery), *machina, machinatio.*

work, v. (**1**) intransit. *laborare* (= to exert oneself), *(in re) elaborare* (strenuously), *operari* (= to be busy): to — at night, *lucubrare*; to — for wages, *operam suam locare* (Pl.); to — upon a person's feelings, *hominem (com)movēre*; see also SUCCEED. (**2**) transit. = to exercise, ply, *exercēre,*

exercitare; = to till, *colĕre, subigĕre*; = to effect, do, *facĕre, efficĕre, perficĕre, fabricari* (= to fashion).

work-basket, *quasillum* or *quasillus.*

working, subst. *tractatio* (= handling), *cultus (-ūs)* or *cultio* (of the soil), *effectus (-ūs*; = effect).

working, adj.: a — day, *dies profestus.*

workman, *opifex, operarius, artifex* (esp. of craftsmen, artists, etc.), *faber* (esp. of smiths, carpenters, etc), *sellularius* (= a mechanic), *operae (-arum,* plur. = labourers, hands).

workmanship, *ars, artificium, opus (-ĕris,* n.).

workshop, *officina.*

world. (**1**) in gen. *rerum natura* or *mundus* (= the visible universe), *orbis terrarum* or *terrae* (= the globe so far as it was known to the Romans), *orbis* alone (poet.), *terra* (= the earth as a planet), *terrae (-arum,* plur.; = all countries): our —, *haec omnia quae videmus*; where in the —? *ubi gentium?* what in the —? *quid tandem?* (**2**) = mankind, *gentes, homines, omnes* (all plur.): the ancient —, *antiquitas, aetas vetus, veteres (-um,* plur.); the learned —, *docti* or *litterati homines*; all the — knows, *nemo est quin sciat.* (**3**) = this present life and its affairs, *vita*: to come into the —, *nasci*; to leave the — (= die), *e vita excedĕre*; a man of the —, *homo urbanus* or *rerum peritus*; a citizen of the —, *mundanus.* (**4**) the lower —, *inferi (-orum,* plur.).

worldliness, worldly, render by phrase, such as *rebus quotidianis nimium deditus.*

worm, subst. *vermis, vermiculus* (= little: Lucr., Plin.), *lumbricus* (Pl., Plin.), *teredo* (= boring —: Ov., Plin.), *tinea* (in wood, books, etc.: Verg., Hor.).

worm, v.: to — out, *extorquēre*; to — one's way in, *(se) insinuare.*

wormwood, *absinthium* (Pl., Lucr.).

worn; see WEAR.

worry, subst., see ANXIETY.

worry, v. (**1**) = to tear, maul, *(di)lacerare, (di)laniare.* (**2**) = to harass, *vexare, sollicitare, cruciare, exercēre.*

worse, adj. *peior, deterior* (= less good than before): to grow —, *degenerare* (in character), *ingravescĕre* (of troubles).

worse, adv. *peius, deterius.*

worship, subst. *veneratio, cultus (-ūs)*: divine —, *cultus deorum, res* (plur.) *divinae, sacra (-orum,* plur.); to attend —, *sacris adesse*; your — (as title), *vir optime.*

worship, v. *venerari, colĕre, adorare* (poet. and Tac.).

worshipful, *optimus.*

worshipper, *cultor.*

worst, adj. *pessimus, deterrimus*; of a range of bad things, often *extremus* or *ultimus* (= last, extreme); my — enemy, *homo mihi omnium inimicissimus.*

worst, adv. *pessime.*

worst, v. *vincĕre*; see also CONQUER, DEFEAT.

worsted; see WOOL.

worth, subst. (**1**) = value (real or estimated), *aestimatio, pretium.* (**2**) = goodness, merit, *virtūs (-ūtis,* f.), *dignitas.*

worth, adj. *dignus* (with abl.; = worthy of); more often rendered by genit. of value (e.g. he is — nothing, *nihili est*) or by *valēre* (= to be —): it is — while, *operae pretium est.*

worthily, *digne.*

worthiness, *dignitas.*

worthless, *vilis* (= cheap), *inutilis* (= useless), *inanis* (= empty): morally —, *nequam, levis, inhonestus.*

worthlessness, render by adj.

worthy, *dignus* : — of a thing, *rē dignus* ; — to, with infin., *dignus qui* with subj. (prose), *dignus* with infin. (poet.); — is also often rendered by a gerundive or a verbal adj. in *-bilis,* so that '— of praise' may be translated in any of the following ways : *laude dignus, dignus qui laudetur, laudandus, laudabilis.*

would; as past tense of will; see WILL, WISH; as auxiliary verb, usually rendered by Latin subjunctive; but in the description of actions, '— be' sometimes should be rendered 'is' (e.g. it — be difficult, it — be tedious, to say, *difficile est, longum est, dicere*) ; — that, in wishes, is rendered by *utinam* and subj. (e.g. — that he were here, *utinam adesset*; — that he had been here, *utinam adfuisset*).

wound, subst. *vulnus* (*-ĕris,* n.), *plaga* (= a blow, etc.), *cicatrix* (= scar): to die of a —, *ex vulnere mori.*

wound, v. *vulnerare, sauciare* (severely), *vulnus (homini) infligĕre* : to be mortally —ed, *vulnus mortiferum accipĕre.*

wounded, *vulneratus, saucius.*

wrangle; see QUARREL.

wrap, *involvĕre, velare, amicire.*

wrapper, = cover, *involucrum, tegumentum* ; = cloak, wrap; see CLOAK.

wrath, *ira, iracundia, bilis, stomachus, indignatio.*

wrathful, *iratus, irā incensus* ; see also ANGRY.

wrathfully, *irate, iracunde, per iram.*

wreak; see REVENGE.

wreath. (1) = garland, *corona, serta* (*-orum,* plur.). (2) of smoke, etc., *volumen* (poet.), *vertex.*

wreathe, *nectĕre,* (*con*)*torquēre* (= twist): to — with garlands, *coronare, sertis redimire.*

wreck, wreckage, subst. = the wrecking of a ship, of fortunes, etc., *naufragium* ; = the remains of a wrecked ship, *navis fracta, navis* or *navigii reliquiae* (*-arum,* plur.), rarely *naufragium.*

wreck, v. *frangĕre* (= break): to be —ed, *naufragium facĕre.*

wrecked, *naufragus* (lit. and fig.).

wren, *regulus* (late Latin).

wrench, wrest: to — a thing from a person, *rem homini extorquēre* or *eripĕre* ; fig., to — words, etc., out of their proper sense, *detorquēre, perverse interpretari.*

wrestle, *luctari.*

wrestler, *luctator* (Ov., Sen.), *athleta* (= athlete, in gen.).

wrestling, subst. *luctatio, luctatus* (*-ūs* : Plin.).

wretch, *homo miser, nequam,* etc.; see also WRETCHED.

wretched. (1) as a term of pity = unfortunate, *miser, miserabilis, maestus, tristis.* (2) as a term of reproach = bad, *malus, nequam, perditus.*

wretchedly, *misere, miserabiliter, male* (= badly).

wretchedness, *miseria, aerumna* ; see also MISERY.

wriggle, *se torquēre, torquēri.*

wring: to — one's hands, *manus tollĕre* (strictly = to raise the hands in astonishment); to —

the neck, *gulam frangĕre* ; to — the soul, *hominem* or *animum cruciare* ; to — out clothes, *aquam exprimĕre linteis.*

wrinkle, subst. *ruga*: full of —s, *rugosus* (poet.).

wrinkle, v.: to — the face or forehead, *frontem contrahĕre* or *adducĕre.*

wrinkled, *rugosus* (poet.).

wrist, render by *manus* (*-ūs* ; = hand).

writ. (1) Holy —, *Litterae* (*-arum,* plur.) *Sanctae, Sacrae* or *Divinae* (eccl.). (2) as legal t. t., *mandatum, praescriptum.*

write, *scribĕre*: to — out, *describĕre* ; to — out in full, *perscribĕre, exscribĕre*; to — on a thing, *(in) re inscribĕre* ; to — a book, *librum* (*con*)*scribĕre* ; to — out, *describĕre* ; to — (a letter) to a person about a thing, (*litteras, epistulam*) *scribĕre ad hominem de re*; to — back, *rescribĕre,* sometimes *respondēre* ; to — often, *scriptitare* ; to — a good hand, *lepidis litteris conscribĕre* (Pl.).

writer, *scriptor, auctor, scriba* (professional); or render by relat. clause, with *scribĕre.*

writhe, *torquēri.*

writing, subst. (1) as an act, *scriptio, scriptura*: the art of —, *ars scribendi.* (2) = a thing written, *scriptum, scriptura* (Ter.), *litterae* (*-arum,* plur.): to put a thing in —, *rem litteris mandare.*

writing-case, *scrinium* (Sall. and poet.).

writing-desk, render by *scrinium,* or by the verb *scribĕre.*

writing-paper, *charta.*

writing-tablet, *tabula, cera* (covered with wax).

wrong, subst., = an injury, *iniuria*; = wickedness, in gen., *nefas* : to do —, *peccare, delinquĕre.*

wrong, adj. *falsus* (= false), *perversus,* or *pravus* (= perverse, distorted), *iniquus* (= unfair), *iniustus* (= unjust): to be — (i.e. mistaken), *se fallĕre, falli, errare.*

wrong, wrongly, adv. *male, perperam, prave, falso* (= falsely), *vitiose* (= faultily), *inique* or *iniuria* (= unjustly), *immerito* (= undeservedly), *nequiter* (= worthlessly).

wrong, v. *iniuriam (homini) inferre, iniuriā (hominem) adficĕre.*

wrongdoer, *malefactor* (Pl.); *homo maleficus, scelerosus,* etc.; or render by the verb *peccare* or *delinquĕre.*

wrongful, *iniustus, iniuriosus*; see also WRONG.

wrongfully, *iniuste, iniuriose*; see also WRONG, WRONGLY.

wrongheaded, *perversus, praeposterus.*

wroth, *iratus* ; see also ANGRY.

wrought, *factus, confectus.*

wry, *distortus, perversus, pravus.*

wryneck, *iynx* (Plin.).

Y

yacht, *celox.*

yard. (1) the measure, *tres pedes* (*-um,* plur.): a — long or wide, *tripedalis.* (2) = court, court- —, *area, cohors* (esp. for cattle or poultry: Cato, Ov.), (*aedium*) *propatulum.* (3) on a ship, a sail- —, *antenna.*

yardstick; see STANDARD.

yarn, subst. (1) the thread, render by *filum lanae* (= wool thread). (2) = story, *fabula.*

yarn, v. = to chat, exchange stories, (*con*)-*fabulari* (Pl.), *sermocinari.*

yawl, *navis, scapha.*

yawn, subst. *oscitatio* (Mart.).
yawn, v. *oscitare*; in gen. = to open wide, *scindi, hiare.*
ye; see YOU.
yea; see YES.
year, *annus, annuum tempus, anni spatium*: lasting a —, or recurring every —, adj. *annuus*; lasting half a —, *semestris*; a full —, *annus solidus*; for a — (i.e. to last for a —, for the — to come), *in annum*; a — after, *post annum, anno post*; after the lapse of a —, *anno peracto* or *intermisso*; last —, *superiore* or *priore* or *proximo anno*; next —, *proximo anno*; at the beginning of the —, *initio anni, incipiente* or *ineunte anno*; at the end of the —, *extremo* or *exeunte anno*; every —, each —, *singulis annis, quotannis*; every other —, *alternis annis*; every three —s, *tertio quōque anno*; a period of two —s, *biennium*; of three —s, *triennium*; of four —s, *quadrennium*; of five —s, *quinquennium, lustrum*; getting on in —s, *aetate provectus.*
yearly, adj. *annuus, anniversarius.*
yearly, adv. *quotannis, singulis annis, in singulos annos* (= for every year).
yearn: to — for, *desiderare.*
yearning, *desiderium.*
yeast, *fermentum* (Cels.).
yell, subst. *ululatus (-ūs), eiulatio.*
yell, v. *ululare, eiulare.*
yellow, *flavus* (poet.), *flavens* (poet.), *luteus* (poet.), *fulvus* (= brownish —; poet.), *luridus* (= pale —, wan), *aureus* (= golden; poet.), *croceus* (= saffron coloured; poet.), *gilvus* (= pale —: Verg.): to turn —, *flavescĕre* (poet.).
yellowish, *sufflavus* (Suet.).
yelp, yelping, subst. *gannitus (-ūs*: Lucr.).
yelp, v. *gannire* (poet.).
yeoman, perhaps *colonus.*
yes, *ita, ita est, sic, certe, vero, etiam, sane* (= of course, to be sure); *immo* (= — indeed); more often rendered by repetition of some word in the question (suitably inflected), e.g. will you come? —!, *veniesne? veniam!*; I say —, *aio*; to answer — or no, *aut etiam aut non respondēre.*
yesterday; as adv. *heri, hesterno die*; as subst. *hesternus dies*: of —, adj. *hesternus*; — evening, *heri vesperi*; — morning, *heri mane.*
yet. (**1**) as an adversative particle = nevertheless, *tamen, attamen, verum tamen, sed, at*; see also HOWEVER, NEVERTHELESS. (**2**) of time = even now, *etiamnunc, adhuc*: not —, *nondum, adhuc non*. (**3**) with comparatives = even, *etiam.*
yew, *taxus.*
yield, subst. *fructus (-ūs)*; in money, *reditus (-ūs).*
yield, v. (**1**) transit., of soil, trees, etc. = to produce, *(ef)ferre, (ef)fundĕre* (freely); = to give, offer, *dare, praebēre*; = to surrender, *dedĕre, (con)cedĕre*. (**2**) intransit. *(con)cedĕre* or *obsequi* (with dat.).
yielding, subst. *(con)cessio*; or render by verb.
yielding, adj., of temper, etc., *facilis, obsequens, indulgens.*
yoke, subst. *iugum*: the — of slavery, *iugum servitutis, iugum servile.*
yoke, v. *(con)iungĕre.*
yokefellow, *socius* (= companion, in gen.), *coniunx* (= husband or wife).

yolk, (of an egg) *vitellus.*
yon, yonder, adj. *ille, iste, illic* (Pl., Ter.).
youder, adv. *illic, istic* (= there where you are).
yore: of —, *olim, quondam, antea* (= before); days of —, *tempora (-um*, plur.) *antiqua*; men of —, *antiqui, veteres, viri prisci.*
York, *Eboracum.*
you, often not expressed in Latin, so long as the form of the verb or the general context makes it clear what person is referred to; otherwise *tu, te*, etc. (sing.), *vos*, etc. (plur.); one of you, in commands, *aliquis* (used with plur. imperat. by Pl.).
young, subst. *partus (-ūs*; = the offspring of any creature), *fetus (-ūs*; = brood), *proles* (= brood; mainly poet.), *pullus* (= any individual — animal), *catulus* (= an individual puppy, cub, etc.).
young, adj. *parvus* or *parvulus* (= little), *infans* (= unable to speak), *adulescens* (= growing up), *iuvenis* (rare as adj.), *novus* (= fresh, new), *novellus* (esp. of trees): a — child, *infans*; a — lad, *puer*; a — lass, *puella*; a — man, *adulescens, adulescentulus, iuvenis*; — people; see YOUTH.
younger, *iunior, (natu) minor.*
youngest, *(natu) minimus.*
your, yours, *tuus* (of a sing. owner; = thy), *vester* (of a plur. owner): that of —, *iste.*
yourself, *tu ipse, tute, tutemet.*
yourselves, *vos ipsi, vosmet (ipsi).*
youth. (**1**) as a time of life, *pueritia* or *aetas puerilis* (= boyhood), *adulescentia* (from about fifteen to thirty); *iuventūs (-ūtis*, f.) or *iuventa* (mainly poet.) or (poet.) *iuventas* (from about twenty to forty-five); more generally, *prima* or *bona aetas* or *flos aetatis*: — personified, *Iuventas*; from one's — up, *ab ineunte aetate, a puero, ab adulescentia*. (**2**) collective, the —, = young people, *iuventūs (-ūtis*, f.), *iuvenes (-um*, plur.), *pubes (-is*; = grown males). (**3**) a —, = a young man, *puer, adulescentulus, adulescens iuvenis*; for the ages covered by these, see above.
youthful, *iuvenilis, iuvenalis, puerilis* (= boyish); see also YOUNG.
youthfully, *iuveniliter, iuvenum more.*

Z

zany, = buffoon, *sannio.*
zeal, *studium, ardor, fervor, industria* (= diligence), *alacritas* (= readiness).
zealot, render by adj.; see ZEALOUS.
zealous, *studiosus* (with genit.), *acer, ardens*; see also EAGER.
zealously, *studiose, summo studio, acriter, ardenter, enixe, intente, industrie.*
zenith, *vertex.*
zephyr, *Zephyrus* (poet.), *Favonius.*
zero, render by *nihil.*
zest, *studium.*
zigzag; see WINDING.
zodiac, *orbis* or *circulus signifer.*
zone. (**1**) = girdle, *cingulum, zona* (poet.); see also GIRDLE. (**2**) = a region, a belt of earth or sky, *orbis, regio, plaga* (poet.), *zona* (poet.): the torrid —, *zona torrida* (Plin.); the temperate —, *orbis medius, temperatae (caeli) regiones (-um*, plur.).
zoology, render by phrase, such as *animantium descriptio.*